Contents

Contents

A Note from Peterson's® Editors

Peterson's Private Secondary Schools 2016–17 is the authoritative source of information for parents and students who are exploring the alternative of privately provided education. In this edition, you will find information for more than 1,000 schools worldwide. The data published in this guide are obtained directly from the schools themselves to help you make a fully informed decision.

If you've decided to look into private schooling for your son or daughter but aren't sure how to begin, relax. You won't have to go it alone. **What You Should Know About Private Education** can help you plan your search and demystify the admission process. In the articles that follow, you'll find valuable advice from admission experts about applying to private secondary schools and choosing the school that's right for your child.

In "Why Choose an Independent School?" Donna Orem, Interim President of the National Association of Independent Schools (NAIS), describes the reasons why an increasing number of families are considering private schooling.

If you want a private education for your child but are hesitant about sending him or her away to a boarding school, read our new article, "Independent Day Schools: The Best of Both Worlds," which discusses the benefits of day schools.

If you are considering attending a boarding school, you will want to read our insightful article, "Why Boarding School: Reasons I Chose This Path and Why You Might Too," by Justin Muchnick, a boarding school student at Phillips Academy Andover. Or check out the article, "Study Confirms Benefits of Boarding School," with valuable data from The Association of Boarding Schools (TABS).

Mark Meyer-Braun, Former Head of School at the Outdoor Academy, offers "Semester Schools: Great Opportunities," which explores various options for students to spend an exciting semester in a new "school-away-from-school."

Schools will be pleased to know that Peterson's helped you in your private secondary school selection.

If you are considering a special needs or therapeutic school for your child, you will want to read "Why a Therapeutic or Special Needs School?" by Diederik van Renesse, an educational consultant who specializes in this area.

To help you compare private schools and make the best choice for your child, check out "Finding the Perfect Match" by Helene Reynolds, a former educational planning and placement counselor.

"Plan a Successful School Search" gives you an overview of the admission process.

If the admission application forms have you baffled and confused, read "Admissions Applications for Private Secondary Schools," by Tom Sheppard, Dean of Admissions and Financial Aid.

For the lowdown on standardized testing, Heather Hoerle, Executive Director of the Secondary School Admission Test Board (SSATB), describes the two tests most often required by private schools and the role that tests play in admission decisions in "About Admission Tests and the SSAT." In addition, you can read about another private schools admissions test in the "About the Independent School Entrance Exam (ISEE)" article.

In "Paying for a Private Education," Mark Mitchell, Vice President, School and Student Services at NAIS, shares some thoughts on financing options.

Finally, "How to Use This Guide" gives you all the information you need on how to make *Peterson's Private Secondary Schools 2016–17* work for you!

Next up, the **Quick-Reference Chart**, "Private Secondary Schools At-a-Glance," lists schools by state, U.S. territory, or country and provides essential information about a school's students, range of grade levels, enrollment figures, faculty, and special offerings.

A Note from Peterson's® Editors

The **School Profiles** follow, and it's here you can learn more about particular schools. *Peterson's Private Secondary Schools 2016–17* contains three **School Profiles** sections—one for traditional college-preparatory and general academic schools, one for special needs schools that serve students with a variety of special learning and social needs, and one for junior boarding schools that serve students in middle school grades. Many schools have chosen to submit a display ad, which appears near their profile and offers specific information the school wants you to know.

Close-Ups follow each **School Profiles** section and feature expanded two-page school descriptions written exclusively for this guide. There is a reference at the end of a profile directing you to that school's **Close-Up.**

The **Specialized Directories** are generated from responses to Peterson's annual school survey. These directories group schools by the categories considered most important when choosing a private school, including type, entrance requirements, curricula, financial aid data, and special programs.

Finally, in the **Index** you'll find the "Alphabetical Listing of Schools" for the page references of schools that have already piqued your interest.

Peterson's publishes a full line of resources to help guide you and your family through the private secondary school admission process. Peterson's publications can be found at your local bookstore and library and your school guidance office, and you can access us online at www.petersons.com. Peterson's books are also available as ebooks.

We welcome any comments or suggestions you may have about this publication. Please send us an e-mail at custsvc@petersons.com. Your feedback will help us make your educational dreams possible.

Schools will be pleased to know that Peterson's helped you in your private secondary school selection. Admission staff members are more than happy to answer questions, address specific problems, and help in any way they can. The editors at Peterson's wish you great success in your search!

NOTICE: Certain portions of or information contained in this book have been submitted and paid for by the educational institution identified, and such institutions take full responsibility for the accuracy, timeliness, completeness and functionality of such content. Such portions or information include (i) each display ad in the "Profiles" sections, which comprise a half page of information covering a single educational institution, and (ii) each two-page description in the "Close-Up" sections, which include Traditional Day and Boarding Schools and Junior Boarding Schools.

What You Should Know About Private Education

Why Choose an Independent School?

Donna Orem
Interim President of the National Association of Independent Schools (NAIS)

What does the ideal school for your child look like? Is it small or large? Competitive, or more nurturing? Are there aptitudes or interests that you'd like to foster in your child? Or challenges that you'd like to address? Are you looking for a school in a particular area, or is living away from home at a boarding school appealing to your child?

Each independent school has a unique mission that guides its offerings. You can choose a school where the philosophy, values, and teaching approach are right for your child.

Independent schools nurture students' intellectual abilities, curiosity, social growth, and civic conscience. Opportunities extend well beyond the classroom to athletic competitions, artistic pursuits, and school leadership experiences.

Students are deeply engaged in learning at independent schools. More than twice as many students at the schools belonging to the National Association of Independent Schools (NAIS) reported that they received helpful feedback from teachers on assignments compared to students at all other types of schools, according to *The High School Survey of Student Engagement*. In addition, students who attended NAIS schools were more than twice as likely as students at other schools to

> *Independent schools nurture not just students' intellectual ability and curiosity but also their personal and social growth and civic conscience.*

say that the school contributed "very much" to their growth in critical thinking.

Graduates of NAIS schools felt more prepared for the academic demands of college than their public school counterparts, according to *The Freshman Survey Trends Report*, an annual study conducted by the Higher Education Research Institute. In addition, as college freshmen, NAIS graduates reported that they were more likely to ask questions in their college classes and explore topics on their own, even though it was not required for a class.

The diverse range of independent school types allows parents to find schools that best meet each child's needs. Once you identify schools of interest, look at each and ask:

- What is the school's mission, and does its philosophy appeal to me?
- What types of learning experiences are available—in class, on the playing field, in extracurricular activities, and in community service? Would these experiences fit my child's needs?
- Does the school offer before- or after-school care or transportation (if necessary)?
- What are the deadlines for admission and financial aid applications?

For tips on applying to independent schools, timelines, and more, visit http://parents.nais.org.

Independent Day Schools: The Best of Both Worlds

It's a common dilemma. You want more for your student than public schools have to offer, but a boarding school isn't the right option either. That's when an independent day school can be the perfect solution—one that benefits both students and their families.

"An independent day school provides a college-prep environment, where kids can get an education similar to the best boarding schools but without having to leave home," says Susan Grodman, Director of Enrollment and Global Programs for Derryfield School in Manchester, New Hampshire. "They can still be home for dinner each night." She says the typical family that chooses an independent day school is one that emphasizes the importance of education and also wants to be involved with their child and their school and activities.

Jen Groen, Director of Admissions and Strategic Engagement for Jack M. Barrack Hebrew Academy in Bryn Mawr, Pennsylvania agrees. "An independent day school offers a self-selected group of families and students a safe, nurturing, college-prep setting. And because they're not bound to some of the things that public schools are required to do, such as testing, independent day schools have the freedom to offer unique, specialized instruction."

"Education is a team effort, and parents are a part of that team. The family is a big part of the development of the child," says Elizabeth Norton, Director of Enrollment and Financial Aid at York Preparatory School in New York City. "The personal connection you get at a day school is incredible. It's like being part of a small town, with much more of a human element."

Independent day schools have the freedom to offer unique, specialized instruction.

What Makes an Independent Day School Special?

Because they are independent, each school has the freedom to establish a unique identity that is suited to the needs of the students and families it serves.

For instance, Barrack Hebrew Academy incorporates the Jewish calendar into the academic year, allowing for easy practice of faith without conflict. "This helps students feel more whole in their identity," says Groen.

Many independent day schools have smaller populations, which helps students develop a strong self-image, self-concept, and self-advocacy skills. The small size also fosters involvement in a range of extracurricular activities; students can explore and try many things.

"There's not a lot of labeling here—no one is a 'jock' or a 'theater geek' and there aren't a lot of cliques," says Grodman. "The kids make a lot of connections with one another as well."

Groen agrees that there is a high level of intimacy and strong relationships are formed at an independent day school, due in part to the fact that the students come from the same geographic area and may share the same faith or another common bond. "Friendships that are made here are those that truly last a lifetime."

Norton pointed out that because students have a wide range of learning styles, an independent day school may be able to serve those with unique needs better because of the smaller number of students.

Of course, there's another big benefit to an independent day school that's close to home. Parents and other family members are able to easily attend athletic events, concerts, plays, and other programs their students are involved with.

Academics and College Prep

Academics are still the heart of every independent day school, with college entrance being the primary focus.

"While placement is the primary goal, the way they get there varies. We seek an appropriate, challenging college acceptance path for each student," says Norton. She adds that schools address the subject of challenge differently. "Some are more aggressive at pushing children to the point where it's almost like college, but we think developmentally that's not where these young people are. We want to challenge them but also teach them to use the tools that they have available, such as how to have contact with their teachers. It's a progression."

"Homework doesn't necessarily equate rigor; we strive to develop a well-rounded child. Honing outside interests and talents is important for the long term, for life. This also helps distinguish each student during the college entrance process," Norton says.

The smaller student population of most independent day schools again is a factor. Grodman points out that independent day schools allow students to develop relationships with teachers that they might not be able to have in other settings. Sharon Levin, Head of School at Barack Academy reports their students perform as well, if not better, at college than those from larger schools.

"Kids find their passion here—it's so much easier to find what they love," says Derryfield's Grodman. "Students come back and report that they were well-prepared for college. They know how to manage their time, how to study effectively, how to advocate for themselves, and how to approach teachers."

Time management is an especially important skill for students at independent day schools. Some will commute an hour or more to get to and from their school. They get up early and often stay late for extracurricular activities, so self-discipline and effective use of time are key components to their success.

Independent day schools also pride themselves on the degree of college guidance their students receive. For instance, at York Preparatory Academy, Norton says that most students have everything in place—the schools they want to attend, applications filled out, essays complete—at the end of their junior year. When students return for senior year they simply review and polish up their materials before applying, so there's no last-minute pressure or rush.

Not Just for Students, But a Community for the Family

One of the hallmarks that sets independent day schools apart is the opportunity to involve the entire family in the school and its activities.

Levin asserts that this is one of the main reasons families choose Barack Hebrew Academy. "People are looking for community and relationships, and this goes beyond just the students. We offer family and community with a Jewish soul."

Families who choose independent day schools tend to be very committed in terms of time, participation, and finances. Most schools have organizations to help facilitate involvement on a variety of levels.

The focus of York's parent organization is also building community. "We want to help these families feel like they're part of our family," Norton states. They have social activities, get-togethers for parents of each grade level, an international dinner where families bring foods that represent their culture and heritage, baseball and volleyball games, picnics, and even a class for parents taught by one of the school's history teachers.

Grodman says that some of the strong sense of community at Derryfield is because students are at the school a long time each day. With required sports participation and many other extracurricular activities, the school day lasts well past the time when classes end. It builds strong relationships, which leads to a lot of parental involvement: they volunteer in the library, serve as parent ambassadors who help with admissions, and help however they can. "Even those who can't get to the school regularly still find ways to be involved," she says.

At Barack Hebrew Academy, parental involvement includes the school's board and numerous committees: technology, recruitment, finances and investments, athletics support, drama boosters, and more. Parents help with learning enrichment and learning support. The Home-School Association provides a large volunteer presence at the school, with some grandparents involved, too. "They know how much the school has given to their kids. This is their way of giving back," Levin states.

Diverse and Accessible

Even though some independent day schools may be affiliated with a particular faith or draw students from a fairly small geographic area, they also strive to make their school community diverse.

"We have a great deal of cultural diversity but also a range of diverse learning styles and diversity of talents as well. It makes for a very interesting community—more the way the real world looks," says Norton. "That's why we celebrate diversity here at York."

Groen describes Barack Hebrew Academy as an incubator for future world leaders, and because of that they stress an attitude of tolerance and diversity within the school's population. They are intentionally pluralistic and promote respect for what everyone stands for and believes.

There is also economic diversity. While an independent day school is often more accessible financially, it can still be a challenge. "Derryfield families have made sacrifices in order to provide this kind of education for their child," explained Grodman. "They want their kids to have a broad, well-rounded education: world issues, travel, different perspectives, the arts, sciences, athletics, and more—not just an emphasis on one of those areas."

Friendships that are made here are those that truly last a lifetime.

Independent day schools work with families to make attendance affordable; often, a large percentage of students receive some type of scholarship.

Much to Offer

Students at independent day schools benefit from top-flight academics; personalized college guidance; small, diverse student populations with strong bonds; and opportunities to participate and thrive in extracurricular activities. But parents and families also benefit, by being able to be present, involved, and engaged with their student's school on a day-to-day, hands-on basis. These are just some of the reasons why independent day schools are a valuable option on the spectrum of education choice available for students today.

Why Boarding School: Reasons I Chose This Path and Why You Might, Too

Justin Muchnick

My seventh-grade literature class changed my life. To be more exact, Mr. Rogers, my seventh-grade literature teacher, changed my life. Only a temporary substitute teacher (the regular faculty member took the year off for maternity leave), Mr. Rogers entered the classroom on the first day of school and did something remarkable: he asked his students to have a conversation about a book we had read over the summer. My school's traditional "raise your hand and wait to be called on" style of learning had left me completely unprepared for a teacher who *wanted* me to talk. Nevertheless, I relished the opportunity to learn in this interesting and dynamic classroom environment, and I certainly jumped at a chance to voice my opinions without fear of being chastised for speaking out of turn.

Within a few weeks, active participation had fully cemented its reputation as the primary way of learning in Mr. Rogers' class. Instead of employing a standard row-and-column classroom seating pattern, Mr. Rogers positioned our seats in a large circle. This "Harkness" method encouraged free-flowing conversations in which Mr. Rogers would serve only as a mediator and participant. Rather than writing bland responses to even blander study questions, my class honed its public speaking skills by participating in spur-of-the-moment

debates about these topics. Mr. Rogers' classroom, reminiscent of a scene out of *Dead Poets Society*, allowed the act of learning to intellectually stretch and stimulate me.

As Mr. Rogers became my friend and mentor as well as my teacher, I learned that he had previously worked as the Writer in Residence at Phillips Exeter Academy, a boarding school in New England. At that time, I thought that boarding school meant a place where disobedient children were sent to resolve their behavioral issues. Mr. Rogers, though, spoke glowingly of the East Coast boarding school system and told me that schools like Exeter utilize an active, discussion-based, Mr. Rogers-esque style of teaching. Soon, I started dreaming of a school full of teachers like Mr. Rogers, full of intellectually curious students, and full of eager learners. I did some research about Exeter and other New England schools, and in the spring of my seventh-grade year, I presented the boarding school idea to my mom and dad.

At first, my parents commended me on the excellent joke I had pulled on them; however, they quickly realized that I was serious. They began to think that I wanted to get away from them or that I disliked my family. But after extensive negotiations, I was able to convince them that this was not the case, and by midway through the summer after seventh grade, they fully backed my decision. Once my family agreed that I was in fact going to pursue the boarding school idea, we made it our mission to select the schools to which I would apply. I devised a list of qualities I was looking for in a boarding school. At this point in the application process, you, too, should create a list of criteria—you can save yourself the wasted time and effort of applying to the "wrong" schools by knowing what kinds of schools best suit you. Though your personal list may be very different, mine was as follows:

Size: I tried to find a relatively big school. At my primary school, the average grade size was about 50 students, and, as time wore on, my desire to expand beyond my small group of classmates grew stronger. By applying to larger schools, I felt that I could both broaden my social experience and avoid another "small school burnout."

Uniform Policy: My former school enforced a strict dress code. Since collared shirts and I never really hit if off, I had definitely worn a uniform for long enough. Thus, I did not want to spend my high school years wearing a blazer and slacks.

> *For me, the process of applying to and selecting boarding schools was fueled by my innate passion for learning: I simply wanted to find a place where it was "cool to be smart."*

7

Single-Sex or Coed: I didn't really want to spend my high school years at an all-boys school.

Location: For me, the East Coast seemed like the best place to find a boarding school. After all, that's what Mr. Rogers had recommended.

Academics: I have an unquenchable thirst for knowledge. I did not wish to "dehydrate" myself at a school with a less-than-excellent academic reputation.

Proximity to an Airport: My mom thought of this one. She suggested that I should apply to schools located near a major airport that offered nonstop flights from Los Angeles. Cross-country flights are tough enough; complicating matters with a connecting flight seemed unnecessary.

Here are some other things that you might want to consider:

Religious Affiliation: Do you want religion to play a large part in your high school experience, or would you rather go to a nondenominational school?

Specialty Schools: Do you want to apply to schools that focus on a specific aspect or method of learning? Are you particularly talented in a certain field? If so, look into arts, math and sciences, or military schools.

Athletics: If you play a sport, you might try to look for schools with strong teams and exceptional athletic facilities. One good way to do this is to contact a school's coach or athletic director. As both a soccer player and a wrestler, I talked to many coaches from a number of different boarding schools to get a sense of each school's athletic program.

Cost/Financial Aid Policy: Obviously, some schools are more expensive than others. In addition to looking at the tuition, you may want to find out which schools offer need-based financial aid or any merit-based scholarships.

By comparing various schools to my personal list of attributes, I was able to find four schools that really matched my requirements. I sent applications to Choate Rosemary Hall, The Lawrenceville School, Phillips Exeter Academy, and Phillips Academy Andover, and I was fortunate enough to have been accepted by all four schools. After taking the SSAT, writing applications, and interviewing with admission officers, little did I realize that I would still have one last, equally significant hurdle to jump. The choice that I was about to make would directly impact the next four years of my life, so my parents and I did everything in our power to ensure that my decision was the correct one. By obtaining contact information from admission offices as well as school counselors and friends of friends, we sought out current students who lived locally and attended each of the schools. We scheduled face-to-face meetings with as many of them as we could, during which we "grilled"

them on the pros and cons of their schools. We spent hours reading websites, blogs, and Facebook pages in hopes of getting students' unsolicited perspectives of their schools. Most importantly, however, we attended the revisit days for each of the schools. For those at this stage of the boarding school process, I would highly recommend going to the admitted students events if you have the financial means and your schedule permits. At any given revisit day, I was truly able to get a feel for the campus and environment and see if I could envision myself as a student at that school next year—sometimes my gut instinct would tell me "yes," and other times it would tell me "no." While on campus, I also had the opportunity to ask countless current students about their high school experiences. Don't be afraid to ask tough questions. By doing so, you can better understand the general campus vibe. After the revisit days, I was able to make my decision with confidence. I was going to Andover!

You might choose to apply to boarding schools for different reasons than I did. No two cases are exactly alike, but many applicants fall into these categories.

Ready to Leave Home: Whether it's a desire for independence, friction within the household, or any other reason, waiting until college to live on your own isn't the best option for you.

Family Tradition: As a baby, you wore a boarding school bib around your neck. Your favorite shirt is one emblazoned with a particular school's emblem. A few older family members have paved the way, or, perhaps, generations of relatives have attended. Boarding school is in your blood.

Diversity: You have grown up in a homogenous community, or you yearn for difference in both tradition and mindset. Today's boarding schools afford you interaction with peers of all racial, financial, geographical, and religious backgrounds—conducive to a multicultural educational experience.

Love of Learning: Is your nose perpetually stuck in a book? Do you stay after class to delve deeper into a conversation with your teacher? Is your idea of a fun weekend activity reading up on political affairs or the latest scientific breakthrough? Do you love learning for learning's sake? If so, boarding school is undoubtedly worth exploring.

For me, the process of applying to and selecting boarding schools was fueled by my innate passion for learning: I simply wanted to find a place where it was "cool to be smart." When I look back at this initial notion, I realize that it was certainly idealistic and a bit naïve, but Andover has come about as close as possible. Though busy work and uninteresting conversations bog me down from time to time, they are more than made up for by engaging writing prompts, stimulating discussions, and inspirational teachers that would make even Mr. Rogers proud.

To learn more about boarding schools, look for Peterson's *The Boarding School Survival Guide*, by Justin Muchnick, available in stores, online, and as an ebook.

Top 10 Tips To Know Before Your Teen Leaves for Boarding School
by Justin Muchnick

Reprinted with permission by Ten to Twenty Parenting (Tentotwentyparenting.com)

1. Only let your son or daughter go away to boarding school if he or she really wants it for the right reasons. Sending you teen off to boarding school as a punishment or because your child thinks it will be an extended camp experience are not good reasons.

2. Don't be worried that your teen isn't under constant parental supervision at school, but definitely try to stay connected through text, Skype, phone calls, or e-mail.

3. That said, cherish the time you spend over school breaks together. Breaks are good opportunities to "make up for lost time."

4. Pack a small "first-aid kit" that includes Neosporin®, Band-Aids®, Tylenol®, TUMS®, and some throat lozenges. A few of these essential medical items can spare your teen an unnecessary trip to the infirmary.

5. To complement the medical kit, make sure to send your teen to school with some nonperishable snacks for late-night study sessions. Some dorm favorites include fruit leathers, microwavable noodles and mac and cheese, and granola bars.

6. Even if you are used to cheering on your child at every Little League game or musical theater production, don't feel guilty about missing many sporting events or other extracurricular activities once your teen is in boarding school. Student bodies at boarding schools are incredibly supportive, and your teen will most likely have a few friends or even teachers on the sidelines or in the audience.

7. Teach your son or daughter the basics of laundry, personal finance, and efficient packing. These skills, however trivial they might seem, are important ones to master before leaving home.

8. Chances are, the boarding school your teen attends is one of the most, if not the very most, diverse communities he or she will be a part of. Be very excited about this and open to this unique aspect of boarding school.

9. Never underestimate the power of a care package! Sometimes, receiving a little pick-me-up in the mail can really brighten up your teen's day.

10. Finally be sure to pick up a copy of *The Boarding School Survival Guide* for additional insights, tips, and strategies about boarding school life, written by students for students (and parents, too!).

Justin Muchnick is a student at Phillips Academy Andover in Massachusetts. He is a four-year varsity wrestler and two-time captain, serves on the Athletic Advisory Bord, works as a senior proctor, participates in the chess club, and works as a campus tour guide. A passionate learner, Justin enjoys reading, writing, Latin, and modern American history. He co-authored Straight-A Study Skills *(Adams Media, January 2013) and is the author of* Teens' Guide to College and Career Planning *(Peterson's 2016). He is the youngest journalist for The Bootleg® (http://stanford.scout.com), Stanford University's sports news website, where he writes articles about college football. When he is not at boarding school, Justin resides in Newport Beach, California, with his parents and three younger siblings. To contact Justin, visit his website www.justinmuchnick.com. He can also be reached via Twitter: @BoardingSchl or Facebook: https://www.facebook.com/TheBoardingSchoolSurvivalGuide.*

Study Confirms Benefits of Boarding School

Many people have long sung the praises of the boarding school experience. The high-level academics, the friendships, and the life lessons learned are without rival at private day or public schools, they say.

A study released by The Association of Boarding Schools (TABS), a nonprofit organization of independent, college-preparatory schools, validates these claims. Not only do boarding school students spend more time studying (and less time watching TV), they are also better prepared for college and progress more quickly in their careers than their counterparts who attended private day or public schools.

The survey, which was conducted by the Baltimore-based research firm the Art & Science Group, involved interviews with 1,000 students and alumni from boarding schools, 1,100 from public schools, and 600 from private day schools (including independent day and parochial schools).

The results not only affirm the benefits enjoyed by boarding school graduates but those bestowed upon current boarding school students as well. "The study helps us better understand how the opportunities for interaction and learning beyond the classroom found at boarding schools impact a student's life at school and into adulthood," explained Steve Ruzicka, former TABS executive director. Ruzicka said the survey also provides boarding school alumni with empirical data to help when considering their children's educational options.

Rigorous Academics Prevail

Why do students apply to boarding schools? The TABS study found that the primary motivation for both applicants and their parents is the promise of a better education. And, happily, the vast majority of current and past students surveyed reported that their schools deliver on this promise. Current students indicated significantly higher levels of satisfaction with their academic experience at boarding schools than their peers at public and private day schools by more than ten percentage points (54 percent of boarding students versus 42 percent of private day students and 40 percent of public school students). Boarders reported in greater relative percentages that they find their schools academically challenging, that their peers are more motivated, and the quality of teaching is very high.

But the boarding environment is valued just as much for the opportunities for interaction and learning beyond the classroom. Interactions in the dining room, the dormitory, and on the playing field both complement and supplement academics, exposing students to a broad geographic and socioeconomic spectrum, challenging their boundaries, and broadening their vision of the world.

The Boarding School Boost

The 24/7 life at boarding schools also gives students a significant leg up when they attend college, the survey documents.

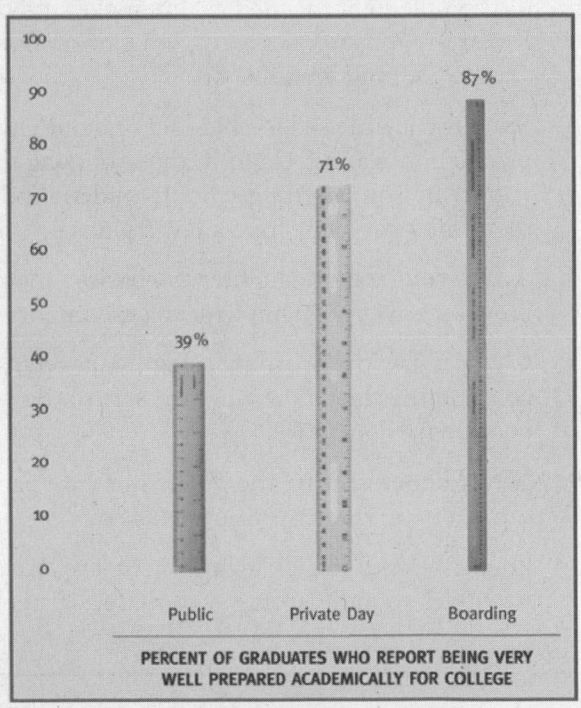

PERCENT OF GRADUATES WHO REPORT BEING VERY WELL PREPARED ACADEMICALLY FOR COLLEGE

Some 87 percent of boarding school graduates said they were very well prepared academically for college, with only 71 percent of private day and just 39 percent of public school alumni saying the same. And 78 percent of boarders reported that their schools also helped better prepare them to face the nonacademic aspects of college life, such as independence, social life, and time management. Only 36 percent of private day graduates and 23 percent of public school graduates said the same.

The TABS survey also documented that a larger percentage of boarding school graduates go on to earn advanced degrees once they finish college: 50 percent, versus 36 percent of private day and 21 percent of public school alumni.

Beyond college, boarding school graduates also reap greater benefits from their on-campus experiences, advancing faster and further in their careers comparatively. The study scrutinized former boarders versus private day and public school graduates in terms of achieving positions in top management and found that by midcareer, 44 percent of boarding school graduates had reached positions in top management versus 33 percent of private day school graduates and 27 percent of public school graduates.

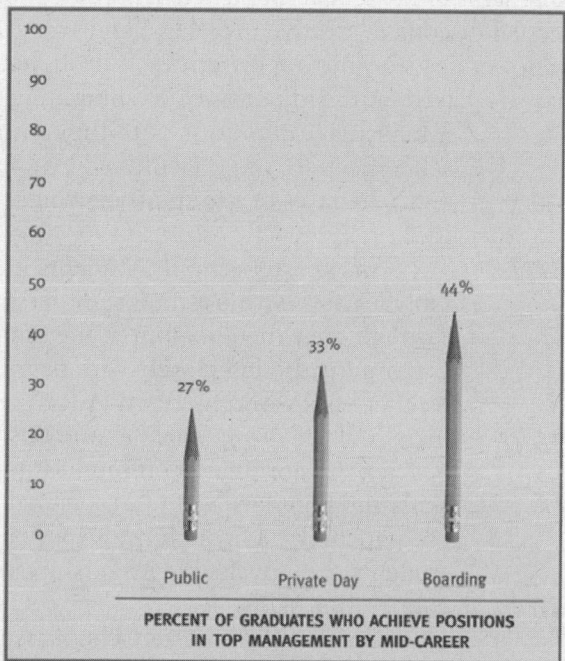

PERCENT OF GRADUATES WHO ACHIEVE POSITIONS
IN TOP MANAGEMENT BY MID-CAREER

By late in their careers, more than half of the surveyed boarding school sample, 52 percent, held positions in top management as opposed to 39 percent of private day and 27 percent of public school graduates.

But perhaps the most compelling statistic that the study produced is the extremely high percentage—some 90 percent—of boarding school alumni who say they would, if given the opportunity, repeat their boarding school experience. This alone is a strong argument that validates the enduring value of the boarding school model. It is hoped that the study will help dispel many of the myths and stereotypes that have dogged the image of boarding schools over the last century and spread the good news that boarding schools today are diverse, exciting places for bright, well-adjusted students who are looking for success in their academic lives—and beyond.

For more information on TABS visit the Web site at www.schools.com.

Used by permission of The Association of Boarding Schools.

Semester Schools: Great Opportunities

Mark Meyer-Braun
Former Head of School, The Outdoor Academy

Over the last twenty years, there has been tremendous growth in the range of educational opportunities available to young Americans. The advent of semester schools has played no small part in this trend. Similar in many ways to semester-abroad programs, semester schools provide secondary school students the opportunity to leave their home school for half an academic year to have a very different kind of experience—the experience of living and learning within a small community, among diverse students, and in a new and different place. The curricula of such schools tend to be thematic, interdisciplinary, rigorous, and experiential.

What Are the Benefits?

As a starting point for their programs, semester schools have embraced many of the qualities typical of independent schools. In fact, a number of semester schools were developed as extension programs by existing independent schools, providing unusual opportunities to their own students and those from other schools. Other semester schools have grown from independent educational organizations or foundations that bring their own educational interests and expertise to their semester programs. In both cases, semester schools provide the kind of challenging environment for which independent schools are known.

Across the board, semester school programs provide students with exceptional opportunities for contact with their teachers. Individual instruction and intimate classes are common, as is contact with teachers outside the classroom. At semester schools, students have a full-immersion experience in a tightly knit learning community. In such a setting, teachers are able

At semester schools, students have a full-immersion experience in a tightly knit learning community.

to challenge each student in his or her own area of need, mentoring students to both academic and personal fulfillment.

Semester schools have developed around specialized curricular interests, often involving unique offerings or nontraditional subjects. In almost every case, these specialized curricula are related to the school's location. Indeed, place-based learning is a common thread in semester school education. Whether in New York City or the Appalachian Mountains, semester schools enable students to cultivate a sense of place and develop greater sensitivity to their surroundings. This is often accomplished through a combination of experiential education and traditional instruction. Students develop academic knowledge and practical skills in tandem through active participation in intellectual discourse, creative projects, hands-on exercises, and service learning opportunities. Throughout, emphasis is placed on the importance of combining intellectual exploration with thoughtful self-reflection, often facilitated by journaling exercises or group processing activities.

At semester schools, students inevitably learn their most important lessons through their membership in the school community. Living closely with peers and teachers and working together for the benefit of the group enables students to develop extraordinary communication skills and high levels of interpersonal accountability. Through this experience, students gain invaluable leadership and cooperation skills.

Ultimately, semester schools seek to impart translatable skills to their students. The common goal is for students to return to their schools and families with greater motivation, empathy, self-knowledge, and self-determination. These skills help to prepare students for the college experience and beyond. In addition, semester school participants report that their experiences helped to distinguish them in the college application process. Semester school programs are certainly not for everybody, but they serve an important role for students who are seeking something beyond the ordinary—students who wish to know themselves and the world in a profound way. All of the following semester school programs manifest these same values in their own distinctive way.

CITYterm

CITYterm, founded in 1996, is an interdisciplinary, experience-based program that takes 30 juniors and seniors from across the country and engages them in a semester-long study of New York City. CITYterm students typically spend three days a week in the classroom, reading, writing, and thinking about New York City, and three days a week in the city working on projects, studying diverse neighborhoods, or meeting with politicians, urban historians, authors, artists, actors, and various city experts. Much of the excitement of CITYterm comes from experiencing firsthand in the city what has been studied in the classroom. Many of the projects are done in collaborative teams where the groups engage not only in formal academic research at the city's libraries but also use the resources of New York City's residents and institutions to gather the information necessary for presentations. Students come to see themselves as the active creators of their own learning both in the classroom and in the world. Learn more about CITYterm by visiting www.cityterm.org.

Conserve School

Conserve School is a semester school for high school juniors that is focused on the theme of environmental stewardship. Attending Conserve School gives high school students a one-semester opportunity to step out of their regular school and into a unique educational setting, while still continuing their required academic studies. Conserve School's challenging, college-prep curriculum immerses high school juniors in environmental history, nature literature, and the science of conservation. Because Conserve School is located on a 1,200-acre wilderness campus, a significant portion of the curriculum is delivered via outdoors, hands-on, active learning. Conserve School is located just west of Land O' Lakes, Wisconsin, near the border of Michigan's Upper Peninsula. Learn more about the Conserve School at www.conserveschool.org/.

The Island School

The Island School, founded in 1999 by The Lawrenceville School, is an independent academic program in the Bahamas for high school sophomores or juniors. The fourteen-week academic course of study includes honors classes in science, field research (a laboratory science), history, math, art, English literature, and physical/outdoor education and a weekly community service component. All courses are place-based and explicitly linked, taking advantage of the school's surroundings to both deepen understandings of complex academic and social issues and to make those understandings lasting by connecting course content with experience. Students apply their investigative, interpretive, and problem-solving skills during four- and eight-day kayaking expeditions, SCUBA diving opportunities, teaching environmental issues to local students, and in daily life at the school. In addition to traditional

classroom assessments, students conduct research on mangrove communities, coastal management, artificial reefs, permaculture, and marine protected areas. These projects support national research and are conducted under the auspices of the Bahamian government. At the conclusion of the semester, students present their work to a panel of visiting scientists and educators, including local and national government officials from the Bahamas. The opportunity to interact with the local community through research, outreach, and the rigorous physical and academic schedule creates a transformative experience for students. The admissions process is competitive, and selected students demonstrate solid academic performance, leadership potential, and a high degree of self-motivation. Contact The Island School for more information at www.islandschool.org.

Chewonki Semester School

The Chewonki Semester School (formerly Maine Coast Semester) offers a small group of eleventh-grade students the chance to live and work on a 400-acre saltwater peninsula with the goal of exploring the natural world through courses in natural science, environmental issues, literature and writing, art, history, mathematics, and foreign language. Since 1988, this semester school has welcomed students from more than 230 public and private schools across the country and in Canada. The Chewonki community is small—39 students and 20 faculty members—and the application process is competitive. In addition to their studies, students work for several hours each afternoon on an organic farm, in a wood lot, or on maintenance and construction projects. Students who attend are highly motivated, capable, and willing to take the risk of leaving friends and family for a portion of their high school career. They enjoy hard work, both intellectual and physical, and they demonstrate a tangible desire to contribute to the world. Chewonki students return to their schools with self-confidence, an appreciation for the struggles and rewards of community living, and an increased sense of ownership of their education. For information on the Chewonki Semester School, go to www.chewonki.org.

The High Mountain Institute Semester

The High Mountain Institute (HMI) Semester is a unique opportunity for juniors and some seniors in high school to spend a semester living, traveling, and studying in the mountains of central Colorado and the canyons of southeastern Utah. The school combines some of the best qualities of an academic program at a rigorous boarding school with the adventure of a summer backpacking expedition. The HMI Semester offers an honors and AP-level curriculum to prepare students to thrive during their senior year and in college. Courses are designed to match the content and rigor of the sending schools to ensure smooth transitions for HMI graduates. The High Mountain Institute is accredited by the Association of Colorado Independent Schools.

Interested students can learn more about The High Mountain Institute Semester at http://www.hminet.org/.

The Mountain School

The Mountain School of Milton Academy, founded in 1984, hosts 45 high school juniors from private and public schools throughout the United States who have chosen to spend four months on a working organic farm in Vermont. Courses provide a demanding and integrated learning experience, taking full advantage of the school's small size and mountain campus. Students and adults develop a social contract of mutual trust that expects individual and communal responsibility, models the values of simplicity and sustainability, and challenges teenagers to engage in meaningful work. Students live with teachers in small houses and help make important decisions concerning how to live together and manage the farm. Courses offered include English, environmental science, U.S. history, and all levels of math, physics, chemistry, Spanish, French, Latin, studio art, and humanities. To learn more, please visit the Web site at www. mountainschool.org.

The Outdoor Academy of the Southern Appalachians

The Outdoor Academy offers tenth-grade and select eleventh-grade students from across the country a semester away in the mountains of North Carolina. Arising from more than eighty years of experiential education at Eagle's Nest Foundation, this school-away-from-school provides a college-preparatory curriculum along with special offerings in environmental education, outdoor leadership, the arts, and community service. Each semester, up to 35 students embrace the Southern Appalachians as a unique ecological, historical, and cultural American region. In this setting, students and teachers live as a close-knit community, and lessons of cooperation and responsibility abound. Students develop a healthy work ethic as course work and projects are pursued both in and out of the classroom. Courses in English, mathematics, science, history, foreign language, visual and performing arts, and music emphasize hands-on and cooperative learning. Classes often meet outside on the 180-acre wooded campus or in nearby national wilderness areas, where the natural world enhances intellectual pursuits. On weekends and extended trips, the outdoor leadership program teaches hiking, backpacking, caving, canoeing, and rock-climbing skills. The Outdoor Academy is open to students from both public and private secondary schools and is accredited by the Southern Association of Colleges and Schools. Learn more about The Outdoor Academy at www.enf.org/outdoor_academy/.

The Oxbow School

The Oxbow School in Napa, California, is a one-semester visual arts program for high school juniors and seniors from public and private schools nationwide. Oxbow offers students a unique educational experience focused on in-depth study in sculpture, printmaking, drawing and painting, and photography and digital media, including animation. The interdisciplinary, project-based curriculum emphasizes experiential learning, critical thinking, and the development of research skills as a means of focused artistic inquiry. Each semester, 2 Visiting Artists are invited to work collaboratively with students and teachers. By engaging students in the creative process, Oxbow fosters a deep appreciation for creativity in all areas of life beyond the classroom. Since its founding in 1998, students who have spent a semester at The Oxbow School have matriculated to leading universities, colleges, and independent colleges of art and design around the country. Learn more at www.oxbowschool.org.

The Traveling School

Through The Traveling School (TTS), 15- to 18-year-old girls have the opportunity to go overseas for an academic semester that enables them experience the world and reconnect with their childhood curiosity of learning.

TTS Fall Semester programs run from the end of August through the beginning of December and alternate between South-East Africa and South-West Africa. The South-East Africa semester travels through Zambia, Mozambique, and South Africa. Starting on the

Zambian side of Victoria Falls, students and faculty journey through rural villages to the South Luangwa National Park. Students discover Mozambique's palm-fringed coasts, where they have the opportunity to earn their open water scuba certificates and experience small towns and colorful markets. In addition, students volunteer in schools, orphanages, and villages during the semester.

In the South-West Africa semester, students travel through South Africa, Namibia, and Botswana—exploring from the tip of Cape Horn to the Skeleton Coast in Namibia to the massive elephant herds in Botswana's Okavango Delta. Students stay with local families outside of Cape Town, hike Table Mountain, and meet with freedom fighters who helped to bring an end to Apartheid in South Africa. Students climb rocks, listen to African drums in ancient villages, help with service projects, and experience a river trip on the gentle Orange River between Namibia and South Africa.

TTS Spring semesters run from the start of February through mid-May in Central or South America. In Central America, students travel throughout Guatemala, Chiapas Mexico, and Nicaragua. Students visit ancient Mayan ruins, learn to scuba dive in the turquoise waters of the Corn Islands of Nicaragua, and try out surfing skills on the coast. Students have the opportunity to live in an indigenous community while doing service projects with a local woman's cooperative. In the alternating Spring Semester in South America, students travel through Ecuador, the Galapagos Islands, Peru, and Bolivia, with equally exciting adventures and learning opportunities.

Throughout the TTS semester, students take a full academic course load, including English, a foreign language, global studies, history, math, physical education, and science. The courses focus on the region where the students are traveling and are rigorous, relevant, and inspiring.

For more information on TTS, visit www.travelingschool.com.

The Woolman Semester School

The Woolman Semester School is a progressive academic school for young people who want to make a difference in the world. Students in their junior, senior, or gap year come for a "semester away" to take charge of their education and study the issues that matter most to them. Woolman students earn transferable high school credits while taking an active role in their learning experience through community work, organic gardening and cooking, permaculture, art, wilderness exploration, service work, and by doing advocacy and activism work with real issues of peace, justice, and sustainability in the world.

The academic foundation of the semester school consists of three core academic classes: Peace Studies, Environmental Science, and Global Issues as well as two academic electives, math (Algebra II and Pre-Calculus), and Spanish II and III. All students take Art, Nonviolent Communication, and Farm to Table classes. In addition, students who do not need math or Spanish may choose from nonacdemic electives, which are offered each semester. In the past, these courses have included Art as Activism, Wilderness Training, Permaculture, the History of American Music and others.

Three times a semester, Woolman learning goes on the road. The backpacking trip along the wild and scenic Yuba River orients students to the natural world that is Woolman's backyard. During the Food Intensive, students and teachers travel to the San Francisco Bay area and California's Central Valley for a week-long exploration of food systems as part of the Environmental Science curriculum. The Peace Studies–Global Issues trip integrates peace with social and environmental justice by traveling to the Bay area to connect with and learn from activists living what they believe.

Students at Woolman live and learn with their classmates and teachers exploring the 230 acres and the nearby Yuba River. They connect with environmental and peace organizations in the local communities of Grass Valley and Nevada City. Through their experience at Woolman, students become engaged citizens with skills to begin addressing issues of peace, social justice, and sustainability on a local and global scale.

For more information on The Woolman Semester School, visit http://semester.woolman.org/.

The author wishes to acknowledge and thank all the semester school programs for contributing their school profiles and collaborating in order to spread the word about semester school education.

Why a Therapeutic or Special Needs School?

Diederik van Renesse

Families contact me when a son or daughter is experiencing increased difficulties in school or has shown a real change in attitude at home. Upon further discussion, parents often share the fact that they have spoken with their child's teachers and have held meetings to establish support systems in the school and at home. Evaluations, medications, therapists, and motivational counseling are but a few of the multiple approaches that parents and educators take—yet in some cases, the downward spiral continues. Anxiety builds in the student and family members; school avoidance and increased family turmoil reach a point where the situation is intolerable, and alternatives must be explored—be it a special needs school, a therapeutic school, or a combination of both.

But should that school be a day or residential school, and how do parents decide which will best meet their child's needs? Resources such as *Peterson's Private Secondary Schools*, the Internet, guidance/school counselors, and therapists are valuable; however, the subtle nuances involved in determining the environment that will best serve the child are difficult to ascertain. Some families seek the help of an independent education consultant to identify the most appropriate setting. Many independent education consultants specialize in working with children who have special needs such as learning differences, anxiety disorders, emotional issues, ADHD, opposition, defiance, school phobia, drug or alcohol abuse, Asperger Syndrome, autism, and more. Consultants have frequent contact with the schools, and they

Some families seek the help of an independent education consultant to identify the most appropriate setting.

work closely with parents during the enrollment process.

Given the broad spectrum of needs presented by individual students, many parents question whether there is indeed a day school that can meet the needs of their child. The answer often depends on location, space availability, willingness to relocate, and appropriateness of the options. While there are many day school options throughout the United States, there are even more residential or boarding options. Clearly the decision to have your child attend a residential school is not made easily. As a family you may feel as though you do not have a choice—but you should undertake a thorough assessment of all the day options and how they might meet the majority of your child's needs.

When the primary concerns are learning differences, many local options (though often small and issue-specific) are available to families. Local counselors are often valuable resources as are local chapters of national LD organizations. If you come up with a variety of options, carefully compare them by visiting the schools and meeting with the specialists at each school—those individuals who will work directly with your child.

With the day options, it is important to keep the following factors in mind: program and staff credentials, transportation time to and from the school, availability of additional resources (support services) in or outside the school setting, sports and extracurricular offerings, facilities and accessibility, and your child's potential peer group. You will also need to assess many of these factors when considering residential schools, although most residential schools are more self-contained than day schools. Also significant is whether the school has been approved by and accepts funding from its state and/or school district.

For families who cannot avail themselves of local day options or whose child is best served in a residential setting, an even greater spectrum of options is available. These range from traditional boarding schools with built-in academic support services to therapeutic boarding schools, wilderness or outdoor therapeutic programs, emotional growth or behavior modification schools, transitional or independent living programs, and even residential treatment centers, hospitals, or other health facilities.

Given the breadth of the residential schools or programs, most families are best served by a team that includes not only the parents (and at times the student), but also the professionals who have taught, counseled, and worked closely with the child. Together, the team can identify the specific needs, deficits, or behavioral issues that must be addressed, and they can work together to match those with the appropriate schools. As with day schools, you should arrange to visit the facilities so that you are well-informed about each option and will be comfortable with your final decision. These visits are not only opportunities for you to meet the staff and students, but also for you and your child to begin a relationship that will continue when your child is enrolled.

There is no question that seeking alternative options, whether they are special needs or therapeutic, is a daunting task. However, with the help of expert resources and reliable professionals, the right school can make a significant and lasting impact on your child's health and well-being.

Diederik van Renesse is a Senior Partner at Steinbrecher & Partners Educational Consulting Services in Westport, Connecticut. A former teacher, admission director, and private school counselor, he now specializes in helping families throughout the United States and abroad with youngsters who require special needs or alternative schools or who need interventions and therapeutic settings.

Finding the Perfect Match

Helene Reynolds

One of the real benefits of independent education is that it allows you to deliberately seek out and choose a school community for your child. If you are like most parents, you want your child's school years to reflect an appropriate balance of academic challenge, social development, and exploration into athletics and the arts. You hope that through exposure to new ideas and sound mentoring your child will develop an awareness of individual social responsibility, as well as the study skills and work ethic to make a contribution to his or her world. It is every parent's fondest wish to have the school experience spark those areas of competence that can be pursued toward excellence and distinction.

An increasing number of parents realize that this ideal education is found outside their public school system, that shrinking budgets, divisive school boards, and overcrowded classrooms have resulted in schools where other agendas vie with education for attention and money. In this environment there is less time and energy for teachers to focus on individual needs.

The decision to choose a private school can be made for as many different reasons as there are families making the choice. Perhaps your child would benefit from smaller classes or accelerated instruction. Perhaps your child has needs or abilities that can be more appropriately addressed in a specialized environment. Perhaps you are concerned about the academic quality of your local public school and the impact it may have on your child's academic future. Or perhaps you feel that a private school education is a gift you can give your child to guide him or her toward a more successful future.

Every child is an individual, and this makes school choice a process unique to each family. The fact that your father attended a top-flight Eastern boarding school to prepare for the Ivy League does not necessarily make this educational course suitable for all of his grandchildren. In addition to determining the school's overall quality, you must explore the appropriateness of philosophy, curriculum, level of academic difficulty, and style before making your selection. The right school is the school where your child will thrive, and a famous name and a hallowed reputation are not necessarily the factors that define the right environment. The challenge is in discovering what the factors are that make the match between your child and his or her school the right one.

No matter how good its quality and reputation, a single school is unlikely to be able to meet the needs of all children. The question remains: How do families begin their search with confidence so they will find what they are looking for? How do they make the right connection?

As a parent, there are a number of steps you can follow to establish a reasoned and objective course of information gathering that will lead to a subjective discussion of this information and the way it applies to the student in question. This can only occur if the first step is done thoroughly and in an orderly manner. Ultimately, targeting a small group of schools, any of which could be an excellent choice, is only possible after information gathering and discussion have taken place. With work and a little luck, the result of this process is a school with an academically sound and challenging program based on an educational philosophy that is an extension of the family's views and which will provide an emotionally and socially supportive milieu for the child.

Step 1: Identify Student Needs

Often the decision to change schools seems to come out of the blue, but, in retrospect, it can be seen as a decision the family has been leading up to for some time. I would urge parents to decide on their own goals for the search first and to make sure, if possible, that they can work in concert toward meeting these goals before introducing the idea to their child. These goals are as different as the parents who hold them. For one parent, finding a school with a state-of-the-art computer program is a high priority. For another, finding a school with a full dance and music program is important. Others will be most concerned about finding a school that has the best record of college acceptances and highest SAT® or ACT® scores.

Once you have decided your own goals for the search, bring the child into the discussion. I often say to parents that the decision to explore is *not* the decision to change schools but only the decision to gather information and consider options. It is important to be aware that everyone has an individual style of decision making and that the decision to make a change is loaded with concerns, many of which will not be discovered until the process has begun.

If you have already made the decision to change your child's school, it is important to let your child know that this aspect of the decision is open to discussion but not to negotiation. It is equally important that you let your child know that he or she will have responsibility in choosing the specific school. Without that knowledge, your son or daughter may feel that he or she has no control over the course of his or her own life.

Some students are responsible enough to take the lead in the exploration; some are too young to do so. But in all cases, children need reassurance about their future and clarity about the reasons for considering other school settings. Sometimes the situation is fraught with disparate opinions that can turn school choice into a family battleground, one in which the child is the ultimate casualty. It is always important to keep in mind that the welfare of the child is the primary goal.

The knowledge that each individual has his or her own agenda and way of making decisions should be warning enough to pursue some preliminary discussion so that you, as parents, can avoid the pitfall of conflicting goals and maintain a united front and a reasonably directed course of action. The family discussion should be energetic, and differences of opinion should be encouraged as healthy and necessary and expressed in a climate of trust and respect.

There are many reasons why you may, at this point, decide to involve a professional educational consultant. Often this choice is made to provide a neutral ground where you and your child can both speak and be heard. Another reason is to make sure that you have established a sound course of exploration that takes both your own and your child's needs into consideration. Consultants who are up-to-date on school information, who have visited each campus, and who are familiar with

> *If you have already made the decision to change your child's school, it is important to let your child know that this aspect of the decision is open to discussion but not to negotiation.*

the situations of their clients can add immeasurably to the process. They can provide a reality check, reinforcement of personal impressions, and experience-based information support for people who are doing a search of this type for the first time. All the research in the world cannot replace the experience and industry knowledge of a seasoned professional. In addition, if the specific circumstances of the placement are delicate, the educational consultant is in a position to advocate for your child during the placement process. There are also situations in which a family in crisis doesn't have the time or the ability to approach school choice in a deliberate and objective manner.

These are some of the many reasons to engage the services of a consultant, but it is the family guidance aspect that most families overlook at the start of the process and value most highly after they have completed it. A good consultant provides neutral ground and information backup that are invaluable.

Step 2: Evaluate Your Child's Academic Profile

If your child's academic profile raises questions about his or her ability, learning style, or emotional profile, get a professional evaluation to make sure that your expectations for your child are congruent with the child's actual abilities and needs.

Start gathering information about your child from the current school. Ask guidance counselors and teachers for their observations, and request a formal meeting to review the standardized testing that virtually every school administers. Question their views of your child's behavior, attentiveness, and areas of strength and weakness. Make sure you fully understand the reasons behind their recommendations. Do not feel shy about calling back to ask questions at a later date, after you have had time to think and consider this important information. Your child's future may depend on the decisions you are making; don't hesitate to keep asking until you have the information you need.

If a picture of concern emerges, ask the guidance counselor, other parents, or your pediatrician for suggestions regarding learning specialists or psychologists in the community who work with children and can provide an evaluation of their academic ability, academic achievement, and learning style. The evaluation should be reviewed in-depth with the specialist, who should be asked about specific recommendations for changes in the youngster's schooling.

Remember, as the parent, it is ultimately your responsibility to weigh the ideas of others and to decide if the difficulty lies with your child or the environment, either of which could indicate a need for a change of school.

Step 3: Review the Goals of Placement

Discuss your differences of opinion about making a change. Identify a list of schools that creates a ballpark of educational possibilities. (An educational consultant can also be helpful at this stage.)

It is important that both you and your child take the time to consider what characteristics, large and small, you would like in the new school and which you would like to avoid. As you each make lists of priorities and discuss them, the process of school choice enters the subjective arena. The impersonal descriptions of school environments transform into very personal visualizations of the ways you and your child view the child in a new setting.

A chance to play ice hockey, a series of courses in Mandarin Chinese, the opportunity to take private flute lessons, or a desire to meet others from all over the world may sound like a bizarre mix of criteria, but the desire to explore and find all of these options in a single environment expresses the expansiveness of the student's mind and the areas he or she wants to perfect, try out, or explore. Don't expect perfectly logical thinking from your child as he or she considers options; don't take everything he or she says literally or too seriously. Open and respectful discussion will allow a child to embrace a new possibility one day and reject it the next—this is part of the process of decision making and affirmation and part of the fun of exploration.

Step 4: Set an Itinerary

Set an itinerary for visits and interviews so that you and your child can compare campuses and test your preconceived ideas of the schools you have researched against the reality of the campus community; forward standardized testing scores and transcripts to the schools prior to visits so that the admission office has pertinent information in advance of your meeting.

In order to allow your child the freedom to form opinions about the schools you visit, you may want to keep these pointers in mind:

- Parents should allow their child to be front and center during the visits and interviews—allow your child to answer questions, even if they leave out details you think are important.

- Parents should stay in the background and have confidence that the admission officers know how to engage kids in conversation.

- This may be the first time your child has been treated by a school as an individual and responsible person—enjoy watching him or her adjust to this as an observer, not as a protector or participant.

- Don't let your own anxiety ruin your child's experience.

- Discuss dress in advance so it doesn't become the issue and focus of the trip.

Keep your ideas and impressions to yourself and allow your child first shot at verbalizing opinions. Remember that immediate reactions are not final decisions; often the first response is only an attempt to process the experience.

Step 5: Use the Application Process for Personal Guidance

Make sure your child uses the application process not only to satisfy the school's need for information but also to continue the personal guidance process of working through and truly understanding his or her goals and expectations.

Application questions demand your child's personal insight and exploration. Addressing questions about significant experiences, people who have influenced his or her life, or selecting four words that best describe him or her are ways of coming to grips with who your child is and what he or she wants to accomplish both at the new school and in life. Although parents want their children to complete seamless and perfect applications, it is important to remember that the application must be the work of the child and that the parent has an excellent opportunity to discuss the questions and answers to help guide the student in a positive and objective self-review.

It is more important that the application essays accurately reflect the personality and values of the student than that they be technically flawless. Since the school is basing part of its acceptance decision on the contents of the application, the school needs to meet the real student in the application. The child's own determination of what it is important for the school to know about them is crucial to this process. That being said, parents can play an important role in helping the child understand the difference between unnecessarily brutal honesty and putting his or her best foot forward.

Step 6: Trust Your Observations

Although the process of school exploration depends on objectivity, it is rare that a family will embrace a school solely because of its computer labs, endowment, library, SAT or ACT scores, or football team. These objective criteria frame the search, but it tends to be the intangibles that determine the decision. It is the subjective—instinctive responses to events on campus, people met, quality of interview, unfathomable vibes—that makes the match.

It is important to review what aspects of the school environment made you feel at home. These questions apply equally to parent and child. Did you like the people you met on campus? Was the tour informational but informal, with students stopping to greet you or the tour guide? Was the tone of the campus (austere or homey, modern or traditional) consistent with the kind of educational atmosphere you are looking for? Are the sports facilities beyond your wildest expectation? Does the college-sending record give you confidence that your child will find an intellectually comfortable peer group? How long do the teachers tend to stay with the school, and do they send their own children there? If it is a boarding school, do teachers live on campus? How homey is the dorm setup?

The most fundamental questions are: Do people in the school community like where they are, trust each other, have respect for each other, and feel comfortable there? Is it a family you would care to join? These subjective responses will help you recognize which schools will make your child feel he or she is part of the community, where he or she will fit in and be respected for who he or she is and wants to become.

Helene Reynolds is a former educational consultant from Princeton, New Jersey.

Tips for a Successful School Search

You'd like to have your child attend a private school—but making that decision is just the first step on the process. From researching and touring, to applying and acceptance, there's a lot to consider along the way. Here are some things to keep in mind as you and your student head toward that exciting first day at a new school!

First of all, don't wait until the last minute. Searching and finding the right school for your student can be a lengthy process. Ideally, you should start searching at least a year before your student will be attending.

Research: Which Schools Do You Want to Consider and Why?

When it comes to private schools, there are hundreds to choose from and many options to consider. Day school or boarding school? A school that offers general college prep or one with a specific focus or specialty, whether it's the arts or athletics? Close to home or across the country? Co-ed or single-sex? What is your child's learning style? Answering some of these questions first will help narrow your search.

You may already have some schools in mind: those that you're familiar with because they're in your area or those that you've heard about from other families. Whether you're conducting a broad search or have a short list of possibilities, books like this one are a great place to start familiarizing yourself with what schools are available and what they have to offer.

Once you have identified some potential schools, start looking more closely at each one. A school's website is a great place to start; it can offer a wealth of information and pictures. You can also request a catalog and application packet from each school, too.

Tips from the Experts:

Be realistic about your child. Don't search in terms of bragging rights instead of your child's needs and abilities. Children are better served if their parents think about what their real needs are. How much pressure can they handle? What kind of structure does your child need?

~Elizabeth Norton, Director of Enrollment and Financial Aid, York Preparatory School

It is important to understand the strengths and weaknesses of your child in order to be able to do the appropriate research and make the most suitable decision on the right school for your family.

~Dr. Douglas Laurie, Vice President, American Heritage School

Students must first determine if the school's academic curriculum is in line with their personal goals. Next, students should consider the school's culture and its values, from daily activities to annual celebrations.

~Emily McKee, Associate Director of Admissions, TASIS The American School in Switzerland

Don't just look at test scores or lists of colleges that the school's students go on to. That doesn't really tell you about the school.

~Susan Grodman, Director of Enrollment and Global Programs, Derryfield School

A year, or even a semester, abroad can be a life-enhancing experience, broadening a student's world perspective as well as helping their college application stand out. You may want to look for an international school with an academic program that complements your child's current curriculum to ease the transition in both directions.

~Karen House, Director of Admissions, TASIS The American School in England

The biggest mistake families can make is creating their list of schools based only on perceived prestige. This process is not about brand names; it is about fit. Being a big fish in a small pond might provide the right student with a needed burst of confidence during these developmentally critical years, and it might be a better choice than ending up at a school where the child might struggle for four years.

~Beth Whitney, Director of Admission, Fay School, Southborough, MA

Visiting: See for Yourself

A website or brochure can only convey so much—if at all possible, you and your child need to visit each school you're considering in person. Most schools have special visit days for prospective families several times throughout the year. If you're not able to make it to a specific event, schedule an appointment to check out the school in person.

Be prepared for the visit. Review the school's website and materials. Write down any questions you may have. Are there specific things you and your student want to see, such as a particular sports facility, dormitory rooms, or the concert hall?

Will your student be interviewed during the visit? If so, help them prepare by practicing answering questions that they might be asked, such as why they want to attend the school or what their educational goals are for the future. Encourage them to relax and be themselves.

Take part in as much as possible during your visit: tours, presentations from administrators and teachers, question and answer sessions, other activities, meals, etc. Take notes about your observations.

Tips from the Experts:

Visit! The best way to know if you have found your home is to experience the place firsthand. It is difficult to differentiate schools on paper or on screen, and visits give students the opportunity to experience classes, extracurricular activities, and, perhaps most importantly, the school's culture and vibe.

~Emily McKee, Associate Director of Admissions, TASIS–The American School in Switzerland

Be open-minded when looking at schools. Don't dismiss a school because you think it might be too rigid, or not athletic enough, or too large, and so on. It could prove to be just right once you actually visit and see it firsthand.

~Sharon Levin, Head of School, Jack M. Barack Hebrew Academy

We host Open Houses two times each year for prospective families, and we also encourage people to schedule a personal tour. We believe that by visiting our campus and seeing firsthand the diversity of our curriculum and the energy of our student body, a family will better understand our school's philosophy and vision so as to make an informed decision whether our school is the right fit for their child.

~Dr. Douglas Laurie, Vice President, American Heritage School

If possible, don't just come for the official tour and the interview. Come to other events, like concerts or ball games, and talk to other parents. Observe the students, too.

~Susan Grodman, Director of Enrollment and Global Programs, Derryfield School

On a campus visit, focus on your feelings and impressions. This is a time for you to "smell" the school's culture and not concern yourself with facts and figures. Before you arrive, read the school's mission and ask your hosts to describe how the school fulfills that mission.

~Tom Sheppard, Dean of Admission and Financial Aid, Lawrenceville School

What would it actually be like to go to this school, to be a member of this learning community? Only by walking around the campus, talking with students and teachers, and observing school life firsthand can this question begin to be answered in an authentic way.

~Beth Whitney, Director of Admission, Fay School

It's Time to Apply

After the research, tours, visits, interviews, and conversations with administrators and teachers at the various schools, you have a lot of information to consider. Your field of possibilities may have been narrowed to just one or two, or you may still have several choices.

Weigh all the options involved: academics, extracurricular activities, size, financial viability, transportation expenses, distance, and so on. Don't forget that important, but vague quality known as "fit." You may just have a gut feeling that a certain school is right—or wrong—for your student.

Then you and your child need to carefully fill out and submit all the required forms and materials for the school or schools that top your list. In addition to the

> *Most schools have January or February deadlines, so it pays to begin filling out forms in November.*

application, schools may request the student's academic records, references from teachers, a student statement, a writing sample or essay, an application fee, and medical history. Some or all of this may be completed and submitted online.

Most schools have deadlines in January or February for the academic year that starts the following fall, so gathering materials and references and filling out the forms should be underway in November.

Tips from the Experts:

One of the biggest mistakes people make when applying is not meeting deadlines or thinking they don't matter. Deadlines are there for a reason; they help both the school and student plan and be prepared. For instance, if a student needs a little help in a certain subject area they can work on that over the summer.

~Jen Groen, Director of Admissions and Strategic Engagement, Jack M. Barack Hebrew Academy

Deadlines are important for many reasons, but perhaps the biggest reason is basic respect. When a student meets all deadlines in the application process, it's a sign that the decision to apply has been well thought-out and that the applicant's family is serious about wanting to join the school community. When the deadlines aren't met, the admission officer is left asking him or herself "Will this child be able to turn in his homework on time at our school next year?" On the other hand, if you learn of a school after the deadline has passed, call the school to find out if applying late is an option. Many schools will welcome a late application if there is still space available in that grade.

~Beth Whitney, Director of Admission, Fay School

Narrowing choices to a manageable and realistic number is most important, along with utilizing common applications, which teachers who are writing recommendations will appreciate. Admissions offices are a helpful resource to ensure students are presenting their best selves. Also, deadlines are critical, and they vary from school to school. Organization is key to ensuring applications are received on time, especially at schools where space is limited.

~Emily McKee, Associate Director of Admissions, TASIS–The American School in Switzerland

While children should have input on the decision, it's okay for parents to make the final call.

~Sharon Levin, Head of School, Jack M. Barack Hebrew Academy

The application process can feel arduous, but seize it as an opportunity for the student to reflect on him or herself as a learner and as a person. Find moments for the whole family to bask in the child's stories of those challenges overcome and accomplishments celebrated that go into the application. And in the end, remember that all of your efforts will end up significantly enhancing the life of the student by matching him/her to an amazing school.

~Beth Whitney, Director of Admission, Fay School

The Decision

Much as you may want your student to attend a particular school, once you've applied, the decision is not yours to make. Sometimes a school will say yes and everyone will be happy, but other times, the answer is no.

Realistically, private schools can't admit every student who applies. It's important to remind your child that being turned down by a school is not a statement about his or her worth. You need to be gracious and look at other possibilities; perhaps reconsidering another school on your list or looking at other choices.

If you apply and your student is accepted at more than one school, then you need to make a final decision and notify the schools that the student chooses not to attend, so their spot could be given to another student.

Tips from the Experts:

A good fit is a two-way street. The school has to be right for the student, and the student has to be right for the school.

~Jen Groen, Director of Admissions and Strategic Engagement, Jack M. Barack Hebrew Academy

We work hard to be honest when families might not be a good fit for the school and even suggest ways to help a student possibly gain admission down the road.

~Susan Grodman, Director of Enrollment and Global Programs, Derryfield School

With any luck, you have been accepted to more than one school . . . and they're all great choices because you pre-screened them before even applying. So at this point, follow your gut. And the corollary is also true: don't ignore your gut.

~Beth Whitney, Director of
Admission, Fay School

A Final Thought

The search for the right private school requires time and effort, but the end result—finding the school that fits your child and his or her needs—is worth it. And there's another benefit. You'll be practiced and prepared when it's time to go through this same process and search for colleges in just a few years!

Admissions Applications for Private Secondary Schools

Tom Sheppard

Dean of Admissions and Financial Aid
Lawrenceville School
Lawrenceville, New Jersey

Enrollment at an independent secondary school is one of the most important educational decisions a family can make. The process of finding the school (or schools) that will be the most appropriate educational fit for any child takes on many dimensions including an application process that can be time consuming and lengthy. However, with careful planning and an understanding of a few important considerations, this process can also serve as important means for parents and children to reflect upon the educational needs of the child.

The most significant development in the application process for secondary schools in recent years has been the integration of technology into what had been a paper-driven process. Advances in technology have enabled the application process for independent schools to evolve rapidly, and, in numerous ways, some of these advances have proven to be helpful to the applicant and their families. At the same time, some developments have resulted in additional challenges and options that the applicant must navigate throughout the application process.

With each passing year, the admission process at secondary schools continues its transition from a paper-based process to a digital process. As this transition continues, more and more schools have adopted at least one form of a digital application to replace or parallel any paper applications that were previously accepted. To complicate matters, there are several applications that are common to many schools, but no application is uni-versally accepted by all independent schools. Some commonly utilized application processes include the following:

- Standard Application Online by SSAT (SAO)—Accepted by over 500 boarding and day schools (http://www.ssat.org/admission/the-sao)
- Gateway to Prep Schools—Accepted by 60 boarding schools (https://www.gatewaytoprepschools.com)
- TABS Admission Application--PDF Application forms accepted by many boarding schools (http://www.boardingschools.com/

Besides the above noted options, families may discover that clusters of schools offer regionally accepted applications or common recommendation forms that are used in an effort to reduce duplication of efforts among teachers who write numerous letters of recommendation.

The variety of application options and the lack of a single application that is common to all independent schools have resulted in an application process that may require extra time and research on the part of families applying to independent schools. In addition, due dates for applications and other required materials can vary widely. The cumulative effect of the various possible application pathways and due dates is that families will be well served and best able to manage the application process with forethought and attention to detail. Whether or not time and advances in technology bring greater clarity and uniformity to this process remains to be seen.

While any one application may have its own unique requirements, applications often include:

- A request for biographical information
- One or more student essays or short answer questions
- One or more recommendations to be completed by teachers or others who know the applicant
- A transcript request form
- that the applicant submits to his or her current school
- An interview with any school to which a student is applying
- Submission of standardized testing required by the schools

The exact type of testing required can vary widely depending upon region and grade level. Many secondary schools utilize the Secondary School Admission Test (SSAT) and/or the Independent School Entrance Exam (ISEE). These same schools may also accept the PSAT/

NMSQT® or the SAT® for older students. Ultimately, the exact nature of the testing that is part of any application process should be clearly explained on a school's website. Unfortunately, since there is no universal test that covers all grades and all areas of the country, there may be instances in which the list of schools to which a family decides to apply is limited by time available to take one or more required tests.

If the above variables seem like they would make the application process a daunting one, be assured it does not need to be. In an attempt to demystify this process, it may be helpful to hear directly from educational consultants and placement directors who have helped thousands families to successfully navigate the secondary school application process for many years.

What advice would you give to students and parents who are beginning the application process to secondary schools for the first time?

Jennifer Evans and Brady Weinstock, Educational Consultants, Virginia Bush and Associates (www.virginiabush.com):

Take the time to do the process right. It is a process to determine the right school fit for you and your child. Investigate schools on their websites to help define your choices. Make appointments to tour and interview on the campuses. Learn from the tour guides, and meet with the admissions officers to best discover what is right for you and your child. When visiting schools, observe the teacher/student interaction on campuses. Reflect on the campus cultures and offerings. Notice the sense of structure and community. Then try to relate that to your own values and set of expectations and goals for your child's future.

There are many extraordinary school options with extremely passionate teachers who are fully dedicated to enriching children's lives every day. Finding the school that is going to best maximize your child's learning process—socially, emotionally and academically—is the key to his or her future success.

The families with whom we work look back on this journey and are amazed at their child's growth and development throughout the process. Students begin to take ownership and gain a sense of inde-

Using a common application makes the process of applying to multiple schools a much more manageable endeavor.

pendence and autonomy while writing their applications, talking to friends, and visiting and interviewing at the schools. It is a time in life when students are given this amazing opportunity to learn, explore, grow, and self-reflect. If the process is done correctly, it can be a transformational experience. Furthermore it gives students the advantage of gaining so much maturity and perspective about themselves and the world around them. This journey of self-discovery is a wonderful asset to have when entering a new school.

Fran Ryan, Assistant Headmaster and Director of Secondary School Placement, Rumsey Hall School:

Whether a family has professional guidance throughout the process or not, the parents must make the decision about the list of schools to which a child may apply. If the parents are relatively satisfied with any of the schools on the list, then the child can, hopefully, choose from among those schools. By framing the process in this way, the parents are secure in any of the school choices, and the child completely owns the decision in the end.

How can families manage the application process since there isn't one application that can work for all schools?

Cammie Bertram, Educational Consultant, The Bertram Group (http://thebertramgroup.com):

As a result of the confusion associated with secondary school applications, many of our candidates approach the process with fear rather than enthusiasm. Our families struggle to determine which application will be the "right" one to file in order for their sons or daughters to present themselves in the most positive light.

SSATB's most recent parental survey featured in *The Ride to Independent Schools* (http://admission.org/whytheyapply) reports that parents of students attending boarding schools tend to experience the highest level of anxiety about the application process. Our goal is for our candidates to take pride in creating their individual profiles and in developing their unique personal stories and essays. Our team strives to simplify the process to allow our students to maintain their busy lifestyles in and out of the classroom yet still devote quality time to the application process one step at a time—a delicate balance.

At The Bertram Group we believe that streamlining the method by which our candidates apply to schools has significantly reduced the amount of anxiety associated with filing applications. Because most schools now accept the SAO and/or Gateway forms, there is no longer an emphasis on completing individual schools' applications. However, there still are some institutions that continue to require candidates to submit their own application forms.

We encourage our families to navigate the application process in a manner that best suits their child's learning style. It is often helpful to print out the forms and supplements and create a roadmap so the candidate knows how to target the questions and then discuss what to emphasize in his or her answers. Clustering similar essay topics and then choosing a different opening or closing paragraph often serves as a way to modify an essay so it can be used more than once. Candidates should be well acquainted with the schools to which they are applying and be able to echo themes of importance in their essays. Their interests and accomplishments should dovetail with the philosophy of the schools to which they are applying. We encourage our students to demonstrate how they can be contributors on every level throughout the application process. At the end of the day we want this chapter in our children's lives to be a healthy and rewarding experience.

Jennifer Evans and Brady Weinstock, Educational Consultants, Virginia Bush and Associates:

Take a deep breath! Be organized. This part of the process is difficult to navigate. Everything in this part of the process varies—from application deadlines, to the essays, to the parent statements, to the supplements, and to the teacher recommendations.

Make a chart of which schools take which applications: Most schools list which applications they accept in the How to Apply section of their website, but some do not show all of the options. Calling the schools is the most accurate way to determine which applications they take, if the website does not make it explicitly clear. Parents can also look

directly on the SSAT website for schools that accept the SAO application and on the Gateway to Prep Schools site for member schools. Some schools do not use a common application but will often accept common recommendation forms. Contact the schools directly for information on which forms to use. You may also be able to use the TABS application for TABS member schools.

Once you have chosen which applications to use, you will need to sort out the requirements and recommendations. Again, refer to the How to Apply pages on the schools' websites for instructions, as well as the pages on Gateway and SAO for each school where applicable. Creating a chart of required and optional items to submit will help keep things clear and organized—and we highly recommend doing this!

In the end, the application process may require an investment of time and effort on the part of families interested in independent schools. At the same time this investment will be more likely to ensure that children enroll at an independent school well suited for their educational needs. As a result of such a careful and detailed process, these same schools are well positioned to effectively serve families and provide an important option in today's educational landscape that includes more options than ever before.

About Admission Tests and the SSAT

Heather Hoerle
Executive Director
Secondary School Admission Test Board (SSATB)

Mention the word "testing" to even the most capable student, and he or she is likely to become anxious. It's no wonder, then, that testing in the independent school admission process causes nail-biting among students and parents alike.

It is important to remember, though, that results of admission testing, while integral to an application, are just one of many factors considered by admission officers when determining if your child and their schools make a great match. The degree of emphasis placed on scores depends on the school and on other information, such as the transcript and teacher recommendations. For the vast majority of schools, students with a wide range of SSAT scores are admitted.

The most important thing to remember about admission tests is that they are different from other kinds of tests. Admission tests, while "standardized," are different from aptitude and achievement tests. A classroom math test, for example, is an achievement test: The teacher specifically designed it to evaluate how much you know about what has been covered in class. The SSAT, on the other hand, is designed to measure the verbal, quantitative, and reading skills you have acquired over time, instead of focusing on your mastery of particular course materials. The SSAT provides independent school admission professionals with meaningful information about the possible academic success of

> *It's important to remember that results of admission testing, while integral to an application, are just one of many factors considered by admission officers.*

potential students like you at their institutions, regardless of students' background or experience.

Admission tests are also different from classroom and achievement tests, because they are "norm-referenced." This means that your child's score is interpreted relative to the group of students taking the test (the *norm group*). For example, if you are a student in the sixth grade, and your percentile rank on the SSAT verbal section is 70 percent, it means that 70 percent of all the other sixth-grade students' (who have taken the test for the first time on one of the students' Standard SSAT administrations in the USA and Canada in the last three years) verbal scaled scores fall below your scaled score. Therefore, the same scaled score on the SSAT may have a different percentile rank from year to year. In contrast, your percent correct from a classroom math test is 90 percent because you answered 90 percent of the questions correctly. Your score is not referenced to the performance of anyone else in your class.

Finally, admission tests are constructed so that only about half of the examinees will get the average test question correct. This is so that the test will effectively differentiate among test-takers, who vary in their level of skills. Therefore, "average" on the SSAT (50 percent) is different than "average" on your child's math test. Many parents express concern that their child's SSAT percentile is lower than they typically score on other tests such as standardized achievement tests and school exams. It is important to remember that SSAT test takers are members of a small and highly competitive group of students who plan to attend some of the world's best private/independent schools. Being in the middle of this group is still impressive!

Taking the SSAT

There are three levels of the SSAT administered. The Upper Level is administered to students in grades 8–12. The Middle Level is administered to grades 5–7, and the Elementary Level is administered to grades 3 and 4. The Middle and Upper Level exams are both approximately 3 hours in length, while the Elementary Level test is just short of 2 hours. Each test has verbal, reading, and quantitative sections that are constructed in a multiple-choice format, as well as an unscored writing sample.

The two mathematics sections of the Middle and Upper Level SSAT measure a student's knowledge of algebra, geometry, and other quantitative concepts and consists of two 25-question sections. The Elementary Level SSAT test measures knowledge of elementary arithmetic, algebra, and geometry in one 30-minute, 30-question section.

The reading comprehension section of the test measures a student's ability to understand what they have read. After reading a passage, the student will be asked questions about its content or about the author's style, intent, or point of view. The goals are to discern the main idea of the piece, to identify the important details that move the narrative along or create a mood or tone, or to identify the details that support the writer's opinion. The Upper and Middle level tests contain 40 questions, while the Elementary Level test consists of 28 reading comprehension questions.

The verbal section asks students to identify synonyms and interpret analogies. The synonym questions test the strength of the student's vocabulary, while the analogy questions measure a student's ability to relate ideas to each other logically. The Upper and Middle Level SSATs consist of 60 verbal questions, while the Elementary Level test has just 30 verbal section questions.

In addition, the exams contain a writing sample that is not scored but is provided to schools to offer a sense of the student's writing skills. The writing sample section varies based on the level of test. The Upper and Middle Level SSATs offer a choice of two writing prompts. In the Upper Level SSAT, one prompt is a creative prompt and the other an essay prompt. On the Middle Level exam, both are creative prompt choices. The Elementary Level exam offers a picture, and the student must write a story about what is happening in the picture.

There are two types of SSAT test administrations: Standard and Flex. The Standard administrations are given eight Saturdays during the academic year (October, November, December, January, February, March, April, and June) at various test locations around the world. Students also have the option of "on demand" Flex testing through member schools and educational consultants. Students can take up to all eight of the Standard tests, but they may only take the Flex test once.

Test takers can arrange to have SSAT scores sent to different schools and have the option to select school score recipients either during test registration or after receiving their scores. Students can learn more about the test, research schools, find a test center, and register for the SSAT online at ssat.org or by calling 609-683-4440. In addition, students can order the *Official Guide to the SSAT* for the Middle and Upper Level tests. *The Official Guide to the SSAT* is the only study guide written by the SSAT test development team. *The Official Guide to*

the Elementary Level SSAT is available for free download on ssat.org.

SSAT.org also offers a wealth of resources for the independent school applicant, including free webinars, advice on the process, and an online application that can make applying to schools much easier.

How is the SSAT Scored?

The SSAT uses a method of scoring known in the testing industry as "formula scoring." Students earn one point for every correct answer, receive no points for omitted questions, and lose ¼ point for each incorrect answer (each question has five choices). This is different from "right scoring," which computes the total score by counting the number of correct answers, with no penalty for incorrect answers. Formula scoring is used to remove the test taker's expected gain from random guessing.

Test takers are instructed to omit questions for which they cannot make an educated guess. Since most students have not encountered this kind of test before, it is an important concept for students to understand and have some experience with prior to taking the SSAT. SSAT score reports provide detailed information by section on the number of questions right, wrong, and not answered to aid families and schools in understanding the student's test-taking strategy and scores.

> *The SSAT is designed to measure the verbal, quantitative, and reading skills you have acquired over time.*

How Important Are the Tests?

The SSAT norm group is a highly competitive group. Your child is being compared to all the other students (same grade and same grade/gender) who are taking this test for admission into independent schools—some of which can be the most selective schools in the world. I can assure you, though, that in 100 percent of independent schools, the test is just one part of the selection process. This is vital for students and families to remember, as it relieves the "test-taking pressure" we've read so much about in the media and heard from families, teachers, and the educational community. Admission officers are tasked with finding the right students that not only fit the academic pace of their school, but also the culture and community that is unique to each independent school environment. The SSAT is not designed to measure other characteristics such as motivation, persistence, or creativity that a student may contribute to a particular school's community environment.

That said, parents should be partners in the test-preparation process, both as tutors and reassuring voices for the student. This same relationship should extend to partnering with your student to submit an application that highlights a student's schoolwork portfolios and other academic achievements, recommendations, and

elements that are just as critical to the selection process. Remember, admission officers must find applicants that are the right academic AND social/cultural fit for their school. The SSAT can only assist in determining one element of this process.

Heather Hoerle's career began in independent schools as an administrator, student advisor, and teacher at George School (Newtown, PA) and Westtown School (Westchester, PA). She then embarked on a successful 23-year tenure in leadership roles with two of the world's largest nonprofit independent school associations: first as associate director of The Association of Boarding Schools (TABS), then as director of admission and marketing services for The National Association of Independent Schools (NAIS), leading to a vice presidency at NAIS overseeing membership, corporate affiliations, customer service, and the annual NAIS Conference.

Heather holds a B.A. in art history from Mount Holyoke College and a M.Ed. in educational administration from Harvard University. She has been a board member for Westtown School (her alma mater) and is presently a trustee for the National Business Officers Association, Princeton Academy of the Sacred Heart, and New Jersey Association of Independent Schools. Heather currently resides in Hopewell, New Jersey with her husband; she has one daughter, a student at Skidmore College.

10 Tips for Doing Your Best on the SSAT

1. Practice, practice, practice—early!

For the SSAT, just like other standardized tests, if you practice, you will feel more confident that you'll do well. Purchase the *Official Guide to the SSAT* a couple of months before you plan to take the test, if possible.

2. Read—a lot!

The best way to build your vocabulary and to get a better sense for the meanings of unfamiliar words is to see them in the context of other words.

3. If you know you're weak in a particular subject, get help before you take the test.

If you know that math is your weakest subject, make sure you address it as soon as you can. Begin early and practice every day if possible until your skills improve. Look to teachers, tutors, or your parents for advice and assistance.

4. Be prepared.

The night before the test, gather everything you need: your admission ticket, pencils, a snack, and so on. This will allow you time in the morning to eat a healthy breakfast and review, if necessary.

5. Get a good night's rest.

We can't stress enough the importance of trying to relax and get plenty of sleep the night before your exam.

6. Arrive at the test center early on test day and come prepared.

Arrive 30 minutes early. Be sure to have your admission ticket, three #2 pencils, a snack in a clear plastic bag, and water. Leave your cell phone and backpack at home, if possible!

7. Relax!

Your attitude and outlook will be reflected in the outcome of the test. Stay confident and calm throughout your exam. If you start to feel nervous or anxious, take a few deep breaths to collect yourself.

8. Set a pace.

Don't spend too much time on one question, and don't speed through carelessly. If you get stuck on a question, skip it, and return to it later if you have time—be sure to leave the bubble unmarked on your answer sheet for this question! Read each question carefully, and answer accurately.

9. Remember your test-taking strategy!

You receive one point for every correct answer and lose ¼ of a point for each wrong answer on a question. You don't lose points by skipping a question. If you can't eliminate at least one or two of the choices in a question and take an "educated guess," it's better to leave the question unanswered. This strategy can help you receive the highest possible score.

10. Remember: The SSAT is one piece of the admission picture!

The SSAT is just one piece of your admission application. Schools will look at your grades, recommendations, test scores, your interview, and more to decide if you are a fit for their school.

Good luck!

About the Independent School Entrance Exam (ISEE)

Elizabeth Mangas

Vice President, Admission Testing
Educational Records Bureau (ERB)

If you have chosen to take the ISEE or a school to which you are applying requires it, we want you to know as much as possible about our admission test. We understand that there is often much anxiety involved in testing, but knowledge about the makeup of the test may help to ease your concerns. In the following paragraphs, we will try to summarize information about the ISEE. However, a very detailed description of the test may be found on our website, www.iseetest.org, under "Preparing for the ISEE." There you will see preparation guides called *What to Expect on the ISEE* that are available to you at no cost online. By looking at these guides, you will have a clear idea of the types of items in each section, a full practice test, sample essays, a copy of an actual answer sheet, and other important components of the test.

Modalities and Availability

You may take the ISEE either as a paper-and-pencil test or online. In 42 cities in the United States, groups of schools have joined together to offer the ISEE on a variety of testing dates. They also offer it on some dates before and after the busy part of the admission season. To see which schools offer the test online, check the website mentioned in the previous paragraph.

You may also take an online ISEE at a Prometric Test Center. Prometric is a subsidiary of ETS and has testing centers in over 400 cities in both the United States and abroad. For more information, visit our website.

Levels and Content

There are four levels on the ISEE: Primary, Lower, Middle, and Upper. The Lower Level is for entrance to grades 5 and 6, Middle Level for entrance to grades 7 and 8, and Upper Level for entrance to grades 9–12. Each of these levels contains four multiple choice sections and an essay, which is unscored.

Two of the multiple choice sections, Verbal Reasoning and Quantitative Reasoning, measure your capability for learning a subject. The Reading Comprehension and Mathematics Achievement multiple choice sections provide a school with specific information about your strengths and weaknesses in these areas. The essay is not scored and is meant to show schools how well you write in response to an essay prompt appropriate for your age.

Even more specifically, the **Verbal Reasoning** section consists of two types of items: vocabulary (synonyms) and sentence completion. The **Quantitative Reasoning** consists of word problems, and for the Middle and Upper levels, quantitative comparisons. The **Reading Comprehension** section consists of reading passages and questions specific to those passages. For example, you may be asked to find the main idea of the passage or inferences that may be made from the author's choice of words. The **Mathematics Achievement** section consists of items that require one or more steps in calculating the answer. These items may cover topics such as algebraic concepts, decimals, and measurement.

Again, it is best to go to the *What to Expect on the ISEE* guide books on our website to see specific examples of ISEE test items and essay questions. You will feel much more comfortable when you sit down to take the ISEE if you do this.

Timing

The Lower Level test is 2 hours 20 minutes in length, and the Middle and Upper level tests are 2 hours 40 minutes in length. The essay section for all three levels is 30 minutes. Once "time" is called, you may not return to a completed section. There is a 5-minute warning before the end of each of the multiple-choice sections, and there is both a 15-minute and a 5-minute warning in the essay section. There are two 5-minute breaks, one after the second section of the test and one after the fourth section.

Non-Standard Administrations

We make every effort to arrange ISEE administrations to accommodate you if you are unable to take the ISEE under standard conditions because of a documented learning difference or physical challenge and you are given accommodations in your current school. Detailed instructions and requirements for seeking approval for accommodations may be found at www.iseetest.org under "ISEE," then "Accommodations."

Parent/Student Portal

You and your family will be able use a portal that is accessed with a password to find test site locations, register for the test, make changes to your registration, and order special services such as expedited score reports.

Scoring

The schools you have selected when you register for the test will generally receive your ISEE score reports electronically within 48 hours of the scoring process. Your family will not receive a copy of your essay because of the security of our essay prompts. The schools will receive a copy of your essay along with your ISEE score report.

You will receive credit only for correct answers. There are no points taken off for incorrect answers.

Your score on each section of the ISEE is based on a pool of students in your same grade who have taken the ISEE over the past three years—the ISEE norming population. Therefore, remember that you are not being compared to the children who took the test at your test site or other students who tested the same day. You should keep in mind that students taking the ISEE are also applying to independent schools and that they tend to be a select and possibly higher achieving group than those who take tests with a wider norming population. Therefore, your scores may be as much as 20 to 40 percentile points lower than you are used to receiving on nationally normed tests. The schools to which you are applying are aware of this difference.

You may ask to have score reports sent to extra schools after you have tested. Your registration includes the sending of score reports to six schools plus your family.

You may wonder what a "good" or "bad" score is. These terms are relative and may only be determined by the specific school looking at your score report.

Fee waivers

Fee waivers are available to cover the cost of an ISEE at a school or a Prometric site. These waivers are granted

by a school's admission office, not by Educational Records Bureau (ERB).

Testing Policy

Identification for a tester is required at check-in on the day of testing. If a student's identity is in question before, during, or after the exam, ERB will not release test scores and reserves the right to investigate the matter at the expense of the family. ERB may, at is discretion, disclose the results of any such investigation to the schools to which the test results were to be sent and to all appropriate government regulators.

How Schools Use Your Information

It is important to remember that each school to which you are applying will use other information about you, besides your ISEE scores, as they evaluate your application. This information may include your transcript, teacher recommendations, scores from other standardized tests, and lists of extracurricular activities and interests. Most important, they will be considering *you*, the person they met at an open house, at a day visit, and/or at an interview. You are the most important part of the admission process.

> *Keep your perspective and remember that the schools will be looking at many items in your application folder—not just your ISEE scores.*

Other Important Information

When using the ISEE as your admission test of choice, please remember the following:

- Test sites and Prometric sites fill up rapidly *and are on a first-come, first-served basis.*
- The test-preparation guides called *What to Expect on the ISEE* are your best preparation for the test. They are online, free of charge, and contain answers to just about everything you ever wanted to know about the test. (You may purchase a copy for $20 if you wish.)
- Check the Verification Letter you will receive after you register for the test. It will be your admission ticket on the day of the test along with some personal identification, such as a library card, passport, or green card. The Verification Letter will give you details about the address of the school, the arrival time for the test, and the start time. You don't want to arrive late for the test.

- *If you are taking a paper-based test*, make sure to bring two #2 pencils for the multiple choice sections and a blue or black pen for the essay. (You may use an erasable pen.) You may also bring a light snack for the two 5-minute breaks.
- Get a good night's sleep the night before, and eat a regular, healthy breakfast that morning.
- Keep your perspective and remember that the schools will be looking at many items in your application folder—not just your ISEE scores.

We wish you the best of luck in the admission process. If you have any questions about registering, please call 800-446-0320 (toll-free). If you have any questions about your score reports, please feel free to call 800-989-3721, Ext. 2620.

ERB (Educational Records Bureau) is a global not-for-profit organization providing admission and achievement assessment as well as instructional services for PreK–Grade 12. For over 85 years, and with over 2,000 member schools and districts around the world, ERB continues to be a trusted source to inform admission decisions and/or to support curriculum and instruction. Collaborating with both independent and public schools around the world to build communities, guide instruction, and put assessment insights into action, ERB is dedicated to supporting student learning.

Paying for a Private School Education

Mark J. Mitchell

Vice President, School and Student Services
National Association of Independent
Schools (NAIS)

Imagine being able to buy a $23,000 car for $12,000 because that is all you can afford. When you buy a car, you know that you will be paying more than it cost to design, build, ship, and sell the car. The sales staff will not offer you a price based on your income. At best, you may receive discounts, rebates, or other incentives that allow you to pay the lowest price the dealer is willing to accept. No matter how you look at it, you pay more than the car cost to make.

Tuition at many private schools can approach the cost of a new car, but paying for a private school education is not the same as buying a car. One difference is the availability of financial aid at thousands of schools in the United States and abroad. Financial aid helps offset the cost of tuition. Learning about the financing options and procedures available can make private school a reality for many families.

Need-Based Financial Aid

Many private schools offer assistance to families who demonstrate financial need. In fact, for a recent academic year, schools that belonged to the National Association of Independent Schools (NAIS) provided more than $2 trillion in need-based financial aid to more than 24 percent of their students. For 2015–16, the median grant for boarding school students was $31,363 and the median grant for day school students was $12,753. These need-based grants do not need to be repaid and are used to offset the school's tuition. Schools make this substantial commitment as one way of ensuring a socio-economically diverse student body and to help ensure that every student qualified for admission has the best chance to enroll, regardless of his or her financial circumstances.

How Financial Need Is Determined

Many schools use a process of determining financial need that requires the completion of applications and the submission of tax forms and other documentation to help them decide how much help each family needs. Currently, more than 2,100 schools nationwide ask families to complete The School and Student Services (SSS by NAIS) Parents' Financial Statement (PFS) online at http://SSSbyNAIS.org to determine eligibility for aid. The Parents' Financial Statement gathers information about family size, income and expenses, parents' assets and indebtedness, and the child's assets. From this and other information, schools are provided with an estimate of the amount of discretionary income (after several allowances are made for basic necessities) available for education costs. Schools review each case individually and use this estimate, along with such supporting documentation as most recent income tax forms, to make a final decision on a family's need for a financial aid grant. For more information, please visit http://sssbynais.org.

The amount of a need-based financial aid award varies from person to person and school to school. Just as individuals have different financial resources and obligations that dictate their need for assistance, schools have different resources and policies that dictate their ability to meet your financial need. Tuition costs, endowment incomes, and the school's philosophy about financial aid are a few of the things that can affect how much aid a school can offer. If your decision to send your child to a private school depends heavily on getting financial help, you would benefit from applying for aid at more than one school.

Merit-Based Awards

While the majority of aid offered is based on a family's financial situation, not everyone who receives financial assistance must demonstrate financial need. Private schools offer millions of dollars in merit-based scholarships to thousands of students. In the 2015–16 academic year, 525 NAIS-member schools granted a median annual merit award worth $4,232 to students, totaling more than $84.1 million. Even with this level of commitment, such awards are rare (just 8.3 percent of students enrolled at schools that offer this type of aid received a merit-based grant) and, therefore, highly competitive. They may serve to reward demonstrated talents or achievements in areas ranging from academics to athletics to the arts.

Some additional resources may be available from organizations and agencies in your community. Civic and religious groups, foundations, and even your employer may sponsor scholarships for students at private schools. Unfortunately, these options tend to be few and far between, and limited in number and size of award. Be sure to ask a financial aid officer at the school(s) in which you are interested if he or she is aware of such organizations and opportunities. Whether it is offered by the school or a local organization, understanding the requirements or conditions on which a merit-based scholarship is based is critical. Ask if the award is renewable and, if so, under what conditions. Often, certain criteria must be met (such as minimum GPA, community service, or participation in activities) to ensure renewal of the award in subsequent years, and some merit awards are available for just one year.

Tuition Financing Options

Whether or not you qualify for grants or scholarships, another way to get financial help involves finding ways to make tuition payments easier on your family's monthly budget. One common option is the tuition payment plan. These plans allow you to spread tuition payments (less any forms of financial aid you receive) over a period of eight to ten months. In most cases, payments start before the school year begins, but this method can be more feasible than coming up with one or two lump sum payments before the beginning of the school year. Payment plans may be administered by the schools themselves or by a private company approved by the school. They do not normally require credit checks or charge interest; however, they typically charge an application or service fee, which may include tuition insurance. Additional information about tuition payment plans is available on the NAIS website at http://sssbynais.org.

Since a high-quality education is one of the best investments they can make in their child's future, many parents finance the cost just as they would any other important expense. A number of schools, banks, and other agencies offer tuition loan programs specifically for elementary and secondary school expenses. While such loans are subject to credit checks and must be repaid with interest, they tend to offer rates and terms that are more favorable than those of other consumer loans. It pays to compare the details of more than one type of loan program to find the best one for your needs. Although they should always be regarded as an option of last resort, tuition loan programs can be helpful. Of course, every family must consider both the short- and long-term costs of borrowing and make its decision part of a larger plan for education financing.

A Final Word

Although the primary responsibility to pay for school costs rests with the family, there are options available if you need help. As you can see, financing a private school education can result in a partnership between the family, the school, and sometimes outside agencies or companies, with each making an effort to provide ways to meet the costs. The financial aid officer at the school is the best source of information about your options and is willing to help you in every way he or she can. Always go to the financial aid officer at a school in which you are interested whenever you have any questions or concerns about programs or the application process. Understanding your responsibilities, meeting deadlines, and learning about the full range of options are your best strategies for obtaining assistance. Although there are no guarantees, with proper planning and by asking the right questions, your family just might get the high-quality private education for less.

> *The financial aid officer at the school is the best source of information about your options.*

How to Use This Guide

Quick-Reference Chart

"Private Secondary Schools At-a-Glance" presents data listed in alphabetical order by state and U.S. territories; schools in Canada and other countries follow state listings. If your search is limited to a specific state, turn to the appropriate section and scan the chart for quick information about each school in that state: Are students boarding, day, or both? Is it coeducational? What grade levels are offered? How many students are enrolled? What is the student/faculty ratio? How many sports are offered? Does the school offer Advanced Placement test preparation?

School Profiles and Displays

The **School Profiles** and **Displays** contain basic information about the schools and are listed alphabetically in each section. An outline of a **School Profile** follows. The items of information found under each section heading are defined and displayed. Any item discussed below that is omitted from a **School Profile** either does not apply to that particular school or is one for which no information was supplied.

> **Heading** Name and address of school, along with the name of the Head of School.

> **General Information** Type (boys', girls', coeducational, boarding/day, distance learning) and academic emphasis, religious affiliation, grades, founding date, campus setting, nearest major city, housing, campus size, total number of buildings, accreditation and memberships, languages of instruction, endowment, enrollment, upper school average class size, upper school faculty-student ratio, number of required school days per year (Upper School), number of days per week Upper School students typically attend, and length of the average school day.

> **Upper School Student Profile** Breakdown by grade, gender, boarding/day, geography, and religion.

> **Faculty** Total number; breakdown by gender, number with advanced degrees, and number who reside on campus.

> **Subjects Offered** Academic and general subjects.

> **Graduation Requirements** Subjects and other requirements, including community service.

> **Special Academic Programs** Honors and Advanced Placement courses, accelerated programs, study at local college for college credit, study abroad, independent study, ESL programs, programs for gifted/ remedial students and students with learning disabilities.

> **College Admission Counseling** Number of recent graduates, representative list of colleges attended. May include mean or median SAT®/ACT® scores and percentage of students scoring over 600 on each section of the SAT, over 1800 on the combined SAT (scores for the redesigned SAT® were not available at the time of this printing), or over 26 on the composite ACT®.

> **Student Life** Dress code, student council, discipline, and religious service attendance requirements.

> **Summer Programs** Programs offered and focus; location; open to boys, girls, or both and availability to students from other schools; usual enrollment; program dates and application deadlines.

> **Tuition and Aid** Costs, available financial aid.

> **Admissions** New-student figures, admissions requirements, application deadlines, fees.

> **Athletics** Sports, levels, and gender; number of PE instructors, coaches, and athletic trainers.

> **Computers** List of classes that use computers, campus technology, and availability of student e-mail accounts, online student grades, and a published electronic and media policy.

> **Contact** Person to whom inquiries should be addressed.

> **Displays,** provided by school administrators, present information designed to complement the data already appearing in the **School Profile.**

Close-Ups

Close-Ups, written expressly for Peterson's by school administrators, provide in-depth information about the schools that have chosen to submit them. These descriptions are all in the same format to provide maximum comparability. **Close-Ups** follow each **School Profile** section; there is a page reference at the end of a **School Profile** directing you to that school's **Close-Up,** if one was provided. Schools are listed alphabetically in each section.

Special Needs Schools

One of the great strengths of private schools is their variety. This section is dedicated to the belief that there is an appropriate school setting for every child, one in which he or she will thrive academically, socially, and emotionally. The task for parents, counselors, and educators is to know the child's needs and the schools' resources well enough to make the right match.

Schools in this section serve those students who may have special challenges, including learning differences, dyslexia, language delay, attention deficit disorders, social maladjustment to family and surroundings, or emotional disturbances; these students may need individual attention or are underachieving for some other reason. Parents of children who lag significantly behind their grade level in basic academic skills or who have little or no motivation for schoolwork will also want to consult this section. (For easy reference, schools that offer extra help for students are identified in two directories: "Schools Reporting Programs for Students with Special Needs" and "Schools Reporting That They Accommodate Underachievers.") The schools included here chose to be in this section because they consider special needs education to be their primary focus. It is the mission of these schools, whose curricula and methodologies vary widely, to uncover a student's strengths and, with appropriate academic, social, and psychological counseling, enable him or her to succeed.

Junior Boarding Schools

As parents know, the early adolescent years are ones of tremendous physical and emotional change. Junior boarding schools specialize in this crucial period by taking advantage of children's natural curiosity, zest for learning, and growing self-awareness. While junior boarding schools enroll students with a wide range of academic abilities and levels of emotional self-assurance, their goal is to meet each youngster's individual needs within a supportive community. They accomplish this through low student-teacher ratios and enrollment numbers deliberately kept low.

The boarding schools featured in this section serve students in the middle school grades (6–9); some offer primary programs as well. For more information about junior boarding schools, visit the Junior Boarding Schools Association Web site at www.jbsa.org.

Specialized Directories

These directories are compiled from the information gathered in *Peterson's Annual Survey of Private Secondary Schools.* The schools that did not return a survey or provided incomplete data are not fully represented in these directories. For ease of reference, the directories are grouped by category: type, curricula, financial data, special programs, and special needs.

Index

The "Alphabetical Listing of Schools" shows page numbers for School Profiles in regular type, page numbers for Displays in italics, and page numbers for Close-Ups in boldface type.

Data Collection Procedures

The data contained in *Peterson's Private Secondary Schools 2016–17* **School Profiles, Quick-Reference Chart, Specialized Directories,** and **Index** were collected through *Peterson's Annual Survey of Private Secondary Schools* during summer and fall 2015. Also included were schools that submitted information for the 2014–15 data collection effort but did not submit updates in the summer/fall of 2015. Questionnaires were posted online. With minor exceptions, data for those schools that responded to the questionnaire were submitted by officials at the schools themselves. All usable information received in time for publication has been included. The omission of a particular item from a **School Profile** means that it is either not applicable to that school or not available or usable. Because of Peterson's extensive system of checking data, we believe that the information presented in this guide is accurate. However, errors and omissions are possible in a data collection and processing endeavor of this scope. Therefore, students and parents should check with a specific school at the time of application to verify all pertinent information.

Criteria for Inclusion in This Book

Most schools in this book have curricula that are primarily college preparatory. If a school is accredited or is a candidate for accreditation by a regional accrediting group, including the European Council of Schools, and/or is approved by a state Department of Education, and/or is a member of the National Association of Independent Schools or the European Council of Schools, then such accreditation, approval, or membership is stated. Schools appearing in the **Special Needs Schools** section may not have such accreditation or approval.

Quick-Reference Chart

Private Secondary Schools At-a-Glance

| | STUDENTS ACCEPTED | | | | GRADES | | | STUDENT/FACULTY | | | SCHOOL OFFERINGS | |
| | BOARDING | | DAY | | | | | | | | | |
	Boys	Girls	Boys	Girls	Lower	Middle	Upper	Total	Upper	Student/Faculty Ratio	Advanced Placement Preparation	Sports
UNITED STATES												
Alabama												
American Christian Academy, Tuscaloosa			X	X	K–6	7–9	10–12	958	240	12:1	X	40
Athens Bible School, Athens			X	X	K–6	–	7–12	270	162			
Briarwood Christian High School, Birmingham			X	X	K–6	7–8	9–12	1,912	562	23:1	X	19
The Donoho School, Anniston			X	X	PK–6	7–8	9–12	357	139	12:1	X	10
Houston Academy, Dothan			X	X	3–6	–	7–12	621	345	13:1	X	12
Indian Springs School, Indian Springs	X	X	X	X	–	–	8–12	299	299	7:1	X	18
Lyman Ward Military Academy, Camp Hill	X				6–8	–	9–12	115	85	15:1	X	41
Marion Academy, Marion			X	X	K–3	4–6	7–12	53	29	8:1		8
Mars Hill Bible School, Florence			X	X	K4–4	5–8	9–12	525	169	14:1		11
Pickens Academy, Carrollton			X	X	K4–6	–	7–12	267	138	20:1		12
Randolph School, Huntsville			X	X	K–4	5–8	9–12	969	376	10:1	X	18
Tuscaloosa Academy, Tuscaloosa			X	X	PK–4	5–8	9–12	438	154	15:1		14
Alaska												
Grace Christian School, Anchorage			X	X	K–6	7–8	9–12	532	185	14:1	X	8
Arizona												
Blueprint Education, Glendale					–	–	7–12					
Brophy College Preparatory, Phoenix			X		–	6–8	9–12	1,391	1,319	15:1	X	44
Green Fields Country Day School, Tucson			X	X	K–5	6–8	9–12	105	34	4:1	X	13
Phoenix Christian Unified Schools, Phoenix			X	X	PS–5	6–8	9–12	385	185	24:1	X	12
Phoenix Country Day School, Paradise Valley			X	X	PK–4	5–8	9–12	750	280	8:1	X	24
Saint Mary's High School, Phoenix			X	X	–	–	9–12	541	541	15:1	X	17
Salpointe Catholic High School, Tucson			X	X	–	–	9–12	1,093	1,093	15:1	X	17
Tri-City Christian Academy, Chandler			X	X	K–6	7–8	9–12	276	106	7:1		5
Xavier College Preparatory, Phoenix				X	–	–	9–12	1,196	1,196	22:1	X	34
Arkansas												
Episcopal Collegiate School, Little Rock			X	X	PK–5	6–8	9–12	784	205	10:1	X	16
California												
Academy of Our Lady of Peace, San Diego				X	–	–	9–12	748	748	13:1	X	15
Alma Heights Christian High School, Pacifica			X	X	K–5	6–8	9–12	303	147	10:1	X	10
Archbishop Mitty High School, San Jose			X	X	–	–	9–12	1,723	1,723	17:1	X	27
Arete Preparatory Academy, Los Angeles			X	X	–	–	9–12	58	58	2:1		1
Army and Navy Academy, Carlsbad	X		X		7–9	–	10–12	267		15:1	X	30
Bakersfield Christian High School, Bakersfield			X	X	–	–	9–12	488	488	17:1	X	17
The Bay School of San Francisco, San Francisco			X	X	–	–	9–12	355	355	8:1		18
Bentley School, Lafayette			X	X	K–5	6–8	9–12	684	325	8:1	X	17
Berean Christian High School, Walnut Creek			X	X	–	–	9–12	411	411	20:1	X	11
Besant Hill School, Ojai	X	X	X	X	–	–	9–PG	100	100	4:1	X	44
Bishop Montgomery High School, Torrance			X	X	–	–	9–12	946	946	22:1	X	17
Bishop Mora Salesian High School, Los Angeles			X		–	–	9–12	480	480	16:1		21
The Bishop's School, La Jolla			X	X	–	6–8	9–12	811	552	9:1	X	18
Brentwood School, Los Angeles			X	X	K–6	7–8	9–12	995	465	8:1	X	39
Bridges Academy, Studio City			X	X	–	4–8	9–12	170	87	8:1		3
The Buckley School, Sherman Oaks			X	X	K–5	6–8	9–12	830	345	8:1	X	12
California Crosspoint High School, Alameda	X	X	X	X	–	–	9–12	200	200	8:1	X	14
California Lutheran High School, Wildomar	X	X			–	–	9–12	85	85	8:1	X	7
Calvin Christian High School, Escondido			X	X	PK–5	6–8	9–12	470	150	17:1	X	11
Campbell Hall (Episcopal), North Hollywood			X	X	K–6	7–8	9–12	1,125	548	8:1	X	20
Capistrano Valley Christian Schools, San Juan Capistrano			X	X	JK–6	7–8	9–12	435	205	13:1	X	16
Carondelet High School, Concord				X	–	–	9–12	800	800	15:1	X	23
Castilleja School, Palo Alto				X	–	6–8	9–12	438	249	6:1	X	14
Cate School, Carpinteria	X	X	X	X	–	–	9–12	270	270	5:1	X	50
Central Catholic High School, Modesto			X	X	–	–	9–12	372	372	16:1	X	15
Chadwick School, Palos Verdes Peninsula			X	X	K–6	7–8	9–12	835	354	5:1	X	20
Chaminade College Preparatory, West Hills			X	X	–	6–8	9–12	2,030	1,322	16:1	X	25
Crossroads School for Arts & Sciences, Santa Monica			X	X	K–5	6–8	9–12	1,174	521	11:1	X	21
Crystal Springs Uplands School, Hillsborough			X	X	–	6–8	9–12	350	250	9:1		24
Damien High School, La Verne			X		–	–	9–12	936	936	17:1	X	24
De La Salle High School, Concord			X		–	–	9–12	1,038	1,038	28:1	X	22
Eldorado Emerson Private School, Orange			X	X	–	–	–	166	111	18:1	X	8

Private Secondary Schools At-a-Glance

	STUDENTS ACCEPTED				GRADES			STUDENT/FACULTY			SCHOOL OFFERINGS	
	BOARDING		DAY									
	Boys	Girls	Boys	Girls	Lower	Middle	Upper	Total	Upper	Student/Faculty Ratio	Advanced Placement Preparation	Sports
Flintridge Preparatory School, La Canada Flintridge			X	X	–	7–8	9–12	500	400	8:1	X	16
Fresno Christian Schools, Fresno			X	X	K–6	7–8	9–12	464	174	10:1	X	16
The Grauer School, Encinitas			X	X	–	7–8	9–12	164	109	7:1		28
Halstrom Academy, Beverly Hills			X	X	–	6–8	9–12	9	7	1:1	X	
Halstrom Academy, Calsbad			X	X	–	6–8	9–12	51	47	1:1	X	
Halstrom Academy, Cupertino			X	X	–	6–8	9–12	19	15	1:1	X	
Halstrom Academy, Huntington Beach			X	X	–	6–8	9–12	32	26	1:1	X	
Halstrom Academy, Irvine			X	X	–	6–8	9–12	31	26	1:1	X	
Halstrom Academy, Los Angeles			X	X	–	6–8	9–12	13	10	1:1	X	
Halstrom Academy, Manhattan Beach			X	X	–	6–8	9–12	20	15	1:1	X	
Halstrom Academy, Mission Viejo			X	X	–	6–8	9–12	44	36	1:1	X	
Halstrom Academy, Orange			X	X	–	6–8	9–12	37	31	1:1	X	
Halstrom Academy, Pasadena			X	X	–	6–8	9–12	27	23	1:1	X	
Halstrom Academy, San Diego			X	X	–	6–8	9–12	37	31	1:1	X	
Halstrom Academy, San Mateo			X	X	–	6–8	9–12	11	6	1:1	X	
Halstrom Academy, Walnut Creek			X	X	–	6–8	9–12	12	10	1:1	X	
Halstrom Academy, Westlake Village			X	X	–	6–8	9–12	30	27	1:1	X	
Halstrom Academy, Woodland Hills			X	X	–	6–8	9–12	40	32	1:1	X	
The Harker School, San Jose			X	X	K–5	6–8	9–12	1,911	767	10:1	X	21
Harvard-Westlake School, Studio City			X	X	–	7–8	9–12	1,592	1,161	8:1	X	20
Hebrew Academy, Huntington Beach		X	X	X	N–5	6–8	9–12	257	26	4:1	X	14
Immaculate Heart High School and Middle School, Los Angeles				X	–	6–8	9–12	700	500	17:1	X	10
International High School, San Francisco			X	X	PK–5	6–8	9–12	1,077	363	10:1		15
Jewish Community High School of the Bay, San Francisco					–	–	–				X	10
Junipero Serra High School, San Mateo			X		–	–	9–12	881	881	27:1	X	29
La Cheim School, Antioch			X	X	–	6–8	9–12	8	3			2
La Jolla Country Day School, La Jolla			X	X	N–4	5–8	9–12	1,118	459	16:1	X	24
La Salle High School, Pasadena			X	X	–	–	9–12	650	650	10:1	X	20
Le Lycee Francais de Los Angeles, Los Angeles			X	X	PS–5	6–8	9–12	819	217	3:1	X	23
Liberty Christian School, Huntington Beach			X	X	K–6	7–8	9–12	112	28	6:1		4
Louisville High School, Woodland Hills				X	–	–	9–12	337	337	25:1	X	16
Lutheran High School of San Diego, Chula Vista			X	X	–	–	9–12	101	101	12:1	X	6
Maranatha High School, Pasadena			X	X	–	–	9–12	680	680	16:1	X	20
Marymount High School, Los Angeles				X	–	–	9–12	396	396	7:1	X	20
Menlo School, Atherton			X	X	–	6–8	9–12	795	580	10:1	X	16
Mesa Grande Seventh-Day Academy, Calimesa			X	X	K–6	7–8	9–12	252	90	10:1		11
Midland School, Los Olivos	X	X			–	–	9–12	81	81	4:1	X	17
Moreau Catholic High School, Hayward			X	X	–	–	9–12	945	945	18:1	X	22
Mountain View Academy, Mountain View			X	X	–	–	9–12	150	150	14:1	X	5
Notre Dame High School, Belmont				X	–	–	9–12	450	450	14:1	X	24
Notre Dame High School, Riverside			X	X	–	–	9–12	629	629	19:1	X	15
Notre Dame High School, San Jose				X	–	–	9–12	631	631	11:1	X	12
Orinda Academy, Orinda			X	X	–	8–8	9–12	78	75	9:1	X	5
Palma School, Salinas			X		–	7–8	9–12	428	326	15:1	X	27
Palo Alto Preparatory School, Mountain View			X	X	–	–	8–12	75	75	8:1	X	
Paradise Adventist Academy, Paradise			X	X	K–4	5–8	9–12	143	51	6:1		4
Patten Academy of Christian Education, Oakland			X	X	K–5	6–8	9–12	119	54	8:1		4
Polytechnic School, Pasadena			X	X	K–5	6–8	9–12	858	374	6:1	X	25
Providence High School, Burbank			X	X	–	–	9–12	435	435	8:1	X	9
Ramona Convent Secondary School, Alhambra				X	–	–	9–12	250	250	9:1	X	8
Redwood Christian Schools, Castro Valley			X	X	K–5	6–8	9–12	650	281	14:1	X	8
Riverside Christian Schools, Riverside			X	X	K–6	7–8	9–12	253	103	10:1	X	7
Rolling Hills Preparatory School, San Pedro			X	X	–	6–8	9–12	256	181	9:1	X	22
Sacramento Country Day School, Sacramento			X	X	PK–5	6–8	9–12	503	142	9:1	X	15
Sacramento Waldorf School, Fair Oaks			X	X	PK–8	–	9–12	441	159	6:1		19
Sacred Heart High School, Los Angeles				X	–	–	9–12	250	250	20:1	X	6
Sage Hill School, Newport Coast			X	X	–	–	9–12	521	521	10:1	X	16
St. Bernard High School, Playa del Rey			X	X	–	–	9–12	260	260	20:1	X	22
St. Bernard's Catholic School, Eureka	X	X	X	X	PK	7–8	9–12	231	170	12:1	X	11
Saint Francis High School, La Canada Flintridge			X		–	–	9–12	663	663	12:1	X	12
Saint Francis High School, Mountain View			X	X	–	–	9–12	1,761	1,761	27:1	X	30
Saint Joseph Academy, San Marcos			X	X	K–5	6–8	9–12	302	65	16:1	X	5
St. Michael's Preparatory School of the Norbertine Fathers, Silverado	X				–	–	9–12	64	64	3:1	X	19
San Domenico School, San Anselmo	X	X	X	X	K–5	6–8	9–12	621	183	5:1	X	14
San Francisco University High School, San Francisco			X	X	–	–	9–12	403	403	8:1	X	24
Santa Catalina School, Monterey		X		X	–		9–12	244	244	8:1	X	31

Private Secondary Schools At-a-Glance

Private Secondary Schools	STUDENTS ACCEPTED				GRADES			STUDENT/FACULTY			SCHOOL OFFERINGS	
	BOARDING		DAY									
	Boys	Girls	Boys	Girls	Lower	Middle	Upper	Total	Upper	Student/Faculty Ratio	Advanced Placement Preparation	Sports
Santa Margarita Catholic High School, Rancho Santa Margarita			X	X	–	–	9–12	1,755	1,755	15:1	X	40
Servite High School, Anaheim			X		–	–	9–12	905	905	15:1	X	16
Sierra Canyon School, Chatsworth					K–6	7–8	9–12	1,000	410	11:1	X	21
Sonoma Academy, Santa Rosa			X	X	–	–	9–12	284		10:1	X	28
Squaw Valley Academy, Olympic Valley	X	X	X	X	–	–	9–12	100	100	8:1	X	68
Stevenson School, Pebble Beach	X	X	X	X	PK–4	5–8	9–12	747	498	10:1	X	38
Summerfield Waldorf School, Santa Rosa			X	X	K–6	7–8	9–12	409	106	7:1		4
The Thacher School, Ojai	X	X	X	X	–	–	9–12	252	252	5:1	X	46
Valley Christian High School, San Jose			X	X	K–5	6–8	9–12	2,668	1,514	11:1	X	24
Victor Valley Christian School, Victorville			X	X	K–6	7–8	9–12	275	78	20:1	X	12
Viewpoint School, Calabasas			X	X	K–5	6–8	9–12	1,215	545	10:1	X	41
The Webb Schools, Claremont	X	X	X	X	–	–	9–12	408	408	8:1	X	20
Westmark School, Encino			X	X	2–5	6–8	9–12	228	98	12:1		14
Woodside Priory School, Portola Valley	X	X	X	X	–	6–8	9–12	386	278	9:1	X	20
York School, Monterey			X	X	–	–	8–12	228	228	7:1	X	20
Colorado												
Alexander Dawson School, Lafayette			X	X	K–4	5–8	9–12	517	246	8:1	X	43
The Colorado Rocky Mountain School, Carbondale	X	X	X	X	–	–	9–12	176	176	5:1	X	47
The Colorado Springs School, Colorado Springs			X	X	PK–5	6–8	9–12	274	98	7:1	X	24
Denver Academy, Denver			X	X	1–6	7–8	9–12	378	206	8:1		27
Fountain Valley School of Colorado, Colorado Springs	X	X	X	X	–	–	9–12	236	236	5:1	X	40
Front Range Christian High School, Littleton			X	X	PK–6	7–8	9–12	437	172	6:1	X	24
Kent Denver School, Englewood			X	X	–	6–8	9–12	698	476	13:1	X	28
Regis Jesuit High School, Boys Division, Aurora			X		–	–	9–12	944	944	12:1	X	35
Regis Jesuit High School, Girls Division, Aurora				X	–	–	9–12	738	738	12:1	X	26
Steamboat Mountain School, Steamboat Springs	X	X	X	X	–	–	9–12	46	46	8:1	X	60
Connecticut												
Academy of the Holy Family, Baltic		X		X	–	–	9–12	29	29	6:1		4
Bridgeport International Academy, Bridgeport	X	X	X	X	–	–	9–12	60	60	6:1		7
Brunswick School, Greenwich			X		PK–4	5–8	9–12	962	380	5:1	X	20
Canterbury School, New Milford	X	X	X	X	–	–	9–PG	350	350	6:1	X	28
Choate Rosemary Hall, Wallingford	X	X	X	X	–	–	9–12	867	867	6:1	X	42
Christian Heritage School, Trumbull			X	X	K–5	6–8	9–12	450	150	9:1	X	7
Eagle Hill School, Greenwich	X	X	X	X	1–6	–	6–9	250	136	4:1		33
Fairfield College Preparatory School, Fairfield			X		–	–	9–12	901	901	18:1	X	31
Franklin Academy, East Haddam	X	X	X	X	–	–	8–PG	85	85	2:1		34
The Glenholme School, Devereux Connecticut, Washington	X	X	X	X	5–6	7–8	9–PG	95	79	10:1		43
The Gunnery, Washington	X	X	X	X	–	–	9–PG	287	287	6:1	X	21
Holy Cross High School, Waterbury			X	X	–	–	9–12	489	489	11:1	X	24
Hyde School, Woodstock	X	X	X	X	–	–	9–12	151	151	6:1	X	21
Kent School, Kent	X	X	X	X	–	–	9–PG	570	570	7:1	X	43
King Low Heywood Thomas, Stamford			X	X	PK–5	6–8	9–12	674	351	8:1	X	21
Kingswood-Oxford School, West Hartford			X	X	–	6–8	9–12	507	341	8:1	X	18
Lauralton Hall, Milford				X	–	–	9–12	467	467	12:1		18
Marianapolis Preparatory School, Thompson	X	X	X	X	–	–	9–PG	400	400	8:1	X	41
The Marvelwood School, Kent	X	X	X	X	–	–	9–12	172	172	4:1	X	45
Mercy High School, Middletown				X	–	–	9–12	573	573	13:1	X	16
Miss Porter's School, Farmington		X		X	–	–	9–12	323	323	8:1	X	45
Northwest Catholic High School, West Hartford			X	X	–	–	9–12	587	587	12:1	X	34
The Norwich Free Academy, Norwich			X	X	–	–	9–12	2,280	2,280	13:1	X	36
The Oxford Academy, Westbrook	X				–	–	9–PG	45	45	1:1	X	31
The Rectory School, Pomfret	X	X	X	X	K–4	5–9	–	243	173	4:1		41
Rumsey Hall School, Washington Depot	X	X	X	X	K–5	6–9	–	420		5:1		48
St. Bernard High School, Uncasville			X	X	–	6–8	9–12	322	232	10:1		25
St. Joseph High School, Trumbull			X	X	–	–	9–12		800	11:1	X	17
St. Luke's School, New Canaan			X	X	–	5–8	9–12	551	308	8:1	X	20
The Taft School, Watertown	X	X	X	X	–	–	9–PG	594	594	5:1	X	48
Trinity Catholic High School, Stamford			X	X	–	–	9–12	429	429	13:1	X	13
Watkinson School, Hartford			X	X	–	6–8	9–PG	240	180	6:1		30
Wellspring Foundation, Bethlehem	X	X	X	X	1–6	–	7–12	51				
Westminster School, Simsbury	X	X	X	X	–	–	9–PG	394	394	5:1	X	38
Westover School, Middlebury		X		X	–	–	9–12	210	210	8:1	X	49
The Woodhall School, Bethlehem	X		X		–	–	9–12	42	42	3:1	X	25
Wooster School, Danbury			X	X	PK–5	6–8	9–12	383	180	10:1	X	20
Delaware												
Archmere Academy, Claymont			X	X	–	–	9–12	505	505	10:1	X	20
Padua Academy, Wilmington				X	–	–	9–12	600	600	11:1	X	15

Private Secondary Schools At-a-Glance

| | STUDENTS ACCEPTED | | | | GRADES | | | STUDENT/FACULTY | | | SCHOOL OFFERINGS | |
| | BOARDING | | DAY | | | | | | | | | |
	Boys	Girls	Boys	Girls	Lower	Middle	Upper	Total	Upper	Student/Faculty Ratio	Advanced Placement Preparation	Sports
St. Andrew's School, Middletown	X	X			–	–	9–12	310	310	5:1		34
Salesianum School, Wilmington			X		–	–	9–12	1,035	1,035	12:1	X	23
Tower Hill School, Wilmington			X	X	PS–4	5–8	9–12	703	260	6:1	X	24
Wilmington Christian School, Hockessin			X	X	PK–5	6–8	9–12	500	210	15:1	X	12
Wilmington Friends School, Wilmington			X	X	PS–5	6–8	9–12	736	286	10:1	X	15
District of Columbia												
British International School of Washington, Washington			X	X	PS–5	6–8	9–12	460	115	12:1		27
Edmund Burke School, Washington			X	X	–	6–8	9–12	297	212	6:1	X	18
Gonzaga College High School, Washington			X				9–12	962	962	13:1	X	27
National Cathedral School, Washington				X	4–6	7–8	9–12	590	313	7:1	X	43
St. Albans School, Washington	X		X		4–8	–	9–12	593	324	7:1	X	35
Washington International School, Washington			X	X	PS–5	6–8	9–12	920		7:1		9
Florida												
Academy at the Lakes, Land O'Lakes			X	X	PK–4	5–8	9–12	466	166	5:1	X	17
Admiral Farragut Academy, St. Petersburg	X	X	X	X	P3–7	–	8–12	436	299	8:1	X	35
Allison Academy, North Miami Beach			X	X	–	6–8	9–12	105	85	10:1	X	21
All Saints' Academy, Winter Haven			X	X	PS–5	6–8	9–12	600			X	17
American Heritage School, Delray Beach			X	X	PK–5	6–8	9–12	1,226	682	8:1	X	26
American Heritage School, Plantation			X	X	PK–6	–	7–12	2,400	1,679	8:1	X	22
Atlantis Academy, Miami			X	X	K–3	4–6	7–12	156	103	8:1		7
Belen Jesuit Preparatory School, Miami			X		–	6–8	9–12	1,479	880	13:1	X	19
The Benjamin School, North Palm Beach			X	X	PK–5	6–8	9–12	1,081	420	8:1	X	24
Berkeley Preparatory School, Tampa			X	X	PK–5	6–8	9–12	1,300	575	9:1	X	28
Bishop John J. Snyder High School, Jacksonville			X	X	–	–	9–12	470	470	15:1	X	18
Bishop Verot High School, Fort Myers			X	X	–	–	9–12	673	673	14:1	X	15
Boca Prep International School, Boca Raton			X	X	PK–5	6–8	9–12	243	103	24:1		3
The Bolles School, Jacksonville	X	X	X	X	PK–5	6–8	9–12	1,637	779	12:1	X	18
Canterbury School, Fort Myers			X	X	PK–6	7–8	9–12	620	240	12:1	X	13
The Canterbury School of Florida, St. Petersburg			X	X	PK–4	5–8	9–12	480	161	7:1	X	35
Cardinal Mooney Catholic High School, Sarasota			X	X	–	–	9–12	474	474	13:1	X	20
Cardinal Newman High School, West Palm Beach			X	X	–	–	9–12	544	544	25:1	X	18
Carrollton School of the Sacred Heart, Miami				X	PK–3	4–6	7–12	800	432	9:1	X	14
Chaminade-Madonna College Preparatory, Hollywood			X	X	–	–	9–12	545	545	19:1	X	14
Christopher Columbus High School, Miami			X		–	–	9–12	1,579	1,579	15:1	X	18
The Community School of Naples, Naples			X	X	PK–5	6–8	9–12	807	312	9:1	X	16
The Crenshaw School, Gotha			X	X	PK–5	6–8	9–12	102	50	10:1		
Donna Klein Jewish Academy, Boca Raton			X	X	K–5	6–8	9–12	580	156	6:1	X	15
Episcopal High School of Jacksonville, Jacksonville			X	X	–	6–8	9–12	857	566	10:1	X	22
Father Lopez High School, Daytona Beach			X	X	–	–	9–12	474	474	13:1	X	18
The First Academy, Orlando			X	X	K4–6	7–8	9–12	990	410	17:1	X	22
Forest Lake Academy, Apopka	X	X	X	X	–	–	9–12	397	397	12:1		13
Foundation Academy, Winter Garden			X	X	K–6	7–8	9–12	677	241	9:1	X	14
Glades Day School, Belle Glade			X	X	PK–6	7–8	9–12	289	123	15:1	X	10
Gulliver Preparatory School, Miami			X	X	1–4	5–8	9–12	2,014	986	8:1	X	38
Immaculata-La Salle High School, Miami			X	X	–	–	9–12	832	832	18:1	X	18
Jesuit High School of Tampa, Tampa			X		–	–	9–12	775	775	12:1	X	17
John Paul II Catholic High School, Tallahassee			X	X	–	–	9–12	169	169	12:1	X	11
Miami Country Day School, Miami			X	X	PK–5	6–8	9–12	1,250	417	10:1	X	24
Mount Dora Christian Academy, Mount Dora			X	X	PK–5	6–8	9–12	557	176	13:1	X	15
The North Broward Preparatory Upper School, Coconut Creek	X	X	X	X	PK–5	6–8	9–12	1,550	895	18:1	X	26
Orangewood Christian School, Maitland			X	X	K4–6	7–8	9–12	732	287	11:1	X	23
Out-Of-Door-Academy, Sarasota			X	X	PK–5	6–8	9–12	723	274	7:1	X	20
PACE/Brantley Hall High School, Longwood			X	X	1–5	6–8	9–12	171	83	12:1	X	11
Pensacola Catholic High School, Pensacola			X	X	–	–	9–12	599	599	18:1	X	16
Ransom Everglades School, Miami			X	X	–	6–8	9–12	1,085	612	9:1	X	22
Saddlebrook Preparatory School, Wesley Chapel	X	X	X	X	3–5	6–8	9–12	80	63	8:1		
Saint Andrew's School, Boca Raton	X	X	X	X	JK–5	6–8	9–12	1,285	585	9:1	X	23
St. Brendan High School, Miami			X	X	–	–	9–12	1,145	1,145	16:1	X	15
St. John Neumann High School, Naples			X	X	–	–	9–12	213	213	12:1	X	13
St. Joseph Academy, St. Augustine			X	X	–	–	9–12	318	318	11:1	X	17
St. Thomas Aquinas High School, Fort Lauderdale			X	X	–	–	9–12	2,171	2,171	18:1	X	31
Scheck Hillel Community School, North Miami Beach			X	X	PK–5	6–8	9–12	1,045	291	15:1	X	13
Shorecrest Preparatory School, Saint Petersburg			X	X	PK–4	5–8	9–12	940	311	12:1	X	14
Tampa Preparatory School, Tampa			X	X	–	6–8	9–12	650	460	16:1	X	18
Trinity Preparatory School, Winter Park			X	X	–	6–8	9–12	861	516	10:1	X	21
The Vanguard School, Lake Wales	X	X	X	X	–	6–8	9–12	95	78	6:1		22
Westminster Academy, Fort Lauderdale					PK–5	6–8	9–12	966	356	11:1		14
Westminster Christian School, Palmetto Bay			X	X	PK–5	6–8	9–12	1,244	502	15:1	X	19

Private Secondary Schools At-a-Glance

| | STUDENTS ACCEPTED | | | | GRADES | | | STUDENT/FACULTY | | | SCHOOL OFFERINGS | |
| | BOARDING | | DAY | | | | | | | | | |
	Boys	Girls	Boys	Girls	Lower	Middle	Upper	Total	Upper	Student/Faculty Ratio	Advanced Placement Preparation	Sports
Windermere Preparatory School, Windermere	X		X	X	PK–5	6–8	9–12	1,200	462	14:1	X	24
Georgia												
Advanced Academy of Georgia, Carrollton	X	X			–	–	10–12	83	83	14:1		8
Aquinas High School, Augusta			X	X	–	–	9–12	244	244	10:1	X	17
Athens Academy, Athens			X	X	N–4	5–8	9–12	963	327	8:1	X	12
Atlanta International School, Atlanta			X	X	PK–5	6–8	9–12	1,160	346	15:1		11
Augusta Christian School, Martinez			X	X	PK–5	6–8	9–12	561	229	11:1	X	13
Ben Franklin Academy, Atlanta			X	X	–	–	9–12	125	125	3:1	X	6
Blessed Trinity High School, Roswell			X	X	–	–	9–12	975	975	13:1	X	16
Brandon Hall School, Atlanta	X	X	X	X	–	6–8	9–12	155	127	8:1	X	14
Calvary Day School, Savannah			X	X	PK–5	6–8	9–12	767	362	17:1	X	16
Chatham Academy, Savannah			X	X	1–5	6–8	9–12	81	38	10:1		18
Eaton Academy, Roswell			X	X	K–5	6–8	9–12	80	40	5:1		34
First Presbyterian Day School, Macon	X	X	X	X	PK–5	6–8	9–12	962	389	8:1	X	21
The Galloway School, Atlanta			X	X	P3–4	5–8	9–12	750	292	12:1	X	11
George Walton Academy, Monroe			X	X	K4–5	6–8	9–12	850	308	12:1	X	20
Greater Atlanta Christian Schools, Norcross			X	X	P3–5	6–8	9–12	1,815	776	13:1	X	29
The Howard School, Atlanta			X	X	K–5	6–8	9–12	264	89	8:1		7
John Hancock Academy, Sparta			X	X	K–5	6–8	9–12	150	50	10:1		11
Landmark Christian School, Fairburn			X	X	K4–5	6–8	9–12	807	224	8:1	X	16
The Lovett School, Atlanta			X	X	K–5	6–8	9–12	1,673	644	8:1	X	43
Mill Springs Academy, Alpharetta			X	X	1–5	6–8	9–12	355	181	6:1		23
Mount Vernon Presbyterian School, Atlanta			X	X	K–4	5–8	9–12	932	308	10:1	X	28
Pace Academy, Atlanta			X	X	K–5	6–8	9–12	1,015	372	7:1	X	25
Piedmont Academy, Monticello			X	X	1–5	6–8	9–12	259	118	13:1		10
Pinecrest Academy, Cumming			X	X	PK–5	6–8	9–12	807	285	8:1	X	12
Rabun Gap-Nacoochee School, Rabun Gap	X	X	X	X	–	5–8	9–12	423	319	10:1	X	42
St. Andrew's School, Savannah			X	X	PK–4	5–8	9–12	457	136	6:1		20
St. Francis School, Milton			X	X	K–5	6–8	9–12	778	317	14:1	X	19
Savannah Christian Preparatory School, Savannah			X	X	PK–5	6–8	9–12	1,227	402	14:1	X	15
The Savannah Country Day School, Savannah			X	X	1–5	6–8	9 12	893	268	6:1	X	26
Stratford Academy, Macon			X	X	1–5	6–8	9–12	896	319	13:1	X	23
Valwood School, Hahira			X	X	PK–5	6–8	9–12	509	174	12:1	X	12
The Weber School, Sandy Springs			X	X	–	–	9–12	226	226	8:1	X	18
Wesleyan School, Peachtree Corners			X	X	K–4	5–8	9–12	1,132	483	14:1	X	17
The Westminster Schools, Atlanta			X	X	K–5	6–8	9–12	1,858	812	8:1	X	34
Westminster Schools of Augusta, Augusta			X	X	PK–5	6–8	9–12	605	217	7:1	X	10
Guam												
Father Duenas Memorial School, Hagatna			X		–	–	9–12	435	435	25:1	X	15
Hawaii												
ASSETS School, Honolulu			X	X	K–8	–	9–12	323	132	8:1		30
Hawaii Baptist Academy, Honolulu			X	X	K–6	7–8	9–12	1,060	460	16:1	X	22
Hawai`i Preparatory Academy, Kamuela	X	X	X	X	K–5	6–8	9–12	628	379	13:1	X	35
Ho'Ala School, Wahiawa			X	X	K–6	7–8	9–12	93	27	5:1	X	7
Kauai Christian Academy, Kilauea			X	X	PS–3	4–6	7–12	79	16	8:1		3
Lutheran High School of Hawaii, Honolulu			X	X	–	6–8	9–12	39	38	7:1		24
Maui Preparatory Academy, Lahaina	X	X	X	X	PK–5	6–8	9–12	187	62	4:1	X	14
Mid-Pacific Institute, Honolulu			X	X	K–5	6–8	9–12	1,556	840	20:1	X	31
Punahou School, Honolulu			X	X	K–5	6–8	9–12	3,768	1,741	11:1	X	21
Seabury Hall, Makawao			X	X	–	6–8	9–12	455	321	11:1	X	25
Idaho												
Bishop Kelly High School, Boise			X	X	–	–	9–12	794	794	19:1	X	22
The Community School, Sun Valley	X	X	X	X	K–5	6–8	9–12	400	166	8:1	X	43
Nampa Christian Schools, Nampa			X	X	PK–5	6–8	9–12	586	197	18:1		16
Riverstone International School, Boise			X	X	PS–5	6–8	9–12	325	102	5:1		25
Illinois												
Brehm Preparatory School, Carbondale	X	X	X	X	–	6–8	9–PG	85	75	4:1		19
Elgin Academy, Elgin			X	X	PS–4	5–8	9–12	323	121	7:1	X	9
The Governor French Academy, Belleville	X	X	X	X	K–8	–	9–12	155	41	6:1	X	5
Hales Franciscan High School, Chicago			X		–	–	9–12	45	45	8:1		12
Holy Trinity High School, Chicago			X	X	–	–	9–12	331	331	12:1	X	14
Illiana Christian High School, Lansing			X	X	–	–	9–12	520	520	18:1	X	13
Josephinum Academy, Chicago				X	–	–	9–12	200	200	10:1	X	9
Marian Central Catholic High School, Woodstock			X	X	–	–	9–12	687	687	19:1	X	16
Mater Dei High School, Breese					–	–	9–12	414	414	18:1	X	12
Mooseheart High School, Mooseheart	X	X	X	X	K–5	6–8	9–12	199	109	6:1	X	15
Mother McAuley High School, Chicago				X	–	–	9–12	1,027	1,027	17:1	X	21

Private Secondary Schools At-a-Glance

	STUDENTS ACCEPTED				GRADES			STUDENT/FACULTY			SCHOOL OFFERINGS	
	BOARDING		DAY									
	Boys	Girls	Boys	Girls	Lower	Middle	Upper	Total	Upper	Student/Faculty Ratio	Advanced Placement Preparation	Sports
Nazareth Academy, LaGrange Park			X	X	–	–	9–12	763	763	17:1	X	16
North Shore Country Day School, Winnetka			X	X	PK–5	6–8	9–12	525	215	8:1	X	15
Sacred Heart/Griffin High School, Springfield			X	X	–	–	9–12	725	725	15:1	X	16
Saint Anthony High School, Effingham			X	X	–	–	9–12	190	190	10:1	X	12
Saint Patrick High School, Chicago			X		–	–	9–12	648	648	17:1	X	20
Timothy Christian High School, Elmhurst			X	X	K–6	7–8	9–12	990	355	10:1	X	12
University of Chicago Laboratory Schools, Chicago			X	X	N–5	6–8	9–12	2,007	516	10:1	X	16
Wheaton Academy, West Chicago			X	X	–	–	9–12	640	640	15:1	X	35
The Willows Academy, Des Plaines				X	–	6–8	9–12	230	150	10:1	X	8
Indiana												
Concordia Lutheran High School, Fort Wayne			X	X	–	–	9–12	772	772	15:1	X	23
The Culver Academies, Culver	X	X	X	X	–	–	9–PG		811	9:1	X	99
La Lumiere School, La Porte	X	X	X	X	–	–	9–PG	230	230	7:1	X	13
Marian High School, Mishawaka			X	X	–	–	9–12	690	690	24:1	X	30
Iowa												
Alpha Omega Academy, Rock Rapids			X	X	K–5	6–8	9–12	2,350	1,600			
Dowling Catholic High School, West Des Moines			X	X	–	–	9–12	1,438	1,438	18:1	X	22
Saint Albert Junior-Senior High School, Council Bluffs			X	X	PK–5	6–8	9–12	720	210	11:1	X	16
Scattergood Friends School, West Branch	X	X	X	X	–	–	9–12	35	35	3:1		28
Kansas												
Bishop Miege High School, Shawnee Mission			X	X	–	–	9–12	721	721	16:1	X	17
Hyman Brand Hebrew Academy of Greater Kansas City, Overland Park			X	X	K–5	6–8	9–12	232	42	5:1	X	4
Immaculata High School, Leavenworth			X	X	–	–	9–12	74	74	9:1		14
Independent School, Wichita			X	X	PK–5	6–8	9–12	538	196	7:1	X	17
Maur Hill-Mount Academy, Atchison	X	X	X	X	–	–	9–12	195	195	9:1	X	37
Saint Thomas Aquinas High School, Overland Park			X	X	–	–	9–12	900	900	15:1	X	20
Wichita Collegiate School, Wichita			X	X	PS–4	5–8	9–12	935	264	8:1	X	15
Kentucky												
Academy for Individual Excellence, Louisville			X	X	K–6	7–8	9–12	368	180	9:1		8
Beth Haven Christian School, Louisville			X	X	K–5	6–8	9–12	178	58	7:1		6
Bishop Brossart High School, Alexandria			X	X	–	–	9–12	382	382	16:1		10
Community Christian Academy, Independence			X	X	PS–6	7–8	9–12	269	58	15:1		6
Kentucky Country Day School, Louisville			X	X	JK–4	5–8	9–12	914	313	7:1	X	20
Landmark Christian Academy, Louisville			X	X	K4–6	7–8	9–12	144	26	6:1		4
Lexington Catholic High School, Lexington			X	X	–	–	9–12	874	874	13:1	X	21
Lexington Christian Academy, Lexington			X	X	PS–6	7–8	9–12	1,445	448	16:1	X	16
Louisville Collegiate School, Louisville			X	X	JK–5	6–8	9–12	676		77:1	X	15
Oneida Baptist Institute, Oneida	X	X	X	X	K–5	6–8	9–12	320	207	11:1	X	11
Sacred Heart Academy, Louisville				X	–	–	–	835	835	15:1	X	12
Trinity High School, Louisville			X		–	–	9–12	1,230	1,230	12:1	X	48
Villa Madonna Academy, Covington			X	X	K–6	7–8	9–12	421	139	8:1	X	12
Whitefield Academy, Louisville			X	X	PS–5	6–8	9–12	711	192	11:1	X	17
Louisiana												
Archbishop Shaw High School, Marrero			X		–	8–12		472	472	24:1	X	13
Holy Cross School, New Orleans			X		PK–4	5–7	8–12	1,140	762	12:1	X	28
Holy Savior Menard Catholic High School, Alexandria			X	X	–	7–8	9–12	510	349	14:1	X	15
Isidore Newman School, New Orleans			X	X	PK–5	6–8	9–12	1,005		17:1	X	15
Notre Dame High School, Crowley			X	X	–	–	9–12	450	450	25:1		14
Parkview Baptist School, Baton Rouge					PK–4	5–8	9–12			21:1		
Pope John Paul II High School, Slidell			X	X	–	–	8–12	346	346	11:1	X	18
St. Joseph's Academy, Baton Rouge				X	–	–	9–12	1,070	1,070	15:1	X	22
St. Martin's Episcopal School, Metairie			X	X	PK–5	6–8	9–12	473	174	6:1	X	16
Saint Thomas More Catholic High School, Lafayette			X	X	–	–	9–12	1,050	1,050	12:1	X	26
Teurlings Catholic High School, Lafayette			X	X	–	–	9–12	779	779	17:1		22
Westminster Christian Academy, Opelousas			X	X	PK–6	7–8	9–12	1,059	213	13:1	X	16
Maine												
Bangor Christian School, Bangor			X	X	K4–5	6–8	9–12	310	80	10:1		14
Cheverus High School, Portland			X	X	–	–	9–12	470	470	10:1	X	27
Erskine Academy, South China			X	X	–	–	9–12	589	589	15:1	X	15
George Stevens Academy, Blue Hill	X	X	X	X	–	–	9–12	325	325	10:1	X	54
Hyde School, Bath	X	X	X	X	–	–	9–12	150	150	6:1	X	42
Lincoln Academy, Newcastle	X	X	X	X	–	–	9–12	588	588	17:1	X	33
Pine Tree Academy, Freeport	X	X	X	X	K–4	5–8	9–12	121	63	6:1		2
Saint Dominic Academy, Auburn			X	X	PK–6	7–8	9–12	571	203	12:1	X	14
Waynflete School, Portland			X	X	PK–5	6–8	9–12	583	263	12:1		23

Private Secondary Schools At-a-Glance

| | STUDENTS ACCEPTED | | | | GRADES | | | STUDENT/FACULTY | | | SCHOOL OFFERINGS | |
| | BOARDING | | DAY | | | | | | | | | |
	Boys	Girls	Boys	Girls	Lower	Middle	Upper	Total	Upper	Student/Faculty Ratio	Advanced Placement Preparation	Sports
Maryland												
Academy of the Holy Cross, Kensington				X	–	–	9–12	500	500	11:1	X	18
Archbishop Curley High School, Baltimore			X		–	–	9–12	535	535	14:1	X	21
The Baltimore Actors' Theatre Conservatory, Baltimore			X	X	1–5	6–8	9–12	22	10	3:1	X	
Bishop McNamara High School, Forestville			X	X	–	–	9–12	880	880	10:1	X	17
Bishop Walsh Middle High School, Cumberland			X	X	PK–5	6–8	9–12	320	140	15:1	X	14
The Bryn Mawr School for Girls, Baltimore			X	X	K–5	6–8	9–12	681	309	6:1	X	41
Calvert Hall College High School, Baltimore			X		–	–	9–12	1,160	1,160	11:1	X	36
Chelsea School, Hyattsville			X	X	–	5–8	9–12	65	43	8:1		4
DeMatha Catholic High School, Hyattsville			X		–	–	9–12	815	815	12:1	X	24
Elizabeth Seton High School, Bladensburg				X	–	–	9–12	563	563	11:1	X	34
Garrison Forest School, Owings Mills		X	X	X	N–5	6–8	9–12	614	280	8:1	X	28
Gilman School, Baltimore			X		K–5	6–8	9–12	1,017	466	7:1	X	27
Griggs International Academy, Silver Spring			X	X	PK–6	7–8	9–12	1,559	920	21:1		
The Gunston School, Centreville			X	X	–	–	9–12	182	182	6:1	X	11
The Heights School, Potomac			X		3–5	6–8	9–12	538	255	7:1	X	17
Indian Creek School, Crownsville			X	X	PK–5	6–8	9–12	621	228	7:1	X	18
The Key School, Annapolis			X	X	PK–4	5–8	9–12	630	210	7:1	X	28
Loyola-Blakefield, Baltimore			X		–	6–8	9–12	956	733	10:1	X	24
McDonogh School, Owings Mills	X	X	X	X	PK–4	5–8	9–12	1,350	603	9:1	X	28
The Nora School, Silver Spring			X	X	–	–	9–12	66	65	5:1		29
Our Lady of Good Counsel High School, Olney			X	X	–	–	9–12	1,240	1,240	13:1	X	33
The Park School of Baltimore, Baltimore			X	X	PK–5	6–8	9–12	788	333	7:1	X	16
Roland Park Country School, Baltimore			X	X	PS–5	6–8	9–12	644	312	7:1	X	26
St. Andrew's Episcopal School, Potomac			X	X	PS–5	6–8	9–12	553	297	7:1	X	20
Saint James School, Hagerstown	X	X	X	X	–	8–8	9–12	237	208	7:1	X	26
St. John's Catholic Prep, Buckeystown			X		–	–	9–12	260	260	9:1	X	22
St. Timothy's School, Stevenson		X		X	–	–	9–12	199	199	6:1		24
Sandy Spring Friends School, Sandy Spring	X	X	X	X	PK–5	6–8	9–12	577	285	8:1	X	43
Severn School, Severna Park			X	X	PS–5	6–8	9–12	843	418	8:1	X	27
Stone Ridge School of the Sacred Heart, Bethesda			X	X	PS–4	5–8	9–12	719	335	7:1	X	28
Takoma Academy, Takoma Park			X	X	–	–	9–12	226	226	11:1	X	5
Tome School, North East			X	X	K–4	5–8	9–12	480	149	10:1	X	20
Worcester Preparatory School, Berlin			X	X	PK–5	6–8	9–12	542	207	9:1	X	14
Massachusetts												
The Academy at Charlemont, Charlemont			X	X	–	7–8	9–PG	88	56	4:1		15
Academy of Notre Dame, Tyngsboro			X	X	K–5	6–8	9–12	610	169	12:1	X	12
Austin Preparatory School, Reading			X	X	–	6–8	9–12	210	514	15:1	X	21
Berkshire School, Sheffield	X	X	X	X	–	–	9–PG	405	405	5:1	X	42
Bishop Connolly High School, Fall River			X	X	–	–	9–12	280	280	16:1	X	17
Bishop Stang High School, North Dartmouth			X	X	–	–	9–12	620	620	13:1	X	30
Boston University Academy, Boston			X	X	–	–	9–12	170	170	8:1		12
Brimmer and May School, Chestnut Hill			X	X	PK–5	6–8	9–12	387	139	6:1	X	20
British International School of Boston, Boston			X	X	PK–5	6–8	9–12	421		4:1		20
Brooks School, North Andover	X	X	X	X	–	–	9–12	373	373	6:1	X	23
Buxton School, Williamstown	X	X	X	X	–	–	9–12	90	90	4:1		25
Cathedral High School, Boston			X	X	–	7–8	9–12	325	252	18:1		9
Central Catholic High School, Lawrence			X	X	–	–	9–12	1,330	1,330	24:1	X	32
Commonwealth School, Boston			X	X	–	–	9–12	145	145	5:1	X	16
Concord Academy, Concord	X	X	X	X	–	–	9–12	378	378	6:1		35
Cushing Academy, Ashburnham	X	X	X	X	–	–	9–PG	400	400	8:1	X	35
Dana Hall School, Wellesley		X		X	–	5–8	9–12	464	361	6:1	X	37
Deerfield Academy, Deerfield	X	X	X	X	–	–	9–PG	638	638	6:1	X	49
Eaglebrook School, Deerfield	X		X		–	6–9	–	250	230	4:1		66
Elizabeth Seton Academy, Dorchester Lower Mills				X	–	–	9–12		98	10:1		
Falmouth Academy, Falmouth			X	X	–	7–8	9–12	200	125	4:1	X	3
Fay School, Southborough	X	X	X	X	PK–2	3–6	7–9	475	235	6:1		21
Fontbonne Academy, Milton				X	–	–	9–12	335	335	10:1	X	29
Gann Academy (The New Jewish High School of Greater Boston), Waltham			X	X	–	–	9–12	277	277	5:1	X	17
The Governor's Academy, Byfield	X	X	X	X	–	–	9–12	405	405	5:1	X	22
Groton School, Groton	X	X	X	X	–	–	8–12	380	380	5:1	X	38
Holyoke Catholic High School, Chicopee			X	X	–	–	9–12	245	245	10:1	X	16
The John Dewey Academy, Great Barrington	X	X			–	–	10–PG	20	20	3:1		
Landmark School, Prides Crossing	X	X	X	X	2–5	6–8	9–12	471	314	3:1		20
Malden Catholic High School, Malden			X		–	–	9–12	562	562	13:1	X	36
Marian High School, Framingham			X	X	–	–	9–12	260	260	13:1	X	18
Matignon High School, Cambridge			X	X	–	–	9–12	462	462	18:1	X	25
Middlesex School, Concord	X	X	X	X	–	–	9–12	384	384	4:1	X	22

Private Secondary Schools At-a-Glance

| | STUDENTS ACCEPTED | | | | GRADES | | | STUDENT/FACULTY | | | SCHOOL OFFERINGS | |
| | BOARDING | | DAY | | | | | | | | | |
	Boys	Girls	Boys	Girls	Lower	Middle	Upper	Total	Upper	Student/Faculty Ratio	Advanced Placement Preparation	Sports
Milton Academy, Milton	X	X	X	X	K–5	6–8	9–12	1,000	695	5:1	X	28
Miss Hall's School, Pittsfield		X		X	–	–	9–PG	214	214	6:1	X	32
Montrose School, Medfield				X	–	6–8	9–12	217	148	6:1	X	13
Noble and Greenough School, Dedham	X	X	X	X	–	7–8	9–12	615	498	7:1	X	20
Northfield Mount Hermon School, Mount Hermon	X	X	X	X	–	–	9–PG	650	650	5:1	X	51
Phillips Academy (Andover), Andover	X	X	X	X	–	–	9–PG	1,131	1,131	5:1	X	48
The Pingree School, South Hamilton			X	X	–	–	9–12	364	364	6:1	X	32
Pioneer Valley Christian Academy, Springfield			X	X	PS–5	6–8	9–12	293	90	6:1	X	10
Redemption Christian Academy, Northfield	X	X	X	X	K–5	6–8	9–PG			8:1	X	7
The Rivers School, Weston			X	X	–	6–8	9–12	490	367	6:1	X	21
The Roxbury Latin School, West Roxbury			X		–		7–12	303	303	7:1	X	10
St. John's Preparatory School, Danvers			X		–	6–8	9–12	1,450	1,150	11:1	X	53
The Sudbury Valley School, Framingham			X	X	–	–	–	160		16:1		
Valley View School, North Brookfield	X				–	6–8	9–12	33	18	4:1		50
Walnut Hill School for the Arts, Natick	X	X	X	X	–	–	9–12	285	285	6:1		16
Whitinsville Christian School, Whitinsville			X	X	PK–5	6–8	9–12	474	176	8:1	X	10
The Williston Northampton School, Easthampton	X	X	X	X	–	7–8	9–PG	528	431	6:1	X	39
The Woodward School, Quincy				X	–	6–8	9–12	120	77	8:1	X	3
Michigan												
Academy of the Sacred Heart, Bloomfield Hills			X	X	N–4	5–8	9–12	478	145	7:1	X	10
Brother Rice High School, Bloomfield Hills			X		–	–	9–12	640	640	13:1	X	27
Catholic Central High School, Novi			X		–	–	9–12	1,070	1,070	17:1	X	18
Detroit Country Day School, Beverly Hills			X	X	PK–5	6–8	9–12	1,523	695	8:1	X	49
Gabriel Richard Catholic High School, Riverview			X	X	–	–	9–12	323	323	17:1	X	17
Jean and Samuel Frankel Jewish Academy of Metropolitan Detroit, West Bloomfield			X	X	–	–	9–12	225	225		X	
Kalamazoo Christian High School, Kalamazoo			X	X	–	–	9–12	234	234	12:1	X	17
The Leelanau School, Glen Arbor	X	X	X	X	–	–	9–12	50	50	5:1	X	49
Lutheran High School Northwest, Rochester Hills			X	X	–	–	9–12	177	177	9:1	X	21
Powers Catholic High School, Flint			X	X	–	–	9–12	605	605	17:1	X	29
The Roeper School, Bloomfield Hills			X	X	PK–5	6–8	9–12	579	149	8:1	X	11
Rudolf Steiner School of Ann Arbor, Ann Arbor			X	X	–	6–8	9–12	345	120	10:1		21
St. Mary's Preparatory School, Orchard Lake	X		X		–	–	9–12	540	540	10:1	X	44
Southfield Christian High School, Southfield			X	X	PK–5	6–8	9–12	588	181	20:1	X	12
The Valley School, Swartz Creek			X	X	PK–4	5–8	9–12	64	19	8:1		8
Minnesota												
The Blake School, Hopkins			X	X	PK–5	6–8	9–12	1,363	527	8:1	X	15
Breck School, Golden Valley			X	X	PK–4	5–8	9–12	1,185	430	16:1	X	19
Concordia Academy, St. Paul			X	X	–	–	9–12	241	241	15:1		15
DeLaSalle High School, Minneapolis			X	X			9–12	760	760	14:1	X	23
Marshall School, Duluth			X	X	–	4–8	9–12	446	270	11:1	X	28
Mounds Park Academy, Maplewood			X	X	PK–4	5–8	9–12	480	215	9:1	X	16
St. Croix Schools, West St. Paul	X	X	X	X	–	6–8	9–12	500	440	13:1	X	40
Saint John's Preparatory School, Collegeville	X	X	X	X	6–6	7–8	9–PG	285	205	10:1	X	50
St. Paul Academy and Summit School, St. Paul			X	X	K–5	6–8	9–12	918	419	8:1		25
St. Paul Preparatory School, Saint Paul			X	X	–	–	9–12	166	166	12:1	X	8
Mississippi												
Lee Academy, Clarksdale			X	X	1–5	6–8	9–12	321	139	20:1		7
Northpoint Christian School, Southaven			X	X	PK–6	–	7–12	1,084	476	13:1	X	16
St. Andrew's Episcopal School, Ridgeland			X	X	PK–4	5–8	9–12	1,217	345	9:1	X	25
St. Patrick Catholic High School, Biloxi			X	X	–	–	7–12	441	441	13:1	X	18
Vicksburg Catholic School, Vicksburg			X	X	PK–6	–	7–12	536	272	11:1	X	13
Missouri												
John Burroughs School, St. Louis			X	X	–	7–8	9–12	600	400	7:1	X	27
John F. Kennedy Catholic High School, Manchester			X	X	–	–	9–12	255	255	10:1	X	16
Lutheran High School, Kansas City			X	X	–	–	9–12	128	128	10:1	X	19
Lutheran High School North, St. Louis			X	X	–	–	9–12	286	286	14:1	X	17
Mary Institute and St. Louis Country Day School (MICDS), St. Louis			X	X	JK–4	5–8	9–12	1,250	650	8:1	X	27
Missouri Military Academy, Mexico	X		X		–	6–8	9–PG	228	191	11:1	X	44
Nerinx Hall, Webster Groves				X	–	–	9–12	597	597	9:1	X	13
New Covenant Academy, Springfield			X	X	JK–6	7–8	9–12	478	118	10:1	X	9
Notre Dame High School, St. Louis				X	–	–	9–12	205	205	12:1	X	20
Rockhurst High School, Kansas City			X		–	–	9–12		1,016	13:1	X	20
Rosati-Kain High School, St. Louis				X	–	–	9–12	300	300	12:1	X	17
St. Louis University High School, St. Louis			X		–	–	9–12	1,071	1,071	12:1	X	31
Saint Paul Lutheran High School, Concordia	X	X	X	X	–	–	9–12	189	189	9:1		19

Private Secondary Schools At-a-Glance

	STUDENTS ACCEPTED				GRADES			STUDENT/FACULTY			SCHOOL OFFERINGS	
	BOARDING		DAY									
	Boys	Girls	Boys	Girls	Lower	Middle	Upper	Total	Upper	Student/Faculty Ratio	Advanced Placement Preparation	Sports
Saint Teresa's Academy, Kansas City				X	–	–	9–12	596	596	12:1	X	25
Thomas Jefferson School, St. Louis	X	X	X	X	–	7–8	9–PG	91	68	7:1	X	9
Villa Duchesne and Oak Hill School, St. Louis			X	X	JK–6	7–8	9–12	585	298	8:1	X	12
Visitation Academy, St. Louis			X	X	PK–5	6–8	9–12	553	306	6:1	X	14
Whitfield School, St. Louis			X	X	–	6–8	9–12	409	298	7:1	X	21
Montana												
Butte Central Catholic High School, Butte	X		X	X	–	–	9–12	145	145	10:1	X	11
Manhattan Christian High School, Manhattan			X	X	PK–5	6–8	9–12	304	93	11:1	X	12
Summit Preparatory School, Kalispell	X	X			–	–	9–12	62	62	8:1		62
Nebraska												
Nebraska Christian Schools, Central City	X	X	X	X	K–6	7–8	9–12	201	118	10:1		7
Pius X High School, Lincoln			X	X	–		9–12	1,224	1,224	23:1	X	18
Nevada												
The Dr. Miriam and Sheldon G. Adelson Educational Campus, The Adelson Upper School, Las Vegas			X	X	PS–4	5–8	9–12	419	131	14:1	X	15
Faith Lutheran High School, Las Vegas			X	X	–	6–8	9–12	1,572	844	17:1	X	22
The Meadows School, Las Vegas			X	X	PK–5	6–8	9–12	871	252	11:1	X	12
Sage Ridge School, Reno			X	X	–	5–8	9–12	220	105	8:1	X	15
New Hampshire												
Bishop Brady High School, Concord			X	X	–	–	9–12	349	349	16:1	X	30
Bishop Guertin High School, Nashua			X	X	–	–	9–12	800	800	14:1	X	38
Cardigan Mountain School, Canaan	X		X		–	6–9	–	215	204	4:1		42
The Derryfield School, Manchester			X	X	–	6–8	9–12	387	271	8:1	X	28
Dublin Christian Academy, Dublin	X	X	X	X	K–6	7–8	9–12	98	35	9:1	X	6
Dublin School, Dublin	X	X	X	X	–	–	9–12	152	152	5:1	X	70
Hampshire Country School, Rindge	X				3–6	–	7–12	20	14	2:1		22
Portsmouth Christian Academy, Dover			X	X	PK–5	6–8	9–12	551	204	9:1	X	21
Proctor Academy, Andover	X	X	X	X	–	–	9–12	360	360	5:1	X	43
St. Paul's School, Concord	X	X			–	–	9–12	541	541	5:1	X	32
St. Thomas Aquinas High School, Dover			X	X	–	–	9–12	526	526	13:1	X	17
Tilton School, Tilton	X	X	X	X	–	–	9–PG	233	233	6:1	X	28
Trinity High School, Manchester			X	X	–	–	9–12	398	398	12:1	X	23
New Jersey												
Baptist Regional School, Haddon Heights			X	X	K–6	7–8	9–12	*253	135	10:1	X	12
Bishop Eustace Preparatory School, Pennsauken			X	X	–	–	9–12	675	675	12:1	X	22
Blair Academy, Blairstown	X	X	X	X	–	–	9–PG	460	460	6:1	X	43
Christian Brothers Academy, Lincroft			X		–	–	9–12	999	999	14:1	X	23
Community High School, Teaneck			X	X	–	–	–	181	181	5:1		7
Delbarton School, Morristown			X		–	7–8	9–12	573	507	15:1	X	28
Doane Academy, Burlington			X	X	PK–6	–	7–12	226	126	6:1	X	14
Donovan Catholic, Toms River			X	X	–	–	9–12	689	689	15:1	X	23
The Hudson School, Hoboken			X	X	–	5–8	9–12	187	68	4:1	X	11
The Hun School of Princeton, Princeton	X	X	X	X	–	6–8	9–PG	630	535	8:1	X	35
Immaculata High School, Somerville			X	X	–	–	9–12	690	690	13:1	X	12
Immaculate Conception High School, Lodi			X		–	–	9–12	208	208	11:1		17
The King's Christian High School, Cherry Hill			X	X	P3–6	7–8	9–12	311	126	6:1	X	10
The Lawrenceville School, Lawrenceville	X	X	X	X	–	–	9–PG	815	815	8:1	X	52
Moorestown Friends School, Moorestown			X	X	PS–4	5–8	9–12	730	295	7:1	X	18
Newark Academy, Livingston			X	X	–	6–8	9–12	580	403	12:1	X	32
Notre Dame High School, Lawrenceville			X	X	–	–	9–12	1,292	1,292	13:1	X	31
Oratory Preparatory School, Summit			X		–	7–8	9–12	359	317	9:1	X	28
Our Lady of Mercy Academy, Newfield				X	–	–	9–12	128	128	11:1	X	17
Peddie School, Hightstown	X	X	X	X	–	–	9–PG	542	542	6:1	X	26
The Pennington School, Pennington	X	X	X	X	–	6–8	9–12	500	398	6:1	X	24
The Pingry School, Basking Ridge			X	X	K–5	6–8	9–12	1,116	557	7:1	X	25
Pope John XXIII Regional High School, Sparta			X	X	–	–	8–12	953	953	12:1	X	19
Rutgers Preparatory School, Somerset			X	X	PK–5	6–8	9–12	640	380	7:1	X	23
Saint Augustine Preparatory School, Richland			X		–	–	9–12	695	695	12:1	X	27
Saint Joseph High School, Metuchen			X		–	–	9–12	683	683	12:1	X	24
Saint Joseph Regional High School, Montvale			X		–	–	9–12	516	516	12:1	X	28
St. Peter's Preparatory School, Jersey City			X		–	–	9–12	931	931	12:1	X	31
SciCore Academy, Hightstown			X	X	K–4	5–8	9–12	95	30	7:1	X	9
Timothy Christian School, Piscataway			X	X	K4–5	6–8	9–12	465	148	11:1	X	9
Villa Walsh Academy, Morristown				X	–	7–8	9–12	238	208	8:1	X	11
New Mexico												
Albuquerque Academy, Albuquerque			X	X	–	6–7	8–12	1,121	802	9:1	X	28
Desert Academy, Santa Fe			X	X	–	6–8	9–12	190	140	7:1		10

Private Secondary Schools At-a-Glance

	Students Accepted — Boarding Boys	Boarding Girls	Day Boys	Day Girls	Grades — Lower	Middle	Upper	Student/Faculty — Total	Upper	Student/Faculty Ratio	Advanced Placement Preparation	Sports
The United World College - USA, Montezuma	X	X			–	–	11–12	229	229	9:1		52
New York												
All Hallows High School, Bronx			X		–	–	9–12	600	600	25:1		15
Bay Ridge Preparatory School, Brooklyn			X	X	K–5	6–8	9–12	396	210	7:1	X	13
The Beekman School, New York			X	X	–	–	9–PG	80	80	8:1	X	
Berkeley Carroll School, Brooklyn			X	X	N–4	5–8	9–12	942	285	6:1		10
The Birch Wathen Lenox School, New York			X	X	K–5	6–8	9–12	570	170	15:1	X	26
The Browning School, New York			X		K–4	5–8	9–12	399	107	4:1	X	9
Buffalo Seminary, Buffalo		X		X	–		9–12	219	219	7:1	X	31
Cascadilla School, Ithaca	X	X	X	X	–	–	9–PG		36	5:1	X	52
Cathedral High School, New York				X	–	–	9–12	660	660	17:1	X	11
Catholic Central High School, Troy			X	X	–	7–8	9–12	379	319	14:1	X	17
Charles Finney School, Penfield			X	X	K–5	6–8	9–12	301			X	7
Christian Central Academy, Williamsville			X	X	K–5	6–8	9–12	335	113	10:1	X	11
Darrow School, New Lebanon	X	X	X		–	–	9–12	118	118	4:1	X	27
Dominican Academy, New York				X	–	–	9–12	216	216	8:1	X	9
The Dwight School, New York			X	X	PS–5	6–8	9–12			6:1	X	19
Fordham Preparatory School, Bronx			X		–	–	9–12	985	985	12:1	X	26
Friends Academy, Locust Valley			X	X	N–5	6–8	9–12	781	369	7:1	X	19
The Gow School, South Wales	X	X	X	X	–	7–9	10–12	145	106	4:1		46
Green Meadow Waldorf School, Chestnut Ridge			X	X	N–8	–	9–12	375	100	9:1		20
The Harvey School, Katonah	X	X	X	X	–	6–8	9–12	365	285	6:1	X	23
Hebrew Academy of the Five Towns & Rockaway, Cedarhurst			X	X	–	–	9–12	388	388		X	7
Holy Trinity Diocesan High School, Hicksville			X	X	–	–	9–12	1,003	1,003	17:1	X	25
Houghton Academy, Houghton	X	X	X	X	–	7–8	9–12	124	109	7:1	X	14
The Knox School, St. James	X	X	X	X	–	6–8	9–12	150	120	5:1	X	21
Maplebrook School, Amenia	X	X	X	X	–	–	–	75	62	8:1		41
Martin Luther High School, Maspeth			X	X	–	7–8	9–12	225	200	12:1	X	18
Marymount School of New York, New York				X	N–3	4–8	9–12	744	227	5:1	X	22
The Masters School, Dobbs Ferry	X	X	X	X	–	5–8	9–12	665	490	7:1	X	34
Mount Mercy Academy, Buffalo				X	–	–	9–12	229	229	20:1		13
Norman Howard School, Rochester			X	X	–	5–8	9–12	121	82	3:1		4
North Country School, Lake Placid	X	X	X	X	–	4–9	–	80	61	3:1		54
Notre Dame High School, Elmira			X	X	–	7–8	9–12	373	265	15:1	X	12
The Packer Collegiate Institute, Brooklyn			X	X	PK–4	5–8	9–12	941	306	7:1		4
Portledge School, Locust Valley			X	X	N–5	6–8	9–12	475	210	8:1		15
Poughkeepsie Day School, Poughkeepsie			X	X	PK–5	6–8	9–12	264	106	7:1	X	24
Preston High School, Bronx				X	–	–	9–12	511	511	25:1	X	7
Professional Children's School, New York			X	X	–	6–8	9–12	198	168	8:1		
Regis High School, New York			X		–	–	9–12	532	532	15:1	X	9
Riverdale Country School, Bronx			X	X	PK–5	6–8	9–12	1,150	505	8:1		21
Rockland Country Day School, Congers	X	X	X	X	PK–4	5–8	9–12	117	64	8:1	X	10
Saint Agnes Academic High School, College Point					–							
St. Thomas Choir School, New York	X				3–6	–	7–8	29	11	5:1		21
Smith School, New York			X	X	–	7–8	9–12	57	42	4:1		14
Soundview Preparatory School, Yorktown Heights			X	X	–	6–8	9–12	70	57	5:1	X	4
The Spence School, New York				X	K–4	5–8	9–12	738	249	6:1	X	14
The Stony Brook School, Stony Brook	X	X	X	X	–	7–8	9–12	360	293	7:1	X	20
The Storm King School, Cornwall-on-Hudson	X	X	X	X	–	8–8	9–PG	167	154	4:1	X	63
THINK Global School, New York	X	X			–	–	10–12	44	44	3:1		1
Trinity-Pawling School, Pawling	X		X		–	7–8	9–PG	285	264	8:1	X	40
United Nations International School, New York			X	X	K–4	5–8	9–12	1,570	453	4:1		49
The Waldorf School of Saratoga Springs, Saratoga Springs			X	X	PK–8	–	9–12	248	44	13:1		19
The Windsor School, Flushing			X	X	–	6–8	9–13	110	100	14:1	X	12
Winston Preparatory School, New York			X	X	–	4–8	9–12	227	146	3:1		16
North Carolina												
Arendell Parrott Academy, Kinston			X	X	PK–5	6–8	9–12	721	245	17:1	X	20
Arthur Morgan School, Burnsville	X	X	X	X	–	7–9	–	27	22	2:1		28
Cape Fear Academy, Wilmington			X	X	PK–5	6–8	9–12	599	229	7:1	X	13
Cardinal Gibbons High School, Raleigh			X	X	–	–	9–12	1,428	1,428	13:1	X	34
Charlotte Country Day School, Charlotte			X	X	PK–4	5–8	9–12	1,660	518	7:1		21
Charlotte Latin School, Charlotte			X	X	K–5	6–8	9–12	1,413	492	10:1	X	20
Durham Academy, Durham			X	X	PK–4	5–8	9–12	1,183	419	8:1	X	25
Fayetteville Academy, Fayetteville			X	X	PK–5	6–8	9–12	370	139	14:1	X	11
Harrells Christian Academy, Harrells			X	X	K–5	6–8	9–12	363	134	11:1	X	9
The Hill Center, Durham Academy, Durham			X	X	K–5	6–8	9–12	175	61	4:1		
Noble Academy, Greensboro			X	X	K–6	7–9	10–12	160	64	9:1		10

Private Secondary Schools At-a-Glance

| | STUDENTS ACCEPTED | | | | GRADES | | | STUDENT/FACULTY | | | SCHOOL OFFERINGS | |
| | BOARDING | | DAY | | | | | | | | | |
	Boys	Girls	Boys	Girls	Lower	Middle	Upper	Total	Upper	Student/Faculty Ratio	Advanced Placement Preparation	Sports
The O'Neal School, Southern Pines			X	X	PK–5	6–8	9–12	411	154	12:1	X	10
Providence Day School, Charlotte			X	X	PK–5	6–8	9–12	1,580	570	9:1	X	24
Ravenscroft School, Raleigh			X	X	PK–5	6–8	9–12	1,169	461	8:1	X	22
Saint Mary's School, Raleigh		X		X	–	–	9–12	262	262	8:1	X	15
Salem Academy, Winston-Salem		X		X	–	–	9–12	160	160	7:1	X	22
North Dakota												
Shanley High School, Fargo			X	X	–	–	9–12	327	327	18:1	X	14
Ohio												
Andrews Osborne Academy, Willoughby	X	X	X	X	PK–5	6–8	9–12	347	151	8:1	X	14
Archbishop Hoban High School, Akron			X	X	–	–	9–12	856	856	13:1	X	23
Benedictine High School, Cleveland			X		–	–	9–12	380	380	11:1	X	22
The Columbus Academy, Gahanna			X	X	PK–4	5–8	9–12	1,080	377	8:1	X	15
Columbus School for Girls, Columbus				X	PK–5	6–8	9–12	562	199	8:1	X	16
Delphos Saint John's High School, Delphos			X	X	–	–	7–12	310	310	15:1		12
Elyria Catholic High School, Elyria			X	X	–	–	9–12	434	434	14:1	X	17
Gilmour Academy, Gates Mills	X	X	X	X	PK–6	7–8	9–12	656	436	9:1	X	37
Hathaway Brown School, Shaker Heights			X	X	PS–4	5–8	9–12	848	385	8:1	X	19
Hawken School, Gates Mills			X	X	PS–5	6–8	9–12	1,011	433	9:1	X	17
Laurel School, Shaker Heights			X	X	–	5–8	9–12	640	272	8:1	X	12
Lawrence School, Sagamore Hills			X	X	K–6	7–8	9–12	344	171	11:1		12
Lehman High School, Sidney			X	X	–	–	9–12	202	202	15:1	X	15
Maumee Valley Country Day School, Toledo	X	X	X	X	P3–6	7–8	9–12	532	207	9:1	X	13
The Miami Valley School, Dayton			X	X	PK–5	6–8	9–12	474	196	8:1	X	15
Notre Dame-Cathedral Latin School, Chardon			X	X	–	–	9–12	678	678	15:1	X	30
Saint Ursula Academy, Cincinnati			X		–	–	9–12					
Saint Ursula Academy, Toledo			X		–	6–8	9–12	552	447	10:1	X	31
Saint Xavier High School, Cincinnati			X		–	–	9–12	1,600	1,600	15:1	X	21
The Seven Hills School, Cincinnati			X	X	PK–5	6–8	9–12	1,017	340	9:1	X	14
Stephen T. Badin High School, Hamilton			X	X	–	–	9–12	543	543	19:1	X	13
The Summit Country Day School, Cincinnati			X	X	PK–4	5–8	9–12	1,011	399	9:1	X	19
Trinity High School, Garfield Heights			X	X	–	–	9–12	327	327	10:1	X	15
Oklahoma												
Casady School, Oklahoma City			X	X	PK–4	5–8	9–12	905	316	15:1	X	29
Cascia Hall Preparatory School, Tulsa			X	X	–	6–8	9–12	527	345	12:1	X	23
Holland Hall, Tulsa			X	X	PK–3	4–8	9–12	995	333	9:1	X	20
Rejoice Christian Schools, Owasso			X	X	P3–5	6–8	9–12	873	171	15:1		11
Oregon												
Blanchet School, Salem			X	X	–	6–8	9–12	367	231	17:1	X	16
The Catlin Gabel School, Portland			X	X	PK–5	6–8	9–12	759	311	7:1		53
Christa McAuliffe Academy School of Arts and Sciences, Lake Oswego			X	X	K–5	6–8	9–12	263	185	20:1	X	
C.S. Lewis Academy, Newberg			X	X	PK–5	6–8	9–12	150	46	7:1		5
De La Salle North Catholic High School, Portland			X	X	–	–	9–12	311	311	17:1	X	5
North Clackamas Christian School, Oregon City			X	X	PK–6	7–8	9–12	258	63	20:1		5
Northwest Academy, Portland			X	X	–	6–8	9–12	211	104	5:1		13
Oak Hill School, Eugene			X	X	K–5	6–8	9–12	151	34	10:1	X	23
Oregon Episcopal School, Portland	X	X	X	X	PK–5	6–8	9–12	870	314	7:1	X	20
Pacific Crest Community School, Portland			X	X	–	6–8	9–12	95	65	9:1		11
St. Mary's School, Medford	X	X	X	X	–	6–8	9–12	467	322	10:1	X	31
Salem Academy, Salem			X	X	K–5	6–8	9–12	646	233	13:1		14
Pennsylvania												
Academy of the New Church Boys' School, Bryn Athyn	X		X		–	–	9–12	121	121	8:1	X	6
Academy of the New Church Girls' School, Bryn Athyn		X		X	–	–	9–12	96	96	8:1	X	9
The Agnes Irwin School, Rosemont				X	PK–4	5–8	9–12	666	285	5:1	X	22
Allentown Central Catholic High School, Allentown			X	X	–	–	9–12	810	810	14:1	X	24
Bishop McCort High School, Johnstown					–	–	–					
Camphill Special School, Glenmoore	X	X	X	X	K–5	6–8	9–13	120	67	7:1		
Central Catholic High School, Pittsburgh			X		–	–	9–12	857	857	16:1	X	26
Christopher Dock Mennonite High School, Lansdale	X	X	X	X	–	–	9–12	375	375	11:1	X	12
Delaware Valley Friends School, Paoli			X	X	–	6–8	9–12	149	114	5:1		18
Devon Preparatory School, Devon			X		–	6–8	9–12	272	210	10:1	X	11
The Ellis School, Pittsburgh				X	PK–4	5–8	9–12	393	135		X	22
Friends' Central School, Wynnewood			X	X	N–5	6–8	9–12	788	378	8:1		25
Friends Select School, Philadelphia			X	X	PK–4	5–8	9–12	558	186	15:1	X	9
George School, Newtown	X	X	X	X	–	–	9–12	540	540	7:1	X	25
Girard College, Philadelphia	X	X			1–6	–	7–12	270	135	16:1	X	20
Grier School, Tyrone		X		X	–	–	7–PG	309	309	7:1	X	50
The Haverford School, Haverford			X		PK–5	6–8	9–12	977	425	8:1		25
Holy Ghost Preparatory School, Bensalem			X		–	–	9–12	467	467	11:1	X	19

Private Secondary Schools At-a-Glance

| | STUDENTS ACCEPTED | | | | GRADES | | | STUDENT/FACULTY | | | SCHOOL OFFERINGS | |
| | BOARDING | | DAY | | | | | | | | | |
	Boys	Girls	Boys	Girls	Lower	Middle	Upper	Total	Upper	Student/Faculty Ratio	Advanced Placement Preparation	Sports
The Keystone School, Bloomsburg					–	6–8	9–12	12,000	9,000			
Lancaster Catholic High School, Lancaster			X	X	–	–	9–12	630	630		X	24
Lancaster Mennonite High School, Lancaster	X	X	X	X	PK–5	6–8	9–12	1,393	591	15:1	X	14
Lansdale Catholic High School, Lansdale			X	X	–	–	9–12	703	703	21:1	X	23
Lehigh Valley Christian High School, Allentown			X	X	–	–	9–12	53	53	5:1	X	5
Malvern Preparatory School, Malvern			X		–	6–8	9–12	654	496	9:1	X	23
Mercersburg Academy, Mercersburg	X	X	X	X	–	–	9–PG	430	430	5:1	X	58
Merion Mercy Academy, Merion Station				X	–	–	9–12	484	484	9:1	X	15
MMI Preparatory School, Freeland			X	X	–	6–8	9–12	252	154	11:1	X	11
Moravian Academy, Bethlehem			X	X	PK–5	6–8	9–12	734	314	7:1	X	15
Mount Saint Joseph Academy, Flourtown				X	–	–	9–12	531	531	10:1	X	14
Notre Dame Junior/Senior High School, East Stroudsburg			X	X	–	–	7–12	317	317	15:1	X	9
The Pathway School, Jeffersonville			X	X	–	–	–	135	65	5:1		5
Perkiomen School, Pennsburg	X	X	X	X	–	6–8	9–PG	350	300	7:1	X	18
The Phelps School, Malvern	X		X		–	–	6–PG	97	97	4:1	X	28
Philadelphia-Montgomery Christian Academy, Erdenheim			X	X	K–5	6–8	9–12	252	124	10:1		8
St. Joseph's Preparatory School, Philadelphia			X		–	–	9–12	890	890	16:1	X	35
Sewickley Academy, Sewickley			X	X	PK–5	6–8	9–12	657	267	7:1	X	15
Shady Side Academy, Pittsburgh	X	X	X	X	PK–5	6–8	9–12	945	509	8:1	X	23
Solebury School, New Hope	X	X	X	X	–	7–8	9–12	223	205	12:1	X	33
Springside Chestnut Hill Academy, Philadelphia			X	X	PK–5	6–8	9–12	1,059	460	9:1	X	22
Westtown School, West Chester	X	X	X	X	PK–5	6–8	9–12	636	366	8:1	X	36
Woodlynde School, Strafford			X	X	K–5	6–8	9–12	270	151	5:1	X	15
Wyoming Seminary, Kingston	X	X	X	X	–	–	9–PG	790	442	8:1	X	25
York Country Day School, York			X	X	PS–5	6–8	9–12	246	63	6:1	X	12
Puerto Rico												
Fowlers Academy, Guaynabo			X	X	–	7–8	9–12	71	47	15:1		8
Guamani Private School, Guayama			X	X	1–6	7–8	9–12	606	164	13:1	X	6
Wesleyan Academy, Guaynabo			X	X	PK–6	7–8	9–12	903	246	25:1	X	11
Rhode Island												
La Salle Academy, Providence			X	X	–	7–8	9–12	1,462	1,377	11:1	X	25
Lincoln School, Providence			X	X	N–5	6–8	9–12	350	170	4:1	X	9
Mount Saint Charles Academy, Woonsocket			X	X	–	6–8	9–12	627	478	14:1	X	27
Portsmouth Abbey School, Portsmouth	X	X	X	X	–	–	9–12	354	354	7:1	X	24
The Prout School, Wakefield			X	X	–	–	9–12	500	500	18:1	X	27
Providence Country Day School, East Providence			X	X	–	6–8	9–12	208	165	8:1	X	19
St. Andrew's School, Barrington	X	X	X	X	–	6–8	9–PG	205	175	5:1	X	32
St. George's School, Middletown	X	X	X	X	–	–	9–12	370	370	6:1	X	22
The Wheeler School, Providence			X	X	N–5	6–8	9–12	819	371	7:1	X	15
South Carolina												
Ashley Hall, Charleston			X	X	PS–4	5–6	7–12	682	313	8:1	X	41
Beaufort Academy, Beaufort			X	X	PK–4	5–8	9–12	260	80	10:1	X	18
Camden Military Academy, Camden	X				–	7–8	9–12	295	230	12:1	X	7
Christ Church Episcopal School, Greenville			X	X	K–4	5–8	9–12	1,128	421	10:1		32
Heritage Academy, Hilton Head Island	X	X	X	X	–	5–8	9–12	116	100	9:1	X	1
Orangeburg Preparatory Schools, Inc., Orangeburg			X	X	K4–5	6–8	9–12	678	190	12:1	X	17
St. Joseph's Catholic School, Greenville			X	X	–	6–8	9–12	677	423	10:1	X	15
Wilson Hall, Sumter			X	X	PS–5	6–8	9–12	781	245	13:1	X	34
South Dakota												
Sunshine Bible Academy, Miller	X	X	X	X	K–5	6–8	9–12	85	59	9:1		12
Tennessee												
Battle Ground Academy, Franklin			X	X	K–4	5–8	9–12	754	347	8:1	X	23
Boyd-Buchanan School, Chattanooga			X	X	PK–5	6–8	9–12	868	270	12:1	X	13
Briarcrest Christian High School, Eads			X	X	PK–5	6–8	9–12	1,657	576	12:1	X	20
Chattanooga Christian School, Chattanooga			X	X	K–5	6–8	9–12	1,143	440	17:1	X	19
Clarksville Academy, Clarksville			X	X	PK–5	6–8	9–12	650	218	12:1	X	13
Collegedale Academy, Collegedale			X	X	–	–	9–12	310	310	18:1		11
Columbia Academy, Columbia			X	X	K–6	–	7–12	748	374	12:1	X	13
Currey Ingram Academy, Brentwood			X	X	K–4	5–8	9–12	307	98			8
Donelson Christian Academy, Nashville			X	X	PS–5	6–8	9–12	818	205	9:1	X	19
Ezell-Harding Christian School, Antioch			X	X	PK–4	5–8	9–12	431	169	9:1	X	14
Father Ryan High School, Nashville			X	X	–	–	9–12	948	948	12:1	X	30
Franklin Road Academy, Nashville			X	X	PK–4	5–8	9–12	720	264	7:1	X	23
Friendship Christian School, Lebanon			X	X	PK–4	5–8	9–12	539	226	15:1	X	8
Grace Baptist Academy, Chattanooga			X	X	K4–5	6–8	9–12	469	161	12:1	X	18

Private Secondary Schools At-a-Glance

| | STUDENTS ACCEPTED | | | | GRADES | | | STUDENT/FACULTY | | | SCHOOL OFFERINGS | |
| | BOARDING | | DAY | | | | | | | | | |
	Boys	Girls	Boys	Girls	Lower	Middle	Upper	Total	Upper	Student/Faculty Ratio	Advanced Placement Preparation	Sports
The Harpeth Hall School, Nashville				X	–	5–8	9–12	690	410	8:1	X	39
Jackson Christian School, Jackson			X	X	JK–5	6–8	9–12	857	286	19:1		10
Memphis Catholic High School and Middle School, Memphis			X	X		7–8	9–12	275	185	13:1		
Memphis University School, Memphis			X			7–8	9–12	633	421	8:1	X	14
Middle Tennessee Christian School, Murfreesboro			X	X	PK–6	7–8	9–12	668	232	18:1	X	13
Montgomery Bell Academy, Nashville			X		–	7–8	9–12	752	514	7:1	X	38
Nashville Christian School, Nashville			X	X	K–5	6–8	9–12	467	233	18:1	X	21
Notre Dame High School, Chattanooga			X	X	–	–	9–12	423	423	10:1	X	42
Saint Agnes Academy–St. Dominic School, Memphis			X	X	PK–6	7–8	9–12	847	346	8:1	X	11
St. Andrew's–Sewanee School, Sewanee	X	X	X	X	–	6–8	9–12	230	147	6:1	X	46
St. Benedict at Auburndale, Cordova			X	X	–	–	9–12	945	945	16:1	X	24
St. George's Independent School, Collierville			X	X	PK–5	6–8	9–12	1,188	418	9:1	X	19
St. Mary's Episcopal School, Memphis				X	PK–4	5–8	9–12	837	254	9:1	X	14
University School of Jackson, Jackson			X	X	PK–5	6–8	9–12	1,124	333	13:1	X	17
Webb School of Knoxville, Knoxville			X	X	K–5	6–8	9–12	989	448	11:1	X	25
Texas												
Allen Academy, Bryan	X	X	X	X	PK–5	6–8	9–12	323	87	8:1	X	16
Austin Waldorf School, Austin			X	X	K–5	6–8	9–12	390	81	20:1		12
The Brook Hill School, Bullard	X	X	X	X	PK–5	6–8	9–12	645	300	9:1	X	24
Episcopal High School, Bellaire			X	X	–	–	9–12	680	680	9:1	X	23
First Baptist Academy, Dallas			X	X	PK–5	6–8	9–12	200	81	8:1	X	13
Fort Worth Country Day School, Fort Worth			X	X	K–4	5–8	9–12	1,110	403	10:1	X	26
Greenhill School, Addison			X	X	PK–4	5–8	9–12	1,280	467	7:1	X	28
The Hockaday School, Dallas		X		X	PK–4	5–8	9–12	1,096		10:1	X	42
Huntington-Surrey School, Austin			X	X	–	–	9–12	36	36	4:1		1
Incarnate Word Academy, Houston				X	–	–	9–12	272	272	9:1	X	13
Jesuit College Preparatory School, Dallas			X		–	–	9–12	1,107	1,107	11:1	X	28
Keystone School, San Antonio			X	X	K–4	5–8	9–12	425	138	10:1	X	8
Lakehill Preparatory School, Dallas			X	X	K–4	5–8	9–12	405	116	10:1	X	19
Marine Military Academy, Harlingen	X				–	–	8–PG	262	262	13:1	X	40
Memorial Hall School, Houston			X	X	–	6–8	9–12	91	90	14:1		11
The Monarch School, Houston			X		K–8	–	5–12	135	67	2:1	X	
North Central Texas Academy, Granbury	X	X	X	X	K–5	6–8	9–12	175	58	7:1		17
Presbyterian Pan American School, Kingsville	X	X	X	X	–	–	9–12	168	168	10:1	X	19
Prestonwood Christian Academy, Plano			X	X	PK–4	5–8	9–12	1,551	507	12:1	X	13
Providence Catholic School, The College Preparatory School for Girls Grades 6-12, San Antonio				X	–	6–8	9–12	301	183	12:1	X	20
River Oaks Baptist School, Houston			X	X	K–4	5–8	–	732	160	16:1		
St. Mark's School of Texas, Dallas			X		1–4	5–8	9–12	863	372	8:1	X	41
St. Pius X High School, Houston			X	X	–	–	9–12	682	682	13:1	X	19
St. Stephen's Episcopal School, Austin	X	X	X	X	–	6–8	9–12	688	490	8:1	X	41
San Marcos Baptist Academy, San Marcos	X	X	X	X	–	6–8	9–12	270	207	9:1	X	25
Shelton School and Evaluation Center, Dallas			X	X	PS–5	6–8	9–12	895	278	10:1		14
Southwest Christian School, Inc., Fort Worth			X	X	PK–6	7–8	9–12	820		10:1	X	21
Spring Creek Academy, Plano	X	X	X	X	K–5	6–8	9–12	136	78	6:1	X	
The Tenney School, Houston			X	X	–	6–8	9–12	57	37	2:1	X	
TMI - The Episcopal School of Texas, San Antonio	X	X	X	X	–	6–8	9–12	472	337	9:1	X	24
Trinity School of Texas, Longview			X	X	PK–5	6–8	9–12	265	65	8:1	X	12
Tyler Street Christian Academy, Dallas			X	X	P3–5	6–8	9–12	161	44	11:1	X	13
The Ursuline Academy of Dallas, Dallas				X	–	–	9–12	843	843	10:1	X	14
Westbury Christian School, Houston			X	X	PK–4	5–8	9–12	464	223	10:1	X	14
The Winston School, Dallas			X	X	–	–	–		51	5:1		20
The Winston School San Antonio, San Antonio			X	X	K–6	7–8	9–12	201	86	8:1		15
The Woodlands Christian Academy, The Woodlands			X	X	PK–4	5–8	9–12	579	171	7:1	X	13
Utah												
Alpine Academy, Erda		X			–	7–8	9–12	61	58	4:1		36
Judge Memorial Catholic High School, Salt Lake City			X	X	–	–	9–12				X	17
Realms of Inquiry, Murray			X	X	–	6–8	9–12	32	21	8:1		50
Wasatch Academy, Mt. Pleasant	X	X	X	X	–	7–8	9–PG	319	249	10:1	X	65
The Waterford School, Sandy			X	X	PK–5	6–8	9–12	880	286	4:1	X	29
Vermont												
Burr and Burton Academy, Manchester	X	X	X	X	–	–	9–12	668	668	12:1	X	26
Long Trail School, Dorset			X	X	–	6–8	9–12	155	93	8:1		26
Rock Point School, Burlington	X	X	X	X	–	–	9–12	26	26	5:1		37
Virgin Islands												
Good Hope Country Day School, Kingshill			X	X	N–6	7–8	9–12	360	130	12:1	X	12

Private Secondary Schools At-a-Glance

	STUDENTS ACCEPTED				GRADES			STUDENT/FACULTY			SCHOOL OFFERINGS	
	BOARDING		DAY									
	Boys	Girls	Boys	Girls	Lower	Middle	Upper	Total	Upper	Student/Faculty Ratio	Advanced Placement Preparation	Sports
Virginia												
Bishop Denis J. O'Connell High School, Arlington			X	X	–	–	9–12	1,100	1,100	12:1	X	24
Bishop Ireton High School, Alexandria			X	X	–	–	9–12	813	813	11:1	X	26
Blessed Sacrament Huguenot Catholic School, Powhatan			X	X	PS–5	6–8	9–12	316		6:1	X	13
Cape Henry Collegiate School, Virginia Beach			X	X	PK–5	6–8	9–12	895	370	10:1	X	40
Carlisle School, Axton	X	X	X	X	PK–5	6–8	9–12	390	132	8:1	X	18
Christchurch School, Christchurch	X	X	X	X	1–4	5–8	9–12	196	196	6:1	X	35
The Collegiate School, Richmond			X	X	JK–4	5–8	9–12	1,644	525	15:1	X	31
Eastern Mennonite High School, Harrisonburg			X	X	K–5	6–8	9–12	379	180	12:1	X	14
Episcopal High School, Alexandria	X	X			–	–	9–12	435	435	5:1	X	44
Flint Hill School, Oakton			X	X	JK–4	5–8	9–12	1,086	529	7:1	X	36
Foxcroft School, Middleburg		X		X	–	–	9–12	167	167	7:1	X	34
Fredericksburg Academy, Fredericksburg			X	X	PK–5	6–8	9–12	357	97	7:1	X	10
Fuqua School, Farmville			X	X	PK–5	6–8	9–12	379	151	7:1	X	13
Hargrave Military Academy, Chatham	X		X		–	7–9	10–PG	230	190	12:1	X	50
Holy Cross Regional Catholic School, Lynchburg			X	X	PK–5	6–8	9–12	197	55	7:1		6
Little Keswick School, Keswick	X				–	6–8	9–11	34	9	3:1		24
Loudoun School for the Gifted, Ashburn			X	X	–	6–8	9–12	35	23	3:1	X	
The Madeira School, McLean		X		X	–	–	9–12	308	308	10:1	X	22
Massanutten Military Academy, Woodstock	X	X	X	X	–	6–8	9–PG	99	90	8:1	X	45
Oakland School, Troy	X	X	X	X	–	–	–			5:1		45
The Potomac School, McLean			X	X	K–3	4–8	9–12	1,032	441	6:1	X	27
Randolph-Macon Academy, Front Royal	X	X	X	X	–	6–8	9–PG	293	241	7:1	X	27
St. Anne's–Belfield School, Charlottesville	X	X	X	X	PK–4	5–8	9–12	910	365	8:1	X	22
St. Catherine's School, Richmond				X	JK–4	5–8	9–12	985	313		X	36
St. Christopher's School, Richmond			X		JK–5	6–8	9–12	1,006	337	6:1	X	28
Saint Gertrude High School, Richmond				X	–	–	9–12	247	247	9:1	X	12
Stuart Hall, Staunton	X	X	X	X	PK–5	6–8	9–12	302	139	8:1	X	10
Tandem Friends School, Charlottesville			X	X		5–8	9–12		110	6:1	X	10
Trinity Episcopal School, Richmond			X	X	–	–	8–12	495	495	9:1	X	46
Washington												
Chrysalis School, Woodinville			X	X	K–6	7–8	9–12	185	125	3:1		
Explorations Academy, Bellingham			X	X	–	–	9–12	35	35	7:1	X	
Holy Names Academy, Seattle				X	–	–	9–12	690	690	14:1		
The Northwest School, Seattle	X	X	X	X	–	6–8	9–12	506	350	9:1		16
Northwest Yeshiva High School, Mercer Island			X	X	–	–	9–12	60	60	4:1		6
Seattle Academy of Arts and Sciences, Seattle			X	X	–	6–8	9–12	764	493	6:1		26
Seattle Lutheran High School, Seattle			X	X	–	–	9–12	128	128	9:1	X	18
Shoreline Christian, Shoreline			X	X	PS–6	7–8	9–12	199	55	8:1		6
University Prep, Seattle			X	X	–	6–8	9–12	545	312	9:1		33
Walla Walla Valley Academy, College			X	X	–	–	9–12	178	178	9:1	X	12
West Sound Academy, Poulsbo	X	X	X	X	–	6–8	9–12	113	70	6:1		19
Wisconsin												
Catholic Central High School, Burlington			X	X	–	–	9–12	185	185	11:1	X	26
Marquette University High School, Milwaukee			X		–	–	9–12	1,074	1,074	13:1	X	29
Racine Lutheran High School, Racine					–	–	–				X	11
Saint Joan Antida High School, Milwaukee				X	–	–	9–12	163	163	14:1		3
St. Lawrence Seminary High School, Mount Calvary	X				–	–	9–12	203	203	9:1		26
Wyoming												
The Journeys School of Teton Science School, Jackson			X	X	K–5	6–8	9–12	159	36	7:1		30
Noah Webster Christian School, Cheyenne			X	X	K–6	7–8	9–12	52	3	12:1		1
CANADA												
The Academy for Gifted Children (PACE), Richmond Hill, ON			X	X	1–3	4–7	8–12	307	114	15:1	X	43
Académie Ste Cécile International School, Windsor, ON	X	X	X	X	JK–8	–	9–12	296	151	15:1	X	24
Armbrae Academy, Halifax, NS			X	X	K–6	–	7–12	250	120	9:1	X	12
Balmoral Hall School, Winnipeg, MB		X		X	N–5	6–8	9–12	504	178	18:1	X	64
Banbury Crossroads School, Calgary, AB			X	X	–	4–6	7–12	41	22	10:1	X	28
Bearspaw Christian School, Calgary, AB			X	X	K–6	7–9	10–12	729	106	10:1		15
Bishop's College School, Sherbrooke, QC	X	X	X	X	–	7–9	10–12	239	156	8:1	X	57
Bodwell High School, North Vancouver, BC	X	X	X	X	–	8–9	10–12	538	348	15:1	X	49
Branksome Hall, Toronto, ON		X		X	JK–6	7–8	9–12	895	456	9:1		50
Brentwood College School, Mill Bay, BC	X	X	X	X	–	–	9–12	510	510	9:1	X	43

Private Secondary Schools At-a-Glance	STUDENTS ACCEPTED				GRADES			STUDENT/FACULTY			SCHOOL OFFERINGS	
	BOARDING		DAY									
	Boys	Girls	Boys	Girls	Lower	Middle	Upper	Total	Upper	Student/Faculty Ratio	Advanced Placement Preparation	Sports
Calgary Academy, Calgary, AB			X	X	2–6	7–9	10–12	370	140	8:1		17
Calgary Academy Collegiate, Calgary, AB			X	X	6–6	7–9	10–12	176	80	8:1	X	27
Campbell River Christian School, Campbell River, BC			X	X	K–7	–	8–12	159	62	15:1		6
Central Alberta Christian High School, Lacombe, AB			X	X	–	–	10–12	97	97	13:1		27
The Country Day School, King City, ON			X	X	JK–6	7–8	9–12	700	300	9:1	X	34
Covenant Canadian Reformed School, County of Barrhead, AB			X	X	K–6	7–9	10–12	244	39	10:1		17
Crawford Adventist Academy, Willowdale, ON			X	X	JK–6	7–8	9–12	361	127	14:1	X	15
Crescent School, Toronto, ON			X		3–6	7–8	9–12	715	365	10:1	X	24
De La Salle College, Toronto, ON			X	X	5–6	7–8	9–12	627	434	15:1	X	21
Edison School, Okotoks, AB			X	X	K–4	5–8	9–12	236	48	12:1	X	5
Elmwood School, Ottawa, ON				X	JK–5	6–8	9–12	340	110	8:1		29
Fredericton Christian Academy, Fredericton, NB			X	X	K–5	6–8	9–12	156	62	14:1		6
Great Lakes Christian High School, Beamsville, ON	X	X	X	X	–	–	9–12	124	124	8:1		22
Highroad Academy, Chilliwack, BC			X	X	K–6	7–8	9–12	427	141	13:1		
Holy Trinity School, Richmond Hill, ON			X	X	JK–6	7–8	9–12	750	400	17:1	X	26
Hope Christian School, Champion, AB			X	X	1–6	7–9	10–12	24	2	12:1		
King's-Edgehill School, Windsor, NS	X	X	X	X	–	6–9	10–12	332	218	10:1		33
Kingsway College, Oshawa, ON	X	X	X	X	–	–	9–12	214	214	13:1		16
Lakefield College School, Lakefield, ON	X	X	X	X	–	–	9–12	365	365	7:1	X	43
Landmark East School, Wolfville, NS	X	X	X	X	3–6	6–9	10–12	71	40	2:1		52
The Laureate Academy, Winnipeg, MB			X	X	1–5	6–8	9–12	80	28	6:1		36
Luther College High School, Regina, SK	X	X	X	X	–	–	9–12	440	440	17:1		21
Lycee Claudel, Ottawa, ON			X	X	–	6–9	10–12	1,010	209	10:1	X	30
Miss Edgar's and Miss Cramp's School, Montreal, QC				X	K–5	6–8	9–11	320	100	9:1	X	26
Niagara Christian Community of Schools, Fort Erie, ON	X	X	X	X	–	6–8	9–12	205	180	16:1		20
North Toronto Christian School, Toronto, ON			X	X	JK–6	7–8	9–12	407	166	15:1		26
Parkview Adventist Academy, Lacombe, AB	X	X	X	X	–	–	10–12	107	107	10:1		8
Peoples Christian Academy, Markham, ON			X	X	JK–5	6–8	9–12	376	107	10:1	X	9
Pickering College, Newmarket, ON	X	X	X	X	JK–5	6–8	9–12	423	252	8:1	X	51
Queen Margaret's School, Duncan, BC		X	X	X	PS–3	4–7	8–12	339	141	8:1	X	73
Quinte Christian High School, Belleville, ON			X	X	–	–	9–12	148	148	15:1		8
Redeemer Christian High School, Ottawa, ON			X	X	–	–	9–12	149	149	9:1		
Ridley College, St. Catharines, ON	X	X	X	X	JK–8	–	9–PG	649	485	8:1		82
Rockway Mennonite Collegiate, Kitchener, ON	X	X	X	X	–	7–8	9–12	265	223	10:1		24
Rosseau Lake College, Rosseau, ON	X	X	X	X	–	7–8	9–12	84	74	6:1		82
Rothesay Netherwood School, Rothesay, NB	X	X	X	X	–	6–8	9–12	271	215	8:1		47
Royal Canadian College, Vancouver, BC			X	X	–	9–10	11–12	149	122	20:1		8
Rundle College, Calgary, AB			X	X	K–6	7–9	10–12	811	246	14:1		23
St. Andrew's Regional High School, Victoria, BC			X	X	–	8–9	10–12	335	189	14:1	X	11
St. Clement's School, Toronto, ON				X	1–6	7–9	10–12	470		7:1	X	29
St. George's School, Vancouver, BC	X		X		1–7	–	8–12	1,150	774	8:1	X	47
St. Margaret's School, Victoria, BC		X		X	JK–6	–	7–12	346	226	8:1	X	62
St. Michael's College School, Toronto, ON			X		–	7–8	9–12	1,029	824	16:1	X	31
St. Patrick's Regional Secondary, Vancouver, BC			X	X	–	–	8–12	500	500		X	8
St. Paul's High School, Winnipeg, MB			X		–	–	9–12	554	554	14:1	X	23
Shawnigan Lake School, Shawnigan Lake, BC	X	X	X	X	–	–	8–12	493	493	8:1	X	54
Signet Christian School, North York, ON			X	X	JK–8	–	9–12	30	10	5:1		9
Smithville Christian High School, Smithville, ON			X	X	–	–	9–12	220	220	11:1		14
Southern Ontario College, Hamilton, ON			X	X	–	–	9–12			15:1		
Stanstead College, Stanstead, QC	X	X	X	X	–	7–9	10–12	220	157	8:1	X	45
The Study, Westmount, Montreal, QC				X	K–3	4–6	7–11	327	134	8:1	X	33
Tapply Binet College, Ancaster, ON			X	X	–	–	–	17	11	3:1		1
Traditional Learning Academy, Coquitlam, BC			X	X	K–3	4–7	8–12	200	47	10:1		15
Trinity College School, Port Hope, ON	X	X	X	X	–	5–8	9–12	562	460	8:1	X	37
United Mennonite Educational Institute, Leamington, ON			X	X	–	–	9–12	48	48	8:1		19
Upper Canada College, Toronto, ON	X		X		K–7	–	8–12	1,166	650	8:1		59
Venta Preparatory School, Ottawa, ON	X	X	X	X	JK–7	–	8–10	66	11	6:1		18
West Island College, Calgary, AB			X	X	–	7–9	10–12	533	229	17:1	X	35
The York School, Toronto, ON			X	X	JK–5	6–8	9–12	600	235	16:1		26

INTERNATIONAL

Colombia

Colegio Bolivar, Cali			X	X	PK–5	6–8	9–12	1,269	345	9:1	X	13

France

The Lycee International, American Section, Saint-Germain-en-Laye Cedex			X	X	PK–5	6–9	10–12	705	200	18:1	X	17

Private Secondary Schools At-a-Glance

| | STUDENTS ACCEPTED | | | | GRADES | | | STUDENT/FACULTY | | | SCHOOL OFFERINGS | |
| | BOARDING | | DAY | | | | | | | | | |
	Boys	Girls	Boys	Girls	Lower	Middle	Upper	Total	Upper	Student/Faculty Ratio	Advanced Placement Preparation	Sports
Germany												
International School Hamburg, Hamburg			X	X	PK–5	6–8	9–12	755	249	8:1		19
Italy												
CCI The Renaissance School, Lanciano	X	X	X	X	–	–	9–12	70	70	7:1		33
St. Stephen's School, Rome, Rome	X	X	X	X	–	–	9–PG	287	287	7:1	X	7
Japan												
The American School in Japan, Tokyo			X	X	N–5	6–8	9–12	1,620	584	10:1	X	18
Columbia International School, Tokorozawa, Saitama	X	X	X	X	1–6	7–9	10–12	225	76	12:1	X	48
Saint Maur International School, Yokohama			X	X	PK–5	6–8	9–12	446	143	4:1	X	6
Seisen International School, Tokyo			X	X	K–6	7–8	9–12	646	194	6:1		12
Luxembourg												
International School of Luxembourg, L-1430 Luxembourg			X	X	PK–5	–	6–12	1,356	724	8:1		19
Mexico												
The American School Foundation, Mexico City, D.F.			X	X	1–5	6–8	9–12	2,530	716	11:1	X	16
The American School of Puerto Vallarta, Puerto Vallarta, Jalisco			X	X	K–6	7–9	10–12	343	68	7:1	X	11
Netherlands												
Rotterdam International Secondary School, Wolfert van Borselen, Rotterdam			X	X	6–8	9–10	11–12	278	81	10:1		8
Portugal												
Carlucci American International School of Lisbon, Linhó, Sintra			X	X	PK–5	6–8	9–12	640	216	8:1		11
Switzerland												
Institut Monte Rosa, Montreux	X	X	X	X	–	–	–			5:1	X	39
International School of Zug and Luzern (ISZL), Baar			X	X	1–5	6–8	9–12	1,189	269	6:1	X	36
Leysin American School in Switzerland, Leysin	X	X			–	7–10	11–PG	340	340	8:1		67
TASIS, The American School in Switzerland, Montagnola-Lugano	X	X	X	X	K–5	6–8	9–PG	722	386	6:1	X	38
Zurich International School, Wädenswil			X	X	PS–5	6–8	9–13	1,422	497	7:1	X	30
Taiwan												
Taipei American School, Taipei			X	X	PK–5	6–8	9–12	2,323	887	8:1	X	12
Thailand												
International School Bangkok, Pakkret			X	X	PK–5	6–8	9–12	1,946	705	10:1	X	15
Trinidad and Tobago												
International School of Port-of-Spain, Westmoorings			X	X	PK–5	6–8	9–12	466	171	12:1	X	11
United Kingdom												
The International School of Aberdeen, Aberdeen			X	X	PK–5	6–8	9–12	439	118	5:1		55
St Leonards School and Sixth Form College, Fife, Scotland	X	X	X	X	1–7	8–11	12–13	453	126	9:1		56
TASIS The American School in England, Thorpe, Surrey	X	X	X	X	N–4	5–8	9–13	750	400	7:1	X	41
Venezuela												
Escuela Campo Alegre, Caracas			X	X	N–5	6–8	9–12	480	145	6:1		5
Zambia												
American International School, Lusaka, Lusaka			X	X	6–8	9–10	11–12	280	73	7:1		19

Traditional Day and Boarding Schools

THE ACADEMY AT CHARLEMONT

1359 Route 2
The Mohawk Trail
Charlemont, Massachusetts 01339

Head of School: Dr. Brian B. Bloomfield

General Information Coeducational day college-preparatory and arts school. Grades 7–PG. Founded: 1981. Setting: rural. Nearest major city is Northampton. 52-acre campus. 2 buildings on campus. Approved or accredited by Association of Independent Schools in New England, New England Association of Schools and Colleges, and Massachusetts Department of Education. Member of National Association of Independent Schools and Secondary School Admission Test Board. Endowment: $1.1 million. Total enrollment: 88. Upper school average class size: 14. Upper school faculty-student ratio: 1:4. There are 164 required school days per year for Upper School students. Upper School students typically attend 5 days per week. The average school day consists of 7 hours and 15 minutes.

Upper School Student Profile Grade 9: 15 students (8 boys, 7 girls); Grade 10: 13 students (7 boys, 6 girls); Grade 11: 11 students (7 boys, 4 girls); Grade 12: 17 students (7 boys, 10 girls).

Faculty School total: 25. In upper school: 9 men, 7 women; 13 have advanced degrees.

Subjects Offered 3-dimensional art, 3-dimensional design, algebra, American legal systems, American literature, architectural drawing, art, art history, biology, calculus, ceramics, chemistry, choral music, civics, computer programming, creative writing, dance, drama, drawing, earth science, ecology, English, English literature, environmental science, ethics, European history, expository writing, film, fine arts, French, geography, geometry, government/civics, grammar, Greek, health, history, jazz band, journalism, Latin, mathematics, music, music appreciation, philosophy, photography, physical education, physics, pre-algebra, pre-calculus, publications, publishing, religion, science, senior humanities, senior project, social studies, Spanish, speech, theater, trigonometry, world history, world literature, yearbook.

Graduation Requirements Algebra, American government, American literature, American studies, arts and fine arts (art, music, dance, drama), biology, calculus, chemistry, civics, computer literacy, English, foreign language, four units of summer reading, geography, geometry, Latin, mathematics, physics, pre-calculus, science, senior project, social studies (includes history), year-long independent senior project equal to one full course, requiring outside evaluation and a presentation.

Special Academic Programs Independent study; term-away projects; study abroad; special instructional classes for deaf students, blind students; ESL (4 students enrolled).

College Admission Counseling 12 students graduated in 2015; 10 went to college, including Brown University; Mount Holyoke College; Northeastern University; Sarah Lawrence College; University of Vermont; Vassar College. Other: 1 entered a postgraduate year, 1 had other specific plans. Mean SAT critical reading: 673, mean SAT math: 585, mean SAT writing: 621, mean combined SAT: 1879, mean composite ACT: 28.

Student Life Upper grades have specified standards of dress, student council, honor system. Discipline rests equally with students and faculty.

Summer Programs Sports, art/fine arts programs offered; session focuses on drama, soccer, visual arts; held on campus; accepts boys and girls; open to students from other schools. 24 students usually enrolled. 2016 schedule: July 11 to August 12. Application deadline: June 15.

Tuition and Aid Day student tuition: $22,500. Tuition installment plan (monthly payment plans, individually arranged payment plans). Need-based scholarship grants available. In 2015–16, 62% of upper-school students received aid. Total amount of financial aid awarded in 2015–16: $419,375.

Admissions Traditional secondary-level entrance grade is 9. For fall 2015, 13 students applied for upper-level admission, 13 were accepted, 6 enrolled. Deadline for receipt of application materials: February 1. Application fee required: $50. On-campus interview required.

Athletics Interscholastic: alpine skiing (boys, girls), baseball (b,g), basketball (b,g), cross-country running (b,g), lacrosse (g), skiing (downhill) (b,g), soccer (b,g), ultimate Frisbee (b,g); intramural: independent competitive sports (b,g); coed interscholastic: baseball, cross-country running, soccer, ultimate Frisbee; coed intramural: alpine skiing, hiking/backpacking, outdoor activities, outdoor recreation, rafting, tennis, yoga. 7 coaches.

Computers Computers are regularly used in all classes. Computer network features include on-campus library services, Internet access, wireless campus network, Internet filtering or blocking technology, school Web site for schedules and other administrative information. Student e-mail accounts and computer access in designated common areas are available to students. Students grades are available online. The school has a published electronic and media policy.

Contact Martha Tirk, Director of Admissions and Advancement. 413-339-4912 Ext. 113. Fax: 413-339-4324. E-mail: mtirk@charlemont.org. Website: www.charlemont.org

ACADEMY AT THE LAKES

2331 Collier Parkway
Land O'Lakes, Florida 34639

Head of School: Mr. Mark Heller

General Information Coeducational day college-preparatory, arts, and technology school. Grades PK–12. Founded: 1992. Setting: suburban. Nearest major city is Tampa.

11-acre campus. 10 buildings on campus. Approved or accredited by Florida Council of Independent Schools, Southern Association of Colleges and Schools, and Florida Department of Education. Member of National Association of Independent Schools and Secondary School Admission Test Board. Total enrollment: 466. Upper school average class size: 14. Upper school faculty-student ratio: 1:5. There are 175 required school days per year for Upper School students. Upper School students typically attend 5 days per week. The average school day consists of 7 hours and 15 minutes.

Faculty School total: 69. In upper school: 10 men, 18 women; 19 have advanced degrees.

Graduation Requirements Standard curriculum.

Special Academic Programs 17 Advanced Placement exams for which test preparation is offered; honors section; ESL.

College Admission Counseling 28 students graduated in 2015; all went to college.

Student Life Upper grades have specified standards of dress, student council, honor system. Discipline rests primarily with faculty.

Summer Programs Enrichment, sports, art/fine arts, computer instruction programs offered; held on campus; accepts boys and girls; open to students from other schools. 350 students usually enrolled. 2016 schedule: June to August.

Tuition and Aid Day student tuition: $10,190–$20,375. Tuition installment plan (monthly payment plans). Need-based scholarship grants available.

Admissions Traditional secondary-level entrance grade is 9. For fall 2015, 76 students applied for upper-level admission, 50 were accepted, 30 enrolled. SSAT required. Deadline for receipt of application materials: February 19. Application fee required: $75. Interview required.

Athletics Interscholastic: baseball (boys), basketball (b,g), cheering (g), cross-country running (b,g), football (b), golf (b,g), physical fitness (b,g), physical training (b,g), soccer (b,g), softball (g), strength & conditioning (b,g), swimming and diving (b,g), tennis (b,g), track and field (b,g), volleyball (g), weight training (b,g), winter soccer (b,g); coed interscholastic: physical fitness, physical training, soccer, strength & conditioning, weight training. 3 PE instructors, 12 coaches, 1 athletic trainer.

Computers Computer network features include on-campus library services, Internet access, wireless campus network, Internet filtering or blocking technology. Student e-mail accounts are available to students. Students grades are available online. The school has a published electronic and media policy.

Contact Mrs. Melissa Starkey, Associate Director of Admissions. 813-909-7919. Fax: 813-949-0563. E-mail: mstarkey@academyatthelakes.org. Website: www.academyatthelakes.org/

THE ACADEMY FOR GIFTED CHILDREN (PACE)

12 Bond Crescent
Richmond Hill, Ontario L4E 3K2, Canada

Head of School: Barbara Rosenberg

General Information Coeducational day college-preparatory and differentiated curriculum for Intellectually gifted students school. Grades 1–12. Founded: 1993. Setting: suburban. Nearest major city is Toronto, Canada. 3-acre campus. 2 buildings on campus. Approved or accredited by Ontario Ministry of Education and Ontario Department of Education. Language of instruction: English. Total enrollment: 307. Upper school average class size: 20. Upper school faculty-student ratio: 1:15. There are 187 required school days per year for Upper School students. Upper School students typically attend 5 days per week. The average school day consists of 6 hours and 45 minutes.

Upper School Student Profile Grade 6: 32 students (14 boys, 18 girls); Grade 7: 31 students (23 boys, 8 girls); Grade 8: 38 students (20 boys, 18 girls); Grade 9: 19 students (11 boys, 8 girls); Grade 10: 18 students (12 boys, 6 girls); Grade 11: 21 students (10 boys, 11 girls); Grade 12: 18 students (10 boys, 8 girls).

Faculty School total: 28. In upper school: 5 men, 7 women; 4 have advanced degrees.

Subjects Offered 20th century world history, Advanced Placement courses, algebra, analytic geometry, biology, calculus, calculus-AP, Canadian geography, Canadian history, Canadian law, career education, chemistry, chemistry-AP, civics, computer programming, computer science, computer science-AP, computer studies, dramatic arts, English, finite math, French, French as a second language, geometry, health and wellness, health education, language, law, literature, mathematics, modern Western civilization, music, philosophy, physical education, physics, science, sociology, visual arts, world civilizations, writing.

Graduation Requirements Advanced chemistry, advanced math, algebra, analytic geometry, biology, calculus, Canadian geography, Canadian history, Canadian literature, career education, chemistry, civics, English literature, French as a second language, healthful living, law, music, philosophy, pre-algebra, pre-calculus, science, scuba diving, senior humanities, social sciences, sociology, theater arts, visual arts, minimum of 40 hours of community service, OSSLT.

Special Academic Programs 5 Advanced Placement exams for which test preparation is offered; honors section; independent study; academic accommodation for the gifted.

College Admission Counseling 21 students graduated in 2015; all went to college, including Harvard University; McMaster University; Queen's University at Kingston; The University of Western Ontario; University of Toronto; University of Waterloo. Median SAT critical reading: 780, median SAT math: 800, median SAT writing: 780, median combined SAT: 2360, median composite ACT: 31. 100% scored over 600 on SAT critical reading, 100% scored over 600 on SAT math, 100% scored over 600 on

SAT writing, 100% scored over 1800 on combined SAT, 100% scored over 26 on composite ACT.

Student Life Upper grades have specified standards of dress, student council, honor system. Discipline rests primarily with faculty.

Tuition and Aid Day student tuition: CAN$12,000. Tuition installment plan (monthly payment plans).

Admissions Traditional secondary-level entrance grade is 8. For fall 2015, 12 students applied for upper-level admission, 7 were accepted, 7 enrolled. Psychoeducational evaluation, Wechsler Individual Achievement Test and WISC III or other aptitude measures; standardized achievement test required. Deadline for receipt of application materials: none. No application fee required. On-campus interview required.

Athletics Interscholastic: badminton (boys, girls), ball hockey (b), baseball (b,g), basketball (b,g), flag football (b), floor hockey (b), golf (b,g), independent competitive sports (b,g), indoor soccer (b,g), sailboarding (b,g), soccer (b,g), softball (b,g), tennis (b,g), track and field (b,g), volleyball (b,g), winter soccer (b,g); intramural: badminton (b,g), basketball (b,g), soccer (b,g), softball (b,g); coed interscholastic: badminton, baseball, bowling, cross-country running, flag football, indoor soccer, sailboarding, tennis, track and field, ultimate Frisbee; coed intramural: alpine skiing, badminton, ball hockey, baseball, basketball, blading, climbing, cooperative games, cross-country running, curling, dance, fitness, floor hockey, handball, ice skating, indoor soccer, jogging, jump rope, life saving, outdoor activities, outdoor education, outdoor skills, physical fitness, rock climbing, ropes courses, scuba diving, skiing (cross-country), skiing (downhill), snowboarding, snowshoeing, track and field, ultimate Frisbee, volleyball, wall climbing. 2 PE instructors, 10 coaches.

Computers Computers are regularly used in career exploration, desktop publishing, digital applications, English, information technology, keyboarding, news writing, newspaper, programming, science, technology, theater, writing, yearbook classes. Computer network features include Internet access, wireless campus network, Internet filtering or blocking technology. Computer access in designated common areas is available to students. The school has a published electronic and media policy.

Contact Barbara Rosenberg, Director. 905-773-3997. Fax: 905-773-4722. Website: www.pace.on.ca

ACADEMY FOR INDIVIDUAL EXCELLENCE

3101Bluebird Lane
Louisville, Kentucky 40299

Head of School: Mr. John Savage

General Information Coeducational day college-preparatory and general academic school. Grades K–12. Founded: 1984. Setting: suburban. 9-acre campus. 1 building on campus. Approved or accredited by Kentucky Department of Education. Total enrollment: 368. Upper school average class size: 16. Upper school faculty-student ratio: 1:9. There are 174 required school days per year for Upper School students. Upper School students typically attend 5 days per week. The average school day consists of 6 hours and 10 minutes.

Upper School Student Profile Grade 9: 47 students (25 boys, 22 girls); Grade 10: 51 students (30 boys, 21 girls); Grade 11: 45 students (31 boys, 14 girls); Grade 12: 39 students (31 boys, 8 girls).

Faculty School total: 46. In upper school: 10 men, 10 women; 12 have advanced degrees.

Subjects Offered Algebra, American government, American history, American literature, American sign language, art, art appreciation, biology, business mathematics, calculus, chemistry, composition, computer applications, creative writing, critical thinking, drama, English, English literature, foreign language, general math, general science, geography, geometry, government, health, music appreciation, personal finance, physical education, psychology, world history.

College Admission Counseling 45 students graduated in 2015; 24 went to college, including Harding University; Lipscomb University; Northern Kentucky University; University of Louisville; Western Kentucky University. Other: 14 went to work, 4 entered a postgraduate year, 3 had other specific plans.

Student Life Upper grades have specified standards of dress. Discipline rests primarily with faculty.

Tuition and Aid Day student tuition: $8395. Tuition installment plan (monthly payment plans). Need-based scholarship grants available. In 2015–16, 7% of upper-school students received aid.

Admissions Traditional secondary-level entrance grade is 9. For fall 2015, 42 students applied for upper-level admission, 37 were accepted, 37 enrolled. Deadline for receipt of application materials: none. No application fee required. On-campus interview required.

Athletics Interscholastic: baseball (boys), basketball (b,g), softball (g), volleyball (g); coed interscholastic: archery, soccer; coed intramural: bowling, horseback riding. 1 PE instructor.

Computers Computers are regularly used in computer applications classes. Computer network features include Internet filtering or blocking technology. Computer access in designated common areas is available to students. The school has a published electronic and media policy.

Contact 502-267-6187. Fax: 502-261-9687. Website: www.aiexcellence.com

ACADEMY OF HOLY ANGELS

6600 Nicollet Avenue South
Richfield, Minnesota 55423-2498

Head of School: Mr. Thomas C. Shipley

General Information Coeducational day college-preparatory, arts, business, religious studies, and technology school, affiliated with Roman Catholic Church. Grades 9–12. Founded: 1877. Setting: suburban. Nearest major city is Minneapolis. 26-acre campus. 2 buildings on campus. Approved or accredited by North Central Association of Colleges and Schools. Endowment: $1 million. Total enrollment: 613. Upper school average class size: 20. Upper school faculty-student ratio: 1:13. The average school day consists of 7 hours.

Upper School Student Profile 80% of students are Roman Catholic.

Faculty School total: 63. In upper school: 30 men, 30 women; 29 have advanced degrees.

Subjects Offered Algebra, American history, American literature, anatomy, art, art history, astronomy, Bible studies, biology, broadcasting, business, business skills, calculus, ceramics, chemistry, computer math, computer programming, computer science, dance, drafting, drama, economics, electronics, English, English literature, environmental science, ethics, European history, expository writing, fine arts, French, geography, geometry, German, government/civics, grammar, health, history, home economics, industrial arts, journalism, mathematics, mechanical drawing, music, photography, physical education, physics, physiology, psychology, religion, Russian, science, social sciences, social studies, sociology, Spanish, speech, theater, theology, trigonometry, typing, world history, world literature, writing.

Graduation Requirements Arts and fine arts (art, music, dance, drama), business skills (includes word processing), English, mathematics, physical education (includes health), religion (includes Bible studies and theology), science, social sciences, social studies (includes history).

Special Academic Programs Advanced Placement exam preparation; honors section; independent study; study at local college for college credit; study abroad; academic accommodation for the gifted, the musically talented, and the artistically talented.

College Admission Counseling 183 students graduated in 2014; 174 went to college, including College of Saint Benedict; Iowa State University of Science and Technology; Saint John's University; University of Minnesota, Duluth; University of Minnesota, Twin Cities Campus; University of Wisconsin–Madison. Other: 2 went to work, 2 entered military service, 5 had other specific plans. Mean SAT critical reading: 577, mean SAT math: 606, mean composite ACT: 25.

Student Life Upper grades have uniform requirement, student council, honor system. Discipline rests equally with students and faculty. Attendance at religious services is required.

Tuition and Aid Day student tuition: $13,670. Tuition installment plan (monthly payment plans, individually arranged payment plans, quarterly payment plan). Need-based scholarship grants, minority student scholarships, single-parent family scholarships available. In 2014–15, 37% of upper-school students received aid. Total amount of financial aid awarded in 2014–15: $1,000,000.

Admissions Traditional secondary-level entrance grade is 9. ACT-Explore required. Deadline for receipt of application materials: January 17. No application fee required. Interview recommended.

Athletics Interscholastic: baseball (boys), basketball (b,g), cross-country running (b,g), danceline (g), football (b), golf (b,g), ice hockey (b,g), soccer (b,g), softball (g), tennis (b,g), track and field (b,g), volleyball (g); intramural: lacrosse (g); coed interscholastic: bowling; coed intramural: football. 3 PE instructors, 27 coaches, 1 athletic trainer.

Computers Computers are regularly used in English, foreign language, mathematics, science, yearbook classes. Computer network features include on-campus library services, online commercial services, Internet access. The school has a published electronic and media policy.

Contact Mrs. Meg Angevine, Assistant Director of Admissions. 612-798-0764. Fax: 612-798-2610. E-mail: mangevine@academyofholyangels.org. Website: www.academyofholyangels.org

ACADEMY OF NOTRE DAME

180 Middlesex Road
Tyngsboro, Massachusetts 01879-1598

Head of School: Ms. Maureen P. Appel

General Information Coeducational day college-preparatory, arts, religious studies, and technology school, affiliated with Roman Catholic Church. Boys grades K–8, girls grades K–12. Founded: 1854. Setting: small town. Nearest major city is Boston. 195-acre campus. 2 buildings on campus. Approved or accredited by National Catholic Education Association, New England Association of Schools and Colleges, and Massachusetts Department of Education. Endowment: $1.6 million. Total enrollment: 610. Upper school average class size: 14. Upper school faculty-student ratio: 1:12. Upper School students typically attend 5 days per week. The average school day consists of 6 hours and 35 minutes.

Upper School Student Profile Grade 9: 38 students (38 girls); Grade 10: 57 students (57 girls); Grade 11: 36 students (36 girls); Grade 12: 38 students (38 girls). 44% of students are Roman Catholic.

Faculty School total: 20. In upper school: 5 men, 15 women; 15 have advanced degrees.

Subjects Offered Advanced biology, advanced chemistry, advanced math, Advanced Placement courses, algebra, American history, American history-AP, American literature, anatomy and physiology, ancient world history, art, art appreciation, art history, Bible studies, biology, biology-AP, British literature, British literature (honors), business mathematics, calculus, calculus-AP, campus ministry, career education internship, career exploration, career/college preparation, chemistry, chemistry-AP, choir, Christian and Hebrew scripture, Christian scripture, Christian testament, church history, college admission preparation, college awareness, college counseling, college placement, college planning, college writing, computer art, desktop publishing, drama workshop, English language and composition-AP, ethics, finite math, fitness, forensics, French, freshman seminar, geometry, government and politics-AP, government/civics, guidance, health and wellness, Hebrew scripture, history, history of the Catholic Church, honors algebra, honors English, honors geometry, honors U.S. history, honors world history, intro to computers, junior and senior seminars, mathematics, music, personal finance, physical education, physical science, physics, piano, poetry, pre-calculus, religion, SAT/ACT preparation, science, social justice, Spanish, Spanish language-AP, statistics, studio art, study skills, U.S. history-AP, United States government-AP, world history, world literature, world religions.

Graduation Requirements Algebra, American literature, ancient world history, art appreciation, biology, British literature, chemistry, Christian and Hebrew scripture, Christian ethics, church history, computer literacy, English, ethics, foreign language, geometry, health and wellness, history of the Catholic Church, literary genres, modern world history, music appreciation, New Testament, physical education (includes health), physical science, pre-calculus, social justice, theology, U.S. history, world literature, world religions, Technology Portfolio Requirement.

Special Academic Programs Advanced Placement exam preparation; honors section; academic accommodation for the gifted.

College Admission Counseling 51 students graduated in 2015; all went to college, including Boston University; Rutgers, The State University of New Jersey, Newark; The Ohio State University; University of Massachusetts Amherst; University of Vermont. Mean SAT critical reading: 572, mean SAT math: 556, mean SAT writing: 581. 44% scored over 600 on SAT critical reading, 38% scored over 600 on SAT math, 38% scored over 600 on SAT writing, 38% scored over 1800 on combined SAT, 50% scored over 26 on composite ACT.

Student Life Upper grades have uniform requirement, student council, honor system. Discipline rests primarily with faculty. Attendance at religious services is required.

Tuition and Aid Day student tuition: $9165. Tuition installment plan (FACTS Tuition Payment Plan, monthly payment plans). Merit scholarship grants available. In 2015–16, 65% of upper-school students received aid; total upper-school merit-scholarship money awarded: $10,000.

Admissions Traditional secondary-level entrance grade is 9. For fall 2015, 162 students applied for upper-level admission, 84 were accepted, 40 enrolled. Archdiocese of Boston High School entrance exam provided by STS required. Deadline for receipt of application materials: December 31. Application fee required: $50.

Athletics Interscholastic: basketball, cross-country running, diving, indoor track & field, soccer, softball, swimming and diving, tennis, track and field, volleyball, winter (indoor) track; intramural: rowing. 1 PE instructor, 17 coaches.

Computers Computers are regularly used in all academic, college planning, independent study, library, media, newspaper, publications, research skills, SAT preparation, study skills, yearbook classes. Computer network features include on-campus library services, Internet access, wireless campus network, Internet filtering or blocking technology. Student e-mail accounts and computer access in designated common areas are available to students. The school has a published electronic and media policy.

Contact Ms. Jocelyn Mendonsa, Vice President of Enrollment Management & Marketing. 978-649-7611 Ext. 327. Fax: 978-649-2909. E-mail: jmendonsa@ndatyngsboro.org. Website: www.ndatyngsboro.org

ACADEMY OF OUR LADY OF PEACE

4860 Oregon Street
San Diego, California 92116-1393

Head of School: Lauren Lek

General Information Girls' day college-preparatory, arts, religious studies, and technology school, affiliated with Roman Catholic Church. Grades 9–12. Founded: 1882. Setting: urban. 20-acre campus. 7 buildings on campus. Approved or accredited by National Catholic Education Association, Western Association of Schools and Colleges, Western Catholic Education Association, and California Department of Education. Endowment: $250,000. Total enrollment: 748. Upper school average class size: 28. Upper school faculty-student ratio: 1:13. There are 180 required school days per year for Upper School students. Upper School students typically attend 5 days per week. The average school day consists of 6 hours and 45 minutes.

Upper School Student Profile Grade 9: 199 students (199 girls); Grade 10: 196 students (196 girls); Grade 11: 189 students (189 girls); Grade 12: 164 students (164 girls). 91% of students are Roman Catholic.

Faculty School total: 69. In upper school: 11 men, 58 women; 48 have advanced degrees.

Subjects Offered Algebra, American literature, art, Bible studies, biology, biology-AP, British literature, calculus, calculus-AP, campus ministry, ceramics, chemistry, chemistry-AP, computer science-AP, dance, drama, economics, engineering, English, English language and composition-AP, English literature and composition-AP, environmental science-AP, ethics, fitness, French, French language-AP, French-AP, genetics, geometry, government, graphic arts, health, honors algebra, marine science, music appreciation, music theory-AP, painting, physical education, physics, physics-AP, pre-calculus, psychology, Spanish, Spanish language-AP, Spanish literature-AP, speech, studio art-AP, study skills, U.S. government and politics-AP, U.S. history, U.S. history-AP, video film production, Western civilization, yearbook, yoga.

Graduation Requirements Arts and fine arts (art, music, dance, drama), English, foreign language, mathematics, physical education (includes health), religion (includes Bible studies and theology), science, social sciences, social studies (includes history), speech, 75 hours of community service, 9-11 reflection paper required for seniors.

Special Academic Programs 16 Advanced Placement exams for which test preparation is offered; honors section.

College Admission Counseling 169 students graduated in 2015; 165 went to college, including Gonzaga University; Northern Arizona University; San Diego State University; San Francisco State University; University of California, Santa Barbara; University of San Francisco. Other: 4 had other specific plans.

Student Life Upper grades have uniform requirement, student council, honor system. Discipline rests equally with students and faculty. Attendance at religious services is required.

Summer Programs Remediation, enrichment, advancement, sports programs offered; session focuses on advancement and remediation/make-up; held on campus; accepts girls; open to students from other schools. 200 students usually enrolled. 2016 schedule: June 13 to July 22. Application deadline: May 1.

Tuition and Aid Day student tuition: $16,880. Tuition installment plan (FACTS Tuition Payment Plan). Merit scholarship grants, need-based scholarship grants available. In 2015–16, 52% of upper-school students received aid; total upper-school merit-scholarship money awarded: $50,000. Total amount of financial aid awarded in 2015–16: $2,600,000.

Admissions Traditional secondary-level entrance grade is 9. For fall 2015, 270 students applied for upper-level admission, 231 were accepted, 199 enrolled. High School Placement Test required. Deadline for receipt of application materials: January 18. Application fee required: $55. On-campus interview required.

Athletics Interscholastic: basketball, cheering, cross-country running, diving, golf, gymnastics, lacrosse, sand volleyball, soccer, softball, surfing, swimming and diving, tennis, track and field, volleyball. 5 PE instructors, 16 coaches, 1 athletic trainer.

Computers Computers are regularly used in all academic, computer applications, media production, music, music technology, photography, Web site design, word processing classes. Computer network features include on-campus library services, online commercial services, Internet access, wireless campus network, Internet filtering or blocking technology. Campus intranet, student e-mail accounts, and computer access in designated common areas are available to students. Students grades are available online. The school has a published electronic and media policy.

Contact Melissa Acosta, Admissions Assistant. 619-725-9118. Fax: 619-297-2473. E-mail: admissions@aolp.org. Website: www.aolp.org

ACADEMY OF THE HOLY CROSS

4920 Strathmore Avenue
Kensington, Maryland 20895-1299

Head of School: Ms. Kathleen R. Prebble

General Information Girls' day college-preparatory, arts, and religious studies school, affiliated with Roman Catholic Church. Grades 9–12. Founded: 1868. Setting: suburban. Nearest major city is Rockville. 28-acre campus. 2 buildings on campus. Approved or accredited by Association of Independent Schools of Greater Washington, Middle States Association of Colleges and Schools, National Catholic Education Association, The College Board, and Maryland Department of Education. Upper school average class size: 19. Upper school faculty-student ratio: 1:11. There are 174 required school days per year for Upper School students. Upper School students typically attend 5 days per week. The average school day consists of 7 hours.

Upper School Student Profile Grade 9: 131 students (131 girls); Grade 10: 120 students (120 girls); Grade 11: 124 students (124 girls); Grade 12: 120 students (120 girls).

Faculty School total: 49. In upper school: 8 men, 41 women.

Subjects Offered Acting, Advanced Placement courses, algebra, American history, American literature, art, art history-AP, Asian studies, biology, biology-AP, calculus, calculus-AP, ceramics, chemistry, chemistry-AP, Christian scripture, computer science, concert choir, creative writing, design, drama, drawing, earth science, economics, English, English language and composition-AP, English literature, English literature and composition-AP, environmental science, ethnic studies, expository writing, fine arts, forensics, French, geography, geometry, government/civics, grammar, health,

Hebrew scripture, history, history of the Catholic Church, honors English, honors geometry, humanities, instrumental music, jazz dance, Latin, Latin American studies, madrigals, mathematics, moral theology, music, music appreciation, musical theater, musical theater dance, painting, peace studies, personal finance, photography, physical education, physical science, physics, physiology, pre-calculus, psychology, public speaking, religion, science, sculpture, Shakespeare, social sciences, social studies, Spanish, sports medicine, statistics, studio art, studio art-AP, tap dance, technology, theater, theater design and production, theology, trigonometry, U.S. government, U.S. government and politics-AP, U.S. history, U.S. history-AP, Web site design, world history, world studies.

Graduation Requirements Art, electives, English, foreign language, mathematics, performing arts, physical education (includes health), science, senior project, social sciences, social studies (includes history), technology, theology, Christian service commitment, senior project internship.

Special Academic Programs International Baccalaureate program; Advanced Placement exam preparation; honors section; independent study; academic accommodation for the gifted and the artistically talented.

College Admission Counseling 136 students graduated in 2015; all went to college, including American University; Penn State University Park; Saint Joseph's University; The Catholic University of America; Towson University; University of Maryland, College Park. Mean SAT critical reading: 563, mean SAT math: 543, mean SAT writing: 572, mean combined SAT: 1678, mean composite ACT: 25. 36% scored over 600 on SAT critical reading, 28% scored over 600 on SAT math, 41% scored over 600 on SAT writing, 30% scored over 1800 on combined SAT, 31% scored over 26 on composite ACT.

Student Life Upper grades have uniform requirement, student council, honor system. Discipline rests equally with students and faculty. Attendance at religious services is required.

Summer Programs Enrichment, advancement, sports, art/fine arts, computer instruction programs offered; session focuses on enrichment and athletic skill-building; held on campus; accepts girls; open to students from other schools. 200 students usually enrolled. 2016 schedule: June 13 to July 1. Application deadline: May 31.

Tuition and Aid Day student tuition: $21,575. Tuition installment plan (FACTS Tuition Payment Plan). Tuition reduction for siblings, merit scholarship grants, need-based scholarship grants, alumnae stipends available. In 2015–16, 31% of upper-school students received aid.

Admissions Traditional secondary-level entrance grade is 9. High School Placement Test required. Deadline for receipt of application materials: December 14. Application fee required: $60.

Athletics Interscholastic: basketball, cheering, crew, cross-country running, dance team, diving, equestrian sports, field hockey, ice hockey, lacrosse, soccer, softball, swimming and diving, tennis, track and field, volleyball; intramural: archery, basketball, soccer; coed interscholastic: golf. 2 PE instructors, 35 coaches, 1 athletic trainer.

Computers Computers are regularly used in art, foreign language, mathematics, science, social sciences classes. Computer network features include on-campus library services, online commercial services, Internet access, wireless campus network, Internet filtering or blocking technology. Campus intranet, student e-mail accounts, and computer access in designated common areas are available to students. Students grades are available online. The school has a published electronic and media policy.

Contact Mrs. Louise Hendon, Director of Admissions. 301-929-6442. Fax: 301-929-6440. E-mail: admissions@academyoftheholycross.org. Website: www.ahctartans.org

ACADEMY OF THE HOLY FAMILY

54 West Main Street
PO Box 691
Baltic, Connecticut 06330-0691

Head of School: Mother Mary David, SCMC

General Information Girls' boarding and day college-preparatory, arts, religious studies, and technology school, affiliated with Roman Catholic Church. Grades 9–12. Founded: 1874. Setting: small town. Nearest major city is New London. Students are housed in single-sex dormitories. 15-acre campus. 3 buildings on campus. Approved or accredited by Association of Independent Schools in New England, Connecticut Association of Independent Schools, National Catholic Education Association, New England Association of Schools and Colleges, and Connecticut Department of Education. Endowment: $300,000. Total enrollment: 29. Upper school average class size: 7. Upper school faculty-student ratio: 1:6. There are 180 required school days per year for Upper School students. Upper School students typically attend 5 days per week. The average school day consists of 6 hours.

Upper School Student Profile Grade 9: 4 students (4 girls); Grade 10: 13 students (13 girls); Grade 11: 12 students (12 girls); Grade 12: 4 students (4 girls). 60% of students are boarding students. 59% are state residents. 9 states are represented in upper school student body. 7% are international students. International students from China, Colombia, Mexico, Republic of Korea, United Arab Emirates, and United Kingdom. 70% of students are Roman Catholic.

Faculty School total: 12. In upper school: 1 man, 11 women; 8 have advanced degrees; 8 reside on campus.

Subjects Offered Algebra, American history, American literature, art, biology, calculus, calculus-AP, Catholic belief and practice, chemistry, church history, civics, community service, computer applications, computer programming, creative writing, economics, English, English literature, English-AP, ESL, family studies, fine arts, foods, geometry, health, honors algebra, honors English, honors geometry, honors U.S. history, honors world history, life skills, mathematics, music, painting, parenting, personal finance, physical education, physical science, practical arts, pre-calculus, religion, SAT preparation, science, scripture, sculpture, senior project, Spanish, theater design and production, U.S. government, vocal jazz, Web site design, world history, world literature.

Graduation Requirements Arts and fine arts (art, music, dance, drama), computer science, English, foreign language, life skills, mathematics, physical education (includes health), religion (includes Bible studies and theology), science, social studies (includes history), vocational arts. Community service is required.

Special Academic Programs Honors section; independent study; study at local college for college credit; academic accommodation for the gifted and the musically talented; remedial reading and/or remedial writing; remedial math; ESL (1 student enrolled).

College Admission Counseling 10 students graduated in 2015; all went to college, including Eastern Connecticut State University; Rhode Island College; Seton Hall University; St. Bonaventure University; University of Connecticut. Median SAT critical reading: 580, median SAT math: 610, median SAT writing: 510, median combined SAT: 1550. 24% scored over 600 on SAT critical reading, 33% scored over 600 on SAT math, 22% scored over 600 on SAT writing, 20% scored over 1800 on combined SAT.

Student Life Upper grades have uniform requirement, student council, honor system. Discipline rests primarily with faculty. Attendance at religious services is required.

Summer Programs Remediation programs offered; session focuses on remediation/make-up courses; held on campus; accepts boys and girls; open to students from other schools. 20 students usually enrolled. 2016 schedule: July 5 to August 5. Application deadline: June 25.

Tuition and Aid Day student tuition: $9000; 5-day tuition and room/board: $25,000; 7-day tuition and room/board: $28,000. Guaranteed tuition plan. Tuition installment plan (FACTS Tuition Payment Plan, individually arranged payment plans, Tuition Management Services). Tuition reduction for siblings, need-based scholarship grants available. In 2015–16, 30% of upper-school students received aid. Total amount of financial aid awarded in 2015–16: $86,600.

Admissions Traditional secondary-level entrance grade is 9. For fall 2015, 19 students applied for upper-level admission, 17 were accepted, 10 enrolled. Admissions testing or STS required. Deadline for receipt of application materials: none. Application fee required: $50. Interview required.

Athletics Interscholastic: basketball, physical fitness, soccer, softball. 1 PE instructor, 3 coaches.

Computers Computers are regularly used in business applications, foreign language, French, graphic arts, independent study, journalism, media production, newspaper, programming, SAT preparation, yearbook classes. Computer network features include on-campus library services, Internet access, wireless campus network, Internet filtering or blocking technology, laptops. Student e-mail accounts and computer access in designated common areas are available to students. Students grades are available online. The school has a published electronic and media policy.

Contact Sr. Mark Mary Orsulak, SCMC, Admissions. 860-822-6279. Fax: 860-822-1318. E-mail: admissions@ahfbaltic.org. Website: www.ahfbaltic.org

ACADEMY OF THE NEW CHURCH BOYS' SCHOOL

2815 Benade Circle
Box 707
Bryn Athyn, Pennsylvania 19009

Head of School: Mr. Jeremy T. Irwin

General Information Boys' boarding and day college-preparatory, arts, and religious studies school, affiliated with Church of the New Jerusalem. Grades 9–12. Founded: 1887. Setting: suburban. Nearest major city is Philadelphia. Students are housed in single-sex dormitories. 200-acre campus. 8 buildings on campus. Approved or accredited by Middle States Association of Colleges and Schools and Pennsylvania Department of Education. Member of National Association of Independent Schools. Endowment: $200 million. Total enrollment: 121. Upper school average class size: 15. Upper school faculty-student ratio: 1:8. There are 180 required school days per year for Upper School students. Upper School students typically attend 5 days per week. The average school day consists of 7 hours and 15 minutes.

Upper School Student Profile Grade 9: 23 students (23 boys); Grade 10: 36 students (36 boys); Grade 11: 34 students (34 boys); Grade 12: 27 students (27 boys). 36% of students are boarding students. 75% are state residents. 17 states are represented in upper school student body. 7% are international students. International students from Canada, China, and Republic of Korea. 85% of students are Church of the New Jerusalem.

Faculty School total: 40. In upper school: 18 men, 18 women; 33 have advanced degrees; 10 reside on campus.

Subjects Offered Advanced chemistry, Advanced Placement courses, African-American literature, algebra, American history, American history-AP, American literature, American literature-AP, anatomy, anatomy and physiology, ancient world history, art, art history, Bible studies, biology, British literature, calculus, calculus-AP, ceramics, chemistry, civics, computer programming, computer science, creative writing, dance, drama, ecology, English, English literature, English literature-AP, environmental science, European history, expository writing, fine arts, French, geometry, German, government/civics, grammar, health, history, honors U.S. history, industrial arts, journalism, Latin, mathematics, music, music theater, musical theater, philosophy, photography, physical education, physical science, physics, physiology, portfolio art, pre-calculus, printmaking, probability and statistics, religion, religious education, religious studies, science, sculpture, senior project, social sciences, social studies, sociology, Spanish, speech, statistics, studio art, theater, theater arts, theater design and production, theater production, theology, trigonometry, U.S. history-AP, vocal ensemble, vocal music, women in literature, world history, world literature.

Graduation Requirements Arts and fine arts (art, music, dance, drama), English, foreign language, mathematics, physical education (includes health), religion (includes Bible studies and theology), science, social sciences, social studies (includes history).

Special Academic Programs Advanced Placement exam preparation; honors section; independent study; study at local college for college credit; academic accommodation for the gifted, the musically talented, and the artistically talented; remedial reading and/or remedial writing; remedial math; programs in English, mathematics, general development for dyslexic students; ESL (6 students enrolled).

College Admission Counseling 36 students graduated in 2015; 34 went to college, including Arcadia University; Bryn Athyn College of the New Church; Gettysburg College; Millersville University of Pennsylvania; Penn State University Park; West Chester University of Pennsylvania. Other: 2 entered military service. Median SAT critical reading: 540, median SAT math: 560, median SAT writing: 530, median combined SAT: 1630. 28% scored over 600 on SAT critical reading, 33% scored over 600 on SAT math, 31% scored over 600 on SAT writing, 31% scored over 1800 on combined SAT.

Student Life Upper grades have specified standards of dress, student council. Discipline rests primarily with faculty. Attendance at religious services is required.

Summer Programs Sports programs offered; held on campus; accepts boys and girls; open to students from other schools. 110 students usually enrolled. 2016 schedule: July 11 to August 1. Application deadline: June 1.

Tuition and Aid Day student tuition: $15,400; 7-day tuition and room/board: $22,850. Tuition installment plan (monthly payment plans, individually arranged payment plans, term payment plan). Need-based scholarship grants available. In 2015–16, 60% of upper-school students received aid. Total amount of financial aid awarded in 2015–16: $750,000.

Admissions Traditional secondary-level entrance grade is 9. For fall 2015, 55 students applied for upper-level admission, 38 were accepted, 32 enrolled. Iowa Subtests, PSAT or SAT required. Deadline for receipt of application materials: none. Application fee required: $50. Interview required.

Athletics Interscholastic: baseball, basketball, football, ice hockey, lacrosse, wrestling. 1 PE instructor, 6 coaches, 1 athletic trainer.

Computers Computers are regularly used in English, foreign language, history, mathematics, science classes. Computer network features include on-campus library services, online commercial services, Internet access, wireless campus network, Internet filtering or blocking technology. Campus intranet, student e-mail accounts, and computer access in designated common areas are available to students. Students grades are available online. The school has a published electronic and media policy.

Contact Denise DiFiglia, Director of Admissions. 267-502-4855. Website: www.ancss.org

ACADEMY OF THE NEW CHURCH GIRLS' SCHOOL

2815 Benade Circle
Box 707
Bryn Athyn, Pennsylvania 19009

Head of School: Susan O. Odhner

General Information Girls' boarding and day college-preparatory, general academic, arts, and religious studies school, affiliated with Church of the New Jerusalem, Christian faith. Grades 9–12. Founded: 1884. Setting: suburban. Nearest major city is Philadelphia. Students are housed in single-sex dormitories. 200-acre campus. 8 buildings on campus. Approved or accredited by Middle States Association of Colleges and Schools, Pennsylvania Association of Independent Schools, and Pennsylvania Department of Education. Member of National Association of Independent Schools. Endowment: $200 million. Total enrollment: 96. Upper school average class size: 15. Upper school faculty-student ratio: 1:8. There are 180 required school days per year for Upper School students. Upper School students typically attend 5 days per week. The average school day consists of 7 hours and 15 minutes.

Upper School Student Profile Grade 9: 18 students (18 girls); Grade 10: 27 students (27 girls); Grade 11: 25 students (25 girls); Grade 12: 26 students (26 girls). 24% of students are boarding students. 76% are state residents. 10 states are represented in upper school student body. 9% are international students. International students from Belize, China, and Republic of Korea. 85% of students are Church of the New Jerusalem, Christian.

Faculty School total: 39. In upper school: 18 men, 18 women; 33 have advanced degrees; 10 reside on campus.

Subjects Offered Advanced chemistry, Advanced Placement courses, African-American literature, algebra, American history, American history-AP, American literature, anatomy, ancient history, ancient world history, art, art history, Bible studies, biology, British literature, calculus, calculus-AP, chemistry, civics, computer science, creative writing, drafting, drama, dramatic arts, drawing, ecology, ecology, environmental systems, economics, English, English literature, English literature-AP, English-AP, European history, expository writing, film studies, fine arts, French, geometry, government/civics, grammar, health, history, honors algebra, honors English, honors geometry, honors U.S. history, human anatomy, Latin, mathematics, medieval history, music, painting, philosophy, photography, physical education, physical science, physics, physiology, pre-calculus, printmaking, religion, science, sculpture, senior project, social sciences, social studies, Spanish, speech, stained glass, statistics-AP, theater, theology, trigonometry, women in literature, world history, world literature.

Graduation Requirements Arts and fine arts (art, music, dance, drama), English, foreign language, mathematics, physical education (includes health), religion (includes Bible studies and theology), science, social sciences, social studies (includes history).

Special Academic Programs 5 Advanced Placement exams for which test preparation is offered; honors section; independent study; study at local college for college credit; academic accommodation for the gifted, the musically talented, and the artistically talented; remedial reading and/or remedial writing; remedial math; special instructional classes for students with Attention Deficit Disorder and learning-disabled children; ESL (10 students enrolled).

College Admission Counseling 24 students graduated in 2015; all went to college, including Bloomsburg University of Pennsylvania; Bryn Athyn College of the New Church; Connecticut College; Salisbury University. Median SAT critical reading: 537, median SAT math: 560, median SAT writing: 530, median combined SAT: 1630. 28% scored over 600 on SAT critical reading, 33% scored over 600 on SAT math, 31% scored over 600 on SAT writing, 31% scored over 1800 on combined SAT.

Student Life Upper grades have uniform requirement, student council. Discipline rests primarily with faculty. Attendance at religious services is required.

Summer Programs Sports programs offered; held on campus; accepts boys and girls; open to students from other schools. 130 students usually enrolled. 2016 schedule: July 11 to August 1. Application deadline: June 1.

Tuition and Aid Day student tuition: $15,400; 7-day tuition and room/board: $22,850. Tuition installment plan (monthly payment plans, individually arranged payment plans, term payment plan). Need-based scholarship grants available. In 2014–15, 60% of upper-school students received aid. Total amount of financial aid awarded in 2014–15: $1,200,000.

Admissions Traditional secondary-level entrance grade is 9. For fall 2015, 85 students applied for upper-level admission, 67 were accepted, 56 enrolled. Iowa Subtests, PSAT or SAT required. Deadline for receipt of application materials: none. Application fee required: $50. Interview required.

Athletics Interscholastic: basketball, dance team, field hockey, ice hockey, lacrosse, soccer, softball, tennis, volleyball. 1 PE instructor, 6 coaches, 1 athletic trainer.

Computers Computers are regularly used in English, foreign language, history, Latin, mathematics, science classes. Computer network features include on-campus library services, online commercial services, Internet access, wireless campus network, Internet filtering or blocking technology. Campus intranet and student e-mail accounts are available to students. Students grades are available online.

Contact Denise DiFiglia, Director of Admissions. 267-502-4855. Fax: 267-502-2617. E mail: denise.difiglia@ancss.org. Website: www.ancss.org

ACADEMY OF THE SACRED HEART

4521 St. Charles Avenue
New Orleans, Louisiana 70115-4831

Head of School: Sr. Melanie A. Guste, RSCJ

General Information Girls' day college-preparatory, arts, religious studies, bilingual studies, and technology school, affiliated with Roman Catholic Church. Grades PK–12. Founded: 1887. Setting: urban. 7-acre campus. 3 buildings on campus. Approved or accredited by Independent Schools Association of the Southwest, National Catholic Education Association, Network of Sacred Heart Schools, Southern Association of Colleges and Schools, and Louisiana Department of Education. Member of National Association of Independent Schools. Endowment: $8.8 million. Total enrollment: 614. Upper school average class size: 16. Upper school faculty-student ratio: 1:16. There are 178 required school days per year for Upper School students. Upper School students typically attend 5 days per week. The average school day consists of 6 hours and 30 minutes.

Upper School Student Profile Grade 9: 67 students (67 girls); Grade 10: 59 students (59 girls); Grade 11: 46 students (46 girls); Grade 12: 48 students (48 girls). 88% of students are Roman Catholic.

Faculty School total: 106. In upper school: 8 men, 21 women; 18 have advanced degrees.

Subjects Offered Advanced chemistry, algebra, American government, American history, American history-AP, American literature, American literature-AP, anatomy and physiology, art, astronomy, athletics, baseball, basketball, biology, biology-AP, British literature, British literature-AP, broadcasting, calculus, calculus-AP, campus ministry, Catholic belief and practice, ceramics, cheerleading, chemistry, chemistry-AP, clayworking, college admission preparation, college awareness, college counseling, college planning, computer applications, computer education, computer processing, computer resources, computer science, computer skills, computer studies, creative writing, drama, drawing, electives, English, English literature, English literature-AP, English-AP, fine arts, foreign language, French, French-AP, geometry, government, government-AP, guidance, handbells, history of the Catholic Church, honors algebra, honors English, honors geometry, honors U.S. history, honors world history, painting, peer counseling, physics, physics-AP, physiology, pre-calculus, religion, robotics, social justice, Spanish, Spanish-AP, statistics, statistics-AP, television, U.S. government, U.S. government and politics, U.S. government and politics-AP, U.S. history, U.S. history-AP, U.S. literature, video communication, Web site design, world history, world history-AP, world religions.

Graduation Requirements 1 1/2 elective credits, Advanced Placement courses, algebra, American government, American history, American literature, arts, arts and fine arts (art, music, dance, drama), athletics, Basic programming, biology, British literature, calculus, campus ministry, career/college preparation, ceramics, chemistry, church history, civics, computer applications, computer literacy, computers, drawing, electives, English, foreign language, French, geometry, government/civics, guidance, health and wellness, history of the Catholic Church, moral theology, painting, peer counseling, physical education (includes health), physics, pre-calculus, religion (includes Bible studies and theology), science, scripture, senior project, social justice, social studies (includes history), Spanish, statistics, U.S. government, U.S. government and politics, U.S. history, United States government-AP, world geography, world history, world literature, world religions, senior project, 50 hours of required community service.

Special Academic Programs Advanced Placement exam preparation; honors section; study at local college for college credit; domestic exchange program (with Network of Sacred Heart Schools, Network of Sacred Heart Schools).

College Admission Counseling 55 students graduated in 2014; all went to college, including High Point University; Louisiana State University and Agricultural & Mechanical College; Rhodes College; Sewanee: The University of the South; University of Georgia; University of Mississippi.

Student Life Upper grades have uniform requirement, student council, honor system. Discipline rests equally with students and faculty. Attendance at religious services is required.

Tuition and Aid Day student tuition: $15,300. Tuition installment plan (The Tuition Plan, individually arranged payment plans, bank loan). Merit scholarship grants, need-based scholarship grants available. In 2014–15, 28% of upper-school students received aid; total upper-school merit-scholarship money awarded: $35,600. Total amount of financial aid awarded in 2014–15: $342,850.

Admissions Traditional secondary-level entrance grade is 9. For fall 2014, 17 students applied for upper-level admission, 14 were accepted, 10 enrolled. Achievement tests, admissions testing, ERB, OLSAT/Stanford or PSAT or SAT for applicants to grade 11 and 12 required. Deadline for receipt of application materials: none. Application fee required: $50. Interview required.

Athletics Interscholastic: aerobics, ballet, baseball, basketball, cheering, cross-country running, fitness, golf, indoor track & field, physical fitness, soccer, softball, strength & conditioning, swimming and diving, tennis, track and field, volleyball; intramural: aerobics, cooperative games, fitness, jogging, jump rope, kickball, modern dance, outdoor activities, outdoor recreation, physical fitness, running, volleyball, walking, yoga. 5 PE instructors, 14 coaches, 1 athletic trainer.

Computers Computers are regularly used in all classes. Computer network features include on-campus library services, online commercial services, Internet access, wireless campus network, Internet filtering or blocking technology. Campus intranet, student e-mail accounts, and computer access in designated common areas are available to students. Students grades are available online. The school has a published electronic and media policy.

Contact Ms. Christy Sevante, Admission Director. 504-269-1214. Fax: 504-896-7880. E-mail: csevante@ashrosary.org. Website: www.ashrosary.org

ACADEMY OF THE SACRED HEART

1250 Kensington Road
Bloomfield Hills, Michigan 48304-3029
Head of School: Bridget Bearss, RSCJ

General Information Coeducational day college-preparatory, arts, religious studies, technology, experiential learning, and community service school, affiliated with Roman Catholic Church. Boys grades N–8, girls grades N–12. Founded: 1851. Setting: suburban. Nearest major city is Detroit. 44-acre campus. 1 building on campus. Approved or accredited by Independent Schools Association of the Central States, Network of Sacred Heart Schools, and Michigan Department of Education. Endowment: $3.8 million. Total enrollment: 478. Upper school average class size: 12. Upper school faculty-student ratio: 1:7. There are 180 required school days per year for Upper School students. Upper School students typically attend 5 days per week. The average school day consists of 7 hours.

Upper School Student Profile Grade 9: 40 students (40 girls); Grade 10: 43 students (43 girls); Grade 11: 28 students (28 girls); Grade 12: 34 students (34 girls). 80% of students are Roman Catholic.

Faculty School total: 66. In upper school: 6 men, 16 women; 11 have advanced degrees.

Subjects Offered 20th century history, Advanced Placement courses, algebra, American literature, art, art history, biology, calculus, calculus-AP, chemistry, child development, choir, clayworking, communication arts, community service, computer applications, computer graphics, concert band, concert choir, crafts, creative writing, earth science, economics, English literature, English literature-AP, English-AP, environmental science, European history, European history-AP, forensics, French, genetics, geometry, global studies, government/civics, health, health and wellness, honors algebra, honors geometry, humanities, interior design, jewelry making, Latin, literature, mathematics, photography, physical education, physical science, physics, pre-calculus, psychology, publications, robotics, social justice, social studies, sociology, Spanish, theater, theology, U.S. history, U.S. history-AP, video, Web site design, women's studies, world history, world literature, writing.

Graduation Requirements Arts and fine arts (art, music, dance, drama), computer applications, foreign language, government, health and wellness, literature, mathematics, physical education (includes health), science, social studies (includes history), theology, U.S. government, U.S. history, world history, world literature, Project Term, First Year Experience (arts lab). Community service is required.

Special Academic Programs 5 Advanced Placement exams for which test preparation is offered; honors section; independent study; term-away projects; domestic exchange program (with Network of Sacred Heart Schools); academic accommodation for the gifted, the musically talented, and the artistically talented.

College Admission Counseling 34 students graduated in 2015; all went to college, including Columbia College Chicago; Grand Valley State University; Loyola University Chicago; Michigan State University; Oakland University; University of Michigan. Mean composite ACT: 26.

Student Life Upper grades have uniform requirement, student council, honor system. Discipline rests primarily with faculty. Attendance at religious services is required.

Tuition and Aid Day student tuition: $22,995. Tuition installment plan (FACTS Tuition Payment Plan). Tuition reduction for siblings, merit scholarship grants, need-based scholarship grants available. In 2015–16, 40% of upper-school students received aid; total upper-school merit-scholarship money awarded: $7000. Total amount of financial aid awarded in 2015–16: $626,915.

Admissions Traditional secondary-level entrance grade is 9. For fall 2015, 29 students applied for upper-level admission, 22 were accepted, 14 enrolled. Scholastic Testing Service High School Placement Test or Stanford Achievement Test required. Deadline for receipt of application materials: none. Application fee required: $50. On-campus interview required.

Athletics Interscholastic: basketball, bowling, dance team, field hockey, figure skating, golf, lacrosse, skiing (downhill), tennis, volleyball. 1 PE instructor, 21 coaches, 1 athletic trainer.

Computers Computers are regularly used in all academic classes. Computer network features include on-campus library services, online commercial services, Internet access, wireless campus network, Internet filtering or blocking technology, tablet PC program with wireless network and print services, classroom multimedia services, computer in each classroom. Campus intranet, student e-mail accounts, and computer access in designated common areas are available to students. Students grades are available online. The school has a published electronic and media policy.

Contact Kris Sanders, Director of Admissions. 248-646-8900 Ext. 129. Fax: 248-646-4143. E-mail: ksanders@ashmi.org. Website: www.ashmi.org

ACADÉMIE STE CÉCILE INTERNATIONAL SCHOOL

925 Cousineau Road
Windsor, Ontario N9G 1V8, Canada
Head of School: Mr. Jim Minello

General Information Coeducational boarding and day college-preparatory, arts, bilingual studies, and technology school, affiliated with Roman Catholic Church. Boarding grades 6–12, day grades JK–12. Founded: 1993. Setting: suburban. Nearest major city is Toronto, Canada. Students are housed in single-sex by floor dormitories. 30-acre campus. 5 buildings on campus. Approved or accredited by International Baccalaureate Organization, Ontario Ministry of Education, The Association of Boarding Schools, and Ontario Department of Education. Languages of instruction: English and French. Total enrollment: 296. Upper school average class size: 15. Upper school faculty-student ratio: 1:15. There are 180 required school days per year for Upper School students. Upper School students typically attend 5 days per week. The average school day consists of 6 hours and 15 minutes.

Upper School Student Profile Grade 9: 12 students (6 boys, 6 girls); Grade 10: 27 students (17 boys, 10 girls); Grade 11: 48 students (20 boys, 28 girls); Grade 12: 54 students (29 boys, 25 girls). 45% of students are boarding students. 2% are province residents. 2 provinces are represented in upper school student body. 45% are international students. International students from Brazil, China, Hong Kong, Mexico, Taiwan, and United States; 2 other countries represented in student body. 40% of students are Roman Catholic.

Faculty School total: 50. In upper school: 13 men, 11 women; 10 have advanced degrees; 4 reside on campus.

Subjects Offered Accounting, advanced chemistry, advanced computer applications, advanced math, algebra, art, art education, art history, audio visual/media, ballet, basketball, biology, business technology, calculus, campus ministry, career education, careers, Catholic belief and practice, chemistry, choir, choral music, civics, classical music, computer information systems, computer programming, computer science, concert band, concert bell choir, concert choir, creative dance, creative drama, creative thinking, creative writing, critical thinking, critical writing, dance, dance performance, decision making skills, desktop publishing, desktop publishing, ESL, discrete mathematics, drama performance, drama workshop, dramatic arts, drawing, drawing and design, driver education, earth science, economics, English, English literature, environmental studies, ethics, expository writing, family living, French, French studies, geography, geometry, German, golf, handbells, health and wellness, health education, history, history of dance, history of music, history of religion, history of the Catholic Church, honors algebra, honors English, honors geometry, honors world history, instrumental music, International Baccalaureate courses, Internet, Internet research, intro to computers, Italian, jazz band, jazz dance, journalism, keyboarding, Latin, leadership, library skills, Life of Christ, literature, literature and composition-AP, mathematics, media studies, music, music appreciation, music composition, music history, music performance, music theory, organ, painting, philosophy, photography, physical education, physics, piano, poetry, prayer/spirituality, pre-algebra, pre-calculus, probability and statistics, public speaking, reading, reading/study skills, religion, research skills, SAT preparation, science, sculpture, Shakespeare, social studies, softball, Spanish, stage and body movement, stained glass, strings, student government, swimming, tennis, TOEFL preparation, track and field, values and decisions, visual arts, vocal ensemble, voice, volleyball, wind ensemble, wind instruments, world religions, writing, yearbook.

Graduation Requirements Ontario Ministry of Education requirements.

Special Academic Programs International Baccalaureate program; Advanced Placement exam preparation; honors section; accelerated programs; academic accommodation for the gifted, the musically talented, and the artistically talented; remedial reading and/or remedial writing; remedial math; ESL (30 students enrolled).

College Admission Counseling 52 students graduated in 2015; they went to McMaster University; The University of British Columbia; The University of Western Ontario; University of Toronto; University of Waterloo; University of Windsor. Other: 52 entered a postgraduate year. Mean SAT critical reading: 593, mean SAT math: 724, mean SAT writing: 615. 67% scored over 600 on SAT critical reading, 83% scored over 600 on SAT math, 67% scored over 600 on SAT writing.

Student Life Upper grades have uniform requirement, student council, honor system. Discipline rests primarily with faculty.

Summer Programs Remediation, enrichment, advancement, ESL, art/fine arts programs offered; session focuses on ESL; held on campus; accepts boys and girls; open to students from other schools. 25 students usually enrolled. 2016 schedule: July 11 to August 12. Application deadline: May 1.

Tuition and Aid Day student tuition: CAN$13,750; 7-day tuition and room/board: CAN$45,500. Tuition installment plan (Insured Tuition Payment Plan). Tuition reduction for siblings, merit scholarship grants available. Total upper-school merit-scholarship money awarded for 2015–16: CAN$4500.

Admissions Traditional secondary-level entrance grade is 9. For fall 2015, 25 students applied for upper-level admission, 21 were accepted, 18 enrolled. CAT, International English Language Test or TOEFL required. Deadline for receipt of application materials: none. Application fee required: CAN$300. Interview recommended.

Athletics Interscholastic: aquatics (boys, girls), badminton (b,g), basketball (b,g), cross-country running (b,g), equestrian sports (b,g), golf (b,g), horseback riding (b,g), independent competitive sports (b,g), modern dance (b,g), physical fitness (b,g), soccer (b,g), softball (b,g), swimming and diving (b,g), tennis (b,g), volleyball (b,g); intramural: aquatics (b,g), badminton (b,g), ballet (g), basketball (b,g), bowling (b,g), cross-country running (b,g), dance (b,g), dressage (b,g), equestrian sports (b,g), golf (b,g), horseback riding (b,g), paddle tennis (b,g), soccer (b,g), softball (b,g), swimming and diving (b,g), table tennis (b,g), tennis (b,g), volleyball (b,g); coed interscholastic: aquatics, badminton, basketball, cross-country running, dressage, equestrian sports, fitness, golf, horseback riding, indoor track & field, modern dance, physical fitness, soccer, softball, swimming and diving, tennis, volleyball; coed intramural: aquatics, badminton, basketball, bowling, cross-country running, dance, dressage, equestrian sports, floor hockey, golf, horseback riding, modern dance, soccer, softball, swimming and diving, tennis, volleyball. 2 PE instructors, 8 coaches.

Computers Computers are regularly used in accounting, business, desktop publishing, ESL, information technology, mathematics classes. Computer network features include Internet access, wireless campus network. Computer access in designated common areas is available to students.

Contact Ms. Gwen A. Gatt, Admissions Clerk. 519-969-1291. Fax: 519-969-7953. E-mail: admissions@stececile.ca. Website: www.stececile.ca

ADMIRAL FARRAGUT ACADEMY

501 Park Street North
St. Petersburg, Florida 33710

Head of School: Capt. Robert J. Fine Jr.

General Information Coeducational boarding and day college-preparatory, Naval Junior ROTC, Aviation, Sailing, Marine Science, Engineering, Scuba, and military

school. Boarding grades 8–12, day grades P3–12. Founded: 1933. Setting: suburban. Students are housed in single-sex by floor dormitories. 35-acre campus. 20 buildings on campus. Approved or accredited by Florida Council of Independent Schools, Southern Association of Colleges and Schools, The Association of Boarding Schools, and Florida Department of Education. Member of National Association of Independent Schools and Secondary School Admission Test Board. Endowment: $4 million. Total enrollment: 436. Upper school average class size: 17. Upper school faculty-student ratio: 1:8. There are 189 required school days per year for Upper School students. Upper School students typically attend 5 days per week. The average school day consists of 7 hours.

Upper School Student Profile 50% of students are boarding students. 73% are state residents. 17 states are represented in upper school student body. 30% are international students. International students from China, Czech Republic, Japan, Mexico, Republic of Korea, and Russian Federation; 20 other countries represented in student body.

Faculty School total: 63. In upper school: 20 men, 14 women; 20 have advanced degrees; 20 reside on campus.

Subjects Offered ACT preparation, advanced math, algebra, American history, American literature, analytic geometry, anatomy and physiology, art, art history, aviation, band, biology, boating, British literature, business communications, calculus, calculus-AP, chemistry, Chinese, chorus, community service, computer programming, computer science, computer science-AP, creative writing, drama, driver education, earth science, economics, English, English composition, English language-AP, English literature, environmental science, ESL, ethics and responsibility, fine arts, French, geography, geometry, government/civics, grammar, health, history, journalism, keyboarding, Latin, library assistant, marching band, marine biology, mathematics, meteorology, military science, music, music history, navigation, NJROTC, oceanography, physical education, physics, pre-algebra, science, sign language, social studies, sociology, Spanish, Spanish language-AP, speech, statistics, swimming test, trigonometry, world history, world literature, yearbook.

Graduation Requirements Arts and fine arts (art, music, dance, drama), economics, English, ethics, foreign language, government, health education, mathematics, NJROTC, physical education (includes health), science, social studies (includes history), U.S. history, world history, Qualified Boat Handler (QBH) test, 80 hours of community service.

Special Academic Programs Advanced Placement exam preparation; honors section; study at local college for college credit; academic accommodation for the gifted; remedial reading and/or remedial writing; remedial math; ESL (15 students enrolled).

College Admission Counseling 63 students graduated in 2015; they went to Florida State University; Georgia Institute of Technology; Syracuse University; United States Naval Academy; University of Florida; University of South Florida. Other: 1 entered military service. Mean SAT critical reading: 488, mean SAT math: 520, mean SAT writing: 478, mean composite ACT: 20. 10% scored over 600 on SAT critical reading, 20% scored over 600 on SAT math, 3% scored over 600 on SAT writing, 15% scored over 26 on composite ACT.

Student Life Upper grades have uniform requirement, student council. Discipline rests equally with students and faculty.

Summer Programs Remediation, enrichment, advancement, ESL programs offered; held on campus; accepts boys and girls; open to students from other schools. 55 students usually enrolled. 2016 schedule: July 2 to August 13.

Tuition and Aid Day student tuition: $8610–$21,325; 5-day tuition and room/board: $37,000–$40,000; 7-day tuition and room/board: $43,850–$46,850. Tuition installment plan (monthly payment plans). Tuition reduction for siblings, need-based scholarship grants, tuition reduction for children of faculty available. In 2015–16, 22% of upper-school students received aid. Total amount of financial aid awarded in 2015–16: $500,000.

Admissions Any standardized test required. Deadline for receipt of application materials: none. Application fee required: $100. Interview required.

Athletics Interscholastic: aquatics (boys, girls), baseball (b), basketball (b,g), cheering (g), cross-country running (b,g), diving (b,g), drill team (b,g), football (b,g), golf (b,g), riflery (b,g), soccer (b,g), softball (g), swimming and diving (b,g), tennis (b,g), track and field (b,g), volleyball (g), wrestling (b,g); intramural: kayaking (b,g), riflery (b,g), running (b,g), weight training (b,g); coed interscholastic: aquatics, drill team, football, golf, JROTC drill, marksmanship, riflery, sailing; coed intramural: basketball, bicycling, billiards, canoeing/kayaking, fishing, fitness, martial arts, outdoor recreation, outdoors, pillo polo, scuba diving, strength & conditioning, table tennis, volleyball. 1 PE instructor, 3 coaches, 1 athletic trainer.

Computers Computers are regularly used in aerospace science, aviation, computer applications, English, foreign language, history, keyboarding, NJROTC, programming, science, writing, yearbook classes. Computer network features include on-campus library services, online commercial services, Internet access, wireless campus network, Internet filtering or blocking technology. Students grades are available online. The school has a published electronic and media policy.

Contact Cosmo Kunzelmann, Admissions Office Manager. 727-384-5500 Ext. 220. Fax: 727-347-5160. E-mail: admissions@farragut.org. Website: www.farragut.org

ADVANCED ACADEMY OF GEORGIA

Honors House
University of West Georgia
Carrollton, Georgia 30118

Head of School: Ms. Adriana Stanley

General Information Coeducational boarding college-preparatory, arts, business, bilingual studies, technology, and mathematics, science, and humanities school. Grades 10–12. Founded: 1995. Setting: small town. Nearest major city is Atlanta. 394-acre campus. 89 buildings on campus. Approved or accredited by Georgia Department of Education. Total enrollment: 83. Upper school average class size: 14. Upper school faculty-student ratio: 1:14.

Upper School Student Profile 4 states are represented in upper school student body. 8% are international students.

Faculty School total: 270. In upper school: 149 men, 121 women; all have advanced degrees.

Subjects Offered Accounting, acting, advanced chemistry, advanced math, advanced studio art-AP, African American studies, algebra, American foreign policy, American government, American literature, American history, American sign language, analysis and differential calculus, analytic geometry, anatomy, ancient world history, ancient/medieval philosophy, anthropology, art and culture, art history, astronomy, athletics, band, biochemistry, biology, business applications, business communications, business education, business skills, business studies, calculus, chemistry, choir, civil rights, civil war history, classical civilization, communications, comparative politics, computer applications, computer art, computer graphics, computer processing, computer programming, computer science, consumer economics, critical writing, data analysis, debate, desktop publishing, drama, drawing, earth science, East European studies, ecology, economics, education, English, English composition, English literature, environmental science, ethics, European history, film studies, forensics, French, geography, geology, geometry, German, German literature, global studies, government/civics, graphic design, Holocaust studies, honors algebra, honors English, honors geometry, honors U.S. history, honors world history, Japanese, language arts, Latin, law studies, linear algebra, marine biology, marketing, media communications, microbiology, microeconomics, model United Nations, modern world history, money management, music, Native American history, North American literature, organic chemistry, performing arts, personal finance, philosophy, photography, physical education, physics, political science, post-calculus, pre-calculus, probability and statistics, psychology, public policy, public speaking, religion and culture, religious studies, science and technology, Shakespeare, social studies, sociology, Spanish, speech and debate, statistics, studio art, telecommunications, U.S. government, U.S. government and politics, U.S. history, U.S. literature, U.S. Presidents, visual and performing arts, Western civilization, women's studies, world history, writing.

Graduation Requirements Students must complete Georgia high school requirements which are satisfied through equivalent college courses offered by the university.

Special Academic Programs Honors section; independent study; study at local college for college credit; study abroad; academic accommodation for the gifted, the musically talented, and the artistically talented.

College Admission Counseling 32 students graduated in 2015; all went to college, including Agnes Scott College; Brown University; Georgia Institute of Technology; Georgia State University; Savannah College of Art and Design; University of Georgia. Mean SAT critical reading: 648, mean SAT math: 645. 79% scored over 600 on SAT critical reading, 75% scored over 600 on SAT math.

Student Life Upper grades have student council, honor system. Discipline rests equally with students and faculty.

Summer Programs Enrichment, advancement, art/fine arts programs offered; session focuses on arts and humanities, mathematics and science; held on campus; accepts boys and girls; open to students from other schools. 2016 schedule: July 11 to July 24. Application deadline: June 1.

Tuition and Aid Merit scholarship grants, need-based scholarship grants, paying campus jobs available. In 2015–16, 65% of upper-school students received aid; total upper-school merit-scholarship money awarded: $56,000. Total amount of financial aid awarded in 2015–16: $109,000.

Admissions Traditional secondary-level entrance grade is 11. ACT or SAT required. Deadline for receipt of application materials: June 1. Application fee required: $40.

Athletics Coed Intramural: aerobics, basketball, flag football, Frisbee, paint ball, soccer, softball, ultimate Frisbee.

Computers Computers are regularly used in all classes. Computer network features include on-campus library services, online commercial services, Internet access, wireless campus network, Internet filtering or blocking technology. Student e-mail accounts are available to students. Students grades are available online. The school has a published electronic and media policy.

Contact Adriana Stanley, Director. 678-839-0634. Fax: 678-839-2685. E-mail: astanley@westga.edu. Website: www.advancedacademy.org

THE AGNES IRWIN SCHOOL

Ithan Avenue and Conestoga Road
Rosemont, Pennsylvania 19010

Head of School: Dr. Wendy L. Hill

General Information Girls' day college-preparatory school. Grades PK–12. Founded: 1869. Setting: suburban. Nearest major city is Philadelphia. 18-acre campus. 5 buildings on campus. Approved or accredited by Middle States Association of Colleges and Schools, Pennsylvania Association of Independent Schools, and Pennsylvania Department of Education. Member of National Association of Independent Schools, Secondary School Admission Test Board, and National Coalition of Girls' Schools. Endowment: $21.2 million. Total enrollment: 666. Upper school average class size: 15. Upper school faculty-student ratio: 1:5. There are 162 required school days per year for Upper School students. Upper School students typically attend 5 days per week. The average school day consists of 6 hours and 45 minutes.

Upper School Student Profile Grade 9: 80 students (80 girls); Grade 10: 71 students (71 girls); Grade 11: 66 students (66 girls); Grade 12: 68 students (68 girls).

Faculty School total: 104. In upper school: 17 men, 44 women; 37 have advanced degrees.

Subjects Offered 20th century world history, advanced studio art-AP, African-American history, algebra, American history, American history-AP, Ancient Greek, art history, Asian studies, bioethics, bioethics, DNA and culture, biology, biology-AP, calculus, calculus-AP, chemistry, chemistry-AP, choreography, computer programming, dance, drama, English, English language and composition-AP, English language-AP, English literature, English literature and composition-AP, English-AP, environmental science-AP, European history, European history-AP, film history, French, French-AP, geometry, Greek, health, history, honors algebra, honors English, honors geometry, honors U.S. history, honors world history, independent study, international relations, Latin, mathematics-AP, media arts, Middle East, Middle Eastern history, music theory, photography, physical education, physics, physics-AP, pre-calculus, public speaking, robotics, Spanish, Spanish-AP, statistics, studio art, theater arts, trigonometry.

Graduation Requirements Arts and fine arts (art, music, dance, drama), English, foreign language, history, mathematics, media literacy, physical education (includes health), science, senior assembly given by each girl before graduation. Community service is required.

Special Academic Programs 12 Advanced Placement exams for which test preparation is offered; honors section; independent study; term-away projects; study abroad; academic accommodation for the gifted.

College Admission Counseling 83 students graduated in 2015; all went to college, including Drexel University; Georgetown University; Penn State University Park; The George Washington University; University of Pennsylvania.

Student Life Upper grades have uniform requirement, student council, honor system. Discipline rests equally with students and faculty.

Summer Programs Remediation, enrichment, advancement, sports, art/fine arts, computer instruction programs offered; session focuses on arts, academics, and athletics; held on campus; accepts boys and girls; open to students from other schools. 340 students usually enrolled. 2016 schedule: June 15 to July 31. Application deadline: none.

Tuition and Aid Day student tuition: $34,200. Tuition installment plan (monthly payment plans). Need-based scholarship grants available. In 2014–15, 27% of upper-school students received aid. Total amount of financial aid awarded in 2014–15: $176,025.

Admissions Traditional secondary-level entrance grade is 9. For fall 2015, 79 students applied for upper-level admission, 37 were accepted, 20 enrolled. ISEE, SSAT or WISC-R or WISC-III required. Deadline for receipt of application materials: December 14. Application fee required: $50. Interview required.

Athletics Interscholastic: basketball, crew, cross-country running, diving, field hockey, golf, independent competitive sports, lacrosse, soccer, softball, squash, swimming and diving, tennis, track and field, volleyball; intramural: crew, dance, fitness, modern dance, physical fitness, physical training, strength & conditioning, weight training. 4 PE instructors, 21 coaches, 1 athletic trainer.

Computers Computers are regularly used in art, drawing and design, English, foreign language, history, mathematics, media arts, photography, science, yearbook classes. Computer network features include on-campus library services, online commercial services, Internet access, wireless campus network, online databases. Campus intranet, student e-mail accounts, and computer access in designated common areas are available to students. The school has a published electronic and media policy.

Contact Mrs. Claire Lewis, Admission Office Manager. 610-526-1667. Fax: 610-581-0495. E-mail: clewis@agnesirwin.org. Website: www.agnesirwin.org

ALBUQUERQUE ACADEMY

6400 Wyoming Boulevard NE
Albuquerque, New Mexico 87109

Head of School: Andrew Watson

General Information Coeducational day college-preparatory, arts, technology, experiential education, and global languages school. Grades 6–12. Founded: 1955. Setting: suburban. 312-acre campus. 9 buildings on campus. Approved or accredited by Independent Schools Association of the Southwest and New Mexico Department of

Education. Member of National Association of Independent Schools and Secondary School Admission Test Board. Endowment: $87 million. Total enrollment: 1,121. Upper school average class size: 15. Upper school faculty-student ratio: 1:9. There are 171 required school days per year for Upper School students. Upper School students typically attend 5 days per week. The average school day consists of 7 hours and 30 minutes.

Upper School Student Profile Grade 8: 145 students (73 boys, 72 girls); Grade 9: 162 students (81 boys, 81 girls); Grade 10: 169 students (81 boys, 88 girls); Grade 11: 160 students (75 boys, 85 girls); Grade 12: 166 students (78 boys, 88 girls).

Faculty School total: 180. In upper school: 66 men, 61 women; 100 have advanced degrees.

Subjects Offered Advanced Placement courses, algebra, American history, anatomy, Arabic, art, art history, astronomy, band, biochemistry, biology, calculus, chemistry, chemistry-AP, computer science, creative writing, dance, drama, drawing, earth science, economics, electronics, English, English-AP, European history, fine arts, French, French language-AP, genetics, geometry, German, government/civics, history, history-AP, horticulture, Japanese, jazz, Latin American history, law, library studies, Mandarin, mathematics, media, music, outdoor education, painting, philosophy, photography, physical education, physics, physiology, printmaking, psychology, religion, robotics, Russian, science, social studies, Spanish, speech, swimming, theater, trigonometry, weight training, women's studies, world history, writing.

Graduation Requirements English, experiential education, foreign language, mathematics, physical education (includes health), science, social studies (includes history), experiential education (environmental and outdoor activities).

Special Academic Programs 18 Advanced Placement exams for which test preparation is offered; independent study; term-away projects; study abroad.

College Admission Counseling 166 students graduated in 2015; all went to college, including Arizona State University at the Tempe campus; Colorado State University; The University of Texas at Austin; University of New Mexico; Washington University in St. Louis. Mean SAT critical reading: 663, mean SAT math: 660, mean SAT writing: 650, mean combined SAT: 1973, mean composite ACT: 29.

Student Life Upper grades have specified standards of dress, student council, honor system. Discipline rests primarily with faculty.

Summer Programs Remediation, enrichment, advancement, sports, art/fine arts, computer instruction programs offered; session focuses on enrichment; held on campus; accepts boys and girls; open to students from other schools. 1,900 students usually enrolled. 2016 schedule: June 2 to July 11. Application deadline: none.

Tuition and Aid Day student tuition: $21,450. Tuition installment plan (FACTS Tuition Payment Plan). Need-based scholarship grants available. In 2015–16, 22% of upper-school students received aid. Total amount of financial aid awarded in 2015–16: $3,526,266.

Admissions Traditional secondary-level entrance grade is 9. For fall 2015, 117 students applied for upper-level admission, 68 were accepted, 35 enrolled. ISEE, school's own exam or SSAT required. Deadline for receipt of application materials: February 5. Application fee required: $65. Interview required.

Athletics Interscholastic: baseball (boys), basketball (b,g), cross-country running (b,g), dance (b,g), diving (b,g), football (b), golf (b,g), hiking/backpacking (b,g), life saving (b,g), modern dance (b,g), outdoor education (b,g), outdoor skills (b,g), physical training (b,g), rafting (b,g), rappelling (b,g), rock climbing (b,g), soccer (b,g), softball (g), swimming and diving (b,g), tennis (b,g), track and field (b,g), volleyball (g), wrestling (b,g); intramural: bowling (b,g); coed intramural: ballet, basketball, canoeing/kayaking, wilderness, wilderness survival. 9 PE instructors, 84 coaches, 3 athletic trainers.

Computers Computers are regularly used in foreign language, history, library science, mathematics classes. Computer network features include on-campus library services, online commercial services, Internet access, wireless campus network, Internet filtering or blocking technology. Campus intranet and student e-mail accounts are available to students. The school has a published electronic and media policy.

Contact Amy Eglinton Keller, Director of Admission. 505-828-3208. Fax: 505-828-3128. E-mail: keller@aa.edu. Website: www.aa.edu

ALEXANDER DAWSON SCHOOL

10455 Dawson Drive
Lafayette, Colorado 80026

Head of School: Mr. George Moore

General Information Coeducational day college-preparatory, arts, technology, and engineering, global studies, robotics school. Grades K–12. Founded: 1970. Setting: rural. Nearest major city is Boulder. 108-acre campus. 11 buildings on campus. Approved or accredited by Association of Colorado Independent Schools and Colorado Department of Education. Member of National Association of Independent Schools and Secondary School Admission Test Board. Total enrollment: 517. Upper school average class size: 15. Upper school faculty-student ratio: 1:8. There are 168 required school days per year for Upper School students. Upper School students typically attend 5 days per week. The average school day consists of 9 hours and 30 minutes.

Upper School Student Profile Grade 9: 67 students (33 boys, 34 girls); Grade 10: 57 students (31 boys, 26 girls); Grade 11: 61 students (28 boys, 33 girls); Grade 12: 61 students (33 boys, 28 girls).

Faculty School total: 55. In upper school: 17 men, 10 women; 25 have advanced degrees.

Subjects Offered Algebra, American history, American literature, art, art history, biology, calculus, ceramics, chemistry, Chinese, computer math, computer multimedia, computer programming, computer science, creative writing, dance, drafting, drama, earth science, economics, English, English literature, European history, expository writing, fine arts, French, geography, geometry, government-AP, government/civics, grammar, health, history, industrial arts, journalism, Latin, mathematics, mechanical drawing, music, photography, physical education, physics, science, social sciences, social studies, Spanish, speech, theater, trigonometry, world history, world literature, writing.

Graduation Requirements Arts and fine arts (art, music, dance, drama), computer science, English, foreign language, history, mathematics, science, sports.

Special Academic Programs 15 Advanced Placement exams for which test preparation is offered; honors section; independent study; term-away projects; study at local college for college credit; study abroad; academic accommodation for the gifted, the musically talented, and the artistically talented; remedial reading and/or remedial writing; remedial math; special instructional classes for deaf students.

College Admission Counseling 57 students graduated in 2015; all went to college, including Middlebury College; Pomona College; University of Denver; Wellesley College. Mean SAT critical reading: 625, mean SAT math: 630, mean SAT writing: 630, mean composite ACT: 27.

Student Life Upper school grades have specified standards of dress, student council, honor system. Discipline rests equally with students and faculty.

Tuition and Aid Day student tuition: $23,950. Tuition installment plan (Insured Tuition Payment Plan, monthly payment plans, individually arranged payment plans). Need-based scholarship grants, need-based loans available. In 2015–16, 21% of upper-school students received aid. Total amount of financial aid awarded in 2015–16: $1,450,000.

Admissions Traditional secondary-level entrance grade is 9. For fall 2015, 108 students applied for upper-level admission, 70 were accepted, 56 enrolled. Deadline for receipt of application materials: none. Application fee required: $75. Interview required.

Athletics Interscholastic: baseball (boys), basketball (b,g), lacrosse (b), soccer (b,g), swimming and diving (b,g), synchronized swimming (g), tennis (b,g), track and field (b,g), volleyball (g); intramural: lacrosse (b); coed interscholastic: bicycling, canoeing/kayaking, cross-country running, equestrian sports, golf, kayaking, martial arts, paddling, skiing (downhill), Special Olympics; coed intramural: aerobics, aerobics/dance, backpacking, Circus, climbing, dance, equestrian sports, fitness, flag football, football, Frisbee, golf, hiking/backpacking, indoor soccer, martial arts, modern dance, outdoor activities, outdoor education, outdoor recreation, outdoor skills, physical fitness, rafting, rock climbing, ropes courses, running, strength & conditioning, weight lifting. 3 PE instructors, 22 coaches, 1 athletic trainer.

Computers Computers are regularly used in art, engineering, mathematics, science classes. Computer network features include on-campus library services, online commercial services, Internet access, wireless campus network, Internet filtering or blocking technology. Campus intranet, student e-mail accounts, and computer access in designated common areas are available to students. Students grades are available online. The school has a published electronic and media policy.

Contact Ms. Denise LaRusch, Assistant to the Director of Admissions. 303-665-6679. Fax: 303-381-0415. E-mail: dlarusch@dawsonschool.org. Website: www.dawsonschool.org

ALLEN ACADEMY

3201 Boonville Road
Bryan, Texas 77802

Head of School: Dr. Matthew J. Rush

General Information Coeducational boarding and day college-preparatory and ESL school. Boarding grades 9–12, day grades PK–12. Founded: 1886. Setting: small town. Nearest major city is Houston. 40-acre campus. 4 buildings on campus. Approved or accredited by Independent Schools Association of the Southwest, Southern Association of Colleges and Schools, and Texas Education Agency. Member of National Association of Independent Schools. Total enrollment: 323. Upper school average class size: 18. Upper school faculty-student ratio: 1:8. There are 175 required school days per year for Upper School students. Upper School students typically attend 5 days per week. The average school day consists of 7 hours and 30 minutes.

Upper School Student Profile Grade 9: 22 students (12 boys, 10 girls); Grade 10: 20 students (13 boys, 7 girls); Grade 11: 22 students (10 boys, 12 girls); Grade 12: 23 students (15 boys, 8 girls). 17% of students are boarding students. 1 state is represented in upper school student body. 100% are international students. International students from China and Republic of Korea; 3 other countries represented in student body.

Faculty School total: 50. In upper school: 8 men, 11 women; 9 have advanced degrees.

Subjects Offered Algebra, American history, American history-AP, American literature, art, band, biology, biology-AP, calculus, calculus-AP, chemistry, choir, drama, drawing, English language-AP, English literature, English literature and composition-AP, English literature-AP, ESL, European history, European history-AP, French, French-AP, geometry, honors English, keyboarding, multimedia, painting, physical education, physics-AP, pre-calculus, Spanish, Spanish-AP, video film production, world history, yearbook.

Graduation Requirements Algebra, American history, American literature, arts and fine arts (art, music, dance, drama), biology, chemistry, English composition, English literature, European history, geometry, physics, pre-calculus, world history, 48 hours of community service (12 per year).

Special Academic Programs Advanced Placement exam preparation; honors section; study at local college for college credit; ESL (12 students enrolled).

College Admission Counseling 21 students graduated in 2015; 19 went to college, including Baylor University; Indiana University Bloomington; Sam Houston State University; St. Edward's University; Texas A&M University; The University of Texas at Austin. Other: 1 went to work, 1 entered a postgraduate year. Median SAT critical reading: 525, median SAT math: 625, median SAT writing: 560, median combined SAT: 1710, median composite ACT: 26. 30% scored over 600 on SAT critical reading, 60% scored over 600 on SAT math, 40% scored over 600 on SAT writing, 20% scored over 1800 on combined SAT, 58% scored over 26 on composite ACT.

Student Life Upper grades have uniform requirement, student council, honor system. Discipline rests equally with students and faculty.

Summer Programs Session focuses on academics; held on campus; accepts boys and girls; open to students from other schools. 80 students usually enrolled. 2016 schedule: June 13 to July 29. Application deadline: June 1.

Tuition and Aid Day student tuition: $8066–$12,051; 7-day tuition and room/board: $36,240. Tuition installment plan (FACTS Tuition Payment Plan, monthly and quarterly payment plans). Need-based scholarship grants available. In 2015–16, 23% of upper-school students received aid. Total amount of financial aid awarded in 2015–16: $40,950.

Admissions Traditional secondary-level entrance grade is 9. Any standardized test, Archdiocese of Washington Entrance Exam, ERB CTP IV, ISEE, PSAT, PSAT, SAT, or ACT for applicants to grade 11 and 12 or writing sample required. Deadline for receipt of application materials: none. Application fee required: $250. Interview required.

Athletics Interscholastic: baseball (boys), basketball (b,g), cheering (g), cross-country running (b,g), football (b), golf (b,g), softball (g), tennis (b,g), track and field (b,g), volleyball (g); coed interscholastic: fitness, soccer, strength & conditioning, weight training, winter soccer; coed intramural: basketball, combined training, weight training. 2 PE instructors, 4 coaches, 2 athletic trainers.

Computers Computers are regularly used in keyboarding, multimedia classes. Computer network features include online commercial services, Internet access, wireless campus network, Internet filtering or blocking technology. Campus intranet, student e-mail accounts, and computer access in designated common areas are available to students. Students grades are available online. The school has a published electronic and media policy.

Contact Mrs. Anne Prescott, Director of Admission. 979-776-0731. Fax: 979-774-7769. E-mail: aprescott@allenacademy.org. Website: www.allenacademy.org

ALLENTOWN CENTRAL CATHOLIC HIGH SCHOOL

301 North Fourth Street
Allentown, Pennsylvania 18102-3098
Head of School: Mr. Blair A. Tiger

General Information Coeducational day college-preparatory, arts, business, religious studies, and technology school, affiliated with Roman Catholic Church. Grades 9–12. Founded: 1927. Setting: urban. 3-acre campus. 3 buildings on campus. Approved or accredited by Middle States Association of Colleges and Schools, National Catholic Education Association, and Pennsylvania Department of Education. Endowment: $100,000. Total enrollment: 810. Upper school average class size: 25. Upper school faculty-student ratio: 1:14. There are 190 required school days per year for Upper School students. Upper School students typically attend 5 days per week. The average school day consists of 6 hours and 50 minutes.

Upper School Student Profile Grade 9: 172 students (90 boys, 82 girls); Grade 10: 224 students (119 boys, 105 girls); Grade 11: 222 students (129 boys, 93 girls); Grade 12: 191 students (100 boys, 91 girls). 87% of students are Roman Catholic.

Faculty School total: 55. In upper school: 27 men, 28 women; 22 have advanced degrees.

Subjects Offered Advanced biology, advanced chemistry, advanced math, Advanced Placement courses, algebra, American culture, American government, American history, American history-AP, American legal systems, American literature, American literature-AP, analysis, analysis and differential calculus, analysis of data, anatomy, anatomy and physiology, art, athletics, band, Basic programming, biology, biology-AP, British literature, British literature (honors), broadcast journalism, business, business applications, business technology, calculus, calculus-AP, campus ministry, Catholic belief and practice, chemistry, chemistry-AP, choir, choral music, church history, comparative government and politics-AP, composition-AP, computer graphics, computer programming, concert band, criminal justice, desktop publishing, ecology, environmental systems, economics, economics-AP, English language and composition-AP, English language-AP, English literature, English literature and composition-AP, English literature-AP, environmental science, environmental science-AP, foreign language, French, geography, geometry, German, government, government and politics-AP, government-AP, graphic design, health education, history of the Catholic Church, history-AP, honors algebra, honors English, honors geometry, honors U.S. history, honors world history, human anatomy, internship, jazz band, journalism, Latin, library assistant, literature and composition-AP, macro/microeconomics-AP, marching

band, math analysis, modern history, moral theology, music appreciation, New Testament, physical education, physics, physics-AP, physiology, pre-calculus, psychology, psychology-AP, sign language, Spanish, Spanish language-AP, speech and debate, statistics-AP, studio art, theology, U.S. government, U.S. government and politics, U.S. government and politics-AP, U.S. history, U.S. history-AP, United States government-AP.

Graduation Requirements Algebra, American government, American studies, biology, chemistry, English, foreign language, geometry, theology, world studies, Community Services for each grade level, Attend two retreats per year.

Special Academic Programs 15 Advanced Placement exams for which test preparation is offered; honors section; independent study; study at local college for college credit; academic accommodation for the gifted; programs in English, mathematics for dyslexic students; special instructional classes for deaf students, blind students.

College Admission Counseling 188 students graduated in 2015; 170 went to college, including Moravian College; Penn State University Park; Temple University; University of Pittsburgh; West Chester University of Pennsylvania. Median SAT critical reading: 580, median SAT math: 540, median SAT writing: 520, median combined SAT: 1640, median composite ACT: 25.

Student Life Upper grades have uniform requirement, student council, honor system. Discipline rests primarily with faculty. Attendance at religious services is required.

Tuition and Aid Day student tuition: $8750. Tuition installment plan (The Tuition Plan, FACTS Tuition Payment Plan). Tuition reduction for siblings, paying campus jobs available. In 2015–16, 46% of upper-school students received aid. Total amount of financial aid awarded in 2015–16: $923,830.

Admissions Traditional secondary-level entrance grade is 9. For fall 2015, 2,015 students applied for upper-level admission, 210 were accepted, 190 enrolled. Placement test required. Deadline for receipt of application materials: none. Application fee required: $250. Interview recommended.

Athletics Interscholastic: aerobics/dance (girls), aerobics/Nautilus (b), baseball (b), basketball (b,g), cross-country running (b,g), dance team (g), field hockey (g), football (b), lacrosse (b,g), power lifting (b), soccer (b,g), swimming and diving (b,g), tennis (b,g), track and field (b,g), volleyball (g), weight lifting (b); coed interscholastic: cheering, diving, drill team, golf; coed intramural: alpine skiing, skiing (downhill), snowboarding, yoga. 2 PE instructors, 17 coaches, 2 athletic trainers.

Computers Computers are regularly used in all classes. Computer network features include on-campus library services, Internet access, wireless campus network, Internet filtering or blocking technology. Campus intranet, student e-mail accounts, and computer access in designated common areas are available to students. Students grades are available online. The school has a published electronic and media policy.

Contact Ms. Ashley Pittman, Director of Admissions. 610-437-4601 Ext. 148. Fax: 610-437-6760. E-mail: apittman@acchs.info. Website: www.acchs.info

ALL HALLOWS HIGH SCHOOL

111 All Hallows Way
Bronx, New York 10452-9402
Head of School: Mr. Ron Schutte

General Information Boys' day college-preparatory, general academic, business, religious studies, and technology school, affiliated with Roman Catholic Church. Grades 9–12. Founded: 1909. Setting: urban. 1 building on campus. Approved or accredited by Christian Brothers Association, Middle States Association of Colleges and Schools, and New York Department of Education. Total enrollment: 600. Upper school average class size: 25. Upper school faculty-student ratio: 1:25. There are 180 required school days per year for Upper School students. Upper School students typically attend 5 days per week. The average school day consists of 6 hours and 8 minutes.

Upper School Student Profile Grade 9: 151 students (151 boys); Grade 10: 157 students (157 boys); Grade 11: 159 students (159 boys); Grade 12: 133 students (133 boys). 85% of students are Roman Catholic.

Faculty School total: 42. In upper school: 37 men, 5 women; 33 have advanced degrees.

Subjects Offered Algebra, American history, art, Bible studies, biology, calculus, chemistry, computer science, economics, English, English literature, environmental science, geometry, government/civics, grammar, history, humanities, Latin, mathematics, media studies, physical education, physics, political science, religion, science, social studies, Spanish, speech, trigonometry.

Graduation Requirements Arts and fine arts (art, music, dance, drama), business skills (includes word processing), computer science, English, foreign language, mathematics, physical education (includes health), religion (includes Bible studies and theology), science, social sciences, social studies (includes history), 100 Christian Service hours accumulated over the 4 years of study. Community service is required.

Special Academic Programs Study at local college for college credit; remedial reading and/or remedial writing; remedial math.

College Admission Counseling 154 students graduated in 2015; all went to college.

Student Life Upper grades have specified standards of dress, student council, honor system. Discipline rests primarily with faculty. Attendance at religious services is required.

Summer Programs Remediation programs offered; held on campus; accepts boys; not open to students from other schools.

Tuition and Aid Day student tuition: $6200. Tuition installment plan (SMART Tuition Payment Plan). Tuition reduction for siblings, merit scholarship grants available.

Admissions Traditional secondary-level entrance grade is 9. For fall 2015, 475 students applied for upper-level admission, 289 were accepted, 151 enrolled. School's own exam required. Deadline for receipt of application materials: none. No application fee required. On-campus interview required.

Athletics Interscholastic: baseball, basketball, bowling, cross-country running, fencing, golf, indoor track & field, soccer, track and field, winter (indoor) track; intramural: basketball, field hockey, flag football, floor hockey, indoor soccer, lacrosse. 1 PE instructor, 4 coaches.

Computers Computers are regularly used in English, history, mathematics, media studies, science classes. Computer resources include Internet access, wireless campus network, Internet filtering or blocking technology.

Contact Mr. Sean Sullivan, Principal. 718-293-4545. Fax: 718-293-8634. E-mail: ssullivan@allhallows.org. Website: www.allhallows.org

ALLISON ACADEMY

1881 Northeast 164th Street

North Miami Beach, Florida 33162

Head of School: Dr. Sarah F. Allison

General Information Coeducational day college-preparatory, general academic, arts, business, and English for Speakers of Other Languages school; primarily serves students with learning disabilities, individuals with Attention Deficit Disorder, dyslexic students, and Aspergers. Grades 6–12. Founded: 1983. Setting: urban. Nearest major city is Miami. 1-acre campus. 2 buildings on campus. Approved or accredited by Association of Independent Schools of Florida, Middle States Association of Colleges and Schools, National Council for Private School Accreditation, Southern Association of Colleges and Schools, and Florida Department of Education. Total enrollment: 105. Upper school average class size: 15. Upper school faculty-student ratio: 1:10. There are 180 required school days per year for Upper School students. Upper School students typically attend 5 days per week. The average school day consists of 5 hours and 50 minutes.

Upper School Student Profile Grade 6: 4 students (3 boys, 1 girl); Grade 7: 9 students (6 boys, 3 girls); Grade 8: 7 students (5 boys, 2 girls); Grade 9: 22 students (15 boys, 7 girls); Grade 10: 21 students (15 boys, 6 girls); Grade 11: 20 students (15 boys, 5 girls); Grade 12: 22 students (17 boys, 5 girls).

Faculty School total: 11. In upper school: 5 men, 6 women; 4 have advanced degrees.

Subjects Offered Advanced Placement courses, algebra, American government, American history, anthropology, arts, basketball, biology, chemistry, computer science, consumer mathematics, creative drama, current events, digital photography, drafting, drama, drama workshop, drawing, ecology, environmental systems, economics, economics and history, English, English language and composition-AP, English literature, environmental science, ESL, fine arts, forensics, French, general math, geography, geometry, health education, history, humanities, law studies, life management skills, life skills, mathematics, painting, participation in sports, peer counseling, personal finance, physical education, physical science, physics, pre-calculus, psychology, reading, reading/study skills, SAT/ACT preparation, science, social sciences, social studies, Spanish, sports, trigonometry, world cultures, writing, yearbook.

Graduation Requirements Algebra, American government, American history, applied arts, arts and fine arts (art, music, dance, drama), biology, business skills (includes word processing), chemistry, computer applications, computer science, creative writing, current events, drama, earth and space science, economics, English, English literature, environmental education, foreign language, geometry, health education, life management skills, mathematics, physical education (includes health), psychology, SAT/ACT preparation, science, social sciences, social studies (includes history), Spanish, U.S. history, world history, 75 hours minimum of community service.

Special Academic Programs 1 Advanced Placement exam for which test preparation is offered; honors section; accelerated programs; study at local college for college credit; academic accommodation for the gifted, the musically talented, and the artistically talented; remedial reading and/or remedial writing; remedial math; programs in English, mathematics, general development for dyslexic students; special instructional classes for students with learning disabilities, dyslexia, and Attention Deficit Disorder; ESL (2 students enrolled).

College Admission Counseling 17 students graduated in 2015; all went to college, including Barry University; Broward College; Florida International University; Lynn University; Miami Dade College; University of Miami. Median SAT critical reading: 500, median SAT math: 510, median composite ACT: 19. 16% scored over 600 on SAT critical reading, 15% scored over 600 on SAT math, 8% scored over 26 on composite ACT.

Student Life Upper grades have uniform requirement, student council. Discipline rests primarily with faculty.

Summer Programs Remediation, enrichment, advancement, ESL programs offered; session focuses on academics for credit courses, remedial reading, and ESL; held on campus; accepts boys and girls; open to students from other schools. 30 students usually enrolled. 2016 schedule: June 13 to July 22. Application deadline: June 6.

Tuition and Aid Day student tuition: $17,000. Tuition installment plan (monthly payment plans, individually arranged payment plans). Tuition reduction for siblings, merit scholarship grants, need-based scholarship grants available. In 2015–16, 26% of upper-school students received aid; total upper-school merit-scholarship money awarded: $50,000. Total amount of financial aid awarded in 2015–16: $170,000.

Admissions Traditional secondary-level entrance grade is 9. For fall 2015, 25 students applied for upper-level admission, 20 were accepted, 20 enrolled. Admissions testing, CTBS (or similar from their school), school placement exam, standardized test scores or Woodcock-Johnson Revised Achievement Test required. Deadline for receipt of application materials: none. Application fee required: $450. Interview required.

Athletics Interscholastic: basketball (boys), cross-country running (b), flag football (b), swimming and diving (b), tennis (b,g), volleyball (b,g), walking (g), weight training (b); intramural: basketball (b,g), cross-country running (b), flag football (b), kickball (b), martial arts (b,g), soccer (b,g), softball (b,g), swimming and diving (b,g), table tennis (b,g), tennis (b,g), volleyball (b,g), walking (g); coed interscholastic: bowling, kickball, physical fitness, tennis, track and field, volleyball; coed intramural: badminton, indoor soccer, indoor track, martial arts, paddle tennis, physical fitness, soccer, softball, swimming and diving, table tennis, tennis, track and field, volleyball, yoga. 2 PE instructors, 3 coaches.

Computers Computers are regularly used in art, business applications, computer applications, current events, drawing and design, English, foreign language, geography, health, history, journalism, keyboarding, life skills, mathematics, news writing, newspaper, psychology, reading, SAT preparation, science, Spanish, word processing, yearbook classes. Computer network features include on-campus library services, online commercial services, Internet access, wireless campus network, Internet filtering or blocking technology, each student has their own Netbooks to access textbooks, etc. Student e-mail accounts and computer access in designated common areas are available to students. Students grades are available online. The school has a published electronic and media policy.

Contact Margaret Sheriff, Administrator. 305-940-3922. Fax: 305-940-1820. E-mail: msheriff@allisonacademy.com. Website: www.allisonacademy.com

ALL SAINTS' ACADEMY

5001 State Road 540 West

Winter Haven, Florida 33880

Head of School: Mrs. Carolyn Baldwin

General Information Coeducational day college-preparatory, arts, technology, and project-based learning school, affiliated with Episcopal Church. Grades PS–12. Setting: suburban. Nearest major city is Orlando. 60-acre campus. 7 buildings on campus. Approved or accredited by Florida Council of Independent Schools, National Association of Episcopal Schools, and Florida Department of Education. Member of National Association of Independent Schools and Secondary School Admission Test Board. Total enrollment: 600. Upper school average class size: 13. Upper School students typically attend 5 days per week.

Special Academic Programs 17 Advanced Placement exams for which test preparation is offered; honors section.

College Admission Counseling 43 students graduated in 2015; all went to college.

Student Life Upper grades have uniform requirement, student council, honor system. Discipline rests primarily with faculty. Attendance at religious services is required.

Summer Programs Enrichment, advancement, sports, art/fine arts, computer instruction programs offered; session focuses on enrichment; held on campus; accepts boys and girls; open to students from other schools. 150 students usually enrolled.

Tuition and Aid Tuition installment plan (FACTS Tuition Payment Plan). Tuition reduction for siblings, need-based scholarship grants available.

Admissions Deadline for receipt of application materials: none. Application fee required: $30.

Athletics Interscholastic: baseball (boys), basketball (b,g), cheering (g), cross-country running (b,g), dance (g), diving (b,g), football (b), golf (b,g), lacrosse (b,g), soccer (b,g), softball (g), swimming and diving (b,g), tennis (b,g), track and field (b,g), volleyball (g); coed interscholastic: dance; coed intramural: strength & conditioning, weight training.

Computers Computers are regularly used in all classes. Computer network features include on-campus library services, Internet access, wireless campus network, Internet filtering or blocking technology. Campus intranet, student e-mail accounts, and computer access in designated common areas are available to students. Students grades are available online. The school has a published electronic and media policy.

Contact Ms. Evelyn Schwalb, Director of Admission. 863-293-5980 Ext. 2239. Fax: 863-595-1163. E-mail: eschwalb@allsaintsacademy.com. Website: www.allsaintsacademy.com

ALMA HEIGHTS CHRISTIAN HIGH SCHOOL

1030 Linda Mar Boulevard
Pacifica, California 94044

Head of School: Dr. David Gross

General Information Coeducational day college-preparatory, general academic, arts, religious studies, and technology school, affiliated with Christian faith. Grades K–12. Founded: 1955. Setting: suburban. Nearest major city is San Francisco. 36-acre campus. 5 buildings on campus. Approved or accredited by Association of Christian Schools International, Western Association of Schools and Colleges, and California Department of Education. Total enrollment: 303. Upper school average class size: 22. Upper school faculty-student ratio: 1:10. There are 176 required school days per year for Upper School students. Upper School students typically attend 5 days per week. The average school day consists of 7 hours and 25 minutes.

Upper School Student Profile Grade 6: 18 students (13 boys, 5 girls); Grade 7: 21 students (5 boys, 16 girls); Grade 8: 14 students (9 boys, 5 girls); Grade 9: 25 students (11 boys, 14 girls); Grade 10: 29 students (14 boys, 15 girls); Grade 11: 45 students (21 boys, 24 girls); Grade 12: 44 students (28 boys, 16 girls). 80% of students are Christian.

Faculty School total: 50. In upper school: 10 men, 9 women; 7 have advanced degrees.

Subjects Offered Advanced Placement courses.

Special Academic Programs International Baccalaureate program; 6 Advanced Placement exams for which test preparation is offered; honors section; accelerated programs; study at local college for college credit; special instructional classes for students with ADD and dyslexia; ESL (19 students enrolled).

College Admission Counseling 45 students graduated in 2015; 40 went to college, including Academy of Art University; Biola University; University of California, Berkeley; University of California, Davis; University of California, Irvine. Other: 5 went to work. Mean SAT critical reading: 494, mean SAT math: 529, mean SAT writing: 503.

Student Life Upper grades have uniform requirement, student council, honor system. Discipline rests primarily with faculty.

Tuition and Aid Day student tuition: $12,800. Tuition installment plan (SMART Tuition Payment Plan). Need-based scholarship grants available. In 2015–16, 25% of upper-school students received aid.

Admissions Traditional secondary-level entrance grade is 9. ISEE required. Deadline for receipt of application materials: January 15. Application fee required: $50. Interview required.

Athletics Interscholastic: baseball (boys), basketball (b,g), cheering (g), football (b), soccer (b), softball (g), strength & conditioning (b), volleyball (b,g); intramural: flag football (b); coed interscholastic: cross-country running, soccer. 3 PE instructors, 6 coaches.

Computers Computer network features include on-campus library services, online commercial services, Internet access, wireless campus network, Internet filtering or blocking technology. Campus intranet, student e-mail accounts, and computer access in designated common areas are available to students. Students grades are available online. The school has a published electronic and media policy.

Contact Anna Valladares, High School Admissions Coordinator. 650-355-1935 Ext. 106. Fax: 650-355-3488. E-mail: avalladares@almaheights.ort. Website: www.almaheights.org

ALPHA OMEGA ACADEMY

804 North Second Avenue East
Rock Rapids, Iowa 51246

Head of School: Mr. Joseph A. Bakker

General Information Coeducational day and distance learning college-preparatory, general academic, and distance learning school, affiliated with Christian faith. Grades K–12. Distance learning grades K–12. Founded: 1992. Setting: small town. Approved or accredited by CITA (Commission on International and Trans-Regional Accreditation) and North Central Association of Colleges and Schools. Total enrollment: 2,350. Upper School students typically attend 5 days per week.

Faculty School total: 46. In upper school: 12 men, 34 women; 6 have advanced degrees.

Subjects Offered 20th century history, accounting, algebra, American Civil War, American government, American history, American literature, art, Bible, biology, British literature, calculus, career planning, chemistry, civics, computer information systems, computer multimedia, computer skills, computer technologies, computer tools, computers, consumer mathematics, digital art, earth science, English, English composition, English literature, French, general math, general science, geography, geometry, health, history, home economics, language arts, mathematics, music appreciation, music theory, physical education, physical fitness, programming, science, Spanish, state history, Vietnam War, world geography, world history.

Graduation Requirements 1 1/2 elective credits, algebra, biology, chemistry, language arts, mathematics, physical education (includes health), science, social studies (includes history), one credit of Bible.

Special Academic Programs Accelerated programs; independent study; remedial math.

College Admission Counseling 351 students graduated in 2015.

Student Life Upper grades have honor system. Discipline rests primarily with faculty.

Summer Programs Remediation, advancement, art/fine arts, computer instruction programs offered; accepts boys and girls; open to students from other schools.

Tuition and Aid Day student tuition: $600–$3000. Tuition installment plan (six month payment plan, two payment plan). Tuition reduction for siblings, need-based scholarship grants available.

Admissions Math and English placement tests or placement test required. Deadline for receipt of application materials: none. Application fee required: $185. Interview required.

Athletics 2 PE instructors.

Computers Computers are regularly used in accounting, Bible studies, business skills, career technology, college planning, English, foreign language, French, geography, health, history, mathematics, music, science, social sciences, social studies, Spanish classes. Students grades are available online. The school has a published electronic and media policy.

Contact Mrs. Robin Inlow, Continuous Improvement Coordinator. 800-682-7396 Ext. 6253. Fax: 712-472-6830. E-mail: rinlow@aoacademy.com. Website: www.aoacademy.com

ALPINE ACADEMY

Erda, Utah
See Special Needs Schools section.

ALVERNO HIGH SCHOOL

200 North Michillinda Avenue
Sierra Madre, California 91024

Head of School: Ms. Julia V. Fanara

General Information Girls' day college-preparatory, arts, religious studies, and technology school, affiliated with Roman Catholic Church; primarily serves individuals with Attention Deficit Disorder. Grades 9–12. Founded: 1960. Setting: suburban. Nearest major city is Pasadena. 13-acre campus. 8 buildings on campus. Approved or accredited by California Association of Independent Schools, National Catholic Education Association, and California Department of Education. Total enrollment: 170. Upper school average class size: 15. Upper school faculty-student ratio: 1:12. There are 181 required school days per year for Upper School students. Upper School students typically attend 5 days per week. The average school day consists of 7 hours and 45 minutes.

Upper School Student Profile Grade 9: 41 students (41 girls); Grade 10: 49 students (49 girls); Grade 11: 47 students (47 girls); Grade 12: 36 students (36 girls). 65% of students are Roman Catholic.

Faculty School total: 17. In upper school: 4 men, 13 women; 11 have advanced degrees.

Subjects Offered ACT preparation, advanced biology, advanced chemistry, advanced studio art-AP, algebra, American literature, band, biology-AP, British literature (honors), calculus AP, Catholic belief and practice, ceramics, choir, college counseling, conceptual physics, dance, dramatic arts, driver education, earth science, English language-AP, English literature-AP, European history-AP, finite math, fitness, freshman seminar, geometry, health, history of the Catholic Church, honors algebra, honors English, honors geometry, honors U.S. history, honors world history, human geography - AP, improvisation, language-AP, leadership and service, literature and composition-AP, literature-AP, Mandarin, modern European history-AP, multicultural studies, musical theater, photography, pre-calculus, religion, SAT preparation, science, senior project, Shakespeare, social studies, softball, Spanish-AP, sports conditioning, stagecraft, student government, studio art-AP, technology/design, theater arts, theater design and production, track and field, trigonometry, U.S. history-AP, United States government-AP, video film production, visual and performing arts, world literature, world religions, writing, yearbook, zoology.

Graduation Requirements ACT preparation, algebra, American government, American history, American literature, ancient world history, art, Bible, biology, British literature, campus ministry, chemistry, civics, electives, English, English literature, ethics, European history, foreign language, geography, geometry, government, health, history, history of the Catholic Church, SAT preparation, Spanish, theology, U.S. government, U.S. history, world history, world religions, completion of 140 service hours.

Special Academic Programs 10 Advanced Placement exams for which test preparation is offered; honors section; independent study; academic accommodation for the gifted; remedial reading and/or remedial writing; remedial math; programs in English, mathematics, general development for dyslexic students.

College Admission Counseling 36 students graduated in 2014; all went to college, including California State Polytechnic University, Pomona; Northern Arizona University; University of California, Los Angeles; University of California, San Diego.

Student Life Upper grades have uniform requirement, student council, honor system. Discipline rests primarily with faculty. Attendance at religious services is required.

Tuition and Aid Day student tuition: $14,950. Tuition installment plan (FACTS Tuition Payment Plan, monthly payment plans). Tuition reduction for siblings, merit scholarship grants, need-based scholarship grants available. In 2014–15, 52% of upper-school students received aid; total upper-school merit-scholarship money awarded: $172,198. Total amount of financial aid awarded in 2014–15: $253,313.

Admissions Traditional secondary-level entrance grade is 9. For fall 2014, 75 students applied for upper-level admission, 60 were accepted, 41 enrolled. High School Placement Test (closed version) from Scholastic Testing Service or ISEE required. Deadline for receipt of application materials: January 30. Application fee required: $75. On-campus interview required.

Athletics Interscholastic: aquatics, basketball, cross-country running, soccer, softball, volleyball; intramural: aerobics/dance, dance, modern dance, self defense. 1 PE instructor, 4 coaches.

Computers Computers are regularly used in all academic classes. Computer network features include on-campus library services, Internet access, wireless campus network, Internet filtering or blocking technology. Campus intranet and computer access in designated common areas are available to students. Students grades are available online. The school has a published electronic and media policy.

Contact Ms. Sara McCarthy, Director of Admissions and Public Relations. 626-355-3463 Ext. 235. Fax: 626-355-3153. E-mail: smccarthy@alverno-hs.org. Website: www.myalverno.org/

AMERICAN ACADEMY

Plantation, Florida
See Special Needs Schools section.

AMERICAN CHRISTIAN ACADEMY

2300 Veterans Memorial Parkway
Tuscaloosa, Alabama 35404

Head of School: Dr. Dan Carden

General Information Coeducational day college-preparatory, arts, religious studies, and technology school, affiliated with Christian faith; primarily serves individuals with Attention Deficit Disorder. Grades K–12. Founded: 1979. Setting: small town. 20-acre campus. 6 buildings on campus. Approved or accredited by Association of Christian Schools International and Southern Association of Colleges and Schools. Endowment: $200,000. Total enrollment: 958. Upper school average class size: 20. Upper school faculty-student ratio: 1:12. There are 170 required school days per year for Upper School students. Upper School students typically attend 5 days per week. The average school day consists of 7 hours and 40 minutes.

Upper School Student Profile Grade 6: 62 students (32 boys, 30 girls); Grade 7: 71 students (35 boys, 36 girls); Grade 8: 72 students (41 boys, 31 girls); Grade 9: 60 students (28 boys, 32 girls); Grade 10: 74 students (32 boys, 42 girls); Grade 11: 69 students (37 boys, 32 girls); Grade 12: 55 students (29 boys, 26 girls). 75% of students are Christian.

Faculty School total: 72. In upper school: 30 men, 42 women; 26 have advanced degrees.

Subjects Offered ACT preparation, algebra, anatomy, Bible, biology, calculus, chemistry, computers, earth science, economics, English, English-AP, fine arts, geography, geology, government, health, history, life science, marine biology, mathematics, physical education, physics, reading, science, Southern literature, Spanish, typing, world history.

Graduation Requirements Arts and fine arts (art, music, dance, drama), business skills (includes word processing), computer science, English, foreign language, mathematics, physical education (includes health), religion (includes Bible studies and theology), science, social sciences, social studies (includes history), accelerated reading is required in all grades, religion classes required in all grades. Community service is required.

Special Academic Programs Advanced Placement exam preparation; honors section; accelerated programs; independent study; study at local college for college credit; study abroad; special instructional classes for deaf students.

College Admission Counseling 64 students graduated in 2015; 63 went to college, including Auburn University; Birmingham-Southern College; Samford University; Shelton State Community College; The University of Alabama; University of South Alabama. Other: 1 went to work. Median composite ACT: 25. 41% scored over 26 on composite ACT.

Student Life Upper grades have specified standards of dress, student council, honor system. Discipline rests primarily with faculty. Attendance at religious services is required.

Tuition and Aid Day student tuition: $5900. Tuition installment plan (monthly payment plans, individually arranged payment plans). Tuition reduction for siblings, need-based scholarship grants, paying campus jobs available. In 2015–16, 15% of upper-school students received aid. Total amount of financial aid awarded in 2015–16: $85,000.

Admissions Traditional secondary-level entrance grade is 10. For fall 2015, 156 students applied for upper-level admission, 127 were accepted, 121 enrolled. Scholastic Achievement Test or TerraNova required. Deadline for receipt of application materials: none. Application fee required: $200. Interview required.

Athletics Interscholastic: baseball (boys), basketball (b,g), bowling (b,g), cheering (g), cross-country running (b,g), dance squad (g), dance team (g), danceline (g), diving (b,g), fishing (b,g), fly fishing (b), football (b), golf (b,g), indoor track (b,g), indoor track & field (b,g), power lifting (b), soccer (b,g), softball (g), strength & conditioning (b,g), swimming and diving (b,g), tennis (b,g), track and field (b,g), volleyball (g),

weight lifting (b,g), weight training (b,g), winter (indoor) track (b,g), wrestling (b); intramural: aerobics (g), aerobics/dance (g), basketball (b,g), cheering (g), dance squad (g), dance team (g), danceline (g), fishing (b,g), flag football (b,g), gymnastics (g), in-line skating (b,g), kickball (b,g), outdoor activities (b,g), paint ball (b), physical training (b,g), roller blading (b,g), softball (g), strength & conditioning (b,g), swimming and diving (b,g), touch football (b,g); coed intramural: outdoor activities, physical fitness, running. 3 PE instructors, 12 coaches, 1 athletic trainer.

Computers Computers are regularly used in computer applications, foreign language, mathematics, typing, video film production classes. Computer network features include on-campus library services, Internet access, wireless campus network, Internet filtering or blocking technology. Campus intranet, student e-mail accounts, and computer access in designated common areas are available to students. Students grades are available online.

Contact Nancy Hastings, Director of Admissions. 205-553-5963 Ext. 12. Fax: 205-553-5942. E-mail: nhastings@acacademy.com. Website: www.acacademy.com

AMERICAN HERITAGE SCHOOL

6200 Linton Boulevard
Delray Beach, Florida 33484

Head of School: William Laurie

General Information Coeducational day college-preparatory, arts, technology, and Pre-Medical, Pre-Law, Pre-Engineering, Bio-Medical, Robotics school. Grades PK–12. Founded: 1999. Setting: suburban. Nearest major city is Boca Raton. 40-acre campus. 9 buildings on campus. Approved or accredited by Association of Independent Schools of Florida, Middle States Association of Colleges and Schools, Southern Association of Colleges and Schools, Southern Association of Independent Schools, The College Board, and Florida Department of Education. Member of National Association of Independent Schools. Total enrollment: 1,226. Upper school average class size: 17. Upper school faculty-student ratio: 1:8. There are 175 required school days per year for Upper School students. Upper School students typically attend 5 days per week. The average school day consists of 7 hours and 15 minutes.

Upper School Student Profile Grade 6: 73 students (40 boys, 33 girls); Grade 7: 99 students (51 boys, 48 girls); Grade 8: 104 students (57 boys, 47 girls); Grade 9: 187 students (94 boys, 93 girls); Grade 10: 155 students (92 boys, 63 girls); Grade 11: 174 students (103 boys, 71 girls); Grade 12: 166 students (88 boys, 78 girls).

Faculty School total: 124. In upper school: 24 men, 52 women; 60 have advanced degrees.

Subjects Offered Acting, advanced biology, advanced chemistry, advanced math, Advanced Placement courses, algebra, American government, American history, American history-AP, American legal systems, American literature, American literature-AP, anatomy and physiology, aquatics, architectural drawing, architecture, art, audio visual/media, ballet, band, baseball, basketball, biology, biology-AP, broadcasting, business, business law, business technology, calculus-AP, cartooning/animation, ceramics, cheerleading, chemistry, chemistry-AP, Chinese, choir, chorus, college counseling, community service, computer graphics, computer science, computer science-AP, constitutional law, costumes and make-up, creative writing, criminal justice, critical thinking, dance, digital photography, drama, drama performance, drawing, drawing and design, earth science, economics, economics-AP, electives, engineering, English, English language and composition-AP, English literature, English literature and composition-AP, English literature-AP, English-AP, environmental science, environmental science-AP, equestrian sports, ESL, ethnic literature, film and literature, fine arts, forensics, French, French-AP, geometry, government-AP, graphic arts, graphic design, guidance, guitar, history-AP, honors algebra, honors English, honors geometry, honors U.S. history, honors world history, jazz band, journalism, law, law and the legal system, law studies, library, Mandarin, mathematics, mathematics-AP, media, media production, multimedia, multimedia design, music theory, music theory-AP, musical productions, news writing, newspaper, oceanography, orchestra, painting, photo shop, photography, photojournalism, physical education, physics, physics-AP, piano, portfolio art, pottery, pre-algebra, pre-calculus, probability and statistics, psychology, psychology-AP, public policy, publications, research skills, SAT/ACT preparation, science, sculpture, set design, Spanish, Spanish language-AP, Spanish-AP, speech and debate, stagecraft, statistics, statistics-AP, strings, student government, student publications, studio art, swimming, television, tennis, theater, theater production, track and field, U.S. government, U.S. government and politics-AP, U.S. history, U.S. history-AP, video, video film production, vocal music, volleyball, Web site design, weight training, world history, world history-AP, world literature, writing, writing, yearbook.

Graduation Requirements Arts and fine arts (art, music, dance, drama), English, foreign language, mathematics, physical education (includes health), science, social studies (includes history), acceptance to a 4-year college, community service requirement. Community service is required.

Special Academic Programs 19 Advanced Placement exams for which test preparation is offered; academic accommodation for the gifted, the musically talented, and the artistically talented; remedial reading and/or remedial writing; remedial math; programs in English, mathematics, general development for dyslexic students; special instructional classes for deaf students, blind students; ESL (108 students enrolled).

College Admission Counseling 127 students graduated in 2014; all went to college, including Florida State University; University of Central Florida; University of

Florida; University of Miami. Mean SAT critical reading: 570, mean SAT math: 580, mean SAT writing: 580, mean composite ACT: 26. 36% scored over 600 on SAT critical reading, 44% scored over 600 on SAT math, 49% scored over 600 on SAT writing, 43% scored over 26 on composite ACT.

Student Life Upper grades have uniform requirement, student council, honor system. Discipline rests primarily with faculty.

Tuition and Aid Day student tuition: $20,000. Tuition installment plan (monthly payment plans, semester payment plan, yearly). Tuition reduction for siblings, merit scholarship grants, need-based scholarship grants available.

Admissions Traditional secondary-level entrance grade is 9. Slossen Intelligence and Stanford Achievement Test required. Deadline for receipt of application materials: none. Application fee required: $100. Interview required.

Athletics Interscholastic: baseball (boys), basketball (b,g), broomball (g), cheering (g), cross-country running (b,g), dance (b,g), dance squad (g), dance team (g), diving (b,g), football (b), golf (b,g), lacrosse (b), polo (b), soccer (b,g), softball (g), volleyball (g), water polo (b), weight training (b,g), winter soccer (b,g), wrestling (b); coed interscholastic: cheering, equestrian sports, physical fitness, swimming and diving, tennis, track and field, yoga. 4 PE instructors, 40 coaches, 1 athletic trainer.

Computers Computers are regularly used in all academic, animation, architecture, art, business, classics, college planning, computer applications, creative writing, dance, desktop publishing, digital applications, drawing and design, economics, engineering, English, ESL, foreign language, French, geography, graphic arts, graphic design, graphics, history, human geography - AP, journalism, keyboarding, library, literary magazine, mathematics, media, media arts, media production, multimedia, music, music technology, newspaper, philosophy, photography, photojournalism, programming, psychology, publications, publishing, reading, SAT preparation, science, social sciences, social studies, Spanish, speech, theater, theater arts, video film production, Web site design, writing, writing, yearbook classes. Computer network features include on-campus library services, online commercial services, Internet access, wireless campus network, Internet filtering or blocking technology, Questia, Lexis-Nexis, ProQuest/SIRS, Cengage Learning Gale, EBSCOhost, Jstor, Worldbook, Discovery Education, Nettrekker, Scientific American, Noodle Tools, Turnitin, Books & Authors, Learning Today, Quia, Accelerated Reader, Naviance. Student e-mail accounts and computer access in designated common areas are available to students. Students grades are available online. The school has a published electronic and media policy.

Contact Mr. Robert Stone, DD, Headmaster. 561-495-7272. E-mail: judy.charles@ahschool.com. Website: www.ahschool.com

See Display below and Close-Up on page 580.

AMERICAN HERITAGE SCHOOL

12200 West Broward Boulevard
Plantation, Florida 33325

Head of School: William R. Laurie

General Information Coeducational day college-preparatory, arts, technology, pre-medical, pre-law, pre-engineering, bio-medical, arts, and journalism, broadcasting school. Grades PK–12. Founded: 1965. Setting: suburban. Nearest major city is Fort Lauderdale. 40-acre campus. 12 buildings on campus. Approved or accredited by Association of Independent Schools of Florida, Middle States Association of Colleges and Schools, Southern Association of Colleges and Schools, Southern Association of Independent Schools, The College Board, and Florida Department of Education. Total enrollment: 2,400. Upper school average class size: 17. Upper school faculty-student ratio: 1:8. There are 175 required school days per year for Upper School students. Upper School students typically attend 5 days per week. The average school day consists of 7 hours and 15 minutes.

Upper School Student Profile Grade 7: 177 students (94 boys, 83 girls); Grade 8: 187 students (88 boys, 99 girls); Grade 9: 326 students (154 boys, 172 girls); Grade 10: 332 students (169 boys, 163 girls); Grade 11: 340 students (181 boys, 159 girls); Grade 12: 317 students (183 boys, 134 girls).

Faculty School total: 188. In upper school: 45 men, 83 women; 64 have advanced degrees.

Subjects Offered Acting, algebra, American government, American history, American history-AP, American legal systems, American literature, American literature-AP, anatomy and physiology, architectural drawing, architecture, art, band, biology, biology-AP, business law, calculus-AP, ceramics, chemistry, chemistry-AP, Chinese, chorus, community service, computer graphics, computer science, computer science-AP, constitutional law, costumes and make-up, creative writing, dance, drama, drawing, economics, economics-AP, engineering, English, English language and composition-AP, English literature, English literature and composition-AP, environmental science, environmental science-AP, ESL, European history-AP, fine arts, forensics, French, French language-AP, French-AP, geometry, government-AP, graphic design, guitar, honors algebra, honors English, honors geometry, honors U.S. history, honors world history, human geography - AP, journalism, law studies, literary magazine, mathematics, music theory, music theory-AP, oceanography, orchestra, organic chemistry, painting, photography, physical education, physics, physics-AP, portfolio art, pre-algebra, pre-calculus, probability and statistics, psychology, psychology-AP, public speaking, research, research skills, SAT preparation, SAT/ACT preparation, science, sculpture, set design, sociology, Spanish, Spanish-AP, speech and debate, stage design, stagecraft, statistics-AP, studio art, technical theater, theater, U.S. government and politics-AP, video film production, visual arts, vocal music, Web site

Plantation Campus

Boca/Delray Campus

AMERICAN HERITAGE SCHOOL

College Preparatory School for PK3—Grade 12

Plantation Campus
12200 W. Broward Blvd.
Plantation, FL 33325
(954) 472-0022

design, weight training, world history, world history-AP, world literature, writing, writing, yearbook.

Graduation Requirements Arts and fine arts (art, music, dance, drama), English, foreign language, mathematics, physical education (includes health), science, social studies (includes history), acceptance to a 4-year college, community service requirement. Community service is required.

Special Academic Programs Advanced Placement exam preparation; honors section; academic accommodation for the gifted, the musically talented, and the artistically talented; ESL (47 students enrolled).

College Admission Counseling 373 students graduated in 2014; all went to college, including Florida Atlantic University; Florida International University; Florida State University; Nova Southeastern University; University of Florida; University of Miami. Mean SAT critical reading: 592, mean SAT math: 613, mean SAT writing: 599, mean composite ACT: 29. 43% scored over 600 on SAT critical reading, 49% scored over 600 on SAT math, 49% scored over 600 on SAT writing, 48% scored over 26 on composite ACT.

Student Life Upper grades have uniform requirement, student council, honor system. Discipline rests primarily with faculty.

Tuition and Aid Day student tuition: $20,662–$26,008. Tuition installment plan (monthly payment plans, Semester payment plan, yearly). Tuition reduction for siblings, merit scholarship grants, need-based scholarship grants available.

Admissions Traditional secondary-level entrance grade is 9. Slossen Intelligence and Stanford Achievement Test required. Deadline for receipt of application materials: none. Application fee required: $100. On-campus interview required.

Athletics Interscholastic: baseball (boys), basketball (b,g), cross-country running (b,g), diving (b,g), football (b), golf (b,g), ice hockey (b), lacrosse (b,g), soccer (b,g), softball (g), swimming and diving (b,g), tennis (b,g), track and field (b,g), volleyball (b,g), weight training (b,g), winter soccer (b,g), wrestling (b); coed interscholastic: cheering, dance team, physical fitness, physical training, strength & conditioning. 4 PE instructors, 6 coaches.

Computers Computers are regularly used in all academic classes. Computer network features include on-campus library services, online commercial services, Internet access, wireless campus network, Internet filtering or blocking technology, Questia, Lexis-Nexis, ProQuest/SIRS, Cengage Learning Gale, EBSCOhost, Jstor, Worldbook, Discovery, Education, Nettrekkcr, Scientific American, Noodle Tools, Turnitin, Books & Authors, Learning Today, Quia, Accelerated Reader, Naviance. Campus intranet, student e-mail accounts, and computer access in designated common areas are available to students. Students grades are available online. The school has a published electronic and media policy.

Contact William R. Laurie, President. 954-472-0022 Ext. 3062. Fax: 954-472-3088. E-mail: admissions@ahschool.com. Website: www.ahschool.com

See Display on previous page and Close-Up on page 580.
See Display on previous page and Close-Up on page 580.

AMERICAN INTERNATIONAL SCHOOL, LUSAKA

PO Box 320176
Lusaka, Zambia

Head of School: Mr. Thomas J. Pado

General Information Coeducational day college-preparatory school. Grades 6–12. Founded: 1986. Setting: suburban. 12-acre campus. 11 buildings on campus. Approved or accredited by Council of International Schools, International Baccalaureate Organization, and Middle States Association of Colleges and Schools. Member of European Council of International Schools. Language of instruction: English. Total enrollment: 280. Upper school average class size: 20. Upper school faculty-student ratio: 1:7. There are 180 required school days per year for Upper School students. Upper School students typically attend 5 days per week. The average school day consists of 7 hours and 5 minutes.

Upper School Student Profile Grade 6: 43 students (25 boys, 18 girls); Grade 7: 42 students (24 boys, 18 girls); Grade 8: 44 students (20 boys, 24 girls); Grade 9: 43 students (27 boys, 16 girls); Grade 10: 35 students (18 boys, 17 girls); Grade 11: 44 students (27 boys, 17 girls); Grade 12: 29 students (16 boys, 13 girls).

Faculty School total: 40. In upper school: 20 men, 20 women; 13 have advanced degrees.

Subjects Offered International Baccalaureate courses.

Graduation Requirements International Baccalaureate courses.

Special Academic Programs International Baccalaureate program; ESL (16 students enrolled).

College Admission Counseling 37 students graduated in 2015; 35 went to college. Other: 2 had other specific plans. Median SAT critical reading: 530, median SAT math: 520, median SAT writing: 540, median combined SAT: 1610, median composite ACT: 23. 26.7% scored over 600 on SAT critical reading, 26.7% scored over 600 on SAT math, 40% scored over 600 on SAT writing, 33.3% scored over 1800 on combined SAT, 27.8% scored over 26 on composite ACT.

Student Life Upper grades have student council, honor system. Discipline rests primarily with faculty.

Tuition and Aid Day student tuition: $18,150. Need-based scholarship grants available. In 2015–16, 1% of upper-school students received aid.

Admissions Traditional secondary-level entrance grade is 11. Admissions testing or English Composition Test for ESL students required. Deadline for receipt of application materials: none. No application fee required.

Athletics Intramural: badminton (boys, girls), basketball (b,g), cross-country running (b,g), dance (b,g), field hockey (b,g), fitness (b,g), floor hockey (b,g), Frisbee (b,g), indoor soccer (b,g), physical fitness (b,g), rugby (b), soccer (b,g), swimming and diving (b,g), tennis (b,g), triathlon (b,g), ultimate Frisbee (b,g), volleyball (b,g), water polo (b,g), weight training (b,g); coed intramural: badminton, basketball, cross-country running, dance, field hockey, fitness, floor hockey, Frisbee, indoor soccer, physical fitness, soccer, swimming and diving, tennis, triathlon, ultimate Frisbee, volleyball, water polo, weight training. 3 PE instructors, 14 coaches.

Computers Computers are regularly used in all classes. Computer network features include on-campus library services, online commercial services, Internet access, wireless campus network, Internet filtering or blocking technology. Campus intranet and student e-mail accounts are available to students. Students grades are available online. The school has a published electronic and media policy.

THE AMERICAN SCHOOL FOUNDATION

Bondojito 215
Colonia Las Americas
Mexico City, D.F. 01120, Mexico

Head of School: Mr. Paul Williams

General Information Coeducational day college-preparatory, Mexican Program Curriculum, and U.S. program curriculum school. Grades PK–12. Founded: 1888. Setting: urban. Nearest major city is Mexico City, Mexico. 17-acre campus. 4 buildings on campus. Approved or accredited by International Baccalaureate Organization, Southern Association of Colleges and Schools, and Southern Association of Independent Schools. Affiliate member of National Association of Independent Schools; member of Secondary School Admission Test Board. Languages of instruction: English and Spanish. Endowment: 191.1 million Mexican pesos. Total enrollment: 2,530. Upper school average class size: 18. Upper school faculty-student ratio: 1:11. There are 180 required school days per year for Upper School students. Upper School students typically attend 5 days per week. The average school day consists of 6 hours and 45 minutes.

Upper School Student Profile Grade 9: 179 students (77 boys, 102 girls); Grade 10: 176 students (74 boys, 102 girls); Grade 11: 168 students (79 boys, 89 girls); Grade 12: 193 students (103 boys, 90 girls).

Faculty School total: 94. In upper school: 34 men, 40 women; 52 have advanced degrees.

Subjects Offered Advanced Placement courses, algebra, American history, American literature, American studies, anatomy, art, art history, biology, calculus, ceramics, chemistry, computer programming, computer science, drafting, drama, earth science, ecology, economics, English, English literature, European history, expository writing, film, fine arts, French, geography, geometry, government/civics, grammar, health, history, humanities, journalism, mathematics, Mexican history, music, philosophy, photography, physical education, physics, physiology, psychology, science, social sciences, social studies, Spanish, speech, statistics, trigonometry, world history, world literature, writing.

Graduation Requirements Art, English, foreign language, health, humanities, mathematics, physical education (includes health), science, social studies (includes history), technology, International Baccalaureate Personal Project (grade 10), Week Without Walls (grade 9).

Special Academic Programs International Baccalaureate program; 13 Advanced Placement exams for which test preparation is offered; independent study; study abroad; remedial reading and/or remedial writing; programs in English, mathematics, general development for dyslexic students; special instructional classes for deaf students, blind students, learning disabilities (LD), Attention Deficit Hyperactivity Disorder (ADHD), and speech and language disorders.

College Admission Counseling 183 students graduated in 2015; 151 went to college, including Boston University; Georgia Institute of Technology; Northeastern University; Stanford University; The University of Texas at Austin; University of Colorado Boulder. Other: 32 had other specific plans. Median SAT critical reading: 610, median SAT math: 620, median SAT writing: 590. 59% scored over 600 on SAT critical reading, 60% scored over 600 on SAT math, 40% scored over 600 on SAT writing.

Student Life Upper grades have specified standards of dress, student council. Discipline rests primarily with faculty.

Tuition and Aid Day student tuition: 184,150 Mexican pesos. Tuition installment plan (monthly payment plans, Tuition Insurance). Need-based scholarship grants available. In 2015–16, 17% of upper-school students received aid. Total amount of financial aid awarded in 2015–16: 13,997,103 Mexican pesos.

Admissions Traditional secondary-level entrance grade is 10. For fall 2015, 216 students applied for upper-level admission, 99 were accepted, 87 enrolled. Essay required. Deadline for receipt of application materials: January 8. Application fee required: 1000 Mexican pesos. On-campus interview required.

Athletics Interscholastic: aquatics (boys, girls), artistic gym (b,g), basketball (b,g), flag football (b), football (b), gymnastics (b,g), soccer (b,g), swimming and diving (b,g), tennis (b,g), track and field (b,g), volleyball (g); intramural: aquatics (b,g), artistic gym (b,g), dance team (g), flag football (b), football (g), gymnastics (b,g), strength &

conditioning (b,g); coed interscholastic: cross-country running, running, tennis, track and field; coed intramural: aerobics/dance, basketball, cross-country running, running, strength & conditioning. 11 PE instructors, 46 coaches, 1 athletic trainer.

Computers Computers are regularly used in all classes. Computer network features include on-campus library services, online commercial services, Internet access, wireless campus network, Internet filtering or blocking technology. Campus intranet, student e-mail accounts, and computer access in designated common areas are available to students. Students grades are available online. The school has a published electronic and media policy.

Contact Patricia Hubp, Director of Admission. 52-555-227-4900. Fax: 52-55273-4357. E-mail: martindehubp@asf.edu.mx. Website: www.asf.edu.mx

THE AMERICAN SCHOOL IN JAPAN

1-1, Nomizu 1-chome

Chofu-shi

Tokyo 182-0031, Japan

Head of School: Ed Ladd

General Information Coeducational day college-preparatory school. Grades N–12. Founded: 1902. Setting: suburban. 14-acre campus. 5 buildings on campus. Approved or accredited by US Department of State and Western Association of Schools and Colleges. Affiliate member of National Association of Independent Schools. Language of instruction: English. Endowment: $29 million. Total enrollment: 1,620. Upper school average class size: 18. Upper school faculty-student ratio: 1:10. There are 176 required school days per year for Upper School students. Upper School students typically attend 5 days per week. The average school day consists of 6 hours and 30 minutes.

Upper School Student Profile Grade 6: 140 students (70 boys, 70 girls); Grade 7: 146 students (72 boys, 74 girls); Grade 8: 130 students (58 boys, 72 girls); Grade 9: 154 students (74 boys, 80 girls); Grade 10: 139 students (64 boys, 75 girls); Grade 11: 141 students (68 boys, 73 girls); Grade 12: 150 students (60 boys, 90 girls).

Faculty School total: 150. In upper school: 40 men, 40 women; 66 have advanced degrees.

Subjects Offered Algebra, American history, American literature, applied music, art, art-AP, arts and crafts, Asian studies, astronomy, biology, biology-AP, calculus-AP, ceramics, chemistry, chemistry-AP, choir, computer graphics, computer programming, computer science-AP, conceptual physics, concert band, creative writing, digital photography, drama, economics, economics-AP, English, English literature, environmental science-AP, European history, European history-AP, expository writing, French, French-AP, geometry, health, honors English, independent living, international foods, Japanese, Japanese as Second Language, Japanese history, Japanese literature, Japanese studies, jazz band, jewelry making, journalism, Mandarin, marine biology, mathematics, metalworking, music composition, mythology, news writing, orchestra, personal fitness, photography, physical education, physics, physics-AP, poetry, pre-calculus, probability and statistics, psychology, science fiction, Spanish, Spanish language-AP, speech, stagecraft, stained glass, statistics-AP, strings, symphonic band, theater arts, trigonometry, U.S. history-AP, video film production, vocal jazz, weightlifting, world history, world literature, writing.

Graduation Requirements Arts and fine arts (art, music, dance, drama), computer applications, English, foreign language, health, Japanese studies, mathematics, physical education (includes health), science, social studies (includes history), one semester of Japanese studies.

Special Academic Programs 15 Advanced Placement exams for which test preparation is offered; honors section; independent study.

College Admission Counseling 143 students graduated in 2015; 141 went to college, including Brigham Young University; Brown University; New York University; Tufts University; University of California, Los Angeles. Other: 2 had other specific plans. Mean SAT critical reading: 589, mean SAT math: 632, mean SAT writing: 580. 50% scored over 600 on SAT critical reading, 60% scored over 600 on SAT math, 60% scored over 600 on SAT writing.

Student Life Upper grades have specified standards of dress, student council. Discipline rests primarily with faculty.

Summer Programs Enrichment, art/fine arts, computer instruction programs offered; session focuses on enrichment; held on campus; accepts boys and girls; open to students from other schools. 75 students usually enrolled. 2016 schedule: June 15 to July 3. Application deadline: April 1.

Tuition and Aid Day student tuition: ¥2,356,000. Tuition installment plan (individually arranged payment plans). Need-based scholarship grants available. In 2015–16, 3% of upper-school students received aid.

Admissions Traditional secondary-level entrance grade is 9. Any standardized test required. Deadline for receipt of application materials: none. Application fee required: ¥20,000. On-campus interview recommended.

Athletics Interscholastic: baseball (boys), basketball (b,g), cross-country running (b,g), field hockey (g), football (b), soccer (b,g), swimming and diving (b,g), tennis (b,g), track and field (b,g), volleyball (g), wrestling (b); coed interscholastic: cheering;

coed intramural: aerobics/dance, badminton, dance, golf, judo, martial arts. 6 PE instructors, 2 coaches, 1 athletic trainer.

Computers Computer network features include on-campus library services, online commercial services, Internet access, wireless campus network, Blackboard, Destiny. Campus intranet and student e-mail accounts are available to students. Students grades are available online. The school has a published electronic and media policy.

Contact Mary Margaret Mallat, Director of Admissions. 81-422-34-5300 Ext. 779. Fax: 81-422-34-5339. E-mail: enroll@asij.ac.jp. Website: http://www.asij.ac.jp/

AMERICAN SCHOOL OF PARIS

41 rue Pasteur

BP 82

Saint Cloud 92210, France

Head of School: Mr. Mark E. Ulfers

General Information Coeducational day college-preparatory school. Grades PK–13. Founded: 1946. Setting: suburban. Nearest major city is Paris, France. 12-acre campus. 7 buildings on campus. Approved or accredited by Council of International Schools and Middle States Association of Colleges and Schools. Affiliate member of National Association of Independent Schools; member of Secondary School Admission Test Board and European Council of International Schools. Language of instruction: English. Total enrollment: 752. Upper school average class size: 18. Upper school faculty-student ratio: 1:7. There are 172 required school days per year for Upper School students. Upper School students typically attend 5 days per week. The average school day consists of 7 hours and 15 minutes.

Upper School Student Profile Grade 6: 52 students (35 boys, 17 girls); Grade 7: 63 students (30 boys, 33 girls); Grade 8: 69 students (40 boys, 29 girls); Grade 9: 77 students (43 boys, 34 girls); Grade 10: 90 students (48 boys, 42 girls); Grade 11: 90 students (45 boys, 45 girls); Grade 12: 86 students (45 boys, 41 girls).

Faculty School total: 112. In upper school: 25 men, 30 women; 41 have advanced degrees.

Subjects Offered Algebra, American history, American literature, art, band, biology, calculus, ceramics, chemistry, choir, computer graphics, computer programming, computer science, drawing, economics, English, English literature, environmental science, European history, film and new technologies, filmmaking, French, geometry, global issues, global studies, graphic arts, health, humanities, information technology, music, music technology, painting, photography, physical education, physics, pre-calculus, psychology, science, sculpture, social studies, Spanish, theater, theory of knowledge, trigonometry, Web site design, world history, world literature, writing.

Graduation Requirements Arts and fine arts (art, music, dance, drama), computer science, English, foreign language, mathematics, performing arts, physical education (includes health), science, social studies (includes history).

Special Academic Programs International Baccalaureate program; Advanced Placement exam preparation; honors section; independent study; programs in English, mathematics for dyslexic students; ESL (100 students enrolled).

College Admission Counseling 106 students graduated in 2014; 100 went to college, including Emory University; Mount Holyoke College; New York University; Purdue University; The American University of Paris. Other: 2 entered military service, 4 had other specific plans. Mean SAT critical reading: 622, mean SAT math: 630, mean SAT writing: 610.

Student Life Upper grades have specified standards of dress, student council. Discipline rests primarily with faculty.

Tuition and Aid Day student tuition: €29,980. Tuition installment plan (monthly payment plans, individually arranged payment plans). Need-based scholarship grants available. In 2014–15, 3% of upper-school students received aid. Total amount of financial aid awarded in 2014–15: €13,000.

Admissions Traditional secondary-level entrance grade is 9. For fall 2014, 91 students applied for upper-level admission, 90 were accepted, 85 enrolled. English for Non-native Speakers required. Deadline for receipt of application materials: none. Application fee required: €1120. Interview recommended.

Athletics Interscholastic: baseball (boys), basketball (b,g), cross-country running (b,g), dance team (g), golf (b,g), rugby (b), soccer (b,g), softball (g), swimming and diving (b,g), tennis (b,g), track and field (b,g), volleyball (b,g); coed interscholastic: golf; coed intramural: basketball, climbing, soccer, softball, track and field. 4 PE instructors, 6 coaches.

Computers Computers are regularly used in English, foreign language, graphic arts, information technology, mathematics, music, science classes. Computer network features include on-campus library services, online commercial services, Internet access, wireless campus network, Internet filtering or blocking technology, online learning platform. Campus intranet, student e-mail accounts, and computer access in designated common areas are available to students. Students grades are available online.

Contact Mrs. Philipa Lane, Admissions Assistant. 331-41-12-86-55. Fax: 331-41-12-82-47. E-mail: admissions@asparis.fr. Website: www.asparis.org

The American School of Puerto Vallarta

THE AMERICAN SCHOOL OF PUERTO VALLARTA

Albatros # 129

Marina Vallarta

Puerto Vallarta, Jalisco 48335, Mexico

Head of School: Mr. Gerald Selitzer

General Information Coeducational day college-preparatory, arts, bilingual studies, and technology school. Grades N–12. Founded: 1986. Setting: small town. 7-acre campus. 4 buildings on campus. Approved or accredited by Council of Accreditation and School Improvement, Southern Association of Colleges and Schools, Southern Association of Independent Schools, The College Board, US Department of State, and state department of education. Affiliate member of National Association of Independent Schools. Languages of instruction: English and Spanish. Endowment: 2 million Mexican pesos. Total enrollment: 343. Upper school average class size: 25. Upper school faculty-student ratio: 1:7. There are 185 required school days per year for Upper School students. Upper School students typically attend 5 days per week. The average school day consists of 6 hours and 40 minutes.

Upper School Student Profile Grade 7: 26 students (11 boys, 15 girls); Grade 8: 26 students (12 boys, 14 girls); Grade 9: 24 students (15 boys, 9 girls); Grade 10: 24 students (13 boys, 11 girls); Grade 11: 24 students (11 boys, 13 girls); Grade 12: 20 students (11 boys, 9 girls).

Faculty School total: 47. In upper school: 11 men, 10 women; 14 have advanced degrees.

Subjects Offered Advanced Placement courses, advanced studio art-AP, algebra, American literature, anatomy, art, biology, British literature, business mathematics, calculus, chemistry, chorus, civics, comparative government and politics-AP, computer science, computers, conceptual physics, earth science, economics-AP, English, English literature, English literature and composition-AP, etymology, geography, journalism, law, life science, literature, literature and composition-AP, mathematics, Mexican history, Mexican literature, philosophy, physical science, physics, pre-algebra, pre-calculus, robotics, Spanish, Spanish language-AP, Spanish literature, Spanish literature-AP, statistics-AP, studio art-AP, trigonometry, U.S. history, U.S. history-AP, world history.

Graduation Requirements American literature, art, art education, biology, British literature, calculus, chemistry, computer education, conceptual physics, economics, English literature, mathematics, Mexican history, Mexican literature, physical education (includes health), pre-calculus, Spanish, Spanish literature, U.S. history.

Special Academic Programs Advanced Placement exam preparation; independent study; remedial reading and/or remedial writing; remedial math; ESL (1 student enrolled).

College Admission Counseling 24 students graduated in 2015; they went to Antelope Valley College; Boise State University; Simon Fraser University; The University of British Columbia; University of California, Santa Cruz; University of Victoria.

Student Life Upper grades have uniform requirement, student council, honor system. Discipline rests primarily with faculty.

Summer Programs Remediation, ESL programs offered; session focuses on remediation and make-up; held on campus; accepts boys and girls; open to students from other schools. 5 students usually enrolled. 2016 schedule: July 8 to August 15. Application deadline: none.

Tuition and Aid Day student tuition: $6589–$7052. Tuition installment plan (monthly payment plans, individually arranged payment plans). Tuition reduction for siblings available. In 2015–16, 10% of upper-school students received aid.

Admissions Traditional secondary-level entrance grade is 10. For fall 2015, 20 students applied for upper-level admission, 12 were accepted, 8 enrolled. Achievement tests, admissions testing, English language, math and English placement tests, Math Placement Exam and math, reading, and mental ability tests required. Deadline for receipt of application materials: none. No application fee required. Interview required.

Athletics Interscholastic: basketball (boys, girls), golf (b,g), sailing (g), soccer (b,g), tennis (b,g); intramural: baseball (b), basketball (b,g), dance (g), jump rope (g), modern dance (g), soccer (b,g), swimming and diving (b,g), tennis (b,g), track and field (b,g). 3 PE instructors, 4 coaches, 3 athletic trainers.

Computers Computers are regularly used in computer applications, history, keyboarding, lab/keyboard, music, science, social studies, Spanish, technology, yearbook classes. Computer network features include on-campus library services, Internet access, wireless campus network, Internet filtering or blocking technology. Campus intranet, student e-mail accounts, and computer access in designated common areas are available to students. Students grades are available online. The school has a published electronic and media policy.

Contact Ms. Elise Langley, Director of Admissions and College Guidance. 52-322 226 7672. Fax: 52-322 226 7677. E-mail: llangley@aspv.edu.mx. Website: www.aspv.edu.mx

ANDREWS OSBORNE ACADEMY

38588 Mentor Avenue

Willoughby, Ohio 44094

Head of School: Dr. Larry Goodman

General Information Coeducational boarding and day college-preparatory and arts school. Boarding grades 7–12, day grades PK–12. Founded: 1910. Setting: suburban. Nearest major city is Cleveland. Students are housed in single-sex dormitories. 300-acre campus. 12 buildings on campus. Approved or accredited by Independent Schools Association of the Central States, Midwest Association of Boarding Schools, Ohio Association of Independent Schools, The Association of Boarding Schools, and Ohio Department of Education. Member of National Association of Independent Schools and Secondary School Admission Test Board. Endowment: $12 million. Total enrollment: 347. Upper school average class size: 10. Upper school faculty-student ratio: 1:8. The average school day consists of 8 hours.

Upper School Student Profile Grade 9: 19 students (19 girls); Grade 10: 15 students (15 girls); Grade 11: 31 students (31 girls); Grade 12: 24 students (24 girls). 14 states are represented in upper school student body.

Faculty School total: 25. In upper school: 7 men, 18 women; 18 have advanced degrees; 10 reside on campus.

Subjects Offered Algebra, American government, American literature, art, astronomy, biology, biology-AP, calculus, calculus-AP, ceramics, chemistry, chemistry-AP, choir, choral music, community service, CPR, drama, economics, English, English composition, English language-AP, English literature, English literature and composition-AP, environmental science, equine science, ESL, ethics, film history, fine arts, first aid, French, French language-AP, geometry with art applications, government, grammar, health science, history, honors algebra, honors English, honors geometry, independent study, instrumental music, Mandarin, mathematics, music, painting, physical education, physics, portfolio art, pre-calculus, probability and statistics, science, social studies, Spanish, Spanish language-AP, speech, studio art, textiles, theater, TOEFL preparation, U.S. history, U.S. history-AP, women in literature, world history.

Graduation Requirements Algebra, arts and fine arts (art, music, dance, drama), biology, computer literacy, CPR, English, foreign language, geometry, mathematics, physical education (includes health), science, social studies (includes history), speech, acceptance into at least one U.S. college or university. Community service is required.

Special Academic Programs Advanced Placement exam preparation; honors section; independent study; study at local college for college credit; academic accommodation for the gifted, the musically talented, and the artistically talented; ESL (35 students enrolled).

College Admission Counseling 50 students graduated in 2015; all went to college, including DePaul University; Emory University; John Carroll University; Mercyhurst University; The Ohio State University. Mean SAT critical reading: 561, mean SAT math: 548, mean SAT writing: 537, mean combined SAT: 1646, mean composite ACT: 24.

Student Life Upper grades have uniform requirement, student council, honor system. Discipline rests primarily with faculty.

Summer Programs ESL, sports programs offered; session focuses on sports/science/ESL; held on campus; accepts boys and girls; open to students from other schools. 30 students usually enrolled.

Tuition and Aid Day student tuition: $16,050; 5-day tuition and room/board: $23,100; 7-day tuition and room/board: $28,350. Tuition installment plan (monthly payment plans, individually arranged payment plans). Merit scholarship grants, need-based scholarship grants available. In 2015–16, 50% of upper-school students received aid; total upper-school merit-scholarship money awarded: $87,190. Total amount of financial aid awarded in 2015–16: $401,000.

Admissions Traditional secondary-level entrance grade is 9. ISEE, SSAT, TOEFL or SLEP or writing sample required. Deadline for receipt of application materials: none. Application fee required: $50. Interview required.

Athletics Interscholastic: baseball (boys), basketball (b), lacrosse (b), soccer (b), softball, tennis (b), volleyball; intramural: flag football, table tennis; coed interscholastic: equestrian sports, horseback riding; coed intramural: alpine skiing, equestrian sports, horseback riding, skiing (downhill), snowboarding. 1 PE instructor, 1 coach, 1 athletic trainer.

Computers Computers are regularly used in art, English, foreign language, history, mathematics, music, science classes. Computer network features include on-campus library services, online commercial services, Internet access, Internet filtering or blocking technology. Student e-mail accounts and computer access in designated common areas are available to students. Students grades are available online. The school has a published electronic and media policy.

Contact Mrs. Rachelle Sundberg, Director of Lower and Middle School Admissions. 440-942-3600 Ext. 114. Fax: 440-942-3660. E-mail: rsundberg@andrewsosborne.org. Website: www.AndrewsOsborne.org

AQUINAS HIGH SCHOOL

1920 Highland Avenue
Augusta, Georgia 30904-5303

Head of School: Mrs. Maureen G. Lewis

General Information Coeducational day college-preparatory school, affiliated with Roman Catholic Church. Grades 9–12. Founded: 1957. Setting: urban. Nearest major city is Atlanta. 25-acre campus. 4 buildings on campus. Approved or accredited by Southern Association of Colleges and Schools. Total enrollment: 244. Upper school average class size: 20. Upper school faculty-student ratio: 1:10. There are 180 required school days per year for Upper School students. Upper School students typically attend 5 days per week. The average school day consists of 6 hours and 40 minutes.

Upper School Student Profile Grade 9: 66 students (33 boys, 33 girls); Grade 10: 64 students (38 boys, 26 girls); Grade 11: 58 students (27 boys, 31 girls); Grade 12: 56 students (22 boys, 34 girls). 77% of students are Roman Catholic.

Faculty School total: 25. In upper school: 14 men, 11 women; 9 have advanced degrees.

Subjects Offered 3-dimensional art, advanced biology, advanced chemistry, Advanced Placement courses, advanced studio art-AP, algebra, American history, American literature, anatomy and physiology, art, Bible studies, biology, biology-AP, British literature, British literature (honors), broadcasting, calculus, calculus-AP, campus ministry, Catholic belief and practice, chemistry, chemistry-AP, choir, computer applications, computer programming, computer science, computer technologies, creative writing, digital art, digital photography, drama, economics, economics and history, economics-AP, English, English language and composition-AP, English literature, English literature and composition-AP, environmental science, ethics, European history, expository writing, foreign language, French, French language-AP, geography, geometry, government, government and politics-AP, government/civics, health, health education, history, honors algebra, honors English, honors geometry, honors U.S. history, honors world history, horticulture, human anatomy, human geography - AP, instruments, language, language and composition, Latin, literature and composition-AP, macroeconomics-AP, mathematics, moral theology, music, music theory, performing arts, philosophy, photography, physical education, physics, physics-AP, play production, prayer/spirituality, religion, religion and culture, religious education, science, social studies, software design, Spanish, Spanish language-AP, speech, statistics-AP, theater, theology, trigonometry, U.S. government and politics, U.S. government and politics-AP, weightlifting, wilderness education, wilderness experience, world geography, world history, world history-AP, world literature, writing, yearbook, yoga, zoology.

Graduation Requirements 20th century American writers, arts and fine arts (art, music, dance, drama), computer science, English, foreign language, mathematics, physical education (includes health), religion (includes Bible studies and theology), science, social studies (includes history). Community service is required.

Special Academic Programs 12 Advanced Placement exams for which test preparation is offered; honors section; independent study; study abroad; special instructional classes for students with learning disabilities, Attention Deficit Disorder, and dyslexia.

College Admission Counseling 60 students graduated in 2015; 57 went to college, including Augusta State University; Georgia Southern University; Kennesaw State University; University of Georgia; University of South Carolina; Valdosta State University. Other: 2 went to work, 1 entered military service.

Student Life Upper grades have uniform requirement, student council. Discipline rests equally with students and faculty. Attendance at religious services is required.

Tuition and Aid Day student tuition: $11,220. Tuition installment plan (FACTS Tuition Payment Plan). Tuition reduction for siblings, merit scholarship grants, need-based scholarship grants, paying campus jobs available. In 2015–16, 28% of upper-school students received aid. Total amount of financial aid awarded in 2015–16: $257,379.

Admissions Traditional secondary-level entrance grade is 9. For fall 2015, 69 students applied for upper-level admission, 66 were accepted, 66 enrolled. High School Placement Test (closed version) from Scholastic Testing Service required. Deadline for receipt of application materials: none. No application fee required. On-campus interview recommended.

Athletics Interscholastic: baseball (boys), basketball (b,g), cheering (g), football (b), golf (b,g), soccer (b,g), softball (g), tennis (b,g), track and field (b,g), volleyball (g), weight training (b,g); coed interscholastic: cross-country running, diving, outdoor education, riflery, swimming and diving, yoga. 2 PE instructors, 20 coaches, 1 athletic trainer.

Computers Computers are regularly used in all academic classes. Computer resources include on-campus library services, Internet access, wireless campus network, Internet filtering or blocking technology. Student e-mail accounts are available to students. Students grades are available online. The school has a published electronic and media policy.

Contact Mrs. Shannon Williams, Assistant Principal. 706-736-5516. Fax: 706-736-2678. E-mail: swilliams@aquinashigh.org. Website: www.aquinashigh.org

ARCHBISHOP CURLEY HIGH SCHOOL

3701 Sinclair Lane
Baltimore, Maryland 21213

Head of School: Fr. Donald Grzymski

General Information Boys' day college-preparatory, arts, business, religious studies, and technology school, affiliated with Roman Catholic Church. Grades 9–12. Founded: 1961. Setting: urban. 33-acre campus. 3 buildings on campus. Approved or accredited by Southern Association of Independent Schools and Maryland Department of Education. Endowment: $4.2 million. Total enrollment: 535. Upper school average class size: 22. Upper school faculty-student ratio: 1:14. There are 180 required school days per year for Upper School students. Upper School students typically attend 5 days per week. The average school day consists of 6 hours and 30 minutes.

Upper School Student Profile Grade 9: 141 students (141 boys); Grade 10: 147 students (147 boys); Grade 11: 133 students (133 boys); Grade 12: 114 students (114 boys). 65% of students are Roman Catholic.

Faculty School total: 46. In upper school: 35 men, 11 women; 24 have advanced degrees.

Subjects Offered 20th century world history, 3-dimensional design, accounting, advanced biology, advanced chemistry, advanced computer applications, advanced math, Advanced Placement courses, algebra, American government, American history, American history-AP, American literature, analytic geometry, art, art appreciation, arts appreciation, astronomy, band, Basic programming, biology, biology-AP, British literature, British literature (honors), British literature-AP, business communications, business law, business mathematics, business technology, calculus, calculus-AP, campus ministry, Catholic belief and practice, chemistry, chemistry-AP, choir, choral music, chorus, Christian and Hebrew scripture, Christian doctrine, Christian ethics, college admission preparation, college awareness, college counseling, college planning, computer applications, computer studies, computer technologies, concert band, consumer law, consumer mathematics, creative writing, earth science, engineering, English, English literature and composition-AP, environmental science, ethical decision making, European history, fine arts, French, freshman seminar, geography, geometry, government, government-AP, health, history of the Catholic Church, HTML design, instrumental music, jazz band, journalism, keyboarding, Latin, Life of Christ, music theory, photography, physical science, physics, physics-AP, pre-algebra, pre-calculus, probability and statistics, psychology, psychology-AP, reading/study skills, SAT/ACT preparation, Spanish, Spanish language-AP, U.S. government and politics-AP.

Graduation Requirements Algebra, American government, American history, art appreciation, biology, British literature, chemistry, church history, computer applications, English, foreign language, geometry, Life of Christ, physical fitness, physics, world history, world religions, 30 hours of community service with a written paper.

Special Academic Programs Advanced Placement exam preparation; honors section; independent study; study at local college for college credit; remedial reading and/or remedial writing; remedial math; programs in English, mathematics for dyslexic students.

College Admission Counseling 120 students graduated in 2015; they went to Loyola University Maryland; Mount St. Mary's University; Stevenson University; Towson University; University of Maryland, Baltimore County; University of Maryland, College Park.

Student Life Upper grades have specified standards of dress, student council, honor system. Discipline rests primarily with faculty. Attendance at religious services is required.

Summer Programs Remediation, enrichment, advancement, sports, art/fine arts, computer instruction programs offered; held on campus; accepts boys and girls; open to students from other schools. 2016 schedule: June 15 to August 9. Application deadline: June 15.

Tuition and Aid Day student tuition: $12,625. Tuition installment plan (FACTS Tuition Payment Plan, individually arranged payment plans). Tuition reduction for siblings, merit scholarship grants, need-based scholarship grants, paying campus jobs available.

Admissions Traditional secondary-level entrance grade is 9. For fall 2015, 300 students applied for upper-level admission, 141 enrolled. High School Placement Test (closed version) from Scholastic Testing Service required. Deadline for receipt of application materials: December 15. Application fee required: $25. Interview required.

Athletics Interscholastic: baseball, basketball, cross-country running, football, golf, ice hockey, indoor track & field, lacrosse, soccer, swimming and diving, tennis, track and field, volleyball, wrestling; intramural: flag football, Frisbee, handball, martial arts, touch football, weight lifting, weight training. 2 PE instructors, 32 coaches, 1 athletic trainer.

Computers Computers are regularly used in all classes. Computer network features include on-campus library services, Internet access, wireless campus network, Internet filtering or blocking technology, 1:1 iPad program. Campus intranet and student e-mail accounts are available to students. Students grades are available online. The school has a published electronic and media policy.

Contact Mr. Nick Brownlee, Admissions Director. 410-485-5000 Ext. 289. Fax: 410-485-6493. E-mail: nbrownlee@archbishopcurley.org. Website: www.archbishopcurley.org

ARCHBISHOP HOBAN HIGH SCHOOL

1 Holy Cross Boulevard
Akron, Ohio 44306

Head of School: Dr. Todd R. Sweda, EdD

General Information Coeducational day college-preparatory, arts, religious studies, and technology school, affiliated with Roman Catholic Church. Grades 9–12. Founded: 1953. Setting: urban. 75-acre campus. 3 buildings on campus. Approved or accredited by National Catholic Education Association, North Central Association of Colleges and Schools, Ohio Catholic Schools Accreditation Association (OCSAA), and Ohio Department of Education. Endowment: $10.5 million. Total enrollment: 856. Upper school average class size: 23. Upper school faculty-student ratio: 1:13. There are 178 required school days per year for Upper School students. Upper School students typically attend 5 days per week. The average school day consists of 6 hours and 55 minutes.

Upper School Student Profile Grade 9: 217 students (110 boys, 107 girls); Grade 10: 215 students (116 boys, 99 girls); Grade 11: 227 students (116 boys, 111 girls); Grade 12: 197 students (98 boys, 99 girls). 78% of students are Roman Catholic.

Faculty School total: 59. In upper school: 31 men, 28 women; 42 have advanced degrees.

Subjects Offered ACT preparation, advanced math, Advanced Placement courses, advanced studio art-AP, algebra, American literature, anatomy and physiology, archaeology, art, art history-AP, art-AP, biology, biology-AP, British literature, calculus-AP, Catholic belief and practice, ceramics, chemistry, chemistry-AP, Chinese, Christian and Hebrew scripture, church history, computer applications, computer graphics, computer science, conceptual physics, concert choir, digital imaging, digital music, drawing, economics, electronic music, electronic publishing, engineering, English, English language and composition-AP, English literature and composition-AP, English literature-AP, ensembles, environmental science, environmental studies, European history-AP, fine arts, French, French language-AP, geometry, government, health, health education, honors algebra, honors English, honors geometry, human anatomy, Italian, Latin, leadership, leadership and service, learning strategies, Mandarin, moral and social development, newspaper, orchestra, organic chemistry, painting, physical education, physics, physics-AP, pre-calculus, printmaking, psychology, psychology-AP, social justice, Spanish, statistics-AP, studio art, television, trigonometry, U.S. government, U.S. history, U.S. history-AP, values and decisions, Web site design, world cultures, world literature, yearbook.

Graduation Requirements Algebra, arts and fine arts (art, music, dance, drama), biology, economics, electives, English, health education, mathematics, physical education (includes health), religious studies, science, social studies (includes history), U.S. government, Christian service totaling 75 hours over four years.

Special Academic Programs 15 Advanced Placement exams for which test preparation is offered; honors section; study at local college for college credit; academic accommodation for the gifted and the artistically talented; remedial reading and/or remedial writing; remedial math; programs in general development for dyslexic students.

College Admission Counseling 198 students graduated in 2015; 192 went to college, including Kent State University; Ohio University; The Ohio State University; The University of Akron; The University of Toledo; University of Dayton. Other: 2 went to work, 4 had other specific plans. Median SAT critical reading: 590, median SAT math: 560, median SAT writing: 580, median composite ACT: 25. 48% scored over 600 on SAT critical reading, 42% scored over 600 on SAT math, 38% scored over 600 on SAT writing, 37% scored over 1800 on combined SAT, 42% scored over 26 on composite ACT.

Student Life Upper grades have specified standards of dress, student council, honor system. Discipline rests primarily with faculty. Attendance at religious services is required.

Summer Programs Advancement programs offered; session focuses on physical education; held on campus; accepts boys and girls; not open to students from other schools. 100 students usually enrolled. 2016 schedule: June 10 to June 30. Application deadline: March.

Tuition and Aid Tuition installment plan (FACTS Tuition Payment Plan). Tuition reduction for siblings, merit scholarship grants, need-based scholarship grants, paying campus jobs available. In 2015–16, 66% of upper-school students received aid.

Admissions Traditional secondary-level entrance grade is 9. For fall 2015, 304 students applied for upper-level admission, 243 were accepted, 217 enrolled. High School Placement Test required. Deadline for receipt of application materials: none. No application fee required. Interview recommended.

Athletics Interscholastic: baseball (boys), basketball (b,g), bowling (b,g), cross-country running (b,g), football (b), golf (b,g), gymnastics (g), indoor track & field (b,g), lacrosse (b,g), soccer (b,g), softball (g), swimming and diving (b,g), tennis (b,g), track and field (b,g), volleyball (b,g), winter (indoor) track (b,g), wrestling (b); intramural: flag football (g); coed interscholastic: cheering, dance team; coed intramural: basketball, strength & conditioning, ultimate Frisbee, weight training. 1 PE instructor, 1 athletic trainer.

Computers Computers are regularly used in graphic arts, literary magazine, newspaper, photography, science, video film production, Web site design, yearbook classes. Computer network features include on-campus library services, Internet access, wireless campus network, Internet filtering or blocking technology. Campus intranet, student e-mail accounts, and computer access in designated common areas are available to students. Students grades are available online. The school has a published electronic and media policy.

Contact Mr. Christopher Fahey, Admissions Counselor. 330-773-6658 Ext. 215. Fax: 330-773-9100. E-mail: Faheyc@hoban.org. Website: www.hoban.org

ARCHBISHOP MITTY HIGH SCHOOL

5000 Mitty Avenue
San Jose, California 95129

Head of School: Mr. Tim Brosnan

General Information Coeducational day college-preparatory, arts, religious studies, and technology school, affiliated with Roman Catholic Church. Grades 9–12. Founded: 1964. Setting: suburban. 24-acre campus. 11 buildings on campus. Approved or accredited by National Catholic Education Association, Western Association of Schools and Colleges, and California Department of Education. Endowment: $12 million. Total enrollment: 1,723. Upper school average class size: 27. Upper school faculty-student ratio: 1:17. There are 180 required school days per year for Upper School students. Upper School students typically attend 5 days per week. The average school day consists of 6 hours and 45 minutes.

Upper School Student Profile Grade 9: 435 students (208 boys, 227 girls); Grade 10: 443 students (215 boys, 228 girls); Grade 11: 424 students (213 boys, 211 girls); Grade 12: 421 students (215 boys, 206 girls). 75% of students are Roman Catholic.

Faculty School total: 110. In upper school: 55 men, 55 women; 75 have advanced degrees.

Subjects Offered 3-dimensional art, acting, American history-AP, American literature-AP, ancient world history, art, biology, biology-AP, British literature, calculus, calculus-AP, Catholic belief and practice, chemistry, chemistry-AP, choral music, chorus, church history, college placement, college writing, community service, computer graphics, computer multimedia, concert band, concert choir, drawing, economics and history, English, English language and composition-AP, English literature, English literature-AP, French, French language-AP, French literature-AP, French studies, French-AP, geometry, history-AP, honors algebra, honors English, honors geometry, honors U.S. history, honors world history, music, music appreciation, music theory-AP, philosophy, physics, physics-AP, political science, religion, social sciences, Spanish, Spanish language-AP, Spanish literature, Spanish literature-AP, student government, theater arts, U.S. government and politics, U.S. government and politics-AP, U.S. history, U.S. history-AP, U.S. literature, visual and performing arts, visual arts, world history.

Graduation Requirements Art, English, foreign language, mathematics, philosophy, physical education (includes health), religious studies, science, social sciences, 80 hours of Christian service.

Special Academic Programs 18 Advanced Placement exams for which test preparation is offered; honors section; study at local college for college credit; academic accommodation for the gifted, the musically talented, and the artistically talented.

College Admission Counseling 425 students graduated in 2015; all went to college, including California Polytechnic State University, San Luis Obispo; Santa Clara University; Stanford University; University of California, Berkeley; University of California, Davis; University of California, Los Angeles. Mean SAT critical reading: 613, mean SAT math: 622, mean SAT writing: 633, mean combined SAT: 1868, mean composite ACT: 27.

Student Life Upper grades have specified standards of dress, student council, honor system. Discipline rests primarily with faculty. Attendance at religious services is required.

Summer Programs Remediation, enrichment, advancement, sports, art/fine arts, computer instruction programs offered; session focuses on academics and athletics; held on campus; accepts boys and girls; open to students from other schools. 500 students usually enrolled. 2016 schedule: June 13 to July 21. Application deadline: May 31.

Tuition and Aid Day student tuition: $17,955. Tuition installment plan (SMART Tuition Payment Plan). Need-based scholarship grants, paying campus jobs available. In 2015–16, 30% of upper-school students received aid. Total amount of financial aid awarded in 2015–16: $3,750,000.

Admissions Traditional secondary-level entrance grade is 9. For fall 2015, 1,500 students applied for upper-level admission, 440 were accepted, 440 enrolled. High School Placement Test required. Deadline for receipt of application materials: December 11. Application fee required: $75.

Athletics Interscholastic: aquatics (boys, girls), badminton (b,g), baseball (b), basketball (b,g), cross-country running (b,g), dance team (g), diving (b,g), field hockey (g), football (b), golf (b,g), lacrosse (b,g), soccer (b,g), softball (g), swimming and diving (b,g), tennis (b,g), track and field (b,g), volleyball (b,g), water polo (b,g), weight training (b,g), winter soccer (b,g); intramural: roller hockey (b,g); coed interscholastic: physical fitness, strength & conditioning, wrestling; coed intramural: basketball, ice hockey, in-line hockey, table tennis. 4 PE instructors, 110 coaches, 2 athletic trainers.

Computers Computers are regularly used in all classes. Computer network features include on-campus library services, online commercial services, Internet access, wireless campus network, Internet filtering or blocking technology. Campus intranet, student e-mail accounts, and computer access in designated common areas are available to students. Students grades are available online. The school has a published electronic and media policy.

Contact Mrs. Lori Robowski, Assistant for Admissions. 408-342-4300. Fax: 408-342-4308. E-mail: admissions@mitty.com. Website: www.mitty.com/

ARCHBISHOP SHAW HIGH SCHOOL
1000 Barataria Boulevard
Marrero, Louisiana 70072-3052
Head of School: Rev. Louis J. Molinelli, SDB

General Information Boys' day college-preparatory, arts, religious studies, and technology school, affiliated with Roman Catholic Church. Grades 8–12. Founded: 1962. Setting: suburban. Nearest major city is New Orleans. 71-acre campus. 5 buildings on campus. Approved or accredited by National Catholic Education Association, Southern Association of Colleges and Schools, and Louisiana Department of Education. Total enrollment: 472. Upper school average class size: 24. Upper school faculty-student ratio: 1:24. There are 178 required school days per year for Upper School students. Upper School students typically attend 5 days per week. The average school day consists of 7 hours.

Upper School Student Profile Grade 8: 96 students (96 boys); Grade 9: 97 students (97 boys); Grade 10: 98 students (98 boys); Grade 11: 98 students (98 boys); Grade 12: 83 students (83 boys). 85% of students are Roman Catholic.

Faculty School total: 45. In upper school: 26 men, 9 women; 30 have advanced degrees.

Subjects Offered 20th century history, accounting, advanced math, algebra, art, band, Bible studies, biology, British literature, business law, calculus, calculus-AP, Catholic belief and practice, chemistry, Christian and Hebrew scripture, Christian doctrine, Christian ethics, Christian testament, Christianity, civics, civics/free enterprise, college counseling, college writing, community service, composition, computer applications, computer literacy, computer science-AP, concert band, driver education, earth science, economics, English, English composition, English literature, ethical decision making, fitness, French, geometry, guidance, health, history, history of the Catholic Church, history-AP, honors algebra, honors English, honors geometry, honors world history, human sexuality, instrumental music, Internet, jazz band, keyboarding, lab science, marching band, moral theology, music, physical education, physics, pre-algebra, pre-calculus, psychology, religious studies, SAT/ACT preparation, Spanish, symphonic band, U.S. history, U.S. history-AP, wind instruments, world geography, world history.

Graduation Requirements Algebra, American history, biology, chemistry, civics/free enterprise, earth science, English composition, English literature, foreign language, geometry, health, mathematics, physical fitness, physical science, religious studies, world geography, world history, 50 service hours.

Special Academic Programs Advanced Placement exam preparation; honors section; study at local college for college credit.

College Admission Counseling 110 students graduated in 2015; 95 went to college, including Louisiana State University and Agricultural & Mechanical College; Louisiana Tech University; University of Louisiana at Lafayette; University of New Orleans. Other: 10 went to work, 5 had other specific plans. Median composite ACT: 21. 15% scored over 26 on composite ACT.

Student Life Upper grades have uniform requirement, student council, honor system. Discipline rests primarily with faculty. Attendance at religious services is required.

Tuition and Aid Day student tuition: $7800. Tuition installment plan (monthly payment plans, individually arranged payment plans, local bank). Merit scholarship grants, need-based scholarship grants, paying campus jobs, educational bank loan financing available. In 2015–16, 10% of upper-school students received aid.

Admissions Traditional secondary-level entrance grade is 10. For fall 2015, 222 students applied for upper-level admission, 217 were accepted, 197 enrolled. High School Placement Test (closed version) from Scholastic Testing Service required. Deadline for receipt of application materials: none. Application fee required: $20. On-campus interview required.

Athletics Interscholastic: baseball, basketball, bowling, cross-country running, football, golf, running, soccer, track and field, wrestling; intramural: basketball, flag football, football, rugby, volleyball. 3 PE instructors, 9 coaches, 1 athletic trainer.

Computers Computers are regularly used in all academic classes. Computer network features include on-campus library services, online commercial services, Internet access, wireless campus network, Internet filtering or blocking technology. Students grades are available online. The school has a published electronic and media policy.

Contact Mr. Matthew Ducote, Admissions Director. 504-340-6727 Ext. 52. Fax: 504-347-9883. E-mail: shawadm@archdiocese-no.org. Website: www.archbishopshaw.org

ARCHMERE ACADEMY
3600 Philadelphia Pike
Claymont, Delaware 19703
Head of School: Dr. Michael Marinelli

General Information Coeducational day college-preparatory, arts, religious studies, and technology school, affiliated with Roman Catholic Church. Grades 9–12. Founded: 1932. Setting: suburban. Nearest major city is Wilmington. 38-acre campus. 6 buildings on campus. Approved or accredited by Middle States Association of Colleges and Schools, National Catholic Education Association, and Delaware Department of Education. Member of National Association of Independent Schools. Endowment: $12 million. Total enrollment: 505. Upper school average class size: 16. Upper school faculty-student ratio: 1:10. The average school day consists of 6 hours and 30 minutes.

Upper School Student Profile 75% of students are Roman Catholic.

Faculty School total: 62. In upper school: 31 men, 25 women; 51 have advanced degrees.

Subjects Offered Algebra, American history, American literature, architecture, art, art history, Bible studies, biology, calculus, chemistry, Chinese, computer programming, computer science, creative writing, drama, driver education, ecology, economics, English, English literature, environmental science, ethics, European history, expository writing, French, geometry, German, government/civics, grammar, health, history, mathematics, music, philosophy, physical education, physics, psychology, reading, religion, science, social studies, Spanish, speech, statistics, theater, theology, trigonometry, world history, writing.

Graduation Requirements Computer science, English, foreign language, mathematics, physical education (includes health), religion (includes Bible studies and theology), science, social studies (includes history), speech.

Special Academic Programs Advanced Placement exam preparation; honors section; independent study; study abroad; academic accommodation for the gifted, the musically talented, and the artistically talented; programs in English, mathematics for dyslexic students.

College Admission Counseling 124 students graduated in 2015; all went to college, including Boston University; Hofstra University; Penn State University Park; Saint Joseph's University; University of Delaware; University of Maryland, College Park. Median SAT critical reading: 595, median SAT math: 600, median SAT writing: 615. 48% scored over 600 on SAT critical reading, 48% scored over 600 on SAT math, 52% scored over 600 on SAT writing.

Student Life Upper grades have uniform requirement, student council, honor system. Discipline rests primarily with faculty. Attendance at religious services is required.

Tuition and Aid Day student tuition: $23,380. Tuition installment plan (10-month Automatic Debit Plan). Merit scholarship grants, need-based scholarship grants, grants for children of faculty and staff, minority scholarships/grants available. In 2015–16, 65% of upper-school students received aid; total upper-school merit-scholarship money awarded: $2,000,000. Total amount of financial aid awarded in 2015–16: $2,000,000.

Admissions Traditional secondary-level entrance grade is 9. For fall 2015, 300 students applied for upper-level admission, 250 were accepted, 135 enrolled. Deadline for receipt of application materials: March 1. Application fee required: $50. On-campus interview required.

Athletics Interscholastic: baseball (boys), basketball (b,g), cheering (g), cross-country running (b,g), field hockey (g), football (b), golf (b,g), ice hockey (b,g), indoor track (b,g), lacrosse (b,g), soccer (b,g), softball (g), swimming and diving (b,g), tennis (b,g), track and field (b,g), volleyball (g), wrestling (b); coed interscholastic: winter (indoor) track; coed intramural: basketball, bowling, fencing. 1 PE instructor, 16 coaches, 2 athletic trainers.

Computers Computers are regularly used in art, English, foreign language, history, mathematics, multimedia, science classes. Computer network features include on-campus library services, online commercial services, Internet access, wireless campus network. Student e-mail accounts are available to students. The school has a published electronic and media policy.

Contact Mrs. Kristin B. Mumford, Director of Admissions. 302-798-6632 Ext. 781. E-mail: kmumford@archmereacademy.com. Website: www.archmereacademy.com

ARENDELL PARROTT ACADEMY
PO Box 1297
Kinston, North Carolina 28503-1297
Head of School: Dr. Bert S. Bright Jr.

General Information Coeducational day college-preparatory and arts school. Grades PK–12. Founded: 1964. Setting: small town. Nearest major city is Greenville. 80-acre campus. 6 buildings on campus. Approved or accredited by North Carolina Association of Independent Schools, Southern Association of Colleges and Schools, and North Carolina Department of Education. Member of National Association of Independent Schools. Total enrollment: 721. Upper school average class size: 18. Upper school faculty-student ratio: 1:17. There are 178 required school days per year for Upper School students. Upper School students typically attend 5 days per week. The average school day consists of 6 hours and 20 minutes.

Upper School Student Profile Grade 9: 62 students (30 boys, 32 girls); Grade 10: 70 students (34 boys, 36 girls); Grade 11: 54 students (28 boys, 26 girls); Grade 12: 59 students (30 boys, 29 girls).

Faculty School total: 60. In upper school: 10 men, 21 women; 20 have advanced degrees.

Special Academic Programs Advanced Placement exam preparation; honors section; study at local college for college credit.

College Admission Counseling 59 students graduated in 2015; 58 went to college, including Duke University; East Carolina University; North Carolina State University; The University of North Carolina at Chapel Hill; University of Mississippi; University of South Carolina. Other: 1 entered military service. Mean SAT critical reading: 555, mean SAT math: 568, mean SAT writing: 546, mean combined SAT: 1669, mean composite ACT: 25.

Student Life Upper grades have specified standards of dress, student council, honor system. Discipline rests primarily with faculty.

Tuition and Aid Day student tuition: $10,150. Tuition installment plan (monthly payment plans, individually arranged payment plans). Need-based scholarship grants available. In 2015–16, 17% of upper-school students received aid. Total amount of financial aid awarded in 2015–16: $260,000.

Admissions Traditional secondary-level entrance grade is 9. For fall 2015, 26 students applied for upper-level admission, 13 were accepted, 13 enrolled. Deadline for receipt of application materials: February 15. Application fee required: $550. Interview required.

Athletics Interscholastic: baseball (boys), basketball (b,g), cheering (g), cross-country running (b,g), dance squad (g), field hockey (g), football (b), lacrosse (b), soccer (b,g), softball (g), swimming and diving (b,g), tennis (b,g), volleyball (g); coed interscholastic: dance, fitness, golf, physical fitness, physical training, strength & conditioning; coed intramural: archery. 5 PE instructors, 4 coaches, 1 athletic trainer.

Computers Computer network features include on-campus library services, Internet access, wireless campus network, Internet filtering or blocking technology. Computer access in designated common areas is available to students. Students grades are available online. The school has a published electronic and media policy.

Contact Nancy Gilmore, Director of Admissions. 252-522-0410 Ext. 202. Fax: 919-522-0672. E-mail: ngilmore@parrottacademy.org. Website: www.parrottacademy.org

ARETE PREPARATORY ACADEMY

11500 West Olympic Boulevard
Suite 318
Los Angeles, California 90064

Head of School: Jim Hahn

General Information Coeducational day college-preparatory and general academic school. Grades 9–12. Founded: 2008. Setting: urban. Approved or accredited by Western Association of Schools and Colleges and California Department of Education. Total enrollment: 58. Upper school average class size: 5. Upper school faculty-student ratio: 1:2. Upper School students typically attend 5 days per week. The average school day consists of 7 hours and 40 minutes.

Upper School Student Profile Grade 9: 16 students (9 boys, 7 girls); Grade 10: 5 students (3 boys, 2 girls); Grade 11: 19 students (11 boys, 8 girls); Grade 12: 14 students (6 boys, 8 girls).

Faculty School total: 22. In upper school: 9 men, 12 women; 12 have advanced degrees.

Subjects Offered 20th century world history, advanced chemistry, algebra, American history, American literature, art, band, biology, calculus, chemistry, college counseling, comparative government and politics, composition, creative writing, critical thinking, critical writing, discrete mathematics, drama, electives, electronics, English, English composition, English literature, environmental science, ethics, ethics and responsibility, film history, foreign language, French, geometry, global issues, great issues, honors English, honors U.S. history, honors world history, humanities, independent study, introduction to literature, Japanese, Japanese studies, language and composition, linguistics, literary magazine, literature, logic, modern civilization, moral reasoning, multicultural literature, neuroscience, participation in sports, philosophy, physical education, physics, poetry, politics, pre-calculus, science, senior composition, senior project, social sciences, social studies, Southern literature, Spanish, sports, strategies for success, theater, theory of knowledge, trigonometry, U.S. constitutional history, U.S. history, U.S. literature, world civilizations, world history.

Special Academic Programs Honors section; accelerated programs; independent study; study at local college for college credit; academic accommodation for the gifted; remedial reading and/or remedial writing; remedial math; programs in English, mathematics, general development for dyslexic students.

College Admission Counseling 17 students graduated in 2015; 15 went to college. Other: 2 had other specific plans.

Student Life Upper grades have student council, honor system. Discipline rests primarily with faculty.

Summer Programs Remediation, enrichment, advancement programs offered; held on campus; accepts boys and girls; open to students from other schools.

Tuition and Aid Day student tuition: $45,000. Need-based scholarship grants available. In 2015–16, 40% of upper-school students received aid.

Admissions Traditional secondary-level entrance grade is 9. For fall 2015, 25 students applied for upper-level admission, 20 were accepted, 17 enrolled. Deadline for receipt of application materials: none. Application fee required: $100. On-campus interview required.

Athletics Interscholastic: cross-country running (boys, girls); coed interscholastic: cross-country running. 2 PE instructors, 2 coaches.

Computers Computer network features include Internet access, wireless campus network, Internet filtering or blocking technology. Campus intranet and student e-mail accounts are available to students. The school has a published electronic and media policy.

Contact Clark Brandon, Dean of Students. 310-478-9900. E-mail: clark@areteprep.org. Website: www.areteprep.org

ARMBRAE ACADEMY

1400 Oxford Street
Halifax, Nova Scotia B3H 3Y8, Canada

Head of School: Gary O'Meara

General Information Coeducational day college-preparatory school. Grades K–12. Founded: 1887. Setting: urban. 2-acre campus. 3 buildings on campus. Approved or accredited by Canadian Association of Independent Schools, Canadian Educational Standards Institute, and Nova Scotia Department of Education. Language of instruction: English. Endowment: CAN$1 million. Total enrollment: 250. Upper school average class size: 22. Upper school faculty-student ratio: 1:9. There are 185 required school days per year for Upper School students. Upper School students typically attend 5 days per week. The average school day consists of 5 hours and 30 minutes.

Faculty School total: 35. In upper school: 5 men, 8 women; 5 have advanced degrees.

Subjects Offered Algebra, American history, art, biology, calculus, chemistry, computer science, earth science, economics, English, English literature, European history, French, geography, geology, geometry, government/civics, grammar, health, history, keyboarding, Mandarin, mathematics, music, physical education, physics, science, social studies, study skills, trigonometry, world literature, writing.

Graduation Requirements Computer science, English, foreign language, mathematics, physical education (includes health), science, social studies (includes history), 6 courses each in grades 11 and 12.

Special Academic Programs Advanced Placement exam preparation; accelerated programs; study at local college for college credit; academic accommodation for the artistically talented.

College Admission Counseling 20 students graduated in 2015; they went to Acadia University; Carleton University; Dalhousie University; McGill University; Queen's University at Kingston; St. Francis Xavier University.

Student Life Upper grades have uniform requirement, student council. Discipline rests equally with students and faculty.

Tuition and Aid Day student tuition: CAN$13,870. Tuition installment plan (monthly payment plans, term payment plan). Tuition reduction for siblings, bursaries, merit scholarship grants available. In 2015–16, 4% of upper-school students received aid; total upper-school merit-scholarship money awarded: CAN$2000. Total amount of financial aid awarded in 2015–16: CAN$60,000.

Admissions Traditional secondary-level entrance grade is 10. For fall 2015, 25 students applied for upper-level admission, 22 were accepted, 15 enrolled. CTBS (or similar from their school) required. Deadline for receipt of application materials: none. Application fee required: CAN$150. On-campus interview required.

Athletics Interscholastic: badminton (boys, girls), basketball (b,g), cross-country running (b,g), field hockey (g), ice hockey (b), soccer (b,g), swimming and diving (b,g), tennis (b,g), track and field (b,g), volleyball (b,g), yoga (b,g); intramural: badminton (b,g), cross-country running (b,g); coed interscholastic: curling, ice hockey; coed intramural: ice hockey. 2 PE instructors, 4 coaches.

Computers Computers are regularly used in all classes. Computer network features include on-campus library services, online commercial services, Internet access, wireless campus network. Campus intranet, student e-mail accounts, and computer access in designated common areas are available to students. Students grades are available online. The school has a published electronic and media policy.

Contact Gary D. O'Meara, Headmaster. 902-423-7920. Fax: 902-423-9731. E-mail: head@armbrae.ns.ca. Website: www.armbrae.ns.ca

ARMY AND NAVY ACADEMY

2605 Carlsbad Boulevard
PO Box 3000
Carlsbad, California 92018-3000

Head of School: Maj. Gen. Arthur M. Bartell, Retd.

General Information Boys' boarding and day college-preparatory, Junior ROTC, and military school. Grades 7–12. Founded: 1910. Setting: small town. Nearest major city is San Diego. Students are housed in single-sex dormitories. 16-acre campus. 34 buildings on campus. Approved or accredited by California Association of Independent Schools and Western Association of Schools and Colleges. Member of National Association of Independent Schools and Secondary School Admission Test Board. Endowment: $637,605. Total enrollment: 267. Upper school average class size: 15. Upper school faculty-student ratio: 1:15. There are 180 required school days per year for Upper School students. Upper School students typically attend 5 days per week. The average school day consists of 7 hours.

Upper School Student Profile 67% of students are boarding students. 44% are state residents. 14 states are represented in upper school student body. 20% are international students. International students from China, Mexico, Nigeria, Republic of Korea, Russian Federation, and Ukraine; 14 other countries represented in student body.

Faculty School total: 33. In upper school: 14 men, 19 women; 16 have advanced degrees.

Subjects Offered Algebra, art, astronomy, biology, biology-AP, calculus-AP, chemistry, chemistry-AP, composition-AP, drama, economics, economics-AP, English, English literature-AP, English-AP, ESL, European history-AP, French, geography, geometry, German, guitar, independent study, JROTC, Mandarin, marching band, music technology, photography, physical education, physics, physics-AP, pre-calculus, psychology-AP, Spanish, Spanish-AP, sports psychology, studio art-AP, study skills, U.S. government, U.S. history, U.S. history-AP, video film production, weight training, world history, yearbook.

Graduation Requirements Arts and fine arts (art, music, dance, drama), electives, English, foreign language, lab science, leadership education training, mathematics, physical education (includes health), social studies (includes history).

Special Academic Programs 7 Advanced Placement exams for which test preparation is offered; honors section; independent study; special instructional classes for students with Attention Deficit Disorder and learning disabilities; ESL (37 students enrolled).

College Admission Counseling 67 students graduated in 2015; 64 went to college, including Arizona State University at the Tempe campus; California State University, Chico; California State University, San Marcos; Penn State University Park; University of California, Irvine; University of Colorado Boulder. Other: 3 entered military service. Median SAT critical reading: 488, median SAT math: 543, median SAT writing: 483.

Student Life Upper grades have uniform requirement, student council, honor system. Discipline rests primarily with faculty.

Summer Programs Enrichment, ESL, sports, computer instruction programs offered; session focuses on academic, JROTC leadership, and recreation; held on campus; accepts boys and girls; open to students from other schools. 300 students usually enrolled. 2016 schedule: July 5 to August 1. Application deadline: none.

Tuition and Aid Day student tuition: $20,850; 7-day tuition and room/board: $35,400. Tuition installment plan (individually arranged payment plans). Tuition reduction for siblings, need-based scholarship grants, military discount available. In 2015–16, 15% of upper-school students received aid. Total amount of financial aid awarded in 2015–16: $382,500.

Admissions Traditional secondary-level entrance grade is 10. For fall 2015, 203 students applied for upper-level admission, 61 were accepted, 46 enrolled. ISEE, Otis-Lennon School Ability Test, SSAT, Star-9 or TOEFL required. Deadline for receipt of application materials: none. Application fee required: $100. Interview required.

Athletics Interscholastic: aquatics, baseball, basketball, cross-country running, drill team, flag football, football, golf, lacrosse, marksmanship, soccer, swimming and diving, tennis, track and field, water polo, wrestling; intramural: badminton, combined training, fitness, hockey, independent competitive sports, JROTC drill, outdoor activities, outdoor recreation, physical fitness, physical training, riflery, strength & conditioning, surfing, weight lifting. 15 coaches, 1 athletic trainer.

Computers Computers are regularly used in music technology, video film production, yearbook classes. Computer network features include on-campus library services, Internet access, wireless campus network, Internet filtering or blocking technology. Computer access in designated common areas is available to students. Students grades are available online. The school has a published electronic and media policy.

Contact Candice Heidenrich, Director of Admissions. 888-762-2338. Fax: 760-434-5948. E-mail: admissions@armyandnavyacademy.org. Website: www.armyandnavyacademy.org

ARTHUR MORGAN SCHOOL

Burnsville, North Carolina
See Junior Boarding Schools section.

ASHBURY COLLEGE

362 Mariposa Avenue
Ottawa, Ontario K1M 0T3, Canada

Head of School: Mr. Norman Southward

General Information Coeducational boarding and day college-preparatory, bilingual studies, and International Baccalaureate school. Boarding grades 9–12, day grades 4–12. Founded: 1891. Setting: urban. Students are housed in single-sex dormitories. 13-acre campus. 3 buildings on campus. Approved or accredited by Canadian Association of Independent Schools, Canadian Educational Standards Institute, Conference of Independent Schools of Ontario, International Baccalaureate Organization, Ontario Ministry of Education, and The Association of Boarding Schools. Affiliate member of National Association of Independent Schools. Languages of instruction: English and French. Endowment: CAN$6.5 million. Total enrollment: 690. Upper school average class size: 17. Upper school faculty-student ratio: 1:9. There are 180 required school days per year for Upper School students. Upper School students typically attend 5 days per week. The average school day consists of 6 hours and 5 minutes.

Upper School Student Profile Grade 6: 35 students (35 boys); Grade 7: 50 students (50 boys); Grade 8: 50 students (50 boys); Grade 9: 118 students (68 boys, 50 girls); Grade 10: 125 students (61 boys, 64 girls); Grade 11: 141 students (71 boys, 70 girls); Grade 12: 141 students (81 boys, 60 girls). 20% of students are boarding students. 75% are province residents. 7 provinces are represented in upper school student body. 15% are international students. International students from Germany, Hong Kong, Japan, Mexico, Nigeria, and United States; 40 other countries represented in student body.

Faculty School total: 60. In upper school: 30 men, 30 women; 45 have advanced degrees; 15 reside on campus.

Subjects Offered Accounting, advanced chemistry, advanced math, algebra, American history, art, art history, biology, business, business skills, calculus, Canadian geography, Canadian history, chemistry, computer applications, computer programming, computer science, creative writing, drama, driver education, economics, English, English literature, environmental science, ESL, European history, fine arts, French, geography, geometry, health, history, mathematics, music, physical education, physics, science, social studies, sociology, Spanish, theater, theory of knowledge, world history, world literature.

Graduation Requirements English, mathematics, science. Community service is required.

Special Academic Programs International Baccalaureate program; independent study; term-away projects; study abroad; ESL (22 students enrolled).

College Admission Counseling 138 students graduated in 2014; all went to college, including Dalhousie University; McGill University; Queen's University at Kingston; The University of Western Ontario; University of Ottawa; University of Toronto. Mean SAT critical reading: 600, mean SAT math: 644, mean SAT writing: 591.

Student Life Upper grades have uniform requirement, student council, honor system. Discipline rests primarily with faculty.

Tuition and Aid Day student tuition: CAN$21,740; 7-day tuition and room/board: CAN$52,600. Tuition installment plan (monthly payment plans, individually arranged payment plans). Tuition reduction for siblings, bursaries, merit scholarship grants available. In 2014–15, 20% of upper-school students received aid; total upper-school merit-scholarship money awarded: CAN$9000. Total amount of financial aid awarded in 2014–15: CAN$470,000.

Admissions Traditional secondary-level entrance grade is 9. For fall 2014, 350 students applied for upper-level admission, 266 were accepted, 123 enrolled. Canadian Standardized Test, SLEP or TOEFL required. Deadline for receipt of application materials: none. Application fee required: CAN$100. Interview required.

Athletics Interscholastic: alpine skiing (boys, girls), badminton (b,g), basketball (b,g), cross-country running (b,g), field hockey (g), football (b), golf (b,g), hockey (b), ice hockey (b), independent competitive sports (b,g), rowing (b,g), rugby (b,g), skiing (downhill) (b,g), soccer (b,g), tennis (b,g), track and field (b,g), volleyball (b,g); intramural: badminton (b,g), ball hockey (b,g), basketball (b,g), ice hockey (b), modern dance (b), outdoor education (b,g), rugby (b,g); coed interscholastic: baseball, running; coed intramural: alpine skiing, basketball, canoeing/kayaking, climbing, cooperative games, fitness, flag football, Frisbee, hiking/backpacking, indoor soccer, life saving, martial arts, Nautilus, nordic skiing, outdoor activities, physical fitness, physical training, skiing (cross-country), skiing (downhill), snowboarding, soccer, softball, strength & conditioning, tennis, track and field, ultimate Frisbee, volleyball, weight training, yoga. 5 PE instructors, 10 coaches.

Computers Computers are regularly used in art, business applications, business education, data processing, economics, geography, graphic arts, humanities, information technology, mathematics, music, science, yearbook classes. Computer network features include on-campus library services, Internet access, wireless campus network, Internet filtering or blocking technology. Campus intranet, student e-mail accounts, and computer access in designated common areas are available to students. Students grades are available online. The school has a published electronic and media policy.

Contact Mrs. Padme Raina, Assistant Director of Admissions, Boarding. 613-749-5954 Ext. 368. Fax: 613-749 9724. E-mail: praina@ashbury.ca. Website: www.ashbury.ca

ASHLEY HALL

172 Rutledge Avenue
Charleston, South Carolina 29403-5877

Head of School: Jill Swisher Muti

General Information Coeducational day (boys' only in lower grades) college-preparatory, arts, technology, and science, mathematics school. Boys grades PS–K, girls grades PS–12. Founded: 1909. Setting: urban. 5-acre campus. 8 buildings on campus. Approved or accredited by South Carolina Independent School Association, Southern Association of Colleges and Schools, and Southern Association of Independent Schools. Member of National Association of Independent Schools. Endowment: $12 million. Total enrollment: 682. Upper school average class size: 16. Upper school faculty-student ratio: 1:8. Upper School students typically attend 5 days per week. The average school day consists of 7 hours.

Upper School Student Profile Grade 7: 45 students (45 girls); Grade 8: 42 students (42 girls); Grade 9: 64 students (64 girls); Grade 10: 54 students (54 girls); Grade 11: 54 students (54 girls); Grade 12: 54 students (54 girls).

Faculty School total: 95. In upper school: 8 men, 20 women; 18 have advanced degrees.

Subjects Offered 3-dimensional design, algebra, American history, American history-AP, American literature, art, art history, art history-AP, bioethics, biology, biology-AP, calculus, calculus-AP, ceramics, chemistry, chemistry-AP, choir, computer science, creative writing, desktop publishing, drama, economics, economics and history, English, English literature, English-AP, European history, European history-AP, forensics, foundations of civilization, French, French-AP, geography, geometry, government/civics, history, Internet, keyboarding, Latin, Latin-AP, marine biology, mathematics, microeconomics-AP, music, photo shop, photography, physical education, physical science, physics, physics-AP, pre-calculus, programming, psychology, social studies, Spanish, Spanish-AP, speech, statistics, statistics-AP, studio art, studio art-AP, technology, trigonometry, U.S. government and politics-AP, Web site design, world history.

Graduation Requirements Advanced Placement courses, arts and fine arts (art, music, dance, drama), English, foreign language, history, mathematics, physical education (includes health), science.

Special Academic Programs Advanced Placement exam preparation; honors section; independent study; term-away projects; study at local college for college credit; study abroad; academic accommodation for the gifted, the musically talented, and the artistically talented.

College Admission Counseling 50 students graduated in 2015; all went to college, including Clemson University; College of Charleston; Sewanee: The University of the South; The University of North Carolina at Chapel Hill; University of South Carolina.

Student Life Upper grades have uniform requirement, student council, honor system. Discipline rests equally with students and faculty.

Summer Programs Enrichment, sports, art/fine arts, computer instruction programs offered; session focuses on enrichment, athletics, adventure, and day camps; held on campus; accepts boys and girls; open to students from other schools. 900 students usually enrolled. 2016 schedule: June 1 to July 28. Application deadline: none.

Tuition and Aid Day student tuition: $14,460–$20,735. Tuition installment plan (FACTS Tuition Payment Plan). Need-based scholarship grants, paying campus jobs available. In 2015–16, 23% of upper-school students received aid. Total amount of financial aid awarded in 2015–16: $1,215,000.

Admissions Traditional secondary-level entrance grade is 9. For fall 2015, 47 students applied for upper-level admission, 45 were accepted, 24 enrolled. ISEE, Kaufman Test of Educational Achievement or SSAT required. Deadline for receipt of application materials: February 7. Application fee required: $75. Interview required.

Athletics Interscholastic: basketball, cross-country running, running, sailing, soccer, softball, strength & conditioning, swimming and diving, tennis, track and field, volleyball; intramural: aerobics/dance, aquatics, backpacking, basketball, canoeing/kayaking, climbing, cross-country running, dance, dance squad, dance team, equestrian sports, fitness, golf, hiking/backpacking, horseback riding, jogging, judo, jump rope, kayaking, kickball, life saving, martial arts, mountain biking, mountaineering, outdoor adventure, outdoor education, outdoor skills, physical fitness, physical training, rock climbing, running, soccer, softball, strength & conditioning, swimming and diving, tennis, track and field, volleyball, walking, weight training. 2 PE instructors, 4 coaches, 1 athletic trainer.

Computers Computers are regularly used in animation, art, career exploration, college planning, desktop publishing, graphic design, independent study, introduction to technology, library skills, newspaper, photography, research skills, SAT preparation, video film production, Web site design, yearbook classes. Computer network features include on-campus library services, online commercial services, Internet access, wireless campus network, Internet filtering or blocking technology. The school has a published electronic and media policy.

Contact Frances Magee, Assistant Director of Admissions. 843-965-8501. Fax: 843-720-2868. E-mail: mageef@ashleyhall.org. Website: www.ashleyhall.org

ASSETS SCHOOL

Honolulu, Hawaii
See Special Needs Schools section.

ATHENS ACADEMY

1281 Spartan Lane
PO Box 6548
Athens, Georgia 30604

Head of School: Mr. John Thorsen

General Information Coeducational day college-preparatory and technology school. Grades N–12. Founded: 1967. Setting: suburban. Nearest major city is Atlanta. 154-acre campus. 11 buildings on campus. Approved or accredited by Georgia Independent School Association, Southern Association of Colleges and Schools, Southern Association of Independent Schools, and Georgia Department of Education. Member of National Association of Independent Schools and Secondary School Admission Test Board. Endowment: $6.5 million. Total enrollment: 963. Upper school average class size: 18. Upper school faculty-student ratio: 1:8.

Upper School Student Profile Grade 9: 82 students (42 boys, 40 girls); Grade 10: 79 students (38 boys, 41 girls); Grade 11: 93 students (42 boys, 51 girls); Grade 12: 72 students (46 boys, 26 girls).

Faculty School total: 102. In upper school: 22 men, 20 women; 31 have advanced degrees.

Subjects Offered Advanced math, advanced studio art-AP, algebra, American history, American history-AP, American literature, anatomy, art, art history, band, biology, biology-AP, calculus, calculus-AP, ceramics, chemistry, chemistry-AP, choral music, creative writing, drama, ecology, economics, English, English literature, English-AP, European history, expository writing, fine arts, French, geography, geometry, government/civics, grammar, health, history, Latin, Latin-AP, mathematics, music, photography, physical education, physics, physics-AP, physiology, robotics, science, social studies, Spanish, statistics, theater, trigonometry, world history, world literature.

Graduation Requirements Arts and fine arts (art, music, dance, drama), English, foreign language, mathematics, physical education (includes health), science, social studies (includes history).

Special Academic Programs 13 Advanced Placement exams for which test preparation is offered; honors section; independent study.

College Admission Counseling 66 students graduated in 2015; 65 went to college, including Georgia Institute of Technology; University of Georgia. Other: 1 had other specific plans. Median SAT critical reading: 616, median SAT math: 628, median SAT writing: 604, median combined SAT: 1848, median composite ACT: 27.

Student Life Upper grades have specified standards of dress, student council, honor system. Discipline rests primarily with faculty.

Summer Programs Remediation, enrichment, sports, art/fine arts, computer instruction programs offered; session focuses on enrichment and review; held on campus; accepts boys and girls; open to students from other schools. 250 students usually enrolled. 2016 schedule: June 15 to August 13. Application deadline: none.

Tuition and Aid Day student tuition: $8300–$16,825. Tuition installment plan (Insured Tuition Payment Plan, monthly payment plans). Tuition reduction for siblings, need-based scholarship grants available. In 2015–16, 20% of upper-school students received aid. Total amount of financial aid awarded in 2015–16: $12,000,000.

Admissions Traditional secondary-level entrance grade is 9. For fall 2015, 39 students applied for upper-level admission, 27 were accepted, 25 enrolled. CTP III and Otis-Lennon School Ability Test, ERB CPT III required. Deadline for receipt of application materials: February 12. Application fee required: $85. On-campus interview required.

Athletics Interscholastic: baseball (boys), basketball (b,g), cheering (g), cross-country running (b,g), football (b), soccer (b,g), swimming and diving (b,g), tennis (b,g), track and field (b,g), volleyball (g), wrestling (b); coed interscholastic: cross-country running, golf, swimming and diving, tennis, track and field. 6 PE instructors, 5 coaches.

Computers Computers are regularly used in English, French, history, Latin, mathematics, science, Spanish classes. Computer network features include on-campus library services, online commercial services, Internet access, wireless campus network. Student e-mail accounts are available to students. The school has a published electronic and media policy.

Contact Mr. Geoffrey R. Walton, Director of Admission. 706-549-9225. Fax: 706-354-3775. E-mail: gwalton@athensacademy.org. Website: www.athensacademy.org/

ATHENS BIBLE SCHOOL

507 South Hoffman Street
Athens, Alabama 35611

Head of School: Mr. Randall L. Adams

General Information Coeducational day college-preparatory school. Grades K–12. Founded: 1943. Setting: small town. Nearest major city is Huntsville. 2 buildings on campus. Approved or accredited by Southern Association of Colleges and Schools and Alabama Department of Education. Total enrollment: 270. Upper school average class size: 30. There are 180 required school days per year for Upper School students. The average school day consists of 6 hours and 11 minutes.

Upper School Student Profile Grade 7: 9 students (9 boys).

Subjects Offered 1968.

Student Life Upper grades have specified standards of dress, student council. Discipline rests primarily with faculty.

Admissions No application fee required. Interview required.

Contact Mrs. Jill Duke, Secretary/Receptionist. 256-232-3525. Fax: 256-232-5417 Ext. 221. E-mail: jill.duke@athensbibleschool.org.

Website: www.athensbibleschool.org

ATLANTA INTERNATIONAL SCHOOL

2890 North Fulton Drive
Atlanta, Georgia 30305

Head of School: Mr. Kevin Glass

General Information Coeducational day college-preparatory, arts, bilingual studies, technology, International Baccalaureate Diploma Programme (Grades 11-12), and International Baccalaureate Middle Years (Grades 9-10) school. Grades PK–12. Founded: 1984. Setting: urban. 14-acre campus. 4 buildings on campus. Approved or accredited by French Ministry of Education, Georgia Independent School Association, International Baccalaureate Organization, National Independent Private Schools Association, Southern Association of Colleges and Schools, Southern Association of Independent Schools, and Georgia Department of Education. Member of National Association of Independent Schools and European Council of International Schools. Total enrollment: 1,160. Upper school average class size: 15. Upper school faculty-student ratio: 1:15. There are 182 required school days per year for Upper School students. Upper School students typically attend 5 days per week. The average school day consists of 7 hours and 30 minutes.

Upper School Student Profile Grade 9: 90 students (39 boys, 51 girls); Grade 10: 96 students (51 boys, 45 girls); Grade 11: 76 students (28 boys, 48 girls); Grade 12: 84 students (36 boys, 48 girls).

Faculty School total: 186.

Subjects Offered American history, art, biology, chemistry, Chinese, choir, chorus, computer science, contemporary issues, design, economics, English, English literature, ESL, fine arts, French, French as a second language, geography, German, health, integrated mathematics, International Baccalaureate courses, jazz band, lab/keyboard, Latin, math methods, mathematics, model United Nations, physical education, physics, robotics, SAT preparation, science, science and technology, social studies, Spanish, theater, theater arts, theory of knowledge, world history, yearbook.

Graduation Requirements Extended essay/research project.

Special Academic Programs International Baccalaureate program; independent study; term-away projects; study abroad; ESL.

College Admission Counseling 80 students graduated in 2015; 78 went to college, including Emory University; Georgia Institute of Technology; Georgia State University; McGill University; New York University; University of Georgia. Other: 2 had other specific plans. Mean SAT critical reading: 623, mean SAT math: 623.

Student Life Upper grades have specified standards of dress, student council, honor system. Discipline rests primarily with faculty.

Summer Programs Enrichment, advancement, ESL, sports, art/fine arts, computer instruction programs offered; session focuses on language acquisition (French, Spanish, German, Chinese, ESL), day camps, sport camps, theater, robotics, chess; held on campus; accepts boys and girls; open to students from other schools. 150 students usually enrolled. 2016 schedule: June 13 to July 29. Application deadline: April 30.

Tuition and Aid Day student tuition: $20,647–$23,570. Tuition installment plan (Insured Tuition Payment Plan). Need-based scholarship grants available. In 2015–16, 11% of upper-school students received aid.

Admissions Traditional secondary-level entrance grade is 9. SSAT required. Deadline for receipt of application materials: none. Application fee required: $100. Interview recommended.

Athletics Interscholastic: basketball (boys, girls), cross-country running (b,g), soccer (b,g), swimming and diving (b,g), tennis (b,g), track and field (b,g), ultimate Frisbee (b,g), volleyball (g); intramural: strength & conditioning (b,g); coed interscholastic: golf, sailing; coed intramural: basketball, soccer, volleyball. 9 PE instructors, 7 coaches, 3 athletic trainers.

Computers Computers are regularly used in all academic classes. Computer network features include on-campus library services, Internet access, wireless campus network, Internet filtering or blocking technology, server space for file storage, online classroom, multi-user learning software. Student e-mail accounts and computer access in designated common areas are available to students. Students grades are available online. The school has a published electronic and media policy.

Contact Ms. Nici Robinson, Associate Director of Admission and Financial Aid. 404-841-3891. Fax: 404-841-3873. E-mail: nrobinson@aischool.org.
Website: www.aischool.org

ATLANTIS ACADEMY

Miami, Florida
See Special Needs Schools section.

AUGUSTA CHRISTIAN SCHOOL

313 Baston Road
Martinez, Georgia 30907

Head of School: Mr. Les Walden

General Information Coeducational day college-preparatory, arts, religious studies, and technology school. Grades K–12. Founded: 1958. Setting: suburban. Nearest major city is Augusta. 26-acre campus. 10 buildings on campus. Approved or accredited by Association of Christian Schools International, South Carolina Independent School Association, Southern Association of Colleges and Schools, and Georgia Department of Education. Total enrollment: 561. Upper school average class size: 11. Upper school faculty-student ratio: 1:11. There are 180 required school days per year for Upper School students. Upper School students typically attend 5 days per week. The average school day consists of 7 hours and 5 minutes.

Upper School Student Profile Grade 9: 43 students (32 boys, 11 girls); Grade 10: 51 students (34 boys, 17 girls); Grade 11: 72 students (38 boys, 34 girls); Grade 12: 65 students (36 boys, 29 girls).

Faculty School total: 62. In upper school: 12 men, 18 women; 11 have advanced degrees.

Subjects Offered Advanced chemistry, advanced computer applications, advanced math, Advanced Placement courses, algebra, American government, American history, American history-AP, American literature, anatomy and physiology, art, athletic training, athletics, band, baseball, basketball, Bible, Bible studies, biology, biology-AP, British literature, British literature-AP, calculus-AP, ceramics, cheerleading, chemistry, choir, choral music, chorus, Christian education, Christian studies, college counseling, comparative religion, computer education, computer skills, drama, drama performance, earth science, ecology, economics and history, electives, English, English composition, English literature, English literature-AP, English-AP, European history, French, general science, geography, geometry, government, grammar, health, health science, history, instrumental music, keyboarding, life skills, mathematics, mathematics-AP, music appreciation, musical productions, New Testament, physics, piano, pre-algebra, pre-

calculus, public speaking, reading, remedial/makeup course work, SAT preparation, science, social studies, Spanish, speech, sports, state history, student government, swimming, U.S. government, U.S. history, U.S. history AP, U.S. literature, volleyball, weight training, weightlifting, world history, wrestling, yearbook.

Graduation Requirements Bible, computers, electives, English, foreign language, mathematics, physical education (includes health), science, social studies (includes history), speech.

Special Academic Programs Advanced Placement exam preparation; honors section; study at local college for college credit; programs in English, mathematics for dyslexic students; ESL (18 students enrolled).

College Admission Counseling 75 students graduated in 2015; all went to college, including Augusta State University; Georgia Institute of Technology; Georgia Southern University; University of Georgia.

Student Life Upper grades have specified standards of dress, student council. Discipline rests primarily with faculty. Attendance at religious services is required.

Summer Programs Remediation, enrichment, advancement programs offered; session focuses on academics; held on campus; accepts boys and girls; open to students from other schools.

Tuition and Aid Day student tuition: $1872–$12,948. Tuition installment plan (Insured Tuition Payment Plan, monthly payment plans, individually arranged payment plans). Tuition reduction for siblings, need-based scholarship grants available.

Admissions Traditional secondary-level entrance grade is 9. Stanford Achievement Test required. Deadline for receipt of application materials: none. Application fee required: $100. Interview required.

Athletics Interscholastic: baseball (boys), basketball (b,g), cross-country running (b,g), football (b), soccer (b,g), softball (g), swimming and diving (b,g), tennis (b,g), track and field (b,g), volleyball (g), wrestling (b); coed interscholastic: cheering, golf. 3 PE instructors.

Computers Computers are regularly used in computer applications, keyboarding, yearbook classes. Computer network features include on-campus library services, Internet access, wireless campus network, Internet filtering or blocking technology. Campus intranet is available to students. Students grades are available online. The school has a published electronic and media policy.

Contact Mrs. Lauren Banks, Director of Admissions. 706-863-2905 Ext. 206. Fax: 706-860-6618. E-mail: laurenbanks@augustachristian.org. Website: www.augustachristian.org

AUSTIN PREPARATORY SCHOOL

101 Willow Street
Reading, Massachusetts 01867

Head of School: Dr. James Hickey

General Information Coeducational day college-preparatory, arts, religious studies, and technology school, affiliated with Roman Catholic Church. Grades 6–12. Founded: 1961. Setting: suburban. Nearest major city is Boston. 42-acre campus. 3 buildings on campus. Approved or accredited by New England Association of Schools and Colleges and Massachusetts Department of Education. Member of National Association of Independent Schools. Upper school average class size: 15. Upper school faculty-student ratio: 1:15. There are 168 required school days per year for Upper School students. Upper School students typically attend 5 days per week. The average school day consists of 6 hours and 30 minutes.

Upper School Student Profile Grade 9: 128 students (59 boys, 69 girls); Grade 10: 117 students (56 boys, 61 girls); Grade 11: 125 students (64 boys, 61 girls); Grade 12: 144 students (60 boys, 84 girls). 85% of students are Roman Catholic.

Faculty School total: 64. In upper school: 25 men, 15 women.

Subjects Offered Algebra, American history, American literature, anatomy, arts, Bible studies, biology, botany, business, calculus, chemistry, computer math, computer programming, computer science, creative writing, earth science, economics, English, English literature, environmental science, French, geography, geology, geometry, government/civics, grammar, history, Latin, marine biology, mathematics, oceanography, physics, physiology, religion, Russian, science, social studies, sociology, Spanish, statistics, technology, trigonometry, writing.

Graduation Requirements English, foreign language, humanities, mathematics, religion (includes Bible studies and theology), science, social studies (includes history). Community service is required.

Special Academic Programs 18 Advanced Placement exams for which test preparation is offered; honors section; study at local college for college credit.

College Admission Counseling 114 students graduated in 2015; all went to college, including Assumption College; Boston College; Boston University; Merrimack College; Northeastern University; University of Massachusetts Lowell. 30% scored over 600 on SAT critical reading, 30% scored over 600 on SAT math.

Student Life Upper grades have uniform requirement, student council. Discipline rests primarily with faculty. Attendance at religious services is required.

Summer Programs Enrichment, sports, art/fine arts programs offered; held on campus; accepts boys and girls; open to students from other schools.

Tuition and Aid Day student tuition: $17,650. Tuition installment plan (Academic Management Services Plan, SMART Tuition Payment Plan, monthly payment plans, see school Web site for full description). Tuition reduction for siblings, merit scholarship grants, need-based scholarship grants available. In 2015–16, 28% of upper-school students received aid.

Admissions Traditional secondary-level entrance grade is 9. Archdiocese of Boston or STS, High School Placement Test, ISEE or SSAT required. Deadline for receipt of application materials: December 18. Application fee required: $40. Interview recommended.

Athletics Interscholastic: baseball (boys), basketball (b,g), cheering (g), cross-country running (b,g), dance team (g), football (b), golf (b,g), ice hockey (b,g), lacrosse (b,g), skiing (downhill) (b,g), soccer (b,g), softball (g), swimming and diving (b,g), tennis (b,g), track and field (b,g), volleyball (g), winter (indoor) track (b,g); intramural: basketball (b,g), skiing (downhill) (b,g), softball (b,g); coed interscholastic: golf, indoor track & field, skiing (downhill), swimming and diving; coed intramural: basketball, dance, equestrian sports, skiing (downhill), softball, yoga. 52 coaches, 1 athletic trainer.

Computers Computers are regularly used in art, creative writing, English, foreign language, French, geography, history, humanities, Latin, library, mathematics, media, music technology, psychology, religion, science, Spanish, writing, yearbook classes. Computer network features include on-campus library services, online commercial services, Internet access, wireless campus network, Internet filtering or blocking technology. Student e-mail accounts are available to students. Students grades are available online. The school has a published electronic and media policy.

Contact Mrs. Elizabeth Flynn, Director of Enrollment. 781-944-4900 Ext. 834. Fax: 781-942-0918. E-mail: eflynn@austinprep.org. Website: www.austinprep.org

AUSTIN WALDORF SCHOOL

8700 South View Road
Austin, Texas 78737

Head of School: Ms. Kathy McElveen

General Information Coeducational day college-preparatory, arts, bilingual studies, and music school. Grades K–12. Founded: 1980. Setting: rural. 19-acre campus. 14 buildings on campus. Approved or accredited by Association of Waldorf Schools of North America, Independent Schools Association of the Southwest, and Texas Department of Education. Total enrollment: 390. Upper school average class size: 30. Upper school faculty-student ratio: 1:20. There are 185 required school days per year for Upper School students. Upper School students typically attend 5 days per week. The average school day consists of 6 hours.

Upper School Student Profile Grade 6: 27 students (11 boys, 16 girls); Grade 7: 32 students (20 boys, 12 girls); Grade 8: 31 students (9 boys, 22 girls); Grade 9: 28 students (7 boys, 21 girls); Grade 10: 20 students (10 boys, 10 girls); Grade 11: 17 students (8 boys, 9 girls); Grade 12: 16 students (9 boys, 7 girls).

Faculty School total: 50. In upper school: 10 have advanced degrees.

Subjects Offered 20th century American writers, 20th century history, 20th century physics, 20th century world history, 3-dimensional art, 3-dimensional design, acting, advanced biology, advanced chemistry, advanced computer applications, advanced math, African American history, African American studies, African-American literature, agriculture, algebra, American biography, American Civil War, American culture, American democracy, American foreign policy, American government, American history, American literature, American studies, analysis, analysis and differential calculus, analytic geometry, anatomy, anatomy and physiology, Ancient Greek, ancient history, ancient world history, ancient/medieval philosophy, anthropology, applied arts, applied music, art, art and culture, art appreciation, art education, art history, Asian history, Asian literature, Asian studies, astronomy, athletics, atomic theory, band, basic language skills, Basic programming, basketball, Bible as literature, biochemistry, biology, bookbinding, botany, British literature, business mathematics, calculus, career education internship, career/college preparation, cell biology, Central and Eastern European history, ceramics, chemistry, child development, choral music, chorus, circus acts, Civil War, classical language, classical studies, clayworking, college admission preparation, college counseling, college planning, communication skills, community garden, community service, comparative civilizations, comparative government and politics, comparative religion, composition, computer animation, computer applications, computer art, computer education, computer graphics, computer information systems, computer literacy, computer math, computer multimedia, computer processing, computer programming, computer resources, computer science, computer skills, computer studies, computer technologies, computer-aided design, constitutional history of U.S., consumer economics, critical thinking, critical writing, cultural geography, current events, current history, data analysis, debate, decision making skills, democracy in America, desktop publishing, digital applications, diversity studies, drama, drawing, East European studies, ecology, environmental systems, economics and history, electives, English, English composition, English literature, environmental education, environmental science, environmental studies, ethics, etymology, European civilization, European history, European literature, eurythmy, expository writing, fiber arts, fiction, film and literature, finance, fine arts, finite math, food and nutrition, foreign language, foundations of civilization, four units of summer reading, gardening, general business, general science, genetics, geography, geology, geometry, German, global studies, golf, government, grammar, Greek culture, health and wellness, history, human anatomy, human biology, human development, humanities, illustration, instrumental music, interactive media, interdisciplinary studies, Internet research, internship, interpersonal skills, intro to computers, jazz band, language and composition, language arts, Latin American history, library research, linear algebra, literature, logarithms, logic, mathematics, mechanics of writing, medieval history, medieval/Renaissance history, metalworking, modern politics,

multicultural studies, music, Native American history, nature study, newspaper, novels, oil painting, oral communications, orchestra, organic chemistry, painting, participation in sports, performing arts, physical education, physics, physiology, poetry, political science, pottery, practical arts, pre-algebra, pre-calculus, projective geometry, public speaking, qualitative analysis, religion and culture, remedial study skills, research, Roman civilization, SAT preparation, sculpture, senior composition, senior internship, senior project, Shakespeare, social studies, Spanish, sports, stage design, stained glass, state government, stone carving, strings, student government, student publications, studio art, swimming, Texas history, textiles, the Web, theater arts, theater design and production, theater production, trigonometry, twentieth century ethnic conflicts, U.S. constitutional history, U.S. government and politics, visual arts, water color painting, weaving, Web site design, Western civilization, Western literature, Western philosophy, woodworking, work experience, world civilizations, writing, yearbook, zoology.

Special Academic Programs Study abroad.

College Admission Counseling 22 students graduated in 2015; 19 went to college, including Southwestern University; Texas State University; The University of Texas at Austin; The University of Texas at San Antonio; University of California, Berkeley. Other: 3 went to work.

Student Life Upper grades have specified standards of dress, student council. Discipline rests primarily with faculty.

Tuition and Aid Day student tuition: $15,000. Tuition installment plan (FACTS Tuition Payment Plan). Need-based scholarship grants available. In 2015–16, 30% of upper-school students received aid.

Admissions Traditional secondary-level entrance grade is 9. For fall 2015, 13 students applied for upper-level admission, 8 were accepted, 8 enrolled. Achievement tests required. Deadline for receipt of application materials: none. Application fee required: $75. Interview required.

Athletics Interscholastic: basketball (boys, girls), cross-country running (b,g), flag football (b), golf (b), independent competitive sports (b,g), running (b,g), swimming and diving (b,g), tennis (b), touch football (b), track and field (b,g), volleyball (g); coed interscholastic: soccer. 2 PE instructors, 4 coaches.

Computers Computer resources include Internet access. Computer access in designated common areas is available to students. Students grades are available online.

Contact Ms. Kim DeVittorio, Enrollment Director. 512-288-5942 Ext. 103. Fax: 512-301-8997. E-mail: enroll@austinwaldorf.org. Website: www.austinwaldorf.org/

BAKERSFIELD CHRISTIAN HIGH SCHOOL

12775 Stockdale Highway
Bakersfield, California 93314

Head of School: Mr. Stephen Dinger

General Information Coeducational day college-preparatory, religious studies, and agriculture science school, affiliated with Christian faith. Grades 9–12. Founded: 1979. Setting: suburban. 47-acre campus. 9 buildings on campus. Approved or accredited by Association of Christian Schools International, Western Association of Schools and Colleges, and California Department of Education. Endowment: $500,000. Total enrollment: 488. Upper school average class size: 22. Upper school faculty-student ratio: 1:17. There are 180 required school days per year for Upper School students. Upper School students typically attend 5 days per week. The average school day consists of 6 hours and 30 minutes.

Upper School Student Profile Postgraduate: 100 students (51 boys, 49 girls).

Faculty School total: 44. In upper school: 21 men, 23 women; 7 have advanced degrees.

Subjects Offered Advanced Placement courses, advanced studio art-AP, agriculture, American literature, American literature-AP, Bible, biology, biology-AP, British literature, British literature-AP, calculus, calculus-AP, chemistry, chemistry-AP, choir, Christian ethics, comparative religion, computer animation, contemporary issues, digital photography, drama, economics, economics-AP, English, English literature, English literature-AP, English-AP, European history, European history-AP, foreign language, forensics, French, history-AP, human anatomy, introduction to literature, jazz band, performing arts, photography, physical science, physics, physics-AP, precalculus, Spanish, Spanish-AP, statistics, statistics-AP, studio art, studio art-AP, U.S. history, U.S. history-AP, video and animation, world history, world literature.

Graduation Requirements 40 hours community service, religious courses.

Special Academic Programs Advanced Placement exam preparation; study at local college for college credit.

College Admission Counseling 92 students graduated in 2015; all went to college, including Azusa Pacific University; California Polytechnic State University, San Luis Obispo; Penn State University Park; United States Naval Academy; University of California, Davis.

Student Life Upper grades have specified standards of dress, student council, honor system. Discipline rests primarily with faculty. Attendance at religious services is required.

Summer Programs Remediation, enrichment, advancement, sports, art/fine arts programs offered; held on campus; accepts boys and girls; open to students from other schools. 300 students usually enrolled. 2016 schedule: June 10 to July 19. Application deadline: May 31.

Tuition and Aid Day student tuition: $12,394. Tuition installment plan (Insured Tuition Payment Plan, FACTS Tuition Payment Plan, monthly payment plans, individually arranged payment plans). Tuition reduction for siblings, need-based scholarship grants, need-based financial aid available. In 2015–16, 31% of upper-school students received aid. Total amount of financial aid awarded in 2015–16: $160,000.

Admissions Traditional secondary-level entrance grade is 9. For fall 2015, 195 students applied for upper-level admission, 181 were accepted, 170 enrolled. Deadline for receipt of application materials: none. Application fee required: $100. On-campus interview required.

Athletics Interscholastic: aquatics (boys, girls), baseball (b), basketball (b,g), cheering (g), football (b), golf (b,g), soccer (b,g), softball (g), tennis (b,g), volleyball (g), water polo (b,g), weight training (b,g), wrestling (b); coed interscholastic: cross-country running, diving, swimming and diving, track and field. 2 PE instructors, 10 coaches, 1 athletic trainer.

Computers Computers are regularly used in all classes. Computer network features include on-campus library services, Internet access, Internet filtering or blocking technology. Student e-mail accounts and computer access in designated common areas are available to students. Students grades are available online. The school has a published electronic and media policy.

Contact Mrs. Alice E. Abril, Director of Admissions. 661-410-7000. Fax: 661-410-7007. E-mail: aabril@bakersfieldchristian.com. Website: www.bakersfieldchristian.com

BALBOA CITY SCHOOL

San Diego, California
See Special Needs Schools section.

THE BALDWIN SCHOOL

701 Montgomery Avenue
Bryn Mawr, Pennsylvania 19010

Head of School: Mrs. Sally M. Powell

General Information Girls' day college-preparatory, arts, technology, and athletics school. Grades PK–12. Founded: 1888. Setting: suburban. Nearest major city is Philadelphia. 25-acre campus. 5 buildings on campus. Approved or accredited by Middle States Association of Colleges and Schools and Pennsylvania Association of Independent Schools. Member of National Association of Independent Schools and Secondary School Admission Test Board. Endowment: $12 million. Total enrollment: 565. Upper school average class size: 14. Upper school faculty-student ratio: 1:5. There are 171 required school days per year for Upper School students. Upper School students typically attend 5 days per week. The average school day consists of 7 hours.

Upper School Student Profile Grade 9: 69 students (69 girls); Grade 10: 64 students (64 girls); Grade 11: 63 students (63 girls); Grade 12: 52 students (52 girls).

Faculty School total: 96. In upper school: 10 men, 46 women; 31 have advanced degrees.

Subjects Offered Advanced Placement courses, algebra, American history, American literature, anthropology, architecture, art, art history, athletics, basketball, bell choir, biology, calculus, ceramics, chemistry, chorus, classical Greek literature, college admission preparation, college counseling, community service, computer resources, computer science, computer studies, contemporary issues, creative writing, current history, dance, digital photography, drama, drama performance, dramatic arts, earth and space science, earth science, English, English literature, environmental studies, ethics, European history, fine arts, French, geometry, golf, handbells, health, health education, history, history-AP, honors algebra, human development, Latin, library skills, life science, Mandarin, mathematics, mentorship program, model United Nations, music, peer counseling, performing arts, photography, photojournalism, physical education, physics, play production, playwriting, public speaking, SAT preparation, science, senior internship, social studies, softball, Spanish, speech, squash, swimming, swimming competency, tennis, theater, trigonometry, U.S. history, vocal ensemble, volleyball, world history, world literature.

Graduation Requirements Arts, English, foreign language, history, life skills, mathematics, physical education (includes health), science, U.S. history.

Special Academic Programs Advanced Placement exam preparation; honors section; independent study; academic accommodation for the gifted, the musically talented, and the artistically talented.

College Admission Counseling 52 students graduated in 2014; all went to college, including Bucknell University; Columbia University; Franklin & Marshall College; Hobart and William Smith Colleges; University of Pennsylvania; Yale University. Median SAT critical reading: 630, median SAT math: 640, median SAT writing: 680, median combined SAT: 1930, median composite ACT: 27. 57% scored over 600 on SAT critical reading, 61% scored over 600 on SAT math, 72% scored over 600 on SAT writing, 65% scored over 1800 on combined SAT, 52% scored over 26 on composite ACT.

Student Life Upper grades have uniform requirement, student council, honor system. Discipline rests equally with students and faculty.

Tuition and Aid Day student tuition: $32,778. Tuition installment plan (monthly payment plans, individually arranged payment plans). Need-based scholarship grants available. In 2014–15, 31% of upper-school students received aid. Total amount of financial aid awarded in 2014–15: $1,611,825.

Admissions Traditional secondary-level entrance grade is 9. ISEE, SSAT, Wechsler Intelligence Scale for Children or writing sample required. Deadline for receipt of application materials: December 1. Application fee required: $50. On-campus interview required.

Athletics Interscholastic: aquatics, basketball, crew, cross-country running, dance, field hockey, golf, independent competitive sports, indoor track, lacrosse, rowing, running, sailing, soccer, softball, squash, swimming and diving, tennis, volleyball, winter (indoor) track. 4 PE instructors, 78 coaches, 1 athletic trainer.

Computers Computers are regularly used in all academic classes. Computer network features include on-campus library services, Internet access, wireless campus network. Campus intranet, student e-mail accounts, and computer access in designated common areas are available to students. The school has a published electronic and media policy.

Contact Sarah J. Goebel, Director of Enrollment Management and Financial Aid. 610-525-2700 Ext. 251. Fax: 610-581-7231. E-mail: sgoebel@baldwinschool.org. Website: www.baldwinschool.org

BALMORAL HALL SCHOOL

630 Westminster Avenue
Winnipeg, Manitoba R3C 3S1, Canada

Head of School: Mrs. Joanne Kamins

General Information Girls' boarding and day college-preparatory, arts, technology, and athletics/prep hockey school. Boarding grades 6–12, day grades N–12. Founded: 1901. Setting: urban. Students are housed in apartment-style residence. 12-acre campus. 2 buildings on campus. Approved or accredited by Canadian Association of Independent Schools, Canadian Educational Standards Institute, International Baccalaureate Organization, The Association of Boarding Schools, and Manitoba Department of Education. Affiliate member of National Association of Independent Schools; member of Secondary School Admission Test Board. Language of instruction: English. Endowment: CAN$1 million. Total enrollment: 504. Upper school average class size: 18. Upper school faculty-student ratio: 1:18. There are 182 required school days per year for Upper School students. Upper School students typically attend 5 days per week. The average school day consists of 5 hours.

Upper School Student Profile Grade 9: 44 students (44 girls); Grade 10: 49 students (49 girls); Grade 11: 49 students (49 girls); Grade 12: 36 students (36 girls). 24% of students are boarding students. 80% are province residents. 2 provinces are represented in upper school student body. 18% are international students. International students from China, Japan, Mexico, Nigeria, Taiwan, and United States.

Faculty School total: 47. In upper school: 6 men, 15 women; 7 have advanced degrees.

Subjects Offered Acting, advanced math, Advanced Placement courses, advanced studio art-AP, advanced TOEFL/grammar, art, biology, biology-AP, calculus, calculus-AP, career and personal planning, career/college preparation, chemistry, chemistry-AP, choir, college planning, communications, community service, computer science, consumer mathematics, dance performance, debate, desktop publishing, digital art, digital photography, drama, English, English language and composition-AP, English literature, English literature and composition-AP, English literature-AP, English/composition-AP, ESL, ethics, French, French language-AP, French literature-AP, general science, geography, health, history, history-AP, mathematics, mathematics-AP, media arts, modern Western civilization, multimedia, music, musical theater, performing arts, personal development, physical education, physics, physics-AP, pre-calculus, psychology-AP, SAT/ACT preparation, science, social studies, Spanish, Spanish-AP, studio art-AP, technology, vocal ensemble, world affairs, world history.

Graduation Requirements English composition, mathematics, science, minimum of 10 hours per year of Service Learning participation in grades 9 through 12.

Special Academic Programs Advanced Placement exam preparation; honors section; accelerated programs; study at local college for college credit; academic accommodation for the gifted; ESL (60 students enrolled).

College Admission Counseling 41 students graduated in 2015; 40 went to college, including McGill University; The University of British Columbia; The University of Western Ontario; The University of Winnipeg; University of Manitoba; University of Toronto. Other: 1 had other specific plans.

Student Life Upper grades have uniform requirement, student council, honor system. Discipline rests primarily with faculty.

Tuition and Aid Day student tuition: CAN$15,325; 5-day tuition and room/board: CAN$31,000; 7-day tuition and room/board: CAN$33,600. Tuition installment plan (The Tuition Plan). Tuition reduction for siblings, bursaries, merit scholarship grants available. In 2015–16, 23% of upper-school students received aid; total upper-school merit-scholarship money awarded: CAN$14,000. Total amount of financial aid awarded in 2015–16: CAN$253,096.

Admissions Traditional secondary-level entrance grade is 9. School's own exam required. Deadline for receipt of application materials: none. Application fee required: CAN$150. Interview required.

Athletics Interscholastic: badminton, basketball, cross-country running, curling, Frisbee, golf, ice hockey, indoor track & field, outdoor skills, running, soccer, speedskating, track and field, ultimate Frisbee, volleyball; intramural: aerobics, aerobics/dance, aerobics/Nautilus, aquatics, archery, badminton, ballet, baseball, basketball, bicycling, bowling, broomball, cooperative games, cross-country running, curling, dance, dance team, diving, fencing, field hockey, figure skating, fitness, fitness walking, floor hockey, Frisbee, golf, gymnastics, handball, hockey, ice hockey, ice skating, in-line skating, indoor hockey, indoor track & field, jogging, jump rope, modern dance, outdoor activities, outdoor education, outdoor skills, physical fitness, physical training, roller blading, rowing, rugby, running, skiing (cross-country), skiing (downhill), snowboarding, snowshoeing, soccer, softball, speedskating, strength & conditioning, swimming and diving, table tennis, tennis, track and field, ultimate Frisbee, volleyball, walking, wall climbing, weight training, yoga. 2 PE instructors, 4 coaches.

Computers Computers are regularly used in all classes. Computer network features include on-campus library services, Internet access, wireless campus network, Internet filtering or blocking technology. Campus intranet, student e-mail accounts, and computer access in designated common areas are available to students. Students grades are available online. The school has a published electronic and media policy.

Contact Ms. Bin Dong Jiang, Admissions Officer. 204-784-1608. Fax: 204-774-5534. E-mail: bdjiang@balmoralhall.net. Website: www.balmoralhall.com

THE BALTIMORE ACTORS' THEATRE CONSERVATORY

The Dumbarton House
300 Dumbarton Road
Baltimore, Maryland 21212-1532

Head of School: Walter E. Anderson

General Information Coeducational day and distance learning college-preparatory and arts school. Grades K–12. Distance learning grades 9–12. Founded: 1979. Setting: suburban. 35-acre campus. 3 buildings on campus. Approved or accredited by Middle States Association of Colleges and Schools and Maryland Department of Education. Endowment: $200,000. Total enrollment: 22. Upper school average class size: 6. Upper school faculty-student ratio: 1:3. There are 175 required school days per year for Upper School students. Upper School students typically attend 5 days per week. The average school day consists of 7 hours and 30 minutes.

Upper School Student Profile Grade 10: 3 students (1 boy, 2 girls); Grade 11: 4 students (4 girls); Grade 12: 2 students (1 boy, 1 girl); Postgraduate: 3 students (1 boy, 2 girls).

Faculty School total: 12. In upper school: 2 men, 8 women; 9 have advanced degrees.

Subjects Offered Acting, algebra, American history-AP, ballet, biology-AP, British literature, chemistry, English language-AP, environmental science-AP, French, geometry, health science, music history, music theory-AP, novels, physics, pre-calculus, psychology, sociology, theater history, trigonometry, world history, world history-AP.

Graduation Requirements Algebra, American history, ballet, chemistry, English, French, geometry, jazz dance, modern dance, music history, physical science, psychology, sociology, theater history, world history, students are required to complete graduation requirements in the three performing arts areas of music, drama, and dance.

Special Academic Programs Advanced Placement exam preparation; honors section; accelerated programs; independent study; study at local college for college credit; academic accommodation for the gifted, the musically talented, and the artistically talented; programs in English for dyslexic students.

College Admission Counseling 4 students graduated in 2015; all went to college, including University of Maryland, Baltimore County. Median SAT critical reading: 600, median SAT math: 570, median composite ACT: 26.

Student Life Upper grades have uniform requirement, student council, honor system. Discipline rests primarily with faculty.

Summer Programs Remediation, art/fine arts programs offered; session focuses on music, drama, dance, and art; held off campus; held at theater in Oregon Ridge Park, Hunt Valley, Maryland; accepts boys and girls; open to students from other schools. 30 students usually enrolled. 2016 schedule: July 25 to August 9. Application deadline: none.

Tuition and Aid Day student tuition: $12,000. Tuition installment plan (individually arranged payment plans). Need-based scholarship grants available. In 2015–16, 10% of upper-school students received aid. Total amount of financial aid awarded in 2015–16: $18,000.

Admissions Traditional secondary-level entrance grade is 9. For fall 2015, 50 students applied for upper-level admission, 15 were accepted, 7 enrolled. Any standardized test, English, French, and math proficiency and writing sample required. Deadline for receipt of application materials: April 3. Application fee required: $100. On-campus interview required.

Computers Computers are regularly used in college planning, creative writing, dance, desktop publishing, English, historical foundations for arts, history, independent study, introduction to technology, keyboarding, music, music technology, psychology, senior seminar, theater, theater arts, word processing, writing classes. Computer network features include Internet access, wireless campus network, Internet filtering or blocking technology. Student e-mail accounts are available to students. The school has a published electronic and media policy.

Contact Mr. Walter E. Anderson, Headmaster. 410-337-8519. Fax: 410-337-8582. E-mail: batpro@baltimoreactorstheatre.org. Website: www.baltimoreactorstheatre.org

BANBURY CROSSROADS SCHOOL

2451 Dieppe Avenue SW, #201
Calgary, Alberta T3E 7K1, Canada

Head of School: Diane Swiatek

General Information Coeducational day college-preparatory and general academic school. Grades 1–12. Founded: 1979. Setting: urban. 1 building on campus. Approved or accredited by Alberta Department of Education. Language of instruction: English. Total enrollment: 41. Upper school average class size: 10. Upper school faculty-student ratio: 1:10. The average school day consists of 6 hours and 30 minutes.

Upper School Student Profile Grade 6: 1 student (1 boy); Grade 8: 4 students (3 boys, 1 girl); Grade 9: 4 students (4 boys); Grade 10: 3 students (3 boys); Grade 11: 6 students (1 boy, 5 girls); Grade 12: 5 students (2 boys, 3 girls).

Faculty School total: 9. In upper school: 1 man, 3 women.

Subjects Offered 20th century world history, adolescent issues, advanced math, algebra, American culture, American democracy, American foreign policy, American government, American literature, American sign language, American studies, anatomy and physiology, Ancient Greek, ancient history, ancient world history, art, art history, arts and crafts, Asian history, Asian literature, Asian studies, athletic training, batik, biology, body human, Brazilian history, Brazilian social studies, Brazilian studies, British history, British literature, calculus, Canadian geography, Canadian history, Canadian law, Canadian literature, career and personal planning, career education, career experience, career/college preparation, cell biology, Central and Eastern European history, chemistry, China/Japan history, cinematography, civil rights, Civil War, civil war history, classical Greek literature, comparative civilizations, comparative cultures, comparative government and politics, comparative religion, computer information systems, computer literacy, contemporary studies, creative dance, creative drama, creative thinking, creative writing, critical thinking, critical writing, culinary arts, cultural arts, current events, current history, dance, decision making skills, democracy in America, design, Eastern religion and philosophy, Eastern world civilizations, ecology, Egyptian history, English, English composition, English literature, English literature and composition-AP, environmental studies, environmental systems, ESL, ethics, European civilization, European history, evolution, expressive arts, family living, family studies, Far Eastern history, film and literature, film history, film studies, food and nutrition, foods, French as a second language, geography, geometry, global issues, global studies, government, government/civics, grammar, Greek culture, Greek drama, health, health and safety, history, history of China and Japan, history of drama, history of England, history of religion, history of rock and roll, home economics, human anatomy, human biology, human issues, human sexuality, integrated mathematics, integrated physics, integrated science, Italian history, language arts, law and the legal system, law studies, life issues, life management skills, literacy, mathematics, mechanics of writing, Middle East, modern politics, modern problems, modern Western civilization.

Graduation Requirements Ballet technique.

Special Academic Programs Accelerated programs; independent study; ESL (6 students enrolled).

College Admission Counseling 1 student graduated in 2015 and went to The University of Western Ontario. Other: 1 entered a postgraduate year.

Student Life Upper grades have student council, honor system. Discipline rests equally with students and faculty.

Tuition and Aid Day student tuition: CAN$9000–CAN$13,000. Tuition installment plan (monthly payment plans). Bursaries available. In 2015–16, 3% of upper-school students received aid. Total amount of financial aid awarded in 2015–16: CAN$10,500.

Admissions Traditional secondary-level entrance grade is 7. Deadline for receipt of application materials: none. Application fee required: CAN$350. Interview required.

Athletics Coed Intramural: aerobics/dance, archery, backpacking, badminton, basketball, bowling, cooperative games, dance, field hockey, fitness walking, floor hockey, Frisbee, golf, gymnastics, horseback riding, ice skating, outdoor recreation, outdoor skills, roller blading, skiing (downhill), soccer, street hockey, swimming and diving, tennis, volleyball, wall climbing, winter walking, yoga. 1 PE instructor.

Computers Computers are regularly used in all academic classes. Computer network features include Internet access.

Contact Anne Bransby-Williams, Office Administrator. 403-270-7787. Fax: 403-270-7486. E-mail: general@banburycrossroads.com. Website: www.banburycrossroads.com

BANCROFT SCHOOL

110 Shore Drive
Worcester, Massachusetts 01605

Head of School: Mr. James (Trey) P. Cassidy III

General Information Coeducational day college-preparatory school. Grades PK–12. Founded: 1900. Setting: suburban. Nearest major city is Boston. 33-acre campus. 7 buildings on campus. Approved or accredited by Association of Independent Schools in New England, New England Association of Schools and Colleges, and Massachusetts Department of Education. Member of National Association of Independent Schools and Secondary School Admission Test Board. Endowment: $28 million. Total enrollment: 463. Upper school average class size: 12. Upper school faculty-student ratio: 1:8.

Upper School Student Profile Grade 6: 36 students (16 boys, 20 girls); Grade 7: 37 students (18 boys, 19 girls); Grade 8: 36 students (15 boys, 21 girls); Grade 9: 56

students (27 boys, 29 girls); Grade 10: 46 students (20 boys, 26 girls); Grade 11: 52 students (25 boys, 27 girls); Grade 12: 58 students (25 boys, 33 girls).

Faculty School total: 75. In upper school: 20 men, 15 women; 28 have advanced degrees.

Subjects Offered Acting, Advanced Placement courses, advanced studio art-AP, algebra, American history, American history-AP, American literature, art, art history, art history-AP, biology, biology-AP, biotechnology, calculus, calculus-AP, ceramics, chamber groups, chemistry, chemistry-AP, chorus, community service, computer graphics, computer science, DNA, drama, dramatic arts, English, English language and composition-AP, English literature, English literature and composition-AP, ethics, European history, European history-AP, French, French-AP, geometry, health, history, jazz band, Latin, Latin-AP, literature by women, marine biology, music, music appreciation, photography, physical education, physics, pre-calculus, psychology, science, senior project, Shakespeare, Spanish, Spanish-AP, theater, theater production, trigonometry, U.S. history-AP, women in world history, world history.

Graduation Requirements Arts and fine arts (art, music, dance, drama), English, foreign language, mathematics, physical education (includes health), science, senior project, social studies (includes history), senior thesis and spring senior project. Community service is required.

Special Academic Programs Advanced Placement exam preparation; honors section; independent study; study at local college for college credit; study abroad; programs in English, mathematics, general development for dyslexic students; ESL (16 students enrolled).

College Admission Counseling 55 students graduated in 2014; all went to college, including Connecticut College; Harvard University; Rensselaer Polytechnic Institute; The George Washington University; Tufts University; University of Pennsylvania. Median SAT critical reading: 650, median SAT math: 650.

Student Life Upper grades have specified standards of dress, student council, honor system. Discipline rests primarily with faculty.

Tuition and Aid Day student tuition: $30,530. Tuition installment plan (Insured Tuition Payment Plan, SMART Tuition Payment Plan, monthly payment plans, individually arranged payment plans). Need-based scholarship grants, scholarship for Worcester residents available. In 2014–15, 33% of upper-school students received aid. Total amount of financial aid awarded in 2014–15: $360,000.

Admissions Traditional secondary-level entrance grade is 9. For fall 2014, 49 students applied for upper-level admission, 37 were accepted, 22 enrolled. ISEE or SSAT required. Deadline for receipt of application materials: February 1. Application fee required: $50. On-campus interview required.

Athletics Interscholastic: alpine skiing (boys, girls), baseball (b), basketball (b,g), crew (b,g), cross-country running (b,g), field hockey (g), lacrosse (b,g), soccer (b,g), softball (g), tennis (b,g), volleyball (g), wrestling (b); coed interscholastic: golf, skiing (downhill), swimming and diving, yoga; coed intramural: dance, track and field. 5 PE instructors, 9 coaches, 1 athletic trainer.

Computers Computers are regularly used in all classes. Computer network features include on-campus library services, online commercial services, Internet access, wireless campus network, Internet filtering or blocking technology. Student e-mail accounts and computer access in designated common areas are available to students. Students grades are available online. The school has a published electronic and media policy.

Contact Mrs. Stephanie Des Chenes, Admission Assistant. 508-854-9227. Fax: 508-853-7824. E-mail: sdeschenes@bancroftschool.org. Website: www.bancroftschool.org

BANGOR CHRISTIAN SCHOOL

1476 Broadway
Bangor, Maine 04401

Head of School: Dr. Jeffrey Benjamin

General Information Coeducational day college-preparatory, arts, business, vocational, religious studies, bilingual studies, and technology school, affiliated with Baptist Church. Grades K4–12. Founded: 1970. Setting: suburban. 35-acre campus. 3 buildings on campus. Approved or accredited by New England Association of Schools and Colleges and Maine Department of Education. Total enrollment: 310. Upper school average class size: 20. Upper school faculty-student ratio: 1:10. There are 175 required school days per year for Upper School students. Upper School students typically attend 5 days per week. The average school day consists of 6 hours and 45 minutes.

Upper School Student Profile Grade 6: 15 students (6 boys, 9 girls); Grade 7: 22 students (11 boys, 11 girls); Grade 8: 29 students (12 boys, 17 girls); Grade 9: 20 students (7 boys, 13 girls); Grade 10: 20 students (4 boys, 16 girls); Grade 11: 17 students (4 boys, 13 girls); Grade 12: 23 students (14 boys, 9 girls). 55% of students are Baptist.

Faculty School total: 23. In upper school: 5 men, 8 women; 5 have advanced degrees.

Special Academic Programs ESL (3 students enrolled).

College Admission Counseling 22 students graduated in 2015; 18 went to college, including Rensselaer Polytechnic Institute; University of Maine. Other: 2 went to work, 2 entered military service.

Student Life Upper grades have specified standards of dress, student council, honor system. Discipline rests primarily with faculty. Attendance at religious services is required.

Tuition and Aid Day student tuition: $4800. Guaranteed tuition plan. Tuition installment plan (monthly payment plans). Tuition reduction for siblings, need-based scholarship grants available.

Admissions Traditional secondary-level entrance grade is 9. Deadline for receipt of application materials: none. Application fee required: $100. Interview required.

Athletics Interscholastic: baseball (boys), basketball (b,g), cheering (g), cross-country running (b,g), hockey (b,g), indoor track & field (b,g), skiing (cross-country) (b,g), skiing (downhill) (b,g), soccer (b,g), softball (g), swimming and diving (b,g), tennis (b,g), track and field (b,g), winter (indoor) track (b,g). 2 PE instructors, 12 coaches.

Computers Computers are regularly used in introduction to technology, keyboarding, lab/keyboard, research skills, typing, word processing, yearbook classes. Computer network features include on-campus library services, Internet access, wireless campus network, Internet filtering or blocking technology. Student e-mail accounts are available to students. Students grades are available online. The school has a published electronic and media policy.

Contact Mrs. Nicky Benjamin, Main Office Secretary. 207-947-7356 Ext. 331. Fax: 207-262-9528. E-mail: nbenjamin@bangorchristian.org. Website: www.bangorchristian.com

BAPTIST REGIONAL SCHOOL

300 Station Avenue
Haddon Heights, New Jersey 08035

Head of School: Mrs. Lynn L. Conahan

General Information Coeducational day college-preparatory, general academic, arts, business, religious studies, and technology school, affiliated with General Association of Regular Baptist Churches. Grades K–12. Founded: 1972. Setting: small town. Nearest major city is Philadelphia, PA. 1 building on campus. Approved or accredited by Association of Christian Schools International, Middle States Association of Colleges and Schools, and New Jersey Department of Education. Total enrollment: 253. Upper school average class size: 25. Upper school faculty-student ratio: 1:10. There are 188 required school days per year for Upper School students. The average school day consists of 6 hours and 35 minutes.

Upper School Student Profile Grade 9: 24 students (13 boys, 11 girls); Grade 10: 36 students (16 boys, 20 girls); Grade 11: 31 students (13 boys, 18 girls); Grade 12: 42 students (20 boys, 22 girls). 60% of students are General Association of Regular Baptist Churches.

Faculty School total: 21. In upper school: 8 men, 13 women; 6 have advanced degrees.

Subjects Offered Accounting, advanced chemistry, advanced computer applications, advanced math, algebra, American government, American history-AP, American literature-AP, analytic geometry, anatomy and physiology, applied music, art, art and culture, art appreciation, arts, Basic programming, Bible studies, biology, business mathematics, calculus, calculus-AP, chemistry, choir, church history, civics, communication skills, computer applications, computer programming, creative writing, desktop publishing, dramatic arts, economics, English composition, English literature, English literature and composition-AP, ethics, foreign language, French, general math, general science, geometry, grammar, health, history, jazz band, keyboarding, physics, pre-algebra, pre-calculus, SAT preparation, Spanish, speech, Western civilization, women's health, world history, world history-AP, yearbook.

Graduation Requirements 20th century history, 20th century world history, algebra, American government, American literature, arts appreciation, Bible, biology, British literature, chemistry, computer science, economics, electives, English composition, English literature, ethics, geometry, health, Holocaust studies, lab/keyboard, physical science.

Special Academic Programs Advanced Placement exam preparation; honors section; study at local college for college credit; remedial reading and/or remedial writing; remedial math; ESL (13 students enrolled).

College Admission Counseling 34 students graduated in 2015; 32 went to college, including Cedarville University; Drexel University; Liberty University; Penn State University Park; Rowan University; Rutgers, The State University of New Jersey; Rutgers College. Other: 2 went to work. Mean SAT critical reading: 540, mean SAT math: 550, mean SAT writing: 570. 32% scored over 600 on SAT critical reading, 32% scored over 600 on SAT math, 19% scored over 600 on SAT writing.

Student Life Upper grades have specified standards of dress, student council, honor system. Discipline rests primarily with faculty. Attendance at religious services is required.

Summer Programs Sports, computer instruction programs offered; session focuses on skill-building; held on campus; accepts boys and girls; open to students from other schools. 50 students usually enrolled. 2016 schedule: June 18 to August 31.

Tuition and Aid Day student tuition: $8300. Tuition installment plan (SMART Tuition Payment Plan). Tuition reduction for siblings, need-based scholarship grants available. In 2015–16, 8% of upper-school students received aid. Total amount of financial aid awarded in 2015–16: $100,000.

Admissions Traditional secondary-level entrance grade is 9. Comprehensive educational evaluation required. Deadline for receipt of application materials: none. Application fee required: $100. Interview required.

Athletics Interscholastic: baseball (boys), basketball (b,g), cheering (g), soccer (b,g), softball (g); intramural: floor hockey (b), indoor hockey (b,g), indoor soccer (b); coed interscholastic: cross-country running, golf, track and field; coed intramural: volleyball. 2 PE instructors, 11 coaches.

Computers Computers are regularly used in accounting, art, business applications, mathematics classes. Computer network features include on-campus library services, Internet access, Internet filtering or blocking technology. The school has a published electronic and media policy.

Contact Mrs. Betty Ryder, School Secretary. 856-547-2996 Ext. 0. Fax: 856-547-6584. E-mail: brsschoolsecretary@gmail.com. Website: www.baptistregional.org

BARNSTABLE ACADEMY

8 Wright Way

Oakland, New Jersey 07436

Head of School: Mrs. Danielle M. Ryckman

General Information Coeducational day college-preparatory, general academic, arts, and technology school; primarily serves students with learning disabilities, individuals with Attention Deficit Disorder, dyslexic students, and Executive Function. Grades 5–12. Founded: 1978. Setting: suburban. Nearest major city is New York, NY. 4-acre campus. 1 building on campus. Approved or accredited by Middle States Association of Colleges and Schools, National Independent Private Schools Association, and New Jersey Department of Education. Total enrollment: 100. Upper school average class size: 8. Upper school faculty-student ratio: 1:7. There are 174 required school days per year for Upper School students. The average school day consists of 6 hours.

Upper School Student Profile Grade 6: 5 students (3 boys, 2 girls); Grade 7: 5 students (4 boys, 1 girl); Grade 8: 11 students (8 boys, 3 girls); Grade 9: 13 students (8 boys, 5 girls); Grade 10: 22 students (15 boys, 7 girls); Grade 11: 22 students (15 boys, 7 girls); Grade 12: 20 students (11 boys, 9 girls).

Faculty School total: 20. In upper school: 6 men, 11 women; 12 have advanced degrees.

Subjects Offered Advanced math, algebra, American culture, American government, American history, American legal systems, art, Basic programming, biology, business applications, business mathematics, calculus, chemistry, computer applications, contemporary issues, economics, English literature, English-AP, French, geometry, Latin, physical education, physics, psychology, Spanish, U.S. constitutional history, U.S. government, U.S. history, world history.

Special Academic Programs Advanced Placement exam preparation; honors section; accelerated programs; independent study; study at local college for college credit; academic accommodation for the gifted, the musically talented, and the artistically talented; remedial reading and/or remedial writing; remedial math; programs in English, general development for dyslexic students; special instructional classes for students with learning disabilities and Attention Deficit Disorder, the fragile emotionally disturbed; ESL (8 students enrolled).

College Admission Counseling 20 students graduated in 2014; 17 went to college, including Drew University; Fairleigh Dickinson University, College at Florham; The College of New Jersey. Other: 1 went to work, 1 entered a postgraduate year, 1 had other specific plans. Median SAT critical reading: 520, median SAT math: 530, median SAT writing: 560, median composite ACT: 24. 25% scored over 600 on SAT critical reading, 25% scored over 600 on SAT math, 25% scored over 600 on SAT writing, 25% scored over 1800 on combined SAT.

Student Life Upper grades have specified standards of dress, student council. Discipline rests primarily with faculty.

Tuition and Aid Day student tuition: $23,750–$31,000. Tuition installment plan (monthly payment plans, individually arranged payment plans). Merit scholarship grants, need-based scholarship grants available. In 2014–15, 30% of upper-school students received aid; total upper-school merit-scholarship money awarded: $150,000. Total amount of financial aid awarded in 2014–15: $200,000.

Admissions Traditional secondary-level entrance grade is 11. For fall 2014, 300 students applied for upper-level admission, 100 were accepted, 35 enrolled. Deadline for receipt of application materials: none. No application fee required. On-campus interview required.

Athletics Interscholastic: baseball (boys), cheering (g), softball (g); coed interscholastic: basketball, dance team, horseback riding, Nautilus, soccer; coed intramural: aerobics, aerobics/dance, aerobics/Nautilus, alpine skiing, billiards, bowling, dance, fitness, fitness walking, flag football, golf, hiking/backpacking, physical fitness, snowboarding, swimming and diving, tennis, track and field, volleyball, weight training, yoga. 2 PE instructors, 3 coaches.

Computers Computers are regularly used in computer applications, reading classes. Computer network features include on-campus library services, Internet access, wireless campus network, Internet filtering or blocking technology. Campus intranet and student e-mail accounts are available to students. Students grades are available online. The school has a published electronic and media policy.

Contact Ms. Lizanne M. Coyne, Director of Student Achievement. 201-651-0200 Ext. 103. Fax: 201-337-9797. E-mail: lcoyne@barnstableacademy.com. Website: www.barnstableacademy.com

BARRIE SCHOOL

13500 Layhill Road

Silver Spring, Maryland 20906

Head of School: Mr. Charles Abelmann

General Information Coeducational day college-preparatory, arts, and technology school. Grades N–12. Founded: 1932. Setting: suburban. Nearest major city is Washington, DC. 45-acre campus. 8 buildings on campus. Approved or accredited by Middle States Association of Colleges and Schools and Maryland Department of Education. Member of National Association of Independent Schools and Secondary School Admission Test Board. Endowment: $320,000. Total enrollment: 330. Upper school average class size: 15. Upper school faculty-student ratio: 1:8. There are 175 required school days per year for Upper School students. Upper School students typically attend 5 days per week. The average school day consists of 7 hours and 20 minutes.

Upper School Student Profile Grade 9: 20 students (5 boys, 15 girls); Grade 10: 18 students (10 boys, 8 girls); Grade 11: 20 students (15 boys, 5 girls); Grade 12: 17 students (11 boys, 6 girls).

Faculty School total: 34: In upper school: 9 men, 14 women; 18 have advanced degrees.

Subjects Offered Algebra, art, biology, calculus, calculus-AP, ceramics, chemistry, community service, drama, drawing, environmental science-AP, fitness, French, French-AP, geometry, health, health and wellness, history, humanities, illustration, instrumental music, music, painting, performing arts, physics, pre-calculus, sculpture, service learning/internship, Spanish, statistics-AP, studio art, world geography, world history, writing, yearbook.

Graduation Requirements Algebra, art, biology, chemistry, English, foreign language, health, history, humanities, mathematics, physics, pre-algebra, science, sports, U.S. history, 96 hours of community service.

Special Academic Programs 13 Advanced Placement exams for which test preparation is offered; independent study.

College Admission Counseling 13 students graduated in 2014; all went to college, including Babson College; Earlham College; St. Mary's College of Maryland; The College of Wooster; University of Maryland, Baltimore County; University of Maryland, College Park. Mean SAT critical reading: 536, mean SAT math: 525, mean SAT writing: 541, mean combined SAT: 1602, mean composite ACT: 25. 21% scored over 600 on SAT critical reading, 26% scored over 600 on SAT math, 21% scored over 600 on SAT writing, 21% scored over 1800 on combined SAT, 17% scored over 26 on composite ACT.

Student Life Upper grades have student council. Discipline rests primarily with faculty.

Tuition and Aid Day student tuition: $27,810. Tuition installment plan (FACTS Tuition Payment Plan, monthly payment plans, The Tuition Refund Plan). Need-based scholarship grants, need-based financial aid grants available. In 2014–15, 47% of upper-school students received aid. Total amount of financial aid awarded in 2014–15: $539,950.

Admissions Traditional secondary-level entrance grade is 9. For fall 2014, 37 students applied for upper-level admission, 12 were accepted, 9 enrolled. ISEE, SSAT or TOEFL or SLEP required. Deadline for receipt of application materials: January 16. Application fee required: $50. Interview required.

Athletics Interscholastic: basketball (boys, girls), soccer (b); coed interscholastic: cross-country running, equestrian sports, horseback riding, outdoor activities, physical fitness, running, tennis, track and field, ultimate Frisbee. 4 coaches.

Computers Computers are regularly used in all classes. Computer network features include Internet access, wireless campus network, Internet filtering or blocking technology. Campus intranet, student e-mail accounts, and computer access in designated common areas are available to students. The school has a published electronic and media policy.

Contact Ms. Alyssa Jahn, Director of Admission. 301-576-2839. Fax: 301-576-2803. E-mail: ajahn@barrie.org. Website: www.barrie.org

BATTLE GROUND ACADEMY

336 Ernest Rice Lane

Franklin, Tennessee 37069

Head of School: Mr. Will Kesler

General Information Coeducational day college-preparatory, arts, and technology school. Grades K–12. Founded: 1889. Setting: suburban. Nearest major city is Nashville. 67-acre campus. 13 buildings on campus. Approved or accredited by Southern Association of Colleges and Schools, Southern Association of Independent Schools, and Tennessee Department of Education. Member of National Association of Independent Schools. Endowment: $11 million. Total enrollment: 754. Upper school average class size: 15. Upper school faculty-student ratio: 1:8. There are 180 required school days per year for Upper School students. Upper School students typically attend 5 days per week. The average school day consists of 7 hours and 15 minutes.

Upper School Student Profile Grade 9: 91 students (44 boys, 47 girls); Grade 10: 94 students (45 boys, 49 girls); Grade 11: 84 students (40 boys, 44 girls); Grade 12: 77 students (43 boys, 34 girls).

Faculty School total: 86. In upper school: 19 men, 20 women; 32 have advanced degrees.

Subjects Offered Accounting, algebra, American history, American literature, art, art history, biology, calculus, chemistry, chorus, computer applications, computer programming, computer science, drama, early childhood, economics, English, English literature, English literature and composition-AP, entrepreneurship, European history, fine arts, French, French-AP, geography, geometry, government/civics, grammar, health, history, Latin, mathematics, modern European history-AP, music, music history, physical education, physics, science, social studies, Spanish, speech, technical theater, theater, trigonometry, U.S. history, U.S. history-AP, world history, world history-AP, world literature, writing.

Graduation Requirements Arts and fine arts (art, music, dance, drama), computer science, English, foreign language, mathematics, physical education (includes health), science, social studies (includes history), speech. Community service is required.

Special Academic Programs Advanced Placement exam preparation; honors section.

College Admission Counseling 77 students graduated in 2015; all went to college, including Auburn University; Belmont University; The University of Tennessee; The University of Tennessee at Chattanooga; University of Mississippi. Mean SAT critical reading: 641, mean SAT math: 601, mean SAT writing: 639, mean combined SAT: 1881, mean composite ACT: 26.

Student Life Upper grades have uniform requirement, student council, honor system. Discipline rests equally with students and faculty.

Summer Programs Remediation, enrichment, sports, art/fine arts, computer instruction programs offered; session focuses on remediation, enrichment, and sports; held both on and off campus; held at local farm; accepts boys and girls; open to students from other schools. 550 students usually enrolled. 2016 schedule: June 1 to July 31. Application deadline: none.

Tuition and Aid Day student tuition: $21,890. Tuition installment plan (The Tuition Plan, FACTS Tuition Payment Plan, individually arranged payment plans). Merit scholarship grants, need-based scholarship grants available. In 2015–16, 22% of upper-school students received aid; total upper-school merit-scholarship money awarded: $100,600. Total amount of financial aid awarded in 2015–16: $657,135.

Admissions Traditional secondary-level entrance grade is 9. For fall 2015, 41 students applied for upper-level admission, 41 were accepted, 35 enrolled. ISEE required. Deadline for receipt of application materials: none. Application fee required: $50. Interview required.

Athletics Interscholastic: aquatics (boys, girls), baseball (b), basketball (b,g), cheering (g), cross-country running (b,g), dance team (g), fitness (b,g), football (b), golf (b,g), soccer (b,g), softball (g), strength & conditioning (b,g), swimming and diving (b,g), tennis (b,g), track and field (b,g); volleyball (g), weight training (b,g), wrestling (b); intramural: baseball (b,g), basketball (b,g), fitness (b,g), football (b), softball (g); coed interscholastic: fitness, trap and skeet; coed intramural: fitness, flag football, physical training, rock climbing, ropes courses, soccer. 1 PE instructor, 4 coaches, 1 athletic trainer.

Computers Computers are regularly used in art, college planning, desktop publishing, English, foreign language, geography, history, library, literary magazine, mathematics, newspaper, photography, SAT preparation, science, social studies, Spanish, study skills, technology, theater, writing classes. Computer network features include on-campus library services, online commercial services, Internet access, wireless campus network, Internet filtering or blocking technology. Campus intranet, student e-mail accounts, and computer access in designated common areas are available to students. Students grades are available online. The school has a published electronic and media policy.

Contact Robin Goertz, Director of Admissions. 615-567-9014. E-mail: robin.goertz@mybga.org. Website: www.battlegroundacademy.org

BAY RIDGE PREPARATORY SCHOOL

7420 Fourth Avenue
Brooklyn, New York 11209

Head of School: Dr. Michael T. Dealy

General Information Coeducational day college-preparatory, general academic, and arts school. Grades K–12. Founded: 1998. Setting: urban. 1 building on campus. Approved or accredited by New York State Association of Independent Schools, New York State Board of Regents, and New York Department of Education. Member of National Association of Independent Schools. Total enrollment: 396. Upper school average class size: 17. Upper school faculty-student ratio: 1:7. There are 165 required school days per year for Upper School students. Upper School students typically attend 5 days per week. The average school day consists of 6 hours and 15 minutes.

Upper School Student Profile Grade 9: 34 students (18 boys, 16 girls); Grade 10: 44 students (32 boys, 12 girls); Grade 11: 66 students (34 boys, 32 girls); Grade 12: 66 students (37 boys, 29 girls).

Faculty School total: 45. In upper school: 43 have advanced degrees.

Subjects Offered Algebra, American government, American history, American literature, ancient world history, art, art history, biology, calculus, chemistry, college admission preparation, college counseling, college writing, computer science, creative writing, earth science, economics, English, English literature, European history, European literature, geometry, health education, journalism, microbiology, modern history, music composition, physics, SAT preparation, Shakespeare, Spanish, statistics, U.S. government and politics.

Special Academic Programs Advanced Placement exam preparation; honors section; independent study; study at local college for college credit; academic accommodation for the gifted, the musically talented, and the artistically talented; remedial reading and/or remedial writing; remedial math; programs in English, mathematics, general development for dyslexic students.

College Admission Counseling 56 students graduated in 2015; 55 went to college. Other: 1 entered military service.

Student Life Upper grades have specified standards of dress, honor system. Discipline rests primarily with faculty.

Tuition and Aid Tuition installment plan (FACTS Tuition Payment Plan, monthly payment plans). Tuition reduction for siblings, merit scholarship grants available.

Admissions Traditional secondary-level entrance grade is 9. For fall 2015, 125 students applied for upper-level admission, 32 were accepted, 25 enrolled. Deadline for receipt of application materials: none. Application fee required: $60. Interview required.

Athletics Interscholastic: baseball (boys), basketball (b,g), soccer (b,g); intramural: baseball (b), basketball (g), cheering (g), hockey (b), soccer (b,g), softball (g); coed interscholastic: squash; coed intramural: cross-country running, dance, dance squad, martial arts, squash, track and field, yoga. 4 PE instructors, 7 coaches.

Computers Computer network features include Internet access, wireless campus network. Student e-mail accounts and computer access in designated common areas are available to students. Students grades are available online.

Contact Ms. Alissa Roeder, Admissions Director. 718-833-9090 Ext. 8305. Fax: 718-833-6680. E-mail: admissions@bayridgeprep.org. Website: www.bayridgeprep.org

THE BAY SCHOOL OF SAN FRANCISCO

35 Keyes Avenue, The Presidio of San Francisco
San Francisco, California 94129

Head of School: Mr. Luke Felker

General Information Coeducational day college-preparatory school. Grades 9–12. Founded: 2004. Setting: urban. 2 buildings on campus. Approved or accredited by California Association of Independent Schools, Western Association of Schools and Colleges, and California Department of Education. Member of National Association of Independent Schools and Secondary School Admission Test Board. Total enrollment: 355. Upper school average class size: 14. Upper school faculty-student ratio: 1:8. The average school day consists of 6 hours and 40 minutes.

Faculty School total: 43. In upper school: 18 men, 25 women; 29 have advanced degrees.

Graduation Requirements Senior signature project.

College Admission Counseling 74 students graduated in 2015; all went to college.

Student Life Upper grades have student council. Discipline rests equally with students and faculty.

Tuition and Aid Day student tuition: $40,740. Tuition installment plan (Insured Tuition Payment Plan, monthly payment plans). Need-based scholarship grants available. In 2015–16, 30% of upper-school students received aid.

Admissions Traditional secondary-level entrance grade is 9. ISEE, PSAT or SAT for applicants to grade 11 and 12 or SSAT required. Deadline for receipt of application materials: January 15. Application fee required: $90. Interview required.

Athletics Interscholastic: baseball (boys), basketball (b,g), climbing (b,g), golf (b,g), lacrosse (b), tennis (b,g); coed interscholastic: cross-country running, sailing, track and field, volleyball; coed intramural: aerobics, aerobics/dance, backpacking, dance, dance squad, hiking/backpacking, rock climbing, yoga.

Computers Computer network features include on-campus library services, Internet access, wireless campus network, Internet filtering or blocking technology. Student e-mail accounts are available to students.

Contact Ms. Magaly Coronado, Admission Associate. 415-684-8949. Fax: 415-561-5808. E-mail: admission@bayschoolsf.org. Website: www.bayschoolsf.org/

BAYVIEW GLEN SCHOOL

275 Duncan Mill Road
Toronto, Ontario M3B 3H9, Canada

Head of School: Mrs. Eileen Daunt

General Information Coeducational day college-preparatory, general academic, arts, business, technology, and athletics school. Grades PK–12. Founded: 1962. Setting: urban. 40-acre campus. 1 building on campus. Approved or accredited by Canadian Association of Independent Schools, Conference of Independent Schools of Ontario, and Ontario Department of Education. Language of instruction: English. Total enrollment: 1,042. Upper school average class size: 22. Upper school faculty-student ratio: 1:22. There are 175 required school days per year for Upper School students. Upper School students typically attend 5 days per week. The average school day consists of 7 hours.

Faculty School total: 100. In upper school: 18 men, 14 women.

Subjects Offered Advanced Placement courses, all academic.

Graduation Requirements Outdoor Leadership trips grade 9 to 11, Grade 10 Physical Education.

Special Academic Programs Advanced Placement exam preparation.

College Admission Counseling 80 students graduated in 2014; they went to Carleton University; McGill University; McMaster University; Queen's University at Kingston; The University of Western Ontario; University of Toronto.

Student Life Upper grades have uniform requirement, student council, honor system. Discipline rests primarily with faculty.

Tuition and Aid Day student tuition: CAN$15,800–CAN$22,600. Tuition installment plan (monthly payment plans, individually arranged payment plans). Bursaries, need-based scholarship grants available.

Admissions Admissions testing required. Deadline for receipt of application materials: December. Application fee required: CAN$100. Interview required.

Athletics Interscholastic: badminton (boys, girls); basketball (b,g), cross-country running (b,g), field hockey (g), soccer (b,g), softball (b,g), tennis (b,g), track and field (b,g), ultimate Frisbee (b,g), volleyball (b,g).

Computers Computers are regularly used in all academic classes. Computer network features include on-campus library services, Internet access, wireless campus network, Internet filtering or blocking technology. Campus intranet, student e-mail accounts, and computer access in designated common areas are available to students. Students grades are available online. The school has a published electronic and media policy.

Contact Mrs. Judy Maxwell, Director of Admissions. 416-443-1030 Ext. 605. Fax: 416-443-1032. E-mail: jmaxwell@bayviewglen.ca. Website: www.bayviewglen.ca/

BEARSPAW CHRISTIAN SCHOOL

15001 69 Street NW
Calgary, Alberta T3R 1C5, Canada

Head of School: Mr. Kelly Blake

General Information Coeducational day and distance learning college-preparatory, general academic, business, and religious studies school, affiliated with Christian faith. Grades K–12. Distance learning grades 1–12. Founded: 1991. Setting: rural. 40-acre campus. 3 buildings on campus. Approved or accredited by Association of Christian Schools International, Association of Independent Schools and Colleges of Alberta, and Alberta Department of Education. Language of instruction: English. Total enrollment: 729. Upper school average class size: 21. Upper school faculty-student ratio: 1:10. There are 177 required school days per year for Upper School students. The average school day consists of 6 hours and 45 minutes.

Upper School Student Profile Grade 10: 24 students (12 boys, 12 girls); Grade 11: 47 students (14 boys, 33 girls); Grade 12: 35 students (23 boys, 12 girls). 95% of students are Christian faith.

Faculty School total: 24. In upper school: 6 men, 18 women; 2 have advanced degrees.

Subjects Offered 20th century history, 20th century world history, acting, advanced chemistry, advanced math, algebra, applied music, art, athletic training, athletics, Bible studies, biology, business, business communications, business education, business law, calculus, Canadian history, Canadian law, career and personal planning, career education, chemistry, Christian education, Christianity, communication skills, computer applications, English composition, food and nutrition, foreign language, French as a second language, general math, health and wellness, keyboarding, media arts, physical education, physics, science, social studies, Spanish, world history.

Graduation Requirements Bible, English, mathematics, science, social studies (includes history).

Special Academic Programs Honors section; independent study; remedial math; special instructional classes for students with learning disabilities, Attention Deficit Disorder, emotional problems, and dyslexia.

College Admission Counseling 34 students graduated in 2015; they went to Trinity Western University; University of Alberta; University of Calgary; University of Victoria.

Student Life Upper grades have uniform requirement, student council, honor system. Discipline rests primarily with faculty. Attendance at religious services is required.

Summer Programs Sports programs offered; session focuses on basketball, volleyball, strength training; held on campus; accepts boys and girls; open to students from other schools. 60 students usually enrolled. 2016 schedule: July 15 to August 15. Application deadline: July 15.

Tuition and Aid Day student tuition: CAN$6200. Tuition installment plan (monthly payment plans, individually arranged payment plans). Tuition reduction for siblings, need-based scholarship grants available. In 2015–16, 16% of upper-school students received aid. Total amount of financial aid awarded in 2015–16: CAN$108,314.

Admissions Traditional secondary-level entrance grade is 10. Achievement tests, admissions testing, CTB/McGraw-Hill/Macmillan Co-op Test, WAIS, WICS, Woodcock-Johnson and writing sample required. Deadline for receipt of application materials: September 30. Application fee required: CAN$150. Interview required.

Athletics Interscholastic: badminton (boys, girls), basketball (b,g), cross-country running (b,g), floor hockey (b,g), golf (b,g), indoor soccer (b,g), track and field (b,g), volleyball (b,g), wrestling (b); intramural: aerobics/dance (b,g), badminton (b,g), basketball (b,g), cross-country running (b,g), flag football (b,g), floor hockey (b,g), track and field (b,g), volleyball (b,g), wrestling (b,g); coed interscholastic: badminton,

indoor soccer, soccer; coed intramural: aerobics/dance, badminton, ball hockey, basketball, flag football, floor hockey, handball, indoor soccer, strength & conditioning, volleyball. 2 PE instructors, 1 athletic trainer.

Computers Computers are regularly used in all academic classes. Computer network features include Internet access, wireless campus network, Internet filtering or blocking technology. Student e-mail accounts and computer access in designated common areas are available to students. Students grades are available online. The school has a published electronic and media policy.

Contact Mrs. Sherri Patzer, Registrar. 403-295-2566 Ext. 1102. Fax: 403-275-8170. E-mail: spatzer@bearspawschool.com. Website: www.bearspawschool.com

BEAUFORT ACADEMY

240 Sams Point Road
Beaufort, South Carolina 29907

Head of School: Stephen Schools

General Information Coeducational day college-preparatory and technology school. Grades PK–12. Founded: 1965. Setting: small town. Nearest major city is Savannah, GA. 35-acre campus. 3 buildings on campus. Approved or accredited by South Carolina Independent School Association, Southern Association of Colleges and Schools, Southern Association of Independent Schools, and The College Board. Member of National Association of Independent Schools. Endowment: $650,000. Total enrollment: 260. Upper school average class size: 12. Upper school faculty-student ratio: 1:10. The average school day consists of 7 hours.

Upper School Student Profile Grade 9: 27 students (6 boys, 21 girls); Grade 10: 31 students (15 boys, 16 girls); Grade 11: 23 students (8 boys, 15 girls); Grade 12: 18 students (12 boys, 6 girls).

Faculty School total: 48. In upper school: 4 men, 13 women; 16 have advanced degrees.

Subjects Offered Algebra, American history, American literature, anatomy, art, art history, biology, calculus, chemistry, composition, computer programming, computer science, creative writing, debate, drama, earth science, economics, English, English literature, environmental science, European history, fine arts, French, geometry, government/civics, grammar, health, history, journalism, Latin, marine biology, mathematics, modern world history, music, physical education, physics, physiology, pre-calculus, science, social studies, Spanish, speech, trigonometry, U.S. history, Western civilization, world literature, writing workshop.

Graduation Requirements Arts and fine arts (art, music, dance, drama), computer science, English, ethics and responsibility, foreign language, mathematics, physical education (includes health), science, social studies (includes history), senior seminar (ethics and philosophy).

Special Academic Programs Advanced Placement exam preparation; honors section; independent study; study at local college for college credit; study abroad; academic accommodation for the gifted; programs in general development for dyslexic students.

College Admission Counseling 17 students graduated in 2015; 16 went to college, including Clemson University; College of Charleston; University of South Carolina; Wofford College. Other: 1 entered a postgraduate year. Median SAT critical reading: 579, median SAT math: 586. 33% scored over 600 on SAT critical reading, 25% scored over 600 on SAT math.

Student Life Upper grades have specified standards of dress, honor system. Discipline rests primarily with faculty.

Summer Programs Sports programs offered; session focuses on sports/soccer; held on campus; accepts boys and girls; open to students from other schools. 30 students usually enrolled. 2016 schedule: June 4 to June 15.

Tuition and Aid Day student tuition: $5400–$11,725. Tuition installment plan (Insured Tuition Payment Plan, monthly payment plans, individually arranged payment plans). Tuition reduction for siblings, need-based scholarship grants, tuition remission for children of faculty available. In 2015–16, 25% of upper-school students received aid. Total amount of financial aid awarded in 2015–16: $72,600.

Admissions Traditional secondary-level entrance grade is 9. For fall 2015, 31 students applied for upper-level admission, 19 were accepted, 16 enrolled. CTP III, ERB CTP III, OLSAT, Stanford Achievement Test or school's own exam or coop required. Deadline for receipt of application materials: none. Application fee required: $75. Interview required.

Athletics Interscholastic: baseball (boys), basketball (b,g), cheering (g), football (b), lacrosse (b), soccer (b,g), softball (g), swimming and diving (b,g), tennis (b,g), volleyball (g); coed interscholastic: crew, golf, physical fitness, soccer, swimming and diving, track and field; coed intramural: crew, fitness, floor hockey, rowing, softball, touch football. 2 PE instructors, 8 coaches, 1 athletic trainer.

Computers Computers are regularly used in English, history, journalism, library skills, media, newspaper, publishing, science, yearbook classes. Computer network features include on-campus library services, online commercial services, Internet access.

Contact MJ Simmons, Director of Admissions. 843-524-3393. Fax: 843-524-1171. E-mail: mjsimmons@beaufortacademy.org. Website: www.beaufortacademy.org

BEAVER COUNTRY DAY SCHOOL

791 Hammond Street
Chestnut Hill, Massachusetts 02467

Head of School: Peter R. Hutton

General Information Coeducational day college-preparatory and arts school. Grades 6–12. Founded: 1920. Setting: suburban. Nearest major city is Boston. 17-acre campus. 3 buildings on campus. Approved or accredited by Association of Independent Schools in New England, New England Association of Schools and Colleges, The College Board, and Massachusetts Department of Education. Member of National Association of Independent Schools and Secondary School Admission Test Board. Endowment: $11 million. Total enrollment: 451. Upper school average class size: 15. Upper school faculty-student ratio: 1:8. Upper School students typically attend 5 days per week. The average school day consists of 7 hours and 40 minutes.

Upper School Student Profile Grade 9: 70 students (41 boys, 29 girls); Grade 10: 90 students (48 boys, 42 girls); Grade 11: 80 students (40 boys, 40 girls); Grade 12: 86 students (40 boys, 46 girls).

Faculty School total: 71. In upper school: 24 men, 34 women; 41 have advanced degrees.

Subjects Offered 20th century American writers, 20th century history, 20th century world history, 3-dimensional art, 3-dimensional design, acting, advanced biology, advanced chemistry, advanced math, algebra, American Civil War, American democracy, American foreign policy, American government, American history, American literature, American studies, anatomy and physiology, art, art history, arts, astronomy, athletics, bioethics, bioethics, DNA and culture, biology, biotechnology, business communications, business skills, calculus, career education internship, cell biology, ceramics, chamber groups, chemistry, child development, Chinese history, chorus, civil rights, Civil War, civil war history, classical music, college counseling, college placement, college writing, community service, comparative civilizations, comparative cultures, comparative government and politics, comparative politics, comparative religion, computer graphics, computer math, computer programming, computer skills, constitutional history of U.S., contemporary history, contemporary issues in science, costumes and make-up, creative writing, current history, dance, decision making skills, digital photography, diversity studies, DNA, drama, drawing and design, driver education, economics, English, English literature, equality and freedom, European civilization, European history, expository writing, fine arts, foreign language, foreign policy, French, French as a second language, French studies, functions, gender and religion, gender issues, general math, geography, geometry, geometry with art applications, government, government/civics, grammar, great books, health, history, Holocaust and other genocides, Holocaust studies, honors algebra, honors English, honors geometry, honors U.S. history, human biology, human sexuality, independent study, integrated mathematics, international affairs, jazz, jazz band, journalism, junior and senior seminars, Latin American history, Latin American studies, marketing, mathematics, Middle Eastern history, modern European history, music, musical theater, painting, peer counseling, philosophy, photography, physical education, physics, play production, poetry, pre-calculus, programming, psychology, science, Shakespeare, social justice, social studies, society, politics and law, Spanish, Spanish literature, squash, statistics, studio art, study skills, theater, trigonometry, typing, U.S. history, world history, writing.

Graduation Requirements Arts, English, foreign language, history, interdisciplinary studies, mathematics, science, 40 hours of community service.

Special Academic Programs Honors section; independent study.

College Admission Counseling 78 students graduated in 2014; all went to college, including Amherst College; Bates College; Brown University; Occidental College; Syracuse University; Trinity College.

Student Life Upper grades have student council, honor system. Discipline rests equally with students and faculty.

Tuition and Aid Day student tuition: $41,750. Tuition installment plan (Academic Management Services Plan, Key Tuition Payment Plan, monthly payment plans, individually arranged payment plans). Need-based scholarship grants available. In 2014–15, 26% of upper-school students received aid. Total amount of financial aid awarded in 2014–15: $3,335,098.

Admissions Traditional secondary-level entrance grade is 9. For fall 2014, 433 students applied for upper-level admission, 326 were accepted, 97 enrolled. ISEE or SSAT required. Deadline for receipt of application materials: January 15. Application fee required: $45. Interview required.

Athletics Interscholastic: baseball (boys), basketball (b,g), cross-country running (b,g), field hockey (g), ice hockey (g), lacrosse (b,g), soccer (b,g), softball (g), tennis (b,g), volleyball (g), wrestling (b); coed interscholastic: cross-country running, fencing, fitness, Frisbee, golf, squash, ultimate Frisbee; coed intramural: dance team, flag football, floor hockey, physical fitness, strength & conditioning, yoga. 108 coaches, 1 athletic trainer.

Computers Computers are regularly used in art, English, foreign language, history, independent study, mathematics, science, social studies classes. Computer network features include on-campus library services, online commercial services, Internet access, wireless campus network, Internet filtering or blocking technology. Student e-mail accounts are available to students. Students grades are available online. The school has a published electronic and media policy.

Contact Nedda Bonassera, Admission Office Manager. 617-738-2725. Fax: 617-738-2767. E-mail: admission@bcdschool.org. Website: www.bcdschool.org

THE BEEKMAN SCHOOL

220 East 50th Street
New York, New York 10022

Head of School: George Higgins

General Information Coeducational day and distance learning college-preparatory, general academic, arts, and technology school. Grades 9–PG. Distance learning grades 9–12. Founded: 1925. Setting: urban.. 1 building on campus. Approved or accredited by New York State Board of Regents and New York Department of Education. Total enrollment: 80. Upper school average class size: 8. Upper school faculty-student ratio: 1:8. There are 165 required school days per year for Upper School students. Upper School students typically attend 5 days per week. The average school day consists of 6 hours and 15 minutes.

Upper School Student Profile Grade 9: 15 students (8 boys, 7 girls); Grade 10: 19 students (11 boys, 8 girls); Grade 11: 21 students (12 boys, 9 girls); Grade 12: 25 students (13 boys, 12 girls); Postgraduate: 2 students (1 boy, 1 girl).

Faculty School total: 12. In upper school: 4 men, 8 women; 10 have advanced degrees.

Subjects Offered Advanced Placement courses, algebra, American history, anatomy and physiology, ancient world history, art, astronomy, bioethics, biology, business mathematics, calculus, calculus-AP, chemistry, computer animation, computer art, computer science, conceptual physics, creative writing, drama, drawing, Eastern religion and philosophy, ecology, economics, English, environmental science, ESL, European history, film, French, geometry, government, health, modern politics, modern world history, photography, physical education, physical science, physics, poetry, pre-calculus, psychology, SAT preparation, sculpture, Spanish, TOEFL preparation, trigonometry, U.S. history, video film production, Web site design, Western philosophy.

Graduation Requirements Art, computer technologies, electives, English, foreign language, health education, mathematics, physical education (includes health), science, social studies (includes history).

Special Academic Programs 30 Advanced Placement exams for which test preparation is offered; honors section; accelerated programs; independent study; academic accommodation for the gifted, the musically talented, and the artistically talented; remedial reading and/or remedial writing; remedial math; programs in English, mathematics, general development for dyslexic students; ESL (4 students enrolled).

College Admission Counseling 28 students graduated in 2015; 27 went to college, including Arizona State University at the Tempe campus; Boston University; Fordham University; New York University; Sarah Lawrence College; University of Vermont. Other: 1 had other specific plans. Mean SAT critical reading: 558, mean SAT math: 519, mean SAT writing: 540. 33% scored over 600 on SAT critical reading, 27% scored over 600 on SAT math, 30% scored over 600 on SAT writing.

Student Life Upper grades have student council, honor system. Discipline rests primarily with faculty.

Summer Programs Remediation, enrichment, advancement, ESL programs offered; session focuses on academics; held on campus; accepts boys and girls; open to students from other schools. 35 students usually enrolled. 2016 schedule: July 5 to August 15. Application deadline: June 30.

Tuition and Aid Day student tuition: $37,500. Tuition installment plan (monthly payment plans, individually arranged payment plans). Merit scholarship grants available. Total upper-school merit-scholarship money awarded for 2015–16: $18,000.

Admissions Traditional secondary-level entrance grade is 9. For fall 2015, 39 students applied for upper-level admission, 38 were accepted, 33 enrolled. Deadline for receipt of application materials: none. No application fee required. On-campus interview required.

Athletics 1 PE instructor.

Computers Computer network features include Internet access, wireless campus network, Internet filtering or blocking technology. Campus intranet and computer access in designated common areas are available to students. The school has a published electronic and media policy.

Contact George Higgins, Headmaster. 212-755-6666. Fax: 212-888-6085. E-mail: georgeh@beekmanschool.org. Website: www.BeekmanSchool.org

BELEN JESUIT PREPARATORY SCHOOL

500 Southwest 127th Avenue
Miami, Florida 33184

Head of School: Fr. Pedro A. Suarez, SJ

General Information Boys' day college-preparatory and religious studies school, affiliated with Roman Catholic Church. Grades 6–12. Founded: 1854. Setting: urban. 32-acre campus. 3 buildings on campus. Approved or accredited by CITA (Commission on International and Trans-Regional Accreditation), Jesuit Secondary Education Association, National Catholic Education Association, Southern Association of Colleges and Schools, and Florida Department of Education. Endowment: $8 million. Total enrollment: 1,479. Upper school average class size: 25. Upper school faculty-student ratio: 1:13. There are 175 required school days per year for Upper School students. Upper School students typically attend 5 days per week. The average school day consists of 8 hours.

Upper School Student Profile Grade 9: 225 students (225 boys); Grade 10: 243 students (243 boys); Grade 11: 185 students (185 boys); Grade 12: 227 students (227 boys). 98% of students are Roman Catholic.

Faculty School total: 106. In upper school: 49 men, 27 women; 57 have advanced degrees.

Subjects Offered Advanced Placement courses, art, art history, biology, chemistry, composition, computers, English, English literature, French, history, mathematics, music, philosophy, physical education, physics, religion, science, social studies, Spanish.

Graduation Requirements Arts and fine arts (art, music, dance, drama), electives, English, foreign language, mathematics, philosophy, physical education (includes health), religion (includes Bible studies and theology), science, social sciences, social studies (includes history). Community service is required.

Special Academic Programs Advanced Placement exam preparation; honors section; study at local college for college credit.

College Admission Counseling 227 students graduated in 2015; 226 went to college, including Florida International University; Florida State University; Miami Dade College; Santa Fe College; University of Florida; University of Miami. Other: 1 entered military service. Mean SAT critical reading: 591, mean SAT math: 587, mean SAT writing: 560, mean combined SAT: 1738, mean composite ACT: 26. 31% scored over 1800 on combined SAT, 40% scored over 26 on composite ACT.

Student Life Upper grades have uniform requirement, student council. Discipline rests primarily with faculty.

Summer Programs Remediation, enrichment programs offered; session focuses on make-up courses; held on campus; accepts boys; not open to students from other schools. 120 students usually enrolled. 2016 schedule: June 27 to July 22.

Tuition and Aid Day student tuition: $14,500. Tuition installment plan (monthly payment plans). Need-based scholarship grants available. In 2015–16, 12% of upper-school students received aid. Total amount of financial aid awarded in 2015–16: $514,810.

Admissions Traditional secondary-level entrance grade is 9. For fall 2015, 119 students applied for upper-level admission, 80 were accepted, 44 enrolled. School's own exam required. Deadline for receipt of application materials: December 12. Application fee required: $75.

Athletics Interscholastic: baseball, basketball, bowling, crew, cross-country running, football, golf, lacrosse, soccer, swimming and diving, tennis, track and field, volleyball, water polo, wrestling; intramural: fencing, fishing, in-line hockey, weight training. 7 PE instructors, 22 coaches, 1 athletic trainer.

Computers Computers are regularly used in art, English, foreign language, history, mathematics, music, science classes. Computer network features include on-campus library services, online commercial services, Internet access, wireless campus network, Internet filtering or blocking technology. Campus intranet and student e-mail accounts are available to students. Students grades are available online. The school has a published electronic and media policy.

Contact Mrs. Chris Besil, Admissions Secretary. 786-621-4032. Fax: 786-621-4033. E-mail: admissions@belenjesuit.org. Website: www.belenjesuit.org

BELLARMINE COLLEGE PREPARATORY

960 West Hedding Street
San Jose, California 95126

Head of School: Mr. Chris Meyercord

General Information Boys' day college-preparatory, arts, religious studies, and technology school, affiliated with Roman Catholic Church. Grades 9–12. Founded: 1851. Setting: suburban. 26-acre campus. 14 buildings on campus. Approved or accredited by National Catholic Education Association and Western Association of Schools and Colleges. Endowment: $57 million. Total enrollment: 1,600. Upper school average class size: 25. Upper school faculty-student ratio: 1:13. There are 170 required school days per year for Upper School students. Upper School students typically attend 5 days per week. The average school day consists of 6 hours and 40 minutes.

Upper School Student Profile Grade 9: 415 students (415 boys); Grade 10: 410 students (410 boys); Grade 11: 390 students (390 boys); Grade 12: 385 students (385 boys). 75% of students are Roman Catholic.

Faculty School total: 99. In upper school: 70 men, 29 women; 65 have advanced degrees.

Subjects Offered Algebra, American history, American literature, American sign language, anatomy, art, arts, biology, calculus, ceramics, chemistry, community service, computer science, drama, English, English literature, ethics, European history, expository writing, fine arts, French, geography, geometry, government/civics, history, international relations, Latin, Mandarin, mathematics, music, physical education, physics, psychology, religion, science, social sciences, social studies, Spanish, speech, theater, theology, trigonometry, world history, world literature, writing.

Graduation Requirements Arts and fine arts (art, music, dance, drama), English, foreign language, mathematics, physical education (includes health), religion (includes Bible studies and theology), science, social sciences, social studies (includes history), 75 hours of Christian service.

Special Academic Programs Advanced Placement exam preparation; honors section; independent study; special instructional classes for students with learning disabilities and Attention Deficit Disorder.

College Admission Counseling 392 students graduated in 2014; 390 went to college, including California Polytechnic State University, San Luis Obispo; Gonzaga University; Loyola Marymount University; San Jose State University; Santa Clara University; Seattle University. Other: 2 had other specific plans. Mean SAT critical reading: 618, mean SAT math: 643, mean SAT writing: 628, mean combined SAT: 1889, mean composite ACT: 28.

Student Life Upper grades have specified standards of dress, student council, honor system. Discipline rests primarily with faculty. Attendance at religious services is required.

Tuition and Aid Day student tuition: $18,260. Tuition installment plan (SMART Tuition Payment Plan, semester payment plan, 11 installment plan). Need-based scholarship grants available. In 2014–15, 24% of upper-school students received aid. Total amount of financial aid awarded in 2014–15: $3,800,000.

Admissions Traditional secondary-level entrance grade is 9. For fall 2014, 1,121 students applied for upper-level admission, 513 were accepted, 425 enrolled. High School Placement Test required. Deadline for receipt of application materials: December 19. Application fee required: $75.

Athletics Interscholastic: aquatics, baseball, basketball, cross-country running, diving, football, golf, ice hockey, lacrosse, soccer, swimming and diving, tennis, track and field, volleyball, water polo, wrestling; intramural: basketball, flag football, Frisbee, in-line hockey, indoor hockey, roller hockey, rugby, soccer, tai chi, touch football, yoga. 4 PE instructors, 15 coaches, 2 athletic trainers.

Computers Computers are regularly used in all classes. Computer network features include on-campus library services, online commercial services, Internet access, wireless campus network. Student e-mail accounts are available to students. Students grades are available online. The school has a published electronic and media policy.

Contact Terry Council, Admissions Assistant. 408-294-9224. Fax: 408-294-1894. E-mail: admissions@bcp.org. Website: www.bcp.org

BELLARMINE-JEFFERSON HIGH SCHOOL

465 East Olive Avenue
Burbank, California 91501-2176

Head of School: Mr. Michael Stumpf

General Information Coeducational day college-preparatory, arts, business, religious studies, and technology school, affiliated with Roman Catholic Church. Grades 9–12. Founded: 1944. Setting: suburban. Nearest major city is Los Angeles. 4 buildings on campus. Approved or accredited by Western Association of Schools and Colleges and California Department of Education. Upper school average class size: 20.

Upper School Student Profile 75% of students are Roman Catholic.

Faculty School total: 15. In upper school: all have advanced degrees.

Special Academic Programs International Baccalaureate program; 7 Advanced Placement exams for which test preparation is offered; honors section; ESL (15 students enrolled).

College Admission Counseling Colleges students went to include California State University, Fullerton; California State University, Long Beach; California State University, Los Angeles; California State University, Monterey Bay; California State University, Northridge; California State University, Sacramento.

Student Life Upper grades have uniform requirement, student council, honor system. Discipline rests primarily with faculty. Attendance at religious services is required.

Tuition and Aid Tuition installment plan (The Tuition Plan). Tuition reduction for siblings, merit scholarship grants, need-based scholarship grants available. In 2014–15, 50% of upper-school students received aid.

Admissions High School Placement Test required. Deadline for receipt of application materials: January 30. Application fee required: $75. Interview required.

Athletics Interscholastic: baseball (boys), basketball (b,g), cheering (g), football (b), soccer (b,g), softball (g), track and field (b,g), volleyball (b,g); coed interscholastic: cross-country running, dance, fitness walking, golf, physical fitness, physical training, weight training.

Computers Computer network features include Internet access, wireless campus network. Student e-mail accounts are available to students. Students grades are available online. The school has a published electronic and media policy.

Contact Mrs. Alison Dirstine, Director of Marketing and Public Relations. 818-972-1408. Fax: 818-559-8796. E-mail: adirstine@bell-jeff.net. Website: www.bell-jeff.net

BENEDICTINE HIGH SCHOOL

2900 Martin Luther King, Jr. Drive
Cleveland, Ohio 44104

Head of School: Fr. Michael Brunovsky, OSB

General Information Boys' day college-preparatory and religious studies school, affiliated with Roman Catholic Church. Grades 9–12. Founded: 1927. Setting: urban. 13-acre campus. 3 buildings on campus. Approved or accredited by National Catholic Education Association, North Central Association of Colleges and Schools, and Ohio Department of Education. Total enrollment: 380. Upper school average class size: 20. Upper school faculty-student ratio: 1:11. There are 180 required school days per year for Upper School students. Upper School students typically attend 5 days per week. The average school day consists of 6 hours and 50 minutes.

Upper School Student Profile Grade 9: 112 students (112 boys); Grade 10: 89 students (89 boys); Grade 11: 109 students (109 boys); Grade 12: 92 students (92 boys). 70% of students are Roman Catholic.

Faculty School total: 37. In upper school: 32 men, 5 women; 31 have advanced degrees.

Subjects Offered Advanced chemistry, advanced math, Advanced Placement courses, aesthetics, algebra, American literature, American literature-AP, analysis and differential calculus, analytic geometry, Ancient Greek, ancient history, art, athletic training, band, Basic programming, Bible studies, biology, biology-AP, British literature-AP, business education, business law, calculus, calculus-AP, Catholic belief and practice, ceramics, chemistry, choir, chorus, church history, Civil War, civil war history, classical Greek literature, classical language, computer graphics, computer information systems, computer literacy, computer skills, computer-aided design, concert band, concert choir, current events, drawing, drawing and design, economics, electives, English, English literature and composition-AP, European history-AP, film studies, foreign language, French, geometry, German, government, government-AP, government/civics, government/civics-AP, graphic design, health, honors algebra, honors English, honors geometry, honors U.S. history, honors world history, human geography - AP, jazz band, journalism, keyboarding, lab science, Latin, Latin-AP, Life of Christ, marching band, marketing, moral theology, music, music appreciation, New Testament, painting, physical education, pre-calculus, probability and statistics, psychology, Russian, Shakespeare.

Graduation Requirements 1 1/2 elective credits, 20th century American writers, 20th century history, 20th century world history, algebra, American government, American history, American literature, ancient history, ancient world history, art, biology, British literature, chemistry, church history, computer applications, English, foreign language, geometry, physical education (includes health), physics, senior project, theology, U.S. history, world history, community service hours.

Special Academic Programs 9 Advanced Placement exams for which test preparation is offered; honors section; independent study; study at local college for college credit; study abroad.

College Admission Counseling 71 students graduated in 2015; 65 went to college, including Bowling Green State University; Case Western Reserve University; Cleveland State University; Kent State University; The University of Akron; University of Dayton. Other: 5 went to work, 1 entered military service. Mean SAT critical reading: 512, mean SAT math: 498, mean SAT writing: 492, mean composite ACT: 22.

Student Life Upper grades have specified standards of dress, student council, honor system. Discipline rests primarily with faculty. Attendance at religious services is required.

Summer Programs Enrichment, sports, computer instruction programs offered; session focuses on enrichment; held on campus; accepts boys and girls; open to students from other schools. 150 students usually enrolled. 2016 schedule: June 8 to July 24. Application deadline: June 1.

Tuition and Aid Day student tuition: $9000. Tuition installment plan (monthly payment plans, individually arranged payment plans). Tuition reduction for siblings, merit scholarship grants, need-based scholarship grants, paying campus jobs available. In 2014–15, 73% of upper-school students received aid.

Admissions Traditional secondary-level entrance grade is 9. For fall 2015, 250 students applied for upper-level admission, 175 were accepted, 112 enrolled. High School Placement Test required. Deadline for receipt of application materials: none. No application fee required. Interview recommended.

Athletics Interscholastic: baseball, basketball, bowling, cross-country running, football, golf, ice hockey, lacrosse, soccer, swimming and diving, track and field, wrestling; intramural: baseball, basketball, flag football, football, physical fitness, physical training, skiing (downhill), snowboarding, strength & conditioning, touch football, volleyball, weight lifting, weight training. 3 PE instructors, 10 coaches, 1 athletic trainer.

Computers Computers are regularly used in all academic, computer applications, creative writing, current events, data processing, design, English, graphic design, history, independent study, information technology, library, mathematics, newspaper, technical drawing, yearbook classes. Computer network features include on-campus library services, online commercial services, Internet access, wireless campus network, Internet filtering or blocking technology, every student has a laptop. Campus intranet and student e-mail accounts are available to students. Students grades are available online. The school has a published electronic and media policy.

Contact Mr. Joe Laffey, Admissions Director. 216-421-2080 Ext. 356. Fax: 216-421-1100. E-mail: laffey@cbhs.edu. Website: www.cbhs.net

BENET ACADEMY

2200 Maple Avenue
Lisle, Illinois 60532

Head of School: Mr. Stephen A. Marth

General Information Coeducational day college-preparatory, arts, and religious studies school, affiliated with Roman Catholic Church. Grades 9–12. Founded: 1887. Setting: suburban. Nearest major city is Chicago. 54-acre campus. 8 buildings on campus. Approved or accredited by National Catholic Education Association, North Central Association of Colleges and Schools, and Illinois Department of Education. Total enrollment: 1,333. Upper school average class size: 27. Upper school faculty-

student ratio: 1:18. There are 177 required school days per year for Upper School students. Upper School students typically attend 5 days per week. The average school day consists of 6 hours and 59 minutes.

Upper School Student Profile Grade 9: 324 students (170 boys, 154 girls); Grade 10: 352 students (182 boys, 170 girls); Grade 11: 326 students (158 boys, 168 girls); Grade 12: 331 students (172 boys, 159 girls). 97% of students are Roman Catholic.

Faculty School total: 76. In upper school: 45 men, 31 women; 67 have advanced degrees.

Subjects Offered Algebra, American history, American literature, art history, biology, business, calculus, chemistry, computer programming, computer science, creative writing, drama, driver education, economics, English, European history, French, geography, geometry, German, government/civics, health, history, Latin, mathematics, music, physical education, physics, religion, science, Spanish, speech, statistics, trigonometry, U.S. history-AP, world history, world literature, writing.

Graduation Requirements Computer science, English, foreign language, mathematics, physical education (includes health), religion (includes Bible studies and theology), science, social studies (includes history).

Special Academic Programs 21 Advanced Placement exams for which test preparation is offered; honors section; study at local college for college credit; academic accommodation for the gifted.

College Admission Counseling 330 students graduated in 2014; all went to college, including Indiana University–Purdue University Fort Wayne; Marquette University; Miami University; University of Illinois; University of Missouri; University of Notre Dame. Mean SAT critical reading: 626, mean SAT math: 626, mean SAT writing: 627, mean composite ACT: 28. 62% scored over 600 on SAT critical reading, 70% scored over 600 on SAT math, 62% scored over 600 on SAT writing, 83% scored over 26 on composite ACT.

Student Life Upper grades have uniform requirement, student council. Discipline rests primarily with faculty. Attendance at religious services is required.

Tuition and Aid Day student tuition: $10,350. Tuition installment plan (monthly payment plans). Tuition reduction for siblings, need-based scholarship grants available. In 2014–15, 5% of upper-school students received aid. Total amount of financial aid awarded in 2014–15: $175,000.

Admissions Traditional secondary-level entrance grade is 9. For fall 2014, 475 students applied for upper-level admission, 400 were accepted, 324 enrolled. High School Placement Test required. Deadline for receipt of application materials: January 10. Application fee required: $35. On-campus interview required.

Athletics Interscholastic: baseball (boys), basketball (b,g), cheering (g), cross-country running (b,g), dance team (g), fishing (b), football (b), golf (b,g), lacrosse (b,g), pom squad (g), soccer (b,g), softball (g), strength & conditioning (b), swimming and diving (b,g), tennis (b,g), track and field (b,g), volleyball (b,g); intramural: weight training (b,g), yoga (g); coed interscholastic: ice hockey; coed intramural: bowling, flag football, Frisbee. 4 PE instructors, 30 coaches, 1 athletic trainer.

Computers Computers are regularly used in English, history, mathematics, science, Spanish classes. Computer network features include on-campus library services, online commercial services, Internet access, wireless campus network, Internet filtering or blocking technology. Campus intranet and student e-mail accounts are available to students. Students grades are available online. The school has a published electronic and media policy.

Contact Mr. James E. Brown, Assistant Principal. 630-719-2782. Fax: 630-719-2849. E-mail: jbrown@benet.org. Website: www.benet.org/

BEN FRANKLIN ACADEMY

1585 Clifton Road
Atlanta, Georgia 30329

Head of School: Dr. Martha B. Burdette

General Information Coeducational day college-preparatory school. Grades 9–12. Founded: 1987. Setting: urban. 3-acre campus. 2 buildings on campus. Approved or accredited by Georgia Independent School Association, Southern Association of Colleges and Schools, Southern Association of Independent Schools, and Georgia Department of Education. Total enrollment: 125. Upper school average class size: 3. Upper school faculty-student ratio: 1:3. There are 180 required school days per year for Upper School students. Upper School students typically attend 5 days per week. The average school day consists of 6 hours.

Faculty School total: 29. In upper school: 12 men, 17 women; 15 have advanced degrees.

Subjects Offered 1 1/2 elective credits.

Graduation Requirements A work-study component in addition to the academic requirements.

Special Academic Programs Advanced Placement exam preparation; honors section; accelerated programs; academic accommodation for the gifted.

College Admission Counseling 40 students graduated in 2015; all went to college.

Student Life Upper grades have specified standards of dress. Discipline rests primarily with faculty.

Tuition and Aid Day student tuition: $25,500–$34,500. Tuition installment plan (individually arranged payment plans). Tuition reduction for siblings, need-based scholarship grants available. In 2015–16, 10% of upper-school students received aid.

Admissions Traditional secondary-level entrance grade is 9. Deadline for receipt of application materials: none. No application fee required. On-campus interview required.

Athletics Interscholastic: cross-country running (boys, girls), golf (b,g); coed interscholastic: basketball, cross-country running, Frisbee, golf, tennis, ultimate Frisbee.

Computers Computer resources include on-campus library services, Internet access, Internet filtering or blocking technology. Campus intranet and student e-mail accounts are available to students. The school has a published electronic and media policy.

Contact Mrs. Amy H. Barnes, Registrar. 404-633-7404. Fax: 404-321-0610. E-mail: abarnes@benfranklinacademy.org. Website: www.benfranklinacademy.org

THE BENJAMIN SCHOOL

11000 Ellison Wilson Road
North Palm Beach, Florida 33408

Head of School: Mr. Robert S. Goldberg

General Information Coeducational day college-preparatory, arts, and technology school. Grades PK–12. Founded: 1960. Setting: suburban. Nearest major city is West Palm Beach. 50-acre campus. 6 buildings on campus. Approved or accredited by Florida Council of Independent Schools, Southern Association of Colleges and Schools, and Florida Department of Education. Member of National Association of Independent Schools and Secondary School Admission Test Board. Endowment: $5.6 million. Total enrollment: 1,081. Upper school average class size: 16. Upper school faculty-student ratio: 1:8. There are 175 required school days per year for Upper School students. Upper School students typically attend 5 days per week. The average school day consists of 5 hours and 30 minutes.

Upper School Student Profile Grade 9: 102 students (47 boys, 55 girls); Grade 10: 105 students (55 boys, 50 girls); Grade 11: 113 students (64 boys, 49 girls); Grade 12: 100 students (52 boys, 48 girls).

Faculty School total: 141. In upper school: 20 men, 23 women; 35 have advanced degrees.

Subjects Offered 3-dimensional art, acting, advanced studio art-AP, algebra, American history, art, art history, art history-AP, Asian studies, band, biology, biology-AP, biotechnology, calculus, calculus-AP, Caribbean history, ceramics, chemistry, chemistry-AP, choral music, chorus, comparative government and politics-AP, computer programming, computer science, computer science-AP, critical studies in film, current events, dance, drama, economics, engineering, English, English language and composition-AP, English literature, English literature and composition-AP, environmental science, environmental studies, European history-AP, expository writing, film appreciation, film studies, French, French language-AP, French-AP, geometry, government/civics, honors English, honors geometry, human biology, human geography - AP, intro to computers, law, law studies, macro/microeconomics-AP, Mandarin, marine biology, modern dance, modern European history-AP, music theory-AP, painting, physical education, physics, physics-AP, piano, pre-calculus, SAT preparation, sculpture, Spanish, Spanish language-AP, Spanish literature-AP, speech, speech communications, statistics-AP, studio art-AP, theater, U.S. government, U.S. government and politics-AP, U.S. history-AP, video film production, world history.

Graduation Requirements Arts and fine arts (art, music, dance, drama), computer science, English, foreign language, mathematics, physical education (includes health), science, social sciences, social studies (includes history), work program for seniors.

Special Academic Programs 22 Advanced Placement exams for which test preparation is offered; honors section.

College Admission Counseling 113 students graduated in 2015; 112 went to college, including Florida State University; Harvard University; The University of Alabama; University of Florida; University of Miami; Wake Forest University. Mean SAT critical reading: 574, mean SAT math: 579, mean SAT writing: 598, mean composite ACT: 26.

Student Life Upper grades have uniform requirement, student council, honor system. Discipline rests primarily with faculty.

Summer Programs Enrichment, advancement, sports, art/fine arts, computer instruction programs offered; session focuses on academic advancement; held on campus; accepts boys and girls; open to students from other schools. 350 students usually enrolled. 2016 schedule: June 1 to August 15. Application deadline: May 1.

Tuition and Aid Day student tuition: $24,500. Tuition installment plan (monthly payment plans, The Tuition Solution). Merit scholarship grants, need-based scholarship grants, need-based loans available. In 2015–16, 24% of upper-school students received aid; total upper-school merit-scholarship money awarded: $24,500. Total amount of financial aid awarded in 2015–16: $1,388,838.

Admissions Traditional secondary-level entrance grade is 9. For fall 2015, 83 students applied for upper-level admission, 76 were accepted, 42 enrolled. ERB or SSAT required. Deadline for receipt of application materials: February 1. Application fee required: $100. On-campus interview required.

Athletics Interscholastic: ballet (girls), baseball (b), basketball (b,g), bowling (b,g), cross-country running (b,g), dance (g), dance team (g), diving (b,g), football (b), golf (b,g), lacrosse (b,g), modern dance (g), soccer (b,g), softball (g), tennis (b,g), track and field (b,g), volleyball (g), winter soccer (b,g), wrestling (b); coed interscholastic: aerobics/dance, cheering, strength & conditioning, swimming and diving, weight training. 1 PE instructor, 40 coaches, 1 athletic trainer.

Computers Computers are regularly used in art, computer applications, English, foreign language, history, mathematics, science classes. Computer network features include on-campus library services, online commercial services, Internet access, wireless campus network, Internet filtering or blocking technology, tablet laptop program for grades 9 to 12. Student e-mail accounts are available to students. Students grades are available online. The school has a published electronic and media policy.

Contact Mrs. Mary Lou Primm, Director of Admission. 561-472-3451. Fax: 561-472-3410. E-mail: marylou.primm@thebenjaminschool.org. Website: www.thebenjaminschool.org

BENTLEY SCHOOL

1000 Upper Happy Valley Road
Bentley School
Lafayette, California 94549

Head of School: Arlene Hogan

General Information Coeducational day college-preparatory, arts, and technology school. Grades K–12. Founded: 1920. Setting: suburban. 12-acre campus. 4 buildings on campus. Approved or accredited by California Association of Independent Schools and California Department of Education. Candidate for accreditation by Western Association of Schools and Colleges. Member of National Association of Independent Schools. Total enrollment: 684. Upper school average class size: 12. Upper school faculty-student ratio: 1:8.

Upper School Student Profile Grade 6: 41 students (20 boys, 21 girls); Grade 7: 52 students (23 boys, 29 girls); Grade 8: 36 students (19 boys, 17 girls); Grade 9: 93 students (52 boys, 41 girls); Grade 10: 87 students (44 boys, 43 girls); Grade 11: 72 students (47 boys, 25 girls); Grade 12: 73 students (39 boys, 34 girls).

Faculty School total: 76. In upper school: 15 men, 25 women; 20 have advanced degrees.

Subjects Offered 20th century history, American literature, art history, biology, British literature, computer science, European history, geometry, modern European history, physics, public speaking, senior internship, U.S. history, visual and performing arts.

Special Academic Programs Advanced Placement exam preparation; honors section; independent study; study at local college for college credit; domestic exchange program (with The Putney School, The Network Program Schools).

College Admission Counseling 80 students graduated in 2015; all went to college, including Brown University; New York University; Oberlin College; University of California, Berkeley; University of Michigan; University of Southern California. Mean SAT critical reading: 623, mean SAT math: 622, mean SAT writing: 624, mean composite ACT: 27.

Student Life Upper grades have specified standards of dress, student council, honor system. Discipline rests equally with students and faculty.

Tuition and Aid Day student tuition: $35,450. Tuition installment plan (The Tuition Plan, SMART Tuition Payment Plan, monthly payment plans, individually arranged payment plans). Need-based scholarship grants available. In 2015–16, 25% of upper-school students received aid.

Admissions Traditional secondary-level entrance grade is 9. For fall 2015, 220 students applied for upper-level admission, 145 were accepted, 69 enrolled. ISEE or SSAT required. Deadline for receipt of application materials: January 14. Application fee required: $100. Interview required.

Athletics Interscholastic: baseball (boys), basketball (b,g), cross-country running (b,g), soccer (b,g), swimming and diving (b,g), tennis (b,g), volleyball (b,g); coed interscholastic: golf, track and field; coed intramural: equestrian sports, fencing, fitness, Frisbee, physical fitness, ultimate Frisbee, weight training, yoga. 19 coaches.

Computers Computers are regularly used in science classes. Computer network features include on-campus library services, online commercial services, Internet access, wireless campus network. Campus intranet, student e-mail accounts, and computer access in designated common areas are available to students. Students grades are available online.

Contact Colleen Curran, Admissions Associate, 9-12. 925-900-4038. Fax: 510-843-5162. E-mail: ccurran@bentleyschool.net. Website: www.bentleyschool.net

BEREAN CHRISTIAN HIGH SCHOOL

245 El Divisadero Avenue
Walnut Creek, California 94598

Head of School: Mr. Nelson M. Noriega

General Information Coeducational day college-preparatory and religious studies school, affiliated with Baptist Church. Grades 9–12. Founded: 1969. Setting: suburban. Nearest major city is Oakland. 5-acre campus. 5 buildings on campus. Approved or accredited by Association of Christian Schools International, Western Association of Schools and Colleges, and California Department of Education. Total enrollment: 411. Upper school average class size: 20. Upper school faculty-student ratio: 1:20. There are 180 required school days per year for Upper School students. Upper School students typically attend 5 days per week. The average school day consists of 6 hours and 30 minutes.

Upper School Student Profile Grade 9: 97 students (51 boys, 46 girls); Grade 10: 105 students (59 boys, 46 girls); Grade 11: 105 students (51 boys, 54 girls); Grade 12: 104 students (49 boys, 55 girls). 50% of students are Baptist.

Faculty School total: 34. In upper school: 12 men, 22 women; 12 have advanced degrees.

Subjects Offered Algebra, American literature, anatomy, art, arts, Bible studies, biology, chemistry, choir, computer literacy, computer science, drama, economics, English, ethics, fine arts, geometry, government, health, mathematics, physical education, physics, physiology, pre-calculus, religion, science, social studies, Spanish, trigonometry, U.S. history, world history, world religions.

Graduation Requirements U.S. history, U.S. history-AP, world history.

Special Academic Programs Advanced Placement exam preparation; study at local college for college credit.

College Admission Counseling 115 students graduated in 2015; 113 went to college. Other: 1 went to work.

Student Life Upper grades have specified standards of dress, student council, honor system. Discipline rests primarily with faculty. Attendance at religious services is required.

Summer Programs Session focuses on biology; held on campus; accepts boys and girls; not open to students from other schools. 25 students usually enrolled. 2016 schedule: May 31 to June 30.

Tuition and Aid Day student tuition: $9500. Tuition installment plan (SMART Tuition Payment Plan). Tuition reduction for siblings, merit scholarship grants, need-based scholarship grants available. In 2015–16, 17% of upper-school students received aid; total upper-school merit-scholarship money awarded: $250. Total amount of financial aid awarded in 2015–16: $286,000.

Admissions Traditional secondary-level entrance grade is 9. For fall 2015, 411 students applied for upper-level admission, 411 were accepted, 411 enrolled. Math Placement Exam required. Deadline for receipt of application materials: none. Application fee required: $95. On-campus interview required.

Athletics Interscholastic: baseball (boys), basketball (b,g), cheering (g), cross-country running (b,g), football (b), soccer (b,g), softball (g), swimming and diving (b,g), tennis (g), volleyball (b,g); coed interscholastic: golf. 2 PE instructors, 42 coaches.

Computers Computers are regularly used in all academic classes. Computer network features include Internet access, wireless campus network, Internet filtering or blocking technology. Campus intranet and student e-mail accounts are available to students. Students grades are available online.

Contact Shelley M. Elson, Acct/HR Assistant. 925-945-6464 Ext. 22. Fax: 925-945-7473. E-mail: selson@berean-eagles.org. Website: www.berean-eagles.org

BERKELEY CARROLL SCHOOL

181 Lincoln Place
Brooklyn, New York 11217

Head of School: Mr. Robert D. Vitalo

General Information Coeducational day college-preparatory school. Grades N–12. Founded: 1886. Setting: urban. Nearest major city is New York. 3 buildings on campus. Approved or accredited by New York State Association of Independent Schools and New York Department of Education. Member of National Association of Independent Schools. Endowment: $2.5 million. Total enrollment: 942. Upper school average class size: 15. Upper school faculty-student ratio: 1:6. There are 174 required school days per year for Upper School students. Upper School students typically attend 5 days per week. The average school day consists of 6 hours and 30 minutes.

Upper School Student Profile Grade 9: 78 students (37 boys, 41 girls); Grade 10: 71 students (32 boys, 39 girls); Grade 11: 80 students (37 boys, 43 girls); Grade 12: 56 students (29 boys, 27 girls).

Faculty School total: 132. In upper school: 28 men, 27 women; 47 have advanced degrees.

Subjects Offered 3-dimensional art, 3-dimensional design, acting, advanced biology, advanced computer applications, advanced math, aerobics, African history, African-American literature, algebra, American studies, analysis and differential calculus, analysis of data, anatomy and physiology, Arabic, art, art history, Asian history, Asian studies, athletic training, athletics, band, Basic programming, bioethics, biology, calculus, ceramics, chamber groups, chemistry, Chinese, choir, choreography, chorus, community service, computer programming, computer science, computer technologies, conceptual physics, concert choir, contemporary women writers, creative writing, dance, dance performance, debate, digital art, digital music, digital photography, drama performance, drawing, earth and space science, earth science, ecology, economics, economics and history, electives, engineering, English, English literature, ensembles, environmental science, equality and freedom, ethics, fine arts, fitness, foreign language, French, French as a second language, geology, geometry, health education, Hispanic literature, history, Holocaust, honors algebra, honors geometry, human anatomy, human biology, humanities, instrumental music, instruments, integrated science, jazz band, Latin, Latin American history, Mandarin, modern world history, painting, participation in sports, peer counseling, philosophy, physical education, physics, play production, playwriting and directing, poetry, portfolio art, pre-algebra, pre-calculus, probability and statistics, science, science and technology, science research, senior composition, senior project, set design, Spanish, Spanish literature, speech and debate, sports

conditioning, statistics, technical theater, theater design and production, video, visual and performing arts, weight training, world religions, writing.

Graduation Requirements Arts and fine arts (art, music, dance, drama), computer science, English, foreign language, mathematics, physical education (includes health), science, social sciences, 2-week Spring Intensives, senior speaker program, Community Service. Community service is required.

Special Academic Programs Honors section; independent study; term-away projects; study at local college for college credit; study abroad.

College Admission Counseling 63 students graduated in 2015; all went to college, including Boston University; Bowdoin College; Columbia University; Drexel University; Ithaca College; Wesleyan University. Median SAT critical reading: 680, median SAT math: 610, median SAT writing: 650, median combined SAT: 1950, median composite ACT: 26. 73% scored over 600 on SAT critical reading, 60% scored over 600 on SAT math, 81% scored over 600 on SAT writing, 76% scored over 1800 on combined SAT, 40% scored over 26 on composite ACT.

Student Life Upper grades have student council, honor system. Discipline rests equally with students and faculty.

Summer Programs Enrichment, sports, art/fine arts, computer instruction programs offered; session focuses on creative arts, athletics, field trips, academics; held on campus; accepts boys and girls; open to students from other schools. 250 students usually enrolled. 2016 schedule: June 28 to August 5. Application deadline: none.

Tuition and Aid Day student tuition: $40,215. Tuition installment plan (Insured Tuition Payment Plan, Academic Management Services Plan, SMART Tuition Payment Plan, monthly payment plans, individually arranged payment plans). Need-based scholarship grants available. In 2015–16, 40% of upper-school students received aid. Total amount of financial aid awarded in 2015–16: $2,957,561.

Admissions Traditional secondary-level entrance grade is 9. ISEE, PSAT and SAT for applicants to grade 11 and 12, SSAT, SSAT, ERB, PSAT, SAT, PLAN or ACT, TOEFL or SLEP or writing sample required. Deadline for receipt of application materials: December 1. Application fee required: $100. On-campus interview required.

Athletics Interscholastic: baseball (boys), basketball (b,g), cross-country running (b,g), soccer (b,g), softball (g), swimming and diving (b,g), tennis (b,g), track and field (b,g), volleyball (b,g); intramural: ultimate Frisbee (b,g); coed intramural: swimming and diving. 8 PE instructors, 30 coaches, 1 athletic trainer.

Computers Computers are regularly used in all classes. Computer network features include on-campus library services, online commercial services, Internet access, wireless campus network, Internet filtering or blocking technology, free iPad for every student, staffed Knowledge Bar for help with iPads and apps. Campus intranet, student e-mail accounts, and computer access in designated common areas are available to students. Students grades are available online. The school has a published electronic and media policy.

Contact Ms. Jennifer Brown, Administrative Assistant for Upper School Admissions. 718-789-6060 Ext. 6527. Fax: 718-398-3640. E-mail: jbrown@berkeleycarroll.org. Website: www.berkeleycarroll.org

BERKELEY PREPARATORY SCHOOL

4811 Kelly Road
Tampa, Florida 33615

Head of School: Joseph W. Seivold

General Information Coeducational day college-preparatory, arts, religious studies, bilingual studies, and technology school, affiliated with Episcopal Church. Grades PK–12. Founded: 1960. Setting: suburban. 80-acre campus. 10 buildings on campus. Approved or accredited by Florida Council of Independent Schools, National Association of Episcopal Schools, Southern Association of Colleges and Schools, Southern Association of Independent Schools, The College Board, and Florida Department of Education. Member of National Association of Independent Schools and Secondary School Admission Test Board. Endowment: $15.8 million. Total enrollment: 1,300. Upper school average class size: 15. Upper school faculty-student ratio: 1:9. Upper School students typically attend 5 days per week. The average school day consists of 7 hours.

Faculty School total: 225.

Subjects Offered African history, algebra, American government, American history, American literature, art, art history, biology, biology-AP, calculus, calculus-AP, ceramics, chemistry, chemistry-AP, China/Japan history, community service, computer math, computer programming, computer science, creative writing, dance, drama, drama performance, drama workshop, early childhood, economics, English, English literature, English-AP, environmental science-AP, etymology, European history, expository writing, fine arts, French, French-AP, freshman seminar, geography, geometry, government/civics, grammar, guitar, health, history, history of China and Japan, honors algebra, honors English, honors geometry, instruments, Latin, Latin American history, Latin-AP, logic, Mandarin, math analysis, mathematics, media arts, microbiology, modern European history, modern European history-AP, music, performing arts, philosophy, physical education, physics, physics-AP, pre-calculus, psychology, religious studies, SAT preparation, science, social studies, Spanish, Spanish-AP, speech, stage design, statistics, statistics-AP, technical theater, television, theater, theater production, U.S. history, U.S. history-AP, video, video film production, Western civilization, world history, world literature, writing.

Graduation Requirements Arts and fine arts (art, music, dance, drama), computer science, English, foreign language, mathematics, physical education (includes health), religious studies, science, social studies (includes history). Community service is required.

Special Academic Programs Advanced Placement exam preparation; honors section; independent study; study abroad.

College Admission Counseling 142 students graduated in 2014; all went to college, including Boston College; Duke University; Florida State University; Harvard University; University of Florida; Wake Forest University. Mean SAT critical reading: 618, mean SAT math: 621, mean SAT writing: 608, mean combined SAT: 1847, mean composite ACT: 28.

Student Life Upper grades have uniform requirement, student council, honor system. Discipline rests equally with students and faculty. Attendance at religious services is required.

Tuition and Aid Day student tuition: $21,800. Guaranteed tuition plan. Tuition installment plan (8-installment plan). Merit scholarship grants, need-based scholarship grants available. Total upper-school merit-scholarship money awarded for 2014–15: $8,600,000.

Admissions Traditional secondary-level entrance grade is 9. Otis-Lennon Mental Ability Test and SSAT required. Deadline for receipt of application materials: January 30. Application fee required: $75. On-campus interview required.

Athletics Interscholastic: baseball (boys), basketball (b,g), cheering (g), crew (b,g), cross-country running (b,g), dance squad (g), dance team (g), diving (b,g), football (b), golf (b,g), ice hockey (b), lacrosse (b), rowing (b,g), soccer (b,g), softball (g), swimming and diving (b,g), tennis (b,g), track and field (b,g), volleyball (b,g); coed interscholastic: weight lifting, wrestling; coed intramural: physical fitness, physical training, power lifting, project adventure, strength & conditioning, wall climbing, weight training. 14 PE instructors, 74 coaches, 2 athletic trainers.

Computers Computers are regularly used in art, English, foreign language, history, mathematics, music, science classes. Computer network features include on-campus library services, online commercial services, Internet access, wireless campus network, Internet filtering or blocking technology. Student e-mail accounts are available to students. Students grades are available online. The school has a published electronic and media policy.

Contact Janie McIlvaine, Director of Admissions. 813-885-1673. Fax: 813-886-6933. E-mail: mcilvjan@berkeleyprep.org. Website: www.berkeleyprep.org

See Display below and Close-Up on page 582.

BERKSHIRE SCHOOL

245 North Undermountain Road
Sheffield, Massachusetts 01257

Head of School: Pieter M. Mulder

General Information Coeducational boarding and day college-preparatory, arts, technology, advanced math/science research, and Advanced Humanities Research school. Grades 9–PG. Founded: 1907. Setting: rural. Nearest major city is Hartford, CT. Students are housed in single-sex dormitories. 400-acre campus. 37 buildings on campus. Approved or accredited by Association of Independent Schools in New England, New England Association of Schools and Colleges, and The Association of Boarding Schools. Member of National Association of Independent Schools and Secondary School Admission Test Board. Endowment: $126 million. Total enrollment: 405. Upper school average class size: 12. Upper school faculty-student ratio: 1:5. There are 187 required school days per year for Upper School students. Upper School students typically attend 6 days per week. The average school day consists of 6 hours and 45 minutes.

Upper School Student Profile Grade 9: 67 students (30 boys, 37 girls); Grade 10: 97 students (58 boys, 39 girls); Grade 11: 118 students (69 boys, 49 girls); Grade 12: 112 students (60 boys, 52 girls); Postgraduate: 11 students (10 boys, 1 girl). 91% of students are boarding students. 8% are state residents. 30 states are represented in upper school student body. 17% are international students. International students from Bermuda, Canada, China, Germany, Hong Kong, and Republic of Korea; 22 other countries represented in student body.

Faculty School total: 59. In upper school: 33 men, 26 women; 50 have advanced degrees; 43 reside on campus.

Subjects Offered 3-dimensional design, acting, Advanced Placement courses, algebra, American government, American history, American literature, art, art history, astronomy, aviation, biology, calculus, ceramics, chamber groups, chemistry, Chinese, choral music, chorus, comparative religion, computer programming, constitutional law, creative writing, dance, digital art, drama, drawing and design, economics, English, English literature, environmental science, ESL, ethics, European history, expository writing, French, geometry, health, history, improvisation, independent study, instrumental music, jazz ensemble, journalism, Latin, mathematics, modern world history, music, music technology, music theory, painting, philosophy, photography, physics, pre-calculus, psychology, science, sculpture, Spanish, statistics, studio art, theater, trigonometry, world history, writing.

Graduation Requirements Arts and fine arts (art, music, dance, drama), English, foreign language, history, mathematics, science. Community service is required.

Special Academic Programs 17 Advanced Placement exams for which test preparation is offered; honors section; independent study; study abroad; ESL.

College Admission Counseling 110 students graduated in 2015; all went to college, including Boston College; Colby College; Elon University; Rollins College; St. Lawrence University; Trinity College.

Student Life Upper grades have specified standards of dress, student council, honor system. Discipline rests equally with students and faculty.

Tuition and Aid Day student tuition: $44,700; 7-day tuition and room/board: $56,150. Tuition installment plan (Key Tuition Payment Plan, monthly payment plans). Need-based scholarship grants available. In 2015–16, 30% of upper-school students received aid. Total amount of financial aid awarded in 2015–16: $4,984,000.

Admissions Traditional secondary-level entrance grade is 9. For fall 2015, 1,202 students applied for upper-level admission, 317 were accepted, 143 enrolled. ACT, PSAT, SAT, SSAT or TOEFL required. Deadline for receipt of application materials: January 15. Application fee required: $100. Interview required.

Athletics Interscholastic: baseball (boys), basketball (b,g), crew (b,g), cross-country running (b,g), field hockey (g), football (b), ice hockey (b,g), lacrosse (b,g), rowing (b,g), skiing (downhill) (b,g), soccer (b,g), softball (g), squash (b,g), tennis (b,g), track and field (b,g), volleyball (g); coed interscholastic: alpine skiing, golf, mountain biking; coed intramural: alpine skiing, bicycling, canoeing/kayaking, climbing, combined training, dance, fly fishing, hiking/backpacking, kayaking, modern dance, mountaineering, nordic skiing, outdoor adventure, outdoor education, outdoor skills, rappelling, rock climbing, ropes courses, skiing (cross-country), snowboarding, wall climbing, weight training, wilderness, wilderness survival. 2 athletic trainers.

Computers Computers are regularly used in all classes. Computer network features include on-campus library services, online commercial services, Internet access, wireless campus network, Internet filtering or blocking technology, network printing, interactive Polyvision white boards (Smart boards). Campus intranet, student e-mail accounts, and computer access in designated common areas are available to students. Students grades are available online. The school has a published electronic and media policy.

Contact Ms. Danielle Francoline, Assistant to Director of Admission. 413-229-1253. Fax: 413-229-1016. E-mail: admission@berkshireschool.org. Website: www.berkshireschool.org

See Display below and Close-Up on page 584.

BERWICK ACADEMY

31 Academy Street
South Berwick, Maine 03908

Head of School: Gregory J. Schneider

General Information Coeducational day college-preparatory and arts school. Grades PK–PG. Founded: 1791. Setting: small town. Nearest major city is Portsmouth, NH. 72-acre campus. 11 buildings on campus. Approved or accredited by Association of Independent Schools in New England, Independent Schools of Northern New England, New England Association of Schools and Colleges, and Maine Department of Education. Member of National Association of Independent Schools and Secondary School Admission Test Board. Endowment: $21 million. Total enrollment: 593. Upper school average class size: 14. Upper school faculty-student ratio: 1:12. There are 169 required school days per year for Upper School students.

Upper School Student Profile Grade 9: 77 students (37 boys, 40 girls); Grade 10: 70 students (32 boys, 38 girls); Grade 11: 62 students (38 boys, 24 girls); Grade 12: 63 students (29 boys, 34 girls); Postgraduate: 3 students (2 boys, 1 girl).

Faculty School total: 89. In upper school: 13 men, 18 women; 23 have advanced degrees.

Subjects Offered Algebra, American history, American literature, art, art history, biology, calculus, chemistry, computer math, computer programming, computer science, dance, English, ethics, European history, fine arts, French, geometry, government/civics, health, history, journalism, Latin, mathematics, metalworking, music, physical education, physics, science, social studies, Spanish, statistics, theater arts, trigonometry, world history.

Graduation Requirements Algebra, analysis, arts and fine arts (art, music, dance, drama), biology, chemistry, computer science, English, English literature, European civilization, foreign language, languages, mathematics, physical education (includes health), physics, science, social studies (includes history).

Special Academic Programs Advanced Placement exam preparation; honors section; independent study; term-away projects; study abroad; academic accommodation for the gifted, the musically talented, and the artistically talented; special instructional classes for deaf students.

College Admission Counseling 63 students graduated in 2014; 59 went to college, including Bates College; Brown University; Rensselaer Polytechnic Institute; University of New Hampshire; University of Vermont; Worcester Polytechnic Institute. Other: 2 entered a postgraduate year, 2 had other specific plans. Mean SAT critical reading: 611, mean SAT math: 613, mean SAT writing: 627.

Student Life Upper grades have specified standards of dress, student council, honor system. Discipline rests equally with students and faculty.

Tuition and Aid Day student tuition: $31,380. Tuition installment plan (FACTS Tuition Payment Plan). Need-based scholarship grants, need-based loans available. In 2014–15, 37% of upper-school students received aid. Total amount of financial aid awarded in 2014–15: $2,200,000.

Admissions Traditional secondary-level entrance grade is 9. For fall 2014, 317 students applied for upper-level admission, 153 were accepted, 117 enrolled. SSAT required. Deadline for receipt of application materials: January 15. Application fee required: $50. Interview required.

Athletics Interscholastic: baseball (boys), basketball (b,g), cross-country running (b,g), dance (b,g), field hockey (g), golf (b,g), hockey (b,g), ice hockey (b,g), lacrosse (b,g), modern dance (b,g), soccer (b,g), softball (g), tennis (b,g); intramural: wilderness (g); coed interscholastic: ballet, crew, dance squad, dance team, diving, rowing; coed intramural: bicycling, Frisbee, hiking/backpacking, physical fitness, wilderness, yoga. 3 PE instructors, 4 coaches, 2 athletic trainers.

Computers Computers are regularly used in art, dance, English, foreign language, graphic design, history, humanities, independent study, library, mathematics, SAT preparation, science, social studies, theater arts, writing, yearbook classes. Computer network features include on-campus library services, Internet access, wireless campus network, Internet filtering or blocking technology. Campus intranet and student e-mail accounts are available to students. Students grades are available online. The school has a published electronic and media policy.

Contact Andrew R. Bishop, Director of Admission and Financial Aid. 207-384-2164 Ext. 2301. Fax: 207-384-3332. E-mail: abishop@berwickacademy.org. Website: www.berwickacademy.org

BESANT HILL SCHOOL

8585 Ojai Santa Paula Road
PO Box 850
Ojai, California 93024

Head of School: Mr. Randy Bertin

General Information Coeducational boarding and day college-preparatory and arts school; primarily serves students with learning disabilities, individuals with Attention Deficit Disorder, and dyslexic students. Grades 9–PG. Founded: 1946. Setting: small town. Nearest major city is Los Angeles. Students are housed in single-sex dormitories. 500-acre campus. 14 buildings on campus. Approved or accredited by Western Association of Schools and Colleges and California Department of Education. Member of National Association of Independent Schools and Secondary School Admission Test Board. Endowment: $1 million. Total enrollment: 100. Upper school average class size: 10. Upper school faculty-student ratio: 1:4. Upper School students typically attend 5 days per week. The average school day consists of 8 hours.

Upper School Student Profile Grade 9: 17 students (9 boys, 8 girls); Grade 10: 26 students (14 boys, 12 girls); Grade 11: 29 students (16 boys, 13 girls); Grade 12: 28 students (14 boys, 14 girls). 84% of students are boarding students. 40% are state residents. 12 states are represented in upper school student body. 40% are international students. International students from China, Germany, Japan, Mexico, Russian Federation, and Taiwan; 12 other countries represented in student body.

Faculty School total: 25. In upper school: 13 men, 12 women; 12 have advanced degrees; 24 reside on campus.

Subjects Offered Acting, addiction, adolescent issues, algebra, American history, art, art history, astronomy, biology, calculus, calculus-AP, ceramics, chemistry, computer science, digital art, drama, English, English as a foreign language, English language and composition-AP, English literature, English-AP, environmental science, ESL, ethics, expository writing, film, fine arts, geography, geometry, government/civics, history, mathematics, music, music history, music theory, music theory-AP, philosophy, photography, physical education, physics, psychology, scene study, science, social sciences, social studies, Spanish, theater, world history.

Graduation Requirements Arts and fine arts (art, music, dance, drama), English, foreign language, mathematics, physical education (includes health), science, social sciences, social studies (includes history).

Special Academic Programs 4 Advanced Placement exams for which test preparation is offered; honors section; independent study; study at local college for college credit; academic accommodation for the musically talented and the artistically talented; programs in English, mathematics, general development for dyslexic students; ESL (22 students enrolled).

College Admission Counseling 27 students graduated in 2015; 26 went to college, including San Diego State University; Sarah Lawrence College; University of California, Santa Barbara; University of California, Santa Cruz; University of Colorado Boulder. Other: 1 had other specific plans. Median SAT critical reading: 580, median SAT math: 550, median SAT writing: 500. 18% scored over 600 on SAT critical reading, 10% scored over 600 on SAT math, 15% scored over 600 on SAT writing.

Student Life Upper grades have student council, honor system. Discipline rests equally with students and faculty.

Summer Programs ESL programs offered; session focuses on ESL; held on campus; accepts boys and girls; open to students from other schools. 30 students usually enrolled. 2016 schedule: June 27 to August 1. Application deadline: May 1.

Tuition and Aid Day student tuition: $22,000; 7-day tuition and room/board: $47,950. Tuition installment plan (Academic Management Services Plan, Key Tuition Payment Plan). Tuition reduction for siblings, need-based scholarship grants available. In 2015–16, 25% of upper-school students received aid. Total amount of financial aid awarded in 2015–16: $450,000.

Admissions Traditional secondary-level entrance grade is 9. For fall 2015, 245 students applied for upper-level admission, 86 were accepted, 37 enrolled. Deadline for receipt of application materials: February 1. Application fee required: $75. Interview required.

Athletics Interscholastic: basketball (boys), soccer (b,g), volleyball (g); intramural: baseball (b), basketball (b), soccer (b,g), softball (b), wrestling (b); coed interscholastic:

aerobics/dance, backpacking, cross-country running, dance, fitness, fitness walking, Frisbee, golf, hiking/backpacking, modern dance, mountain biking, outdoor activities, outdoor adventure, outdoor education, outdoor skills, paddle tennis, physical training, ropes courses, skeet shooting; coed intramural: bicycling, billiards, climbing, jogging, kayaking, running, skateboarding, skiing (downhill), surfing, swimming and diving, table tennis, tennis, track and field, ultimate Frisbee, walking, wall climbing, weight lifting, wilderness, yoga. 2 coaches, 1 athletic trainer.

Computers Computers are regularly used in desktop publishing, graphic arts, graphic design, mathematics, media arts, publications, video film production classes. Computer network features include on-campus library services, online commercial services, Internet access, wireless campus network, Internet filtering or blocking technology. Campus intranet, student e-mail accounts, and computer access in designated common areas are available to students. Students grades are available online.

Contact Terra Furguiel, Associate Director of Admissions. 805-646-4343 Ext. 111. Fax: 805-646-4371. E-mail: tfurguiel@besanthill.org. Website: www.besanthill.org

BETH HAVEN CHRISTIAN SCHOOL

5515 Johnsontown Road
Louisville, Kentucky 40272

Head of School: Mrs. Diana Cahill

General Information Coeducational day college-preparatory and religious studies school, affiliated with Baptist Church. Grades K–12. Founded: 1971. Setting: suburban. 2-acre campus. 2 buildings on campus. Approved or accredited by Association of Christian Schools International and Kentucky Department of Education. Total enrollment: 178. Upper school average class size: 15. Upper school faculty-student ratio: 1:7. There are 175 required school days per year for Upper School students. Upper School students typically attend 5 days per week. The average school day consists of 7 hours.

Upper School Student Profile Grade 9: 12 students (6 boys, 6 girls); Grade 10: 16 students (12 boys, 4 girls); Grade 11: 16 students (7 boys, 9 girls); Grade 12: 14 students (9 boys, 5 girls). 55% of students are Baptist.

Faculty School total: 17. In upper school: 6 men, 3 women; 4 have advanced degrees.

Subjects Offered ACT preparation, algebra, American history, American literature, analytic geometry, Bible studies, biology, chemistry, computer applications, drama, dramatic arts, earth science, English, English composition, health, journalism, lab science, senior seminar, Spanish, trigonometry, weight fitness, world geography, world history, yearbook.

Graduation Requirements ACT preparation, algebra, American government, American history, American literature, analytic geometry, arts appreciation, Bible, biology, British literature, chemistry, earth science, economics, English, language, physical education (includes health), Spanish, world geography, world history.

Special Academic Programs Study at local college for college credit.

College Admission Counseling 12 students graduated in 2015; all went to college, including Bellarmine University; Jefferson Community and Technical College; University of Kentucky; University of Louisville. Median composite ACT: 20.

Student Life Upper grades have uniform requirement, student council, honor system. Discipline rests primarily with faculty. Attendance at religious services is required.

Summer Programs Remediation programs offered; held off campus; held at Way of Wisdom Tutoring Center; accepts boys and girls; not open to students from other schools. 2016 schedule: June 3 to August 16. Application deadline: June 3.

Tuition and Aid Day student tuition: $5200. Tuition installment plan (FACTS Tuition Payment Plan). Tuition reduction for siblings, need-based scholarship grants, two full-tuition memorial scholarships are awarded each year based on a combination of merit and need available. In 2015–16, 5% of upper-school students received aid. Total amount of financial aid awarded in 2015–16: $10,150.

Admissions Traditional secondary-level entrance grade is 9. California Achievement Test required. Deadline for receipt of application materials: none. Application fee required: $250. Interview required.

Athletics Interscholastic: baseball (boys), basketball (b,g), cheering (g), softball (g), volleyball (g); coed interscholastic: golf. 1 PE instructor, 6 coaches.

Computers Computers are regularly used in computer applications, journalism, yearbook classes. Computer network features include Internet access, Internet filtering or blocking technology. Computer access in designated common areas is available to students. Students grades are available online. The school has a published electronic and media policy.

Contact Ms. Jessica Piercey, Registrar/Secretary. 502-937-3516. Fax: 502-937-3364. E-mail: jpiercey@bethhaven.com. Website: www.bethhaven.com/

THE BIRCH WATHEN LENOX SCHOOL

210 East 77th Street
New York, New York 10075

Head of School: Mr. Frank J. Carnabuci III

General Information Coeducational day college-preparatory school. Grades K–12. Founded: 1916. Setting: urban. 1 building on campus. Approved or accredited by New York Department of Education. Member of National Association of Independent Schools. Endowment: $7.2 million. Total enrollment: 570. Upper school average class size: 17. Upper school faculty-student ratio: 1:15. Upper School students typically attend 5 days per week. The average school day consists of 7 hours.

Upper School Student Profile Grade 9: 46 students (24 boys, 22 girls); Grade 10: 45 students (25 boys, 20 girls); Grade 11: 46 students (23 boys, 23 girls); Grade 12: 48 students (22 boys, 26 girls).

Faculty School total: 120. In upper school: 30 men, 85 women; 115 have advanced degrees.

Subjects Offered Algebra, American history, American history-AP, American literature, American literature-AP, art, art history, biology, calculus, ceramics, chemistry, community service, computer math, computer science, creative writing, dance, drama, driver education, economics, English, English literature, environmental science, European history, expository writing, fine arts, French, geography, geology, geometry, government/civics, grammar, industrial arts, Japanese, journalism, mathematics, music, philosophy, photography, physical education, physics, science, Shakespeare, social studies, Spanish, speech, swimming, theater, trigonometry, typing, world history, writing.

Graduation Requirements 20th century world history, arts and fine arts (art, music, dance, drama), computer science, English, foreign language, mathematics, physical education (includes health), science, social studies (includes history). Community service is required.

Special Academic Programs Advanced Placement exam preparation; honors section; independent study; study abroad; academic accommodation for the gifted, the musically talented, and the artistically talented.

College Admission Counseling 44 students graduated in 2015; all went to college, including Bowdoin College; Cornell University; Princeton University; University of Pennsylvania; Vanderbilt University; Wesleyan University. Mean SAT critical reading: 680, mean SAT math: 700, mean SAT writing: 700.

Student Life Upper grades have uniform requirement, student council, honor system. Discipline rests equally with students and faculty.

Summer Programs Enrichment programs offered; session focuses on math and science; not open to students from other schools.

Tuition and Aid Day student tuition: $40,898. Tuition installment plan (Key Tuition Payment Plan, monthly payment plans, individually arranged payment plans). Merit scholarship grants, need-based scholarship grants available. In 2015–16, 18% of upper-school students received aid. Total amount of financial aid awarded in 2015–16: $1,500,000.

Admissions Traditional secondary-level entrance grade is 9. For fall 2015, 200 students applied for upper-level admission, 85 were accepted, 62 enrolled. ERB, ISEE, Math Placement Exam or writing sample required. Deadline for receipt of application materials: none. Application fee required: $50. On-campus interview required.

Athletics Interscholastic: baseball (boys), basketball (b,g), cross-country running (b,g), field hockey (g), hockey (b), ice hockey (b), lacrosse (b), soccer (b,g), softball (g), squash (b,g), swimming and diving (b,g), tennis (b,g), track and field (b,g), volleyball (g); intramural: aerobics (b,g), badminton (g), baseball (b), basketball (b,g), dance (b), ice hockey (b), indoor soccer (b), running (b,g), skiing (downhill) (b,g), soccer (b,g), softball (g), swimming and diving (b,g), tennis (b,g), track and field (b,g), volleyball (b,g); coed interscholastic: cross-country running, Frisbee, golf, ice hockey, indoor track & field, lacrosse, squash; coed intramural: bicycling, dance, golf, gymnastics, indoor track & field, skiing (cross-country), skiing (downhill). 5 PE instructors, 8 coaches.

Computers Computers are regularly used in all academic classes. Computer network features include on-campus library services, Internet access, wireless campus network, MOBY, Smartboard. Student e-mail accounts are available to students.

Contact Billie Williams, Admissions Coordinator. 212-861-0404. Fax: 212-879-3388. E-mail: bwilliams@bwl.org. Website: www.bwl.org

BISHOP BRADY HIGH SCHOOL

25 Columbus Avenue
Concord, New Hampshire 03301

Head of School: Ms. Andrea Elliot

General Information Coeducational day college-preparatory school, affiliated with Roman Catholic Church. Grades 9–12. Founded: 1963. Setting: suburban. 8-acre campus. 1 building on campus. Approved or accredited by National Catholic Education Association, New England Association of Schools and Colleges, and New Hampshire Department of Education. Endowment: $100,000. Total enrollment: 349. Upper school average class size: 17. Upper school faculty-student ratio: 1:16. There are 179 required school days per year for Upper School students. Upper School students typically attend 5 days per week. The average school day consists of 6 hours and 30 minutes.

Upper School Student Profile Grade 9: 73 students (30 boys, 43 girls); Grade 10: 87 students (40 boys, 47 girls); Grade 11: 101 students (63 boys, 38 girls); Grade 12: 88 students (48 boys, 40 girls). 55% of students are Roman Catholic.

Faculty School total: 32. In upper school: 13 men, 19 women; 25 have advanced degrees.

Subjects Offered Advanced chemistry, advanced math, Advanced Placement courses, algebra, anatomy and physiology, art appreciation, arts, biology, biology-AP, calculus-AP, career/college preparation, chemistry, chemistry-AP, Christian scripture, civics, college awareness, college counseling, computer education, computer programming, conceptual physics, drama, engineering, English, English literature-AP,

English-AP, ethics, film studies, forensics, French-AP, freshman seminar, geometry, guidance, health education, history, history-AP, honors English, Latin, moral theology, music appreciation, musical theater, physical education, physics-AP, pre calculus, probability and statistics, psychology, religious studies, research and reference, SAT preparation, social justice, Spanish-AP, theology, trigonometry, U.S. history-AP, world religions, writing.

Graduation Requirements Algebra, American literature, arts and fine arts (art, music, dance, drama), biology, chemistry, civics, computer education, economics, English, geometry, languages, literature, mathematics, physical education (includes health), science, theology, U.S. history, wellness, world history, 100 hours of community service.

Special Academic Programs 10 Advanced Placement exams for which test preparation is offered; honors section; independent study; study at local college for college credit; academic accommodation for the gifted; special instructional classes for deaf students; ESL (34 students enrolled).

College Admission Counseling 78 students graduated in 2015; 75 went to college, including Merrimack College; Plymouth State University; Purdue University; Saint Anselm College; University of New Hampshire; University of Vermont. Other: 2 went to work, 1 entered a postgraduate year. Mean SAT critical reading: 542, mean SAT math: 564, mean SAT writing: 542, mean composite ACT: 24. 30% scored over 600 on SAT critical reading, 30% scored over 600 on SAT math.

Student Life Upper grades have specified standards of dress, student council, honor system. Discipline rests primarily with faculty. Attendance at religious services is required.

Summer Programs Remediation, enrichment, advancement, ESL, sports, art/fine arts, computer instruction programs offered; session focuses on SAT prep, sports training, high school transition; held on campus; accepts boys and girls; open to students from other schools. 75 students usually enrolled. 2016 schedule: July 10 to August 15.

Tuition and Aid Day student tuition: $11,565. Tuition installment plan (Insured Tuition Payment Plan, FACTS Tuition Payment Plan, monthly payment plans, individually arranged payment plans). Tuition reduction for siblings, merit scholarship grants, need-based scholarship grants available. In 2015–16, 34% of upper-school students received aid; total upper-school merit-scholarship money awarded: $4000. Total amount of financial aid awarded in 2015–16: $550,000.

Admissions Traditional secondary-level entrance grade is 9. For fall 2015, 179 students applied for upper-level admission, 167 were accepted, 101 enrolled. SSAT, STS Examination or TOEFL or SLEP required. Deadline for receipt of application materials: none. Application fee required: $45. Interview required.

Athletics Interscholastic: alpine skiing (boys, girls), baseball (b), basketball (b,g), cross-country running (b,g), field hockey (g), fishing (b), football (b), golf (b,g), ice hockey (b,g), indoor track & field (b,g), lacrosse (b,g), nordic skiing (b,g), skiing (cross-country) (b,g), skiing (downhill) (b,g), soccer (b,g), softball (g), swimming and diving (b,g), tennis (b,g), track and field (b,g); coed interscholastic: equestrian sports, juggling, physical fitness; coed intramural: crew, rock climbing, snowboarding, strength & conditioning, table tennis, volleyball, weight lifting, weight training. 1 PE instructor.

Computers Computers are regularly used in business applications, college planning, computer applications, journalism, literary magazine, newspaper classes. Computer network features include on-campus library services, online commercial services, Internet access, wireless campus network, Internet filtering or blocking technology. Student e-mail accounts and computer access in designated common areas are available to students. Students grades are available online. The school has a published electronic and media policy.

Contact Mrs. Lonna J. Abbott, Director of Admissions and Enrollment. 603-224-7419. Fax: 603-228-6664. E-mail: labbott@bishopbrady.edu. Website: www.bishopbrady.edu

BISHOP BROSSART HIGH SCHOOL

4 Grove Street
Alexandria, Kentucky 41001

Head of School: Mr. Dan Ridder

General Information Coeducational day college-preparatory school, affiliated with Roman Catholic Church. Grades 9–12. Founded: 1950. Setting: small town. Nearest major city is Cincinnati, OH. 1 building on campus. Approved or accredited by National Catholic Education Association, Southern Association of Colleges and Schools, and Kentucky Department of Education. Total enrollment: 382. Upper school average class size: 25. Upper school faculty-student ratio: 1:16. There are 177 required school days per year for Upper School students. Upper School students typically attend 5 days per week. The average school day consists of 6 hours and 10 minutes.

Upper School Student Profile Grade 9: 71 students (44 boys, 27 girls); Grade 10: 55 students (25 boys, 30 girls); Grade 11: 65 students (25 boys, 40 girls); Grade 12: 86 students (54 boys, 32 girls). 98% of students are Roman Catholic.

Faculty School total: 27. In upper school: 11 men, 16 women; 25 have advanced degrees.

Subjects Offered Advanced Placement courses, anatomy, art, arts appreciation, biology, business, calculus-AP, chemistry, chorus, communication arts, computer programming, computer technologies, discrete mathematics, earth science, economics, English, English language-AP, English literature-AP, English-AP, European history-AP, film, finance, foreign language, French, French language-AP, French-AP, geometry, global issues, government, health, history-AP, instrumental music, introduction to technology, physics, religion, science, social studies, Spanish, Spanish-AP, theater, U.S. history, U.S. history-AP.

Special Academic Programs Honors section.

College Admission Counseling 108 students graduated in 2015; 101 went to college, including Northern Kentucky University; University of Cincinnati; University of Kentucky; University of Louisville. Other: 7 had other specific plans.

Student Life Upper grades have uniform requirement, student council, honor system. Discipline rests primarily with faculty. Attendance at religious services is required.

Tuition and Aid Day student tuition: $6290. Tuition installment plan (FACTS Tuition Payment Plan, monthly payment plans, individually arranged payment plans). Tuition reduction for siblings, merit scholarship grants, need-based scholarship grants available.

Admissions Traditional secondary-level entrance grade is 9. High School Placement Test required. Application fee required: $100.

Athletics Interscholastic: baseball (boys), basketball (b,g), bowling (b,g), cheering (g), dance team (g), golf (b,g), indoor track & field (b,g), soccer (b,g), track and field (b,g), volleyball (g). 5 coaches.

Computers Computers are regularly used in all academic classes. Computer network features include Internet access. The school has a published electronic and media policy.

Contact Admissions. 859-635-2108. Fax: 859-635-2135. E-mail: info@bishopbrossart.org. Website: bishopbrossart.org

BISHOP CONNOLLY HIGH SCHOOL

373 Elsbree Street
Fall River, Massachusetts 02720

Head of School: Mr. Christopher Myron

General Information Coeducational day college-preparatory and religious studies school, affiliated with Roman Catholic Church. Grades 9–12. Founded: 1966. Setting: suburban. 72-acre campus. 1 building on campus. Approved or accredited by New England Association of Schools and Colleges and Massachusetts Department of Education. Total enrollment: 280. Upper school average class size: 16. Upper school faculty-student ratio: 1:16. There are 185 required school days per year for Upper School students. Upper School students typically attend 5 days per week. The average school day consists of 6 hours and 30 minutes.

Upper School Student Profile 95% of students are Roman Catholic.

Faculty School total: 26. In upper school: 13 men, 13 women; 22 have advanced degrees.

Subjects Offered Advanced Placement courses, algebra, American literature, American studies, anatomy and physiology, art, art history, Bible studies, biology, biology-AP, British literature, British literature (honors), calculus, calculus-AP, campus ministry, chemistry, chemistry-AP, choir, chorus, community service, computer programming, creative writing, desktop publishing, drama, English, English literature, English-AP, environmental science, European history-AP, French, French-AP, geometry, health, history, honors algebra, honors English, honors geometry, honors U.S. history, honors world history, human biology, instrumental music, keyboarding, math analysis, mathematics, music, music history, music theory, physical education, physics, Portuguese, psychology, religion, science, social studies, Spanish, theology, trigonometry, U.S. history-AP, world history, world literature.

Graduation Requirements English, foreign language, mathematics, religion (includes Bible studies and theology), science, social studies (includes history). Community service is required.

Special Academic Programs Advanced Placement exam preparation; honors section; independent study; study at local college for college credit.

College Admission Counseling 72 students graduated in 2015; 70 went to college, including Bridgewater State University; Northeastern University; Providence College; Quinnipiac University; University of Massachusetts Dartmouth; University of Rhode Island. Other: 2 entered military service. Mean SAT critical reading: 511, mean SAT math: 508, mean SAT writing: 522.

Student Life Upper grades have uniform requirement, student council, honor system. Discipline rests primarily with faculty. Attendance at religious services is required.

Tuition and Aid Day student tuition: $8900. Tuition installment plan (FACTS Tuition Payment Plan, monthly payment plans). Merit scholarship grants, need-based scholarship grants available.

Admissions Traditional secondary-level entrance grade is 9. High School Placement Test required. Deadline for receipt of application materials: none. No application fee required. Interview recommended.

Athletics Interscholastic: baseball (boys), basketball (b,g), cheering (g), cross-country running (b,g), field hockey (g), football (b), ice hockey (b), lacrosse (b), soccer (b,g), softball (g), tennis (b,g), track and field (b,g), volleyball (g), winter (indoor) track (b,g); intramural: field hockey (g); coed interscholastic: golf, indoor soccer, indoor track & field. 1 PE instructor, 18 coaches, 1 athletic trainer.

Computers Computers are regularly used in all classes. Computer network features include online commercial services, Internet access, wireless campus network, Internet filtering or blocking technology. Computer access in designated common areas is available to students. The school has a published electronic and media policy.

Contact Mr. Anthony C. Ciampanelli, Director of Admissions/Alumni. 508-676-1071 Ext. 333. Fax: 508-676-8594. E-mail: aciampanelli@bchs.dfrcs.org. Website: www.bishopconnolly.com

BISHOP DENIS J. O'CONNELL HIGH SCHOOL

6600 Little Falls Road
Arlington, Virginia 22213

Head of School: Dr. Joseph Vorbach III

General Information Coeducational day college-preparatory, arts, business, religious studies, bilingual studies, and technology school, affiliated with Roman Catholic Church. Grades 9–12. Founded: 1957. Setting: suburban. Nearest major city is Washington, DC. 28-acre campus. 1 building on campus. Approved or accredited by National Catholic Education Association, Southern Association of Colleges and Schools, Southern Association of Independent Schools, and Virginia Department of Education. Member of Secondary School Admission Test Board. Total enrollment: 1,100. Upper school average class size: 17. Upper school faculty-student ratio: 1:12. There are 180 required school days per year for Upper School students. Upper School students typically attend 5 days per week. The average school day consists of 7 hours and 15 minutes.

Upper School Student Profile 80% of students are Roman Catholic.

Faculty School total: 110. In upper school: 71 have advanced degrees.

Subjects Offered Accounting, African American history, African-American history, algebra, American history, American history-AP, American literature, analysis, art, art history, athletic training, Basic programming, Bible studies, biology, biology-AP, business, business technology, calculus, calculus-AP, chemistry, chemistry-AP, choir, choral music, chorus, church history, comparative government and politics-AP, comparative political systems-AP, computer graphics, computer multimedia, computer music, computer programming, computer science, computer science-AP, computer skills, creative writing, digital art, dramatic arts, driver education, earth science, East Asian history, ecology, economics, economics-AP, English, English language-AP, English literature, English literature-AP, environmental science-AP, European history, European history-AP, fine arts, forensics, French, French language-AP, French-AP, geography, geometry, German, German-AP, government and politics-AP, government-AP, government/civics, guitar, health, history, history of the Catholic Church, honors English, honors geometry, honors U.S. history, honors world history, introduction to theater, Italian, jazz band, journalism, Latin, Latin-AP, literature-AP, macro/microeconomics-AP, macroeconomics-AP, marketing, mathematics, media arts, microeconomics-AP, modern European history-AP, music, music theory-AP, music-AP, New Testament, newspaper, orchestra, painting, personal finance, personal fitness, photo shop, photography, photojournalism, physical education, physical fitness, physics, physics-AP, piano, play production, pre-calculus, probability, psychology, psychology-AP, public speaking, religion, remedial study skills, science, science research, social sciences, social studies, sociology, Spanish, Spanish language-AP, Spanish literature-AP, Spanish-AP, speech, speech and debate, sports conditioning, sports psychology, statistics, statistics-AP, student government, studio art-AP, theater arts, theater design and production, theology, trigonometry, U.S. and Virginia government-AP, U.S. and Virginia history, U.S. government, U.S. government and politics-AP, U.S. history, U.S. history-AP, United States government-AP, video film production, voice ensemble, Web site design, weight training, weightlifting, world history, world literature.

Graduation Requirements Arts and fine arts (art, music, dance, drama), computer science, English, foreign language, mathematics, physical education (includes health), religion (includes Bible studies and theology), science, social sciences, social studies (includes history), community service program incorporated into graduation requirements.

Special Academic Programs 26 Advanced Placement exams for which test preparation is offered; honors section; independent study; study at local college for college credit; academic accommodation for the gifted; remedial math; programs in general development for dyslexic students; ESL (20 students enrolled).

College Admission Counseling 310 students graduated in 2015; 306 went to college, including George Mason University; James Madison University; The College of William and Mary; University of Virginia; Virginia Commonwealth University; Virginia Polytechnic Institute and State University. Other: 4 entered military service. Median SAT critical reading: 560, median SAT math: 560, median SAT writing: 555, median combined SAT: 1675, median composite ACT: 29.

Student Life Upper grades have uniform requirement, student council, honor system. Discipline rests equally with students and faculty. Attendance at religious services is required.

Summer Programs Remediation, enrichment, advancement, sports, art/fine arts, computer instruction programs offered; held on campus; accepts boys and girls; open to students from other schools. 200 students usually enrolled. 2016 schedule: June 15 to August 15. Application deadline: none.

Tuition and Aid Day student tuition: $13,995–$15,995. Tuition installment plan (FACTS Tuition Payment Plan). Tuition reduction for siblings, merit scholarship grants, need-based scholarship grants, scholarship competition only for eighth graders currently enrolled in a Diocese of Arlington Catholic school available. In 2015–16, 30% of upper-school students received aid; total upper-school merit-scholarship money awarded: $50,000. Total amount of financial aid awarded in 2015–16: $2,100,000.

Admissions High School Placement Test required. Deadline for receipt of application materials: January 15. Application fee required: $50.

Athletics Interscholastic: baseball (boys), basketball (b,g), crew (b,g), cross-country running (b,g), dance team (g), diving (b,g), field hockey (g), football (b), ice hockey (b), lacrosse (b,g), soccer (b,g), softball (g), swimming and diving (b,g), tennis (b,g), track and field (b,g), volleyball (g), weight lifting (b,g), weight training (b,g), winter (indoor) track (b,g), wrestling (b); intramural: basketball (b,g), weight lifting (b,g); coed interscholastic: golf, ice hockey, sailing; coed intramural: crew, flag football, softball, ultimate Frisbee, volleyball. 7 PE instructors, 7 coaches, 1 athletic trainer.

Computers Computers are regularly used in accounting, all academic, art, business, computer applications, English, foreign language, health, history, mathematics, science, social sciences classes. Computer network features include on-campus library services, online commercial services, Internet access, wireless campus network, Internet filtering or blocking technology. Campus intranet, student e-mail accounts, and computer access in designated common areas are available to students. Students grades are available online. The school has a published electronic and media policy.

Contact Mr. Michael Cresson, Director of Admissions. 703-237-1433. Fax: 703-241-4297. E-mail: mcresson@bishopoconnell.org. Website: www.bishopoconnell.org

BISHOP EUSTACE PREPARATORY SCHOOL

5552 Route 70
Pennsauken, New Jersey 08109-4798

Head of School: Br. James Beamesderfer, SAC

General Information Coeducational day college-preparatory, arts, religious studies, and technology school, affiliated with Roman Catholic Church. Grades 9–12. Founded: 1954. Setting: suburban. Nearest major city is Philadelphia, PA. 32-acre campus. 7 buildings on campus. Approved or accredited by Middle States Association of Colleges and Schools and New Jersey Department of Education. Member of National Association of Independent Schools. Endowment: $4.8 million. Total enrollment: 675. Upper school average class size: 19. Upper school faculty-student ratio: 1:12. There are 165 required school days per year for Upper School students. Upper School students typically attend 5 days per week. The average school day consists of 6 hours and 20 minutes.

Upper School Student Profile 88% of students are Roman Catholic.

Faculty School total: 54. In upper school: 25 men, 29 women; 43 have advanced degrees.

Subjects Offered Advanced chemistry, advanced computer applications, Advanced Placement courses, algebra, American history, American history-AP, American literature, anatomy, anatomy and physiology, applied music, art and culture, art history, band, Bible studies, biology, biology-AP, British literature, British literature (honors), calculus, calculus-AP, campus ministry, career education, career exploration, career/college preparation, chemistry, chemistry-AP, choir, Christian doctrine, Christian education, Christian ethics, Christian scripture, clinical chemistry, college counseling, college placement, college planning, comparative religion, computer education, computer science, creative writing, driver education, economics and history, electives, English, English literature, English literature and composition-AP, environmental science, environmental science-AP, ethics, European history-AP, film, film and literature, fine arts, French, French as a second language, gender issues, genetics, geometry, German, government and politics-AP, government/civics, grammar, health, history, honors algebra, honors English, honors geometry, honors U.S. history, honors world history, instrumental music, journalism, Latin, law, law studies, macroeconomics-AP, mathematics, mathematics-AP, music, music composition, music history, music theory, music theory-AP, physical education, physical science, physics, physics-AP, physiology, pre-calculus, psychology, psychology-AP, science, sex education, social studies, sociology, Spanish, Spanish-AP, statistics-AP, theology, trigonometry, U.S. government and politics-AP, U.S. history, U.S. history-AP, vocal music, women's studies, world affairs, world history, world religions.

Graduation Requirements Art history, arts and fine arts (art, music, dance, drama), career exploration, computer science, English, foreign language, mathematics, physical education (includes health), religion (includes Bible studies and theology), science, social studies (includes history). Community service is required.

Special Academic Programs 17 Advanced Placement exams for which test preparation is offered; honors section; independent study; study at local college for college credit; academic accommodation for the gifted and the musically talented.

College Admission Counseling 160 students graduated in 2015; 156 went to college, including Drexel University; Penn State University Park; Rutgers, The State University of New Jersey, New Brunswick; Saint Joseph's University; University of Delaware; Villanova University. Other: 1 entered a postgraduate year, 3 had other specific plans. Mean SAT critical reading: 564, mean SAT math: 574, mean SAT writing: 566. 33.5% scored over 600 on SAT critical reading, 37.5% scored over 600 on SAT math, 35.5% scored over 600 on SAT writing.

Student Life Upper grades have uniform requirement, student council, honor system. Discipline rests primarily with faculty. Attendance at religious services is required.

Summer Programs Enrichment, advancement, sports programs offered; session focuses on student recruitment and enrichment for middle school students; advancement in math for current students; held on campus; accepts boys and girls; open to students from other schools. 150 students usually enrolled. 2016 schedule: June 20 to July 28. Application deadline: June 20.

Tuition and Aid Day student tuition: $16,400. Tuition installment plan (FACTS Tuition Payment Plan). Merit scholarship grants, need-based scholarship grants available. In 2015–16, 35% of upper-school students received aid; total upper-school merit-scholarship money awarded: $295,200. Total amount of financial aid awarded in 2015–16: $800,000.

Admissions Traditional secondary-level entrance grade is 9. For fall 2015, 400 students applied for upper-level admission, 335 were accepted, 170 enrolled. High School Placement Test, math and English placement tests or placement test required. Deadline for receipt of application materials: none. Application fee required: $60.

Athletics Interscholastic: baseball (boys), basketball (b,g), bowling (b,g), cheering (g), crew (b,g), cross-country running (b,g), field hockey (g), football (b), golf (b,g), ice hockey (b), indoor track (b,g), indoor track & field (b,g), lacrosse (b,g), running (b,g), soccer (b,g), softball (g), swimming and diving (b,g), tennis (b,g), track and field (b,g); coed interscholastic: aquatics, diving, golf; coed intramural: ultimate Frisbee. 3 PE instructors, 59 coaches, 1 athletic trainer.

Computers Computers are regularly used in all academic classes. Computer network features include on-campus library services, online commercial services, Internet access, wireless campus network, Internet filtering or blocking technology. Campus intranet and computer access in designated common areas are available to students. Students grades are available online. The school has a published electronic and media policy.

Contact Mr. Nicholas Italiano, Dean of Admissions. 856-662-2160 Ext. 240. Fax: 856-662-0025. E-mail: admissions@eustace.org. Website: www.eustace.org

BISHOP FENWICK HIGH SCHOOL

4855 State Route 122
Franklin, Ohio 45005

Head of School: Mr. Andrew J. Barczak

General Information Coeducational day college-preparatory, arts, religious studies, technology, and engineering school, affiliated with Roman Catholic Church. Grades 9–12. Founded: 1952. Setting: suburban. Nearest major city is Cincinnati. 66-acre campus. 1 building on campus. Approved or accredited by National Catholic Education Association, North Central Association of Colleges and Schools, Ohio Catholic Schools Accreditation Association (OCSAA), and Ohio Department of Education. Upper school average class size: 24. Upper school faculty-student ratio: 1:14. There are 184 required school days per year for Upper School students. Upper School students typically attend 5 days per week. The average school day consists of 6 hours and 35 minutes.

Upper School Student Profile Grade 9: 130 students (78 boys, 52 girls); Grade 10: 142 students (73 boys, 69 girls); Grade 11: 144 students (77 boys, 67 girls); Grade 12: 123 students (68 boys, 55 girls). 85% of students are Roman Catholic.

Faculty School total: 38. In upper school: 17 men, 21 women; 23 have advanced degrees.

Subjects Offered Accounting, ACT preparation, algebra, American democracy, art, art-AP, athletic training, biology, botany, calculus-AP, career planning, cell biology, chemistry, choir, chorus, church history, college admission preparation, computer graphics, computer programming, concert band, creative writing, economics, engineering, English, English-AP, ensembles, film and literature, fine arts, French, functions, general business, geometry, government, government/civics-AP, health, honors algebra, honors English, honors geometry, integrated mathematics, jazz band, Latin, Latin-AP, leadership, marching band, mathematics, multimedia, music appreciation, mythology, physical education, physical science, physics, physiology, portfolio art, pre-algebra, psychology, publications, religion, science, social studies, Spanish, statistics, study skills, technology, theater, theater arts, trigonometry, U.S. history, U.S. history-AP, Web site design, world geography, world history, writing, yearbook, zoology.

Graduation Requirements Arts and fine arts (art, music, dance, drama), English, foreign language, mathematics, physical education (includes health), religion (includes Bible studies and theology), science, social studies (includes history), technology, community service, retreats, must pass the Ohio Graduation Test.

Special Academic Programs Advanced Placement exam preparation; honors section; study at local college for college credit; academic accommodation for the gifted.

College Admission Counseling 150 students graduated in 2014; 148 went to college, including Miami University; Ohio University; The Ohio State University; University of Cincinnati; University of Dayton; Xavier University. Other: 1 went to work, 1 entered military service. Median SAT critical reading: 575, median SAT math: 580, median SAT writing: 556, median combined SAT: 1711, median composite ACT: 24.

Student Life Upper grades have uniform requirement, student council, honor system. Discipline rests primarily with faculty. Attendance at religious services is required.

Tuition and Aid Day student tuition: $9100. Tuition installment plan (FACTS Tuition Payment Plan). Tuition reduction for siblings, merit scholarship grants, need-based scholarship grants, paying campus jobs available. In 2014–15, 19% of upper-school students received aid.

Admissions Traditional secondary-level entrance grade is 9. High School Placement Test required. Deadline for receipt of application materials: November 24. No application fee required.

Athletics Interscholastic: baseball (boys), basketball (b,g), bowling (b,g), cheering (g), cross-country running (b,g), dance team (g), football (b), golf (b,g), lacrosse (b,g), soccer (b,g), softball (g), tennis (b,g), volleyball (b,g), weight training (b,g), wrestling (b); intramural: basketball (b), weight training (b,g); coed interscholastic: in-line hockey, roller hockey, swimming and diving, track and field; coed intramural: freestyle skiing, paint ball, skiing (downhill), snowboarding, strength & conditioning. 1 PE instructor, 62 coaches, 2 athletic trainers.

Computers Computers are regularly used in career exploration, career technology, college planning, engineering, graphic arts, graphic design, introduction to technology, multimedia, photography, publications, technology, video film production, Web site design, yearbook classes. Computer network features include on-campus library services, Internet access, wireless campus network, Internet filtering or blocking technology, laptop carts, iPad cart, Kindles. Campus intranet and computer access in designated common areas are available to students. Students grades are available online. The school has a published electronic and media policy.

Contact Mrs. Betty Turvy, Director of Admissions. 513-428-0525. Fax: 513-727-1501. E-mail: bturvy@fenwickfalcons.org. Website: www.fenwickfalcons.org

BISHOP GUERTIN HIGH SCHOOL

194 Lund Road
Nashua, New Hampshire 03060-4398

Head of School: Mrs. Linda Brodeur

General Information Coeducational day college-preparatory, arts, business, religious studies, and technology school, affiliated with Roman Catholic Church. Grades 9–12. Founded: 1963. Setting: suburban. Nearest major city is Boston, MA. 1 building on campus. Approved or accredited by National Catholic Education Association, New England Association of Schools and Colleges, and New Hampshire Department of Education. Total enrollment: 800. Upper school average class size: 19. Upper school faculty-student ratio: 1:14. There are 180 required school days per year for Upper School students. Upper School students typically attend 5 days per week. The average school day consists of 6 hours and 30 minutes.

Upper School Student Profile 70% of students are Roman Catholic.

Faculty School total: 72.

Subjects Offered 20th century history, 20th century world history, acting, advanced biology, advanced chemistry, advanced computer applications, advanced math, Advanced Placement courses, algebra, American history-AP, American literature, American literature-AP, analysis and differential calculus, anatomy and physiology, ancient world history, art appreciation, art history, band, Bible studies, biology, biology-AP, British history, British literature, British literature (honors), business applications, business law, calculus, calculus-AP, campus ministry, career/college preparation, chemistry, chemistry-AP, chorus, Christian and Hebrew scripture, Christian doctrine, Christian education, Christian ethics, Christianity, church history, civics, college admission preparation, college counseling, college writing, community service, comparative government and politics, comparative government and politics-AP, comparative religion, computer applications, computer art, computer education, computer literacy, computer multimedia, computer processing, computer programming, computer programming-AP, computer science, computer science-AP, computer technologies, computer-aided design, concert band, concert choir, constitutional history of U.S., consumer economics, contemporary history, CPR, creative writing, death and loss, debate, desktop publishing, digital photography, discrete mathematics, dramatic arts, drawing, driver education, economics, emergency medicine, English, English composition, English literature, English literature and composition-AP, English literature-AP, English-AP, environmental science, environmental science-AP, ethics, European history, film studies, fine arts, foreign language, French, French-AP, geography, geometry, government and politics-AP, government/civics, grammar, Greek, health, health and wellness, health education, health enhancement, healthful living, history, Holocaust and other genocides, honors geometry, honors U.S. history, honors world history, human anatomy, human biology, human sexuality, instrumental music, introduction to literature, jazz band, journalism, Latin, Latin-AP, law, literary magazine, marching band, mechanics of writing, moral reasoning, moral theology, music, music appreciation, philosophy, photography, physical education, physics, physics-AP, pre-calculus, psychology, religion, religious studies, science, senior seminar, Shakespeare, social justice, social studies, Spanish, Spanish-AP, statistics, studio art, studio art-AP, The 20th Century, theater, trigonometry, U.S. government and politics, U.S. government and politics-AP, U.S. history, U.S. history-AP, U.S. literature, world history, world literature, yearbook.

Graduation Requirements Arts and fine arts (art, music, dance, drama), computer science, English, foreign language, mathematics, physical education (includes health), religion (includes Bible studies and theology), science, social studies (includes history).

Special Academic Programs 16 Advanced Placement exams for which test preparation is offered; honors section; study at local college for college credit; academic accommodation for the gifted.

College Admission Counseling 209 students graduated in 2015; 208 went to college, including Boston College; College of the Holy Cross; Dartmouth College; Saint Anselm College; University of Massachusetts Amherst; University of New Hampshire. Other: 1 entered military service. Median combined SAT: 1720, median composite ACT: 26.

Student Life Upper grades have uniform requirement, student council, honor system. Discipline rests primarily with faculty. Attendance at religious services is required.

Summer Programs Remediation, enrichment, advancement programs offered; held on campus; accepts boys and girls; not open to students from other schools. 40 students usually enrolled. 2016 schedule: July 1 to July 31. Application deadline: May 1.

Tuition and Aid Day student tuition: $13,495. Tuition installment plan (FACTS Tuition Payment Plan, individually arranged payment plans). Merit scholarship grants, need-based scholarship grants available. In 2015–16, 21% of upper-school students received aid. Total amount of financial aid awarded in 2015–16: $600,000.

Admissions Traditional secondary-level entrance grade is 9. High School Placement Test required. Deadline for receipt of application materials: January 15. Application fee required: $30.

Athletics Interscholastic: baseball (boys), basketball (b,g), cheering (b,g), cross-country running (b,g), field hockey (g), football (b), gymnastics (g), hockey (b,g), ice hockey (b,g), lacrosse (b,g), skiing (downhill) (b,g), soccer (b,g), softball (g), swimming and diving (b,g), tennis (b,g), track and field (b,g), volleyball (b,g), wrestling (b); intramural: crew (b,g); coed interscholastic: alpine skiing, aquatics, bowling, cheering, fishing, golf, ice hockey, indoor track, nordic skiing, skiing (downhill); coed intramural: aerobics/dance, basketball, bowling, crew, dance, fishing, fly fishing, freestyle skiing, golf, mountain biking, outdoor education, physical fitness, skiing (downhill), strength & conditioning, swimming and diving, table tennis, tennis, ultimate Frisbee, volleyball, weight lifting, weight training. 4 PE instructors, 55 coaches, 2 athletic trainers.

Computers Computers are regularly used in career education, career exploration, career technology, college planning, data processing, desktop publishing, independent study, information technology, introduction to technology, library, library science, library skills, literary magazine, multimedia, music, news writing, newspaper, programming, publications, publishing, research skills, stock market, technology, Web site design, word processing, yearbook classes. Computer network features include on-campus library services, online commercial services, Internet access, wireless campus network, Internet filtering or blocking technology. Student e-mail accounts and computer access in designated common areas are available to students. Students grades are available online. The school has a published electronic and media policy.

Contact Mrs. Joni McCabe, Admissions Coordinator. 603-889-4107 Ext. 4304. Fax: 603-889-0701. E-mail: admit@bghs.org. Website: www.bghs.org

BISHOP HENDRICKEN HIGH SCHOOL

2615 Warwick Avenue
Warwick, Rhode Island 02889

Head of School: Mr. John A. Jackson

General Information Boys' day college-preparatory, arts, business, religious studies, and technology school, affiliated with Roman Catholic Church. Grades 9–12. Founded: 1959. Setting: suburban. Nearest major city is Providence. 34-acre campus. 1 building on campus. Approved or accredited by National Catholic Education Association, New England Association of Schools and Colleges, and Rhode Island Department of Education. Endowment: $1.2 million. Total enrollment: 948. Upper school average class size: 24. Upper school faculty-student ratio: 1:12. There are 180 required school days per year for Upper School students. Upper School students typically attend 5 days per week. The average school day consists of 6 hours and 20 minutes.

Upper School Student Profile Grade 9: 226 students (226 boys); Grade 10: 225 students (225 boys); Grade 11: 236 students (236 boys); Grade 12: 244 students (244 boys). 78% of students are Roman Catholic.

Faculty School total: 70. In upper school: 38 men, 32 women; 32 have advanced degrees.

Subjects Offered Accounting, advanced biology, advanced chemistry, advanced computer applications, advanced math, Advanced Placement courses, algebra, American history, American history-AP, American literature, American literature-AP, analysis, art, Basic programming, biochemistry, biology, biology-AP, British literature, British literature (honors), British literature-AP, business, calculus, calculus-AP, cell biology, chemistry, chemistry-AP, college writing, computer programming, computer programming-AP, computer-aided design, criminology, drama, drama performance, drama workshop, drawing, drawing and design, economics, English, English language and composition-AP, English literature, English literature and composition-AP, European history, European history-AP, film and new technologies, filmmaking, finance, fine arts, foreign language, French, French language-AP, French-AP, geometry, graphic arts, graphic design, health, history of rock and roll, history-AP, honors algebra, honors English, honors geometry, honors U.S. history, honors world history, instrumental music, introduction to technology, introduction to theater, Italian, jazz, jazz ensemble, linear algebra, media arts, music, music theory-AP, physics-AP, psychology, SAT preparation, Spanish, Spanish-AP, theater arts, theology, U.S. history-AP, video film production, visual and performing arts, visual arts, world civilizations.

Graduation Requirements Algebra, American history, American literature, arts, biology, British literature, chemistry, computer science, geometry, grammar, health and wellness, literature, mathematics, modern languages, physical education (includes health), science, senior career experience, theology, world cultures, world literature.

Special Academic Programs 16 Advanced Placement exams for which test preparation is offered; honors section; remedial reading and/or remedial writing; remedial math; programs in English, mathematics, general development for dyslexic students; special instructional classes for deaf students, blind students, Options Program, with select Admissions criteria and minimal available support.

College Admission Counseling 218 students graduated in 2014; 208 went to college, including Boston College; Bryant University; Johnson & Wales University; Providence College; Quinnipiac University; University of Rhode Island. Other: 3 went to work, 2 entered military service, 2 entered a postgraduate year, 3 had other specific plans. Mean SAT critical reading: 532, mean SAT math: 543, mean SAT writing: 537.

Student Life Upper grades have specified standards of dress, student council, honor system. Discipline rests primarily with faculty. Attendance at religious services is required.

Tuition and Aid Day student tuition: $12,750. Tuition installment plan (monthly payment plans, individually arranged payment plans). Merit scholarship grants, need-based scholarship grants available. In 2014–15, 63% of upper-school students received aid; total upper-school merit-scholarship money awarded: $80,000. Total amount of financial aid awarded in 2014–15: $1,700,000.

Admissions Traditional secondary-level entrance grade is 9. For fall 2014, 387 students applied for upper-level admission, 370 were accepted, 237 enrolled. Catholic High School Entrance Examination and High School Placement Test (closed version) from Scholastic Testing Service required. Deadline for receipt of application materials: January 1. Application fee required: $50.

Athletics Interscholastic: baseball, basketball, cross-country running, diving, football, golf, ice hockey, indoor track, indoor track & field, lacrosse, rugby, sailing, soccer, Special Olympics, swimming and diving, tennis, track and field, volleyball, winter (indoor) track, wrestling; intramural: archery, badminton, billiards, bocce, bowling, flag football, fly fishing, golf, hiking/backpacking, outdoors, paddle tennis, physical training, skiing (downhill), surfing, table tennis, water polo, whiffle ball. 3 PE instructors, 14 coaches, 1 athletic trainer.

Computers Computers are regularly used in aviation, computer applications, desktop publishing, digital applications, drafting, graphic design, introduction to technology, library skills, media arts, music technology, programming, video film production, Web site design classes. Computer resources include on-campus library services, Internet access, wireless campus network, Internet filtering or blocking technology. Computer access in designated common areas is available to students. Students grades are available online. The school has a published electronic and media policy.

Contact Mrs. Catherine A. Solomon, Director of Admissions. 401-739-3450 Ext. 163. Fax: 401-732-8261. E-mail: csolomon@hendricken.com. Website: www.hendricken.com

BISHOP IRETON HIGH SCHOOL

201 Cambridge Road
Alexandria, Virginia 22314-4899

Head of School: Dr. Thomas J. Curry

General Information Coeducational day college-preparatory, arts, religious studies, and technology school, affiliated with Roman Catholic Church. Grades 9–12. Founded: 1964. Setting: suburban. 12-acre campus. 1 building on campus. Approved or accredited by National Catholic Education Association and Southern Association of Colleges and Schools. Total enrollment: 813. Upper school average class size: 24. Upper school faculty-student ratio: 1:11. There are 180 required school days per year for Upper School students. Upper School students typically attend 5 days per week. The average school day consists of 7 hours.

Upper School Student Profile Grade 9: 201 students (90 boys, 111 girls); Grade 10: 216 students (100 boys, 116 girls); Grade 11: 194 students (84 boys, 110 girls); Grade 12: 202 students (94 boys, 108 girls). 87% of students are Roman Catholic.

Faculty School total: 83. In upper school: 36 men, 47 women; 50 have advanced degrees.

Subjects Offered Advanced Placement courses, Catholic belief and practice, computer science, driver education, English, film, fine arts, foreign language, health, law, mathematics, physical education, psychology, religion, science, social studies, World War II.

Graduation Requirements Arts and fine arts (art, music, dance, drama), computer science, English, foreign language, mathematics, physical education (includes health), religion (includes Bible studies and theology), science, social studies (includes history), 60 hours of community service. Community service is required.

Special Academic Programs 16 Advanced Placement exams for which test preparation is offered; honors section; academic accommodation for the musically talented; special instructional classes for students with Attention Deficit Disorder.

College Admission Counseling 194 students graduated in 2015; 188 went to college, including George Mason University; James Madison University; The Catholic University of America; University of Virginia; Virginia Commonwealth University; Virginia Polytechnic Institute and State University. Other: 1 went to work, 1 entered military service, 2 entered a postgraduate year, 2 had other specific plans. Mean SAT critical reading: 586, mean SAT math: 562, mean SAT writing: 577, mean combined SAT: 1725, mean composite ACT: 25.

Student Life Upper grades have uniform requirement, student council, honor system. Discipline rests primarily with faculty. Attendance at religious services is required.

Summer Programs Remediation, enrichment, art/fine arts, computer instruction programs offered; session focuses on remediation; held on campus; accepts boys and girls; open to students from other schools. 50 students usually enrolled. 2016 schedule: June to July.

Tuition and Aid Day student tuition: $13,545–$18,600. Tuition installment plan (FACTS Tuition Payment Plan, monthly payment plans). Tuition reduction for siblings, merit scholarship grants, need-based scholarship grants available. In 2015–16, 15% of upper-school students received aid; total upper-school merit-scholarship money awarded: $143,000. Total amount of financial aid awarded in 2015–16: $757,000.

Admissions Traditional secondary-level entrance grade is 9. For fall 2015, 433 students applied for upper-level admission, 395 were accepted, 228 enrolled. High School Placement Test (closed version) from Scholastic Testing Service required. Deadline for receipt of application materials: January 15. Application fee required: $50.

Athletics Interscholastic: baseball (boys), basketball (b,g), field hockey (g), football (b), lacrosse (b,g), soccer (b,g), softball (g), swimming and diving (b,g), tennis (b,g), track and field (b,g), volleyball (g), water polo (b), winter (indoor) track (b,g), wrestling (b); intramural: weight training (b,g); coed interscholastic: cheering, crew, cross-country running, diving, golf, ice hockey, indoor track, ultimate Frisbee, water polo, weight training; coed intramural: Frisbee, skiing (downhill), table tennis. 4 PE instructors, 2 athletic trainers.

Computers Computers are regularly used in all academic classes. Computer network features include on-campus library services, online commercial services, Internet access, wireless campus network, Internet filtering or blocking technology. Student e-mail accounts and computer access in designated common areas are available to students. Students grades are available online. The school has a published electronic and media policy.

Contact Mr. Peter J. Hamer, Director of Admissions and Financial Aid. 703-212-5190. Fax: 703-212-8173. E-mail: hamerp@bishopireton.org. Website: www.bishopireton.org

BISHOP JOHN J. SNYDER HIGH SCHOOL

5001 Samaritan Way
Jacksonville, Florida 32210

Head of School: Deacon David Yazdiya

General Information Coeducational day college-preparatory school, affiliated with Roman Catholic Church. Grades 9–12. Founded: 2002. Setting: suburban. 50-acre campus. 15 buildings on campus. Approved or accredited by Council of Accreditation and School Improvement, National Catholic Education Association, Southern Association of Colleges and Schools, and Florida Department of Education. Upper school average class size: 16. Upper school faculty-student ratio: 1:15. There are 180 required school days per year for Upper School students. Upper School students typically attend 5 days per week. The average school day consists of 6 hours and 47 minutes.

Upper School Student Profile Grade 9: 119 students (60 boys, 59 girls); Grade 10: 125 students (64 boys, 61 girls); Grade 11: 109 students (61 boys, 48 girls); Grade 12: 108 students (50 boys, 58 girls). 74% of students are Roman Catholic.

Faculty School total: 32. In upper school: 16 men, 16 women; 15 have advanced degrees.

Subjects Offered Advanced biology, advanced chemistry, Advanced Placement courses, algebra, American government, American history, American history-AP, American literature, American literature AP, anatomy and physiology, applied skills, art, athletics, Basic programming, Bible, biology, biology-AP, British literature, British literature (honors), calculus-AP, campus ministry, chemistry-AP, Chinese, choir, choral music, Christian doctrine, church history, college admission preparation, college awareness, college counseling, college planning, composition-AP, computer skills, creative writing, debate, economics, economics-AP, English, English composition, English language and composition-AP, English literature and composition-AP, French, geography, geometry, government, government-AP, guidance, healthful living, history of the Catholic Church, honors algebra, honors English, honors geometry, honors U.S. history, honors world history, Latin, marine science, physics, religious education, Spanish, speech and debate, statistics, studio art, the Web, U.S. history, U.S. history-AP, world history, world history-AP.

Graduation Requirements 20th century world history, algebra, American government, American history, chemistry, economics, English, English composition, English literature, foreign language, geometry, government, world history, all students must complete 25 hours of off-campus Christian service to the community.

Special Academic Programs 9 Advanced Placement exams for which test preparation is offered.

College Admission Counseling 104 students graduated in 2015; 100 went to college, including Florida Gulf Coast University; Florida State University; University of Central Florida; University of Florida; University of North Florida; University of South Florida. Other: 2 went to work, 1 entered military service, 1 had other specific plans.

Student Life Upper grades have uniform requirement, student council, honor system. Discipline rests primarily with faculty. Attendance at religious services is required.

Summer Programs Remediation programs offered; held on campus; accepts boys and girls; not open to students from other schools. 15 students usually enrolled. 2016 schedule: June to July.

Tuition and Aid Day student tuition: $7400. Tuition installment plan (FACTS Tuition Payment Plan). Tuition reduction for siblings, need-based scholarship grants, Step Up for Students, McKay Scholarship available. In 2015–16, 35% of upper-school students received aid. Total amount of financial aid awarded in 2015–16: $325,000.

Admissions Traditional secondary-level entrance grade is 9. For fall 2015, 475 students applied for upper-level admission, 472 were accepted, 470 enrolled. High School Placement Test required. Deadline for receipt of application materials: none. Application fee required: $375. Interview recommended.

Athletics Interscholastic: baseball (boys), basketball (b,g), cheering (b,g), cross-country running (b,g), dance team (g), diving (b,g), drill team (b,g), football (b), golf (b,g), lacrosse (b), soccer (b,g), softball (g), swimming and diving (b,g), tennis (b,g), track and field (b,g), volleyball (g), weight lifting (b,g), wrestling (b). 3 PE instructors, 23 coaches, 1 athletic trainer.

Computers Computers are regularly used in all academic classes. Computer network features include on-campus library services, Internet access, wireless campus network, Internet filtering or blocking technology. Campus intranet, student e-mail accounts, and computer access in designated common areas are available to students. Students grades are available online. The school has a published electronic and media policy.

Contact Mrs. Mary Anne Briggs, Assistant to the Principal. 904-771-1029. Fax: 904-908-8988. E-mail: maryannebriggs@bishopsnyder.org. Website: www.bishopsnyder.org

BISHOP KELLY HIGH SCHOOL

7009 Franklin Road
Boise, Idaho 83709-0922

Head of School: Mr. Mike Caldwell

General Information Coeducational day college-preparatory and religious studies school, affiliated with Roman Catholic Church. Grades 9–12. Founded: 1964. Setting: urban. 68-acre campus. 2 buildings on campus. Approved or accredited by National Catholic Education Association, Northwest Accreditation Commission, Western Catholic Education Association, and Idaho Department of Education. Endowment: $8.1 million. Total enrollment: 794. Upper school average class size: 21. Upper school faculty-student ratio: 1:19. There are 175 required school days per year for Upper School students. Upper School students typically attend 5 days per week. The average school day consists of 7 hours.

Upper School Student Profile Grade 9: 231 students (119 boys, 112 girls); Grade 10: 175 students (85 boys, 90 girls); Grade 11: 200 students (113 boys, 87 girls); Grade 12: 187 students (97 boys, 90 girls); Grade 13: 1 student (1 girl). 76% of students are Roman Catholic.

Faculty School total: 52. In upper school: 25 men, 27 women; 43 have advanced degrees.

Subjects Offered Advanced Placement courses, algebra, American government, American history-AP, art, art-AP, ASB Leadership, band, biology, biology-AP, calculus-AP, campus ministry, Catholic belief and practice, ceramics, chemistry, chemistry-AP, choir, Christianity, comparative religion, computer applications, computer programming, computer science-AP, conceptual physics, creative writing, drawing, economics, engineering, English, English language and composition-AP, English-AP, fitness, French, geometry, guitar, health, history of the Catholic Church, horticulture, human anatomy, instrumental music, Latin, literature, moral reasoning, painting, physical education, physics, physics-AP, physiology, pre-calculus, psychology, reading/study skills, religious education, religious studies, senior seminar, service learning/internship, social justice, Spanish, Spanish-AP, speech, speech and debate, sports medicine, statistics-AP, theater, theater arts, theology, U.S. history, weight training, world history, yearbook.

Graduation Requirements Computer science, English, foreign language, mathematics, physical education (includes health), religion (includes Bible studies and theology), science, social studies (includes history), 30 hours of community service.

Special Academic Programs Advanced Placement exam preparation; honors section; independent study; study at local college for college credit.

College Admission Counseling 181 students graduated in 2015; 178 went to college, including Boise State University; Gonzaga University; Idaho State University; The College of Idaho; University of Idaho; University of Utah. Other: 1 went to work, 2 had other specific plans. Mean SAT critical reading: 585, mean SAT math: 610, mean SAT writing: 577, mean combined SAT: 1772, mean composite ACT: 25.

Student Life Upper grades have specified standards of dress, student council, honor system. Discipline rests primarily with faculty. Attendance at religious services is required.

Tuition and Aid Day student tuition: $7650. Tuition installment plan (The Tuition Plan, monthly payment plans, individually arranged payment plans). Need-based scholarship grants available. In 2015–16, 75% of upper-school students received aid. Total amount of financial aid awarded in 2015–16: $1,412,691.

Admissions Traditional secondary-level entrance grade is 9. For fall 2015, 794 students applied for upper-level admission, 794 were accepted, 794 enrolled. Deadline for receipt of application materials: none. Application fee required: $205.

Athletics Interscholastic: baseball (boys), basketball (b,g), cheering (g), cross-country running (b,g), fitness (b,g), football (b), golf (b,g), lacrosse (b,g), physical fitness (b,g), skiing (downhill) (b,g), snowboarding (b,g), soccer (b,g), softball (g), swimming and diving (b,g), tennis (b,g), track and field (b,g), volleyball (g), weight lifting (b,g), weight training (b,g), wrestling (b); coed interscholastic: ice hockey, water polo. 3 PE instructors, 12 coaches, 1 athletic trainer.

Computers Computers are regularly used in computer applications, economics, English, foreign language, history, journalism, mathematics, science classes. Computer network features include on-campus library services, Internet access, wireless campus

network, Internet filtering or blocking technology, Blackboard, 1:1 Technology-Bring Your Own Device. Student e-mail accounts and computer access in designated common areas are available to students. Students grades are available online. The school has a published electronic and media policy.

Contact Mrs. Kelly Shockey, Director of Admissions. 208-375-6010. Fax: 208-375-3626. E-mail: kshockey@bk.org. Website: www.bk.org

BISHOP KENNY HIGH SCHOOL

1055 Kingman Avenue
Jacksonville, Florida 32207

Head of School: Rev. Michael R. Houle

General Information Coeducational day college-preparatory and college prep, Honors, AP school, affiliated with Roman Catholic Church. Grades 9–12. Founded: 1952. Setting: urban. 55-acre campus. 10 buildings on campus. Approved or accredited by Southern Association of Colleges and Schools. Upper school average class size: 23. Upper school faculty-student ratio: 1:15. There are 180 required school days per year for Upper School students. Upper School students typically attend 5 days per week. The average school day consists of 6 hours and 30 minutes.

Upper School Student Profile 83% of students are Roman Catholic.

Faculty School total: 71. In upper school: 24 men, 47 women; 49 have advanced degrees.

Subjects Offered Accounting, desktop publishing, psychology, technology, word processing.

Graduation Requirements Electives, English, foreign language, health, mathematics, performing arts, personal fitness, practical arts, religion (includes Bible studies and theology), science, social studies (includes history), service hour requirements.

Special Academic Programs 12 Advanced Placement exams for which test preparation is offered; honors section.

College Admission Counseling 278 students graduated in 2014; 275 went to college, including Florida Gulf Coast University; Florida State University; University of Central Florida; University of Florida; University of North Florida. Other: 1 entered military service, 2 had other specific plans. Median SAT critical reading: 530, median SAT math: 530, median SAT writing: 520, median combined SAT: 1600, median composite ACT: 25. 19% scored over 600 on SAT critical reading, 23% scored over 600 on SAT math, 17% scored over 600 on SAT writing, 16% scored over 1800 on combined SAT, 27% scored over 26 on composite ACT.

Student Life Upper grades have uniform requirement, student council, honor system. Discipline rests primarily with faculty. Attendance at religious services is required.

Tuition and Aid Day student tuition: $7700–$10,845. Tuition installment plan (FACTS Tuition Payment Plan, individually arranged payment plans). Tuition reduction for siblings, need-based scholarship grants available. In 2014–15, 25% of upper-school students received aid.

Admissions Traditional secondary-level entrance grade is 9. ACT-Explore or Explore required. Deadline for receipt of application materials: none. No application fee required. Interview required.

Athletics Interscholastic: baseball (boys), basketball (b,g), cheering (g), cross-country running (b,g), diving (b,g), drill team (g), football (b), golf (b,g), JROTC drill (b,g), riflery (b,g), soccer (b,g), softball (g), swimming and diving (b,g), tennis (b,g), track and field (b,g), volleyball (g), weight lifting (b), wrestling (b). 4 PE instructors, 55 coaches, 3 athletic trainers.

Computers Computers are regularly used in journalism, newspaper, writing, yearbook classes. Computer network features include on-campus library services, Internet access, wireless campus network, Internet filtering or blocking technology, design software for Journalism and MultiMedia, CS4 Suite, 5 computer labs. Campus intranet and student e-mail accounts are available to students. Students grades are available online. The school has a published electronic and media policy.

Contact Mr. Caleb Kitchings, Director of Admissions. 904-398-7545. Fax: 904-398-5728. E-mail: admissions@bishopkenny.org. Website: www.bishopkenny.org

BISHOP MCCORT HIGH SCHOOL

25 Osborne Street
Johnstown, Pennsylvania 15905

Head of School: Mr. Thomas P. Fleming Jr.

General Information College-preparatory school, affiliated with Roman Catholic Church. Founded: 1922. Setting: small town. Nearest major city is Pittsburgh. 1 building on campus. Approved or accredited by North Central Association of Colleges and Schools and Pennsylvania Department of Education. Upper school average class size: 20.

Upper School Student Profile 80% of students are Roman Catholic.

Student Life Upper grades have uniform requirement, student council, honor system. Discipline rests primarily with faculty. Attendance at religious services is required.

Admissions No application fee required.

Contact Sarah Golden, Administrative Assistant. 814-536-8991. Fax: 724-535-4118. E-mail: sgolden@mccort.org. Website: www.mccort.org

BISHOP MCGUINNESS CATHOLIC HIGH SCHOOL

1725 NC Highway 66 South
Kernersville, North Carolina 27284

Head of School: Mr. George L. Repass

General Information Coeducational day college-preparatory, arts, religious studies, and technology school, affiliated with Roman Catholic Church. Grades 9–12. Founded: 1959. Setting: small town. Nearest major city is Winston-Salem/Greensboro. 42-acre campus. 1 building on campus. Approved or accredited by National Catholic Education Association, Southern Association of Colleges and Schools, The College Board, and North Carolina Department of Education. Member of National Association of Independent Schools. Endowment: $298,869. Total enrollment: 458. Upper school average class size: 18. Upper school faculty-student ratio: 1:15. There are 180 required school days per year for Upper School students. Upper School students typically attend 5 days per week. The average school day consists of 6 hours and 50 minutes.

Upper School Student Profile Grade 9: 93 students (55 boys, 38 girls); Grade 10: 111 students (53 boys, 58 girls); Grade 11: 124 students (54 boys, 70 girls); Grade 12: 130 students (75 boys, 55 girls). 82% of students are Roman Catholic.

Faculty School total: 35. In upper school: 17 men, 18 women; 30 have advanced degrees.

Subjects Offered Algebra, American history, anatomy, art history, arts, biology, biology-AP, calculus, calculus-AP, chemistry, chemistry-AP, computer science, computer science-AP, English, English language-AP, English literature and composition-AP, environmental science, European history-AP, French, French language-AP, geometry, health, honors algebra, honors English, honors geometry, honors U.S. history, honors world history, Latin, Latin-AP, mathematics, music, music theory-AP, peer ministry, photography, physical education, physics, pre-calculus, psychology-AP, religion, science, social studies, Spanish, Spanish-AP, statistics-AP, trigonometry, U.S. government and politics, U.S. history-AP, weightlifting, world history, yearbook.

Graduation Requirements English, foreign language, mathematics, physical education (includes health), religion (includes Bible studies and theology), science, social studies (includes history), all students must attend retreat for each grade level; all students must complete 15 hours, of community service each year; all seniors must complete 30 hours of a senior career project.

Special Academic Programs 17 Advanced Placement exams for which test preparation is offered; honors section; independent study; term-away projects.

College Admission Counseling 131 students graduated in 2014; all went to college, including Appalachian State University; East Carolina University; North Carolina State University; The University of North Carolina at Chapel Hill; The University of North Carolina at Charlotte; The University of North Carolina Wilmington. Mean SAT critical reading: 560, mean SAT math: 554, mean SAT writing: 555, mean combined SAT: 1669, mean composite ACT: 25. 35% scored over 600 on SAT critical reading, 33% scored over 600 on SAT math, 43% scored over 600 on SAT writing, 32% scored over 1800 on combined SAT, 65% scored over 26 on composite ACT.

Student Life Upper grades have specified standards of dress, student council, honor system. Discipline rests primarily with faculty. Attendance at religious services is required.

Tuition and Aid Tuition installment plan (monthly payment plans, yearly, semester, and quarterly payment plans). Tuition reduction for siblings, need-based scholarship grants available. In 2014–15, 22% of upper-school students received aid. Total amount of financial aid awarded in 2014–15: $337,500.

Admissions Traditional secondary-level entrance grade is 9. For fall 2014, 135 students applied for upper-level admission, 120 were accepted, 102 enrolled. High School Placement Test required. Deadline for receipt of application materials: none. Application fee required: $75. On-campus interview required.

Athletics Interscholastic: baseball (boys), basketball (b,g), cheering (g), fencing (b), football (b), lacrosse (b), soccer (b,g), softball (g), tennis (b,g), volleyball (g), wrestling (b); coed interscholastic: cross-country running, golf, swimming and diving, track and field, weight training. 3 PE instructors, 40 coaches, 1 athletic trainer.

Computers Computer resources include on-campus library services, Internet access, Internet filtering or blocking technology. Student e-mail accounts and computer access in designated common areas are available to students. Students grades are available online. The school has a published electronic and media policy.

Contact Mr. Robert Belcher, Admissions Director. 336-564-1011. Fax: 336-564-1060. E-mail: rb@bmhs.us. Website: www.bmhs.us

BISHOP MCGUINNESS CATHOLIC HIGH SCHOOL

801 Northwest 50th Street
Oklahoma City, Oklahoma 73118-6001

Head of School: Mr. David L. Morton

General Information Coeducational day college-preparatory, arts, business, religious studies, bilingual studies, and technology school, affiliated with Roman Catholic Church. Grades 9–12. Founded: 1950. Setting: urban. 20-acre campus. 4 buildings on campus. Approved or accredited by North Central Association of Colleges and Schools, Oklahoma Private Schools Accreditation Commission, and Oklahoma Department of Education. Total enrollment: 714. Upper school average class size: 13.

Upper school faculty-student ratio: 1:12. There are 177 required school days per year for Upper School students. Upper School students typically attend 5 days per week. The average school day consists of 6 hours and 10 minutes.

Upper School Student Profile Grade 11: 160 students (78 boys, 82 girls); Grade 12: 164 students (73 boys, 91 girls). 75% of students are Roman Catholic.

Faculty School total: 57. In upper school: 14 men, 13 women; 20 have advanced degrees.

Subjects Offered Algebra, American literature, art, band, Bible, biology, biology-AP, broadcasting, business, calculus-AP, Catholic belief and practice, ceramics, chemistry, chemistry-AP, Chinese studies, chorus, church history, computer technologies, creative writing, culinary arts, current events, dance, debate, digital photography, drama, drawing, drawing and design, electives, English, English language and composition-AP, English literature, English literature and composition-AP, French, geometry, German, government, health and wellness, history of the Catholic Church, honors algebra, honors English, honors geometry, human geography - AP, introduction to theater, Latin, Latin-AP, leadership, learning lab, Life of Christ, macroeconomics-AP, media production, music appreciation, newspaper, painting, personal finance, photography, physical education, physical science, physics, physics-AP, physiology, practical arts, prayer/spirituality, pre-calculus, psychology, psychology-AP, scripture, social justice, sociology, Spanish, Spanish-AP, speech, stagecraft, state history, statistics-AP, strategies for success, theater, trigonometry, U.S. government and politics-AP, U.S. history, U.S. history-AP, weight training, world history, world history-AP, world religions, writing workshop, yearbook.

Graduation Requirements Arts and fine arts (art, music, dance, drama), electives, English, foreign language, mathematics, physical education (includes health), practical arts, science, social studies (includes history), theology, 90 hours of Christian service.

Special Academic Programs 16 Advanced Placement exams for which test preparation is offered; honors section; academic accommodation for the gifted and the artistically talented; programs in English, mathematics for dyslexic students; special instructional classes for students with learning differences.

College Admission Counseling 167 students graduated in 2014; 163 went to college, including Colorado School of Mines; Oklahoma State University; Texas Christian University; University of Arkansas; University of Oklahoma. Other: 4 had other specific plans. Median SAT critical reading: 610, median SAT math: 570, median SAT writing: 585, median combined SAT: 1770, median composite ACT: 25. 65% scored over 600 on SAT critical reading, 25% scored over 600 on SAT math, 40% scored over 600 on SAT writing, 40% scored over 1800 on combined SAT, 41% scored over 26 on composite ACT.

Student Life Upper grades have uniform requirement, student council, honor system. Discipline rests primarily with faculty. Attendance at religious services is required.

Tuition and Aid Day student tuition: $8600. Tuition installment plan (FACTS Tuition Payment Plan). Need-based scholarship grants, paying campus jobs available. In 2014–15, 19% of upper school students received aid. Total amount of financial aid awarded in 2014–15: $237,350.

Admissions For fall 2014, 7 students applied for upper-level admission, 7 were accepted, 7 enrolled. STS or writing sample required. Deadline for receipt of application materials: May 1. Application fee required: $400. On-campus interview required.

Athletics Interscholastic: baseball (boys), basketball (b,g), bowling (b,g), cheering (g), cross-country running (b,g), football (b), golf (b,g), soccer (b,g), softball (g), swimming and diving (b,g), tennis (b,g), track and field (b,g), volleyball (g), weight training (b,g), winter (indoor) track (b,g), wrestling (b); coed interscholastic: dance team, physical fitness. 30 coaches, 1 athletic trainer.

Computers Computers are regularly used in all academic classes. Computer network features include on-campus library services, online commercial services, Internet access, wireless campus network, Internet filtering or blocking technology, laptop classroom carts, wireless printing, eBooks, and My Road, Digital Citizenship classes, each student has an iPad. Student e-mail accounts and computer access in designated common areas are available to students. Students grades are available online. The school has a published electronic and media policy.

Contact Mrs. Laura O'Hara, 9th Grade Counselor. 405-842-6638 Ext. 225. Fax: 405-858-9550. E-mail: Lohara@bmchs.org. Website: www.bmchs.org

BISHOP MCNAMARA HIGH SCHOOL

6800 Marlboro Pike
Forestville, Maryland 20747

Head of School: Dr. Robert Van der Waag

General Information Coeducational day college-preparatory and arts school, affiliated with Roman Catholic Church; primarily serves individuals with Attention Deficit Disorder. Grades 9–12. Founded: 1964. Setting: suburban. Nearest major city is Washington, DC. 16-acre campus. 3 buildings on campus. Approved or accredited by Middle States Association of Colleges and Schools, National Catholic Education Association, and Maryland Department of Education. Endowment: $2.6 million. Total enrollment: 880. Upper school average class size: 21. Upper school faculty-student ratio: 1:10. There are 180 required school days per year for Upper School students. Upper School students typically attend 5 days per week. The average school day consists of 6 hours.

Upper School Student Profile Grade 9: 224 students (105 boys, 119 girls); Grade 10: 223 students (105 boys, 118 girls); Grade 11: 227 students (94 boys, 133 girls); Grade 12: 211 students (90 boys, 121 girls). 50% of students are Roman Catholic.

Faculty School total: 88. In upper school: 39 men, 49 women; 50 have advanced degrees.

Subjects Offered 3-dimensional design.

Special Academic Programs Advanced Placement exam preparation; honors section; study at local college for college credit; academic accommodation for the gifted.

College Admission Counseling 197 students graduated in 2015; 190 went to college. Other: 6 entered military service.

Student Life Upper grades have uniform requirement, student council, honor system. Discipline rests primarily with faculty. Attendance at religious services is required.

Summer Programs Enrichment, sports, art/fine arts, computer instruction programs offered; session focuses on summer school is remediation, camps are enrichment; held on campus; accepts boys and girls; open to students from other schools. 2016 schedule: June 22 to August 14.

Tuition and Aid Day student tuition: $13,250. Tuition installment plan (FACTS Tuition Payment Plan). Tuition reduction for siblings, merit scholarship grants, need-based scholarship grants available.

Admissions Traditional secondary-level entrance grade is 9. For fall 2015, 800 students applied for upper-level admission, 275 were accepted, 225 enrolled. High School Placement Test required. Deadline for receipt of application materials: December 15. Application fee required: $50. Interview recommended.

Athletics Interscholastic: baseball (boys), cheering (g), football (b), pom squad (g), softball (g), volleyball (g), wrestling (b); coed interscholastic: basketball, cross-country running, horseback riding, indoor track & field, soccer, swimming and diving, tennis, track and field, winter (indoor) track; coed intramural: bowling. 3 PE instructors, 2 athletic trainers.

Computers Computers are regularly used in aerospace science, all academic classes. Computer network features include on-campus library services, online commercial services, Internet access, wireless campus network. Student e-mail accounts and computer access in designated common areas are available to students. Students grades are available online.

Contact Mr. Jeffrey Southworth, Associate Director of Admissions. 301-735-8401 Ext. 102. Fax: 301-735-0934. E-mail: jeffrey.southworth@bmhs.org. Website: www.bmhs.org

BISHOP MIEGE HIGH SCHOOL

5041 Reinhardt Drive
Shawnee Mission, Kansas 66205-1599

Head of School: Dr. Joseph Passantino

General Information Coeducational day college-preparatory, religious studies, and technology school, affiliated with Roman Catholic Church. Grades 9–12. Founded: 1958. Setting: suburban. Nearest major city is Roeland Park. 25-acre campus. 1 building on campus. Approved or accredited by National Catholic Education Association and Kansas Department of Education. Total enrollment: 721. Upper school average class size: 16. Upper school faculty-student ratio: 1:16. There are 170 required school days per year for Upper School students. Upper School students typically attend 5 days per week. The average school day consists of 8 hours.

Upper School Student Profile Grade 9: 182 students (100 boys, 82 girls); Grade 10: 173 students (93 boys, 80 girls); Grade 11: 205 students (110 boys, 95 girls); Grade 12: 161 students (82 boys, 79 girls). 81% of students are Roman Catholic.

Faculty School total: 43. In upper school: 19 men, 24 women; 38 have advanced degrees.

Special Academic Programs Advanced Placement exam preparation; honors section; independent study; study at local college for college credit.

College Admission Counseling 160 students graduated in 2015; 157 went to college, including Kansas State University; The University of Kansas.

Student Life Upper grades have uniform requirement, student council. Discipline rests primarily with faculty. Attendance at religious services is required.

Summer Programs Remediation, computer instruction programs offered; held on campus; accepts boys and girls; open to students from other schools. 140 students usually enrolled. 2016 schedule: June to July. Application deadline: May 1.

Tuition and Aid Day student tuition: $9850. Tuition installment plan (SMART Tuition Payment Plan). Tuition reduction for siblings, merit scholarship grants, need-based scholarship grants, paying campus jobs available. In 2015–16, 35% of upper-school students received aid. Total amount of financial aid awarded in 2015–16: $1,000,000.

Admissions Traditional secondary-level entrance grade is 9. Scholastic Testing Service High School Placement Test or STS required. Deadline for receipt of application materials: February 20. Application fee required: $630. Interview required.

Athletics Interscholastic: baseball (boys), basketball (b,g), cheering (g), cross-country running (b,g), dance team (g), diving (b,g), fitness (b,g), football (b), golf (b,g), soccer (b,g), softball (g), strength & conditioning (b,g), swimming and diving (b,g), tennis (b,g), track and field (b,g), volleyball (g), wrestling (b). 3 PE instructors, 23 coaches, 1 athletic trainer.

Computers Computer network features include on-campus library services, online commercial services, Internet access.

Contact Mrs. Patti Marnett, Director of Admissions. 913-262-2701 Ext. 226. Fax: 913-262-2752. E-mail: pmarnett@bishopmiege.com. Website: www.bishopmiege.com

BISHOP MONTGOMERY HIGH SCHOOL

5430 Torrance Boulevard
Torrance, California 90503

Head of School: Ms. Rosemary Distaso-Libbon

General Information Coeducational day college-preparatory, arts, religious studies, and technology school, affiliated with Roman Catholic Church. Grades 9–12. Founded: 1957. Setting: suburban. Nearest major city is Los Angeles. 27-acre campus. 9 buildings on campus. Approved or accredited by National Catholic Education Association, Western Association of Schools and Colleges, Western Catholic Education Association, and California Department of Education. Total enrollment: 946. Upper school average class size: 22. Upper school faculty-student ratio: 1:22. There are 180 required school days per year for Upper School students. Upper School students typically attend 5 days per week. The average school day consists of 6 hours and 10 minutes.

Upper School Student Profile Grade 9: 240 students (103 boys, 137 girls); Grade 10: 257 students (133 boys, 124 girls); Grade 11: 247 students (112 boys, 135 girls); Grade 12: 202 students (107 boys, 95 girls). 75% of students are Roman Catholic.

Faculty School total: 60. In upper school: 26 men, 34 women; 22 have advanced degrees.

Subjects Offered Advanced Placement courses, algebra, American history, American history-AP, American literature, anatomy, art, Bible studies, biology, calculus, chemistry, chorus, composition, computer science, drama, economics, English, English literature, English literature-AP, fine arts, French, geometry, government/civics, health, history, languages, literature, mathematics, physical education, physics, physics-AP, physiology, religion, science, social studies, Spanish, statistics, theater, weight training, world history, yearbook.

Graduation Requirements Arts and fine arts (art, music, dance, drama), business skills (includes word processing), computer science, English, mathematics, physical education (includes health), religion (includes Bible studies and theology), science, social studies (includes history).

Special Academic Programs Advanced Placement exam preparation; honors section; ESL (27 students enrolled).

College Admission Counseling 240 students graduated in 2015; 237 went to college, including California State University, Long Beach; Loyola Marymount University; University of California, Irvine; University of California, Los Angeles; University of California, Riverside. Other: 3 had other specific plans. Mean combined SAT: 1900, mean composite ACT: 25.

Student Life Upper grades have uniform requirement, student council, honor system. Discipline rests primarily with faculty. Attendance at religious services is required.

Summer Programs Remediation, enrichment, advancement, sports, art/fine arts, computer instruction programs offered; session focuses on academic enrichment/remediation and athletic conditioning; held on campus; accepts boys and girls; not open to students from other schools. 900 students usually enrolled. 2016 schedule: June 15 to July 19. Application deadline: June 14.

Tuition and Aid Day student tuition: $9400. Tuition installment plan (SMART Tuition Payment Plan). Tuition reduction for siblings, merit scholarship grants, need-based scholarship grants, financial need available. In 2015–16, 4% of upper-school students received aid; total upper-school merit-scholarship money awarded: $38,000. Total amount of financial aid awarded in 2015–16: $68,000.

Admissions Traditional secondary-level entrance grade is 9. For fall 2015, 455 students applied for upper-level admission, 380 were accepted, 248 enrolled. High School Placement Test, Iowa Tests of Basic Skills, Stanford 9 and Star-9 required. Deadline for receipt of application materials: January 14. Application fee required: $80.

Athletics Interscholastic: baseball (boys), basketball (b,g), cheering (g), cross-country running (b,g), dance (g), dance team (g), football (b), golf (b,g), soccer (b,g), softball (g), strength & conditioning (b,g), tennis (b,g), volleyball (b,g); coed interscholastic: aerobics, surfing, swimming and diving, track and field. 3 PE instructors, 32 coaches, 2 athletic trainers.

Computers Computers are regularly used in library, newspaper, programming, publications, technology, Web site design classes. Computer network features include on-campus library services, Internet access, wireless campus network, Internet filtering or blocking technology. Student e-mail accounts are available to students. Students grades are available online. The school has a published electronic and media policy.

Contact Mrs. Casey Dunn, Director of Admissions. 310-540-2021 Ext. 227. Fax: 310-543-5102. E-mail: cdunn@bmhs-la.org. Website: www.bmhs-la.org

BISHOP MORA SALESIAN HIGH SCHOOL

960 South Soto Street
Los Angeles, California 90023

Head of School: Mr. Alex Chacon

General Information Boys' day college-preparatory, general academic, and religious studies school, affiliated with Roman Catholic Church. Grades 9–12. Founded: 1958. Setting: urban. 2 buildings on campus. Approved or accredited by Accrediting

Commission for Schools, Western Association of Schools and Colleges, Western Catholic Education Association, and California Department of Education. Upper school average class size: 28. Upper school faculty-student ratio: 1:16. There are 188 required school days per year for Upper School students. The average school day consists of 6 hours and 50 minutes.

Upper School Student Profile Grade 9: 125 students (125 boys); Grade 10: 90 students (90 boys); Grade 11: 141 students (141 boys); Grade 12: 122 students (122 boys). 98% of students are Roman Catholic.

Faculty School total: 32. In upper school: 24 men, 8 women; 28 have advanced degrees.

Subjects Offered Advanced biology, advanced chemistry, advanced math, Advanced Placement courses, algebra, American history, American history-AP, American literature, anatomy and physiology, applied music, art, arts appreciation, athletic training, athletics, baseball, basketball, Bible studies, biology, biology-AP, British history, British literature, British literature (honors), business, calculus, calculus-AP, Catholic belief and practice, chemistry, chemistry-AP, Christianity, church history, cinematography, college admission preparation, college awareness, college counseling, college placement, college planning, computer applications, computer science, creative writing, drama, drawing, economics, economics-AP, English, English literature, English-AP, environmental science, ethics, European history, expository writing, fine arts, geometry, government/civics, grammar, health, health education, Hispanic literature, history, mathematics, music, physical education, physical science, physics, physics-AP, pre-algebra, pre-calculus, psychology, psychology-AP, religion, science, social studies, Spanish, Spanish-AP, speech and debate, theater, trigonometry, U.S. government and politics-AP, volleyball, weight training, world history, world literature, writing.

Graduation Requirements Arts and fine arts (art, music, dance, drama), computer science, English, foreign language, mathematics, physical education (includes health), religion (includes Bible studies and theology), religious studies, science, social studies (includes history), Christian service program.

Special Academic Programs Study at local college for college credit; academic accommodation for the musically talented and the artistically talented; remedial reading and/or remedial writing.

College Admission Counseling 87 students graduated in 2015; 86 went to college, including California State University, Los Angeles; Loyola Marymount University; San Francisco State University; University of California, Los Angeles; University of California, Riverside; Whittier College. Other: 1 entered military service.

Student Life Upper grades have uniform requirement, student council, honor system. Discipline rests equally with students and faculty. Attendance at religious services is required.

Summer Programs Remediation, enrichment, advancement, sports, art/fine arts, rigorous outdoor training, computer instruction programs offered; session focuses on refresher course; held on campus; accepts boys and girls; open to students from other schools. 200 students usually enrolled. 2016 schedule: June 19 to July 31. Application deadline: May 1.

Tuition and Aid Day student tuition: $8500. Tuition installment plan (FACTS Tuition Payment Plan, monthly payment plans, individually arranged payment plans). Tuition reduction for siblings, merit scholarship grants, need-based scholarship grants available. In 2015–16, 85% of upper-school students received aid; total upper-school merit scholarship money awarded: $2500. Total amount of financial aid awarded in 2015–16: $1,548,500.

Admissions Traditional secondary-level entrance grade is 9. ETS high school placement exam required. Deadline for receipt of application materials: none. Application fee required: $60. On-campus interview required.

Athletics Interscholastic: baseball, basketball, bicycling, cross-country running, football, golf, physical fitness, physical training, power lifting, running, soccer, track and field, volleyball, weight training, wrestling; intramural: aerobics/Nautilus, basketball, billiards, cheering, dance squad, dance team, soccer, yoga. 12 coaches, 1 athletic trainer.

Computers Computers are regularly used in design, desktop publishing, English, mathematics, word processing, writing, writing, yearbook classes. Computer network features include Internet access. Campus intranet and student e-mail accounts are available to students. The school has a published electronic and media policy.

Contact Ms. Adriana Bronzina, Vice Principal/Director of Curriculum. 323-261-7124 Ext. 236. Fax: 323-261-7600. E-mail: bronzina@mustangsla.org. Website: www.mustangsla.org

BISHOP'S COLLEGE SCHOOL

80 Moulton Hill Road
Sherbrooke, Quebec J1M 1Z8, Canada

Head of School: Mr. Tyler Lewis

General Information Coeducational boarding and day college-preparatory, arts, and bilingual studies school. Grades 7–12. Founded: 1836. Setting: small town. Nearest major city is Montreal, Canada. Students are housed in single-sex dormitories. 240-acre campus. 30 buildings on campus. Approved or accredited by Canadian Association of Independent Schools, Canadian Educational Standards Institute, Quebec Association of Independent Schools, The Association of Boarding Schools, and Quebec Department of Education. Affiliate member of National Association of Independent Schools; member of Secondary School Admission Test Board. Languages of instruction: English and

French. Endowment: CAN$15.6 million. Total enrollment: 239. Upper school average class size: 15. Upper school faculty-student ratio: 1:8. There are 180 required school days per year for Upper School students. Upper School students typically attend 5 days per week. The average school day consists of 7 hours.

Upper School Student Profile Grade 10: 59 students (36 boys, 23 girls); Grade 11: 66 students (39 boys, 27 girls); Grade 12: 44 students (31 boys, 13 girls). 75% of students are boarding students. 44% are province residents. 15 provinces are represented in upper school student body. 45% are international students. International students from China, France, Germany, Mexico, Saudi Arabia, and United States; 34 other countries represented in student body.

Faculty School total: 30. In upper school: 17 men, 13 women; 15 reside on campus.

Subjects Offered Acting, Advanced Placement courses, algebra, art, band, biology, calculus, chemistry, college counseling, college placement, computer science, creative writing, dance, drama, economics, English, environmental science, ESL, ethics, finite math, French, French as a second language, geography, geometry, history, mathematics, music, philosophy, physical education, physical science, physics, political science, religion, robotics, science, sociology, study skills, technology, theater, trigonometry, world history.

Graduation Requirements Follow Ministry of Quebec guidelines, follow Ministry of New Brunswick guidelines, follow International Bacclaureate (IB) guidelines.

Special Academic Programs 6 Advanced Placement exams for which test preparation is offered; term-away projects; study at local college for college credit; study abroad; academic accommodation for the gifted; remedial reading and/or remedial writing; remedial math; ESL (31 students enrolled).

College Admission Counseling 40 students graduated in 2015; 39 went to college, including Bishop's University; Carleton University; McGill University; Ryerson University; University of Guelph; University of Toronto. Other: 1 entered a postgraduate year.

Student Life Upper grades have uniform requirement, student council, honor system. Discipline rests equally with students and faculty.

Summer Programs ESL programs offered; session focuses on English or French as a Second Language; held on campus; accepts boys and girls; open to students from other schools. 150 students usually enrolled. 2016 schedule: July 3 to July 30. Application deadline: none.

Tuition and Aid Day student tuition: CAN$21,800; 7-day tuition and room/board: CAN$54,700. Tuition installment plan (monthly payment plans, individually arranged payment plans, single payment plan). Tuition reduction for siblings, bursaries, merit scholarship grants, need-based scholarship grants, need-based loans available. In 2015–16, 40% of upper-school students received aid. Total amount of financial aid awarded in 2015–16: CAN$900,000.

Admissions Admissions testing or English for Non-native Speakers required. Deadline for receipt of application materials: none. Application fee required: CAN$100. Interview required.

Athletics Interscholastic: baseball (boys), football (b), gymnastics (g), hockey (b,g), ice hockey (b), softball (g); intramural: football (g); coed interscholastic: alpine skiing, aquatics, basketball, bicycling, climbing, combined training, cross-country running, equestrian sports, golf, horseback riding, independent competitive sports, nordic skiing, outdoor adventure, rugby, skiing (cross-country), skiing (downhill), soccer, swimming and diving, tennis; coed intramural: aerobics, alpine skiing, backpacking, badminton, basketball, canoeing/kayaking, climbing, Cosom hockey, curling, dance, figure skating, fitness; fitness walking, floor hockey, freestyle skiing, hiking/backpacking, hockey, horseback riding, ice hockey, ice skating, indoor hockey, jogging, mountain biking, outdoor activities, outdoor education, outdoor skills, physical fitness, racquetball, rock climbing, snowboarding, snowshoeing, soccer, squash, strength & conditioning, table tennis, tennis, wall climbing, weight training, wilderness survival, yoga. 1 PE instructor, 10 coaches, 1 athletic trainer.

Computers Computer network features include on-campus library services, Internet access, wireless campus network, Internet filtering or blocking technology, school-wide laptop initiative (included in tuition), fiber optic network. Campus intranet and student e-mail accounts are available to students. Students grades are available online. The school has a published electronic and media policy.

Contact Mr. Greg McConnell, Director of Admissions. 819-566-0227 Ext. 296. Fax: 819-566-8123. E-mail: gmcconnell@bishopscollegeschool.com. Website: www.bishopscollegeschool.com

THE BISHOP'S SCHOOL

7607 La Jolla Boulevard
La Jolla, California 92037

Head of School: Aimeclaire Roche

General Information Coeducational day college-preparatory, arts, religious studies, and technology school, affiliated with Episcopal Church. Grades 6–12. Founded: 1909. Setting: suburban. Nearest major city is San Diego. 11-acre campus. 9 buildings on campus. Approved or accredited by California Association of Independent Schools, National Association of Episcopal Schools, Western Association of Schools and Colleges, and California Department of Education. Member of National Association of Independent Schools. Endowment: $40.1 million. Total enrollment: 811. Upper school average class size: 14. Upper school faculty-student ratio: 1:9. There are 165 required school days per year for Upper School students. Upper School students typically attend 5 days per week. The average school day consists of 7 hours.

Faculty School total: 105. In upper school: 44 men, 36 women; 64 have advanced degrees.

Subjects Offered Acting, Advanced Placement courses, advanced studio art-AP, algebra, American history, American literature, art history, art history-AP, arts, ASB Leadership, biology, biology-AP, calculus, calculus-AP, ceramics, chemistry, chemistry-AP, Chinese, Chinese studies, chorus, community service, comparative government and politics-AP, comparative religion, computer programming, computer science, creative writing, dance, discrete mathematics, drama, drawing, earth science, ecology, economics, economics and history, economics-AP, English, English literature, English-AP, environmental science, ethics, European history, European history-AP, forensics, French, French language-AP, French literature-AP, genetics, geography, geometry, government/civics, health, history, human anatomy, humanities, integrated mathematics, Internet, jazz band, journalism, Latin, Latin American studies, Latin-AP, literature and composition-AP, literature-AP, macro/microeconomics-AP, marine biology, mathematics, music, painting, philosophy, photography, physical education, physical science, physics, physics-AP, physiology, pre-algebra, pre-calculus, probability, programming, religious studies, Shakespeare, social studies, Spanish, Spanish language-AP, Spanish literature-AP, speech, speech and debate, stained glass, statistics, statistics-AP, studio art-AP, tap dance, theater, theater design and production, typing, U.S. government and politics-AP, U.S. history, U.S. history-AP, visual reality, world history, yearbook.

Graduation Requirements Arts and fine arts (art, music, dance, drama), computer science, English, foreign language, mathematics, physical education (includes health), religion (includes Bible studies and theology), science, social sciences, social studies (includes history), swimming test, computer proficiency. Community service is required.

Special Academic Programs Advanced Placement exam preparation; honors section; independent study; study abroad.

College Admission Counseling 137 students graduated in 2015; 133 went to college, including New York University; Stanford University; University of Chicago; University of Southern California. Other: 4 had other specific plans. Median SAT critical reading: 690, median SAT math: 700, median SAT writing: 700, median combined SAT: 2110, median composite ACT: 31. 82.9% scored over 600 on SAT critical reading, 82.9% scored over 600 on SAT math, 87.4% scored over 600 on SAT writing, 88.3% scored over 1800 on combined SAT, 86.9% scored over 26 on composite ACT.

Student Life Upper grades have uniform requirement, student council, honor system. Discipline rests equally with students and faculty. Attendance at religious services is required.

Summer Programs Remediation, enrichment, advancement, sports, art/fine arts, computer instruction programs offered; held on campus; accepts boys and girls; open to students from other schools. 270 students usually enrolled. 2016 schedule: June 6 to July 25. Application deadline: June 6.

Tuition and Aid Day student tuition: $32,500. Tuition installment plan (FACTS Tuition Payment Plan, semester payment plans, Key Resources Achiever Loan). Need-based scholarship grants available. In 2015–16, 21% of upper-school students received aid.

Admissions Traditional secondary-level entrance grade is 9. ISEE required. Deadline for receipt of application materials: February 1. Application fee required: $100. On-campus interview required.

Athletics Interscholastic: baseball (boys), basketball (b,g), cross-country running (b,g), equestrian sports (b,g), field hockey (g), football (b), golf (b,g), gymnastics (g), lacrosse (b,g), soccer (b,g), softball (g), swimming and diving (b,g), tennis (b,g), track and field (b,g), volleyball (b,g), water polo (b,g); intramural: weight training (b,g); coed interscholastic: sailing. 4 PE instructors, 58 coaches, 1 athletic trainer.

Computers Computers are regularly used in English, foreign language, history, journalism, library, music, science, yearbook classes. Computer network features include on-campus library services, online commercial services, Internet access, wireless campus network. Student e-mail accounts and computer access in designated common areas are available to students. Students grades are available online.

Contact Kim Peckham, Director of Admissions and Financial Aid. 858-875-0809. Fax: 858-459-2990. E-mail: peckhamk@bishops.com. Website: www.bishops.com

BISHOP STANG HIGH SCHOOL

500 Slocum Road
North Dartmouth, Massachusetts 02747-2999

Head of School: Mr. Peter V. Shaughnessy

General Information Coeducational day college-preparatory, arts, business, religious studies, technology, and science school, affiliated with Roman Catholic Church. Grades 9–12. Founded: 1959. Setting: suburban. Nearest major city is New Bedford. 8-acre campus. 1 building on campus. Approved or accredited by New England Association of Schools and Colleges and Massachusetts Department of Education. Endowment: $2 million. Total enrollment: 620. Upper school average class size: 19. Upper school faculty-student ratio: 1:13. There are 180 required school days

per year for Upper School students. Upper School students typically attend 5 days per week. The average school day consists of 6 hours and 30 minutes.

Upper School Student Profile Grade 9: 145 students (77 boys, 68 girls); Grade 10: 172 students (74 boys, 98 girls); Grade 11: 145 students (59 boys, 86 girls); Grade 12: 156 students (77 boys, 79 girls). 75% of students are Roman Catholic.

Faculty School total: 50. In upper school: 21 men, 29 women; 31 have advanced degrees.

Subjects Offered 20th century American writers, 20th century world history, 3-dimensional art, 3-dimensional design, advanced biology, advanced chemistry, advanced math, Advanced Placement courses, algebra, alternative physical education, American history, American history-AP, American literature, American literature-AP, anatomy and physiology, art, athletics, biochemistry, bioethics, biology, biology-AP, business law, calculus, calculus-AP, campus ministry, career and personal planning, career/college preparation, Catholic belief and practice, chemistry, chemistry-AP, chorus, church history, clayworking, collage and assemblage, college admission preparation, college awareness, college counseling, college placement, college planning, college writing, communications, community service, comparative religion, computer education, computer literacy, computer science, computer technologies, concert band, criminal justice, criminology, death and loss, drama, drama performance, dramatic arts, drawing, drawing and design, driver education, ecology, English, English language and composition-AP, English literature, English literature-AP, English-AP, environmental science, fine arts, French, geometry, government/civics, health, health science, history, history of the Catholic Church, honors algebra, honors English, honors geometry, honors U.S. history, honors world history, human biology, human development, instrumental music, introduction to theater, jazz band, lab science, Latin, leadership and service, Life of Christ, marine biology, marketing, mathematics, mechanical drawing, media production, modern European history, modern European history-AP, moral theology, music, oceanography, painting, photography, physical education, physics, physics-AP, physiology, Portuguese, prayer/spirituality, psychology, psychology-AP, public service, public speaking, religion, religious studies, SAT/ACT preparation, science, social sciences, social studies, sociology, Spanish, study skills, technical drawing, theater arts, trigonometry, U.S. history-AP, Web authoring, Web site design, world history, world literature, writing, yearbook.

Graduation Requirements Arts and fine arts (art, music, dance, drama), English, foreign language, mathematics, physical education (includes health), religion (includes Bible studies and theology), science, social sciences, social studies (includes history), U.S. history, world history, service project. Community service is required.

Special Academic Programs 11 Advanced Placement exams for which test preparation is offered; honors section; remedial reading and/or remedial writing; remedial math; programs in English, mathematics, general development for dyslexic students.

College Admission Counseling 169 students graduated in 2015; 167 went to college, including Bridgewater State University; Plymouth State University; Roger Williams University; Salve Regina University; University of Massachusetts Amherst; University of Massachusetts Dartmouth. Other: 1 went to work. Mean SAT critical reading: 552, mean SAT math: 534, mean SAT writing: 542, mean combined SAT: 1628.

Student Life Upper grades have uniform requirement, student council, honor system. Discipline rests primarily with faculty. Attendance at religious services is required.

Summer Programs Enrichment, advancement, sports, art/fine arts, computer instruction programs offered; session focuses on sport and activity camps; held on campus; accepts boys and girls; open to students from other schools. 200 students usually enrolled. 2016 schedule: July 1 to August 19. Application deadline: June 1.

Tuition and Aid Day student tuition: $9300. Tuition installment plan (FACTS Tuition Payment Plan, monthly payment plans). Merit scholarship grants, need-based scholarship grants available. In 2014–15, 26% of upper-school students received aid; total upper-school merit-scholarship money awarded: $10,000. Total amount of financial aid awarded in 2014–15: $500,000.

Admissions Traditional secondary-level entrance grade is 9. For fall 2015, 228 students applied for upper-level admission, 220 were accepted, 145 enrolled. Scholastic Testing Service High School Placement Test or SSAT required. Deadline for receipt of application materials: none. No application fee required. On-campus interview recommended.

Athletics Interscholastic: aquatics (boys, girls), baseball (b), basketball (b,g), cheering (g), cross-country running (b,g), diving (b,g), field hockey (g), fitness (b,g), football (b), ice hockey (b,g), indoor track (b,g), lacrosse (b,g), soccer (b,g), softball (g), swimming and diving (b,g), tennis (b,g), track and field (b,g), volleyball (g), winter (indoor) track (b,g); intramural: volleyball (b); coed interscholastic: golf, sailing, strength & conditioning; coed intramural: climbing, crew, Frisbee, physical training, rowing, sailing, strength & conditioning, ultimate Frisbee, weight lifting, weight training. 1 PE instructor, 13 coaches, 1 athletic trainer.

Computers Computers are regularly used in all classes. Computer network features include on-campus library services, online commercial services, Internet access, wireless campus network, Internet filtering or blocking technology, iPads used by all students in grades 9-11. Campus intranet, student e-mail accounts, and computer access in designated common areas are available to students. Students grades are available online. The school has a published electronic and media policy.

Contact Mrs. Christine Payette, Admissions Director. 508-996-5602 Ext. 424. Fax: 508-994-6756. E-mail: admissions@bishopstang.org. Website: www.bishopstang.org

BISHOP VEROT HIGH SCHOOL

5598 Sunrise Drive
Fort Myers, Florida 33919-1799

Head of School: Dr. Denny Denison

General Information Coeducational day college-preparatory, arts, religious studies, technology, honors, and Advanced Placement school, affiliated with Roman Catholic Church. Grades 9–12. Founded: 1962. Setting: suburban. Nearest major city is Tampa. 20-acre campus. 8 buildings on campus. Approved or accredited by Southern Association of Colleges and Schools and Florida Department of Education. Endowment: $800,000. Total enrollment: 673. Upper school average class size: 25. Upper school faculty-student ratio: 1:14. There are 182 required school days per year for Upper School students. Upper School students typically attend 5 days per week. The average school day consists of 7 hours.

Upper School Student Profile Grade 9: 170 students (91 boys, 79 girls); Grade 10: 179 students (103 boys, 76 girls); Grade 11: 176 students (91 boys, 85 girls); Grade 12: 148 students (76 boys, 72 girls). 60% of students are Roman Catholic.

Faculty School total: 50. In upper school: 19 men, 31 women; 33 have advanced degrees.

Subjects Offered Acting, Advanced Placement courses, algebra, American government, American history, American history-AP, American literature, American sign language, art, athletic training, band, Bible studies, biology, biology-AP, British literature, British literature (honors), broadcast journalism, business, calculus-AP, career planning, career/college preparation, ceramics, chemistry, chemistry-AP, choir, church history, college admission preparation, college counseling, comparative government and politics-AP, computer studies, creative writing, drafting, drama, drawing, driver education, economics, electives, English, English literature and composition-AP, English literature-AP, environmental science, European history-AP, fine arts, foreign language, French, geometry, government, government-AP, health education, history, history of the Catholic Church, history-AP, honors algebra, honors English, honors geometry, honors U.S. history, honors world history, industrial arts, law studies, marine biology, mathematics, painting, personal fitness, photography, physical education, physics, physics-AP, pottery, practical arts, pre-algebra, pre-calculus, probability and statistics, psychology, SAT preparation, Spanish, Spanish language-AP, speech, studio art, television, theater, U.S. government and politics-AP, U.S. history, U.S. history-AP, weightlifting, world history, world history-AP, writing, yearbook.

Graduation Requirements Algebra, American government, arts and fine arts (art, music, dance, drama), biology, British literature, chemistry, economics, electives, English, English composition, foreign language, geometry, health education, mathematics, moral theology, personal fitness, physics, practical arts, psychology, religion (includes Bible studies and theology), science, U.S. history, world history, world literature.

Special Academic Programs Advanced Placement exam preparation; honors section; independent study; study at local college for college credit.

College Admission Counseling 154 students graduated in 2015; 153 went to college, including Florida Atlantic University; Florida Gulf Coast University; Florida State University; University of Central Florida; University of Florida. Other: 1 had other specific plans. Mean SAT critical reading: 518, mean SAT math: 539, mean SAT writing: 520, mean combined SAT: 1577, mean composite ACT: 24.

Student Life Upper grades have specified standards of dress, student council, honor system. Discipline rests primarily with faculty. Attendance at religious services is required.

Summer Programs Enrichment, sports, rigorous outdoor training programs offered; session focuses on enrichment; held on campus; accepts boys and girls; not open to students from other schools.

Tuition and Aid Day student tuition: $9625. Tuition installment plan (FACTS Tuition Payment Plan, monthly payment plans, individually arranged payment plans, quarterly payment plan). Merit scholarship grants, need-based scholarship grants, tuition reduction for contributing Catholic families available. In 2015–16, 40% of upper-school students received aid.

Admissions High School Placement Test required. Deadline for receipt of application materials: none. Application fee required: $75.

Athletics Interscholastic: baseball (boys), basketball (b,g), cheering (g), cross-country running (b,g), diving (b,g), football (b), golf (b,g), lacrosse (b,g), soccer (b,g), softball (g), swimming and diving (b,g), tennis (b,g), track and field (b,g), volleyball (g); coed interscholastic: strength & conditioning. 2 PE instructors, 20 coaches, 1 athletic trainer.

Computers Computers are regularly used in career exploration, college planning, drafting, information technology, media production, media services, photography, publications, SAT preparation, technology, vocational-technical courses, Web site design, yearbook classes. Computer network features include Internet access, wireless campus network, Internet filtering or blocking technology, Naviance Family Connection—college and career planning. Student e-mail accounts are available to students. Students grades are available online. The school has a published electronic and media policy.

Contact Mrs. Jill Rhone, Director of Admission. 239-274-6760. Fax: 239-274-6795. E-mail: jill.rhone@bvhs.org. Website: www.bvhs.org/

BISHOP WALSH MIDDLE HIGH SCHOOL

Bishop Walsh School
700 Bishop Walsh Road
Cumberland, Maryland 21502

Head of School: Mrs. Ann Workmeister

General Information Coeducational day college-preparatory school, affiliated with Roman Catholic Church. Grades PK–12. Founded: 1966. Setting: small town. 10-acre campus. 1 building on campus. Approved or accredited by National Catholic Education Association and Maryland Department of Education. Total enrollment: 320. Upper school average class size: 20. Upper school faculty-student ratio: 1:15. There are 190 required school days per year for Upper School students. Upper School students typically attend 5 days per week. The average school day consists of 6 hours and 5 minutes.

Upper School Student Profile 70% of students are Roman Catholic.

Faculty School total: 40. In upper school: 8 men, 12 women; 15 have advanced degrees.

Subjects Offered 3-dimensional design, advanced biology, advanced chemistry, algebra, American government, American history, American history-AP, American literature, art, art history-AP, biology, biology-AP, British literature, British literature-AP, calculus, calculus-AP, campus ministry, Catholic belief and practice, chemistry, chemistry-AP, Christian and Hebrew scripture, Christian ethics, computer applications, computer science, English language and composition-AP, English language-AP, English literature, English literature and composition-AP, English literature-AP, environmental science, environmental science-AP, ESL, ESL, geography, geometry, government and politics-AP, government-AP, Hausa, health, Hebrew scripture, history-AP, honors algebra, honors English, honors geometry, honors U.S. history, honors world history, Internet, lab science, literature and composition-AP, model United Nations, music, music appreciation, New Testament, physical education, physics, psychology, scripture, social justice, Spanish, statistics, statistics-AP, U.S. government, U.S. government and politics, U.S. government and politics-AP, U.S. history, U.S. history-AP, United States government-AP, Web site design, weight training, weightlifting, Western civilization, world civilizations, yearbook.

Special Academic Programs 10 Advanced Placement exams for which test preparation is offered; honors section; remedial reading and/or remedial writing; programs in English, general development for dyslexic students; ESL (10 students enrolled).

College Admission Counseling 30 students graduated in 2015; 29 went to college, including Frostburg State University; West Virginia University. Other: 1 entered military service. Median SAT critical reading: 505, median SAT math: 504, median SAT writing: 500, median combined SAT: 1509, median composite ACT: 25.

Student Life Upper grades have uniform requirement, student council. Discipline rests primarily with faculty. Attendance at religious services is required.

Tuition and Aid Day student tuition: $5500. Tuition installment plan (FACTS Tuition Payment Plan, monthly payment plans). Need-based scholarship grants available. In 2015–16, 50% of upper-school students received aid. Total amount of financial aid awarded in 2015–16: $30,000.

Admissions Traditional secondary-level entrance grade is 9. High School Placement Test (closed version) from Scholastic Testing Service required. Deadline for receipt of application materials: none. Application fee required: $60. Interview required.

Athletics Interscholastic: baseball (boys), basketball (b,g), bowling (b,g), cheering (g), golf (b), horseback riding (b,g), soccer (b,g), softball (g), tennis (b,g), volleyball (g), weight training (b,g); coed interscholastic: cross-country running, track and field; coed intramural: table tennis. 1 PE instructor, 8 coaches, 1 athletic trainer.

Computers Computer network features include Internet access, wireless campus network. Student e-mail accounts are available to students. Students grades are available online. The school has a published electronic and media policy.

Contact Mrs. Erin Dale, Administrative Assistant. 301-724-5360 Ext. 104. Fax: 301-722-0555. E-mail: edale@bishopwalsh.org. Website: www.bishopwalsh.org

BLAIR ACADEMY

2 Park Street
Blairstown, New Jersey 07825

Head of School: Christopher Fortunato, JD

General Information Coeducational boarding and day college-preparatory, arts, and technology school. Boarding grades 9–PG, day grades 9–12. Founded: 1848. Setting: rural. Nearest major city is New York, NY. Students are housed in single-sex dormitories. 425-acre campus. 42 buildings on campus. Approved or accredited by Middle States Association of Colleges and Schools, The Association of Boarding Schools, and New Jersey Department of Education. Member of National Association of Independent Schools and Secondary School Admission Test Board. Endowment: $90 million. Total enrollment: 460. Upper school average class size: 11. Upper school faculty-student ratio: 1:6. Upper School students typically attend 6 days per week. The average school day consists of 6 hours and 45 minutes.

Upper School Student Profile 80% of students are boarding students. 30% are state residents. 26 states are represented in upper school student body. 17% are international students. International students from China, Hong Kong, Republic of Korea, Spain, Thailand, and United Kingdom; 20 other countries represented in student body.

Blair Academy

Faculty School total: 90. In upper school: 50 men, 40 women; 57 have advanced degrees; 83 reside on campus.

Subjects Offered 3-dimensional art, 3-dimensional design, advanced math, Advanced Placement courses, advanced studio art-AP, African history, algebra, American government, American history, American history-AP, American literature, anatomy, architectural drawing, architecture, art, art history-AP, art-AP, Asian studies, biochemistry, biology, biology-AP, biotechnology, calculus, calculus-AP, ceramics, chemistry, chemistry-AP, Chinese, comparative government and politics-AP, computer programming, computer science, computer science-AP, creative writing, dance, drafting, drama, drawing, drawing and design, driver education, economics, economics and history, economics-AP, English, English language-AP, English literature, English literature-AP, environmental science, environmental science-AP, ethics, European history, European history-AP, filmmaking, fine arts, French, French language-AP, geometry, government/civics, health, history, Japanese history, jazz band, Latin, marine biology, marine science, mathematics, mechanical drawing, music, music theory-AP, painting, philosophy, photography, physics, pre-calculus, psychology, religion, robotics, science, social studies, Spanish, Spanish language-AP, statistics-AP, theater, theology, world history, world history-AP, world literature, writing.

Graduation Requirements Arts and fine arts (art, music, dance, drama), biology, English, foreign language, mathematics, performing arts, religion (includes Bible studies and theology), science, social studies (includes history), U.S. history, athletic requirement.

Special Academic Programs 23 Advanced Placement exams for which test preparation is offered; honors section; independent study; study abroad.

College Admission Counseling 135 students graduated in 2015; all went to college, including Boston College; Cornell University; Lehigh University; New York University; Syracuse University; University of Pennsylvania.

Student Life Upper grades have specified standards of dress, student council, honor system. Discipline rests equally with students and faculty. Attendance at religious services is required.

Tuition and Aid Day student tuition: $35,600; 7-day tuition and room/board: $49,500. Tuition installment plan (Key Tuition Payment Plan, monthly payment plans). Need-based scholarship grants, need-based loans available. In 2015–16, 32% of upper-school students received aid. Total amount of financial aid awarded in 2015–16: $5,100,000.

Admissions Traditional secondary-level entrance grade is 9. For fall 2015, 991 students applied for upper-level admission, 241 were accepted, 154 enrolled. SSAT or TOEFL required. Deadline for receipt of application materials: January 15. Application fee required: $50. On-campus interview required.

Athletics Interscholastic: alpine skiing (boys, girls), baseball (b), basketball (b,g), crew (b,g), cross-country running (b,g), field hockey (g), football (b), golf (b,g), indoor track (b,g), lacrosse (b,g), rowing (b,g), running (b,g), skiing (downhill) (b,g), soccer (b,g), softball (g), squash (b,g), swimming and diving (b,g), tennis (b,g), track and field (b,g), volleyball (g), winter (indoor) track (b,g), wrestling (b); intramural: basketball (b,g), crew (b,g), ice hockey (b,g), rowing (b,g), volleyball (g); coed intramural: alpine skiing, bicycling, canoeing/kayaking, dance, equestrian sports, fitness, flag football, golf, horseback riding, kayaking, life saving, modern dance, mountaineering, outdoor activities, outdoor adventure, outdoor education, outdoor skills, physical fitness, skiing (downhill), snowboarding, squash, swimming and diving, tennis, weight lifting, weight training, wrestling, yoga. 3 athletic trainers.

Computers Computers are regularly used in architecture, drawing and design, English, foreign language, graphic arts, graphic design, history, information technology, mathematics, media production, science, video film production, writing classes. Computer network features include on-campus library services, online commercial services, Internet access, Internet filtering or blocking technology. Campus intranet, student e-mail accounts, and computer access in designated common areas are available to students. The school has a published electronic and media policy.

Contact Nancy Klein, Administrative Assistant. 800-462-5247. Fax: 908-362-7975. E-mail: admissions@blair.edu. Website: www.blair.edu

THE BLAKE SCHOOL

110 Blake Road South
Hopkins, Minnesota 55343

Head of School: Dr. Anne E. Stavney

General Information Coeducational day college-preparatory school. Grades PK–12. Founded: 1900. Setting: urban. Nearest major city is Minneapolis. 5-acre campus. 1 building on campus. Approved or accredited by Independent Schools Association of the Central States. Member of National Association of Independent Schools. Endowment: $63.8 million. Total enrollment: 1,363. Upper school average class size: 16. Upper school faculty-student ratio: 1:8. There are 176 required school days per year for Upper School students. Upper School students typically attend 5 days per week. The average school day consists of 7 hours and 30 minutes.

Upper School Student Profile Grade 9: 130 students (66 boys, 64 girls); Grade 10: 134 students (68 boys, 66 girls); Grade 11: 136 students (71 boys, 65 girls); Grade 12: 129 students (63 boys, 66 girls).

Faculty School total: 135. In upper school: 31 men, 34 women; 37 have advanced degrees.

Subjects Offered Advanced chemistry, African-American literature, algebra, American history, American literature, art, Asian studies, astronomy, band, biology, biology-AP, calculus, calculus-AP, ceramics, chemistry, chemistry-AP, Chinese, choir, chorus, communication arts, communications, computer math, creative writing, debate, design, drama, drawing, economics, English, English literature, English-AP, ethics, European history, European history-AP, fine arts, French, French language-AP, French literature-AP, geology, geometry, German-AP, government/civics, history, instrumental music, jazz ensemble, journalism, Latin, mathematics, multicultural studies, music, painting, performing arts, photography, physical education, physics, physics-AP, policy and value, political science, printmaking, psychology, religion, science, sculpture, senior project, social psychology, social studies, Spanish, Spanish language-AP, speech, statistics, statistics-AP, studio art, studio art-AP, theater, theater arts, trigonometry, visual and performing arts, vocal ensemble, women's studies, world cultures, world history, world literature, writing.

Graduation Requirements Arts and fine arts (art, music, dance, drama), communications, English, foreign language, mathematics, physical education (includes health), science, social studies (includes history), senior speech.

Special Academic Programs 14 Advanced Placement exams for which test preparation is offered; honors section; term-away projects; study at local college for college credit; study abroad.

College Admission Counseling 134 students graduated in 2015; 129 went to college, including Abilene Christian University; Carleton University; Northwestern University; St. Olaf College; University of Minnesota, Twin Cities Campus; University of Wisconsin–Madison. Other: 4 had other specific plans. Median SAT critical reading: 665, median SAT math: 660, median SAT writing: 680, median combined SAT: 2005, median composite ACT: 29. 68% scored over 600 on SAT critical reading, 64% scored over 600 on SAT math, 69% scored over 600 on SAT writing, 75% scored over 26 on composite ACT.

Student Life Upper grades have specified standards of dress, student council, honor system. Discipline rests primarily with faculty.

Summer Programs Remediation, enrichment, advancement, sports, art/fine arts programs offered; session focuses on broad-based program including academics, arts, and sports; held both on and off campus; held at local lakes and beaches, museums, other locations; accepts boys and girls; open to students from other schools. 250 students usually enrolled. 2016 schedule: June 24 to August 9.

Tuition and Aid Day student tuition: $25,525. Tuition installment plan (Insured Tuition Payment Plan, monthly payment plans, local bank-arranged plan). Need-based scholarship grants, need-based loans, tuition remission for children of faculty available. In 2015–16, 22% of upper-school students received aid. Total amount of financial aid awarded in 2015–16: $2,321,797.

Admissions Traditional secondary-level entrance grade is 9. For fall 2015, 90 students applied for upper-level admission, 59 were accepted, 34 enrolled. ERB required. Deadline for receipt of application materials: January 31. Application fee required: $100. On-campus interview required.

Athletics Interscholastic: alpine skiing (boys, girls), baseball (b), basketball (b,g), cross-country running (b,g), diving (b,g), football (b), golf (b,g), ice hockey (b,g), lacrosse (b,g), skiing (cross-country) (b,g), skiing (downhill) (b,g), soccer (b,g), softball (g), swimming and diving (b,g); coed interscholastic: fencing. 1 PE instructor, 45 coaches, 1 athletic trainer.

Computers Computers are regularly used in all classes. Computer network features include on-campus library services, online commercial services, Internet access, wireless campus network, Internet filtering or blocking technology, laptops. Campus intranet, student e-mail accounts, and computer access in designated common areas are available to students. Students grades are available online. The school has a published electronic and media policy.

Contact Joseph Silvestri, Director of Admissions. 952-988-3422. Fax: 952-988-3455. E-mail: jsilvestri@blakeschool.org. Website: www.blakeschool.org

BLANCHET SCHOOL

4373 Market Street NE
Salem, Oregon 97305

Head of School: Mr. Anthony Guevara

General Information Coeducational day college-preparatory, arts, and religious studies school, affiliated with Roman Catholic Church. Grades 6–12. Founded: 1995. Setting: suburban. 22-acre campus. 2 buildings on campus. Approved or accredited by National Catholic Education Association, Northwest Accreditation Commission, Northwest Association of Schools and Colleges, and Oregon Department of Education. Endowment: $285,000. Total enrollment: 367. Upper school average class size: 18. Upper school faculty-student ratio: 1:17. There are 175 required school days per year for Upper School students. Upper School students typically attend 5 days per week. The average school day consists of 7 hours.

Upper School Student Profile 70% of students are Roman Catholic.

Faculty School total: 30. In upper school: 13 men, 15 women; 23 have advanced degrees.

Subjects Offered Advanced Placement courses, algebra, American government, American history-AP, American literature, anatomy, anatomy and physiology, art, art education, band, Bible studies, biology, calculus, campus ministry, career and personal planning, Catholic belief and practice, chemistry, chemistry-AP, choir, civics, college counseling, college placement, comparative religion, composition, critical thinking, critical writing, debate, digital photography, drama, economics, economics and history, English literature, English literature and composition-AP, first aid, fitness, French, geometry, global studies, government, great books, health, health and safety, health and wellness, health education, history of the Catholic Church, history-AP, lab science, leadership, literature and composition-AP, mathematics, media production, music, personal finance, physical education, physical fitness, physical science, physics, pre-algebra, pre-calculus, psychology, publications, religion, religion and culture, SAT/ACT preparation, sociology, Spanish, speech and debate, U.S. government, U.S. history, U.S. history-AP, weight training, world history, world religions, World War II.

Graduation Requirements Applied arts, arts and fine arts (art, music, dance, drama), electives, English, foreign language, mathematics, physical education (includes health), religion (includes Bible studies and theology), science, social studies (includes history), 20 hours of community service for each year in attendance.

Special Academic Programs 2 Advanced Placement exams for which test preparation is offered; honors section; study at local college for college credit; special instructional classes for deaf students; ESL (6 students enrolled).

College Admission Counseling 65 students graduated in 2015; all went to college, including Chemeketa Community College; Gonzaga University; Linfield College; Oregon State University; University of Portland; Willamette University. Mean SAT critical reading: 553, mean SAT math: 535, mean SAT writing: 534, mean composite ACT: 25.

Student Life Upper grades have specified standards of dress, student council. Discipline rests primarily with faculty. Attendance at religious services is required.

Summer Programs Enrichment, sports programs offered; session focuses on preparation for the next academic year, athletic training; held on campus; accepts boys and girls; open to students from other schools. 75 students usually enrolled. 2016 schedule: June 13 to August 31.

Tuition and Aid Day student tuition: $8260. Tuition installment plan (FACTS Tuition Payment Plan). Tuition reduction for siblings, need-based scholarship grants available. In 2015–16, 35% of upper-school students received aid. Total amount of financial aid awarded in 2015–16: $250,000.

Admissions Traditional secondary-level entrance grade is 9. For fall 2015, 100 students applied for upper-level admission, 97 were accepted, 95 enrolled. Math Placement Exam required. Deadline for receipt of application materials: none. Application fee required: $100. Interview recommended.

Athletics Interscholastic: baseball (boys), basketball (b,g), cheering (g), cross-country running (b,g), fencing (b,g), football (b), golf (b,g), physical fitness (b,g), soccer (b,g), softball (g), swimming and diving (b,g), tennis (b,g), track and field (b,g), volleyball (g), weight training (b,g); intramural: weight training (b,g); coed intramural: badminton. 4 PE instructors, 60 coaches.

Computers Computers are regularly used in business, media production, photography, science, social studies classes. Computer network features include online commercial services, Internet access, wireless campus network, Internet filtering or blocking technology. Computer access in designated common areas is available to students. Students grades are available online. The school has a published electronic and media policy.

Contact Mrs. Megan Johnston, Admissions Office. 503-485-4491. Fax: 503-399-1259. E-mail: admissions@blanchetcatholicschool.com. Website: www.blanchetcatholicschool.com

BLESSED SACRAMENT HUGUENOT CATHOLIC SCHOOL

2501 Academy Road
Powhatan, Virginia 23139

Head of School: Mrs. Paula Ledbetter

General Information Coeducational day college-preparatory and religious studies school, affiliated with Roman Catholic Church. Grades PS–12. Founded: 1954. Setting: rural. Nearest major city is Richmond. 46-acre campus. 5 buildings on campus. Approved or accredited by National Catholic Education Association, Southern Association of Colleges and Schools, Virginia Association of Independent Schools, and Virginia Department of Education. Total enrollment: 316. Upper school average class size: 12. Upper school faculty-student ratio: 1:6. There are 180 required school days per year for Upper School students. Upper School students typically attend 5 days per week. The average school day consists of 7 hours.

Upper School Student Profile 33% of students are Roman Catholic.

Faculty School total: 36. In upper school: 5 men, 9 women; 6 have advanced degrees.

Subjects Offered Advanced math, Advanced Placement courses, algebra, American government, American history, American history-AP, American literature-AP, art, athletics, baseball, basketball, biology, calculus, calculus-AP, Central and Eastern European history, cheerleading, chemistry, Christian education, college admission preparation, college awareness, college counseling, college planning, college writing, community service, conceptual physics, drama, drama performance, English, English-AP, European history, foreign language, geography, geometry, government-AP, history of the Catholic Church, history-AP, honors algebra, honors English, honors geometry, honors U.S. history, honors world history, Latin, modern European history, physical education, religious education, SAT preparation, Spanish, student government,

swimming, tennis, theology, trigonometry, U.S. and Virginia government, U.S. and Virginia government-AP, U.S. history-AP, world history.

Graduation Requirements Admission to a 4-year institution, community service hours, state diploma standards.

Special Academic Programs Advanced Placement exam preparation; honors section.

College Admission Counseling 33 students graduated in 2015; all went to college, including Hampden-Sydney College; James Madison University; Johns Hopkins University; Radford University; Virginia Polytechnic Institute and State University. Median SAT critical reading: 540, median SAT math: 500, median composite ACT: 22.

Student Life Upper grades have uniform requirement, student council, honor system. Discipline rests equally with students and faculty. Attendance at religious services is required.

Summer Programs Enrichment, sports, art/fine arts, computer instruction programs offered; session focuses on extracurricular activities, art enrichment, and sports enrichment; held on campus; accepts boys and girls; open to students from other schools. 50 students usually enrolled. 2016 schedule: June 11 to August 24. Application deadline: none.

Tuition and Aid Day student tuition: $12,000. Tuition installment plan (FACTS Tuition Payment Plan). Tuition reduction for siblings, need-based scholarship grants available. In 2015–16, 30% of upper-school students received aid. Total amount of financial aid awarded in 2015–16: $150,000.

Admissions Traditional secondary-level entrance grade is 9. For fall 2015, 25 students applied for upper-level admission, 20 were accepted, 16 enrolled. Deadline for receipt of application materials: none. Application fee required: $50. Interview recommended.

Athletics Interscholastic: baseball (boys), basketball (b,g), football (b), softball (g), volleyball (g); intramural: basketball (b,g), football (b), softball (g), Special Olympics (b,g), volleyball (g); coed interscholastic: cheering, cross-country running, field hockey, golf, soccer, swimming and diving, tennis; coed intramural: cross-country running, soccer, swimming and diving, tennis. 2 PE instructors, 20 coaches, 1 athletic trainer.

Computers Computer network features include on-campus library services, online commercial services, Internet access, wireless campus network, Internet filtering or blocking technology. Campus intranet and student e-mail accounts are available to students. Students grades are available online. The school has a published electronic and media policy.

Contact Mrs. Jennifer Bussmann, Director of Admissions. 804-598-4211. Fax: 804-598-1053. E-mail: jbussman@bshknights.org. Website: www.bshknights.org

BLESSED TRINITY HIGH SCHOOL

11320 Woodstock Road
Roswell, Georgia 30075

Head of School: Mr. Frank Moore

General Information Coeducational day college-preparatory and religious studies school, affiliated with Roman Catholic Church. Grades 9–12. Founded: 2000. Setting: suburban. Nearest major city is Atlanta. 68-acre campus. 2 buildings on campus. Approved or accredited by Georgia Independent School Association, Southern Association of Colleges and Schools, Southern Association of Independent Schools, and Georgia Department of Education. Member of National Association of Independent Schools and Secondary School Admission Test Board. Upper school average class size: 20. Upper school faculty-student ratio: 1:13. There are 180 required school days per year for Upper School students. Upper School students typically attend 5 days per week. The average school day consists of 7 hours.

Upper School Student Profile Grade 9: 255 students (129 boys, 126 girls); Grade 10: 252 students (117 boys, 135 girls); Grade 11: 242 students (117 boys, 125 girls); Grade 12: 226 students (91 boys, 135 girls). 86% of students are Roman Catholic.

Faculty School total: 83. In upper school: 40 men, 43 women; 56 have advanced degrees.

Graduation Requirements Advanced math, algebra, American government, American history, American literature, ancient world history, arts and fine arts (art, music, dance, drama), biology, British literature, chemistry, economics, foreign language, geometry, health, personal finance, physics, theology, world history.

Special Academic Programs 23 Advanced Placement exams for which test preparation is offered; honors section.

College Admission Counseling 236 students graduated in 2015; all went to college, including Auburn University; Georgia College & State University; Georgia Institute of Technology; Georgia Southern University; The University of Alabama; University of Georgia.

Student Life Upper grades have uniform requirement, student council, honor system. Discipline rests primarily with faculty. Attendance at religious services is required.

Tuition and Aid Day student tuition: $11,850. Tuition installment plan (FACTS Tuition Payment Plan). Need-based scholarship grants available. In 2015–16, 19% of upper-school students received aid.

Admissions Traditional secondary-level entrance grade is 9. SSAT required. Deadline for receipt of application materials: February 1. Application fee required: $100.

Athletics Interscholastic: baseball (boys), basketball (b,g), cheering (g), cross-country running (b,g), dance (b,g), dance team (g), football (b), golf (b,g), lacrosse (b,g), soccer (b,g), softball (g), swimming and diving (b,g), tennis (b,g), track and field (b,g), volleyball (g), wrestling (b). 5 PE instructors, 2 athletic trainers.

Computers Computer network features include on-campus library services, Internet access, wireless campus network. Campus intranet and student e-mail accounts are available to students. Students grades are available online.

Contact Mr. Paul Stevens, Director of Admissions. 678-277-9083 Ext. 531. Fax: 678-277-9756. E-mail: pstevens@btcatholic.org. Website: www.btcatholic.org

BLUEPRINT EDUCATION

5651 West Talavi Boulevard
Suite 170
Glendale, Arizona 85306

Head of School: Mr. Mark French

General Information Distance learning only college-preparatory, general academic, vocational, technology, and distance learning school. Distance learning grades 7–12. Founded: 1969. Approved or accredited by CITA (Commission on International and Trans-Regional Accreditation), North Central Association of Colleges and Schools, and Arizona Department of Education.

Faculty School total: 4. In upper school: 1 man, 3 women; all have advanced degrees.

Subjects Offered 3-dimensional art, algebra, American government, American history, animation, art, art appreciation, art history, audio visual/media, auto mechanics, biology, business studies, calculus, career experience, career exploration, career planning, careers, chemistry, Chinese, computer applications, computer education, digital art, earth science, economics, English, entrepreneurship, foreign language, French, general business, geometry, German, government, health and wellness, health education, health science, information technology, interpersonal skills, literacy, mathematics, personal development, personal finance, physical education, physical fitness, physics, pre-algebra, psychology, reading, remedial/makeup course work, sociology, Spanish, speech communications, statistics, travel, trigonometry, U.S. government, U.S. history, work experience, world geography, world history.

Graduation Requirements Arts and fine arts (art, music, dance, drama), computers, economics, English, foreign language, geography, health, mathematics, science, social studies (includes history), speech.

Special Academic Programs Honors section; accelerated programs; independent study; academic accommodation for the musically talented and the artistically talented; remedial reading and/or remedial writing; remedial math.

College Admission Counseling Colleges students went to include Arizona State University at the Tempe campus; Northern Arizona University; Pima Community College; The University of Arizona.

Student Life Upper grades have honor system.

Summer Programs Remediation, advancement programs offered; session focuses on remediation and advancement; held off campus; held at various locations for independent study; accepts boys and girls; open to students from other schools.

Admissions Deadline for receipt of application materials: none. No application fee required.

Computers Computers are regularly used in all academic classes. Computer resources include Internet access. Students grades are available online. The school has a published electronic and media policy.

Contact Admissions. 800-426-4952. Fax: 602-943-9700. Website: www.blueprinteducation.org

BOCA PREP INTERNATIONAL SCHOOL

10333 Diego Drive South
Boca Raton, Florida 33428

Head of School: Mr. Stan L. Daniel

General Information Coeducational day college-preparatory school. Grades PK–12. Founded: 1998. Setting: suburban. Students are housed in Their own homes. 1.5-acre campus. 2 buildings on campus. Approved or accredited by Florida Council of Independent Schools, Southern Association of Colleges and Schools, and Florida Department of Education. Total enrollment: 243. Upper school average class size: 22. Upper school faculty-student ratio: 1:24. There are 186 required school days per year for Upper School students. Upper School students typically attend 5 days per week. The average school day consists of 7 hours and 10 minutes.

Upper School Student Profile Grade 6: 20 students (9 boys, 11 girls); Grade 7: 23 students (15 boys, 8 girls); Grade 8: 17 students (7 boys, 10 girls); Grade 9: 28 students (19 boys, 9 girls); Grade 10: 23 students (12 boys, 11 girls); Grade 11: 20 students (7 boys, 13 girls); Grade 12: 31 students (19 boys, 12 girls).

Faculty School total: 28. In upper school: 9 men, 19 women; 19 have advanced degrees.

Special Academic Programs International Baccalaureate program.

Student Life Upper grades have uniform requirement, student council, honor system. Discipline rests primarily with faculty.

Tuition and Aid Tuition installment plan (monthly payment plans). Tuition reduction for siblings, bursaries, merit scholarship grants, need-based scholarship grants available.

Admissions Traditional secondary-level entrance grade is 9. Deadline for receipt of application materials: none. Application fee required: $250. Interview required.

Athletics Coed Interscholastic: physical fitness, soccer, swimming and diving. 1 PE instructor, 3 coaches.

Computers Computer network features include on-campus library services, Internet access, Internet filtering or blocking technology. Campus intranet and student e-mail accounts are available to students. Students grades are available online. The school has a published electronic and media policy.

Contact Mrs. Lesley F. Fisher, Director of Admissions and Marketing. 561-852-1410 Ext. 222. Fax: 561-470-6124. E-mail: lesley.fisher@iesmail.com. Website: www.bocaprep.net

BODWELL HIGH SCHOOL

955 Harbourside Drive
North Vancouver, British Columbia V7P 3S4, Canada

Head of School: Ms. Cathy Lee

General Information Coeducational boarding and day college-preparatory, arts, business, and technology school. Grades 8–12. Founded: 1991. Setting: suburban. Students are housed in single-sex by floor dormitories. 2-acre campus. 1 building on campus. Approved or accredited by British Columbia Department of Education. Language of instruction: English. Total enrollment: 538. Upper school average class size: 17. Upper school faculty-student ratio: 1:15. There are 290 required school days per year for Upper School students. Upper School students typically attend 6 days per week. The average school day consists of 5 hours and 50 minutes.

Upper School Student Profile 80% of students are boarding students. 25% are province residents. 8 provinces are represented in upper school student body. 75% are international students. International students from Brazil, China, Japan, Mexico, Nigeria, and Russian Federation; 40 other countries represented in student body.

Faculty School total: 40. In upper school: 17 men, 23 women; 15 have advanced degrees; 2 reside on campus.

Subjects Offered 3-dimensional art, Advanced Placement courses, art, band, biology, calculus, chemistry, choral music, communications, composition, computer applications, drama, economics, English, entrepreneurship, ESL, French as a second language, geography, global studies, health and wellness, history, information technology, Japanese, leadership, Mandarin, mathematics, music, physical education, physics, psychology, science, social studies, Spanish, sports, studio art.

Graduation Requirements British Columbia Ministry of Education Requirements.

Special Academic Programs Advanced Placement exam preparation; accelerated programs; academic accommodation for the gifted; ESL (150 students enrolled).

College Admission Counseling 161 students graduated in 2015; 120 went to college, including Simon Fraser University; The University of British Columbia; University of Toronto; University of Victoria. Other: 41 had other specific plans.

Student Life Upper grades have uniform requirement, student council, honor system. Discipline rests primarily with faculty.

Summer Programs Advancement, ESL, sports, art/fine arts, computer instruction programs offered; session focuses on ESL and Activities; held both on and off campus; held at University of British Columbia, University of Victoria, and Quest University; accepts boys and girls; open to students from other schools. 400 students usually enrolled. 2016 schedule: July 10 to August 13. Application deadline: June 3.

Tuition and Aid Day student tuition: CAN$16,650; 7-day tuition and room/board: CAN$33,650. Merit scholarship grants available. In 2015–16, 2% of upper-school students received aid; total upper-school merit-scholarship money awarded: CAN$50,000.

Admissions Traditional secondary-level entrance grade is 10. For fall 2015, 299 students applied for upper-level admission, 249 were accepted, 219 enrolled. English proficiency required. Deadline for receipt of application materials: none. Application fee required: CAN$300. Interview required.

Athletics Interscholastic: aquatics (boys, girls), baseball (b), basketball (b,g), soccer (b), swimming and diving (b,g), volleyball (b,g); intramural: aquatics (b,g), badminton (b,g), baseball (b,g), basketball (b,g), cheering (g), fitness (b,g), floor hockey (b,g), hiking/backpacking (b,g), ice skating (b,g), indoor soccer (b), martial arts (b), mountain biking (b,g), outdoor activities (b,g), outdoor education (b,g), outdoor recreation (b,g), running (b,g), skiing (downhill) (b,g), snowboarding (b,g), snowshoeing (b,g), soccer (b), swimming and diving (b,g), table tennis (b,g), tennis (b,g), track and field (b,g), triathlon (b), ultimate Frisbee (b), volleyball (b,g), wrestling (b); coed interscholastic: aerobics/dance, aquatics, backpacking, badminton, ball hockey, bicycling, cross-country running, fitness, floor hockey, swimming and diving; coed intramural: aquatics, badminton, bicycling, bowling, canoeing/kayaking, climbing, cross-country running, dance, fishing, fitness, floor hockey, golf, hiking/backpacking, ice skating, indoor hockey, indoor soccer, kayaking, martial arts, mountain biking, outdoor activities, outdoor education, outdoor recreation, physical fitness, rock climbing, running, skiing (downhill), snowboarding, snowshoeing, soccer, strength & conditioning, swimming and diving, table tennis, tennis, track and field, ultimate Frisbee, volleyball, wall climbing, weight training, wilderness, wilderness survival, wrestling, yoga. 3 PE instructors, 5 coaches.

Computers Computers are regularly used in all academic classes. Computer network features include on-campus library services, Internet access, wireless campus network, Internet filtering or blocking technology. Campus intranet and student e-mail accounts are available to students. Students grades are available online. The school has a published electronic and media policy.

Contact Ms. Rachel Wong, Registration Manager. 604-998-1000. Fax: 604-998-1150. E-mail: office@bodwell.edu. Website: www.bodwell.edu

THE BOLLES SCHOOL
7400 San Jose Boulevard
Jacksonville, Florida 32217-3499
Head of School: David J. Farace

General Information Coeducational boarding and day college-preparatory and arts school. Boarding grades 7–PG, day grades PK–PG. Founded: 1933. Setting: suburban. Students are housed in single-sex dormitories. 52-acre campus. 12 buildings on campus. Approved or accredited by Florida Council of Independent Schools, National Independent Private Schools Association, Southern Association of Colleges and Schools, Southern Association of Independent Schools, The Association of Boarding Schools, and Florida Department of Education. Member of National Association of Independent Schools and Secondary School Admission Test Board. Endowment: $10.7 million. Total enrollment: 1,637. Upper school average class size: 17. Upper school faculty-student ratio: 1:12. There are 175 required school days per year for Upper School students. Upper School students typically attend 5 days per week. The average school day consists of 6 hours.

Upper School Student Profile Grade 9: 186 students (106 boys, 80 girls); Grade 10: 202 students (102 boys, 100 girls); Grade 11: 201 students (102 boys, 99 girls); Grade 12: 190 students (117 boys, 73 girls). 11% of students are boarding students. 88% are state residents. 4 states are represented in upper school student body. 12% are international students. International students from Brazil, China, Colombia, Democratic People's Republic of Korea, Germany, and Mexico; 16 other countries represented in student body.

Faculty School total: 157. In upper school: 54 men, 103 women; 69 have advanced degrees; 9 reside on campus.

Subjects Offered Acting, algebra, American government, American history, American history-AP, American literature, anatomy, art, art history, art history-AP, art-AP, band, biology, biology-AP, calculus, calculus-AP, ceramics, chemistry, chemistry-AP, Chinese, Chinese studies, chorus, comparative government and politics-AP, composition, computer science, contemporary history, dance, data analysis, design, directing, drama, drawing, driver education, ecology, economics, English, environmental science, ESL, European history, fine arts, fitness, French, French language-AP, French-AP, geography, geometry, government/civics, health, history, history-AP, humanities, Japanese, journalism, Latin, Latin-AP, life management skills, life skills, literature, marine science, mathematics, Middle Eastern history, modern European history-AP, multimedia, music, mythology, neurobiology, painting, performing arts, photography, physical education, physics, physics-AP, portfolio art, pre-algebra, pre-calculus, programming, psychology, public speaking, publications, science, sculpture, social sciences, social studies, Spanish, Spanish language-AP, Spanish-AP, speech and debate, statistics, statistics-AP, studio art, theater, U.S. government and politics-AP, U.S. history, U.S. history-AP, visual arts, Web site design, weight training, world cultures, world history.

Graduation Requirements Arts and fine arts (art, music, dance, drama), English, foreign language, mathematics, physical education (includes health), science, social studies (includes history).

Special Academic Programs International Baccalaureate program; Advanced Placement exam preparation; honors section; independent study; term-away projects; study at local college for college credit; ESL (45 students enrolled).

College Admission Counseling 197 students graduated in 2015; 194 went to college, including Florida State University; University of Florida; University of Mississippi; University of South Carolina; University of Virginia; Wake Forest University. Other: 1 entered a postgraduate year, 2 had other specific plans. 50% scored over 600 on SAT critical reading, 50% scored over 600 on SAT math, 49% scored over 600 on SAT writing, 47% scored over 1800 on combined SAT, 50% scored over 26 on composite ACT.

Student Life Upper grades have specified standards of dress, student council, honor system. Discipline rests equally with students and faculty.

Summer Programs Enrichment, ESL, art/fine arts, computer instruction programs offered; session focuses on Enrichment; held on campus; accepts boys and girls; open to students from other schools. 150 students usually enrolled. 2016 schedule: June 6 to July 22.

Tuition and Aid Day student tuition: $23,870; 7-day tuition and room/board: $48,750. Tuition installment plan (FACTS Tuition Payment Plan). Need-based scholarship grants, faculty tuition remission available. In 2015–16, 21% of upper-school students received aid. Total amount of financial aid awarded in 2015–16: $3,841,539.

Admissions Traditional secondary-level entrance grade is 9. For fall 2015, 485 students applied for upper-level admission, 351 were accepted, 243 enrolled. ISEE required. Deadline for receipt of application materials: none. Application fee required: $45. Interview required.

Athletics Interscholastic: baseball (boys), basketball (b,g), cheering (g), crew (b,g), cross-country running (b,g), dance (b,g), diving (b,g), football (b), golf (b,g), lacrosse (b,g), soccer (b,g), softball (g), swimming and diving (b,g), tennis (b,g), track and field (b,g), volleyball (g), weight lifting (b), wrestling (b). 2 PE instructors, 5 coaches, 1 athletic trainer.

Computers Computers are regularly used in all academic classes. Computer network features include on-campus library services, online commercial services, Internet access, wireless campus network, Internet filtering or blocking technology. Campus intranet, student e-mail accounts, and computer access in designated common areas are available to students. Students grades are available online. The school has a published electronic and media policy.

Contact Mark I. Frampton, Director of Upper School and Boarding Admission. 904-256-5032. Fax: 904-739-9929. E-mail: framptonm@bolles.org. Website: www.bolles.org

BOSTON TRINITY ACADEMY
17 Hale Street
Boston, Massachusetts 02136
Head of School: Mr. Frank Guerra

General Information Coeducational day college-preparatory school, affiliated with Christian faith. Grades 6–12. Founded: 2002. Setting: urban. 5-acre campus. 1 building on campus. Approved or accredited by Association of Independent Schools in New England, New England Association of Schools and Colleges, and Massachusetts Department of Education. Member of National Association of Independent Schools and Secondary School Admission Test Board. Total enrollment: 233. Upper school average class size: 14. Upper school faculty-student ratio: 1:8. There are 169 required school days per year for Upper School students. Upper School students typically attend 5 days per week. The average school day consists of 6 hours and 30 minutes.

Upper School Student Profile 80% of students are Christian faith.

Faculty School total: 34. In upper school: 11 men, 18 women; 19 have advanced degrees.

Special Academic Programs 12 Advanced Placement exams for which test preparation is offered; ESL.

College Admission Counseling 45 students graduated in 2014; all went to college.

Student Life Upper grades have uniform requirement, student council, honor system. Discipline rests primarily with faculty. Attendance at religious services is required.

Tuition and Aid Day student tuition: $16,500. Tuition installment plan (FACTS Tuition Payment Plan). Need-based scholarship grants available.

Admissions Traditional secondary level entrance grade is 9. ISEE or SSAT required. Deadline for receipt of application materials: January 31. Application fee required: $50. Interview required.

Athletics Interscholastic: baseball (boys), basketball (b,g), cross-country running (b,g), lacrosse (b,g), soccer (b,g), softball (g), tennis (b,g), wrestling (b); intramural: physical fitness (b,g), table tennis (b,g).

Computers Computer network features include on-campus library services, Internet access, wireless campus network, Internet filtering or blocking technology. Campus intranet and computer access in designated common areas are available to students. Students grades are available online. The school has a published electronic and media policy.

Contact Ms. Bisi Oloko, Associate Director of Admission. 617-364-3700. Fax: 617-364-3800. E-mail: boloko@bostontrinity.org. Website: www.bostontrinity.org

BOSTON UNIVERSITY ACADEMY
One University Road
Boston, Massachusetts 02215
Head of School: Dr. Ari M. Betof

General Information Coeducational day college-preparatory and arts school. Grades 9–12. Founded: 1993. Setting: urban. 132-acre campus. 1 building on campus. Approved or accredited by Association of Independent Schools in New England, New England Association of Schools and Colleges, and Massachusetts Department of Education. Member of National Association of Independent Schools and Secondary School Admission Test Board. Total enrollment: 170. Upper school average class size: 12. Upper school faculty-student ratio: 1:8. There are 164 required school days per year for Upper School students. Upper School students typically attend 5 days per week. The average school day consists of 7 hours.

Upper School Student Profile Grade 9: 38 students (23 boys, 15 girls); Grade 10: 55 students (35 boys, 20 girls); Grade 11: 33 students (17 boys, 16 girls); Grade 12: 44 students (26 boys, 18 girls).

Faculty School total: 20. In upper school: 12 men, 8 women; 18 have advanced degrees.

Subjects Offered Advanced math, African American studies, algebra, American history, American literature, Ancient Greek, ancient history, anthropology, Arabic, archaeology, art, art history, astronomy, biochemistry, biology, calculus, chemistry, Chinese, classical studies, college counseling, community service, computer programming, drama, English, English literature, European history, French, geometry, German, Hebrew, history, Italian, Japanese, Latin, music, physical education, physics, robotics, Russian, sculpture, senior project, Spanish, statistics, theater, trigonometry, women's studies, writing.

Graduation Requirements Ancient Greek, arts and fine arts (art, music, dance, drama), chemistry, English, history, Latin, mathematics, physical education (includes health), physics, two-semester senior thesis project, coursework at Boston University. Community service is required.

Special Academic Programs Honors section; accelerated programs; independent study; study at local college for college credit; academic accommodation for the gifted.

College Admission Counseling 41 students graduated in 2015; 40 went to college, including Boston University; Brown University; Rensselaer Polytechnic Institute; University of California, Berkeley; University of Rochester. Other: 1 went to work. Median SAT critical reading: 735, median SAT math: 720, median SAT writing: 730, median combined SAT: 2205. 97.5% scored over 600 on SAT critical reading, 97.5% scored over 600 on SAT math, 97.5% scored over 600 on SAT writing, 97.5% scored over 1800 on combined SAT.

Student Life Upper grades have student council, honor system. Discipline rests equally with students and faculty.

Tuition and Aid Day student tuition: $39,483. Tuition installment plan (Insured Tuition Payment Plan, monthly payment plans, individually arranged payment plans, Tuition Management Systems). Need-based scholarship grants available. In 2015–16, 40% of upper-school students received aid. Total amount of financial aid awarded in 2015–16: $1,514,582.

Admissions Traditional secondary-level entrance grade is 9. For fall 2015, 189 students applied for upper-level admission, 106 were accepted, 46 enrolled. SSAT required. Deadline for receipt of application materials: January 31. Application fee required: $50. On-campus interview required.

Athletics Interscholastic: basketball (boys, girls), crew (b,g); intramural: volleyball (g); coed interscholastic: cross-country running, fencing, soccer, tennis, ultimate Frisbee; coed intramural: climbing, dance, sailing, softball. 10 PE instructors, 7 coaches.

Computers Computers are regularly used in art, English, foreign language, history, mathematics, science classes. Computer network features include on-campus library services, online commercial services, Internet access, wireless campus network, Internet filtering or blocking technology, internal electronic bulletin board system. Campus intranet and student e-mail accounts are available to students. Students grades are available online. The school has a published electronic and media policy.

Contact Ms. Nastaran Hakimi, Associate Director of Admission. 617-358-2493. Fax: 617-353-8999. E-mail: nrhakimi@bu.edu. Website: www.buacademy.org

BOURGADE CATHOLIC HIGH SCHOOL

4602 North 31st Avenue
Phoenix, Arizona 85017

Head of School: Ms. Kathryn Rother

General Information Coeducational day college-preparatory, arts, religious studies, and English Pre-AP curriculum for 9th and 10th grade students school, affiliated with Roman Catholic Church. Grades 9–12. Founded: 1962. Setting: urban. 27-acre campus. 6 buildings on campus. Approved or accredited by North Central Association of Colleges and Schools, Western Catholic Education Association, and Arizona Department of Education. Total enrollment: 401. Upper school average class size: 32. Upper school faculty-student ratio: 1:20. There are 184 required school days per year for Upper School students. Upper School students typically attend 5 days per week. The average school day consists of 6 hours.

Upper School Student Profile Grade 9: 106 students (55 boys, 51 girls); Grade 10: 103 students (54 boys, 49 girls); Grade 11: 88 students (43 boys, 45 girls); Grade 12: 104 students (49 boys, 55 girls). 94% of students are Roman Catholic.

Faculty School total: 27. In upper school: 12 men, 15 women; 22 have advanced degrees.

Subjects Offered Acting, advanced biology, advanced chemistry, algebra, American government, American history, American history-AP, ancient world history, art, band, bell choir, biology, calculus, calculus-AP, Catholic belief and practice, chemistry, chemistry-AP, choir, Christian and Hebrew scripture, Christian doctrine, Christian ethics, church history, college admission preparation, computer graphics, constitutional history of U.S., creative dance, dance, desktop publishing, digital photography, drama performance, earth science, economics, English, English composition, foreign language, general science, geography, government, graphic design, health education, Hebrew scripture, honors algebra, honors English, honors geometry, honors U.S. history, honors world history, leadership and service, modern dance, New Testament, photography, pre-algebra, psychology, reading, social justice, Spanish, Spanish-AP, speech, study skills, theater arts, U.S. government, U.S. history, U.S. history-AP, world religions, yearbook.

Graduation Requirements Advanced Placement courses, arts and fine arts (art, music, dance, drama), English, foreign language, mathematics, physical education (includes health), religion (includes Bible studies and theology), science, Christian Service requirement of 20 service hours each year.

Special Academic Programs Advanced Placement exam preparation; honors section; study at local college for college credit; ESL (8 students enrolled).

College Admission Counseling 83 students graduated in 2014; all went to college, including Arizona State University at the Tempe campus; Grand Canyon University; Northern Arizona University; The University of Arizona.

Student Life Upper grades have uniform requirement, student council, honor system. Discipline rests primarily with faculty. Attendance at religious services is required.

Tuition and Aid Day student tuition: $12,920. Tuition installment plan (FACTS Tuition Payment Plan, monthly payment plans, individually arranged payment plans). Merit scholarship grants, need-based scholarship grants, paying campus jobs, Catholic Education Arizona (CEA) available. In 2014–15, 85% of upper-school students received aid. Total amount of financial aid awarded in 2014–15: $1,600,000.

Admissions Traditional secondary-level entrance grade is 9. For fall 2014, 410 students applied for upper-level admission, 410 were accepted, 401 enrolled. ETS high school placement exam or Stanford 9 required. Deadline for receipt of application materials: January 31. Application fee required: $40. On-campus interview required.

Athletics Interscholastic: baseball (boys), basketball (b,g), cheering (g), dance (g), danceline (g), football (b), golf (b), soccer (b), softball (g), strength & conditioning (b,g), swimming and diving (b,g), tennis (b,g), track and field (b,g), volleyball (g), wrestling (b); intramural: weight training (b,g). 2 PE instructors, 2 coaches, 1 athletic trainer.

Computers Computers are regularly used in all academic, art, college planning, design, foreign language, French, graphic arts, media, newspaper, photography, publications, SAT preparation classes. Computer network features include on-campus library services, Internet access, wireless campus network, Internet filtering or blocking technology. Campus intranet and student e-mail accounts are available to students. Students grades are available online. The school has a published electronic and media policy.

Contact Ms. Mary Ann Burns, Admissions Coordinator. 602-973-4000 Ext. 116. Fax: 602-973-5854. E-mail: maburns@bourgadecatholic.org. Website: www.bourgadecatholic.org

BOYD-BUCHANAN SCHOOL

4650 Buccaneer Trail
Chattanooga, Tennessee 37411

Head of School: Mrs. Jill Hartness

General Information Coeducational day college-preparatory and religious studies school, affiliated with Church of Christ. Grades PK–12. Founded: 1952. Setting: urban. 50-acre campus. 7 buildings on campus. Approved or accredited by National Christian School Association, Southern Association of Colleges and Schools, Tennessee Association of Independent Schools, and Tennessee Department of Education. Endowment: $3 million. Total enrollment: 868. Upper school average class size: 18. Upper school faculty-student ratio: 1:12. There are 177 required school days per year for Upper School students. Upper School students typically attend 5 days per week. The average school day consists of 6 hours.

Upper School Student Profile 30% of students are members of Church of Christ.

Faculty School total: 74. In upper school: 13 men, 17 women; 18 have advanced degrees.

Subjects Offered ACT preparation, Advanced Placement courses, algebra, American government, American history, American studies, art, band, Bible, biology, biology-AP, calculus, calculus-AP, chemistry, chemistry-AP, choir, choral music, chorus, computer applications, computer programming, concert choir, contemporary issues, contemporary problems, data processing, desktop publishing, ecology, economics, English, English composition, English language-AP, English literature, English literature and composition-AP, fitness, French, French-AP, geometry, government, health and wellness, honors algebra, honors English, honors geometry, integrated arts, jazz band, journalism, library assistant, music appreciation, music theory, physical science, physics, pre-algebra, pre-calculus, probability and statistics, psychology, SAT/ACT preparation, sociology, Spanish, Spanish-AP, theater arts, trigonometry, U.S. history, U.S. history-AP, Web site design, wellness, world geography, world history, yearbook.

Graduation Requirements Arts and fine arts (art, music, dance, drama), Bible, electives, English, foreign language, health and wellness, mathematics, physical education (includes health), physics, science, social sciences.

Special Academic Programs 11 Advanced Placement exams for which test preparation is offered; honors section.

College Admission Counseling 95 students graduated in 2015; all went to college, including Chattanooga State Community College; Lipscomb University; Middle Tennessee State University; Tennessee Technological University; The University of Tennessee; The University of Tennessee at Chattanooga.

Student Life Upper grades have uniform requirement, student council, honor system. Discipline rests primarily with faculty. Attendance at religious services is required.

Summer Programs Remediation, enrichment, sports programs offered; session focuses on sports and enrichment; held on campus; accepts boys and girls; open to students from other schools. 150 students usually enrolled. 2016 schedule: May 25 to June 30. Application deadline: May 25.

Tuition and Aid Day student tuition: $7480–$10,090. Tuition installment plan (FACTS Tuition Payment Plan, Tuition Bank). Tuition reduction for siblings, need-based scholarship grants, paying campus jobs available. In 2015–16, 4% of upper-school students received aid. Total amount of financial aid awarded in 2015–16: $80,000.

Admissions Traditional secondary-level entrance grade is 9. ISEE required. Deadline for receipt of application materials: none. Application fee required: $50. Interview required.

Athletics Interscholastic: baseball (boys), basketball (b,g), cheering (g), cross-country running (b,g), football (b), golf (b,g), soccer (b,g), softball (g), swimming and diving (b,g), tennis (b,g), volleyball (g), wrestling (b); coed interscholastic: archery. 3 PE instructors, 18 coaches, 1 athletic trainer.

Computers Computers are regularly used in creative writing, data processing, desktop publishing, journalism, keyboarding, newspaper, programming, study skills, technology, Web site design, word processing, writing, yearbook classes. Computer network features include on-campus library services, online commercial services, Internet access, wireless campus network, Internet filtering or blocking technology. Campus intranet, student e-mail accounts, and computer access in designated common areas are available to students. Students grades are available online. The school has a published electronic and media policy.

Contact Mrs. Heather Wamack, Secondary Admissions Director. 423-629-7610 Ext. 249. Fax: 423-508-2218. E-mail: hwamack@bbschool.org. Website: www.bbschool.org

BOYLAN CENTRAL CATHOLIC HIGH SCHOOL

4000 Saint Francis Drive
Rockford, Illinois 61103-1699

Head of School: Mr. Jerry Kerrigan

General Information Coeducational day and distance learning college-preparatory, general academic, arts, business, vocational, religious studies, bilingual studies, and technology school, affiliated with Roman Catholic Church. Grades 9–12. Distance learning grades 9–12. Founded: 1960. Setting: urban. Nearest major city is Chicago. 60-acre campus. 3 buildings on campus. Approved or accredited by National Catholic Education Association, North Central Association of Colleges and Schools, and Illinois Department of Education. Endowment: $3 million. Total enrollment: 1,012. Upper school average class size: 24. Upper school faculty-student ratio: 1:12. There are 176 required school days per year for Upper School students. Upper School students typically attend 5 days per week. The average school day consists of 7 hours.

Upper School Student Profile Grade 9: 252 students (133 boys, 119 girls); Grade 10: 243 students (116 boys, 127 girls); Grade 11: 255 students (129 boys, 126 girls); Grade 12: 262 students (126 boys, 136 girls). 90% of students are Roman Catholic.

Faculty School total: 71. In upper school: 27 men, 44 women; 55 have advanced degrees.

Subjects Offered 20th century history, 3-dimensional art, accounting, ACT preparation, acting, advanced computer applications, Advanced Placement courses, advanced studio art-AP, algebra, American history, American history-AP, American literature-AP, analysis and differential calculus, analytic geometry, anatomy and physiology, architectural drawing, architecture, art, art history, art history-AP, art-AP, athletics, band, biology, biology-AP, botany, British literature, British literature (honors), broadcasting, business, business education, business law, calculus, calculus-AP, career education, career exploration, career planning, Catholic belief and practice, cheerleading, chemistry, chemistry-AP, child development, Chinese, choir, chorus, Christian and Hebrew scripture, Christian doctrine, Christian ethics, church history, college counseling, communications, comparative religion, composition-AP, computer multimedia, computer-aided design, concert band, concert choir, consumer economics, consumer education, consumer mathematics, contemporary history, contemporary issues, contemporary studies, creative writing, critical thinking, culinary arts, debate, drafting, drama, dramatic arts, earth and space science, earth science, economics-AP, English, English language-AP, English literature-AP, English/composition-AP, environmental science, European history, European history-AP, family and consumer science, family living, fashion, fiction, finite math, foods, French, French as a second language, French literature-AP, French-AP, general math, geography, geometry, German, government, government and politics-AP, government-AP, graphics, guitar, health, health education, history of music, illustration, industrial technology, information processing, integrated science, jazz band, keyboarding, library assistant, marketing, music appreciation, music composition, music history, music technology, music theory, music theory-AP, physical science, physics, physics-AP, pre-algebra, pre-calculus, psychology, psychology-AP, religion, senior composition, Spanish, Spanish literature, Spanish-AP, statistics, studio art, swimming, technological applications, technology/design, trigonometry, U.S. history, vocal music, Web authoring, Web site design, world geography, world history, world literature, writing, yearbook, zoology.

Graduation Requirements Consumer education, critical thinking, English, mathematics, physical education (includes health), religious studies, science, social studies (includes history), fine and applied arts, community service.

Special Academic Programs 14 Advanced Placement exams for which test preparation is offered; honors section; independent study; academic accommodation for the gifted, the musically talented, and the artistically talented; remedial reading and/or remedial writing; remedial math; programs in general development for dyslexic students; special instructional classes for deaf students, blind students.

College Admission Counseling 254 students graduated in 2014; 230 went to college, including Illinois State University; Iowa State University of Science and Technology; Marquette University; Northern Illinois University; University of Illinois at Urbana–Champaign; University of Missouri. Other: 1 went to work, 1 entered military service, 22 had other specific plans. 26% scored over 26 on composite ACT.

Student Life Upper grades have uniform requirement, student council. Discipline rests primarily with faculty. Attendance at religious services is required.

Tuition and Aid Day student tuition: $5900. Tuition installment plan (monthly payment plans, individually arranged payment plans, full-year or semester payment plan). Tuition reduction for siblings, need-based scholarship grants, paying campus jobs available. In 2014–15, 30% of upper-school students received aid. Total amount of financial aid awarded in 2014–15: $562,000.

Admissions Traditional secondary-level entrance grade is 9. For fall 2014, 270 students applied for upper-level admission, 270 were accepted, 252 enrolled. ETS HSPT (closed) required. Deadline for receipt of application materials: none. Application fee required: $100. Interview required.

Athletics Interscholastic: aerobics/dance (girls), baseball (b), basketball (b,g), bowling (b,g), cheering (g), cross-country running (b,g), dance (g), dance team (g), diving (b,g), fishing (b,g), football (b), golf (b,g), soccer (b,g), softball (g), swimming and diving (b,g), tennis (b,g), track and field (b,g), volleyball (b,g), wrestling (b); intramural: outdoor education (b,g), physical fitness (b,g), physical training (b,g), running (b,g), strength & conditioning (b,g), weight training (b,g); coed intramural: Frisbee, ultimate Frisbee. 4 PE instructors, 1 athletic trainer.

Computers Computers are regularly used in all academic, architecture, business applications, computer applications, desktop publishing, drawing and design, keyboarding, music technology, photography, publications, technical drawing, technology, video film production, Web site design, word processing, yearbook classes. Computer network features include on-campus library services, online commercial services, Internet access, wireless campus network, Internet filtering or blocking technology. Campus intranet, student e-mail accounts, and computer access in designated common areas are available to students. Students grades are available online. The school has a published electronic and media policy.

Contact Mrs. Penny Yurkew, Assistant Principal. 815-877-0531 Ext. 227. Fax: 815-877-2544. E-mail: pyurkew@boylan.org. Website: www.boylan.org

BRANDON HALL SCHOOL

Atlanta, Georgia
See Special Needs Schools section.

BRANKSOME HALL

10 Elm Avenue
Toronto, Ontario M4W 1N4, Canada

Head of School: Ms. Karen L. Jurjevich

General Information Girls' boarding and day college-preparatory and arts school. Boarding grades 7–12, day grades JK–12. Founded: 1903. Setting: urban. Students are housed in single-sex dormitories. 13-acre campus. 6 buildings on campus. Approved or accredited by Canadian Association of Independent Schools, Canadian Educational Standards Institute, International Baccalaureate Organization, Ontario Ministry of Education, The Association of Boarding Schools, and Ontario Department of Education. Affiliate member of National Association of Independent Schools; member of Secondary School Admission Test Board. Language of instruction: English. Endowment: CAN$17 million. Total enrollment: 895. Upper school average class size: 20. Upper school faculty-student ratio: 1:9. There are 180 required school days per year for Upper School students. Upper School students typically attend 5 days per week. The average school day consists of 8 hours.

Upper School Student Profile Grade 9: 113 students (113 girls); Grade 10: 117 students (117 girls); Grade 11: 116 students (116 girls); Grade 12: 111 students (111 girls). 12% of students are boarding students. 87% are province residents. 8 provinces are represented in upper school student body. 13% are international students. International students from China, Germany, India, Mexico, Nigeria, and United States; 12 other countries represented in student body.

Faculty School total: 130. In upper school: 14 men, 81 women; 25 have advanced degrees; 6 reside on campus.

Subjects Offered Accounting, acting, advanced math, algebra, American history, American literature, ancient history, ancient world history, Arabic, art, art and culture, art history, arts, athletics, band, biology, British history, British literature, business, calculus, Canadian geography, Canadian history, Canadian law, Canadian literature, Cantonese, career and personal planning, career exploration, career/college preparation, chemistry, Chinese, Chinese studies, classical civilization, classical Greek literature, computer multimedia, computer programming, computer science, critical thinking, critical writing, drama, drawing, economics, economics and history, English, English literature, environmental science, environmental systems, ethics, European history, European literature, expository writing, film studies, fine arts, food science, French, French studies, geography, geometry, German, government/civics, health, history, home economics, independent study, interdisciplinary studies, Latin, Mandarin, mathematics, music, physical education, physics, science, social sciences, social studies, Spanish, theater, theory of knowledge, trigonometry, vocal ensemble, vocal music, world affairs, world arts, world civilizations, world cultures, world geography, world governments, world history, world issues, world literature, world religions, world studies, writing, writing workshop, yearbook.

Graduation Requirements Arts and fine arts (art, music, dance, drama), business skills (includes word processing), English, International Baccalaureate courses, language, mathematics, physical education (includes health), science, social sciences, social studies (includes history), International Baccalaureate diploma or certificate requirements.

Special Academic Programs International Baccalaureate program; honors section; academic accommodation for the gifted, the musically talented, and the artistically talented; ESL (38 students enrolled).

College Admission Counseling 111 students graduated in 2015; all went to college, including Dalhousie University; McGill University; Queen's University at Kingston; The University of Western Ontario; University of Southern California; University of Toronto. Mean SAT critical reading: 605, mean SAT math: 632, mean SAT writing: 621, mean combined SAT: 1858, mean composite ACT: 26.

Student Life Upper grades have uniform requirement, student council, honor system. Discipline rests primarily with faculty.

Tuition and Aid Day student tuition: CAN$29,590; 7-day tuition and room/board: CAN$54,605. Tuition installment plan (Insured Tuition Payment Plan, monthly payment plans, tri-annual payment, early payment option ($500 savings)). Bursaries, merit scholarship grants available. In 2015–16, 8% of upper-school students received aid; total upper-school merit-scholarship money awarded: CAN$192,500. Total amount of financial aid awarded in 2015–16: CAN$600,000.

Admissions Traditional secondary-level entrance grade is 9. For fall 2015, 251 students applied for upper-level admission, 74 were accepted, 56 enrolled. English entrance exam, Math Placement Exam or SSAT required. Deadline for receipt of application materials: December 4. Application fee required: CAN$210. Interview required.

Athletics Interscholastic: alpine skiing, aquatics, badminton, baseball, basketball, crew, cross-country running, dance, dance team, field hockey, golf, hockey, ice hockey, indoor track, indoor track & field, nordic skiing, rowing, skiing (downhill), soccer, softball, swimming and diving, synchronized swimming, tennis, track and field, volleyball; intramural: aerobics, aerobics/dance, aquatics, badminton, ball hockey, ballet, basketball, climbing, cooperative games, cross-country running, dance, dance squad, fitness, fitness walking, floor hockey, Frisbee, gymnastics, jogging, modern dance, nordic skiing, outdoor activities, paddle tennis, physical fitness, physical training, rock climbing, rugby, soccer, softball, squash, strength & conditioning, swimming and diving, table tennis, tennis, track and field, triathlon, volleyball, yoga. 6 PE instructors, 2 coaches, 1 athletic trainer.

Computers Computers are regularly used in all academic classes. Computer network features include on-campus library services, Internet access, wireless campus network, Internet filtering or blocking technology. Campus intranet, student e-mail accounts, and computer access in designated common areas are available to students. The school has a published electronic and media policy.

Contact Kimberly Carter, Director of Enrolment Management. 416-920-6265 Ext. 136. Fax: 416-920-5390. E-mail: admissions@branksome.on.ca. Website: www.branksome.on.ca

BRECK SCHOOL

123 Ottawa Avenue North
Golden Valley, Minnesota 55422

Head of School: Edward Kim

General Information Coeducational day college-preparatory, arts, religious studies, and service school, affiliated with Episcopal Church. Grades PK–12. Founded: 1886. Setting: suburban. Nearest major city is Minneapolis. 53-acre campus. 1 building on campus. Approved or accredited by Independent Schools Association of the Central States. Member of National Association of Independent Schools and Secondary School Admission Test Board. Total enrollment: 1,185. Upper school average class size: 16. Upper school faculty-student ratio: 1:16. The average school day consists of 6 hours and 15 minutes.

Upper School Student Profile 10% of students are members of Episcopal Church.

Faculty School total: 145. In upper school: 12 men, 17 women; 22 have advanced degrees.

Subjects Offered Algebra, American history, American literature, art, astronomy, biology, calculus, ceramics, chemistry, Chinese, chorus, community service, computer math, computer programming, creative writing, dance, drama, ecology, economics, English, English literature, environmental science, ethics, European history, expository writing, fine arts, French, geometry, health, history, mathematics, music, orchestra, physical education, physics, religion, science, social studies, Spanish, statistics, theater, theology, trigonometry, world history, world literature, writing.

Graduation Requirements Arts and fine arts (art, music, dance, drama), English, foreign language, mathematics, physical education (includes health), religion (includes Bible studies and theology), science, social studies (includes history), senior speech, May Program, service. Community service is required.

Special Academic Programs Advanced Placement exam preparation; honors section; independent study; term-away projects; academic accommodation for the gifted, the musically talented, and the artistically talented.

College Admission Counseling 106 students graduated in 2015; 105 went to college, including Bowdoin College; Carleton College; Colgate University; Pepperdine University; Washington University in St. Louis; Williams College. Median SAT critical reading: 640, median SAT math: 640, median SAT writing: 650, median combined SAT: 1910, median composite ACT: 29. 64% scored over 600 on SAT critical reading, 67% scored over 600 on SAT math, 67% scored over 600 on SAT writing, 67% scored over 1800 on combined SAT, 70% scored over 26 on composite ACT.

Student Life Upper grades have specified standards of dress, student council, honor system. Discipline rests equally with students and faculty. Attendance at religious services is required.

Tuition and Aid Day student tuition: $27,995. Tuition installment plan (Key Tuition Payment Plan). Need-based scholarship grants available. In 2015–16, 23% of upper-school students received aid.

Admissions Traditional secondary-level entrance grade is 9. CTP III required. Deadline for receipt of application materials: February 1. Application fee required: $75. On-campus interview required.

Athletics Interscholastic: alpine skiing (boys, girls), baseball (b), basketball (b,g), cross-country running (b,g), diving (b,g), football (b), golf (b,g), gymnastics (g), ice hockey (b,g), lacrosse (b,g), nordic skiing (b,g), skiing (cross-country) (b,g), skiing (downhill) (b,g), soccer (b,g), softball (g), swimming and diving (b,g), tennis (b,g), track and field (b,g), volleyball (g). 6 PE instructors, 82 coaches, 1 athletic trainer.

Computers Computers are regularly used in all classes. Computer network features include on-campus library services, online commercial services, Internet access, wireless campus network, Internet filtering or blocking technology, multimedia imaging, video presentation, student laptop program. Campus intranet and student e-mail accounts are available to students. Students grades are available online. The school has a published electronic and media policy.

Contact Scott D. Wade, Director of Admissions. 763-381-8200. Fax: 763-381-8288. E-mail: scott.wade@breckschool.org. Website: www.breckschool.org

BREHM PREPARATORY SCHOOL

Carbondale, Illinois
See Special Needs Schools section.

BRENTWOOD COLLEGE SCHOOL

2735 Mount Baker Road
Mill Bay, British Columbia V0R 2P1, Canada

Head of School: Mr. Bud Patel

General Information Coeducational boarding and day college-preparatory, arts, and athletics, leadership, and citizenship school. Grades 9–12. Founded: 1923. Setting: small town. Nearest major city is Victoria, Canada. Students are housed in single-sex dormitories. 77-acre campus. 16 buildings on campus. Approved or accredited by The Association of Boarding Schools, Western Boarding Schools Association, and British Columbia Department of Education. Affiliate member of National Association of Independent Schools. Language of instruction: English. Endowment: CAN$10 million. Total enrollment: 510. Upper school average class size: 16. Upper school faculty-student ratio: 1:9. Upper School students typically attend 6 days per week. The average school day consists of 6 hours.

Upper School Student Profile Grade 9: 73 students (37 boys, 36 girls); Grade 10: 142 students (77 boys, 65 girls); Grade 11: 148 students (60 boys, 88 girls); Grade 12: 147 students (79 boys, 68 girls). 81% of students are boarding students. 58% are province residents. 20 provinces are represented in upper school student body. 27% are international students. International students from Germany, Hong Kong, Mexico, Republic of Korea, Saudi Arabia, and United States; 21 other countries represented in student body.

Faculty School total: 50. In upper school: 28 men, 22 women; 39 have advanced degrees; 30 reside on campus.

Subjects Offered Advanced Placement courses, algebra, art history-AP, athletics, audio visual/media, band, basketball, biology, biology-AP, business, calculus, calculus-AP, Canadian geography, Canadian history, Canadian law, career and personal planning, ceramics, chemistry, chemistry-AP, choir, choreography, computer graphics, computer science, dance, dance performance, debate, design, drafting, drama, dramatic arts, drawing, economics, economics-AP, English, English literature, English literature-AP, French, French language-AP, geography, geometry, golf, government and politics-AP, health and wellness, history, human geography - AP, information technology, instrumental music, international studies, jazz band, jazz ensemble, marketing, mathematics, musical productions, musical theater, orchestra, outdoor education, painting, photography, physics, physics-AP, pottery, psychology, psychology-AP, public speaking, science, sculpture, sex education, social studies, Spanish, Spanish-AP, stagecraft, technical theater, tennis, theater design and production, video film production, visual and performing arts, vocal jazz, volleyball, yearbook.

Graduation Requirements Arts and fine arts (art, music, dance, drama), career and personal planning, English, foreign language, mathematics, physical education (includes health), science, social studies (includes history).

Special Academic Programs Advanced Placement exam preparation.

College Admission Counseling 112 students graduated in 2015; all went to college, including Duke University; McGill University; Queen's University at Kingston; The University of British Columbia; University of California, Berkeley; University of California, Los Angeles.

Student Life Upper grades have uniform requirement, student council, honor system. Discipline rests primarily with faculty.

Summer Programs Sports programs offered; session focuses on athletics and arts; held on campus; accepts boys and girls; open to students from other schools. 30 students usually enrolled. 2016 schedule: July to July. Application deadline: July.

Tuition and Aid Day student tuition: CAN$23,800; 7-day tuition and room/board: CAN$44,500–CAN$60,500. Tuition installment plan (The Tuition Plan). Tuition reduction for siblings available. In 2015–16, 20% of upper-school students received aid.

Admissions Traditional secondary-level entrance grade is 9. Henmon-Nelson or SSAT required. Deadline for receipt of application materials: none. Application fee required: CAN$2500. Interview required.

Athletics Interscholastic: basketball (boys, girls), crew (b,g), cross-country running (b,g), field hockey (g), hockey (g), rowing (b,g), rugby (b,g), running (b,g), soccer (b,g), squash (b,g), tennis (b,g), volleyball (g); intramural: crew (b,g), cross-country running (b,g), field hockey (g), indoor hockey (g), soccer (b,g), squash (b,g), tennis (b,g), track and field (b,g), volleyball (g), weight training (g); coed interscholastic: badminton, ballet, canoeing/kayaking, fitness, golf, ice hockey, judo, kayaking, modern dance, ocean paddling, outdoor activities, rock climbing, sailing; coed intramural: aerobics, aerobics/dance, badminton, canoeing/kayaking, cooperative games, dance, fitness, floor hockey, hiking/backpacking, indoor soccer, kayaking, outdoor activities, physical fitness, physical training, rowing, rugby, running, skiing (downhill), snowboarding, strength & conditioning, table tennis, touch football, weight lifting, weight training. 6 PE instructors, 36 coaches.

Computers Computers are regularly used in photojournalism, video film production classes. Computer network features include on-campus library services, Internet access, wireless campus network, Internet filtering or blocking technology. Campus intranet and student e-mail accounts are available to students. The school has a published electronic and media policy.

Contact Mr. Clayton Johnston, Director of Admissions. 250-743-5521. Fax: 250-743-2911. E-mail: admissions@brentwood.bc.ca. Website: www.brentwood.bc.ca

BRENTWOOD SCHOOL

100 South Barrington Place
Los Angeles, California 90049

Head of School: Dr. Michael Riera

General Information Coeducational day college-preparatory school. Grades K–12. Founded: 1972. Setting: suburban. 30-acre campus. 12 buildings on campus. Approved or accredited by California Association of Independent Schools, Northwest Association of Independent Schools, Western Association of Schools and Colleges, and Western Catholic Education Association. Member of National Association of Independent Schools and Secondary School Admission Test Board. Endowment: $13 million. Total enrollment: 995. Upper school average class size: 17. Upper school faculty-student ratio: 1:8. There are 170 required school days per year for Upper School students. Upper School students typically attend 5 days per week. The average school day consists of 8 hours.

Upper School Student Profile Grade 9: 126 students (65 boys, 61 girls); Grade 10: 122 students (63 boys, 59 girls); Grade 11: 115 students (63 boys, 52 girls); Grade 12: 103 students (52 boys, 51 girls).

Faculty School total: 130. In upper school: 45 men, 49 women; 60 have advanced degrees.

Subjects Offered Acting, Advanced Placement courses, advanced studio art-AP, algebra, American history, American literature, Ancient Greek, anthropology, art, art history, art history-AP, art-AP, astronomy, biology, biology-AP, calculus, calculus-AP, ceramics, chemistry, chemistry-AP, Chinese, choir, choral music, chorus, community service, comparative government and politics-AP, computer programming, computer programming-AP, computer science, computer science-AP, concert choir, creative writing, dance, digital photography, directing, drama, drawing, ecology, economics, economics-AP, English, English literature, environmental science-AP, European history, filmmaking, fine arts, French, French-AP, geometry, global studies, government and politics-AP, government-AP, history, honors algebra, honors English, honors geometry, human development, human geography - AP, Japanese, jazz band, jazz dance, journalism, language-AP, Latin, Latin-AP, literature-AP, math analysis, mathematics, music, music theater, music theory-AP, orchestra, organic chemistry, philosophy, photography, physical education, physics, physics-AP, probability and statistics, robotics, science, senior seminar, senior thesis, social sciences, social studies, Spanish, Spanish-AP, speech, speech and debate, stagecraft, stained glass, statistics-AP, studio art-AP, theater, U.S. government and politics-AP, U.S. history-AP, video, word processing, world history, world literature.

Graduation Requirements Arts and fine arts (art, music, dance, drama), English, foreign language, mathematics, physical education (includes health), science, social sciences, social studies (includes history). Community service is required.

Special Academic Programs 26 Advanced Placement exams for which test preparation is offered; honors section; independent study; study at local college for college credit; academic accommodation for the gifted and the artistically talented.

College Admission Counseling 103 students graduated in 2015; all went to college, including New York University; Northwestern University; University of Michigan; University of Pennsylvania; University of Southern California; Yale University. Mean SAT critical reading: 660, mean SAT math: 660, mean SAT writing: 683, mean combined SAT: 2003, mean composite ACT: 31.

Student Life Upper grades have specified standards of dress, student council, honor system. Discipline rests primarily with faculty.

Summer Programs Remediation, enrichment, advancement, sports, art/fine arts, computer instruction programs offered; session focuses on academic enrichment and sports; held on campus; accepts boys and girls; open to students from other schools. 350 students usually enrolled. 2016 schedule: June 20 to August 5. Application deadline: none.

Tuition and Aid Day student tuition: $37,725. Tuition installment plan (Insured Tuition Payment Plan, monthly payment plans, individually arranged payment plans). Need-based scholarship grants available. In 2015–16, 15% of upper-school students received aid. Total amount of financial aid awarded in 2015–16: $3,500,000.

Admissions Traditional secondary-level entrance grade is 9. For fall 2015, 200 students applied for upper-level admission, 12 were accepted, 8 enrolled. ISEE required. Deadline for receipt of application materials: January 11. Application fee required: $125. Interview required.

Athletics Interscholastic: baseball (boys), basketball (b,g), cheering (g), cross-country running (b,g), dance squad (g), dance team (g), football (b), independent competitive sports (b,g), lacrosse (b,g), soccer (b,g), softball (g), swimming and diving (b,g), tennis (b,g), track and field (b,g), volleyball (b,g), water polo (b), wrestling (b); intramural: modern dance (g), ultimate Frisbee (b); coed interscholastic: dance, drill team, equestrian sports, fencing, football, golf, swimming and diving, water polo; coed intramural: fitness, Frisbee, jogging, mountain biking, outdoor activities, physical fitness, physical training, running, sailing, surfing, table tennis, ultimate Frisbee, weight lifting, weight training, wilderness, yoga. 6 PE instructors, 40 coaches, 2 athletic trainers.

Computers Computers are regularly used in college planning, computer applications, desktop publishing, digital applications, foreign language, graphic design, introduction to technology, journalism, literary magazine, mathematics, media arts, media production, photojournalism, programming, publications, research skills, science, technical drawing, technology, video film production, Web site design classes. Computer network features include on-campus library services, online commercial services, Internet access, wireless campus network, Internet filtering or blocking technology, Schoology (learning management system). Campus intranet, student e-mail accounts, and computer access in designated common areas are available to students. Students grades are available online. The school has a published electronic and media policy.

Contact Ms. Melissa Gruenthal, Admissions Administrative Assistant. 310-889-2657. Fax: 310-476-4087. E-mail: mgruenthal@bwscampus.com. Website: www.bwscampus.com

BRENTWOOD SCHOOL

PO Box 955
725 Linton Road
Sandersville, Georgia 31082

Head of School: Mr. Layne A. Brennick

General Information Coeducational day college preparatory school. Grades PK–12. Founded: 1969. Setting: rural. Nearest major city is Macon. 20-acre campus. 2 buildings on campus. Approved or accredited by Southern Association of Colleges and Schools and Southern Association of Independent Schools. Endowment: $8 million. Total enrollment: 324. Upper school average class size: 16. Upper school faculty-student ratio: 1:11. There are 180 required school days per year for Upper School students. Upper School students typically attend 5 days per week. The average school day consists of 6 hours.

Upper School Student Profile Grade 6: 25 students (21 boys, 4 girls); Grade 7: 30 students (14 boys, 16 girls); Grade 8: 31 students (12 boys, 19 girls); Grade 9: 18 students (7 boys, 11 girls); Grade 10: 16 students (6 boys, 10 girls); Grade 11: 27 students (11 boys, 16 girls); Grade 12: 31 students (18 boys, 13 girls).

Faculty School total: 30. In upper school: 3 men, 11 women; 9 have advanced degrees.

Subjects Offered Advanced Placement courses, algebra, American history, American literature, art, art history, biology, calculus, chemistry, computer science, earth science, economics, English, English literature, environmental science, French, geography, geometry, government/civics, grammar, history, mathematics, music appreciation, physical education, physics, psychology, science, social studies, statistics, trigonometry, world history, world literature.

Graduation Requirements Algebra, American government, American history, American literature, biology, British literature, chemistry, composition, computer applications, economics, electives, English, English composition, environmental science, foreign language, French, geography, geometry, mathematics, physical education (includes health), physical science, science, social studies (includes history), world history.

Special Academic Programs 3 Advanced Placement exams for which test preparation is offered.

College Admission Counseling 37 students graduated in 2014; all went to college, including Georgia College & State University; Georgia Southern University; Mercer University; University of Georgia; Valdosta State University. Median SAT critical reading: 530, median SAT math: 530, median SAT writing: 580, median combined SAT: 1650. 17% scored over 600 on SAT critical reading, 14% scored over 600 on SAT math, 38% scored over 600 on SAT writing, 28% scored over 1800 on combined SAT.

Student Life Upper grades have specified standards of dress, student council, honor system. Discipline rests primarily with faculty.

Tuition and Aid Day student tuition: $6500. Tuition installment plan (monthly payment plans). Tuition reduction for siblings, need-based scholarship grants available.

Admissions Traditional secondary-level entrance grade is 9. For fall 2014, 2 students applied for upper-level admission, 2 were accepted, 2 enrolled. Admissions testing required. Deadline for receipt of application materials: none. Application fee required: $100. On-campus interview required.

Athletics Interscholastic: baseball (boys), basketball (b,g), cheering (g), cross-country running (b,g), dance team (g), football (b), golf (b,g), softball (g), tennis (b,g), track and field (b,g); coed interscholastic: cross-country running. 4 PE instructors, 4 coaches, 1 athletic trainer.

Computers Computers are regularly used in computer applications classes. Computer network features include on-campus library services, Internet access, wireless campus network, Internet filtering or blocking technology. Campus intranet and computer access in designated common areas are available to students. Students grades are available online. The school has a published electronic and media policy.

Contact Mrs. Anne R. Brantley, Assistant Head of School. 478-552-5136. Fax: 478-552-2947. E-mail: abrantley@brentwoodschool.org. Website: www.brentwoodschool.org

BRETHREN CHRISTIAN JUNIOR AND SENIOR HIGH SCHOOLS

21141 Strathmoor Lane
Huntington Beach, California 92646

Head of School: Mr. Rick Niswonger

General Information Coeducational day college-preparatory, arts, and religious studies school, affiliated with Christian faith; primarily serves students with learning disabilities. Grades 6–12. Founded: 1947. Setting: suburban. 15-acre campus. 1 building on campus. Approved or accredited by Association of Christian Schools International, Western Association of Schools and Colleges, and California Department of Education. Endowment: $250,000. Total enrollment: 313. Upper school average class size: 19. Upper school faculty-student ratio: 1:13. There are 174 required school days per year for Upper School students. Upper School students typically attend 5 days per week. The average school day consists of 6 hours and 35 minutes.

Upper School Student Profile Grade 9: 53 students (28 boys, 25 girls); Grade 10: 75 students (45 boys, 30 girls); Grade 11: 46 students (24 boys, 22 girls); Grade 12: 61 students (36 boys, 25 girls). 95% of students are Christian.

Faculty School total: 30. In upper school: 10 men, 16 women; 7 have advanced degrees.

Subjects Offered Algebra, American government, American literature, anatomy and physiology, art, ASB Leadership, athletics, band, basketball, Bible, biology, biology-AP, calculus-AP, cheerleading, chemistry, choir, Christian ethics, comedy, concert band, drama, drama performance, drama workshop, economics, English literature, English literature and composition-AP, fitness, golf, government, jazz band, keyboarding, math analysis, physical education, physics, pre-algebra, Spanish, studio art, theater, U.S. history, U.S. history-AP, volleyball, weightlifting, world history-AP.

Graduation Requirements Algebra, American literature, arts and fine arts (art, music, dance, drama), Bible, biology, chemistry, computer applications, economics, English composition, English literature, geometry, physical education (includes health), physics, U.S. government, U.S. history, world history, geography and current issues.

Special Academic Programs 6 Advanced Placement exams for which test preparation is offered; accelerated programs; academic accommodation for the gifted; remedial reading and/or remedial writing; remedial math; special instructional classes for deaf students, blind students.

College Admission Counseling 63 students graduated in 2014; 58 went to college, including Azusa Pacific University; Biola University; California State University, Long Beach; Chapman University; Grand Canyon University; University of California, Irvine. Other: 4 went to work, 1 had other specific plans. Mean SAT critical reading: 521, mean SAT math: 574, mean SAT writing: 511. 27% scored over 600 on SAT critical reading, 41% scored over 600 on SAT math, 22% scored over 600 on SAT writing.

Student Life Upper grades have specified standards of dress, student council. Discipline rests primarily with faculty. Attendance at religious services is required.

Tuition and Aid Tuition installment plan (monthly payment plans, individually arranged payment plans, pre-payment discount). Need-based scholarship grants, need- and merit-based financial aid available. In 2014–15, 25% of upper-school students received aid. Total amount of financial aid awarded in 2014–15: $7500.

Admissions Traditional secondary-level entrance grade is 9. For fall 2014, 68 students applied for upper-level admission, 63 were accepted, 62 enrolled. Achievement tests, Math Placement Exam and PSAT required. Deadline for receipt of application materials: none. Application fee required: $395. On-campus interview required.

Athletics Interscholastic: baseball (boys), basketball (b,g), cheering (g), cross-country running (b,g), dance (b,g), flag football (b), football (b), golf (b), physical fitness (b,g), soccer (b,g), softball (g), strength & conditioning (g), track and field (b,g), volleyball (b,g). 2 PE instructors, 14 coaches, 1 athletic trainer.

Computers Computers are regularly used in computer applications classes. Computer network features include on-campus library services, online commercial services, Internet access, wireless campus network, Internet filtering or blocking technology. Student e-mail accounts and computer access in designated common areas are available

to students. Students grades are available online. The school has a published electronic and media policy.

Contact Mrs. June Helton, Records Secretary. 714-962-6617 Ext. 14. Fax: 714-962-3171. E-mail: jhelton@bchs.net. Website: www.bchs.net

BREWSTER ACADEMY

80 Academy Drive
Wolfeboro, New Hampshire 03894

Head of School: Dr. Michael E. Cooper

General Information Coeducational boarding and day college-preparatory, arts, and technology school. Grades 9–PG. Founded: 1820. Setting: small town. Nearest major city is Boston, MA. Students are housed in single-sex dormitories. 91-acre campus. 39 buildings on campus. Approved or accredited by Independent Schools of Northern New England, New England Association of Schools and Colleges, and The Association of Boarding Schools. Member of National Association of Independent Schools and Secondary School Admission Test Board. Endowment: $15 million. Total enrollment: 358. Upper school average class size: 12. Upper school faculty-student ratio: 1:6. There are 165 required school days per year for Upper School students. Upper School students typically attend 6 days per week. The average school day consists of 6 hours.

Upper School Student Profile Grade 9: 50 students (27 boys, 23 girls); Grade 10: 97 students (49 boys, 48 girls); Grade 11: 97 students (60 boys, 37 girls); Grade 12: 87 students (49 boys, 38 girls); Postgraduate: 27 students (25 boys, 2 girls). 83% of students are boarding students. 26% are state residents. 27 states are represented in upper school student body. 20% are international students. International students from Canada, China, Japan, Mexico, Republic of Korea, and Spain; 9 other countries represented in student body.

Faculty School total: 54. In upper school: 31 men, 23 women; 28 have advanced degrees; 40 reside on campus.

Subjects Offered 3-dimensional design, acting, algebra, art, art history, astronomy, biology, biology-AP, calculus, calculus-AP, chemistry, chorus, community service, computer graphics, computer programming, creative writing, dance, dance performance, digital photography, drama, driver education, ecology, environmental systems, economics, English, English language and composition-AP, English literature, English literature-AP, environmental science, ESL, filmmaking, French, geometry, humanities, jazz band, journalism, macroeconomics-AP, mathematics, media arts, music, music history, music technology, music theory, orchestra, physics, pottery, science, Spanish, statistics-AP, studio art, theater, U.S. history, U.S. history-AP, Web authoring, Web site design, wind ensemble, world history, writing.

Graduation Requirements English, foreign language, mathematics, science, social studies (includes history).

Special Academic Programs 8 Advanced Placement exams for which test preparation is offered; honors section; programs in English, mathematics, general development for dyslexic students; ESL (20 students enrolled).

College Admission Counseling 117 students graduated in 2014; 114 went to college, including Boston University; Bryant University; Denison University; Hobart and William Smith Colleges; Lehigh University; University of California, Los Angeles. Other: 1 entered a postgraduate year, 2 had other specific plans. Median SAT critical reading: 500, median SAT math: 520, median SAT writing: 500, median combined SAT: 1520, median composite ACT: 22. 14% scored over 600 on SAT critical reading, 28% scored over 600 on SAT math, 12% scored over 600 on SAT writing, 13% scored over 1800 on combined SAT, 20% scored over 26 on composite ACT.

Student Life Upper grades have specified standards of dress, student council, honor system. Discipline rests primarily with faculty.

Tuition and Aid Day student tuition: $31,700; 7-day tuition and room/board: $51,400. Tuition installment plan (FACTS Tuition Payment Plan). Need-based scholarship grants available. In 2014–15, 32% of upper-school students received aid. Total amount of financial aid awarded in 2014–15: $3,400,000.

Admissions Traditional secondary-level entrance grade is 9. For fall 2014, 546 students applied for upper-level admission, 280 were accepted, 143 enrolled. SSAT or TOEFL or SLEP required. Deadline for receipt of application materials: February 1. Application fee required: $50. On-campus interview required.

Athletics Interscholastic: alpine skiing (boys, girls), baseball (b), basketball (b,g), crew (b,g), cross-country running (b,g), field hockey (g), ice hockey (b,g), lacrosse (b,g), running (b,g), skiing (downhill) (b,g), soccer (b,g), tennis (b,g); coed interscholastic: equestrian sports, golf, sailing, snowboarding; coed intramural: alpine skiing, ballet, climbing, dance, dance team, fitness, golf, outdoor skills, rock climbing, sailing, skiing (downhill), snowboarding, strength & conditioning, table tennis, tennis, touch football, ultimate Frisbee, wall climbing, weight training, yoga. 2 athletic trainers.

Computers Computers are regularly used in all classes. Computer network features include on-campus library services, online commercial services, Internet access, wireless campus network, Internet filtering or blocking technology. Campus intranet, student e-mail accounts, and computer access in designated common areas are available to students. Students grades are available online. The school has a published electronic and media policy.

Contact Mary Roetger, Admission Coordinator. 603-569-7200. Fax: 603-569-7272. E-mail: mary_roetger@brewsteracademy.org. Website: www.brewsteracademy.org

BRIARCREST CHRISTIAN HIGH SCHOOL

76 S. Houston Levee Road
Eads, Tennessee 38028

Head of School: Mr. Eric Sullivan

General Information Coeducational day college-preparatory, arts, religious studies, and technology school, affiliated with Christian faith. Grades 9–12. Founded: 1973. Setting: suburban. Nearest major city is Memphis. 100-acre campus. 1 building on campus. Approved or accredited by Southern Association of Colleges and Schools and Southern Association of Independent Schools. Member of National Association of Independent Schools. Total enrollment: 1,657. Upper school average class size: 18. Upper school faculty-student ratio: 1:12. There are 176 required school days per year for Upper School students. Upper School students typically attend 5 days per week. The average school day consists of 7 hours and 30 minutes.

Upper School Student Profile Grade 9: 156 students (71 boys, 85 girls); Grade 10: 157 students (81 boys, 76 girls); Grade 11: 130 students (72 boys, 58 girls); Grade 12: 133 students (72 boys, 61 girls). 92% of students are Christian.

Faculty School total: 42. In upper school: 19 men, 23 women; 29 have advanced degrees.

Subjects Offered ACT preparation, Advanced Placement courses, algebra, American history, American literature, anatomy, art, Bible studies, biology, business, calculus, chemistry, computer math, computer programming, computer science, creative writing, drama, driver education, English, English literature, environmental science, European history, expository writing, French, geography, geometry, government/civics, grammar, health, history, Latin, mathematics, music, physical education, physics, physiology, psychology, religion, science, social sciences, social studies, sociology, Spanish, speech, sports conditioning, theater, trigonometry, typing, world history, writing.

Graduation Requirements Arts and fine arts (art, music, dance, drama), business skills (includes word processing), English, foreign language, mathematics, physical education (includes health), religion (includes Bible studies and theology), science, social sciences, social studies (includes history).

Special Academic Programs Advanced Placement exam preparation; honors section; study at local college for college credit; academic accommodation for the gifted, the musically talented, and the artistically talented; programs in English, mathematics, general development for dyslexic students.

College Admission Counseling 138 students graduated in 2015; 134 went to college, including Mississippi State University; The University of Tennessee; The University of Tennessee at Chattanooga; University of Arkansas; University of Memphis; University of Mississippi. Other: 2 entered military service, 2 had other specific plans. Median composite ACT: 25. 39% scored over 26 on composite ACT.

Student Life Upper grades have uniform requirement, student council, honor system. Discipline rests primarily with faculty. Attendance at religious services is required.

Tuition and Aid Day student tuition: $14,295. Tuition installment plan (Insured Tuition Payment Plan, SMART Tuition Payment Plan, monthly payment plans, individually arranged payment plans, 2-payment plan). Tuition reduction for siblings, need-based tuition assistance available. In 2015–16, 12% of upper-school students received aid.

Admissions Traditional secondary-level entrance grade is 9. ISEE required. Deadline for receipt of application materials: none. Application fee required: $50. On-campus interview required.

Athletics Interscholastic: baseball (boys), basketball (b,g), cheering (g), cross-country running (b,g), drill team (g), football (b), golf (b,g), lacrosse (b,g), pom squad (g), soccer (b,g), softball (g), strength & conditioning (b), swimming and diving (b,g), tennis (b,g), track and field (b,g), trap and skeet (b,g), volleyball (g), weight lifting (b), wrestling (b); coed interscholastic: bowling, cross-country running, swimming and diving. 2 PE instructors.

Computers Computers are regularly used in accounting, art, English, history, journalism, keyboarding, lab/keyboard, language development, mathematics, newspaper, science, social sciences, social studies, Spanish, speech, yearbook classes. Computer network features include on-campus library services, Internet access, wireless campus network, Internet filtering or blocking technology. Campus intranet, student e-mail accounts, and computer access in designated common areas are available to students. Students grades are available online. The school has a published electronic and media policy.

Contact Mrs. Claire Foster, Admissions Coordinator. 901-765-4605. Fax: 901-765-4667. E-mail: cofoster@briarcrest.com. Website: www.briarcrest.com

BRIARWOOD CHRISTIAN HIGH SCHOOL

6255 Cahaba Valley Road
Birmingham, Alabama 35242

Head of School: Dr. Barrett L. Mosbacker

General Information Coeducational day college-preparatory, arts, and religious studies school, affiliated with Presbyterian Church in America. Grades K4–12. Founded: 1964. Setting: suburban. 85-acre campus. 6 buildings on campus. Approved or accredited by Association of Christian Schools International, Southern Association of Colleges and Schools, and Alabama Department of Education. Endowment: $500,000. Total enrollment: 1,912. Upper school average class size: 23. Upper school faculty-student ratio: 1:23. There are 177 required school days per year for Upper

School students. Upper School students typically attend 5 days per week. The average school day consists of 6 hours and 10 minutes.

Upper School Student Profile Grade 9: 146 students (80 boys, 66 girls); Grade 10: 148 students (80 boys, 68 girls); Grade 11: 132 students (69 boys, 63 girls); Grade 12: 136 students (64 boys, 72 girls). 22% of students are Presbyterian Church in America.

Faculty School total: 125. In upper school: 30 men, 25 women; 35 have advanced degrees.

Subjects Offered Accounting, algebra, American history, American literature, art, band, Bible studies, biology, calculus, chemistry, community service, computer science, creative writing, debate, drama, driver education, economics, electives, English, English literature, ethics, European history, film history, French, geometry, government, grammar, health, history, Latin, Mandarin, mathematics, music, philosophy, photo shop, physical education, physics, psychology, religion, robotics, science, social sciences, social studies, Spanish, speech, trigonometry, world history, world literature.

Graduation Requirements 20th century history, business skills (includes word processing), computer science, English, foreign language, mathematics, physical education (includes health), religion (includes Bible studies and theology), science, social sciences, social studies (includes history). Community service is required.

Special Academic Programs Advanced Placement exam preparation; honors section; academic accommodation for the gifted; special instructional classes for students with learning disabilities, students Attention Deficit Disorder.

College Admission Counseling 136 students graduated in 2015; 135 went to college, including Auburn University; Mississippi State University; Samford University; The University of Alabama; Troy University; University of Mississippi. Other: 1 went to work. Mean combined SAT: 1186, mean composite ACT: 26.

Student Life Upper grades have specified standards of dress, student council. Discipline rests primarily with faculty. Attendance at religious services is required.

Summer Programs Remediation, advancement programs offered; session focuses on social studies and mathematics; held on campus; accepts boys and girls; not open to students from other schools. 50 students usually enrolled. 2016 schedule: June 11 to July 28. Application deadline: March 1.

Tuition and Aid Day student tuition: $7500. Tuition installment plan (monthly payment plans). Tuition reduction for siblings available. In 2015–16, 3% of upper-school students received aid. Total amount of financial aid awarded in 2015–16: $5000.

Admissions Traditional secondary-level entrance grade is 9. For fall 2015, 62 students applied for upper-level admission, 28 were accepted, 26 enrolled. SSAT required. Deadline for receipt of application materials: none. Application fee required: $75. On campus interview required.

Athletics Interscholastic: baseball (boys), basketball (b,g), cheering (g), cross-country running (b,g), dance team (g), fishing (b), football (b), golf (b,g), indoor track (b,g), indoor track & field (b,g), outdoor activities (b,g), physical fitness (b,g), soccer (b,g), softball (g), strength & conditioning (b), swimming and diving (b,g), tennis (b,g), track and field (b,g), volleyball (g). 5 PE instructors, 15 coaches, 1 athletic trainer.

Computers Computers are regularly used in computer applications classes. Computer network features include on-campus library services, online commercial services, Internet access, wireless campus network, each student is issued an iPad for their use for the academic school year. Students grades are available online. The school has a published electronic and media policy.

Contact Mrs. Kelly McCarthy Mooney, Director of Admissions. 205-776-5812. Fax: 205-776-5816. E-mail: kmooney@bcsk12.org. Website: www.bcsk12.org

BRIDGEPORT INTERNATIONAL ACADEMY

285 Lafayette Street
Bridgeport, Connecticut 06604

Head of School: Dr. Frank LaGrotteria

General Information Coeducational boarding and day college-preparatory and arts school. Grades 9–12. Founded: 1997. Setting: urban. Nearest major city is New York, NY. Students are housed in single-sex dormitories. 2 buildings on campus. Approved or accredited by New England Association of Schools and Colleges and Connecticut Department of Education. Total enrollment: 60. Upper school average class size: 15. Upper school faculty-student ratio: 1:6. There are 180 required school days per year for Upper School students. Upper School students typically attend 5 days per week. The average school day consists of 7 hours.

Upper School Student Profile Grade 9: 9 students (6 boys, 3 girls); Grade 10: 11 students (3 boys, 8 girls); Grade 11: 20 students (11 boys, 9 girls); Grade 12: 20 students (8 boys, 12 girls). 27% of students are boarding students. 60% are state residents. 1 state is represented in upper school student body. 40% are international students. International students from Australia, China, Congo, Japan, Republic of Korea, and Viet Nam; 2 other countries represented in student body.

Faculty School total: 10. In upper school: 5 men, 5 women; 3 have advanced degrees; 7 reside on campus.

Subjects Offered Algebra, American government, American history, American literature, analytic geometry, applied arts, arts, band, basketball, biology, British literature, business mathematics, career/college preparation, character education, chemistry, Chinese, college admission preparation, college counseling, college writing, communication arts, computer applications, computer science, computer-aided design, dance, digital art, earth science, electives, English, English as a foreign language, English composition, English literature, ESL, expository writing, filmmaking, fine arts, geometry, guidance, health, history, human biology, introduction to theater, Japanese, journalism, keyboarding, language arts, learning lab, literature, media communications, modern civilization, oil painting, painting, performing arts, personal fitness, physics, play production, pre-calculus, psychology, public speaking, SAT/ACT preparation, social studies, Spanish, sports, stagecraft, theater, U.S. government, U.S. history, world cultures, world religions.

Graduation Requirements American government, American history, character education, 25 hours of community service per year.

Special Academic Programs Accelerated programs; study at local college for college credit; ESL (8 students enrolled).

College Admission Counseling 19 students graduated in 2015; all went to college, including Babson College; Boston University; Fairfield University; Sacred Heart University; Southern Connecticut State University; University of Connecticut. Mean SAT critical reading: 544, mean SAT math: 540, mean SAT writing: 524, mean combined SAT: 1608, mean composite ACT: 25. 30% scored over 600 on SAT critical reading, 38% scored over 600 on SAT math, 24% scored over 600 on SAT writing, 23% scored over 1800 on combined SAT, 42% scored over 26 on composite ACT.

Student Life Upper grades have specified standards of dress, student council, honor system. Discipline rests primarily with faculty.

Tuition and Aid Day student tuition: $7000; 7-day tuition and room/board: $36,000. Tuition installment plan (SMART Tuition Payment Plan, monthly payment plans, individually arranged payment plans). Tuition reduction for siblings, merit scholarship grants available. In 2015–16, 25% of upper-school students received aid.

Admissions Traditional secondary-level entrance grade is 9. For fall 2015, 30 students applied for upper-level admission, 25 were accepted, 17 enrolled. Writing sample required. Deadline for receipt of application materials: June 30. Application fee required: $125. Interview recommended.

Athletics Intramural: basketball (boys, girls), dance (g), modern dance (g), soccer (b), softball (b,g), volleyball (b,g); coed intramural: table tennis, volleyball. 1 PE instructor, 1 coach.

Computers Computers are regularly used in all classes. Computer network features include Internet access, wireless campus network. Campus intranet, student e-mail accounts, and computer access in designated common areas are available to students. Students grades are available online. The school has a published electronic and media policy.

Contact Dr. Frederick Swarts, Academic Dean. 203-334-3434. Fax: 203-334-8651. E-mail: fswarts@bridgeportacademy.org. Website: http://www.bridgeportacademy.org/

BRIDGES ACADEMY

Studio City, California
See Special Needs Schools section.

BRIMMER AND MAY SCHOOL

69 Middlesex Road
Chestnut Hill, Massachusetts 02467

Head of School: Mrs. Judy Guild

General Information Coeducational day college-preparatory, arts, technology, Creative Arts diploma program, and Global Studies diploma program, STEAM diploma program school. Grades PK–12. Founded: 1880. Setting: suburban. Nearest major city is Boston. 7-acre campus. 7 buildings on campus. Approved or accredited by New England Association of Schools and Colleges. Member of National Association of Independent Schools and Secondary School Admission Test Board. Endowment: $13 million. Total enrollment: 387. Upper school average class size: 12. Upper school faculty-student ratio: 1:6. There are 175 required school days per year for Upper School students. Upper School students typically attend 5 days per week. The average school day consists of 7 hours and 20 minutes.

Upper School Student Profile Grade 9: 39 students (18 boys, 21 girls); Grade 10: 36 students (20 boys, 16 girls); Grade 11: 29 students (15 boys, 14 girls); Grade 12: 35 students (18 boys, 17 girls).

Faculty School total: 67. In upper school: 15 men, 12 women; 22 have advanced degrees.

Subjects Offered Acting, adolescent issues, Advanced Placement courses, advanced studio art-AP, algebra, American history, American literature, art, biology, biology-AP, calculus, calculus-AP, ceramics, chamber groups, chemistry, chorus, college counseling, community service, computer education, creative arts, creative writing, desktop publishing, drama, economics, economics-AP, English, English literature, English literature-AP, ESL, European history, expository writing, fine arts, French, French language-AP, geometry, grammar, health, health education, history, humanities, literature and composition-AP, Mandarin, mathematics, microeconomics-AP, music, music theater, music theory, musical theater, newspaper, participation in sports, performing arts, photography, physical education, physical science, physics, physics-AP, psychology, social studies, Spanish, Spanish language-AP, statistics-AP, theater, trigonometry, typing, U.S. history, video film production, world history, world history-AP, world literature, writing, yearbook.

Graduation Requirements Creative arts, English, foreign language, history, mathematics, physical education (includes health), science, technology, senior independent project, senior thesis defense. Community service is required.

Special Academic Programs 16 Advanced Placement exams for which test preparation is offered; honors section; independent study; study at local college for college credit; ESL (18 students enrolled).

College Admission Counseling 37 students graduated in 2015; all went to college, including Bates College; Brown University; Harvard University; Hobart and William Smith Colleges; Lehigh University.

Student Life Upper grades have specified standards of dress, student council, honor system. Discipline rests equally with students and faculty.

Summer Programs Enrichment, sports, art/fine arts programs offered; session focuses on coed day camp for students ages 3-10 and select enrichment programs for middle and high school students; held both on and off campus; held at local area; accepts boys and girls; open to students from other schools. 300 students usually enrolled. 2016 schedule: June 20 to August 19. Application deadline: none.

Tuition and Aid Day student tuition: $43,000. Tuition installment plan (SMART Tuition Payment Plan, monthly payment plans). Need-based scholarship grants available. In 2015–16, 40% of upper-school students received aid. Total amount of financial aid awarded in 2015–16: $1,606,150.

Admissions Traditional secondary-level entrance grade is 9. For fall 2015, 113 students applied for upper-level admission, 73 were accepted, 23 enrolled. ISEE, SSAT or TOEFL or SLEP required. Deadline for receipt of application materials: January 16. Application fee required: $50. Interview required.

Athletics Interscholastic: baseball (boys), basketball (b,g), field hockey (g), lacrosse (b,g), soccer (b,g), softball (g), tennis (b,g); coed interscholastic: cross-country running, curling, golf; coed intramural: alpine skiing, fitness, Frisbee, outdoor education, physical fitness, running, skiing (downhill), snowboarding, strength & conditioning, tennis, weight training. 3 PE instructors, 20 coaches, 1 athletic trainer.

Computers Computers are regularly used in architecture, desktop publishing, foreign language, graphic design, humanities, journalism, media production, technology, typing, video film production, Web site design, yearbook classes. Computer network features include on-campus library services, online commercial services, Internet access, wireless campus network, Internet filtering or blocking technology. Campus intranet, student e-mail accounts, and computer access in designated common areas are available to students. Students grades are available online. The school has a published electronic and media policy.

Contact Ms. Myra Korin, Admissions Coordinator. 617-738-8695. Fax: 617-734-5147. E-mail: admissions@brimmer.org. Website: www.brimmerandmay.org

BRITISH INTERNATIONAL SCHOOL OF BOSTON

416 Pond Street
Boston, Massachusetts 02130

Head of School: Mr. Paul Wiseman, OBE

General Information Coeducational day college-preparatory, International Baccalaureate Diploma Programme, and International Primary Curriculum/International Middle Years school. Grades PK–12. Founded: 2000. Setting: suburban. 40-acre campus. 2 buildings on campus. Approved or accredited by Council of International Schools, International Baccalaureate Organization, New England Association of Schools and Colleges, and Massachusetts Department of Education. Member of National Association of Independent Schools and Secondary School Admission Test Board. Total enrollment: 421. Upper school average class size: 10. Upper school faculty-student ratio: 1:4. There are 180 required school days per year for Upper School students. Upper School students typically attend 5 days per week. The average school day consists of 7 hours.

Faculty School total: 60. In upper school: 14 men, 11 women.

Subjects Offered ACT preparation, arts, British National Curriculum, business, career and personal planning, career education internship, choir, college counseling, college placement, college planning, computer education, computer science, English, English as a foreign language, French, geography, history, International Baccalaureate courses, language, life management skills, mathematics, research skills, science, Spanish, sports, study skills.

Graduation Requirements International Baccalaureate courses.

Special Academic Programs International Baccalaureate program; academic accommodation for the gifted; ESL.

College Admission Counseling 15 students graduated in 2015; 13 went to college. Other: 2 went to work.

Student Life Upper grades have specified standards of dress, student council, honor system. Discipline rests equally with students and faculty.

Tuition and Aid Day student tuition: $30,800. Tuition installment plan (individually arranged payment plans). Tuition reduction for siblings, merit scholarship grants, discounts for students who enroll for full four years of high school available.

Admissions Traditional secondary-level entrance grade is 9. ISEE or SSAT required. Deadline for receipt of application materials: February 1. Application fee required: $150. Interview required.

Athletics Interscholastic: basketball (boys, girls), cross-country running (b,g), independent competitive sports (b), soccer (b,g), swimming and diving (b,g), tennis (b,g); intramural: basketball (b,g); coed interscholastic: curling, rugby, soccer; coed intramural: alpine skiing, backpacking, combined training, cross-country running, fitness, golf, hiking/backpacking, life saving, outdoor activities, outdoor education, outdoors, sailing, strength & conditioning. 2 PE instructors.

Computers Computers are regularly used in all classes. Computer network features include Internet access, wireless campus network. Student e-mail accounts and computer access in designated common areas are available to students. Students grades are available online. The school has a published electronic and media policy.

Contact Ms. Anique Seldon, Director of Admissions and Marketing. 617-522-2261 Ext. 141. Fax: 617-522-0385. E-mail: anique.seldon@bisboston.org. Website: www.bisboston.org

BRITISH INTERNATIONAL SCHOOL OF WASHINGTON

2001 Wisconsin Avenue NW
Washington, District of Columbia 20007

Head of School: David Rowsell

General Information Coeducational day college-preparatory and arts school. Grades PS–12. Founded: 1998. Setting: urban. 1 building on campus. Approved or accredited by Council of International Schools, International Baccalaureate Organization, and District of Columbia Department of Education. Candidate for accreditation by Middle States Association of Colleges and Schools. Member of National Association of Independent Schools and European Council of International Schools. Total enrollment: 460. Upper school average class size: 15. Upper school faculty-student ratio: 1:12. There are 180 required school days per year for Upper School students. Upper School students typically attend 5 days per week. The average school day consists of 7 hours and 15 minutes.

Upper School Student Profile Grade 6: 45 students (20 boys, 25 girls); Grade 7: 30 students (15 boys, 15 girls); Grade 8: 45 students (25 boys, 20 girls); Grade 9: 35 students (15 boys, 20 girls); Grade 10: 35 students (20 boys, 15 girls); Grade 11: 25 students (10 boys, 15 girls); Grade 12: 20 students (10 boys, 10 girls).

Special Academic Programs International Baccalaureate program; independent study; ESL (20 students enrolled).

College Admission Counseling 23 students graduated in 2015; all went to college, including Savannah College of Art and Design; The George Washington University; University of California, San Diego.

Student Life Upper grades have uniform requirement, student council. Discipline rests equally with students and faculty.

Admissions Application fee required: $150.

Athletics Coed Interscholastic: basketball, cross-country running, flag football, Frisbee, kickball, soccer, squash, swimming and diving, track and field, triathlon, ultimate Frisbee, volleyball; coed intramural: aerobics/dance, backpacking, basketball, cross-country running, dance, field hockey, fitness, flag football, golf, gymnastics, handball, physical fitness, rounders, rugby, self defense, skiing (downhill), soccer, softball, table tennis, track and field, ultimate Frisbee, volleyball. 3 PE instructors.

Computers Computer resources include Internet access, wireless campus network, Internet filtering or blocking technology. Student e-mail accounts are available to students. Students grades are available online. The school has a published electronic and media policy.

Contact Admissions Office. 202-829-3700. Fax: 202-829-6522. E-mail: admissions@BISWashington.org. Website: www.BISWashington.org

THE BROOK HILL SCHOOL

1051 N. Houston
Bullard, Texas 75757

Head of School: Rod Fletcher

General Information Coeducational boarding and day college-preparatory and arts school, affiliated with Christian faith. Boarding grades 8–12, day grades PK–12. Founded: 1997. Setting: small town. Nearest major city is Dallas. Students are housed in single-sex dormitories. 280-acre campus. 9 buildings on campus. Approved or accredited by Association of Christian Schools International, Southern Association of Colleges and Schools, The Association of Boarding Schools, and The College Board. Member of National Association of Independent Schools. Endowment: $1 million. Total enrollment: 645. Upper school average class size: 11. Upper school faculty-student ratio: 1:9. There are 176 required school days per year for Upper School students. Upper School students typically attend 5 days per week. The average school day consists of 6 hours and 30 minutes.

Upper School Student Profile Grade 6: 37 students (24 boys, 13 girls); Grade 7: 48 students (26 boys, 22 girls); Grade 8: 37 students (20 boys, 17 girls); Grade 9: 62 students (26 boys, 36 girls); Grade 10: 68 students (32 boys, 36 girls); Grade 11: 66 students (34 boys, 32 girls); Grade 12: 55 students (28 boys, 27 girls). 30% of students are boarding students. 65% are state residents. 5 states are represented in upper school student body. 20% are international students. International students from China, Nigeria, Republic of Korea, Saudi Arabia, South Africa, and Viet Nam; 21 other countries represented in student body. 70% of students are Christian faith.

Faculty School total: 50. In upper school: 14 men, 17 women; 25 have advanced degrees; 6 reside on campus.

Subjects Offered Accounting, ACT preparation, advanced biology, advanced chemistry, advanced math, Advanced Placement courses, advanced studio art-AP, advanced TOEFL/grammar, algebra, American government, American history, American history-AP, American literature, American literature-AP, analysis and differential calculus, anatomy and physiology, ancient history, ancient world history, art, art-AP, athletics, baseball, basketball, Bible as literature, Bible studies, biology, British literature, British literature-AP, business, calculus, calculus-AP, career/college preparation, chemistry, chemistry-AP, choir, choral music, Christian ethics, Christian studies, Christianity, church history, civics/free enterprise, classics, college admission preparation, college awareness, college writing, communication skills, communications, community service, comparative religion, composition, composition-AP, computer applications, computer art, computer education, conceptual physics, concert choir, creation science, dance, dance performance, digital art, digital photography, drama, drama performance, dramatic arts, drawing, economics, economics-AP, English, English composition, English language and composition-AP, English language-AP, English literature, English literature and composition-AP, English literature-AP, English/composition-AP, ensembles, environmental science, epic literature, ESL, European history, European history-AP, European literature, finance, fine arts, foreign language, four units of summer reading, French, French as a second language, geometry, government, government and politics-AP, government-AP, great books, health, history-AP, honors algebra, honors English, honors geometry, human biology, lab science, Latin, leadership and service, literary genres, literature and composition-AP, literature-AP, logic, logic, rhetoric, and debate, macro/microeconomics-AP, macroeconomics-AP, mathematics-AP, microeconomics-AP, modern European history-AP, modern languages, orchestra, painting, physical education, physics, physics-AP, pre-calculus, public speaking, religion, rhetoric, SAT preparation, SAT/ACT preparation, senior project, Spanish, Spanish language-AP, Spanish literature-AP, Spanish-AP, speech communications, stagecraft, statistics-AP, strings, student government, student publications, studio art-AP, theater arts, TOEFL preparation, U.S. government and politics, U.S. government and politics-AP, U.S. history, U.S. history-AP, volleyball, yearbook.

Graduation Requirements Arts and fine arts (art, music, dance, drama), Bible, college admission preparation, economics, electives, English, foreign language, government, history, lab science, leadership, mathematics, physical education (includes health). Community service is required.

Special Academic Programs 12 Advanced Placement exams for which test preparation is offered; honors section; study at local college for college credit; academic accommodation for the gifted and the artistically talented; ESL (15 students enrolled).

College Admission Counseling 50 students graduated in 2015; all went to college, including Baylor University; Texas A&M University; Texas Tech University; The University of Texas at Austin; University of Mississippi; Wheaton College. Median SAT critical reading: 630, median SAT math: 632, median SAT writing: 611, median combined SAT: 1873, median composite ACT: 28. 67% scored over 600 on SAT critical reading, 67% scored over 600 on SAT math, 65% scored over 600 on SAT writing, 65% scored over 1800 on combined SAT, 67% scored over 26 on composite ACT.

Student Life Upper grades have uniform requirement, student council, honor system. Discipline rests primarily with faculty. Attendance at religious services is required.

Summer Programs Remediation, enrichment, advancement, ESL, sports, art/fine arts programs offered; session focuses on enrichment; held on campus; accepts boys and girls; open to students from other schools. 125 students usually enrolled. 2016 schedule: June 1 to August 10. Application deadline: none.

Tuition and Aid Day student tuition: $10,350; 7-day tuition and room/board: $37,350. Tuition installment plan (FACTS Tuition Payment Plan, individually arranged payment plans). Tuition reduction for siblings, need-based scholarship grants available. In 2015–16, 40% of upper-school students received aid. Total amount of financial aid awarded in 2015–16: $850,000.

Admissions Traditional secondary-level entrance grade is 9. For fall 2015, 170 students applied for upper-level admission, 100 were accepted, 95 enrolled. International English Language Test, Iowa Test, CTBS, or TAP, Iowa Tests of Basic Skills, SSAT, Stanford Achievement Test, Otis-Lennon School Ability Test, TOEFL or TOEFL or SLEP required. Deadline for receipt of application materials: none. Application fee required: $75. Interview recommended.

Athletics Interscholastic: baseball (boys, girls), basketball (b,g), cheering (g), cross-country running (b,g), dance (g), dance squad (g), dance team (g), football (b), golf (b,g), independent competitive sports (b,g), physical fitness (b,g), physical training (b,g), soccer (b,g), softball (g), strength & conditioning (b,g), swimming and diving (b,g), tennis (b,g), track and field (b,g), volleyball (g), weight training (b,g); intramural: baseball (b,g), basketball (b,g), fishing (b,g), flag football (b,g), Frisbee (b,g), ultimate Frisbee (b,g); coed interscholastic: cheering, dance, dance squad, dance team, tennis; coed intramural: fishing, flag football, Frisbee. 1 PE instructor, 2 coaches, 1 athletic trainer.

Computers Computers are regularly used in all academic, art classes. Computer network features include on-campus library services, Internet access, wireless campus network, Internet filtering or blocking technology. Computer access in designated common areas is available to students. Students grades are available online. The school has a published electronic and media policy.

Contact Mr. Landry Humphries, Associate Director of Admissions, Boarding. 903-894-5000 Ext. 1042. Fax: 903-894-6332. E-mail: Landry.humphries@brookhill.org. Website: www.brookhill.org/

BROOKS SCHOOL

1160 Great Pond Road
North Andover, Massachusetts 01845-1298

Head of School: Mr. John R. Packard

General Information Coeducational boarding and day college-preparatory school, affiliated with Episcopal Church. Grades 9–12. Founded: 1926. Setting: suburban. Nearest major city is Boston. Students are housed in single-sex dormitories. 251-acre campus. 40 buildings on campus. Approved or accredited by Association of Independent Schools in New England, National Association of Episcopal Schools, New England Association of Schools and Colleges, The Association of Boarding Schools, and Massachusetts Department of Education. Member of National Association of Independent Schools and Secondary School Admission Test Board. Endowment: $75 million. Total enrollment: 373. Upper school average class size: 12. Upper school faculty-student ratio: 1:6. There are 180 required school days per year for Upper School students. Upper School students typically attend 6 days per week. The average school day consists of 7 hours.

Upper School Student Profile Grade 9: 78 students (39 boys, 39 girls); Grade 10: 106 students (63 boys, 43 girls); Grade 11: 104 students (61 boys, 43 girls); Grade 12: 86 students (51 boys, 35 girls). 67% of students are boarding students. 60% are state residents. 23 states are represented in upper school student body. 14% are international students. International students from Bermuda, Canada, China, Germany, Republic of Korea, and Thailand; 8 other countries represented in student body.

Faculty School total: 87. In upper school: 30 men, 32 women; 47 have advanced degrees; 47 reside on campus.

Subjects Offered Advanced Placement courses, algebra, American history, American history-AP, American literature, anatomy and physiology, art, art history, art history-AP, astronomy, Bible studies, biology, biology-AP, business, calculus, calculus-AP, ceramics, chemistry, chemistry-AP, Chinese, chorus, computer math, creative writing, drama, driver education, earth science, English, English literature, English-AP, environmental science-AP, ethics, European history, expository writing, film, fine arts, French, French language-AP, French literature-AP, French-AP, geometry, government and politics-AP, grammar, Greek, health, history, history-AP, honors algebra, honors geometry, honors world history, integrated arts, journalism, Latin, Latin-AP, life skills, Mandarin, mathematics, mathematics-AP, Middle East, model United Nations, music, music theory, music theory-AP, painting, photography, physics, physics-AP, playwriting, poetry, psychology, public speaking, religion, rhetoric, robotics, senior project, senior seminar, Southern literature, Spanish, Spanish language-AP, Spanish literature, Spanish literature-AP, Spanish-AP, statistics, studio art, theater, theater design and production, theology, trigonometry, U.S. government and politics-AP, U.S. history-AP, visual arts, world history, world history-AP, world literature, writing.

Graduation Requirements Arts and fine arts (art, music, dance, drama), English, foreign language, health, history, mathematics, religion (includes Bible studies and theology), science. Community service is required.

Special Academic Programs 15 Advanced Placement exams for which test preparation is offered; honors section; independent study; term-away projects; study abroad.

College Admission Counseling 106 students graduated in 2015; all went to college, including Bates College; Boston University; Elon University; Northeastern University; The George Washington University; Trinity College. Mean SAT critical reading: 598, mean SAT math: 626, mean SAT writing: 603, mean combined SAT: 1827.

Student Life Upper grades have specified standards of dress, student council. Discipline rests primarily with faculty. Attendance at religious services is required.

Summer Programs Enrichment, advancement, sports, computer instruction programs offered; session focuses on English, mathematics, SSAT and SAT preparation; held on campus; accepts boys and girls; open to students from other schools. 70 students usually enrolled. 2016 schedule: June 29 to August 21. Application deadline: none.

Tuition and Aid Day student tuition: $42,450; 7-day tuition and room/board: $55,560. Tuition installment plan (Academic Management Services Plan, FACTS Tuition Payment Plan, individually arranged payment plans). Need-based scholarship grants available. In 2015–16, 25% of upper-school students received aid. Total amount of financial aid awarded in 2015–16: $3,767,435.

Admissions Traditional secondary-level entrance grade is 9. For fall 2015, 964 students applied for upper-level admission, 269 were accepted, 113 enrolled. ISEE, SSAT, ERB, PSAT, SAT, PLAN or ACT or TOEFL required. Deadline for receipt of application materials: January 15. Application fee required: $60. Interview required.

Athletics Interscholastic: baseball (boys), basketball (b,g), crew (b,g), cross-country running (b,g), field hockey (g), football (b), ice hockey (b,g), lacrosse (b,g), soccer (b,g), softball (g), squash (b,g), tennis (b,g), wrestling (b); coed interscholastic: golf; coed intramural: dance, fitness, Frisbee, modern dance, physical fitness, sailing, skiing (downhill), weight training, yoga. 2 athletic trainers.

Computers Computers are regularly used in all academic classes. Computer network features include on-campus library services, online commercial services, Internet access, wireless campus network, Internet filtering or blocking technology. Campus intranet, student e-mail accounts, and computer access in designated common areas are available to students. Students grades are available online. The school has a published electronic and media policy.

Contact Mrs. Bini Egertson, Director of Admission. 978-725-6272. Fax: 978-725-6298. E-mail: admission@brooksschool.org. Website: www.brooksschool.org

BROPHY COLLEGE PREPARATORY

4701 North Central Avenue
Phoenix, Arizona 85012-1797

Head of School: Mr. Robert E. Ryan III

General Information Boys' day college-preparatory, arts, religious studies, and technology school, affiliated with Roman Catholic Church (Jesuit order). Grades 6–12. Founded: 1928. Setting: urban. 38-acre campus. 9 buildings on campus. Approved or accredited by Jesuit Secondary Education Association, National Catholic Education Association, and Western Catholic Education Association. Endowment: $19 million. Total enrollment: 1,391. Upper school average class size: 24. Upper school faculty-student ratio: 1:15. There are 180 required school days per year for Upper School students. Upper School students typically attend 5 days per week. The average school day consists of 6 hours and 40 minutes.

Upper School Student Profile Grade 9: 353 students (353 boys); Grade 10: 330 students (330 boys); Grade 11: 338 students (338 boys); Grade 12: 298 students (298 boys). 66% of students are Roman Catholic Church (Jesuit order).

Faculty School total: 97. In upper school: 71 men, 20 women; 70 have advanced degrees.

Subjects Offered Advanced Placement courses, advanced studio art-AP, algebra, American history, American literature, anatomy, art, Bible studies, biology, business, calculus, chemistry, community service, computer math, computer programming, computer science, creative writing, drama, earth science, economics, engineering, English, English literature, ethics, European history, expository writing, fine arts, French, geography, geometry, government/civics, health, history, Latin, mathematics, mechanical drawing, music, physical education, physics, probability and statistics, psychology, religion, science, social sciences, social studies, sociology, Spanish, speech, theater, theology, trigonometry, video film production, world history, world literature.

Graduation Requirements Arts and fine arts (art, music, dance, drama), English, foreign language, mathematics, physical education (includes health), religion (includes Bible studies and theology), science, social studies (includes history). Community service is required.

Special Academic Programs Advanced Placement exam preparation; honors section; study at local college for college credit; study abroad.

College Admission Counseling 295 students graduated in 2015; 290 went to college, including Arizona State University at the Tempe campus; Creighton University; Gonzaga University; Northern Arizona University; Santa Clara University; The University of Arizona. Other: 1 entered military service, 4 had other specific plans. Median SAT critical reading: 609, median SAT math: 607, median SAT writing: 588, median combined SAT: 1804, median composite ACT: 27.

Student Life Upper grades have specified standards of dress, student council, honor system. Discipline rests primarily with faculty. Attendance at religious services is required.

Summer Programs Enrichment, advancement, sports, art/fine arts, computer instruction programs offered; session focuses on academic skills and sports; held both on and off campus; held at Manresa Retreat (Sedona, AZ) and Brophy Sports Campus; accepts boys and girls; open to students from other schools. 1,300 students usually enrolled. 2016 schedule: May 31 to July 1. Application deadline: May 27.

Tuition and Aid Day student tuition: $14,200. Tuition installment plan (The Tuition Plan, monthly payment plans, individually arranged payment plans). Need-based scholarship grants, paying campus jobs available. In 2015–16, 22% of upper-school students received aid. Total amount of financial aid awarded in 2015–16: $3,841,050.

Admissions Traditional secondary-level entrance grade is 9. For fall 2015, 630 students applied for upper-level admission, 383 were accepted, 353 enrolled. STS required. Deadline for receipt of application materials: January 29. Application fee required: $75. On-campus interview required.

Athletics Interscholastic: aquatics, baseball, basketball, cross-country running, diving, flagball, football, golf, ice hockey, lacrosse, soccer, swimming and diving, tennis, track and field, volleyball, wrestling; intramural: aquatics, badminton, baseball, basketball, bicycling, bowling, cheering, climbing, crew, cricket, fishing, fitness, flag football, Frisbee, golf, handball, hockey, ice hockey, lacrosse, mountain biking, outdoor activities, physical fitness, physical training, rock climbing, skiing (downhill), softball, strength & conditioning, table tennis, touch football, ultimate Frisbee, volleyball, wall climbing, water polo, weight lifting, weight training. 2 PE instructors, 15 coaches, 3 athletic trainers.

Computers Computers are regularly used in all academic classes. Computer network features include on-campus library services, online commercial services, Internet access, wireless campus network, Blackboard, computer tablets, iPads. Student e-mail accounts are available to students. Students grades are available online. The school has a published electronic and media policy.

Contact Ms. Shelly Scheuring, Assistant to Director of Admissions. 602-264-5291 Ext. 6233. Fax: 602-234-1669. E-mail: sscheuring@brophyprep.org. Website: www.brophyprep.org/

BROTHER RICE HIGH SCHOOL

7101 Lahser Road

Bloomfield Hills, Michigan 48301

Head of School: Mr. John Birney

General Information Boys' day college-preparatory, arts, business, religious studies, and technology school, affiliated with Roman Catholic Church. Grades 9–12. Founded: 1960. Setting: suburban. Nearest major city is Detroit. 20-acre campus. 1 building on campus. Approved or accredited by North Central Association of Colleges and Schools and Michigan Department of Education. Endowment: $2 million. Total enrollment: 640. Upper school average class size: 22. Upper school faculty-student ratio: 1:13. Upper School students typically attend 5 days per week. The average school day consists of 6 hours and 51 minutes.

Upper School Student Profile Grade 9: 165 students (165 boys); Grade 10: 162 students (162 boys); Grade 11: 159 students (159 boys); Grade 12: 148 students (148 boys). 75% of students are Roman Catholic.

Faculty School total: 60. In upper school: 32 men, 10 women; 36 have advanced degrees.

Subjects Offered 20th century world history, accounting, algebra, American government, anatomy, anthropology, architectural drawing, art, band, biology, biology-AP, business law, calculus, calculus-AP, chemistry, Chinese, choir, church history, computer science, computer science-AP, computers, concert band, creative writing, death and loss, debate, drama, earth science, economics, electronics, engineering, English, English composition, English language-AP, ensembles, European history, family living, forensics, French, French-AP, geometry, German, global science, health, jazz band, Latin, library science, literature, mathematics, mechanical drawing, music, music history, music theory, organic chemistry, photography, photojournalism, physical education, physics, physiology, pre-calculus, probability and statistics, psychology, social justice, Spanish, Spanish-AP, speech, studio art-AP, theology, trigonometry, U.S. government and politics-AP, U.S. history, U.S. history-AP, Western civilization, world geography, world religions.

Graduation Requirements Computer science, electives, English, foreign language, mathematics, physical education (includes health), science, social studies (includes history), speech, theology.

Special Academic Programs 13 Advanced Placement exams for which test preparation is offered; honors section; remedial reading and/or remedial writing; remedial math.

College Admission Counseling 168 students graduated in 2015; 162 went to college, including Central Michigan University; Michigan State University; Oakland University; University of Michigan; Wayne State University. Other: 6 had other specific plans. Median combined SAT: 1838, median composite ACT: 25.

Student Life Upper grades have specified standards of dress, student council, honor system. Discipline rests primarily with faculty. Attendance at religious services is required.

Summer Programs Remediation, enrichment, art/fine arts programs offered; session focuses on camps and enrichment; held on campus; accepts boys and girls; open to students from other schools. 550 students usually enrolled. 2016 schedule: June to August.

Tuition and Aid Day student tuition: $11,750. Tuition installment plan (SMART Tuition Payment Plan, monthly payment plans, individually arranged payment plans). Tuition reduction for siblings, merit scholarship grants, need-based scholarship grants available. In 2015–16, 40% of upper-school students received aid; total upper-school merit-scholarship money awarded: $600,000. Total amount of financial aid awarded in 2015–16: $900,000.

Admissions Traditional secondary-level entrance grade is 9. For fall 2015, 476 students applied for upper-level admission, 300 were accepted, 165 enrolled. High School Placement Test (closed version) from Scholastic Testing Service or SAS, STS-HSPT required. Deadline for receipt of application materials: none. No application fee required. Interview required.

Athletics Interscholastic: alpine skiing, baseball, basketball, bowling, cross-country running, diving, football, golf, hockey, ice hockey, lacrosse, skiing (downhill), soccer, swimming and diving, tennis, track and field, wrestling; intramural: basketball, bowling, fishing, fitness, flag football, football, mountain biking, paint ball, skiing (downhill), snowboarding, strength & conditioning, touch football, ultimate Frisbee, winter (indoor) track. 50 coaches, 1 athletic trainer.

Computers Computers are regularly used in computer applications, drafting, drawing and design, engineering, keyboarding, lab/keyboard, newspaper, publications, video film production, yearbook classes. Computer resources include online commercial services, Internet access, wireless campus network, Internet filtering or blocking technology. Campus intranet and student e-mail accounts are available to students. Students grades are available online. The school has a published electronic and media policy.

Contact Mr. Brendan F. Robinson, Director of Admissions. 248-833-2022. Fax: 248-833-2011. E-mail: robinson@brrice.edu. Website: www.brrice.edu

THE BROWNING SCHOOL

52 East 62nd Street

New York, New York 10065

Head of School: Stephen M. Clement III

General Information Boys' day college-preparatory school. Grades K–12. Founded: 1888. Setting: urban. 1 building on campus. Approved or accredited by New York State Association of Independent Schools and New York State University. Member of National Association of Independent Schools and Secondary School Admission Test Board. Endowment: $50 million. Total enrollment: 399. Upper school average class size: 15. Upper school faculty-student ratio: 1:4. There are 164 required school days per year for Upper School students. Upper School students typically attend 5 days per week. The average school day consists of 6 hours and 54 minutes.

Upper School Student Profile Grade 9: 26 students (26 boys); Grade 10: 29 students (29 boys); Grade 11: 26 students (26 boys); Grade 12: 26 students (26 boys).

Faculty School total: 60. In upper school: 22 men, 10 women; 32 have advanced degrees.

Subjects Offered Adolescent issues, advanced biology, advanced chemistry, advanced math, Advanced Placement courses, advanced studio art-AP, African drumming, algebra, American history, American history-AP, American literature, American literature-AP, anatomy and physiology, Ancient Greek, ancient world history, applied arts, applied music, art, art history, athletics, baseball, basketball, bell choir, biology, biology-AP, calculus, calculus-AP, ceramics, chemistry, chemistry-AP, chorus, college admission preparation, computer math, computer music, computer programming, computer science, drama, dramatic arts, English, English literature, English-AP, environmental science, environmental studies, ethics, European history, European history-AP, expository writing, fencing, filmmaking, fine arts, French, French language-AP, general science, geography, geometry, golf, government/civics, grammar, Greek, handbells, health, history, instruments, jazz ensemble, language arts, Latin, Latin-AP, mathematics, medieval/Renaissance history, mentorship program, model United Nations, music, peer counseling, philosophy, physical education, physics, physics-AP, political science, public speaking, science, senior project, social sciences, social studies, Spanish, Spanish language-AP, squash, statistics, technology, tennis, theater, track and field, trigonometry, U.S. history-AP, video film production, visual arts, wrestling, yearbook.

Graduation Requirements Arts and fine arts (art, music, dance, drama), computer science, English, foreign language, mathematics, physical education (includes health), public speaking, science, social sciences, social studies (includes history), senior community service project.

Special Academic Programs Advanced Placement exam preparation; honors section; independent study; academic accommodation for the gifted and the musically talented.

College Admission Counseling 25 students graduated in 2015; all went to college, including Brown University; Cornell University; Dartmouth College; University of Virginia. Median SAT critical reading: 636, median SAT math: 654, median SAT writing: 664, median combined SAT: 1954, median composite ACT: 27. 71% scored over 600 on SAT critical reading, 71% scored over 600 on SAT math, 83% scored over 600 on SAT writing, 75% scored over 1800 on combined SAT, 57% scored over 26 on composite ACT.

Student Life Upper grades have specified standards of dress, student council, honor system. Discipline rests primarily with faculty.

Tuition and Aid Day student tuition: $44,500. Need-based scholarship grants available. In 2015–16, 32% of upper-school students received aid. Total amount of financial aid awarded in 2015–16: $953,900.

Admissions Traditional secondary-level entrance grade is 9. For fall 2015, 75 students applied for upper-level admission, 16 were accepted, 8 enrolled. ISEE and SSAT required. Deadline for receipt of application materials: January 15. Application fee required: $75. On-campus interview required.

Athletics Interscholastic: baseball, basketball, soccer, tennis; intramural: basketball, cross-country running, ice hockey, soccer, softball, tai chi; coed intramural: fencing. 4 PE instructors, 6 coaches.

Computers Computers are regularly used in English, foreign language, history, mathematics, music technology, science, video film production classes. Computer network features include on-campus library services, online commercial services, Internet access, wireless campus network. Student e-mail accounts are available to students. The school has a published electronic and media policy.

Contact Janetta Lien, Director of Middle and Upper School Admission. 212-838-6280 Ext. 105. Fax: 212-355-5602. E-mail: jlien@browning.edu.

Website: www.browning.edu

BRUNSWICK SCHOOL

100 Maher Avenue

Greenwich, Connecticut 06830

Head of School: Thomas W. Philip

General Information Boys' day college-preparatory school. Grades PK–12. Founded: 1902. Setting: suburban. Nearest major city is New York, NY. 10-acre campus. 1 building on campus. Approved or accredited by New England Association of Schools and Colleges and Connecticut Department of Education. Member of National

Association of Independent Schools. Endowment: $118.3 million. Total enrollment: 962. Upper school average class size: 15. Upper school faculty-student ratio: 1:5. There are 167 required school days per year for Upper School students. Upper School students typically attend 5 days per week. The average school day consists of 6 hours and 30 minutes.

Upper School Student Profile Grade 9: 93 students (93 boys); Grade 10: 95 students (95 boys); Grade 11: 95 students (95 boys); Grade 12: 97 students (97 boys).

Faculty School total: 171. In upper school: 42 men, 14 women; 47 have advanced degrees.

Subjects Offered 20th century history, 3-dimensional design, acting, advanced chemistry, African-American literature, algebra, American history, American history-AP, American literature, anthropology, Arabic, architecture, art, art history, art history-AP, astronomy, biology, biology-AP, calculus, calculus-AP, ceramics, chemistry, chemistry-AP, Chinese, choir, community service, computer graphics, computer programming, computer programming-AP, creative writing, digital art, digital music, drama, earth science, economics, economics-AP, English, environmental science-AP, ethics, European history, European history-AP, film and literature, fine arts, French, French language-AP, French literature-AP, geometry, government-AP, Greek, Greek culture, health, history, honors algebra, honors geometry, human geography - AP, Italian, Japanese history, jazz, jazz band, jazz ensemble, Latin, Latin American literature, Latin-AP, mathematics, media studies, microeconomics, military history, music, oceanography, philosophy, photography, physical education, physics, physics-AP, poetry, pre-calculus, psychology, psychology-AP, science, senior seminar, Shakespeare, short story, social studies, Spanish, Spanish language-AP, Spanish literature-AP, speech and debate, statistics-AP, studio art, studio art-AP, theater, trigonometry, U.S. government and politics-AP, U.S. history-AP, world cultures, world history-AP, writing.

Graduation Requirements Arts and fine arts (art, music, dance, drama), English, foreign language, mathematics, physical education (includes health), science, social studies (includes history). Community service is required.

Special Academic Programs Advanced Placement exam preparation; honors section; independent study; term-away projects; study abroad.

College Admission Counseling 96 students graduated in 2015; all went to college, including Cornell University; Dartmouth College; Duke University; Georgetown University; University of Virginia; Yale University. Mean SAT critical reading: 660, mean SAT math: 665, mean SAT writing: 670, mean combined SAT: 1985. 75% scored over 600 on SAT critical reading, 87% scored over 600 on SAT math, 88% scored over 600 on SAT writing, 85% scored over 1800 on combined SAT.

Student Life Upper grades have specified standards of dress, student council, honor system. Discipline rests equally with students and faculty.

Summer Programs Enrichment programs offered; session focuses on academic enrichment; held on campus; accepts boys and girls; open to students from other schools. 2016 schedule: June 13 to July 8. Application deadline: April 1.

Tuition and Aid Day student tuition: $39,250. Tuition installment plan (Key Tuition Payment Plan, monthly payment plans). Need-based scholarship grants available. In 2015–16, 11% of upper-school students received aid. Total amount of financial aid awarded in 2015–16: $1,250,000.

Admissions Traditional secondary-level entrance grade is 9. For fall 2015, 162 students applied for upper-level admission, 38 were accepted, 33 enrolled. ISEE, PSAT or SSAT required. Deadline for receipt of application materials: December 15. Application fee required: $75. On-campus interview required.

Athletics Interscholastic: baseball, basketball, crew, cross-country running, fencing, fitness, football, golf, ice hockey, lacrosse, sailing, soccer, squash, tennis, track and field, water polo, wrestling; intramural: basketball, softball, squash, touch football, ultimate Frisbee. 4 PE instructors, 2 coaches, 4 athletic trainers.

Computers Computers are regularly used in career technology classes. Computer network features include on-campus library services, online commercial services, Internet access, wireless campus network, Internet filtering or blocking technology. Campus intranet and student e-mail accounts are available to students. Students grades are available online. The school has a published electronic and media policy.

Contact Tucker Hastings, Director, Upper School Admission. 203-625-5842. Fax: 203-625-5863. E-mail: thastings@brunswickschool.org. Website: www.brunswickschool.org

THE BRYN MAWR SCHOOL FOR GIRLS

109 West Melrose Avenue
Baltimore, Maryland 21210

Head of School: Maureen E. Walsh

General Information Coeducational day (boys' only in lower grades) college-preparatory, arts, and technology school. Boys grade PK, girls grades PK–12. Founded: 1885. Setting: suburban. 26-acre campus. 9 buildings on campus. Approved or accredited by Association of Independent Maryland Schools and Maryland Department of Education. Member of National Association of Independent Schools and Secondary School Admission Test Board. Endowment: $31.8 million. Total enrollment: 681.

Upper school average class size: 15. Upper school faculty-student ratio: 1:6. There are 180 required school days per year for Upper School students. Upper School students typically attend 5 days per week. The average school day consists of 7 hours.

Upper School Student Profile Grade 9: 82 students (82 girls); Grade 10: 73 students (73 girls); Grade 11: 74 students (74 girls); Grade 12: 66 students (66 girls).

Faculty School total: 130. In upper school: 16 men, 33 women; 23 have advanced degrees.

Subjects Offered 20th century American writers, accounting, acting, African-American history, African-American literature, algebra, American history, American literature, anatomy, anatomy and physiology, Arabic, architectural drawing, art, art history, art history-AP, astronomy, biology, biology-AP, British literature, calculus, ceramics, chemistry, chemistry-AP, Chinese, comparative government and politics-AP, comparative religion, computer programming, computer science, computer science-AP, creative writing, dance, design, digital art, digital photography, drama, drawing, ecology, economics, emerging technology, English, English literature, English-AP, environmental science-AP, ethics, European history, fine arts, forensics, French, French literature-AP, genetics, geography, geology, geometry, grammar, Greek, health, Holocaust studies, human geography - AP, Irish literature, Latin, Latin American history, mathematics, mechanical drawing, moral theology, music, music theory, mythology, Native American studies, orchestra, painting, personal finance, photography, physical education, physics, physics-AP, poetry, pre-calculus, public speaking, rite of passage, Russian, science, Shakespearean histories, short story, social studies, Spanish, statistics, strings, technology, theater, trigonometry, U.S. government and politics-AP, U.S. history, urban studies, Vietnam War, world history, world history-AP, world literature, World War I, World War II, writing.

Graduation Requirements Arts and fine arts (art, music, dance, drama), emerging technology, English, foreign language, history, mathematics, physical education (includes health), public speaking, science, 50 hours of community service, convocation speech.

Special Academic Programs 27 Advanced Placement exams for which test preparation is offered; honors section; independent study; term-away projects; study abroad; academic accommodation for the gifted, the musically talented, and the artistically talented.

College Admission Counseling 66 students graduated in 2015; all went to college, including American University; Columbia University; Howard University; Stanford University; University of Chicago; University of Maryland, College Park. Median SAT critical reading: 660, median SAT math: 650, median SAT writing: 680, median combined SAT: 2000, median composite ACT: 29. 76.6% scored over 600 on SAT critical reading, 75% scored over 600 on SAT math, 84.4% scored over 600 on SAT writing, 82.3% scored over 1800 on combined SAT, 60% scored over 26 on composite ACT.

Student Life Upper grades have uniform requirement, student council, honor system. Discipline rests equally with students and faculty.

Summer Programs Enrichment, sports, art/fine arts programs offered; session focuses on arts, crafts, language, culture, and sports; held on campus; accepts boys and girls; open to students from other schools. 350 students usually enrolled. 2016 schedule: June 13 to July 29. Application deadline: none.

Tuition and Aid Day student tuition: $28,400. Tuition installment plan (FACTS Tuition Payment Plan, individual payment 65% due August 1st and remaining 35% December 1st, semi-monthly payroll deduction (for employees only)). Merit scholarship grants, need-based scholarship grants available. In 2015–16, 32% of upper-school students received aid; total upper-school merit-scholarship money awarded: $35,000. Total amount of financial aid awarded in 2015–16: $1,797,988.

Admissions Traditional secondary-level entrance grade is 9. For fall 2015, 116 students applied for upper-level admission, 68 were accepted, 37 enrolled. ISEE, Otis-Lennon Ability or Stanford Achievement Test, school's own exam, SSAT, TOEFL or writing sample required. Deadline for receipt of application materials: December 15. Application fee required: $60. On-campus interview required.

Athletics Interscholastic: badminton, ballet, basketball, crew, cross-country running, dance, field hockey, hockey, indoor soccer, indoor track & field, lacrosse, rowing, running, soccer, softball, squash, tennis, track and field, volleyball, winter (indoor) track, winter soccer; intramural: aerobics, aerobics/dance, aerobics/Nautilus, archery, badminton, ball hockey, basketball, bowling, cooperative games, croquet, cross-country running, dance, fitness, flag football, floor hockey, ice hockey, jogging, outdoor activities, physical training, pillo polo, ropes courses, running, strength & conditioning, tennis, touch football, weight training. 5 PE instructors, 27 coaches, 2 athletic trainers.

Computers Computers are regularly used in all academic, animation, art, computer applications, Web site design classes. Computer network features include on-campus library services, online commercial services, Internet access, wireless campus network, Internet filtering or blocking technology, off-campus email. Student e-mail accounts and computer access in designated common areas are available to students. Students grades are available online. The school has a published electronic and media policy.

Contact Rebekah Jackson, Director of Enrollment Management. 410-323-8800 Ext. 1237. Fax: 410-435-4678. E-mail: jacksonr@brynmawrschool.org. Website: www.brynmawrschool.org

THE BUCKLEY SCHOOL

3900 Stansbury Avenue
Sherman Oaks, California 91423

Head of School: Mr. James Busby

General Information Coeducational day college-preparatory, arts, technology, and full college preparatory program school. Grades K–12. Founded: 1933. Setting: suburban. Nearest major city is Los Angeles. 20-acre campus. 8 buildings on campus. Approved or accredited by California Association of Independent Schools, National Association of Episcopal Schools, Western Association of Schools and Colleges, and California Department of Education. Member of National Association of Independent Schools. Total enrollment: 830. Upper school average class size: 14. Upper school faculty-student ratio: 1:8. There are 180 required school days per year for Upper School students. Upper School students typically attend 5 days per week. The average school day consists of 6 hours.

Upper School Student Profile Grade 9: 86 students (47 boys, 39 girls); Grade 10: 83 students (45 boys, 38 girls); Grade 11: 90 students (45 boys, 45 girls); Grade 12: 86 students (42 boys, 44 girls).

Faculty School total: 110. In upper school: 28 men, 27 women; 31 have advanced degrees.

Subjects Offered Algebra, American history, American literature, art history, biology, calculus, ceramics, chemistry, chorus, computer graphics, computer science, creative writing, dance, drama, ecology, English, English literature, fine arts, French, geology, geometry, government/civics, humanities, journalism, Latin, mathematics, music, music theory, orchestra, photography, physical education, physics, science, social sciences, Spanish, theater, trigonometry, world history, world literature, yoga.

Graduation Requirements Arts and fine arts (art, music, dance, drama), computer science, English, foreign language, humanities, mathematics, performing arts, physical education (includes health), science, social sciences. Community service is required.

Special Academic Programs Advanced Placement exam preparation; honors section; independent study; study abroad.

College Admission Counseling 74 students graduated in 2015; all went to college, including New York University; Stanford University; University of California, Berkeley; University of California, Los Angeles; University of Southern California.

Student Life Upper grades have uniform requirement, student council, honor system. Discipline rests primarily with faculty.

Summer Programs Enrichment, advancement, art/fine arts, computer instruction programs offered; session focuses on college preparatory courses and enrichment; held on campus; accepts boys and girls; open to students from other schools. 100 students usually enrolled. 2016 schedule: June 20 to July 22.

Tuition and Aid Day student tuition: $36,003. Tuition installment plan (monthly payment plans, individually arranged payment plans, reduced payments for families receiving financial aid). Need-based scholarship grants available. In 2015–16, 14% of upper-school students received aid. Total amount of financial aid awarded in 2015–16: $530,000.

Admissions Traditional secondary-level entrance grade is 9. For fall 2015, 176 students applied for upper-level admission, 58 were accepted, 28 enrolled. ISEE or SSAT required. Deadline for receipt of application materials: January 10. Application fee required: $125. On-campus interview required.

Athletics Interscholastic: baseball (boys), softball (g), volleyball (g); coed interscholastic: basketball, cross-country running, dance, dance team, equestrian sports, horseback riding, soccer, swimming and diving, tennis. 12 PE instructors, 11 coaches, 2 athletic trainers.

Computers Computers are regularly used in art, English, foreign language, graphic design, music, science, video film production, yearbook classes. Computer network features include on-campus library services, online commercial services, Internet access, wireless campus network, Internet filtering or blocking technology, Web page design, online syllabi. Campus intranet, student e-mail accounts, and computer access in designated common areas are available to students. Students grades are available online. The school has a published electronic and media policy.

Contact Mr. Stephen D. Milich, Director of Admission and Financial Aid. 818-461-6719. Fax: 818-461-6714. E-mail: admissions@buckley.org. Website: www.buckley.org

BUFFALO SEMINARY

205 Bidwell Parkway
Buffalo, New York 14222

Head of School: Jody Douglass

General Information Girls' boarding and day college-preparatory, arts, technology, and Community Service school. Grades 9–12. Founded: 1851. Setting: urban. Students are housed in single-sex dormitories. 3-acre campus. 6 buildings on campus. Approved or accredited by New York Department of Education, New York State Association of Independent Schools, The Association of Boarding Schools, and New York Department of Education. Member of National Association of Independent Schools and Secondary School Admission Test Board. Endowment: $7 million. Total enrollment: 219. Upper school average class size: 11. Upper school faculty-student ratio: 1:7. There are 168 required school days per year for Upper School students. Upper School students typically attend 5 days per week. The average school day consists of 7 hours and 35 minutes.

Upper School Student Profile Grade 9: 49 students (49 girls); Grade 10: 61 students (61 girls); Grade 11: 63 students (63 girls); Grade 12: 43 students (43 girls). 22% of students are boarding students. 80% are state residents. 3 states are represented in upper school student body. 17% are international students. International students from China, France, Germany, Republic of Korea, and United States; 3 other countries represented in student body.

Faculty School total: 37. In upper school: 4 men, 33 women; 23 have advanced degrees; 7 reside on campus.

Subjects Offered 20th century American writers, 20th century history, 20th century physics, 20th century world history, 3-dimensional art, 3-dimensional design, acting, advanced biology, advanced chemistry, advanced computer applications, advanced math, Advanced Placement courses, algebra, American biography, American culture, American democracy, American history, American history-AP, American literature, anatomy, ancient history, ancient world history, applied arts, applied music, art, art and culture, art appreciation, arts appreciation, astronomy, athletics, biology, biology-AP, British literature (honors), calculus, calculus-AP, career education internship, chemistry, Chinese, choral music, chorus, cinematography, community service, computer applications, computer literacy, computer science, computer skills, conceptual physics, contemporary women writers, creative writing, dance, digital art, digital photography, drama, drama workshop, dramatic arts, drawing, driver education, ecology, engineering, English, English language-AP, English literature, English literature and composition-AP, environmental science, European history, European literature, expository writing, film and literature, fine arts, foreign language, French, French language-AP, French literature-AP, French-AP, geometry, government and politics-AP, grammar, health and wellness, honors English, honors U.S. history, honors world history, Latin, leadership and service, literary magazine, mathematics, mathematics-AP, modern European history, music, photography, physical education, physics, physics-AP, play production, public speaking, science, senior internship, Shakespeare, social studies, society and culture, South African history, Spanish, Spanish language-AP, statistics, student government, theater, trigonometry, U.S. government and politics-AP, U.S. history-AP, United States government-AP, visual and performing arts, visual arts, vocal ensemble, women's health, women's literature, women's studies, world history, world history-AP, world literature, writing.

Graduation Requirements Arts and fine arts (art, music, dance, drama), computer science, English, foreign language, health education, history, mathematics, physical education (includes health), science, senior internship. Community service is required.

Special Academic Programs Advanced Placement exam preparation; honors section; independent study; academic accommodation for the gifted.

College Admission Counseling 66 students graduated in 2015; all went to college, including Boston University; Canisius College; Hobart and William Smith Colleges; Loyola University Chicago; University of Pittsburgh; University of Toronto. Mean SAT critical reading: 545, mean SAT math: 575, mean SAT writing: 557, mean composite ACT: 27. 71% scored over 600 on SAT critical reading, 65% scored over 600 on SAT math.

Student Life Upper grades have specified standards of dress, student council, honor system. Discipline rests equally with students and faculty.

Summer Programs Sports programs offered; session focuses on Squash, Soccer, and Lacrosse clinics; held on campus; accepts girls; open to students from other schools. 2016 schedule: July 5 to August 7. Application deadline: June 30.

Tuition and Aid Day student tuition: $19,840; 5-day tuition and room/board: $42,715; 7-day tuition and room/board: $46,715. Tuition installment plan (FACTS Tuition Payment Plan, monthly payment plans, individually arranged payment plans, 2-payment plan, prepayment discount plan). Tuition reduction for siblings, merit scholarship grants, need-based scholarship grants, faculty remission available. In 2015–16, 58% of upper-school students received aid; total upper-school merit-scholarship money awarded: $400,000. Total amount of financial aid awarded in 2015–16: $1,074,305.

Admissions Traditional secondary-level entrance grade is 9. For fall 2015, 140 students applied for upper-level admission, 120 were accepted, 58 enrolled. School placement exam, school's own exam, TOEFL and writing sample required. Deadline for receipt of application materials: none. Application fee required: $35. Interview required.

Athletics Interscholastic: basketball, bowling, crew, fencing, field hockey, golf, independent competitive sports, lacrosse, rowing, sailing, soccer, squash, swimming and diving, tennis; intramural: aerobics, dance, drill team, fitness, fitness walking, lacrosse, Nautilus, outdoors, paddle tennis, physical fitness, physical training, self defense, skiing (downhill), snowboarding, strength & conditioning, tai chi, volleyball, yoga. 2 PE instructors, 20 coaches, 1 athletic trainer.

Computers Computers are regularly used in digital applications classes. Computer network features include on-campus library services, online commercial services, Internet access, wireless campus network, Internet filtering or blocking technology. Campus intranet, student e-mail accounts, and computer access in designated common areas are available to students. Students grades are available online. The school has a published electronic and media policy.

Contact Ms. Laura Munson, Director of Admission. 716-885-6780 Ext. 253. Fax: 716-885-6785. E-mail: lmunson@buffaloseminary.org. Website: www.buffaloseminary.org

Bulloch Academy

BULLOCH ACADEMY

873 Westside Road
Statesboro, Georgia 30458

Head of School: Mrs. Leisa Houghton

General Information Coeducational day college-preparatory, arts, and technology school, affiliated with Protestant faith, Baptist Church. Grades PK–12. Founded: 1971. Setting: small town. Nearest major city is Savannah. 35-acre campus. 4 buildings on campus. Approved or accredited by Georgia Accrediting Commission, Georgia Independent School Association, Southern Association of Colleges and Schools, and Southern Association of Independent Schools. Member of National Association of Independent Schools. Total enrollment: 498. Upper school average class size: 17. Upper school faculty-student ratio: 1:17. There are 180 required school days per year for Upper School students. Upper School students typically attend 5 days per week. The average school day consists of 8 hours.

Upper School Student Profile Grade 9: 35 students (19 boys, 16 girls); Grade 10: 36 students (20 boys, 16 girls); Grade 11: 42 students (19 boys, 23 girls); Grade 12: 45 students (20 boys, 25 girls). 90% of students are Protestant, Baptist.

Faculty School total: 31. In upper school: 4 men, 11 women; 4 have advanced degrees.

Subjects Offered Advanced Placement courses, American government, American history, anatomy and physiology, art, art education, biology, calculus, chemistry, computer applications, computer science, earth science, economics, economics and history, English, ethics, geometry, government, government-AP, government/civics, health education, journalism, language and composition, language arts, literature-AP, mathematics-AP, music, performing arts, physical education, physics, pre-algebra, pre-calculus, research skills, science, social sciences, Spanish, speech and debate, technology, U.S. government and politics-AP, U.S. history, Web site design, world geography, world history.

Graduation Requirements Computer science, English, foreign language, mathematics, physical education (includes health), science, social sciences, social studies (includes history).

Special Academic Programs 6 Advanced Placement exams for which test preparation is offered; honors section; independent study; study at local college for college credit; academic accommodation for the gifted, the musically talented, and the artistically talented.

College Admission Counseling 46 students graduated in 2014; all went to college, including DePaul University; Georgia Institute of Technology; Georgia Southern University; Mercer University; The University of Alabama; University of Georgia. Median SAT critical reading: 497, median SAT math: 513, median SAT writing: 487, median combined SAT: 1497, median composite ACT: 22.

Student Life Upper grades have specified standards of dress, student council, honor system. Discipline rests primarily with faculty.

Tuition and Aid Day student tuition: $6940. Tuition installment plan (monthly payment plans, individually arranged payment plans). Tuition reduction for siblings, need-based scholarship grants, tuition assistance available. In 2014–15, 15% of upper-school students received aid. Total amount of financial aid awarded in 2014–15: $50,000.

Admissions Traditional secondary-level entrance grade is 9. For fall 2014, 25 students applied for upper-level admission, 24 were accepted, 24 enrolled. Any standardized test required. Deadline for receipt of application materials: none. Application fee required: $375. Interview recommended.

Athletics Interscholastic: baseball (boys), basketball (b,g), cheering (g), cross-country running (b,g), dance team (g), football (b), golf (b,g), physical fitness (b,g), running (b,g), soccer (b,g), softball (g), strength & conditioning (b,g), tennis (b,g), track and field (b,g), weight lifting (b,g), weight training (b,g), wrestling (b); intramural: cheering (g), cross-country running (b,g), football (b), physical fitness (b,g); coed interscholastic: archery, physical fitness, skeet shooting, trap and skeet; coed intramural: basketball, football, physical fitness. 3 PE instructors, 7 coaches, 3 athletic trainers.

Computers Computers are regularly used in art, career education, career exploration, computer applications, creative writing, desktop publishing, economics, geography, history, independent study, keyboarding, technology classes. Computer network features include on-campus library services, online commercial services, Internet access, wireless campus network, Internet filtering or blocking technology. Student e-mail accounts are available to students. Students grades are available online. The school has a published electronic and media policy.

Contact Mr. Leisa Houghton, Head of School. 912-764-6297. Fax: 912-764-3165. E-mail: lhoughton@bullochacademy.com. Website: www.bullochacademy.com

BURR AND BURTON ACADEMY

57 Seminary Avenue
Manchester, Vermont 05254

Head of School: Mr. Mark Tashjian

General Information Coeducational boarding and day college-preparatory, general academic, arts, and technology school. Grades 9–12. Founded: 1829. Setting: small town. Nearest major city is Albany, NY. Students are housed in single-sex dormitories and homes of host families. 49-acre campus. 7 buildings on campus. Approved or accredited by Independent Schools of Northern New England, New England Association of Schools and Colleges, and Vermont Department of Education. Member

of National Association of Independent Schools. Total enrollment: 668. Upper school average class size: 19. Upper school faculty-student ratio: 1:12. There are 175 required school days per year for Upper School students. Upper School students typically attend 5 days per week. The average school day consists of 6 hours and 40 minutes.

Upper School Student Profile Grade 9: 164 students (72 boys, 92 girls); Grade 10: 156 students (74 boys, 82 girls); Grade 11: 175 students (88 boys, 87 girls); Grade 12: 173 students (80 boys, 93 girls). 8% of students are boarding students. 8% are international students. International students from China, Germany, Japan, Republic of Korea, Spain, and Taiwan; 3 other countries represented in student body.

Faculty School total: 60. In upper school: 35 men, 25 women; 30 have advanced degrees.

Subjects Offered Algebra, American history, American literature, anatomy, art, art history, biology, business, calculus, chemistry, computer math, computer science, drafting, drama, driver education, earth science, ecology, English, English literature, environmental science, expository writing, French, geometry, German, government/civics, health, history, mathematics, music, photography, physical education, physics, psychology, science, social studies, Spanish, theater, trigonometry, world history, world literature.

Graduation Requirements Arts, computer literacy, English, mathematics, physical education (includes health), science, social studies (includes history), U.S. history. Community service is required.

Special Academic Programs 14 Advanced Placement exams for which test preparation is offered; honors section; independent study; term-away projects; study abroad; remedial reading and/or remedial writing; remedial math; programs in English, mathematics, general development for dyslexic students; special instructional classes for deaf students, blind students; ESL (20 students enrolled).

College Admission Counseling 188 students graduated in 2015; 154 went to college, including Michigan State University; University of Vermont. Other: 22 went to work, 3 entered military service, 9 had other specific plans.

Student Life Upper grades have specified standards of dress, student council. Discipline rests primarily with faculty.

Tuition and Aid Tuition installment plan (individually arranged payment plans). Financial aid available to upper-school students. In 2015–16, 10% of upper-school students received aid.

Admissions Traditional secondary-level entrance grade is 9. School's own test and TOEFL or SLEP required. Deadline for receipt of application materials: none. No application fee required. Interview required.

Athletics Interscholastic: alpine skiing (boys, girls), baseball (b), basketball (b,g), cross-country running (b,g), dance team (g), field hockey (g), football (b), golf (b,g), hockey (b,g), ice hockey (b,g), lacrosse (b,g), nordic skiing (b,g), skiing (cross-country) (b,g), skiing (downhill) (b,g), snowboarding (b,g), soccer (b,g), softball (g), tennis (b,g), track and field (b,g), wrestling (b,g); coed intramural: equestrian sports, floor hockey, outdoor adventure, outdoor education, volleyball, weight training. 4 PE instructors, 1 athletic trainer.

Computers Computers are regularly used in drafting, drawing and design, English, foreign language, graphic design, history, information technology, mathematics, science, video film production, Web site design, yearbook classes. Computer network features include on-campus library services, Internet access, wireless campus network, Internet filtering or blocking technology. Campus intranet, student e-mail accounts, and computer access in designated common areas are available to students.

Contact Mr. Kirk R. Knutson, Director of Admissions and School Counseling. 802-362-1775 Ext. 125. Fax: 802-362-0574. E-mail: kknutson@burrburton.org. Website: www.burrburton.org

BUTTE CENTRAL CATHOLIC HIGH SCHOOL

9 South Idaho Street
Butte, Montana 59701

Head of School: Mr. Kevin St. John

General Information Boys' boarding and coeducational day college-preparatory, arts, business, vocational, religious studies, and technology school, affiliated with Roman Catholic Church. Boarding boys grades 9–12, day boys grades 9–12, day girls grades 9–12. Founded: 1892. Setting: small town. Nearest major city is Bozeman. 6-acre campus. 1 building on campus. Approved or accredited by National Catholic Education Association, Western Catholic Education Association, and Montana Department of Education. Endowment: $300,000. Total enrollment: 145. Upper school average class size: 20. Upper school faculty-student ratio: 1:10. There are 180 required school days per year for Upper School students. Upper School students typically attend 5 days per week. The average school day consists of 7 hours.

Upper School Student Profile Grade 9: 27 students (15 boys, 12 girls); Grade 10: 44 students (25 boys, 19 girls); Grade 11: 37 students (18 boys, 19 girls); Grade 12: 37 students (16 boys, 21 girls). 4% of students are boarding students. 93% are state residents. 1 state is represented in upper school student body. 5% are international students. International students from China and Taiwan; 5 other countries represented in student body. 75% of students are Roman Catholic.

Faculty School total: 17. In upper school: 6 men, 11 women; 3 have advanced degrees; 1 resides on campus.

Subjects Offered Accounting, advanced math, Advanced Placement courses, algebra, American literature-AP, animal behavior, art, athletic training, biology, calculus,

calculus-AP, career education, chemistry, choir, college counseling, college placement, college planning, college writing, community service, computer science, computers, debate, desktop publishing, drama, English, English literature and composition-AP, foreign language, French, French as a second language, geometry, government/civics, health, history, honors algebra, honors English, honors geometry, human biology, integrated mathematics, keyboarding, mathematics, model United Nations, physical education, physics, pre-calculus, public speaking, reading, religion, science, social studies, Spanish, student government, trigonometry, Web site design, weightlifting, world history, writing, yearbook.

Graduation Requirements American government, American history, arts and fine arts (art, music, dance, drama), electives, English, foreign language, global studies, health education, keyboarding, mathematics, physical education (includes health), religion (includes Bible studies and theology), science, social studies (includes history), writing. Community service is required.

Special Academic Programs 2 Advanced Placement exams for which test preparation is offered; honors section; independent study; study at local college for college credit; remedial reading and/or remedial writing; remedial math.

College Admission Counseling 32 students graduated in 2015; 30 went to college, including Carroll University; Division of Technology of Montana Tech of The University of Montana; Gonzaga University; Montana State University; The University of Montana Western. Other: 1 went to work, 1 entered military service. Median composite ACT: 20. 7% scored over 26 on composite ACT.

Student Life Upper grades have specified standards of dress, student council, honor system. Discipline rests primarily with faculty. Attendance at religious services is required.

Tuition and Aid Day student tuition: $4000–$8000; 7-day tuition and room/board: $10,000–$15,000. Guaranteed tuition plan. Tuition installment plan (FACTS Tuition Payment Plan, monthly payment plans, individually arranged payment plans). Tuition reduction for siblings, need-based scholarship grants available. In 2015–16, 25% of upper-school students received aid. Total amount of financial aid awarded in 2015–16: $68,000.

Admissions Traditional secondary-level entrance grade is 9. For fall 2015, 145 students applied for upper-level admission, 145 were accepted, 145 enrolled. Admissions testing required. Deadline for receipt of application materials: none. Application fee required: $150. Interview required.

Athletics Interscholastic: basketball (boys, girls), cheering (g), cross-country running (b,g), football (b), golf (b,g), softball (g), strength & conditioning (b,g), tennis (b,g), track and field (b,g), volleyball (g), wrestling (b). 1 PE instructor, 30 coaches, 1 athletic trainer.

Computers Computer network features include on-campus library services, Internet access, Internet filtering or blocking technology. The school has a published electronic and media policy.

Contact Mr. Kevin St. John, Principal. 406-782-6761. Fax: 406-723-3873. E-mail: ksj@buttecentralschools.org. Website: www.buttecentralschools.org

BUXTON SCHOOL

291 South Street
Williamstown, Massachusetts 01267

Head of School: Peter Smith '74

General Information Coeducational boarding and day college-preparatory and arts school. Grades 9–12. Founded: 1928. Setting: small town. Nearest major city is Boston. Students are housed in single-sex dormitories. 120-acre campus. 18 buildings on campus. Approved or accredited by Association of Independent Schools in New England, New England Association of Schools and Colleges, The Association of Boarding Schools, and Massachusetts Department of Education. Member of National Association of Independent Schools and Secondary School Admission Test Board. Endowment: $3 million. Total enrollment: 90. Upper school average class size: 9. Upper school faculty-student ratio: 1:4. There are 222 required school days per year for Upper School students. Upper School students typically attend 7 days per week. The average school day consists of 5 hours and 15 minutes.

Upper School Student Profile Grade 9: 17 students (8 boys, 9 girls); Grade 10: 23 students (11 boys, 12 girls); Grade 11: 25 students (12 boys, 13 girls); Grade 12: 25 students (12 boys, 13 girls). 91% of students are boarding students. 26% are state residents. 12 states are represented in upper school student body. 17% are international students. International students from China, Mexico, Nicaragua, Spain, and United Kingdom.

Faculty School total: 22. In upper school: 11 men, 11 women; 8 have advanced degrees; 13 reside on campus.

Subjects Offered Advanced math, African dance, African drumming, African studies, algebra, American history, American literature, anatomy and physiology, anthropology, architecture, astronomy, biology, British literature, calculus, cell biology, ceramics, chemistry, civil rights, costumes and make-up, creative writing, critical writing, dance performance, drama, drama performance, drawing, economics, education, English, English literature, ensembles, ESL, European history, expository writing, fiction, film history, French, geometry, grammar, history, improvisation, independent study, instruments, lab science, linear algebra, literary genres, literature, marine biology, medieval/Renaissance history, music, music composition, music performance, music theory, mythology, oceanography, painting, performing arts,

philosophy, photography, physics, poetry, pre-calculus, printmaking, psychology, religion, set design, social sciences, Spanish, studio art, technical theater, TOEFL preparation, trigonometry, video film production, voice, Western civilization, writing workshop.

Graduation Requirements American history, English, foreign language, lab science, mathematics, social sciences.

Special Academic Programs Honors section; independent study; study at local college for college credit; academic accommodation for the gifted, the musically talented, and the artistically talented; ESL (7 students enrolled).

College Admission Counseling 27 students graduated in 2015; 26 went to college, including Bard College; Ithaca College; Mount Holyoke College; Pitzer College; Reed College; Sarah Lawrence College. Other: 1 went to work.

Student Life Discipline rests primarily with faculty.

Tuition and Aid Day student tuition: $31,000; 7-day tuition and room/board: $51,000. Tuition installment plan (individually arranged payment plans, Tuition Management Systems). Need-based scholarship grants, need-based loans with limited in-house financing available. In 2015–16, 49% of upper-school students received aid. Total amount of financial aid awarded in 2015–16: $1,600,000.

Admissions Traditional secondary-level entrance grade is 9. SSAT or TOEFL or SLEP required. Deadline for receipt of application materials: February 1. Application fee required: $50. Interview required.

Athletics Interscholastic: soccer (boys, girls); intramural: cheering (g), soccer (b,g); coed interscholastic: basketball, ultimate Frisbee; coed intramural: basketball, bicycling, dance, fitness, hiking/backpacking, horseback riding, ice skating, indoor soccer, jogging, martial arts, mountain biking, outdoor activities, running, skateboarding, skiing (cross-country), skiing (downhill), snowboarding, soccer, table tennis, ultimate Frisbee, volleyball, walking, weight lifting, yoga.

Computers Computers are regularly used in architecture, ESL, language development, mathematics, media production, multimedia, music, photography, science, Spanish, video film production, writing, yearbook classes. Computer network features include Internet access, wireless campus network, Internet filtering or blocking technology. Campus intranet and computer access in designated common areas are available to students. The school has a published electronic and media policy.

Contact Admissions Office. 413-458-3919. Fax: 413-458-9428.
E-mail: Admissions@BuxtonSchool.org. Website: www.BuxtonSchool.org

CALGARY ACADEMY

9400 17 Avenue SW
Calgary, Alberta T3H 4A6, Canada

Head of School: Ms. Dana Braunberger

General Information Coeducational day college preparatory, arts, and technology school; primarily serves underachievers, students with learning disabilities, individuals with Attention Deficit Disorder, and dyslexic students. Grades 2–12. Founded: 1981. Setting: suburban. 17 acre campus. 3 buildings on campus. Approved or accredited by Association of Independent Schools and Colleges of Alberta and Alberta Department of Education. Language of instruction: English. Endowment: CAN$3 million. Total enrollment: 370. Upper school average class size: 16. Upper school faculty-student ratio: 1:8. There are 188 required school days per year for Upper School students. Upper School students typically attend 5 days per week. The average school day consists of 6 hours and 10 minutes.

Upper School Student Profile Grade 10: 41 students (21 boys, 20 girls); Grade 11: 49 students (29 boys, 20 girls); Grade 12: 50 students (32 boys, 18 girls).

Faculty School total: 25. In upper school: 10 men, 15 women; 10 have advanced degrees.

Subjects Offered Art history, athletics, band, biology, calculus, career and personal planning, character education, chemistry, computer animation, computer multimedia, creative drama, drama, English composition, English literature, general science, grammar, language arts, mathematics, outdoor education, physical education, physics, psychology, reading/study skills, remedial study skills, sociology, Spanish, study skills.

Graduation Requirements Biology, chemistry, English, mathematics, physics, science, social studies (includes history).

Special Academic Programs Remedial reading and/or remedial writing; remedial math; programs in English, mathematics for dyslexic students.

College Admission Counseling 64 students graduated in 2015; 55 went to college, including Mount Royal University; University of Alberta; University of Calgary; University of Lethbridge. Other: 5 went to work, 4 had other specific plans.

Student Life Upper grades have specified standards of dress, student council, honor system. Discipline rests primarily with faculty.

Tuition and Aid Day student tuition: CAN$18,000. Tuition installment plan (monthly payment plans, individually arranged payment plans). Bursaries available. In 2015–16, 5% of upper-school students received aid. Total amount of financial aid awarded in 2015–16: CAN$300,000.

Admissions Traditional secondary-level entrance grade is 10. For fall 2015, 100 students applied for upper-level admission, 30 were accepted, 25 enrolled. Achievement tests, Wechsler Individual Achievement Test and Wechsler Intelligence Scale for Children III required. Deadline for receipt of application materials: none. Application fee required: CAN$1500. On-campus interview required.

Athletics Interscholastic: badminton (boys, girls), ball hockey (b), basketball (b,g), cross-country running (b,g), floor hockey (b), golf (b,g), handball (b,g), track and field (b,g), volleyball (b,g), wrestling (b,g); intramural: fly fishing (b), ice hockey (b,g); coed interscholastic: badminton, curling, golf, soccer; coed intramural: alpine skiing, outdoor recreation, triathlon. 6 PE instructors.

Computers Computers are regularly used in all academic classes. Computer network features include on-campus library services, Internet access, wireless campus network, Internet filtering or blocking technology. Campus intranet and computer access in designated common areas are available to students. Students grades are available online. The school has a published electronic and media policy.

Contact Ms. Irina Dart, Director of Admissions. 403-686-6444 Ext. 236. Fax: 403-240-3427. E-mail: idart@calgaryacademy.com. Website: www.calgaryacademy.com

CALGARY ACADEMY COLLEGIATE

1677 93rd St Sw
Calgary, Alberta T3H 0R3, Canada
Head of School: Ms. Jessica Richmond

General Information Coeducational day college-preparatory, arts, and technology school; primarily serves students with learning disabilities, individuals with Attention Deficit Disorder, and dyslexic students. Grades 6–12. Founded: 1981. Setting: urban. 17-acre campus. 3 buildings on campus. Approved or accredited by Association of Independent Schools and Colleges of Alberta and Alberta Department of Education. Language of instruction: English. Endowment: CAN$15 million. Total enrollment: 176. Upper school average class size: 17. Upper school faculty-student ratio: 1:8. There are 188 required school days per year for Upper School students. Upper School students typically attend 5 days per week. The average school day consists of 6 hours and 10 minutes.

Upper School Student Profile Grade 10: 30 students (20 boys, 10 girls); Grade 11: 30 students (19 boys, 11 girls); Grade 12: 35 students (21 boys, 14 girls).

Faculty School total: 25. In upper school: 10 men, 15 women; 20 have advanced degrees.

Subjects Offered Art history, athletics, band, biology, calculus, career and personal planning, character education, chemistry, computer animation, computer multimedia, drama, English composition, English literature, grammar, language arts, mathematics, outdoor education, physical education, physics, psychology, social studies, sociology, Spanish, study skills.

Graduation Requirements Biology, chemistry, English, mathematics, physics, social studies (includes history).

Special Academic Programs International Baccalaureate program; 1 Advanced Placement exam for which test preparation is offered.

College Admission Counseling 39 students graduated in 2015; 38 went to college, including Mount Royal University; University of Alberta; University of Calgary; University of Lethbridge. Other: 1 went to work.

Student Life Upper grades have specified standards of dress, student council, honor system. Discipline rests primarily with faculty.

Tuition and Aid Day student tuition: CAN$18,000. Tuition installment plan (monthly payment plans, individually arranged payment plans). Bursaries, need-based scholarship grants available. In 2015–16, 5% of upper-school students received aid. Total amount of financial aid awarded in 2015–16: CAN$300,000.

Admissions Traditional secondary-level entrance grade is 10. For fall 2015, 50 students applied for upper-level admission, 30 were accepted, 20 enrolled. Achievement tests, Wechsler Individual Achievement Test or Wechsler Intelligence Scale for Children III required. Deadline for receipt of application materials: none. Application fee required: CAN$1600. On-campus interview required.

Athletics Interscholastic: badminton (boys, girls), ball hockey (b), basketball (b,g), cross-country running (b,g), golf (b,g), handball (b,g), rugby (b), track and field (b,g), volleyball (b,g), wrestling (b,g); intramural: ice hockey (b,g); coed interscholastic: badminton, cheering, curling, soccer; coed intramural: aerobics/Nautilus, bicycling, canoeing/kayaking, martial arts, mountain biking, outdoor activities, outdoor education, outdoor recreation, rock climbing, skiing (cross-country), skiing (downhill), triathlon, wall climbing. 6 PE instructors, 30 coaches.

Computers Computers are regularly used in all academic classes. Computer network features include on-campus library services, Internet access, wireless campus network, Internet filtering or blocking technology. Computer access in designated common areas is available to students. Students grades are available online. The school has a published electronic and media policy.

Contact Ms. Irina Dart, Director of Admissions. 403-686-6444 Ext. 236. Fax: 403-686-3427. E-mail: idart@calgaryacademy.com. Website: http://www.calgaryacademy.com/

CALIFORNIA CROSSPOINT HIGH SCHOOL

1501 Harbor Bay Parkway
Alameda, California 94502
Head of School: Mr. Robin S. Hom

General Information Coeducational boarding and day college-preparatory and religious studies school, affiliated with Bible Fellowship Church,

Evangelical/Fundamental faith. Grades 9–12. Founded: 1979. Setting: suburban. Nearest major city is Oakland. Students are housed in student residences. 10-acre campus. 2 buildings on campus. Approved or accredited by Association of Christian Schools International, The College Board, US Department of State, Western Association of Schools and Colleges, and California Department of Education. Endowment: $100,000. Total enrollment: 200. Upper school average class size: 15. Upper school faculty-student ratio: 1:8. There are 173 required school days per year for Upper School students. Upper School students typically attend 5 days per week. The average school day consists of 7 hours and 5 minutes.

Upper School Student Profile Grade 9: 40 students (21 boys, 19 girls); Grade 10: 59 students (36 boys, 23 girls); Grade 11: 40 students (19 boys, 21 girls); Grade 12: 59 students (23 boys, 36 girls). 20% of students are Bible Fellowship Church, Evangelical/Fundamental faith.

Faculty School total: 38. In upper school: 15 men, 20 women; 14 have advanced degrees.

Subjects Offered Advanced computer applications, Advanced Placement courses, aerobics, algebra, American government, American history, American history-AP, American literature, American literature-AP, applied music, art, art-AP, audio visual/media, Basic programming, basketball, Bible, Bible studies, biology, biology-AP, British literature, calculus, calculus-AP, career/college preparation, chemistry, Chinese, Chinese studies, choir, choral music, Christian doctrine, Christian ethics, Christian studies, civics, civics/free enterprise, college counseling, college placement, college planning, communications, community service, comparative religion, computer applications, computer graphics, computer science, computer science-AP, CPR, debate, drama, driver education, economics, economics-AP, electives, English, English language-AP, English literature, English literature-AP, ESL, European history-AP, first aid, foreign language, general science, geometry, government, government and politics-AP, government-AP, graphic arts, honors English, intro to computers, language arts, leadership and service, learning strategies, library assistant, literature and composition-AP, literature-AP, macro/microeconomics-AP, Mandarin, marching band, marine science, martial arts, mathematics-AP, microeconomics, microeconomics-AP, music, newspaper, participation in sports, physical education, physics, physics-AP, pre-algebra, pre-calculus, probability and statistics, psychology-AP, public speaking, religious education, religious studies, ROTC (for boys), SAT preparation, SAT/ACT preparation, science, science research, Spanish, speech, speech and debate, speech communications, sports, state history, statistics, student government, theater, theater arts, trigonometry, U.S. government, U.S. government and politics-AP, U.S. history, U.S. history-AP, visual and performing arts, volleyball, Web authoring, world history, world wide web design, yearbook.

Graduation Requirements Algebra, American government, American history, Bible, Chinese, CPR, driver education, economics, English, first aid, foreign language, geometry, history, lab science, Life of Christ, mathematics, physical education (includes health), physics, pre-algebra, science, visual and performing arts, world history, Mandarin I or Chinese Culture class.

Special Academic Programs 15 Advanced Placement exams for which test preparation is offered; honors section; term-away projects; study at local college for college credit; study abroad; academic accommodation for the gifted; remedial reading and/or remedial writing; ESL (30 students enrolled).

College Admission Counseling 55 students graduated in 2015; all went to college, including San Jose State University; University of California, Davis; University of California, Irvine; University of California, Riverside; University of California, Santa Cruz; University of the Pacific. Mean SAT critical reading: 584, mean SAT math: 685, mean SAT writing: 598, mean combined SAT: 1866. 45% scored over 600 on SAT critical reading, 85% scored over 600 on SAT math, 50% scored over 600 on SAT writing, 60% scored over 1800 on combined SAT.

Student Life Upper grades have uniform requirement, student council. Discipline rests primarily with faculty. Attendance at religious services is required.

Summer Programs Remediation, enrichment, advancement, ESL, sports programs offered; session focuses on academic enrichment or remediation; held on campus; accepts boys and girls; open to students from other schools. 40 students usually enrolled. 2016 schedule: June 10 to July 24. Application deadline: May 15.

Tuition and Aid Day student tuition: $9750–$11,750. Tuition installment plan (monthly payment plans, individually arranged payment plans, eTuition automatic electronic deposit). Tuition reduction for siblings, merit scholarship grants, need-based scholarship grants, paying campus jobs, tuition reduction for staff children, tuition reduction for children of full-time Christian ministers of like faith available. In 2015–16, 15% of upper-school students received aid; total upper-school merit-scholarship money awarded: $25,000. Total amount of financial aid awarded in 2015–16: $205,000.

Admissions Traditional secondary-level entrance grade is 9. For fall 2015, 40 students applied for upper-level admission, 40 were accepted, 31 enrolled. Achievement/Aptitude/Writing, admissions testing, California Achievement Test, CTBS (or similar from their school), Math Placement Exam, Stanford Achievement Test or writing sample required. Deadline for receipt of application materials: none. No application fee required. Interview required.

Athletics Interscholastic: badminton (boys, girls), basketball (b,g), cross-country running (b,g), golf (b,g), soccer (b,g), tennis (b), track and field (b,g), volleyball (b,g); intramural: basketball (b,g), outdoor education (b,g), outdoor recreation (b,g), soccer (b,g), table tennis (b,g), tennis (g), volleyball (b,g); coed interscholastic: badminton, golf, swimming and diving; coed intramural: backpacking, outdoor education, outdoor recreation, softball, table tennis, volleyball. 2 PE instructors, 1 coach.

Computers Computers are regularly used in lab/keyboard, programming, science, senior seminar, Web site design classes. Computer network features include on-campus library services, Internet access, wireless campus network, Internet filtering or blocking technology. Student e-mail accounts are available to students. Students grades are available online. The school has a published electronic and media policy.
Contact Mrs. Christine Hom, Admissions Director. 510-995-5333. Fax: 510-995-5333. E-mail: ChristineHom@cchsrams.org. Website: www.cchsrams.org

CALIFORNIA LUTHERAN HIGH SCHOOL

31970 Central Avenue
PO Box 1570
Wildomar, California 92595
Head of School: Mr. Steven Rosenbaum

General Information Coeducational boarding college-preparatory and religious studies school, affiliated with Wisconsin Evangelical Lutheran Synod. Grades 9–12. Founded: 1977. Setting: small town. Nearest major city is Temecula. Students are housed in single-sex dormitories. 6-acre campus. 4 buildings on campus. Approved or accredited by Western Association of Schools and Colleges and California Department of Education. Total enrollment: 85. Upper school average class size: 15. Upper school faculty-student ratio: 1:8. There are 175 required school days per year for Upper School students. Upper School students typically attend 5 days per week. The average school day consists of 7 hours.
Upper School Student Profile Grade 9: 22 students (11 boys, 11 girls); Grade 10: 28 students (15 boys, 13 girls); Grade 11: 16 students (9 boys, 7 girls); Grade 12: 19 students (12 boys, 7 girls). 54% of students are boarding students. 76% are state residents. 1 state is represented in upper school student body. 24% are international students. International students from China and Japan; 1 other country represented in student body. 59% of students are Wisconsin Evangelical Lutheran Synod.
Faculty School total: 11. In upper school: 7 men, 4 women; 2 have advanced degrees; 3 reside on campus.
Special Academic Programs International Baccalaureate program; Advanced Placement exam preparation; honors section; ESL (20 students enrolled).
College Admission Counseling 17 students graduated in 2015; 12 went to college. Other: 1 entered military service, 1 had other specific plans.
Student Life Upper grades have specified standards of dress, student council, honor system. Discipline rests primarily with faculty. Attendance at religious services is required.
Tuition and Aid Tuition installment plan (FACTS Tuition Payment Plan). Tuition reduction for siblings, need-based scholarship grants available. In 2015–16, 40% of upper-school students received aid.
Admissions Traditional secondary-level entrance grade is 9. For fall 2015, 26 students applied for upper level admission, 26 were accepted, 26 enrolled. Math and English placement tests required. Deadline for receipt of application materials: none. Application fee required: $100. Interview required.
Athletics Interscholastic: baseball (boys), basketball (b,g), football (b), softball (g), track and field (b,g), volleyball (g); coed interscholastic: cross-country running.
Computers Computers are regularly used in yearbook classes. Computer network features include Internet access, wireless campus network, Internet filtering or blocking technology. Student e-mail accounts and computer access in designated common areas are available to students. Students grades are available online.
Contact Sarah Garvin, Secretary. 951-678-7000. Fax: 951-678-0172. E-mail: sgarvin@clhsonline.net. Website: www.clhsonline.net

CALVARY DAY SCHOOL

4625 Waters Avenue
Savannah, Georgia 31404
Head of School: Dr. James Taylor

General Information Coeducational day college-preparatory, arts, religious studies, and technology school, affiliated with Baptist Church. Grades PK–12. Founded: 1961. Setting: suburban. 22-acre campus. 6 buildings on campus. Approved or accredited by Southern Association of Colleges and Schools and Georgia Department of Education. Total enrollment: 767. Upper school average class size: 17. Upper school faculty-student ratio: 1:17. There are 180 required school days per year for Upper School students. Upper School students typically attend 5 days per week. The average school day consists of 6 hours and 45 minutes.
Upper School Student Profile 10% of students are Baptist.
Faculty School total: 72. In upper school: 22 men, 28 women; 32 have advanced degrees.
Subjects Offered 20th century history, 20th century world history, accounting, acting, advanced biology, advanced chemistry, advanced math, Advanced Placement courses, algebra, American government, American history, American history-AP, American literature, American literature-AP, analysis and differential calculus, anatomy and physiology, ancient world history, art, band, Bible, biochemistry, biology, biology-AP, calculus-AP, chemistry, chemistry-AP, Chinese, chorus, composition-AP, computer applications, data processing, economics, English, English language and composition-

AP, European history-AP, French, geometry, government, government/civics-AP, mathematics-AP, physical education, physical science, physics, pre-calculus, religion, Spanish, U.S. history, weight training, world history.
Graduation Requirements Business skills (includes word processing), computer science, English, foreign language, history, mathematics, physical education (includes health), religion (includes Bible studies and theology), science, social sciences, social studies (includes history), technology.
Special Academic Programs 11 Advanced Placement exams for which test preparation is offered; honors section; accelerated programs; independent study; study at local college for college credit; domestic exchange program; academic accommodation for the gifted; remedial reading and/or remedial writing; remedial math.
College Admission Counseling 76 students graduated in 2015; 75 went to college, including Armstrong State University; Georgia Institute of Technology; Georgia Southern University; Liberty University; Mercer University; University of Georgia. Other: 1 went to work. 38% scored over 600 on SAT critical reading, 27% scored over 600 on SAT math.
Student Life Upper grades have uniform requirement, student council, honor system. Discipline rests primarily with faculty. Attendance at religious services is required.
Summer Programs Enrichment, sports, art/fine arts programs offered; session focuses on Enrichment; held both on and off campus; held at Appalachian Mountains; accepts boys and girls; open to students from other schools. 35 students usually enrolled. 2016 schedule: June 1 to July 30. Application deadline: May 30.
Tuition and Aid Day student tuition: $8400. Tuition installment plan (Insured Tuition Payment Plan, monthly payment plans, individually arranged payment plans). Tuition reduction for siblings, merit scholarship grants, need-based scholarship grants available. In 2015–16, 10% of upper-school students received aid; total upper-school merit-scholarship money awarded: $5000. Total amount of financial aid awarded in 2015–16: $183,000.
Admissions Traditional secondary-level entrance grade is 9. For fall 2015, 112 students applied for upper-level admission, 74 were accepted, 73 enrolled. Otis-Lennon School Ability Test, Reading for Understanding, Stanford Achievement Test, Otis-Lennon School Ability Test or WRAT required. Deadline for receipt of application materials: none. Application fee required: $100. Interview required.
Athletics Interscholastic: aquatics (boys, girls), baseball (b), basketball (b,g), cross-country running (b,g), equestrian sports (b,g), football (b), golf (b,g), soccer (b,g), softball (g), tennis (b,g), track and field (b,g), volleyball (g), weight lifting (b,g); intramural: backpacking (b,g), physical fitness (b,g), physical training (b,g); coed intramural: physical fitness, physical training. 4 PE instructors, 4 coaches, 1 athletic trainer.
Computers Computers are regularly used in all academic classes. Computer network features include on-campus library services, online commercial services, Internet access, wireless campus network, Internet filtering or blocking technology. Campus intranet, student e-mail accounts, and computer access in designated common areas are available to students. Students grades are available online. The school has a published electronic and media policy.
Contact Kim Rice, Admissions Director. 912-351-2299 Ext. 112. Fax: 912-351-2280. E-mail: KRice@calvarydayschool.com. Website: http://www.calvarydayschool.com/

CALVERT HALL COLLEGE HIGH SCHOOL

8102 LaSalle Road
Baltimore, Maryland 21286
Head of School: Br. John Kane, FSC

General Information Boys' day college-preparatory, arts, religious studies, and technology school, affiliated with Roman Catholic Church. Grades 9–12. Founded: 1845. Setting: suburban. 32-acre campus. 6 buildings on campus. Approved or accredited by Christian Brothers Association, Middle States Association of Colleges and Schools, National Catholic Education Association, and Maryland Department of Education. Member of National Association of Independent Schools. Endowment: $8.5 million. Total enrollment: 1,160. Upper school average class size: 18. Upper school faculty-student ratio: 1:11. There are 174 required school days per year for Upper School students. Upper School students typically attend 5 days per week. The average school day consists of 6 hours and 20 minutes.
Upper School Student Profile Grade 9: 286 students (286 boys); Grade 10: 305 students (305 boys); Grade 11: 284 students (284 boys); Grade 12: 285 students (285 boys). 64% of students are Roman Catholic.
Faculty School total: 106. In upper school: 72 men, 32 women; 70 have advanced degrees.
Subjects Offered Accounting, algebra, American history, American literature, art, art history, band, Bible studies, biology, business, business skills, calculus, chemistry, chorus, computer programming, computer science, creative writing, drama, earth science, economics, engineering, English, English literature, ethics, European history, fine arts, French, geography, geometry, German, government/civics, graphic arts, history, journalism, Latin, leadership, mathematics, music, painting, philosophy, physical education, physics, psychology, religion, science, sculpture, social sciences, social studies, Spanish, speech, statistics, theater, theology, typing, world history, world literature, writing.

Graduation Requirements Arts and fine arts (art, music, dance, drama), English, foreign language, mathematics, physical education (includes health), religion (includes Bible studies and theology), science, social sciences, social studies (includes history).

Special Academic Programs 22 Advanced Placement exams for which test preparation is offered; honors section; academic accommodation for the gifted, the musically talented, and the artistically talented; programs in English, mathematics, general development for dyslexic students.

College Admission Counseling Colleges students went to include Loyola University Maryland; Salisbury University; Towson University; University of Maryland, College Park; York College of Pennsylvania. Median SAT critical reading: 565, median SAT math: 575, median SAT writing: 545, median combined SAT: 1685, median composite ACT: 24. 31% scored over 600 on SAT critical reading, 42% scored over 600 on SAT math, 31% scored over 600 on SAT writing, 36% scored over 1800 on combined SAT, 35% scored over 26 on composite ACT.

Student Life Upper grades have specified standards of dress, student council, honor system. Discipline rests primarily with faculty. Attendance at religious services is required.

Summer Programs Remediation, enrichment, sports, art/fine arts, computer instruction programs offered; session focuses on remediation and make-up courses; held on campus; accepts boys and girls; open to students from other schools. 250 students usually enrolled. 2016 schedule: June 24 to July 26. Application deadline: June 15.

Tuition and Aid Day student tuition: $13,700. Tuition installment plan (monthly payment plans, individually arranged payment plans). Merit scholarship grants, need-based scholarship grants available. In 2015–16, 55% of upper-school students received aid; total upper-school merit-scholarship money awarded: $830,850. Total amount of financial aid awarded in 2015–16: $2,668,735.

Admissions Traditional secondary-level entrance grade is 9. High School Placement Test (closed version) from Scholastic Testing Service required. Deadline for receipt of application materials: none. Application fee required: $25. Interview recommended.

Athletics Interscholastic: aquatics, baseball, basketball, cross-country running, football, golf, hockey, ice hockey, indoor track & field, lacrosse, rugby, soccer, squash, swimming and diving, tennis, track and field, volleyball, water polo, winter (indoor) track, wrestling; intramural: basketball, bicycling, billiards, bocce, bowling, fitness, flag football, freestyle skiing, Frisbee, martial arts, outdoor adventure, rock climbing, rugby, sailing, skiing (downhill), table tennis, ultimate Frisbee, weight lifting. 2 PE instructors, 11 coaches, 1 athletic trainer.

Computers Computers are regularly used in accounting, business, college planning, computer applications, digital applications, economics, English, foreign language, graphic design, history, independent study, journalism, keyboarding, library, literary magazine, mathematics, music, programming, religion, SAT preparation, science, social sciences, stock market, video film production, writing, yearbook classes. Computer network features include on-campus library services, Internet access, wireless campus network, Internet filtering or blocking technology. Campus intranet, student e-mail accounts, and computer access in designated common areas are available to students. Students grades are available online. The school has a published electronic and media policy.

Contact Chris Bengel, Director of Admissions. 410-825-4266 Ext. 126. Fax: 410-825-6826. E-mail: bengelc@calverthall.com. Website: www.calverthall.com

CALVIN CHRISTIAN HIGH SCHOOL

2000 North Broadway
Escondido, California 92026

Head of School: Mr. Terry D. Kok

General Information Coeducational day college-preparatory, arts, and religious studies school, affiliated with Reformed Church. Grades PK–12. Founded: 1980. Setting: suburban. Nearest major city is San Diego. 24-acre campus. 2 buildings on campus. Approved or accredited by Christian Schools International, Western Association of Schools and Colleges, and California Department of Education. Endowment: $1 million. Total enrollment: 470. Upper school average class size: 18. Upper school faculty-student ratio: 1:17. There are 175 required school days per year for Upper School students. Upper School students typically attend 5 days per week. The average school day consists of 6 hours and 25 minutes.

Upper School Student Profile Grade 9: 34 students (15 boys, 19 girls); Grade 10: 32 students (16 boys, 16 girls); Grade 11: 42 students (24 boys, 18 girls); Grade 12: 42 students (27 boys, 15 girls). 30% of students are Reformed.

Faculty School total: 15. In upper school: 8 men, 7 women; 8 have advanced degrees.

Subjects Offered Advanced Placement courses, algebra, American government, art, band, Bible, biology, biology-AP, business mathematics, calculus-AP, chemistry, choir, Christian doctrine, Christian ethics, Christian studies, church history, computer applications, computer programming, computers, dramatic arts, economics, electives, English, English literature-AP, geometry, health, instrumental music, intro to computers, media, modern history, photography, physical education, physical science, physics, pre-calculus, psychology, robotics, Spanish, Spanish-AP, speech, U.S. history, U.S. history-AP, world history, World War II, yearbook.

Graduation Requirements Advanced Placement courses, arts and fine arts (art, music, dance, drama), English, foreign language, mathematics, media, physical education (includes health), religion (includes Bible studies and theology), science, social studies (includes history), technology, service-learning requirements.

Special Academic Programs 6 Advanced Placement exams for which test preparation is offered; remedial reading and/or remedial writing.

College Admission Counseling 43 students graduated in 2015; 41 went to college, including California State University, San Marcos; Calvin College; Dordt College; Point Loma Nazarene University; Trinity Christian College; University of California, San Diego. Other: 1 went to work, 1 entered military service. Mean SAT critical reading: 568, mean SAT math: 570, mean SAT writing: 549, mean composite ACT: 24. 43% scored over 600 on SAT critical reading, 36% scored over 600 on SAT math, 29% scored over 600 on SAT writing.

Student Life Upper grades have specified standards of dress, student council, honor system. Discipline rests primarily with faculty. Attendance at religious services is required.

Summer Programs Remediation, advancement, sports programs offered; session focuses on Bible courses and/or athletics; held on campus; accepts boys and girls; open to students from other schools. 60 students usually enrolled. 2016 schedule: June 10 to July 31. Application deadline: May 31.

Tuition and Aid Day student tuition: $9995. Tuition installment plan (monthly payment plans, individually arranged payment plans). Need-based scholarship grants, need-based loans available. In 2015–16, 30% of upper-school students received aid. Total amount of financial aid awarded in 2015–16: $275,000.

Admissions For fall 2015, 20 students applied for upper-level admission, 18 were accepted, 18 enrolled. Deadline for receipt of application materials: none. Application fee required: $300. Interview required.

Athletics Interscholastic: baseball (boys), basketball (b,g), cross-country running (b,g), football (b), soccer (b,g), softball (g), track and field (b,g), volleyball (g); coed interscholastic: golf; coed intramural: swimming and diving, weight training. 2 PE instructors, 16 coaches.

Computers Computers are regularly used in computer applications, keyboarding, photography, programming, science, yearbook classes. Computer network features include on-campus library services, Internet access, wireless campus network, Internet filtering or blocking technology. Student e-mail accounts are available to students. Students grades are available online. The school has a published electronic and media policy.

Contact Mr. Frank Steidl, Principal. 760-489-6430. Fax: 760-489-7055. E-mail: franksteidl@calvinchristianescondido.org. Website: www.calvinchristianescondido.org

THE CAMBRIDGE SCHOOL OF WESTON

45 Georgian Road
Weston, Massachusetts 02493

Head of School: Jane Moulding

General Information Coeducational boarding and day college-preparatory and arts school. Grades 9–PG. Founded: 1886. Setting: suburban. Nearest major city is Boston. Students are housed in single-sex dormitories. 65-acre campus. 25 buildings on campus. Approved or accredited by Association of Independent Schools in New England, New England Association of Schools and Colleges, The Association of Boarding Schools, and The College Board. Member of National Association of Independent Schools and Secondary School Admission Test Board. Endowment: $7.8 million. Total enrollment: 338. Upper school average class size: 14. Upper school faculty-student ratio: 1:6. There are 160 required school days per year for Upper School students. Upper School students typically attend 5 days per week. The average school day consists of 6 hours.

Upper School Student Profile Grade 9: 66 students (27 boys, 39 girls); Grade 10: 88 students (36 boys, 52 girls); Grade 11: 91 students (42 boys, 49 girls); Grade 12: 93 students (39 boys, 54 girls). 30% of students are boarding students. 81% are state residents. 12 states are represented in upper school student body. 12% are international students. International students from China, Germany, Mexico, Republic of Korea, Taiwan, and Thailand; 7 other countries represented in student body.

Faculty School total: 60. In upper school: 25 men, 25 women; 40 have advanced degrees; 15 reside on campus.

Subjects Offered 20th century physics, 3-dimensional art, acting, Advanced Placement courses, aerospace science, African dance, African history, African literature, African studies, African-American history, African-American literature, African-American studies, algebra, American Civil War, American democracy, American history, American literature, American sign language, analytic geometry, anatomy, anatomy and physiology, animal behavior, animal science, art, art and culture, art history, Asian literature, athletics, backpacking, ballet, ballet technique, baseball, basketball, Bible as literature, biology, botany, calculus, calculus-AP, cell biology, ceramics, chemistry, child development, Chinese history, choir, choreography, chorus, Civil War, collage and assemblage, community service, computer animation, computer math, computer programming, computer science, computer skills, constitutional history of U.S., creative writing, dance, death and loss, digital art, digital photography, discrete mathematics, drama, drama performance, drawing, driver education, earth science, ecology, economics, electronic music, English, English composition, English literature, environmental science, environmental systems, ethics, ethnic literature, European history, European literature, expository writing, fashion, field ecology, film history, film studies, filmmaking, fine arts, foods, French, geography, geometry, government/civics, grammar, great books, Harlem Renaissance, health, health and wellness, history, history of ideas, history of music, history of science, independent study, interdisciplinary studies, Islamic history, Japanese history, jazz, jazz dance, jazz ensemble, jewelry making, journalism, keyboarding, Latin, Latin American history, Latin American literature, leadership education training, literature by women, logic, Mandarin, marine biology, martial arts, mathematical modeling, mathematics, Middle East, model United Nations, music, music theory, musical theater, musicianship, mythology, ornithology, painting, philosophy, photography, physical education, physics, physiology, playwriting, poetry, pre-calculus, printmaking, psychology, religion, Roman civilization, science, sculpture, senior project, set design, Shakespeare, short story, social studies, sociology, Spanish, sports nutrition, stagecraft, statistics, the Presidency, theater, trigonometry, U.S. constitutional history, U.S. history, Vietnam War, weight training, wilderness education, wilderness experience, woodworking, world history, world literature, World War II, writing, yearbook, zoology.

Graduation Requirements Arts and fine arts (art, music, dance, drama), English, foreign language, health education, history, mathematics, performing arts, physical education (includes health), science, senior project, Social Justice. Community service is required.

Special Academic Programs Advanced Placement exam preparation; independent study; term-away projects; study abroad.

College Admission Counseling 80 students graduated in 2014; 79 went to college, including Brown University; Oberlin College; Rhode Island School of Design; Skidmore College; Smith College; The George Washington University. Other: 1 had other specific plans.

Student Life Upper grades have student council. Discipline rests equally with students and faculty.

Tuition and Aid Day student tuition: $41,900; 7-day tuition and room/board: $54,400. Tuition installment plan (Insured Tuition Payment Plan, FACTS Tuition Payment Plan, monthly payment plans, individually arranged payment plans). Tuition reduction for siblings, need-based scholarship grants, paying campus jobs available. In 2014–15, 27% of upper-school students received aid. Total amount of financial aid awarded in 2014–15: $2,700,000.

Admissions Traditional secondary-level entrance grade is 9. For fall 2014, 421 students applied for upper-level admission, 214 were accepted, 96 enrolled. ISEE, PSAT, SAT, SSAT or TOEFL required. Deadline for receipt of application materials: February 1. Application fee required: $50. Interview required.

Athletics Interscholastic: basketball (boys, girls), field hockey (g), lacrosse (g), soccer (b,g); coed interscholastic: baseball, cross-country running, Frisbee, running, tennis, ultimate Frisbee; coed intramural: alpine skiing, backpacking, ballet, bicycling, canoeing/kayaking, climbing, dance, dance team, fencing, fitness, fitness walking, Frisbee, golf, hiking/backpacking, indoor soccer, kayaking, martial arts, modern dance, nordic skiing, outdoor activities, outdoor adventure, outdoor education, outdoor skills, physical fitness, physical training, rafting, rock climbing, running, skateboarding, skiing (downhill), snowboarding, snowshoeing, soccer, strength & conditioning, table tennis, tai chi, tennis, triathlon, ultimate Frisbee, volleyball, weight training, wilderness, yoga.

Computers Computers are regularly used in art, college planning, English, ESL, ethics, French, graphic design, history, humanities, independent study, journalism, keyboarding, Latin, library, literary magazine, mathematics, music, newspaper, photography, programming, psychology, publications, science, Spanish, word processing, writing, yearbook classes. Computer network features include on-campus library services, online commercial services, Internet access, wireless campus network, Internet filtering or blocking technology, laptops available for use in-class, language lab, media lab. Campus intranet, student e-mail accounts, and computer access in designated common areas are available to students. Students grades are available online.

Contact Trish Saunders, Director of Admissions. 781-642-8650. Fax: 781-398-8344. E-mail: admissions@csw.org. Website: www.csw.org

CAMDEN MILITARY ACADEMY
520 Highway 1 North
Camden, South Carolina 29020

Head of School: Col. Eric Boland

General Information Boys' boarding college-preparatory and military school; primarily serves students with learning disabilities, individuals with Attention Deficit Disorder, individuals with emotional and behavioral problems, and dyslexic students. Grades 7–PG. Founded: 1892. Setting: small town. Nearest major city is Columbia. Students are housed in single-sex dormitories. 40-acre campus. 15 buildings on campus. Approved or accredited by South Carolina Independent School Association, Southern Association of Colleges and Schools, and Southern Association of Independent Schools. Member of National Association of Independent Schools. Total enrollment: 295. Upper school average class size: 15. Upper school faculty-student ratio: 1:12. Upper School students typically attend 5 days per week. The average school day consists of 6 hours.

Upper School Student Profile Grade 9: 55 students (55 boys); Grade 10: 55 students (55 boys); Grade 11: 60 students (60 boys); Grade 12: 60 students (60 boys). 100% of students are boarding students. 39% are state residents. 23 states are represented in upper school student body. International students from Bermuda, Cayman Islands, Ghana, Mexico, and Trinidad and Tobago.

Faculty School total: 49. In upper school: 35 men, 3 women; 23 have advanced degrees; 9 reside on campus.

Subjects Offered Algebra, American government, anatomy and physiology, band, biology, calculus, chemistry, computer applications, computer literacy, driver education, economics, English, French, geometry, humanities, physical science, physics, pre-calculus, psychology, sociology, Spanish, U.S. history, world geography, world history.

Graduation Requirements Computer literacy, English, foreign language, history, JROTC, mathematics, science.

Special Academic Programs Advanced Placement exam preparation; honors section; study at local college for college credit; remedial reading and/or remedial writing.

College Admission Counseling 58 students graduated in 2015; 56 went to college, including University of South Carolina. Other: 2 entered military service.

Student Life Upper grades have uniform requirement, student council, honor system. Discipline rests primarily with faculty.

Summer Programs Remediation, advancement, ESL programs offered; session focuses on academics; held on campus; accepts boys; open to students from other schools. 100 students usually enrolled. 2016 schedule: June 20 to July 28.

Tuition and Aid 7-day tuition and room/board: $17,595. Tuition installment plan (monthly payment plans, individually arranged payment plans). Tuition reduction for siblings, need-based scholarship grants available. In 2015–16, 20% of upper-school students received aid.

Admissions Traditional secondary-level entrance grade is 10. Deadline for receipt of application materials: none. Application fee required: $100. Interview required.

Athletics Interscholastic: baseball, basketball, cross-country running, football, golf; intramural: aerobics, aquatics. 2 PE instructors, 15 coaches, 1 athletic trainer.

Computers Computers are regularly used in all academic classes. Computer resources include on-campus library services, Internet access. Student e-mail accounts are available to students.

Contact Mr. Casey Robinson, Director of Admissions. 803-432-6001. Fax: 803-425-1020. E-mail: admissions@camdenmilitary.com. Website: www.camdenmilitary.com

CAMPBELL HALL (EPISCOPAL)
4533 Laurel Canyon Boulevard
North Hollywood, California 91607

Head of School: Rev. Canon Julian Bull

General Information Coeducational day college-preparatory, arts, and technology school, affiliated with Episcopal Church. Grades K–12. Founded: 1944. Setting: suburban. Nearest major city is Los Angeles. 15-acre campus. 12 buildings on campus. Approved or accredited by National Association of Episcopal Schools, The College Board, Western Association of Schools and Colleges, and California Department of Education. Member of National Association of Independent Schools. Endowment: $10 million. Total enrollment: 1,125. Upper school average class size: 15. Upper school faculty-student ratio: 1:8. There are 140 required school days per year for Upper School students. Upper School students typically attend 5 days per week. The average school day consists of 7 hours and 15 minutes.

Upper School Student Profile Grade 7: 116 students (61 boys, 55 girls), Grade 8: 119 students (62 boys, 57 girls); Grade 9: 141 students (67 boys, 74 girls); Grade 10: 136 students (71 boys, 65 girls); Grade 11: 125 students (71 boys, 54 girls); Grade 12: 146 students (79 boys, 67 girls). 7% of students are members of Episcopal Church.

Faculty School total: 110. In upper school: 23 men, 32 women; 30 have advanced degrees.

Subjects Offered Algebra, American history, American literature, American studies, ancient history, art, art history, astronomy, band, biology, calculus, ceramics, chemistry, Chinese, community service, computer programming, computer science, creative writing, dance, drama, drawing, earth science, ecology, economics, English, English literature, environmental science, ethics, European history, filmmaking, fine arts, French, geography, geometry, government/civics, history, human development, humanities, instrumental music, Japanese, law, mathematics, music, orchestra, painting, philosophy, photography, physical education, physics, physiology, pre-calculus, printmaking, psychology, science, sculpture, senior seminar, social studies, sociology, Spanish, speech, statistics, theater, theater arts, trigonometry, voice, yearbook.

Graduation Requirements Arts and fine arts (art, music, dance, drama), English, foreign language, mathematics, music history, physical education (includes health), science, social studies (includes history). Community service is required.

Special Academic Programs Advanced Placement exam preparation; honors section; independent study; study at local college for college credit.

College Admission Counseling 132 students graduated in 2015; all went to college, including Boston University; Indiana University Bloomington; New York University; University of California, Los Angeles; University of Michigan; University of Southern California.

Student Life Upper grades have uniform requirement, student council, honor system. Discipline rests equally with students and faculty. Attendance at religious services is required.

Summer Programs Enrichment, advancement, sports, art/fine arts, computer instruction programs offered; session focuses on creative arts and sports; held on campus; accepts boys and girls; open to students from other schools. 200 students usually enrolled. 2016 schedule: June 13 to August 17. Application deadline: May 1.

Tuition and Aid Day student tuition: $34,400. Tuition installment plan (Insured Tuition Payment Plan, monthly payment plans, individually arranged payment plans).

Need-based scholarship grants, Episcopal Credit Union tuition loans available. In 2015–16, 25% of upper-school students received aid. Total amount of financial aid awarded in 2015–16: $5,400,000.

Admissions Traditional secondary-level entrance grade is 9. ISEE required. Deadline for receipt of application materials: December 16. Application fee required: $135. Interview required.

Athletics Interscholastic: aerobics/dance (boys, girls), ballet (b,g), baseball (b), basketball (b,g), cheering (b,g), cross-country running (b,g), dance (b,g), dance squad (b,g), equestrian sports (b,g), flag football (b,g), football (b), golf (b,g), horseback riding (b,g), modern dance (b,g), soccer (b,g), softball (g), tennis (b,g), track and field (b,g), volleyball (b,g); intramural: weight lifting (b,g); coed interscholastic: aerobics/dance, ballet, cheering, cross-country running, dance, dance squad, golf, horseback riding, modern dance, track and field. 5 PE instructors, 13 coaches, 2 athletic trainers.

Computers Computers are regularly used in all classes. Computer network features include on-campus library services, online commercial services, Internet access, wireless campus network, Internet filtering or blocking technology. Campus intranet, student e-mail accounts, and computer access in designated common areas are available to students. The school has a published electronic and media policy.

Contact Mr. George White, Director of Admissions & Enrollment Management. 818-980-7280. Fax: 818-762-3269. E-mail: whiteg@campbellhall.org. Website: www.campbellhall.org

CAMPBELL RIVER CHRISTIAN SCHOOL

250 South Dogwood Street
Campbell River, British Columbia V9W 6Y7, Canada

Head of School: Mr. Christian Klaue

General Information Coeducational day college-preparatory, arts, religious studies, and technology school, affiliated with Baptist Church. Grades K–12. Founded: 1981. Setting: small town. Nearest major city is Nanaimo, Canada. 3-acre campus. 1 building on campus. Approved or accredited by Association of Christian Schools International and British Columbia Department of Education. Language of instruction: English. Upper school average class size: 15. Upper school faculty-student ratio: 1:15. There are 178 required school days per year for Upper School students. Upper School students typically attend 5 days per week. The average school day consists of 6 hours and 15 minutes.

Upper School Student Profile Grade 8: 16 students (7 boys, 9 girls); Grade 9: 10 students (6 boys, 4 girls); Grade 10: 12 students (10 boys, 2 girls); Grade 11: 11 students (5 boys, 6 girls); Grade 12: 13 students (8 boys, 5 girls). 50% of students are Baptist.

Faculty School total: 177. In upper school: 6 men, 3 women; 1 has an advanced degree.

Subjects Offered All academic.

Graduation Requirements Bible, Canadian history, career and personal planning, English.

College Admission Counseling Colleges students went to include Trinity Western University.

Student Life Upper grades have specified standards of dress. Discipline rests primarily with faculty. Attendance at religious services is required.

Admissions For fall 2015, 62 students applied for upper-level admission, 62 were accepted, 62 enrolled. Deadline for receipt of application materials: none. Application fee required: CAN$100. Interview required.

Athletics Interscholastic: basketball (boys, girls), cross-country running (b,g), track and field (b,g), volleyball (b,g), wrestling (b); coed intramural: outdoor education. 1 PE instructor, 1 coach.

Computers Computers are regularly used in all academic classes. Computer network features include on-campus library services, Internet access, wireless campus network, Internet filtering or blocking technology. Campus intranet and student e-mail accounts are available to students. The school has a published electronic and media policy.

Contact Mr. Christian Klaue, Principal. 250-287-4266. Fax: 250-287-4266. E-mail: principal@crcs.bc.ca. Website: http://www.crcs.bc.ca/

CAMPHILL SPECIAL SCHOOL

Glenmoore, Pennsylvania
See Special Needs Schools section.

CANTERBURY SCHOOL

101 Aspetuck Avenue
New Milford, Connecticut 06776

Head of School: Thomas J. Sheehey III

General Information Coeducational boarding and day college-preparatory, arts, business, religious studies, bilingual studies, and technology school, affiliated with Roman Catholic Church. Grades 9–PG. Founded: 1915. Setting: small town. Nearest major city is Hartford. Students are housed in single-sex dormitories. 150-acre campus. 20 buildings on campus. Approved or accredited by New England Association of Schools and Colleges, The Association of Boarding Schools, and Connecticut

Department of Education. Member of National Association of Independent Schools and Secondary School Admission Test Board. Endowment: $25 million. Total enrollment: 350. Upper school average class size: 11. Upper school faculty-student ratio: 1:6.

Upper School Student Profile Grade 9: 50 students (30 boys, 20 girls); Grade 10: 82 students (39 boys, 43 girls); Grade 11: 108 students (63 boys, 45 girls); Grade 12: 107 students (62 boys, 45 girls); Postgraduate: 21 students (19 boys, 2 girls). 70% of students are boarding students. 50% are state residents. 18 states are represented in upper school student body. 17% are international students. International students from Australia, China, Germany, Republic of Korea, Spain, and Taiwan; 12 other countries represented in student body. 65% of students are Roman Catholic.

Faculty School total: 76. In upper school: 40 men, 36 women; 45 have advanced degrees; 56 reside on campus.

Subjects Offered 1 1/2 elective credits, adolescent issues, algebra, American history, American literature, anthropology, art, art history, astronomy, biochemistry, biology, calculus, ceramics, chemistry, civil rights, computer programming, computer science, creative writing, dance, drama, driver education, earth science, economics, English, English literature, environmental science, ethics, European history, expository writing, fine arts, French, geography, geology, geometry, grammar, history, Irish studies, Latin, marine biology, mathematics, microbiology, music, oceanography, philosophy, photography, physics, physiology, religion, science, social studies, Spanish, Spanish literature, speech, statistics, theater, theology, trigonometry, women's studies, world history, world literature, writing.

Graduation Requirements Arts and fine arts (art, music, dance, drama), computer science, English, foreign language, mathematics, New Testament, religion (includes Bible studies and theology), science, social studies (includes history).

Special Academic Programs Advanced Placement exam preparation; honors section; independent study; ESL (15 students enrolled).

College Admission Counseling 108 students graduated in 2015; all went to college, including Boston University; Hobart and William Smith Colleges; Sacred Heart University; University of Connecticut. 25% scored over 600 on SAT critical reading, 35% scored over 600 on SAT math.

Student Life Upper grades have specified standards of dress, student council, honor system. Discipline rests primarily with faculty. Attendance at religious services is required.

Summer Programs Sports programs offered; session focuses on basketball and football camps; held on campus; accepts boys and girls; open to students from other schools. 70 students usually enrolled.

Tuition and Aid Day student tuition: $33,000; 7-day tuition and room/board: $42,500. Tuition installment plan (Academic Management Services Plan, Key Tuition Payment Plan). Need-based scholarship grants, need-based loans, middle-income loans available. In 2015–16, 36% of upper-school students received aid. Total amount of financial aid awarded in 2015–16: $3,500,000.

Admissions Traditional secondary-level entrance grade is 9. For fall 2015, 700 students applied for upper-level admission, 250 were accepted, 125 enrolled. SLEP, SSAT, TOEFL and writing sample required. Deadline for receipt of application materials: January 31. Application fee required: $50. Interview required.

Athletics Interscholastic: baseball (boys), basketball (b,g), cross-country running (b,g), diving (b,g), field hockey (g), football (b), ice hockey (b,g), lacrosse (b,g), soccer (b,g), softball (g), squash (b,g), swimming and diving (b,g), tennis (b,g), track and field (b,g), volleyball (g); intramural: dance (g), equestrian sports (g), hockey (b,g), horseback riding (b,g); coed interscholastic: crew, golf, water polo, wrestling; coed intramural: fitness, softball, Special Olympics, strength & conditioning, weight lifting, weight training. 40 coaches, 2 athletic trainers.

Computers Computers are regularly used in accounting, English, mathematics, multimedia, science classes. Computer network features include on-campus library services, Internet access, wireless campus network, Internet filtering or blocking technology. Student e-mail accounts and computer access in designated common areas are available to students. Students grades are available online. The school has a published electronic and media policy.

Contact Mr. Matt Mulhern, Director of Admission. 860-210-3836. Fax: 860-350-1120. E-mail: mmulhern@cbury.org. Website: www.cbury.org

CANTERBURY SCHOOL

8141 College Parkway
Fort Myers, Florida 33919

Head of School: Mr. Rick Kirschner

General Information Coeducational day college-preparatory and liberal arts school. Grades PK–12. Founded: 1964. Setting: suburban. 33-acre campus. 7 buildings on campus. Approved or accredited by Council of Accreditation and School Improvement, Florida Council of Independent Schools, Southern Association of Colleges and Schools, Southern Association of Independent Schools, The College Board, and Florida Department of Education. Member of National Association of Independent Schools and Secondary School Admission Test Board. Endowment: $6.4 million. Total enrollment: 620. Upper school average class size: 18. Upper school faculty-student ratio: 1:12. There are 181 required school days per year for Upper School students. Upper School students typically attend 5 days per week. The average school day consists of 6 hours and 30 minutes.

Upper School Student Profile Grade 9: 55 students (31 boys, 24 girls); Grade 10: 72 students (35 boys, 37 girls); Grade 11: 51 students (31 boys, 20 girls); Grade 12: 62 students (31 boys, 31 girls).

Faculty School total: 91. In upper school: 19 men, 14 women; 16 have advanced degrees.

Subjects Offered Advanced Placement courses, algebra, American history, American history-AP, American literature, anatomy, art, art history, biology, biology-AP, British literature, calculus, calculus-AP, ceramics, chemistry, chemistry-AP, comparative government and politics-AP, computer programming, constitutional law, creative writing, critical writing, drama, earth science, ecology, economics, English, English literature, English literature-AP, environmental science-AP, European history, fine arts, French, French language-AP, geography, geometry, government-AP, government/civics, grammar, health, history, Latin, leadership, macroeconomics-AP, marine biology, mathematics, music, nationalism and ethnic conflict, photography, physical education, physics, physics-AP, physiology, SAT preparation, science, social studies, sociology, Spanish, Spanish language-AP, speech, statistics, theater, U.S. government and politics-AP, U.S. history, United Nations and international issues, world history, world literature, writing, yearbook.

Graduation Requirements Arts and fine arts (art, music, dance, drama), English, foreign language, mathematics, physical education (includes health), science, social studies (includes history), speech, required community service hours.

Special Academic Programs 16 Advanced Placement exams for which test preparation is offered; independent study; study at local college for college credit; ESL (19 students enrolled).

College Admission Counseling 52 students graduated in 2015; all went to college, including Boston College; Duke University; Florida State University; Georgia Institute of Technology; Middlebury College; University of Florida. Mean SAT critical reading: 607, mean SAT math: 587, mean SAT writing: 587, mean combined SAT: 1781, mean composite ACT: 26.

Student Life Upper grades have specified standards of dress, student council, honor system. Discipline rests primarily with faculty.

Summer Programs Remediation, enrichment, advancement, sports, art/fine arts programs offered; session focuses on academic enrichment; held on campus; accepts boys and girls; open to students from other schools. 125 students usually enrolled. 2016 schedule: June 6 to July 30. Application deadline: none.

Tuition and Aid Day student tuition: $22,220. Tuition installment plan (Insured Tuition Payment Plan, monthly payment plans, individually arranged payment plans, quarterly payment plan). Need-based scholarship grants available. In 2015–16, 38% of upper-school students received aid. Total amount of financial aid awarded in 2015–16: $1,273,045.

Admissions Traditional secondary-level entrance grade is 9. For fall 2015, 69 students applied for upper-level admission, 49 were accepted, 39 enrolled. ERB CTP IV or SSAT required. Deadline for receipt of application materials: none. Application fee required: $100. Interview required.

Athletics Interscholastic: baseball (boys), basketball (b,g), cheering (g), football (b), lacrosse (b,g), soccer (b,g), volleyball (g), winter soccer (b,g); intramural: volleyball (b); coed interscholastic: cross-country running, golf, swimming and diving, tennis, track and field. 6 PE instructors, 26 coaches, 1 athletic trainer.

Computers Computers are regularly used in art, college planning, English, foreign language, French, history, independent study, journalism, Latin, library, mathematics, science, social sciences, Spanish, speech, theater arts, yearbook classes. Computer network features include on-campus library services, Internet access, wireless campus network, Internet filtering or blocking technology. Campus intranet, student e-mail accounts, and computer access in designated common areas are available to students. Students grades are available online. The school has a published electronic and media policy.

Contact Ms. Julie A. Peters, Director of Admission. 239-415-8945. Fax: 239-481-8339. E-mail: jpeters@canterburyfortmyers.org. Website: www.canterburyfortmyers.org

See Display below and Close-Up on page 586.

THE CANTERBURY SCHOOL OF FLORIDA

990 62nd Avenue NE
St. Petersburg, Florida 33702

Head of School: Mr. Mac H. Hall

General Information Coeducational day college-preparatory, arts, and marine studies, international studies, educational tech school, affiliated with Episcopal Church. Grades PK–12. Founded: 1968. Setting: suburban. 20-acre campus. 5 buildings on campus. Approved or accredited by Florida Council of Independent Schools, The College Board, and Florida Department of Education. Member of National Association of Independent Schools. Total enrollment: 480. Upper school average class size: 15. Upper school faculty-student ratio: 1:7. There are 174 required school days per year for Upper School students. Upper School students typically attend 5 days per week. The average school day consists of 7 hours and 23 minutes.

Upper School Student Profile Grade 9: 46 students (22 boys, 24 girls); Grade 10: 34 students (15 boys, 19 girls); Grade 11: 43 students (18 boys, 25 girls); Grade 12: 38 students (19 boys, 19 girls). 20% of students are members of Episcopal Church.

Faculty School total: 90. In upper school: 10 men, 11 women; 17 have advanced degrees.

CANTERBURY SCHOOL

EDUCATION • CHARACTER • LEADERSHIP • SERVICE

8141 College Parkway Fort Myers, Florida 33919 • (239) 481-4323
www.canterburyfortmyers.org

Subjects Offered 20th century world history, advanced computer applications, Advanced Placement courses, advanced studio art-AP, algebra, American government, American history-AP, American literature, anatomy, Ancient Greek, ancient world history, art, art history, art history-AP, astronomy, athletics, band, Basic programming, biology, biology-AP, British literature, British literature (honors), calculus, calculus-AP, ceramics, character education, chemistry, chemistry-AP, choir, choral music, chorus, classical language, classical studies, college counseling, college placement, communication skills, community service, comparative government and politics-AP, competitive science projects, computer multimedia, computer science, computer science-AP, computer skills, contemporary issues, creative writing, critical thinking, dance, dance performance, digital imaging, drama, earth science, economics, economics-AP, English, English composition, English language and composition-AP, English literature, English literature and composition-AP, English literature-AP, environmental science, environmental science-AP, environmental studies, ethics, European history, expository writing, fine arts, finite math, foreign language, French, French-AP, freshman seminar, geography, geometry, golf, government and politics-AP, government/civics, grammar, Greek culture, guitar, health, history, history of music, history-AP, honors algebra, honors geometry, honors U.S. history, honors world history, human geography - AP, independent living, interdisciplinary studies, keyboarding, Latin, Latin-AP, leadership, leadership and service, library, library research, library skills, life management skills, life science, life skills, macro/microeconomics-AP, macroeconomics-AP, Mandarin, marine biology, marine ecology, marine science, marine studies, mathematics, mathematics-AP, mechanical drawing, mentorship program, modern world history, music, musical productions, musical theater, oceanography, outdoor education, personal and social education, personal fitness, photojournalism, physical education, physical science, physics, physics-AP, play production, portfolio art, pre-algebra, pre-calculus, pre-college orientation, psychology, psychology-AP, reading/study skills, robotics, SAT preparation, SAT/ACT preparation, science, senior composition, senior seminar, senior thesis, social sciences, social studies, Spanish, Spanish language-AP, Spanish literature-AP, Spanish-AP, speech, speech and debate, sports conditioning, stagecraft, statistics-AP, student government, student publications, student teaching, studio art-AP, swimming, technical theater, tennis, theater arts, theater design and production, theater history, theater production, track and field, typing, U.S. history, U.S. history-AP, values and decisions, visual and performing arts, volleyball, weight fitness, weight training, Western philosophy, world history, world literature, world religions, yearbook, yoga.

Graduation Requirements Arts and fine arts (art, music, dance, drama), career/college preparation, electives, English, ethics, foreign language, history, mathematics, physical education (includes health), research, science, senior seminar, writing, community service hours, mini-term, character education. Community service is required.

Special Academic Programs 25 Advanced Placement exams for which test preparation is offered; honors section; independent study; term-away projects; study at local college for college credit; ESL (2 students enrolled).

College Admission Counseling 36 students graduated in 2015; all went to college, including Florida Gulf Coast University; The University of North Carolina at Chapel Hill; University of Florida; University of South Florida; Washington and Lee University. Mean SAT critical reading: 559, mean SAT math: 542, mean SAT writing: 542, mean composite ACT: 24. 28% scored over 600 on SAT critical reading, 22% scored over 600 on SAT math, 25% scored over 600 on SAT writing, 28% scored over 26 on composite ACT.

Student Life Upper grades have specified standards of dress, student council, honor system. Discipline rests equally with students and faculty. Attendance at religious services is required.

Summer Programs Remediation, enrichment, advancement, sports, art/fine arts, computer instruction programs offered; session focuses on fun, enrichment, multi-discipline skills and abilities; held both on and off campus; held at some of the Marine Studies camps are held at Tampa Bay beaches, estuaries, and islands; accepts boys and girls; open to students from other schools. 330 students usually enrolled. 2016 schedule: June 8 to August 7. Application deadline: March 15.

Tuition and Aid Day student tuition: $8050–$19,000. Tuition installment plan (Insured Tuition Payment Plan, monthly payment plans, individually arranged payment plans). Tuition reduction for siblings, need-based scholarship grants available. In 2015–16, 16% of upper-school students received aid. Total amount of financial aid awarded in 2015–16: $480,442.

Admissions Traditional secondary-level entrance grade is 9. For fall 2015, 30 students applied for upper-level admission, 25 were accepted, 23 enrolled. 3-R Achievement Test, any standardized test, ERB, SSAT or TOEFL required. Deadline for receipt of application materials: none. Application fee required: $75. On-campus interview required.

Athletics Interscholastic: baseball (boys), basketball (b,g), cross-country running (b,g), dance (g), dance team (g), diving (b,g), football (b), golf (b,g), soccer (b,g), softball (g), swimming and diving (b,g), tennis (b,g), track and field (b,g), volleyball (g); intramural: yoga (g); coed interscholastic: cheering, soccer; coed intramural: canoeing/kayaking, fitness, flag football, floor hockey, hiking/backpacking, kayaking, kickball, modern dance, outdoor activities, outdoor adventure, outdoor education, paddle tennis, physical fitness, ropes courses, running, scuba diving, strength & conditioning, ultimate Frisbee, weight training. 3 PE instructors, 20 coaches.

Computers Computers are regularly used in all academic classes. Computer network features include on-campus library services, online commercial services, Internet

access, wireless campus network, Internet filtering or blocking technology, 1:1 iPad program for grades 3-7 (each child receives an iPad), 1:1 Chromebooks for grade 8, 2 makerspaces. Computer access in designated common areas is available to students. Students grades are available online. The school has a published electronic and media policy.

Contact Mrs. Michelle Robinson, Director of Advancement and Admission. 727-521-5903. Fax: 727-525-2545. E-mail: mrobinson@canterburyflorida.org. Website: www.canterburyflorida.org

CAPE FEAR ACADEMY

3900 South College Road
Wilmington, North Carolina 28412

Head of School: Mr. Donald Berger

General Information Coeducational day college-preparatory and arts school. Grades PK–12. Founded: 1967. Setting: suburban. 27-acre campus. 4 buildings on campus. Approved or accredited by Southern Association of Colleges and Schools, Southern Association of Independent Schools, and North Carolina Department of Education. Member of National Association of Independent Schools. Endowment: $881,340. Total enrollment: 599. Upper school average class size: 17. Upper school faculty-student ratio: 1:7. There are 177 required school days per year for Upper School students. Upper School students typically attend 5 days per week. The average school day consists of 7 hours and 20 minutes.

Upper School Student Profile Grade 9: 64 students (29 boys, 35 girls); Grade 10: 45 students (24 boys, 21 girls); Grade 11: 61 students (34 boys, 27 girls); Grade 12: 59 students (24 boys, 35 girls).

Faculty School total: 70. In upper school: 12 men, 19 women; 13 have advanced degrees.

Subjects Offered 3-dimensional art, Advanced Placement courses, algebra, American history, American history-AP, American literature, analysis, art, art history, band, biology, biology-AP, British literature, calculus-AP, chemistry, choral music, comparative government and politics-AP, computer science, conceptual physics, critical studies in film, discrete mathematics, drama, earth and space science, English, English language-AP, English literature, English literature-AP, environmental science, environmental science-AP, European history, European history-AP, film studies, finance, fine arts, geometry, global studies, government and politics-AP, government-AP, history, honors geometry, human anatomy, independent study, journalism, language, literature, marine science, mathematics, music, music theory-AP, musical theater, newspaper, organizational studies, photography, physical education, physics, pre-calculus, psychology, publications, religion, SAT preparation, science, sculpture, social studies, Spanish, student publications, theater, video film production, vocal ensemble, weight training, world history.

Graduation Requirements Arts and fine arts (art, music, dance, drama), biology, English, foreign language, mathematics, physical education (includes health), science, social studies (includes history), U.S. government, U.S. history, 72 hours of community service over 4 years. Community service is required.

Special Academic Programs 12 Advanced Placement exams for which test preparation is offered; honors section; independent study; study at local college for college credit; study abroad; ESL (4 students enrolled).

College Admission Counseling 66 students graduated in 2015; all went to college, including East Carolina University; North Carolina State University; The University of North Carolina at Chapel Hill; The University of North Carolina Wilmington. Mean combined SAT: 1686, mean composite ACT: 25.

Student Life Upper grades have specified standards of dress, student council, honor system. Discipline rests primarily with faculty.

Summer Programs Enrichment, advancement, sports, art/fine arts, computer instruction programs offered; session focuses on enrichment and sports; held on campus; accepts boys and girls; open to students from other schools. 525 students usually enrolled. 2016 schedule: June 12 to August 8. Application deadline: none.

Tuition and Aid Day student tuition: $15,975. Tuition installment plan (Insured Tuition Payment Plan, FACTS Tuition Payment Plan, monthly payment plans). Merit scholarship grants, need-based scholarship grants available. In 2015–16, 14% of upper-school students received aid; total upper-school merit-scholarship money awarded: $70,507. Total amount of financial aid awarded in 2015–16: $331,999.

Admissions Traditional secondary-level entrance grade is 9. For fall 2015, 57 students applied for upper-level admission, 45 were accepted, 26 enrolled. ERB, ISEE, PSAT or SAT or SSAT required. Deadline for receipt of application materials: none. Application fee required: $80. On-campus interview recommended.

Athletics Interscholastic: basketball (boys, girls), cheering (g), field hockey (g), lacrosse (b,g), soccer (b,g), tennis (b,g), volleyball (g); coed interscholastic: cross-country running, golf, outdoor education, outdoor recreation, surfing, swimming and diving. 2 PE instructors, 11 coaches, 1 athletic trainer.

Computers Computers are regularly used in all academic classes. Computer network features include on-campus library services, online commercial services, Internet access, wireless campus network, Internet filtering or blocking technology. Campus intranet, student e-mail accounts, and computer access in designated common areas are available to students. Students grades are available online. The school has a published electronic and media policy.

Contact Mrs. Nelda Nutter, Director of Admission. 910-791-0287 Ext. 1015. Fax: 910-791-0290. E-mail: nelda.nutter@capefearacademy.org. Website: www.capefearacademy.org

CAPE HENRY COLLEGIATE SCHOOL

1320 Mill Dam Road
Virginia Beach, Virginia 23454-2306

Head of School: Dr. Christopher Garran

General Information Coeducational day college-preparatory, arts, technology, and global education school. Grades PK–12. Founded: 1924. Setting: suburban. 30-acre campus. 9 buildings on campus. Approved or accredited by Southern Association of Colleges and Schools, Southern Association of Independent Schools, Virginia Association of Independent Schools, and Virginia Department of Education. Member of National Association of Independent Schools. Endowment: $16 million. Total enrollment: 895. Upper school average class size: 14. Upper school faculty-student ratio: 1:10. There are 176 required school days per year for Upper School students. Upper School students typically attend 5 days per week. The average school day consists of 7 hours and 20 minutes.

Upper School Student Profile Grade 6: 67 students (38 boys, 29 girls); Grade 7: 70 students (35 boys, 35 girls); Grade 8: 65 students (40 boys, 25 girls); Grade 9: 98 students (48 boys, 50 girls); Grade 10: 90 students (59 boys, 31 girls); Grade 11: 73 students (42 boys, 31 girls); Grade 12: 104 students (60 boys, 44 girls).

Faculty School total: 117. In upper school: 20 men, 23 women; 32 have advanced degrees.

Subjects Offered Algebra, American history, American literature, art, art history, biology, botany, business skills, calculus, ceramics, chemistry, community service, computer programming, computer science, creative writing, drama, driver education, earth science, ecology, economics, English, English literature, environmental science, European history, expository writing, fine arts, French, geography, geology, geometry, government/civics, health, history, journalism, Latin, law, marine biology, mathematics, music, oceanography, photography, physical education, physics, science, social sciences, social studies, sociology, Spanish, speech, statistics, theater, trigonometry, world history, world literature, writing.

Graduation Requirements Arts and fine arts (art, music, dance, drama), computer science, English, foreign language, mathematics, physical education (includes health), science, social sciences, social studies (includes history). Community service is required.

Special Academic Programs Advanced Placement exam preparation; honors section; independent study; academic accommodation for the gifted, the musically talented, and the artistically talented; ESL (10 students enrolled).

College Admission Counseling 106 students graduated in 2015; all went to college, including Duke University; James Madison University; The College of William and Mary; University of Virginia; Virginia Polytechnic Institute and State University; Washington and Lee University.

Student Life Upper grades have specified standards of dress, student council, honor system. Discipline rests equally with students and faculty.

Summer Programs Enrichment, advancement, ESL, sports, art/fine arts, computer instruction programs offered; session focuses on academics and enrichment; held on campus; accepts boys and girls; open to students from other schools. 1,200 students usually enrolled. 2016 schedule: June 9 to August 15. Application deadline: none.

Tuition and Aid Day student tuition: $19,250. Tuition installment plan (The Tuition Plan, Insured Tuition Payment Plan, monthly payment plans, individually arranged payment plans, 3-payment plan). Merit scholarship grants, need-based scholarship grants available. In 2015–16, 25% of upper-school students received aid.

Admissions Traditional secondary-level entrance grade is 9. For fall 2015, 85 students applied for upper-level admission, 60 were accepted, 35 enrolled. ERB CTP, ISEE, Scholastic Achievement Test, SSAT, ERB, PSAT, SAT, PLAN or ACT, TOEFL or writing sample required. Deadline for receipt of application materials: none. Application fee required: $50. Interview required.

Athletics Interscholastic: baseball (boys), basketball (b,g), crew (b,g), cross-country running (b,g), field hockey (g), golf (b,g), lacrosse (b,g), physical fitness (b,g), soccer (b,g), softball (g), tennis (b,g), volleyball (b,g), wrestling (b); intramural: field hockey (g), fitness (b,g), floor hockey (b,g), wrestling (b); coed interscholastic: cheering, dance, dance team, swimming and diving, track and field; coed intramural: badminton, ballet, dance, fishing, fitness, fitness walking, flag football, golf, hiking/backpacking, jogging, kayaking, lacrosse, modern dance, ocean paddling, outdoor activities, outdoor adventure, physical fitness, physical training, soccer, strength & conditioning, surfing, swimming and diving, table tennis, tennis, volleyball, weight lifting, weight training, wilderness, yoga. 3 PE instructors, 25 coaches, 1 athletic trainer.

Computers Computers are regularly used in computer applications, desktop publishing, graphic arts, information technology, literary magazine, newspaper, publications, technology, video film production, Web site design, word processing, yearbook classes. Computer network features include on-campus library services, online commercial services, Internet access, wireless campus network, Internet filtering or blocking technology. Campus intranet, student e-mail accounts, and computer access in designated common areas are available to students. Students grades are available online. The school has a published electronic and media policy.

Contact Mrs. Angie Finley, Admissions Associate. 757-963-8234. Fax: 757-481-9194. E-mail: angiefinley@capehenry.org. Website: www.capehenrycollegiate.org

CAPISTRANO VALLEY CHRISTIAN SCHOOLS

32032 Del Obispo Street
San Juan Capistrano, California 92675

Head of School: Dr. Ron Sipus

General Information Coeducational day college-preparatory, arts, business, vocational, religious studies, bilingual studies, and technology school, affiliated with Christian faith. Grades JK–12. Founded: 1972. Setting: suburban. 8-acre campus. 3 buildings on campus. Approved or accredited by Association of Christian Schools International, The College Board, Western Association of Schools and Colleges, and California Department of Education. Total enrollment: 435. Upper school average class size: 18. Upper school faculty-student ratio: 1:13. There are 180 required school days per year for Upper School students. Upper School students typically attend 5 days per week. The average school day consists of 6 hours.

Upper School Student Profile Grade 9: 35 students (19 boys, 16 girls); Grade 10: 57 students (33 boys, 24 girls); Grade 11: 49 students (28 boys, 21 girls); Grade 12: 51 students (30 boys, 21 girls). 80% of students are Christian faith.

Faculty School total: 55. In upper school: 16 men, 18 women; 11 have advanced degrees.

Subjects Offered Advanced biology, advanced chemistry, advanced computer applications, advanced math, Advanced Placement courses, advanced TOEFL/grammar, algebra, American government, American history, American history-AP, American literature, American literature-AP, anatomy, art, ASB Leadership, athletic training, athletics, Bible, Bible studies, biology, biology-AP, business, business applications, business communications, business education, business law, business skills, business studies, calculus, calculus-AP, career planning, chemistry, choir, chorus, Christian doctrine, Christian ethics, Christian scripture, Christian studies, Christian testament, Christianity, church history, college admission preparation, college counseling, college placement, college planning, comparative government and politics-AP, competitive science projects, composition, composition-AP, computer applications, computer education, computer information systems, computer literacy, computer multimedia, computer skills, computer technologies, dance, desktop publishing, drama performance, economics, English, English literature-AP, English-AP, ESL, European history, geometry, government, health, history, honors algebra, honors English, independent study, Internet, intro to computers, journalism, keyboarding, kinesiology, lab science, leadership, photography, physical education, physical science, physics, public speaking, research skills, Spanish, sports medicine, sports nutrition, statistics, statistics-AP, student government, TOEFL preparation, U.S. government and politics-AP, U.S. history-AP, Web site design, world cultures, writing, yearbook.

Graduation Requirements Algebra, American government, American history, American literature, arts and fine arts (art, music, dance, drama), Bible, biology, composition, computer skills, economics, electives, English, European history, foreign language, freshman foundations, geometry, physical education (includes health), research skills, speech, graduation requirements meet UC and CSU entrance requirements.

Special Academic Programs 11 Advanced Placement exams for which test preparation is offered; honors section; independent study; study at local college for college credit; special instructional classes for Opportunity School Program; ESL (20 students enrolled).

College Admission Counseling 42 students graduated in 2015; 41 went to college, including Biola University; University of California, Irvine; University of California, Los Angeles; Westmont College. Other: 1 entered military service. Median SAT critical reading: 552, median SAT math: 584, median SAT writing: 521, median combined SAT: 1657, median composite ACT: 23.

Student Life Upper grades have uniform requirement, student council, honor system. Discipline rests primarily with faculty. Attendance at religious services is required.

Summer Programs Remediation, enrichment, advancement, sports, art/fine arts programs offered; session focuses on advancement; held on campus; accepts boys and girls; open to students from other schools. 25 students usually enrolled. 2016 schedule: July 11 to August 5. Application deadline: May 1.

Tuition and Aid Day student tuition: $13,120. Tuition installment plan (FACTS Tuition Payment Plan, individually arranged payment plans, payroll deductions). Tuition reduction for siblings, need-based scholarship grants available. In 2015–16, 30% of upper-school students received aid. Total amount of financial aid awarded in 2015–16: $250,000.

Admissions Traditional secondary-level entrance grade is 9. For fall 2015, 51 students applied for upper-level admission, 47 were accepted, 45 enrolled. Admissions testing, ESOL English Proficiency Test, High School Placement Test, Stanford Test of Academic Skills or TOEFL required. Deadline for receipt of application materials: none. Application fee required: $100. On-campus interview required.

Athletics Interscholastic: baseball (boys), basketball (b,g), cheering (g), combined training (b,g), cross-country running (b,g), football (b), soccer (b,g), softball (g), tennis (g), volleyball (b,g); coed interscholastic: equestrian sports, golf, physical training, strength & conditioning, track and field, weight training. 3 PE instructors, 14 coaches, 4 athletic trainers.

Computers Computers are regularly used in all academic, data processing, design, journalism, writing, yearbook classes. Computer network features include on-campus library services, Internet access, wireless campus network, Internet filtering or blocking technology, 1:1 tablet PC program. Campus intranet, student e-mail accounts, and computer access in designated common areas are available to students. Students grades are available online. The school has a published electronic and media policy.

Contact Mrs. Jo Beveridge, Director of Admissions. 949-493-5683 Ext. 109. Fax: 949-493-6057. E-mail: jbeveridge@cvcs.org. Website: www.cvcs.org

THE CAPITOL SCHOOL, INC.

2828 Sixth Street
Tuscaloosa, Alabama 35401

Head of School: Dr. Barbara Starnes Rountree

General Information Coeducational boarding and day college-preparatory, arts, business, bilingual studies, and technology school. Grades PK–12. Founded: 1993. Setting: urban. 3-acre campus. 3 buildings on campus. Approved or accredited by Southern Association of Colleges and Schools and Alabama Department of Education. Languages of instruction: English, German, and Spanish. Total enrollment: 220. Upper school average class size: 12. Upper school faculty-student ratio: 1:16. There are 175 required school days per year for Upper School students. Upper School students typically attend 5 days per week. The average school day consists of 7 hours.

Faculty School total: 24. In upper school: 2 men, 4 women; 5 have advanced degrees.

Subjects Offered All.

Special Academic Programs International Baccalaureate program; accelerated programs; study at local college for college credit; study abroad; academic accommodation for the gifted, the musically talented, and the artistically talented.

College Admission Counseling 5 students graduated in 2014; 4 went to college, including The University of Alabama. Other: 1 went to work. 100% scored over 26 on composite ACT.

Student Life Upper grades have honor system. Discipline rests primarily with faculty.

Tuition and Aid Tuition installment plan (SMART Tuition Payment Plan).

Admissions Deadline for receipt of application materials: none. Application fee required: $975. Interview required.

Athletics Interscholastic: cross-country running (boys, girls), golf (b,g), indoor track & field (b,g), soccer (b,g), tennis (b,g), volleyball (b,g); coed interscholastic: bowling. 1 PE instructor, 10 coaches, 4 athletic trainers.

Computers Computer network features include on-campus library services, Internet access, wireless campus network, Internet filtering or blocking technology. Student e-mail accounts and computer access in designated common areas are available to students. Students grades are available online. The school has a published electronic and media policy.

Contact Dr. Barbara Starnes Rountree, Director. 205-758-2828. Fax: 205-750-0280. E-mail: brountree@thecapitolschool.com. Website: www.thecapitolschool.com

CARDIGAN MOUNTAIN SCHOOL

Canaan, New Hampshire
See Junior Boarding Schools section.

CARDINAL GIBBONS HIGH SCHOOL

1401 Edwards Mill Road
Raleigh, North Carolina 27607

Head of School: Mr. Jason Curtis

General Information Coeducational day college-preparatory, arts, business, religious studies, and technology school, affiliated with Roman Catholic Church. Grades 9–12. Founded: 1909. Setting: suburban. 36-acre campus. 1 building on campus. Approved or accredited by Southern Association of Colleges and Schools. Endowment: $750,000. Total enrollment: 1,428. Upper school faculty-student ratio: 1:13. Upper School students typically attend 5 days per week. The average school day consists of 7 hours.

Upper School Student Profile Grade 9: 425 students (229 boys, 196 girls); Grade 10: 367 students (196 boys, 171 girls); Grade 11: 334 students (163 boys, 171 girls); Grade 12: 302 students (138 boys, 164 girls). 86% of students are Roman Catholic.

Faculty School total: 100. In upper school: 51 men, 49 women.

Special Academic Programs Advanced Placement exam preparation; honors section; accelerated programs; independent study.

College Admission Counseling 302 students graduated in 2015; all went to college, including Appalachian State University; University of Notre Dame.

Student Life Upper grades have uniform requirement, student council. Discipline rests primarily with faculty. Attendance at religious services is required.

Summer Programs Enrichment, advancement, sports, art/fine arts programs offered; session focuses on sports, music, theatre; held on campus; accepts boys and girls; open to students from other schools. 2016 schedule: June to August.

Tuition and Aid Day student tuition: $10,140–$14,200. Tuition installment plan (FACTS Tuition Payment Plan). Need-based scholarship grants available.

Admissions Traditional secondary-level entrance grade is 9. Application fee required: $100. On-campus interview required.

Athletics Interscholastic: aerobics/dance (boys, girls), ballet (g), baseball (b,g), basketball (b,g), cheering (g), cross-country running (b,g), dance (g), dance squad (g), dance team (g), diving (b,g), field hockey (g), football (b), golf (b,g), kickball (b,g), lacrosse (b,g), modern dance (g), mountain biking (b,g), outdoor education (b,g), physical fitness (b,g), physical training (b,g), roller hockey (b), running (b,g), soccer (b,g), softball (g), strength & conditioning (b), surfing (b,g), swimming and diving (b,g), tennis (b,g), track and field (b,g), ultimate Frisbee (b,g), volleyball (g), weight lifting (b,g), weight training (g), wrestling (b). 85 coaches.

Computers Computers are regularly used in accounting classes. Computer network features include Internet access, wireless campus network, Internet filtering or blocking technology. Campus intranet, student e-mail accounts, and computer access in designated common areas are available to students. Students grades are available online.

Contact Mrs. Marianne McCarty, Admissions Director. 919-834-1625 Ext. 209. Fax: 919-834-9771. E-mail: mmccarty@cghsnc.org. Website: www.cghsnc.org

CARDINAL HAYES HIGH SCHOOL

650 Grand Concourse
Bronx, New York 10451

Head of School: Mr. William Daniel Lessa

General Information College-preparatory school, affiliated with Roman Catholic Church. Founded: 1941. Setting: urban. Nearest major city is New York City. 1 building on campus. Approved or accredited by Middle States Association of Colleges and Schools and New York Department of Education. Upper school average class size: 23. The average school day consists of 6 hours and 17 minutes.

Upper School Student Profile 50% of students are Roman Catholic.

Special Academic Programs 4 Advanced Placement exams for which test preparation is offered.

College Admission Counseling 226 students graduated in 2014; 222 went to college. Other: 3 entered military service, 1 entered a postgraduate year.

Student Life Upper grades have uniform requirement, student council. Discipline rests primarily with faculty. Attendance at religious services is required.

Admissions No application fee required.

Athletics Interscholastic: baseball (boys), basketball (b), football (b), golf (b), indoor track (b), indoor track & field (b), soccer (b).

Computers The school has a published electronic and media policy.

Contact 718-292-6100. Fax: 718-292-5607. Website: www.cardinalhayes.org

CARDINAL MOONEY CATHOLIC COLLEGE PREPARATORY HIGH SCHOOL

660 South Water Street
Marine City, Michigan 48039

Head of School: Mr. Jason Petrella

General Information Coeducational day college-preparatory school, affiliated with Roman Catholic Church. Grades 9–12. Founded: 1977. Setting: small town. Nearest major city is Mount Clemens. 1-acre campus. 1 building on campus. Approved or accredited by North Central Association of Colleges and Schools and Michigan Department of Education. Total enrollment: 150. Upper school average class size: 22. Upper school faculty-student ratio: 1:9. There are 186 required school days per year for Upper School students. Upper School students typically attend 5 days per week. The average school day consists of 6 hours and 25 minutes.

Upper School Student Profile Grade 9: 39 students (24 boys, 15 girls); Grade 10: 26 students (7 boys, 19 girls); Grade 11: 45 students (21 boys, 24 girls); Grade 12: 40 students (19 boys, 21 girls). 90% of students are Roman Catholic.

Faculty School total: 20. In upper school: 5 men, 13 women; 10 have advanced degrees.

Subjects Offered Advanced Placement courses, algebra, American literature, anatomy, art, biology, biology-AP, British literature, calculus, Catholic belief and practice, chemistry, choir, computer applications, computer skills, drama, economics, English, fiction, French, French language-AP, geography, geometry, government, government-AP, health, humanities, Italian, library science, moral and social development, mythology, philosophy, physical education, physical science, physics, poetry, pre-calculus, psychology-AP, Spanish, Spanish language-AP, statistics, study skills, U.S. history, U.S. history-AP, world history, world literature, yearbook.

Special Academic Programs 8 Advanced Placement exams for which test preparation is offered; honors section.

College Admission Counseling 45 students graduated in 2014; 42 went to college, including Central Michigan University; Grand Valley State University; Michigan State University; Oakland University; University of Detroit Mercy; University of Michigan. Other: 1 went to work, 2 entered military service.

Student Life Upper grades have uniform requirement, student council, honor system. Discipline rests primarily with faculty. Attendance at religious services is required.

Tuition and Aid Tuition installment plan (FACTS Tuition Payment Plan, monthly payment plans). Tuition reduction for siblings, merit scholarship grants available. In 2014–15, 40% of upper-school students received aid.

Admissions Traditional secondary-level entrance grade is 9. For fall 2014, 39 students applied for upper-level admission, 39 were accepted, 39 enrolled. High School Placement Test required. Deadline for receipt of application materials: none. Application fee required: $250. Interview required.

Athletics Interscholastic: baseball (boys), basketball (b,g), bowling (b,g), cheering (g), cross-country running (b,g), equestrian sports (b,g), football (b), golf (b,g), horseback riding (b,g), soccer (b,g), softball (g), volleyball (g); coed interscholastic: cross-country running, track and field. 2 PE instructors, 6 coaches.

Computers Computers are regularly used in all academic, art, computer applications, desktop publishing, digital applications, drawing and design, graphic arts, graphic design, independent study, word processing, yearbook classes. Computer network features include on-campus library services, Internet access, wireless campus network, Internet filtering or blocking technology. Computer access in designated common areas is available to students. Students grades are available online. The school has a published electronic and media policy.

Contact Ms. Christine Alongi-Arnold, Director of Admissions. 810-765-8825 Ext. 11. Fax: 810-765-7164. E-mail: calongi@cardinalmooney.org. Website: www.cardinalmooney.org/

CARDINAL MOONEY CATHOLIC HIGH SCHOOL

4171 Fruitville Road
Sarasota, Florida 34232

Head of School: Mr. Stephen J. Christie

General Information Coeducational day college-preparatory, arts, religious studies, and technology school, affiliated with Roman Catholic Church. Grades 9–12. Founded: 1959. Setting: suburban. Nearest major city is Tampa. 36-acre campus. 5 buildings on campus. Approved or accredited by Southern Association of Colleges and Schools. Endowment: $1.8 million. Total enrollment: 474. Upper school average class size: 18. Upper school faculty-student ratio: 1:13. There are 180 required school days per year for Upper School students. Upper School students typically attend 5 days per week. The average school day consists of 6 hours and 35 minutes.

Upper School Student Profile Grade 9: 126 students (76 boys, 50 girls); Grade 10: 145 students (75 boys, 70 girls); Grade 11: 132 students (69 boys, 63 girls); Grade 12: 110 students (60 boys, 50 girls). 75% of students are Roman Catholic.

Faculty School total: 50. In upper school: 12 men, 26 women; 25 have advanced degrees.

Subjects Offered Algebra, American government, American history, anatomy, art, biology, business, calculus, ceramics, chemistry, chorus, Christian and Hebrew scripture, community service, computer applications, computer graphics, contemporary history, creative writing, drama, earth science, economics, economics and history, English, English literature, environmental science, fine arts, French, geometry, guitar, health, history, instrumental music, integrated mathematics, journalism, keyboarding, learning strategies, marine biology, mathematics, music, physical education, physics, psychology, science, social justice, social studies, sociology, Spanish, speech, theology, trigonometry, U.S. government and politics-AP, world history, world literature, world religions.

Graduation Requirements Arts and fine arts (art, music, dance, drama), electives, English, foreign language, mathematics, physical education (includes health), religion (includes Bible studies and theology), science, social studies (includes history), 100 hours of community service.

Special Academic Programs 8 Advanced Placement exams for which test preparation is offered; honors section; remedial reading and/or remedial writing; remedial math; programs in English, mathematics for dyslexic students.

College Admission Counseling 123 students graduated in 2015; all went to college, including Auburn University; Florida Gulf Coast University; Florida State University; University of Central Florida; University of Florida. Median SAT critical reading: 512, median SAT math: 507, median SAT writing: 506, median composite ACT: 23. 31% scored over 600 on SAT critical reading, 41% scored over 600 on SAT math, 35% scored over 600 on SAT writing, 38% scored over 26 on composite ACT.

Student Life Upper grades have specified standards of dress, student council. Discipline rests primarily with faculty. Attendance at religious services is required.

Tuition and Aid Tuition installment plan (monthly payment plans, semester payment plan). Tuition reduction for siblings, merit scholarship grants, need-based scholarship grants available. In 2015–16, 25% of upper-school students received aid. Total amount of financial aid awarded in 2015–16: $200,000.

Admissions Traditional secondary-level entrance grade is 9. For fall 2015, 180 students applied for upper-level admission, 180 were accepted, 128 enrolled. Placement test required. Deadline for receipt of application materials: none. No application fee required. On-campus interview required.

Athletics Interscholastic: baseball (boys), basketball (b,g), cheering (g), cross-country running (b,g), dance team (g), diving (b,g), football (b), golf (b,g), lacrosse (b,g), modern dance (g), physical fitness (b,g), soccer (b,g), softball (g), strength & conditioning (b,g), swimming and diving (b,g), track and field (b,g), volleyball (g), weight lifting (b,g), weight training (b,g); intramural: basketball (b,g), volleyball (b,g);

coed interscholastic: aquatics; coed intramural: volleyball. 4 PE instructors, 66 coaches, 4 athletic trainers.

Computers Computers are regularly used in art, basic skills, Christian doctrine, computer applications, creative writing, English, foreign language, French, history, mathematics, religious studies, remedial study skills, science, social sciences, social studies, Spanish, technology, theater arts, video film production, writing, yearbook classes. Computer network features include on-campus library services, Internet access, wireless campus network. Student e-mail accounts are available to students. Students grades are available online. The school has a published electronic and media policy.

Contact Mrs. Joanne Mades, Registrar. 941-371-4917. Fax: 941-371-6924 Ext. 135. E-mail: jmades@cmhs-sarasota.org. Website: www.cmhs-sarasota.org

CARDINAL NEWMAN HIGH SCHOOL

512 Spencer Drive
West Palm Beach, Florida 33409-3699

Head of School: Fr. David W. Carr

General Information Coeducational day college-preparatory and International Baccalaureate school, affiliated with Roman Catholic Church. Grades 9–12. Founded: 1961. Setting: suburban. Nearest major city is Miami. 50-acre campus. 5 buildings on campus. Approved or accredited by National Catholic Education Association, Southern Association of Colleges and Schools, and Florida Department of Education. Total enrollment: 544. Upper school average class size: 25. Upper school faculty-student ratio: 1:25. There are 180 required school days per year for Upper School students. Upper School students typically attend 5 days per week. The average school day consists of 6 hours and 40 minutes.

Upper School Student Profile Grade 9: 137 students (66 boys, 71 girls); Grade 10: 139 students (74 boys, 65 girls); Grade 11: 143 students (69 boys, 74 girls); Grade 12: 125 students (62 boys, 63 girls). 80% of students are Roman Catholic.

Faculty School total: 43. In upper school: 15 men, 28 women; 33 have advanced degrees.

Subjects Offered Algebra, American government, American history, American literature, anatomy and physiology, art, band, Bible studies, biology, biology-AP, calculus, calculus-AP, chemistry, chorus, church history, computer applications, computer science, desktop publishing, drama, economics, English, English literature, English-AP, ethics, European history, fine arts, French, French-AP, geometry, government/civics, health, history, honors algebra, honors English, honors geometry, integrated science, International Baccalaureate courses, journalism, leadership, marine biology, mathematics, physical education, physics, political science, pre-calculus, probability and statistics, religion, social justice, social studies, Spanish, speech, world history, world literature, writing, yearbook.

Graduation Requirements Arts and fine arts (art, music, dance, drama), English, foreign language, mathematics, physical education (includes health), religion (includes Bible studies and theology), science, social studies (includes history), 100-hour community service requirement.

Special Academic Programs International Baccalaureate program; Advanced Placement exam preparation; honors section; study at local college for college credit; academic accommodation for the gifted; remedial reading and/or remedial writing; remedial math.

College Admission Counseling 116 students graduated in 2015; 115 went to college, including Florida Atlantic University; Florida Gulf Coast University; Florida State University; Palm Beach State College; University of Central Florida; University of Florida. Other: 1 entered military service.

Student Life Upper grades have uniform requirement, student council, honor system. Discipline rests primarily with faculty. Attendance at religious services is required.

Summer Programs Remediation, enrichment, sports programs offered; session focuses on freshman preparation; held on campus; accepts boys and girls; not open to students from other schools. 75 students usually enrolled. 2016 schedule: June 15 to June 30.

Tuition and Aid Day student tuition: $11,800–$12,800. Tuition installment plan (FACTS Tuition Payment Plan). Need-based scholarship grants available. In 2015–16, 18% of upper-school students received aid.

Admissions Traditional secondary-level entrance grade is 9. STS required. Deadline for receipt of application materials: none. Application fee required: $50. On-campus interview recommended.

Athletics Interscholastic: baseball (boys), basketball (b,g), bowling (b,g), cheering (g), cross-country running (b,g), dance team (b,g), diving (b,g), football (b), golf (b,g), lacrosse (b,g), physical fitness (b,g), soccer (b,g), softball (g), swimming and diving (b,g), tennis (b,g), track and field (b,g), volleyball (g), wrestling (b). 2 PE instructors, 1 athletic trainer.

Computers Computers are regularly used in all academic, Bible studies, social studies, yearbook classes. Computer network features include on-campus library services, online commercial services, Internet access, wireless campus network, Internet filtering or blocking technology. Student e-mail accounts are available to students. Students grades are available online. The school has a published electronic and media policy.

Contact Miss Anna Christie, Admissions Director. 561-683-6266 Ext. 1050. Fax: 561-683-7307. E-mail: anna.christie@cardinalnewman.com. Website: www.cardinalnewman.com

CARLISLE SCHOOL

300 Carlisle Road
Axton, Virginia 24054

Head of School: Mr. Thomas P. Hudgins Jr.

General Information Coeducational boarding and day college-preparatory school. Boarding grades 9–12, day grades PK–12. Founded: 1968. Setting: rural. Nearest major city is Danville. Students are housed in single-sex dormitories and hosted by local families. 32-acre campus. 5 buildings on campus. Approved or accredited by Southern Association of Colleges and Schools, Southern Association of Independent Schools, Virginia Association of Independent Schools, and Virginia Department of Education. Member of National Association of Independent Schools. Endowment: $1.9 million. Total enrollment: 390. Upper school average class size: 15. Upper school faculty-student ratio: 1:8. There are 177 required school days per year for Upper School students. Upper School students typically attend 5 days per week. The average school day consists of 6 hours and 45 minutes.

Upper School Student Profile Grade 9: 25 students (13 boys, 12 girls); Grade 10: 35 students (19 boys, 16 girls); Grade 11: 33 students (16 boys, 17 girls); Grade 12: 39 students (21 boys, 18 girls). 9% of students are boarding students. 75% are state residents. 2 states are represented in upper school student body. 25% are international students. International students from Canada, China, Colombia, Japan, Republic of Korea, and Yemen.

Faculty School total: 42. In upper school: 4 men, 14 women; 8 have advanced degrees; 4 reside on campus.

Subjects Offered Advanced computer applications, advanced math, Advanced Placement courses, algebra, American government, American history, American history-AP, American literature, art, arts, band, biology, biology-AP, calculus, calculus-AP, chemistry, chemistry-AP, choir, composition-AP, computer information systems, computer programming, computer science, computer science-AP, concert band, creative dance, creative drama, creative writing, dance, drama, earth science, economics, economics-AP, English, English language and composition-AP, English literature, English literature and composition-AP, English literature-AP, ESL, film studies, fine arts, geometry, government, government/civics, health, health and wellness, history, history of the Americas, honors algebra, honors English, honors geometry, HTML design, independent study, International Baccalaureate courses, intro to computers, jazz band, jazz ensemble, journalism, lab science, madrigals, mathematics, mathematics-AP, music, physical education, physics, play production, pre-algebra, pre-calculus, psychology, psychology-AP, publications, robotics, science, senior project, social studies, Spanish, statistics, statistics-AP, studio art, theater, theory of knowledge, U.S. government and politics-AP, U.S. history-AP, wind ensemble, world civilizations, world history, world history-AP, world wide web design, yearbook.

Graduation Requirements Advanced math, algebra, arts and fine arts (art, music, dance, drama), computer science, electives, English, foreign language, mathematics, physical education (includes health), science, social studies (includes history), U.S. and Virginia history, U.S. government, community service, senior project.

Special Academic Programs Advanced Placement exam preparation; honors section; independent study; term-away projects; study at local college for college credit; ESL (17 students enrolled).

College Admission Counseling 41 students graduated in 2015; all went to college, including George Mason University; Old Dominion University; University of Virginia; Virginia Commonwealth University; Virginia Polytechnic Institute and State University. Median SAT critical reading: 510, median SAT math: 520, median SAT writing: 500, median combined SAT: 1560, median composite ACT: 23. 18% scored over 600 on SAT critical reading, 24% scored over 600 on SAT math, 29% scored over 600 on SAT writing, 24% scored over 1800 on combined SAT, 13% scored over 26 on composite ACT.

Student Life Upper grades have specified standards of dress, student council, honor system. Discipline rests equally with students and faculty.

Summer Programs Remediation, enrichment, advancement, ESL, sports, art/fine arts, computer instruction programs offered; session focuses on enrichment, academics, sports, fun; held on campus; accepts boys and girls; open to students from other schools. 60 students usually enrolled. 2016 schedule: June 15 to August 15. Application deadline: June 1.

Tuition and Aid Day student tuition: $11,490; 5-day tuition and room/board: $28,000; 7-day tuition and room/board: $36,810. Tuition installment plan (Insured Tuition Payment Plan, FACTS Tuition Payment Plan). Need-based scholarship grants available. In 2015–16, 39% of upper-school students received aid. Total amount of financial aid awarded in 2015–16: $372,479.

Admissions Traditional secondary-level entrance grade is 9. Nelson-Denny Reading Test, TOEFL or SLEP, Woodcock-Johnson or writing sample required. Deadline for receipt of application materials: none. Application fee required: $65. Interview required.

Athletics Interscholastic: basketball (boys, girls), cheering (g), field hockey (g), soccer (b,g), softball (g), tennis (b,g), volleyball (g); intramural: basketball (b,g), cheering (g), softball (g); coed interscholastic: baseball, cross-country running, dance, fencing, golf; coed intramural: aerobics/Nautilus, archery, basketball, Frisbee, swimming and diving, table tennis, weight lifting. 2 PE instructors, 29 coaches, 1 athletic trainer.

Computers Computers are regularly used in all academic classes. Computer network features include on-campus library services, online commercial services, Internet access, wireless campus network, Internet filtering or blocking technology. Campus intranet, student e-mail accounts, and computer access in designated common areas are available to students. Students grades are available online. The school has a published electronic and media policy.

Contact Ms. Cindy Pike, International Student Affairs Coordinator, Admissions Assistant. 276-632-7288 Ext. 221. Fax: 276-632-9545. E-mail: cpike@carlisleschool.org. Website: www.carlisleschool.org

CARLUCCI AMERICAN INTERNATIONAL SCHOOL OF LISBON

Rua António dos Reis, 95
Linhó, Sintra 2710-301, Portugal

Head of School: Ms. Blannie M. Curtis

General Information Coeducational day college-preparatory school. Grades PK–12. Founded: 1956. Setting: suburban. Nearest major city is Lisbon, Portugal. 4-hectare campus. 4 buildings on campus. Approved or accredited by Council of International Schools, International Baccalaureate Organization, New England Association of Schools and Colleges, US Department of State, and state department of education. Member of European Council of International Schools. Language of instruction: English. Total enrollment: 640. Upper school average class size: 15. Upper school faculty-student ratio: 1:8. There are 179 required school days per year for Upper School students. Upper School students typically attend 5 days per week. The average school day consists of 5 hours and 30 minutes.

Upper School Student Profile Grade 9: 59 students (34 boys, 25 girls); Grade 10: 52 students (28 boys, 24 girls); Grade 11: 51 students (22 boys, 29 girls); Grade 12: 54 students (26 boys, 28 girls).

Faculty School total: 78. In upper school: 12 men, 15 women; 25 have advanced degrees.

Subjects Offered Algebra, art, biology, business studies, chemistry, choir, computer applications, computer art, economics, English, European history, French, geography, geometry, International Baccalaureate courses, journalism, model United Nations, modern civilization, music, physical education, physics, Portuguese, Portuguese literature, Spanish, theory of knowledge, U.S. history, U.S. literature, writing workshop, yearbook.

Graduation Requirements Arts and fine arts (art, music, dance, drama), computer science, electives, English, foreign language, mathematics, physical education (includes health), science, social studies (includes history), International Baccalaureate diploma candidates have to complete 150 Community Action Service hours, plus Theory of Knowledge and Extended Essay.

Special Academic Programs International Baccalaureate program; honors section; independent study; programs in general development for dyslexic students; ESL (68 students enrolled).

College Admission Counseling 39 students graduated in 2015; 35 went to college, including Amherst College; Boston University; California State University, Fullerton; Rensselaer Polytechnic Institute; Rollins College; Suffolk University. Other: 4 had other specific plans.

Student Life Upper grades have specified standards of dress, student council, honor system. Discipline rests primarily with faculty.

Tuition and Aid Day student tuition: €7596–€17,716. Tuition installment plan (monthly payment plans, individually arranged payment plans, early payment discount, quarterly payment plan). Tuition reduction for siblings, merit scholarship grants, Merit-based scholarships are available to student residents in Sintra, Portugal only available.

Admissions English for Non-native Speakers or Math Placement Exam required. Deadline for receipt of application materials: none. No application fee required.

Athletics Interscholastic: basketball (boys, girls), cross-country running (b,g), soccer (b,g), track and field (b,g), volleyball (b,g); intramural: basketball (b,g), soccer (b,g); coed interscholastic: baseball; coed intramural: ballet, fitness, gymnastics, modern dance, mountain biking, volleyball. 4 PE instructors, 6 coaches.

Computers Computers are regularly used in computer applications, digital applications, graphic design classes. Computer network features include on-campus library services, Internet access, wireless campus network, Internet filtering or blocking technology. Campus intranet, student e-mail accounts, and computer access in designated common areas are available to students. Students grades are available online. The school has a published electronic and media policy.

Contact Ms. Maria Barral, DMC Manager. 351-21-923-9800. Fax: 351-21-923-9809. E-mail: admissions@caislisbon.org. Website: www.caislisbon.org

CARMEL HIGH SCHOOL

One Carmel Parkway
Mundelein, Illinois 60060-2499

Head of School: Sr. Mary Frances McLaughlin, PhD

General Information Coeducational day college-preparatory, arts, business, religious studies, and technology school, affiliated with Roman Catholic Church. Grades 9–12. Founded: 1962. Setting: suburban. Nearest major city is Libertyville. 45-acre campus. 1 building on campus. Approved or accredited by National Catholic Education Association and Illinois Department of Education. Total enrollment: 1,340. Upper school average class size: 25. Upper school faculty-student ratio: 1:16. Upper

School students typically attend 5 days per week. The average school day consists of 7 hours.

Upper School Student Profile 83% of students are Roman Catholic.

Faculty School total: 90. In upper school: 33 men, 57 women; 63 have advanced degrees.

Subjects Offered 20th century world history, accounting, advanced chemistry, advanced math, Advanced Placement courses, advanced studio art-AP, algebra, American government, American history, American literature, American literature-AP, anatomy and physiology, art, athletic training, band, biology, biology-AP, biotechnology, botany, British literature, British literature (honors), business, calculus, calculus-AP, chemistry, chemistry-AP, choir, choral music, chorus, community service, computer applications, computer programming, computer programming-AP, concert band, drama, drama performance, drawing, economics, English, English composition, English language and composition-AP, English literature, English literature-AP, European history-AP, French, French language-AP, French-AP, geography, geometry, government, government-AP, history of religion, honors algebra, honors English, honors geometry, honors U.S. history, honors world history, instrumental music, Internet research, intro to computers, jazz band, journalism, Latin, Latin-AP, Mandarin, marching band, music, music composition, music theory-AP, orchestra, performing arts, physical education, physical science, physics, physics-AP, pre-algebra, pre-calculus, probability and statistics, psychology, reading/study skills, religion, religious education, scripture, sociology, Spanish, strings, student government, student publications, student teaching, studio art, studio art-AP, theater arts, trigonometry, U.S. government and politics-AP, U.S. history, U.S. history-AP, Web site design, wind ensemble, women spirituality and faith, world history, world history-AP, world literature, yearbook, zoology.

Graduation Requirements Ministry requirement, 20 hours of ministry service per semester.

Special Academic Programs 19 Advanced Placement exams for which test preparation is offered; honors section; special instructional classes for deaf students, blind students.

College Admission Counseling 320 students graduated in 2014; 316 went to college, including Marquette University; Purdue University; The University of Iowa; University of Illinois at Urbana–Champaign. Other: 1 went to work, 3 entered military service. Mean composite ACT: 26.

Student Life Upper grades have uniform requirement, student council. Discipline rests primarily with faculty. Attendance at religious services is required.

Tuition and Aid Day student tuition: $10,350. Tuition installment plan (FACTS Tuition Payment Plan). Merit scholarship grants, need-based scholarship grants available. In 2014–15, 13% of upper-school students received aid; total upper-school merit-scholarship money awarded: $16,000. Total amount of financial aid awarded in 2014–15: $1,200,000.

Admissions Traditional secondary-level entrance grade is 9. High School Placement Test required. Deadline for receipt of application materials: January 23. Application fee required: $400.

Athletics Interscholastic: baseball (boys), basketball (b,g), cheering (g), cross-country running (b,g), football (b), golf (b,g), gymnastics (g), ice hockey (b), lacrosse (b,g), pom squad (g), soccer (b,g), softball (g), tennis (b,g), track and field (b,g), volleyball (b,g), wrestling (b); intramural: basketball (b,g); coed intramural: Frisbee, volleyball, winter soccer, yoga.

Computers Computers are regularly used in all academic classes. Computer network features include on-campus library services, Internet access, wireless campus network. Student e-mail accounts are available to students. Students grades are available online. The school has a published electronic and media policy.

Contact Mr. Brian Stith, Director of Admissions. 847-388-3320. Fax: 847-566-8465. E-mail: bstith@carmelhs.org. Website: www.carmelhs.org

CAROLINA DAY SCHOOL

1345 Hendersonville Road
Asheville, North Carolina 28803

Head of School: Kirk Duncan

General Information Coeducational day college-preparatory school. Grades PK–12. Founded: 1987. Setting: suburban. 60-acre campus. 9 buildings on campus. Approved or accredited by North Carolina Association of Independent Schools, Southern Association of Colleges and Schools, Southern Association of Independent Schools, and North Carolina Department of Education. Member of National Association of Independent Schools and Secondary School Admission Test Board. Endowment: $3.4 million. Total enrollment: 625. Upper school average class size: 14. Upper school faculty-student ratio: 1:9. There are 180 required school days per year for Upper School students. Upper School students typically attend 5 days per week. The average school day consists of 6 hours and 25 minutes.

Upper School Student Profile Grade 9: 49 students (23 boys, 26 girls); Grade 10: 50 students (28 boys, 22 girls); Grade 11: 42 students (19 boys, 23 girls); Grade 12: 48 students (30 boys, 18 girls).

Faculty School total: 114. In upper school: 11 men, 12 women; 17 have advanced degrees.

Subjects Offered 3-dimensional art, 3-dimensional design, acting, advanced biology, advanced chemistry, advanced studio art-AP, algebra, American literature, art history,

art history-AP, biology, biology-AP, calculus, calculus-AP, ceramics, chemistry, chemistry-AP, chorus, CPR, creative writing, debate, ecology, English language and composition-AP, English literature, environmental science-AP, European history-AP, fiction, French, geometry, global studies, history, industrial arts, language and composition, linear algebra, linguistics, literature, literature and composition-AP, martial arts, music theory, music theory-AP, photography, physical education, physics, physics-AP, pre-calculus, psychology-AP, reading/study skills, research, science, Spanish, Spanish-AP, speech, statistics-AP, studio art, theater, U.S. government and politics-AP, U.S. history, U.S. history-AP, world literature.

Graduation Requirements Algebra, arts and fine arts (art, music, dance, drama), biology, chemistry, electives, English, geometry, global studies, modern languages, physical education (includes health), public speaking, social studies (includes history), U.S. history, CPR/First Aid (non-credit class).

Special Academic Programs 15 Advanced Placement exams for which test preparation is offered; independent study.

College Admission Counseling 37 students graduated in 2014; all went to college, including Boston College; Georgetown University; The College of Wooster; The University of North Carolina at Chapel Hill; University of North Carolina at Asheville; University of Pennsylvania. Mean SAT critical reading: 595, mean SAT math: 618, mean SAT writing: 617, mean combined SAT: 1830, mean composite ACT: 27.

Student Life Upper grades have specified standards of dress, student council, honor system. Discipline rests equally with students and faculty.

Tuition and Aid Day student tuition: $21,350–$22,675. Tuition installment plan (Insured Tuition Payment Plan, FACTS Tuition Payment Plan, monthly payment plans, individually arranged payment plans, 1-payment plan or 2-installments plan (August and January)). Merit scholarship grants, need-based scholarship grants available. In 2014–15, 45% of upper-school students received aid; total upper-school merit-scholarship money awarded: $237,503. Total amount of financial aid awarded in 2014–15: $722,070.

Admissions Traditional secondary-level entrance grade is 9. For fall 2014, 58 students applied for upper-level admission, 47 were accepted, 37 enrolled. ERB, ISEE, PSAT or SAT or SSAT required. Deadline for receipt of application materials: none. Application fee required: $100. On-campus interview required.

Athletics Interscholastic: baseball (boys), basketball (b,g), cross-country running (b,g), field hockey (g), soccer (b,g), swimming and diving (b,g), tennis (b,g), track and field (b,g), volleyball (g); intramural: softball (g); coed interscholastic: alpine skiing, archery, golf; coed intramural: basketball, lacrosse, martial arts, skiing (downhill), snowboarding, table tennis. 3 PE instructors, 11 coaches, 1 athletic trainer.

Computers Computers are regularly used in all academic classes. Computer network features include on-campus library services, online commercial services, Internet access, wireless campus network, Internet filtering or blocking technology. Campus intranet, student e-mail accounts, and computer access in designated common areas are available to students. The school has a published electronic and media policy.

Contact Carole Hilderbran, Admission Associate. 828-274-0757 Ext. 141. Fax: 828-274-0756. E-mail: childerbran@carolinaday.org. Website: www.carolinaday.org

CARONDELET HIGH SCHOOL

1133 Winton Drive
Concord, California 94518

Head of School: Bonnie Cotter

General Information Girls' day college-preparatory, arts, religious studies, and technology school, affiliated with Roman Catholic Church. Grades 9–12. Founded: 1965. Setting: suburban. Nearest major city is Oakland. 9-acre campus. 5 buildings on campus. Approved or accredited by Western Association of Schools and Colleges and Western Catholic Education Association. Member of National Association of Independent Schools. Endowment: $9 million. Total enrollment: 800. Upper school average class size: 26. Upper school faculty-student ratio: 1:15. There are 176 required school days per year for Upper School students. Upper School students typically attend 5 days per week. The average school day consists of 7 hours and 30 minutes.

Upper School Student Profile Grade 9: 200 students (200 girls); Grade 10: 200 students (200 girls); Grade 11: 200 students (200 girls); Grade 12: 200 students (200 girls). 85% of students are Roman Catholic.

Faculty School total: 65. In upper school: 13 men, 48 women; 30 have advanced degrees.

Subjects Offered Algebra, American studies, animation, architectural drawing, art, band, biology, calculus, calculus-AP, cartooning/animation, chemistry, chorus, church history, civics, community service, computer applications, concert band, concert choir, creative writing, criminal justice, dance, design, drafting, drawing, economics, English, English-AP, ethics, finite math, fitness, French, geometry, government-AP, health, honors algebra, honors English, honors geometry, Italian, jazz band, journalism, Latin, marching band, marine biology, music history, music theory, musical theater, orchestra, painting, physical education, physics, physics-AP, physiology, pre-algebra, pre-calculus, psychology, psychology-AP, relationships, sculpture, Spanish, Spanish-AP, sports medicine, statistics, studio art-AP, technical drawing, transition mathematics, U.S. history, U.S. history-AP, water color painting, Web site design, women's health, world arts, world civilizations, world religions, writing, yearbook.

Graduation Requirements Computer literacy, English, mathematics, modern languages, physical education (includes health), religious studies, science, social studies (includes history), visual and performing arts.

Special Academic Programs 12 Advanced Placement exams for which test preparation is offered; honors section; independent study; academic accommodation for the gifted.

College Admission Counseling 199 students graduated in 2015; all went to college, including California Polytechnic State University, San Luis Obispo; California State University, Chico; Loyola Marymount University; Saint Mary's College of California; University of California, Berkeley. Mean SAT critical reading: 548, mean SAT math: 538, mean SAT writing: 556, mean composite ACT: 24.

Student Life Upper grades have uniform requirement, honor system. Discipline rests primarily with faculty. Attendance at religious services is required.

Summer Programs Remediation, enrichment, sports programs offered; session focuses on academics, sports, and fun; held on campus; accepts boys and girls; open to students from other schools. 60 students usually enrolled. 2016 schedule: June to July. Application deadline: May.

Tuition and Aid Day student tuition: $16,500. Tuition installment plan (SMART Tuition Payment Plan, monthly payment plans, prepayment plan, semester or quarterly payment plans). Need-based scholarship grants available. In 2015–16, 25% of upper-school students received aid. Total amount of financial aid awarded in 2015–16: $1,300,000.

Admissions Traditional secondary-level entrance grade is 9. For fall 2015, 380 students applied for upper-level admission, 240 were accepted, 220 enrolled. High School Placement Test (closed version) from Scholastic Testing Service required. Deadline for receipt of application materials: December 2. Application fee required: $100. On-campus interview required.

Athletics Interscholastic: aquatics, badminton, basketball, cheering, combined training, cross-country running, dance squad, dance team, diving, golf, lacrosse, soccer, softball, swimming and diving, tennis, track and field, volleyball, water polo; intramural: badminton, basketball, broomball, flag football, physical fitness, physical training, touch football, volleyball. 3 PE instructors, 40 coaches, 1 athletic trainer.

Computers Computers are regularly used in all academic, computer applications classes. Computer network features include on-campus library services, Internet access, wireless campus network, Internet filtering or blocking technology. Campus intranet, student e-mail accounts, and computer access in designated common areas are available to students. Students grades are available online. The school has a published electronic and media policy.

Contact Ms. Jess Mix, Assistant Principal. 925-686-5353. Fax: 925-671-9429. E-mail: jmix@carondeleths.org. Website: www.carondelet.net

CARRABASSETT VALLEY ACADEMY

3197 Carrabassett Drive
Carrabassett Valley, Maine 04947

Head of School: Kate W. Punderson

General Information Coeducational boarding and day college-preparatory and arts school. Grades 7–PG. Founded: 1982. Setting: rural. Nearest major city is Waterville. Students are housed in single-sex by floor dormitories. 8-acre campus. 4 buildings on campus. Approved or accredited by New England Association of Schools and Colleges and Maine Department of Education. Total enrollment: 89. Upper school average class size: 12. Upper school faculty-student ratio: 1:6. There are 171 required school days per year for Upper School students. Upper School students typically attend 5 days per week.

Upper School Student Profile Grade 9: 20 students (14 boys, 6 girls); Grade 10: 10 students (7 boys, 3 girls); Grade 11: 26 students (17 boys, 9 girls); Grade 12: 21 students (14 boys, 7 girls); Grade 13: 1 student (1 boy). 76% of students are boarding students. 61% are state residents. 5 states are represented in upper school student body. 1% are international students. International students from Canada, Ireland, Japan, Spain, and United Kingdom.

Faculty School total: 14. In upper school: 2 men, 9 women; 5 have advanced degrees; 9 reside on campus.

Subjects Offered Algebra, American history, American literature, athletic training, athletics, biology, calculus, chemistry, earth science, English, environmental science, ESL, European history, fine arts, French, freshman foundations, geography, geometry, health, history, mathematics, music, music performance, physical education, physics, pre-calculus, publications, science, senior seminar, social psychology, social studies, Spanish, sports conditioning, sports nutrition, sports performance development, sports psychology, studio art, world history.

Graduation Requirements Algebra, American history, applied arts, arts and fine arts (art, music, dance, drama), athletic training, athletics, biology, chemistry, earth science, English, foreign language, geometry, health education, physical education (includes health), science, social studies (includes history), Western civilization, world cultures, participation and training in alpine racing, freestyle skiing, snowboarding, or ALPS. We are a ski/snowboard academy that balances athletics and academics daily.

Special Academic Programs Honors section; ESL (2 students enrolled).

College Admission Counseling 19 students graduated in 2014; 13 went to college, including Clarkson University; Plymouth State University; Saint Anselm College; St. Lawrence University; University of Colorado Boulder; University of Maine. Other: 4

entered a postgraduate year, 2 had other specific plans. Mean SAT critical reading: 517, mean SAT math: 529, mean SAT writing: 497.

Student Life Upper grades have specified standards of dress, student council, honor system. Discipline rests primarily with faculty.

Tuition and Aid Day student tuition: $35,500; 7-day tuition and room/board: $46,800. Tuition installment plan (monthly payment plans, individually arranged payment plans). Need-based scholarship grants available. In 2014–15, 43% of upper-school students received aid.

Admissions Traditional secondary-level entrance grade is 10. For fall 2014, 42 students applied for upper-level admission, 42 were accepted, 34 enrolled. Deadline for receipt of application materials: March 31. Application fee required: $40. Interview required.

Athletics Interscholastic: alpine skiing (boys, girls), freestyle skiing (b,g), skiing (downhill) (b,g), snowboarding (b,g); intramural: weight lifting (b,g), weight training (b,g); coed intramural: backpacking, canoeing/kayaking, climbing, combined training, fitness, golf, hiking/backpacking, in-line skating, kayaking, mountain biking, mountaineering, outdoor activities, physical fitness, physical training, rappelling, roller blading, running, skateboarding, soccer, Special Olympics, tennis, ultimate Frisbee, volleyball, wall climbing, wilderness. 17 coaches, 1 athletic trainer.

Computers Computers are regularly used in English, ESL, foreign language, history, mathematics, publications, science, social sciences classes. Computer network features include online commercial services, Internet access, wireless campus network, Internet filtering or blocking technology, iPads, Ebackpack. Student e-mail accounts and computer access in designated common areas are available to students. Students grades are available online. The school has a published electronic and media policy.

Contact Dawn Smith, Director of Admissions. 207-237-2250. Fax: 207-237-2213. E-mail: dsmith@gocva.com. Website: www.gocva.com

CARROLLTON CHRISTIAN ACADEMY

2205 East Hebron Parkway
Carrollton, Texas 75010

Head of School: Mr. David Culpepper

General Information Coeducational day college-preparatory, arts, religious studies, and technology school, affiliated with United Methodist Church. Grades K–12. Founded: 1980. Setting: suburban. Nearest major city is Dallas/Fort Worth. 25-acre campus. 1 building on campus. Approved or accredited by Association of Christian Schools International, Southern Association of Colleges and Schools, University Senate of United Methodist Church, and Texas Department of Education. Language of instruction: English. Total enrollment: 230. Upper school average class size: 20. The average school day consists of 7 hours.

Subjects Offered ACT preparation, acting, advanced biology, advanced chemistry, Advanced Placement courses, algebra, anatomy and physiology, art, athletics, band, baseball, basketball, Bible, biology, biology-AP, calculus, chemistry, chemistry-AP, computer skills, computer studies, digital photography, economics-AP, English, English-AP, fine arts, foreign language, geometry, golf, government-AP.

Special Academic Programs Honors section; study at local college for college credit.

Student Life Upper grades have uniform requirement, student council, honor system. Discipline rests primarily with faculty. Attendance at religious services is required.

Tuition and Aid Day student tuition: $11,800. Tuition installment plan (FACTS Tuition Payment Plan). Tuition reduction for siblings, need-based scholarship grants available.

Admissions Stanford Achievement Test or TerraNova required. Application fee required: $125. Interview required.

Athletics Interscholastic: baseball (boys), basketball (b,g), cheering (g), cross-country running (b,g), dance team (g), football (b), golf (b,g), soccer (b,g), softball (g), strength & conditioning (b,g), tennis (b,g), track and field (b,g), volleyball (g), winter soccer (b,g).

Computers Computer resources include on-campus library services, wireless campus network. Campus intranet and computer access in designated common areas are available to students. Students grades are available online.

Contact Ms. Jane Funk, Admissions Coordinator. 972-242-6688 Ext. 1360. Fax: 469-568-1396. E-mail: jane.funk@ccasaints.org. Website: www.ccasaints.org

CARROLLTON SCHOOL OF THE SACRED HEART

3747 Main Highway
Miami, Florida 33133

Head of School: Mr. Olen Kalkus

General Information Girls' day college-preparatory, arts, religious studies, bilingual studies, and technology school, affiliated with Roman Catholic Church. Grades PK–12. Founded: 1961. Setting: urban. 17-acre campus. 5 buildings on campus. Approved or accredited by Florida Council of Independent Schools, Network of Sacred Heart Schools, and Southern Association of Colleges and Schools. Member of National Association of Independent Schools and Secondary School Admission Test Board. Endowment: $2 million. Total enrollment: 800. Upper school average class size: 16. Upper school faculty-student ratio: 1:9. There are 180 required school days per year for

Upper School students. Upper School students typically attend 5 days per week. The average school day consists of 8 hours.

Upper School Student Profile 87% of students are Roman Catholic.

Faculty School total: 74. In upper school: 9 men, 24 women; 20 have advanced degrees.

Subjects Offered Algebra, American history, American literature, anatomy and physiology, art, art history, Bible studies, biology, British literature, calculus, chemistry, computer science, debate, drama, earth systems analysis, economics, English, English literature, environmental science, ethics, expository writing, fine arts, French, general science, geometry, government/civics, grammar, health, history, humanities, journalism, mathematics, music, photography, physical education, physical science, physics, pre-calculus, psychology, religion, science, scripture, social sciences, social studies, Spanish, speech, theater, trigonometry, vocal ensemble, world history, world literature.

Graduation Requirements Arts and fine arts (art, music, dance, drama), computer science, English, foreign language, mathematics, physical education (includes health), religion (includes Bible studies and theology), science, social studies (includes history). Community service is required.

Special Academic Programs International Baccalaureate program; Advanced Placement exam preparation; honors section; independent study; study at local college for college credit; domestic exchange program; study abroad.

College Admission Counseling 70 students graduated in 2015; all went to college, including Boston College; Massachusetts Institute of Technology; Northwestern University; University of Miami; Vanderbilt University. Median SAT math: 590, median composite ACT: 24. Mean SAT critical reading: 590. 51% scored over 600 on SAT critical reading, 47% scored over 600 on SAT math, 30% scored over 26 on composite ACT.

Student Life Upper grades have uniform requirement, student council, honor system. Discipline rests primarily with faculty. Attendance at religious services is required.

Tuition and Aid Day student tuition: $30,350. Tuition installment plan (Insured Tuition Payment Plan, monthly payment plans). Merit scholarship grants, need-based scholarship grants available. In 2015–16, 25% of upper-school students received aid; total upper-school merit-scholarship money awarded: $45,000. Total amount of financial aid awarded in 2015–16: $920,000.

Admissions Traditional secondary-level entrance grade is 9. For fall 2015, 132 students applied for upper-level admission, 37 were accepted, 30 enrolled. Admissions testing or ISEE required. Deadline for receipt of application materials: February 1. Application fee required: $50. On-campus interview required.

Athletics Interscholastic: aquatics, basketball, crew, cross-country running, golf, sailing, soccer, softball, swimming and diving, tennis, track and field, volleyball, water polo, winter soccer. 6 PE instructors, 30 coaches, 3 athletic trainers.

Computers Computers are regularly used in all academic classes. Computer network features include on-campus library services, online commercial services, Internet access, wireless campus network, Internet filtering or blocking technology, laptop program. Student e-mail accounts are available to students. The school has a published electronic and media policy.

Contact Ms. Ana J. Roye, Director of Admission and Financial Aid. 305-446-5673 Ext. 1224. Fax: 305-446-4160. E-mail: aroye@carrollton.org. Website: www.carrollton.org

CASADY SCHOOL

9500 North Pennsylvania Avenue
Oklahoma City, Oklahoma 73120

Head of School: Mr. Nathan Sheldon

General Information Coeducational day college-preparatory and arts school, affiliated with Episcopal Church. Grades PK–12. Founded: 1947. Setting: suburban. 80-acre campus. 30 buildings on campus. Approved or accredited by Independent Schools Association of the Southwest, National Independent Private Schools Association, Southwest Association of Episcopal Schools, and The College Board. Member of National Association of Independent Schools and Secondary School Admission Test Board. Endowment: $16 million. Total enrollment: 905. Upper school average class size: 15. Upper school faculty-student ratio: 1:15.

Upper School Student Profile Grade 6: 65 students (33 boys, 32 girls); Grade 7: 63 students (31 boys, 32 girls); Grade 8: 71 students (39 boys, 32 girls); Grade 9: 82 students (39 boys, 43 girls); Grade 10: 80 students (40 boys, 40 girls); Grade 11: 77 students (46 boys, 31 girls); Grade 12: 77 students (37 boys, 40 girls). 30% of students are members of Episcopal Church.

Faculty School total: 115. In upper school: 32 men, 21 women; 35 have advanced degrees.

Subjects Offered African-American studies, algebra, American history, American literature, art, art history, Asian history, athletic training, band, Bible studies, biochemistry, biology, biology-AP, British literature, calculus, calculus-AP, ceramics, chemistry, chemistry-AP, Chinese, choir, choral music, college counseling, college placement, college planning, computer applications, computer programming, computer science, creative writing, data processing, digital imaging, drama, drama performance, drawing, driver education, earth science, economics, English, English language-AP, English literature, English literature-AP, environmental science, European history, expository writing, fine arts, French, French language-AP, French literature-AP, freshman seminar, functions, geology, geometry, German, government/civics, grammar,

Greek, health, history, human anatomy, journalism, Latin, Latin-AP, mathematics, Middle Eastern history, modern languages, music, mythology, Native American history, painting, photography, physical education, physics, physiology, religion, Russian history, science, social studies, Spanish, Spanish language-AP, Spanish literature-AP, speech, statistics, theater, theology, trigonometry, U.S. history-AP, water color painting, weight training, word processing, world history, world literature, writing, yearbook.

Graduation Requirements Arts and fine arts (art, music, dance, drama), computer science, English, foreign language, mathematics, physical education (includes health), science, social studies (includes history); service learning.

Special Academic Programs Advanced Placement exam preparation; independent study; study abroad; academic accommodation for the gifted, the musically talented, and the artistically talented.

College Admission Counseling 70 students graduated in 2015; all went to college, including Brown University; Duke University; Oklahoma State University; Texas Christian University; University of Oklahoma. Median SAT critical reading: 625, median SAT math: 630, median SAT writing: 608, median combined SAT: 1234. 55% scored over 600 on SAT critical reading, 55% scored over 600 on SAT math.

Student Life Upper grades have specified standards of dress, student council, honor system. Discipline rests equally with students and faculty. Attendance at religious services is required.

Summer Programs Remediation, enrichment, advancement, sports, art/fine arts, computer instruction programs offered; held on campus; accepts boys and girls; open to students from other schools. 500 students usually enrolled. 2016 schedule: June 11 to July 13. Application deadline: June 1.

Tuition and Aid Day student tuition: $3145–$19,900. Tuition installment plan (The Tuition Plan, Insured Tuition Payment Plan, FACTS Tuition Payment Plan, monthly payment plans, individually arranged payment plans, 2-installment plan). Merit scholarship grants, need-based scholarship grants available. In 2015–16, 11% of upper-school students received aid; total upper-school merit-scholarship money awarded: $4000. Total amount of financial aid awarded in 2015–16: $400,000.

Admissions Traditional secondary-level entrance grade is 9. For fall 2015, 60 students applied for upper-level admission, 45 were accepted, 27 enrolled. CTP, ERB - verbal abilities, reading comprehension, quantitative abilities (level F, form 1) and school's own exam required. Deadline for receipt of application materials: none. Application fee required: $50. On-campus interview required.

Athletics Interscholastic: baseball (boys), basketball (b,g), cheering (g), cross-country running (b,g), field hockey (g), football (b), golf (b,g), soccer (b,g), softball (g), swimming and diving (b,g), tennis (b,g), track and field (b,g), volleyball (b,g), wrestling (b); intramural: aerobics/dance (g), dance (g), martial arts (b,g), modern dance (g), physical fitness (b,g), physical training (b,g); coed intramural: aerobics, bowling, climbing, fencing, fitness walking, racquetball, sailing, weight lifting, yoga. 9 PE instructors, 23 coaches, 2 athletic trainers.

Computers Computers are regularly used in all academic classes. Computer resources include on-campus library services, Internet access, wireless campus network, Internet filtering or blocking technology. Campus intranet and student e-mail accounts are available to students. Students grades are available online.

Contact Mrs. Lacy Leggett, Advancement Office Coordinator. 405-749-3185. Fax: 405-749-3223. E-mail: leggettl@casady.org. Website: www.casady.org

CASCADILLA SCHOOL

116 Summit Street
Ithaca, New York 14850

Head of School: Patricia T. Kendall

General Information Coeducational boarding and day college-preparatory, arts, bilingual studies, English/language arts (The Cascadilla Seminar/Cornell Univ.), and mathematics school. Grades 9–PG. Founded: 1876. Setting: urban. Nearest major city is Syracuse. Students are housed in single-sex dormitories. 2-acre campus. 3 buildings on campus. Approved or accredited by New York Department of Education, New York State Board of Regents, New York State University, The College Board, US Department of State, and New York Department of Education. Endowment: $1.5 million. Upper school average class size: 7. Upper school faculty-student ratio: 1:5. There are 185 required school days per year for Upper School students. Upper School students typically attend 5 days per week. The average school day consists of 8 hours.

Upper School Student Profile Grade 9: 9 students (5 boys, 4 girls); Grade 10: 3 students (1 boy, 2 girls); Grade 11: 13 students (9 boys, 4 girls); Grade 12: 11 students (4 boys, 7 girls). 30% of students are boarding students. 45% are state residents. 4 states are represented in upper school student body. 55% are international students. International students from Angola, China, Portugal, and Republic of Korea.

Faculty School total: 13. In upper school: 5 men, 8 women; 12 have advanced degrees; 4 reside on campus.

Subjects Offered Advanced biology, advanced chemistry, advanced math, Advanced Placement courses, advanced TOEFL/grammar, African literature, algebra, alternative physical education, American government, American history, American history-AP, American literature, analysis and differential calculus, analytic geometry, art, biochemistry, biology, biology-AP, calculus, calculus-AP, career/college preparation, ceramics, chemistry, chemistry-AP, civics, classical language, college admission preparation, college awareness, college counseling, college placement, college planning, college writing, computer programming, computer science, creative writing, decision making skills, desktop publishing, digital photography, DNA science lab, earth science, economics, electives, English, English composition, English literature, English literature and composition-AP, English literature-AP, environmental education, environmental science, ethics, expository writing, fabric arts, French, French as a second language, geometry, government/civics, graphic design, health, health and wellness, health education, history, honors algebra, honors English, honors geometry, honors U.S. history, honors world history, journalism, lab science, Latin, leadership, library research, library skills, literary magazine, mathematics, philosophy, photography, photojournalism, physical education, physics, pre-calculus, psychology, public speaking, reading, reading/study skills, SAT preparation, SAT/ACT preparation, science, senior composition, senior humanities, senior seminar, senior thesis, Shakespeare, social studies, Spanish, statistics, statistics-AP, TOEFL preparation, trigonometry, U.S. government, U.S. government and politics, U.S. history, U.S. history-AP, U.S. literature, video film production, world history, world history-AP, world literature, writing, yearbook, zoology.

Graduation Requirements Alternative physical education, arts, arts and fine arts (art, music, dance, drama), computer science, current events, debate, economics, economics and history, English, European history, foreign language, government, health education, international affairs, mathematics, physical education (includes health), political science, public speaking, research, research and reference, research seminar, science, senior seminar, social studies (includes history), study skills, U.S. government and politics, English V-The Cascadilla Seminar (preparation for college writing and research). Community service is required.

Special Academic Programs 16 Advanced Placement exams for which test preparation is offered; honors section; accelerated programs; independent study; term-away projects; study at local college for college credit; academic accommodation for the gifted, the musically talented, and the artistically talented; remedial reading and/or remedial writing; remedial math; programs in English, mathematics for dyslexic students; special instructional classes for students with learning disabilities and Attention Deficit Disorder.

College Admission Counseling 11 students graduated in 2015; all went to college, including Barry University; Ithaca College; Pace University; University of California, Riverside; University of Missouri; University of Pittsburgh. Median SAT critical reading: 630, median SAT math: 610, median SAT writing: 510, median combined SAT: 1800. 60% scored over 600 on SAT critical reading, 60% scored over 600 on SAT math, 20% scored over 600 on SAT writing, 20% scored over 1800 on combined SAT.

Student Life Upper grades have specified standards of dress, student council, honor system. Discipline rests equally with students and faculty.

Summer Programs Remediation, enrichment, advancement, art/fine arts programs offered; session focuses on academics; held on campus; accepts boys and girls; open to students from other schools. 10 students usually enrolled. 2016 schedule: July 1 to August 16. Application deadline: June 30.

Tuition and Aid Day student tuition: $14,550; 7-day tuition and room/board: $39,950. Tuition installment plan (monthly payment plans, individually arranged payment plans). Tuition reduction for siblings, merit scholarship grants, need-based scholarship grants available. In 2015–16, 40% of upper-school students received aid; total upper-school merit-scholarship money awarded: $50,000. Total amount of financial aid awarded in 2015–16: $60,000.

Admissions Traditional secondary-level entrance grade is 10. For fall 2015, 70 students applied for upper-level admission, 16 were accepted, 14 enrolled. English Composition Test for ESL students, English entrance exam, English for Non-native Speakers, English language, English proficiency, High School Placement Test, math and English placement tests, mathematics proficiency exam, non-standardized placement tests, Reading for Understanding, school's own exam or writing sample required. Deadline for receipt of application materials: none. Application fee required: $75. Interview recommended.

Athletics Interscholastic: crew (boys, girls), modern dance (g); intramural: crew (b,g), fencing (b), independent competitive sports (b,g), rowing (b,g), sailing (b,g), skiing (cross-country) (b,g), skiing (downhill) (b,g), soccer (b,g), tennis (b,g); coed interscholastic: aerobics, aerobics/Nautilus, alpine skiing, aquatics, backpacking, badminton, ballet, basketball, billiards, blading, bowling, climbing, combined training, fencing, fitness, fitness walking, Frisbee, hiking/backpacking, jogging, kayaking, nordic skiing, outdoor activities, outdoor adventure, outdoor education, physical fitness, physical training, swimming and diving, table tennis, weight lifting, yoga; coed intramural: aerobics, aerobics/dance, badminton, basketball, blading, bowling, equestrian sports, horseback riding, independent competitive sports, jogging, Nautilus, nordic skiing, outdoor activities, outdoor adventure, physical fitness, physical training, pillo polo, racquetball, rowing, sailboarding, skiing (cross-country), skiing (downhill), snowboarding, soccer, strength & conditioning, tennis, volleyball, walking, wall climbing, windsurfing. 3 PE instructors.

Computers Computers are regularly used in career exploration, college planning, creative writing, desktop publishing, economics, English, foreign language, graphic design, journalism, language development, library skills, literary magazine, mathematics, media arts, news writing, newspaper, photography, photojournalism, publications, publishing, research skills, SAT preparation, senior seminar, Spanish, stock market, theater, theater arts, video film production, Web site design, word processing, writing, yearbook classes. Computer network features include on-campus library services, online commercial services, Internet access, wireless campus network, Internet filtering or blocking technology, dormitories are fitted for high speed Internet.

Student e-mail accounts and computer access in designated common areas are available to students. Students grades are available online.
Contact Mary B. Lorson, Assistant Director of Admissions. 607-272-3110. Fax: 607-272-0747. E-mail: admissions@cascadillaschool.org. Website: www.cascadillaschool.org

See Display on next page and Close-Up on page 588.

CASCIA HALL PREPARATORY SCHOOL

2520 South Yorktown Avenue
Tulsa, Oklahoma 74114-2803

Head of School: Mr. Roger C. Carter

General Information Coeducational day college-preparatory and liberal arts school, affiliated with Roman Catholic Church. Grades 6–12. Founded: 1926. Setting: urban. 40-acre campus. 10 buildings on campus. Approved or accredited by North Central Association of Colleges and Schools, Southern Association of Colleges and Schools, and Oklahoma Department of Education. Endowment: $8 million. Total enrollment: 527. Upper school average class size: 18. Upper school faculty-student ratio: 1:12. There are 180 required school days per year for Upper School students. Upper School students typically attend 5 days per week. The average school day consists of 6 hours and 30 minutes.

Upper School Student Profile Grade 9: 105 students (55 boys, 50 girls); Grade 10: 76 students (40 boys, 36 girls); Grade 11: 78 students (38 boys, 40 girls); Grade 12: 86 students (40 boys, 46 girls). 45% of students are Roman Catholic.

Faculty School total: 48. In upper school: 19 men, 20 women; 32 have advanced degrees.

Subjects Offered 20th century physics, ACT preparation, Advanced Placement courses, advanced studio art-AP, algebra, American history-AP, American literature, anatomy and physiology, ancient world history, art, art-AP, Asian studies, astronomy, Basic programming, Bible studies, biology, business, calculus, calculus-AP, career experience, career exploration, Catholic belief and practice, Central and Eastern European history, chemistry, chemistry-AP, Chinese, Chinese studies, chorus, Christian ethics, church history, college admission preparation, composition, computer science, CPR, creative writing, digital photography, drama, drawing, driver education, English language and composition-AP, English literature and composition-AP, environmental studies, ethics, European history, European history-AP, French, geography, geometry, German, government-AP, grammar, health, history of the Catholic Church, Holocaust studies, independent study, Latin, literature, philosophy, photography, physical science, physics, physics-AP, pre-calculus, probability and statistics, psychology, Russian studies, SAT/ACT preparation, senior seminar, senior thesis, Shakespeare, Spanish, Spanish language-AP, speech, speech and debate, theater, theology, trigonometry, U.S. government and politics-AP, U.S. history, world history, yearbook.

Graduation Requirements Arts and fine arts (art, music, dance, drama), career exploration, college admission preparation, computer science, English, foreign language, mathematics, religion (includes Bible studies and theology), science, senior seminar, social sciences, social studies (includes history), community service.

Special Academic Programs 12 Advanced Placement exams for which test preparation is offered; honors section; independent study; study at local college for college credit; study abroad; academic accommodation for the gifted.

College Admission Counseling 86 students graduated in 2015; all went to college, including Kansas State University; Oklahoma State University; Texas Christian University; The University of Tulsa; University of Arkansas; University of Oklahoma. Median SAT critical reading: 611, median SAT math: 602, median SAT writing: 600, median composite ACT: 26. 56% scored over 600 on SAT critical reading, 56% scored over 600 on SAT math, 53% scored over 600 on SAT writing, 45% scored over 26 on composite ACT.

Student Life Upper grades have uniform requirement, student council. Discipline rests primarily with faculty. Attendance at religious services is required.

Summer Programs Remediation, enrichment, advancement, sports, art/fine arts programs offered; session focuses on sports camp, driver's education, and performing arts, English Enrichment, College essay writing; held on campus; accepts boys and girls; open to students from other schools. 500 students usually enrolled. 2016 schedule: June to August. Application deadline: May 1.

Tuition and Aid Day student tuition: $1,312,500. Tuition installment plan (monthly payment plans). Tuition reduction for siblings, need-based scholarship grants available. In 2015–16, 20% of upper-school students received aid. Total amount of financial aid awarded in 2015–16: $75,000.

Admissions Traditional secondary-level entrance grade is 9. For fall 2015, 75 students applied for upper-level admission, 59 were accepted, 44 enrolled. STS - Educational Development Series required. Deadline for receipt of application materials: none. Application fee required: $25. On-campus interview required.

Athletics Interscholastic: baseball (boys), basketball (b,g), bowling (b), cheering (g), cross-country running (b,g), dance team (g), football (b), golf (b,g), power lifting (b,g), soccer (b,g), softball (g), strength & conditioning (b,g), tennis (b,g), track and field (b,g), volleyball (g), weight training (b,g), wrestling (b); coed intramural: bowling, crew, lacrosse, outdoor recreation, rowing, rugby, ultimate Frisbee. 1 PE instructor, 17 coaches, 1 athletic trainer.

Computers Computer network features include on-campus library services, online commercial services, Internet access, wireless campus network, Internet filtering or blocking technology, InfoTrac Search Bank, Internet access to local and state university library catalogues. Campus intranet, student e-mail accounts, and computer access in designated common areas are available to students. Students grades are available online. The school has a published electronic and media policy.

Contact Mrs. Patricia A. Wilson, Coordinator of Admissions. 918-746-2604. Fax: 918-746-2640. E-mail: pwilson@casciahall.com. Website: www.casciahall.com

CASTILLEJA SCHOOL

1310 Bryant Street
Palo Alto, California 94301

Head of School: Nanci Z. Kauffman

General Information Girls' day college-preparatory, arts, and technology school. Grades 6–12. Founded: 1907. Setting: suburban. Nearest major city is San Francisco/San Jose. 5-acre campus. 7 buildings on campus. Approved or accredited by California Association of Independent Schools, National Council for Private School Accreditation, and Western Association of Schools and Colleges. Member of National Association of Independent Schools and Secondary School Admission Test Board. Endowment: $42 million. Total enrollment: 438. Upper school average class size: 14. Upper school faculty-student ratio: 1:6. Upper School students typically attend 5 days per week. The average school day consists of 7 hours.

Upper School Student Profile Grade 9: 65 students (65 girls); Grade 10: 60 students (60 girls); Grade 11: 57 students (57 girls); Grade 12: 67 students (67 girls).

Faculty School total: 75. In upper school: 12 men, 34 women; 40 have advanced degrees.

Subjects Offered Advanced Placement courses, African studies, algebra, American history, American literature, art, art history, biology, calculus, ceramics, chemistry, computer math, computer science, creative writing, drama, economics, English, English literature, environmental science, European history, expository writing, fine arts, French, geometry, global issues, government/civics, grammar, health, history, journalism, Latin, marine biology, mathematics, music, philosophy, physical education, physics, psychology, Russian history, science, social studies, Spanish, speech, statistics, theater, trigonometry, world history, writing.

Graduation Requirements Arts and fine arts (art, music, dance, drama), English, foreign language, health and wellness, mathematics, science, social studies (includes history).

Special Academic Programs 13 Advanced Placement exams for which test preparation is offered; honors section; independent study; academic accommodation for the gifted.

College Admission Counseling 62 students graduated in 2015; all went to college, including Brown University; Dartmouth College; Northwestern University; Stanford University; University of Southern California. Mean SAT critical reading: 710, mean SAT math: 704, mean SAT writing: 730.

Student Life Upper grades have uniform requirement, student council, honor system. Discipline rests equally with students and faculty.

Tuition and Aid Day student tuition: $40,930. Tuition installment plan (monthly payment plans, individually arranged payment plans). Need-based scholarship grants available. In 2015–16, 20% of upper-school students received aid. Total amount of financial aid awarded in 2015–16: $2,200,000.

Admissions Traditional secondary-level entrance grade is 9. ISEE, SSAT or TOEFL required. Deadline for receipt of application materials: January 14. Application fee required: $75. On-campus interview required.

Athletics Interscholastic: basketball, cross-country running, golf, lacrosse, soccer, softball, swimming and diving, tennis, track and field, volleyball, water polo; intramural: climbing, fitness, rock climbing. 6 PE instructors, 15 coaches, 1 athletic trainer.

Computers Computers are regularly used in art, English, foreign language, history, mathematics, science classes. Computer network features include on-campus library services, online commercial services, Internet access, wireless campus network, Internet filtering or blocking technology, one-to-one laptop program, iPads. Campus intranet and student e-mail accounts are available to students. Students grades are available online. The school has a published electronic and media policy.

Contact Jill V.W. Lee, Director of Admission. 650-470-7731. Fax: 650-326-8036. E-mail: jlee@castilleja.org. Website: www.castilleja.org

CATE SCHOOL

1960 Cate Mesa Road
Carpinteria, California 93013

Head of School: Benjamin D. Williams, IV

General Information Coeducational boarding and day college-preparatory school. Grades 9–12. Founded: 1910. Setting: small town. Nearest major city is Santa Barbara. Students are housed in single-sex dormitories. 150-acre campus. 18 buildings on campus. Approved or accredited by California Association of Independent Schools, The Association of Boarding Schools, and Western Association of Schools and Colleges. Member of National Association of Independent Schools and Secondary School Admission Test Board. Endowment: $60 million. Total enrollment: 270. Upper school average class size: 10. Upper school faculty-student ratio: 1:5. There are 184 required

school days per year for Upper School students. Upper School students typically attend 6 days per week. The average school day consists of 6 hours and 45 minutes.

Upper School Student Profile Grade 9: 55 students (27 boys, 28 girls); Grade 10: 70 students (35 boys, 35 girls); Grade 11: 70 students (35 boys, 35 girls); Grade 12: 70 students (35 boys, 35 girls). 83% of students are boarding students. 45% are state residents. 31 states are represented in upper school student body. 16% are international students. International students from China, Hong Kong, Republic of Korea, Saudi Arabia, Switzerland, and Taiwan; 11 other countries represented in student body.

Faculty School total: 52. In upper school: 34 men, 18 women; 43 have advanced degrees; 51 reside on campus.

Subjects Offered Advanced studio art-AP, African American history, algebra, American history, American literature, anatomy and physiology, art, art history-AP, Asian history, astronomy, biology, biology-AP, calculus, California writers, ceramics, chemistry, chemistry-AP, Chinese, choir, computer programming, computer science, computer science-AP, creative writing, digital art, drama, drama performance, economics-AP, English, English literature, environmental science-AP, ethics, European history, finance, fine arts, French, French language-AP, French literature-AP, French-AP, freshman seminar, genetics, geometry, government-AP, human development, international relations, Japanese, marine biology, Middle Eastern history, multimedia, music, photography, photojournalism, physics, physics-AP, pre-calculus, psychology, research skills, Russian literature, Spanish, Spanish language-AP, Spanish literature-AP, Spanish-AP, statistics, statistics-AP, studio art-AP, the Sixties, theater, trigonometry, U.S. government and politics-AP, U.S. history-AP, world history, writing.

Graduation Requirements 1 1/2 elective credits, arts and fine arts (art, music, dance, drama), English, foreign language, history, human development, mathematics, science, social sciences.

Special Academic Programs 19 Advanced Placement exams for which test preparation is offered; honors section; independent study; term-away projects; study abroad; academic accommodation for the gifted, the musically talented, and the artistically talented; special instructional classes for deaf students.

College Admission Counseling 70 students graduated in 2015; all went to college, including Barnard College; New York University; Stanford University; University of Chicago; University of Pennsylvania; University of Southern California. Median SAT critical reading: 660, median SAT math: 660, median SAT writing: 680, median combined SAT: 1970. 81% scored over 600 on SAT critical reading, 81% scored over 600 on SAT math, 83% scored over 600 on SAT writing, 82% scored over 1800 on combined SAT.

Student Life Upper grades have student council, honor system. Discipline rests equally with students and faculty.

Tuition and Aid Day student tuition: $44,260; 7-day tuition and room/board: $55,550. Tuition installment plan (The Tuition Plan, Insured Tuition Payment Plan, Key Tuition Payment Plan, monthly payment plans). Need-based scholarship grants available. In 2015–16, 35% of upper-school students received aid. Total amount of financial aid awarded in 2015–16: $3,200,000.

Admissions Traditional secondary-level entrance grade is 9. For fall 2015, 700 students applied for upper-level admission, 110 were accepted, 61 enrolled. ISEE, PSAT and SAT for applicants to grade 11 and 12, SSAT, ERB, PSAT, SAT, PLAN or ACT or TOEFL required. Deadline for receipt of application materials: January 15. Application fee required: $85. On-campus interview required.

Athletics Interscholastic: aquatics (boys, girls), baseball (b), basketball (b,g), cross-country running (b,g), football (b), lacrosse (b,g), running (b,g), soccer (b,g), softball (g), squash (b,g), tennis (b,g), track and field (b,g), volleyball (b,g), water polo (b,g); intramural: flag football (g), independent competitive sports (b,g); coed interscholastic: aquatics, cross-country running, golf, swimming and diving; coed intramural: aerobics, aerobics/dance, backpacking, ballet, bicycling, canoeing/kayaking, climbing, dance, dance team, fitness, Frisbee, hiking/backpacking, independent competitive sports, indoor soccer, kayaking, martial arts, modern dance, mountain biking, ocean paddling, outdoor activities, outdoor education, outdoor recreation, outdoor skills, outdoors, physical fitness, physical training, rock climbing, ropes courses, scuba diving, surfing, ultimate Frisbee, wall climbing, yoga. 3 coaches, 1 athletic trainer.

Computers Computers are regularly used in English, history, humanities, literary magazine, mathematics, media arts, media production, multimedia, music, newspaper, photography, science, yearbook classes. Computer network features include on-campus library services, online commercial services, Internet access, wireless campus network, Internet filtering or blocking technology. Campus intranet, student e-mail accounts, and computer access in designated common areas are available to students. Students grades are available online. The school has a published electronic and media policy.

Contact Charlotte Brownlee, Director of Admission. 805-684-8409 Ext. 216. Fax: 805-684-2279. E-mail: charlotte_brownlee@cate.org. Website: www.cate.org

CATHEDRAL HIGH SCHOOL

74 Union Park Street
Boston, Massachusetts 02118

Head of School: Dr. Oscar Santos

General Information Coeducational day college-preparatory school, affiliated with Roman Catholic Church. Grades 7–12. Founded: 1926. Setting: urban. 2 buildings on campus. Approved or accredited by New England Association of Schools and Colleges and Massachusetts Department of Education. Total enrollment: 325. Upper school average class size: 18. Upper school faculty-student ratio: 1:18. There are 180 required school days per year for Upper School students. Upper School students typically attend 5 days per week. The average school day consists of 7 hours.

Upper School Student Profile 40% of students are Roman Catholic.

Faculty School total: 23. In upper school: 12 men, 11 women; 13 have advanced degrees.

College Admission Counseling 46 students graduated in 2015; all went to college.

Student Life Upper grades have uniform requirement, student council. Discipline rests primarily with faculty. Attendance at religious services is required.

Summer Programs Enrichment programs offered; session focuses on Mathematics; held on campus; accepts boys and girls; not open to students from other schools. 100 students usually enrolled. 2016 schedule: August 1 to August 21.

Tuition and Aid Tuition installment plan (FACTS Tuition Payment Plan). Need-based scholarship grants available.

Admissions Traditional secondary-level entrance grade is 9. Archdiocese of Boston High School entrance exam provided by STS required. Deadline for receipt of application materials: none. No application fee required. Interview required.

Athletics Interscholastic: baseball (boys), basketball (b,g), cheering (g), football (b), physical fitness (b,g), softball (g), volleyball (g); coed interscholastic: soccer, track and field. 1 PE instructor.

Computers Computer resources include Internet access, wireless campus network, Internet filtering or blocking technology. Campus intranet and student e-mail accounts are available to students. Students grades are available online. The school has a published electronic and media policy.

Contact 617-542-2325. Fax: 617-542-1745. Website: www.cathedralhighschool.net/

CATHEDRAL HIGH SCHOOL

350 East 56th Street
New York, New York 10022-4199

Head of School: Ms. Maria Spagnuolo

General Information Girls' day college-preparatory, arts, business, religious studies, and technology school, affiliated with Roman Catholic Church. Grades 9–12. Founded: 1905. Setting: urban. 1 building on campus. Approved or accredited by Middle States Association of Colleges and Schools, National Catholic Education Association, New York Department of Education, New York State Board of Regents, The College Board, and New York Department of Education. Total enrollment: 660. Upper school average class size: 30. Upper school faculty-student ratio: 1:17. There are 180 required school days per year for Upper School students. Upper School students typically attend 5 days per week. The average school day consists of 7 hours.

Upper School Student Profile Grade 9: 160 students (160 girls); Grade 10: 180 students (180 girls); Grade 11: 150 students (150 girls); Grade 12: 170 students (170 girls). 75% of students are Roman Catholic.

Faculty School total: 48.

Subjects Offered Advanced Placement courses, algebra, American sign language, art, band, biology, biology-AP, broadcasting, business law, business skills, business studies, calculus, calculus-AP, campus ministry, career education internship, career exploration, Catholic belief and practice, chemistry, choir, chorus, Christian doctrine, college admission preparation, college counseling, computer education, computer graphics, computers, constitutional history of U.S., crafts, drama, earth science, economics, electives, English composition, English literature, English-AP, English/composition-AP, fashion, fitness, foreign language, general math, geometry, government, guidance, health, health education, honors algebra, honors English, honors geometry, honors U.S. history, honors world history, HTML design, integrated mathematics, internship, journalism, lab science, Latin, law and the legal system, literature, Mandarin, mathematics-AP, photography, physics, physics-AP, physiology, portfolio art, pre-algebra, pre-calculus, psychology, psychology-AP, religion, robotics, science, science and technology, social education, sociology, Spanish literature, Spanish-AP, statistics-AP, studio art, U.S. government, U.S. government and politics-AP, U.S. history, U.S. history-AP, Web site design, women's studies, world history, world history-AP, world wide web design, writing workshop.

Graduation Requirements Art, electives, English, foreign language, health, mathematics, music, physical education (includes health), religion (includes Bible studies and theology), science, social studies (includes history), New York State Regents.

Special Academic Programs 10 Advanced Placement exams for which test preparation is offered; honors section; study at local college for college credit.

College Admission Counseling 120 students graduated in 2015; all went to college, including Barnard College; College of the Holy Cross; Columbia University; Cornell University; New York University; University of Pennsylvania.

Student Life Upper grades have uniform requirement, student council, honor system. Discipline rests primarily with faculty. Attendance at religious services is required.

Summer Programs Remediation, sports programs offered; held on campus; accepts boys and girls; open to students from other schools. 2016 schedule: July to August.

Tuition and Aid Day student tuition: $7900. Tuition installment plan (FACTS Tuition Payment Plan). Tuition reduction for siblings, merit scholarship grants, need-based scholarship grants available.

Admissions Traditional secondary-level entrance grade is 9. Admissions testing and Catholic High School Entrance Examination required. Deadline for receipt of application materials: none. No application fee required. Interview recommended.

Athletics Interscholastic: basketball, cheering, cross-country running, indoor track, lacrosse, soccer, softball, track and field, volleyball; intramural: basketball, fitness, swimming and diving. 1 PE instructor, 7 coaches.

Computers Computers are regularly used in all academic classes. Computer network features include on-campus library services, Internet access, wireless campus network, Internet filtering or blocking technology. Campus intranet, student e-mail accounts, and computer access in designated common areas are available to students. Students grades are available online.

Contact Mrs. Johanna Velez, Director of Admissions. 212-688-1545 Ext. 224. Fax: 212-754-2024. E-mail: jcastex@cathedralhs.org. Website: www.cathedralhs.org

CATHOLIC CENTRAL HIGH SCHOOL

27225 Wixom Road

Novi, Michigan 48374

Head of School: Fr. Dennis Noelke, CSB

General Information Boys' day college-preparatory, arts, business, vocational, religious studies, and technology school, affiliated with Roman Catholic Church. Grades 9–12. Founded: 1928. Setting: suburban. Nearest major city is Detroit. 113-acre campus. 1 building on campus. Approved or accredited by North Central Association of Colleges and Schools and Michigan Department of Education. Endowment: $3 million. Total enrollment: 1,070. Upper school average class size: 25. Upper school faculty-student ratio: 1:17. Upper School students typically attend 5 days per week. The average school day consists of 6 hours and 45 minutes.

Upper School Student Profile Grade 9: 280 students (280 boys); Grade 10: 273 students (273 boys); Grade 11: 247 students (247 boys); Grade 12: 270 students (270 boys). 81% of students are Roman Catholic.

Faculty School total: 68. In upper school: 35 men, 24 women; 59 have advanced degrees.

Subjects Offered Advanced biology, advanced chemistry, advanced computer applications, advanced math, Advanced Placement courses, algebra, American Civil War, American government, American history, American history-AP, anatomy and physiology, art, art history, biology, biology-AP, Catholic belief and practice, chemistry, chemistry-AP, Chinese, church history, Civil War, civil war history, computer science-AP, drawing, English, environmental science, European history-AP, French, geometry, health, history, journalism, keyboarding, Latin, mathematics, microeconomics, painting, physics, pre-calculus, psychology, science, sculpture, social justice, sociology, Spanish, Spanish-AP, theology, trigonometry, U.S. government and politics-AP, U.S. history, Web site design, world history.

Special Academic Programs 14 Advanced Placement exams for which test preparation is offered; honors section.

College Admission Counseling 264 students graduated in 2015; 262 went to college, including Central Michigan University; Michigan State University; Oakland University; University of Detroit Mercy; University of Michigan; University of Notre Dame. Other: 1 went to work, 1 entered military service. Mean SAT critical reading: 668, mean SAT math: 681, mean SAT writing: 636, mean composite ACT: 26.

Student Life Upper grades have specified standards of dress, student council, honor system. Discipline rests equally with students and faculty. Attendance at religious services is required.

Tuition and Aid Day student tuition: $11,200. Tuition installment plan (monthly payment plans, individually arranged payment plans). Tuition reduction for siblings, merit scholarship grants, need-based scholarship grants available. In 2015–16, 30% of upper-school students received aid; total upper-school merit-scholarship money awarded: $50,000. Total amount of financial aid awarded in 2015–16: $1,100,000.

Admissions Traditional secondary-level entrance grade is 9. For fall 2015, 533 students applied for upper-level admission, 458 were accepted, 281 enrolled. STS required. Deadline for receipt of application materials: March 22. No application fee required. Interview recommended.

Athletics Interscholastic: alpine skiing, baseball, basketball, bowling, cross-country running, diving, ice hockey, lacrosse, physical fitness, physical training, skiing (downhill), soccer, swimming and diving, tennis, track and field, wrestling; intramural: basketball, cross-country running, flag football, ice hockey, touch football. 3 PE instructors, 54 coaches, 1 athletic trainer.

Computers Computer network features include on-campus library services, Internet access. The school has a published electronic and media policy.

Contact Mr. Jake Marmul, Director of Admissions. 248-596-3874. Fax: 248-596-3839. E-mail: jmarmul@catholiccentral.net. Website: www.catholiccentral.net

CATHOLIC CENTRAL HIGH SCHOOL

625 Seventh Avenue

Troy, New York 12182-2595

Head of School: Mr. Christopher Bott

General Information Coeducational day college-preparatory, arts, business, and religious studies school, affiliated with Roman Catholic Church. Grades 7–12. Founded: 1924. Setting: suburban. 4-acre campus. 2 buildings on campus. Approved or accredited by National Catholic Education Association and New York State Board of Regents. Endowment: $50,000. Total enrollment: 379. Upper school average class size: 16. Upper school faculty-student ratio: 1:14. There are 168 required school days per year for Upper School students. Upper School students typically attend 5 days per week. The average school day consists of 6 hours and 40 minutes.

Upper School Student Profile Grade 7: 36 students (15 boys, 21 girls); Grade 8: 32 students (13 boys, 19 girls); Grade 9: 80 students (32 boys, 48 girls); Grade 10: 81 students (32 boys, 49 girls); Grade 11: 83 students (30 boys, 53 girls); Grade 12: 81 students (33 boys, 48 girls). 85% of students are Roman Catholic.

Faculty School total: 36. In upper school: 15 men, 21 women; 24 have advanced degrees.

Subjects Offered Accounting, algebra, anatomy and physiology, art, band, biology, business communications, business law, calculus, Catholic belief and practice, chemistry, chorus, computer art, computer programming, computer science, drama, drawing and design, driver education, earth science, economics, English, English language-AP, global studies, government, health, history, honors English, honors U.S. history, Internet, library skills, mathematics, physics, pre-calculus, religion, social studies, Spanish, technology, U.S. history.

Graduation Requirements Art, English, mathematics, physical education (includes health), science, social studies (includes history), theology.

Special Academic Programs Advanced Placement exam preparation; remedial reading and/or remedial writing; remedial math; ESL (12 students enrolled).

College Admission Counseling 85 students graduated in 2015; 84 went to college, including Binghamton University, State University of New York; Le Moyne College; Siena College; State University of New York at New Paltz; State University of New York College at Geneseo; University at Albany, State University of New York. Other: 1 went to work.

Student Life Upper grades have uniform requirement, student council. Discipline rests primarily with faculty. Attendance at religious services is required.

Tuition and Aid Day student tuition: $6800. Tuition installment plan (FACTS Tuition Payment Plan). Need-based scholarship grants, paying campus jobs available. In 2015–16, 26% of upper-school students received aid. Total amount of financial aid awarded in 2015–16: $240,000.

Admissions Traditional secondary-level entrance grade is 9. Scholastic Testing Service High School Placement Test required. Deadline for receipt of application materials: none. Application fee required: $100. Interview recommended.

Athletics Interscholastic: baseball (boys), basketball (b,g), bowling (b,g), cross-country running (b,g), dance squad (g), football (b), golf (b), indoor track & field (b,g), lacrosse (g), soccer (b,g), softball (g), tennis (b,g), track and field (b,g), volleyball (g); intramural: figure skating (g); coed interscholastic: cheering; coed intramural: Frisbee. 2 PE instructors, 8 coaches, 1 athletic trainer.

Computers Computers are regularly used in accounting, art, business applications, graphic design, programming classes. Computer network features include on-campus library services, Internet access, Internet filtering or blocking technology. Computer access in designated common areas is available to students. Students grades are available online.

Contact Mrs. Teresa Mainello, Publicity Director. 518-235-7100 Ext. 224. Fax: 518-237-1796. E-mail: tmainello@cchstroy.org. Website: www.cchstroy.org

CATHOLIC CENTRAL HIGH SCHOOL

148 McHenry Street

Burlington, Wisconsin 53105

Head of School: Mr. David Wieters

General Information Coeducational day college-preparatory, arts, business, religious studies, and technology school, affiliated with Roman Catholic Church; primarily serves students with learning disabilities and individuals with Attention Deficit Disorder. Grades 9–12. Founded: 1924. Setting: small town. Nearest major city is Milwaukee. 25-acre campus. 2 buildings on campus. Approved or accredited by Academy of Orton-Gillingham Practitioners and Educators, National Catholic Education Association, North Central Association of Colleges and Schools, and Wisconsin Department of Education. Endowment: $1.5 million. Total enrollment: 185. Upper school average class size: 12. Upper school faculty-student ratio: 1:11. There are 180 required school days per year for Upper School students. Upper School students typically attend 5 days per week. The average school day consists of 6 hours and 45 minutes.

Upper School Student Profile Grade 9: 35 students (16 boys, 19 girls); Grade 10: 33 students (18 boys, 15 girls); Grade 11: 42 students (21 boys, 21 girls); Grade 12: 52 students (23 boys, 29 girls). 86% of students are Roman Catholic.

Faculty School total: 24. In upper school: 8 men, 16 women; 11 have advanced degrees.

Subjects Offered 20th century history, 3-dimensional art, 3-dimensional design, accounting, advanced biology, advanced chemistry, advanced computer applications, advanced math, Advanced Placement courses, African-American history, algebra, American government, American history, American literature, American literature-AP, analytic geometry, anatomy, anatomy and physiology, animation, Arabic, art, band, Bible, Bible studies, biology, biology-AP, biotechnology, botany, business, business education, business technology, calculus, calculus-AP, cartooning/animation, Catholic belief and practice, ceramics, chemistry, Chinese, choir, church history, college admission preparation, college planning, composition, composition-AP, computer animation, computer graphics, computer skills, consumer education, digital photography, diversity studies, drawing, earth science, economics, English, English literature-AP, environmental science, finance, forensics, French, geography, geometry, government, health, history of religion, history of the Catholic Church, human anatomy, human biology, integrated science, intro to computers, Italian, journalism, language-AP, marketing, mathematics-AP, music theory, New Testament, painting, personal finance, personal fitness, photography, physical fitness, physics, physiology, pre-calculus, probability and statistics, psychology, psychology-AP, religion, religious studies, skills for success, social justice, sociology, Spanish, speech, statistics, study skills, theology, trigonometry, U.S. history, video and animation, world religions, zoology.

Graduation Requirements 20th century history, American government, American history, health, personal finance, physical education (includes health), religious education, speech, community service hours required.

Special Academic Programs 3 Advanced Placement exams for which test preparation is offered; honors section; independent study; study at local college for college credit; academic accommodation for the gifted and the artistically talented.

College Admission Counseling 42 students graduated in 2015; all went to college, including University of Wisconsin–Eau Claire; University of Wisconsin–Green Bay; University of Wisconsin–Madison; University of Wisconsin–Oshkosh; University of Wisconsin–Stevens Point; University of Wisconsin–Whitewater. Median composite ACT: 22. 7% scored over 26 on composite ACT.

Student Life Upper grades have specified standards of dress, student council, honor system. Discipline rests primarily with faculty. Attendance at religious services is required.

Summer Programs Sports programs offered; session focuses on basketball, football; held on campus; accepts boys and girls; open to students from other schools. 150 students usually enrolled. 2016 schedule: June 15 to July 31. Application deadline: June 15.

Tuition and Aid Day student tuition: $7750–$12,000. Tuition installment plan (FACTS Tuition Payment Plan, individually arranged payment plans). Tuition reduction for siblings, need-based scholarship grants available. In 2015–16, 40% of upper-school students received aid. Total amount of financial aid awarded in 2015–16: $140,000.

Admissions For fall 2015, 168 students applied for upper-level admission, 163 were accepted, 162 enrolled. ACT-Explore required. Deadline for receipt of application materials: none. Application fee required: $100. On-campus interview required.

Athletics Interscholastic: baseball (boys), basketball (b,g), dance team (g), football (b), golf (b), softball (g), tennis (g), volleyball (g), wrestling (b); coed interscholastic: cheering, cross-country running, fishing, fitness, gymnastics, swimming and diving, track and field; coed intramural: bicycling, bowling, dance, dance squad, physical fitness, physical training, strength & conditioning, table tennis, ultimate Frisbee, weight training. 1 PE instructor, 31 coaches, 1 athletic trainer.

Computers Computers are regularly used in accounting, business, economics, graphic design, journalism, multimedia, newspaper, photography, typing, video film production, Web site design, writing classes. Computer network features include Internet access, wireless campus network, Internet filtering or blocking technology. Student e-mail accounts and computer access in designated common areas are available to students. Students grades are available online. The school has a published electronic and media policy.

Contact Mrs. Karen Schwenn, Admissions Director. 262-763-1510 Ext. 225. Fax: 262-763-1509. E-mail: kschwenn@cchsnet.org. Website: www.cchsnet.org

THE CATLIN GABEL SCHOOL

8825 SW Barnes Road
Portland, Oregon 97225

Head of School: Mr. Tim Bazemore

General Information Coeducational day college-preparatory, arts, technology, and sciences school. Grades PK–12. Founded: 1957. Setting: suburban. 63-acre campus. 13 buildings on campus. Approved or accredited by Northwest Accreditation Commission and Northwest Association of Independent Schools. Member of National Association of Independent Schools and Secondary School Admission Test Board. Endowment: $30 million. Total enrollment: 759. Upper school average class size: 15. Upper school faculty-student ratio: 1:7. There are 170 required school days per year for Upper School students. Upper School students typically attend 5 days per week. The average school day consists of 7 hours and 15 minutes.

Upper School Student Profile Grade 9: 77 students (35 boys, 42 girls); Grade 10: 78 students (46 boys, 32 girls); Grade 11: 79 students (41 boys, 38 girls); Grade 12: 77 students (40 boys, 37 girls).

Faculty School total: 97. In upper school: 26 men, 27 women; 38 have advanced degrees.

Subjects Offered 20th century history, 20th century world history, 3-dimensional art, advanced biology, algebra, American democracy, American foreign policy, American government, American history, American literature, American studies, analysis and differential calculus, analytic geometry, anatomy and physiology, ancient world history, art, art and culture, art appreciation, art history, astronomy, athletics, audio visual/media, audition methods, basketball, bioethics, biology, calculus, career/college preparation, ceramics, chemistry, chorus, civil rights, Civil War, civil war history, classics, college writing, communication skills, community service, composition, computer programming, computer science, computer skills, contemporary history, creative arts, creative writing, critical thinking, critical writing, cultural geography, current events, debate, desktop publishing, digital photography, drama, drawing and design, ecology, economics, engineering, English, English composition, English literature, environmental science, equality and freedom, ethics and responsibility, European history, expository writing, fiction, film and literature, film history, film studies, fine arts, fitness, food and nutrition, foreign language, foreign policy, French, French as a second language, French studies, geometry, global studies, government, government/civics, graphic design, health, history, honors algebra, honors geometry, human biology, humanities, independent study, inorganic chemistry, instrumental music, interdisciplinary studies, international relations, jazz band, language and composition, leadership, life science, linear algebra, literary magazine, literature, literature seminar, logic, marketing, math applications, mathematics, mechanics, media studies, microbiology, minority studies, model United Nations, modern European history, modern Western civilization, music, musical theater, neurobiology, neuroscience, news writing, non-Western societies, organic chemistry, outdoor education, painting, performing arts, photography, photojournalism, physical education, physical science, physics, physiology, play/screen writing, poetry, political science, portfolio art, pre-calculus, probability and statistics, psychology, public policy, public speaking, publishing, research skills, science, science fiction, Shakespeare, social studies, socioeconomic problems, software design, Spanish, speech and debate, statistics, student government, student publications, swimming, theater arts, trigonometry, U.S. constitutional history, U.S. government, U.S. government and politics, U.S. history, U.S. literature, video and animation, video film production, visual and performing arts, visual arts, Western civilization, world affairs, world history, world literature, writing.

Graduation Requirements Arts, biology, chemistry, English, foreign language, health, history, mathematics, physical education (includes health), physics, senior project, U.S. history.

Special Academic Programs Honors section; independent study; study abroad; academic accommodation for the gifted.

College Admission Counseling 77 students graduated in 2015; 74 went to college, including Northeastern University; Occidental College; Stanford University; University of Oregon; Whitman College; Worcester Polytechnic Institute. Other: 3 had other specific plans. Median SAT critical reading: 680, median SAT math: 660, median SAT writing: 660, median combined SAT: 1985, median composite ACT: 30. 100% scored over 600 on SAT critical reading, 100% scored over 600 on SAT math, 100% scored over 600 on SAT writing, 100% scored over 1800 on combined SAT, 100% scored over 26 on composite ACT.

Student Life Upper grades have specified standards of dress, student council, honor system. Discipline rests equally with students and faculty.

Summer Programs Enrichment, art/fine arts, computer instruction programs offered; session focuses on academic enrichment and offerings to experience the 63-acre campus for kids ages 4-18; held both on and off campus; held at various outdoor areas—hiking, climbing, biking, etc; accepts boys and girls; open to students from other schools. 500 students usually enrolled. 2016 schedule: June 22 to July 31.

Tuition and Aid Day student tuition: $21,050–$28,250. Tuition installment plan (Insured Tuition Payment Plan, monthly payment plans, individually arranged payment plans). Merit scholarship grants, need-based scholarship grants available. In 2015–16, 28% of upper-school students received aid. Total amount of financial aid awarded in 2015–16: $18,119.

Admissions Traditional secondary-level entrance grade is 9. SSAT required. Deadline for receipt of application materials: January 19. Application fee required: $75. Interview required.

Athletics Interscholastic: aquatics (boys, girls), baseball (b,g), basketball (b,g), cross-country running (b,g), golf (b,g), racquetball (b,g), skiing (downhill) (b,g), soccer (b,g), swimming and diving (b,g), tennis (b,g), track and field (b,g), volleyball (g); coed interscholastic: racquetball; coed intramural: aerobics/dance, alpine skiing, backpacking, bicycling, bowling, canoeing/kayaking, climbing, dance team, fishing, fitness, Frisbee, hiking/backpacking, jogging, kayaking, mountain biking, mountaineering, nordic skiing, ocean paddling, outdoor activities, outdoor adventure, outdoor education, outdoor recreation, outdoors, physical fitness, physical training, rafting, rock climbing, ropes courses, running, skiing (cross-country), skiing (downhill), snowshoeing, strength & conditioning, telemark skiing, ultimate Frisbee, walking, wall climbing, weight lifting, weight training, wilderness, wilderness survival, yoga. 6 PE instructors, 20 coaches.

Computers Computers are regularly used in all classes. Computer network features include on-campus library services, online commercial services, Internet access, wireless campus network, all students attending the Upper School have laptops, video conferencing capabilities are available on campus, SmartBoards or projectors are installed in most classrooms. Campus intranet, student e-mail accounts, and computer access in designated common areas are available to students. The school has a published electronic and media policy.

Contact Ms. Sara Nordhoff, Director of Admission and Financial Aid. 503-297-1894 Ext. 345. Fax: 503-297-0139. E-mail: nordhoffs@catlin.edu. Website: www.catlin.edu

CCI THE RENAISSANCE SCHOOL

Via Cavour 13
Lanciano 66034, Italy

Head of School: Marisa Di Carlo D'Alessandro

General Information Coeducational boarding and day college-preparatory, arts, and science school. Grades 9–12. Founded: 1995. Setting: small town. Nearest major city is Rome, Italy. Students are housed in single-sex residences. 5 buildings on campus. Approved or accredited by Ontario Ministry of Education and state department of education. Member of European Council of International Schools. Language of instruction: English. Total enrollment: 70. Upper school average class size: 16. Upper school faculty-student ratio: 1:7.

Upper School Student Profile 99% of students are boarding students. 99% are international students. International students from Canada, Mexico, Russian Federation, and United States; 4 other countries represented in student body.

Faculty School total: 12. In upper school: 7 men, 5 women; 8 have advanced degrees; 10 reside on campus.

Subjects Offered Algebra, anthropology, art, biology, calculus, Canadian history, career exploration, chemistry, civics, classical civilization, community service, computers, creative writing, data analysis, drama, economics, English, English literature, environmental science, expository writing, finite math, geometry, government/civics, history, information technology, Italian, literature, mathematics, physics, politics, psychology, science, social studies, sociology, trigonometry, world history, world issues, world literature, writing.

Graduation Requirements English, foreign language, mathematics, physical education (includes health), science, social studies (includes history). Community service is required.

Special Academic Programs Study abroad.

College Admission Counseling 30 students graduated in 2015; all went to college, including Acadia University; Dalhousie University; McGill University; Queen's University at Kingston; The University of Western Ontario; University of Toronto.

Student Life Upper grades have uniform requirement, student council, honor system. Discipline rests equally with students and faculty.

Summer Programs Art/fine arts programs offered; session focuses on credit courses in social sciences, Italian, and art; held on campus; accepts boys and girls; open to students from other schools. 70 students usually enrolled. 2016 schedule: July 2 to July 31. Application deadline: April 1.

Tuition and Aid 7-day tuition and room/board: €33,000. Tuition installment plan (monthly payment plans, individually arranged payment plans). Bursaries, need-based scholarship grants available. In 2015–16, 5% of upper-school students received aid. Total amount of financial aid awarded in 2015–16: €30,000.

Admissions Achievement/Aptitude/Writing required. Deadline for receipt of application materials: none. Application fee required: $100. Interview recommended.

Athletics Intramural: dance (girls), modern dance (g); coed intramural: aerobics, aerobics/dance, alpine skiing, aquatics, ball hockey, basketball, bicycling, climbing, cross-country running, equestrian sports, fitness, fitness walking, flag football, hiking/backpacking, horseback riding, jogging, mountain biking, outdoor activities, outdoor recreation, physical fitness, running, skiing (downhill), snowboarding, soccer, softball, swimming and diving, tennis, touch football, walking, weight training, yoga. 3 coaches.

Computers Computers are regularly used in yearbook classes. Computer resources include on-campus library services, online commercial services, Internet access. Computer access in designated common areas is available to students. Students grades are available online. The school has a published electronic and media policy.

Contact Jocelyn Manchee, Admissions Officer. 905-508-7108. Fax: 905-508-5480. E-mail: cciren@rogers.com. Website: www.ccilanciano.com

CENTRAL ALBERTA CHRISTIAN HIGH SCHOOL

22 Eagle Road
Lacombe, Alberta T4L 1G7, Canada

Head of School: Mr. Mel Brandsma

General Information Coeducational day college-preparatory, general academic, religious studies, and bilingual studies school, affiliated with Christian Reformed Church. Grades 10–12. Founded: 1989. Setting: rural. Nearest major city is Red Deer, Canada. 12-acre campus. 1 building on campus. Approved or accredited by Association of Independent Schools and Colleges of Alberta, Christian Schools International, and Alberta Department of Education. Language of instruction: English. Total enrollment: 97. Upper school average class size: 97. Upper school faculty-student ratio: 1:13. There are 181 required school days per year for Upper School students. Upper School students typically attend 5 days per week. The average school day consists of 6 hours and 25 minutes.

Upper School Student Profile Grade 10: 34 students (20 boys, 14 girls); Grade 11: 30 students (20 boys, 10 girls); Grade 12: 33 students (17 boys, 16 girls). 75% of students are members of Christian Reformed Church.

Faculty School total: 8. In upper school: 5 men, 3 women; 2 have advanced degrees.

Subjects Offered Accounting, agriculture, art, career education, Christian ethics, computer education, drafting, foods, French as a second language, photography, physical education, work experience.

Graduation Requirements All academic, French.

College Admission Counseling 32 students graduated in 2015; they went to Nicholls State University.

Student Life Upper grades have student council, honor system. Discipline rests primarily with faculty. Attendance at religious services is required.

Tuition and Aid Day student tuition: CAN$5850. Tuition installment plan (monthly payment plans, individually arranged payment plans). Tuition reduction for siblings available.

Admissions Traditional secondary-level entrance grade is 10. Deadline for receipt of application materials: none. No application fee required. Interview recommended.

Athletics Coed Interscholastic: badminton, basketball, bowling, climbing, cross-country running, fitness, golf, ice skating, jogging, outdoor activities, physical fitness, physical training, running, soccer, softball, swimming and diving, track and field, volleyball, wall climbing, weight training, whiffle ball; coed intramural: basketball, broomball, cooperative games, hiking/backpacking, outdoor adventure, outdoor education, outdoor recreation. 1 PE instructor, 1 coach.

Computers Computers are regularly used in all classes. Computer network features include Internet access, wireless campus network, Internet filtering or blocking technology. Campus intranet is available to students.

Contact Office. 403-782-4535. Fax: 403-782-5425. E-mail: office@cachs.ca. Website: www.cachs.ca/

CENTRAL CATHOLIC HIGH SCHOOL

200 South Carpenter Road
Modesto, California 95351

Head of School: Jim Pecchenino

General Information Coeducational day college-preparatory, arts, religious studies, and bilingual studies school, affiliated with Roman Catholic Church. Grades 9–12. Founded: 1966. Setting: urban. Nearest major city is Sacramento. 21-acre campus. 13 buildings on campus. Approved or accredited by National Catholic Education Association, Western Association of Schools and Colleges, and Western Catholic Education Association. Endowment: $2.2 million. Total enrollment: 372. Upper school average class size: 22. Upper school faculty-student ratio: 1:16. There are 180 required school days per year for Upper School students. Upper School students typically attend 5 days per week. The average school day consists of 6 hours and 50 minutes.

Upper School Student Profile Grade 9: 98 students (53 boys, 45 girls); Grade 10: 95 students (43 boys, 52 girls); Grade 11: 92 students (50 boys, 42 girls); Grade 12: 87 students (58 boys, 29 girls). 82% of students are Roman Catholic.

Faculty School total: 28. In upper school: 5 men, 23 women; 15 have advanced degrees.

Subjects Offered Agriculture, algebra, American history, American literature, animal science, art, Bible studies, biology, broadcast journalism, calculus, chemistry, dance, drama, drawing and design, economics, English, English literature, environmental science, ethics, European history, geometry, government/civics, health, mathematics, music, physical education, physical science, physics, pre-calculus, Spanish, speech, theology, vocal ensemble, world history, world literature, yearbook.

Graduation Requirements Arts and fine arts (art, music, dance, drama), English, geography, mathematics, physical education (includes health), religion (includes Bible studies and theology), science, social studies (includes history), speech, 100 Christian service hours.

Special Academic Programs Advanced Placement exam preparation; honors section; study at local college for college credit; remedial reading and/or remedial writing; remedial math; programs in English, mathematics, general development for dyslexic students.

College Admission Counseling 87 students graduated in 2015; 85 went to college, including California Polytechnic State University, San Luis Obispo; California State University, Chico; California State University, Fresno; California State University, Stanislaus; University of California, Berkeley. Other: 2 entered military service. Median SAT critical reading: 510, median SAT math: 500, median SAT writing: 520, median combined SAT: 1530. 14% scored over 600 on SAT critical reading, 23% scored over 600 on SAT math, 19% scored over 600 on SAT writing, 17% scored over 1800 on combined SAT.

Student Life Upper grades have specified standards of dress, student council. Discipline rests primarily with faculty. Attendance at religious services is required.

Summer Programs Remediation programs offered; session focuses on remediation and SAT prep; held on campus; accepts boys and girls; open to students from other schools. 100 students usually enrolled. 2016 schedule: June 4 to July 6. Application deadline: May 11.

Tuition and Aid Day student tuition: $9835–$10,290. Tuition installment plan (FACTS Tuition Payment Plan, monthly payment plans, individually arranged payment plans, quarterly and semiannual payment plans). Tuition reduction for siblings, merit scholarship grants, need-based scholarship grants, paying campus jobs available. In 2015–16, 40% of upper-school students received aid; total upper-school merit-scholarship money awarded: $14,250. Total amount of financial aid awarded in 2015–16: $541,705.

Admissions Traditional secondary-level entrance grade is 9. For fall 2015, 125 students applied for upper-level admission, 98 were accepted, 98 enrolled. ETS HSPT (closed), Otis-Lennon School Ability Test or Otis-Lennon School Ability Test, ERB CPT III required. Deadline for receipt of application materials: none. Application fee required: $45. On-campus interview required.

Athletics Interscholastic: baseball (boys), basketball (b,g), cross-country running (b,g), football (b), golf (b,g), soccer (b,g), softball (g), tennis (b,g), track and field (b,g), volleyball (g), water polo (b,g), wrestling (b,g); intramural: cheering (g); coed intramural: dance, yoga. 1 PE instructor, 90 coaches.

Computers Computers are regularly used in graphic arts, literacy, yearbook classes. Computer network features include on-campus library services, Internet access, wireless campus network, Internet filtering or blocking technology. Computer access in designated common areas is available to students. Students grades are available online. The school has a published electronic and media policy.

Contact Jodi Tybor, Admissions Coordinator/Registrar. 209-524-9611 Ext. 113. Fax: 209-524-4913. E-mail: tybor@cchsca.org. Website: www.cchsca.org

CENTRAL CATHOLIC HIGH SCHOOL

300 Hampshire Street
Lawrence, Massachusetts 01841

Head of School: Mrs. Doreen A. Keller

General Information Coeducational day and distance learning college-preparatory, arts, business, religious studies, and technology school, affiliated with Roman Catholic Church. Grades 9–12. Distance learning grades 11–12. Founded: 1935. Setting: urban. Nearest major city is Boston. 11-acre campus. 1 building on campus. Approved or accredited by Commission on Independent Schools, New England Association of Schools and Colleges, and Massachusetts Department of Education. Member of National Association of Independent Schools. Endowment: $11 million. Total enrollment: 1,330. Upper school average class size: 25. Upper school faculty-student ratio: 1:24. There are 168 required school days per year for Upper School students. Upper School students typically attend 5 days per week. The average school day consists of 6 hours and 15 minutes.

Upper School Student Profile Grade 9: 319 students (174 boys, 145 girls); Grade 10: 350 students (176 boys, 174 girls); Grade 11: 318 students (133 boys, 185 girls); Grade 12: 343 students (169 boys, 174 girls). 80% of students are Roman Catholic.

Faculty School total: 87. In upper school: 40 men, 47 women; 60 have advanced degrees.

Subjects Offered Art, arts, computer science, English, fine arts, French, health, mathematics, physical education, religion, science, social studies, Spanish.

Graduation Requirements Arts and fine arts (art, music, dance, drama), computer science, English, foreign language, mathematics, religion (includes Bible studies and theology), science, social studies (includes history).

Special Academic Programs International Baccalaureate program; Advanced Placement exam preparation; honors section; study at local college for college credit.

College Admission Counseling 306 students graduated in 2015; 299 went to college, including Boston University; University of Massachusetts Amherst; University of Massachusetts Lowell; University of New Hampshire. Other: 5 entered a postgraduate year, 2 had other specific plans. Mean SAT critical reading: 536, mean SAT math: 558, mean SAT writing: 537, mean combined SAT: 1631, mean composite ACT: 23. 21% scored over 600 on SAT critical reading, 37% scored over 600 on SAT math, 28% scored over 600 on SAT writing, 34% scored over 26 on composite ACT.

Student Life Upper grades have uniform requirement, student council, honor system. Discipline rests primarily with faculty. Attendance at religious services is required.

Summer Programs Remediation, enrichment, advancement, art/fine arts, computer instruction programs offered; session focuses on remediation/advancement; held on campus; accepts boys and girls; open to students from other schools. 300 students usually enrolled. 2016 schedule: June 27 to August 2.

Tuition and Aid Day student tuition: $12,690. Tuition installment plan (monthly payment plans). Merit scholarship grants, need-based scholarship grants available. In 2015–16, 28% of upper-school students received aid; total upper-school merit-scholarship money awarded: $105,115. Total amount of financial aid awarded in 2015–16: $1,689,766.

Admissions Traditional secondary-level entrance grade is 9. For fall 2015, 646 students applied for upper-level admission, 613 were accepted, 317 enrolled. Archdiocese of Boston High School entrance exam provided by STS, High School Placement Test and High School Placement Test (closed version) from Scholastic Testing Service required. Deadline for receipt of application materials: none. No application fee required. Interview required.

Athletics Interscholastic: baseball (boys), basketball (b,g), bowling (b,g), cheering (g), cross-country running (b,g), dance squad (b,g), diving (b,g), field hockey (g), figure skating (g), fishing (b,g), football (b), golf (b), gymnastics (g), hockey (b), ice hockey (b), ice skating (g), indoor hockey (g), indoor track (b,g), indoor track & field (b,g), lacrosse (b,g), martial arts (b,g), modern dance (b,g), soccer (b,g), softball (g), swimming and diving (b,g), tennis (b,g), track and field (b,g), volleyball (b,g), wall

climbing (b,g), winter (indoor) track (b,g), wrestling (b); intramural: basketball (b,g); coed interscholastic: dance team. 2 PE instructors, 80 coaches, 1 athletic trainer.

Computers Computer network features include on-campus library services, Internet access, wireless campus network, Internet filtering or blocking technology. Campus intranet, student e-mail accounts, and computer access in designated common areas are available to students. The school has a published electronic and media policy.

Contact Ms. Elizabeth Schroth, Assistant Director of Admissions. 978-682-0260 Ext. 626. Fax: 978-685-2707. E-mail: elyons@centralcatholic.net. Website: www.centralcatholic.net

CENTRAL CATHOLIC HIGH SCHOOL

4720 Fifth Avenue
Pittsburgh, Pennsylvania 15213

Head of School: Br. Robert Schaefer, FSC

General Information Boys' day college-preparatory, arts, business, religious studies, and technology school, affiliated with Roman Catholic Church. Grades 9–12. Founded: 1927. Setting: urban. 3 buildings on campus. Approved or accredited by Christian Brothers Association, Middle States Association of Colleges and Schools, National Catholic Education Association, and Pennsylvania Department of Education. Endowment: $10.1 million. Total enrollment: 857. Upper school average class size: 21. Upper school faculty-student ratio: 1:16. There are 180 required school days per year for Upper School students. Upper School students typically attend 5 days per week. The average school day consists of 6 hours and 40 minutes.

Upper School Student Profile Grade 9: 201 students (201 boys); Grade 10: 222 students (222 boys); Grade 11: 229 students (229 boys); Grade 12: 205 students (205 boys). 83% of students are Roman Catholic.

Faculty School total: 68. In upper school: 53 men, 11 women; 49 have advanced degrees.

Subjects Offered 20th century history, 20th century world history, 3-dimensional design, accounting, advanced computer applications, Advanced Placement courses, algebra, American government, American history, American history-AP, American literature, art, athletic training, band, bioethics, DNA and culture, biology, biology-AP, biotechnology, British literature, British literature (honors), business, business mathematics, calculus, calculus-AP, Catholic belief and practice, chemistry, chemistry-AP, chorus, civics, college admission preparation, comparative government and politics, computer programming, computer science, computer-aided design, computers, concert band, concert choir, consumer education, cultural geography, debate, digital applications, economics-AP, electives, English, English language and composition-AP, English-AP, environmental science, European history-AP, film and literature, fitness, foreign language, French, geometry, government, government-AP, health, health education, history, honors algebra, honors English, honors geometry, human geography - AP, instrumental music, introduction to technology, Italian, jazz band, journalism, Latin, Latin-AP, law, math analysis, mathematics, modern world history, music, music theory, physical education, physics, physics-AP, pre-calculus, probability and statistics, programming, psychology, religion, robotics, SAT/ACT preparation, science, senior seminar, social studies, sociology, Spanish, Spanish language-AP, Spanish-AP, speech and debate, statistics-AP, studio art, The 20th Century, theater arts, trigonometry, U.S. government, U.S. government and politics-AP, U.S. history, U.S. history-AP, vocal music, wellness, world history, world literature, writing.

Special Academic Programs 16 Advanced Placement exams for which test preparation is offered; honors section; study at local college for college credit; academic accommodation for the gifted.

College Admission Counseling 209 students graduated in 2015; 203 went to college, including Carnegie Mellon University; Duquesne University; Miami University; Penn State University Park; University of Chicago; University of Pittsburgh. Other: 3 entered military service, 3 had other specific plans. Mean SAT critical reading: 560, mean SAT math: 560, mean SAT writing: 570, mean combined SAT: 1690, mean composite ACT: 24.

Student Life Upper grades have specified standards of dress, student council. Discipline rests primarily with faculty. Attendance at religious services is required.

Tuition and Aid Day student tuition: $10,920. Tuition installment plan (SMART Tuition Payment Plan). Merit scholarship grants, need-based scholarship grants available. In 2015–16, 37% of upper-school students received aid; total upper-school merit-scholarship money awarded: $109,200. Total amount of financial aid awarded in 2015–16: $1,600,000.

Admissions Traditional secondary-level entrance grade is 9. For fall 2015, 320 students applied for upper-level admission, 272 were accepted, 221 enrolled. Scholastic Testing Service High School Placement Test required. Deadline for receipt of application materials: none. No application fee required. Interview recommended.

Athletics Interscholastic: baseball, basketball, bowling, crew, cross-country running, fencing, football, golf, hockey, ice hockey, in-line hockey, indoor track, lacrosse, rowing, rugby, soccer, squash, swimming and diving, tennis, track and field, ultimate Frisbee, volleyball, wrestling; intramural: basketball, flag football, football, Frisbee, touch football. 2 PE instructors, 17 coaches, 2 athletic trainers.

Computers Computers are regularly used in all academic classes. Computer network features include on-campus library services, online commercial services, Internet access, wireless campus network, Internet filtering or blocking technology. Campus intranet, student e-mail accounts, and computer access in designated common areas are

available to students. Students grades are available online. The school has a published electronic and media policy.

Contact Mr. Brian Miller, Director of Admissions. 412-621-7505. Fax: 412-208-0555. E-mail: bmiller@centralcatholichs.com. Website: www.centralcatholichs.com

CENTRAL CATHOLIC HIGH SCHOOL

1403 North St. Mary's Street
San Antonio, Texas 78215-1785

Head of School: Rev. Richard G.T. Wosman, S.M.

General Information Boys' day college-preparatory school, affiliated with Roman Catholic Church. Grades 9–12. Founded: 1852. Setting: urban. 11-acre campus. 3 buildings on campus. Approved or accredited by National Catholic Education Association, Southern Association of Colleges and Schools, Texas Catholic Conference, and Texas Department of Education. Endowment: $6.1 million. Total enrollment: 520. Upper school average class size: 23. Upper school faculty-student ratio: 1:17. There are 180 required school days per year for Upper School students. Upper School students typically attend 5 days per week. The average school day consists of 6 hours and 30 minutes.

Upper School Student Profile Grade 9: 121 students (121 boys); Grade 10: 127 students (127 boys); Grade 11: 131 students (131 boys); Grade 12: 124 students (124 boys). 90% of students are Roman Catholic.

Faculty School total: 43. In upper school: 33 men, 10 women; 35 have advanced degrees.

Subjects Offered Algebra, American government, American history-AP, anatomy, art, biology, calculus-AP, ceramics, chemistry, chemistry-AP, chorus, Christian and Hebrew scripture, church history, community service, computer science, concert band, economics, English, English language and composition-AP, English language-AP, English literature and composition-AP, English literature-AP, environmental science, fine arts, geometry, health, honors algebra, honors English, honors geometry, honors world history, humanities, information technology, jazz band, journalism, JROTC, languages, Latin, marching band, physics, pre-calculus, probability and statistics, psychology, religion, science, social studies, Spanish, Spanish literature-AP, speech, trigonometry, world geography, world history.

Graduation Requirements Algebra, American government, American history, arts and fine arts (art, music, dance, drama), biology, chemistry, Christian and Hebrew scripture, Christian doctrine, computer information systems, computer science, economics, English, foreign language, geometry, health, JROTC, moral reasoning, religion (includes Bible studies and theology), religious education, social justice, speech, trigonometry, world civilizations, world geography, world history, world religions, different requirements for Marianist Honors Diploma. Community service is required.

Special Academic Programs 10 Advanced Placement exams for which test preparation is offered; honors section; study at local college for college credit.

College Admission Counseling 127 students graduated in 2014; 126 went to college, including Saint Mary's University; Texas A&M University; Texas Tech University; The University of Texas at Austin; The University of Texas at San Antonio; University of the Incarnate Word. Other: 1 entered military service. Mean SAT critical reading: 536, mean SAT math: 532, mean SAT writing: 525, mean composite ACT: 25.

Student Life Upper grades have specified standards of dress, student council, honor system. Discipline rests primarily with faculty. Attendance at religious services is required.

Tuition and Aid Day student tuition: $10,500. Tuition installment plan (FACTS Tuition Payment Plan, monthly payment plans, individually arranged payment plans, semester payment plan, Tuition Management Systems). Tuition reduction for siblings, merit scholarship grants, need-based scholarship grants available. In 2014–15, 28% of upper-school students received aid; total upper-school merit-scholarship money awarded: $125,000. Total amount of financial aid awarded in 2014–15: $425,000.

Admissions Traditional secondary-level entrance grade is 9. For fall 2014, 130 students applied for upper-level admission, 126 were accepted, 121 enrolled. Essay, Scholastic Testing Service High School Placement Test and writing sample required. Deadline for receipt of application materials: none. No application fee required. On-campus interview required.

Athletics Interscholastic: baseball, basketball, cheering (g), cross-country running, drill team, football, golf, JROTC drill, lacrosse, physical training, riflery, soccer, swimming and diving; intramural: basketball, bowling, football. 1 PE instructor, 26 coaches, 1 athletic trainer.

Computers Computers are regularly used in college planning, computer applications, drawing and design, engineering, English, foreign language, information technology, journalism, newspaper, NJROTC, religion, science, social studies, Spanish, technology, Web site design, wilderness education, yearbook classes. Computer network features include on-campus library services, Internet access, wireless campus network, Internet filtering or blocking technology, access to other libraries through Texas Library Connection. Student e-mail accounts are available to students. Students grades are available online. The school has a published electronic and media policy.

Contact Mr. Christopher Cantu, Director of Admissions. 210-225-6794 Ext. 227. Fax: 210-227-9353. E-mail: ccantu@cchs-satx.org. Website: www.cchs-satx.org

CENTRAL CATHOLIC MID-HIGH SCHOOL

1200 Ruby Avenue
Grand Island, Nebraska 68803-3799

Head of School: Mr. Steve M. Osborn

General Information Coeducational day college-preparatory and religious studies school, affiliated with Roman Catholic Church. Grades 6–12. Founded: 1956. Setting: suburban. 1 building on campus. Approved or accredited by National Catholic Education Association, North Central Association of Colleges and Schools, The College Board, and Nebraska Department of Education. Total enrollment: 332. Upper school average class size: 17. Upper school faculty-student ratio: 1:12. There are 175 required school days per year for Upper School students. Upper School students typically attend 5 days per week. The average school day consists of 7 hours.

Upper School Student Profile Grade 9: 49 students (22 boys, 27 girls); Grade 10: 48 students (25 boys, 23 girls); Grade 11: 38 students (20 boys, 18 girls); Grade 12: 25 students (11 boys, 14 girls). 98% of students are Roman Catholic.

Faculty School total: 36. In upper school: 8 men, 27 women; 14 have advanced degrees.

Subjects Offered ACT preparation, advanced chemistry, Advanced Placement courses, algebra, American government, American history, American history-AP, art, audio visual/media, basketball, biology, calculus-AP, career education, careers, Catholic belief and practice, cheerleading, chemistry, college writing, commercial art, computer applications, concert band, concert choir, contemporary problems, CPR, desktop publishing, drama, driver education, economics, English, English composition, English/composition-AP, environmental science, general science, golf, government, guidance, health, history, human biology, instrumental music, jazz band, journalism, marching band, music, music theory, newspaper, physical education, physics, pre-algebra, pre-calculus, psychology, public speaking, religious studies, senior seminar, sociology, Spanish, speech, tennis, U.S. government, video film production, vocal music, volleyball, Web site design, weight training, world history, world history-AP, wrestling, yearbook.

Graduation Requirements American government, American history, American literature, biology, composition, computer applications, English, English composition, English literature, English literature and composition-AP, English/composition-AP, geography, government, history, mathematics, physical education (includes health), religion (includes Bible studies and theology), science, senior seminar, world history, world history-AP, community service.

Special Academic Programs 3 Advanced Placement exams for which test preparation is offered; study at local college for college credit.

College Admission Counseling 36 students graduated in 2014; 34 went to college, including University of Nebraska–Lincoln; University of Nebraska at Kearney; University of Nebraska at Omaha. Other: 1 went to work, 1 entered military service. Median composite ACT: 24. 43% scored over 26 on composite ACT.

Student Life Upper grades have uniform requirement, student council. Discipline rests primarily with faculty. Attendance at religious services is required.

Tuition and Aid Tuition installment plan (monthly payment plans). Tuition reduction for siblings, need-based scholarship grants, paying campus jobs available.

Admissions Traditional secondary-level entrance grade is 9. Deadline for receipt of application materials: none. Application fee required: $100. Interview recommended.

Athletics Interscholastic: baseball (boys), basketball (b,g), cheering (g), cross-country running (b,g), dance team (g), football (b), golf (b,g), physical fitness (b,g). 2 PE instructors.

Computers Computers are regularly used in computer applications, desktop publishing, English, journalism, keyboarding, Web site design, writing, yearbook classes. Computer network features include on-campus library services, Internet access, Internet filtering or blocking technology. Computer access in designated common areas is available to students. Students grades are available online. The school has a published electronic and media policy.

Contact Admissions. 308-384-2440. Fax: 308-389-3274. Website: www.gicentralcatholic.org/

CENTRAL CHRISTIAN HIGH SCHOOL

3970 Kidron Road
PO Box 9
Kidron, Ohio 44636

Head of School: Mr. Eugene Miller

General Information Coeducational day college-preparatory, general academic, arts, business, religious studies, and bilingual studies school, affiliated with Mennonite Church; primarily serves students with learning disabilities, individuals with Attention Deficit Disorder, individuals with emotional and behavioral problems, and dyslexic students. Grades K–12. Founded: 1962. Setting: rural. Nearest major city is Wooster. 60-acre campus. 1 building on campus. Approved or accredited by Mennonite Schools Council, Southern Association of Colleges and Schools, and Ohio Department of Education. Endowment: $750,000. Total enrollment: 322. Upper school average class size: 18. Upper school faculty-student ratio: 1:13. There are 180 required school days per year for Upper School students. Upper School students typically attend 5 days per week. The average school day consists of 7 hours.

Upper School Student Profile Grade 9: 28 students (13 boys, 15 girls); Grade 10: 29 students (10 boys, 19 girls); Grade 11: 39 students (16 boys, 23 girls); Grade 12: 39 students (22 boys, 17 girls). 50% of students are Mennonite.

Faculty School total: 31. In upper school: 8 men, 7 women; 6 have advanced degrees.

Subjects Offered Algebra, American government, American history, American literature, anatomy, art, Bible studies, biology, business, business skills, ceramics, chemistry, child development, community service, current events, ecology, English, English literature, environmental science, European history, fine arts, general science, geography, geometry, government/civics, grammar, health, history, home economics, human development, industrial arts, journalism, mathematics, music, photography, physical education, physics, pre-calculus, religion, Romantic period literature, science, sculpture, social sciences, social studies, sociology, Spanish, trigonometry, world history, world literature, writing.

Graduation Requirements Arts and fine arts (art, music, dance, drama), business skills (includes word processing), English, foreign language, mathematics, physical education (includes health), religion (includes Bible studies and theology), science, social sciences, social studies (includes history). Community service is required.

Special Academic Programs International Baccalaureate program; Advanced Placement exam preparation; honors section; independent study; term-away projects; study at local college for college credit; academic accommodation for the gifted and the musically talented; remedial reading and/or remedial writing; remedial math; programs in English, mathematics for dyslexic students; ESL (5 students enrolled).

College Admission Counseling 35 students graduated in 2014; 21 went to college, including Bluffton University; Eastern Mennonite University; Goshen College; Malone University; The University of Akron. Other: 5 went to work, 2 entered military service, 3 had other specific plans. 14% scored over 1800 on combined SAT.

Student Life Upper grades have specified standards of dress, student council, honor system. Discipline rests primarily with faculty.

Tuition and Aid Day student tuition: $4999–$7499. Tuition installment plan (monthly payment plans, individually arranged payment plans). Tuition reduction for siblings, need-based scholarship grants available. In 2014–15, 45% of upper-school students received aid.

Admissions Traditional secondary-level entrance grade is 9. TOEFL or SLEP required. Deadline for receipt of application materials: none. Application fee required: $50. Interview required.

Athletics Interscholastic: archery (girls), baseball (b), basketball (b,g), cross-country running (b,g), golf (b,g), running (b,g), soccer (b,g), softball (g), tennis (b,g), volleyball (g); intramural: basketball (b,g), flag football (b,g), kickball (b,g), soccer (b,g), softball (b,g), tennis (b,g), volleyball (b,g), weight lifting (b,g); coed interscholastic: archery, golf, running; coed intramural: field hockey, fitness, flag football, floor hockey, Frisbee, golf, indoor hockey, kickball, physical fitness, roller skating, running, skiing (downhill), soccer, softball, table tennis, tennis, volleyball. 2 PE instructors, 20 coaches.

Computers Computers are regularly used in classics, desktop publishing, English, keyboarding, science classes. Computer network features include on-campus library services, Internet access, wireless campus network, Internet filtering or blocking technology. Campus intranet is available to students. Students grades are available online. The school has a published electronic and media policy.

Contact Christina Lowe, Enrollment. 330-857-7311 Ext. 224. Fax: 330-857-7331. E-mail: ChristinaL@CentralChristianSchool.org. Website: www.ccscomets.org

CHADWICK SCHOOL

26800 South Academy Drive
Palos Verdes Peninsula, California 90274

Head of School: Frederick T. Hill

General Information Coeducational day college-preparatory, arts, and technology school. Grades K–12. Founded: 1935. Setting: suburban. Nearest major city is Los Angeles. 45-acre campus. 5 buildings on campus. Approved or accredited by Association for Experiential Education, The College Board, Western Association of Schools and Colleges, and California Department of Education. Member of National Association of Independent Schools and Secondary School Admission Test Board. Endowment: $30 million. Total enrollment: 835. Upper school average class size: 17. Upper school faculty-student ratio: 1:5. There are 170 required school days per year for Upper School students. Upper School students typically attend 5 days per week. The average school day consists of 7 hours and 45 minutes.

Upper School Student Profile Grade 9: 105 students (49 boys, 56 girls); Grade 10: 68 students (38 boys, 30 girls); Grade 11: 95 students (39 boys, 56 girls); Grade 12: 86 students (35 boys, 51 girls).

Faculty School total: 74. In upper school: 32 men, 40 women; 54 have advanced degrees.

Subjects Offered 3-dimensional art, Advanced Placement courses, African history, algebra, American history, American literature, American studies, art, art history-AP, art-AP, Asian history, biology, calculus, calculus-AP, ceramics, chemistry, chemistry-AP, choral music, comparative government and politics-AP, computer math, computer programming, computer science-AP, constitutional law, creative writing, dance, drama, economics, English, English literature, English literature-AP, environmental science, environmental science-AP, European history, expository writing, fine arts, forensics, French, French-AP, geometry, grammar, health, history, honors algebra, honors geometry, instrumental music, integrated science, Latin, Latin American history, Latin

American studies, life science, Mandarin, marine biology, mathematics, Middle East, Middle Eastern history, music, music theory-AP, outdoor education, photography, physical education, physics, pre-calculus, probability, robotics, science, social studies, South African history, Spanish, Spanish-AP, speech, statistics, statistics-AP, theater, trigonometry, U.S. history-AP, wilderness education, world history, world literature, writing, yearbook.

Graduation Requirements Arts and fine arts (art, music, dance, drama), English, foreign language, history, mathematics, outdoor education, performing arts, physical education (includes health), science.

Special Academic Programs Advanced Placement exam preparation; honors section; independent study; term-away projects; study abroad; academic accommodation for the gifted, the musically talented, and the artistically talented.

College Admission Counseling 82 students graduated in 2015; all went to college, including Johns Hopkins University; University of California, Berkeley; University of California, Los Angeles; University of Michigan; University of Southern California. Mean SAT critical reading: 646, mean SAT math: 665, mean SAT writing: 678, mean combined SAT: 1989, mean composite ACT: 29.

Student Life Upper grades have specified standards of dress, student council, honor system. Discipline rests equally with students and faculty.

Summer Programs Sports, art/fine arts, computer instruction programs offered; session focuses on visual and performing arts, academics, athletics, academic enrichment; held on campus; accepts boys and girls; open to students from other schools. 500 students usually enrolled. 2016 schedule: June 20 to July 22. Application deadline: March 1.

Tuition and Aid Day student tuition: $32,950. Tuition installment plan (monthly payment plans, individually arranged payment plans). Need-based scholarship grants, Malone Scholarship (need/merit-based), MacFarlane Leadership Scholarship (need/merit-based) available. In 2015–16, 22% of upper-school students received aid. Total amount of financial aid awarded in 2015–16: $1,647,415.

Admissions Traditional secondary-level entrance grade is 9. ISEE required. Deadline for receipt of application materials: January 11. Application fee required: $125. On-campus interview required.

Athletics Interscholastic: baseball (boys), basketball (b,g), cheering (g), cross-country running (b,g), diving (b,g), football (b), golf (b,g), lacrosse (b,g), soccer (b,g), softball (g), swimming and diving (b,g), tennis (b,g), track and field (b,g), volleyball (b,g), water polo (b,g); intramural: aerobics/dance (g), dance (g), horseback riding (g); coed interscholastic: cheering, equestrian sports; coed intramural: fencing. 1 PE instructor, 11 coaches, 3 athletic trainers.

Computers Computers are regularly used in art, college planning, computer applications, creative writing, drawing and design, economics, engineering, English, foreign language, geography, graphic arts, health, history, humanities, journalism, mathematics, music, newspaper, photography, photojournalism, programming, publications, research skills, science, social studies, theater arts, Web site design, wilderness education, writing, yearbook classes. Computer network features include on-campus library services, Internet access, wireless campus network, Internet filtering or blocking technology. Campus intranet, student e-mail accounts, and computer access in designated common areas are available to students. Students grades are available online. The school has a published electronic and media policy.

Contact Vivian Ham, Admission Manager. 310-377-1543 Ext. 4025. Fax: 310-377-0380. E-mail: admissions@chadwickschool.org. Website: www.chadwickschool.org

CHAMINADE COLLEGE PREPARATORY

7500 Chaminade Avenue
West Hills, California 91304

Head of School: Ms. Cynthia Colόn

General Information Coeducational day college-preparatory, arts, business, religious studies, and technology school, affiliated with Roman Catholic Church. Grades 9–12. Founded: 1952. Setting: suburban. Nearest major city is Los Angeles. 21-acre campus. 15 buildings on campus. Approved or accredited by Western Association of Schools and Colleges, Western Catholic Education Association, and California Department of Education. Endowment: $6.8 million. Total enrollment: 2,030. Upper school average class size: 27. Upper school faculty-student ratio: 1:16. There are 180 required school days per year for Upper School students. Upper School students typically attend 5 days per week. The average school day consists of 6 hours and 25 minutes.

Upper School Student Profile Grade 9: 347 students (174 boys, 173 girls); Grade 10: 337 students (180 boys, 157 girls); Grade 11: 317 students (169 boys, 148 girls); Grade 12: 321 students (174 boys, 147 girls). 49% of students are Roman Catholic.

Faculty School total: 82. In upper school: 33 men, 49 women; 66 have advanced degrees.

Subjects Offered Algebra, American history, American literature, anatomy, art, art history, athletic training, band, baseball, basketball, biology, biology-AP, British literature, British literature (honors), calculus, calculus-AP, chemistry, chemistry-AP, Chinese, Christian and Hebrew scripture, community service, comparative government and politics-AP, composition, computer programming, computer programming-AP, computer science, creative writing, dance, dance performance, debate, drama, drawing, driver education, economics, economics and history, English, English language-AP, English literature and composition-AP, environmental science-AP, ethics, European history, expository writing, film studies, finance, fine arts, finite math, French, French language-AP, French literature-AP, geography, geometry, government-AP, government/civics, guitar, human geography - AP, jazz ensemble, journalism, Latin, Latin-AP, literature and composition-AP, macroeconomics-AP, marching band, mathematics, modern European history-AP, music, music appreciation, music performance, mythology, physical education, physical science, physics, physics-AP, physiology, play/screen writing, probability and statistics, psychology, psychology-AP, religion, science, science fiction, scripture, Shakespeare, social studies, Spanish, Spanish language-AP, Spanish literature-AP, speech, speech and debate, sports medicine, statistics-AP, studio art, theater, trigonometry, U.S. government, U.S. history, U.S. history-AP, United States government-AP, visual and performing arts, visual arts, Western philosophy, Western religions, women's studies, world history, world history-AP, world literature, writing.

Graduation Requirements Arts and fine arts (art, music, dance, drama), college writing, computer science, English, foreign language, mathematics, physical education (includes health), religious studies, science, social studies (includes history), speech. Community service is required.

Special Academic Programs 18 Advanced Placement exams for which test preparation is offered; honors section.

College Admission Counseling 332 students graduated in 2015; 325 went to college, including California Lutheran University; California State University, Northridge; Chapman University; The University of Arizona; University of California, Los Angeles; University of Oregon. Other: 1 entered military service, 6 had other specific plans. Mean SAT critical reading: 570, mean SAT math: 567, mean SAT writing: 577, mean combined SAT: 1714, mean composite ACT: 25. 39% scored over 600 on SAT critical reading, 40% scored over 600 on SAT math, 44% scored over 600 on SAT writing, 41% scored over 1800 on combined SAT, 39% scored over 26 on composite ACT.

Student Life Upper grades have uniform requirement, student council, honor system. Discipline rests primarily with faculty. Attendance at religious services is required.

Summer Programs Remediation, enrichment, advancement, sports, art/fine arts, computer instruction programs offered; session focuses on remediation; held on campus; accepts boys and girls; open to students from other schools. 400 students usually enrolled. 2016 schedule: June 6 to July 15. Application deadline: none.

Tuition and Aid Day student tuition: $14,875. Tuition installment plan (monthly payment plans, 2-payment plan, discounted one-payment plan). Merit scholarship grants, need-based scholarship grants available. In 2015–16, 25% of upper-school students received aid; total upper-school merit-scholarship money awarded: $18,000. Total amount of financial aid awarded in 2015–16: $2,390,407.

Admissions Traditional secondary-level entrance grade is 9. For fall 2015, 394 students applied for upper-level admission, 319 were accepted, 190 enrolled. Non-standardized placement tests required. Deadline for receipt of application materials: January 16. Application fee required: $100. On-campus interview required.

Athletics Interscholastic: aquatics (boys, girls), baseball (b), basketball (b,g), cross-country running (b,g), equestrian sports (b,g), fencing (b,g), field hockey (g), football (b), golf (b,g), lacrosse (b,g), soccer (b,g), softball (g), strength & conditioning (b,g), swimming and diving (b,g), tennis (b,g), track and field (b,g), volleyball (b,g), weight training (b,g), wrestling (b); coed interscholastic: cheering, dance, equestrian sports, physical fitness, strength & conditioning, weight training; coed intramural: dance team, hiking/backpacking, table tennis. 3 PE instructors, 85 coaches, 2 athletic trainers.

Computers Computers are regularly used in all classes. Computer network features include on-campus library services, online commercial services, Internet access, wireless campus network, Internet filtering or blocking technology, laptops are issued to students in grades 9-12, Blackboard online learning system, Dyno. Student e-mail accounts are available to students. Students grades are available online. The school has a published electronic and media policy.

Contact Mrs. Yolanda Uramoto, Assistant to Admissions and Registrar. 818-347-8300 Ext. 355. Fax: 818-348-8374. E-mail: yuramoto@chaminade.org. Website: www.chaminade.org

CHAMINADE-MADONNA COLLEGE PREPARATORY

500 Chaminade Drive
Hollywood, Florida 33021-5800

Head of School: Mrs. Raiza Echemendia

General Information Coeducational day college-preparatory, arts, business, religious studies, and technology school, affiliated with Roman Catholic Church. Grades 9–12. Founded: 1960. Setting: suburban. Nearest major city is Fort Lauderdale. 13-acre campus. 10 buildings on campus. Approved or accredited by Southern Association of Colleges and Schools and Florida Department of Education. Total enrollment: 545. Upper school average class size: 26. Upper school faculty-student ratio: 1:19. There are 180 required school days per year for Upper School students. Upper School students typically attend 5 days per week. The average school day consists of 6 hours and 45 minutes.

Upper School Student Profile Grade 9: 124 students (66 boys, 58 girls); Grade 10: 148 students (76 boys, 72 girls); Grade 11: 156 students (98 boys, 58 girls); Grade 12: 117 students (69 boys, 48 girls). 70% of students are Roman Catholic.

Faculty School total: 36. In upper school: 14 men, 22 women.

Subjects Offered Advanced chemistry, advanced computer applications, advanced math, Advanced Placement courses, advanced studio art-AP, algebra, American government, American history, American history-AP, American literature, American literature-AP, anatomy, art, art history, athletic training, band, biology, business skills, calculus, calculus-AP, campus ministry, Catholic belief and practice, ceramics, chemistry, chemistry-AP, choir, chorus, college placement, community service, computer applications, computer graphics, computer skills, creative writing, dance, dance performance, design, directing, drama, drama performance, dramatic arts, economics, English, English composition, English language and composition-AP, English literature and composition-AP, ethics, European history-AP, film studies, fine arts, foreign language, French, French-AP, geography, geometry, government/civics, health, health and wellness, history, history of the Catholic Church, history-AP, honors algebra, honors English, honors geometry, honors U.S. history, honors world history, international relations, journalism, keyboarding, leadership, macro/microeconomics-AP, marine biology, mathematics, model United Nations, music, music history, music theater, musical productions, New Testament, newspaper, peace and justice, philosophy, physical education, physics, physics-AP, physiology, play production, practical arts, pre-calculus, psychology, public speaking, reading, religion, SAT/ACT preparation, science, Shakespeare, social studies, sociology, Spanish, Spanish language-AP, Spanish literature-AP, speech, sports medicine, stagecraft, theater, trigonometry, U.S. history-AP, weight training, word processing, world history, writing, yearbook.

Graduation Requirements Arts and fine arts (art, music, dance, drama), business skills (includes word processing), English, foreign language, mathematics, physical education (includes health), practical arts, religion (includes Bible studies and theology), science, social studies (includes history), 80 community service hours.

Special Academic Programs 10 Advanced Placement exams for which test preparation is offered; honors section; study at local college for college credit; academic accommodation for the gifted, the musically talented, and the artistically talented; remedial reading and/or remedial writing; remedial math; programs in general development for dyslexic students; special instructional classes for students with learning disabilities, Attention Deficit Disorder, and dyslexia.

College Admission Counseling 137 students graduated in 2015; all went to college, including Florida Atlantic University; Florida Gulf Coast University; Florida International University; Florida State University; University of Central Florida; University of Florida. Mean composite ACT: 22.

Student Life Upper grades have uniform requirement, student council, honor system. Discipline rests primarily with faculty. Attendance at religious services is required.

Summer Programs Remediation, enrichment programs offered; session focuses on remediation/make-up; held on campus; accepts boys and girls; not open to students from other schools.

Tuition and Aid Day student tuition: $10,645. Tuition installment plan (FACTS Tuition Payment Plan). Merit scholarship grants, need-based scholarship grants, need-based loans available. In 2015–16, 33% of upper-school students received aid.

Admissions Traditional secondary-level entrance grade is 9. For fall 2015, 250 students applied for upper-level admission, 200 were accepted, 152 enrolled. High School Placement Test (closed version) from Scholastic Testing Service required. Deadline for receipt of application materials: none. Application fee required: $50. Interview required.

Athletics Interscholastic: baseball (boys), basketball (b,g), cheering (g), cross-country running (b,g), dance (g), dance team (g), football (b), golf (b,g), soccer (b,g), softball (g), swimming and diving (b,g), track and field (b,g), volleyball (b,g), wrestling (b). 2 PE instructors, 1 athletic trainer.

Computers Computers are regularly used in all classes. Computer network features include on-campus library services, online commercial services, Internet access, wireless campus network, Internet filtering or blocking technology. Student e-mail accounts are available to students. The school has a published electronic and media policy.

Contact Ms. Tainah Georges, Director of Admissions. 954-989-5150 Ext. 103. Fax: 954-983-4663. E-mail: tgeorges@cmlions.org. Website: www.cmlions.org

CHARLES FINNEY SCHOOL

2070 Five Mile Line Road
Penfield, New York 14526

Head of School: Mr. Michael VanLeeuwen

General Information Coeducational day college-preparatory, arts, religious studies, bilingual studies, and technology school, affiliated with Christian faith. Grades K–12. Founded: 1992. Setting: suburban. Nearest major city is Rochester. 8-acre campus. 1 building on campus. Approved or accredited by New York Department of Education. Total enrollment: 301. Upper school average class size: 25.

Faculty School total: 35.

Special Academic Programs Advanced Placement exam preparation; honors section; study at local college for college credit.

Student Life Upper grades have uniform requirement, student council, honor system. Discipline rests primarily with faculty. Attendance at religious services is required.

Tuition and Aid Tuition installment plan (monthly payment plans). Tuition reduction for siblings, need-based scholarship grants available.

Admissions Traditional secondary-level entrance grade is 9. Deadline for receipt of application materials: none. Application fee required: $40. Interview required.

Athletics Interscholastic: baseball (boys), basketball (b,g), football (b), soccer (b,g), softball (g), volleyball (g); coed interscholastic: track and field. 1 PE instructor.

Computers Computer network features include on-campus library services, Internet access, wireless campus network, Internet filtering or blocking technology. Students grades are available online. The school has a published electronic and media policy.

Contact Ms. Tara Bator, Director of Admissions and Recruitment. 585-387-3770. Fax: 585-387-3771. E-mail: info@finneyschool.org. Website: www.finneyschool.org

CHARLOTTE CHRISTIAN SCHOOL

7301 Sardis Road
Charlotte, North Carolina 28270
Head of School: Mr. Barry Giller

General Information Coeducational day college-preparatory, arts, and religious studies school, affiliated with Christian faith. Grades JK–12. Founded: 1950. Setting: suburban. 55-acre campus. 5 buildings on campus. Approved or accredited by Southern Association of Colleges and Schools and North Carolina Department of Education. Total enrollment: 1,035. Upper school average class size: 20. Upper school faculty-student ratio: 1:11. There are 172 required school days per year for Upper School students. Upper School students typically attend 5 days per week. The average school day consists of 7 hours.

Upper School Student Profile Grade 9: 104 students (63 boys, 41 girls); Grade 10: 107 students (46 boys, 61 girls); Grade 11: 102 students (60 boys, 42 girls); Grade 12: 101 students (58 boys, 43 girls). 100% of students are Christian faith.

Faculty School total: 121. In upper school: 18 men, 18 women; 14 have advanced degrees.

Subjects Offered 20th century physics, accounting, ACT preparation, acting, advanced biology, advanced chemistry, advanced computer applications, advanced math, Advanced Placement courses, advanced studio art-AP, algebra, American culture, American government, American literature, anatomy and physiology, art, art history-AP, athletic training, band, biology, biology-AP, British literature, broadcasting, business, business law, calculus, calculus-AP, chamber groups, chemistry, choir, choreography, Christian doctrine, Christian education, Christian ethics, church history, civil war history, computer applications, computer science-AP, computer-aided design, economics, English literature, environmental science-AP, European history-AP, French, French-AP, geometry, German, graphic arts, graphic design, health and wellness, language-AP, Latin, leadership, learning strategies, Life of Christ, literature and composition-AP, marketing, math applications, music composition, music theory-AP, newspaper, painting, photo shop, photography, physical education, physical science, physics, physics-AP, pre-calculus, psychology, psychology-AP, public speaking, research skills, SAT preparation, Spanish, Spanish-AP, speech and debate, sports medicine, stage design, statistics-AP, studio art-AP, technology/design, theater, theater design and production, trigonometry, U.S. government and politics-AP, U.S. history, U.S. history-AP, video film production, voice, voice and diction, Web site design, weight training, Western civilization, wind ensemble, world civilizations, world literature, world religions, World War II, yearbook.

Graduation Requirements Arts and fine arts (art, music, dance, drama), Bible studies, English, foreign language, mathematics, physical education (includes health), SAT preparation, science, social studies (includes history), speech, service hours.

Special Academic Programs Advanced Placement exam preparation; honors section; term-away projects; study at local college for college credit.

College Admission Counseling 96 students graduated in 2014; 95 went to college, including Clemson University; North Carolina State University; The University of North Carolina at Chapel Hill; The University of Tennessee; University of Mississippi; Wake Forest University. Other: 1 entered military service.

Student Life Upper grades have specified standards of dress, student council, honor system. Discipline rests primarily with faculty. Attendance at religious services is required.

Tuition and Aid Day student tuition: $12,825–$18,580. Tuition installment plan (The Tuition Plan, Insured Tuition Payment Plan, monthly payment plans, individually arranged payment plans). Tuition reduction for siblings, need-based scholarship grants available. In 2014–15, 20% of upper-school students received aid. Total amount of financial aid awarded in 2014–15: $389,150.

Admissions Traditional secondary-level entrance grade is 9. Admissions testing, ISEE, Wechsler Intelligence Scale for Children III or Woodcock-Johnson required. Deadline for receipt of application materials: none. Application fee required: $90. On-campus interview required.

Athletics Interscholastic: baseball (boys), basketball (b,g), cheering (g), cross-country running (b,g), dance team (g), football (b), golf (b), indoor track (b,g), lacrosse (b), soccer (b,g), softball (g), swimming and diving (b,g), tennis (b,g), track and field (b,g), volleyball (g), wrestling (b); intramural: basketball (b,g), cheering (g), ultimate Frisbee (b); coed interscholastic: physical fitness, physical training, strength & conditioning, weight training; coed intramural: basketball. 2 PE instructors, 25 coaches, 2 athletic trainers.

Computers Computers are regularly used in computer applications, journalism, keyboarding, Latin, media arts, newspaper, photography, publications, video film production, yearbook classes. Computer network features include on-campus library

services, Internet access, wireless campus network, Internet filtering or blocking technology, NewsBank InfoWeb. Student e-mail accounts are available to students. Students grades are available online. The school has a published electronic and media policy.

Contact Mrs. Cathie Broocks, Director of Admissions. 704-366-5657. Fax: 704-366-5678. E-mail: cathie.broocks@charchrist.com. Website: www.charlottechristian.com

CHARLOTTE COUNTRY DAY SCHOOL

1440 Carmel Road
Charlotte, North Carolina 28226
Head of School: Mr. Mark Reed

General Information Coeducational day college-preparatory school. Grades JK–12. Founded: 1941. Setting: suburban. 60-acre campus. 10 buildings on campus. Approved or accredited by Southern Association of Colleges and Schools, Southern Association of Independent Schools, and North Carolina Department of Education. Member of National Association of Independent Schools and Secondary School Admission Test Board. Endowment: $50.1 million. Total enrollment: 1,660. Upper school average class size: 12. Upper school faculty-student ratio: 1:7. There are 170 required school days per year for Upper School students. Upper School students typically attend 5 days per week. The average school day consists of 7 hours and 15 minutes.

Upper School Student Profile Grade 6: 134 students (59 boys, 75 girls); Grade 7: 133 students (69 boys, 64 girls); Grade 8: 133 students (74 boys, 59 girls); Grade 9: 139 students (78 boys, 61 girls); Grade 10: 132 students (50 boys, 82 girls); Grade 11: 128 students (54 boys, 74 girls); Grade 12: 119 students (57 boys, 62 girls).

Faculty School total: 228. In upper school: 33 men, 42 women; 49 have advanced degrees.

Subjects Offered Algebra, American history, American history-AP, anatomy, art, art history-AP, astronomy, biology, biology-AP, biotechnology, calculus-AP, ceramics, chemistry, chemistry-AP, Chinese, computer graphics, computer science, computer science-AP, creative writing, dance, debate, discrete mathematics, drama, ecology, economics, English, English literature, English-AP, environmental science-AP, ESL, European history, European history-AP, French, French-AP, geography, geometry, German, German-AP, Japanese, journalism, Latin, Latin-AP, library studies, music, novels, photography, physical education, physics, physics-AP, physiology, poetry, political science, pre-calculus, probability and statistics, psychology-AP, sculpture, Shakespeare, short story, Spanish, Spanish-AP, studio art-AP, theater, theory of knowledge, trigonometry, visual arts, yearbook.

Graduation Requirements Arts and fine arts (art, music, dance, drama), computer science, English, foreign language, mathematics, physical education (includes health), science, social sciences, social studies (includes history). Community service is required.

Special Academic Programs International Baccalaureate program; honors section; independent study; term-away projects; study abroad; academic accommodation for the gifted; ESL (20 students enrolled).

College Admission Counseling 128 students graduated in 2015; all went to college, including Elon University; North Carolina State University; The University of North Carolina at Chapel Hill; University of Georgia; University of Virginia; Wake Forest University. Median SAT critical reading: 660, median SAT math: 680, median SAT writing: 670, median combined SAT: 2020, median composite ACT: 31. 54% scored over 600 on SAT critical reading, 62% scored over 600 on SAT math, 65% scored over 600 on SAT writing, 57% scored over 1800 on combined SAT, 78% scored over 26 on composite ACT.

Student Life Upper grades have specified standards of dress, student council, honor system. Discipline rests primarily with faculty.

Summer Programs Remediation, enrichment, advancement, sports, art/fine arts, computer instruction programs offered; session focuses on enrichment classes, academic courses, and sports camps; held on campus; accepts boys and girls; open to students from other schools. 200 students usually enrolled. 2016 schedule: June 13 to July 29. Application deadline: none.

Tuition and Aid Day student tuition: $22,085. Tuition installment plan (The Tuition Plan, Insured Tuition Payment Plan, monthly payment plans). Need-based scholarship grants available. In 2015–16, 17% of upper-school students received aid. Total amount of financial aid awarded in 2015–16: $1,275,523.

Admissions Traditional secondary-level entrance grade is 9. For fall 2015, 126 students applied for upper-level admission, 76 were accepted, 45 enrolled. CTP III, ERB or ISEE required. Deadline for receipt of application materials: January 15. Application fee required: $90. On-campus interview required.

Athletics Interscholastic: baseball (boys), basketball (b,g), cheering (g), crew (g), cross-country running (b,g), dance (g), dance team (g), field hockey (g), fitness (b,g), football (b), golf (b,g), lacrosse (b,g), soccer (b,g), softball (g), strength & conditioning (b,g), swimming and diving (b,g), tennis (b,g), track and field (b,g), volleyball (g), weight training (b,g), wrestling (b). 1 PE instructor, 38 coaches, 3 athletic trainers.

Computers Computers are regularly used in art, computer applications, English, foreign language, mathematics, photography, science, yearbook classes. Computer network features include on-campus library services, online commercial services, Internet access, wireless campus network, Internet filtering or blocking technology. Campus intranet and student e-mail accounts are available to students. Students grades are available online. The school has a published electronic and media policy.

Contact Nancy R. Ehringhaus, Director of Admissions. 704-943-4530 Ext. 4531. Fax: 704-943-4536. E-mail: nancy.ehringhaus@charlottecountryday.org. Website: www.charlottecountryday.org

CHARLOTTE LATIN SCHOOL

9502 Providence Road
Charlotte, North Carolina 28277-8695

Head of School: Mr. Arch N. McIntosh Jr.

General Information Coeducational day college-preparatory school. Grades K–12. Founded: 1970. Setting: suburban. 122-acre campus. 7 buildings on campus. Approved or accredited by Southern Association of Colleges and Schools, Southern Association of Independent Schools, and North Carolina Department of Education. Member of National Association of Independent Schools and Secondary School Admission Test Board. Endowment: $29.1 million. Total enrollment: 1,413. Upper school average class size: 14. Upper school faculty-student ratio: 1:10. There are 176 required school days per year for Upper School students. Upper School students typically attend 5 days per week. The average school day consists of 7 hours and 5 minutes.

Upper School Student Profile Grade 9: 131 students (74 boys, 57 girls); Grade 10: 129 students (69 boys, 60 girls); Grade 11: 117 students (56 boys, 61 girls); Grade 12: 115 students (55 boys, 60 girls).

Faculty School total: 194. In upper school: 42 men, 30 women; 42 have advanced degrees.

Subjects Offered 20th century American writers, 20th century history, 20th century physics, 20th century world history, 3-dimensional art, acting, advanced chemistry, Advanced Placement courses, algebra, American culture, American foreign policy, American government, American history, American history-AP, American literature, American studies, anatomy, anatomy and physiology, art, biology, biology-AP, British literature, calculus, calculus-AP, ceramics, chemistry, chemistry-AP, choir, college admission preparation, college counseling, composition-AP, computer applications, computer math, computer programming, computer science, computer science-AP, computer technology certification, conceptual physics, concert band, concert choir, creative writing, debate, discrete mathematics, drama, dramatic arts, earth science, ecology, ecology, environmental systems, economics, economics and history, engineering, English, English literature, English literature and composition-AP, English-AP, environmental science, environmental science-AP, European history, European history-AP, expository writing, finite math, French, French-AP, geography, geology, geometry, global studies, government and politics-AP, government/civics, grammar, Greek, health, history, Holocaust and other genocides, honors algebra, honors English, honors geometry, human anatomy, human rights, hydrology, international relations, international studies, Irish literature, journalism, Latin, Latin-AP, leadership and service, mathematics, media literacy, music, music theory, music theory-AP, physical education, physical fitness, physics, physics-AP, pre-calculus, programming, psychology, psychology-AP, science, social studies, Southern literature, Spanish, Spanish language-AP, Spanish-AP, speech, sports medicine, statistics-AP, studio art, technical theater, theater, trigonometry, U.S. government and politics-AP, U.S. history-AP, United States government-AP, visual arts, Web site design, wind ensemble, world history, world literature, world religions, writing, yearbook.

Graduation Requirements Electives, English, foreign language, history, mathematics, physical education (includes health), science.

Special Academic Programs 19 Advanced Placement exams for which test preparation is offered; honors section; study abroad; academic accommodation for the gifted.

College Admission Counseling 128 students graduated in 2015; all went to college, including Clemson University; Duke University; The University of North Carolina at Chapel Hill; University of Georgia; University of South Carolina; Wake Forest University. Mean SAT critical reading: 639, mean SAT math: 650, mean SAT writing: 639, mean combined SAT: 1928, mean composite ACT: 29. 65% scored over 600 on SAT critical reading, 78% scored over 600 on SAT math, 70% scored over 600 on SAT writing, 73% scored over 1800 on combined SAT, 77% scored over 26 on composite ACT.

Student Life Upper grades have specified standards of dress, student council, honor system. Discipline rests primarily with faculty.

Summer Programs Enrichment, sports, art/fine arts, computer instruction programs offered; session focuses on STEM, enrichment, sports; held both on and off campus; held at various trips to local venues; accepts boys and girls; open to students from other schools. 2,700 students usually enrolled. 2016 schedule: June 13 to July 29. Application deadline: none.

Tuition and Aid Day student tuition: $21,280. Tuition installment plan (Insured Tuition Payment Plan, FACTS Tuition Payment Plan, monthly payment plans, individually arranged payment plans). Merit scholarship grants, need-based scholarship grants available. In 2015–16, 19% of upper-school students received aid; total upper-school merit-scholarship money awarded: $243,500. Total amount of financial aid awarded in 2015–16: $1,091,140.

Admissions Traditional secondary-level entrance grade is 9. For fall 2015, 143 students applied for upper-level admission, 68 were accepted, 43 enrolled. ERB, ISEE, Wechsler Intelligence Scale for Children or Woodcock-Johnson required. Deadline for receipt of application materials: none. Application fee required: $90. On-campus interview required.

Athletics Interscholastic: aquatics (boys, girls); baseball (b); basketball (b,g); cross-country running (b,g); dance team (g); field hockey (g); football (b); golf (b,g); independent competitive sports (b,g); indoor track (b,g); lacrosse (b,g); soccer (b,g); softball (g); swimming and diving (b,g); tennis (b,g); track and field (b,g); volleyball (g); wrestling (b); intramural: basketball (b,g); outdoor activities (b,g); coed interscholastic: ultimate Frisbee; coed intramural: outdoor activities. 9 PE instructors, 47 coaches, 3 athletic trainers.

Computers Computers are regularly used in all academic classes. Computer network features include on-campus library services, online commercial services, Internet access, wireless campus network. Student e-mail accounts and computer access in designated common areas are available to students. The school has a published electronic and media policy.

Contact Mrs. Mary Yorke Oates, Director of Admissions. 704-846-7207. Fax: 704-849-0503. E-mail: moates@charlottelatin.org. Website: www.charlottelatin.org

See Display on next page and Close-Up on page 590.

CHATHAM ACADEMY

Savannah, Georgia
See Special Needs Schools section.

CHATTANOOGA CHRISTIAN SCHOOL

3354 Charger Drive
Chattanooga, Tennessee 37409

Head of School: Mr. Chad Dirkse

General Information Coeducational day college-preparatory, arts, religious studies, technology, college-level (AP) courses, and dual enrollment courses school, affiliated with Christian faith. Grades K–12. Founded: 1970. Setting: urban. Nearest major city is Atlanta, GA. 60-acre campus. 6 buildings on campus. Approved or accredited by Christian Schools International, Southern Association of Colleges and Schools, Southern Association of Independent Schools, and Tennessee Department of Education. Endowment: $8 million. Total enrollment: 1,143. Upper school average class size: 20. Upper school faculty-student ratio: 1:17. There are 175 required school days per year for Upper School students. Upper School students typically attend 5 days per week. The average school day consists of 7 hours.

Upper School Student Profile Grade 6: 119 students (58 boys, 61 girls); Grade 7: 112 students (62 boys, 50 girls); Grade 8: 106 students (48 boys, 58 girls); Grade 9: 124 students (65 boys, 59 girls); Grade 10: 105 students (44 boys, 61 girls); Grade 11: 103 students (43 boys, 60 girls); Grade 12: 108 students (52 boys, 56 girls). 100% of students are Christian faith.

Faculty School total: 104. In upper school: 33 men, 35 women; 19 have advanced degrees.

Subjects Offered Advanced biology, advanced chemistry, advanced studio art-AP, algebra, American government, American history, American literature, anatomy and physiology, ancient history, art, art and culture, art appreciation, art history, art-AP, astronomy, band, Bible, Bible studies, biology, biology-AP, calculus, calculus-AP, chemistry, choir, civil rights, community service, computer applications, computer programming, computer-aided design, concert band, concert choir, creative writing, current events, dance, drama, drama performance, earth science, Eastern world civilizations, economics, English, English literature, English-AP, environmental science, environmental studies, ethics, European history, European history-AP, fine arts, foreign language, French, geometry, German, government, health, honors geometry, industrial arts, introduction to theater, Latin, leadership education training, life science, mathematics, mathematics-AP, mechanical drawing, Microsoft, modern dance, modern European history-AP, music, music theory, New Testament, personal finance, physical education, physical science, physics, physics-AP, physiology, psychology, religion, science, shop, Spanish, statistics-AP, studio art-AP, theater, trigonometry, U.S. history-AP, Web site design, weight training, wellness, world literature, writing.

Graduation Requirements Arts and fine arts (art, music, dance, drama), computer science, English, foreign language, mathematics, physical education (includes health), religion (includes Bible studies and theology), science, social sciences, social studies (includes history). Community service is required.

Special Academic Programs Advanced Placement exam preparation; honors section; independent study; study at local college for college credit; academic accommodation for the gifted and the artistically talented; remedial reading and/or remedial writing; remedial math.

College Admission Counseling 104 students graduated in 2015; 98 went to college, including Chattanooga State Community College; Covenant College; Samford University; Tennessee Technological University; The University of Tennessee; The University of Tennessee at Chattanooga. Other: 4 went to work, 1 entered a postgraduate year, 1 had other specific plans. Mean SAT critical reading: 560, mean SAT math: 540, mean SAT writing: 530, mean combined SAT: 1650, mean composite ACT: 25. 35% scored over 600 on SAT critical reading, 22% scored over 600 on SAT math, 29% scored over 600 on SAT writing, 26% scored over 1800 on combined SAT, 35% scored over 26 on composite ACT.

Student Life Upper grades have specified standards of dress, student council, honor system. Discipline rests primarily with faculty. Attendance at religious services is required.

Summer Programs Remediation, enrichment, sports, art/fine arts programs offered; session focuses on sports camps and arts camps; held on campus; accepts boys and girls; open to students from other schools. 100 students usually enrolled. 2016 schedule: June 6 to July 29. Application deadline: May 31.

Tuition and Aid Day student tuition: $9990. Tuition installment plan (monthly payment plans, individually arranged payment plans). Tuition reduction for siblings, need-based scholarship grants, paying campus jobs available. In 2015–16, 20% of upper-school students received aid. Total amount of financial aid awarded in 2015–16: $500,000.

Admissions For fall 2015, 153 students applied for upper-level admission, 115 were accepted, 95 enrolled. Deadline for receipt of application materials: none. Application fee required: $100. Interview required.

Athletics Interscholastic: baseball (boys), basketball (b,g), bowling (b,g), cheering (g), cross-country running (b,g), football (b), golf (b,g), soccer (b,g), softball (g), strength & conditioning (b,g), swimming and diving (b,g), tennis (b,g), track and field (b,g), volleyball (g), weight lifting (b,g), weight training (b,g), wrestling (b); intramural: basketball (b,g), flag football (g); coed intramural: aerobics/dance, swimming and diving. 5 PE instructors, 15 coaches, 2 athletic trainers.

Computers Computers are regularly used in all academic, drawing and design, English, foreign language, history, lab/keyboard, library, mathematics, psychology, science, technology classes. Computer network features include on-campus library services, online commercial services, Internet access, wireless campus network, Internet filtering or blocking technology. Student e-mail accounts are available to students. Students grades are available online. The school has a published electronic and media policy.

Contact Mrs. Charlene Wolfe, Admission Director. 423-265-6411 Ext. 209. Fax: 423-756-4044. E-mail: cwolfe@ccsk12.com. Website: www.ccsk12.com

CHELSEA SCHOOL

Hyattsville, Maryland

See Special Needs Schools section.

CHESHIRE ACADEMY

10 Main Street
Cheshire, Connecticut 06410

Head of School: Mr. John D. Nozell

General Information Coeducational boarding and day college-preparatory, general academic, arts, and bilingual studies school; primarily serves students with learning disabilities, individuals with Attention Deficit Disorder, and dyslexic students. Grades 8–PG. Founded: 1794. Setting: small town. Nearest major city is New Haven. Students are housed in single-sex dormitories. 104-acre campus. 24 buildings on campus. Approved or accredited by Connecticut Association of Independent Schools, International Baccalaureate Organization, New England Association of Schools and Colleges, and The Association of Boarding Schools. Member of National Association of Independent Schools and Secondary School Admission Test Board. Endowment: $8 million. Total enrollment: 400. Upper school average class size: 12. Upper school faculty-student ratio: 1:7. There are 171 required school days per year for Upper School students. Upper School students typically attend 5 days per week.

Upper School Student Profile Grade 8: 19 students (17 boys, 2 girls); Grade 9: 73 students (33 boys, 40 girls); Grade 10: 89 students (54 boys, 35 girls); Grade 11: 99 students (62 boys, 37 girls); Grade 12: 94 students (49 boys, 45 girls); Postgraduate: 26 students (24 boys, 2 girls). 62% of students are boarding students. 46% are state residents. 17 states are represented in upper school student body. 40% are international students. International students from China, Democratic People's Republic of Korea, Jamaica, and Taiwan; 29 other countries represented in student body.

Faculty School total: 74. In upper school: 26 men, 41 women; 50 have advanced degrees; 47 reside on campus.

Subjects Offered 3-dimensional art, 3-dimensional design, acting, advanced math, Advanced Placement courses, African-American studies, algebra, American government, American history, American history-AP, American literature, American literature-AP, anatomy, anatomy and physiology, ancient world history, animation, art, art history, art-AP, arts, Asian studies, biology, calculus, calculus-AP, ceramics, chemistry, chemistry-AP, Chinese, community service, computer programming, computer science, creative writing, digital art, digital imaging, digital photography, discrete mathematics, drama, drama performance, dramatic arts, drawing, drawing and design, earth and space science, earth science, ecology, economics, electives, engineering, English, English language and composition-AP, English literature, English/composition-AP, environmental science, environmental studies, ESL, FSL, European history, experimental science, expository writing, fencing, film and literature, fine arts, French, French studies, functions, geography, geometry, government-AP, government/civics, grammar, guitar, health, history, honors English, honors geometry, honors world history, illustration, independent study, instrumental music, integrated mathematics, interdisciplinary studies, International Baccalaureate courses, internship,

...*lives well lived*

www.charlottelatin.org

Charlotte Latin School is an independent, non-sectarian, coeducational, college-preparatory day school for students in transitional kindergarten through twelfth grade. Financial assistance is available.

CHARLOTTE LATIN SCHOOL
9502 Providence Road, Charlotte, NC 28277

jazz ensemble, language arts, Latin American studies, mathematics, music, music theory-AP, nutrition, orchestra, painting, performing arts, philosophy, photography, physical education, physics, physiology, portfolio art, pre-calculus, psychology, psychology-AP, public speaking, reading, science, social sciences, social studies, Spanish, speech, statistics, statistics-AP, theater, Vietnam, world history, world literature, writing.

Graduation Requirements Arts and fine arts (art, music, dance, drama), computer science, electives, English, foreign language, mathematics, science, social sciences, social studies (includes history), senior speech.

Special Academic Programs International Baccalaureate program; Advanced Placement exam preparation; honors section; independent study; academic accommodation for the gifted, the musically talented, and the artistically talented; remedial reading and/or remedial writing; remedial math; programs in English, mathematics, general development for dyslexic students; ESL (45 students enrolled).

College Admission Counseling 112 students graduated in 2014; 105 went to college, including Boston College; Boston University; Cornell University; Emory University; Trinity College; University of Rochester. Other: 3 entered a postgraduate year, 4 had other specific plans. Median SAT critical reading: 540, median SAT math: 570, median SAT writing: 550, median combined SAT: 1690. 22.8% scored over 600 on SAT critical reading, 45.7% scored over 600 on SAT math, 33.3% scored over 600 on SAT writing, 38% scored over 1800 on combined SAT.

Student Life Upper grades have specified standards of dress, student council, honor system. Discipline rests primarily with faculty.

Tuition and Aid Day student tuition: $32,360; 7-day tuition and room/board: $45,385. Tuition installment plan (Key Tuition Payment Plan, monthly payment plans). Merit scholarship grants, need-based scholarship grants, need-based loans available. In 2014–15, 40% of upper-school students received aid; total upper-school merit-scholarship money awarded: $250,000. Total amount of financial aid awarded in 2014–15: $3,300,000.

Admissions Traditional secondary-level entrance grade is 9. ACT, ISEE, PSAT, SAT, SSAT or TOEFL required. Deadline for receipt of application materials: none. Application fee required: $50. Interview required.

Athletics Interscholastic: baseball (boys), basketball (b,g), cross-country running (b,g), field hockey (g), football (b), hockey (b), ice hockey (b), lacrosse (b,g), soccer (b,g), softball (g), swimming and diving (b,g), tennis (b,g), track and field (b,g), volleyball (g), wrestling (b); coed interscholastic: fencing, golf, ultimate Frisbee; coed intramural: dance, fitness, physical fitness, physical training, ropes courses, skiing (downhill), snowboarding, strength & conditioning, weight training, yoga. 1 PE instructor, 9 coaches, 2 athletic trainers.

Computers Computers are regularly used in all classes. Computer network features include on-campus library services, online commercial services, Internet access, wireless campus network, Internet filtering or blocking technology, 1:1 iPad program. Campus intranet, student e-mail accounts, and computer access in designated common areas are available to students. Students grades are available online. The school has a published electronic and media policy.

Contact Kristen A. Mariotti, Associate Director of Admission. 203-471-7404 Ext. 455. Fax: 203-493-7601. E-mail: kristen.mariotti@cheshireacademy.org. Website: www.cheshireacademy.org

CHEVERUS HIGH SCHOOL

267 Ocean Avenue
Portland, Maine 04103

Head of School: Mr. John H.R. Mullen

General Information Coeducational day college-preparatory, religious studies, technology, honors, and AP courses school, affiliated with Roman Catholic Church (Jesuit order). Grades 9–12. Founded: 1917. Setting: suburban. 32-acre campus. 2 buildings on campus. Approved or accredited by Association of Independent Schools in New England, Independent Schools of Northern New England, Jesuit Secondary Education Association, New England Association of Schools and Colleges, The College Board, and Maine Department of Education. Endowment: $3 million. Total enrollment: 470. Upper school average class size: 22. Upper school faculty-student ratio: 1:10. There are 173 required school days per year for Upper School students. Upper School students typically attend 5 days per week. The average school day consists of 6 hours and 30 minutes.

Upper School Student Profile Grade 9: 124 students (71 boys, 53 girls); Grade 10: 111 students (58 boys, 53 girls); Grade 11: 116 students (65 boys, 51 girls); Grade 12: 119 students (80 boys, 39 girls). 65% of students are Roman Catholic Church (Jesuit order).

Faculty School total: 55. In upper school: 31 men, 24 women; 28 have advanced degrees.

Subjects Offered Advanced Placement courses, algebra, American history, art, biology, calculus, chemistry, college counseling, creative writing, economics, English, European history, fine arts, French, geography, geometry, government/civics, history, journalism, Latin, library skills, mathematics, music, physics, religion, science, social studies, Spanish, statistics, trigonometry, world history, yearbook.

Graduation Requirements Arts and fine arts (art, music, dance, drama), computer science, English, foreign language, health, mathematics, science, social studies

(includes history), theology, all seniors are required to fill a community service requirement. Community service is required.

Special Academic Programs Advanced Placement exam preparation; honors section; study at local college for college credit; programs in general development for dyslexic students.

College Admission Counseling 119 students graduated in 2015; 117 went to college, including Maine Maritime Academy; Saint Joseph's College of Maine; Saint Louis University; The Catholic University of America; University of Maine; University of Southern Maine. Other: 2 went to work. Median SAT critical reading: 574, median SAT math: 604, median SAT writing: 559.

Student Life Upper grades have specified standards of dress, student council, honor system. Discipline rests primarily with faculty. Attendance at religious services is required.

Summer Programs Enrichment, sports programs offered; session focuses on enrichment; held on campus; accepts boys and girls; open to students from other schools. 75 students usually enrolled. 2016 schedule: June 21 to August 8. Application deadline: June 1.

Tuition and Aid Day student tuition: $17,500. Tuition installment plan (FACTS Tuition Payment Plan, monthly payment plans, individually arranged payment plans). Tuition reduction for siblings, merit scholarship grants, need-based scholarship grants, paying campus jobs available. In 2015–16, 68% of upper-school students received aid; total upper-school merit-scholarship money awarded: $15,000. Total amount of financial aid awarded in 2015–16: $2,298,173.

Admissions Traditional secondary-level entrance grade is 9. For fall 2015, 234 students applied for upper-level admission, 169 were accepted, 125 enrolled. English language and Math Placement Exam required. Deadline for receipt of application materials: none. Application fee required: $50. On-campus interview required.

Athletics Interscholastic: baseball (boys), basketball (b,g), cross-country running (b,g), diving (b,g), field hockey (g), football (b), golf (b,g), ice hockey (b,g), indoor track & field (b,g), lacrosse (b,g), sailing (b,g), skiing (downhill), soccer (b,g), softball (g), swimming and diving (b,g), tennis (b,g), track and field (b,g), ultimate Frisbee (b), volleyball (g), winter (indoor) track (b,g), wrestling (b); intramural: basketball (b,g), flag football (b,g); coed interscholastic: alpine skiing, outdoor adventure; coed intramural: basketball, bicycling, flag football, hiking/backpacking, table tennis, volleyball. 89 coaches, 2 athletic trainers.

Computers Computers are regularly used in creative writing, economics, history, information technology, journalism, mathematics, SAT preparation, science, word processing, yearbook classes. Computer network features include on-campus library services, online commercial services, Internet access, wireless campus network. Student e-mail accounts and computer access in designated common areas are available to students. Students grades are available online. The school has a published electronic and media policy.

Contact Mrs. Ruth Summers, Director of Admissions. 207-774-6238 Ext. 190. Fax: 207-774-8461. E-mail: summers@cheverus.org. Website: www.cheverus.org

THE CHICAGO ACADEMY FOR THE ARTS

1010 West Chicago Avenue
Chicago, Illinois 60642

Head of School: Mr. Jason Patera

General Information Coeducational day college-preparatory and arts school. Grades 9–12. Founded: 1981. Setting: urban. 1-acre campus. 1 building on campus. Approved or accredited by Independent Schools Association of the Central States and Illinois Department of Education. Member of National Association of Independent Schools. Total enrollment: 143. Upper school average class size: 12. Upper school faculty-student ratio: 1:10. There are 163 required school days per year for Upper School students. Upper School students typically attend 5 days per week. The average school day consists of 8 hours.

Upper School Student Profile Grade 9: 38 students (10 boys, 28 girls); Grade 10: 37 students (10 boys, 27 girls); Grade 11: 25 students (7 boys, 18 girls); Grade 12: 43 students (18 boys, 25 girls).

Faculty School total: 56. In upper school: 26 men, 30 women; 21 have advanced degrees.

Subjects Offered Advanced math, Advanced Placement courses, African-American literature, algebra, American history, American literature, anatomy, anatomy and physiology, art, art history, art history-AP, arts, ballet, ballet technique, biology, biology-AP, Broadway dance, business law, calculus, calculus-AP, chemistry, choreography, cinematography, classical music, college counseling, consumer law, creative writing, critical studies in film, dance, dance performance, digital art, digital music, discrete mathematics, drama, drawing, drawing and design, English, English literature and composition-AP, European history-AP, film, film history, film studies, filmmaking, fine arts, French, French language-AP, geometry, geometry with art applications, global issues, global studies, graphic arts, guitar, historical foundations for arts, history of dance, history of drama, history of music, honors English, honors geometry, humanities, instrumental music, jazz, jazz band, jazz theory, keyboarding, Latin American literature, mathematics, mathematics-AP, media arts, modern dance, music, music composition, music for dance, music history, music performance, music theater, music theory, physics, play production, play/screen writing, playwriting and directing, poetry, printmaking, public speaking, scene study, science, sculpture, senior internship, set design, Shakespeare, shop, social sciences, Spanish, Spanish language-AP, speech, stage design, stagecraft, statistics-AP, studio art, study skills, theater, theater design and production, theater history, U.S. history, U.S. literature, urban design, video, video and animation, video film production, visual and performing arts, visual arts, vocal ensemble, vocal jazz, vocal music, voice, wind ensemble, wind instruments, world affairs, world history, world religions, World War I.

Graduation Requirements Arts and fine arts (art, music, dance, drama), English, foreign language, mathematics, science, social sciences, U.S. history, requirements vary according to arts discipline.

Special Academic Programs 10 Advanced Placement exams for which test preparation is offered; honors section; independent study; academic accommodation for the musically talented and the artistically talented; programs in general development for dyslexic students.

College Admission Counseling 41 students graduated in 2014; 39 went to college, including Berklee College of Music; California Institute of the Arts; Parsons School of Design; Rhode Island School of Design; The Juilliard School; University of Southern California. Other: 2 went to work. Median composite ACT: 26.

Student Life Upper grades have honor system. Discipline rests equally with students and faculty.

Tuition and Aid Day student tuition: $24,720. Tuition installment plan (FACTS Tuition Payment Plan, monthly payment plans). Merit scholarship grants, need-based scholarship grants available. In 2014–15, 70% of upper-school students received aid; total upper-school merit-scholarship money awarded: $253,000. Total amount of financial aid awarded in 2014–15: $903,620.

Admissions Traditional secondary-level entrance grade is 9. For fall 2014, 125 students applied for upper-level admission, 74 were accepted, 53 enrolled. ISEE required. Deadline for receipt of application materials: December 4. Application fee required: $65. On-campus interview required.

Computers Computers are regularly used in animation, college planning, commercial art, English, graphic arts, graphics, historical foundations for arts, media arts, media production, music technology, video film production classes. Computer resources include online commercial services, Internet access, wireless campus network, graphic design and production, animation, filmmaking and production. Computer access in designated common areas is available to students. Students grades are available online.

Contact Ms. Hannah Stromberg, Admissions Assistant. 312-421-0202 Ext. 32. Fax: 312-421-3816. E-mail: hstromberg@chicagoartsacademy.org.
Website: www.chicagoartsacademy.org

CHILDREN'S CREATIVE AND PERFORMING ARTS ACADEMY OF SAN DIEGO

3051 El Cajon Boulevard
San Diego, California 92104

Head of School: Mrs. Janet M. Cherif

General Information Coeducational boarding and day college-preparatory, arts, mathematics, and science school. Boarding grades 6–12, day grades K–12. Founded: 1981. Setting: urban. Students are housed in homestay families. 1-acre campus. 1 building on campus. Approved or accredited by Western Association of Schools and Colleges and California Department of Education. Total enrollment: 262. Upper school average class size: 18. Upper school faculty-student ratio: 1:18. There are 186 required school days per year for Upper School students. Upper School students typically attend 5 days per week. The average school day consists of 7 hours and 30 minutes.

Upper School Student Profile Grade 6: 18 students (8 boys, 10 girls); Grade 7: 18 students (9 boys, 9 girls); Grade 8: 18 students (8 boys, 10 girls); Grade 9: 25 students (10 boys, 15 girls); Grade 10: 27 students (12 boys, 15 girls); Grade 11: 23 students (11 boys, 12 girls); Grade 12: 25 students (13 boys, 12 girls). 20% of students are boarding students. 70% are state residents. 1 state is represented in upper school student body. 30% are international students. International students from Brazil, China, Germany, Mexico, Republic of Korea, and Viet Nam; 3 other countries represented in student body.

Faculty School total: 30. In upper school: 3 men, 14 women; 10 have advanced degrees.

Subjects Offered 3-dimensional art, 3-dimensional design, algebra, American government, anatomy and physiology, art, art history, art history-AP, art-AP, audition methods, ballet, band, biology, business skills, calculus, calculus-AP, ceramics, chamber groups, cheerleading, chemistry, Chinese, choir, choreography, chorus, communications, comparative government and politics-AP, computer applications, computer literacy, computer programming-AP, concert band, concert choir, creative writing, dance performance, digital photography, drama, drama performance, earth science, English, English literature-AP, English-AP, English/composition-AP, ensembles, environmental science-AP, ESL, European history-AP, film, fitness, French, French language-AP, geometry, government and politics-AP, government/civics, government/civics-AP, graphic design, gymnastics, health, history of music, history-AP, honors algebra, honors English, honors geometry, honors U.S. history, honors world history, HTML design, human anatomy, instrumental music, Japanese, jazz band, jazz dance, jazz ensemble, journalism, Latin, mathematics, mathematics-AP, modern dance, music history, music performance, music theory-AP, orchestra, performing arts, physical education, physics, physics-AP, playwriting and directing, political science, portfolio art, pottery, pre-algebra, pre-calculus, reading/study skills, SAT preparation,

SAT/ACT preparation, science, senior seminar, social sciences, social studies, Spanish, Spanish language-AP, Spanish literature-AP, speech, sports, stage design, statistics, studio art-AP, tap dance, theater design and production, TOEFL preparation, track and field, trigonometry, U.S. government and politics-AP, U.S. history, U.S. history-AP, vocal ensemble, vocal jazz, voice ensemble, volleyball, Web site design, Western civilization, world history, world history-AP, writing, writing workshop, yearbook.

Graduation Requirements Algebra, arts, biology, business skills (includes word processing), chemistry, choir, chorus, computer applications, computer skills, English, English composition, English literature, foreign language, government/civics, history, mathematics, modern world history, music, physical education (includes health), physics, science, social sciences, Spanish, sports, TOEFL preparation, trigonometry, U.S. government, U.S. history, visual and performing arts, senior recital or project, 30 hours of community service per year of attendance. Community service is required.

Special Academic Programs 14 Advanced Placement exams for which test preparation is offered; honors section; accelerated programs; independent study; academic accommodation for the gifted, the musically talented, and the artistically talented; remedial reading and/or remedial writing; remedial math; ESL (20 students enrolled).

College Admission Counseling 24 students graduated in 2014; all went to college, including California Polytechnic State University, San Luis Obispo; California State University, San Marcos; San Diego State University; University of California, Berkeley; University of California, Davis; University of California, San Diego. Median SAT critical reading: 520, median SAT math: 650, median SAT writing: 590, median combined SAT: 1760. 8.3% scored over 600 on SAT critical reading, 57.1% scored over 600 on SAT math, 16.7% scored over 600 on SAT writing, 16.7% scored over 1800 on combined SAT.

Student Life Upper grades have uniform requirement, student council, honor system. Discipline rests primarily with faculty.

Tuition and Aid Day student tuition: $10,750; 7-day tuition and room/board: $19,650. Tuition installment plan (individually arranged payment plans, Pay by semester). Tuition reduction for siblings, merit scholarship grants, need-based scholarship grants, paying campus jobs, music scholarships, science and math scholarships available. In 2014–15, 20% of upper-school students received aid; total upper-school merit-scholarship money awarded: $10,000. Total amount of financial aid awarded in 2014–15: $25,000.

Admissions Traditional secondary-level entrance grade is 10. For fall 2014, 20 students applied for upper-level admission, 17 were accepted, 17 enrolled. Admissions testing, any standardized test, audition, math and English placement tests, Math Placement Exam, TOEFL or SLEP or writing sample required. Deadline for receipt of application materials: none. Application fee required: $300. Interview recommended.

Athletics Interscholastic: badminton (boys, girls), baseball (b,g), basketball (b,g), cross-country running (b,g), flag football (b), indoor soccer (b,g), soccer (b,g), softball (g), track and field (b,g), volleyball (b,g); intramural: aerobics/dance (b,g), badminton (b,g), ballet (b,g), baseball (b,g), basketball (b,g), bowling (b,g), cheering (g), dance (b,g), dance squad (b,g), dance team (b,g), field hockey (b,g), fitness (b,g), flag football (b,g), gymnastics (b,g), hiking/backpacking (b,g), horseback riding (b,g), indoor soccer (b,g), jump rope (b,g), modern dance (b,g), outdoor activities (b,g), outdoor education (b,g), physical fitness (b,g), soccer (b,g), softball (b,g), surfing (b,g), swimming and diving (b,g), table tennis (b,g), tennis (b,g), track and field (b,g), volleyball (b,g); coed interscholastic: indoor soccer; coed intramural: aerobics/dance, badminton, ballet, baseball, bowling, dance, dance squad, dance team, fitness, flag football, hiking/backpacking, indoor soccer, jump rope, modern dance, outdoor activities, outdoor education, physical fitness, softball, surfing, swimming and diving, table tennis, track and field. 2 PE instructors, 2 coaches.

Computers Computers are regularly used in architecture, business skills, creative writing, desktop publishing, drawing and design, journalism, keyboarding, media arts, music, programming, SAT preparation, typing, video film production, Web site design, word processing, yearbook classes. Computer network features include Internet access, college credit classes online.

Contact Mrs. Kelly McMorrow, Admissions Department. 619-584-2454. Fax: 619-584-2422. E-mail: jmcherif@yahoo.com. Website: www.ccpaasd.com

CHOATE ROSEMARY HALL

333 Christian Street
Wallingford, Connecticut 06492-3800

Head of School: Alex D. Curtis, PhD

General Information Coeducational boarding and day college-preparatory school. Grades 9–PG. Founded: 1890. Setting: small town. Nearest major city is New Haven. Students are housed in single-sex dormitories. 458-acre campus. 121 buildings on campus. Approved or accredited by Connecticut Association of Independent Schools, New England Association of Schools and Colleges, The Association of Boarding Schools, and Connecticut Department of Education. Member of National Association of Independent Schools and Secondary School Admission Test Board. Endowment: $346 million. Total enrollment: 867. Upper school average class size: 12. Upper school faculty-student ratio: 1:6. There are 159 required school days per year for Upper School students. Upper School students typically attend 5 days per week. The average school day consists of 5 hours.

Upper School Student Profile Grade 9: 174 students (87 boys, 87 girls); Grade 10: 215 students (100 boys, 115 girls); Grade 11: 242 students (124 boys, 118 girls); Grade 12: 214 students (110 boys, 104 girls); Postgraduate: 22 students (19 boys, 3 girls). 75% of students are boarding students. 37% are state residents. 42 states are represented in upper school student body. 18% are international students. International students from Canada, China, Hong Kong, Japan, Republic of Korea, and Thailand; 39 other countries represented in student body.

Faculty School total: 140. In upper school: 71 men, 69 women; 138 have advanced degrees; all reside on campus.

Subjects Offered Algebra, American history, American literature, anatomy, Arabic, architecture, art, astronomy, biology, British history, calculus, calculus-AP, ceramics, chemistry, chemistry-AP, child development, Chinese, computer programming, computer science, computer science-AP, creative writing, dance, design, drama, ecology, economics, English, English literature, environmental science, environmental science-AP, European history-AP, fine arts, French, French language-AP, French studies, geometry, government and politics-AP, history, history-AP, Holocaust, interdisciplinary studies, international studies, Italian, language, Latin, Latin-AP, linear algebra, macroeconomics-AP, marine biology, mathematics, microbiology, microeconomics-AP, music, music composition, music history, music performance, music technology, music theater, music theory-AP, music-AP, musical productions, musical theater, musical theater dance, musicianship, philosophy, photography, physics, physics-AP, psychology, psychology-AP, public speaking, religion, Spanish, Spanish language-AP, Spanish literature, Spanish literature-AP, Spanish-AP, statistics, statistics-AP, studio art, theater, trigonometry, U.S. history, U.S. history-AP, visual arts, world history, world literature, world religions, world studies, wrestling, writing, writing, writing workshop.

Graduation Requirements Art, English, foreign language, global studies, history, mathematics, philosophy, physical education (includes health), science, 30 hours of community service.

Special Academic Programs 25 Advanced Placement exams for which test preparation is offered; honors section; independent study; term-away projects; study abroad; academic accommodation for the gifted, the musically talented, and the artistically talented.

College Admission Counseling 255 students graduated in 2015; 247 went to college, including Boston College; Columbia University; Cornell College; New York University; University of Michigan; Yale University. Other: 8 had other specific plans. Mean SAT critical reading: 660, mean SAT math: 677, mean SAT writing: 669, mean combined SAT: 2006, mean composite ACT: 29.

Student Life Upper grades have specified standards of dress, student council, honor system. Discipline rests primarily with faculty.

Summer Programs Enrichment, advancement, ESL, sports, art/fine arts programs offered; session focuses on academic growth and enrichment; held both on and off campus; held at China, France, Jordan, and Spain; accepts boys and girls; open to students from other schools. 575 students usually enrolled. 2016 schedule: June 22 to July 22. Application deadline: May 1.

Tuition and Aid Day student tuition: $42,080; 7-day tuition and room/board: $54,450. Tuition installment plan (Higher One). Need-based scholarship grants available. In 2015–16, 34% of upper-school students received aid. Total amount of financial aid awarded in 2015–16: $11,300,000.

Admissions Traditional secondary-level entrance grade is 9. For fall 2015, 2,040 students applied for upper-level admission, 458 were accepted, 270 enrolled. ACT, ISEE, PSAT or SAT for applicants to grade 11 and 12, SSAT or TOEFL required. Deadline for receipt of application materials: January 10. Application fee required: $75. Interview required.

Athletics Interscholastic: baseball (boys), basketball (b,g), crew (b,g), cross-country running (b,g), diving (b,g), field hockey (g), football (b), golf (b,g), ice hockey (b,g), lacrosse (b,g), soccer (b,g), softball (g), squash (b,g), swimming and diving (b,g), tennis (b,g), track and field (b,g), volleyball (b,g), water polo (b,g); intramural: crew (b,g), squash (b,g); coed interscholastic: archery, sailing, ultimate Frisbee, wrestling; coed intramural: aerobics, aerobics/dance, aerobics/Nautilus, ballet, basketball, dance, dance squad, fitness, martial arts, modern dance, Nautilus, outdoor activities, physical fitness, physical training, rock climbing, running, soccer, softball, strength & conditioning, swimming and diving, tennis, ultimate Frisbee, volleyball, wall climbing, weight training, winter (indoor) track, yoga. 10 coaches, 3 athletic trainers.

Computers Computers are regularly used in all academic, art, college planning, computer applications, desktop publishing, drawing and design, graphic design, information technology, library skills, literary magazine, media production, music, newspaper, photography, programming, stock market, study skills, theater arts, video film production, word processing, yearbook classes. Computer network features include on-campus library services, online commercial services, Internet access, wireless campus network, Internet filtering or blocking technology. Campus intranet, student e-mail accounts, and computer access in designated common areas are available to students. Students grades are available online. The school has a published electronic and media policy.

Contact Raymond M. Diffley III, Director of Admission. 203-697-2239. Fax: 203-697-2629. E-mail: admission@choate.edu. Website: www.choate.edu

CHRISTA MCAULIFFE ACADEMY SCHOOL OF ARTS AND SCIENCES

5200 SW Meadows Road, Ste 150
Lake Oswego, Oregon 97035

Head of School: Christopher M. Geis

General Information Coeducational day and distance learning college-preparatory, general academic, arts, vocational, technology, and Advanced Placement, honors school. Grades K–12. Distance learning grades K–12. Founded: 2009. Setting: small town. Nearest major city is Portland. 1 building on campus. Approved or accredited by Northwest Accreditation Commission, Northwest Association of Schools and Colleges, and Oregon Department of Education. Total enrollment: 263. Upper school average class size: 25. Upper school faculty-student ratio: 1:20. There are 195 required school days per year for Upper School students. Upper School students typically attend 5 days per week. The average school day consists of 5 hours.

Faculty School total: 18. In upper school: 1 man, 17 women; 4 have advanced degrees.

Subjects Offered ACT preparation, alternative physical education, American government, American history, American literature, American sign language, art, art appreciation, art history, astronomy, Bible studies, British literature, British literature (honors), career education, chemistry, child development, Chinese, civics, computer literacy, economics, electives, English, English composition, environmental science, foreign language, forensics, French, geography, geometry, German, government, health, Japanese, keyboarding, Latin, mathematics, music, occupational education, physical education, science, social studies, standard curriculum, technology.

Graduation Requirements Art, career exploration, computer applications, English, mathematics, music, pre-vocational education, science, social studies (includes history).

Special Academic Programs Advanced Placement exam preparation; honors section; accelerated programs; independent study; academic accommodation for the gifted, the musically talented, and the artistically talented; remedial reading and/or remedial writing; remedial math; programs in general development for dyslexic students.

College Admission Counseling 20 students graduated in 2015; 15 went to college. Other: 5 went to work. Mean SAT critical reading: 601, mean SAT math: 523, mean SAT writing: 540, mean combined SAT: 1663, mean composite ACT: 25.

Student Life Upper grades have student council, honor system. Discipline rests equally with students and faculty.

Summer Programs Remediation, enrichment, advancement, computer instruction programs offered; session focuses on make-up and advancement; held both on and off campus; held at student's homes; accepts boys and girls; open to students from other schools. 40 students usually enrolled. 2016 schedule: July 1 to August 31. Application deadline: none.

Tuition and Aid Day student tuition: $5795. Guaranteed tuition plan. Tuition installment plan (monthly payment plans, individually arranged payment plans). Tuition reduction for siblings available.

Admissions Traditional secondary-level entrance grade is 9. Achievement/Aptitude/Writing required. Deadline for receipt of application materials: none. Application fee required: $250.

Computers Computer resources include Internet access. The school has a published electronic and media policy.

Contact Lauren Goodrich, Director of Administrative Services. 888-832-9437 Ext. 3. Fax: 866-920-1619. E-mail: lgoodrich@cmasas.org. Website: www.cmasas.org

CHRIST CHURCH EPISCOPAL SCHOOL

245 Cavalier Drive
Greenville, South Carolina 29607

Head of School: Dr. Leonard Kupersmith

General Information Coeducational day college-preparatory, arts, religious studies, bilingual studies, and technology school, affiliated with Episcopal Church. Grades K–12. Founded: 1959. Setting: suburban. Nearest major city is Greenville/Spartanburg. 72-acre campus. 8 buildings on campus. Approved or accredited by International Baccalaureate Organization, National Association of Episcopal Schools, South Carolina Independent School Association, Southern Association of Colleges and Schools, Southern Association of Independent Schools, and The College Board. Member of National Association of Independent Schools. Endowment: $485,000. Total enrollment: 1,128. Upper school average class size: 13. Upper school faculty-student ratio: 1:10. There are 175 required school days per year for Upper School students. Upper School students typically attend 5 days per week. The average school day consists of 7 hours.

Upper School Student Profile 24% of students are members of Episcopal Church.

Faculty School total: 140. In upper school: 29 men, 26 women; 32 have advanced degrees.

Subjects Offered 20th century world history, algebra, Ancient Greek, ancient history, archaeology, art, art-AP, band, Bible studies, biology, biology-AP, calculus, calculus-AP, ceramics, chemistry, chemistry-AP, China/Japan history, comparative government and politics-AP, computer applications, computer graphics, computer programming, computer science, computer science-AP, contemporary issues, creative writing, digital applications, digital art, digital photography, economics, English, environmental science, environmental science-AP, environmental systems, ESL, ethics, European history, European history-AP, film appreciation, French, French-AP, geometry, German, government and politics-AP, government/civics, graphic arts, honors English, instrumental music, International Baccalaureate courses, journalism, Latin, Latin-AP, literature-AP, Mandarin, mathematics, military history, modern European history, music, music history, music theory, music theory-AP, orchestra, physical education, physical fitness, physics, physics-AP, pre-calculus, probability and statistics, psychology, psychology-AP, religion, sculpture, senior thesis, service learning/internship, Southern literature, Spanish, Spanish-AP, sports conditioning, statistics, statistics-AP, theater, theater design and production, theology, theory of knowledge, U.S. history, U.S. history-AP, video communication, visual and performing arts, visual arts, voice, voice ensemble, Web authoring, world religions, World War II, yearbook.

Graduation Requirements American history, arts and fine arts (art, music, dance, drama), electives, English, foreign language, mathematics, physical education (includes health), religion (includes Bible studies and theology), science, senior thesis, service learning/internship, extended essay (for IB diploma candidates), sophomore project (all students), senior thesis (for non-IB diploma candidates).

Special Academic Programs International Baccalaureate program; honors section; independent study; academic accommodation for the gifted; remedial reading and/or remedial writing; remedial math; ESL (40 students enrolled).

College Admission Counseling 90 students graduated in 2015; all went to college, including Clemson University; College of Charleston; Furman University; The University of Alabama; University of South Carolina; Wofford College. Mean SAT critical reading: 603, mean SAT math: 606, mean SAT writing: 605, mean combined SAT: 1815, mean composite ACT: 27.

Student Life Upper grades have specified standards of dress, student council, honor system. Discipline rests equally with students and faculty. Attendance at religious services is required.

Summer Programs Enrichment, advancement, sports programs offered; session focuses on enrichment, athletics, academics; held both on and off campus; held at field trips to other locations; accepts boys and girls; open to students from other schools. 1,036 students usually enrolled. 2016 schedule: June 1 to August 14.

Tuition and Aid Day student tuition: $18,810. Tuition installment plan (Insured Tuition Payment Plan, FACTS Tuition Payment Plan, monthly payment plans). Merit scholarship grants, need-based scholarship grants available. In 2015–16, 21% of upper-school students received aid; total upper-school merit-scholarship money awarded: $127,786. Total amount of financial aid awarded in 2015–16: $626,210.

Admissions Traditional secondary-level entrance grade is 9. For fall 2015, 80 students applied for upper-level admission, 64 were accepted, 34 enrolled. ERB or PSAT required. Deadline for receipt of application materials: December 1. Application fee required: $150. On-campus interview required.

Athletics Interscholastic: aquatics (boys, girls), baseball (b), basketball (b,g), boxing (b), cheering (g), cross-country running (b,g), dance team (g), field hockey (g), football (b), golf (b,g), gymnastics (g), lacrosse (b,g), soccer (b,g), softball (g), swimming and diving (b,g), tennis (b,g), track and field (b,g), volleyball (g), wrestling (b); intramural: dance team (g); coed interscholastic: fitness, physical fitness; coed intramural: bicycling, dance, dance squad, flag football, hiking/backpacking, lacrosse, martial arts, physical training, roller skating, strength & conditioning, weight lifting, weight training. 2 PE instructors, 59 coaches, 1 athletic trainer.

Computers Computers are regularly used in all academic classes. Computer network features include on-campus library services, online commercial services, Internet access, wireless campus network, Internet filtering or blocking technology, classroom computers, 6-8th grade 1:1 iPad program. Student e-mail accounts and computer access in designated common areas are available to students. Students grades are available online. The school has a published electronic and media policy.

Contact Mrs. Kathy Jones, Director of Admission. 864-299-1522 Ext. 1208. Fax: 864-299-8861. E-mail: jonesk@cces.org. Website: www.cces.org

CHRISTCHURCH SCHOOL

49 Seahorse Lane
Christchurch, Virginia 23031

Head of School: Mr. John E. Byers

General Information Coeducational boarding and day college-preparatory, marine and environmental sciences, and ESL school, affiliated with Episcopal Church. Grades 9–12. Founded: 1921. Setting: rural. Nearest major city is Richmond. Students are housed in single-sex by floor dormitories and single-sex dormitories. 125-acre campus. 15 buildings on campus. Approved or accredited by National Association of Episcopal Schools, The Association of Boarding Schools, The College Board, Virginia Association of Independent Schools, and Virginia Department of Education. Member of National Association of Independent Schools and Secondary School Admission Test Board. Endowment: $4 million. Total enrollment: 196. Upper school average class size: 12. Upper school faculty-student ratio: 1:6. There are 165 required school days per year for Upper School students. Upper School students typically attend 5 days per week. The average school day consists of 9 hours.

Upper School Student Profile Grade 9: 34 students (21 boys, 13 girls); Grade 10: 58 students (39 boys, 19 girls); Grade 11: 56 students (39 boys, 17 girls); Grade 12: 48 students (34 boys, 14 girls). 68% of students are boarding students. 47% are state residents. 17 states are represented in upper school student body. 35% are international

students. International students from Bahamas, China, Guatemala, Republic of Korea, Turkey, and Viet Nam; 7 other countries represented in student body. 12% of students are members of Episcopal Church.

Faculty School total: 38. In upper school: 20 men, 18 women; 27 have advanced degrees; 25 reside on campus.

Subjects Offered Advanced biology, advanced chemistry, algebra, ancient world history, art, biology, calculus, chemistry, Chesapeake Bay studies, Chinese, computer art, computer-aided design, conceptual physics, digital art, drawing and design, economics, English, English language and composition-AP, English literature and composition-AP, environmental science, environmental science-AP, ESL, fine arts, finite math, geography, geometry, health and wellness, honors U.S. history, honors world history, marine biology, modern world history, physical education, physics, pre-calculus, probability and statistics, SAT/ACT preparation, Spanish, Spanish-AP, technology/design, theology, U.S. government, U.S. government and politics-AP, U.S. history, U.S. history-AP, world geography, world history.

Graduation Requirements Arts and fine arts (art, music, dance, drama), English, foreign language, health and wellness, mathematics, physical education (includes health), religion (includes Bible studies and theology), science, social studies (includes history), theology, Great Journeys Integrated Work.

Special Academic Programs 11 Advanced Placement exams for which test preparation is offered; honors section; independent study; academic accommodation for the gifted; ESL (36 students enrolled).

College Admission Counseling 61 students graduated in 2015; all went to college, including Hampden-Sydney College; Randolph-Macon College; University of Mississippi. Mean SAT critical reading: 505, mean SAT math: 555, mean SAT writing: 510, mean combined SAT: 1545. 25% scored over 600 on SAT critical reading, 25% scored over 600 on SAT math.

Student Life Upper grades have specified standards of dress, student council, honor system. Discipline rests equally with students and faculty. Attendance at religious services is required.

Summer Programs Enrichment, sports programs offered; session focuses on marine and environmental science, sailing, camping, fishing, outdoor adventure; held on campus; accepts boys and girls; open to students from other schools. 75 students usually enrolled. 2016 schedule: June 21 to August 1. Application deadline: none.

Tuition and Aid Day student tuition: $20,100; 7-day tuition and room/board: $46,900. Tuition installment plan (monthly payment plans, individually arranged payment plans, 10 month plan, 1st payment due 6/15, 4-payment plan, first payment due 6/15, 2-payment plan, first payment due 6/15). Need-based scholarship grants available. In 2015–16, 54% of upper-school students received aid. Total amount of financial aid awarded in 2015–16: $2,204,840.

Admissions Traditional secondary-level entrance grade is 9. For fall 2015, 286 students applied for upper-level admission, 145 were accepted, 68 enrolled. SSAT or TOEFL required. Deadline for receipt of application materials: none. Application fee required: $50. Interview required.

Athletics Interscholastic: baseball (boys), basketball (b,g), crew (b,g), field hockey (g), football (b), golf (b), indoor track (b), lacrosse (b), sailing (b,g), soccer (b,g), volleyball (g), winter (indoor) track (b); intramural: weight training (b,g); coed interscholastic: cross-country running, golf, indoor track, lacrosse, sailing, swimming and diving, winter (indoor) track; coed intramural: backpacking, canoeing/kayaking, fishing, fly fishing, Frisbee, hiking/backpacking, indoor soccer, outdoor activities, outdoor adventure, outdoor education, outdoor recreation, outdoor skills, paint ball, physical training, rock climbing, sailing, skateboarding, skeet shooting, soccer, strength & conditioning, tennis, yoga. 1 athletic trainer.

Computers Computers are regularly used in all academic classes. Computer network features include on-campus library services, online commercial services, Internet access, wireless campus network, Internet filtering or blocking technology. Campus intranet, student e-mail accounts, and computer access in designated common areas are available to students. Students grades are available online. The school has a published electronic and media policy.

Contact Mrs. Kelly Espy-Page, Senior Associate Director of Admission. 804-758-2306. Fax: 804-758-0721. E-mail: admission@christchurchschool.org. Website: www.christchurchschool.org

CHRISTIAN BROTHERS ACADEMY

850 Newman Springs Road
Lincroft, New Jersey 07738

Head of School: Mr. Ross Fales

General Information Boys' day college-preparatory and religious studies school, affiliated with Roman Catholic Church. Grades 9–12. Founded: 1959. Setting: suburban. Nearest major city is New York, NY. 157-acre campus. 3 buildings on campus. Approved or accredited by Middle States Association of Colleges and Schools. Endowment: $16 million. Total enrollment: 999. Upper school average class size: 24. Upper school faculty-student ratio: 1:14. There are 180 required school days per year for Upper School students. Upper School students typically attend 5 days per week. The average school day consists of 6 hours and 15 minutes.

Upper School Student Profile Grade 9: 265 students (265 boys); Grade 10: 240 students (240 boys); Grade 11: 238 students (238 boys); Grade 12: 256 students (256 boys). 86% of students are Roman Catholic.

Faculty School total: 79. In upper school: 54 men, 25 women; 53 have advanced degrees.

Subjects Offered 20th century history, algebra, American Civil War, American government, American history, anatomy and physiology, Arabic, art history-AP, Bible studies, biology, biology-AP, business, business skills, calculus, calculus-AP, chemistry, chemistry-AP, Civil War, computer science, computer science-AP, creative writing, driver education, economics, English, English language-AP, English literature-AP, environmental science, environmental science-AP, European history, European history-AP, French, geometry, health, history, honors algebra, honors English, honors geometry, honors U.S. history, human geography - AP, journalism, Latin, Latin-AP, linear algebra, macro/microeconomics-AP, mathematics, mythology, peer ministry, physical education, physics, physics-AP, pre-calculus, psychology, psychology-AP, religion, science, social sciences, social studies, Spanish, Spanish-AP, statistics-AP, theology, trigonometry, U.S. history, world history, world literature, writing.

Graduation Requirements Business skills (includes word processing), computer science, English, foreign language, mathematics, physical education (includes health), religion (includes Bible studies and theology), science, social studies (includes history).

Special Academic Programs Advanced Placement exam preparation; honors section.

College Admission Counseling 219 students graduated in 2015; 214 went to college, including Boston College; Manhattan College; Penn State University Park; Saint Joseph's University; Stevens Institute of Technology; Villanova University. Other: 1 entered military service, 4 had other specific plans. Median SAT critical reading: 590, median SAT math: 610, median SAT writing: 600, median combined SAT: 1800.

Student Life Upper grades have specified standards of dress, student council. Discipline rests primarily with faculty. Attendance at religious services is required.

Tuition and Aid Day student tuition: $14,975. Tuition installment plan (FACTS Tuition Payment Plan, individually arranged payment plans, 1-Time, Bi-Annual, 8-Pmts, 10-Pmts). Merit scholarship grants, need-based scholarship grants available. In 2014–15, 18% of upper-school students received aid; total upper-school merit-scholarship money awarded: $498,575. Total amount of financial aid awarded in 2014–15: $700,000.

Admissions Traditional secondary-level entrance grade is 9. For fall 2015, 494 students applied for upper-level admission, 365 were accepted, 265 enrolled. School's own test required. Deadline for receipt of application materials: November 7. Application fee required: $75.

Athletics Interscholastic: baseball, basketball, bowling, crew, cross-country running, fencing, golf, ice hockey, indoor track & field, lacrosse, rugby, sailing, soccer, swimming and diving, tennis, track and field, volleyball, winter (indoor) track, wrestling; intramural: baseball, basketball, bowling, flag football, Frisbee, soccer, squash, tennis, ultimate Frisbee, volleyball. 3 PE instructors, 22 coaches, 1 athletic trainer.

Computers Computers are regularly used in all academic, mathematics, science classes. Computer network features include on-campus library services, online commercial services, Internet access, wireless campus network, Internet filtering or blocking technology. Campus intranet, student e-mail accounts, and computer access in designated common areas are available to students. Students grades are available online. The school has a published electronic and media policy.

Contact Mr. Kevin Donahue, Director of Admissions. 732-747-1959 Ext. 217. Fax: 732-576-8057. Website: www.cbalincroftnj.org

CHRISTIAN BROTHERS ACADEMY

6245 Randall Road
Syracuse, New York 13214

Head of School: Br. Joseph Jozwiak, FSC

General Information Coeducational day college-preparatory and religious studies school, affiliated with Roman Catholic Church. Grades 7–12. Founded: 1900. Setting: suburban. 40-acre campus. 1 building on campus. Approved or accredited by Christian Brothers Association, Middle States Association of Colleges and Schools, and New York State Board of Regents. Endowment: $800,000. Total enrollment: 750. Upper school average class size: 25.

Upper School Student Profile 85% of students are Roman Catholic.

Faculty School total: 62. In upper school: 28 men, 34 women; 58 have advanced degrees.

Subjects Offered Advanced Placement courses, American history, American literature, art, biology, business, calculus, chemistry, chemistry-AP, earth science, economics, English, English literature, European history, expository writing, fine arts, French, government/civics, grammar, health, history, mathematics, music, physical education, physics, pre-calculus, psychology, religion, science, social sciences, social studies, Spanish, theology, world history, world literature.

Graduation Requirements Arts and fine arts (art, music, dance, drama), English, foreign language, mathematics, physical education (includes health), religion (includes Bible studies and theology), science, social sciences, social studies (includes history), community service for seniors.

Special Academic Programs Advanced Placement exam preparation; honors section.

College Admission Counseling 122 students graduated in 2014; 121 went to college, including Le Moyne College; Loyola University Maryland; New York

University; Saint Joseph's University; Syracuse University. Other: 1 entered a postgraduate year. Mean SAT critical reading: 567, mean SAT math: 573, mean SAT writing: 547, mean combined SAT: 1687, mean composite ACT: 25.

Student Life Upper grades have specified standards of dress, student council. Discipline rests primarily with faculty. Attendance at religious services is required.

Tuition and Aid Day student tuition: $9405. Tuition installment plan (SMART Tuition Payment Plan, individually arranged payment plans). Merit scholarship grants, need-based scholarship grants available. In 2014–15, 95% of upper-school students received aid; total upper-school merit-scholarship money awarded: $650,000.

Admissions Traditional secondary-level entrance grade is 9. For fall 2014, 50 students applied for upper-level admission, 38 were accepted, 38 enrolled. Admissions testing required. Deadline for receipt of application materials: February 1. Application fee required: $40. Interview recommended.

Athletics Interscholastic: baseball (boys), basketball (b,g), cheering (g), cross-country running (b,g), diving (b,g), football (b), golf (b,g), gymnastics (b), ice hockey (b), lacrosse (b,g), soccer (b,g), softball (g), swimming and diving (b,g), tennis (b,g), track and field (b,g), volleyball (g), wrestling (b); coed interscholastic: bowling. 3 PE instructors, 1 athletic trainer.

Computers Computer network features include on-campus library services, Internet access, Internet filtering or blocking technology. Students grades are available online. The school has a published electronic and media policy.

Contact Mr. Mark Person, Assistant Principal for Student Affairs. 315-446-5960 Ext. 1227. Fax: 315-446-3393. E-mail: mperson@cbasyracuse.org. Website: www.cbasyracuse.org

CHRISTIAN CENTRAL ACADEMY

39 Academy Street
Williamsville, New York 14221

Head of School: Mr. Thad Gaebelein

General Information Coeducational day college-preparatory, arts, religious studies, and technology school, affiliated with Christian faith. Grades K–12. Founded: 1949. Setting: suburban. Nearest major city is Buffalo. 5-acre campus. 4 buildings on campus. Approved or accredited by Association of Christian Schools International, Middle States Association of Colleges and Schools, New York State Association of Independent Schools, New York State Board of Regents, and New York Department of Education. Member of Secondary School Admission Test Board. Endowment: $1.1 million. Total enrollment: 335. Upper school average class size: 15. Upper school faculty-student ratio: 1:10. There are 180 required school days per year for Upper School students. Upper School students typically attend 5 days per week. The average school day consists of 7 hours.

Upper School Student Profile Grade 9: 23 students (9 boys, 14 girls); Grade 10: 32 students (17 boys, 15 girls); Grade 11: 28 students (14 boys, 14 girls); Grade 12: 30 students (14 boys, 16 girls). 100% of students are Christian faith.

Faculty School total: 42. In upper school: 6 men, 15 women; 10 have advanced degrees.

Subjects Offered Advanced computer applications, advertising design, algebra, art, band, Bible, biology, biology-AP, business mathematics, calculus-AP, chemistry, chorus, communications, computer skills, drawing, driver education, earth science, economics, English, English language-AP, English literature-AP, European history-AP, geometry, global studies, government, government-AP, health, Holocaust, independent study, journalism, mathematics, music, music theory, orchestra, painting, physical education, physics, physics-AP, pre-calculus, Spanish, studio art, trigonometry, U.S. history, U.S. history-AP, yearbook.

Graduation Requirements Algebra, American government, American history, arts and fine arts (art, music, dance, drama), Bible, biology, chemistry, earth science, economics, English, English literature, geometry, global studies, physical education (includes health), physics, Spanish, trigonometry, community service hours for all four years, completion of standardized NYS Regents exams, honors and high honors diplomas have more rigorous requirements.

Special Academic Programs 8 Advanced Placement exams for which test preparation is offered; honors section; independent study.

College Admission Counseling 24 students graduated in 2015; 23 went to college, including Daemen College; Niagara County Community College; University at Buffalo, the State University of New York. Other: 1 entered a postgraduate year. Median SAT critical reading: 550, median SAT math: 570, median SAT writing: 570, median combined SAT: 1690. 46% scored over 600 on SAT critical reading, 38% scored over 600 on SAT math, 33% scored over 600 on SAT writing, 29% scored over 1800 on combined SAT.

Student Life Upper grades have specified standards of dress, student council, honor system. Discipline rests primarily with faculty. Attendance at religious services is required.

Summer Programs Sports programs offered; session focuses on basketball and soccer camps and training; held on campus; accepts boys and girls; not open to students from other schools. 30 students usually enrolled. 2016 schedule: July 6 to July 10. Application deadline: June 30.

Tuition and Aid Day student tuition: $8990. Tuition installment plan (FACTS Tuition Payment Plan, monthly payment plans, prepayment discount plans, multiple-student discounts, pastors/full-time Christian service discounts). Tuition reduction for siblings, merit scholarship grants available. In 2015–16, 43% of upper-school students received aid; total upper-school merit-scholarship money awarded: $5500. Total amount of financial aid awarded in 2015–16: $124,961.

Admissions Traditional secondary-level entrance grade is 9. For fall 2015, 21 students applied for upper-level admission, 18 were accepted, 18 enrolled. Admissions testing, Brigance Test of Basic Skills, essay, Iowa Subtests, school's own test or writing sample required. Deadline for receipt of application materials: none. Application fee required: $50. Interview recommended.

Athletics Interscholastic: baseball (boys), basketball (b,g), flag football (b), golf (b), soccer (b,g), softball (g), volleyball (g); intramural: basketball (b,g), physical fitness (b,g), soccer (b,g); coed interscholastic: bowling, cross-country running, soccer; coed intramural: basketball, track and field, volleyball. 2 PE instructors, 15 coaches.

Computers Computers are regularly used in college planning, computer applications, desktop publishing, drawing and design, English, journalism, library skills, photojournalism, yearbook classes. Computer network features include on-campus library services, Internet access, wireless campus network, Internet filtering or blocking technology, teacher-guided use of programs in various subject areas. Student e-mail accounts and computer access in designated common areas are available to students. Students grades are available online. The school has a published electronic and media policy.

Contact Mrs. Susan Fagan, Admissions Office Manager. 716-634-4821 Ext. 151. Fax: 716-634-5851. E-mail: sfagan@christianca.com. Website: www.christianca.com

CHRISTIAN HERITAGE SCHOOL

575 White Plains Road
Trumbull, Connecticut 06611-4898

Head of School: Mr. Brian Modarelli, PhD

General Information Coeducational day college-preparatory, religious studies, and technology school. Grades K–12. Founded: 1977. Setting: suburban. Nearest major city is Bridgeport. 12-acre campus. 7 buildings on campus. Approved or accredited by Association of Christian Schools International, New England Association of Schools and Colleges, The College Board, and Connecticut Department of Education. Member of European Council of International Schools. Endowment: $15 million. Total enrollment: 450. Upper school average class size: 19. Upper school faculty-student ratio: 1:9. There are 170 required school days per year for Upper School students. Upper School students typically attend 5 days per week. The average school day consists of 7 hours and 15 minutes.

Upper School Student Profile Grade 6: 32 students (17 boys, 15 girls); Grade 7: 34 students (18 boys, 16 girls); Grade 8: 39 students (18 boys, 21 girls); Grade 9: 53 students (27 boys, 26 girls); Grade 10: 36 students (19 boys, 17 girls); Grade 11: 44 students (25 boys, 19 girls); Grade 12: 46 students (20 boys, 26 girls).

Faculty School total: 59. In upper school: 18 men, 13 women; 23 have advanced degrees.

Subjects Offered 20th century American writers, 20th century history, 20th century physics, 20th century world history, advanced chemistry, advanced math, Advanced Placement courses, algebra, American democracy, American foreign policy, American government, American history, American history-AP, American literature, applied music, art, athletics, band, Basic programming, Bible, Bible studies, biology, biology-AP, British literature, business, calculus, calculus-AP, career and personal planning, career exploration, career/college preparation, chamber groups, chemistry, choir, choral music, chorus, Christian and Hebrew scripture, Christian doctrine, Christian education, Christian ethics, Christian scripture, Christian studies, Christian testament, Christianity, church history, classical Greek literature, classics, college admission preparation, college awareness, college counseling, college placement, college planning, college writing, communication skills, comparative government and politics, computer education, computer processing, computer programming, computer programming-AP, computer science, computer skills, computer technologies, concert band, concert choir, constitutional history of U.S., consumer mathematics, contemporary history, contemporary issues, contemporary issues in science, creative arts, current events, current history, data processing, desktop publishing, drama performance, drawing, earth science, English, English composition, English language-AP, English literature, English literature-AP, ensembles, ethics, ethics and responsibility, expository writing, functions, general science, geography, geometry, government/civics, grammar, health and wellness, health education, history, history-AP, honors algebra, honors English, honors geometry, honors U.S. history, human anatomy, human biology, instrumental music, instruments, intro to computers, journalism, keyboarding, language and composition, life issues, Life of Christ, life science, literature, mathematics, mathematics-AP, moral reasoning, music, music theory, musical productions, newspaper, novels, painting, philosophy, physical education, physical science, physics, poetry, prayer/spirituality, pre-algebra, pre-calculus, public speaking, publications, reading/study skills, religion, religious education, science, science project, Shakespeare, social studies, Spanish, Spanish-AP, speech, statistics, student government, student publications, U.S. government, U.S. history-AP, vocal ensemble, vocal music, volleyball, work experience, world affairs, world history, writing, yearbook.

Graduation Requirements Electives, English, foreign language, mathematics, physical education (includes health), religion (includes Bible studies and theology), science, social studies (includes history), community service hours.

Special Academic Programs Advanced Placement exam preparation; honors section; accelerated programs; independent study; term-away projects; academic accommodation for the gifted; ESL (9 students enrolled).

College Admission Counseling 44 students graduated in 2015; 42 went to college, including Southern Connecticut State University; University of Connecticut; Wheaton College. Other: 2 entered military service. Median SAT critical reading: 579, median SAT math: 597, median SAT writing: 588, median combined SAT: 1695, median composite ACT: 25. 9% scored over 600 on SAT critical reading, 9% scored over 600 on SAT math, 8% scored over 600 on SAT writing, 10% scored over 1800 on combined SAT.

Student Life Upper grades have specified standards of dress, student council, honor system. Discipline rests primarily with faculty. Attendance at religious services is required.

Tuition and Aid Day student tuition: $17,400. Tuition installment plan (FACTS Tuition Payment Plan, monthly payment plans, individually arranged payment plans, Tuition Management Systems). Need-based scholarship grants available. In 2015–16, 46% of upper-school students received aid. Total amount of financial aid awarded in 2015–16: $500,000.

Admissions Traditional secondary-level entrance grade is 9. For fall 2015, 56 students applied for upper-level admission, 43 were accepted, 38 enrolled. Admissions testing, ISEE, Otis-Lennon School Ability Test or Stanford Achievement Test required. Deadline for receipt of application materials: none. Application fee required: $50. Interview required.

Athletics Interscholastic: baseball (boys), basketball (b,g), cross-country running (b,g), soccer (b,g), tennis (b,g), volleyball (g); intramural: soccer (b,g), softball (g). 4 PE instructors, 31 coaches.

Computers Computers are regularly used in business education, college planning, data processing, desktop publishing, journalism, keyboarding, mathematics, newspaper, programming, word processing, yearbook classes. Computer network features include on-campus library services, online commercial services, Internet access, wireless campus network, Internet filtering or blocking technology, iPads for all high school students. Campus intranet and student e-mail accounts are available to students. Students grades are available online. The school has a published electronic and media policy.

Contact Mrs. Robin Parrish, Director of Admissions. 203-261-6230 Ext. 555. Fax: 203-268-1046. E-mail: admissions@kingsmen.org. Website: www.kingsmen.org

CHRISTOPHER COLUMBUS HIGH SCHOOL

3000 Southwest 87th Avenue
Miami, Florida 33165-3293

Head of School: Mr. David Pugh II

General Information Boys' day college-preparatory school, affiliated with Roman Catholic Church. Grades 9–12. Founded: 1958. Setting: suburban. 19-acre campus. 10 buildings on campus. Approved or accredited by National Catholic Education Association, Southern Association of Colleges and Schools, and Florida Department of Education. Total enrollment: 1,579. Upper school average class size: 25. Upper school faculty-student ratio: 1:15. There are 180 required school days per year for Upper School students. Upper School students typically attend 5 days per week. The average school day consists of 6 hours and 25 minutes.

Upper School Student Profile Grade 9: 421 students (421 boys); Grade 10: 407 students (407 boys); Grade 11: 384 students (384 boys); Grade 12: 367 students (367 boys). 95% of students are Roman Catholic.

Faculty School total: 82. In upper school: 56 men, 26 women; 35 have advanced degrees.

Subjects Offered 3-dimensional art, accounting, acting, advanced biology, advanced chemistry, advanced computer applications, advanced math, Advanced Placement courses, algebra, American government, American history, American history-AP, American literature, analysis, anatomy, ancient world history, architectural drawing, art, athletic training, athletics, band, Basic programming, Bible, biology, biology-AP, British literature (honors), business law, business skills, calculus, calculus-AP, campus ministry, Catholic belief and practice, chemistry, chemistry-AP, Christian and Hebrew scripture, Christian doctrine, Christian ethics, church history, college counseling, composition-AP, computer applications, computer information systems, computer programming, computer science, computer science-AP, computer-aided design, contemporary history, debate, drama, economics, economics-AP, English, English language and composition-AP, English literature, English literature-AP, English-AP, ethics, European history, European history-AP, French, French language-AP, French-AP, geometry, global studies, government, government and politics-AP, health, history of the Catholic Church, Holocaust studies, keyboarding, library assistant, marine biology, physical education, physical fitness, physics, physics-AP, pre-algebra, pre-calculus, psychology, Spanish, Spanish language-AP, Spanish literature, Spanish literature-AP, speech, U.S. government, U.S. government and politics, U.S. government and politics-AP, U.S. history, U.S. history-AP, Vietnam War, word processing, world governments, yearbook.

Graduation Requirements Algebra, arts and fine arts (art, music, dance, drama), computer applications, English, lab science, language, mathematics, personal fitness, physical education (includes health), practical arts, religion (includes Bible studies and theology), science, social studies (includes history), students must earn a Florida scale

GPA of 2.0, students must complete 100 hours of community service during their four years of high school.

Special Academic Programs Advanced Placement exam preparation; honors section; study at local college for college credit; academic accommodation for the gifted; remedial reading and/or remedial writing.

College Admission Counseling 355 students graduated in 2015; 354 went to college, including Florida International University; Florida State University; University of Central Florida; University of Florida; University of Miami; University of South Florida. Other: 1 entered military service. Mean SAT critical reading: 530, mean SAT math: 540, mean SAT writing: 520, mean combined SAT: 1590, mean composite ACT: 24. 25% scored over 600 on SAT critical reading, 25% scored over 600 on SAT math, 25% scored over 600 on SAT writing, 25% scored over 1800 on combined SAT, 30% scored over 26 on composite ACT.

Student Life Upper grades have uniform requirement, student council, honor system. Discipline rests primarily with faculty. Attendance at religious services is required.

Summer Programs Remediation, enrichment programs offered; session focuses on enrichment, remediation, and study skills; held on campus; accepts boys; not open to students from other schools. 154 students usually enrolled. 2016 schedule: June 11 to June 29. Application deadline: January 18.

Tuition and Aid Tuition installment plan (monthly payment plans, individually arranged payment plans). Bursaries available.

Admissions Traditional secondary-level entrance grade is 9. High School Placement Test required. Deadline for receipt of application materials: none. Application fee required: $50.

Athletics Interscholastic: baseball, basketball, bowling, cross-country running, football, golf, lacrosse, soccer, swimming and diving, tennis, track and field, volleyball, water polo, wrestling; intramural: basketball, flag football, power lifting, roller hockey, weight training. 2 PE instructors, 25 coaches, 2 athletic trainers.

Computers Computers are regularly used in architecture, computer applications, history, journalism, keyboarding, media production, science, yearbook classes. Computer network features include on-campus library services, online commercial services, Internet access, wireless campus network, Internet filtering or blocking technology. Campus intranet, student e-mail accounts, and computer access in designated common areas are available to students. Students grades are available online. The school has a published electronic and media policy.

Contact Mrs. Rebecca Rafuls, Registrar. 305-223-5650 Ext. 2239. Fax: 305-559-4306. E-mail: rrafuls@columbushs.com. Website: www.columbushs.com

CHRISTOPHER DOCK MENNONITE HIGH SCHOOL

1000 Forty Foot Road
Lansdale, Pennsylvania 19446

Head of School: Dr. Conrad J. Swartzentruber

General Information Coeducational boarding and day college-preparatory, general academic, arts, business, vocational, religious studies, and technology school, affiliated with Christian faith, Mennonite Church. Grades 9–12. Founded: 1954. Setting: suburban. Nearest major city is Philadelphia. Students are housed in homes. 75-acre campus. 6 buildings on campus. Approved or accredited by Mennonite Education Agency and Pennsylvania Department of Education. Endowment: $3.8 million. Total enrollment: 375. Upper school average class size: 16. Upper school faculty-student ratio: 1:11. There are 180 required school days per year for Upper School students. Upper School students typically attend 5 days per week. The average school day consists of 6 hours and 55 minutes.

Upper School Student Profile Grade 9: 91 students (56 boys, 35 girls); Grade 10: 109 students (52 boys, 57 girls); Grade 11: 81 students (37 boys, 44 girls); Grade 12: 95 students (50 boys, 45 girls). 4% of students are boarding students. 84% are state residents. 1 state is represented in upper school student body. 16% are international students. International students from Albania, China, Colombia, and Republic of Korea. 43% of students are Christian, Mennonite.

Faculty School total: 33. In upper school: 19 men, 14 women; 23 have advanced degrees.

Subjects Offered Accounting, advanced biology, advanced chemistry, advanced math, Advanced Placement courses, algebra, American government, American history, American literature, anatomy, anatomy and physiology, art, art history, arts, arts appreciation, athletic training, athletics, Basic programming, Bible, Bible studies, biology, British literature, business, business mathematics, business skills, calculus, calculus-AP, career education internship, career technology, ceramics, chemistry, child development, choir, choral music, chorus, Christian and Hebrew scripture, Christian doctrine, Christian education, Christian ethics, Christian scripture, Christian studies, Christian testament, Christianity, church history, communication skills, communications, composition-AP, computer graphics, computer information systems, computer literacy, computer programming, computer science, computer skills, computer technologies, computers, concert choir, consumer economics, creative writing, design, digital art, digital imaging, digital music, digital photography, drama, driver education, early childhood, earth science, ecology, environmental systems, economics, economics and history, economics-AP, English, English language and composition-AP, English literature, environmental science, European history, family and consumer science, family living, family studies, fine arts, food science, foreign language, forensics, genetics, geography, geology, geometry, global studies,

government-AP, government/civics, grammar, graphic design, guitar, health, health and wellness, health education, history, honors English, honors geometry, instrumental music, instruments, international foods, jazz band, journalism, keyboarding, language and composition, Life of Christ, life saving, life science, mathematics, mathematics-AP, music, New Testament, oral communications, parent/child development, peace and justice, peace education, peace studies, personal finance, photography, physical education, physics, religion, religion and culture, religious education, religious studies, research and reference, rhetoric, science, science research, scripture, sculpture, senior internship, service learning/internship, social sciences, social studies, Spanish, Spanish language-AP, Spanish literature-AP, Spanish-AP, speech, speech communications, sports team management, stage and body movement, statistics, student government, student publications, theater, trigonometry, U.S. government, U.S. history, U.S. literature, Vietnam, vocal ensemble, vocal music, vocational skills, vocational-technical courses, Web site design, word processing, work-study, world cultures, world history, world literature.

Graduation Requirements Arts and fine arts (art, music, dance, drama), business skills (includes word processing), computer science, English, family and consumer science, mathematics, physical education (includes health), religion (includes Bible studies and theology), science, social sciences, social studies (includes history), three-day urban experience, senior independent study/service experience (one week), senior presentation.

Special Academic Programs 16 Advanced Placement exams for which test preparation is offered; honors section; term-away projects; study at local college for college credit; remedial reading and/or remedial writing; programs in English for dyslexic students.

College Admission Counseling 88 students graduated in 2015; 84 went to college, including Liberty University; Messiah College; Montgomery County Community College; Penn State University Park. Other: 2 went to work, 2 had other specific plans. Mean SAT critical reading: 507, mean SAT math: 563, mean SAT writing: 517, mean combined SAT: 1587, mean composite ACT: 25. 25% scored over 600 on SAT critical reading, 45% scored over 600 on SAT math, 24% scored over 600 on SAT writing, 29% scored over 1800 on combined SAT.

Student Life Upper grades have specified standards of dress, student council, honor system. Discipline rests primarily with faculty. Attendance at religious services is required.

Tuition and Aid Day student tuition: $15,440; 7-day tuition and room/board: $30,440. Tuition installment plan (monthly payment plans). Tuition reduction for siblings, need-based scholarship grants available. In 2015–16, 64% of upper-school students received aid. Total amount of financial aid awarded in 2015–16: $621,600.

Admissions Traditional secondary-level entrance grade is 9. For fall 2015, 163 students applied for upper-level admission, 130 were accepted, 123 enrolled. Deadline for receipt of application materials: none. Application fee required: $50. Interview required.

Athletics Interscholastic: baseball (boys), basketball (b,g), bowling (b,g), cheering (g), cross-country running (b,g), field hockey (g), golf (b,g), soccer (b,g), softball (g), tennis (b,g), track and field (b,g), volleyball (b,g); coed interscholastic: bowling, cross-country running. 3 PE instructors, 37 coaches, 1 athletic trainer.

Computers Computers are regularly used in accounting, art, computer applications, design, digital applications, graphic design, journalism, keyboarding, lab/keyboard, library, library skills, mathematics, music, music technology, programming, research skills, SAT preparation, science, technology, Web site design, word processing, yearbook classes. Computer network features include on-campus library services, online commercial services, Internet access, wireless campus network, Internet filtering or blocking technology, PowerSchool, WinSNAP, 1:1 iPad program. Campus intranet, student e-mail accounts, and computer access in designated common areas are available to students. Students grades are available online. The school has a published electronic and media policy.

Contact Doug Hackman, Admissions Director. 215-362-2675 Ext. 106. Fax: 215-362-2943. E-mail: dhackman@dockhs.org. Website: www.dockhs.org

CHRYSALIS SCHOOL

14241 North East Woodinville-Duvall Road
PMB 243
Woodinville, Washington 98072

Head of School: Karen Fogle

General Information Coeducational day college-preparatory, general academic, arts, and technology school. Grades 1–12. Founded: 1983. Setting: suburban. Nearest major city is Seattle. 1.5-acre campus. 1 building on campus. Approved or accredited by Northwest Association of Schools and Colleges and Washington Department of Education. Total enrollment: 185. Upper school average class size: 10. Upper school faculty-student ratio: 1:3. Upper School students typically attend 4 days per week. The average school day consists of 5 hours.

Upper School Student Profile Grade 9: 20 students (12 boys, 8 girls); Grade 10: 30 students (19 boys, 11 girls); Grade 11: 33 students (16 boys, 17 girls); Grade 12: 40 students (23 boys, 17 girls).

Faculty School total: 46. In upper school: 17 men, 26 women; 18 have advanced degrees.

Chrysalis School

Subjects Offered Advanced biology, advanced chemistry, advanced computer applications, advanced math, art, audio visual/media, career planning, college counseling, computer technologies, drama, English, filmmaking, French, geography, German, graphics, history, Japanese, mathematics, physical education, SAT preparation, science, social sciences, Spanish.

Graduation Requirements Career and personal planning, computer literacy, English, foreign language, history, mathematics, physical education (includes health), science, portfolio.

Special Academic Programs Honors section; accelerated programs; study at local college for college credit; academic accommodation for the gifted; programs in English, mathematics, general development for dyslexic students; special instructional classes for students with learning challenges.

College Admission Counseling 39 students graduated in 2015; 32 went to college, including Bellevue College; Central Washington University; University of Washington; Washington State University; Western Washington University. Other: 3 went to work, 4 had other specific plans.

Student Life Upper grades have specified standards of dress, honor system. Discipline rests primarily with faculty.

Summer Programs Remediation, enrichment, advancement, computer instruction programs offered; session focuses on enrichment; held on campus; accepts boys and girls; open to students from other schools. 10 students usually enrolled. 2016 schedule: July 12 to August 25. Application deadline: June 1.

Tuition and Aid Tuition installment plan (monthly payment plans).

Admissions Traditional secondary-level entrance grade is 9. For fall 2015, 96 students applied for upper-level admission, 92 were accepted, 90 enrolled. Deadline for receipt of application materials: none. Application fee required: $1000. On-campus interview required.

Computers Computers are regularly used in computer applications, English, foreign language, graphic arts, history, information technology, introduction to technology, keyboarding, mathematics, media, science, video film production, Web site design, word processing, yearbook classes. Computer resources include on-campus library services, online commercial services, Internet access, wireless campus network, Internet filtering or blocking technology. Computer access in designated common areas is available to students. The school has a published electronic and media policy.

Contact Wanda Metcalfe, Director of Student Services. 425-481-2228. Fax: 425-486-8107. E-mail: wanda@chrysalis-school.com. Website: www.chrysalis-school.com

CINCINNATI COUNTRY DAY SCHOOL

6905 Given Road
Cincinnati, Ohio 45243-2898

Head of School: Dr. Robert P. Macrae

General Information Coeducational day college-preparatory, arts, and technology school. Grades PK–12. Founded: 1926. Setting: suburban. 62-acre campus. 8 buildings on campus. Approved or accredited by Independent Schools Association of the Central States and Ohio Department of Education. Member of National Association of Independent Schools and Secondary School Admission Test Board. Endowment: $20 million. Total enrollment: 850. Upper school average class size: 15. Upper school faculty-student ratio: 1:9. There are 180 required school days per year for Upper School students. Upper School students typically attend 5 days per week. The average school day consists of 7 hours.

Upper School Student Profile Grade 9: 77 students (38 boys, 39 girls); Grade 10: 69 students (36 boys, 33 girls); Grade 11: 69 students (32 boys, 37 girls); Grade 12: 73 students (35 boys, 38 girls).

Faculty School total: 110. In upper school: 25 men, 18 women; 37 have advanced degrees.

Subjects Offered Acting, algebra, American history, American history-AP, American literature, analysis, art, art history, biology, biology-AP, calculus, calculus-AP, ceramics, chemistry, chemistry-AP, choir, computer graphics, computer programming, computer science, CPR, creative writing, dance, drama, earth science, engineering, English, English literature, European history, fine arts, French, French language-AP, French literature-AP, genetics, geometry, health, humanities, music, photography, physical education, physics, psychology, public speaking, Spanish, Spanish language-AP, Spanish literature-AP, speech, statistics, theater, trigonometry, world history.

Graduation Requirements Arts and fine arts (art, music, dance, drama), computer science, English, foreign language, history, mathematics, physical education (includes health), science, senior project. Community service is required.

Special Academic Programs Advanced Placement exam preparation; honors section; independent study; study abroad.

College Admission Counseling 70 students graduated in 2014; all went to college, including Butler University; Elon University; Indiana University Bloomington; Miami University; The Ohio State University. Mean SAT critical reading: 630, mean SAT math: 630, mean SAT writing: 640, mean combined SAT: 1900, mean composite ACT: 27.

Student Life Upper grades have specified standards of dress, student council, honor system. Discipline rests equally with students and faculty.

Tuition and Aid Day student tuition: $21,920. Tuition installment plan (Insured Tuition Payment Plan, FACTS Tuition Payment Plan, monthly payment plans, individually arranged payment plans). Merit scholarship grants, need-based scholarship

grants, parent loans, Sallie Mae loans available. In 2014–15, 38% of upper-school students received aid; total upper-school merit-scholarship money awarded: $750,000. Total amount of financial aid awarded in 2014–15: $1,600,000.

Admissions Traditional secondary-level entrance grade is 9. For fall 2014, 61 students applied for upper-level admission, 37 were accepted, 25 enrolled. ISEE, Otis-Lennon Ability or Stanford Achievement Test or SSAT, ERB, PSAT, SAT, PLAN or ACT required. Deadline for receipt of application materials: February 15. Application fee required: $25. Interview recommended.

Athletics Interscholastic: baseball (boys), basketball (b,g), crew (b,g), cross-country running (b,g), football (b), golf (b,g), gymnastics (g), lacrosse (b,g), soccer (b,g), softball (g), swimming and diving (b,g), tennis (b,g), track and field (b,g); intramural: cheering (g); coed interscholastic: crew, dance squad. 4 PE instructors, 1 athletic trainer.

Computers Computers are regularly used in all academic classes. Computer network features include on-campus library services, online commercial services, Internet access, wireless campus network, Internet filtering or blocking technology. Campus intranet, student e-mail accounts, and computer access in designated common areas are available to students. Students grades are available online. The school has a published electronic and media policy.

Contact Mr. Aaron B. Kellenberger, Director of Admission. 513-979-0220. Fax: 513-527-7614. E-mail: kellenbea@countryday.net. Website: www.countryday.net

CISTERCIAN PREPARATORY SCHOOL

3660 Cistercian Road
Irving, Texas 75039

Head of School: Fr. Paul McCormick

General Information Boys' day college-preparatory, arts, and religious studies school, affiliated with Roman Catholic Church. Grades 5–12. Founded: 1962. Setting: suburban. Nearest major city is Dallas. 80-acre campus. 7 buildings on campus. Approved or accredited by Independent Schools Association of the Southwest, Texas Catholic Conference, and Texas Department of Education. Member of National Association of Independent Schools. Endowment: $6.9 million. Total enrollment: 355. Upper school average class size: 22. Upper school faculty-student ratio: 1:5. There are 180 required school days per year for Upper School students. Upper School students typically attend 5 days per week. The average school day consists of 8 hours.

Upper School Student Profile Grade 9: 47 students (47 boys); Grade 10: 46 students (46 boys); Grade 11: 44 students (44 boys); Grade 12: 44 students (44 boys). 82% of students are Roman Catholic.

Faculty School total: 52. In upper school: 32 men, 5 women; 31 have advanced degrees.

Subjects Offered Advanced biology, advanced chemistry, algebra, American history, American literature, art, athletics, baseball, basketball, biology, calculus, chemistry, computer science, creative writing, digital applications, drama, earth science, ecology, economics, English, English composition, English literature, epic literature, ethics, European history, expository writing, fine arts, French, geometry, government/civics, grammar, health, history, history of the Catholic Church, Latin, modern world history, music, performing arts, photography, physical education, physics, pre-algebra, pre-calculus, religion, science, senior project, social studies, Spanish, speech, studio art, swimming, tennis, Texas history, theology, trigonometry, world history, world literature.

Graduation Requirements Arts and fine arts (art, music, dance, drama), electives, English, foreign language, mathematics, physical education (includes health), science, senior project, social studies (includes history), theology, completion of an independent senior project during fourth quarter of senior year.

Special Academic Programs 18 Advanced Placement exams for which test preparation is offered; independent study; study at local college for college credit.

College Admission Counseling 43 students graduated in 2014; all went to college, including Baylor University; Texas A&M University; The University of Texas at Austin; University of Michigan. Median SAT critical reading: 700, median SAT math: 700, median SAT writing: 690, median combined SAT: 2070, median composite ACT: 30. 92% scored over 600 on SAT critical reading, 97% scored over 600 on SAT math, 95% scored over 600 on SAT writing, 97% scored over 1800 on combined SAT, 93% scored over 26 on composite ACT.

Student Life Upper grades have uniform requirement, student council. Discipline rests primarily with faculty. Attendance at religious services is required.

Tuition and Aid Day student tuition: $16,450–$17,750. Tuition installment plan (FACTS Tuition Payment Plan). Need-based scholarship grants available. In 2014–15, 21% of upper-school students received aid. Total amount of financial aid awarded in 2014–15: $354,250.

Admissions Traditional secondary-level entrance grade is 9. For fall 2014, 26 students applied for upper-level admission, 2 were accepted, 2 enrolled. English language, High School Placement Test, Iowa Tests of Basic Skills, ITBS achievement test, Kuhlmann-Anderson, mathematics proficiency exam or writing sample required. Deadline for receipt of application materials: January 19. Application fee required: $100.

Athletics Interscholastic: baseball, basketball, cross-country running, football, physical training, soccer, swimming and diving, tennis, track and field; intramural: basketball, physical training, soccer, strength & conditioning, ultimate Frisbee, volleyball, weight lifting, weight training. 5 coaches, 1 athletic trainer.

Computers Computers are regularly used in college planning, computer applications, digital applications, library, literary magazine, newspaper, photography, programming, publications, yearbook classes. Computer network features include on-campus library services, Internet access, Internet filtering or blocking technology, online college applications, numerous online databases, reference sources, Moodle. Student e-mail accounts and computer access in designated common areas are available to students. The school has a published electronic and media policy.

Contact Mrs. Lisa Richard, Assistant to Headmaster/Registrar. 469-499-5402. Fax: 469-499-5440. E-mail: lrichard@cistercian.org. Website: www.cistercian.org

CLARKSVILLE ACADEMY

710 North Second Street
Clarksville, Tennessee 37040-2998

Head of School: Mrs. Kay D. Drew

General Information Coeducational day college-preparatory, 1:1 Apple program, and FUSE school. Grades PK–12. Founded: 1970. Setting: urban. 31-acre campus. 7 buildings on campus. Approved or accredited by Southern Association of Colleges and Schools, Tennessee Association of Independent Schools, and Tennessee Department of Education. Member of National Association of Independent Schools. Endowment: $1 million. Total enrollment: 650. Upper school average class size: 15. Upper school faculty-student ratio: 1:12. There are 175 required school days per year for Upper School students. Upper School students typically attend 5 days per week. The average school day consists of 7 hours and 10 minutes.

Upper School Student Profile Grade 9: 67 students (34 boys, 33 girls); Grade 10: 58 students (28 boys, 30 girls); Grade 11: 51 students (22 boys, 29 girls); Grade 12: 42 students (21 boys, 21 girls).

Faculty School total: 60. In upper school: 12 men, 18 women; 18 have advanced degrees.

Subjects Offered ACT preparation, American history, art, art appreciation, art history, Bible as literature, biology, biology-AP, calculus, calculus-AP, calligraphy, ceramics, chemistry, chemistry-AP, choir, chorus, college writing, computer education, debate, drama, driver education, ecology, economics, economics and history, English language and composition-AP, English literature and composition-AP, European history-AP, fitness, French, geometry, government, graphic design, guitar, health, health education, honors algebra, honors English, honors geometry, honors U.S. history, honors world history, Italian, Latin, leadership, literature, logic, rhetoric, and debate, media arts, modern history, multimedia design, music, mythology, personal finance, physical education, physical fitness, physics, piano, political science, pre-calculus, printmaking, psychology, publications, sculpture, Spanish, speech, statistics, studio art, study skills, trigonometry, U.S. history, U.S. history-AP, weight training, wellness, women's health, world history, writing, yearbook.

Graduation Requirements Arts and fine arts (art, music, dance, drama), debate, electives, English, foreign language, mathematics, personal finance, science, social studies (includes history), speech, wellness, 24 credit, 4 years of high school math required.

Special Academic Programs 7 Advanced Placement exams for which test preparation is offered; honors section; independent study; study at local college for college credit.

College Admission Counseling 37 students graduated in 2015; all went to college, including Austin Peay State University; Belmont University; Emory University; High Point University; Samford University; The University of Tennessee.

Student Life Upper grades have specified standards of dress, student council, honor system. Discipline rests primarily with faculty.

Summer Programs Remediation, enrichment, sports, art/fine arts, computer instruction programs offered; session focuses on enrichment and remediation; held both on and off campus; held at sports complex; accepts boys and girls; open to students from other schools. 2016 schedule: June 1 to August 3. Application deadline: May 20.

Tuition and Aid Tuition installment plan (monthly payment plans). Tuition reduction for siblings, paying campus jobs available.

Admissions Traditional secondary-level entrance grade is 9. For fall 2015, 18 students applied for upper-level admission, 18 were accepted, 13 enrolled. Brigance Test of Basic Skills, Otis-Lennon School Ability Test and writing sample required. Deadline for receipt of application materials: none. Application fee required: $75. On-campus interview required.

Athletics Interscholastic: baseball (boys), basketball (b,g), cheering (g), dance team (g), football (b), soccer (b,g), softball (g), volleyball (g); coed interscholastic: archery, bowling, cross-country running, golf, tennis. 4 coaches.

Computers Computers are regularly used in all classes. Computer network features include on-campus library services, Internet access, wireless campus network, Internet filtering or blocking technology, 1:1 Apple MacBook program, 1:1 Apple iPad program, 1:1 Apple iPad mini program. Campus intranet, student e-mail accounts, and computer access in designated common areas are available to students. Students grades are available online. The school has a published electronic and media policy.

Contact Mrs. Angie Henson, Business Office and Enrollment. 931-647-6311. Fax: 931-906-0610. E-mail: ahenson@clarksvilleacademy.com. Website: www.clarksvilleacademy.com

CLEARWATER CENTRAL CATHOLIC HIGH SCHOOL

2750 Haines Bayshore Road
Clearwater, Florida 33760

Head of School: Dr. John A. Venturella

General Information Coeducational day college-preparatory, arts, religious studies, technology, and International Baccalaureate diploma program school, affiliated with Roman Catholic Church. Grades 9–12. Founded: 1962. Setting: suburban. Nearest major city is Tampa. 40-acre campus. 8 buildings on campus. Approved or accredited by International Baccalaureate Organization, National Catholic Education Association, Southern Association of Colleges and Schools, The College Board, and Florida Department of Education. Upper school average class size: 25. Upper school faculty-student ratio: 1:13. There are 190 required school days per year for Upper School students. Upper School students typically attend 5 days per week. The average school day consists of 6 hours and 13 minutes.

Upper School Student Profile 80% of students are Roman Catholic.

Faculty School total: 41. In upper school: 14 men, 27 women; 32 have advanced degrees.

Subjects Offered Acting, advanced chemistry, Advanced Placement courses, aerobics, algebra, American government, American history, American history-AP, American literature, American literature-AP, American sign language, anatomy, architecture, Bible studies, biology, biology-AP, British literature, British literature (honors), calculus, calculus-AP, campus ministry, chemistry, chemistry-AP, choral music, chorus, church history, composition, computer processing, creative writing, desktop publishing, discrete mathematics, drama, drawing, drawing and design, ecology, economics, English, English literature and composition-AP, foreign language, French, general science, geometry, health, honors algebra, honors English, honors geometry, honors U.S. history, honors world history, information technology, journalism, keyboarding, language arts, law, law studies, leadership, learning strategies, life management skills, marine biology, music appreciation, oral communications, painting, personal fitness, philosophy, physical education, physics, pre-algebra, probability and statistics, psychology, sociology, Spanish, Spanish language-AP, speech, speech and debate, theater, theology, trigonometry, U.S. government, U.S. government and politics-AP, U.S. history, U.S. history-AP, video, volleyball, Web site design, wellness, world history.

Graduation Requirements Algebra, biology, ceramics, chemistry, comparative government and politics-AP, economics, English, general science, geometry, global studies, physical education (includes health), physical fitness, physical science, physics, Spanish, theology, U.S. government, U.S. history, United States government-AP, visual and performing arts, world geography, world history, world religions, yearbook.

Special Academic Programs International Baccalaureate program; Advanced Placement exam preparation; honors section; study at local college for college credit; programs in English, mathematics, general development for dyslexic students.

College Admission Counseling 130 students graduated in 2014; all went to college, including Florida State University; University of Central Florida; University of Florida; University of South Florida.

Student Life Upper grades have uniform requirement, student council, honor system. Discipline rests primarily with faculty. Attendance at religious services is required.

Tuition and Aid Day student tuition: $10,700–$12,625. Tuition installment plan (FACTS Tuition Payment Plan). Tuition reduction for siblings, need-based scholarship grants available. In 2014–15, 20% of upper-school students received aid. Total amount of financial aid awarded in 2014–15: $830,000.

Admissions Traditional secondary-level entrance grade is 9. For fall 2014, 230 students applied for upper-level admission, 200 were accepted, 170 enrolled. ACT-Explore and Explore required. Deadline for receipt of application materials: none. Application fee required: $100. Interview recommended.

Athletics Interscholastic: baseball (boys), basketball (b,g), cheering (g), cross-country running (b,g), diving (b,g), football (b), golf (b,g), physical fitness (b,g), running (b,g), soccer (b,g), softball (g), swimming and diving (b,g), tennis (b,g), track and field (b,g), volleyball (g), weight lifting (b,g), weight training (b,g), winter soccer (b,g), wrestling (b). 1 PE instructor, 43 coaches, 1 athletic trainer.

Computers Computer network features include on-campus library services, online commercial services, Internet access, wireless campus network, all students utilize iPad Technology. Campus intranet and student e-mail accounts are available to students. Students grades are available online. The school has a published electronic and media policy.

Contact Mrs. Tara Shea McLaughlin, Director of Admissions and Enrollment Management. 727-531-1449 Ext. 304. Fax: 727-451-0101. E-mail: tsheamclaughlin@ccchs.org. Website: www.ccchs.org

COLEGIO BOLIVAR

Calle 5 # 122-21 Via a Pance
Cali, Colombia

Head of School: Dr. Joseph John Nagy

General Information Coeducational day college-preparatory, bilingual studies, and technology school. Grades PK–12. Founded: 1947. Setting: suburban. 14-hectare campus. 7 buildings on campus. Approved or accredited by Association of American Schools in South America, Colombian Ministry of Education, and Southern Association of Colleges and Schools. Languages of instruction: English and Spanish. Total enrollment: 1,269. Upper school average class size: 18. Upper school faculty-student ratio: 1:9. There are 180 required school days per year for Upper School students. The average school day consists of 7 hours.

Upper School Student Profile Grade 9: 85 students (48 boys, 37 girls); Grade 10: 92 students (43 boys, 49 girls); Grade 11: 81 students (26 boys, 55 girls); Grade 12: 87 students (45 boys, 42 girls).

Faculty School total: 163. In upper school: 20 men, 22 women; 31 have advanced degrees.

Subjects Offered Advanced chemistry, Advanced Placement courses, algebra, American history, American literature, art, art history, biology, business, calculus, chemistry, computer science, dance, drama, English, English literature, environmental science, ESL, ethics, French, geology, government/civics, graphic design, history, journalism, mathematics, music, philosophy, photography, physical education, physics, programming, psychology, religion, robotics, social studies, Spanish, theater, trigonometry, world literature.

Graduation Requirements Algebra, American history, American literature, art, biology, calculus, chemistry, computer education, economics, electives, geography, geometry, history of the Americas, music, physical education (includes health), physics, political science, pre-calculus, senior project, Spanish, Spanish literature, trigonometry, world history, world literature, writing, social service hours, senior project.

Special Academic Programs Advanced Placement exam preparation; independent study; remedial reading and/or remedial writing; remedial math; ESL.

College Admission Counseling 85 students graduated in 2015; 66 went to college, including Georgia Institute of Technology; Northwestern State University of Louisiana; University of Miami. Other: 19 had other specific plans.

Student Life Upper grades have specified standards of dress, student council, honor system. Discipline rests equally with students and faculty.

Summer Programs Remediation programs offered; session focuses on math camp; held on campus; accepts boys and girls; not open to students from other schools. 20 students usually enrolled. 2016 schedule: June 27 to July 11.

Tuition and Aid Day student tuition: 17,000,000 Colombian pesos–25,000,000 Colombian pesos. Tuition installment plan (monthly payment plans, annual payment plan). Need-based scholarship grants available.

Admissions Traditional secondary-level entrance grade is 9. For fall 2015, 157 students applied for upper-level admission, 100 were accepted, 90 enrolled. School's own exam required. Deadline for receipt of application materials: none. Application fee required: 80,000 Colombian pesos. On-campus interview required.

Athletics Interscholastic: aerobics/dance (girls), baseball (b), basketball (b,g), dance (g), equestrian sports (b,g), gymnastics (b,g), horseback riding (b,g), running (b,g), soccer (b,g), swimming and diving (b,g), track and field (b,g), volleyball (b,g); intramural: gymnastics (b,g), soccer (b,g), softball (b), swimming and diving (b,g), track and field (b,g), volleyball (b,g). 11 PE instructors, 25 coaches.

Computers Computers are regularly used in graphic design, photography, Web site design, yearbook classes. Computer network features include Internet access, Internet filtering or blocking technology. The school has a published electronic and media policy.

Contact Mrs. Patricia Nasser, Admissions Assistant. 57-2 485 5050 Ext. 274. Fax: 57-2-4850453. E-mail: pnasser@colegiobolivar.edu.co. Website: www.colegiobolivar.edu.co

COLEGIO SAN JOSE

PO Box 21300
San Juan, Puerto Rico 00928-1300

Head of School: Br. Francisco T. Gonzalez, MD

General Information Boys' day college-preparatory, arts, business, religious studies, bilingual studies, technology, science, anatomy, and environmental science, and psychology, humanities, health, economy, political science school, affiliated with Roman Catholic Church. Grades 7–12. Founded: 1938. Setting: urban. 6-acre campus. 2 buildings on campus. Approved or accredited by Middle States Association of Colleges and Schools, National Catholic Education Association, The College Board, and Puerto Rico Department of Education. Languages of instruction: English and Spanish. Endowment: $293,000. Total enrollment: 489. Upper school average class size: 22. Upper School students typically attend 5 days per week. The average school day consists of 6 hours and 50 minutes.

Upper School Student Profile Grade 9: 97 students (97 boys); Grade 10: 81 students (81 boys); Grade 11: 62 students (62 boys); Grade 12: 90 students (90 boys). 90% of students are Roman Catholic.

Faculty School total: 45. In upper school: 24 men, 21 women; 24 have advanced degrees.

Subjects Offered Accounting, algebra, American history, American literature, anatomy, art, art history, biology, biology-AP, broadcasting, business skills, calculus, chemistry, choir, Christian ethics, computer education, computer science, ecology, English, English literature, ethics, European history, French, French as a second language, geography, geometry, government/civics, grammar, health, history,

instrumental music, keyboarding, mathematics, music, physical education, physics, pre-calculus, psychology, religion, science, social studies, Spanish, world history.

Graduation Requirements Business skills (includes word processing), computer science, English, foreign language, history, mathematics, physical education (includes health), religion (includes Bible studies and theology), science, social studies (includes history), Spanish, 40 hours of Christian community service.

Special Academic Programs International Baccalaureate program; Advanced Placement exam preparation; honors section.

College Admission Counseling 108 students graduated in 2014; all went to college, including University of Dayton; University of Puerto Rico, Mayagüez Campus; University of Puerto Rico, Río Piedras Campus.

Student Life Upper grades have uniform requirement, student council, honor system. Discipline rests equally with students and faculty. Attendance at religious services is required.

Tuition and Aid Day student tuition: $7050. Tuition installment plan (The Tuition Plan, individually arranged payment plans). Need-based scholarship grants available. In 2014–15, 13% of upper-school students received aid. Total amount of financial aid awarded in 2014–15: $293,000.

Admissions Traditional secondary-level entrance grade is 9. Catholic High School Entrance Examination required. Deadline for receipt of application materials: February 28. Application fee required: $10. On-campus interview required.

Athletics Interscholastic: baseball, basketball, bowling, cross-country running, fitness, golf, indoor soccer, physical fitness, soccer, swimming and diving, tennis, track and field, volleyball; intramural: cross-country running, indoor soccer, soccer, swimming and diving, tennis, track and field, volleyball. 4 PE instructors, 6 coaches, 1 athletic trainer.

Computers Computers are regularly used in accounting, art, data processing, English, foreign language, keyboarding, mathematics, music, psychology, science, Spanish, yearbook classes. Computer network features include on-campus library services, online commercial services, Internet access, wireless campus network, Internet filtering or blocking technology, Edline, Rediker. Campus intranet and student e-mail accounts are available to students. Students grades are available online. The school has a published electronic and media policy.

Contact Mrs. María E. Guzmán, Guidance Advisor. 787-751-8177 Ext. 229. Fax: 866-955-7646. E-mail: mguzman@csj-rpi.org. Website: www.csj-rpi.org

COLE VALLEY CHRISTIAN HIGH SCHOOL

200 East Carlton Avenue
Meridian, Idaho 83642

Head of School: Mr. Bradley Carr

General Information Coeducational day college-preparatory, general academic, arts, religious studies, and technology school, affiliated with Christian faith. Grades PK–12. Founded: 1990. Setting: suburban. Nearest major city is Boise. 5-acre campus. 3 buildings on campus. Approved or accredited by Association of Christian Schools International, Northwest Accreditation Commission, and Idaho Department of Education. Total enrollment: 793. Upper school average class size: 24. Upper school faculty-student ratio: 1:10. There are 180 required school days per year for Upper School students. Upper School students typically attend 5 days per week. The average school day consists of 5 hours and 50 minutes.

Upper School Student Profile Grade 9: 56 students (28 boys, 28 girls); Grade 10: 64 students (31 boys, 33 girls); Grade 11: 71 students (40 boys, 31 girls); Grade 12: 51 students (28 boys, 23 girls). 95% of students are Christian.

Faculty School total: 29. In upper school: 11 men, 18 women; 5 have advanced degrees.

Subjects Offered 20th century history, acting, algebra, American government, American literature, art, Bible, biology, British literature, business mathematics, calculus-AP, chemistry, choral music, computer literacy, economics, English, English literature, French, geometry, honors English, physical education, physical science, physics, pre-algebra, pre-calculus, Spanish, speech, U.S. history, world history, yearbook.

Graduation Requirements 20th century history, American government, economics, English, mathematics, physical education (includes health), religion (includes Bible studies and theology), science, social studies (includes history), speech, Bible classes.

Special Academic Programs Advanced Placement exam preparation; honors section; independent study; study at local college for college credit.

College Admission Counseling 55 students graduated in 2014; 52 went to college, including Boise State University; Grand Canyon University; Northwest Nazarene University; The College of Idaho; University of Idaho. Other: 3 went to work.

Student Life Upper grades have specified standards of dress, student council, honor system. Discipline rests primarily with faculty. Attendance at religious services is required.

Tuition and Aid Day student tuition: $6500. Tuition installment plan (SMART Tuition Payment Plan, monthly payment plans, individually arranged payment plans). Tuition reduction for siblings, need-based scholarship grants available. In 2014–15, 20% of upper-school students received aid.

Admissions Traditional secondary-level entrance grade is 9. Deadline for receipt of application materials: none. Application fee required: $140. Interview required.

Athletics Interscholastic: basketball (boys, girls), cheering (g), cross-country running (b,g), football (b), track and field (b,g), volleyball (g), wrestling (b); intramural: skiing (cross-country) (b,g), skiing (downhill) (b,g), snowboarding (b,g). 3 PE instructors, 12 coaches.

Computers Computers are regularly used in all academic classes. Computer network features include on-campus library services, Internet access, wireless campus network, Internet filtering or blocking technology. Student e-mail accounts are available to students. Students grades are available online. The school has a published electronic and media policy.

Contact Mrs. Robin Didriksen, Administrative Assistant to the Guidance Counselor/Registrar. 208-947-1212 Ext. 1210. Fax: 208-898-9016. E-mail: rdidriksen@cvcsonline.org. Website: www.colevalleychristian.org

COLLEGEDALE ACADEMY

PO Box 628
4855 College Drive East
Collegedale, Tennessee 37315

Head of School: Mr. Brent Baldwin

General Information Coeducational day college-preparatory and arts school, affiliated with Seventh-day Adventists. Grades 9–12. Founded: 1892. Setting: small town. Nearest major city is Chattanooga. 20-acre campus. 3 buildings on campus. Approved or accredited by Middle States Association of Colleges and Schools, Southern Association of Colleges and Schools, and Tennessee Department of Education. Endowment: $725,000. Total enrollment: 310. Upper school average class size: 25. Upper school faculty-student ratio: 1:18. There are 180 required school days per year for Upper School students. Upper School students typically attend 5 days per week. The average school day consists of 8 hours and 15 minutes.

Upper School Student Profile Grade 9: 103 students (62 boys, 41 girls); Grade 10: 74 students (29 boys, 45 girls); Grade 11: 66 students (39 boys, 27 girls); Grade 12: 67 students (38 boys, 29 girls). 98% of students are Seventh-day Adventists.

Faculty School total: 39. In upper school: 18 men, 17 women; 28 have advanced degrees.

Graduation Requirements Arts and fine arts (art, music, dance, drama), computer science, English, foreign language, mathematics, physical education (includes health), religion (includes Bible studies and theology), science, social studies (includes history).

Special Academic Programs 1 Advanced Placement exam for which test preparation is offered; honors section; accelerated programs; study at local college for college credit.

College Admission Counseling 75 students graduated in 2015; 74 went to college. Other: 1 went to work. 34% scored over 26 on composite ACT.

Student Life Upper grades have uniform requirement, student council, honor system. Discipline rests primarily with faculty. Attendance at religious services is required.

Summer Programs Advancement programs offered; session focuses on U.S. history; held on campus; accepts boys and girls; open to students from other schools. 20 students usually enrolled. 2016 schedule: June 1 to July 3. Application deadline: none.

Tuition and Aid Day student tuition: $8760. Tuition installment plan (monthly payment plans). Need-based scholarship grants available. In 2015–16, 20% of upper-school students received aid. Total amount of financial aid awarded in 2015–16: $55,000.

Admissions Traditional secondary-level entrance grade is 9. For fall 2015, 317 students applied for upper-level admission, 310 were accepted, 310 enrolled. Mathematics proficiency exam required. Deadline for receipt of application materials: August 1. Application fee required: $125. On-campus interview required.

Athletics Interscholastic: cross-country running (boys, girls), golf (b,g), tennis (b,g); intramural: basketball (b,g), soccer (b,g), track and field (b,g), volleyball (b,g); coed intramural: flag football, gymnastics, hiking/backpacking, paddle tennis, volleyball. 2 PE instructors, 2 coaches.

Computers Computers are regularly used in Bible studies, history, mathematics, publications, social studies, study skills, writing classes. Computer network features include on-campus library services, Internet access, wireless campus network, Internet filtering or blocking technology. Student e-mail accounts and computer access in designated common areas are available to students. Students grades are available online. The school has a published electronic and media policy.

Contact Miss Kerre Conerly, Registrar. 423-396-2124 Ext. 5421. Fax: 423-396-3363. E-mail: kconerly@collegedaleacademy.com. Website: www.collegedaleacademy.com

THE COLLEGE PREPARATORY SCHOOL

6100 Broadway
Oakland, California 94618

Head of School: Monique DeVane

General Information Coeducational day college-preparatory school. Grades 9–12. Founded: 1960. Setting: urban. 5-acre campus. 15 buildings on campus. Approved or accredited by California Association of Independent Schools, Western Association of Schools and Colleges, and California Department of Education. Member of National Association of Independent Schools and Secondary School Admission Test Board.

Endowment: $19.6 million. Total enrollment: 360. Upper school average class size: 14. Upper school faculty-student ratio: 1:7. Upper School students typically attend 5 days per week.

Upper School Student Profile Grade 9: 94 students (46 boys, 48 girls); Grade 10: 92 students (44 boys, 48 girls); Grade 11: 89 students (42 boys, 47 girls); Grade 12: 85 students (39 boys, 46 girls).

Faculty School total: 55. In upper school: 25 men, 30 women; 46 have advanced degrees.

Subjects Offered 20th century American writers, 3-dimensional art, acting, advanced math, Advanced Placement courses, algebra, American government, American history, American literature, animal behavior, art, art-AP, astronomy, audio visual/media, biology, biology-AP, calculus, calculus-AP, chemistry, chemistry-AP, Chinese, Chinese literature, chorus, comparative religion, computer science, contemporary issues in science, creative writing, dance, dance performance, debate, digital applications, drama, drama performance, drawing and design, economics, English, English literature, environmental science-AP, European history, forensics, French, French literature-AP, French-AP, freshman foundations, genetics, geometry, health education, history, independent study, instruments, Japanese, jazz band, junior and senior seminars, language-AP, Latin, Latin American literature, Latin-AP, linguistics, mathematics, music, music theory-AP, orchestra, peer counseling, philosophy, photography, physical education, physical science, physics, physics-AP, poetry, psychology, science, Shakespeare, Spanish, Spanish-AP, stagecraft, statistics, statistics-AP, theater, theater design and production, U.S. government, vocal ensemble, Western civilization, women's studies, world civilizations, zoology.

Graduation Requirements Arts, English, foreign language, history, mathematics, physical education (includes health), science.

Special Academic Programs Advanced Placement exam preparation; honors section; independent study.

College Admission Counseling 99 students graduated in 2014; all went to college, including Barnard College; Carleton College; Columbia University; Oberlin College; Williams College. Mean SAT critical reading: 710, mean SAT math: 727, mean SAT writing: 728.

Student Life Upper grades have student council. Discipline rests primarily with faculty.

Tuition and Aid Day student tuition: $37,090. Tuition installment plan (FACTS Tuition Payment Plan, monthly payment plans). Need-based scholarship grants available. In 2014–15, 25% of upper-school students received aid. Total amount of financial aid awarded in 2014–15: $2,075,000.

Admissions Traditional secondary-level entrance grade is 9. For fall 2014, 340 students applied for upper-level admission, 126 were accepted, 98 enrolled. ISEE or SSAT required. Deadline for receipt of application materials: January 15. Application fee required: $75. Interview required.

Athletics Interscholastic: baseball (boys), basketball (b,g), cross-country running (b,g), outdoor recreation (b,g), soccer (b,g), softball (g), swimming and diving (b,g), tennis (b,g), track and field (b,g), volleyball (b,g); intramural: dance (b,g); coed interscholastic: golf; coed intramural: badminton, basketball, cross-country running, dance, golf, outdoor recreation, soccer, volleyball. 4 PE instructors, 21 coaches.

Computers Computers are regularly used in art, drawing and design, mathematics, music, newspaper, science, theater arts, video film production, yearbook classes. Computer network features include on-campus library services, online commercial services, Internet access, wireless campus network, remote access to library services, Web publishing, remote file-server access, video recording and editing. Campus intranet, student e-mail accounts, and computer access in designated common areas are available to students. Students grades are available online. The school has a published electronic and media policy.

Contact Jonathan Zucker, Director of Admission and Financial Aid. 510-652-4364 Ext. 2. Fax: 510-652-7467. E-mail: jonathan@college-prep.org. Website: www.college-prep.org

THE COLLEGIATE SCHOOL

103 North Mooreland Road
Richmond, Virginia 23229

Head of School: Stephen D. Hickman

General Information Coeducational day college-preparatory, arts, and technology school. Grades K–12. Founded: 1915. Setting: suburban. 211-acre campus. 13 buildings on campus. Approved or accredited by Southern Association of Colleges and Schools, Virginia Association of Independent Schools, and Virginia Department of Education. Member of National Association of Independent Schools and Secondary School Admission Test Board. Endowment: $59.1 million. Total enrollment: 1,644. Upper school average class size: 15. Upper school faculty-student ratio: 1:15. There are 174 required school days per year for Upper School students. Upper School students typically attend 5 days per week. The average school day consists of 7 hours.

Upper School Student Profile Grade 9: 136 students (69 boys, 67 girls); Grade 10: 131 students (66 boys, 65 girls); Grade 11: 133 students (69 boys, 64 girls); Grade 12: 125 students (59 boys, 66 girls).

Faculty School total: 196. In upper school: 31 men, 35 women; 42 have advanced degrees.

Subjects Offered 20th century history, acting, advanced chemistry, African studies, algebra, American Civil War, American history, American history-AP, American literature, art, Asian literature, Bible as literature, biology, biology-AP, calculus-AP, ceramics, chemistry, chemistry-AP, community service, computer applications, creative writing, drama, driver education, earth science, economics, economics-AP, English, English literature, ethics, European history, film and literature, fine arts, French, French-AP, geometry, government and politics-AP, government/civics, health, journalism, Latin, music, photography, physics, physics-AP, religion, robotics, Russian literature, senior project, senior seminar, Spanish, Spanish language-AP, statistics, theater, trigonometry, world history, World War II.

Graduation Requirements Arts and fine arts (art, music, dance, drama), English, ethics, foreign language, government, history, mathematics, physical education (includes health), religion (includes Bible studies and theology), science, sports, senior speech, senior project. Community service is required.

Special Academic Programs 16 Advanced Placement exams for which test preparation is offered; honors section; independent study; study at local college for college credit; programs in general development for dyslexic students.

College Admission Counseling 136 students graduated in 2015; all went to college, including James Madison University; University of South Carolina; University of Virginia; Virginia Commonwealth University; Virginia Polytechnic Institute and State University. Mean SAT critical reading: 627, mean SAT math: 648, mean SAT writing: 623, mean combined SAT: 1897, mean composite ACT: 28. 66% scored over 600 on SAT critical reading, 77% scored over 600 on SAT math, 63% scored over 600 on SAT writing, 66% scored over 1800 on combined SAT, 80% scored over 26 on composite ACT.

Student Life Upper grades have specified standards of dress, student council, honor system. Discipline rests equally with students and faculty.

Summer Programs Remediation, enrichment, advancement, sports, art/fine arts, computer instruction programs offered; session focuses on advancement, remediation, sports; held both on and off campus; held at various locations in metro Richmond; accepts boys and girls; open to students from other schools. 1,334 students usually enrolled. 2016 schedule: June 13 to August 12. Application deadline: none.

Tuition and Aid Day student tuition: $23,610. Tuition installment plan (Insured Tuition Payment Plan, monthly payment plans). Need-based scholarship grants available.

Admissions Traditional secondary-level entrance grade is 9. For fall 2015, 124 students applied for upper-level admission, 53 were accepted, 28 enrolled. PSAT and SAT for applicants to grade 11 and 12, SSAT or writing sample required. Deadline for receipt of application materials: none. Application fee required: $50. Interview required.

Athletics Interscholastic: baseball (boys), basketball (b,g), cross-country running (b,g), diving (b,g), field hockey (g), football (b), indoor track & field (b,g), lacrosse (b,g), soccer (b,g), softball (g), swimming and diving (b,g), tennis (b,g), track and field (b,g), volleyball (g), winter (indoor) track (b,g), wrestling (b); coed interscholastic: golf, indoor soccer; coed intramural: combined training, dance, dance squad, dance team, fitness, hiking/backpacking, modern dance, mountain biking, outdoor activities, outdoor adventure, strength & conditioning, weight lifting, yoga. 5 PE instructors, 50 coaches, 2 athletic trainers.

Computers Computers are regularly used in all academic classes. Computer network features include on-campus library services, Internet access, wireless campus network, Internet filtering or blocking technology. Campus intranet, student e-mail accounts, and computer access in designated common areas are available to students. Students grades are available online. The school has a published electronic and media policy.

Contact John R. Wilson, Director of Admission. 804-741-5472. Fax: 804-754-4326. E-mail: john_wilson@collegiate-va.org. Website: www.collegiate-va.org/

THE COLORADO ROCKY MOUNTAIN SCHOOL

500 Holden Way
Carbondale, Colorado 81623

Head of School: Jeff Leahy

General Information Coeducational boarding and day college-preparatory and arts school. Grades 9–12. Founded: 1953. Setting: small town. Nearest major city is Denver. Students are housed in single-sex dormitories. 350-acre campus. 23 buildings on campus. Approved or accredited by Association for Experiential Education, Association of Colorado Independent Schools, The Association of Boarding Schools, and Colorado Department of Education. Member of National Association of Independent Schools and Secondary School Admission Test Board. Endowment: $20 million. Total enrollment: 176. Upper school average class size: 12. Upper school faculty-student ratio: 1:5. There are 175 required school days per year for Upper School students. Upper School students typically attend 5 days per week. The average school day consists of 8 hours.

Upper School Student Profile Grade 9: 43 students (23 boys, 20 girls); Grade 10: 46 students (26 boys, 20 girls); Grade 11: 38 students (21 boys, 17 girls); Grade 12: 49 students (30 boys, 19 girls). 57% of students are boarding students. 59% are state residents. 22 states are represented in upper school student body. 20% are international students. International students from China, Germany, Japan, Macedonia, Mexico, and Mongolia; 6 other countries represented in student body.

Faculty School total: 35. In upper school: 20 men, 15 women; 19 have advanced degrees; 33 reside on campus.

Subjects Offered Advanced Placement courses, algebra, American literature, art, art history, biology, calculus, ceramics, chemistry, computer programming, computer science, creative writing, drama, ecology, English, English literature, environmental science, ESL, ethics, European history, fine arts, gardening, geography, geology, geometry, geopolitics, government/civics, grammar, graphic design, guitar, history, history of ideas, journalism, mathematics, music, philosophy, photography, physical education, physics, physiology, religion, robotics, science, senior project, Shakespeare, social studies, Spanish, theater, trigonometry, video film production, Western civilization, world history, world literature, writing.

Graduation Requirements Arts and fine arts (art, music, dance, drama), biology, chemistry, English, foreign language, mathematics, science, senior project, social studies (includes history), wilderness experience, participation in wilderness orientation. Community service is required.

Special Academic Programs 5 Advanced Placement exams for which test preparation is offered; independent study; academic accommodation for the gifted, the musically talented, and the artistically talented; ESL (10 students enrolled).

College Admission Counseling 39 students graduated in 2015; 37 went to college, including Lewis & Clark College; Middlebury College; The Colorado College; University of Colorado Boulder; University of Pennsylvania. Other: 2 entered military service. Mean SAT critical reading: 520, mean SAT math: 525, mean SAT writing: 515, mean combined SAT: 1561, mean composite ACT: 24. 23% scored over 600 on SAT critical reading, 23% scored over 600 on SAT math, 8% scored over 600 on SAT writing, 13% scored over 1800 on combined SAT, 28% scored over 26 on composite ACT.

Student Life Upper grades have student council, honor system. Discipline rests equally with students and faculty.

Tuition and Aid Day student tuition: $32,500; 7-day tuition and room/board: $52,000. Tuition installment plan (monthly payment plans, individually arranged payment plans, 3rd party loan options). Merit scholarship grants, need-based scholarship grants available. In 2015–16, 30% of upper-school students received aid; total upper-school merit-scholarship money awarded: $45,500. Total amount of financial aid awarded in 2015–16: $2,072,750.

Admissions Traditional secondary-level entrance grade is 9. For fall 2015, 157 students applied for upper-level admission, 100 were accepted, 70 enrolled. PSAT or SAT, SSAT or TOEFL required. Deadline for receipt of application materials: February 15. Application fee required: $75. Interview required.

Athletics Intramural: aerobics/dance (girls), basketball (b,g), dance (b,g), fly fishing (b,g), freestyle skiing (b,g); coed interscholastic: alpine skiing, bicycling, canoeing/kayaking, climbing, cross-country running, independent competitive sports, kayaking, mountain biking, nordic skiing, rock climbing, running, skiing (downhill), snowboarding, telemark skiing, wall climbing; coed intramural: alpine skiing, backpacking, basketball, bicycling, canoeing/kayaking, climbing, cross-country running, dance, fishing, fitness, floor hockey, fly fishing, freestyle skiing, Frisbee, hiking/backpacking, horseback riding, horseshoes, jogging, kayaking, martial arts, mountain biking, mountaineering, nordic skiing, outdoor activities, outdoor adventure, outdoor education, outdoor recreation, outdoor skills, outdoors, physical fitness, physical training, rafting, rock climbing, running, skiing (cross-country), skiing (downhill), snowboarding, strength & conditioning, swimming and diving, telemark skiing, wall climbing, weight lifting, wilderness, wilderness survival, yoga. 4 coaches.

Computers Computers are regularly used in art, college planning, ESL, mathematics, science classes. Computer network features include on-campus library services, online commercial services, Internet access, wireless campus network, Internet filtering or blocking technology. Student e-mail accounts are available to students. Students grades are available online. The school has a published electronic and media policy.

Contact Molly Dorais, Director of Admission and Financial Aid. 970-963-2562. Fax: 970-963-9865. E-mail: mdorais@crms.org. Website: www.crms.org

THE COLORADO SPRINGS SCHOOL

21 Broadmoor Avenue
Colorado Springs, Colorado 80906

Head of School: Mr. Aaron Schubach

General Information Coeducational day college-preparatory, arts, experiential and project-based learning, and global perspectives school. Grades PK–12. Founded: 1962. Setting: suburban. 30-acre campus. 7 buildings on campus. Approved or accredited by Association of Colorado Independent Schools. Member of National Association of Independent Schools and National Association for College Admission Counseling. Endowment: $3.1 million. Total enrollment: 274. Upper school average class size: 16. Upper school faculty-student ratio: 1:7. There are 169 required school days per year for Upper School students. Upper School students typically attend 5 days per week. The average school day consists of 6 hours and 30 minutes.

Upper School Student Profile Grade 9: 21 students (11 boys, 10 girls); Grade 10: 22 students (11 boys, 11 girls); Grade 11: 32 students (14 boys, 18 girls); Grade 12: 23 students (12 boys, 11 girls).

Faculty School total: 46. In upper school: 11 men, 13 women; 18 have advanced degrees.

Subjects Offered 20th century history, 3-dimensional art, 3-dimensional design, ACT preparation, acting, adolescent issues, advanced chemistry, advanced math, Advanced Placement courses, advanced studio art-AP, African history, African studies, algebra, American government, American history, American history-AP, American literature, American literature-AP, American studies, analysis and differential calculus, anatomy and physiology, art history, art-AP, athletics, band, biology, biology-AP, botany, British literature-AP, calculus, calculus-AP, career education internship, career/college preparation, ceramics, chemistry, choir, choral music, clayworking, college admission preparation, college counseling, community service, comparative government and politics, comparative government and politics-AP, composition, computer applications, concert band, costumes and make-up, creative arts, digital art, digital photography, directing, discrete mathematics, drama, drawing, economics, economics-AP, English, English literature, English literature and composition-AP, English literature-AP, environmental science, environmental science-AP, environmental studies, equality and freedom, ethics, European history-AP, European literature, experiential education, filmmaking, fine arts, French, French language-AP, French literature-AP, French-AP, functions, gardening, geography, geology, geometry, glassblowing, global studies, government and politics-AP, grammar, health and wellness, history, history-AP, Latin American history, literature, macro/microeconomics-AP, microeconomics, music, music appreciation, musical productions, painting, philosophy, photography, photojournalism, physical education, physics, physics-AP, playwriting, post-calculus, pottery, pre-algebra, pre-calculus, printmaking, SAT/ACT preparation, science, sculpture, Spanish, Spanish literature, Spanish literature-AP, speech, statistics, statistics-AP, stone carving, studio art, studio art-AP, textiles, theater, theater arts, theater production, trigonometry, U.S. history, U.S. history-AP, welding, Western civilization, wilderness education, wilderness experience, world affairs, world civilizations, world cultures, world geography, world governments, world history, world history-AP, world issues, world literature, world religions, writing, writing workshop, yearbook.

Graduation Requirements Arts and fine arts (art, music, dance, drama), athletics, college admission preparation, English, experiential education, foreign language, mathematics, science, social studies (includes history), speech and oral interpretations, experience-centered seminar each year, college overview course, 24 hours of community service per each year of high school.

Special Academic Programs Advanced Placement exam preparation; honors section; independent study; term-away projects; academic accommodation for the gifted; programs in general development for dyslexic students; special instructional classes for deaf students.

College Admission Counseling 26 students graduated in 2015; 25 went to college, including University of Colorado Boulder. Other: 1 had other specific plans. Mean combined SAT: 1952, mean composite ACT: 27.

Student Life Upper grades have specified standards of dress, student council, honor system. Discipline rests equally with students and faculty.

Tuition and Aid Day student tuition: $20,850. Tuition installment plan (Insured Tuition Payment Plan, monthly payment plans, individually arranged payment plans). Merit scholarship grants, need-based scholarship grants available. In 2014–15, 46% of upper-school students received aid; total upper-school merit-scholarship money awarded: $165,750. Total amount of financial aid awarded in 2014–15: $347,902.

Admissions Traditional secondary-level entrance grade is 9. For fall 2015, 11 students applied for upper-level admission, 10 were accepted, 9 enrolled. Standardized test scores or TOEFL required. Deadline for receipt of application materials: none. Application fee required: $75. On-campus interview required.

Athletics Interscholastic: basketball (boys, girls), cross-country running (b,g), golf (b), lacrosse (b), soccer (b,g), tennis (b,g), volleyball (b,g); intramural: archery (b,g), climbing (b,g), Frisbee (b,g), physical fitness (b,g), physical training (b,g); coed interscholastic: mountain biking; coed intramural: fly fishing, golf, mountaineering, outdoor activities, outdoor adventure, outdoor education, paddle tennis, rock climbing, skiing (cross-country), skiing (downhill), wilderness, yoga. 2 PE instructors, 8 coaches.

Computers Computer network features include on-campus library services, online commercial services, Internet access, wireless campus network, Internet filtering or blocking technology. Campus intranet, student e-mail accounts, and computer access in designated common areas are available to students. Students grades are available online. The school has a published electronic and media policy.

Contact Ms. Lisa Kleintjes Kamemoto, Director of Admission and Marketing. 719-434-3500. Fax: 719-475-9864. E-mail: lisakk@css.org. Website: www.css.org

COLUMBIA ACADEMY

1101 West 7th Street
Columbia, Tennessee 38401

Head of School: Dr. James Thomas

General Information Coeducational day college-preparatory, arts, business, religious studies, and technology school, affiliated with Church of Christ. Grades K–12. Founded: 1978. Setting: small town. Nearest major city is Nashville. 67-acre campus. 6 buildings on campus. Approved or accredited by National Christian School Association, Southern Association of Colleges and Schools, and Tennessee Department of Education. Endowment: $2.7 million. Total enrollment: 748. Upper school average class size: 17. Upper school faculty-student ratio: 1:12. There are 175 required school

days per year for Upper School students. Upper School students typically attend 5 days per week. The average school day consists of 7 hours.

Upper School Student Profile Grade 7: 53 students (27 boys, 26 girls); Grade 8: 71 students (43 boys, 28 girls); Grade 9: 83 students (52 boys, 31 girls); Grade 10: 74 students (43 boys, 31 girls); Grade 11: 52 students (23 boys, 29 girls); Grade 12: 41 students (19 boys, 22 girls). 60% of students are members of Church of Christ.

Faculty School total: 30. In upper school: 15 men, 15 women; 13 have advanced degrees.

Subjects Offered Accounting, ACT preparation, advanced math, algebra, American history, American literature, anatomy and physiology, art, band, Bible, biology, British literature, calculus, chemistry, computer applications, economics, English, English literature and composition-AP, environmental science, fine arts, geometry, government/civics, grammar, health, keyboarding, math review, music, personal finance, physical education, physics, pre-calculus, religion, Spanish, speech, U.S. history-AP, world geography, world history.

Graduation Requirements ACT preparation, arts and fine arts (art, music, dance, drama), computer applications, economics, electives, English, foreign language, mathematics, physical education (includes health), religion (includes Bible studies and theology), science, social sciences, social studies (includes history), speech, four hours of approved service required for each quarter enrolled.

Special Academic Programs Advanced Placement exam preparation; honors section; independent study; study at local college for college credit.

College Admission Counseling 51 students graduated in 2015; 50 went to college, including Columbia State Community College; Freed-Hardeman University; The University of Alabama; The University of Tennessee; The University of Tennessee at Chattanooga; The University of Tennessee at Martin. Other: 1 went to work. Median composite ACT: 24. 37% scored over 26 on composite ACT.

Student Life Upper grades have specified standards of dress, student council, honor system. Discipline rests primarily with faculty.

Summer Programs Remediation programs offered; session focuses on make-up or credit recovery for failing grades during the semesters; held on campus; accepts boys and girls; not open to students from other schools. 5 students usually enrolled. 2016 schedule: May 29 to June 20. Application deadline: May 11.

Tuition and Aid Day student tuition: $7400. Tuition installment plan (monthly payment plans, individually arranged payment plans). Tuition reduction for siblings, need-based scholarship grants, paying campus jobs available. In 2015–16, 5% of upper-school students received aid. Total amount of financial aid awarded in 2015–16: $32,250.

Admissions Traditional secondary-level entrance grade is 9. For fall 2015, 45 students applied for upper-level admission, 44 were accepted, 39 enrolled. Otis-Lennon School Ability Test or WISC-R required. Deadline for receipt of application materials: none. Application fee required: $50. On-campus interview recommended.

Athletics Interscholastic: baseball (boys), basketball (b,g), cheering (g), football (b), golf (b,g), soccer (b,g), softball (g), tennis (b,g), trap and skeet (b,g), volleyball (g); coed interscholastic: bowling, cross-country running, marksmanship.

Computers Computers are regularly used in all academic, computer applications, keyboarding, library, yearbook classes. Computer network features include on-campus library services, Internet access, wireless campus network, Internet filtering or blocking technology, students in grades 7-12 are issued iPads. Campus intranet, student e-mail accounts, and computer access in designated common areas are available to students. Students grades are available online. The school has a published electronic and media policy.

Contact Mrs. Emily Lansdell, Director of Admissions. 931-398-5355. Fax: 931-398-5359. E-mail: emily.lansdell@cabulldogs.org. Website: www.columbia-academy.net

COLUMBIA INTERNATIONAL COLLEGE OF CANADA

1003 Main Street West
Hamilton, Ontario L8S 4P3, Canada

Head of School: Mr. Ron Rambarran

General Information Coeducational boarding and day college-preparatory, general academic, arts, business, technology, science, and mathematics school. Grades 7–12. Founded: 1979. Setting: urban. Nearest major city is Toronto, Canada. Students are housed in single-sex dormitories. 12-acre campus. 7 buildings on campus. Approved or accredited by Ontario Ministry of Education and Ontario Department of Education. Language of instruction: English. Endowment: CAN$1 million. Total enrollment: 1,804. Upper school average class size: 20. Upper school faculty-student ratio: 1:20. There are 208 required school days per year for Upper School students. Upper School students typically attend 5 days per week. The average school day consists of 7 hours and 15 minutes.

Upper School Student Profile 80% of students are boarding students. 5% are province residents. 5 provinces are represented in upper school student body. 95% are international students. International students from China, Indonesia, Mexico, Nigeria, Russian Federation, and Viet Nam; 70 other countries represented in student body.

Faculty School total: 125. In upper school: 38 men, 57 women; 35 have advanced degrees.

Columbia International College of Canada

Subjects Offered 20th century world history, accounting, advanced TOEFL/grammar, algebra, analytic geometry, anthropology, applied arts, art, band, biology, business, calculus, calculus-AP, Canadian geography, Canadian history, career education, character education, chemistry, Chinese, choir, civics, computer programming, computer science, computer technologies, dance, discrete mathematics, dramatic arts, economics, English, English composition, English literature, ESL, family studies, food and nutrition, French, French as a second language, general business, general math, general science, geography, geometry, history, intro to computers, kinesiology, Korean, lab science, language arts, law, law studies, leadership, leadership and service, life skills, Mandarin, marketing, math applications, mathematics, mathematics-AP, media studies, model United Nations, music, outdoor education, physical education, physics, psychology, society challenge and change, sociology, Spanish, visual arts.

Graduation Requirements Arts, business, English, mathematics, science, social studies (includes history), community volunteer hours, Ontario Secondary School Literacy Test.

Special Academic Programs 4 Advanced Placement exams for which test preparation is offered; accelerated programs; study at local college for college credit; academic accommodation for the gifted; ESL.

College Admission Counseling Colleges students went to include Brock University; McMaster University; The University of Western Ontario; University of Toronto; University of Waterloo; York University.

Student Life Upper grades have uniform requirement, student council. Discipline rests primarily with faculty.

Tuition and Aid Day student tuition: CAN$17,896–CAN$29,791; 7-day tuition and room/board: CAN$21,435–CAN$36,871. Tuition reduction for siblings, merit scholarship grants, tuition reduction for Canadian citizens and permanent residents available.

Admissions Traditional secondary-level entrance grade is 11. English proficiency, Math Placement Exam and SLEP required. Deadline for receipt of application materials: none. Application fee required: CAN$200. Interview recommended.

Athletics Interscholastic: badminton (boys, girls), basketball (b), indoor soccer (b), soccer (b); intramural: aerobics (g), aerobics/dance (g), aquatics (b,g), badminton (b,g), ball hockey (g), basketball (b,g), cheering (g), dance (g), field hockey (b,g), fitness (b,g), floor hockey (b), football (b), hockey (b,g), indoor hockey (b,g), indoor soccer (b,g), jump rope (b,g), martial arts (b), outdoor activities (b,g), outdoor adventure (b,g), outdoor education (b,g), physical fitness (b,g), soccer (b,g), squash (b), strength & conditioning (b), swimming and diving (b,g), table tennis (b,g), track and field (b,g), volleyball (b,g), weight training (b,g), winter walking (b,g); coed interscholastic: badminton, indoor track & field; coed intramural: aquatics, badminton, ball hockey, canoeing/kayaking, cooperative games, cross-country running, fitness, floor hockey, golf, hiking/backpacking, hockey, in-line skating, indoor hockey, indoor track & field, jogging, jump rope, kayaking, martial arts, outdoor activities, outdoor adventure, outdoor education, physical fitness, physical training, roller blading, ropes courses, running, self defense, skiing (cross-country), snowshoeing, squash, strength & conditioning, swimming and diving, table tennis, track and field, volleyball, wallyball, weight training, wilderness, wilderness survival, winter walking, yoga. 3 PE instructors, 4 coaches.

Computers Computers are regularly used in accounting, business, business applications, career education, economics, English, ESL, geography, information technology, music, SAT preparation, science classes. Computer network features include Internet access, wireless campus network. Computer access in designated common areas is available to students. Students grades are available online.

Contact Ms. Marina Rosas, Admissions Officer. 905-572-7883 Ext. 2835. Fax: 905-572-9332. E-mail: admissions02@cic-totalcare.com. Website: www.cic-TotalCare.com

COLUMBIA INTERNATIONAL SCHOOL

153 Matsugo
Tokorozawa, Saitama 359-0027, Japan

Head of School: Mr. Barrie McCliggott

General Information Coeducational boarding and day and distance learning college-preparatory, business, bilingual studies, and technology school. Boarding grades 7–12, day grades 1–12. Distance learning grade X. Founded: 1988. Setting: suburban. Nearest major city is Tokyo, Japan. Students are housed in coed dormitories. 2-acre campus. 3 buildings on campus. Approved or accredited by Western Association of Schools and Colleges and state department of education. Language of instruction: English. Endowment: ¥100 million. Total enrollment: 225. Upper school average class size: 15. Upper school faculty-student ratio: 1:12. There are 180 required school days per year for Upper School students. Upper School students typically attend 5 days per week. The average school day consists of 5 hours and 30 minutes.

Upper School Student Profile Grade 10: 32 students (16 boys, 16 girls); Grade 11: 26 students (16 boys, 10 girls); Grade 12: 18 students (8 boys, 10 girls). 25% of students are boarding students. 20% are international students. International students from Canada, China, Philippines, Republic of Korea, United Kingdom, and United States; 10 other countries represented in student body.

Faculty School total: 24. In upper school: 12 men, 2 women; 7 have advanced degrees; 3 reside on campus.

Subjects Offered 1 1/2 elective credits, 20th century world history, advanced TOEFL/grammar, algebra, ancient world history, art, Asian history, biology, business, calculus, Canadian geography, Canadian history, chemistry, communications, community service, computer science, computers, economics, English, ESL, foreign language, geography, geometry, global issues, history, Internet, keyboarding, literacy, mathematics, media studies, physical education, reading, TOEFL preparation, world issues, yearbook.

Graduation Requirements 20th century history, arts, Asian history, biology, chemistry, economics, English, geography, humanities, law, mathematics, physical education (includes health), science, social sciences, Ontario Literacy Test, 40 hours of community involvement activities.

Special Academic Programs Advanced Placement exam preparation; honors section; accelerated programs; independent study; study abroad; remedial reading and/or remedial writing; remedial math; ESL (70 students enrolled).

College Admission Counseling 21 students graduated in 2015; 19 went to college, including Queen's University at Kingston; Temple University; The University of British Columbia; University of Saskatchewan; University of Victoria; Western Michigan University. Other: 2 had other specific plans.

Student Life Upper grades have uniform requirement, student council, honor system. Discipline rests primarily with faculty.

Summer Programs Remediation, enrichment, advancement, ESL, sports, art/fine arts, computer instruction programs offered; session focuses on ESL, computers, science, and art; held both on and off campus; held at Tokyo, Japan, Edmonton, Canada, and Gold Coast, Australia; accepts boys and girls; open to students from other schools. 350 students usually enrolled. 2016 schedule: July 5 to August 31. Application deadline: June 30.

Tuition and Aid Day student tuition: ¥1,575,000; 7-day tuition and room/board: ¥2,805,000. Tuition installment plan (individually arranged payment plans, term payment plans). Tuition reduction for siblings, merit scholarship grants available. In 2015–16, 5% of upper-school students received aid; total upper-school merit-scholarship money awarded: ¥2,735,000. Total amount of financial aid awarded in 2015–16: ¥3,360,000.

Admissions Traditional secondary-level entrance grade is 10. For fall 2015, 53 students applied for upper-level admission, 30 were accepted, 26 enrolled. Any standardized test required. Deadline for receipt of application materials: none. Application fee required: ¥25,000. Interview required.

Athletics Coed Interscholastic: basketball, dance, football, soccer; coed intramural: aerobics, alpine skiing, artistic gym, badminton, ball hockey, baseball, bicycling, bowling, climbing, cooperative games, dance team, field hockey, fitness, flag football, floor hockey, freestyle skiing, Frisbee, golf, hiking/backpacking, hockey, horseback riding, indoor hockey, indoor soccer, juggling, kickball, life saving, mountain biking, outdoor activities, physical fitness, power lifting, rock climbing, self defense, ski jumping, skiing (downhill), snowboarding, softball, table tennis, team handball, tennis, volleyball, wall climbing, weight lifting, weight training, yoga. 2 PE instructors.

Computers Computers are regularly used in all classes. Computer network features include Internet access, wireless campus network, Internet filtering or blocking technology, repair service. Campus intranet and student e-mail accounts are available to students. The school has a published electronic and media policy.

Contact Mr. Tetsuya Morimata, Administrator. 81-4-2946-1911. Fax: 81-4-2946-1955. E-mail: morimata@columbia-ca.co.jp. Website: www.columbia-ca.co.jp

THE COLUMBUS ACADEMY

4300 Cherry Bottom Road
Gahanna, Ohio 43230

Head of School: Melissa B. Soderberg

General Information Coeducational day college-preparatory school. Grades PK–12. Founded: 1911. Setting: suburban. Nearest major city is Columbus. 231-acre campus. 16 buildings on campus. Approved or accredited by Independent Schools Association of the Central States and Ohio Department of Education. Member of National Association of Independent Schools and Secondary School Admission Test Board. Endowment: $30 million. Total enrollment: 1,080. Upper school average class size: 14. Upper school faculty-student ratio: 1:8. The average school day consists of 7 hours and 5 minutes.

Upper School Student Profile Grade 9: 98 students (49 boys, 49 girls); Grade 10: 96 students (52 boys, 44 girls); Grade 11: 90 students (45 boys, 45 girls); Grade 12: 93 students (43 boys, 50 girls).

Faculty School total: 148. In upper school: 25 men, 22 women; 36 have advanced degrees.

Subjects Offered Advanced chemistry, advanced computer applications, advanced math, Advanced Placement courses, advanced studio art-AP, algebra, American history, American history-AP, American literature, analysis and differential calculus, art history, biology, biology-AP, British literature, calculus, calculus-AP, career/college preparation, ceramics, chemistry, chemistry-AP, Chinese, choir, choral music, chorus, college counseling, comparative government and politics-AP, comparative political systems-AP, computer applications, computer education, computer science, computer science-AP, concert band, concert choir, creative writing, drawing and design, economics, economics-AP, English, European history, fine arts, French-AP, geology, geometry, government and politics-AP, government-AP, health education, history of

China and Japan, instrumental music, Latin, Latin-AP, military history, photography, physical education, physics, physics-AP, pre-calculus, robotics, senior career experience, South African history, Spanish, Spanish language-AP, Spanish literature-AP, speech, statistics-AP, strings, theater, trigonometry, U.S. government and politics-AP, U.S. history-AP, United States government-AP, weight training, world history, world religions.

Graduation Requirements Arts and fine arts (art, music, dance, drama), English, foreign language, mathematics, science, social studies (includes history), formal speech delivered to the students and faculty of the upper school during junior year, community service requirement.

Special Academic Programs 21 Advanced Placement exams for which test preparation is offered; honors section; independent study; academic accommodation for the gifted.

College Admission Counseling 93 students graduated in 2015; all went to college, including Columbia University; Harvard University; Miami University; The Ohio State University; Washington University in St. Louis. Mean SAT critical reading: 643, mean SAT math: 656, mean SAT writing: 639, mean combined SAT: 1974, mean composite ACT: 29.

Student Life Upper grades have specified standards of dress, student council. Discipline rests equally with students and faculty.

Summer Programs Remediation, enrichment, advancement, art/fine arts, computer instruction programs offered; session focuses on academic enrichment, fine arts, fun and games; held on campus; accepts boys and girls; open to students from other schools. 400 students usually enrolled. 2016 schedule: June 15 to August 22.

Tuition and Aid Day student tuition: $21,600. Tuition installment plan (The Tuition Plan, Academic Management Services Plan, Tuition Management Systems Plan). Merit scholarship grants, need-based scholarship grants available. In 2015–16, 21% of upper-school students received aid. Total amount of financial aid awarded in 2015–16: $1,000,000.

Admissions Traditional secondary-level entrance grade is 9. For fall 2015, 79 students applied for upper-level admission, 33 were accepted, 24 enrolled. ISEE or SSAT required. Deadline for receipt of application materials: February 10. Application fee required: $50. On-campus interview required.

Athletics Interscholastic: baseball (boys), basketball (b,g), bowling (b,g), cross-country running (b,g), diving (b,g), field hockey (g), football (b), lacrosse (b,g), soccer (b,g), swimming and diving (b,g), tennis (b,g), track and field (b,g), volleyball (g), wrestling (b); coed intramural: bicycling. 3 PE instructors, 2 athletic trainers.

Computers Computers are regularly used in college planning, current events, economics, English, foreign language, humanities, journalism, Latin, learning cognition, library skills, mathematics, media production, multimedia, music, photography, publications, reading, research skills, SAT preparation, science, technology, theater, writing, yearbook classes. Computer network features include on-campus library services, online commercial services, Internet access, wireless campus network. Campus intranet, student e-mail accounts, and computer access in designated common areas are available to students. The school has a published electronic and media policy.

Contact John Wuorinen, Director of Admissions and Financial Aid. 614-509-2220. Fax: 614-475-0396. E-mail: admissions@columbusacademy.org. Website: www.ColumbusAcademy.org

COLUMBUS SCHOOL FOR GIRLS
56 South Columbia Avenue
Columbus, Ohio 43209

Head of School: Mrs. Jennifer Ciccarelli

General Information Girls' day college-preparatory, arts, technology, and STEM school. Grades PK–12. Founded: 1898. Setting: urban. 80-acre campus. 1 building on campus. Approved or accredited by Independent Schools Association of the Central States and Ohio Association of Independent Schools. Member of National Association of Independent Schools. Endowment: $18.2 million. Total enrollment: 562. Upper school average class size: 13. Upper school faculty-student ratio: 1:8. There are 175 required school days per year for Upper School students. Upper School students typically attend 5 days per week. The average school day consists of 7 hours and 30 minutes.

Upper School Student Profile Grade 6: 53 students (53 girls); Grade 7: 41 students (41 girls); Grade 8: 42 students (42 girls); Grade 9: 55 students (55 girls); Grade 10: 50 students (50 girls); Grade 11: 41 students (41 girls); Grade 12: 53 students (53 girls).

Faculty School total: 68. In upper school: 9 men, 17 women; 21 have advanced degrees.

Subjects Offered Acting, Advanced Placement courses, algebra, American literature, astronomy, band, biology, biology-AP, British literature, calculus, calculus-AP, ceramics, chemistry, chemistry-AP, civics, college admission preparation, comparative government and politics-AP, computer science, concert choir, digital photography, discrete mathematics, drawing, economics, English, English language and composition-AP, English literature and composition-AP, European history-AP, fine arts, geometry, German, health, lab science, Latin, Latin-AP, Mandarin, modern European history-AP, music theory-AP, newspaper, philosophy, photography, physical education, physics, physics-AP, pre-calculus, public speaking, robotics, senior seminar, Spanish, Spanish language-AP, statistics, strings, studio art-AP, theater, trigonometry, U.S. government

and politics-AP, U.S. history, visual arts, vocal ensemble, world history, world literature, world religions, yearbook.

Graduation Requirements Algebra, arts and fine arts (art, music, dance, drama), biology, chemistry, civics, college planning, electives, English, foreign language, geometry, health, physical education (includes health), physics, public speaking, self-defense, senior project, technology, U.S. history, world history, senior May program, service hours, water safety.

Special Academic Programs Advanced Placement exam preparation; honors section; independent study; study at local college for college credit.

College Admission Counseling 43 students graduated in 2015; all went to college, including Miami University; Northwestern University; Princeton University; The Ohio State University; University of Pennsylvania; Vanderbilt University. Median SAT critical reading: 640, median SAT math: 640, median SAT writing: 640, median combined SAT: 1930, median composite ACT: 29. 79% scored over 600 on SAT critical reading, 61% scored over 600 on SAT math, 79% scored over 600 on SAT writing, 76% scored over 1800 on combined SAT, 76% scored over 26 on composite ACT.

Student Life Upper grades have uniform requirement, student council, honor system. Discipline rests primarily with faculty.

Summer Programs Remediation, enrichment, advancement, sports, art/fine arts, rigorous outdoor training, computer instruction programs offered; session focuses on academic areas; held both on and off campus; held at various sites in community and CSG's Kirk Athletic Campus; accepts boys and girls; open to students from other schools. 391 students usually enrolled. 2016 schedule: June 13 to August 5. Application deadline: June 13.

Tuition and Aid Day student tuition: $19,800–$22,775. Merit scholarship grants, need-based scholarship grants, tuition reduction for three or more siblings available. In 2015–16, 29% of upper-school students received aid; total upper-school merit-scholarship money awarded: $62,000. Total amount of financial aid awarded in 2015–16: $630,518.

Admissions Traditional secondary-level entrance grade is 9. For fall 2015, 47 students applied for upper-level admission, 23 were accepted, 19 enrolled. ISEE or school's own test required. Deadline for receipt of application materials: February 8. Application fee required: $50. On-campus interview required.

Athletics Interscholastic: basketball, cross-country running, diving, field hockey, golf, independent competitive sports, lacrosse, running, soccer, swimming and diving, tennis, track and field, volleyball; intramural: aquatics, basketball, field hockey, golf, lacrosse, martial arts, running, self defense, soccer, swimming and diving, tennis, track and field, volleyball. 1 PE instructor, 26 coaches, 1 athletic trainer.

Computers Computers are regularly used in art, English, foreign language, freshman foundations, health, history, mathematics, music, publications, science, technology, theater, yearbook classes. Computer network features include on-campus library services, online commercial services, Internet access, wireless campus network, Internet filtering or blocking technology. Campus intranet, student e-mail accounts, and computer access in designated common areas are available to students. Students grades are available online. The school has a published electronic and media policy.

Contact Jenni Biehn, Director of Admission and Financial Aid. 614-252-0781 Ext. 104. Fax: 614-252-0571. E-mail: jbiehn@columbusschoolforgirls.org. Website: www.columbusschoolforgirls.org

COMMONWEALTH SCHOOL
151 Commonwealth Avenue
Boston, Massachusetts 02116

Head of School: Mr. William D. Wharton

General Information Coeducational day college-preparatory school. Grades 9–12. Founded: 1957. Setting: urban. 1 building on campus. Approved or accredited by Association of Independent Schools in New England, New England Association of Schools and Colleges, and Massachusetts Department of Education. Member of National Association of Independent Schools and Secondary School Admission Test Board. Endowment: $16 million. Total enrollment: 145. Upper school average class size: 12. Upper school faculty-student ratio: 1:5. Upper School students typically attend 5 days per week. The average school day consists of 6 hours and 30 minutes.

Upper School Student Profile Grade 9: 43 students (24 boys, 19 girls); Grade 10: 37 students (23 boys, 14 girls); Grade 11: 28 students (8 boys, 20 girls); Grade 12: 39 students (19 boys, 20 girls).

Faculty School total: 36. In upper school: 14 men, 22 women; 27 have advanced degrees.

Subjects Offered 20th century American writers, 20th century history, acting, advanced biology, advanced chemistry, advanced computer applications, advanced math, Advanced Placement courses, African-American literature, algebra, American history, American history-AP, American literature, ancient history, ancient world history, art, art history, biology, biology-AP, calculus, calculus-AP, ceramics, chamber groups, chemistry, chemistry-AP, choral music, chorus, classics, computer programming, computer science, creative writing, dance, drama, drawing, economics, economics-AP, English, English literature, English-AP, environmental science, environmental studies, ethics, European history, European history-AP, expository writing, film, film history, film studies, fine arts, foreign language, French, French language-AP, French literature-AP, French studies, French-AP, geometry, health and safety, Hispanic literature, history of the Americas, Japanese history, jazz, jazz band, jazz ensemble, jazz theory, Latin, Latin American history, Latin-AP, mathematics, mathematics-AP, medieval history, medieval/Renaissance history, modern European history-AP, music, music theory, music theory-AP, orchestra, organic chemistry, painting, performing arts, philosophy, photography, physical education, physics, physics-AP, pottery, pre-calculus, printmaking, probability and statistics, psychology, Russian literature, science, short story, society, politics and law, Spanish, Spanish language-AP, Spanish literature, Spanish literature-AP, Spanish-AP, studio art, theater, U.S. history-AP, visual and performing arts, visual arts, voice ensemble, writing.

Graduation Requirements Algebra, ancient history, art, biology, calculus, chemistry, English, ethics, foreign language, geometry, medieval history, physical education (includes health), physics, U.S. history, City of Boston course, completion of a one- to three-week project each year (with report), Health and Community. Community service is required.

Special Academic Programs Advanced Placement exam preparation; honors section; independent study; term-away projects; study abroad; academic accommodation for the gifted, the musically talented, and the artistically talented.

College Admission Counseling 35 students graduated in 2015; all went to college, including Cornell University; Harvard University; Princeton University; University of Chicago; University of Massachusetts Amherst; Yale University. Mean SAT critical reading: 748, mean SAT math: 730, mean SAT writing: 728.

Student Life Discipline rests primarily with faculty.

Tuition and Aid Day student tuition: $36,868. Tuition installment plan (Key Tuition Payment Plan). Need-based scholarship grants, need-based loans available. In 2015–16, 32% of upper-school students received aid. Total amount of financial aid awarded in 2015–16: $1,288,730.

Admissions Traditional secondary-level entrance grade is 9. For fall 2015, 214 students applied for upper-level admission, 90 were accepted, 45 enrolled. ISEE or SSAT required. Deadline for receipt of application materials: February 1. Application fee required: $60. On-campus interview required.

Athletics Interscholastic: basketball (boys, girls), independent competitive sports (b,g), soccer (b,g); coed interscholastic: baseball, cross-country running, fencing, squash, ultimate Frisbee; coed intramural: aerobics/Nautilus, ballet, cross-country running, dance, fencing, fitness, martial arts, sailing, squash, tai chi, yoga. 12 coaches.

Computers Computers are regularly used in computer applications, photography, programming classes. Computer network features include on-campus library services, online commercial services, Internet access, wireless campus network, Internet filtering or blocking technology. Campus intranet, student e-mail accounts, and computer access in designated common areas are available to students. The school has a published electronic and media policy.

Contact Ms. Carrie Healy, Director of Admissions and Financial Aid. 617-266-7525. Fax: 617-266-5769. E-mail: admissions@commschool.org. Website: www.commschool.org

COMMUNITY CHRISTIAN ACADEMY

11875 Taylor Mill Road
Independence, Kentucky 41051

Head of School: Tara Montez Bates

General Information Coeducational day college-preparatory and religious studies school, affiliated with Pentecostal Church. Grades PS–12. Founded: 1983. Setting: rural. Nearest major city is Cincinnati, OH. 112-acre campus. 2 buildings on campus. Approved or accredited by International Christian Accrediting Association and Kentucky Department of Education. Total enrollment: 269. Upper school average class size: 15. Upper school faculty-student ratio: 1:15. There are 175 required school days per year for Upper School students. Upper School students typically attend 5 days per week. The average school day consists of 6 hours.

Upper School Student Profile Grade 9: 18 students (8 boys, 10 girls); Grade 10: 13 students (5 boys, 8 girls); Grade 11: 12 students (5 boys, 7 girls); Grade 12: 15 students (6 boys, 9 girls). 50% of students are Pentecostal.

Faculty School total: 14. In upper school: 3 men, 3 women; 2 have advanced degrees.

Subjects Offered Advanced biology, advanced math, algebra, American history, art appreciation, Bible, biology, business skills, calculus, chemistry, choral music, computer applications, cultural geography, English, geography, health, integrated science, life skills, literature, pre-algebra, pre-calculus, Spanish.

Graduation Requirements Bible, electives, English, foreign language, mathematics, physical education (includes health), science, social studies (includes history), statistics, visual and performing arts.

College Admission Counseling 12 students graduated in 2015; 10 went to college, including Cincinnati State Technical and Community College; Morehead State University; Northern Kentucky University; Oral Roberts University; University of Cincinnati. Other: 2 went to work. Mean composite ACT: 21. 20% scored over 26 on composite ACT.

Student Life Upper grades have uniform requirement, student council, honor system. Discipline rests primarily with faculty. Attendance at religious services is required.

Tuition and Aid Day student tuition: $3349. Guaranteed tuition plan. Tuition installment plan (The Tuition Plan, monthly payment plans). Financial aid available to upper-school students. In 2015–16, 5% of upper-school students received aid. Total amount of financial aid awarded in 2015–16: $9000.

Admissions Traditional secondary-level entrance grade is 9. For fall 2015, 16 students applied for upper-level admission, 11 were accepted, 11 enrolled. Admissions testing required. Deadline for receipt of application materials: none. Application fee required: $50. Interview required.

Athletics Interscholastic: baseball (boys), basketball (b,g), cheering (g), softball (g), volleyball (g); coed interscholastic: cross-country running. 2 PE instructors, 13 coaches.

Computers Computers are regularly used in foreign language classes. Computer network features include Internet access.

Contact Edie Carkeek, Secretary. 859-356-7990 Ext. 112. Fax: 859-356-7991. E-mail: edie.carkeek@ccaky.org. Website: www.ccaky.org

COMMUNITY HIGH SCHOOL

Teaneck, New Jersey
See Special Needs Schools section.

THE COMMUNITY SCHOOL

PO Box 2118
Sun Valley, Idaho 83353

Head of School: Ben Pettit

General Information Coeducational boarding and day college-preparatory, arts, and technology school. Boarding grades 9–12, day grades K–12. Founded: 1973. Setting: small town. Nearest major city is Boise. 45-acre campus. 4 buildings on campus. Approved or accredited by Northwest Association of Independent Schools and Idaho Department of Education. Member of National Association of Independent Schools, Secondary School Admission Test Board, and Council for the Advancement and Support of Education. Endowment: $3.4 million. Total enrollment: 400. Upper school average class size: 12. Upper school faculty-student ratio: 1:8. Upper School students typically attend 5 days per week. The average school day consists of 6 hours and 30 minutes.

Upper School Student Profile Grade 9: 33 students (12 boys, 21 girls); Grade 10: 38 students (19 boys, 19 girls); Grade 11: 46 students (21 boys, 25 girls); Grade 12: 47 students (28 boys, 19 girls). 13% of students are boarding students. 87% are state residents. 10 states are represented in upper school student body. 3% are international students. International students from Bermuda, Brazil, and China.

Faculty School total: 64. In upper school: 11 men, 6 women; 13 have advanced degrees.

Subjects Offered Algebra, American history, American literature, art, biology, calculus, ceramics, chemistry, computer graphics, computer math, computer programming, computer science, constitutional law, creative writing, drama, earth science, ecology, economics, English, English literature, environmental science, ethics, European history, expository writing, fine arts, forensics, French, geography, geology, geometry, government/civics, history, human development, information technology, mathematics, music, musical productions, philosophy, photography, physical education, physics, science, social studies, Spanish, speech, statistics, theater, trigonometry, world history, world literature, writing.

Graduation Requirements Arts and fine arts (art, music, dance, drama), computer science, English, foreign language, mathematics, outdoor education, physical education (includes health), science, social studies (includes history), speech, senior project presentation, senior speech, outdoor program.

Special Academic Programs Advanced Placement exam preparation; honors section; independent study; term-away projects; domestic exchange program; academic accommodation for the gifted; programs in English, mathematics, general development for dyslexic students; ESL (8 students enrolled).

College Admission Counseling 34 students graduated in 2015; 33 went to college, including Dartmouth College; Harvard University; The Colorado College; Tufts University; University of Colorado Boulder; University of Virginia. Other: 1 entered military service. Mean SAT critical reading: 604, mean SAT math: 582, mean SAT writing: 591. 51% scored over 600 on SAT critical reading, 54% scored over 600 on SAT math, 54% scored over 600 on SAT writing.

Student Life Upper grades have specified standards of dress, student council, honor system. Discipline rests primarily with faculty.

Summer Programs Enrichment, sports, art/fine arts, rigorous outdoor training, computer instruction programs offered; session focuses on academics, arts, outdoor education; held both on and off campus; held at various sites for swimming, hiking, and exploring local mountains; accepts boys and girls; open to students from other schools. 150 students usually enrolled. 2016 schedule: June 15 to July 30. Application deadline: none.

Tuition and Aid Day student tuition: $26,500; 7-day tuition and room/board: $43,500. Tuition installment plan (individually arranged payment plans). Merit scholarship grants, need-based scholarship grants available. In 2015–16, 41% of upper-school students received aid; total upper-school merit-scholarship money awarded: $153,650. Total amount of financial aid awarded in 2015–16: $599,175.

Admissions Traditional secondary-level entrance grade is 9. PSAT and SAT for applicants to grade 11 and 12, SSAT and writing sample required. Deadline for receipt of application materials: February 25. Application fee required: $50. Interview required.

Athletics Interscholastic: alpine skiing (boys, girls), basketball (b,g), cross-country running (b,g), freestyle skiing (b,g), golf (b,g), ice hockey (b,g), ice skating (b,g), lacrosse (b), nordic skiing (b,g), physical fitness (b,g), rock climbing (b,g), skiing (cross-country) (b,g), skiing (downhill) (b,g), snowboarding (b,g), soccer (b,g), swimming and diving (g), tennis (b,g), track and field (b,g), volleyball (g); coed interscholastic: backpacking, bicycling, canoeing/kayaking, climbing, cooperative games, equestrian sports, figure skating, fitness, hiking/backpacking, independent competitive sports, kayaking, mountain biking, mountaineering, outdoor activities, outdoor adventure, outdoor education, outdoor skills, physical fitness, rafting, rock climbing, ropes courses, snowshoeing, strength & conditioning, telemark skiing, tennis, wilderness, wilderness survival. 2 PE instructors, 9 coaches, 1 athletic trainer.

Computers Computers are regularly used in English, foreign language, independent study, science, yearbook classes. Computer network features include on-campus library services, online commercial services, Internet access, wireless campus network, Internet filtering or blocking technology. Student e-mail accounts and computer access in designated common areas are available to students. Students grades are available online. The school has a published electronic and media policy.

Contact Katie Robins, Director of Admission. 208-622-3960 Ext. 117. Fax: 208-622-3962. E-mail: krobins@communityschool.org. Website: www.communityschool.org

THE COMMUNITY SCHOOL OF NAPLES

13275 Livingston Road
Naples, Florida 34109

Head of School: Dr. David Watson

General Information Coeducational day college-preparatory and arts school. Grades PK–12. Founded: 1982. Setting: suburban. Nearest major city is Miami. 77-acre campus. 4 buildings on campus. Approved or accredited by Florida Council of Independent Schools. Member of National Association of Independent Schools and Secondary School Admission Test Board. Endowment: $9.6 million. Total enrollment: 807. Upper school average class size: 13. Upper school faculty-student ratio: 1:9. There are 172 required school days per year for Upper School students. Upper School students typically attend 5 days per week. The average school day consists of 5 hours and 15 minutes.

Upper School Student Profile Grade 9: 64 students (37 boys, 27 girls); Grade 10: 81 students (42 boys, 39 girls); Grade 11: 82 students (35 boys, 47 girls); Grade 12: 85 students (50 boys, 35 girls).

Faculty School total: 99. In upper school: 15 men, 26 women; 35 have advanced degrees.

Subjects Offered 3-dimensional art, 3-dimensional design, advanced computer applications, advanced math, Advanced Placement courses, advanced studio art-AP, algebra, American government, American history, American literature, American literature AP, American sign language, anatomy and physiology, art, art history, art history-AP, art-AP, band, biology, biology-AP, biotechnology, calculus, calculus-AP, chemistry, chemistry-AP, chorus, clayworking, comparative government and politics-AP, composition, composition-AP, computer graphics, computer programming, computer programming-AP, computer science, computer science-AP, creative writing, digital photography, drama performance, dramatic arts, drawing, drawing and design, economics, economics-AP, electives, English, English composition, English language and composition-AP, English language-AP, English literature, English literature and composition-AP, English literature-AP, English-AP, English/composition-AP, environmental science, environmental science-AP, fine arts, French, French language-AP, French literature-AP, French-AP, geometry, government, government and politics-AP, government-AP, government/civics, government/civics-AP, graphic design, health, history, history-AP, honors algebra, honors English, honors geometry, honors U.S. history, honors world history, human geography - AP, jazz band, Latin, literature, literature and composition-AP, literature-AP, macro/microeconomics-AP, macroeconomics-AP, marine biology, marine science, mathematics, mathematics-AP, microeconomics, microeconomics-AP, modern European history-AP, music, music theory-AP, oceanography, painting, performing arts, personal fitness, photography, physical education, physical fitness, physics, physics-AP, portfolio art, pre-algebra, pre-calculus, psychology, psychology-AP, robotics, science, senior project, Spanish, Spanish language-AP, Spanish literature-AP, Spanish-AP, statistics-AP, strings, studio art-AP, theater, U.S. government and politics, U.S. government and politics-AP, U.S. history, U.S. history-AP, United States government-AP, visual and performing arts, visual arts, vocal music, Web site design, world history, world history-AP, world literature.

Graduation Requirements Arts and fine arts (art, music, dance, drama), computer science, electives, English, foreign language, history, mathematics, physical education (includes health), science, community service hours (25 per year).

Special Academic Programs 26 Advanced Placement exams for which test preparation is offered; honors section; independent study; study at local college for college credit; study abroad; academic accommodation for the gifted.

College Admission Counseling 84 students graduated in 2015; all went to college, including Boston University; Southern Methodist University; University of Central Florida; University of Colorado Boulder; University of Florida; University of Michigan. Median SAT critical reading: 597, median SAT math: 634, median SAT writing: 589, median composite ACT: 26. 13% scored over 600 on SAT critical reading, 32% scored over 600 on SAT math, 16% scored over 600 on SAT writing.

Student Life Upper grades have specified standards of dress, student council, honor system. Discipline rests equally with students and faculty.

Summer Programs Enrichment, sports programs offered, session focuses on mathematics, English, and SAT preparation, sports; held on campus; accepts boys and girls; open to students from other schools. 25 students usually enrolled. 2016 schedule: June 8 to August 8. Application deadline: June 1.

Tuition and Aid Day student tuition: $25,360. Tuition installment plan (Insured Tuition Payment Plan, monthly payment plans, individually arranged payment plans). Need-based scholarship grants available. In 2015–16, 22% of upper-school students received aid. Total amount of financial aid awarded in 2015–16: $1,199,038.

Admissions Traditional secondary-level entrance grade is 9. For fall 2015, 65 students applied for upper-level admission, 50 were accepted, 45 enrolled. Math, reading, and mental ability tests or SSAT required. Deadline for receipt of application materials: February 1. Application fee required: $100. Interview recommended.

Athletics Interscholastic: baseball (boys), basketball (b,g), cross-country running (b,g), diving (b,g), football (b), golf (b,g), lacrosse (b,g), soccer (b,g), softball (g), swimming and diving (b,g), tennis (b,g), track and field (b,g), volleyball (g), winter soccer (b,g); coed intramural: cheering, sailing. 1 PE instructor, 67 coaches, 1 athletic trainer.

Computers Computers are regularly used in art, computer applications, creative writing, design, desktop publishing, digital applications, English, foreign language, history, mathematics, music, science, Web site design, writing, writing, yearbook classes. Computer network features include on-campus library services, online commercial services, Internet access, wireless campus network, Internet filtering or blocking technology. Campus intranet, student e-mail accounts, and computer access in designated common areas are available to students. Students grades are available online. The school has a published electronic and media policy.

Contact Ms. Franchesca Gannon, Administrative Assistant, Admissions. 239-597-7575 Ext. 133. Fax: 239-598-2973. E-mail: FGannont@communityschoolnaples.org. Website: www.communityschoolnaples.org

CONCORD ACADEMY

166 Main Street
Concord, Massachusetts 01742

Head of School: Mr. Rick Hardy

General Information Coeducational boarding and day college-preparatory, arts, and technology school. Grades 9–12. Founded: 1922. Setting: suburban. Nearest major city is Boston. Students are housed in single-sex dormitories. 39-acre campus. 29 buildings on campus. Approved or accredited by New England Association of Schools and Colleges, The Association of Boarding Schools, and Massachusetts Department of Education. Member of National Association of Independent Schools and Secondary School Admission Test Board. Endowment: $66.4 million. Total enrollment: 378. Upper school average class size: 12. Upper School faculty-student ratio: 1:6. Upper School students typically attend 5 days per week. The average school day consists of 6 hours and 30 minutes.

Upper School Student Profile Grade 9: 94 students (49 boys, 45 girls); Grade 10: 99 students (48 boys, 51 girls); Grade 11: 94 students (42 boys, 52 girls); Grade 12: 90 students (43 boys, 47 girls). 40% of students are boarding students. 71% are state residents. 18 states are represented in upper school student body. 10% are international students. International students from Canada, China, Hong Kong, Republic of Korea, Thailand, and United Kingdom; 5 other countries represented in student body.

Faculty School total: 64. In upper school: 27 men, 37 women; 55 have advanced degrees; 26 reside on campus.

Subjects Offered 20th century American writers, 3-dimensional art, advanced chemistry, advanced math, African history, African-American literature, algebra, American history, American literature, ancient history, ancient world history, anthropology, applied music, architecture, art, art history, Asian history, astronomy, astrophysics, batik, Bible as literature, biochemistry, biology, bookmaking, British literature, calculus, ceramics, chamber groups, chemistry, Chinese history, choreography, chorus, classical civilization, classical Greek literature, classical language, computer multimedia, computer programming, computer science, computer studies, creative writing, critical studies in film, dance, dance performance, digital imaging, directing, drama, drama performance, drawing, earth science, economics, English, English literature, environmental science, environmental studies, European history, experimental science, expository writing, fiber arts, fiction, film, film history, filmmaking, forensics, French, freshman seminar, geology, geometry, German, German literature, guitar, health and wellness, history, history of China and Japan, history of music, Holocaust, HTML design, improvisation, instruments, introduction to digital multitrack recording techniques, Irish literature, Islamic history, jazz ensemble, journalism, Latin, Latin American history, Latin American literature, life management skills, literature seminar, math analysis, mathematics, medieval/Renaissance history, Middle East, Middle Eastern history, model United Nations, modern dance, modern European history, modern languages, music, music composition, music history, music technology, music theory, musical productions, neuroscience, newspaper, novels, oceanography, orchestra, painting, performing arts, philosophy, photography, physical education, physics, piano, play/screen writing, poetry, post-calculus, pre-calculus, printmaking, probability and statistics, Roman civilization, science, science fiction, sculpture, senior project, sex education, Shakespeare, Spanish, Spanish literature, statistics, student publications, studio art, technical theater, theater, theater design and production, theater history, trigonometry, U.S. history, urban studies, visual arts, voice, Web site design, wind ensemble, writing.

Graduation Requirements Computer science, English, foreign language, history, mathematics, performing arts, physical education (includes health), science, visual arts.

Special Academic Programs Honors section; independent study; term-away projects; study abroad; academic accommodation for the gifted, the musically talented, and the artistically talented.

College Admission Counseling 90 students graduated in 2015; all went to college, including Barnard College; Brown University; Connecticut College; New York University; Tufts University; Yale University. Mean SAT critical reading: 694, mean SAT math: 697, mean SAT writing: 694, mean combined SAT: 2085.

Student Life Upper grades have student council, honor system. Discipline rests equally with students and faculty.

Tuition and Aid Day student tuition: $45,390; 7-day tuition and room/board: $56,360. Tuition installment plan (Key Tuition Payment Plan, monthly payment plans). Need-based scholarship grants, need-based loans available. In 2015–16, 25% of upper-school students received aid. Total amount of financial aid awarded in 2015–16: $3,900,000.

Admissions Traditional secondary-level entrance grade is 9. For fall 2015, 811 students applied for upper-level admission, 225 were accepted, 101 enrolled. ISEE, SSAT or TOEFL required. Deadline for receipt of application materials: January 15. Application fee required: $50. Interview recommended.

Athletics Interscholastic: baseball (boys), basketball (b,g), cross-country running (b,g), field hockey (g), lacrosse (g), skiing (downhill) (b,g), soccer (b,g), squash (g), tennis (b,g), volleyball (g), wrestling (b); intramural: softball (g), squash (b); coed interscholastic: alpine skiing, golf, lacrosse, ultimate Frisbee; coed intramural: aerobics, aerobics/dance, ballet, canoeing/kayaking, combined training, cross-country running, dance, fencing, fitness, jogging, martial arts, modern dance, outdoor activities, physical fitness, physical training, sailing, self defense, skiing (downhill), strength & conditioning, track and field, ultimate Frisbee, weight training, yoga. 8 PE instructors, 35 coaches, 2 athletic trainers.

Computers Computers are regularly used in English, foreign language, history, library skills, mathematics, music, newspaper, science, social studies, technology, video film production, Web site design, yearbook classes. Computer network features include on-campus library services, online commercial services, Internet access, wireless campus network, Internet filtering or blocking technology. Campus intranet, student e-mail accounts, and computer access in designated common areas are available to students. Students grades are available online. The school has a published electronic and media policy.

Contact Marie D. Myers, Director of Admissions. 978-402-2250. Fax: 978-402-2345. E-mail: admissions@concordacademy.org. Website: www.concordacademy.org

CONCORDIA ACADEMY

2400 North Dale Street
St. Paul, Minnesota 55113

Head of School: Rev. Dr. Timothy Berner

General Information Coeducational day college-preparatory, arts, and religious studies school, affiliated with Lutheran Church–Missouri Synod. Grades 9–12. Founded: 1893. Setting: suburban. 14-acre campus. 1 building on campus. Approved or accredited by National Lutheran School Accreditation, North Central Association of Colleges and Schools, and Minnesota Department of Education. Endowment: $300,000. Total enrollment: 241. Upper school average class size: 18. Upper school faculty-student ratio: 1:15. There are 175 required school days per year for Upper School students. Upper School students typically attend 5 days per week. The average school day consists of 6 hours and 45 minutes.

Upper School Student Profile Grade 9: 55 students (32 boys, 23 girls); Grade 10: 67 students (41 boys, 26 girls); Grade 11: 62 students (32 boys, 30 girls); Grade 12: 57 students (28 boys, 29 girls). 45% of students are Lutheran Church–Missouri Synod.

Faculty School total: 27. In upper school: 15 men, 12 women; 16 have advanced degrees.

Subjects Offered Algebra, American history, American literature, American sign language, anatomy and physiology, art, Bible studies, biology, business, business skills, calculus, ceramics, chamber groups, chemistry, choir, chorus, communications, computer programming, computer science, concert band, concert choir, consumer mathematics, creative writing, earth science, English, English literature, European history, fine arts, geography, geometry, government/civics, health, history, honors algebra, honors English, mathematics, modern world history, music, music appreciation, physical education, physics, pre-algebra, pre-calculus, psychology, religion, robotics, science, social sciences, social studies, Spanish, speech, theology, world literature, writing.

Graduation Requirements Arts and fine arts (art, music, dance, drama), Christian scripture, English, health, mathematics, physical education (includes health), science, social studies (includes history).

Special Academic Programs Honors section; study at local college for college credit; remedial reading and/or remedial writing; remedial math; programs in general development for dyslexic students; special instructional classes for deaf students.

College Admission Counseling 72 students graduated in 2015; 70 went to college, including Concordia College; University of Minnesota, Twin Cities Campus. Other: 1 went to work, 1 entered military service. Median composite ACT: 24. 55% scored over 26 on composite ACT.

Student Life Upper grades have specified standards of dress, student council. Discipline rests primarily with faculty. Attendance at religious services is required.

Summer Programs Sports, art/fine arts, computer instruction programs offered; held on campus; accepts boys and girls; open to students from other schools. 150 students usually enrolled. 2016 schedule: June 6 to August 5.

Tuition and Aid Day student tuition: $9800–$17,000. Tuition installment plan (monthly payment plans, quarterly payment plan, semi-annual payment plan, 10 monthly payments (through TADS)). Merit scholarship grants, need-based scholarship grants available. In 2015–16, 37% of upper-school students received aid; total upper-school merit-scholarship money awarded: $98,500. Total amount of financial aid awarded in 2015–16: $334,804.

Admissions Traditional secondary-level entrance grade is 9. For fall 2015, 540 students applied for upper-level admission, 520 were accepted, 476 enrolled. Math and English placement tests required. Deadline for receipt of application materials: none. Application fee required: $100. On-campus interview required.

Athletics Interscholastic: baseball (boys), basketball (b,g), cross-country running (b,g), dance team (g), football (b), golf (b), ice hockey (b), lacrosse (b), soccer (b,g), softball (g), strength & conditioning (b,g), track and field (b,g), volleyball (g), wrestling (b); intramural: basketball (b,g), weight training (b,g). 1 PE instructor, 30 coaches, 1 athletic trainer.

Computers Computers are regularly used in Christian doctrine, creative writing, English, foreign language, freshman foundations, graphic design, history, mathematics, music, photography, remedial study skills, science, speech, writing, yearbook classes. Computer resources include online commercial services, Internet access, wireless campus network, Internet filtering or blocking technology. Campus intranet, student e-mail accounts, and computer access in designated common areas are available to students. Students grades are available online. The school has a published electronic and media policy.

Contact Mrs. Sofia Humphries, Director of Admissions. 651-484-8429 Ext. 679. Fax: 651-484-0594. E-mail: sofia.humphries@concordiaacademy.com. Website: www.concordiaacademy.com

CONCORDIA LUTHERAN HIGH SCHOOL

1601 Saint Joe River Drive
Fort Wayne, Indiana 46805

Head of School: Mr. Terry Breininger

General Information Coeducational day college-preparatory and religious studies school, affiliated with Lutheran Church–Missouri Synod. Grades 9–12. Founded: 1935. Setting: urban. Nearest major city is Indianapolis. 3 buildings on campus. Approved or accredited by National Lutheran School Accreditation, North Central Association of Colleges and Schools, and Indiana Department of Education. Total enrollment: 772. Upper school average class size: 21. Upper school faculty-student ratio: 1:15. There are 180 required school days per year for Upper School students. Upper School students typically attend 5 days per week. The average school day consists of 7 hours and 5 minutes.

Upper School Student Profile Grade 9: 207 students (101 boys, 106 girls); Grade 10: 203 students (100 boys, 103 girls); Grade 11: 207 students (102 boys, 105 girls); Grade 12: 155 students (72 boys, 83 girls). 76% of students are Lutheran Church–Missouri Synod.

Faculty School total: 58. In upper school: 25 men, 26 women; 22 have advanced degrees.

Subjects Offered 3-dimensional art, Advanced Placement courses, algebra, American history, American history-AP, American literature, anatomy and physiology, art, band, Bible studies, biology, biology-AP, broadcasting, business, calculus, calculus-AP, ceramics, chemistry, chemistry-AP, choir, computer science, creative writing, driver education, earth science, economics, English, English literature, English literature and composition-AP, entrepreneurship, environmental science, ethics, expository writing, family and consumer science, food and nutrition, geography, geometry, German, government/civics, grammar, health, health and safety, history, home economics, honors algebra, honors English, honors geometry, internship, journalism, JROTC, JROTC or LEAD (Leadership Education and Development), Latin, marching band, mathematics, media arts, media communications, microeconomics-AP, music, newspaper, painting, physical education, physics, physics-AP, psychology, religion, science, social sciences, social studies, sociology, Spanish, speech, statistics-AP, theater, theater arts, theology, U.S. government, U.S. history, U.S. history-AP, video film production, weight training, world history, world literature, writing, yearbook.

Graduation Requirements English, foreign language, health education, mathematics, physical education (includes health), religion (includes Bible studies and theology), science, social sciences, social studies (includes history). Community service is required.

Special Academic Programs Advanced Placement exam preparation; honors section; independent study; study at local college for college credit; programs in English, mathematics, general development for dyslexic students.

College Admission Counseling 162 students graduated in 2015; 145 went to college, including Ball State University; Concordia University Chicago; Indiana University-Purdue University Fort Wayne; Indiana University Bloomington; Purdue University; Valparaiso University. Other: 13 went to work, 4 entered military service. Mean SAT critical reading: 516, mean SAT math: 539, mean SAT writing: 498, mean composite ACT: 24.

Student Life Upper grades have uniform requirement, student council. Discipline rests primarily with faculty. Attendance at religious services is required.

Summer Programs Remediation, advancement, sports, art/fine arts, computer instruction programs offered; session focuses on summer classes, drivers education, summer conditioning, and sports camps; held both on and off campus; held at various locations based on sport; accepts boys and girls; open to students from other schools. 700 students usually enrolled. 2016 schedule: June to August.

Tuition and Aid Day student tuition: $7800–$9250. Tuition installment plan (FACTS Tuition Payment Plan, monthly payment plans, individually arranged payment plans, bank loan). Tuition reduction for siblings, merit scholarship grants, need-based scholarship grants, Indiana Choice Scholarships available. In 2015–16, 97% of upper-school students received aid; total upper-school merit-scholarship money awarded: $499,000. Total amount of financial aid awarded in 2015–16: $3,163,000.

Admissions Traditional secondary-level entrance grade is 9. Deadline for receipt of application materials: none. Application fee required: $35. On-campus interview recommended.

Athletics Interscholastic: baseball (boys), basketball (b,g), cheering (g), cross-country running (b,g), football (b), golf (b,g), gymnastics (g), lacrosse (b), soccer (b,g), softball (g), swimming and diving (b,g), tennis (b,g), track and field (b,g), volleyball (g), wrestling (b); coed interscholastic: bowling, crew, dance team, JROTC drill, outdoor adventure, rappelling, riflery, rowing; coed intramural: volleyball. 3 PE instructors, 70 coaches, 2 athletic trainers.

Computers Computers are regularly used in all classes. Computer network features include on-campus library services, online commercial services, Internet access, wireless campus network, Internet filtering or blocking technology. Student e-mail accounts and computer access in designated common areas are available to students. Students grades are available online.

Contact Mrs. Krista Friend, Director of Enrollment and Retention. 260-483-1102. Fax: 260-471-0180. E-mail: kfriend@clhscadets.com. Website: www.clhscadets.com

CONVENT OF THE SACRED HEART

1177 King Street
Greenwich, Connecticut 06831

Head of School: Mrs. Pamela Juan Hayes

General Information Coeducational day (boys only in lower grades) and distance learning college-preparatory, arts, religious studies, technology, STEM (Science, Technology,Engineering, Math), and World Languages school, affiliated with Roman Catholic Church. Boys grades PS–PK, girls grades PS–12. Distance learning grades 9–12. Founded: 1848. Setting: suburban. Nearest major city is New York, NY. 118-acre campus. 10 buildings on campus. Approved or accredited by Connecticut Association of Independent Schools, Network of Sacred Heart Schools, New England Association of Schools and Colleges, and Connecticut Department of Education. Member of National Association of Independent Schools and Secondary School Admission Test Board. Endowment: $29.9 million. Total enrollment: 750. Upper school average class size: 13. Upper school faculty-student ratio: 1:7. There are 163 required school days per year for Upper School students. Upper School students typically attend 5 days per week. The average school day consists of 7 hours and 15 minutes.

Upper School Student Profile Grade 6: 65 students (65 girls); Grade 7: 71 students (71 girls); Grade 8: 79 students (79 girls); Grade 9: 78 students (78 girls); Grade 10: 76 students (76 girls); Grade 11: 77 students (77 girls); Grade 12: 82 students (82 girls). 70% of students are Roman Catholic.

Faculty School total: 123. In upper school: 10 men, 40 women; 39 have advanced degrees.

Subjects Offered 20th century world history, advanced biology, advanced chemistry, advanced math, Advanced Placement courses, advanced studio art-AP, algebra, American literature, American literature-AP, Arabic, biology, biology-AP, broadcast journalism, calculus, calculus-AP, Catholic belief and practice, chemistry, chemistry-AP, Chinese, choir, choral music, Christian and Hebrew scripture, Christian education, Christian ethics, Christianity, college counseling, community service, comparative government and politics-AP, computer science, concert bell choir, design, drama, drawing, English language and composition-AP, English literature, English literature and composition-AP, environmental science-AP, ethics, European history, European history-AP, fine arts, French, French language-AP, geometry, health, honors algebra, honors geometry, honors U.S. history, HTML design, instrumental music, journalism, Latin, literary magazine, photography, physical education, physics, physics-AP, pre-calculus, SAT/ACT preparation, Spanish, Spanish language-AP, Spanish literature-AP, statistics-AP, theology, trigonometry, U.S. history, U.S. history-AP, world cultures, world literature.

Graduation Requirements Electives, English, foreign language, mathematics, physical education (includes health), science, theology, 100 hours of community service by graduation. Community service is required.

Special Academic Programs 19 Advanced Placement exams for which test preparation is offered; honors section; independent study; term-away projects; domestic exchange program (with Network of Sacred Heart Schools); study abroad; academic accommodation for the gifted and the artistically talented.

College Admission Counseling 60 students graduated in 2014; all went to college, including Boston College; Cornell University; Fordham University; Georgetown University; University of Notre Dame; University of Pennsylvania.

Student Life Upper grades have uniform requirement, student council, honor system. Discipline rests primarily with faculty. Attendance at religious services is required.

Tuition and Aid Day student tuition: $37,300. Tuition installment plan (Sallie May Payment Plan). Merit scholarship grants, need-based scholarship grants available. In 2014–15, 20% of upper-school students received aid.

Admissions Traditional secondary-level entrance grade is 9. For fall 2014, 111 students applied for upper-level admission, 56 were accepted, 28 enrolled. ISEE or SSAT required. Deadline for receipt of application materials: February 1. Application fee required: $50. On-campus interview required.

Athletics Interscholastic: basketball, cooperative games, crew, cross-country running, dance, diving, field hockey, fitness, golf, jogging, lacrosse, physical fitness, running, soccer, softball, squash, swimming and diving, tennis, volleyball; intramural: fitness, independent competitive sports, physical training, strength & conditioning. 4 PE instructors, 34 coaches, 1 athletic trainer.

Computers Computers are regularly used in all academic classes. Computer network features include on-campus library services, online commercial services, Internet access, wireless campus network, Internet filtering or blocking technology, course selection online; grades online; CSH is a member of the Online School for Girls, laptops mandatory for students in grades 6 to 12. Campus intranet, student e-mail accounts, and computer access in designated common areas are available to students. Students grades are available online. The school has a published electronic and media policy.

Contact Mrs. Catherine Cullinane, Director of Admission. 203-532-3534. Fax: 203-532-3301. E-mail: admission@cshct.org. Website: www.cshgreenwich.org

CONVENT OF THE SACRED HEART

1 East 91st Street
New York, New York 10128-0689

Head of School: Dr. Joseph J. Ciancaglini

General Information Girls' day college-preparatory, arts, religious studies, bilingual studies, and technology school, affiliated with Roman Catholic Church. Grades PK–12. Founded: 1881. Setting: urban. 2 buildings on campus. Approved or accredited by Network of Sacred Heart Schools, New York State Board of Regents, and New York Department of Education. Member of National Association of Independent Schools and Secondary School Admission Test Board. Endowment: $37.5 million. Total enrollment: 700. Upper school average class size: 14. Upper school faculty-student ratio: 1:10. Upper School students typically attend 5 days per week. The average school day consists of 7 hours.

Upper School Student Profile Grade 9: 56 students (56 girls); Grade 10: 57 students (57 girls); Grade 11: 45 students (45 girls); Grade 12: 45 students (45 girls). 65% of students are Roman Catholic.

Faculty School total: 110. In upper school: 10 men, 30 women; 38 have advanced degrees.

Subjects Offered Advanced studio art-AP, algebra, American history, American literature, art, audio visual/media, biology, biology-AP, calculus, calculus-AP, campus ministry, ceramics, chemistry, chemistry-AP, chorus, computer applications, computer multimedia, creative writing, dance, desktop publishing, digital photography, drama, earth science, East European studies, English, English literature, English literature-AP, environmental science, ethics, European history, expository writing, film history, fine arts, finite math, forensics, French, French-AP, functions, geography, geometry, government/civics, handbells, health, history, journalism, Latin, madrigals, mathematics, model United Nations, multicultural literature, multimedia design, music, musical theater, performing arts, photography, physical education, physical science, physics, physics-AP, portfolio art, pottery, pre-calculus, religion, science, science research, social studies, Spanish, Spanish-AP, speech, statistics, statistics-AP, theater, theology, trigonometry, U.S. history-AP, visual arts, women's literature, world history, world issues, world literature, world religions, writing.

Graduation Requirements Arts and fine arts (art, music, dance, drama), computer science, English, foreign language, history, mathematics, physical education (includes health), religion (includes Bible studies and theology), science, social studies (includes history).

Special Academic Programs 18 Advanced Placement exams for which test preparation is offered; honors section; independent study; term-away projects; domestic exchange program (with Network of Sacred Heart Schools); study abroad.

College Admission Counseling 45 students graduated in 2014; all went to college, including Columbia University; Dartmouth College; Georgetown University; Harvard University; University of Pennsylvania; Yale University. Mean SAT critical reading: 698, mean SAT math: 669.

Student Life Upper grades have uniform requirement, student council. Discipline rests primarily with faculty. Attendance at religious services is required.

Tuition and Aid Day student tuition: $42,810. Tuition installment plan (monthly payment plans). Need-based scholarship grants available. In 2014–15, 38% of upper-school students received aid. Total amount of financial aid awarded in 2014–15: $2,300,000.

Admissions Traditional secondary-level entrance grade is 9. For fall 2014, 200 students applied for upper-level admission, 35 were accepted, 16 enrolled. ERB or ISEE required. Deadline for receipt of application materials: December 1. Application fee required: $65. On-campus interview required.

Athletics Interscholastic: basketball, cross-country running, indoor track & field, lacrosse, soccer, softball, swimming and diving, tennis, track and field, volleyball, winter (indoor) track; intramural: aerobics/dance, aerobics/Nautilus, aquatics, ballet, basketball, dance, fitness, fitness walking, gymnastics, jogging, life saving, martial arts, physical fitness, physical training, roller blading, running, self defense, soccer, softball, strength & conditioning, swimming and diving, tennis, track and field, volleyball, weight lifting, weight training, yoga. 8 PE instructors, 8 coaches, 1 athletic trainer.

Computers Computers are regularly used in all academic classes. Computer network features include on-campus library services, online commercial services, Internet access, wireless campus network, Internet filtering or blocking technology. Campus intranet, student e-mail accounts, and computer access in designated common areas are available to students. The school has a published electronic and media policy.

Contact Amanda Rosenthal, Admissions Office Coordinator. 212-722-4745 Ext. 105. Fax: 212-996-1784. E-mail: arosenthal@cshnyc.org. Website: www.cshnyc.org

COTTER SCHOOLS

1115 West Broadway
Winona, Minnesota 55987-1399

Head of School: Sr. Judith Schaefer, OP

General Information Coeducational boarding and day college-preparatory, general academic, arts, religious studies, technology, and ESL school, affiliated with Roman Catholic Church. Boarding grades 9–12, day grades 7–12. Founded: 1911. Setting: small town. Nearest major city is Minneapolis. Students are housed in single-sex by floor dormitories. 45-acre campus. 7 buildings on campus. Approved or accredited by Midwest Association of Boarding Schools, National Catholic Education Association, North Central Association of Colleges and Schools, The Association of Boarding Schools, and Minnesota Department of Education. Member of Secondary School Admission Test Board. Endowment: $15 million. Total enrollment: 362. Upper school average class size: 18. Upper school faculty-student ratio: 1:11. There are 176 required school days per year for Upper School students. Upper School students typically attend 5 days per week. The average school day consists of 5 hours and 55 minutes.

Upper School Student Profile Grade 9: 61 students (31 boys, 30 girls); Grade 10: 82 students (44 boys, 38 girls); Grade 11: 59 students (37 boys, 22 girls); Grade 12: 75 students (42 boys, 33 girls). 31% of students are boarding students. 65% are state residents. 4 states are represented in upper school student body. 30% are international students. International students from China, Japan, Mexico, Republic of Korea, Taiwan, and Viet Nam; 7 other countries represented in student body. 62% of students are Roman Catholic.

Faculty School total: 36. In upper school: 17 men, 19 women; 32 have advanced degrees; 5 reside on campus.

Subjects Offered Algebra, American history, anatomy, art, band, Bible, biology, calculus, calculus-AP, campus ministry, chemistry, chorus, Christian and Hebrew scripture, Christian ethics, community service, computer science, death and loss, economics, English, environmental science, ESL, German, health, Hebrew scripture, honors English, learning lab, linear algebra, literature and composition-AP, math analysis, mathematics, media, painting, physical education, physical science, physics, psychology, science, Spanish, statistics, U.S. history, U.S. history-AP, visual arts, world geography, world religions.

Graduation Requirements English, foreign language, mathematics, performing arts, physical education (includes health), religion (includes Bible studies and theology), science, social studies (includes history), visual arts, 80 hours of community service.

Special Academic Programs 13 Advanced Placement exams for which test preparation is offered; honors section; accelerated programs; independent study; term-away projects; study at local college for college credit; study abroad; academic accommodation for the gifted, the musically talented, and the artistically talented; remedial reading and/or remedial writing; remedial math; programs in English, mathematics for dyslexic students; ESL (25 students enrolled).

College Admission Counseling 85 students graduated in 2014; 84 went to college, including Indiana University Bloomington; Saint John's University; University of Illinois at Urbana–Champaign; University of Minnesota, Twin Cities Campus; University of St. Thomas; University of Wisconsin–Madison. Other: 1 had other specific plans. Median combined SAT: 1722, median composite ACT: 24. 50% scored over 26 on composite ACT.

Student Life Upper grades have specified standards of dress, student council. Discipline rests primarily with faculty. Attendance at religious services is required.

Tuition and Aid Day student tuition: $12,075; 7-day tuition and room/board: $32,300. Tuition installment plan (FACTS Tuition Payment Plan, monthly payment plans, individually arranged payment plans). Tuition reduction for siblings, merit

scholarship grants, need-based scholarship grants available. In 2014–15, 60% of upper-school students received aid.

Admissions Traditional secondary-level entrance grade is 9. For fall 2014, 96 students applied for upper-level admission, 75 were accepted, 51 enrolled. SLEP for foreign students or TOEFL required. Deadline for receipt of application materials: none. Application fee required: $100. Interview required.

Athletics Interscholastic: aerobics/dance (girls), baseball (b), basketball (b,g), cheering (g), cross-country running (b,g), dance (g), dance team (g), danceline (g), football (b), gymnastics (g), hockey (b,g), ice hockey (b,g), skiing (cross-country) (b,g), soccer (b,g), softball (g), swimming and diving (b,g), tennis (b,g), track and field (b,g), volleyball (g), weight lifting (b,g), weight training (b,g), wrestling (b); intramural: basketball (b,g), indoor soccer (b), skiing (downhill) (b,g), snowboarding (b,g), yoga (b,g); coed interscholastic: weight lifting, weight training; coed intramural: alpine skiing, badminton, basketball, canoeing/kayaking, curling, indoor soccer, skiing (downhill), snowboarding, yoga. 2 PE instructors, 66 coaches, 1 athletic trainer.

Computers Computers are regularly used in art, freshman foundations, graphic arts, graphic design, introduction to technology, journalism, photography, technology, video film production classes. Computer network features include on-campus library services, Internet access, wireless campus network, Internet filtering or blocking technology. Campus intranet, student e-mail accounts, and computer access in designated common areas are available to students. Students grades are available online. The school has a published electronic and media policy.

Contact Mr. Will Gibson, Director of Admissions. 507-453-5403. Fax: 507-453-5006. E-mail: wgibson@cotterschools.org. Website: www.cotterschools.org

THE COUNTRY DAY SCHOOL

13415 Dufferin Street
King City, Ontario L7B 1K5, Canada

Head of School: Mr. John Liggett

General Information Coeducational day college-preparatory, arts, business, and technology school. Grades JK–12. Founded: 1972. Setting: rural. Nearest major city is Toronto, Canada. 100-acre campus. 3 buildings on campus. Approved or accredited by Canadian Association of Independent Schools, Canadian Educational Standards Institute, Conference of Independent Schools of Ontario, and Ontario Department of Education. Affiliate member of National Association of Independent Schools. Language of instruction: English. Total enrollment: 700. Upper school average class size: 17. Upper school faculty-student ratio: 1:9. Upper School students typically attend 5 days per week. The average school day consists of 6 hours and 25 minutes.

Upper School Student Profile Grade 9: 75 students (30 boys, 45 girls); Grade 10: 75 students (30 boys, 45 girls); Grade 11: 75 students (30 boys, 45 girls); Grade 12: 91 students (46 boys, 45 girls).

Faculty School total: 81. In upper school: 28 men, 20 women.

Subjects Offered Advanced chemistry, advanced computer applications, advanced math, algebra, American history, anatomy and physiology, ancient history, ancient/medieval philosophy, art and culture, art history, athletics, band, biology, business studies, Canadian geography, Canadian history, Canadian literature, career education, career/college preparation, choir, comparative politics, computer programming, creative writing, English, environmental geography, European history, French, government/civics, history, languages, mathematics, modern Western civilization, performing arts, philosophy, physical education, physics, politics, science, society, world history.

Graduation Requirements Ministry Grade 10 Literacy Test (Government of Ontario).

Special Academic Programs Advanced Placement exam preparation; study abroad.

College Admission Counseling 91 students graduated in 2015; all went to college, including McGill University; McMaster University; Queen's University at Kingston; The University of Western Ontario; University of Toronto; Wilfrid Laurier University.

Student Life Upper grades have uniform requirement, student council, honor system. Discipline rests primarily with faculty.

Summer Programs Advancement, sports, art/fine arts programs offered; session focuses on advancement; held both on and off campus; held at Costa Rica, England, and Greece and Italy; accepts boys and girls; open to students from other schools. 20 students usually enrolled. 2016 schedule: July 4 to July 29. Application deadline: March 1.

Tuition and Aid Day student tuition: CAN$27,100. Bursaries, need-based scholarship grants available.

Admissions Traditional secondary-level entrance grade is 9. For fall 2015, 97 students applied for upper-level admission, 58 were accepted, 37 enrolled. CAT 5 or SSAT required. Deadline for receipt of application materials: none. Application fee required: CAN$125. On-campus interview required.

Athletics Interscholastic: baseball (girls), basketball (b,g), cross-country running (b,g), golf (b,g), hockey (b,g), ice hockey (b,g), rugby (b,g), running (b,g), soccer (b,g), softball (b,g), tennis (b,g), track and field (b,g), volleyball (b,g); intramural: badminton (b,g), basketball (b,g), bowling (b,g), ice hockey (b), ice skating (b,g), physical fitness (b,g), skiing (downhill) (b,g), snowboarding (b,g), soccer (b,g), softball (b,g), volleyball (b,g); coed interscholastic: alpine skiing, skiing (cross-country); coed intramural: bicycling, curling, Frisbee, mountain biking, nordic skiing, outdoor activities, outdoor education, physical fitness, physical training, strength & conditioning, swimming and diving, table tennis, weight training, yoga. 5 PE instructors.

Computers Computers are regularly used in accounting, business, career education, English, geography, history, mathematics, media, music, writing, yearbook classes. Computer network features include on-campus library services, Internet access, wireless campus network, Internet filtering or blocking technology, access to online library resources from home, access to homework online via Blackboard Software. Campus intranet is available to students.

Contact Mr. David Huckvale, Director of Admission. 905-833-1220. Fax: 905-833-1350. E-mail: admissions@cds.on.ca. Website: www.cds.on.ca/

COUNTRY DAY SCHOOL OF THE SACRED HEART

480 Bryn Mawr Avenue

Bryn Mawr, Pennsylvania 19010

Head of School: Sr. Matthew Anita MacDonald, SSJ

General Information Girls' day college-preparatory, arts, religious studies, and technology school, affiliated with Roman Catholic Church. Grades PK–12. Founded: 1865. Setting: suburban. Nearest major city is Philadelphia. 16-acre campus. 3 buildings on campus. Approved or accredited by Middle States Association of Colleges and Schools, Network of Sacred Heart Schools, and Pennsylvania Department of Education. Member of National Association of Independent Schools. Total enrollment: 314. Upper school average class size: 15. Upper school faculty-student ratio: 1:8. There are 180 required school days per year for Upper School students. The average school day consists of 7 hours.

Upper School Student Profile Grade 9: 49 students (49 girls); Grade 10: 38 students (38 girls); Grade 11: 40 students (40 girls); Grade 12: 44 students (44 girls). 75% of students are Roman Catholic.

Faculty School total: 44. In upper school: 3 men, 30 women; 25 have advanced degrees.

Subjects Offered Algebra, American history, American history-AP, American literature, art, arts, Bible studies, biology, calculus, chemistry, composition, computer science, economics, English, English literature, environmental science, ethics, European history, film, fine arts, French, geometry, government/civics, health, Latin, mathematics, media studies, physical education, physics, pre-calculus, religion, science, social sciences, social studies, Spanish, trigonometry, word processing, world history, world literature.

Graduation Requirements Arts and fine arts (art, music, dance, drama), English, foreign language, mathematics, physical education (includes health), religion (includes Bible studies and theology), science, social studies (includes history), two weeks of senior independent study with a working professional, 25 hours of community service per year.

Special Academic Programs 7 Advanced Placement exams for which test preparation is offered; honors section; independent study; term-away projects; study at local college for college credit; domestic exchange program (with Network of Sacred Heart Schools); study abroad; academic accommodation for the musically talented.

College Admission Counseling 37 went to college, including Drexel University; Fordham University; Georgetown University; Saint Joseph's University; The Catholic University of America; University of Pittsburgh. Mean SAT critical reading: 620, mean SAT math: 580, mean SAT writing: 650. 45% scored over 600 on SAT critical reading, 40% scored over 600 on SAT math, 50% scored over 600 on SAT writing.

Student Life Upper grades have uniform requirement, student council. Discipline rests equally with students and faculty. Attendance at religious services is required.

Tuition and Aid Day student tuition: $17,500. Tuition installment plan (SMART Tuition Payment Plan). Tuition reduction for siblings, merit scholarship grants, need-based scholarship grants available. In 2014–15, 75% of upper-school students received aid; total upper-school merit-scholarship money awarded: $415,900. Total amount of financial aid awarded in 2014–15: $424,500.

Admissions Traditional secondary-level entrance grade is 9. For fall 2014, 90 students applied for upper-level admission, 65 were accepted, 32 enrolled. High School Placement Test required. Deadline for receipt of application materials: none. Application fee required: $35. Interview required.

Athletics Interscholastic: basketball, crew, cross-country running, field hockey, golf, lacrosse, softball, tennis, track and field, volleyball; intramural: fitness walking. 2 PE instructors, 12 coaches, 1 athletic trainer.

Computers Computers are regularly used in English, foreign language, history, mathematics, science, technology classes. Computer network features include on-campus library services, online commercial services, Internet access, wireless campus network. Student e-mail accounts are available to students. Students grades are available online. The school has a published electronic and media policy.

Contact Mrs. Mary Lee FitzPatrick, Director of Admissions. 610-527-3915 Ext. 214. Fax: 610-527-0942. E-mail: mfitzpatrick@cdssh.org. Website: www.cdssh.org

COVENANT CANADIAN REFORMED SCHOOL

3030 TWP Road 615A

County of Barrhead, Alberta T0G 1R2, Canada

Head of School: Mr. James Meinen

General Information Coeducational day college-preparatory, general academic, business, religious studies, and technology school, affiliated with Reformed Church. Grades K–12. Founded: 1977. Setting: rural. Nearest major city is Edmonton, Canada. 5-acre campus. 2 buildings on campus. Approved or accredited by Association of Independent Schools and Colleges of Alberta and Alberta Department of Education. Language of instruction: English. Total enrollment: 244. Upper school average class size: 10. Upper school faculty-student ratio: 1:10. There are 167 required school days per year for Upper School students. Upper School students typically attend 4 days per week. The average school day consists of 6 hours and 10 minutes.

Upper School Student Profile Grade 10: 15 students (8 boys, 7 girls); Grade 11: 14 students (7 boys, 7 girls); Grade 12: 10 students (6 boys, 4 girls). 100% of students are Reformed.

Faculty School total: 16. In upper school: 5 men, 4 women.

Subjects Offered Accounting, architectural drawing, Bible studies, biology, Canadian geography, career and personal planning, career technology, chemistry, child development, Christian education, computer information systems, computer skills, computer studies, consumer law, desktop publishing, digital photography, drama, drawing and design, early childhood, electronic publishing, English, ESL, French as a second language, geology, health education, history, HTML design, information processing, intro to computers, introduction to technology, keyboarding, mathematics, physical education, physics, prayer/spirituality, religious studies, science, sewing, social studies, theology and the arts, Web site design, Western religions, work experience, world geography, world religions, yearbook.

Graduation Requirements Must pass religious studies courses offered in grades 10, 11, and 12 for years attended.

Special Academic Programs Independent study; remedial reading and/or remedial writing; remedial math.

College Admission Counseling 8 students graduated in 2015; 2 went to college, including Stevenson University; University of Alberta; University of Calgary; University of Lethbridge. Other: 6 went to work.

Student Life Upper grades have specified standards of dress, student council. Discipline rests primarily with faculty.

Tuition and Aid Day student tuition: CAN$6900. Tuition installment plan (monthly payment plans, individually arranged payment plans). Tuition rates per family available.

Admissions Traditional secondary-level entrance grade is 10. For fall 2015, 1 student applied for upper-level admission, 1 was accepted, 1 enrolled. Achievement tests or Saltus Achievement Test required. Deadline for receipt of application materials: none. No application fee required. Interview required.

Athletics Interscholastic: track and field (boys, girls), volleyball (b,g); coed intramural: badminton, ball hockey, baseball, basketball, flag football, floor hockey, football, Frisbee, hockey, ice hockey, indoor hockey, indoor soccer, lacrosse, soccer, softball, volleyball. 4 PE instructors, 6 coaches.

Computers Computers are regularly used in all classes. Computer network features include on-campus library services, Internet access, Internet filtering or blocking technology. Computer access in designated common areas is available to students. The school has a published electronic and media policy.

Contact Mr. James Meinen, Principal. 780-674-4774. Fax: 780-401-3295. E-mail: principal@covenantschool.ca. Website: www.covenantschool.ca/

CRAWFORD ADVENTIST ACADEMY

531 Finch Avenue West

Willowdale, Ontario M2R 3X2, Canada

Head of School: Mr. Norman Brown

General Information Coeducational day college-preparatory, arts, business, religious studies, bilingual studies, and technology school, affiliated with Seventh-day Adventist Church. Grades JK–12. Founded: 1954. Setting: urban. Nearest major city is Toronto, Canada. 5-acre campus. 1 building on campus. Approved or accredited by National Council for Private School Accreditation, Ontario Ministry of Education, and Ontario Department of Education. Language of instruction: English. Total enrollment: 361. Upper school average class size: 25. Upper school faculty-student ratio: 1:14. There are 196 required school days per year for Upper School students. Upper School students typically attend 5 days per week. The average school day consists of 7 hours and 15 minutes.

Upper School Student Profile Grade 9: 36 students (15 boys, 21 girls); Grade 10: 31 students (12 boys, 19 girls); Grade 11: 30 students (17 boys, 13 girls); Grade 12: 30 students (13 boys, 17 girls). 90% of students are Seventh-day Adventists.

Faculty School total: 17. In upper school: 12 men, 5 women; 13 have advanced degrees.

Subjects Offered Advanced computer applications, band, Bible, biology, business, business technology, calculus, Canadian geography, Canadian history, chemistry, choir, civics, community service, computer applications, computer information systems, drama, dramatic arts, earth and space science, English, English composition, French,

French as a second language, geography, guidance, independent study, information technology, marketing, mathematics, physical education, physics, religion, science, writing, yearbook.

Graduation Requirements French as a second language, complete 40 community service hours, must pass the Ontario Secondary School Literacy Test.

Special Academic Programs 3 Advanced Placement exams for which test preparation is offered; remedial reading and/or remedial writing; programs in English for dyslexic students; ESL.

College Admission Counseling 30 students graduated in 2015; 4 went to college, including Andrews University; Oakwood University; Ryerson University; University of Toronto; University of Waterloo; York University. Other: 26 entered a postgraduate year. Median composite ACT: 20. 22% scored over 26 on composite ACT.

Student Life Upper grades have uniform requirement, student council, honor system. Discipline rests primarily with faculty. Attendance at religious services is required.

Tuition and Aid Day student tuition: CAN$8500. Tuition installment plan (monthly payment plans, individually arranged payment plans). Tuition reduction for siblings, need-based scholarship grants, paying campus jobs available. In 2015–16, 25% of upper-school students received aid. Total amount of financial aid awarded in 2015–16: CAN$40,000.

Admissions Traditional secondary-level entrance grade is 9. CAT, CAT 2, CCAT, CTBS (or similar from their school) or Learn Aid Aptitude Test required. Deadline for receipt of application materials: none. Application fee required: CAN$50. On-campus interview required.

Athletics Interscholastic: basketball (boys, girls), weight lifting (b,g); intramural: basketball (b,g); coed interscholastic: cooperative games, outdoor recreation; coed intramural: basketball, flag football, floor hockey, indoor hockey, indoor soccer, outdoor education, outdoor recreation, physical fitness, physical training, snowboarding, soccer, table tennis, volleyball. 1 PE instructor, 2 coaches.

Computers Computers are regularly used in accounting, business, computer applications, yearbook classes. Computer network features include Internet access, wireless campus network, Internet filtering or blocking technology. Student e-mail accounts and computer access in designated common areas are available to students. Students grades are available online. The school has a published electronic and media policy.

Contact Mr. Andrew Mark Thomas, Principal, 9-12. 416-633-0090 Ext. 223. Fax: 416-633-0467. E-mail: athomas@caasda.com. Website: www.tadsb.com/

THE CRENSHAW SCHOOL

2342 Hempel Ave.

Gotha, Florida 34734

Head of School: Mrs. Brenda Crenshaw

General Information Coeducational day college-preparatory school. Grades PK–12. Founded: 1999. Setting: suburban. Nearest major city is Orlando. 2 buildings on campus. Approved or accredited by Association of Independent Schools of Florida, National Council for Private School Accreditation, Southern Association of Colleges and Schools, and Florida Department of Education. Total enrollment: 102. Upper school average class size: 10. Upper school faculty-student ratio: 1:10. There are 180 required school days per year for Upper School students. Upper School students typically attend 5 days per week. The average school day consists of 6 hours.

Faculty School total: 18. In upper school: 2 men, 6 women; 3 have advanced degrees.

Subjects Offered 1968.

Special Academic Programs Honors section; accelerated programs; study at local college for college credit; academic accommodation for the gifted; ESL (10 students enrolled).

College Admission Counseling 16 students graduated in 2015; 1 went to college, including University of Central Florida; University of South Florida; Valencia College. Other: 1 had other specific plans.

Student Life Upper grades have uniform requirement, student council, honor system. Discipline rests equally with students and faculty.

Summer Programs Advancement programs offered; session focuses on private course classes; held on campus; accepts boys and girls; not open to students from other schools. 2016 schedule: June 1 to June 30.

Admissions For fall 2015, 25 students applied for upper-level admission, 20 were accepted, 20 enrolled. Deadline for receipt of application materials: none. Application fee required: $1250. Interview required.

Athletics 1 coach.

Computers Computer resources include wireless campus network. Students grades are available online. The school has a published electronic and media policy.

Contact Mrs. Brenda Crenshaw, Head of School. 407-877-7412. Fax: 407-877-0541. E-mail: bcrenshaw@crenshawschool.com. Website: www.crenshawschool.com/

CRESCENT SCHOOL

2365 Bayview Avenue

Toronto, Ontario M2L 1A2, Canada

Head of School: Michael Fellin

General Information Boys' day college-preparatory school. Grades 3–12. Founded: 1913. Setting: urban. 30-acre campus. 2 buildings on campus. Approved or accredited by Canadian Association of Independent Schools, Canadian Educational Standards Institute, Conference of Independent Schools of Ontario, Ontario Ministry of Education, and Ontario Department of Education. Affiliate member of National Association of Independent Schools; member of Secondary School Admission Test Board. Language of instruction: English. Endowment: CAN$10.2 million. Total enrollment: 715. Upper school average class size: 22. Upper school faculty-student ratio: 1:10. The average school day consists of 6 hours and 50 minutes.

Upper School Student Profile Grade 9: 101 students (101 boys); Grade 10: 87 students (87 boys); Grade 11: 90 students (90 boys); Grade 12: 87 students (87 boys).

Faculty School total: 68. In upper school: 31 men, 11 women; 9 have advanced degrees.

Subjects Offered Accounting, algebra, American history, art, biology, business skills, calculus, chemistry, computer programming, computer science, creative writing, drama, economics, English, English literature, entrepreneurship, fine arts, finite math, French, geography, health, history, information technology, law, leadership, mathematics, media arts, music, philosophy, physical education, physics, political science, robotics, science, social studies, Spanish, technology/design, theater, world history.

Graduation Requirements Arts and fine arts (art, music, dance, drama), business skills (includes word processing), English, foreign language, mathematics, physical education (includes health), science, social studies (includes history).

Special Academic Programs Advanced Placement exam preparation; honors section; accelerated programs.

College Admission Counseling 86 students graduated in 2015; 82 went to college, including Dalhousie University; McGill University; Queen's University at Kingston; The University of Western Ontario; University of Waterloo; Wilfrid Laurier University. Other: 4 had other specific plans. 75% scored over 600 on SAT critical reading, 80% scored over 600 on SAT math.

Student Life Upper grades have uniform requirement, student council. Discipline rests primarily with faculty.

Summer Programs Advancement programs offered; session focuses on earning additional credits; held on campus; accepts boys and girls; open to students from other schools. 135 students usually enrolled. 2016 schedule: June 27 to July 29. Application deadline: May 1.

Tuition and Aid Day student tuition: CAN$30,750. Tuition installment plan (monthly payment plans, individually arranged payment plans). Bursaries, merit scholarship grants, need-based scholarship grants available. In 2015–16, 3% of upper-school students received aid; total upper-school merit-scholarship money awarded: CAN$30,000. Total amount of financial aid awarded in 2015–16: CAN$680,000.

Admissions Traditional secondary-level entrance grade is 9. For fall 2015, 81 students applied for upper-level admission, 50 were accepted, 31 enrolled. CAT, ERB CTP III, school's own exam or SSAT required. Deadline for receipt of application materials: December 4. Application fee required: CAN$200. On-campus interview required.

Athletics Interscholastic: alpine skiing, badminton, basketball, cross-country running, golf, ice hockey, judo, rugby, skiing (downhill), snowboarding, soccer, softball, squash, swimming and diving, table tennis, tennis, track and field, volleyball; intramural: ball hockey, basketball, curling, flag football, Frisbee, golf, ice hockey, mountain biking, soccer, softball, squash, table tennis, tennis, track and field, volleyball, weight lifting. 3 PE instructors.

Computers Computers are regularly used in accounting, art, business, computer applications, creative writing, economics, English, foreign language, French, geography, history, human geography - AP, information technology, mathematics, media arts, music, science, technology, yearbook classes. Computer network features include on-campus library services, online commercial services, Internet access, wireless campus network. Student e-mail accounts are available to students. Students grades are available online. The school has a published electronic and media policy.

Contact Angela Van Straubenzee, Admissions Coordinator. 416-449-2556 Ext. 476. Fax: 416-449-7950. E-mail: avanstraubenzee@crescentschool.org. Website: www.crescentschool.org

CROSSROADS SCHOOL FOR ARTS & SCIENCES

1714 21st Street

Santa Monica, California 90404-3917

Head of School: Bob Riddle

General Information Coeducational day college-preparatory, arts, and technology school. Grades K–12. Founded: 1971. Setting: urban. Nearest major city is Los Angeles. 3-acre campus. 20 buildings on campus. Approved or accredited by California Association of Independent Schools, Western Association of Schools and Colleges, and California Department of Education. Member of National Association of Independent Schools. Endowment: $17.9 million. Total enrollment: 1,174. Upper school average class size: 17. Upper school faculty-student ratio: 1:11. There are 164 required school days per year for Upper School students. Upper School students typically attend 5 days per week. The average school day consists of 7 hours.

Upper School Student Profile Grade 9: 133 students (59 boys, 74 girls), Grade 10: 130 students (64 boys, 66 girls); Grade 11: 127 students (67 boys, 60 girls); Grade 12: 131 students (64 boys, 67 girls).

Faculty School total: 165. In upper school: 42 men, 45 women; 73 have advanced degrees.

Subjects Offered Algebra, American history, American studies, art history, biology, calculus, ceramics, chemistry, community service, computer programming, computer science, creative writing, critical studies in film, cultural arts, dance, earth and space science, English, environmental education, film studies, French, gender issues, geometry, graphic design, great books, Greek, human development, Japanese, jazz ensemble, jazz theory, journalism, Latin, marine biology, marine ecology, music appreciation, music theory, orchestra, photography, physical education, physics, physiology, pre-calculus, sculpture, Spanish, statistics, studio art, theater, trigonometry, video film production, world civilizations, yoga.

Graduation Requirements Arts and fine arts (art, music, dance, drama), English, foreign language, human development, mathematics, physical education (includes health), science, social studies (includes history), community service hours, senior project. Community service is required.

Special Academic Programs Honors section; term-away projects; academic accommodation for the gifted, the musically talented, and the artistically talented.

College Admission Counseling 126 students graduated in 2015; all went to college, including New York University; The George Washington University; Tulane University; University of California, Los Angeles; University of Michigan; University of Southern California. Median SAT critical reading: 640, median SAT math: 630, median SAT writing: 670, median combined SAT: 1930, median composite ACT: 29. 69% scored over 600 on SAT critical reading, 60% scored over 600 on SAT math, 77% scored over 600 on SAT writing, 69% scored over 1800 on combined SAT, 82% scored over 26 on composite ACT.

Student Life Upper grades have student council. Discipline rests primarily with faculty.

Summer Programs Remediation, enrichment, advancement, sports, art/fine arts, computer instruction programs offered; session focuses on enrichment, academics, day care, aquatics, arts, musical productions, jazz camp; held on campus; accepts boys and girls; open to students from other schools. 950 students usually enrolled. 2016 schedule: June 20 to August 5. Application deadline: March 1.

Tuition and Aid Day student tuition: $36,000. Tuition installment plan (individually arranged payment plans, in-house only—2 payment plan for full pay students, and 10 payment plan exclusively for financial aid students only). Need-based scholarship grants, tuition reduction fund, need-based financial aid available. In 2015–16, 25% of upper-school students received aid. Total amount of financial aid awarded in 2015–16: $3,490,851.

Admissions Traditional secondary-level entrance grade is 9. For fall 2015, 140 students applied for upper-level admission, 28 were accepted, 20 enrolled. ISEE required. Deadline for receipt of application materials: December 2. Application fee required: $150. On-campus interview required.

Athletics Interscholastic: baseball (boys), basketball (b,g), cross-country running (b,g), soccer (b,g), softball (g), tennis (b,g), track and field (b,g), volleyball (b,g); coed interscholastic: flag football, golf, swimming and diving; coed intramural: canoeing/kayaking, climbing, hiking/backpacking, kayaking, outdoor activities, outdoor education, rock climbing, ropes courses, snowshoeing, table tennis. 7 PE instructors, 24 coaches, 3 athletic trainers.

Computers Computers are regularly used in college planning, creative writing, foreign language, graphic design, journalism, mathematics, music, newspaper, programming, science classes. Computer network features include on-campus library services, online commercial services, Internet access, wireless campus network. Student e-mail accounts and computer access in designated common areas are available to students. Students grades are available online. The school has a published electronic and media policy.

Contact Eric Barber, Director of Enrollment Management. 310-829-7391 Ext. 525. Fax: 310-828-5636. E-mail: Ebarber@xrds.org. Website: www.xrds.org

CRYSTAL SPRINGS UPLANDS SCHOOL

400 Uplands Drive
Hillsborough, California 94010

Head of School: Ms. Amy Richards

General Information Coeducational day college-preparatory school. Grades 6–12. Founded: 1952. Setting: suburban. Nearest major city is San Francisco. 10-acre campus. 4 buildings on campus. Approved or accredited by American Association of Christian Schools, Western Association of Schools and Colleges, and California Department of Education. Member of National Association of Independent Schools and Secondary School Admission Test Board. Endowment: $15 million. Total enrollment: 350. Upper school average class size: 14. Upper school faculty-student ratio: 1:9. Upper School students typically attend 5 days per week. The average school day consists of 7 hours.

Faculty School total: 44. In upper school: 18 men, 26 women; 24 have advanced degrees.

Subjects Offered Acting, advanced computer applications, algebra, American history, American literature, art, astronomy, biology, calculus, ceramics, chamber groups, chemistry, chorus, comparative cultures, computer math, computer programming, computer science, concert bell choir, creative writing, dance, dance performance, drama, English, English literature, ensembles, European history, fine arts, French, geometry, graphic design, health, history, mathematics, multicultural literature, music, photography, physical education, physics, poetry, post-calculus, pre-calculus, science, Shakespeare, Spanish, statistics, theater, video film production, wellness, world history, world literature, writing.

Graduation Requirements Arts and fine arts (art, music, dance, drama), English, foreign language, history, mathematics, physical education (includes health), science, senior project.

Special Academic Programs Honors section; independent study; term-away projects; domestic exchange program; study abroad.

College Admission Counseling 61 students graduated in 2015; all went to college, including Stanford University; University of California, Los Angeles; University of California, San Diego; University of Pennsylvania; University of Southern California. Mean SAT critical reading: 674, mean SAT math: 703, mean SAT writing: 688, mean combined SAT: 2067, mean composite ACT: 29.

Student Life Upper grades have specified standards of dress, student council, honor system. Discipline rests equally with students and faculty.

Tuition and Aid Day student tuition: $37,485. Tuition installment plan (Insured Tuition Payment Plan, monthly payment plans, Tuition Management Systems Plan). Need-based scholarship grants available. In 2015–16, 20% of upper-school students received aid. Total amount of financial aid awarded in 2015–16: $2,200,000.

Admissions Traditional secondary-level entrance grade is 9. For fall 2015, 477 students applied for upper-level admission, 137 were accepted, 77 enrolled. ISEE or SSAT required. Deadline for receipt of application materials: January 14. Application fee required: $85. On-campus interview required.

Athletics Interscholastic: baseball (boys), basketball (b,g), cross-country running (b,g), football (b), soccer (b,g), softball (g), swimming and diving (b,g), tennis (b,g), track and field (b,g), volleyball (g); coed interscholastic: badminton, dance, golf, running, strength & conditioning; coed intramural: dance, fitness, Frisbee, hiking/backpacking, outdoors, rock climbing, table tennis, ultimate Frisbee, weight lifting, weight training. 3 PE instructors, 14 coaches, 1 athletic trainer.

Computers Computers are regularly used in all academic classes. Computer network features include on-campus library services, online commercial services, Internet access, wireless campus network, Internet filtering or blocking technology. Campus intranet, student e-mail accounts, and computer access in designated common areas are available to students. Students grades are available online. The school has a published electronic and media policy.

Contact Admission Office. 650-342-4175. Fax: 650-342-7611. E-mail: admission@csus.org. Website: www.csus.org

C.S. LEWIS ACADEMY

PO Box 3250
Newberg, Oregon 97132

Head of School: Mr. Mike Wenger

General Information Coeducational day college-preparatory and general academic school, affiliated with Christian faith, Christian faith. Grades 9–12. Founded: 1985. Setting: small town. Nearest major city is Portland. 8-acre campus. 3 buildings on campus. Approved or accredited by Northwest Accreditation Commission, Northwest Association of Independent Schools, and Oregon Department of Education. Total enrollment: 150. Upper school average class size: 10. Upper school faculty-student ratio: 1:7. There are 170 required school days per year for Upper School students. Upper School students typically attend 5 days per week. The average school day consists of 7 hours.

Upper School Student Profile Grade 9: 9 students (6 boys, 3 girls); Grade 10: 11 students (3 boys, 8 girls); Grade 11: 15 students (5 boys, 10 girls); Grade 12: 11 students (6 boys, 5 girls).

Faculty School total: 25. In upper school: 3 men, 7 women; 5 have advanced degrees.

Subjects Offered Algebra, American literature, ancient world history, art, band, Bible, Bible studies, biology, career/college preparation, chemistry, choir, consumer education, creative writing, drama, economics, English, European literature, food science, general science, geometry, government, health, history, home economics, journalism, language arts, physical education, physics, pre-algebra, pre-calculus, social studies, Spanish, speech, U.S. history, Western civilization, yearbook.

College Admission Counseling 22 students graduated in 2015; 19 went to college, including Chemeketa Community College; George Fox University; Portland Community College; Western Oregon University. Other: 1 went to work, 2 entered military service. Mean combined SAT: 1721, mean composite ACT: 30. 43% scored over 600 on SAT critical reading, 29% scored over 600 on SAT math, 43% scored over 600 on SAT writing, 43% scored over 1800 on combined SAT, 50% scored over 26 on composite ACT.

Student Life Upper grades have specified standards of dress, student council. Discipline rests primarily with faculty. Attendance at religious services is required.

Tuition and Aid Day student tuition: $7250. Tuition installment plan (FACTS Tuition Payment Plan, individually arranged payment plans). Tuition reduction for siblings, need-based scholarship grants available. In 2015–16, 9% of upper-school students received aid. Total amount of financial aid awarded in 2015–16: $22,113.

Admissions Traditional secondary-level entrance grade is 9. Deadline for receipt of application materials: none. Application fee required: $75. Interview required.

Athletics Interscholastic: basketball (boys, girls), track and field (b,g), volleyball (g); coed interscholastic: golf, soccer. 1 PE instructor, 10 coaches.

Computers Computer network features include Internet access, wireless campus network, Internet filtering or blocking technology. Students grades are available online. The school has a published electronic and media policy.

Contact Ms. Dianne Sargent, Administrative Assistant. 503-538-0114. Fax: 503-538-4113. E-mail: highschool@cslewisacademy.com. Website: www.cslewisacademy.com

THE CULVER ACADEMIES

1300 Academy Road
Culver, Indiana 46511

Head of School: Mr. John N. Buxton

General Information Coeducational boarding and day college-preparatory, arts, and business school. Grades 9–PG. Founded: 1894. Setting: small town. Nearest major city is South Bend. Students are housed in single-sex dormitories. 1,700-acre campus. 38 buildings on campus. Approved or accredited by Independent Schools Association of the Central States and Indiana Department of Education. Member of National Association of Independent Schools and Secondary School Admission Test Board. Endowment: $385 million. Upper school average class size: 13. Upper school faculty-student ratio: 1:9. There are 185 required school days per year for Upper School students. Upper School students typically attend 5 days per week. The average school day consists of 6 hours.

Upper School Student Profile Grade 9: 163 students (95 boys, 68 girls); Grade 10: 228 students (136 boys, 92 girls); Grade 11: 210 students (121 boys, 89 girls); Grade 12: 208 students (120 boys, 88 girls); Postgraduate: 2 students (2 girls). 92% of students are boarding students. 30% are state residents. 43 states are represented in upper school student body. 32% are international students. International students from Canada, China, Mexico, Republic of Korea, Saudi Arabia, and Switzerland; 18 other countries represented in student body.

Faculty School total: 97. In upper school: 53 men, 44 women; 83 have advanced degrees; 16 reside on campus.

Subjects Offered Acting, advanced math, African-American history, algebra, American government, American history, American history-AP, American literature, anatomy, anatomy and physiology, art, art history, arts, ballet, Basic programming, biology, biology-AP, calculus, calculus-AP, career/college preparation, ceramics, character education, chemistry, chemistry-AP, Chinese, choir, church history, college admission preparation, college placement, college planning, comparative government and politics-AP, comparative religion, computer math, computer programming, computer science, computer science-AP, dance, drama, dramatic arts, driver education, economics, economics-AP, English, English language-AP, English literature, entrepreneurship, equestrian sports, equine science, equitation, ESL, ethics and responsibility, European history, film studies, fine arts, fitness, French, French-AP, geology, geometry, German, German literature, German-AP, global studies, government, government-AP, government/civics, health and wellness, honors English, honors geometry, humanities, instrumental music, integrated mathematics, integrated science, jazz band, Latin, Latin-AP, leadership, library research, macro/microeconomics-AP, mathematics, mentorship program, music, music theory, music theory-AP, photography, physical education, physics, physics-AP, physiology, piano, play production, pottery, pre-algebra, pre-calculus, science, science research, Shakespeare, social studies, Spanish, Spanish language-AP, Spanish-AP, speech, statistics-AP, strings, theater, trigonometry, U.S. government and politics-AP, U.S. history-AP, world history, world religions.

Graduation Requirements Arts and fine arts (art, music, dance, drama), English, foreign language, health education, history, leadership, mathematics, science, senior community service project.

Special Academic Programs 25 Advanced Placement exams for which test preparation is offered; honors section; study abroad; academic accommodation for the gifted, the musically talented, and the artistically talented; ESL (24 students enrolled).

College Admission Counseling 204 students graduated in 2015; 192 went to college, including Indiana University Bloomington; Princeton University; Purdue University; United States Military Academy; United States Naval Academy. Other: 6 entered a postgraduate year, 6 had other specific plans.

Student Life Upper grades have uniform requirement, student council, honor system. Discipline rests primarily with students. Attendance at religious services is required.

Summer Programs Enrichment, advancement, ESL, sports, art/fine arts, rigorous outdoor training, computer instruction programs offered; session focuses on leadership training, citizenship, lifetime interests, and skills development; held on campus; accepts boys and girls; open to students from other schools. 1,385 students usually enrolled. 2016 schedule: June 18 to July 29. Application deadline: April 1.

Tuition and Aid Day student tuition: $44,500; 7-day tuition and room/board: $34,500. Tuition installment plan (Key Tuition Payment Plan). Merit scholarship grants, need-based scholarship grants available. In 2015–16, 48% of upper-school students received aid; total upper-school merit-scholarship money awarded: $7,850,000. Total amount of financial aid awarded in 2015–16: $8,900,000.

Admissions Traditional secondary-level entrance grade is 9. SSAT or TOEFL required. Deadline for receipt of application materials: June 1. Application fee required: $30. Interview required.

Athletics Interscholastic: baseball (boys), basketball (b,g), crew (b,g), cross-country running (b,g), diving (b,g), equestrian sports (b,g), fencing (b,g), football (b), golf (b,g), hockey (b,g), ice hockey (b,g), indoor track & field (b,g), lacrosse (b,g), polo (b,g), rowing (b,g), rugby (b,g), soccer (b,g), softball (g), swimming and diving (b,g), tennis (b,g), track and field (b,g), volleyball (g), winter (indoor) track (b,g), wrestling (b,g); intramural: basketball (b), dance team (g), drill team (b,g), flag football (b), ice hockey (b,g), indoor soccer (b,g), modern dance (b,g), paint ball (b,g), soccer (b); coed interscholastic: cheering, dressage, equestrian sports, sailing, trap and skeet; coed intramural: aerobics, aerobics/dance, aerobics/Nautilus, alpine skiing, aquatics, archery, backpacking, badminton, ballet, bicycling, bowling, broomball, canoeing/kayaking, climbing, combined training, cooperative games, cross-country running, dance, figure skating, fishing, fitness, fitness walking, fly fishing, Frisbee, handball, hiking/backpacking, horseback riding, ice skating, independent competitive sports, indoor track & field, jogging, kickball, life saving, marksmanship, Nautilus, outdoor activities, outdoor adventure, outdoor education, outdoor recreation, outdoor skills, outdoors, paddling, physical fitness, physical training, power lifting, project adventure, racquetball, riflery, ropes courses, running, scuba diving, skeet shooting, skiing (cross-country), skiing (downhill), snowboarding, squash, strength & conditioning, swimming and diving, table tennis, tai chi, ultimate Frisbee, volleyball, walking, wall climbing, weight lifting, weight training, wilderness, winter walking, yoga. 8 PE instructors, 4 athletic trainers.

Computers Computers are regularly used in all classes. Computer network features include on-campus library services, online commercial services, Internet access, wireless campus network, Internet filtering or blocking technology, each student is issued a tablet. Campus intranet, student e-mail accounts, and computer access in designated common areas are available to students. Students grades are available online. The school has a published electronic and media policy.

Contact Mr. Michael Turnbull, Director of Admissions. 574-842-7100. Fax: 574-842-8066. E-mail: Michael.Turnbull@culver.org. Website: www.culver.org

CURREY INGRAM ACADEMY

6544 Murray Lane
Brentwood, Tennessee 37027

Head of School: Dr. Jeffrey Mitchell

General Information Coeducational day college-preparatory, arts, technology, ethics and character education, and service learning school; primarily serves students with learning disabilities, individuals with Attention Deficit Disorder, dyslexic students, non-verbal learning disabilities, and speech and language disabilities. Grades K–12. Founded: 1968. Setting: suburban. Nearest major city is Nashville. 83-acre campus. 3 buildings on campus. Approved or accredited by Council of Accreditation and School Improvement, Southern Association of Colleges and Schools, Southern Association of Independent Schools, and Tennessee Department of Education. Member of National Association of Independent Schools. Total enrollment: 307. Upper school average class size: 7. There are 175 required school days per year for Upper School students. Upper School students typically attend 5 days per week. The average school day consists of 7 hours and 30 minutes.

Subjects Offered Algebra, American government, art, basic language skills, biology, British literature, character education, chemistry, cinematography, college admission preparation, college awareness, college counseling, college planning, community service, digital music, digital photography, drama performance, earth science, economics, electives, English composition, English literature, environmental science, ethics and responsibility, government, health, history, integrated technology fundamentals, learning strategies, life skills, literature, modern world history, music, newspaper, physical education, physics, pragmatics, pre-calculus, reading/study skills, social studies, sports, studio art, technology, video film production, vocal music, writing, writing workshop, yearbook.

Graduation Requirements Arts and fine arts (art, music, dance, drama), electives, English, ethics, foreign language, mathematics, physical education (includes health), science, social studies (includes history), students who need remediation in reading/writing take reading/writing workshop instead of foreign language, seniors must complete Service Learning credit plus 30 hours of community service.

Special Academic Programs Honors section; independent study; academic accommodation for the gifted, the musically talented, and the artistically talented; remedial reading and/or remedial writing; programs in English, mathematics, general development for dyslexic students.

College Admission Counseling 12 students graduated in 2015; 11 went to college, including Austin Peay State University; Chattanooga State Community College; High Point University; Lipscomb University; Lynn University; Reinhardt University. Other: 1 entered military service.

Student Life Upper grades have uniform requirement, student council, honor system. Discipline rests primarily with faculty.

Summer Programs Enrichment, art/fine arts programs offered; session focuses on theatre and music camp; held on campus; accepts boys and girls; open to students from other schools.

Tuition and Aid Day student tuition: $37,380–$38,524. Tuition installment plan (Insured Tuition Payment Plan, monthly payment plans). Need-based scholarship grants available. In 2015–16, 35% of upper-school students received aid. Total amount of financial aid awarded in 2015–16: $1,750,000.

Admissions Traditional secondary-level entrance grade is 9. Psychoeducational evaluation required. Deadline for receipt of application materials: none. Application fee required: $250. Interview required.

Athletics Interscholastic: basketball (boys), cheering (g), volleyball (g); intramural: fitness (b,g); coed interscholastic: cross-country running, golf, soccer, tennis.

Computers Computers are regularly used in all academic classes. Computer network features include on-campus library services, Internet access, wireless campus network, Internet filtering or blocking technology, iPods for instructional use in classrooms, 1:1 laptop and/or iPad program, assistive technology. Campus intranet and student e-mail accounts are available to students. Students grades are available online. The school has a published electronic and media policy.

Contact Mrs. Kathy Boles, Director of Admission. 615-507-3173 Ext. 250. Fax: 615-507-3170. E-mail: kathy.boles@curreyingram.org. Website: www.curreyingram.org

CUSHING ACADEMY

39 School Street
Ashburnham, Massachusetts 01430-8000

Head of School: Mr. Christopher Torino

General Information Coeducational boarding and day college-preparatory, arts, technology, Cushing Scholars, and academic support, ESL school. Grades 9–PG. Founded: 1865. Setting: small town. Nearest major city is Boston. Students are housed in single-sex dormitories. 162-acre campus. 32 buildings on campus. Approved or accredited by Association of Independent Schools in New England, New England Association of Schools and Colleges, and Massachusetts Department of Education. Member of National Association of Independent Schools and Secondary School Admission Test Board. Endowment: $45 million. Total enrollment: 400. Upper school average class size: 12. Upper school faculty-student ratio: 1:8. There are 152 required school days per year for Upper School students. Upper School students typically attend 5 days per week. The average school day consists of 7 hours.

Upper School Student Profile Grade 9: 49 students (20 boys, 29 girls); Grade 10: 94 students (52 boys, 42 girls); Grade 11: 122 students (70 boys, 52 girls); Grade 12: 116 students (65 boys, 51 girls); Postgraduate: 19 students (18 boys, 1 girl). 85% of students are boarding students. 31% are state residents. 28 states are represented in upper school student body. 30% are international students. International students from China, Japan, Mexico, Republic of Korea, Spain, and Taiwan; 24 other countries represented in student body.

Faculty School total: 64. In upper school: 27 men, 37 women; 37 have advanced degrees; 47 reside on campus.

Subjects Offered Advanced biology, advanced math, Advanced Placement courses, aerobics, algebra, American government, American history, American literature, American literature-AP, anatomy, anatomy and physiology, architectural drawing, art, art history, athletic training, bioethics, biology, biology-AP, calculus, calculus-AP, career education internship, chemistry, chemistry-AP, Chinese, chorus, Civil War, community service, computer programming, computer science, creative arts, creative drama, creative writing, dance, developmental language skills, digital photography, discrete mathematics, drafting, drama, drawing, driver education, earth and space science, ecology, ecology, environmental systems, economics, economics and history, economics-AP, English, English literature, environmental science, ESL, ethics, European history, expository writing, fine arts, French, geometry, government/civics, grammar, graphic arts, health, health and wellness, history, honors algebra, honors English, honors geometry, honors U.S. history, honors world history, Latin, Latin-AP, Mandarin, marine biology, mathematics, mechanical drawing, music, music history, music theory, musical theater, photography, physics, physiology, pre-calculus, probability and statistics, psychology, SAT preparation, science, social studies, sociology, Spanish, Spanish-AP, speech, stagecraft, statistics-AP, student government, technology, The 20th Century, theater, theater history, trigonometry, U.S. government and politics-AP, U.S. history, United Nations and international issues, Vietnam War, visual arts, vocal music, wind instruments, world history, world literature, World-Wide-Web publishing, writing.

Graduation Requirements Art, English, foreign language, mathematics, science, social studies (includes history).

Special Academic Programs 14 Advanced Placement exams for which test preparation is offered; honors section; independent study; term-away projects; academic accommodation for the gifted, the musically talented, and the artistically talented; remedial reading and/or remedial writing; remedial math; programs in English, mathematics, general development for dyslexic students; ESL (55 students enrolled).

College Admission Counseling 131 students graduated in 2015; 124 went to college, including Boston University; Hobart and William Smith Colleges; Ithaca College; Northeastern University; Skidmore College; Syracuse University. Other: 1 entered a postgraduate year, 6 had other specific plans.

Student Life Upper grades have specified standards of dress, student council, honor system. Discipline rests equally with students and faculty.

Summer Programs Remediation, enrichment, advancement, ESL, sports, art/fine arts, computer instruction programs offered; session focuses on enrichment; held on campus; accepts boys and girls; open to students from other schools. 280 students usually enrolled. 2016 schedule: July 3 to August 5.

Tuition and Aid Day student tuition: $39,900; 7-day tuition and room/board: $55,850. Tuition installment plan (monthly payment plans). Merit scholarship grants, need-based scholarship grants available. In 2015–16, 26% of upper-school students received aid; total upper-school merit-scholarship money awarded: $100,000. Total amount of financial aid awarded in 2015–16: $3,100,000.

Admissions Traditional secondary-level entrance grade is 9. For fall 2015, 804 students applied for upper-level admission, 505 were accepted, 153 enrolled. ACT, PSAT, SAT, SSAT, TOEFL or TOEFL Junior required. Deadline for receipt of application materials: January 15. Application fee required: $50. Interview required.

Athletics Interscholastic: baseball (boys), basketball (b,g), field hockey (g), football (b), hockey (b,g), ice hockey (b,g), lacrosse (b,g), running (b,g), skiing (downhill) (b,g), soccer (b,g), softball (g), tennis (b,g), track and field (b,g), volleyball (g); coed interscholastic: alpine skiing, cross-country running, golf, running; coed intramural: aerobics, aerobics/dance, alpine skiing, dance, equestrian sports, figure skating, fitness, horseback riding, ice hockey, ice skating, independent competitive sports, martial arts, modern dance, mountain biking, physical fitness, physical training, skiing (downhill), snowboarding, strength & conditioning, weight training, yoga. 3 coaches, 2 athletic trainers.

Computers Computers are regularly used in all academic classes. Computer network features include on-campus library services, online commercial services, Internet access, wireless campus network, Internet filtering or blocking technology, CushNet (on-campus network), digital library, live webcasting. Campus intranet, student e-mail accounts, and computer access in designated common areas are available to students. Students grades are available online. The school has a published electronic and media policy.

Contact Mrs. Deborah A. Gustafson, Director of Admissions. 978-827-7300. Fax: 978-827-6253. E-mail: admissions@cushing.org. Website: www.cushing.org

DAMIEN HIGH SCHOOL

2280 Damien Avenue
La Verne, California 91750

Head of School: Dr. Merritt Hemenway

General Information Boys' day college-preparatory, Project Lead The Way: 4-year pre-engineering program, and Interscholastic Debate school, affiliated with Roman Catholic Church. Grades 9–12. Founded: 1959. Setting: suburban. Nearest major city is Los Angeles. 28-acre campus. 9 buildings on campus. Approved or accredited by Western Association of Schools and Colleges, Western Catholic Education Association, and California Department of Education. Endowment: $450,000. Total enrollment: 936. Upper school average class size: 26. Upper school faculty-student ratio: 1:17. There are 180 required school days per year for Upper School students. Upper School students typically attend 5 days per week. The average school day consists of 7 hours.

Upper School Student Profile Grade 9: 210 students (210 boys); Grade 10: 270 students (270 boys); Grade 11: 229 students (229 boys); Grade 12: 227 students (227 boys). 68% of students are Roman Catholic.

Faculty School total: 54. In upper school: 43 men, 11 women; 29 have advanced degrees.

Subjects Offered Advanced biology, advanced chemistry, Advanced Placement courses, advanced studio art-AP, algebra, American history, American history-AP, American literature, American literature-AP, anatomy and physiology, ancient world history, art history, art history-AP, band, biology, biology-AP, calculus-AP, chemistry, chemistry-AP, Chinese, comparative government and politics-AP, comparative religion, computer applications, computer programming, computer science-AP, debate, earth science, economics, economics-AP, English composition, English language and composition-AP, English literature, English literature and composition-AP, environmental science-AP, European history-AP, fitness, French, French language-AP, German, German-AP, government, health, honors geometry, human geography - AP, macroeconomics-AP, mathematics, microeconomics-AP, music, physics, physics-AP, pre-calculus, social issues, Spanish, Spanish-AP, sports medicine, statistics-AP, theology, U.S. government and politics, U.S. history, visual arts, weight training, Western civilization, world history.

Graduation Requirements Algebra, American government, American history, ancient world history, art, biology, Catholic belief and practice, chemistry, Christian and Hebrew scripture, Christian doctrine, Christian ethics, Christian scripture, economics, English, English composition, foreign language, geometry, government, health and wellness, history of the Catholic Church, language and composition, modern world history, New Testament, U.S. history, world history, world literature, 100 hours of community service.

Special Academic Programs 25 Advanced Placement exams for which test preparation is offered; honors section; ESL (30 students enrolled).

College Admission Counseling 221 students graduated in 2015; 214 went to college, including Arizona State University at the Tempe campus; California State Polytechnic University, Pomona; The University of Arizona; University of California, Riverside; University of Oregon; University of San Diego. Other: 1 entered military service, 6 had other specific plans. Mean SAT critical reading: 528, mean SAT math:

539, mean SAT writing: 519, mean combined SAT: 1586, mean composite ACT: 25. 27% scored over 600 on SAT critical reading, 29% scored over 600 on SAT math, 19% scored over 600 on SAT writing, 25% scored over 1800 on combined SAT, 37% scored over 26 on composite ACT.

Student Life Upper grades have uniform requirement, student council. Discipline rests primarily with faculty. Attendance at religious services is required.

Summer Programs Remediation, enrichment, advancement, sports, art/fine arts, computer instruction programs offered; session focuses on academic advancement, remediation; held on campus; accepts boys and girls; open to students from other schools. 600 students usually enrolled. 2016 schedule: June 13 to July 15. Application deadline: June 1.

Tuition and Aid Day student tuition: $7900. Tuition installment plan (FACTS Tuition Payment Plan). Tuition reduction for siblings, merit scholarship grants, need-based scholarship grants available. In 2015–16, 52% of upper-school students received aid; total upper-school merit-scholarship money awarded: $80,000. Total amount of financial aid awarded in 2015–16: $745,000.

Admissions Traditional secondary-level entrance grade is 9. For fall 2015, 264 students applied for upper-level admission, 260 were accepted, 210 enrolled. High School Placement Test (closed version) from Scholastic Testing Service required. Deadline for receipt of application materials: none. Application fee required: $75. On-campus interview required.

Athletics Interscholastic: baseball, basketball, bicycling, cross-country running, football, golf, hockey, ice hockey, in-line skating, lacrosse, mountain biking, roller hockey, soccer, swimming and diving, tennis, track and field, volleyball, water polo, wrestling; intramural: bocce, bowling, fishing, hiking/backpacking, surfing. 2 PE instructors, 30 coaches, 2 athletic trainers.

Computers Computers are regularly used in all academic classes. Computer network features include online commercial services, Internet access, wireless campus network, Internet filtering or blocking technology. Campus intranet, student e-mail accounts, and computer access in designated common areas are available to students. Students grades are available online. The school has a published electronic and media policy.

Contact Mrs. Christina Provenzano, Admissions Coordinator. 909-596-1946 Ext. 247. Fax: 909-596-6112. E-mail: christina@damien-hs.edu. Website: www.damien-hs.edu

DANA HALL SCHOOL

45 Dana Road
Wellesley, Massachusetts 02482

Head of School: Ms. Caroline Erisman, JD

General Information Girls' boarding and day college-preparatory, Forum-Life Skills, and leadership school. Boarding grades 9–12, day grades 5–12. Founded: 1881. Setting: suburban. Nearest major city is Boston. Students are housed in single-sex dormitories. 55-acre campus. 34 buildings on campus. Approved or accredited by Association of Independent Schools in New England, Massachusetts Department of Education, New England Association of Schools and Colleges, The Association of Boarding Schools, and Massachusetts Department of Education. Member of National Association of Independent Schools and Secondary School Admission Test Board. Endowment: $47.8 million. Total enrollment: 464. Upper school average class size: 12. Upper school faculty-student ratio: 1:6. There are 165 required school days per year for Upper School students. Upper School students typically attend 5 days per week. The average school day consists of 7 hours and 30 minutes.

Upper School Student Profile Grade 9: 89 students (89 girls); Grade 10: 90 students (90 girls); Grade 11: 89 students (89 girls); Grade 12: 93 students (93 girls). 40% of students are boarding students. 76% are state residents. 13 states are represented in upper school student body. 16% are international students. International students from China, Hong Kong, Mexico, Republic of Korea, Taiwan, and Thailand; 4 other countries represented in student body.

Faculty School total: 65. In upper school: 17 men, 29 women; 34 have advanced degrees; 37 reside on campus.

Subjects Offered 20th century history, acting, African history, African studies, algebra, American history, American literature, architecture, art, art history, art-AP, astronomy, biology, calculus, ceramics, chemistry, chorus, community service, computer programming, computer science, computer science-AP, creative writing, dance, dance performance, drama, drama workshop, drawing, East Asian history, economics, electives, engineering, English, English composition, English language and composition-AP, English/composition-AP, European history, European history-AP, fitness, French, French language-AP, French literature-AP, freshman foundations, geometry, government, government/civics, health, journalism, Latin, Latin American history, Latin-AP, leadership education training, library, Mandarin, marine biology, mathematics-AP, Middle Eastern history, music, music composition, music performance, music theory, photography, physics, physics-AP, public speaking, Russian studies, Spanish, Spanish-AP, statistics-AP, trigonometry, U.S. history-AP, U.S. literature, weight training, Western civilization, women in the classical world.

Graduation Requirements American history, area studies, English, fitness, foreign language, health and wellness, mathematics, performing arts, science, social studies (includes history), visual arts, 20 hours of community service. Community service is required.

Special Academic Programs 17 Advanced Placement exams for which test preparation is offered; honors section; independent study; term-away projects; study abroad.

College Admission Counseling 76 students graduated in 2015; all went to college, including Boston University; Georgetown University; Gettysburg College; New York University; Syracuse University; The George Washington University. Mean SAT critical reading: 631, mean SAT math: 663, mean SAT writing: 656, mean combined SAT: 1950, mean composite ACT: 29.

Student Life Upper grades have specified standards of dress, student council, honor system. Discipline rests equally with students and faculty.

Summer Programs Enrichment programs offered; session focuses on leadership training and confidence building for girls entering high school; held on campus; accepts girls; open to students from other schools. 40 students usually enrolled. 2016 schedule: June 25 to July 1. Application deadline: none.

Tuition and Aid Day student tuition: $43,200; 7-day tuition and room/board: $57,700. Tuition installment plan (monthly payment plans). Merit scholarship grants, need-based scholarship grants available. In 2015–16, 28% of upper-school students received aid; total upper-school merit-scholarship money awarded: $10,000. Total amount of financial aid awarded in 2015–16: $3,895,640.

Admissions Traditional secondary-level entrance grade is 9. For fall 2015, 583 students applied for upper-level admission, 262 were accepted, 119 enrolled. ISEE, SSAT or TOEFL required. Deadline for receipt of application materials: January 15. Application fee required: $50. Interview required.

Athletics Interscholastic: basketball, cross-country running, equestrian sports, fencing, field hockey, golf, horseback riding, ice hockey, lacrosse, modern dance, soccer, softball, squash, swimming and diving, tennis, volleyball; intramural: aquatics, ballet, crew, dance, equestrian sports, fitness, Frisbee, golf, hiking/backpacking, horseback riding, indoor track, life saving, martial arts, modern dance, Nautilus, outdoor activities, physical fitness, physical training, rock climbing, self defense, squash, strength & conditioning, swimming and diving, tennis, ultimate Frisbee, weight lifting, weight training, yoga. 3 PE instructors, 33 coaches, 2 athletic trainers.

Computers Computers are regularly used in all academic, art, English, French, history, Latin, mathematics, science, Spanish, Web site design, yearbook classes. Computer network features include on-campus library services, online commercial services, Internet access, wireless campus network, Internet filtering or blocking technology, grades available online to students only. Campus intranet, student e-mail accounts, and computer access in designated common areas are available to students. Students grades are available online. The school has a published electronic and media policy.

Contact Mrs. Bethann Coppi, Admission Office Manager/Database Coordinator. 781-235-3010 Ext. 2531. Fax: 781-239-1383. E-mail: admission@danahall.org. Website: www.danahall.org

DARLINGTON SCHOOL

1014 Cave Spring Road, SW
Rome, Georgia 30161-4700

Head of School: Mr. Brent Bell

General Information Coeducational boarding and day college-preparatory, arts, and technology school, affiliated with Christian faith. Boarding grades 9–PG, day grades PK–PG. Founded: 1905. Setting: small town. Nearest major city is Atlanta. Students are housed in single-sex dormitories. 500-acre campus. 15 buildings on campus. Approved or accredited by Georgia Independent School Association, Southern Association of Colleges and Schools, Southern Association of Independent Schools, The Association of Boarding Schools, The College Board, and Georgia Department of Education. Member of National Association of Independent Schools and Secondary School Admission Test Board. Endowment: $34.9 million. Total enrollment: 789. Upper school average class size: 13. Upper school faculty-student ratio: 1:15. There are 176 required school days per year for Upper School students. Upper School students typically attend 5 days per week. The average school day consists of 7 hours and 30 minutes.

Upper School Student Profile Grade 6: 38 students (21 boys, 17 girls); Grade 7: 52 students (26 boys, 26 girls); Grade 8: 57 students (33 boys, 24 girls); Grade 9: 87 students (39 boys, 48 girls); Grade 10: 127 students (75 boys, 52 girls); Grade 11: 119 students (70 boys, 49 girls); Grade 12: 121 students (60 boys, 61 girls); Postgraduate: 2 students (1 boy, 1 girl). 40% of students are boarding students. 72% are state residents. 15 states are represented in upper school student body. 18% are international students. International students from Bahamas, Bermuda, China, Germany, Mexico, and Republic of Korea; 19 other countries represented in student body.

Faculty School total: 71. In upper school: 34 men, 37 women; 47 have advanced degrees; 57 reside on campus.

Subjects Offered Advanced biology, advanced chemistry, Advanced Placement courses, advanced studio art-AP, algebra, ancient world history, art, art history, art history-AP, band, biology, biology-AP, calculus, calculus-AP, chemistry, chemistry-AP, choir, chorus, college counseling, computer programming, computer science, concert choir, creative writing, drama, drawing, economics, economics-AP, English, English language and composition-AP, English language-AP, English literature, English literature-AP, English-AP, ensembles, environmental science, environmental science-AP, ESL, fine arts, French, geometry, government-AP, graphic arts, graphic design, health, honors algebra, honors English, honors geometry, honors world history, humanities, jazz ensemble, journalism, lab science, macro/microeconomics-AP, macroeconomics-AP, modern European history-AP, music, music theory-AP, musical theater, newspaper, personal fitness, physical education, physics, physics-AP, pre-calculus, probability and statistics, psychology-AP, robotics, Spanish, Spanish language-AP, Spanish literature-AP, Spanish-AP, statistics-AP, studio art-AP, trigonometry, U.S. history, U.S. history-AP, video, video film production, vocal ensemble, wind ensemble, world cultures, world history, world history-AP, yearbook.

Graduation Requirements Arts and fine arts (art, music, dance, drama), English, foreign language, information technology, mathematics, physical education (includes health), science, social studies (includes history), community service/servant leadership program, after school activity.

Special Academic Programs 21 Advanced Placement exams for which test preparation is offered; honors section; academic accommodation for the musically talented; ESL (18 students enrolled).

College Admission Counseling 135 students graduated in 2014; all went to college, including Auburn University; Emory University, Oxford College; Georgia Institute of Technology; Georgia Southern University; New York University; University of Georgia. Median SAT critical reading: 520, median SAT math: 571, median SAT writing: 527, median combined SAT: 1614, median composite ACT: 19.

Student Life Upper grades have uniform requirement, student council, honor system. Discipline rests equally with students and faculty.

Tuition and Aid Day student tuition: $19,000; 7-day tuition and room/board: $44,900–$50,700. Tuition installment plan (FACTS Tuition Payment Plan, monthly payment plans, individually arranged payment plans). Merit scholarship grants, need-based scholarship grants available. In 2014–15, 43% of upper-school students received aid; total upper-school merit-scholarship money awarded: $749,800. Total amount of financial aid awarded in 2014–15: $2,566,200.

Admissions Traditional secondary-level entrance grade is 9. For fall 2014, 341 students applied for upper-level admission, 213 were accepted, 160 enrolled. PSAT and SAT for applicants to grade 11 and 12, SSAT, SSAT or WISC III or TOEFL required. Deadline for receipt of application materials: February 1. Application fee required: $100. Interview required.

Athletics Interscholastic: baseball (boys), basketball (b,g), cheering (g), crew (b,g), cross-country running (b,g), diving (b,g), football (b), golf (b,g), lacrosse (b,g), rowing (b,g), soccer (b,g), softball (g), swimming and diving (b,g), tennis (b,g), track and field (b,g), volleyball (g), wrestling (b); intramural: aerobics/dance (g), aquatics (b,g), basketball (b,g), cheering (g), dance squad (g), fitness (b,g), flag football (b,g), flagball (b,g), running (b,g), tennis (b,g), volleyball (b,g); coed intramural: aerobics, fishing, fly fishing, Frisbee, independent competitive sports, outdoor activities, outdoor education, outdoor recreation, physical fitness, physical training, soccer, speleology, strength & conditioning, table tennis, ultimate Frisbee, water volleyball, weight lifting, weight training. 2 PE instructors, 11 coaches, 2 athletic trainers.

Computers Computers are regularly used in computer applications, English, foreign language, history, mathematics, science, Web site design classes. Computer network features include on-campus library services, Internet access, wireless campus network, Internet filtering or blocking technology. Campus intranet, student e-mail accounts, and computer access in designated common areas are available to students. Students grades are available online. The school has a published electronic and media policy.

Contact Mrs. Darla Betts, Assistant Director of Boarding Admission. 706-236-0421. Fax: 706-232-3600. E-mail: dbetts@darlingtonschool.org. Website: www.darlingtonschool.org

DARROW SCHOOL

110 Darrow Road
New Lebanon, New York 12125

Head of School: Mr. Simon Holzapfel

General Information Coeducational boarding and day college-preparatory, arts, hands-on learning, and sustainability school. Grades 9–12. Founded: 1932. Setting: rural. Nearest major city is Pittsfield, MA. Students are housed in single-sex dormitories. 365.5-acre campus. 26 buildings on campus. Approved or accredited by Middle States Association of Colleges and Schools, New York State Association of Independent Schools, The Association of Boarding Schools, and New York Department of Education. Member of National Association of Independent Schools and Secondary School Admission Test Board. Endowment: $4.6 million. Upper school average class size: 9. Upper school faculty-student ratio: 1:4. There are 220 required school days per year for Upper School students. Upper School students typically attend 6 days per week. The average school day consists of 6 hours.

Upper School Student Profile Grade 9: 19 students (11 boys, 8 girls); Grade 10: 35 students (18 boys, 17 girls); Grade 11: 29 students (17 boys, 12 girls); Grade 12: 35 students (20 boys, 15 girls). 80% of students are boarding students. 52% are state residents. 15 states are represented in upper school student body. 25% are international students. International students from Bahamas, China, Ghana, Japan, Taiwan, and Turkey; 4 other countries represented in student body.

Faculty School total: 33. In upper school: 18 men, 15 women; 24 have advanced degrees; 30 reside on campus.

Subjects Offered 3-dimensional art, advanced math, African drumming, African-American literature, algebra, American literature, art, art history, athletics, biology, calculus, ceramics, chemistry, civil rights, clayworking, computer graphics, creative

writing, critical writing, culinary arts, design, digital art, drama, drawing, drawing and design, ecology, economics, English, English literature, ensembles, environmental education, environmental science, environmental studies, ESL, ethics, experiential education, fine arts, French, geometry, health and wellness, history, independent study, Latin American literature, leadership, literature, mathematics, microeconomics, multicultural studies, music appreciation, music theory, oil painting, photo shop, photography, physics, play production, poetry, portfolio art, pottery, pre-calculus, reading/study skills, Russian literature, science, social studies, Spanish, Spanish literature, sports, studio art, study skills, theater, U.S. history, Western civilization, women's literature, woodworking, writing, yearbook.

Graduation Requirements Arts, arts and fine arts (art, music, dance, drama), electives, English, foreign language, history, mathematics, physical education (includes health), science.

Special Academic Programs Advanced Placement exam preparation; independent study; term-away projects; academic accommodation for the musically talented and the artistically talented; ESL (12 students enrolled).

College Admission Counseling 30 students graduated in 2015; 29 went to college, including Brandeis University; Clarkson University; Hartwick College; Hobart and William Smith Colleges; Suffolk University; Wheaton College. Other: 1 went to work. Mean composite ACT: 25.

Student Life Upper grades have specified standards of dress, student council, honor system. Discipline rests with students and faculty.

Summer Programs ESL programs offered; session focuses on ESOL immersion; held both on and off campus; held at home stays, day trips; accepts boys and girls; not open to students from other schools. 8 students usually enrolled. 2016 schedule: August 15 to August 30.

Tuition and Aid Day student tuition: $31,200; 7-day tuition and room/board: $54,700. Tuition installment plan (Academic Management Services Plan, SMART Tuition Payment Plan, individually arranged payment plans). Need-based scholarship grants available. In 2015–16, 40% of upper-school students received aid. Total amount of financial aid awarded in 2015–16: $1,400,000.

Admissions Traditional secondary-level entrance grade is 9. For fall 2015, 145 students applied for upper-level admission, 93 were accepted, 33 enrolled. SLEP for foreign students or TOEFL or SLEP required. Deadline for receipt of application materials: none. Application fee required: $75. On-campus interview required.

Athletics Interscholastic: basketball (boys, girls), cross-country running (b,g), soccer (b,g), softball (g), tennis (b,g); coed interscholastic: cross-country running, Frisbee, lacrosse, tennis, ultimate Frisbee; coed intramural: aerobics/dance, alpine skiing, backpacking, dance, equestrian sports, fitness, freestyle skiing, hiking/backpacking, lacrosse, martial arts, outdoor activities, outdoor education, physical fitness, rock climbing, self defense, skiing (downhill), snowboarding, telemark skiing, weight lifting, yoga. 1 coach.

Computers Computers are regularly used in graphic design, photography, video film production classes. Computer network features include on-campus library services, Internet access, wireless campus network, Internet filtering or blocking technology. Campus intranet, student e-mail accounts, and computer access in designated common areas are available to students. Students grades are available online. The school has a published electronic and media policy.

Contact Ms. Betsy Strickler, Director of Admission. 518-794-6008. Fax: 518-794-7065. E-mail: stricklerb@darrowschool.org. Website: www.darrowschool.org

DAVIDSON ACADEMY

1414 W. Old Hickory Boulevard
Nashville, Tennessee 37207-1098

Head of School: Dr. Bill Chaney

General Information Coeducational day college-preparatory, arts, religious studies, technology, and science, mathematics school, affiliated with Christian faith. Grades PK–12. Founded: 1980. Setting: suburban. 67-acre campus. 1 building on campus. Approved or accredited by Association of Christian Schools International, Southern Association of Colleges and Schools, and Tennessee Department of Education. Endowment: $25,000. Total enrollment: 750. Upper school average class size: 15. Upper school faculty-student ratio: 1:15. There are 180 required school days per year for Upper School students. Upper School students typically attend 5 days per week. The average school day consists of 5 hours and 50 minutes.

Upper School Student Profile 99.9% of students are Christian faith.

Faculty School total: 34. In upper school: 16 men, 18 women.

Subjects Offered 3-dimensional art, ACT preparation, advanced math, Advanced Placement courses, algebra, American government, American history, American history-AP, art, art appreciation, audio visual/media, band, Bible, Bible studies, biology, calculus, calculus-AP, cheerleading, chemistry, choral music, chorus, church history, college admission preparation, college counseling, college placement, composition-AP, computer applications, computer skills, conceptual physics, concert band, concert choir, consumer economics, creative writing, drama, drama performance, dramatic arts, earth science, economics, English, English literature-AP, English-AP, English/composition-AP, European history-AP, film and new technologies, geography, geometry, government-AP, health and wellness, history, honors algebra, honors English, honors geometry, human anatomy, independent study, Latin, leadership and service, Life of Christ, literature, marching band, mathematics, mathematics-AP, music, musical productions, New Testament, newspaper, physical education, physical fitness, physical science, physics, physics-AP, poetry, pre-algebra, pre-calculus, pre-college orientation, probability and statistics, psychology, reading, religious studies, science, senior project, Spanish, speech, speech communications, trigonometry, U.S. history, U.S. history-AP, video film production, wellness, world geography, world history, writing, yearbook.

Graduation Requirements Algebra, art, biology, calculus, chemistry, computer technologies, drama, economics, electives, English, English composition, English literature, foreign language, geometry, government, literature, physical science, physics, senior project, trigonometry, U.S. history, wellness, world history, Senior Research Project, Bible.

Special Academic Programs 3 Advanced Placement exams for which test preparation is offered; honors section; independent study; study at local college for college credit; programs in general development for dyslexic students; ESL (15 students enrolled).

College Admission Counseling 54 students graduated in 2014; all went to college, including Belmont University; Lipscomb University; Tennessee Technological University; The University of Tennessee; The University of Tennessee at Chattanooga; Western Kentucky University.

Student Life Upper grades have uniform requirement, student council, honor system. Discipline rests primarily with faculty.

Tuition and Aid Day student tuition: $9300. Tuition installment plan (monthly payment plans, individually arranged payment plans). Tuition reduction for siblings, need-based scholarship grants, need-based financial aid, tuition reduction for children of faculty and staff available. In 2014–15, 20% of upper-school students received aid.

Admissions Traditional secondary-level entrance grade is 9. Admissions testing, any standardized test and WRAT required. Deadline for receipt of application materials: none. Application fee required: $75.

Athletics Interscholastic: baseball (boys), basketball (b,g), cheering (g), cross-country running (b,g), dance team (g), football (b), golf (b,g), soccer (b,g), softball (g), tennis (b,g), track and field (b,g), volleyball (g), wrestling (b); intramural: ballet (g), dance (g), weight training (b); coed interscholastic: bowling. 2 PE instructors, 1 athletic trainer.

Computers Computers are regularly used in computer applications, English, graphic arts, history, mathematics, media production, yearbook classes. Computer network features include on-campus library services, Internet access, wireless campus network, Internet filtering or blocking technology, RenWeb, Accelerated Reader, CollegeView. Computer access in designated common areas is available to students. Students grades are available online. The school has a published electronic and media policy.

Contact Mr. Jason McGehee, Director of Admission. 615-860-5317. Fax: 615-860-7631. E-mail: jason.mcgehee@davidsonacademy.com. Website: www.davidsonacademy.com

DEERFIELD ACADEMY

7 Boyden Lane
Deerfield, Massachusetts 01342

Head of School: Dr. Margarita O'Byrne Curtis

General Information Coeducational boarding and day college-preparatory school. Grades 9–PG. Founded: 1797. Setting: rural. Nearest major city is Hartford, CT. Students are housed in single-sex dormitories. 280-acre campus. 81 buildings on campus. Approved or accredited by Association of Independent Schools in New England, National Independent Private Schools Association, New England Association of Schools and Colleges, and Massachusetts Department of Education. Member of National Association of Independent Schools and Secondary School Admission Test Board. Endowment: $500 million. Total enrollment: 638. Upper school average class size: 12. Upper school faculty-student ratio: 1:6. There are 150 required school days per year for Upper School students. Upper School students typically attend 5 days per week. The average school day consists of 5 hours and 25 minutes.

Upper School Student Profile Grade 9: 115 students (56 boys, 59 girls); Grade 10: 155 students (74 boys, 81 girls); Grade 11: 177 students (93 boys, 84 girls); Grade 12: 166 students (85 boys, 81 girls); Postgraduate: 25 students (22 boys, 3 girls). 89% of students are boarding students. 22% are state residents. 42 states are represented in upper school student body. 18% are international students. International students from Canada, China, Hong Kong, Jamaica, Republic of Korea, and Singapore; 28 other countries represented in student body.

Faculty School total: 100. In upper school: 53 men, 42 women; 88 have advanced degrees; 120 reside on campus.

Subjects Offered Advanced chemistry, advanced computer applications, advanced math, advanced studio art-AP, algebra, American government, American history-AP, American studies, analytic geometry, anatomy, applied arts, applied music, Arabic, architectural drawing, architecture, art, art history, art history-AP, Asian history, Asian literature, Asian studies, astronomy, Basic programming, biochemistry, biology, biology-AP, Black history, calculus, calculus-AP, chemistry, chemistry-AP, Chinese, computer applications, computer math, computer programming, computer science, computer science-AP, concert band, creative writing, dance, dance performance, discrete mathematics, drama, drama performance, drama workshop, drawing and design, earth science, Eastern religion and philosophy, economics, economics-AP, English, English literature, English literature-AP, English-AP, environmental science, ethics, European history, expository writing, fine arts, French, geology, geometry, Greek, health, health education, history, instrumental music, journalism, Latin, literature, mathematics, modern European history, music, philosophy, photography,

physics, physics-AP, physiology, probability and statistics, religion, science, social studies, Spanish, Spanish literature, statistics, studio art, studio art-AP, theater, theater arts, trigonometry, U.S. history, U.S. literature, video, vocal music, Western civilization, world civilizations, world governments, world history, world literature, world religions, writing.

Graduation Requirements Arts and fine arts (art, music, dance, drama), English, foreign language, history, mathematics, philosophy, science.

Special Academic Programs Advanced Placement exam preparation; honors section; independent study; term-away projects; study abroad; academic accommodation for the gifted, the musically talented, and the artistically talented; ESL (6 students enrolled).

College Admission Counseling 193 students graduated in 2015; 186 went to college, including Bowdoin College; Columbia University; Georgetown University; Princeton University; University of Chicago; University of Virginia. Other: 2 entered a postgraduate year, 5 had other specific plans. Mean SAT critical reading: 663, mean SAT math: 679, mean SAT writing: 666, mean combined SAT: 2008, mean composite ACT: 30.

Student Life Upper grades have specified standards of dress, student council, honor system. Discipline rests equally with students and faculty.

Summer Programs Enrichment programs offered; session focuses on Interdisciplinary, project-based learning; held on campus; accepts boys and girls; open to students from other schools. 75 students usually enrolled. 2016 schedule: July 10 to August 6. Application deadline: May 1.

Tuition and Aid Day student tuition: $39,220; 7-day tuition and room/board: $54,720. Tuition installment plan (SMART Tuition Payment Plan, Educational Data Systems, Inc). Need-based scholarship grants available. In 2015–16, 33% of upper-school students received aid. Total amount of financial aid awarded in 2015–16: $8,985,000.

Admissions Traditional secondary-level entrance grade is 9. For fall 2015, 1,972 students applied for upper-level admission, 344 were accepted, 217 enrolled. ACT, ISEE, PSAT, SAT, SSAT or TOEFL required. Deadline for receipt of application materials: January 15. Application fee required: $60. Interview required.

Athletics Interscholastic: alpine skiing (boys, girls), baseball (b), basketball (b,g), crew (b,g), cross-country running (b,g), diving (b,g), field hockey (g), football (b), golf (b), hockey (b,g), ice hockey (b,g), lacrosse (b,g), rowing (b,g), skiing (downhill) (b,g), soccer (b,g), softball (g), squash (b,g), swimming and diving (b,g), tennis (b,g), track and field (b,g), volleyball (g), water polo (b,g), wrestling (b); intramural: dance (b,g), fitness (b,g), modern dance (b,g); coed interscholastic: bicycling, diving, golf, indoor track & field, swimming and diving; coed intramural: aerobics/dance, aerobics/Nautilus, alpine skiing, aquatics, ballet, canoeing/kayaking, combined training, dance, dance team, fitness, hiking/backpacking, life saving, modern dance, nordic skiing, outdoor activities, outdoor adventure, outdoor recreation, outdoor skills, paddle tennis, sailing, skiing (cross-country), skiing (downhill), snowboarding, soccer, squash, strength & conditioning, swimming and diving, tennis, volleyball, weight lifting, weight training. 1 coach, 2 athletic trainers.

Computers Computers are regularly used in architecture, mathematics, programming, science classes. Computer network features include on-campus library services, online commercial services, Internet access, wireless campus network, Internet filtering or blocking technology. Campus intranet, student e-mail accounts, and computer access in designated common areas are available to students. Students grades are available online. The school has a published electronic and media policy.

Contact Pam Safford, Dean of Admission and Financial Aid. 413-774-1400. Fax: 413-772-1100. E-mail: admission@deerfield.edu. Website: www.deerfield.edu

See Display on next page and Close-Up on page 592.

DE LA SALLE COLLEGE

131 Farnham Avenue
Toronto, Ontario M4V 1H7, Canada

Head of School: Br. Domenic Viggiani, FSC

General Information Coeducational day college-preparatory, arts, business, and Advanced Placement courses school, affiliated with Roman Catholic Church. Grades 5–12. Founded: 1851. Setting: urban. 12-acre campus. 4 buildings on campus. Approved or accredited by Conference of Independent Schools of Ontario, Western Catholic Education Association, and Ontario Department of Education. Language of instruction: English. Total enrollment: 627. Upper school average class size: 22. Upper school faculty-student ratio: 1:15. The average school day consists of 5 hours and 40 minutes.

Upper School Student Profile 90% of students are Roman Catholic.

Faculty School total: 51. In upper school: 36 men, 15 women.

Subjects Offered Advanced Placement courses.

Special Academic Programs Advanced Placement exam preparation; accelerated programs.

College Admission Counseling 100 students graduated in 2015; all went to college, including McGill University; McMaster University; Queen's University at Kingston; The University of Western Ontario; University of Toronto; York University.

Student Life Upper grades have uniform requirement, student council, honor system. Discipline rests primarily with faculty. Attendance at religious services is required.

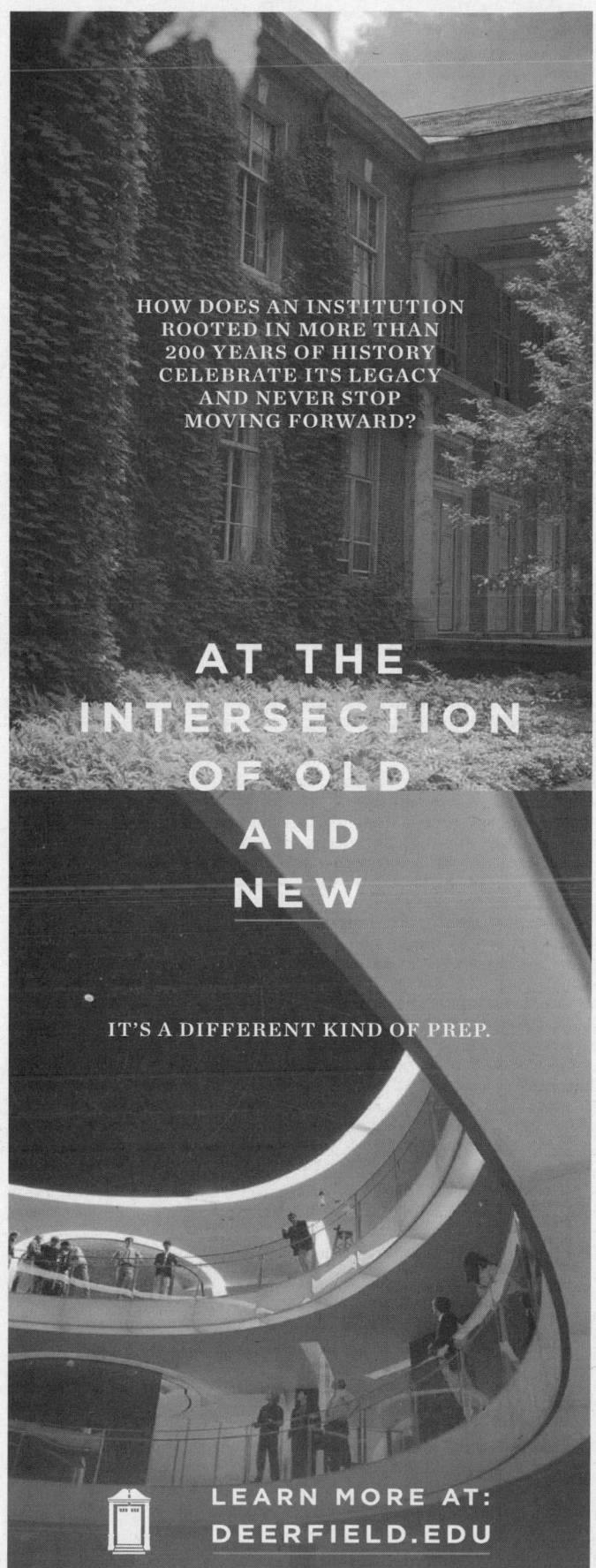

Summer Programs Enrichment, advancement programs offered; held on campus; accepts boys and girls; open to students from other schools. 75 students usually enrolled. 2016 schedule: July 1 to August 25. Application deadline: June 15.

Tuition and Aid Day student tuition: CAN$13,750. Tuition installment plan (monthly payment plans). Bursaries, need-based scholarship grants available. In 2015–16, 15% of upper-school students received aid.

Admissions Traditional secondary-level entrance grade is 9. For fall 2015, 150 students applied for upper-level admission, 75 were accepted, 50 enrolled. Canadian Standardized Test required. Deadline for receipt of application materials: December 4. Application fee required: CAN$100. Interview required.

Athletics Interscholastic: baseball (boys), basketball (b,g), field hockey (g), ice hockey (b,g), rugby (g), soccer (b,g), softball (b,g), volleyball (b); coed interscholastic: alpine skiing, aquatics, badminton, cross-country running, golf, skiing (downhill), swimming and diving, track and field, ultimate Frisbee; coed intramural: ball hockey, physical fitness, physical training, strength & conditioning. 4 PE instructors.

Computers Computer network features include on-campus library services, Internet access, wireless campus network, Internet filtering or blocking technology. Student e-mail accounts are available to students. The school has a published electronic and media policy.

Contact Mrs. Kim Sibley, Principal of the Junior School. 416-969-8771 Ext. 231. Fax: 416-969-9175. E-mail: ksibley@delasalle.ca. Website: www.delasalle.ca

DE LA SALLE HIGH SCHOOL

1130 Winton Drive
Concord, California 94518-3528

Head of School: Br. Robert J. Wickman, FSC

General Information Boys' day college-preparatory, arts, and religious studies school, affiliated with Roman Catholic Church; primarily serves students with learning disabilities, individuals with Attention Deficit Disorder, dyslexic students, and Autism (Asperger's). Grades 9–12. Founded: 1965. Setting: suburban. Nearest major city is Oakland. 25-acre campus. 11 buildings on campus. Approved or accredited by Western Association of Schools and Colleges and Western Catholic Education Association. Endowment: $8.4 million. Total enrollment: 1,038. Upper school average class size: 30. Upper school faculty-student ratio: 1:28. There are 172 required school days per year for Upper School students. Upper School students typically attend 5 days per week. The average school day consists of 6 hours and 5 minutes.

Upper School Student Profile Grade 9: 273 students (273 boys); Grade 10: 257 students (257 boys); Grade 11: 267 students (267 boys); Grade 12: 241 students (241 boys). 80% of students are Roman Catholic.

Faculty School total: 73. In upper school: 50 men, 23 women; 40 have advanced degrees.

Subjects Offered Advanced Placement courses, advanced studio art-AP, algebra, American history, anatomy, art, band, Bible studies, biology, calculus, chemistry, chorus, design, drafting, drawing, economics, English, English-AP, ethics, fine arts, first aid, French, geometry, government/civics, health, history, Italian, jazz, Latin, literature, marine biology, mathematics, music theory, painting, physical education, physics, physiology, pre-calculus, psychology, religion, science, sculpture, social studies, Spanish, Spanish-AP, sports medicine, statistics, statistics-AP, trigonometry, world history, world religions, writing.

Graduation Requirements Arts and fine arts (art, music, dance, drama), English, foreign language, mathematics, physical education (includes health), religion (includes Bible studies and theology), science, social studies (includes history).

Special Academic Programs Advanced Placement exam preparation; honors section; independent study; remedial math.

College Admission Counseling 245 students graduated in 2015; 241 went to college, including California Polytechnic State University, San Luis Obispo; Saint Mary's College of California; San Diego State University; San Francisco State University; Santa Clara University; The University of Arizona. Other: 1 entered military service, 1 had other specific plans. Mean SAT critical reading: 551, mean SAT math: 560, mean SAT writing: 533, mean combined SAT: 1644, mean composite ACT: 25. 30% scored over 600 on SAT critical reading, 38% scored over 600 on SAT math, 25% scored over 600 on SAT writing, 32% scored over 1800 on combined SAT, 36% scored over 26 on composite ACT.

Student Life Upper grades have specified standards of dress, student council, honor system. Discipline rests primarily with faculty. Attendance at religious services is required.

Summer Programs Remediation, sports programs offered; session focuses on make-up for current students, sports programs for local kids, conditionally accepted study skills program; held on campus; accepts boys and girls; not open to students from other schools. 40 students usually enrolled. 2016 schedule: June 13 to August 3. Application deadline: June 1.

Tuition and Aid Day student tuition: $16,800. Tuition installment plan (individually arranged payment plans, 10-month). Need-based scholarship grants, need-based grants available. In 2015–16, 32% of upper-school students received aid. Total amount of financial aid awarded in 2015–16: $2,330,000.

Admissions Traditional secondary-level entrance grade is 9. For fall 2015, 436 students applied for upper-level admission, 341 were accepted, 273 enrolled. High

School Placement Test required. Deadline for receipt of application materials: December 4. Application fee required: $100. On-campus interview required.

Athletics Interscholastic: badminton, baseball, basketball, cross-country running, diving, football, golf, ice hockey, lacrosse, rugby, soccer, swimming and diving, tennis, track and field, volleyball, water polo, wrestling; intramural: basketball, flag football, floor hockey, football, indoor soccer, street hockey, ultimate Frisbee. 5 PE instructors, 120 coaches, 3 athletic trainers.

Computers Computers are regularly used in all classes. Computer network features include on-campus library services, Internet access, wireless campus network, Internet filtering or blocking technology, Learning Management System/Schoology. Student e-mail accounts and computer access in designated common areas are available to students. Students grades are available online. The school has a published electronic and media policy.

Contact Mr. Joseph Grantham, Director of Admissions. 925-288-8102. Fax: 925-686-3474. E-mail: granthamj@dlshs.org. Website: www.dlshs.org

DELASALLE HIGH SCHOOL

One DeLaSalle Drive
Minneapolis, Minnesota 55401-1597

Head of School: Mr. Barry Lieske

General Information Coeducational day college-preparatory, arts, business, religious studies, and technology school, affiliated with Roman Catholic Church. Grades 9–12. Founded: 1900. Setting: urban. 10-acre campus. 3 buildings on campus. Approved or accredited by National Catholic Education Association, North Central Association of Colleges and Schools, and Minnesota Department of Education. Endowment: $3.9 million. Total enrollment: 760. Upper school average class size: 23. Upper school faculty-student ratio: 1:14. There are 175 required school days per year for Upper School students. Upper School students typically attend 5 days per week. The average school day consists of 6 hours and 30 minutes.

Upper School Student Profile Grade 9: 215 students (112 boys, 103 girls); Grade 10: 193 students (93 boys, 100 girls); Grade 11: 198 students (96 boys, 102 girls); Grade 12: 156 students (75 boys, 81 girls). 70% of students are Roman Catholic.

Faculty School total: 53. In upper school: 26 men, 27 women; 46 have advanced degrees.

Subjects Offered 20th century history, 20th century world history, advanced computer applications, advanced studio art-AP, African literature, algebra, American government, American history, American history-AP, ancient world history, anthropology, art, band, Bible, biology, biology-AP, business applications, calculus, calculus-AP, campus ministry, Catholic belief and practice, chamber groups, chemistry, chemistry-AP, Chinese, choir, Christian and Hebrew scripture, Christian ethics, comparative religion, computer graphics, concert band, concert choir, creative writing, economics, English, English language and composition-AP, English language-AP, English literature-AP, environmental studies, ethics, European history, European history-AP, first aid, fitness, forensics, French, geography, geometry, government, graphic arts, graphic design, health and wellness, history of the Catholic Church, history-AP, honors algebra, honors English, honors geometry, honors U.S. history, honors world history, instrumental music, journalism, mathematics, mathematics-AP, moral and social development, personal finance, philosophy, physical education, physical science, physics, physics-AP, pre-calculus, psychology, psychology-AP, social justice, Spanish, Spanish language-AP, speech, street law, studio art-AP, U.S. government and politics-AP, Western civilization, world geography, world religions, World War II, writing.

Graduation Requirements Arts and fine arts (art, music, dance, drama), English, foreign language, mathematics, physical education (includes health), religious studies, science, social studies (includes history), 60 hours of documented Christian service.

Special Academic Programs Advanced Placement exam preparation; honors section; independent study; study at local college for college credit; study abroad.

College Admission Counseling 204 students graduated in 2015; 202 went to college, including College of Saint Benedict; Marquette University; Saint John's University; University of Minnesota, Twin Cities Campus; University of St. Thomas; University of Wisconsin–Madison. Other: 1 went to work, 1 entered military service. Mean composite ACT: 25. 61% scored over 26 on composite ACT.

Student Life Upper grades have uniform requirement, student council, honor system. Discipline rests primarily with faculty. Attendance at religious services is required.

Summer Programs Enrichment, advancement programs offered; held on campus; accepts boys and girls; open to students from other schools. 350 students usually enrolled. 2016 schedule: June 8 to July 30. Application deadline: June 1.

Tuition and Aid Day student tuition: $12,345. Tuition installment plan (monthly payment plans). Merit scholarship grants, need-based scholarship grants, off-campus work programs for tuition benefit available. In 2015–16, 53% of upper-school students received aid; total upper-school merit-scholarship money awarded: $383,000. Total amount of financial aid awarded in 2015–16: $24,600,000.

Admissions Traditional secondary-level entrance grade is 9. For fall 2015, 409 students applied for upper-level admission, 289 were accepted, 215 enrolled. Academic Profile Tests or High School Placement Test required. Deadline for receipt of application materials: none. No application fee required. Interview required.

Athletics Interscholastic: baseball (boys), basketball (b,g), cross-country running (b,g), football (b), golf (b,g), hockey (b,g), lacrosse (b,g), soccer (b,g), softball (g), swimming and diving (g), tennis (b,g), track and field (b,g), volleyball (g), wrestling (b); coed interscholastic: cheering, dance team, rowing, weight training; coed intramural: aerobics, archery, bowling, dance, dance team, strength & conditioning. 2 PE instructors, 63 coaches, 1 athletic trainer.

Computers Computers are regularly used in all academic, art, business, English, French, graphic design, independent study, journalism, media, media production, music, science, social studies, Spanish, writing classes. Computer network features include on-campus library services, online commercial services, Internet access, wireless campus network, Internet filtering or blocking technology, one-to-one iPad technology for all students. Student e-mail accounts are available to students. Students grades are available online. The school has a published electronic and media policy.

Contact Mr. Patrick Felicetta, Director of Admission. 612-676-7605. Fax: 612-676-7699. E-mail: patrick.felicetta@delasalle.com. Website: www.delasalle.com

DE LA SALLE NORTH CATHOLIC HIGH SCHOOL

7528 N. Fenwick Avenue
Portland, Oregon 97217

Head of School: Mr. Tim Joy

General Information Coeducational day college-preparatory, business, and religious studies school, affiliated with Roman Catholic Church. Grades 9–12. Founded: 2000. Setting: urban. 1 building on campus. Approved or accredited by Northwest Accreditation Commission and Oregon Department of Education. Endowment: $289,297. Total enrollment: 311. Upper school average class size: 21. Upper school faculty-student ratio: 1:17. There are 178 required school days per year for Upper School students. Upper School students typically attend 5 days per week. The average school day consists of 7 hours and 30 minutes.

Upper School Student Profile Grade 9: 98 students (56 boys, 42 girls); Grade 10: 89 students (38 boys, 51 girls); Grade 11: 60 students (21 boys, 39 girls); Grade 12: 64 students (29 boys, 35 girls). 38% of students are Roman Catholic.

Faculty School total: 22. In upper school: 13 men, 9 women; 12 have advanced degrees.

Subjects Offered Acting.

Graduation Requirements English, health education, mathematics, religion (includes Bible studies and theology), social studies (includes history), World Language, Corporate Work Study.

Special Academic Programs 2 Advanced Placement exams for which test preparation is offered; honors section; independent study; remedial reading and/or remedial writing; remedial math.

College Admission Counseling 62 students graduated in 2015; 58 went to college, including George Fox University; Georgetown University; Oregon State University; Portland Community College; Portland State University; University of Oregon. Other: 1 entered military service, 2 had other specific plans.

Student Life Upper grades have uniform requirement, student council, honor system. Discipline rests primarily with faculty. Attendance at religious services is required.

Summer Programs Remediation, enrichment programs offered; session focuses on academic preparation and work-study training program; held on campus; accepts boys and girls; not open to students from other schools. 120 students usually enrolled. 2016 schedule: June 27 to August 5.

Tuition and Aid Day student tuition: $2995. Tuition installment plan (monthly payment plans, individually arranged payment plans). Need-based scholarship grants available. In 2015–16, 85% of upper-school students received aid. Total amount of financial aid awarded in 2015–16: $294,820.

Admissions Traditional secondary-level entrance grade is 9. Catholic High School Entrance Examination and Measures of Academic Progress® (MAP®). Deadline for receipt of application materials: none. No application fee required. On-campus interview required.

Athletics Interscholastic: basketball (boys, girls), soccer (b,g), track and field (b,g), volleyball (g), wrestling (b,g); coed interscholastic: wrestling. 2 PE instructors, 7 coaches.

Computers Computer network features include Internet access, wireless campus network, Internet filtering or blocking technology. Student e-mail accounts and computer access in designated common areas are available to students. Students grades are available online. The school has a published electronic and media policy.

Contact Ms. Rocio Arreola, Admissions Coordinator. 503-285-9385 Ext. 135. Fax: 503-285-9546. E-mail: admissions@dlsnc.org. Website: www.delasallenorth.org/

DELAWARE COUNTY CHRISTIAN SCHOOL

462 Malin Road
Newtown Square, Pennsylvania 19073-3499

Head of School: Dr. Timothy P. Wiens

General Information Coeducational day college-preparatory and arts school, affiliated with Protestant-Evangelical faith. Grades PK–12. Founded: 1950. Setting: suburban. Nearest major city is Philadelphia. 26-acre campus. 6 buildings on campus. Approved or accredited by Association of Christian Schools International, Middle States Association of Colleges and Schools, and Pennsylvania Department of Education. Member of National Association of Independent Schools. Endowment: $3.8

million. Total enrollment: 810. Upper school average class size: 21. Upper school faculty-student ratio: 1:12. The average school day consists of 6 hours and 30 minutes.

Upper School Student Profile Grade 9: 91 students (48 boys, 43 girls); Grade 10: 87 students (39 boys, 48 girls); Grade 11: 79 students (35 boys, 44 girls); Grade 12: 83 students (42 boys, 41 girls). 100% of students are Protestant-Evangelical faith.

Faculty School total: 100. In upper school: 28 men, 32 women; 45 have advanced degrees.

Subjects Offered Algebra, American history, American literature, art, Bible studies, biology, calculus, chemistry, choir, choral music, concert band, concert bell choir, concert choir, creative writing, digital art, discrete mathematics, drama, earth science, economics, English, English literature, English literature and composition-AP, European history-AP, fine arts, geography, geometry, German, German-AP, government/civics, grammar, graphics, handbells, journalism, literature, mathematics, music, music theory, physical education, physics, physics-AP, religion, science, social studies, Spanish, Spanish-AP, theater, trigonometry, U.S. history-AP, world history, writing workshop, yearbook.

Graduation Requirements Arts and fine arts (art, music, dance, drama), computer science, English, foreign language, mathematics, physical education (includes health), religion (includes Bible studies and theology), science, social studies (includes history).

Special Academic Programs Advanced Placement exam preparation; honors section; study abroad; academic accommodation for the gifted, the musically talented, and the artistically talented.

College Admission Counseling 95 students graduated in 2014; 86 went to college, including Eastern University; Penn State University Park; Temple University. Other: 2 went to work, 1 had other specific plans. Mean SAT critical reading: 577, mean SAT math: 555, mean SAT writing: 566, mean combined SAT: 1698.

Student Life Upper grades have uniform requirement, student council, honor system. Discipline rests primarily with faculty. Attendance at religious services is required.

Tuition and Aid Day student tuition: $11,319. Tuition installment plan (monthly payment plans). Tuition reduction for siblings, merit scholarship grants, need-based scholarship grants available. In 2014–15, 33% of upper-school students received aid; total upper-school merit-scholarship money awarded: $18,000. Total amount of financial aid awarded in 2014–15: $800,000.

Admissions Traditional secondary-level entrance grade is 9. ERB required. Deadline for receipt of application materials: none. Application fee required: $50. On-campus interview required.

Athletics Interscholastic: baseball (boys), basketball (b,g), cheering (g), cross-country running (b,g), field hockey (g), football (b), golf (b,g), ice hockey (b), lacrosse (b), soccer (b,g), softball (g), tennis (b,g), track and field (b,g), wrestling (b); intramural: ice hockey (b); coed interscholastic: life saving. 3 PE instructors, 1 athletic trainer.

Computers Computers are regularly used in art, English, journalism, library, literary magazine, mathematics, newspaper, photography, photojournalism, publications, SAT preparation, science, technology, video film production, writing, writing, yearbook classes. Computer network features include on-campus library services, Internet access, wireless campus network, Internet filtering or blocking technology. Students grades are available online. The school has a published electronic and media policy.

Contact Mrs. Arlene J. Warmhold, Admissions Administrative Assistant. 610-353-6522 Ext. 2285. Fax: 610-356-9684. E-mail: awarmhold@dccs.org. Website: www.dccs.org

DELAWARE VALLEY FRIENDS SCHOOL

Paoli, Pennsylvania
See Special Needs Schools section.

DELBARTON SCHOOL

230 Mendham Road
Morristown, New Jersey 07960

Head of School: Br. Paul Diveny, OSB

General Information Boys' day college-preparatory, arts, religious studies, and technology school, affiliated with Roman Catholic Church. Grades 7–12. Founded: 1939. Setting: suburban. Nearest major city is New York, NY. 200-acre campus. 7 buildings on campus. Approved or accredited by Middle States Association of Colleges and Schools, National Catholic Education Association, New Jersey Association of Independent Schools, and New Jersey Department of Education. Member of National Association of Independent Schools and Secondary School Admission Test Board. Endowment: $26 million. Total enrollment: 573. Upper school average class size: 15. Upper school faculty-student ratio: 1:15. There are 165 required school days per year for Upper School students. Upper School students typically attend 5 days per week. The average school day consists of 6 hours and 15 minutes.

Upper School Student Profile Grade 9: 134 students (134 boys); Grade 10: 129 students (129 boys); Grade 11: 127 students (127 boys); Grade 12: 117 students (117 boys). 78% of students are Roman Catholic.

Faculty School total: 78. In upper school: 60 men, 18 women; 57 have advanced degrees.

Subjects Offered Accounting, advanced chemistry, algebra, American history, American literature, art, art history, astronomy, biology, calculus, chemistry, computer math, computer programming, computer science, creative writing, driver education, economics, English, English literature, environmental science, ethics, European history, fine arts, French, geography, geometry, German, grammar, health, history, international relations, Latin, mathematics, music, philosophy, physical education, physics, religion, Russian, social studies, Spanish, speech, trigonometry, world history.

Graduation Requirements Arts and fine arts (art, music, dance, drama), computer science, English, foreign language, mathematics, physical education (includes health), religion (includes Bible studies and theology), science, social studies (includes history), speech.

Special Academic Programs Advanced Placement exam preparation; independent study.

College Admission Counseling 117 students graduated in 2015; all went to college, including Boston College; Columbia University; Georgetown University; Loyola University Maryland; Princeton University; Villanova University.

Student Life Upper grades have specified standards of dress, student council, honor system. Discipline rests primarily with faculty. Attendance at religious services is required.

Summer Programs Enrichment, advancement, sports, computer instruction programs offered; session focuses on summer school (coed) and summer sports (boys); held on campus; accepts boys and girls; open to students from other schools. 1,200 students usually enrolled. 2016 schedule: June 22 to July 29. Application deadline: June 1.

Tuition and Aid Day student tuition: $35,500. Tuition installment plan (monthly payment plans, individually arranged payment plans). Need-based scholarship grants available. In 2015–16, 15% of upper-school students received aid. Total amount of financial aid awarded in 2015–16: $2,294,000.

Admissions Traditional secondary-level entrance grade is 9. For fall 2015, 409 students applied for upper-level admission, 161 were accepted, 141 enrolled. Stanford Achievement Test, Otis-Lennon School Ability Test, school's own exam required. Deadline for receipt of application materials: November 20. Application fee required: $65. On-campus interview required.

Athletics Interscholastic: baseball, basketball, bowling, cross-country running, football, golf, ice hockey, indoor track, lacrosse, soccer, squash, swimming and diving, tennis, track and field, winter (indoor) track, wrestling; intramural: bicycling, combined training, fitness, flag football, Frisbee, independent competitive sports, mountain biking, skiing (downhill), strength & conditioning, ultimate Frisbee, weight lifting, weight training. 3 PE instructors, 2 athletic trainers.

Computers Computers are regularly used in computer applications, music, science, word processing classes. Computer network features include on-campus library services, online commercial services, Internet access, wireless campus network. Student e-mail accounts are available to students. Students grades are available online.

Contact Mrs. Connie Curnow, Administrative Assistant, Office of Admissions. 973-538-3231 Ext. 3019. Fax: 973-538-8836. E-mail: ccurnow@delbarton.org. Website: www.delbarton.org

See Display on next page and Close-Up on page 594.

THE DELPHIAN SCHOOL

20950 Southwest Rock Creek Road
Sheridan, Oregon 97378

Head of School: Rosemary Didear

General Information Coeducational boarding and day college-preparatory, general academic, arts, business, technology, and computer technology, career orientation, community outreach school. Boarding grades 4–12, day grades K–12. Founded: 1976. Setting: rural. Nearest major city is Salem. Students are housed in single-sex dormitories. 800-acre campus. 4 buildings on campus. Approved or accredited by Northwest Accreditation Commission, Northwest Association of Independent Schools, The Association of Boarding Schools, and Oregon Department of Education. Member of National Association of Independent Schools. Total enrollment: 266. Upper school average class size: 17. Upper School students typically attend 5 days per week. The average school day consists of 7 hours.

Upper School Student Profile 80% of students are boarding students. 10% are state residents. 15 states are represented in upper school student body. 40% are international students. International students from Canada, China, Germany, Japan, Mexico, and Taiwan; 18 other countries represented in student body.

Faculty School total: 55. In upper school: 48 reside on campus.

Subjects Offered Advanced chemistry, advanced computer applications, algebra, American history, American literature, anatomy and physiology, art, arts and crafts, biology, biology-AP, business, business applications, business skills, calculus, calculus-AP, career and personal planning, career/college preparation, ceramics, cheerleading, chemistry, choir, communication skills, comparative religion, computer programming, computer science, computer skills, concert choir, creative writing, drama, drawing, economics, economics-AP, electronics, English, English composition, English language and composition-AP, English literature and composition-AP, ESL, ethical decision making, ethics, ethics and responsibility, fine arts, first aid, French, geography, geometry, government, grammar, health, language arts, leadership, logic, mathematics, music, music history, nutrition, personal money management, photography, physical education, physical fitness, physical science, physics, public speaking, research skills,

SAT preparation, science, Shakespeare, social studies, Spanish, student government, study skills, trigonometry, U.S. constitutional history, U.S. government, volleyball, world history, yearbook, yoga.

Graduation Requirements American history, anatomy and physiology, business skills (includes word processing), career/college preparation, communication skills, composition, computer science, current events, economics, English, ethics, foreign language, leadership, literature, logic, mathematics, mathematics-AP, physical education (includes health), public speaking, science, social studies (includes history), student government, U.S. government, world history, specific graduation requirements which students are required to meet in order to complete each equivalent grade level. Community service is required.

Special Academic Programs Advanced Placement exam preparation; accelerated programs; independent study; academic accommodation for the gifted, the musically talented, and the artistically talented; ESL (38 students enrolled).

College Admission Counseling 39 students graduated in 2014; they went to Berklee College of Music; Johns Hopkins University; New York University; Parsons School of Design; University of California, Davis; University of Oregon.

Student Life Upper grades have specified standards of dress, student council, honor system. Discipline rests equally with students and faculty.

Tuition and Aid Day student tuition: $13,050–$27,525; 7-day tuition and room/board: $43,530–$45,940. Tuition installment plan (monthly payment plans, individually arranged payment plans, Your Tuition Solution). Tuition reduction for siblings, merit scholarship grants, need-based scholarship grants, need-based loans available. In 2014–15, 41% of upper-school students received aid; total upper-school merit-scholarship money awarded: $150,000. Total amount of financial aid awarded in 2014–15: $315,000.

Admissions Traditional secondary-level entrance grade is 9. Admissions testing and any standardized test required. Deadline for receipt of application materials: none. Application fee required: $100. On-campus interview required.

Athletics Interscholastic: baseball (boys), basketball (b,g), cheering (g), soccer (b), softball (g), tennis (b,g), volleyball (g); coed intramural: archery, fitness, flag football, hiking/backpacking, jogging, jump rope, kickball, martial arts, outdoors, physical fitness, physical training, racquetball, running, strength & conditioning, tennis, walking, weight lifting, weight training, yoga. 4 PE instructors, 15 coaches.

Computers Computers are regularly used in art, business applications, business skills, career education, college planning, computer applications, creative writing, design, digital applications, foreign language, graphic design, mathematics, media arts, media production, multimedia, music, publications, research skills, technology, typing, video film production, Web site design, writing, yearbook classes. Computer network features include on-campus library services, Internet access, wireless campus network, Internet filtering or blocking technology. Campus intranet, student e-mail accounts, and computer access in designated common areas are available to students. The school has a published electronic and media policy.

Contact Sue MacKenzie, Admissions Assistant. 800-626-6610. Fax: 503-843-4158. E-mail: info@delphian.org. Website: www.delphian.org

DELPHOS SAINT JOHN'S HIGH SCHOOL

515 East Second Street
Delphos, Ohio 45833

Head of School: Mr. Adam J. Lee

General Information Coeducational day college-preparatory, general academic, arts, business, religious studies, bilingual studies, and technology school, affiliated with Roman Catholic Church; primarily serves underachievers. Grades 7–12. Founded: 1912. Setting: rural. Nearest major city is Toledo. 2 buildings on campus. Approved or accredited by National Catholic Education Association, Ohio Catholic Schools Accreditation Association (OCSAA), and Ohio Department of Education. Total enrollment: 310. Upper school average class size: 15. Upper school faculty-student ratio: 1:15. There are 180 required school days per year for Upper School students. Upper School students typically attend 5 days per week. The average school day consists of 6 hours and 30 minutes.

Upper School Student Profile 98% of students are Roman Catholic.

Faculty School total: 25. In upper school: 10 men, 15 women; 15 have advanced degrees.

College Admission Counseling 50 students graduated in 2015; 48 went to college, including Bowling Green State University; The Ohio State University; The University of Toledo; University of Cincinnati; University of Dayton. Other: 2 went to work.

Student Life Upper grades have uniform requirement, student council, honor system. Discipline rests primarily with faculty. Attendance at religious services is required.

Tuition and Aid Tuition installment plan (SMART Tuition Payment Plan, monthly payment plans, individually arranged payment plans). Tuition reduction for siblings, need-based scholarship grants available.

Admissions Deadline for receipt of application materials: none. No application fee required. Interview required.

Athletics Interscholastic: basketball (boys, girls), cheering (g), cross-country running (b,g), football (b), golf (b,g), indoor track (b,g), soccer (g), strength & conditioning (b), volleyball (g), weight lifting (b,g), weight training (b,g); intramural: baseball (b), basketball (b), strength & conditioning (b,g), volleyball (b,g). 12 coaches, 1 athletic trainer.

Computers Computers are regularly used in all academic classes. Computer network features include on-campus library services, online commercial services, Internet access, wireless campus network, Internet filtering or blocking technology. Campus intranet and student e-mail accounts are available to students. Students grades are available online. The school has a published electronic and media policy.
Contact Mr. Alan Unterbrink, Guidance Counselor. 419-692-5371 Ext. 1135. Fax: 419-879-6874. E-mail: unterbrink@delphosstjohns.org. Website: www.delphosstjohns.org/

DEMATHA CATHOLIC HIGH SCHOOL

4313 Madison Street
Hyattsville, Maryland 20781

Head of School: Daniel J. McMahon, PhD

General Information Boys' day college-preparatory, arts, business, religious studies, technology, and music (instrumental and choral) school, affiliated with Roman Catholic Church. Grades 9–12. Founded: 1946. Setting: suburban. Nearest major city is Washington, DC. 6-acre campus. 5 buildings on campus. Approved or accredited by National Catholic Education Association and Maryland Department of Education. Endowment: $4.1 million. Total enrollment: 815. Upper school average class size: 22. Upper school faculty-student ratio: 1:12. There are 175 required school days per year for Upper School students. Upper School students typically attend 5 days per week. The average school day consists of 6 hours.
Upper School Student Profile Grade 9: 254 students (254 boys); Grade 10: 203 students (203 boys); Grade 11: 173 students (173 boys); Grade 12: 185 students (185 boys). 52% of students are Roman Catholic.
Faculty School total: 73. In upper school: 54 men, 19 women; 44 have advanced degrees.
Subjects Offered Accounting, Advanced Placement courses, algebra, American government, American history, American history-AP, anatomy and physiology, art, art history, art-AP, astronomy, band, biology, biology-AP, British literature, British literature-AP, business, business law, calculus, calculus-AP, campus ministry, chemistry, chemistry-AP, Chinese, choral music, chorus, Christian ethics, church history, college admission preparation, community service, computer applications, computer programming, computer science, computer science-AP, computer skills, computer studies, contemporary art, digital photography, English, English composition, English literature, environmental science, film studies, French, French language-AP, geology, geometry, German, German-AP, government, government-AP, Greek, health, health education, history, history of religion, history of rock and roll, honors algebra, honors English, honors geometry, honors U.S. history, honors world history, instrumental music, jazz, journalism, Latin, Latin American studies, Latin-AP, literature-AP, mathematics, modern languages, music, music performance, mythology, newspaper, photography, photojournalism, physical education, physical science, physics, physics-AP, pre-calculus, psychology, SAT preparation, science, science research, social studies, Spanish, Spanish-AP, speech, sports medicine, statistics, studio art, studio art-AP, study skills, symphonic band, theology, trigonometry, U.S. government, U.S. government and politics-AP, U.S. history, U.S. literature, vocal music, world history, writing, yearbook.
Graduation Requirements Arts, computer science, English, foreign language, mathematics, physical education (includes health), science, social studies (includes history), theology, 55 hours of Christian service, service reflection paper.
Special Academic Programs 13 Advanced Placement exams for which test preparation is offered; honors section; independent study; academic accommodation for the gifted, the musically talented, and the artistically talented; remedial reading and/or remedial writing.
College Admission Counseling 184 students graduated in 2015; 180 went to college, including Bowie State University; Hampton University; The Catholic University of America; Towson University; University of Maryland, Baltimore County; University of Maryland, College Park. Other: 3 went to work, 1 entered military service. 23% scored over 600 on SAT critical reading, 29% scored over 600 on SAT math, 20% scored over 600 on SAT writing, 24% scored over 1800 on combined SAT, 28% scored over 26 on composite ACT.
Student Life Upper grades have uniform requirement, student council, honor system. Discipline rests primarily with faculty. Attendance at religious services is required.
Summer Programs Remediation, enrichment, sports, art/fine arts, computer instruction programs offered; session focuses on remediation/enrichment; held on campus; accepts boys and girls; open to students from other schools. 400 students usually enrolled. 2016 schedule: June 20 to July 22. Application deadline: June 17.
Tuition and Aid Day student tuition: $15,600. Tuition installment plan (FACTS Tuition Payment Plan). Tuition reduction for siblings, merit scholarship grants, need-based scholarship grants, paying campus jobs available. In 2015–16, 55% of upper-school students received aid; total upper-school merit-scholarship money awarded: $694,600. Total amount of financial aid awarded in 2015–16: $1,632,348.
Admissions Traditional secondary-level entrance grade is 9. For fall 2015, 511 students applied for upper-level admission, 367 were accepted, 254 enrolled. High School Placement Test required. Deadline for receipt of application materials: December 15. Application fee required: $50.
Athletics Interscholastic: baseball, basketball, crew, cross-country running, diving, football, golf, hockey, ice hockey, indoor track, indoor track & field, lacrosse, rugby,

soccer, swimming and diving, tennis, track and field, ultimate Frisbee, water polo, winter (indoor) track, wrestling; intramural: basketball, paddle tennis, strength & conditioning, table tennis. 2 PE instructors, 1 coach, 2 athletic trainers.
Computers Computers are regularly used in business, computer applications, digital applications, English, foreign language, independent study, lab/keyboard, library, mathematics, newspaper, publishing, religious studies, science, technology, Web site design, word processing, yearbook classes. Computer network features include on-campus library services, Internet access, wireless campus network, Internet filtering or blocking technology, ProQuest, SIRS, World Book, Veracross. Student e-mail accounts and computer access in designated common areas are available to students. Students grades are available online. The school has a published electronic and media policy.
Contact Mrs. Christine Thomas, Assistant Director of Admissions. 240-764-2210. Fax: 240-764-2277. E-mail: cthomas@dematha.org. Website: www.dematha.org

DENVER ACADEMY

Denver, Colorado
See Special Needs Schools section.

DENVER CHRISTIAN HIGH SCHOOL

3898 S. Teller Street
Lakewood, Colorado 80235

Head of School: Mr. Steve Kortenhoeven

General Information Coeducational day college-preparatory, general academic, arts, business, religious studies, bilingual studies, and technology school, affiliated with Christian Reformed Church. Grades PK–12. Founded: 1950. Setting: suburban. 20-acre campus. 1 building on campus. Approved or accredited by Association of Christian Schools International, Christian Schools International, North Central Association of Colleges and Schools, and Colorado Department of Education. Endowment: $1.5 million. Total enrollment: 417. Upper school average class size: 20. Upper school faculty-student ratio: 1:19. There are 180 required school days per year for Upper School students. Upper School students typically attend 5 days per week. The average school day consists of 6 hours and 45 minutes.
Upper School Student Profile Grade 9: 45 students (26 boys, 19 girls); Grade 10: 38 students (16 boys, 22 girls); Grade 11: 29 students (18 boys, 11 girls); Grade 12: 30 students (18 boys, 12 girls). 20% of students are members of Christian Reformed Church.
Faculty School total: 17. In upper school: 8 men, 9 women; 16 have advanced degrees.
Subjects Offered Acting, advanced biology, advanced chemistry, advanced computer applications, advanced math, algebra, American government, American history, American literature, art, band, Bible, biology, British literature, calculus, chamber groups, chemistry, choir, Christian doctrine, Christian scripture, church history, composition, computer applications, concert band, concert choir, consumer economics, drama, driver education, earth science, European history, general math, government, grammar, health, introduction to literature, jazz band, keyboarding, personal fitness, physical education, physical fitness, physics, poetry, pre-algebra, pre-calculus, psychology, research, senior seminar, Shakespeare, Spanish, speech, studio art, symphonic band, the Web, trigonometry, U.S. government, U.S. history, Web site design, weight fitness, Western civilization, world geography, world history, yearbook.
Graduation Requirements Bible studies.
Special Academic Programs Honors section; independent study; special instructional classes for deaf students.
College Admission Counseling 29 students graduated in 2014; all went to college, including Baylor University; Calvin College; Colorado State University; Dordt College; University of Northern Colorado. Mean SAT critical reading: 560, mean SAT math: 545, mean composite ACT: 24.
Student Life Upper grades have specified standards of dress, student council. Discipline rests primarily with faculty. Attendance at religious services is required.
Tuition and Aid Day student tuition: $10,650. Tuition installment plan (FACTS Tuition Payment Plan, monthly payment plans). Tuition reduction for siblings, merit scholarship grants, need-based scholarship grants available. In 2014–15, 40% of upper-school students received aid; total upper-school merit-scholarship money awarded: $1500. Total amount of financial aid awarded in 2014–15: $30,000.
Admissions Traditional secondary-level entrance grade is 9. For fall 2014, 18 students applied for upper-level admission, 15 were accepted, 13 enrolled. WISC-III and Woodcock-Johnson, WISC/Woodcock-Johnson or Woodcock-Johnson Educational Evaluation, WISC III required. Deadline for receipt of application materials: none. Application fee required: $500. Interview required.
Athletics Interscholastic: baseball (boys), basketball (b,g), cheering (g), cross-country running (b,g), football (b), golf (b), soccer (b,g), track and field (b,g), volleyball (g); coed interscholastic: physical training, strength & conditioning, weight training. 3 PE instructors, 24 coaches, 1 athletic trainer.
Computers Computer network features include on-campus library services, Internet access, wireless campus network, Internet filtering or blocking technology. Student e-mail accounts and computer access in designated common areas are available to students. Students grades are available online. The school has a published electronic and media policy.

Contact Mrs. Sandie Posthumus, Administrative Assistant. 303-763-7922. Fax: 303-733-7734. E-mail: sposthumus@denverchristian.org. Website: www.denverchristian.org

DEPAUL CATHOLIC HIGH SCHOOL

1512 Alps Road
Wayne, New Jersey 07470

Head of School: Mr. Joseph Tweed

General Information Coeducational day college-preparatory, arts, religious studies, and technology school, affiliated with Roman Catholic Church. Grades 8–12. Founded: 1956. Setting: suburban. Nearest major city is New York, NY. 5-acre campus. 2 buildings on campus. Approved or accredited by National Catholic Education Association and New Jersey Department of Education. Total enrollment: 650. Upper school average class size: 22. Upper school faculty-student ratio: 1:19. There are 185 required school days per year for Upper School students. Upper School students typically attend 5 days per week. The average school day consists of 7 hours.

Upper School Student Profile 90% of students are Roman Catholic.

Faculty School total: 65. In upper school: 25 men, 40 women; 40 have advanced degrees.

Special Academic Programs International Baccalaureate program; Advanced Placement exam preparation; honors section; accelerated programs; independent study; remedial reading and/or remedial writing; remedial math; programs in general development for dyslexic students; special instructional classes for deaf students, blind students.

College Admission Counseling 169 students graduated in 2014; all went to college.

Student Life Upper grades have uniform requirement, student council, honor system. Discipline rests equally with students and faculty. Attendance at religious services is required.

Tuition and Aid Day student tuition: $11,500. Tuition installment plan (SMART Tuition Payment Plan, FACTS Tuition Payment Plan, monthly payment plans, individually arranged payment plans). Tuition reduction for siblings, merit scholarship grants, need-based scholarship grants available.

Admissions Traditional secondary-level entrance grade is 9. For fall 2014, 550 students applied for upper-level admission, 350 were accepted, 150 enrolled. Deadline for receipt of application materials: none. No application fee required. Interview recommended.

Athletics Interscholastic: baseball (boys), basketball (b,g), cheering (g), cross-country running (b,g), dance (g), dance squad (g), dance team (g), danceline (g), figure skating (g), football (b), gymnastics (g), ice skating (g), independent competitive sports (b,g), indoor track (b,g), indoor track & field (b,g), lacrosse (b,g), modern dance (g), soccer (b,g), softball (b), swimming and diving (b,g), tennis (b,g), track and field (b,g), volleyball (b,g), weight lifting (b,g), weight training (b,g), winter (indoor) track (b,g), wrestling (b); intramural: aerobics/dance (g), equestrian sports (g), strength & conditioning (b,g); coed interscholastic: alpine skiing, bowling, drill team, golf, ice hockey, skiing (downhill); coed intramural: backpacking, hiking/backpacking. 5 PE instructors, 40 coaches, 1 athletic trainer.

Computers Computer network features include on-campus library services, Internet access, wireless campus network, Internet filtering or blocking technology. Campus intranet, student e-mail accounts, and computer access in designated common areas are available to students. Students grades are available online. The school has a published electronic and media policy.

Contact Mr. Kenneth Jennings, Principal. 973-694-3702 Ext. 221. Fax: 973-694-3525. E-mail: jenningsk@dpchs.org. Website: www.depaulcatholic.org

THE DERRYFIELD SCHOOL

2108 River Road
Manchester, New Hampshire 03104-1302

Head of School: Mrs. Mary Halpin Carter, PhD

General Information Coeducational day college-preparatory school. Grades 6–12. Founded: 1964. Setting: suburban. Nearest major city is Boston, MA. 84-acre campus. 4 buildings on campus. Approved or accredited by Association of Independent Schools in New England, Independent Schools of Northern New England, New England Association of Schools and Colleges, and New Hampshire Department of Education. Member of National Association of Independent Schools and Secondary School Admission Test Board. Endowment: $5 million. Total enrollment: 387. Upper school average class size: 13. Upper school faculty-student ratio: 1:8. There are 163 required school days per year for Upper School students. Upper School students typically attend 5 days per week. The average school day consists of 6 hours and 45 minutes.

Upper School Student Profile Grade 9: 75 students (35 boys, 40 girls); Grade 10: 59 students (37 boys, 22 girls); Grade 11: 70 students (35 boys, 35 girls); Grade 12: 67 students (35 boys, 32 girls).

Faculty School total: 46. In upper school: 20 men, 15 women; 23 have advanced degrees.

Subjects Offered 20th century history, 3-dimensional art, algebra, American literature, anatomy and physiology, ancient world history, art, athletic training, biology, British literature, calculus, calculus-AP, chemistry, chemistry-AP, China/Japan history, Chinese, chorus, computer science, contemporary issues, creative writing, drafting, drama, driver education, earth science, economics, economics and history, engineering, English, English composition, English language and composition-AP, English literature, English literature-AP, environmental studies, European history, expository writing, film, fine arts, freshman foundations, geography, geometry, global issues, government/civics, graphics, Greek, health, history, Holocaust, honors English, independent study, international relations, Latin, Latin-AP, Mandarin, marketing, mathematics, media, music, music theory, mythology, organic biochemistry, organic chemistry, physical education, physics, physics-AP, pre-calculus, public speaking, robotics, science, sculpture, senior project, social studies, Spanish, Spanish language-AP, Spanish literature-AP, Spanish-AP, speech, stage design, statistics, statistics-AP, studio art, theater, trigonometry, U.S. history-AP, Western civilization, world history, world literature, writing.

Graduation Requirements Arts and fine arts (art, music, dance, drama), athletics, English, foreign language, health and wellness, history, mathematics, science.

Special Academic Programs 14 Advanced Placement exams for which test preparation is offered; honors section; independent study; term-away projects; study abroad.

College Admission Counseling 57 students graduated in 2014; 56 went to college, including College of the Holy Cross; Connecticut College; Georgetown University; Rochester Institute of Technology; Wheaton College; Worcester Polytechnic Institute. Other: 1 entered a postgraduate year. Mean SAT critical reading: 606, mean SAT math: 618, mean SAT writing: 619, mean combined SAT: 1843, mean composite ACT: 27.

Student Life Upper grades have specified standards of dress, student council. Discipline rests equally with students and faculty.

Tuition and Aid Day student tuition: $29,650. Tuition installment plan (SMART Tuition Payment Plan). Merit scholarship grants, need-based scholarship grants, Malone Family Foundation grants available. In 2014–15, 23% of upper-school students received aid; total upper-school merit-scholarship money awarded: $244,230. Total amount of financial aid awarded in 2014–15: $1,692,264.

Admissions Traditional secondary-level entrance grade is 9. SSAT required. Deadline for receipt of application materials: January 30. Application fee required: $50. On-campus interview required.

Athletics Interscholastic: alpine skiing (boys, girls), baseball (b), basketball (b,g), crew (b,g), cross-country running (b,g), diving (b), field hockey (g), independent competitive sports (b,g), lacrosse (b,g), skiing (cross-country) (b,g), skiing (downhill) (b,g), soccer (b,g), softball (g), tennis (b,g); coed interscholastic: equestrian sports, fishing, golf, ice hockey, swimming and diving; coed intramural: aerobics, cooperative games, dance, flag football, physical training, ropes courses, strength & conditioning, weight training, yoga. 1 PE instructor, 10 coaches, 1 athletic trainer.

Computers Computers are regularly used in all academic, college planning classes. Computer network features include on-campus library services, online commercial services, Internet access, wireless campus network, online computer linked to New Hampshire State Library. Campus intranet, student e-mail accounts, and computer access in designated common areas are available to students. Students grades are available online. The school has a published electronic and media policy.

Contact Ms. Kathleen Rutty-Fey, Director of Admission. 603-669-4524. Fax: 603-641-9521. E-mail: krutty@derryfield.org. Website: www.derryfield.org

See Display on next page and Close-Up on page 596.

DESERT ACADEMY

7300 Old Santa Fe Trail
Santa Fe, New Mexico 87505

Head of School: Mr. Terry Passalacqua

General Information Coeducational day college-preparatory, arts, and technology school. Grades 6–12. Founded: 1994. Setting: urban. 26-acre campus. 4 buildings on campus. Approved or accredited by International Baccalaureate Organization, North Central Association of Colleges and Schools, and New Mexico Department of Education. Candidate for accreditation by Independent Schools Association of the Southwest. Member of National Association of Independent Schools. Endowment: $12,000. Total enrollment: 190. Upper school average class size: 13. Upper school faculty-student ratio: 1:7. There are 180 required school days per year for Upper School students. The average school day consists of 7 hours and 30 minutes.

Upper School Student Profile Grade 6: 12 students (10 boys, 2 girls); Grade 7: 40 students (20 boys, 20 girls); Grade 8: 30 students (15 boys, 15 girls); Grade 9: 23 students (12 boys, 11 girls); Grade 10: 33 students (17 boys, 16 girls); Grade 11: 30 students (15 boys, 15 girls); Grade 12: 22 students (9 boys, 13 girls).

Faculty School total: 26. In upper school: 11 men, 11 women; 10 have advanced degrees.

Subjects Offered Acting, advanced chemistry, algebra, American history, American literature, American sign language, anatomy, applied music, art, Basic programming, biology, business mathematics, calculus, chemistry, Chinese, chorus, civics, computer graphics, computer programming, culinary arts, current events, digital photography, drama, drama performance, earth science, electives, French, geometry, government, honors algebra, honors English, honors geometry, honors U.S. history, honors world history, independent study, keyboarding, language and composition, Latin, literature, modern world history, musical productions, newspaper, performing arts, photography, physical education, physical science, physics, poetry, pre-algebra, pre-calculus, reading/study skills, SAT/ACT preparation, social studies, Spanish, U.S. history, Web site design, world history, writing, yearbook.

Graduation Requirements Algebra, biology, electives, English, foreign language, geometry, mathematics, science, social studies (includes history). Community service is required.

Special Academic Programs International Baccalaureate program; honors section; independent study; remedial reading and/or remedial writing; remedial math; ESL (6 students enrolled).

College Admission Counseling 16 students graduated in 2015; 10 went to college, including Adams State University; Austin College; Montana State University; University of California, Santa Cruz; University of Denver; University of New Mexico. Other: 4 went to work, 2 had other specific plans.

Student Life Upper grades have specified standards of dress, student council, honor system. Discipline rests primarily with faculty.

Summer Programs Remediation, computer instruction programs offered; session focuses on technology; held on campus; accepts boys and girls; open to students from other schools. 20 students usually enrolled.

Tuition and Aid Day student tuition: $14,600. Tuition installment plan (monthly payment plans, two annual payments). Tuition reduction for siblings, merit scholarship grants, need-based scholarship grants available. In 2015–16, 29% of upper-school students received aid; total upper-school merit-scholarship money awarded: $83,000. Total amount of financial aid awarded in 2015–16: $180,000.

Admissions Traditional secondary-level entrance grade is 9. For fall 2015, 48 students applied for upper-level admission, 40 were accepted, 20 enrolled. Deadline for receipt of application materials: none. Application fee required: $65. Interview recommended.

Athletics Interscholastic: basketball (boys, girls), cross-country running (b,g), golf (b), soccer (b,g), swimming and diving (b,g), track and field (b,g), volleyball (g); coed intramural: alpine skiing, backpacking, weight training. 1 PE instructor, 8 coaches.

Computers Computers are regularly used in current events, English, geography, graphic design, history, journalism, literary magazine, newspaper, photography, science, social sciences, social studies, Web site design, writing, yearbook classes. Computer network features include Internet access, wireless campus network, Internet filtering or blocking technology, DSL Internet access. Students grades are available online. The school has a published electronic and media policy.

Contact Jennifer Warren, Director of Admissions. 505-992-8284 Ext. 22. Fax: 505-992-8270. E-mail: admissions@desertacademy.org. Website: www.desertacademy.org

DETROIT COUNTRY DAY SCHOOL

22305 West Thirteen Mile Road
Beverly Hills, Michigan 48025-4435
Head of School: Glen P. Shilling

General Information Coeducational day college-preparatory, arts, and global communities school. Grades PK–12. Founded: 1914. Setting: suburban. Nearest major city is Detroit. 100-acre campus. 1 building on campus. Approved or accredited by Independent Schools Association of the Central States and Michigan Department of Education. Member of National Association of Independent Schools. Endowment: $36 million. Total enrollment: 1,523. Upper school average class size: 15. Upper school faculty-student ratio: 1:8.

Upper School Student Profile Grade 6: 114 students (61 boys, 53 girls); Grade 7: 133 students (81 boys, 52 girls); Grade 8: 116 students (59 boys, 57 girls); Grade 9: 182 students (86 boys, 96 girls); Grade 10: 172 students (103 boys, 69 girls); Grade 11: 155 students (84 boys, 71 girls); Grade 12: 183 students (103 boys, 80 girls).

Faculty School total: 202. In upper school: 35 men, 37 women; 60 have advanced degrees.

Subjects Offered African-American studies, algebra, American history, American literature, American studies, analytic geometry, anatomy, anatomy and physiology, ancient history, art, art and culture, art appreciation, art-AP, astronomy, band, biology, botany, calculus, ceramics, chemistry, Chinese, chorus, college counseling, community service, composition, computer programming, computer science, current events, design, drama, drawing, ecology, economics, economics and history, English, English literature, environmental science, European history, fine arts, finite math, French, genetics, geometry, German, government/civics, grammar, graphic arts, health, history, humanities, Japanese, Latin, literature, mathematics, media, metalworking, microbiology, music, music history, music theory, natural history, orchestra, painting, photography, physical education, physical science, physics, physiology, poetry, pre-calculus, printmaking, science, sculpture, social studies, Spanish, speech, statistics, study skills, theater, theory of knowledge, Western civilization, world literature, zoology.

Graduation Requirements American government, American history, arts and fine arts (art, music, dance, drama), English, foreign language, mathematics, science, speech, athletic participation, skill-oriented activities, service-oriented activities.

Special Academic Programs International Baccalaureate program; Advanced Placement exam preparation; honors section; independent study; academic accommodation for the gifted, the musically talented, and the artistically talented; programs in English, mathematics, general development for dyslexic students.

College Admission Counseling 178 students graduated in 2015; all went to college, including Michigan State University; University of Michigan. Mean SAT

critical reading: 664, mean SAT math: 687, mean SAT writing: 664, mean combined SAT: 2015, mean composite ACT: 29.

Student Life Upper grades have uniform requirement, student council, honor system. Discipline rests primarily with faculty.

Summer Programs Enrichment, advancement, sports, art/fine arts, computer instruction programs offered; session focuses on academic enrichment and sports camps; held on campus; accepts boys and girls; open to students from other schools. 300 students usually enrolled. 2016 schedule: June 18 to August 3.

Tuition and Aid Day student tuition: $28,000. Tuition installment plan (The Tuition Plan, Insured Tuition Payment Plan, Academic Management Services Plan, Key Tuition Payment Plan, SMART Tuition Payment Plan, FACTS Tuition Payment Plan, Dewar Tuition Refund Plan). Need-based scholarship grants available.

Admissions Traditional secondary-level entrance grade is 9. ISEE and Otis-Lennon School Ability Test required. Deadline for receipt of application materials: none. Application fee required: $50. Interview required.

Athletics Interscholastic: aerobics/dance (girls), alpine skiing (b,g), ball hockey (g), baseball (b), basketball (b,g), bicycling (b,g), bowling (b,g), cross-country running (b,g), dance squad (g), dance team (g), diving (b,g), field hockey (g), football (b), golf (b,g), hockey (b), ice hockey (b,g), lacrosse (b,g), skiing (downhill) (b,g), soccer (b,g), softball (g), swimming and diving (b,g), tennis (b,g), track and field (b,g), volleyball (g), wrestling (b); intramural: weight lifting (b,g), weight training (b,g); coed interscholastic: cheering, modern dance, mountain biking, outdoor adventure, running, sailing, snowboarding; coed intramural: basketball, climbing, crew, figure skating, Frisbee, hiking/backpacking, kickball, mountaineering, outdoor education, outdoor skills, project adventure, rock climbing, running, strength & conditioning, ultimate Frisbee, volleyball, wall climbing, weight training, yoga. 4 coaches, 3 athletic trainers.

Computers Computers are regularly used in all classes. Computer network features include on-campus library services, online commercial services, Internet access, wireless campus network, Internet filtering or blocking technology. Campus intranet and student e-mail accounts are available to students. Students grades are available online. The school has a published electronic and media policy.

Contact Michele Reimer, Enrollment and Admissions Manager. 248-430-3587. Fax: 248-203-2184. E-mail: mreimer@dcds.edu. Website: www.dcds.edu

DEVON PREPARATORY SCHOOL

363 North Valley Forge Road

Devon, Pennsylvania 19333-1299

Head of School: Rev. Francisco J. Aisa, Sch.P.

General Information Boys' day college-preparatory school, affiliated with Roman Catholic Church. Grades 6–12. Founded: 1956. Setting: suburban. Nearest major city is Philadelphia. 20-acre campus. 7 buildings on campus. Approved or accredited by Middle States Association of Colleges and Schools, National Catholic Education Association, Pennsylvania Association of Independent Schools, and Pennsylvania Department of Education. Member of National Association of Independent Schools. Endowment: $600,000. Total enrollment: 272. Upper school average class size: 15. Upper school faculty-student ratio: 1:10. There are 180 required school days per year for Upper School students. Upper School students typically attend 5 days per week. The average school day consists of 6 hours.

Upper School Student Profile Grade 9: 51 students (51 boys); Grade 10: 62 students (62 boys); Grade 11: 46 students (46 boys); Grade 12: 51 students (51 boys). 84% of students are Roman Catholic.

Faculty School total: 34. In upper school: 18 men, 8 women; 23 have advanced degrees.

Subjects Offered Accounting, ACT preparation, Advanced Placement courses, algebra, American history, American literature, anatomy and physiology, art, biology, biology-AP, British literature, calculus, calculus-AP, chemistry, chemistry-AP, community service, computer science, computer science-AP, economics, English, environmental science, environmental science-AP, European history, forensics, French, French language-AP, geography, geometry, German, German-AP, health, human geography - AP, journalism, language-AP, Latin, literature and composition-AP, mathematics, modern European history, physical education, physics, physics-AP, political science, pre-calculus, public speaking, religion, science, social studies, Spanish, Spanish-AP, study skills, trigonometry, U.S. history-AP, world cultures, world literature.

Graduation Requirements Computer science, English, foreign language, geography, Latin, mathematics, physical education (includes health), political science, religion (includes Bible studies and theology), science, social studies (includes history). Community service is required.

Special Academic Programs 21 Advanced Placement exams for which test preparation is offered.

College Admission Counseling 49 students graduated in 2015; 40 went to college, including Drexel University; Loyola University Maryland; Penn State University Park; University of Pennsylvania; University of Pittsburgh; Villanova University. Other: 1 had other specific plans. Median SAT critical reading: 643, median SAT math: 636, median SAT writing: 625, median combined SAT: 1904.

Student Life Upper grades have student council. Discipline rests primarily with faculty. Attendance at religious services is required.

Tuition and Aid Day student tuition: $22,200. Tuition installment plan (monthly payment plans). Tuition reduction for siblings, merit scholarship grants, need-based scholarship grants available. In 2015–16, 65% of upper-school students received aid; total upper-school merit-scholarship money awarded: $660,000. Total amount of financial aid awarded in 2015–16: $1,030,000.

Admissions Traditional secondary-level entrance grade is 9. For fall 2015, 220 students applied for upper-level admission, 85 were accepted, 40 enrolled. Math and English placement tests required. Deadline for receipt of application materials: none. Application fee required: $50. On-campus interview recommended.

Athletics Interscholastic: baseball, basketball, bowling, cross-country running, golf, indoor track & field, lacrosse, soccer, swimming and diving, tennis, track and field. 2 PE instructors, 11 coaches, 2 athletic trainers.

Computers Computers are regularly used in all academic, newspaper, technology, writing, yearbook classes. Computer network features include on-campus library services, Internet access, wireless campus network, Internet filtering or blocking technology. Student e-mail accounts and computer access in designated common areas are available to students. Students grades are available online. The school has a published electronic and media policy.

Contact Mr. Patrick Kane, Director of Admissions. 610-688-7337 Ext. 129. Fax: 610-688-2409. E-mail: pkane@devonprep.com. Website: www.devonprep.com

DEXTER SOUTHFIELD

20 Newton Street

Brookline, Massachusetts 02445

Head of School: Mr. Todd A. Vincent

General Information Coeducational day college-preparatory and arts school. Grades PK–12. Founded: 1926. Setting: suburban. Nearest major city is Boston. 36-acre campus. 4 buildings on campus. Approved or accredited by Association of Independent Schools in New England, Michigan Association of Non-Public Schools, and Massachusetts Department of Education. Candidate for accreditation by New England Association of Schools and Colleges. Member of National Association of Independent Schools and Secondary School Admission Test Board. Endowment: $30 million. Total enrollment: 794. Upper school average class size: 16. Upper school faculty-student ratio: 1:7. There are 172 required school days per year for Upper School students. Upper School students typically attend 5 days per week. The average school day consists of 6 hours and 45 minutes.

Upper School Student Profile Grade 9: 78 students (43 boys, 35 girls); Grade 10: 50 students (29 boys, 21 girls); Grade 11: 47 students (26 boys, 21 girls); Grade 12: 62 students (39 boys, 23 girls).

Faculty School total: 110. In upper school: 26 men, 23 women; 31 have advanced degrees.

Subjects Offered Acting, advanced studio art-AP, algebra, American government, American history-AP, American literature, American literature-AP, analysis and differential calculus, Ancient Greek, ancient history, art, art history, art history-AP, art-AP, astronomy, biology, biology-AP, British literature, British literature-AP, calculus, calculus-AP, Central and Eastern European history, ceramics, character education, chemistry, chemistry-AP, Chinese history, choral music, community service, computer graphics, computer music, conceptual physics, constitutional law, digital photography, drama workshop, earth and space science, economics, electronic music, engineering, English, English language-AP, English literature-AP, environmental science, ethics, European history, European history-AP, European literature, Far Eastern history, French, French language-AP, French literature-AP, French-AP, geometry, grammar, graphic arts, history of China and Japan, history of England, history of music, honors algebra, honors English, honors geometry, honors U.S. history, independent study, instrumental music, jazz ensemble, Latin, Latin-AP, marine biology, medieval history, Middle Eastern history, modern European history, music, music composition, music history, music technology, music theory, music theory-AP, music-AP, photography, physics, physics-AP, probability and statistics, public speaking, robotics, Russian history, SAT preparation, Spanish, Spanish language-AP, Spanish literature-AP, Spanish-AP, statistics, studio art, studio art-AP, U.S. history, U.S. history-AP, vocal music, woodworking, writing workshop.

Special Academic Programs 15 Advanced Placement exams for which test preparation is offered; honors section; independent study.

College Admission Counseling 52 students graduated in 2014; 50 went to college, including Boston College; Bowdoin College; Colgate University; Harvard University; Middlebury College; Trinity College. Other: 1 entered a postgraduate year, 1 had other specific plans.

Student Life Upper grades have specified standards of dress, student council, honor system. Discipline rests equally with students and faculty. Attendance at religious services is required.

Tuition and Aid Day student tuition: $42,120. Tuition installment plan (monthly payment plans). Need-based scholarship grants available. In 2014–15, 21% of upper-school students received aid. Total amount of financial aid awarded in 2014–15: $3,000,000.

Admissions Traditional secondary-level entrance grade is 9. For fall 2014, 161 students applied for upper-level admission, 81 were accepted, 40 enrolled. ISEE, PSAT and SAT for applicants to grade 11 and 12, SSAT or TOEFL required. Deadline for receipt of application materials: February 1. Application fee required: $50. Interview required.

Athletics Interscholastic: baseball (boys), basketball (b,g), crew (b,g), cross-country running (b,g), curling (b,g), field hockey (g), fitness (b,g), football (b), golf (b,g), ice hockey (b,g), lacrosse (b,g), soccer (b,g), softball (g), squash (b,g), strength & conditioning (b,g), swimming and diving (b,g), tennis (b,g). 6 coaches, 2 athletic trainers.

Computers Computers are regularly used in all classes. Computer network features include on-campus library services, online commercial services, Internet access, wireless campus network, Internet filtering or blocking technology, one-to-one laptop program. Campus intranet, student e-mail accounts, and computer access in designated common areas are available to students. The school has a published electronic and media policy.

Contact Mrs. Jennifer DaPonte, Admissions Office Manager. 617-454-2721. Fax: 617-928-7691. E-mail: admissions@dextersouthfield.org. Website: www.dextersouthfield.org

DEXTER SOUTHFIELD

20 Newton Street
Brookline, Massachusetts 02445

Head of School: Mr. Todd A. Vincent

General Information Coeducational day college-preparatory and arts school. Grades PK–12. Founded: 1926. Setting: suburban. Nearest major city is Boston. 36-acre campus. 4 buildings on campus. Approved or accredited by Association of Independent Schools in New England and Massachusetts Department of Education. Candidate for accreditation by New England Association of Schools and Colleges. Member of National Association of Independent Schools and Secondary School Admission Test Board. Endowment: $30 million. Total enrollment: 792. Upper school average class size: 14. Upper school faculty-student ratio: 1:7. There are 172 required school days per year for Upper School students. Upper School students typically attend 5 days per week. The average school day consists of 6 hours and 45 minutes.

Upper School Student Profile Grade 9: 78 students (43 boys, 35 girls); Grade 10: 50 students (29 boys, 21 girls); Grade 11: 47 students (26 boys, 21 girls); Grade 12: 61 students (38 boys, 23 girls).

Faculty School total: 110. In upper school: 26 men, 23 women; 31 have advanced degrees.

Subjects Offered Advanced studio art-AP, algebra, American government, American history, American history-AP, American literature, anatomy and physiology, Ancient Greek, ancient world history, art, art history, astronomy, biology, biology-AP, British history, British literature, British literature (honors), calculus-AP, chemistry, chemistry-AP, Chinese history, choir, college counseling, community service, computer music, constitutional history of U.S., digital imaging, digital photography, drama performance, drama workshop, earth and space science, English, English language-AP, English literature-AP, environmental science, equality and freedom, ethics, European history, European history-AP, French, French-AP, geometry, grammar, health and wellness, honors algebra, honors English, honors geometry, human anatomy, jazz ensemble, Latin, Latin-AP, marine biology, music technology, music theory-AP, painting, physics, physics-AP, physiology, pre-calculus, probability and statistics, public speaking, SAT preparation, senior project, shop, space and physical sciences, Spanish, Spanish language-AP, statistics-AP, studio art, studio art-AP, The 20th Century, U.S. history, U.S. history-AP, world history, world history-AP.

Special Academic Programs 13 Advanced Placement exams for which test preparation is offered; honors section; independent study.

College Admission Counseling 52 students graduated in 2014; 51 went to college, including Columbia University; Dartmouth College; Harvard University; Massachusetts Institute of Technology; The George Washington University; Trinity College. Other: 1 entered military service.

Student Life Upper grades have specified standards of dress, student council, honor system. Discipline rests equally with students and faculty. Attendance at religious services is required.

Tuition and Aid Day student tuition: $42,120. Tuition installment plan (monthly payment plans). Need-based scholarship grants available. In 2014–15, 27% of upper-school students received aid. Total amount of financial aid awarded in 2014–15: $3,000,000.

Admissions Traditional secondary-level entrance grade is 9. For fall 2014, 146 students applied for upper-level admission, 81 were accepted, 41 enrolled. ISEE, PSAT and SAT for applicants to grade 11 and 12, SSAT or TOEFL required. Deadline for receipt of application materials: February 1. Application fee required: $50. Interview required.

Athletics Interscholastic: basketball (boys, girls), crew (b,g), cross-country running (b,g), curling (b,g), field hockey (g), football (b), ice hockey (b,g), independent competitive sports (b,g), lacrosse (b,g), physical fitness (b,g), rowing (b,g), soccer (b,g), softball (g), squash (b,g), tennis (b,g), weight training (b,g); intramural: dance (g), hiking/backpacking (g), life saving (g). 4 coaches, 2 athletic trainers.

Computers Computers are regularly used in all classes. Computer network features include on-campus library services, online commercial services, Internet access,

wireless campus network, Internet filtering or blocking technology, one-to-one device program. Campus intranet and student e-mail accounts are available to students. The school has a published electronic and media policy.

Contact Mrs. Jennifer DaPonte, Admissions Office Manager. 617-454-2721. Fax: 617-928-7691. E-mail: admissions@dextersouthfield.org. Website: www.dextersouthfield.org

DOANE ACADEMY

350 Riverbank
Burlington, New Jersey 08016-2199

Head of School: Mr. George B. Sanderson

General Information Coeducational day college-preparatory and arts school, affiliated with Episcopal Church. Grades PK–12. Founded: 1837. Setting: suburban. Nearest major city is Philadelphia, PA. 10-acre campus. 4 buildings on campus. Approved or accredited by Middle States Association of Colleges and Schools and National Association of Episcopal Schools. Member of National Association of Independent Schools. Endowment: $1 million. Total enrollment: 226. Upper school average class size: 12. Upper school faculty-student ratio: 1:6. There are 177 required school days per year for Upper School students. Upper School students typically attend 5 days per week. The average school day consists of 7 hours.

Upper School Student Profile Grade 6: 14 students (9 boys, 5 girls); Grade 7: 20 students (12 boys, 8 girls); Grade 8: 9 students (6 boys, 3 girls); Grade 9: 19 students (11 boys, 8 girls); Grade 10: 25 students (16 boys, 9 girls); Grade 11: 23 students (8 boys, 15 girls); Grade 12: 28 students (17 boys, 11 girls).

Faculty School total: 30. In upper school: 6 men, 11 women; 5 have advanced degrees.

Subjects Offered African American history, algebra, American Civil War, American literature, ancient world history, arts and crafts, band, biology, biology-AP, British literature, calculus, calculus-AP, chemistry, chemistry-AP, choir, Civil War, computer graphics, computer literacy, computer science, creative writing, cultural geography, digital photography, drama, drawing, economics, English literature and composition-AP, environmental science, ethics, European history, European history-AP, French, geometry, government-AP, graphic design, health and wellness, honors algebra, instrumental music, Latin, Latin-AP, life science, music, novels, painting, physical education, physical science, physics, piano, poetry, pre-algebra, psychology, psychology-AP, research skills, SAT preparation, sculpture, Shakespeare, short story, Spanish, Spanish-AP, speech and debate, studio art-AP, trigonometry, U.S. history, U.S. history-AP, Web site design, world history, world literature, world religions, writing.

Graduation Requirements Arts and fine arts (art, music, dance, drama), computer skills, English, ethics, foreign language, lab science, mathematics, physical education (includes health), science, social studies (includes history), world religions, one semester of ethics and world religions.

Special Academic Programs Advanced Placement exam preparation; honors section; independent study; study at local college for college credit; academic accommodation for the gifted, the musically talented, and the artistically talented; remedial reading and/or remedial writing; remedial math.

College Admission Counseling 18 students graduated in 2015; all went to college, including Haverford College; Lehigh University; The College of New Jersey; Wellesley College.

Student Life Upper grades have uniform requirement, student council, honor system. Discipline rests primarily with faculty. Attendance at religious services is required.

Tuition and Aid Day student tuition: $13,700–$15,900. Tuition installment plan (FACTS Tuition Payment Plan, monthly payment plans). Tuition reduction for siblings, merit scholarship grants, need-based scholarship grants, tuition remission for children of faculty and staff available. In 2015–16, 30% of upper-school students received aid; total upper-school merit-scholarship money awarded: $20,000. Total amount of financial aid awarded in 2015–16: $120,000.

Admissions Traditional secondary-level entrance grade is 9. For fall 2015, 40 students applied for upper-level admission, 32 were accepted, 32 enrolled. ISEE or SSAT required. Deadline for receipt of application materials: none. Application fee required: $35. On-campus interview required.

Athletics Interscholastic: baseball (boys), basketball (b,g), crew (b,g), cross-country running (b,g), golf (b,g), soccer (b,g), softball (g); coed interscholastic: outdoor adventure, soccer, strength & conditioning; coed intramural: alpine skiing, basketball, kickball, outdoor activities, soccer, softball, table tennis, volleyball. 2 PE instructors, 11 coaches.

Computers Computers are regularly used in graphic design, lab/keyboard, mathematics, photography, research skills, SAT preparation, science, Web site design, yearbook classes. Computer network features include on-campus library services, Internet access, wireless campus network, Internet filtering or blocking technology, homework assignments available online. Campus intranet is available to students. Students grades are available online. The school has a published electronic and media policy.

Contact Miss Lacy Hall, Dean of Admission. 609-386-3500 Ext. 115. Fax: 609-386-5878. E-mail: lhall@doaneacademy.org. Website: www.doaneacademy.org

DOANE STUART SCHOOL

199 Washington Avenue
Rensselaer, New York 12144

Head of School: Mrs. Pamela J. Clarke

General Information Coeducational day college-preparatory, arts, religious studies, Irish and peace studies, and Bioethics school, affiliated with Episcopal Church. Grades N–12. Founded: 1852. Setting: urban. Nearest major city is Albany. 27-acre campus. 1 building on campus. Approved or accredited by National Association of Episcopal Schools, New York State Association of Independent Schools, and New York Department of Education. Member of National Association of Independent Schools. Endowment: $1 million. Total enrollment: 295. Upper school average class size: 15. Upper school faculty-student ratio: 1:8. Upper School students typically attend 5 days per week. The average school day consists of 7 hours and 30 minutes.

Upper School Student Profile Grade 9: 34 students (16 boys, 18 girls); Grade 10: 39 students (24 boys, 15 girls); Grade 11: 38 students (14 boys, 24 girls); Grade 12: 51 students (25 boys, 26 girls). 10% of students are members of Episcopal Church.

Faculty School total: 50. In upper school: 10 men, 11 women; 13 have advanced degrees.

Subjects Offered 3-dimensional art, 3-dimensional design, accounting, advanced biology, advanced chemistry, advanced math, advanced studio art-AP, algebra, American history, American literature, art, bioethics, biology, Buddhism, calculus, campus ministry, ceramics, chemistry, choral music, college admission preparation, college counseling, college placement, college planning, college writing, community service, computer science, creative writing, earth science, economics, English, English literature, environmental science, ethics, fencing, fine arts, French, geometry, government/civics, health, history, independent study, instrumental music, instruments, international studies, internship, Irish literature, Irish studies, jazz band, jazz ensemble, journalism, literature, mathematics, mechanical drawing, media arts, medieval/Renaissance history, mentorship program, microeconomics, Middle Eastern history, music, music composition, music performance, music theory, newspaper, oil painting, oral communications, oral expression, organ, painting, peace and justice, peace education, peace studies, performing arts, photography, physical education, physical fitness, physical science, physics, play production, playwriting, poetry, political economy, political science, politics, portfolio art, portfolio writing, pre-algebra, pre-calculus, psychology, psychology-AP, public service, public speaking, religion, SAT preparation, science, senior seminar, Shakespeare, social studies, Spanish, theater, trigonometry, world history, writing.

Graduation Requirements American history, biology, health, religion (includes Bible studies and theology).

Special Academic Programs 30 Advanced Placement exams for which test preparation is offered; honors section; independent study; term-away projects; study at local college for college credit; study abroad; academic accommodation for the gifted, the musically talented, and the artistically talented.

College Admission Counseling 34 students graduated in 2014; all went to college, including Brandeis University; Mount Holyoke College; Union College; Worcester Polytechnic Institute.

Student Life Upper grades have uniform requirement, student council. Discipline rests primarily with faculty. Attendance at religious services is required.

Tuition and Aid Day student tuition: $20,702–$22,895. Tuition installment plan (Insured Tuition Payment Plan, Academic Management Services Plan, FACTS Tuition Payment Plan). Merit scholarship grants, need-based scholarship grants available. In 2014–15, 60% of upper-school students received aid; total upper-school merit-scholarship money awarded: $25,422. Total amount of financial aid awarded in 2014–15: $1,783,059.

Admissions Traditional secondary-level entrance grade is 9. For fall 2014, 230 students applied for upper-level admission, 118 were accepted, 49 enrolled. School's own test or SLEP for foreign students required. Deadline for receipt of application materials: none. Application fee required: $75. On-campus interview required.

Athletics Interscholastic: baseball (boys), basketball (b,g), crew (b,g), indoor track (b,g), indoor track & field (b,g), soccer (b,g), softball (g), tennis (b,g), track and field (b,g), volleyball (g); intramural: backpacking (b,g), badminton (b,g), independent competitive sports (b,g); coed interscholastic: crew, cross-country running, independent competitive sports, indoor track, indoor track & field, tennis, track and field; coed intramural: backpacking, badminton, crew, cross-country running, fencing, Frisbee, hiking/backpacking, independent competitive sports, jogging, outdoor adventure, outdoors, physical fitness, running, sailing, soccer, strength & conditioning, tai chi, ultimate Frisbee, walking, weight lifting, weight training, yoga. 3 PE instructors, 8 coaches.

Computers Computers are regularly used in accounting, architecture, art, basic skills, business, career exploration, college planning, creative writing, current events, data processing, desktop publishing, drawing and design, economics, English, ethics, foreign language, freshman foundations, geography, graphic arts, graphic design, graphics, health, historical foundations for arts, history, humanities, independent study, introduction to technology, journalism, keyboarding, language development, learning cognition, library science, library skills, literary magazine, mathematics, media arts, media production, mentorship program, multimedia, music, music technology, news writing, newspaper, philosophy, photography, programming, psychology, publications, publishing, reading, religion, religious studies, remedial study skills, research skills, SAT preparation, science, senior seminar, social sciences, social studies, study skills,

technology, theater, theater arts, video film production, Web site design, writing, writing, yearbook classes. Computer resources include on-campus library services, online commercial services, Internet access, wireless campus network. Computer access in designated common areas is available to students. The school has a published electronic and media policy.

Contact Mr. Geoffrey Bowman, Director of Admission. 518-465-5222 Ext. 241. Fax: 518-465-5230. E-mail: gbowman@doanestuart.org. Website: www.doanestuart.org

THE DR. MIRIAM AND SHELDON G. ADELSON EDUCATIONAL CAMPUS, THE ADELSON UPPER SCHOOL

9700 West Hillpointe Road
Las Vegas, Nevada 89134

Head of School: Dr. Joyce Raynor

General Information Coeducational day college-preparatory, arts, religious studies, bilingual studies, and technology school, affiliated with Jewish faith. Grades PS–12. Founded: 1979. Setting: suburban. 30-acre campus. 1 building on campus. Approved or accredited by Northwest Association of Independent Schools and Nevada Department of Education. Member of National Association of Independent Schools. Total enrollment: 419. Upper school average class size: 16. Upper school faculty-student ratio: 1:14. There are 185 required school days per year for Upper School students. Upper School students typically attend 5 days per week. The average school day consists of 7 hours and 10 minutes.

Upper School Student Profile Grade 9: 23 students (14 boys, 9 girls); Grade 10: 36 students (19 boys, 17 girls); Grade 11: 41 students (18 boys, 23 girls); Grade 12: 31 students (15 boys, 16 girls). 80% of students are Jewish.

Faculty School total: 31. In upper school: 14 men, 17 women; all have advanced degrees.

Graduation Requirements Jewish studies.

Special Academic Programs 13 Advanced Placement exams for which test preparation is offered; honors section; study at local college for college credit; study abroad; academic accommodation for the gifted; programs in English, mathematics for dyslexic students; ESL (5 students enrolled).

Student Life Upper grades have uniform requirement, student council, honor system. Discipline rests primarily with faculty. Attendance at religious services is required.

Tuition and Aid Day student tuition: $20,850. Tuition installment plan (monthly payment plans, individually arranged payment plans). Need-based scholarship grants available. In 2015–16, 35% of upper-school students received aid. Total amount of financial aid awarded in 2015–16: $1,000,000.

Admissions Traditional secondary-level entrance grade is 9. For fall 2015, 16 students applied for upper-level admission, 11 were accepted, 10 enrolled. Admissions testing and ERB (CTP-Verbal, Quantitative) required. Deadline for receipt of application materials: none. No application fee required. Interview required.

Athletics Interscholastic: aerobics/dance (girls), baseball (b), basketball (b,g), cheering (g), cross-country running (b,g), dance (b,g), dance team (b,g), fencing (b,g), modern dance (b,g), soccer (b,g), swimming and diving (b,g), tennis (b,g), volleyball (b,g); coed interscholastic: aquatics, golf. 6 PE instructors, 10 coaches.

Computers Computer network features include on-campus library services, Internet access, wireless campus network, Internet filtering or blocking technology. Student e-mail accounts and computer access in designated common areas are available to students. Students grades are available online. The school has a published electronic and media policy.

Contact Mrs. Alli Abrahamson, Director of Admissions. 702-255-4500. Fax: 702-255-7232. E-mail: alli.abrahamson@adelsoncampus.org. Website: www.adelsoncampus.org

DOMINICAN ACADEMY

44 East 68th Street
New York, New York 10065

Head of School: Sr. Margaret Ormond, OP

General Information Girls' day college-preparatory, arts, religious studies, and technology school, affiliated with Roman Catholic Church. Grades 9–12. Founded: 1897. Setting: urban. 1 building on campus. Approved or accredited by Middle States Association of Colleges and Schools, National Catholic Education Association, New York State Board of Regents, and New York Department of Education. Member of National Association of Independent Schools and Secondary School Admission Test Board. Total enrollment: 216. Upper school average class size: 18. Upper school faculty-student ratio: 1:8. There are 180 required school days per year for Upper School students. Upper School students typically attend 5 days per week. The average school day consists of 6 hours and 30 minutes.

Upper School Student Profile Grade 9: 42 students (42 girls); Grade 10: 58 students (58 girls); Grade 11: 58 students (58 girls); Grade 12: 59 students (59 girls). 80% of students are Roman Catholic.

Faculty School total: 27. In upper school: 3 men, 24 women; 20 have advanced degrees.

Subjects Offered Algebra, American history, American history-AP, American literature, art history-AP, biology, biology-AP, calculus, calculus-AP, chemistry, chemistry-AP, Chinese, chorus, communications, computer science, creative writing, dance, debate, drama, economics, economics-AP, English, English literature, English-AP, European history-AP, forensics, French, French-AP, geometry, global studies, government and politics-AP, government/civics, health, history, Latin, Latin-AP, library studies, logic, mathematics, music, music theory, physical education, physics, physics-AP, pre-calculus, psychology, religion, science, social studies, Spanish, Spanish-AP, world history.

Graduation Requirements Alternative physical education, arts and fine arts (art, music, dance, drama), English, foreign language, Latin, mathematics, religion (includes Bible studies and theology), science, social studies (includes history), 5 years of language including 2 years minimum of both Latin and a Modern Language.

Special Academic Programs 12 Advanced Placement exams for which test preparation is offered; honors section; ESL (6 students enrolled).

College Admission Counseling 39 students graduated in 2015; all went to college, including Middlebury College; Northeastern University; Princeton University. Mean combined SAT: 1835.

Student Life Upper grades have uniform requirement, student council. Discipline rests primarily with faculty. Attendance at religious services is required.

Summer Programs Remediation, enrichment, advancement programs offered; session focuses on prospective student and math prep; held on campus; accepts girls; open to students from other schools. 80 students usually enrolled. 2016 schedule: July 6 to August 14. Application deadline: June 15.

Tuition and Aid Day student tuition: $14,925. Tuition installment plan (FACTS Tuition Payment Plan, individually arranged payment plans, quarterly payment plan, semester payment plan). Tuition reduction for siblings, merit scholarship grants, need-based scholarship grants, paying campus jobs available. In 2015–16, 33% of upper-school students received aid.

Admissions Traditional secondary-level entrance grade is 9. For fall 2015, 390 students applied for upper-level admission, 215 were accepted, 42 enrolled. Catholic High School Entrance Examination or Differential Aptitude Test required. Deadline for receipt of application materials: December 15. Application fee required: $150.

Athletics Interscholastic: basketball, cross-country running, soccer, softball, tennis, track and field, volleyball; intramural: billiards, dance, soccer, track and field, volleyball. 1 PE instructor.

Computers Computers are regularly used in economics, health, history, Latin, library science, library studies, mathematics, religious studies, science, technology classes. Computer network features include on-campus library services, online commercial services, Internet access, wireless campus network, Internet filtering or blocking technology, T1 fiber optic network. Campus intranet, student e-mail accounts, and computer access in designated common areas are available to students. The school has a published electronic and media policy.

Contact Ms. Madeleine Metzler, Director of Admissions. 212-744-0195 Ext. 31. Fax: 212-744-0375. E-mail: mmetzler@dominicanacademy.org. Website: www.dominicanacademy.org

DON BOSCO PREPARATORY HIGH SCHOOL

492 North Franklin Turnpike
Ramsey, New Jersey 07446

Head of School: Fr. James Heuser

General Information Boys' day college-preparatory, arts, business, religious studies, and technology school, affiliated with Roman Catholic Church. Grades 9–12. Founded: 1915. Setting: suburban. Nearest major city is New York, NY. 35-acre campus. 3 buildings on campus. Approved or accredited by Middle States Association of Colleges and Schools, National Catholic Education Association, and New Jersey Department of Education. Upper school average class size: 23. Upper school faculty-student ratio: 1:14. There are 190 required school days per year for Upper School students. Upper School students typically attend 5 days per week. The average school day consists of 6 hours.

Faculty In upper school: 43 men, 24 women.

Subjects Offered Zoology.

Special Academic Programs International Baccalaureate program; Advanced Placement exam preparation; programs in English, mathematics, general development for dyslexic students.

College Admission Counseling 232 students graduated in 2014; all went to college, including Union College. Mean combined SAT: 1743.

Student Life Upper grades have uniform requirement, student council, honor system. Discipline rests primarily with faculty. Attendance at religious services is required.

Tuition and Aid Day student tuition: $14,200. Tuition installment plan (FACTS Tuition Payment Plan, monthly payment plans). Tuition reduction for siblings, merit scholarship grants, need-based scholarship grants, need-based loans available.

Admissions Traditional secondary-level entrance grade is 9. Catholic High School Entrance Examination required. Deadline for receipt of application materials: December. No application fee required.

Athletics Interscholastic: baseball, basketball, bowling, crew, cross-country running, fencing, football, golf, hockey, ice hockey, indoor track & field, lacrosse, skiing (downhill), soccer, swimming and diving, tennis, track and field, volleyball, winter (indoor) track, wrestling.

Computers Computer network features include on-campus library services, Internet access, Internet filtering or blocking technology. Campus intranet, student e-mail accounts, and computer access in designated common areas are available to students. Students grades are available online. The school has a published electronic and media policy.

Contact Mr. George Mihalik, Admissions Director. 201-327-8003 Ext. 102. Fax: 201-327-3397. E-mail: gmihalik@donboscoprep.org. Website: www.donboscoprep.org

DONELSON CHRISTIAN ACADEMY

300 Danyacrest Drive
Nashville, Tennessee 37214

Head of School: Mr. Keith M. Singer

General Information Coeducational day college-preparatory, arts, religious studies, and technology school, affiliated with Christian faith. Grades PS–12. Founded: 1971. Setting: suburban. 50-acre campus. 1 building on campus. Approved or accredited by Association of Christian Schools International, Southern Association of Colleges and Schools, Tennessee Association of Independent Schools, and Tennessee Department of Education. Member of National Association of Independent Schools. Endowment: $78,000. Total enrollment: 818. Upper school average class size: 14. Upper school faculty-student ratio: 1:9. There are 175 required school days per year for Upper School students. Upper School students typically attend 5 days per week. The average school day consists of 7 hours and 20 minutes.

Upper School Student Profile Grade 9: 53 students (28 boys, 25 girls); Grade 10: 66 students (34 boys, 32 girls); Grade 11: 44 students (23 boys, 21 girls); Grade 12: 42 students (17 boys, 25 girls). 90% of students are Christian faith.

Faculty School total: 60. In upper school: 15 men, 20 women; 20 have advanced degrees.

Subjects Offered 3-dimensional art, ACT preparation, Advanced Placement courses, advanced studio art-AP, algebra, American history, American history-AP, American literature, American literature-AP, anatomy, art, athletic training, Bible studies, biology, biology-AP, business, calculus, calculus-AP, chemistry, chemistry-AP, Chinese, choir, community service, computer science, creative writing, drama, earth science, ecology, economics, English, English language and composition-AP, English literature, English literature and composition-AP, environmental science, ESL, European history-AP, fine arts, French, geography, geometry, government/civics, grammar, health, history, honors algebra, honors English, honors geometry, honors U.S. history, journalism, keyboarding, Latin, Latin-AP, mathematics, music, personal finance, physical education, physics, physiology, psychology, religion, science, social sciences, social studies, sociology, Spanish, speech, theater, U.S. history-AP, world history, world literature, yearbook.

Graduation Requirements Arts and fine arts (art, music, dance, drama), Bible, chemistry, consumer economics, electives, English, foreign language, mathematics, physical education (includes health), science, social sciences, social studies (includes history), wellness, senior service (community service for 12th grade students).

Special Academic Programs 6 Advanced Placement exams for which test preparation is offered; independent study; study at local college for college credit; ESL (4 students enrolled).

College Admission Counseling Median composite ACT: 24. 27% scored over 26 on composite ACT.

Student Life Upper grades have uniform requirement, student council, honor system. Discipline rests primarily with faculty. Attendance at religious services is required.

Summer Programs Sports, art/fine arts programs offered; session focuses on to enhance in the areas of academics, the arts, and athletics; held on campus; accepts boys and girls; not open to students from other schools. 75 students usually enrolled. 2016 schedule: May 30 to July 31.

Tuition and Aid Day student tuition: $11,175. Tuition installment plan (FACTS Tuition Payment Plan). Need-based scholarship grants available. In 2015–16, 27% of upper-school students received aid. Total amount of financial aid awarded in 2015–16: $169,053.

Admissions Traditional secondary-level entrance grade is 9. For fall 2015, 25 students applied for upper-level admission, 18 were accepted, 15 enrolled. Admissions testing required. Deadline for receipt of application materials: none. Application fee required: $40. On-campus interview required.

Athletics Interscholastic: baseball (boys), basketball (b,g), bowling (b,g), cheering (g), cross-country running (b,g), football (b), golf (b,g), soccer (b,g), softball (g), tennis (b,g), track and field (b,g), volleyball (g), wrestling (b); intramural: basketball (b,g), football (b); coed interscholastic: fitness, physical fitness, swimming and diving, weight training; coed intramural: fitness, kickball, rappelling. 1 PE instructor, 2 coaches, 1 athletic trainer.

Computers Computers are regularly used in all academic, career exploration, college planning, creative writing, English, French, history, journalism, library, mathematics, newspaper, science, social sciences, Spanish, technology, yearbook classes. Computer network features include on-campus library services, Internet access, wireless campus network, Internet filtering or blocking technology. Campus intranet and student e-mail accounts are available to students. Students grades are available online. The school has a published electronic and media policy.

Contact Mrs. Nicole Schierling, Assistant to Advancement. 615-577-1215. Fax: 615-883-2998. E-mail: nschierling@dcawildcats.org. Website: www.dcawildcats.org

DONNA KLEIN JEWISH ACADEMY

9701 Donna Klein Boulevard

Boca Raton, Florida 33428-1524

Head of School: Helena Levine

General Information Coeducational day college-preparatory, arts, religious studies, and bilingual studies school, affiliated with Jewish faith. Grades K–12. Founded: 1979. Setting: suburban. 23-acre campus. 1 building on campus. Approved or accredited by Florida Council of Independent Schools, Southern Association of Colleges and Schools, and Florida Department of Education. Member of National Association of Independent Schools and Secondary School Admission Test Board. Languages of instruction: English and Hebrew. Endowment: $1 million. Total enrollment: 580. Upper school average class size: 15. Upper school faculty-student ratio: 1:6. There are 172 required school days per year for Upper School students. Upper School students typically attend 5 days per week. The average school day consists of 7 hours and 30 minutes.

Upper School Student Profile Grade 6: 53 students (30 boys, 23 girls); Grade 7: 53 students (19 boys, 34 girls); Grade 8: 50 students (25 boys, 25 girls); Grade 9: 47 students (18 boys, 29 girls); Grade 10: 40 students (28 boys, 12 girls); Grade 11: 25 students (12 boys, 13 girls); Grade 12: 46 students (19 boys, 27 girls). 100% of students are Jewish.

Faculty School total: 24. In upper school: 11 men, 13 women; 11 have advanced degrees.

Subjects Offered Advanced biology, advanced chemistry, advanced math, Advanced Placement courses, advanced studio art-AP, anatomy and physiology, art, band, basketball, Bible studies, biology, calculus, calculus-AP, chemistry, college counseling, computer programming, computer skills, computer tools, dance, debate, drama, economics, English, English language and composition-AP, English literature and composition-AP, environmental science, environmental science-AP, French studies, geometry, government, government-AP, guidance, health, Hebrew, honors English, honors geometry, honors U.S. history, honors world history, Jewish history, journalism, Judaic studies, literature and composition-AP, model United Nations, physical education, pre-calculus, psychology-AP, SAT/ACT preparation, softball, Spanish, statistics, statistics-AP, student government, studio art-AP, theater production, U.S. government and politics, U.S. history-AP, visual arts, volleyball, world history, world history-AP, writing, yearbook.

Graduation Requirements Electives, English, foreign language, history, Judaic studies, mathematics, physical education (includes health), science, writing, completion of 225 hours of community service.

Special Academic Programs 15 Advanced Placement exams for which test preparation is offered; honors section; independent study; study at local college for college credit; study abroad.

College Admission Counseling 25 students graduated in 2015; 23 went to college, including Boston University; Florida Atlantic University; Florida State University; University of Central Florida; University of Florida; University of Miami. Other: 2 went to work. Median combined SAT: 1090, median composite ACT: 25.

Student Life Upper grades have specified standards of dress, student council, honor system. Discipline rests primarily with faculty. Attendance at religious services is required.

Tuition and Aid Day student tuition: $23,125. Tuition installment plan (FACTS Tuition Payment Plan, monthly payment plans, individually arranged payment plans). Merit scholarship grants, need-based scholarship grants available. In 2015–16, 50% of upper-school students received aid; total upper-school merit-scholarship money awarded: $33,000. Total amount of financial aid awarded in 2015–16: $840,465.

Admissions Traditional secondary-level entrance grade is 9. For fall 2015, 30 students applied for upper-level admission, 14 were accepted, 14 enrolled. SSAT and SSAT, ERB, PSAT, SAT, PLAN or ACT required. Deadline for receipt of application materials: none. Application fee required: $100. On-campus interview required.

Athletics Interscholastic: baseball (boys), basketball (b,g), dance team (g), golf (b), soccer (b,g), softball (g), volleyball (g); coed interscholastic: cross-country running, tennis; coed intramural: dance team, fitness, scuba diving, self defense, swimming and diving, tennis, weight lifting, weight training. 1 PE instructor, 6 coaches.

Computers Computers are regularly used in all classes. Computer network features include Internet access, wireless campus network, Internet filtering or blocking technology. Campus intranet and student e-mail accounts are available to students. Students grades are available online. The school has a published electronic and media policy.

Contact Mrs. Jodi Orshan. 561-852-3310. Fax: 561-852-3327. E-mail: orshanj@dkja.net. Website: www.dkja.org

THE DONOHO SCHOOL

2501 Henry Road

Anniston, Alabama 36207

Head of School: Dr. James Hutchins

General Information Coeducational day college-preparatory and arts school. Grades PK–12. Founded: 1963. Setting: suburban. Nearest major city is Birmingham. 73-acre campus. 4 buildings on campus. Approved or accredited by Southern Association of Colleges and Schools and Alabama Department of Education. Member of National Association of Independent Schools. Total enrollment: 357. Upper school average class size: 12. Upper school faculty-student ratio: 1:12. There are 180 required school days per year for Upper School students. Upper School students typically attend 5 days per week. The average school day consists of 5 hours and 25 minutes.

Upper School Student Profile Grade 9: 40 students (23 boys, 17 girls); Grade 10: 27 students (17 boys, 10 girls); Grade 11: 38 students (18 boys, 20 girls); Grade 12: 34 students (13 boys, 21 girls).

Faculty School total: 33. In upper school: 6 men, 12 women; 12 have advanced degrees.

Subjects Offered Algebra, American history, American literature, anatomy, art, arts, band, biology, calculus, chemistry, chorus, computer science, drama, economics, English, English literature, European history, fine arts, French, geography, geometry, government/civics, grammar, health, history, journalism, Latin, mathematics, music, physical education, physics, physiology, public speaking, robotics, science, social studies, Spanish, speech, theater, world history.

Graduation Requirements Arts and fine arts (art, music, dance, drama), English, foreign language, mathematics, physical education (includes health), public speaking, science, social sciences, social studies (includes history).

Special Academic Programs Advanced Placement exam preparation; honors section; term-away projects; study at local college for college credit; ESL (6 students enrolled).

College Admission Counseling 22 students graduated in 2015; all went to college, including Auburn University; Birmingham-Southern College; Samford University; University of Montevallo; Vanderbilt University. Mean SAT critical reading: 625, mean SAT math: 631, mean SAT writing: 633, mean combined SAT: 1889, mean composite ACT: 27.

Student Life Upper grades have specified standards of dress, student council, honor system. Discipline rests primarily with faculty.

Summer Programs Remediation, enrichment programs offered; session focuses on enrichment; held on campus; accepts boys and girls; open to students from other schools. 50 students usually enrolled. 2016 schedule: June 6 to July 29. Application deadline: May 13.

Tuition and Aid Day student tuition: $4630–$9245. Tuition installment plan (FACTS Tuition Payment Plan, monthly payment plans). Need-based scholarship grants available. In 2015–16, 18% of upper-school students received aid.

Admissions Traditional secondary-level entrance grade is 10. For fall 2015, 14 students applied for upper-level admission, 11 were accepted, 11 enrolled. Admissions testing, Woodcock-Johnson and writing sample required. Deadline for receipt of application materials: none. Application fee required: $50. Interview required.

Athletics Interscholastic: baseball (boys), basketball (b,g), cheering (g), cross-country running (b,g), football (b), golf (b,g), soccer (b,g), tennis (b,g), track and field (b,g), volleyball (g). 2 coaches.

Computers Computers are regularly used in English, foreign language, mathematics, science classes. Computer network features include on-campus library services, online commercial services, Internet access, wireless campus network, Internet filtering or blocking technology, laptop and iPad use welcomed on campus. Student e-mail accounts and computer access in designated common areas are available to students. Students grades are available online. The school has a published electronic and media policy.

Contact Mrs. Jean Jaudon, Lower School Director. 256-236-4459 Ext. 108. Fax: 256-237-6474. E-mail: jean.jaudon@donohoschool.com. Website: www.donohoschool.com/

DONOVAN CATHOLIC

711 Hooper Avenue

Toms River, New Jersey 08753

Head of School: Dr. Edward Gere

General Information Coeducational day college-preparatory, arts, business, religious studies, and technology school, affiliated with Roman Catholic Church. Grades 9–12. Founded: 1962. Setting: suburban. Nearest major city is New York City, NY. 5-acre campus. 1 building on campus. Approved or accredited by National Catholic Education Association and New Jersey Department of Education. Total enrollment: 689. Upper school average class size: 23. Upper school faculty-student ratio: 1:15. There are 180 required school days per year for Upper School students. Upper School students typically attend 5 days per week. The average school day consists of 6 hours.

Upper School Student Profile Grade 9: 165 students (85 boys, 80 girls); Grade 10: 167 students (91 boys, 76 girls); Grade 11: 187 students (99 boys, 88 girls); Grade 12: 183 students (80 boys, 103 girls). 85% of students are Roman Catholic.

Faculty School total: 61. In upper school: 28 men, 33 women; 23 have advanced degrees.

Subjects Offered 1968.

Special Academic Programs Advanced Placement exam preparation; honors section; independent study; study at local college for college credit; academic accommodation for the gifted, the musically talented, and the artistically talented; remedial reading and/or remedial writing; remedial math.

College Admission Counseling 182 students graduated in 2015.

Student Life Upper grades have uniform requirement, student council, honor system. Discipline rests equally with students and faculty. Attendance at religious services is required.

Tuition and Aid Day student tuition: $11,570. Tuition installment plan (SMART Tuition Payment Plan, monthly payment plans). Merit scholarship grants, need-based scholarship grants, paying campus jobs available. In 2015–16, 20% of upper-school students received aid. Total amount of financial aid awarded in 2015–16: $400,000.

Admissions Traditional secondary-level entrance grade is 9. Scholastic Testing Service High School Placement Test required. Deadline for receipt of application materials: October 31. No application fee required. On-campus interview recommended.

Athletics Interscholastic: baseball (boys), cheering (g), football (b), golf (b), ice hockey (b), lacrosse (g), softball (g), wrestling (b); coed interscholastic: basketball, bowling, cross-country running, dance, hiking/backpacking, sailing, skiing (cross-country), snowboarding, soccer, strength & conditioning, surfing, swimming and diving, tennis, weight lifting, weight training. 5 PE instructors, 22 coaches, 1 athletic trainer.

Computers Computers are regularly used in all academic classes. Computer network features include on-campus library services, Internet access, wireless campus network, Internet filtering or blocking technology. Student e-mail accounts are available to students. Students grades are available online. The school has a published electronic and media policy.

Contact Mrs. Tara Mulligan, Registrar. 732-349-8801 Ext. 2426. Fax: 732-505-8014. E-mail: tmulligan@donovancatholic.org. Website: www.donovancatholic.org

DOWLING CATHOLIC HIGH SCHOOL

1400 Buffalo Road
West Des Moines, Iowa 50265

Head of School: Dr. Jerry M. Deegan

General Information Coeducational day college-preparatory, general academic, arts, business, religious studies, bilingual studies, technology, performing arts, and Advanced Placement school, affiliated with Roman Catholic Church. Grades 9–12. Founded: 1918. Setting: suburban. 60-acre campus. 1 building on campus. Approved or accredited by Iowa Department of Education. Endowment: $9 million. Total enrollment: 1,438. Upper school average class size: 25. Upper school faculty-student ratio: 1:18. The average school day consists of 6 hours and 30 minutes.

Upper School Student Profile 94% of students are Roman Catholic.

Faculty School total: 101. In upper school: 55 have advanced degrees.

Subjects Offered 20th century world history, accounting, ACT preparation, acting, advanced chemistry, advanced computer applications, advanced math, Advanced Placement courses, advertising design, algebra, American government, American history, American history-AP, American literature, American literature-AP, applied arts, aquatics, art, art history, athletics, band, baseball, Basic programming, biology, biology-AP, brass choir, British literature, business, business communications, business law, calculus, calculus-AP, career and personal planning, career planning, career/college preparation, ceramics, chamber groups, cheerleading, chemistry, chemistry-AP, choir, choral music, chorus, church history, college counseling, college planning, composition, composition-AP, computer applications, computer information systems, computer processing, computer programming, computers, concert band, concert choir, creative writing, digital photography, drama, economics, economics-AP, engineering, English, English composition, English language and composition-AP, English literature, environmental science, European history, European history-AP, finance, fine arts, foreign language, French, general business, general science, geography, geometry, German, government, government-AP, health, health education, history, history-AP, honors algebra, honors English, honors geometry, honors U.S. history, honors world history, humanities, information processing, integrated mathematics, jazz band, journalism, keyboarding, Latin, life saving, literature, literature-AP, marching band, metalworking, modern European history, newspaper, painting, personal finance, physical education, physics, physics-AP, play production, poetry, pottery, pre-algebra, pre-calculus, probability and statistics, programming, religion, SAT/ACT preparation, scuba diving, social justice, sociology, Spanish, Spanish language-AP, speech and debate, swimming, tennis, theater production, theology, U.S. government, U.S. government and politics-AP, U.S. history, U.S. history-AP, visual arts, vocal jazz, weight training, world religions, yearbook.

Graduation Requirements Arts, business, electives, English, mathematics, reading, science, social studies (includes history), theology, Reading Across the Curriculum (RAC), 10 Christian service hours per semester/20 per year, 10.5 credits of electives. Community service is required.

Special Academic Programs Advanced Placement exam preparation; study at local college for college credit; academic accommodation for the gifted, the musically

talented, and the artistically talented; remedial reading and/or remedial writing; remedial math; special instructional classes for blind students.

College Admission Counseling 326 students graduated in 2015; 323 went to college, including Creighton University; Iowa State University of Science and Technology; Loras College; The University of Iowa; University of Northern Iowa. Median SAT critical reading: 629, median SAT math: 648, median SAT writing: 634, median composite ACT: 24.

Student Life Upper grades have uniform requirement, student council, honor system. Discipline rests primarily with faculty. Attendance at religious services is required.

Summer Programs Enrichment, advancement, sports, art/fine arts, computer instruction programs offered; session focuses on advancement for the purpose of freeing up a slot in the schedule to take an elective; held on campus; accepts boys and girls; not open to students from other schools. 500 students usually enrolled. 2016 schedule: June 1 to June 30.

Tuition and Aid Day student tuition: $7256. Tuition installment plan (monthly payment plans, individually arranged payment plans). Need-based scholarship grants available. In 2015–16, 40% of upper-school students received aid. Total amount of financial aid awarded in 2015–16: $1,000,000.

Admissions Traditional secondary-level entrance grade is 9. High School Placement Test required. Deadline for receipt of application materials: none. Application fee required: $95.

Athletics Interscholastic: aerobics/dance (girls), aquatics (b,g), baseball (b), basketball (b,g), bowling (b,g), cheering (g), cross-country running (b,g), dance (g), dance team (g), diving (g), drill team (g), football (b), golf (b,g), soccer (b,g), softball (g), swimming and diving (b,g), tennis (b,g), track and field (b,g), volleyball (g), wrestling (b); coed interscholastic: cheering, running; coed intramural: ultimate Frisbee.

Computers Computers are regularly used in keyboarding classes. Computer network features include on-campus library services, Internet access, wireless campus network, Internet filtering or blocking technology. Computer access in designated common areas is available to students. Students grades are available online.

Contact Mrs. Tatia Eischeid, Admissions Director. 515-222-1025. Fax: 515-222-1056. E-mail: teischei@dowlingcatholic.org. Website: www.dowlingcatholic.org

DUBLIN CHRISTIAN ACADEMY

106 Page Road
Dublin, New Hampshire 03444

Head of School: Mr. Eric J. Moody

General Information Coeducational boarding and day college-preparatory, arts, business, and religious studies school, affiliated with Christian faith, Christian faith. Boarding grades 7–12, day grades K–12. Founded: 1964. Setting: rural. Nearest major city is Boston, MA. Students are housed in single-sex dormitories. 200-acre campus. 5 buildings on campus. Approved or accredited by American Association of Christian Schools and New Hampshire Department of Education. Total enrollment: 98. Upper school average class size: 15. Upper school faculty-student ratio: 1:9. There are 170 required school days per year for Upper School students. Upper School students typically attend 5 days per week. The average school day consists of 7 hours.

Upper School Student Profile Grade 7: 3 students (1 boy, 2 girls); Grade 8: 8 students (5 boys, 3 girls); Grade 9: 5 students (1 boy, 4 girls); Grade 10: 13 students (8 boys, 5 girls); Grade 11: 5 students (1 boy, 4 girls); Grade 12: 12 students (8 boys, 4 girls). 5% of students are boarding students. 50% are state residents. 2 states are represented in upper school student body. 80% of students are Christian faith, Christian.

Faculty School total: 17. In upper school: 5 men, 6 women; 7 have advanced degrees; 14 reside on campus.

Subjects Offered Accounting, algebra, art, Bible studies, biology, business, calculus, calculus-AP, ceramics, chemistry, chorus, computer literacy, consumer mathematics, economics, English, geometry, history, home economics, instrumental music, law, mathematics, music, physics, piano, religion, science, social studies, Spanish, speech, studio art, study skills, U.S. history, voice, word processing, world history.

Graduation Requirements English, foreign language, mathematics, religion (includes Bible studies and theology), science, social studies (includes history), speech.

Special Academic Programs International Baccalaureate program; Advanced Placement exam preparation; independent study; academic accommodation for the musically talented and the artistically talented; remedial reading and/or remedial writing; remedial math.

College Admission Counseling 14 students graduated in 2015; all went to college, including Bob Jones University; Clearwater Christian College; Grove City College; Liberty University; The Master's College and Seminary. Mean SAT critical reading: 620, mean SAT math: 560, mean SAT writing: 510, mean composite ACT: 23.

Student Life Upper grades have uniform requirement, student council, honor system. Discipline rests primarily with faculty. Attendance at religious services is required.

Tuition and Aid Day student tuition: $7025; 7-day tuition and room/board: $13,675. Tuition installment plan (FACTS Tuition Payment Plan). Need-based scholarship grants available. In 2015–16, 20% of upper-school students received aid. Total amount of financial aid awarded in 2015–16: $150,000.

Admissions Traditional secondary-level entrance grade is 9. For fall 2015, 15 students applied for upper-level admission, 15 were accepted, 8 enrolled. SLEP for foreign students, Stanford Diagnostic Test, TOEFL Junior or TOEFL or SLEP required.

Deadline for receipt of application materials: July 31. Application fee required: $35. Interview required.

Athletics Interscholastic: basketball (boys, girls), soccer (b), volleyball (g); coed intramural: alpine skiing, ice skating, snowboarding. 1 PE instructor, 2 coaches.

Computers Computers are regularly used in accounting, business, English, foreign language, history, mathematics, music, science classes. Computer network features include on-campus library services, Internet access, Internet filtering or blocking technology. Students grades are available online.

Contact Miss JoAnna Guilliams, Assistant to Head of School. 603-563-8505 Ext. 15. Fax: 603-563-8008. E-mail: jguilliams@dublinchristian.org. Website: www.dublinchristian.org

DUBLIN SCHOOL

Box 522
18 Lehmann Way
Dublin, New Hampshire 03444-0522

Head of School: Bradford D. Bates

General Information Coeducational boarding and day college-preparatory, arts, and technology school; primarily serves students with learning disabilities, individuals with Attention Deficit Disorder, and dyslexic students. Grades 9–12. Founded: 1935. Setting: rural. Nearest major city is Boston, MA. Students are housed in single-sex dormitories. 400-acre campus. 22 buildings on campus. Approved or accredited by Independent Schools of Northern New England, New England Association of Schools and Colleges, and The Association of Boarding Schools. Member of National Association of Independent Schools and Secondary School Admission Test Board. Endowment: $2.2 million. Total enrollment: 152. Upper school average class size: 10. Upper school faculty-student ratio: 1:5. Upper School students typically attend 5 days per week. The average school day consists of 5 hours.

Upper School Student Profile 80% of students are boarding students. 30% are state residents. 19 states are represented in upper school student body. 15% are international students. International students from Bahamas, China, Finland, Mexico, Republic of Korea, and Spain; 3 other countries represented in student body.

Faculty School total: 42. In upper school: 15 men, 20 women; 35 have advanced degrees; 33 reside on campus.

Subjects Offered Acting, advanced biology, advanced math, algebra, American foreign policy, American literature, anatomy and physiology, ancient world history, art, arts, biology, biology-AP, calculus, calculus-AP, carpentry, ceramics, chemistry, choir, chorus, college counseling, college placement, community service, computer education, computer literacy, computer programming, costumes and make-up, creative arts, creative dance, creative drama, cultural arts, dance performance, digital music, drama, drama performance, dramatic arts, drawing and design, electronic music, English, English composition, English literature, ESL, European civilization, European history, film history, fine arts, foreign policy, French, geology, geometry, guitar, honors U.S. history, instrumental music, Latin, library research, library skills, literature, marine biology, mathematics, modern dance, modern European history, music, music composition, music performance, music technology, music theory, musical productions, musical theater, musical theater dance, painting, personal and social education, personal development, philosophy, photography, physics, poetry, pre-calculus, psychology, research, science, senior project, Shakespeare, social studies, Spanish, stagecraft, statistics, student government, studio art, study skills, theater, theater arts, U.S. government and politics, U.S. history, U.S. history-AP, video film production, vocal ensemble, voice, voice ensemble, Web site design, weight training, white-water trips, wilderness experience, women's studies, woodworking, world literature, writing, writing workshop, yearbook.

Graduation Requirements Art, computer skills, English, general science, history, languages, mathematics, senior presentation, graduation requirements for honors diploma different.

Special Academic Programs 10 Advanced Placement exams for which test preparation is offered; honors section; independent study; term-away projects; study at local college for college credit; academic accommodation for the gifted; programs in general development for dyslexic students; ESL (10 students enrolled).

College Admission Counseling 35 students graduated in 2015; all went to college, including Berklee College of Music; Boston University; Hamilton College; Hobart and William Smith Colleges; Johns Hopkins University; St. Lawrence University. Median SAT critical reading: 480, median SAT math: 605, median SAT writing: 525, median combined SAT: 1610, median composite ACT: 24.

Student Life Upper grades have specified standards of dress, student council, honor system. Discipline rests equally with students and faculty.

Tuition and Aid Day student tuition: $31,000; 7-day tuition and room/board: $54,000. Tuition installment plan (monthly payment plans). Need-based scholarship grants, loans and payment plans are through a third party available. In 2015–16, 32% of upper-school students received aid. Total amount of financial aid awarded in 2015–16: $1,490,000.

Admissions Traditional secondary-level entrance grade is 9. For fall 2015, 143 students applied for upper-level admission, 97 were accepted, 48 enrolled. SSAT, SSAT, ERB, PSAT, SAT, PLAN or ACT or TOEFL or SLEP required. Deadline for receipt of application materials: January 31. Application fee required: $50. Interview required.

Athletics Interscholastic: basketball (boys, girls), crew (b,g), cross-country running (b,g), lacrosse (b,g), mountain biking (b), nordic skiing (b,g), rowing (b,g), running (b,g), sailing (b,g), skiing (cross-country) (b,g), skiing (downhill) (b,g), snowboarding (b,g), soccer (b,g), tennis (b,g); coed interscholastic: aerobics/dance, alpine skiing, ballet, crew, cross-country running, dance, dance team, equestrian sports, golf, modern dance, mountain biking, nordic skiing, rowing, running, sailing, skiing (cross-country), skiing (downhill), snowboarding; coed intramural: aerobics/dance, alpine skiing, archery, backpacking, badminton, basketball, biathlon, bicycling, billiards, bowling, canoeing/kayaking, climbing, cooperative games, equestrian sports, fencing, fishing, fitness, flag football, flagball, fly fishing, freestyle skiing, Frisbee, golf, hiking/backpacking, horseback riding, ice hockey, indoor soccer, kayaking, martial arts, outdoor activities, outdoor adventure, outdoor education, outdoor recreation, paddle tennis, physical fitness, physical training, rafting, rock climbing, ropes courses, rowing, sailing, skateboarding, skiing (cross-country), skiing (downhill), snowshoeing, softball, strength & conditioning, table tennis, telemark skiing, tennis, ultimate Frisbee, volleyball, wall climbing, weight lifting, weight training, whiffle ball, wrestling, yoga. 20 coaches, 1 athletic trainer.

Computers Computers are regularly used in all academic classes. Computer network features include on-campus library services, online commercial services, Internet access, wireless campus network, Internet filtering or blocking technology. Campus intranet, student e-mail accounts, and computer access in designated common areas are available to students. Students grades are available online. The school has a published electronic and media policy.

Contact Jill Hutchins, Director of Admission and Financial Aid. 603-563-1233. Fax: 603-563-8671. E-mail: admission@dublinschool.org. Website: www.dublinschool.org/

DURHAM ACADEMY

3601 Ridge Road
Durham, North Carolina 27705

Head of School: Mr. Michael Ulku-Steiner

General Information Coeducational day college-preparatory, arts, and technology school. Grades PK–12. Founded: 1933. Setting: suburban. 75-acre campus. 10 buildings on campus. Approved or accredited by Southern Association of Colleges and Schools, Southern Association of Independent Schools, and North Carolina Department of Education. Member of National Association of Independent Schools and Secondary School Admission Test Board. Endowment: $10.5 million. Total enrollment: 1,183. Upper school average class size: 15. Upper school faculty-student ratio: 1:8. There are 179 required school days per year for Upper School students. Upper School students typically attend 5 days per week. The average school day consists of 6 hours.

Upper School Student Profile Grade 9: 110 students (59 boys, 51 girls); Grade 10: 107 students (58 boys, 49 girls); Grade 11: 102 students (50 boys, 52 girls); Grade 12: 100 students (48 boys, 52 girls).

Faculty School total: 196. In upper school: 26 men, 30 women; 47 have advanced degrees.

Subjects Offered 3-dimensional art, accounting, acting, advanced biology, advanced chemistry, advanced computer applications, advanced math, Advanced Placement courses, advanced studio art-AP, algebra, American history, American literature, art, art history, art history-AP, astronomy, biology, calculus, ceramics, chemistry, chemistry-AP, Chinese, Chinese studies, chorus, community service, computer graphics, computer programming, computer science, computer science-AP, concert band, creative writing, dance, drama, ecology, economics, engineering, English, English language and composition-AP, English literature, English literature and composition-AP, environmental science, environmental science-AP, fine arts, finite math, forensics, French, French language-AP, French-AP, geometry, German, history, Latin, literature and composition-AP, mathematics, mathematics-AP, modern European history-AP, music, outdoor education, physical education, physics, psychology, robotics, science, social studies, Spanish, statistics, studio art-AP, theater, U.S. government and politics-AP, U.S. history-AP.

Graduation Requirements Arts and fine arts (art, music, dance, drama), computer science, English, foreign language, mathematics, outdoor education, physical education (includes health), science, senior project, social studies (includes history), community service hours required for graduation, senior project required for graduation.

Special Academic Programs Advanced Placement exam preparation; honors section; independent study; special instructional classes for students with learning disabilities and Attention Deficit Disorder.

College Admission Counseling 103 students graduated in 2015; 101 went to college, including Duke University; Elon University; Furman University; North Carolina State University; Stanford University; The University of North Carolina at Chapel Hill. Other: 2 had other specific plans. Mean SAT critical reading: 655, mean SAT math: 660, mean SAT writing: 656.

Student Life Upper grades have specified standards of dress, student council, honor system. Discipline rests equally with students and faculty.

Summer Programs Remediation, enrichment, sports, art/fine arts, computer instruction programs offered; session focuses on academic enrichment, non-academic activities; held on campus; accepts boys and girls; open to students from other schools. 847 students usually enrolled. 2016 schedule: June 9 to July 25. Application deadline: none.

Tuition and Aid Day student tuition: $23,205. Tuition installment plan (FACTS Tuition Payment Plan). Need-based scholarship grants available. In 2015–16, 14% of upper-school students received aid. Total amount of financial aid awarded in 2015–16: $1,442,738.

Admissions Traditional secondary-level entrance grade is 9. For fall 2015, 99 students applied for upper-level admission, 51 were accepted, 32 enrolled. ISEE required. Deadline for receipt of application materials: January 8. Application fee required: $55. Interview required.

Athletics Interscholastic: aquatics (boys, girls), baseball (b), basketball (b,g), cross-country running (b,g), dance team (g), field hockey (g), golf (b,g), lacrosse (b,g), soccer (b,g), softball (g), swimming and diving (b,g), tennis (b,g), track and field (b,g), volleyball (g), weight training (b,g); coed interscholastic: outdoor adventure, outdoor education, ultimate Frisbee, weight training; coed intramural: indoor soccer, judo, martial arts, modern dance, physical fitness, physical training, winter soccer. 1 PE instructor, 3 coaches, 2 athletic trainers.

Computers Computers are regularly used in all academic, animation, computer applications, graphic arts, graphic design, introduction to technology, video film production, Web site design classes. Computer network features include on-campus library services, online commercial services, Internet access, wireless campus network, Internet filtering or blocking technology. Student e-mail accounts and computer access in designated common areas are available to students. Students grades are available online. The school has a published electronic and media policy.

Contact Ms. S. Victoria Muradi, Director of Admission and Financial Aid. 919-493-5787. Fax: 919-489-4893. E-mail: admissions@da.org. Website: www.da.org

THE DWIGHT SCHOOL

291 Central Park West
New York, New York 10024

Head of School: Mrs. Dianne Drew

General Information Coeducational day college-preparatory, arts, business, bilingual studies, and technology school. Grades PK–12. Founded: 1880. Setting: urban. 3 buildings on campus. Approved or accredited by International Baccalaureate Organization, Middle States Association of Colleges and Schools, and New York Department of Education. Member of National Association of Independent Schools, Secondary School Admission Test Board, and European Council of International Schools. Upper school average class size: 15. Upper school faculty-student ratio: 1:6.

Faculty School total: 93. In upper school: 24 men, 26 women; 32 have advanced degrees.

Subjects Offered Algebra, American history, American literature, art, art history, biology, calculus, chemistry, community service, computer math, computer science, creative writing, dance, drama, economics, English, English literature, environmental science, ethics, European history, expository writing, film, fine arts, French, geometry, government/civics, grammar, health, history, Italian, Japanese, journalism, Latin, mathematics, music, philosophy, photography, physical education, physics, physiology, psychology, science, social studies, Spanish, technology/design, theater, theory of knowledge, trigonometry, typing, world history, world literature, writing.

Graduation Requirements Arts and fine arts (art, music, dance, drama), computer science, English, foreign language, mathematics, physical education (includes health), science, social studies (includes history). Community service is required.

Special Academic Programs International Baccalaureate program; Advanced Placement exam preparation; honors section; independent study; term-away projects; study abroad; academic accommodation for the gifted, the musically talented, and the artistically talented; remedial reading and/or remedial writing; remedial math; programs in English for dyslexic students; special instructional classes for students with learning disabilities; ESL (15 students enrolled).

College Admission Counseling 65 students graduated in 2015; 61 went to college, including Brown University; Dartmouth College; New York University; Northwestern University; The George Washington University; Trinity College. Other: 4 went to work.

Student Life Upper grades have specified standards of dress, student council, honor system. Discipline rests equally with students and faculty.

Summer Programs Remediation, enrichment, ESL programs offered; held on campus; accepts boys and girls; not open to students from other schools.

Tuition and Aid Day student tuition: $43,675. Tuition installment plan (The Tuition Plan, Insured Tuition Payment Plan, monthly payment plans, individually arranged payment plans). Need-based scholarship grants, prepGATE loans available. In 2014–15, 20% of upper-school students received aid.

Admissions Traditional secondary-level entrance grade is 9. ERB or ISEE required. Deadline for receipt of application materials: none. Application fee required: $65. On-campus interview required.

Athletics Interscholastic: baseball (boys), basketball (b,g), cross-country running (b,g), dance (g), fencing (b,g); intramural: basketball (b,g), boxing (b,g), fencing (b,g); coed interscholastic: aquatics, fencing, golf, running, swimming and diving, tennis; coed intramural: aerobics/dance, boxing, dance squad, dance team, fencing, fitness, skateboarding, weight lifting, weight training, yoga.

Computers Computers are regularly used in foreign language, mathematics, music, science classes. Computer network features include on-campus library services, online commercial services, Internet access, wireless campus network, Internet filtering or blocking technology. Students grades are available online.

Contact Ellana Mandell, Admissions Associate. 212-724-6360 Ext. 201. Fax: 212-724-2539. E-mail: admissions@dwight.edu. Website: www.dwight.edu

EAGLEBROOK SCHOOL

Deerfield, Massachusetts
See Junior Boarding Schools section.

EAGLE HILL SCHOOL

Greenwich, Connecticut
See Special Needs Schools section.

EASTERN MENNONITE HIGH SCHOOL

801 Parkwood Drive
Harrisonburg, Virginia 22802

Head of School: Mr. Paul G. Leaman

General Information Coeducational day college-preparatory, general academic, arts, religious studies, and technology school, affiliated with Mennonite Church. Grades K–12. Founded: 1917. Setting: small town. Nearest major city is Washington, DC. 24-acre campus. 1 building on campus. Approved or accredited by Mennonite Education Agency, Southern Association of Colleges and Schools, Virginia Association of Independent Schools, and Virginia Department of Education. Member of National Association of Independent Schools. Endowment: $3 million. Total enrollment: 379. Upper school average class size: 15. Upper school faculty-student ratio: 1:12. There are 180 required school days per year for Upper School students. Upper School students typically attend 5 days per week. The average school day consists of 7 hours.

Upper School Student Profile Grade 6: 30 students (15 boys, 15 girls); Grade 7: 36 students (20 boys, 16 girls); Grade 8: 40 students (22 boys, 18 girls); Grade 9: 34 students (20 boys, 14 girls); Grade 10: 42 students (23 boys, 19 girls); Grade 11: 43 students (23 boys, 20 girls); Grade 12: 57 students (32 boys, 25 girls). 60% of students are Mennonite.

Faculty School total: 40. In upper school: 14 men, 17 women; 24 have advanced degrees.

Subjects Offered Acting, advanced math, algebra, American government, American history, American literature, analysis, applied music, art, art history, band, bell choir, Bible studies, biology, British literature, British literature (honors), business, business skills, ceramics, chemistry, choir, choral music, chorus, Christian and Hebrew scripture, Christian doctrine, Christian ethics, Christian studies, Christian testament, Christianity, church history, community service, computer education, computer science, concert choir, consumer mathematics, creative writing, desktop publishing, drama, drawing, driver education, earth science, economics, engineering, English, English composition, English literature, family and consumer science, fiction, fine arts, food and nutrition, food science, French, general science, geography, geometry, government, grammar, guitar, handbells, health, health education, history, home economics, honors English, human development, industrial arts, industrial technology, instrumental music, interior design, keyboarding, Latin, mathematics, mechanical drawing, music, music composition, music theory, novels, oil painting, orchestra, outdoor education, painting, photography, physical education, physical science, physics, poetry, pottery, pre-algebra, religion, religious education, research skills, science, sculpture, sewing, shop, social sciences, social studies, sociology, Spanish, speech, speech communications, stained glass, study skills, theater, typing, U.S. government, U.S. history, vocal music, voice, water color painting, woodworking, world cultures, world history, writing.

Graduation Requirements Arts and fine arts (art, music, dance, drama), electives, English, foreign language, history, home economics, keyboarding, mathematics, physical education (includes health), religion (includes Bible studies and theology), science, social studies (includes history), technical arts, experiential learning credit annually.

Special Academic Programs 5 Advanced Placement exams for which test preparation is offered; honors section; independent study; term-away projects; study at local college for college credit; study abroad; academic accommodation for the gifted; remedial reading and/or remedial writing; remedial math; ESL (6 students enrolled).

College Admission Counseling 58 students graduated in 2015; 54 went to college, including Eastern Mennonite University; James Madison University; The College of William and Mary; The College of Wooster; University of Richmond; Virginia Polytechnic Institute and State University. Other: 4 went to work. Median SAT critical reading: 585, median SAT math: 606, median SAT writing: 567, median combined SAT: 1758. 47% scored over 600 on SAT critical reading, 43% scored over 600 on SAT math, 46% scored over 600 on SAT writing, 60% scored over 1800 on combined SAT.

Student Life Upper grades have specified standards of dress, student council, honor system. Discipline rests primarily with faculty. Attendance at religious services is required.

Tuition and Aid Day student tuition: $6695–$13,895. Tuition installment plan (monthly payment plans, individually arranged payment plans). Need-based scholarship grants, paying campus jobs, VDOE Education Improvement Scholarship available. In

2015–16, 70% of upper-school students received aid. Total amount of financial aid awarded in 2015–16: $200,000.

Admissions Traditional secondary-level entrance grade is 9. For fall 2015, 42 students applied for upper-level admission, 37 were accepted, 32 enrolled. Any standardized test required. Deadline for receipt of application materials: none. Application fee required: $50. Interview recommended.

Athletics Interscholastic: baseball (boys), basketball (b,g), cheering (g), cross-country running (b,g), soccer (b,g), softball (g), tennis (b,g), track and field (b,g), volleyball (g); intramural: baseball (b), basketball (b,g), soccer (g), wrestling (b); coed interscholastic: baseball, cross-country running, golf; coed intramural: Frisbee, table tennis, ultimate Frisbee, volleyball. 3 PE instructors, 9 coaches, 2 athletic trainers.

Computers Computers are regularly used in Bible studies, business skills, Christian doctrine, college planning, computer applications, construction, creative writing, current events, design, desktop publishing, digital applications, economics, English, foreign language, graphic arts, graphic design, history, independent study, industrial technology, information technology, introduction to technology, keyboarding, library, literary magazine, mathematics, media arts, music, photography, psychology, publications, publishing, religious studies, research skills, science, social sciences, social studies, Spanish, speech, study skills, technology, Web site design, word processing, writing, yearbook classes. Computer resources include on-campus library services, online commercial services, Internet access, wireless campus network, Internet filtering or blocking technology. Campus intranet, student e-mail accounts, and computer access in designated common areas are available to students. Students grades are available online. The school has a published electronic and media policy.

Contact Mrs. Marsha Thomas, Admissions Counselor. 540-236-6021. Fax: 540-236-6028. E-mail: thomasm@emhs.net. Website: www.emhs.net

EASTSIDE CATHOLIC SCHOOL

232 228th Avenue SE
Sammamish, Washington 98074

Head of School: Tom Lord

General Information Coeducational day college-preparatory, arts, business, religious studies, and technology school, affiliated with Roman Catholic Church. Grades 6–12. Founded: 1980. Setting: suburban. 50-acre campus. 2 buildings on campus. Approved or accredited by National Catholic Education Association, Northwest Association of Independent Schools, and Washington Department of Education. Upper school average class size: 20. Upper school faculty-student ratio: 1:13. There are 180 required school days per year for Upper School students. Upper School students typically attend 5 days per week. The average school day consists of 7 hours.

Upper School Student Profile 60% of students are Roman Catholic.

Faculty School total: 65. In upper school: 22 men, 30 women; 38 have advanced degrees.

Subjects Offered 3-dimensional art, acting, Advanced Placement courses, algebra, American government, American history, American literature, anatomy and physiology, art, ASB Leadership, athletic training, band, biology, biology-AP, British literature, calculus, calculus-AP, campus ministry, Catholic belief and practice, ceramics, chemistry, chemistry-AP, choir, church history, community service, computers, contemporary issues, creative writing, debate, digital photography, drama, drawing, economics, English, English literature, environmental science-AP, French, French-AP, geometry, government and politics-AP, graphic design, health, history, honors algebra, honors English, honors geometry, honors U.S. history, honors world history, journalism, law, literature and composition-AP, Mandarin, math analysis, music, music theory-AP, painting, performing arts, physical education, physics, physics-AP, religious education, social justice, Spanish, Spanish-AP, speech and debate, statistics-AP, studio art, studio art-AP, theology, trigonometry, U.S. government and politics-AP, U.S. history, U.S. history-AP, Web site design, world history, world history-AP, yearbook, yoga.

Graduation Requirements Arts and fine arts (art, music, dance, drama), business education, English, foreign language, health, history, information technology, lab science, mathematics, physical education (includes health), science, social sciences, theology, 100 hours of community service (over 4 years).

Special Academic Programs Advanced Placement exam preparation; honors section; study at local college for college credit; academic accommodation for the gifted; programs in English, mathematics, general development for dyslexic students.

College Admission Counseling 144 students graduated in 2014; 142 went to college, including Gonzaga University; Santa Clara University; University of Colorado Boulder; University of Portland; University of Washington; Washington State University. Other: 1 entered a postgraduate year, 1 had other specific plans.

Student Life Upper grades have specified standards of dress, student council, honor system. Discipline rests primarily with faculty. Attendance at religious services is required.

Tuition and Aid Day student tuition: $17,260. Tuition installment plan (monthly payment plans). Tuition reduction for siblings, merit scholarship grants, need-based scholarship grants available.

Admissions Traditional secondary-level entrance grade is 9. ISEE required. Deadline for receipt of application materials: January 12. Application fee required: $25. Interview recommended.

Athletics Interscholastic: baseball (boys), basketball (b,g), cheering (g), cross-country running (b,g), drill team (g), football (b), golf (b,g), lacrosse (b,g), soccer (b,g), softball (g), swimming and diving (b,g), tennis (b,g), track and field (b,g), volleyball (g), wrestling (b); coed interscholastic: Special Olympics; coed intramural: strength & conditioning, weight lifting, weight training. 2 PE instructors, 43 coaches, 1 athletic trainer.

Computers Computers are regularly used in business education, digital applications, graphic design, newspaper, technology, yearbook classes. Computer network features include on-campus library services, online commercial services, Internet access, wireless campus network, Internet filtering or blocking technology. Students grades are available online.

Contact Lori Maughan, Associate Director of Admissions. 425-295-3017. Fax: 425-392-5160. E-mail: lmaughan@eastsidecatholic.org. Website: www.eastsidecatholic.org

EATON ACADEMY

1000 Old Roswell Lakes Parkway
Roswell, Georgia 30076

Head of School: Ms. Bridgit Eaton-Partalis

General Information Coeducational day and distance learning college-preparatory school. Grades K–12. Distance learning grades 5–12. Founded: 1995. Setting: suburban. Nearest major city is Atlanta. 12-acre campus. 1 building on campus. Approved or accredited by Southern Association of Colleges and Schools, Southern Association of Independent Schools, and Georgia Department of Education. Total enrollment: 80. Upper school average class size: 5. Upper school faculty-student ratio: 1:5. There are 180 required school days per year for Upper School students. Upper School students typically attend 5 days per week. The average school day consists of 6 hours and 45 minutes.

Upper School Student Profile Grade 9: 8 students (6 boys, 2 girls); Grade 10: 8 students (6 boys, 2 girls); Grade 11: 8 students (6 boys, 2 girls); Grade 12: 8 students (6 boys, 2 girls).

Faculty School total: 35. In upper school: 3 men, 6 women; 6 have advanced degrees.

Subjects Offered All academic.

Special Academic Programs Honors section; accelerated programs; independent study; academic accommodation for the gifted, the musically talented, and the artistically talented; remedial reading and/or remedial writing; remedial math; special instructional classes for deaf students.

College Admission Counseling 22 students graduated in 2015; all went to college, including Georgia College & State University; Georgia Institute of Technology; Georgia Perimeter College; Georgia Southern University; Kennesaw State University; University of Georgia.

Student Life Upper grades have specified standards of dress. Discipline rests primarily with faculty.

Summer Programs Remediation, enrichment, advancement, ESL, sports, art/fine arts, computer instruction programs offered; session focuses on academic acceleration and remediation; held both on and off campus; held at local sports facilities; accepts boys and girls; open to students from other schools. 35 students usually enrolled. 2016 schedule: June 3 to July 26. Application deadline: none.

Tuition and Aid Day student tuition: $20,500.

Admissions For fall 2015, 50 students applied for upper-level admission, 25 were accepted, 20 enrolled. Deadline for receipt of application materials: none. Application fee required: $250. Interview required.

Athletics Coed Intramural: aquatics, artistic gym, basketball, bowling, canoeing/kayaking, crew, cross-country running, equestrian sports, field hockey, fitness walking, flag football, floor hockey, Frisbee, golf, gymnastics, hockey, horseback riding, ice hockey, ice skating, jogging, kayaking, martial arts, modern dance, outdoor activities, physical fitness, racquetball, rock climbing, ropes courses, running, scuba diving, strength & conditioning, tennis, volleyball, weight training. 3 PE instructors.

Computers Computers are regularly used in all academic classes. Computer network features include Internet access, wireless campus network, Internet filtering or blocking technology. Student e-mail accounts are available to students. Students grades are available online. The school has a published electronic and media policy.

Contact Ms. Margie Cohan, Admissions Director. 770-645-2673 Ext. 242. Fax: 770-645-2711. E-mail: mcohan@eatonacademy.org. Website: www.eatonacademy.org

EDGEWOOD ACADEMY

5475 Elmore Road
PO Box 160
Elmore, Alabama 36025

Head of School: Mr. Clint Welch

General Information Coeducational day college-preparatory, arts, business, religious studies, bilingual studies, and technology school. Grades PK–12. Founded: 1967. Setting: small town. Nearest major city is Montgomery. 30-acre campus. 4 buildings on campus. Approved or accredited by CITA (Commission on International and Trans-Regional Accreditation), National Council for Private School Accreditation, Southern Association of Colleges and Schools, and Alabama Department of Education. Total enrollment: 320. Upper school average class size: 18. Upper school faculty-student ratio: 1:11. There are 177 required school days per year for Upper School students. Upper School students typically attend 5 days per week. The average school day consists of 5 hours and 45 minutes.

Upper School Student Profile Grade 9: 30 students (16 boys, 14 girls); Grade 10: 26 students (19 boys, 7 girls); Grade 11: 23 students (14 boys, 9 girls); Grade 12: 42 students (24 boys, 18 girls).

Faculty School total: 24. In upper school: 4 men, 7 women; 7 have advanced degrees.

Graduation Requirements Advanced diploma requires 100 hours of community service, standard diplomas requires 50 hours of community service.

Special Academic Programs Advanced Placement exam preparation; study at local college for college credit.

College Admission Counseling 34 students graduated in 2014; they went to Auburn University; Auburn University at Montgomery; The University of Alabama. Median composite ACT: 25.

Student Life Upper grades have specified standards of dress, student council.

Tuition and Aid Day student tuition: $6500. Tuition installment plan (SMART Tuition Payment Plan). Tuition reduction for siblings available.

Admissions Admissions testing required. Deadline for receipt of application materials: none. No application fee required. Interview required.

Athletics Interscholastic: baseball (boys), basketball (b,g), cheering (g), football (b), physical fitness (b,g), physical training (b,g), softball (g), volleyball (g), weight lifting (b), weight training (b,g); coed interscholastic: fishing, golf, track and field. 2 PE instructors, 4 coaches.

Computers Computers are regularly used in lab/keyboard, yearbook classes. Computer network features include on-campus library services, Internet access, wireless campus network, Internet filtering or blocking technology, SmartBoard Technology. Campus intranet and student e-mail accounts are available to students. Students grades are available online. The school has a published electronic and media policy.

Contact Carole Angus, Office Manager. 334-567-5102 Ext. 201. Fax: 334-567-8316. E-mail: cangus@edgewoodacademy.org. Website: www.edgewoodacademy.org/

EDISON SCHOOL

Box 2, Site 11, RR2
Okotoks, Alberta T1S 1A2, Canada

Head of School: Mrs. Beth Chernoff

General Information Coeducational day college-preparatory and general academic school. Grades K–12. Founded: 1993. Setting: small town. Nearest major city is Calgary, Canada. 10-acre campus. 3 buildings on campus. Approved or accredited by Association of Independent Schools and Colleges of Alberta and Alberta Department of Education. Language of instruction: English. Total enrollment: 236. Upper school average class size: 12. Upper school faculty-student ratio: 1:12. There are 185 required school days per year for Upper School students. Upper School students typically attend 5 days per week. The average school day consists of 6 hours and 15 minutes.

Upper School Student Profile Grade 9: 20 students (10 boys, 10 girls); Grade 10: 12 students (6 boys, 6 girls); Grade 11: 12 students (6 boys, 6 girls); Grade 12: 12 students (6 boys, 6 girls).

Faculty School total: 22. In upper school: 3 men, 3 women; 4 have advanced degrees.

Subjects Offered Advanced Placement courses, art, biology, chemistry, English, French, mathematics, physical education, physics, science, social studies, Spanish, standard curriculum.

Graduation Requirements Alberta Learning requirements.

Special Academic Programs 11 Advanced Placement exams for which test preparation is offered; accelerated programs; independent study; study at local college for college credit; academic accommodation for the gifted.

College Admission Counseling 10 students graduated in 2015; 9 went to college, including Queen's University at Kingston; The University of British Columbia; University of Alberta; University of Calgary; University of Waterloo. Other: 1 went to work. Median composite ACT: 26. 58% scored over 26 on composite ACT.

Student Life Upper grades have uniform requirement, student council, honor system. Discipline rests primarily with faculty.

Tuition and Aid Day student tuition: CAN$7000. Tuition installment plan (monthly payment plans). Tuition reduction for siblings available.

Admissions Traditional secondary-level entrance grade is 9. For fall 2015, 20 students applied for upper-level admission, 4 were accepted, 4 enrolled. Achievement tests or admissions testing required. Deadline for receipt of application materials: none. No application fee required. On-campus interview required.

Athletics Interscholastic: badminton (boys, girls), basketball (b,g), cross-country running (b,g); intramural: badminton (b,g), basketball (b,g), cross-country running (b,g); coed interscholastic: badminton, flag football; coed intramural: badminton, flag football, outdoor education. 1 PE instructor, 1 coach.

Computers Computers are regularly used in all classes. Computer resources include Internet access, wireless campus network. Computer access in designated common areas is available to students. Students grades are available online.

Contact Mrs. Beth Chernoff, Headmistress. 403-938-7670. Fax: 403-938-7224 Ext. 200. E-mail: office@edisonschool.ca. Website: www.edisonschool.ca

EDMONTON ACADEMY

Edmonton, Alberta, Canada
See Special Needs Schools section.

EDMUND BURKE SCHOOL

4101 Connecticut Avenue NW
Washington, District of Columbia 20008

Head of School: Damian Jones

General Information Coeducational day college-preparatory and arts school. Grades 6–12. Founded: 1968. Setting: urban. 2 buildings on campus. Approved or accredited by Association of Independent Maryland Schools, Association of Independent Schools of Greater Washington, Middle States Association of Colleges and Schools, and District of Columbia Department of Education. Member of National Association of Independent Schools and Secondary School Admission Test Board. Endowment: $829,556. Total enrollment: 297. Upper school average class size: 12. Upper school faculty-student ratio: 1:6. There are 176 required school days per year for Upper School students. Upper School students typically attend 5 days per week. The average school day consists of 5 hours.

Upper School Student Profile Grade 9: 42 students (19 boys, 23 girls); Grade 10: 52 students (29 boys, 23 girls); Grade 11: 53 students (30 boys, 23 girls); Grade 12: 60 students (29 boys, 31 girls).

Faculty School total: 50. In upper school: 19 men, 19 women; 25 have advanced degrees.

Subjects Offered African-American literature, algebra, American history, American literature, anatomy, anthropology, biology, calculus, ceramics, chemistry, computer science, creative writing, economics, English, English literature, European history, French, geography, geometry, health, history, journalism, Latin, linguistics, music, performing arts, philosophy, photography, physical education, physics, senior seminar, Spanish, theater, trigonometry, values and decisions, visual arts, women's studies, world history, writing.

Graduation Requirements English, foreign language, history, mathematics, physical education (includes health), science, social sciences, values and decisions, visual and performing arts, senior research seminar, senior project. Community service is required.

Special Academic Programs Advanced Placement exam preparation; independent study; term-away projects.

College Admission Counseling 65 students graduated in 2015; all went to college, including New York University; University of New Hampshire; University of Pittsburgh; University of Rhode Island; Wesleyan University. Median SAT critical reading: 651, median SAT math: 641, median SAT writing: 648.

Student Life Upper grades have student council, honor system. Discipline rests primarily with faculty.

Summer Programs Remediation, enrichment, advancement, ESL, art/fine arts, computer instruction programs offered; session focuses on academic programs and visual arts; held on campus; accepts boys and girls; open to students from other schools. 50 students usually enrolled. 2016 schedule: June 20 to August 21. Application deadline: none.

Tuition and Aid Day student tuition: $36,875. Tuition installment plan (The Tuition Plan, Insured Tuition Payment Plan, Academic Management Services Plan, individually arranged payment plans). Need-based scholarship grants available. In 2015–16, 29% of upper-school students received aid. Total amount of financial aid awarded in 2015–16: $978,185.

Admissions Traditional secondary-level entrance grade is 9. For fall 2015, 130 students applied for upper-level admission, 86 were accepted, 45 enrolled. ISEE or SSAT required. Deadline for receipt of application materials: January 4. Application fee required: $60. Interview required.

Athletics Interscholastic: aquatics (boys, girls), baseball (b), basketball (b,g), cross-country running (b,g), golf (b,g), soccer (b,g), softball (g), swimming and diving (g), track and field (b,g), volleyball (b,g), wrestling (b,g); intramural: dance team (b,g), Frisbee (b,g), martial arts (b,g), physical fitness (b,g), weight lifting (b,g); coed interscholastic: swimming and diving; coed intramural: indoor soccer, jogging. 2 PE instructors, 2 coaches.

Computers Computers are regularly used in creative writing, English, foreign language, French, graphic arts, history, journalism, mathematics, science classes. Computer network features include on-campus library services, online commercial services, Internet access. Students grades are available online. The school has a published electronic and media policy.

Contact Admissions Office. 202-362-8882 Ext. 670. Fax: 202-362-1914. E-mail: admissions@burkeschool.org. Website: www.burkeschool.org

ELDORADO EMERSON PRIVATE SCHOOL

4100 East Walnut Street
Orange, California 92869
Head of School: Mr. Sean Kelley

General Information Coeducational day college-preparatory, general academic, and arts school. Grades K–12. Founded: 1958. Setting: suburban. Nearest major city is Los Angeles. 5-acre campus. 8 buildings on campus. Approved or accredited by Western Association of Schools and Colleges and California Department of Education. Total enrollment: 166. Upper school average class size: 20. Upper school faculty-student ratio: 1:18. There are 167 required school days per year for Upper School students. Upper School students typically attend 5 days per week. The average school day consists of 6 hours.

Upper School Student Profile Grade 7: 7 students (3 boys, 4 girls); Grade 8: 7 students (1 boy, 6 girls); Grade 9: 18 students (14 boys, 4 girls); Grade 10: 21 students (16 boys, 5 girls); Grade 11: 36 students (28 boys, 8 girls); Grade 12: 22 students (16 boys, 6 girls).

Faculty School total: 25. In upper school: 7 men, 5 women; 10 have advanced degrees.

Subjects Offered Acting, advanced chemistry, advanced math, advanced TOEFL/grammar, algebra, American government, American history-AP, analysis and differential calculus, anatomy, ancient world history, applied arts, applied music, Arabic, art, art and culture, art appreciation, art education, art history, Basic programming, biology, biology-AP, calculus, calculus-AP, cell biology, ceramics, chemistry, chemistry-AP, Chinese, civil war history, classical civilization, classical Greek literature, classical music, classics, clayworking, computer processing, computer programming, computer skills, concert band, contemporary art, contemporary history, creative drama, creative writing, cultural geography, current events, current history, drama workshop, drawing, earth science, economics and history, Egyptian history, English, English literature, ESL, fine arts, gardening, general math, geography, geometry, grammar, jazz band, keyboarding, library skills, Mandarin, math analysis, physics, physics-AP, pre-algebra, pre-calculus, reading, SAT preparation, science, Shakespeare, Spanish, TOEFL preparation, U.S. government and politics-AP, U.S. history, world history.

Graduation Requirements Art, English, foreign language, mathematics, music, physical education (includes health), science, social studies (includes history). Community service is required.

Special Academic Programs Advanced Placement exam preparation; honors section; accelerated programs; independent study; study at local college for college credit; academic accommodation for the gifted, the musically talented, and the artistically talented; ESL (50 students enrolled).

College Admission Counseling 30 students graduated in 2015; they went to California State University, Fullerton; Chapman University; Johns Hopkins University; Occidental College; Purdue University; University of California, Santa Cruz.

Student Life Upper grades have specified standards of dress, honor system. Discipline rests equally with students and faculty.

Summer Programs Enrichment, sports, art/fine arts programs offered. 2016 schedule: June 21 to July 22. Application deadline: June 1.

Tuition and Aid Day student tuition: $12,150. Tuition installment plan (monthly payment plans, individually arranged payment plans). Tuition reduction for siblings, need-based scholarship grants available. In 2015–16, 10% of upper-school students received aid. Total amount of financial aid awarded in 2015–16: $50,000.

Admissions Achievement tests or any standardized test required. Deadline for receipt of application materials: none. Application fee required: $250. Interview required.

Athletics Interscholastic: basketball (boys, girls), flag football (b), soccer (b), volleyball (g); coed interscholastic: cross-country running, fitness, flag football, physical fitness, physical training, soccer. 1 PE instructor, 3 coaches.

Computers Computers are regularly used in desktop publishing, graphic design, keyboarding, Web site design, word processing, yearbook classes. Computer resources include Internet access, Internet filtering or blocking technology.

Contact Ms. Jackie Fogle, Administration. 714-633-4774. Fax: 714-744-3304. E-mail: jfogle@eldoradoemerson.org. Website: www.eldorado-emerson.org

ELGIN ACADEMY

350 Park Street
Elgin, Illinois 60120
Head of School: Mr. Seth L. Hanford

General Information Coeducational day college-preparatory, arts, and technology school. Grades PS–12. Founded: 1839. Setting: suburban. Nearest major city is Chicago. 20-acre campus. 8 buildings on campus. Approved or accredited by Independent Schools Association of the Central States and Illinois Department of Education. Member of National Association of Independent Schools. Endowment: $8 million. Total enrollment: 323. Upper school average class size: 12. Upper school faculty-student ratio: 1:7. There are 173 required school days per year for Upper School students. Upper School students typically attend 5 days per week. The average school day consists of 6 hours and 30 minutes.

Upper School Student Profile Grade 9: 16 students (7 boys, 9 girls); Grade 10: 33 students (16 boys, 17 girls); Grade 11: 40 students (19 boys, 21 girls); Grade 12: 33 students (15 boys, 18 girls).

Faculty School total: 54. In upper school: 13 men, 11 women; 21 have advanced degrees.

Subjects Offered Algebra, American history, American literature, art, art history, biology, calculus, ceramics, chemistry, computer programming, computer science, creative writing, drama, English, English literature, environmental science, European history, expository writing, fine arts, finite math, French, geometry, government/civics, grammar, history, Latin, Latin-AP, mathematics, music, painting, photography, physical education, psychology, psychology-AP, science, social studies, Spanish, statistics, theater, trigonometry, video film production, world history, world literature, writing.

Graduation Requirements Arts and fine arts (art, music, dance, drama), English, foreign language, mathematics, physical education (includes health), science, social studies (includes history).

Special Academic Programs 16 Advanced Placement exams for which test preparation is offered; honors section; independent study; ESL.

College Admission Counseling 32 students graduated in 2015; all went to college, including Georgia Institute of Technology; Indiana University Bloomington; Marquette University; Northwestern University; University of Illinois at Urbana–Champaign; University of Michigan. Mean SAT critical reading: 591, mean SAT math: 609, mean SAT writing: 578, mean combined SAT: 1778, mean composite ACT: 27.

Student Life Upper grades have specified standards of dress, student council, honor system. Discipline rests primarily with faculty.

Summer Programs Enrichment, sports, art/fine arts programs offered; session focuses on college prep work, academics, athletics, art, music; held both on and off campus; held at Centre of Elgin and Gail Borden Library; accepts boys and girls; open to students from other schools. 140 students usually enrolled. 2016 schedule: June 1 to August 30.

Tuition and Aid Day student tuition: $25,480. Tuition installment plan (FACTS Tuition Payment Plan). Tuition reduction for siblings, merit scholarship grants, need-based scholarship grants available. In 2015–16, 40% of upper-school students received aid; total upper-school merit-scholarship money awarded: $50,000. Total amount of financial aid awarded in 2015–16: $800,000.

Admissions Traditional secondary-level entrance grade is 9. For fall 2015, 34 students applied for upper-level admission, 21 were accepted, 16 enrolled. ISEE and TOEFL required. Deadline for receipt of application materials: none. Application fee required: $50. Interview required.

Athletics Interscholastic: baseball (boys), basketball (b,g), cross-country running (b,g), field hockey (g), soccer (b,g), tennis (b,g), track and field (b,g), volleyball (g); coed interscholastic: cross-country running, golf. 2 PE instructors.

Computers Computers are regularly used in art, English, foreign language, mathematics, science, social studies, video film production classes. Computer network features include on-campus library services, online commercial services, Internet access, wireless campus network, Internet filtering or blocking technology. Campus intranet, student e-mail accounts, and computer access in designated common areas are available to students. Students grades are available online. The school has a published electronic and media policy.

Contact Dr. Diane R. Schael, Interim Director of Admissions. 847-695-0309 Ext. 243. Fax: 847-695-5017. E-mail: dschael@elginacademy.org. Website: www.elginacademy.org

ELIZABETH SETON ACADEMY

2220 Dorchester Avenue
Dorchester Lower Mills, Massachusetts 02124-5607
Head of School: Mr. Michael Christopher Bonina

General Information Girls' day college-preparatory school, affiliated with Roman Catholic Church. Grades 9–12. Founded: 2003. Setting: urban. Nearest major city is Boston. 2 buildings on campus. Approved or accredited by New England Association of Schools and Colleges and Massachusetts Department of Education. Upper school average class size: 25. Upper school faculty-student ratio: 1:10. Upper School students typically attend 5 days per week. The average school day consists of 7 hours.

Upper School Student Profile Grade 9: 23 students (23 girls); Grade 10: 20 students (20 girls); Grade 11: 26 students (26 girls); Grade 12: 29 students (29 girls). 70% of students are Roman Catholic.

Faculty School total: 12. In upper school: 3 men, 7 women; 9 have advanced degrees.

Student Life Upper grades have uniform requirement, student council. Attendance at religious services is required.

Tuition and Aid Day student tuition: $8200. Tuition installment plan (FACTS Tuition Payment Plan). Merit scholarship grants, need-based scholarship grants available. In 2015–16, 70% of upper-school students received aid.

Admissions High School Placement Test (closed version) from Scholastic Testing Service required. Deadline for receipt of application materials: December 31. No application fee required.

Contact Admissions Team. 617-296-1087 Ext. 10. E-mail: admissions@esaboston.com. Website: http://esaboston.com/

ELIZABETH SETON HIGH SCHOOL

5715 Emerson Street
Bladensburg, Maryland 20710-1844
Head of School: Sr. Ellen Marie Hagar

General Information Girls' day college-preparatory, arts, religious studies, bilingual studies, technology, and engineering, law, pharmacy school, affiliated with Roman Catholic Church. Grades 9–12. Founded: 1959. Setting: suburban. Nearest major city is Washington, DC. 24-acre campus. 2 buildings on campus. Approved or accredited by Middle States Association of Colleges and Schools, National Catholic Education Association, and Maryland Department of Education. Total enrollment: 563. Upper school average class size: 16. Upper school faculty-student ratio: 1:11. There are 180 required school days per year for Upper School students. Upper School students typically attend 5 days per week. The average school day consists of 6 hours and 30 minutes.

Upper School Student Profile Grade 9: 144 students (144 girls); Grade 10: 115 students (115 girls); Grade 11: 158 students (158 girls); Grade 12: 146 students (146 girls). 50% of students are Roman Catholic.

Faculty School total: 58. In upper school: 3 men, 45 women; 35 have advanced degrees.

Subjects Offered 3-dimensional design, advanced biology, advanced chemistry, advanced math, advanced studio art-AP, algebra, American history, American history-AP, American legal systems, American literature, American sign language, analytic geometry, anatomy, art, art-AP, band, bioethics, biology, biology-AP, British literature-AP, calculus, calculus-AP, Catholic belief and practice, ceramics, chemistry, chemistry-AP, choir, choral music, chorus, Christian and Hebrew scripture, Christianity, church history, college counseling, college planning, college writing, computer multimedia, computer programming, computer science, computer skills, computer technologies, concert band, concert choir, constitutional history of U.S., dance, dance performance, desktop publishing, drama performance, drama workshop, dramatic arts, drawing, drawing and design, earth science, economics, engineering, English, English literature, English literature and composition-AP, English literature-AP, environmental science, environmental science-AP, ethics, European history, film and literature, fine arts, foreign language, French, French-AP, genetics, geography, geometry, government-AP, government/civics, government/civics-AP, grammar, health, health science, history, Holocaust studies, honors algebra, honors English, honors geometry, HTML design, introduction to theater, journalism, keyboarding, Latin, life management skills, mathematics, music, newspaper, orchestra, philosophy, photography, physical education, physics, physiology, pre-calculus, probability and statistics, psychology, psychology-AP, religion, religious education, robotics, science, social studies, sociology, Spanish, speech, statistics-AP, symphonic band, theater arts, theater production, theology, trigonometry, U.S. government and politics-AP, U.S. history-AP, Web site design, weightlifting, wind ensemble, women in literature, world history, world history-AP, world literature, writing.

Graduation Requirements 1 1/2 elective credits, arts and fine arts (art, music, dance, drama), English, foreign language, health education, mathematics, physical education (includes health), religion (includes Bible studies and theology), science, social studies (includes history), technology. Community service is required.

Special Academic Programs Advanced Placement exam preparation; honors section; independent study; academic accommodation for the gifted, the musically talented, and the artistically talented; programs in general development for dyslexic students; special instructional classes for students with mild learning disabilities, organizational deficiencies, Attention Deficit Disorder, and dyslexia.

College Admission Counseling 109 students graduated in 2015; all went to college, including George Mason University; Hampton University; Mount St. Mary's University; The Catholic University of America; Towson University; University of Maryland, Baltimore County. Mean SAT critical reading: 589, mean SAT math: 573, mean SAT writing: 585.

Student Life Upper grades have uniform requirement, student council, honor system. Discipline rests equally with students and faculty. Attendance at religious services is required.

Summer Programs Remediation, enrichment, sports, art/fine arts, computer instruction programs offered; held on campus; accepts girls; open to students from other schools. 2016 schedule: June to August.

Tuition and Aid Day student tuition: $12,750. Tuition installment plan (FACTS Tuition Payment Plan, monthly payment plans, one, two, or ten payments). Tuition reduction for siblings, merit scholarship grants, need-based scholarship grants, paying campus jobs available. In 2015–16, 35% of upper-school students received aid; total upper-school merit-scholarship money awarded: $104,000. Total amount of financial aid awarded in 2015–16: $500,000.

Admissions Traditional secondary-level entrance grade is 9. High School Placement Test required. Deadline for receipt of application materials: December 3. Application fee required: $50. On-campus interview required.

Athletics Interscholastic: aerobics/dance, archery, badminton, basketball, cheering, crew, cross-country running, dance, dance squad, dance team, equestrian sports, field hockey, flag football, golf, horseback riding, indoor track, indoor track & field, lacrosse, martial arts, rowing, running, self defense, soccer, softball, swimming and diving, tennis, touch football, volleyball, winter (indoor) track; intramural: dance, flag football, martial arts, outdoor recreation, physical fitness, strength & conditioning, weight lifting, weight training. 3 PE instructors, 56 coaches, 1 athletic trainer.

Computers Computers are regularly used in all academic, computer applications, desktop publishing, graphic design, independent study, lab/keyboard, literary magazine, multimedia, photojournalism, programming, research skills, writing, yearbook classes. Computer network features include on-campus library services, online commercial services, Internet access, wireless campus network, Internet filtering or blocking technology. Campus intranet and student e-mail accounts are available to students. Students grades are available online. The school has a published electronic and media policy.

Contact Mrs. Melissa Davey Landini, Dean of Admissions. 301-864-4532 Ext. 7015. Fax: 301-864-8946. E-mail: mlandini@setonhs.org. Website: www.setonhs.org

THE ELLIS SCHOOL

6425 Fifth Avenue
Pittsburgh, Pennsylvania 15206
Head of School: Mrs. Robin Newham

General Information Girls' day and distance learning college-preparatory, arts, STEM, and integrated studies school. Grades PK–12. Distance learning grades 9–12. Founded: 1916. Setting: urban. 8-acre campus. 5 buildings on campus. Approved or accredited by Pennsylvania Association of Independent Schools and Pennsylvania Department of Education. Member of National Association of Independent Schools. Endowment: $24 million. Total enrollment: 393. Upper school average class size: 15. There are 167 required school days per year for Upper School students. Upper School students typically attend 5 days per week. The average school day consists of 6 hours and 20 minutes.

Upper School Student Profile Grade 6: 29 students (29 girls); Grade 7: 36 students (36 girls); Grade 8: 20 students (20 girls); Grade 9: 37 students (37 girls); Grade 10: 38 students (38 girls); Grade 11: 31 students (31 girls); Grade 12: 29 students (29 girls).

Faculty School total: 68.

Subjects Offered Acting, advanced studio art-AP, algebra, American history, American literature, anthropology, art, art history, Basic programming, biology, calculus, calculus-AP, ceramics, chemistry, chemistry-AP, chorus, college admission preparation, college counseling, computer graphics, computer science, creative writing, dance, digital art, digital music, discrete mathematics, drama, English, English language and composition-AP, English literature, environmental science, European history, expository writing, fine arts, French, French language-AP, geometry, global issues, government/civics, health, history, human anatomy, journalism, Latin, Latin-AP, mathematics, music, musical productions, photography, physical education, physics, public service, SAT/ACT preparation, social studies, Spanish, Spanish language-AP, speech, statistics, theater, trigonometry, U.S. government and politics-AP, U.S. history-AP, video, voice, world history, world literature, writing.

Graduation Requirements Arts and fine arts (art, music, dance, drama), computer literacy, English, first aid, foreign language, health education, mathematics, physical education (includes health), science, social studies (includes history), completion of three-week mini-course program (grades 9-11), senior projects.

Special Academic Programs 14 Advanced Placement exams for which test preparation is offered; honors section; independent study; term-away projects; study at local college for college credit; study abroad; academic accommodation for the gifted and the musically talented.

College Admission Counseling 30 students graduated in 2015; all went to college, including Duquesne University; Harvard University; Johns Hopkins University; Stanford University; University of Pittsburgh; Yale University. Mean SAT critical reading: 639, mean SAT math: 628, mean SAT writing: 657, mean combined SAT: 1924, mean composite ACT: 30.

Student Life Upper grades have uniform requirement, student council, honor system. Discipline rests primarily with faculty.

Summer Programs Computer instruction programs offered; session focuses on STEM and robotics; held on campus; accepts girls; open to students from other schools. 15 students usually enrolled.

Tuition and Aid Day student tuition: $9100–$27,500. Tuition installment plan (FACTS Tuition Payment Plan, 10-month payment plan; two-payment plan). Tuition reduction for siblings, merit scholarship grants, need-based scholarship grants, need-based financial aid available. In 2015–16, 37% of upper-school students received aid.

Admissions Traditional secondary-level entrance grade is 9. For fall 2015, 46 students applied for upper-level admission, 32 were accepted, 18 enrolled. ISEE required. Deadline for receipt of application materials: none. Application fee required: $50. Interview required.

Athletics Interscholastic: basketball, crew, cross-country running, field hockey, gymnastics, lacrosse, soccer, softball, swimming and diving, tennis, track and field; intramural: aerobics/dance, archery, badminton, ball hockey, ballet, cooperative games, crew, field hockey, fitness, indoor soccer, lacrosse, outdoor activities, physical fitness, running. 2 PE instructors, 4 coaches, 1 athletic trainer.

Computers Computers are regularly used in all classes. Computer network features include on-campus library services, online commercial services, Internet access, wireless campus network, Internet filtering or blocking technology, blended learning and flipped classrooms, Google Glass/Labcasts. Campus intranet and student e-mail accounts are available to students. The school has a published electronic and media policy.

Contact Ms. Bayh Sullivan, Director of Admission and Financial Aid. 412-661-4880. Fax: 412-661-7634. E-mail: admissions@theellisschool.org. Website: www.theellisschool.org

ELMWOOD SCHOOL

261 Buena Vista Road
Ottawa, Ontario K1M 0V9, Canada

Head of School: Ms. Cheryl Boughton

General Information Girls' day college-preparatory, arts, business, bilingual studies, and technology school. Grades JK–12. Founded: 1915. Setting: suburban. 2-acre campus. 1 building on campus. Approved or accredited by Canadian Association of Independent Schools, Canadian Educational Standards Institute, Conference of Independent Schools of Ontario, International Baccalaureate Organization, Ontario Ministry of Education, and Ontario Department of Education. Language of instruction: English. Total enrollment: 340. Upper school average class size: 10. Upper school faculty-student ratio: 1:8. There are 178 required school days per year for Upper School students. The average school day consists of 6 hours and 45 minutes.

Faculty School total: 50. In upper school: 8 men, 20 women; 14 have advanced degrees.

Subjects Offered Algebra, art, art history, biology, business, calculus, Canadian geography, Canadian history, chemistry, communications, computer math, computer science, creative writing, drama, economics, English, English literature, environmental science, ESL, European history, fine arts, French, geography, geometry, German, grammar, health, history, Latin, mathematics, music, philosophy, physical education, physics, science, social studies, Spanish, theater, theory of knowledge, trigonometry, typing, world history, world literature.

Graduation Requirements Arts and fine arts (art, music, dance, drama), business skills (includes word processing), Canadian geography, Canadian history, English, foreign language, mathematics, physical education (includes health), science, social studies (includes history).

Special Academic Programs International Baccalaureate program; academic accommodation for the gifted; ESL.

College Admission Counseling 31 students graduated in 2015; all went to college, including McGill University; Nova Southeastern University; Queen's University at Kingston; The University of Western Ontario; University of Ottawa; University of Toronto.

Student Life Upper grades have uniform requirement, student council, honor system. Discipline rests primarily with faculty.

Summer Programs ESL, sports, art/fine arts programs offered; held on campus; accepts girls; open to students from other schools. 2016 schedule: June 20 to August 26.

Tuition and Aid Day student tuition: CAN$12,956–CAN$23,640. Tuition installment plan (monthly payment plans, individually arranged payment plans, 4 payment plan and 11 month payment plan). Bursaries, merit scholarship grants, need-based scholarship grants available. In 2015–16, 10% of upper-school students received aid; total upper-school merit-scholarship money awarded: CAN$80,000. Total amount of financial aid awarded in 2015–16: CAN$250,000.

Admissions School's own exam required. Deadline for receipt of application materials: none. Application fee required: CAN$150. Interview required.

Athletics Interscholastic: alpine skiing, aquatics, badminton, basketball, cross-country running, field hockey, golf, nordic skiing, rowing, rugby, skiing (cross-country), skiing (downhill), snowboarding, soccer, swimming and diving, tennis, ultimate Frisbee, volleyball, water polo; intramural: aerobics/dance, aerobics/Nautilus, badminton, ball hockey, ballet, dance, hiking/backpacking, outdoor adventure, ropes courses, wilderness, yoga. 4 PE instructors, 1 coach.

Computers Computers are regularly used in all classes. Computer network features include on-campus library services, Internet access, wireless campus network, Internet filtering or blocking technology. Campus intranet, student e-mail accounts, and computer access in designated common areas are available to students. The school has a published electronic and media policy.

Contact Ms. Elise Aylen, Director of Admissions. 613-744-7783. Fax: 613-741-8210. E-mail: admissions@elmwood.ca. Website: www.elmwood.ca

ELYRIA CATHOLIC HIGH SCHOOL

725 Gulf Road
Elyria, Ohio 44035-3697

Head of School: Mrs. Amy Butler

General Information Coeducational day college-preparatory, arts, business, religious studies, bilingual studies, and technology school, affiliated with Roman Catholic Church; primarily serves students with learning disabilities, individuals with Attention Deficit Disorder, and dyslexic students. Grades 9–12. Founded: 1948. Setting: suburban. Nearest major city is Cleveland. 16-acre campus. 2 buildings on campus. Approved or accredited by North Central Association of Colleges and Schools and Ohio Department of Education. Endowment: $3 million. Total enrollment: 434. Upper school average class size: 24. Upper school faculty-student ratio: 1:14. There are 180 required school days per year for Upper School students. Upper School students typically attend 5 days per week. The average school day consists of 6 hours and 45 minutes.

Upper School Student Profile Grade 9: 103 students (54 boys, 49 girls); Grade 10: 105 students (52 boys, 53 girls); Grade 11: 117 students (56 boys, 61 girls); Grade 12: 109 students (48 boys, 61 girls). 90% of students are Roman Catholic.

Faculty School total: 37. In upper school: 18 men, 19 women; 22 have advanced degrees.

Subjects Offered Accounting, advanced math, algebra, American government, American history, American history-AP, analysis of data, anatomy and physiology, ancient world history, art, band, biology, business, calculus, calculus-AP, campus ministry, Catholic belief and practice, chemistry, choir, Christian and Hebrew scripture, Christian doctrine, Christian ethics, church history, computer applications, concert band, concert choir, current events, data analysis, drama, drama performance, earth science, English, fine arts, French, French language-AP, geometry, German, health, history, honors English, industrial arts, introduction to theater, journalism, leadership, life issues, marching band, music appreciation, parent/child development, peer ministry, physical fitness, physics, prayer/spirituality, pre-calculus, psychology, reading/study skills, social justice, Spanish, Spanish language-AP, theater, world religions, yearbook.

Graduation Requirements Arts and fine arts (art, music, dance, drama), computers, English, mathematics, physical education (includes health), religion (includes Bible studies and theology), science, social studies (includes history), school and community service hours, Ohio Proficiency Test.

Special Academic Programs Advanced Placement exam preparation; honors section; study at local college for college credit; remedial reading and/or remedial writing; remedial math; programs in English, mathematics, general development for dyslexic students; special instructional classes for students with learning disabilities and Attention Deficit Disorder; ESL (5 students enrolled).

College Admission Counseling 92 students graduated in 2015; 91 went to college, including Baldwin Wallace University; Bowling Green State University; John Carroll University; Kent State University; The Ohio State University; The University of Toledo. Other: 1 entered military service. Mean SAT critical reading: 570, mean SAT math: 557.

Student Life Upper grades have specified standards of dress, student council, honor system. Discipline rests primarily with faculty. Attendance at religious services is required.

Summer Programs Sports programs offered; session focuses on sports; held on campus; accepts boys and girls; open to students from other schools. 300 students usually enrolled. 2016 schedule: June 12 to July 31. Application deadline: April 15.

Tuition and Aid Day student tuition: $7750. Tuition installment plan (FACTS Tuition Payment Plan). Tuition reduction for siblings, merit scholarship grants, need-based scholarship grants, paying campus jobs available. In 2015–16, 54% of upper-school students received aid; total upper-school merit-scholarship money awarded: $15,750. Total amount of financial aid awarded in 2015–16: $250,300.

Admissions Traditional secondary-level entrance grade is 9. High School Placement Test (closed version) from Scholastic Testing Service required. Deadline for receipt of application materials: January 14. No application fee required. Interview recommended.

Athletics Interscholastic: baseball (boys), basketball (b,g), cross-country running (b,g), diving (b,g), football (b), golf (b), rugby (b), soccer (b,g), softball (g), tennis (b,g), volleyball (g), wrestling (b); coed interscholastic: bowling, cheering, ice hockey, swimming and diving, track and field. 1 PE instructor, 47 coaches, 1 athletic trainer.

Computers Computers are regularly used in business studies, journalism, newspaper, typing, word processing, yearbook classes. Computer network features include on-campus library services, online commercial services, Internet access, wireless campus network, Internet filtering or blocking technology, 1:1 Google Chromebook Initiative. Campus intranet and student e-mail accounts are available to students. Students grades are available online. The school has a published electronic and media policy.

Contact Mrs. Annie Cunningham, Director of Admissions/Marketing. 440-365-1821 Ext. 116. Fax: 440-365-7536. E-mail: annie.cunningham@elyriacatholic.com. Website: www.elyriacatholic.com

THE ENGLISH COLLEGE IN PRAGUE

Sokolovska 320
Prague 190 00, Czech Republic

Head of School: Mr. Simon Marshall

General Information Coeducational day college-preparatory and arts school. Grades 8–13. Founded: 1994. Setting: urban. 1-acre campus. 2 buildings on campus. Approved or accredited by Department of Education and Employment, United Kingdom, Headmasters' Conference, Independent Schools Council (UK), and International Baccalaureate Organization. Language of instruction: English. Total enrollment: 360. Upper school average class size: 13. Upper school faculty-student ratio: 1:11. The average school day consists of 7 hours and 30 minutes.

Faculty School total: 40. In upper school: 20 men, 20 women.

Subjects Offered Independent study, International Baccalaureate courses.

Graduation Requirements International Baccalaureate courses, Czech maturita for Czech students.

Special Academic Programs International Baccalaureate program; independent study; academic accommodation for the gifted, the musically talented, and the artistically talented; programs in English for dyslexic students; ESL (30 students enrolled).

College Admission Counseling 67 students graduated in 2014; 64 went to college. Other: 1 went to work, 2 had other specific plans.

Student Life Upper grades have student council, honor system. Discipline rests primarily with faculty.

Tuition and Aid Tuition reduction for siblings, bursaries, merit scholarship grants, need-based scholarship grants available. In 2014–15, 30% of upper-school students received aid.

Admissions Traditional secondary-level entrance grade is 12. For fall 2014, 15 students applied for upper-level admission, 6 were accepted, 6 enrolled. English entrance exam and mathematics proficiency exam required. Deadline for receipt of application materials: May 1. Application fee required: 500 Czech korun. Interview required.

Athletics 2 PE instructors.

Computers Computers are regularly used in all academic classes. Computer network features include on-campus library services, online commercial services, Internet access, wireless campus network, Internet filtering or blocking technology. Campus intranet, student e-mail accounts, and computer access in designated common areas are available to students. Students grades are available online.

Contact Mrs. Iva Rozkosna, Admissions Registrar. 420-283893113. Fax: 420-283890118. E-mail: office@englishcollege.cz. Website: www.englishcollege.cz

EPISCOPAL COLLEGIATE SCHOOL

Jackson T. Stephens Campus
1701 Cantrell Road
Little Rock, Arkansas 72201

Head of School: Mr. Christopher Tompkins

General Information Coeducational day college-preparatory, arts, and technology school, affiliated with Episcopal Church. Grades PK–12. Founded: 1998. Setting: suburban. 34-acre campus. 3 buildings on campus. Approved or accredited by Arkansas Nonpublic School Accrediting Association, National Association of Episcopal Schools, Southern Association of Colleges and Schools, Southern Association of Independent Schools, and Southwest Association of Episcopal Schools. Member of National Association of Independent Schools. Endowment: $72 million. Total enrollment: 784. Upper school average class size: 15. Upper school faculty-student ratio: 1:10. There are 179 required school days per year for Upper School students. Upper School students typically attend 5 days per week. The average school day consists of 7 hours and 30 minutes.

Upper School Student Profile Grade 9: 49 students (23 boys, 26 girls); Grade 10: 49 students (25 boys, 24 girls); Grade 11: 51 students (22 boys, 29 girls); Grade 12: 56 students (22 boys, 34 girls). 35% of students are members of Episcopal Church.

Faculty School total: 103. In upper school: 15 men, 25 women; 33 have advanced degrees.

Graduation Requirements Senior chapel talk.

Special Academic Programs 16 Advanced Placement exams for which test preparation is offered; honors section; independent study.

College Admission Counseling 56 students graduated in 2015; all went to college, including Hendrix College; Louisiana State University and Agricultural & Mechanical College; Ouachita Baptist University; University of Arkansas; University of Mississippi. Mean SAT critical reading: 637, mean SAT math: 610, mean SAT writing: 633, mean combined SAT: 1879, mean composite ACT: 27. 66% scored over 600 on SAT critical reading, 47% scored over 600 on SAT math, 63% scored over 600 on SAT writing, 63% scored over 1800 on combined SAT, 43% scored over 26 on composite ACT.

Student Life Upper grades have uniform requirement, student council, honor system. Discipline rests primarily with faculty. Attendance at religious services is required.

Summer Programs Enrichment, sports, art/fine arts, computer instruction programs offered; session focuses on enrichment; held on campus; accepts boys and girls; open to students from other schools. 150 students usually enrolled. 2016 schedule: June 1 to July 31. Application deadline: May 30.

Tuition and Aid Day student tuition: $12,570. Tuition installment plan (FACTS Tuition Payment Plan). Need-based scholarship grants available. In 2015–16, 17% of upper-school students received aid. Total amount of financial aid awarded in 2015–16: $482,000.

Admissions Traditional secondary-level entrance grade is 9. For fall 2015, 36 students applied for upper-level admission, 15 were accepted, 14 enrolled. Stanford 9 required. Deadline for receipt of application materials: none. Application fee required: $50. Interview required.

Athletics Interscholastic: baseball (boys), basketball (b,g), cross-country running (b,g), fishing (b,g), fitness (b,g), football (b), golf (b,g), physical fitness (b,g), physical training (b,g), soccer (b,g), tennis (b,g), track and field (b,g), volleyball (g), weight training (b,g), wrestling (b,g); coed interscholastic: cheering. 5 PE instructors, 10 coaches, 2 athletic trainers.

Computers Computers are regularly used in all academic classes. Computer network features include on-campus library services, online commercial services, Internet access, wireless campus network, Internet filtering or blocking technology. Campus intranet, student e-mail accounts, and computer access in designated common areas are available to students. Students grades are available online. The school has a published electronic and media policy.

Contact Ms. Ashley Honeywell, Director of Admission. 501-372-1194 Ext. 2406. Fax: 501-372-2160. E-mail: ahoneywell@episcopalcollegiate.org. Website: www.episcopalcollegiate.org

EPISCOPAL HIGH SCHOOL

4650 Bissonnet
Bellaire, Texas 77401

Head of School: Mr. C. Edward Smith

General Information Coeducational day college-preparatory, arts, religious studies, and technology school, affiliated with Episcopal Church. Grades 9–12. Founded: 1984. Setting: urban. Nearest major city is Houston. 35-acre campus. 7 buildings on campus. Approved or accredited by Independent Schools Association of the Southwest, National Association of Episcopal Schools, The College Board, and Texas Department of Education. Member of National Association of Independent Schools and Secondary School Admission Test Board. Total enrollment: 680. Upper school average class size: 15. Upper school faculty-student ratio: 1:9. Upper School students typically attend 5 days per week. The average school day consists of 8 hours.

Upper School Student Profile Grade 9: 172 students (81 boys, 91 girls); Grade 10: 175 students (77 boys, 98 girls); Grade 11: 162 students (91 boys, 71 girls); Grade 12: 171 students (95 boys, 76 girls). 20.9% of students are members of Episcopal Church.

Faculty School total: 90. In upper school: 42 men, 48 women; 54 have advanced degrees.

Subjects Offered Acting, algebra, anatomy, ancient history, art appreciation, art history, band, Bible studies, biology, biology-AP, calculus-AP, ceramics, chemistry, choir, civil rights, dance, debate, design, drawing, English, English-AP, ethics, European history, French, French-AP, geography, geology, geometry, government, government-AP, graphic design, health, history of science, instrumental music, journalism, Latin, Latin American studies, music theory, newspaper, oceanography, orchestra, painting, photography, physical education, physics, physics-AP, physiology, pre-calculus, sculpture, Spanish, Spanish-AP, speech, stagecraft, statistics, theater, theology, U.S. history, U.S. history-AP, video film production, Vietnam War, world religions, World War II, writing, yearbook.

Graduation Requirements Arts and fine arts (art, music, dance, drama), English, foreign language, mathematics, physical education (includes health), religion (includes Bible studies and theology), religious studies, science, social studies (includes history).

Special Academic Programs 14 Advanced Placement exams for which test preparation is offered; honors section; independent study; study at local college for college credit.

College Admission Counseling 161 students graduated in 2015; all went to college, including Southern Methodist University; Texas A&M University; Texas Christian University; The University of Texas at Austin; Washington and Lee University. Mean SAT critical reading: 580, mean SAT math: 594, mean SAT writing: 576, mean combined SAT: 1750, mean composite ACT: 32.

Student Life Upper grades have uniform requirement, student council, honor system. Discipline rests equally with students and faculty. Attendance at religious services is required.

Summer Programs Remediation, enrichment, advancement, art/fine arts programs offered; session focuses on remediation, advancement, enrichment; held on campus; accepts boys and girls; open to students from other schools. 250 students usually enrolled. 2016 schedule: June 6 to July 16. Application deadline: May 15.

Tuition and Aid Day student tuition: $26,100. Tuition installment plan (Insured Tuition Payment Plan, SMART Tuition Payment Plan, monthly payment plans). Need-based scholarship grants, middle-income loans available. In 2015–16, 17% of upper-school students received aid. Total amount of financial aid awarded in 2015–16: $1,700,000.

Admissions Traditional secondary-level entrance grade is 9. For fall 2015, 546 students applied for upper-level admission, 349 were accepted, 188 enrolled. ISEE and Otis-Lennon Ability or Stanford Achievement Test required. Deadline for receipt of application materials: December 15. Application fee required: $75. On-campus interview required.

Athletics Interscholastic: ballet (boys, girls), baseball (b), basketball (b,g), cheering (b,g), cross-country running (b,g), dance (b,g), drill team (g), field hockey (g), fitness (b,g), football (b), golf (b,g), lacrosse (b,g), physical fitness (b,g), running (b,g), soccer (b,g), softball (g), strength & conditioning (b,g), swimming and diving (b,g), tennis (b,g), track and field (b,g), volleyball (b,g), weight training (b,g), wrestling (b). 7 PE instructors, 8 coaches, 1 athletic trainer.

Computers Computers are regularly used in art, English, foreign language, history, mathematics, music, religion, science classes. Computer network features include on-campus library services, online commercial services, Internet access, wireless campus network, CollegeView. Student e-mail accounts are available to students. Students grades are available online. The school has a published electronic and media policy.

Contact Audrey Koehler, Director of Admission. 713-512-3400. Fax: 713-512-3603. E-mail: akoehler@ehshouston.org. Website: www.ehshouston.org/

EPISCOPAL HIGH SCHOOL

1200 North Quaker Lane
Alexandria, Virginia 22302

Head of School: Mr. F. Robertson Hershey

General Information Coeducational boarding college-preparatory, arts, business, religious studies, and technology school, affiliated with Episcopal Church. Grades 9–12. Founded: 1839. Setting: urban. Nearest major city is Washington, DC. Students are housed in single-sex dormitories. 130-acre campus. 26 buildings on campus. Approved or accredited by Southern Association of Colleges and Schools, Virginia Association of Independent Schools, and Virginia Department of Education. Member of National Association of Independent Schools and Secondary School Admission Test Board. Endowment: $214 million. Total enrollment: 435. Upper school average class size: 11. Upper school faculty-student ratio: 1:5. Upper School students typically attend 5 days per week. The average school day consists of 7 hours.

Upper School Student Profile Grade 9: 100 students (52 boys, 48 girls); Grade 10: 115 students (52 boys, 63 girls); Grade 11: 113 students (56 boys, 57 girls); Grade 12: 124 students (59 boys, 65 girls). 100% of students are boarding students. 29% are state residents. 31 states are represented in upper school student body. 13% are international students. International students from Canada, China, Republic of Korea, and Taiwan; 15 other countries represented in student body.

Faculty School total: 68. In upper school: 38 men, 30 women; 56 have advanced degrees; 61 reside on campus.

Subjects Offered 3-dimensional art, 3-dimensional design, acting, advanced biology, advanced chemistry, advanced computer applications, advanced math, aesthetics, algebra, American government, American history, American literature, anatomy and physiology, Ancient Greek, ancient history, ancient world history, art, art and culture, art history, arts, astronomy, ballet, Bible studies, biology, biotechnology, calculus, ceramics, chemistry, Chinese, Chinese history, Chinese literature, Chinese studies, choir, Christian education, comparative religion, computer programming, computer science, computer studies, conceptual physics, dance, digital photography, drama, drawing, drawing and design, ecology, ecology, environmental systems, economics, electives, engineering, English, English composition, English literature, equality and freedom, forensics, French, French studies, genetics, geology, geometry, German, German literature, global studies, government, government/civics, Greek, guitar, health and wellness, honors algebra, honors English, honors geometry, independent study, intro to computers, introduction to digital multitrack recording techniques, Latin, linear algebra, modern politics, music theory, orchestra, painting, photography, physics, portfolio art, pre-calculus, Shakespeare, Spanish, Spanish literature, statistics, studio art, technology, theater, theater arts, theater design and production, theater production, theology, U.S. history.

Graduation Requirements Arts and fine arts (art, music, dance, drama), computer studies, English, foreign language, mathematics, physical education (includes health), science, social studies (includes history), theology.

Special Academic Programs Advanced Placement exam preparation; honors section; independent study; term-away projects; study abroad; academic accommodation for the gifted, the musically talented, and the artistically talented.

College Admission Counseling 126 students graduated in 2015; all went to college, including Sewanee: The University of the South; Southern Methodist University; The University of North Carolina at Chapel Hill; University of Georgia; University of Virginia. Median SAT critical reading: 620, median SAT math: 610, median SAT writing: 640, median combined SAT: 1860, median composite ACT: 27. 64% scored over 600 on SAT critical reading, 56% scored over 600 on SAT math, 71% scored over 600 on SAT writing, 63% scored over 1800 on combined SAT, 57% scored over 26 on composite ACT.

Student Life Upper grades have specified standards of dress, student council, honor system. Discipline rests primarily with faculty. Attendance at religious services is required.

Summer Programs Enrichment, advancement, sports, art/fine arts programs offered; session focuses on academic enrichment and athletic skills; held on campus; accepts boys and girls; open to students from other schools. 2016 schedule: June 12 to July 31.

Tuition and Aid 7-day tuition and room/board: $51,750. Tuition installment plan (Insured Tuition Payment Plan, monthly payment plans). Merit scholarship grants, need-based scholarship grants, paying campus jobs available. In 2015–16, 32% of upper-school students received aid; total upper-school merit-scholarship money awarded: $189,500. Total amount of financial aid awarded in 2015–16: $6,000,000.

Admissions Traditional secondary-level entrance grade is 9. For fall 2015, 657 students applied for upper-level admission, 242 were accepted, 147 enrolled. ISEE, PSAT or SAT or SSAT required. Deadline for receipt of application materials: January 15. Application fee required: $60. Interview required.

Athletics Interscholastic: baseball (boys), basketball (b,g), crew (g), cross-country running (b,g), field hockey (g), football (b), golf (b), indoor track (b,g), indoor track & field (b,g), lacrosse (b,g), rowing (g), soccer (b,g), softball (g), squash (b,g), tennis (b,g), track and field (b,g), volleyball (g), winter (indoor) track (b,g), wrestling (b); intramural: strength & conditioning (b,g); coed interscholastic: climbing, fitness, outdoor education, outdoor recreation, outdoors, physical fitness, physical training, rock climbing, strength & conditioning, weight lifting, weight training; coed intramural: aerobics, aerobics/dance, aerobics/Nautilus, backpacking, ballet, canoeing/kayaking, climbing, dance, fitness, hiking/backpacking, kayaking, modern dance, outdoor activities, outdoor adventure, physical fitness, physical training, power lifting, rock climbing, soccer, wall climbing, weight lifting, weight training. 4 coaches, 2 athletic trainers.

Computers Computers are regularly used in all academic classes. Computer network features include on-campus library services, online commercial services, Internet access, wireless campus network, Internet filtering or blocking technology. Campus intranet and student e-mail accounts are available to students. Students grades are available online. The school has a published electronic and media policy.

Contact Mr. Scott Conklin, Director of Admission. 703-933-4062. Fax: 703-933-3016. E-mail: admissions@episcopalhighschool.org. Website: www.episcopalhighschool.org

EPISCOPAL HIGH SCHOOL OF JACKSONVILLE

Episcopal School of Jacksonville
4455 Atlantic Boulevard
Jacksonville, Florida 32207

Head of School: Charles F. Zimmer

General Information Coeducational day college-preparatory, arts, religious studies, and technology school, affiliated with Episcopal Church. Grades 6–12. Founded: 1966. Setting: urban. 88-acre campus. 25 buildings on campus. Approved or accredited by Florida Council of Independent Schools, National Association of Episcopal Schools, Southern Association of Colleges and Schools, and Southern Association of Independent Schools. Member of National Association of Independent Schools. Endowment: $15.4 million. Total enrollment: 857. Upper school average class size: 17. Upper school faculty-student ratio: 1:10. There are 175 required school days per year for Upper School students. Upper School students typically attend 5 days per week. The average school day consists of 6 hours and 50 minutes.

Upper School Student Profile Grade 9: 140 students (76 boys, 64 girls); Grade 10: 142 students (73 boys, 69 girls); Grade 11: 140 students (73 boys, 67 girls); Grade 12: 144 students (77 boys, 67 girls). 33% of students are members of Episcopal Church.

Faculty School total: 100. In upper school: 35 men, 58 women; 53 have advanced degrees.

Subjects Offered Advanced studio art-AP, algebra, American history, American history-AP, American literature, ancient history, art, art history, art history-AP, band, Basic programming, biology, biology-AP, calculus, calculus-AP, ceramics, chemistry, chemistry-AP, Chinese, computer programming, computer science, computer science-AP, dance, drama, earth science, economics, electronic publishing, English, English language and composition-AP, English literature and composition-AP, English/composition-AP, environmental science-AP, European history-AP, fine arts, French, French language-AP, geography, geometry, German, German-AP, government and politics-AP, government/civics, health, history, journalism, Latin, Latin-AP, marine biology, mathematics, music, music history, music theory, music theory-AP, photography, physical education, physics, physics-AP, public speaking, religion, religious studies, science, social studies, Spanish, Spanish language-AP, statistics, statistics-AP, studio art-AP, technical theater, theater, theology, trigonometry, U.S. government and politics-AP, U.S. history-AP, world history, writing, yearbook.

Graduation Requirements Arts and fine arts (art, music, dance, drama), computer science, English, foreign language, leadership, library skills, mathematics, physical education (includes health), religion (includes Bible studies and theology), science, social studies (includes history), 75 community service hours. Community service is required.

Special Academic Programs Advanced Placement exam preparation; honors section; independent study; study abroad; academic accommodation for the gifted.

College Admission Counseling 156 students graduated in 2015; all went to college, including Florida State University; University of Florida; University of North Florida. Median SAT critical reading: 579, median SAT math: 584, median SAT writing: 567, median combined SAT: 1729, median composite ACT: 26.

Student Life Upper grades have uniform requirement, student council, honor system. Discipline rests equally with students and faculty. Attendance at religious services is required.

Summer Programs Remediation, enrichment, advancement, sports, art/fine arts, rigorous outdoor training, computer instruction programs offered; session focuses on academics, athletics, fine arts, specialty programs; held both on and off campus; held at beach for fishing camp, paint ball facility, ice skating facility, golf course; accepts boys and girls; open to students from other schools. 500 students usually enrolled. 2016 schedule: May 27 to August 5. Application deadline: none.

Tuition and Aid Day student tuition: $18,500. Tuition installment plan (Insured Tuition Payment Plan, monthly payment plans). Need-based scholarship grants available. In 2014–15, 23% of upper-school students received aid. Total amount of financial aid awarded in 2014–15: $2,000,000.

Admissions Traditional secondary-level entrance grade is 9. For fall 2015, 89 students applied for upper-level admission, 58 were accepted, 38 enrolled. ISEE required. Deadline for receipt of application materials: January 1. Application fee required: $50. On-campus interview required.

Athletics Interscholastic: baseball (boys), basketball (b,g), crew (b,g), cross-country running (b,g), football (b), golf (b,g), lacrosse (b,g), modern dance (b,g), soccer (b,g), softball (g), swimming and diving (b,g), tennis (b,g), track and field (b,g), volleyball (g), weight lifting (b), weight training (b), wrestling (b); intramural: dance (g); coed interscholastic: cheering, dance, dance squad, dance team, wrestling; coed intramural: fencing. 7 PE instructors, 100 coaches, 4 athletic trainers.

Computers Computers are regularly used in all classes. Computer network features include on-campus library services, online commercial services, Internet access, wireless campus network, Internet filtering or blocking technology, Senior Systems: My BackPack online grading and student accounts, online parent portals, RSS feeds. Campus intranet, student e-mail accounts, and computer access in designated common areas are available to students. Students grades are available online. The school has a published electronic and media policy.

Contact Sam Hyde, Director of Admissions. 904-396-7104. Fax: 904-396-0981. E-mail: hydes@esj.org. Website: www.episcopalhigh.org

THE EPISCOPAL SCHOOL OF ACADIANA
PO Box 380
Cade, Louisiana 70519
Head of School: Dr. Paul Baker, PhD
General Information Coeducational day college-preparatory and arts school, affiliated with Episcopal Church. Grades PK–12. Founded: 1979. Setting: rural. Nearest major city is Lafayette. 90-acre campus. 15 buildings on campus. Approved or accredited by Independent Schools Association of the Southwest, National Association of Episcopal Schools, and Louisiana Department of Education. Member of National Association of Independent Schools. Endowment: $265,000. Total enrollment: 496. Upper school average class size: 11. Upper school faculty-student ratio: 1:6. The average school day consists of 7 hours and 30 minutes.

Upper School Student Profile Grade 9: 53 students (33 boys, 20 girls); Grade 10: 45 students (26 boys, 19 girls); Grade 11: 36 students (19 boys, 17 girls); Grade 12: 42 students (24 boys, 18 girls). 20% of students are members of Episcopal Church.

Faculty School total: 58. In upper school: 17 men, 14 women; 16 have advanced degrees.

Subjects Offered Advanced chemistry, algebra, American history, American history-AP, American literature, architectural drawing, art, biology, biology-AP, calculus, calculus-AP, ceramics, chemistry, chemistry-AP, civics, computer programming, computer science, drama, drawing, earth science, English, English literature, environmental science, fine arts, French, French language-AP, French-AP, geography, geometry, government/civics, grammar, honors English, honors geometry, interpersonal skills, mathematics, music, photography, physical education, physics, pre-calculus, public speaking, reading, science, social studies, speech, studio art, U.S. history, Western civilization, world history, writing.

Graduation Requirements Algebra, American history, American literature, arts and fine arts (art, music, dance, drama), biology, British literature, British literature (honors), chemistry, computer science, electives, English, foreign language, geometry, mathematics, physical education (includes health), physics, pre-calculus, Western civilization.

Special Academic Programs Advanced Placement exam preparation; honors section; independent study; academic accommodation for the gifted; programs in general development for dyslexic students.

College Admission Counseling 43 students graduated in 2014; all went to college, including Louisiana State University and Agricultural & Mechanical College; Loyola University New Orleans; Sewanee: The University of the South; The University of Alabama; Tulane University; University of Louisiana at Lafayette. Median SAT critical reading: 580, median SAT math: 610, median composite ACT: 27. 49% scored over 600 on SAT critical reading, 54% scored over 600 on SAT math, 68% scored over 26 on composite ACT.

Student Life Upper grades have specified standards of dress, student council, honor system. Discipline rests equally with students and faculty. Attendance at religious services is required.

Tuition and Aid Day student tuition: $15,850. Tuition installment plan (monthly payment plans, 2-payment plan, 4-payment plan). Need-based scholarship grants, faculty tuition remission available. In 2014–15, 23% of upper-school students received aid. Total amount of financial aid awarded in 2014–15: $500,000.

Admissions Traditional secondary-level entrance grade is 9. For fall 2014, 34 students applied for upper-level admission, 25 were accepted, 23 enrolled. ERB Reading and Math, Otis-Lennon School Ability Test or writing sample required. Deadline for receipt of application materials: none. Application fee required: $50. On-campus interview required.

Athletics Interscholastic: baseball (boys), basketball (b), cheering (g), cross-country running (b,g), indoor track & field (b,g), rugby (b), soccer (b,g), swimming and diving (b,g), tennis (b,g), track and field (b,g), volleyball (g); coed interscholastic: golf, outdoor adventure; coed intramural: backpacking, canoeing/kayaking, fly fishing, hiking/backpacking, kayaking. 5 PE instructors, 1 coach, 1 athletic trainer.

Computers Computers are regularly used in all academic, art classes. Computer network features include on-campus library services, online commercial services, Internet access, wireless campus network, Internet filtering or blocking technology, university library link. Campus intranet and student e-mail accounts are available to students. Students grades are available online. The school has a published electronic and media policy.

Contact Mr. Jon D. Berthelot, Director of Admissions. 337-365-1416. Fax: 337-367-9841. E-mail: jonberthelot@ESAcadiana.com. Website: www.ESAcadiana.com

ERSKINE ACADEMY
309 Windsor Road
South China, Maine 04358
Head of School: Michael McQuarrie
General Information Coeducational day college-preparatory, general academic, vocational, and technology school. Grades 9–12. Founded: 1893. Setting: rural. Nearest major city is Augusta. 29-acre campus. 3 buildings on campus. Approved or accredited by New England Association of Schools and Colleges and Maine Department of Education. Total enrollment: 589. Upper school average class size: 15. Upper school faculty-student ratio: 1:15. There are 175 required school days per year for Upper School students. Upper School students typically attend 5 days per week. The average school day consists of 6 hours and 30 minutes.

Upper School Student Profile Grade 9: 156 students (89 boys, 67 girls); Grade 10: 159 students (79 boys, 80 girls); Grade 11: 125 students (60 boys, 65 girls); Grade 12: 149 students (63 boys, 86 girls).

Faculty School total: 44. In upper school: 18 men, 26 women; 23 have advanced degrees.

Subjects Offered Accounting, advanced biology, advanced chemistry, advanced math, Advanced Placement courses, algebra, art, calculus, calculus-AP, chemistry, college admission preparation, composition-AP, concert band, drama, English, English composition, English language and composition-AP, English language-AP, English literature, ESL, French, geometry, German, global studies, government, health, health education, history, Latin, Latin-AP, life science, physics, physics-AP, psychology, psychology-AP, Russian, Spanish, Spanish-AP, speech and debate, U.S. government, U.S. history-AP, vocal ensemble, vocal jazz, world history.

Special Academic Programs 30 Advanced Placement exams for which test preparation is offered; honors section; study at local college for college credit; ESL (5 students enrolled).

College Admission Counseling 131 students graduated in 2015; 103 went to college, including University of Maine; University of Maine at Farmington; University of Southern Maine. Other: 22 went to work, 6 entered military service. Median SAT critical reading: 470, median SAT math: 480, median SAT writing: 450. 9% scored over 600 on SAT critical reading, 17% scored over 600 on SAT math, 7% scored over 600 on SAT writing.

Student Life Upper grades have honor system. Discipline rests primarily with faculty.

Tuition and Aid 7-day tuition and room/board: $39,300. Guaranteed tuition plan. Tuition installment plan (Insured Tuition Payment Plan).

Admissions Traditional secondary-level entrance grade is 9. For fall 2015, 156 students applied for upper-level admission, 156 were accepted, 156 enrolled. TOEFL or SLEP required. Deadline for receipt of application materials: none. Application fee required: $75. Interview required.

Athletics Interscholastic: baseball (boys), basketball (b,g), cheering (g), cross-country running (b,g), field hockey (g), indoor track (b,g), lacrosse (b,g), soccer (b,g), softball (g), swimming and diving (b,g), tennis (b,g), winter (indoor) track (b,g); coed interscholastic: golf, wrestling; coed intramural: skiing (downhill). 2 PE instructors, 1 athletic trainer.

Computers Computers are regularly used in all academic classes. Computer resources include on-campus library services, Internet access, wireless campus network, Internet filtering or blocking technology. Student e-mail accounts are available to students. Students grades are available online. The school has a published electronic and media policy.

Contact Jamie Soule, Associate Headmaster. 207-445-2962 Ext. 1109. Fax: 207-445-5520. E-mail: jsoule@erskine247.com. Website: www.erskineacademy.org/

ESCOLA AMERICANA DE CAMPINAS
Rua Cajamar, 35
Chácara da Barra
Campinas-SP 13090-860, Brazil
Head of School: Stephen A. Herrera
General Information Coeducational day college-preparatory, arts, bilingual studies, and technology school. Grades PK–12. Founded: 1956. Setting: urban. Nearest major city is São Paulo, Brazil. 4-acre campus. 4 buildings on campus. Approved or accredited by Association of American Schools in South America. Affiliate member of National Association of Independent Schools; member of European Council of International Schools. Languages of instruction: English and Portuguese. Endowment: $358,000. Total enrollment: 713. Upper school average class size: 20. Upper school faculty-student ratio: 1:7.

Upper School Student Profile Grade 6: 51 students (21 boys, 30 girls); Grade 7: 54 students (23 boys, 31 girls); Grade 8: 49 students (27 boys, 22 girls); Grade 9: 31 students (15 boys, 16 girls); Grade 10: 49 students (27 boys, 22 girls); Grade 11: 22 students (13 boys, 9 girls); Grade 12: 33 students (17 boys, 16 girls).

Faculty School total: 83. In upper school: 18 men, 21 women; 39 have advanced degrees.

Subjects Offered Algebra, American history, American literature, art, biology, calculus, chemistry, computer science, creative writing, drama, economics, English, English literature, fine arts, geography, geometry, government/civics, grammar, history, journalism, mathematics, music, physical education, physics, Portuguese, psychology, science, social studies, speech, trigonometry, world history, world literature, writing.

Graduation Requirements Arts and fine arts (art, music, dance, drama), computer science, English, foreign language, mathematics, physical education (includes health), science, social studies (includes history). Community service is required.

Special Academic Programs Advanced Placement exam preparation; honors section; term-away projects; study at local college for college credit; study abroad; special instructional classes for students with mild learning differences; ESL (5 students enrolled).

College Admission Counseling 17 students graduated in 2014; 16 went to college, including Emerson College; Northwestern University; Southwestern University; The University of Tampa. Other: 1 entered a postgraduate year. Median SAT critical reading: 610, median SAT math: 640, median SAT writing: 540, median combined SAT: 1790.

Student Life Upper grades have student council, honor system. Discipline rests equally with students and faculty.

Tuition and Aid Day student tuition: 70,299 Brazilian reals. Tuition installment plan (monthly payment plans). Need-based scholarship grants available. In 2014–15, 10% of upper-school students received aid. Total amount of financial aid awarded in 2014–15: $51,000.

Admissions Traditional secondary-level entrance grade is 9. For fall 2014, 57 students applied for upper-level admission, 33 were accepted, 28 enrolled. Admissions testing, English Composition Test for ESL students, ERB CTP IV, Iowa Test, CTBS, or TAP, SAT and writing sample required. Deadline for receipt of application materials: September 3. No application fee required. On-campus interview required.

Athletics Interscholastic: basketball (boys, girls), canoeing/kayaking (g), cheering (g), indoor soccer (b,g), soccer (b,g), volleyball (g); intramural: ballet (g), basketball (b,g), canoeing/kayaking (g), cheering (g), climbing (b,g), indoor soccer (b,g), soccer (b,g); coed intramural: aerobics, baseball, basketball, climbing, cooperative games, fitness, flag football, Frisbee, gymnastics, handball, indoor soccer, jogging, judo, kickball, martial arts, physical fitness, self defense, soccer, softball, strength & conditioning, table tennis, track and field, ultimate Frisbee, volleyball. 5 PE instructors, 12 coaches.

Computers Computers are regularly used in art, English, history, independent study, mathematics, science, yearbook classes. Computer network features include on-campus library services, online commercial services, Internet access. Campus intranet is available to students. .

Contact Mr. Peter Steedman, High School Principal. 55-19-2102-1006. Fax: 55-19-2102-1016. E-mail: pete.steedman@eac.com.br. Website: www.eac.com.br

ESCUELA CAMPO ALEGRE

Final Calle La Cinta Las Mercedes
Caracas, Venezuela

Head of School: Dr. Gregory Hedger

General Information Coeducational day college-preparatory, arts, and business school; primarily serves N/A. Grades N–12. Founded: 1937. Setting: urban. 7-acre campus. 4 buildings on campus. Approved or accredited by Council of International Schools and Middle States Association of Colleges and Schools. Language of instruction: English. Total enrollment: 480. Upper school average class size: 14. Upper school faculty-student ratio: 1:6. There are 183 required school days per year for Upper School students. Upper School students typically attend 5 days per week. The average school day consists of 1 hours and 30 minutes.

Upper School Student Profile Grade 9: 38 students (25 boys, 13 girls); Grade 10: 39 students (16 boys, 23 girls); Grade 11: 25 students (12 boys, 13 girls); Grade 12: 38 students (12 boys, 26 girls).

Faculty School total: 72. In upper school: 15 men, 14 women; 25 have advanced degrees.

Special Academic Programs International Baccalaureate program; ESL (95 students enrolled).

College Admission Counseling 44 students graduated in 2015; 42 went to college, including Boston University; Florida International University; Georgetown University; Georgia Institute of Technology; New York University; Northeastern University. Other: 2 had other specific plans.

Student Life Upper grades have uniform requirement. Discipline rests primarily with faculty.

Tuition and Aid Day student tuition: $28,700.

Admissions Traditional secondary-level entrance grade is 10. For fall 2015, 10 students applied for upper-level admission, 10 were accepted, 10 enrolled. No application fee required. Interview required.

Athletics Interscholastic: basketball (boys, girls), soccer (b,g), volleyball (b,g); intramural: basketball (b,g), soccer (b,g), volleyball (b,g); coed interscholastic: swimming and diving; coed intramural: cooperative games. 3 PE instructors.

Computers Computer network features include on-campus library services, Internet access, Internet filtering or blocking technology. Campus intranet and student e-mail accounts are available to students. Students grades are available online.

Contact Mrs. MONICA RIVERO, DIRECTOR OF ADMISSIONS. 58-2129933922 Ext. 1011. E-mail: admissions@ecak12.com. Website: http://www.ecak12.com/

THE ETHEL WALKER SCHOOL

230 Bushy Hill Road
Simsbury, Connecticut 06070

Head of School: Mrs. Elizabeth Cromwell Speers

General Information Girls' boarding and day college-preparatory and arts school. Boarding grades 9–12, day grades 6–12. Founded: 1911. Setting: suburban. Nearest major city is Hartford. Students are housed in single-sex dormitories. 300-acre campus. 9 buildings on campus. Approved or accredited by Connecticut Association of Independent Schools, New England Association of Schools and Colleges, The Association of Boarding Schools, and Connecticut Department of Education. Member of National Association of Independent Schools and Secondary School Admission Test Board. Endowment: $15.9 million. Total enrollment: 252. Upper school average class size: 12. Upper school faculty-student ratio: 1:5. There are 180 required school days per year for Upper School students. Upper School students typically attend 5 days per week. The average school day consists of 7 hours.

Upper School Student Profile Grade 9: 58 students (58 girls); Grade 10: 49 students (49 girls); Grade 11: 49 students (49 girls); Grade 12: 64 students (64 girls). 61% of students are boarding students. 43% are state residents. 16 states are represented in upper school student body. 19% are international students. International students from Afghanistan, China, Germany, Republic of Korea, Somalia, and Spain; 9 other countries represented in student body.

Faculty School total: 45. In upper school: 12 men, 31 women; 33 have advanced degrees; 30 reside on campus.

Subjects Offered 3-dimensional art, acting, advanced studio art-AP, African history, African literature, African studies, algebra, American government, American history, American history-AP, American literature, anatomy and physiology, Ancient Greek, ancient world history, art, art history, art-AP, Asian history, astronomy, bell choir, biology, biology-AP, calculus, calculus-AP, Caribbean history, ceramics, chemistry, chemistry-AP, Chinese, choir, choral music, choreography, civil rights, computer literacy, computer science, computer science-AP, conceptual physics, concert bell choir, concert choir, creative writing, digital photography, directing, diversity studies, drama, drama performance, dramatic arts, drawing, drawing and design, East Asian history, economics, economics-AP, English, English composition, English literature, English literature and composition-AP, English literature-AP, environmental science, environmental science-AP, environmental studies, equine science, ethics, European history, European history-AP, fiber arts, fiction, fine arts, forensics, French language-AP, geography, geometry, graphic design, health and wellness, history, history-AP, honors algebra, honors English, honors geometry, honors U.S. history, honors world history, independent study, instrumental music, Islamic studies, justice seminar, Latin, Latin American history, Latin-AP, leadership, macro/microeconomics-AP, Mandarin, Middle Eastern history, modern civilization, modern European history, modern European history-AP, music, music theory, musical theater, mythology, newspaper, painting, peace and justice, philosophy of government, photography, physics, physics-AP, playwriting, poetry, pre-calculus, psychology, psychology-AP, public speaking, religion and culture, Russian studies, sculpture, senior project, set design, Shakespeare, social justice, Spanish, Spanish language-AP, Spanish literature-AP, statistics-AP, student publications, studio art-AP, the Web, theater, trigonometry, U.S. history, U.S. history-AP, visual and performing arts, voice, Western civilization, women in literature, women's health, world history, world literature, world religions, writing, yearbook.

Graduation Requirements Arts and fine arts (art, music, dance, drama), English, ethics, foreign language, history, leadership, mathematics, performing arts, science, women's health, Junior/Senior project, community service hours. Community service is required.

Special Academic Programs 19 Advanced Placement exams for which test preparation is offered; honors section; independent study; term-away projects; study at local college for college credit; study abroad; academic accommodation for the gifted, the musically talented, and the artistically talented; ESL (12 students enrolled).

College Admission Counseling 66 students graduated in 2014; all went to college, including Barnard College; Bates College; Boston University; Carnegie Mellon University; Colgate University; Harvard University. Mean SAT critical reading: 569, mean SAT math: 576, mean SAT writing: 575, mean composite ACT: 24.

Student Life Upper grades have specified standards of dress, student council, honor system. Discipline rests equally with students and faculty.

Tuition and Aid Day student tuition: $38,600; 7-day tuition and room/board: $53,550. Tuition installment plan (monthly payment plans, individually arranged payment plans, 1-, 2-, and 10-payment plans). Need-based scholarship grants available. In 2014–15, 42% of upper-school students received aid. Total amount of financial aid awarded in 2014–15: $3,058,789.

Admissions Traditional secondary-level entrance grade is 9. For fall 2014, 316 students applied for upper-level admission, 181 were accepted, 77 enrolled. SSAT and TOEFL required. Deadline for receipt of application materials: January 15. Application fee required: $60. Interview required.

Athletics Interscholastic: alpine skiing, basketball, dance, dressage, equestrian sports, field hockey, golf, horseback riding, independent competitive sports, lacrosse, modern dance, nordic skiing, skiing (downhill), soccer, softball, squash, swimming and diving, tennis, volleyball; intramural: ballet, climbing, combined training, cross-country running, dance, dance team, equestrian sports, fitness, hiking/backpacking, jogging, kayaking, mountain biking, mountaineering, Nautilus, outdoor activities, outdoor adventure, physical fitness, physical training, rock climbing, ropes courses, running, strength & conditioning, wall climbing, weight lifting, weight training, yoga. 5 coaches, 1 athletic trainer.

Computers Computer network features include on-campus library services, online commercial services, Internet access, wireless campus network, Internet filtering or blocking technology. Student e-mail accounts and computer access in designated common areas are available to students. Students grades are available online. The school has a published electronic and media policy.

Contact Ms. Missy Shea, Director of Admission. 860-408-4200. Fax: 860-408-4201. E-mail: mshea@ethelwalker.org. Website: www.ethelwalker.org

ETON ACADEMY

Birmingham, Michigan

See Special Needs Schools section.

EXCEL CHRISTIAN ACADEMY

325 Old Mill Road

Cartersville, Georgia 30120

Head of School: Tommy Harris

General Information Coeducational day college-preparatory school, affiliated with Christian faith. Grades K–12. Founded: 1993. Setting: suburban. 15-acre campus. 3 buildings on campus. Approved or accredited by Association of Christian Schools International, Southern Association of Colleges and Schools, and Georgia Department of Education. Total enrollment: 297. Upper school average class size: 20. Upper school faculty-student ratio: 1:18. There are 177 required school days per year for Upper School students. Upper School students typically attend 5 days per week. The average school day consists of 7 hours and 25 minutes.

Upper School Student Profile Grade 9: 21 students (9 boys, 12 girls); Grade 10: 30 students (13 boys, 17 girls); Grade 11: 26 students (16 boys, 10 girls); Grade 12: 24 students (9 boys, 15 girls). 99% of students are Christian.

Faculty School total: 29. In upper school: 10 men, 10 women; 10 have advanced degrees.

Subjects Offered Algebra, American government, anatomy, art, band, Bible, British literature, broadcast journalism, business education, calculus-AP, chemistry, choir, chorus, computer applications, concert band, dance, drama, earth science, electives, English, English literature, foreign language, government, health, history, life science, literature, mathematics, music, personal fitness, physical education, physical science, physics, pre-algebra, psychology, reading, science, social studies, Spanish, trigonometry, U.S. government, U.S. history, U.S. history-AP, world geography, world history.

Graduation Requirements Advanced Placement courses, Bible, computer technologies, electives, English, foreign language, history, mathematics, physical education (includes health), science.

Special Academic Programs 2 Advanced Placement exams for which test preparation is offered; honors section; study at local college for college credit.

College Admission Counseling 18 students graduated in 2014; 17 went to college, including Georgia Institute of Technology; Kennesaw State University; Truett-McConnell College; Valdosta State University. Other: 1 had other specific plans. Median SAT critical reading: 480, median SAT math: 490, median SAT writing: 470. Mean combined SAT: 1481. 11% scored over 600 on SAT critical reading, 17% scored over 600 on SAT math, 17% scored over 600 on SAT writing, 17% scored over 1800 on combined SAT.

Student Life Upper grades have uniform requirement, student council, honor system. Discipline rests primarily with faculty.

Tuition and Aid Day student tuition: $8640. Tuition installment plan (monthly payment plans). Need-based scholarship grants available.

Admissions Traditional secondary-level entrance grade is 9. For fall 2014, 21 students applied for upper-level admission, 21 were accepted, 17 enrolled. Any standardized test required. Deadline for receipt of application materials: none. Application fee required: $1125. Interview required.

Athletics Interscholastic: baseball (boys), basketball (b,g), cheering (g), cross-country running (b,g), softball (g); intramural: football (b); coed interscholastic: soccer. 2 PE instructors, 4 coaches.

Computers Computers are regularly used in business applications, computer applications, newspaper, yearbook classes. Computer network features include Internet access, wireless campus network, Internet filtering or blocking technology. Computer access in designated common areas is available to students. Students grades are available online. The school has a published electronic and media policy.

Contact Mrs. Ann Fox, Administrator. 770-382-9488. Fax: 770-606-9884. E-mail: afox@excelca.org. Website: www.excelca.org

EXPLORATIONS ACADEMY

PO Box 3014

Bellingham, Washington 98227

Head of School: Daniel Kirkpatrick

General Information Coeducational day and distance learning college-preparatory, experiential education, and international field study expeditions school. Ungraded, ages 11–18. Distance learning grades 9–12. Founded: 1995. Setting: urban. Nearest major city is Vancouver, BC, Canada. 1-acre campus. 1 building on campus. Approved or accredited by Northwest Accreditation Commission, Northwest Association of Independent Schools, Northwest Association of Schools and Colleges, and Washington Department of Education. Total enrollment: 35. Upper school average class size: 10. Upper school faculty-student ratio: 1:7. There are 177 required school days per year for Upper School students. Upper School students typically attend 5 days per week. The average school day consists of 6 hours.

Faculty School total: 11. In upper school: 5 men, 6 women; 7 have advanced degrees.

Subjects Offered Agriculture, American literature, anatomy and physiology, anthropology, archaeology, art, boat building, botany, calculus, carpentry, chemistry, Chinese, computer graphics, computer programming, conflict resolution, construction, creative writing, desktop publishing, drawing, earth science, ecology, environmental science, first aid, gardening, gender issues, geology, government, health, horticulture, human relations, journalism, Latin American studies, leadership, marine biology, media, meteorology, microbiology, music, music history, painting, philosophy, photography, physical education, physics, poetry, political science, printmaking, psychology, sculpture, sexuality, short story, Spanish, technology, theater design and production, video film production, world cultures, world geography, world history, world literature, writing.

Graduation Requirements Arts and fine arts (art, music, dance, drama), computer science, English, foreign language, human relations, lab science, mathematics, occupational education, physical education (includes health), science, social sciences, social studies (includes history), U.S. government and politics, Washington State and Northwest History, world history, one term of self-designed interdisciplinary studies, one month-long international study/service expedition. Community service is required.

Special Academic Programs Advanced Placement exam preparation; honors section; accelerated programs; independent study; term-away projects; academic accommodation for the gifted.

College Admission Counseling 6 students graduated in 2015; 5 went to college, including The Evergreen State College; University of Washington; Western Washington University. Other: 1 went to work.

Student Life Upper grades have honor system. Discipline rests primarily with faculty.

Summer Programs Enrichment, advancement, art/fine arts, rigorous outdoor training, computer instruction programs offered; session focuses on experiential learning; held both on and off campus; held at local urban and wilderness areas; accepts boys and girls; open to students from other schools. 12 students usually enrolled. 2016 schedule: July 8 to August 16. Application deadline: none.

Tuition and Aid Day student tuition: $15,400. Tuition installment plan (monthly payment plans, individually arranged payment plans, school's own payment plan). Merit scholarship grants, need-based scholarship grants, need-based loans, low-interest loans with deferred payment available. In 2015–16, 48% of upper-school students received aid; total upper-school merit-scholarship money awarded: $35,000. Total amount of financial aid awarded in 2015–16: $200,000.

Admissions Traditional secondary-level entrance age is 14. For fall 2015, 42 students applied for upper-level admission, 40 were accepted, 35 enrolled. Non-standardized placement tests required. Deadline for receipt of application materials: none. Application fee required: $60. Interview required.

Computers Computers are regularly used in animation, art, English, French, graphics, mathematics, media production, publications, SAT preparation, science, writing, yearbook classes. Computer network features include online commercial services, Internet access, wireless campus network. Computer access in designated common areas is available to students. The school has a published electronic and media policy.

Contact Jeanie Tran, Outreach and Admissions Coordinator. 360-671-8085. Fax: 360-671-2521. E-mail: info@explorationsacademy.org. Website: www.ExplorationsAcademy.org

EZELL-HARDING CHRISTIAN SCHOOL

574 Bell Road

Antioch, Tennessee 37013

Head of School: Mrs. Belvia Pruitt

General Information Coeducational day college-preparatory, religious studies, and STEM school, affiliated with Church of Christ. Grades PK–12. Founded: 1973. Setting: suburban. Nearest major city is Nashville. 30-acre campus. 1 building on campus. Approved or accredited by National Christian School Association, Southern Association of Colleges and Schools, and Tennessee Association of Independent Schools. Endowment: $100,000. Total enrollment: 431. Upper school average class size: 17. Upper school faculty-student ratio: 1:9. There are 176 required school days per year for Upper School students. Upper School students typically attend 5 days per week. The average school day consists of 7 hours.

Upper School Student Profile Grade 9: 39 students (14 boys, 25 girls); Grade 10: 47 students (24 boys, 23 girls); Grade 11: 46 students (28 boys, 18 girls); Grade 12: 37 students (23 boys, 14 girls). 25% of students are members of Church of Christ.

Faculty School total: 21. In upper school: 10 men, 11 women; 16 have advanced degrees.

Subjects Offered ACT preparation, advanced biology, advanced chemistry, advanced math, Advanced Placement courses, algebra, American history, American history-AP, anatomy and physiology, art, band, Bible, biology, biotechnology, calculus, calculus-AP, chemistry, chorus, computer applications, economics, English literature and composition-AP, European history-AP, fitness, geography, geometry, government, grammar, keyboarding, physical science, psychology, science, Spanish, statistics-AP, trigonometry, weight training, wellness, world history.

Graduation Requirements All academic, Bible.

Special Academic Programs 5 Advanced Placement exams for which test preparation is offered; honors section; independent study; study at local college for college credit.

College Admission Counseling 36 students graduated in 2015; 34 went to college, including Lipscomb University; Middle Tennessee State University; The University of Tennessee; The University of Tennessee at Chattanooga. Other: 2 had other specific plans. Median composite ACT: 24. 34% scored over 26 on composite ACT.

Student Life Upper grades have uniform requirement, student council. Discipline rests primarily with faculty.

Tuition and Aid Day student tuition: $9000. Tuition installment plan (The Tuition Plan, monthly payment plans). Need-based scholarship grants available. In 2015–16, 31% of upper-school students received aid. Total amount of financial aid awarded in 2015–16: $136,000.

Admissions Traditional secondary-level entrance grade is 9. For fall 2015, 21 students applied for upper-level admission, 17 were accepted, 9 enrolled. MAT 7 Metropolitan Achievement Test, TOEFL or SLEP or writing sample required. Deadline for receipt of application materials: none. Application fee required: $75. Interview required.

Athletics Interscholastic: baseball (boys), basketball (b,g), bowling (b,g), cheering (g), cross-country running (b,g), drill team (g), football (b), golf (b,g), soccer (b,g), softball (g), tennis (b,g), track and field (b,g), volleyball (g), weight training (b,g). 1 PE instructor, 6 coaches, 1 athletic trainer.

Computers Computers are regularly used in all academic classes. Computer network features include on-campus library services, Internet access, wireless campus network, Internet filtering or blocking technology. Student e-mail accounts are available to students. Students grades are available online. The school has a published electronic and media policy.

Contact Mrs. Lisa Phillips, Admissions Officer. 615-367-0532 Ext. 109. Fax: 615-399-8747. E-mail: lphillips@ezellharding.com. Website: www.ezellharding.com

FAIRFIELD COLLEGE PREPARATORY SCHOOL

1073 North Benson Road
Fairfield, Connecticut 06824-5157

Head of School: Rev. John J. Hanwell, SJ

General Information Boys' day college-preparatory, arts, religious studies, and technology school, affiliated with Roman Catholic Church. Grades 9–12. Founded: 1942. Setting: suburban. Nearest major city is Bridgeport. 220-acre campus. 4 buildings on campus. Approved or accredited by Jesuit Secondary Education Association, New England Association of Schools and Colleges, and Connecticut Department of Education. Member of National Association of Independent Schools. Endowment: $17 million. Total enrollment: 901. Upper school average class size: 21. Upper school faculty-student ratio: 1:18. There are 182 required school days per year for Upper School students. Upper School students typically attend 5 days per week. The average school day consists of 5 hours and 50 minutes.

Upper School Student Profile Grade 9: 249 students (249 boys); Grade 10: 211 students (211 boys); Grade 11: 222 students (222 boys); Grade 12: 219 students (219 boys). 68% of students are Roman Catholic.

Faculty School total: 55. In upper school: 33 men, 22 women; 49 have advanced degrees.

Subjects Offered Advanced Placement courses, algebra, American Civil War, American government, American history, American history-AP, American literature, American literature-AP, art, Asian studies, band, biology, biology-AP, British literature, British literature-AP, calculus, calculus-AP, career exploration, chemistry, chemistry-AP, choir, chorus, Christian education, Christian ethics, Christian scripture, Christian studies, Christianity, civil rights, Civil War, college admission preparation, college planning, community service, computer education, computer literacy, computer science, constitutional history of U.S., constitutional law, creative writing, drama, drama workshop, drawing and design, driver education, economics, English, English literature, English literature and composition-AP, English literature-AP, English-AP, environmental science, ethical decision making, ethics and responsibility, European history, European history-AP, expository writing, fine arts, French, French language-AP, French literature-AP, French-AP, geometry, government-AP, grammar, graphics, guidance, history, history of religion, history of the Catholic Church, honors algebra, honors English, honors geometry, honors U.S. history, introduction to theater, jazz band, journalism, language and composition, language arts, language structure, Latin, Latin-AP, Life of Christ, literary magazine, mathematics, Middle East, modern European history-AP, moral theology, music, musical productions, musical theater, physics, physics-AP, pre-calculus, religion, remedial study skills, SAT preparation, science, social justice, social studies, sociology, Spanish, Spanish language-AP, Spanish-AP, student government, studio art, symphonic band, technical drawing, theater, theater arts, theology, trigonometry, U.S. constitutional history, U.S. history-AP, United States government-AP, values and decisions, visual and performing arts, visual arts, Web site design, Western civilization, wind ensemble, word processing, world history, world literature, world religions, world religions, world studies, World War I, World War II, writing.

Graduation Requirements Arts and fine arts (art, music, dance, drama), computer science, English, foreign language, mathematics, religion (includes Bible studies and theology), science, social studies (includes history), senior comprehensive exercises. Community service is required.

Special Academic Programs Advanced Placement exam preparation; honors section; study at local college for college credit.

College Admission Counseling 201 students graduated in 2015; 193 went to college, including College of the Holy Cross; Loyola University Maryland; Saint Joseph's University; University of Connecticut; University of Notre Dame; Villanova University. Other: 8 entered a postgraduate year. Mean SAT critical reading: 588, mean SAT math: 604, mean SAT writing: 594, mean combined SAT: 1786.

Student Life Upper grades have specified standards of dress, student council. Discipline rests primarily with faculty. Attendance at religious services is required.

Summer Programs Remediation, enrichment, sports, computer instruction programs offered; session focuses on enrichment; held on campus; accepts boys and girls; open to students from other schools. 160 students usually enrolled. 2016 schedule: June 30 to July 25.

Tuition and Aid Day student tuition: $18,675. Tuition installment plan (FACTS Tuition Payment Plan). Need-based scholarship grants available. In 2015–16, 29% of upper-school students received aid. Total amount of financial aid awarded in 2015–16: $2,163,000.

Admissions Traditional secondary-level entrance grade is 9. For fall 2015, 481 students applied for upper-level admission, 249 enrolled. High School Placement Test required. Deadline for receipt of application materials: December 1. Application fee required: $60.

Athletics Interscholastic: baseball, basketball, bowling, crew, cross-country running, diving, fencing, football, golf, ice hockey, indoor track & field, lacrosse, rugby, sailing, skiing (downhill), soccer, strength & conditioning, swimming and diving, tennis, track and field, weight training, winter (indoor) track, wrestling; intramural: alpine skiing, basketball, bicycling, fitness, flag football, mountain biking, skiing (downhill), strength & conditioning, table tennis, weight lifting, weight training, whiffle ball. 33 coaches, 2 athletic trainers.

Computers Computers are regularly used in art, English, foreign language, history, mathematics, science, technology, theology classes. Computer network features include on-campus library services, online commercial services, Internet access, Internet filtering or blocking technology. Student e-mail accounts are available to students. Students grades are available online. The school has a published electronic and media policy.

Contact Mr. Andrew M. Davenport, Admissions Counselor. 203-254-4210. Fax: 203-254-4108. E-mail: adavenport@fairfieldprep.org. Website: www.fairfieldprep.org

FAITH CHRISTIAN HIGH SCHOOL

3105 Colusa Highway
Yuba City, California 95993

Head of School: Mr. Stephen Finlay

General Information Coeducational day college-preparatory, arts, religious studies, and technology school, affiliated with Christian faith. Grades 9–12. Founded: 1975. Setting: small town. Nearest major city is Sacramento. 10-acre campus. 4 buildings on campus. Approved or accredited by Association of Christian Schools International, Western Association of Schools and Colleges, and California Department of Education. Total enrollment: 77. Upper school average class size: 25. Upper school faculty-student ratio: 1:12. There are 175 required school days per year for Upper School students. Upper School students typically attend 5 days per week. The average school day consists of 5 hours and 30 minutes.

Upper School Student Profile Grade 9: 15 students (8 boys, 7 girls); Grade 10: 22 students (10 boys, 12 girls); Grade 11: 21 students (10 boys, 11 girls); Grade 12: 19 students (12 boys, 7 girls). 85% of students are Christian.

Faculty School total: 16. In upper school: 10 men, 6 women; 4 have advanced degrees.

Subjects Offered Algebra, arts, Bible, biology, biology-AP, British literature, calculus-AP, chemistry, civics, computer science, computer studies, concert band, drama, economics, English, English composition, English literature, English-AP, geography, geometry, government, health, honors English, physical education, physical science, pre-calculus, senior project, Spanish, U.S. history, world geography, world history, yearbook.

Graduation Requirements Algebra, Bible, biology, civics, economics, English, geometry, health, physical science, senior project, U.S. history, world geography, world history.

Special Academic Programs Advanced Placement exam preparation; study at local college for college credit.

College Admission Counseling 22 students graduated in 2014; 20 went to college, including Azusa Pacific University; Texas Christian University; University of California, Davis; University of California, Irvine; University of Nevada, Reno; University of the Pacific. Other: 1 went to work, 1 entered military service. Median SAT critical reading: 580, median SAT math: 540, median SAT writing: 550, median combined SAT: 1640, median composite ACT: 20. 30% scored over 600 on SAT critical reading, 20% scored over 600 on SAT math, 30% scored over 600 on SAT writing, 30% scored over 1800 on combined SAT, 25% scored over 26 on composite ACT.

Student Life Upper grades have specified standards of dress, student council, honor system. Discipline rests primarily with faculty. Attendance at religious services is required.

Tuition and Aid Day student tuition: $7460. Tuition installment plan (monthly payment plans). Tuition reduction for siblings, need-based scholarship grants available. In 2014–15, 20% of upper-school students received aid. Total amount of financial aid awarded in 2014–15: $50,000.

Admissions Traditional secondary-level entrance grade is 9. For fall 2014, 18 students applied for upper-level admission, 17 were accepted, 17 enrolled. Achievement tests required. Deadline for receipt of application materials: none. Application fee required: $50. Interview required.

Athletics Interscholastic: baseball (boys), basketball (b,g), cheering (g), soccer (b), softball (g), volleyball (g); coed interscholastic: golf. 1 PE instructor, 8 coaches.

Computers Computers are regularly used in all academic classes. Computer network features include on-campus library services, Internet access, Internet filtering or blocking technology. Students grades are available online. The school has a published electronic and media policy.

Contact Mrs. Sue Shorey, Secretary. 530-674-5474. Fax: 530-674-0194. E-mail: sshorey@fcs-k12.org. Website: www.fcs-k12.org

FAITH CHRISTIAN SCHOOL

7464 E Main St
Mesa, Arizona 85207

Head of School: Mr. Dick Buckingham

General Information Coeducational day college-preparatory, general academic, and religious studies school, affiliated with Christian faith. Grades K–12. Founded: 1988. Setting: suburban. 1 building on campus. Approved or accredited by Association of Christian Schools International, Christian Schools International, and North Central Association of Colleges and Schools. Upper school average class size: 20. Upper school faculty-student ratio: 1:15. There are 185 required school days per year for Upper School students. Upper School students typically attend 5 days per week. The average school day consists of 6 hours and 20 minutes.

Upper School Student Profile 90% of students are Christian faith.

Faculty School total: 14. In upper school: 4 men, 3 women; 4 have advanced degrees.

Subjects Offered Algebra, American government, American literature, art, Basic programming, Bible, biology, chemistry, chorus, Christian and Hebrew scripture, Christian ethics, Christian testament, civics/free enterprise, computer applications, debate, English, general math, Greek, math applications, physical education, pre-calculus, Spanish, world cultures, world religions, yearbook.

College Admission Counseling 6 students graduated in 2014; all went to college, including Arizona State University at the Tempe campus; Grand Canyon University.

Student Life Upper grades have uniform requirement, student council. Discipline rests primarily with faculty. Attendance at religious services is required.

Tuition and Aid Day student tuition: $7160. Tuition installment plan (FACTS Tuition Payment Plan). Tuition reduction for siblings, need-based scholarship grants available.

Admissions Traditional secondary-level entrance grade is 9. Deadline for receipt of application materials: none. Application fee required: $250.

Athletics Interscholastic: basketball (boys, girls), soccer (b,g), volleyball (g). 2 PE instructors, 2 coaches.

Computers Computers are regularly used in computer applications, keyboarding, word processing, yearbook classes. Computer network features include Internet access, Internet filtering or blocking technology. Students grades are available online.

Contact Admissions. 480-833-1983. Fax: 480-361-2075. E-mail: admissions@faith-christian.org. Website: www.faith-christian.org

FAITH LUTHERAN HIGH SCHOOL

2015 South Hualapai Way
Las Vegas, Nevada 89117-6949

Head of School: Dr. Steven J. Buuck

General Information Coeducational day college-preparatory and religious studies school, affiliated with Lutheran Church–Missouri Synod, Evangelical Lutheran Church in America. Grades 6–12. Founded: 1979. Setting: suburban. 49-acre campus. 5 buildings on campus. Approved or accredited by National Lutheran School Accreditation, Northwest Accreditation Commission, Northwest Association of Schools and Colleges, and Nevada Department of Education. Endowment: $1 million. Total enrollment: 1,572. Upper school average class size: 25. Upper school faculty-student ratio: 1:17. There are 180 required school days per year for Upper School students. Upper School students typically attend 5 days per week. The average school day consists of 7 hours.

Upper School Student Profile Grade 6: 242 students (125 boys, 117 girls); Grade 7: 276 students (147 boys, 129 girls); Grade 8: 248 students (132 boys, 116 girls); Grade 9: 247 students (129 boys, 118 girls); Grade 10: 239 students (120 boys, 119 girls); Grade 11: 207 students (105 boys, 102 girls); Grade 12: 227 students (117 boys, 110 girls). 24% of students are Lutheran Church–Missouri Synod, Evangelical Lutheran Church in America.

Faculty School total: 109. In upper school: 44 men, 65 women; 71 have advanced degrees.

Subjects Offered Advanced Placement courses, algebra, American history, art, biology, chemistry, computer science, earth science, English, fine arts, fitness, geometry, German, health, mathematics, music, physical education, physical science, religion, SAT/ACT preparation, science, social studies, Spanish.

Graduation Requirements American history, arts and fine arts (art, music, dance, drama), computer science, English, foreign language, mathematics, physical education (includes health), religion (includes Bible studies and theology), science, social studies (includes history), community service.

Special Academic Programs 7 Advanced Placement exams for which test preparation is offered; honors section; independent study; study at local college for college credit; academic accommodation for the musically talented.

College Admission Counseling 177 students graduated in 2015; 173 went to college, including Concordia University Irvine; Grand Canyon University; University of Nevada, Las Vegas; University of Nevada, Reno. Other: 2 went to work, 2 entered military service. Median SAT critical reading: 534, median SAT math: 534, median SAT writing: 537, median combined SAT: 1605, median composite ACT: 24. 25% scored over 600 on SAT critical reading, 25% scored over 600 on SAT math, 20% scored over 600 on SAT writing, 23% scored over 1800 on combined SAT, 30% scored over 26 on composite ACT.

Student Life Upper grades have uniform requirement, student council. Discipline rests primarily with faculty. Attendance at religious services is required.

Summer Programs Remediation programs offered; held on campus; accepts boys and girls; not open to students from other schools. 125 students usually enrolled.

Tuition and Aid Day student tuition: $11,100. Tuition installment plan (monthly payment plans, individually arranged payment plans). Tuition reduction for siblings, need-based scholarship grants available. In 2015–16, 12% of upper-school students received aid. Total amount of financial aid awarded in 2015–16: $555,000.

Admissions Traditional secondary-level entrance grade is 9. For fall 2015, 161 students applied for upper-level admission, 151 were accepted, 145 enrolled. High School Placement Test and Stanford 9 required. Deadline for receipt of application materials: none. Application fee required: $350. Interview required.

Athletics Interscholastic: aerobics/dance (girls), aquatics (b,g), baseball (b), basketball (b,g), cheering (g), cross-country running (b,g), dance team (g), football (b), golf (b,g), lacrosse (b,g), soccer (b,g), softball (g), swimming and diving (b,g), tennis (b,g), track and field (b,g), volleyball (g), wrestling (b); intramural: strength & conditioning (b,g), weight training (b,g); coed interscholastic: strength & conditioning; coed intramural: skiing (downhill), snowboarding, ultimate Frisbee. 7 PE instructors, 26 coaches, 1 athletic trainer.

Computers Computers are regularly used in keyboarding, yearbook classes. Computer network features include on-campus library services, online commercial services, Internet access, wireless campus network, Internet filtering or blocking technology. Student e-mail accounts and computer access in designated common areas are available to students. Students grades are available online. The school has a published electronic and media policy.

Contact Mr. Joel Arnold, Director of Admissions. 702-804-4413. Fax: 702-562-7728. E-mail: arnoldj@flhsemail.org. Website: www.faithlutheranlv.org

FALMOUTH ACADEMY

7 Highfield Drive
Falmouth, Massachusetts 02540

Head of School: Mr. Stephen A. Duffy

General Information Coeducational day college-preparatory and arts school. Grades 7–12. Founded: 1976. Setting: small town. Nearest major city is Boston. 34-acre campus. 2 buildings on campus. Approved or accredited by New England Association of Schools and Colleges. Member of National Association of Independent Schools and Secondary School Admission Test Board. Endowment: $5 million. Total enrollment: 200. Upper school average class size: 12. Upper school faculty-student ratio: 1:4. There are 167 required school days per year for Upper School students. Upper School students typically attend 5 days per week. The average school day consists of 7 hours and 5 minutes.

Upper School Student Profile Grade 9: 34 students (20 boys, 14 girls); Grade 10: 31 students (14 boys, 17 girls); Grade 11: 26 students (13 boys, 13 girls); Grade 12: 33 students (19 boys, 14 girls).

Faculty School total: 40. In upper school: 10 men, 19 women; 22 have advanced degrees.

Subjects Offered Algebra, American history, American literature, art, biology, calculus, ceramics, chemistry, creative writing, drama, earth science, ecology, English, English literature, environmental science, European history, expository writing, fine arts, French, geography, geology, geometry, German, grammar, health, history, journalism, mathematics, music, photography, physical education, physics, science, sculpture, social studies, statistics, theater, trigonometry, woodworking, world history, world literature, writing.

Graduation Requirements Arts and fine arts (art, music, dance, drama), English, foreign language, history, mathematics, science.

Special Academic Programs 5 Advanced Placement exams for which test preparation is offered; independent study; term-away projects; study abroad.

College Admission Counseling 22 students graduated in 2015; all went to college, including Connecticut College; University of Massachusetts Amherst. Mean SAT critical reading: 679, mean SAT math: 651, mean SAT writing: 660.

Student Life Upper grades have specified standards of dress, student council, honor system. Discipline rests primarily with faculty.

Summer Programs Enrichment, sports, art/fine arts programs offered; held on campus; accepts boys and girls; open to students from other schools. 150 students usually enrolled. 2016 schedule: June 29 to August 14.

Tuition and Aid Day student tuition: $26,990. Merit scholarship grants, need-based scholarship grants, need-based loans available. In 2015–16, 45% of upper-school students received aid; total upper-school merit-scholarship money awarded: $3000. Total amount of financial aid awarded in 2015–16: $928,000.

Admissions Traditional secondary-level entrance grade is 9. For fall 2015, 29 students applied for upper-level admission, 26 were accepted, 9 enrolled. SSAT required. Deadline for receipt of application materials: February 15. Application fee required: $65. On-campus interview required.

Athletics Interscholastic: basketball (boys, girls), lacrosse (b,g), soccer (b,g). 1 PE instructor, 2 coaches, 1 athletic trainer.

Computers Computers are regularly used in design, English, foreign language, humanities, mathematics, science classes. Computer resources include on-campus library services, Internet access, wireless campus network, Internet filtering or blocking technology. The school has a published electronic and media policy.

Contact Ms. Karen A. Loder, Director of Admission and Enrollment Management. 508-457-9696 Ext. 236. Fax: 508-457-4112. E-mail: kloder@falmouthacademy.org. Website: www.falmouthacademy.org

FATHER DUENAS MEMORIAL SCHOOL

Mangilao
PO Box FD
Hagatna, Guam 96910
Head of School: Fr. Jeffrey San Nicolas

General Information Boys' day college-preparatory and College Preparatory school, affiliated with Roman Catholic Church. Grades 9–12. Founded: 1948. Setting: rural. 9 buildings on campus. Approved or accredited by Western Association of Schools and Colleges, Western Catholic Education Association, and Guam Department of Education. Member of Secondary School Admission Test Board. Total enrollment: 435. Upper school average class size: 25. Upper school faculty-student ratio: 1:25. There are 180 required school days per year for Upper School students. Upper School students typically attend 5 days per week. The average school day consists of 7 hours.

Upper School Student Profile Grade 10: 93 students (93 boys); Grade 11: 120 students (120 boys); Grade 12: 123 students (123 boys); Grade 13: 99 students (99 boys). 70% of students are Roman Catholic.

Faculty School total: 27. In upper school: 20 men, 7 women; 10 have advanced degrees.

Subjects Offered Accounting, algebra, American government, American literature, biology, biology-AP, British literature, calculus-AP, chemistry, chemistry-AP, chorus, church history, composition, computer science, English literature and composition-AP, environmental studies, fine arts, general science, geography, geometry, government and politics-AP, introduction to literature, Japanese, methods of research, naval science, oral communications, physical education, physics, pre-calculus, psychology, scripture, Spanish, theology, U.S. history, U.S. history-AP, world history, world literature.

Special Academic Programs Advanced Placement exam preparation; study at local college for college credit.

College Admission Counseling 101 students graduated in 2015; 90 went to college. Other: 5 went to work, 4 entered military service, 1 had other specific plans.

Student Life Upper grades have uniform requirement, student council, honor system. Discipline rests primarily with faculty. Attendance at religious services is required.

Summer Programs Remediation programs offered; held on campus; accepts boys and girls; open to students from other schools. 2016 schedule: June 1 to July 7.

Tuition and Aid Day student tuition: $8000. Tuition reduction for siblings, merit scholarship grants, need-based scholarship grants available.

Admissions Traditional secondary-level entrance grade is 9. Otis-Lennon Mental Ability Test, Reading for Understanding and WRAT required. Deadline for receipt of application materials: May 30. Application fee required: $50. Interview recommended.

Athletics Interscholastic: baseball, basketball, canoeing/kayaking, cross-country running, drill team, football, JROTC drill, rugby, soccer, tennis, track and field, volleyball, wrestling; intramural: basketball, indoor soccer, table tennis, volleyball. 4 PE instructors, 30 coaches.

Computers Computer network features include on-campus library services, online commercial services, Internet access, wireless campus network, Internet filtering or

blocking technology. Student e-mail accounts are available to students. Students grades are available online. The school has a published electronic and media policy.
Contact 671-734-2261. Fax: 671-734-5738. Website: www.fatherduenas.com

FATHER LOPEZ HIGH SCHOOL

3918 LPGA Boulevard
Daytona Beach, Florida 32124
Head of School: Dr. Michael J. Coury

General Information Coeducational day college-preparatory and religious studies school, affiliated with Roman Catholic Church. Grades 9–12. Founded: 1959. Setting: suburban. 90-acre campus. 7 buildings on campus. Approved or accredited by National Catholic Education Association, Southern Association of Colleges and Schools, and Florida Department of Education. Total enrollment: 474. Upper school average class size: 16. Upper school faculty-student ratio: 1:13. There are 181 required school days per year for Upper School students. Upper School students typically attend 5 days per week. The average school day consists of 7 hours.

Upper School Student Profile Grade 9: 152 students (78 boys, 74 girls); Grade 10: 129 students (62 boys, 67 girls); Grade 11: 101 students (44 boys, 57 girls); Grade 12: 91 students (47 boys, 44 girls). 64% of students are Roman Catholic.

Faculty School total: 36. In upper school: 14 men, 22 women; 19 have advanced degrees.

Subjects Offered Advanced biology, advanced chemistry, advanced math, Advanced Placement courses, algebra, American history, American history-AP, American literature, anatomy and physiology, applied skills, art, art-AP, audio visual/media, basketball, biology, biology-AP, British literature, calculus, calculus-AP, Catholic belief and practice, chemistry, chemistry-AP, Chinese, Christian and Hebrew scripture, Christian studies, church history, classical Greek literature, college writing, communication skills, computer applications, computer art, computer graphics, computer technology certification, computer-aided design, consumer mathematics, critical writing, culinary arts, dance, dance performance, death and loss, design, digital art, digital photography, drama, drama performance, dramatic arts, drawing, economics, English, English as a foreign language, English literature, English literature and composition-AP, environmental science-AP, ESL, film, film and literature, filmmaking, French, French-AP, geometry, global studies, government, grammar, graphic design, health education, honors algebra, honors English, honors geometry, honors U.S. history, honors world history, human geography - AP, journalism, marine science, mathematics, moral and social development, philosophy, photography, physical education, physical science, physics, physics-AP, pre-calculus, psychology, psychology-AP, SAT/ACT preparation, senior science survey, senior seminar, senior thesis, social justice, sociology, Spanish, speech, statistics, studio art-AP, television, tennis, theology, trigonometry, U.S. government and politics-AP, U.S. history, U.S. history-AP, video film production, Web authoring, Web site design, weight training, weightlifting, world geography, world history, world history-AP, world religions, writing, yearbook.

Graduation Requirements Algebra, American history, American literature, arts, arts and fine arts (art, music, dance, drama), biology, British literature, chemistry, economics, electives, English, English literature, foreign language, geometry, health and wellness, mathematics, physical education (includes health), physics, science, theology, U.S. government, world history, 100 hours of community service.

Special Academic Programs 13 Advanced Placement exams for which test preparation is offered; honors section; study at local college for college credit; ESL (16 students enrolled).

College Admission Counseling 124 students graduated in 2015; 123 went to college, including Florida State University; Stetson University; University of Florida; University of North Florida; University of South Florida. Other: 1 entered military service. Mean SAT critical reading: 501, mean SAT math: 509, mean SAT writing: 492, mean composite ACT: 22. 14.4% scored over 600 on SAT critical reading, 19.5% scored over 600 on SAT math, 12.7% scored over 600 on SAT writing, 13.5% scored over 26 on composite ACT.

Student Life Upper grades have uniform requirement, student council, honor system. Discipline rests primarily with faculty. Attendance at religious services is required.

Tuition and Aid Day student tuition: $10,500. Tuition installment plan (FACTS Tuition Payment Plan). Tuition reduction for siblings, merit scholarship grants, need-based scholarship grants, tiered tuition rate based on income available. In 2015–16, 62% of upper-school students received aid. Total amount of financial aid awarded in 2015–16: $1,230,000.

Admissions Traditional secondary-level entrance grade is 9. For fall 2015, 186 students applied for upper-level admission, 169 were accepted, 145 enrolled. High School Placement Test required. Deadline for receipt of application materials: none. Application fee required: $50.

Athletics Interscholastic: baseball (boys), basketball (b,g), cross-country running (b,g), football (b), golf (b,g), lacrosse (b), soccer (b,g), softball (g), swimming and diving (b,g), tennis (b,g), track and field (b,g), volleyball (g), weight lifting (b,g); coed intramural: cheering, dance team, pom squad, table tennis, weight training. 2 PE instructors, 37 coaches, 1 athletic trainer.

Computers Computers are regularly used in all academic, art, computer applications, graphic design, media production, photography, video film production, yearbook classes. Computer network features include Internet access, wireless campus network, Internet filtering or blocking technology. Student e-mail accounts and computer access in designated common areas are available to students. Students grades are available online. The school has a published electronic and media policy.

Contact Mrs. Carmen Rivera, Admissions Coordinator. 386-253-5213 Ext. 325. Fax: 386-252-6101. E-mail: crivera@fatherlopez.org. Website: www.fatherlopez.org

FATHER RYAN HIGH SCHOOL

700 Norwood Drive
Nashville, Tennessee 37204

Head of School: Mr. Jim McIntyre

General Information Coeducational day college-preparatory, arts, and religious studies school, affiliated with Roman Catholic Church. Grades 9–12. Founded: 1925. Setting: suburban. 40-acre campus. 9 buildings on campus. Approved or accredited by National Catholic Education Association, Southern Association of Colleges and Schools, Southern Association of Independent Schools, Tennessee Association of Independent Schools, and The College Board. Endowment: $5 million. Total enrollment: 948. Upper school average class size: 20. Upper school faculty-student ratio: 1:12. There are 180 required school days per year for Upper School students. Upper School students typically attend 5 days per week. The average school day consists of 7 hours and 10 minutes.

Upper School Student Profile Grade 9: 254 students (149 boys, 105 girls); Grade 10: 240 students (141 boys, 99 girls); Grade 11: 227 students (134 boys, 93 girls); Grade 12: 227 students (132 boys, 95 girls). 90% of students are Roman Catholic.

Faculty School total: 84. In upper school: 43 men, 41 women; 48 have advanced degrees.

Subjects Offered 3-dimensional design, Advanced Placement courses, aerobics, algebra, American government, American history, American history-AP, American literature, anatomy, art, art history, art-AP, Bible studies, biology, British literature, calculus, calculus-AP, Catholic belief and practice, chemistry, chemistry-AP, Chinese, Chinese studies, chorus, church history, college counseling, college planning, college writing, computer programming, computer science, computer studies, dance, dance performance, drama, drama performance, driver education, economics, English, English literature, English-AP, European history, European history-AP, film studies, French, French-AP, geography, geometry, government-AP, government/civics, grammar, health, history, honors geometry, honors U.S. history, journalism, Latin, mathematics, music, physical education, physics, physics-AP, physiology, psychology, psychology-AP, religion, SAT preparation, science, Shakespeare, social studies, Spanish, Spanish-AP, speech, statistics-AP, theater, theater production, theology, trigonometry, U.S. government and politics-AP, Web site design, wind ensemble, world history, world literature, world religions, writing.

Graduation Requirements Arts and fine arts (art, music, dance, drama), computer science, English, foreign language, health education, mathematics, physical education (includes health), religion (includes Bible studies and theology), science, social studies (includes history), service hours required each year.

Special Academic Programs 27 Advanced Placement exams for which test preparation is offered; honors section; academic accommodation for the gifted, the musically talented, and the artistically talented; programs in English, mathematics for dyslexic students.

College Admission Counseling 211 students graduated in 2015; all went to college, including Belmont University; Middle Tennessee State University; Tennessee Technological University; The University of Tennessee; The University of Tennessee at Chattanooga; Western Kentucky University. Median SAT critical reading: 553, median SAT math: 524, median composite ACT: 24. 20% scored over 26 on composite ACT.

Student Life Upper grades have uniform requirement, student council. Discipline rests primarily with faculty. Attendance at religious services is required.

Summer Programs Remediation, enrichment, advancement, sports, art/fine arts, computer instruction programs offered; held on campus; accepts boys and girls; open to students from other schools. 240 students usually enrolled. 2016 schedule: June 1 to June 30. Application deadline: none.

Tuition and Aid Day student tuition: $13,275. Tuition installment plan (FACTS Tuition Payment Plan, individually arranged payment plans). Tuition reduction for siblings, need-based scholarship grants available. In 2014–15, 13% of upper-school students received aid. Total amount of financial aid awarded in 2014–15: $550,000.

Admissions Traditional secondary-level entrance grade is 9. For fall 2015, 347 students applied for upper-level admission, 278 were accepted, 251 enrolled. High School Placement Test required. Deadline for receipt of application materials: none. Application fee required: $85. On-campus interview required.

Athletics Interscholastic: aquatics (boys, girls), baseball (b), basketball (b,g), bowling (b,g), cheering (g), cross-country running (b,g), dance (b,g), dance squad (b), dance team (g), diving (b,g), football (b), golf (b,g), ice hockey (b), lacrosse (b,g), modern dance (g), power lifting (b), soccer (b,g), softball (g), Special Olympics (b,g), strength & conditioning (b,g), swimming and diving (b,g), tennis (b,g), track and field (b,g), volleyball (g), weight lifting (b,g), weight training (b,g), wrestling (b); intramural: fishing (b,g), indoor soccer (b,g), physical fitness (b,g). 1 athletic trainer.

Computers Computers are regularly used in all classes. Computer network features include on-campus library services, online commercial services, Internet access, wireless campus network, Internet filtering or blocking technology. Computer access in

designated common areas is available to students. Students grades are available online. The school has a published electronic and media policy.

Contact Mrs. Marisol Preston, Director of Admission. 615-383-4200. Fax: 615-783-0264. E-mail: prestonm@fatherryan.org. Website: www.fatherryan.org

FAYETTEVILLE ACADEMY

3200 Cliffdale Road
Fayetteville, North Carolina 28303

Head of School: Mr. Ray J. Quesnel

General Information Coeducational day college-preparatory, arts, and technology school. Grades PK–12. Founded: 1970. Setting: suburban. 30-acre campus. 10 buildings on campus. Approved or accredited by North Carolina Association of Independent Schools, Southern Association of Colleges and Schools, Southern Association of Independent Schools, The College Board, and North Carolina Department of Education. Member of National Association of Independent Schools. Endowment: $604,473. Total enrollment: 370. Upper school average class size: 14. Upper school faculty-student ratio: 1:14. There are 175 required school days per year for Upper School students. Upper School students typically attend 5 days per week. The average school day consists of 6 hours and 55 minutes.

Upper School Student Profile Grade 9: 37 students (27 boys, 10 girls); Grade 10: 34 students (19 boys, 15 girls); Grade 11: 40 students (16 boys, 24 girls); Grade 12: 30 students (16 boys, 14 girls).

Faculty School total: 62. In upper school: 6 men, 16 women; 11 have advanced degrees.

Subjects Offered Algebra, American history, American literature, anatomy, art, band, biology, biology-AP, calculus, calculus-AP, chemistry, chemistry-AP, chorus, communications, ecology, English, English language and composition-AP, English literature, English literature-AP, European history, European history-AP, geography, geometry, government/civics, history, honors geometry, mathematics, music, physical education, physics, physiology, pre-calculus, psychology, science, social studies, Spanish, Spanish-AP, statistics-AP, trigonometry, typing, U.S. history-AP, weight training, world history, world history-AP, yearbook.

Graduation Requirements Arts and fine arts (art, music, dance, drama), English, foreign language, history, lab science, mathematics, physical education (includes health), senior projects.

Special Academic Programs Advanced Placement exam preparation; honors section; independent study; study at local college for college credit.

College Admission Counseling 41 students graduated in 2015; all went to college, including Duke University; East Carolina University; Meredith College; North Carolina State University; The University of North Carolina at Chapel Hill; Wake Forest University. Median SAT critical reading: 560, median SAT math: 570, median SAT writing: 540, median combined SAT: 1670, median composite ACT: 26. 39% scored over 600 on SAT critical reading, 39% scored over 600 on SAT math, 39% scored over 600 on SAT writing, 39% scored over 1800 on combined SAT, 37% scored over 26 on composite ACT.

Student Life Upper grades have specified standards of dress, student council, honor system. Discipline rests primarily with faculty.

Summer Programs Enrichment, sports, art/fine arts, computer instruction programs offered; session focuses on enrichment; held on campus; accepts boys and girls; open to students from other schools. 200 students usually enrolled. 2016 schedule: June 12 to August 1.

Tuition and Aid Day student tuition: $14,400. Tuition installment plan (monthly payment plans, payment in full, 3 payment plan). Need-based scholarship grants available. In 2015–16, 30% of upper-school students received aid. Total amount of financial aid awarded in 2015–16: $204,000.

Admissions Traditional secondary-level entrance grade is 9. For fall 2015, 37 students applied for upper-level admission, 32 were accepted, 27 enrolled. Admissions testing, ERB, SSAT or TOEFL required. Deadline for receipt of application materials: none. Application fee required: $75. On-campus interview recommended.

Athletics Interscholastic: baseball (boys), basketball (b,g), cheering (g), cross-country running (b,g), soccer (b,g), softball (g), tennis (b,g), track and field (b,g), volleyball (g); coed interscholastic: golf, swimming and diving. 2 PE instructors, 10 coaches, 1 athletic trainer.

Computers Computers are regularly used in all classes. Computer network features include on-campus library services, online commercial services, Internet access, wireless campus network. Computer access in designated common areas is available to students. Students grades are available online. The school has a published electronic and media policy.

Contact Ms. Barbara E. Lambert, Director of Admissions. 910-868-5131 Ext. 3311. Fax: 910-868-7351. E-mail: blambert@fayettevilleacademy.com. Website: www.fayettevilleacademy.com

FAY SCHOOL

Southborough, Massachusetts
See Junior Boarding Schools section.

THE FIRST ACADEMY

2667 Bruton Boulevard
Orlando, Florida 32805

Head of School: Dr. Steve D. Whitaker

General Information Coeducational day college-preparatory, arts, religious studies, and technology school, affiliated with Christian faith. Grades K4–12. Founded: 1986. Setting: suburban. 140-acre campus. 1 building on campus. Approved or accredited by Association of Christian Schools International, Association of Independent Schools of Florida, Southern Association of Colleges and Schools, Southern Association of Independent Schools, and Florida Department of Education. Member of National Association of Independent Schools and Secondary School Admission Test Board. Endowment: $2.5 million. Total enrollment: 990. Upper school average class size: 15. Upper school faculty-student ratio: 1:17. There are 180 required school days per year for Upper School students. Upper School students typically attend 5 days per week. The average school day consists of 6 hours and 30 minutes.

Upper School Student Profile Grade 9: 94 students (41 boys, 53 girls); Grade 10: 111 students (50 boys, 61 girls); Grade 11: 110 students (64 boys, 46 girls); Grade 12: 95 students (48 boys, 47 girls). 100% of students are Christian.

Faculty School total: 90. In upper school: 17 men, 17 women; 14 have advanced degrees.

Subjects Offered Advanced chemistry, advanced computer applications, advanced math, Advanced Placement courses, advanced studio art-AP, algebra, American government, American history, American history-AP, American literature, American literature-AP, analytic geometry, anatomy, ancient world history, art, art-AP, athletics, audio visual/media, band, Bible, Bible studies, biology, biology-AP, broadcasting, calculus, calculus-AP, chemistry, chemistry-AP, choir, Christian doctrine, Christian ethics, Christian testament, comparative government and politics, composition, computer programming, computer science, creative writing, drama, economics, economics and history, electives, English, English composition, English literature, English literature-AP, English-AP, ethics, European history, European history-AP, expository writing, fine arts, genetics, geometry, government, grammar, health, history, history-AP, honors algebra, honors English, honors geometry, honors U.S. history, honors world history, integrated mathematics, journalism, keyboarding, Latin, life skills, literature, literature-AP, marine biology, mathematics, media communications, music, newspaper, physical education, physical science, physics, politics, pottery, pre-algebra, pre-calculus, psychology, psychology-AP, religion, SAT/ACT preparation, science, social sciences, social studies, Spanish, Spanish-AP, speech, speech and debate, theater, trigonometry, U.S. government, U.S. government and politics-AP, world history, world history-AP, world literature, writing, yearbook.

Graduation Requirements Arts and fine arts (art, music, dance, drama), computer science, English, foreign language, mathematics, physical education (includes health), religion (includes Bible studies and theology), science, social sciences, social studies (includes history).

Special Academic Programs Advanced Placement exam preparation; honors section; study at local college for college credit.

College Admission Counseling 86 students graduated in 2015; all went to college, including Auburn University at Montgomery; Clemson University; Florida State University; Samford University; University of Central Florida; University of Florida.

Student Life Upper grades have uniform requirement, student council, honor system. Discipline rests primarily with faculty. Attendance at religious services is required.

Summer Programs Enrichment, advancement, sports, art/fine arts programs offered; session focuses on academics and athletic camps; held on campus; accepts boys and girls; open to students from other schools. 200 students usually enrolled. 2016 schedule: June 1 to July 31. Application deadline: March 1.

Tuition and Aid Day student tuition: $14,000. Tuition installment plan (SMART Tuition Payment Plan). Need-based scholarship grants available.

Admissions Traditional secondary-level entrance grade is 9. CTBS, Stanford Achievement Test, any other standardized test and TerraNova required. Deadline for receipt of application materials: none. Application fee required: $125. On-campus interview required.

Athletics Interscholastic: baseball (boys), basketball (b,g), cheering (g), cross-country running (b,g), diving (b,g), flag football (b), football (b), golf (b,g), lacrosse (b), physical fitness (b,g), physical training (b,g), power lifting (b), running (b,g), soccer (b,g), softball (g), strength & conditioning (b,g), swimming and diving (b,g), tennis (b,g), track and field (b,g), volleyball (g), weight lifting (b), wrestling (b). 6 PE instructors, 18 coaches, 1 athletic trainer.

Computers Computers are regularly used in all classes. Computer network features include on-campus library services, Internet access, wireless campus network, Internet filtering or blocking technology. Campus intranet and student e-mail accounts are available to students. Students grades are available online. The school has a published electronic and media policy.

Contact Kristi Summers, Assistant Director of Admissions. 407-206-8818. Fax: 407-206-8700. E-mail: kristisummers@thefirstacademy.org. Website: www.TheFirstAcademy.org

FIRST BAPTIST ACADEMY

PO Box 868
Dallas, Texas 75221

Head of School: Mr. Jason Lovvorn

General Information Coeducational day college-preparatory, arts, religious studies, and technology school, affiliated with Baptist Church, Southern Baptist Convention. Grades PK–12. Founded: 1972. Setting: urban. 1 building on campus. Approved or accredited by Accreditation Commission of the Texas Association of Baptist Schools, Association of Christian Schools International, and Texas Department of Education. Total enrollment: 200. Upper school average class size: 15. Upper school faculty-student ratio: 1:8. There are 175 required school days per year for Upper School students. Upper School students typically attend 5 days per week. The average school day consists of 7 hours.

Upper School Student Profile 50% of students are Baptist, Southern Baptist Convention.

Faculty School total: 33.

Subjects Offered Algebra, American history, architecture, Bible, biology, calculus, calculus-AP, chemistry, choir, computer skills, concert band, desktop publishing, drawing, economics, English, English literature-AP, English-AP, fine arts, geometry, government-AP, history, math analysis, photography, physics, pre-calculus, Spanish, speech and debate, theater arts, world history.

Graduation Requirements Algebra, American history, arts and fine arts (art, music, dance, drama), Basic programming, Bible studies, biology, chemistry, economics, electives, English, foreign language, government, history, keyboarding, mathematics, physical education (includes health), physics, science, U.S. history, world geography, service hours are required for graduation. Community service is required.

Special Academic Programs 4 Advanced Placement exams for which test preparation is offered; honors section.

College Admission Counseling Colleges students went to include Baylor University; Texas A&M University; Texas Tech University; The University of Texas at Austin; University of Mississippi; University of Oklahoma.

Student Life Upper grades have uniform requirement, student council, honor system. Discipline rests primarily with faculty. Attendance at religious services is required.

Tuition and Aid Day student tuition: $13,950. Tuition installment plan (FACTS Tuition Payment Plan). Need-based scholarship grants available.

Admissions Traditional secondary-level entrance grade is 9. ERB (grade level), ISEE or Stanford Achievement Test required. Deadline for receipt of application materials: none. Application fee required: $100. Interview required.

Athletics Interscholastic: baseball (boys), basketball (b,g), cheering (g), drill team (g), football (b), golf (b,g), softball (g), strength & conditioning (b,g), swimming and diving (b,g), tennis (b,g), track and field (b,g), volleyball (g), wrestling (b). 1 PE instructor, 25 coaches.

Computers Computers are regularly used in computer applications, desktop publishing, yearbook classes. Computer resources include on-campus library services, Internet access. Students grades are available online. The school has a published electronic and media policy.

Contact Elizabeth Gore, Director of Admissions and Marketing. 214-969-7861. Fax: 214-969-7797. E-mail: egore@firstdallas.org. Website: www.fbacademy.com

FIRST PRESBYTERIAN DAY SCHOOL

5671 Calvin Drive
Macon, Georgia 31210

Head of School: Mr. Gregg E. Thompson

General Information Coeducational boarding and day college-preparatory, arts, religious studies, and technology school, affiliated with Christian faith, Presbyterian Church in America. Boarding grades 9–12, day grades PK–12. Founded: 1970. Setting: suburban. Nearest major city is Atlanta. Students are housed in single-sex dormitories. 104-acre campus. 7 buildings on campus. Approved or accredited by Council of Accreditation and School Improvement, Georgia Independent School Association, Southern Association of Colleges and Schools, Southern Association of Independent Schools, and Georgia Department of Education. Endowment: $4.2 million. Total enrollment: 962. Upper school average class size: 18. Upper school faculty-student ratio: 1:8. There are 180 required school days per year for Upper School students. Upper School students typically attend 5 days per week. The average school day consists of 7 hours.

Upper School Student Profile Grade 9: 103 students (55 boys, 48 girls); Grade 10: 92 students (42 boys, 50 girls); Grade 11: 97 students (51 boys, 46 girls); Grade 12: 90 students (37 boys, 53 girls). 3% of students are boarding students. 97% are state residents. 1 state is represented in upper school student body. 3% are international students. International students from China, Japan, and Viet Nam. 89% of students are Christian, Presbyterian Church in America.

Faculty School total: 103. In upper school: 29 men, 29 women; 46 have advanced degrees; 2 reside on campus.

Subjects Offered 3-dimensional design, accounting, advanced biology, advanced chemistry, Advanced Placement courses, advanced studio art-AP, algebra, American literature, anatomy and physiology, art, art appreciation, art-AP, band, Bible, biology, biology-AP, British literature, calculus-AP, chemistry, chemistry-AP, chorus, comparative religion, computer applications, computer programming, computer programming-AP, computer science, computer science-AP, dance, debate, economics, English, English language and composition-AP, English literature and composition-AP, family living, French, geometry, government, government-AP, honors algebra, honors English, honors geometry, journalism, Latin, Latin-AP, logic, model United Nations, modern European history, music appreciation, physical science, physics, physics-AP, pre-calculus, psychology, Spanish, statistics, studio art-AP, theater, U.S. government and politics-AP, U.S. history, U.S. history-AP, world history.

Graduation Requirements Arts and fine arts (art, music, dance, drama), Bible, computer skills, electives, English, foreign language, mathematics, physical education (includes health), science, social studies (includes history), service to distressed populations.

Special Academic Programs 18 Advanced Placement exams for which test preparation is offered; honors section; ESL (12 students enrolled).

College Admission Counseling 92 students graduated in 2015; all went to college, including Auburn University; Georgia College & State University; Georgia Institute of Technology; Mercer University; Samford University; University of Georgia. 35% scored over 600 on SAT critical reading, 47% scored over 600 on SAT math, 38% scored over 600 on SAT writing, 43% scored over 1800 on combined SAT, 36% scored over 26 on composite ACT.

Student Life Upper grades have uniform requirement, student council, honor system. Discipline rests primarily with faculty. Attendance at religious services is required.

Summer Programs Remediation, enrichment, sports, art/fine arts, computer instruction programs offered; session focuses on reading and study skills, mathematics enrichment, science, sports, recreation; held on campus; accepts boys and girls; open to students from other schools. 200 students usually enrolled. 2016 schedule: June 10 to July 30. Application deadline: May 15.

Tuition and Aid Day student tuition: $13,330. Tuition installment plan (monthly payment plans). Merit scholarship grants, need-based scholarship grants available. In 2015–16, 40% of upper-school students received aid; total upper-school merit-scholarship money awarded: $28,000. Total amount of financial aid awarded in 2015–16: $874,000.

Admissions Traditional secondary-level entrance grade is 9. CTP, English proficiency, ISEE, Math Placement Exam or writing sample required. Deadline for receipt of application materials: February 1. Application fee required: $50. Interview recommended.

Athletics Interscholastic: baseball (boys), basketball (b,g), cheering (g), cross-country running (b,g), dance (b,g), dance team (g), football (b), golf (b,g), gymnastics (g), lacrosse (b,g), skeet shooting (b,g), soccer (b,g), softball (g), swimming and diving (b,g), tennis (b,g), track and field (b,g), volleyball (g), wrestling (b,g); intramural: cheering (g), football (b), indoor soccer (b,g), soccer (b,g), strength & conditioning (b,g), weight training (b,g); coed intramural: cross-country running. 3 PE instructors, 6 coaches, 1 athletic trainer.

Computers Computers are regularly used in all classes. Computer network features include on-campus library services, online commercial services, Internet access, wireless campus network, Internet filtering or blocking technology, students issued convertible tablet PC. Campus intranet, student e-mail accounts, and computer access in designated common areas are available to students. Students grades are available online. The school has a published electronic and media policy.

Contact Mrs. Cheri Frame, Director of Admissions. 478-477-6505 Ext. 107. Fax: 478-477-2804. E-mail: admissions@fpdmacon.org. Website: www.fpdmacon.org

FLINT HILL SCHOOL

3320 Jermantown Road
Oakton, Virginia 22124

Head of School: Mr. John Thomas

General Information Coeducational day college-preparatory, arts, technology, and athletics, community service school. Grades JK–12. Founded: 1956. Setting: suburban. Nearest major city is Washington, DC. 45-acre campus. 1 building on campus. Approved or accredited by Virginia Association of Independent Schools and Virginia Department of Education. Member of National Association of Independent Schools and Secondary School Admission Test Board. Endowment: $2.3 million. Total enrollment: 1,086. Upper school average class size: 12. Upper school faculty-student ratio: 1:7. There are 168 required school days per year for Upper School students. Upper School students typically attend 5 days per week. The average school day consists of 6 hours and 30 minutes.

Upper School Student Profile Grade 9: 135 students (68 boys, 67 girls); Grade 10: 132 students (64 boys, 68 girls); Grade 11: 139 students (76 boys, 63 girls); Grade 12: 123 students (62 boys, 61 girls).

Faculty School total: 161. In upper school: 29 men, 43 women; 53 have advanced degrees.

Subjects Offered 20th century history, advanced chemistry, algebra, anatomy, art, ballet, biology, biology-AP, British literature, calculus, calculus-AP, ceramics, chemistry, chemistry-AP, Chinese, choir, choral music, chorus, civil rights, community service, computer animation, computer graphics, computer programming, computer science-AP, concert band, concert choir, creative writing, digital imaging, discrete mathematics, drama, drawing, drawing and design, earth science, economics-AP, English, English literature, English literature and composition-AP, English-AP,

environmental science, environmental science-AP, environmental studies, European civilization, European history, fine arts, French, French language-AP, French literature-AP, geometry, government-AP, history, history of music, honors English, improvisation, jazz band, jazz dance, Latin, Latin American studies, Latin-AP, macro/microeconomics-AP, marine science, modern European history-AP, music, music history, music theory, music theory-AP, orchestra, ornithology, photography, physical education, physics, physics-AP, physiology, playwriting, pre-calculus, psychology, psychology-AP, science, sculpture, senior project, Shakespeare, short story, Spanish, Spanish-AP, statistics-AP, studio art, study skills, symphonic band, theater, trigonometry, U.S. history, U.S. history-AP, world religions.

Graduation Requirements Arts and fine arts (art, music, dance, drama), athletics, English, foreign language, history, mathematics, physical education (includes health), science, senior project. Community service is required.

Special Academic Programs 23 Advanced Placement exams for which test preparation is offered; honors section; academic accommodation for the musically talented and the artistically talented.

College Admission Counseling 137 students graduated in 2015; all went to college, including Duke University; Elon University; James Madison University; The College of William and Mary; University of Virginia; Virginia Polytechnic Institute and State University. Median SAT critical reading: 580, median SAT math: 620, median SAT writing: 590, median combined SAT: 1790, median composite ACT: 27. 44% scored over 600 on SAT critical reading, 56% scored over 600 on SAT math, 48% scored over 600 on SAT writing, 48% scored over 1800 on combined SAT, 56% scored over 26 on composite ACT.

Student Life Upper grades have specified standards of dress, student council, honor system. Discipline rests primarily with faculty.

Summer Programs Remediation, enrichment, advancement, ESL, sports, art/fine arts, rigorous outdoor training, computer instruction programs offered; session focuses on academics, arts, enrichment, travel, athletics, and service; held both on and off campus; held at various domestic and international locations; accepts boys and girls; open to students from other schools. 815 students usually enrolled. 2016 schedule: June 20 to July 29. Application deadline: none.

Tuition and Aid Day student tuition: $37,280. Tuition installment plan (Insured Tuition Payment Plan, FACTS Tuition Payment Plan, monthly payment plans, one payment, two payments, or ten payments). Need-based scholarship grants available. In 2015–16, 17% of upper-school students received aid. Total amount of financial aid awarded in 2015–16: $2,089,701.

Admissions Traditional secondary-level entrance grade is 9. For fall 2015, 296 students applied for upper-level admission, 189 were accepted, 100 enrolled. PSAT, SAT, SSAT or Wechsler Intelligence Scale for Children required. Deadline for receipt of application materials: January 23. Application fee required: $50. On-campus interview required.

Athletics Interscholastic: aerobics/dance (girls), baseball (b), basketball (b,g), cross-country running (b,g), dance (g), dance team (g), diving (b,g), field hockey (g), football (b), lacrosse (b,g), self defense (g), soccer (b,g), softball (g), swimming and diving (b,g), tennis (b,g), track and field (b,g), volleyball (g); coed interscholastic: golf, hockey, ice hockey, independent competitive sports, physical fitness, running, strength & conditioning, yoga; coed intramural: aerobics/dance, canoeing/kayaking, climbing, dance, fitness, modern dance, mountaineering, outdoor activities, outdoor education, physical fitness, physical training, strength & conditioning, wall climbing, weight training, winter soccer. 16 coaches, 2 athletic trainers.

Computers Computers are regularly used in all academic classes. Computer network features include on-campus library services, online commercial services, Internet access, wireless campus network, Internet filtering or blocking technology. Campus intranet, student e-mail accounts, and computer access in designated common areas are available to students. Students grades are available online. The school has a published electronic and media policy.

Contact Ms. Lisa Knight, Director of Admission and Financial Aid. 703-584-2300. Fax: 703-242-0718. E-mail: lknight@flinthill.org. Website: www.flinthill.org

FLINTRIDGE PREPARATORY SCHOOL

4543 Crown Avenue
La Canada Flintridge, California 91011

Head of School: Mr. Peter H. Bachmann

General Information Coeducational day college-preparatory school. Grades 7–12. Founded: 1933. Setting: suburban. Nearest major city is Los Angeles. 7-acre campus. 8 buildings on campus. Approved or accredited by California Association of Independent Schools, The College Board, and Western Association of Schools and Colleges. Member of National Association of Independent Schools. Total enrollment: 500. Upper school average class size: 12. Upper school faculty-student ratio: 1:8. Upper School students typically attend 5 days per week. The average school day consists of 6 hours and 20 minutes.

Faculty School total: 66. In upper school: 37 men, 29 women; 46 have advanced degrees.

Subjects Offered Algebra, American history, American literature, analysis and differential calculus, anatomy and physiology, art, art history, art history-AP, art-AP, Basic programming, Bible as literature, biology, biology-AP, British literature-AP, business applications, calculus, calculus-AP, ceramics, chemistry, chemistry-AP, choral music, college counseling, computer literacy, computer programming, creative writing, dance, drama, earth science, economics, English, English literature-AP, environmental studies, European history, expository writing, fine arts, French, French language-AP, geography, geometry, government/civics, grammar, great books, history, jazz band, Latin, mathematics, music, photography, physical education, physics, physics-AP, psychology, science, social studies, Spanish, Spanish literature-AP, Spanish-AP, statistics, statistics-AP, theater, trigonometry, U.S. government and politics-AP, U.S. history-AP, world history, world literature, writing.

Graduation Requirements Arts and fine arts (art, music, dance, drama), English, foreign language, mathematics, science, social studies (includes history), community service.

Special Academic Programs 18 Advanced Placement exams for which test preparation is offered; honors section; independent study.

College Admission Counseling 96 students graduated in 2015; 95 went to college, including New York University; University of California, Berkeley; University of California, Los Angeles; University of Michigan; University of Southern California. Mean SAT critical reading: 684, mean SAT math: 693, mean SAT writing: 684, mean combined SAT: 2061.

Student Life Upper grades have specified standards of dress, student council, honor system. Discipline rests equally with students and faculty.

Summer Programs Remediation, enrichment, advancement, sports, art/fine arts, computer instruction programs offered; session focuses on academic enrichment/advancement, fine arts, and athletics; held on campus; accepts boys and girls; open to students from other schools. 300 students usually enrolled. 2016 schedule: June 23 to August 1. Application deadline: June 23.

Tuition and Aid Day student tuition: $31,000. Tuition installment plan (FACTS Tuition Payment Plan, Tuition Management Systems). Need-based scholarship grants available. In 2014–15, 30% of upper-school students received aid. Total amount of financial aid awarded in 2014–15: $2,286,100.

Admissions Traditional secondary-level entrance grade is 9. ISEE required. Deadline for receipt of application materials: January 15. Application fee required: $100. On-campus interview required.

Athletics Interscholastic: aquatics (boys, girls), baseball (b), basketball (b,g), cheering (g), cross-country running (b,g), diving (b,g), football (b), soccer (b,g), softball (g), swimming and diving (b,g), tennis (b,g), track and field (b,g), volleyball (b,g), water polo (b,g), winter soccer (b,g); coed interscholastic: golf. 4 PE instructors, 41 coaches, 1 athletic trainer.

Computers Computers are regularly used in all academic, foreign language, mathematics, photography, science classes. Computer network features include on-campus library services, online commercial services, Internet access, wireless campus network, Internet filtering or blocking technology. Campus intranet, student e-mail accounts, and computer access in designated common areas are available to students. Students grades are available online. The school has a published electronic and media policy.

Contact Ms. Dana Valentino, Admissions Assistant. 818-949-5514. Fax: 818-952-6247. E-mail: dvalentino@flintridgeprep.org. Website: www.flintridgeprep.org

FONTBONNE ACADEMY

930 Brook Road
Milton, Massachusetts 02186

Head of School: Ms. Susan Degnan

General Information Girls' day college-preparatory, arts, religious studies, and technology school, affiliated with Roman Catholic Church. Grades 9–12. Founded: 1954. Setting: suburban. Nearest major city is Boston. 6-acre campus. 1 building on campus. Approved or accredited by Association of Independent Schools in New England, New England Association of Schools and Colleges, and Massachusetts Department of Education. Total enrollment: 335. Upper school average class size: 18. Upper school faculty-student ratio: 1:10. There are 180 required school days per year for Upper School students. Upper School students typically attend 5 days per week. The average school day consists of 6 hours and 15 minutes.

Upper School Student Profile Grade 9: 78 students (78 girls); Grade 10: 94 students (94 girls); Grade 11: 69 students (69 girls); Grade 12: 94 students (94 girls). 73.2% of students are Roman Catholic.

Faculty School total: 42. In upper school: 7 men, 30 women; 35 have advanced degrees.

Subjects Offered 20th century American writers, advanced computer applications, algebra, American history, American history-AP, American literature, analytic geometry, applied music, art, art-AP, biology, biology-AP, British literature (honors), calculus-AP, career/college preparation, Catholic belief and practice, chemistry, choral music, chorus, church history, college admission preparation, college counseling, computer music, computer programming, conceptual physics, ecology, environmental systems, electronic music, English, English literature, English-AP, fine arts, French, French-AP, geometry, guidance, health, instrumental music, integrated mathematics, jazz ensemble, Latin, law and the legal system, library research, literature by women, media communications, physical education, physics, physiology, pre-calculus, research skills, science, social justice, social studies, Spanish, Spanish-AP, theater production, theology, trigonometry, U.S. history-AP, vocal jazz, women's literature, world history.

Graduation Requirements Arts and fine arts (art, music, dance, drama), English, foreign language, health, mathematics, physical education (includes health), science, theology, U.S. history, world history, 100 hours of community service.

Special Academic Programs Advanced Placement exam preparation; honors section; independent study; study at local college for college credit.

College Admission Counseling 72 students graduated in 2015; all went to college, including Boston University; Quinnipiac University; Saint Anselm College; Saint Michael's College; University of Connecticut.

Student Life Upper grades have uniform requirement, student council, honor system. Discipline rests primarily with faculty. Attendance at religious services is required.

Summer Programs Sports, art/fine arts programs offered; held on campus; accepts boys and girls; open to students from other schools. 100 students usually enrolled. 2016 schedule: July 11 to August 5. Application deadline: none.

Tuition and Aid Day student tuition: $15,600. Tuition installment plan (FACTS Tuition Payment Plan). Merit scholarship grants, need-based scholarship grants, tuition reduction for daughters of employees, work-study positions available.

Admissions Traditional secondary-level entrance grade is 9. Archdiocese of Boston High School entrance exam provided by STS, High School Placement Test or standardized test scores required. Deadline for receipt of application materials: December 15. Application fee required: $35.

Athletics Interscholastic: basketball, cheering, cross-country running, golf, hockey, ice hockey, indoor track, indoor track & field, lacrosse, soccer, softball, tennis, track and field, volleyball, winter (indoor) track; intramural: aerobics/Nautilus, alpine skiing, archery, basketball, dance, fitness, fitness walking, flag football, physical fitness, physical training, skiing (downhill), snowboarding, strength & conditioning, weight training, yoga. 2 PE instructors, 27 coaches, 3 athletic trainers.

Computers Computers are regularly used in all classes. Computer network features include on-campus library services, online commercial services, Internet access, wireless campus network, Internet filtering or blocking technology. Student e-mail accounts and computer access in designated common areas are available to students. Students grades are available online. The school has a published electronic and media policy.

Contact Christin Schow, Director of Admissions. 617-615-3014. Fax: 617-696-7688. E-mail: admissions@fontbonneacademy.org. Website: www.fontbonneacademy.org

FORDHAM PREPARATORY SCHOOL

441 East Fordham Road
Bronx, New York 10458-5175

Head of School: Rev. Christopher Devron, SJ

General Information Boys' day college-preparatory school, affiliated with Roman Catholic Church. Grades 9–12. Founded: 1841. Setting: urban. Nearest major city is New York. 5-acre campus. 2 buildings on campus. Approved or accredited by Jesuit Secondary Education Association, Middle States Association of Colleges and Schools, National Catholic Education Association, New York State Association of Independent Schools, and New York Department of Education. Member of National Association of Independent Schools. Endowment: $31 million. Total enrollment: 985. Upper school average class size: 24. Upper school faculty-student ratio: 1:12. There are 157 required school days per year for Upper School students. Upper School students typically attend 5 days per week. The average school day consists of 6 hours.

Upper School Student Profile Grade 9: 262 students (262 boys); Grade 10: 293 students (293 boys); Grade 11: 221 students (221 boys); Grade 12: 209 students (209 boys). 75% of students are Roman Catholic.

Faculty School total: 85. In upper school: 59 men, 26 women; 75 have advanced degrees.

Subjects Offered Advanced chemistry, American history, American history-AP, American literature, Ancient Greek, Arabic, architectural drawing, art history-AP, biochemistry, biology, biology-AP, calculus, calculus-AP, chemistry, chemistry-AP, Chinese, computer graphics, computer programming, creative writing, drama, economics, English, English language and composition-AP, English literature-AP, European history-AP, forensics, French, geometry, German, global studies, government and politics-AP, graphic design, health, Italian, Latin, Latin-AP, macroeconomics-AP, media communications, meteorology, modern history, music, physical education, physics, physics-AP, pre-calculus, religious studies, short story, Spanish, Spanish language-AP, Spanish literature-AP, statistics-AP, studio art, studio art-AP, trigonometry, world history-AP.

Graduation Requirements Arts and fine arts (art, music, dance, drama), English, foreign language, mathematics, physical education (includes health), religious studies, science, social studies (includes history), service requirement each year enrolled.

Special Academic Programs 17 Advanced Placement exams for which test preparation is offered; honors section; term-away projects; study at local college for college credit; study abroad.

College Admission Counseling 242 students graduated in 2015; 240 went to college, including Boston College; College of the Holy Cross; Fordham University; Georgetown University; New York University; Providence College. Other: 2 had other specific plans. Mean SAT critical reading: 604, mean SAT math: 605, mean SAT writing: 604, mean combined SAT: 1813, mean composite ACT: 27.

Student Life Upper grades have specified standards of dress. Discipline rests primarily with faculty. Attendance at religious services is required.

Tuition and Aid Day student tuition: $18,410. Tuition installment plan (monthly payment plans). Merit scholarship grants, need-based scholarship grants available. In 2015–16, 45% of upper-school students received aid; total upper-school merit-scholarship money awarded: $480,000. Total amount of financial aid awarded in 2015–16: $2,980,000.

Admissions Traditional secondary-level entrance grade is 9. For fall 2015, 1,073 students applied for upper-level admission, 688 were accepted, 262 enrolled. Cooperative Entrance Exam (McGraw-Hill), Diocesan Entrance Exam, High School Placement Test, ISEE, SSAT or STS required. Deadline for receipt of application materials: December 15. No application fee required.

Athletics Interscholastic: baseball, basketball, bowling, crew, cross-country running, diving, football, golf, ice hockey, indoor track, lacrosse, rugby, soccer, swimming and diving, tennis, track and field, volleyball, winter (indoor) track, wrestling; intramural: basketball, fitness, Frisbee, skiing (downhill), soccer, strength & conditioning, weight lifting, weight training, wilderness. 2 PE instructors, 16 coaches.

Computers Computers are regularly used in all classes. Computer network features include on-campus library services, online commercial services, Internet access, wireless campus network, Internet filtering or blocking technology, Rosetta Stone. Student e-mail accounts are available to students. Students grades are available online. The school has a published electronic and media policy.

Contact Mr. Bradley J. Serton, Director of Admissions. 718-584-8367. Fax: 718-367-7598. E-mail: admissions@fordhamprep.org. Website: www.fordhamprep.org

FOREST LAKE ACADEMY

500 Education Loop
Apopka, Florida 32703

Head of School: Mr. David Denton

General Information Coeducational boarding and day and distance learning college-preparatory, arts, religious studies, and bilingual studies school, affiliated with Seventh-day Adventists. Grades 9–12. Distance learning grades 9–12. Founded: 1918. Setting: suburban. Nearest major city is Orlando. Students are housed in single-sex dormitories. 6 buildings on campus. Approved or accredited by CITA (Commission on International and Trans-Regional Accreditation), Middle States Association of Colleges and Schools, National Council for Private School Accreditation, and Florida Department of Education. Total enrollment: 397. Upper school average class size: 22. Upper school faculty-student ratio: 1:12. There are 179 required school days per year for Upper School students. Upper School students typically attend 5 days per week. The average school day consists of 6 hours.

Upper School Student Profile 8% of students are boarding students. 84% are state residents. 13 states are represented in upper school student body. 1% are international students. International students from Argentina, Bermuda, Brazil, China, Italy, and Spain; 3 other countries represented in student body. 95% of students are Seventh-day Adventists.

Faculty School total: 32. In upper school: 20 men, 12 women; 15 have advanced degrees; 4 reside on campus.

Subjects Offered Algebra, American government, American literature, art, band, bell choir, Bible studies, biology, calculus, chemistry, choir, church history, computer applications, desktop publishing, digital photography, economics, English, environmental science, geometry, health, honors algebra, honors English, honors geometry, honors world history, integrated mathematics, life management skills, physical science, physics, play production, pre-calculus, psychology, SAT preparation, senior project, Spanish, statistics, strings, swimming, tennis, U.S. history, video film production, world geography, world history, world literature, writing, yearbook.

Graduation Requirements Algebra, American government, American literature, arts and fine arts (art, music, dance, drama), Bible studies, biology, chemistry, computer applications, computer science, economics, English, environmental science, fitness, foreign language, geometry, health education, life management skills, physical education (includes health), physical science, pre-calculus, religion (includes Bible studies and theology), science, social studies (includes history), Spanish, statistics, U.S. history, world history, world literature, writing, 20 hours of community service activity for each year enrolled.

Special Academic Programs Honors section; study at local college for college credit; ESL (22 students enrolled).

College Admission Counseling 94 students graduated in 2015; all went to college, including Adventist University of Health Sciences; Andrews University; Oakwood University; Seminole State College of Florida; Southern Adventist University; University of Central Florida.

Student Life Upper grades have uniform requirement, student council, honor system. Discipline rests primarily with faculty.

Summer Programs ESL programs offered; held on campus; accepts boys and girls; open to students from other schools. 200 students usually enrolled. Application deadline: none.

Tuition and Aid Day student tuition: $12,610; 7-day tuition and room/board: $24,400. Tuition installment plan (FACTS Tuition Payment Plan, monthly payment plans, individually arranged payment plans). Merit scholarship grants, need-based scholarship grants, paying campus jobs available. In 2015–16, 37% of upper-school students received aid; total upper-school merit-scholarship money awarded: $75,000. Total amount of financial aid awarded in 2015–16: $347,000.

Admissions Traditional secondary-level entrance grade is 9. WRAT required. Deadline for receipt of application materials: none. Application fee required: $75. Interview recommended.

Athletics Interscholastic: basketball (boys, girls), golf (b), volleyball (g); intramural: golf (b); coed interscholastic: aquatics, life saving, physical fitness, strength & conditioning, tennis; coed intramural: basketball, flag football, floor hockey, indoor hockey, indoor soccer, soccer, tennis, volleyball. 2 PE instructors, 1 coach.

Computers Computers are regularly used in desktop publishing, photography, Web site design, writing, yearbook classes. Computer resources include on-campus library services, Internet access, wireless campus network, Internet filtering or blocking technology, financial aid and grant search programs for college. Campus intranet, student e-mail accounts, and computer access in designated common areas are available to students. Students grades are available online. The school has a published electronic and media policy.

Contact Mrs. Claudia Dure C. Osorio, Director of Student Records. 407-862-8411 Ext. 743. Fax: 407-862-7050. E-mail: osorioc@forestlake.org. Website: www.forestlakeacademy.org

THE FORMAN SCHOOL

Litchfield, Connecticut
See Special Needs Schools section.

FORSYTH COUNTRY DAY SCHOOL

5501 Shallowford Road
PO Box 549
Lewisville, North Carolina 27023-0549

Head of School: Dr. Vincent M. Stumpo

General Information Coeducational day college-preparatory school. Grades PK–12. Founded: 1970. Setting: suburban. Nearest major city is Winston-Salem. 80-acre campus. 7 buildings on campus. Approved or accredited by North Carolina Association of Independent Schools, Southern Association of Colleges and Schools, Southern Association of Independent Schools, The College Board, and North Carolina Department of Education. Member of National Association of Independent Schools. Endowment: $13 million. Total enrollment: 702. Upper school average class size: 15. Upper school faculty-student ratio: 1:12. There are 175 required school days per year for Upper School students. Upper School students typically attend 5 days per week. The average school day consists of 6 hours.

Upper School Student Profile Grade 9: 65 students (36 boys, 29 girls); Grade 10: 81 students (50 boys, 31 girls); Grade 11: 75 students (42 boys, 33 girls); Grade 12: 77 students (42 boys, 35 girls).

Faculty School total: 175. In upper school: 18 men, 29 women; 24 have advanced degrees.

Subjects Offered Advanced Placement courses, advanced studio art-AP, algebra, American history, American history-AP, American literature, art, astronomy, biology, calculus, calculus-AP, ceramics, chemistry, Chinese studies, community service, computer math, computer programming, computer science, creative writing, digital art, drama, English, English literature, European history, fine arts, foreign policy, French, freshman seminar, geometry, grammar, health, history, history of science, humanities, international relations, Japanese studies, journalism, Latin, Mandarin, mathematics, Middle Eastern history, music, photography, physical education, physics, psychology, SAT/ACT preparation, science, social studies, Spanish, statistics-AP, theater, yearbook.

Graduation Requirements Arts and fine arts (art, music, dance, drama), English, foreign language, history, mathematics, physical education (includes health), physical fitness, science. Community service is required.

Special Academic Programs 18 Advanced Placement exams for which test preparation is offered; honors section; academic accommodation for the gifted; programs in English, general development for dyslexic students; ESL (7 students enrolled).

College Admission Counseling 89 students graduated in 2014; all went to college, including Duke University; Elon University; North Carolina State University; The University of North Carolina at Chapel Hill; The University of North Carolina Wilmington; Wake Forest University. Median SAT critical reading: 600, median SAT math: 615, 70% scored over 600 on SAT critical reading, 68% scored over 600 on SAT math.

Student Life Upper grades have specified standards of dress, student council, honor system. Discipline rests equally with students and faculty.

Tuition and Aid Day student tuition: $20,308. Tuition installment plan (Insured Tuition Payment Plan, monthly payment plans). Merit scholarship grants, need-based scholarship grants available. In 2014–15, 28% of upper-school students received aid; total upper-school merit-scholarship money awarded: $88,882. Total amount of financial aid awarded in 2014–15: $890,296.

Admissions Traditional secondary-level entrance grade is 9. For fall 2014, 74 students applied for upper-level admission, 46 were accepted, 28 enrolled. ERB CTP IV, WRAT and writing sample required. Deadline for receipt of application materials: none. Application fee required: $100. On-campus interview recommended.

Athletics Interscholastic: baseball (boys), basketball (b,g), cheering (g), cross-country running (b,g), field hockey (g), football (b), golf (b,g), lacrosse (b,g), physical fitness (b,g), soccer (b,g), softball (g), tennis (b,g), track and field (b,g), volleyball (g), wrestling (b); coed interscholastic: swimming and diving; coed intramural: sailing. 4 PE instructors, 4 coaches, 2 athletic trainers.

Computers Computers are regularly used in art, English, foreign language, history, mathematics, music, science classes. Computer network features include on-campus library services, online commercial services, Internet access, wireless campus network, Internet filtering or blocking technology. Campus intranet, student e-mail accounts, and computer access in designated common areas are available to students. Students grades are available online. The school has a published electronic and media policy.

Contact Peter C. Egan, Director of Admission and Financial Aid. 336-945-3151 Ext. 340. Fax: 336-945-2907. E-mail: peteregan@fcds.org. Website: www.fcds.org

FORT WORTH CHRISTIAN SCHOOL

6200 Holiday Lane
North Richland Hills, Texas 76180

Head of School: Mr. Kelly Moore

General Information Coeducational day college-preparatory, arts, religious studies, and technology school, affiliated with Christian faith, Christian faith. Grades PK–12. Founded: 1958. Setting: suburban. 40-acre campus. 6 buildings on campus. Approved or accredited by National Christian School Association, Southern Association of Colleges and Schools, Texas Private School Accreditation Commission, and Texas Department of Education. Endowment: $600,000. Total enrollment: 835. Upper school average class size: 17. Upper school faculty-student ratio: 1:14. There are 175 required school days per year for Upper School students. Upper School students typically attend 5 days per week. The average school day consists of 6 hours and 40 minutes.

Upper School Student Profile Grade 6: 82 students (39 boys, 43 girls); Grade 7: 88 students (42 boys, 46 girls); Grade 8: 75 students (34 boys, 41 girls); Grade 9: 74 students (36 boys, 38 girls); Grade 10: 79 students (40 boys, 39 girls); Grade 11: 90 students (48 boys, 42 girls); Grade 12: 94 students (47 boys, 47 girls). 80% of students are Christian faith, Christian.

Faculty School total: 108. In upper school: 12 men, 21 women; 12 have advanced degrees.

Subjects Offered Advanced Placement courses, African drumming, algebra, anatomy and physiology, art, band, Bible studies, biology, biology-AP, calculus, calculus-AP, chemistry, chemistry-AP, chorus, computer applications, computer information systems, computer science-AP, drama, economics, economics and history, economics-AP, English, English language and composition-AP, English literature and composition-AP, ethics, family studies, geometry, golf, government, government/civics, Latin, physical education, physics, pre-calculus, robotics, SAT/ACT preparation, Spanish, strings, theater arts, U.S. history, U.S. history-AP, video, world geography, world history, world history-AP, yearbook.

Graduation Requirements Arts and fine arts (art, music, dance, drama), business skills (includes word processing), computer science, electives, English, foreign language, history, mathematics, physical education (includes health), religion (includes Bible studies and theology), science, social sciences, social studies (includes history), world geography, community service hours.

Special Academic Programs 12 Advanced Placement exams for which test preparation is offered; honors section; independent study; study at local college for college credit.

College Admission Counseling 91 students graduated in 2014; all went to college, including Abilene Christian University; Baylor University; Harding University; Oklahoma State University; Texas A&M University; University of North Texas. Mean SAT critical reading: 511, mean SAT math: 538, mean SAT writing: 506, mean combined SAT: 1555, mean composite ACT: 24. 49% scored over 600 on SAT critical reading, 59% scored over 600 on SAT math, 46% scored over 600 on SAT writing, 21% scored over 1800 on combined SAT, 37% scored over 26 on composite ACT.

Student Life Upper grades have uniform requirement, student council, honor system. Discipline rests primarily with faculty. Attendance at religious services is required.

Tuition and Aid Day student tuition: $12,600. Tuition installment plan (FACTS Tuition Payment Plan, monthly payment plans). Tuition reduction for siblings, need-based scholarship grants, tuition reduction for children of faculty and staff available. In 2014–15, 13% of upper-school students received aid. Total amount of financial aid awarded in 2014–15: $111,000.

Admissions Traditional secondary-level entrance grade is 9. For fall 2014, 58 students applied for upper-level admission, 52 were accepted, 52 enrolled. Stanford Achievement Test required. Deadline for receipt of application materials: none. Application fee required: $100. On-campus interview required.

Athletics Interscholastic: baseball (boys), basketball (b,g), cheering (g), cross-country running (b,g), football (b), golf (b,g), physical fitness (b,g), physical training (b,g), rodeo (b,g), running (b,g), soccer (b,g), softball (g), strength & conditioning (b,g), swimming and diving (b,g), tennis (b,g), track and field (b,g), volleyball (g). 8 coaches, 1 athletic trainer.

Computers Computers are regularly used in computer applications, desktop publishing, independent study, media production, newspaper, technology, word processing, yearbook classes. Computer network features include on-campus library services, Internet access, wireless campus network, Internet filtering or blocking

technology, online courses. Student e-mail accounts and computer access in designated common areas are available to students. Students grades are available online. The school has a published electronic and media policy.

Contact Mrs. Shirley Atkinson, Director of Admissions. 817-520-6561. Fax: 817-281-7063. E-mail: satkinson@fwc.org. Website: www.fwc.org

FORT WORTH COUNTRY DAY SCHOOL

4200 Country Day Lane
Fort Worth, Texas 76109-4299

Head of School: Eric V. Lombardi

General Information Coeducational day and distance learning college-preparatory, arts, and technology school. Grades K–12. Distance learning grades 11–12. Founded: 1962. Setting: suburban. 100-acre campus. 13 buildings on campus. Approved or accredited by Independent Schools Association of the Southwest. Member of National Association of Independent Schools. Endowment: $42 million. Total enrollment: 1,110. Upper school average class size: 14. Upper school faculty-student ratio: 1:10. There are 174 required school days per year for Upper School students. Upper School students typically attend 5 days per week. The average school day consists of 8 hours.

Upper School Student Profile Grade 9: 90 students (46 boys, 44 girls); Grade 10: 104 students (50 boys, 54 girls); Grade 11: 110 students (53 boys, 57 girls); Grade 12: 99 students (50 boys, 49 girls).

Faculty School total: 137. In upper school: 16 men, 21 women; 12 have advanced degrees.

Subjects Offered 3-dimensional art, algebra, American history, American history-AP, American literature, art, art history, biology, calculus, ceramics, chemistry, comparative religion, computer math, computer programming, computer science, computer technologies, creative writing, dance, drama, earth science, economics, English, English literature, European history, fine arts, French, geography, geology, geometry, government/civics, health, history, journalism, Latin, mathematics, modern problems, music, music history, photography, physical education, physics, science, social studies, Spanish, technology, theater, trigonometry, world history, writing.

Graduation Requirements Algebra, American government, arts and fine arts (art, music, dance, drama), biology, English, foreign language, lab science, mathematics, physical education (includes health), science, social studies (includes history), participation in athletics, completion of a two-year College Counseling Course. Community service is required.

Special Academic Programs 22 Advanced Placement exams for which test preparation is offered; study at local college for college credit; academic accommodation for the gifted, the musically talented, and the artistically talented.

College Admission Counseling 102 students graduated in 2015; all went to college, including Baylor University; Texas A&M University; Texas Christian University; Texas Tech University; The University of Texas at Austin; University of Oklahoma.

Student Life Upper grades have uniform requirement, student council, honor system. Discipline rests equally with students and faculty.

Summer Programs Remediation, enrichment, sports, art/fine arts programs offered; session focuses on athletics and enrichment; held both on and off campus; held at local golf course (for enrichment golf and golf team practice); accepts boys and girls; open to students from other schools. 300 students usually enrolled. 2016 schedule: June 1 to July 31. Application deadline: May 30.

Tuition and Aid Day student tuition: $19,505. Tuition installment plan (monthly payment plans, individually arranged payment plans). Merit scholarship grants, need-based scholarship grants, Malone Scholars Program, Betty Reese Memorial, Vicki and Edward P. Bass Scholarship, Reilly Breakthrough Scholarship, Joey Pollard Memorial Scholarship, Joann Chandler Thompson Memorial Scholarship available. In 2015–16, 22% of upper-school students received aid; total upper-school merit-scholarship money awarded: $176,482. Total amount of financial aid awarded in 2015–16: $980,225.

Admissions Traditional secondary-level entrance grade is 9. For fall 2015, 65 students applied for upper-level admission, 38 were accepted, 27 enrolled. ERB or ISEE required. Deadline for receipt of application materials: March 3. Application fee required: $75. Interview required.

Athletics Interscholastic: ballet (boys, girls), baseball (b), basketball (b,g), cheering (g), field hockey (g), football (b), lacrosse (b), track and field (b,g), volleyball (b,g), winter soccer (b,g), wrestling (b); intramural: lacrosse (b); coed interscholastic: ballet, cross-country running, dance, dance team, fitness, golf, independent competitive sports, outdoor education, outdoor recreation, physical fitness, physical training, ropes courses, strength & conditioning, swimming and diving, tennis, weight training. 12 PE instructors, 45 coaches, 2 athletic trainers.

Computers Computers are regularly used in architecture, college planning, computer applications, creative writing, desktop publishing, engineering, English, foreign language, history, humanities, introduction to technology, journalism, library skills, life skills, mathematics, music, newspaper, photography, publications, reading, religion, science, Spanish, theater, Web site design, writing, yearbook classes. Computer network features include on-campus library services, online commercial services, Internet access, wireless campus network, Internet filtering or blocking technology. Campus intranet, student e-mail accounts, and computer access in designated common areas are available to students. Students grades are available online. The school has a published electronic and media policy.

Contact Yolanda Espinoza, Admission Associate. 817-302-3209. Fax: 817-377-3425. E-mail: yolanda.espinoza@fwcd.com. Website: www.fwcd.org

FOUNDATION ACADEMY

15304 Tilden Road
Winter Garden, Florida 34787

Head of School: Dr. Lorne Wenzel

General Information Coeducational day college-preparatory and arts school, affiliated with Baptist Church. Grades 7–12. Founded: 1958. Setting: suburban. Nearest major city is Orlando. 75-acre campus. 3 buildings on campus. Approved or accredited by Association of Christian Schools International, Southern Association of Colleges and Schools, and Florida Department of Education. Total enrollment: 677. Upper school average class size: 17. Upper school faculty-student ratio: 1:9. There are 180 required school days per year for Upper School students. Upper School students typically attend 5 days per week. The average school day consists of 6 hours and 20 minutes.

Upper School Student Profile Grade 7: 63 students (35 boys, 28 girls); Grade 8: 59 students (34 boys, 25 girls); Grade 9: 68 students (42 boys, 26 girls); Grade 10: 63 students (34 boys, 29 girls); Grade 11: 72 students (42 boys, 30 girls); Grade 12: 43 students (16 boys, 27 girls). 20% of students are Baptist.

Faculty School total: 41. In upper school: 12 men, 29 women; 12 have advanced degrees.

Subjects Offered Advanced math, Advanced Placement courses, algebra, American government, American literature, anatomy and physiology, art, band, Bible, biology, biology-AP, business law, business mathematics, calculus, calculus-AP, career/college preparation, chemistry, chemistry-AP, choir, Christian education, college admission preparation, communication skills, computer processing, drama, ecology, economics and history, English, English composition, English language-AP, English literature, English literature-AP, environmental science, environmental science-AP, geometry, government, health and wellness, health education, history-AP, honors algebra, honors English, honors geometry, honors U.S. history, honors world history, human anatomy, human biology, human geography - AP, journalism, life science, marine biology, personal fitness, photography, physical education, physical fitness, pre-algebra, pre-calculus, SAT preparation, SAT/ACT preparation, science, science project, Spanish, speech, speech and debate, speech communications, sports conditioning, statistics, statistics-AP, studio art-AP, U.S. government and politics-AP, U.S. history, weight training, weightlifting, yearbook.

Graduation Requirements Algebra, American government, American history, American literature, arts and fine arts (art, music, dance, drama), Bible, Bible studies, biology, chemistry, economics and history, English, English composition, English literature, geography, geometry, government, health and wellness, history, languages, pre-calculus, science, U.S. history.

Special Academic Programs Advanced Placement exam preparation; honors section; independent study; study at local college for college credit; programs in English, mathematics for dyslexic students.

College Admission Counseling 29 students graduated in 2015; 28 went to college, including Florida State University; Palm Beach Atlantic University; Rollins College; University of Florida; Valencia College. Other: 1 went to work.

Student Life Upper grades have uniform requirement, student council. Discipline rests primarily with faculty. Attendance at religious services is required.

Summer Programs Remediation, enrichment, sports, art/fine arts programs offered; session focuses on sports camps, art, drama, academic; held on campus; accepts boys and girls; open to students from other schools. 100 students usually enrolled. 2016 schedule: June 1 to July 31.

Tuition and Aid Day student tuition: $10,815–$11,335. Tuition installment plan (FACTS Tuition Payment Plan). Tuition reduction for siblings, need-based scholarship grants available. In 2015–16, 20% of upper-school students received aid. Total amount of financial aid awarded in 2015–16: $250,000.

Admissions Traditional secondary-level entrance grade is 9. For fall 2015, 106 students applied for upper-level admission, 90 were accepted, 80 enrolled. Admissions testing, Gates MacGinite Reading Tests, Math Placement Exam and Wide Range Achievement Test required. Deadline for receipt of application materials: none. Application fee required: $150. Interview required.

Athletics Interscholastic: baseball (boys), basketball (b,g), bowling (b,g), boxing (b,g), cheering (g), cross-country running (b,g), football (b), golf (b,g), soccer (b,g), softball (g), tennis (b,g), track and field (b,g), volleyball (g); coed intramural: archery. 2 PE instructors, 1 athletic trainer.

Computers Computers are regularly used in career exploration, college planning, computer applications, health, independent study, keyboarding, mathematics, music, SAT preparation, word processing, writing, yearbook classes. Computer network features include Internet access, wireless campus network, Internet filtering or blocking technology. Campus intranet and student e-mail accounts are available to students. Students grades are available online.

Contact Mrs. Michelle Campbell, Admissions Director. 407-877-2744 Ext. 223. Fax: 407-877-1985. E-mail: michelle.campbell@foundationacademy.net. Website: www.foundationacademy.net

FOUNTAIN VALLEY SCHOOL OF COLORADO

6155 Fountain Valley School Road
Colorado Springs, Colorado 80911

Head of School: William V. Webb

General Information Coeducational boarding and day college-preparatory, arts, and global education school. Grades 9–12. Founded: 1930. Setting: suburban. Students are housed in single-sex dormitories. 1,100-acre campus. 42 buildings on campus. Approved or accredited by Association of Colorado Independent Schools, The Association of Boarding Schools, and Colorado Department of Education. Member of National Association of Independent Schools and Secondary School Admission Test Board. Endowment: $36 million. Total enrollment: 236. Upper school average class size: 11. Upper school faculty-student ratio: 1:5. There are 155 required school days per year for Upper School students. Upper School students typically attend 5 days per week. The average school day consists of 9 hours and 15 minutes.

Upper School Student Profile Grade 9: 45 students (17 boys, 28 girls); Grade 10: 62 students (37 boys, 25 girls); Grade 11: 66 students (31 boys, 35 girls); Grade 12: 63 students (35 boys, 28 girls). 64% of students are boarding students. 49% are state residents. 27 states are represented in upper school student body. 26% are international students. International students from China, Germany, Japan, Mexico, Republic of Korea, and Saudi Arabia; 15 other countries represented in student body.

Faculty School total: 43. In upper school: 22 men, 21 women; 30 have advanced degrees; 25 reside on campus.

Subjects Offered 3-dimensional art, 3-dimensional design, ACT preparation, advanced chemistry, Advanced Placement courses, advanced studio art-AP, algebra, American history, American history-AP, American literature, band, biology, biology-AP, British literature, calculus, calculus-AP, ceramics, chamber groups, chemistry, chemistry-AP, college counseling, Colorado ecology, composition, computer applications, computer multimedia, computer programming, creative writing, drama, English, English literature and composition-AP, environmental science-AP, ESL, fiction, film and literature, French, French language-AP, geology, geometry, global issues, honors algebra, honors English, honors geometry, instrumental music, jewelry making, literature, Mandarin, music theory, musical productions, outdoor education, photography, physics, physics-AP, pre-calculus, probability and statistics, senior project, senior seminar, Shakespeare, Shakespearean histories, short story, Spanish, Spanish language-AP, statistics-AP, strings, student government, student publications, studio art, studio art-AP, U.S. government and politics-AP, visual and performing arts, vocal ensemble, wilderness education, wind ensemble, world history, world history-AP, world literature, writing.

Graduation Requirements Arts and fine arts (art, music, dance, drama), computer science, English, foreign language, history, mathematics, physical education (includes health), science, social studies (includes history), senior seminar. Community service is required.

Special Academic Programs 20 Advanced Placement exams for which test preparation is offered; honors section; independent study; study abroad; ESL (17 students enrolled).

College Admission Counseling 67 students graduated in 2015; 56 went to college, including Mount Holyoke College; Tufts University; University of California, San Diego; University of Colorado Boulder, University of Puget Sound. Other: 9 had other specific plans. Mean SAT critical reading: 600, mean SAT math: 610, mean SAT writing: 590, mean composite ACT: 27.

Student Life Upper grades have specified standards of dress, student council, honor system. Discipline rests equally with students and faculty.

Tuition and Aid Day student tuition: $26,796; 7-day tuition and room/board: $50,650. Tuition installment plan (Key Tuition Payment Plan, monthly payment plans, individually arranged payment plans). Merit scholarship grants, need-based scholarship grants available. In 2015–16, 43% of upper-school students received aid. Total amount of financial aid awarded in 2015–16: $2,354,978.

Admissions Traditional secondary-level entrance grade is 9. For fall 2015, 225 students applied for upper-level admission, 150 were accepted, 96 enrolled. SSAT or TOEFL required. Deadline for receipt of application materials: February 1. Application fee required: $50. Interview required.

Athletics Interscholastic: basketball (boys, girls), cross-country running (b,g), diving (g), hockey (b), ice hockey (b), lacrosse (b), soccer (b,g), swimming and diving (g), tennis (b,g), track and field (b,g), volleyball (b,g), winter soccer (g); coed interscholastic: climbing, equestrian sports, horseback riding, independent competitive sports, mountain biking, rock climbing, rodeo, skiing (downhill), snowboarding, telemark skiing, wall climbing; coed intramural: alpine skiing, backpacking, bicycling, climbing, equestrian sports, fitness, hiking/backpacking, horseback riding, mountain biking, mountaineering, outdoor activities, outdoor adventure, outdoor education, outdoor recreation, outdoor skills, physical fitness, rock climbing, skiing (downhill), snowboarding, strength & conditioning, table tennis, telemark skiing, tennis, wall climbing, weight lifting, weight training, wilderness. 2 coaches, 1 athletic trainer.

Computers Computers are regularly used in all academic, college planning, multimedia, news writing, photography, publications, yearbook classes. Computer network features include on-campus library services, online commercial services, Internet access, wireless campus network, Internet filtering or blocking technology, live webcasts of select athletic events. Campus intranet, student e-mail accounts, and computer access in designated common areas are available to students. Students grades are available online. The school has a published electronic and media policy.

Contact Kila McCann, Director of Admission. 719-390-7035 Ext. 297. Fax: 719-390-7762. E-mail: kmccan@fvs.edu. Website: www.fvs.edu

FOWLERS ACADEMY

PO Box 921
Guaynabo, Puerto Rico 00970-0921
Head of School: Mr. Jared Ramos

General Information Coeducational day general academic, arts, religious studies, technology, music, and graphic art design school, affiliated with Christian faith; primarily serves underachievers, students with learning disabilities, individuals with Attention Deficit Disorder, dyslexic students, highly-functional autism, and Asperger's Syndrome. Grades 7–12. Founded: 1986. Setting: suburban. 2-acre campus. 2 buildings on campus. Approved or accredited by Comisión Acreditadora de Instituciones Educativas, The College Board, and Puerto Rico Department of Education. Languages of instruction: English and Spanish. Total enrollment: 71. Upper school average class size: 15. Upper school faculty-student ratio: 1:15. There are 160 required school days per year for Upper School students. Upper School students typically attend 5 days per week. The average school day consists of 6 hours and 50 minutes.

Upper School Student Profile Grade 7: 11 students (9 boys, 2 girls); Grade 8: 13 students (9 boys, 4 girls); Grade 9: 13 students (9 boys, 4 girls); Grade 10: 14 students (9 boys, 5 girls); Grade 11: 6 students (5 boys, 1 girl); Grade 12: 14 students (9 boys, 5 girls).

Faculty School total: 8. In upper school: 5 men, 3 women; 4 have advanced degrees.

Subjects Offered Algebra, American history, ancient world history, art, athletics, basketball, Bible, character education, chemistry, Christian education, Christian ethics, Christian scripture, computer applications, computer art, computer education, computer graphics, computer literacy, computer skills, drama, drawing, earth science, electives, English, film appreciation, geometry, history, instrumental music, keyboarding, Latin American history, leadership, leadership and service, martial arts, mathematics, music, physical education, physics, pre-algebra, pre-college orientation, Puerto Rican history, science, sex education, Spanish, Spanish literature, theater, U.S. history, world history.

Graduation Requirements Algebra, ancient world history, biology, chemistry, Christian education, electives, English, geometry, physical education (includes health), physical science, physics, pre-college orientation, Puerto Rican history, Spanish, U.S. history, world history.

Special Academic Programs Accelerated programs; special instructional classes for students with ADD and LD.

College Admission Counseling 9 students graduated in 2015; all went to college, including University of Puerto Rico, Río Piedras Campus; University of Puerto Rico in Carolina.

Student Life Upper grades have uniform requirement, honor system. Discipline rests primarily with faculty. Attendance at religious services is required.

Summer Programs Remediation, enrichment, advancement, ESL programs offered; session focuses on academic courses and remediation; held on campus; accepts boys and girls; open to students from other schools. 35 students usually enrolled. 2016 schedule: June 1 to June 26. Application deadline: May 31.

Tuition and Aid Day student tuition: $6300. Tuition installment plan (monthly payment plans, individually arranged payment plans). Tuition reduction for siblings, need-based scholarship grants available. In 2015–16, 15% of upper-school students received aid. Total amount of financial aid awarded in 2015–16: $35,000.

Admissions Traditional secondary-level entrance grade is 9. For fall 2015, 11 students applied for upper-level admission, 10 were accepted, 9 enrolled. Achievement tests or psychoeducational evaluation required. Deadline for receipt of application materials: none. No application fee required. On-campus interview required.

Athletics Interscholastic: basketball (boys); intramural: basketball (b); coed interscholastic: archery, cooperative games, physical fitness; coed intramural: archery, fitness, physical fitness, soccer, table tennis, volleyball. 1 PE instructor.

Computers Computers are regularly used in English, graphic arts, graphic design, keyboarding, mathematics, religious studies, science, Spanish classes. Computer resources include Internet access, Internet filtering or blocking technology. Computer access in designated common areas is available to students.

Contact Mr. Lynette Montes, Registrar. 787-787-1350. Fax: 787-789-0055. E-mail: academiafowler@gmail.com. Website: www.academiafowler.com/

FOXCROFT SCHOOL

22407 Foxhound Lane
P.O. Box 5555
Middleburg, Virginia 20118
Head of School: Mrs. Catherine S. McGehee

General Information Girls' boarding and day college-preparatory, technology, and STEM school. Grades 9–12. Founded: 1914. Setting: rural. Nearest major city is Washington, DC. Students are housed in single-sex dormitories. 500-acre campus. 32 buildings on campus. Approved or accredited by The Association of Boarding Schools, The College Board, Virginia Association of Independent Schools, and Virginia

Department of Education. Member of National Association of Independent Schools and Secondary School Admission Test Board. Endowment: $60 million. Total enrollment: 167. Upper school average class size: 12. Upper school faculty-student ratio: 1:7. There are 185 required school days per year for Upper School students. Upper School students typically attend 5 days per week. The average school day consists of 7 hours and 15 minutes.

Upper School Student Profile Grade 9: 45 students (45 girls); Grade 10: 40 students (40 girls); Grade 11: 34 students (34 girls); Grade 12: 47 students (47 girls); Postgraduate: 1 student (1 girl). 72% of students are boarding students. 46% are state residents. 19 states are represented in upper school student body. 24% are international students. International students from Australia, China, Germany, Japan, Mexico, and Republic of Korea; 9 other countries represented in student body.

Faculty School total: 23. In upper school: 6 men, 17 women; 17 have advanced degrees; 17 reside on campus.

Subjects Offered 3-dimensional art, acting, advanced chemistry, algebra, American literature, anatomy and physiology, ancient world history, architecture, art, art history, astronomy, biology, British literature, calculus, calculus-AP, cell biology, ceramics, chemistry, chemistry-AP, choir, chorus, college counseling, community service, comparative religion, computer graphics, computer science, conceptual physics, constitutional law, creative dance, creative drama, creative writing, current events, dance, debate, digital photography, discrete mathematics, drama, drawing and design, economics, economics-AP, electives, English, English composition, English literature, English literature-AP, environmental science, European civilization, European history, European literature, expository writing, fine arts, fitness, French, French language-AP, general science, geology, geometry, grammar, health education, history, human anatomy, independent study, leadership, library, macroeconomics-AP, mathematics, microbiology, music, music theory, music theory-AP, painting, performing arts, photography, physical education, physics, piano, poetry, pottery, pre-calculus, probability and statistics, production, public speaking, SAT preparation, sculpture, senior project, social studies, Spanish, Spanish language-AP, Spanish literature, Spanish literature-AP, studio art, studio art-AP, technology, The 20th Century, trigonometry, U.S. history, U.S. history-AP, vocal ensemble, world cultures, world literature, writing, yearbook, yoga.

Graduation Requirements Arts and fine arts (art, music, dance, drama), English, foreign language, history, mathematics, physical education (includes health), science, senior thesis if student is not enrolled in AP English.

Special Academic Programs 11 Advanced Placement exams for which test preparation is offered; independent study; term-away projects; study abroad; academic accommodation for the gifted, the musically talented, and the artistically talented; ESL (25 students enrolled).

College Admission Counseling 34 students graduated in 2015; all went to college, including Carnegie Mellon University; Emory University; High Point University; Rhode Island School of Design; The College of William and Mary; University of Virginia.

Student Life Upper grades have specified standards of dress, student council, honor system. Discipline rests equally with students and faculty.

Tuition and Aid Day student tuition: $43,760; 7-day tuition and room/board: $51,900. Tuition installment plan (Insured Tuition Payment Plan, Tuition Management Systems Plan (Monthly Payment Plan)). Merit scholarship grants, need-based scholarship grants, merit-based scholarship grants are offered to prospective 9th grade students available. In 2015–16, 30% of upper-school students received aid; total upper-school merit-scholarship money awarded: $31,000. Total amount of financial aid awarded in 2015–16: $1,589,890.

Admissions Traditional secondary-level entrance grade is 9. For fall 2015, 218 students applied for upper-level admission, 145 were accepted, 65 enrolled. SSAT or TOEFL required. Deadline for receipt of application materials: February 1. Application fee required: $75. Interview required.

Athletics Interscholastic: basketball, cross-country running, dressage, equestrian sports, field hockey, horseback riding, lacrosse, running, soccer, softball, tennis, volleyball; intramural: aerobics, aerobics/dance, basketball, climbing, combined training, dance, dance team, dressage, equestrian sports, field hockey, fitness, horseback riding, indoor soccer, indoor track, lacrosse, modern dance, outdoor activities, physical fitness, physical training, rock climbing, ropes courses, running, squash, strength & conditioning, swimming and diving, tennis, volleyball, walking, weight lifting, weight training, yoga. 3 coaches, 1 athletic trainer.

Computers Computers are regularly used in all classes. Computer resources include on-campus library services, online commercial services, Internet access, wireless campus network, Internet filtering or blocking technology. Campus intranet, student e-mail accounts, and computer access in designated common areas are available to students. The school has a published electronic and media policy.

Contact Gina B. Finn, Director of Admission and Financial Aid. 540-687-4340. Fax: 540-687-3627. E-mail: gina.finn@foxcroft.org. Website: www.foxcroft.org

FRANKLIN ACADEMY

East Haddam, Connecticut
See Special Needs Schools section.

FRANKLIN ROAD ACADEMY

4700 Franklin Road
Nashville, Tennessee 37220

Head of School: Mr. Sean Casey

General Information Coeducational day college-preparatory, arts, religious studies, and technology school; primarily serves students with learning disabilities and ASPIRE—Student Learning Services Program. Grades PK–12. Founded: 1971. Setting: suburban. 57-acre campus. 5 buildings on campus. Approved or accredited by Southern Association of Colleges and Schools, Southern Association of Independent Schools, and Tennessee Department of Education. Member of National Association of Independent Schools. Total enrollment: 720. Upper school average class size: 15. Upper school faculty-student ratio: 1:7. There are 185 required school days per year for Upper School students. Upper School students typically attend 5 days per week. The average school day consists of 6 hours and 30 minutes.

Upper School Student Profile Grade 9: 67 students (33 boys, 34 girls); Grade 10: 67 students (34 boys, 33 girls); Grade 11: 63 students (31 boys, 32 girls); Grade 12: 67 students (33 boys, 34 girls).

Faculty School total: 105. In upper school: 21 men, 14 women; 24 have advanced degrees.

Subjects Offered ACT preparation, advanced chemistry, Advanced Placement courses, algebra, American history, American literature, anatomy and physiology, art, art-AP, band, baseball, basketball, Bible, Bible studies, biology, biology-AP, calculus, calculus-AP, chemistry, chemistry-AP, choral music, Civil War, college counseling, computer education, computer music, computer programming, computer science, current events, dance, drama, dramatic arts, economics, economics and history, electronic music, English, English language-AP, English literature, English literature-AP, environmental science, European history, European history-AP, fine arts, French, French language-AP, French literature-AP, geometry, government/civics, grammar, history, history-AP, honors algebra, honors English, honors geometry, honors U.S. history, human anatomy, jazz band, keyboarding, Latin, Latin-AP, Life of Christ, mathematics, mathematics-AP, model United Nations, music, music theory, personal development, physical education, physics, physics-AP, pottery, pre-calculus, SAT preparation, SAT/ACT preparation, science, social sciences, social studies, Spanish, Spanish language-AP, Spanish literature-AP, speech, statistics, statistics-AP, student government, student publications, technical theater, theater, theater production, track and field, trigonometry, U.S. government, U.S. history, U.S. history-AP, vocal music, volleyball, weight training, world history, world literature, wrestling, writing.

Graduation Requirements Algebra, arts and fine arts (art, music, dance, drama), computer science, English, foreign language, mathematics, physical education (includes health), religion (includes Bible studies and theology), science, social studies (includes history), community service hours required for graduation. Community service is required.

Special Academic Programs Advanced Placement exam preparation; honors section; independent study; term-away projects; academic accommodation for the gifted, the musically talented, and the artistically talented; programs in general development for dyslexic students.

College Admission Counseling 63 students graduated in 2015; all went to college, including Belmont University; DePaul University; Mississippi State University; The University of Alabama; The University of Tennessee; The University of Tennessee at Chattanooga. 45% scored over 600 on SAT critical reading, 55% scored over 600 on SAT math, 55% scored over 26 on composite ACT.

Student Life Upper grades have uniform requirement, student council, honor system. Discipline rests primarily with faculty.

Summer Programs Enrichment, sports, art/fine arts, computer instruction programs offered; session focuses on day camps, the arts, technology, and sports; held both on and off campus; held at area swimming pool; accepts boys and girls; open to students from other schools. 400 students usually enrolled. 2016 schedule: June 1 to July 17.

Tuition and Aid Day student tuition: $19,320. Tuition installment plan (Insured Tuition Payment Plan, FACTS Tuition Payment Plan, individually arranged payment plans). Need-based scholarship grants available. In 2015–16, 20% of upper-school students received aid. Total amount of financial aid awarded in 2015–16: $500,000.

Admissions Traditional secondary-level entrance grade is 9. Admissions testing, ISEE and writing sample required. Deadline for receipt of application materials: none. Application fee required: $40. On-campus interview required.

Athletics Interscholastic: baseball (boys), basketball (b,g), bowling (b,g), cheering (g), cross-country running (b,g), dance (g), diving (b,g), football (b), golf (b,g), hockey (b), ice hockey (b), soccer (b,g), softball (g), swimming and diving (b,g), tennis (b,g), track and field (b,g), volleyball (g), wrestling (b); intramural: aerobics/dance (g), physical fitness (b,g), physical training (b,g), power lifting (b), strength & conditioning (b,g); coed intramural: aerobics/dance. 2 PE instructors, 2 coaches, 1 athletic trainer.

Computers Computers are regularly used in art, Bible studies, college planning, creative writing, economics, English, foreign language, French, history, journalism, keyboarding, Latin, library skills, literary magazine, mathematics, music, religious studies, science, social sciences, Spanish, technology, theater, theater arts, Web site design, writing, yearbook classes. Computer network features include on-campus library services, online commercial services, Internet access, wireless campus network, Internet filtering or blocking technology, networked instructional software. Campus intranet, student e-mail accounts, and computer access in designated common areas are available to students. Students grades are available online. The school has a published electronic and media policy.

Contact Mrs. Courtney Williamson, Director of Admissions. 615-832-8845. Fax: 615-834-8845. E-mail: williamsonc@franklinroadacademy.com. Website: www.franklinroadacademy.com

FREDERICKSBURG ACADEMY

10800 Academy Drive
Fredericksburg, Virginia 22408-1931

Head of School: Ms. Karen A. Moschetto

General Information Coeducational day college-preparatory, arts, and technology school. Grades PK–12. Founded: 1992. Setting: suburban. Nearest major city is Washington, DC. 45-acre campus. 3 buildings on campus. Approved or accredited by Virginia Association of Independent Specialized Education Facilities and Virginia Department of Education. Member of National Association of Independent Schools. Endowment: $61,400. Total enrollment: 357. Upper school average class size: 12. Upper school faculty-student ratio: 1:7. There are 173 required school days per year for Upper School students. Upper School students typically attend 5 days per week. The average school day consists of 6 hours and 20 minutes.

Upper School Student Profile Grade 6: 20 students (10 boys, 10 girls); Grade 7: 37 students (17 boys, 20 girls); Grade 8: 32 students (22 boys, 10 girls); Grade 9: 24 students (17 boys, 7 girls); Grade 10: 33 students (14 boys, 19 girls); Grade 11: 30 students (14 boys, 16 girls); Grade 12: 10 students (6 boys, 4 girls).

Faculty School total: 43. In upper school: 7 men, 10 women; 9 have advanced degrees.

Subjects Offered Advanced Placement courses, advanced studio art-AP, algebra, American government, American history, American history-AP, American literature-AP, anatomy and physiology, art, art-AP, band, biology, biology-AP, British literature, British literature (honors), calculus, calculus-AP, chemistry, Chesapeake Bay studies, choral music, chorus, classical civilization, classics, computer science, computer skills, computer tools, concert band, creative writing, critical thinking, cultural arts, drama, earth science, English, English literature, English-AP, expository writing, fine arts, foreign language, French, geometry, health, health education, history, history-AP, instrumental music, journalism, language arts, Latin, Latin History, life science, mathematics, music, music history, newspaper, oral communications, orchestra, physical education, physics, probability and statistics, programming, reading, Roman civilization, science, senior seminar, Shakespeare, social studies, Spanish, studio art, studio art-AP, technical writing, technology, trigonometry, U.S. history, U.S. history-AP, world geography, world history, world literature, writing, writing workshop, yearbook.

Graduation Requirements Arts, electives, English, foreign language, history, lab science, mathematics, independent exhibit-research project and presentation.

Special Academic Programs Advanced Placement exam preparation; independent study.

College Admission Counseling 19 students graduated in 2015; all went to college, including Denison University; George Mason University; Purdue University; The College of William and Mary; University of Virginia; Virginia Polytechnic Institute and State University. Median combined SAT: 1700, median composite ACT: 24. 26% scored over 1800 on combined SAT, 26% scored over 26 on composite ACT.

Student Life Upper grades have specified standards of dress, student council, honor system. Discipline rests equally with students and faculty.

Summer Programs Enrichment, sports, art/fine arts programs offered; session focuses on enrichment, arts, and athletic opportunities; held on campus; accepts boys and girls; open to students from other schools. 200 students usually enrolled. 2016 schedule: June 15 to August 14. Application deadline: June 1.

Tuition and Aid Day student tuition: $21,270. Tuition installment plan (FACTS Tuition Payment Plan). Merit scholarship grants, need-based scholarship grants available. In 2015–16, 39% of upper-school students received aid; total upper-school merit-scholarship money awarded: $107,010. Total amount of financial aid awarded in 2015–16: $366,400.

Admissions Traditional secondary-level entrance grade is 9. For fall 2015, 25 students applied for upper-level admission, 10 were accepted, 7 enrolled. Admissions testing required. Deadline for receipt of application materials: none. Application fee required: $50. Interview required.

Athletics Interscholastic: basketball (boys, girls), cross-country running (b,g), field hockey (g), lacrosse (b,g), soccer (b,g), swimming and diving (b,g), tennis (b,g); coed interscholastic: aquatics, fitness, physical training. 6 coaches.

Computers Computers are regularly used in English, foreign language, French, history, journalism, Latin, mathematics, newspaper, publications, science, Spanish, writing, yearbook classes. Computer network features include on-campus library services, online commercial services, Internet access, wireless campus network, Internet filtering or blocking technology, syllabi and assignments online. Student e-mail accounts are available to students. Students grades are available online. The school has a published electronic and media policy.

Contact Mrs. Marnie Schattgen, Assistant Director of Admission. 540-898-0020 Ext. 228. Fax: 540-898-0440. E-mail: mschattgen@fredericksburgacademy.org. Website: www.fredericksburgacademy.org

FREDERICTON CHRISTIAN ACADEMY

778 MacLaren Ave
Fredericton, New Brunswick E3A 5J8, Canada

Head of School: Mr. Jonathan McAloon

General Information Coeducational day and distance learning college-preparatory, general academic, arts, religious studies, and technology school, affiliated with Baptist Church, Evangelical Christian Church; primarily serves students with learning disabilities. Grades 1–12. Distance learning grades 8–12. Founded: 1979. Setting: suburban. 5-acre campus. 1 building on campus. Approved or accredited by Association of Christian Schools International and New Brunswick Department of Education. Language of instruction: English. Total enrollment: 156. Upper school average class size: 15. Upper school faculty-student ratio: 1:14. Upper School students typically attend 5 days per week. The average school day consists of 7 hours.

Upper School Student Profile Grade 6: 12 students (6 boys, 6 girls); Grade 7: 9 students (2 boys, 7 girls); Grade 8: 11 students (5 boys, 6 girls); Grade 9: 7 students (6 boys, 1 girl); Grade 10: 21 students (10 boys, 11 girls); Grade 11: 17 students (9 boys, 8 girls); Grade 12: 17 students (8 boys, 9 girls). 30% of students are Baptist, members of Evangelical Christian Church.

Faculty School total: 13. In upper school: 4 men, 4 women; 1 has an advanced degree.

Subjects Offered All academic.

Special Academic Programs Accelerated programs; independent study; study at local college for college credit; academic accommodation for the gifted; remedial reading and/or remedial writing; remedial math; ESL (10 students enrolled).

College Admission Counseling 15 students graduated in 2015; 13 went to college. Other: 2 went to work.

Student Life Upper grades have specified standards of dress, student council, honor system. Discipline rests primarily with faculty. Attendance at religious services is required.

Tuition and Aid Tuition installment plan (monthly payment plans, individually arranged payment plans). Tuition reduction for siblings, bursaries, need-based scholarship grants available. In 2015–16, 10% of upper-school students received aid.

Admissions Traditional secondary-level entrance grade is 10. For fall 2015, 10 students applied for upper-level admission, 9 were accepted, 9 enrolled. Deadline for receipt of application materials: August 15. Application fee required: CAN$50. Interview required.

Athletics Interscholastic: basketball (boys, girls), cross-country running (b,g); intramural: aerobics/dance (b,g), badminton (b,g), ball hockey (b,g), basketball (b,g), soccer (b,g); coed intramural: aerobics/dance, badminton, ball hockey, soccer.

Computers Computer resources include Internet access, wireless campus network. Student e-mail accounts are available to students. Students grades are available online.

Contact Mrs. Sandra Amos, Administrator. 506-458-9379. Fax: 506-458-8702. E-mail: office@fcae.ca. Website: https://www.fcae.ca/

FREEMAN ACADEMY

748 South Main Street
PO Box 1000
Freeman, South Dakota 57029

Head of School: Mrs. Katie Minster

General Information Coeducational boarding and day college-preparatory, arts, and religious studies school, affiliated with Mennonite Church. Boarding grades 9–12, day grades 1–12. Founded: 1900. Setting: rural. Nearest major city is Sioux Falls. Students are housed in coed dormitories and host family homes. 80-acre campus. 6 buildings on campus. Approved or accredited by Mennonite Schools Council, North Central Association of Colleges and Schools, and South Dakota Department of Education. Endowment: $450,000. Total enrollment: 85. Upper school average class size: 9. Upper school faculty-student ratio: 1:5. There are 180 required school days per year for Upper School students. Upper School students typically attend 5 days per week. The average school day consists of 8 hours.

Upper School Student Profile Grade 9: 9 students (6 boys, 3 girls); Grade 10: 7 students (4 boys, 3 girls); Grade 11: 12 students (5 boys, 7 girls); Grade 12: 11 students (4 boys, 7 girls). 1 state is represented in upper school student body. 55% of students are Mennonite.

Faculty School total: 10. In upper school: 4 men, 6 women; 3 have advanced degrees.

Subjects Offered Computer science, English, fine arts, humanities, mathematics, music, religion, science, social sciences.

Graduation Requirements Arts and fine arts (art, music, dance, drama), computer science, English, foreign language, mathematics, religion (includes Bible studies and theology), science, social studies (includes history), humanities.

Special Academic Programs Independent study; academic accommodation for the musically talented and the artistically talented.

College Admission Counseling 6 students graduated in 2014; all went to college, including Goshen College; Hesston College; The University of South Dakota. Median composite ACT: 25. 31% scored over 26 on composite ACT.

Student Life Upper grades have specified standards of dress, honor system. Discipline rests primarily with faculty. Attendance at religious services is required.

Tuition and Aid Day student tuition: $6485; 7-day tuition and room/board: $22,500. Tuition installment plan (FACTS Tuition Payment Plan, monthly payment plans, individually arranged payment plans, semester payment plan). Tuition reduction for siblings, merit scholarship grants, need-based scholarship grants available. In 2014–15, 30% of upper-school students received aid; total upper-school merit-scholarship money awarded: $500. Total amount of financial aid awarded in 2014–15: $30,000.

Admissions Traditional secondary-level entrance grade is 9. For fall 2014, 6 students applied for upper-level admission, 5 were accepted, 4 enrolled. Secondary Level English Proficiency required. Deadline for receipt of application materials: none. No application fee required. Interview recommended.

Athletics Interscholastic: basketball (boys, girls), cheering (g), cross-country running (b,g), golf (b,g), soccer (b,g), track and field (b,g), volleyball (g); coed interscholastic: soccer. 4 coaches.

Computers Computers are regularly used in English, keyboarding, mathematics, religion, science, social studies, speech, yearbook classes. Computer network features include on-campus library services, Internet access, wireless campus network, Internet filtering or blocking technology. Student e-mail accounts and computer access in designated common areas are available to students. Students grades are available online. The school has a published electronic and media policy.

Contact Ms. Nanette Hofer, Enrollment Director and International Student Coordinator. 605-925-4237 Ext. 225. Fax: 605-925-4271. E-mail: nhofer@freemanacademy.org. Website: www.freemanacademy.org

FRENCH-AMERICAN SCHOOL OF NEW YORK

525 Fenimore Road
Mamaroneck, New York 10543

Head of School: Mr. Joël Peinado

General Information Coeducational day college-preparatory and bilingual studies school. Grades N–12. Founded: 1980. Setting: suburban. Nearest major city is White Plains. 1 building on campus. Approved or accredited by New York State Association of Independent Schools and New York Department of Education. Member of National Association of Independent Schools. Languages of instruction: English and French. Total enrollment: 842. Upper school average class size: 17. Upper school faculty-student ratio: 1:6. There are 169 required school days per year for Upper School students. Upper School students typically attend 5 days per week. The average school day consists of 7 hours and 45 minutes.

Upper School Student Profile Grade 9: 50 students (27 boys, 23 girls); Grade 10: 64 students (36 boys, 28 girls); Grade 11: 38 students (22 boys, 16 girls); Grade 12: 55 students (22 boys, 33 girls).

Faculty School total: 82. In upper school: 18 men, 32 women; 33 have advanced degrees.

Subjects Offered Algebra, American history, American literature, art, biology, choir, civics, computer applications, computer multimedia, current events, earth science, ecology, economics, English, ESL, European history, expository writing, French, French language-AP, French literature-AP, French studies, geometry, German, government, health, Latin, mathematics, multimedia, music, newspaper, philosophy, physical education, physics, physics-AP, public speaking, science, social studies, Spanish, Spanish language-AP, world history, world literature, writing, yearbook.

Graduation Requirements 20th century history, algebra, American history, biology, calculus, chemistry, civics, computer studies, current events, English, European history, foreign language, French, geography, geology, geometry, mathematics, music, philosophy, physical education (includes health), physics, pre-algebra, pre-calculus, research seminar, social studies (includes history). Community service is required.

Special Academic Programs Advanced Placement exam preparation; honors section; ESL (38 students enrolled).

College Admission Counseling 47 students graduated in 2014; all went to college, including Georgetown University; Georgia Institute of Technology; McGill University; Stanford University. Mean SAT critical reading: 626, mean SAT math: 651, mean SAT writing: 650.

Student Life Upper grades have specified standards of dress, student council. Discipline rests primarily with faculty.

Tuition and Aid Day student tuition: $27,150–$28,200. Tuition installment plan (Academic Management Services Plan). Need-based scholarship grants available. In 2014–15, 5% of upper-school students received aid. Total amount of financial aid awarded in 2014–15: $290,314.

Admissions Traditional secondary-level entrance grade is 9. For fall 2014, 302 students applied for upper-level admission, 295 were accepted, 175 enrolled. English, French, and math proficiency required. Deadline for receipt of application materials: none. Application fee required: $150. Interview recommended.

Athletics Interscholastic: baseball (boys), basketball (b,g), cross-country running (b,g), rugby (b,g), soccer (b,g), softball (g), tennis (b,g); coed intramural: fencing. 4 PE instructors, 4 coaches.

Computers Computers are regularly used in art, English, foreign language, French, history, mathematics, music, publications, science classes. Computer network features include on-campus library services, Internet access, Internet filtering or blocking technology, laptop use (in certain classes), new iPad program in seventh grade. Student e-mail accounts are available to students. The school has a published electronic and media policy.

Contact Mr. Clyde Javois, Director of Admissions. 914-250-0400. Fax: 914-940-2214. E-mail: cjavois@fasny.org. Website: www.fasny.org

FRESNO CHRISTIAN SCHOOLS

7280 North Cedar Avenue
Fresno, California 93720

Head of School: Mr. Jeremy Brown

General Information Coeducational day college-preparatory, arts, religious studies, and technology school, affiliated with Protestant-Evangelical faith. Grades K–12. Founded: 1977. Setting: suburban. 27-acre campus. 4 buildings on campus. Approved or accredited by Association of Christian Schools International, Western Association of Schools and Colleges, and California Department of Education. Endowment: $200,000. Total enrollment: 464. Upper school average class size: 20. Upper school faculty-student ratio: 1:10. There are 176 required school days per year for Upper School students. Upper School students typically attend 5 days per week. The average school day consists of 5 hours and 20 minutes.

Upper School Student Profile Grade 9: 36 students (18 boys, 18 girls); Grade 10: 39 students (20 boys, 19 girls); Grade 11: 49 students (29 boys, 20 girls); Grade 12: 52 students (22 boys, 30 girls). 90% of students are Protestant-Evangelical faith.

Faculty School total: 26. In upper school: 8 men, 9 women; 5 have advanced degrees.

Subjects Offered Advanced Placement courses, algebra, alternative physical education, American government, American history, American history-AP, art, athletics, band, baseball, basketball, Bible, Bible studies, biology, biology-AP, British literature, calculus-AP, cheerleading, chemistry, Chinese, choir, choral music, Christian education, civics, composition-AP, concert band, concert choir, drama, drama performance, economics, economics and history, English, English language and composition-AP, English literature and composition-AP, English-AP, ensembles, European history-AP, geometry, golf, home economics, honors algebra, honors English, honors geometry, humanities, jazz band, journalism, leadership, marching band, mathematics, mathematics-AP, physical education, physical science, physics, pre-calculus, softball, Spanish, sports, statistics-AP, student government, tennis, track and field, trigonometry, U.S. history, video film production, vocal music, volleyball, woodworking, work experience, world history, yearbook.

Graduation Requirements Arts and fine arts (art, music, dance, drama), electives, English, mathematics, physical education (includes health), religion (includes Bible studies and theology), science, social studies (includes history), 4 years of Biblical Studies classes, 4 years of physical education.

Special Academic Programs 7 Advanced Placement exams for which test preparation is offered; honors section; independent study; study at local college for college credit; remedial reading and/or remedial writing; remedial math; special instructional classes for students with learning disabilities.

College Admission Counseling 50 students graduated in 2015; 46 went to college, including California State University, Fresno; Fresno City College. Other: 1 went to work, 1 entered military service, 2 had other specific plans. Mean SAT critical reading: 494, mean SAT math: 513, mean SAT writing: 479, mean combined SAT: 1486, mean composite ACT: 24.

Student Life Upper grades have specified standards of dress, student council, honor system. Discipline rests primarily with faculty. Attendance at religious services is required.

Tuition and Aid Day student tuition: $8275. Tuition installment plan (monthly payment plans, individually arranged payment plans). Tuition reduction for siblings, merit scholarship grants, need-based scholarship grants available. In 2015–16, 29% of upper-school students received aid; total upper-school merit-scholarship money awarded: $27,984. Total amount of financial aid awarded in 2015–16: $262,944.

Admissions Traditional secondary-level entrance grade is 9. Stanford Achievement Test required. Deadline for receipt of application materials: none. Application fee required: $100. Interview required.

Athletics Interscholastic: baseball (boys), basketball (b,g), cheering (g), cross-country running (b,g), drill team (g), football (b), soccer (b,g), softball (g), strength & conditioning (b,g), tennis (b,g), track and field (b,g), volleyball (g), weight training (b,g); coed interscholastic: golf, physical training; coed intramural: outdoor recreation, volleyball. 1 PE instructor, 16 coaches.

Computers Computers are regularly used in media production, publications, yearbook classes. Computer network features include on-campus library services, online commercial services, Internet access, wireless campus network, Internet filtering or blocking technology. Computer access in designated common areas is available to students. Students grades are available online. The school has a published electronic and media policy.

Contact Mrs. Kerry Roberts, Registrar. 559-299-1695 Ext. 102. Fax: 559-299-1051. E-mail: kroberts@fresnochristian.com. Website: www.fresnochristian.com

FRIENDS ACADEMY

270 Duck Pond Road
Locust Valley, New York 11560

Head of School: William Morris

General Information Coeducational day college-preparatory, arts, and religious studies school, affiliated with Society of Friends. Grades N–12. Founded: 1876. Setting: suburban. Nearest major city is New York. 65-acre campus. 8 buildings on campus. Approved or accredited by New York State Association of Independent Schools and New York Department of Education. Member of National Association of Independent Schools and Secondary School Admission Test Board. Endowment: $30 million. Total enrollment: 781. Upper school average class size: 15. Upper school faculty-student ratio: 1:7. There are 165 required school days per year for Upper School students. Upper School students typically attend 5 days per week. The average school day consists of 7 hours and 15 minutes.

Upper School Student Profile Grade 9: 93 students (42 boys, 51 girls); Grade 10: 89 students (46 boys, 43 girls); Grade 11: 92 students (57 boys, 35 girls); Grade 12: 95 students (40 boys, 55 girls). 1% of students are members of Society of Friends.

Faculty School total: 111. In upper school: 23 men, 34 women; 48 have advanced degrees.

Subjects Offered Advanced Placement courses, African studies, algebra, American history, American literature, art, art history, Bible studies, biology, calculus, ceramics, chemistry, community service, computer literacy, computer programming, computer science, creative writing, drama, driver education, English, English literature, environmental science, ethics, European history, expository writing, fine arts, French, geography, geometry, grammar, Greek, health, history, Italian, Latin, logic, mathematics, mechanical drawing, music, outdoor education, photography, physical education, physics, psychology, religion, science, social sciences, social studies, Spanish, speech, theater, trigonometry, Western civilization, world literature, writing.

Graduation Requirements Arts and fine arts (art, music, dance, drama), computer literacy, English, foreign language, mathematics, outdoor education, physical education (includes health), religion (includes Bible studies and theology), science, social sciences, social studies (includes history), speech, participation in on-campus work crew program, independent service program. Community service is required.

Special Academic Programs 18 Advanced Placement exams for which test preparation is offered; honors section; independent study; remedial reading and/or remedial writing; remedial math.

College Admission Counseling 98 students graduated in 2015; all went to college, including Boston College; Dartmouth College; New York University; Towson University; University of Southern California; Washington University in St. Louis.

Student Life Upper grades have specified standards of dress, student council, honor system. Discipline rests equally with students and faculty. Attendance at religious services is required.

Summer Programs Art/fine arts programs offered; session focuses on arts and sports; held both on and off campus; held at off-campus for golf, sailing, and riding and off-campus field trips; accepts boys and girls; open to students from other schools. 500 students usually enrolled. 2016 schedule: June 27 to August 19.

Tuition and Aid Day student tuition: $31,700. Tuition installment plan (Insured Tuition Payment Plan, monthly payment plans). Need-based scholarship grants, Quaker grants, tuition remission for children of faculty and staff available. In 2015–16, 20% of upper-school students received aid.

Admissions Traditional secondary-level entrance grade is 9. For fall 2015, 118 students applied for upper-level admission, 49 were accepted, 36 enrolled. SSAT required. Deadline for receipt of application materials: January 13. Application fee required: $55. Interview required.

Athletics Interscholastic: baseball (boys), basketball (b,g), crew (b,g), cross-country running (b,g), field hockey (g), fitness (b,g), football (b), golf (b,g), ice hockey (b), indoor track & field (b,g), lacrosse (b,g), soccer (b,g), softball (g), tennis (b,g), track and field (b,g), winter (indoor) track (b,g); coed interscholastic: squash; coed intramural: dance, volleyball. 9 PE instructors, 1 athletic trainer.

Computers Computers are regularly used in English, mathematics, science, technology classes. Computer network features include on-campus library services, online commercial services, Internet access, wireless campus network, Internet filtering or blocking technology, iPad program for middle school students. Campus intranet, student e-mail accounts, and computer access in designated common areas are available to students. Students grades are available online. The school has a published electronic and media policy.

Contact Joanna Kim, Associate Director of Admissions. 516-393-4244. Fax: 516-465-1718. E-mail: joanna_kim@fa.org. Website: www.fa.org

FRIENDS' CENTRAL SCHOOL

1101 City Avenue
Wynnewood, Pennsylvania 19096

Head of School: Craig N. Sellers

General Information Coeducational day college-preparatory school, affiliated with Society of Friends. Grades N–12. Founded: 1845. Setting: suburban. Nearest major city is Philadelphia. 23-acre campus. 7 buildings on campus. Approved or accredited by Pennsylvania Department of Education. Member of National Association of Independent Schools and Secondary School Admission Test Board. Endowment: $25 million. Total enrollment: 788. Upper school average class size: 18. Upper school faculty-student ratio: 1:8. There are 170 required school days per year for Upper School students. Upper School students typically attend 5 days per week. The average school day consists of 6 hours and 40 minutes.

Upper School Student Profile Grade 9: 83 students (44 boys, 39 girls); Grade 10: 95 students (48 boys, 47 girls); Grade 11: 102 students (51 boys, 51 girls); Grade 12: 98 students (50 boys, 48 girls). 3% of students are members of Society of Friends.

Faculty School total: 115. In upper school: 22 men, 23 women; 34 have advanced degrees.

Friends' Central School

Subjects Offered Advanced biology, advanced chemistry, advanced math, algebra, American history, American literature, architecture, art history, Bible, biology, botany, calculus, ceramics, chemistry, chorus, computer applications, computer multimedia, computer programming, computer-aided design, conflict resolution, digital photography, drama, English, equality and freedom, film studies, French, geometry, German, health education, instrumental music, international relations, jazz band, Latin, life skills, media studies, modern European history, modern history, music history, music theory, philosophy, photography, physical education, physical science, physics, pre-calculus, psychology, Quakerism and ethics, senior project, sexuality, Spanish, statistics, studio art, study skills, Western literature, women in world history, woodworking, world history, writing workshop.

Graduation Requirements Arts and fine arts (art, music, dance, drama), English, foreign language, mathematics, science, service learning/internship, U.S. history, world cultures.

Special Academic Programs Independent study; term-away projects; study abroad.

College Admission Counseling 95 students graduated in 2015; all went to college, including Brown University; Bucknell University; Syracuse University; The George Washington University; University of Pennsylvania; Washington University in St. Louis. Mean SAT critical reading: 642, mean SAT math: 638, mean SAT writing: 640.

Student Life Upper grades have specified standards of dress, student council, honor system. Discipline rests primarily with faculty. Attendance at religious services is required.

Summer Programs Remediation, advancement programs offered; held on campus; accepts boys and girls; open to students from other schools. 37 students usually enrolled. 2016 schedule: June 23 to August 1.

Tuition and Aid Day student tuition: $17,000–$32,800. Tuition installment plan (FACTS Tuition Payment Plan, monthly payment plans, Higher Education Service, Inc). Need-based scholarship grants available. In 2015–16, 36% of upper-school students received aid. Total amount of financial aid awarded in 2015–16: $2,581,380.

Admissions Traditional secondary-level entrance grade is 9. For fall 2015, 211 students applied for upper-level admission, 95 were accepted, 44 enrolled. ISEE, SSAT or Wechsler Intelligence Scale for Children required. Deadline for receipt of application materials: January 8. Application fee required: $50. On-campus interview required.

Athletics Interscholastic: aquatics (boys, girls), baseball (b), basketball (b,g), cross-country running (b,g), field hockey (g), indoor track (b,g), lacrosse (g), soccer (b,g), softball (g), tennis (b,g), track and field (b,g), winter (indoor) track (b,g), wrestling (b,g); coed interscholastic: golf, squash, water polo; coed intramural: aerobics, aerobics/dance, aerobics/Nautilus, cheering, dance, fitness, flag football, life saving, table tennis. 8 PE instructors, 10 coaches, 1 athletic trainer.

Computers Computers are regularly used in college planning, foreign language, French, health, information technology, introduction to technology, Latin, mathematics, publishing, science, Spanish, technology, Web site design, yearbook classes. Computer network features include on-campus library services, online commercial services, Internet access, wireless campus network, Internet filtering or blocking technology, Intranet collaboration. Campus intranet, student e-mail accounts, and computer access in designated common areas are available to students. Students grades are available online. The school has a published electronic and media policy.

Contact Dr. Susan Robinson, Director of Enrollment Management. 610-645-5032. Fax: 610-658-5644. E-mail: admission@friendscentral.org. Website: www.friendscentral.org

FRIENDSHIP CHRISTIAN SCHOOL

5400 Coles Ferry Pike
Lebanon, Tennessee 37087

Head of School: Mr. Jon Shoulders

General Information Coeducational day college-preparatory, arts, business, religious studies, technology, and dual enrollment school, affiliated with Christian faith. Grades PK–12. Founded: 1973. Setting: rural. Nearest major city is Nashville. 50-acre campus. 6 buildings on campus. Approved or accredited by National Christian School Association, Southern Association of Colleges and Schools, and Tennessee Department of Education. Member of National Association of Independent Schools. Total enrollment: 539. Upper school average class size: 20. Upper school faculty-student ratio: 1:15. There are 175 required school days per year for Upper School students. Upper School students typically attend 5 days per week. The average school day consists of 6 hours and 35 minutes.

Upper School Student Profile Grade 9: 56 students (34 boys, 22 girls); Grade 10: 57 students (31 boys, 26 girls); Grade 11: 50 students (27 boys, 23 girls); Grade 12: 63 students (35 boys, 28 girls). 80% of students are Christian faith.

Faculty School total: 50. In upper school: 9 men, 12 women; 18 have advanced degrees.

Subjects Offered Accounting, ACT preparation, advanced biology, advanced chemistry, advanced math, Advanced Placement courses, agriculture, algebra, American government, anatomy and physiology, Ancient Greek, art, athletic training, backpacking, band, Bible, Bible studies, biology, bowling, British literature (honors), business applications, calculus, calculus-AP, chemistry, choral music, chorus, college placement, college planning, computers, creative writing, drama, driver education, earth science, economics, English, English-AP, environmental science, geometry, honors algebra, honors English, honors geometry, Internet, journalism, keyboarding,

mathematics, modern history, physical education, physical science, physics, physiology, pre-algebra, psychology, science project, science research, Spanish, speech, swimming, trigonometry, U.S. constitutional history, U.S. government, U.S. history, U.S. history-AP, U.S. Presidents, weight training, wellness, world geography, world history, yearbook.

Graduation Requirements ACT preparation, advanced chemistry, advanced math, Advanced Placement courses, algebra, American government, American history, American history-AP, applied arts, arts and fine arts (art, music, dance, drama), Bible, biology, chemistry, chemistry-AP, ecology, English language and composition-AP, English literature-AP, English-AP, foreign language, French, honors U.S. history, keyboarding, physical education (includes health), physics, pre-calculus, U.S. government and politics-AP, U.S. history-AP, weight training.

Special Academic Programs Advanced Placement exam preparation; honors section; study at local college for college credit.

College Admission Counseling 55 students graduated in 2015; 54 went to college, including Cumberland University; Lipscomb University; Tennessee Technological University; The University of Tennessee; The University of Tennessee at Chattanooga; United States Naval Academy. Other: 1 entered military service. Mean composite ACT: 25. 50% scored over 26 on composite ACT.

Student Life Upper grades have uniform requirement, student council, honor system. Discipline rests primarily with faculty.

Tuition and Aid Day student tuition: $9120. Tuition installment plan (FACTS Tuition Payment Plan). Tuition reduction for siblings, need-based scholarship grants, paying campus jobs available. In 2015–16, 2% of upper-school students received aid. Total amount of financial aid awarded in 2015–16: $5000.

Admissions Traditional secondary-level entrance grade is 9. For fall 2015, 25 students applied for upper-level admission, 19 were accepted, 19 enrolled. Otis-Lennon School Ability Test required. Deadline for receipt of application materials: none. Application fee required: $75. Interview recommended.

Athletics Interscholastic: baseball (boys), basketball (b,g), cheering (g), football (b), golf (b,g), physical fitness (b,g); coed interscholastic: bowling, cross-country running, golf, physical fitness. 2 PE instructors, 13 coaches, 1 athletic trainer.

Computers Computers are regularly used in accounting, business, college planning, creative writing, journalism, keyboarding, library, media, multimedia, newspaper, reading, remedial study skills, science, typing classes. Computer network features include on-campus library services, online commercial services, Internet access, wireless campus network, Internet filtering or blocking technology. Student e-mail accounts and computer access in designated common areas are available to students. Students grades are available online. The school has a published electronic and media policy.

Contact Terresia Williams, Director of Admissions. 615-449-1573 Ext. 207. Fax: 615-449-2769. E-mail: twilliams@friendshipchristian.org.
Website: www.friendshipchristian.org

FRIENDS SELECT SCHOOL

17th & Benjamin Franklin Parkway
Philadelphia, Pennsylvania 19103-1284

Head of School: Ms. Rose Hagan

General Information Coeducational day college-preparatory, arts, and religious studies school, affiliated with Society of Friends. Grades PK–12. Founded: 1689. Setting: urban. 1-acre campus. 2 buildings on campus. Member of National Association of Independent Schools and Secondary School Admission Test Board. Endowment: $10 million. Total enrollment: 558. Upper school average class size: 15. Upper school faculty-student ratio: 1:15. There are 167 required school days per year for Upper School students. Upper School students typically attend 5 days per week. The average school day consists of 6 hours and 20 minutes.

Upper School Student Profile 5% of students are members of Society of Friends.

Faculty School total: 83. In upper school: 12 men, 23 women; 27 have advanced degrees.

Subjects Offered 20th century American writers, 3-dimensional art, algebra, American history, American literature, art, art history, biology, calculus, chemistry, computer math, computer programming, computer science, creative writing, drama, drawing, earth science, ecology, economics, electronics, English, English literature, ethics, European history, expository writing, fine arts, French, geography, geology, geometry, government/civics, grammar, health, history, Italian, Latin, marine biology, mathematics, music, photography, physical education, physics, religion, science, sculpture, social studies, Spanish, statistics, theater, trigonometry, world history, world literature, writing.

Graduation Requirements Arts and fine arts (art, music, dance, drama), English, foreign language, history, mathematics, physical education (includes health), religion (includes Bible studies and theology), science, senior project, social studies (includes history), junior internship.

Special Academic Programs Advanced Placement exam preparation; independent study; academic accommodation for the musically talented and the artistically talented; ESL (10 students enrolled).

College Admission Counseling Colleges students went to include Cornell University; Drexel University; New York University; School of the Art Institute of Chicago; The George Washington University; University of Pittsburgh.

Student Life Upper grades have student council. Discipline rests primarily with faculty. Attendance at religious services is required.

Summer Programs Remediation, enrichment, advancement, art/fine arts, computer instruction programs offered; session focuses on enrichment and advancement; held on campus; accepts boys and girls; open to students from other schools. 50 students usually enrolled. 2016 schedule: June 27 to August 5. Application deadline: June 6.

Tuition and Aid Day student tuition: $31,000. Tuition installment plan (10-month payment plan, 2-payment plan). Tuition reduction for siblings, need-based scholarship grants, need-based loans, K-12 Family Education Loan Program (SLM Financial Group), AchieverLoans (Key Education Resources), tuition reduction for 3-plus siblings from same family, 5% reduction for children of alumni/alumnae available. In 2015–16, 43% of upper-school students received aid. Total amount of financial aid awarded in 2015–16: $888,000.

Admissions Traditional secondary-level entrance grade is 9. ERB CTP IV, ISEE, PSAT and SAT for applicants to grade 11 and 12, SSAT or WISC or WAIS required. Deadline for receipt of application materials: none. Application fee required: $60. On-campus interview required.

Athletics Interscholastic: baseball (boys), basketball (b,g), crew (b,g), cross-country running (b,g), field hockey (g), soccer (b,g), softball (g); coed interscholastic: crew, cross-country running, swimming and diving, tennis. 3 PE instructors, 28 coaches, 1 athletic trainer.

Computers Computers are regularly used in all academic, English, foreign language, mathematics, science classes. Computer network features include on-campus library services, online commercial services, Internet access, online learning center. Campus intranet, student e-mail accounts, and computer access in designated common areas are available to students. The school has a published electronic and media policy.

Contact Annemiek Young, Director of Admission and Enrollment Management. 215-561-5900 Ext. 102. Fax: 215-864-2979. E-mail: annemieky@friends-select.org. Website: www.friends-select.org

FRONT RANGE CHRISTIAN HIGH SCHOOL

6637 West Ottawa Avenue
Littleton, Colorado 80128

Head of School: David Cooper

General Information Coeducational day college-preparatory, general academic, arts, business, vocational, religious studies, bilingual studies, technology, and science, math, language arts, media, Spanish school, affiliated with Christian faith. Grades PK–12. Founded: 1994. Setting: suburban. Nearest major city is Denver. 20-acre campus. 3 buildings on campus. Approved or accredited by Association of Christian Schools International, North Central Association of Colleges and Schools, Northwest Accreditation Commission, Southern Association of Colleges and Schools, and Colorado Department of Education. Total enrollment: 437. Upper school average class size: 13. Upper school faculty-student ratio: 1:6. There are 175 required school days per year for Upper School students. Upper School students typically attend 5 days per week. The average school day consists of 7 hours and 20 minutes.

Upper School Student Profile Grade 9: 38 students (14 boys, 24 girls); Grade 10: 39 students (21 boys, 18 girls); Grade 11: 44 students (27 boys, 17 girls); Grade 12: 48 students (24 boys, 24 girls). 99% of students are Christian faith.

Faculty School total: 56. In upper school: 13 men, 16 women; 14 have advanced degrees.

Subjects Offered ACT preparation, acting, advanced biology, advanced math, Advanced Placement courses, algebra, American history, American literature, anatomy and physiology, ancient world history, art, athletics, band, baseball, basketball, Bible, biology, biology-AP, British literature, calculus, career and personal planning, career/college preparation, chemistry, choir, Christian doctrine, Christian scripture, composition, drama, drama performance, earth science, electives, foreign language, forensics, geometry, golf, grammar, guitar, health education, home economics, honors algebra, honors English, honors U.S. history, honors world history, junior and senior seminars, lab science, language arts, leadership and service, Life of Christ, literature and composition-AP, music, musical productions, participation in sports, performing arts, photojournalism, physical education, physical fitness, physics, pre-calculus, probability and statistics, psychology, Spanish, speech, speech and oral interpretations, sports, statistics, trigonometry, video and animation, video film production, visual arts, vocal ensemble, volleyball, world religions, yearbook.

Graduation Requirements Algebra, career planning, college planning, history, language arts, science, Spanish, speech, participation in annual Spring Practicum, participation in monthly service projects (called GO!).

Special Academic Programs 5 Advanced Placement exams for which test preparation is offered; honors section; study at local college for college credit; academic accommodation for the gifted; remedial reading and/or remedial writing; remedial math; programs in English, mathematics, general development for dyslexic students.

College Admission Counseling 45 students graduated in 2015; 40 went to college, including Bethel College; Colorado Christian University; Dordt College; Grand Canyon University. Other: 2 went to work, 1 entered military service, 2 had other specific plans. Median SAT critical reading: 460, median SAT math: 590, median SAT writing: 490, median combined SAT: 1560, median composite ACT: 23. 8% scored over 600 on SAT critical reading, 48% scored over 600 on SAT math, 4% scored over 600 on SAT writing, 30% scored over 26 on composite ACT.

Student Life Upper grades have specified standards of dress, student council, honor system. Discipline rests equally with students and faculty. Attendance at religious services is required.

Summer Programs Remediation, enrichment, sports, art/fine arts programs offered; session focuses on keeping students ready for academics and competition over the long break; held on campus; accepts boys and girls; open to students from other schools. 50 students usually enrolled. 2016 schedule: June to August.

Tuition and Aid Day student tuition: $9975. Tuition installment plan (FACTS Tuition Payment Plan). Merit scholarship grants, need-based scholarship grants, employee discounts for parents with students who attend available. In 2015–16, 25% of upper-school students received aid; total upper-school merit-scholarship money awarded: $5000. Total amount of financial aid awarded in 2015–16: $181,000.

Admissions Traditional secondary-level entrance grade is 9. For fall 2015, 122 students applied for upper-level admission, 113 were accepted, 98 enrolled. Essay and Math Placement Exam required. Deadline for receipt of application materials: none. Application fee required: $50. Interview required.

Athletics Interscholastic: baseball (boys), basketball (b,g), football (b), golf (b), soccer (b,g), volleyball (g); intramural: basketball (b,g), cheering (g), golf (g), volleyball (g); coed interscholastic: cross-country running, track and field; coed intramural: aerobics, bicycling, combined training, dance, fitness, modern dance, mountain biking, outdoor recreation, outdoor skills, physical fitness, physical training, rock climbing, skiing (downhill), snowboarding, weight training. 2 PE instructors, 23 coaches.

Computers Computers are regularly used in all academic, basic skills, introduction to technology, media arts, multimedia, yearbook classes. Computer network features include Internet access, wireless campus network, Internet filtering or blocking technology, RenWeb parents and student access, 1:1 iPad program, Moodle for classrooms. Campus intranet, student e-mail accounts, and computer access in designated common areas are available to students. Students grades are available online. The school has a published electronic and media policy.

Contact Jennifer Dodd, Admissions Manager. 303-531-4522. Fax: 720-922-3296. E-mail: admissions@frcs.org. Website: www.frcs.org

THE FROSTIG SCHOOL

Pasadena, California
See Special Needs Schools section.

FUQUA SCHOOL

605 Fuqua Drive
PO Box 328
Farmville, Virginia 23901

Head of School: Mr. John H. Melton

General Information Coeducational day college-preparatory and arts school. Grades PK–12. Founded: 1993. Setting: small town. Nearest major city is Richmond. 65-acre campus. 19 buildings on campus. Approved or accredited by Southern Association of Colleges and Schools, Virginia Association of Independent Schools, and Virginia Department of Education. Member of National Association of Independent Schools and Secondary School Admission Test Board. Endowment: $5.1 million. Total enrollment: 379. Upper school average class size: 15. Upper school faculty-student ratio: 1:7. There are 180 required school days per year for Upper School students. Upper School students typically attend 5 days per week. The average school day consists of 6 hours.

Upper School Student Profile Grade 9: 40 students (20 boys, 20 girls); Grade 10: 44 students (24 boys, 20 girls); Grade 11: 28 students (13 boys, 15 girls); Grade 12: 39 students (20 boys, 19 girls).

Faculty School total: 42. In upper school: 10 men, 11 women; 6 have advanced degrees.

Subjects Offered Agriculture, algebra, art, band, biology-AP, calculus-AP, chemistry, chemistry-AP, communications, composition, computer information systems, driver education, economics, English composition, English literature-AP, English-AP, environmental science, environmental studies, ethics, fitness, general business, geometry, government-AP, grammar, health, history-AP, industrial technology, personal finance, physics, pre-calculus, psychology, Spanish, theater, U.S. government, U.S. history-AP, United States government-AP, weight training, world religions, yearbook, zoology.

Graduation Requirements Arts and fine arts (art, music, dance, drama), communications, composition, computer information systems, driver education, English, fitness, foreign language, grammar, health education, mathematics, physical education (includes health), science, social studies (includes history). Community service is required.

Special Academic Programs Advanced Placement exam preparation; honors section; accelerated programs; independent study; study at local college for college credit; ESL (6 students enrolled).

College Admission Counseling 41 students graduated in 2015; all went to college, including Hampden-Sydney College; James Madison University; Longwood University; The College of William and Mary; University of Virginia; Virginia Polytechnic Institute and State University. Median SAT critical reading: 530, median SAT math: 520, median SAT writing: 520, median combined SAT: 1610, median composite ACT: 23. 25% scored over 600 on SAT critical reading, 35% scored over 600 on SAT math, 38% scored over 600 on SAT writing, 38% scored over 1800 on combined SAT, 40% scored over 26 on composite ACT.

Student Life Upper grades have specified standards of dress, student council, honor system. Discipline rests primarily with faculty.

Summer Programs Enrichment, sports, art/fine arts programs offered; session focuses on sports and sport skills, arts, enrichment; held on campus; accepts boys and girls; open to students from other schools. 75 students usually enrolled. 2016 schedule: June 15 to July 31. Application deadline: May 15.

Tuition and Aid Day student tuition: $7750. Tuition installment plan (The Tuition Plan, monthly payment plans, individually arranged payment plans). Tuition reduction for siblings, merit scholarship grants, need-based scholarship grants available. In 2014–15, 40% of upper-school students received aid; total upper-school merit-scholarship money awarded: $6000. Total amount of financial aid awarded in 2014–15: $67,636.

Admissions Traditional secondary-level entrance grade is 9. For fall 2015, 32 students applied for upper-level admission, 30 were accepted, 30 enrolled. Placement test required. Deadline for receipt of application materials: none. Application fee required: $100. On-campus interview required.

Athletics Interscholastic: baseball (boys), basketball (b,g), cheering (g), football (b), lacrosse (b,g), softball (g), tennis (g), volleyball (g); coed interscholastic: cross-country running, golf, soccer, swimming and diving, track and field; coed intramural: basketball. 4 PE instructors, 38 coaches, 1 athletic trainer.

Computers Computers are regularly used in desktop publishing classes. Computer network features include on-campus library services, online commercial services, Internet access, wireless campus network, Internet filtering or blocking technology. Student e-mail accounts and computer access in designated common areas are available to students. The school has a published electronic and media policy.

Contact Mrs. Christy M. Murphy, Director of Admissions. 434-392-4131 Ext. 273. Fax: 434-392-5062. E-mail: murphycm@fuquaschool.com. Website: www.FuquaSchool.com

GABRIEL RICHARD CATHOLIC HIGH SCHOOL

15325 Pennsylvania Road
Riverview, Michigan 48193

Head of School: Mr. Joseph J. Whalen

General Information Coeducational day college-preparatory, arts, business, and religious studies school, affiliated with Roman Catholic Church. Grades 9–12. Founded: 1965. Setting: suburban. Nearest major city is Detroit. 23-acre campus. 1 building on campus. Approved or accredited by North Central Association of Colleges and Schools and Michigan Department of Education. Total enrollment: 323. Upper school average class size: 17. Upper school faculty-student ratio: 1:17. There are 180 required school days per year for Upper School students. Upper School students typically attend 5 days per week. The average school day consists of 7 hours and 5 minutes.

Upper School Student Profile Grade 9: 98 students (52 boys, 46 girls); Grade 10: 68 students (37 boys, 31 girls); Grade 11: 77 students (41 boys, 36 girls); Grade 12: 80 students (44 boys, 36 girls); Postgraduate: 323 students (174 boys, 149 girls). 90% of students are Roman Catholic.

Faculty School total: 18. In upper school: 4 men, 14 women; 13 have advanced degrees.

Subjects Offered 1 1/2 elective credits, 20th century American writers, 20th century history, 20th century world history, accounting, acting, advanced chemistry, advanced math, Advanced Placement courses, advanced studio art-AP, algebra, American Civil War, American democracy, American government, American history, American history-AP, American literature, American literature-AP, anatomy, anatomy and physiology, ancient history, ancient world history, animal science, art, band, basic language skills, biology, biology-AP, British literature (honors), business law, calculus, calculus-AP, campus ministry, Catholic belief and practice, ceramics, chemistry, chemistry-AP, Christian doctrine, Christian education, Christian scripture, Christian testament, Christianity, church history, Civil War, civil war history, clayworking, college planning, communications, comparative politics, comparative religion, constitutional history of U.S., constitutional law, digital art, digital photography, drama, drawing, earth science, economics, English literature, English-AP, environmental science, European history-AP, family living, forensics, French, general science, geography, geometry, government, government-AP, health, history, history of the Catholic Church, history-AP, honors algebra, honors English, human anatomy, humanities, lab science, logic, New Testament, participation in sports, peace and justice, peer ministry, photography, physical fitness, physics, physics-AP, portfolio art, psychology-AP, publications, research, senior composition, sociology, Spanish, speech, sports, studio art-AP, theater arts, U.S. government and politics-AP, U.S. history, U.S. history-AP, United States government-AP, weight training, zoology.

Graduation Requirements Arts and fine arts (art, music, dance, drama), English, mathematics, physical education (includes health), science, social studies (includes history), speech, theology.

Special Academic Programs Advanced Placement exam preparation; honors section; independent study.

College Admission Counseling 79 students graduated in 2015; all went to college. Median composite ACT: 24. 32% scored over 26 on composite ACT.

Student Life Upper grades have uniform requirement, student council, honor system. Discipline rests primarily with faculty. Attendance at religious services is required.

Tuition and Aid Tuition installment plan (The Tuition Plan, Academic Management Services Plan). Tuition reduction for siblings, merit scholarship grants, need-based scholarship grants available.

Admissions Traditional secondary-level entrance grade is 9. For fall 2015, 98 students applied for upper-level admission, 98 were accepted, 98 enrolled. High School Placement Test required. Deadline for receipt of application materials: none. Application fee required: $100. Interview required.

Athletics Interscholastic: baseball (boys), basketball (b,g), cheering (g), cross-country running (b,g), football (b), ice hockey (b), pom squad (g), soccer (b,g), softball (g), tennis (b,g), track and field (b,g), volleyball (g), wrestling (b); coed interscholastic: bowling, equestrian sports, figure skating, golf. 1 PE instructor.

Computers Computers are regularly used in digital applications, research skills, speech classes. Computer network features include on-campus library services, Internet access, Internet filtering or blocking technology. Computer access in designated common areas is available to students. Students grades are available online.

Contact Mr. Joseph J. Whalen, Principal. 734-284-1875. Fax: 734-284-9304. E-mail: whalenj@gabrielrichard.org. Website: www.gabrielrichard.org

THE GALLOWAY SCHOOL

215 West Wieuca Road NW
Atlanta, Georgia 30342

Head of School: Suzanna Jemsby

General Information Coeducational day college-preparatory, arts, and technology school. Grades P3–12. Founded: 1969. Setting: suburban. 8-acre campus. 5 buildings on campus. Approved or accredited by Academy of Orton-Gillingham Practitioners and Educators, Georgia Independent School Association, Southern Association of Colleges and Schools, Southern Association of Independent Schools, and Georgia Department of Education. Member of National Association of Independent Schools and Secondary School Admission Test Board. Endowment: $17 million. Total enrollment: 750. Upper school average class size: 12. Upper school faculty-student ratio: 1:12. There are 170 required school days per year for Upper School students. Upper School students typically attend 5 days per week. The average school day consists of 7 hours.

Upper School Student Profile Grade 6: 68 students (30 boys, 38 girls); Grade 7: 72 students (31 boys, 41 girls); Grade 8: 69 students (40 boys, 29 girls); Grade 9: 76 students (33 boys, 43 girls); Grade 10: 75 students (36 boys, 39 girls); Grade 11: 77 students (35 boys, 42 girls); Grade 12: 64 students (23 boys, 41 girls).

Faculty School total: 100. In upper school: 16 men, 27 women; 32 have advanced degrees.

Subjects Offered 20th century American writers, 20th century history, 20th century world history, 3-dimensional design, acting, advanced biology, advanced chemistry, advanced computer applications, advanced math, Advanced Placement courses, advanced studio art-AP, algebra, American Civil War, American culture, American government, American history, American history-AP, American literature, American literature-AP, analytic geometry, animation, art history, audio visual/media, band, biology, biology-AP, British literature, British literature-AP, calculus, calculus-AP, ceramics, chemistry, chemistry-AP, chorus, comparative government and politics-AP, composition-AP, computer animation, computer applications, computer graphics, concert band, desktop publishing, digital art, digital music, digital photography, drama, economics, electives, English, English-AP, filmmaking, fine arts, French, geometry, guidance, history, integrated physics, language arts, Latin, library, mathematics, music, physical education, physical science, political science, pre-calculus, public speaking, science, senior composition, social studies, Spanish, technology, U.S. government and politics-AP, visual arts, world geography, world history, world literature.

Graduation Requirements Arts and fine arts (art, music, dance, drama), computers, electives, English, foreign language, health and wellness, mathematics, science, social studies (includes history).

Special Academic Programs Advanced Placement exam preparation; accelerated programs; independent study; term-away projects; study at local college for college credit; academic accommodation for the gifted, the musically talented, and the artistically talented.

College Admission Counseling 57 students graduated in 2015; 56 went to college, including Georgia Institute of Technology; Haverford College; New York University; The George Washington University; University of Colorado Boulder; Vanderbilt University. Other: 1 had other specific plans. Median SAT critical reading: 650, median SAT math: 600, median SAT writing: 630, median combined SAT: 1850, median composite ACT: 27. 71% scored over 600 on SAT critical reading, 53% scored over 600 on SAT math, 63% scored over 600 on SAT writing, 59% scored over 1800 on combined SAT, 59% scored over 26 on composite ACT.

Student Life Upper grades have student council, honor system. Discipline rests primarily with faculty.

Summer Programs Remediation, enrichment, advancement, sports, art/fine arts, computer instruction programs offered; session focuses on enrichment; held both on and off campus; held at athletics complex; accepts boys and girls; open to students from other schools. 55 students usually enrolled. 2016 schedule: June 6 to August 5. Application deadline: June 3.

Tuition and Aid Day student tuition: $24,900. Tuition installment plan (FACTS Tuition Payment Plan, 50/50—twice a year payments, payroll deductions, special arrangements provided to families based upon their circumstances). Need-based scholarship grants available. In 2015–16, 23% of upper-school students received aid. Total amount of financial aid awarded in 2015–16: $847,611.

Admissions Traditional secondary-level entrance grade is 9. For fall 2015, 127 students applied for upper-level admission, 47 were accepted, 36 enrolled. Admissions testing and SSAT required. Deadline for receipt of application materials: February 1. Application fee required: $85. On-campus interview required.

Athletics Interscholastic: baseball (boys), basketball (b,g), golf (b,g), soccer (b,g), softball (g), swimming and diving (b,g), tennis (b,g), track and field (b,g), volleyball (g); coed interscholastic: cross-country running, ultimate Frisbee. 1 PE instructor, 3 coaches, 1 athletic trainer.

Computers Computers are regularly used in art, desktop publishing, drawing and design, English, graphic arts, information technology, introduction to technology, journalism, keyboarding, literary magazine, mathematics, multimedia, music, newspaper, photography, publishing, research skills, science, technology, theater, Web site design, yearbook classes. Computer network features include on-campus library services, online commercial services, Internet access, wireless campus network, Internet filtering or blocking technology, print sharing. Campus intranet, student e-mail accounts, and computer access in designated common areas are available to students. Students grades are available online. The school has a published electronic and media policy.

Contact Elizabeth King, Director of Admissions. 404-252-8389 Ext. 106. Fax: 404-252-7770. E-mail: e.king@gallowayschool.org. Website: www.gallowayschool.org

GANN ACADEMY (THE NEW JEWISH HIGH SCHOOL OF GREATER BOSTON)

333 Forest Street
Waltham, Massachusetts 02452

Head of School: Rabbi Marc A. Baker

General Information Coeducational day college-preparatory, arts, and religious studies school, affiliated with Jewish faith. Grades 9–12. Founded: 1997. Setting: suburban. Nearest major city is Boston. 20-acre campus. 2 buildings on campus. Approved or accredited by Association of Independent Schools in New England, New England Association of Schools and Colleges, and Massachusetts Department of Education. Member of National Association of Independent Schools. Endowment: $9 million. Total enrollment: 277. Upper school average class size: 14. Upper school faculty-student ratio: 1:5. There are 165 required school days per year for Upper School students. Upper School students typically attend 5 days per week. The average school day consists of 8 hours.

Upper School Student Profile Grade 9: 70 students (37 boys, 33 girls); Grade 10: 68 students (33 boys, 35 girls); Grade 11: 73 students (34 boys, 39 girls); Grade 12: 66 students (32 boys, 34 girls). 100% of students are Jewish.

Faculty School total: 59. In upper school: 25 men, 34 women; 44 have advanced degrees.

Subjects Offered Advanced Placement courses, algebra, American history-AP, American literature-AP, art history, arts, Bible as literature, biology, calculus, calculus-AP, chemistry, computer science, creative arts, creative writing, drama, English, geometry, health and wellness, Hebrew, history, Holocaust, Jewish history, Judaic studies, Mandarin, modern dance, music, photography, physics, pre-calculus, Rabbinic literature, robotics, Spanish.

Graduation Requirements Arts, athletics, Bible as literature, English, health, Hebrew, history, mathematics, Rabbinic literature, science.

Special Academic Programs Advanced Placement exam preparation; study abroad.

College Admission Counseling 86 students graduated in 2015; 84 went to college, including Brandeis University; The George Washington University; Tulane University; University of Maryland, College Park; University of Massachusetts Amherst; University of Pennsylvania. Other: 2 had other specific plans. Mean SAT critical reading: 640, mean SAT math: 650, mean SAT writing: 655, mean combined SAT: 1945, mean composite ACT: 27.

Student Life Upper grades have specified standards of dress, student council, honor system. Discipline rests primarily with faculty. Attendance at religious services is required.

Tuition and Aid Day student tuition: $37,750. Guaranteed tuition plan. Tuition installment plan (FACTS Tuition Payment Plan). Need-based scholarship grants available. In 2015–16, 48% of upper-school students received aid. Total amount of financial aid awarded in 2015–16: $2,300,000.

Admissions Traditional secondary-level entrance grade is 9. For fall 2015, 126 students applied for upper-level admission, 114 were accepted, 84 enrolled. SSAT required. Deadline for receipt of application materials: January 15. Application fee required: $100. On-campus interview required.

Athletics Interscholastic: baseball (boys), basketball (b,g), cross-country running (b,g), dance team (g), lacrosse (b,g), soccer (b,g), softball (g), tennis (b,g), volleyball (g); intramural: basketball (b,g), dance team (g), tennis (b,g), volleyball (g); coed interscholastic: fitness, juggling, martial arts, ultimate Frisbee; coed intramural: fitness, golf, modern dance, table tennis, yoga. 26 coaches, 1 athletic trainer.

Computers Computers are regularly used in all classes. Computer network features include on-campus library services, Internet access, wireless campus network, Internet filtering or blocking technology, computer lab. Campus intranet, student e-mail accounts, and computer access in designated common areas are available to students. Students grades are available online. The school has a published electronic and media policy.

Contact Farrah Rubenstein, Director of Enrollment Management. 781-642-6800. Fax: 781-642-6805. E-mail: frubenstein@gannacademy.org. Website: www.gannacademy.org/

GARCES MEMORIAL HIGH SCHOOL

2800 Loma Linda Drive
Bakersfield, California 93305

Head of School: Dr. Richard Tucker

General Information Coeducational day college-preparatory school, affiliated with Roman Catholic Church. Grades 9–12. Founded: 1947. Setting: suburban. Nearest major city is Los Angeles. 32-acre campus. 18 buildings on campus. Approved or accredited by Western Association of Schools and Colleges and Western Catholic Education Association. Endowment: $560,000. Total enrollment: 582. Upper school average class size: 25. Upper school faculty-student ratio: 1:28. There are 180 required school days per year for Upper School students. Upper School students typically attend 5 days per week. The average school day consists of 6 hours and 15 minutes.

Upper School Student Profile Grade 9: 138 students (75 boys, 63 girls); Grade 10: 152 students (76 boys, 76 girls); Grade 11: 146 students (65 boys, 81 girls); Grade 12: 146 students (67 boys, 79 girls). 75% of students are Roman Catholic.

Faculty School total: 41. In upper school: 21 men, 20 women; 24 have advanced degrees.

Subjects Offered Algebra, American history, American literature, anatomy, art, biology, calculus, chemistry, community service, computer science, creative writing, drama, economics, English, English literature, ethics, European history-AP, fine arts, French, geography, geometry, government/civics, graphic arts, health, history, mathematics, music, physical education, physics, physiology, psychology, religion, science, social studies, Spanish, theater, world history, world literature.

Graduation Requirements Arts and fine arts (art, music, dance, drama), computer literacy, English, foreign language, health education, mathematics, physical education (includes health), religion (includes Bible studies and theology), science, social studies (includes history), 60 hours of community service.

Special Academic Programs 13 Advanced Placement exams for which test preparation is offered; honors section; study at local college for college credit.

College Admission Counseling 128 students graduated in 2014; all went to college, including Bakersfield College; California Polytechnic State University, San Luis Obispo; California State University, Bakersfield; Texas Christian University; University of California, Santa Barbara. Mean SAT critical reading: 538, mean SAT math: 525, mean SAT writing: 529, mean composite ACT: 24. 15.3% scored over 600 on SAT critical reading, 16.9% scored over 600 on SAT math.

Student Life Upper grades have uniform requirement, student council. Discipline rests primarily with faculty. Attendance at religious services is required.

Tuition and Aid Day student tuition: $8500–$9500. Tuition installment plan (SMART Tuition Payment Plan, monthly payment plans, individually arranged payment plans). Merit scholarship grants, need-based scholarship grants available. In 2014–15, 32% of upper-school students received aid; total upper-school merit-scholarship money awarded: $9035. Total amount of financial aid awarded in 2014–15: $312,000.

Admissions Traditional secondary-level entrance grade is 9. For fall 2014, 185 students applied for upper-level admission, 175 were accepted, 162 enrolled. CTBS/4 required. Deadline for receipt of application materials: January 31. Application fee required: $75. Interview required.

Athletics Interscholastic: baseball (boys), basketball (b,g), cheering (g), cross-country running (b,g), dance (g), dance squad (g), dance team (g), diving (b,g), football (b), golf (b,g), soccer (b,g), softball (g), swimming and diving (b,g), tennis (b,g), track and field (b,g), volleyball (g), water polo (b,g). 3 PE instructors, 28 coaches, 1 athletic trainer.

Computers Computers are regularly used in graphic arts, keyboarding classes. Computer resources include on-campus library services, Internet access. Student e-mail accounts are available to students.

Contact Mrs. Joan M. Richardson, Registrar. 661-327-2578 Ext. 109. Fax: 661-327-5427. E-mail: jrichardson@garces.org. Website: www.garces.org

GARRISON FOREST SCHOOL

300 Garrison Forest Road
Owings Mills, Maryland 21117

Head of School: Dr. Kimberley J. Roberts

General Information Girls' boarding and day (coeducational in lower grades) college-preparatory, arts, technology, and Women in Science & Engineering (WISE) school. Boarding girls grades 8–12, day boys grades N–PK, day girls grades N–12. Founded: 1910. Setting: suburban. Nearest major city is Baltimore. Students are housed in single-sex dormitories. 110-acre campus. 18 buildings on campus. Approved or accredited by Association of Independent Maryland Schools, Middle States Association of Colleges and Schools, The Association of Boarding Schools, and Maryland Department of Education. Member of National Association of Independent Schools and Secondary School Admission Test Board. Endowment: $42 million. Total enrollment: 614. Upper school average class size: 14. Upper school faculty-student ratio: 1:8. There are 173 required school days per year for Upper School students. Upper School students typically attend 5 days per week. The average school day consists of 7 hours.

Upper School Student Profile Grade 9: 76 students (76 girls); Grade 10: 68 students (68 girls); Grade 11: 58 students (58 girls); Grade 12: 78 students (78 girls). 26% of students are boarding students. 85% are state residents. 11 states are represented in upper school student body. 12% are international students. International students from British Virgin Islands, China, Germany, Mexico, Republic of Korea, and Spain; 6 other countries represented in student body.

Faculty School total: 86. In upper school: 5 men, 38 women; 35 have advanced degrees; 22 reside on campus.

Subjects Offered 3-dimensional art, 3-dimensional design, advanced chemistry, advanced math, algebra, American foreign policy, American government, American history, American history-AP, American literature, anatomy, ancient world history, animation, applied music, art, art history, art history-AP, arts and crafts, biology, calculus, calculus-AP, ceramics, chemistry, chemistry-AP, Chinese, Chinese studies, choral music, college counseling, college placement, college planning, computer science, computer skills, creative writing, dance, decision making skills, design, desktop publishing, digital applications, digital art, digital imaging, digital photography, drama, drawing, ecology, English, English composition, English literature, English-AP, environmental science-AP, environmental studies, equestrian sports, equine science, equitation, ESL, ethics, film studies, filmmaking, fine arts, French, French language-AP, French-AP, geometry, health and safety, health and wellness, history-AP, jewelry making, Latin, Latin-AP, leadership and service, life skills, mathematics, music, musical productions, painting, peace studies, peer counseling, philosophy, photography, physical education, physics, physics-AP, play production, portfolio art, pre-calculus, psychology-AP, public policy, public policy issues and action, public service, public speaking, publications, science, science project, science research, sculpture, social justice, Spanish, Spanish language-AP, Spanish-AP, sports, stage design, statistics, student government, study skills, technological applications, technology, technology/design, theater, trigonometry, U.S. history-AP, values and decisions, voice ensemble, world history, writing, yearbook.

Graduation Requirements Arts and fine arts (art, music, dance, drama), decision making skills, English, foreign language, mathematics, physical education (includes health), science, social studies (includes history).

Special Academic Programs 12 Advanced Placement exams for which test preparation is offered; honors section; independent study; term-away projects; academic accommodation for the gifted, the musically talented, and the artistically talented; ESL (22 students enrolled).

College Admission Counseling 68 students graduated in 2015; all went to college, including Boston University; Columbia University; Johns Hopkins University; University of Maryland, College Park; University of South Carolina; University of Virginia. 50% scored over 600 on SAT critical reading, 50% scored over 600 on SAT math, 50% scored over 600 on SAT writing, 50% scored over 26 on composite ACT.

Student Life Upper grades have uniform requirement, student council, honor system. Discipline rests equally with students and faculty.

Summer Programs Sports, art/fine arts programs offered; session focuses on extracurricular activities and young children; held on campus; accepts boys and girls; open to students from other schools. 400 students usually enrolled. 2016 schedule: June 16 to August 22. Application deadline: June 1.

Tuition and Aid Day student tuition: $27,810; 7-day tuition and room/board: $52,540. Tuition installment plan (FACTS Tuition Payment Plan). Merit scholarship grants, need-based scholarship grants, merit-based Legacy Scholarship available. In 2015–16, 34% of upper-school students received aid; total upper-school merit-scholarship money awarded: $20,000. Total amount of financial aid awarded in 2015–16: $377,600.

Admissions Traditional secondary-level entrance grade is 9. For fall 2015, 174 students applied for upper-level admission, 86 were accepted, 36 enrolled. Admissions testing, ISEE, SSAT, TOEFL or WISC-R or WISC-III required. Deadline for receipt of application materials: December 11. Application fee required: $50. Interview required.

Athletics Interscholastic: badminton, basketball, cross-country running, equestrian sports, field hockey, golf, horseback riding, indoor soccer, indoor track, lacrosse, polo, soccer, softball, tennis, track and field, winter (indoor) track, winter soccer; intramural: aerobics, aerobics/dance, bowling, dance, fitness, horseback riding, modern dance, physical fitness, squash, strength & conditioning, volleyball, yoga. 5 PE instructors, 12 coaches, 1 athletic trainer.

Computers Computers are regularly used in animation, art, college planning, design, desktop publishing, digital applications, English, ESL, foreign language, French, history, humanities, literary magazine, mathematics, newspaper, photography, publications, science, Spanish, study skills, technology, word processing, writing, yearbook classes. Computer network features include on-campus library services, Internet access, wireless campus network, Internet filtering or blocking technology, Moodle. Student e-mail accounts and computer access in designated common areas are available to students. Students grades are available online. The school has a published electronic and media policy.

Contact Ms. Alison C. Greer, Director of Admission. 410-559-3110. Fax: 410-363-8441. E-mail: admission@gfs.org. Website: www.gfs.org

GASTON DAY SCHOOL

2001 Gaston Day School Road
Gastonia, North Carolina 28056

Head of School: Dr. Richard E. Rankin

General Information Coeducational day college-preparatory and arts school. Grades PS–12. Founded: 1967. Setting: suburban. Nearest major city is Charlotte. 60-acre campus. 4 buildings on campus. Approved or accredited by North Carolina Association of Independent Schools, Southern Association of Colleges and Schools, Southern Association of Independent Schools, and North Carolina Department of Education. Member of National Association of Independent Schools. Endowment: $2.3 million. Total enrollment: 481. Upper school average class size: 12. Upper school faculty-student ratio: 1:8. There are 180 required school days per year for Upper School students. Upper School students typically attend 5 days per week. The average school day consists of 7 hours and 15 minutes.

Upper School Student Profile Grade 9: 32 students (8 boys, 24 girls); Grade 10: 42 students (16 boys, 26 girls); Grade 11: 45 students (18 boys, 27 girls); Grade 12: 36 students (19 boys, 17 girls).

Faculty School total: 54. In upper school: 8 men, 12 women; 12 have advanced degrees.

Subjects Offered Advanced chemistry, Advanced Placement courses, advanced studio art-AP, algebra, American history-AP, American literature, anatomy and physiology, art, band, biology, biology-AP, British literature, British literature (honors), calculus-AP, chemistry, chemistry-AP, choral music, chorus, creative writing, drama, English language and composition-AP, English language-AP, English literature and composition-AP, environmental science, environmental science-AP, film and literature, fine arts, French, general science, geometry, government/civics, honors algebra, honors English, honors geometry, honors U.S. history, honors world history, jazz band, journalism, learning lab, physics, pre-calculus, senior internship, Spanish, Spanish-AP, statistics-AP, student government, studio art-AP, study skills, U.S. government, U.S. history, U.S. history-AP, United States government-AP, visual arts, weight training, world literature, yearbook.

Graduation Requirements Arts and fine arts (art, music, dance, drama), electives, English, foreign language, mathematics, physical education (includes health), science, social studies (includes history), 25 hours of community service per year, seniors must complete a senior project.

Special Academic Programs Advanced Placement exam preparation; honors section; independent study; academic accommodation for the gifted; ESL (6 students enrolled).

College Admission Counseling 33 students graduated in 2014; all went to college, including Clemson University; East Carolina University; North Carolina State University; The University of North Carolina at Chapel Hill; University of South Carolina; Washington and Lee University. Mean SAT critical reading: 569, mean SAT math: 612, mean SAT writing: 583, mean combined SAT: 1765, mean composite ACT: 25.

Student Life Upper grades have specified standards of dress, student council, honor system. Discipline rests primarily with faculty.

Tuition and Aid Day student tuition: $15,550. Tuition installment plan (monthly payment plans, individually arranged payment plans). Merit scholarship grants, need-based scholarship grants available. In 2014–15, 60% of upper-school students received aid; total upper-school merit-scholarship money awarded: $106,700. Total amount of financial aid awarded in 2014–15: $203,858.

Admissions Traditional secondary-level entrance grade is 9. For fall 2014, 53 students applied for upper-level admission, 36 were accepted, 31 enrolled. ACT, ISEE, PSAT or SAT required. Deadline for receipt of application materials: none. Application fee required: $50. On-campus interview required.

Athletics Interscholastic: baseball (boys), basketball (b,g), cheering (g), cross-country running (b,g), golf (b), soccer (b,g), swimming and diving (b,g), tennis (b,g), track and field (b,g), volleyball (g); intramural: fitness (b,g); coed intramural: crew, rowing. 1 PE instructor, 7 coaches, 1 athletic trainer.

Computers Computers are regularly used in art, English, foreign language, history, journalism, mathematics, newspaper, science, yearbook classes. Computer network features include on-campus library services, online commercial services, Internet access, wireless campus network, Internet filtering or blocking technology, iPads issued to each middle and upper school student. Student e-mail accounts and computer access in designated common areas are available to students. Students grades are available online. The school has a published electronic and media policy.

Contact Mrs. Martha Jayne Rhyne, Director of Admission. 704-864-7744 Ext. 174. Fax: 704-865-3813. E-mail: mrhyne@gastonday.org. Website: www.gastonday.org

GATEWAY SCHOOL

Arlington, Texas
See Special Needs Schools section.

GEORGE SCHOOL

1690 Newtown Langhorne Road
PO Box 4460
Newtown, Pennsylvania 18940

Head of School: Nancy O. Starmer

General Information Coeducational boarding and day college-preparatory, arts, religious studies, and International Baccalaureate school, affiliated with Society of Friends. Grades 9–12. Founded: 1893. Setting: suburban. Nearest major city is Philadelphia. Students are housed in single-sex dormitories. 265-acre campus. 19 buildings on campus. Approved or accredited by Friends Council on Education, International Baccalaureate Organization, Middle States Association of Colleges and Schools, The Association of Boarding Schools, The College Board, and Pennsylvania Department of Education. Member of National Association of Independent Schools and Secondary School Admission Test Board. Endowment: $150.6 million. Total enrollment: 540. Upper school average class size: 14. Upper school faculty-student ratio: 1:7. There are 165 required school days per year for Upper School students. Upper School students typically attend 5 days per week. The average school day consists of 6 hours.

Upper School Student Profile Grade 9: 112 students (54 boys, 58 girls); Grade 10: 142 students (74 boys, 68 girls); Grade 11: 142 students (73 boys, 69 girls); Grade 12: 144 students (80 boys, 64 girls). 53% of students are boarding students. 49% are state residents. 22 states are represented in upper school student body. 24% are international students. International students from China, Mexico, Republic of Korea, Taiwan, United Kingdom, and Viet Nam; 46 other countries represented in student body. 12% of students are members of Society of Friends.

Faculty School total: 80. In upper school: 32 men, 48 women; 57 have advanced degrees; 53 reside on campus.

Subjects Offered 3-dimensional art, acting, advanced biology, advanced chemistry, advanced math, Advanced Placement courses, advanced studio art-AP, African American history, African-American history, algebra, American history, American history-AP, American literature, analysis, analysis and differential calculus, ancient world history, art, art-AP, arts, Asian history, astronomy, athletic training, athletics, biology, biology-AP, calculus, calculus-AP, cell biology, ceramics, chemistry, chemistry-AP, Chinese, choral music, classical language, clayworking, community service, composition, computer science, computer science-AP, conceptual physics, creative arts, dance, dance performance, desktop publishing, digital imaging, drama, drama performance, drawing, driver education, economics-AP, electives, English, English as a foreign language, English composition, English language and composition AP, English language-AP, English literature, English literature and composition-AP, English literature-AP, English-AP, English/composition-AP, ensembles, environmental science, environmental systems, equality and freedom, ESL, fine arts, foreign language, French, French as a second language, French language-AP, French literature-AP, French-AP, functions, gardening, general science, geography, geometry, global studies, health, health and wellness, health education, history, history-AP, honors algebra, honors English, honors geometry, honors U.S. history, honors world history, horticulture, human geography - AP, inorganic chemistry, instrumental music, International Baccalaureate courses, jazz band, jazz ensemble, journalism, lab science, language, language and composition, language-AP, languages, Latin, Latin-AP, life science, literature, literature and composition-AP, literature-AP, management information systems, Mandarin, marine science, mathematics, mathematics-AP, microcomputer technology applications, microeconomics-AP, modern dance, modern European history, modern history, modern languages, modern world history, music, music performance, musical productions, musical theater, newspaper, non-Western literature, orchestra, painting, peace and justice, peace education, peace studies, performing arts, photography, physical education, physical fitness, physics, physics-AP, portfolio art, pre-calculus, probability and statistics, programming, publications, Quakerism and ethics, religion, religious studies, robotics, science, sculpture, set design, Spanish, Spanish language-AP, Spanish literature, Spanish literature-AP, Spanish-AP, stage design, stagecraft, statistics, statistics-AP, studio art, studio art-AP, theater, theater arts, theory of knowledge, trigonometry, U.S. history, U.S. history-AP, video, video film production, visual arts, vocal ensemble, vocal music, wellness, Western religions, wind ensemble, woodworking, work camp program, world civilizations, world history, world literature, world religions, world religions, writing, yearbook, yoga.

Graduation Requirements Arts and fine arts (art, music, dance, drama), English, foreign language, geometry, mathematics, performing arts, religion (includes Bible studies and theology), science, social studies (includes history), 65 hours of community service.

Special Academic Programs International Baccalaureate program; Advanced Placement exam preparation; honors section; ESL (16 students enrolled).

College Admission Counseling 135 students graduated in 2015; 134 went to college, including Drexel University; Elon University; New York University; Temple University; University of Colorado Boulder; Vassar College. Other: 1 had other specific plans. Mean SAT critical reading: 625, mean SAT math: 621, mean SAT writing: 609, mean combined SAT: 1855, mean composite ACT: 27. 66% scored over 600 on SAT critical reading, 58% scored over 600 on SAT math, 56% scored over 600 on SAT writing, 61% scored over 1800 on combined SAT, 67% scored over 26 on composite ACT.

Student Life Upper grades have specified standards of dress, student council, honor system. Discipline rests equally with students and faculty. Attendance at religious services is required.

Summer Programs Enrichment, advancement, ESL programs offered; session focuses on academic and social preparation; held on campus; accepts boys and girls; not open to students from other schools. 80 students usually enrolled.

Tuition and Aid Day student tuition: $36,975; 7-day tuition and room/board: $54,600. Tuition installment plan (monthly payment plans, individually arranged payment plans). Merit scholarship grants, need-based scholarship grants available. In 2015–16, 50% of upper-school students received aid; total upper-school merit-scholarship money awarded: $225,000. Total amount of financial aid awarded in 2015–16: $8,500,000.

Admissions Traditional secondary-level entrance grade is 9. For fall 2015, 709 students applied for upper-level admission, 324 were accepted, 152 enrolled. ERB, SSAT or TOEFL or SLEP required. Deadline for receipt of application materials: February 1. Application fee required: $60. Interview required.

Athletics Interscholastic: baseball (boys), basketball (b,g), cross-country running (b,g), field hockey (g), football (b), hockey (g), lacrosse (b,g), soccer (b,g), softball (g), swimming and diving (b,g), tennis (b,g), track and field (b,g), volleyball (g), wrestling (b,g); coed interscholastic: cheering, equestrian sports, golf, horseback riding, indoor track, modern dance, winter (indoor) track; coed intramural: aerobics/dance, dance, horseback riding, strength & conditioning, yoga. 5 PE instructors, 5 coaches, 1 athletic trainer.

Computers Computers are regularly used in English, ESL, foreign language, history, mathematics, newspaper, photography, science, yearbook classes. Computer network features include on-campus library services, online commercial services, Internet access, wireless campus network, Internet filtering or blocking technology. Campus intranet, student e-mail accounts, and computer access in designated common areas are available to students. Students grades are available online. The school has a published electronic and media policy.

Contact Monica Isserman, Admission Services Coordinator. 215-579-6548. Fax: 215-579-6549. E-mail: misserman@georgeschool.org. Website: www.georgeschool.org

GEORGE STEVENS ACADEMY

23 Union Street
Blue Hill, Maine 04614

Head of School: Mr. Timothy Seeley

General Information Coeducational boarding and day college preparatory and general academic school. Grades 9–12. Founded: 1803. Setting: small town. Nearest major city is Bangor. Students are housed in single-sex dormitories and host family homes. 300-acre campus. 7 buildings on campus. Approved or accredited by Independent Schools of Northern New England, New England Association of Schools and Colleges, The Association of Boarding Schools, The College Board, and Maine Department of Education. Member of National Association of Independent Schools and Secondary School Admission Test Board. Endowment: $7 million. Total enrollment: 325. Upper school average class size: 15. Upper school faculty-student ratio: 1:10. There are 180 required school days per year for Upper School students. Upper School students typically attend 5 days per week. The average school day consists of 6 hours and 30 minutes.

Upper School Student Profile Grade 9: 74 students (32 boys, 42 girls); Grade 10: 82 students (40 boys, 42 girls); Grade 11: 90 students (46 boys, 44 girls); Grade 12: 79 students (37 boys, 42 girls). 13% of students are boarding students. 87% are state residents. 1 state is represented in upper school student body. 13% are international students. International students from China, Italy, Jamaica, Russian Federation, Turkey, and Viet Nam; 3 other countries represented in student body.

Faculty School total: 34. In upper school: 15 men, 19 women; 18 have advanced degrees; 2 reside on campus.

Subjects Offered 20th century history, 3-dimensional design, advanced chemistry, advanced math, Advanced Placement courses, algebra, American literature, American literature-AP, art, art history, art-AP, arts and crafts, band, biology, British literature (honors), business mathematics, calculus-AP, carpentry, chamber groups, chemistry, computer applications, computer literacy, creative writing, critical thinking, desktop publishing, developmental language skills, drafting, drawing, driver education, earth science, electives, English, English-AP, environmental science, environmental science-AP, ESL, European history, fine arts, foreign language, forensics, French, general math, general science, geometry, German, health education, history, history-AP, honors algebra, honors English, honors geometry, honors U.S. history, human geography - AP, humanities, independent study, industrial arts, industrial technology, instrumental music, internship, jazz band, jazz ensemble, lab science, languages, Latin, literature, literature-AP, marine science, mathematics, mathematics-AP, mechanics, model United Nations, modern history, modern languages, modern problems, music, music theory, musical productions, mythology, personal fitness, photo shop, photography, physical education, physics, pre-algebra, pre-calculus, printmaking, psychology, reading/study skills, remedial study skills, science, senior project, shop, small engine repair, social issues, social sciences, Spanish, speech and debate, sports, statistics-AP, street law, student government, technology/design, TOEFL preparation, transportation technology, U.S. history, U.S. history-AP, Western civilization, wilderness education, woodworking, work-study, World-Wide-Web publishing, writing.

Graduation Requirements Arts and fine arts (art, music, dance, drama), electives, English, history, mathematics, physical education (includes health), science, social sciences, U.S. history, senior debate.

Special Academic Programs 9 Advanced Placement exams for which test preparation is offered; honors section; accelerated programs; independent study; term-away projects; study at local college for college credit; study abroad; academic accommodation for the gifted, the musically talented, and the artistically talented; remedial reading and/or remedial writing; remedial math; special instructional classes for deaf students, blind students; ESL (24 students enrolled).

College Admission Counseling 84 students graduated in 2015; 75 went to college, including Bowdoin College; Emory University; Maine Maritime Academy; Simmons College; University of Maine; University of Southern Maine. Other: 5 went to work, 4 had other specific plans. Mean SAT critical reading: 499, mean SAT math: 526, mean SAT writing: 508.

Student Life Upper grades have student council. Discipline rests primarily with faculty.

Tuition and Aid Day student tuition: $10,500; 7-day tuition and room/board: $42,500. Tuition installment plan (monthly payment plans, individually arranged payment plans). Need-based scholarship grants available. In 2015–16, 1% of upper-school students received aid. Total amount of financial aid awarded in 2015–16: $100,000.

Admissions Traditional secondary-level entrance grade is 9. International English Language Test, SSAT, TAP or TOEFL or SLEP required. Deadline for receipt of application materials: none. Application fee required: $75. Interview required.

Athletics Interscholastic: baseball (boys); basketball (b,g); cheering (b,g); cross-country running (b,g); golf (b,g); independent competitive sports (b,g); running (b,g); sailing (b,g); soccer (b,g); softball (g); swimming and diving (b,g); tennis (b,g); track and field (b,g); volleyball (g); wrestling (b); coed interscholastic: indoor track; coed intramural: backpacking, bocce, canoeing/kayaking, croquet, dance, dance team, fitness, fitness walking, flag football, floor hockey, Frisbee, hiking/backpacking, jogging, kayaking, modern dance, ocean paddling, outdoor activities, outdoor adventure, outdoor education, outdoor recreation, outdoor skills, paddle tennis, physical fitness, physical training, running, sailing, skateboarding, skiing (cross-country), skiing (downhill), snowboarding, snowshoeing, strength & conditioning, table tennis, ultimate Frisbee, volleyball, walking, weight lifting, weight training, wilderness, winter walking, yoga. 2 PE instructors, 26 coaches.

Computers Computers are regularly used in all classes. Computer network features include on-campus library services, online commercial services, Internet access, wireless campus network, Internet filtering or blocking technology, All students receive a MacBook Air laptop to work on. Student e-mail accounts and computer access in designated common areas are available to students. Students grades are available online. The school has a published electronic and media policy.

Contact Mrs. Joanna Evans, Director of Admissions. 207-374-2808 Ext. 134. Fax: 207-374-2982. E-mail: j.evans@georgestevens.info. Website: www.georgestevensacademy.org

GEORGETOWN PREPARATORY SCHOOL

10900 Rockville Pike
North Bethesda, Maryland 20852-3299

Head of School: Fr. Scott Pilarz

General Information Boys' boarding and day college-preparatory, arts, religious studies, and technology school, affiliated with Roman Catholic Church. Grades 9–12. Founded: 1789. Setting: suburban. Nearest major city is Washington, DC. Students are housed in single-sex dormitories. 92-acre campus. 8 buildings on campus. Approved or accredited by Jesuit Secondary Education Association, Middle States Association of Colleges and Schools, National Catholic Education Association, The Association of Boarding Schools, and Maryland Department of Education. Member of National Association of Independent Schools and Secondary School Admission Test Board. Endowment: $20 million. Total enrollment: 490. Upper school average class size: 16. Upper school faculty-student ratio: 1:8. There are 150 required school days per year for Upper School students. Upper School students typically attend 5 days per week. The average school day consists of 6 hours and 30 minutes.

Upper School Student Profile Grade 9: 118 students (118 boys); Grade 10: 117 students (117 boys); Grade 11: 129 students (129 boys); Grade 12: 126 students (126 boys). 20% of students are boarding students. 60% are state residents. 18 states are represented in upper school student body. 30% are international students. International students from China, Mexico, Nigeria, Republic of Korea, Spain, and Taiwan; 24 other countries represented in student body. 70% of students are Roman Catholic.

Faculty School total: 60. In upper school: 40 men, 20 women; 55 have advanced degrees; 18 reside on campus.

Subjects Offered Algebra, American history, American literature, art, art history, Bible studies, biology, calculus, chemistry, computer programming, computer science, drama, driver education, economics, English, English literature, ESL, ethics, European history, fine arts, French, geometry, German, government/civics, history, journalism, Latin, mathematics, music, philosophy, physical education, physics, psychology, religion, science, social studies, Spanish, speech, stained glass, theater, theology, trigonometry, world history, world literature.

Graduation Requirements Arts and fine arts (art, music, dance, drama), classics, English, foreign language, mathematics, music theory, religion (includes Bible studies and theology), science, social studies (includes history), two years of Latin. Community service is required.

Special Academic Programs 24 Advanced Placement exams for which test preparation is offered; honors section; independent study; term-away projects; study abroad; academic accommodation for the gifted; ESL (14 students enrolled).

College Admission Counseling 111 students graduated in 2014; 110 went to college, including Boston College; Georgetown University; Stanford University; University of Notre Dame; University of Pennsylvania; University of Virginia. Other: 1 entered a postgraduate year. Mean SAT critical reading: 680, mean SAT math: 683, mean SAT writing: 637, mean combined SAT: 2000, mean composite ACT: 27.

Student Life Upper grades have specified standards of dress, student council. Discipline rests primarily with faculty. Attendance at religious services is required.

Tuition and Aid Day student tuition: $32,120; 7-day tuition and room/board: $54,820. Tuition installment plan (FACTS Tuition Payment Plan). Need-based scholarship grants, middle-income loans available. In 2014–15, 25% of upper-school students received aid. Total amount of financial aid awarded in 2014–15: $2,000,000.

Admissions Traditional secondary-level entrance grade is 9. For fall 2014, 400 students applied for upper-level admission, 160 were accepted, 129 enrolled. SSAT required. Deadline for receipt of application materials: January 5. Application fee required: $100. Interview required.

Athletics Interscholastic: baseball, basketball, cross-country running, diving, fencing, football, golf, ice hockey, indoor soccer, indoor track & field, lacrosse, rugby, running, soccer, swimming and diving, tennis, track and field, winter (indoor) track, wrestling; intramural: basketball, canoeing/kayaking, fitness, flag football, floor hockey, Frisbee, hiking/backpacking, ice skating, indoor hockey, kayaking, life saving, martial arts, mountain biking, Nautilus, ocean paddling, paddle tennis, paint ball, physical fitness, physical training, power lifting, racquetball, rappelling, rock climbing, ropes courses, scuba diving, skiing (downhill), snowboarding, soccer, softball, strength & conditioning, table tennis, tennis, ultimate Frisbee, volleyball, weight training. 16 coaches, 3 athletic trainers.

Computers Computers are regularly used in art, classics, data processing, English, French, history, Latin, mathematics, music, religious studies, science, Spanish, writing classes. Computer network features include on-campus library services, online commercial services, Internet access, wireless campus network, Internet filtering or blocking technology. Campus intranet, student e-mail accounts, and computer access in designated common areas are available to students. Students grades are available online. The school has a published electronic and media policy.

Contact Mr. Brian J. Gilbert, Dean of Admissions. 301-214-1215. Fax: 301-493-6128. E-mail: admissions@gprep.org. Website: www.gprep.org

GEORGETOWN VISITATION PREPARATORY SCHOOL

1524 35th Street NW
Washington, District of Columbia 20007

Head of School: Daniel M. Kerns Jr.

General Information Girls' day college-preparatory school, affiliated with Roman Catholic Church. Grades 9–12. Founded: 1799. Setting: urban. 23-acre campus. 7 buildings on campus. Approved or accredited by Association of Independent Schools of Greater Washington, Middle States Association of Colleges and Schools, National Catholic Education Association, National Independent Private Schools Association, and District of Columbia Department of Education. Member of National Association of Independent Schools. Endowment: $16.7 million. Total enrollment: 490. Upper school average class size: 15. Upper school faculty-student ratio: 1:11. There are 181 required school days per year for Upper School students. Upper School students typically attend 5 days per week. The average school day consists of 5 hours and 30 minutes.

Upper School Student Profile Grade 9: 125 students (125 girls); Grade 10: 124 students (124 girls); Grade 11: 120 students (120 girls); Grade 12: 121 students (121 girls). 93% of students are Roman Catholic.

Faculty School total: 54. In upper school: 14 men, 40 women; 40 have advanced degrees.

Subjects Offered Advanced Placement courses, advanced studio art-AP, algebra, American history, American literature, anatomy, ancient world history, anthropology, art, art history, art history-AP, art-AP, Bible studies, biochemistry, bioethics, biology, biology-AP, calculus, calculus-AP, Catholic belief and practice, chemistry, chemistry-AP, chorus, comparative political systems-AP, computer science, conceptual physics, creative writing, dance, economics, electives, English, English language and composition-AP, English literature, English literature and composition-AP, English literature-AP, English/composition-AP, environmental science, environmental science-AP, ethics, European history, European history-AP, expository writing, fine arts, French, French-AP, geometry, government-AP, government/civics, health, health and wellness, history, Latin, madrigals, mathematics, music, music theory-AP, neuroscience, personal development, physical education, physical fitness, physics, physics-AP, pre-calculus, psychology, psychology-AP, religion, science, social sciences, social studies, Spanish, Spanish-AP, speech, speech communications, statistics-AP, studio art-AP, theology, trigonometry, U.S. government and politics-AP, U.S. history-AP, world history.

Graduation Requirements Arts and fine arts (art, music, dance, drama), English, foreign language, history, mathematics, physical education (includes health), religion (includes Bible studies and theology), science, social studies (includes history), speech, 80 hours of community service.

Special Academic Programs 19 Advanced Placement exams for which test preparation is offered; honors section; independent study; study at local college for college credit.

College Admission Counseling 125 students graduated in 2014; all went to college, including Boston University; The College of William and Mary; University of Maryland, College Park; University of Virginia; Virginia Polytechnic Institute and State University. Mean SAT critical reading: 654, mean SAT math: 626, mean SAT writing: 672.

Student Life Upper grades have uniform requirement, student council, honor system. Discipline rests primarily with faculty. Attendance at religious services is required.

Tuition and Aid Day student tuition: $26,500. Tuition installment plan (FACTS Tuition Payment Plan). Merit scholarship grants, need-based scholarship grants available. In 2014–15, 29% of upper-school students received aid; total upper-school merit-scholarship money awarded: $55,000. Total amount of financial aid awarded in 2014–15: $1,900,000.

Admissions Traditional secondary-level entrance grade is 9. High School Placement Test or High School Placement Test (closed version) from Scholastic Testing Service required. Deadline for receipt of application materials: December 5. Application fee required: $50. On-campus interview required.

Athletics Interscholastic: basketball, crew, cross-country running, diving, field hockey, indoor track, indoor track & field, lacrosse, soccer, softball, swimming and diving, tennis, track and field, volleyball, winter (indoor) track; intramural: aerobics/dance, dance, equestrian sports, fitness, horseback riding, ice hockey, modern dance, pom squad, strength & conditioning. 3 PE instructors, 23 coaches, 1 athletic trainer.

Computers Computers are regularly used in all academic, art, English, French, history, mathematics, religion, science, Spanish classes. Computer network features include on-campus library services, online commercial services, Internet access, wireless campus network, Internet filtering or blocking technology. Campus intranet and student e-mail accounts are available to students. Students grades are available online. The school has a published electronic and media policy.

Contact Janet Keller, Director of Admissions. 202-337-3350 Ext. 2241. Fax: 202-333-3522. E-mail: jkeller@visi.org. Website: www.visi.org

GEORGE WALTON ACADEMY

One Bulldog Drive
Monroe, Georgia 30655

Head of School: Mr. William M. Nicholson

General Information Coeducational day college-preparatory, arts, and technology school. Grades K4–12. Founded: 1969. Setting: small town. Nearest major city is Atlanta. 63-acre campus. 12 buildings on campus. Approved or accredited by Georgia Independent School Association, Southern Association of Colleges and Schools, Southern Association of Independent Schools, and Georgia Department of Education. Total enrollment: 850. Upper school average class size: 17. Upper school faculty-student ratio: 1:12. There are 180 required school days per year for Upper School students. Upper School students typically attend 5 days per week. The average school day consists of 6 hours and 45 minutes.

Upper School Student Profile Grade 9: 75 students (45 boys, 30 girls); Grade 10: 71 students (36 boys, 35 girls); Grade 11: 92 students (44 boys, 48 girls); Grade 12: 78 students (41 boys, 37 girls).

Faculty School total: 85. In upper school: 15 men, 38 women; 20 have advanced degrees.

Subjects Offered Algebra, American history, American literature, anatomy, art, art history, Bible studies, biology, calculus, chemistry, creative writing, drama, economics, English, English literature, environmental science, European history, fine arts, geography, geometry, government/civics, grammar, health, history, journalism, Latin, mathematics, music, photography, physical education, physics, psychology, science, social sciences, social studies, sociology, Spanish, trigonometry, world history, world literature, writing.

Graduation Requirements Arts and fine arts (art, music, dance, drama), composition, English, foreign language, mathematics, physical education (includes health), science, social sciences, social studies (includes history), all students must be accepted to a college or university to graduate.

Special Academic Programs 13 Advanced Placement exams for which test preparation is offered; honors section; academic accommodation for the gifted, the musically talented, and the artistically talented.

College Admission Counseling 68 students graduated in 2015; all went to college, including Georgia College & State University; Georgia Institute of Technology; Georgia Southern University; Georgia State University; University of Georgia; University of North Georgia. Median combined SAT: 1720.

Student Life Upper grades have uniform requirement, student council, honor system. Discipline rests primarily with faculty.

Summer Programs Enrichment, advancement, sports, art/fine arts, computer instruction programs offered; session focuses on academic and athletic enrichment; held on campus; accepts boys and girls; open to students from other schools. 500 students usually enrolled. 2016 schedule: May 25 to July 31.

Tuition and Aid Day student tuition: $10,485. Tuition installment plan (monthly payment plans). Tuition reduction for siblings, need-based scholarship grants available. In 2015–16, 1% of upper-school students received aid.

Admissions Traditional secondary-level entrance grade is 9. ACT, CAT 5, CTBS, Stanford Achievement Test, any other standardized test, Otis-Lennon, Stanford Achievement Test, PSAT or SAT required. Deadline for receipt of application materials: none. Application fee required: $175. On-campus interview recommended.

Athletics Interscholastic: aquatics (boys, girls), baseball (b), basketball (b,g), cheering (g), cross-country running (b,g), dance squad (g), drill team (g), football (b), golf (b), physical fitness (b,g), soccer (b,g), softball (g), swimming and diving (b,g), tennis (b,g), track and field (b,g), volleyball (g), weight lifting (b), weight training (b,g), wrestling (b); coed interscholastic: equestrian sports. 3 PE instructors, 8 coaches.

Computers Computers are regularly used in all academic classes. Computer network features include on-campus library services, online commercial services, Internet access, wireless campus network, Internet filtering or blocking technology. Student e-mail accounts and computer access in designated common areas are available to students. Students grades are available online. The school has a published electronic and media policy.

Contact Ms. Cari Bailey, Director of Admissions. 770-207-5172 Ext. 254. Fax: 770-267-4023. E-mail: cbailey@gwa.com. Website: www.gwa.com

GERMANTOWN FRIENDS SCHOOL

31 West Coulter Street
Philadelphia, Pennsylvania 19144

Head of School: Dana O. Weeks

General Information Coeducational day college-preparatory, arts, and technology school, affiliated with Society of Friends. Grades K–12. Founded: 1845. Setting: urban. 21-acre campus. 21 buildings on campus. Approved or accredited by Friends Council on Education, National Independent Private Schools Association, and Pennsylvania Association of Independent Schools. Member of National Association of Independent Schools and Secondary School Admission Test Board. Endowment: $27.3 million. Total enrollment: 864. Upper school average class size: 18. Upper school faculty-student ratio: 1:9. There are 172 required school days per year for Upper School students. Upper School students typically attend 5 days per week. The average school day consists of 6 hours and 25 minutes.

Upper School Student Profile Grade 9: 133 students (44 boys, 89 girls); Grade 10: 124 students (45 boys, 79 girls); Grade 11: 129 students (43 boys, 86 girls); Grade 12: 135 students (39 boys, 96 girls). 5.9% of students are members of Society of Friends.

Faculty School total: 136. In upper school: 28 men, 30 women; 46 have advanced degrees.

Subjects Offered 3-dimensional art, advanced chemistry, advanced math, algebra, American history, ancient history, art, art history, bioethics, biology, calculus, chemistry, choir, chorus, comparative cultures, computer applications, computer programming, creative writing, drama, dramatic arts, drawing, English, environmental education, environmental science, European history, French, geometry, Greek, health, human sexuality, independent study, instrumental music, jazz ensemble, Latin, Latin History, madrigals, Mandarin, mathematics, music, music theory, orchestra, painting, philosophy, photography, physical education, physics, pre-calculus, science, social studies, Spanish, sports, stagecraft, statistics, studio art, theater, trigonometry, vocal music.

Graduation Requirements English, foreign language, history, lab science, mathematics, music, physical education (includes health), month-long off-campus independent project, January Intercession Program.

Special Academic Programs Honors section; independent study; term-away projects; domestic exchange program (with The Network Program Schools, The Catlin Gabel School); study abroad; academic accommodation for the gifted, the musically talented, and the artistically talented; ESL (6 students enrolled).

College Admission Counseling 86 students graduated in 2014; 85 went to college, including Brown University; Johns Hopkins University; Temple University; University of Chicago; University of Pennsylvania; Yale University. Mean SAT critical reading: 670, mean SAT math: 657, mean SAT writing: 659, mean composite ACT: 31.

Student Life Upper grades have student council. Discipline rests primarily with faculty. Attendance at religious services is required.

Tuition and Aid Day student tuition: $29,520. Tuition installment plan (FACTS Tuition Payment Plan). Need-based scholarship grants available. In 2014–15, 29% of upper-school students received aid. Total amount of financial aid awarded in 2014–15: $1,879,209.

Admissions Traditional secondary-level entrance grade is 9. For fall 2014, 134 students applied for upper-level admission, 64 were accepted, 34 enrolled. ISEE or SSAT required. Deadline for receipt of application materials: December 6. Application fee required: $40. On-campus interview required.

Athletics Interscholastic: baseball (boys), basketball (b,g), cross-country running (b,g), field hockey (g), indoor track & field (b,g), lacrosse (g), soccer (b,g), softball (g), squash (b,g), tennis (b,g), track and field (b,g), wrestling (b); intramural: flag football (b), rugby (b); coed interscholastic: crew; coed intramural: physical training, strength & conditioning, weight training. 7 PE instructors, 37 coaches, 2 athletic trainers.

Computers Computers are regularly used in art, English, foreign language, history, mathematics, music, photography, publications, science classes. Computer network features include on-campus library services, online commercial services, Internet access, wireless campus network, Internet filtering or blocking technology. Campus intranet, student e-mail accounts, and computer access in designated common areas are available to students. Students grades are available online.

Contact Laura Sharpless Myran, Director, Enrollment and Financial Aid. 215-951-2346. Fax: 215-951-2370. E-mail: lauram@germantownfriends.org. Website: www.germantownfriends.org

GILMAN SCHOOL

5407 Roland Avenue
Baltimore, Maryland 21210

Head of School: Mr. Henry P.A. Smyth

General Information Boys' day college-preparatory school. Grades K–12. Founded: 1897. Setting: suburban. 68-acre campus. 6 buildings on campus. Approved or accredited by Association of Independent Maryland Schools and Maryland Department of Education. Member of National Association of Independent Schools and Secondary School Admission Test Board. Endowment: $110 million. Total enrollment: 1,017. Upper school average class size: 16. Upper school faculty-student ratio: 1:7. There are 172 required school days per year for Upper School students. Upper School students typically attend 5 days per week. The average school day consists of 9 hours.

Upper School Student Profile Grade 6: 79 students (79 boys); Grade 7: 82 students (82 boys); Grade 8: 96 students (96 boys); Grade 9: 121 students (121 boys); Grade 10: 120 students (120 boys); Grade 11: 113 students (113 boys); Grade 12: 112 students (112 boys).

Faculty School total: 147. In upper school: 59 men, 9 women; 57 have advanced degrees.

Subjects Offered Advanced Placement courses, advanced studio art-AP, algebra, American history, American literature, anatomy, Arabic, architectural drawing, art, art history, biology, calculus, chemistry, Chinese, community service, computer math, computer programming, computer science, creative writing, drafting, drama, ecology, economics, English, English literature, environmental science, European history, expository writing, fine arts, French, geometry, German, government/civics, Greek, history, industrial arts, Latin, mathematics, mechanical drawing, music, photography, physical education, physics, physiology, religion, Russian, science, social studies, Spanish, speech, statistics, theater, trigonometry, writing.

Graduation Requirements Art history, athletics, English, foreign language, history, mathematics, music appreciation, religion (includes Bible studies and theology), science, senior project.

Special Academic Programs 30 Advanced Placement exams for which test preparation is offered; honors section; independent study; term-away projects; academic accommodation for the gifted, the musically talented, and the artistically talented.

College Admission Counseling 114 students graduated in 2015; 113 went to college, including Harvard University; Johns Hopkins University; Princeton University; University of Maryland, College Park; University of Virginia. Other: 1 entered a postgraduate year. Mean SAT critical reading: 638, mean SAT math: 660, mean SAT writing: 637.

Student Life Upper grades have specified standards of dress, student council, honor system. Discipline rests equally with students and faculty.

Summer Programs Remediation, enrichment, advancement, sports, art/fine arts, rigorous outdoor training, computer instruction programs offered; session focuses on remediation and enrichment; held on campus; accepts boys and girls; open to students from other schools. 250 students usually enrolled. 2016 schedule: June 18 to July 26. Application deadline: June 18.

Tuition and Aid Day student tuition: $28,110. Tuition installment plan (Insured Tuition Payment Plan, FACTS Tuition Payment Plan, monthly payment plans). Need-based scholarship grants, need-based loans available. In 2015–16, 25% of upper-school students received aid. Total amount of financial aid awarded in 2015–16: $1,839,100.

Admissions Traditional secondary-level entrance grade is 9. For fall 2015, 164 students applied for upper-level admission, 70 were accepted, 41 enrolled. ISEE required. Deadline for receipt of application materials: December 16. Application fee required: $50. On-campus interview required.

Athletics Interscholastic: baseball, basketball, cross-country running, football, golf, ice hockey, indoor track, lacrosse, soccer, squash, swimming and diving, tennis, track and field, volleyball, water polo, winter (indoor) track, wrestling; intramural: basketball, bicycling, climbing, cross-country running, fitness, flag football, Frisbee, golf, physical fitness, rugby, table tennis, tennis, touch football, weight lifting. 3 PE instructors, 2 athletic trainers.

Computers Computers are regularly used in all academic, computer applications, design, digital applications classes. Computer network features include on-campus library services, Internet access, wireless campus network, Internet filtering or blocking technology. Campus intranet, student e-mail accounts, and computer access in designated common areas are available to students. Students grades are available online. The school has a published electronic and media policy.

Contact Danielle Moran, Admissions Assistant. 410-323-7169. Fax: 410-864-2825. E-mail: dmoran@gilman.edu. Website: www.gilman.edu

GILMOUR ACADEMY

34001 Cedar Road
Gates Mills, Ohio 44040-9356

Head of School: Kathleen C. Kenny

General Information Coeducational boarding and day and distance learning college-preparatory, arts, business, religious studies, and technology school, affiliated with Roman Catholic Church. Boarding grades 7–12, day grades PK–12. Distance learning grades 9–12. Founded: 1946. Setting: suburban. Nearest major city is Cleveland. Students are housed in coed dormitories and boy's wing and girl's wing dormitory. 144-acre campus. 15 buildings on campus. Approved or accredited by Independent Schools Association of the Central States, Midwest Association of Boarding Schools, National Catholic Education Association, The Association of Boarding Schools, and Ohio Department of Education. Member of National Association of Independent Schools and Secondary School Admission Test Board. Endowment: $30 million. Total enrollment: 656. Upper school average class size: 15. Upper school faculty-student ratio: 1:9. There are 169 required school days per year for Upper School students. Upper School students typically attend 5 days per week. The average school day consists of 7 hours and 20 minutes.

Upper School Student Profile Grade 9: 103 students (52 boys, 51 girls); Grade 10: 121 students (63 boys, 58 girls); Grade 11: 98 students (55 boys, 43 girls); Grade 12: 115 students (60 boys, 55 girls). 15% of students are boarding students. 86% are state residents. 14 states are represented in upper school student body. 8% are international students. International students from Canada, China, Republic of Korea, and Switzerland. 80% of students are Roman Catholic.

Faculty School total: 70. In upper school: 34 men, 36 women; 55 have advanced degrees; 4 reside on campus.

Subjects Offered Advanced Placement courses, advanced studio art-AP, algebra, American government, American history, American literature, anatomy and physiology, architecture, art, audio visual/media, band, Bible, biology, biology-AP, British literature, broadcast journalism, calculus, calculus-AP, ceramics, chemistry, chemistry-AP, chorus, community service, computer programming, computer science, computer science-AP, constitutional law, creative writing, drama, drawing, economics, economics and history, English, English literature, English-AP, ensembles, entrepreneurship, ethics, European history, European history-AP, fashion, fine arts, forensics, French, French as a second language, French language-AP, French-AP, functions, genetics, geometry, geometry with art applications, government, government-AP, government/civics, health, history, history of rock and roll, independent study, jazz ensemble, journalism, Latin, Latin-AP, law, leadership, literature and composition-AP, Mandarin, mathematics, mathematics-AP, model United Nations, modern European history-AP, music, music theory-AP, musical productions, mythology, oceanography, oil painting, painting, photography, physical education, physical fitness, physics, physics-AP, pre-algebra, pre-calculus, programming, religion, religious studies, robotics, SAT/ACT preparation, science, social studies, Spanish, Spanish language-AP, speech, speech and debate, sports medicine, statistics-AP, student government, student publications, studio art, studio art-AP, swimming, theater, trigonometry, U.S. government, U.S. government and politics-AP, U.S. history, U.S. history-AP, weight training, work-study, world history, world history-AP, writing, writing workshop, yearbook.

Graduation Requirements Arts and fine arts (art, music, dance, drama), English, foreign language, mathematics, physical education (includes health), religion (includes Bible studies and theology), science, social studies (includes history), speech, senior project. Community service is required.

Special Academic Programs 14 Advanced Placement exams for which test preparation is offered; accelerated programs; independent study; study at local college for college credit; academic accommodation for the gifted, the musically talented, and the artistically talented.

College Admission Counseling 122 students graduated in 2015; 114 went to college, including John Carroll University; Miami University; Ohio University; The Ohio State University; University of Cincinnati; University of Dayton. Other: 1 went to work, 1 entered military service, 6 had other specific plans. Median SAT critical reading: 570, median SAT math: 540, median SAT writing: 560, median combined SAT: 1720, median composite ACT: 26. 24% scored over 600 on SAT critical reading, 28% scored over 600 on SAT math, 24% scored over 600 on SAT writing, 29% scored over 1800 on combined SAT, 35% scored over 26 on composite ACT.

Student Life Upper grades have specified standards of dress, student council, honor system. Discipline rests equally with students and faculty. Attendance at religious services is required.

Summer Programs Enrichment, advancement, sports programs offered; session focuses on academic enrichment; held both on and off campus; held at some universities; accepts boys and girls; open to students from other schools. 75 students usually enrolled. 2016 schedule: June to July. Application deadline: none.

Tuition and Aid Day student tuition: $10,360–$29,500; 7-day tuition and room/board: $43,500. Tuition installment plan (monthly payment plans, Tuition Management Systems). Tuition reduction for siblings, merit scholarship grants, need-based scholarship grants, need-based loans, paying campus jobs, endowed scholarships with criteria specified by donors available. In 2015–16, 50% of upper-school students received aid; total upper-school merit-scholarship money awarded: $95,000. Total amount of financial aid awarded in 2015–16: $3,682,304.

Admissions Traditional secondary-level entrance grade is 9. ACT, ACT-Explore, ISEE, PSAT, SAT, SSAT or TOEFL required. Deadline for receipt of application materials: none. No application fee required. Interview required.

Athletics Interscholastic: baseball (boys), basketball (b,g), cross-country running (b,g), diving (g), football (b), hockey (b,g), ice hockey (b,g), lacrosse (b,g), running (b,g), soccer (b,g), softball (g), swimming and diving (b,g), tennis (b,g), track and field (b,g), volleyball (g); intramural: cheering (g), indoor soccer (b,g); coed interscholastic: figure skating, golf, indoor track, indoor track & field, winter (indoor) track; coed intramural: aerobics, alpine skiing, aquatics, basketball, bowling, broomball, figure skating, fitness, golf, ice skating, indoor track, paddle tennis, physical fitness, physical training, skiing (downhill), snowboarding, soccer, strength & conditioning, swimming and diving, tennis, volleyball, weight training, winter (indoor) track, winter soccer. 2 PE instructors, 16 coaches, 2 athletic trainers.

Computers Computers are regularly used in all academic classes. Computer network features include on-campus library services, online commercial services, Internet access, wireless campus network, Internet filtering or blocking technology. Campus intranet, student e-mail accounts, and computer access in designated common areas are available to students. Students grades are available online. The school has a published electronic and media policy.

Contact Jeanne Tippen, Admission Administrative Assistant. 440-473-8050. Fax: 440-473-8010. E-mail: admission@gilmour.org. Website: www.gilmour.org

GIRARD COLLEGE

2101 South College Avenue
Philadelphia, Pennsylvania 19121-4857

Head of School: Mr. Clarence D. Armbrister

General Information Coeducational boarding college-preparatory and general academic school. Grades 1–12. Founded: 1848. Setting: urban. Students are housed in single-sex dormitories. 43-acre campus. 10 buildings on campus. Approved or accredited by Middle States Association of Colleges and Schools, The Association of Boarding Schools, and Pennsylvania Department of Education. Member of National Association of Independent Schools. Endowment: $450 million. Total enrollment: 270. Upper school average class size: 17. Upper school faculty-student ratio: 1:16. There are 180 required school days per year for Upper School students. Upper School students typically attend 5 days per week. The average school day consists of 6 hours and 30 minutes.

Upper School Student Profile Grade 7: 28 students (11 boys, 17 girls); Grade 8: 21 students (9 boys, 12 girls); Grade 9: 35 students (14 boys, 21 girls); Grade 10: 16 students (9 boys, 7 girls); Grade 11: 8 students (4 boys, 4 girls); Grade 12: 27 students (10 boys, 17 girls). 100% of students are boarding students. 73% are state residents. 6 states are represented in upper school student body.

Faculty School total: 60. In upper school: 4 men, 12 women; 9 have advanced degrees; 20 reside on campus.

Subjects Offered Algebra, American history, American literature, anatomy, art, biology, calculus, chemistry, choir, college counseling, community service, computer literacy, earth science, English, English literature, European history, French, geometry, government/civics, health, honors algebra, honors English, honors geometry, honors U.S. history, instrumental music, jazz band, life management skills, mathematics, multicultural studies, music appreciation, physical education, physics, poetry, pre-calculus, SAT preparation, senior project, social studies, sociology, Spanish, video film production, world cultures.

Graduation Requirements American politics in film, college counseling, computer literacy, English, foreign language, mathematics, physical education (includes health), science, senior career experience, senior project, social sciences, social studies (includes history). Community service is required.

Special Academic Programs 1 Advanced Placement exam for which test preparation is offered; honors section; study at local college for college credit; remedial reading and/or remedial writing; remedial math.

College Admission Counseling 33 students graduated in 2015; 29 went to college, including Penn State University Park; Penn State University Park; Penn State University Park; Temple University; University of Pennsylvania; University of Pittsburgh. Other: 1 went to work, 2 entered military service, 1 had other specific plans.

Student Life Upper grades have uniform requirement, student council, honor system. Discipline rests primarily with faculty.

Summer Programs Remediation programs offered; session focuses on remediation; held on campus; accepts boys and girls; not open to students from other schools. 40 students usually enrolled. 2016 schedule: June to August.

Tuition and Aid Tuition installment plan (full scholarships awarded if admission requirements are met). Full scholarships awarded if admission requirements are met available.

Admissions For fall 2015, 162 students applied for upper-level admission, 33 were accepted, 32 enrolled. ISEE, SSAT, Wechsler Intelligence Scale for Children or Wide Range Achievement Test required. Deadline for receipt of application materials: none. No application fee required. On-campus interview required.

Athletics Interscholastic: baseball (boys), basketball (b,g), cross-country running (b,g), soccer (b,g), softball (g); intramural: aquatics (b,g), strength & conditioning (b,g), swimming and diving (b,g), yoga (b,g); coed intramural: dance, fitness, flag football,

jogging, jump rope, outdoor activities, outdoor adventure, physical fitness, running, touch football, walking. 1 PE instructor, 11 coaches.

Computers Computers are regularly used in college planning, English, foreign language, history, library, mathematics, newspaper, reading, research skills, SAT preparation, science, social studies, study skills, word processing, writing, yearbook classes. Computer network features include on-campus library services, online commercial services, Internet access, wireless campus network, Internet filtering or blocking technology. Student e-mail accounts are available to students. The school has a published electronic and media policy.

Contact Admissions. 215-787-2621. Fax: 215-787-4402. E-mail: admissions@girardcollege.edu. Website: www.girardcollege.edu

GLADES DAY SCHOOL

400 Gator Boulevard
Belle Glade, Florida 33430

Head of School: Mrs. Amie Pitts

General Information Coeducational day college-preparatory, general academic, vocational, and agriscience school. Grades PK–12. Founded: 1965. Setting: small town. Nearest major city is West Palm Beach. 21-acre campus. 4 buildings on campus. Approved or accredited by Florida Council of Independent Schools. Total enrollment: 289. Upper school average class size: 20. Upper school faculty-student ratio: 1:15. There are 180 required school days per year for Upper School students. Upper School students typically attend 5 days per week. The average school day consists of 6 hours and 35 minutes.

Upper School Student Profile Grade 9: 26 students (16 boys, 10 girls); Grade 10: 31 students (15 boys, 16 girls); Grade 11: 37 students (21 boys, 16 girls); Grade 12: 29 students (22 boys, 7 girls).

Faculty School total: 18. In upper school: 7 men, 11 women; 3 have advanced degrees.

Subjects Offered ACT preparation, agriculture, algebra, American government, American history, American literature, anatomy, ancient history, art, Bible studies, biology, biology-AP, calculus, calculus-AP, chemistry, computer applications, computer skills, computer technologies, earth science, economics, English, English language and composition-AP, English literature, English literature and composition-AP, environmental science, European history, general math, geometry, government and politics-AP, grammar, health, health education, human geography - AP, journalism, keyboarding, literature and composition-AP, macroeconomics-AP, marine biology, modern world history, music performance, physical education, pre-calculus, SAT/ACT preparation, Spanish, Spanish-AP, trigonometry, U.S. government and politics-AP, U.S. history, U.S. history-AP, weightlifting, world geography, world history, world history-AP, yearbook.

Graduation Requirements Algebra, American government, American literature, anatomy, ancient world history, arts and fine arts (art, music, dance, drama), biology, calculus, chemistry, computer applications, economics, English, English composition, English literature, geometry, health education, keyboarding, macroeconomics-AP, marine biology, modern world history, physical education (includes health), physical fitness, physical science, physics, pre-calculus, Spanish, U.S. history, world geography, world history.

Special Academic Programs 8 Advanced Placement exams for which test preparation is offered; honors section; independent study; study at local college for college credit; programs in general development for dyslexic students.

College Admission Counseling 32 students graduated in 2015; 27 went to college, including Florida Gulf Coast University; Florida State University; Palm Beach State College; Santa Fe College; University of Central Florida; University of Florida. Other: 2 went to work, 3 entered military service.

Student Life Upper grades have uniform requirement, student council, honor system. Discipline rests primarily with faculty.

Summer Programs Remediation programs offered; session focuses on remediation; held on campus; accepts boys and girls; not open to students from other schools. 7 students usually enrolled. 2016 schedule: June 7 to July 15. Application deadline: June 4.

Tuition and Aid Day student tuition: $6900–$8750. Tuition installment plan (FACTS Tuition Payment Plan, monthly payment plans, individually arranged payment plans). Tuition reduction for siblings, need-based scholarship grants available. In 2015–16, 10% of upper-school students received aid.

Admissions Traditional secondary-level entrance grade is 9. For fall 2015, 18 students applied for upper-level admission, 17 were accepted, 14 enrolled. Deadline for receipt of application materials: none. Application fee required: $400. On-campus interview required.

Athletics Interscholastic: baseball (boys), basketball (b,g), cheering (g), football (b), soccer (b,g), softball (g), track and field (b,g), volleyball (g); intramural: strength & conditioning (b,g), weight training (b,g). 2 PE instructors, 2 coaches.

Computers Computers are regularly used in English, journalism, newspaper, science, Spanish, word processing, yearbook classes. Computer network features include on-campus library services, Internet access, wireless campus network. Campus intranet and student e-mail accounts are available to students. Students grades are available online. The school has a published electronic and media policy.

Contact Mrs. Krista Carter, High School Secretary. 561-996-6769 Ext. 10. Fax: 561-992-9274. E-mail: kcarter@gladesdayschool.com. Website: www.gladesdayschool.com

GLEN EDEN SCHOOL

Richmond, British Columbia, Canada
See Special Needs Schools section.

GLENELG COUNTRY SCHOOL

12793 Folly Quarter Road
Ellicott City, Maryland 21042

Head of School: Mr. Gregory J. Ventre

General Information Coeducational day college-preparatory, arts, and technology school. Grades PK–12. Founded: 1954. Setting: suburban. Nearest major city is Baltimore. 90-acre campus. 1 building on campus. Approved or accredited by Association of Independent Maryland Schools, Middle States Association of Colleges and Schools, and Maryland Department of Education. Member of National Association of Independent Schools. Endowment: $1 million. Total enrollment: 751. Upper school average class size: 15. Upper school faculty-student ratio: 1:6. There are 175 required school days per year for Upper School students. Upper School students typically attend 5 days per week. The average school day consists of 7 hours.

Upper School Student Profile Grade 9: 65 students (36 boys, 29 girls); Grade 10: 81 students (41 boys, 40 girls); Grade 11: 66 students (36 boys, 30 girls); Grade 12: 69 students (34 boys, 35 girls).

Faculty School total: 125. In upper school: 24 men, 22 women; 39 have advanced degrees.

Subjects Offered 3-dimensional art, 3-dimensional design, advanced biology, advanced computer applications, advanced math, Advanced Placement courses, advanced studio art-AP, African American studies, algebra, American history, American literature, American literature-AP, American sign language, American studies, analysis, anatomy and physiology, Ancient Greek, ancient history, art, art history, astronomy, athletics, band, basketball, biology, biology-AP, broadcast journalism, business studies, calculus, calculus-AP, character education, chemistry, chemistry-AP, Chinese, Chinese studies, choir, chorus, college counseling, college planning, community garden, community service, computer applications, computer programming, computer science, computer science-AP, CPR, creative writing, digital photography, drama, dramatic arts, economics-AP, English, English literature, English literature-AP, English-AP, environmental science-AP, equestrian sports, European history, expository writing, forensics, French, French literature-AP, French-AP, geometry, golf, history, honors geometry, honors U.S. history, humanities, integrative seminar, interdisciplinary studies, internship, interpersonal skills, introduction to theater, Islamic studies, Latin, Latin-AP, leadership education training, Mandarin, mathematics, modern world history, photography, physical education, physical science, physics, physics-AP, pre-calculus, psychology, publications, radio broadcasting, research seminar, science, senior project, senior thesis, social studies, Spanish, Spanish language-AP, Spanish literature-AP, Spanish-AP, stagecraft, statistics, studio art, theater, travel, trigonometry, video, volleyball, Web site design, Western civilization, Western literature, world affairs, wrestling, yearbook.

Graduation Requirements Civics, English, foreign language, integrative seminar, mathematics, physical education (includes health), science, social studies (includes history), participation in Civic Leadership Program, 25 hours of community service per year.

Special Academic Programs 18 Advanced Placement exams for which test preparation is offered; honors section; independent study; academic accommodation for the gifted.

College Admission Counseling 66 students graduated in 2014; all went to college, including University of Maryland, College Park; University of South Carolina; Wake Forest University. Mean SAT critical reading: 600, mean SAT math: 624, mean SAT writing: 608, mean combined SAT: 1832. 51% scored over 600 on SAT critical reading, 53% scored over 600 on SAT math, 56% scored over 600 on SAT writing, 57% scored over 1800 on combined SAT.

Student Life Upper grades have uniform requirement, student council, honor system. Discipline rests equally with students and faculty.

Tuition and Aid Day student tuition: $25,650. Tuition installment plan (monthly payment plans, individually arranged payment plans, 2-payment plan). Merit scholarship grants, need-based scholarship grants available. In 2014–15, 40% of upper-school students received aid; total upper-school merit-scholarship money awarded: $300,000. Total amount of financial aid awarded in 2014–15: $2,000,000.

Admissions Traditional secondary-level entrance grade is 9. For fall 2014, 68 students applied for upper-level admission, 52 were accepted, 40 enrolled. ISEE, PSAT or SAT for applicants to grade 11 and 12, SSAT or TOEFL required. Deadline for receipt of application materials: January 15. Application fee required: $75. On-campus interview required.

Athletics Interscholastic: baseball (boys), basketball (b,g), cross-country running (b,g), field hockey (g), golf (b,g), ice hockey (b), indoor soccer (g), indoor track (b,g), lacrosse (b,g), soccer (b,g), tennis (b,g), volleyball (g), winter soccer (g), wrestling (b); coed interscholastic: equestrian sports, golf, ice hockey, strength & conditioning; coed intramural: aerobics, aerobics/dance, dance, fitness, flag football, Frisbee, physical fitness, physical training, skiing (downhill), strength & conditioning, ultimate Frisbee, weight training, yoga. 5 PE instructors, 12 coaches, 1 athletic trainer.

Computers Computers are regularly used in all academic classes. Computer network features include on-campus library services, Internet access, wireless campus network.

Campus intranet, student e-mail accounts, and computer access in designated common areas are available to students. Students grades are available online. The school has a published electronic and media policy.

Contact Mrs. Karen K. Wootton, Director of Admission and Financial Aid. 410-531-7346 Ext. 2203. Fax: 410-531-7363. E-mail: wootton@glenelg.org. Website: www.glenelg.org

THE GLENHOLME SCHOOL, DEVEREUX CONNECTICUT

Washington, Connecticut
See Special Needs Schools section.

GONZAGA COLLEGE HIGH SCHOOL

19 Eye Street NW
Washington, District of Columbia 20001

Head of School: Mr. Thomas K. Every II

General Information Boys' day college-preparatory, arts, religious studies, and technology school, affiliated with Roman Catholic Church. Grades 9–12. Founded: 1821. Setting: urban. 1-acre campus. 9 buildings on campus. Approved or accredited by Association of Independent Schools of Greater Washington, Jesuit Secondary Education Association, and District of Columbia Department of Education. Member of National Association of Independent Schools. Endowment: $9.1 million. Total enrollment: 962. Upper school average class size: 26. Upper school faculty-student ratio: 1:13. There are 164 required school days per year for Upper School students. Upper School students typically attend 5 days per week. The average school day consists of 6 hours and 35 minutes.

Upper School Student Profile Grade 9: 245 students (245 boys); Grade 10: 244 students (244 boys); Grade 11: 236 students (236 boys); Grade 12: 237 students (237 boys). 85% of students are Roman Catholic.

Faculty School total: 73. In upper school: 52 men, 21 women; all have advanced degrees.

Subjects Offered Acting, Advanced Placement courses, African-American literature, algebra, American history, American literature, applied music, art, band, biology, broadcasting, calculus, calculus-AP, Catholic belief and practice, chemistry, chemistry-AP, Chinese, choir, choral music, Christian and Hebrew scripture, Christian ethics, Christian scripture, communications, community service, computer applications, computer math, computer programming, computer science, concert band, concert choir, creative writing, earth science, economics, economics-AP, English, English literature, English literature and composition-AP, English literature-AP, English-AP, environmental science-AP, ethics, ethics and responsibility, European history, European history-AP, expository writing, film appreciation, film studies, fine arts, French, French-AP, functions, geometry, government, government/civics, grammar, Greek, health, health education, history, honors algebra, honors English, honors geometry, human geography - AP, independent study, Irish literature, jazz ensemble, Latin, Latin-AP, mathematics, media communications, music, musicianship, orchestra, philosophy, photography, physical education, physics, physics-AP, piano, poetry, political science, political systems, psychology, psychology-AP, religion, science, social justice, social sciences, social studies, Spanish, Spanish-AP, statistics, statistics-AP, studio art-AP, symphonic band, theology, trigonometry, U.S. government and politics-AP, Web site design, world history, world literature.

Graduation Requirements Arts and fine arts (art, music, dance, drama), English, ethics, foreign language, mathematics, physical education (includes health), religion (includes Bible studies and theology), science, social justice, social sciences, social studies (includes history). Community service is required.

Special Academic Programs Advanced Placement exam preparation; honors section.

College Admission Counseling 226 students graduated in 2015; 222 went to college, including James Madison University; Miami University; University of Maryland, College Park; University of South Carolina; University of Virginia; Virginia Polytechnic Institute and State University. Other: 4 had other specific plans.

Student Life Upper grades have specified standards of dress, student council, honor system. Discipline rests primarily with faculty. Attendance at religious services is required.

Summer Programs Remediation, enrichment programs offered; session focuses on new student remediation, enrichment, and SAT preparation; held on campus; accepts boys and girls; open to students from other schools. 200 students usually enrolled. 2016 schedule: June to July. Application deadline: June 1.

Tuition and Aid Day student tuition: $20,800. Tuition installment plan (Insured Tuition Payment Plan, monthly payment plans). Merit scholarship grants, need-based scholarship grants available. In 2015–16, 33% of upper-school students received aid; total upper-school merit-scholarship money awarded: $100,000. Total amount of financial aid awarded in 2015–16: $2,900,000.

Admissions Traditional secondary-level entrance grade is 9. For fall 2015, 640 students applied for upper-level admission, 325 were accepted, 245 enrolled. High School Placement Test (closed version) from Scholastic Testing Service required.

Deadline for receipt of application materials: December 10. Application fee required: $35.

Athletics Interscholastic: baseball, basketball, crew, cross-country running, diving, football, golf, ice hockey, indoor track & field, lacrosse, rugby, soccer, squash, swimming and diving, tennis, track and field, water polo, winter (indoor) track, wrestling; intramural: basketball, fencing, fitness, football, physical training, skiing (downhill), strength & conditioning, table tennis, weight lifting, whiffle ball. 2 PE instructors, 30 coaches, 2 athletic trainers.

Computers Computer network features include on-campus library services, Internet access, wireless campus network. Campus intranet and student e-mail accounts are available to students. Students grades are available online. The school has a published electronic and media policy.

Contact Mr. Andrew C. Battaile, Dean of Admissions and Financial Aid. 202-336-7101. Fax: 202-454-1188. E-mail: abattaile@gonzaga.org. Website: www.gonzaga.org

GOOD HOPE COUNTRY DAY SCHOOL

RR #1, Box 6199

Kingshill, Virgin Islands 00850-9807

Head of School: Mr. Kari Loya

General Information Coeducational day college-preparatory and technology school. Grades N–12. Founded: 1964. Setting: rural. Nearest major city is Christiansted, U.S. Virgin Islands. 34-acre campus. 6 buildings on campus. Approved or accredited by Middle States Association of Colleges and Schools and Virgin Islands Department of Education. Member of National Association of Independent Schools. Endowment: $574,000. Total enrollment: 360. Upper school average class size: 14. Upper school faculty-student ratio: 1:12. Upper School students typically attend 5 days per week. The average school day consists of 7 hours.

Upper School Student Profile Grade 9: 34 students (18 boys, 16 girls); Grade 10: 31 students (11 boys, 20 girls); Grade 11: 26 students (14 boys, 12 girls); Grade 12: 38 students (21 boys, 17 girls).

Faculty School total: 51. In upper school: 6 men, 17 women; 20 have advanced degrees.

Subjects Offered Algebra, American history, American literature, art, art history, arts, band, biology, calculus, ceramics, chemistry, chorus, community service, computer programming, computer science, creative writing, current events, dance, drama, earth science, ecology, economics, electronics, English, English literature, film, fine arts, French, geometry, government/civics, health, history, journalism, keyboarding, marine biology, mathematics, music, Native American studies, photography, physical education, physical science, physics, pre-calculus, psychology, public speaking, science, social studies, sociology, Spanish, statistics, swimming, theater, trigonometry, world history.

Graduation Requirements Arts and fine arts (art, music, dance, drama), computer science, English, foreign language, mathematics, physical education (includes health), science, social studies (includes history), swimming, typing. Community service is required.

Special Academic Programs Advanced Placement exam preparation.

College Admission Counseling Colleges students went to include Michigan Technological University; University of Pennsylvania; University of Pittsburgh; Vassar College. Median SAT critical reading: 520, median SAT math: 540, median composite ACT: 22. 35% scored over 600 on SAT critical reading, 25% scored over 600 on SAT math, 19% scored over 26 on composite ACT.

Student Life Upper grades have specified standards of dress, student council, honor system. Discipline rests primarily with faculty.

Tuition and Aid Day student tuition: $14,000. Tuition installment plan (monthly payment plans, individually arranged payment plans, semiannual and annual payment plans). Merit scholarship grants, need-based scholarship grants available. In 2015–16, 41% of upper-school students received aid; total upper-school merit-scholarship money awarded: $24,250. Total amount of financial aid awarded in 2015–16: $311,550.

Admissions Traditional secondary-level entrance grade is 9. For fall 2015, 25 students applied for upper-level admission, 10 were accepted, 10 enrolled. Essay and Test of Achievement and Proficiency required. Deadline for receipt of application materials: none. Application fee required: $150. On-campus interview required.

Athletics Interscholastic: baseball (boys), basketball (b,g), football (b), softball (g), tennis (b,g), volleyball (b,g); intramural: volleyball (b,g); coed interscholastic: aerobics, aquatics, basketball, cross-country running, sailing, soccer; coed intramural: basketball, soccer, ultimate Frisbee. 3 PE instructors, 3 coaches.

Computers Computers are regularly used in mathematics, music, science, yearbook classes. Computer network features include on-campus library services, online commercial services, Internet access. The school has a published electronic and media policy.

Contact Mrs. Alma V. Castro-Nieves, Registrar. 340-778-1974 Ext. 2108. Fax: 340-779-3331. E-mail: acastronieves@ghcds.org. Website: www.ghcds.org/

THE GOVERNOR FRENCH ACADEMY

219 West Main Street

Belleville, Illinois 62220-1537

Head of School: Mr. Phillip E. Paeltz

General Information Coeducational boarding and day college-preparatory school. Boarding grades 9–12, day grades K–12. Founded: 1983. Setting: urban. Nearest major city is St. Louis, MO. Students are housed in homes of local families. 3 buildings on campus. Approved or accredited by North Central Association of Colleges and Schools and Illinois Department of Education. Endowment: $100,000. Total enrollment: 155. Upper school average class size: 15. Upper school faculty-student ratio: 1:6. There are 176 required school days per year for Upper School students. Upper School students typically attend 5 days per week. The average school day consists of 6 hours and 45 minutes.

Upper School Student Profile Grade 9: 12 students (3 boys, 9 girls); Grade 10: 10 students (7 boys, 3 girls); Grade 11: 13 students (5 boys, 8 girls); Grade 12: 6 students (3 boys, 3 girls). 2% of students are boarding students. 97% are state residents. 1 state is represented in upper school student body. 3% are international students. International students from China and Republic of Korea.

Faculty School total: 13. In upper school: 3 men, 4 women; 4 have advanced degrees.

Subjects Offered Algebra, American history, American literature, biology, biology-AP, calculus, chemistry, creative writing, ecology, economics, engineering, English, English literature, environmental science, European history, expository writing, geometry, government/civics, history, mathematics, physical education, physics, psychology, science, social sciences, statistics, theater arts, trigonometry, world history, world literature.

Graduation Requirements English, foreign language, history, mathematics, science, social sciences, vote of faculty.

Special Academic Programs 10 Advanced Placement exams for which test preparation is offered; accelerated programs; independent study; academic accommodation for the gifted; programs in English for dyslexic students; ESL.

College Admission Counseling 14 students graduated in 2015; all went to college, including Colorado State University; Saint Louis University; South Dakota School of Mines and Technology; Southern Illinois University Edwardsville; University of Chicago; University of Missouri. Median composite ACT: 26. 50% scored over 26 on composite ACT.

Student Life Upper grades have uniform requirement, student council, honor system. Discipline rests primarily with faculty.

Summer Programs Remediation, enrichment, advancement programs offered; session focuses on academics; held on campus; accepts boys and girls; open to students from other schools. 25 students usually enrolled. 2016 schedule: June 15 to July 29. Application deadline: none.

Tuition and Aid Day student tuition: $6000; 7-day tuition and room/board: $22,200. Tuition installment plan (monthly payment plans). Tuition reduction for siblings available.

Admissions Traditional secondary-level entrance grade is 9. For fall 2015, 15 students applied for upper-level admission, 12 were accepted, 9 enrolled. School placement exam required. Deadline for receipt of application materials: none. No application fee required. Interview required.

Athletics Interscholastic: basketball (boys, girls), volleyball (b,g); coed interscholastic: cross-country running; coed intramural: independent competitive sports, softball.

Computers Computers are regularly used in computer applications, science, yearbook classes. Computer network features include Internet access, wireless campus network, Internet filtering or blocking technology. Computer access in designated common areas is available to students. The school has a published electronic and media policy.

Contact Ms. Carol S. Wilson, Dean of Admissions. 618-233-7542. Fax: 618-233-0541. E-mail: admiss@governorfrench.com. Website: www.governorfrench.com

THE GOVERNOR'S ACADEMY

1 Elm Street

Byfield, Massachusetts 01922

Head of School: Dr. Peter H. Quimby

General Information Coeducational boarding and day college-preparatory and arts school. Grades 9–12. Founded: 1763. Setting: rural. Nearest major city is Boston. Students are housed in single-sex dormitories. 450-acre campus. 48 buildings on campus. Approved or accredited by Association of Independent Schools in New England, New England Association of Schools and Colleges, The Association of Boarding Schools, and Massachusetts Department of Education. Member of National Association of Independent Schools and Secondary School Admission Test Board. Endowment: $70 million. Total enrollment: 405. Upper school average class size: 12. Upper school faculty-student ratio: 1:5. There are 158 required school days per year for Upper School students. Upper School students typically attend 5 days per week. The average school day consists of 7 hours.

Upper School Student Profile Grade 9: 93 students (51 boys, 42 girls); Grade 10: 102 students (51 boys, 51 girls); Grade 11: 105 students (56 boys, 49 girls); Grade 12: 105 students (57 boys, 48 girls). 65% of students are boarding students. 50% are state residents. 25 states are represented in upper school student body. 14% are international

The Governor's Academy

students. International students from Bermuda, China, Republic of Korea, Singapore, Taiwan, and Thailand; 17 other countries represented in student body.

Faculty School total: 82. In upper school: 46 men, 36 women; 54 have advanced degrees; 60 reside on campus.

Subjects Offered Advanced chemistry, algebra, American history, American history-AP, American literature, anatomy, art, band, biology, biology-AP, calculus-AP, ceramics, chemistry, chemistry-AP, Chinese, chorus, civics, computer graphics, computer math, computer programming, computer science, computer science-AP, constitutional law, creative writing, dance, drama, driver education, ecology, economics, economics-AP, English language-AP, English literature, English literature and composition-AP, environmental science, ESL, European history, European history-AP, expository writing, filmmaking, fine arts, French, French-AP, geometry, German, health, history, Holocaust and other genocides, honors algebra, jazz band, Latin, Latin-AP, marine biology, marine science, mathematics, Middle Eastern history, modern European history, modern European history-AP, music, music history, music theory, photography, physics, physics-AP, psychology, religion, science, social studies, Spanish, Spanish language-AP, Spanish literature-AP, statistics-AP, studio art-AP, theater, trigonometry, visual and performing arts, women in society, women's studies, writing.

Graduation Requirements Arts and fine arts (art, music, dance, drama), English, foreign language, history, mathematics, science, 100 hours of community service. Community service is required.

Special Academic Programs 27 Advanced Placement exams for which test preparation is offered; honors section; independent study; term-away projects; study abroad.

College Admission Counseling 105 students graduated in 2015; all went to college, including Bates College; Colby College; The University of North Carolina at Chapel Hill. Mean SAT critical reading: 602, mean SAT math: 633, mean SAT writing: 603, mean combined SAT: 1829. 38% scored over 600 on SAT critical reading, 50% scored over 600 on SAT math, 42% scored over 600 on SAT writing, 42% scored over 1800 on combined SAT.

Student Life Upper grades have specified standards of dress, student council, honor system. Discipline rests primarily with faculty.

Summer Programs Enrichment, advancement, sports, art/fine arts programs offered; session focuses on exploration and development of skills, talents, and interests; held on campus; accepts boys and girls; open to students from other schools. 500 students usually enrolled. 2016 schedule: June 15 to August 15. Application deadline: none.

Tuition and Aid Day student tuition: $44,500; 7-day tuition and room/board: $55,900. Tuition installment plan (Insured Tuition Payment Plan, FACTS Tuition Payment Plan, monthly payment plans). Need-based scholarship grants available. In 2015–16, 30% of upper-school students received aid. Total amount of financial aid awarded in 2015–16: $4,400,000.

Admissions Traditional secondary-level entrance grade is 9. For fall 2015, 995 students applied for upper-level admission, 240 were accepted, 121 enrolled. ISEE, SSAT or TOEFL required. Deadline for receipt of application materials: January 31. Application fee required: $60. Interview required.

Athletics Interscholastic: alpine skiing (boys, girls), baseball (b), basketball (b,g), cross-country running (b,g), field hockey (g), football (b), ice hockey (b,g), indoor track & field (b,g), lacrosse (b,g), soccer (b,g), softball (g), tennis (b,g), track and field (b,g), volleyball (g), wrestling (b); intramural: dance (g); coed interscholastic: golf; coed intramural: aerobics/dance, alpine skiing, dance, outdoor activities, outdoor recreation, skiing (downhill), tennis, yoga. 2 athletic trainers.

Computers Computers are regularly used in art, English, foreign language, history, mathematics, music, science classes. Computer network features include on-campus library services, online commercial services, Internet access, wireless campus network, Internet filtering or blocking technology, laptop sign-out in student center and library, Moodle Web site for teachers and students to share course data, events, and discussions. Campus intranet, student e-mail accounts, and computer access in designated common areas are available to students. Students grades are available online. The school has a published electronic and media policy.

Contact Michael Kinnealey, Director of Admission, Director of Financial Aid. 978-499-3120. Fax: 978-462-1278. E-mail: admissions@govsacademy.org. Website: www.thegovernorsacademy.org

THE GOW SCHOOL

South Wales, New York
See Special Needs Schools section.

GRACE BAPTIST ACADEMY

7815 Shallowford Road
Chattanooga, Tennessee 37421

Head of School: Mr. Matthew Pollock

General Information Coeducational day college-preparatory and religious studies school, affiliated with Baptist Church; primarily serves students with learning disabilities, individuals with Attention Deficit Disorder, and dyslexic students. Grades K4–12. Founded: 1985. Setting: suburban. 2 buildings on campus. Approved or accredited by Association of Christian Schools International, Southern Association of Colleges and Schools, and Tennessee Department of Education. Total enrollment: 469. Upper school average class size: 18. Upper school faculty-student ratio: 1:12. Upper School students typically attend 5 days per week. The average school day consists of 7 hours.

Upper School Student Profile Grade 6: 41 students (20 boys, 21 girls); Grade 7: 33 students (12 boys, 21 girls); Grade 8: 29 students (8 boys, 21 girls); Grade 9: 40 students (20 boys, 20 girls); Grade 10: 29 students (13 boys, 16 girls); Grade 11: 42 students (18 boys, 24 girls); Grade 12: 32 students (15 boys, 17 girls). 75% of students are Baptist.

Faculty School total: 50. In upper school: 16 men, 17 women; 10 have advanced degrees.

Subjects Offered Advanced biology, advanced math, Advanced Placement courses, algebra, American government, American history, American literature, art, band, Bible, Bible studies, biology, biology-AP, calculus, calculus-AP, career exploration, career/college preparation, chemistry, choir, Christian doctrine, Christian ethics, Christian testament, computer applications, consumer mathematics, drama performance, dramatic arts, economics, English, English composition, English literature, fitness, general math, general science, geometry, global studies, health, health and safety, honors English, honors world history, keyboarding, language arts, mathematics, music, New Testament, painting, personal finance, physical education, physical fitness, physics, pre-algebra, pre-calculus, senior internship, senior project, Spanish, speech, state history, statistics-AP, study skills, U.S. government and politics, U.S. history, U.S. history-AP, weight training, world geography, world religions, yearbook.

Graduation Requirements Algebra, Bible, biology, chemistry, economics, English, English literature, geometry, global studies, physical education (includes health), senior project, Spanish, speech, trigonometry, U.S. government, U.S. history, visual and performing arts, world geography.

Special Academic Programs 2 Advanced Placement exams for which test preparation is offered; honors section; study at local college for college credit.

College Admission Counseling 41 students graduated in 2015; all went to college, including Chattanooga State Community College; Middle Tennessee State University; Tennessee Technological University; The University of Tennessee; The University of Tennessee at Chattanooga. Mean composite ACT: 24.

Student Life Upper grades have uniform requirement, student council, honor system. Discipline rests primarily with faculty. Attendance at religious services is required.

Tuition and Aid Tuition installment plan (SMART Tuition Payment Plan, monthly payment plans, individually arranged payment plans, bank draft). Tuition reduction for siblings, need-based scholarship grants available.

Admissions Traditional secondary-level entrance grade is 9. Kaufman Test of Educational Achievement or latest standardized score from previous school required. Deadline for receipt of application materials: none. Application fee required: $50. On-campus interview required.

Athletics Interscholastic: baseball (boys), basketball (b,g), cheering (g), cross-country running (b,g), drill team (g), football (b), soccer (b,g), softball (g), tennis (b,g), track and field (b,g), volleyball (g), weight training (b,g); intramural: physical training (b,g), strength & conditioning (b,g), weight lifting (b), weight training (b); coed interscholastic: archery, golf, running. 2 PE instructors, 5 coaches, 1 athletic trainer.

Computers Computers are regularly used in all academic, career education, career exploration, college planning, computer applications, keyboarding, mathematics, programming, science, senior seminar, video film production, yearbook classes. Computer network features include on-campus library services, Internet access, wireless campus network, Internet filtering or blocking technology. Student e-mail accounts and computer access in designated common areas are available to students. Students grades are available online. The school has a published electronic and media policy.

Contact Miss Taylor Walker, Advancement. 423-892-8224 Ext. 202. Fax: 423-892-1194. E-mail: twalker@mygracechatt.org. Website: www.gracechatt.org

GRACE CHRISTIAN SCHOOL

12407 Pintail Street
Anchorage, Alaska 99516

Head of School: Mr. Randy Karlberg

General Information Coeducational day college-preparatory, arts, religious studies, and technology school, affiliated with Christian faith. Grades K–12. Founded: 1980. Setting: urban. 7-acre campus. 1 building on campus. Approved or accredited by Northwest Accreditation Commission and Northwest Association of Schools and Colleges. Total enrollment: 532. Upper school average class size: 13. Upper school faculty-student ratio: 1:14. There are 170 required school days per year for Upper School students. Upper School students typically attend 5 days per week. The average school day consists of 6 hours and 50 minutes.

Upper School Student Profile Grade 7: 43 students (14 boys, 29 girls); Grade 8: 50 students (28 boys, 22 girls); Grade 9: 56 students (34 boys, 22 girls); Grade 10: 49 students (20 boys, 29 girls); Grade 11: 43 students (22 boys, 21 girls); Grade 12: 37 students (19 boys, 18 girls). 99% of students are Christian faith.

Faculty School total: 47. In upper school: 13 men, 18 women; 12 have advanced degrees.

Subjects Offered Algebra, American government, American history, American history-AP, art, astronomy, Bible, biology, biology-AP, calculus-AP, chemistry, chemistry-AP, choir, computer science, computer skills, computer technologies, creative writing, drama, economics, English, English language and composition-AP, English literature and composition-AP, English literature-AP, English/composition-AP, film, fine arts, geology, geometry, government-AP, health, leadership and service, literature, media, meteorology, music theory-AP, oceanography, physical education, physical science, physics, psychology, publications, science, social studies, Spanish, speech, trigonometry, U.S. history, U.S. history-AP, weightlifting, world history, yearbook.

Graduation Requirements Algebra, American government, American literature, biology, British literature, consumer economics, electives, English composition, English literature, geometry, literary genres, literature, physical education (includes health), physical science, practical arts, U.S. history, world history, one year of Bible for every year attending, Old Testament survey in 9th grade, 10th grade—New Testament survey, 11th grade—Life and Times of Christ/Marriage and Family, 12th grade—Defending Your Faith/Understanding the Times.

Special Academic Programs Advanced Placement exam preparation.

College Admission Counseling 59 students graduated in 2015; 55 went to college, including Corban University; Montana State University; United States Air Force Academy; University of Alaska Anchorage; University of Alaska Fairbanks; Wheaton College. Other: 2 went to work, 2 had other specific plans. Mean SAT critical reading: 577, mean SAT math: 536, mean SAT writing: 544, mean combined SAT: 1657, mean composite ACT: 25.

Student Life Upper grades have specified standards of dress, student council, honor system. Discipline rests primarily with faculty. Attendance at religious services is required.

Summer Programs Enrichment programs offered; session focuses on science/forensics; held on campus; accepts boys and girls; open to students from other schools. 30 students usually enrolled. 2016 schedule: June 6 to June 10.

Tuition and Aid Day student tuition: $9500. Tuition installment plan (FACTS Tuition Payment Plan). Tuition reduction for siblings, need-based scholarship grants available. In 2015–16, 15% of upper-school students received aid. Total amount of financial aid awarded in 2015–16: $200,000.

Admissions Traditional secondary-level entrance grade is 9. For fall 2015, 41 students applied for upper-level admission, 30 were accepted, 29 enrolled. Math and English placement tests, school's own exam or Stanford Achievement Test required. Deadline for receipt of application materials: none. Application fee required: $50. Interview required.

Athletics Interscholastic: basketball (boys, girls), cheering (g), cross-country running (b,g), skiing (cross-country) (b,g), soccer (b,g), track and field (b,g), volleyball (g), wrestling (b). 2 PE instructors, 15 coaches, 1 athletic trainer.

Computers Computers are regularly used in computer applications, media, publications, technology, yearbook classes. Computer network features include on-campus library services, online commercial services, Internet access, wireless campus network, Internet filtering or blocking technology. Students grades are available online.

Contact Admissions, 907-345-4814 Fax: 907-644-2260. E-mail: admissions@gracechristianalaska.org. Website: www.gracechristianalaska.org

GRACE CHRISTIAN SCHOOL

50 Kirkdale Road
Charlottetown, Prince Edward Island C1E 1N6, Canada

Head of School: Mr. Jason Biech

General Information Coeducational day college-preparatory, arts, religious studies, and technology school, affiliated with Baptist Church, Evangelical faith. Grades JK–12. Founded: 1980. Setting: small town. 6-acre campus. 1 building on campus. Approved or accredited by Christian Schools International and Prince Edward Island Department of Education. Language of instruction: English. Endowment: CAN$100,000. Total enrollment: 124. Upper school average class size: 10. Upper school faculty-student ratio: 1:10. There are 185 required school days per year for Upper School students. Upper School students typically attend 5 days per week. The average school day consists of 6 hours.

Upper School Student Profile Grade 6: 14 students (4 boys, 10 girls); Grade 7: 13 students (7 boys, 6 girls); Grade 8: 10 students (5 boys, 5 girls); Grade 9: 12 students (8 boys, 4 girls); Grade 10: 8 students (5 boys, 3 girls); Grade 11: 7 students (1 boy, 6 girls); Grade 12: 10 students (5 boys, 5 girls). 70% of students are Baptist, members of Evangelical faith.

Faculty School total: 12. In upper school: 4 men, 4 women.

Subjects Offered American literature, American literature-AP, Bible, biology, British literature, business technology, Canadian history, chemistry, computer science.

Graduation Requirements Bible, language, mathematics, Christian service requirements.

Special Academic Programs 2 Advanced Placement exams for which test preparation is offered; ESL (21 students enrolled).

College Admission Counseling 10 students graduated in 2014; 9 went to college, including Acadia University. Other: 1 went to work.

Student Life Upper grades have specified standards of dress, student council. Discipline rests primarily with faculty. Attendance at religious services is required.

Tuition and Aid Day student tuition: CAN$4740. Tuition installment plan (monthly payment plans). Tuition reduction for siblings, bursaries available. In 2014–15, 5% of upper-school students received aid. Total amount of financial aid awarded in 2014–15: CAN$4000.

Admissions Traditional secondary-level entrance grade is 10. For fall 2014, 6 students applied for upper-level admission, 6 were accepted, 6 enrolled. Deadline for receipt of application materials: June 25. Application fee required: CAN$250. On-campus interview required.

Athletics Interscholastic: cross-country running (boys, girls), soccer (b,g); coed interscholastic: aerobics, alpine skiing, aquatics, badminton, basketball, cross-country running, golf, track and field; coed intramural: cross-country running, track and field. 1 PE instructor.

Computers Computers are regularly used in information technology classes. Computer network features include Internet access, wireless campus network. Students grades are available online.

Contact Mr. Jason Biech, Administrator. 902-628-1668 Ext. 223. Fax: 902-628-1668. E-mail: principal@gracechristianschool.ca. Website: www.gracechristianschool.ca/

THE GRAND RIVER ACADEMY

3042 College Street
Austinburg, Ohio 44010

Head of School: Mr. Tim Viands

General Information Boys' boarding college-preparatory, arts, technology, ESL, and Foundations of Learning Program school; primarily serves underachievers, students with learning disabilities, individuals with Attention Deficit Disorder, and dyslexic students. Grades 9–PG. Founded: 1831. Setting: small town. Nearest major city is Cleveland. Students are housed in single-sex dormitories. 200-acre campus. 11 buildings on campus. Approved or accredited by Independent Schools Association of the Central States, Midwest Association of Boarding Schools, Ohio Association of Independent Schools, The Association of Boarding Schools, and Ohio Department of Education. Member of National Association of Independent Schools and Secondary School Admission Test Board. Endowment: $23 million. Total enrollment: 109. Upper school average class size: 7. Upper school faculty-student ratio: 1:6.

Upper School Student Profile Grade 9: 10 students (10 boys); Grade 10: 27 students (27 boys); Grade 11: 31 students (31 boys); Grade 12: 41 students (41 boys). 100% of students are boarding students. 30% are state residents. 18 states are represented in upper school student body. 30% are international students. International students from Brazil, China, Republic of Korea, Russian Federation, Spain, and Thailand; 2 other countries represented in student body.

Faculty School total: 24. In upper school: 17 men, 7 women; 15 have advanced degrees; 21 reside on campus.

Subjects Offered 20th century American writers, 20th century history, 20th century world history, Advanced Placement courses, algebra, American history, American literature, art, biology, British literature (honors), calculus, calculus-AP, chemistry, civics, college writing, Coming of Age in the 20th Century, community service, comparative government and politics, computer science, creative writing, criminology, digital imaging, digital photography, economics, English, English as a foreign language, English literature, environmental science, ESL, ESL, European literature, fine arts, forensics, geography, government, government/civics, grammar, graphic design, health, history, integrated science, lab science, mathematics, music theory, photography, physical education, physics, physics-AP, pre-calculus, psychology, public speaking, science, social studies, Spanish, speech, TOEFL preparation, video and animation, video film production, Web site design, world civilizations, world history, world issues, world literature, yearbook.

Graduation Requirements Arts and fine arts (art, music, dance, drama), computer science, English, mathematics, physical education (includes health), science, social studies (includes history), all students must gain college acceptance. Community service is required.

Special Academic Programs 9 Advanced Placement exams for which test preparation is offered; honors section; independent study; study at local college for college credit; academic accommodation for the gifted; remedial reading and/or remedial writing; programs in English, mathematics for dyslexic students; special instructional classes for students with Attention Deficit Disorder, students with Executive Functioning Disorder; ESL (18 students enrolled).

College Admission Counseling 29 students graduated in 2014; all went to college, including Arizona State University at the Tempe campus; Baldwin Wallace University; Case Western Reserve University; John Carroll University; Penn State Erie, The Behrend College; Penn State University Park.

Student Life Upper grades have uniform requirement, student council, honor system. Discipline rests primarily with faculty.

Tuition and Aid 5-day tuition and room/board: $39,100; 7-day tuition and room/board: $40,700. Need-based scholarship grants, prepGATE Loans available. In 2014–15, 10% of upper-school students received aid. Total amount of financial aid awarded in 2014–15: $205,000.

Admissions Traditional secondary-level entrance grade is 9. For fall 2014, 67 students applied for upper-level admission, 55 were accepted, 43 enrolled. Deadline for receipt of application materials: none. Application fee required: $35. Interview required.

Athletics Interscholastic: baseball, basketball, cross-country running, golf, horseback riding, ice hockey, independent competitive sports, indoor soccer, soccer, swimming and diving, tennis, wrestling; intramural: backpacking, baseball, basketball, bicycling, billiards, bocce, bowling, canoeing/kayaking, equestrian sports, fishing, fitness, fitness walking, flag football, fly fishing, football, freestyle skiing, Frisbee, golf, hiking/backpacking, horseback riding, horseshoes, ice hockey, jogging, martial arts, mountain biking, Nautilus, outdoor activities, outdoor recreation, outdoor skills, paddle tennis, paint ball, physical fitness, physical training, power lifting, rafting, roller blading, roller skating, ropes courses, running, self defense, skateboarding, skiing (cross-country), skiing (downhill), snowboarding, soccer, softball, strength & conditioning, table tennis, tennis, touch football, ultimate Frisbee, volleyball, walking, weight lifting, weight training, whiffle ball, wrestling. 1 PE instructor, 10 coaches.

Computers Computers are regularly used in English, ESL, foreign language, history, mathematics, science classes. Computer network features include on-campus library services, online commercial services, Internet access, wireless campus network, Internet filtering or blocking technology, 1:1 program, Class Owl (Online Assignment Notifications), SmartBoards technology. Campus intranet and student e-mail accounts are available to students. Students grades are available online. The school has a published electronic and media policy.

Contact Glenn Singer, Director of Admission. 440-275-2811 Ext. 225. Fax: 440-275-1825. E-mail: admissions@grandriver.org. Website: www.grandriver.org

THE GRAUER SCHOOL

1500 South El Camino Real
Encinitas, California 92024

Head of School: Dr. Stuart Robert Grauer

General Information Coeducational day college-preparatory and arts school. Grades 7–12. Founded: 1991. Setting: suburban. Nearest major city is San Diego. 5-acre campus. 2 buildings on campus. Approved or accredited by Western Association of Schools and Colleges and California Department of Education. Member of National Association of Independent Schools. Endowment: $250,000. Total enrollment: 164. Upper school average class size: 12. Upper school faculty-student ratio: 1:7. There are 178 required school days per year for Upper School students. Upper School students typically attend 5 days per week. The average school day consists of 6 hours and 30 minutes.

Upper School Student Profile Grade 7: 26 students (13 boys, 13 girls); Grade 8: 29 students (14 boys, 15 girls); Grade 9: 22 students (12 boys, 10 girls); Grade 10: 28 students (11 boys, 17 girls); Grade 11: 28 students (16 boys, 12 girls); Grade 12: 30 students (11 boys, 19 girls).

Faculty School total: 32. In upper school: 14 men, 16 women; 25 have advanced degrees.

Subjects Offered ACT preparation, advanced biology, advanced chemistry, advanced math, algebra, alternative physical education, American government, American history, American sign language, anatomy and physiology, ancient history, applied music, art, art appreciation, art history, ASB Leadership, athletic training, audio visual/media, basketball, biology, business mathematics, calculus, character education, chemistry, Chinese, choir, civics, classical music, college admission preparation, college planning, community service, computer applications, computer education, computer multimedia, computers, creative writing, culinary arts, drama, dramatic arts, economics, English literature, environmental education, ESL, experiential education, film studies, filmmaking, fitness, French, gardening, geography, geometry, global studies, health, high adventure outdoor program, honors algebra, honors English, honors geometry, honors U.S. history, honors world history, Japanese, keyboarding, leadership and service, marine science, multimedia, music, music appreciation, music performance, outdoor education, peace studies, personal fitness, photo shop, photography, physical education, physics, pre-algebra, pre-calculus, religion, religion and culture, robotics, Spanish, speech and debate, studio art, study skills, surfing, tennis, theater arts, trigonometry, U.S. government, U.S. history, U.S. literature, world geography, world history, world religions.

Graduation Requirements Economics, electives, English, experiential education, foreign language, geography, health, mathematics, physical education (includes health), science, senior project, U.S. government, U.S. history, visual and performing arts, world history, world religions, expeditionary learning in the field and 50 hours community service, all students graduate with distinction in a subject of their choice. Community service is required.

Special Academic Programs Honors section; independent study; study abroad; academic accommodation for the gifted, the musically talented, and the artistically talented; ESL (3 students enrolled).

College Admission Counseling 27 students graduated in 2015; all went to college, including Lewis & Clark College; University of San Diego. Median SAT critical reading: 600, median SAT math: 560, median SAT writing: 600, median combined SAT: 1760, median composite ACT: 27.

Student Life Upper grades have specified standards of dress, student council, honor system. Discipline rests equally with students and faculty.

Summer Programs Remediation, enrichment, advancement, ESL, sports, art/fine arts, rigorous outdoor training, computer instruction programs offered; session focuses on academics and enrichment; held on campus; accepts boys and girls; open to students from other schools. 60 students usually enrolled.

Tuition and Aid Day student tuition: $22,583. Tuition installment plan (individually arranged payment plans, 3 payment plans). Need-based scholarship grants available. In 2015–16, 13% of upper-school students received aid. Total amount of financial aid awarded in 2015–16: $160,877.

Admissions Traditional secondary-level entrance grade is 9. Deadline for receipt of application materials: February 1. Application fee required: $100. Interview required.

Athletics Interscholastic: baseball (boys), basketball (b,g), field hockey (g), football (b), golf (b,g), indoor soccer (b,g), lacrosse (b,g), soccer (b,g), softball (g), tennis (b,g), volleyball (b,g), water polo (b,g); intramural: soccer (b,g); coed interscholastic: archery, cross-country running, flag football, gymnastics, indoor soccer, surfing, swimming and diving, tennis, track and field, wrestling; coed intramural: basketball, cross-country running, flag football, independent competitive sports, outdoor activities, outdoor adventure, outdoor education, outdoor recreation, outdoor skills, outdoors, skateboarding, soccer, surfing, tennis, track and field. 2 PE instructors.

Computers Computers are regularly used in all classes. Computer network features include Internet access, wireless campus network, Internet filtering or blocking technology, online text books, online portfolios, all students required to have computers. Campus intranet, student e-mail accounts, and computer access in designated common areas are available to students. Students grades are available online. The school has a published electronic and media policy.

Contact Mrs. Olivia Kleinrath, Senior Admissions Associate. 760-274-2116. Fax: 760-944-6784. E-mail: admissions@grauerschool.com. Website: www.grauerschool.com

GREATER ATLANTA CHRISTIAN SCHOOLS

1575 Indian Trail Road
Norcross, Georgia 30093

Head of School: Dr. David Fincher

General Information Coeducational day college-preparatory, arts, religious studies, and technology school, affiliated with Christian faith, Christian faith. Grades P3–12. Founded: 1961. Setting: suburban. Nearest major city is Atlanta. 88-acre campus. 22 buildings on campus. Approved or accredited by Georgia Independent School Association, National Christian School Association, Southern Association of Colleges and Schools, Southern Association of Independent Schools, The College Board, and Georgia Department of Education. Member of National Association of Independent Schools and Secondary School Admission Test Board. Endowment: $28.5 million. Total enrollment: 1,815. Upper school average class size: 18. Upper school faculty-student ratio: 1:13. There are 180 required school days per year for Upper School students. Upper School students typically attend 5 days per week. The average school day consists of 7 hours and 10 minutes.

Upper School Student Profile Grade 9: 204 students (106 boys, 98 girls); Grade 10: 203 students (103 boys, 100 girls); Grade 11: 175 students (103 boys, 72 girls); Grade 12: 195 students (103 boys, 92 girls). 97% of students are Christian, Christian.

Faculty School total: 150. In upper school: 39 men, 27 women; 42 have advanced degrees.

Subjects Offered 3-dimensional art, accounting, Advanced Placement courses, advanced studio art-AP, algebra, American government, American history, American history-AP, American literature, analysis, anatomy, anatomy and physiology, art, art appreciation, art history, art-AP, audio visual/media, band, Bible, biology, biology-AP, British literature, British literature (honors), broadcast journalism, business, calculus, calculus-AP, chemistry, chemistry-AP, Chinese, choir, chorus, church history, composition, computer applications, computer math, computer programming, computer science-AP, concert choir, dance, drama, dramatic arts, economics-AP, English language and composition-AP, English literature-AP, environmental science, environmental science-AP, environmental studies, ethics, European history, European history-AP, expository writing, foreign language, French, French as a second language, French-AP, geometry, government-AP, government/civics-AP, graphic design, health, home economics, honors English, jazz band, journalism, language arts, Latin, Latin-AP, literature-AP, Mandarin, marching band, mathematics-AP, music appreciation, music theory-AP, music-AP, musical theater, newspaper, orchestra, painting, personal finance, philosophy, photography, physics, physics-AP, physiology, pre-calculus, psychology-AP, religion, SAT preparation, sculpture, sociology, Spanish, Spanish-AP, speech, speech communications, statistics, statistics-AP, studio art-AP, symphonic band, theology, trigonometry, U.S. history, U.S. history-AP, video, video film production, visual arts, Web site design, world history-AP, world literature, yearbook.

Graduation Requirements English, foreign language, mathematics, physical education (includes health), religious studies, science, social sciences, social studies (includes history), one year of Bible for each year of attendance.

Special Academic Programs 23 Advanced Placement exams for which test preparation is offered; honors section; study abroad; academic accommodation for the gifted, the musically talented, and the artistically talented.

College Admission Counseling 168 students graduated in 2015; all went to college, including Auburn University; Georgia Institute of Technology; Lipscomb University; Samford University; The University of Alabama; University of Georgia. Median SAT critical reading: 566, median SAT math: 581, median SAT writing: 568, median combined SAT: 1715, median composite ACT: 26.

Student Life Upper grades have uniform requirement, student council, honor system. Discipline rests primarily with faculty. Attendance at religious services is required.

Summer Programs Enrichment, sports, art/fine arts programs offered; session focuses on recreation; held on campus; accepts boys and girls; open to students from other schools. 150 students usually enrolled. 2016 schedule: June 1 to August 1.

Tuition and Aid Day student tuition: $17,900. Tuition installment plan (monthly payment plans, quarterly payment plan). Need-based scholarship grants available. In 2015–16, 33% of upper-school students received aid.

Admissions Traditional secondary-level entrance grade is 9. OLSAT and English Exam or SSAT required. Deadline for receipt of application materials: none. Application fee required: $90. On-campus interview required.

Athletics Interscholastic: baseball (boys), dance team (g), flag football (b), football (b), golf (b,g), lacrosse (b,g), soccer (b,g), softball (g), tennis (b,g), volleyball (g), wrestling (b); intramural: aerobics (g), aerobics/dance (g), ballet (g), cheering (g), combined training (b,g), dance (g), physical fitness (b,g), strength & conditioning (b,g), weight lifting (b), weight training (b,g); coed interscholastic: aquatics, basketball, cross-country running, diving, swimming and diving, track and field, water polo; coed intramural: Frisbee. 5 PE instructors, 1 athletic trainer.

Computers Computers are regularly used in all academic, college planning classes. Computer network features include on-campus library services, online commercial services, Internet access, wireless campus network, Internet filtering or blocking technology. Campus intranet is available to students. Students grades are available online. The school has a published electronic and media policy.

Contact Mrs. Mary Helen Bryant, Director of Admissions and Enrollment. 770-243-2274. Fax: 770-243-2213. E-mail: mbryant@greateratlantachristian.org. Website: www.greateratlantachristian.org

GREAT LAKES CHRISTIAN HIGH SCHOOL

4875 King Street
Beamsville, Ontario L0R 1B6, Canada

Head of School: Mr. Don Rose

General Information Coeducational boarding and day college-preparatory, general academic, arts, religious studies, bilingual studies, and technology school, affiliated with Church of Christ. Grades 9–12. Founded: 1952. Setting: small town. Nearest major city is St. Catherines, Canada. Students are housed in single-sex dormitories. 8-acre campus. 6 buildings on campus. Approved or accredited by Ontario Ministry of Education and Ontario Department of Education. Language of instruction: English. Endowment: CAN$500,000. Total enrollment: 124. Upper school average class size: 22. Upper school faculty-student ratio: 1:8. There are 252 required school days per year for Upper School students. Upper School students typically attend 5 days per week. The average school day consists of 6 hours and 10 minutes.

Upper School Student Profile Grade 9: 26 students (13 boys, 13 girls); Grade 10: 23 students (14 boys, 9 girls); Grade 11: 25 students (15 boys, 10 girls); Grade 12: 50 students (26 boys, 24 girls). 45% of students are boarding students. 40% are province residents. 7 provinces are represented in upper school student body. 55% are international students. International students from Canada, China, Hong Kong, Nigeria, Republic of Korea, and United States; 3 other countries represented in student body. 40% of students are members of Church of Christ.

Faculty School total: 14. In upper school: 8 men, 6 women; 4 have advanced degrees; 3 reside on campus.

Subjects Offered 20th century world history, accounting, algebra, anthropology, arts appreciation, Bible, biology, calculus, career and personal planning, chemistry, computer science, computer technologies, dramatic arts, economics, English, English composition, English language and composition-AP, English literature, English-AP, ESL, family studies, foods, French, functions, geography, history, mathematics, mathematics-AP, media, media arts, music, physical education, physics, psychology, society, sociology, technology, visual arts, world issues.

Graduation Requirements 20th century history, advanced math, art, Bible, business, Canadian geography, Canadian history, Canadian literature, career planning, civics, computer information systems, conceptual physics, critical thinking, current events, economics, English, English composition, English literature, French as a second language, geography, mathematics, physical education (includes health), science, society challenge and change, world geography, world history.

Special Academic Programs Independent study; ESL (20 students enrolled).

College Admission Counseling 36 students graduated in 2015; 27 went to college, including Carleton University; McMaster University; University of Ottawa; University of Toronto; University of Waterloo; Wilfrid Laurier University. Other: 9 went to work.

Student Life Upper grades have uniform requirement, student council, honor system. Discipline rests primarily with faculty. Attendance at religious services is required.

Summer Programs Enrichment, rigorous outdoor training programs offered; session focuses on skill levels improvement; held on campus; accepts boys and girls; not open to students from other schools. 6 students usually enrolled. 2016 schedule: June 19 to August 31. Application deadline: May 8.

Tuition and Aid Day student tuition: CAN$8800; 5-day tuition and room/board: CAN$15,200; 7-day tuition and room/board: CAN$17,500. Tuition installment plan (monthly payment plans, individually arranged payment plans). Tuition reduction for siblings, bursaries, merit scholarship grants, need-based scholarship grants, need-based loans, middle-income loans, paying campus jobs available. In 2014–15, 55% of upper-school students received aid; total upper-school merit-scholarship money awarded: CAN$8000. Total amount of financial aid awarded in 2014–15: CAN$225,000.

Admissions Traditional secondary-level entrance grade is 9. For fall 2015, 134 students applied for upper-level admission, 126 were accepted, 124 enrolled. CAT and SLEP required. Deadline for receipt of application materials: none. Application fee required: CAN$100. Interview recommended.

Athletics Interscholastic: badminton (boys, girls), basketball (b,g), cross-country running (b,g), golf (b), ice hockey (b,g), soccer (b,g), tennis (b,g), track and field (b,g), volleyball (b,g); intramural: aerobics (g), badminton (b,g), basketball (b,g), cooperative games (b,g), Cosom hockey (b,g), fitness (b,g), ice hockey (b,g), indoor hockey (b,g), indoor soccer (b,g), lacrosse (b,g), soccer (b,g), softball (b,g), table tennis (b,g), tennis (b,g), volleyball (b,g); coed interscholastic: badminton, tennis; coed intramural: badminton, ball hockey, baseball, basketball, cooperative games, Cosom hockey, floor hockey, hockey, indoor soccer, lacrosse, table tennis, tennis, volleyball. 2 PE instructors, 2 coaches.

Computers Computers are regularly used in accounting, business, computer applications, introduction to technology, technology, typing classes. Computer network features include on-campus library services, Internet access, wireless campus network, Internet filtering or blocking technology, Edsby system. Campus intranet and computer access in designated common areas are available to students. Students grades are available online. The school has a published electronic and media policy.

Contact Mrs. Ingrid Kielstra, Director of Domestic Admissions. 905-563-5374 Ext. 212. Fax: 905-563-0818. E-mail: study@glchs.on.ca. Website: www.glchs.on.ca

GREENFIELD SCHOOL

3351 NC Hwy 42 W
Wilson, North Carolina 27893

Head of School: Dr. Vincent M. Janney

General Information Coeducational day and distance learning college-preparatory school. Grades PS–12. Distance learning grades 11–12. Founded: 1969. Setting: small town. Nearest major city is Raleigh. 61-acre campus. 9 buildings on campus. Approved or accredited by Southern Association of Colleges and Schools and North Carolina Department of Education. Member of National Association of Independent Schools. Total enrollment: 250. Upper school average class size: 17. Upper school faculty-student ratio: 1:3. There are 178 required school days per year for Upper School students. Upper School students typically attend 5 days per week. The average school day consists of 6 hours and 45 minutes.

Upper School Student Profile Grade 9: 15 students (10 boys, 5 girls); Grade 10: 15 students (8 boys, 7 girls); Grade 11: 21 students (17 boys, 4 girls); Grade 12: 18 students (10 boys, 8 girls)

Faculty School total: 56. In upper school: 9 men, 16 women; 13 have advanced degrees.

Subjects Offered Advanced computer applications, advanced math, Advanced Placement courses, algebra, American history, American literature, ancient world history, art, athletics, biology, British literature, calculus, calculus-AP, chemistry, chorus, college awareness, community service, computer applications, computer education, computer graphics, computer information systems, computer math, computer multimedia, computer processing, computer programming, computer programming-AP, computer science, computer skills, computer technologies, desktop publishing, drama, earth science, economics, electives, English, English literature, fine arts, foreign language, geography, geometry, government/civics, grammar, health, history, honors algebra, honors English, honors geometry, honors world history, keyboarding, language arts, mathematics, music, physical education, physical science, physics, pre-algebra, pre-calculus, SAT preparation, science, social studies, Spanish, sports conditioning, trigonometry, Web site design, world geography, world history, writing, yearbook.

Graduation Requirements Arts and fine arts (art, music, dance, drama), computer science, English, foreign language, mathematics, physical education (includes health), science, social studies (includes history). Community service is required.

Special Academic Programs 5 Advanced Placement exams for which test preparation is offered; honors section; independent study; academic accommodation for the gifted; remedial reading and/or remedial writing; remedial math; programs in English, general development for dyslexic students.

College Admission Counseling 23 students graduated in 2014; all went to college, including Appalachian State University; East Carolina University; Meredith College; North Carolina State University; The University of North Carolina at Chapel Hill. Median SAT critical reading: 520, median SAT math: 510, median SAT writing: 500, median combined SAT: 1540, median composite ACT: 23. 18% scored over 600 on SAT critical reading, 24% scored over 600 on SAT math, 29% scored over 600 on SAT writing, 24% scored over 1800 on combined SAT, 38% scored over 26 on composite ACT.

Student Life Upper grades have specified standards of dress, student council, honor system. Discipline rests primarily with faculty.

Tuition and Aid Day student tuition: $9900. Tuition installment plan (monthly payment plans). Tuition reduction for siblings, merit scholarship grants, need-based scholarship grants available. In 2014–15, 20% of upper-school students received aid; total upper-school merit-scholarship money awarded: $28,500. Total amount of financial aid awarded in 2014–15: $28,500.

Admissions Traditional secondary-level entrance grade is 9. For fall 2014, 15 students applied for upper-level admission, 12 were accepted, 7 enrolled. Brigance Test of Basic

Skills, Comprehensive Test of Basic Skills or CTP III required. Deadline for receipt of application materials: none. Application fee required: $100. On-campus interview required.

Athletics Interscholastic: baseball (boys), basketball (b,g), cross-country running (g), golf (b), soccer (b,g), tennis (b,g), volleyball (g); coed interscholastic: golf. 3 PE instructors, 11 coaches.

Computers Computers are regularly used in all academic classes. Computer resources include on-campus library services, Internet access, wireless campus network, Internet filtering or blocking technology. Computer access in designated common areas is available to students. The school has a published electronic and media policy.

Contact Robin Hauser, Director of Advancement. 252-237-8046. Fax: 252-237-1825. E-mail: hauserr@greenfieldschool.org. Website: www.greenfieldschool.org

GREEN FIELDS COUNTRY DAY SCHOOL

6000 North Camino de la Tierra
Tucson, Arizona 85741

Head of School: Rebecca Cordier

General Information Coeducational day college-preparatory and arts school. Grades K–12. Founded: 1933. Setting: suburban. 22-acre campus. 15 buildings on campus. Approved or accredited by Arizona Association of Independent Schools. Member of National Association of Independent Schools. Total enrollment: 105. Upper school average class size: 12. Upper school faculty-student ratio: 1:4. The average school day consists of 7 hours.

Upper School Student Profile Grade 6: 9 students (1 boy, 8 girls); Grade 7: 6 students (5 boys, 1 girl); Grade 8: 13 students (6 boys, 7 girls); Grade 9: 9 students (4 boys, 5 girls); Grade 10: 9 students (3 boys, 6 girls); Grade 11: 10 students (6 boys, 4 girls); Grade 12: 7 students (3 boys, 4 girls).

Faculty School total: 29. In upper school: 9 men, 9 women; 12 have advanced degrees.

Subjects Offered 3-dimensional art, advanced chemistry, advanced computer applications, advanced math, Advanced Placement courses, advanced studio art-AP, algebra, American government, American history, American history-AP, American literature, anatomy and physiology, art, art-AP, Basic programming, biology, biology-AP, British literature (honors), British literature-AP, calculus, calculus-AP, ceramics, chemistry, chorus, college placement, computer programming, computer science, conceptual physics, drama, drama performance, English, environmental science-AP, European history, European history-AP, expository writing, fine arts, French, French language-AP, French literature-AP, French-AP, geography, geometry, government and politics-AP, government-AP, independent study, journalism, music theory, musical theater, newspaper, physical education, physics, political science, pre-calculus, probability and statistics, social studies, Spanish, Spanish-AP, studio art-AP, trigonometry, U.S. government and politics-AP, U.S. history-AP, Web site design, world history, writing, yearbook.

Graduation Requirements Advanced math, algebra, American history, American literature, arts and fine arts (art, music, dance, drama), biology, chemistry, computer skills, electives, English, English literature, foreign language, geometry, mathematics, physical education (includes health), science, social studies (includes history), world history, writing.

Special Academic Programs Advanced Placement exam preparation; independent study; study abroad.

College Admission Counseling 12 students graduated in 2015; 11 went to college, including California Institute of Technology; Connecticut College; Northern Arizona University; The University of Arizona.

Student Life Upper grades have specified standards of dress, student council, honor system. Discipline rests primarily with faculty.

Summer Programs Enrichment, sports, art/fine arts programs offered; session focuses on basketball and volleyball; held on campus; accepts boys and girls; open to students from other schools. 2016 schedule: June 7 to August 5.

Tuition and Aid Day student tuition: $14,600. Guaranteed tuition plan. Tuition installment plan (SMART Tuition Payment Plan, individually arranged payment plans, semester payment plan). Merit scholarship grants, need-based scholarship grants available. In 2015–16, 40% of upper-school students received aid; total upper-school merit-scholarship money awarded: $20,317. Total amount of financial aid awarded in 2015–16: $187,987.

Admissions Traditional secondary-level entrance grade is 9. Achievement tests or Achievement/Aptitude/Writing required. Deadline for receipt of application materials: none. Application fee required: $50. On-campus interview required.

Athletics Interscholastic: aquatics (girls), basketball (b,g), cross-country running (b,g), tennis (b), volleyball (b,g); coed interscholastic: flag football, physical fitness, physical training, running, soccer, track and field; coed intramural: rock climbing, tennis, yoga. 1 PE instructor, 8 coaches.

Computers Computers are regularly used in English, mathematics, newspaper, science, yearbook classes. Computer network features include on-campus library services, online commercial services, Internet access, wireless campus network, Internet filtering or blocking technology. Campus intranet, student e-mail accounts, and computer access in designated common areas are available to students. The school has a published electronic and media policy.

Contact Rebecca Cordier, Director of Admission. 520-297-2288 Ext. 7105. Fax: 520-618-2599. E-mail: admissions@greenfields.org. Website: www.greenfields.org

GREENHILL SCHOOL

4141 Spring Valley Road
Addison, Texas 75001

Head of School: Scott A. Griggs

General Information Coeducational day college-preparatory school. Grades PK–12. Founded: 1950. Setting: suburban. Nearest major city is Dallas. 78-acre campus. 8 buildings on campus. Approved or accredited by Independent Schools Association of the Southwest and Texas Department of Education. Member of National Association of Independent Schools and Secondary School Admission Test Board. Endowment: $34 million. Total enrollment: 1,280. Upper school average class size: 16. Upper school faculty-student ratio: 1:7. Upper School students typically attend 5 days per week. The average school day consists of 7 hours and 45 minutes.

Upper School Student Profile Grade 9: 116 students (58 boys, 58 girls); Grade 10: 116 students (54 boys, 62 girls); Grade 11: 115 students (62 boys, 53 girls); Grade 12: 120 students (60 boys, 60 girls).

Faculty School total: 171. In upper school: 45 men, 37 women; 52 have advanced degrees.

Subjects Offered Algebra, American history, American literature, art, art history, biology, calculus, ceramics, chemistry, Chinese, computer programming, computer science, creative writing, dance, drama, ecology, economics, English, English literature, European history, fine arts, French, geometry, government/civics, health, history, journalism, Latin, mathematics, music, philosophy, photography, physical education, physics, robotics, science, social studies, Spanish, speech, theater, trigonometry, wellness.

Graduation Requirements Arts and fine arts (art, music, dance, drama), classical language, computer studies, English, history, mathematics, modern languages, physical education (includes health), science. Community service is required.

Special Academic Programs Advanced Placement exam preparation; honors section; independent study; term-away projects; study abroad.

College Admission Counseling 118 students graduated in 2015; all went to college, including Duke University; Hendrix College; The University of Texas at Austin; University of Michigan; University of Southern California.

Student Life Upper grades have specified standards of dress, student council, honor system. Discipline rests primarily with faculty.

Summer Programs Enrichment, sports, art/fine arts, computer instruction programs offered; session focuses on enrichment and sports; held on campus; accepts boys and girls; open to students from other schools. 1,300 students usually enrolled. 2016 schedule: June 6 to August 5. Application deadline: none.

Tuition and Aid Day student tuition: $27,100. Need-based scholarship grants available. In 2015–16, 18% of upper-school students received aid. Total amount of financial aid awarded in 2015–16: $1,727,046.

Admissions Traditional secondary-level entrance grade is 9. For fall 2015, 197 students applied for upper-level admission, 86 were accepted, 56 enrolled. ISEE required. Deadline for receipt of application materials: January 8. Application fee required: $175. Interview required.

Athletics Interscholastic: aquatics (boys, girls), baseball (b), basketball (b,g), cross-country running (b,g), field hockey (g), football (b), golf (b,g), lacrosse (b,g), running (b,g), soccer (b,g), softball (g), swimming and diving (b,g), tennis (b,g), track and field (b,g), volleyball (b,g), winter soccer (b,g); intramural: baseball (b), basketball (b,g), field hockey (g), fitness (b,g), football (b), lacrosse (b,g), physical fitness (b,g), running (b,g), soccer (b,g), softball (g), strength & conditioning (b,g), swimming and diving (b,g), tennis (b,g), track and field (b,g), volleyball (b,g), weight lifting (b,g), winter soccer (b,g); coed interscholastic: cheering; coed intramural: aquatics, ballet, cross-country running, dance, fitness, Frisbee, golf, physical fitness, running, soccer, strength & conditioning, swimming and diving, tai chi, tennis, track and field, ultimate Frisbee, volleyball, weight lifting, weight training, winter soccer, yoga. 15 PE instructors, 4 athletic trainers.

Computers Computers are regularly used in computer applications, digital applications, independent study, programming, video film production, Web site design classes. Computer network features include on-campus library services, online commercial services, Internet access, wireless campus network, Internet filtering or blocking technology. Campus intranet, student e-mail accounts, and computer access in designated common areas are available to students. Students grades are available online. The school has a published electronic and media policy.

Contact Sarah Markhovsky, Director of Admission. 972-628-5910. Fax: 972-404-8217. E-mail: admission@greenhill.org. Website: www.greenhill.org

GREENHILLS SCHOOL

850 Greenhills Drive
Ann Arbor, Michigan 48105

Head of School: Carl J. Pelofsky

General Information Coeducational day college-preparatory and arts school. Grades 6–12. Founded: 1968. Setting: suburban. Nearest major city is Detroit. 30-acre campus. 1 building on campus. Approved or accredited by Independent Schools Association of the Central States and Michigan Department of Education. Member of National Association of Independent Schools and Secondary School Admission Test Board. Endowment: $7 million. Total enrollment: 574. Upper school average class size: 16.

Upper school faculty-student ratio: 1:8. There are 165 required school days per year for Upper School students. Upper School students typically attend 5 days per week. The average school day consists of 7 hours.

Upper School Student Profile Grade 9: 87 students (41 boys, 46 girls); Grade 10: 85 students (42 boys, 43 girls); Grade 11: 80 students (43 boys, 37 girls); Grade 12: 88 students (43 boys, 45 girls).

Faculty School total: 69. In upper school: 26 men, 43 women; 54 have advanced degrees.

Subjects Offered 3-dimensional art, advanced chemistry, Advanced Placement courses, African-American literature, algebra, American history, American literature, ancient history, art, astronomy, biology, calculus, calculus-AP, ceramics, chemistry, Chinese, Chinese studies, chorus, community service, creative writing, discrete mathematics, drama, drawing, economics, economics and history, English, English literature, ethics, European history, expository writing, fine arts, French, geometry, government, health, history, jazz, journalism, Latin, mathematics, music, orchestra, painting, photography, physical education, physical science, physics, science, social studies, Spanish, theater, trigonometry, world history, world literature, writing.

Graduation Requirements Arts and fine arts (art, music, dance, drama), English, foreign language, mathematics, physical education (includes health), science, social studies (includes history), senior project. Community service is required.

Special Academic Programs Advanced Placement exam preparation; honors section; independent study; programs in English, mathematics for dyslexic students; special instructional classes for blind students.

College Admission Counseling 74 students graduated in 2014; all went to college, including Brown University; Johns Hopkins University; Michigan State University; Stanford University; The College of Wooster; University of Michigan. Mean SAT critical reading: 645, mean SAT math: 650, mean SAT writing: 653, mean combined SAT: 1948, mean composite ACT: 28.

Student Life Upper grades have specified standards of dress, student council, honor system. Discipline rests equally with students and faculty.

Tuition and Aid Day student tuition: $21,120. Tuition installment plan (SMART Tuition Payment Plan, monthly payment plans). Need-based scholarship grants available. In 2014–15, 18% of upper-school students received aid. Total amount of financial aid awarded in 2014–15: $10,011,500.

Admissions Traditional secondary-level entrance grade is 9. For fall 2014, 87 students applied for upper-level admission, 49 were accepted, 34 enrolled. SSAT or TOEFL required. Deadline for receipt of application materials: none. Application fee required: $50. Interview required.

Athletics Interscholastic: baseball (boys), basketball (b,g), cross country running (b,g), field hockey (g), golf (b,g), ice hockey (b), lacrosse (b), soccer (b,g), softball (g), tennis (b,g), track and field (b,g), volleyball (g); intramural: basketball (b,g), cross-country running (b,g), field hockey (g), soccer (b,g); coed interscholastic: swimming and diving; coed intramural: hiking/backpacking, horseback riding, outdoor activities, outdoor education, physical fitness. 3 PE instructors, 36 coaches, 1 athletic trainer.

Computers Computers are regularly used in all academic classes. Computer network features include on-campus library services, online commercial services, Internet access, wireless campus network, Internet filtering or blocking technology. Campus intranet, student e-mail accounts, and computer access in designated common areas are available to students. Students grades are available online. The school has a published electronic and media policy.

Contact Betsy Ellsworth, Director of Admission and Financial Aid. 734-205-4061. Fax: 734-205-4056. E-mail: admission@greenhillsschool.org. Website: www.greenhillsschool.org

GREEN MEADOW WALDORF SCHOOL

307 Hungry Hollow Road
Chestnut Ridge, New York 10977

Head of School: Bill Pernice

General Information Coeducational day college-preparatory, general academic, and arts school. Grades N–12. Founded: 1950. Setting: suburban. Nearest major city is New York. 11-acre campus. 3 buildings on campus. Approved or accredited by Association of Waldorf Schools of North America, New York State Association of Independent Schools, and New York Department of Education. Total enrollment: 375. Upper school average class size: 25. Upper school faculty-student ratio: 1:9. There are 171 required school days per year for Upper School students. Upper School students typically attend 5 days per week. The average school day consists of 7 hours.

Upper School Student Profile Grade 9: 21 students (8 boys, 13 girls); Grade 10: 24 students (12 boys, 12 girls); Grade 11: 25 students (9 boys, 16 girls); Grade 12: 30 students (11 boys, 19 girls).

Faculty School total: 60. In upper school: 8 men, 12 women; 11 have advanced degrees.

Subjects Offered 20th century American writers, 20th century history, 20th century physics, 20th century world history, 3-dimensional art, 3-dimensional design, ACT preparation, acting, adolescent issues, African American history, African history, African literature, African-American history, African-American literature, agriculture, algebra, American Civil War, American government, American history, American literature, analytic geometry, anatomy, anatomy and physiology, ancient history, ancient world history, ancient/medieval philosophy, applied arts, applied music, architecture,

art, art history, arts, Bible studies, biology, botany, calculus, chemistry, computer math, computer science, creative writing, dance, drama, earth science, English, English literature, ethics, European history, expository writing, fine arts, French, geography, geology, geometry, German, government/civics, grammar, health, history, history of ideas, history of science, logic, marine biology, mathematics, music, orchestra, philosophy, physical education, physics, physiology, poetry, Russian literature, science, sculpture, social studies, Spanish, speech, theater, trigonometry, woodworking, world history, world literature, writing, zoology.

Graduation Requirements Arts and fine arts (art, music, dance, drama), English, foreign language, mathematics, physical education (includes health), science, social studies (includes history).

Special Academic Programs Independent study; term-away projects; study abroad; remedial reading and/or remedial writing; remedial math; programs in English, general development for dyslexic students; ESL (12 students enrolled).

College Admission Counseling 22 students graduated in 2015; 20 went to college, including Brandeis University; Cornell University; Eugene Lang College of Liberal Arts; Fordham University; Hampshire College; Northeastern University. Other: 1 went to work, 1 entered military service. 31% scored over 600 on SAT critical reading, 27% scored over 600 on SAT math.

Student Life Upper grades have specified standards of dress, student council, honor system. Discipline rests primarily with faculty.

Tuition and Aid Day student tuition: $23,100. Guaranteed tuition plan. Tuition installment plan (Insured Tuition Payment Plan, monthly payment plans). Tuition reduction for siblings, need-based scholarship grants available. In 2015–16, 35% of upper-school students received aid.

Admissions Traditional secondary-level entrance grade is 9. Deadline for receipt of application materials: none. Application fee required: $50. Interview required.

Athletics Interscholastic: baseball (boys), basketball (b,g), running (g), softball (g), tennis (g), volleyball (g); intramural: basketball (b,g); coed interscholastic: Circus, cooperative games, cross-country running, equestrian sports, horseback riding, outdoor activities, outdoor adventure, outdoor education, outdoor recreation, outdoor skills, outdoors, physical fitness, running, tennis, volleyball, wilderness, wilderness survival; coed intramural: cooperative games, cross-country running, running, volleyball. 2 PE instructors, 5 coaches.

Computers Computers are regularly used in mathematics classes. Computer resources include Internet access, wireless campus network, Internet filtering or blocking technology. Computer access in designated common areas is available to students. Students grades are available online. The school has a published electronic and media policy.

Contact Melissa McDonagh, Director of Admissions, Grades 1-12. 845-356-2514 Ext. 302. Fax: 845-371-2358. E-mail: mmcdonagh@gmws.org. Website: www.gmws.org

GRIER SCHOOL

PO Box 308
Tyrone, Pennsylvania 16686-0308

Head of School: Mrs. Gina Borst

General Information Girls' boarding and day college-preparatory, arts, and business school. Boarding grades 7–PG, day grades 7–12. Founded: 1853. Setting: rural. Nearest major city is Pittsburgh. Students are housed in single-sex dormitories. 320-acre campus. 6 buildings on campus. Approved or accredited by Middle States Association of Colleges and Schools, Pennsylvania Association of Independent Schools, and The Association of Boarding Schools. Member of National Association of Independent Schools and Secondary School Admission Test Board. Endowment: $20 million. Total enrollment: 309. Upper school average class size: 10. Upper school faculty-student ratio: 1:7. There are 160 required school days per year for Upper School students. Upper School students typically attend 5 days per week. The average school day consists of 7 hours.

Upper School Student Profile Grade 7: 16 students (16 girls); Grade 8: 34 students (34 girls); Grade 9: 53 students (53 girls); Grade 10: 78 students (78 girls); Grade 11: 67 students (67 girls); Grade 12: 61 students (61 girls). 85% of students are boarding students. 20% are state residents. 19 states are represented in upper school student body. 50% are international students. International students from China, Germany, Mexico, Republic of Korea, Russian Federation, and Viet Nam; 10 other countries represented in student body.

Faculty School total: 63. In upper school: 18 men, 45 women; 37 have advanced degrees; 19 reside on campus.

Subjects Offered 3-dimensional art, acting, advanced biology, advanced chemistry, advanced studio art-AP, advanced TOEFL/grammar, algebra, American history, American history-AP, American literature, anatomy, art, art history-AP, art-AP, ballet, ballet technique, batik, biology, biology-AP, British literature, British literature (honors), Broadway dance, calculus, calculus-AP, ceramics, chemistry, chemistry-AP, Chinese, choir, choral music, choreography, civics, community service, comparative religion, computer graphics, computer math, computer programming, computer-aided design, costumes and make-up, creative writing, criminology, current events, dance, desktop publishing, digital art, digital photography, directing, drama, drama performance, dramatic arts, drawing, earth science, ecology, economics, economics-AP, English, English as a foreign language, English literature, English literature and composition-AP, English literature-AP, environmental science, environmental science-AP, equine science, ESL, European history, European history-AP, fabric arts, fashion, fiber arts, filmmaking, finance, fine arts, French, French language-AP, French-AP, geography, geometry, government, government/civics, government/civics-AP, graphic arts, guitar, health, health and wellness, history, honors algebra, honors English, honors geometry, honors U.S. history, honors world history, human anatomy, human biology, instrumental music, international relations, jazz band, jazz dance, journalism, linguistics, macro/microeconomics-AP, macroeconomics-AP, marine biology, mathematics, microeconomics-AP, model United Nations, modern dance, music, music technology, music theater, music theory, music theory-AP, musical theater, musical theater dance, newspaper, oil painting, painting, personal finance, philosophy, photography, physical education, physics, physics-AP, physiology, piano, portfolio art, pre-algebra, pre-calculus, printmaking, probability and statistics, psychology, psychology-AP, science, scuba diving, social studies, Spanish, Spanish language-AP, stagecraft, statistics-AP, studio art-AP, symphonic band, tap dance, theater, TOEFL preparation, trigonometry, typing, video film production, vocal ensemble, voice, weaving, women's studies, world history, world history-AP, world literature, writing, writing, writing workshop, yearbook.

Graduation Requirements Arts and fine arts (art, music, dance, drama), English, foreign language, mathematics, physical education (includes health), science, social sciences, social studies (includes history).

Special Academic Programs 20 Advanced Placement exams for which test preparation is offered; honors section; independent study; study abroad; academic accommodation for the gifted, the musically talented, and the artistically talented; remedial reading and/or remedial writing; remedial math; programs in English, general development for dyslexic students; special instructional classes for students with learning disabilities, Attention Deficit Disorder, and dyslexia; ESL (60 students enrolled).

College Admission Counseling 76 students graduated in 2015; 75 went to college, including Boston University; Grinnell College; New York University; Penn State University Park; The University of Arizona; University of Wisconsin–Madison. Other: 1 had other specific plans. Median SAT critical reading: 600, median SAT math: 640. 25% scored over 600 on SAT critical reading, 20% scored over 600 on SAT math.

Student Life Upper grades have specified standards of dress, student council, honor system. Discipline rests primarily with faculty.

Summer Programs Enrichment, ESL, sports, art/fine arts programs offered; session focuses on recreation and ESL; held on campus; accepts girls; open to students from other schools. 100 students usually enrolled. 2016 schedule: June 26 to September 7. Application deadline: none.

Tuition and Aid Day student tuition: $18,000; 7-day tuition and room/board: $50,500. Tuition installment plan (individually arranged payment plans). Tuition reduction for siblings, merit scholarship grants, need-based scholarship grants, need-based loans, paying campus jobs available. In 2015–16, 51% of upper-school students received aid; total upper-school merit-scholarship money awarded: $800,000. Total amount of financial aid awarded in 2015–16: $2,000,000.

Admissions Traditional secondary-level entrance grade is 9. For fall 2015, 320 students applied for upper-level admission, 200 were accepted, 140 enrolled. SSAT or WISC III required. Deadline for receipt of application materials: none. Application fee required: $50. Interview recommended.

Athletics Interscholastic: basketball, dance, equestrian sports, fencing, skiing (downhill), soccer, tennis, volleyball; intramural: aerobics, aerobics/dance, alpine skiing, aquatics, archery, badminton, ballet, basketball, bicycling, bowling, canoeing/kayaking, cheering, cross-country running, dance, dressage, equestrian sports, fencing, figure skating, fitness, fitness walking, fly fishing, golf, gymnastics, hiking/backpacking, horseback riding, jogging, jump rope, kayaking, martial arts, modern dance, mountain biking, nordic skiing, outdoor adventure, outdoor recreation, paddle tennis, physical fitness, physical training, ropes courses, running, scuba diving, skiing (cross-country), skiing (downhill), snowboarding, soccer, swimming and diving, tennis, volleyball, walking, weight training, yoga. 3 PE instructors, 3 coaches, 3 athletic trainers.

Computers Computers are regularly used in creative writing, English, foreign language, graphic arts, mathematics, music technology, newspaper, science, yearbook classes. Computer network features include on-campus library services, online commercial services, Internet access, wireless campus network, Internet filtering or blocking technology. Campus intranet and student e-mail accounts are available to students. Students grades are available online. The school has a published electronic and media policy.

Contact Mrs. Jennifer D. Neely, Admissions Director. 814-684-3000 Ext. 7006. Fax: 814-684-2177. E-mail: admissions@grier.org. Website: www.grier.org

See Display below and Close-Up on page 598.

GRIGGS INTERNATIONAL ACADEMY

12501 Old Columbia Pike
Silver Spring, Maryland 20904-6600

Head of School: Ms. LaRonda Forsey

General Information Coeducational day and distance learning college-preparatory, general academic, and religious studies school, affiliated with Seventh-day Adventist Church. Grades PK–PG. Distance learning grades K–12. Founded: 1909. Setting: suburban. Nearest major city is Washington, DC. 1 building on campus. Approved or accredited by Board of Regents, General Conference of Seventh-day Adventists, CITA (Commission on International and Trans-Regional Accreditation), Distance Education Accrediting Commission, Middle States Association of Colleges and Schools, Southern

GRIER school | grades 7-12
summer camps | ages 6-17

A boarding school for girls in grades 7-12 that features a diverse student body and a comprehensive college preparatory curriculum offering both academic rigor and learning support

admissions@grier.org | www.grier.org | 814.684.3000

Association of Colleges and Schools, and Maryland Department of Education. Total enrollment: 1,559. Upper school faculty-student ratio: 1:21.

Upper School Student Profile 60% of students are Seventh-day Adventists.

Faculty School total: 30. In upper school: 7 men, 19 women; 24 have advanced degrees.

Subjects Offered Accounting, algebra, American government, American history, American literature, art appreciation, art history, arts, Bible studies, biology, business skills, chemistry, digital photography, earth science, English, English literature, fine arts, food science, French, geography, geometry, government/civics, health, Holocaust, home economics, keyboarding, mathematics, Microsoft, music appreciation, physical education, physical science, physics, pre-algebra, science, social studies, Spanish, word processing, world history, writing.

Graduation Requirements American government, arts and fine arts (art, music, dance, drama), English, health, history, keyboarding, language, mathematics, physical education (includes health), religion (includes Bible studies and theology), science, social studies (includes history), requirements for standard diploma differ. Community service is required.

Special Academic Programs Accelerated programs; independent study; study at local college for college credit.

College Admission Counseling 422 students graduated in 2015; they went to Andrews University; Loma Linda University; Southern Adventist University; Towson University; University of Maryland, Baltimore County; Washington Adventist University.

Student Life Upper grades have honor system. Discipline rests primarily with faculty.

Summer Programs Remediation, enrichment programs offered; held on campus; accepts boys and girls; open to students from other schools.

Tuition and Aid Day student tuition: $2000–$3000. Tuition installment plan (monthly payment plans, individually arranged payment plans).

Admissions Stanford Achievement Test required. Deadline for receipt of application materials: none. Application fee required: $100.

Computers Computers are regularly used in computer applications, keyboarding, word processing classes. Students grades are available online.

Contact Ms. Gabriela Melgar, Enrollment Coordinator. 269-471-6529. Fax: 301-680-5157. E-mail: enrollgia@andrews.edu. Website: www.griggs.edu

GROTON SCHOOL

Box 991
Farmers Row
Groton, Massachusetts 01450

Head of School: Temba B. Maqubela

General Information Coeducational boarding and day college preparatory, arts, and religious studies school, affiliated with Episcopal Church. Grades 8–12. Founded: 1884. Setting: rural. Nearest major city is Boston. Students are housed in single-sex dormitories. 410-acre campus. 17 buildings on campus. Approved or accredited by Association of Independent Schools in New England, New England Association of Schools and Colleges, and The Association of Boarding Schools. Member of National Association of Independent Schools and Secondary School Admission Test Board. Endowment: $350 million. Total enrollment: 380. Upper school average class size: 12. Upper school faculty-student ratio: 1:5. There are 182 required school days per year for Upper School students. Upper School students typically attend 6 days per week. The average school day consists of 6 hours and 30 minutes.

Upper School Student Profile Grade 8: 26 students (15 boys, 11 girls); Grade 9: 84 students (43 boys, 41 girls); Grade 10: 94 students (52 boys, 42 girls); Grade 11: 92 students (44 boys, 48 girls); Grade 12: 84 students (40 boys, 44 girls). 84% of students are boarding students. 32% are state residents. 33 states are represented in upper school student body. 15% are international students. International students from Canada, China, Hong Kong, Mexico, Republic of Korea, and South Africa; 11 other countries represented in student body.

Faculty School total: 69. In upper school: 40 men, 29 women; 52 have advanced degrees; 58 reside on campus.

Subjects Offered Advanced chemistry, advanced math, Advanced Placement courses, algebra, American literature, American literature-AP, analytic geometry, Ancient Greek, ancient world history, archaeology, art, art history, art history-AP, Bible studies, biology, biology-AP, botany, Buddhism, calculus, calculus-AP, cell biology, Central and Eastern European history, ceramics, chemistry, chemistry-AP, Chinese, choir, choral music, civil rights, Civil War, civil war history, classical Greek literature, classical language, classics, composition, composition-AP, creative writing, dance, discrete mathematics, drawing, earth science, ecology, environmental systems, economics, English, English composition, English-AP, environmental science, environmental science-AP, environmental studies, ethics, ethics and responsibility, European history, European history-AP, expository writing, fine arts, fractal geometry, French, French language-AP, French literature-AP, geography, geometry, government, grammar, Greek, health, history, Holocaust, honors algebra, honors English, honors geometry, honors U.S. history, honors world history, independent study, lab science, language-AP, Latin, Latin-AP, linear algebra, literature, literature and composition-AP, mathematics, mathematics-AP, modern European history, modern European history-AP, modern history, modern languages, modern world history, music, music history, music

theory, music theory-AP, organic biochemistry, painting, philosophy, photo shop, photography, physical science, physics, physics-AP, pre-algebra, pre-calculus, psychology, religion, religious education, religious studies, science, Shakespeare, social sciences, Spanish, Spanish language-AP, Spanish literature, Spanish literature-AP, sports medicine, statistics, studio art, studio art-AP, theology, trigonometry, U.S. constitutional history, U.S. government, U.S. government and politics, U.S. government and politics-AP, U.S. history, U.S. history-AP, vocal music, Western civilization, wood lab, woodworking, world history, world history-AP, writing.

Graduation Requirements Arts and fine arts (art, music, dance, drama), classical language, English, foreign language, mathematics, religious studies, science, social studies (includes history).

Special Academic Programs 13 Advanced Placement exams for which test preparation is offered; honors section; term-away projects; study abroad; academic accommodation for the gifted, the musically talented, and the artistically talented.

College Admission Counseling 88 students graduated in 2015; 86 went to college, including Bowdoin College; Brown University; Dartmouth College; Georgetown University; Harvard University; Yale University. Other: 2 had other specific plans. Median SAT critical reading: 710, median SAT math: 700, median SAT writing: 710, median combined SAT: 2110, median composite ACT: 31. 87% scored over 600 on SAT critical reading, 91% scored over 600 on SAT math, 92% scored over 600 on SAT writing, 92% scored over 1800 on combined SAT, 86% scored over 26 on composite ACT.

Student Life Upper grades have specified standards of dress, student council, honor system. Discipline rests equally with students and faculty. Attendance at religious services is required.

Tuition and Aid Day student tuition: $43,990; 7-day tuition and room/board: $56,700. Tuition installment plan (Insured Tuition Payment Plan, Key Tuition Payment Plan, monthly payment plans, individually arranged payment plans). Need-based scholarship grants, Key Education Resources available. In 2015–16, 39% of upper-school students received aid. Total amount of financial aid awarded in 2015–16: $6,200,000.

Admissions Traditional secondary-level entrance grade is 9. For fall 2015, 1,560 students applied for upper-level admission, 158 were accepted, 98 enrolled. ISEE, SSAT or TOEFL required. Deadline for receipt of application materials: January 15. Application fee required: $50. Interview required.

Athletics Interscholastic: baseball (boys), basketball (b,g), crew (b,g), cross-country running (b,g), field hockey (g), Fives (b,g), football (b), hockey (b,g), ice hockey (b,g), lacrosse (b,g), rowing (b,g), soccer (b,g), squash (b,g), tennis (b,g); intramural: self defense (g), weight training (b,g); coed intramural: aerobics/dance, alpine skiing, dance, fitness, Fives, Frisbee, golf, ice skating, modern dance, nordic skiing, outdoor activities, physical training, running, skeet shooting, skiing (cross-country), skiing (downhill), snowboarding, strength & conditioning, swimming and diving, track and field, trap and skeet, ultimate Frisbee, yoga. 2 coaches, 1 athletic trainer.

Computers Computers are regularly used in all academic classes. Computer network features include on-campus library services, Internet access, wireless campus network, Internet filtering or blocking technology, campus-wide wireless environment. Campus intranet and student e-mail accounts are available to students. Students grades are available online. The school has a published electronic and media policy.

Contact Mr. Ian Gracey, Director of Admission. 978-448-7510. Fax: 978-448-9623. E-mail: igracey@groton.org. Website: www.groton.org

GUAMANI PRIVATE SCHOOL

PO Box 3000
Guayama, Puerto Rico 00785

Head of School: Mr. Eduardo Delgado

General Information Coeducational day college-preparatory and bilingual studies school. Grades 1–12. Founded: 1914. Setting: urban. Nearest major city is Caguas. 1-acre campus. 1 building on campus. Approved or accredited by Middle States Association of Colleges and Schools, National Catholic Education Association, and Puerto Rico Department of Education. Total enrollment: 606. Upper school average class size: 20. Upper school faculty-student ratio: 1:13.

Faculty School total: 32. In upper school: 10 men, 10 women; 3 have advanced degrees.

Subjects Offered Advanced math, Advanced Placement courses, algebra, American government, American history, analysis and differential calculus, chemistry, civics, pre-algebra, pre-calculus, science project, science research, social sciences, social studies, sociology, Spanish, Spanish language-AP, U.S. literature, visual arts, world geography, world history.

Graduation Requirements Mathematics, science, social sciences, Spanish, acceptance into a college or university. Community service is required.

Special Academic Programs Advanced Placement exam preparation; honors section; independent study.

College Admission Counseling 23 students graduated in 2015; they went to Embry-Riddle Aeronautical University–Daytona; Syracuse University; University of Puerto Rico, Mayagüez Campus; University of Puerto Rico, Río Piedras Campus; University of Puerto Rico in Cayey. Other: 23 entered a postgraduate year.

Student Life Upper grades have uniform requirement, student council, honor system. Discipline rests primarily with faculty.

Summer Programs Remediation, ESL programs offered; held on campus; accepts boys and girls; open to students from other schools. 30 students usually enrolled. 2016 schedule: June 1 to June 30. Application deadline: May 27.

Admissions Traditional secondary-level entrance grade is 9. For fall 2015, 30 students applied for upper-level admission, 21 were accepted, 20 enrolled. School's own test or Test of Achievement and Proficiency required. Deadline for receipt of application materials: none. Application fee required: $30. Interview required.

Athletics Interscholastic: aerobics/dance (girls), basketball (b,g), cheering (g), dance squad (g), volleyball (b,g); coed interscholastic: dance team. 3 PE instructors, 2 coaches.

Computers Computers are regularly used in aviation, English, mathematics, science, social sciences, Spanish, word processing classes. Computer resources include on-campus library services, Internet access, wireless campus network, Internet filtering or blocking technology. The school has a published electronic and media policy.

Contact Mrs. Digna Torres, Secretary. 787-864-6880. Fax: 787-866-4947. Website: www.guamani.com

GULLIVER PREPARATORY SCHOOL

6575 North Kendall Drive
Miami, Florida 33156

Head of School: Mr. Frank Steel

General Information Coeducational day college-preparatory, arts, business, technology, International Baccalaureate, architectural design, and pre-engineering, law and litigation, Biomedical sciences school. Grades PK–12. Founded: 1926. Setting: suburban. 14-acre campus. 11 buildings on campus. Approved or accredited by CITA (Commission on International and Trans-Regional Accreditation), Florida Council of Independent Schools, Southern Association of Colleges and Schools, Southern Association of Independent Schools, and Florida Department of Education. Member of National Association of Independent Schools and Secondary School Admission Test Board. Total enrollment: 2,014. Upper school average class size: 14. Upper school faculty-student ratio: 1:8. There are 172 required school days per year for Upper School students. Upper School students typically attend 5 days per week. The average school day consists of 7 hours and 5 minutes.

Upper School Student Profile Grade 6: 168 students (97 boys, 71 girls); Grade 7: 171 students (95 boys, 76 girls); Grade 8: 157 students (83 boys, 74 girls); Grade 9: 215 students (113 boys, 102 girls); Grade 10: 245 students (122 boys, 123 girls); Grade 11: 278 students (145 boys, 133 girls); Grade 12: 248 students (125 boys, 123 girls).

Faculty School total: 102. In upper school: 49 men, 53 women; 71 have advanced degrees.

Subjects Offered Algebra, American history, American literature, anatomy, architectural drawing, architecture, art, art history, biology, calculus, ceramics, chemistry, college admission preparation, college writing, computer animation, computer applications, computer processing, computer programming, computer programming-AP, computer science, computer science-AP, computer skills, computer studies, concert band, concert choir, creative writing, dance, desktop publishing, drafting, drama, economics, engineering, English, English literature, European history, fine arts, French, geometry, government/civics, history, Italian, keyboarding, Latin, marine biology, mathematics, mechanical drawing, music, newspaper, physical education, physics, psychology, science, social studies, Spanish, speech, statistics, theater, trigonometry, video, world history, world literature, yearbook, zoology.

Graduation Requirements Arts and fine arts (art, music, dance, drama), computer science, English, foreign language, mathematics, physical education (includes health), science, social studies (includes history). Community service is required.

Special Academic Programs International Baccalaureate program; Advanced Placement exam preparation; honors section; study at local college for college credit; academic accommodation for the gifted, the musically talented, and the artistically talented.

College Admission Counseling 180 students graduated in 2015; all went to college, including Boston University; Florida International University; New York University; The George Washington University; University of Florida; University of Miami. Median SAT critical reading: 564, median SAT math: 579, median SAT writing: 573, median combined SAT: 1716, median composite ACT: 25. 29% scored over 600 on SAT critical reading, 39% scored over 600 on SAT math, 35% scored over 600 on SAT writing, 36% scored over 1800 on combined SAT, 24% scored over 26 on composite ACT.

Student Life Upper grades have specified standards of dress, student council, honor system. Discipline rests primarily with faculty.

Summer Programs Remediation, enrichment, advancement, sports, art/fine arts, rigorous outdoor training, computer instruction programs offered; session focuses on enrichment and reinforcement; held on campus; accepts boys and girls; not open to students from other schools. 189 students usually enrolled. 2016 schedule: June 6 to July 15. Application deadline: May 13.

Tuition and Aid Day student tuition: $14,030–$31,030. Tuition installment plan (monthly payment plans, school's own tuition recovery plan). Tuition reduction for siblings, need-based scholarship grants, application and matriculation fee waived for children of alumni available.

Admissions Traditional secondary-level entrance grade is 9. For fall 2015, 340 students applied for upper-level admission, 242 were accepted, 134 enrolled. School's own exam and SSAT required. Deadline for receipt of application materials: February 23. Application fee required: $100. Interview recommended.

Athletics Interscholastic: aerobics/Nautilus (girls), baseball (b), basketball (b,g), cross-country running (b,g), dance (g), dance squad (g), dance team (g), diving (b,g), football (b), golf (b,g), gymnastics (b,g), lacrosse (b), physical training (b,g), running (b,g), soccer (b,g), softball (g), swimming and diving (b,g), tennis (b,g), track and field (b,g), volleyball (g), water polo (b,g); intramural: boxing (b,g), weight training (b,g); coed interscholastic: aerobics, bowling, cheering, modern dance, yoga; coed intramural: aerobics/dance, aerobics/Nautilus, badminton, dance, dance squad, dance team, fitness, flag football, Frisbee, kickball, modern dance, netball, physical fitness, running, strength & conditioning, touch football, yoga. 4 PE instructors, 68 coaches, 3 athletic trainers.

Computers Computers are regularly used in architecture, art, college planning, drafting, English, graphic arts, graphic design, keyboarding, newspaper, programming, science, technology, word processing, yearbook classes. Computer network features include on-campus library services, online commercial services, Internet access, wireless campus network, Internet filtering or blocking technology, modified laptop program, SmartBoards and Audio enhancement systems. Students grades are available online. The school has a published electronic and media policy.

Contact Carol A. Bowen, Director of Admission. 305-666-7937 Ext. 1408. Fax: 305-665-3791. E-mail: bowc@gulliverschools.org. Website: www.gulliverschools.org

THE GUNNERY

99 Green Hill Road
Washington, Connecticut 06793

Head of School: Peter W.E. Becker

General Information Coeducational boarding and day college-preparatory, arts, and technology school. Boarding grades 9–PG, day grades 9–12. Founded: 1850. Setting: rural. Nearest major city is Hartford. Students are housed in single-sex dormitories. 220-acre campus. 27 buildings on campus. Approved or accredited by National Commission of Accreditation of Special Education Services, New England Association of Schools and Colleges, The Association of Boarding Schools, and Connecticut Department of Education. Member of National Association of Independent Schools and Secondary School Admission Test Board. Endowment: $22 million. Total enrollment: 287. Upper school average class size: 12. Upper school faculty-student ratio: 1:6. Upper School students typically attend 6 days per week.

Upper School Student Profile Grade 9: 40 students (24 boys, 16 girls); Grade 10: 72 students (41 boys, 31 girls); Grade 11: 94 students (62 boys, 32 girls); Grade 12: 79 students (50 boys, 29 girls); Postgraduate: 5 students (3 boys, 2 girls). 70% of students are boarding students. 50% are state residents. 19 states are represented in upper school student body. 20% are international students. International students from China, China, France, Germany, Japan, and Taiwan; 19 other countries represented in student body.

Faculty School total: 57. In upper school: 32 men, 23 women; 39 have advanced degrees; 50 reside on campus.

Subjects Offered Advanced chemistry, algebra, American history, American history-AP, American literature, anatomy, art, art history, biology, calculus, ceramics, chemistry, computer graphics, computer math, computer programming, computer science, creative writing, drama, drawing, earth science, economics, economics-AP, English, English language-AP, English literature, English literature-AP, environmental science, environmental studies, ESL, ethics, ethics and responsibility, European history, European history-AP, expository writing, fine arts, French, geometry, government/civics, grammar, health, history, history of rock and roll, honors algebra, honors English, honors geometry, human development, instruments, marine biology, mathematics, modern European history-AP, music, music composition, mythology, painting, photography, physical education, physical science, physics, physics-AP, physiology, political science, pottery, pre-calculus, psychology, public speaking, science, social studies, sociology, Spanish, Spanish language-AP, Spanish literature-AP, speech, studio art, theater, trigonometry, U.S. history-AP, values and decisions, voice, world history, world literature, writing.

Graduation Requirements Arts and fine arts (art, music, dance, drama), English, ethics and responsibility, foreign language, history, human development, mathematics, physical education (includes health), public speaking, science, speech, senior Capstone—30 hours of community service.

Special Academic Programs Advanced Placement exam preparation; honors section; independent study; term-away projects; study abroad; academic accommodation for the gifted, the musically talented, and the artistically talented; ESL (5 students enrolled).

College Admission Counseling 84 students graduated in 2015; 82 went to college, including Boston University; Hobart and William Smith Colleges; New York University; Northeastern University; United States Naval Academy; University of Wisconsin–Madison. Other: 2 had other specific plans.

Student Life Upper grades have specified standards of dress, student council, honor system. Discipline rests equally with students and faculty.

Summer Programs Sports programs offered; held both on and off campus; held at Lake Waramaug; accepts boys and girls; open to students from other schools. 40 students usually enrolled. 2016 schedule: July 1 to August 15. Application deadline: March 15.

Tuition and Aid Day student tuition: $38,500; 7-day tuition and room/board: $51,200. Tuition installment plan (Insured Tuition Payment Plan, monthly payment plans). Merit scholarship grants, need-based scholarship grants, need-based loans available. In 2015–16, 45% of upper-school students received aid. Total amount of financial aid awarded in 2015–16: $3,500,000.

Admissions Traditional secondary-level entrance grade is 9. For fall 2015, 575 students applied for upper-level admission, 330 were accepted, 109 enrolled. ACT, PSAT or SAT or SSAT required. Deadline for receipt of application materials: January 31. Application fee required: $50. On-campus interview required.

Athletics Interscholastic: baseball (boys), basketball (b,g), crew (b,g), cross-country running (b,g), field hockey (g), football (b), ice hockey (b,g), lacrosse (b,g), skiing (downhill) (b,g), soccer (b,g), softball (g), strength & conditioning (b,g), tennis (b,g); intramural: yoga (g); coed interscholastic: alpine skiing, Frisbee, golf; coed intramural: dance team, fitness, outdoor education, ultimate Frisbee. 2 coaches, 1 athletic trainer.

Computers Computers are regularly used in art, English, foreign language, history, mathematics, music, science classes. Computer network features include on-campus library services, Internet access, wireless campus network. Campus intranet and student e-mail accounts are available to students. Students grades are available online. The school has a published electronic and media policy.

Contact Sara Lynn Levenworth, Director of Admissions. 860-868-7334. Fax: 860-868-1614. E-mail: admissions@gunnery.org. Website: www.gunnery.org

THE GUNSTON SCHOOL

911 Gunston Road
PO Box 200
Centreville, Maryland 21617

Head of School: Mr. John A. Lewis, IV

General Information Coeducational day college-preparatory, arts, and technology school. Grades 9–12. Founded: 1911. Setting: rural. Nearest major city is Annapolis. 32-acre campus. 4 buildings on campus. Approved or accredited by Association of Independent Maryland Schools and Maryland Department of Education. Member of National Association of Independent Schools and Secondary School Admission Test Board. Endowment: $1 million. Total enrollment: 182. Upper school average class size: 10. Upper school faculty-student ratio: 1:6. There are 170 required school days per year for Upper School students. Upper School students typically attend 5 days per week. The average school day consists of 8 hours.

Upper School Student Profile Grade 9: 51 students (23 boys, 28 girls); Grade 10: 45 students (27 boys, 18 girls); Grade 11: 47 students (27 boys, 20 girls); Grade 12: 39 students (18 boys, 21 girls).

Faculty School total: 23. In upper school: 12 men, 11 women; 14 have advanced degrees.

Subjects Offered Advanced biology, advanced chemistry, advanced math, Advanced Placement courses, advanced studio art-AP, algebra, American government, American history, American literature, anatomy and physiology, ancient history, applied arts, art, art history, art history-AP, biology, biology-AP, British literature, British literature (honors), calculus, calculus-AP, calligraphy, ceramics, chemistry, chemistry-AP, Chesapeake Bay studies, Chinese literature, chorus, college counseling, college placement, college planning, community service, computer applications, computer science, digital photography, drama performance, economics, English, English as a foreign language, English literature, environmental science, environmental science-AP, ethical decision making, ethics, European history-AP, fine arts, fitness, freshman seminar, geometry, golf, government, government-AP, government/civics, health, health and wellness, history, history-AP, honors algebra, honors English, honors geometry, ideas, lab science, Latin, Latin-AP, mathematics, mathematics-AP, medieval history, Microsoft, music, music appreciation, music composition, music theory, painting, performing arts, photography, physics, physics-AP, play production, poetry, pottery, pre-calculus, pre-college orientation, printmaking, psychology, SAT preparation, SAT/ACT preparation, science, sculpture, senior internship, senior project, senior thesis, short story, silk screening, Spanish, Spanish-AP, sports, studio art, studio art-AP, swimming, tennis, trigonometry, U.S. government, U.S. government and politics-AP, U.S. history, U.S. history-AP, weight training, wellness, woodworking, world history, writing workshop.

Graduation Requirements Arts and fine arts (art, music, dance, drama), athletics, computer science, English, foreign language, history, mathematics, science, social sciences, wellness. Community service is required.

Special Academic Programs 12 Advanced Placement exams for which test preparation is offered; honors section; independent study; term-away projects; study at local college for college credit; study abroad; academic accommodation for the gifted, the musically talented, and the artistically talented; ESL (27 students enrolled).

College Admission Counseling 41 students graduated in 2015; all went to college, including Dickinson College; Lehigh University; St. Mary's College of Maryland; University of Maryland, College Park; Virginia Polytechnic Institute and State University; Washington College. Mean SAT critical reading: 575, mean SAT math: 528, mean SAT writing: 546, mean combined SAT: 1649.

Student Life Upper grades have specified standards of dress, student council, honor system. Discipline rests primarily with faculty.

Summer Programs Enrichment, advancement, sports, computer instruction programs offered; session focuses on student activities for ages 6-18; held on campus; accepts boys and girls; open to students from other schools. 75 students usually enrolled. 2016 schedule: June 13 to August 19. Application deadline: none.

Tuition and Aid Day student tuition: $23,500. Tuition installment plan (monthly payment plans, individually arranged payment plans, Sallie Mae, Tuition Management Solutions). Merit scholarship grants, need-based scholarship grants available. In 2015–16, 70% of upper-school students received aid; total upper-school merit-scholarship money awarded: $12,000. Total amount of financial aid awarded in 2015–16: $1,350,000.

Admissions Traditional secondary-level entrance grade is 9. For fall 2015, 90 students applied for upper-level admission, 86 were accepted, 55 enrolled. ISEE, SSAT or TOEFL or SLEP required. Deadline for receipt of application materials: none. Application fee required: $50. On-campus interview required.

Athletics Interscholastic: basketball (boys, girls), field hockey (g), lacrosse (b,g), soccer (b,g), tennis (b,g); intramural: independent competitive sports (b,g), tennis (b,g); coed interscholastic: crew, sailing, tennis; coed intramural: fitness, independent competitive sports, strength & conditioning, tennis, weight training. 4 coaches.

Computers Computers are regularly used in all academic classes. Computer network features include on-campus library services, Internet access, wireless campus network, Internet filtering or blocking technology. Campus intranet, student e-mail accounts, and computer access in designated common areas are available to students.

Contact David Henry, Director of Admission and Financial Aid. 410-758-0620. Fax: 410-758-0628. E-mail: dhenry@gunston.org. Website: www.gunston.org

HALES FRANCISCAN HIGH SCHOOL

4930 South Cottage Grove Avenue
Chicago, Illinois 60615

Head of School: Mrs. Nichole Jackson

General Information Boys' day college-preparatory, general academic, arts, business, religious studies, and technology school, affiliated with Roman Catholic Church. Grades 9–12. Founded: 1962. Setting: urban. 4-acre campus. 2 buildings on campus. Approved or accredited by National Catholic Education Association, North Central Association of Colleges and Schools, and Illinois Department of Education. Total enrollment: 45. Upper school average class size: 8. Upper school faculty-student ratio: 1:8. Upper School students typically attend 5 days per week. The average school day consists of 7 hours and 15 minutes.

Upper School Student Profile Grade 9: 12 students (12 boys); Grade 10: 11 students (11 boys); Grade 11: 6 students (6 boys); Grade 12: 16 students (16 boys). 100% of students are Roman Catholic.

Faculty School total: 7. In upper school: 7 men; 5 have advanced degrees.

Subjects Offered Advanced computer applications, Advanced Placement courses, African-American history, African-American literature, algebra, American government, American literature, art, Bible studies, biology, biology-AP, business skills, calculus-AP, chemistry, community service, computer science, English, fine arts, geography, health, literature, mathematics, physical education, physics, pre-calculus, religion, SAT/ACT preparation, science, social sciences, social studies, speech, trigonometry, word processing, world history, writing.

Graduation Requirements Arts and fine arts (art, music, dance, drama), business skills (includes word processing), computer science, English, foreign language, mathematics, physical education (includes health), religion (includes Bible studies and theology), science, social sciences, social studies (includes history). Community service is required.

Special Academic Programs International Baccalaureate program; academic accommodation for the gifted.

College Admission Counseling 55 students graduated in 2015; 45 went to college, including Chicago State University; Earlham College; Eastern Michigan University; University of California, Berkeley; University of Chicago; University of Illinois at Urbana–Champaign. Other: 2 went to work, 8 had other specific plans. Median composite ACT: 17. 1% scored over 26 on composite ACT.

Student Life Upper grades have uniform requirement, student council, honor system. Discipline rests equally with students and faculty. Attendance at religious services is required.

Summer Programs Remediation, enrichment, sports, computer instruction programs offered; session focuses on writing, reading, math, and study skills; held on campus; accepts boys; open to students from other schools. 65 students usually enrolled. 2016 schedule: June 21 to August 10. Application deadline: none.

Tuition and Aid Day student tuition: $7500. Tuition installment plan (SMART Tuition Payment Plan, monthly payment plans, individually arranged payment plans). Tuition reduction for siblings, merit scholarship grants, need-based scholarship grants, paying campus jobs available. In 2015–16, 95% of upper-school students received aid; total upper-school merit-scholarship money awarded: $25,000. Total amount of financial aid awarded in 2015–16: $1,500,000.

Admissions Traditional secondary-level entrance grade is 9. For fall 2015, 45 students applied for upper-level admission, 20 were accepted, 12 enrolled. Academic Profile Tests and TerraNova required. Deadline for receipt of application materials: none. No application fee required. On-campus interview required.

Athletics Interscholastic: baseball, basketball, football, indoor track, indoor track & field, strength & conditioning, track and field, weight lifting, weight training; intramural: basketball, flag football, strength & conditioning, touch football, weight lifting, weight training; coed interscholastic: cheering. 1 PE instructor, 19 coaches, 1 athletic trainer.

Computers Computers are regularly used in basic skills, business education, business skills, introduction to technology, library skills, publications classes. Computer network features include on-campus library services, online commercial services, Internet access, wireless campus network. Student e-mail accounts are available to students. Students grades are available online.

Contact Mr. Daniel Szymanski, Business Manager. 773-285-8400. Fax: 773-285-7025. E-mail: daniel.szymanski@halesfranciscan.org. Website: www.halesfranciscanhs.org

HALSTROM ACADEMY

8484 Wilshire Blvd., Ste. 220
Beverly Hills, California 90211

Head of School: Ms. Chanel Grant

General Information Coeducational day and distance learning college-preparatory and general academic school; primarily serves underachievers, students with learning disabilities, individuals with Attention Deficit Disorder, dyslexic students, Mild learning disabilities, and Social anxiety. Grades 6–12. Distance learning grades 6–12. Founded: 1985. Setting: urban. Nearest major city is Los Angeles. 1 building on campus. Approved or accredited by Western Association of Schools and Colleges and California Department of Education. Upper school average class size: 1. Upper school faculty-student ratio: 1:1. The average school day consists of 4 hours.

Faculty School total: 6. In upper school: 3 men, 3 women; 2 have advanced degrees.

Subjects Offered Algebra, American literature, anatomy and physiology, art appreciation, arts, biology, British literature, business mathematics, calculus, career/college preparation, chemistry, computer applications, contemporary issues, economics, English, fine arts, French, geometry, health, history, Latin, mathematics, physical education, physics, pre-calculus, science, social sciences, Spanish, trigonometry, U.S. government, U.S. history, world history.

Graduation Requirements Arts and fine arts (art, music, dance, drama), English, foreign language, mathematics, personal development, physical education (includes health), science, social sciences, portfolio presentation, proficiency exams, volunteer credit hours. Community service is required.

Special Academic Programs Advanced Placement exam preparation; honors section; accelerated programs; study at local college for college credit; academic accommodation for the gifted, the musically talented, and the artistically talented; remedial reading and/or remedial writing; remedial math; programs in English, mathematics, general development for dyslexic students; special instructional classes for students with mild learning disabilities and Attention Deficit Disorder, Social anxiety.

Student Life Upper grades have specified standards of dress, student council, honor system. Discipline rests equally with students and faculty.

Summer Programs Remediation, enrichment, advancement, art/fine arts programs offered; session focuses on advancement and remedial academic work; held both on and off campus; held at on campus and online; accepts boys and girls; open to students from other schools. 130 students usually enrolled. 2016 schedule: June 6 to August 19. Application deadline: June 1.

Tuition and Aid Tuition installment plan (monthly payment plans, individually arranged payment plans). Tuition reduction for siblings available.

Admissions Traditional secondary-level entrance grade is 10. For fall 2015, 9 students applied for upper-level admission, 9 were accepted, 9 enrolled. English language and Math Placement Exam required. Deadline for receipt of application materials: none. No application fee required. On-campus interview required.

Computers Computers are regularly used in English, foreign language, history, mathematics, social studies classes. Computer network features include Internet access, wireless campus network, Internet filtering or blocking technology. Student e-mail accounts and computer access in designated common areas are available to students. Students grades are available online. The school has a published electronic and media policy.

HALSTROM ACADEMY

705 Palomar Airport Rd., Ste. 350
Calsbad, California 92011

Head of School: Ms. Rosamaria Pagarigan

General Information Coeducational day and distance learning college-preparatory and general academic school. Grades 6–12. Distance learning grades 6–12. Founded: 1985. Setting: suburban. Nearest major city is San Diego. 1 building on campus. Approved or accredited by Western Association of Schools and Colleges and California Department of Education. Total enrollment: 51. Upper school average class size: 1. Upper school faculty-student ratio: 1:1. The average school day consists of 4 hours.

Faculty School total: 9. In upper school: 4 men, 5 women; 4 have advanced degrees.

Subjects Offered Algebra, American literature, anatomy and physiology, art appreciation, arts, biology, British literature, business mathematics, calculus, career/college preparation, chemistry, computer applications, contemporary issues, economics, English, fine arts, French, geometry, health, Latin, literature, mathematics, physical education, physics, pre-calculus, social studies, Spanish, trigonometry, U.S. government, U.S. history, world history.

Graduation Requirements Arts and fine arts (art, music, dance, drama), English, foreign language, mathematics, personal development, physical education (includes health), science, social sciences, portfolio presentation, proficiency exams, volunteer credit hours. Community service is required.

Special Academic Programs Advanced Placement exam preparation; honors section; accelerated programs; independent study; study at local college for college credit; academic accommodation for the gifted, the musically talented, and the artistically talented; remedial reading and/or remedial writing; remedial math; programs in English, mathematics, general development for dyslexic students; special instructional classes for Mild learning disabilities, Social anxiety.

College Admission Counseling 3 students graduated in 2015; all went to college, including San Diego State University.

Student Life Upper grades have specified standards of dress, student council, honor system. Discipline rests equally with students and faculty.

Summer Programs Remediation, enrichment, advancement, art/fine arts programs offered; session focuses on advancement and remedial academic work; held both on and off campus; held at On campus and online; accepts boys and girls; open to students from other schools. 130 students usually enrolled. 2016 schedule: June 6 to August 19. Application deadline: June 1.

Tuition and Aid Tuition installment plan (monthly payment plans, individually arranged payment plans). Tuition reduction for siblings available.

Admissions Traditional secondary-level entrance grade is 9. For fall 2015, 51 students applied for upper-level admission, 51 were accepted, 51 enrolled. English language and Math Placement Exam required. Deadline for receipt of application materials: none. Application fee required. On-campus interview required.

Computers Computers are regularly used in English, foreign language, history, mathematics, science classes. Computer network features include Internet access, wireless campus network, Internet filtering or blocking technology. Computer access in designated common areas is available to students. Students grades are available online. The school has a published electronic and media policy.

HALSTROM ACADEMY

19638 Stevens Creek Blvd., Suite 230
Cupertino, California 95014

Head of School: Ms. Grace Lee

General Information Coeducational day and distance learning college-preparatory and general academic school; primarily serves underachievers, students with learning disabilities, individuals with Attention Deficit Disorder, dyslexic students, Mild learning disabilities, and Social anxiety. Grades 6–12. Distance learning grades 6–12. Founded: 1985. Setting: suburban. 1 building on campus. Approved or accredited by Western Association of Schools and Colleges and California Department of Education. Total enrollment: 19. Upper school average class size: 1. Upper school faculty-student ratio: 1:1. The average school day consists of 4 hours.

Faculty School total: 5. In upper school: 3 men, 2 women; 2 have advanced degrees.

Subjects Offered Algebra, American literature, anatomy and physiology, art appreciation, arts, biology, British literature, business mathematics, calculus, career/college preparation, chemistry, computer applications, contemporary issues, drawing, economics, English, fine arts, French, geometry, health, history, Latin, mathematics, physical education, physics, pre-calculus, social sciences, social studies, Spanish, trigonometry, U.S. government, U.S. history, world history.

Graduation Requirements Arts and fine arts (art, music, dance, drama), English, foreign language, mathematics, personal development, physical education (includes health), science, social sciences, portfolio presentation, proficiency exams, volunteer credit hours. Community service is required.

Special Academic Programs Advanced Placement exam preparation; honors section; accelerated programs; study at local college for college credit; academic accommodation for the gifted, the musically talented, and the artistically talented; remedial reading and/or remedial writing; remedial math; programs in English, mathematics, general development for dyslexic students; special instructional classes for Mild learning disabilities, Social anxiety.

Student Life Upper grades have specified standards of dress, student council, honor system. Discipline rests equally with students and faculty.

Summer Programs Remediation, enrichment, advancement, art/fine arts programs offered; session focuses on Advancement and remedial academic work; held both on and off campus; held at On campus and onlne; accepts boys and girls; open to students from other schools. 130 students usually enrolled. 2016 schedule: June 6 to August 19. Application deadline: June 1.

Tuition and Aid Tuition installment plan (monthly payment plans, individually arranged payment plans).

Admissions Traditional secondary-level entrance grade is 9. For fall 2015, 19 students applied for upper-level admission, 19 were accepted, 19 enrolled. English language and

Math Placement Exam required. Deadline for receipt of application materials: none. Application fee required. On-campus interview required.

Computers Computers are regularly used in English, foreign language, history, mathematics, science classes. Computer network features include Internet access, wireless campus network, Internet filtering or blocking technology. Student e-mail accounts and computer access in designated common areas are available to students. Students grades are available online. The school has a published electronic and media policy.

HALSTROM ACADEMY

2100 Main St., Ste. 260
Huntington Beach, California 92648

Head of School: Ms. Gina Johnson

General Information Coeducational day and distance learning college-preparatory and general academic school; primarily serves underachievers, students with learning disabilities, individuals with Attention Deficit Disorder, dyslexic students, Mild learning disabilities, and Social anxiety. Grades 6–12. Distance learning grades 6–12. Founded: 1985. Setting: suburban. 1 building on campus. Approved or accredited by Western Association of Schools and Colleges and California Department of Education. Total enrollment: 32. Upper school average class size: 1. Upper school faculty-student ratio: 1:1. The average school day consists of 4 hours.

Faculty School total: 9. In upper school: 5 men, 4 women; 4 have advanced degrees.

Subjects Offered Algebra, American literature, anatomy and physiology, art appreciation, arts, biology, British literature, business mathematics, calculus, career/college preparation, chemistry, computer applications, contemporary issues, economics, English, fine arts, French, geometry, health, history, Latin, mathematics, physical education, physics, pre-calculus, science, social sciences, Spanish, trigonometry, U.S. government, U.S. history, world history.

Graduation Requirements Arts and fine arts (art, music, dance, drama), English, foreign language, mathematics, personal development, physical education (includes health), science, social sciences, portfolio presentation, proficiency exams, volunteer credit hours. Community service is required.

Special Academic Programs Advanced Placement exam preparation; honors section; accelerated programs; study at local college for college credit; academic accommodation for the gifted, the musically talented, and the artistically talented; remedial reading and/or remedial writing; remedial math; programs in English, mathematics, general development for dyslexic students; special instructional classes for students with mild learning disabilities and Attention Deficit Disorder, Social anxiety.

College Admission Counseling 13 students graduated in 2015; 12 went to college, including California State University, Los Angeles; Humboldt State University; Triton College; University of California, Santa Barbara; University of Southern California. Other: 1 had other specific plans.

Student Life Upper grades have specified standards of dress, student council, honor system. Discipline rests equally with students and faculty.

Summer Programs Remediation, enrichment, advancement, art/fine arts programs offered; held both on and off campus; held at on campus and online; accepts boys and girls; open to students from other schools. 130 students usually enrolled. 2016 schedule: June 6 to August 19. Application deadline: June 1.

Tuition and Aid Tuition installment plan (monthly payment plans, individually arranged payment plans). Tuition reduction for siblings available.

Admissions Traditional secondary-level entrance grade is 10. For fall 2015, 32 students applied for upper-level admission, 32 were accepted, 32 enrolled. English language and Math Placement Exam required. Deadline for receipt of application materials: none. Application fee required. On-campus interview required.

Computers Computers are regularly used in English, foreign language, history, mathematics, science classes. Computer network features include Internet access, wireless campus network, Internet filtering or blocking technology. Student e-mail accounts and computer access in designated common areas are available to students. Students grades are available online. The school has a published electronic and media policy.

HALSTROM ACADEMY

2302 Martin St., Ste. 100, Colton Plaza
Irvine, California 92612

Head of School: Ms. June Tseng

General Information Coeducational day and distance learning college-preparatory and general academic school; primarily serves underachievers, students with learning disabilities, individuals with Attention Deficit Disorder, dyslexic students, Mild learning disabilities, and Social anxiety. Grades 6–12. Distance learning grades 6–12. Founded: 1985. Setting: suburban. 1 building on campus. Approved or accredited by Western Association of Schools and Colleges and California Department of Education. Total enrollment: 31. Upper school average class size: 1. Upper school faculty-student ratio: 1:1. The average school day consists of 4 hours.

Faculty School total: 6. In upper school: 3 men, 3 women; 2 have advanced degrees.

Subjects Offered Art appreciation, arts, biology, British literature, business mathematics, calculus, career/college preparation, chemistry, computer applications, contemporary issues, economics, English, fine arts, French, geometry, health, history, Latin, mathematics, physical education, physics, pre-calculus, science, social sciences, social studies, Spanish, trigonometry, U.S. government, U.S. history, world history.

Graduation Requirements Arts and fine arts (art, music, dance, drama), English, foreign language, mathematics, personal development, physical education (includes health), science, social sciences, portfolio presentation, proficiency exams, volunteer credit hours. Community service is required.

Special Academic Programs Advanced Placement exam preparation; honors section; accelerated programs; study at local college for college credit; academic accommodation for the gifted, the musically talented, and the artistically talented; remedial reading and/or remedial writing; remedial math; programs in English, mathematics, general development for dyslexic students; special instructional classes for students with mild learning disabilities and Attention Deficit Disorder, Social anxiety.

College Admission Counseling 2 students graduated in 2015; all went to college.

Student Life Upper grades have specified standards of dress, student council, honor system. Discipline rests equally with students and faculty.

Summer Programs Remediation, enrichment, advancement, art/fine arts programs offered; held both on and off campus; held at on campus and online; accepts boys and girls; open to students from other schools. 130 students usually enrolled. 2016 schedule: June 6 to August 19. Application deadline: June 1.

Tuition and Aid Tuition installment plan (monthly payment plans, individually arranged payment plans). Tuition reduction for siblings available.

Admissions Traditional secondary-level entrance grade is 10. For fall 2015, 31 students applied for upper-level admission, 31 were accepted, 31 enrolled. English language and Math Placement Exam required. Deadline for receipt of application materials: none. No application fee required. On-campus interview required.

Computers Computers are regularly used in English, foreign language, history, mathematics, science classes. Computer network features include Internet access, wireless campus network, Internet filtering or blocking technology. Student e-mail accounts and computer access in designated common areas are available to students. Students grades are available online. The school has a published electronic and media policy.

HALSTROM ACADEMY

12300 Wilshire Blvd., Ste.110
Los Angeles, California 90025

Head of School: Ms. Lena Liu

General Information Coeducational day and distance learning college-preparatory and general academic school; primarily serves underachievers, students with learning disabilities, individuals with Attention Deficit Disorder, dyslexic students, Mild learning disabilities, and Social anxiety. Grades 6–12. Distance learning grades 6–12. Founded: 1985. Setting: urban. 1 building on campus. Approved or accredited by Western Association of Schools and Colleges and California Department of Education. Total enrollment: 13. Upper school average class size: 1. Upper school faculty-student ratio: 1:1. The average school day consists of 4 hours.

Faculty School total: 12. In upper school: 8 men, 4 women; 4 have advanced degrees.

Subjects Offered Tropical biology, U.S. government, U.S. history, world history.

Graduation Requirements Social sciences, portfolio presentation, proficiency exams, volunteer credit hours.

Special Academic Programs Advanced Placement exam preparation; honors section; accelerated programs; study at local college for college credit; academic accommodation for the gifted, the musically talented, and the artistically talented; remedial reading and/or remedial writing; remedial math; programs in English, mathematics, general development for dyslexic students; special instructional classes for students with mild learning disabilities and Attention Deficit Disorder, Social anxiety.

College Admission Counseling 3 students graduated in 2015; all went to college, including DePaul University; Santa Monica College; University of California, Santa Cruz.

Summer Programs Enrichment, advancement, art/fine arts programs offered; session focuses on advancement and remedial academic work; held both on and off campus; held at on campus and online; accepts boys and girls; open to students from other schools. 130 students usually enrolled. 2016 schedule: June 6 to August. Application deadline: June 1.

Tuition and Aid Tuition installment plan (monthly payment plans, individually arranged payment plans). Tuition reduction for siblings available.

Admissions For fall 2015, 13 students applied for upper-level admission, 13 were accepted, 13 enrolled. English language and Math Placement Exam required. Deadline for receipt of application materials: none. Application fee required. On-campus interview required.

Computers Computers are regularly used in English, foreign language, history, mathematics, science classes. Computer network features include Internet access, wireless campus network, Internet filtering or blocking technology. Student e-mail accounts and computer access in designated common areas are available to students.

Students grades are available online. The school has a published electronic and media policy.

HALSTROM ACADEMY

2101 Rosecrans Avenue, Ste. 1225
Manhattan Beach, California 90245

Head of School: Ms. Mary Donielson

General Information Coeducational day and distance learning college-preparatory and general academic school; primarily serves underachievers, students with learning disabilities, individuals with Attention Deficit Disorder, dyslexic students, Mild learning disabilities, and Social anxiety. Grades 6–12. Distance learning grades 6–12. Founded: 1985. Setting: suburban. 1 building on campus. Approved or accredited by Western Association of Schools and Colleges and California Department of Education. Total enrollment: 20. Upper school average class size: 1. Upper school faculty-student ratio: 1:1. The average school day consists of 4 hours.

Faculty School total: 9. In upper school: 4 men, 5 women; 3 have advanced degrees.

Subjects Offered Fine arts, French, geometry, health, history, Latin, mathematics, physical education, physics, pre-calculus, science, social sciences, social studies, Spanish, trigonometry, U.S. government, U.S. history, world history.

Graduation Requirements English, foreign language, mathematics, personal development, physical education (includes health), science, social sciences, portfolio presentation, proficiency exams, volunteer credit hours. Community service is required.

Special Academic Programs Advanced Placement exam preparation; honors section; accelerated programs; study at local college for college credit; academic accommodation for the gifted, the musically talented, and the artistically talented; remedial reading and/or remedial writing; remedial math; programs in English, mathematics, general development for dyslexic students; special instructional classes for students with mild learning disabilities and Attention Deficit Disorder, Social anxiety.

College Admission Counseling 3 students graduated in 2015; all went to college, including Austin College; California State University, Long Beach; Long Beach City College.

Student Life Upper grades have specified standards of dress, student council, honor system. Discipline rests equally with students and faculty.

Summer Programs Remediation, enrichment, advancement, art/fine arts programs offered; session focuses on advancement and remedial academic work; held both on and off campus; held at on campus and online; accepts boys and girls; open to students from other schools. 130 students usually enrolled. 2016 schedule: June 6 to August 19. Application deadline: June 1.

Tuition and Aid Tuition installment plan (monthly payment plans, individually arranged payment plans). Tuition reduction for siblings available.

Admissions Traditional secondary-level entrance grade is 10. For fall 2015, 20 students applied for upper-level admission, 20 were accepted, 20 enrolled. English language and Math Placement Exam required. Deadline for receipt of application materials: none. Application fee required. On-campus interview required.

Computers Computers are regularly used in English, foreign language, history, mathematics, science classes. Computer network features include Internet access, wireless campus network, Internet filtering or blocking technology. Student e-mail accounts and computer access in designated common areas are available to students. Students grades are available online. The school has a published electronic and media policy.

HALSTROM ACADEMY

26440 La Alameda, Suite 350
Mission Viejo, California 92691-6319

Head of School: Ms. Julie Arlotti

General Information Coeducational day and distance learning college-preparatory and general academic school; primarily serves students with learning disabilities, individuals with Attention Deficit Disorder, individuals with emotional and behavioral problems, dyslexic students, Mild learning disabilities, and Social anxiety. Grades 6–12. Distance learning grades 6–12. Founded: 1985. Setting: suburban. 1 building on campus. Approved or accredited by Western Association of Schools and Colleges and California Department of Education. Upper school average class size: 1. Upper school faculty-student ratio: 1:1. The average school day consists of 4 hours.

Faculty School total: 16. In upper school: 8 men, 8 women; 5 have advanced degrees.

Subjects Offered ACT preparation, Advanced Placement courses, algebra, American history, anatomy, art appreciation, astronomy, biology, business mathematics, business skills, calculus, chemistry, community service, computer applications, computer science, consumer mathematics, earth science, economics, English, French, geography, geometry, government, Latin, life science, mathematics, music appreciation, physical education, physics, physiology, pre-algebra, pre-calculus, science, social sciences, social studies, Spanish, trigonometry, world history.

Graduation Requirements Arts and fine arts (art, music, dance, drama), foreign language, mathematics, personal development, physical education (includes health), science, social sciences, portfolio presentation, proficiency exams, volunteer credit hours. Community service is required.

Special Academic Programs Advanced Placement exam preparation; honors section; accelerated programs; study at local college for college credit; academic accommodation for the gifted, the musically talented, and the artistically talented; remedial reading and/or remedial writing; remedial math; programs in English, mathematics, general development for dyslexic students; special instructional classes for students with mild learning disabilities and Attention Deficit Disorder.

College Admission Counseling 31 students graduated in 2015; 29 went to college, including California State Polytechnic University, Pomona; Loyola Marymount University; Seattle Pacific University; The University of Arizona; University of California, Los Angeles; Utah State University. Other: 1 went to work, 1 entered military service.

Student Life Upper grades have specified standards of dress, student council, honor system. Discipline rests equally with students and faculty.

Summer Programs Remediation, enrichment, advancement, art/fine arts programs offered; session focuses on Acceleration and remediation; held both on and off campus; held at Online program; accepts boys and girls; open to students from other schools. 130 students usually enrolled. 2016 schedule: June 6 to August 19. Application deadline: June 1.

Tuition and Aid Tuition installment plan (monthly payment plans, individually arranged payment plans). Tuition reduction for siblings available.

Admissions Traditional secondary-level entrance grade is 10. For fall 2015, 44 students applied for upper-level admission, 44 were accepted, 44 enrolled. English language and Math Placement Exam required. Deadline for receipt of application materials: none. Application fee required. On-campus interview required.

Computers Computers are regularly used in English, foreign language, history, mathematics, science classes. Computer network features include Internet access, wireless campus network, Internet filtering or blocking technology. Student e-mail accounts and computer access in designated common areas are available to students. Students grades are available online. The school has a published electronic and media policy.

Contact Ms. Kate Mocciaro, Administrative Assistant. 866-814-4354. E-mail: MissionViejo@futures.edu. Website: www.halstromacademy.org

HALSTROM ACADEMY

3111 N. Tustin St., Ste. 240
Orange, California 92865

Head of School: Ms. Mary Paliescheskey

General Information Coeducational day and distance learning college-preparatory and general academic school; primarily serves underachievers, students with learning disabilities, individuals with Attention Deficit Disorder, dyslexic students, Mild learning disabilities, and Social anxiety. Grades 6–12. Distance learning grades 6–12. Founded: 1985. Setting: suburban. 1 building on campus. Approved or accredited by Western Association of Schools and Colleges and California Department of Education. Upper school average class size: 1. Upper school faculty-student ratio: 1:1. The average school day consists of 4 hours.

Faculty School total: 8. In upper school: 5 men, 3 women; 3 have advanced degrees.

Subjects Offered Algebra, American literature, anatomy and physiology, art appreciation, arts, biology, British literature, business mathematics, calculus, career/college preparation, chemistry, computer applications, contemporary issues, economics, fine arts, French, geometry, health, history, Latin, mathematics, physical education, pre-calculus, science, social issues, social sciences, social studies, Spanish, trigonometry, U.S. government, U.S. history, world history.

Graduation Requirements Arts and fine arts (art, music, dance, drama), English, foreign language, mathematics, personal development, physical education (includes health), science, social sciences, portfolio presentation, proficiency exams, volunteer credit hours. Community service is required.

Special Academic Programs Advanced Placement exam preparation; honors section; accelerated programs; study at local college for college credit; academic accommodation for the gifted, the musically talented, and the artistically talented; remedial reading and/or remedial writing; remedial math; programs in English, mathematics, general development for dyslexic students.

College Admission Counseling 7 students graduated in 2015; 5 went to college, including California State University, Fullerton; Chapman University; San Francisco State University; University of Redlands. Other: 2 entered military service.

Student Life Upper grades have specified standards of dress, student council, honor system. Discipline rests equally with students and faculty.

Summer Programs Remediation, enrichment, advancement, art/fine arts programs offered; session focuses on advancement and remedial academic work; held both on and off campus; held at on campus and online; accepts boys and girls; open to students from other schools. 130 students usually enrolled. 2016 schedule: June 6 to August 19. Application deadline: June 1.

Tuition and Aid Tuition installment plan (monthly payment plans, individually arranged payment plans). Tuition reduction for siblings available.

Admissions Traditional secondary-level entrance grade is 10. For fall 2015, 37 students applied for upper-level admission, 37 were accepted, 37 enrolled. English language and Math Placement Exam required. Deadline for receipt of application materials: none. Application fee required.

Computers Computers are regularly used in English, foreign language, history, mathematics, science classes. Computer network features include Internet access, wireless campus network, Internet filtering or blocking technology. Student e-mail accounts and computer access in designated common areas are available to students. Students grades are available online. The school has a published electronic and media policy.

HALSTROM ACADEMY

35 N. Lake Ave., Ste. 250
Pasadena, California 91101

Head of School: Ms. Ani Zeneian

General Information Coeducational day and distance learning college-preparatory and general academic school; primarily serves underachievers, students with learning disabilities, individuals with Attention Deficit Disorder, dyslexic students, Mild learning disabilities, and Social anxiety. Grades 6–12. Distance learning grades 6–12. Founded: 1985. Setting: urban. 1 building on campus. Approved or accredited by Western Association of Schools and Colleges and California Department of Education. Total enrollment: 27. Upper school average class size: 1. Upper school faculty-student ratio: 1:1. The average school day consists of 4 hours.

Faculty School total: 8. In upper school: 2 men, 6 women; 3 have advanced degrees.

Subjects Offered Algebra, American literature, anatomy and physiology, art appreciation, arts, biology, British literature, business mathematics, calculus, career/college preparation, chemistry, computer applications, contemporary issues, economics, fiber arts, French, geometry, health, history, Latin, mathematics, physical education, physics, pre-calculus, science, social sciences, social studies, Spanish, trigonometry, U.S. government, U.S. history, world history.

Graduation Requirements Arts and fine arts (art, music, dance, drama), English, foreign language, mathematics, personal development, physical education (includes health), science, social sciences, portfolio presentation, proficiency exams, volunteer credit hours. Community service is required.

Special Academic Programs Advanced Placement exam preparation; honors section; accelerated programs; study at local college for college credit; academic accommodation for the gifted, the musically talented, and the artistically talented; remedial reading and/or remedial writing; remedial math; programs in English, mathematics, general development for dyslexic students; special instructional classes for students with mild learning disabilities and Attention Deficit Disorder, Social anxiety.

College Admission Counseling 6 students graduated in 2015; all went to college, including California State University, Los Angeles; Willamette University; William Peace University.

Student Life Upper grades have specified standards of dress, student council, honor system. Discipline rests equally with students and faculty.

Summer Programs Remediation, enrichment, advancement, art/fine arts programs offered; session focuses on Advancement and remedial academic work; held both on and off campus; held at On campus and online; accepts boys and girls; open to students from other schools. 2016 schedule: June 6 to August 19. Application deadline: June 1.

Tuition and Aid Tuition installment plan (monthly payment plans, individually arranged payment plans). Tuition reduction for siblings available.

Admissions Traditional secondary-level entrance grade is 10. For fall 2015, 27 students applied for upper-level admission, 27 were accepted, 27 enrolled. English language and Math Placement Exam required. Deadline for receipt of application materials: none. Application fee required.

Computers Computers are regularly used in English, foreign language, history, mathematics, science classes. Computer network features include Internet access, wireless campus network, Internet filtering or blocking technology. Student e-mail accounts and computer access in designated common areas are available to students. Students grades are available online. The school has a published electronic and media policy.

HALSTROM ACADEMY

9915 Mira Mesa Boulevard
Suite 210
San Diego, California 92131

Head of School: Mr. Eduardo Ceja

General Information Coeducational day and distance learning college-preparatory, general academic, and vocational school; primarily serves underachievers, students with learning disabilities, individuals with Attention Deficit Disorder, dyslexic students, Mild learning disabilities, and Social anxiety. Grades 6–12. Distance learning grades 6–12. Founded: 1985. Setting: urban. 1 building on campus. Approved or accredited by Western Association of Schools and Colleges and California Department of Education. Upper school average class size: 1. Upper school faculty-student ratio: 1:1. The average school day consists of 4 hours.

Faculty School total: 12. In upper school: 6 men, 6 women; 5 have advanced degrees.

Subjects Offered Algebra, American literature, anatomy and physiology, art appreciation, arts, biology, British literature, business mathematics, calculus, career/college preparation, chemistry, computer applications, contemporary issues, economics, English, fine arts, French, geometry, health, mathematics, physical education, physics, pre-calculus, social studies, Spanish, trigonometry, U.S. government, U.S. history, world history.

Graduation Requirements Arts and fine arts (art, music, dance, drama), English, foreign language, mathematics, personal development, physical education (includes health), science, social sciences, portfolio presentation, proficiency exams, volunteer credit hours. Community service is required.

Special Academic Programs Advanced Placement exam preparation; honors section; accelerated programs; study at local college for college credit; academic accommodation for the gifted, the musically talented, and the artistically talented; remedial reading and/or remedial writing; remedial math; programs in English, mathematics, general development for dyslexic students; special instructional classes for students with mild learning disabilities and Attention Deficit Disorder.

College Admission Counseling 12 students graduated in 2015; 11 went to college, including Arizona State University at the Tempe campus; Carnegie Mellon University; MiraCosta College; University of San Diego. Other: 1 went to work.

Student Life Upper grades have honor system. Discipline rests equally with students and faculty.

Summer Programs Remediation, enrichment, advancement, art/fine arts, computer instruction programs offered; session focuses on advancement and remedial academic work; held both on and off campus; held at On campus and online; accepts boys and girls; open to students from other schools. 130 students usually enrolled. 2016 schedule: June 6 to August 19. Application deadline: June 1.

Tuition and Aid Tuition installment plan (monthly payment plans, individually arranged payment plans). Tuition reduction for siblings available.

Admissions Traditional secondary-level entrance grade is 10. For fall 2015, 37 students applied for upper-level admission, 37 were accepted, 37 enrolled. English language and Math Placement Exam required. Deadline for receipt of application materials: none. Application fee required. On-campus interview required.

Computers Computers are regularly used in English, foreign language, history, mathematics, science classes. Computer network features include Internet access, wireless campus network, Internet filtering or blocking technology. Computer access in designated common areas is available to students. Students grades are available online. The school has a published electronic and media policy.

Contact Lorena Moreno, Administrative Assistant. 866-814-4354. Fax: 858-549-6292. E-mail: sandiego@futures.edu. Website: www.halstromacademy.org

HALSTROM ACADEMY

1840 Gateway Dr., Ste. 100
San Mateo, California 94404

Head of School: Ms. Jayne Cho

General Information Coeducational day and distance learning college-preparatory and general academic school; primarily serves underachievers, students with learning disabilities, individuals with Attention Deficit Disorder, dyslexic students, Mild learning disabilities, and Social anxiety. Grades 6–12. Distance learning grades 6–12. Founded: 1985. Setting: suburban. 1 building on campus. Approved or accredited by Western Association of Schools and Colleges and California Department of Education. Total enrollment: 11. Upper school average class size: 1. Upper school faculty-student ratio: 1:1. The average school day consists of 4 hours.

Faculty School total: 4. In upper school: 2 men, 2 women; 1 has an advanced degree.

Subjects Offered Algebra, American literature, anatomy and physiology, art appreciation, arts, biology, British literature, business mathematics, calculus, career/college preparation, chemistry, computer applications, contemporary issues, economics, English, fine arts, French, geometry, health, history, Latin, mathematics, physical education, physics, pre-calculus, social sciences, social studies, Spanish, trigonometry, U.S. government, U.S. history, world history.

Graduation Requirements Sculpture, social sciences, portfolio presentation, proficiency exams, volunteer credit hours.

Special Academic Programs Advanced Placement exam preparation; honors section; accelerated programs; study at local college for college credit; academic accommodation for the gifted, the musically talented, and the artistically talented; remedial reading and/or remedial writing; remedial math; programs in English, mathematics, general development for dyslexic students; special instructional classes for students with mild learning disabilities and Attention Deficit Disorder, Social anxiety.

Student Life Upper grades have specified standards of dress, student council, honor system. Discipline rests equally with students and faculty.

Summer Programs Remediation, enrichment, advancement, art/fine arts programs offered; session focuses on Advancement and remedial academic work; held both on and off campus; held at On campus and online; accepts boys and girls; open to students from other schools. 130 students usually enrolled. 2016 schedule: June 6 to August 19. Application deadline: June 1.

Tuition and Aid Tuition installment plan (monthly payment plans, individually arranged payment plans). Tuition reduction for siblings available.

Admissions Traditional secondary-level entrance grade is 9. For fall 2015, 11 students applied for upper-level admission, 11 were accepted, 11 enrolled. English language and

Math Placement Exam required. Deadline for receipt of application materials: none. Application fee required. On-campus interview required.

Computers Computers are regularly used in English, foreign language, history, mathematics, science classes. Computer network features include Internet access, wireless campus network, Internet filtering or blocking technology. Student e-mail accounts and computer access in designated common areas are available to students. Students grades are available online. The school has a published electronic and media policy.

HALSTROM ACADEMY
101 Ygnacio Valley Road
Suite 345
Walnut Creek, California 94596
Head of School: Ms. Carol Rupp

General Information Coeducational day and distance learning college-preparatory and general academic school; primarily serves underachievers, students with learning disabilities, individuals with Attention Deficit Disorder, and dyslexic students. Grades 6–12. Distance learning grades 6–12. Founded: 1985. Setting: suburban. 1 building on campus. Approved or accredited by Western Association of Schools and Colleges and California Department of Education. Total enrollment: 12. Upper school average class size: 1. Upper school faculty-student ratio: 1:1. The average school day consists of 4 hours.

Faculty School total: 6. In upper school: 2 men, 4 women; 2 have advanced degrees.

Subjects Offered Algebra, American literature, anatomy and physiology, art appreciation, arts, biology, British literature, business mathematics, calculus, career/college preparation, chemistry, computer applications, contemporary issues, economics, English, fine arts, French, geometry, health, history, Latin, mathematics, physical education, physics, pre-calculus, science, social sciences, social studies, Spanish, trigonometry, U.S. government, U.S. history, world history.

Graduation Requirements Arts and fine arts (art, music, dance, drama), English, foreign language, mathematics, personal development, physical education (includes health), science, social sciences, portfolio presentation, proficiency exams, volunteer credit hours. Community service is required.

Special Academic Programs Advanced Placement exam preparation; honors section; accelerated programs; study at local college for college credit; academic accommodation for the gifted, the musically talented, and the artistically talented; remedial reading and/or remedial writing; remedial math; programs in English, mathematics, general development for dyslexic students; special instructional classes for students with mild learning disabilities and Attention Deficit Disorder, Social anxiety.

Student Life Upper grades have specified standards of dress, student council, honor system. Discipline rests equally with students and faculty.

Summer Programs Remediation, enrichment, advancement, art/fine arts programs offered; session focuses on advancement and remedial academic work; held both on and off campus; held at on campus and online; accepts boys and girls; open to students from other schools. 130 students usually enrolled. 2016 schedule: June 6 to August 19. Application deadline: June 1.

Tuition and Aid Tuition installment plan (monthly payment plans, individually arranged payment plans). Tuition reduction for siblings available.

Admissions Traditional secondary-level entrance grade is 10. For fall 2015, 12 students applied for upper-level admission, 12 were accepted, 12 enrolled. English language and Math Placement Exam required. Deadline for receipt of application materials: none. Application fee required. On-campus interview required.

Computers Computers are regularly used in English, foreign language, history, mathematics, science classes. Computer resources include Internet access, wireless campus network, Internet filtering or blocking technology. Student e-mail accounts and computer access in designated common areas are available to students. Students grades are available online. The school has a published electronic and media policy.

HALSTROM ACADEMY
30700 Russell Ranch Rd., Ste. 180
Westlake Village, California 91362
Head of School: Ms. Kiersten Rugg

General Information Coeducational day and distance learning college-preparatory and general academic school; primarily serves underachievers, students with learning disabilities, individuals with Attention Deficit Disorder, and dyslexic students. Grades 6–12. Distance learning grades 6–12. Founded: 1985. Setting: suburban. 1 building on campus. Approved or accredited by Western Association of Schools and Colleges and California Department of Education. Upper school average class size: 1. Upper school faculty-student ratio: 1:1. The average school day consists of 4 hours.

Faculty School total: 11. In upper school: 4 men, 7 women; 5 have advanced degrees.

Subjects Offered Algebra, American literature, art appreciation, arts, biology, British literature, business mathematics, calculus, career/college preparation, chemistry, computer applications, contemporary issues, economics, English, fine arts, French, geometry, health, Latin, literature, mathematics, physical education, physics, pre-

calculus, science, social sciences, social studies, Spanish, trigonometry, U.S. government, U.S. history, world history.

Graduation Requirements Arts and fine arts (art, music, dance, drama), English, foreign language, mathematics, personal development, physical education (includes health), science, social sciences, portfolio presentation, proficiency exams, volunteer credit hours. Community service is required.

Special Academic Programs Advanced Placement exam preparation; honors section; accelerated programs; study at local college for college credit; academic accommodation for the gifted, the musically talented, and the artistically talented; remedial reading and/or remedial writing; programs in English, mathematics, general development for dyslexic students; special instructional classes for Mild learning disabilities, Social anxiety.

Student Life Upper grades have specified standards of dress, student council, honor system. Discipline rests equally with students and faculty.

Summer Programs Remediation, enrichment, advancement, art/fine arts programs offered; held both on and off campus; held at On campus and online; accepts boys and girls; open to students from other schools. 130 students usually enrolled. 2016 schedule: June 6 to August 19. Application deadline: June 1.

Tuition and Aid Tuition installment plan (monthly payment plans, individually arranged payment plans).

Admissions Traditional secondary-level entrance grade is 10. For fall 2015, 30 students applied for upper-level admission, 30 were accepted, 30 enrolled. English language and Math Placement Exam required. Deadline for receipt of application materials: none. No application fee required. On-campus interview required.

Computers Computers are regularly used in English, foreign language, history, mathematics, science classes. Computer network features include Internet access, wireless campus network, Internet filtering or blocking technology. Student e-mail accounts and computer access in designated common areas are available to students. Students grades are available online. The school has a published electronic and media policy.

HALSTROM ACADEMY
21800 Oxnard St., Ste. 270
Woodland Hills, California 91367
Head of School: Mr. Joseph Harper

General Information Coeducational day and distance learning college-preparatory and general academic school; primarily serves underachievers, students with learning disabilities, individuals with Attention Deficit Disorder, dyslexic students, Mild learning disabilities, and Social anxiety. Grades 6–12. Distance learning grades 6–12. Founded: 1985. Setting: suburban. 1 building on campus. Approved or accredited by Western Association of Schools and Colleges and California Department of Education. Total enrollment: 40. Upper school average class size: 1. Upper school faculty-student ratio: 1:1. The average school day consists of 4 hours.

Faculty School total: 12. In upper school: 5 men, 7 women; 4 have advanced degrees.

Subjects Offered Algebra, American literature, anatomy and physiology, art appreciation, arts, biology, British literature, business mathematics, calculus, career/college preparation, chemistry, computer applications, contemporary issues, economics, English, fine arts, French, geometry, health, history, Latin, mathematics, physical education, physics, pre-calculus, science, social sciences, social studies, Spanish, trigonometry, U.S. government, U.S. history, world history.

Graduation Requirements Arts and fine arts (art, music, dance, drama), English, foreign language, mathematics, personal development, physical education (includes health), science, social sciences, portfolio presentation, proficiency exams, volunteer credit hours. Community service is required.

Special Academic Programs Advanced Placement exam preparation; honors section; accelerated programs; study at local college for college credit; academic accommodation for the gifted, the musically talented, and the artistically talented; remedial reading and/or remedial writing; remedial math; programs in English, mathematics, general development for dyslexic students; special instructional classes for Mild learning disabilities, Social anxiety.

College Admission Counseling 8 students graduated in 2015; all went to college, including American University; Azusa Pacific University; California State University, Fullerton; University of Colorado Boulder.

Student Life Upper grades have specified standards of dress, student council, honor system. Discipline rests equally with students and faculty.

Summer Programs Remediation, enrichment, advancement, art/fine arts programs offered; session focuses on advancement and remedial academic work; held both on and off campus; held at On campus and online; accepts boys and girls; open to students from other schools. 130 students usually enrolled. 2016 schedule: June 6 to August 19. Application deadline: June 1.

Tuition and Aid Tuition installment plan (monthly payment plans, individually arranged payment plans).

Admissions Traditional secondary-level entrance grade is 10. For fall 2015, 40 students applied for upper-level admission, 40 were accepted, 40 enrolled. English language and Math Placement Exam required. Deadline for receipt of application materials: none. No application fee required. On-campus interview required.

Computers Computers are regularly used in English, foreign language, history, mathematics, science classes. Computer network features include Internet access, wireless campus network, Internet filtering or blocking technology. Student e-mail accounts and computer access in designated common areas are available to students. Students grades are available online. The school has a published electronic and media policy.

HAMILTON DISTRICT CHRISTIAN HIGH

92 Glancaster Road
Ancaster, Ontario L9G 3K9, Canada
Head of School: Mr. Nathan Siebenga
General Information Coeducational day college-preparatory, general academic, arts, business, vocational, religious studies, and technology school, affiliated with Christian faith. Grades 9–12. Founded: 1956. Setting: suburban. Nearest major city is Hamilton, Canada. 22-acre campus. 1 building on campus. Approved or accredited by Christian Schools International, Ontario Ministry of Education, and Ontario Department of Education. Language of instruction: English. Total enrollment: 480. Upper school average class size: 19. Upper school faculty-student ratio: 1:19. There are 180 required school days per year for Upper School students. Upper School students typically attend 5 days per week. The average school day consists of 6 hours.
Upper School Student Profile Grade 9: 120 students (60 boys, 60 girls); Grade 10: 100 students (50 boys, 50 girls); Grade 11: 130 students (65 boys, 65 girls); Grade 12: 130 students (65 boys, 65 girls). 100% of students are Christian faith.
Faculty School total: 37. In upper school: 24 men, 13 women; 9 have advanced degrees.
Subjects Offered 20th century history, 3-dimensional art, 3-dimensional design, accounting, acting, adolescent issues, advanced chemistry, advanced computer applications, advanced math, ancient history, ancient world history, applied arts, architectural drawing, art, art history, Bible, biology, business technology, calculus, Canadian geography, Canadian history, Canadian law, career experience, carpentry, chemistry, choir, civics, computer applications, computer multimedia, computer programming, computer technologies, computer-aided design, concert band, creative writing, drafting, drama, economics, English literature, environmental science, ESL, family and consumer science, finite math, food and nutrition, French, geometry, guidance, history, instrumental music, keyboarding, leadership, mathematics, media, modern Western civilization, music, peer counseling, personal finance, physical education, physics, religious studies, science, sociology, trigonometry, woodworking.
Graduation Requirements Art, Bible, Canadian geography, Canadian history, career education, civics, English, French, history, keyboarding, mathematics, science, 40 hours of community service.
Special Academic Programs 6 Advanced Placement exams for which test preparation is offered; independent study; term-away projects; academic accommodation for the musically talented and the artistically talented; remedial reading and/or remedial writing; remedial math; ESL (20 students enrolled).
College Admission Counseling 108 students graduated in 2014; 95 went to college, including McMaster University; Queen's University at Kingston; Redeemer University College; The University of Western Ontario; University of Waterloo; Wilfrid Laurier University. Other: 8 went to work, 5 had other specific plans. Median composite ACT: 23. 25% scored over 26 on composite ACT.
Student Life Upper grades have uniform requirement, student council. Discipline rests primarily with faculty.
Tuition and Aid Day student tuition: CAN$12,940. Tuition installment plan (monthly payment plans, individually arranged payment plans). Merit scholarship grants, need-based scholarship grants, tuition assistance fund, family rate tuition (additional children at no extra charge), reduced rate for two-school tuition families and home school families available. In 2014–15, 10% of upper-school students received aid; total upper-school merit-scholarship money awarded: CAN$4000. Total amount of financial aid awarded in 2014–15: CAN$200,000.
Admissions Traditional secondary-level entrance grade is 9. For fall 2014, 140 students applied for upper-level admission, 139 were accepted, 130 enrolled. Deadline for receipt of application materials: none. No application fee required. Interview required.
Athletics Interscholastic: badminton (boys, girls), baseball (g), basketball (b,g), cross-country running (b,g), golf (b,g), hockey (b), ice hockey (b), lacrosse (b,g), running (b,g), soccer (b,g), softball (g), touch football (b), track and field (b,g), volleyball (b,g); intramural: ball hockey (b,g), basketball (b,g), flag football (b,g), floor hockey (b,g), volleyball (b,g), wallyball (b,g), whiffle ball (b,g); coed interscholastic: badminton, canoeing/kayaking, rafting, swimming and diving, ultimate Frisbee; coed intramural: floor hockey, horseback riding, indoor soccer, mountain biking, weight lifting, weight training. 5 PE instructors, 6 coaches.
Computers Computers are regularly used in art, business studies, career education, career exploration, college planning, current events, desktop publishing, drafting, economics, English, ESL, ethics, geography, graphic arts, graphic design, history, independent study, keyboarding, library, literary magazine, mathematics, media production, music, news writing, newspaper, photography, religious studies, research skills, science, video film production, Web site design, writing, yearbook classes. Computer network features include on-campus library services, online commercial services, Internet access, wireless campus network, Internet filtering or blocking technology, course Web pages, course chat rooms. Campus intranet, student e-mail accounts, and computer access in designated common areas are available to students.

Students grades are available online. The school has a published electronic and media policy.
Contact Mr. Harry Meester, Director of Recruitment. 905-648-6655 Ext. 113. Fax: 905-648-3139. E-mail: jhagen@hdch.org. Website: www.hdch.org

HAMMOND SCHOOL

854 Galway Lane
Columbia, South Carolina 29209
Head of School: Mr. Chris Angel
General Information Coeducational day college-preparatory, arts, and technology school. Grades PK–12. Founded: 1966. Setting: suburban. 108-acre campus. 20 buildings on campus. Approved or accredited by New England Association of Schools and Colleges, South Carolina Independent School Association, Southern Association of Colleges and Schools, and Southern Association of Independent Schools. Member of National Association of Independent Schools and Secondary School Admission Test Board. Endowment: $2 million. Total enrollment: 898. Upper school average class size: 15. Upper school faculty-student ratio: 1:9. There are 180 required school days per year for Upper School students. Upper School students typically attend 5 days per week. The average school day consists of 7 hours and 20 minutes.
Upper School Student Profile Grade 9: 67 students (26 boys, 41 girls); Grade 10: 74 students (38 boys, 36 girls); Grade 11: 76 students (45 boys, 31 girls); Grade 12: 84 students (47 boys, 37 girls).
Faculty School total: 112. In upper school: 22 men, 22 women; 24 have advanced degrees.
Subjects Offered Advanced Placement courses, African American history, algebra, American government, American history, American literature, art, art history, biology, calculus, chemistry, choir, chorus, computer programming, computer science, creative writing, drama, earth science, economics, electives, English, English literature, European history, film studies, finite math, French, geometry, government/civics, history, journalism, Latin, mathematics, music, physical education, physics, science, social studies, Spanish, speech, trigonometry, world history, world literature.
Graduation Requirements Arts and fine arts (art, music, dance, drama), English, foreign language, mathematics, physical education (includes health), science, social studies (includes history).
Special Academic Programs Advanced Placement exam preparation; honors section; independent study; study abroad; academic accommodation for the gifted, the musically talented, and the artistically talented; remedial reading and/or remedial writing; programs in general development for dyslexic students.
College Admission Counseling 64 students graduated in 2014; all went to college, including Clemson University; Furman University; University of Georgia; University of South Carolina; Washington and Lee University; Wofford College. Mean SAT critical reading: 585, mean SAT math: 612, mean SAT writing: 586, mean combined SAT: 1783, mean composite ACT: 27. 45% scored over 600 on SAT critical reading, 55% scored over 600 on SAT math, 45% scored over 600 on SAT writing, 55% scored over 26 on composite ACT.
Student Life Upper grades have uniform requirement, student council, honor system. Discipline rests primarily with faculty.
Tuition and Aid Day student tuition: $16,444. Tuition installment plan (Insured Tuition Payment Plan). Merit scholarship grants, need-based scholarship grants available. In 2014–15, 23% of upper-school students received aid; total upper-school merit-scholarship money awarded: $91,000. Total amount of financial aid awarded in 2014–15: $1,400,000.
Admissions Traditional secondary-level entrance grade is 9. For fall 2014, 37 students applied for upper-level admission, 28 were accepted, 22 enrolled. ACT, any standardized test, ISEE, PSAT or SSAT required. Deadline for receipt of application materials: none. Application fee required: $75. Interview required.
Athletics Interscholastic: backpacking (boys, girls), ballet (b,g), baseball (b), basketball (b,g), canoeing/kayaking (b,g), cheering (b,g), climbing (b,g), combined training (b,g), cross-country running (b,g), dance (b,g), dance squad (g), equestrian sports (b,g), fitness (b,g), football (b), golf (b,g), hiking/backpacking (b,g), horseback riding (b,g), kayaking (b,g), lacrosse (b), physical fitness (b,g), physical training (b,g), pom squad (g), rafting (b,g), rappelling (b,g), rock climbing (b,g), ropes courses (b,g), running (b,g), skeet shooting (b,g), soccer (b,g), softball (g), strength & conditioning (b,g), swimming and diving (b,g), tennis (b,g), track and field (b,g), trap and skeet (b,g), ultimate Frisbee (b,g), volleyball (g), wall climbing (b,g), weight lifting (b,g), weight training (b,g), wilderness (b,g), wrestling (b); coed interscholastic: aerobics/dance, aquatics, ballet, cheering, cross-country running, dance, equestrian sports, golf, horseback riding, outdoor activities, physical fitness, physical training, pom squad, skeet shooting, soccer, trap and skeet, ultimate Frisbee. 1 PE instructor, 73 coaches, 2 athletic trainers.
Computers Computers are regularly used in all classes. Computer network features include on-campus library services, online commercial services, Internet access, wireless campus network, Internet filtering or blocking technology. Campus intranet and student e-mail accounts are available to students. Students grades are available online. The school has a published electronic and media policy.
Contact Mrs. Carson O. McQueen, Admission Counselor. 803-776-0295 Ext. 1. Fax: 803-776-0122. E-mail: cmcqueen@hammondschool.org. Website: www.hammondschool.org

HAMPSHIRE COUNTRY SCHOOL

Rindge, New Hampshire
See Junior Boarding Schools section.

HAMPTON ROADS ACADEMY

739 Academy Lane
Newport News, Virginia 23602

Head of School: Mr. Peter Mertz

General Information Coeducational day college-preparatory school. Grades PK–12. Founded: 1959. Setting: suburban. 52-acre campus. 4 buildings on campus. Approved or accredited by Virginia Association of Independent Schools and Virginia Department of Education. Member of National Association of Independent Schools. Total enrollment: 606. Upper school average class size: 14. Upper school faculty-student ratio: 1:10. Upper School students typically attend 5 days per week. The average school day consists of 6 hours and 30 minutes.

Upper School Student Profile Grade 9: 53 students (25 boys, 28 girls); Grade 10: 62 students (35 boys, 27 girls); Grade 11: 64 students (40 boys, 24 girls); Grade 12: 67 students (34 boys, 33 girls).

Faculty School total: 70. In upper school: 13 men, 17 women; 19 have advanced degrees.

Subjects Offered Algebra, American history, American literature, anatomy, art, biology, calculus, ceramics, chemistry, creative writing, drama, earth science, economics, English, English literature, European history, expository writing, fine arts, French, geography, geometry, government/civics, grammar, health, history, Latin, mathematics, music, photography, physical education, physics, physiology, science, social studies, Spanish, speech, statistics, theater, trigonometry, world history, world literature, writing.

Graduation Requirements Arts and fine arts (art, music, dance, drama), English, foreign language, mathematics, physical education (includes health), science, social studies (includes history), community service, Senior Project. Community service is required.

Special Academic Programs 19 Advanced Placement exams for which test preparation is offered; honors section; independent study; ESL (10 students enrolled).

College Admission Counseling 69 students graduated in 2014; all went to college, including James Madison University; The College of William and Mary; University of South Carolina; University of Virginia; Virginia Polytechnic Institute and State University. Median SAT critical reading: 600, median SAT math: 600, median SAT writing: 600, median combined SAT: 1800, median composite ACT: 22. 60% scored over 600 on SAT critical reading, 54% scored over 600 on SAT math, 56% scored over 600 on SAT writing, 57% scored over 1800 on combined SAT, 36% scored over 26 on composite ACT.

Student Life Upper grades have specified standards of dress, student council, honor system. Discipline rests primarily with faculty.

Tuition and Aid Day student tuition: $16,600. Tuition installment plan (SMART Tuition Payment Plan). Need-based scholarship grants available. In 2014–15, 20% of upper-school students received aid. Total amount of financial aid awarded in 2014–15: $700,000.

Admissions Traditional secondary-level entrance grade is 9. For fall 2014, 47 students applied for upper-level admission, 40 were accepted, 37 enrolled. ERB, school's own test and writing sample required. Deadline for receipt of application materials: none. Application fee required: $75. On-campus interview required.

Athletics Interscholastic: ball hockey (girls), baseball (b), basketball (b,g), cheering (g), cross-country running (b,g), equestrian sports (b,g), field hockey (g), football (b), golf (b,g), lacrosse (b), physical training (b,g), running (b,g), sailing (b,g), soccer (b,g), softball (g), swimming and diving (b,g), tennis (b,g), track and field (b,g), volleyball (g), weight training (b,g); intramural: hiking/backpacking (b,g), outdoor adventure (b,g), outdoor education (b,g), outdoor recreation (b,g), outdoor skills (b,g), outdoors (b,g), strength & conditioning (b,g); coed interscholastic: aquatics, cheering, equestrian sports, running; coed intramural: archery, equestrian sports, fitness, hiking/backpacking, outdoor adventure, outdoor education, outdoor recreation, outdoor skills, outdoors, paddle tennis, physical fitness, physical training, ropes courses, strength & conditioning, table tennis, ultimate Frisbee, weight training. 3 PE instructors, 44 coaches, 1 athletic trainer.

Computers Computers are regularly used in English, history, mathematics, music, science, social sciences, social studies, technology, writing, writing, yearbook classes. Computer network features include on-campus library services, online commercial services, Internet access, wireless campus network, Internet filtering or blocking technology. Student e-mail accounts and computer access in designated common areas are available to students. Students grades are available online. The school has a published electronic and media policy.

Contact Genelda Burke, Admission Associate. 757-884-9148. Fax: 757-884-9137. E-mail: admissions@hra.org. Website: www.hra.org

HARDING ACADEMY

Box 10775, Harding University
1529 East Park Avenue
Searcy, Arkansas 72149

Head of School: James Simmons

General Information Coeducational boarding and day college-preparatory, arts, business, vocational, religious studies, bilingual studies, and technology school, affiliated with Church of Christ. Boarding grades 9–12, day grades K–12. Founded: 1924. Setting: small town. Nearest major city is Little Rock. Students are housed in single-sex dormitories. 15-acre campus. 1 building on campus. Approved or accredited by Arkansas Nonpublic School Accrediting Association, National Christian School Association, North Central Association of Colleges and Schools, and Arkansas Department of Education. Total enrollment: 598. Upper school average class size: 25. Upper school faculty-student ratio: 1:11. There are 180 required school days per year for Upper School students. Upper School students typically attend 5 days per week. The average school day consists of 7 hours and 25 minutes.

Upper School Student Profile Grade 7: 47 students (21 boys, 26 girls); Grade 8: 62 students (31 boys, 31 girls); Grade 9: 64 students (30 boys, 34 girls); Grade 10: 50 students (25 boys, 25 girls); Grade 11: 55 students (30 boys, 25 girls); Grade 12: 49 students (24 boys, 25 girls). 4% of students are boarding students. 96% are state residents. 1 state is represented in upper school student body. 4% are international students. International students from China, Indonesia, Japan, and Republic of Korea. 78% of students are members of Church of Christ.

Faculty School total: 55. In upper school: 16 men, 15 women; 20 have advanced degrees; 1 resides on campus.

Subjects Offered Accounting, ACT preparation, advanced chemistry, advanced math, algebra, American history, anatomy, art, athletic training, Bible, Bible studies, biology, calculus-AP, chemistry, chorus, civics, computer applications, computer programming, consumer education, drama, engineering, English, English-AP, family living, geography, geometry, health, history, history-AP, human anatomy, journalism, keyboarding, life skills, Mandarin, mathematics, modern world history, music appreciation, physical education, physical science, physics-AP, pre-calculus, psychology, robotics, science, Spanish, speech, statistics, study skills, wellness.

Special Academic Programs Advanced Placement exam preparation; study at local college for college credit; ESL (4 students enrolled).

College Admission Counseling 63 students graduated in 2014; 60 went to college, including Arkansas State University; Freed-Hardeman University; Harding University; Northpoint Bible College; Ouachita Baptist University; University of Arkansas. Other: 2 went to work, 1 entered military service. Median composite ACT: 24.

Student Life Upper grades have specified standards of dress, student council, honor system. Discipline rests primarily with faculty. Attendance at religious services is required.

Tuition and Aid Tuition installment plan (monthly payment plans). Tuition reduction for siblings, need-based scholarship grants available.

Admissions Traditional secondary-level entrance grade is 7. Any standardized test or TOEFL required. Deadline for receipt of application materials: none. Application fee required: $50. Interview required.

Athletics Interscholastic: baseball (boys), basketball (b,g), cheering (g), cross-country running (b,g), football (b), golf (b,g), softball (g), tennis (b,g), track and field (b,g), volleyball (g), weight lifting (b). 4 PE instructors, 10 coaches, 1 athletic trainer.

Computers Computers are regularly used in all academic classes. Computer network features include on-campus library services, Internet access, wireless campus network, Internet filtering or blocking technology. Student e-mail accounts are available to students. Students grades are available online. The school has a published electronic and media policy.

Contact Darren Mathews, High School Principal. 501-279-7201. Fax: 501-279-7213. E-mail: dmathews@harding.edu. Website: academy.harding.edu/

HARGRAVE MILITARY ACADEMY

200 Military Drive
Chatham, Virginia 24531

Head of School: Brig. Gen. Don Broome, USA (Ret.)

General Information Boys' boarding and day college-preparatory, general academic, arts, religious studies, bilingual studies, technology, academic postgraduate, leadership and ethics, and military school, affiliated with Baptist General Association of Virginia. Grades 7–PG. Founded: 1909. Setting: small town. Nearest major city is Danville. Students are housed in single-sex dormitories. 214-acre campus. 29 buildings on campus. Approved or accredited by Southern Association of Colleges and Schools, The Association of Boarding Schools, and Virginia Association of Independent Schools. Member of National Association of Independent Schools. Endowment: $3.5 million. Total enrollment: 230. Upper school average class size: 11. Upper school faculty-student ratio: 1:12. Upper School students typically attend 5 days per week.

Upper School Student Profile 24 states are represented in upper school student body. 20% of students are Baptist General Association of Virginia.

Faculty School total: 30. In upper school: 17 men, 13 women; 7 have advanced degrees; 6 reside on campus.

Subjects Offered Advanced biology, advanced chemistry, advanced math, Advanced Placement courses, algebra, American government, American history, American literature, art, astronomy, Bible studies, biology, calculus, chemistry, creative writing, debate, English, English literature, environmental science, ESL, functions, geometry, government/civics, health, history, journalism, leadership, leadership and service, leadership education training, Mandarin, mathematics, media production, physical education, physics, psychology, reading, religion, SAT/ACT preparation, science, social studies, sociology, Spanish, speech, study skills, TOEFL preparation, trigonometry.

Graduation Requirements English, foreign language, mathematics, physical education (includes health), religion (includes Bible studies and theology), science, social studies (includes history).

Special Academic Programs Advanced Placement exam preparation; honors section; independent study; study at local college for college credit; remedial reading and/or remedial writing; remedial math; programs in general development for dyslexic students; special instructional classes for students with Attention Deficit Disorder; ESL (8 students enrolled).

College Admission Counseling 62 students graduated in 2015; all went to college, including Hampden-Sydney College; The University of North Carolina at Charlotte; United States Military Academy; Virginia Military Institute; Virginia Polytechnic Institute and State University.

Student Life Upper grades have uniform requirement, student council, honor system. Discipline rests equally with students and faculty. Attendance at religious services is required.

Summer Programs Remediation, enrichment, advancement, ESL, sports, rigorous outdoor training, computer instruction programs offered; session focuses on academics/sports camps; held on campus; accepts boys; open to students from other schools. 140 students usually enrolled. 2016 schedule: June 26 to July 24. Application deadline: June 26.

Tuition and Aid Day student tuition: $12,900; 5-day tuition and room/board: $30,800; 7-day tuition and room/board: $30,800. Guaranteed tuition plan. Tuition installment plan (monthly payment plans, individually arranged payment plans). Tuition reduction for siblings, merit scholarship grants, need-based scholarship grants, need-based loans, Sallie Mae loans available. In 2015–16, 35% of upper-school students received aid; total upper-school merit-scholarship money awarded: $52,000. Total amount of financial aid awarded in 2015–16: $525,000.

Admissions Traditional secondary-level entrance grade is 10. Math and English placement tests required. Deadline for receipt of application materials: none. Application fee required: $75. Interview recommended.

Athletics Interscholastic: aquatics, baseball, basketball, cross-country running, football, golf, independent competitive sports, lacrosse, marksmanship, riflery, soccer, swimming and diving, tennis, track and field, wrestling; intramural: aquatics, billiards, canoeing/kayaking, climbing, cross-country running, drill team, fishing, fitness, fitness walking, hiking/backpacking, independent competitive sports, jogging, jump rope, kayaking, lacrosse, life saving, marksmanship, mountaineering, Nautilus, outdoor activities, outdoor adventure, outdoor recreation, paint ball, physical fitness, physical training, power lifting, rappelling, riflery, rock climbing, ropes courses, running, scuba diving, skeet shooting, skiing (downhill), strength & conditioning, swimming and diving, table tennis, tennis, trap and skeet, walking, water polo, weight lifting, weight training. 1 PE instructor, 10 coaches, 1 athletic trainer.

Computers Computers are regularly used in all academic, photography classes. Computer network features include on-campus library services, online commercial services, Internet access, wireless campus network, Internet filtering or blocking technology. Campus intranet, student e-mail accounts, and computer access in designated common areas are available to students. Students grades are available online. The school has a published electronic and media policy.

Contact Mr. Thomas Messinger, Director of Admissions. 800-432-2480. Fax: 434-432-3129. E-mail: admissions@hargrave.edu. Website: www.hargrave.edu

THE HARKER SCHOOL

500 Saratoga Avenue
San Jose, California 95129

Head of School: Christopher Nikoloff

General Information Coeducational day college-preparatory, arts, business, technology, and gifted students school. Grades K–12. Founded: 1893. Setting: urban. 16-acre campus. 7 buildings on campus. Approved or accredited by California Association of Independent Schools, Western Association of Schools and Colleges, and California Department of Education. Member of National Association of Independent Schools. Total enrollment: 1,911. Upper school average class size: 18. Upper school faculty-student ratio: 1:10. Upper School students typically attend 5 days per week. The average school day consists of 7 hours and 13 minutes.

Upper School Student Profile Grade 9: 197 students (93 boys, 104 girls); Grade 10: 193 students (97 boys, 96 girls); Grade 11: 190 students (93 boys, 97 girls); Grade 12: 187 students (89 boys, 98 girls).

Faculty School total: 222. In upper school: 43 men, 47 women; 69 have advanced degrees.

Subjects Offered 20th century American writers, acting, advanced math, algebra, American literature, anatomy and physiology, architecture, art history, art history-AP, Asian history, astronomy, baseball, basketball, biology, biology-AP, biotechnology, British literature, British literature (honors), calculus-AP, ceramics, cheerleading, chemistry, chemistry-AP, choreography, classical studies, college counseling, community service, computer science-AP, dance, dance performance, debate, digital photography, discrete mathematics, drawing, ecology, economics, electronics, engineering, English literature and composition-AP, English literature-AP, environmental science-AP, ethics, European history-AP, evolution, expository writing, film and literature, fitness, forensics, French, French language-AP, French literature-AP, geometry, golf, graphic arts, graphic design, great books, history of dance, Holocaust seminar, honors algebra, honors geometry, human geography - AP, Japanese, Japanese literature, jazz band, journalism, Latin, Latin-AP, linear algebra, literary magazine, Mandarin, medieval literature, mentorship program, music appreciation, music theory-AP, newspaper, orchestra, organic chemistry, painting, photography, physics, physics-AP, play production, poetry, political thought, pre-calculus, programming, psychology, psychology-AP, public policy, public speaking, research, robotics, scene study, sculpture, Shakespeare, softball, Spanish, Spanish language-AP, Spanish literature-AP, statistics, statistics-AP, stone carving, student government, studio art-AP, study skills, swimming, technical theater, tennis, theater arts, theater history, track and field, trigonometry, U.S. government and politics-AP, U.S. history, U.S. history-AP, video and animation, visual arts, vocal ensemble, volleyball, water polo, weight training, Western philosophy, world history, world history-AP, world religions, wrestling, yearbook, yoga.

Graduation Requirements Arts and fine arts (art, music, dance, drama), biology, chemistry, computer science, English, foreign language, mathematics, physical education (includes health), physics, public speaking, U.S. history, world history, 30 total hours of community service, one year arts survey theater, dance, music or visual arts.

Special Academic Programs Advanced Placement exam preparation; honors section; independent study; academic accommodation for the gifted.

College Admission Counseling 187 students graduated in 2015; all went to college, including Cornell University; Stanford University; University of California, Berkeley; University of Chicago; University of Southern California; Yale University. Mean SAT critical reading: 710, mean SAT math: 736, mean SAT writing: 736.

Student Life Upper grades have specified standards of dress, student council, honor system. Discipline rests primarily with faculty.

Summer Programs Enrichment, advancement, ESL, sports programs offered; session focuses on academics, sports, enrichment, research; held both on and off campus; held at abroad for upper school research and language students and field trips to local historical and cultural sites; accepts boys and girls; open to students from other schools. 1,112 students usually enrolled. 2016 schedule: June 22 to August 7.

Tuition and Aid Day student tuition: $41,432. Need-based scholarship grants, need-based loans available. In 2015–16, 10% of upper-school students received aid.

Admissions Traditional secondary-level entrance grade is 9. ERB CTP IV, essay, ISEE or SSAT required. Deadline for receipt of application materials: January 14. Application fee required: $100. Interview required.

Athletics Interscholastic: baseball (boys), basketball (b,g), cross-country running (b,g), football (b), golf (b,g), lacrosse (g), soccer (b,g), softball (g), swimming and diving (b,g), tennis (b,g), track and field (b,g), volleyball (b,g), water polo (b,g); coed interscholastic: cheering, wrestling; coed intramural: aerobics/dance, dance, fencing, fitness, physical fitness, tennis, yoga. 4 PE instructors, 27 coaches, 1 athletic trainer.

Computers Computers are regularly used in all academic, business, college planning, graphic arts, newspaper, yearbook classes. Computer network features include on-campus library services, online commercial services, Internet access, wireless campus network, Internet filtering or blocking technology, ProQuest, Gale Group, InfoTrac, Facts On File. Campus intranet and student e-mail accounts are available to students. The school has a published electronic and media policy.

Contact Christianne Marra, Assistant to the Director of Admission. 408-249-2510. Fax: 408-984-2325. E-mail: christianne.marra@harker.org. Website: www.harker.org

THE HARLEY SCHOOL

1981 Clover Street
Rochester, New York 14618

Head of School: Mr. Ward J. Ghory

General Information Coeducational day college-preparatory and arts school. Grades N–12. Founded: 1917. Setting: suburban. 25-acre campus. 5 buildings on campus. Approved or accredited by National Independent Private Schools Association and New York State Association of Independent Schools. Member of National Association of Independent Schools. Endowment: $10.4 million. Total enrollment: 537. Upper school average class size: 8. Upper school faculty-student ratio: 1:8. There are 180 required school days per year for Upper School students. Upper School students typically attend 5 days per week. The average school day consists of 6 hours and 50 minutes.

Upper School Student Profile Grade 9: 47 students (20 boys, 27 girls); Grade 10: 47 students (16 boys, 31 girls); Grade 11: 49 students (21 boys, 28 girls); Grade 12: 45 students (21 boys, 24 girls).

Faculty School total: 90. In upper school: 14 men, 14 women; 28 have advanced degrees.

Subjects Offered 3-dimensional art, Advanced Placement courses, algebra, American history, anthropology, art, art history, art-AP, band, biology, calculus, calculus-AP, ceramics, chamber groups, chemistry, Chinese, choir, chorus, community service, comparative government and politics-AP, computer graphics, computer math, computer programming, computer science, creative writing, debate, desktop publishing, drama, drawing, driver education, economics-AP, English, English language and composition-AP, English literature, environmental science, ethics, European history, expository writing, film, fine arts, foreign language, French, gardening, geometry, graphic arts, Greek, health, jazz band, language-AP, Latin, mathematics, multimedia, music, music theory, orchestra, organic gardening, outdoor education, photography, physical education, physics, psychology, SAT preparation, science, Shakespeare, social studies, Spanish, speech, student government, study skills, theater, theater arts, theater production, U.S. history-AP, voice, world history, writing, yoga.

Graduation Requirements Arts and fine arts (art, music, dance, drama), computer science, English, foreign language, internship, mathematics, physical education (includes health), science, social studies (includes history), participation in team sports, community service. Community service is required.

Special Academic Programs 17 Advanced Placement exams for which test preparation is offered.

College Admission Counseling 43 students graduated in 2014; all went to college, including Northwestern University; Oberlin College; Rochester Institute of Technology; University of Michigan; University of Pittsburgh; University of Rochester. Mean SAT critical reading: 628, mean SAT math: 621, mean SAT writing: 619.

Student Life Upper grades have student council, honor system. Discipline rests primarily with faculty.

Tuition and Aid Day student tuition: $18,500–$23,750. Tuition installment plan (Insured Tuition Payment Plan, monthly payment plans, 2-payment plan, prepaid discount plan). Tuition reduction for siblings, need-based scholarship grants available. In 2014–15, 33% of upper-school students received aid.

Admissions Traditional secondary-level entrance grade is 9. For fall 2014, 38 students applied for upper-level admission, 17 were accepted, 14 enrolled. Essay and Math Placement Exam required. Deadline for receipt of application materials: none. Application fee required: $50. On-campus interview required.

Athletics Interscholastic: baseball (boys), basketball (b,g), bowling (b,g), golf (b), skiing (downhill) (b,g), soccer (b,g), softball (b,g), swimming and diving (b,g), tennis (b,g), track and field (b,g), volleyball (b,g); coed interscholastic: cross-country running, outdoor education, running, yoga. 3 PE instructors, 11 coaches.

Computers Computers are regularly used in all academic, art classes. Computer network features include Internet access, wireless campus network. The school has a published electronic and media policy.

Contact Mrs. Ivone Foisy, Director of Admissions. 585-442-1770 Ext. 3009. Fax: 585-442-5758. E-mail: ifoisy@harleyschool.org. Website: www.harleyschool.org

THE HARPETH HALL SCHOOL

3801 Hobbs Road
PO Box 150207
Nashville, Tennessee 37215-0207

Head of School: Dr. Stephanie Balmer

General Information Girls' day college-preparatory, arts, and technology school. Grades 5–12. Founded: 1951. Setting: suburban. 45-acre campus. 7 buildings on campus. Approved or accredited by Southern Association of Colleges and Schools, Southern Association of Independent Schools, and Tennessee Association of Independent Schools. Member of National Association of Independent Schools. Endowment: $41.3 million. Total enrollment: 690. Upper school average class size: 16. Upper school faculty-student ratio: 1:8. There are 180 required school days per year for Upper School students. Upper School students typically attend 5 days per week. The average school day consists of 6 hours.

Upper School Student Profile Grade 9: 102 students (102 girls); Grade 10: 102 students (102 girls); Grade 11: 103 students (103 girls); Grade 12: 103 students (103 girls).

Faculty School total: 92. In upper school: 16 men, 53 women; 53 have advanced degrees.

Subjects Offered Advanced Placement courses, algebra, American government, American history, American history-AP, American literature, art, art history, art history-AP, athletics, audio visual/media, biology, biology-AP, calculus, chamber groups, chemistry, chemistry-AP, Chinese, choir, choral music, college admission preparation, college counseling, comparative politics, computer math, computer programming, computer science, conceptual physics, contemporary issues, creative writing, dance, digital art, drama, ecology, English, English literature, environmental science, environmental studies, European history, European history-AP, expository writing, fine arts, French, French language-AP, French literature-AP, functions, geometry, government/civics, grammar, health, history, honors algebra, honors English, Latin, Latin-AP, life skills, Mandarin, mathematics, media arts, music, photography, physical education, physics, physics-AP, probability and statistics, psychology, science, social sciences, social studies, Spanish, Spanish language-AP, Spanish literature-AP, speech, statistics-AP, studio art-AP, theater, theater arts, trigonometry, video, world history, world history-AP, world literature, writing.

Graduation Requirements Arts and fine arts (art, music, dance, drama), electives, English, foreign language, mathematics, physical education (includes health), science, social sciences, participation in Winterim program each year.

Special Academic Programs Advanced Placement exam preparation; honors section; independent study; term-away projects; study abroad; academic accommodation for the gifted, the musically talented, and the artistically talented.

College Admission Counseling 96 students graduated in 2015; 94 went to college, including Furman University; Southern Methodist University; The University of Tennessee; University of Georgia; Vanderbilt University. Other: 2 had other specific plans.

Student Life Upper grades have uniform requirement, student council, honor system. Discipline rests primarily with faculty.

Summer Programs Enrichment, sports, art/fine arts, computer instruction programs offered; session focuses on enrichment classes and sports; held on campus; accepts girls; open to students from other schools. 750 students usually enrolled. 2016 schedule: June 6 to August 5. Application deadline: none.

Tuition and Aid Day student tuition: $25,380. Tuition installment plan (monthly payment plans, individually arranged payment plans, Tuition Management Systems Plan). Need-based scholarship grants available. In 2015–16, 17% of upper-school students received aid. Total amount of financial aid awarded in 2015–16: $1,000,000.

Admissions Traditional secondary-level entrance grade is 9. For fall 2015, 53 students applied for upper-level admission, 39 were accepted, 26 enrolled. ISEE required. Deadline for receipt of application materials: January 4. Application fee required: $50. Interview required.

Athletics Interscholastic: aquatics, basketball, bowling, crew, cross-country running, diving, golf, lacrosse, running, soccer, softball, swimming and diving, tennis, track and field, volleyball; intramural: aerobics/dance, cheering, climbing, cooperative games, dance, fitness, flag football, jogging, modern dance, outdoor activities, outdoor adventure, outdoor education, outdoor recreation, outdoor skills, physical training, rock climbing, self defense, strength & conditioning, ultimate Frisbee, walking, wall climbing, weight training, yoga; coed intramural: riflery. 4 PE instructors, 20 coaches, 1 athletic trainer.

Computers Computers are regularly used in all academic classes. Computer network features include on-campus library services, online commercial services, Internet access, wireless campus network, Internet filtering or blocking technology. Campus intranet and student e-mail accounts are available to students. Students grades are available online. The school has a published electronic and media policy.

Contact Sandy Binkley, Admission Coordinator. 615-346-0126. Fax: 615-647-0724. E-mail: binkley@harpethhall.org. Website: www.harpethhall.org

HARRELLS CHRISTIAN ACADEMY

360 Tomahawk Highway
PO Box 88
Harrells, North Carolina 28444

Head of School: Mr. Kevin M. Kunst

General Information Coeducational day college-preparatory school, affiliated with Christian faith. Grades K–12. Founded: 1969. Setting: rural. Nearest major city is Wilmington. 32-acre campus. 7 buildings on campus. Approved or accredited by North Carolina Association of Independent Schools, Southern Association of Colleges and Schools, Southern Association of Independent Schools, and North Carolina Department of Education. Total enrollment: 363. Upper school average class size: 12. Upper school faculty-student ratio: 1:11. There are 180 required school days per year for Upper School students. Upper School students typically attend 5 days per week. The average school day consists of 5 hours and 23 minutes.

Upper School Student Profile Grade 9: 28 students (16 boys, 12 girls); Grade 10: 27 students (18 boys, 9 girls); Grade 11: 35 students (20 boys, 15 girls); Grade 12: 44 students (23 boys, 21 girls). 96% of students are Christian.

Faculty School total: 15. In upper school: 4 men, 10 women; 4 have advanced degrees.

Subjects Offered Algebra, animal science, art, art education, biology, biology-AP, calculus, ceramics, chemistry, chemistry-AP, computer art, earth science, English, English language and composition-AP, English literature, English literature and composition-AP, environmental science-AP, French, government/civics, history, journalism, mathematics, painting, physical education, religion, social studies, Spanish, U.S. history-AP, weightlifting, world history-AP, yearbook.

Graduation Requirements Biology, computer applications, electives, English, environmental science, foreign language, mathematics, physical education (includes health), physical science, religious studies, science, social studies (includes history).

Special Academic Programs 5 Advanced Placement exams for which test preparation is offered; honors section; study at local college for college credit; programs in English, mathematics, general development for dyslexic students.

College Admission Counseling 38 students graduated in 2015; 22 went to college, including College of Charleston; East Carolina University; North Carolina State University; The University of North Carolina at Chapel Hill; The University of North Carolina Wilmington; University of Mississippi. Other: 1 went to work, 14 entered a postgraduate year, 1 had other specific plans. Median SAT critical reading: 460, median SAT math: 470, median SAT writing: 460, median combined SAT: 1390, median composite ACT: 21. 4% scored over 600 on SAT critical reading, 11% scored over 600 on SAT math, 6% scored over 26 on composite ACT.

Student Life Upper grades have specified standards of dress, honor system. Discipline rests primarily with faculty. Attendance at religious services is required.

Tuition and Aid Day student tuition: $8510. Tuition installment plan (SMART Tuition Payment Plan). Tuition reduction for siblings, need-based scholarship grants available. In 2015–16, 15% of upper-school students received aid. Total amount of financial aid awarded in 2015–16: $61,378.

Admissions Traditional secondary-level entrance grade is 9. For fall 2015, 24 students applied for upper-level admission, 20 were accepted, 18 enrolled. Achievement tests required. Deadline for receipt of application materials: none. Application fee required: $75. On-campus interview required.

Athletics Interscholastic: baseball (boys), basketball (b,g), cheering (g), football (b), soccer (b,g), softball (g), tennis (g), volleyball (g); coed interscholastic: golf. 1 PE instructor, 1 coach.

Computers Computers are regularly used in art, English, journalism, yearbook classes. Computer resources include Internet access, wireless campus network, Internet filtering or blocking technology. Students grades are available online. The school has a published electronic and media policy.

Contact Mrs. Susan Frederick, Administrative Assistant. 910-532-4575 Ext. 221. Fax: 910-532-2958. E-mail: sfrederick@harrellsca.com. Website: www.harrellschristianacademy.com

HARVARD-WESTLAKE SCHOOL

3700 Coldwater Canyon
Studio City, California 91604

Head of School: Richard B. Commons

General Information Coeducational day college-preparatory school. Grades 7–12. Founded: 1989. Setting: urban. Nearest major city is Los Angeles. 26-acre campus. 12 buildings on campus. Approved or accredited by Western Association of Schools and Colleges. Member of National Association of Independent Schools. Endowment: $92.7 million. Total enrollment: 1,592. Upper school average class size: 16. Upper school faculty-student ratio: 1:8. Upper School students typically attend 5 days per week. The average school day consists of 6 hours and 35 minutes.

Upper School Student Profile Grade 9: 295 students (151 boys, 144 girls); Grade 10: 288 students (158 boys, 130 girls); Grade 11: 292 students (158 boys, 134 girls); Grade 12: 286 students (159 boys, 127 girls).

Faculty School total: 122. In upper school: 72 men, 50 women; 85 have advanced degrees.

Subjects Offered 3-dimensional art, advanced studio art-AP, algebra, American history, American history-AP, American literature, American literature-AP, anatomy, architecture, art, art history, art history-AP, art-AP, Asian studies, astronomy, biology, biology-AP, calculus, calculus-AP, ceramics, chemistry, chemistry-AP, Chinese, choreography, chorus, classics, community service, comparative government and politics-AP, composition-AP, computer animation, computer programming, computer science, computer science-AP, creative writing, dance, dance performance, drama, drawing, economics, economics-AP, electronics, English, English language and composition-AP, English language-AP, English literature, English literature and composition-AP, English literature-AP, environmental science, environmental science-AP, European history, expository writing, film, film studies, fine arts, French, French language-AP, French literature-AP, French-AP, geography, geology, geometry, government and politics-AP, government-AP, government/civics, grammar, health, human development, human geography - AP, Japanese, jazz, jazz band, journalism, Latin, Latin-AP, law and the legal system, logic, macro/microeconomics-AP, Mandarin, mathematics, music, music history, music theory-AP, oceanography, orchestra, painting, photography, physical education, physics, physics-AP, physiology, political science, pre-calculus, psychology, Russian, science, senior project, Shakespeare, social studies, Spanish, Spanish language-AP, Spanish literature-AP, Spanish-AP, statistics, statistics-AP, studio art-AP, technical theater, theater, trigonometry, U.S. government and politics-AP, U.S. history, U.S. history-AP, video, women's studies, world history, world history-AP, world literature, yearbook, zoology.

Graduation Requirements English, foreign language, history, human development, mathematics, performing arts, physical education (includes health), science, technical skills, visual arts. Community service is required.

Special Academic Programs 30 Advanced Placement exams for which test preparation is offered; honors section; independent study; term-away projects; study abroad; academic accommodation for the gifted, the musically talented, and the artistically talented.

College Admission Counseling 283 students graduated in 2015; 281 went to college, including Brown University; Harvard University; New York University; University of Michigan; University of Pennsylvania; University of Southern California. Other: 2 had other specific plans. Mean SAT critical reading: 700, mean SAT math: 716, mean SAT writing: 720. 93% scored over 600 on SAT critical reading, 95% scored over 600 on SAT math, 93% scored over 600 on SAT writing, 93% scored over 1800 on combined SAT, 93% scored over 26 on composite ACT.

Student Life Upper grades have specified standards of dress, student council, honor system. Discipline rests primarily with faculty.

Summer Programs Enrichment, sports, art/fine arts, rigorous outdoor training, computer instruction programs offered; session focuses on enrichment and sports; held on campus; accepts boys and girls; open to students from other schools. 1,392 students usually enrolled. 2016 schedule: June 13 to August 12. Application deadline: none.

Tuition and Aid Day student tuition: $34,700. Tuition installment plan (monthly payment plans, semi-annual payment plan, triennial payment plan). Need-based scholarship grants available. In 2015–16, 19% of upper-school students received aid. Total amount of financial aid awarded in 2015–16: $7,636,700.

Admissions Traditional secondary-level entrance grade is 9. For fall 2015, 597 students applied for upper-level admission, 134 were accepted, 106 enrolled. ISEE required. Deadline for receipt of application materials: January 15. Application fee required: $200. On-campus interview required.

Athletics Interscholastic: baseball (boys), basketball (b,g), cross-country running (b,g), field hockey (g), football (b), golf (b,g), gymnastics (g), lacrosse (b), soccer (b,g), softball (g), swimming and diving (b,g), tennis (b,g), track and field (b,g), volleyball (b,g), water polo (b,g), wrestling (b); coed interscholastic: diving, equestrian sports, fencing, martial arts. 6 PE instructors, 32 coaches, 4 athletic trainers.

Computers Computers are regularly used in art, English, foreign language, history, mathematics, music, science classes. Computer resources include on-campus library services, Internet access, wireless campus network, 1:1 laptop program, music composition and editing, foreign language lab, science lab. Campus intranet, student e-mail accounts, and computer access in designated common areas are available to students. Students grades are available online. The school has a published electronic and media policy.

Contact Elizabeth Gregory, Director of Admission. 310-274-7281. Fax: 310-288-3212. E-mail: egregory@hw.com. Website: www.hw.com

THE HARVEY SCHOOL

260 Jay Street
Katonah, New York 10536

Head of School: Mr. Barry W. Fenstermacher

General Information Coeducational boarding and day and distance learning college-preparatory school. Boarding grades 9–12, day grades 6–12. Distance learning grades 6–12. Founded: 1916. Setting: small town. Students are housed in single-sex dormitories. 125-acre campus. 14 buildings on campus. Approved or accredited by New York State Association of Independent Schools. Member of National Association of Independent Schools. Endowment: $3 million. Total enrollment: 365. Upper school average class size: 10. Upper school faculty-student ratio: 1:6. There are 165 required school days per year for Upper School students. Upper School students typically attend 5 days per week. The average school day consists of 8 hours and 50 minutes.

Upper School Student Profile Grade 9: 76 students (43 boys, 33 girls); Grade 10: 67 students (39 boys, 28 girls); Grade 11: 73 students (39 boys, 34 girls); Grade 12: 69 students (36 boys, 33 girls). 10% of students are boarding students. 75% are state residents. 3 states are represented in upper school student body. 4% are international students. International students from China, France, Samoa, and Taiwan.

Faculty School total: 61. In upper school: 26 men, 24 women; 30 have advanced degrees; 22 reside on campus.

Subjects Offered 3-dimensional design, algebra, American history, American literature, art, art history, biology, calculus, ceramics, chemistry, composition AP, computer programming-AP, creative writing, drama, English, English literature, European history, expository writing, fine arts, general science, geology, geometry, government/civics, grammar, history, Japanese, Latin, mathematics, music, photography, physics, religion, science, social studies, Spanish, theater, trigonometry, world history, writing.

Graduation Requirements Arts and fine arts (art, music, dance, drama), computer literacy, English, foreign language, mathematics, science, social sciences, social studies (includes history).

Special Academic Programs 10 Advanced Placement exams for which test preparation is offered; honors section; independent study.

College Admission Counseling 69 students graduated in 2015; all went to college, including Barnard College; Bentley University; Cornell University; University of Connecticut; Villanova University.

Student Life Upper grades have specified standards of dress, student council. Discipline rests primarily with faculty.

Summer Programs Remediation, advancement programs offered; session focuses on online academic course; held both on and off campus; held at via distance learning; accepts boys and girls; open to students from other schools. 2016 schedule: June 20 to August 10. Application deadline: May 1.

Tuition and Aid Day student tuition: $33,150–$36,150; 5-day tuition and room/board: $42,850–$44,150. Tuition installment plan (FACTS Tuition Payment Plan, individually arranged payment plans). Need-based scholarship grants available. In 2015–16, 26% of upper-school students received aid. Total amount of financial aid awarded in 2015–16: $2,080,000.

Admissions Traditional secondary-level entrance grade is 9. For fall 2015, 187 students applied for upper-level admission, 101 were accepted, 54 enrolled. Deadline for receipt of application materials: none. Application fee required: $50. Interview required.

Athletics Interscholastic: baseball (boys), basketball (b,g), football (b), ice hockey (b), lacrosse (b,g), rugby (b), soccer (b,g), softball (g), tennis (b,g), volleyball (g); coed interscholastic: cross-country running, weight lifting, yoga; coed intramural: aerobics, dance, figure skating, fitness, fitness walking, Frisbee, golf, modern dance, strength & conditioning, tai chi, yoga. 20 coaches, 1 athletic trainer.

Computers Computers are regularly used in English, foreign language, history, mathematics, science classes. Computer resources include on-campus library services, online commercial services, Internet access. The school has a published electronic and media policy.

Contact Mr. William Porter, Director of Admissions. 914-232-3161 Ext. 113. Fax: 914-232-6034. E-mail: wporter@harveyschool.org. Website: www.harveyschool.org

HATHAWAY BROWN SCHOOL

19600 North Park Boulevard
Shaker Heights, Ohio 44122

Head of School: H. William Christ

General Information Coeducational day (boys' only in lower grades) college-preparatory, arts, business, and technology school. Boys grade PS, girls grades PS–12. Founded: 1876. Setting: suburban. Nearest major city is Cleveland. 16-acre campus. 1 building on campus. Approved or accredited by Independent Schools Association of the Central States, Ohio Association of Independent Schools, and Ohio Department of Education. Member of National Association of Independent Schools. Endowment: $53.5 million. Total enrollment: 848. Upper school average class size: 18. Upper school faculty-student ratio: 1:8. There are 186 required school days per year for Upper School students. Upper School students typically attend 5 days per week. The average school day consists of 7 hours and 17 minutes.

Upper School Student Profile Grade 9: 96 students (96 girls); Grade 10: 108 students (108 girls); Grade 11: 96 students (96 girls); Grade 12: 85 students (85 girls).

Faculty School total: 143. In upper school: 19 men, 48 women; 37 have advanced degrees.

Subjects Offered Advanced Placement courses, algebra, American history, American literature, anatomy, art, art history, biology, biology-AP, calculus, ceramics, chemistry, chemistry-AP, communications, community service, computer math, computer programming, computer science, creative writing, dance, drama, economics, engineering, English, English literature, environmental science, ethics, European history, expository writing, fine arts, French, geography, geometry, government/civics, graphic design, health, history, international relations, journalism, Latin, mathematics, microbiology, music, outdoor education, photography, physical education, physics, physics-AP, physiology, psychology, research seminar, science, social studies, Spanish, statistics, statistics-AP, theater, trigonometry, U.S. history, U.S. history-AP, woodworking, world history, writing.

Graduation Requirements Arts and fine arts (art, music, dance, drama), computer applications, computer science, English, foreign language, history, mathematics, physical education (includes health), science, senior speech, senior project.

Special Academic Programs 16 Advanced Placement exams for which test preparation is offered; honors section; independent study; term-away projects; study at local college for college credit; study abroad; academic accommodation for the gifted and the musically talented; remedial reading and/or remedial writing; remedial math; programs in general development for dyslexic students; special instructional classes for deaf students.

College Admission Counseling 85 students graduated in 2015; all went to college, including Bates College; Brown University; Columbia College; Miami University; Yale University. Mean SAT critical reading: 633, mean SAT math: 631, mean SAT writing: 653, mean combined SAT: 1917.

Student Life Upper grades have specified standards of dress, student council, honor system. Discipline rests equally with students and faculty.

Summer Programs Enrichment, advancement, sports programs offered; session focuses on science and foreign language advancement, humanities and mathematics enrichment; held on campus; accepts boys and girls; open to students from other schools. 60 students usually enrolled. 2016 schedule: June 1 to August 10. Application deadline: none.

Tuition and Aid Day student tuition: $26,100–$27,400. Tuition installment plan (Academic Management Services Plan, Key Tuition Payment Plan). Merit scholarship grants, need-based scholarship grants available. In 2015–16, 30% of upper-school students received aid. Total amount of financial aid awarded in 2015–16: $3,100,000.

Admissions Traditional secondary-level entrance grade is 9. For fall 2015, 150 students applied for upper-level admission, 40 enrolled. ISEE required. Deadline for receipt of application materials: none. Application fee required: $35. Interview required.

Athletics Interscholastic: basketball, cross-country running, diving, field hockey, golf, indoor track & field, lacrosse, soccer, softball, swimming and diving, tennis, track and field, volleyball; intramural: modern dance, outdoor adventure, physical fitness, physical training, ropes courses, strength & conditioning. 6 PE instructors, 22 coaches, 1 athletic trainer.

Computers Computers are regularly used in all academic classes. Computer network features include on-campus library services, online commercial services, Internet access, wireless campus network, Internet filtering or blocking technology. Student e-mail accounts and computer access in designated common areas are available to students. The school has a published electronic and media policy.

Contact Tina Reifsnyder, Admission Coordinator. 216-320-8767. Fax: 216-371-1501. E-mail: treifsnyder@hb.edu. Website: www.hb.edu

THE HAVERFORD SCHOOL

450 Lancaster Avenue
Haverford, Pennsylvania 19041

Head of School: Dr. John A. Nagl

General Information Boys' day college-preparatory, arts, and bilingual studies school. Grades PK–12. Founded: 1884. Setting: suburban. Nearest major city is Philadelphia. 30-acre campus. 7 buildings on campus. Approved or accredited by Middle States Association of Colleges and Schools, Pennsylvania Association of Independent Schools, and Pennsylvania Department of Education. Member of National Association of Independent Schools and Secondary School Admission Test Board. Endowment: $65.5 million. Total enrollment: 977. Upper school average class size: 16. Upper school faculty-student ratio: 1:8. There are 170 required school days per year for Upper School students. Upper School students typically attend 5 days per week. The average school day consists of 6 hours and 45 minutes.

Upper School Student Profile Grade 9: 106 students (106 boys); Grade 10: 106 students (106 boys); Grade 11: 110 students (110 boys); Grade 12: 103 students (103 boys).

Faculty School total: 124. In upper school: 37 men, 19 women; 40 have advanced degrees.

Subjects Offered 3-dimensional art, algebra, ancient world history, biology, calculus, chemistry, Chinese, clayworking, engineering, geometry, Latin, modern world history, physical education, physics, Spanish, theater, U.S. history, video and animation, visual and performing arts, world history.

Graduation Requirements Arts and fine arts (art, music, dance, drama), English, foreign language, mathematics, physical education (includes health), science, social studies (includes history).

Special Academic Programs Honors section; independent study; term-away projects; academic accommodation for the gifted; remedial reading and/or remedial writing; remedial math.

College Admission Counseling 117 students graduated in 2015; all went to college, including Dickinson College; Penn State University Park; The George Washington University; University of Colorado Boulder; University of Pennsylvania; Wake Forest University. Mean SAT critical reading: 630, mean SAT math: 640, mean SAT writing: 640, mean combined SAT: 1910, mean composite ACT: 26. 41% scored over 600 on SAT critical reading, 48% scored over 600 on SAT math, 42% scored over 600 on SAT writing.

Student Life Upper grades have specified standards of dress, student council, honor system. Discipline rests equally with students and faculty.

Tuition and Aid Day student tuition: $37,500. Tuition installment plan (Insured Tuition Payment Plan, monthly payment plans, individually arranged payment plans). Merit scholarship grants, need-based scholarship grants available. In 2015–16, 31% of upper-school students received aid; total upper-school merit-scholarship money awarded: $20,000. Total amount of financial aid awarded in 2015–16: $2,614,756.

Admissions Traditional secondary-level entrance grade is 9. For fall 2015, 193 students applied for upper-level admission, 68 were accepted, 39 enrolled. ISEE, SSAT or Wechsler Intelligence Scale for Children required. Deadline for receipt of application materials: none. Application fee required: $40. Interview required.

Athletics Interscholastic: aquatics, baseball, basketball, crew, cross-country running, football, golf, ice hockey, indoor track, lacrosse, rowing, soccer, squash, swimming and diving, tennis, track and field, ultimate Frisbee, water polo, winter (indoor) track, wrestling; intramural: fitness, physical fitness, physical training, strength & conditioning, weight training. 2 PE instructors, 2 coaches, 2 athletic trainers.

Computers Computers are regularly used in art, English, history, mathematics, music, science classes. Computer network features include on-campus library services, online commercial services, Internet access, wireless campus network, Internet filtering or blocking technology. Campus intranet, student e-mail accounts, and computer access in designated common areas are available to students. Students grades are available online. The school has a published electronic and media policy.

Contact Mr. Kevin Seits, Interim Director of Admissions. 610-642-3020 Ext. 1457. Fax: 610-642-8724. E-mail: kseits@haverford.org. Website: www.haverford.org

HAWAIIAN MISSION ACADEMY

1438 Pensacola Street
Honolulu, Hawaii 96822

Head of School: Mr. Roland Graham

General Information Coeducational boarding and day college-preparatory, general academic, arts, business, religious studies, bilingual studies, and technology school, affiliated with Seventh-day Adventist Church. Grades 9–12. Founded: 1895. Setting: urban. Students are housed in single-sex by floor dormitories. 4-acre campus. 4 buildings on campus. Approved or accredited by The Hawaii Council of Private Schools, Western Association of Schools and Colleges, and Hawaii Department of Education. Member of National Association of Independent Schools. Total enrollment: 106. Upper school average class size: 25. Upper school faculty-student ratio: 1:15. There are 180 required school days per year for Upper School students. Upper School students typically attend 5 days per week. The average school day consists of 6 hours and 50 minutes.

Upper School Student Profile Grade 9: 20 students (11 boys, 9 girls); Grade 10: 31 students (23 boys, 8 girls); Grade 11: 22 students (14 boys, 8 girls); Grade 12: 33 students (14 boys, 19 girls). 20% of students are boarding students. 46% are state residents. 2 states are represented in upper school student body. 30% are international students. International students from China, Japan, and Republic of Korea. 80% of students are Seventh-day Adventists.

Faculty School total: 9. In upper school: 6 men, 3 women; 4 have advanced degrees; 3 reside on campus.

Subjects Offered Algebra, anatomy and physiology, art, band, bell choir, Bible, biology, British literature, business, business education, business skills, calculus, chemistry, choir, Christianity, community service, computer literacy, computer science, conceptual physics, concert choir, desktop publishing, digital art, drama, economics, economics and history, electives, English, ESL, family and consumer science, family living, general science, geometry, grammar, Hawaiian history, health, independent living, interactive media, journalism, keyboarding, lab science, library, Microsoft, personal finance, physical education, pre-algebra, pre-calculus, Spanish, student government, student publications, U.S. government, U.S. history, video film production, weight training, work experience, work-study, world history, yearbook.

Graduation Requirements Algebra, arts and fine arts (art, music, dance, drama), Bible, biology, chemistry, computer literacy, English, foreign language, geometry, Hawaiian history, keyboarding, physical education (includes health), physics, practical arts, religion (includes Bible studies and theology), social studies (includes history), U.S. government, work experience, world history, 25 hours of community service per year, 100 hours of work experience throughout the 4 years combined. Community service is required.

Special Academic Programs Advanced Placement exam preparation; honors section; ESL (8 students enrolled).

College Admission Counseling 35 students graduated in 2014; all went to college, including Hawai`i Pacific University; Kapiolani Community College; La Sierra University; Pacific Union College; Southern Adventist University; University of Hawaii at Manoa. Mean SAT critical reading: 505, mean SAT math: 535.

Student Life Upper grades have specified standards of dress, student council. Discipline rests primarily with faculty. Attendance at religious services is required.

Tuition and Aid Tuition installment plan (Insured Tuition Payment Plan, monthly payment plans, individually arranged payment plans). Tuition reduction for siblings, need-based scholarship grants, paying campus jobs available. In 2014–15, 25% of upper-school students received aid.

Admissions Traditional secondary-level entrance grade is 9. Placement test and TOEFL required. Deadline for receipt of application materials: none. Application fee required: $25. Interview recommended.

Athletics Interscholastic: basketball (boys, girls), golf (b,g), volleyball (b,g). 2 PE instructors, 6 coaches.

Computers Computers are regularly used in desktop publishing, economics, graphic arts, journalism, keyboarding, media production, newspaper, publications, science, video film production, word processing, yearbook classes. Computer network features include on-campus library services, Internet access, wireless campus network. Students grades are available online.

Contact Mrs. Nenny Safotu, Registrar. 808-536-2207 Ext. 652. Fax: 808-524-3294. E-mail: registrar@hawaiianmissionacademy.org.
Website: www.hawaiianmissionacademy.org

HAWAII BAPTIST ACADEMY

2429 Pali Highway
Honolulu, Hawaii 96817

Head of School: Richard Bento

General Information Coeducational day college-preparatory and Christian education school, affiliated with Southern Baptist Convention. Grades K–12. Founded: 1949. Setting: urban. 13-acre campus. 5 buildings on campus. Approved or accredited by Association of Christian Schools International and Western Association of Schools and Colleges. Member of National Association of Independent Schools and Secondary School Admission Test Board. Endowment: $5.4 million. Total enrollment: 1,060. Upper school average class size: 16. Upper school faculty-student ratio: 1:16. There are 176 required school days per year for Upper School students. Upper School students typically attend 5 days per week. The average school day consists of 6 hours.

Upper School Student Profile Grade 9: 121 students (50 boys, 71 girls); Grade 10: 117 students (60 boys, 57 girls); Grade 11: 113 students (51 boys, 62 girls); Grade 12: 109 students (45 boys, 64 girls). 12% of students are Southern Baptist Convention.

Faculty School total: 88. In upper school: 19 men, 25 women; 22 have advanced degrees.

Subjects Offered Advanced Placement courses, algebra, American history, American literature, ancient world history, art, Bible studies, biology, biology-AP, British literature, calculus-AP, chemistry, chemistry-AP, Chinese, Christian education, Christian ethics, Christian studies, communication skills, concert band, digital photography, discrete mathematics, drafting, drama, drama performance, drawing, economics, English, English language and composition-AP, English literature, English literature-AP, environmental science, film, film history, fine arts, geometry, handbells, Japanese, journalism, mathematics, modern world history, music theory-AP, oceanography, physical education, physics, physics-AP, political science, pre-calculus,

psychology, religion, science, social studies, Spanish, speech, statistics, statistics-AP, trigonometry, U.S. history-AP, world history, world literature, writing.

Graduation Requirements Algebra, ancient history, arts and fine arts (art, music, dance, drama), Bible studies, biology, communication skills, computer applications, economics, English, foreign language, mathematics, physical education (includes health), political science, science, social studies (includes history), U.S. history, world history.

Special Academic Programs 9 Advanced Placement exams for which test preparation is offered; independent study.

College Admission Counseling 114 students graduated in 2015; all went to college, including Azusa Pacific University; Chapman University; Seattle University; University of Hawaii at Manoa; University of Nevada, Las Vegas; University of Portland. Mean SAT critical reading: 567, mean SAT math: 601, mean SAT writing: 575, mean composite ACT: 24.

Student Life Upper grades have uniform requirement, student council. Discipline rests primarily with faculty. Attendance at religious services is required.

Summer Programs Remediation, enrichment, sports, art/fine arts, computer instruction programs offered; session focuses on academic/social preparation for entrance to regular school, instruction/remediation, and personal growth; held both on and off campus; held at various recreation sites; accepts boys and girls; open to students from other schools. 270 students usually enrolled. 2016 schedule: June 16 to July 12. Application deadline: March 28.

Tuition and Aid Day student tuition: $15,500. Guaranteed tuition plan. Tuition installment plan (Insured Tuition Payment Plan, monthly payment plans). Need-based scholarship grants available. In 2015–16, 19% of upper-school students received aid. Total amount of financial aid awarded in 2015–16: $405,465.

Admissions Traditional secondary-level entrance grade is 9. For fall 2015, 30 students applied for upper-level admission, 28 were accepted, 19 enrolled. Achievement tests and SSAT required. Deadline for receipt of application materials: December 31. Application fee required: $75. On-campus interview required.

Athletics Interscholastic: aquatics (boys, girls), baseball (b), basketball (b,g), bowling (b,g), canoeing/kayaking (b,g), cheering (g), cross-country running (b,g), diving (b,g), football (b), golf (b,g), judo (b,g), kayaking (b,g), riflery (b,g), soccer (b,g), softball (g), swimming and diving (b,g), tennis (b,g), track and field (b,g), volleyball (b,g), water polo (b,g), wrestling (b,g); coed interscholastic: canoeing/kayaking, cheering, golf, sailing. 3 PE instructors, 30 coaches, 2 athletic trainers.

Computers Computers are regularly used in all academic, college planning, digital applications, graphic design, journalism, keyboarding, media production, newspaper, video film production, word processing, yearbook classes. Computer network features include on-campus library services, online commercial services, Internet access, wireless campus network, Internet filtering or blocking technology, one-to-one iPads. Campus intranet, student e-mail accounts, and computer access in designated common areas are available to students. Students grades are available online. The school has a published electronic and media policy.

Contact Mrs. Katherine Lee, Director of Admissions. 808-595-7585. Fax: 808-564-0332. E-mail: klee@hba.net. Website: www.hba.net

HAWAI`I PREPARATORY ACADEMY

65-1692 Kohala Mountain Road
Kamuela, Hawaii 96743-8476

Head of School: Mr. Robert McKendry Jr.

General Information Coeducational boarding and day college-preparatory, arts, and technology school; primarily serves students with learning disabilities. Boarding grades 9–PG, day grades K–8. Founded: 1949. Setting: small town. Nearest major city is Kona. Students are housed in single-sex by floor dormitories and single-sex dormitories. 220-acre campus. 22 buildings on campus. Approved or accredited by The Association of Boarding Schools and Western Association of Schools and Colleges. Member of National Association of Independent Schools and Secondary School Admission Test Board. Endowment: $16.4 million. Total enrollment: 628. Upper school average class size: 15. Upper school faculty-student ratio: 1:13. There are 163 required school days per year for Upper School students. Upper School students typically attend 5 days per week. The average school day consists of 8 hours.

Upper School Student Profile Grade 9: 85 students (42 boys, 43 girls); Grade 10: 83 students (46 boys, 37 girls); Grade 11: 96 students (42 boys, 54 girls); Grade 12: 115 students (51 boys, 64 girls); Postgraduate: 1 student (1 girl). 50% of students are boarding students. 50% are state residents. 17 states are represented in upper school student body. 20% are international students. International students from China, Germany, Italy, Japan, Kazakhstan, and Republic of Korea; 18 other countries represented in student body.

Faculty School total: 66. In upper school: 21 men, 20 women; 32 have advanced degrees; 22 reside on campus.

Subjects Offered 3-dimensional art, advanced computer applications, Advanced Placement courses, algebra, American literature, art history-AP, astronomy, band, biology, biology-AP, calculus, calculus-AP, ceramics, chemistry, chemistry-AP, choir, comparative government and politics-AP, composition-AP, computer literacy, computer programming, creative writing, digital photography, drama, drama performance, drawing, driver education, economics, English, environmental science, environmental science-AP, ESL, ethnic studies, film, fine arts, forensics, geology, geometry, Hawaiian history, Hawaiian language, honors world history, human geography - AP, instrumental music, Japanese, literary genres, literature-AP, Mandarin, marine biology, marine science, math applications, mathematics, music theater, orchestra, photography, physical education, physical science, physics, physics-AP, pre-calculus, probability and statistics, psychology, psychology-AP, robotics, science research, Spanish, statistics, statistics-AP, strings, studio art, theater arts, theater production, trigonometry, U.S. history, U.S. history-AP, video film production, visual arts, vocal music, Web site design, woodworking, world cultures, world history, world literature, yearbook.

Graduation Requirements Arts and fine arts (art, music, dance, drama), electives, English, mathematics, modern languages, science, social studies (includes history), sports, technology.

Special Academic Programs 17 Advanced Placement exams for which test preparation is offered; honors section; independent study; study at local college for college credit; ESL (15 students enrolled).

College Admission Counseling 110 students graduated in 2015; all went to college, including Chapman University; Lehigh University; Stanford University; University of Hawaii at Manoa; University of San Diego; Willamette University. Median SAT critical reading: 490, median SAT math: 520, median SAT writing: 480, median combined SAT: 1490. Mean composite ACT: 22. 12% scored over 600 on SAT critical reading, 37% scored over 600 on SAT math, 27% scored over 600 on SAT writing, 31% scored over 1800 on combined SAT, 17% scored over 26 on composite ACT.

Student Life Upper grades have specified standards of dress, student council, honor system. Discipline rests equally with students and faculty.

Summer Programs Enrichment, ESL, sports, art/fine arts, computer instruction programs offered; session focuses on academic enrichment; held on campus; accepts boys and girls; open to students from other schools. 100 students usually enrolled. 2016 schedule: June 22 to July 17. Application deadline: April 15.

Tuition and Aid Day student tuition: $23,900; 5-day tuition and room/board: $42,700; 7-day tuition and room/board: $47,200. Tuition installment plan (monthly payment plans, prepayment plan, 2-payment plan, 4-payment plan). Merit scholarship grants, need-based scholarship grants, Hawaii residential boarding grants, merit-based scholarship (75% demonstrated need to apply) available. In 2015–16, 50% of upper-school students received aid; total upper-school merit-scholarship money awarded: $600,000. Total amount of financial aid awarded in 2015–16: $4,000,000.

Admissions Traditional secondary-level entrance grade is 9. Any standardized test, ISEE or SSAT required. Deadline for receipt of application materials: February 8. Application fee required: $50. Interview required.

Athletics Interscholastic: baseball (boys), basketball (b,g), cross-country running (b,g), ocean paddling (b,g), soccer (b,g), softball (g), swimming and diving (b,g), tennis (b,g), track and field (b,g), volleyball (b,g), water polo (g), wrestling (b,g); intramural: baseball (b); coed interscholastic: canoeing/kayaking, cheering, diving, dressage, football, golf, horseback riding; coed intramural: archery, badminton, basketball, dance, dressage, golf, hockey, horseback riding, lacrosse, life saving, outdoor adventure, outdoor recreation, polo, rugby, scuba diving, soccer, strength & conditioning, surfing, swimming and diving, tennis, ultimate Frisbee, volleyball, weight lifting, yoga. 1 PE instructor, 5 coaches, 1 athletic trainer.

Computers Computers are regularly used in computer applications, digital applications, science, video film production, yearbook classes. Computer network features include on-campus library services, online commercial services, Internet access, wireless campus network, Internet filtering or blocking technology. Campus intranet, student e-mail accounts, and computer access in designated common areas are available to students. Students grades are available online. The school has a published electronic and media policy.

Contact Mr. Joshua D. Clark, Director of Admission. 808-881-4074. Fax: 808-881-4003. E-mail: admissions@hpa.edu. Website: www.hpa.edu/

HAWKEN SCHOOL

12465 County Line Road
PO Box 8002
Gates Mills, Ohio 44040-8002

Head of School: D. Scott Looney

General Information Coeducational day college-preparatory, arts, business, STEMM (Science, Technology, Engineering, Math, Medicine), and experiential and service learning school. Grades PS–12. Founded: 1915. Setting: suburban. Nearest major city is Cleveland. 325-acre campus. 5 buildings on campus. Approved or accredited by Ohio Association of Independent Schools and Ohio Department of Education. Member of National Association of Independent Schools. Endowment: $43.6 million. Total enrollment: 1,011. Upper school average class size: 15. Upper school faculty-student ratio: 1:9. There are 176 required school days per year for Upper School students. Upper School students typically attend 5 days per week. The average school day consists of 5 hours and 54 minutes.

Upper School Student Profile Grade 9: 112 students (68 boys, 44 girls); Grade 10: 111 students (57 boys, 54 girls); Grade 11: 118 students (61 boys, 57 girls); Grade 12: 92 students (50 boys, 42 girls).

Faculty School total: 143. In upper school: 29 men, 31 women; 43 have advanced degrees.

Subjects Offered 20th century world history, accounting, acting, advanced chemistry, advanced math, Advanced Placement courses, advanced studio art-AP, African-American literature, algebra, American Civil War, American history, American history-AP, American literature, animal science, art, art appreciation, art history, band, Bible as literature, biology, business, calculus, calculus-AP, ceramics, chemistry, chemistry-AP, Chinese, choir, choral music, chorus, Civil War, classical Greek literature, creative dance, creative writing, dance, dance performance, drama, drawing, ecology, economics, economics and history, engineering, English, English literature, English-AP, entrepreneurship, environmental science-AP, ethics, European history, experiential education, field ecology, film, film studies, fine arts, first aid, French, French studies, French-AP, geography, geometry, government/civics, graphic design, health, history, Holocaust and other genocides, humanities, improvisation, Latin, Latin-AP, mathematics, mathematics-AP, music, music theory, outdoor education, painting, performing arts, philosophy, photography, physical education, physics, physics-AP, physiology, poetry, probability and statistics, science, science research, sculpture, senior project, service learning/internship, social sciences, social studies, Spanish, Spanish literature-AP, speech, statistics-AP, strings, studio art-AP, swimming, theater, theater arts, theater design and production, theater production, trigonometry, U.S. history, U.S. history-AP, world history, world literature, World War I, World War II, writing.

Graduation Requirements Arts and fine arts (art, music, dance, drama), computer science, English, foreign language, history, mathematics, physical education (includes health), science. Community service is required.

Special Academic Programs 16 Advanced Placement exams for which test preparation is offered; honors section; accelerated programs; independent study; term-away projects; study abroad.

College Admission Counseling 90 students graduated in 2015; all went to college, including Case Western Reserve University; Miami University; The College of Wooster; The George Washington University; The Ohio State University; Washington University in St. Louis. Median SAT critical reading: 635, median SAT math: 641, median SAT writing: 647, median combined SAT: 1913, median composite ACT: 28. 58% scored over 600 on SAT critical reading, 69% scored over 600 on SAT math, 61% scored over 600 on SAT writing, 64% scored over 1800 on combined SAT, 70% scored over 26 on composite ACT.

Student Life Upper grades have specified standards of dress, student council, honor system. Discipline rests equally with students and faculty.

Summer Programs Remediation, enrichment, advancement, computer instruction programs offered; session focuses on credit, review, preview, and enrichment in English, math, computer studies, and health; held on campus; accepts boys and girls; open to students from other schools. 133 students usually enrolled. 2016 schedule: June 10 to August 9. Application deadline: none.

Tuition and Aid Day student tuition: $23,115–$25,570. Tuition installment plan (Key Tuition Payment Plan, individually arranged payment plans, installment payment plan (60 percent by 8/15 and 40 percent by 1/15), AchieverLoans (Key Education Resources)). Merit scholarship grants, need-based scholarship grants, need-based loans available. In 2015–16, 37% of upper-school students received aid; total upper-school merit-scholarship money awarded: $162,000. Total amount of financial aid awarded in 2015–16: $5,102,962.

Admissions Traditional secondary-level entrance grade is 9. For fall 2015, 128 students applied for upper-level admission, 91 were accepted, 60 enrolled. ISEE required. Deadline for receipt of application materials: December 15. Application fee required: $50. On-campus interview required.

Athletics Interscholastic: baseball (boys), basketball (b,g), cross-country running (b,g), diving (b,g), field hockey (g), football (b), golf (b,g), lacrosse (b,g), soccer (b,g), softball (g), swimming and diving (b,g), tennis (b,g), track and field (b,g), wrestling (b); intramural: basketball (b); coed intramural: dance, life saving, outdoor skills. 3 PE instructors, 33 coaches, 1 athletic trainer.

Computers Computers are regularly used in all classes. Computer network features include on-campus library services, Internet access, wireless campus network, Internet filtering or blocking technology. Campus intranet and student e-mail accounts are available to students. Students grades are available online. The school has a published electronic and media policy.

Contact Heather Willis Daly, Director of Admission and Financial Assistance. 440-423-2955. Fax: 440-423-2994. E-mail: hdaly@hawken.edu. Website: www.hawken.edu/

HAWTHORNE CHRISTIAN ACADEMY

2000 Route 208
Hawthorne, New Jersey 07506

Head of School: Mr. David Seidman

General Information Coeducational day college-preparatory, arts, religious studies, technology, music, and missions school, affiliated with Christian faith, Christian faith. Grades PS–12. Founded: 1981. Setting: suburban. Nearest major city is New York, NY. 22-acre campus. 4 buildings on campus. Approved or accredited by Association of Christian Schools International, Middle States Association of Colleges and Schools, and New Jersey Department of Education. Total enrollment: 482. Upper school average class size: 20. Upper school faculty-student ratio: 1:7. There are 180 required school days per year for Upper School students. Upper School students typically attend 5 days per week. The average school day consists of 6 hours and 40 minutes.

Upper School Student Profile Grade 9: 48 students (23 boys, 25 girls); Grade 10: 29 students (8 boys, 21 girls); Grade 11: 36 students (22 boys, 14 girls); Grade 12: 32 students (16 boys, 16 girls). 100% of students are Christian faith, Christian.

Faculty School total: 60. In upper school: 8 men, 14 women; 7 have advanced degrees.

Subjects Offered Accounting, advanced computer applications, Advanced Placement courses, algebra, anatomy and physiology, art and culture, band, Basic programming, bell choir, Bible, biology, business applications, calculus, calculus-AP, chemistry, choir, choral music, chorus, Christian ethics, composition, computer information systems, computer programming, computer programming-AP, computers, contemporary issues, creative writing, current events, drama, electives, English literature, English literature-AP, ensembles, foreign language, geometry, government, guidance, handbells, health, information technology, instrumental music, instruments, intro to computers, law, mathematics, music, music appreciation, music history, music theory, physical education, physical science, physics, politics, pre-calculus, psychology, Spanish, studio art, U.S. government, U.S. government and politics-AP, U.S. history-AP, video, visual arts, voice, Web site design, world history, yearbook.

Graduation Requirements Algebra, Bible, biology, chemistry, English literature, English literature-AP, geometry, intro to computers, mathematics, physical education (includes health), physical science, pre-calculus, Spanish, U.S. government, U.S. history, U.S. history-AP, world history, Christian service hours, Apologetics and Current Issues, specified number of Academic Elective Courses.

Special Academic Programs 5 Advanced Placement exams for which test preparation is offered.

College Admission Counseling 45 students graduated in 2014; 43 went to college, including Bergen Community College; Gordon College; Messiah College; Montclair State University; William Paterson University of New Jersey. Other: 1 went to work, 1 had other specific plans. Mean SAT critical reading: 568, mean SAT math: 543, mean SAT writing: 569, mean combined SAT: 1111.

Student Life Upper grades have specified standards of dress, student council. Discipline rests primarily with faculty. Attendance at religious services is required.

Tuition and Aid Tuition installment plan (FACTS Tuition Payment Plan, monthly payment plans). Tuition reduction for siblings, merit scholarship grants, need-based scholarship grants, pastoral discounts, teacher/employee discounts available. In 2014–15, 30% of upper-school students received aid; total upper-school merit-scholarship money awarded: $23,000. Total amount of financial aid awarded in 2014–15: $74,440.

Admissions Traditional secondary-level entrance grade is 9. Admissions testing, BASIS, Math Placement Exam or Otis-Lennon School Ability Test required. Deadline for receipt of application materials: none. Application fee required: $100. On-campus interview required.

Athletics Interscholastic: baseball (boys), basketball (b,g), soccer (b,g), softball (g), volleyball (g); coed interscholastic: bowling, cross-country running, track and field; coed intramural: strength & conditioning. 2 PE instructors.

Computers Computers are regularly used in computer applications, information technology, introduction to technology, lab/keyboard, library, technology, Web site design, yearbook classes. Computer network features include on-campus library services, Internet access, Internet filtering or blocking technology. Campus intranet is available to students. Students grades are available online. The school has a published electronic and media policy.

Contact Mrs. Judith De Boer, Admissions Coordinator. 973-423-3331 Ext. 261. Fax: 973-238-1718. E-mail: jdeboer@hca.org. Website: www.hca.org/

HEAD-ROYCE SCHOOL

4315 Lincoln Avenue
Oakland, California 94602

Head of School: Robert Lake

General Information Coeducational day college-preparatory, arts, technology, and STEM, robotics, Global Online Academy school. Grades K–12. Founded: 1887. Setting: urban. 22-acre campus. 8 buildings on campus. Approved or accredited by Western Association of Schools and Colleges and California Department of Education. Member of National Association of Independent Schools. Endowment: $30 million. Total enrollment: 876. Upper school average class size: 16. Upper school faculty-student ratio: 1:9. There are 175 required school days per year for Upper School students. Upper School students typically attend 5 days per week. The average school day consists of 7 hours.

Upper School Student Profile Grade 9: 90 students (43 boys, 47 girls); Grade 10: 94 students (45 boys, 49 girls); Grade 11: 91 students (37 boys, 54 girls); Grade 12: 85 students (44 boys, 41 girls).

Faculty School total: 95. In upper school: 24 men, 19 women; 29 have advanced degrees.

Subjects Offered Algebra, American history, American literature, art, art history, astronomy, biology, calculus, ceramics, chemistry, Chinese, community service, computer programming, computer science, creative writing, debate, drama, ecology, English, English literature, European history, expository writing, fine arts, French, geometry, graphic arts, health, history, journalism, Latin, marine biology, mathematics, music, neurobiology, photography, physical education, physics, psychology, science, social studies, Spanish, theater, trigonometry, typing, video, world history, world literature, writing.

Graduation Requirements Art history, arts and fine arts (art, music, dance, drama), computer science, English, foreign language, mathematics, physical education (includes health), science, social studies (includes history), 40 hours of community service.

Special Academic Programs 24 Advanced Placement exams for which test preparation is offered; honors section; independent study; term-away projects; study at local college for college credit; study abroad; academic accommodation for the gifted, the musically talented, and the artistically talented.

College Admission Counseling 86 students graduated in 2014; all went to college, including Occidental College; Stanford University; University of California, Berkeley; University of California, Davis; University of California, Los Angeles; University of Southern California. Mean SAT critical reading: 691, mean SAT math: 689, mean SAT writing: 712.

Student Life Upper grades have specified standards of dress, student council, honor system. Discipline rests primarily with faculty.

Tuition and Aid Day student tuition: $35,455. Tuition installment plan (SMART Tuition Payment Plan, monthly payment plans). Need-based scholarship grants, paying campus jobs, tuition remission for children of faculty and staff available. In 2014–15, 25% of upper-school students received aid. Total amount of financial aid awarded in 2014–15: $3,100,000.

Admissions Traditional secondary-level entrance grade is 9. For fall 2014, 204 students applied for upper-level admission, 67 were accepted, 25 enrolled. ISEE or SSAT required. Deadline for receipt of application materials: January 15. Application fee required: $100. On-campus interview required.

Athletics Interscholastic: baseball (boys), basketball (b,g), cross-country running (b,g), dance squad (g), golf (b,g), lacrosse (b), modern dance (g), outdoor education (b,g), physical fitness (b,g), soccer (b,g), softball (g), strength & conditioning (b,g), swimming and diving (b,g), tennis (b,g), volleyball (b,g), weight lifting (b,g), weight training (b,g); coed interscholastic: cross-country running, golf, outdoor education, physical fitness, strength & conditioning, swimming and diving; coed intramural: bicycling, dance, ultimate Frisbee. 6 PE instructors, 39 coaches.

Computers Computers are regularly used in all academic, English, graphics, mathematics, science, yearbook classes. Computer network features include on-campus library services, online commercial services, Internet access, wireless campus network, laptop carts, Smartboards, iPad carts. Student e-mail accounts and computer access in designated common areas are available to students. Students grades are available online. The school has a published electronic and media policy.

Contact Mr. Christian Donovan, Director of Admissions & Financial Aid. 510-531-1300. Fax: 510-530-8329. E-mail: cdonovan@headroyce.org. Website: www.headroyce.org

HEBREW ACADEMY

14401 Willow Lane
Huntington Beach, California 92647

Head of School: Dr. Megan Carlson

General Information Girls' boarding and coeducational day college-preparatory, general academic, religious studies, and technology school, affiliated with Jewish faith. Boarding girls grades 9–12, day boys grades N–8, day girls grades N–12. Founded: 1969. Setting: suburban. Students are housed in single-sex dormitories. 11-acre campus. 11 buildings on campus. Approved or accredited by Accrediting Commission for Schools and Western Association of Schools and Colleges. Total enrollment: 257. Upper school average class size: 10. Upper school faculty-student ratio: 1:4. There are 176 required school days per year for Upper School students. Upper School students typically attend 5 days per week. The average school day consists of 7 hours and 30 minutes.

Upper School Student Profile Grade 9: 7 students (7 girls); Grade 10: 5 students (5 girls); Grade 11: 9 students (9 girls); Grade 12: 5 students (5 girls). 40% of students are boarding students. 73% are state residents. 5 states are represented in upper school student body. 100% of students are Jewish.

Faculty School total: 41. In upper school: 6 men, 12 women; 2 have advanced degrees.

Subjects Offered Algebra, American history, American literature, art history, biology, earth science, economics, English, English literature, geography, government/civics, grammar, Hebrew, history, mathematics, physical education, physics, physiology, psychology, religion, science, social sciences, social studies, theology, world cultures, world history, writing.

Graduation Requirements Computer science, English, foreign language, mathematics, physical education (includes health), religion (includes Bible studies and theology), science, social sciences, social studies (includes history).

Special Academic Programs International Baccalaureate program; 5 Advanced Placement exams for which test preparation is offered; honors section; independent study; remedial reading and/or remedial writing; remedial math; programs in general development for dyslexic students.

Student Life Upper grades have uniform requirement, student council. Discipline rests primarily with faculty. Attendance at religious services is required.

Tuition and Aid Day student tuition: $15,400. Guaranteed tuition plan. Tuition installment plan (monthly payment plans, individually arranged payment plans). Tuition reduction for siblings, need-based scholarship grants available. In 2015–16, 30% of upper-school students received aid. Total amount of financial aid awarded in 2015–16: $30,000.

Admissions Traditional secondary-level entrance grade is 9. For fall 2015, 8 students applied for upper-level admission, 5 were accepted, 5 enrolled. Deadline for receipt of application materials: none. Application fee required: $100. On-campus interview required.

Athletics Interscholastic: aerobics/dance, aerobics/Nautilus, aquatics (b), archery (b), badminton, baseball (b), basketball (b), dance, jogging (b), physical fitness (b), soccer (b), softball (b), swimming and diving (b), volleyball. 2 PE instructors, 1 coach.

Computers Computers are regularly used in English, foreign language, science, technology classes. Computer network features include on-campus library services, online commercial services, Internet access, multimedia, including laser disks, digital cameras. Computer access in designated common areas is available to students. The school has a published electronic and media policy.

Contact Mrs. Nelli Greenspan, Enrollment Manager. 714-898-0051 Ext. 284. Fax: 714-898-0633. E-mail: nelli@hacds.org. Website: www.hebrewacademyhb.com

HEBREW ACADEMY OF THE FIVE TOWNS & ROCKAWAY

635 Central Avenue
Cedarhurst, New York 11516
Head of School: Ms. Naomi Lippman

General Information Coeducational day college-preparatory, arts, business, and religious studies school, affiliated with Jewish faith. Grades 9–12. Founded: 1978. Setting: suburban. Nearest major city is New York. 1 building on campus. Approved or accredited by Middle States Association of Colleges and Schools, The College Board, and New York Department of Education. Languages of instruction: English and Hebrew. Total enrollment: 388. Upper school average class size: 20. The average school day consists of 9 hours and 15 minutes.

Upper School Student Profile 100% of students are Jewish.

Faculty School total: 60.

Subjects Offered Advanced Placement courses, arts, English, fine arts, foreign language, Jewish studies, Judaic studies, mathematics, physical education, religion, science, social sciences, social studies.

Graduation Requirements Arts and fine arts (art, music, dance, drama), English, foreign language, Judaic studies, mathematics, physical education (includes health), religion (includes Bible studies and theology), science, social sciences, social studies (includes history), community service requirement.

Special Academic Programs 11 Advanced Placement exams for which test preparation is offered; honors section; independent study; study abroad; academic accommodation for the artistically talented.

College Admission Counseling 82 students graduated in 2015; all went to college, including Binghamton University, State University of New York; Columbia University; Cornell University; New York University; Queens College of the City University of New York; Yeshiva University. Median SAT critical reading: 590, median SAT math: 610, median SAT writing: 570. 48% scored over 600 on SAT critical reading, 56% scored over 600 on SAT math, 41% scored over 600 on SAT writing.

Student Life Upper grades have specified standards of dress, student council, honor system. Discipline rests primarily with faculty. Attendance at religious services is required.

Tuition and Aid Tuition installment plan (monthly payment plans, individually arranged payment plans). Need-based scholarship grants available.

Admissions Traditional secondary-level entrance grade is 9. Board of Jewish Education Entrance Exam required. Deadline for receipt of application materials: March 15. Application fee required. On-campus interview required.

Athletics Interscholastic: baseball (boys, girls), basketball (b,g), field hockey (b), softball (b,g), tennis (b,g), volleyball (g); coed intramural: skiing (downhill). 2 PE instructors, 8 coaches.

Computers Computers are regularly used in computer applications classes. Computer resources include on-campus library services, online commercial services, Internet access, Internet filtering or blocking technology. Student e-mail accounts are available to students. Students grades are available online. The school has a published electronic and media policy.

Contact Ms. Naomi Lippman, Principal, General Studies. 516-569-3807. Fax: 516-374-5761. Website: www.haftr.org

HEBRON ACADEMY

PO Box 309
Hebron, Maine 04238
Head of School: Mr. John J. King

General Information Coeducational boarding and day college-preparatory, arts, technology, Public Speaking, and honors and AP Courses school. Boarding grades 9–PG, day grades 6–PG. Founded: 1804. Setting: rural. Nearest major city is Portland. Students are housed in single-sex dormitories. 1,500-acre campus. 22 buildings on campus. Approved or accredited by Independent Schools of Northern New England, New England Association of Schools and Colleges, The Association of Boarding Schools, and Maine Department of Education. Member of National Association of Independent Schools and Secondary School Admission Test Board. Endowment: $14

million. Total enrollment: 268. Upper school average class size: 12. Upper school faculty-student ratio: 1:7. There are 175 required school days per year for Upper School students. Upper School students typically attend 5 days per week. The average school day consists of 5 hours and 45 minutes.

Upper School Student Profile Grade 9: 42 students (28 boys, 14 girls); Grade 10: 47 students (28 boys, 19 girls); Grade 11: 65 students (45 boys, 20 girls); Grade 12: 73 students (46 boys, 27 girls); Postgraduate: 14 students (13 boys, 1 girl). 75% of students are boarding students. 43% are state residents. 20 states are represented in upper school student body. 30% are international students. International students from Canada, China, Germany, Mexico, Republic of Korea, and Spain; 11 other countries represented in student body.

Faculty School total: 44. In upper school: 19 men, 22 women; 16 have advanced degrees; 28 reside on campus.

Subjects Offered Algebra, anatomy and physiology, art, art-AP, biology, business studies, calculus, calculus-AP, chemistry, chemistry-AP, college counseling, composition, composition-AP, computer multimedia, computer programming, computer science, computer studies, current events, digital photography, drama, drawing, drawing and design, English, environmental science, ESL, ethics, French, functions, geology, geometry, health and wellness, history, independent study, international relations, jazz, Latin, leadership, music, music theory, painting, personal fitness, photography, physics, piano, portfolio art, pottery, programming, psychology, sculpture, Spanish, studio art, U.S. history, wilderness education, world history, world religions.

Graduation Requirements Algebra, art, biology, chemistry, English, foreign language, geometry, U.S. history.

Special Academic Programs Advanced Placement exam preparation; honors section; independent study; academic accommodation for the gifted, the musically talented, and the artistically talented; programs in general development for dyslexic students; ESL (32 students enrolled).

College Admission Counseling 79 students graduated in 2014; 76 went to college, including Bucknell University; Johnson & Wales University; Siena College; United States Military Academy; University of Maine; University of Rhode Island. Median SAT critical reading: 470, median SAT math: 530, median SAT writing: 470, median combined SAT: 1470, median composite ACT: 22. 5% scored over 600 on SAT critical reading, 19% scored over 600 on SAT math, 6% scored over 600 on SAT writing, 9% scored over 1800 on combined SAT, 7% scored over 26 on composite ACT.

Student Life Upper grades have specified standards of dress, student council, honor system. Discipline rests primarily with faculty.

Tuition and Aid Day student tuition: $29,600; 7-day tuition and room/board: $53,900. Tuition installment plan (Insured Tuition Payment Plan, FACTS Tuition Payment Plan, monthly payment plans). Merit scholarship grants, need-based scholarship grants, prepGATE loans available. In 2014–15, 60% of upper-school students received aid; total upper-school merit-scholarship money awarded: $250,000. Total amount of financial aid awarded in 2014–15: $2,000,000.

Admissions Traditional secondary-level entrance grade is 9. For fall 2014, 323 students applied for upper-level admission, 249 were accepted, 108 enrolled. PSAT or SAT for applicants to grade 11 and 12, SSAT or TOEFL or SLEP required. Deadline for receipt of application materials: February 1. Application fee required: $50. Interview required.

Athletics Interscholastic: alpine skiing (boys, girls), baseball (b), basketball (b,g), cross-country running (b,g), field hockey (g), football (b), ice hockey (b,g), lacrosse (b,g), mountain biking (b,g), outdoor education (b,g), outdoor skills (b,g), physical fitness (b,g), running (b,g), skiing (downhill) (b,g), snowboarding (b,g), soccer (b,g), softball (b,g), tennis (b,g), track and field (b,g), wall climbing (b,g); coed interscholastic: fitness, golf; coed intramural: aerobics/dance, broomball, canoeing/kayaking, dance, fitness, Frisbee, outdoor activities, outdoor education, outdoor skills, rock climbing, roller hockey, squash, yoga.

Computers Computers are regularly used in art, ESL, graphic design, introduction to technology, mathematics, media production, research skills, science, writing, yearbook classes. Computer network features include on-campus library services, online commercial services, Internet access, wireless campus network, Internet filtering or blocking technology. Campus intranet, student e-mail accounts, and computer access in designated common areas are available to students. Students grades are available online. The school has a published electronic and media policy.

Contact Mr. Joseph M. Hemmings, Assistant Head of School for Enrollment. 207-966-2100 Ext. 225. Fax: 207-966-1111. E-mail: admissions@hebronacademy.org. Website: www.hebronacademy.org

THE HEIGHTS SCHOOL

10400 Seven Locks Road
Potomac, Maryland 20854
Head of School: Mr. Alvaro J. de Vicente

General Information Boys' day college-preparatory and religious studies school, affiliated with Roman Catholic Church. Grades 3–12. Founded: 1969. Setting: suburban. Nearest major city is Washington, DC. 20-acre campus. 5 buildings on campus. Approved or accredited by Association of Independent Maryland Schools, Association of Independent Schools of Greater Washington, and Maryland Department of Education. Member of National Association of Independent Schools and Secondary

School Admission Test Board. Total enrollment: 538. Upper school average class size: 16. Upper school faculty-student ratio: 1:7. There are 173 required school days per year for Upper School students. Upper School students typically attend 5 days per week. The average school day consists of 6 hours and 45 minutes.

Upper School Student Profile Grade 6: 59 students (59 boys); Grade 7: 60 students (60 boys); Grade 8: 54 students (54 boys); Grade 9: 70 students (70 boys); Grade 10: 66 students (66 boys); Grade 11: 60 students (60 boys); Grade 12: 59 students (59 boys). 90% of students are Roman Catholic.

Faculty School total: 64. In upper school: 64 men; 35 have advanced degrees.

Subjects Offered Algebra, American history, American literature, American literature-AP, Ancient Greek, art history-AP, bioethics, biology, biology-AP, calculus, calculus-AP, chemistry, chemistry-AP, chorus, computer programming, computer science, drama, economics, economics-AP, English, English literature, ethics, European history, European history-AP, geology, geometry, government-AP, history, Latin, Latin-AP, macro/microeconomics-AP, macroeconomics-AP, mathematics, medieval history, music, philosophy, physical education, physics, physics-AP, post-calculus, religion, science, Spanish, Spanish language-AP, Spanish literature-AP, statistics-AP, studio art-AP, trigonometry, world literature, World War II, writing.

Graduation Requirements Athletics, electives, English, foreign language, history, mathematics, religion (includes Bible studies and theology), science.

Special Academic Programs Advanced Placement exam preparation; independent study; academic accommodation for the gifted, the musically talented, and the artistically talented.

College Admission Counseling 59 students graduated in 2015; 54 went to college, including The Catholic University of America; University of Dallas; University of Maryland, College Park; University of Notre Dame; University of Virginia; Virginia Polytechnic Institute and State University. Other: 1 went to work, 3 had other specific plans.

Student Life Upper grades have specified standards of dress, student council. Discipline rests primarily with faculty.

Summer Programs Remediation, enrichment, advancement, sports, art/fine arts, rigorous outdoor training, computer instruction programs offered; session focuses on academic enrichment and outdoor adventure; held both on and off campus; held at various D.C. area locations; accepts boys; open to students from other schools. 200 students usually enrolled. 2016 schedule: June 8 to August 21. Application deadline: June 1.

Tuition and Aid Tuition installment plan (FACTS Tuition Payment Plan, monthly payment plans). Need-based scholarship grants available. In 2015–16, 45% of upper-school students received aid. Total amount of financial aid awarded in 2015–16: $1,000,000.

Admissions Traditional secondary-level entrance grade is 9. For fall 2015, 89 students applied for upper-level admission, 46 were accepted, 25 enrolled. High School Placement Test or SSAT required. Deadline for receipt of application materials: January 25. Application fee required: $50. On-campus interview required.

Athletics Interscholastic: aquatics, baseball, basketball, cross-country running, diving, golf, lacrosse, rugby, soccer, squash, swimming and diving, tennis, track and field, wrestling; intramural: archery, basketball, cross-country running, rock climbing, skateboarding. 2 PE instructors, 1 athletic trainer.

Computers Computers are regularly used in computer applications, journalism, library skills, newspaper, programming, yearbook classes. Computer network features include on-campus library services, online commercial services, Internet access, wireless campus network, Internet filtering or blocking technology. Computer access in designated common areas is available to students.

Contact Mr. George Che Martin, Admissions Associate. 301-765-2093. Fax: 301-365-4303. E-mail: gmartin@heights.edu. Website: www.heights.edu

HERITAGE ACADEMY

11 New Orleans Road
Hilton Head Island, South Carolina 29928

Head of School: Gloria Sprouse

General Information Coeducational boarding and day college-preparatory school. Grades 5–PG. Founded: 1993. Setting: small town. Nearest major city is Savannah, GA. Students are housed in single-sex condos. 3-acre campus. 1 building on campus. Approved or accredited by South Carolina Independent School Association, Southern Association of Colleges and Schools, and South Carolina Department of Education. Total enrollment: 116. Upper school average class size: 9. Upper school faculty-student ratio: 1:9. There are 175 required school days per year for Upper School students. Upper School students typically attend 5 days per week. The average school day consists of 4 hours and 30 minutes.

Upper School Student Profile Grade 6: 5 students (4 boys, 1 girl); Grade 7: 3 students (2 boys, 1 girl); Grade 8: 5 students (4 boys, 1 girl); Grade 9: 15 students (7 boys, 8 girls); Grade 10: 22 students (17 boys, 5 girls); Grade 11: 32 students (25 boys, 7 girls); Grade 12: 29 students (18 boys, 11 girls); Postgraduate: 1 student (1 boy). 59% of students are boarding students. 32% are state residents. 18 states are represented in upper school student body. 47% are international students. International students from Brazil, China, India, Japan, Mexico, and Thailand; 19 other countries represented in student body.

Faculty School total: 19. In upper school: 3 men, 13 women; 1 resides on campus.

Special Academic Programs Advanced Placement exam preparation; honors section; academic accommodation for the gifted; ESL (15 students enrolled).

College Admission Counseling 36 students graduated in 2015; 35 went to college, including Arizona State University at the Tempe campus; Indiana University Bloomington; The University of North Carolina at Chapel Hill; University of South Carolina; University of Washington; University of Wisconsin–Madison. Other: 1 entered a postgraduate year.

Student Life Upper grades have specified standards of dress, student council, honor system. Discipline rests primarily with faculty.

Tuition and Aid Day student tuition: $16,600; 7-day tuition and room/board: $35,900. Tuition installment plan (individually arranged payment plans). Tuition reduction for siblings, need-based scholarship grants available.

Admissions Deadline for receipt of application materials: none. Application fee required: $195. Interview recommended.

Athletics Interscholastic: golf (boys, girls).

Computers Computers are regularly used in all classes. Computer resources include Internet access, wireless campus network. Computer access in designated common areas is available to students. Students grades are available online.

Contact Tina Sprouse, Director of Admissions. 843-842-8600 Ext. 1. Fax: 843-842-9620. E-mail: tina.sprouse@heritagehhi.com. Website: www.heritagehhi.com

HERITAGE CHRISTIAN SCHOOL

9825 Woodley Avenue
North Hills, California 91343

Head of School: Mr. Lance Haliday

General Information Coeducational day college-preparatory, arts, religious studies, and technology school, affiliated with Christian faith. Grades 7–12. Founded: 1962. Setting: suburban. Nearest major city is Los Angeles. 11-acre campus. 5 buildings on campus. Approved or accredited by Association of Christian Schools International and Western Association of Schools and Colleges. Total enrollment: 707. Upper school average class size: 30. Upper school faculty-student ratio: 1:22. There are 180 required school days per year for Upper School students. Upper School students typically attend 5 days per week. The average school day consists of 6 hours and 45 minutes.

Upper School Student Profile Grade 9: 137 students (71 boys, 66 girls); Grade 10: 128 students (63 boys, 65 girls); Grade 11: 146 students (64 boys, 82 girls); Grade 12: 170 students (96 boys, 74 girls).

Faculty School total: 38. In upper school: 16 men, 20 women; 26 have advanced degrees.

Subjects Offered 3-dimensional design, advanced computer applications, algebra, American history, American literature, analysis and differential calculus, anatomy and physiology, art, ASB Leadership, band, Bible studies, biology, biology-AP, biotechnology, calculus-AP, ceramics, chemistry, choir, choral music, Christian doctrine, Christian education, Christian ethics, computer applications, computer education, computer graphics, computer programming, computer science, computer skills, computer technologies, digital photography, drama, drama performance, economics, English, English literature, English-AP, expository writing, fine arts, food and nutrition, French, French-AP, geography, geometry, government/civics, HTML design, intro to computers, jazz band, journalism, mathematics, music, photography, physical education, physics, physics-AP, pre-calculus, psychology, psychology-AP, science, social studies, Spanish, Spanish-AP, statistics, statistics-AP, studio art, theater arts, trigonometry, U.S. history-AP, world history, world history-AP.

Graduation Requirements Arts and fine arts (art, music, dance, drama), English, foreign language, mathematics, physical education (includes health), practical arts, religion (includes Bible studies and theology), science, social studies (includes history).

Special Academic Programs Advanced Placement exam preparation; honors section; ESL (16 students enrolled).

College Admission Counseling 172 students graduated in 2014; 169 went to college, including Biola University; California Lutheran University; California State University, Northridge; Grand Canyon University; University of California, Los Angeles; University of California, Santa Barbara. Other: 2 went to work, 1 entered military service. Median composite ACT: 24. Mean SAT critical reading: 512, mean SAT math: 539, mean SAT writing: 516.

Student Life Upper grades have uniform requirement, student council, honor system. Discipline rests primarily with faculty. Attendance at religious services is required.

Tuition and Aid Day student tuition: $9218. Tuition installment plan (FACTS Tuition Payment Plan, monthly payment plans, 2-semester payment plan, annual payment plan). Need-based scholarship grants available. In 2014–15, 30% of upper-school students received aid. Total amount of financial aid awarded in 2014–15: $520,000.

Admissions Traditional secondary-level entrance grade is 9. For fall 2014, 110 students applied for upper-level admission, 95 were accepted, 81 enrolled. QUIC required. Deadline for receipt of application materials: August 1. Application fee required: $120. On-campus interview required.

Athletics Interscholastic: baseball (boys), basketball (b,g), cheering (g), cross-country running (b,g), football (b), golf (b), soccer (b,g), softball (g), tennis (g), track and field (b,g), volleyball (b,g). 3 PE instructors, 40 coaches.

Computers Computers are regularly used in animation, business applications, career technology, graphic design, graphics, introduction to technology, keyboarding, lab/keyboard, programming, technology, typing, Web site design, word processing classes. Computer network features include on-campus library services, Internet access, Internet filtering or blocking technology. The school has a published electronic and media policy.

Contact Mrs. Penny Lade, South Campus Registrar. 818-894-5742 Ext. 324. Fax: 818-892-5018. E-mail: plade@heritage-schools.org. Website: www.heritage-schools.org

HERITAGE CHRISTIAN SCHOOL

2850 Fourth Avenue
PO Box 400
Jordan, Ontario L0R 1S0, Canada

Head of School: Mr. A. Ben Harsevoort

General Information Coeducational day college-preparatory, general academic, arts, and religious studies school, affiliated with Reformed Church. Grades K–12. Founded: 1992. Setting: rural. Nearest major city is St. Catharines, Canada. 26-acre campus. 1 building on campus. Approved or accredited by Ontario Department of Education. Language of instruction: English. Total enrollment: 638. Upper school average class size: 50. Upper school faculty-student ratio: 1:15. There are 185 required school days per year for Upper School students. Upper School students typically attend 5 days per week. The average school day consists of 5 hours.

Upper School Student Profile Grade 9: 40 students (20 boys, 20 girls); Grade 10: 51 students (25 boys, 26 girls); Grade 11: 45 students (22 boys, 23 girls); Grade 12: 45 students (23 boys, 22 girls). 95% of students are Reformed.

Faculty School total: 35. In upper school: 11 men, 4 women; 4 have advanced degrees.

Subjects Offered 20th century American writers, 20th century physics, 20th century world history, advanced chemistry, advanced math, algebra, analysis and differential calculus, art, Bible, biology, bookkeeping, British literature, business mathematics, business studies, calculus, Canadian geography, Canadian history, Canadian law, Canadian literature, career education, chemistry, choral music, Christian and Hebrew scripture, Christian doctrine, Christian education, Christian ethics, Christian studies, Christian testament, Christianity, church history, civics, classical civilization, computer education, computer programming, computer skills, consumer mathematics, creative writing, culinary arts, drafting, English, English composition, English literature, entrepreneurship, environmental education, ethics, European civilization, European history, family studies, finite math, foods, foundations of civilization, French as a second language, general math, geography, geometry, grammar, health, history, honors algebra, honors English, honors geometry, honors world history, humanities, independent living, keyboarding, language and composition, language arts, law and the legal system, life science, literature, marketing, mathematics, media literacy, modern civilization, modern European history, modern Western civilization, music, music appreciation, novels, personal finance, physical education, physics, practicum, public speaking, religion and culture, religious education, religious studies, Shakespeare, society challenge and change, speech communications, technical drawing, vocal music, word processing, world civilizations, world literature, writing.

Graduation Requirements Ontario Secondary School Diploma requirements.

Special Academic Programs Remedial reading and/or remedial writing; remedial math.

College Admission Counseling 53 students graduated in 2014; 47 went to college, including Calvin College; Covenant College. Other: 6 went to work.

Student Life Upper grades have uniform requirement, student council. Discipline rests primarily with faculty. Attendance at religious services is required.

Tuition and Aid Day student tuition: CAN$15,000. Tuition installment plan (monthly payment plans).

Admissions Traditional secondary-level entrance grade is 9. Deadline for receipt of application materials: none. No application fee required. On-campus interview required.

Athletics Interscholastic: badminton (boys, girls), basketball (b,g), ice hockey (b), soccer (b,g), volleyball (b,g). 3 coaches.

Computers Computers are regularly used in accounting, business, economics, information technology, keyboarding, mathematics, newspaper, typing, yearbook classes. The school has a published electronic and media policy.

Contact Mrs. Mariam Sinke, Administrative Assistant. 905-562-7303 Ext. 221. Fax: 905-562-0020. E-mail: heritage@hcsjordan.ca. Website: www.hcsjordan.ca

THE HEWITT SCHOOL

45 East 75th Street
New York, New York 10021

Head of School: Ms. Joan Z. Lonergan

General Information Girls' day college-preparatory school. Grades K–12. Founded: 1920. Setting: urban. 1 building on campus. Approved or accredited by National Independent Private Schools Association, New York State Association of Independent Schools, and New York Department of Education. Member of National Association of Independent Schools and Secondary School Admission Test Board. Total enrollment: 517. Upper school average class size: 15. Upper school faculty-student ratio: 1:7. Upper School students typically attend 5 days per week. The average school day consists of 7 hours.

Upper School Student Profile Grade 9: 41 students (41 girls); Grade 10: 32 students (32 girls); Grade 11: 23 students (23 girls); Grade 12: 29 students (29 girls).

Faculty School total: 82. In upper school: 14 men, 16 women; 24 have advanced degrees.

Subjects Offered Algebra, American history, American literature, anatomy and physiology, art, biology, calculus, chemistry, computers, drama, earth science, English, English literature, European history, fine arts, French, genetics, geometry, history, Latin, mathematics, music, photography, physical education, physics, pre-calculus, science, Spanish, world history.

Graduation Requirements Creative arts, English, foreign language, history, mathematics, physical education (includes health), science, technology.

Special Academic Programs Advanced Placement exam preparation; honors section; independent study; term-away projects; study abroad.

College Admission Counseling 24 students graduated in 2014; all went to college, including Bard College; Barnard College; Bates College; Syracuse University; University of Michigan; University of Pennsylvania.

Student Life Upper grades have uniform requirement, student council. Discipline rests primarily with faculty.

Tuition and Aid Day student tuition: $42,500. Guaranteed tuition plan. Tuition installment plan (Insured Tuition Payment Plan, Key Tuition Payment Plan, monthly payment plans). Need-based scholarship grants available. In 2014–15, 22% of upper-school students received aid. Total amount of financial aid awarded in 2014–15: $1,394,709.

Admissions Traditional secondary-level entrance grade is 9. ERB and ISEE required. Deadline for receipt of application materials: December 1. Application fee required: $75. On-campus interview required.

Athletics Interscholastic: badminton, basketball, cross-country running, soccer, squash, swimming and diving, tennis, track and field, volleyball; intramural: badminton, basketball, crew, cross-country running, lacrosse, soccer, swimming and diving, tennis, track and field, volleyball. 4 PE instructors.

Computers Computers are regularly used in all academic, architecture, art, English, foreign language, history, humanities, mathematics, music, science classes. Computer network features include on-campus library services, online commercial services, Internet access, wireless campus network, Internet filtering or blocking technology. Campus intranet, student e-mail accounts, and computer access in designated common areas are available to students. The school has a published electronic and media policy.

Contact Ms. Miriam Miller, Assistant Director of Middle and Upper School Admissions. 212-994-2623. Fax: 212-472-7531. E-mail: mmiller@hewittschool.org. Website: www.hewittschool.org

HIGHLAND HALL WALDORF SCHOOL

17100 Superior Street
Northridge, California 91325

Head of School: Lynn Kern

General Information Coeducational day college-preparatory and arts school. Grades N–12. Founded: 1955. Setting: suburban. Nearest major city is Los Angeles. 11-acre campus. 4 buildings on campus. Approved or accredited by Association of Waldorf Schools of North America, Western Association of Schools and Colleges, and California Department of Education. Total enrollment: 243. Upper school average class size: 25. Upper school faculty-student ratio: 1:6. There are 175 required school days per year for Upper School students. Upper School students typically attend 5 days per week. The average school day consists of 7 hours and 10 minutes.

Upper School Student Profile Grade 9: 17 students (10 boys, 7 girls); Grade 10: 25 students (11 boys, 14 girls); Grade 11: 23 students (8 boys, 15 girls); Grade 12: 17 students (2 boys, 15 girls).

Faculty School total: 37. In upper school: 13 men, 9 women; 7 have advanced degrees.

Subjects Offered Algebra, American history, American literature, anatomy, ancient history, architecture, art, art history, astronomy, biology, bookbinding, botany, calculus, career/college preparation, cell biology, chemistry, choral music, chorus, clayworking, conflict resolution, CPR, creative writing, drama, drawing, earth science, economics, English, English literature, ethnic studies, European history, eurythmy, expository writing, geography, geology, geometry, German, government/civics, grammar, guidance, guitar, handbells, health, history, honors U.S. history, jazz ensemble, marine biology, mathematics, metalworking, music, music history, Native American history, orchestra, painting, physical education, physics, physiology, pre-algebra, pre-calculus, SAT preparation, sculpture, sewing, social studies, Spanish, speech, stone carving, theater, trigonometry, woodworking, world history, world literature, writing, yearbook, zoology.

Graduation Requirements 20th century world history, 20th century world history, acting, algebra, American Civil War, anatomy, ancient history, ancient world history, architecture, art, art history, arts and crafts, arts and fine arts (art, music, dance, drama), atomic theory, bell choir, biology, bookbinding, botany, calculus, cell biology, chemistry, choral music, clayworking, college counseling, comparative religion, constitutional history of U.S., CPR, crafts, drama, drawing, earth science, economics, English, English composition, eurythmy, first aid, food and nutrition, foreign language, geography, geometry, German, government, health, history of architecture, history of music, human anatomy, human biology, human sexuality, inorganic chemistry, instrumental music, mathematics, music, music history, Native American history, novels, optics, orchestra, organic chemistry, physical education (includes health), physics, physiology, poetry, pre-calculus, probability, projective geometry, research skills, science, sculpture, sewing, Shakespeare, society and culture, Spanish, speech, student government, U.S. history, utopia, woodworking, world history, zoology. Community service is required.

Special Academic Programs Independent study; study abroad.

College Admission Counseling 22 students graduated in 2014; 20 went to college, including Berklee College of Music; Lewis & Clark College; Marlboro College; Middlebury College; Sarah Lawrence College; Vassar College. Other: 2 went to work. Mean SAT critical reading: 645, mean SAT math: 550, mean composite ACT: 27. 50% scored over 600 on SAT critical reading, 60% scored over 600 on SAT math, 50% scored over 26 on composite ACT.

Student Life Upper grades have specified standards of dress, student council. Discipline rests primarily with faculty.

Tuition and Aid Day student tuition: $22,965. Tuition installment plan (Insured Tuition Payment Plan, FACTS Tuition Payment Plan, monthly payment plans). Need-based scholarship grants available. In 2014–15, 38% of upper-school students received aid. Total amount of financial aid awarded in 2014–15: $204,600.

Admissions Traditional secondary-level entrance grade is 9. For fall 2014, 51 students applied for upper-level admission, 36 were accepted, 19 enrolled. Essay, math and English placement tests and writing sample required. Deadline for receipt of application materials: January 31. Application fee required: $100. Interview required.

Athletics Interscholastic: baseball (boys), basketball (b,g), softball (g), volleyball (b,g); coed interscholastic: soccer; coed intramural: artistic gym. 2 PE instructors, 2 coaches.

Computers Computers are regularly used in library skills, newspaper, yearbook classes. Computer network features include on-campus library services, Internet access, wireless campus network.

Contact Lynn van Schilfgaarde, Enrollment Director. 818-349-1394 Ext. 211. Fax: 818-349-2390. E-mail: lvs@highlandhall.org. Website: www.highlandhall.org

HIGH MOWING SCHOOL

222 Isaac Frye Highway
Wilton, New Hampshire 03086

Head of School: Rea Gill

General Information Coeducational boarding and day college-preparatory, arts, Naturalist / Environmental Program, and horticultural/farming and gardening program school. Grades 9–12. Founded: 1942. Setting: rural. Nearest major city is Boston, MA. Students are housed in single-sex dormitories. 250-acre campus. 17 buildings on campus. Approved or accredited by Association of Independent Schools in New England, Association of Waldorf Schools of North America, Independent Schools of Northern New England, New England Association of Schools and Colleges, The Association of Boarding Schools, and New Hampshire Department of Education. Member of National Association of Independent Schools and Secondary School Admission Test Board. Endowment: $1.7 million. Total enrollment: 91. Upper school average class size: 8. Upper school faculty-student ratio: 1:5. There are 165 required school days per year for Upper School students. Upper School students typically attend 5 days per week. The average school day consists of 6 hours.

Upper School Student Profile Grade 9: 15 students (7 boys, 8 girls); Grade 10: 32 students (8 boys, 24 girls); Grade 11: 17 students (6 boys, 11 girls); Grade 12: 27 students (14 boys, 13 girls). 56% of students are boarding students. 50% are state residents. 13 states are represented in upper school student body. 17% are international students. International students from China, France, Germany, Mexico, Spain, and Switzerland; 2 other countries represented in student body.

Faculty School total: 28. In upper school: 13 men, 15 women; 20 have advanced degrees; 10 reside on campus.

Subjects Offered Advanced chemistry, algebra, American history, American literature, anatomy, ancient history, ancient world history, art, art appreciation, art history, arts, batik, biochemistry, biology, botany, calculus, ceramics, chemistry, chorus, community service, computer programming, creative writing, digital art, drama, driver education, earth science, ecology, economics, English, English literature, environmental science, ESL, ethics, European history, eurythmy, expository writing, fiber arts, filmmaking, fine arts, French, geography, geology, geometry, government/civics, grammar, graphic arts, graphic design, health, health education, history, history of science, jazz band, mathematics, meteorology, music, mythology, nature study, optics, philosophy, photography, physical education, physics, physiology, probability and statistics, projective geometry, Russian literature, science, social sciences, social studies, Spanish, speech, studio art, theater, theory of knowledge, trigonometry, video film production, wilderness education, world history, world literature, writing, zoology.

Graduation Requirements Algebra, arts and fine arts (art, music, dance, drama), economics, English, foreign language, geometry, government, health, language arts, mathematics, performing arts, physical education (includes health), physics, science, social sciences, social studies (includes history), studio art, U.S. history. Community service is required.

Special Academic Programs Advanced Placement exam preparation; honors section; independent study; term-away projects; study at local college for college credit; study abroad; academic accommodation for the musically talented and the artistically

talented; remedial math; programs in mathematics for dyslexic students; ESL (12 students enrolled).

College Admission Counseling 33 students graduated in 2014; 26 went to college. Other: 1 entered a postgraduate year, 6 had other specific plans. Mean SAT critical reading: 595, mean SAT math: 531, mean SAT writing: 568, mean combined SAT: 1694, mean composite ACT: 22.

Student Life Upper grades have specified standards of dress, student council. Discipline rests equally with students and faculty.

Tuition and Aid Day student tuition: $29,500; 7-day tuition and room/board: $47,000. Tuition installment plan (FACTS Tuition Payment Plan). Merit scholarship grants, need-based scholarship grants available. In 2014–15, 45% of upper-school students received aid; total upper-school merit-scholarship money awarded: $150,000. Total amount of financial aid awarded in 2014–15: $900,000.

Admissions Traditional secondary-level entrance grade is 9. For fall 2014, 50 students applied for upper-level admission, 48 were accepted, 40 enrolled. Deadline for receipt of application materials: February 1. Application fee required: $50. Interview required.

Athletics Interscholastic: baseball (boys), basketball (b,g), cross-country running (b,g), lacrosse (g), soccer (b,g); coed intramural: aerobics, alpine skiing, backpacking, bicycling, broomball, Circus, climbing, cross-country running, dance, fitness, fitness walking, Frisbee, hiking/backpacking, jogging, juggling, outdoor activities, outdoor education, outdoor recreation, outdoor skills, outdoors, physical fitness, physical training, rock climbing, running, skiing (cross-country), skiing (downhill), snowboarding, snowshoeing, tennis, ultimate Frisbee, volleyball, walking, wall climbing, wilderness, wilderness survival, wildernessways, yoga. 1 PE instructor, 8 coaches.

Computers Computers are regularly used in drawing and design, graphic arts, graphic design, mathematics, science, technology classes. Computer resources include on-campus library services, Internet access, wireless campus network. The school has a published electronic and media policy.

Contact Patricia Meissner, Director of Admissions. 603-654-2391 Ext. 109. Fax: 603-654-6588. E-mail: admissions@highmowing.org. Website: www.highmowing.org

HIGHROAD ACADEMY

46641 Chilliwack Central Road
Chilliwack, British Columbia V2P 1K3, Canada

Head of School: Mr. Stuart Morris

General Information Coeducational day college-preparatory and religious studies school, affiliated with Christian faith; primarily serves students with learning disabilities, individuals with Attention Deficit Disorder, individuals with emotional and behavioral problems, and dyslexic students. Grades K–12. Founded: 1978. Setting: small town. Nearest major city is Vancouver, Canada. 45-acre campus. 1 building on campus. Approved or accredited by Christian Schools International and British Columbia Department of Education. Language of instruction: English. Total enrollment: 427. Upper school average class size: 25. Upper school faculty-student ratio: 1:13. Upper School students typically attend 5 days per week. The average school day consists of 5 hours.

Upper School Student Profile Grade 6: 34 students (16 boys, 18 girls); Grade 7: 31 students (15 boys, 16 girls); Grade 8: 29 students (17 boys, 12 girls); Grade 9: 27 students (12 boys, 15 girls); Grade 10: 44 students (25 boys, 19 girls); Grade 11: 35 students (15 boys, 20 girls); Grade 12: 35 students (16 boys, 19 girls). 100% of students are Christian.

Faculty School total: 29. In upper school: 9 men, 6 women.

Graduation Requirements Bible.

Special Academic Programs Independent study; study at local college for college credit; ESL (24 students enrolled).

College Admission Counseling 26 students graduated in 2015; 7 went to college, including The University of British Columbia. Other: 14 went to work, 4 entered a postgraduate year.

Student Life Upper grades have uniform requirement, student council, honor system. Discipline rests primarily with faculty. Attendance at religious services is required.

Tuition and Aid Tuition installment plan (monthly payment plans).

Admissions Traditional secondary-level entrance grade is 10. Deadline for receipt of application materials: none. Application fee required: CAN$100. Interview required.

Athletics 1 PE instructor, 6 coaches.

Computers Computer network features include Internet access, wireless campus network, Internet filtering or blocking technology. Computer access in designated common areas is available to students. Students grades are available online.

Contact Mrs. Denise Kraubner, Office Manager. 604-792-4680. Fax: 604-792-2465. E-mail: dkraubner@highroadacademy.com. Website: www.highroadacademy.com

THE HILL CENTER, DURHAM ACADEMY

Durham, North Carolina
See Special Needs Schools section.

HILLSIDE SCHOOL

Marlborough, Massachusetts
See Junior Boarding Schools section.

HO'ALA SCHOOL

1067A California Avenue
Wahiawa, Hawaii 96786

Head of School: Linda Perry

General Information Coeducational day college-preparatory, arts, and service learning school. Grades K–12. Founded: 1986. Setting: rural. Nearest major city is Honolulu. 1-acre campus. 1 building on campus. Approved or accredited by Western Association of Schools and Colleges and Hawaii Department of Education. Total enrollment: 93. Upper school average class size: 7. Upper school faculty-student ratio: 1:5. There are 183 required school days per year for Upper School students. Upper School students typically attend 5 days per week. The average school day consists of 5 hours and 30 minutes.

Upper School Student Profile Grade 6: 12 students (8 boys, 4 girls); Grade 7: 7 students (1 boy, 6 girls); Grade 8: 9 students (2 boys, 7 girls); Grade 9: 10 students (5 boys, 5 girls); Grade 10: 4 students (2 boys, 2 girls); Grade 11: 6 students (3 boys, 3 girls); Grade 12: 6 students (2 boys, 4 girls).

Faculty School total: 11. In upper school: 2 men, 4 women; 3 have advanced degrees.

Subjects Offered 1 1/2 elective credits, 20th century history, 20th century physics, 20th century world history, advanced biology, advanced chemistry, advanced computer applications, advanced math, Advanced Placement courses, advanced studio art-AP, algebra, alternative physical education, American Civil War, American government, American history, American history-AP, American literature, American literature-AP, analytic geometry, anthropology, art, art appreciation, art education, art history, art history-AP, athletics, basketball, biology, biology-AP, bowling, calculus, calculus-AP, character education, chemistry, chemistry-AP, civics, Civil War, civil war history, college admission preparation, college awareness, college counseling, college placement, college planning, college writing, community service, composition, composition-AP, computer applications, contemporary art, creative arts, creative dance, creative drama, creative thinking, creative writing, dance, drama, drama performance, drawing, drawing and design, English, English composition, English language and composition-AP, English language-AP, English literature and composition-AP, English literature-AP, English-AP, English/composition-AP, environmental science, environmental studies, fine arts, foreign language, general science, geometry, government/civics, government/civics-AP, grammar, guidance, Hawaiian history, health, health and safety, health and wellness, health education, history, home economics, honors algebra, honors English, honors geometry, honors U.S. history, honors world history, Internet, Internet research, lab science, language, language and composition, language-AP, life management skills, life skills, marine biology, marine science, mathematics-AP, mentorship program, modern dance, modern history, painting, personal and social education, physical education, physics, physics-AP, post-calculus, pre-algebra, pre-calculus, pre-college orientation, SAT/ACT preparation, science, scuba diving, senior career experience, senior project, service learning/internship, sewing, social sciences, social studies, Spanish, Spanish language-AP, Spanish-AP, student government, student teaching, studio art-AP, study skills, theater arts, volleyball, world geography, world governments, world history, world history-AP, writing, yearbook.

Special Academic Programs Advanced Placement exam preparation; honors section; academic accommodation for the gifted and the artistically talented; remedial reading and/or remedial writing; remedial math; programs in general development for dyslexic students.

Student Life Upper grades have uniform requirement, student council, honor system. Discipline rests primarily with faculty.

Tuition and Aid Day student tuition: $9900. Tuition installment plan (monthly payment plans, individually arranged payment plans). Tuition reduction for siblings, merit scholarship grants, need-based scholarship grants available. In 2015–16, 30% of upper-school students received aid. Total amount of financial aid awarded in 2015–16: $21,600.

Admissions Traditional secondary-level entrance grade is 9. For fall 2015, 11 students applied for upper-level admission, 10 were accepted, 10 enrolled. Admissions testing, High School Placement Test, school's own exam and writing sample required. Deadline for receipt of application materials: none. Application fee required: $50. Interview recommended.

Athletics Interscholastic: basketball (boys), cross-country running (b,g), golf (b), physical fitness (b), swimming and diving (b,g), track and field (b,g), volleyball (b); intramural: basketball (b). 5 PE instructors, 1 coach.

Computers Computers are regularly used in college planning, computer applications, English, health, history, keyboarding, lab/keyboard, mentorship program, science, Web site design, yearbook classes. Computer network features include wireless campus network. Students grades are available online.

Contact Mickie Hettema, Admissions Clerk. 808-621-1898. Fax: 808-622-3615. E-mail: Mickie@hoalaschool.org. Website: www.hoalaschool.org/

THE HOCKADAY SCHOOL

11600 Welch Road
Dallas, Texas 75229-2999

Head of School: Liza Lee

General Information Girls' boarding and day and distance learning college-preparatory, arts, and technology school. Boarding grades 8–12, day grades PK–12. Distance learning grades 3–12. Founded: 1913. Setting: suburban. Students are housed in single-sex dormitories. 88-acre campus. 12 buildings on campus. Approved or accredited by Independent Schools Association of the Southwest, The Association of Boarding Schools, Virginia Association of Independent Schools, and Virginia Association of Independent Specialized Education Facilities. Member of National Association of Independent Schools and Secondary School Admission Test Board. Endowment: $145 million. Total enrollment: 1,096. Upper school average class size: 15. Upper school faculty-student ratio: 1:10. There are 160 required school days per year for Upper School students. Upper School students typically attend 5 days per week. The average school day consists of 6 hours and 40 minutes.

Upper School Student Profile 15% of students are boarding students. 91% are state residents. 5 states are represented in upper school student body. 9% are international students. International students from Canada, China, Jamaica, Mexico, Republic of Korea, and Russian Federation; 7 other countries represented in student body.

Faculty School total: 128. In upper school: 18 men, 41 women; 48 have advanced degrees; 4 reside on campus.

Subjects Offered Acting, advanced math, advanced studio art-AP, algebra, American history, American history-AP, American literature, analytic geometry, anatomy, applied arts, applied music, art history, astronomy, athletics, audio visual/media, ballet, basketball, biology, biology-AP, body human, British literature, broadcast journalism, broadcasting, Broadway dance, calculus, calculus-AP, cell biology, ceramics, chemistry, chemistry-AP, college counseling, comparative religion, computer applications, computer science, computer science-AP, concert choir, consumer economics, CPR, creative writing, current events, dance, dance performance, debate, digital art, digital imaging, digital music, digital photography, directing, discrete mathematics, drawing and design, ecology, environmental systems, economics-AP, English, English literature, English literature and composition-AP, English-AP, environmental science, environmental science-AP, ESL, ESL, fencing, fine arts, finite math, first aid, French, French language-AP, French literature-AP, genetics, geometry, guitar, health, health and wellness, honors English, humanities, information technology, interdisciplinary studies, journalism, Latin, Latin-AP, madrigals, Mandarin, microbiology, modern European history-AP, newspaper, non-Western literature, orchestra, philosophy, photography, physical education, physical fitness, physics, physics-AP, piano, pre-calculus, printmaking, probability and statistics, psychology, psychology-AP, self-defense, senior internship, set design, short story, Spanish, Spanish language-AP, Spanish literature-AP, stagecraft, studio art, studio art-AP, swimming, technology, tennis, track and field, U.S. government, U.S. history, U.S. history-AP, voice, volleyball, Web site design, wellness, world history, yearbook.

Graduation Requirements Algebra, American literature, art history, audio visual/media, biology-AP, chemistry, computer literacy, computer skills, English, English literature, geometry, history of music, information technology, languages, physical education (includes health), physics, senior project, U.S. government, U.S. history, world history, one semester of History of Art and Music, 60 hours of community service.

Special Academic Programs Advanced Placement exam preparation; honors section; independent study; term-away projects; study abroad; ESL (12 students enrolled).

College Admission Counseling 121 students graduated in 2015; all went to college, including Cornell University; Georgetown University; Northwestern University; Stanford University; Vanderbilt University. Mean SAT critical reading: 700, mean SAT math: 695, mean SAT writing: 705.

Student Life Upper grades have uniform requirement, student council, honor system. Discipline rests primarily with faculty.

Summer Programs Enrichment, advancement, ESL, sports, art/fine arts, computer instruction programs offered; session focuses on enrichment; held on campus; accepts boys and girls; open to students from other schools. 900 students usually enrolled. 2016 schedule: June 8 to July 17. Application deadline: none.

Tuition and Aid Day student tuition: $27,070–$27,095; 7-day tuition and room/board: $48,099–$52,855. Need-based scholarship grants, need-based financial aid available. In 2015–16, 18% of upper-school students received aid. Total amount of financial aid awarded in 2015–16: $3,400,000.

Admissions Traditional secondary-level entrance grade is 9. For fall 2015, 239 students applied for upper-level admission, 70 were accepted, 44 enrolled. Admissions testing required. Deadline for receipt of application materials: none. Application fee required: $175. Interview required.

Athletics Interscholastic: basketball (girls), crew (g), cross-country running (g), fencing (g), field hockey (g), golf (g), independent competitive sports (g), jogging (g), lacrosse (g), rowing (g), running (g), soccer (g), softball (g), swimming and diving (g), tennis (g), track and field (g), volleyball (g), winter soccer (g); intramural: aerobics (g), aerobics/dance (g), aquatics (g), archery (g), ballet (g), basketball (g), cheering (g), cooperative games (g), dance (g), fitness (g), independent competitive sports (g), jogging (g), life saving (g), martial arts (g), modern dance (g), outdoor skills (g), physical fitness (g), physical training (g), project adventure (g), racquetball (g), ropes

courses (g), running (g), self defense (g), strength & conditioning (g), swimming and diving (g), tennis (g), track and field (g), ultimate Frisbee (g), volleyball (g), weight lifting (g), weight training (g), yoga (g). 13 PE instructors, 9 coaches, 3 athletic trainers.
Computers Computers are regularly used in animation, art, computer applications, creative writing, dance, engineering, English, French, health, history, humanities, information technology, introduction to technology, journalism, Latin, mathematics, media, media production, media services, multimedia, music, newspaper, photography, photojournalism, psychology, publications, publishing, science, Spanish, technology, Web site design, yearbook classes. Computer network features include on-campus library services, online commercial services, Internet access, wireless campus network, Internet filtering or blocking technology. Campus intranet, student e-mail accounts, and computer access in designated common areas are available to students. Students grades are available online. The school has a published electronic and media policy.
Contact Maryanna Phipps, Director of Admission. 214-363-6311. Fax: 214-265-1649. E-mail: admissions@hockaday.org. Website: www.hockaday.org

HOLDERNESS SCHOOL

Chapel Lane
PO Box 1879
Plymouth, New Hampshire 03264-1879

Head of School: Mr. R. Phillip Peck

General Information Coeducational boarding and day college-preparatory, arts, religious studies, bilingual studies, and technology school, affiliated with Episcopal Church. Grades 9–PG. Founded: 1879. Setting: small town. Nearest major city is Boston, MA. Students are housed in single-sex dormitories. 620-acre campus. 35 buildings on campus. Approved or accredited by Association of Independent Schools in New England, New England Association of Schools and Colleges, The Association of Boarding Schools, and New Hampshire Department of Education. Member of National Association of Independent Schools and Secondary School Admission Test Board. Endowment: $44 million. Total enrollment: 281. Upper school average class size: 12. Upper school faculty-student ratio: 1:6. Upper School students typically attend 6 days per week.
Upper School Student Profile Grade 9: 49 students (27 boys, 22 girls); Grade 10: 66 students (42 boys, 24 girls); Grade 11: 87 students (47 boys, 40 girls); Grade 12: 76 students (48 boys, 28 girls); Postgraduate: 3 students (3 boys). 79% of students are boarding students. 36% are state residents. 24 states are represented in upper school student body. 13% are international students. International students from Canada, China, Lithuania, Republic of Korea, Saudi Arabia, and Spain; 7 other countries represented in student body. 20% of students are members of Episcopal Church.
Faculty School total: 49. In upper school: 29 men, 20 women; 29 have advanced degrees, 29 reside on campus.
Subjects Offered Advanced chemistry, Advanced Placement courses, algebra, anatomy and physiology, art, art history, Bible studies, biology, calculus, ceramics, chemistry, chorus, community service, drama, drawing, driver education, economics, economics and history, English, environmental science, ethics, ethics and responsibility, European history, fine arts, French, geometry, government/civics, history, human anatomy, human development, humanities, jazz band, Latin, mathematics, music, music composition, music theory, music theory-AP, painting, photography, physics, pre-calculus, religion, science, society and culture, Spanish, statistics, theater, theater arts, theater production, theology, trigonometry, U.S. history, women in world history, women's studies, world history, world religions, writing.
Graduation Requirements Arts and fine arts (art, music, dance, drama), English, foreign language, history, human development, humanities, mathematics, science, theology. Community service is required.
Special Academic Programs Advanced Placement exam preparation; honors section; independent study; term-away projects; study abroad; academic accommodation for the gifted, the musically talented, and the artistically talented.
College Admission Counseling 78 students graduated in 2014; 77 went to college, including Bates College; Dartmouth College; St. Lawrence University; University of New Hampshire; University of Vermont. Other: 1 entered a postgraduate year. Mean SAT critical reading: 555, mean SAT math: 577, mean SAT writing: 555. 37% scored over 600 on SAT critical reading, 39% scored over 600 on SAT math.
Student Life Upper grades have specified standards of dress, student council, honor system. Discipline rests equally with students and faculty. Attendance at religious services is required.
Tuition and Aid Day student tuition: $25,360; 7-day tuition and room/board: $42,670. Tuition installment plan (Insured Tuition Payment Plan, Key Tuition Payment Plan, monthly payment plans). Need-based scholarship grants available. In 2014–15, 41% of upper-school students received aid. Total amount of financial aid awarded in 2014–15: $2,577,890.
Admissions Traditional secondary-level entrance grade is 9. For fall 2014, 425 students applied for upper-level admission, 204 were accepted, 104 enrolled. SSAT or WISC III or TOEFL required. Deadline for receipt of application materials: February 1. Application fee required: $50. Interview required.
Athletics Interscholastic: alpine skiing (boys, girls), baseball (b), basketball (b,g), bicycling (b,g), cross-country running (b,g), field hockey (g), football (b), freestyle skiing (b,g), ice hockey (b,g), lacrosse (b,g), nordic skiing (b,g), skiing (cross-country)

(b,g), skiing (downhill) (b,g), snowboarding (b,g), soccer (b,g), softball (g), tennis (b,g); coed interscholastic: golf, running, ski jumping; coed intramural: aerobics/dance, backpacking, canoeing/kayaking, climbing, dance, equestrian sports, fishing, fly fishing, Frisbee, hiking/backpacking, horseback riding, ice hockey, kayaking, mountain biking, mountaineering, outdoor activities, outdoor skills, physical fitness, rock climbing, skiing (cross-country), skiing (downhill), snowboarding, snowshoeing, softball, squash, strength & conditioning, table tennis, ultimate Frisbee, wall climbing, weight lifting, weight training, wilderness, wilderness survival. 21 coaches, 1 athletic trainer.
Computers Computers are regularly used in Bible studies, creative writing, English, foreign language, graphic arts, history, library, mathematics, music, photography, religious studies, science, technology, theater, video film production, Web site design, yearbook classes. Computer network features include on-campus library services, Internet access, wireless campus network, Internet filtering or blocking technology, four computer labs (3 PC, 1 Mac). Campus intranet, student e-mail accounts, and computer access in designated common areas are available to students. The school has a published electronic and media policy.
Contact Ms. Nancy Dalley, Director of Financial Aid and Admission Operations. 603-536-1747. Fax: 603-536-2125. E-mail: admissions@holderness.org. Website: www.holderness.org

HOLLAND HALL

5666 East 81st Street
Tulsa, Oklahoma 74137-2099

Head of School: J.P. Culley

General Information Coeducational day college-preparatory, arts, religious studies, and technology school, affiliated with Episcopal Church. Grades PK–12. Founded: 1922. Setting: suburban. 162-acre campus. 5 buildings on campus. Approved or accredited by Independent Schools Association of the Southwest, National Association of Episcopal Schools, and Oklahoma Department of Education. Member of National Association of Independent Schools. Endowment: $68 million. Total enrollment: 995. Upper school average class size: 13. Upper school faculty-student ratio: 1:9. There are 172 required school days per year for Upper School students. Upper School students typically attend 5 days per week. The average school day consists of 6 hours and 52 minutes.
Upper School Student Profile Grade 6: 77 students (32 boys, 45 girls); Grade 7: 63 students (31 boys, 32 girls); Grade 8: 64 students (36 boys, 28 girls); Grade 9: 77 students (40 boys, 37 girls); Grade 10: 90 students (44 boys, 46 girls); Grade 11: 95 students (55 boys, 40 girls); Grade 12: 71 students (38 boys, 33 girls). 7% of students are members of Episcopal Church.
Faculty School total: 93. In upper school: 23 men, 19 women; 28 have advanced degrees.
Subjects Offered Algebra, American history, American studies, art, biology, calculus, calculus-AP, ceramics, chemistry, chemistry-AP, Chinese, computer programming, computer science, creative writing, dance, drama, driver education, ecology, economics, English, English literature, ethics, fine arts, French, geology, geometry, government/civics, history, journalism, Latin, leadership, mathematics, music, photography, physical education, physics, religion, science, social studies, Spanish, statistics-AP, theater, trigonometry, writing.
Graduation Requirements Arts and fine arts (art, music, dance, drama), English, foreign language, mathematics, physical education (includes health), religion (includes Bible studies and theology), science, social studies (includes history), senior intern program, 9th/12th grade wellness, college seminar.
Special Academic Programs Advanced Placement exam preparation; honors section; independent study; study at local college for college credit; study abroad.
College Admission Counseling 85 students graduated in 2015; all went to college, including Oklahoma State University; Southern Methodist University; The University of Tulsa; University of Oklahoma. Median SAT critical reading: 640, median SAT math: 640, median SAT writing: 620, median combined SAT: 1900, median composite ACT: 28.
Student Life Upper grades have uniform requirement, student council, honor system. Discipline rests equally with students and faculty.
Summer Programs Enrichment, advancement, sports, art/fine arts, computer instruction programs offered; session focuses on academic enrichment; held on campus; accepts boys and girls; open to students from other schools. 830 students usually enrolled. 2016 schedule: June 3 to July 26. Application deadline: June 1.
Tuition and Aid Day student tuition: $18,850. Tuition installment plan (monthly payment plans, school's own payment plan). Merit scholarship grants, need-based scholarship grants available. In 2015–16, 28% of upper-school students received aid; total upper-school merit-scholarship money awarded: $154,900. Total amount of financial aid awarded in 2015–16: $928,525.
Admissions Traditional secondary-level entrance grade is 9. Admissions testing and ISEE required. Deadline for receipt of application materials: none. Application fee required: $25. On-campus interview required.
Athletics Interscholastic: baseball (boys), basketball (b,g), cheering (g), cross-country running (b,g), field hockey (g), football (b), golf (b,g), modern dance (b,g), soccer (b,g), softball (g), tennis (b,g), track and field (b,g), volleyball (g); intramural: aerobics (b,g), dance (b,g), modern dance (b,g), soccer (b,g); coed interscholastic: cheering, crew,

modern dance, physical training, strength & conditioning; coed intramural: fitness, modern dance, physical training, soccer, weight lifting. 39 coaches, 1 athletic trainer.

Computers Computers are regularly used in art, English, foreign language, history, journalism, library, mathematics, science, yearbook classes. Computer network features include on-campus library services, online commercial services, Internet access, wireless campus network, Internet filtering or blocking technology. Student e-mail accounts and computer access in designated common areas are available to students. Students grades are available online. The school has a published electronic and media policy.

Contact Olivia Martin, Director of Admission and Financial Aid. 918-481-1111. Ext. 740. Fax: 918-481-1145. E-mail: omartin@hollandhall.org. Website: www.hollandhall.org

HOLY CROSS HIGH SCHOOL

587 Oronoke Road
Waterbury, Connecticut 06708

Head of School: Mr. Frank Samuelson Jr.

General Information Coeducational day college-preparatory, arts, religious studies, and technology school, affiliated with Roman Catholic Church. Grades 9–12. Founded: 1968. Setting: suburban. 37-acre campus. 1 building on campus. Approved or accredited by National Catholic Education Association, New England Association of Schools and Colleges, and Connecticut Department of Education. Total enrollment: 489. Upper school average class size: 20. Upper school faculty-student ratio: 1:11. There are 160 required school days per year for Upper School students. Upper School students typically attend 5 days per week. The average school day consists of 6 hours.

Upper School Student Profile Grade 9: 123 students (61 boys, 62 girls); Grade 10: 124 students (61 boys, 63 girls); Grade 11: 115 students (59 boys, 56 girls); Grade 12: 127 students (60 boys, 67 girls). 70% of students are Roman Catholic.

Faculty School total: 60. In upper school: 28 men, 32 women; 37 have advanced degrees.

Subjects Offered Advanced biology, advanced math, Advanced Placement courses, advanced studio art-AP, algebra, American history, American history-AP, American literature, American literature-AP, American studies, anatomy, anatomy and physiology, art, art-AP, arts, band, Basic programming, biology, biology-AP, British literature, British literature-AP, business, business law, calculus, calculus-AP, campus ministry, Catholic belief and practice, chamber groups, chemistry, chemistry-AP, choir, computer applications, computer programming, computer science, concert band, concert choir, CPR, creative writing, drama, driver education, economics, economics and history, English, English literature, English-AP, environmental science, French, geometry, history, mathematics, music, physical education, physics, physiology, psychology, religion, science, social studies, Spanish, statistics, theater, theology, trigonometry, word processing, world history, world literature.

Graduation Requirements English, foreign language, mathematics, physical education (includes health), religion (includes Bible studies and theology), science, social studies (includes history).

Special Academic Programs Advanced Placement exam preparation; honors section; independent study; study at local college for college credit.

College Admission Counseling 151 students graduated in 2015; 144 went to college, including Central Connecticut State University; Naugatuck Valley Community College; Southern Connecticut State University; University of Connecticut; Western Connecticut State University. Other: 1 went to work, 3 entered military service, 3 entered a postgraduate year.

Student Life Upper grades have specified standards of dress, student council. Discipline rests primarily with faculty. Attendance at religious services is required.

Summer Programs Sports, art/fine arts programs offered; session focuses on basketball, volleyball, theatre; held on campus; accepts boys and girls; open to students from other schools.

Tuition and Aid Day student tuition: $12,950. Tuition installment plan (monthly payment plans, individually arranged payment plans, Tuition Management Systems (TMS)). Merit scholarship grants, need-based scholarship grants available. In 2015–16, 30% of upper-school students received aid; total upper-school merit-scholarship money awarded: $135,000. Total amount of financial aid awarded in 2015–16: $650,000.

Admissions Traditional secondary-level entrance grade is 9. For fall 2015, 292 students applied for upper-level admission, 262 were accepted, 123 enrolled. ETS HSPT (closed) required. Deadline for receipt of application materials: none. Application fee required: $25.

Athletics Interscholastic: baseball (boys), basketball (b,g), cheering (g), cross-country running (b,g), dance team (g), diving (b,g), football (b), golf (b,g), gymnastics (g), lacrosse (b,g), soccer (b,g), softball (g), swimming and diving (b,g), tennis (b,g), track and field (b,g), volleyball (g), winter (indoor) track (b,g), wrestling (b); intramural: basketball (b), skiing (downhill) (b,g), weight lifting (b); coed intramural: bowling, table tennis, ultimate Frisbee, yoga. 3 PE instructors, 22 coaches, 1 athletic trainer.

Computers Computers are regularly used in accounting, business, computer applications, creative writing, English, foreign language, French, history, mathematics, music technology, psychology, religious studies, science, social sciences, social studies, Spanish, technology, theology, Web site design, word processing, writing, writing, yearbook classes. Computer network features include on-campus library services, online commercial services, Internet access, wireless campus network. Campus intranet

and computer access in designated common areas are available to students. Students grades are available online.

Contact Mrs. Jodie LaCava McGarrity, Director of Admissions. 203-757-9248. Fax: 203-757-3423. E-mail: jmcgarrity@holycrosshs-ct.com. Website: www.holycrosshs-ct.com

HOLY CROSS REGIONAL CATHOLIC SCHOOL

2125 Langhorne Road
Lynchburg, Virginia 24501-1449

Head of School: Ms. Mary Sherry

General Information Coeducational day college-preparatory, religious studies, and STEAM school, affiliated with Roman Catholic Church. Grades PK–12. Founded: 1879. Setting: small town. 1 building on campus. Approved or accredited by National Catholic Education Association, Southern Association of Colleges and Schools, and Virginia Department of Education. Upper school average class size: 14. Upper school faculty-student ratio: 1:7. There are 183 required school days per year for Upper School students. Upper School students typically attend 5 days per week. The average school day consists of 7 hours and 5 minutes.

Upper School Student Profile Grade 6: 14 students (6 boys, 8 girls); Grade 7: 17 students (8 boys, 9 girls); Grade 8: 11 students (5 boys, 6 girls); Grade 9: 18 students (8 boys, 10 girls); Grade 10: 10 students (4 boys, 6 girls); Grade 11: 8 students (6 boys, 2 girls); Grade 12: 19 students (9 boys, 10 girls). 62% of students are Roman Catholic.

Faculty School total: 24. In upper school: 3 men, 8 women; 4 have advanced degrees.

Subjects Offered Advanced biology, advanced chemistry, advanced math, Advanced Placement courses, algebra, American government, American history, biology, British literature, British literature-AP, calculus-AP, chemistry, composition-AP, dramatic arts, earth science, English literature and composition-AP, government-AP, health science, honors English, honors geometry, honors U.S. history, honors world history, Latin, physics, pre-algebra, pre-calculus, psychology, religious studies, Spanish, U.S. and Virginia government-AP.

Graduation Requirements Community service hour requirements.

Special Academic Programs Independent study; study at local college for college credit.

College Admission Counseling 13 students graduated in 2015; all went to college, including Christopher Newport University; Elon University; Stony Brook University, State University of New York; Virginia Military Institute; Virginia Polytechnic Institute and State University; Washington and Lee University. Mean SAT critical reading: 567, mean SAT math: 574, mean SAT writing: 559.

Student Life Upper grades have uniform requirement, student council, honor system. Discipline rests primarily with faculty. Attendance at religious services is required.

Tuition and Aid Tuition installment plan (FACTS Tuition Payment Plan). Tuition reduction for siblings available.

Admissions Traditional secondary-level entrance grade is 9. For fall 2015, 12 students applied for upper-level admission, 11 were accepted, 11 enrolled. TOEFL required. Deadline for receipt of application materials: none. Application fee required: $50. Interview required.

Athletics Interscholastic: baseball (boys), basketball (b,g), soccer (b), tennis (g), volleyball (g); coed interscholastic: golf. 1 PE instructor, 11 coaches.

Computers Computers are regularly used in computer applications, writing, yearbook classes. Computer network features include Internet access, Internet filtering or blocking technology. Student e-mail accounts are available to students. Students grades are available online. The school has a published electronic and media policy.

Contact Ms. Catherine Chapman Mosley, Director of School Relations and Advancement. 434-847-5436. Fax: 434-847-4156. E-mail: cmosley@hcfaculty.com. Website: http://hcrs-va.org/

HOLY CROSS SCHOOL

5500 Paris Avenue
New Orleans, Louisiana 70122

Head of School: Mr. Charles DiGange

General Information Boys' day college-preparatory, arts, religious studies, and technology school, affiliated with Roman Catholic Church. Grades PK–12. Founded: 1849. Setting: suburban. 20-acre campus. 5 buildings on campus. Approved or accredited by National Catholic Education Association, Southern Association of Colleges and Schools, and Louisiana Department of Education. Total enrollment: 1,140. Upper school average class size: 21. Upper school faculty-student ratio: 1:12. There are 184 required school days per year for Upper School students. Upper School students typically attend 5 days per week. The average school day consists of 6 hours and 35 minutes.

Upper School Student Profile Grade 6: 79 students (79 boys); Grade 7: 121 students (121 boys); Grade 8: 144 students (144 boys); Grade 9: 161 students (161 boys); Grade 10: 162 students (162 boys); Grade 11: 153 students (153 boys); Grade 12: 142 students (142 boys). 80% of students are Roman Catholic.

Faculty School total: 86. In upper school: 37 men, 10 women; 22 have advanced degrees.

Graduation Requirements Community service requirement.

Special Academic Programs 14 Advanced Placement exams for which test preparation is offered; honors section; study at local college for college credit; academic accommodation for the gifted, the musically talented, and the artistically talented.

College Admission Counseling 132 students graduated in 2015; all went to college, including Louisiana State University and Agricultural & Mechanical College; Loyola University New Orleans; St. Edward's University; Tulane University; University of Louisiana at Lafayette; University of Southern Mississippi. Median composite ACT: 23. 25% scored over 26 on composite ACT.

Student Life Upper grades have uniform requirement, student council, honor system. Discipline rests primarily with faculty. Attendance at religious services is required.

Summer Programs Remediation, enrichment, computer instruction programs offered; session focuses on enrichment; held on campus; accepts boys; not open to students from other schools. 75 students usually enrolled. 2016 schedule: July 14 to July 28. Application deadline: May 31.

Tuition and Aid Day student tuition: $8000. Tuition installment plan (monthly payment plans). Tuition reduction for siblings, merit scholarship grants, need-based scholarship grants, paying campus jobs available. In 2015–16, 5% of upper-school students received aid; total upper-school merit-scholarship money awarded: $50,000.

Admissions Traditional secondary-level entrance grade is 8. For fall 2015, 350 students applied for upper-level admission, 235 were accepted, 210 enrolled. ACT-Explore, High School Placement Test, High School Placement Test (closed version) from Scholastic Testing Service or Iowa Subtests required. Deadline for receipt of application materials: November 15. Application fee required: $20. Interview required.

Athletics Interscholastic: baseball, basketball, bowling, cheering, cross-country running, football, golf, indoor track, indoor track & field, power lifting, soccer, swimming and diving, tennis, wrestling; intramural: baseball, basketball, bicycling, fishing, flag football, football, Frisbee, lacrosse, martial arts, physical training, sailing, skateboarding, soccer, softball, strength & conditioning, ultimate Frisbee, volleyball, weight training. 10 PE instructors, 38 coaches, 2 athletic trainers.

Computers Computers are regularly used in all classes. Computer network features include on-campus library services, online commercial services, Internet access, wireless campus network, Internet filtering or blocking technology. Student e-mail accounts and computer access in designated common areas are available to students. Students grades are available online. The school has a published electronic and media policy.

Contact Mr. Brian Kitchen, Director of Admissions. 504-942-3100. Fax: 504-284-3424. E-mail: bkitchen@holycrosstigers.com. Website: www.holycrosstigers.com

HOLY GHOST PREPARATORY SCHOOL

2429 Bristol Pike
Bensalem, Pennsylvania 19020

Head of School: Mr. Gregory J. Geruson

General Information Boys' day college-preparatory, arts, and technology school, affiliated with Roman Catholic Church. Grades 9–12. Founded: 1897. Setting: suburban. Nearest major city is Philadelphia. 53-acre campus. 5 buildings on campus. Approved or accredited by Middle States Association of Colleges and Schools, National Catholic Education Association, and Pennsylvania Association of Independent Schools. Member of National Association of Independent Schools. Endowment: $2 million. Total enrollment: 467. Upper school average class size: 17. Upper school faculty-student ratio: 1:11. The average school day consists of 6 hours and 30 minutes.

Upper School Student Profile Grade 9: 126 students (126 boys); Grade 10: 120 students (120 boys); Grade 11: 120 students (120 boys); Grade 12: 101 students (101 boys). 94% of students are Roman Catholic.

Faculty School total: 50. In upper school: 32 men, 18 women; 36 have advanced degrees.

Subjects Offered 3-dimensional art, Advanced Placement courses, advanced studio art-AP, algebra, American government, American history, American history-AP, American literature, analysis, anatomy and physiology, art, Bible, biology, biology-AP, calculus, calculus-AP, campus ministry, career/college preparation, careers, ceremonies of life, chemistry, Chinese history, choral music, church history, college admission preparation, college counseling, communication arts, communication skills, computer programming-AP, computer science, computer science-AP, creative writing, drama performance, earth science, economics, English, English language and composition-AP, English literature, English literature and composition-AP, environmental science, European history, European history-AP, film, fine arts, French, French language-AP, geometry, government and politics-AP, government/civics, health, history, journalism, language-AP, Latin, Latin-AP, mathematics, modern European history-AP, music, music theory-AP, oral communications, physical education, physics, public speaking, religion, science, sexuality, social studies, Spanish, Spanish language-AP, Spanish-AP, speech, statistics, trigonometry, U.S. history-AP, United States government-AP, world cultures, world history, world history-AP, world literature, writing, yearbook.

Graduation Requirements Arts and fine arts (art, music, dance, drama), computer science, English, foreign language, mathematics, physical education (includes health), religion (includes Bible studies and theology), science, social studies (includes history), summer reading. Community service is required.

Special Academic Programs Advanced Placement exam preparation; honors section; independent study; study abroad.

College Admission Counseling 118 students graduated in 2015; all went to college, including Boston College; Duquesne University; Penn State University Park; Saint Joseph's University; University of Pennsylvania; Villanova University. Median SAT critical reading: 610, median SAT math: 640.

Student Life Upper grades have specified standards of dress, student council, honor system. Discipline rests primarily with faculty.

Summer Programs Enrichment, advancement, sports, computer instruction programs offered; session focuses on entrance exam preparation; held on campus; accepts boys and girls; open to students from other schools. 100 students usually enrolled. 2016 schedule: June 22 to July 24. Application deadline: June 15.

Tuition and Aid Day student tuition: $16,700. Tuition installment plan (monthly payment plans, quarterly and semi-annual payment plans). Merit scholarship grants, need-based scholarship grants, music scholarships, minority scholarships, art scholarships available. In 2015–16, 40% of upper-school students received aid; total upper-school merit-scholarship money awarded: $1,000,000. Total amount of financial aid awarded in 2015–16: $1,000,000.

Admissions Traditional secondary-level entrance grade is 9. For fall 2015, 398 students applied for upper-level admission, 158 were accepted, 106 enrolled. High School Placement Test (closed version) from Scholastic Testing Service required. Deadline for receipt of application materials: none. Application fee required: $60. On-campus interview required.

Athletics Interscholastic: baseball, basketball, bowling, cross-country running, golf, ice hockey, indoor track & field, lacrosse, soccer, Special Olympics, swimming and diving, tennis, track and field; intramural: basketball, fitness walking, flag football, football, Frisbee, soccer, street hockey, tennis, ultimate Frisbee. 10 coaches, 1 athletic trainer.

Computers Computers are regularly used in college planning, English, foreign language, mathematics, programming, publications, science, speech, yearbook classes. Computer network features include on-campus library services, online commercial services, Internet access, wireless campus network, Internet filtering or blocking technology. Student e-mail accounts are available to students. The school has a published electronic and media policy.

Contact Mr. Ryan T. Abramson, Director of Admissions. 215-639-0811. Fax: 215-639-4225. E-mail: rabramson@holyghostprep.org. Website: www.holyghostprep.org

HOLY INNOCENTS' EPISCOPAL SCHOOL

805 Mount Vernon Highway NW
Atlanta, Georgia 30327

Head of School: Mr. Paul A. Barton

General Information Coeducational day college-preparatory, arts, religious studies, and technology school, affiliated with Episcopal Church. Grades PS–12. Founded: 1959. Setting: suburban. 42-acre campus. 4 buildings on campus. Approved or accredited by Georgia Independent School Association, National Association of Episcopal Schools, Southern Association of Colleges and Schools, and Georgia Department of Education. Member of National Association of Independent Schools and Secondary School Admission Test Board. Endowment: $17 million. Total enrollment: 1,360. Upper school average class size: 14. Upper school faculty-student ratio: 1:7. There are 173 required school days per year for Upper School students. Upper School students typically attend 5 days per week. The average school day consists of 7 hours and 15 minutes.

Upper School Student Profile 22% of students are members of Episcopal Church.

Faculty School total: 180. In upper school: 29 men, 32 women; 45 have advanced degrees.

Subjects Offered 3-dimensional art, 3-dimensional design, advanced biology, advanced chemistry, advanced math, Advanced Placement courses, advanced studio art-AP, algebra, American government, American history, American history-AP, American literature, American literature-AP, anatomy, anatomy and physiology, ancient world history, applied music, art, art-AP, athletics, band, baseball, basketball, Bible, Bible studies, biology, biology-AP, calculus, calculus-AP, cheerleading, chemistry, chemistry-AP, choir, choral music, chorus, college counseling, college placement, community service, composition, computer animation, computer education, computer graphics, computer resources, computer science-AP, concert band, concert choir, creative writing, drama, drama performance, drawing and design, earth science, economics, electives, English, English composition, English language-AP, English literature, English literature-AP, English-AP, environmental studies, ethics, European history, European history-AP, fine arts, French, French language-AP, French-AP, geometry, golf, government, government and politics-AP, government/civics, Greek, guidance, health and wellness, history, honors algebra, honors English, honors geometry, honors U.S. history, honors world history, human geography - AP, Jewish history, Jewish studies, language arts, Latin, Latin-AP, mathematics, New Testament, orchestra, peer counseling, performing arts, personal finance, photography, physical education, physics, physics-AP, pre-calculus, psychology, religion, religious studies, SAT preparation, SAT/ACT preparation, science, science project, sex education, social studies, Spanish, Spanish language-AP, speech and debate, sports, study skills, swimming, U.S. history, U.S. history-AP, visual arts, world history, writing workshop, yearbook.

Graduation Requirements Arts and fine arts (art, music, dance, drama), electives, English, foreign language, history, mathematics, physical education (includes health), physical fitness, religion (includes Bible studies and theology), science, 15 hours of community service each year, plus additional hours for NHS students.

Special Academic Programs Advanced Placement exam preparation; honors section; term-away projects; study abroad; academic accommodation for the gifted, the musically talented, and the artistically talented.

College Admission Counseling 110 students graduated in 2014; all went to college, including Auburn University; Clemson University; Georgia Institute of Technology; The University of Alabama; The University of North Carolina at Chapel Hill; University of Georgia. Mean SAT critical reading: 600, mean SAT math: 610, mean SAT writing: 620, mean composite ACT: 26.

Student Life Upper grades have uniform requirement, student council, honor system. Discipline rests equally with students and faculty. Attendance at religious services is required.

Tuition and Aid Day student tuition: $23,300. Tuition installment plan (Insured Tuition Payment Plan, FACTS Tuition Payment Plan, monthly payment plans). Need-based scholarship grants available. In 2014–15, 20% of upper-school students received aid. Total amount of financial aid awarded in 2014–15: $1,800,000.

Admissions Traditional secondary-level entrance grade is 9. For fall 2014, 116 students applied for upper-level admission, 59 were accepted, 33 enrolled. Essay, ISEE, mathematics proficiency exam, school's own test and SSAT required. Deadline for receipt of application materials: February 1. Application fee required: $95. Interview required.

Athletics Interscholastic: baseball (boys), basketball (b,g), cheering (g), cross-country running (b,g), equestrian sports (g), football (b), golf (b,g), lacrosse (b,g), physical fitness (b,g), physical training (b,g), soccer (b,g), softball (g), swimming and diving (b,g), tennis (b,g), track and field (b,g), volleyball (g), wrestling (b); intramural: combined training (b,g), fitness (b,g), ultimate Frisbee (b); coed intramural: combined training, fitness. 9 PE instructors, 120 coaches, 1 athletic trainer.

Computers Computers are regularly used in all academic classes. Computer network features include on-campus library services, Internet access, wireless campus network, Internet filtering or blocking technology, 1:1 student laptops (grades 5-12), two computer labs, and various individual classroom computers. Campus intranet and student e-mail accounts are available to students. Students grades are available online. The school has a published electronic and media policy.

Contact Mr. Chris Pomar, Assistant Head of School for Enrollment and Planning. 404-255-4026 Ext. 203. Fax: 404-847-1156. E-mail: chris.pomar@hies.org. Website: www.hies.org

HOLY NAME CENTRAL CATHOLIC HIGH SCHOOL

144 Granite St.
Worcester, Massachusetts 01604

Head of School: Mr. Edward Reynolds

General Information Coeducational day college-preparatory school, affiliated with Roman Catholic Church. Grades 7–12. Founded: 1942. Setting: urban. 1 building on campus. Approved or accredited by New England Association of Schools and Colleges. There are 180 required school days per year for Upper School students. Upper School students typically attend 5 days per week. The average school day consists of 6 hours and 20 minutes.

Faculty School total: 40. In upper school: 14 men, 26 women; 24 have advanced degrees.

Student Life Upper grades have uniform requirement.

Tuition and Aid Day student tuition: $7755. Tuition installment plan (FACTS Tuition Payment Plan).

Admissions Traditional secondary-level entrance grade is 9. No application fee required.

Contact Mr. Scott Anderson, Admissions Director. 508-753-6371. Fax: 508-831-1287. E-mail: sanderson@holyname.net. Website: www.holyname.net

HOLY NAMES ACADEMY

728 21st Avenue East
Seattle, Washington 98112

Head of School: Elizabeth Swift

General Information Girls' day college-preparatory school, affiliated with Roman Catholic Church. Grades 9–12. Founded: 1880. Setting: urban. 1 building on campus. Approved or accredited by Northwest Association of Independent Schools and Washington Department of Education. Member of National Association of Independent Schools. Upper school average class size: 14. Upper school faculty-student ratio: 1:14. There are 180 required school days per year for Upper School students. Upper School students typically attend 5 days per week. The average school day consists of 6 hours.

Upper School Student Profile 74% of students are Roman Catholic.

Faculty School total: 52. In upper school: 10 men, 42 women; 46 have advanced degrees.

College Admission Counseling 160 students graduated in 2015; all went to college.

Student Life Upper grades have specified standards of dress. Attendance at religious services is required.

Tuition and Aid Day student tuition: $14,856. Financial aid available to upper-school students. In 2015–16, 31% of upper-school students received aid.

Admissions Traditional secondary-level entrance grade is 9. TerraNova required. Deadline for receipt of application materials: January 11. Application fee required: $30.

Contact 206-323-4272. Website: www.holynames-sea.org

HOLYOKE CATHOLIC HIGH SCHOOL

134 Springfield Street
Chicopee, Massachusetts 01013

Head of School: Mrs. Maryann Lennihan

General Information Coeducational day college-preparatory and arts school, affiliated with Roman Catholic Church. Grades 9–12. Founded: 1963. Setting: urban. Nearest major city is Springfield. 1 building on campus. Approved or accredited by New England Association of Schools and Colleges and Massachusetts Department of Education. Total enrollment: 245. Upper school average class size: 15. Upper school faculty-student ratio: 1:10. There are 180 required school days per year for Upper School students. Upper School students typically attend 5 days per week. The average school day consists of 6 hours.

Upper School Student Profile Grade 9: 64 students (25 boys, 39 girls); Grade 10: 49 students (20 boys, 29 girls); Grade 11: 63 students (25 boys, 38 girls); Grade 12: 69 students (34 boys, 35 girls). 84% of students are Roman Catholic.

Faculty School total: 25. In upper school: 8 men, 17 women; 16 have advanced degrees.

Subjects Offered Advanced biology, advanced math, algebra, American literature, American literature-AP, art, biology, calculus, calculus-AP, Catholic belief and practice, chemistry, English, English literature, environmental science, forensics, French, geometry, Latin, literature-AP, moral theology, multimedia design, physics, pottery, pre-calculus, psychology, social sciences, Spanish, studio art, The 20th Century, U.S. history, U.S. history-AP, Web site design, world civilizations, world history, world religions.

Graduation Requirements Electives, English, foreign language, mathematics, religion (includes Bible studies and theology), science, social studies (includes history), U.S. literature, community service hours at each grade level, English research paper at each level, senior internship program.

Special Academic Programs 5 Advanced Placement exams for which test preparation is offered; honors section; independent study; study at local college for college credit; ESL (9 students enrolled).

College Admission Counseling 76 students graduated in 2015; 74 went to college, including Bryant University; Elms College; Holyoke Community College; Merrimack College; Siena College; Western New England University. Other: 1 entered military service, 1 had other specific plans. Median SAT critical reading: 534, median SAT math: 501, median SAT writing: 531. 48% scored over 600 on SAT critical reading, 46% scored over 600 on SAT math, 41% scored over 600 on SAT writing.

Student Life Upper grades have uniform requirement, student council. Discipline rests primarily with faculty. Attendance at religious services is required.

Summer Programs Enrichment programs offered; session focuses on study skills, essay writing, SAT prep, Algebra review; held on campus; accepts boys and girls; not open to students from other schools. 25 students usually enrolled. 2016 schedule: July 30 to August 17. Application deadline: July 2.

Tuition and Aid Day student tuition: $8800. Tuition installment plan (FACTS Tuition Payment Plan, Your Tuition Solution Loan Program (YTS)). Need-based scholarship grants available. In 2015–16, 32% of upper-school students received aid. Total amount of financial aid awarded in 2015–16: $150,000.

Admissions Traditional secondary-level entrance grade is 9. Scholastic Testing Service High School Placement Test required. Deadline for receipt of application materials: none. Application fee required: $50. Interview required.

Athletics Interscholastic: baseball (boys), basketball (b,g), cross-country running (b,g), football (b), indoor track & field (b,g), lacrosse (b,g), soccer (b,g), softball (g), winter (indoor) track (b,g); coed interscholastic: dance, golf, hiking/backpacking, juggling, outdoor adventure, swimming and diving, tennis. 10 coaches.

Computers Computers are regularly used in multimedia classes. Computer network features include on-campus library services, Internet access, Internet filtering or blocking technology. Campus intranet and student e-mail accounts are available to students. Students grades are available online. The school has a published electronic and media policy.

Contact Mrs. Ann M. Rivers, Director of Admissions. 413-331-2480 Ext. 1132. Fax: 413-331-2708. E-mail: arivers@holyokecatholichigh.org. Website: www.holyokecatholichigh.org

HOLY SAVIOR MENARD CATHOLIC HIGH SCHOOL

4603 Coliseum Boulevard
Alexandria, Louisiana 71303

Head of School: Mr. Joel Desselle

General Information Coeducational day college-preparatory and religious studies school, affiliated with Roman Catholic Church. Grades 7–12. Founded: 1930. Setting: suburban. 5-acre campus. 5 buildings on campus. Approved or accredited by National

Catholic Education Association, Southern Association of Colleges and Schools, The College Board, and Louisiana Department of Education. Total enrollment: 510. Upper school average class size: 20. Upper school faculty-student ratio: 1:14. There are 178 required school days per year for Upper School students. Upper School students typically attend 5 days per week. The average school day consists of 7 hours and 15 minutes.

Upper School Student Profile Grade 9: 96 students (49 boys, 47 girls); Grade 10: 107 students (60 boys, 47 girls); Grade 11: 69 students (30 boys, 39 girls); Grade 12: 78 students (38 boys, 40 girls). 79% of students are Roman Catholic.

Faculty School total: 38. In upper school: 10 men, 22 women; 13 have advanced degrees.

Subjects Offered Advanced math, algebra, American history, anatomy and physiology, art, athletics, biology, biology-AP, British literature, British literature (honors), calculus-AP, campus ministry, Catholic belief and practice, cheerleading, chemistry, civics/free enterprise, computer applications, computer science, digital photography, English, English composition, English literature, English literature-AP, fine arts, French, general science, geometry, health, honors algebra, honors English, honors geometry, honors U.S. history, honors world history, journalism, language arts, law studies, moral reasoning, New Testament, newspaper, philosophy, physical education, physical science, physics, pre-algebra, pre-calculus, psychology, publications, reading/study skills, religion, sociology, Spanish, speech, world geography, world history, yearbook.

Graduation Requirements Algebra, American history, arts and fine arts (art, music, dance, drama), biology, chemistry, civics/free enterprise, computer applications, English, foreign language, geometry, physical science, religion (includes Bible studies and theology), world history, 27 credits required.

Special Academic Programs 4 Advanced Placement exams for which test preparation is offered; honors section; independent study; study at local college for college credit.

College Admission Counseling 77 students graduated in 2015; 72 went to college, including Louisiana State University and Agricultural & Mechanical College; Louisiana Tech University; Northwestern State University of Louisiana; University of Louisiana at Lafayette; University of New Orleans. Other: 2 went to work, 2 entered a postgraduate year, 1 had other specific plans. Mean composite ACT: 24. 19% scored over 26 on composite ACT.

Student Life Upper grades have uniform requirement, student council, honor system. Discipline rests primarily with faculty. Attendance at religious services is required.

Tuition and Aid Day student tuition: $5900. Tuition installment plan (FACTS Tuition Payment Plan, monthly payment plans, individually arranged payment plans). Tuition reduction for siblings, merit scholarship grants, need-based scholarship grants available. In 2015–16, 12% of upper-school students received aid; total upper-school merit-scholarship money awarded: $5000. Total amount of financial aid awarded in 2015–16: $150,000.

Admissions Traditional secondary-level entrance grade is 9. For fall 2015, 38 students applied for upper-level admission, 38 were accepted, 38 enrolled. ACT or CTBS, Stanford Achievement Test, any other standardized test required. Deadline for receipt of application materials: March 15. Application fee required: $500. On-campus interview required.

Athletics Interscholastic: baseball (boys), basketball (b,g), cheering (g), cross country running (b,g), danceline (g), football (b), golf (b,g), power lifting (b,g), running (b,g), soccer (b,g), softball (g), tennis (b,g), track and field (b,g); intramural: paddle tennis (b,g); coed interscholastic: swimming and diving; coed intramural: paddle tennis. 3 PE instructors, 3 coaches.

Computers Computers are regularly used in computer applications, English, journalism, mathematics, photography, publications, science, Web site design classes. Computer network features include on-campus library services, Internet access, wireless campus network, Internet filtering or blocking technology. Computer access in designated common areas is available to students. Students grades are available online.

Contact Mrs. Ashley Meadows, Guidance Secretary. 318-445-8233. Fax: 318-448-8170. E-mail: ameadows@holysaviormenard.com. Website: www.holysaviormenard.com

HOLY TRINITY DIOCESAN HIGH SCHOOL

98 Cherry Lane
Hicksville, New York 11801

Head of School: Mr. Gene Fennell

General Information Coeducational day college-preparatory school, affiliated with Roman Catholic Church. Grades 9–12. Founded: 1967. Setting: suburban. Nearest major city is New York. 1 building on campus. Approved or accredited by Middle States Association of Colleges and Schools, National Council for Private School Accreditation, New York State Board of Regents, The College Board, and New York Department of Education. Total enrollment: 1,003. Upper school average class size: 32. Upper school faculty-student ratio: 1:17. There are 180 required school days per year for Upper School students. Upper School students typically attend 5 days per week. The average school day consists of 6 hours and 30 minutes.

Upper School Student Profile Grade 9: 225 students (105 boys, 120 girls); Grade 10: 226 students (108 boys, 118 girls); Grade 11: 272 students (118 boys, 154 girls); Grade 12: 222 students (108 boys, 114 girls). 90% of students are Roman Catholic.

Faculty School total: 61. In upper school: 25 men, 36 women; 59 have advanced degrees.

Subjects Offered Accounting, advanced math, Advanced Placement courses, American government, American history, American history-AP, American literature, American literature-AP, anatomy and physiology, architectural drawing, art, band, biology, biology-AP, British literature, British literature (honors), calculus, calculus-AP, campus ministry, ceramics, chemistry, chemistry-AP, chorus, Christian scripture, Christian studies, Christian testament, comparative religion, composition, concert band, criminology, critical studies in film, dance, desktop publishing, earth science, economics, English, English composition, English language and composition-AP, English literature, English literature-AP, environmental science, food and nutrition, French, government and politics-AP, health, honors English, honors U.S. history, honors world history, intro to computers, jazz theory, keyboarding, literature and composition-AP, mathematics, music, performing arts, physical education, physics, physics-AP, pre-calculus, public speaking, religion, Spanish, Spanish language-AP, stagecraft, statistics, theater arts, theology, U.S. government and politics, U.S. government and politics-AP, U.S. history, U.S. history-AP, world wide web design.

Graduation Requirements Arts and fine arts (art, music, dance, drama), economics, English, foreign language, mathematics, physical education (includes health), religion (includes Bible studies and theology), science, U.S. government and politics.

Special Academic Programs Advanced Placement exam preparation; honors section; study at local college for college credit.

College Admission Counseling 318 students graduated in 2015; 279 went to college, including Adelphi University; Hofstra University; Nassau Community College; State University of New York College at Cortland; Stony Brook University, State University of New York. Other: 2 went to work, 2 entered military service, 5 entered a postgraduate year, 30 had other specific plans. Mean SAT critical reading: 484, mean SAT math: 484, mean SAT writing: 484.

Student Life Upper grades have uniform requirement, student council. Discipline rests primarily with faculty.

Tuition and Aid Day student tuition: $9400. Tuition installment plan (monthly payment plans, individually arranged payment plans, 10-month tuition plan, 3-payment plan). Merit scholarship grants, need-based scholarship grants available. In 2014–15, 8% of upper-school students received aid.

Admissions Traditional secondary-level entrance grade is 9. Catholic High School Entrance Examination required. Deadline for receipt of application materials: none. Application fee required: $50. Interview recommended.

Athletics Interscholastic: badminton (girls), baseball (b), basketball (b,g), cheering (g), cross-country running (b,g), dance team (g), football (b), gymnastics (g), indoor track (b,g), lacrosse (b,g), soccer (b,g), softball (g), swimming and diving (b,g), tennis (b,g), track and field (b,g), volleyball (b,g), weight lifting (b), weight training (b), winter (indoor) track (b,g), wrestling (b); intramural: physical training (b), weight training (b); coed interscholastic: bowling, fitness, golf; coed intramural: modern dance. 3 PE instructors, 1 athletic trainer.

Computers Computers are regularly used in college planning, computer applications, desktop publishing, drawing and design, economics, English, foreign language, graphic design, history, journalism, library, music technology, newspaper, occupational education, programming, research skills, SAT preparation, science, social studies, theater, Web site design, writing, yearbook classes. Computer network features include on-campus library services, Internet access, wireless campus network, Internet filtering or blocking technology. Student e-mail accounts and computer access in designated common areas are available to students. Students grades are available online. The school has a published electronic and media policy.

Contact Admissions. 516-433-2900. Fax: 516-433-2827. E-mail: hths98@holytrinityhs.org. Website: www.holytrinityhs.org

HOLY TRINITY HIGH SCHOOL

1443 West Division Street
Chicago, Illinois 60642

Head of School: Mr. Timothy M. Bopp

General Information Coeducational day college-preparatory, arts, business, religious studies, bilingual studies, technology, and business, STEM school, affiliated with Roman Catholic Church. Grades 9–12. Founded: 1910. Setting: urban. 1 building on campus. Approved or accredited by North Central Association of Colleges and Schools and Illinois Department of Education. Total enrollment: 331. Upper school average class size: 20. Upper school faculty-student ratio: 1:12. There are 180 required school days per year for Upper School students. The average school day consists of 6 hours and 52 minutes.

Upper School Student Profile Grade 9: 96 students (46 boys, 50 girls); Grade 10: 85 students (45 boys, 40 girls); Grade 11: 65 students (32 boys, 33 girls); Grade 12: 87 students (42 boys, 45 girls). 60% of students are Roman Catholic.

Faculty School total: 27. In upper school: 12 men, 15 women; 17 have advanced degrees.

Subjects Offered Advanced Placement courses, band, French.

Graduation Requirements Business, English, mathematics, modern languages, physical education (includes health), religion (includes Bible studies and theology), science, social studies (includes history), visual and performing arts.

Special Academic Programs 6 Advanced Placement exams for which test preparation is offered; honors section; study at local college for college credit; remedial reading and/or remedial writing; ESL (25 students enrolled).

College Admission Counseling 60 students graduated in 2015; 50 went to college, including Knox College; Northeastern Illinois University; Northern Illinois University; Triton College; Western Illinois University. Other: 8 went to work, 1 entered military service, 1 entered a postgraduate year.

Student Life Upper grades have uniform requirement, student council, honor system. Discipline rests equally with students and faculty. Attendance at religious services is required.

Tuition and Aid Day student tuition: $7600. Tuition installment plan (SMART Tuition Payment Plan, monthly payment plans). Tuition reduction for siblings, merit scholarship grants, need-based scholarship grants available. In 2015–16, 85% of upper-school students received aid; total upper-school merit-scholarship money awarded: $125,000. Total amount of financial aid awarded in 2015–16: $600,000.

Admissions Traditional secondary-level entrance grade is 9. For fall 2015, 175 students applied for upper-level admission, 160 were accepted, 96 enrolled. High School Placement Test required. Deadline for receipt of application materials: none. Application fee required: $25. Interview recommended.

Athletics Interscholastic: baseball (boys), basketball (b,g), soccer (b,g), softball (g), volleyball (b,g); coed interscholastic: cheering, cross-country running, flag football, track and field; coed intramural: dance, dance team, fitness, physical fitness, weight lifting. 2 PE instructors, 4 coaches.

Computers Computers are regularly used in animation, business education, business skills, college planning, keyboarding classes. Computer network features include on-campus library services, online commercial services, Internet access, wireless campus network, Internet filtering or blocking technology. Student e-mail accounts and computer access in designated common areas are available to students. Students grades are available online. The school has a published electronic and media policy.

Contact Ms. Samara Galvan, Admission Coordinator. 773-278-4212 Ext. 3025. Fax: 773-278-0144. E-mail: sglavan@holytrinity-hs.org. Website: www.holytrinity-hs.org

HOLY TRINITY SCHOOL

11300 Bayview Avenue
Richmond Hill, Ontario L4S 1L4, Canada

Head of School: Mr. Barry Hughes

General Information Coeducational day college-preparatory, arts, and business school, affiliated with Anglican Church of Canada. Grades JK–12. Founded: 1981. Setting: suburban. 37-acre campus. 1 building on campus. Approved or accredited by Canadian Association of Independent Schools, Conference of Independent Schools of Ontario, and Ontario Department of Education. Member of Secondary School Admission Test Board. Language of instruction: English. Endowment: CAN$6 million. Total enrollment: 750. Upper school average class size: 22. Upper school faculty-student ratio: 1:17. Upper School students typically attend 5 days per week. The average school day consists of 6 hours.

Upper School Student Profile Grade 9: 88 students (44 boys, 44 girls); Grade 10: 88 students (44 boys, 44 girls); Grade 11: 80 students (45 boys, 35 girls); Grade 12: 88 students (44 boys, 44 girls). 10% of students are members of Anglican Church of Canada.

Faculty School total: 80. In upper school: 30 men, 20 women; 25 have advanced degrees.

Special Academic Programs 8 Advanced Placement exams for which test preparation is offered.

College Admission Counseling 99 students graduated in 2015; all went to college, including McMaster University; Queen's University at Kingston; The University of Western Ontario; University of Toronto; University of Waterloo.

Student Life Upper grades have uniform requirement, student council, honor system. Discipline rests primarily with faculty. Attendance at religious services is required.

Summer Programs Enrichment, sports programs offered; held on campus; accepts boys and girls; open to students from other schools. 400 students usually enrolled. 2016 schedule: July 1 to August 7. Application deadline: April 30.

Tuition and Aid Day student tuition: CAN$25,000. Bursaries, need-based scholarship grants available. In 2015–16, 5% of upper-school students received aid. Total amount of financial aid awarded in 2015–16: CAN$40,000.

Admissions Traditional secondary-level entrance grade is 9. For fall 2015, 110 students applied for upper-level admission, 50 were accepted, 35 enrolled. Canada Quick Individual Educational Test or SSAT required. Deadline for receipt of application materials: December. Application fee required: CAN$125. Interview required.

Athletics Interscholastic: badminton (boys, girls), baseball (b,g), basketball (b,g), cross-country running (b,g), field hockey (g), fitness (b,g), golf (b,g), hockey (b), ice hockey (b), indoor track (b,g), indoor track & field (b,g), outdoor education (b,g), outdoor recreation (b,g), rugby (b,g), soccer (b,g), softball (b,g), squash (b,g), tennis (b,g), track and field (b,g), ultimate Frisbee (b,g), volleyball (b,g); intramural: table tennis (b,g); coed interscholastic: Frisbee, ultimate Frisbee; coed intramural: floor hockey, horseback riding, street hockey, table tennis. 4 PE instructors, 25 coaches, 1 athletic trainer.

Computers Computer network features include on-campus library services, Internet access, wireless campus network, Internet filtering or blocking technology. Campus intranet, student e-mail accounts, and computer access in designated common areas are available to students. Students grades are available online.

Contact Mrs. Jennifer Gibbons, Admission Coordinator. 905-737-1115 Ext. 1. Fax: 905-737-5187. E-mail: jgibbons@hts.on.ca. Website: www.hts.on.ca

HOPE CHRISTIAN SCHOOL

PO Box 235
Champion, Alberta T0L 0R0, Canada

Head of School: Mr. Dale Anger

General Information Coeducational day and distance learning college-preparatory, general academic, arts, vocational, and religious studies school, affiliated with Evangelical Free Church of America. Grades 1–12. Distance learning grades 1–12. Founded: 1980. Setting: small town. Nearest major city is Lethbridge, Canada. 1-acre campus. 2 buildings on campus. Approved or accredited by Alberta Department of Education. Language of instruction: English. Total enrollment: 24. Upper school average class size: 10. Upper school faculty-student ratio: 1:12. There are 160 required school days per year for Upper School students. Upper School students typically attend 4 days per week. The average school day consists of 6 hours and 45 minutes.

Upper School Student Profile Grade 6: 1 student (1 girl); Grade 7: 1 student (1 girl); Grade 8: 1 student (1 girl). 2% of students are members of Evangelical Free Church of America.

Faculty School total: 4. In upper school: 2 men.

Subjects Offered All academic.

College Admission Counseling 1 student graduated in 2015. Other: 1 went to work.

Student Life Upper grades have uniform requirement, student council. Discipline rests primarily with faculty. Attendance at religious services is required.

Admissions Placement test required. Deadline for receipt of application materials: none. No application fee required. Interview required.

Computers Computer resources include Internet filtering or blocking technology. Campus intranet and computer access in designated common areas are available to students. Students grades are available online.

Contact Mr. Dale Anger, Principal. 403-897-3019. Fax: 403-897-2392. E-mail: principal@hopechristianschool.ca. Website: www.hopechristianschool.ca

HOPKINS SCHOOL

986 Forest Road
New Haven, Connecticut 06515

Head of School: Ms. Barbara M. Riley

General Information Coeducational day college-preparatory school. Grades 7–12. Founded: 1660. Setting: urban. Nearest major city is New York, NY. 108-acre campus. 10 buildings on campus. Approved or accredited by New England Association of Schools and Colleges and Connecticut Department of Education. Member of National Association of Independent Schools. Endowment: $88.3 million. Total enrollment: 710. Upper school average class size: 12. Upper school faculty-student ratio: 1:6. There are 170 required school days per year for Upper School students. Upper School students typically attend 5 days per week. The average school day consists of 7 hours and 30 minutes.

Upper School Student Profile Grade 9: 139 students (69 boys, 70 girls); Grade 10: 140 students (72 boys, 68 girls); Grade 11: 142 students (71 boys, 71 girls); Grade 12: 134 students (67 boys, 67 girls).

Faculty School total: 129. In upper school: 62 men, 67 women; 92 have advanced degrees.

Subjects Offered African-American history, algebra, American history, American literature, anatomy and physiology, ancient history, art, art history, art history-AP, Asian studies, biochemistry, biology, biology-AP, calculus, calculus-AP, ceramics, chemistry, chemistry-AP, Chinese, chorus, classical music, computer programming, creative writing, drama, earth science, economics, English, English literature, environmental science-AP, European history, European history-AP, expository writing, film, fine arts, forensics, French, French-AP, geometry, government/civics, graphic design, Greek, history, Holocaust studies, HTML design, human geography - AP, human sexuality, Islamic history, Italian, jazz, Latin, Latin American history, Latin-AP, linear algebra, mathematics, military history, music, music theory, music theory-AP, philosophy, photography, physics, physics-AP, politics, probability and statistics, psychology, Spanish, Spanish-AP, statistics-AP, studio art, studio art-AP, theater, trigonometry, U.S. history-AP, urban studies, video, Web site design, woodworking, world literature, writing.

Graduation Requirements Arts and fine arts (art, music, dance, drama), English, foreign language, mathematics, physical education (includes health), science, social studies (includes history), swimming, grade 12 community service project.

Special Academic Programs Advanced Placement exam preparation; honors section; independent study; term-away projects; study abroad.

College Admission Counseling 137 students graduated in 2014; all went to college, including Brown University; Georgetown University; Johns Hopkins University; Tufts University; University of Chicago; Yale University. Mean SAT critical reading: 690, mean SAT math: 697, mean SAT writing: 703, mean combined SAT: 2090, mean composite ACT: 30.

Student Life Upper grades have specified standards of dress, student council, honor system. Discipline rests equally with students and faculty.

Tuition and Aid Day student tuition: $37,550. Tuition installment plan (FACTS Tuition Payment Plan). Need-based scholarship grants available. In 2014–15, 20% of upper-school students received aid. Total amount of financial aid awarded in 2014–15: $3,276,165.

Admissions Traditional secondary-level entrance grade is 9. For fall 2014, 282 students applied for upper-level admission, 113 were accepted, 71 enrolled. ISEE or SSAT required. Deadline for receipt of application materials: January 15. Application fee required: $75. On-campus interview required.

Athletics Interscholastic: aquatics (boys, girls), baseball (b), basketball (b,g), crew (b,g), cross-country running (b,g), diving (b,g), fencing (b,g), field hockey (g), football (b), golf (b,g), independent competitive sports (b,g), indoor track (b,g), lacrosse (b,g), soccer (b,g), softball (g), squash (b,g), swimming and diving (b,g), tennis (b,g), track and field (b,g), volleyball (g), water polo (b,g), winter (indoor) track (b,g), wrestling (b); intramural: independent competitive sports (b,g); coed interscholastic: independent competitive sports; coed intramural: aerobics, basketball, cooperative games, fencing, fitness, floor hockey, Frisbee, independent competitive sports, Nautilus, outdoor adventure, project adventure, ropes courses, squash, tennis, weight lifting, weight training, wilderness, yoga. 4 coaches, 3 athletic trainers.

Computers Computers are regularly used in art, English, foreign language, history, mathematics, science classes. Computer network features include on-campus library services, Internet access, wireless campus network, Internet filtering or blocking technology. Campus intranet and student e-mail accounts are available to students. The school has a published electronic and media policy.

Contact Ms. Gena Eggert, Administrative Assistant to Director of Admissions. 203-397-1001 Ext. 211. Fax: 203-389-2249. E-mail: admissions@hopkins.edu. Website: www.hopkins.edu

THE HOTCHKISS SCHOOL

11 Interlaken Road
Lakeville, Connecticut 06039

Head of School: Mr. Kevin H. Hicks

General Information Coeducational boarding and day college-preparatory school. Grades 9–PG. Founded: 1891. Setting: rural. Nearest major city is Hartford. Students are housed in single-sex dormitories. 810-acre campus. 80 buildings on campus. Approved or accredited by Connecticut Association of Independent Schools, New England Association of Schools and Colleges, The Association of Boarding Schools, and Connecticut Department of Education. Member of National Association of Independent Schools and Secondary School Admission Test Board. Endowment: $444.1 million. Total enrollment: 598. Upper school average class size: 12. Upper school faculty-student ratio: 1:5. There are 172 required school days per year for Upper School students. Upper School students typically attend 6 days per week. The average school day consists of 6 hours and 50 minutes.

Upper School Student Profile Grade 9: 118 students (49 boys, 69 girls); Grade 10: 156 students (79 boys, 77 girls); Grade 11: 157 students (79 boys, 78 girls); Grade 12: 151 students (78 boys, 73 girls); Postgraduate: 16 students (13 boys, 3 girls). 92% of students are boarding students. 15% are state residents. 41 states are represented in upper school student body. 22% are international students. International students from Canada, China, Ghana, Hong Kong, Republic of Korea, and United Kingdom; 28 other countries represented in student body.

Faculty School total: 152. In upper school: 77 men, 75 women; 111 have advanced degrees; 94 reside on campus.

Subjects Offered 3-dimensional design, acting, advanced math, Advanced Placement courses, advanced studio art-AP, African studies, algebra, American history, American history-AP, American literature, anatomy and physiology, Ancient Greek, ancient history, architecture, art, art history-AP, astronomy, ballet, Bible, bioethics, biology, biology-AP, calculus, calculus-AP, ceramics, chemistry, chemistry-AP, China/Japan history, Chinese, chorus, classics, college counseling, comparative government and politics-AP, computer programming, computer science, computer science-AP, conceptual physics, constitutional history of U.S., creative writing, dance, digital photography, discrete mathematics, drama, drawing, economics, economics-AP, English, English-AP, environmental science, environmental science-AP, ethics, European history, European history-AP, expository writing, fine arts, French, French language-AP, French literature-AP, geometry, German, Greek, history of music, Holocaust, humanities, independent study, jazz dance, jazz ensemble, Latin, Latin American history, Latin-AP, limnology, mathematics, Middle East, music, music history, music technology, music theory, music theory-AP, musical productions, non-Western literature, orchestra, organic chemistry, philosophy, photography, physics, physics-AP, playwriting, pre-calculus, public speaking, religion, science, Spanish, Spanish language-AP, Spanish literature-AP, statistics-AP, studio art, theater, trigonometry, video, voice, world literature, writing.

Graduation Requirements American history, arts and fine arts (art, music, dance, drama), English, foreign language, mathematics, science.

Special Academic Programs Advanced Placement exam preparation; honors section; independent study; term-away projects; study abroad; academic accommodation for the gifted, the musically talented, and the artistically talented.

College Admission Counseling 173 students graduated in 2014; they went to Bucknell University; Georgetown University; Harvard University; Hobart and William Smith Colleges; Princeton University; Yale University. Median SAT critical reading: 660, median SAT math: 670, median SAT writing: 670, median combined SAT: 2000, median composite ACT: 29. 79% scored over 600 on SAT critical reading, 79% scored over 600 on SAT math, 77% scored over 600 on SAT writing, 81% scored over 1800 on combined SAT, 72% scored over 26 on composite ACT.

Student Life Upper grades have specified standards of dress, student council. Discipline rests equally with students and faculty.

Tuition and Aid Day student tuition: $44,575; 7-day tuition and room/board: $52,430. Tuition installment plan (Your Tuition Solution Loan Program). Need-based scholarship grants, need-based loans available. In 2014–15, 34% of upper-school students received aid. Total amount of financial aid awarded in 2014–15: $8,282,945.

Admissions Traditional secondary-level entrance grade is 9. For fall 2014, 1,745 students applied for upper-level admission, 365 were accepted, 198 enrolled. ACT, ISEE, PSAT, SAT, or ACT for applicants to grade 11 and 12, SSAT or TOEFL required. Deadline for receipt of application materials: January 15. Application fee required: $70. Interview required.

Athletics Interscholastic: baseball (boys), basketball (b,g), cross-country running (b,g), diving (b,g), field hockey (g), football (b), golf (b,g), ice hockey (b,g), lacrosse (b,g), soccer (b,g), softball (g), squash (b,g), swimming and diving (b,g), tennis (b,g), touch football (b), track and field (b,g), volleyball (g), water polo (b), wrestling (b); coed interscholastic: Frisbee, sailing, ultimate Frisbee; coed intramural: aerobics, aerobics/Nautilus, ballet, basketball, canoeing/kayaking, climbing, combined training, dance, drill team, fitness, fitness walking, Frisbee, golf, hiking/backpacking, ice hockey, jogging, Nautilus, outdoor education, paddle tennis, physical fitness, physical training, rock climbing, running, squash, strength & conditioning, tennis, ultimate Frisbee, volleyball, walking, wall climbing, water polo, weight lifting, yoga. 2 coaches, 2 athletic trainers.

Computers Computers are regularly used in all academic classes. Computer network features include on-campus library services, online commercial services, Internet access, wireless campus network, Internet filtering or blocking technology. Campus intranet, student e-mail accounts, and computer access in designated common areas are available to students. Students grades are available online. The school has a published electronic and media policy.

Contact Ms. Heather Eckert, Director of Admission Operations. 860-435-3102. Fax: 860-435-0042. E-mail: admission@hotchkiss.org. Website: www.hotchkiss.org

HOUGHTON ACADEMY

9790 Thayer Street
Houghton, New York 14744

Head of School: Mr. John Nelson

General Information Coeducational boarding and day college-preparatory and religious studies school, affiliated with Christian faith. Grades 7–12. Founded: 1883. Setting: rural. Nearest major city is Buffalo. Students are housed in single-sex dormitories and staff house, townhouse. 25-acre campus. 6 buildings on campus. Approved or accredited by Association of Christian Schools International, Middle States Association of Colleges and Schools, and New York Department of Education. Member of National Association of Independent Schools and Secondary School Admission Test Board. Endowment: $90,000. Total enrollment: 124. Upper school average class size: 16. Upper school faculty-student ratio: 1:7. There are 176 required school days per year for Upper School students. Upper School students typically attend 5 days per week. The average school day consists of 6 hours and 40 minutes.

Upper School Student Profile Grade 9: 20 students (9 boys, 11 girls); Grade 10: 29 students (18 boys, 11 girls); Grade 11: 23 students (11 boys, 12 girls); Grade 12: 37 students (16 boys, 21 girls). 53% of students are boarding students. 49% are state residents. 2 states are represented in upper school student body. 50% are international students. International students from Cameroon, China, Nigeria, Republic of Korea, Rwanda, and Viet Nam; 3 other countries represented in student body.

Faculty School total: 18. In upper school: 7 men, 11 women; 12 have advanced degrees; 1 resides on campus.

Subjects Offered Algebra, American history, American literature, art, band, Bible, Bible studies, biology, business, calculus, chemistry, chorus, community service, computer science, creative writing, desktop publishing, earth science, economics, English, English literature, environmental science, ESL, ethics, fine arts, geography, geometry, government/civics, grammar, history, mathematics, music, photography, physical education, physics, science, social sciences, social studies, Spanish, speech, trigonometry, word processing, world history, writing.

Graduation Requirements Arts and fine arts (art, music, dance, drama), Bible, electives, English, mathematics, physical education (includes health), science, social studies (includes history).

Special Academic Programs 5 Advanced Placement exams for which test preparation is offered; honors section; independent study; study at local college for college credit; ESL (15 students enrolled).

College Admission Counseling 38 students graduated in 2015; 36 went to college, including Houghton College; Indiana University Bloomington; Johnson & Wales University; Rochester Institute of Technology; University at Buffalo, the State University of New York; University of Massachusetts Boston. Other: 1 entered military service, 1 had other specific plans.

Student Life Upper grades have uniform requirement, student council. Discipline rests primarily with faculty. Attendance at religious services is required.

Tuition and Aid Day student tuition: $6310; 7-day tuition and room/board: $30,735. Tuition installment plan (FACTS Tuition Payment Plan). Need-based scholarship grants available. In 2015–16, 25% of upper-school students received aid. Total amount of financial aid awarded in 2015–16: $95,000.

Admissions Traditional secondary-level entrance grade is 9. For fall 2015, 97 students applied for upper-level admission, 34 were accepted, 23 enrolled. PSAT or SAT, SSAT or TOEFL required. Deadline for receipt of application materials: February 12. Application fee required: $100. Interview required.

Athletics Interscholastic: basketball (boys, girls), cheering (g), soccer (b), volleyball (g); intramural: badminton (b,g), basketball (b,g), floor hockey (b,g), golf (b,g), indoor soccer (b,g), paddle tennis (b,g), racquetball (b,g), skiing (downhill) (b,g), soccer (b,g), table tennis (b,g), tennis (b,g), volleyball (b,g); coed interscholastic: golf; coed intramural: badminton, golf, indoor soccer, paddle tennis, skiing (downhill), softball, table tennis, tennis, volleyball. 2 PE instructors, 1 athletic trainer.

Computers Computers are regularly used in accounting, Bible studies, college planning, English, graphic design, keyboarding, mathematics, multimedia, SAT preparation, science, word processing, yearbook classes. Computer network features include on-campus library services, Internet access, Internet filtering or blocking technology, electronic access to Houghton College Library holdings. Student e-mail accounts and computer access in designated common areas are available to students. Students grades are available online. The school has a published electronic and media policy.

Contact Mrs. Sandy Merrill, Admission Coordinator. 585-567-8115. Fax: 585-567-8048. E-mail: admissions@houghton.academy. Website: www.houghtonacademy.org

HOUSTON ACADEMY

901 Buena Vista Drive
Dothan, Alabama 36303

Head of School: Dr. Scott P. Phillipps

General Information Coeducational day college-preparatory, arts, and technology school. Grades P3–12. Founded: 1970. Setting: small town. Nearest major city is Montgomery. 19-acre campus. 5 buildings on campus. Approved or accredited by Southern Association of Colleges and Schools, Southern Association of Independent Schools, and The College Board. Member of National Association of Independent Schools. Endowment: $700,000. Total enrollment: 621. Upper school average class size: 18. Upper school faculty-student ratio: 1:13. There are 175 required school days per year for Upper School students. Upper School students typically attend 5 days per week. The average school day consists of 7 hours and 15 minutes.

Upper School Student Profile Grade 6: 49 students (24 boys, 25 girls); Grade 7: 67 students (33 boys, 34 girls); Grade 8: 55 students (29 boys, 26 girls); Grade 9: 52 students (33 boys, 19 girls); Grade 10: 64 students (37 boys, 27 girls); Grade 11: 56 students (31 boys, 25 girls); Grade 12: 51 students (25 boys, 26 girls).

Faculty School total: 60. In upper school: 12 men, 22 women; 17 have advanced degrees.

Subjects Offered 20th century history, advanced chemistry, advanced computer applications, advanced math, Advanced Placement courses, algebra, American government, American history, American history-AP, American literature, analysis and differential calculus, art, Basic programming, biology, calculus, calculus-AP, career/college preparation, chemistry, chemistry-AP, chorus, communication skills, composition-AP, computer education, computer information systems, computer programming-AP, computer science, drama, driver education, earth and space science, earth science, economics, English, English composition, English language and composition-AP, English literature and composition-AP, European history, foreign language, French, French-AP, geography, geometry, German, German-AP, government/civics, history, history-AP, honors algebra, honors English, honors geometry, honors U.S. history, human anatomy, jazz band, journalism, Latin, Latin-AP, marching band, math review, mathematics, mathematics-AP, music, music theory-AP, physical education, physics, physics-AP, psychology, reading/study skills, SAT/ACT preparation, science, senior internship, social studies, Spanish, Spanish language-AP, theater, trigonometry, U.S. government, U.S. history-AP, United Nations and international issues, video communication, world history.

Graduation Requirements English, foreign language, mathematics, physical education (includes health), science, social studies (includes history).

Special Academic Programs Advanced Placement exam preparation; honors section; academic accommodation for the gifted and the musically talented; programs in general development for dyslexic students.

College Admission Counseling 38 students graduated in 2015; all went to college, including Auburn University; Birmingham-Southern College; The University of Alabama; The University of Alabama at Birmingham; Vanderbilt University.

Student Life Upper grades have uniform requirement, student council, honor system. Discipline rests primarily with faculty.

Summer Programs Remediation, enrichment, advancement, sports programs offered; session focuses on Academic improvement and Enrichment; held on campus; accepts boys and girls; open to students from other schools. 150 students usually enrolled. 2016 schedule: June to August. Application deadline: March.

Tuition and Aid Day student tuition: $10,365–$10,700. Guaranteed tuition plan. Tuition installment plan (SMART Tuition Payment Plan, monthly payment plans, two-payment plan). Merit scholarship grants, need-based scholarship grants available. In 2015–16, 30% of upper-school students received aid; total upper-school merit-scholarship money awarded: $152,637. Total amount of financial aid awarded in 2015–16: $408,049.

Admissions Traditional secondary-level entrance grade is 7. For fall 2015, 23 students applied for upper-level admission, 21 were accepted, 20 enrolled. OLSAT, Stanford Achievement Test required. Deadline for receipt of application materials: none. Application fee required: $75. On-campus interview required.

Athletics Interscholastic: baseball (boys), basketball (b,g), bowling (b,g), cross-country running (b,g), football (b), golf (b,g), soccer (b,g), softball (g), tennis (b,g), volleyball (g); intramural: cheering (g), dance team (g). 2 PE instructors, 5 coaches, 1 athletic trainer.

Computers Computers are regularly used in all academic classes. Computer network features include on-campus library services, Internet access, Internet filtering or blocking technology. Campus intranet, student e-mail accounts, and computer access in designated common areas are available to students. The school has a published electronic and media policy.

Contact Mrs. Leanne M. Todd, Director of Admissions. 334-794-4106. Fax: 334-793-4053. E-mail: toddl@houstonacademy.com. Website: www.houstonacademy.com

THE HOWARD SCHOOL

Atlanta, Georgia
See Special Needs Schools section.

HOWE MILITARY ACADEMY

PO Box 240
Howe, Indiana 46746

Head of School: Col. George Douglass

General Information Coeducational boarding and day college-preparatory, religious studies, bilingual studies, Junior ROTC, and military school, affiliated with Episcopal Church. Grades 7–12. Founded: 1884. Setting: rural. Nearest major city is South Bend. Students are housed in single-sex dormitories. 100-acre campus. 15 buildings on campus. Approved or accredited by North Central Association of Colleges and Schools, The Association of Boarding Schools, and Indiana Department of Education. Member of National Association of Independent Schools. Total enrollment: 60. Upper school average class size: 10. Upper school faculty-student ratio: 1:9. There are 180 required school days per year for Upper School students. Upper School students typically attend 5 days per week. The average school day consists of 7 hours.

Upper School Student Profile Grade 7: 1 student (1 boy); Grade 8: 7 students (5 boys, 2 girls); Grade 9: 9 students (6 boys, 3 girls); Grade 10: 15 students (13 boys, 2 girls); Grade 11: 13 students (12 boys, 1 girl); Grade 12: 15 students (11 boys, 4 girls). 83% of students are boarding students. 39% are state residents. 16 states are represented in upper school student body. 17% are international students. International students from Belarus, China, Mexico, and Saudi Arabia. 4% of students are members of Episcopal Church.

Faculty School total: 16. In upper school: 8 men, 7 women; 5 have advanced degrees; 6 reside on campus.

Subjects Offered ACT preparation, algebra, American history, American literature, band, biology, calculus-AP, chemistry, chorus, comparative religion, computer graphics, economics, English, English literature, geometry, government/civics, JROTC or LEAD (Leadership Education and Development), Latin, music, music appreciation, photography, physical education, SAT preparation, senior project, sociology, Spanish, speech communications, student publications, TOEFL preparation, trigonometry, U.S. history, world geography, world history, world literature, world religions, yearbook.

Graduation Requirements Computer education, English, foreign language, health, JROTC, mathematics, physical education (includes health), religion (includes Bible studies and theology), science, social studies (includes history), speech.

Special Academic Programs Advanced Placement exam preparation; honors section; study at local college for college credit; ESL (9 students enrolled).

College Admission Counseling 16 students graduated in 2014; 12 went to college, including Indiana University–Purdue University Fort Wayne; Michigan State University; Rose-Hulman Institute of Technology; The Citadel, The Military College of South Carolina; Wittenberg University. Other: 1 went to work, 3 entered military service.

Student Life Upper grades have uniform requirement, student council, honor system. Discipline rests primarily with faculty. Attendance at religious services is required.

Tuition and Aid Day student tuition: $17,745; 5-day tuition and room/board: $24,493; 7-day tuition and room/board: $33,000. Tuition installment plan (monthly payment plans, individually arranged payment plans). Tuition reduction for siblings, merit scholarship grants, need-based scholarship grants available. In 2014–15, 40% of upper-school students received aid; total upper-school merit-scholarship money awarded: $86,000. Total amount of financial aid awarded in 2014–15: $215,000.

Admissions Traditional secondary-level entrance grade is 9. OLSAT, Stanford Achievement Test and TOEFL or SLEP required. Deadline for receipt of application materials: none. Application fee required: $100. Interview required.

Athletics Interscholastic: baseball (boys), basketball (b,g), football (b), lacrosse (b), tennis (g), track and field (b), volleyball (g); intramural: baseball (b), physical training (b), softball (b); coed interscholastic: baseball, basketball, football, golf, JROTC drill, marksmanship, riflery, soccer; coed intramural: basketball, horseback riding, outdoor adventure, outdoor recreation, paint ball, physical fitness, scuba diving, self defense, soccer, swimming and diving, volleyball. 1 PE instructor, 1 coach.

Computers Computers are regularly used in JROTC classes. Computer network features include on-campus library services, Internet access, wireless campus network, Internet filtering or blocking technology, Microsoft Office. Campus intranet and student e-mail accounts are available to students. Students grades are available online. The school has a published electronic and media policy.

Contact Mrs. Marisue Barton, Office Manager/Admissions Representative. 260-562-2131 Ext. 220. Fax: 260-562-3678. E-mail: mbarton@howemilitary.org. Website: www.howemilitary.org

THE HUDSON SCHOOL

601 Park Avenue
Hoboken, New Jersey 07030

Head of School: Mrs. Suellen F. Newman

General Information Coeducational day college-preparatory, arts, and music, theater, foreign languages school. Grades 5–12. Founded: 1978. Setting: urban. Nearest major city is New York, NY. 1 building on campus. Approved or accredited by Middle States Association of Colleges and Schools, New Jersey Association of Independent Schools, and New Jersey Department of Education. Member of National Association of Independent Schools. Endowment: $2.5 million. Total enrollment: 187. Upper school average class size: 18. Upper school faculty-student ratio: 1:4. There are 175 required school days per year for Upper School students. Upper School students typically attend 5 days per week. The average school day consists of 7 hours.

Upper School Student Profile Grade 9: 20 students (6 boys, 14 girls); Grade 10: 17 students (6 boys, 11 girls); Grade 11: 17 students (4 boys, 13 girls); Grade 12: 14 students (8 boys, 6 girls).

Faculty School total: 50. In upper school: 11 men, 19 women; 19 have advanced degrees.

Subjects Offered 3-dimensional design, acting, advanced biology, advanced chemistry, advanced math, Advanced Placement courses, advanced studio art-AP, African drumming, algebra, American literature, American sign language, analysis of data, Ancient Greek, art, art and culture, art history, art history-AP, art-AP, athletics, biology, biology-AP, British literature, calculus, calculus-AP, chamber groups, chemistry, chemistry-AP, Chinese, chorus, community service, computer graphics, computer science, computers, contemporary issues, creative writing, dance, electives, English, English literature, English-AP, environmental education, ESL, ethics, film, French, geometry, German, German literature, guitar, health, history of music, HTML design, humanities, instrumental music, Japanese, jazz band, language arts, Latin, learning strategies, Mandarin, mathematical modeling, mathematics, music, music history, performing arts, personal finance, personal money management, photo shop, photography, physical education, physics, poetry, post-calculus, pre-algebra, pre-calculus, psychology, public speaking, reading/study skills, robotics, Russian, science, science fiction, sculpture, senior project, senior seminar, skills for success, social justice, social sciences, Spanish, statistics, studio art, theater, trigonometry, U.S. history, visual arts, voice, world civilizations, world cultures, world geography, world governments, world history, world literature, writing, yoga.

Graduation Requirements American history, art, art history, biology, chemistry, computer science, English, foreign language, Latin, mathematics, music history, personal finance, physical education (includes health), physics, science, world history. Community service is required.

Special Academic Programs Advanced Placement exam preparation; honors section; accelerated programs; independent study; study at local college for college credit; study abroad; academic accommodation for the gifted, the musically talented, and the artistically talented; remedial reading and/or remedial writing; remedial math; ESL (3 students enrolled).

College Admission Counseling 24 students graduated in 2015; 23 went to college, including Bard College; Drexel University; Franklin & Marshall College; Northeastern University; Rutgers, The State University of New Jersey, New Brunswick; University of Vermont. Other: 1 had other specific plans. Median SAT critical reading: 590, median SAT math: 590, median SAT writing: 600, median combined SAT: 1780. Mean composite ACT: 29. 37% scored over 600 on SAT critical reading, 32% scored over 600 on SAT math, 47% scored over 600 on SAT writing, 37% scored over 1800 on combined SAT, 86% scored over 26 on composite ACT.

Student Life Upper grades have student council, honor system. Discipline rests primarily with faculty.

Summer Programs Art/fine arts programs offered; session focuses on theater; held on campus; accepts boys and girls; open to students from other schools. 25 students usually enrolled. 2016 schedule: July 1 to July 31. Application deadline: May 1.

Tuition and Aid Day student tuition: $18,510. Tuition installment plan (monthly payment plans, individually arranged payment plans, semiannual and annual payment plans, quarterly by special arrangement). Need-based scholarship grants available. In 2015–16, 36% of upper-school students received aid. Total amount of financial aid awarded in 2015–16: $308,710.

Admissions Traditional secondary-level entrance grade is 9. For fall 2015, 53 students applied for upper-level admission, 38 were accepted, 15 enrolled. ERB, ISEE or SSAT required. Deadline for receipt of application materials: December 31. Application fee required: $60. On-campus interview required.

Athletics Interscholastic: basketball (boys, girls), soccer (b,g), softball (g); coed interscholastic: track and field; coed intramural: aerobics/dance, dance, fencing, modern dance, outdoor education, physical fitness, yoga. 2 PE instructors, 4 coaches.

Computers Computers are regularly used in business education, college planning, creative writing, desktop publishing, ESL, English, ethics, French, history, humanities, mathematics, music, newspaper, philosophy, photography, photojournalism, programming, publications, Spanish, technology, theater, Web site design, word processing, writing, yearbook classes. Computer network features include on-campus library services, Internet access, wireless campus network, Internet filtering or blocking technology, Chrome books provided to students, free of charge. Campus intranet, student e-mail accounts, and computer access in designated common areas are available to students. Students grades are available online. The school has a published electronic and media policy.

Contact Mrs. Janet F. Wright, Admissions Assistant. 201-659-8335 Ext. 326. Fax: 201-222-3669. E-mail: admissions@thehudsonschool.org. Website: www.thehudsonschool.org

HUMANEX ACADEMY

Englewood, Colorado
See Special Needs Schools section.

THE HUN SCHOOL OF PRINCETON

176 Edgerstoune Road
Princeton, New Jersey 08540

Head of School: Mr. Jonathan Brougham

General Information Coeducational boarding and day college-preparatory school. Boarding grades 9–PG, day grades 6–PG. Founded: 1914. Setting: suburban. Nearest major city is New York, NY. Students are housed in single-sex dormitories. 45-acre campus. 7 buildings on campus. Approved or accredited by Middle States Association of Colleges and Schools, New England Association of Schools and Colleges, New Jersey Association of Independent Schools, New Jersey Department of Education, The Association of Boarding Schools, and New Jersey Department of Education. Member of National Association of Independent Schools and Secondary School Admission Test Board. Endowment: $18 million. Total enrollment: 630. Upper school average class size: 13. Upper school faculty-student ratio: 1:8. Upper School students typically attend 5 days per week.

Upper School Student Profile Grade 9: 106 students (56 boys, 50 girls); Grade 10: 128 students (73 boys, 55 girls); Grade 11: 134 students (84 boys, 50 girls); Grade 12: 121 students (75 boys, 46 girls); Postgraduate: 13 students (12 boys, 1 girl). 35% of students are boarding students. 18 states are represented in upper school student body. 13% are international students. International students from China, Russian Federation, Saudi Arabia, Taiwan, United Kingdom, and Venezuela; 24 other countries represented in student body.

Faculty School total: 117. In upper school: 60 men, 57 women; 52 have advanced degrees; 29 reside on campus.

Subjects Offered 3-dimensional art, 3-dimensional design, advanced computer applications, Advanced Placement courses, advanced TOEFL/grammar, algebra, American government, American history, American history-AP, American literature, anatomy, architectural drawing, architecture, art, art history, art history-AP, astrophysics, biology, biology-AP, calculus, calculus-AP, ceramics, chemistry, chemistry-AP, chorus, community service, computer programming, computer science, drama, driver education, economics, engineering, English, English-AP, ESL, European history, fine arts, forensics, French, French-AP, geometry, government/civics, health, history, interdisciplinary studies, jazz band, Latin, Latin-AP, marine biology, mathematics, mechanical drawing, music, photography, physical education, physics, physics-AP, physiology, public speaking, science, social studies, Spanish, Spanish-AP, statistics-AP, television, theater, trigonometry, U.S. history-AP, video, video film production, world history.

Graduation Requirements Arts and fine arts (art, music, dance, drama), computer science, English, foreign language, health, history, mathematics, science, 10-20 hours of community service per year, extracurricular activities.

Special Academic Programs Advanced Placement exam preparation; honors section; academic accommodation for the gifted; programs in general development for dyslexic students; ESL (35 students enrolled).

College Admission Counseling 151 students graduated in 2015; all went to college, including Boston University; Lehigh University; Penn State University Park;

Princeton University; Syracuse University. Median SAT critical reading: 590, median SAT math: 620, median SAT writing: 610, median composite ACT: 27.

Student Life Upper grades have specified standards of dress, student council, honor system. Discipline rests equally with students and faculty.

Summer Programs Remediation, enrichment, advancement, ESL, sports, art/fine arts, computer instruction programs offered; session focuses on make-up courses, enrichment, SAT and TOEFL preparation; held on campus; accepts boys and girls; open to students from other schools. 110 students usually enrolled. 2016 schedule: June 28 to July 23. Application deadline: none.

Tuition and Aid Day student tuition: $37,850; 7-day tuition and room/board: $55,050. Tuition installment plan (Insured Tuition Payment Plan, Academic Management Services Plan, FACTS Tuition Payment Plan, individually arranged payment plans). Need-based scholarship grants, prepGATE loans available. In 2015–16, 30% of upper-school students received aid. Total amount of financial aid awarded in 2015–16: $4,000,000.

Admissions Traditional secondary-level entrance grade is 9. PSAT or SAT for applicants to grade 11 and 12, SSAT or TOEFL required. Deadline for receipt of application materials: January 31. Application fee required: $75. Interview required.

Athletics Interscholastic: baseball (boys), basketball (b,g), crew (b,g), cross-country running (b,g), fencing (b,g), field hockey (g), football (b), lacrosse (b,g), soccer (b,g), softball (g), tennis (b,g); intramural: dance squad (g), soccer (b,g), weight training (b,g); coed interscholastic: golf, ice hockey, swimming and diving, track and field; coed intramural: aerobics/dance, aerobics/Nautilus, ballet, basketball, cross-country running, dance, fitness, flag football, Frisbee, jogging, Nautilus, paint ball, physical fitness, running, skiing (downhill), strength & conditioning, touch football, ultimate Frisbee, volleyball, weight lifting. 3 coaches, 1 athletic trainer.

Computers Computers are regularly used in all academic classes. Computer network features include on-campus library services, online commercial services, Internet access, wireless campus network, Internet filtering or blocking technology. Campus intranet, student e-mail accounts, and computer access in designated common areas are available to students. Students grades are available online. The school has a published electronic and media policy.

Contact Mr. Steven C. Bristol, Director of Admissions. 609-921-7600. Fax: 609-279-9398. E-mail: admiss@hunschool.org. Website: www.hunschool.org

HUNTINGTON-SURREY SCHOOL

5206 Balcones Drive
Austin, Texas 78731

Head of School: Dr. Light Bailey German

General Information Coeducational day college-preparatory and writing school. Grades 9–12. Founded: 1973. Setting: urban. 1 building on campus. Approved or accredited by Southern Association of Colleges and Schools, The College Board, and Texas Department of Education. Total enrollment: 36. Upper school average class size: 8. Upper school faculty-student ratio: 1:4. There are 160 required school days per year for Upper School students. Upper School students typically attend 5 days per week. The average school day consists of 4 hours and 50 minutes.

Upper School Student Profile Grade 9: 5 students (5 boys); Grade 10: 8 students (5 boys, 3 girls); Grade 11: 10 students (8 boys, 2 girls); Grade 12: 13 students (5 boys, 8 girls).

Faculty In upper school: 6 men, 12 women; 11 have advanced degrees.

Subjects Offered Algebra, art, biology, calculus, chemistry, college planning, comparative religion, creative drama, discrete mathematics, drama, ecology, environmental systems, English, French, geometry, German, history, Latin, literature, math analysis, math review, mathematics, philosophy, physical science, physics, portfolio art, pre-algebra, pre-calculus, senior science survey, social studies, Spanish, student publications, study skills, theater arts, trigonometry, U.S. history, work-study, world history, writing, yearbook, yoga.

Graduation Requirements American literature, biology, British literature, economics, foreign language, mathematics, science, U.S. government, U.S. history, world history, world literature, writing, senior research project, school exit examinations: assertion with proof essay exam and mathematical competency exam, senior advisory course.

Special Academic Programs Accelerated programs; academic accommodation for the gifted.

College Admission Counseling 10 students graduated in 2015; all went to college, including Colorado State University; Concordia University Texas; Hofstra University; Loyola University New Orleans; Southwestern University; St. Mary's University. Median SAT critical reading: 510, median SAT math: 460, median SAT writing: 460, median combined SAT: 1430. 25% scored over 600 on SAT critical reading, 12% scored over 600 on SAT math, 6% scored over 1800 on combined SAT.

Student Life Upper grades have student council, honor system. Discipline rests primarily with faculty.

Summer Programs Remediation, enrichment, advancement programs offered; session focuses on one-on-one teaching, or small classes, college preparation; held on campus; accepts boys and girls; open to students from other schools. 12 students usually enrolled. 2016 schedule: June 6 to July 29. Application deadline: May 2.

Tuition and Aid Day student tuition: $1350. Tuition installment plan (monthly payment plans).

Admissions Traditional secondary-level entrance grade is 9. For fall 2015, 8 students applied for upper-level admission, 6 were accepted, 6 enrolled. Deadline for receipt of application materials: none. No application fee required. On-campus interview required.

Athletics Coed Intramural: yoga. 1 PE instructor.

Computers Computers are regularly used in science, study skills, writing classes. Computer resources include study hall computers and printers (available for student use). Computer access in designated common areas is available to students.

Contact Ms. Johni Walker-Little, Assistant Director. 512-478-4743. Fax: 512-457-0235. Website: www.huntingtonsurrey.com

HYDE SCHOOL

PO Box 237
150 Route 169
Woodstock, Connecticut 06281

Head of School: Bob Felt

General Information Coeducational boarding and day college-preparatory, general academic, arts, and leadership school. Grades 9–12. Founded: 1996. Setting: rural. Nearest major city is Providence, RI. Students are housed in single-sex dormitories. 120-acre campus. 7 buildings on campus. Approved or accredited by Association of Independent Schools in New England, Connecticut Association of Independent Schools, New England Association of Schools and Colleges, The Association of Boarding Schools, and Connecticut Department of Education. Member of National Association of Independent Schools. Endowment: $8 million. Total enrollment: 151. Upper school average class size: 8. Upper school faculty-student ratio: 1:6. There are 222 required school days per year for Upper School students. Upper School students typically attend 6 days per week. The average school day consists of 6 hours and 30 minutes.

Upper School Student Profile Grade 9: 12 students (8 boys, 4 girls); Grade 10: 25 students (18 boys, 7 girls); Grade 11: 54 students (38 boys, 16 girls); Grade 12: 58 students (40 boys, 18 girls); Postgraduate: 2 students (2 boys). 98% of students are boarding students. 24% are state residents. 21 states are represented in upper school student body. 27% are international students. International students from Canada, China, Russian Federation, Senegal, Spain, and Switzerland; 1 other country represented in student body.

Faculty School total: 23. In upper school: 15 men, 8 women; 11 have advanced degrees; all reside on campus.

Subjects Offered 20th century history, advanced chemistry, Advanced Placement courses, algebra, athletics, biology, calculus, calculus-AP, character education, chemistry, English, English language and composition-AP, English language-AP, English literature, environmental science-AP, ethics, geometry, global issues, independent study, media arts, physics, pre-calculus, Spanish, Spanish-AP, sports, U.S. history, U.S. history-AP, wilderness education, wilderness experience.

Graduation Requirements Electives, English, foreign language, mathematics, science, social studies (includes history), Hyde's graduation requirements embody academic achievement and character development. Character growth is determined through an intense 40-hour, evaluation process involving all members of the senior class and faculty. All students make a speech at graduation representing their principles.

Special Academic Programs 5 Advanced Placement exams for which test preparation is offered; honors section; independent study; remedial reading and/or remedial writing; remedial math; ESL (26 students enrolled).

College Admission Counseling 55 students graduated in 2015; 53 went to college, including Boston University; Drexel University; Eastern Connecticut State University; Rutgers, The State University of New Jersey, New Brunswick; University of Illinois at Urbana–Champaign; Wheaton College. Other: 2 entered a postgraduate year. Median SAT critical reading: 488, median SAT math: 536, median SAT writing: 481, median combined SAT: 1505, median composite ACT: 20.

Student Life Upper grades have specified standards of dress, honor system. Discipline rests equally with students and faculty.

Summer Programs Remediation, enrichment, advancement, sports, art/fine arts, rigorous outdoor training programs offered; session focuses on orientation for the fall and summer enrichment; held both on and off campus; held at Hyde's Wilderness Campus in Eustis, ME; accepts boys and girls; open to students from other schools. 50 students usually enrolled. 2016 schedule: July 13 to August 9. Application deadline: none.

Tuition and Aid Day student tuition: $28,000; 5-day tuition and room/board: $52,000; 7-day tuition and room/board: $52,000. Tuition installment plan (monthly payment plans, individually arranged payment plans). Tuition reduction for siblings, need-based scholarship grants available. In 2015–16, 30% of upper-school students received aid. Total amount of financial aid awarded in 2015–16: $258,000.

Admissions Traditional secondary-level entrance grade is 11. For fall 2015, 151 students applied for upper-level admission, 106 were accepted, 94 enrolled. Deadline for receipt of application materials: none. Application fee required: $100. Interview required.

Athletics Interscholastic: basketball (boys, girls), cross-country running (b,g), football (b), lacrosse (b,g), soccer (b,g), tennis (b,g), track and field (b,g), wrestling (b); coed interscholastic: equestrian sports, ropes courses, winter (indoor) track, wrestling; coed intramural: backpacking, canoeing/kayaking, climbing, dance team, hiking/backpacking, outdoor activities, outdoor adventure, outdoor skills, rafting, ropes courses, wilderness. 2 athletic trainers.

Computers Computers are regularly used in art, design, digital applications, drawing and design, graphic design classes. Computer network features include on-campus library services, online commercial services, Internet access, wireless campus network, Internet filtering or blocking technology. Student e-mail accounts and computer access in designated common areas are available to students. Students grades are available online. The school has a published electronic and media policy.

Contact Jason Warnick, Director of Admission. 860-963-4721. Fax: 860-928-0612. E-mail: jwarnick@hyde.edu. Website: www.hyde.edu

HYDE SCHOOL

616 High Street
Bath, Maine 04530

Head of School: Laura Gauld

General Information Coeducational boarding and day college-preparatory and arts school. Grades 9–12. Founded: 1966. Setting: small town. Nearest major city is Portland. Students are housed in single-sex dormitories. 145-acre campus. 32 buildings on campus. Approved or accredited by Association of Independent Schools in New England, Independent Schools of Northern New England, New England Association of Schools and Colleges, and The Association of Boarding Schools. Member of National Association of Independent Schools. Endowment: $16.5 million. Total enrollment: 150. Upper school average class size: 7. Upper school faculty-student ratio: 1:6. There are 191 required school days per year for Upper School students. Upper School students typically attend 6 days per week. The average school day consists of 7 hours.

Upper School Student Profile Grade 9: 7 students (3 boys, 4 girls); Grade 10: 20 students (15 boys, 5 girls); Grade 11: 52 students (38 boys, 14 girls); Grade 12: 46 students (24 boys, 22 girls); Postgraduate: 4 students (3 boys, 1 girl). 99% of students are boarding students. 21% are state residents. 27 states are represented in upper school student body. 21% are international students. International students from Brazil, Canada, China, Democratic People's Republic of Korea, Spain, and United Kingdom; 7 other countries represented in student body.

Faculty School total: 23. In upper school: 12 men, 7 women; 16 have advanced degrees; 21 reside on campus.

Subjects Offered 20th century history, 3-dimensional design, acting, advanced biology, advanced chemistry, advanced math, Advanced Placement courses, advanced studio art-AP, advanced TOEFL/grammar, algebra, American government, American history, American history-AP, American literature-AP, ancient history, art, backpacking, band, biology, biology-AP, calculus, calculus-AP, chemistry, chemistry-AP, Chinese, college admission preparation, college counseling, college placement, college planning, college writing, communication skills, communications, comparative government and politics, comparative government and politics-AP, composition-AP, creative writing, early childhood, economics, English, European history, geometry, government, history, music, physical education, physics-AP, pre-calculus, public policy, religion and culture, Spanish, statistics, technical theater, U.S. history, U.S. history-AP.

Graduation Requirements Electives, English, foreign language, history, mathematics, science, Hyde's graduation requirements embody academic achievement and character development. Character growth is determined through an intense 40-hour, evaluation process involving all members of the senior class and faculty. All students make a speech at graduation representing their principles.

Special Academic Programs Advanced Placement exam preparation; honors section; independent study; study at local college for college credit; academic accommodation for the gifted, the musically talented, and the artistically talented; remedial reading and/or remedial writing; remedial math; programs in English, mathematics, general development for dyslexic students; ESL (18 students enrolled).

College Admission Counseling 53 students graduated in 2015; 51 went to college, including Brandeis University; Columbia University; Cornell University; Stanford University; Tufts University; United States Military Academy. Other: 1 went to work, 1 entered military service. Mean SAT critical reading: 530, mean SAT math: 520, mean SAT writing: 520, mean combined SAT: 1570, mean composite ACT: 21. 25% scored over 600 on SAT critical reading, 17% scored over 600 on SAT math, 14% scored over 600 on SAT writing, 18% scored over 1800 on combined SAT, 16% scored over 26 on composite ACT.

Student Life Upper grades have specified standards of dress, student council, honor system. Discipline rests equally with students and faculty.

Summer Programs Remediation, enrichment, advancement, ESL, sports, art/fine arts, rigorous outdoor training, computer instruction programs offered; session focuses on to offer a unique summer experience for teens; held both on and off campus; held at Bath, ME and Woodstock, CT campuses, New York, NY; Washington, D.C.; Philadelphia, PA, and wilderness preserve in Eustis, ME; accepts boys and girls; open to students from other schools. 50 students usually enrolled. 2016 schedule: May 31 to August 31. Application deadline: none.

Tuition and Aid Day student tuition: $28,000; 7-day tuition and room/board: $52,000. Tuition installment plan (The Tuition Plan, individually arranged payment plans). Tuition reduction for siblings, merit scholarship grants, need-based scholarship grants available. In 2015–16, 33% of upper-school students received aid. Total amount of financial aid awarded in 2015–16: $1,300,000.

Admissions Traditional secondary-level entrance grade is 9. For fall 2015, 137 students applied for upper-level admission, 83 were accepted, 68 enrolled. Deadline for receipt of application materials: none. Application fee required: $100. Interview required.

Athletics Interscholastic: basketball (boys, girls), crew (b,g), cross-country running (b,g), dance team (g), field hockey (g), football (b), lacrosse (b,g), rowing (b), soccer (b,g), swimming and diving (b,g), tennis (b,g), track and field (b,g), ultimate Frisbee (b); coed interscholastic: aerobics, aerobics/dance, aerobics/Nautilus, aquatics, climbing, dance, equestrian sports, hiking/backpacking, indoor track, nordic skiing, rock climbing, ropes courses, wrestling; coed intramural: hiking/backpacking, kayaking, life saving, outdoor adventure, outdoor skills, physical fitness, physical training, project adventure, ropes courses, skateboarding, skiing (downhill), snowshoeing, strength & conditioning, ultimate Frisbee, walking, weight lifting, weight training, wilderness, wilderness survival. 8 coaches, 1 athletic trainer.

Computers Computers are regularly used in graphic design, video film production classes. Computer network features include on-campus library services, online commercial services, Internet access, wireless campus network, Internet filtering or blocking technology. Student e-mail accounts are available to students. Students grades are available online. The school has a published electronic and media policy.

Contact Wanda Smith, Admission Assistant. 207-443-7101. Fax: 207-442-9346. E-mail: wsmith@hyde.edu. Website: www.hyde.edu

HYMAN BRAND HEBREW ACADEMY OF GREATER KANSAS CITY

5801 West 115th Street
Overland Park, Kansas 66211

Head of School: Mr. Howard Haas

General Information Coeducational day college-preparatory, general academic, and religious studies school, affiliated with Jewish faith. Grades K–12. Founded: 1966. Setting: suburban. Nearest major city is Kansas City, MO. 32-acre campus. 1 building on campus. Approved or accredited by Independent Schools Association of the Central States. Languages of instruction: English and Hebrew. Endowment: $10.1 million. Total enrollment: 232. Upper school average class size: 11. Upper school faculty-student ratio: 1:5. There are 178 required school days per year for Upper School students. Upper School students typically attend 5 days per week. The average school day consists of 7 hours and 45 minutes.

Upper School Student Profile Grade 9: 12 students (10 boys, 2 girls); Grade 10: 14 students (4 boys, 10 girls); Grade 11: 5 students (2 boys, 3 girls); Grade 12: 11 students (5 boys, 6 girls). 100% of students are Jewish.

Faculty School total: 42. In upper school: 7 men, 9 women; 16 have advanced degrees.

Subjects Offered 3-dimensional design, algebra, American government, American history, American history-AP, American literature, anatomy and physiology, art, art history, Bible studies, biology, British literature, calculus AP, chemistry, community service, computer applications, computer science, digital art, economics, English, English language and composition-AP, English literature, English literature and composition-AP, environmental science, ethics, European history, fine arts, geometry, health, Hebrew, Hebrew scripture, Holocaust seminar, Jewish studies, model United Nations, physical education, physics, statistics-AP, Talmud, trigonometry, U.S. government and politics-AP, world history, world literature, yearbook.

Graduation Requirements Arts and fine arts (art, music, dance, drama), English, foreign language, mathematics, physical education (includes health), religion (includes Bible studies and theology), science, social studies (includes history). Community service is required.

Special Academic Programs 6 Advanced Placement exams for which test preparation is offered; honors section; independent study; study at local college for college credit; academic accommodation for the gifted.

College Admission Counseling 9 students graduated in 2015; all went to college, including Chapman University; Johns Hopkins University; The University of Kansas; Tulane University; Yeshiva University. Median composite ACT: 28. 77% scored over 26 on composite ACT.

Student Life Upper grades have specified standards of dress, student council. Discipline rests primarily with faculty. Attendance at religious services is required.

Tuition and Aid Day student tuition: $8400. Tuition installment plan (FACTS Tuition Payment Plan). Need-based scholarship grants available. In 2015–16, 30% of upper-school students received aid. Total amount of financial aid awarded in 2015–16: $63,235.

Admissions Traditional secondary-level entrance grade is 9. Writing sample required. Deadline for receipt of application materials: none. Application fee required: $50.

Athletics Interscholastic: basketball (boys, girls), soccer (b,g), tennis (b,g); coed interscholastic: cross-country running. 2 PE instructors, 6 coaches.

Computers Computers are regularly used in computer applications, desktop publishing, digital applications, economics, English, foreign language, humanities, journalism, mathematics, newspaper, psychology, religious studies, science, social studies, writing, yearbook classes. Computer network features include on-campus library services, online commercial services, Internet access, wireless campus network, Internet filtering or blocking technology. Student e-mail accounts and computer access in designated common areas are available to students. Students grades are available online. The school has a published electronic and media policy.

Contact Mrs. Tamara Lawson Schuster, Director of Admissions. 913-327-8135. Fax: 913-327-8180. E-mail: tschuster@hbha.edu. Website: www.hbha.edu

ILLIANA CHRISTIAN HIGH SCHOOL

2261 Indiana Avenue
Lansing, Illinois 60438

Head of School: Peter Boonstra

General Information Coeducational day college-preparatory, general academic, arts, business, vocational, religious studies, bilingual studies, and technology school, affiliated with Christian Reformed Church, Reformed Church in America. Grades 9–12. Founded: 1945. Setting: suburban. Nearest major city is Chicago. 15-acre campus. 1 building on campus. Approved or accredited by Association of Christian Schools International, North Central Association of Colleges and Schools, and Illinois Department of Education. Endowment: $17 million. Total enrollment: 520. Upper school average class size: 21. Upper school faculty-student ratio: 1:18. Upper School students typically attend 5 days per week. The average school day consists of 7 hours and 10 minutes.

Upper School Student Profile Grade 9: 155 students (87 boys, 68 girls); Grade 10: 187 students (97 boys, 90 girls); Grade 11: 170 students (92 boys, 78 girls); Grade 12: 163 students (75 boys, 88 girls). 70% of students are members of Christian Reformed Church, Reformed Church in America.

Faculty School total: 41. In upper school: 20 men, 21 women; 32 have advanced degrees.

Subjects Offered Algebra, American history, American literature, art, arts, Bible studies, biology, botany, business, business skills, calculus, ceramics, chemistry, computer programming, computer science, drama, earth science, economics, English, environmental science, European history, expository writing, fine arts, geometry, German, government/civics, history, home economics, industrial arts, journalism, mathematics, music, physical education, physics, psychology, social studies, sociology, Spanish, theater, typing, world history, world literature, zoology.

Graduation Requirements Arts and fine arts (art, music, dance, drama), business skills (includes word processing), English, foreign language, mathematics, physical education (includes health), practical arts, religion (includes Bible studies and theology), science, social studies (includes history).

Special Academic Programs Advanced Placement exam preparation; honors section; remedial reading and/or remedial writing; remedial math; programs in English, mathematics for dyslexic students.

College Admission Counseling 155 students graduated in 2015; 121 went to college, including Calvin College; Dordt College; Hope College; Olivet Nazarene University; Purdue University; Trinity Christian College. Other: 3 entered military service, 31 had other specific plans.

Student Life Upper grades have specified standards of dress, student council. Discipline rests primarily with faculty. Attendance at religious services is required.

Summer Programs Sports, art/fine arts programs offered; session focuses on educational and recreational programs; held on campus; accepts boys and girls; open to students from other schools. 100 students usually enrolled. 2016 schedule: June 9 to July 18. Application deadline: none.

Tuition and Aid Day student tuition: $8400. Tuition installment plan (monthly payment plans). Need-based scholarship grants available.

Admissions Traditional secondary-level entrance grade is 9. ACT-Explore required. Deadline for receipt of application materials: none. No application fee required. On-campus interview required.

Athletics Interscholastic: baseball (boys), basketball (b,g), cheering (g), cross-country running (b,g), golf (b), indoor track & field (b,g), soccer (b,g), softball (g), tennis (b,g), track and field (b,g), volleyball (b,g), wrestling (b); coed intramural: bowling. 3 PE instructors, 37 coaches, 1 athletic trainer.

Computers Computers are regularly used in business applications, drawing and design, information technology classes. Computer network features include on-campus library services, online commercial services, Internet access. Students grades are available online.

Contact Elly Makowski, Admissions Counselor. 708-474-0515 Ext. 49. Fax: 708-474-0581. E-mail: elly.makowski@illianachristian.org. Website: www.illianachristian.org/

IMMACULATA HIGH SCHOOL

600 Shawnee
Leavenworth, Kansas 66048

Head of School: Mr. Richard V. Geraci

General Information Coeducational day college-preparatory, arts, business, religious studies, and technology school, affiliated with Roman Catholic Church. Grades 9–12. Founded: 1924. Setting: suburban. Nearest major city is Kansas City. 2-acre campus. 1 building on campus. Approved or accredited by North Central Association of Colleges and Schools and Kansas Department of Education. Total enrollment: 74. Upper school average class size: 10. Upper school faculty-student ratio: 1:9. There are 171 required school days per year for Upper School students. Upper

School students typically attend 5 days per week. The average school day consists of 7 hours and 30 minutes.

Upper School Student Profile 82% of students are Roman Catholic.

Faculty School total: 15. In upper school: 6 men, 9 women; 7 have advanced degrees.

Special Academic Programs Honors section; study at local college for college credit.

College Admission Counseling 26 students graduated in 2015; 24 went to college, including Johnson County Community College.

Student Life Upper grades have uniform requirement, student council. Discipline rests primarily with faculty. Attendance at religious services is required.

Admissions Traditional secondary-level entrance grade is 9. Achievement tests required. Deadline for receipt of application materials: none. Application fee required. Interview recommended.

Athletics Interscholastic: baseball (boys), basketball (b,g), cheering (g), dance team (g), football (b), golf (b), power lifting (b,g), soccer (b,g), softball (g), swimming and diving (b), tennis (b,g), track and field (b,g), volleyball (g), wrestling (b). 2 PE instructors, 4 coaches.

Computers Computers are regularly used in business education classes. Computer network features include Internet access, wireless campus network. Campus intranet is available to students. Students grades are available online.

Contact Ms. Sarah Wise, Academic Advisor. 913-682-3900. Fax: 913-682-9036. E-mail: swise@archkckcs.org. Website: www.leavenworthcatholicschools.org

IMMACULATA HIGH SCHOOL

240 Mountain Avenue
Somerville, New Jersey 08876

Head of School: Mrs. Jean Kline

General Information Coeducational day college-preparatory and religious studies school, affiliated with Roman Catholic Church. Grades 9–12. Founded: 1962. Setting: suburban. 19-acre campus. 3 buildings on campus. Approved or accredited by National Catholic Education Association and New Jersey Department of Education. Total enrollment: 690. Upper school average class size: 22. Upper school faculty-student ratio: 1:13. There are 180 required school days per year for Upper School students. Upper School students typically attend 5 days per week. The average school day consists of 6 hours and 30 minutes.

Upper School Student Profile Grade 9: 148 students (73 boys, 75 girls); Grade 10: 176 students (82 boys, 94 girls); Grade 11: 183 students (99 boys, 84 girls); Grade 12: 183 students (96 boys, 87 girls). 92% of students are Roman Catholic.

Faculty School total: 71. In upper school: 20 men, 51 women; 43 have advanced degrees.

Subjects Offered Accounting, advanced chemistry, advanced math, Advanced Placement courses, algebra, American history, American literature, anatomy, ancient world history, art, art history-AP, biology, British literature, business, calculus, calculus-AP, chemistry, chemistry-AP, creative writing, drama, drawing and design, driver education, Eastern world civilizations, ecology, English-AP, environmental science, environmental studies, European history-AP, film history, foreign language, French language-AP, geometry, global issues, global studies, graphic design, health, honors algebra, honors English, honors geometry, marching band, music theory, religious education, science, social studies, speech, trigonometry, U.S. history-AP.

Graduation Requirements Algebra, American literature, biology, British literature, chemistry, driver education, foreign language, geometry, health education, physical education (includes health), physics, theology, U.S. history.

Special Academic Programs Advanced Placement exam preparation; honors section; academic accommodation for the musically talented.

College Admission Counseling 191 students graduated in 2015; 187 went to college, including Loyola University Maryland; Penn State University Park; Rutgers, The State University of New Jersey, New Brunswick; Saint Joseph's University; Seton Hall University; The University of Scranton. Other: 2 entered military service, 2 had other specific plans. Mean SAT critical reading: 532, mean SAT math: 540, mean SAT writing: 554.

Student Life Upper grades have uniform requirement. Discipline rests primarily with faculty. Attendance at religious services is required.

Tuition and Aid Day student tuition: $10,400. Tuition installment plan (FACTS Tuition Payment Plan).

Admissions Traditional secondary-level entrance grade is 9. For fall 2015, 225 students applied for upper-level admission, 175 were accepted, 148 enrolled. High School Placement Test required. Deadline for receipt of application materials: December 31. Application fee required: $150. On-campus interview required.

Athletics Interscholastic: baseball (boys), basketball (b,g), cheering (g), cross-country running (b,g), football (b), lacrosse (b,g), soccer (b,g), softball (g), tennis (b,g); coed interscholastic: bowling, golf, swimming and diving. 4 PE instructors, 50 coaches, 1 athletic trainer.

Computers Computers are regularly used in graphic design, journalism, yearbook classes. Computer network features include on-campus library services, online commercial services, Internet access. Students grades are available online.

Contact Mr. Joseph Conry, Assistant Principal/Academic Dean. 908-722-0200 Ext. 118. Fax: 908-218-7765. E-mail: jconry@immaculatahighschool.org. Website: www.immaculatahighschool.org

IMMACULATA-LA SALLE HIGH SCHOOL

3601 South Miami Avenue
Miami, Florida 33133

Head of School: Sr. Kim Keraitis, FMA

General Information Coeducational day college-preparatory, arts, business, religious studies, and technology school, affiliated with Roman Catholic Church. Grades 9–12. Founded: 1958. Setting: urban. 13-acre campus. 7 buildings on campus. Approved or accredited by National Catholic Education Association, Southern Association of Colleges and Schools, The College Board, and Florida Department of Education. Endowment: $109,345. Total enrollment: 832. Upper school average class size: 18. Upper school faculty-student ratio: 1:18. There are 180 required school days per year for Upper School students. Upper School students typically attend 5 days per week. The average school day consists of 6 hours and 30 minutes.

Upper School Student Profile Grade 9: 222 students (78 boys, 144 girls); Grade 10: 224 students (95 boys, 129 girls); Grade 11: 207 students (86 boys, 121 girls); Grade 12: 179 students (73 boys, 106 girls). 95% of students are Roman Catholic.

Faculty School total: 60. In upper school: 24 men, 36 women; 25 have advanced degrees.

Subjects Offered 3-dimensional art, algebra, American government, American history, American history-AP, analytic geometry, anatomy, anatomy and physiology, art, band, Bible studies, biology, business technology, calculus, chemistry, chemistry-AP, Chinese, chorus, church history, comparative government and politics-AP, computer science, computer technology certification, creative writing, critical thinking, desktop publishing, digital photography, drama, driver education, economics, electronics, emerging technology, engineering, English, English language and composition-AP, English literature and composition-AP, environmental science-AP, ethics, European history-AP, filmmaking, finance, fine arts, first aid, French, French language-AP, geometry, government and politics-AP, government/civics, graphic design, health, health and wellness, history, honors algebra, honors English, honors geometry, honors U.S. history, honors world history, keyboarding, marine biology, mathematics, music appreciation, physical education, physics, psychology, religion, science, social studies, sociology, Spanish, U.S. government, U.S. government and politics-AP, U.S. history, U.S. history-AP, video film production, weight training, world history, world religions, yearbook.

Graduation Requirements Arts and fine arts (art, music, dance, drama), business skills (includes word processing), English, foreign language, geometry, mathematics, physical education (includes health), religion (includes Bible studies and theology), science, social studies (includes history), 100 hours of community service.

Special Academic Programs Advanced Placement exam preparation; honors section; independent study; study at local college for college credit.

College Admission Counseling 197 students graduated in 2015; all went to college, including Florida International University; Florida State University; Loyola University Chicago; Miami Dade College; University of Florida; University of Miami. Median SAT critical reading: 486, median SAT math: 511, median SAT writing: 484, median combined SAT: 1481, median composite ACT: 21. 20% scored over 600 on SAT critical reading, 22% scored over 600 on SAT math, 21% scored over 600 on SAT writing, 21% scored over 1800 on combined SAT, 25% scored over 26 on composite ACT.

Student Life Upper grades have uniform requirement, student council, honor system. Discipline rests equally with students and faculty. Attendance at religious services is required.

Summer Programs Remediation, enrichment, advancement programs offered; session focuses on remediation and advancement; held on campus; accepts boys and girls; open to students from other schools. 168 students usually enrolled. 2016 schedule: June 20 to July 15. Application deadline: June 13.

Tuition and Aid Day student tuition: $14,090. Tuition installment plan (FACTS Tuition Payment Plan, monthly payment plans). Merit scholarship grants, paying campus jobs available. In 2015–16, 17% of upper-school students received aid. Total amount of financial aid awarded in 2015–16: $490,471.

Admissions Traditional secondary-level entrance grade is 9. For fall 2015, 366 students applied for upper-level admission, 304 were accepted, 269 enrolled. Catholic High School Entrance Examination and High School Placement Test (closed version) from Scholastic Testing Service required. Deadline for receipt of application materials: none. Application fee required: $50. On-campus interview required.

Athletics Interscholastic: aerobics/dance (girls), baseball (b), basketball (b,g), cheering (g), cross-country running (b,g), dance team (g), football (b), golf (b,g), lacrosse (b), soccer (b,g), softball (g), swimming and diving (b,g), tennis (b,g), track and field (b,g), volleyball (b,g), weight training (b,g), winter soccer (b,g); coed intramural: physical fitness. 1 PE instructor, 12 coaches, 1 athletic trainer.

Computers Computers are regularly used in business, business applications, economics, French, health, history, journalism, mathematics, programming, psychology, religion, science, technology, video film production, word processing, yearbook classes. Computer network features include on-campus library services, online commercial services, Internet access, wireless campus network, Internet filtering or blocking technology. Campus intranet and student e-mail accounts are available to students. Students grades are available online. The school has a published electronic and media policy.

Contact Ms. Catherine Campos, Admissions Director. 305-854-2334 Ext. 130. Fax: 305-858-5971. E-mail: admissions@ilsroyals.com. Website: www.ilsroyals.com

IMMACULATE CONCEPTION HIGH SCHOOL

258 South Main Street
Lodi, New Jersey 07644-2199

Head of School: Mr. Joseph Robert Azzolino

General Information Girls' day college-preparatory, arts, business, and religious studies school, affiliated with Roman Catholic Church. Grades 9–12. Founded: 1915. Setting: suburban. Nearest major city is New York. 3-acre campus. 1 building on campus. Approved or accredited by Middle States Association of Colleges and Schools and New Jersey Department of Education. Upper school average class size: 18. Upper school faculty-student ratio: 1:11. There are 185 required school days per year for Upper School students. Upper School students typically attend 5 days per week. The average school day consists of 6 hours and 20 minutes.

Upper School Student Profile Grade 9: 49 students (49 girls); Grade 10: 52 students (52 girls); Grade 11: 59 students (59 girls); Grade 12: 48 students (48 girls). 85% of students are Roman Catholic.

Faculty School total: 22. In upper school: 6 men, 16 women; 20 have advanced degrees.

Subjects Offered Advanced math, algebra, American government, American history, American history-AP, American literature, anatomy and physiology, art, Bible studies, biology, British literature, character education, chemistry, communications, computer graphics, computer skills, driver education, English, French, genetics, geometry, health and safety, honors algebra, honors English, honors geometry, honors U.S. history, lab science, musical productions, organic chemistry, performing arts, photography, physical education, physical science, pre-calculus, psychology, religious education, social psychology, Spanish, women in society, world cultures, writing.

Graduation Requirements English, foreign language, lab science, mathematics, physical education (includes health), religious studies, social studies (includes history), service requirement. Community service is required.

Special Academic Programs Honors section; study at local college for college credit; ESL (4 students enrolled).

College Admission Counseling 48 students graduated in 2015; all went to college, including Bergen Community College; Felician University; Ramapo College of New Jersey; Rutgers, The State University of New Jersey, New Brunswick; Seton Hall University; William Paterson University of New Jersey. Mean SAT critical reading: 525, mean SAT math: 495, mean SAT writing: 545, mean combined SAT: 1565, mean composite ACT: 19. 3% scored over 600 on SAT critical reading, 2% scored over 600 on SAT math, 5% scored over 600 on SAT writing.

Student Life Upper grades have uniform requirement, student council. Discipline rests primarily with faculty. Attendance at religious services is required.

Summer Programs Enrichment, advancement programs offered; session focuses on Jump Start Program for incoming freshmen; held on campus; accepts girls; not open to students from other schools. 15 students usually enrolled. 2016 schedule: July 11 to July 28. Application deadline: May 20.

Tuition and Aid Day student tuition: $10,484. Tuition installment plan (FACTS Tuition Payment Plan, annual payment plan). Tuition reduction for siblings, merit scholarship grants, need-based scholarship grants available. In 2015–16, 45% of upper-school students received aid; total upper-school merit-scholarship money awarded: $54,500. Total amount of financial aid awarded in 2015–16: $155,000.

Admissions Traditional secondary-level entrance grade is 9. For fall 2015, 225 students applied for upper-level admission, 220 were accepted, 58 enrolled. Cooperative Entrance Exam (McGraw-Hill) required. Deadline for receipt of application materials: none. No application fee required. Interview recommended.

Athletics Interscholastic: basketball, cheering, cross-country running, soccer, softball, swimming and diving, tennis, volleyball; intramural: aerobics, basketball, fitness, fitness walking, floor hockey, physical fitness, physical training, tennis, volleyball, walking; coed interscholastic: indoor track, indoor track & field. 2 PE instructors, 12 coaches, 1 athletic trainer.

Computers Computers are regularly used in graphics, newspaper, photography, word processing, yearbook classes. Computer resources include Internet access, Internet filtering or blocking technology. Computer access in designated common areas is available to students. Students grades are available online. The school has a published electronic and media policy.

Contact Ms. Nicole Mineo, Director of Enrollment Management. 973-773-2665. Fax: 973-614-0893. E-mail: nmineo@ichslodi.org. Website: www.ichslodi.org

IMMACULATE HEART HIGH SCHOOL AND MIDDLE SCHOOL

5515 Franklin Avenue
Los Angeles, California 90028-5999

Head of School: Ms. Virginia Hurst

General Information Girls' day college-preparatory school, affiliated with Roman Catholic Church. Grades 6–12. Founded: 1906. Setting: urban. 5-acre campus. 7 buildings on campus. Approved or accredited by California Association of Independent Schools, Western Association of Schools and Colleges, and California Department of Education. Upper school average class size: 18. Upper school faculty-student ratio: 1:17.

Faculty School total: 45. In upper school: 36 have advanced degrees.

Subjects Offered Advanced biology, advanced chemistry, advanced computer applications, advanced math, Advanced Placement courses, advanced studio art-AP, algebra, American history-AP, ancient world history, art history-AP, ASB Leadership, athletics, biology-AP, British literature, British literature (honors), British literature-AP, calculus-AP, chemistry, chemistry-AP, chorus, Christian and Hebrew scripture, Christian testament, church history, college planning, computer graphics, computer programming, creative writing, dance, debate, drama, drama performance, drama workshop, dramatic arts, economics, English, English language-AP, English literature-AP, European history, European history-AP, French, French-AP, geometry, health and wellness, health education, history-AP, honors algebra, honors English, honors geometry, honors U.S. history, honors world history, journalism, marine biology, physics, physics-AP, physiology, pre-calculus, printmaking, probability and statistics, psychology-AP, robotics, Shakespeare, Spanish, Spanish language-AP, Spanish literature-AP, speech and debate, sports conditioning, statistics, statistics-AP, theology, U.S. history, U.S. history-AP, visual and performing arts, visual arts, women in literature, women spirituality and faith, world civilizations, writing workshop, yearbook.

Special Academic Programs Advanced Placement exam preparation; honors section; independent study.

Student Life Upper grades have uniform requirement, student council, honor system. Discipline rests primarily with faculty. Attendance at religious services is required.

Summer Programs Remediation, enrichment, sports, art/fine arts programs offered; held on campus; accepts boys and girls; open to students from other schools.

Tuition and Aid Tuition installment plan (The Tuition Plan). Merit scholarship grants, need-based scholarship grants available.

Admissions High School Placement Test or High School Placement Test (closed version) from Scholastic Testing Service required. Deadline for receipt of application materials: January 8. Application fee required: $75. On-campus interview required.

Athletics Interscholastic: basketball, cheering, cross-country running, equestrian sports, soccer, softball, swimming and diving, track and field, volleyball, yoga.

Computers Computers are regularly used in all academic classes. Computer network features include Internet access, wireless campus network, Internet filtering or blocking technology. Campus intranet and student e-mail accounts are available to students. Students grades are available online.

Contact Ms. Jennie Lee, Director of Admissions. 323-461-3651 Ext. 240. Fax: 323-462-0610. E-mail: jlee@immaculateheart.org. Website: www.immaculateheart.org

INCARNATE WORD ACADEMY

609 Crawford
Houston, Texas 77002-3668

Head of School: Ms. Mary Aamodt

General Information Girls' day college-preparatory, arts, religious studies, and leadership school, affiliated with Roman Catholic Church. Grades 9–12. Founded: 1873. Setting: urban. 1 building on campus. Approved or accredited by Southern Association of Colleges and Schools, Texas Catholic Conference, Texas Education Agency, and Texas Department of Education. Total enrollment: 272. Upper school average class size: 16. Upper school faculty-student ratio: 1:9. There are 180 required school days per year for Upper School students. Upper School students typically attend 5 days per week. The average school day consists of 7 hours and 20 minutes.

Upper School Student Profile Grade 9: 85 students (85 girls); Grade 10: 85 students (85 girls); Grade 11: 72 students (72 girls); Grade 12: 70 students (70 girls). 85% of students are Roman Catholic.

Faculty School total: 36. In upper school: 7 men, 29 women; 25 have advanced degrees.

Subjects Offered Algebra, American government, American history, American history-AP, American literature, American literature-AP, art, biology, biology-AP, British literature, British literature-AP, calculus, chemistry, chemistry-AP, concert choir, drama, English composition, English literature, English literature and composition-AP, English literature-AP, English-AP, English/composition-AP, environmental science-AP, French, government and politics-AP, government-AP, health, history-AP, honors algebra, honors English, honors geometry, honors U.S. history, honors world history, Latin, Latin-AP, leadership and service, leadership education training, literature and composition-AP, literature-AP, microeconomics, microeconomics-AP, modern dance, newspaper, physical education, physics, pre-calculus, psychology, publications, SAT/ACT preparation, social studies, Spanish, Spanish language-AP, Spanish literature-AP, Spanish-AP, theater arts, theater production, theology, trigonometry, U.S. government and politics, U.S. government and politics-AP, U.S. history, U.S. history-AP, U.S. literature, United States government-AP, video and animation, Web site design, world geography, world history, world literature, world religions, world studies, world wide web design, World-Wide-Web publishing, yearbook.

Graduation Requirements 75 hours of community service.

Special Academic Programs Advanced Placement exam preparation; honors section; study at local college for college credit.

College Admission Counseling 64 students graduated in 2015; all went to college, including Baylor University; Texas A&M University; The University of Texas at Austin; University of Houston.

Student Life Upper grades have uniform requirement, student council, honor system. Discipline rests primarily with faculty. Attendance at religious services is required.

Summer Programs Sports programs offered; session focuses on sports conditioning camp; held both on and off campus; held at University of St. Thomas and St. Thomas High School; accepts girls; open to students from other schools. 45 students usually enrolled. 2016 schedule: July 28 to August 1.

Tuition and Aid Day student tuition: $12,000. Tuition installment plan (monthly payment plans). Merit scholarship grants, need-based scholarship grants, paying campus jobs available. In 2015–16, 30% of upper-school students received aid.

Admissions Traditional secondary-level entrance grade is 9. For fall 2015, 230 students applied for upper-level admission, 180 were accepted, 85 enrolled. High School Placement Test (closed version) from Scholastic Testing Service or ISEE required. Deadline for receipt of application materials: January 15. Application fee required: $75. Interview recommended.

Athletics Interscholastic: basketball, cheering, cross-country running, dance, dance team, golf, running, soccer, softball, track and field, volleyball; intramural: fitness, physical fitness. 2 PE instructors, 6 coaches, 1 athletic trainer.

Computers Computers are regularly used in all classes. Computer network features include on-campus library services, online commercial services, Internet access, wireless campus network, Internet filtering or blocking technology, 1:1 iPad program. Student e-mail accounts and computer access in designated common areas are available to students. Students grades are available online. The school has a published electronic and media policy.

Contact Ms. Kate O'Brien, Director of Admissions. 713-227-3637 Ext. 117. Fax: 713-227-1014. E-mail: kobrien@incarnateword.org. Website: www.incarnateword.org

INDEPENDENT SCHOOL

8317 East Douglas
Wichita, Kansas 67207

Head of School: Dr. Milt Dougherty

General Information Coeducational day college-preparatory, arts, and technology school. Grades PK–12. Founded: 1980. Setting: suburban. 22-acre campus. 2 buildings on campus. Approved or accredited by Independent Schools Association of the Central States. Total enrollment: 538. Upper school average class size: 12. Upper school faculty-student ratio: 1:7. There are 160 required school days per year for Upper School students. Upper School students typically attend 5 days per week. The average school day consists of 6 hours.

Upper School Student Profile Grade 9: 42 students (22 boys, 20 girls); Grade 10: 46 students (26 boys, 20 girls); Grade 11: 52 students (29 boys, 23 girls); Grade 12: 56 students (26 boys, 30 girls).

Faculty School total: 60. In upper school: 15 men, 14 women; 18 have advanced degrees.

Subjects Offered 3-dimensional art, advanced chemistry, advanced math, Advanced Placement courses, algebra, American government, American history, American history-AP, American literature, anatomy and physiology, art, art history, astronomy, biology, biology-AP, British literature, British literature (honors), business law, calculus, calculus-AP, ceramics, chemistry, chemistry-AP, choir, choral music, computer applications, computer art, computer programming, concert band, creative writing, debate, drama, driver education, economics, engineering, English literature-AP, film and new technologies, foreign language, forensics, geometry, government, graphic design, health, health and wellness, journalism, Latin, Latin American literature, madrigals, music, music theory, music theory-AP, music-AP, newspaper, physics, physics-AP, psychology, psychology-AP, Spanish, Spanish-AP, statistics-AP, theater, theater arts, trigonometry, U.S. government and politics-AP, Web site design, weight training, yearbook, zoology.

Graduation Requirements Algebra, American government, American history, American literature, arts and fine arts (art, music, dance, drama), biology, British literature, chemistry, computer applications, computer literacy, English, foreign language, geography, geometry, humanities, physical education (includes health), world history, world literature, 50 hours of community service.

Special Academic Programs 14 Advanced Placement exams for which test preparation is offered; honors section; independent study; study at local college for college credit; academic accommodation for the gifted, the musically talented, and the artistically talented.

College Admission Counseling 54 students graduated in 2015; 53 went to college, including Belmont University; Kansas State University; Oklahoma State University; Texas A&M University; The University of Kansas; The University of Tulsa.

Student Life Upper grades have specified standards of dress, student council, honor system. Discipline rests primarily with faculty.

Summer Programs Enrichment, advancement, sports, art/fine arts, computer instruction programs offered; held on campus; accepts boys and girls; open to students from other schools. 391 students usually enrolled. 2016 schedule: May 20 to August 15.

Tuition and Aid Day student tuition: $10,950. Tuition installment plan (monthly payment plans). Need-based scholarship grants available. In 2015–16, 26% of upper-school students received aid.

Admissions Traditional secondary-level entrance grade is 9. For fall 2015, 41 students applied for upper-level admission, 33 were accepted, 29 enrolled. Admissions testing, non-standardized placement tests and Otis-Lennon Ability or Stanford Achievement

Test required. Deadline for receipt of application materials: none. Application fee required: $40. Interview recommended.

Athletics Interscholastic: baseball (boys), basketball (b,g), bowling (b,g), cheering (g), cross-country running (b,g), dance team (g), football (b), golf (b,g), soccer (b,g), softball (g), strength & conditioning (b,g), swimming and diving (b,g), tennis (b,g), track and field (b,g), volleyball (g), weight training (b,g), wrestling (b); coed interscholastic: strength & conditioning, weight training. 2 PE instructors, 5 coaches, 1 athletic trainer.

Computers Computers are regularly used in art, college planning, economics, English, humanities, introduction to technology, library, literary magazine, mathematics, newspaper, photography, publications, Web site design, yearbook classes. Computer network features include on-campus library services, Internet access, wireless campus network, Internet filtering or blocking technology, homework online. Student e-mail accounts and computer access in designated common areas are available to students. Students grades are available online. The school has a published electronic and media policy.

Contact Beth Sturm, Director of Admissions. 316-686-0152 Ext. 405. Fax: 316-686-3918. E-mail: beth.sturm@theindependentschool.com. Website: www.theindependentschool.com

INDIAN CREEK SCHOOL

Lower, Middle Schools: 680 Evergreen Road
Upper School-1130 Anne Chambers Way
Crownsville, Maryland 21032

Head of School: Dr. Rick Branson

General Information Coeducational day college-preparatory school. Grades PK–12. Founded: 1973. Setting: suburban. Nearest major city is Annapolis. 114-acre campus. 3 buildings on campus. Approved or accredited by Association of Independent Maryland Schools, National Independent Private Schools Association, and Maryland Department of Education. Member of National Association of Independent Schools. Endowment: $35 million. Total enrollment: 621. Upper school average class size: 16. Upper school faculty-student ratio: 1:7. There are 179 required school days per year for Upper School students. Upper School students typically attend 5 days per week. The average school day consists of 8 hours.

Upper School Student Profile Grade 9: 58 students (28 boys, 30 girls); Grade 10: 57 students (30 boys, 27 girls); Grade 11: 65 students (36 boys, 29 girls); Grade 12: 48 students (24 boys, 24 girls).

Faculty School total: 94. In upper school: 13 men, 23 women; 23 have advanced degrees.

Special Academic Programs 18 Advanced Placement exams for which test preparation is offered; independent study; academic accommodation for the gifted; remedial reading and/or remedial writing.

College Admission Counseling 49 students graduated in 2015; all went to college.

Student Life Upper grades have uniform requirement, student council. Discipline rests primarily with faculty.

Summer Programs Enrichment, sports, art/fine arts programs offered; held on campus; accepts boys and girls; open to students from other schools. 300 students usually enrolled. 2016 schedule: June 16 to August 1.

Tuition and Aid Day student tuition: $8000 $22,800. Tuition installment plan (Insured Tuition Payment Plan, SMART Tuition Payment Plan, monthly payment plans, individually arranged payment plans). Merit scholarship grants, need-based scholarship grants available. In 2015–16, 22% of upper-school students received aid.

Admissions Traditional secondary-level entrance grade is 9. Math and English placement tests or writing sample required. Deadline for receipt of application materials: none. Application fee required: $50. Interview required.

Athletics Interscholastic: basketball (boys, girls), cross-country running (b,g), field hockey (g), lacrosse (b,g), soccer (b,g); intramural: baseball (b); coed interscholastic: dressage, equestrian sports, golf, horseback riding, sailing, tennis; coed intramural: aerobics/dance, aquatics, dance, martial arts, weight training, yoga. 15 coaches, 1 athletic trainer.

Computers Computers are regularly used in all academic classes. Computer network features include on-campus library services, online commercial services, Internet access, wireless campus network, Internet filtering or blocking technology. Campus intranet, student e-mail accounts, and computer access in designated common areas are available to students. Students grades are available online. The school has a published electronic and media policy.

Contact Ms. Melissa Haber, Director of Admission for Lower and Middle Schools. 410-923-3660. Fax: 410-923-0670. E-mail: mhaber@indiancreekschool.org. Website: www.indiancreekschool.org

INDIAN MOUNTAIN SCHOOL

Lakeville, Connecticut
See Junior Boarding Schools section.

INDIAN SPRINGS SCHOOL

190 Woodward Drive
Indian Springs, Alabama 35124

Head of School: Mr. Gareth Vaughan

General Information Coeducational boarding and day college-preparatory and arts school. Grades 8–12. Founded: 1952. Setting: suburban. Nearest major city is Birmingham. Students are housed in single-sex dormitories. 350-acre campus. 38 buildings on campus. Approved or accredited by Southern Association of Colleges and Schools, Southern Association of Independent Schools, The Association of Boarding Schools, and Alabama Department of Education. Member of National Association of Independent Schools and Secondary School Admission Test Board. Endowment: $18 million. Total enrollment: 299. Upper school average class size: 12. Upper school faculty-student ratio: 1:7. There are 175 required school days per year for Upper School students. Upper School students typically attend 5 days per week. The average school day consists of 6 hours and 20 minutes.

Upper School Student Profile Grade 8: 36 students (22 boys, 14 girls); Grade 9: 63 students (34 boys, 29 girls); Grade 10: 71 students (31 boys, 40 girls); Grade 11: 61 students (34 boys, 27 girls); Grade 12: 68 students (33 boys, 35 girls). 28% of students are boarding students. 75% are state residents. 13 states are represented in upper school student body. 15% are international students. International students from China, Czech Republic, Ethiopia, Germany, Republic of Korea, and Spain; 13 other countries represented in student body.

Faculty School total: 43. In upper school: 20 men, 21 women; 34 have advanced degrees; 23 reside on campus.

Subjects Offered Advanced Placement courses, algebra, American history, American literature, art, art history, astronomy, athletics, biology, biology-AP, calculus, calculus-AP, ceramics, chemistry, chemistry-AP, Chinese, computer applications, computer multimedia, concert choir, constitutional law, contemporary issues, creative writing, drama, economics, economics-AP, English, English literature, English-AP, environmental science-AP, European history, expository writing, film studies, fine arts, French, French-AP, geology, geometry, government-AP, government/civics, history, jazz, jazz ensemble, keyboarding, Latin, Latin-AP, mathematics, music, painting, philosophy, photo shop, physical education, physical fitness, physics, play production, pre-calculus, science, Shakespeare, social studies, Spanish, Spanish-AP, statistics-AP, theater, trigonometry, U.S. government and politics-AP, world history, world literature, world religions, writing, yearbook.

Graduation Requirements Arts and fine arts (art, music, dance, drama), English, foreign language, mathematics, physical education (includes health), science, social studies (includes history), art or music history.

Special Academic Programs Advanced Placement exam preparation; independent study; academic accommodation for the gifted and the musically talented.

College Admission Counseling 68 students graduated in 2015; all went to college, including Auburn University; Birmingham-Southern College; Brandeis University; Pomona College; Rhodes College; The University of Alabama. Median SAT critical reading: 670, median SAT math: 650, median SAT writing: 630, median combined SAT: 1950, median composite ACT: 28. 77% scored over 600 on SAT critical reading, 64% scored over 600 on SAT math, 70% scored over 600 on SAT writing, 70% scored over 1800 on combined SAT, 55% scored over 26 on composite ACT.

Student Life Upper grades have student council, honor system. Discipline rests equally with students and faculty.

Summer Programs Remediation, enrichment, sports, art/fine arts programs offered; session focuses on middle school students; held on campus; accepts boys and girls; open to students from other schools. 2016 schedule: June 16 to August 3. Application deadline: June 1.

Tuition and Aid Day student tuition: $20,250; 5-day tuition and room/board: $37,500; 7-day tuition and room/board: $44,000. Tuition installment plan (FACTS Tuition Payment Plan, monthly payment plans). Need-based scholarship grants available. In 2015–16, 27% of upper-school students received aid. Total amount of financial aid awarded in 2015–16: $1,000,000.

Admissions Traditional secondary-level entrance grade is 9. For fall 2015, 209 students applied for upper-level admission, 127 were accepted, 99 enrolled. SSAT or TOEFL required. Deadline for receipt of application materials: January 16. Application fee required: $75. Interview required.

Athletics Interscholastic: baseball (boys), basketball (b,g), soccer (b,g), softball (g), tennis (b,g), volleyball (g); intramural: basketball (b,g), flag football (b), soccer (b,g); coed interscholastic: cross-country running, golf, ultimate Frisbee; coed intramural: aerobics, aerobics/Nautilus, outdoor activities, paint ball, physical fitness, strength & conditioning, table tennis, ultimate Frisbee, yoga. 2 PE instructors, 5 coaches, 1 athletic trainer.

Computers Computers are regularly used in all academic classes. Computer network features include on-campus library services, online commercial services, Internet access, wireless campus network, Internet filtering or blocking technology. Campus intranet, student e-mail accounts, and computer access in designated common areas are available to students. Students grades are available online.

Contact Mrs. Christine Copeland, Assistant Director of Admission and Financial Aid. 205-332-0582. Fax: 205-988-3797. E-mail: ccopeland@indiansprings.org. Website: www.indiansprings.org

INSTITUT MONTE ROSA

57 Av. de Chillon
Montreux 1820, Switzerland

Head of School: Mr. Bernhard Gademann

General Information Coeducational boarding and day college-preparatory, business, and bilingual studies school. Grades 7–12. Founded: 1874. Setting: small town. Students are housed in single-sex dormitories. 6-hectare campus. 2 buildings on campus. Approved or accredited by Swiss Federation of Private Schools. Languages of instruction: English and French. Upper school average class size: 8. Upper school faculty-student ratio: 1:5.

Special Academic Programs Advanced Placement exam preparation; ESL.

Student Life Upper grades have specified standards of dress, honor system. Discipline rests equally with students and faculty.

Summer Programs ESL, sports programs offered; session focuses on languages; held on campus; accepts boys and girls; open to students from other schools. 100 students usually enrolled.

Admissions Math and English placement tests required. Deadline for receipt of application materials: none. Application fee required: 800 Swiss francs. Interview recommended.

Athletics Coed Intramural: aerobics/dance, alpine skiing, aquatics, archery, badminton, basketball, bicycling, canoeing/kayaking, climbing, dance, equestrian sports, fitness, football, freestyle skiing, golf, gymnastics, handball, horseback riding, ice hockey, ice skating, indoor soccer, kayaking, modern dance, mountain biking, mountaineering, outdoor activities, outdoor education, outdoor recreation, paddling, physical fitness, physical training, rafting, skiing (cross-country), skiing (downhill), snowboarding, soccer, swimming and diving, tennis, water skiing.

Computers Computer resources include Internet access, wireless campus network, Internet filtering or blocking technology.

INTERMOUNTAIN CHRISTIAN SCHOOL

6515 South Lion Lane
Salt Lake City, Utah 84121

Head of School: Mr. Mitch Menning

General Information Coeducational day college-preparatory, general academic, arts, business, and religious studies school, affiliated with Evangelical Free Church of America, Christian faith. Boys grades PK–8, girls grades PK–12. Founded: 1982. Setting: suburban. 6-acre campus. 1 building on campus. Approved or accredited by Association of Christian Schools International, Northwest Association of Schools and Colleges, and Utah Department of Education. Endowment: $79,000. Total enrollment: 285. Upper school average class size: 19. Upper school faculty-student ratio: 1:9. There are 180 required school days per year for Upper School students. Upper School students typically attend 5 days per week. The average school day consists of 7 hours.

Upper School Student Profile Grade 6: 24 students (11 boys, 13 girls); Grade 7: 19 students (6 boys, 13 girls); Grade 8: 17 students (5 boys, 12 girls); Grade 9: 19 students (12 boys, 7 girls); Grade 10: 22 students (11 boys, 11 girls); Grade 11: 13 students (5 boys, 8 girls); Grade 12: 10 students (4 boys, 6 girls). 92% of students are members of Evangelical Free Church of America, Christian.

Faculty School total: 33. In upper school: 8 men, 6 women; 9 have advanced degrees.

Subjects Offered Advanced Placement courses, algebra, American government, American history, American literature, American literature-AP, art, athletics, baseball, basketball, bell choir, Bible, biology, calculus, career education, ceramics, chemistry, choir, chorus, Christian doctrine, church history, community service, composition, computer science, computer skills, concert band, concert bell choir, concert choir, current events, debate, drama, drama performance, economics, economics and history, electives, English, English literature-AP, environmental science-AP, European history, European literature, family and consumer science, finance, fine arts, food science, geometry, government, handbells, health, history, independent study, instrumental music, jazz band, keyboarding, leadership and service, Life of Christ, mathematics, peer ministry, physical education, physics, pre-algebra, pre-calculus, science, senior seminar, sex education, social studies, Spanish, statistics, U.S. government, U.S. history, vocal ensemble, volleyball, world geography, world history.

Graduation Requirements Arts and fine arts (art, music, dance, drama), Bible, computer science, English, finance, foreign language, mathematics, physical education (includes health), science, social studies (includes history), class trips. Community service is required.

Special Academic Programs 3 Advanced Placement exams for which test preparation is offered; honors section; study at local college for college credit.

College Admission Counseling 10 students graduated in 2014; 8 went to college, including Clemson University; Grand Canyon University; Northwest Nazarene University; Texas Christian University; The University of Alabama; University of Utah. Other: 2 went to work. Mean SAT critical reading: 581, mean SAT math: 590, mean SAT writing: 543, mean combined SAT: 1714, mean composite ACT: 25. 33% scored over 600 on SAT critical reading, 44% scored over 600 on SAT math, 22% scored over 600 on SAT writing, 44% scored over 1800 on combined SAT, 38% scored over 26 on composite ACT.

Student Life Upper grades have specified standards of dress, student council, honor system. Discipline rests primarily with faculty. Attendance at religious services is required.

Tuition and Aid Day student tuition: $7120. Tuition installment plan (Insured Tuition Payment Plan, monthly payment plans, discounted up-front tuition payment). Tuition reduction for siblings, need-based scholarship grants available. In 2014–15, 19% of upper-school students received aid. Total amount of financial aid awarded in 2014–15: $24,904.

Admissions Traditional secondary-level entrance grade is 9. For fall 2014, 5 students applied for upper-level admission, 5 were accepted, 5 enrolled. School's own test required. Deadline for receipt of application materials: none. Application fee required: $95. On-campus interview required.

Athletics Interscholastic: baseball (boys), basketball (b,g), golf (b,g), soccer (b,g), volleyball (g). 1 PE instructor, 4 coaches.

Computers Computers are regularly used in art, computer applications, technology, writing classes. Computer network features include Internet access, wireless campus network, Internet filtering or blocking technology. Students grades are available online. The school has a published electronic and media policy.

Contact Tiffany McDermaid, Registrar. 801-365-0370. Fax: 801-942-8813. E-mail: mcdermaid_t@slcics.org. Website: www.slcics.org

INTERNATIONAL HIGH SCHOOL

150 Oak Street
San Francisco, California 94102

Head of School: Ms. Melinda Bihn

General Information Coeducational day college-preparatory, arts, business, bilingual studies, technology, and philosophy school. Grades PK–12. Founded: 1962. Setting: urban. 3-acre campus. 3 buildings on campus. Approved or accredited by Council of International Schools, French Ministry of Education, Western Association of Schools and Colleges, and California Department of Education. Member of National Association of Independent Schools, Secondary School Admission Test Board, and European Council of International Schools. Languages of instruction: English and French. Endowment: $6 million. Total enrollment: 1,077. Upper school average class size: 17. Upper school faculty-student ratio: 1:10. There are 165 required school days per year for Upper School students. Upper School students typically attend 5 days per week. The average school day consists of 7 hours.

Upper School Student Profile Grade 9: 98 students (45 boys, 53 girls); Grade 10: 100 students (43 boys, 57 girls); Grade 11: 94 students (46 boys, 48 girls); Grade 12: 72 students (35 boys, 37 girls).

Faculty School total: 139. In upper school: 33 men, 30 women; 35 have advanced degrees.

Subjects Offered Advanced chemistry, advanced math, algebra, American history, American literature, art, biology, calculus, chemistry, community service, current events, drama, earth science, economics, English, English literature, environmental science, ESL, European history, fine arts, French, geography, geometry, German, government/civics, history, International Baccalaureate courses, Mandarin, mathematics, music, philosophy, physical education, physics, psychology, science, social studies, Spanish, theater, theory of knowledge, trigonometry, world history, world literature, writing.

Graduation Requirements Arts and fine arts (art, music, dance, drama), English, foreign language, International Baccalaureate courses, mathematics, physical education (includes health), science, social studies (includes history), theory of knowledge, extended essay, 150 hours of CAS.

Special Academic Programs International Baccalaureate program; honors section; independent study; term-away projects; study abroad; academic accommodation for the gifted, the musically talented, and the artistically talented; ESL (12 students enrolled).

College Admission Counseling 85 students graduated in 2015; 83 went to college, including New York University; Stanford University; University of California, Berkeley; University of California, Los Angeles; University of Chicago; University of Washington. Other: 2 had other specific plans. Mean SAT critical reading: 639, mean SAT math: 642, mean SAT writing: 623.

Student Life Upper grades have student council. Discipline rests equally with students and faculty.

Summer Programs Remediation, enrichment, advancement programs offered; session focuses on enrichment; held on campus; accepts boys and girls; open to students from other schools. 15 students usually enrolled.

Tuition and Aid Day student tuition: $36,670. Tuition installment plan (FACTS Tuition Payment Plan). Need-based scholarship grants, French bourse available. In 2015–16, 25% of upper-school students received aid. Total amount of financial aid awarded in 2015–16: $748,000.

Admissions Traditional secondary-level entrance grade is 9. For fall 2015, 265 students applied for upper-level admission, 179 were accepted, 59 enrolled. Any standardized test, SSAT or writing sample required. Deadline for receipt of application materials: January 14. Application fee required: $100. Interview required.

Athletics Interscholastic: baseball (boys, girls), basketball (b,g), soccer (b,g), volleyball (b,g); intramural: baseball (b), basketball (b,g), soccer (b,g), tennis (b,g), volleyball (b,g); coed interscholastic: badminton, cross-country running, sailing, swimming and diving, tennis, track and field; coed intramural: badminton, cross-country running, fencing, outdoor activities, outdoor adventure, physical fitness, physical training, sailing, swimming and diving, track and field. 4 PE instructors, 8 coaches, 2 athletic trainers.

Computers Computers are regularly used in all academic classes. Computer network features include on-campus library services, online commercial services, Internet access, wireless campus network, iPad program for all high school students. Campus intranet, student e-mail accounts, and computer access in designated common areas are available to students. Students grades are available online. The school has a published electronic and media policy.

Contact Ms. Erin Cronin, Associate Director of Admission. 415-558-2093. Fax: 415-558-2085. E-mail: erinc@internationalsf.org. Website: www.internationalsf.org

INTERNATIONAL SCHOOL BANGKOK

39/7 Soi Nichada Thani, Samakee Road
Pakkret 11120, Thailand

Head of School: Dr. Andrew Davies

General Information Coeducational day college-preparatory, arts, and technology school. Grades PK–12. Founded: 1951. Setting: suburban. Nearest major city is Bangkok, Thailand. 37-acre campus. 2 buildings on campus. Approved or accredited by International Baccalaureate Organization, Ministry of Education (Thailand), and Western Association of Schools and Colleges. Affiliate member of National Association of Independent Schools. Language of instruction: English. Total enrollment: 1,946. Upper school average class size: 18. Upper school faculty-student ratio: 1:10. There are 182 required school days per year for Upper School students. Upper School students typically attend 5 days per week. The average school day consists of 6 hours.

Faculty School total: 242. In upper school: 57 men, 37 women; 74 have advanced degrees.

Subjects Offered 3-dimensional design, algebra, American history, American literature, art, art history, biology, business, business education, business studies, calculus, calculus-AP, chemistry, choir, computer science, concert band, creative writing, dance, drama, drawing, drawing and design, Dutch, earth science, ecology, economics, economics and history, electives, English, English literature, environmental education, environmental science, environmental studies, ESL, European history, expository writing, fine arts, French, French studies, geography, geology, geometry, German, government/civics, health, history, humanities, industrial arts, Japanese, journalism, language arts, languages, mathematics, music, performing arts, photography, physical education, physics, psychology, reading, robotics, science, social studies, sociology, Spanish, speech, statistics, Thai, theater, theory of knowledge, trigonometry, world history, world literature, writing.

Graduation Requirements Arts and fine arts (art, music, dance, drama), electives, English, health, mathematics, physical education (includes health), science, social studies (includes history), theory of knowledge, community service hours, Senior Seminar, Global Citizenship Week, Thailand and Southeast Asia course. Community service is required.

Special Academic Programs International Baccalaureate program; Advanced Placement exam preparation; ESL.

College Admission Counseling 178 students graduated in 2015; all went to college, including Boston University; Northeastern University; Penn State University Park; Syracuse University; University of California, Davis; University of Illinois at Urbana–Champaign. Mean SAT critical reading: 575, mean SAT math: 655, mean SAT writing: 592, mean combined SAT: 1822, mean composite ACT: 25.

Student Life Upper grades have uniform requirement, student council, honor system. Discipline rests primarily with faculty.

Summer Programs Remediation, enrichment, ESL, art/fine arts programs offered; held on campus; accepts boys and girls; open to students from other schools. 400 students usually enrolled. 2016 schedule: June to July. Application deadline: June 3.

Tuition and Aid Day student tuition: 869,000 Thai bahts. Tuition installment plan (individually arranged payment plans).

Admissions Math and English placement tests and school's own exam required. Deadline for receipt of application materials: none. Application fee required: 4500 Thai bahts. On-campus interview required.

Athletics Interscholastic: aquatics (boys, girls), badminton (b,g), basketball (b,g), cross-country running (b,g), dance (b,g), rugby (b,g), running (b,g), soccer (b,g), softball (b,g), swimming and diving (b,g), tennis (b,g), track and field (b,g), volleyball (b,g); intramural: aquatics (b,g), badminton (b,g), basketball (b,g), cross-country running (b,g), dance (b,g), fencing (b), rugby (b,g), running (b,g), soccer (b,g), softball (b,g), swimming and diving (b,g), tennis (b,g), track and field (b,g), volleyball (b,g); coed interscholastic: dance team. 5 PE instructors.

Computers Computers are regularly used in all academic classes. Computer network features include on-campus library services, Internet access, wireless campus network, Internet filtering or blocking technology. Campus intranet, student e-mail accounts, and computer access in designated common areas are available to students. Students grades are available online. The school has a published electronic and media policy.

Contact Ms. Wendy Van Bramer, Admissions Director. 662-963-5800. Fax: 662-960-4103. E-mail: register@isb.ac.th. Website: www.isb.ac.th

INTERNATIONAL SCHOOL HAMBURG

Hemmingstedter Weg 130
Hamburg 22609, Germany

Head of School: Mr. Andreas Swoboda

General Information Coeducational day college-preparatory, arts, and technology school. Grades PK–12. Founded: 1957. Setting: suburban. 3-acre campus. 1 building on campus. Approved or accredited by Council of International Schools and New England Association of Schools and Colleges. Member of European Council of International Schools. Language of instruction: English. Total enrollment: 755. Upper school average class size: 20. Upper school faculty-student ratio: 1:8. Upper School students typically attend 5 days per week.

Upper School Student Profile Grade 9: 69 students (43 boys, 26 girls); Grade 10: 51 students (29 boys, 22 girls); Grade 11: 46 students (25 boys, 21 girls); Grade 12: 47 students (22 boys, 25 girls).

Faculty School total: 90. In upper school: 47 men, 25 women; 40 have advanced degrees.

Subjects Offered 20th century world history, 3-dimensional art, 3-dimensional design, advanced biology, advanced chemistry, art, biology, chemistry, computer math, drama, English, ESL, European history, fine arts, French, geography, German, history, mathematics, model United Nations, music, photography, physical education, physics, science, social studies, Spanish, theater, theory of knowledge, world history.

Graduation Requirements All academic, arts and fine arts (art, music, dance, drama), English, foreign language, mathematics, physical education (includes health), science, social studies (includes history).

Special Academic Programs International Baccalaureate program; programs in English, mathematics for dyslexic students; ESL (80 students enrolled).

College Admission Counseling 50 students graduated in 2015; 45 went to college, including Boston University; Columbia University; McGill University; University of Edinburgh; Yale University. Other: 3 had other specific plans.

Student Life Upper grades have student council. Discipline rests primarily with faculty.

Tuition and Aid Day student tuition: €15,440–€19,230. Tuition installment plan (2-payment plan). Financial aid available to upper-school students. In 2015–16, 1% of upper-school students received aid.

Admissions Traditional secondary-level entrance grade is 9. For fall 2015, 60 students applied for upper-level admission, 60 were accepted, 59 enrolled. ACT, CTBS, Stanford Achievement Test, any other standardized test or PSAT and SAT for applicants to grade 11 and 12 required. Deadline for receipt of application materials: none. Application fee required: €100. On-campus interview required.

Athletics Interscholastic: badminton (boys, girls), basketball (b,g), canoeing/kayaking (b,g), climbing (b,g), cross-country running (b,g), floor hockey (b,g), football (b,g), indoor hockey (b,g), indoor soccer (b,g), netball (b,g), physical training (b,g), rowing (b,g), running (b,g), sailing (b,g), soccer (b,g), tennis (b,g), track and field (b,g), volleyball (b,g); intramural: basketball (b,g), cross-country running (b,g), field hockey (b,g), football (b,g), soccer (b,g), tennis (b,g), track and field (b,g), volleyball (b,g); coed interscholastic: badminton, canoeing/kayaking, climbing, cross-country running, floor hockey, football, indoor hockey, indoor soccer, netball, running, sailing, soccer, tennis, track and field, volleyball; coed intramural: cross-country running, football, soccer, tennis, track and field, volleyball. 5 PE instructors, 4 coaches.

Computers Computers are regularly used in business studies, English, ESL, foreign language, French, geography, history, humanities, library, mathematics, music, science, Spanish, yearbook classes. Computer network features include on-campus library services, online commercial services, Internet access, wireless campus network, Internet filtering or blocking technology. Campus intranet and student e-mail accounts are available to students. Students grades are available online. The school has a published electronic and media policy.

Contact Catherine Bissonnet, Director of Admissions. 49-40-800050-133. Fax: 49-40-881-1405. E-mail: cbissonnet@ishamburg.org. Website: www.ishamburg.org

INTERNATIONAL SCHOOL MANILA

University Parkway
Fort Bonifacio
1634 Taguig City, Philippines

Head of School: David Toze

General Information Coeducational day college-preparatory, arts, business, bilingual studies, and technology school. Grades PS–12. Founded: 1920. Setting: urban. Nearest major city is Manila, Philippines. 7-hectare campus. 1 building on campus. Approved or accredited by Council of International Schools. Affiliate member of National Association of Independent Schools; member of Secondary School Admission Test Board. Language of instruction: English. Endowment: $2 million. Total enrollment: 2,169. Upper school average class size: 16. Upper school faculty-student ratio: 1:9. There are 180 required school days per year for Upper School students. Upper School students typically attend 5 days per week. The average school day consists of 5 hours and 50 minutes.

Upper School Student Profile Grade 6: 168 students (69 boys, 99 girls); Grade 7: 176 students (93 boys, 83 girls); Grade 8: 192 students (101 boys, 91 girls); Grade 9:

186 students (98 boys, 88 girls); Grade 10: 196 students (90 boys, 106 girls); Grade 11: 184 students (94 boys, 90 girls); Grade 12: 178 students (98 boys, 80 girls).

Faculty School total: 220. In upper school: 47 men, 39 women; 60 have advanced degrees.

Subjects Offered Acting, anthropology, art, athletic training, band, Basic programming, biology, business, calculus-AP, chemistry, Chinese, choir, college admission preparation, college awareness, college counseling, college placement, college planning, computer applications, computer graphics, computer literacy, computer multimedia, computer programming, computer science, creative writing, critical writing, dance, desktop publishing, digital photography, economics, economics and history, English, environmental science, ESL, film, filmmaking, foreign language, French, French as a second language, general science, geography, graphic design, health, health and wellness, health education, information technology, integrated mathematics, International Baccalaureate courses, international relations, Japanese, Japanese as Second Language, jazz band, leadership, math applications, math methods, mathematics, media studies, music, orchestra, parenting, peer counseling, personal fitness, Philippine culture, physical science, physics, political science, pre-calculus, programming, psychology, reading/study skills, remedial study skills, research, service learning/internship, sex education, Spanish, theater, theater arts, theory of knowledge, track and field, U.S. history, U.S. history-AP, video film production, visual and performing arts, visual arts, weight fitness, weight training, world history, world religions, writing.

Special Academic Programs International Baccalaureate program; Advanced Placement exam preparation; honors section; accelerated programs; independent study; academic accommodation for the gifted, the musically talented, and the artistically talented; remedial reading and/or remedial writing; remedial math; programs in English, mathematics, general development for dyslexic students; special instructional classes for deaf students; ESL (257 students enrolled).

College Admission Counseling 187 students graduated in 2014; all went to college, including McGill University; New York University; The University of British Columbia; University of California, Berkeley; University of Toronto. Mean SAT critical reading: 604, mean SAT math: 646, mean SAT writing: 613, mean combined SAT: 1863, mean composite ACT: 27.

Student Life Upper grades have uniform requirement, student council, honor system. Discipline rests primarily with faculty.

Tuition and Aid Day student tuition: $24,000. Tuition installment plan (monthly payment plans, individually arranged payment plans, quarterly payment plan). Scholarships for low-income local students available.

Admissions Traditional secondary-level entrance grade is 9. For fall 2014, 120 students applied for upper-level admission, 74 were accepted, 74 enrolled. Iowa Tests of Basic Skills required. Deadline for receipt of application materials: none. Application fee required: $500. On-campus interview recommended.

Athletics Interscholastic: badminton (boys, girls), basketball (b,g), cheering (g), cross-country running (b,g), golf (b,g), gymnastics (b,g), martial arts (b,g), rugby (b,g), soccer (b,g), softball (b,g), swimming and diving (b,g), table tennis (b,g), tennis (b,g), track and field (b,g), volleyball (b,g), wall climbing (b,g); intramural: rugby (b,g), wall climbing (b,g), water polo (b,g); coed interscholastic: dance, wall climbing; coed intramural: volleyball, wall climbing. 5 PE instructors, 10 coaches.

Computers Computers are regularly used in art, English, foreign language, history, mathematics, music, science classes. Computer network features include on-campus library services, online commercial services, Internet access, wireless campus network, Internet filtering or blocking technology. Campus intranet, student e-mail accounts, and computer access in designated common areas are available to students. Students grades are available online. The school has a published electronic and media policy.

Contact Stephanie Hagedorn, Director of Admissions and Advancement. 63-2-840-8488. Fax: 63-2-840-8489. E-mail: admission@ismanila.org. Website: www.ismanila.org

THE INTERNATIONAL SCHOOL OF ABERDEEN

Pitfodels House
North Deeside Road
Pitfodels, Cults
Aberdeen AB15 9PN, United Kingdom

Head of School: Dr. Daniel A. Hovde

General Information Coeducational day college-preparatory and general academic school. Grades PK–12. Founded: 1972. Setting: suburban. 14-acre campus. 1 building on campus. Approved or accredited by Council of International Schools, International Baccalaureate Organization, and Middle States Association of Colleges and Schools. Member of European Council of International Schools. Language of instruction: English. Total enrollment: 439. Upper school average class size: 18. Upper school faculty-student ratio: 1:5. There are 170 required school days per year for Upper School students. Upper School students typically attend 5 days per week. The average school day consists of 5 hours and 50 minutes.

Upper School Student Profile Grade 6: 28 students (17 boys, 11 girls); Grade 7: 30 students (17 boys, 13 girls); Grade 8: 26 students (13 boys, 13 girls); Grade 9: 19 students (8 boys, 11 girls); Grade 10: 35 students (21 boys, 14 girls); Grade 11: 29 students (11 boys, 18 girls); Grade 12: 35 students (19 boys, 16 girls).

Faculty School total: 61. In upper school: 18 men, 21 women; 29 have advanced degrees.

Subjects Offered Algebra, art, band, biology, chemistry, choir, computer applications, computer information systems, computer science, desktop publishing, drama, Dutch, earth science, ecology, environmental systems, economics, English, ESL, fitness, French, French as a second language, geography, geometry, government/civics, health education, history, information technology, international relations, language arts, library studies, mathematics, model United Nations, music, music composition, music performance, performing arts, physical education, physics, science, social studies, Spanish, technical theater.

Graduation Requirements Arts and fine arts (art, music, dance, drama), computer science, electives, English, foreign language, mathematics, physical education (includes health), science, social studies (includes history).

Special Academic Programs International Baccalaureate program; independent study; ESL (35 students enrolled).

College Admission Counseling 29 students graduated in 2015; 27 went to college, including Baylor University; Kansas State University; Penn State University Park; Texas A&M University; The University of Texas at San Antonio; University of Colorado Boulder. Other: 2 had other specific plans.

Student Life Upper grades have student council, honor system. Discipline rests primarily with faculty.

Summer Programs Sports, art/fine arts, computer instruction programs offered; held on campus; accepts boys and girls; open to students from other schools. 2016 schedule: July to August. Application deadline: March.

Tuition and Aid Day student tuition: £20,420. Tuition installment plan (monthly payment plans, individually arranged payment plans). Bursaries, merit scholarship grants, need-based scholarship grants available.

Admissions Admissions testing or English for Non-native Speakers required. Deadline for receipt of application materials: none. Application fee required: £500. On-campus interview required.

Athletics Interscholastic: badminton (boys, girls), ball hockey (b,g), basketball (b,g), football (b,g), golf (b,g), soccer (b,g), volleyball (b,g); intramural: aerobics (g), aerobics/dance (g), badminton (b,g), ball hockey (b,g), ballet (b,g), baseball (b), basketball (b,g), Circus (b,g), climbing (b,g), football (b,g), handball (b,g), hockey (b,g), lacrosse (b,g), soccer (b,g), softball (b,g), table tennis (b,g), track and field (b,g), ultimate Frisbee (b,g), unicycling (b,g), volleyball (b,g); coed interscholastic: aquatics, archery, badminton, ball hockey, basketball, canoeing/kayaking, Circus, climbing, combined training, cross-country running, field hockey, fitness, kayaking, lacrosse, physical fitness, physical training, roller blading, roller skating, running, skateboarding, softball, swimming and diving, table tennis, tennis, track and field, wall climbing; coed intramural: aquatics, archery, badminton, ball hockey, basketball, bocce, canoeing/kayaking, Circus, climbing, combined training, croquet, cross-country running, fencing, fitness, Frisbee, gymnastics, indoor hockey, juggling, jump rope, kayaking, lacrosse, life saving, martial arts, outdoor activities, outdoor adventure, outdoor education, outdoor recreation, outdoor skills, physical fitness, physical training, roller blading, roller hockey, roller skating, running, skateboarding, soccer, softball, swimming and diving, table tennis, tennis, triathlon, ultimate Frisbee, wall climbing. 4 PE instructors, 10 coaches.

Computers Computers are regularly used in all academic, English, foreign language, mathematics, science classes. Computer network features include on campus library services, Internet access, wireless campus network, Internet filtering or blocking technology. Campus intranet and student e-mail accounts are available to students. Students grades are available online. The school has a published electronic and media policy.

Contact Mrs. Sheila Sibley, Admissions. 44-1224 730300. Fax: 44-1224 865558. E-mail: sheila.sibley@isa.aberdeen.sch.uk. Website: www.isa.aberdeen.sch.uk

INTERNATIONAL SCHOOL OF AMSTERDAM

Sportlaan 45
Amstelveen 1185 TB, Netherlands

Head of School: Dr. Ed Greene

General Information Coeducational day college-preparatory, arts, bilingual studies, and technology school. Grades PS–12. Founded: 1964. Setting: suburban. Nearest major city is Amsterdam, Netherlands. 1-acre campus. 3 buildings on campus. Member of European Council of International Schools. Language of instruction: English. Total enrollment: 1,166. Upper school average class size: 20. Upper school faculty-student ratio: 1:5. There are 181 required school days per year for Upper School students. Upper School students typically attend 5 days per week. The average school day consists of 7 hours.

Upper School Student Profile Grade 9: 79 students (43 boys, 36 girls); Grade 10: 68 students (38 boys, 30 girls); Grade 11: 70 students (41 boys, 29 girls); Grade 12: 56 students (35 boys, 21 girls).

Faculty School total: 180. In upper school: 31 men, 49 women; 28 have advanced degrees.

Subjects Offered Addiction, advanced math, algebra, American literature, art, biology, calculus, chemistry, community service, computer programming, computer science, drama, Dutch, economics, English, English literature, ESL, European history, food science, French, geography, geometry, history, Japanese, Mandarin, mathematics, music, photography, physical education, physics, science, social sciences, social studies, Spanish, technology, theater, theory of knowledge, trigonometry, world history, world literature.

Graduation Requirements Arts, computer science, English, foreign language, mathematics, physical education (includes health), science, social sciences, social studies (includes history). Community service is required.

Special Academic Programs International Baccalaureate program; independent study; academic accommodation for the gifted, the musically talented, and the artistically talented; remedial reading and/or remedial writing; remedial math; programs in English, mathematics, general development for dyslexic students; ESL (23 students enrolled).

College Admission Counseling 61 students graduated in 2014; 38 went to college, including University of Arkansas. Other: 1 entered military service, 9 had other specific plans. Median SAT critical reading: 600, median SAT math: 660, median SAT writing: 610, median combined SAT: 1870. Mean composite ACT: 31. 44% scored over 600 on SAT critical reading, 67% scored over 600 on SAT math, 56% scored over 600 on SAT writing, 61% scored over 1800 on combined SAT, 100% scored over 26 on composite ACT.

Student Life Upper grades have specified standards of dress, student council, honor system. Discipline rests primarily with faculty.

Tuition and Aid Day student tuition: €22,375–€23,050. Tuition installment plan (monthly payment plans, individually arranged payment plans).

Admissions Traditional secondary-level entrance grade is 9. For fall 2014, 100 students applied for upper-level admission, 71 were accepted, 46 enrolled. Deadline for receipt of application materials: none. No application fee required. On-campus interview required.

Athletics Interscholastic: basketball (boys, girls), soccer (b,g), softball (b,g), swimming and diving (b,g), tennis (b,g), track and field (b,g), volleyball (g); coed intramural: aerobics, aerobics/dance, badminton, basketball, cricket, fitness, handball, hockey, netball, rugby, running, soccer, softball, tennis, track and field, volleyball. 7 PE instructors, 14 coaches, 14 athletic trainers.

Computers Computers are regularly used in art, drawing and design, English, foreign language, information technology, keyboarding, library, mathematics, music, science, yearbook classes. Computer network features include on-campus library services, online commercial services, Internet access, wireless campus network, Internet filtering or blocking technology. Campus intranet and student e-mail accounts are available to students.

Contact Julia True, Director of Admissions. 31-20-347-1111. Fax: 31-20-347-1105. E-mail: admissions@isa.nl. Website: www.isa.nl

THE INTERNATIONAL SCHOOL OF KUALA LUMPUR

Jalan Kerja Ayer Lama
Ampang, Selangor 68000, Malaysia
Head of School: Dr. Norma J. Hudson

General Information Coeducational day college-preparatory school. Grades PK–12. Founded: 1965. Setting: suburban. Nearest major city is Kuala Lumpur, Malaysia. 13-acre campus. 1 building on campus. Approved or accredited by Council of International Schools, International Baccalaureate Organization, and Western Association of Schools and Colleges. Language of instruction: English. Total enrollment: 1,591. Upper school average class size: 22. Upper school faculty-student ratio: 1:7. There are 178 required school days per year for Upper School students.

Upper School Student Profile Grade 6: 113 students (51 boys, 62 girls); Grade 7: 135 students (61 boys, 74 girls); Grade 8: 128 students (64 boys, 64 girls); Grade 9: 153 students (85 boys, 68 girls); Grade 10: 147 students (68 boys, 79 girls); Grade 11: 162 students (71 boys, 91 girls); Grade 12: 158 students (71 boys, 87 girls).

Faculty School total: 212. In upper school: 39 men, 40 women.

Subjects Offered Advanced chemistry, advanced math, Advanced Placement courses, anthropology, applied arts, architecture, art, Asian history, biology, calculus-AP, ceramics, chemistry, computer multimedia, computer science, concert band, concert choir, economics, English, English literature, English-AP, environmental science, ESL, film studies, fine arts, French, graphic design, guitar, health, history, information technology, integrated mathematics, integrated science, International Baccalaureate courses, Japanese, jazz band, journalism, Korean, Malay, Mandarin, math analysis, mathematics, music theory, photography, physical education, physics, pre-calculus, psychology, science, Spanish, stagecraft, statistics-AP, theater, theory of knowledge, U.S. history-AP, vocal ensemble, world studies, world wide web design, yearbook.

Graduation Requirements Art, English, foreign language, health, mathematics, physical education (includes health), science, social studies (includes history).

Special Academic Programs International Baccalaureate program; Advanced Placement exam preparation; honors section; accelerated programs; independent study; term-away projects; special instructional classes for students with mild learning disabilities; ESL (100 students enrolled).

College Admission Counseling 143 students graduated in 2014; 137 went to college, including Boston University; McGill University; School of the Art Institute of Chicago; The University of British Columbia; University of Toronto; University of Washington. Other: 1 went to work, 3 entered military service, 2 had other specific

plans. Mean SAT critical reading: 559, mean SAT math: 632, mean SAT writing: 568, mean combined SAT: 1759, mean composite ACT: 25.

Student Life Upper grades have uniform requirement, student council, honor system. Discipline rests primarily with faculty.

Tuition and Aid Day student tuition: 82,810 Malaysian ringgits. Tuition installment plan (individually arranged payment plans). IB scholarships offered to 2 Malaysian students each year available.

Admissions Traditional secondary-level entrance grade is 9. For fall 2014, 282 students applied for upper-level admission, 205 were accepted, 164 enrolled. English for Non-native Speakers, Gates MacGinite Reading Tests or Math Placement Exam required. Deadline for receipt of application materials: none. Application fee required: 960 Malaysian ringgits. Interview recommended.

Athletics Interscholastic: aerobics/dance (boys, girls), aquatics (b,g), badminton (b,g), basketball (b,g), cross-country running (b,g), dance (b,g), dance team (b,g), golf (b,g), rugby (b), running (b,g), soccer (b,g), softball (b,g), swimming and diving (b,g), tennis (b,g), touch football (b,g), track and field (b,g), volleyball (b,g); intramural: aerobics/dance (b,g), aquatics (b,g), badminton (b,g), basketball (b,g), climbing (b,g), cooperative games (b,g), dance (b,g), fitness (b,g), Frisbee (b,g), judo (b,g), martial arts (b,g), outdoor education (b,g), paddle tennis (b,g), physical fitness (b,g), rock climbing (b,g), rugby (b), soccer (b,g), softball (b,g), swimming and diving (b,g), tennis (b,g), touch football (b,g), track and field (b,g), ultimate Frisbee (b,g), volleyball (b,g), water polo (b,g), water volleyball (b,g), weight training (b,g); coed interscholastic: aerobics/dance, aquatics, badminton, climbing, dance, dance team, running, swimming and diving, track and field, triathlon, wall climbing; coed intramural: aerobics, aerobics/dance, aerobics/Nautilus, aquatics, badminton, ball hockey, basketball, climbing, cooperative games, Cosom hockey, cross-country running, dance, field hockey, fitness, flag football, floor hockey, football, Frisbee, golf, kickball, life saving, outdoor activities, outdoor education, outdoor recreation, outdoor skills, paddle tennis, physical fitness, rappelling, rock climbing, self defense, soccer, softball, strength & conditioning, swimming and diving, touch football, track and field, triathlon, ultimate Frisbee, volleyball, wall climbing, weight training, yoga. 4 PE instructors, 67 coaches, 1 athletic trainer.

Computers Computers are regularly used in all academic, computer applications, graphic design, multimedia, newspaper, photography, programming, publications, video film production, Web site design, yearbook classes. Computer network features include on-campus library services, online commercial services, Internet access, wireless campus network, Internet filtering or blocking technology, Microsoft Office. Campus intranet, student e-mail accounts, and computer access in designated common areas are available to students. Students grades are available online. The school has a published electronic and media policy.

Contact Ms. Wendy Wong, Admissions Officer. 603-4259 5600 Ext. 5628. Fax: 603-4259 5738. E-mail: wwongteo@iskl.edu.my. Website: www.iskl.edu.my

INTERNATIONAL SCHOOL OF LUXEMBOURG

36 Boulevard Pierre Dupong
L-1430 Luxembourg, Luxembourg
Head of School: Mrs. Nicki Crush

General Information Coeducational day college-preparatory, arts, bilingual studies, technology, and global issues and awareness school. Grades PK–12. Founded: 1963. Setting: suburban. Nearest major city is Luxembourg City, Luxembourg. 3-acre campus. 2 buildings on campus. Approved or accredited by Council of International Schools, International Baccalaureate Organization, and Middle States Association of Colleges and Schools. Affiliate member of National Association of Independent Schools; member of European Council of International Schools. Language of instruction: English. Total enrollment: 1,356. Upper school average class size: 18. Upper school faculty-student ratio: 1:8. There are 186 required school days per year for Upper School students. The average school day consists of 8 hours.

Upper School Student Profile Grade 6: 108 students (61 boys, 47 girls); Grade 7: 108 students (57 boys, 51 girls); Grade 8: 113 students (61 boys, 52 girls); Grade 9: 100 students (44 boys, 56 girls); Grade 10: 102 students (56 boys, 46 girls); Grade 11: 101 students (52 boys, 49 girls); Grade 12: 92 students (50 boys, 42 girls).

Faculty School total: 153. In upper school: 58 men, 95 women; 70 have advanced degrees.

Subjects Offered Advanced math, algebra, art, art history, biology, chemistry, computers, drama, earth science, English, English literature, ESL, European history, French, geography, geometry, German, health, history, International Baccalaureate courses, mathematics, music, physical education, physics, science, social studies, study skills, theory of knowledge, trigonometry, world history, world literature.

Graduation Requirements English, foreign language, mathematics, physical education (includes health), science, social studies (includes history). Community service is required.

Special Academic Programs International Baccalaureate program; ESL (165 students enrolled).

College Admission Counseling 74 students graduated in 2015; 67 went to college, including McGill University; Northeastern University; University of Victoria; Worcester Polytechnic Institute. Other: 7 had other specific plans. Median SAT critical reading: 570, median SAT math: 610, median SAT writing: 570, median combined SAT: 1770, median composite ACT: 26. 41% scored over 600 on SAT critical reading, 59%

scored over 600 on SAT math, 38% scored over 600 on SAT writing, 44% scored over 1800 on combined SAT, 83% scored over 26 on composite ACT.

Student Life Upper grades have student council, honor system. Discipline rests primarily with faculty.

Tuition and Aid Day student tuition: €18,765.

Admissions For fall 2015, 131 students applied for upper-level admission, 75 were accepted, 60 enrolled. Admissions testing and math and English placement tests required. Deadline for receipt of application materials: none. Application fee required: €300. On-campus interview required.

Athletics Interscholastic: baseball (boys), basketball (b,g), soccer (b,g), swimming and diving (b,g), tennis (b,g), track and field (b,g), volleyball (g); intramural: basketball (b,g), soccer (b,g), track and field (b,g), volleyball (g); coed interscholastic: golf, rugby, skiing (downhill), soccer; coed intramural: badminton, fitness, gymnastics, modern dance, Nautilus, physical fitness, strength & conditioning, swimming and diving, triathlon, weight training. 5 PE instructors.

Computers Computers are regularly used in all academic classes. Computer network features include on-campus library services, Internet access, wireless campus network, Internet filtering or blocking technology. Student e-mail accounts are available to students. Students grades are available online. The school has a published electronic and media policy.

Contact Mrs. Henriette Rosenkvist, Head of Admissions. 352-260440. E-mail: admissions@islux.lu. Website: www.islux.lu

INTERNATIONAL SCHOOL OF PORT-OF-SPAIN

1 International Drive
Westmoorings, Trinidad and Tobago
Head of School: Ms. Annabel Majendie

General Information Coeducational day college-preparatory, general academic, and arts school. Grades PK–12. Founded: 1994. Setting: suburban. Nearest major city is Port of Spain, Trinidad and Tobago. 3-acre campus. 2 buildings on campus. Approved or accredited by Southern Association of Independent Schools. Language of instruction: English. Total enrollment: 466. Upper school average class size: 13. Upper school faculty student ratio: 1:12. There are 180 required school days per year for Upper School students. The average school day consists of 5 hours and 45 minutes.

Upper School Student Profile Grade 9: 41 students (16 boys, 25 girls); Grade 10: 40 students (22 boys, 18 girls); Grade 11: 40 students (17 boys, 23 girls); Grade 12: 50 students (27 boys, 23 girls).

Faculty School total: 29. In upper school: 15 men, 14 women; 13 have advanced degrees.

Subjects Offered Advanced Placement courses, algebra, American history, American history-AP, ancient world history, art, biology, biology-AP, calculus-AP, chemistry, chemistry-AP, computer literacy, computers, contemporary studies, dance, drama, economics, English, English literature and composition-AP, environmental science, French, geometry, human geography - AP, leadership, model United Nations, modern world history, music, physical education, physics, physics-AP, pre-calculus, psychology-AP, Spanish, Spanish language-AP, statistics-AP, studio art-AP, theater arts, theater production, U.S. history, video film production.

Graduation Requirements Algebra, ancient world history, biology, English, foreign language, geometry, modern world history, physical education (includes health), physical science, technology.

Special Academic Programs Advanced Placement exam preparation.

College Admission Counseling 43 students graduated in 2015; 36 went to college, including Boston University; Florida Institute of Technology; Penn State University Park; Savannah College of Art and Design; The University of Texas at Austin; Villanova University. Other: 1 went to work, 6 had other specific plans. Mean SAT critical reading: 535, mean SAT math: 531, mean SAT writing: 531, mean combined SAT: 1597. 25% scored over 600 on SAT critical reading, 17% scored over 600 on SAT math, 25% scored over 600 on SAT writing, 25% scored over 1800 on combined SAT.

Student Life Upper grades have uniform requirement, student council, honor system. Discipline rests primarily with faculty.

Tuition and Aid Day student tuition: $17,927. Merit scholarship grants, need-based scholarship grants available. In 2015–16, 10% of upper-school students received aid; total upper-school merit-scholarship money awarded: $42,000. Total amount of financial aid awarded in 2015–16: $42,000.

Admissions Traditional secondary-level entrance grade is 9. For fall 2015, 45 students applied for upper-level admission, 38 were accepted, 35 enrolled. Math Placement Exam and writing sample required. Deadline for receipt of application materials: none. Application fee required: $100. Interview required.

Athletics Coed Interscholastic: basketball, rugby, soccer, volleyball; coed intramural: archery, baseball, basketball, cheering, cricket, martial arts, rugby, soccer, softball, ultimate Frisbee, volleyball. 3 PE instructors, 1 coach.

Computers Computers are regularly used in all classes. Computer network features include on-campus library services, online commercial services, Internet access. Student e-mail accounts are available to students.

Contact Mrs. Jackie Fung-Kee-Fung, Director of Admission, Communication & Marketing. 868-632-4591 Ext. 411. Fax: 868-632-4033. E-mail: jfungkeefung@isps.edu.tt. Website: www.isps.edu.tt

INTERNATIONAL SCHOOL OF ZUG AND LUZERN (ISZL)

Walterswil
Baar 6340, Switzerland
Head of School: Dominic Currer

General Information Coeducational day college-preparatory, International Baccalaureate (PYP, MYP, DP), and Advanced Placement school. Founded: 1961. Setting: small town. Nearest major city is Zurich, Switzerland. 5-hectare campus. 1 building on campus. Approved or accredited by International Baccalaureate Organization, New England Association of Schools and Colleges, and The College Board. Member of European Council of International Schools. Language of instruction: English. Total enrollment: 1,189. Upper school average class size: 18. Upper school faculty-student ratio: 1:6. There are 180 required school days per year for Upper School students. Upper School students typically attend 5 days per week. The average school day consists of 7 hours.

Faculty School total: 200. In upper school: 16 men, 28 women.

Subjects Offered Art, art history-AP, biology, biology-AP, calculus-AP, chemistry, chemistry-AP, computer graphics, computer science-AP, dance, drama, English, English language and composition-AP, English literature and composition-AP, environmental science-AP, ESL, European history-AP, French, French language-AP, German, German-AP, human geography - AP, humanities, integrated mathematics, integrated science, macro/microeconomics-AP, music, physical education, physics, physics-AP, pre-calculus, studio art-AP, technology/design.

Graduation Requirements Art, art history-AP, biology-AP, calculus-AP, chemistry-AP, choir, college counseling, computer programming-AP, computer science-AP, computers, dance, drama, economics-AP, English, English language-AP, English literature-AP, environmental science-AP, ESL, European history-AP, foreign language, French, French language-AP, German, German-AP, health education, human geography - AP, International Baccalaureate courses, lab science, macro/microeconomics-AP, macroeconomics-AP, mathematics, model United Nations, modern European history-AP, music, physical education (includes health), physics-AP, pre-calculus, SAT/ACT preparation, social sciences, Spanish, studio art-AP, yearbook. Community service is required.

Special Academic Programs International Baccalaureate program; Advanced Placement exam preparation; accelerated programs; independent study; ESL (40 students enrolled).

College Admission Counseling 33 students graduated in 2015; 26 went to college, including Pace University; Pepperdine University; Stanford University; Villanova University; Yale University. Other: 3 entered a postgraduate year, 4 had other specific plans.

Student Life Upper grades have specified standards of dress, student council. Discipline rests primarily with faculty.

Summer Programs ESL, sports, rigorous outdoor training programs offered; session focuses on sports and language; held both on and off campus; held at outdoor Activity Centre; accepts boys and girls; not open to students from other schools.

Tuition and Aid Day student tuition: 21,500 Swiss francs–32,000 Swiss francs. Tuition installment plan (monthly payment plans, individually arranged payment plans, semester payment plan). Discounts for children of staff and reciprocal arrangements with international primary school available.

Admissions English for Non-native Speakers or math and English placement tests required. Deadline for receipt of application materials: none. Application fee required: 5000 Swiss francs. Interview recommended.

Athletics Interscholastic: aerobics/dance (girls), alpine skiing (b,g), basketball (b,g), cross-country running (b,g), golf (b,g), indoor soccer (b,g), rugby (b), skiing (downhill) (b,g), soccer (b,g), swimming and diving (b,g), track and field (b,g), volleyball (b,g); intramural: alpine skiing (b,g), basketball (b,g), cross-country running (b,g), indoor soccer (b,g), soccer (b,g), track and field (b,g); coed interscholastic: canoeing/kayaking, climbing, softball; coed intramural: aerobics/dance, backpacking, badminton, ball hockey, bicycling, canoeing/kayaking, climbing, dance, field hockey, golf, hiking/backpacking, ice skating, kayaking, martial arts, mountain biking, outdoor activities, outdoor education, racquetball, rowing, running, sailing, skiing (downhill), snowboarding, soccer, softball, swimming and diving, tennis, walking, winter walking. 2 PE instructors, 2 coaches, 2 athletic trainers.

Computers Computers are regularly used in college planning classes. Computer network features include Internet access, Internet filtering or blocking technology. Campus intranet, student e-mail accounts, and computer access in designated common areas are available to students. The school has a published electronic and media policy.

Contact Urs Kappeler, Business Director. 41-41-768 2950. Fax: 41-41-768 2951. E-mail: urs.kappeler@iszl.ch. Website: www.iszl.ch

INTERNATIONAL SCHOOL SINGAPORE

21 Preston Road
Singapore 109355, Singapore
Head of School: Dr. Margaret Alvarez

General Information Coeducational day college-preparatory, arts, business, and technology school. Grades K–12. Founded: 1981. Setting: urban. 5 buildings on campus. Approved or accredited by Council of International Schools, International

Baccalaureate Organization, Ministry of Education, Singapore, and Western Association of Schools and Colleges. Member of European Council of International Schools. Language of instruction: English. Upper school average class size: 20. Upper school faculty-student ratio: 1:10. Upper School students typically attend 5 days per week. The average school day consists of 7 hours and 30 minutes.

Faculty School total: 75. In upper school: 23 men, 44 women; 22 have advanced degrees.

Subjects Offered Algebra, American history, art, art history, biology, business, business skills, chemistry, Chinese, computer science, creative writing, dance, drama, economics, English, environmental science, ESL, European history, expository writing, fine arts, French, geography, geometry, health, history, Japanese, keyboarding, mathematics, music, physical education, physics, science, social studies, speech, theater, world history, world literature, writing.

Graduation Requirements Arts and fine arts (art, music, dance, drama), computer science, English, foreign language, mathematics, physical education (includes health), science, social studies (includes history), participation in annual interim semester program (activity week), satisfactory completion of a 2-year balance extra curricular program.

Special Academic Programs International Baccalaureate program; honors section; accelerated programs; independent study; academic accommodation for the gifted; remedial reading and/or remedial writing; remedial math; programs in English, mathematics, general development for dyslexic students; ESL (62 students enrolled).

College Admission Counseling 47 students graduated in 2014; 42 went to college, including Pepperdine University; Queen's University at Kingston; University of California, Davis; University of Michigan; University of Toronto. Other: 5 entered military service.

Student Life Upper grades have uniform requirement, student council, honor system. Discipline rests equally with students and faculty.

Tuition and Aid Day student tuition: 10,000 Singapore dollars–21,000 Singapore dollars. Tuition installment plan (monthly payment plans, individually arranged payment plans). Tuition reduction for siblings, discount for third child in family available. In 2014–15, 3% of upper-school students received aid.

Admissions Traditional secondary-level entrance grade is 9. Macalaitus Test of English or school's own exam required. Deadline for receipt of application materials: none. Application fee required: 1545 Singapore dollars. Interview recommended.

Athletics Interscholastic: badminton (boys, girls), baseball (b), basketball (b,g), cross-country running (b,g), football (b,g), netball (g), rugby (b), soccer (b,g), tennis (b,g), track and field (b,g), volleyball (b,g); intramural: aerobics/dance (b,g), badminton (b,g), basketball (b,g), bicycling (b,g), cross-country running (b,g), dance (b,g), fitness (b,g), football (b,g), golf (b,g), hiking/backpacking (b,g), independent competitive sports (b,g), modern dance (b,g), netball (g), outdoor activities (b,g), outdoor adventure (b,g), outdoor education (b,g), outdoor recreation (b,g), outdoor skills (b,g), physical fitness (b,g), physical training (b,g), rugby (b,g), sailing (b,g), scuba diving (b,g), soccer (b,g), swimming and diving (b,g), table tennis (b,g), track and field (b,g), volleyball (b,g); coed interscholastic: Frisbee, netball, ultimate Frisbee, volleyball; coed intramural: backpacking, badminton, canoeing/kayaking, climbing, dance, fitness, Frisbee, hiking/backpacking, jogging, modern dance, netball, outdoor activities, outdoor adventure, outdoor education, outdoor recreation, outdoor skills, physical fitness, physical training, rugby, table tennis, ultimate Frisbee, volleyball. 2 PE instructors, 2 coaches.

Computers Computers are regularly used in art, business education, economics, English, ESL, French, French as a second language, geography, history, humanities, library, mathematics, music, science, social sciences, Spanish classes. Computer network features include on-campus library services, online commercial services, Internet access, wireless campus network. Student e-mail accounts are available to students. Students grades are available online. The school has a published electronic and media policy.

Contact Ms. Angelia Toh, Director of Admissions. 65-6475-4188 Ext. 438. Fax: 65-6273-7065. E-mail: admissions@iss.edu.sg. Website: www.iss.edu.sg

IOLANI SCHOOL

563 Kamoku Street
Honolulu, Hawaii 96826

Head of School: Dr. Timothy Cottrell

General Information Coeducational day college-preparatory, arts, and technology school, affiliated with Episcopal Church. Grades K–12. Founded: 1863. Setting: urban. 25-acre campus. 8 buildings on campus. Approved or accredited by National Association of Episcopal Schools, Western Association of Schools and Colleges, and Hawaii Department of Education. Member of National Association of Independent Schools and Secondary School Admission Test Board. Endowment: $100 million. Total enrollment: 1,885. Upper school average class size: 16. Upper school faculty-student ratio: 1:12. There are 178 required school days per year for Upper School students. Upper School students typically attend 5 days per week. The average school day consists of 6 hours.

Upper School Student Profile Grade 7: 181 students (84 boys, 97 girls); Grade 8: 196 students (99 boys, 97 girls); Grade 9: 244 students (120 boys, 124 girls); Grade 10: 242 students (113 boys, 129 girls); Grade 11: 233 students (109 boys, 124 girls); Grade 12: 230 students (114 boys, 116 girls).

Faculty School total: 185. In upper school: 63 men, 68 women; 90 have advanced degrees.

Subjects Offered 3-dimensional design, Advanced Placement courses, advanced studio art-AP, African American history, algebra, American history, American history-AP, American literature, American literature-AP, art, Asian studies, band, Basic programming, Bible, Bible studies, biology, biology-AP, British literature, calculus, calculus-AP, ceramics, chemistry, chemistry-AP, Chinese, chorus, computer programming, computer programming-AP, computer science, computer science-AP, conceptual physics, concert band, creative writing, dance, drama, earth science, economics, economics-AP, English, English as a foreign language, English language and composition-AP, English literature, English literature and composition-AP, English literature-AP, European history, European history-AP, expository writing, film and literature, fine arts, French, French language-AP, French literature-AP, geography, geometry, government-AP, government/civics, Hawaiian history, health, health education, history, Japanese, Japanese studies, jazz band, jazz ensemble, journalism, Latin, Latin-AP, leadership, macro/microeconomics-AP, macroeconomics-AP, Mandarin, marching band, mathematics, money management, music, newspaper, orchestra, photography, physical education, physics, physics-AP, pre-calculus, psychology, psychology-AP, religion, science, Shakespeare, social studies, Spanish, Spanish-AP, speech, statistics, statistics-AP, studio art-AP, theater, trigonometry, U.S. government and politics-AP, Web site design, world affairs, world history, world literature, writing.

Graduation Requirements Algebra, arts and fine arts (art, music, dance, drama), Bible, biology, chemistry, computer science, English, European history, foreign language, geometry, literature, physical education (includes health), physics, U.S. history.

Special Academic Programs Advanced Placement exam preparation; honors section; independent study; academic accommodation for the gifted, the musically talented, and the artistically talented.

College Admission Counseling 223 students graduated in 2014; all went to college, including Oregon State University; Santa Clara University; University of Hawaii at Manoa; University of Southern California; University of Washington.

Student Life Upper grades have specified standards of dress, student council. Discipline rests primarily with faculty. Attendance at religious services is required.

Tuition and Aid Day student tuition: $20,100. Tuition installment plan (monthly payment plans, semester and annual payment plans). Need-based scholarship grants available. In 2014–15, 23% of upper-school students received aid. Total amount of financial aid awarded in 2014–15: $3,900,000.

Admissions Traditional secondary-level entrance grade is 7. For fall 2014, 696 students applied for upper-level admission, 188 were accepted, 132 enrolled. SSAT required. Deadline for receipt of application materials: December 1. Application fee required: $125. Interview recommended.

Athletics Interscholastic: aerobics/dance (girls), baseball (b), basketball (b,g), bowling (b,g), canoeing/kayaking (b,g), cross-country running (b,g), dance (b,g), dance team (g), diving (b,g), football (b), kayaking (b,g), modern dance (g), ocean paddling (b,g), soccer (b,g), softball (g), strength & conditioning (b,g), swimming and diving (b,g), tennis (b,g), track and field (b,g), volleyball (b,g), water polo (b,g), weight training (b,g), wrestling (b,g); coed interscholastic: ballet, cheering, golf, judo, tennis. 6 PE instructors, 170 coaches, 3 athletic trainers.

Computers Computers are regularly used in all academic classes. Computer network features include on-campus library services, online commercial services, Internet access, wireless campus network, Internet filtering or blocking technology. Student e-mail accounts and computer access in designated common areas are available to students. The school has a published electronic and media policy.

Contact Kelly Monaco, Director of Admission. 808-949-5355. Fax: 808-943-2375. E-mail: admission@iolani.org. Website: www.iolani.org

ISIDORE NEWMAN SCHOOL

1903 Jefferson Avenue
New Orleans, Louisiana 70115

Head of School: Dr. Dale M. Smith

General Information Coeducational day college-preparatory school. Grades PK–12. Founded: 1903. Setting: urban. 11-acre campus. 10 buildings on campus. Approved or accredited by Independent Schools Association of the Southwest and Louisiana Department of Education. Member of National Association of Independent Schools and Secondary School Admission Test Board. Endowment: $3.3 million. Total enrollment: 1,005. Upper school average class size: 16. Upper school faculty-student ratio: 1:17. There are 175 required school days per year for Upper School students. Upper School students typically attend 5 days per week. The average school day consists of 7 hours and 50 minutes.

Subjects Offered Advanced computer applications, Advanced Placement courses, algebra, American history, American history-AP, American literature, anatomy, art, art history, biology, biology-AP, calculus, calculus-AP, ceramics, chemistry, Chinese, choral music, chorus, civics, communications, computer science-AP, dance, drama, English, English literature, environmental science, European history-AP, film, film history, fine arts, French, French language-AP, French literature-AP, French-AP, genetics, geometry, government/civics, history, human development, humanities, Latin, Latin-AP, mathematics, modern European history, modern European history-AP, music,

music theory, peer counseling, photojournalism, physical education, physics, physics-AP, physiology, science, sculpture, social studies, Spanish, Spanish language-AP, Spanish literature-AP, speech, statistics-AP, technical theater, theater, trigonometry, U.S. government and politics-AP, U.S. history, U.S. history-AP, world history.

Graduation Requirements Arts and fine arts (art, music, dance, drama), computer science, English, foreign language, mathematics, physical education (includes health), science, social studies (includes history), speech, senior Capstone Elective–one class each semester of senior year.

Special Academic Programs Advanced Placement exam preparation; honors section; independent study; term-away projects.

Student Life Upper grades have specified standards of dress, student council, honor system. Discipline rests equally with students and faculty.

Summer Programs Remediation, enrichment, sports, art/fine arts, computer instruction programs offered; held on campus; accepts boys and girls; open to students from other schools. 2016 schedule: June to July. Application deadline: none.

Tuition and Aid Tuition installment plan (Sallie Mae tuition loans). Need-based scholarship grants, Sallie Mae loans available.

Admissions Traditional secondary-level entrance grade is 9. ERB (CTP-Verbal, Quantitative), ERB CTP III, independent norms, Individual IQ, Achievement and behavior rating scale, ISEE, school's own test and writing sample required. Deadline for receipt of application materials: none. Application fee required: $50. Interview required.

Athletics Interscholastic: aquatics (boys, girls), baseball (b), basketball (b,g), cross-country running (b,g), football (b), golf (b,g), gymnastics (b,g), indoor track & field (b), soccer (b,g), softball (g), swimming and diving (b,g), tennis (b,g), track and field (b,g), volleyball (g); coed interscholastic: cheering. 2 athletic trainers.

Computers Computers are regularly used in all academic classes. Computer network features include on-campus library services, online commercial services, Internet access, wireless campus network, Internet filtering or blocking technology. Campus intranet and student e-mail accounts are available to students. Students grades are available online. The school has a published electronic and media policy.

Contact Mrs. Kenley Breckenridge, Admission Coordinator. 504-896-6323. Fax: 504-896-8597. E-mail: kenleybreckenridge@newmanschool.org. Website: www.newmanschool.org

JACKSON CHRISTIAN SCHOOL

832 Country Club Lane
Jackson, Tennessee 38305

Head of School: Dr. Mark Benton

General Information Coeducational day college-preparatory, arts, religious studies, bilingual studies, and technology school, affiliated with Church of Christ. Grades JK–12. Founded: 1976. Setting: suburban. 30-acre campus. 6 buildings on campus. Approved or accredited by National Christian School Association, Southern Association of Colleges and Schools, and Tennessee Department of Education. Endowment: $875,000. Total enrollment: 857. Upper school average class size: 19. Upper school faculty-student ratio: 1:19. There are 180 required school days per year for Upper School students. Upper School students typically attend 5 days per week. The average school day consists of 6 hours.

Upper School Student Profile Grade 6: 86 students (39 boys, 47 girls); Grade 7: 72 students (41 boys, 31 girls); Grade 8: 58 students (30 boys, 28 girls); Grade 9: 79 students (40 boys, 39 girls); Grade 10: 60 students (28 boys, 32 girls); Grade 11: 77 students (38 boys, 39 girls); Grade 12: 70 students (40 boys, 30 girls). 34% of students are members of Church of Christ.

Faculty School total: 65. In upper school: 14 men, 24 women; 13 have advanced degrees.

Subjects Offered Advanced chemistry, advanced computer applications, algebra, American government, American history, anatomy and physiology, art, baseball, basketball, Bible, Bible studies, biology, calculus, chemistry, choir, chorus, current events, ecology, economics, English, English composition, geometry, government, government/civics, honors English, journalism, keyboarding, life science, physical education, physical science, physics, pre-calculus, psychology, Spanish, state history, theater, theater arts, trigonometry, U.S. government, U.S. history, world geography, world history.

Graduation Requirements 20th century world history, arts and fine arts (art, music, dance, drama), English, foreign language, mathematics, physical education (includes health), religion (includes Bible studies and theology), science, social studies (includes history), must take the ACT test.

Special Academic Programs Honors section; study at local college for college credit; programs in English, mathematics for dyslexic students.

College Admission Counseling 68 students graduated in 2015; 66 went to college, including Freed-Hardeman University; Harding University; Jackson State Community College; The University of Tennessee at Chattanooga; Union University. Other: 2 went to work. Median composite ACT: 24. 35% scored over 26 on composite ACT.

Student Life Upper grades have uniform requirement, student council, honor system. Discipline rests primarily with faculty.

Summer Programs Remediation programs offered; session focuses on make-up failed courses; held on campus; accepts boys and girls; not open to students from other schools. 8 students usually enrolled. 2016 schedule: June to July.

Tuition and Aid Day student tuition: $7200. Tuition installment plan (FACTS Tuition Payment Plan, monthly payment plans, individually arranged payment plans, quarterly payment plan, semester payment plan, pay-in-full discount). Tuition reduction for siblings, need-based scholarship grants available. In 2015–16, 15% of upper-school students received aid. Total amount of financial aid awarded in 2015–16: $15,218.

Admissions Traditional secondary-level entrance grade is 9. For fall 2015, 40 students applied for upper-level admission, 32 were accepted, 31 enrolled. Math and English placement tests required. Deadline for receipt of application materials: none. Application fee required: $100. Interview required.

Athletics Interscholastic: baseball (boys), basketball (b,g), cheering (g), cross-country running (b,g), football (b), golf (b,g), soccer (b,g), softball (g), tennis (b,g), track and field (b,g); coed interscholastic: cheering. 3 PE instructors, 10 coaches.

Computers Computers are regularly used in business applications, computer applications, desktop publishing, library, multimedia, programming, science, Web site design classes. Computer network features include online commercial services, Internet access, wireless campus network, Internet filtering or blocking technology. Campus intranet, student e-mail accounts, and computer access in designated common areas are available to students. Students grades are available online. The school has a published electronic and media policy.

Contact Jill Joiner, Director of Admissions. 731-300-4578. Fax: 731-664-5763. E-mail: jill.joiner@jcseagles.org. Website: www.jcseagles.org

JACKSON PREPARATORY SCHOOL

3100 Lakeland Drive
Jackson, Mississippi 39232

Head of School: Dr. Jason L. Walton, PhD

General Information Coeducational day college-preparatory school. Grades 6–12. Founded: 1970. Setting: urban. 74-acre campus. 6 buildings on campus. Approved or accredited by Mississippi Private School Association, Southern Association of Colleges and Schools, Southern Association of Independent Schools, and The College Board. Member of National Association of Independent Schools. Endowment: $993,373. Total enrollment: 806. Upper school average class size: 17. Upper school faculty-student ratio: 1:13. There are 176 required school days per year for Upper School students. Upper School students typically attend 5 days per week. The average school day consists of 6 hours and 45 minutes.

Upper School Student Profile Grade 10: 136 students (71 boys, 65 girls); Grade 11: 125 students (54 boys, 71 girls); Grade 12: 118 students (61 boys, 57 girls).

Faculty School total: 90. In upper school: 26 men, 49 women; 42 have advanced degrees.

Subjects Offered Accounting, advanced chemistry, Advanced Placement courses, algebra, American government, American history, American history-AP, American literature, art, Asian studies, Bible as literature, biology, biology-AP, British literature, calculus, calculus-AP, chemistry, chemistry-AP, choral music, civics, classical studies, computer science, creative writing, debate, discrete mathematics, drama, driver education, earth science, economics, English, English literature, English literature-AP, European history, film, fine arts, finite math, French, geography, geometry, government AP, government/civics, grammar, Greek, Greek culture, history, honors algebra, honors English, honors geometry, journalism, Latin, Latin-AP, mathematics, music, physical education, physics, physics-AP, pre-algebra, pre-calculus, science, social studies, Spanish, trigonometry, U.S. government, U.S. government and politics-AP, U.S. history, U.S. history-AP, world history, world literature.

Graduation Requirements Arts and fine arts (art, music, dance, drama), computer applications, English, foreign language, mathematics, science, social studies (includes history).

Special Academic Programs Advanced Placement exam preparation; honors section; academic accommodation for the gifted, the musically talented, and the artistically talented; programs in English, mathematics, general development for dyslexic students.

College Admission Counseling 129 students graduated in 2014; all went to college, including Louisiana State University in Shreveport; Millsaps College; Mississippi College; Mississippi State University; The University of Alabama; University of Mississippi. Mean SAT critical reading: 610, mean SAT math: 615, mean SAT writing: 580, mean composite ACT: 26. 48% scored over 26 on composite ACT.

Student Life Upper grades have uniform requirement, student council, honor system. Discipline rests primarily with faculty.

Tuition and Aid Day student tuition: $12,543. Tuition installment plan (monthly payment plans). Need-based scholarship grants available. In 2014–15, 12% of upper-school students received aid. Total amount of financial aid awarded in 2014–15: $195,000.

Admissions Traditional secondary-level entrance grade is 10. For fall 2014, 15 students applied for upper-level admission, 9 were accepted, 7 enrolled. Nonstandardized placement tests and OLSAT, Stanford Achievement Test required. Deadline for receipt of application materials: none. Application fee required: $40. Interview required.

Athletics Interscholastic: baseball (boys), basketball (b,g), cheering (g), cross-country running (b,g), dance team (g), football (b), Frisbee (b), soccer (b,g), softball (g), swimming and diving (b,g), tennis (b,g), track and field (b,g), ultimate Frisbee (b), volleyball (g); intramural: basketball (b,g), Frisbee (b), soccer (b,g), volleyball (b,g); coed interscholastic: cheering, golf. 4 coaches.

Computers Computers are regularly used in all classes. Computer network features include on-campus library services, online commercial services, Internet access, Electric Library, EBSCOhost®, GaleNet, Grolier Online, NewsBank, online subscription services. The school has a published electronic and media policy.

Contact Lesley W. Morton, Director of Admission. 601-932-8106 Ext. 1. Fax: 601-936-4068. E-mail: lmorton@jacksonprep.net. Website: www.jacksonprep.net

JEAN AND SAMUEL FRANKEL JEWISH ACADEMY OF METROPOLITAN DETROIT

6600 West Maple Road
West Bloomfield, Michigan 48322

Head of School: Rabbi Azaryah Cohen

General Information Coeducational day college-preparatory, arts, business, and religious studies school, affiliated with Jewish faith. Grades 9–12. Founded: 2000. Setting: suburban. Nearest major city is West Bloomfield-Metro Detroit. 1 building on campus. Approved or accredited by Independent Schools Association of the Central States and Michigan Department of Education. Member of National Association of Independent Schools. Languages of instruction: English and Hebrew. Upper school average class size: 13. The average school day consists of 8 hours.

Upper School Student Profile Grade 9: 60 students (30 boys, 30 girls); Grade 10: 60 students (30 boys, 30 girls); Grade 11: 60 students (30 boys, 30 girls); Grade 12: 60 students (30 boys, 30 girls). 100% of students are Jewish.

Faculty In upper school: 30 have advanced degrees.

Special Academic Programs Advanced Placement exam preparation; honors section; study abroad; academic accommodation for the gifted; remedial reading and/or remedial writing; remedial math; special instructional classes for deaf students, blind students.

College Admission Counseling 56 went to college, including Michigan State University; University of Michigan–Dearborn.

Student Life Upper grades have specified standards of dress, student council, honor system. Discipline rests primarily with faculty. Attendance at religious services is required.

Tuition and Aid Day student tuition: $21,000. Tuition reduction for siblings, need-based scholarship grants available.

Admissions Traditional secondary-level entrance grade is 9. High School Placement Test required. Deadline for receipt of application materials: January 30. Application fee required: $100. Interview required.

Athletics 2 PE instructors, 8 coaches.

Computers Computer network features include on-campus library services, online commercial services, Internet access, wireless campus network, all students are given issued an iPad. Campus intranet and student e-mail accounts are available to students. Students grades are available online. The school has a published electronic and media policy.

Contact Lisa Gilan, Director of Admissions. 248-592-5263. Fax: 248-592-0022. E-mail: lgilan@frankelja.org. Website: www.frankelja.org/

JESUIT COLLEGE PREPARATORY SCHOOL

12345 Inwood Road
Dallas, Texas 75244

Head of School: Mr. Tom Garrison

General Information Boys' day college-preparatory school, affiliated with Roman Catholic Church (Jesuit order). Grades 9–12. Founded: 1942. Setting: suburban. 27-acre campus. 2 buildings on campus. Approved or accredited by Jesuit Secondary Education Association, National Catholic Education Association, Southern Association of Colleges and Schools, Texas Catholic Conference, and Texas Department of Education. Endowment: $25.6 million. Total enrollment: 1,107. Upper school average class size: 17. Upper school faculty-student ratio: 1:11. There are 190 required school days per year for Upper School students. Upper School students typically attend 5 days per week. The average school day consists of 6 hours.

Upper School Student Profile Grade 9: 285 students (285 boys); Grade 10: 277 students (277 boys); Grade 11: 271 students (271 boys); Grade 12: 274 students (274 boys). 81% of students are Roman Catholic Church (Jesuit order).

Faculty School total: 115. In upper school: 85 men, 30 women; 56 have advanced degrees.

Subjects Offered Advanced chemistry, advanced computer applications, advanced math, American literature-AP, American studies, art, art appreciation, art-AP, arts, band, Bible, biology, biology-AP, British literature, British literature-AP, calculus, calculus-AP, Catholic belief and practice, ceramics, chemistry, chemistry-AP, choir, Christian ethics, church history, civics, college counseling, community service, composition, composition-AP, computer applications, computer graphics, computer science, computer science-AP, contemporary issues, discrete mathematics, drama, drama performance, drama workshop, drawing, drawing and design, driver education, earth science, economics, economics-AP, English, English composition, English language and composition-AP, English language-AP, English literature, English literature and composition-AP, English literature-AP, English-AP, English/composition-AP, ethical decision making, European history, fine arts, French, French-AP, general science, geometry, government, government-AP, grammar, guitar, health, history, history-AP, honors algebra, honors English, honors geometry, honors U.S. history, honors world history, instrumental music, jazz band, journalism, Latin, literature and composition-AP, marching band, mathematics, mathematics-AP, microcomputer technology applications, music, music appreciation, musical productions, orchestra, peace and justice, peer ministry, performing arts, physical education, physics, physics-AP, pottery, prayer/spirituality, pre-calculus, psychology, public speaking, publications, religion, scripture, social studies, Spanish, Spanish language-AP, Spanish literature-AP, Spanish-AP, speech, speech and debate, speech and oral interpretations, statistics, student government, student publications, studio art, studio art-AP, symphonic band, theater, theology, U.S. government, U.S. government and politics-AP, U.S. history, U.S. history-AP, U.S. literature, world history, world history-AP.

Graduation Requirements Arts and fine arts (art, music, dance, drama), computer science, English, foreign language, mathematics, physical education (includes health), science, social studies (includes history), theology. Community service is required.

Special Academic Programs 18 Advanced Placement exams for which test preparation is offered; honors section; independent study; study at local college for college credit.

College Admission Counseling 256 students graduated in 2015; 254 went to college, including Saint Louis University; Southern Methodist University; Texas A&M University; Texas Christian University; The University of Alabama; The University of Texas at Austin. Other: 2 had other specific plans. Mean SAT critical reading: 598, mean SAT math: 618, mean SAT writing: 595.

Student Life Upper grades have specified standards of dress, student council, honor system. Discipline rests primarily with faculty. Attendance at religious services is required.

Summer Programs Remediation, enrichment, advancement, sports, art/fine arts, computer instruction programs offered; session focuses on youth recreation; held on campus; accepts boys and girls; open to students from other schools. 800 students usually enrolled. 2016 schedule: June 15 to July 10. Application deadline: May 30.

Tuition and Aid Day student tuition: $16,300. Tuition installment plan (FACTS Tuition Payment Plan). Merit scholarship grants, need-based scholarship grants, paying campus jobs available. In 2015–16, 25% of upper-school students received aid; total upper-school merit-scholarship money awarded: $56,000. Total amount of financial aid awarded in 2015–16: $1,233,850.

Admissions Traditional secondary-level entrance grade is 9. For fall 2015, 525 students applied for upper-level admission, 326 were accepted, 285 enrolled. ISEE required. Deadline for receipt of application materials: January 15. Application fee required: $100. Interview required.

Athletics Interscholastic: baseball, basketball, bowling, crew, cross-country running, diving, fencing, football, golf, ice hockey, lacrosse, power lifting, rugby, soccer, swimming and diving, tennis, track and field, volleyball, water polo, wrestling; intramural: basketball, bicycling, broomball, flagball, floor hockey, indoor soccer, ultimate Frisbee, volleyball; coed interscholastic: cheering, drill team. 6 PE instructors, 30 coaches, 2 athletic trainers.

Computers Computers are regularly used in college planning, desktop publishing, digital applications, engineering, English, foreign language, graphic design, graphics, humanities, introduction to technology, journalism, literary magazine, mathematics, media production, multimedia, newspaper, programming, publications, science, social studies, technology, video film production, Web site design, writing, yearbook classes. Computer network features include on-campus library services, online commercial services, Internet access, wireless campus network, Internet filtering or blocking technology. Campus intranet, student e-mail accounts, and computer access in designated common areas are available to students. Students grades are available online. The school has a published electronic and media policy.

Contact Mrs. Marueen Miramontes, Admissions Assistant. 972-387-8700 Ext. 453. Fax: 972-980-6707. E-mail: mmiramontes@jesuitcp.org. Website: www.jesuitcp.org

JESUIT HIGH SCHOOL OF TAMPA

4701 North Himes Avenue
Tampa, Florida 33614-6694

Head of School: Mr. Barry Neuburger

General Information Boys' day college-preparatory school, affiliated with Roman Catholic Church. Grades 9–12. Founded: 1899. Setting: urban. 40-acre campus. 9 buildings on campus. Approved or accredited by Jesuit Secondary Education Association, National Catholic Education Association, Southern Association of Colleges and Schools, and Florida Department of Education. Total enrollment: 775. Upper school average class size: 20. Upper school faculty-student ratio: 1:12. There are 178 required school days per year for Upper School students. Upper School students typically attend 5 days per week. The average school day consists of 7 hours and 23 minutes.

Upper School Student Profile Grade 9: 196 students (196 boys); Grade 10: 208 students (208 boys); Grade 11: 181 students (181 boys); Grade 12: 190 students (190 boys). 80% of students are Roman Catholic.

Faculty School total: 62. In upper school: 44 men, 18 women; 42 have advanced degrees.

Subjects Offered Algebra, American foreign policy, American government, American history, analytic geometry, anatomy, ancient world history, art, biology, biology-AP, calculus, calculus-AP, chemistry, chemistry-AP, chorus, computer programming, computer science, computer science-AP, economics, English, English language and composition-AP, English literature and composition-AP, environmental science, ethics, European history-AP, French, geometry, health, human geography - AP, journalism, Latin, Latin-AP, marine biology, music, physical education, physics, physics-AP, physiology, pre-calculus, psychology-AP, Spanish, Spanish language-AP, speech, statistics-AP, studio art-AP, theology, trigonometry, U.S. government and politics-AP, U.S. history-AP, world history, world history-AP.

Graduation Requirements Arts and fine arts (art, music, dance, drama), English, foreign language, mathematics, physical education (includes health), science, social studies (includes history), theology, 150 hours of community service.

Special Academic Programs 16 Advanced Placement exams for which test preparation is offered; honors section.

College Admission Counseling 178 students graduated in 2015; all went to college, including Florida State University; The University of Tampa; University of Central Florida; University of Florida; University of Miami; University of South Florida. Median SAT critical reading: 600, median SAT math: 620, median SAT writing: 600, median combined SAT: 1785, median composite ACT: 27. 48% scored over 600 on SAT critical reading, 61% scored over 600 on SAT math, 46% scored over 600 on SAT writing, 46% scored over 1800 on combined SAT, 51% scored over 26 on composite ACT.

Student Life Upper grades have specified standards of dress, student council. Discipline rests primarily with faculty. Attendance at religious services is required.

Summer Programs Remediation programs offered; session focuses on remediation; held on campus; accepts boys; not open to students from other schools. 60 students usually enrolled. 2016 schedule: June 13 to July 15.

Tuition and Aid Day student tuition: $14,400. Tuition installment plan (FACTS Tuition Payment Plan). Merit scholarship grants, need-based scholarship grants available. In 2015–16, 25% of upper-school students received aid; total upper-school merit-scholarship money awarded: $28,800. Total amount of financial aid awarded in 2015–16: $1,687,085.

Admissions Traditional secondary-level entrance grade is 9. For fall 2015, 394 students applied for upper-level admission, 235 were accepted, 196 enrolled. High School Placement Test (closed version) from Scholastic Testing Service required. Deadline for receipt of application materials: January 9. Application fee required: $50.

Athletics Interscholastic: baseball, basketball, bowling, cross-country running, football, golf, ice hockey, lacrosse, soccer, swimming and diving, tennis, track and field, wrestling; intramural: basketball, football, Frisbee, kickball, softball, ultimate Frisbee. 1 PE instructor, 4 coaches, 1 athletic trainer.

Computers Computers are regularly used in all academic classes. Computer network features include on-campus library services, online commercial services, Internet access, wireless campus network, Internet filtering or blocking technology, 1:1 iPad program, Learning Management Systems—Canvas. Campus intranet, student e-mail accounts, and computer access in designated common areas are available to students. Students grades are available online. The school has a published electronic and media policy.

Contact Mr. Steve Matesich, Director of Admissions. 813-877-5344 Ext. 509. Fax: 813-872-1853. E-mail: smatesich@jesuittampa.org. Website: www.jesuittampa.org

JEWISH COMMUNITY HIGH SCHOOL OF THE BAY

1835 Ellis Street
San Francisco, California 94115

Head of School: Rabbi Howard Ruben

General Information College-preparatory, arts, religious studies, and bilingual studies school, affiliated with Jewish faith. Founded: 2001. Setting: urban. 1 building on campus. Approved or accredited by California Association of Independent Schools, Western Association of Schools and Colleges, and California Department of Education. Member of National Association of Independent Schools. Languages of instruction: English, Hebrew, and Spanish. Upper school average class size: 14.

Upper School Student Profile 100% of students are Jewish.

Special Academic Programs Advanced Placement exam preparation; honors section.

Student Life Upper grades have specified standards of dress, student council. Discipline rests primarily with faculty. Attendance at religious services is required.

Admissions Deadline for receipt of application materials: January 14. Application fee required: $90. On-campus interview required.

Athletics Interscholastic: basketball (boys, girls), soccer (b,g), volleyball (g); coed interscholastic: baseball, cross-country running, swimming and diving, tennis; coed intramural: dance team, ultimate Frisbee, yoga.

Computers Computer resources include on-campus library services, online commercial services, Internet access, wireless campus network, Internet filtering or blocking technology. Campus Intranet, student e-mail accounts, and computer access in designated common areas are available to students. Students grades are available online. The school has a published electronic and media policy.

Contact Michelle Kushnir, Admissions Assistant. 415-345-9777 Ext. 112. Fax: 415-345-1888. E-mail: rbuonaiuto@jchsofthebay.org. Website: www.jchsofthebay.org/

JOHN BURROUGHS SCHOOL

755 South Price Road
St. Louis, Missouri 63124

Head of School: Andy Abbott

General Information Coeducational day college-preparatory school. Grades 7–12. Founded: 1923. Setting: suburban. 47-acre campus. 7 buildings on campus. Approved or accredited by Independent Schools Association of the Central States. Member of National Association of Independent Schools and Secondary School Admission Test Board. Endowment: $47.4 million. Total enrollment: 600. Upper school average class size: 13. Upper school faculty-student ratio: 1:7. There are 164 required school days per year for Upper School students. Upper School students typically attend 5 days per week. The average school day consists of 8 hours.

Upper School Student Profile Grade 9: 103 students (53 boys, 50 girls); Grade 10: 100 students (50 boys, 50 girls); Grade 11: 99 students (49 boys, 50 girls); Grade 12: 98 students (49 boys, 49 girls).

Faculty School total: 125. In upper school: 54 men, 71 women; 92 have advanced degrees.

Subjects Offered Acting, Advanced Placement courses, African American history, algebra, American history, American literature, Ancient Greek, ancient world history, applied arts, architectural drawing, art, art history, art history-AP, astronomy, bioethics, biology, biology-AP, calculus, calculus-AP, ceramics, chemistry, chemistry-AP, Chinese, choral music, chorus, classical language, community service, comparative religion, computer math, computer science, computer skills, computer-aided design, creative writing, dance, debate, drama, earth science, ecology, economics, engineering, English, English literature, environmental science, environmental systems, expository writing, fine arts, finite math, foreign language, French, French language-AP, gardening, geology, geometry, German, global issues, global studies, Greek, Greek culture, health, history, home economics, honors English, industrial arts, jazz, jazz band, keyboarding, lab science, Latin, Latin-AP, mathematics, mechanical drawing, meteorology, model United Nations, music, orchestra, organic chemistry, personal finance, photography, physical education, physics-AP, poetry, pre-algebra, pre-calculus, probability and statistics, psychology, public speaking, reading/study skills, religion, Russian, science, social sciences, social studies, Spanish, Spanish-AP, speech and debate, statistics, trigonometry, vocal music, word processing, world civilizations, world history, world literature, world religions, writing.

Graduation Requirements Arts and fine arts (art, music, dance, drama), English, foreign language, history, mathematics, performing arts, physical education (includes health), practical arts, science, senior May project, sophomore Diversity seminar, freshman health.

Special Academic Programs 9 Advanced Placement exams for which test preparation is offered; honors section; independent study.

College Admission Counseling 98 students graduated in 2015; all went to college, including Harvard University; New York University; Southern Methodist University; Tulane University; Vanderbilt University; Washington University in St. Louis. Median SAT critical reading: 690, median SAT math: 700, median SAT writing: 700, median combined SAT: 2090, median composite ACT: 32. 88% scored over 600 on SAT critical reading, 88% scored over 600 on SAT math, 89% scored over 600 on SAT writing, 89% scored over 1800 on combined SAT, 92% scored over 26 on composite ACT.

Student Life Upper grades have student council, honor system. Discipline rests equally with students and faculty.

Tuition and Aid Day student tuition: $25,650. Tuition installment plan (monthly payment plans). Need-based scholarship grants, need-based loans available. In 2015–16, 22% of upper-school students received aid. Total amount of financial aid awarded in 2015–16: $2,431,278.

Admissions Traditional secondary-level entrance grade is 9. For fall 2015, 90 students applied for upper-level admission, 14 were accepted, 12 enrolled. SSAT required. Deadline for receipt of application materials: December 18. Application fee required: $40. On-campus interview required.

Athletics Interscholastic: baseball (boys), basketball (b,g), cheering (b,g), cross-country running (b,g), dance (b,g), dance squad (b,g), diving (b,g), field hockey (g), fitness (b,g), football (b), golf (b,g), ice hockey (b), independent competitive sports (b,g), lacrosse (b,g), modern dance (b,g), outdoor education (b,g), physical fitness (b,g), physical training (b,g), soccer (b,g), strength & conditioning (b,g), swimming and diving (b,g), tennis (b,g), track and field (b,g), volleyball (g), water polo (b), wrestling (b), yoga (b,g); coed interscholastic: baseball, cheering, dance, dance squad, football, ice hockey, modern dance, outdoor education, physical fitness, physical training, strength & conditioning, water polo, wrestling, yoga. 53 coaches, 1 athletic trainer.

Computers Computers are regularly used in all academic, animation, architecture, art, basic skills, cabinet making, classics, college planning, current events, desktop publishing, digital applications, drafting, drawing and design, economics, engineering, English, foreign language, French, French as a second language, health, history, humanities, independent study, industrial technology, journalism, keyboarding, lab/keyboard, library, library skills, literary magazine, mathematics, media production, multimedia, music, music technology, news writing, newspaper, photography, photojournalism, programming, publications, reading, remedial study skills, research skills, science, senior seminar, social sciences, social studies, Spanish, speech, study skills, technical drawing, technology, theater, typing, video film production, Web site design, woodworking, word processing, writing, writing, yearbook classes. Computer network features include on-campus library services, online commercial services, Internet access, wireless campus network, access to Google Apps, access to necessary curricular software, iPad/laptop check out from library. Campus intranet, student e-mail accounts, and computer access in designated common areas are available to students. The school has a published electronic and media policy.

Contact Caroline LaVigne, Director of Admissions and Tuition Aid. 314-993-4040. Fax: 314-567-2896. E-mail: clavigne@jburroughs.org. Website: www.jburroughs.org

THE JOHN DEWEY ACADEMY

Great Barrington, Massachusetts
See Special Needs Schools section.

JOHN F. KENNEDY CATHOLIC HIGH SCHOOL

500 Woods Mill Road
Manchester, Missouri 63011

Head of School: Fr. Richard Wosman

General Information Coeducational day college-preparatory, religious studies, and technology school, affiliated with Roman Catholic Church. Grades 9–12. Founded: 1968. Setting: suburban. Nearest major city is St. Louis. 26-acre campus. 2 buildings on campus. Approved or accredited by New England Association of Schools and Colleges, North Central Association of Colleges and Schools, and Missouri Department of Education. Total enrollment: 255. Upper school average class size: 20. Upper school faculty-student ratio: 1:10. Upper School students typically attend 5 days per week. The average school day consists of 7 hours.

Upper School Student Profile Grade 9: 51 students (20 boys, 31 girls); Grade 10: 59 students (19 boys, 40 girls); Grade 11: 76 students (37 boys, 39 girls); Grade 12: 69 students (30 boys, 39 girls). 96% of students are Roman Catholic.

Faculty School total: 41. In upper school: 14 men, 27 women; 15 have advanced degrees.

Special Academic Programs 4 Advanced Placement exams for which test preparation is offered; honors section.

College Admission Counseling 82 students graduated in 2015; 81 went to college. Other: 1 entered military service. Mean composite ACT: 24.

Student Life Upper grades have uniform requirement, student council, honor system. Discipline rests primarily with faculty. Attendance at religious services is required.

Summer Programs Sports programs offered; held on campus; accepts boys and girls; open to students from other schools.

Tuition and Aid Day student tuition: $12,000. Tuition installment plan (FACTS Tuition Payment Plan, monthly payment plans, individually arranged payment plans). Tuition reduction for siblings, merit scholarship grants, need-based scholarship grants, paying campus jobs available. In 2015–16, 35% of upper-school students received aid.

Admissions Traditional secondary-level entrance grade is 9. For fall 2015, 67 students applied for upper-level admission, 66 were accepted, 55 enrolled. Deadline for receipt of application materials: none. No application fee required. On-campus interview recommended.

Athletics Interscholastic: baseball (boys), basketball (b,g), cheering (g), cross-country running (b,g), dance squad (g), dance team (g), diving (b,g), football (b), pom squad (g), soccer (b,g), softball (g), swimming and diving (g), tennis (b,g), track and field (b,g), volleyball (g); coed interscholastic: golf.

Computers Computer network features include on-campus library services, Internet access, wireless campus network, Internet filtering or blocking technology, every student receives a personal lap top computer. Campus intranet, student e-mail accounts, and computer access in designated common areas are available to students. Students grades are available online.

Contact Mr. Mark Clynes, Director of Enrollment. 636-227-5900 Ext. 104. Fax: 636-227-0298. E-mail: mclynes@kennedycatholic.net. Website: www.kennedycatholic.net

JOHN F. KENNEDY CATHOLIC HIGH SCHOOL

140 South 140th Street
Burien, Washington 98168-3496

Head of School: Mr. Michael L. Prato

General Information Coeducational boarding and day college-preparatory and religious studies school, affiliated with Roman Catholic Church. Grades 9–12. Founded: 1966. Setting: suburban. Nearest major city is Seattle. Students are housed in single-sex dormitories and one dorm for international boys. 25-acre campus. 4 buildings on campus. Approved or accredited by CITA (Commission on International and Trans-Regional Accreditation), National Catholic Education Association, Northwest Accreditation Commission, The College Board, and Washington Department of Education. Endowment: $3.9 million. Total enrollment: 836. Upper school average class size: 23. Upper school faculty-student ratio: 1:17. There are 180 required school

days per year for Upper School students. Upper School students typically attend 5 days per week. The average school day consists of 6 hours and 45 minutes.

Upper School Student Profile Grade 9: 219 students (119 boys, 100 girls); Grade 10: 204 students (121 boys, 83 girls); Grade 11: 209 students (109 boys, 100 girls); Grade 12: 204 students (108 boys, 96 girls). 2% of students are boarding students. 98% are international students. International students from China, Japan, Republic of Korea, Taiwan, Thailand, and Viet Nam; 4 other countries represented in student body. 70% of students are Roman Catholic.

Faculty School total: 70. In upper school: 37 men, 33 women; 25 have advanced degrees.

Subjects Offered Accounting, acting, Advanced Placement courses, advanced TOEFL/grammar, algebra, American sign language, art, art appreciation, art history, astronomy, basic skills, Bible, biology, business mathematics, calculus, Catholic belief and practice, chemistry, Christian doctrine, Christian ethics, Christian scripture, clayworking, community service, comparative religion, composition-AP, computer applications, computer-aided design, concert band, concert choir, contemporary issues, creative writing, current events, drama, economics, English, English composition, English language and composition-AP, English literature, ESL, ethical decision making, fiction, filmmaking, fine arts, French, French-AP, general business, geometry, German, health, Hebrew scripture, honors algebra, honors English, honors geometry, honors U.S. history, ideas, integrated science, interdisciplinary studies, international studies, jazz ensemble, journalism, language arts, Latin, Latin-AP, law, leadership, marching band, marine biology, mathematics, media, personal fitness, physical education, physical fitness, physics, public policy, public service, publications, sculpture, sign language, social justice, Spanish, speech, symphonic band, trigonometry, U.S. history, U.S. history-AP, video, Washington State and Northwest History, world history, world religions, yearbook.

Graduation Requirements Arts and fine arts (art, music, dance, drama), English, foreign language, mathematics, physical education (includes health), religion (includes Bible studies and theology), religious education, science, social studies (includes history), culminating project, education plan (high school-college) or alternative.

Special Academic Programs International Baccalaureate program; Advanced Placement exam preparation; honors section; study at local college for college credit; academic accommodation for the gifted, the musically talented, and the artistically talented; remedial reading and/or remedial writing; remedial math; programs in English, mathematics, general development for dyslexic students; ESL (41 students enrolled).

College Admission Counseling 201 went to college, including Central Washington University; Gonzaga University; Seattle University; University of Washington; Washington State University; Western Washington University. Other: 2 went to work, 1 entered military service. Mean SAT critical reading: 506, mean SAT math: 518, mean SAT writing: 500, mean combined SAT: 1524. 20% scored over 600 on SAT critical reading, 21% scored over 600 on SAT math, 17% scored over 600 on SAT writing.

Student Life Upper grades have specified standards of dress, student council. Discipline rests primarily with faculty. Attendance at religious services is required.

Tuition and Aid Day student tuition: $10,950–$11,675; 7-day tuition and room/board: $19,350. Tuition installment plan (monthly payment plans, individually arranged payment plans). Tuition reduction for siblings, merit scholarship grants, need-based scholarship grants, paying campus jobs available. In 2014–15, 19% of upper-school students received aid; total upper-school merit-scholarship money awarded: $9780. Total amount of financial aid awarded in 2014–15: $390,000.

Admissions Traditional secondary-level entrance grade is 9. Scholastic Testing Service High School Placement Test required. Deadline for receipt of application materials: none. Application fee required: $25. Interview recommended.

Athletics Interscholastic: aquatics (boys, girls), baseball (b), basketball (b,g), cheering (g), cross-country running (b,g), diving (b,g), drill team (g), football (b), golf (b,g), gymnastics (g), lacrosse (b,g), soccer (b,g), softball (g), swimming and diving (b,g), tennis (b,g), track and field (b,g), volleyball (b,g), wrestling (b); intramural: basketball (b,g), combined training (b), Frisbee (b,g), physical training (b,g), strength & conditioning (b,g), table tennis (b,g), ultimate Frisbee (b,g), volleyball (b,g), weight lifting (b,g), weight training (b,g); coed intramural: table tennis, ultimate Frisbee. 3 PE instructors, 53 coaches, 1 athletic trainer.

Computers Computers are regularly used in all academic, English, foreign language, history, science, technology, video film production classes. Computer network features include on-campus library services, Internet access, wireless campus network. Students grades are available online. The school has a published electronic and media policy.

Contact Mrs. Amy Hall, Director of Advancement. 206-246-0500 Ext. 404. Fax: 206-242-0831. E-mail: halla@kennedyhs.org. Website: www.kennedyhs.org

JOHN HANCOCK ACADEMY

PO Drawer E
Sparta, Georgia 31087

Head of School: Mr. Steve James

General Information Coeducational day college-preparatory, general academic, arts, religious studies, and technology school, affiliated with Baptist Church, United Methodist Church. Grades K–12. Founded: 1966. Setting: rural. Nearest major city is Macon. 1 building on campus. Approved or accredited by Georgia Accrediting Commission, Georgia Independent School Association, and Georgia Department of

Education. Total enrollment: 150. Upper school average class size: 10. Upper school faculty-student ratio: 1:10. There are 180 required school days per year for Upper School students. Upper School students typically attend 5 days per week. The average school day consists of 8 hours.

Upper School Student Profile Grade 9: 20 students (9 boys, 11 girls); Grade 10: 8 students (5 boys, 3 girls); Grade 11: 14 students (10 boys, 4 girls); Grade 12: 8 students (6 boys, 2 girls). 80% of students are Baptist, United Methodist Church.

Faculty School total: 18. In upper school: 2 men, 4 women; 2 have advanced degrees.

Subjects Offered Advanced math, algebra, American government, American history, American literature, anatomy, art history, Bible, biology, botany, chemistry, computer applications, data processing, earth science, economics, English, English literature, environmental science, general math, geography, geometry, government, health, history, journalism, keyboarding, language arts, physical education, physical science, physics, pre-algebra, science, social studies, Spanish, state history, statistics, trigonometry, U.S. government, U.S. history, Web site design, weight training, world geography, world history, yearbook.

Special Academic Programs International Baccalaureate program; honors section; independent study; study at local college for college credit.

College Admission Counseling 13 students graduated in 2015; 5 went to college, including Georgia Southern University; University of Georgia.

Student Life Upper grades have specified standards of dress, student council, honor system. Discipline rests primarily with faculty.

Summer Programs Remediation programs offered; session focuses on make-up work; held on campus; accepts boys and girls; open to students from other schools. 10 students usually enrolled. 2016 schedule: June 1 to July 7.

Tuition and Aid Day student tuition: $4400. Tuition installment plan (monthly payment plans, individually arranged payment plans). Tuition reduction for siblings available.

Admissions Traditional secondary-level entrance grade is 9. ACT, any standardized test, OLSAT, Stanford Achievement Test, Otis-Lennon Ability or Stanford Achievement Test, PSAT or SAT required. Deadline for receipt of application materials: none. Application fee required: $100. Interview required.

Athletics Interscholastic: baseball (boys), basketball (b,g), cheering (g), football (b), running (b,g), softball (g), tennis (b,g), track and field (b,g), volleyball (g), weight lifting (b,g); coed interscholastic: physical fitness. 2 PE instructors, 5 coaches.

Computers Computers are regularly used in keyboarding, Web site design, yearbook classes. Computer network features include Internet access.

Contact Ms. Nancy Roach, Secretary. 706-444-6470. Fax: 706-444-6933. E-mail: johnhancockad@bellsouth.net. Website: www.johnhancockacademy.com/

JOHN PAUL II CATHOLIC HIGH SCHOOL

5100 Terrebone Drive
Tallahassee, Florida 32311-7848

Head of School: Mr. Tommy Bridges

General Information Coeducational day college-preparatory, general academic, and religious studies school, affiliated with Roman Catholic Church. Grades 9–12. Founded: 2001. Setting: suburban. 37-acre campus. 3 buildings on campus. Approved or accredited by Academy of Orton-Gillingham Practitioners and Educators, Accreditation Commission of the Texas Association of Baptist Schools, American Association of Christian Schools, Arizona Association of Independent Schools, Association for Experiential Education, Association of American Schools in South America, Association of Christian Schools International, Association of Colorado Independent Schools, Association of Independent Maryland Schools, Association of Independent Schools and Colleges of Alberta, Association of Independent Schools in New England, Association of Independent Schools of Florida, Association of Independent Schools of Greater Washington, Southern Association of Colleges and Schools, and Florida Department of Education. Total enrollment: 169. Upper school average class size: 15. Upper school faculty-student ratio: 1:12. There are 180 required school days per year for Upper School students. Upper School students typically attend 5 days per week. The average school day consists of 7 hours and 12 minutes.

Upper School Student Profile Grade 9: 35 students (19 boys, 16 girls); Grade 10: 41 students (24 boys, 17 girls); Grade 11: 51 students (27 boys, 24 girls); Grade 12: 41 students (22 boys, 19 girls). 75% of students are Roman Catholic.

Faculty School total: 22. In upper school: 9 men, 12 women; 14 have advanced degrees.

Subjects Offered All academic, Bible, English language and composition-AP, English literature and composition-AP, history of the Catholic Church, Latin, music, Spanish, Spanish language-AP, strings, world history-AP.

Graduation Requirements Algebra, American government, American history, biology, Christian doctrine, economics, English, fitness, foreign language, health, world history.

Special Academic Programs 12 Advanced Placement exams for which test preparation is offered; honors section; study at local college for college credit.

College Admission Counseling 43 students graduated in 2015; 42 went to college, including Florida State University; Tallahassee Community College; The University of North Carolina at Chapel Hill; University of Florida; University of South Florida. Other: 1 entered military service. Mean SAT critical reading: 559, mean SAT math: 544,

mean SAT writing: 535. 50% scored over 600 on SAT critical reading, 48% scored over 600 on SAT math, 45% scored over 600 on SAT writing.

Student Life Upper grades have uniform requirement, student council. Discipline rests primarily with faculty. Attendance at religious services is required.

Tuition and Aid Day student tuition: $12,000. Tuition installment plan (SMART Tuition Payment Plan, monthly payment plans, individually arranged payment plans). Need-based scholarship grants available. In 2015–16, 40% of upper-school students received aid.

Admissions Traditional secondary-level entrance grade is 9. High School Placement Test or High School Placement Test (closed version) from Scholastic Testing Service required. Deadline for receipt of application materials: none. Application fee required: $250. On-campus interview recommended.

Athletics Interscholastic: baseball (boys), basketball (b,g), cross-country running (b,g), football (b), golf (b,g), soccer (b,g), softball (g), tennis (b,g), track and field (b,g), volleyball (g), weight training (b,g). 1 PE instructor, 14 coaches, 1 athletic trainer.

Computers Computers are regularly used in all academic, drawing and design, technology classes. Computer network features include on-campus library services, Internet access, wireless campus network, Internet filtering or blocking technology. Campus intranet and student e-mail accounts are available to students. Students grades are available online. The school has a published electronic and media policy.

Contact Mrs. Sharon Strohl, Office Administrator. 850-201-5744. Fax: 850-205-3299. E-mail: sstrohl@jpiichs.org. Website: www.jpiichs.org

JOSEPHINUM ACADEMY

1501 North Oakley Boulevard
Chicago, Illinois 60622

Head of School: Mrs. Julie Raino

General Information Girls' day college-preparatory, arts, religious studies, and technology school, affiliated with Roman Catholic Church. Grades 9–12. Founded: 1890. Setting: urban. 2-acre campus. 1 building on campus. Approved or accredited by International Baccalaureate Organization, National Catholic Education Association, Network of Sacred Heart Schools, North Central Association of Colleges and Schools, and Illinois Department of Education. Endowment: $1.5 million. Total enrollment: 200. Upper school average class size: 18. Upper school faculty-student ratio: 1:10. There are 176 required school days per year for Upper School students. Upper School students typically attend 5 days per week. The average school day consists of 7 hours and 30 minutes.

Upper School Student Profile Grade 9: 48 students (48 girls); Grade 10: 58 students (58 girls); Grade 11: 54 students (54 girls); Grade 12: 39 students (39 girls). 50% of students are Roman Catholic.

Faculty School total: 24. In upper school: 6 men, 14 women; 16 have advanced degrees.

Subjects Offered ACT preparation, acting, advanced biology, advanced chemistry, Advanced Placement courses, algebra, American literature, applied arts, art, athletics, basketball, biology, biology-AP, business education, calculus-AP, campus ministry, Catholic belief and practice, chemistry, Christian studies, civics, college admission preparation, college awareness, college counseling, college placement, college planning, community garden, community service, computer education, constitutional history of U.S., consumer economics, consumer education, current events, drama, drama performance, electives, English, English literature-AP, English-AP, environmental science, fitness, foreign language, French, French as a second language, freshman seminar, geometry, global issues, global studies, health, health and wellness, history of the Americas, honors English, honors geometry, honors U.S. history, honors world history, Life of Christ, literature by women, modern history, moral theology, peer counseling, performing arts, physical education, physical science, physics, pre-calculus, religious studies, research seminar, senior project, senior thesis, Shakespeare, social justice, softball, Spanish, Spanish literature, Spanish-AP, speech, U.S. history, volleyball, water color painting, women's literature, women's studies, world history, world literature, world religions, world religions, writing, yearbook.

Graduation Requirements Algebra, arts and fine arts (art, music, dance, drama), biology, college admission preparation, computer science, consumer education, English, foreign language, health, mathematics, physical education (includes health), religion (includes Bible studies and theology), science, social sciences, social studies (includes history), technology, senior Capstone project, portfolio projects. Community service is required.

Special Academic Programs 6 Advanced Placement exams for which test preparation is offered; honors section; independent study; term-away projects; domestic exchange program (with Network of Sacred Heart Schools); study abroad; remedial reading and/or remedial writing; remedial math.

College Admission Counseling 55 students graduated in 2015; 50 went to college, including Carleton College; DePaul University; Grand Valley State University; Loyola University Chicago; University of Illinois at Chicago; University of Illinois at Urbana–Champaign. Other: 5 had other specific plans.

Student Life Upper grades have uniform requirement, student council, honor system. Discipline rests primarily with faculty. Attendance at religious services is required.

Summer Programs Remediation, enrichment, sports, art/fine arts, computer instruction programs offered; session focuses on community service and educational advancement; held both on and off campus; held at Sacred Heart schools; accepts girls; open to students from other schools. 40 students usually enrolled.

Tuition and Aid Day student tuition: $4900. Tuition installment plan (FACTS Tuition Payment Plan, monthly payment plans, individually arranged payment plans). Tuition reduction for siblings, merit scholarship grants, need-based scholarship grants available. In 2015–16, 89% of upper-school students received aid.

Admissions Traditional secondary-level entrance grade is 9. Catholic High School Entrance Examination required. Deadline for receipt of application materials: none. No application fee required. Interview recommended.

Athletics Interscholastic: basketball, soccer, softball, volleyball; intramural: dance team, fitness, football, track and field, weight training. 2 PE instructors, 5 coaches.

Computers Computers are regularly used in all academic classes. Computer network features include on-campus library services, online commercial services, Internet access, wireless campus network, Internet filtering or blocking technology, all students provided with iPads. Campus intranet, student e-mail accounts, and computer access in designated common areas are available to students. Students grades are available online. The school has a published electronic and media policy.

Contact Mrs. Stephanie Castrounis, Director of Admissions. 773-276-1261 Ext. 234. Fax: 773-292-3963. E-mail: stephanie.castrounis@josephinum.org. Website: www.josephinum.org

THE JOURNEYS SCHOOL OF TETON SCIENCE SCHOOL

700 Coyote Canyon Road
Jackson, Wyoming 83001

Head of School: Nancy Lang

General Information Coeducational day college-preparatory school. Grades K–12. Founded: 2001. Setting: rural. 800-acre campus. 1 building on campus. Approved or accredited by International Baccalaureate Organization, Northwest Association of Independent Schools, and Wyoming Department of Education. Member of National Association of Independent Schools. Endowment: $12 million. Total enrollment: 159. Upper school average class size: 10. Upper school faculty-student ratio: 1:7. There are 175 required school days per year for Upper School students. Upper School students typically attend 5 days per week. The average school day consists of 7 hours and 45 minutes.

Upper School Student Profile Grade 6: 20 students (14 boys, 6 girls); Grade 7: 16 students (6 boys, 10 girls); Grade 8: 25 students (14 boys, 11 girls); Grade 9: 11 students (4 boys, 7 girls); Grade 10: 7 students (5 boys, 2 girls); Grade 11: 9 students (5 boys, 4 girls); Grade 12: 10 students (2 boys, 8 girls).

Faculty School total: 40. In upper school: 8 men, 11 women; 13 have advanced degrees.

Subjects Offered International Baccalaureate courses.

Graduation Requirements International Baccalaureate courses.

Special Academic Programs International Baccalaureate program; academic accommodation for the gifted.

College Admission Counseling 10 students graduated in 2015; all went to college.

Student Life Upper grades have student council. Discipline rests equally with students and faculty.

Tuition and Aid Day student tuition: $21,550. Tuition installment plan (monthly payment plans, individually arranged payment plans). Need-based scholarship grants available. In 2015–16, 43% of upper-school students received aid. Total amount of financial aid awarded in 2015–16: $240,150.

Admissions Deadline for receipt of application materials: none. Application fee required: $50. Interview required.

Athletics Interscholastic: aerobics/dance (girls), alpine skiing (b,g), aquatics (g), baseball (b), basketball (b,g), cheering (g), cross-country running (b,g), dance (g), football (b), gymnastics (g), ice hockey (b,g), indoor track & field (g), martial arts (b,g), nordic skiing (b,g), soccer (b,g), swimming and diving (g), tennis (b,g), volleyball (g); intramural: dressage (g), equestrian sports (g), freestyle skiing (b,g), horseback riding (g), lacrosse (b,g), snowboarding (b,g); coed interscholastic: backpacking, skiing (cross-country), skiing (downhill), track and field; coed intramural: climbing, soccer, wall climbing. 1 PE instructor.

Computers Computer network features include Internet access, wireless campus network, Internet filtering or blocking technology. Campus intranet and student e-mail accounts are available to students. Students grades are available online.

Contact Warren Samuels, Director of Admissions. 307-732-7745. Fax: 307-733-3340. E-mail: warren.samuels@journeysschool.org. Website: www.tetonscience.org/journeys-school/home

JUDGE MEMORIAL CATHOLIC HIGH SCHOOL

650 South 1100 East
Salt Lake City, Utah 84102

Head of School: Mr. Patrick Lambert

General Information Coeducational day college-preparatory school, affiliated with Roman Catholic Church. Grades 9–12. Founded: 1921. Setting: urban. Approved or accredited by Western Association of Schools and Colleges, Western Catholic Education Association, and Utah Department of Education. Upper school average class size: 20.

Upper School Student Profile 60% of students are Roman Catholic.

Special Academic Programs Advanced Placement exam preparation; honors section.

Student Life Upper grades have uniform requirement, student council. Discipline rests primarily with faculty. Attendance at religious services is required.

Summer Programs Enrichment, advancement, sports, art/fine arts, computer instruction programs offered.

Tuition and Aid Tuition installment plan (FACTS Tuition Payment Plan).

Admissions Application fee required.

Athletics Interscholastic: baseball (boys), basketball (b,g), bowling (b,g), cheering (g), cross-country running (b,g), football (b), golf (b,g), lacrosse (b,g), running (b,g), soccer (b,g), softball (g), swimming and diving (b), tennis (b,g), track and field (b,g), volleyball (g); coed interscholastic: hockey, ice hockey.

Contact Mrs. Suzanne Rainwater, Director of Admissions. 801-363-8895. Fax: 801-517-2190. E-mail: srainwater@judgememorial.com. Website: www.judgememorial.com/

JUNIPERO SERRA HIGH SCHOOL

14830 South Van Ness Avenue
Gardena, California 90249

Head of School: Mr. Jeffrey Guzman

General Information Coeducational day college-preparatory, arts, and religious studies school, affiliated with Roman Catholic Church. Grades 9–12. Founded: 1950. Setting: urban. 24-acre campus. 10 buildings on campus. Approved or accredited by National Catholic Education Association, Western Association of Schools and Colleges, Western Catholic Education Association, and California Department of Education. Member of Secondary School Admission Test Board. Endowment: $200,000. Total enrollment: 675. Upper school average class size: 27. Upper school faculty-student ratio: 1:27. There are 180 required school days per year for Upper School students. Upper School students typically attend 5 days per week. The average school day consists of 5 hours and 45 minutes.

Upper School Student Profile Grade 9: 150 students (75 boys, 75 girls); Grade 10: 150 students (75 boys, 75 girls); Grade 11: 140 students (70 boys, 70 girls); Grade 12: 130 students (65 boys, 65 girls). 25% of students are Roman Catholic.

Faculty School total: 36. In upper school: 22 men, 14 women; 30 have advanced degrees.

Subjects Offered Acting, advanced math, advanced studio art-AP, algebra, American history-AP, American literature, anatomy, biology, biology-AP, calculus-AP, chemistry, choir, computer science, drama, economics, English, English literature, English literature-AP, fine arts, geometry, government, journalism, mathematics, music, photography, physical education, physics, physiology, pre-calculus, religion, science, social studies, Spanish, Spanish-AP, theater, theology, U.S. history, world history, writing.

Graduation Requirements Arts and fine arts (art, music, dance, drama), computer science, English, foreign language, mathematics, physical education (includes health), religion (includes Bible studies and theology), science, social studies (includes history), completion of an SAT or ACT test preparation program, completion of 80 service hours, school does not accept D and F grades as passing. Community service is required.

Special Academic Programs Advanced Placement exam preparation; honors section; study at local college for college credit; academic accommodation for the gifted; remedial reading and/or remedial writing; remedial math; ESL (20 students enrolled).

College Admission Counseling 135 students graduated in 2014; 134 went to college, including California State University; El Camino College; Loyola Marymount University; University of California, Los Angeles. Other: 1 entered military service. Mean SAT critical reading: 464, mean SAT math: 452, mean SAT writing: 455, mean composite ACT: 21. 10% scored over 600 on SAT critical reading, 10% scored over 600 on SAT math, 10% scored over 600 on SAT writing, 7% scored over 26 on composite ACT.

Student Life Upper grades have uniform requirement, student council, honor system. Discipline rests primarily with faculty. Attendance at religious services is required.

Tuition and Aid Day student tuition: $7510. Tuition installment plan (FACTS Tuition Payment Plan). Tuition reduction for siblings, merit scholarship grants, need-based scholarship grants available. In 2014–15, 65% of upper-school students received aid; total upper-school merit-scholarship money awarded: $35,000. Total amount of financial aid awarded in 2014–15: $400,000.

Admissions Traditional secondary-level entrance grade is 9. For fall 2014, 450 students applied for upper-level admission, 350 were accepted, 150 enrolled. High School Placement Test required. Deadline for receipt of application materials: none. No application fee required. On-campus interview required.

Athletics Interscholastic: baseball (boys), basketball (b,g), cheering (g), cross-country running (b,g), football (b), golf (b,g), soccer (b,g), softball (g), tennis (b,g), track and field (b,g), volleyball (b,g), winter soccer (b,g), wrestling (b); coed interscholastic: swimming and diving, track and field; coed intramural: basketball, volleyball. 2 PE instructors, 23 coaches, 2 athletic trainers.

Computers Computers are regularly used in art, English, foreign language, history, mathematics, music, science classes. Computer network features include on-campus library services, Internet access, wireless campus network, Internet filtering or blocking technology. Computer access in designated common areas is available to students. Students grades are available online. The school has a published electronic and media policy.

Contact Mr. John Posatko, Director of Marketing and Admissions. 310-324-6675 Ext. 1015. Fax: 310-352-4953. E-mail: jposatko@la-serrahs.org. Website: www.la-serrahs.org

JUNIPERO SERRA HIGH SCHOOL

451 West 20th Avenue
San Mateo, California 94403-1385

Head of School: Mr. Lars Lund

General Information Boys' day college-preparatory, arts, business, religious studies, and technology school, affiliated with Roman Catholic Church. Grades 9–12. Founded: 1944. Setting: suburban. Nearest major city is San Francisco. 13-acre campus. 9 buildings on campus. Approved or accredited by Western Association of Schools and Colleges and Western Catholic Education Association. Endowment: $9.4 million. Total enrollment: 881. Upper school average class size: 25. Upper school faculty-student ratio: 1:27. There are 180 required school days per year for Upper School students. Upper School students typically attend 5 days per week. The average school day consists of 6 hours and 35 minutes.

Upper School Student Profile Grade 9: 240 students (240 boys); Grade 10: 239 students (239 boys); Grade 11: 193 students (193 boys); Grade 12: 209 students (209 boys). 67% of students are Roman Catholic.

Faculty School total: 76. In upper school: 51 men, 24 women; 57 have advanced degrees.

Subjects Offered Advanced biology, advanced chemistry, advanced computer applications, advanced math, Advanced Placement courses, algebra, American history, American history-AP, American literature, analytic geometry, architectural drawing, architecture, art, art history-AP, athletic training, athletics, band, biology, biology-AP, business, business communications, calculus, calculus-AP, ceramics, chemistry, chemistry-AP, Chinese, chorus, church history, college admission preparation, college counseling, college placement, college planning, college writing, community service, computer programming, computer programming-AP, computer science, concert band, creative writing, dance, drama, dramatic arts, driver education, ecology, environmental systems, economics, English, English language-AP, English literature, English literature-AP, English-AP, ethics, European history, film appreciation, fine arts, French, French language-AP, French-AP, geography, geometry, German, government/civics, grammar, health education, history, honors algebra, honors English, honors geometry, honors world history, instrumental music, jazz band, journalism, keyboarding, leadership and service, library skills, Mandarin, marketing, mathematics, music, musical productions, newspaper, performing arts, photography, physical education, physics, physics-AP, pre-calculus, psychology, psychology-AP, publications, religious studies, SAT preparation, science, social justice, social sciences, social studies, Spanish, Spanish language-AP, Spanish-AP, speech, sports conditioning, statistics, statistics-AP, student government, theater, trigonometry, U.S. government, U.S. government and politics, U.S. government and politics-AP, U.S. history, U.S. history-AP, visual and performing arts, world history, writing.

Graduation Requirements All academic, arts and fine arts (art, music, dance, drama), computer science, English, foreign language, literature, mathematics, physical education (includes health), political systems, religion (includes Bible studies and theology), science, social sciences, social studies (includes history), 80 hours of community service. Community service is required.

Special Academic Programs 19 Advanced Placement exams for which test preparation is offered; honors section; study at local college for college credit.

College Admission Counseling 202 students graduated in 2015; 201 went to college, including Loyola Marymount University; Santa Clara University; The University of Arizona; University of California, Davis; University of California, San Diego; University of Oregon. Other: 1 went to work.

Student Life Upper grades have specified standards of dress, student council, honor system. Discipline rests primarily with faculty. Attendance at religious services is required.

Summer Programs Remediation, enrichment, advancement, sports, art/fine arts, computer instruction programs offered; session focuses on enrichment and remediation; held on campus; accepts boys and girls; open to students from other schools. 480 students usually enrolled. 2016 schedule: June 13 to July 15. Application deadline: June 9.

Tuition and Aid Day student tuition: $18,990. Tuition installment plan (monthly payment plans, semester payment plan, annual payment plan, direct debit plan). Merit scholarship grants, need-based scholarship grants available. In 2015–16, 30% of upper-school students received aid; total upper-school merit-scholarship money awarded: $65,000. Total amount of financial aid awarded in 2015–16: $2,400,000.

Admissions Traditional secondary-level entrance grade is 9. For fall 2015, 476 students applied for upper-level admission, 330 were accepted, 240 enrolled. High School Placement Test required. Deadline for receipt of application materials: January 6. Application fee required: $75. On-campus interview required.

Athletics Interscholastic: baseball, basketball, crew, cross-country running, diving, football, golf, lacrosse, rowing, soccer, swimming and diving, tennis, track and field, volleyball, water polo, wrestling; intramural: basketball, bicycling, bowling, fishing, fitness, mountain biking, physical training, rock climbing, soccer, softball, strength & conditioning, surfing, touch football, weight lifting, weight training. 1 PE instructor, 48 coaches, 1 athletic trainer.

Computers Computers are regularly used in all academic classes. Computer network features include on-campus library services, Internet access, wireless campus network, Internet filtering or blocking technology. Campus intranet and student e-mail accounts are available to students. Students grades are available online. The school has a published electronic and media policy.

Contact Mr. Randy Vogel, Director of Admissions. 650-345-8242. Fax: 650-573-6638. E-mail: rvogel@serrahs.com. Website: www.serrahs.com

KALAMAZOO CHRISTIAN HIGH SCHOOL

2121 Stadium Drive
Kalamazoo, Michigan 49008-1692

Head of School: Mr. Bartel James Huizenga

General Information Coeducational day college-preparatory, general academic, arts, business, vocational, religious studies, bilingual studies, and technology school, affiliated with Christian Reformed Church, Reformed Church in America. Grades 9–12. Founded: 1877. Setting: urban. 3-acre campus. 1 building on campus. Approved or accredited by Christian Schools International, North Central Association of Colleges and Schools, and Michigan Department of Education. Endowment: $1 million. Upper school average class size: 22. Upper school faculty-student ratio: 1:12. There are 172 required school days per year for Upper School students. Upper School students typically attend 5 days per week. The average school day consists of 6 hours and 45 minutes.

Upper School Student Profile Grade 9: 64 students (39 boys, 25 girls); Grade 10: 45 students (24 boys, 21 girls); Grade 11: 65 students (30 boys, 35 girls); Grade 12: 60 students (30 boys, 30 girls). 30% of students are members of Christian Reformed Church, Reformed Church in America.

Faculty School total: 20. In upper school: 14 men, 6 women; 10 have advanced degrees.

Graduation Requirements 50 hours of community service.

Special Academic Programs Advanced Placement exam preparation; honors section; study at local college for college credit.

College Admission Counseling 52 students graduated in 2015; they went to Calvin College; Grand Valley State University; Hope College; University of Michigan; Western Michigan University. Median composite ACT: 23. 27% scored over 26 on composite ACT.

Student Life Upper grades have specified standards of dress, student council, honor system. Discipline rests primarily with faculty. Attendance at religious services is required.

Tuition and Aid Day student tuition: $8970. Tuition installment plan (FACTS Tuition Payment Plan, monthly payment plans, individually arranged payment plans). Tuition reduction for siblings, need-based scholarship grants available. In 2015–16, 50% of upper-school students received aid.

Admissions Traditional secondary-level entrance grade is 9. Deadline for receipt of application materials: none. Application fee required: $150. Interview required.

Athletics Interscholastic: baseball (boys), basketball (b,g), bowling (b,g), cheering (g), cross-country running (b,g), football (b), golf (b,g), hockey (b), physical fitness (b,g), soccer (b,g), softball (g), strength & conditioning (b,g), tennis (b,g), track and field (b,g), volleyball (g), weight lifting (b,g), weight training (b,g). 2 PE instructors, 32 coaches, 1 athletic trainer.

Computers Computers are regularly used in accounting, business, business applications, business skills, data processing, graphic arts, graphic design, keyboarding, lab/keyboard classes. Computer network features include on-campus library services, online commercial services, Internet access. The school has a published electronic and media policy.

Contact Mr. Bartel James Huizenga, Principal. 269-381-2250 Ext. 114. Fax: 269-381-0319. E-mail: bhuizenga@kcsa.org. Website: www.kcsa.org

KAUAI CHRISTIAN ACADEMY

PO Box 1121
4000 Kilauea Road
Kilauea, Hawaii 96754

Head of School: Daniel A. Plunkett

General Information Coeducational day college-preparatory, general academic, arts, religious studies, bilingual studies, and technology school, affiliated with Protestant-Evangelical faith, Christian faith. Grades PS–12. Founded: 1973. Setting: rural. Nearest major city is Lihue. 10-acre campus. 3 buildings on campus. Approved or accredited by American Association of Christian Schools and Hawaii Department of Education. Total enrollment: 79. Upper school average class size: 8. Upper school faculty-student ratio: 1:8. There are 181 required school days per year for Upper School students. Upper

School students typically attend 5 days per week. The average school day consists of 6 hours and 30 minutes.

Upper School Student Profile Grade 7: 3 students (3 boys); Grade 8: 2 students (2 girls); Grade 9: 2 students (1 boy, 1 girl); Grade 10: 2 students (2 boys); Grade 11: 5 students (5 girls); Grade 12: 2 students (2 girls). 75% of students are Protestant-Evangelical faith, Christian faith.

Faculty School total: 10. In upper school: 4 men, 2 women; 1 has an advanced degree.

Subjects Offered Advanced math, agriculture, algebra, American government, American history, ancient history, art, arts, athletics, Basic programming, Bible, Bible as literature, Bible studies, biology, botany, calculus, chemistry, Christian and Hebrew scripture, economics, economics-AP, electives, English, English literature, English literature and composition-AP, family living, geography, geometry, government, history, Latin, music, physical science, pre-algebra, speech, world geography, world history.

Graduation Requirements Arts and fine arts (art, music, dance, drama), computer science, English, Latin, mathematics, science, social studies (includes history), speech, one year of Bible for each year enrolled.

Special Academic Programs Accelerated programs; independent study; remedial reading and/or remedial writing; remedial math.

College Admission Counseling 3 students graduated in 2015; 2 went to college, including Columbia International University; Montana State University. Other: 1 went to work. Median SAT critical reading: 570, median SAT math: 530, median SAT writing: 550, median combined SAT: 1705, median composite ACT: 24. 50% scored over 600 on SAT critical reading, 50% scored over 600 on SAT writing.

Student Life Upper grades have specified standards of dress, honor system. Discipline rests primarily with faculty.

Summer Programs Remediation programs offered; session focuses on make-up; held on campus; accepts boys and girls; not open to students from other schools. 2016 schedule: June 13 to July 8. Application deadline: May 31.

Tuition and Aid Day student tuition: $6300. Tuition installment plan (monthly payment plans, 10-month payment plan). Tuition reduction for siblings, need-based scholarship grants, paying campus jobs available. In 2015–16, 40% of upper-school students received aid. Total amount of financial aid awarded in 2015–16: $40,000.

Admissions Traditional secondary-level entrance grade is 7. For fall 2015, 12 students applied for upper-level admission, 12 were accepted, 12 enrolled. Cognitive Abilities Test, Iowa Test of Educational Development or OLSAT, Stanford Achievement Test required. Deadline for receipt of application materials: none. Application fee required: $100. Interview recommended.

Athletics Interscholastic: cross-country running (boys, girls), golf (b,g), track and field (b,g). 1 PE instructor, 2 coaches.

Computers Computers are regularly used in computer applications, typing classes. Computer network features include Internet access, wireless campus network, Internet filtering or blocking technology. Campus intranet and computer access in designated common areas are available to students.

Contact Daniel A. Plunkett, Principal. 808-828-0047. Fax: 808-828-1850. E-mail: dplunkett@kcaschool.net. Website: www.kcaschool.net

KENT DENVER SCHOOL

4000 East Quincy Avenue
Englewood, Colorado 80113

Head of School: Dr. Randal Harrington

General Information Coeducational day college-preparatory and arts school. Grades 6–12. Founded: 1922. Setting: suburban. Nearest major city is Denver. 220-acre campus. 6 buildings on campus. Approved or accredited by Association of Colorado Independent Schools and Colorado Department of Education. Member of National Association of Independent Schools and Secondary School Admission Test Board. Endowment: $54.4 million. Total enrollment: 698. Upper school average class size: 14. Upper school faculty-student ratio: 1:13. There are 172 required school days per year for Upper School students. Upper School students typically attend 5 days per week. The average school day consists of 7 hours.

Upper School Student Profile Grade 6: 70 students (35 boys, 35 girls); Grade 7: 78 students (39 boys, 39 girls); Grade 8: 74 students (40 boys, 34 girls); Grade 9: 124 students (60 boys, 64 girls); Grade 10: 121 students (65 boys, 56 girls); Grade 11: 118 students (61 boys, 57 girls); Grade 12: 113 students (59 boys, 54 girls).

Faculty School total: 86. In upper school: 57 have advanced degrees.

Subjects Offered African-American literature, algebra, American history, American history-AP, American literature, art, art history, art history-AP, Asian studies, biology, calculus, calculus-AP, career education internship, ceramics, chemistry, choir, clayworking, college counseling, community service, computer math, computer programming, computer programming-AP, computer science, creative writing, drama, earth science, economics, English, English literature, English literature and composition-AP, environmental science, European history, European history-AP, fine arts, French, French language-AP, French literature-AP, French-AP, general science, genetics, geography, geology, geometry, government/civics, grammar, guitar, health and wellness, history, history-AP, human development, independent study, jazz band, Latin, Mandarin, mathematics, music, music performance, mythology, photography, physical education, physics, pre-calculus, science, social studies, Spanish, Spanish language-AP,

Spanish literature-AP, statistics, studio art-AP, theater, Web site design, world history, world literature, writing.

Graduation Requirements Arts and fine arts (art, music, dance, drama), English, foreign language, history, internship, mathematics, participation in sports, science. Community service is required.

Special Academic Programs 20 Advanced Placement exams for which test preparation is offered; honors section; independent study; programs in general development for dyslexic students.

College Admission Counseling 118 students graduated in 2015; all went to college, including Brown University; Stanford University; The University of Texas at Austin; University of Denver; University of Southern California; Wake Forest University. Mean SAT critical reading: 620, mean SAT math: 653, mean SAT writing: 637, mean composite ACT: 29.

Student Life Upper grades have specified standards of dress, student council. Discipline rests equally with students and faculty.

Summer Programs Enrichment, sports, art/fine arts, computer instruction programs offered; session focuses on skill-building, arts, enrichment, athletics; held on campus; accepts boys and girls; open to students from other schools. 1,400 students usually enrolled. 2016 schedule: June 8 to July 24. Application deadline: none.

Tuition and Aid Day student tuition: $24,170. Tuition installment plan (Insured Tuition Payment Plan, Key Tuition Payment Plan, monthly payment plans). Need-based scholarship grants available. In 2015–16, 23% of upper-school students received aid. Total amount of financial aid awarded in 2015–16: $2,200,000.

Admissions Traditional secondary-level entrance grade is 9. For fall 2015, 190 students applied for upper-level admission, 92 were accepted, 60 enrolled. ISEE or SSAT required. Deadline for receipt of application materials: January 31. Application fee required: $60. Interview required.

Athletics Interscholastic: baseball (boys), basketball (b,g), cross-country running (b,g), diving (g), field hockey (g), football (b), golf (b,g), hockey (b), ice hockey (b), lacrosse (b,g), soccer (b,g), swimming and diving (g), tennis (b,g), track and field (b,g), volleyball (g); coed interscholastic: independent competitive sports, outdoor education, yoga; coed intramural: aerobics/Nautilus, bicycling, fitness, mountain biking, outdoor adventure, outdoor education, outdoor skills, physical fitness, physical training, strength & conditioning, weight lifting. 3 PE instructors, 17 coaches, 1 athletic trainer.

Computers Computers are regularly used in all classes. Computer network features include on-campus library services, online commercial services, Internet access, wireless campus network, Internet filtering or blocking technology. Student e-mail accounts and computer access in designated common areas are available to students. Students grades are available online. The school has a published electronic and media policy.

Contact Susan Green, Admission Office Manager. 303-770-7660 Ext. 237. Fax: 303-770-1398. E-mail: sgreen@kentdenver.org. Website: www.kentdenver.org

KENT PLACE SCHOOL

42 Norwood Avenue
Summit, New Jersey 07902-0308

Head of School: Mrs. Susan C. Bosland

General Information Coeducational day (boys' only in lower grades) college-preparatory school. Boys grades N–PK, girls grades N–12. Founded: 1894. Setting: suburban. Nearest major city is New York, NY. 26-acre campus. 6 buildings on campus. Approved or accredited by Middle States Association of Colleges and Schools and New Jersey Association of Independent Schools. Member of National Association of Independent Schools and Secondary School Admission Test Board. Endowment: $15 million. Total enrollment: 636. Upper school average class size: 16. Upper school faculty-student ratio: 1:7. There are 167 required school days per year for Upper School students. Upper School students typically attend 5 days per week. The average school day consists of 6 hours and 55 minutes.

Upper School Student Profile Grade 9: 69 students (69 girls); Grade 10: 78 students (78 girls); Grade 11: 67 students (67 girls); Grade 12: 63 students (63 girls).

Faculty School total: 119. In upper school: 7 men, 36 women; 35 have advanced degrees.

Subjects Offered Advanced Placement courses, algebra, American history, American history-AP, American literature, anatomy and physiology, art, art history-AP, biology, biology-AP, calculus, calculus-AP, ceramics, chemistry, chemistry-AP, computer literacy, computer programming-AP, computer science, creative writing, dance, drama, driver education, economics, English, English language-AP, English literature, English literature-AP, environmental science, environmental science-AP, European history, expository writing, fine arts, French, French language-AP, French literature-AP, geometry, government/civics, grammar, health, history, independent study, Latin, Latin-AP, macroeconomics-AP, mathematics, modern European history-AP, music, music theory-AP, photography, physical education, physics, science, social studies, Spanish, Spanish language-AP, Spanish literature-AP, statistics, statistics-AP, theater, trigonometry, world history.

Graduation Requirements Arts and fine arts (art, music, dance, drama), English, foreign language, history, mathematics, physical education (includes health), science.

Special Academic Programs 22 Advanced Placement exams for which test preparation is offered; independent study.

College Admission Counseling 66 students graduated in 2014; all went to college, including Boston College; Colgate University; Cornell University; Princeton University; University of Pennsylvania; Yale University.

Student Life Upper grades have specified standards of dress, student council, honor system. Discipline rests equally with students and faculty.

Tuition and Aid Day student tuition: $38,100. Tuition installment plan (Insured Tuition Payment Plan, Key Tuition Payment Plan, monthly payment plans). Need-based scholarship grants available. In 2014–15, 20% of upper-school students received aid. Total amount of financial aid awarded in 2014–15: $1,299,061.

Admissions Traditional secondary-level entrance grade is 9. ISEE or SSAT required. Deadline for receipt of application materials: January 9. Application fee required: $75. On-campus interview required.

Athletics Interscholastic: basketball, cross-country running, field hockey, indoor track, lacrosse, soccer, softball, swimming and diving, tennis, track and field, volleyball, winter (indoor) track; intramural: dance, fencing, modern dance, physical fitness, squash. 4 PE instructors, 19 coaches, 1 athletic trainer.

Computers Computers are regularly used in all classes. Computer network features include on-campus library services, online commercial services, Internet access, wireless campus network, Internet filtering or blocking technology. Campus intranet, student e-mail accounts, and computer access in designated common areas are available to students. The school has a published electronic and media policy.

Contact Mrs. Julia Wall, Director of Admission and Financial Aid. 908-273-0900 Ext. 254. Fax: 908-273-9390. E-mail: admission@kentplace.org. Website: www.kentplace.org

KENT SCHOOL

PO Box 2006
Kent, Connecticut 06757

Head of School: Rev. Richardson W. Schell

General Information Coeducational boarding and day college-preparatory, arts, religious studies, technology, Pre-Engineering, and Entrepreneurship school, affiliated with Episcopal Church. Grades 9–PG. Founded: 1906. Setting: small town. Nearest major city is Hartford. Students are housed in single-sex dormitories. 1,200-acre campus. 17 buildings on campus. Approved or accredited by Association of Independent Schools in New England, Connecticut Association of Independent Schools, National Association of Episcopal Schools, New England Association of Schools and Colleges, New York State Association of Independent Schools, The Association of Boarding Schools, and Connecticut Department of Education. Member of National Association of Independent Schools and Secondary School Admission Test Board. Endowment: $80 million. Total enrollment: 570. Upper school average class size: 12. Upper school faculty-student ratio: 1:7. Upper School students typically attend 6 days per week.

Upper School Student Profile Grade 9: 96 students (52 boys, 44 girls); Grade 10: 142 students (62 boys, 80 girls); Grade 11: 169 students (96 boys, 73 girls); Grade 12: 138 students (68 boys, 70 girls); Postgraduate: 25 students (17 boys, 8 girls). 90% of students are boarding students. 22% are state residents. 35 states are represented in upper school student body. 28% are international students. International students from Canada, China, Hong Kong, Republic of Korea, Russian Federation, and Thailand; 40 other countries represented in student body.

Faculty School total: 73. In upper school: 43 men, 30 women; 55 have advanced degrees; 66 reside on campus.

Subjects Offered Advanced studio art-AP, African-American history, algebra, American history, American history-AP, American literature, architecture, art, art history-AP, Asian history, astronomy, Bible studies, biology, biology-AP, biotechnology, calculus, calculus-AP, ceramics, chemistry, chemistry-AP, Chinese, classical Greek literature, classical studies, composition-AP, computer math, computer programming, computer science, computer science-AP, digital imaging, drama, ecology, economics, English, English literature, English literature-AP, environmental science-AP, environmental studies, European history, European history-AP, expository writing, fine arts, French, French language-AP, French literature-AP, genetics, geology, geometry, German, German-AP, government and politics-AP, Greek, history, Latin, Latin American history, Latin-AP, law and the legal system, mathematics, meteorology, Middle Eastern history, modern European history-AP, music, music theory-AP, photography, physical education, physics, physics-AP, probability and statistics, psychology-AP, religion, science, sculpture, social studies, Spanish, Spanish language-AP, Spanish literature-AP, statistics-AP, theater, theology, trigonometry, U.S. government and politics-AP, world geography, world history, world literature.

Graduation Requirements Arts and fine arts (art, music, dance, drama), English, foreign language, history, mathematics, music, religion (includes Bible studies and theology), science, U.S. history.

Special Academic Programs 26 Advanced Placement exams for which test preparation is offered; honors section; independent study; academic accommodation for the gifted, the musically talented, and the artistically talented; ESL.

College Admission Counseling 171 students graduated in 2015; all went to college, including Boston University; Carnegie Mellon University; Colgate University; Cornell University; Princeton University; St. Lawrence University.

Student Life Upper grades have specified standards of dress, student council, honor system. Discipline rests equally with students and faculty. Attendance at religious services is required.

Summer Programs Enrichment programs offered; session focuses on Summer Educational Experience at Kent; held on campus; accepts boys and girls; open to students from other schools. 50 students usually enrolled. Application deadline: none.

Tuition and Aid Day student tuition: $44,500; 7-day tuition and room/board: $56,500. Tuition installment plan (Key Tuition Payment Plan, monthly payment plans, individually arranged payment plans). Merit scholarship grants, need-based scholarship grants, need-based loans available. In 2015–16, 42% of upper-school students received aid. Total amount of financial aid awarded in 2015–16: $8,400,000.

Admissions Traditional secondary-level entrance grade is 9. For fall 2015, 1,372 students applied for upper-level admission, 567 were accepted, 226 enrolled. ACT, PSAT or SAT for applicants to grade 11 and 12, SSAT or TOEFL required. Deadline for receipt of application materials: January 15. Application fee required: $80. Interview required.

Athletics Interscholastic: baseball (boys), basketball (b,g), crew (b,g), cross-country running (b,g), diving (b,g), field hockey (g), football (b), golf (b,g), hockey (b,g), ice hockey (b,g), lacrosse (b,g), rowing (b,g), soccer (b,g), softball (g), squash (b,g), swimming and diving (b,g), tennis (b,g); intramural: basketball (b), crew (b,g), rowing (b,g); coed interscholastic: crew, dressage, equestrian sports, golf, horseback riding; coed intramural: aerobics/dance, aerobics/Nautilus, alpine skiing, ballet, bicycling, combined training, dance, dressage, equestrian sports, figure skating, fitness, hockey, horseback riding, ice skating, life saving, modern dance, mountain biking, physical fitness, physical training, ropes courses, sailing, skiing (downhill), snowboarding, soccer, squash, strength & conditioning, swimming and diving, tennis, ultimate Frisbee, weight training, yoga. 2 athletic trainers.

Computers Computers are regularly used in all academic, journalism, newspaper, yearbook classes. Computer network features include on-campus library services, online commercial services, Internet access, wireless campus network, students have online storage for schoolwork, Adobe Creative Suite, Autodesk, Mathcad, and Microsoft Office Software for all students. Campus intranet, student e-mail accounts, and computer access in designated common areas are available to students. The school has a published electronic and media policy.

Contact Ms. Sarah Gleason Ross, Director of Admissions. 860-927-6111. Fax: 860-927-6109. E-mail: admissions@kent-school.edu. Website: www.kent-school.edu

KENTUCKY COUNTRY DAY SCHOOL

4100 Springdale Road
Louisville, Kentucky 40241

Head of School: Mr. Bradley E. Lyman

General Information Coeducational day college-preparatory, arts, technology, and honors program, independent study school. Grades JK–12. Founded: 1972. Setting: suburban. 85-acre campus. 3 buildings on campus. Approved or accredited by Independent Schools Association of the Central States. Member of National Association of Independent Schools. Endowment: $10.3 million. Total enrollment: 914. Upper school average class size: 16. Upper school faculty-student ratio: 1:7. There are 170 required school days per year for Upper School students. Upper School students typically attend 5 days per week. The average school day consists of 7 hours and 5 minutes.

Faculty School total: 125. In upper school: 19 men, 21 women; 36 have advanced degrees.

Subjects Offered Algebra, American history, American literature, art, biology, calculus, ceramics, chemistry, choral music, communications, computer math, computer programming, computer science, drama, economics, English, English literature, European history, fine arts, French, geology, geometry, government/civics, history, humanities, instrumental music, Latin, law, mathematics, multimedia, music, physical education, physics, play production, psychology, psychology-AP, science, sculpture, senior internship, senior project, social sciences, social studies, Spanish, Spanish language-AP, speech, stagecraft, statistics, studio art-AP, technical theater, theater, trigonometry, U.S. government and politics-AP, U.S. history-AP.

Graduation Requirements Arts and fine arts (art, music, dance, drama), communications, English, foreign language, mathematics, physical education (includes health), science, social studies (includes history).

Special Academic Programs 20 Advanced Placement exams for which test preparation is offered; honors section; independent study; term-away projects; study abroad; academic accommodation for the gifted, the musically talented, and the artistically talented.

College Admission Counseling 67 students graduated in 2015; 66 went to college, including Brown University; Indiana University Bloomington; Miami University; University of Cincinnati; University of Kentucky; University of Louisville. Other: 1 had other specific plans. Median SAT critical reading: 610, median SAT math: 640, median SAT writing: 640, median combined SAT: 1900, median composite ACT: 27. 58% scored over 600 on SAT critical reading, 58% scored over 600 on SAT math, 58% scored over 600 on SAT writing, 64% scored over 1800 on combined SAT, 58% scored over 26 on composite ACT.

Student Life Upper grades have specified standards of dress, student council, honor system. Discipline rests equally with students and faculty.

Summary Programs Remediation, enrichment, advancement, sports, art/fine arts, rigorous outdoor training, computer instruction programs offered; session focuses on enrichment; held on campus; accepts boys and girls; open to students from other schools. 200 students usually enrolled. 2016 schedule: June 6 to August 18. Application deadline: none.

Tuition and Aid Day student tuition: $19,950. Tuition installment plan (FACTS Tuition Payment Plan). Merit scholarship grants, need-based scholarship grants available. In 2015–16, 24% of upper-school students received aid; total upper-school merit-scholarship money awarded: $63,610.

Admissions Traditional secondary-level entrance grade is 9. For fall 2015, 58 students applied for upper-level admission, 36 were accepted, 26 enrolled. ERB Reading and Math required. Deadline for receipt of application materials: none. Application fee required: $75. On-campus interview required.

Athletics Interscholastic: baseball (boys), basketball (b,g), cross-country running (b,g), diving (b,g), field hockey (g), football (b), golf (b,g), lacrosse (b,g), soccer (b,g), softball (g), swimming and diving (b,g), tennis (b,g), track and field (b,g), volleyball (g), winter (indoor) track (b,g); coed interscholastic: weight training; coed intramural: bowling, project adventure, ropes courses, weight lifting. 8 PE instructors, 86 coaches, 1 athletic trainer.

Computers Computers are regularly used in all classes. Computer network features include on-campus library services, online commercial services, Internet access, wireless campus network, Internet filtering or blocking technology. Campus intranet and student e-mail accounts are available to students. Students grades are available online. The school has a published electronic and media policy.

Contact Mr. Jeff Holbrook, Director of Admissions. 502-814-4375. Fax: 502-814-4381. E-mail: admissions@kcd.org. Website: www.kcd.org

THE KEY SCHOOL

534 Hillsmere Drive
Annapolis, Maryland 21403

Head of School: Matthew Nespole

General Information Coeducational day college-preparatory, arts, and outdoor education school. Grades PK–12. Founded: 1958. Setting: suburban. Nearest major city is Washington, DC. 15-acre campus. 10 buildings on campus. Approved or accredited by Association of Independent Maryland Schools and Maryland Department of Education. Member of National Association of Independent Schools. Endowment: $10 million. Total enrollment: 630. Upper school average class size: 14. Upper school faculty-student ratio: 1:7. There are 173 required school days per year for Upper School students. Upper School students typically attend 5 days per week. The average school day consists of 7 hours and 20 minutes.

Upper School Student Profile Grade 9: 60 students (33 boys, 27 girls); Grade 10: 49 students (19 boys, 30 girls); Grade 11: 52 students (24 boys, 28 girls); Grade 12: 49 students (22 boys, 27 girls).

Faculty School total: 107. In upper school: 17 men, 25 women; 23 have advanced degrees.

Subjects Offered Acting, advanced biology, advanced chemistry, advanced math, algebra, American studies, ancient history, art, art history, biology, calculus, ceramics, chemistry, Chesapeake Bay studies, choir, computer education, computer literacy, computer science, computer skills, conceptual physics, creative writing, dance, digital art, digital photography, drama, drama performance, drawing, economics, English, English literature, European history, fine arts, French, geometry, journalism, Latin, literature by women, music, photography, physical education, physics, physiology, playwriting, pre-calculus, printmaking, Russian literature, sculpture, Shakespeare, Spanish, Spanish literature, statistics, studio art, theater, theater production, trigonometry.

Graduation Requirements Arts and fine arts (art, music, dance, drama), English, foreign language, history, mathematics, performing arts, physical education (includes health), science.

Special Academic Programs Advanced Placement exam preparation; honors section; independent study; academic accommodation for the gifted.

College Admission Counseling 47 students graduated in 2015; all went to college, including American University; College of Charleston; New York University; Smith College; University of Maryland, College Park; University of South Carolina.

Student Life Discipline rests equally with students and faculty.

Summer Programs Remediation, enrichment, sports, art/fine arts, rigorous outdoor training, computer instruction programs offered; held both on and off campus; held at area pools, area parks, and other off-site locations; accepts boys and girls; open to students from other schools. 900 students usually enrolled. 2016 schedule: June 20 to August 12.

Tuition and Aid Day student tuition: $26,300. Tuition installment plan (FACTS Tuition Payment Plan, monthly payment plans, Tuition Refund Plan (TRP)). Tuition reduction for siblings, need-based scholarship grants available. In 2015–16, 25% of upper-school students received aid. Total amount of financial aid awarded in 2015–16: $667,300.

Admissions Traditional secondary-level entrance grade is 9. For fall 2015, 47 students applied for upper-level admission, 32 were accepted, 20 enrolled. ISEE, PSAT and SAT for applicants to grade 11 and 12 or SAT for students entering as juniors required.

Deadline for receipt of application materials: February 15. Application fee required: $55. Interview required.

Athletics Interscholastic: baseball (boys), basketball (b,g), field hockey (g), indoor soccer (g), lacrosse (b,g), soccer (b,g), volleyball (g); intramural: field hockey (g), lacrosse (b,g); coed interscholastic: baseball, cross-country running, equestrian sports, golf, sailing, tennis; coed intramural: backpacking, basketball, canoeing/kayaking, climbing, cooperative games, dance, fitness, fitness walking, golf, hiking/backpacking, kayaking, kickball, modern dance, Newcombe ball, outdoor activities, project adventure, roller blading, running. 1 PE instructor, 44 coaches, 1 athletic trainer.

Computers Computers are regularly used in all academic classes. Computer network features include on-campus library services, online commercial services, Internet access, wireless campus network, online supplementary course materials. Campus intranet, student e-mail accounts, and computer access in designated common areas are available to students. Students grades are available online. The school has a published electronic and media policy.

Contact Tom Rossini, Director of Enrollment and Outreach. 410-263-9231 Ext. 1226. Fax: 410-280-5516. E-mail: trossini@keyschool.org. Website: www.keyschool.org

THE KEYSTONE SCHOOL

920 Central Road
Bloomsburg, Pennsylvania 17815

Head of School: Erica Rhone

General Information Distance learning only college-preparatory, general academic, arts, business, technology, and Distance Learning and Online Learning school. Distance learning grades 6–12. Founded: 1995. Setting: small town. Nearest major city is Harrisburg. Approved or accredited by Middle States Association of Colleges and Schools, Northwest Accreditation Commission, and Pennsylvania Department of Education. Total enrollment: 12,000.

Faculty School total: 100. In upper school: 40 men, 60 women.

Subjects Offered Advanced Placement courses, algebra, alternative physical education, American government, American history, American literature, art and culture, art appreciation, biology, British literature, business law, career and personal planning, chemistry, civics, composition, computer applications, computer technologies, consumer law, contemporary math, creative writing, earth science, economics, English, English composition, English literature, environmental science, fitness, foreign language, general math, geography, government, grammar, health, health education, history, independent study, intro to computers, lab science, life skills, marketing, math review, mathematics, microcomputer technology applications, music, music appreciation, physical science, physics, pre-algebra, pre-calculus, psychology, science, skills for success, social studies, sociology, trigonometry, wellness, work experience, world arts, writing.

Graduation Requirements Algebra, art, electives, English, health, mathematics, science, social sciences, 21 total credits required for graduation with a minimum of 5 coming from Keystone.

Special Academic Programs Accelerated programs; independent study; study at local college for college credit; academic accommodation for the gifted, the musically talented, and the artistically talented.

Student Life Upper grades have student council, honor system. Discipline rests equally with students and faculty.

Summer Programs Remediation, enrichment, advancement, art/fine arts, computer instruction programs offered; session focuses on credit remediation or acceleration; held off campus; held at Courses offered for at home work; accepts boys and girls; open to students from other schools.

Tuition and Aid Tuition installment plan (monthly payment plans). Tuition reduction for siblings available.

Admissions Deadline for receipt of application materials: none. No application fee required.

Computers Computers are regularly used in all classes. Computer resources include on-campus library services, Internet access, Internet filtering or blocking technology. Students grades are available online. The school has a published electronic and media policy.

Contact Elizabeth Letteer, Student Admissions Supervisor. 570-784-5220 Ext. 5512. Fax: 570-784-2129. E-mail: eletteer@keystonehighschool.com. Website: www.keystoneschoolonline.com

KEYSTONE SCHOOL

119 East Craig Place
San Antonio, Texas 78212-3497

Head of School: Mr. Brian Yager

General Information Coeducational day college-preparatory and accelerated curriculum school. Grades PK–12. Founded: 1948. Setting: urban. 3-acre campus. 12 buildings on campus. Approved or accredited by Independent Schools Association of the Southwest and Texas Department of Education. Member of National Association of Independent Schools. Endowment: $920,000. Total enrollment: 425. Upper school average class size: 16. Upper school faculty-student ratio: 1:10. Upper School students typically attend 5 days per week. The average school day consists of 7 hours and 15 minutes.

Upper School Student Profile Grade 9: 39 students (17 boys, 22 girls); Grade 10: 36 students (19 boys, 17 girls); Grade 11: 32 students (13 boys, 19 girls); Grade 12: 31 students (21 boys, 10 girls).

Faculty School total: 49. In upper school: 10 men, 11 women; 14 have advanced degrees.

Subjects Offered Advanced Placement courses, algebra, American history, American history-AP, anatomy and physiology, biology, biology-AP, calculus-AP, chemistry, chemistry-AP, civics, community service, computer science-AP, creative writing, digital imaging, English, English language and composition-AP, English literature and composition-AP, English-AP, environmental science-AP, European history-AP, French, French language-AP, French-AP, geometry, health, history, history-AP, mathematics, performing arts, photojournalism, physical education, physics, physics-AP, political science, psychology, science, social studies, Spanish, Spanish literature-AP, Spanish-AP, statistics-AP, studio art, theater, theater arts, U.S. history-AP, world history.

Graduation Requirements Arts and fine arts (art, music, dance, drama), English, foreign language, mathematics, physical education (includes health), science, social studies (includes history), 4 Advanced Placement courses. Community service is required.

Special Academic Programs Advanced Placement exam preparation; honors section; academic accommodation for the gifted.

College Admission Counseling 36 students graduated in 2015; 35 went to college, including Georgia Institute of Technology; Stanford University; The University of Texas at Austin; University of Southern California; Vanderbilt University; Washington University in St. Louis. Other: 1 had other specific plans. Mean SAT critical reading: 689, mean SAT math: 679, mean SAT writing: 694, mean combined SAT: 2062, mean composite ACT: 31.

Student Life Upper grades have student council. Discipline rests primarily with faculty.

Summer Programs Enrichment, sports programs offered; session focuses on Sports Camps, Writing Workshop, and Advanced Mammalian Dissection; held on campus; accepts boys and girls; not open to students from other schools. 60 students usually enrolled. 2016 schedule: June 2 to July 30. Application deadline: none.

Tuition and Aid Day student tuition: $17,535–$18,620. Tuition installment plan (monthly payment plans). Need-based scholarship grants available. In 2015–16, 15% of upper-school students received aid.

Admissions Traditional secondary-level entrance grade is 9. For fall 2015, 23 students applied for upper-level admission, 11 were accepted, 10 enrolled. ISEE, standardized test scores and writing sample required. Deadline for receipt of application materials: none. Application fee required: $50. On-campus interview required.

Athletics Interscholastic: basketball (boys, girls), golf (b,g), softball (g), tennis (b,g), volleyball (g); coed interscholastic: cross-country running, soccer; coed intramural: outdoor education. 3 PE instructors, 4 coaches.

Computers Computer network features include on-campus library services, online commercial services, Internet access, wireless campus network, Internet filtering or blocking technology, ProQuest Platinum. Computer access in designated common areas is available to students. Students grades are available online. The school has a published electronic and media policy.

Contact Mrs. Zina Wormley, Director of Admissions and Financial Aid. 210-735-4022. Fax: 210-732-4905. E-mail: zwormley@keystoneschool.org. Website: www.keystoneschool.org

KILDONAN SCHOOL

Amenia, New York
See Special Needs Schools section.

KING DAVID HIGH SCHOOL

5718 Willow Street
Vancouver, British Columbia V5Z 4S9, Canada

Head of School: Mr. Russ Klein

General Information Coeducational day college-preparatory, general academic, arts, business, religious studies, bilingual studies, technology, and fine arts school, affiliated with Jewish faith. Grades 8–12. Founded: 1986. Setting: suburban. 2-acre campus. 1 building on campus. Approved or accredited by Canadian Association of Independent Schools and British Columbia Department of Education. Languages of instruction: English and Hebrew. Total enrollment: 205. Upper school average class size: 20. Upper school faculty-student ratio: 1:7. There are 176 required school days per year for Upper School students. Upper School students typically attend 5 days per week. The average school day consists of 6 hours and 15 minutes.

Upper School Student Profile 100% of students are Jewish.

Faculty School total: 27. In upper school: 9 men, 17 women; 6 have advanced degrees.

Subjects Offered 20th century history, acting, adolescent issues, aquatics, art, art appreciation, art education, art history, arts and crafts, athletics, Bible studies, biology, British literature, business education, calculus, Canadian geography, Canadian history, career and personal planning, career planning, chemistry, computer education, computer graphics, computer literacy, computer science, computer skills, concert band,

contemporary art, critical thinking, critical writing, culinary arts, current events, current history, debate, decision making skills, drama, drama performance, East Asian history, English, English composition, English literature, fashion, food science, foods, foreign language, French as a second language, general math, geography, geometry, government, guitar, Hebrew, Hebrew scripture, Holocaust, Holocaust and other genocides, home economics, information technology, instrumental music, Jewish history, Judaic studies, keyboarding, language and composition, modern languages, music, music appreciation, music composition, newspaper, novels, oral expression, painting, peer counseling, performing arts, physical education, physical fitness, physics, poetry, reading/study skills, religion and culture, religious education, sex education, Shakespeare, short story, social studies, Spanish, Spanish language-AP, Talmud, technology, The 20th Century, theater arts, visual arts, volleyball, World War I, World War II, writing, yearbook.

Special Academic Programs Programs in English, general development for dyslexic students; special instructional classes for deaf students; ESL (2 students enrolled).

College Admission Counseling Colleges students went to include McGill University; Queen's University at Kingston; The University of British Columbia; The University of Western Ontario; University of Victoria.

Student Life Upper grades have uniform requirement, student council, honor system. Discipline rests primarily with faculty.

Tuition and Aid Tuition installment plan (monthly payment plans, individually arranged payment plans). Tuition reduction for siblings, need-based scholarship grants, sliding scale available.

Admissions Traditional secondary-level entrance grade is 8. For fall 2014, 54 students applied for upper-level admission, 54 were accepted, 54 enrolled. Deadline for receipt of application materials: February. Application fee required. On-campus interview recommended.

Athletics Interscholastic: badminton (boys, girls), basketball (b,g), floor hockey (b), Frisbee (b,g), golf (b,g), soccer (b,g), track and field (b,g), volleyball (g); coed interscholastic: independent competitive sports, softball. 3 PE instructors, 9 coaches.

Computers Computer network features include on-campus library services, Internet access, wireless campus network, Internet filtering or blocking technology. Campus intranet and student e-mail accounts are available to students. Students grades are available online.

Contact Ms. Debbie Appelbaum, Director of Admissions. 604-263-9700. Fax: 604-263-4848. E-mail: dappelbaum@kdhs.org. Website: www.kdhs.org

KING LOW HEYWOOD THOMAS

1450 Newfield Avenue
Stamford, Connecticut 06905

Head of School: Thomas B. Main

General Information Coeducational day college-preparatory, global studies distinction, language distinction, and independent study school. Grades PK–12. Founded: 1865. Setting: suburban. Nearest major city is New York, NY. 40-acre campus. 3 buildings on campus. Approved or accredited by Connecticut Association of Independent Schools and New England Association of Schools and Colleges. Member of National Association of Independent Schools. Endowment: $23.5 million. Total enrollment: 674. Upper school average class size: 13. Upper school faculty-student ratio: 1:8. There are 167 required school days per year for Upper School students. Upper School students typically attend 5 days per week. The average school day consists of 7 hours.

Upper School Student Profile Grade 9: 86 students (44 boys, 42 girls); Grade 10: 85 students (44 boys, 41 girls); Grade 11: 91 students (50 boys, 41 girls); Grade 12: 89 students (45 boys, 44 girls).

Faculty School total: 105. In upper school: 29 men, 28 women; 47 have advanced degrees.

Subjects Offered Acting, advanced chemistry, advanced computer applications, advanced math, Advanced Placement courses, algebra, American history, ancient history, ancient world history, ancient/medieval philosophy, anthropology, archaeology, art, biology, calculus, calculus-AP, chemistry, chemistry-AP, Chinese, choral music, college counseling, college planning, computer multimedia, computer programming, computer science-AP, digital photography, economics, economics-AP, English, English language and composition-AP, English literature, English literature-AP, environmental studies, ethics, European history, European history-AP, fine arts, French, French language-AP, general science, geometry, global studies, government, history, honors algebra, honors geometry, honors U.S. history, honors world history, independent study, life skills, literature and composition-AP, macroeconomics-AP, mathematics, microeconomics-AP, model United Nations, modern European history-AP, modern languages, music theory-AP, musical productions, musical theater, oceanography, performing arts, philosophy, physics, physics-AP, play production, pre-calculus, psychology, public speaking, robotics, SAT preparation, SAT/ACT preparation, social studies, Spanish, Spanish language-AP, Spanish literature, Spanish literature-AP, statistics, statistics-AP, student government, student publications, studio art, theater arts, trigonometry, U.S. history-AP, U.S. literature, world history, world religions.

Graduation Requirements Arts and fine arts (art, music, dance, drama), English, ethics, foreign language, history, life skills, mathematics, science, sports, participation in one theater performance before graduation.

Special Academic Programs 17 Advanced Placement exams for which test preparation is offered; honors section; independent study; academic accommodation for the gifted, the musically talented, and the artistically talented.

College Admission Counseling 75 students graduated in 2015; all went to college, including Boston University; Elon University; New York University; University of Richmond; University of Virginia; Wake Forest University. Median SAT critical reading: 585, median SAT math: 610, median SAT writing: 596, median combined SAT: 1791, median composite ACT: 28. 42% scored over 600 on SAT critical reading, 46% scored over 600 on SAT math, 51% scored over 600 on SAT writing, 41% scored over 1800 on combined SAT, 60% scored over 26 on composite ACT.

Student Life Upper grades have specified standards of dress, student council, honor system. Discipline rests primarily with faculty.

Summer Programs Remediation, enrichment, advancement, sports, art/fine arts, computer instruction programs offered; session focuses on academics (grades 6-12), enrichment (elementary school), and sports (grades 4-8) enrichment; held on campus; accepts boys and girls; open to students from other schools. 200 students usually enrolled. 2016 schedule: June 27 to August 5. Application deadline: June 1.

Tuition and Aid Day student tuition: $38,725. Tuition installment plan (Key Tuition Payment Plan). Need-based scholarship grants available. In 2015–16, 14% of upper-school students received aid. Total amount of financial aid awarded in 2015–16: $1,490,540.

Admissions Traditional secondary-level entrance grade is 9. For fall 2015, 211 students applied for upper-level admission, 68 were accepted, 36 enrolled. ISEE, school's own test or SSAT required. Deadline for receipt of application materials: January 1. Application fee required: $75. On-campus interview required.

Athletics Interscholastic: baseball (boys), basketball (b,g), cross-country running (b,g), field hockey (g), football (b), golf (b,g), ice hockey (b), independent competitive sports (b,g), lacrosse (b,g), soccer (b,g), softball (g), squash (b,g), tennis (b,g), volleyball (g); intramural: dance (g), physical training (b,g); coed interscholastic: independent competitive sports, squash; coed intramural: aerobics/dance, dance, fitness, physical training, strength & conditioning, weight lifting, weight training. 4 PE instructors, 27 coaches, 2 athletic trainers.

Computers Computers are regularly used in college planning, economics, English, ethics, foreign language, French, history, mathematics, science, technology, video film production, writing, yearbook classes. Computer network features include on-campus library services, online commercial services, Internet access, wireless campus network, Internet filtering or blocking technology. Campus intranet, student e-mail accounts, and computer access in designated common areas are available to students. The school has a published electronic and media policy.

Contact Carrie Salvatore, Director of Admission and Financial Aid. 203-322-3496 Ext. 352. Fax: 203-505-6288. E-mail: csalvatore@klht.org. Website: www.klht.org

THE KING'S CHRISTIAN HIGH SCHOOL

5 Carnegie Plaza
Cherry Hill, New Jersey 08003-1020

Head of School: John Walsh

General Information Coeducational day and distance learning college-preparatory, arts, business, religious studies, and technology school, affiliated with Christian faith. Grades P3–12. Distance learning grades 6–12. Founded: 1946. Setting: suburban. Nearest major city is Philadelphia, PA. 11-acre campus. 1 building on campus. Approved or accredited by American Association of Christian Schools, Association of Christian Schools International, Middle States Association of Colleges and Schools, and New Jersey Department of Education. Total enrollment: 311. Upper school average class size: 18. Upper school faculty-student ratio: 1:6. There are 180 required school days per year for Upper School students. Upper School students typically attend 5 days per week. The average school day consists of 6 hours and 30 minutes.

Upper School Student Profile Grade 6: 12 students (6 boys, 6 girls); Grade 7: 15 students (7 boys, 8 girls); Grade 8: 39 students (15 boys, 24 girls); Grade 9: 28 students (17 boys, 11 girls); Grade 10: 30 students (17 boys, 13 girls); Grade 11: 43 students (22 boys, 21 girls); Grade 12: 26 students (17 boys, 9 girls). 80% of students are Christian faith.

Faculty School total: 43. In upper school: 7 men, 12 women; 2 have advanced degrees.

Subjects Offered Advanced Placement courses, algebra, American literature, anatomy and physiology, art, art appreciation, band, bell choir, Bible, Bible studies, biology, biology-AP, British literature, calculus, calculus-AP, career and personal planning, career education, career/college preparation, chemistry, choir, Christian ethics, church history, college admission preparation, composition, computer education, computer graphics, computer skills, concert band, concert bell choir, concert choir, consumer mathematics, drama, economics, English literature, environmental science, ESL, fine arts, foreign language, general math, geometry, government-AP, handbells, health and safety, health and wellness, health education, honors algebra, honors English, honors geometry, honors U.S. history, instrumental music, jazz band, language arts, Life of Christ, marine science, music appreciation, music theory, New Testament, physical education, physics, SAT preparation, SAT/ACT preparation, Shakespeare, Spanish, speech, study skills, U.S. government, U.S. history, vocal ensemble, Web site design, world cultures, world history, yearbook.

Graduation Requirements Algebra, arts and fine arts (art, music, dance, drama), Bible, biology, British literature, career education, career technology, chemistry,

Christian ethics, church history, computer technologies, English composition, English literature, ethics, human biology, Life of Christ, physical education (includes health), physical science, public speaking, SAT preparation, senior project, Spanish, study skills, U.S. government, U.S. history, world literature, writing, required volunteer service hours each year for grades 6-12.

Special Academic Programs 7 Advanced Placement exams for which test preparation is offered; honors section; independent study; study at local college for college credit; programs in English, mathematics, general development for dyslexic students; special instructional classes for students with learning disabilities, Attention Deficit Disorder; ESL (35 students enrolled).

College Admission Counseling 14 students graduated in 2015; all went to college, including Cedarville University; Eastern University; Liberty University; Rutgers, The State University of New Jersey, New Brunswick. Mean SAT critical reading: 540, mean SAT math: 515, mean SAT writing: 522, mean combined SAT: 1577. 21% scored over 600 on SAT critical reading, 18% scored over 600 on SAT math, 15% scored over 600 on SAT writing.

Student Life Upper grades have specified standards of dress, student council, honor system. Discipline rests primarily with faculty. Attendance at religious services is required.

Summer Programs Remediation, enrichment, advancement, sports programs offered; session focuses on summer school programs; held both on and off campus; held at via distance learning; accepts boys and girls; open to students from other schools. 10 students usually enrolled. 2016 schedule: June 27 to August 26. Application deadline: June 21.

Tuition and Aid Day student tuition: $8870. Tuition installment plan (FACTS Tuition Payment Plan, annual and semi-annual payments). Tuition reduction for siblings, merit scholarship grants, need-based scholarship grants, military discount, Ministry Discount available. In 2015–16, 46% of upper-school students received aid.

Admissions Writing sample required. Deadline for receipt of application materials: none. Application fee required: $100. On-campus interview required.

Athletics Interscholastic: baseball (boys), basketball (b,g), cross-country running (b,g), physical fitness (b,g), soccer (b,g), softball (g), tennis (b,g), track and field (b,g); intramural: basketball (b), flag football (b), golf (b,g). 2 PE instructors, 3 coaches.

Computers Computers are regularly used in desktop publishing, graphic design, library, library skills, Web site design, writing, yearbook classes. Computer network features include on-campus library services, Internet access, wireless campus network, Internet filtering or blocking technology. Campus intranet and computer access in designated common areas are available to students. Students grades are available online. The school has a published electronic and media policy.

Contact Mrs. Mimi Magill, Director of Admissions and Development. 856-489-6720 Ext. 228. Fax: 856-489-6727. E-mail: mmagill@tkcs.org. Website: www.tkcs.org

KING'S-EDGEHILL SCHOOL

254 College Road
Windsor, Nova Scotia B0N 2T0, Canada

Head of School: Mr. Joseph Seagram

General Information Coeducational boarding and day college-preparatory school. Grades 6–12. Founded: 1788. Setting: small town. Nearest major city is Halifax, Canada. Students are housed in single-sex dormitories. 65-acre campus. 17 buildings on campus. Approved or accredited by Canadian Educational Standards Institute and Nova Scotia Department of Education. Language of instruction: English. Total enrollment: 332. Upper school average class size: 15. Upper school faculty-student ratio: 1:10. Upper School students typically attend 5 days per week. The average school day consists of 7 hours.

Upper School Student Profile Grade 10: 76 students (44 boys, 32 girls); Grade 11: 85 students (46 boys, 39 girls); Grade 12: 66 students (33 boys, 33 girls). 68% of students are boarding students. 55% are province residents. 13 provinces are represented in upper school student body. 30% are international students. International students from China, Germany, Hong Kong, Mexico, Taiwan, and United States; 13 other countries represented in student body.

Faculty School total: 49. In upper school: 22 men, 23 women; 15 have advanced degrees; 22 reside on campus.

Subjects Offered Art, biology, calculus, chemistry, current events, drama, economics, English, French, geography, geology, history, mathematics, music, physics, political science, religion, science, social sciences, social studies, theater, theory of knowledge, world history.

Graduation Requirements English, foreign language, mathematics, science, social sciences, social studies (includes history).

Special Academic Programs International Baccalaureate program; honors section; term-away projects; study abroad; academic accommodation for the gifted; ESL (22 students enrolled).

College Admission Counseling 70 students graduated in 2015; all went to college, including Dalhousie University; McGill University; Queen's University at Kingston; The University of British Columbia; The University of Western Ontario; University of Toronto.

Student Life Upper grades have uniform requirement, student council, honor system. Discipline rests primarily with faculty. Attendance at religious services is required.

Tuition and Aid Day student tuition: CAN$16,850; 7-day tuition and room/board: CAN$39,600. Tuition installment plan (monthly payment plans, individually arranged payment plans). Bursaries, merit scholarship grants available. In 2015–16, 35% of upper-school students received aid; total upper-school merit-scholarship money awarded: CAN$200,000. Total amount of financial aid awarded in 2015–16: CAN$900,000.

Admissions Traditional secondary-level entrance grade is 10. OLSAT and English Exam required. Deadline for receipt of application materials: none. Application fee required: CAN$100. Interview required.

Athletics Interscholastic: alpine skiing (boys, girls), aquatics (b,g), badminton (b,g), baseball (b,g), basketball (b,g), biathlon (b,g), bicycling (b,g), cross-country running (b,g), equestrian sports (b,g), fitness (b,g), Frisbee (b,g), golf (b,g), ice hockey (b,g), outdoor recreation (b,g), outdoor skills (b,g), physical fitness (b,g), rugby (b,g), skiing (cross-country) (b,g), skiing (downhill) (b,g), snowboarding (b,g), soccer (b,g), softball (b,g), table tennis (b,g), tennis (b,g), track and field (b,g), ultimate Frisbee (b,g), volleyball (b,g), weight lifting (b,g), wrestling (b,g); intramural: basketball (b,g), bicycling (b,g), cross-country running (b,g), golf (b,g), rugby (b,g), skiing (cross-country) (b,g), skiing (downhill) (b,g), snowboarding (b,g), soccer (b,g), softball (b,g), table tennis (b,g), tennis (b,g), track and field (b,g), weight lifting (b,g), yoga (b,g); coed interscholastic: alpine skiing, aquatics, bicycling, equestrian sports, fitness, Frisbee, outdoor recreation, outdoor skills, physical fitness, table tennis; coed intramural: bowling, curling, field hockey, table tennis, yoga. 2 PE instructors, 30 coaches.

Computers Computers are regularly used in computer applications, English, foreign language, mathematics, music, science classes. Computer network features include on-campus library services, online commercial services, Internet access, Internet filtering or blocking technology. Campus intranet, student e-mail accounts, and computer access in designated common areas are available to students.

Contact Mr. Chris B. Strickey, Director of Admission. 902-798-2278. Fax: 902-798-2105. E-mail: strickey@kes.ns.ca. Website: www.kes.ns.ca

KINGSWAY COLLEGE

1200 Leland Road
Oshawa, Ontario L1K 2H4, Canada

Head of School: Mr. Lee Richards

General Information Coeducational boarding and day college-preparatory, general academic, arts, business, religious studies, bilingual studies, and technology school, affiliated with Seventh-day Adventists. Grades 9–12. Founded: 1903. Setting: small town. Nearest major city is Toronto, Canada. Students are housed in single-sex dormitories. 100-acre campus. 9 buildings on campus. Approved or accredited by Ontario Ministry of Education and Ontario Department of Education. Language of instruction: English. Endowment: CAN$1.6 million. Total enrollment: 214. Upper school average class size: 13. Upper school faculty-student ratio: 1:13. There are 180 required school days per year for Upper School students. Upper School students typically attend 5 days per week. The average school day consists of 5 hours and 50 minutes.

Upper School Student Profile Grade 9: 48 students (23 boys, 25 girls); Grade 10: 47 students (28 boys, 19 girls); Grade 11: 53 students (31 boys, 22 girls); Grade 12: 66 students (32 boys, 34 girls). 60% of students are boarding students. 65% are province residents. 5 provinces are represented in upper school student body. 33% are international students. International students from Bermuda, China, Germany, Republic of Korea, Ukraine, and United States; 1 other country represented in student body. 67% of students are Seventh-day Adventists.

Faculty School total: 17. In upper school: 10 men, 7 women; 5 have advanced degrees; 1 resides on campus.

Subjects Offered Accounting, advanced chemistry, advanced computer applications, advanced math, algebra, American history, anthropology, band, biology, business studies, calculus, Canadian geography, Canadian history, Canadian law, career education, ceramics, chemistry, choir, civics, computer applications, computer information systems, computer programming, computer studies, concert band, English, English literature, ESL, French, healthful living, information processing, intro to computers, music, music performance, physical education, physics, psychology, religious education, science, sociology, study skills, U.S. history, visual arts, work-study, world civilizations, world religions.

Graduation Requirements Art, Canadian geography, Canadian history, careers, civics, English, French, mathematics, physical education (includes health), science, all students must take one religion course per year.

Special Academic Programs ESL (63 students enrolled).

College Admission Counseling 48 students graduated in 2015; 45 went to college, including Andrews University; Southern Adventist University; University of Toronto; Walla Walla University. Other: 3 went to work.

Student Life Upper grades have specified standards of dress, student council. Discipline rests primarily with faculty.

Tuition and Aid Day student tuition: CAN$9350; 7-day tuition and room/board: CAN$15,600. Tuition installment plan (monthly payment plans, individually arranged payment plans). Tuition reduction for siblings, merit scholarship grants, need-based scholarship grants, paying campus jobs available. In 2015–16, 30% of upper-school students received aid; total upper-school merit-scholarship money awarded: CAN$5000. Total amount of financial aid awarded in 2015–16: CAN$250,000.

Admissions Traditional secondary-level entrance grade is 9. For fall 2015, 220 students applied for upper-level admission, 215 were accepted, 214 enrolled. Deadline for receipt of application materials: none. No application fee required. Interview recommended.

Athletics Interscholastic: basketball (boys, girls); intramural: basketball (b,g), flag football (b,g), floor hockey (b,g), ice hockey (b), racquetball (b,g), soccer (b,g), softball (b,g), volleyball (b,g); coed interscholastic: backpacking; coed intramural: badminton, canoeing/kayaking, gymnastics, hiking/backpacking, roller skating, skiing (downhill), snowboarding, volleyball. 1 PE instructor, 3 coaches.

Computers Computers are regularly used in accounting, business, career education, computer applications, data processing, English, ESL, history, programming, science, social sciences, yearbook classes. Computer network features include Internet access, wireless campus network, Internet filtering or blocking technology. Student e-mail accounts and computer access in designated common areas are available to students. Students grades are available online. The school has a published electronic and media policy.

Contact Mrs. Jessika Lopez, Communications Assistant. 905-433-1144 Ext. 211. Fax: 905-433-1156. E-mail: admissions@kingswaycollege.on.ca. Website: www.kingswaycollege.on.ca

KINGSWOOD-OXFORD SCHOOL

170 Kingswood Road
West Hartford, Connecticut 06119-1430

Head of School: Mr. Dennis Bisgaard

General Information Coeducational day college-preparatory school. Grades 6–12. Founded: 1909. Setting: suburban. Nearest major city is Hartford. 30-acre campus. 11 buildings on campus. Approved or accredited by New England Association of Schools and Colleges and Connecticut Department of Education. Member of National Association of Independent Schools and Secondary School Admission Test Board. Endowment: $29.9 million. Total enrollment: 507. Upper school average class size: 12. Upper school faculty-student ratio: 1:8. There are 160 required school days per year for Upper School students. Upper School students typically attend 5 days per week. The average school day consists of 7 hours.

Upper School Student Profile Grade 9: 78 students (46 boys, 32 girls); Grade 10: 85 students (53 boys, 32 girls); Grade 11: 82 students (39 boys, 43 girls); Grade 12: 96 students (56 boys, 40 girls).

Faculty School total: 53. In upper school: 27 men, 26 women; 33 have advanced degrees.

Subjects Offered Algebra, American history, American literature, art, art history-AP, band, biology, biology-AP, calculus, calculus-AP, chemistry, chemistry-AP, Chinese, Chinese studies, chorus, composition-AP, computer science, computer science-AP, concert band, concert choir, creative writing, digital music, digital photography, dramatic arts, drawing, economics, economics-AP, English, English language-AP, English literature, English literature-AP, environmental science, fine arts, forensics, French, French language-AP, geography, geometry, government/civics-AP, jazz band, jazz ensemble, journalism, Latin, Latin-AP, marine biology, mathematics, media, music, orchestra, photography, physics, physics-AP, political science, public speaking, social studies, Spanish, Spanish language-AP, Spanish-AP, statistics, statistics-AP, theater, U.S. history-AP, visual arts, world history, world literature, writing.

Graduation Requirements Computer science, English, foreign language, mathematics, performing arts, science, social studies (includes history), technology, visual arts, participation on athletic teams, senior thesis in English, 30 hours of community service. Community service is required.

Special Academic Programs 17 Advanced Placement exams for which test preparation is offered; honors section; independent study; term-away projects; study at local college for college credit; study abroad.

College Admission Counseling 91 students graduated in 2015; all went to college, including Boston University; Trinity College; University of Connecticut. Median SAT critical reading: 615, median SAT math: 595, median SAT writing: 610, median combined SAT: 1820, median composite ACT: 27.

Student Life Upper grades have specified standards of dress, student council, honor system. Discipline rests equally with students and faculty.

Summer Programs Advancement, sports, art/fine arts programs offered; session focuses on academics, sports, and arts; held on campus; accepts boys and girls; open to students from other schools. 45 students usually enrolled.

Tuition and Aid Day student tuition: $37,500. Tuition installment plan (SMART Tuition Payment Plan). Merit scholarship grants, need-based scholarship grants available. In 2015–16, 43% of upper-school students received aid; total upper-school merit-scholarship money awarded: $276,500. Total amount of financial aid awarded in 2015–16: $2,300,000.

Admissions Traditional secondary-level entrance grade is 9. For fall 2015, 212 students applied for upper-level admission, 129 were accepted, 39 enrolled. SSAT required. Deadline for receipt of application materials: February 1. Application fee required: $55. On-campus interview required.

Athletics Interscholastic: baseball (boys), basketball (b,g), cross-country running (b,g), diving (b,g), field hockey (g), football (b), ice hockey (b,g), lacrosse (b,g), soccer (b,g), softball (g), squash (b,g), strength & conditioning (b,g), swimming and diving (b,g), tennis (b,g), track and field (b,g), volleyball (g); intramural: basketball (b,g), ice hockey (b), soccer (b,g), yoga (g); coed interscholastic: golf; coed intramural: strength & conditioning. 9 coaches, 2 athletic trainers.

Computers Computers are regularly used in English, foreign language, history, mathematics, music technology, photography, science classes. Computer resources include on-campus library services, Internet access, wireless campus network. Student e-mail accounts and computer access in designated common areas are available to students. Students grades are available online. The school has a published electronic and media policy.

Contact Ms. Sharon N. Gaskin, Director of Enrollment Management. 860-727-5000. Fax: 860-236-3651. E-mail: gaskin.s@kingswoodoxford.org. Website: www.kingswoodoxford.org

THE KNOX SCHOOL

541 Long Beach Road
St. James, New York 11780

Head of School: Ms. Kristen B. Tillona

General Information Coeducational boarding and day college-preparatory, arts, bilingual studies, and technology school. Grades 6–12. Founded: 1904. Setting: suburban. Students are housed in single-sex dormitories. 48-acre campus. 12 buildings on campus. Approved or accredited by Middle States Association of Colleges and Schools, New York State Association of Independent Schools, New York State Board of Regents, The Association of Boarding Schools, and New York Department of Education. Member of National Association of Independent Schools. Endowment: $5 million. Total enrollment: 150. Upper school average class size: 12. Upper school faculty-student ratio: 1:5. Upper School students typically attend 5 days per week.

Upper School Student Profile Grade 6: 6 students (3 boys, 3 girls); Grade 7: 13 students (8 boys, 5 girls); Grade 8: 10 students (5 boys, 5 girls); Grade 9: 28 students (16 boys, 12 girls); Grade 10: 34 students (11 boys, 23 girls); Grade 11: 27 students (14 boys, 13 girls); Grade 12: 27 students (15 boys, 12 girls). 50% of students are boarding students. 47% are state residents. 5 states are represented in upper school student body. 53% are international students. International students from China, Greece, Republic of Korea, Russian Federation, Spain, and Taiwan; 10 other countries represented in student body.

Faculty School total: 37. In upper school: 12 men, 20 women; 14 have advanced degrees; 20 reside on campus.

Subjects Offered 20th century history, algebra, American literature, art history, biology, biology-AP, British literature, calculus, calculus-AP, ceramics, chemistry, chemistry-AP, computer art, computer science, creative writing, earth science, economics, English, English composition, environmental science, ESL, European history, French, geometry, government, health and wellness, Latin, music, music history, photo shop, photography, physics, physics-AP, pre algebra, pre-calculus, psychology, robotics, Spanish, studio art, theater, U.S. history, vocal music, world history, world literature.

Graduation Requirements Art, computer education, electives, English, foreign language, health, history, lab science, mathematics, senior project, community service.

Special Academic Programs Advanced Placement exam preparation; honors section; independent study; study at local college for college credit; study abroad; academic accommodation for the gifted; ESL (32 students enrolled).

College Admission Counseling 36 students graduated in 2015; 35 went to college, including Boston University; New York University; Syracuse University; The George Washington University; University of Connecticut; University of Maryland, College Park. Other: 1 had other specific plans.

Student Life Upper grades have uniform requirement, student council, honor system. Discipline rests primarily with faculty.

Tuition and Aid Day student tuition: $10,500; 5-day tuition and room/board: $34,500; 7-day tuition and room/board: $45,000. Tuition installment plan (SMART Tuition Payment Plan, individually arranged payment plans). Need-based scholarship grants available. In 2015–16, 25% of upper-school students received aid. Total amount of financial aid awarded in 2015–16: $400,000.

Admissions Traditional secondary-level entrance grade is 9. For fall 2015, 200 students applied for upper-level admission, 133 were accepted, 62 enrolled. ERB, PSAT, SAT, or ACT for applicants to grade 11 and 12, SSAT, TOEFL or TOEFL Junior required. Deadline for receipt of application materials: February 15. Application fee required: $75. Interview required.

Athletics Interscholastic: aerobics/dance (boys, girls), baseball (b), basketball (b,g), soccer (b), softball (g), tennis (b,g), volleyball (g); coed interscholastic: crew, cross-country running, equestrian sports, fencing, golf, horseback riding, soccer; coed intramural: bowling, combined training, dance, dressage, equestrian sports, fitness, golf, horseback riding, outdoor activities, physical training, yoga. 19 coaches.

Computers Computers are regularly used in computer applications, graphic arts, graphic design classes. Computer network features include on-campus library services, Internet access, wireless campus network. Computer access in designated common areas is available to students. Students grades are available online. The school has a published electronic and media policy.

Contact Ms. Brileigh I. Pinkney, Associate Dean of Admission. 631-686-1600 Ext. 413. Fax: 631-686-1650. E-mail: bpinkney@knoxschool.org. Website: www.knoxschool.org

THE LAB SCHOOL OF WASHINGTON

Washington, District of Columbia
See Special Needs Schools section.

LA CHEIM SCHOOL

Antioch, California
See Special Needs Schools section.

LA GRANGE ACADEMY

1501 Vernon Road
La Grange, Georgia 30240

Head of School: Mr. Carl Parke

General Information Coeducational day college-preparatory, arts, and technology school. Grades PK–12. Founded: 1970. Setting: small town. Nearest major city is Atlanta. 15-acre campus. 4 buildings on campus. Approved or accredited by Georgia Independent School Association, Southern Association of Independent Schools, and Georgia Department of Education. Member of National Association of Independent Schools. Total enrollment: 215. Upper school average class size: 15. Upper school faculty-student ratio: 1:17. Upper School students typically attend 5 days per week. The average school day consists of 8 hours.

Upper School Student Profile Grade 9: 16 students (3 boys, 13 girls); Grade 10: 12 students (5 boys, 7 girls); Grade 11: 21 students (10 boys, 11 girls); Grade 12: 17 students (8 boys, 9 girls).

Faculty School total: 28. In upper school: 4 men, 8 women; 6 have advanced degrees.

Subjects Offered Advanced Placement courses, algebra, American history, American history-AP, American literature, anatomy, art, art history, biology, biology-AP, British literature, business, calculus, calculus-AP, chemistry, chemistry-AP, chorus, computer science, driver education, earth science, economics, English, English language and composition-AP, English literature, English literature and composition-AP, environmental science, environmental science-AP, expository writing, geography, geometry, government/civics, grammar, health, health education, history, instrumental music, Latin, mathematics, music, physical education, physics, political science, science, social studies, Spanish, trigonometry, world history, world literature.

Graduation Requirements English, foreign language, mathematics, physical education (includes health), science, social studies (includes history).

Special Academic Programs Advanced Placement exam preparation; honors section; independent study; academic accommodation for the gifted, the musically talented, and the artistically talented.

College Admission Counseling 13 students graduated in 2014; 12 went to college, including Auburn University; LaGrange College; University of Georgia; Villanova University. Other: 1 went to work. Median SAT critical reading: 525, median SAT math: 540, median SAT writing: 510.

Student Life Upper school grades have specified standards of dress, student council, honor system. Discipline rests primarily with faculty.

Tuition and Aid Tuition installment plan (monthly payment plans, quarterly payment plan). Merit scholarship grants, need-based scholarship grants, funded scholarships for specific groups or individuals available. In 2014–15, 20% of upper-school students received aid; total upper-school merit-scholarship money awarded: $25,000. Total amount of financial aid awarded in 2014–15: $159,411.

Admissions School's own exam required. Deadline for receipt of application materials: none. Application fee required: $50. On-campus interview required.

Athletics Interscholastic: baseball (boys), basketball (b,g), cheering (g), soccer (b,g), softball (g), tennis (b,g), weight training (b,g); coed interscholastic: tennis. 3 PE instructors, 8 coaches.

Computers Computers are regularly used in all classes. Computer network features include on-campus library services, Internet access, wireless campus network. Students grades are available online.

Contact Mr. Mike Petite, Director of Admissions. 706-882-8097. Fax: 706-882-8640. E-mail: MikePetite@lagrangeacademy.org. Website: www.lagrangeacademy.org

LA JOLLA COUNTRY DAY SCHOOL

9490 Genesee Avenue
La Jolla, California 92037

Head of School: Dr. Gary Krahn

General Information Coeducational day college-preparatory, arts, and technology school. Grades N–12. Founded: 1926. Setting: suburban. Nearest major city is San Diego. 24-acre campus. 8 buildings on campus. Approved or accredited by California Association of Independent Schools, Western Association of Schools and Colleges, and California Department of Education. Member of National Association of Independent Schools and Secondary School Admission Test Board. Endowment: $24. Total enrollment: 1,118. Upper school average class size: 16. Upper school faculty-student ratio: 1:16. There are 171 required school days per year for Upper School students.

Upper School students typically attend 5 days per week. The average school day consists of 7 hours.

Upper School Student Profile Grade 9: 106 students (57 boys, 49 girls); Grade 10: 118 students (60 boys, 58 girls); Grade 11: 117 students (68 boys, 49 girls); Grade 12: 118 students (55 boys, 63 girls).

Faculty School total: 146. In upper school: 20 men, 20 women; 31 have advanced degrees.

Subjects Offered Advanced studio art-AP, algebra, art, art history-AP, art-AP, ASB Leadership, astronomy, athletic training, band, baseball, basketball, biology, biology-AP, calculus, calculus-AP, ceramics, chemistry, chemistry-AP, choir, choral music, chorus, college counseling, community service, computer graphics, conceptual physics, concert band, creative writing, dance, dance performance, digital photography, drama, economics, English, English literature, English literature and composition-AP, English-AP, environmental science, European history, European history-AP, experiential education, film studies, French, French language-AP, French-AP, freshman seminar, geometry, golf, government, government and politics-AP, government-AP, history-AP, honors algebra, honors geometry, independent study, instrumental music, journalism, linear algebra, madrigals, Mandarin, marine biology, modern European history-AP, music appreciation, music theory, music theory-AP, music-AP, neuroscience, performing arts, photography, physical education, physics, physics-AP, portfolio art, pre-calculus, programming, psychology, psychology-AP, Spanish, Spanish language-AP, Spanish literature-AP, Spanish-AP, speech, statistics-AP, strings, studio art, studio art-AP, technical theater, theater, theater arts, theater history, theater production, U.S. history-AP, world cultures, writing.

Graduation Requirements Arts and fine arts (art, music, dance, drama), English, foreign language, mathematics, performing arts, physical education (includes health), science, senior project, social sciences, speech, 40 hours of community service.

Special Academic Programs Advanced Placement exam preparation; honors section; study abroad.

College Admission Counseling 128 students graduated in 2015; 126 went to college, including Chapman University; The George Washington University; Tulane University; University of California, Berkeley; University of San Diego; University of Southern California. Other: 2 had other specific plans. Median SAT critical reading: 600, median SAT math: 630, median SAT writing: 620, median composite ACT: 29. 48% scored over 600 on SAT critical reading, 61% scored over 600 on SAT math, 57% scored over 600 on SAT writing, 68% scored over 26 on composite ACT.

Student Life Upper grades have specified standards of dress, student council. Discipline rests equally with students and faculty.

Summer Programs Remediation, enrichment, advancement, sports, art/fine arts, computer instruction programs offered; session focuses on academics, summer camp, sports camps; held both on and off campus; held at swimming at the Jewish Community Center; accepts boys and girls; open to students from other schools. 300 students usually enrolled. 2016 schedule: June 22 to July 31. Application deadline: none.

Tuition and Aid Day student tuition: $30,920. Tuition installment plan (FACTS Tuition Payment Plan, monthly payment plans). Need-based scholarship grants available. In 2014–15, 25% of upper-school students received aid. Total amount of financial aid awarded in 2014–15: $2,285,386.

Admissions Traditional secondary-level entrance grade is 9. ERB (grade level), ISEE, TerraNova or writing sample required. Deadline for receipt of application materials: January 30. Application fee required: $125. On-campus interview required.

Athletics Interscholastic: aquatics (boys, girls), baseball (b), basketball (b,g), cross-country running (b,g), dance squad (g), fencing (b,g), football (b), golf (b,g), lacrosse (b,g), soccer (b,g), softball (g), surfing (b,g), swimming and diving (b,g), tennis (b,g), track and field (b,g), volleyball (g), water polo (b,g); intramural: independent competitive sports (b,g); coed interscholastic: cheering, rock climbing, strength & conditioning, ultimate Frisbee; coed intramural: outdoor education, snowboarding. 1 PE instructor, 5 coaches, 1 athletic trainer.

Computers Computers are regularly used in art, English, French, history, mathematics, science, Spanish, technology classes. Computer network features include on-campus library services, online commercial services, Internet access, wireless campus network, Internet filtering or blocking technology, email connection from home. Student e-mail accounts are available to students. The school has a published electronic and media policy.

Contact Ms. Inez Odom, Director of Admission. 858-453-3440 Ext. 273. Fax: 858-453-8210. E-mail: Iodom@ljcds.org. Website: www.ljcds.org

LAKEFIELD COLLEGE SCHOOL

4391 County Road #29
Lakefield, Ontario K0L 2H0, Canada

Head of School: Mr. Struan Robertson

General Information Coeducational boarding and day and distance learning college-preparatory, arts, and athletics, music, outdoor education school, affiliated with Church of England (Anglican). Grades 9–12. Distance learning grades 9–12. Founded: 1879. Setting: small town. Nearest major city is Toronto, Canada. Students are housed in single-sex dormitories. 315-acre campus. 27 buildings on campus. Approved or accredited by Canadian Association of Independent Schools, The Association of Boarding Schools, and Ontario Department of Education. Affiliate member of National Association of Independent Schools; member of Secondary School Admission Test

Board. Language of instruction: English. Endowment: CAN$30.5 million. Total enrollment: 365. Upper school average class size: 16. Upper school faculty-student ratio: 1:7. There are 195 required school days per year for Upper School students. Upper School students typically attend 6 days per week. The average school day consists of 5 hours.

Upper School Student Profile Grade 9: 55 students (28 boys, 27 girls); Grade 10: 96 students (49 boys, 47 girls); Grade 11: 105 students (58 boys, 47 girls); Grade 12: 109 students (53 boys, 56 girls). 70% of students are boarding students. 59% are province residents. 16 provinces are represented in upper school student body. 32% are international students. International students from Barbados, Bermuda, China, Democratic People's Republic of Korea, Germany, and Mexico; 27 other countries represented in student body.

Faculty School total: 53. In upper school: 27 men, 22 women; 12 have advanced degrees; 25 reside on campus.

Subjects Offered Algebra, art, art history, biology, calculus, chemistry, computer science, creative writing, drama, earth science, economics, English, English literature, environmental science, fine arts, French, geography, geometry, government/civics, health, history, kinesiology, mathematics, music, outdoor education, physical education, physics, science, social studies, sociology, Spanish, theater, trigonometry, vocal music, world literature.

Graduation Requirements English, foreign language, mathematics, physical education (includes health), science, social studies (includes history).

Special Academic Programs 8 Advanced Placement exams for which test preparation is offered; term-away projects; study abroad.

College Admission Counseling 103 students graduated in 2015; 98 went to college, including McGill University; Ryerson University; The University of Western Ontario; Trent University; University of Ottawa; University of Toronto. Other: 5 had other specific plans.

Student Life Upper grades have uniform requirement, student council, honor system. Discipline rests equally with students and faculty.

Summer Programs Enrichment programs offered; session focuses on online courses; held both on and off campus; held at via distance learning; accepts boys and girls; open to students from other schools. 100 students usually enrolled. 2016 schedule: June 21 to August 29.

Tuition and Aid Day student tuition: CAN$30,200; 7-day tuition and room/board: CAN$53,950. Tuition installment plan (Insured Tuition Payment Plan, monthly payment plans, individually arranged payment plans, 3-payment plans or custom payment plans if req'd). Bursaries, merit scholarship grants, need-based scholarship grants available. In 2015–16, 25% of upper-school students received aid; total upper-school merit-scholarship money awarded: CAN$40,000. Total amount of financial aid awarded in 2015–16: CAN$180,000.

Admissions Traditional secondary-level entrance grade is 9. For fall 2015, 225 students applied for upper-level admission, 193 were accepted, 140 enrolled. Otis-Lennon School Ability Test or SSAT required. Deadline for receipt of application materials: none. Application fee required: CAN$100. Interview required.

Athletics Interscholastic: alpine skiing (boys, girls), baseball (b), basketball (g), crew (b,g), cross-country running (b,g), field hockey (g), hockey (b,g), ice hockey (b,g), nordic skiing (b,g), outdoor education (b,g), physical fitness (b,g), rock climbing (b,g), ropes courses (b,g), rowing (b,g), rugby (b,g), skiing (cross-country) (b,g), skiing (downhill) (b,g), snowboarding (b,g), soccer (b,g), softball (b), tennis (b), track and field (b,g), volleyball (g); intramural: aerobics/dance (g), basketball (b,g), cross-country running (b,g), fitness (b,g), running (b,g), skiing (cross-country) (b,g), tennis (b,g); coed interscholastic: alpine skiing, badminton, cross-country running, dressage, equestrian sports, Frisbee, hockey, horseback riding, ice hockey, nordic skiing, outdoor education, physical fitness, rock climbing, sailboarding, sailing, skiing (cross-country), skiing (downhill), snowboarding, tennis, track and field, ultimate Frisbee, wall climbing, windsurfing; coed intramural: basketball, canoeing/kayaking, climbing, cross-country running, dance, dance team, equestrian sports, fitness, ice hockey, kayaking, running, sailboarding, sailing, skiing (cross-country), skiing (downhill), softball, tennis, weight training, windsurfing, yoga.

Computers Computers are regularly used in all classes. Computer network features include on-campus library services, online commercial services, Internet access, wireless campus network, Internet filtering or blocking technology. Campus intranet, student e-mail accounts, and computer access in designated common areas are available to students. Students grades are available online. The school has a published electronic and media policy.

Contact Mrs. Barbara M. Rutherford, Assistant Director of Admissions. 705-652-3324 Ext. 345. Fax: 705-652-6320. E-mail: admissions@lcs.on.ca. Website: www.lcs.on.ca

LAKEHILL PREPARATORY SCHOOL

2720 Hillside Drive
Dallas, Texas 75214

Head of School: Roger L. Perry

General Information Coeducational day college-preparatory, arts, bilingual studies, and technology school. Grades K–12. Founded: 1971. Setting: urban. 23-acre campus. 4 buildings on campus. Approved or accredited by Independent Schools Association of the Southwest, Texas Private School Accreditation Commission, The College Board, and Texas Department of Education. Member of National Association of Independent

Schools. Endowment: $300,000. Total enrollment: 405. Upper school average class size: 15. Upper school faculty-student ratio: 1:10. There are 175 required school days per year for Upper School students. Upper School students typically attend 5 days per week. The average school day consists of 7 hours and 30 minutes.

Upper School Student Profile Grade 9: 32 students (15 boys, 17 girls); Grade 10: 25 students (11 boys, 14 girls); Grade 11: 33 students (18 boys, 15 girls); Grade 12: 26 students (12 boys, 14 girls).

Faculty School total: 44. In upper school: 9 men, 13 women; 18 have advanced degrees.

Subjects Offered Advanced Placement courses, advanced studio art-AP, algebra, American history, American history-AP, American literature, art, art history, biology, broadcast journalism, business communications, calculus, calculus-AP, chemistry, college counseling, computer math, computer programming, computer programming-AP, computer science, digital photography, drama, earth science, economics, English, English language and composition-AP, English literature, environmental science-AP, European history, French, French language-AP, geography, geometry, government/civics, grammar, health, history, journalism, Latin, mathematics, music, music theater, physical education, physics, psychology, public speaking, publications, science, senior career experience, Shakespeare, social sciences, social studies, Spanish, Spanish language-AP, Spanish literature-AP, speech, statistics, theater, trigonometry, Western civilization, world history, world literature, writing.

Graduation Requirements Arts and fine arts (art, music, dance, drama), computer science, electives, English, foreign language, mathematics, physical education (includes health), science, social studies (includes history), senior internship program.

Special Academic Programs 14 Advanced Placement exams for which test preparation is offered; honors section; independent study; study abroad.

College Admission Counseling 22 students graduated in 2015; all went to college, including New York University; Rhodes College; Texas A&M University; The University of Texas at Austin. Median SAT critical reading: 595, median SAT math: 562, median SAT writing: 563, median combined SAT: 1719, median composite ACT: 27.

Student Life Upper grades have specified standards of dress, student council, honor system. Discipline rests primarily with faculty.

Summer Programs Enrichment, sports, art/fine arts, computer instruction programs offered; session focuses on enrichment; held on campus; accepts boys and girls; open to students from other schools. 300 students usually enrolled. 2016 schedule: June 6 to August 8. Application deadline: May 15.

Tuition and Aid Day student tuition: $19,900. Tuition installment plan (monthly payment plans). Tuition reduction for siblings, need-based scholarship grants available. In 2015–16, 19% of upper-school students received aid.

Admissions Traditional secondary-level entrance grade is 9. ERB CTP IV, ISEE or Stanford Achievement Test required. Deadline for receipt of application materials: January 15. Application fee required: $100. On-campus interview recommended.

Athletics Interscholastic: baseball (boys), basketball (b,g), cheering (g), crew (b,g), cross-country running (b,g), football (b), golf (b,g), rock climbing (b,g), rowing (b,g), running (b,g), softball (g), strength & conditioning (b,g), swimming and diving (b,g), tennis (b,g), track and field (b,g), volleyball (g), weight training (b,g); coed interscholastic: soccer, swimming and diving, tennis; coed intramural: bowling. 3 PE instructors, 12 coaches, 1 athletic trainer.

Computers Computers are regularly used in all academic, art, college planning, creative writing, English, graphic design, journalism, mathematics, science, speech, Web site design, word processing, writing, yearbook classes. Computer network features include on-campus library services, online commercial services, Internet access, wireless campus network, Internet filtering or blocking technology. Student e-mail accounts and computer access in designated common areas are available to students. Students grades are available online. The school has a published electronic and media policy.

Contact Lisa Bracken, Director of Admission. 214-826-2931. Fax: 214-826-4623. E-mail: lbracken@lakehillprep.org. Website: www.lakehillprep.org

LA LUMIERE SCHOOL
6801 North Wilhelm Road
La Porte, Indiana 46350

Head of School: Dr. Charles F. Clark

General Information Coeducational boarding and day college-preparatory, arts, and religious studies school, affiliated with Roman Catholic Church. Boarding grades 9–PG, day grades 9–12. Founded: 1963. Setting: rural. Nearest major city is Chicago, IL. Students are housed in single-sex dormitories. 190-acre campus. 22 buildings on campus. Approved or accredited by Independent Schools Association of the Central States, Midwest Association of Boarding Schools, North Central Association of Colleges and Schools, and The Association of Boarding Schools. Member of National Association of Independent Schools. Total enrollment: 230. Upper school average class size: 11. Upper school faculty-student ratio: 1:7. There are 174 required school days per year for Upper School students. Upper School students typically attend 5 days per week. The average school day consists of 7 hours and 30 minutes.

Upper School Student Profile Grade 9: 55 students (25 boys, 30 girls); Grade 10: 57 students (33 boys, 24 girls); Grade 11: 60 students (29 boys, 31 girls); Grade 12: 58 students (29 boys, 29 girls). 38% of students are boarding students. 61% are state residents. 9 states are represented in upper school student body. 20% are international students. International students from Australia, Canada, China, Denmark, Japan, and Republic of Korea; 3 other countries represented in student body. 45% of students are Roman Catholic.

Faculty School total: 34. In upper school: 20 men, 14 women; 20 have advanced degrees; 28 reside on campus.

Subjects Offered Acting, advanced biology, advanced chemistry, advanced computer applications, Advanced Placement courses, algebra, American government, American history, American history-AP, American literature, anatomy and physiology, applied music, art, art history, band, Basic programming, Bible, Bible as literature, Bible studies, biochemistry, biology, biology-AP, British literature, calculus, chemistry, Chinese, choir, Christian and Hebrew scripture, Christian studies, college counseling, communications, comparative government and politics, comparative government and politics-AP, computer programming, computer programming-AP, conceptual physics, concert choir, contemporary issues, creative writing, current events, debate, desktop publishing, digital photography, drama, drama performance, drama workshop, economics, economics-AP, English, English as a foreign language, English composition, English literature, English literature-AP, English-AP, entrepreneurship, environmental geography, environmental science, environmental science-AP, environmental studies, equality and freedom, equestrian sports, ESL, ESL, ethical decision making, ethics, ethics and responsibility, fine arts, finite math, fitness, foreign language, French, French as a second language, freshman seminar, geography, geometry, government, government and politics-AP, government-AP, government/civics, graphic design, health, health and safety, health and wellness, health education, Hebrew scripture, history, history-AP, human anatomy, human biology, independent study, instrumental music, international relations, introduction to literature, jazz band, jazz ensemble, language and composition, Latin, leadership, literature, literature-AP, marine biology, marine science, marine studies, moral reasoning, multicultural literature, music, music theory, New Testament, non-Western literature, oceanography, participation in sports, philosophy, photography, physics, physics-AP, physiology, portfolio art, pre-calculus, programming, psychology, psychology-AP, public speaking, SAT/ACT preparation, Spanish, Spanish literature, Spanish-AP, speech, speech and debate, sports, statistics, statistics-AP, studio art, study skills, theology, trigonometry, U.S. government, U.S. government and politics-AP, U.S. history, U.S. history-AP, U.S. literature, Web site design, world history, world literature, world religions, writing, writing, yearbook.

Graduation Requirements American government, American literature, arts and fine arts (art, music, dance, drama), Bible as literature, British literature, economics, electives, English, English composition, English literature, ethics, foreign language, health education, leadership, mathematics, science, social studies (includes history), U.S. history, world history.

Special Academic Programs Advanced Placement exam preparation; honors section; independent study; study at local college for college credit; academic accommodation for the gifted and the artistically talented; ESL (16 students enrolled).

College Admission Counseling 50 students graduated in 2015; all went to college, including Arizona State University at the Tempe campus; Indiana University Bloomington; Loyola University Chicago; Purdue University; University of California, Los Angeles; University of Notre Dame. Median SAT critical reading: 500, median SAT math: 580, median SAT writing: 520, median combined SAT: 1640, median composite ACT: 26. 24% scored over 600 on SAT critical reading, 46% scored over 600 on SAT math, 29% scored over 600 on SAT writing, 27% scored over 1800 on combined SAT, 57% scored over 26 on composite ACT.

Student Life Upper grades have uniform requirement, student council. Discipline rests primarily with faculty.

Summer Programs Enrichment, advancement, ESL, sports programs offered; session focuses on academics; held both on and off campus; held at English Language Institute is held on campus, but also includes trips to 4 U.S. cities and academic and service trips to Italy, Prague, and Taiwan are available to students during the summer; accepts boys and girls; open to students from other schools.

Tuition and Aid Day student tuition: $13,725; 7-day tuition and room/board: $42,230. Tuition installment plan (FACTS Tuition Payment Plan, individually arranged payment plans). Merit scholarship grants, need-based scholarship grants available. In 2015–16, 27% of upper-school students received aid; total upper-school merit-scholarship money awarded: $53,250. Total amount of financial aid awarded in 2015–16: $988,830.

Admissions Traditional secondary-level entrance grade is 9. For fall 2015, 164 students applied for upper-level admission, 99 were accepted, 53 enrolled. SSAT or TOEFL required. Deadline for receipt of application materials: none. Application fee required: $50. Interview required.

Athletics Interscholastic: baseball (boys), basketball (b,g), cheering (b), crew (b,g), cross-country running (b,g), fitness (b,g), football (b), golf (b,g), independent competitive sports (b,g), lacrosse (b), soccer (b,g), track and field (b,g), volleyball (b). 10 coaches, 1 athletic trainer.

Computers Computers are regularly used in all academic, college planning, creative writing, programming, yearbook classes. Computer network features include on-campus library services, Internet access, wireless campus network, Internet filtering or blocking technology. Campus intranet, student e-mail accounts, and computer access in designated common areas are available to students. Students grades are available online. The school has a published electronic and media policy.

Contact Mrs. Alexandra Penry, Director of Admissions. 219-326-7450. Fax: 219-325-3185. E-mail: apenry@lalumiere.org. Website: www.lalumiere.org

LANCASTER CATHOLIC HIGH SCHOOL

650 Juliette Avenue
Lancaster, Pennsylvania 17601

Head of School: Terry J. Klugh

General Information Coeducational day college-preparatory, arts, religious studies, and technology school, affiliated with Roman Catholic Church. Grades 9–12. Founded: 1929. Setting: small town. 1 building on campus. Approved or accredited by Middle States Association of Colleges and Schools, National Catholic Education Association, and Pennsylvania Department of Education. Total enrollment: 630. Upper school average class size: 25. There are 180 required school days per year for Upper School students. Upper School students typically attend 5 days per week. The average school day consists of 6 hours and 56 minutes.

Special Academic Programs Advanced Placement exam preparation; honors section; study at local college for college credit; academic accommodation for the gifted, the musically talented, and the artistically talented; remedial reading and/or remedial writing.

College Admission Counseling 155 students graduated in 2015.

Student Life Upper grades have uniform requirement, student council, honor system. Discipline rests primarily with faculty. Attendance at religious services is required.

Admissions Traditional secondary-level entrance grade is 9. No application fee required.

Athletics Interscholastic: aerobics/dance (girls), aquatics (b,g), ballet (g), baseball (b), basketball (b,g), bowling (b,g), cheering (g), cross-country running (b,g), dance (g), dance team (g), field hockey (g), flag football (g), football (b), golf (b), indoor track & field (b,g), lacrosse (b,g), modern dance (g), soccer (b,g), softball (g), swimming and diving (b,g), table tennis (b,g), tennis (b,g), track and field (b,g), winter (indoor) track (b,g).

Computers Computer resources include Internet access, wireless campus network, Internet filtering or blocking technology. Students grades are available online. The school has a published electronic and media policy.

Contact Kyla Hockley, Admissions Counselor. 717-509-0313. Fax: 717-509-0312. E-mail: khockley@lchsyes.org. Website: www.lchsyes.org/

LANCASTER MENNONITE HIGH SCHOOL

2176 Lincoln Highway East
Lancaster, Pennsylvania 17602

Head of School: Mr. Elvin Kennel

General Information Coeducational boarding and day college-preparatory, general academic, arts, vocational, religious studies, bilingual studies, and agriculture school, affiliated with Mennonite Church. Boarding grades 9–12, day grades 6–12. Founded: 1942. Setting: suburban. Nearest major city is Philadelphia. Students are housed in coed dormitories and single-sex by wings. 100-acre campus. 10 buildings on campus. Approved or accredited by Mennonite Education Agency, Mennonite Schools Council, and Pennsylvania Department of Education. Endowment: $12 million. Total enrollment: 1,393. Upper school average class size: 18. Upper school faculty-student ratio: 1:15. There are 182 required school days per year for Upper School students. Upper School students typically attend 5 days per week. The average school day consists of 6 hours and 30 minutes.

Upper School Student Profile Grade 9: 126 students (59 boys, 67 girls); Grade 10: 144 students (63 boys, 81 girls); Grade 11: 152 students (72 boys, 80 girls); Grade 12: 170 students (93 boys, 77 girls). 8% of students are boarding students. 89% are state residents. 4 states are represented in upper school student body. 11% are international students. International students from China, Ethiopia, Hong Kong, Republic of Korea, Taiwan, and Viet Nam; 13 other countries represented in student body. 30% of students are Mennonite.

Faculty School total: 77. In upper school: 38 men, 37 women; 50 have advanced degrees; 4 reside on campus.

Subjects Offered 1 1/2 elective credits, 3-dimensional art, 3-dimensional design, accounting, advanced biology, advanced chemistry, advanced math, Advanced Placement courses, agriculture, American government, American history, American history-AP, art appreciation, athletics, band, baseball, basketball, bell choir, Bible, Bible as literature, Bible studies, biology, biology-AP, bowling, business, business mathematics, calculus, calculus-AP, career experience, career exploration, career/college preparation, chemistry, chemistry-AP, Chinese, choir, chorus, Christian doctrine, Christian education, Christian scripture, Christian studies, church history, communications, community service, comparative government and politics, comparative government and politics-AP, concert band, concert choir, creative writing, culinary arts, drama, drawing, driver education, ecology, electives, English, English composition, English language and composition-AP, entrepreneurship, environmental science, ESL, European history, family and consumer science, family living, family studies, fashion, foods, foreign language, French, German, guitar, health education, history, human development, instrumental music, jazz band, language arts, Life of Christ, literary magazine, literature-AP, music, music appreciation, music composition,

music performance, music theory, music-AP, musical productions, newspaper, orchestra, painting, parent/child development, participation in sports, performing arts, photography, physical education, physics, physics-AP, psychology, psychology-AP, public speaking, science, senior project, small engine repair, sociology, softball, Spanish, Spanish language-AP, statistics, statistics-AP, strings, student government, student publications, tennis, track and field, U.S. history, U.S. history-AP, U.S. literature, visual and performing arts, visual arts, voice, volleyball, weight training, welding, wind ensemble, wind instruments, woodworking, world history, world history-AP, writing.

Graduation Requirements A certain amount of credits are needed in various academic areas.

Special Academic Programs 13 Advanced Placement exams for which test preparation is offered; honors section; independent study; study at local college for college credit; academic accommodation for the musically talented; remedial reading and/or remedial writing; remedial math; special instructional classes for deaf students, blind students; ESL (40 students enrolled).

College Admission Counseling 170 students graduated in 2015; 127 went to college, including Drexel University; Eastern Mennonite University; Messiah College; Millersville University of Pennsylvania; Penn State University Park. Other: 29 went to work, 14 had other specific plans.

Student Life Upper grades have specified standards of dress, student council. Discipline rests primarily with faculty. Attendance at religious services is required.

Summer Programs Enrichment, sports, art/fine arts programs offered; held on campus; accepts boys and girls; open to students from other schools. 200 students usually enrolled. 2016 schedule: June to August. Application deadline: none.

Tuition and Aid Day student tuition: $8034; 5-day tuition and room/board: $14,334; 7-day tuition and room/board: $18,114. Tuition installment plan (monthly payment plans). Tuition reduction for siblings, merit scholarship grants, need-based scholarship grants, paying campus jobs available. In 2014–15, 40% of upper-school students received aid; total upper-school merit-scholarship money awarded: $20,000. Total amount of financial aid awarded in 2014–15: $3,000,000.

Admissions Traditional secondary-level entrance grade is 9. For fall 2015, 112 students applied for upper-level admission, 112 were accepted, 112 enrolled. Deadline for receipt of application materials: none. Application fee required: $100. Interview recommended.

Athletics Interscholastic: ball hockey (girls), baseball (b), basketball (b,g), cross-country running (b,g), field hockey (g), football (b), golf (b), lacrosse (b), soccer (b,g), softball (g), tennis (b,g), track and field (b,g), volleyball (b,g); coed interscholastic: baseball, bowling. 4 PE instructors, 20 coaches, 1 athletic trainer.

Computers Computers are regularly used in all academic classes. Computer network features include on-campus library services, Internet access, wireless campus network, Internet filtering or blocking technology. Campus intranet and student e-mail accounts are available to students. Students grades are available online. The school has a published electronic and media policy.

Contact Christy L. Horst, Director of Admissions. 717-509-4459 Ext. 312. Fax: 717-299-0823. E-mail: horstcl@lancastermennonite.org. Website: www.lancastermennonite.org

LANDMARK CHRISTIAN ACADEMY

6502 Johnsontown Road
Louisville, Kentucky 40272

Head of School: Mr. Monte L. Ashworth

General Information Coeducational day college-preparatory and religious studies school, affiliated with Baptist Church. Grades K4–12. Founded: 1978. Setting: suburban. 5-acre campus. 1 building on campus. Approved or accredited by American Association of Christian Schools. Total enrollment: 144. Upper school average class size: 8. Upper school faculty-student ratio: 1:6. There are 177 required school days per year for Upper School students. Upper School students typically attend 5 days per week. The average school day consists of 6 hours and 50 minutes.

Upper School Student Profile Grade 9: 5 students (4 boys, 1 girl); Grade 10: 11 students (7 boys, 4 girls); Grade 11: 5 students (1 boy, 4 girls); Grade 12: 5 students (2 boys, 3 girls). 80% of students are Baptist.

Faculty School total: 16. In upper school: 5 men, 4 women; 2 have advanced degrees.

Subjects Offered Advanced math, algebra, American history, American literature, analytic geometry, ancient history, ancient world history, Bible, biology, business mathematics, chemistry, choir, computer technologies, consumer economics, consumer mathematics, economics, English composition, English literature, general science, geography, geometry, grammar, health, history, home economics, keyboarding, modern history, physical education, physics, pre-algebra, pre-calculus, speech, trigonometry, world geography, world history.

Graduation Requirements Bible, computers, English, foreign language, history, mathematics, science, social sciences.

College Admission Counseling 10 students graduated in 2015; 8 went to college, including Indiana University Bloomington; Jefferson Community and Technical College; University of Louisville. Other: 1 went to work, 1 had other specific plans. Mean composite ACT: 22.

Student Life Upper grades have uniform requirement. Discipline rests primarily with faculty.

Tuition and Aid Day student tuition: $3500. Tuition installment plan (FACTS Tuition Payment Plan). Tuition reduction for siblings available.

Admissions Traditional secondary-level entrance grade is 9. For fall 2015, 3 students applied for upper-level admission, 3 were accepted, 3 enrolled. Math and English placement tests required. Deadline for receipt of application materials: none. Application fee required: $275. On-campus interview required.

Athletics Interscholastic: basketball (boys), soccer (b), track and field (b,g), volleyball (g). 1 PE instructor, 3 coaches.

Computers Computers are regularly used in computer applications, keyboarding, Spanish classes. The school has a published electronic and media policy.

Contact Mrs. Gloria G. Hope, School Secretary. 502-933-3000 Ext. 2. Fax: 502-933-5179. E-mail: LCAinfo@libcky.com. Website: www.lcaky.com/main.html

LANDMARK CHRISTIAN SCHOOL

50 SE Broad Street
Fairburn, Georgia 30213
Head of School: Mr. Mike Titus

General Information Coeducational day college-preparatory, arts, and religious studies school, affiliated with Christian faith, Christian faith. Grades K4–12. Founded: 1989. Setting: suburban. Nearest major city is Atlanta. 62-acre campus. 4 buildings on campus. Approved or accredited by Association of Christian Schools International, Southern Association of Colleges and Schools, and Georgia Department of Education. Total enrollment: 807. Upper school average class size: 17. Upper school faculty-student ratio: 1:8. There are 177 required school days per year for Upper School students. Upper School students typically attend 5 days per week. The average school day consists of 7 hours and 15 minutes.

Upper School Student Profile Grade 9: 66 students (25 boys, 41 girls); Grade 10: 81 students (43 boys, 38 girls); Grade 11: 65 students (37 boys, 28 girls); Grade 12: 65 students (31 boys, 34 girls). 100% of students are Christian faith, Christian faith.

Faculty School total: 85. In upper school: 15 men, 34 women; 12 have advanced degrees.

Subjects Offered Advanced biology, advanced chemistry, advanced math, Advanced Placement courses, advanced studio art-AP, algebra, American government, American history, American literature-AP, anatomy and physiology, art, art-AP, athletic training, band, baseball, basketball, Bible, Bible studies, biology, biology-AP, British literature-AP, calculus, calculus-AP, chamber groups, cheerleading, chemistry, chemistry-AP, choral music, chorus, Christian studies, communications, composition, computer literacy, computer skills, computer technologies, computers, concert band, concert choir, drama, drama performance, economics, electives, English, English language and composition-AP, English literature, English literature-AP, English-AP, fine arts, foreign language, forensics, geometry, golf, government/civics-AP, health, health and wellness, history, history-AP, honors algebra, honors English, honors geometry, honors U.S. history, human anatomy, human biology, instrumental music, keyboarding, leadership education training, marine biology, music, music appreciation, music theater, physics, physics-AP, physiology, pre-calculus, social studies, Spanish, Spanish language-AP, Spanish-AP, speech, sports medicine, statistics, swimming, tennis, theater arts, U.S. history, U.S. history-AP, vocal ensemble, volleyball, weight training, writing, yearbook.

Graduation Requirements American government, American history, American literature, arts and fine arts (art, music, dance, drama), Bible, biology, British literature, chemistry, economics, electives, foreign language, geometry, language and composition, personal fitness, physical education (includes health), pre-calculus, world history, world literature.

Special Academic Programs 9 Advanced Placement exams for which test preparation is offered; honors section; study at local college for college credit.

College Admission Counseling 62 students graduated in 2015; all went to college, including Auburn University; Georgia Institute of Technology; Mercer University; Samford University; University of Georgia. Median SAT critical reading: 540, median SAT math: 540, median SAT writing: 540, median combined SAT: 1620, median composite ACT: 24. 27% scored over 600 on SAT critical reading, 26% scored over 600 on SAT math, 26% scored over 600 on SAT writing, 25% scored over 1800 on combined SAT, 35% scored over 26 on composite ACT.

Student Life Upper grades have specified standards of dress, student council, honor system. Discipline rests primarily with faculty. Attendance at religious services is required.

Summer Programs Computer instruction programs offered; held on campus; accepts boys and girls; not open to students from other schools. 20 students usually enrolled. 2016 schedule: June to August.

Tuition and Aid Day student tuition: $14,975. Tuition installment plan (monthly payment plans). Need-based scholarship grants available. In 2015–16, 20% of upper-school students received aid. Total amount of financial aid awarded in 2015–16: $250,000.

Admissions Traditional secondary-level entrance grade is 9. For fall 2015, 50 students applied for upper-level admission, 25 were accepted, 18 enrolled. School placement exam required. Deadline for receipt of application materials: February 15. Application fee required: $100. On-campus interview required.

Athletics Interscholastic: baseball (boys), basketball (b,g), cheering (g), cross-country running (b,g), football (b), golf (b,g), physical training (b,g), soccer (b,g), softball (g), strength & conditioning (b,g), swimming and diving (b,g), tennis (b,g), track and field (b,g), volleyball (g), weight lifting (b,g), wrestling (b). 5 PE instructors, 49 coaches, 2 athletic trainers.

Computers Computers are regularly used in all academic classes. Computer network features include on-campus library services, Internet access, wireless campus network, Internet filtering or blocking technology, class assignments available online. Computer access in designated common areas is available to students. Students grades are available online. The school has a published electronic and media policy.

Contact Mrs. Renee Chastain, Assistant to the Director of Admission. 770-692-6753. Fax: 770-969-6551. E-mail: admissions@landmark-cs.org. Website: www.landmarkchristianschool.org

LANDMARK EAST SCHOOL

Wolfville, Nova Scotia, Canada
See Special Needs Schools section.

LANDMARK SCHOOL

Prides Crossing, Massachusetts
See Special Needs Schools section.

LANDON SCHOOL

6101 Wilson Lane
Bethesda, Maryland 20817
Head of School: Mr. Jim Neill

General Information Boys' day college-preparatory, arts, and music school. Grades 3–12. Founded: 1929. Setting: suburban. Nearest major city is Washington, DC. 75-acre campus. 13 buildings on campus. Approved or accredited by Association of Independent Maryland Schools, Middle States Association of Colleges and Schools, and Maryland Department of Education. Member of National Association of Independent Schools. Endowment: $10.5 million. Total enrollment: 681. Upper school average class size: 12. Upper school faculty-student ratio: 1:6. There are 170 required school days per year for Upper School students. Upper School students typically attend 5 days per week. The average school day consists of 7 hours and 10 minutes.

Upper School Student Profile Grade 9: 99 students (99 boys); Grade 10: 76 students (76 boys); Grade 11: 78 students (78 boys); Grade 12: 87 students (87 boys).

Faculty School total: 108. In upper school: 42 men, 12 women; 35 have advanced degrees.

Subjects Offered Acting, algebra, American Civil War, American foreign policy, American history, American literature, American studies, art, art history-AP, biology, biology-AP, calculus, calculus-AP, ceramics, chemistry, chemistry-AP, Chinese, Chinese history, classics, computer science, computer science-AP, conceptual physics, constitutional law, creative writing, digital art, drama, drawing, earth science, economics-AP, engineering, English, English literature, environmental science AP, environmental studies, ethics, European history, expository writing, fine arts, foreign policy, forensics, French, French language-AP, French literature-AP, French studies, freshman foundations, geography, geology, geometry, government/civics, grammar, handbells, health, history, humanities, international relations, jazz band, journalism, justice seminar, Latin, mathematics, meteorology, Middle Eastern history, music, music history, music theory, music theory-AP, oceanography, painting, performing arts, photography, photojournalism, physical education, physics, physics-AP, pre-calculus, science, sculpture, senior project, Shakespeare, social studies, Spanish, Spanish language-AP, Spanish literature, statistics-AP, strings, technological applications, theater, trigonometry, typing, U.S. history, U.S. history-AP, world history, world literature, writing.

Graduation Requirements American Civil War, American government, arts and fine arts (art, music, dance, drama), biology, chemistry, English, ethics, foreign language, government, humanities, mathematics, music, physical education (includes health), pre-calculus, science, social studies (includes history), Independent senior project, 2-year arts requirement.

Special Academic Programs Advanced Placement exam preparation; honors section; independent study; term-away projects; study abroad.

College Admission Counseling 77 students graduated in 2014; all went to college, including Boston College; Bucknell University; Davidson College; University of Maryland, College Park; University of Virginia; Washington and Lee University. Mean SAT critical reading: 627, mean SAT math: 664, mean SAT writing: 622, mean combined SAT: 1913, mean composite ACT: 28.

Student Life Upper grades have specified standards of dress, student council, honor system. Discipline rests equally with students and faculty.

Tuition and Aid Day student tuition: $36,706. Tuition installment plan (FACTS Tuition Payment Plan, monthly payment plans). Need-based scholarship grants, 50% tuition remission for children of faculty available. In 2014–15, 25% of upper-school students received aid. Total amount of financial aid awarded in 2014–15: $4,000,000.

Admissions Traditional secondary-level entrance grade is 9. ISEE or SSAT required. Deadline for receipt of application materials: January 13. Application fee required: $75. On-campus interview required.

Athletics Interscholastic: baseball, basketball, cross-country running, diving, fencing, football, golf, ice hockey, lacrosse, riflery, rugby, soccer, squash, strength & conditioning, swimming and diving, tennis, track and field, ultimate Frisbee, water polo, winter (indoor) track, wrestling; intramural: basketball, Frisbee, physical fitness, physical training, sailing, strength & conditioning, tennis, ultimate Frisbee, weight training. 13 coaches, 2 athletic trainers.

Computers Computers are regularly used in art, computer applications, photojournalism, technology classes. Computer network features include on-campus library services, online commercial services, Internet access, wireless campus network, Internet filtering or blocking technology, password-accessed Web portals. Campus intranet, student e-mail accounts, and computer access in designated common areas are available to students. Students grades are available online. The school has a published electronic and media policy.

Contact Mr. Len Armstrong Jr., Assistant Headmaster for Enrollment, Admissions & Community. 301-320-1069. Fax: 301-320-1133. E-mail: len_armstrong@landon.net. Website: www.landon.net

LANSDALE CATHOLIC HIGH SCHOOL

700 Lansdale Avenue
Lansdale, Pennsylvania 19446-2995

Head of School: Mrs. Rita McGovern

General Information Coeducational day and distance learning college-preparatory, general academic, and religious studies school, affiliated with Roman Catholic Church. Grades 9–12. Distance learning grades 9–12. Founded: 1949. Setting: suburban. Nearest major city is Philadelphia. 33-acre campus. 1 building on campus. Approved or accredited by Middle States Association of Colleges and Schools, National Catholic Education Association, and Pennsylvania Department of Education. Total enrollment: 703. Upper school average class size: 30. Upper school faculty-student ratio: 1:21. There are 190 required school days per year for Upper School students. Upper School students typically attend 5 days per week. The average school day consists of 6 hours and 45 minutes.

Upper School Student Profile Grade 9: 163 students (68 boys, 95 girls); Grade 10: 175 students (88 boys, 87 girls); Grade 11: 180 students (84 boys, 96 girls); Grade 12: 185 students (90 boys, 95 girls). 99% of students are Roman Catholic.

Faculty School total: 36. In upper school: 10 men, 26 women; 18 have advanced degrees.

Subjects Offered Algebra, American government, American history, American history-AP, American literature, art, art history-AP, art-AP, band, biology-AP, business law, calculus, calculus-AP, career education, career planning, career/college preparation, Catholic belief and practice, chemistry, Chinese, choir, chorus, church history, college counseling, college placement, college planning, composition-AP, computer education, computer programming, drama, English language and composition-AP, English literature and composition-AP, English literature-AP, English/composition-AP, environmental science, European history, European history-AP, French, government-AP, health education, Italian, Latin, mathematics-AP, physical fitness, physical science, physics, pre-calculus, SAT/ACT preparation, Spanish, statistics, statistics-AP, student government, studio art, studio art-AP, The 20th Century, trigonometry, U.S. government and politics, U.S. government and politics-AP, U.S. history, U.S. history-AP, United States government-AP, Western civilization.

Graduation Requirements 30 hour service requirement by the middle of junior year.

Special Academic Programs 17 Advanced Placement exams for which test preparation is offered; honors section; study at local college for college credit.

College Admission Counseling 181 students graduated in 2015; all went to college, including Montgomery County Community College; Penn State University Park; Saint Joseph's University; Temple University; University of Pittsburgh.

Student Life Upper grades have uniform requirement, student council, honor system. Discipline rests primarily with faculty. Attendance at religious services is required.

Summer Programs Remediation, enrichment, advancement, sports, art/fine arts programs offered; held on campus; accepts boys and girls; open to students from other schools. 100 students usually enrolled. 2016 schedule: June to August.

Tuition and Aid Day student tuition: $6800. Tuition installment plan (SMART Tuition Payment Plan). Tuition reduction for siblings, merit scholarship grants, need-based scholarship grants, TAP Program available. In 2015–16, 20% of upper-school students received aid; total upper-school merit-scholarship money awarded: $70,000. Total amount of financial aid awarded in 2015–16: $125,000.

Admissions Traditional secondary-level entrance grade is 9. Deadline for receipt of application materials: none. No application fee required. Interview recommended.

Athletics Interscholastic: baseball (boys), basketball (b,g), cheering (g), cross-country running (b,g), dance squad (b,g), field hockey (g), football (b), golf (b,g), ice hockey (b,g), lacrosse (b,g), soccer (b,g), softball (g), swimming and diving (b,g), tennis (b,g), track and field (b,g), volleyball (g), winter (indoor) track (b,g); intramural: flag football (b), ice hockey (b,g); coed interscholastic: bowling, diving, indoor track, indoor track & field; coed intramural: yoga. 1 PE instructor, 1 athletic trainer.

Computers Computers are regularly used in all classes. Computer network features include on-campus library services, online commercial services, Internet access, wireless campus network, Internet filtering or blocking technology. Computer access in

designated common areas is available to students. Students grades are available online. The school has a published electronic and media policy.

Contact Mr. James Casey, President. 215-362-6160 Ext. 133. Fax: 215-362-5746. E-mail: jcasey@lansdalecatholic.com. Website: www.lansdalecatholic.com

LA SALLE ACADEMY

612 Academy Avenue
Providence, Rhode Island 02908

Head of School: Br. Thomas Gerrow, FSC

General Information Coeducational day college-preparatory, arts, religious studies, and technology school, affiliated with Roman Catholic Church. Grades 7–12. Founded: 1871. Setting: urban. 40-acre campus. 5 buildings on campus. Approved or accredited by New England Association of Schools and Colleges. Member of National Association of Independent Schools. Total enrollment: 1,462. Upper school average class size: 20. Upper school faculty-student ratio: 1:11. There are 185 required school days per year for Upper School students. Upper School students typically attend 5 days per week. The average school day consists of 6 hours and 30 minutes.

Upper School Student Profile 76% of students are Roman Catholic.

Faculty School total: 142. In upper school: 84 men, 58 women; all have advanced degrees.

Subjects Offered Algebra, American history, American literature, anatomy, art, astronomy, biology, business, calculus, ceramics, chemistry, community service, computer programming, computer science, creative writing, dance, drama, drawing, economics, electronics, engineering, English, English literature, environmental science, ESL, film, fine arts, French, geology, geometry, history, Italian, journalism, law, mathematics, microbiology, music, painting, photography, physical education, physical science, physics, physiology, psychology, religion, science, social studies, sociology, Spanish, statistics, theater, trigonometry, world history, world literature, writing.

Graduation Requirements Arts and fine arts (art, music, dance, drama), computer science, English, foreign language, mathematics, physical education (includes health), religion (includes Bible studies and theology), science, social studies (includes history). Community service is required.

Special Academic Programs Advanced Placement exam preparation; honors section; study at local college for college credit; academic accommodation for the gifted, the musically talented, and the artistically talented.

College Admission Counseling 334 students graduated in 2015; 331 went to college, including Boston College; Brown University; Harvard University; United States Military Academy; University of Rhode Island; Yale University. Other: 2 went to work, 1 entered military service.

Student Life Upper grades have uniform requirement, student council, honor system. Discipline rests equally with students and faculty.

Summer Programs Enrichment, sports, art/fine arts, computer instruction programs offered; held on campus; accepts boys and girls; open to students from other schools. 80 students usually enrolled.

Tuition and Aid Day student tuition: $14,100. Tuition installment plan (FACTS Tuition Payment Plan). Merit scholarship grants, need-based scholarship grants available. In 2015–16, 37% of upper-school students received aid; total upper-school merit-scholarship money awarded: $600,000. Total amount of financial aid awarded in 2015–16: $2,200,000.

Admissions Traditional secondary-level entrance grade is 9. For fall 2015, 850 students applied for upper-level admission, 400 were accepted, 350 enrolled. STS, Diocese Test required. Deadline for receipt of application materials: December 31. Application fee required: $50.

Athletics Interscholastic: baseball (boys), basketball (b,g), cross-country running (b,g), field hockey (g), football (b), golf (b,g), gymnastics (b,g), ice hockey (b,g), lacrosse (b,g), sailing (b,g), soccer (b,g), softball (g), swimming and diving (b,g), tennis (b,g), track and field (b,g), volleyball (b,g), wrestling (b,g); coed intramural: fencing, modern dance, physical fitness, physical training, table tennis, touch football, volleyball, walking, whiffle ball. 5 PE instructors, 61 coaches, 4 athletic trainers.

Computers Computers are regularly used in English, foreign language, history, mathematics, music, science classes. Computer network features include on-campus library services, online commercial services, Internet access. Student e-mail accounts are available to students. Students grades are available online.

Contact Mr. George Aldrich, Director of Admissions and Public Relations. 401-351-7750 Ext. 122. Fax: 401-444-1782. E-mail: galdrich@lasalle-academy.org. Website: www.lasalle-academy.org

LA SALLE HIGH SCHOOL

3880 East Sierra Madre Boulevard
Pasadena, California 91107-1996

Head of School: Br. Christopher Brady, FSC

General Information Coeducational day college-preparatory, arts, and religious studies school, affiliated with Roman Catholic Church. Grades 9–12. Founded: 1956. Setting: suburban. Nearest major city is Los Angeles. 10-acre campus. 3 buildings on campus. Approved or accredited by Western Association of Schools and Colleges, Western Catholic Education Association, and California Department of Education.

Member of National Association of Independent Schools. Total enrollment: 650. Upper school average class size: 25. Upper school faculty-student ratio: 1:10. There are 180 required school days per year for Upper School students. Upper School students typically attend 5 days per week. The average school day consists of 6 hours and 30 minutes.

Upper School Student Profile Grade 9: 164 students (82 boys, 82 girls); Grade 10: 154 students (91 boys, 63 girls); Grade 11: 164 students (96 boys, 68 girls); Grade 12: 168 students (97 boys, 71 girls). 60% of students are Roman Catholic.

Faculty School total: 67. In upper school: 37 men, 30 women; 48 have advanced degrees.

Subjects Offered 20th century history, acting, Advanced Placement courses, advanced studio art-AP, algebra, American Civil War, American government, American literature-AP, ancient world history, art, art-AP, ASB Leadership, band, biology-AP, calculus, calculus-AP, campus ministry, Catholic belief and practice, chemistry-AP, chorus, civics, classical civilization, community service, comparative religion, composition, composition-AP, computer applications, computer education, computer graphics, computer literacy, computer programming, constitutional history of U.S., creative writing, dance, dance performance, digital photography, drama, dramatic arts, drawing, ecology, environmental systems, economics, economics-AP, education, electives, English, English composition, English language-AP, English literature, English literature and composition-AP, English-AP, fiction, film, fine arts, foreign language, French, general math, general science, geometry, government, government/civics, government/civics-AP, health and safety, health education, Hispanic literature, history, history-AP, honors algebra, honors English, honors U.S. history, honors world history, integrated mathematics, introduction to theater, jazz band, jazz dance, jazz ensemble, journalism, lab science, lab/keyboard, law and the legal system, leadership, leadership and service, mathematics, mathematics-AP, modern European history-AP, musical productions, newspaper, photo shop, photography, physics, physics-AP, play production, pottery, pre-calculus, religion, religion and culture, religious studies, Roman civilization, science, social justice, Spanish, Spanish-AP, student government, studio art, studio art-AP, study skills, technical theater, television, theater, theater arts, theater design and production, theater production, trigonometry, U.S. government, U.S. government and politics-AP, U.S. history, U.S. history-AP, U.S. literature, video communication, visual and performing arts, visual arts, wind instruments, world history, writing, yearbook.

Graduation Requirements Algebra, American literature, arts and fine arts (art, music, dance, drama), biology, chemistry, Christian doctrine, civics, computer literacy, economics, English, English composition, foreign language, geometry, integrated mathematics, macroeconomics-AP, physical education (includes health), religious studies, U.S. history.

Special Academic Programs 15 Advanced Placement exams for which test preparation is offered; honors section.

College Admission Counseling 170 students graduated in 2015; 168 went to college, including California State University, Northridge; San Diego State University; University of California, Berkeley; University of California, Irvine; University of California, Los Angeles; University of Southern California. Other: 2 had other specific plans. Median SAT critical reading: 570, median SAT math: 545, median SAT writing: 565, median combined SAT: 1710, median composite ACT: 24. 35% scored over 600 on SAT critical reading, 32% scored over 600 on SAT math, 37% scored over 600 on SAT writing, 33% scored over 1800 on combined SAT, 37% scored over 26 on composite ACT.

Student Life Upper grades have uniform requirement, student council, honor system. Discipline rests primarily with faculty. Attendance at religious services is required.

Summer Programs Remediation, enrichment, advancement, sports, art/fine arts, computer instruction programs offered; session focuses on academics and sports camps; held on campus; accepts boys and girls; open to students from other schools. 455 students usually enrolled. 2016 schedule: June 13 to July 22. Application deadline: June 3.

Tuition and Aid Day student tuition: $17,712. Tuition installment plan (monthly payment plans, annual and biannual; ACH Payments recommended). Merit scholarship grants, need-based scholarship grants, San Miguel Program for exceptional Catholic students under the poverty level available. In 2015–16, 48% of upper-school students received aid; total upper-school merit-scholarship money awarded: $340,100. Total amount of financial aid awarded in 2015–16: $2,000,250.

Admissions Traditional secondary-level entrance grade is 9. For fall 2015, 466 students applied for upper-level admission, 346 were accepted, 174 enrolled. High School Placement Test required. Deadline for receipt of application materials: January 15. Application fee required: $85. Interview recommended.

Athletics Interscholastic: aerobics/dance (boys, girls), baseball (b), basketball (b,g), cross-country running (b,g), dance team (g), football (b), golf (b,g), soccer (b,g), softball (g), swimming and diving (b,g), tennis (b,g), track and field (b,g), volleyball (b,g), water polo (b,g); intramural: basketball (b,g), dance team (g), flag football (b); coed interscholastic: aerobics/dance, cheering, physical fitness, weight training; coed intramural: fitness, Frisbee, physical fitness, weight training. 4 PE instructors, 70 coaches, 2 athletic trainers.

Computers Computer network features include on-campus library services, Internet access, wireless campus network, Internet filtering or blocking technology. Campus intranet and student e-mail accounts are available to students. Students grades are available online. The school has a published electronic and media policy.

Contact Mr. Nathan Housman, Assistant Director of Admissions. 626-696-4365. Fax: 626-696-4411. E-mail: nhousman@lasallehs.org. Website: www.lasallehs.org

LA SCUOLA D'ITALIA GUGLIELMO MARCONI
12 East 96th Street
New York, New York 10128

Head of School: Dr. Maria Palandra

General Information Coeducational day college-preparatory and bilingual studies school. Grades PK–12. Founded: 1977. Setting: urban. Nearest major city is Manhattan. 1 building on campus. Approved or accredited by New York State Association of Independent Schools, New York State Board of Regents, and New York Department of Education. Languages of instruction: English, French, and Italian. Total enrollment: 283. Upper school average class size: 10. There are 212 required school days per year for Upper School students. Upper School students typically attend 5 days per week.

Upper School Student Profile Grade 9: 15 students (5 boys, 10 girls); Grade 10: 16 students (7 boys, 9 girls); Grade 11: 15 students (11 boys, 4 girls); Grade 12: 13 students (6 boys, 7 girls).

Faculty School total: 54. In upper school: 6 men, 9 women; 15 have advanced degrees.

Special Academic Programs International Baccalaureate program; Advanced Placement exam preparation; honors section; study at local college for college credit; domestic exchange program; study abroad; remedial reading and/or remedial writing; remedial math; ESL (26 students enrolled).

College Admission Counseling 10 students graduated in 2014; all went to college, including University of Pennsylvania.

Student Life Upper grades have uniform requirement, honor system. Discipline rests equally with students and faculty.

Tuition and Aid Day student tuition: $23,000. Tuition installment plan (The Tuition Plan). Tuition reduction for siblings, merit scholarship grants, need-based scholarship grants, need-based loans available.

Admissions Traditional secondary-level entrance grade is 9. For fall 2014, 13 students applied for upper-level admission, 13 were accepted, 9 enrolled. Deadline for receipt of application materials: none. Application fee required: $100. Interview required.

Athletics Coed Interscholastic: basketball, fencing, scooter football, soccer. 2 PE instructors, 2 coaches, 2 athletic trainers.

Computers Computer network features include on-campus library services, Internet access, Internet filtering or blocking technology. Computer access in designated common areas is available to students. The school has a published electronic and media policy.

Contact Mrs. Pia Pedicini, Deputy Head of School/Director of Admissions. 212-369-3290. Fax: 212-369-1164. E-mail: secretary@lascuoladitalia.org. Website: www.lascuoladitalia.org

LAURALTON HALL
200 High Street
Milford, Connecticut 06460

Head of School: Dr. Antoinette Iadarola

General Information Girls' day college-preparatory, arts, religious studies, and technology school, affiliated with Roman Catholic Church. Grades 9–12. Founded: 1905. Setting: suburban. Nearest major city is New Haven. 30-acre campus. 5 buildings on campus. Approved or accredited by Connecticut Association of Independent Schools, Mercy Secondary Education Association, New England Association of Schools and Colleges, and Connecticut Department of Education. Member of National Association of Independent Schools. Total enrollment: 467. Upper school average class size: 15. Upper school faculty-student ratio: 1:12. There are 165 required school days per year for Upper School students. Upper School students typically attend 5 days per week. The average school day consists of 6 hours and 15 minutes.

Upper School Student Profile Grade 9: 115 students (115 girls); Grade 10: 114 students (114 girls); Grade 11: 130 students (130 girls); Grade 12: 108 students (108 girls). 76% of students are Roman Catholic.

Faculty School total: 43. In upper school: 3 men, 40 women; 29 have advanced degrees.

Subjects Offered Algebra, American history, American literature, anatomy, art, biology, business, calculus, chemistry, Chinese, computer math, computer programming, English, English literature, environmental science, European history, fine arts, French, geometry, government/civics, health, history, journalism, Latin, mathematics, music, physical education, physics, physiology, religion, science, social studies, Spanish, trigonometry, world history, writing.

Graduation Requirements Arts and fine arts (art, music, dance, drama), English, foreign language, mathematics, physical education (includes health), religion (includes Bible studies and theology), science, social studies (includes history). Community service is required.

Special Academic Programs Honors section; study at local college for college credit.

College Admission Counseling 119 students graduated in 2015; all went to college, including Boston College; College of the Holy Cross; Fairfield University;

Loyola University Maryland; Quinnipiac University; University of Connecticut. Mean SAT critical reading: 572, mean SAT math: 538, mean SAT writing: 572.

Student Life Upper grades have uniform requirement, student council, honor system. Discipline rests primarily with faculty. Attendance at religious services is required.

Tuition and Aid Day student tuition: $18,750. Tuition installment plan (FACTS Tuition Payment Plan, 1- and 2-payment plans). Tuition reduction for siblings, merit scholarship grants, need-based scholarship grants available. In 2015–16, 28% of upper-school students received aid; total upper-school merit-scholarship money awarded: $125,000. Total amount of financial aid awarded in 2015–16: $450,000.

Admissions Traditional secondary-level entrance grade is 9. High School Placement Test required. Deadline for receipt of application materials: none. Application fee required: $60.

Athletics Interscholastic: basketball, cheering, cross-country running, diving, field hockey, golf, gymnastics, ice hockey, indoor track, lacrosse, running, skiing (downhill), soccer, softball, swimming and diving, tennis, track and field, volleyball; intramural: basketball. 1 PE instructor, 27 coaches, 1 athletic trainer.

Computers Computers are regularly used in mathematics classes. Computer network features include on-campus library services, online commercial services, Internet access, wireless campus network, Internet filtering or blocking technology. Campus intranet, student e-mail accounts, and computer access in designated common areas are available to students. Students grades are available online. The school has a published electronic and media policy.

Contact Jennifer Casceillo, Dean of Student Development. 203-877-2786 Ext. 123. Fax: 203-876-9760. E-mail: jcasceillo@lauraltonhall.org. Website: www.lauraltonhall.org

See Display below and Close-Up on page 600.

THE LAUREATE ACADEMY

Winnipeg, Manitoba, Canada
See Special Needs Schools section.

LAUREL SCHOOL

One Lyman Circle
Shaker Heights, Ohio 44122

Head of School: Ann V. Klotz

General Information Coeducational day (boys' only in lower grades) college-preparatory school. Boys grades PS–PK, girls grades PS–12. Founded: 1896. Setting: suburban. Nearest major city is Cleveland. 11-acre campus. 1 building on campus. Approved or accredited by Independent Schools Association of the Central States, Ohio

Association of Independent Schools, and Ohio Department of Education. Member of National Association of Independent Schools. Endowment: $50.1 million. Total enrollment: 640. Upper school average class size: 14. Upper school faculty-student ratio: 1:8. Upper School students typically attend 5 days per week. The average school day consists of 7 hours and 18 minutes.

Upper School Student Profile Grade 9: 65 students (65 girls); Grade 10: 73 students (73 girls); Grade 11: 69 students (69 girls); Grade 12: 65 students (65 girls).

Faculty School total: 86. In upper school: 13 men, 24 women; 29 have advanced degrees.

Subjects Offered Algebra, American history, American literature, American literature-AP, anatomy and physiology, art, art history-AP, astronomy, biology, biology-AP, biotechnology, calculus, calculus-AP, ceramics, chemistry, chemistry-AP, choir, choreography, classical studies, classics, community service, computer art, computer multimedia, computer science, creative writing, discrete mathematics, drama, drawing, driver education, earth science, engineering, English, English literature, English-AP, environmental science, European history, European history-AP, experiential education, expository writing, fine arts, forensics, French, French-AP, geography, geology, geometry, government-AP, grammar, health, history, honors algebra, honors English, honors geometry, honors U.S. history, independent study, Latin, Latin-AP, mathematics, music, music theory, orchestra, painting, photography, physical education, physics, physics-AP, pre-calculus, probability and statistics, science, sculpture, senior project, social studies, Spanish, Spanish language-AP, Spanish literature, Spanish literature-AP, Spanish-AP, speech, studio art, studio art-AP, technical theater, theater, trigonometry, U.S. history-AP, world history, writing.

Graduation Requirements Arts and fine arts (art, music, dance, drama), English, foreign language, history, mathematics, physical education (includes health), science, speech, 10-minute speech on a subject of choice to the entire Upper School student body and faculty. Community service is required.

Special Academic Programs Advanced Placement exam preparation; honors section; independent study; term-away projects; study at local college for college credit; study abroad; academic accommodation for the gifted, the musically talented, and the artistically talented.

College Admission Counseling 67 students graduated in 2015; all went to college, including Case Western Reserve University; Purdue University; Syracuse University; Tulane University; University of Cincinnati; Washington University in St. Louis. Mean SAT critical reading: 612, mean SAT math: 609, mean SAT writing: 628, mean composite ACT: 26.

Student Life Upper grades have uniform requirement, student council, honor system. Discipline rests primarily with faculty.

Summer Programs Enrichment, advancement, art/fine arts programs offered; held on campus; accepts boys and girls; open to students from other schools. 30 students usually enrolled. 2016 schedule: June 16 to August 15. Application deadline: May 30.

Lauralton Hall — Connecticut's First Catholic College-Prep School for Girls

Strengthen Your Core

Freshman Physics
Women's Studies
Global Vision

Milford, Connecticut   203.878.3333   LauraltonHall.org
ACADEMY OF OUR LADY OF MERCY

Tuition and Aid Day student tuition: $27,750. Tuition installment plan (monthly payment plans, individually arranged payment plans). Tuition reduction for siblings, merit scholarship grants, need-based scholarship grants available. In 2015–16, 57% of upper-school students received aid; total upper-school merit-scholarship money awarded: $307,500. Total amount of financial aid awarded in 2015–16: $1,875,460.

Admissions Traditional secondary-level entrance grade is 9. For fall 2015, 86 students applied for upper-level admission, 66 were accepted, 30 enrolled. Deadline for receipt of application materials: none. Application fee required: $40. On-campus interview required.

Athletics Interscholastic: basketball, cross-country running, field hockey, golf, lacrosse, soccer, softball, strength & conditioning, swimming and diving, tennis, track and field, volleyball; intramural: basketball, field hockey, lacrosse, soccer, softball, swimming and diving, tennis, volleyball. 26 coaches, 1 athletic trainer.

Computers Computers are regularly used in all academic classes. Computer network features include on-campus library services, Internet access, wireless campus network, Internet filtering or blocking technology. Campus intranet, student e-mail accounts, and computer access in designated common areas are available to students.

Contact Kathryn Purcell, Assistant Head of School - Enrollment Management. 216-464-0946. Fax: 216-464-1446. E-mail: kPurcell@LaurelSchool.org. Website: www.laurelschool.org

LAWRENCE SCHOOL

Sagamore Hills, Ohio
See Special Needs Schools section.

THE LAWRENCEVILLE SCHOOL

PO Box 6008
2500 Main Street
Lawrenceville, New Jersey 08648

Head of School: Stephen S. Murray

General Information Coeducational boarding and day college-preparatory, arts, religious studies, and technology school. Grades 9–PG. Founded: 1810. Setting: small town. Nearest major city is Philadelphia, PA. Students are housed in single-sex dormitories. 700-acre campus. 120 buildings on campus. Approved or accredited by Middle States Association of Colleges and Schools, New Jersey Association of Independent Schools, The Association of Boarding Schools, and New Jersey Department of Education. Member of National Association of Independent Schools and Secondary School Admission Test Board. Endowment: $403 million. Total enrollment: 815. Upper school average class size: 12. Upper school faculty-student ratio: 1:8. There are 169 required school days per year for Upper School students. Upper School students typically attend 6 days per week. The average school day consists of 7 hours.

Upper School Student Profile Grade 9: 158 students (82 boys, 76 girls); Grade 10: 215 students (111 boys, 104 girls); Grade 11: 217 students (113 boys, 104 girls); Grade 12: 209 students (106 boys, 103 girls); Postgraduate: 16 students (13 boys, 3 girls). 69% of students are boarding students. 42% are state residents. 41 states are represented in upper school student body. 14% are international students. International students from China, Hong Kong, Mexico, Republic of Korea, United Kingdom, and Viet Nam; 34 other countries represented in student body.

Faculty In upper school: 73 men, 50 women; 91 have advanced degrees; 140 reside on campus.

Subjects Offered Acting, advanced chemistry, advanced computer applications, Advanced Placement courses, advanced studio art-AP, African-American literature, algebra, American Civil War, American foreign policy, American government, American history, American history-AP, American literature, American studies, architecture, art, art history, art history-AP, art-AP, arts, Asian history, astronomy, Basic programming, Bible, Bible studies, biochemistry, bioethics, bioethics, DNA and culture, biology, biology-AP, Buddhism, calculus, calculus-AP, Central and Eastern European history, ceramics, chamber groups, chemistry, chemistry-AP, China/Japan history, Chinese, Chinese studies, choir, chorus, Christian studies, Civil War, civil war history, classical Greek literature, classical language, comparative government and politics, conceptual physics, constitutional history of U.S., contemporary women writers, critical writing, dance, data analysis, design, digital applications, digital art, drama, dramatic arts, drawing, drawing and design, driver education, Eastern religion and philosophy, ecology, environmental systems, economics, economics-AP, electronic music, English, English literature, English literature-AP, English/composition-AP, environmental science, environmental studies, ethics, European history, European literature, evolution, fiction, field ecology, film and new technologies, film appreciation, film studies, filmmaking, food science, foreign language, foreign policy, French, French language-AP, French studies, geometry, global science, health and wellness, Hebrew scripture, historical foundations for arts, history of China and Japan, Holocaust, honors geometry, honors U.S. history, human biology, humanities, independent study, instruments, interdisciplinary studies, introduction to literature, introduction to theater, Irish literature, Irish studies, Islamic studies, Japanese history, jazz, Jewish studies, journalism, Latin, linear algebra, literature, macro/microeconomics-AP, medieval literature, Middle East, Middle Eastern history, nature study, non-Western societies, orchestra, organic chemistry, painting, participation

in sports, personal development, philosophy, photography, physics, physics-AP, physiology, poetry, pre-calculus, printmaking, probability and statistics, programming, research seminar, robotics, Russian history, science, senior project, set design, Shakespeare, short story, Southern literature, Spanish, Spanish language-AP, Spanish literature, studio art, the Presidency, the Sixties, theater, theater arts, U.S. constitutional history, U.S. government, U.S. government and politics, U.S. history, Vietnam War, visual arts, water color painting, women in world history, world religions, world religions, writing, Zen Buddhism.

Graduation Requirements Arts and fine arts (art, music, dance, drama), English, foreign language, history, interdisciplinary studies, mathematics, religion (includes Bible studies and theology), science, social studies (includes history). Community service is required.

Special Academic Programs Honors section; independent study; term-away projects; study at local college for college credit; study abroad.

College Admission Counseling 231 students graduated in 2015; 228 went to college, including Brown University; Georgetown University; Princeton University; University of Michigan; Williams College; Yale University. Other: 2 entered a postgraduate year, 1 had other specific plans. Mean SAT critical reading: 700, mean SAT math: 714, mean SAT writing: 710, mean combined SAT: 2124, mean composite ACT: 30.

Student Life Upper grades have specified standards of dress, student council, honor system. Discipline rests equally with students and faculty.

Summer Programs Enrichment, advancement, sports, art/fine arts, computer instruction programs offered; session focuses on math advancement and enrichment; held on campus; accepts boys and girls; open to students from other schools. 200 students usually enrolled. 2016 schedule: June 27 to August 5. Application deadline: none.

Tuition and Aid Day student tuition: $47,840; 7-day tuition and room/board: $57,840. Tuition installment plan (FACTS Tuition Payment Plan, one, two, and nine month installment plans are available). Merit scholarship grants, need-based scholarship grants available. In 2014–15, 29% of upper-school students received aid; total upper-school merit-scholarship money awarded: $239,000. Total amount of financial aid awarded in 2014–15: $11,533,470.

Admissions Traditional secondary-level entrance grade is 9. For fall 2015, 1,895 students applied for upper-level admission, 394 were accepted, 253 enrolled. ISEE, PSAT and SAT for applicants to grade 11 and 12, SSAT or TOEFL or SLEP required. Deadline for receipt of application materials: January 15. Application fee required: $50. Interview required.

Athletics Interscholastic: baseball (boys), basketball (b,g), crew (b,g), cross-country running (b,g), fencing (b,g), field hockey (g), football (b), golf (b,g), hockey (b,g), ice hockey (b,g), indoor track (b,g), indoor track & field (b,g), lacrosse (b,g), rowing (b,g), soccer (b,g), softball (g), squash (b,g), swimming and diving (b,g), tennis (b,g), track and field (b,g), volleyball (b,g), water polo (b,g), winter (indoor) track (b,g); intramural: basketball (b,g), Frisbee (g), handball (b,g), team handball (b,g), ultimate Frisbee (g), weight lifting (b,g), weight training (b,g); coed interscholastic: wrestling; coed intramural: aerobics/dance, backpacking, bicycling, broomball, canoeing/kayaking, climbing, cricket, dance, fitness, hiking/backpacking, ice skating, kayaking, modern dance, Nautilus, outdoor activities, physical fitness, physical training, rock climbing, ropes courses, squash, strength & conditioning, wall climbing, yoga. 32 coaches, 5 athletic trainers.

Computers Computers are regularly used in art, English, foreign language, mathematics, music, science, technology classes. Computer network features include on-campus library services, online commercial services, Internet access, wireless campus network, Internet filtering or blocking technology. Campus intranet, student e-mail accounts, and computer access in designated common areas are available to students. Students grades are available online. The school has a published electronic and media policy.

Contact Tom Sheppard, Dean of Admission and Financial Aid. 800-735-2030. Fax: 609-895-2217. E-mail: admission@lawrenceville.org. Website: www.lawrenceville.org

See Display on next page and Close-Up on page 602.

LEE ACADEMY

415 Lee Drive
Clarksdale, Mississippi 38614

Head of School: Tommy Gunn

General Information Coeducational day college-preparatory, arts, and business school. Grades 1–12. Founded: 1970. Setting: small town. Nearest major city is Memphis, TN. 4 buildings on campus. Approved or accredited by Mississippi Private School Association, Southern Association of Colleges and Schools, and Mississippi Department of Education. Total enrollment: 321. Upper school average class size: 22. Upper school faculty-student ratio: 1:20. There are 185 required school days per year for Upper School students. Upper School students typically attend 5 days per week. The average school day consists of 6 hours and 30 minutes.

Upper School Student Profile Grade 6: 9 students (5 boys, 4 girls); Grade 7: 41 students (21 boys, 20 girls); Grade 8: 40 students (17 boys, 23 girls); Grade 9: 33 students (17 boys, 16 girls); Grade 10: 31 students (15 boys, 16 girls); Grade 11: 42 students (21 boys, 21 girls); Grade 12: 40 students (24 boys, 16 girls).

Faculty School total: 45. In upper school: 3 men, 15 women; 8 have advanced degrees.

Subjects Offered ACT preparation, acting, American government, American history, ancient world history, art, athletics, baseball, basketball, Bible, biology, bookkeeping, business, business law, calculus, cheerleading, chemistry, choral music, computer applications, earth and space science, earth science, English, English composition, English literature, foreign language, geography, geometry, guidance, health, Spanish, U.S. history, writing workshop, yearbook.

Graduation Requirements Math methods.

College Admission Counseling 41 students graduated in 2015; all went to college, including Mississippi State University; University of Mississippi.

Student Life Upper grades have uniform requirement, student council. Discipline rests primarily with faculty.

Tuition and Aid Day student tuition: $5500. Tuition installment plan (monthly payment plans). Tuition reduction for siblings, need-based scholarship grants available. In 2015–16, 15% of upper-school students received aid. Total amount of financial aid awarded in 2015–16: $35,000.

Admissions Traditional secondary-level entrance grade is 9. For fall 2015, 80 students applied for upper-level admission, 80 were accepted, 80 enrolled. 3-R Achievement Test required. Deadline for receipt of application materials: February 28. No application fee required.

Athletics Interscholastic: baseball (boys), basketball (b), cheering (g), football (b); coed interscholastic: cross-country running, golf, soccer. 2 PE instructors, 5 coaches.

Computers Computer resources include on-campus library services. Computer access in designated common areas is available to students. Students grades are available online.

Contact Beverly Antici, Counselor. 662-627-7891. Fax: 662-627-7896. E-mail: leeoffice@acbleone.net. Website: www.leeacademycolts.com/

THE LEELANAU SCHOOL

Glen Arbor, Michigan
See Special Needs Schools section.

LEHIGH VALLEY CHRISTIAN HIGH SCHOOL

3436 Winchester Road
Allentown, Pennsylvania 18104

Head of School: Mr. Brendan O'Brien

General Information Coeducational day college-preparatory, general academic, arts, business, religious studies, and technology school, affiliated with Protestant-Evangelical faith. Grades 9–12. Founded: 1988. Setting: urban. 2-acre campus. 1 building on campus. Approved or accredited by Association of Christian Schools International, Middle States Association of Colleges and Schools, and Pennsylvania Department of Education. Endowment: $17,387. Total enrollment: 53. Upper school average class size: 20. Upper school faculty-student ratio: 1:5. There are 180 required school days per year for Upper School students. Upper School students typically attend 5 days per week. The average school day consists of 6 hours and 42 minutes.

Upper School Student Profile Grade 9: 8 students (4 boys, 4 girls); Grade 10: 23 students (12 boys, 11 girls); Grade 11: 15 students (9 boys, 6 girls); Grade 12: 7 students (2 boys, 5 girls). 90% of students are Protestant-Evangelical faith.

Faculty School total: 5. In upper school: 3 men, 2 women; 3 have advanced degrees.

Subjects Offered Accounting, Advanced Placement courses, algebra, American history, ancient world history, art, Bible, biology, calculus-AP, chemistry, chorus, English, geometry, health, history, physical education, physical science, pre-calculus, Spanish, U.S. history, Western civilization.

Graduation Requirements Algebra, American history, American literature, art, Bible, Bible studies, biology, British literature, choir, civics, English, foreign language, geometry, mathematics, physical education (includes health), science, social sciences, Western civilization, general lifestyle not harmful to the testimony of the school as a Christian institution, minimum one year of full-time enrollment in LVCH or another Christian high school.

Special Academic Programs Advanced Placement exam preparation; honors section; accelerated programs; independent study; study at local college for college credit; programs in English, mathematics, general development for dyslexic students; special instructional classes for students needing learning support.

College Admission Counseling 30 went to college, including Albright College; Lehigh University; Liberty University; Moravian College; Penn State University Park; Temple University. Other: 2 went to work. Mean SAT critical reading: 552, mean SAT math: 564, mean SAT writing: 531, mean combined SAT: 1647.

Student Life Upper grades have specified standards of dress, student council. Discipline rests primarily with faculty.

Summer Programs Remediation, advancement programs offered; session focuses on make-up courses; held both on and off campus; held at student's homes (for independent credit); accepts boys and girls; not open to students from other schools. 5 students usually enrolled. 2016 schedule: June 18 to August 21.

Tuition and Aid Day student tuition: $7800. Tuition installment plan (FACTS Tuition Payment Plan, individually arranged payment plans). Tuition reduction for siblings, need-based scholarship grants available. In 2015–16, 24% of upper-school students received aid. Total amount of financial aid awarded in 2015–16: $17,387.

Admissions Traditional secondary-level entrance grade is 9. For fall 2015, 16 students applied for upper-level admission, 16 were accepted, 14 enrolled. Achievement tests, Gates MacGinite Reading Tests or Wide Range Achievement Test required. Deadline

for receipt of application materials: none. Application fee required: $200. On-campus interview required.

Athletics Interscholastic: baseball (boys), basketball (b,g), soccer (b,g), volleyball (g); coed intramural: fitness walking. 1 PE instructor.

Computers Computers are regularly used in accounting, business, college planning, computer applications, creative writing, ESL, foreign language, history, science, social sciences, social studies, Spanish, writing, yearbook classes. Computer network features include on-campus library services, Internet access, wireless campus network, Internet filtering or blocking technology. Campus intranet, student e-mail accounts, and computer access in designated common areas are available to students. Students grades are available online. The school has a published electronic and media policy.

Contact Mrs. Deanna Gehman, Director of Admissions. 610-351-9144 Ext. 102. Fax: 610-351-9187. E-mail: d.gehman@lvchs.org. Website: www.lvchs.org

LEHMAN HIGH SCHOOL

2400 Saint Mary Avenue
Sidney, Ohio 45365

Head of School: Mrs. Denise Stauffer

General Information Coeducational day and distance learning college-preparatory, arts, business, and religious studies school, affiliated with Roman Catholic Church. Grades 9–12. Distance learning grades 10–12. Founded: 1970. Setting: small town. Nearest major city is Dayton. 50-acre campus. 1 building on campus. Approved or accredited by North Central Association of Colleges and Schools, Ohio Catholic Schools Accreditation Association (OCSAA), and Ohio Department of Education. Endowment: $600,000. Total enrollment: 202. Upper school average class size: 15. Upper school faculty-student ratio: 1:15. There are 178 required school days per year for Upper School students. Upper School students typically attend 5 days per week. The average school day consists of 7 hours.

Upper School Student Profile Grade 9: 62 students (28 boys, 34 girls); Grade 10: 55 students (27 boys, 28 girls); Grade 11: 45 students (22 boys, 23 girls); Grade 12: 40 students (16 boys, 24 girls). 93% of students are Roman Catholic.

Faculty School total: 18. In upper school: 8 men, 10 women; 9 have advanced degrees.

Subjects Offered Accounting, algebra, American government, American literature, anatomy and physiology, art, art history, biology, biology-AP, British literature, British literature (honors), business, calculus, calculus-AP, ceramics, chemistry, chemistry-AP, choir, computer applications, concert band, drafting, earth science, English, English literature and composition-AP, environmental science, geography, geometry, government, government-AP, health education, history of the Catholic Church, integrated science, intro to computers, Latin, moral theology, newspaper, painting, peace and justice, physical education, physics, pre-algebra, pre-calculus, psychology, sociology, Spanish, studio art, U.S. history, vocal music, weight fitness, world history, yearbook.

Graduation Requirements Biology, business, computer applications, electives, English composition, English literature, health education, mathematics, physical education (includes health), physical science, religion (includes Bible studies and theology), U.S. government, U.S. history, must attend a senior retreat.

Special Academic Programs Advanced Placement exam preparation; honors section; independent study; study at local college for college credit.

College Admission Counseling 47 students graduated in 2015; 44 went to college, including Bowling Green State University; Miami University; The Ohio State University; University of Cincinnati; University of Dayton; Wright State University. Other: 3 went to work. Median SAT critical reading: 656, median SAT math: 616, median SAT writing: 593, median combined SAT: 1960. Mean composite ACT: 24. 66.6% scored over 600 on SAT critical reading, 66.6% scored over 600 on SAT math, 66.6% scored over 600 on SAT writing, 66.6% scored over 1800 on combined SAT, 21% scored over 26 on composite ACT.

Student Life Upper grades have uniform requirement, student council, honor system. Discipline rests primarily with faculty. Attendance at religious services is required.

Tuition and Aid Day student tuition: $7400. Tuition installment plan (FACTS Tuition Payment Plan). Tuition reduction for siblings, need-based scholarship grants available. In 2015–16, 44% of upper-school students received aid. Total amount of financial aid awarded in 2015–16: $353,850.

Admissions Traditional secondary-level entrance grade is 9. Achievement tests or any standardized test required. Deadline for receipt of application materials: none. Application fee required: $100. Interview recommended.

Athletics Interscholastic: baseball (boys), basketball (b,g), cheering (g), cross-country running (b,g), football (b), golf (b), soccer (b,g), softball (g), swimming and diving (b,g), tennis (b,g), track and field (b,g), volleyball (g), wrestling (b); intramural: strength & conditioning (b,g); coed intramural: indoor track. 1 PE instructor, 35 coaches, 1 athletic trainer.

Computers Computers are regularly used in accounting, computer applications, drafting, newspaper, science, yearbook classes. Computer resources include on-campus library services, Internet access, wireless campus network, Internet filtering or blocking technology. Students grades are available online. The school has a published electronic and media policy.

Contact Mrs. Denise Stauffer, Principal/CEO. 937-498-1161 Ext. 115. Fax: 937-492-9877. E-mail: d.stauffer@lehmancatholic.com. Website: www.lehmancatholic.com/

LE LYCEE FRANCAIS DE LOS ANGELES

3261 Overland Avenue
Los Angeles, California 90034-3589

Head of School: Mrs. Clara-Lisa Kabbaz

General Information Coeducational day college-preparatory, general academic, arts, bilingual studies, technology, Classic French Baccalaureate Exam, and Franco-American Bacc Exam in association w/The College Board school. Grades PS–12. Founded: 1964. Setting: suburban. Nearest major city is Beverly Hills. 2-acre campus. 1 building on campus. Approved or accredited by Western Association of Schools and Colleges and California Department of Education. Member of National Association of Independent Schools. Languages of instruction: English and French. Endowment: $100 million. Total enrollment: 819. Upper school average class size: 17. Upper school faculty-student ratio: 1:3. There are 165 required school days per year for Upper School students. Upper School students typically attend 5 days per week. The average school day consists of 7 hours and 45 minutes.

Upper School Student Profile Grade 6: 43 students (23 boys, 20 girls); Grade 7: 52 students (19 boys, 33 girls); Grade 8: 48 students (19 boys, 29 girls); Grade 9: 65 students (44 boys, 21 girls); Grade 10: 61 students (29 boys, 32 girls); Grade 11: 40 students (18 boys, 22 girls); Grade 12: 51 students (21 boys, 30 girls).

Faculty School total: 105. In upper school: 28 men, 29 women; 30 have advanced degrees.

Subjects Offered 3-dimensional art, acting, advanced biology, advanced chemistry, advanced math, Advanced Placement courses, advanced studio art-AP, algebra, American government, American history, American history-AP, American literature, American literature-AP, analysis, Ancient Greek, ancient world history, applied arts, art, art history, art-AP, arts, athletics, ballet, band, basketball, biology, biology-AP, calculus, calculus-AP, chemistry, chemistry-AP, choir, civics, classical civilization, classical Greek literature, classical music, college admission preparation, college counseling, college writing, computer music, computer science, computer skills, computer technologies, creative arts, creative writing, dance, drama, earth science, economics, English, English language and composition-AP, English literature, environmental science, ESL, European history, expository writing, fencing, fine arts, French, French as a second language, French language-AP, French studies, gardening, geography, geometry, German, government/civics, grammar, history, Latin, Mandarin, mathematics, microeconomics-AP, music, philosophy, physical education, physics, pre-calculus, SAT preparation, science, social sciences, social studies, Spanish, sports, statistics, theater, theater arts, trigonometry, U.S. history, volleyball, world history, world literature, writing.

Graduation Requirements Arts and fine arts (art, music, dance, drama), electives, English, French, mathematics, physical education (includes health), science, U.S. history, world history.

Special Academic Programs International Baccalaureate program; 19 Advanced Placement exams for which test preparation is offered; honors section; remedial reading and/or remedial writing; remedial math; ESL (10 students enrolled).

College Admission Counseling 44 students graduated in 2015; all went to college, including Concordia University Irvine; Loyola Marymount University; McGill University; New York University; University of California, Los Angeles; University of Southern California. Median SAT critical reading: 610, median SAT math: 595, median SAT writing: 590, median combined SAT: 1525, median composite ACT: 28. 51.8% scored over 600 on SAT critical reading, 48.1% scored over 600 on SAT math, 55.5% scored over 600 on SAT writing, 55.5% scored over 1800 on combined SAT, 75% scored over 26 on composite ACT.

Student Life Upper grades have uniform requirement, student council, honor system. Discipline rests primarily with faculty.

Summer Programs Enrichment, sports, art/fine arts, computer instruction programs offered; session focuses on social activities, sports, foreign languages; held both on and off campus; held at field trips, local parks, local beaches; accepts boys and girls; open to students from other schools. 209 students usually enrolled. 2016 schedule: June 20 to July 28. Application deadline: April 1.

Tuition and Aid Day student tuition: $24,800. Tuition installment plan (Insured Tuition Payment Plan, individually arranged payment plans). Merit scholarship grants, need-based scholarship grants available. In 2015–16, 11% of upper-school students received aid. Total amount of financial aid awarded in 2015–16: $460,024.

Admissions Traditional secondary-level entrance grade is 11. For fall 2015, 63 students applied for upper-level admission, 55 were accepted, 26 enrolled. International English Language Test, ISEE, school's own exam or TOEFL required. Deadline for receipt of application materials: none. Application fee required: $100. Interview required.

Athletics Interscholastic: basketball (boys, girls), volleyball (b,g); intramural: ballet (g); coed interscholastic: fencing, soccer; coed intramural: archery, basketball, fencing, fitness, handball, indoor soccer, kickball, life saving, martial arts, modern dance, physical fitness, rock climbing, self defense, soccer, softball, swimming and diving, table tennis, tennis, touch football, track and field, ultimate Frisbee, volleyball. 6 PE instructors, 4 coaches, 1 athletic trainer.

Computers Computers are regularly used in art, English, foreign language, mathematics, science, social studies classes. Computer network features include on-campus library services, Internet access, wireless campus network, Internet filtering or blocking technology, homework is available online/attendance, Student Information System online, Libraries/Internet Café/Computer Labs. Student e-mail accounts and computer access in designated common areas are available to students. Students grades are available online.

Contact Mme. Sophie Darmon, Director of Admissions. 310-836-3464 Ext. 315. Fax: 310-558-8069. E-mail: admissions@lyceela.org. Website: www.LyceeLA.org

LEXINGTON CATHOLIC HIGH SCHOOL

2250 Clays Mill Road
Lexington, Kentucky 40503-1797

Head of School: Dr. Steven Angelucci

General Information Coeducational day college-preparatory and religious studies school, affiliated with Roman Catholic Church. Grades 9–12. Founded: 1823. Setting: urban. 7-acre campus. 3 buildings on campus. Approved or accredited by National Catholic Education Association, Southern Association of Colleges and Schools, and Kentucky Department of Education. Endowment: $500,000. Total enrollment: 874. Upper school average class size: 20. Upper school faculty-student ratio: 1:13. There are 177 required school days per year for Upper School students. Upper School students typically attend 5 days per week. The average school day consists of 7 hours and 15 minutes.

Upper School Student Profile Grade 9: 244 students (127 boys, 117 girls); Grade 10: 226 students (127 boys, 99 girls); Grade 11: 199 students (103 boys, 96 girls); Grade 12: 205 students (96 boys, 109 girls). 74% of students are Roman Catholic.

Faculty School total: 67. In upper school: 34 men, 33 women; 48 have advanced degrees.

Subjects Offered Accounting, advanced chemistry, Advanced Placement courses, advanced studio art-AP, algebra, American government, American history, American history-AP, American literature, anatomy and physiology, art, astronomy, band, Bible as literature, biology, biology-AP, British literature, British literature (honors), calculus, calculus-AP, Catholic belief and practice, ceramics, chemistry, chemistry-AP, choral music, Christian and Hebrew scripture, church history, comparative religion, computer applications, computer programming, creative writing, drama, economics, English-AP, ethics, film, French, French-AP, geography, geology, geometry, government and politics-AP, health, history of the Catholic Church, honors English, honors geometry, honors U.S. history, honors world history, humanities, introduction to literature, Latin, Latin-AP, physical education, physics, psychology, religious studies, sociology, Spanish, Spanish language-AP, U.S. government, U.S. government and politics-AP, U.S. history, U.S. history-AP, world history, world literature.

Graduation Requirements American history, American literature, arts and fine arts (art, music, dance, drama), biology, British literature, Catholic belief and practice, chemistry, church history, computer applications, English, foreign language, mathematics, physical education (includes health), religion (includes Bible studies and theology), science, U.S. government, U.S. government and politics, U.S. history, world history.

Special Academic Programs 18 Advanced Placement exams for which test preparation is offered; honors section.

College Admission Counseling 193 students graduated in 2015; 188 went to college, including University of Kentucky. Other: 2 went to work, 1 entered military service, 1 entered a postgraduate year. Mean SAT critical reading: 592, mean SAT math: 604, mean SAT writing: 552, mean composite ACT: 25. 59% scored over 26 on composite ACT.

Student Life Upper grades have uniform requirement, student council, honor system. Discipline rests primarily with faculty. Attendance at religious services is required.

Summer Programs Computer instruction programs offered; session focuses on health, physical education, and computers; held on campus; accepts boys and girls; not open to students from other schools. 60 students usually enrolled. 2016 schedule: June to July.

Tuition and Aid Day student tuition: $8745. Tuition installment plan (monthly payment plans, individually arranged payment plans). Merit scholarship grants, need-based scholarship grants available. In 2015–16, 18% of upper-school students received aid; total upper-school merit-scholarship money awarded: $5000. Total amount of financial aid awarded in 2015–16: $650,000.

Admissions Traditional secondary-level entrance grade is 9. For fall 2015, 250 students applied for upper-level admission, 248 were accepted, 244 enrolled. Scholastic Testing Service High School Placement Test required. Deadline for receipt of application materials: none. Application fee required: $275.

Athletics Interscholastic: baseball (boys), basketball (b,g), cheering (g), cross-country running (b,g), dance team (g), diving (b,g), football (b), golf (b,g), soccer (b,g), softball (g), swimming and diving (b,g), tennis (b,g), track and field (b,g), volleyball (g); intramural: badminton (b,g), basketball (b,g), flag football (g), lacrosse (b), physical training (b,g); coed interscholastic: bowling, ultimate Frisbee; coed intramural: outdoor activities. 3 PE instructors, 2 athletic trainers.

Computers Computers are regularly used in all academic classes. Computer network features include on-campus library services, Internet access, wireless campus network, Internet filtering or blocking technology. Computer access in designated common areas is available to students. Students grades are available online. The school has a published electronic and media policy.

Contact Ms. Mindy Towles, Admissions Director. 859-277-7183 Ext. 231. Fax: 859-276-5086. E-mail: mtowles@lexingtoncatholic.com. Website: www.lexingtoncatholic.com

LEXINGTON CHRISTIAN ACADEMY

450 West Reynolds Road
Lexington, Kentucky 40503

Head of School: Rick Burslem

General Information Coeducational day college-preparatory school. Grades PK–12. Founded: 1989. Setting: suburban. 1 building on campus. Approved or accredited by Southern Association of Colleges and Schools and Kentucky Department of Education. Total enrollment: 1,445. Upper school average class size: 18. Upper school faculty-student ratio: 1:16. There are 178 required school days per year for Upper School students. Upper School students typically attend 5 days per week. The average school day consists of 6 hours and 40 minutes.

Special Academic Programs Advanced Placement exam preparation; honors section; study at local college for college credit.

College Admission Counseling 109 students graduated in 2015; 105 went to college. Other: 4 had other specific plans.

Student Life Discipline rests primarily with faculty. Attendance at religious services is required.

Admissions Stanford Achievement Test required. Deadline for receipt of application materials: August 1. Application fee required: $100. Interview required.

Athletics Interscholastic: archery (boys, girls), baseball (b), basketball (b,g), cheering (g), cross-country running (b,g), dance team (g), football (b), golf (b,g), soccer (b,g), softball (g), swimming and diving (b,g), track and field (b,g), volleyball (g), wrestling (b); intramural: cheering (g), flag football (g), lacrosse (b).

Contact Mrs. Lesley Sizemore-Hardin, Director of Admissions. 859-422-5733. Fax: 859-223-3769. E-mail: lhardin@lexingtonchristian.org. Website: www.lexingtonchristian.org

LEXINGTON CHRISTIAN ACADEMY

48 Bartlett Avenue
Lexington, Massachusetts 02420

Head of School: Mr. Timothy Russell

General Information Coeducational boarding and day college-preparatory, arts, religious studies, and technology school, affiliated with Christian faith. Boarding grades 9–12, day grades 6–12. Founded: 1946. Setting: suburban. Nearest major city is Boston. Students are housed in single-sex by floor dormitories. 30-acre campus. 2 buildings on campus. Approved or accredited by Association of Christian Schools International, Association of Independent Schools in New England, Christian Schools International, New England Association of Schools and Colleges, and Massachusetts Department of Education. Member of National Association of Independent Schools and Secondary School Admission Test Board. Endowment: $3.6 million. Total enrollment: 317. Upper school average class size: 16. Upper school faculty-student ratio: 1:11. There are 168 required school days per year for Upper School students. Upper School students typically attend 5 days per week. The average school day consists of 7 hours.

Upper School Student Profile Grade 6: 15 students (7 boys, 8 girls); Grade 7: 28 students (11 boys, 17 girls); Grade 8: 30 students (18 boys, 12 girls); Grade 9: 56 students (26 boys, 30 girls); Grade 10: 55 students (27 boys, 28 girls); Grade 11: 74 students (35 boys, 39 girls); Grade 12: 59 students (22 boys, 37 girls). 1 state is represented in upper school student body.

Faculty School total: 42. In upper school: 21 men, 21 women; 29 have advanced degrees; 1 resides on campus.

Subjects Offered Advanced Placement courses, algebra, American history-AP, anatomy, ancient history, art, Bible studies, biology, biology-AP, British literature, British literature-AP, calculus-AP, chemistry, choral music, Christian ethics, college counseling, community service, computer graphics, computer information systems, computer programming, computers, concert band, creative writing, drama, economics, English, English literature, English literature-AP, ESL, European history-AP, French, general science, geography, geometry, health, history, independent study, journalism, Latin, mathematics, modern world history, music, music theory, physical education, physical science, physics, physiology, psychology, religion, science, science research, senior internship, senior project, social studies, Spanish, theater, trigonometry, U.S. government and politics, world history, world literature, writing.

Graduation Requirements Algebra, American history, American literature, ancient world history, Bible, Bible studies, biology, British history, British literature, chemistry, college counseling, college planning, computer literacy, electives, English, English literature, ethics, European history, European literature, foreign language, geometry, health education, keyboarding, lab science, mathematics, physical education (includes health), physics, religion (includes Bible studies and theology), science, senior internship, service learning/internship, social studies (includes history), U.S. history, senior internship (3-week work experience in career of student's choice, including a journal of the experience), Interim (participation each year in one week of special Interim courses). Community service is required.

Special Academic Programs Advanced Placement exam preparation; honors section; independent study; term-away projects; study at local college for college credit; ESL (5 students enrolled).

College Admission Counseling 46 students graduated in 2014; 45 went to college, including Boston University; Furman University; Gordon College; Northeastern

University; Wheaton College. Other: 1 had other specific plans. Mean SAT critical reading: 604, mean SAT math: 617, mean SAT writing: 597.

Student Life Upper grades have specified standards of dress, student council. Discipline rests primarily with faculty. Attendance at religious services is required.

Tuition and Aid Day student tuition: $21,250. Tuition installment plan (Tuition Management Systems). Merit scholarship grants, need-based scholarship grants available. In 2014–15, 45% of upper-school students received aid; total upper-school merit-scholarship money awarded: $223,973. Total amount of financial aid awarded in 2014–15: $739,135.

Admissions Traditional secondary-level entrance grade is 9. For fall 2014, 181 students applied for upper-level admission, 123 were accepted, 67 enrolled. ISEE, SSAT, TOEFL or TOEFL Junior required. Deadline for receipt of application materials: February 1. Application fee required: $50. Interview required.

Athletics Interscholastic: baseball (boys), basketball (b,g), cross-country running (b,g), field hockey (g), lacrosse (b,g), soccer (b,g), softball (g), wrestling (b); intramural: basketball (b,g), gymnastics (b,g), lacrosse (b), physical training (b,g), soccer (b,g), tennis (b,g), volleyball (b,g), wrestling (b); coed interscholastic: golf; coed intramural: fitness, outdoor activities, rock climbing, skiing (downhill), snowboarding, strength & conditioning, ultimate Frisbee, volleyball, wall climbing. 2 PE instructors, 10 coaches, 1 athletic trainer.

Computers Computers are regularly used in all academic, graphic design, library science, literary magazine, mathematics, media arts, music, photography, publications, science, yearbook classes. Computer network features include on-campus library services, online commercial services, Internet access, wireless campus network, Internet filtering or blocking technology. Campus intranet, student e-mail accounts, and computer access in designated common areas are available to students. Students grades are available online. The school has a published electronic and media policy.

Contact Mrs. Cynthia Torjesen, Director of Admission. 781-862-7850 Ext. 152. Fax: 781-863-8503. E-mail: cindy.torjesen@lca.edu. Website: www.lca.edu

LEYSIN AMERICAN SCHOOL IN SWITZERLAND

Belle Epoque Campus
Chemin de la Source 3
Leysin 1854, Switzerland

Head of School: Dr. Marc-Frédéric Ott

General Information Coeducational boarding college-preparatory school. Grades 7–PG. Founded: 1961. Setting: small town. Nearest major city is Geneva, Switzerland. Students are housed in single-sex dormitories. 14 buildings on campus. Approved or accredited by International Baccalaureate Organization, New England Association of Schools and Colleges, Swiss Federation of Private Schools, and The Association of Boarding Schools. Member of Secondary School Admission Test Board. Language of instruction: English. Total enrollment: 340. Upper school average class size: 12. Upper school faculty-student ratio: 1:8. There are 180 required school days per year for Upper School students. Upper School students typically attend 5 days per week. The average school day consists of 5 hours and 55 minutes.

Upper School Student Profile 100% of students are boarding students. 98% are international students. International students from Brazil, Kazakhstan, Mexico, Russian Federation, Saudi Arabia, and United States; 55 other countries represented in student body.

Faculty School total: 72. In upper school: 40 men, 32 women; 42 have advanced degrees; 67 reside on campus.

Subjects Offered Algebra, American history, American literature, ancient history, art, band, biology, business, business studies, calculus, calculus-AP, chemistry, chorus, college counseling, computer programming, computer science, computer technologies, creative arts, current events, dance, drama, ecology, environmental systems, economics, English, English literature, ensembles, ESL, European history, fine arts, fitness, French, French studies, geometry, German, health education, history, history of the Americas, humanities, information technology, International Baccalaureate courses, intro to computers, journalism, language arts, math analysis, math methods, mathematics, mathematics-AP, model United Nations, modern languages, music, music appreciation, performing arts, physical education, physical science, physics, piano, pre-algebra, pre-calculus, psychology, SAT preparation, science, social sciences, social studies, Spanish, Spanish literature, stagecraft, studio art, study skills, theater, theory of knowledge, TOEFL preparation, trigonometry, United Nations and international issues, weightlifting, world history, yearbook.

Graduation Requirements Arts and fine arts (art, music, dance, drama), computer science, English, foreign language, mathematics, physical education (includes health), science, senior humanities, social studies (includes history), Swiss and European cultural trip reports.

Special Academic Programs International Baccalaureate program; honors section; independent study; study abroad; academic accommodation for the gifted, the musically talented, and the artistically talented; ESL (110 students enrolled).

College Admission Counseling 96 students graduated in 2015; 93 went to college, including Boston University; Mount Holyoke College; New York University; Northeastern University; The University of Texas at Austin; University of Virginia. Other: 2 entered a postgraduate year, 1 had other specific plans. Mean SAT critical reading: 496, mean SAT math: 548, mean SAT writing: 509.

Student Life Upper grades have specified standards of dress, student council, honor system. Discipline rests equally with students and faculty.

Summer Programs Remediation, enrichment, advancement, ESL, sports, art/fine arts, rigorous outdoor training, computer instruction programs offered; session focuses on enrichment, theater, chamber music, leadership, European travel, students with dyslexia; held on campus; accepts boys and girls; open to students from other schools. 250 students usually enrolled. 2016 schedule: June 26 to August 13. Application deadline: none.

Tuition and Aid 5-day tuition and room/board: 51,000 Swiss francs; 7-day tuition and room/board: 69,500 Swiss francs. Tuition installment plan (individually arranged payment plans, corporate payment plan). Tuition reduction for siblings, bursaries, merit scholarship grants, need-based scholarship grants, paying campus jobs available. In 2014–15, 10% of upper-school students received aid; total upper-school merit-scholarship money awarded: 250,000 Swiss francs. Total amount of financial aid awarded in 2014–15: 600,000 Swiss francs.

Admissions Traditional secondary-level entrance grade is 10. Achievement/Aptitude/Writing or essay required. Deadline for receipt of application materials: none. Application fee required: 500 Swiss francs. Interview recommended.

Athletics Interscholastic: alpine skiing (boys, girls), basketball (b,g), hockey (b), ice hockey (b), soccer (b,g), tennis (b,g), volleyball (b,g); intramural: basketball (b,g), soccer (b,g), tennis (b,g), volleyball (b,g); coed interscholastic: bicycling, cross-country running, equestrian sports, golf, skiing (cross-country), skiing (downhill), snowboarding, squash, swimming and diving, track and field; coed intramural: aerobics, aerobics/dance, alpine skiing, backpacking, ball hockey, ballet, bicycling, canoeing/kayaking, climbing, cross-country running, curling, dance, dance team, equestrian sports, figure skating, fitness, flag football, floor hockey, freestyle skiing, golf, hiking/backpacking, horseback riding, ice skating, indoor hockey, indoor soccer, jogging, juggling, martial arts, mountain biking, mountaineering, nordic skiing, outdoor activities, outdoor adventure, outdoor education, outdoor recreation, paddle tennis, paint ball, physical fitness, physical training, rafting, rappelling, rock climbing, ropes courses, running, sailing, skiing (cross-country), skiing (downhill), snowboarding, snowshoeing, squash, street hockey, strength & conditioning, swimming and diving, table tennis, track and field, unicycling, walking, wall climbing, weight lifting, weight training, yoga. 1 PE instructor, 2 athletic trainers.

Computers Computers are regularly used in all classes. Computer network features include on-campus library services, online commercial services, Internet access, wireless campus network, Internet filtering or blocking technology. Campus intranet and student e-mail accounts are available to students. Students grades are available online. The school has a published electronic and media policy.

Contact Mrs. Danka Perrauld, Admissions Office Manager. 603-431-4888. E-mail: admissions@las.ch. Website: www.las.ch

LIBERTY CHRISTIAN SCHOOL

7661 Warner Avenue
Huntington Beach, California 92647

Head of School: Mr. David Whitmire

General Information Coeducational day college-preparatory and religious studies school, affiliated with Protestant faith, Baptist Church. Grades K–12. Founded: 1970. Setting: suburban. Nearest major city is Los Angeles. 5-acre campus. 3 buildings on campus. Approved or accredited by Accrediting Commission for Schools, Western Association of Schools and Colleges, and California Department of Education. Total enrollment: 112. Upper school average class size: 10. Upper school faculty-student ratio: 1:6. There are 180 required school days per year for Upper School students. Upper School students typically attend 5 days per week. The average school day consists of 6 hours and 30 minutes.

Upper School Student Profile 90% of students are Protestant, Baptist.

Faculty School total: 14. In upper school: 5 men, 4 women; 1 has an advanced degree.

Subjects Offered American literature, U.S. government.

Graduation Requirements World cultures.

Special Academic Programs Honors section; independent study.

College Admission Counseling 16 students graduated in 2015; 14 went to college, including California State University, Long Beach; Grand Canyon University; Orange Coast College. Other: 1 entered military service.

Student Life Upper grades have specified standards of dress, student council, honor system. Discipline rests primarily with faculty.

Tuition and Aid Day student tuition: $8800. Tuition installment plan (SMART Tuition Payment Plan). Need-based scholarship grants available. In 2015–16, 40% of upper-school students received aid. Total amount of financial aid awarded in 2015–16: $70,000.

Admissions Deadline for receipt of application materials: none. Application fee required: $350. On-campus interview required.

Athletics Interscholastic: basketball (boys, girls), flag football (b), softball (g), volleyball (b,g). 1 coach.

Computers Computers are regularly used in media classes. Computer network features include Internet access, wireless campus network. Computer access in designated common areas is available to students. Students grades are available online. The school has a published electronic and media policy.

Contact Mrs. LeighAnne Lockerbie, Registrar. 714-842-5992. Fax: 714-848-7484. E-mail: info@libertychristian.org. Website: www.libertychristian.org

LIFEGATE SCHOOL

1052 Fairfield Avenue
Eugene, Oregon 97402-2053
Head of School: Mr. Mike McCoy

General Information Coeducational boarding and day and distance learning college-preparatory, general academic, arts, and religious studies school, affiliated with Christian faith; primarily serves students with learning disabilities, individuals with Attention Deficit Disorder, and individuals with emotional and behavioral problems. Grades 6–12. Distance learning grade X. Founded: 1994. Setting: suburban. 1-acre campus. 1 building on campus. Approved or accredited by Northwest Accreditation Commission, Northwest Association of Independent Schools, Northwest Association of Schools and Colleges, Texas Private School Accreditation Commission, and Oregon Department of Education. Languages of instruction: English, Japanese, and Spanish. Total enrollment: 44. Upper school average class size: 8. Upper school faculty-student ratio: 1:10. Upper School students typically attend 5 days per week. The average school day consists of 7 hours and 45 minutes.

Upper School Student Profile Grade 6: 5 students (4 boys, 1 girl); Grade 7: 4 students (2 boys, 2 girls); Grade 8: 5 students (2 boys, 3 girls); Grade 9: 7 students (4 boys, 3 girls); Grade 10: 10 students (5 boys, 5 girls); Grade 11: 9 students (4 boys, 5 girls); Grade 12: 6 students (3 boys, 3 girls). 100% are state residents. 50 states are represented in upper school student body. 95% of students are Christian.

Faculty School total: 10. In upper school: 3 men, 4 women; 5 have advanced degrees.

Subjects Offered Advanced biology, advanced math, Advanced Placement courses, algebra, American government, American history, ancient world history, art, band, Bible, Bible studies, biology, biology-AP, British literature (honors), British literature-AP, calculus, calculus-AP, career and personal planning, chemistry, drama, economics, English, English composition, English language and composition-AP, English literature-AP, geometry, health education, independent study, journalism, keyboarding, leadership, life skills, physical education, physical science, physics, pre-algebra, pre-calculus, reading/study skills, Spanish, world history, writing, yearbook.

Graduation Requirements Bible, English, government, history, keyboarding, life skills, mathematics, physical education (includes health), 25 hours of volunteer work per year.

Special Academic Programs International Baccalaureate program; Advanced Placement exam preparation; honors section; accelerated programs; independent study; academic accommodation for the gifted and the artistically talented; remedial reading and/or remedial writing; remedial math; programs in mathematics, general development for dyslexic students.

College Admission Counseling 12 students graduated in 2014; 9 went to college, including George Fox University; Georgia State University; Lane Community College; Oregon Institute of Technology; Oregon State University; University of Oregon. Other: 1 went to work, 2 entered military service.

Student Life Upper grades have specified standards of dress, student council, honor system. Discipline rests primarily with faculty.

Tuition and Aid Day student tuition: $8000. Tuition installment plan (monthly payment plans). Tuition reduction for siblings, merit scholarship grants, need-based scholarship grants available. In 2014–15, 14% of upper-school students received aid; total upper-school merit-scholarship money awarded: $13,000. Total amount of financial aid awarded in 2014–15: $50,000.

Admissions Traditional secondary-level entrance grade is 9. For fall 2014, 9 students applied for upper-level admission, 9 were accepted, 9 enrolled. Deadline for receipt of application materials: May 15. No application fee required. On-campus interview required.

Athletics Interscholastic: basketball (boys), outdoor activities (b,g), outdoor education (b,g). 1 PE instructor, 1 coach.

Computers Computers are regularly used in desktop publishing, English, lab/keyboard, media arts, writing, yearbook classes. Computer network features include on-campus library services, Internet access, wireless campus network, Internet filtering or blocking technology. Campus intranet and student e-mail accounts are available to students. Students grades are available online.

Contact Ms. Donna Wickwire, Assistant Administrator. 541-689-5847. Fax: 541-689-6028. E-mail: donnaw@lifegatechristian.org. Website: www.lifegatechristian.org

LIGHTHOUSE CHRISTIAN ACADEMY

4290-50th Street
Sylvan Lake, Alberta T4S 0H3, Canada
Head of School: Dion Krause

General Information Coeducational day college-preparatory, general academic, arts, and religious studies school. Grades PK–12. Founded: 1982. Setting: small town. Nearest major city is Red Deer, Canada. 1 building on campus. Approved or accredited by Association of Christian Schools International and Alberta Department of Education. Language of instruction: English. Total enrollment: 93. Upper school average class size: 12. Upper school faculty-student ratio: 1:6. There are 189 required school days per year for Upper School students. Upper School students typically attend 5 days per week. The average school day consists of 5 hours and 30 minutes.

Upper School Student Profile Grade 6: 2 students (2 boys); Grade 7: 6 students (2 boys, 4 girls); Grade 8: 7 students (2 boys, 5 girls); Grade 9: 9 students (3 boys, 6 girls); Grade 10: 4 students (3 boys, 1 girl); Grade 12: 4 students (1 boy, 3 girls).

Faculty School total: 11. In upper school: 2 men, 9 women; 8 have advanced degrees.

College Admission Counseling 7 students graduated in 2014; 2 went to college. Other: 4 went to work, 1 had other specific plans.

Student Life Upper grades have specified standards of dress, honor system.

Tuition and Aid Tuition installment plan (individually arranged payment plans).

Admissions Traditional secondary-level entrance grade is 10. Deadline for receipt of application materials: none. No application fee required. Interview required.

Athletics 1 PE instructor.

Contact Dion Krause, Principal. 403-887-2166. Fax: 403-887-5729. E-mail: lightca@telusplanet.net. Website: www.lighthousechristianacademy.ca/

LINCOLN ACADEMY

81 Academy Hill
Newcastle, Maine 04553
Head of School: Mr. David B. Sturdevant

General Information Coeducational boarding and day college-preparatory, general academic, arts, business, vocational, technology, Advanced Placement, and world languages school; primarily serves students with learning disabilities, individuals with Attention Deficit Disorder, and dyslexic students. Grades 9–12. Founded: 1801. Setting: small town. Nearest major city is Portland. Students are housed in single-sex dormitories. 85-acre campus. 7 buildings on campus. Approved or accredited by Independent Schools of Northern New England, New England Association of Schools and Colleges, The Association of Boarding Schools, and Maine Department of Education. Member of National Association of Independent Schools and Secondary School Admission Test Board. Endowment: $7 million. Total enrollment: 588. Upper school average class size: 18. Upper school faculty-student ratio: 1:17. There are 176 required school days per year for Upper School students. Upper School students typically attend 5 days per week. The average school day consists of 6 hours and 40 minutes.

Upper School Student Profile Grade 9: 136 students (73 boys, 63 girls); Grade 10: 148 students (84 boys, 64 girls); Grade 11: 143 students (72 boys, 71 girls); Grade 12: 161 students (77 boys, 84 girls). 14% of students are boarding students. 86% are state residents. 2 states are represented in upper school student body. 14% are international students. International students from China, Germany, Republic of Korea, Spain, Turkey, and Viet Nam; 11 other countries represented in student body.

Faculty School total: 63. In upper school: 22 men, 23 women; 26 have advanced degrees; 8 reside on campus.

Subjects Offered 3-dimensional art, 3-dimensional design, accounting, ACT preparation, acting, advanced biology, advanced chemistry, advanced math, Advanced Placement courses, advanced studio art-AP, algebra, American history, American history-AP, American literature, American literature-AP, anatomy and physiology, architecture, art-AP, astronomy, athletics, audio visual/media, auto mechanics, band, basic language skills, biology, biology-AP, boat building, bookkeeping, business, cabinet making, calculus, calculus-AP, career experience, career/college preparation, carpentry, ceramics, chemistry, chemistry-AP, child development, choir, chorus, college counseling, computer skills, computer technologies, computer-aided design, conceptual physics, concert band, concert choir, construction, CPR, creative writing, culinary arts, debate, design, desktop publishing, developmental language skills, developmental math, digital applications, digital photography, drafting, drama, drama performance, drawing and design, early childhood, engineering, English composition, English language-AP, English literature-AP, English/composition-AP, environmental science-AP, European history-AP, film, filmmaking, finance, foreign language, French, French-AP, general math, geography, geology, geometry, German, global studies, guitar, health and wellness, history, history of rock and roll, honors algebra, honors English, honors geometry, honors U.S. history, honors world history, industrial arts, instrumental music, integrated physics, internship, Italian, jazz band, jazz ensemble, language arts, language development, leadership, macroeconomics-AP, Mandarin, marching band, marine biology, marine ecology, marine science, marine studies, maritime history, mathematical modeling, mechanical drawing, media production, metal fabrication technology, model United Nations, money management, music theory, music theory-AP, musical productions, Native American studies, oceanography, painting, performing arts, personal finance, photography, physical education, physics, physics-AP, piano, play production, play/screen writing, playwriting and directing, poetry, politics, portfolio art, pre-algebra, pre-calculus, printmaking, probability and statistics, psychology, public speaking, robotics, SAT preparation, scuba diving, sculpture, self-defense, short story, silk screening, small engine repair, social studies, Spanish, Spanish language-AP, studio art, technical drawing, technical education, technology/design, theater production, TOEFL preparation, trigonometry, U.S. government and politics, video film production, visual and performing arts, vocal ensemble, vocal jazz, welding, wind ensemble, woodworking, work-study, world history, world religions, yearbook.

Graduation Requirements English, foreign language, health, mathematics, physical education (includes health), science, social studies (includes history), visual and performing arts, job shadow experiences, community service. Community service is required.

Special Academic Programs 16 Advanced Placement exams for which test preparation is offered; honors section; independent study; study abroad; academic accommodation for the gifted, the musically talented, and the artistically talented; remedial reading and/or remedial writing; remedial math; ESL (28 students enrolled).

College Admission Counseling 109 students graduated in 2015; 80 went to college, including Champlain College; Johnson & Wales University; Plymouth State University; Saint Joseph's College of Maine; University of Maine; University of Rhode Island. Other: 24 went to work, 5 entered military service.

Student Life Upper grades have specified standards of dress, student council. Discipline rests primarily with faculty.

Summer Programs ESL, art/fine arts programs offered; session focuses on English immersion, cultural experience; held on campus; accepts boys and girls; open to students from other schools. 2016 schedule: July 27 to August 14.

Tuition and Aid Day student tuition: $10,046; 7-day tuition and room/board: $37,000. Tuition reduction for siblings, need-based scholarship grants available. In 2015–16, 4% of upper-school students received aid. Total amount of financial aid awarded in 2015–16: $172,000.

Admissions Traditional secondary-level entrance grade is 9. For fall 2015, 107 students applied for upper-level admission, 71 were accepted, 35 enrolled. CTBS or ERB, ERB CTP IV, International English Language Test, PSAT, SSAT, TOEFL or TOEFL Junior required. Deadline for receipt of application materials: none. Application fee required: $50. Interview required.

Athletics Interscholastic: baseball (boys), basketball (b,g), cheering (g), cross-country running (b,g), field hockey (g), golf (b,g), lacrosse (b,g), soccer (b,g), softball (g), swimming and diving (b,g), tennis (b,g), track and field (b,g), wrestling (b,g); intramural: self defense (g); coed interscholastic: indoor track, Special Olympics, winter (indoor) track; coed intramural: canoeing/kayaking, dance team, fly fishing, hiking/backpacking, horseback riding, nordic skiing, outdoor activities, physical fitness, physical training, sailing, skiing (cross-country), skiing (downhill), snowboarding, table tennis, weight lifting, weight training. 3 PE instructors, 34 coaches, 1 athletic trainer.

Computers Computers are regularly used in all classes. Computer network features include on-campus library services, online commercial services, Internet access, wireless campus network. Campus intranet, student e-mail accounts, and computer access in designated common areas are available to students. Students grades are available online. The school has a published electronic and media policy.

Contact Sheryl Stearns, Director of Enrollment and Marketing. 207-563-3596 Ext. 108. Fax: 207-563-1067. E-mail: stearns@lincolnacademy.org. Website: www.lincolnacademy.org

LINCOLN SCHOOL

301 Butler Avenue
Providence, Rhode Island 02906-5556

Head of School: Suzanne Fogarty

General Information Coeducational day (boys' only in lower grades) college-preparatory, arts, and technology school, affiliated with Society of Friends. Boys grades N–PK, girls grades N–12. Founded: 1884. Setting: urban. 46-acre campus. 5 buildings on campus. Approved or accredited by Association of Independent Schools in New England, Friends Council on Education, New England Association of Schools and Colleges, and Rhode Island Department of Education. Member of National Association of Independent Schools and Secondary School Admission Test Board. Endowment: $8 million. Total enrollment: 350. Upper school average class size: 13. Upper school faculty-student ratio: 1:4. Upper School students typically attend 5 days per week. The average school day consists of 7 hours and 13 minutes.

Upper School Student Profile Grade 9: 55 students (55 girls); Grade 10: 32 students (32 girls); Grade 11: 41 students (41 girls); Grade 12: 42 students (42 girls). 1% of students are members of Society of Friends.

Faculty School total: 75. In upper school: 11 men, 35 women; 24 have advanced degrees.

Subjects Offered Algebra, American history, American literature, anatomy, Arabic, art, biology, biology-AP, calculus, calculus-AP, ceramics, chemistry, chemistry-AP, college awareness, community service, computer science, creative writing, dance, English, English literature, environmental science, ethics, European history, European history-AP, French, French-AP, geometry, health, history, Latin, music, photography, physical education, physics, pre-calculus, Spanish, Spanish language-AP, statistics-AP, theater, trigonometry, U.S. history-AP, visual literacy, women's studies, world history, world literature.

Graduation Requirements Arts and fine arts (art, music, dance, drama), college planning, computer science, English, ethics, foreign language, mathematics, physical education (includes health), science, social studies (includes history), senior service trip. Community service is required.

Special Academic Programs Advanced Placement exam preparation; honors section; independent study; term-away projects; study at local college for college credit; study abroad; programs in general development for dyslexic students.

College Admission Counseling 48 students graduated in 2015; all went to college, including Bates College; Boston University; Worcester Polytechnic Institute. Median SAT critical reading: 590, median SAT math: 570, median SAT writing: 609.

Student Life Upper grades have uniform requirement, student council, honor system. Discipline rests equally with students and faculty.

Tuition and Aid Day student tuition: $28,650. Tuition installment plan (FACTS Tuition Payment Plan, Tuition Management Systems Plan). Merit scholarship grants, need-based scholarship grants available. In 2015–16, 40% of upper-school students received aid; total upper-school merit-scholarship money awarded: $15,000. Total amount of financial aid awarded in 2015–16: $2,000,000.

Admissions Traditional secondary-level entrance grade is 9. For fall 2015, 82 students applied for upper-level admission, 59 were accepted, 24 enrolled. ISEE or SSAT required. Deadline for receipt of application materials: February 15. Application fee required: $50. Interview required.

Athletics Interscholastic: basketball, crew, cross-country running, field hockey, lacrosse, soccer, squash, swimming and diving, tennis. 3 PE instructors, 17 coaches, 1 athletic trainer.

Computers Computers are regularly used in English, history, science classes. Computer network features include on-campus library services, Internet access, wireless campus network, Internet filtering or blocking technology. Student e-mail accounts and computer access in designated common areas are available to students. The school has a published electronic and media policy.

Contact Mrs. Diane Mota, Admission Office Administrative Assistant. 401-331-9696 Ext. 3157. Fax: 401-751-6670. E-mail: dmota@lincolnschool.org. Website: www.lincolnschool.org

THE LINSLY SCHOOL

60 Knox Lane
Wheeling, West Virginia 26003-6489

Head of School: Mr. Justin Zimmerman

General Information Coeducational boarding and day college-preparatory, arts, technology, and science, mathematics, humanities, foreign language school. Boarding grades 7–12, day grades 5–12. Founded: 1814. Setting: suburban. Nearest major city is Pittsburgh, PA. Students are housed in single-sex dormitories. 60-acre campus. 19 buildings on campus. Approved or accredited by Independent Schools Association of the Central States, North Central Association of Colleges and Schools, The Association of Boarding Schools, and West Virginia Department of Education. Member of National Association of Independent Schools. Endowment: $16 million. Total enrollment: 443. Upper school average class size: 15. Upper school faculty-student ratio: 1:10. There are 165 required school days per year for Upper School students. Upper School students typically attend 5 days per week. The average school day consists of 6 hours and 30 minutes.

Upper School Student Profile Grade 9: 79 students (42 boys, 37 girls); Grade 10: 72 students (34 boys, 38 girls); Grade 11: 83 students (53 boys, 30 girls); Grade 12: 64 students (32 boys, 32 girls). 27% of students are boarding students. 47% are state residents. 15 states are represented in upper school student body. 10% are international students. International students from Bahamas, China, Mexico, Republic of Korea, Saudi Arabia, and South Africa; 15 other countries represented in student body.

Faculty School total: 60. In upper school: 28 men, 14 women; 27 have advanced degrees; 24 reside on campus.

Subjects Offered Algebra, American history, American literature, art, art history, biology, biology-AP, calculus-AP, character education, chemistry, chemistry-AP, Chinese, chorus, college counseling, communications, computer programming, computer science, concert band, contemporary issues, contemporary studies, creative writing, drama, earth science, economics, English, English language-AP, English literature, English literature-AP, environmental science, expository writing, fine arts, French, geometry, German, government/civics, health, history, human geography - AP, humanities, Latin, mathematics, model United Nations, multimedia design, music, newspaper, physical education, physics, physics-AP, psychology, psychology-AP, science, social studies, Spanish, speech, statistics, technology/design, theater, U.S. history-AP, world history, writing, yearbook, zoology.

Graduation Requirements Arts and fine arts (art, music, dance, drama), computer science, English, foreign language, mathematics, physical education (includes health), science, social studies (includes history), Senior Research Essay.

Special Academic Programs 12 Advanced Placement exams for which test preparation is offered; academic accommodation for the gifted.

College Admission Counseling 64 students graduated in 2014; all went to college, including Duquesne University; Marshall University; New York University; Ohio University; Penn State University Park; West Virginia University. Mean SAT critical reading: 580, mean SAT math: 580, mean SAT writing: 570, mean combined SAT: 1730, mean composite ACT: 26.

Student Life Upper grades have uniform requirement, student council, honor system. Discipline rests primarily with faculty.

Tuition and Aid Day student tuition: $15,590; 5-day tuition and room/board: $32,170; 7-day tuition and room/board: $32,170. Need-based scholarship grants available. In 2014–15, 48% of upper-school students received aid. Total amount of financial aid awarded in 2014–15: $2,345,000.

Admissions Traditional secondary-level entrance grade is 9. Otis-Lennon, Stanford Achievement Test, SSAT or TOEFL or SLEP required. Deadline for receipt of application materials: none. No application fee required. Interview required.

Athletics Interscholastic: baseball (boys), basketball (b,g), cheering (g), cross-country running (b,g), diving (b,g), football (b), golf (b,g), ice hockey (b,g), lacrosse (b), soccer (b,g), softball (g), wrestling (b); intramural: flag football (b,g), floor hockey (b), football (b), hiking/backpacking (b,g), indoor soccer (b,g), indoor track (b,g), indoor track & field (b,g), life saving (b,g), mountain biking (b,g), outdoor activities (b,g), physical fitness (b,g), power lifting (b), rappelling (b,g), rock climbing (b,g), roller blading (b,g), ropes courses (b,g), running (b,g), street hockey (b); coed intramural: backpacking, badminton, bowling, canoeing/kayaking, climbing, combined training, cooperative games, cross-country running, fitness, Frisbee, ice skating, in-line skating, jogging, kayaking, kickball, life saving, mountain biking, Nautilus, physical fitness, physical training, rafting, rock climbing, ropes courses, running, scuba diving, soccer, softball. 4 PE instructors, 4 coaches, 1 athletic trainer.

Computers Computers are regularly used in economics, English, foreign language, humanities, journalism, mathematics, music, psychology, science classes. Computer network features include on-campus library services, online commercial services, Internet access, wireless campus network, Internet filtering or blocking technology. Student e-mail accounts are available to students. The school has a published electronic and media policy.

Contact Mr. Robert J. Zitzelsberger III, Director of Admissions. 304-233-1436. Fax: 304-234-4614. E-mail: admit@linsly.org. Website: www.linsly.org

LITTLE KESWICK SCHOOL

Keswick, Virginia
See Special Needs Schools section.

LONG TRAIL SCHOOL

1045 Kirby Hollow Road
Dorset, Vermont 05251-9776

Head of School: Steven Dear

General Information Coeducational day college-preparatory and arts school. Grades 6–12. Founded: 1975. Setting: rural. Nearest major city is Rutland. 14-acre campus. 1 building on campus. Approved or accredited by International Baccalaureate Organization, New England Association of Schools and Colleges, and Vermont Department of Education. Member of National Association of Independent Schools. Endowment: $4.5 million. Total enrollment: 155. Upper school average class size: 10. Upper school faculty-student ratio: 1:8. There are 175 required school days per year for Upper School students. Upper School students typically attend 5 days per week. The average school day consists of 7 hours.

Upper School Student Profile Grade 6: 12 students (4 boys, 8 girls); Grade 7: 35 students (20 boys, 15 girls); Grade 8: 27 students (9 boys, 18 girls); Grade 9: 30 students (16 boys, 14 girls); Grade 10: 31 students (15 boys, 16 girls); Grade 11: 26 students (14 boys, 12 girls); Grade 12: 22 students (11 boys, 11 girls).

Faculty School total: 32. In upper school: 10 men, 22 women; 16 have advanced degrees.

Subjects Offered 20th century world history, acting, advanced biology, algebra, American literature, American literature-AP, art, band, biology, calculus, calculus-AP, chemistry, chorus, computer information systems, conceptual physics, concert band, drama, drawing, earth science, economics, English, English literature, English literature-AP, environmental science, environmental science-AP, French, geography, geometry, government/civics, history, mathematics, model United Nations, music, physical education, physical science, physics, political science, pre-algebra, pre-calculus, probability and statistics, psychology, psychology-AP, science, social studies, Spanish, statistics, statistics-AP, technical theater, theater, trigonometry, U.S. history, U.S. history-AP, world history, world literature, writing.

Graduation Requirements Arts and fine arts (art, music, dance, drama), computer science, English, foreign language, mathematics, physical education (includes health), science, social studies (includes history), brief graduation ceremony speech. Community service is required.

Special Academic Programs International Baccalaureate program; honors section; independent study; programs in English, mathematics, general development for dyslexic students; ESL (5 students enrolled).

College Admission Counseling 23 students graduated in 2015; 22 went to college, including Colgate University; Cornell University; Manhattanville College; Occidental College; Saint Michael's College; Temple University. Other: 1 went to work. Mean SAT critical reading: 584, mean SAT math: 561, mean SAT writing: 554.

Student Life Upper grades have specified standards of dress, student council, honor system. Discipline rests equally with students and faculty.

Tuition and Aid Day student tuition: $16,950. Tuition installment plan (monthly payment plans, individually arranged payment plans, TADS Financial Management). Merit scholarship grants, need-based scholarship grants available. In 2015–16, 25% of upper-school students received aid; total upper-school merit-scholarship money awarded: $9000. Total amount of financial aid awarded in 2015–16: $99,599.

Admissions Traditional secondary-level entrance grade is 9. For fall 2015, 20 students applied for upper-level admission, 13 were accepted, 9 enrolled. Admissions testing or essay required. Deadline for receipt of application materials: none. Application fee required: $35. On-campus interview required.

Athletics Interscholastic: baseball (boys), basketball (b,g), soccer (b,g), softball (g); coed interscholastic: alpine skiing, cross-country running, dance team, freestyle skiing, golf, rock climbing, skiing (downhill), snowboarding; coed intramural: aerobics/dance, alpine skiing, basketball, bicycling, dance, fitness walking, fly fishing, freestyle skiing, Frisbee, golf, ice skating, indoor soccer, mountain biking, nordic skiing, skiing (downhill), snowboarding, tennis, touch football, ultimate Frisbee, weight lifting. 1 PE instructor, 8 coaches.

Computers Computers are regularly used in art, English, foreign language, history, library, mathematics, music, science, technology, yearbook classes. Computer network features include on-campus library services, online commercial services, Internet access, wireless campus network, Internet filtering or blocking technology. Campus intranet is available to students. The school has a published electronic and media policy.

Contact Katie Redding, Director of Admissions. 802-867-5717 Ext. 106. Fax: 802-867-0147. E-mail: applylts@longtrailschool.org. Website: www.longtrailschool.org

LOUDOUN SCHOOL FOR THE GIFTED

44675 Cape Ct., #105
Ashburn, Virginia 20147

Head of School: Dr. Deep Sran

General Information Coeducational day college-preparatory school. Grades 6–12. Founded: 2008. Setting: suburban. .3-acre campus. 1 building on campus. Approved or accredited by Southern Association of Colleges and Schools and Virginia Department of Education. Total enrollment: 35. Upper school average class size: 7. Upper school faculty-student ratio: 1:3. There are 180 required school days per year for Upper School students. Upper School students typically attend 5 days per week. The average school day consists of 7 hours.

Upper School Student Profile Grade 9: 6 students (4 boys, 2 girls); Grade 10: 12 students (5 boys, 7 girls); Grade 11: 2 students (2 boys); Grade 12: 3 students (1 boy, 2 girls).

Faculty School total: 11. In upper school: 5 men, 6 women; 8 have advanced degrees.

Special Academic Programs Advanced Placement exam preparation; honors section; accelerated programs; academic accommodation for the gifted.

College Admission Counseling 13 students graduated in 2015; all went to college, including Cornell University; Oberlin College; Rochester Institute of Technology; University of California, Berkeley; University of Virginia.

Student Life Discipline rests primarily with faculty.

Tuition and Aid Day student tuition: $23,100. Tuition installment plan (monthly payment plans).

Admissions Traditional secondary-level entrance grade is 9. For fall 2015, 15 students applied for upper-level admission, 9 were accepted, 9 enrolled. Deadline for receipt of application materials: none. No application fee required. Interview required.

Athletics 2 PE instructors.

Computers Computers are regularly used in computer applications classes. Computer network features include Internet access, wireless campus network, Internet filtering or blocking technology. Student e-mail accounts and computer access in designated common areas are available to students. Students grades are available online.

Contact Susan Talbott, Executive Director. 703-956-5020. Fax: 703-858-0843. E-mail: stalbott@idealschools.org. Website: www.loudounschool.org

LOUISVILLE COLLEGIATE SCHOOL

2427 Glenmary Avenue
Louisville, Kentucky 40204

Head of School: Dr. James Calleroz White

General Information Coeducational day college-preparatory, arts, and technology school. Grades JK–12. Founded: 1915. Setting: urban. 11-acre campus. 2 buildings on campus. Approved or accredited by Independent Schools Association of the Central States. Member of National Association of Independent Schools and Secondary School Admission Test Board. Endowment: $5.7 million. Total enrollment: 676. Upper school average class size: 15. Upper school faculty-student ratio: 1:77. The average school day consists of 7 hours.

Faculty School total: 80. In upper school: 12 men, 10 women; 20 have advanced degrees.

Subjects Offered Algebra, American history, American literature, ancient history, art, art history, biology, calculus, chemistry, Chinese, chorus, community service, composition, computer science, creative writing, discrete mathematics, drama, economics, English, English literature, ensembles, environmental science, European history, fine arts, French, geometry, German, history, mathematics, media, music, music history, physical education, physics, physiology, pre-calculus, science, social studies, Spanish, statistics, studio art, theater, trigonometry, world history, world literature, writing.

Graduation Requirements Arts and fine arts (art, music, dance, drama), English, foreign language, mathematics, physical education (includes health), science, social studies (includes history), senior symposium in leadership and service, individual and class service projects, senior speech.

Special Academic Programs Advanced Placement exam preparation; honors section; independent study; term-away projects; study abroad.

College Admission Counseling 53 students graduated in 2015; all went to college, including Centre College; Miami University; Northwestern University; University of Louisville; Vanderbilt University; Wake Forest University. Median SAT critical reading: 602, median SAT math: 662, median SAT writing: 629, median composite ACT: 28.

Student Life Upper grades have uniform requirement, student council, honor system. Discipline rests equally with students and faculty.

Summer Programs Enrichment, advancement, sports, art/fine arts, computer instruction programs offered; session focuses on educational enrichment and sports; held both on and off campus; held at Champion's Trace athletic fields; accepts boys and girls; open to students from other schools. 350 students usually enrolled. 2016 schedule: June 1 to July 31. Application deadline: none.

Tuition and Aid Day student tuition: $22,300. Tuition installment plan (The Tuition Plan, monthly payment plans, individually arranged payment plans). Merit scholarship grants, need-based scholarship grants available. In 2015–16, 31% of upper-school students received aid.

Admissions Traditional secondary-level entrance grade is 9. School's own exam and SSAT required. Deadline for receipt of application materials: none. Application fee required: $50.

Athletics Interscholastic: basketball (boys, girls), crew (g), cross-country running (b,g), field hockey (g), golf (b,g), indoor track (b,g), lacrosse (b,g), rowing (b,g), soccer (b,g), softball (g), strength & conditioning (b,g), swimming and diving (b,g), tennis (b,g), track and field (b,g), winter (indoor) track (b,g); intramural: basketball (b,g), soccer (b,g), tennis (b,g); coed interscholastic: soccer, strength & conditioning; coed intramural: soccer. 4 PE instructors, 60 coaches, 1 athletic trainer.

Computers Computers are regularly used in art, English, foreign language, history, mathematics, science classes. Computer network features include on-campus library services, online commercial services, Internet access, wireless campus network, Internet filtering or blocking technology. Student e-mail accounts and computer access in designated common areas are available to students. Students grades are available online. The school has a published electronic and media policy.

Contact Lynne Age, Admission Office Coordinator. 502-479-0378. Fax: 502-454-0549. E-mail: lage@loucol.com. Website: www.loucol.com

LOUISVILLE HIGH SCHOOL

22300 Mulholland Drive
Woodland Hills, California 91364

Head of School: Mrs. Kathleen Vercillo

General Information Girls' day college-preparatory, arts, religious studies, and technology school, affiliated with Roman Catholic Church. Grades 9–12. Founded: 1960. Setting: suburban. Nearest major city is Tarzana. 17-acre campus. 7 buildings on campus. Approved or accredited by National Catholic Education Association, Western Association of Schools and Colleges, Western Catholic Education Association, and California Department of Education. Total enrollment: 337. Upper school average class size: 25. Upper school faculty-student ratio: 1:25. There are 180 required school days per year for Upper School students. Upper School students typically attend 5 days per week. The average school day consists of 6 hours.

Upper School Student Profile Grade 9: 71 students (71 girls); Grade 10: 74 students (74 girls); Grade 11: 111 students (111 girls); Grade 12: 81 students (81 girls). 73% of students are Roman Catholic.

Faculty School total: 39. In upper school: 6 men, 33 women; 26 have advanced degrees.

Subjects Offered Advanced Placement courses, advanced studio art-AP, algebra, American history, American history-AP, American literature, American literature-AP, anatomy, art, art-AP, Bible studies, biology, calculus, calculus-AP, campus ministry, ceramics, chemistry, choir, computer science, creative writing, dance, drama, earth science, economics, English, English language-AP, English literature, English literature-AP, environmental science-AP, European history, European history-AP, fine arts, French, French language-AP, geography, geometry, government/civics, government/civics-AP, grammar, health, history, journalism, law, mathematics, media production, music, photography, physical education, physics, physics-AP, physiology, probability and statistics, psychology, religion, science, social sciences, social studies, Spanish, Spanish language-AP, speech, theater, theater production, trigonometry, U.S. history-AP, video film production, Web site design, world geography, world history, world literature, yoga.

Graduation Requirements Arts and fine arts (art, music, dance, drama), biology, chemistry, computer science, economics, English, foreign language, health, mathematics, performing arts, physical education (includes health), religion (includes Bible studies and theology), science, social sciences, social studies (includes history), U.S. government, U.S. history, visual arts, world history. Community service is required.

Special Academic Programs Advanced Placement exam preparation; independent study.

College Admission Counseling 101 students graduated in 2015; all went to college, including California Polytechnic State University, San Luis Obispo; California State University, Northridge; Oregon State University; Texas Christian University; University of California, Berkeley; University of Michigan.

Student Life Upper grades have uniform requirement, student council, honor system. Discipline rests equally with students and faculty. Attendance at religious services is required.

Summer Programs Sports programs offered; session focuses on skill development; held both on and off campus; held at Los Angeles Pierce Community College and Balboa Park; accepts girls; open to students from other schools. 200 students usually enrolled. 2016 schedule: June 15 to August 5. Application deadline: May 27.

Tuition and Aid Day student tuition: $15,500. Tuition installment plan (FACTS Tuition Payment Plan). Merit scholarship grants, need-based scholarship grants available. In 2015–16, 35% of upper-school students received aid; total upper-school merit-scholarship money awarded: $95,000. Total amount of financial aid awarded in 2015–16: $564,475.

Admissions Traditional secondary-level entrance grade is 9. For fall 2015, 139 students applied for upper-level admission, 127 were accepted, 71 enrolled. High School Placement Test required. Deadline for receipt of application materials: January 27. Application fee required: $110. On-campus interview required.

Athletics Interscholastic: basketball, cross-country running, equestrian sports, field hockey, golf, lacrosse, soccer, softball, swimming and diving, tennis, track and field, volleyball, water polo; intramural: fitness walking, table tennis, tennis, yoga. 2 PE instructors, 25 coaches, 1 athletic trainer.

Computers Computers are regularly used in all academic, college planning, computer applications, creative writing, economics, English, foreign language, French, graphic design, health, journalism, library, literary magazine, mathematics, media, media production, photography, religion, religious studies, science, social studies, Spanish, speech, technology, yearbook classes. Computer network features include on-campus library services, online commercial services, Internet access, wireless campus network, Internet filtering or blocking technology. Student e-mail accounts are available to students. Students grades are available online. The school has a published electronic and media policy.

Contact Mrs. Linda Klarin, Admissions Coordinator. 818-346-8812 Ext. 1000. Fax: 818-346-9483. E-mail: lklarin@louisvillehs.org. Website: www.louisvillehs.org

THE LOVETT SCHOOL

4075 Paces Ferry Road NW
Atlanta, Georgia 30327

Head of School: William S. Peebles

General Information Coeducational day college-preparatory school. Grades K–12. Founded: 1926. Setting: suburban. 100-acre campus. 8 buildings on campus. Approved or accredited by Southern Association of Colleges and Schools, Southern Association of Independent Schools, and Georgia Department of Education. Member of National Association of Independent Schools and Secondary School Admission Test Board. Endowment: $70.5 million. Total enrollment: 1,673. Upper school average class size: 13. Upper school faculty-student ratio: 1:8. There are 180 required school days per year for Upper School students. Upper School students typically attend 5 days per week. The average school day consists of 6 hours.

Upper School Student Profile Grade 9: 172 students (84 boys, 88 girls); Grade 10: 167 students (88 boys, 79 girls); Grade 11: 159 students (77 boys, 82 girls); Grade 12: 146 students (74 boys, 72 girls).

Faculty School total: 283. In upper school: 40 men, 45 women; 64 have advanced degrees.

Subjects Offered Advanced chemistry, advanced computer applications, advanced math, Advanced Placement courses, African American history, African history, African literature, African-American literature, algebra, American government, American history, American history-AP, American legal systems, American literature, ancient history, ancient world history, architecture, art, art history, Asian history, Asian studies, band, biology, botany, calculus, calculus-AP, career and personal planning, career/college preparation, ceramics, character education, chemistry, chorus, computer art, computer education, computer graphics, computer programming, computer science, creative writing, dance, debate, drama, driver education, earth science, ecology, economics, electronic music, English, English literature, English literature-AP, English-AP, environmental science, ethics, European history, fiction, film history, fine arts, French, French language-AP, French literature-AP, French studies, French-AP, gender issues, genetics, geometry, German, history, human development, jazz dance, journalism, Latin, Latin-AP, leadership, marine biology, mathematics, medieval history, music theory, music theory-AP, newspaper, orchestra, painting, philosophy, photography, physical education, physics, portfolio art, pre-calculus, public speaking, religion, robotics, science, sculpture, social studies, Spanish, Spanish language-AP, Spanish literature-AP, speech, statistics, technical theater, theater, theater arts, trigonometry, U.S. government and politics-AP, video, Western civilization, Western philosophy, world cultures, world history, world literature, world religions, writing workshop, yearbook, zoology.

Graduation Requirements Algebra, American studies, arts and fine arts (art, music, dance, drama), biology, electives, English, foreign language, geometry, history, mathematics, physical education (includes health), religion (includes Bible studies and theology), science, Western civilization.

Special Academic Programs Advanced Placement exam preparation; honors section; independent study; term-away projects; study abroad.

College Admission Counseling 142 students graduated in 2015; all went to college, including Auburn University; Georgia Institute of Technology; Southern Methodist University; The University of Alabama; University of Georgia; University of Mississippi.

Student Life Upper grades have uniform requirement, student council, honor system. Discipline rests primarily with faculty. Attendance at religious services is required.

Summer Programs Remediation, enrichment, advancement programs offered; session focuses on academic course work; held on campus; accepts boys and girls; open to students from other schools. 400 students usually enrolled. 2016 schedule: June 6 to July 22. Application deadline: June 1.

Tuition and Aid Day student tuition: $21,650–$25,630. Tuition installment plan (individually arranged payment plans, 1/2 paid in July and 1/2 paid in November). Need-based scholarship grants available. In 2015–16, 15% of upper-school students received aid. Total amount of financial aid awarded in 2015–16: $1,511,970.

Admissions Traditional secondary-level entrance grade is 9. For fall 2015, 117 students applied for upper-level admission, 25 were accepted, 21 enrolled. SSAT required. Deadline for receipt of application materials: January 15. Application fee required: $75. On-campus interview required.

Athletics Interscholastic: baseball (boys), basketball (b,g), cheering (g), cross-country running (b,g), football (b), golf (b,g), gymnastics (g), lacrosse (b,g), soccer (b,g), softball (g), swimming and diving (b,g), tennis (b,g), track and field (b,g), volleyball (g), wrestling (b); intramural: aerobics/dance (g), ballet (g), dance (g), in-line hockey (b), modern dance (g); coed intramural: backpacking, bicycling, bowling, canoeing/kayaking, climbing, equestrian sports, fitness, flag football, Frisbee, hiking/backpacking, kayaking, mountain biking, outdoor activities, physical fitness, physical training, rappelling, rock climbing, strength & conditioning, ultimate Frisbee, wall climbing, weight lifting, weight training, yoga. 3 PE instructors, 51 coaches, 4 athletic trainers.

Computers Computers are regularly used in all academic classes. Computer network features include on-campus library services, online commercial services, Internet access, wireless campus network, Internet filtering or blocking technology, central file storage. Student e-mail accounts and computer access in designated common areas are available to students. Students grades are available online.

Contact Mrs. Janie Beck, Director of Admission and Enrollment Management. 404-262-3032. Fax: 404-479-8463. E-mail: janie.beck@lovett.org. Website: www.lovett.org

LOWER CANADA COLLEGE

4090 Royal Avenue
Montreal, Quebec H4A 2M5, Canada

Head of School: Mr. Christopher Shannon

General Information Coeducational day college-preparatory, arts, bilingual studies, technology, and mathematics and science school. Grades K–12. Founded: 1861. Setting: urban. 7-acre campus. 4 buildings on campus. Approved or accredited by Canadian Association of Independent Schools, Canadian Educational Standards Institute, National Independent Private Schools Association, Quebec Association of Independent Schools, and Quebec Department of Education. Affiliate member of National Association of Independent Schools; member of Secondary School Admission Test Board. Languages of instruction: English and French. Endowment: CAN$4.4 million. Total enrollment: 775. Upper school average class size: 22. Upper school faculty-student ratio: 1:22.

Upper School Student Profile Grade 9: 93 students (61 boys, 32 girls); Grade 10: 88 students (52 boys, 36 girls); Grade 11: 99 students (49 boys, 50 girls); Grade 12: 52 students (26 boys, 26 girls).

Faculty School total: 87. In upper school: 31 men, 17 women; 20 have advanced degrees.

Subjects Offered Accounting, advanced chemistry, advanced computer applications, advanced math, Advanced Placement courses, algebra, American history, ancient history, ancient world history, ancient/medieval philosophy, art, art history, biology, biology-AP, broadcast journalism, calculus, calculus-AP, Canadian geography, Canadian history, Canadian literature, career/college preparation, chemistry, chemistry-AP, cinematography, college admission preparation, college counseling, community service, computer graphics, computer math, computer multimedia, computer science, computer studies, concert band, creative writing, current events, desktop publishing, drama, earth science, ecology, economics, English, English literature, English-AP, environmental science, ethics, European history, expository writing, filmmaking, fine arts, finite math, French, French language-AP, general science, geography, health, health education, history, independent study, leadership, linear algebra, mathematics, media, music, North American literature, philosophy, physical education, physical fitness, physical science, physics, political science, pre-calculus, psychology, public speaking, robotics, SAT preparation, science, Shakespeare, social sciences, social studies, Spanish, Spanish-AP, theater, video film production, world geography, world history.

Graduation Requirements English, French, mathematics, science, social studies (includes history), overall average of 70%. Community service is required.

Special Academic Programs Advanced Placement exam preparation; honors section; independent study; remedial reading and/or remedial writing; remedial math.

College Admission Counseling 104 students graduated in 2014; all went to college, including Acadia University; Mount Allison University; Queen's University at Kingston; The University of British Columbia; The University of Western Ontario; University of Toronto.

Student Life Upper grades have uniform requirement, student council, honor system. Discipline rests equally with students and faculty.

Tuition and Aid Day student tuition: CAN$14,045. Tuition installment plan (monthly payment plans, individually arranged payment plans). Bursaries, merit scholarship grants, need-based scholarship grants, need-based loans available. In 2014–15, 15% of upper-school students received aid; total upper-school merit-scholarship money awarded: CAN$145,500. Total amount of financial aid awarded in 2014–15: CAN$327,845.

Admissions For fall 2014, 284 students applied for upper-level admission, 149 were accepted, 99 enrolled. School's own exam, SLEP, SSAT or TOEFL required. Deadline for receipt of application materials: none. Application fee required: CAN$50. On-campus interview required.

Athletics Interscholastic: badminton (boys, girls), baseball (b), basketball (b,g), cross-country running (b,g), football (b,g), hockey (b,g), ice hockey (b,g), indoor track & field (b,g), rugby (b,g), running (b,g), skiing (cross-country) (b,g), soccer (b,g), swimming and diving (b,g), tennis (b,g), touch football (g), track and field (b,g), volleyball (b,g); intramural: dance (g); football (b,g); coed interscholastic: aquatics, baseball, cross-country running, curling, football, golf, hockey, ice hockey, martial arts, skiing (cross-country), table tennis; coed intramural: aerobics, aerobics/dance, aerobics/Nautilus, aquatics, archery, backpacking, badminton, baseball, basketball, bowling, broomball, climbing, cooperative games, Cosom hockey, cross-country running, curling, fencing, field hockey, fitness, fitness walking, floor hockey, Frisbee, golf, gymnastics, handball, hiking/backpacking, hockey, ice hockey, ice skating, indoor track & field, judo, life saving, martial arts, outdoor activities, outdoor education, physical fitness, physical training, rappelling, rock climbing, rugby, running, self defense, skiing (cross-country), snowshoeing, soccer, softball, strength & conditioning, swimming and diving, table tennis, tennis, touch football, track and field, ultimate Frisbee, volleyball, wall climbing, weight training. 5 PE instructors, 8 coaches.

Computers Computers are regularly used in animation, basic skills, creative writing, current events, data processing, design, English, French, French as a second language, geography, graphic arts, graphic design, graphics, independent study, mathematics, multimedia, science, technology classes. Computer network features include on-campus library services, Internet access, Internet filtering or blocking technology, audio/video production, DVD production.

Contact Ms. Andrea Burdman, Admission Officer. 514-482-0951 Ext. 237. Fax: 514-482-0195. E-mail: aburdman@lcc.ca. Website: www.lcc.ca

LOYOLA-BLAKEFIELD

PO Box 6819
Baltimore, Maryland 21285-6819

Head of School: Mr. Anthony I. Day

General Information Boys' day college-preparatory, arts, religious studies, and technology school, affiliated with Roman Catholic Church. Grades 6–12. Founded: 1852. Setting: suburban. 60-acre campus. 6 buildings on campus. Approved or accredited by Association of Independent Maryland Schools and Jesuit Secondary Education Association. Endowment: $24.6 million. Total enrollment: 956. Upper school average class size: 18. Upper school faculty-student ratio: 1:10. There are 175 required school days per year for Upper School students. Upper School students typically attend 5 days per week. The average school day consists of 7 hours.

Upper School Student Profile Grade 9: 195 students (195 boys); Grade 10: 184 students (184 boys); Grade 11: 173 students (173 boys); Grade 12: 181 students (181 boys). 75% of students are Roman Catholic.

Faculty School total: 94. In upper school: 51 men, 21 women; 60 have advanced degrees.

Subjects Offered Acting, Advanced Placement courses, algebra, American government, American literature, American literature-AP, architecture, art, art history, band, biology, biology-AP, biotechnology, British literature, British literature (honors), calculus, calculus-AP, chemistry, chemistry-AP, chorus, civil war history, composition, composition-AP, computer graphics, computer programming, computer science, conceptual physics, concert band, drawing, driver education, economics, engineering, English, English language-AP, English literature-AP, film studies, fine arts, forensics, German, German-AP, government and politics-AP, Greek, history, history of music, honors algebra, honors English, honors geometry, honors U.S. history, honors world history, instrumental music, Italian, jazz ensemble, Latin, Latin-AP, marine science, mathematics, music history, oil painting, painting, photography, physical education, physics, physics-AP, poetry, pre-calculus, psychology, religion, Roman civilization, science, Spanish, Spanish language-AP, statistics-AP, theater production, U.S. government and politics-AP, U.S. history, U.S. history-AP, voice ensemble, world religions, World War II, world wide web design.

Graduation Requirements Arts and fine arts (art, music, dance, drama), computer science, English, foreign language, mathematics, physical education (includes health), religion (includes Bible studies and theology), science, social studies (includes history), 40 hours of Christian service.

Special Academic Programs 20 Advanced Placement exams for which test preparation is offered; honors section; academic accommodation for the gifted, the musically talented, and the artistically talented; programs in English, mathematics, general development for dyslexic students.

College Admission Counseling 178 students graduated in 2015; 176 went to college, including James Madison University; Loyola University Maryland; Towson University; University of Maryland, Baltimore County; University of Maryland, College Park; University of South Carolina. Other: 1 went to work, 1 entered military service. Median SAT critical reading: 580, median SAT math: 610, median SAT writing: 580, median combined SAT: 1780, median composite ACT: 25. 46% scored over 600 on SAT critical reading, 52% scored over 600 on SAT math, 46% scored over 600 on SAT writing, 45% scored over 1800 on combined SAT, 44% scored over 26 on composite ACT.

Student Life Upper grades have specified standards of dress, student council, honor system. Discipline rests primarily with faculty. Attendance at religious services is required.

Summer Programs Remediation, enrichment, advancement, sports, art/fine arts, computer instruction programs offered; held on campus; accepts boys and girls; open to students from other schools. 900 students usually enrolled. 2016 schedule: June 13 to August 5. Application deadline: none.

Tuition and Aid Day student tuition: $19,125. Tuition installment plan (FACTS Tuition Payment Plan). Merit scholarship grants, need-based scholarship grants available. In 2015–16, 50% of upper-school students received aid; total upper-school merit-scholarship money awarded: $544,145. Total amount of financial aid awarded in 2015–16: $2,876,095.

Admissions Traditional secondary-level entrance grade is 9. For fall 2015, 312 students applied for upper-level admission, 267 were accepted, 109 enrolled. High School Placement Test or ISEE required. Deadline for receipt of application materials: December 15. Application fee required: $50. On-campus interview required.

Athletics Interscholastic: baseball, basketball, cross-country running, diving, football, golf, ice hockey, indoor track & field, lacrosse, rugby, soccer, squash, swimming and diving, tennis, track and field, volleyball, water polo, winter (indoor) track, wrestling; intramural: basketball, flag football, indoor soccer, lacrosse, martial arts, rock climbing, tennis, ultimate Frisbee. 5 PE instructors, 40 coaches, 1 athletic trainer.

Computers Computers are regularly used in all classes. Computer network features include on-campus library services, online commercial services, Internet access, wireless campus network, Internet filtering or blocking technology. Campus intranet, student e-mail accounts, and computer access in designated common areas are available to students. Students grades are available online. The school has a published electronic and media policy.

Contact Ms. Paddy M. London, Admissions Assistant. 443-841-3680. Fax: 443-841-3105. E-mail: plondon@loyolablakefield.org. Website: www.loyolablakefield.org

LUTHERAN HIGH SCHOOL
3960 Fruit Street
La Verne, California 91750
Head of School: Lance E. Ebel

General Information Coeducational day college preparatory, general academic, arts, religious studies, and technology school, affiliated with Lutheran Church–Missouri Synod. Grades 9–12. Founded: 1973. Setting: suburban. Nearest major city is Los Angeles. 10-acre campus. 7 buildings on campus. Approved or accredited by Association of Christian Schools International, Lutheran School Accreditation Commission, National Lutheran School Accreditation, and Western Association of Schools and Colleges. Total enrollment: 130. Upper school average class size: 15. Upper school faculty-student ratio: 1:9. There are 180 required school days per year for Upper School students. Upper School students typically attend 5 days per week. The average school day consists of 6 hours and 40 minutes.

Upper School Student Profile Grade 9: 35 students (18 boys, 17 girls); Grade 10: 34 students (21 boys, 13 girls); Grade 11: 24 students (16 boys, 8 girls); Grade 12: 37 students (20 boys, 17 girls). 29% of students are Lutheran Church–Missouri Synod.

Faculty School total: 14. In upper school: 5 men, 9 women; 9 have advanced degrees.

Subjects Offered Advanced math, Advanced Placement courses, algebra, American government, American history, American history-AP, American literature, anatomy, anatomy and physiology, art, ASB Leadership, athletics, biology, biology-AP, British literature, calculus, calculus-AP, chemistry, choir, college counseling, community service, comparative religion, composition, computer literacy, computer programming, computer science, computer science-AP, computers, conceptual physics, drama, economics, English, English literature and composition-AP, English literature-AP, fine arts, geography, geometry, government, history-AP, honors algebra, honors English, honors geometry, honors U.S. history, honors world history, human anatomy, keyboarding, mathematics, naval science, NJROTC, physical education, physics, physics-AP, pre-calculus, psychology, religion, science, sign language, social sciences, social studies, Spanish, Spanish language-AP, theology, U.S. government, U.S. government and politics-AP, U.S. history-AP, word processing, world history, world literature, yearbook.

Graduation Requirements Arts and fine arts (art, music, dance, drama), business skills (includes word processing), computer science, English, foreign language, mathematics, physical education (includes health), religion (includes Bible studies and theology), science, social sciences, social studies (includes history), 24 hours per year of service to the community, senior project completion.

Special Academic Programs Advanced Placement exam preparation; honors section; accelerated programs; study at local college for college credit.

College Admission Counseling 31 students graduated in 2014; 30 went to college, including Azusa Pacific University; California State Polytechnic University, Pomona; California State University, Fullerton; Concordia University Irvine; University of California, Berkeley. Other: 1 entered military service. Median SAT critical reading: 485, median SAT math: 495, median SAT writing: 515, median combined SAT: 1465. 18% scored over 600 on SAT critical reading, 14% scored over 600 on SAT math, 9% scored over 600 on SAT writing, 14% scored over 1800 on combined SAT.

Student Life Upper grades have specified standards of dress, student council, honor system. Discipline rests primarily with faculty. Attendance at religious services is required.

Tuition and Aid Day student tuition: $6950–$7450. Tuition installment plan (SMART Tuition Payment Plan, monthly payment plans, individually arranged payment plans, advance payment discounts, credit card payments). Tuition reduction for siblings, merit scholarship grants, need-based scholarship grants available. In 2014–15, 41% of upper-school students received aid; total upper-school merit-scholarship money awarded: $7500. Total amount of financial aid awarded in 2014–15: $79,500.

Admissions Traditional secondary-level entrance grade is 9. High School Placement Test required. Deadline for receipt of application materials: none. Application fee required: $75. Interview required.

Athletics Interscholastic: aerobics/dance (girls), baseball (b), basketball (b,g), cheering (g), cross-country running (b,g), dance squad (g), dance team (g), drill team (b,g), football (b), golf (b,g), softball (g), volleyball (g), wrestling (b); coed interscholastic: golf, JROTC drill, soccer, track and field. 1 PE instructor, 20 coaches.

Computers Computers are regularly used in all academic, English, geography, history, information technology, mathematics, NJROTC, programming, science, Spanish, yearbook classes. Computer network features include online commercial services, Internet access, wireless campus network, Internet filtering or blocking technology. Campus intranet is available to students. Students grades are available online. The school has a published electronic and media policy.

Contact Kathy Johnson, Office Manager. 909-593-4494 Ext. 221. Fax: 909-596-3744. E-mail: kjohnson@lhslv.org. Website: www.lhslv.org

LUTHERAN HIGH SCHOOL
12411 Wornall Road
Kansas City, Missouri 64145-1736
Head of School: Dr. Cary Stelmachowicz

General Information Coeducational day college-preparatory, general academic, and religious studies school, affiliated with Lutheran Church–Missouri Synod. Grades 9–12. Founded: 1980. Setting: suburban. 29-acre campus. 1 building on campus. Approved or accredited by Missouri Independent School Association, National Lutheran School Accreditation, North Central Association of Colleges and Schools, and Missouri Department of Education. Endowment: $97,000. Total enrollment: 128. Upper school average class size: 15. Upper school faculty-student ratio: 1:10. There are 172 required school days per year for Upper School students. Upper School students typically attend 5 days per week. The average school day consists of 6 hours and 45 minutes.

Upper School Student Profile Grade 9: 28 students (15 boys, 13 girls); Grade 10: 28 students (15 boys, 13 girls); Grade 11: 40 students (28 boys, 12 girls); Grade 12: 32 students (16 boys, 16 girls). 80% of students are Lutheran Church–Missouri Synod.

Faculty School total: 15. In upper school: 6 men, 8 women; 5 have advanced degrees.

Subjects Offered Advanced math, algebra, American government, American literature, analysis, analytic geometry, anatomy and physiology, ancient world history, applied music, art, athletics, baseball, basketball, Bible studies, biology, biology-AP, calculus, cheerleading, chemistry, choir, Christian doctrine, Christian education, Christian ethics, Christian scripture, Christianity, church history, college counseling, communication skills, comparative religion, composition, contemporary art, earth science, English composition, English literature, geometry, government, graphic arts, health education, history, history of religion, instrumental music, Internet, Internet research, introduction to literature, keyboarding, Life of Christ, math analysis, New Testament, photography, physical education, physical science, physics, pre-algebra, psychology, sociology, Spanish, speech and oral interpretations, state history, statistics, student government, tennis, theater, theater production, track and field, trigonometry, U.S. government, volleyball, weightlifting.

Graduation Requirements Algebra, American government, American history, American literature, analytic geometry, art, arts and fine arts (art, music, dance, drama), Bible studies, biology, British literature, calculus, chemistry, church history, electives, geometry, health education, math analysis, modern world history, trigonometry, U.S. history.

Special Academic Programs Honors section; independent study; study at local college for college credit; academic accommodation for the artistically talented; remedial math.

College Admission Counseling 26 students graduated in 2015; 25 went to college, including Johnson County Community College; Kansas State University; Northwest Missouri State University; University of Central Missouri; University of Missouri. Other: 1 entered military service. Mean SAT critical reading: 550, mean SAT math: 480, mean composite ACT: 24. 50% scored over 600 on SAT critical reading, 50% scored over 600 on SAT math, 25% scored over 26 on composite ACT.

Student Life Upper grades have specified standards of dress, student council, honor system. Discipline rests primarily with faculty.

Summer Programs Sports programs offered; session focuses on sports skills enrichment; held both on and off campus; held at baseball on Belton Field; accepts boys and girls; not open to students from other schools. 60 students usually enrolled. 2016 schedule: June 1 to July 31. Application deadline: May 30.

Tuition and Aid Day student tuition: $8450–$11,000. Tuition installment plan (monthly payment plans, individually arranged payment plans). Tuition reduction for siblings, need-based scholarship grants available. In 2015–16, 45% of upper-school students received aid. Total amount of financial aid awarded in 2015–16: $153,000.

Admissions Traditional secondary-level entrance grade is 9. For fall 2015, 128 students applied for upper-level admission, 128 were accepted, 128 enrolled. High School Placement Test or SLEP for foreign students required. Deadline for receipt of application materials: none. Application fee required: $275. On-campus interview required.

Athletics Interscholastic: baseball (boys), basketball (b,g), cheering (g), cross-country running (b,g), dance (g), dance team (g), fitness (b,g), golf (b), physical training (b,g), soccer (b,g), tennis (b,g), track and field (b,g), volleyball (g), weight lifting (b,g), weight training (b,g); coed intramural: basketball, bowling, golf, gymnastics, physical fitness, softball, volleyball, weight training. 2 coaches.

Computers Computers are regularly used in data processing, desktop publishing, journalism, photography, word processing classes. Computer network features include on-campus library services, Internet access, wireless campus network, Internet filtering or blocking technology. Campus intranet, student e-mail accounts, and computer access in designated common areas are available to students. Students grades are available online. The school has a published electronic and media policy.

Contact Mrs. Paula Meier, Registrar. 816-241-5478. Fax: 816-876-2069. E-mail: pmeier@lhskc.com. Website: www.lhskc.com/

LUTHERAN HIGH SCHOOL NORTH

5401 Lucas Hunt Road
St. Louis, Missouri 63121

Head of School: Mr. Timothy Brackman

General Information Coeducational day college-preparatory, arts, business, religious studies, bilingual studies, and technology school, affiliated with Lutheran Church–Missouri Synod. Grades 9–12. Founded: 1946. Setting: urban. 47-acre campus. 1 building on campus. Approved or accredited by Lutheran School Accreditation Commission, National Lutheran School Accreditation, North Central Association of Colleges and Schools, and Missouri Department of Education. Endowment: $6.8 million. Total enrollment: 286. Upper school average class size: 19. Upper school faculty-student ratio: 1:14. There are 178 required school days per year for Upper School students. Upper School students typically attend 5 days per week. The average school day consists of 6 hours and 20 minutes.

Upper School Student Profile Grade 9: 78 students (45 boys, 33 girls); Grade 10: 60 students (35 boys, 25 girls); Grade 11: 74 students (38 boys, 36 girls); Grade 12: 74 students (41 boys, 33 girls). 49% of students are Lutheran Church–Missouri Synod.

Faculty School total: 30. In upper school: 16 men, 14 women; 27 have advanced degrees.

Subjects Offered Accounting, advanced chemistry, Advanced Placement courses, algebra, American history, American history-AP, American literature, anatomy, art, Bible studies, biology, business, business law, business skills, calculus, calculus-AP, ceramics, chemistry, child development, choir, Christian doctrine, Christian education, Christian ethics, Christian scripture, Christian studies, Christianity, church history, computer applications, computer multimedia, computer science, concert band, concert choir, data analysis, design, drawing, drawing and design, economics, English, English composition, English literature, English literature-AP, entrepreneurship, European history, family and consumer science, fashion, fine arts, finite math, food and nutrition, foods, French, geography, geometry, government, government/civics, health education, history, human anatomy, keyboarding, literature-AP, Mandarin, marketing, mathematics, media studies, multimedia design, music, organic chemistry, painting, physical education, physics, physiology, practical arts, pre-calculus, printmaking, probability and statistics, psychology, religion, research, science, social studies, society and culture, Spanish, speech, statistics, student publications, theology, U.S. government, U.S. history-AP, world geography, world history, world literature, world religions, writing.

Graduation Requirements American history, arts and fine arts (art, music, dance, drama), English, mathematics, physical education (includes health), practical arts, religion (includes Bible studies and theology), science, social studies (includes history), Saved to Serve (community service hours).

Special Academic Programs Advanced Placement exam preparation; honors section; independent study; study at local college for college credit.

College Admission Counseling 76 students graduated in 2015; 75 went to college, including Missouri State University; Saint Louis University; Truman State University; University of Missouri; University of Missouri–St. Louis. Other: 1 entered military service. 50% scored over 26 on composite ACT.

Student Life Upper grades have uniform requirement, student council, honor system. Discipline rests primarily with faculty. Attendance at religious services is required.

Summer Programs Enrichment, sports programs offered; session focuses on fundamentals and enrichment; held on campus; accepts boys and girls; not open to students from other schools. 150 students usually enrolled. 2016 schedule: June 1 to July 31.

Tuition and Aid Day student tuition: $10,500–$11,750. Tuition installment plan (FACTS Tuition Payment Plan, monthly payment plans, individually arranged payment plans, semester payment plan, full-year payment plan with discount). Tuition reduction for siblings, merit scholarship grants, need-based scholarship grants available. In 2015–16, 72% of upper-school students received aid; total upper-school merit-scholarship money awarded: $22,000. Total amount of financial aid awarded in 2015–16: $820,000.

Admissions Traditional secondary-level entrance grade is 9. For fall 2015, 139 students applied for upper-level admission, 129 were accepted, 98 enrolled. School's own test required. Deadline for receipt of application materials: none. Application fee required: $250. Interview required.

Athletics Interscholastic: baseball (boys), basketball (b,g), cheering (g), cross-country running (b,g), dance squad (g), dance team (g), football (b), golf (b), pom squad (g), soccer (b,g), softball (g), swimming and diving (g), tennis (b,g), track and field (b,g), volleyball (g), wrestling (b); coed interscholastic: table tennis. 2 PE instructors, 15 coaches, 1 athletic trainer.

Computers Computers are regularly used in art, business education, English, history, mathematics, science, social studies, yearbook classes. Computer network features include on-campus library services, Internet access, wireless campus network, Internet filtering or blocking technology, Internet college work program. Campus intranet, student e-mail accounts, and computer access in designated common areas are available to students. Students grades are available online. The school has a published electronic and media policy.

Contact Karen Kersten, Records Clerk. 314-389-3100 Ext. 2934. Fax: 314-389-3103. E-mail: kkersten@lhsnstl.org. Website: www.lhsnstl.org

LUTHERAN HIGH SCHOOL NORTHWEST

1000 Bagley Avenue
Rochester Hills, Michigan 48309

Head of School: Mr. Steve Garrabrant

General Information Coeducational day college-preparatory and religious studies school, affiliated with Lutheran Church–Missouri Synod. Grades 9–12. Founded: 1978. Setting: suburban. Nearest major city is Detroit. 30-acre campus. 1 building on campus. Approved or accredited by National Lutheran School Accreditation, North Central Association of Colleges and Schools, and Michigan Department of Education. Endowment: $1 million. Total enrollment: 177. Upper school average class size: 25. Upper school faculty-student ratio: 1:9. There are 185 required school days per year for Upper School students. Upper School students typically attend 5 days per week. The average school day consists of 7 hours and 20 minutes.

Upper School Student Profile Grade 9: 52 students (29 boys, 23 girls); Grade 10: 82 students (37 boys, 45 girls); Grade 11: 69 students (42 boys, 27 girls); Grade 12: 74 students (35 boys, 39 girls). 75% of students are Lutheran Church–Missouri Synod.

Faculty School total: 21. In upper school: 12 men, 9 women; 14 have advanced degrees.

Subjects Offered 20th century history, accounting, advanced chemistry, algebra, American history, American history-AP, art, audio visual/media, band, Basic programming, biology, biology-AP, bookkeeping, business, business applications, business mathematics, calculus, ceramics, chemistry, choral music, chorus, Christian doctrine, Christian scripture, computer education, computer science, conceptual physics, concert band, concert choir, desktop publishing, drawing, drawing and design, Eastern world civilizations, economics, English, English-AP, environmental science, geography, geometry, German, government/civics, graphic arts, law, mathematics, music, painting, physical education, physical science, physics-AP, psychology, Spanish, statistics-AP, theology, trigonometry, U.S. government and politics-AP, world history.

Graduation Requirements Arts and fine arts (art, music, dance, drama), English, mathematics, physical education (includes health), religion (includes Bible studies and theology), science, social sciences, social studies (includes history). Community service is required.

Special Academic Programs 6 Advanced Placement exams for which test preparation is offered; honors section; independent study; study at local college for college credit.

College Admission Counseling 74 students graduated in 2015; 68 went to college, including Central Michigan University; Concordia University Chicago; Concordia University Wisconsin; Michigan State University; Oakland University; Western Michigan University. Other: 5 went to work, 1 entered military service. Median composite ACT: 24. 38% scored over 26 on composite ACT.

Student Life Upper grades have specified standards of dress, student council. Discipline rests primarily with faculty. Attendance at religious services is required.

Tuition and Aid Day student tuition: $7550. Tuition installment plan (monthly payment plans). Merit scholarship grants, need-based scholarship grants available. In 2015–16, 2% of upper-school students received aid; total upper-school merit-scholarship money awarded: $20,000. Total amount of financial aid awarded in 2015–16: $20,000.

Admissions Traditional secondary-level entrance grade is 9. For fall 2015, 70 students applied for upper-level admission, 70 were accepted, 70 enrolled. High School

Placement Test required. Deadline for receipt of application materials: none. Application fee required: $350. On-campus interview required.

Athletics Interscholastic: baseball (boys), basketball (b,g), cheering (g), cross-country running (b,g), dance team (g), football (b), golf (b,g), hockey (b), soccer (b,g), softball (g), track and field (b,g), volleyball (g), wrestling (b); intramural: indoor soccer (b,g); coed interscholastic: bowling; coed intramural: badminton, fitness, physical fitness, physical training, tennis, weight training. 2 PE instructors.

Computers Computers are regularly used in journalism, keyboarding, mathematics, media, research skills, word processing, yearbook classes. Computer network features include Internet access, wireless campus network, Internet filtering or blocking technology. Student e-mail accounts are available to students. Students grades are available online. The school has a published electronic and media policy.

Contact Mr. Joseph Lower, Admissions Director. 248-852-6677. Fax: 248-852-2667. E-mail: jlower@lhsa.com. Website: www.lhnw.lhsa.com

LUTHERAN HIGH SCHOOL OF HAWAII

1404 University Avenue
Honolulu, Hawaii 96822-2494

Head of School: Daryl S. Utsumi

General Information Coeducational day college-preparatory school, affiliated with Lutheran Church–Missouri Synod. Grades 6–12. Founded: 1988. Setting: urban. 1-acre campus. 3 buildings on campus. Approved or accredited by Lutheran School Accreditation Commission, The Hawaii Council of Private Schools, Western Association of Schools and Colleges, and Hawaii Department of Education. Member of Secondary School Admission Test Board. Endowment: $43,000. Total enrollment: 39. Upper school average class size: 12. Upper school faculty-student ratio: 1:7. There are 178 required school days per year for Upper School students. Upper School students typically attend 5 days per week. The average school day consists of 7 hours and 15 minutes.

Upper School Student Profile Grade 6: 1 student (1 boy); Grade 9: 4 students (3 boys, 1 girl); Grade 10: 12 students (2 boys, 10 girls); Grade 11: 10 students (5 boys, 5 girls); Grade 12: 12 students (5 boys, 7 girls). 10% of students are Lutheran Church–Missouri Synod.

Faculty School total: 12. In upper school: 6 men, 6 women; 5 have advanced degrees.

Subjects Offered 20th century history, 3-dimensional art, Advanced Placement courses, algebra, American government, American history, American literature, analytic geometry, art, art-AP, Bible studies, biology, British literature, calculus, calculus-AP, chemistry, choir, computer applications, computer programming, computer science, concert band, consumer economics, drama, earth science, economics, English, English literature, European history, expository writing, fine arts, food and nutrition, geometry, government/civics, grammar, health, history, home economics, Japanese, journalism, keyboarding, life skills, marine biology, mathematics, music, oceanography, photography, physical education, physics, psychology, religion, science, social sciences, social studies, Spanish, speech, theater, trigonometry, world history, world literature.

Graduation Requirements Arts and fine arts (art, music, dance, drama), computer science, English, health, mathematics, physical education (includes health), religion (includes Bible studies and theology), science, social studies (includes history).

Special Academic Programs Advanced Placement exam preparation; honors section; study at local college for college credit; academic accommodation for the musically talented and the artistically talented.

College Admission Counseling 9 students graduated in 2015; all went to college, including Kapiolani Community College; University of Hawaii at Manoa. Median composite ACT: 23. Mean SAT critical reading: 525, mean SAT math: 530, mean SAT writing: 525. 10% scored over 600 on SAT critical reading, 15% scored over 600 on SAT math.

Student Life Upper grades have uniform requirement, student council, honor system. Discipline rests primarily with faculty. Attendance at religious services is required.

Summer Programs Remediation, enrichment, advancement, sports, art/fine arts, computer instruction programs offered; session focuses on academic advancement; held on campus; accepts boys and girls; open to students from other schools. 15 students usually enrolled. 2016 schedule: May 31 to July 8.

Tuition and Aid Day student tuition: $10,750–$12,240. Tuition installment plan (Insured Tuition Payment Plan). Tuition reduction for siblings, merit scholarship grants, need-based scholarship grants available. In 2015–16, 25% of upper-school students received aid; total upper-school merit-scholarship money awarded: $40,000. Total amount of financial aid awarded in 2015–16: $50,000.

Admissions Traditional secondary-level entrance grade is 9. For fall 2015, 20 students applied for upper-level admission, 19 were accepted, 15 enrolled. SSAT and TOEFL or SLEP required. Deadline for receipt of application materials: none. Application fee required: $50. Interview recommended.

Athletics Interscholastic: baseball (boys), basketball (b,g), bowling (b,g), canoeing/kayaking (b,g), cross-country running (b,g), diving (b,g), golf (b,g), judo (b,g), kayaking (b,g), paddling (b,g), soccer (b,g), softball (g), swimming and diving (b,g), tennis (b,g), track and field (b,g), volleyball (b,g), water polo (b,g), wrestling (b,g); coed interscholastic: cheering, football, gymnastics, JROTC drill, sailing, strength & conditioning. 1 PE instructor, 5 coaches, 1 athletic trainer.

Computers Computers are regularly used in art, business applications, desktop publishing, English, history, journalism, library, mathematics, newspaper, photography, photojournalism, science, yearbook classes. Computer network features include on-campus library services, Internet access, wireless campus network, Internet filtering or blocking technology. Student e-mail accounts are available to students. Students grades are available online. The school has a published electronic and media policy.

Contact Lea Dominici, Admissions Officer. 808-949-5302. Fax: 808-947-3701. E-mail: office@lhshawaii.org. Website: www.lhshawaii.org

LUTHERAN HIGH SCHOOL OF SAN DIEGO

810 Buena Vista Way
Chula Vista, California 91910-6853

Head of School: Mr. Paul Kasaty

General Information Coeducational day college-preparatory, arts, religious studies, and technology school, affiliated with Lutheran Church. Grades 9–12. Founded: 1975. Setting: urban. Nearest major city is San Diego. 9-acre campus. 6 buildings on campus. Approved or accredited by National Lutheran School Accreditation, Western Association of Schools and Colleges, and California Department of Education. Total enrollment: 101. Upper school average class size: 12. Upper school faculty-student ratio: 1:12. There are 180 required school days per year for Upper School students. Upper School students typically attend 5 days per week. The average school day consists of 6 hours and 30 minutes.

Upper School Student Profile Grade 9: 15 students (7 boys, 8 girls); Grade 10: 20 students (10 boys, 10 girls); Grade 11: 31 students (20 boys, 11 girls); Grade 12: 35 students (25 boys, 10 girls). 50% of students are Lutheran.

Faculty School total: 9. In upper school: 5 men, 4 women; 6 have advanced degrees.

Subjects Offered Accounting, acting, Advanced Placement courses, algebra, American government, American history, American literature, American literature-AP, analytic geometry, anatomy and physiology, applied arts, applied music, art, art appreciation, art history-AP, ASB Leadership, athletics, band, baseball, basketball, bell choir, Bible, biology, biology-AP, British literature, British literature-AP, calculus-AP, campus ministry, chemistry, choir, choral music, Christian education, Christian ethics, comparative religion, computer literacy, creative writing, drama, driver education, economics, English, English language and composition-AP, English language-AP, English literature and composition-AP, English literature-AP, English-AP, English/composition-AP, European history-AP, French, geometry, government, health education, history, music appreciation, physical education, physics, pre-calculus, softball, Spanish, Spanish language-AP, speech, student government, U.S. government and politics, yearbook

Graduation Requirements Algebra, arts and fine arts (art, music, dance, drama), electives, English, foreign language, history, physical education (includes health), religion (includes Bible studies and theology), science.

Special Academic Programs Advanced Placement exam preparation.

College Admission Counseling 44 students graduated in 2015; all went to college, including Concordia University Irvine; Pepperdine University; Rutgers, The State University of New Jersey, New Brunswick; Syracuse University; University of California, Davis; University of Connecticut. Mean SAT critical reading: 510, mean SAT math: 556, mean SAT writing: 501, mean combined SAT: 1567.

Student Life Upper grades have specified standards of dress, student council, honor system. Discipline rests primarily with faculty. Attendance at religious services is required.

Tuition and Aid Day student tuition: $8495. Tuition installment plan (monthly payment plans, individually arranged payment plans, Simply Giving—Thrivent Financial for Lutherans, Tuition Solution). Tuition reduction for siblings, merit scholarship grants, need-based scholarship grants available. In 2015–16, 26% of upper-school students received aid; total upper-school merit-scholarship money awarded: $130,000. Total amount of financial aid awarded in 2015–16: $130,000.

Admissions Traditional secondary-level entrance grade is 9. For fall 2015, 103 students applied for upper-level admission, 101 were accepted, 101 enrolled. Admissions testing required. Application fee required: $250. Interview required.

Athletics Interscholastic: baseball (boys), basketball (b,g), cross-country running (b,g), football (b), softball (g), volleyball (b,g). 1 PE instructor, 10 coaches, 1 athletic trainer.

Computers Computers are regularly used in all classes. Computer network features include on-campus library services, Internet access, wireless campus network, Internet filtering or blocking technology. Campus intranet and student e-mail accounts are available to students. Students grades are available online. The school has a published electronic and media policy.

Contact Debbie Heien, Office Manager. 619-262-4444 Ext. 120. Fax: 619-872-0974. E-mail: debbie.heien@lhssd.org. Website: www.lutheranhighsandiego.org

LUTHER COLLEGE HIGH SCHOOL

1500 Royal Street
Regina, Saskatchewan S4T 5A5, Canada

Head of School: Dr. Mark Anderson

General Information Coeducational boarding and day college-preparatory, general academic, arts, International Baccalaureate, and ESL school, affiliated with Lutheran Church. Grades 9–12. Founded: 1913. Setting: urban. Nearest major city is Winnipeg, MB, Canada. Students are housed in single-sex dormitories. 27-acre campus. 7 buildings on campus. Approved or accredited by Saskatchewan Department of Education. Language of instruction: English. Endowment: CAN$600,000. Total enrollment: 440. Upper school average class size: 23. Upper school faculty-student ratio: 1:17. There are 190 required school days per year for Upper School students. Upper School students typically attend 5 days per week. The average school day consists of 7 hours.

Upper School Student Profile 14% of students are boarding students. 86% are province residents. 2 provinces are represented in upper school student body. 14% are international students. International students from China, Hong Kong, Republic of Korea, Taiwan, United States, and Zambia; 6 other countries represented in student body. 22% of students are Lutheran.

Faculty School total: 36. In upper school: 19 men, 17 women; 7 have advanced degrees; 1 resides on campus.

Subjects Offered Band, biology, calculus, chemistry, choir, Christian ethics, computer science, drama, English, ESL, French, German, handbells, history, information processing, International Baccalaureate courses, Latin, mathematics, music, orchestra, physical fitness, physics, psychology, science, video film production.

Graduation Requirements Christian ethics, English, mathematics, science, social studies (includes history).

Special Academic Programs International Baccalaureate program; independent study; study abroad; academic accommodation for the gifted; ESL (30 students enrolled).

College Admission Counseling 91 students graduated in 2015; 75 went to college, including McGill University; University of Alberta; University of Calgary; University of Regina; University of Saskatchewan. Other: 16 went to work. 40% scored over 600 on SAT critical reading, 40% scored over 600 on SAT math, 40% scored over 600 on SAT writing, 20% scored over 1800 on combined SAT.

Student Life Upper grades have specified standards of dress. Discipline rests primarily with faculty. Attendance at religious services is required.

Summer Programs ESL programs offered; session focuses on ESL and cultural experience; held off campus; held at Luther College, University of Regina and Regina, Saskatchewan; accepts boys and girls; open to students from other schools. 7 students usually enrolled. 2016 schedule: July 28 to August 28.

Tuition and Aid Day student tuition: CAN$5760–CAN$14,345; 7-day tuition and room/board: CAN$15,595–CAN$24,180. Tuition installment plan (monthly payment plans, individually arranged payment plans). Tuition reduction for siblings, bursaries, merit scholarship grants, need-based scholarship grants available. In 2015–16, 20% of upper-school students received aid; total upper-school merit-scholarship money awarded: CAN$30,000. Total amount of financial aid awarded in 2015–16: CAN$165,000.

Admissions Traditional secondary-level entrance grade is 9. For fall 2015, 184 students applied for upper-level admission, 174 were accepted, 164 enrolled. English entrance exam required. Deadline for receipt of application materials: March. Application fee required: CAN$400.

Athletics Interscholastic: badminton (boys, girls), baseball (b), basketball (b,g), bicycling (b,g), cross-country running (b,g), curling (b,g), football (b), golf (b,g), hockey (b,g), pom squad (g), soccer (b,g), softball (g), volleyball (g); intramural: soccer (b,g), volleyball (g); coed interscholastic: badminton, cheering, curling, pom squad, track and field, ultimate Frisbee; coed intramural: outdoor education, running, table tennis, weight lifting, yoga. 2 PE instructors, 28 coaches, 2 athletic trainers.

Computers Computer network features include on-campus library services, Internet access, wireless campus network, Internet filtering or blocking technology. Student e-mail accounts and computer access in designated common areas are available to students. Students grades are available online.

Contact Ms. Alanna Kalyniuk, Registrar. 306-791-9154. Fax: 306-359-6962. E-mail: lutherhs@luthercollege.edu. Website: www.luthercollege.edu

LYCEE CLAUDEL

1635 Promenade Riverside
Ottawa, Ontario K1G 0E5, Canada

Head of School: Mme. Pascale Garrec

General Information Coeducational day and distance learning college-preparatory and general academic school. Grades 1–12. Distance learning grade X. Founded: 1962. Setting: urban. 2-hectare campus. 1 building on campus. Approved or accredited by French Ministry of Education. Language of instruction: French. Endowment: CAN$9 million. Total enrollment: 1,010. Upper school average class size: 24. Upper school faculty-student ratio: 1:10. There are 174 required school days per year for Upper School students. Upper School students typically attend 5 days per week. The average school day consists of 7 hours.

Faculty School total: 52. In upper school: 25 men, 27 women.

Subjects Offered 20th century world history, advanced biology, advanced chemistry, advanced math, Advanced Placement courses, algebra, anatomy, anatomy and physiology, ancient world history, applied arts, applied music, art and culture, art history, arts, arts and crafts, audio visual/media, band, biology, botany, calculus, Canadian geography, Canadian history, Canadian literature, chemistry, cinematography, classics, composition, computer education, computer technologies, consumer economics, current history, drawing, ecology, ecology, environmental systems, economics, economics and history, English, English composition, English language and composition-AP, English language-AP, English literature, English literature-AP, English-AP, equality and freedom, ESL, European civilization, European history, experimental science, film and literature, fitness, foreign language, French, French as a second language, French studies, general math, general science, geography, geology, geometry, grammar, gymnastics, health and safety, health education, history, human anatomy, human biology, human issues, human sexuality, lab science, language-AP, Latin, Latin History, literacy, literature and composition-AP, literature-AP, math analysis, math applications, mathematics, music, music history, music performance, oral communications, oral expression, organic chemistry, painting, philosophy, physical education, physics, political economy, reading, reading/study skills, science, science and technology, science project, social education, society, society and culture, sports, technology.

Special Academic Programs Advanced Placement exam preparation; ESL (50 students enrolled).

College Admission Counseling 86 students graduated in 2015; they went to Carleton University; McGill University; Queen's University at Kingston; University of Ottawa; University of Toronto; University of Waterloo. Other: 86 entered a postgraduate year.

Student Life Upper grades have specified standards of dress, student council, honor system. Discipline rests primarily with faculty.

Tuition and Aid Day student tuition: CAN$10,441. Tuition installment plan (monthly payment plans). Bursaries available.

Admissions For fall 2015, 250 students applied for upper-level admission, 200 were accepted, 150 enrolled. Admissions testing required. Deadline for receipt of application materials: June 15. Application fee required: CAN$120. Interview required.

Athletics Interscholastic: badminton (boys, girls), basketball (b), biathlon (b,g), cross-country running (b,g), golf (b), judo (b,g), skiing (downhill) (b), snowboarding (b), soccer (b,g), speedskating (g), track and field (b,g), volleyball (b,g); intramural: cross-country running (b,g), soccer (b,g); coed interscholastic: skiing (cross-country); coed intramural: badminton, basketball, fitness, gymnastics, handball, indoor soccer, indoor track, indoor track & field, jogging, judo, martial arts, Nautilus, physical fitness, physical training, running, soccer, strength & conditioning, swimming and diving, table tennis, tennis, track and field, volleyball, yoga. 4 PE instructors.

Computers Computers are regularly used in computer applications, English, ESL, foreign language, French, French as a second language, geography, graphic arts, graphic design, graphics, history, introduction to technology, mathematics, media, media arts, media production, multimedia, music, photography, programming, science, Spanish, technology, video film production, Web site design classes. Computer network features include on-campus library services, Internet access, wireless campus network. Campus intranet and student e-mail accounts are available to students. The school has a published electronic and media policy.

Contact Mme. Carla Khazzaka, Registrar. 613-733-8522 Ext. 606. Fax: 613-733-3782. E-mail: secretariat.lycee@claudel.org. Website: www.claudel.org/?lang=en

THE LYCEE INTERNATIONAL, AMERICAN SECTION

2 bis rue du Fer-a-Cheval
C.S. 40118
Saint-Germain-en-Laye Cedex 78105, France

Head of School: Mr. Scot Hicks

General Information Coeducational day college-preparatory and bilingual studies school. Grades PK–12. Founded: 1952. Setting: suburban. Nearest major city is Paris, France. 10-acre campus. 6 buildings on campus. Approved or accredited by French Ministry of Education and The College Board. Member of European Council of International Schools. Languages of instruction: English and French. Total enrollment: 705. Upper school average class size: 20. Upper school faculty-student ratio: 1:18. Upper School students typically attend 5 days per week. The average school day consists of 8 hours and 30 minutes.

Upper School Student Profile Grade 10: 63 students (27 boys, 36 girls); Grade 11: 54 students (19 boys, 35 girls); Grade 12: 55 students (19 boys, 36 girls).

Faculty School total: 20. In upper school: 5 men, 3 women; 7 have advanced degrees.

Subjects Offered Algebra, American history, American literature, art, biology, botany, calculus, chemistry, computer math, computer programming, computer science, drama, Dutch, economics, English, English literature, English-AP, European history, French, geography, geometry, German, grammar, Greek, health, history, Italian, Latin, mathematics, music, philosophy, physical education, physics, Russian, science, social sciences, social studies, Spanish, statistics, theater, trigonometry, world history, world literature, writing, zoology.

Graduation Requirements English, foreign language, French, mathematics, philosophy, physical education (includes health), science, social sciences, social studies (includes history), examination (French Baccalauréate with International option).

Special Academic Programs Advanced Placement exam preparation; honors section.

College Admission Counseling 61 students graduated in 2015; all went to college, including Duke University; Pomona College; Stanford University; University of California, Berkeley; University of Toronto; Wellesley College. 73.4% scored over 600 on SAT critical reading, 73.4% scored over 600 on SAT math.

Student Life Upper grades have student council. Discipline rests primarily with faculty.

Tuition and Aid Day student tuition: €5149–€10,155. Tuition installment plan (monthly payment plans). Tuition reduction for siblings, need-based scholarship grants available. In 2015–16, 5% of upper-school students received aid. Total amount of financial aid awarded in 2015–16: €30,000.

Admissions Traditional secondary-level entrance grade is 10. For fall 2015, 34 students applied for upper-level admission, 5 were accepted, 4 enrolled. Admissions testing required. Deadline for receipt of application materials: none. Application fee required: €250. On-campus interview recommended.

Athletics Intramural: badminton (boys, girls), basketball (b,g), climbing (b,g), judo (b), rugby (b), soccer (b,g), tennis (b,g), track and field (b,g), volleyball (b,g), wall climbing (b,g); coed interscholastic: aerobics, aerobics/dance, badminton, basketball, climbing, cross-country running, dance, handball, judo, rugby, soccer, volleyball, wall climbing; coed intramural: swimming and diving, table tennis. 9 PE instructors.

Computers Computers are regularly used in English, foreign language, mathematics, technology classes. Computer resources include on-campus library services, Internet access, Internet filtering or blocking technology. Student e-mail accounts and computer access in designated common areas are available to students. Students grades are available online.

Contact Mrs. Mary Friel, Director of Admissions. 33-1-34-51-90-92. Fax: 33-1 30 87 00 49. E-mail: admissions@americansection.org. Website: www.americansection.org

LYCEE INTERNATIONAL DE LOS ANGELES

1105 W Riverside Drive
Burbank, California 91506

Head of School: Mrs. Anneli Harvey

General Information Coeducational day and distance learning college-preparatory, arts, bilingual studies, technology, Math and Sciences, and International Baccalaureate school. Grades PS–12. Distance learning grades 11–12. Founded: 1978. Setting: urban. Nearest major city is Los Angeles. 5-acre campus. 1 building on campus. Approved or accredited by French Ministry of Education, International Baccalaureate Organization, Western Association of Schools and Colleges, and California Department of Education. Languages of instruction: English and French. Total enrollment: 1,045. Upper school average class size: 15. Upper school faculty-student ratio: 1·9. There are 176 required school days per year for Upper School students. Upper School students typically attend 5 days per week. The average school day consists of 6 hours.

Upper School Student Profile Grade 6: 72 students (37 boys, 35 girls); Grade 7: 54 students (20 boys, 34 girls); Grade 8: 55 students (30 boys, 25 girls); Grade 9: 38 students (20 boys, 18 girls); Grade 10: 31 students (17 boys, 14 girls); Grade 11: 33 students (13 boys, 20 girls); Grade 12: 32 students (9 boys, 23 girls).

Faculty School total: 100. In upper school: 19 men, 18 women; 20 have advanced degrees.

Subjects Offered 20th century world history, advanced biology, advanced chemistry, advanced math, advanced studio art–AP, algebra, analysis and differential calculus, analytic geometry, art, biology, calculus, chemistry, civics, computer applications, economics, English, ESL, European history, film, fine arts, French, geography, geometry, health, history, honors English, industrial arts, integrated arts, integrated mathematics, integrated science, International Baccalaureate courses, lab science, Mandarin, mathematics, music, philosophy, physical education, physical science, physics, psychology, SAT preparation, science, science and technology, social studies, Spanish, technology/design, U.S. government, U.S. history, visual and performing arts, yearbook.

Graduation Requirements Advanced biology, algebra, arts and fine arts (art, music, dance, drama), biology, civics, computer science, English, French, geography, health, integrated mathematics, integrated science, mathematics, music, physical education (includes health), science, social studies (includes history), Spanish, U.S. government, U.S. history, 150 hours of CAS (creativity, action, service).

Special Academic Programs International Baccalaureate program; 3 Advanced Placement exams for which test preparation is offered; honors section; independent study; term-away projects; study abroad; ESL (25 students enrolled).

College Admission Counseling 25 students graduated in 2014; all went to college, including Barnard College; McGill University; New York University; University of California, Berkeley; University of California, Irvine; University of California, Los Angeles. Median SAT critical reading: 580, median SAT math: 550, median SAT writing: 600, median combined SAT: 1800, median composite ACT: 26. 60% scored over 600 on SAT critical reading, 30% scored over 600 on SAT math, 65% scored over 600 on SAT writing, 60% scored over 1800 on combined SAT, 20% scored over 26 on composite ACT.

Student Life Upper grades have specified standards of dress, student council, honor system. Discipline rests equally with students and faculty.

Tuition and Aid Day student tuition: $15,100–$16,200. Tuition installment plan (SMART Tuition Payment Plan). Tuition reduction for siblings, need-based scholarship grants available. In 2014–15, 24% of upper-school students received aid. Total amount of financial aid awarded in 2014–15: $403,316.

Admissions For fall 2014, 279 students applied for upper-level admission, 265 were accepted, 189 enrolled. Admissions testing, math and English placement tests and writing sample required. Deadline for receipt of application materials: none. Application fee required: $125. Interview required.

Athletics Interscholastic: basketball (boys, girls), volleyball (g); intramural: basketball (b,g), cross-country running (b,g), indoor soccer (b), skiing (downhill) (b,g), snowboarding (b,g), soccer (b), table tennis (b,g), volleyball (b,g); coed intramural: basketball, dance, horseback riding, running, swimming and diving, tennis. 2 PE instructors, 3 coaches, 1 athletic trainer.

Computers Computers are regularly used in accounting, art, computer applications, economics, English, ESL, foreign language, French, mathematics, science, technology classes. Computer network features include on-campus library services, Internet access, wireless campus network, Internet filtering or blocking technology, homework assignments available online, SmartBoards, iPads. Campus intranet, student e-mail accounts, and computer access in designated common areas are available to students. Students grades are available online. The school has a published electronic and media policy.

Contact Mme. Juliette Lange, Admissions Director. 626-695-5159. Fax: 818-994-2816. E-mail: juliette.lange@lilaschool.com. Website: www.lilaschool.com

LYMAN WARD MILITARY ACADEMY

PO Drawer 550
174 Ward Circle
Camp Hill, Alabama 36850-0550

Head of School: Col. Roy W. Berwick

General Information Boys' boarding and distance learning college-preparatory, vocational, and military school, affiliated with Christian faith; primarily serves underachievers and individuals with Attention Deficit Disorder. Grades 6–12. Distance learning grades 11–12. Founded: 1898. Setting: small town. Nearest major city is Birmingham. Students are housed in single-sex dormitories. 300-acre campus. 23 buildings on campus. Approved or accredited by Southern Association of Colleges and Schools and Alabama Department of Education. Member of National Association of Independent Schools. Total enrollment: 115. Upper school average class size: 15. Upper school faculty-student ratio: 1:15. There are 185 required school days per year for Upper School students. Upper School students typically attend 5 days per week. The average school day consists of 7 hours.

Upper School Student Profile Grade 9: 20 students (20 boys); Grade 10: 20 students (20 boys); Grade 11: 20 students (20 boys); Grade 12: 25 students (25 boys). 98% of students are boarding students. 50% are state residents. 15 states are represented in upper school student body. 1% are international students. International students from Bermuda, China, Guatemala, Guinea, and Mexico. 85% of students are Christian faith.

Faculty School total: 14. In upper school: 8 men, 4 women; 6 have advanced degrees; 2 reside on campus.

Subjects Offered Advanced Placement courses, algebra, band, biology, chemistry, computers, economics, English, geometry, government, health, JROTC, physical science, physiology, pre-algebra, pre-calculus, reading, Spanish, trigonometry, U.S. history, world history.

Special Academic Programs Advanced Placement exam preparation; honors section; study at local college for college credit; remedial reading and/or remedial writing; remedial math.

College Admission Counseling 18 students graduated in 2015; 15 went to college, including Auburn University; Jacksonville State University; Marion Military Institute; The University of Alabama; Troy University. Other: 3 entered military service. 5% scored over 600 on SAT critical reading, 5% scored over 600 on SAT math, 5% scored over 26 on composite ACT.

Student Life Upper grades have uniform requirement, student council, honor system. Discipline rests primarily with faculty. Attendance at religious services is required.

Summer Programs Remediation, enrichment, advancement, rigorous outdoor training programs offered; session focuses on leadership training through challenging exercises; held both on and off campus; held at Lake Martin, Natahalla River, and Mt. Cheaha; accepts boys; open to students from other schools. 50 students usually enrolled. 2016 schedule: June 19 to July 29. Application deadline: none.

Tuition and Aid Day student tuition: $8990; 7-day tuition and room/board: $21,000. Tuition installment plan (monthly payment plans, individually arranged payment plans). Tuition reduction for siblings, merit scholarship grants, need-based scholarship grants available. In 2015–16, 15% of upper-school students received aid. Total amount of financial aid awarded in 2015–16: $100,000.

Admissions Traditional secondary-level entrance grade is 9. Star-9 required. Deadline for receipt of application materials: none. Application fee required: $250. Interview recommended.

Athletics Interscholastic: baseball, basketball, cross-country running, drill team, football, JROTC drill, marksmanship, riflery, soccer, weight training; intramural: aquatics, archery, basketball, billiards, canoeing/kayaking, cross-country running, drill team, fishing, fitness, flag football, football, Frisbee, hiking/backpacking, JROTC drill, life saving, marksmanship, outdoor activities, outdoor adventure, outdoor recreation, outdoor skills, paint ball, physical fitness, physical training, project adventure, rafting, rappelling, riflery, ropes courses, running, skiing (downhill), soccer, softball, strength & conditioning, swimming and diving, table tennis, tennis, ultimate Frisbee, volleyball, weight lifting. 2 PE instructors, 5 coaches, 1 athletic trainer.

Computers Computers are regularly used in keyboarding classes. Computer resources include on-campus library services, Internet access, Internet filtering or blocking technology. Student e-mail accounts are available to students. The school has a published electronic and media policy.

Contact Maj. Joe C. Watson, Assistant to the President/Admissions. 256-392-8614. Fax: 256-896-4661. E-mail: info@lwma.org. Website: www.lwma.org

THE MACDUFFIE SCHOOL

66 School Street
Granby, Massachusetts 01033

Head of School: Steven Griffin

General Information Coeducational boarding and day college-preparatory, arts, and technology school. Boarding grades 9–12, day grades 6–12. Founded: 1890. Setting: rural. Nearest major city is Northampton. Students are housed in single-sex dormitories. 50-acre campus. 5 buildings on campus. Approved or accredited by Association of Independent Schools in New England, New England Association of Schools and Colleges, The Association of Boarding Schools, and Massachusetts Department of Education. Member of National Association of Independent Schools and Secondary School Admission Test Board. Total enrollment: 210. Upper school average class size: 11. Upper school faculty-student ratio: 1:6. The average school day consists of 7 hours.

Upper School Student Profile Grade 9: 32 students (18 boys, 14 girls); Grade 10: 33 students (18 boys, 15 girls); Grade 11: 53 students (28 boys, 25 girls); Grade 12: 48 students (28 boys, 20 girls). 28% of students are boarding students. 65% are state residents. 2 states are represented in upper school student body. 30% are international students. International students from Brazil, China, Germany, Jamaica, Republic of Korea, and Russian Federation; 7 other countries represented in student body.

Faculty School total: 40. In upper school: 25 have advanced degrees; 7 reside on campus.

Subjects Offered Acting, Advanced Placement courses, African-American history, algebra, American literature, architecture, art, astronomy, biology, British literature, calculus, calculus-AP, chemistry, choreography, computer programming, conceptual physics, creative writing, dance, earth science, East European studies, English, English-AP, environmental science, ESL, European history, film studies, French, geometry, global studies, graphic design, health, journalism, Latin, modern dance, modern European history, modern European history-AP, music, painting, peace studies, physical education, physics, physiology, portfolio art, pre-calculus, psychology, SAT/ACT preparation, sculpture, Spanish, theater, U.S. history, U.S. history-AP, visual arts, Web site design, Western philosophy, women in literature, world literature, yearbook.

Graduation Requirements Algebra, arts and fine arts (art, music, dance, drama), English, foreign language, geometry, history, mathematics, physical education (includes health), science.

Special Academic Programs Advanced Placement exam preparation; honors section; independent study; study at local college for college credit; academic accommodation for the gifted; ESL.

College Admission Counseling 43 students graduated in 2014; all went to college, including Boston College; Boston University; Fordham University; Holy Cross College; Simmons College; Syracuse University.

Student Life Upper grades have specified standards of dress, student council, honor system. Discipline rests primarily with faculty.

Tuition and Aid Day student tuition: $25,950; 5-day tuition and room/board: $48,250; 7-day tuition and room/board: $55,300. Tuition installment plan (Academic Management Services Plan, monthly payment plans, individually arranged payment plans). Merit scholarship grants, need-based scholarship grants, tuition remission for children of faculty available. In 2014–15, 42% of upper-school students received aid; total upper-school merit-scholarship money awarded: $6000. Total amount of financial aid awarded in 2014–15: $500,000.

Admissions Traditional secondary-level entrance grade is 9. For fall 2014, 169 students applied for upper-level admission, 95 were accepted, 66 enrolled. SSAT or TOEFL or SLEP required. Deadline for receipt of application materials: none. Application fee required: $50. Interview required.

Athletics Interscholastic: baseball (boys), basketball (b,g), cross-country running (b,g), field hockey (g), lacrosse (g), soccer (b), softball (g), tennis (b,g), volleyball (g); coed interscholastic: ballet, soccer; coed intramural: aerobics/dance, badminton, ballet, blading, cooperative games, cricket, dance, fitness, fitness walking, flag football, football, Frisbee, handball, in-line skating, jogging, modern dance, physical fitness, pillo polo. 2 PE instructors, 10 coaches, 2 athletic trainers.

Computers Computers are regularly used in all academic classes. Computer network features include on-campus library services, online commercial services, Internet access, wireless campus network, Internet filtering or blocking technology, campus computer labs. Campus intranet, student e-mail accounts, and computer access in designated common areas are available to students. Students grades are available online. The school has a published electronic and media policy.

Contact Ms. Susan Clayton, Director of Boarding Admissions. 413-255-0000. E-mail: sclayton@macduffie.org. Website: www.macduffie.org

THE MADEIRA SCHOOL

8328 Georgetown Pike
McLean, Virginia 22102-1200

Head of School: Ms. Pilar Cabeza de Vaca

General Information Girls' boarding and day college-preparatory, arts, and technology school; primarily serves students with learning disabilities, individuals with Attention Deficit Disorder, individuals with emotional and behavioral problems, and dyslexic students. Grades 9–12. Founded: 1906. Setting: suburban. Nearest major city is Washington, DC. Students are housed in single-sex dormitories. 376-acre campus. 34 buildings on campus. Approved or accredited by Association of Independent Schools of Greater Washington, The Association of Boarding Schools, and Virginia Department of Education. Member of National Association of Independent Schools and Secondary School Admission Test Board. Endowment: $63.4 million. Total enrollment: 308. Upper school average class size: 12. Upper school faculty-student ratio: 1:10. There are 170 required school days per year for Upper School students. Upper School students typically attend 5 days per week. The average school day consists of 7 hours and 15 minutes.

Upper School Student Profile Grade 9: 76 students (76 girls); Grade 10: 88 students (88 girls); Grade 11: 81 students (81 girls); Grade 12: 70 students (70 girls). 54% of students are boarding students. 51% are state residents. 21 states are represented in upper school student body. 18% are international students. International students from China, Jamaica, Mexico, Nigeria, Republic of Korea, and United Arab Emirates; 7 other countries represented in student body.

Faculty School total: 38. In upper school: 7 men, 27 women; 28 have advanced degrees; 15 reside on campus.

Subjects Offered Acting, advanced biology, advanced math, Advanced Placement courses, algebra, American literature, ancient history, Arabic, art history AP, Asian literature, ballet, Basic programming, basketball, biology, biology-AP, British literature, calculus, calculus-AP, career/college preparation, ceramics, chamber groups, character education, chemistry, chemistry-AP, Chinese, chorus, college counseling, comparative religion, computer programming, computer science-AP, conceptual physics, dance, digital photography, English, English composition, English language and composition-AP, English literature, English-AP, environmental science, equestrian sports, equitation, ESL, ethics, European history, European history-AP, expository writing, Farsi, filmmaking, fine arts, forensics, French, French language-AP, geometry, global issues, grammar, graphic design, health, health and wellness, history, jazz dance, junior and senior seminars, Latin, Latin-AP, leadership education training, linear algebra, literature seminar, madrigals, mathematics, media literacy, Middle Eastern history, modern civilization, modern world history, music, musical productions, mythology, orchestra, performing arts, photography, physical education, physics, physics-AP, politics, pre-calculus, public speaking, science, science and technology, sex education, Spanish, Spanish language-AP, sports, statistics, statistics-AP, student government, student publications, studio art, study skills, swimming, technical theater, theater, theater arts, trigonometry, U.S. government and politics-AP, U.S. history, U.S. history-AP, visual and performing arts, world civilizations, world history, world history-AP, world religions, writing, yearbook, yoga.

Graduation Requirements Arts and fine arts (art, music, dance, drama), English, foreign language, history, life management skills, mathematics, physical education (includes health), science, co-curriculum program (off-campus internship program). Community service is required.

Special Academic Programs Advanced Placement exam preparation; independent study; term-away projects; special instructional classes for deaf students; ESL (25 students enrolled).

College Admission Counseling 84 students graduated in 2015; 83 went to college, including Colgate University; New York University; The College of William and Mary; University of Pennsylvania; University of Virginia; Virginia Polytechnic Institute and State University. Other: 1 had other specific plans.

Student Life Upper grades have specified standards of dress, student council, honor system. Discipline rests equally with students and faculty.

Summer Programs Enrichment, advancement, sports, art/fine arts programs offered; session focuses on writing, forensics, fashion design, veterinary science, culinary exploration, athletics, riding, summer camp; held on campus; accepts boys and girls; open to students from other schools. 315 students usually enrolled. 2016 schedule: June 8 to August 8. Application deadline: none.

Tuition and Aid Day student tuition: $42,461; 7-day tuition and room/board: $56,191. Tuition installment plan (Insured Tuition Payment Plan, FACTS Tuition Payment Plan, monthly payment plans). Merit scholarship grants, need-based scholarship grants, need-based loans, middle-income loans available. In 2015–16, 30% of upper-school students received aid; total upper-school merit-scholarship money awarded: $230,000. Total amount of financial aid awarded in 2015–16: $3,043,151.

Admissions Traditional secondary-level entrance grade is 9. For fall 2015, 388 students applied for upper-level admission, 227 were accepted, 104 enrolled. ISEE,

PSAT, SAT, or ACT for applicants to grade 11 and 12, SSAT or TOEFL required. Deadline for receipt of application materials: January 31. Application fee required: $70. Interview required.

Athletics Interscholastic: basketball, cross-country running, dance, equestrian sports, field hockey, fitness, horseback riding, independent competitive sports, indoor track, lacrosse, martial arts, soccer, softball, squash, strength & conditioning, swimming and diving, tennis, track and field, volleyball, winter soccer; intramural: dance, weight training, yoga. 1 PE instructor, 20 coaches, 1 athletic trainer.

Computers Computers are regularly used in art, English, foreign language, history, mathematics, science classes. Computer network features include on-campus library services, online commercial services, Internet access, wireless campus network, Internet filtering or blocking technology, campus interactive network. Campus intranet, student e-mail accounts, and computer access in designated common areas are available to students. Students grades are available online. The school has a published electronic and media policy.

Contact Ms. Mary Herridge, Director of Enrollment Management. 703-556-8273. Fax: 703-821-2845. E-mail: admission@madeira.org. Website: www.madeira.org

MADISON ACADEMY

325 Slaughter Road
Madison, Alabama 35758

Head of School: Dr. Barry F. Kirkland

General Information Coeducational day college-preparatory and religious studies school, affiliated with Church of Christ. Grades PS–12. Founded: 1955. Setting: suburban. Nearest major city is Huntsville. 160-acre campus. 5 buildings on campus. Approved or accredited by Southern Association of Colleges and Schools. Endowment: $2 million. Total enrollment: 850. Upper school average class size: 20. Upper school faculty-student ratio: 1:15. There are 180 required school days per year for Upper School students. Upper School students typically attend 5 days per week. The average school day consists of 6 hours.

Upper School Student Profile 35% of students are members of Church of Christ.

Faculty School total: 75. In upper school: 14 men, 20 women; 14 have advanced degrees.

Subjects Offered Accounting, advanced math, Alabama history and geography, algebra, American literature, anatomy, art, art history, arts, band, Bible studies, biology, calculus, calculus-AP, chemistry, choral music, chorus, Christian education, Christian ethics, Christian scripture, Christian studies, church history, community service, computer science, concert choir, consumer mathematics, creative writing, drama, earth science, economics, English, English literature, English/composition-AP, environmental science, European history, expository writing, French, general math, geography, geology, geometry, government/civics, health, human anatomy, journalism, keyboarding, music, photography, physical education, physical science, physics, physics-AP, physiology, pre-algebra, religion, Spanish, speech, studio art, trigonometry, U.S. government, U.S. government and politics, U.S. history, world geography, world history, world literature.

Graduation Requirements English, foreign language, mathematics, religion (includes Bible studies and theology), science, social sciences.

Special Academic Programs Honors section; accelerated programs; study at local college for college credit.

College Admission Counseling 70 students graduated in 2014; all went to college, including Abilene Christian University; Auburn University; Freed-Hardeman University; Lipscomb University; The University of Alabama. Mean composite ACT: 25.

Student Life Upper grades have uniform requirement, student council, honor system. Discipline rests primarily with faculty. Attendance at religious services is required.

Tuition and Aid Day student tuition: $7250. Tuition installment plan (monthly payment plans). Tuition reduction for siblings, need-based scholarship grants available. In 2014–15, 10% of upper-school students received aid. Total amount of financial aid awarded in 2014–15: $100,000.

Admissions Traditional secondary-level entrance grade is 9. For fall 2014, 100 students applied for upper-level admission, 50 were accepted, 41 enrolled. Stanford Achievement Test required. Deadline for receipt of application materials: none. Application fee required: $200. On-campus interview required.

Athletics Interscholastic: baseball (boys), basketball (b,g), cheering (g), football (b), golf (b,g), softball (g), swimming and diving (b,g), tennis (b,g), volleyball (g). 3 PE instructors, 36 coaches, 1 athletic trainer.

Computers Computers are regularly used in art, foreign language, science classes. Computer network features include on-campus library services, Internet access, wireless campus network, Internet filtering or blocking technology. Student e-mail accounts are available to students. The school has a published electronic and media policy.

Contact Dr. Michael Weimer, High School Principal. 256-469-6402. Fax: 256-649-6408. E-mail: mweimer@macademy.org. Website: www.macademy.org

MADISON COUNTRY DAY SCHOOL

5606 River Road
Waunakee, Wisconsin 53597

Head of School: Luke Felker

General Information Coeducational day college-preparatory and arts school. Grades PK–12. Founded: 1997. Setting: rural. Nearest major city is Madison. 75-acre campus. 1 building on campus. Approved or accredited by Independent Schools Association of the Central States and Wisconsin Department of Education. Member of National Association of Independent Schools. Total enrollment: 400. Upper school faculty-student ratio: 1:6. There are 173 required school days per year for Upper School students. Upper School students typically attend 5 days per week. The average school day consists of 7 hours and 30 minutes.

Upper School Student Profile Grade 9: 40 students (18 boys, 22 girls); Grade 10: 19 students (8 boys, 11 girls); Grade 11: 22 students (9 boys, 13 girls); Grade 12: 14 students (1 boy, 13 girls).

Faculty School total: 50. In upper school: 12 men, 38 women; 15 have advanced degrees.

Special Academic Programs International Baccalaureate program; study abroad.

Student Life Upper grades have specified standards of dress, student council. Discipline rests primarily with students.

Tuition and Aid Tuition installment plan (monthly payment plans, individually arranged payment plans). Tuition reduction for siblings, merit scholarship grants, need-based scholarship grants available. In 2014–15, 37% of upper-school students received aid.

Admissions Traditional secondary-level entrance grade is 9. ISEE required. Deadline for receipt of application materials: none. Application fee required.

Athletics Interscholastic: cross-country running (boys, girls), football (b), Frisbee (b,g), soccer (b,g), volleyball (g).

Computers Computer resources include on-campus library services, Internet access, wireless campus network. Students grades are available online. The school has a published electronic and media policy.

Contact Mrs. Dana Asmuth, Director of Marketing and Admissions. 608-850-6375. Fax: 608-850-6006. E-mail: dasmuth@madisoncountryday.org. Website: www.madisoncountryday.org

MAHARISHI SCHOOL OF THE AGE OF ENLIGHTENMENT

804 Dr. Robert Keith Wallace Drive
Fairfield, Iowa 52556-2200

Head of School: Dr. Richard Beall

General Information Coeducational boarding and day college-preparatory, arts, Science of Creative Intelligence: universal principles, and Transcendental Meditation: Research in Consciousness school. Boarding grades 9–12, day grades PS–12. Founded: 1972. Setting: small town. Nearest major city is Iowa City. Students are housed in host families. 10-acre campus. 5 buildings on campus. Approved or accredited by Independent Schools Association of the Central States and Iowa Department of Education. Member of National Association of Independent Schools. Total enrollment: 204. Upper school average class size: 15. Upper school faculty-student ratio: 1:12. There are 186 required school days per year for Upper School students. Upper School students typically attend 5 days per week. The average school day consists of 9 hours.

Upper School Student Profile Grade 9: 19 students (12 boys, 7 girls); Grade 10: 19 students (7 boys, 12 girls); Grade 11: 17 students (9 boys, 8 girls); Grade 12: 28 students (19 boys, 9 girls). 35% of students are boarding students. 65% are state residents. 4 states are represented in upper school student body. 30% are international students. International students from China, India, Mexico, and South Africa; 20 other countries represented in student body.

Faculty School total: 54. In upper school: 11 men, 17 women; 12 have advanced degrees.

Subjects Offered Algebra, American government, American history, American literature, art, art history, basketball, biology, British literature, business mathematics, ceramics, chemistry, Chinese, Chinese studies, computer science, critical writing, culinary arts, desktop publishing, digital photography, drama performance, driver education, economics, electives, environmental education, environmental studies, ESL, general math, geometry, global studies, integrated mathematics, meditation, music, photography, physical education, physics, physiology, pre-calculus, Sanskrit, science project, senior thesis, Spanish, speech, track and field, Vedic science, vocal music, volleyball, world history, world literature, writing, yoga.

Graduation Requirements Art history, computer science, economics, electives, English, foreign language, mathematics, physical education (includes health), science, senior thesis, social studies (includes history), writing, Science of Creative Intelligence course.

Special Academic Programs Honors section; academic accommodation for the gifted, the musically talented, and the artistically talented; remedial reading and/or remedial writing; remedial math; ESL (21 students enrolled).

College Admission Counseling 29 students graduated in 2014; 27 went to college, including Grinnell College; Maharishi University of Management; Middlebury College;

Purdue University; The University of Iowa; University of Chicago. Other: 2 had other specific plans. Median SAT critical reading: 550, median SAT math: 650, median SAT writing: 530; median combined SAT: 1730, median composite ACT: 24. 29% scored over 600 on SAT critical reading, 59% scored over 600 on SAT math, 29% scored over 600 on SAT writing, 35% scored over 1800 on combined SAT, 25% scored over 26 on composite ACT.

Student Life Upper grades have uniform requirement, student council. Discipline rests primarily with faculty.

Tuition and Aid Day student tuition: $13,900; 7-day tuition and room/board: $28,500–$42,994. Tuition installment plan (two semester payments). Tuition reduction for siblings, need-based scholarship grants available. In 2014–15, 85% of upper-school students received aid.

Admissions Traditional secondary-level entrance grade is 9. For fall 2014, 27 students applied for upper-level admission, 23 were accepted, 19 enrolled. International English Language Test or TOEFL or SLEP required. Deadline for receipt of application materials: none. No application fee required. Interview required.

Athletics Interscholastic: basketball (boys, girls), cheering (g), golf (b), indoor track & field (b,g), soccer (b), tennis (b,g), track and field (b,g), volleyball (g), winter (indoor) track (b,g); intramural: archery (b), badminton (b,g), baseball (b), basketball (b,g), canoeing/kayaking (b,g), dance (g), fitness (b,g), fitness walking (g), handball (b,g), jogging (b,g), life saving (b,g), modern dance (g), outdoor activities (b,g), outdoor recreation (b,g), physical fitness (b,g), physical training (b,g), running (b,g), strength & conditioning (b,g), table tennis (b,g), tennis (b,g), volleyball (g), wall climbing (b,g), winter (indoor) track (b,g), yoga (b,g). 3 PE instructors, 11 coaches.

Computers Computers are regularly used in business education, creative writing, desktop publishing, economics, English, ESL, geography, graphic design, history, independent study, library, library science, library skills, literacy, mathematics, multimedia, photography, programming, publications, science, senior seminar, social sciences, social studies, stock market, typing, video film production, writing classes. Computer network features include Internet access, Internet filtering or blocking technology, file and portfolio management. Campus intranet and computer access in designated common areas are available to students. Students grades are available online. The school has a published electronic and media policy.

Contact Ms. Springli Johnson, Director of International Admissions. 641-472-9400 Ext. 5538. Fax: 641-472-1211. E-mail: sjohnson@msae.edu. Website: www.maharishischooliowa.org

MAINE CENTRAL INSTITUTE

295 Main Street
Pittsfield, Maine 04967

General Information Coeducational boarding and day college-preparatory, general academic, arts, vocational, bilingual studies, technology, humanities, and mathematics, the sciences school. Grades 9–PG. Founded: 1866. Setting: small town. Nearest major city is Portland. Students are housed in single-sex dormitories and honors dorm is coed. 23-acre campus. 19 buildings on campus. Approved or accredited by Independent Schools of Northern New England, New England Association of Schools and Colleges, The Association of Boarding Schools, and Maine Department of Education. Member of National Association of Independent Schools and Secondary School Admission Test Board. Endowment: $5 million. Total enrollment: 455. Upper school average class size: 16. Upper school faculty-student ratio: 1:14. There are 175 required school days per year for Upper School students. Upper School students typically attend 5 days per week. The average school day consists of 7 hours and 15 minutes.

See Display below and Close-Up on page 604.

MALDEN CATHOLIC HIGH SCHOOL

99 Crystal Street
Malden, Massachusetts 02148

Head of School: Mr. Thomas J. Doherty III

General Information Boys' day college-preparatory, arts, business, religious studies, bilingual studies, and technology school, affiliated with Roman Catholic Church; primarily serves students with learning disabilities and individuals with Attention Deficit Disorder. Grades 9–12. Founded: 1932. Setting: urban. Nearest major city is Boston. 15-acre campus. 1 building on campus. Approved or accredited by National Catholic Education Association, New England Association of Schools and Colleges, and Massachusetts Department of Education. Member of National Association of Independent Schools. Endowment: $3 million. Total enrollment: 562. Upper school average class size: 23. Upper school faculty-student ratio: 1:13. There are 168 required school days per year for Upper School students. Upper School students typically attend 5 days per week. The average school day consists of 6 hours.

Upper School Student Profile Grade 9: 121 students (121 boys); Grade 10: 156 students (156 boys); Grade 11: 143 students (143 boys); Grade 12: 142 students (142 boys). 85% of students are Roman Catholic.

Faculty School total: 44. In upper school: 34 men, 10 women; 38 have advanced degrees.

Subjects Offered 20th century history, 3-dimensional art, accounting, advanced chemistry, advanced math, Advanced Placement courses, algebra, American

MAINE CENTRAL INSTITUTE

MCI pledges to provide a rigorous, comprehensive educational program to a multicultural student body, representing 17 countries and 11 U.S. states, with a wide range of abilities and interests. In a safe and caring atmosphere, students will acquire knowledge, self-esteem, social responsibility, and the critical thinking and communication skills necessary for global citizenship and lifelong learning.
MCI—where relationships are formed while achieving the highest level of academics as well as multiple opportunities to participate in extracurriculars.

www.mci-school.org/admissions 207.487.2282

government, American history-AP, American literature, ancient world history, art, art appreciation, art history, Asian history, athletics, basic language skills, Bible studies, biology, British literature, British literature (honors), British literature-AP, business, calculus-AP, campus ministry, Chinese history, Christian and Hebrew scripture, Christian testament, college admission preparation, community service, computer programming, computer skills, desktop publishing, English language and composition-AP, English-AP, European history, European history-AP, fine arts, foreign language, French, French language-AP, genetics, geometry, global studies, government, health and safety, honors algebra, honors English, honors geometry, honors U.S. history, honors world history, independent study, integrated science, language arts, leadership and service, library studies, marine biology, marine science, math analysis, modern European history, music appreciation, physical education, psychology, religion, SAT preparation, Spanish, Spanish language-AP, studio art, the Sixties, U.S. history, U.S. history-AP, world history, world history-AP.

Graduation Requirements Algebra, American literature, arts and fine arts (art, music, dance, drama), biology, British literature, Catholic belief and practice, chemistry, computer skills, foreign language, geometry, global studies, mathematics, physical education (includes health), religion (includes Bible studies and theology), science, social studies (includes history), Christian service.

Special Academic Programs 12 Advanced Placement exams for which test preparation is offered; honors section; independent study; ESL (30 students enrolled).

College Admission Counseling 137 students graduated in 2015; 124 went to college, including Assumption College; Boston College; Boston University; Merrimack College; Saint Anselm College; University of Massachusetts Amherst. Other: 2 went to work, 2 entered military service, 9 entered a postgraduate year. Mean SAT critical reading: 542, mean SAT math: 545, mean SAT writing: 533, mean composite ACT: 25.

Student Life Upper grades have specified standards of dress, student council, honor system. Discipline rests primarily with faculty. Attendance at religious services is required.

Summer Programs Enrichment, advancement, sports programs offered; session focuses on academic preparation/college preparation; held on campus; accepts boys and girls; open to students from other schools. 100 students usually enrolled. 2016 schedule: July 5 to July 28. Application deadline: June 27.

Tuition and Aid Day student tuition: $14,950. Tuition installment plan (FACTS Tuition Payment Plan). Merit scholarship grants, need-based scholarship grants available. In 2015–16, 65% of upper-school students received aid; total upper-school merit-scholarship money awarded: $623,500. Total amount of financial aid awarded in 2015–16: $1,105,973.

Admissions Traditional secondary-level entrance grade is 9. For fall 2015, 275 students applied for upper-level admission, 260 were accepted, 121 enrolled. Archdiocese of Boston High School entrance exam provided by STS required. Deadline for receipt of application materials: December 15. No application fee required. Interview recommended.

Athletics Interscholastic: baseball, basketball, cross-country running, football, golf, hockey, ice hockey, indoor track, indoor track & field, lacrosse, rugby, soccer, swimming and diving, tennis, track and field, winter (indoor) track, wrestling; intramural: alpine skiing, badminton, ball hockey, basketball, fitness, flag football, floor hockey, Frisbee, jogging, lacrosse, life saving, nordic skiing, physical fitness, physical training, power lifting, skiing (downhill), snowboarding, strength & conditioning, table tennis, weight lifting, weight training. 1 PE instructor, 46 coaches, 1 athletic trainer.

Computers Computers are regularly used in all academic, basic skills, business applications, business studies, design, desktop publishing, graphic arts, graphic design, graphics, information technology, journalism, library, library skills, multimedia, news writing, photography, photojournalism, religion, study skills, technology, theology, Web site design, word processing classes. Computer network features include on-campus library services, online commercial services, Internet access, wireless campus network, Internet filtering or blocking technology. Students grades are available online. The school has a published electronic and media policy.

Contact Mr. Matthew O'Neil, Associate Director of Admissions. 781-475-5308. Fax: 781-397-0573. E-mail: oneilm@maldencatholic.org. Website: www.maldencatholic.org

MALVERN PREPARATORY SCHOOL

418 South Warren Avenue
Malvern, Pennsylvania 19355-2707

Head of School: Mr. Christian M. Talbot

General Information Boys' day college-preparatory school, affiliated with Roman Catholic Church. Grades 6–12. Founded: 1842. Setting: suburban. Nearest major city is Philadelphia. 104-acre campus. 18 buildings on campus. Approved or accredited by Pennsylvania Association of Independent Schools and Pennsylvania Department of Education. Member of National Association of Independent Schools. Total enrollment: 654. Upper school average class size: 18. Upper school faculty-student ratio: 1:9. There are 180 required school days per year for Upper School students. Upper School students typically attend 5 days per week. The average school day consists of 7 hours.

Upper School Student Profile 85% of students are Roman Catholic.

Faculty School total: 74. In upper school: 54 men, 20 women; 51 have advanced degrees.

Subjects Offered Algebra, American history, American literature, art, Bible studies, biology, calculus, ceramics, chemistry, Chinese, computer math, computer

programming, computer science, concert band, creative writing, data analysis, drama, earth science, ecology, economics, English, English literature, environmental science, ethics, European history, expository writing, fine arts, French, geography, geometry, government/civics, grammar, health, history, jazz band, journalism, logic, Mandarin, mathematics, music, music performance, music theory, philosophy, photography, physical education, physics, printmaking, religion, science, sculpture, social sciences, social studies, sociology, Spanish, speech, sports medicine, studio art, theater, theology, trigonometry, world history, world literature, writing.

Graduation Requirements Arts and fine arts (art, music, dance, drama), computer science, English, foreign language, mathematics, physical education (includes health), religion (includes Bible studies and theology), science, senior career experience, social sciences, social studies (includes history). Community service is required.

Special Academic Programs Advanced Placement exam preparation; honors section; independent study; study abroad.

College Admission Counseling 112 students graduated in 2015; all went to college, including Georgetown University; Penn State University Park; United States Naval Academy; University of Notre Dame; University of Pennsylvania; Villanova University.

Student Life Upper grades have specified standards of dress, student council, honor system. Discipline rests primarily with faculty.

Summer Programs Remediation, enrichment, advancement, sports, art/fine arts, computer instruction programs offered; session focuses on academics; held on campus; accepts boys and girls; open to students from other schools. 2016 schedule: June 21 to July 30. Application deadline: none.

Tuition and Aid Day student tuition: $27,300–$29,950. Tuition installment plan (Insured Tuition Payment Plan, Bryn Mawr Trust Loan Program). Merit scholarship grants, need-based scholarship grants available. In 2015–16, 35% of upper-school students received aid.

Admissions Traditional secondary-level entrance grade is 9. Deadline for receipt of application materials: none. Application fee required: $35. On-campus interview required.

Athletics Interscholastic: aquatics, baseball, basketball, crew, cross-country running, diving, football, golf, ice hockey, lacrosse, rowing, rugby, soccer, squash, strength & conditioning, swimming and diving, tennis, track and field, water polo, weight lifting, weight training, winter (indoor) track, wrestling. 4 PE instructors, 23 coaches, 1 athletic trainer.

Computers Computers are regularly used in all academic classes. Computer network features include on-campus library services, online commercial services, Internet access. Student e-mail accounts are available to students.

Contact Mr. Sean Kenney, Director of Admissions. 484-595-1181. Fax: 484-595-1104. E-mail: skenney@malvernprep.org. Website: www.malvernprep.org

MANHATTAN CHRISTIAN HIGH SCHOOL

8000 Churchill Road
Manhattan, Montana 59741

Head of School: Mr. Patrick J. De Jong

General Information Coeducational day and distance learning college-preparatory, general academic, arts, business, vocational, religious studies, and technology school, affiliated with Christian Reformed Church, Christian faith; primarily serves students with learning disabilities, individuals with Attention Deficit Disorder, individuals with emotional and behavioral problems, and dyslexic students. Grades PK–12. Distance learning grades 9–12. Founded: 1907. Setting: rural. Nearest major city is Bozeman. 20-acre campus. 1 building on campus. Approved or accredited by Christian Schools International, Office for Standards in Education (OFSTED), The College Board, home study, and Montana Department of Education. Endowment: $5.5 million. Total enrollment: 304. Upper school average class size: 23. Upper school faculty-student ratio: 1:11. There are 178 required school days per year for Upper School students. Upper School students typically attend 5 days per week. The average school day consists of 6 hours and 19 minutes.

Upper School Student Profile Grade 6: 22 students (9 boys, 13 girls); Grade 7: 34 students (15 boys, 19 girls); Grade 8: 25 students (11 boys, 14 girls); Grade 9: 26 students (13 boys, 13 girls); Grade 10: 28 students (17 boys, 11 girls); Grade 11: 22 students (11 boys, 11 girls); Grade 12: 19 students (11 boys, 8 girls). 95% of students are members of Christian Reformed Church, Christian faith.

Faculty School total: 23. In upper school: 3 men, 5 women; 3 have advanced degrees.

Subjects Offered Art, Bible studies, business, community service, English, general science, mathematics, music, physical education, senior project, social studies, Spanish.

Graduation Requirements Arts and fine arts (art, music, dance, drama), business skills (includes word processing), English, mathematics, physical education (includes health), religion (includes Bible studies and theology), science, senior project, social studies (includes history), speech. Community service is required.

Special Academic Programs Advanced Placement exam preparation; honors section; independent study; term-away projects; study at local college for college credit; remedial reading and/or remedial writing; remedial math; programs in English, mathematics, general development for dyslexic students.

College Admission Counseling 14 students graduated in 2015; 12 went to college, including Azusa Pacific University; Dordt College; Montana State University;

Oklahoma State University; The University of Montana Western. Other: 2 went to work. Mean composite ACT: 24.

Student Life Upper grades have specified standards of dress, student council, honor system. Discipline rests primarily with faculty. Attendance at religious services is required.

Summer Programs Enrichment, sports programs offered; session focuses on skill development; held on campus; accepts boys and girls; open to students from other schools. 25 students usually enrolled. 2016 schedule: June 15 to July 3.

Tuition and Aid Day student tuition: $9200. Tuition installment plan (monthly payment plans, individually arranged payment plans). Tuition reduction for siblings, need-based scholarship grants available. In 2015–16, 95% of upper-school students received aid. Total amount of financial aid awarded in 2015–16: $60,000.

Admissions Traditional secondary-level entrance grade is 9. For fall 2015, 17 students applied for upper-level admission, 16 were accepted, 16 enrolled. Academic Profile Tests or any standardized test required. Deadline for receipt of application materials: none. Application fee required: $50. Interview required.

Athletics Interscholastic: baseball (boys), basketball (b,g), cheering (b,g), cross-country running (b,g), dance (g), football (b), golf (b,g), horseback riding (g), marksmanship (g), rodeo (b,g), track and field (b,g), volleyball (g). 1 PE instructor, 6 coaches, 2 athletic trainers.

Computers Computers are regularly used in art, business, English, religious studies, science, senior seminar, social studies classes. Computer network features include on-campus library services, online commercial services, Internet access, wireless campus network, Internet filtering or blocking technology. Student e-mail accounts and computer access in designated common areas are available to students. Students grades are available online. The school has a published electronic and media policy.

Contact Mrs. Gloria Veltkamp, Admissions Director. 406-282-7261. Fax: 406-282-7701. E-mail: gveltkamp@manhattanchristian.org. Website: www.manhattanchristian.org

MAPLEBROOK SCHOOL

Amenia, New York
See Special Needs Schools section.

MARANATHA HIGH SCHOOL

169 South Saint John Avenue
Pasadena, California 91105

Head of School: Dr. Richard Riesen

General Information Coeducational day college-preparatory, religious studies, and liberal arts school, affiliated with Christian faith. Grades 9–12. Founded: 1965. Setting: urban. 9-acre campus. 4 buildings on campus. Approved or accredited by Association of Christian Schools International, Western Association of Schools and Colleges, and California Department of Education. Total enrollment: 680. Upper school average class size: 26. Upper school faculty-student ratio: 1:16. There are 178 required school days per year for Upper School students. Upper School students typically attend 5 days per week. The average school day consists of 7 hours and 5 minutes.

Faculty School total: 42. In upper school: 15 men, 27 women; 16 have advanced degrees.

Subjects Offered Advanced math, algebra, American history, American history-AP, American literature, American sign language, anatomy and physiology, art, ASB Leadership, Bible, biology, biology-AP, calculus, calculus-AP, chemistry, chemistry-AP, choir, composition, conceptual physics, concert choir, drama performance, drawing, economics, English, English language-AP, English literature, English literature-AP, filmmaking, foreign language, French, geometry, government and politics-AP, government-AP, graphic design, honors algebra, honors English, honors U.S. history, jazz dance, learning lab, macroeconomics-AP, math analysis, modern world history, music theory, music theory-AP, musical theater, New Testament, orchestra, performing arts, photography, physical education, physical science, physics, physics-AP, psychology, psychology-AP, sociology, Spanish, Spanish language-AP, Spanish-AP, speech and debate, sports medicine, statistics-AP, studio art-AP, swimming, theater, theater arts, theology, theology and the arts, U.S. government, U.S. history-AP, weight training, world geography, world history, yearbook.

Graduation Requirements English, foreign language, history, life science, mathematics, performing arts, physical education (includes health), physical science, theology, visual arts, theology must be taken every year student attends school. Community service is required.

Special Academic Programs 16 Advanced Placement exams for which test preparation is offered; honors section; study at local college for college credit; academic accommodation for the artistically talented; remedial reading and/or remedial writing; remedial math; special instructional classes for students with learning difficulties and Attention Deficit Disorder.

College Admission Counseling 149 students graduated in 2015; they went to Azusa Pacific University.

Student Life Upper grades have uniform requirement, student council, honor system. Discipline rests primarily with faculty. Attendance at religious services is required.

Summer Programs Remediation, enrichment, advancement, sports, art/fine arts programs offered; session focuses on science and math; held on campus; accepts boys and girls; open to students from other schools. 140 students usually enrolled. 2016 schedule: June 15 to July 24. Application deadline: May 18.

Tuition and Aid Day student tuition: $17,085. Tuition installment plan (SMART Tuition Payment Plan, monthly payment plans). Merit scholarship grants, need-based scholarship grants available. In 2015–16, 30% of upper-school students received aid.

Admissions Traditional secondary-level entrance grade is 9. ISEE required. Deadline for receipt of application materials: none. Application fee required: $75. Interview required.

Athletics Interscholastic: baseball (boys), basketball (b,g), cheering (g), cross-country running (b,g), diving (b,g), football (b), soccer (b,g), softball (g), swimming and diving (b,g), tennis (b,g), track and field (b,g), volleyball (b,g); coed interscholastic: dance team, equestrian sports, golf; coed intramural: hiking/backpacking, kayaking, outdoor activities, outdoor adventure, outdoor skills. 2 PE instructors, 27 coaches, 1 athletic trainer.

Computers Computers are regularly used in college planning, freshman foundations, graphic design, library, photography, research skills, yearbook classes. Computer network features include on-campus library services, online commercial services, Internet access, wireless campus network, Internet filtering or blocking technology, eLibrary, 1:1: iPad program. Campus intranet, student e-mail accounts, and computer access in designated common areas are available to students. Students grades are available online. The school has a published electronic and media policy.

Contact Mrs. Debbie Middlebrook, Admissions Administrative Assistant. 626-817-4021. Fax: 626-817-4040. E-mail: d_middlebrook@mhs-hs.org. Website: www.maranatha-hs.org

MARET SCHOOL

3000 Cathedral Avenue NW
Washington, District of Columbia 20008

Head of School: Marjo Talbott

General Information Coeducational day college-preparatory, arts, and technology school. Grades K–12. Founded: 1911. Setting: urban. 7-acre campus. 6 buildings on campus. Approved or accredited by Association of Independent Maryland Schools, Association of Independent Schools of Greater Washington, and District of Columbia Department of Education. Member of National Association of Independent Schools and Secondary School Admission Test Board. Endowment: $31.8 million. Total enrollment: 645. Upper school average class size: 18. Upper school faculty-student ratio: 1:7. Upper School students typically attend 5 days per week. The average school day consists of 7 hours.

Upper School Student Profile Grade 9: 81 students (44 boys, 37 girls); Grade 10: 81 students (39 boys, 42 girls); Grade 11: 72 students (36 boys, 36 girls); Grade 12: 78 students (38 boys, 40 girls).

Faculty School total: 109. In upper school: 45 men, 64 women; 79 have advanced degrees.

Subjects Offered 20th century history, 20th century world history, 3-dimensional art, acting, advanced biology, advanced chemistry, advanced computer applications, advanced math, advanced studio art-AP, African-American literature, algebra, American Civil War, American government, American history, American legal systems, American literature, Arabic, art, Asian history, Asian literature, Asian studies, astrophysics, biochemistry, bioethics, biology, biotechnology, British literature, Buddhism, calculus, calculus-AP, ceramics, chemistry, Chinese, Chinese literature, Chinese studies, choir, choral music, civil rights, classical civilization, classical language, classics, clayworking, college admission preparation, college counseling, college planning, comedy, comparative religion, computer graphics, computer math, computer programming, computer science, conceptual physics, concert choir, constitutional history of U.S., constitutional law, creative writing, critical thinking, critical writing, digital photography, drama, earth science, ecology, ecology, environmental systems, economics, English, English literature, environmental science, equality and freedom, ethics, European history, evolution, film, film and literature, film history, fine arts, French, gender issues, geometry, global studies, government/civics, Hispanic literature, history, human development, human sexuality, humanities, Islamic history, Islamic studies, jazz band, jazz ensemble, Latin, madrigals, Mandarin, marine biology, marine ecology, mathematics, model United Nations, music, music theory, newspaper, organic chemistry, painting, photography, physical education, physics, pre-algebra, pre-calculus, psychology, science, science fiction, sculpture, senior project, service learning/internship, Shakespeare, Spanish, Spanish literature, statistics, technical theater, technology, trigonometry, world history, world literature, writing.

Graduation Requirements Arts and fine arts (art, music, dance, drama), English, foreign language, history, mathematics, music, performing arts, physical education (includes health), science, 15 hours of community service in grades 9 and 10, additional 15 hours in grades 11 and 12.

Special Academic Programs 16 Advanced Placement exams for which test preparation is offered; honors section; independent study; study abroad; academic accommodation for the gifted, the musically talented, and the artistically talented; remedial reading and/or remedial writing; remedial math.

College Admission Counseling 80 students graduated in 2014; 77 went to college, including Bowdoin College; Dartmouth College; Tufts University; Washington University in St. Louis; Wesleyan University; Williams College. Other: 1 entered military service, 1 entered a postgraduate year, 1 had other specific plans.

Student Life Upper grades have student council. Discipline rests primarily with faculty.

Tuition and Aid Day student tuition: $34,790. Tuition installment plan (Tuition Management Systems (TMS)). Need-based scholarship grants available. In 2014–15, 24% of upper-school students received aid. Total amount of financial aid awarded in 2014–15: $1,821,624.

Admissions Traditional secondary-level entrance grade is 9. For fall 2014, 290 students applied for upper-level admission, 51 were accepted, 29 enrolled. Admissions testing, ISEE, PSAT, SSAT, Wechsler Intelligence Scale for Children, Wechsler Intelligence Scale for Children III or Woodcock-Johnson required. Deadline for receipt of application materials: January 6. Application fee required: $65. Interview required.

Athletics Interscholastic: baseball (boys), basketball (b,g), football (b), lacrosse (b,g), soccer (b,g), softball (g), tennis (b,g), volleyball (g), wrestling (b); intramural: ice hockey (b); coed interscholastic: cross-country running, diving, golf, independent competitive sports, swimming and diving, track and field, ultimate Frisbee; coed intramural: flag football, ultimate Frisbee, weight lifting, weight training, yoga. 6 PE instructors, 25 coaches, 1 athletic trainer.

Computers Computers are regularly used in graphic design, graphics, programming, publications, Web site design classes. Computer network features include on-campus library services, online commercial services, Internet access, wireless campus network, Internet filtering or blocking technology. Campus intranet and student e-mail accounts are available to students. Students grades are available online. The school has a published electronic and media policy.

Contact Annie M. Farquhar, Director of Admission and Financial Aid. 202-939-8814. Fax: 202-939-8845. E-mail: admissions@maret.org. Website: www.maret.org

MARIANAPOLIS PREPARATORY SCHOOL

PO Box 304
26 Chase Road
Thompson, Connecticut 06277-0304

Head of School: Mr. Joseph C. Hanrahan

General Information Coeducational boarding and day and distance learning college-preparatory, arts, religious studies, technology, and ESL school, affiliated with Roman Catholic Church. Grades 9–PG. Distance learning grades 9–12. Founded: 1926. Setting: small town. Nearest major city is Boston, MA. Students are housed in single-sex dormitories. 150-acre campus. 10 buildings on campus. Approved or accredited by Association of Independent Schools in New England, Connecticut Association of Independent Schools, New England Association of Schools and Colleges, The Association of Boarding Schools, and Connecticut Department of Education. Member of National Association of Independent Schools and Secondary School Admission Test Board. Total enrollment: 400. Upper school average class size: 14. Upper school faculty-student ratio: 1:8.

Upper School Student Profile Grade 9: 95 students (43 boys, 52 girls); Grade 10: 98 students (45 boys, 53 girls); Grade 11: 111 students (51 boys, 60 girls); Grade 12: 93 students (50 boys, 43 girls); Postgraduate: 3 students (3 boys). 43% of students are boarding students. 25% are state residents. 10 states are represented in upper school student body. 30% are international students. International students from Austria, Canada, China, Mexico, Republic of Korea, and Russian Federation; 14 other countries represented in student body. 50% of students are Roman Catholic.

Faculty School total: 50. In upper school: 25 men, 25 women; 28 have advanced degrees; 36 reside on campus.

Subjects Offered Algebra, American government, American literature, art, astronomy, Bible as literature, Bible studies, biology, biology-AP, calculus, calculus-AP, chemistry, chemistry-AP, Chinese, choir, chorus, Christian and Hebrew scripture, Christian doctrine, Christian ethics, church history, classical language, comparative religion, composition, composition-AP, computer programming, computer science, conceptual physics, contemporary studies, creative writing, dance, dance performance, digital photography, drawing, drawing and design, economics, English, English composition, English language and composition-AP, English literature, English literature and composition-AP, English literature-AP, English-AP, English/composition-AP, ensembles, environmental science, ESL, ethics, etymology, fine arts, French, geometry, global studies, government, government/civics, guitar, history, honors algebra, honors English, honors geometry, human biology, journalism, literary genres, Mandarin, mathematics, modern European history, modern European history-AP, moral theology, music, music performance, music technology, music theory, painting, photography, physics, physics-AP, piano, pre-calculus, printmaking, probability and statistics, programming, psychology, religion, science, sculpture, social justice, social studies, sociology, Spanish, Spanish-AP, statistics, statistics-AP, theology, trigonometry, U.S. history, U.S. history-AP, Web site design, world history, world history-AP, world literature, world religions.

Graduation Requirements Arts and fine arts (art, music, dance, drama), computer science, electives, English, foreign language, history, mathematics, science, theology.

Special Academic Programs Advanced Placement exam preparation; honors section; independent study; ESL (90 students enrolled).

College Admission Counseling 98 students graduated in 2015; all went to college, including Boston University; Michigan State University; Penn State University Park;

Roger Williams University; University of Connecticut; University of Massachusetts Amherst.

Student Life Upper grades have specified standards of dress, student council. Discipline rests equally with students and faculty. Attendance at religious services is required.

Summer Programs Remediation, enrichment, advancement, ESL programs offered; held off campus; held at online; accepts boys and girls; open to students from other schools. 45 students usually enrolled. 2016 schedule: June 29 to August 9. Application deadline: June 15.

Tuition and Aid Day student tuition: $15,610; 7-day tuition and room/board: $47,633. Tuition installment plan (SMART Tuition Payment Plan, monthly payment plans, individually arranged payment plans). Merit scholarship grants, need-based scholarship grants, tuition reduction for Diocese of Norwich affiliation available. In 2015–16, 43% of upper-school students received aid.

Admissions Traditional secondary-level entrance grade is 9. Common entrance examinations, International English Language Test, PSAT, SAT, SSAT, TOEFL, TOEFL Junior or TOEFL or SLEP required. Deadline for receipt of application materials: January 15. Application fee required: $100. Interview required.

Athletics Interscholastic: baseball (boys), basketball (b,g), crew (b,g), cross-country running (b,g), lacrosse (b,g), soccer (b,g), softball (g), tennis (b,g), volleyball (g); intramural: basketball (b,g), dance (g), modern dance (g); coed interscholastic: badminton, Frisbee, golf, gymnastics, horseback riding, indoor track & field, running, skiing (cross-country), skiing (downhill), track and field, ultimate Frisbee, winter (indoor) track, wrestling; coed intramural: aerobics/dance, alpine skiing, ballet, cross-country running, dance, flag football, Frisbee, independent competitive sports, jogging, judo, martial arts, ropes courses, skiing (cross-country), skiing (downhill), snowboarding, snowshoeing, strength & conditioning, table tennis, tai chi, tennis, ultimate Frisbee, volleyball, weight lifting, weight training, yoga. 1 coach, 1 athletic trainer.

Computers Computers are regularly used in all academic, ESL classes. Computer network features include online commercial services, Internet access, wireless campus network, Internet filtering or blocking technology. Student e-mail accounts are available to students. Students grades are available online. The school has a published electronic and media policy.

Contact Mr. Ray Cross, Director of Admission. 860-923-9245. Fax: 860-923-3730. E-mail: rcross@marianapolis.org. Website: www.marianapolis.org

MARIAN CENTRAL CATHOLIC HIGH SCHOOL

1001 McHenry Avenue
Woodstock, Illinois 60098

Head of School: Mrs. Barbara Villont

General Information Coeducational day college-preparatory, arts, business, religious studies, bilingual studies, and technology school, affiliated with Roman Catholic Church. Grades 9–12. Founded: 1959. Setting: suburban. 42-acre campus. 1 building on campus. Approved or accredited by National Catholic Education Association, North Central Association of Colleges and Schools, and Illinois Department of Education. Endowment: $1.7 million. Total enrollment: 687. Upper school average class size: 21. Upper school faculty-student ratio: 1:19. There are 177 required school days per year for Upper School students. Upper School students typically attend 5 days per week. The average school day consists of 6 hours and 25 minutes.

Upper School Student Profile Grade 9: 170 students (76 boys, 94 girls); Grade 10: 176 students (79 boys, 97 girls); Grade 11: 182 students (89 boys, 93 girls); Grade 12: 159 students (93 boys, 66 girls). 87.8% of students are Roman Catholic.

Faculty School total: 39. In upper school: 18 men, 21 women; 28 have advanced degrees.

Subjects Offered Accounting, advanced biology, advanced chemistry, advanced math, Advanced Placement courses, algebra, American government, art, band, biology, biology-AP, business law, calculus, calculus-AP, chemistry, chemistry-AP, chorus, composition, computer applications, consumer economics, cultural geography, desktop publishing, engineering, English, English composition, English literature-AP, first aid, French, general science, geography, geometry, global issues, government and politics-AP, health, honors algebra, honors English, honors geometry, integrated science, macroeconomics-AP, marketing, photo shop, physical education, physical science, physics, pre-calculus, psychology, psychology-AP, publications, Spanish, speech, statistics-AP, theater, theology, U.S. history, U.S. history-AP, Web site design, world history, world history-AP.

Graduation Requirements Art, biology, consumer economics, electives, English, first aid, foreign language, government, health, mathematics, music, physical education (includes health), science, theology, U.S. history.

Special Academic Programs 10 Advanced Placement exams for which test preparation is offered; honors section; remedial reading and/or remedial writing; remedial math; special instructional classes for deaf students.

College Admission Counseling 182 students graduated in 2015; 178 went to college, including Illinois State University; Loras College; Loyola University Chicago; Northern Illinois University; The University of Iowa; University of Dayton. Other: 2 went to work, 1 entered military service, 1 had other specific plans. Mean composite ACT: 25. 35% scored over 26 on composite ACT.

Student Life Upper grades have uniform requirement, student council. Discipline rests primarily with faculty. Attendance at religious services is required.

Summer Programs Enrichment, sports, art/fine arts, computer instruction programs offered; session focuses on sports camps, study skills, art, band, chorus, media/technology, Model United Nations; held on campus; accepts boys and girls; open to students from other schools. 2016 schedule: June to August.

Tuition and Aid Day student tuition: $6255–$8375. Tuition installment plan (monthly payment plans, quarterly payment plan, semester payment plans, yearly payment plans). Tuition reduction for siblings, need-based scholarship grants, paying campus jobs available. In 2015–16, 17% of upper-school students received aid. Total amount of financial aid awarded in 2015–16: $288,816.

Admissions Traditional secondary-level entrance grade is 9. High School Placement Test (closed version) from Scholastic Testing Service required. Deadline for receipt of application materials: none. No application fee required.

Athletics Interscholastic: baseball (boys), basketball (b,g), cheering (g), cross-country running (b,g), dance team (g), football (b), golf (b,g), soccer (b,g), softball (g), tennis (b,g), volleyball (g), wrestling (b); coed interscholastic: fencing, fishing, track and field; coed intramural: floor hockey. 4 PE instructors, 79 coaches, 1 athletic trainer.

Computers Computers are regularly used in computer applications, desktop publishing, photography, publications, Web site design classes. Computer resources include on-campus library services, online commercial services, Internet access, Internet filtering or blocking technology. Students grades are available online. The school has a published electronic and media policy.

Contact Mr. Michael Maloney, Director of Admissions. 815-338-4220 Ext. 108. Fax: 815-338-4253. E-mail: mmaloney@marian.com. Website: www.marian.com

MARIAN HIGH SCHOOL

1311 South Logan Street
Mishawaka, Indiana 46544

Head of School: Mark Kirzeder

General Information Coeducational day college-preparatory, arts, business, vocational, religious studies, bilingual studies, and technology school, affiliated with Roman Catholic Church. Grades 9–12. Founded: 1965. Setting: suburban. 72-acre campus. 1 building on campus. Approved or accredited by North Central Association of Colleges and Schools, The College Board, and Indiana Department of Education. Total enrollment: 690. Upper school average class size: 27. Upper school faculty-student ratio: 1:24. There are 180 required school days per year for Upper School students. Upper School students typically attend 5 days per week. The average school day consists of 6 hours and 30 minutes.

Upper School Student Profile 83% of students are Roman Catholic.

Faculty School total: 48. In upper school: 18 men, 30 women; 22 have advanced degrees.

Subjects Offered 20th century history, 20th century physics, 20th century world history, 3-dimensional art, 3-dimensional design, accounting, acting, advanced chemistry, advanced computer applications, advanced math, algebra, alternative physical education, American government, American literature, analysis and differential calculus, analytic geometry, anatomy, ancient world history, art, art history, arts and crafts, arts appreciation, business law, calculus, Catholic belief and practice, chemistry, drama, drawing, drawing and design, economics, English composition, English literature-AP, environmental science, environmental studies, environmental systems, family and consumer science, family living, fashion, fine arts, food and nutrition, foods, French, French language-AP, general business, general math, geography, geometry, German, government and politics-AP, government-AP, government/civics, guidance, health, histology, honors world history, independent living, integrated science, keyboarding, Latin, Life of Christ, media, media arts, moral theology, music, music appreciation, nutrition, physics, physics-AP, pre-algebra, pre-calculus, psychology, religion, scripture, senior project, sewing, sociology, Spanish, Spanish language-AP, Spanish-AP, study skills, theology, U.S. government and politics-AP, U.S. history, U.S. history-AP, visual arts, vocal music, Western civilization.

Graduation Requirements Algebra, American government, American history, analytic geometry, arts and fine arts (art, music, dance, drama), biology, chemistry, computer information systems, computer skills, economics, English, English composition, English literature, French, keyboarding, languages, mathematics, science, scripture, writing, four years of theology.

Special Academic Programs Advanced Placement exam preparation; study at local college for college credit; remedial reading and/or remedial writing; remedial math.

College Admission Counseling 162 students graduated in 2015; 155 went to college, including Ball State University; DePaul University; Indiana University–Purdue University Fort Wayne; Indiana University Bloomington; Purdue University; University of Notre Dame. Other: 4 went to work, 1 entered military service, 2 had other specific plans. Mean SAT critical reading: 542, mean SAT math: 541, mean SAT writing: 537, mean composite ACT: 23.

Student Life Upper grades have specified standards of dress, student council, honor system. Discipline rests equally with students and faculty. Attendance at religious services is required.

Summer Programs Sports, art/fine arts, computer instruction programs offered; session focuses on enrichment; held on campus; accepts boys and girls; open to students from other schools. 2016 schedule: June 7 to July 2.

Tuition and Aid Day student tuition: $5575–$6575. Tuition installment plan (The Tuition Plan, FACTS Tuition Payment Plan, individually arranged payment plans). Tuition reduction for siblings, need-based loans available. In 2015–16, 45% of upper-school students received aid. Total amount of financial aid awarded in 2015–16: $350,000.

Admissions Traditional secondary-level entrance grade is 9. For fall 2015, 210 students applied for upper-level admission, 210 were accepted, 199 enrolled. High School Placement Test, Math Placement Exam or placement test required. Deadline for receipt of application materials: September 9. Application fee required: $100. Interview required.

Athletics Interscholastic: aerobics/dance (girls), aquatics (b,g), baseball (b), basketball (b,g), cheering (b,g), Cosom hockey (b), cross-country running (b,g), dance team (g), diving (b,g), flag football (g), football (b), golf (b,g), gymnastics (g), hockey (b), ice hockey (b), indoor hockey (b), lacrosse (b,g), power lifting (b,g), rugby (b), soccer (b,g), softball (g), swimming and diving (b,g), tennis (b,g), track and field (b,g), volleyball (g), weight training (b,g), wrestling (b,g); intramural: basketball (b), flag football (g), pom squad (g); coed interscholastic: cheering, wrestling; coed intramural: alpine skiing, bowling. 2 PE instructors, 42 coaches, 1 athletic trainer.

Computers Computers are regularly used in business education, business skills, career education, commercial art, economics, foreign language, graphic arts, history, library, media arts, occupational education, publications, religion, yearbook classes. Computer network features include on-campus library services, online commercial services, Internet access, Internet filtering or blocking technology. Students grades are available online. The school has a published electronic and media policy.

Contact Mary Kay Dance, Director of Admissions and Public Relations. 574-259-5257 Ext. 319. Fax: 574-258-7668. E-mail: mdance@marianhs.org. Website: www.marianhs.org/

MARIAN HIGH SCHOOL

273 Union Avenue
Framingham, Massachusetts 01702

Head of School: Mr. John J. Ermilio

General Information Coeducational day college-preparatory and arts school, affiliated with Roman Catholic Church; primarily serves students with learning disabilities and individuals with Attention Deficit Disorder. Grades 9–12. Founded: 1956. Setting: urban. Nearest major city is Boston. 2-acre campus. 1 building on campus. Approved or accredited by Massachusetts Department of Education, New England Association of Schools and Colleges, and Massachusetts Department of Education. Endowment: $300,000. Total enrollment: 260. Upper school average class size: 13. Upper school faculty-student ratio: 1:13. There are 172 required school days per year for Upper School students. Upper School students typically attend 5 days per week. The average school day consists of 6 hours and 30 minutes.

Upper School Student Profile Grade 9: 53 students (22 boys, 31 girls); Grade 10: 48 students (16 boys, 32 girls); Grade 11: 84 students (42 boys, 42 girls); Grade 12: 67 students (34 boys, 33 girls). 47% of students are Roman Catholic.

Faculty School total: 23. In upper school: 14 men, 9 women; 22 have advanced degrees.

Subjects Offered 1968.

Graduation Requirements Arts and fine arts (art, music, dance, drama), English, foreign language, mathematics, science, U.S. history, world history, 4 years of Religious studies.

Special Academic Programs Advanced Placement exam preparation; honors section; study at local college for college credit.

College Admission Counseling 72 students graduated in 2015; 70 went to college, including Framingham State University; Sacred Heart University; University of Massachusetts Amherst. Other: 1 went to work, 1 entered a postgraduate year.

Student Life Upper grades have uniform requirement, student council. Discipline rests primarily with faculty. Attendance at religious services is required.

Tuition and Aid Day student tuition: $10,200. Tuition installment plan (FACTS Tuition Payment Plan). Merit scholarship grants, need-based scholarship grants available. In 2015–16, 36% of upper-school students received aid. Total amount of financial aid awarded in 2015–16: $475,000.

Admissions Traditional secondary-level entrance grade is 9. For fall 2015, 75 students applied for upper-level admission, 71 were accepted, 64 enrolled. High School Placement Test required. Deadline for receipt of application materials: January 15. No application fee required. Interview required.

Athletics Interscholastic: baseball (boys), basketball (b,g), cross-country running (b,g), field hockey (g), football (b), hockey (b), ice hockey (b), lacrosse (b,g), soccer (b,g), softball (g), tennis (g), track and field (b,g), volleyball (g), winter (indoor) track (b,g); coed interscholastic: cheering, dance, golf, indoor track. 15 coaches, 1 athletic trainer.

Computers Computer resources include on-campus library services, online commercial services, Internet access, wireless campus network, Internet filtering or blocking technology. Campus intranet, student e-mail accounts, and computer access in designated common areas are available to students. Students grades are available online. The school has a published electronic and media policy.

Contact Ms. Jamie Gaudet, Director of Admissions. 508-875-7646 Ext. 203. Fax: 508-875-0838. E-mail: admissions@marianhigh.org. Website: www.marianhigh.org

MARINE MILITARY ACADEMY

320 Iwo Jima Boulevard
Harlingen, Texas 78550

Head of School: Col. R Glenn Hill, USMC-Retd.

General Information Boys' boarding college-preparatory, general academic, and military school; primarily serves underachievers. Grades 8–PG. Founded: 1965. Setting: small town. Students are housed in single-sex dormitories. 142-acre campus. 43 buildings on campus. Approved or accredited by Military High School and College Association, Southern Association of Colleges and Schools, Southern Association of Independent Schools, and Texas Department of Education. Endowment: $18 million. Total enrollment: 262. Upper school average class size: 11. Upper school faculty-student ratio: 1:13.

Upper School Student Profile Grade 8: 21 students (21 boys); Grade 9: 41 students (41 boys); Grade 10: 90 students (90 boys); Grade 11: 54 students (54 boys); Grade 12: 54 students (54 boys); Postgraduate: 2 students (2 boys). 100% of students are boarding students. 31% are state residents. 23 states are represented in upper school student body. 39% are international students. International students from China, Mexico, Nigeria, Russian Federation, Taiwan, and Venezuela; 5 other countries represented in student body.

Faculty School total: 34. In upper school: 17 men, 17 women; 16 have advanced degrees; 24 reside on campus.

Subjects Offered Aerospace science, algebra, American history, band, biology, calculus, calculus-AP, chemistry, computer programming, computer science, economics, English, environmental science, geography, geometry, government/civics, history, journalism, JROTC, keyboarding, mathematics, military science, physics, physics-AP, political science, SAT preparation, science, social sciences, social studies, Spanish, Spanish-AP, speech, world history.

Graduation Requirements Business skills (includes word processing), computer science, English, foreign language, mathematics, military science, physical education (includes health), science, social sciences, social studies (includes history).

Special Academic Programs Advanced Placement exam preparation; honors section; study at local college for college credit; academic accommodation for the gifted; remedial reading and/or remedial writing; remedial math; ESL (60 students enrolled).

College Admission Counseling 58 students graduated in 2015; 57 went to college, including Texas A&M University; Texas Tech University; The Citadel, The Military College of South Carolina; United States Military Academy; United States Naval Academy; Virginia Military Institute. Other: 1 entered military service. Median SAT critical reading: 470, median SAT math: 470, median SAT writing: 440, median combined SAT: 1400, median composite ACT: 20. 17% scored over 600 on SAT critical reading, 20% scored over 600 on SAT math, 12% scored over 600 on SAT writing, 12% scored over 1800 on combined SAT, 18% scored over 26 on composite ACT.

Student Life Upper grades have uniform requirement, student council, honor system. Discipline rests equally with students and faculty. Attendance at religious services is required.

Summer Programs ESL, sports, rigorous outdoor training programs offered; session focuses on leadership training; held on campus; accepts boys; open to students from other schools. 360 students usually enrolled. 2016 schedule: June 25 to July 23. Application deadline: none.

Tuition and Aid 7-day tuition and room/board: $35,000. Tuition installment plan (FACTS Tuition Payment Plan, monthly payment plans, individually arranged payment plans, Chief Financial Officer authorization required). Tuition reduction for siblings, merit scholarship grants, need-based scholarship grants, parent Active Duty Military Discount, referral reward discount available. In 2015–16, 12% of upper-school students received aid. Total amount of financial aid awarded in 2015–16: $760,000.

Admissions Traditional secondary-level entrance grade is 9. For fall 2015, 213 students applied for upper-level admission, 172 were accepted, 140 enrolled. Deadline for receipt of application materials: none. Application fee required: $100.

Athletics Interscholastic: baseball, basketball, bicycling, boxing, cross-country running, diving, drill team, football, golf, JROTC drill, marksmanship, physical fitness, riflery, running, soccer, swimming and diving, tennis, track and field, winter soccer; intramural: baseball, basketball, boxing, climbing, fitness, flag football, football, judo, kickball, martial arts, outdoor activities, outdoor adventure, paint ball, physical fitness, physical training, power lifting, racquetball, rappelling, rock climbing, running, sailing, scuba diving, soccer, softball, swimming and diving, track and field, volleyball, wall climbing, weight lifting, weight training. 15 coaches, 1 athletic trainer.

Computers Computers are regularly used in English, foreign language, mathematics, science, yearbook classes. Computer network features include on-campus library services, online commercial services, Internet access, Internet filtering or blocking technology. Student e-mail accounts and computer access in designated common areas are available to students. Students grades are available online.

Contact Mrs. Jay Perez, Assistant Admissions Director. 956-423-6006 Ext. 251. Fax: 956-421-9273. E-mail: admissions@mma-tx.org. Website: www.mma-tx.org

THE MARIN SCHOOL

150 N San Pedro Rd.
San Rafael, California 94903

Head of School: Barbara Brown, EdD

General Information Coeducational day college-preparatory, arts, technology, and film, technology, photography school. Grades 9–12. Founded: 1980. Setting: small town. Nearest major city is San Francisco. 7-acre campus. 4 buildings on campus. Approved or accredited by Western Association of Schools and Colleges and California Department of Education. Member of National Association of Independent Schools. Total enrollment: 75. Upper school average class size: 9. Upper school faculty-student ratio: 1:7. There are 174 required school days per year for Upper School students. Upper School students typically attend 5 days per week. The average school day consists of 6 hours and 20 minutes.

Faculty School total: 17. In upper school: 7 men, 7 women; 14 have advanced degrees.

Subjects Offered Algebra, American literature, arts, biology, British literature (honors), calculus, chemistry, civics, community service, composition, drama, earth science, ecology, economics, English, environmental science, fine arts, general science, geography, geometry, health, life science, literature, mathematics, physics, pre-calculus, science, social sciences, social studies, Spanish, trigonometry, U.S. history, visual arts, Western civilization, women's literature.

Graduation Requirements Arts and fine arts (art, music, dance, drama), foreign language, mathematics, physical education (includes health), science, social sciences. Community service is required.

Special Academic Programs Honors section.

College Admission Counseling 25 students graduated in 2014; all went to college, including Bard College; Eugene Lang College of Liberal Arts; Goucher College; Lewis & Clark College; Reed College; The Evergreen State College.

Student Life Upper grades have student council, honor system. Discipline rests primarily with faculty.

Tuition and Aid Day student tuition: $37,270. Tuition installment plan (FACTS Tuition Payment Plan). Need-based scholarship grants available. In 2014–15, 35% of upper-school students received aid.

Admissions Deadline for receipt of application materials: none. No application fee required. On-campus interview required.

Athletics Coed Interscholastic: basketball, dance, soccer; coed intramural: baseball, basketball, bicycling, fencing, soccer.

Computers Computers are regularly used in all classes. Computer network features include on-campus library services, online commercial services, Internet access, wireless campus network, Internet filtering or blocking technology. Campus intranet, student e-mail accounts, and computer access in designated common areas are available to students. Students grades are available online. The school has a published electronic and media policy

Contact Emily Burns, Director of Admissions and Financial Aid. 415-339-9336 Ext. 104. E-mail: eburns@themarinschool.org. Website: www.themarinschool.org

MARION ACADEMY

1820 Prier Drive
Marion, Alabama 36756

Head of School: Mr. Benjamin Catlin Miller

General Information Coeducational day college-preparatory, general academic, arts, religious studies, bilingual studies, and technology school, affiliated with Christian faith. Grades K–12. Founded: 1987. Setting: small town. Nearest major city is Tuscaloosa. 5-acre campus. 1 building on campus. Approved or accredited by Southern Association of Colleges and Schools and Alabama Department of Education. Total enrollment: 53. Upper school average class size: 8. Upper school faculty-student ratio: 1:8. There are 180 required school days per year for Upper School students. Upper School students typically attend 5 days per week. The average school day consists of 6 hours and 30 minutes.

Upper School Student Profile Grade 6: 6 students (3 boys, 3 girls); Grade 7: 6 students (3 boys, 3 girls); Grade 8: 3 students (2 boys, 1 girl); Grade 9: 5 students (2 boys, 3 girls); Grade 10: 5 students (3 boys, 2 girls); Grade 11: 4 students (3 boys, 1 girl); Grade 12: 6 students (4 boys, 2 girls). 98% of students are Christian.

Faculty School total: 19. In upper school: 4 men, 6 women; 2 have advanced degrees.

Subjects Offered 20th century history, 20th century world history, advanced computer applications, advanced math, Alabama history and geography, algebra, American government, anatomy and physiology, art, athletics, basic language skills, Bible studies, biology, cheerleading, college planning, creative writing, drama, earth science, economics, English language and composition-AP, English language-AP, English literature, English literature and composition-AP, foreign language, general math, geography, government, grammar, health education, history, honors algebra, honors English, human anatomy, Internet, language, language and composition, language arts, library, math applications, math methods, math review, mathematics, mathematics-AP, physical education, SAT/ACT preparation, speech, U.S. government, U.S. history.

College Admission Counseling 9 students graduated in 2015; 7 went to college.

Student Life Upper grades have specified standards of dress, student council, honor system. Discipline rests primarily with faculty.

Tuition and Aid Guaranteed tuition plan. Tuition reduction for siblings available.

Admissions Traditional secondary-level entrance grade is 9. Deadline for receipt of application materials: none. Application fee required. Interview required.

Athletics Interscholastic: baseball (boys), basketball (b,g), cheering (g), cross-country running (b,g), football (b), softball (g), track and field (b,g), volleyball (g); coed interscholastic: track and field. 1 PE instructor, 2 coaches.

Computers Computers are regularly used in career education, library skills classes. Computer network features include Internet access. Student e-mail accounts are available to students. Students grades are available online.

Contact Mrs. Margaret S. Hallmon, Secretary. 334-683-8204. Fax: 334-683-4938. E-mail: marionacademy@hotmail.com. Website: www.marion-academy.com

MARIST HIGH SCHOOL

4200 West 115th Street

Chicago, Illinois 60655-4306

Head of School: Br. Hank Hammer, FMS

General Information Coeducational day college-preparatory, arts, business, religious studies, bilingual studies, and technology school, affiliated with Roman Catholic Church. Grades 9–12. Founded: 1963. Setting: suburban. 55-acre campus. 1 building on campus. Approved or accredited by National Catholic Education Association, National Council for Nonpublic Schools, and Illinois Department of Education. Total enrollment: 1,703. Upper school average class size: 27. Upper school faculty-student ratio: 1:18. There are 180 required school days per year for Upper School students. Upper School students typically attend 5 days per week. The average school day consists of 6 hours and 35 minutes.

Upper School Student Profile 93% of students are Roman Catholic.

Faculty School total: 107. In upper school: 61 men, 46 women; 74 have advanced degrees.

Subjects Offered Accounting, algebra, American legal systems, anatomy, architecture, art, art history-AP, band, biology, biology-AP, business mathematics, calculus, calculus-AP, chemistry, chemistry-AP, chorus, computer graphics, computer science, computer science-AP, creative writing, drafting, drawing, economics, English, English language and composition-AP, English literature and composition-AP, English-AP, entrepreneurship, environmental science, film and literature, film studies, forensics, French, French language-AP, French-AP, geometry, information technology, Italian, journalism, macro/microeconomics-AP, music appreciation, painting, peer counseling, philosophy, physics, physics-AP, pottery, psychology, psychology-AP, reading, religious studies, rhetoric, senior humanities, Spanish, Spanish language-AP, Spanish literature-AP, Spanish-AP, studio art, studio art-AP, U.S. government and politics-AP, U.S. history, U.S. history-AP, Web site design, wellness, Western civilization, world geography.

Graduation Requirements Electives, English, foreign language, mathematics, performing arts, physical education (includes health), religion (includes Bible studies and theology), science, social studies (includes history), technology, visual arts.

Special Academic Programs 21 Advanced Placement exams for which test preparation is offered; honors section; study at local college for college credit; study abroad; academic accommodation for the gifted, the musically talented, and the artistically talented; remedial reading and/or remedial writing; remedial math.

College Admission Counseling 438 students graduated in 2014; 430 went to college, including Illinois State University; Loyola University Chicago; Marquette University; Purdue University; The University of Iowa; University of Illinois at Urbana–Champaign. Other: 3 went to work, 5 entered military service. Mean composite ACT: 24.

Student Life Upper grades have uniform requirement, student council, honor system. Discipline rests primarily with faculty. Attendance at religious services is required.

Tuition and Aid Day student tuition: $11,000. Tuition installment plan (monthly payment plans, individually arranged payment plans). Tuition reduction for siblings, merit scholarship grants, need-based scholarship grants, paying campus jobs available. In 2014–15, 33% of upper-school students received aid.

Admissions Traditional secondary-level entrance grade is 9. High School Placement Test required. Deadline for receipt of application materials: January 10. Application fee required: $150.

Athletics Interscholastic: baseball (boys), basketball (b,g), bowling (b,g), boxing (b), cheering (g), cross-country running (b,g), dance team (g), football (b), golf (b,g), indoor track (b,g), indoor track & field (b,g), lacrosse (b,g), pom squad (b), soccer (b,g), softball (g), swimming and diving (g), tennis (b,g), track and field (b,g), volleyball (b,g), wrestling (b); intramural: basketball (b,g), boxing (b), flag football (b,g), volleyball (b,g); coed interscholastic: billiards, fishing, Frisbee, ice hockey; coed intramural: bicycling, bowling, dance, fencing, Frisbee, judo, skiing (downhill), table tennis, volleyball. 3 PE instructors, 5 coaches, 2 athletic trainers.

Computers Computers are regularly used in architecture, business, computer applications, digital applications, drafting, drawing and design, engineering, graphic arts, graphic design, media, newspaper, photography, programming, Web site design, yearbook classes. Computer network features include on-campus library services, online commercial services, Internet access, wireless campus network, Internet filtering

or blocking technology, Marist is a 1:1 school with all freshman and sophomores using iPads. By Fall of 2016, all four levels will use iPads. Student e-mail accounts and computer access in designated common areas are available to students. Students grades are available online. The school has a published electronic and media policy.

Contact Mrs. Alex Brown, Director of Admissions. 773-881-5300 Ext. 5330. Fax: 773-881-0595. E-mail: alex@marist.net. Website: www.marist.net

MARIST SCHOOL

3790 Ashford-Dunwoody Road NE

Atlanta, Georgia 30319-1899

Head of School: Rev. Joel M. Konzen, SM

General Information Coeducational day college-preparatory, arts, business, religious studies, and technology school, affiliated with Roman Catholic Church. Grades 7–12. Founded: 1901. Setting: suburban. 77-acre campus. 18 buildings on campus. Approved or accredited by Southern Association of Colleges and Schools, Southern Association of Independent Schools, and Georgia Department of Education. Member of National Association of Independent Schools and Secondary School Admission Test Board. Endowment: $21.3 million. Total enrollment: 1,088. Upper school average class size: 18. Upper school faculty-student ratio: 1:9. There are 174 required school days per year for Upper School students. Upper School students typically attend 5 days per week. The average school day consists of 5 hours and 30 minutes.

Upper School Student Profile Grade 7: 148 students (74 boys, 74 girls); Grade 8: 149 students (71 boys, 78 girls); Grade 9: 207 students (108 boys, 99 girls); Grade 10: 202 students (103 boys, 99 girls); Grade 11: 188 students (90 boys, 98 girls); Grade 12: 194 students (97 boys, 97 girls). 74% of students are Roman Catholic.

Faculty School total: 101. In upper school: 45 men, 39 women; 66 have advanced degrees.

Subjects Offered Algebra, American history, American literature, ancient history, art, art history, biology, business skills, calculus, ceramics, chemistry, community service, computer programming, computer science, creative writing, dance, drama, driver education, economics, English, English literature, European history, fine arts, French, general science, geography, geology, geometry, German, government/civics, health, history, humanities, journalism, Latin, mathematics, music, peace and justice, philosophy, photography, physical education, physics, religion, science, social studies, Spanish, speech, statistics, studio art, theater, theology, world history, world literature, world religions, writing.

Graduation Requirements Arts and fine arts (art, music, dance, drama), business skills (includes word processing), computer science, English, foreign language, mathematics, physical education (includes health), religion (includes Bible studies and theology), science, social studies (includes history), community service requirements in all grades. Community service is required.

Special Academic Programs 22 Advanced Placement exams for which test preparation is offered; honors section; independent study.

College Admission Counseling 197 students graduated in 2014; all went to college, including Auburn University; Clemson University; Georgia Institute of Technology; The University of Alabama; University of Georgia; University of Virginia. 52% scored over 600 on SAT critical reading, 62% scored over 600 on SAT math, 60% scored over 600 on SAT writing, 60% scored over 1800 on combined SAT, 65% scored over 26 on composite ACT.

Student Life Upper grades have uniform requirement, student council, honor system. Discipline rests primarily with faculty. Attendance at religious services is required.

Tuition and Aid Day student tuition: $17,200. Tuition installment plan (individually arranged payment plans, Tuition Management System). Need-based scholarship grants available. In 2014–15, 18% of upper-school students received aid. Total amount of financial aid awarded in 2014–15: $2,100,000.

Admissions Traditional secondary-level entrance grade is 9. For fall 2014, 297 students applied for upper-level admission, 89 were accepted, 61 enrolled. SSAT required. Deadline for receipt of application materials: January 30. Application fee required: $75. On-campus interview required.

Athletics Interscholastic: baseball (boys), basketball (b,g), cheering (g), cross-country running (b,g), diving (b,g), football (b), golf (b,g), lacrosse (b,g), soccer (b,g), softball (g), swimming and diving (b,g), tennis (b,g), track and field (b,g), volleyball (g), wrestling (b); coed interscholastic: drill team; coed intramural: ultimate Frisbee. 7 PE instructors.

Computers Computers are regularly used in accounting, business applications, computer applications, drawing and design, English, foreign language, mathematics, music, science classes. Computer network features include on-campus library services, online commercial services, Internet access, wireless campus network, Internet filtering or blocking technology, one-to-one computing program, dedicated technical support website, on-site technology training. Student e-mail accounts and computer access in designated common areas are available to students. Students grades are available online. The school has a published electronic and media policy.

Contact Mr. Jim Byrne, Director of Admissions. 770-936-2214. Fax: 770-457-8402. E-mail: admissions@marist.com. Website: www.marist.com

MARLBOROUGH SCHOOL

250 South Rossmore Avenue
Los Angeles, California 90004

Head of School: Ms. Barbara E. Wagner

General Information Girls' day college-preparatory school. Grades 7–12. Founded: 1889. Setting: urban. 4-acre campus. 5 buildings on campus. Approved or accredited by Western Association of Schools and Colleges and California Department of Education. Member of National Association of Independent Schools. Endowment: $36.8 million. Total enrollment: 530. Upper school average class size: 12. Upper school faculty-student ratio: 1:8. There are 166 required school days per year for Upper School students. Upper School students typically attend 5 days per week. The average school day consists of 6 hours and 20 minutes.

Upper School Student Profile Grade 10: 88 students (88 girls); Grade 11: 80 students (80 girls); Grade 12: 95 students (95 girls).

Faculty School total: 77. In upper school: 20 men, 39 women; 47 have advanced degrees.

Subjects Offered Algebra, American literature, American studies, architecture, art history-AP, astronomy, athletic training, ballet technique, biology, biology-AP, calculus, calculus-AP, ceramics, chemistry, chemistry-AP, Chinese history, choral music, choreography, community service, computer programming, creative writing, dance, digital art, drawing, earth systems analysis, economics, English, English literature, English literature and composition-AP, environmental science, environmental science-AP, European history, European history-AP, French, French language-AP, gender issues, geometry, global studies, health, Hispanic literature, instrumental music, internship, journalism, Latin, Latin American literature, Latin-AP, linear algebra, Mandarin, metalworking, modern world history, music theory, newspaper, painting, photography, physical education, physics, physics-AP, political thought, psychology, research, robotics, Russian literature, sculpture, self-defense, social sciences, Spanish, Spanish language-AP, statistics, statistics-AP, studio art-AP, theater, trigonometry, U.S. history, U.S. history-AP, video and animation, world history, world history-AP, world literature, yearbook, yoga.

Graduation Requirements Arts and fine arts (art, music, dance, drama), English, foreign language, history, mathematics, science, social sciences.

Special Academic Programs 21 Advanced Placement exams for which test preparation is offered; honors section; independent study.

College Admission Counseling 99 students graduated in 2014; all went to college, including Brown University; Princeton University; Stanford University; University of Michigan; University of Pennsylvania; University of Southern California.

Student Life Upper grades have uniform requirement, student council, honor system. Discipline rests equally with students and faculty.

Tuition and Aid Day student tuition: $35,050. Tuition installment plan (FACTS Tuition Payment Plan, monthly payment plans). Need-based scholarship grants available. In 2014–15, 18% of upper-school students received aid. Total amount of financial aid awarded in 2014–15: $2,438,000.

Admissions ISEE required. Deadline for receipt of application materials: January 5. Application fee required: $150. On-campus interview required.

Athletics Interscholastic: basketball, cross-country running, equestrian sports, golf, independent competitive sports, soccer, softball, swimming and diving, tennis, track and field, volleyball, water polo. 7 PE instructors, 31 coaches, 1 athletic trainer.

Computers Computers are regularly used in all academic classes. Computer network features include on-campus library services, online commercial services, Internet access, wireless campus network, Internet filtering or blocking technology, videoconferencing. Student e-mail accounts are available to students. Students grades are available online. The school has a published electronic and media policy.

Contact Ms. Jeanette Woo Chitjian, Director of Admissions. 323-964-8450. Fax: 323-933-0542. E-mail: jeanette.woochitjian@marlboroughschool.org. Website: www.marlboroughschool.org

MARQUETTE UNIVERSITY HIGH SCHOOL

3401 West Wisconsin Avenue
Milwaukee, Wisconsin 53208

Head of School: Mr. Jeff Monday

General Information Boys' day college-preparatory school, affiliated with Roman Catholic Church. Grades 9–12. Founded: 1857. Setting: urban. 1 building on campus. Approved or accredited by National Catholic Education Association, North Central Association of Colleges and Schools, and Wisconsin Department of Education. Total enrollment: 1,074. Upper school average class size: 22. Upper school faculty-student ratio: 1:13. Upper School students typically attend 5 days per week. The average school day consists of 8 hours and 10 minutes.

Upper School Student Profile Grade 9: 264 students (264 boys); Grade 10: 289 students (289 boys); Grade 11: 272 students (272 boys); Grade 12: 249 students (249 boys). 85% of students are Roman Catholic.

Faculty School total: 80. In upper school: 55 men, 25 women; 62 have advanced degrees.

Subjects Offered Algebra, American history, American literature, architectural drawing, architecture, art, art-AP, Bible studies, biology, biology-AP, calculus, calculus-AP, ceramics, chemistry, chemistry-AP, choral music, computer math, computer programming, computer science, computer science-AP, creative writing, drama, driver education, economics, English, English language-AP, English literature, English literature-AP, ethics, European history, European history-AP, expository writing, geography, geometry, German, government/civics, grammar, graphic design, health, history, jazz band, Latin, Latin-AP, macroeconomics-AP, mathematics, microeconomics-AP, music, philosophy, photography, physical education, physics, psychology, psychology-AP, religion, social studies, sociology, Spanish, Spanish language-AP, statistics-AP, studio art-AP, theology, trigonometry, U.S. government and politics-AP, U.S. history-AP, world history, world literature, World War I, World War II, writing.

Graduation Requirements Arts and fine arts (art, music, dance, drama), English, foreign language, mathematics, science, social studies (includes history), theology, retreats, community service hours. Community service is required.

Special Academic Programs Advanced Placement exam preparation; honors section.

College Admission Counseling 248 students graduated in 2015; 246 went to college, including Marquette University; Saint Louis University; University of Wisconsin–Madison; University of Wisconsin–Milwaukee; Xavier University. Other: 2 entered military service. Median composite ACT: 27. Mean SAT critical reading: 670, mean SAT math: 690.

Student Life Upper grades have specified standards of dress, student council, honor system. Discipline rests primarily with faculty.

Tuition and Aid Day student tuition: $11,970. Tuition installment plan (SMART Tuition Payment Plan, monthly payment plans, prepaid tuition loan program). Need-based scholarship grants, state-sponsored voucher program available. In 2015–16, 41% of upper-school students received aid. Total amount of financial aid awarded in 2015–16: $2,400,000.

Admissions Traditional secondary-level entrance grade is 9. Essay and STS - Educational Development Series required. Deadline for receipt of application materials: November 1. Application fee required: $25.

Athletics Interscholastic: baseball, basketball, cross-country running, diving, fitness, football, golf, hockey, ice hockey, indoor track, indoor track & field, lacrosse, physical fitness, physical training, power lifting, rugby, sailing, skiing (downhill), soccer, strength & conditioning, swimming and diving, tennis, track and field, volleyball, weight lifting, weight training, wrestling; intramural: basketball, bowling, soccer, softball, volleyball.

Computers Computers are regularly used in architecture, college planning, creative writing, data processing, desktop publishing, economics, English, graphic design, literary magazine, mathematics, music, newspaper, research skills, stock market, Web site design, word processing, writing, yearbook classes. Computer network features include on-campus library services, online commercial services, Internet access, Internet filtering or blocking technology, university and county library systems link. Student e-mail accounts are available to students.

Contact Mr. Sean O'Brien, Director of Admissions. 414-933-7220 Ext. 3046. Fax: 414-933-3086. E-mail: admissions@muhs.edu. Website: www.muhs.edu

MARSHALL SCHOOL

1215 Rice Lake Road
Duluth, Minnesota 55811

Head of School: Kevin Breen

General Information Coeducational day college-preparatory, arts, religious studies, and technology school. Grades 4–12. Founded: 1904. Setting: suburban. Nearest major city is Minneapolis. 40-acre campus. 1 building on campus. Approved or accredited by Independent Schools Association of the Central States. Member of National Association of Independent Schools. Endowment: $5 million. Total enrollment: 446. Upper school average class size: 18. Upper school faculty-student ratio: 1:11.

Upper School Student Profile Grade 9: 80 students (43 boys, 37 girls); Grade 10: 72 students (38 boys, 34 girls); Grade 11: 56 students (34 boys, 22 girls); Grade 12: 62 students (33 boys, 29 girls).

Faculty School total: 51. In upper school: 18 men, 13 women; 13 have advanced degrees.

Subjects Offered Algebra, American history, American literature, anatomy, art, biology, botany, calculus, calculus-AP, chemistry, community service, computer science, computer science-AP, creative writing, drama, earth science, English, English literature, English literature-AP, environmental science, European history, expository writing, fine arts, French, French-AP, geography, geometry, German, government/civics, health, history, law, mathematics, music, outdoor education, physical education, physics, poetry, religion, science, social studies, Spanish, Spanish-AP, speech, theater, theology, trigonometry, world history, world literature, writing.

Graduation Requirements Arts and fine arts (art, music, dance, drama), computer science, English, foreign language, mathematics, outdoor education, physical education (includes health), religion (includes Bible studies and theology), science, social studies (includes history). Community service is required.

Special Academic Programs 10 Advanced Placement exams for which test preparation is offered; honors section; independent study; study abroad; academic accommodation for the gifted; remedial reading and/or remedial writing; remedial math; programs in English, mathematics, general development for dyslexic students; special instructional classes for deaf students.

College Admission Counseling 57 students graduated in 2015; 54 went to college, including University of St. Thomas. Other: 1 entered a postgraduate year, 2 had other specific plans. Median SAT critical reading: 630, median SAT math: 621, median composite ACT: 27.

Student Life Upper grades have student council, honor system. Discipline rests equally with students and faculty.

Summer Programs Enrichment, sports, art/fine arts, computer instruction programs offered; session focuses on enrichment and study skills; held on campus; accepts boys and girls; open to students from other schools. 300 students usually enrolled. 2016 schedule: June to August 18. Application deadline: none.

Tuition and Aid Day student tuition: $16,800. Tuition installment plan (Insured Tuition Payment Plan, monthly payment plans). Need-based scholarship grants, paying campus jobs available. In 2015–16, 45% of upper-school students received aid. Total amount of financial aid awarded in 2015–16: $1,700,000.

Admissions Traditional secondary-level entrance grade is 9. For fall 2015, 61 students applied for upper-level admission, 42 were accepted, 37 enrolled. CTP or ERB required. Deadline for receipt of application materials: none. Application fee required: $50. Interview required.

Athletics Interscholastic: baseball (boys), basketball (b,g), cheering (b,g), cross-country running (b,g), dance (g), dance squad (g), dance team (g), danceline (g), football (b), golf (b,g), hockey (b,g), ice hockey (b,g), nordic skiing (b,g), skiing (cross-country) (b,g), skiing (downhill) (b,g), soccer (b,g), softball (g), tennis (b,g), track and field (b,g), volleyball (g); coed interscholastic: alpine skiing, football; coed intramural: outdoor activities, outdoor adventure, outdoor education, outdoor recreation, outdoors, physical fitness, physical training. 3 PE instructors, 43 coaches, 1 athletic trainer.

Computers Computers are regularly used in English, foreign language, history, mathematics, science classes. Computer network features include on-campus library services, online commercial services, Internet access, wireless campus network, Internet filtering or blocking technology. Campus intranet, student e-mail accounts, and computer access in designated common areas are available to students. Students grades are available online. The school has a published electronic and media policy.

Contact Joe Wicklund, Director of Enrollment. 218-727-7266 Ext. 111. Fax: 218-727-1569. E-mail: joe.wicklund@marshallschool.org. Website: www.marshallschool.org

MARS HILL BIBLE SCHOOL

698 Cox Creek Parkway
Florence, Alabama 35630

Head of School: Mr. Dexter Rutherford

General Information Coeducational day college-preparatory, arts, and religious studies school, affiliated with Church of Christ. Grades K–12. Founded: 1947. Setting: suburban. Nearest major city is Huntsville. 80-acre campus. 7 buildings on campus. Approved or accredited by National Christian School Association and Southern Association of Colleges and Schools. Endowment: $2.7 million. Total enrollment: 525. Upper school average class size: 22. Upper school faculty-student ratio: 1:14. There are 180 required school days per year for Upper School students. Upper School students typically attend 5 days per week. The average school day consists of 7 hours.

Upper School Student Profile Grade 9: 45 students (23 boys, 22 girls); Grade 10: 35 students (20 boys, 15 girls); Grade 11: 38 students (24 boys, 14 girls); Grade 12: 51 students (18 boys, 33 girls). 81% of students are members of Church of Christ.

Faculty School total: 42. In upper school: 11 men, 12 women; 14 have advanced degrees.

Subjects Offered ACT preparation, algebra, American government, American literature, anatomy and physiology, ancient world history, band, Bible studies, biology, biology-AP, calculus, calculus-AP, chemistry, chorus, computer literacy, computer programming, computer science, concert band, concert choir, debate, drama, drama performance, driver education, ecology, economics, English, English composition, English literature, English literature and composition-AP, forensics, geometry, health, honors English, human anatomy, Internet research, jazz band, Life of Christ, marine biology, musical productions, physical education, physical science, physics, pre-algebra, pre-calculus, Spanish, speech, speech and debate, student government, student publications, U.S. history, Western civilization, word processing, world geography, world history, yearbook.

Graduation Requirements Algebra, American government, American history, American literature, ancient world history, art, Bible, biology, chemistry, college writing, computer applications, computer literacy, economics, English composition, foreign language, geometry, health and wellness, introduction to literature, mathematics, physical education (includes health), physical science, science, social studies (includes history). Community service is required.

Special Academic Programs Special instructional classes for students with learning disabilities, Attention Deficit Disorder, and dyslexia.

College Admission Counseling 38 students graduated in 2015; all went to college, including Auburn University; Freed-Hardeman University; Harding University; The University of Alabama; The University of Alabama at Birmingham; University of North Alabama.

Student Life Upper grades have specified standards of dress, student council. Discipline rests primarily with faculty. Attendance at religious services is required.

Summer Programs Enrichment, sports, art/fine arts programs offered; session focuses on athletics, driver education, forensics, show choir, band; held on campus;

accepts boys and girls; open to students from other schools. 180 students usually enrolled. 2016 schedule: June 1 to July 31. Application deadline: June 1.

Tuition and Aid Day student tuition: $6867. Tuition installment plan (FACTS Tuition Payment Plan, monthly payment plans). Tuition reduction for siblings, need-based scholarship grants available. In 2015–16, 20% of upper-school students received aid. Total amount of financial aid awarded in 2015–16: $160,000.

Admissions For fall 2015, 10 students applied for upper-level admission, 9 were accepted, 9 enrolled. Achievement tests, ACT-Explore or PSAT required. Deadline for receipt of application materials: none. Application fee required: $100. Interview required.

Athletics Interscholastic: baseball (boys), basketball (b,g), cheering (g), cross-country running (b,g), football (b), golf (b,g), soccer (b,g), softball (g), tennis (b,g), track and field (b,g), volleyball (g); intramural: basketball (b,g). 3 PE instructors, 7 coaches.

Computers Computers are regularly used in all academic, Bible studies, English, history, remedial study skills, yearbook classes. Computer network features include on-campus library services, online commercial services, Internet access, wireless campus network, Internet filtering or blocking technology. Campus intranet and computer access in designated common areas are available to students. Students grades are available online. The school has a published electronic and media policy.

Contact Mrs. Jeannie Garrett, Director of Admissions. 256-767-1203 Ext. 2005. Fax: 256-767-6304. E-mail: jgarrett@mhbs.org. Website: www.mhbs.org

MARTIN LUTHER HIGH SCHOOL

60-02 Maspeth Avenue
Maspeth, New York 11378

Head of School: Mr. Randy Gast

General Information Coeducational day college-preparatory, arts, business, religious studies, and technology school, affiliated with Lutheran Church. Grades 6–12. Founded: 1960. Setting: urban. Nearest major city is New York. 1-acre campus. 1 building on campus. Approved or accredited by Middle States Association of Colleges and Schools and New York Department of Education. Total enrollment: 225. Upper school average class size: 22. Upper school faculty-student ratio: 1:12.

Upper School Student Profile Grade 9: 44 students (26 boys, 18 girls); Grade 10: 49 students (29 boys, 20 girls); Grade 11: 55 students (38 boys, 17 girls); Grade 12: 52 students (26 boys, 26 girls). 16% of students are Lutheran.

Faculty School total: 21. In upper school: 8 men, 11 women; 11 have advanced degrees.

Subjects Offered Algebra, American history, art, Bible studies, biology, business, business skills, calculus, calculus-AP, chemistry, chemistry-AP, computer programming, computer science, drama, driver education, earth science, economics, English, English literature, English literature-AP, environmental science-AP, ethics, European history, fine arts, French, geography, geometry, German, government/civics, grammar, health, history, journalism, marine biology, mathematics, music, philosophy, photography, physical education, physics, psychology, religion, science, social studies, Spanish, Spanish-AP, speech, theater, theology, trigonometry, U.S. history-AP, world history.

Graduation Requirements 1 1/2 elective credits, arts and fine arts (art, music, dance, drama), computer applications, English, foreign language, health, mathematics, physical education (includes health), religion (includes Bible studies and theology), science, social studies (includes history), service hours.

Special Academic Programs Advanced Placement exam preparation; honors section; independent study; study at local college for college credit; programs in general development for dyslexic students.

College Admission Counseling 53 students graduated in 2015; 51 went to college, including John Jay College of Criminal Justice of the City University of New York; Queens College of the City University of New York; St. Francis College; St. John's University; St. Joseph's College, New York; Stony Brook University, State University of New York. Other: 1 went to work, 1 entered military service. Mean SAT critical reading: 482, mean SAT math: 511, mean SAT writing: 473.

Student Life Upper grades have uniform requirement, student council. Discipline rests primarily with faculty. Attendance at religious services is required.

Summer Programs Remediation, computer instruction programs offered; held on campus; accepts boys and girls; open to students from other schools. 70 students usually enrolled. 2016 schedule: July 2 to August 16. Application deadline: none.

Tuition and Aid Day student tuition: $8150. Tuition installment plan (SMART Tuition Payment Plan, monthly payment plans, quarterly payment plan, one payment plan). Tuition reduction for siblings, merit scholarship grants, need-based scholarship grants available. In 2015–16, 50% of upper-school students received aid; total upper-school merit-scholarship money awarded: $40,800. Total amount of financial aid awarded in 2015–16: $1,955,670.

Admissions Traditional secondary-level entrance grade is 9. Deadline for receipt of application materials: none. Application fee required: $50. On-campus interview required.

Athletics Interscholastic: baseball (boys), basketball (b,g), cross-country running (b,g), fitness (b,g), soccer (b), softball (g), tennis (b,g), track and field (b,g), volleyball (g), wrestling (b,g); intramural: basketball (b,g), cross-country running (b,g), floor hockey (b,g), indoor hockey (b,g), soccer (b,g), weight lifting (b,g), wrestling (b); coed interscholastic: cross-country running, fitness, soccer; coed intramural: archery, badminton, cross-country running, fitness, handball, paddle tennis, racquetball, track and field, volleyball, wrestling. 2 PE instructors, 15 coaches.

Computers Computers are regularly used in business education, career education, Christian doctrine, computer applications, desktop publishing, history, keyboarding, newspaper, SAT preparation, Spanish, Web site design, yearbook classes. Computer resources include on-campus library services, Internet access. Student e-mail accounts are available to students. Students grades are available online.

Contact Ms. Patricia Dee, Admissions Administrator. 718-894-4000 Ext. 122. Fax: 718-894-1469. E-mail: pdee@martinluthernyc.org. Website: www.martinluthernyc.org

THE MARVELWOOD SCHOOL

476 Skiff Mountain Road
PO Box 3001
Kent, Connecticut 06757-3001

Head of School: Mr. Arthur Goodearl

General Information Coeducational boarding and day college-preparatory, arts, technology, field science, and community service, ESL school. Grades 9–12. Founded: 1956. Setting: rural. Nearest major city is Hartford. Students are housed in single-sex dormitories. 83-acre campus. 5 buildings on campus. Approved or accredited by Association for Experiential Education, Association of Independent Schools in New England, Connecticut Association of Independent Schools, New England Association of Schools and Colleges, The Association of Boarding Schools, and Connecticut Department of Education. Member of National Association of Independent Schools and Secondary School Admission Test Board. Endowment: $2.1 million. Total enrollment: 172. Upper school average class size: 10. Upper school faculty-student ratio: 1:4. Upper School students typically attend 6 days per week. The average school day consists of 6 hours and 40 minutes.

Upper School Student Profile Grade 9: 27 students (16 boys, 11 girls); Grade 10: 36 students (26 boys, 10 girls); Grade 11: 47 students (35 boys, 12 girls); Grade 12: 62 students (35 boys, 27 girls). 94% of students are boarding students. 30% are state residents. 14 states are represented in upper school student body. 28% are international students. International students from China, Hong Kong, Japan, Mexico, Republic of Korea, and Spain; 7 other countries represented in student body.

Faculty School total: 49. In upper school: 20 men, 29 women; 24 have advanced degrees; 35 reside on campus.

Subjects Offered Algebra, American history, American literature, anatomy and physiology, art, art history, biology, calculus, ceramics, chemistry, chorus, college writing, community service, creative writing, drama, driver education, English, English literature, ESL, ethology, European history, film, fine arts, forensics, French, geography, geometry, history of China and Japan, Korean literature, limnology, mathematics, music, ornithology, photography, physics, pre-algebra, psychology, religion, SAT preparation, science, Shakespeare, social studies, Spanish, studio art, trigonometry, world cultures, world history, world literature.

Graduation Requirements Arts and fine arts (art, music, dance, drama), English, foreign language, mathematics, science, social studies (includes history), senior service project, weekly community service program.

Special Academic Programs 11 Advanced Placement exams for which test preparation is offered; honors section; independent study; remedial reading and/or remedial writing; remedial math; programs in general development for dyslexic students; ESL (24 students enrolled).

College Admission Counseling 51 students graduated in 2015; 50 went to college, including New York University; Pace University; Penn State University Park; Suffolk University; Syracuse University. Other: 1 went to work. Median SAT critical reading: 458, median SAT math: 424, median SAT writing: 458.

Student Life Upper grades have specified standards of dress, student council. Discipline rests equally with students and faculty.

Summer Programs Remediation, enrichment, ESL, art/fine arts programs offered; session focuses on enrichment; held on campus; accepts boys and girls; open to students from other schools. 25 students usually enrolled. 2016 schedule: July 1 to July 31. Application deadline: March 1.

Tuition and Aid Day student tuition: $35,200; 7-day tuition and room/board: $54,000. Tuition installment plan (Insured Tuition Payment Plan, Academic Management Services Plan, SMART Tuition Payment Plan, individually arranged payment plans). Merit scholarship grants, need-based scholarship grants available. In 2015–16, 24% of upper-school students received aid; total upper-school merit-scholarship money awarded: $54,000. Total amount of financial aid awarded in 2015–16: $1,250,000.

Admissions Traditional secondary-level entrance grade is 9. For fall 2015, 151 students applied for upper-level admission, 90 were accepted, 67 enrolled. SSAT or WISC III required. Deadline for receipt of application materials: none. Application fee required: $50. Interview required.

Athletics Interscholastic: baseball (boys), basketball (b,g), cross-country running (b,g), lacrosse (b), soccer (b,g), softball (g), tennis (b,g), volleyball (g), wrestling (b); coed interscholastic: alpine skiing, Frisbee, golf, hockey, ice hockey, indoor hockey, skiing (downhill), ultimate Frisbee, wrestling; coed intramural: backpacking, bicycling, canoeing/kayaking, climbing, dance, equestrian sports, fishing, fitness, hiking/backpacking, horseback riding, ice skating, kayaking, mountain biking,

mountaineering, outdoor activities, outdoor adventure, outdoor education, outdoor skills, physical training, rappelling, rock climbing, ropes courses, skiing (downhill), snowboarding, strength & conditioning, weight training, wilderness, wildernessways, yoga. 1 coach, 1 athletic trainer.

Computers Computers are regularly used in computer applications, desktop publishing, mathematics, newspaper, photography, science, writing classes. Computer network features include on-campus library services, Internet access, wireless campus network, Internet filtering or blocking technology. Campus intranet, student e-mail accounts, and computer access in designated common areas are available to students. Students grades are available online. The school has a published electronic and media policy.

Contact Mrs. Maureen Smith, Associate Director of Admission. 860-927-0047 Ext. 1005. Fax: 860-927-0021. E-mail: maureen.smith@marvelwood.org. Website: www.marvelwood.org

MARY INSTITUTE AND ST. LOUIS COUNTRY DAY SCHOOL (MICDS)

101 North Warson Road
St. Louis, Missouri 63124

Head of School: Lisa Lyle

General Information Coeducational day college-preparatory school. Grades JK–12. Founded: 1859. Setting: suburban. 100-acre campus. 9 buildings on campus. Approved or accredited by Independent Schools Association of the Central States and Missouri Department of Education. Member of National Association of Independent Schools and Secondary School Admission Test Board. Endowment: $10.1 million. Total enrollment: 1,250. Upper school average class size: 15. Upper school faculty-student ratio: 1:8. There are 170 required school days per year for Upper School students. Upper School students typically attend 5 days per week. The average school day consists of 7 hours and 15 minutes.

Upper School Student Profile Grade 9: 156 students (78 boys, 78 girls); Grade 10: 164 students (78 boys, 86 girls); Grade 11: 161 students (75 boys, 86 girls); Grade 12: 169 students (88 boys, 81 girls).

Faculty School total: 137. In upper school: 36 men, 26 women; 50 have advanced degrees.

Subjects Offered 20th century world history, 3-dimensional design, acting, algebra, American Civil War, analytic geometry, anatomy and physiology, animal behavior, architecture, art history-AP, astronomy, astrophysics, biology-AP, biotechnology, botany, calculus, ceramics, chemistry, chemistry-AP, Chinese, computer science-AP, concert choir, creative writing, design, digital photography, discrete mathematics, drawing, economics, electronics, English, environmental science, environmental science-AP, ethics, European history-AP, forensics, French, genetics, German, health, independent study, instrumental music, integrated mathematics, kinesiology, Latin, Latin-AP, literature, macro/microeconomics-AP, marine biology, music theory-AP, neuroscience, painting, personal finance, physics, physics-AP, psychology-AP, public speaking, robotics, science, sculpture, Spanish, stagecraft, statistics AP, studio art AP, U.S. government and politics-AP, U.S. history, U.S. history-AP, world geography, world history.

Graduation Requirements Arts and fine arts (art, music, dance, drama), English, foreign language, health, mathematics, physical education (includes health), science, social studies (includes history). Community service is required.

Special Academic Programs Advanced Placement exam preparation; honors section; independent study; term-away projects; study abroad; academic accommodation for the gifted.

College Admission Counseling 154 students graduated in 2015; all went to college, including Colgate University; New York University; Saint Louis University; University of Missouri; University of Southern California; Washington University in St. Louis. Median SAT critical reading: 650, median SAT math: 635, median SAT writing: 660, median combined SAT: 1930, median composite ACT: 29.

Student Life Upper grades have specified standards of dress, student council, honor system. Discipline rests equally with students and faculty.

Summer Programs Remediation, enrichment, advancement, sports, art/fine arts, rigorous outdoor training, computer instruction programs offered; session focuses on conditioning/training; held on campus; accepts boys and girls; open to students from other schools. 200 students usually enrolled. 2016 schedule: June 13 to July 26. Application deadline: January 15.

Tuition and Aid Day student tuition: $25,550. Tuition installment plan (FACTS Tuition Payment Plan, monthly plan through FACTS Management, Your Tuition Solution (Loan), credit card payment). Merit scholarship grants, need-based scholarship grants available. In 2015–16, 23% of upper-school students received aid; total upper-school merit-scholarship money awarded: $100,000. Total amount of financial aid awarded in 2015–16: $2,512,985.

Admissions Traditional secondary-level entrance grade is 9. For fall 2015, 112 students applied for upper-level admission, 55 were accepted, 38 enrolled. ISEE or SSAT required. Deadline for receipt of application materials: January 15. Application fee required: $40. Interview required.

Athletics Interscholastic: baseball (boys), cheering (g), crew (b,g), cross-country running (b,g), dance (b,g), diving (b,g), field hockey (g), fitness (b,g), football (b), golf (b,g), ice hockey (b), lacrosse (b,g), soccer (b,g), swimming and diving (b,g), tennis (b,g), track and field (b,g), volleyball (g), water polo (b), wrestling (b); intramural: fitness (b,g), independent competitive sports (b,g), jogging (b,g), modern dance (b,g), physical fitness (b,g), physical training (b,g), strength & conditioning (b,g), weight training (b,g); coed interscholastic: dance, fitness, water polo, wrestling; coed intramural: fitness, independent competitive sports, modern dance, physical fitness, physical training, strength & conditioning, ultimate Frisbee, weight training. 45 coaches.

Computers Computers are regularly used in art, English, foreign language, history, mathematics, music, science classes. Computer network features include on-campus library services, online commercial services, Internet access, wireless campus network, Internet filtering or blocking technology, Intranet services and internet monitoring software. Student e-mail accounts and computer access in designated common areas are available to students. Students grades are available online. The school has a published electronic and media policy.

Contact Peggy B. Laramie, Director of Admission and Financial Aid. 314-995-7367. Fax: 314-872-3257. E-mail: plaramie@micds.org. Website: www.micds.org/home

THE MARY LOUIS ACADEMY

176-21 Wexford Terrace
Jamaica Estates, New York 11432-2926

Head of School: Sr. Kathleen M. McKinney CSJ, EdD

General Information Girls' day college-preparatory, arts, religious studies, and technology school, affiliated with Roman Catholic Church. Grades 9–12. Founded: 1936. Setting: suburban. Nearest major city is New York. 5-acre campus. 8 buildings on campus. Approved or accredited by Middle States Association of Colleges and Schools, National Catholic Education Association, New York Department of Education, New York State Board of Regents, and New York Department of Education. Endowment: $14 million. Total enrollment: 782. Upper school average class size: 25. Upper school faculty-student ratio: 1:13. There are 180 required school days per year for Upper School students. Upper School students typically attend 5 days per week. The average school day consists of 6 hours and 30 minutes.

Upper School Student Profile Grade 9: 172 students (172 girls); Grade 10: 199 students (199 girls); Grade 11: 205 students (205 girls); Grade 12: 206 students (206 girls). 74.5% of students are Roman Catholic.

Faculty School total: 69. In upper school: 14 men, 55 women; all have advanced degrees.

Subjects Offered 20th century American writers, 20th century history, 20th century physics, 20th century world history, 3-dimensional art, 3-dimensional design, advanced biology, advanced chemistry, advanced computer applications, advanced math, Advanced Placement courses, advanced studio art-AP, algebra, American Civil War, American culture, American democracy, American foreign policy, American government, American history, American history-AP, American legal systems, American literature, American literature-AP, analysis and differential calculus, anatomy, anatomy and physiology, ancient history, ancient world history, ancient/medieval philosophy, animation, anthropology, applied arts, applied music, art, art and culture, art appreciation, art education, art history, art history-AP, art in New York, art-AP, astronomy, athletics, audio visual/media, Basic programming, Bible, Bible studies, biology, biology-AP, British history, British literature, business communications, business law, business skills, calculus, calculus-AP, campus ministry, career and personal planning, career exploration, career/college preparation, Catholic belief and practice, chemistry, chemistry-AP, Christian doctrine, Christian ethics, Christian scripture, Christian testament, church history, Civil War, civil war history, classical civilization, classical language, classical music, college admission preparation, college counseling, college placement, college planning, college writing, communication arts, community service, composition, computer animation, computer applications, computer art, computer education, computer graphics, computer information systems, computer literacy, computer programming, computer science, computer skills, computer studies, conflict resolution, constitutional history of U.S., contemporary women writers, creative dance, criminal justice, criminology, cultural geography, current events, current history, digital art, drawing, driver education, earth science, ecology, ecology, environmental systems, economics, economics and history, engineering, English, English composition, English literature, English literature and composition-AP, environmental science, ethics and responsibility, European history, European literature, family studies, female experience in America, fine arts, first aid, forensics, French, government, government/civics, graphic arts, graphic design, guidance, health and wellness, health education, health science, healthful living, heritage of American Women, history, history of music, history of religion, history of the Americas, history of the Catholic Church, history-AP, honors algebra, honors English, honors geometry, honors U.S. history, honors world history, human biology, human development, instrumental music, integrated mathematics, integrated physics, integrated science, Italian, jazz, journalism, language-AP, Latin, Latin-AP, law, leadership, leadership and service, leadership education training, library research, library science, life management skills, life skills, literary magazine, literature, literature by women, literature-AP, mathematics, mathematics-AP, mechanics of writing, medieval history, mentorship program, microbiology, modern European history, modern European history-AP, music, music history, music performance, music theory, music theory-AP, music-AP, New Testament, nutrition, painting, performing

arts, personal money management, physical education, physical science, physics, physics-AP, piano, poetry, political science, pre-calculus, psychology, psychology-AP, religion, robotics, SAT preparation, SAT/ACT preparation, science, science and technology, sculpture, social studies, sociology, Spanish, Spanish-AP, speech and debate, statistics, statistics-AP, studio art, studio art-AP, theater arts, theology, U.S. government and politics-AP, U.S. history, U.S. history-AP, U.S. literature, visual and performing arts, visual arts, vocal ensemble, vocal music, voice, volleyball, wind instruments, women in literature, women in society, women in the classical world, women in world history, women spirituality and faith, women's health, women's literature, women's studies, world history, world history-AP, world literature, world studies, yearbook.

Graduation Requirements Arts and fine arts (art, music, dance, drama), English, foreign language, mathematics, music, physical education (includes health), religion (includes Bible studies and theology), science, social studies (includes history), technology, community service project, Regents Diploma.

Special Academic Programs 17 Advanced Placement exams for which test preparation is offered; honors section; study at local college for college credit; academic accommodation for the gifted, the musically talented, and the artistically talented; programs in general development for dyslexic students.

College Admission Counseling 248 students graduated in 2014; all went to college, including Adelphi University; Binghamton University, State University of New York; Fordham University; Hunter College of the City University of New York; Pace University; St. John's University.

Student Life Upper grades have uniform requirement, student council. Discipline rests primarily with faculty. Attendance at religious services is required.

Tuition and Aid Day student tuition: $8200. Tuition installment plan (monthly payment plans, quarterly payment plan, tuition in full (yearly)). Tuition reduction for siblings, merit scholarship grants, need-based scholarship grants available. In 2014–15, 50% of upper-school students received aid; total upper-school merit-scholarship money awarded: $530,000. Total amount of financial aid awarded in 2014–15: $615,000.

Admissions Traditional secondary-level entrance grade is 9. For fall 2014, 904 students applied for upper-level admission, 452 were accepted, 172 enrolled. Catholic High School Entrance Examination or school's own exam required. Deadline for receipt of application materials: February 1. Application fee required: $450. Interview recommended.

Athletics Interscholastic: aerobics, aerobics/dance, archery, badminton, basketball, billiards, bowling, cheering, cross-country running, dance, dance team, golf, gymnastics, indoor track, indoor track & field, lacrosse, running, self defense, soccer, softball, swimming and diving, tennis, track and field, volleyball, winter (indoor) track, yoga; intramural: basketball, billiards, fitness, self defense, soccer, yoga. 4 PE instructors, 27 coaches.

Computers Computers are regularly used in career exploration, college planning, English, foreign language, graphic design, history, library skills, literary magazine, mathematics, music, newspaper, science classes. Computer network features include on-campus library services, online commercial services, Internet access, wireless campus network, Internet filtering or blocking technology. Campus intranet and student e-mail accounts are available to students. Students grades are available online. The school has a published electronic and media policy.

Contact Sr. Lorraine O'Neill, CSJ, Administrative Secretary. 718-297-2120 Ext. 228. Fax: 718-739-0037. E-mail: loneill@tmla.org. Website: www.tmla.org

MARYMOUNT HIGH SCHOOL

10643 Sunset Boulevard
Los Angeles, California 90077

Head of School: Ms. Jacqueline Landry

General Information Girls' day college-preparatory, arts, religious studies, and technology school, affiliated with Roman Catholic Church. Grades 9–12. Founded: 1923. Setting: suburban. 5-acre campus. 6 buildings on campus. Approved or accredited by Western Association of Schools and Colleges, Western Catholic Education Association, and California Department of Education. Member of National Association of Independent Schools. Endowment: $5.7 million. Total enrollment: 396. Upper school average class size: 17. Upper school faculty-student ratio: 1:7. There are 170 required school days per year for Upper School students. Upper School students typically attend 5 days per week. The average school day consists of 6 hours and 15 minutes.

Upper School Student Profile Grade 9: 94 students (94 girls); Grade 10: 102 students (102 girls); Grade 11: 100 students (100 girls); Grade 12: 100 students (100 girls). 66% of students are Roman Catholic.

Faculty School total: 51. In upper school: 13 men, 38 women; 42 have advanced degrees.

Subjects Offered Acting, advanced studio art-AP, aerobics, African literature, algebra, American history, American legal systems, American literature, anatomy, art, art history, art-AP, biology, biology-AP, British literature, calculus, calculus-AP, ceramics, chemistry, choir, Christian testament, community service, computer literacy, computer science, contemporary issues, dance, death and loss, design, drama, drawing, ecology, economics, English, English literature, environmental science, environmental science-AP, ethics, fencing, film, fine arts, French, French-AP, gender and religion, geography, geometry, government/civics, Hebrew scripture, human development, Japanese literature, jazz ensemble, journalism, language and composition, literary magazine, literature, literature-AP, music, musical productions, oceanography, painting, peace studies, performing arts, photography, physical education, physics, physiology, pre-calculus, printmaking, psychology, religion, religious studies, robotics, science; self-defense, service learning/internship, social justice, social studies, softball, Spanish, Spanish language-AP, Spanish literature-AP, speech, swimming, theology, trigonometry, U.S. government and politics-AP, U.S. history, U.S. history-AP, vocal music, volleyball, women's studies, world religions, writing.

Graduation Requirements Arts and fine arts (art, music, dance, drama), English, foreign language, mathematics, performing arts, physical education (includes health), religion (includes Bible studies and theology), science, social studies (includes history).

Special Academic Programs 18 Advanced Placement exams for which test preparation is offered; honors section; independent study.

College Admission Counseling 92 students graduated in 2015; 91 went to college, including Boston College; Brown University; Santa Clara University; University of California, Berkeley; University of Colorado Boulder; Yale University. Other: 1 had other specific plans. Mean SAT critical reading: 629, mean SAT math: 620, mean SAT writing: 672, mean combined SAT: 1921, mean composite ACT: 27.

Student Life Upper grades have uniform requirement, student council, honor system. Discipline rests equally with students and faculty. Attendance at religious services is required.

Summer Programs Remediation, enrichment, advancement, sports, art/fine arts, computer instruction programs offered; session focuses on enrichment, advancement; held on campus; accepts girls; open to students from other schools. 100 students usually enrolled. 2016 schedule: June 23 to July 25. Application deadline: June 2.

Tuition and Aid Day student tuition: $28,900. Tuition installment plan (FACTS Tuition Payment Plan). Merit scholarship grants, need-based scholarship grants available. In 2015–16, 25% of upper-school students received aid; total upper-school merit-scholarship money awarded: $11,000. Total amount of financial aid awarded in 2015–16: $1,300,000.

Admissions Traditional secondary-level entrance grade is 9. Deadline for receipt of application materials: January 5. Application fee required: $100. On-campus interview required.

Athletics Interscholastic: basketball, cross-country running, equestrian sports, golf, soccer, softball, swimming and diving, tennis, track and field, volleyball, water polo; intramural: aerobics, aerobics/dance, archery, crew, dance, fitness, physical fitness, self defense, strength & conditioning. 1 PE instructor, 31 coaches, 1 athletic trainer.

Computers Computers are regularly used in all academic classes. Computer network features include on-campus library services, online commercial services, Internet access, wireless campus network, Internet filtering or blocking technology, one-to-one student laptop program, access to UCLA Library, Loyola Marymount University Library, 14 independent high school libraries. Campus intranet, student e-mail accounts, and computer access in designated common areas are available to students. Students grades are available online. The school has a published electronic and media policy.

Contact Ms. Patti Lemlein, Director of Admission. 310-472-1205 Ext. 220. Fax: 310-440-4316. E-mail: plemlein@mhs-la.org. Website: www.mhs-la.org

MARYMOUNT INTERNATIONAL SCHOOL

Via di Villa Lauchli 180
Rome 00191, Italy
Head of School: Ms. Maria Castelluccio

General Information Coeducational day college-preparatory school, affiliated with Roman Catholic Church. Grades PK–12. Founded: 1946. Setting: suburban. 16-acre campus. 3 buildings on campus. Approved or accredited by New England Association of Schools and Colleges. Member of European Council of International Schools. Language of instruction: English. Total enrollment: 617. Upper school average class size: 18. Upper school faculty-student ratio: 1:15. There are 170 required school days per year for Upper School students. Upper School students typically attend 5 days per week. The average school day consists of 6 hours and 45 minutes.

Upper School Student Profile Grade 9: 50 students (24 boys, 26 girls); Grade 10: 43 students (25 boys, 18 girls); Grade 11: 53 students (29 boys, 24 girls); Grade 12: 54 students (20 boys, 34 girls). 74% of students are Roman Catholic.

Faculty School total: 90. In upper school: 13 men, 34 women; 40 have advanced degrees.

Subjects Offered Algebra, American history, American literature, art, art history, biology, calculus, ceramics, chemistry, computer science, current events, drama, English, English literature, environmental science, ESL, European history, fine arts, French, geography, geometry, health, history, International Baccalaureate courses, international relations, Italian, mathematics, music, photography, physical education, physics, pre-calculus, psychology, religious education, science, social studies, Spanish, study skills, theater arts, theory of knowledge, trigonometry, world history.

Graduation Requirements Arts and fine arts (art, music, dance, drama), English, foreign language, mathematics, physical education (includes health), religion (includes Bible studies and theology), science, social studies (includes history).

Special Academic Programs International Baccalaureate program; ESL (36 students enrolled).

College Admission Counseling 51 students graduated in 2014; 49 went to college, including New York University; Syracuse University; University of Colorado Boulder; University of Southern California; University of Virginia. Other: 2 had other specific

plans. Median SAT critical reading: 500, median SAT math: 500, median SAT writing: 520. 15% scored over 600 on SAT critical reading, 15% scored over 600 on SAT math, 15% scored over 600 on SAT writing.

Student Life Upper grades have specified standards of dress, student council, honor system. Discipline rests primarily with faculty. Attendance at religious services is required.

Tuition and Aid Day student tuition: €19,000.

Admissions Traditional secondary-level entrance grade is 9. For fall 2014, 57 students applied for upper-level admission, 42 were accepted, 32 enrolled. English proficiency or writing sample required. Deadline for receipt of application materials: none. Application fee required: €350. On-campus interview recommended.

Athletics Interscholastic: basketball (boys, girls), cheering (g), cross-country running (b,g), soccer (b,g), tennis (b,g), track and field (b,g), volleyball (b,g). 2 PE instructors, 9 coaches.

Computers Computers are regularly used in graphic arts classes. Computer network features include on-campus library services, Internet access, wireless campus network, Internet filtering or blocking technology, one-to-one laptop program in the middle school. Student e-mail accounts are available to students.

Contact Ms. Deborah Woods, Admissions Director. 39-063629101 Ext. 212. Fax: 39-0636301738. E-mail: admissions@marymountrome.org.
Website: www.marymountrome.org

MARYMOUNT SCHOOL OF NEW YORK

1026 Fifth Avenue
New York, New York 10028
Head of School: Mrs. Concepcion Alvar, EdD

General Information Coeducational day (boys' only in lower grades) college-preparatory, arts, religious studies, and technology school, affiliated with Roman Catholic Church. Boys grades N–PK, girls grades N–12. Founded: 1926. Setting: urban. 3 buildings on campus. Approved or accredited by New York State Association of Independent Schools. Member of National Association of Independent Schools. Endowment: $8 million. Total enrollment: 744. Upper school average class size: 15. Upper school faculty-student ratio: 1:5. There are 183 required school days per year for Upper School students. Upper School students typically attend 5 days per week. The average school day consists of 7 hours and 30 minutes.

Upper School Student Profile Grade 9: 62 students (62 girls); Grade 10: 56 students (56 girls); Grade 11: 55 students (55 girls); Grade 12: 559 students (559 girls). 67% of students are Roman Catholic.

Faculty School total: 131. In upper school: 12 men, 32 women; 32 have advanced degrees.

Subjects Offered Advanced studio art-AP, algebra, American history, American history-AP, American literature, art, art history, art-AP, astronomy, bell choir, Bible studies, biology, biology-AP, British literature-AP, calculus, chemistry, chemistry-AP, chorus, community service, computer science, computer science-AP, contemporary history, dance, digital applications, DNA research, economics, English, English literature, English literature-AP, ethics, European history, European history-AP, fine arts, fitness, French, French literature-AP, French-AP, geometry, Greek, health, information design technology, integrated technology fundamentals, Latin, Latin-AP, mathematics, music, music history, physical education, physics, political science, religion, science, Spanish, speech, statistics, studio art, studio art-AP, technological applications, technology, theater history, trigonometry, world history, world literature, writing.

Graduation Requirements Arts and fine arts (art, music, dance, drama), computer science, English, foreign language, history, mathematics, physical education (includes health), religion (includes Bible studies and theology), science, speech, senior internships, senior seminars, Class XII retreat. Community service is required.

Special Academic Programs Advanced Placement exam preparation; honors section; study abroad; academic accommodation for the gifted.

College Admission Counseling 52 students graduated in 2015; all went to college, including Boston University; Cornell University; Fordham University; New York University; Princeton University; Villanova University. Mean SAT critical reading: 656, mean SAT math: 625, mean SAT writing: 670.

Student Life Upper grades have uniform requirement, student council, honor system. Discipline rests primarily with faculty. Attendance at religious services is required.

Summer Programs Enrichment, advancement, sports programs offered; session focuses on internships, preseason sports, community service; held both on and off campus; held at copntingent on internship and community service locations; accepts girls; not open to students from other schools. 60 students usually enrolled. 2016 schedule: June 14 to August 31.

Tuition and Aid Day student tuition: $44,630. Tuition installment plan (Key Tuition Payment Plan, individually arranged payment plans). Need-based scholarship grants available. In 2015–16, 23% of upper-school students received aid. Total amount of financial aid awarded in 2015–16: $3,000,000.

Admissions Traditional secondary-level entrance grade is 9. ISEE or SSAT required. Deadline for receipt of application materials: November 30. Application fee required: $70. On-campus interview required.

Athletics Interscholastic: aerobics, badminton, basketball, bicycling, cross-country running, dance, fencing, field hockey, fitness, jogging, lacrosse, modern dance, physical fitness, soccer, softball, swimming and diving, tennis, track and field, volleyball, yoga; intramural: aerobics, badminton, basketball, bicycling, cross-country running, dance, fitness, jogging, lacrosse, martial arts, modern dance, outdoor adventure, physical fitness, soccer, softball, volleyball, yoga. 3 PE instructors, 18 coaches, 1 athletic trainer.

Computers Computers are regularly used in all classes. Computer network features include on-campus library services, online commercial services, Internet access, wireless campus network, Internet filtering or blocking technology. Campus intranet, student e-mail accounts, and computer access in designated common areas are available to students. Students grades are available online. The school has a published electronic and media policy.

Contact Mrs. Lillian Issa, Director of Admissions. 212-744-4486 Ext. 8152. Fax: 212-744-0716. E-mail: lissa@marymountnyc.org. Website: www.marymountnyc.org

See Display below and Close-Up on page 606.

MASSANUTTEN MILITARY ACADEMY

614 South Main Street
Woodstock, Virginia 22664

Head of School: Dr. David Skipper

General Information Coeducational boarding and day college-preparatory, arts, and military school, affiliated with Christian faith. Grades 6–PG. Founded: 1899. Setting: small town. Nearest major city is Washington, DC. Students are housed in single-sex dormitories. 40-acre campus. 11 buildings on campus. Approved or accredited by Southern Association of Colleges and Schools, The Association of Boarding Schools, Virginia Association of Independent Schools, and Virginia Department of Education. Endowment: $13 million. Total enrollment: 99. Upper school average class size: 10. Upper school faculty-student ratio: 1:8.

Upper School Student Profile Grade 7: 3 students (1 boy, 2 girls); Grade 8: 6 students (3 boys, 3 girls); Grade 9: 17 students (14 boys, 3 girls); Grade 10: 24 students (16 boys, 8 girls); Grade 11: 21 students (12 boys, 9 girls); Grade 12: 26 students (16 boys, 10 girls); Postgraduate: 2 students (2 boys). 99% of students are boarding students. 15% are state residents. 17 states are represented in upper school student body. 20% are international students. International students from Canada, China, Egypt, Kuwait, Nigeria, and Saudi Arabia; 2 other countries represented in student body.

Faculty School total: 27. In upper school: 19 men, 8 women; 8 have advanced degrees; 6 reside on campus.

Subjects Offered Algebra, American history, American literature, art, art appreciation, band, biology, calculus, character education, chemistry, computer applications, earth science, English, English literature, ESL, French, geometry, government/civics, grammar, health, history, Internet research, intro to computers, introduction to literature, JROTC, leadership, mathematics, music, news writing,

physical education, physical science, physics, pre-calculus, Russian, science, social sciences, social studies, Spanish, U.S. history, world history, world literature.

Graduation Requirements Arts and fine arts (art, music, dance, drama), computer applications, English, foreign language, JROTC, mathematics, physical education (includes health), science, social studies (includes history), one year of JROTC for each year enrolled.

Special Academic Programs Advanced Placement exam preparation; independent study; study at local college for college credit; remedial reading and/or remedial writing; remedial math; ESL.

College Admission Counseling 24 students graduated in 2015; all went to college, including George Mason University; Mary Baldwin College; Radford University; The Citadel, The Military College of South Carolina; University of Georgia; Virginia Polytechnic Institute and State University.

Student Life Upper grades have uniform requirement, student council, honor system. Discipline rests equally with students and faculty.

Summer Programs Remediation, advancement, ESL, sports, art/fine arts, computer instruction programs offered; session focuses on academics, JROTC program, leadership; held on campus; accepts boys and girls; open to students from other schools. 90 students usually enrolled. 2016 schedule: July 1 to July 30. Application deadline: June 15.

Tuition and Aid Day student tuition: $8200; 7-day tuition and room/board: $32,900. Tuition installment plan (FACTS Tuition Payment Plan, monthly payment plans, individually arranged payment plans). Tuition reduction for siblings, merit scholarship grants, need-based scholarship grants, need-based loans, middle-income loans, USS Education Loan Program, PLATO Loans, legacy discounts available.

Admissions Traditional secondary-level entrance grade is 10. For fall 2015, 140 students applied for upper-level admission, 110 were accepted, 60 enrolled. Deadline for receipt of application materials: none. Application fee required: $50. Interview required.

Athletics Interscholastic: baseball (boys), basketball (b,g), cross-country running (b,g), fitness (b,g), football (b), independent competitive sports (b,g), softball (g), strength & conditioning (b), track and field (b,g), volleyball (g); coed interscholastic: drill team, JROTC drill, lacrosse, marksmanship, pistol, riflery, soccer, tennis, wrestling; coed intramural: billiards, canoeing/kayaking, cheering, cross-country running, drill team, equestrian sports, kickball, marksmanship, outdoor activities, outdoor adventure, outdoor education, outdoor recreation, outdoor skills, outdoors, paddle tennis, physical fitness, physical training, pistol, power lifting, rafting, rappelling, riflery, running, skiing (downhill), snowboarding, snowshoeing, soccer, strength & conditioning, table tennis, tennis, walking, weight lifting, weight training, whiffle ball. 1 PE instructor, 5 coaches, 1 athletic trainer.

Computers Computers are regularly used in all academic, business applications, business skills, business studies, computer applications, journalism, JROTC, SAT

preparation, yearbook classes. Computer network features include on-campus library services, Internet access, wireless campus network, Internet filtering or blocking technology. Computer access in designated common areas is available to students. Students grades are available online. The school has a published electronic and media policy.

Contact Mr. Murali Sinnathamby, Director of Admissions. 877-466-6222. Fax: 540-459-5421. E-mail: admissions@militaryschool.com. Website: www.militaryschool.com

THE MASTERS SCHOOL

49 Clinton Avenue
Dobbs Ferry, New York 10522

Head of School: Laura Danforth

General Information Coeducational boarding and day college-preparatory, arts, and technology school. Boarding grades 9–12, day grades 5 12. Founded: 1877. Setting: suburban. Nearest major city is New York. Students are housed in single-sex dormitories. 100-acre campus. 15 buildings on campus. Approved or accredited by Middle States Association of Colleges and Schools, The Association of Boarding Schools, and New York Department of Education. Member of National Association of Independent Schools and Secondary School Admission Test Board. Endowment: $45 million. Total enrollment: 665. Upper school average class size: 14. Upper school faculty-student ratio: 1:7. Upper School students typically attend 5 days per week. The average school day consists of 6 hours.

Upper School Student Profile Grade 9: 113 students (55 boys, 58 girls); Grade 10: 127 students (65 boys, 62 girls); Grade 11: 130 students (65 boys, 65 girls); Grade 12: 120 students (60 boys, 60 girls). 40% of students are boarding students. 50% are state residents. 20 states are represented in upper school student body. 18% are international students. International students from Canada, China, Germany, Republic of Korea, Russian Federation, and Switzerland; 29 other countries represented in student body.

Faculty School total: 99. In upper school: 45 men, 50 women; 76 have advanced degrees; 60 reside on campus.

Subjects Offered Acting, algebra, American history, American literature, art history, biology, biology-AP, calculus, calculus-AP, ceramics, chemistry, chemistry-AP, computer math, computer programming, computer science, creative writing, dance, drama, driver education, earth science, electronics, English, English language-AP, English literature, English literature-AP, environmental science, ESL, ethics, European history, European history-AP, expository writing, fine arts, French, French language-AP, French literature-AP, geography, geometry, grammar, health, health and wellness, health education, jazz, jazz band, journalism, Latin, Latin-AP, mathematics, meteorology, music, music theory-AP, performing arts, photography, physical education, physics, physics-AP, pre-calculus, religion, science, senior thesis, social studies, Spanish, Spanish language-AP, Spanish literature-AP, speech, statistics, statistics-AP, studio art, studio art-AP, theater, trigonometry, U.S. history, U.S. history-AP, world history, world literature, world religions, writing, yearbook, yoga.

Graduation Requirements Arts and fine arts (art, music, dance, drama), computer science, English, foreign language, health, mathematics, physical education (includes health), public speaking, science, U.S. history, world history, world religions.

Special Academic Programs 19 Advanced Placement exams for which test preparation is offered; honors section; independent study; term-away projects; study at local college for college credit; study abroad; academic accommodation for the gifted, the musically talented, and the artistically talented; ESL (18 students enrolled).

College Admission Counseling 112 students graduated in 2015; all went to college, including Boston University; Cornell University; Middlebury College; New York University; University of Chicago; Williams College. Mean SAT critical reading: 660, mean SAT math: 660, mean SAT writing: 680, mean combined SAT: 2000. 61% scored over 600 on SAT critical reading, 57% scored over 600 on SAT math, 68% scored over 600 on SAT writing, 58% scored over 1800 on combined SAT.

Student Life Upper grades have specified standards of dress, student council, honor system. Discipline rests equally with students and faculty.

Summer Programs Enrichment, sports, art/fine arts, rigorous outdoor training programs offered; session focuses on Various; held on campus; accepts boys and girls; open to students from other schools.

Tuition and Aid Day student tuition: $41,110; 7-day tuition and room/board: $57,810. Tuition installment plan (Insured Tuition Payment Plan, monthly payment plans, individually arranged payment plans). Need-based scholarship grants available. In 2015–16, 25% of upper-school students received aid. Total amount of financial aid awarded in 2015–16: $50,400,000.

Admissions Traditional secondary-level entrance grade is 9. For fall 2015, 610 students applied for upper-level admission, 215 were accepted, 102 enrolled. ISEE, SSAT or TOEFL required. Deadline for receipt of application materials: February 1. Application fee required: $75. Interview required.

Athletics Interscholastic: baseball (boys), basketball (b,g), cross-country running (b,g), fencing (b,g), field hockey (g), lacrosse (b,g), soccer (b,g), softball (g), squash (b,g), tennis (b,g), volleyball (g); intramural: fencing (b,g), squash (b,g), swimming and diving (b,g); coed interscholastic: dance, dance team, golf, indoor track, swimming and diving, track and field; coed intramural: aerobics, aerobics/dance, aerobics/Nautilus, combined training, dance squad, dance team, fitness, Frisbee, martial arts, modern dance, outdoor activities, physical fitness, physical training, strength & conditioning,

ultimate Frisbee, weight lifting, weight training, yoga. 2 PE instructors, 13 coaches, 1 athletic trainer.

Computers Computers are regularly used in computer applications, English, foreign language, graphic arts, graphic design, history, mathematics, newspaper, photography, programming, publications, science, senior seminar, study skills, video film production, Web site design, writing, yearbook classes. Computer network features include on-campus library services, online commercial services, Internet access, wireless campus network, Internet filtering or blocking technology. Campus intranet, student e-mail accounts, and computer access in designated common areas are available to students. The school has a published electronic and media policy.

Contact Office of Admission. 914-479-6420. Fax: 914-693-7295. E-mail: admission@mastersny.org. Website: www.mastersny.org

MATER DEI HIGH SCHOOL

900 North Mater Dei Drive
Breese, Illinois 62230

Head of School: Mr. Dennis Litteken Sr.

General Information College-preparatory, arts, business, vocational, and technology school, affiliated with Roman Catholic Church. Founded: 1954. Setting: small town. Nearest major city is St. Louis, MO. 55-acre campus. 1 building on campus. Approved or accredited by National Christian School Association, North Central Association of Colleges and Schools, and Illinois Department of Education. Endowment: $2 million. Total enrollment: 414. Upper school average class size: 18. Upper school faculty-student ratio: 1:18. There are 178 required school days per year for Upper School students. Upper School students typically attend 5 days per week. The average school day consists of 6 hours and 35 minutes.

Upper School Student Profile Grade 9: 93 students (44 boys, 49 girls); Grade 10: 90 students (47 boys, 43 girls); Grade 11: 119 students (58 boys, 61 girls); Grade 12: 112 students (58 boys, 54 girls). 99% of students are Roman Catholic.

Faculty School total: 43. In upper school: 18 men, 21 women; 22 have advanced degrees.

Graduation Requirements Algebra.

Special Academic Programs Advanced Placement exam preparation; honors section; academic accommodation for the gifted; remedial reading and/or remedial writing; remedial math.

College Admission Counseling 117 students graduated in 2015; 115 went to college, including Albion College. Other: 1 went to work, 1 entered military service. Median composite ACT: 24.

Student Life Upper grades have uniform requirement, student council, honor system. Discipline rests primarily with faculty. Attendance at religious services is required.

Tuition and Aid Day student tuition: $5000. Tuition installment plan (SMART Tuition Payment Plan, monthly payment plans). Tuition reduction for siblings, need-based scholarship grants available. In 2015–16, 51% of upper-school students received aid. Total amount of financial aid awarded in 2015–16: $120,000.

Admissions Traditional secondary-level entrance grade is 9. For fall 2015, 95 students applied for upper-level admission, 93 were accepted, 93 enrolled. Explore required. Deadline for receipt of application materials: February 27. Application fee required: $50.

Athletics Interscholastic: baseball (boys), basketball (b), cheering (g), dance team (g), football (b), golf (b,g), volleyball (g), wrestling (b); intramural: weight lifting (b), weight training (b,g); coed interscholastic: bowling, fishing. 2 PE instructors, 15 coaches, 1 athletic trainer.

Computers Computer network features include on-campus library services, Internet access, wireless campus network, Internet filtering or blocking technology. Campus intranet and student e-mail accounts are available to students. Students grades are available online. The school has a published electronic and media policy.

Contact Mrs. Donna Goetz, Guidance Director. 618-526-7216. Fax: 618-526-8310. E-mail: dgoetz@materdeiknights.org. Website: www.materdeiknights.org

MATIGNON HIGH SCHOOL

One Matignon Road
Cambridge, Massachusetts 02140

Head of School: Mr. Timothy M. Welsh

General Information Coeducational day college-preparatory, arts, business, religious studies, technology, and STEM school, affiliated with Roman Catholic Church. Grades 9–12. Founded: 1945. Setting: suburban. Nearest major city is Boston. 10-acre campus. 3 buildings on campus. Approved or accredited by National Catholic Education Association, New England Association of Schools and Colleges, and Massachusetts Department of Education. Endowment: $150,000. Total enrollment: 462. Upper school average class size: 19. Upper school faculty-student ratio: 1:18. There are 180 required school days per year for Upper School students. Upper School students typically attend 5 days per week. The average school day consists of 7 hours.

Upper School Student Profile Grade 9: 119 students (45 boys, 74 girls); Grade 10: 115 students (57 boys, 58 girls); Grade 11: 107 students (41 boys, 66 girls); Grade 12: 121 students (54 boys, 67 girls). 70% of students are Roman Catholic.

Faculty School total: 33. In upper school: 14 men, 19 women; 25 have advanced degrees.

Subjects Offered 3-dimensional art, 3-dimensional design, accounting, adolescent issues, Advanced Placement courses, algebra, American history, American literature, anatomy and physiology, art, art history, Bible studies, biology, calculus, chemistry, community service, computer science, drawing and design, economics, English, English literature, environmental science, fine arts, French, geometry, government/civics, grammar, health, history, Latin, law, mathematics, physical education, physics, psychology, religion, science, social sciences, social studies, Spanish, theology, trigonometry, world history, writing.

Graduation Requirements 20th century history, accounting, Advanced Placement courses, algebra, American history, anatomy and physiology, arts and fine arts (art, music, dance, drama), chemistry, computer science, English-AP, French, French-AP, geometry, health education, honors algebra, honors English, honors geometry, honors world history, Latin, law, physical education (includes health), psychology, psychology-AP, religious studies, SAT preparation, senior internship, Spanish, Spanish-AP, U.S. history, U.S. history-AP, world cultures, world history, Christian service, 45 hours of community service (before junior year).

Special Academic Programs Advanced Placement exam preparation; honors section; independent study; study at local college for college credit; study abroad; ESL (38 students enrolled).

College Admission Counseling 109 students graduated in 2015; 105 went to college, including Boston University; Merrimack College; Northeastern University; Stonehill College; University of Massachusetts Amherst; University of Massachusetts Boston. Other: 1 went to work, 1 entered military service, 2 entered a postgraduate year. Mean SAT critical reading: 430, mean SAT math: 450, mean SAT writing: 440, mean combined SAT: 1320. 21% scored over 600 on SAT critical reading, 23% scored over 600 on SAT math, 14% scored over 600 on SAT writing, 20% scored over 1800 on combined SAT.

Student Life Upper grades have uniform requirement, student council, honor system. Discipline rests primarily with faculty. Attendance at religious services is required.

Summer Programs Remediation, enrichment programs offered; session focuses on remediation/makeup and enrichment; held on campus; accepts boys and girls; open to students from other schools. 50 students usually enrolled. 2016 schedule: June 20 to July 15. Application deadline: none.

Tuition and Aid Day student tuition: $9650. Tuition installment plan (FACTS Tuition Payment Plan, monthly payment plans). Merit scholarship grants, need-based scholarship grants available. In 2015–16, 50% of upper-school students received aid; total upper-school merit-scholarship money awarded: $475,000. Total amount of financial aid awarded in 2015–16: $600,000.

Admissions Traditional secondary-level entrance grade is 9. For fall 2015, 435 students applied for upper-level admission, 340 were accepted, 119 enrolled. Catholic High School Entrance Examination, SSAT or TOEFL or SLEP required. Deadline for receipt of application materials: none. No application fee required. On-campus interview recommended.

Athletics Interscholastic: baseball (boys), basketball (b,g), cheering (g), cross-country running (b,g), football (b), ice hockey (b,g), lacrosse (b,g), soccer (b,g), softball (g), swimming and diving (b,g), tennis (b,g), track and field (b,g), volleyball (g); intramural: aerobics/dance (b,g), dance (b,g), dance squad (b,g), dance team (b,g), Frisbee (b,g), physical training (b,g), strength & conditioning (b,g), weight lifting (b,g), weight training (b,g); coed interscholastic: golf; coed intramural: table tennis, yoga. 1 PE instructor, 20 coaches, 1 athletic trainer.

Computers Computers are regularly used in all academic classes. Computer network features include on-campus library services, Internet access, wireless campus network, Internet filtering or blocking technology, all academic homework is provided online. Student e-mail accounts and computer access in designated common areas are available to students. Students grades are available online. The school has a published electronic and media policy.

Contact Mr. Joseph A. DiSarcina, Principal. 617-876-1212 Ext. 14. Fax: 617-661-3905. E-mail: jdisarcina@matignon.org. Website: www.matignon.org

MAUI PREPARATORY ACADEMY

5095 Napilihau Street, #109B
PMB #186
Lahaina, Hawaii 96761

Head of School: Dr. Jonathan L. Silver

General Information Coeducational boarding and day college-preparatory, arts, technology, and project-based 21st Century Skills school. Boarding grades 9–12, day grades PK–12. Founded: 2005. Setting: small town. Students are housed in coed dormitories. 22-acre campus. 7 buildings on campus. Approved or accredited by Western Association of Schools and Colleges and Hawaii Department of Education. Member of National Association of Independent Schools. Total enrollment: 187. Upper school average class size: 15. Upper school faculty-student ratio: 1:4. There are 177 required school days per year for Upper School students. Upper School students typically attend 5 days per week. The average school day consists of 7 hours.

Upper School Student Profile Grade 6: 17 students (7 boys, 10 girls); Grade 7: 12 students (8 boys, 4 girls); Grade 8: 17 students (4 boys, 13 girls); Grade 9: 10 students (4 boys, 6 girls); Grade 10: 14 students (6 boys, 8 girls); Grade 11: 26 students (11 boys, 15 girls); Grade 12: 12 students (6 boys, 6 girls). 15% of students are boarding students. 75% are state residents. 2 states are represented in upper school student body. 25% are international students. International students from Brazil, Canada, China, France, Germany, and Japan.

Faculty School total: 22. In upper school: 7 men, 7 women; 10 have advanced degrees; 2 reside on campus.

Subjects Offered Art, biology, calculus, chemistry, English, environmental science, foreign language, health, history, marine science, mathematics, physics, social studies, technology.

Graduation Requirements 1 1/2 elective credits, algebra, art, athletics, biology, calculus-AP, chemistry, college planning, English, foreign language, geometry, physics-AP, science project, 25 hours of community service per year, two varsity teams per year.

Special Academic Programs Advanced Placement exam preparation; independent study; study at local college for college credit; ESL (8 students enrolled).

College Admission Counseling 11 students graduated in 2015; 8 went to college, including Chapman University; Lehigh University; The George Washington University; University of Hawaii at Manoa; University of San Diego; William Paterson University of New Jersey. Other: 3 went to work. Median SAT critical reading: 520, median SAT math: 510, median SAT writing: 490, median combined SAT: 1510. 11% scored over 600 on SAT critical reading, 11% scored over 600 on SAT math, 11% scored over 600 on SAT writing, 11% scored over 1800 on combined SAT.

Student Life Upper grades have uniform requirement, student council, honor system. Discipline rests primarily with faculty.

Summer Programs Enrichment, ESL, sports, rigorous outdoor training programs offered; session focuses on tennis, golf, ocean sports, Hawaiiana; held both on and off campus; held at Tennis Courts, Golf Cours, Ocean; accepts boys and girls; open to students from other schools. 2016 schedule: June 15 to July 31. Application deadline: none.

Tuition and Aid Day student tuition: $17,350; 7-day tuition and room/board: $32,400. Tuition installment plan (Insured Tuition Payment Plan, monthly payment plans, TADS Tuition Payment Plan). Tuition reduction for siblings, merit scholarship grants, need-based scholarship grants available. In 2015–16, 40% of upper-school students received aid; total upper-school merit-scholarship money awarded: $212,801. Total amount of financial aid awarded in 2015–16: $261,776.

Admissions Traditional secondary-level entrance grade is 9. For fall 2015, 24 students applied for upper-level admission, 21 were accepted, 13 enrolled. CTP, ERB Mathematics and TOEFL required. Deadline for receipt of application materials: March 30. Application fee required: $125. Interview required.

Athletics Interscholastic: aquatics (boys, girls), canoeing/kayaking (b,g), cross-country running (b,g), diving (b,g), golf (b,g), independent competitive sports (b,g), ocean paddling (b,g), surfing (b,g), swimming and diving (b,g), tennis (b,g), track and field (b,g), volleyball (g); intramural: basketball (b,g), surfing (b,g); coed interscholastic: ocean paddling; coed intramural: basketball, cross-country running, flag football, golf, surfing. 1 PE instructor, 9 coaches.

Computers Computers are regularly used in all classes. Computer network features include on-campus library services, Internet access, wireless campus network. Campus intranet and student e-mail accounts are available to students. Students grades are available online. The school has a published electronic and media policy.

Contact Mrs. Cathi Minami, Director of Advancement. 808-665-9966. Fax: 808-665-1075. E-mail: cminami@mauiprep.org. Website: www.mauiprep.org

MAUMEE VALLEY COUNTRY DAY SCHOOL

1715 South Reynolds Road
Toledo, Ohio 43614-1499

Head of School: Mr. Gary Boehm

General Information Coeducational boarding and day college-preparatory, arts, and global studies school. Boarding grades 9–12, day grades P3–12. Founded: 1884. Setting: suburban. Students are housed in coed dormitories. 72-acre campus. 4 buildings on campus. Approved or accredited by Independent Schools Association of the Central States, Ohio Association of Independent Schools, The Association of Boarding Schools, and Ohio Department of Education. Member of National Association of Independent Schools. Endowment: $10.5 million. Total enrollment: 532. Upper school average class size: 14. Upper school faculty-student ratio: 1:9. Upper School students typically attend 5 days per week. The average school day consists of 7 hours.

Upper School Student Profile Grade 9: 53 students (25 boys, 28 girls); Grade 10: 58 students (28 boys, 30 girls); Grade 11: 43 students (28 boys, 15 girls); Grade 12: 50 students (24 boys, 26 girls). 20% of students are boarding students. 80% are state residents. 1 state is represented in upper school student body. 20% are international students. International students from China, Germany, Switzerland, and Viet Nam; 4 other countries represented in student body.

Faculty School total: 62. In upper school: 12 men, 10 women; 21 have advanced degrees.

Subjects Offered Algebra, American government, American history, anthropology, art, biology, biology-AP, calculus-AP, chemistry, Chinese, choir, computer graphics, computer science, creative writing, design, drama, earth science, ecology, English, environmental science, European history, expository writing, fine arts, geology, geometry, government/civics, grammar, health, history, human development, humanities, mathematics, microbiology, music, physical education, physics, science, social studies, Spanish, Spanish-AP, speech, statistics, statistics-AP, theater, trigonometry, women's studies, world history.

Graduation Requirements American government, arts and fine arts (art, music, dance, drama), English, foreign language, mathematics, physical education (includes health), science, social studies (includes history). Community service is required.

Special Academic Programs Advanced Placement exam preparation; honors section; independent study; term-away projects; study at local college for college credit; domestic exchange program (with The Athenian School, The Network Program Schools); study abroad; academic accommodation for the gifted, the musically talented, and the artistically talented; ESL (35 students enrolled).

College Admission Counseling 54 students graduated in 2015; all went to college, including Bowling Green State University; Case Western Reserve University; Ohio Wesleyan University; The Ohio State University; The University of Toledo; University of Michigan. Mean SAT critical reading: 634, mean SAT math: 632, mean SAT writing: 621, mean combined SAT: 1887, mean composite ACT: 29. 50% scored over 600 on SAT critical reading, 50% scored over 600 on SAT math.

Student Life Upper grades have specified standards of dress, student council, honor system. Discipline rests equally with students and faculty.

Summer Programs Enrichment, ESL, sports, art/fine arts, computer instruction programs offered; session focuses on day camp, sports camps, ESL camp; held on campus; accepts boys and girls; open to students from other schools. 300 students usually enrolled. 2016 schedule: June 20 to August 12. Application deadline: June 3.

Tuition and Aid Day student tuition: $18,175–$19,175; 7-day tuition and room/board: $39,500. Tuition installment plan (FACTS Tuition Payment Plan, monthly payment plans, individually arranged payment plans). Merit scholarship grants, need-based scholarship grants available. In 2015–16, 50% of upper-school students received aid; total upper-school merit-scholarship money awarded: $136,000. Total amount of financial aid awarded in 2015–16: $454,900.

Admissions Traditional secondary-level entrance grade is 9. For fall 2015, 99 students applied for upper-level admission, 52 were accepted, 33 enrolled. OLSAT, ERB, Otis-Lennon and 2 sections of ERB, SSAT, TOEFL or writing sample required. Deadline for receipt of application materials: none. Application fee required: $50. Interview required.

Athletics Interscholastic: baseball (boys), basketball (b,g), cheering (b,g), cross-country running (b,g), field hockey (g), golf (b,g), lacrosse (g), soccer (b,g), tennis (b,g), track and field (b,g); intramural: indoor soccer (g), lacrosse (g); coed intramural: strength & conditioning, weight training. 3 PE instructors, 10 coaches, 1 athletic trainer.

Computers Computers are regularly used in English, foreign language, graphic design, history, information technology, library skills, literary magazine, mathematics, music, newspaper, science, yearbook classes. Computer network features include on-campus library services, online commercial services, Internet access, wireless campus network, Internet filtering or blocking technology. Student e-mail accounts are available to students. Students grades are available online. The school has a published electronic and media policy.

Contact Sarah Bigenho, Assistant Director of Admission Operations. 419-381-1313 Ext. 105. Fax: 419-381-9941. E-mail: sbigenho@mvcds.org. Website: www.mvcds.org

MAUR HILL-MOUNT ACADEMY

1000 Green Street
Atchison, Kansas 66002

Head of School: Mr. Phil Baniewicz

General Information Coeducational boarding and day college-preparatory, arts, religious studies, bilingual studies, and English as a Second language school, affiliated with Roman Catholic Church. Grades 9–12. Founded: 1863. Setting: small town. Nearest major city is Kansas City, MO. Students are housed in single-sex dormitories. 90-acre campus. 7 buildings on campus. Approved or accredited by National Catholic Education Association, North Central Association of Colleges and Schools, The Association of Boarding Schools, and Kansas Department of Education. Member of Secondary School Admission Test Board. Total enrollment: 195. Upper school average class size: 17. Upper school faculty-student ratio: 1:9. There are 182 required school days per year for Upper School students. Upper School students typically attend 5 days per week. The average school day consists of 6 hours and 30 minutes.

Upper School Student Profile Grade 9: 50 students (26 boys, 24 girls); Grade 10: 53 students (27 boys, 26 girls); Grade 11: 52 students (27 boys, 25 girls); Grade 12: 50 students (24 boys, 26 girls). 40% of students are boarding students. 50% are state residents. 9 states are represented in upper school student body. 30% are international students. International students from China, Mexico, Nigeria, Republic of Korea, Spain, and Viet Nam; 11 other countries represented in student body. 60% of students are Roman Catholic.

Faculty School total: 21. In upper school: 13 men, 8 women; 11 have advanced degrees; 3 reside on campus.

Subjects Offered Algebra, American history, American literature, anatomy, art, Bible studies, biology, calculus, chemistry, computer science, drama, economics, English, English literature, ESL, fine arts, geography, geometry, government/civics, grammar, health, history, journalism, mathematics, music, photography, physical education, physics, physiology, psychology, religion, science, social sciences, social studies, sociology, Spanish, speech, theater, theology, trigonometry, typing, world history, world literature, writing.

Graduation Requirements Arts and fine arts (art, music, dance, drama), business skills (includes word processing), computer science, English, foreign language, mathematics, physical education (includes health), religion (includes Bible studies and theology), science, social sciences, social studies (includes history).

Special Academic Programs Advanced Placement exam preparation; honors section; study at local college for college credit; academic accommodation for the gifted; special instructional classes for students with Attention Deficit Disorder; ESL (15 students enrolled).

College Admission Counseling 53 students graduated in 2015; all went to college, including Benedictine College; Penn State University Park; Saint Louis University; The University of Kansas; The University of Texas at Austin.

Student Life Upper grades have uniform requirement, student council, honor system. Discipline rests primarily with faculty. Attendance at religious services is required.

Summer Programs ESL programs offered; session focuses on activities camp, ESL program; held on campus; accepts boys and girls; open to students from other schools. 17 students usually enrolled. 2016 schedule: July 5 to August 12. Application deadline: June 1.

Tuition and Aid 5-day tuition and room/board: $20,750; 7-day tuition and room/board: $22,250. Tuition installment plan (monthly payment plans, individually arranged payment plans, Sallie Mae). Tuition reduction for siblings, merit scholarship grants, need-based scholarship grants, need-based loans, paying campus jobs available. In 2015–16, 40% of upper-school students received aid. Total amount of financial aid awarded in 2015–16: $275,000.

Admissions Traditional secondary-level entrance grade is 10. For fall 2015, 152 students applied for upper-level admission, 79 were accepted, 71 enrolled. ACT, High School Placement Test, SAT or SSAT required. Deadline for receipt of application materials: none. Application fee required: $50. Interview required.

Athletics Interscholastic: aquatics (girls), baseball (b), basketball (b,g), cheering (g), cross-country running (b,g), dance (g), dance squad (g), dance team (g), drill team (g), football (b), soccer (b), softball (g), swimming and diving (b,g), tennis (b,g), track and field (b,g), volleyball (g); intramural: boxing (b), field hockey (b), fitness (b), flag football (b), floor hockey (b), football (b), running (b,g), skateboarding (b), skiing (downhill) (b,g), soccer (b,g), strength & conditioning (b,g), swimming and diving (b,g), touch football (b), track and field (b,g), weight lifting (b,g), weight training (b,g); coed interscholastic: bowling, golf, physical fitness, physical training, running, soccer, wrestling; coed intramural: baseball, basketball, Nautilus, physical fitness, physical training, roller blading, table tennis, tennis, volleyball, walking. 1 PE instructor, 10 coaches, 1 athletic trainer.

Computers Computer network features include on-campus library services, Internet access, wireless campus network, Internet filtering or blocking technology. Student e-mail accounts are available to students. Students grades are available online. The school has a published electronic and media policy.

Contact Mr. Deke Nolan, Admissions Director. 913-367-5482 Ext. 110. Fax: 913-367-5096. E-mail: admissions@mh-ma.com. Website: www.mh-ma.com

MCAULEY HIGH SCHOOL

6000 Oakwood Avenue
Cincinnati, Ohio 45224-2398

Head of School: Mr. Daniel Minelli

General Information Girls' day college-preparatory school, affiliated with Roman Catholic Church. Grades 9–12. Founded: 1960. Setting: urban. 1 building on campus. Approved or accredited by North Central Association of Colleges and Schools and Ohio Department of Education. Total enrollment: 480.

Upper School Student Profile 95% of students are Roman Catholic.

Special Academic Programs 12 Advanced Placement exams for which test preparation is offered; study at local college for college credit.

Student Life Upper grades have uniform requirement. Discipline rests equally with students and faculty. Attendance at religious services is required.

Admissions High School Placement Test or ICS tests required. Application fee required: $500.

Contact Ms. Maria Schweikert, Director of Admissions. 513-681-1800 Ext. 2272. Fax: 513-681-1802. E-mail: schweikertm@live.mcauleyhs.net. Website: www.mcauleyhs.net

MCDONOGH SCHOOL

8600 McDonogh Road
Owings Mills, Maryland 21117-0380

Head of School: Charles W. Britton

General Information Coeducational boarding and day college-preparatory school. Boarding grades 9–12, day grades PK–12. Founded: 1873. Setting: suburban. Nearest major city is Baltimore. Students are housed in single-sex dormitories. 800-acre campus. 46 buildings on campus. Approved or accredited by Association of Independent Maryland Schools. Member of National Association of Independent Schools. Endowment: $83 million. Total enrollment: 1,350. Upper school average class size: 15. Upper school faculty-student ratio: 1:9. There are 169 required school days per year for Upper School students. Upper School students typically attend 5 days per week. The average school day consists of 6 hours and 10 minutes.

Upper School Student Profile Grade 6: 114 students (60 boys, 54 girls); Grade 7: 98 students (53 boys, 45 girls); Grade 8: 118 students (63 boys, 55 girls); Grade 9: 159 students (87 boys, 72 girls); Grade 10: 155 students (85 boys, 70 girls); Grade 11: 146 students (77 boys, 69 girls); Grade 12: 143 students (73 boys, 70 girls). 5% of students are boarding students. 98% are state residents. 4 states are represented in upper school student body. 1% are international students.

Faculty School total: 177. In upper school: 37 men, 51 women; 60 have advanced degrees; 37 reside on campus.

Subjects Offered 20th century American writers, acting, Advanced Placement courses, African history, African literature, African-American studies, algebra, American history, American history-AP, American literature, American literature-AP, anatomy, art, art history, art-AP, Asian studies, band, biology, biology-AP, botany, calculus, calculus-AP, ceramics, chemistry, chemistry-AP, Chesapeake Bay studies, classical Greek literature, composition-AP, computer animation, computer graphics, computer music, computer programming, computer science, computer science-AP, concert band, concert choir, creative writing, dance, drama, drawing, ecology, economics, economics-AP, electives, engineering, English, English composition, English literature, English literature and composition-AP, English literature-AP, English-AP, English/composition-AP, environmental science, environmental science-AP, ethics, European history, film, film and literature, fine arts, fitness, foreign language, French, French language-AP, French literature-AP, French-AP, genetics, geology, geometry, German, German-AP, government and politics-AP, government-AP, government/civics, health and wellness, history, history-AP, honors algebra, honors English, honors geometry, honors U.S. history, honors world history, jazz band, jazz dance, journalism, language-AP, languages, Latin, Latin American literature, linguistics, literature and composition-AP, literature by women, marine biology, mathematics, Middle Eastern history, music, music theory, music theory-AP, oceanography, photography, physical education, physical fitness, physics, poetry, pre-calculus, psychology, religion, Russian history, science, senior project, set design, Shakespeare, short story, Spanish, Spanish language-AP, Spanish literature, Spanish literature-AP, Spanish-AP, speech, speech communications, statistics-AP, tap dance, theater, trigonometry, U.S. government and politics-AP, U.S. history, U.S. history-AP, video, visual arts, Web site design, woodworking, world history, world history-AP, world religions, world wide web design, writing workshop, yearbook.

Graduation Requirements Arts and fine arts (art, music, dance, drama), English, foreign language, mathematics, physical education (includes health), science, senior project, social studies (includes history). Community service is required.

Special Academic Programs Advanced Placement exam preparation; honors section; independent study; term-away projects.

College Admission Counseling 145 students graduated in 2015; all went to college. Mean SAT critical reading: 615, mean SAT math: 628, mean SAT writing: 606, mean combined SAT: 1850, mean composite ACT: 27.

Student Life Upper grades have uniform requirement, student council, honor system. Discipline rests primarily with faculty.

Summer Programs Enrichment, ESL, sports, art/fine arts, computer instruction programs offered; session focuses on recreation and sports camps; held both on and off campus; held at Gunpowder Falls State Park and Chesapeake Bay; accepts boys and girls; open to students from other schools. 1,700 students usually enrolled. 2016 schedule: June 20 to July 29. Application deadline: May 1.

Tuition and Aid Day student tuition: $28,120; 5-day tuition and room/board: $37,790. Tuition installment plan (Key Tuition Payment Plan, monthly payment plans, individually arranged payment plans). Need-based scholarship grants, need-based loans available. In 2015–16, 28% of upper-school students received aid. Total amount of financial aid awarded in 2015–16: $3,340,390.

Admissions Traditional secondary-level entrance grade is 9. For fall 2015, 377 students applied for upper-level admission, 75 were accepted, 51 enrolled. ISEE required. Deadline for receipt of application materials: December 4. Application fee required: $55. On-campus interview required.

Athletics Interscholastic: aquatics (boys, girls), baseball (b), basketball (b,g), cross-country running (b,g), equestrian sports (b,g), field hockey (g), football (b), golf (b,g), indoor track & field (b,g), lacrosse (b,g), soccer (b,g), softball (g), swimming and diving (b,g), tennis (b,g), volleyball (g), water polo (b,g), winter (indoor) track (b,g), wrestling (b); coed interscholastic: cheering, equestrian sports, horseback riding, indoor track & field, squash, track and field; coed intramural: badminton, ballet, dance, fencing, fitness, squash, ultimate Frisbee. 14 PE instructors, 92 coaches, 2 athletic trainers.

Computers Computers are regularly used in all classes. Computer network features include on-campus library services, online commercial services, Internet access, wireless campus network, Internet filtering or blocking technology. Campus intranet, student e-mail accounts, and computer access in designated common areas are available to students. Students grades are available online. The school has a published electronic and media policy.

Contact Steve Birdsall, Director of Admissions. 443-544-7021. Fax: 443-544-7030. E-mail: sbirdsall@mcdonogh.org. Website: www.mcdonogh.org

MCGILL-TOOLEN CATHOLIC HIGH SCHOOL

1501 Old Shell Road
Mobile, Alabama 36604-2291

Head of School: Mrs. Michelle T. Haas

General Information Coeducational day college-preparatory, arts, religious studies, and technology school, affiliated with Roman Catholic Church. Grades 9–12. Founded: 1896. Setting: urban. 18-acre campus. 5 buildings on campus. Approved or accredited by Southern Association of Colleges and Schools and Alabama Department of Education. Total enrollment: 1,170. Upper school average class size: 21. Upper school faculty-student ratio: 1:14. There are 180 required school days per year for Upper School students. Upper School students typically attend 5 days per week. The average school day consists of 6 hours and 40 minutes.

Upper School Student Profile Grade 9: 325 students (163 boys, 162 girls); Grade 10: 302 students (170 boys, 132 girls); Grade 11: 284 students (159 boys, 125 girls); Grade 12: 259 students (125 boys, 134 girls). 90.4% of students are Roman Catholic.

Faculty School total: 81. In upper school: 37 men, 43 women; 53 have advanced degrees.

Subjects Offered 3-dimensional art, 3-dimensional design, accounting, ACT preparation, advanced biology, advanced chemistry, advanced math, Advanced Placement courses, American government, American history, American history-AP, American literature, analytic geometry, anatomy and physiology, athletic training, band, baseball, basketball, Bible studies, biology, biology-AP, British literature, British literature (honors), calculus, calculus-AP, campus ministry, Catholic belief and practice, ceramics, cheerleading, chemistry, chemistry-AP, choir, choral music, chorus, church history, conceptual physics, concert choir, driver education, economics, English, English composition, English language and composition-AP, English-AP, French, geography, geometry, government, government and politics-AP, graphic design, health, health and wellness, history of the Catholic Church, honors algebra, honors English, honors geometry, honors U.S. history, honors world history, independent study, keyboarding, Latin, marine biology, modern European history-AP, modern world history, multimedia, music appreciation, painting, physical education, physical fitness, physics, physics-AP, pre-algebra, pre-calculus, psychology, reading, reading/study skills, softball, Spanish, Spanish language-AP, speech, studio art, studio art-AP, U.S. government, U.S. government and politics, U.S. government and politics-AP, U.S. history, U.S. history-AP, U.S. literature, video film production, vocal ensemble, volleyball, Web site design, weight fitness, weight training, world geography, world history, world history-AP, world literature, yearbook.

Graduation Requirements Electives, English, keyboarding, mathematics, physical education (includes health), religion (includes Bible studies and theology), science, social studies (includes history).

Special Academic Programs 14 Advanced Placement exams for which test preparation is offered; honors section; remedial reading and/or remedial writing; remedial math.

College Admission Counseling 294 students graduated in 2014; 279 went to college, including Auburn University; Louisiana State University and Agricultural & Mechanical College; Spring Hill College; The University of Alabama; University of South Alabama; University of Southern Mississippi. Other: 9 went to work, 6 entered military service. Median composite ACT: 24. 96% scored over 26 on composite ACT.

Student Life Upper grades have uniform requirement, student council. Discipline rests primarily with faculty. Attendance at religious services is required.

Tuition and Aid Day student tuition: $7000–$8000. Tuition installment plan (monthly payment plans, individually arranged payment plans). Tuition reduction for siblings, need-based scholarship grants available. In 2014–15, 26% of upper-school students received aid. Total amount of financial aid awarded in 2014–15: $958,000.

Admissions Traditional secondary-level entrance grade is 9. ACT-Explore required. Deadline for receipt of application materials: none. Application fee required: $100. On-campus interview recommended.

Athletics Interscholastic: baseball (boys), basketball (b,g), cheering (g), cross-country running (b,g), diving (b,g), football (b), golf (b,g), indoor track (g), soccer (b,g), softball (g), swimming and diving (b,g), tennis (b,g), track and field (b,g), volleyball (g). 4 PE instructors, 3 coaches, 1 athletic trainer.

Computers Computers are regularly used in current events, graphic design, keyboarding, reading, technology, video film production, Web site design, yearbook classes. Computer network features include on-campus library services, Internet access, wireless campus network, Internet filtering or blocking technology. Campus intranet, student e-mail accounts, and computer access in designated common areas are available to students. Students grades are available online. The school has a published electronic and media policy.

Contact Mrs. Jennifer Tolbert, Director of Enrollment. 251-445-2913. Fax: 251-433-8356. E-mail: tolberj@mcgill-toolen.org. Website: www.mcgill-toolen.org/

THE MCLEAN SCHOOL OF MARYLAND, INC.

8224 Lochinver Lane
Potomac, Maryland 20854

Head of School: Mr. Michael Saxenian

General Information Coeducational day college-preparatory school. Grades K–12. Founded: 1954. Setting: suburban. Nearest major city is Washington, DC. 10-acre campus. 1 building on campus. Approved or accredited by Association of Independent Maryland Schools and Maryland Department of Education. Member of National Association of Independent Schools. Endowment: $1.2 million. Total enrollment: 355. Upper school average class size: 9. Upper school faculty-student ratio: 1:9. There are 180 required school days per year for Upper School students. Upper School students typically attend 5 days per week. The average school day consists of 7 hours.

Upper School Student Profile Grade 6: 48 students (29 boys, 19 girls); Grade 7: 51 students (24 boys, 27 girls); Grade 8: 35 students (22 boys, 13 girls); Grade 9: 36 students (24 boys, 12 girls); Grade 10: 38 students (23 boys, 15 girls); Grade 11: 24 students (18 boys, 6 girls); Grade 12: 20 students (14 boys, 6 girls).

Faculty School total: 90. In upper school: 14 men, 15 women; 12 have advanced degrees.

Subjects Offered Advanced Placement courses, all academic, American sign language, Latin, robotics, Spanish.

Graduation Requirements Art, English, foreign language, history, humanities, literature, mathematics, physical education (includes health), science, 40 hours of community services.

Special Academic Programs 9 Advanced Placement exams for which test preparation is offered; honors section; independent study; study at local college for college credit; academic accommodation for the gifted; remedial reading and/or remedial writing; remedial math; programs in English, mathematics for dyslexic students.

College Admission Counseling 20 students graduated in 2014; 19 went to college, including American University; Brandeis University; Duke University; High Point University; Susquehanna University; University of Maryland, College Park. Other: 1 entered a postgraduate year. Mean combined SAT: 1715, mean composite ACT: 24.

Student Life Upper grades have specified standards of dress, student council, honor system. Discipline rests equally with students and faculty.

Tuition and Aid Day student tuition: $36,985. Tuition installment plan (monthly payment plans). Need-based scholarship grants available. In 2014–15, 28% of upper-school students received aid. Total amount of financial aid awarded in 2014–15: $804,593.

Admissions Traditional secondary-level entrance grade is 9. For fall 2014, 32 students applied for upper-level admission, 20 were accepted, 12 enrolled. WISC or WAIS and Woodcock-Johnson required. Deadline for receipt of application materials: none. Application fee required: $100. Interview required.

Athletics Interscholastic: basketball (boys, girls), cross-country running (b,g), lacrosse (b), soccer (b,g), softball (b), track and field (b,g), volleyball (g), wrestling (b,g).

Computers Computer network features include on-campus library services, online commercial services, Internet access, wireless campus network. Campus intranet and student e-mail accounts are available to students. Students grades are available online.

Contact Ms. Cathy Patterson, Director of Admission. 240-395-0698. Fax: 301-299-1639. E-mail: cpatterson@mcleanschool.org. Website: www.mcleanschool.org

MEADOWRIDGE SCHOOL
12224 240th Street
Maple Ridge, British Columbia V4R 1N1, Canada
Head of School: Mr. Hugh Burke

General Information Coeducational day college-preparatory, arts, technology, and International Baccalaureate school. Grades JK–12. Founded: 1985. Setting: rural. Nearest major city is Vancouver, Canada. 27-acre campus. 1 building on campus. Approved or accredited by Canadian Association of Independent Schools, Council of International Schools, International Baccalaureate Organization, and British Columbia Department of Education. Affiliate member of National Association of Independent Schools. Language of instruction: English. Upper school faculty-student ratio: 1:12. Upper School students typically attend 5 days per week. The average school day consists of 7 hours.

Faculty School total: 74.

Subjects Offered Accounting, art, biology, calculus, career and personal planning, chemistry, comparative civilizations, computer technologies, drama, English, English literature, fencing, French, geography, history, humanities, mathematics, photography, physical education, physics, science, Spanish, technology/design, theater, volleyball, weight training.

Graduation Requirements 3 provincially examinable courses, International Baccalaureate Diploma Programme.

Special Academic Programs International Baccalaureate program; study abroad.

College Admission Counseling 42 students graduated in 2014; they went to McGill University; Queen's University at Kingston; Simon Fraser University; The University of British Columbia; University of Toronto; University of Victoria.

Student Life Upper grades have uniform requirement, student council, honor system. Discipline rests equally with students and faculty.

Tuition and Aid Day student tuition: CAN$17,800. Tuition installment plan (Insured Tuition Payment Plan, monthly payment plans). Tuition reduction for siblings, merit scholarship grants available. Total upper-school merit-scholarship money awarded for 2014–15: CAN$24,300.

Admissions Admissions testing and writing sample required. Deadline for receipt of application materials: none. Application fee required: CAN$150. Interview required.

Athletics Interscholastic: aerobics/dance (boys, girls), badminton (b,g), basketball (b,g), fitness (b,g), physical fitness (b,g), rugby (b,g), soccer (b,g), volleyball (b,g); intramural: aerobics/dance (b,g), basketball (b,g); coed interscholastic: aerobics/dance, cross-country running, flag football, golf, jogging, outdoor activities, outdoor education, outdoor recreation, outdoor skills, outdoors, strength & conditioning, swimming and diving, track and field, yoga; coed intramural: aerobics/dance, floor hockey.

Computers Computers are regularly used in all academic, art, English, history, humanities, industrial technology, library, library skills, mathematics, science, yearbook classes. Computer network features include on-campus library services, online commercial services, Internet access, wireless campus network, Internet filtering or blocking technology, Bring Your Own Device Programme. Campus intranet, student e-mail accounts, and computer access in designated common areas are available to students. Students grades are available online.

Contact Ms. Natalie Blomly, Admissions Coordinator. 604-467-4444. Fax: 604-467-4989. E-mail: info@meadowridge.bc.ca. Website: www.meadowridge.bc.ca

THE MEADOWS SCHOOL
8601 Scholar Lane
Las Vegas, Nevada 89128-7302
Head of School: Mr. Jeremy B. Gregersen

General Information Coeducational day college-preparatory, arts, technology, and debate, foreign languages school. Grades PK–12. Founded: 1981. Setting: suburban. 40-acre campus. 11 buildings on campus. Approved or accredited by Northwest Accreditation Commission, Northwest Association of Independent Schools, and Nevada Department of Education. Member of National Association of Independent Schools and Secondary School Admission Test Board. Endowment: $15 million. Total enrollment: 871. Upper school average class size: 12. Upper school faculty-student ratio: 1:11. There are 180 required school days per year for Upper School students. Upper School students typically attend 5 days per week. The average school day consists of 7 hours.

Upper School Student Profile Grade 9: 62 students (24 boys, 38 girls); Grade 10: 62 students (29 boys, 33 girls); Grade 11: 68 students (28 boys, 40 girls); Grade 12: 60 students (27 boys, 33 girls).

Faculty School total: 90. In upper school: 19 men, 22 women; 33 have advanced degrees.

Subjects Offered 20th century American writers, 3-dimensional art, acting, advanced math, Advanced Placement courses, advanced studio art-AP, American literature, anatomy and physiology, Ancient Greek, Arabic, architecture, art, art history, art history-AP, athletics, band, banking, Basic programming, bioethics, biology, biology-AP, British literature, British literature (honors), calculus, calculus-AP, ceramics, chemistry, chemistry-AP, choral music, chorus, composition, computer applications, computer graphics, computer literacy, computer programming, computer science, computer science-AP, concert choir, creative writing, dance, debate, digital art, digital photography, drama, drama performance, drawing, drawing and design, economics, English, English composition, English language and composition-AP, English literature, English literature and composition-AP, European history, European history-AP, film studies, filmmaking, finance, fine arts, finite math, foreign language, forensics, French, French-AP, genetics, geometry, government-AP, health, honors English, honors geometry, honors U.S. history, honors world history, human anatomy, instrumental music, integrated mathematics, international affairs, international relations, Japanese, journalism, keyboarding, Latin, Latin-AP, literature and composition-AP, macro/microeconomics-AP, military history, money management, music theater, music theory-AP, organic chemistry, painting, photography, physics, physics-AP, policy and value, pre-calculus, psychology-AP, Shakespeare, social justice, social sciences, Spanish, Spanish language-AP, Spanish literature, Spanish literature-AP, Spanish-AP, speech, speech and debate, speech and oral interpretations, sports medicine, statistics, statistics-AP, studio art, studio art-AP, technical theater, technology, theater production, trigonometry, U.S. government, U.S. government and politics-AP, U.S. history, U.S. history-AP, yearbook.

Graduation Requirements American literature, ancient world history, art, biology, English, English composition, English literature, European history, foreign language, geometry, mathematics, physical education (includes health), physics, pre-calculus, science, social studies (includes history), technical skills, U.S. government, U.S. history, seniors have a 24-hour per semester community service requirement, grades 9-11 have a 16-hour per semester community service requirement.

Special Academic Programs 26 Advanced Placement exams for which test preparation is offered; honors section; academic accommodation for the gifted, the musically talented, and the artistically talented.

College Admission Counseling 62 students graduated in 2015; all went to college, including Boston University; The University of Arizona; University of California, Los Angeles; University of Nevada, Las Vegas; University of Nevada, Reno; University of Southern California. Median SAT critical reading: 650, median SAT math: 690, median SAT writing: 690, median combined SAT: 2010, median composite ACT: 30. 75% scored over 600 on SAT critical reading, 87% scored over 600 on SAT math, 84% scored over 600 on SAT writing, 83% scored over 1800 on combined SAT, 86% scored over 26 on composite ACT.

Student Life Upper grades have uniform requirement, student council, honor system. Discipline rests equally with students and faculty.

Summer Programs Enrichment, sports, art/fine arts programs offered; session focuses on enrichment; held on campus; accepts boys and girls; open to students from other schools. 50 students usually enrolled. 2016 schedule: June 6 to July 1. Application deadline: June 3.

Tuition and Aid Day student tuition: $23,375. Tuition installment plan (Insured Tuition Payment Plan, monthly payment plans, individually arranged payment plans, 2-payment plan, 70% by July 15 and 30% by February 15, 10 monthly payment plan using electronic withdrawal only). Need-based scholarship grants available. In 2015–16, 14% of upper-school students received aid. Total amount of financial aid awarded in 2015–16: $514,698.

Admissions Traditional secondary-level entrance grade is 9. For fall 2015, 56 students applied for upper-level admission, 41 were accepted, 23 enrolled. ERB, ISEE, PSAT or SSAT required. Deadline for receipt of application materials: none. Application fee required: $100. On-campus interview required.

Athletics Interscholastic: baseball (boys), basketball (b,g), bowling (b,g), cheering (g), cross-country running (b,g), football (b), softball (g), tennis (b,g), track and field (b,g), volleyball (g); coed interscholastic: golf, soccer. 1 athletic trainer.

Computers Computers are regularly used in all academic, art, college planning, desktop publishing, economics, English, foreign language, French, geography, graphic design, history, independent study, introduction to technology, journalism, library, mathematics, music, news writing, photography, photojournalism, programming, publications, publishing, science, speech, technology, yearbook classes. Computer network features include on-campus library services, online commercial services, Internet access, wireless campus network, Internet filtering or blocking technology, SmartBoards in all classrooms, 5 iPad carts, 6 laptop carts, 10 Chromebooks carts, course syllabus and homework available online. Campus intranet, student e-mail accounts, and computer access in designated common areas are available to students. Students grades are available online. The school has a published electronic and media policy.

Contact Mrs. Laura Ommen, Admissions Coordinator/Office of Advancement. 702-254-1610 Ext. 5928. Fax: 702-363-5298. E-mail: lommen@themeadowsschool.org. Website: www.TheMeadowsSchool.org

MEMORIAL HALL SCHOOL

2501 Central Parkway Ste A-19
Houston, Texas 77092

Head of School: Mrs. Kimberly Aurich Taylor

General Information Coeducational day college-preparatory, general academic, and bilingual studies school. Grades 6–12. Founded: 1966. Setting: urban. 1 building on campus. Approved or accredited by Southern Association of Colleges and Schools, Southern Association of Independent Schools, Texas Education Agency, and Texas Department of Education. Total enrollment: 91. Upper school average class size: 14. Upper school faculty-student ratio: 1:14. Upper School students typically attend 4 days per week. The average school day consists of 7 hours and 30 minutes.

Faculty School total: 11. In upper school: 2 men, 9 women; 3 have advanced degrees.

Subjects Offered Algebra, American history, art, biology, business mathematics, business skills, chemistry, computer science, economics, English, ESL, fine arts, geography, geometry, government/civics, health, history, journalism, mathematics, physical education, physics, psychology, science, social sciences, social studies, sociology, Spanish, trigonometry, world history.

Graduation Requirements Arts and crafts, arts and fine arts (art, music, dance, drama), business skills (includes word processing), computer science, English, foreign language, mathematics, physical education (includes health), science, social sciences, social studies (includes history), community service, foreign credit accepted upon completion.

Special Academic Programs Study at local college for college credit; remedial reading and/or remedial writing; remedial math; programs in English, mathematics, general development for dyslexic students; special instructional classes for students with learning disabilities, Attention Deficit Disorder, and dyslexia; ESL (85 students enrolled).

College Admission Counseling 24 students graduated in 2015; 22 went to college, including Houston Community College; Sam Houston State University; St. Thomas University; Texas A&M University; The University of Texas at Austin; University of Houston. Other: 2 went to work.

Student Life Upper grades have uniform requirement, student council, honor system. Discipline rests equally with students and faculty.

Summer Programs Remediation, enrichment, advancement, ESL, computer instruction programs offered; session focuses on additional credit enrichment, study skills; held on campus; accepts boys and girls; open to students from other schools. 40 students usually enrolled. 2016 schedule: June 15 to August 6. Application deadline: none.

Tuition and Aid Day student tuition: $13,700. Tuition installment plan (monthly payment plans, individually arranged payment plans). Tuition reduction for siblings available. In 2015–16, 5% of upper-school students received aid.

Admissions Traditional secondary-level entrance grade is 9. Deadline for receipt of application materials: none. Application fee required: $300. Interview required.

Athletics Interscholastic: aerobics (boys, girls), aerobics/dance (b,g), bowling (b,g), fitness (b,g), fitness walking (b,g), jump rope (b,g), paddle tennis (b,g), yoga (b,g); coed interscholastic: bowling, paddle tennis; coed intramural: dance, outdoor activities, physical fitness. 2 PE instructors.

Computers Computers are regularly used in all academic, basic skills, foreign language classes. Computer resources include wireless campus network. Campus intranet is available to students. The school has a published electronic and media policy.

Contact Mrs. Kimberly Aurich Taylor, Director. 713-688-5566. Fax: 713-956-9751. E-mail: memhallsch@aol.com. Website: www.memorialhall.org

MEMPHIS CATHOLIC HIGH SCHOOL AND MIDDLE SCHOOL

61 North McLean Boulevard
Memphis, Tennessee 38104-2644

Head of School: Mr. Kevin Alexander Kimberly

General Information Coeducational day college-preparatory school, affiliated with Roman Catholic Church. Grades 7–12. Founded: 1954. Setting: urban. 4-acre campus. 1 building on campus. Approved or accredited by Southern Association of Colleges and Schools and Tennessee Department of Education. Total enrollment: 275. Upper school average class size: 20. Upper school faculty-student ratio: 1:13. There are 200 required school days per year for Upper School students. Upper School students typically attend 5 days per week. The average school day consists of 7 hours and 40 minutes.

Upper School Student Profile 38% of students are Roman Catholic.

Faculty School total: 22. In upper school: 12 men, 8 women; 9 have advanced degrees.

Graduation Requirements Four credits of Theology.

Student Life Upper grades have uniform requirement, student council. Discipline rests primarily with faculty. Attendance at religious services is required.

Tuition and Aid Tuition installment plan (SMART Tuition Payment Plan). Tuition reduction for siblings, merit scholarship grants, need-based scholarship grants, paying campus jobs available.

Admissions Traditional secondary-level entrance grade is 9. High School Placement Test required. Deadline for receipt of application materials: none. Application fee required: $25. On-campus interview required.

Athletics 1 PE instructor, 1 coach.

Computers Computer network features include Internet access, wireless campus network, Internet filtering or blocking technology. Student e-mail accounts are available to students. Students grades are available online. The school has a published electronic and media policy.

Contact Mr. Kevin Alexander Kimberly, Principal. 901-276-1221 Ext. 20. Fax: 901-725-1447. E-mail: kkimberly@memphiscatholic.org. Website: www.memphiscatholic.org

MEMPHIS UNIVERSITY SCHOOL

6191 Park Avenue
Memphis, Tennessee 38119-5399

Head of School: Mr. Ellis L. Haguewood

General Information Boys' day college-preparatory school. Grades 7–12. Founded: 1893. Setting: suburban. 94-acre campus. 8 buildings on campus. Approved or accredited by Southern Association of Colleges and Schools, Southern Association of Independent Schools, and Tennessee Association of Independent Schools. Member of National Association of Independent Schools. Endowment: $33.1 million. Total enrollment: 633. Upper school average class size: 14. Upper school faculty-student ratio: 1:8. There are 176 required school days per year for Upper School students. Upper School students typically attend 5 days per week. The average school day consists of 7 hours.

Upper School Student Profile Grade 9: 101 students (101 boys); Grade 10: 105 students (105 boys); Grade 11: 107 students (107 boys); Grade 12: 108 students (108 boys).

Faculty School total: 76. In upper school: 44 men, 14 women; 42 have advanced degrees.

Subjects Offered Algebra, American government, American literature, art, art history, art history-AP, arts and crafts, Bible, biology, biology-AP, British literature, business education, calculus, calculus-AP, chemistry, chemistry-AP, choral music, college counseling, college placement, comparative government and politics-AP, comparative religion, composition-AP, computer education, computer programming, computer science, computer science-AP, driver education, earth science, economics, economics and history, English, English composition, English literature, English literature and composition-AP, environmental science, ethics, ethics and responsibility, European history, European history-AP, expository writing, filmmaking, fine arts, foreign language, French, geometry, global studies, government and politics-AP, government/civics, grammar, health, history, humanities, introduction to theater, keyboarding, language and composition, Latin, library skills, literature, mathematics, music, music appreciation, music composition, music theory, physical education, physical science, physics, physics-AP, pre-algebra, pre-calculus, probability and statistics, psychology, religion, research skills, science, social sciences, social studies, Spanish, speech communications, studio art, study skills, trigonometry, U.S. history,

U.S. history-AP, United States government-AP, Western civilization, world history, writing.

Graduation Requirements Arts and fine arts (art, music, dance, drama), English, foreign language, mathematics, physical education (includes health), religion (includes Bible studies and theology), science, social sciences, social studies (includes history).

Special Academic Programs 18 Advanced Placement exams for which test preparation is offered; honors section; study abroad; academic accommodation for the gifted; remedial reading and/or remedial writing; remedial math.

College Admission Counseling 119 students graduated in 2015; all went to college, including Rhodes College; Sewanee: The University of the South; Southern Methodist University; The University of Alabama; The University of Tennessee; University of Arkansas. Median composite ACT: 30. Mean SAT critical reading: 618, mean SAT math: 619, mean SAT writing: 616. 59% scored over 600 on SAT critical reading, 65% scored over 600 on SAT math, 61% scored over 600 on SAT writing, 61% scored over 1800 on combined SAT, 79% scored over 26 on composite ACT.

Student Life Upper grades have specified standards of dress, student council, honor system. Discipline rests primarily with faculty.

Summer Programs Remediation, enrichment, advancement, sports, computer instruction programs offered; session focuses on academics and athletics; held on campus; accepts boys; open to students from other schools. 460 students usually enrolled. 2016 schedule: June 6 to July 28. Application deadline: none.

Tuition and Aid Day student tuition: $19,950. Tuition installment plan (FACTS Tuition Payment Plan, monthly payment plans). Need-based scholarship grants available. In 2015–16, 30% of upper-school students received aid. Total amount of financial aid awarded in 2015–16: $2,475,000.

Admissions Traditional secondary-level entrance grade is 9. For fall 2015, 29 students applied for upper-level admission, 25 were accepted, 25 enrolled. ISEE required. Deadline for receipt of application materials: December 10. Application fee required: $50. On-campus interview recommended.

Athletics Interscholastic: baseball, basketball, cross-country running, football, golf, lacrosse, soccer, swimming and diving, tennis, track and field, trap and skeet, water polo, weight training, wrestling. 5 PE instructors, 9 coaches, 1 athletic trainer.

Computers Computers are regularly used in all academic, career exploration, college planning, graphic design, library science, newspaper, publications, yearbook classes. Computer network features include on-campus library services, online commercial services, Internet access, wireless campus network, Internet filtering or blocking technology. Campus intranet, student e-mail accounts, and computer access in designated common areas are available to students. Students grades are available online. The school has a published electronic and media policy.

Contact Mrs. Peggy E. Williamson, Director of Admissions. 901-260-1349. Fax: 901-260-1301. E-mail: peggy.williamson@musowls.org. Website: www.musowls.org

MENLO SCHOOL

50 Valparaiso Avenue
Atherton, California 94027
Head of School: Than Healy

General Information Coeducational day college-preparatory school. Grades 6–12. Founded: 1915. Setting: suburban. Nearest major city is San Jose. 35-acre campus. 23 buildings on campus. Approved or accredited by California Association of Independent Schools, Western Association of Schools and Colleges, and California Department of Education. Member of National Association of Independent Schools. Endowment: $37.7 million. Total enrollment: 795. Upper school average class size: 15. Upper school faculty-student ratio: 1:10. There are 170 required school days per year for Upper School students. Upper School students typically attend 5 days per week. The average school day consists of 7 hours.

Faculty School total: 86. In upper school: 34 men, 39 women; 58 have advanced degrees.

Subjects Offered 20th century American writers, advanced biology, advanced chemistry, advanced computer applications, advanced math, algebra, American history, American history-AP, American literature, American literature-AP, analytic geometry, anatomy and physiology, ancient world history, art, art history, art-AP, Asian studies, biology, biology-AP, British literature-AP, calculus, calculus-AP, chemistry, chemistry-AP, chorus, computer graphics, computer literacy, computer multimedia, computer programming, computer science, computer science-AP, creative writing, dance, debate, drama, earth science, economics, economics-AP, engineering, English, English language and composition-AP, English literature, English literature-AP, English-AP, environmental science, ethics, European history, European history-AP, film studies, fine arts, French, French as a second language, French language-AP, French literature-AP, French-AP, freshman seminar, geometry, government and politics-AP, history, honors English, honors geometry, honors U.S. history, intro to computers, Japanese, jazz band, jazz dance, jazz ensemble, journalism, Latin, Latin-AP, law, literature-AP, Mandarin, mathematics, mathematics-AP, methods of research, modern European history, modern world history, multimedia, music, music theory, music theory-AP, music-AP, musical productions, newspaper, orchestra, performing arts, philosophy, photography, physical education, physics, physics-AP, play production, poetry, pre-calculus, rhetoric, robotics, science, science fiction, science research, senior project, Shakespeare, society and culture, Spanish, Spanish language-AP, Spanish literature-AP, Spanish-AP, statistics, statistics-AP, student government, student publications, studio art, studio art-AP,

swimming, U.S. government and politics-AP, U.S. history-AP, video film production, wellness, women's literature, world history, world religions, writing, yearbook.

Graduation Requirements Arts and fine arts (art, music, dance, drama), English, foreign language, mathematics, physical education (includes health), science, social studies (includes history), Freshman seminar, Knight School, senior project (3-week project at the end of senior year). Community service is required.

Special Academic Programs Advanced Placement exam preparation; honors section; independent study.

College Admission Counseling 136 students graduated in 2015; 133 went to college, including Princeton University; Stanford University; University of California, Berkeley; University of California, Los Angeles; University of California, Santa Barbara; University of Southern California. Other: 1 entered a postgraduate year, 2 had other specific plans. Mean SAT critical reading: 655, mean SAT math: 681, mean SAT writing: 673. 74% scored over 600 on SAT critical reading, 88% scored over 600 on SAT math, 80% scored over 600 on SAT writing, 86% scored over 26 on composite ACT.

Student Life Upper grades have student council. Discipline rests equally with students and faculty.

Summer Programs Enrichment programs offered; session focuses on academic enrichment; held on campus; accepts boys and girls; open to students from other schools. 70 students usually enrolled. 2016 schedule: June 15 to July 2. Application deadline: April 30.

Tuition and Aid Day student tuition: $41,100. Tuition installment plan (Key Tuition Payment Plan). Need-based scholarship grants, paying campus jobs available. In 2015–16, 20% of upper-school students received aid. Total amount of financial aid awarded in 2015–16: $4,200,000.

Admissions Traditional secondary-level entrance grade is 9. For fall 2015, 429 students applied for upper-level admission, 77 enrolled. ISEE, SSAT or TOEFL required. Deadline for receipt of application materials: January 14. Application fee required: $85. On-campus interview required.

Athletics Interscholastic: aerobics/dance (girls), baseball (b), basketball (b,g), cross-country running (b,g), dance (g), football (b), golf (b,g), lacrosse (b,g), soccer (b,g), softball (g), swimming and diving (b,g), tennis (b,g), track and field (b,g), volleyball (b,g), water polo (b,g); coed interscholastic: aerobics/dance, dance, martial arts. 67 coaches, 2 athletic trainers.

Computers Computers are regularly used in English, foreign language, history, journalism, mathematics, media arts, multimedia, newspaper, science, yearbook classes. Computer network features include on-campus library services, online commercial services, Internet access, wireless campus network, Internet filtering or blocking technology. Student e-mail accounts and computer access in designated common areas are available to students.

Contact Ms. Melanie Rossi, Admissions Assistant. 650-330-2000 Ext. 2435. Fax: 650-330-2012. E-mail: melanie.rossi@menloschool.org. Website: www.menloschool.org

MENNONITE COLLEGIATE INSTITUTE

Box 250
Gretna, Manitoba R0G 0V0, Canada
Head of School: Mr. Darryl K. Loewen

General Information Coeducational boarding and day college-preparatory, general academic, arts, business, religious studies, and technology school, affiliated with Mennonite Church, Christian faith; primarily serves students with learning disabilities, individuals with Attention Deficit Disorder, individuals with emotional and behavioral problems, and dyslexic students. Boarding grades 9–12, day grades 7–12. Founded: 1889. Setting: small town. Nearest major city is Winnipeg, Canada. Students are housed in single-sex dormitories. 12-acre campus. 5 buildings on campus. Approved or accredited by The College Board and Manitoba Department of Education. Language of instruction: English. Endowment: CAN$500,000. Total enrollment: 131. Upper school average class size: 20. Upper school faculty-student ratio: 1:13. There are 196 required school days per year for Upper School students. Upper School students typically attend 5 days per week. The average school day consists of 7 hours and 10 minutes.

Upper School Student Profile Grade 9: 22 students (12 boys, 10 girls); Grade 10: 23 students (10 boys, 13 girls); Grade 11: 28 students (11 boys, 17 girls); Grade 12: 48 students (23 boys, 25 girls). 42% of students are boarding students. 95% are province residents. 3 provinces are represented in upper school student body. 3% are international students. International students from China, Congo, Democratic People's Republic of Korea, Hong Kong, Kenya, and Mexico; 1 other country represented in student body. 70% of students are Mennonite, Christian.

Faculty School total: 12. In upper school: 7 men, 5 women; 2 have advanced degrees; 2 reside on campus.

Subjects Offered Advanced TOEFL/grammar, agriculture, all academic, jazz ensemble, journalism, music.

Graduation Requirements English, geography, history, mathematics, physical education (includes health), compulsory religion courses at each grade level, compulsory religious history courses at one level.

Special Academic Programs 2 Advanced Placement exams for which test preparation is offered; independent study; academic accommodation for the musically talented; remedial reading and/or remedial writing; remedial math; programs in

Mennonite Collegiate Institute

English, mathematics for dyslexic students; special instructional classes for blind students; ESL (8 students enrolled).

College Admission Counseling 36 students graduated in 2014; 24 went to college, including The University of Winnipeg; University of Manitoba. Other: 10 went to work, 2 had other specific plans.

Student Life Upper grades have uniform requirement, student council, honor system. Discipline rests primarily with faculty. Attendance at religious services is required.

Tuition and Aid Day student tuition: CAN$4800; 7-day tuition and room/board: CAN$18,200. Tuition installment plan (monthly payment plans, individually arranged payment plans). Tuition reduction for siblings, bursaries, merit scholarship grants, need-based scholarship grants, middle-income loans available. In 2014–15, 30% of upper-school students received aid; total upper-school merit-scholarship money awarded: CAN$9000. Total amount of financial aid awarded in 2014–15: CAN$40,000.

Admissions Traditional secondary-level entrance grade is 9. For fall 2014, 138 students applied for upper-level admission, 137 were accepted, 131 enrolled. Deadline for receipt of application materials: none. Application fee required: CAN$200. Interview recommended.

Athletics Interscholastic: badminton (boys, girls), baseball (b,g), basketball (b,g), cross-country running (b,g), curling (b,g), golf (b,g), soccer (b,g), track and field (b,g), volleyball (b,g); intramural: floor hockey (b,g), indoor soccer (b,g), paddle tennis (b,g), soccer (b,g), street hockey (b,g), table tennis (b,g); coed interscholastic: badminton, cross-country running, curling, golf, track and field; coed intramural: floor hockey, indoor soccer, paddle tennis, soccer, street hockey, table tennis. 3 PE instructors, 2 athletic trainers.

Computers Computers are regularly used in all academic classes. Computer network features include on-campus library services, Internet access, wireless campus network, Internet filtering or blocking technology. The school has a published electronic and media policy.

Contact Ms. Shanda Hochstetler, Admissions Counselor. 204-327-5891. Fax: 888-684-5909. E-mail: admissions@mciblues.net. Website: www.mciblues.net

MERCERSBURG ACADEMY

300 East Seminary Street
Mercersburg, Pennsylvania 17236

Head of School: Mr. Doug Hale

General Information Coeducational boarding and day college-preparatory school. Boarding grades 9–PG, day grades 9–11. Founded: 1893. Setting: small town. Nearest major city is Washington, DC. Students are housed in single-sex dormitories. 300-acre campus. 30 buildings on campus. Approved or accredited by Middle States Association of Colleges and Schools and Pennsylvania Department of Education. Member of National Association of Independent Schools and Secondary School Admission Test Board. Endowment: $244 million. Total enrollment: 430. Upper school average class size: 12. Upper school faculty-student ratio: 1:5. Upper School students typically attend 5 days per week. The average school day consists of 7 hours.

Upper School Student Profile Grade 9: 71 students (38 boys, 33 girls); Grade 10: 123 students (69 boys, 54 girls); Grade 11: 122 students (56 boys, 66 girls); Grade 12: 108 students (56 boys, 52 girls); Postgraduate: 18 students (10 boys, 8 girls). 85% of students are boarding students. 27% are state residents. 31 states are represented in upper school student body. 23% are international students. International students from China, Germany, Mexico, Republic of Korea, Spain, and Viet Nam; 36 other countries represented in student body.

Faculty School total: 97. In upper school: 64 men, 33 women; 74 have advanced degrees; 50 reside on campus.

Subjects Offered 20th century American writers, 20th century world history, 3-dimensional art, acting, advanced chemistry, advanced computer applications, Advanced Placement courses, African American history, African dance, African drumming, algebra, American Civil War, American history, American history-AP, American literature, American literature-AP, art, art history, art history-AP, Asian history, astronomy, ballet, band, biology, biology-AP, botany, British literature-AP, Buddhism, calculus, calculus-AP, ceramics, chemistry, chemistry-AP, Chinese, choral music, chorus, comparative government and politics-AP, computer graphics, computer math, computer programming-AP, computer science, computer science-AP, concert band, creative writing, dance, digital art, drama, drawing, economics-AP, English, English literature, English literature and composition-AP, environmental science-AP, ethics, European history, European history-AP, film studies, fine arts, French, French language-AP, French literature-AP, genetics, geometry, German, German-AP, government and politics-AP, health, history, history of music, honors algebra, honors English, honors geometry, honors U.S. history, honors world history, humanities, Islamic studies, jazz band, journalism, Latin, Latin-AP, mathematics, modern European history-AP, music, music composition, music history, musical theater dance, orchestra, painting, personal fitness, physical education, physical science, physics, physics-AP, poetry, public speaking, religion, robotics, SAT preparation, science, sculpture, social studies, Spanish, Spanish language-AP, speech, stagecraft, statistics-AP, strings, studio art, theater, theater design and production, trigonometry, U.S. government and politics-AP, U.S. history-AP, United States government-AP, world history, world history-AP, world literature, yoga.

Graduation Requirements Arts and fine arts (art, music, dance, drama), English, foreign language, history, mathematics, physical education (includes health), religion

(includes Bible studies and theology), science, participation in sports, performing arts, or other activities.

Special Academic Programs Advanced Placement exam preparation; honors section; independent study; term-away projects; study abroad; academic accommodation for the gifted, the musically talented, and the artistically talented.

College Admission Counseling 127 students graduated in 2015; all went to college, including Boston University; Bucknell University; Georgetown University; Northwestern University; United States Naval Academy; University of Pennsylvania.

Student Life Upper grades have specified standards of dress, student council, honor system. Discipline rests primarily with faculty.

Summer Programs Enrichment, ESL, sports, art/fine arts, rigorous outdoor training programs offered; session focuses on enrichment; held on campus; accepts boys and girls; open to students from other schools. 1,500 students usually enrolled. 2016 schedule: June 10 to August 22. Application deadline: none.

Tuition and Aid Day student tuition: $38,000; 7-day tuition and room/board: $54,550. Tuition installment plan (Insured Tuition Payment Plan, Key Tuition Payment Plan, monthly payment plans). Merit scholarship grants, need-based scholarship grants, need-based loans available. In 2015–16, 50% of upper-school students received aid; total upper-school merit-scholarship money awarded: $1,138,175. Total amount of financial aid awarded in 2015–16: $6,178,725.

Admissions Traditional secondary-level entrance grade is 9. For fall 2015, 589 students applied for upper-level admission, 289 were accepted, 155 enrolled. ACT, PSAT and SAT for applicants to grade 11 and 12, SAT, SSAT or TOEFL required. Deadline for receipt of application materials: January 15. Application fee required: $50. Interview required.

Athletics Interscholastic: baseball (boys), basketball (b,g), cross-country running (b,g), diving (b,g), field hockey (g), football (b), lacrosse (b,g), running (b,g), soccer (b,g), softball (g), squash (b,g), swimming and diving (b,g), tennis (b,g), track and field (b,g), volleyball (g), winter (indoor) track (b,g), wrestling (b); coed interscholastic: alpine skiing, golf; coed intramural: aerobics/dance, alpine skiing, backpacking, ballet, bicycling, canoeing/kayaking, climbing, dance, equestrian sports, fitness, freestyle skiing, Frisbee, golf, hiking/backpacking, horseback riding, kayaking, martial arts, modern dance, mountain biking, outdoor activities, outdoor adventure, outdoor education, outdoor recreation, outdoor skills, outdoors, paddling, physical fitness, physical training, rafting, rappelling, rock climbing, skiing (downhill), snowboarding, strength & conditioning, table tennis, ultimate Frisbee, wall climbing, weight lifting, weight training, wilderness survival, yoga. 4 PE instructors, 22 coaches, 2 athletic trainers.

Computers Computers are regularly used in art, English, foreign language, history, mathematics, music, science classes. Computer network features include on-campus library services, online commercial services, Internet access, wireless campus network. Student e-mail accounts and computer access in designated common areas are available to students. The school has a published electronic and media policy.

Contact Mr. Tommy W. Adams, Assistant Head of School for Enrollment. 717-328-6173. Fax: 717-328-6319. E-mail: admission@mercersburg.edu. Website: www.mercersburg.edu

MERCY HIGH SCHOOL

1740 Randolph Road
Middletown, Connecticut 06457-5155

Head of School: Sr. Mary McCarthy, RSM

General Information Girls' day college-preparatory, arts, and religious studies school, affiliated with Roman Catholic Church. Grades 9–12. Founded: 1963. Setting: rural. Nearest major city is Hartford. 26-acre campus. 1 building on campus. Approved or accredited by National Catholic Education Association, New England Association of Schools and Colleges, and Connecticut Department of Education. Total enrollment: 573. Upper school average class size: 21. Upper school faculty-student ratio: 1:13. There are 172 required school days per year for Upper School students. Upper School students typically attend 5 days per week. The average school day consists of 6 hours and 30 minutes.

Upper School Student Profile Grade 9: 134 students (134 girls); Grade 10: 136 students (136 girls); Grade 11: 146 students (146 girls); Grade 12: 157 students (157 girls). 78% of students are Roman Catholic.

Faculty School total: 45. In upper school: 8 men, 37 women; 40 have advanced degrees.

Subjects Offered Accounting, advanced math, algebra, American government, American literature, art, art history, arts and crafts, biochemistry, biology, biology-AP, business, calculus, calculus-AP, Catholic belief and practice, ceramics, chamber groups, chemistry, chemistry-AP, choir, chorus, civics, comparative government and politics, computer applications, concert band, concert choir, creative writing, desktop publishing, digital photography, drawing and design, English, English language-AP, English literature, English literature-AP, European history-AP, forensics, French, French language-AP, French literature-AP, French-AP, geography, geometry, government/civics, health, history, honors algebra, honors English, honors geometry, honors U.S. history, honors world history, humanities, independent study, Italian, journalism, keyboarding, Latin, Latin-AP, law, mathematics, modern history, modern world history, music, neuroscience, photography, physical education, physics, physics-AP, physiology, pottery, pre-calculus, psychology, psychology-AP, public speaking, religious studies, social studies, Spanish, Spanish language-AP, Spanish-AP, statistics, statistics-AP, theater arts, U.S. history, U.S. history-AP, Web site design, wind ensemble, word processing, world geography, world history, world history-AP, world literature, world religions, writing.

Graduation Requirements Civics, computer applications, English, foreign language, health, mathematics, physical education (includes health), science, social studies (includes history), theology, U.S. history, 100 hours of community service.

Special Academic Programs 16 Advanced Placement exams for which test preparation is offered; honors section; independent study; study at local college for college credit.

College Admission Counseling 143 students graduated in 2015; 139 went to college, including Central Connecticut State University; Emmanuel College; Fairfield University; Sacred Heart University; Seton Hall University; University of Connecticut. Other: 1 entered a postgraduate year, 3 had other specific plans. Median SAT critical reading: 530, median SAT math: 520, median SAT writing: 540, median combined SAT: 1590, median composite ACT: 23. 26% scored over 600 on SAT critical reading, 28% scored over 600 on SAT math, 31% scored over 600 on SAT writing, 27% scored over 1800 on combined SAT, 35% scored over 26 on composite ACT.

Student Life Upper grades have uniform requirement, student council. Discipline rests primarily with faculty. Attendance at religious services is required.

Tuition and Aid Day student tuition: $13,000–$13,500. Tuition installment plan (FACTS Tuition Payment Plan, individually arranged payment plans). Tuition reduction for siblings, merit scholarship grants, need-based scholarship grants available.

Admissions Traditional secondary-level entrance grade is 9. For fall 2015, 269 students applied for upper-level admission, 234 were accepted, 143 enrolled. High School Placement Test (closed version) from Scholastic Testing Service required. Deadline for receipt of application materials: none. Application fee required: $50.

Athletics Interscholastic: basketball, cheering, cross-country running, diving, field hockey, golf, gymnastics, ice hockey, indoor track, lacrosse, soccer, softball, swimming and diving, tennis, track and field, volleyball. 1 PE instructor, 33 coaches, 1 athletic trainer.

Computers Computers are regularly used in accounting, all academic, business applications, computer applications, desktop publishing, introduction to technology, journalism, photography, technology, Web site design, word processing classes. Computer network features include on-campus library services, Internet access, wireless campus network, Internet filtering or blocking technology. Campus intranet, student e-mail accounts, and computer access in designated common areas are available to students. Students grades are available online.

Contact Mrs. Diane Santostefano, Director of Admissions. 860-346-6659. Fax: 860-344-9887. E-mail: dsantostefano@mercyhigh.com. Website: www.mercyhigh.com

MERCY HIGH SCHOOL COLLEGE PREPARATORY

3250 19th Avenue
San Francisco, California 94132-2000

Head of School: Dr. Dorothy McCrea

General Information Girls' day college-preparatory, Women In Medicine, and Women in the Art school, affiliated with Roman Catholic Church. Grades 9–12. Founded: 1952. Setting: urban. Nearest major city is Daly City. 6-acre campus. 2 buildings on campus. Approved or accredited by Western Association of Schools and Colleges, Western Catholic Education Association, and California Department of Education. Endowment: $2 million. Total enrollment: 401. Upper school average class size: 25. Upper school faculty-student ratio: 1:15. There are 180 required school days per year for Upper School students. Upper School students typically attend 5 days per week. The average school day consists of 7 hours and 5 minutes.

Upper School Student Profile Grade 9: 120 students (120 girls); Grade 10: 99 students (99 girls); Grade 11: 81 students (81 girls); Grade 12: 101 students (101 girls). 64% of students are Roman Catholic.

Faculty School total: 27. In upper school: 5 men, 22 women; 18 have advanced degrees.

Subjects Offered 3-dimensional art, advanced studio art-AP, algebra, American history, American literature, art, biology, calculus, calculus-AP, ceramics, chemistry, chemistry-AP, chorus, creative writing, dance, dance performance, drama, English, English language-AP, English literature, English literature and composition-AP, environmental science, ethnic studies, expository writing, foreign language, French, geometry, government/civics, mathematics, physical education, physical science, physics, physics-AP, poetry, pre-calculus, religious studies, social justice, social studies, Spanish, speech, statistics, theater, trigonometry, U.S. history, United States government-AP, visual and performing arts, visual arts, world history, world literature.

Graduation Requirements Electives, English, languages, mathematics, physical science, religious studies, science, U.S. government, U.S. history, visual and performing arts, world history, 50 volunteer hours and a senior culminating project, Intersession. Community service is required.

Special Academic Programs Advanced Placement exam preparation; honors section; programs in English, mathematics, general development for dyslexic students; special instructional classes for McAuley Academic Program.

College Admission Counseling 104 students graduated in 2014; all went to college, including College of San Mateo; Dominican University; San Francisco State University; Sonoma State University; University of California, Davis; University of California, Los Angeles. Mean SAT critical reading: 495, mean SAT math: 502, mean SAT writing: 514, mean combined SAT: 1511, mean composite ACT: 22. 16.5% scored over 600 on SAT critical reading, 16.5% scored over 600 on SAT math, 16.5% scored over 600 on SAT writing, 16.5% scored over 1800 on combined SAT, 22.4% scored over 26 on composite ACT.

Student Life Upper grades have uniform requirement, student council, honor system. Discipline rests primarily with faculty. Attendance at religious services is required.

Tuition and Aid Day student tuition: $16,350. Tuition installment plan (SMART Tuition Payment Plan, monthly payment plans, individually arranged payment plans, SMART, 10 months payment (July-April), full pay and semiannual payment (July & December)). Merit scholarship grants, need-based scholarship grants available. In 2014–15, 40% of upper-school students received aid; total upper-school merit-scholarship money awarded: $30,000. Total amount of financial aid awarded in 2014–15: $1,400,000.

Admissions Traditional secondary-level entrance grade is 9. For fall 2014, 270 students applied for upper-level admission, 200 were accepted, 120 enrolled. High School Placement Test required. Deadline for receipt of application materials: December 5. Application fee required: $85. On-campus interview required.

Athletics Interscholastic: basketball, cross-country running, dance, dance squad, self defense, soccer, softball, swimming and diving, tennis, track and field, volleyball. 2 PE instructors, 11 coaches.

Computers Computers are regularly used in all academic classes. Computer network features include on-campus library services, Internet access, wireless campus network, Internet filtering or blocking technology, RenWeb. Campus intranet, student e-mail accounts, and computer access in designated common areas are available to students. Students grades are available online. The school has a published electronic and media policy.

Contact Michelle Ferrari, Director of Community Outreach and Admissions. 415-584-5929. Fax: 415-334-9726. E-mail: mferrari@mercyhs.org. Website: www.mercyhs.org

MERION MERCY ACADEMY

511 Montgomery Avenue
Merion Station, Pennsylvania 19066

Head of School: Sr. Barbara Buckley

General Information Girls' day college-preparatory, arts, and religious studies school, affiliated with Roman Catholic Church. Grades 9–12. Founded: 1884. Setting: suburban. Nearest major city is Philadelphia. 35-acre campus. 7 buildings on campus. Approved or accredited by Middle States Association of Colleges and Schools and National Catholic Education Association. Member of National Association of Independent Schools. Endowment: $11 million. Total enrollment: 484. Upper school average class size: 16. Upper school faculty-student ratio: 1:9. The average school day consists of 6 hours and 7 minutes.

Upper School Student Profile Grade 9: 111 students (111 girls); Grade 10: 124 students (124 girls); Grade 11: 122 students (122 girls); Grade 12: 127 students (127 girls). 90% of students are Roman Catholic.

Faculty School total: 53. In upper school: 6 men, 47 women, 41 have advanced degrees.

Subjects Offered Algebra, American history, American literature, art, art history, biology, business, calculus, chemistry, computer programming, creative writing, drama, economics, English, English literature, environmental science, European history, fine arts, French, geometry, government/civics, grammar, health, history, journalism, Latin, mathematics, music, music history, physical education, physics, physiology, psychology, religion, science, social studies, Spanish, speech, theater, theology, trigonometry, women's studies, world history, world literature, writing.

Graduation Requirements Arts and fine arts (art, music, dance, drama), English, foreign language, mathematics, physical education (includes health), religion (includes Bible studies and theology), science, social studies (includes history).

Special Academic Programs Advanced Placement exam preparation; honors section; study at local college for college credit; academic accommodation for the gifted, the musically talented, and the artistically talented; remedial reading and/or remedial writing; remedial math.

College Admission Counseling 120 students graduated in 2015; all went to college, including Drexel University; Fordham University; Penn State University Park; Saint Joseph's University; University of Pennsylvania; Villanova University. Mean SAT critical reading: 599, mean SAT math: 585, mean SAT writing: 608, mean combined SAT: 1793, mean composite ACT: 25.

Student Life Upper grades have uniform requirement, student council, honor system. Discipline rests primarily with faculty. Attendance at religious services is required.

Summer Programs Enrichment, advancement, sports, art/fine arts programs offered; session focuses on enrichment; held on campus; accepts boys and girls; open to students from other schools. 150 students usually enrolled. 2016 schedule: June 13 to August 5. Application deadline: May 1.

Tuition and Aid Day student tuition: $17,200. Tuition installment plan (The Tuition Plan, monthly payment plans, 2 equal payments plan, one entire payment, 10 payments July-April). Tuition reduction for siblings, merit scholarship grants, need-based scholarship grants, alumnae, Mercy, and music scholarships available. In 2015–16, 45% of upper-school students received aid; total upper-school merit-scholarship money awarded: $397,550. Total amount of financial aid awarded in 2015–16: $1,420,000.

Admissions Traditional secondary-level entrance grade is 9. For fall 2015, 253 students applied for upper-level admission, 240 were accepted, 111 enrolled. High School Placement Test required. Deadline for receipt of application materials: November 6. Application fee required: $60. On-campus interview required.

Athletics Interscholastic: basketball, cheering, crew, cross-country running, field hockey, golf, lacrosse, soccer, softball, swimming and diving, tennis, track and field, volleyball, winter (indoor) track; intramural: basketball, dance, tennis. 2 PE instructors, 19 coaches, 1 athletic trainer.

Computers Computers are regularly used in all academic classes. Computer network features include on-campus library services, online commercial services, Internet access, wireless campus network, Internet filtering or blocking technology. Student e-mail accounts and computer access in designated common areas are available to students.

Contact Eileen Killeen, Director of Admissions. 610-664-6655 Ext. 116. Fax: 610-664-6322. E-mail: ekilleen@merion-mercy.com. Website: www.merion-mercy.com

MESA GRANDE SEVENTH-DAY ACADEMY

975 Fremont Street
Calimesa, California 92320

Head of School: Alfred J. Riddle

General Information Coeducational day college-preparatory, arts, religious studies, bilingual studies, and technology school, affiliated with Seventh-day Adventists, Christian faith. Grades K–12. Founded: 1928. Setting: rural. Nearest major city is San Bernardino. 14-acre campus. 3 buildings on campus. Approved or accredited by Western Association of Schools and Colleges and California Department of Education. Endowment: $650,000. Total enrollment: 252. Upper school average class size: 27. Upper school faculty-student ratio: 1:10. There are 180 required school days per year for Upper School students. Upper School students typically attend 5 days per week. The average school day consists of 8 hours.

Upper School Student Profile Grade 9: 18 students (12 boys, 6 girls); Grade 10: 26 students (12 boys, 14 girls); Grade 11: 27 students (10 boys, 17 girls); Grade 12: 19 students (9 boys, 10 girls). 90% of students are Seventh-day Adventists, Christian.

Faculty School total: 22. In upper school: 6 men, 8 women; 7 have advanced degrees.

Subjects Offered Algebra, American literature, arts, ASB Leadership, auto mechanics, bell choir, biology, British literature, career education, chemistry, choral music, community service, composition, computer applications, computer-aided design, computers, concert choir, desktop publishing, drama, economics, economics and history, English, English composition, family living, fine arts, geometry, government/civics, graphic arts, handbells, health, instrumental music, keyboarding, lab science, marine biology, mathematics, music composition, music theory, physical education, physical science, physics, pre-calculus, relationships, religion, religious education, science, social sciences, social studies, Spanish, U.S. government, U.S. history, video film production, world history, world literature, yearbook.

Graduation Requirements Algebra, American government, applied skills, arts and fine arts (art, music, dance, drama), biology, British literature, career education, chemistry, computer education, computer technologies, economics, English, English composition, family living, industrial technology, keyboarding, mathematics, modern languages, physical education (includes health), physical fitness, physical science, physics, religious studies, science, social studies (includes history), Spanish, technical skills, work experience, community service.

Special Academic Programs ESL (10 students enrolled).

College Admission Counseling Colleges students went to include La Sierra University; Pacific Union College; Southern Adventist University; University of California, Irvine; University of California, Los Angeles; Walla Walla University.

Student Life Upper grades have uniform requirement, student council, honor system. Discipline rests primarily with faculty. Attendance at religious services is required.

Summer Programs Sports programs offered; session focuses on sports; held both on and off campus; held at Drayson Center, Loma Linda, CA; accepts boys and girls; open to students from other schools. 50 students usually enrolled. 2016 schedule: June 8 to August 3. Application deadline: May 5.

Tuition and Aid Day student tuition: $8910. Tuition installment plan (monthly payment plans, individually arranged payment plans). Need-based scholarship grants, need-based loans, middle-income loans available. In 2015–16, 30% of upper-school students received aid. Total amount of financial aid awarded in 2015–16: $35,000.

Admissions Traditional secondary-level entrance grade is 9. For fall 2015, 30 students applied for upper-level admission, 28 were accepted, 28 enrolled. Any standardized test, English proficiency, ITBS-TAP, Math Placement Exam or writing sample required. Deadline for receipt of application materials: none. Application fee required: $50. On-campus interview required.

Athletics Interscholastic: baseball (boys), basketball (b,g), flag football (b,g), football (b), softball (g), volleyball (b,g); coed interscholastic: cross-country running, golf, physical fitness, weight lifting, weight training. 2 PE instructors, 12 coaches, 2 athletic trainers.

Computers Computers are regularly used in art, design, graphic design, science, technical drawing, technology, typing, video film production, writing, yearbook classes. Computer network features include on-campus library services, online commercial services, Internet access, wireless campus network, Internet filtering or blocking technology. Student e-mail accounts and computer access in designated common areas

are available to students. Students grades are available online. The school has a published electronic and media policy.

Contact Lois M. Myhre, Admissions Office. 909-795-1112 Ext. 257. Fax: 909-795-1653. E-mail: lois.myhre@mgak-12.org. Website: www.mesagrandeacademy.org

MIAMI COUNTRY DAY SCHOOL

601 Northeast 107th Street
Miami, Florida 33161

Head of School: Dr. John P. Davies

General Information Coeducational day college-preparatory school. Grades PK–12. Founded: 1938. Setting: suburban. 22-acre campus. 6 buildings on campus. Approved or accredited by Florida Council of Independent Schools, Missouri Independent School Association, Southern Association of Colleges and Schools, Southern Association of Independent Schools, The College Board, and Florida Department of Education. Member of National Association of Independent Schools and Secondary School Admission Test Board. Endowment: $4.5 million. Total enrollment: 1,250. Upper school average class size: 18. Upper school faculty-student ratio: 1:10. There are 179 required school days per year for Upper School students. Upper School students typically attend 5 days per week. The average school day consists of 6 hours and 15 minutes.

Upper School Student Profile Grade 9: 115 students (54 boys, 61 girls); Grade 10: 117 students (60 boys, 57 girls); Grade 11: 97 students (52 boys, 45 girls); Grade 12: 88 students (43 boys, 45 girls).

Faculty School total: 90. In upper school: 28 men, 32 women; 48 have advanced degrees.

Subjects Offered Advanced Placement courses, African-American studies, algebra, American history, American history-AP, American literature, ancient history, art, art history, backpacking, band, biology, calculus, calculus-AP, ceramics, chemistry, community service, composition, computer programming, computer science, conflict resolution, creative writing, design, desktop publishing, DNA science lab, drama, drawing, economics, English, English language and composition-AP, English literature, English literature-AP, environmental science-AP, ESL, European history, film, film and literature, fine arts, French, geography, geometry, government/civics, health, instrumental music, jewelry making, journalism, law, life management skills, literature, marine biology, mathematics, music theory, orchestra, painting, philosophy, photography, physical education, physical science, physics, physics-AP, post-calculus, psychology, public speaking, religion, science, sculpture, social sciences, social studies, Spanish, Spanish language-AP, Spanish literature-AP, theater, trigonometry, U.S. government and politics-AP, video film production, world history, world literature, writing, yearbook.

Graduation Requirements Arts and fine arts (art, music, dance, drama), computer science, electives, English, foreign language, mathematics, philosophy, physical education (includes health), science, social studies (includes history), speech and debate, 100 hours of community service.

Special Academic Programs 24 Advanced Placement exams for which test preparation is offered; honors section; independent study; study at local college for college credit; ESL (9 students enrolled).

College Admission Counseling 97 students graduated in 2015; all went to college, including American University; Boston University; Duke University; Florida State University; University of Florida; University of Miami. Median SAT critical reading: 630, median SAT math: 660, median SAT writing: 630.

Student Life Upper grades have uniform requirement, student council, honor system. Discipline rests equally with students and faculty.

Summer Programs Remediation, enrichment, advancement, ESL, sports, art/fine arts, rigorous outdoor training, computer instruction programs offered; session focuses on academics, enrichment, review, and recreation; held on campus; accepts boys and girls; open to students from other schools. 250 students usually enrolled. 2016 schedule: June 15 to August 14. Application deadline: none.

Tuition and Aid Day student tuition: $29,964. Need-based scholarship grants available. In 2015–16, 21% of upper-school students received aid. Total amount of financial aid awarded in 2015–16: $3,100,000.

Admissions Traditional secondary-level entrance grade is 9. For fall 2015, 161 students applied for upper-level admission, 49 were accepted, 30 enrolled. ISEE or PSAT and SAT for applicants to grade 11 and 12 required. Deadline for receipt of application materials: January 29. Application fee required: $100. Interview required.

Athletics Interscholastic: baseball (boys), basketball (b,g), cheering (g), cross-country running (b,g), football (b), golf (b,g), lacrosse (b), soccer (b,g), softball (g), swimming and diving (b,g), tennis (b,g), track and field (b,g), volleyball (g), water polo (b,g), yoga (b,g); intramural: baseball (b), basketball (b,g), cheering (g), cross-country running (b,g), dance (g), lacrosse (b), volleyball (b), yoga (g); coed intramural: flag football, modern dance, outdoor education, outdoor skills, physical fitness, physical training, soccer, strength & conditioning, weight training. 3 PE instructors, 24 coaches, 1 athletic trainer.

Computers Computers are regularly used in all academic, graphic design, journalism, media, research skills, Web site design, yearbook classes. Computer network features include on-campus library services, online commercial services, Internet access, wireless campus network, Internet filtering or blocking technology, Google Drive. Student e-mail accounts and computer access in designated common areas are available to students. Students grades are available online. The school has a published electronic and media policy.

Contact Ingrid Palmisano, Director of Admission and Financial Aid. 305-779-7230. Fax: 305-397-0370. E-mail: admissions@miamicountryday.org. Website: www.miamicountryday.org

THE MIAMI VALLEY SCHOOL

5151 Denise Drive
Dayton, Ohio 45429

Head of School: Jay Scheurle

General Information Coeducational day college-preparatory, arts, and technology school. Grades PK–12. Founded: 1964. Setting: suburban. 22-acre campus. 1 building on campus. Approved or accredited by Independent Schools Association of the Central States, Ohio Association of Independent Schools, and Ohio Department of Education. Member of National Association of Independent Schools. Endowment: $64 million. Total enrollment: 474. Upper school average class size: 14. Upper school faculty-student ratio: 1:8. There are 180 required school days per year for Upper School students. Upper School students typically attend 5 days per week. The average school day consists of 7 hours and 20 minutes.

Upper School Student Profile Grade 9: 46 students (27 boys, 19 girls); Grade 10: 50 students (29 boys, 21 girls); Grade 11: 51 students (22 boys, 29 girls); Grade 12: 48 students (27 boys, 21 girls).

Faculty School total: 66. In upper school: 12 men, 14 women; 20 have advanced degrees.

Subjects Offered Advanced Placement courses, algebra, American history, American literature, anatomy, art, art history, biology, calculus, ceramics, chemistry, Chinese, Chinese history, choir, college admission preparation, college counseling, community service, computer programming, computer science, creative writing, criminal justice, drama, earth science, Eastern world civilizations, ecology, economics, English, English literature, environmental science, ESL, European history, fine arts, French, gardening, gender issues, genetics, geology, geometry, government/civics, grammar, health, history, human issues, instrumental music, jazz, jazz band, journalism, Latin, Mandarin, marine biology, mathematics, microbiology, model United Nations, modern European history-AP, music, philosophy, photography, physical education, physics, physiology, pottery, pre-algebra, pre-calculus, religion, science, social sciences, social studies, Spanish, speech, statistics, theater, trigonometry, woodworking, word processing, world civilizations, world history, world literature, writing, yearbook.

Graduation Requirements Alternative physical education, arts and fine arts (art, music, dance, drama), English, foreign language, mathematics, science, social sciences, social studies (includes history), immersion term, community service. Community service is required.

Special Academic Programs Advanced Placement exam preparation; honors section; independent study; term-away projects; study at local college for college credit; study abroad; academic accommodation for the gifted, the musically talented, and the artistically talented; ESL (12 students enrolled).

College Admission Counseling 41 students graduated in 2015; all went to college, including Bowdoin College; Case Western Reserve University; Miami University; University of Chicago; Vanderbilt University; Washington University in St. Louis. Median combined SAT: 1802, median composite ACT: 28.

Student Life Upper grades have specified standards of dress, student council, honor system. Discipline rests primarily with faculty.

Summer Programs Remediation, enrichment, ESL, sports, art/fine arts, rigorous outdoor training programs offered; session focuses on general summer day camp; held on campus; accepts boys and girls; open to students from other schools. 150 students usually enrolled. 2016 schedule: June 13 to July 22.

Tuition and Aid Day student tuition: $19,725. Tuition installment plan (FACTS Tuition Payment Plan). Merit scholarship grants, need-based scholarship grants available. In 2015–16, 47% of upper-school students received aid; total upper-school merit-scholarship money awarded: $148,350. Total amount of financial aid awarded in 2015–16: $1,204,171.

Admissions Traditional secondary-level entrance grade is 9. For fall 2015, 39 students applied for upper-level admission, 29 were accepted, 24 enrolled. Achievement/Aptitude/Writing, school's own test, SSAT, Stanford Achievement Test, Otis-Lennon School Ability Test, TOEFL or SLEP or writing sample required. Deadline for receipt of application materials: none. Application fee required: $125. On-campus interview required.

Athletics Interscholastic: basketball (boys, girls), cheering (g), lacrosse (b,g), soccer (b,g), strength & conditioning (b,g), tennis (b,g), track and field (b,g), volleyball (g), weight training (b,g); intramural: squash (b); coed interscholastic: bowling, cross-country running, golf, swimming and diving; coed intramural: crew. 2 PE instructors, 42 coaches, 2 athletic trainers.

Computers Computers are regularly used in literary magazine, mathematics, media production, multimedia, music technology, newspaper, photography, programming, science, social sciences, technology, yearbook classes. Computer network features include on-campus library services, online commercial services, Internet access, wireless campus network, Internet filtering or blocking technology. Campus intranet and student e-mail accounts are available to students. Students grades are available online. The school has a published electronic and media policy.

Contact Susan Strong, Director of Enrollment and Financial Aid. 937-434-4444 Ext. 230. Fax: 937-434-1033. E-mail: susan.strong@mvschool.com. Website: www.mvschool.com

MIDDLESEX SCHOOL

1400 Lowell Road
Concord, Massachusetts 01742

Head of School: Kathleen C. Giles

General Information Coeducational boarding and day college-preparatory and arts school. Grades 9–12. Founded: 1901. Setting: suburban. Nearest major city is Boston. Students are housed in single-sex dormitories. 350-acre campus. 31 buildings on campus. Approved or accredited by New England Association of Schools and Colleges. Member of National Association of Independent Schools and Secondary School Admission Test Board. Endowment: $244 million. Total enrollment: 384. Upper school average class size: 12. Upper school faculty-student ratio: 1:4. There are 180 required school days per year for Upper School students. Upper School students typically attend 6 days per week. The average school day consists of 7 hours and 15 minutes.

Upper School Student Profile Grade 9: 84 students (42 boys, 42 girls); Grade 10: 104 students (54 boys, 50 girls); Grade 11: 103 students (53 boys, 50 girls); Grade 12: 93 students (44 boys, 49 girls). 67% of students are boarding students. 55% are state residents. 26 states are represented in upper school student body. 11% are international students. International students from China, Jamaica, Republic of Korea, Thailand, United Kingdom, and Viet Nam; 9 other countries represented in student body.

Faculty School total: 88. In upper school: 48 men, 40 women; 62 have advanced degrees; 51 reside on campus.

Subjects Offered Acting, advanced biology, advanced chemistry, advanced computer applications, Advanced Placement courses, advanced studio art-AP, African American history, African history, African-American history, algebra, American literature, analytic geometry, art, art history, art history-AP, art-AP, Asian literature, astronomy, biology, biology-AP, British literature, calculus, calculus-AP, ceramics, chemistry, chemistry-AP, Chinese, classical Greek literature, computer programming, computer programming-AP, computer science, computer science-AP, creative writing, discrete mathematics, DNA, drama, economics, economics-AP, English, English literature, English literature and composition-AP, environmental science, environmental science-AP, ethics, European history, European history-AP, finite math, forensics, French, French language-AP, French literature-AP, geometry, Greek, history, history of jazz, Holocaust studies, independent study, jazz band, Latin, Latin-American history, marine studies, mathematics, media, Middle East, Middle Eastern history, model United Nations, music, music theory, music theory-AP, philosophy, photography, physics, physics-AP, political science, religion, Shakespeare, Spanish, Spanish language-AP, Spanish literature-AP, statistics, statistics-AP, studio art-AP, theater, trigonometry, U.S. government and politics-AP, U.S. history, U.S. history-AP, video film production, Vietnam history, Vietnam War, vocal ensemble, women in world history, woodworking, world history, writing, writing workshop.

Graduation Requirements Algebra, analytic geometry, arts, English, English literature and composition-AP, European history, foreign language, geometry, science, trigonometry, U.S. history, each senior completes a hand-carved wooden plaque. Students also attend mindfulness classes, writing workshops, and a math/science/computer science problem solving initiative.

Special Academic Programs 23 Advanced Placement exams for which test preparation is offered; honors section; independent study; academic accommodation for the gifted.

College Admission Counseling 96 students graduated in 2015; all went to college, including Boston College; Brown University; Colby College; Columbia University; Duke University; Georgetown University. Median SAT critical reading: 690, median SAT math: 680, median SAT writing: 700, median combined SAT: 2070, median composite ACT: 29. 93% scored over 600 on SAT critical reading, 92% scored over 600 on SAT math, 94% scored over 600 on SAT writing, 96% scored over 1800 on combined SAT, 90% scored over 26 on composite ACT.

Student Life Upper grades have specified standards of dress, student council, honor system. Discipline rests primarily with faculty.

Tuition and Aid Day student tuition: $44,840; 7-day tuition and room/board: $56,060. Guaranteed tuition plan. Tuition installment plan (Insured Tuition Payment Plan, monthly payment plans, semiannual payment plan). Need-based scholarship grants, need-based loans available. In 2015–16, 30% of upper-school students received aid. Total amount of financial aid awarded in 2015–16: $5,090,000.

Admissions Traditional secondary-level entrance grade is 9. For fall 2015, 1,218 students applied for upper-level admission, 112 enrolled. ISEE, SSAT or TOEFL required. Deadline for receipt of application materials: January 15. Application fee required: $55. Interview recommended.

Athletics Interscholastic: alpine skiing (boys, girls), baseball (b), basketball (b,g), crew (b,g), cross-country running (b,g), field hockey (g), football (b), ice hockey (b,g), lacrosse (b,g), skiing (downhill) (b,g), soccer (b,g), squash (b,g), tennis (b,g), volleyball (g), wrestling (b); coed interscholastic: dance, golf, track and field; coed intramural: dance, fitness, physical training, squash, strength & conditioning, yoga. 1 PE instructor, 23 coaches, 2 athletic trainers.

Computers Computers are regularly used in all classes. Computer network features include on-campus library services, online commercial services, Internet access, wireless campus network, Internet filtering or blocking technology. Campus intranet, student e-mail accounts, and computer access in designated common areas are available to students. Students grades are available online. The school has a published electronic and media policy.

Contact Douglas C. Price, Director of Admissions. 978-371-6524. Fax: 978-402-1400. E-mail: admissions@mxschool.edu. Website: www.mxschool.edu

MIDDLE TENNESSEE CHRISTIAN SCHOOL

100 East MTCS Road
Murfreesboro, Tennessee 37129
Head of School: Dr. Phil Ellenburg

General Information Coeducational day college-preparatory, arts, religious studies, and technology school, affiliated with Church of Christ. Grades PK–12. Founded: 1962. Setting: suburban. Nearest major city is Nashville. 37-acre campus. 3 buildings on campus. Approved or accredited by National Christian School Association, Southern Association of Colleges and Schools, Southern Association of Independent Schools, and Tennessee Department of Education. Member of National Association of Independent Schools. Total enrollment: 668. Upper school average class size: 18. Upper school faculty-student ratio: 1:18. There are 175 required school days per year for Upper School students. Upper School students typically attend 5 days per week. The average school day consists of 7 hours and 15 minutes.

Upper School Student Profile Grade 9: 63 students (30 boys, 33 girls); Grade 10: 63 students (37 boys, 26 girls); Grade 11: 55 students (33 boys, 22 girls); Grade 12: 51 students (31 boys, 20 girls). 49% of students are members of Church of Christ.

Faculty School total: 50. In upper school: 15 men, 15 women; 20 have advanced degrees.

Subjects Offered ACT preparation, advanced math, algebra, American history, American history-AP, American literature, anatomy, art, band, Bible, biology, biology-AP, calculus, chemistry, chorus, computer applications, computer technologies, driver education, economics, electives, English, French, geometry, integrated mathematics, keyboarding, physics, pre-algebra, pre-calculus, Spanish, speech, U.S. government, U.S. history, wellness, yearbook.

Graduation Requirements Algebra, arts, Bible, biology, chemistry, computer applications, economics, electives, English, French, geometry, keyboarding, physical science, pre-algebra, Spanish, speech, U.S. government, U.S. history, wellness, world history.

Special Academic Programs 3 Advanced Placement exams for which test preparation is offered; honors section; study at local college for college credit.

College Admission Counseling 57 students graduated in 2015; 55 went to college, including Freed-Hardeman University; Harding University; Lipscomb University; Middle Tennessee State University; Tennessee Technological University; The University of Tennessee at Chattanooga. Other: 1 went to work, 1 entered military service. Mean composite ACT: 24. 24% scored over 26 on composite ACT.

Student Life Upper grades have specified standards of dress, student council, honor system. Discipline rests primarily with faculty. Attendance at religious services is required.

Tuition and Aid Day student tuition: $8480. Tuition installment plan (monthly payment plans, individually arranged payment plans). Tuition reduction for siblings, need-based scholarship grants available.

Admissions Traditional secondary-level entrance grade is 9. For fall 2015, 31 students applied for upper-level admission, 26 were accepted, 21 enrolled. Achievement tests and OLSAT/Stanford required. Deadline for receipt of application materials: none. Application fee required: $75. Interview required.

Athletics Interscholastic: baseball (boys), basketball (b,g), bowling (b,g), cheering (g), cross-country running (b,g), football (b), golf (b), skeet shooting (b,g), soccer (b,g), softball (g), tennis (b,g), trap and skeet (b,g), volleyball (g). 2 PE instructors.

Computers Computers are regularly used in engineering, keyboarding, mathematics, science, writing, yearbook classes. Computer network features include on-campus library services, Internet access, wireless campus network, Internet filtering or blocking technology. Student e-mail accounts and computer access in designated common areas are available to students. Students grades are available online. The school has a published electronic and media policy.

Contact Mrs. Monica Helton, Admissions and Public Relations. 615-893-0601 Ext. 15. Fax: 615-895-8815. E-mail: monicahelton@mtcscougars.org. Website: www.mtcscougars.org

MIDLAND SCHOOL

PO Box 8
5100 Figueroa Mountain Road
Los Olivos, California 93441
Head of School: Mr. Will Graham

General Information Coeducational boarding college-preparatory and environmental studies school. Grades 9–12. Founded: 1932. Setting: rural. Nearest major city is Santa Barbara. Students are housed in single-sex cabins. 2,860-acre campus. Approved or accredited by California Association of Independent Schools, The Association of Boarding Schools, Western Association of Schools and Colleges, and

California Department of Education. Member of National Association of Independent Schools and Secondary School Admission Test Board. Endowment: $16 million. Total enrollment: 81. Upper school average class size: 10. Upper school faculty-student ratio: 1:4. There are 180 required school days per year for Upper School students. Upper School students typically attend 6 days per week. The average school day consists of 6 hours and 45 minutes.

Upper School Student Profile Grade 9: 17 students (8 boys, 9 girls); Grade 10: 25 students (9 boys, 16 girls); Grade 11: 19 students (10 boys, 9 girls); Grade 12: 20 students (12 boys, 8 girls). 100% of students are boarding students. 70% are state residents. 10 states are represented in upper school student body. 12% are international students. International students from China, India, Mexico, and Saudi Arabia.

Faculty School total: 22. In upper school: 11 men, 11 women; 11 have advanced degrees; all reside on campus.

Subjects Offered 3-dimensional art, advanced chemistry, advanced math, agroecology, algebra, American history, American literature, American studies, anthropology, backpacking, basketball, biology, ceramics, character education, chemistry, clayworking, community service, composition, creative writing, drama, economics, environmental education, environmental studies, equestrian sports, foreign language, gardening, geology, geometry, health education, human sexuality, hydrology, integrated science, land and ranch management, leadership, literature by women, metalworking, music, painting, physics, pre-calculus, senior project, senior seminar, senior thesis, Spanish, Spanish literature, statistics, U.S. history, volleyball, wilderness education, wilderness experience, world studies.

Graduation Requirements Arts and fine arts (art, music, dance, drama), English, foreign language, history, mathematics, science, senior thesis.

Special Academic Programs 9 Advanced Placement exams for which test preparation is offered; honors section; independent study.

College Admission Counseling 17 students graduated in 2015; all went to college, including Harvey Mudd College; Oberlin College; Rensselaer Polytechnic Institute; Smith College; Stanford University; University of Puget Sound. Mean SAT critical reading: 571, mean SAT math: 567, mean SAT writing: 559, mean combined SAT: 1697, mean composite ACT: 25.

Student Life Upper grades have student council. Discipline rests equally with students and faculty.

Tuition and Aid 7-day tuition and room/board: $46,200. Tuition installment plan (monthly payment plans, Your Tuition Solution, Tuition Management Systems). Need-based scholarship grants available. In 2015–16, 47% of upper-school students received aid. Total amount of financial aid awarded in 2015–16: $1,000,000.

Admissions Traditional secondary-level entrance grade is 9. For fall 2015, 77 students applied for upper-level admission, 57 were accepted, 27 enrolled. ISEE, SSAT or TOEFL required. Deadline for receipt of application materials: February 15. Application fee required: $50. On-campus interview required.

Athletics Interscholastic: basketball (boys, girls), cross-country running (b,g), soccer (b,g), softball (g), volleyball (b,g); intramural: table tennis (b,g); coed intramural: backpacking, equestrian sports, fitness, hiking/backpacking, horseback riding, mountain biking, outdoor adventure, outdoor skills, physical fitness, strength & conditioning, yoga.

Computers Computer network features include on-campus library services, online commercial services, Internet access, Internet filtering or blocking technology. Student e-mail accounts and computer access in designated common areas are available to students. The school has a published electronic and media policy.

Contact Amy E. Graham, Assistant Head of School for Enrollment Management. 805-688-5114 Ext. 114. Fax: 805-686-2470. E-mail: admissions@midland-school.org. Website: www.midland-school.org

MID-PACIFIC INSTITUTE

2445 Kaala Street
Honolulu, Hawaii 96822-2299
Head of School: Dr. Paul Turnbull

General Information Coeducational day college-preparatory, arts, bilingual studies, technology, and International Baccalaureate school, affiliated with United Church of Christ. Grades K–12. Founded: 1908. Setting: urban. 42-acre campus. 35 buildings on campus. Approved or accredited by International Baccalaureate Organization and Western Association of Schools and Colleges. Member of National Association of Independent Schools and Secondary School Admission Test Board. Total enrollment: 1,556. Upper school average class size: 20. Upper school faculty-student ratio: 1:20. Upper School students typically attend 5 days per week. The average school day consists of 7 hours and 15 minutes.

Faculty School total: 150. In upper school: 25 have advanced degrees.

Subjects Offered Algebra, American history, American literature, art, art history, astronomy, ballet, band, biology, business skills, calculus, career education, ceramics, chemistry, computer programming, computer science, creative writing, dance, debate, drama, drawing, economics, English, English literature, ESL, film, fine arts, first aid, French, general science, geography, geometry, Hawaiian history, health, history, instrumental music, Japanese, Latin, law, mathematics, oceanography, oral communications, painting, philosophy, photography, physical education, physics, printmaking, psychology, religion, science, sculpture, social sciences, social studies,

Spanish, speech, swimming, swimming competency, technological applications, technology, theater, video, weight training, world history, world literature, writing.

Graduation Requirements Arts and fine arts (art, music, dance, drama), business skills (includes word processing), career education, computer science, English, foreign language, mathematics, oral communications, physical education (includes health), religion (includes Bible studies and theology), science, social sciences, social studies (includes history), speech, swimming competency.

Special Academic Programs International Baccalaureate program; Advanced Placement exam preparation; honors section; study at local college for college credit; academic accommodation for the gifted and the artistically talented; ESL (41 students enrolled).

College Admission Counseling 200 students graduated in 2015; all went to college, including Oregon State University; Seattle University; University of Hawaii at Manoa; University of Oregon; University of Southern California.

Student Life Upper grades have specified standards of dress, student council, honor system. Discipline rests primarily with faculty. Attendance at religious services is required.

Summer Programs Enrichment, advancement, ESL, art/fine arts, computer instruction programs offered; session focuses on physical fitness and skills; held on campus; accepts boys and girls; open to students from other schools. 1,200 students usually enrolled. 2016 schedule: June 5 to July 26. Application deadline: April 5.

Tuition and Aid Day student tuition: $21,050. Tuition installment plan (FACTS Tuition Payment Plan, monthly payment plans, semiannual payment plan). Merit scholarship grants, need-based scholarship grants, paying campus jobs, tuition reduction for children of employees available. In 2015–16, 17% of upper-school students received aid.

Admissions Traditional secondary-level entrance grade is 9. For fall 2015, 700 students applied for upper-level admission, 220 were accepted, 150 enrolled. SAT, SSAT and TOEFL required. Deadline for receipt of application materials: December 1. Application fee required: $125. Interview required.

Athletics Interscholastic: aquatics (boys, girls), baseball (b), basketball (b,g), bowling (b,g), canoeing/kayaking (b,g), cheering (g), cross-country running (b,g), football (b), golf (b,g), gymnastics (g), independent competitive sports (b,g), kayaking (b,g), ocean paddling (b,g), physical fitness (b,g), physical training (b,g), riflery (b,g), soccer (b,g), softball (g), strength & conditioning (b,g), surfing (b,g), swimming and diving (b,g), tennis (b,g), track and field (b,g), volleyball (b,g), water polo (b,g), wrestling (b,g); intramural: badminton (b,g), weight lifting (b,g), weight training (b,g); coed interscholastic: fitness, modern dance; coed intramural: badminton. 7 PE instructors, 50 coaches, 3 athletic trainers.

Computers Computers are regularly used in English, foreign language, history, mathematics, media arts, science classes. Computer network features include on-campus library services, online commercial services, Internet access, wireless campus network, Internet filtering or blocking technology, one-to-one iPad program. Campus intranet, student e-mail accounts, and computer access in designated common areas are available to students. Students grades are available online. The school has a published electronic and media policy.

Contact Ms. Lani Corrie, Admissions Assistant. 808-973-5005. Fax: 808-973-5099. E-mail: admissions@midpac.edu. Website: www.midpac.edu

MID-PENINSULA HIGH SCHOOL

1340 Willow Road
Menlo Park, California 94025-1516

Head of School: Douglas C. Thompson, PhD

General Information Coeducational day college-preparatory, general academic, and arts school; primarily serves underachievers, students with learning disabilities, individuals with Attention Deficit Disorder, individuals with emotional and behavioral problems, dyslexic students, and Asberger's Syndrome. Grades 9–12. Founded: 1979. Setting: suburban. Nearest major city is San Francisco. 2-acre campus. 1 building on campus. Approved or accredited by Western Association of Schools and Colleges and California Department of Education. Member of National Association of Independent Schools. Endowment: $2.4 million. Total enrollment: 117. Upper school average class size: 12. Upper school faculty-student ratio: 1:8. Upper School students typically attend 5 days per week. The average school day consists of 6 hours and 10 minutes.

Upper School Student Profile Grade 9: 25 students (11 boys, 14 girls); Grade 10: 30 students (17 boys, 13 girls); Grade 11: 34 students (22 boys, 12 girls); Grade 12: 27 students (19 boys, 8 girls).

Faculty School total: 18. In upper school: 6 men, 9 women; 5 have advanced degrees.

Subjects Offered Algebra, American sign language, art, biology, calculus, calculus-AP, chemistry, composition, contemporary issues, drama, driver education, English, geometry, government, human relations, mathematics, music performance, physical education, physics, SAT/ACT preparation, science, Spanish, sports, study skills, trigonometry, U.S. history, world studies.

Graduation Requirements American government, government, human relations, mathematics, physical education (includes health), science, social sciences, U.S. history. Community service is required.

Special Academic Programs Accelerated programs; independent study; remedial reading and/or remedial writing; remedial math.

College Admission Counseling Colleges students went to include California State University, Chico; California State University, East Bay; California State University, Monterey Bay; Pacific Lutheran University; University of San Francisco; Whittier College.

Student Life Discipline rests primarily with faculty.

Tuition and Aid Day student tuition: $29,740. Tuition installment plan (monthly payment plans, individually arranged payment plans, 2-payment plan). Need-based scholarship grants available. In 2014–15, 36% of upper-school students received aid.

Admissions Traditional secondary-level entrance grade is 9. Deadline for receipt of application materials: none. No application fee required. On-campus interview required.

Athletics Interscholastic: baseball (boys), basketball (b,g), softball (g), volleyball (b,g); coed interscholastic: cross-country running, soccer, track and field. 1 PE instructor, 4 coaches.

Computers Computers are regularly used in all academic, art, basic skills, college planning, desktop publishing, music, publications, SAT preparation, theater arts classes. Computer network features include Internet access, wireless campus network, Internet filtering or blocking technology. Campus intranet, student e-mail accounts, and computer access in designated common areas are available to students. The school has a published electronic and media policy.

Contact Ms. Andrea Henderson, Director of Admissions. 650-321-1991 Ext. 147. Fax: 650-321-9921. E-mail: andrea@mid-pen.com. Website: www.mid-pen.com

MILLBROOK SCHOOL

131 Millbrook School Road
Millbrook, New York 12545

Head of School: Mr. Drew Casertano

General Information Coeducational boarding and day college-preparatory, arts, environmental stewardship, and community service school. Grades 9–12. Founded: 1931. Setting: rural. Nearest major city is New York. Students are housed in single-sex dormitories. 800-acre campus. 41 buildings on campus. Approved or accredited by New York State Association of Independent Schools, The Association of Boarding Schools, and New York Department of Education. Member of National Association of Independent Schools and Secondary School Admission Test Board. Endowment: $340,000. Total enrollment: 294. Upper school average class size: 14. Upper school faculty-student ratio: 1:5. There are 179 required school days per year for Upper School students. Upper School students typically attend 6 days per week. The average school day consists of 7 hours.

Upper School Student Profile Grade 9: 56 students (29 boys, 27 girls); Grade 10: 77 students (40 boys, 37 girls); Grade 11: 83 students (50 boys, 33 girls); Grade 12: 75 students (35 boys, 40 girls); Postgraduate: 3 students (3 boys). 84% of students are boarding students. 42% are state residents. 23 states are represented in upper school student body. 15% are international students. International students from Canada, China, Germany, Republic of Korea, Spain, and Viet Nam; 14 other countries represented in student body.

Faculty School total: 62. In upper school: 30 men, 32 women; 37 have advanced degrees; 52 reside on campus.

Subjects Offered Acting, advanced biology, advanced chemistry, advanced math, Advanced Placement courses, advanced studio art-AP, aesthetics, algebra, American history, American literature, ancient history, ancient world history, animal behavior, animal science, anthropology, art, art history, astronomy, biology, calculus, calculus-AP, ceramics, chemistry, Chinese, choral music, constitutional law, creative writing, dance, dance performance, digital photography, drama, drama performance, drawing, ecology, English, English language-AP, English literature, English-AP, environmental science, European history, fine arts, forensics, French, French language-AP, French-AP, geometry, global studies, history, honors English, honors geometry, human biology, human development, independent study, instrumental music, jazz band, jazz ensemble, journalism, Mandarin, mathematics, medieval history, Middle Eastern history, music, music appreciation, music history, painting, philosophy, photography, physics, pre-calculus, psychology, science, senior project, social sciences, social studies, Spanish, Spanish-AP, studio art, study skills, theater, trigonometry, world history.

Graduation Requirements Biology, English, foreign language, history, mathematics, science, visual and performing arts.

Special Academic Programs 9 Advanced Placement exams for which test preparation is offered; honors section; independent study; term-away projects; study abroad.

College Admission Counseling 81 students graduated in 2014; 75 went to college, including Elon University; Hamilton College; New York University; St. Lawrence University; Trinity College; Union College. Other: 6 had other specific plans. Mean SAT critical reading: 585, mean SAT math: 586, mean SAT writing: 589, mean combined SAT: 1760, mean composite ACT: 24.

Student Life Upper grades have specified standards of dress, student council. Discipline rests equally with students and faculty.

Tuition and Aid Day student tuition: $40,400; 7-day tuition and room/board: $53,500. Need-based scholarship grants, need-based loans available. In 2014–15, 28% of upper-school students received aid. Total amount of financial aid awarded in 2014–15: $2,841,000.

Admissions Traditional secondary-level entrance grade is 9. For fall 2014, 626 students applied for upper-level admission, 251 were accepted, 112 enrolled. ISEE,

PSAT or SAT for applicants to grade 11 and 12, SSAT, TOEFL or writing sample required. Deadline for receipt of application materials: January 15. Application fee required: $50. Interview required.

Athletics Interscholastic: baseball (boys), basketball (b,g), cross-country running (b,g), field hockey (g), ice hockey (b,g), lacrosse (b,g), soccer (b,g), softball (g), squash (b,g), tennis (b,g); coed interscholastic: golf, track and field; coed intramural: aerobics/dance, aerobics/Nautilus, alpine skiing, badminton, ballet, bicycling, dance, equestrian sports, fitness, hiking/backpacking, horseback riding, modern dance, outdoor education, physical training, running, skiing (downhill), snowboarding, strength & conditioning, weight training, yoga. 1 coach, 1 athletic trainer.

Computers Computers are regularly used in foreign language, French, history, journalism, mathematics, photography, science, Spanish, study skills, video film production, yearbook classes. Computer network features include on-campus library services, online commercial services, Internet access, wireless campus network, Internet filtering or blocking technology. Campus intranet, student e-mail accounts, and computer access in designated common areas are available to students. Students grades are available online. The school has a published electronic and media policy.

Contact Mrs. Wendy Greenfield, Admission Office Assistant. 845-677-8261 Ext. 138. Fax: 845-677-1265. E-mail: admissions@millbrook.org. Website: www.millbrook.org

MILL SPRINGS ACADEMY

Alpharetta, Georgia
See Special Needs Schools section.

MILTON ACADEMY

170 Centre Street
Milton, Massachusetts 02186

Head of School: Todd Bland

General Information Coeducational boarding and day college-preparatory school. Boarding grades 9–12, day grades K–12. Founded: 1798. Setting: suburban. Nearest major city is Boston. Students are housed in single-sex dormitories. 125-acre campus. 25 buildings on campus. Approved or accredited by Association of Independent Schools in New England, New England Association of Schools and Colleges, The Association of Boarding Schools, and Massachusetts Department of Education. Member of National Association of Independent Schools and Secondary School Admission Test Board. Endowment: $244 million. Total enrollment: 1,000. Upper school average class size: 14. Upper school faculty-student ratio: 1:5. There are 162 required school days per year for Upper School students. Upper School students typically attend 5 days per week. The average school day consists of 7 hours.

Upper School Student Profile 50% of students are boarding students. 65% are state residents. 28 states are represented in upper school student body. 11% are international students. International students from Canada, China, Hong Kong, Jamaica, Republic of Korea, and United Kingdom; 16 other countries represented in student body.

Faculty School total: 139. In upper school: 66 men, 73 women; 104 have advanced degrees; 111 reside on campus.

Subjects Offered Algebra, American history, American literature, anatomy, architecture, art, art history, astronomy, biology, calculus, ceramics, chemistry, Chinese, computer math, computer programming, computer science, creative writing, current events, dance, drama, earth science, economics, English, English literature, ethics, European history, expository writing, fine arts, French, geography, geometry, government/civics, grammar, Greek, health, history, Latin, mathematics, music, philosophy, photography, physical education, physics, physiology, psychology, religion, science, social studies, sociology, Spanish, speech, statistics, theater, trigonometry, world history, world literature, writing.

Graduation Requirements Arts and fine arts (art, music, dance, drama), current events, English, foreign language, leadership, mathematics, physical education (includes health), public speaking, science, social studies (includes history).

Special Academic Programs Advanced Placement exam preparation; honors section; independent study; term-away projects; study abroad; academic accommodation for the gifted, the musically talented, and the artistically talented.

College Admission Counseling 171 students graduated in 2014; all went to college, including Boston College; Brown University; Columbia University; The George Washington University; Trinity College; University of Chicago. Mean SAT critical reading: 686, mean SAT math: 693, mean SAT writing: 701.

Student Life Upper grades have student council, honor system. Discipline rests equally with students and faculty.

Tuition and Aid Day student tuition: $42,130; 7-day tuition and room/board: $51,330. Tuition installment plan (The Tuition Management Systems (TMS)). Need-based scholarship grants available. In 2014–15, 30% of upper-school students received aid. Total amount of financial aid awarded in 2014–15: $9,100,000.

Admissions Traditional secondary-level entrance grade is 9. For fall 2014, 1,100 students applied for upper-level admission, 277 were accepted, 150 enrolled. ISEE, PSAT, SAT, SSAT or TOEFL required. Deadline for receipt of application materials: January 15. Application fee required: $50. Interview required.

Athletics Interscholastic: baseball (boys), basketball (b,g), cross-country running (b,g), field hockey (g), football (b), ice hockey (b,g), lacrosse (b,g), soccer (b,g), softball (g), squash (b,g), tennis (b,g), track and field (b,g), volleyball (g); intramural:

basketball (b,g), soccer (b,g), strength & conditioning (b,g); coed interscholastic: alpine skiing, diving, golf, sailing, skiing (downhill), swimming and diving, wrestling; coed intramural: climbing, outdoor activities, outdoor education, project adventure, rock climbing, skiing (downhill), squash, tennis, ultimate Frisbee, yoga. 6 PE instructors, 107 coaches, 3 athletic trainers.

Computers Computers are regularly used in mathematics, science classes. Computer network features include on-campus library services, online commercial services, Internet access, wireless campus network, Internet filtering or blocking technology. Student e-mail accounts and computer access in designated common areas are available to students.

Contact Mrs. Patricia Finn, Admission Assistant. 617-898-2227. Fax: 617-898-1701. E-mail: admissions@milton.edu. Website: www.milton.edu

See Display on next page and Close-Up on page 608.

MILTON HERSHEY SCHOOL

PO Box 830
Hershey, Pennsylvania 17033-0830

General Information Coeducational boarding college-preparatory, general academic, vocational, and technology school. Grades PK–12. Founded: 1909. Setting: rural. Nearest major city is Harrisburg. Students are housed in student homes of 8 to 10 students. 2,640-acre campus. 9 buildings on campus. Approved or accredited by Middle States Association of Colleges and Schools, Pennsylvania Association of Independent Schools, and The Association of Boarding Schools. Member of National Association of Independent Schools. Endowment: $5.5 billion. Total enrollment: 1,301. Upper school average class size: 15. Upper school faculty-student ratio: 1:15.

See Display on page 350 and Close-Up on page 610.

MISS EDGAR'S AND MISS CRAMP'S SCHOOL

525 Mount Pleasant Avenue
Montreal, Quebec H3Y 3H6, Canada

Head of School: Ms. Natalie Little

General Information Girls' day college-preparatory, arts, bilingual studies, and technology school. Grades K–11. Founded: 1909. Setting: urban. 4-acre campus. 1 building on campus. Approved or accredited by Canadian Association of Independent Schools, Quebec Association of Independent Schools, and Quebec Department of Education. Affiliate member of National Association of Independent Schools; member of Secondary School Admission Test Board. Languages of instruction: English and French. Total enrollment: 320. Upper school average class size: 19. Upper school faculty-student ratio: 1:9. There are 180 required school days per year for Upper School students. Upper School students typically attend 5 days per week. The average school day consists of 5 hours.

Upper School Student Profile Grade 9: 38 students (38 girls); Grade 10: 30 students (30 girls); Grade 11: 32 students (32 girls).

Faculty School total: 40. In upper school: 4 men, 14 women; 8 have advanced degrees.

Subjects Offered Art, art history, biology, calculus, career exploration, chemistry, computer science, creative writing, drama, ecology, economics, English, environmental science, European history, French, geography, history, mathematics, media, music, physical education, physics, science, social studies, Spanish, theater, women's studies, world history.

Graduation Requirements English, foreign language, mathematics, science, social studies (includes history).

Special Academic Programs 2 Advanced Placement exams for which test preparation is offered; honors section.

College Admission Counseling 43 students graduated in 2015; all went to college, including John Abbott College; Lower Canada College; Marianopolis College.

Student Life Upper grades have uniform requirement, student council, honor system. Discipline rests primarily with faculty.

Tuition and Aid Day student tuition: CAN$18,500. Tuition installment plan (individually arranged payment plans). Bursaries, merit scholarship grants available. In 2015–16, 18% of upper-school students received aid; total upper-school merit-scholarship money awarded: CAN$80,000. Total amount of financial aid awarded in 2015–16: CAN$135,000.

Admissions Traditional secondary-level entrance grade is 9. For fall 2015, 20 students applied for upper-level admission, 12 were accepted, 5 enrolled. CCAT, SSAT or writing sample required. Deadline for receipt of application materials: none. Application fee required: CAN$50. On-campus interview required.

Athletics Interscholastic: badminton, basketball, cross-country running, golf, hockey, ice hockey, running, soccer, swimming and diving, tennis, touch football, track and field, volleyball; intramural: badminton, baseball, basketball, crew, cross-country running, curling, dance, field hockey, gymnastics, ice hockey, outdoor adventure, outdoor education, outdoor skills, physical fitness, rugby, running, skiing (cross-country), soccer, softball, touch football, track and field, volleyball. 3 PE instructors, 11 coaches.

Computers Computers are regularly used in art, English, French, history, newspaper, writing, yearbook classes. Computer network features include on-campus library services, Internet access, wireless campus network, Internet filtering or blocking technology. Campus intranet, student e-mail accounts, and computer access in designated common areas are available to students. The school has a published electronic and media policy.

Contact Ms. Carla Bolsius, Admissions Coordinator. 514-935-6357 Ext. 254. Fax: 514-935-1099. E-mail: bolsiusc@ecs.qc.ca. Website: www.ecs.qc.ca

MISS HALL'S SCHOOL

492 Holmes Road
Pittsfield, Massachusetts 01201

Head of School: Ms. Julia Nakano Heaton

General Information Girls' boarding and day college-preparatory, arts, technology, community service, and leadership development school. Grades 9–PG. Founded: 1898. Setting: suburban. Nearest major city is Albany, NY. Students are housed in single-sex dormitories. 80-acre campus. 11 buildings on campus. Approved or accredited by Association of Independent Schools in New England, New England Association of Schools and Colleges, The Association of Boarding Schools, The College Board, and Massachusetts Department of Education. Member of National Association of Independent Schools and Secondary School Admission Test Board. Endowment: $19 million. Total enrollment: 214. Upper school average class size: 10. Upper school faculty-student ratio: 1:6. There are 157 required school days per year for Upper School students. Upper School students typically attend 5 days per week. The average school day consists of 6 hours.

Upper School Student Profile Grade 9: 48 students (48 girls); Grade 10: 52 students (52 girls); Grade 11: 52 students (52 girls); Grade 12: 62 students (62 girls). 68% of students are boarding students. 34% are state residents. 18 states are represented in upper school student body. 34% are international students. International students from Bhutan, China, Japan, Republic of Korea, Rwanda, and Viet Nam; 23 other countries represented in student body.

Faculty School total: 36. In upper school: 8 men, 28 women; 25 have advanced degrees; 16 reside on campus.

Subjects Offered 20th century history, 3-dimensional art, acting, advanced biology, advanced chemistry, advanced math, Advanced Placement courses, advanced studio art-AP, African-American literature, algebra, American government, American history, American literature, anatomy, art, art history, athletics, biology, business skills, calculus, career exploration, ceramics, chamber groups, character education, chemistry, Chinese, college counseling, community service, computer science, CPR, creative writing, dance, drama, drawing, driver education, ecology, economics, English, English literature, English-AP, ensembles, entrepreneurship, environmental education, environmental science, environmental science-AP, ESL, ethics, ethics and responsibility, European history, European history-AP, expressive arts, fashion, field ecology, fine arts, forensics, French, French-AP, gardening, geometry, government/civics, Greek culture, health, history, human geography - AP, human sexuality, Italian history, Latin, leadership and service, mathematics, media literacy, music, music history, painting, photography, physics, physiology, political science, psychology, robotics, science, senior internship, service learning/internship, social studies, sociology, Spanish, theater, trigonometry, world cultures, world history.

Graduation Requirements Arts, arts and fine arts (art, music, dance, drama), English, foreign language, history, mathematics, physical education (includes health), science. Community service is required.

Special Academic Programs Advanced Placement exam preparation; honors section; independent study; term-away projects; academic accommodation for the gifted, the musically talented, and the artistically talented; programs in English, mathematics for dyslexic students; special instructional classes for students with mild learning disabilities and Attention Deficit Disorder; ESL (20 students enrolled).

College Admission Counseling 62 students graduated in 2015; all went to college.

Student Life Upper grades have specified standards of dress, student council, honor system. Discipline rests equally with students and faculty.

Tuition and Aid Day student tuition: $33,430; 7-day tuition and room/board: $55,105. Tuition installment plan (Insured Tuition Payment Plan, Academic Management Services Plan, Key Tuition Payment Plan, monthly payment plans, individually arranged payment plans). Merit scholarship grants, need-based scholarship grants available. In 2015–16, 50% of upper-school students received aid; total upper-school merit-scholarship money awarded: $275,000. Total amount of financial aid awarded in 2015–16: $3,000,000.

Admissions Traditional secondary-level entrance grade is 9. For fall 2015, 299 students applied for upper-level admission, 152 were accepted, 74 enrolled. PSAT, SAT, SSAT or TOEFL required. Deadline for receipt of application materials: February 1. Application fee required: $75. Interview required.

Athletics Interscholastic: alpine skiing, basketball, cross-country running, equestrian sports, golf, lacrosse, skiing (downhill), soccer, softball, tennis, volleyball; intramural: aerobics, aerobics/dance, alpine skiing, dance, equestrian sports, fitness, fitness walking, golf, gymnastics, horseback riding, jogging, modern dance, outdoor activities, outdoor education, physical fitness, ropes courses, running, skiing (cross-country), skiing (downhill), snowboarding, swimming and diving, tennis, volleyball, walking, wall climbing, wilderness, yoga. 10 coaches, 1 athletic trainer.

Computers Computers are regularly used in computer applications, English, foreign language, history, mathematics, music, newspaper, photography, science, yearbook classes. Computer network features include on-campus library services, online commercial services, Internet access, wireless campus network, Internet filtering or blocking technology. Campus intranet, student e-mail accounts, and computer access in designated common areas are available to students. Students grades are available online. The school has a published electronic and media policy.

Contact Ms. Julie Bradley, Director of Admission. 413-499-1300. Fax: 413-448-2994. E-mail: info@misshalls.org. Website: www.misshalls.org

Milton Academy

Milton Academy cultivates in its students a passion for learning and a respect for others. Embracing diversity and the pursuit of excellence, we create a community in which individuals develop competence, confidence, and character.

Our active learning environment, in and out of the classroom, develops creative and critical thinkers who are unafraid to express their ideas and are prepared to seek meaningful lifetime success and to live by our motto, "Dare to be true."

For more information, please contact:

Milton Academy
170 Centre Street
Milton, MA 02186
www.milton.edu

MISSOURI MILITARY ACADEMY

204 Grand Avenue
Mexico, Missouri 65265

Head of School: Mr. Charles A. McGeorge

General Information Boys' boarding and day college-preparatory, technology, ESL, military science, and military school, affiliated with Christian faith. Boarding grades 6–PG, day grades 6–12. Founded: 1889. Setting: small town. Nearest major city is St. Louis. Students are housed in single-sex dormitories. 288-acre campus. 19 buildings on campus. Approved or accredited by Independent Schools Association of the Central States and The Association of Boarding Schools. Member of National Association of Independent Schools and Secondary School Admission Test Board. Endowment: $39 million. Total enrollment: 228. Upper school average class size: 10. Upper school faculty-student ratio: 1:11. There are 180 required school days per year for Upper School students. Upper School students typically attend 5 days per week. The average school day consists of 5 hours and 50 minutes.

Upper School Student Profile Grade 9: 34 students (34 boys); Grade 10: 38 students (38 boys); Grade 11: 53 students (53 boys); Grade 12: 65 students (65 boys); Postgraduate: 1 student (1 boy). 99% of students are boarding students. 20% are state residents. 30 states are represented in upper school student body. 40% are international students. International students from China, Mexico, Mongolia, Republic of Korea, Russian Federation, and Taiwan; 13 other countries represented in student body.

Faculty School total: 47. In upper school: 27 men, 8 women; 27 have advanced degrees; 5 reside on campus.

Subjects Offered Algebra, American literature, art, biology, broadcasting, business, business skills, calculus, chemistry, computer science, drama, economics, English, ESL, fine arts, French, geography, geometry, government/civics, history, honors algebra, honors English, honors U.S. history, humanities, instrumental music, Internet, jazz band, journalism, JROTC or LEAD (Leadership Education and Development), keyboarding, languages, Latin American studies, leadership, literary magazine, marching band, mathematics, military science, music, newspaper, physical education, physical science, physics, physics-AP, psychology, science, social studies, sociology, Spanish, speech, statistics, student government, student publications, swimming, theater, track and field, typing, U.S. government, U.S. history, vocal ensemble, vocal music, world history, wrestling, writing, yearbook.

Graduation Requirements Arts and fine arts (art, music, dance, drama), business skills (includes word processing), computer science, English, foreign language, JROTC, mathematics, physical education (includes health), science, social studies (includes history), 20 hours of community service per school year.

Special Academic Programs 9 Advanced Placement exams for which test preparation is offered; honors section; independent study; study at local college for college credit; academic accommodation for the gifted, the musically talented, and the artistically talented; remedial reading and/or remedial writing; remedial math; special instructional classes for students with Attention Deficit Disorder; ESL (33 students enrolled).

College Admission Counseling 67 students graduated in 2015; all went to college, including Texas A&M University; The University of Texas at Austin; University of California, Berkeley; University of Miami; University of Missouri; Washington University in St. Louis. Median SAT critical reading: 467, median SAT math: 547, median combined SAT: 1016, median composite ACT: 21.

Student Life Upper grades have uniform requirement, student council, honor system. Discipline rests equally with students and faculty. Attendance at religious services is required.

Summer Programs Remediation, enrichment, ESL, sports, rigorous outdoor training programs offered; session focuses on academics and leadership; held both on and off campus; held at water park in Jefferson City, MO and Courtois River for float/canoe trips; accepts boys and girls; open to students from other schools. 70 students usually enrolled. 2016 schedule: June 19 to July 15. Application deadline: June 15.

Tuition and Aid Day student tuition: $9100; 7-day tuition and room/board: $34,700. Tuition installment plan (individually arranged payment plans, school's own payment plan). Tuition reduction for siblings, merit scholarship grants, need-based scholarship grants, need-based loans available. In 2015–16, 42% of upper-school students received aid; total upper-school merit-scholarship money awarded: $25,000. Total amount of financial aid awarded in 2015–16: $1,200,000.

Admissions Traditional secondary-level entrance grade is 9. For fall 2015, 252 students applied for upper-level admission, 158 were accepted, 100 enrolled. SSAT or TOEFL or SLEP required. Deadline for receipt of application materials: none. Application fee required: $25. Interview required.

Athletics Interscholastic: baseball, basketball, cross-country running, drill team, football, golf, JROTC drill, lacrosse, marksmanship, outdoor activities, riflery, rugby, soccer, swimming and diving, tennis, track and field, weight training, wrestling; intramural: aquatics, basketball, canoeing/kayaking, equestrian sports, fishing, fitness, fitness walking, flag football, horseback riding, indoor track, marksmanship, martial arts, outdoor activities, outdoor recreation, outdoor skills, paint ball, physical fitness, physical training, rappelling, riflery, roller blading, ropes courses, running, soccer, softball, strength & conditioning, swimming and diving, table tennis, tennis, touch football, track and field, volleyball, weight lifting, weight training, winter (indoor) track, wrestling. 12 coaches, 1 athletic trainer.

Computers Computers are regularly used in business, English, history, journalism, library, mathematics, newspaper, science, yearbook classes. Computer network features include on-campus library services, online commercial services, Internet access, wireless campus network, Internet filtering or blocking technology. Campus intranet, student e-mail accounts, and computer access in designated common areas are available

to students. Students grades are available online. The school has a published electronic and media policy.

Contact Mrs. Michele Schulte, Enrollment Office Coordinator. 573-581-1776 Ext. 321. Fax: 573-581-0081. E-mail: michele.schulte@missourimilitaryacademy.com. Website: www.MissouriMilitaryAcademy.org

MISS PORTER'S SCHOOL

60 Main Street
Farmington, Connecticut 06032

Head of School: Dr. Katherine G. Windsor

General Information Girls' boarding and day college-preparatory and arts school. Grades 9–12. Founded: 1843. Setting: suburban. Nearest major city is Hartford. Students are housed in single-sex dormitories. 50-acre campus. 56 buildings on campus. Approved or accredited by Connecticut Association of Independent Schools, New England Association of Schools and Colleges, The Association of Boarding Schools, and Connecticut Department of Education. Member of National Association of Independent Schools and Secondary School Admission Test Board. Endowment: $111 million. Total enrollment: 323. Upper school average class size: 10. Upper school faculty-student ratio: 1:8. There are 167 required school days per year for Upper School students. Upper School students typically attend 5 days per week. The average school day consists of 7 hours and 20 minutes.

Upper School Student Profile Grade 9: 76 students (76 girls); Grade 10: 83 students (83 girls); Grade 11: 83 students (83 girls); Grade 12: 81 students (81 girls). 66% of students are boarding students. 54% are state residents. 25 states are represented in upper school student body. 18% are international students. International students from China, Hong Kong, Mexico, Republic of Korea, and Russian Federation; 13 other countries represented in student body.

Faculty School total: 49. In upper school: 8 men, 39 women; 32 have advanced degrees; 35 reside on campus.

Subjects Offered Acting, advanced chemistry, advanced computer applications, advanced math, Advanced Placement courses, advanced studio art-AP, African history, algebra, American history, American literature, anatomy and physiology, aquatics, area studies, art history, art history-AP, arts, astronomy, athletics, ballet, biology, biology-AP, British literature, calculus, calculus-AP, career/college preparation, ceramics, chemistry, chemistry-AP, Chinese, Chinese history, classical language, college counseling, college planning, community service, computer applications, computer graphics, computer programming, computer science, concert choir, creative writing, dance, dance performance, desktop publishing, drama, drama performance, economics, economics and history, engineering, English, English literature, environmental science, environmental science-AP, ethical decision making, ethics, European history, European history-AP, experiential education, expository writing, fitness, foreign language, forensics, French, French language-AP, French literature-AP, geometry, global issues, golf, graphic design, health and wellness, healthful living, history, honors geometry, human rights, international relations, intro to computers, Japanese history, jazz, jazz band, jewelry making, languages, Latin, Latin American literature, Latin-AP, leadership, mathematics, Middle Eastern history, model United Nations, modern dance, modern European history-AP, multicultural literature, music, music history, music performance, music theory, participation in sports, performing arts, personal finance, photography, physics, physics-AP, pre-calculus, printmaking, psychology, public speaking, science, Shakespeare, social studies, Spanish, Spanish language-AP, Spanish literature-AP, sports, squash, statistics, statistics-AP, student government, studio art, studio art-AP, swimming, swimming test, tennis, textiles, theater, trigonometry, U.S. history, U.S. history-AP, video film production, visual arts, vocal music, Web site design, Western civilization, writing, yoga.

Graduation Requirements Arts and fine arts (art, music, dance, drama), athletics, computer science, English, experiential education, foreign language, leadership, mathematics, science, social studies (includes history), online course. Community service is required.

Special Academic Programs 26 Advanced Placement exams for which test preparation is offered; honors section; independent study; term-away projects; study abroad; ESL (5 students enrolled).

College Admission Counseling 84 students graduated in 2015; all went to college, including Boston College; Loyola University Maryland; New York University; Pomona College; Smith College; St. Lawrence University. Median SAT critical reading: 620, median SAT math: 610, median SAT writing: 630, median combined SAT: 1880, median composite ACT: 28. 60% scored over 600 on SAT critical reading, 56% scored over 600 on SAT math, 63% scored over 600 on SAT writing, 62% scored over 1800 on combined SAT, 58% scored over 26 on composite ACT.

Student Life Upper grades have specified standards of dress, student council, honor system. Discipline rests equally with students and faculty.

Summer Programs Enrichment, advancement, ESL programs offered; session focuses on for middle school girls: Model UN, leadership, STEAM and CHAT (an English immersion program); held on campus; accepts girls; open to students from other schools. 100 students usually enrolled. 2016 schedule: July 3 to July 23. Application deadline: none.

Tuition and Aid Day student tuition: $43,950; 7-day tuition and room/board: $54,575. Tuition installment plan (monthly payment plans, individually arranged payment plans). Merit scholarship grants, need-based scholarship grants available. In

2015–16, 45% of upper-school students received aid. Total amount of financial aid awarded in 2015–16: $3,700,000.

Admissions Traditional secondary-level entrance grade is 9. For fall 2015, 454 students applied for upper-level admission, 200 were accepted, 96 enrolled. ISEE, PSAT and SAT for applicants to grade 11 and 12, SSAT or TOEFL required. Deadline for receipt of application materials: January 15. Application fee required: $65. Interview required.

Athletics Interscholastic: alpine skiing, badminton, basketball, crew, cross-country running, dance, diving, equestrian sports, field hockey, Frisbee, golf, horseback riding, independent competitive sports, lacrosse, rowing, running, skiing (downhill), soccer, softball, squash, swimming and diving, tennis, track and field, ultimate Frisbee, volleyball; intramural: aerobics, aerobics/Nautilus, ballet, climbing, dance, equestrian sports, fitness, horseback riding, jogging, life saving, martial arts, modern dance, outdoor adventure, outdoor recreation, physical fitness, physical training, rock climbing, running, self defense, skiing (downhill), snowboarding, squash, strength & conditioning, swimming and diving, tennis, wall climbing, weight training, yoga. 9 coaches, 2 athletic trainers.

Computers Computers are regularly used in computer applications, desktop publishing, graphic design, graphics, introduction to technology, publications, Web site design classes. Computer network features include on-campus library services, online commercial services, Internet access, wireless campus network, Internet filtering or blocking technology, online courses. Campus intranet, student e-mail accounts, and computer access in designated common areas are available to students. Students grades are available online. The school has a published electronic and media policy.

Contact Kimberly M. Mount, Director of Admission and Financial Aid. 860-409-3530. Fax: 860-409-3531. E-mail: kim_mount@missporters.org. Website: www.porters.org

MMI PREPARATORY SCHOOL

154 Centre Street
Freeland, Pennsylvania 18224

Head of School: Mr. Thomas G. Hood

General Information Coeducational day college-preparatory, arts, and technology school. Grades 6–12. Founded: 1879. Setting: small town. Nearest major city is Hazleton. 20-acre campus. 1 building on campus. Approved or accredited by Middle States Association of Colleges and Schools and Pennsylvania Department of Education. Member of National Association of Independent Schools. Endowment: $19 million. Total enrollment: 252. Upper school average class size: 16. Upper school faculty-student ratio: 1:11. There are 168 required school days per year for Upper School students. Upper School students typically attend 5 days per week. The average school day consists of 6 hours and 30 minutes.

Upper School Student Profile Grade 9: 42 students (21 boys, 21 girls); Grade 10: 39 students (22 boys, 17 girls); Grade 11: 42 students (24 boys, 18 girls); Grade 12: 31 students (17 boys, 14 girls).

Faculty School total: 28. In upper school: 10 men, 17 women; 18 have advanced degrees.

Subjects Offered 3-dimensional art, algebra, American history, American history-AP, American literature, anatomy, anthropology, art, art-AP, biology, biology-AP, calculus, chemistry, chemistry-AP, Chinese, computer programming, computer programming-AP, computer science, consumer education, creative writing, earth science, economics, English, English language and composition-AP, English literature, English literature and composition-AP, environmental science, European history, European history-AP, expository writing, fine arts, geography, geometry, German, government/civics, grammar, health, history, keyboarding, Latin, marine biology, mathematics, music, physical education, physics, physics-AP, physiology, psychology, science, social studies, Spanish, speech, statistics, trigonometry, world history, world literature.

Graduation Requirements Analysis and differential calculus, arts and fine arts (art, music, dance, drama), college counseling, computer science, consumer education, economics, English, foreign language, mathematics, physical education (includes health), science, social studies (includes history), speech, independent research project presentation every spring, public speaking assembly project every year.

Special Academic Programs 10 Advanced Placement exams for which test preparation is offered; honors section; study at local college for college credit; academic accommodation for the gifted; special instructional classes for blind students.

College Admission Counseling 43 students graduated in 2015; 42 went to college, including Drexel University; Saint Joseph's University; Temple University; The University of Scranton; Ursinus College. Other: 1 went to work. Mean SAT critical reading: 572, mean SAT math: 572, mean SAT writing: 574, mean combined SAT: 1718.

Student Life Upper grades have specified standards of dress, student council. Discipline rests primarily with faculty.

Tuition and Aid Day student tuition: $14,025. Tuition installment plan (FACTS Tuition Payment Plan, monthly payment plans). Merit scholarship grants, need-based scholarship grants, paying campus jobs available. In 2015–16, 68% of upper-school students received aid; total upper-school merit-scholarship money awarded: $93,000. Total amount of financial aid awarded in 2015–16: $619,296.

Admissions Traditional secondary-level entrance grade is 9. For fall 2015, 36 students applied for upper-level admission, 30 were accepted, 17 enrolled. Cognitive Abilities

Test and Iowa Tests of Basic Skills required. Deadline for receipt of application materials: none. Application fee required: $25. On-campus interview required.

Athletics Interscholastic: baseball (boys), basketball (b,g), cross-country running (b,g), soccer (b,g), softball (g), tennis (b,g), volleyball (g); intramural: bowling (b,g); coed interscholastic: golf; coed intramural: skiing (downhill), snowboarding. 2 PE instructors, 15 coaches, 1 athletic trainer.

Computers Computers are regularly used in all classes. Computer network features include on-campus library services, Internet access, wireless campus network, Internet filtering or blocking technology. Computer access in designated common areas is available to students. Students grades are available online. The school has a published electronic and media policy.

Contact Marci Hosier, Director of Admissions and Marketing. 570-636-1108 Ext. 136. Fax: 570-636-0742. E-mail: mhosier@mmiprep.org. Website: www.mmiprep.org

THE MONARCH SCHOOL

Houston, Texas
See Special Needs Schools section.

MONTCLAIR KIMBERLEY ACADEMY

201 Valley Road
Montclair, New Jersey 07042

Head of School: Mr. Thomas W. Nammack

General Information Coeducational day college-preparatory, arts, and technology school. Grades PK–12. Founded: 1887. Setting: suburban. Nearest major city is New York, NY. 28-acre campus. 1 building on campus. Approved or accredited by Middle States Association of Colleges and Schools and New Jersey Association of Independent Schools. Member of National Association of Independent Schools and Secondary School Admission Test Board. Endowment: $12 million. Total enrollment: 990. Upper school average class size: 12. Upper school faculty-student ratio: 1:6. There are 163 required school days per year for Upper School students. Upper School students typically attend 5 days per week. The average school day consists of 6 hours and 30 minutes.

Upper School Student Profile Grade 6: 72 students (43 boys, 29 girls); Grade 7: 93 students (46 boys, 47 girls); Grade 8: 93 students (53 boys, 40 girls); Grade 9: 111 students (59 boys, 52 girls); Grade 10: 102 students (55 boys, 47 girls); Grade 11: 107 students (55 boys, 52 girls); Grade 12: 100 students (50 boys, 50 girls).

Faculty School total: 74. In upper school: 41 men, 33 women; 60 have advanced degrees.

Subjects Offered Acting, advanced chemistry, advanced math, algebra, American history, American literature, architecture, art, astronomy, biology, biology-AP, British literature, calculus, calculus-AP, chemistry, chemistry-AP, Chinese, chorus, communications, concert band, creative writing, dance, digital photography, drama, driver education, ecology, economics, economics-AP, English, English literature, environmental science, ethics, European history, expository writing, fine arts, French, French language-AP, French literature-AP, geometry, government/civics, health, history, Latin, mathematics, music, photography, physical education, physics, physics-AP, post-calculus, Spanish, Spanish language-AP, Spanish literature-AP, statistics-AP, theater, trigonometry, world history, world literature, world wide web design, writing.

Graduation Requirements Art, arts and fine arts (art, music, dance, drama), English, foreign language, history, mathematics, music, physical education (includes health), science, swimming, citizenship. Community service is required.

Special Academic Programs Advanced Placement exam preparation; honors section; independent study; term-away projects; study abroad; academic accommodation for the gifted.

College Admission Counseling 105 students graduated in 2014; 104 went to college, including Boston College; Lehigh University; New York University; University of Pennsylvania; Villanova University; Wesleyan University. Other: 1 entered a postgraduate year. Mean SAT critical reading: 630, mean SAT math: 647. 60% scored over 600 on SAT critical reading, 65% scored over 600 on SAT math.

Student Life Upper grades have specified standards of dress, student council, honor system. Discipline rests equally with students and faculty.

Tuition and Aid Day student tuition: $34,400. Tuition installment plan (Insured Tuition Payment Plan, monthly payment plans, individually arranged payment plans). Need-based scholarship grants available. In 2014–15, 15% of upper-school students received aid. Total amount of financial aid awarded in 2014–15: $1,222,000.

Admissions Traditional secondary-level entrance grade is 9. For fall 2014, 177 students applied for upper-level admission, 67 were accepted, 37 enrolled. ISEE or SSAT required. Deadline for receipt of application materials: February 2. Application fee required: $50. On-campus interview required.

Athletics Interscholastic: baseball (boys), basketball (b,g), cheering (g), cross-country running (b,g), dance (b,g), dance team (b,g), fencing (b,g), field hockey (g), football (b), ice hockey (b), lacrosse (b,g), outdoor activities (b,g), physical fitness (b,g), soccer (b,g), softball (g), swimming and diving (b,g), tennis (b,g), track and field (b,g),

volleyball (g), winter (indoor) track (b,g); coed interscholastic: golf. 5 PE instructors, 9 coaches, 2 athletic trainers.

Computers Computers are regularly used in architecture classes. Computer network features include on-campus library services, online commercial services, Internet access, wireless campus network, Internet filtering or blocking technology, 1:1 laptop school, community Intranet. Campus intranet and student e-mail accounts are available to students. The school has a published electronic and media policy.

Contact Alyson Waldman, Director of Admissions and Financial Aid. 973-509-7930. Fax: 973-509-4526. E-mail: awaldman@mka.org. Website: www.mka.org

MONTEREY BAY ACADEMY

783 San Andreas Road
La Selva Beach, California 95076-1907

Head of School: Mr. Jeffrey M. Deming

General Information Coeducational boarding and day college-preparatory and religious studies school, affiliated with Seventh-day Adventist Church. Grades 9–12. Founded: 1949. Setting: rural. Nearest major city is San Jose. Students are housed in single-sex dormitories. 379-acre campus. 8 buildings on campus. Approved or accredited by Western Association of Schools and Colleges and California Department of Education. Total enrollment: 181. Upper school average class size: 20. Upper school faculty-student ratio: 1:13. There are 180 required school days per year for Upper School students. Upper School students typically attend 5 days per week. The average school day consists of 7 hours.

Upper School Student Profile Grade 9: 34 students (23 boys, 11 girls); Grade 10: 47 students (27 boys, 20 girls); Grade 11: 52 students (30 boys, 22 girls); Grade 12: 48 students (32 boys, 16 girls). 75% of students are boarding students. 66% are state residents. 14 states are represented in upper school student body. 21% are international students. International students from China, Japan, Republic of Korea, Taiwan, Viet Nam, and Zimbabwe; 1 other country represented in student body. 80% of students are Seventh-day Adventists.

Faculty School total: 18. In upper school: 14 men, 4 women; 7 have advanced degrees; all reside on campus.

Subjects Offered Accounting, Advanced Placement courses, algebra, American literature, biology, calculus, chemistry, choir, Christianity, computer applications, computer literacy, drama, economics, English, English language and composition-AP, geometry, graphics, health, instrumental music, marine biology, photography, physical education, physical science, physics, physiology, pre-algebra, pre-calculus, religion, Spanish, technology, U.S. government, U.S. history, U.S. history-AP, voice, weight training, woodworking, world history.

Graduation Requirements Algebra, American literature, arts and fine arts (art, music, dance, drama), biology, chemistry, computer applications, computer science, economics, electives, English, English composition, English literature, geometry, health, mathematics, physical education (includes health), physics, religion (includes Bible studies and theology), U.S. government, U.S. history, work experience, world history, religious studies for each year in a Seventh-day Adventist School.

Special Academic Programs Advanced Placement exam preparation; ESL (15 students enrolled).

College Admission Counseling 45 students graduated in 2014; all went to college, including Amherst College; La Sierra University; Pacific Union College; Southern Adventist University; Walla Walla University; Williams College. Mean SAT critical reading: 558, mean SAT math: 553, mean SAT writing: 543, mean combined SAT: 1654, mean composite ACT: 25. 39% scored over 600 on SAT critical reading, 35% scored over 600 on SAT math, 30% scored over 600 on SAT writing, 30% scored over 1800 on combined SAT, 33% scored over 26 on composite ACT.

Student Life Upper grades have specified standards of dress, student council. Discipline rests primarily with faculty. Attendance at religious services is required.

Tuition and Aid Day student tuition: $9400–$11,570; 7-day tuition and room/board: $15,600–$27,000. Tuition installment plan (SMART Tuition Payment Plan, monthly payment plans). Need-based scholarship grants, paying campus jobs available. In 2014–15, 30% of upper-school students received aid. Total amount of financial aid awarded in 2014–15: $300,000.

Admissions Traditional secondary-level entrance grade is 9. For fall 2014, 190 students applied for upper-level admission, 187 were accepted, 182 enrolled. TOEFL required. Deadline for receipt of application materials: July 15. Application fee required: $50. Interview recommended.

Athletics Interscholastic: basketball (boys, girls), flag football (b,g), softball (b,g), volleyball (b,g); intramural: basketball (b,g), flag football (b,g), volleyball (b,g); coed interscholastic: soccer; coed intramural: soccer, softball. 1 PE instructor, 12 coaches.

Computers Computers are regularly used in accounting, mathematics, science, yearbook classes. Computer resources include Internet access, Internet filtering or blocking technology. Students grades are available online. The school has a published electronic and media policy.

Contact Ms. Donna J. Baerg, Vice Principal for Academic Affairs. 831-728-1481 Ext. 1218. Fax: 831-728-1485. E-mail: academics@montereybayacademy.org. Website: www.montereybayacademy.org

MONTGOMERY BELL ACADEMY

4001 Harding Road
Nashville, Tennessee 37205

Head of School: Bradford Gioia

General Information Boys' day college-preparatory and arts school. Grades 7–12. Founded: 1867. Setting: urban. 43-acre campus. 13 buildings on campus. Approved or accredited by Southern Association of Colleges and Schools, Southern Association of Independent Schools, and Tennessee Association of Independent Schools. Member of National Association of Independent Schools and Secondary School Admission Test Board. Endowment: $59.4 million. Total enrollment: 752. Upper school average class size: 13. Upper school faculty-student ratio: 1:7. There are 180 required school days per year for Upper School students. Upper School students typically attend 5 days per week. The average school day consists of 7 hours and 20 minutes.

Upper School Student Profile Grade 9: 128 students (128 boys); Grade 10: 134 students (134 boys); Grade 11: 126 students (126 boys); Grade 12: 126 students (126 boys).

Faculty School total: 98. In upper school: 57 men, 11 women; 50 have advanced degrees.

Subjects Offered Advanced Placement courses, algebra, American history, American history-AP, American literature, American literature-AP, art, art history, art history-AP, biology, biology-AP, calculus, calculus-AP, chemistry, chemistry-AP, Chinese, computer programming, computer science, computer science-AP, drama, earth science, economics, English, English literature, environmental science-AP, European history, European history-AP, fine arts, French, French language-AP, French literature-AP, French-AP, geography, geology, geometry, German, German-AP, government/civics, grammar, Greek, history, Latin, Latin-AP, mathematics, music, music history, music theory, music theory-AP, physical education, physics, physics-AP, science, social studies, Spanish, Spanish-AP, speech, statistics, statistics-AP, theater, trigonometry, U.S. government and politics-AP, U.S. history-AP, world history, world history-AP, writing.

Graduation Requirements Arts and fine arts (art, music, dance, drama), English, foreign language, mathematics, physical education (includes health), science, social studies (includes history).

Special Academic Programs Advanced Placement exam preparation; honors section; term-away projects; domestic exchange program; study abroad.

College Admission Counseling 120 students graduated in 2015; all went to college, including Auburn University at Montgomery; Sewanee: The University of the South; The University of Alabama; The University of Tennessee; Vanderbilt University; Washington University in St. Louis. Mean combined SAT: 1914, mean composite ACT: 29.

Student Life Upper grades have specified standards of dress, student council, honor system. Discipline rests primarily with faculty.

Summer Programs Remediation, enrichment, sports, art/fine arts, rigorous outdoor training, computer instruction programs offered; session focuses on academics and athletics; held both on and off campus; held at Long Mountain, TN; accepts boys and girls; open to students from other schools. 3,100 students usually enrolled. 2016 schedule: June 1 to July 31.

Tuition and Aid Day student tuition: $24,232. Tuition installment plan (monthly payment plans, Dewar Tuition Refund Plan). Need-based scholarship grants available. In 2015–16, 22% of upper-school students received aid. Total amount of financial aid awarded in 2015–16: $2,035,000.

Admissions Traditional secondary-level entrance grade is 9. For fall 2015, 62 students applied for upper-level admission, 30 were accepted, 26 enrolled. ISEE required. Deadline for receipt of application materials: February 1. Application fee required: $50. Interview required.

Athletics Interscholastic: baseball, basketball, bowling, crew, cross-country running, diving, football, Frisbee, golf, hockey, ice hockey, lacrosse, riflery, rock climbing, rowing, soccer, swimming and diving, tennis, track and field, ultimate Frisbee, wrestling; intramural: backpacking, baseball, basketball, cheering, climbing, crew, cricket, fencing, flag football, fly fishing, football, Frisbee, hiking/backpacking, independent competitive sports, outdoor activities, paddle tennis, running, soccer, strength & conditioning, table tennis, track and field, weight training, wilderness, yoga. 2 PE instructors, 4 coaches, 2 athletic trainers.

Computers Computers are regularly used in all academic classes. Computer network features include on-campus library services, online commercial services, Internet access, wireless campus network, Internet filtering or blocking technology. Student e-mail accounts and computer access in designated common areas are available to students. Students grades are available online. The school has a published electronic and media policy.

Contact Mr. Greg Ferrell, Director, Admission and Financial Aid. 615-369-5311. Fax: 615-369-5316. E-mail: greg.ferrell@montgomerybell.edu. Website: www.montgomerybell.edu

MONTROSE SCHOOL

29 North Street
Medfield, Massachusetts 02052

Head of School: Dr. Karen E. Bohlin

General Information Girls' day college-preparatory school, affiliated with Roman Catholic Church. Grades 6–12. Founded: 1979. Setting: suburban. Nearest major city is Boston. 14-acre campus. 3 buildings on campus. Approved or accredited by Massachusetts Department of Education and New England Association of Schools and Colleges. Member of Secondary School Admission Test Board. Total enrollment: 217. Upper school average class size: 15. Upper school faculty-student ratio: 1:6. There are 180 required school days per year for Upper School students. Upper School students typically attend 5 days per week. The average school day consists of 7 hours and 10 minutes.

Upper School Student Profile Grade 9: 42 students (42 girls); Grade 10: 45 students (45 girls); Grade 11: 20 students (20 girls); Grade 12: 41 students (41 girls). 71% of students are Roman Catholic.

Faculty School total: 48. In upper school: 28 women; 21 have advanced degrees.

Subjects Offered 20th century American writers, 20th century history, advanced biology, advanced math, Advanced Placement courses, algebra, American history-AP, American literature, anatomy and physiology, art, biology, biology-AP, British literature, calculus-AP, chemistry, chorus, church history, comparative politics, composition-AP, computer science, computers, drama, English-AP, French, geometry, Life of Christ, medieval/Renaissance history, modern European history, moral theology, music, physical education, physics, pre-calculus, religion, social doctrine, Spanish, speech, studio art, trigonometry, U.S. history, world history, world literature.

Graduation Requirements Arts and fine arts (art, music, dance, drama), English, foreign language, mathematics, physical education (includes health), religion (includes Bible studies and theology), science, social studies (includes history).

Special Academic Programs 8 Advanced Placement exams for which test preparation is offered; honors section; independent study.

College Admission Counseling 32 students graduated in 2015; all went to college, including Boston University; Fairfield University; Providence College; Stonehill College; University of Notre Dame. Mean SAT critical reading: 640, mean SAT math: 640, mean SAT writing: 680. 53% scored over 600 on SAT critical reading, 53% scored over 600 on SAT math.

Student Life Upper grades have uniform requirement, student council, honor system. Discipline rests primarily with faculty.

Summer Programs Remediation, enrichment, sports, art/fine arts programs offered; held on campus; accepts girls; open to students from other schools. 75 students usually enrolled. 2016 schedule: July 11 to July 29. Application deadline: June 1.

Tuition and Aid Day student tuition: $25,485. Tuition installment plan (SMART Tuition Payment Plan). Merit scholarship grants, need-based scholarship grants available. In 2015–16, 39% of upper-school students received aid; total upper-school merit-scholarship money awarded: $5000. Total amount of financial aid awarded in 2015–16: $500,000.

Admissions Traditional secondary-level entrance grade is 9. Admissions testing, essay, ISEE and SSAT required. Deadline for receipt of application materials: January 31. Application fee required: $50. On-campus interview required.

Athletics Interscholastic: basketball, cross-country running, field hockey, golf, lacrosse, soccer, softball; intramural: dance, fitness, life saving, skiing (downhill), strength & conditioning, volleyball. 1 PE instructor, 7 coaches, 1 athletic trainer.

Computers Computers are regularly used in English, foreign language, history, newspaper, philosophy, religion, Spanish, theology classes. Computer network features include on-campus library services, Internet access, wireless campus network, Internet filtering or blocking technology. Campus intranet and student e-mail accounts are available to students. The school has a published electronic and media policy.

Contact Mrs. Sarah McGowan, Assistant Director of Admissions. 508-359-2423 Ext. 315. Fax: 508-359-2597. E-mail: smcgowan@montroseschool.org. Website: www.montroseschool.org

MOORESTOWN FRIENDS SCHOOL

110 East Main Street
Moorestown, New Jersey 08057

Head of School: Mr. Laurence Van Meter

General Information Coeducational day college-preparatory, arts, religious studies, and technology school, affiliated with Society of Friends. Grades PS–12. Founded: 1785. Setting: suburban. Nearest major city is Philadelphia, PA. 48-acre campus. 9 buildings on campus. Approved or accredited by Friends Council on Education, Middle States Association of Colleges and Schools, and New Jersey Department of Education. Member of National Association of Independent Schools. Endowment: $10.1 million. Total enrollment: 730. Upper school average class size: 14. Upper school faculty-student ratio: 1:7. There are 170 required school days per year for Upper School students. Upper School students typically attend 5 days per week. The average school day consists of 7 hours and 5 minutes.

Upper School Student Profile Grade 9: 67 students (30 boys, 37 girls); Grade 10: 73 students (33 boys, 40 girls); Grade 11: 78 students (37 boys, 41 girls); Grade 12: 77 students (34 boys, 43 girls). 3.4% of students are members of Society of Friends.

Faculty School total: 100. In upper school: 18 men, 26 women; 35 have advanced degrees.

Subjects Offered Algebra, American history, American literature, art, art history, biology, calculus, ceramics, chemistry, Chinese, community service, computer programming, computer science, creative writing, drama, driver education, earth science, economics, English, English literature, environmental science, ethics, European history, expository writing, finance, fine arts, French, geometry, government/civics, grammar, health, history, mathematics, music, philosophy, photography, physical education, physics, psychology, religion, science, social studies, Spanish, theater, trigonometry, world history, writing.

Graduation Requirements Arts and fine arts (art, music, dance, drama), English, foreign language, history, mathematics, physical education (includes health), science, senior project, social studies (includes history). Community service is required.

Special Academic Programs Advanced Placement exam preparation; honors section; independent study; term-away projects; study abroad.

College Admission Counseling 76 students graduated in 2015; all went to college, including Cornell University; Lehigh University; Muhlenberg College; Princeton University; Rutgers, The State University of New Jersey, New Brunswick; The George Washington University. Mean SAT critical reading: 608, mean SAT math: 623, mean SAT writing: 617, mean combined SAT: 1848.

Student Life Upper grades have specified standards of dress, student council, honor system. Discipline rests primarily with faculty. Attendance at religious services is required.

Summer Programs Enrichment, advancement, art/fine arts programs offered; session focuses on academic courses for acceleration, enrichment experiences in video/audio, mock trial, and robotics; held on campus; accepts boys and girls; open to students from other schools. 250 students usually enrolled. 2016 schedule: July 11 to September 2.

Tuition and Aid Day student tuition: $27,450. Tuition installment plan (Academic Management Services Plan, Tuition Refund Plan). Tuition reduction for siblings, merit scholarship grants, need-based scholarship grants, need-based loans, tuition reduction for children of faculty and staff available. In 2015–16, 24% of upper-school students received aid; total upper-school merit-scholarship money awarded: $12,500. Total amount of financial aid awarded in 2015–16: $1,784,855.

Admissions Traditional secondary-level entrance grade is 9. For fall 2015, 75 students applied for upper-level admission, 39 were accepted, 33 enrolled. ERB CTP required. Deadline for receipt of application materials: January 8. Application fee required: $45. On-campus interview required.

Athletics Interscholastic: baseball (boys), basketball (b,g), crew (b,g), cross-country running (b,g), fencing (b,g), field hockey (g), independent competitive sports (b,g), lacrosse (b,g), physical training (b,g), soccer (b,g), swimming and diving (b,g), tennis (b,g); intramural: floor hockey (b), roller hockey (b), street hockey (b), weight training (b,g); coed interscholastic: golf; coed intramural: ultimate Frisbee. 5 PE instructors, 23 coaches, 1 athletic trainer.

Computers Computers are regularly used in English, foreign language, mathematics, media production, music, newspaper, photography, publications, religion, science, social studies, video film production, yearbook classes. Computer network features include on-campus library services, Internet access, wireless campus network, Internet filtering or blocking technology, campus portal. Campus intranet, student e-mail accounts, and computer access in designated common areas are available to students. Students grades are available online. The school has a published electronic and media policy.

Contact Rachel Tilney, Director of Admissions and Financial Aid. 856-235-2900 Ext. 227. Fax: 856-235-6684. E-mail: rtilney@mfriends.org. Website: www.mfriends.org

MOOSEHEART HIGH SCHOOL

255 James J. Davis Drive
Mooseheart, Illinois 60539

Head of School: Dr. Jeffrey Scott Szymczak

General Information Coeducational boarding and day college-preparatory, general academic, arts, business, vocational, religious studies, bilingual studies, technology, automotive, and cosmetology school, affiliated with Protestant faith, Roman Catholic Church; primarily serves underachievers, individuals with Attention Deficit Disorder, and OHI. Grades K–12. Founded: 1913. Setting: small town. Nearest major city is Aurora. Students are housed in single-sex dormitories and family homes. 1,000-acre campus. 40 buildings on campus. Approved or accredited by North Central Association of Colleges and Schools and Illinois Department of Education. Endowment: $2 million. Total enrollment: 199. Upper school average class size: 13. Upper school faculty-student ratio: 1:6. There are 176 required school days per year for Upper School students. Upper School students typically attend 5 days per week. The average school day consists of 6 hours and 45 minutes.

Upper School Student Profile Grade 6: 11 students (9 boys, 2 girls); Grade 7: 16 students (6 boys, 10 girls); Grade 8: 17 students (8 boys, 9 girls); Grade 9: 26 students (16 boys, 10 girls); Grade 10: 32 students (18 boys, 14 girls); Grade 11: 20 students (12 boys, 8 girls); Grade 12: 30 students (18 boys, 12 girls). 100% of students are boarding students. 65% are state residents. 22 states are represented in upper school student body. 6% are international students. International students from Congo, Ghana, Mexico, Nigeria, and Sudan; 4 other countries represented in student body. 95% of students are Protestant, Roman Catholic.

Faculty School total: 45. In upper school: 9 men, 11 women; 6 have advanced degrees; 1 resides on campus.

Subjects Offered Algebra, American government, American history, auto mechanics, biology, business education, business law, career and personal planning, chemistry, child development, computer education, concert band, consumer education, ESL, geometry, government, language arts, mathematics, music technology, NJROTC, pre-algebra, religious education, vocational arts, world geography.

Graduation Requirements Vocational class and NJROTC required.

Special Academic Programs Advanced Placement exam preparation; independent study; remedial reading and/or remedial writing; remedial math; ESL (31 students enrolled).

College Admission Counseling 24 students graduated in 2015; 13 went to college, including Illinois State University; Saint Xavier University; University of Illinois at Urbana–Champaign; University of Wisconsin–Oshkosh; Virginia Military Institute; Waubonsee Community College. Other: 9 went to work, 1 entered military service, 1 had other specific plans. Mean composite ACT: 16.

Student Life Upper grades have specified standards of dress, student council, honor system. Discipline rests primarily with faculty. Attendance at religious services is required.

Summer Programs Remediation, sports programs offered; session focuses on recreation; held both on and off campus; held at camp owned by us and local quarry for swimming; accepts boys and girls; not open to students from other schools. 211 students usually enrolled. 2016 schedule: June 13 to July 22. Application deadline: none.

Admissions Traditional secondary-level entrance grade is 9. Mathematics proficiency exam or writing sample required. Deadline for receipt of application materials: none. No application fee required. Interview required.

Athletics Interscholastic: basketball (boys, girls), cross-country running (g), drill team (b,g), football (b), indoor track & field (b,g), track and field (b,g), volleyball (g), wrestling (b); intramural: aerobics (b), aerobics/dance (g), fitness (b,g); coed interscholastic: JROTC drill, marksmanship; coed intramural: horseback riding, strength & conditioning. 2 PE instructors, 12 coaches.

Computers Computers are regularly used in business education, computer applications, music technology, vocational-technical courses, word processing classes. Computer network features include on-campus library services, Internet access, wireless campus network, Internet filtering or blocking technology. Campus intranet and computer access in designated common areas are available to students. Students grades are available online. The school has a published electronic and media policy.

Contact Kyle Rife, Director of Admission. 630-906-3631 Ext. 3631. Fax: 630-906-3634 Ext. 3634. E-mail: krife@mooseheart.org. Website: www.mooseheart.org/Academic.asp

MORAVIAN ACADEMY

4313 Green Pond Road
Bethlehem, Pennsylvania 18020

Head of School: George N. King Jr.

General Information Coeducational day college-preparatory school, affiliated with Moravian Church. Grades PK–12. Founded: 1742. Setting: rural. Nearest major city is Philadelphia. 120-acre campus. 10 buildings on campus. Approved or accredited by Middle States Association of Colleges and Schools, Pennsylvania Association of Independent Schools, and Pennsylvania Department of Education. Member of National Association of Independent Schools and Secondary School Admission Test Board. Endowment: $14.8 million. Total enrollment: 734. Upper school average class size: 15. Upper school faculty-student ratio: 1:7. There are 173 required school days per year for Upper School students. Upper School students typically attend 5 days per week. The average school day consists of 7 hours and 15 minutes.

Upper School Student Profile Grade 9: 83 students (47 boys, 36 girls); Grade 10: 79 students (44 boys, 35 girls); Grade 11: 72 students (32 boys, 40 girls); Grade 12: 80 students (39 boys, 41 girls).

Faculty School total: 96. In upper school: 18 men, 23 women; 39 have advanced degrees.

Subjects Offered Acting, advanced biology, advanced chemistry, Advanced Placement courses, algebra, American history, American history-AP, anatomy and physiology, ancient history, ancient world history, art, bell choir, biology, biology-AP, calculus, calculus-AP, ceramics, chemistry, chemistry-AP, Chinese, Chinese history, community service, drama, drawing, driver education, ecology, economics, English, English language-AP, English literature-AP, environmental science, environmental science-AP, ethics, European history, European history-AP, film, fine arts, French, French language-AP, geometry, government, health, history, honors geometry, Latin American history, mathematics, Middle East, music, painting, photography, physical education, physics, physics-AP, playwriting, poetry, probability and statistics, religion, science, short story, Spanish, Spanish language-AP, statistics, statistics-AP, theater, trigonometry, U.S. history-AP, woodworking, world history, world literature, Zen Buddhism, zoology.

Graduation Requirements Arts and fine arts (art, music, dance, drama), comedy, English, foreign language, mathematics, physical education (includes health), religion (includes Bible studies and theology), science, social studies (includes history), service project.

Special Academic Programs 13 Advanced Placement exams for which test preparation is offered; honors section; independent study; study at local college for college credit.

College Admission Counseling 67 students graduated in 2015; 66 went to college, including High Point University; Lehigh University; Muhlenberg College; Syracuse University; University of Pennsylvania; University of Pittsburgh. Other: 1 had other specific plans. Median SAT critical reading: 620, median SAT math: 650, median SAT writing: 640, median combined SAT: 1910, median composite ACT: 27.

Student Life Upper grades have specified standards of dress, student council. Discipline rests equally with students and faculty. Attendance at religious services is required.

Summer Programs Enrichment, sports, art/fine arts programs offered; session focuses on enrichment; held on campus; accepts boys and girls; open to students from other schools. 2016 schedule: June 13 to August 5.

Tuition and Aid Day student tuition: $26,790. Tuition installment plan (monthly payment plans). Need-based scholarship grants available. In 2015–16, 30% of upper-school students received aid. Total amount of financial aid awarded in 2015–16: $1,400,160.

Admissions Traditional secondary-level entrance grade is 9. For fall 2015, 57 students applied for upper-level admission, 42 were accepted, 29 enrolled. ERB and Otis-Lennon School Ability Test required. Deadline for receipt of application materials: none. Application fee required: $65. On-campus interview required.

Athletics Interscholastic: baseball (boys), basketball (b,g), field hockey (g), football (b), lacrosse (b,g), soccer (b,g), softball (g), tennis (b,g), track and field (b,g), volleyball (g), wrestling (b); coed interscholastic: cross-country running, golf, swimming and diving; coed intramural: outdoor education. 3 PE instructors, 15 coaches, 1 athletic trainer.

Computers Computers are regularly used in all academic, art, English, foreign language, history, mathematics, music, science classes. Computer resources include on-campus library services, Internet access, wireless campus network, Internet filtering or blocking technology, 1:1 program using MacBook Air computers. Student e-mail accounts and computer access in designated common areas are available to students. The school has a published electronic and media policy.

Contact Daniel Axford, Director of Upper School Admissions. 610-691-1600. Fax: 610-691-3354. E-mail: daxford@moravianacademy.org. Website: www.moravianacademy.org

See Display below and Close-Up on page 612.

MOREAU CATHOLIC HIGH SCHOOL
27170 Mission Boulevard
Hayward, California 94544
Head of School: Mr. Terry Lee

General Information Coeducational day college-preparatory, arts, religious studies, technology, and STEM school, affiliated with Roman Catholic Church. Grades 9–12. Founded: 1965. Setting: suburban. Nearest major city is San Francisco. 14-acre campus. 6 buildings on campus. Approved or accredited by National Catholic Education Association, Western Association of Schools and Colleges, Western Catholic Education Association, and California Department of Education. Total enrollment: 945. Upper school average class size: 24. Upper school faculty-student ratio: 1:18. There are 186 required school days per year for Upper School students. Upper School students typically attend 5 days per week. The average school day consists of 6 hours and 35 minutes.

Upper School Student Profile Grade 9: 250 students (135 boys, 115 girls); Grade 10: 252 students (121 boys, 131 girls); Grade 11: 202 students (89 boys, 113 girls); Grade 12: 241 students (130 boys, 111 girls). 72% of students are Roman Catholic.

Faculty School total: 69. In upper school: 30 men, 23 women; 27 have advanced degrees.

Subjects Offered Advanced Placement courses, algebra, American Civil War, American history, American legal systems, American literature, anatomy, art, ASB Leadership, athletics, Bible as literature, biology, biology-AP, business, business law, calculus, calculus-AP, campus ministry, ceramics, cheerleading, chemistry, choral music, Christian ethics, Christian scripture, Christianity, church history, community service, computer education, computer programming, computer science, concert band, drama, drama performance, economics, engineering, English, English literature, English/composition-AP, ethics, ethics and responsibility, European history, expository writing, fine arts, French, French-AP, geometry, government-AP, government/civics, grammar, health, health education, history, history of the Catholic Church, honors algebra, honors English, honors geometry, honors U.S. history, honors world history, human biology, instrumental music, jazz band, jazz ensemble, journalism, marching band, mathematics, media studies, moral theology, music, music appreciation, newspaper, physical education, physics, physics-AP, physiology, psychology, religion, science, sculpture, social sciences, social studies, Spanish, Spanish language-AP, speech, sports medicine, sports science, student government, student publications, symphonic band, theater, theology, trigonometry, U.S. government, U.S. government and politics-AP, U.S. history, U.S. history-AP, weight training, world history, world literature, writing, yearbook.

Graduation Requirements Arts and fine arts (art, music, dance, drama), English, foreign language, mathematics, physical education (includes health), religion (includes

Bible studies and theology), science, social sciences, social studies (includes history). Community service is required.

Special Academic Programs Advanced Placement exam preparation; honors section; special instructional classes for Saints and Scholars program for students with documented learning disabilities who require accommodations; ESL (14 students enrolled).

College Admission Counseling 233 students graduated in 2015; 232 went to college, including California State University, East Bay; San Francisco State University; University of California, Berkeley; University of California, Davis; University of California, Santa Cruz; University of San Francisco. Other: 1 had other specific plans. Mean SAT critical reading: 530, mean SAT math: 534, mean SAT writing: 531, mean composite ACT: 25.

Student Life Upper grades have specified standards of dress, student council, honor system. Discipline rests primarily with faculty. Attendance at religious services is required.

Summer Programs Remediation, enrichment, sports programs offered; session focuses on enrichment and remediation; held on campus; accepts boys and girls; open to students from other schools. 2016 schedule: June 17 to July 19. Application deadline: June 7.

Tuition and Aid Day student tuition: $16,970. Tuition installment plan (FACTS Tuition Payment Plan, monthly payment plans). Merit scholarship grants, need-based scholarship grants available. In 2015–16, 40% of upper-school students received aid. Total amount of financial aid awarded in 2015–16: $1,700,000.

Admissions Traditional secondary-level entrance grade is 9. Scholastic Testing Service High School Placement Test required. Deadline for receipt of application materials: January 6. Application fee required: $90. On-campus interview required.

Athletics Interscholastic: aquatics (boys, girls), badminton (b,g), baseball (b), basketball (b,g), cheering (g), cross-country running (b,g), dance squad (g), football (b), golf (b,g), soccer (b,g), softball (g), swimming and diving (b,g), tennis (b,g), track and field (b,g), volleyball (b,g), water polo (b,g); intramural: lacrosse (g); coed interscholastic: aerobics/dance, modern dance; coed intramural: equestrian sports, skiing (downhill), strength & conditioning. 5 PE instructors, 50 coaches, 1 athletic trainer.

Computers Computers are regularly used in career exploration, college planning, English, foreign language, history, journalism, mathematics, newspaper, religious studies, science, Spanish, technology, theology, writing, yearbook classes. Computer network features include on-campus library services, online commercial services, Internet access, wireless campus network, PowerSchool grade program, 1:1 student laptop program, laptop included in tuition. Campus intranet, student e-mail accounts, and computer access in designated common areas are available to students. Students grades are available online. The school has a published electronic and media policy.

Contact Patricia Bevilacqua, Admissions Assistant. 510-881-4320. Fax: 510-582-8405. E-mail: admissions@moreaucatholic.org. Website: www.moreaucatholic.org

MOTHER MCAULEY HIGH SCHOOL

3737 West 99th Street

Chicago, Illinois 60655-3133

Head of School: Ms. Eileen Boyce

General Information Girls' day college-preparatory, arts, religious studies, and technology school, affiliated with Roman Catholic Church. Grades 9–12. Founded: 1846. Setting: urban. 21-acre campus. 2 buildings on campus. Approved or accredited by Mercy Secondary Education Association, National Catholic Education Association, North Central Association of Colleges and Schools, The College Board, and Illinois Department of Education. Endowment: $2 million. Total enrollment: 1,027. Upper school average class size: 25. Upper school faculty-student ratio: 1:17. There are 180 required school days per year for Upper School students. Upper School students typically attend 5 days per week. The average school day consists of 6 hours and 30 minutes.

Upper School Student Profile Grade 9: 254 students (254 girls); Grade 10: 237 students (237 girls); Grade 11: 271 students (271 girls); Grade 12: 265 students (265 girls). 87% of students are Roman Catholic.

Faculty School total: 92. In upper school: 12 men, 80 women; 56 have advanced degrees.

Subjects Offered ACT preparation, advanced studio art-AP, anatomy and physiology, art history, art history-AP, biology, biology-AP, calculus, calculus-AP, ceramics, chemistry-AP, child development, chorus, college counseling, comparative government and politics-AP, composition-AP, CPR, English, English language and composition-AP, English literature, English literature and composition-AP, European history-AP, first aid, French, French-AP, general science, geography, geometry, global issues, government/civics-AP, graphic design, honors algebra, honors English, honors geometry, honors U.S. history, honors world history, introduction to theater, journalism, Latin, Latin-AP, marching band, media literacy, music appreciation, newspaper, orchestra, painting, photography, physical education, physics, physics-AP, play production, Spanish, Spanish-AP, speech, studio art, studio art-AP, theater, theology, U.S. history, U.S. history-AP, U.S. literature, Web site design, wind ensemble, women's studies, world history, world history-AP, yearbook.

Graduation Requirements Art history, arts and fine arts (art, music, dance, drama), English, lab science, language, mathematics, music, physical education (includes health), social sciences, technology, theology.

Special Academic Programs 16 Advanced Placement exams for which test preparation is offered; honors section; study at local college for college credit.

College Admission Counseling 279 students graduated in 2015; all went to college, including Eastern Illinois University; Illinois State University; Loyola University Chicago; University of Illinois at Chicago; University of Illinois at Urbana–Champaign. Mean composite ACT: 23.

Student Life Upper grades have uniform requirement, student council. Discipline rests primarily with faculty. Attendance at religious services is required.

Summer Programs Remediation, enrichment, advancement, sports, art/fine arts, computer instruction programs offered; session focuses on academics; held on campus; accepts girls; open to students from other schools. 200 students usually enrolled. 2016 schedule: June 13 to July 23. Application deadline: June 1.

Tuition and Aid Day student tuition: $10,650. Tuition installment plan (monthly payment plans, individually arranged payment plans). Tuition reduction for siblings, merit scholarship grants, need-based scholarship grants, paying campus jobs available. In 2015–16, 56% of upper-school students received aid; total upper-school merit-scholarship money awarded: $30,000. Total amount of financial aid awarded in 2015–16: $1,000,000.

Admissions Traditional secondary-level entrance grade is 9. For fall 2015, 361 students applied for upper-level admission, 312 were accepted, 254 enrolled. High School Placement Test required. Deadline for receipt of application materials: May 1. Application fee required: $300.

Athletics Interscholastic: basketball, bowling, cross-country running, dance team, diving, golf, independent competitive sports, lacrosse, sailing, soccer, softball, swimming and diving, tennis, track and field, volleyball, water polo; intramural: aerobics, basketball, bowling, flag football, Frisbee, softball, touch football, ultimate Frisbee, volleyball. 3 PE instructors, 20 coaches, 1 athletic trainer.

Computers Computers are regularly used in accounting, art, basic skills, business education, drafting, drawing and design, English, foreign language, French, graphics, journalism, Latin, mathematics, music, newspaper, photography, science, social sciences, Spanish, theater, Web site design, writing, yearbook classes. Computer network features include on-campus library services, Internet access, wireless campus network, Internet filtering or blocking technology. Student e-mail accounts and computer access in designated common areas are available to students. Students grades are available online. The school has a published electronic and media policy.

Contact Mrs. Kathryn Klyczek, Director of Admissions and Financial Aid. 773-881-6534. Fax: 773-881-6515. E-mail: kklyczek@mothermcauley.org. Website: www.mothermcauley.org

MOUNDS PARK ACADEMY

2051 Larpenteur Avenue East

Maplewood, Minnesota 55109

Head of School: Dr. William Hudson

General Information Coeducational day college-preparatory, arts, bilingual studies, and technology school. Grades PK–12. Founded: 1982. Setting: suburban. Nearest major city is St. Paul. 32-acre campus. 1 building on campus. Approved or accredited by Independent Schools Association of the Central States, Middle States Association of Colleges and Schools, and Minnesota Department of Education. Member of National Association of Independent Schools. Endowment: $6 million. Total enrollment: 480. Upper school average class size: 16. Upper school faculty-student ratio: 1:9. There are 175 required school days per year for Upper School students. Upper School students typically attend 5 days per week. The average school day consists of 6 hours and 40 minutes.

Upper School Student Profile Grade 9: 52 students (25 boys, 27 girls); Grade 10: 55 students (27 boys, 28 girls); Grade 11: 55 students (27 boys, 28 girls); Grade 12: 57 students (27 boys, 30 girls).

Faculty School total: 76. In upper school: 11 men, 23 women; 16 have advanced degrees.

Subjects Offered Algebra, American history, American literature, anatomy, area studies, art, biology, calculus, ceramics, chemistry, chorus, contemporary women writers, creative writing, debate, design, drama, drawing, economics, English literature, fine arts, French, geometry, health, history, independent study, instrumental music, law, literature, mathematics, media, men's studies, multicultural literature, music, painting, photography, physical education, physical science, physics, physiology, psychology, public policy issues and action, science, senior seminar, social sciences, social studies, Spanish, speech, statistics, theater, trigonometry, vocal music, Western civilization, world literature, writing.

Graduation Requirements Arts and fine arts (art, music, dance, drama), English, foreign language, health education, mathematics, physical education (includes health), science, senior seminar, social studies (includes history), senior performance. Community service is required.

Special Academic Programs 6 Advanced Placement exams for which test preparation is offered; honors section; independent study; study at local college for college credit; programs in general development for dyslexic students; ESL (8 students enrolled).

College Admission Counseling 40 students graduated in 2015; all went to college, including Harvard University; Rice University; St. Olaf College; University of Minnesota, Twin Cities Campus; University of St. Thomas; University of Wisconsin–Madison. Mean SAT critical reading: 628, mean SAT math: 613, mean SAT writing: 607, mean combined SAT: 1848, mean composite ACT: 28.

Student Life Upper grades have specified standards of dress, student council, honor system. Discipline rests equally with students and faculty.

Summer Programs Enrichment, sports, art/fine arts, rigorous outdoor training, computer instruction programs offered; held on campus; accepts boys and girls; open to students from other schools. 350 students usually enrolled. 2016 schedule: June 21 to August 13.

Tuition and Aid Day student tuition: $23,900. Tuition installment plan (monthly payment plans, 2-payment plan, 3-payment plan, 4-payment plan, 8-payment plan). Need-based scholarship grants, Malone Scholarship for qualified applicants available. In 2015–16, 30% of upper-school students received aid. Total amount of financial aid awarded in 2015–16: $1,000,000.

Admissions Traditional secondary-level entrance grade is 9. For fall 2015, 50 students applied for upper-level admission, 40 were accepted, 19 enrolled. Writing sample required. Deadline for receipt of application materials: March 1. Application fee required: $50. Interview required.

Athletics Interscholastic: baseball (boys), basketball (b,g), cross-country running (b,g), dance team (g), equestrian sports (g), football (b), golf (b,g), hockey (b), nordic skiing (b,g), skiing (cross-country) (b,g), soccer (b,g), softball (g), swimming and diving (g), tennis (b,g), track and field (b,g), volleyball (g). 4 PE instructors, 20 coaches.

Computers Computers are regularly used in English, foreign language, mathematics, science, social studies classes. Computer network features include on-campus library services, online commercial services, Internet access, wireless campus network, Internet filtering or blocking technology. Student e-mail accounts are available to students. Students grades are available online. The school has a published electronic and media policy.

Contact Craig Dodson, Director of Admission. 651-748-5577. Fax: 651-748-5534. E-mail: cdodson@moundsparkacademy.org. Website: www.moundsparkacademy.org

MOUNTAIN VIEW ACADEMY

360 South Shoreline Boulevard
Mountain View, California 94041
Head of School: Mr. Gerald Corson

General Information Coeducational day college-preparatory, arts, religious studies, and bilingual studies school, affiliated with Seventh-day Adventist Church. Grades 9–12. Founded: 1923. Setting: urban. Nearest major city is San Jose. 3-acre campus. 4 buildings on campus. Approved or accredited by Western Association of Schools and Colleges and California Department of Education. Total enrollment: 150. Upper school average class size: 20. Upper school faculty-student ratio: 1:14. There are 180 required school days per year for Upper School students. Upper School students typically attend 5 days per week. The average school day consists of 7 hours.

Upper School Student Profile Grade 9: 38 students (24 boys, 14 girls); Grade 10: 35 students (16 boys, 19 girls); Grade 11: 40 students (21 boys, 19 girls); Grade 12: 35 students (16 boys, 19 girls). 70% of students are Seventh-day Adventists.

Faculty School total: 14. In upper school: 7 men, 7 women; 6 have advanced degrees.

Graduation Requirements Algebra, American government, American history, arts and fine arts (art, music, dance, drama), biology, computer literacy, economics, electives, English, English composition, English literature, foreign language, geometry, health, home economics, religion (includes Bible studies and theology), world history, 25 hours of community service per year.

Special Academic Programs Advanced Placement exam preparation; honors section; accelerated programs; remedial math.

College Admission Counseling 34 students graduated in 2015; all went to college, including De Anza College; La Sierra University; Pacific Union College; San Jose State University; University of California, Los Angeles.

Student Life Upper grades have specified standards of dress, student council, honor system. Discipline rests primarily with faculty.

Tuition and Aid Day student tuition: $14,427–$18,407. Tuition installment plan (monthly payment plans). Merit scholarship grants, need-based scholarship grants, paying campus jobs available. In 2015–16, 35% of upper-school students received aid; total upper-school merit-scholarship money awarded: $15,000. Total amount of financial aid awarded in 2015–16: $48,500.

Admissions Traditional secondary-level entrance grade is 9. For fall 2015, 163 students applied for upper-level admission, 158 were accepted, 158 enrolled. TOEFL required. Deadline for receipt of application materials: March 1. No application fee required. Interview required.

Athletics Interscholastic: basketball (boys, girls), flag football (b,g), soccer (b,g), softball (b,g), volleyball (b,g); intramural: basketball (b,g), flag football (b,g), softball (b,g), volleyball (b,g). 1 PE instructor.

Computers Computers are regularly used in basic skills classes. Computer network features include Internet access. Computer access in designated common areas is available to students. Students grades are available online. The school has a published electronic and media policy.

Contact Alyce Schales, Registrar. 650-967-2324 Ext. 6654. Fax: 650-967-6886. E-mail: registrar@mtnviewacademy.org. Website: www.mtnviewacademy.org

MOUNT CARMEL SCHOOL

PO Box 500006
Saipan, Northern Mariana Islands 96950
Head of School: Mr. Galvin S. Deleon Guerrero

General Information Coeducational day college-preparatory, general academic, religious studies, and technology school, affiliated with Roman Catholic Church. Grades 1–12. Founded: 1952. Setting: rural. Nearest major city is Hagatna, GU. 5-acre campus. 1 building on campus. Approved or accredited by National Catholic Education Association and Northern Mariana Islands Department of Education. Candidate for accreditation by North Central Association of Colleges and Schools. Total enrollment: 378. Upper school average class size: 25. Upper school faculty-student ratio: 1:20. There are 180 required school days per year for Upper School students. Upper School students typically attend 5 days per week. The average school day consists of 6 hours and 5 minutes.

Upper School Student Profile Grade 9: 41 students (19 boys, 22 girls); Grade 10: 28 students (16 boys, 12 girls); Grade 11: 40 students (19 boys, 21 girls); Grade 12: 37 students (21 boys, 16 girls). 95% of students are Roman Catholic.

Faculty School total: 20. In upper school: 3 men, 6 women; 4 have advanced degrees.

Subjects Offered Advanced math, algebra, American government, American history, American history-AP, art, biology, British literature, calculus, calculus-AP, campus ministry, Catholic belief and practice, chemistry, Christian doctrine, Christian scripture, civics, composition, computer applications, computer science, drama, English, English literature, English literature-AP, foreign language, gardening, geometry, history of the Catholic Church, HTML design, independent study, Japanese, literature, media production, moral theology, physical education, physics, pre-calculus, Spanish, state history, theology, trigonometry, world history, world literature, world religions, yearbook.

Graduation Requirements Algebra, American history, art, biology, British literature, Catholic belief and practice, chemistry, Christian ethics, Christian scripture, church history, civics, composition, computer applications, English, English literature, foreign language, geometry, physical education (includes health), physics, theology, U.S. literature, world history.

Special Academic Programs 4 Advanced Placement exams for which test preparation is offered; independent study.

College Admission Counseling 45 students graduated in 2014; 25 went to college, including Northern Marianas College. Other: 3 went to work, 2 entered military service.

Student Life Upper grades have uniform requirement, student council, honor system. Discipline rests primarily with faculty. Attendance at religious services is required.

Tuition and Aid Day student tuition: $3530. Tuition installment plan (monthly payment plans). Tuition reduction for siblings, merit scholarship grants, need-based scholarship grants available. In 2014–15, 25% of upper-school students received aid; total upper-school merit-scholarship money awarded: $1000. Total amount of financial aid awarded in 2014–15: $30,000.

Admissions Traditional secondary-level entrance grade is 9. For fall 2014, 79 students applied for upper-level admission, 79 were accepted, 78 enrolled. Deadline for receipt of application materials: none. Application fee required: $50.

Athletics Interscholastic: aquatics (boys, girls), basketball (b,g), canoeing/kayaking (b,g), flag football (b), ocean paddling (b,g), softball (g), track and field (b,g), volleyball (b,g); intramural: badminton (b,g), basketball (b,g), flag football (b,g), floor hockey (b,g), soccer (b,g), volleyball (b,g); coed interscholastic: aquatics, ocean paddling, volleyball; coed intramural: badminton, soccer, volleyball. 1 PE instructor.

Computers Computers are regularly used in all academic, computer applications classes. Computer network features include on-campus library services, online commercial services, Internet access, wireless campus network, Internet filtering or blocking technology. Campus intranet is available to students. Students grades are available online. The school has a published electronic and media policy.

Contact Mr. Galvin S. Deleon Guerrero, President. 670-234-6184. Fax: 670-235-4751. E-mail: president.mcs@pticom.com. Website: www.mountcarmelsaipan.com

MT. DE SALES ACADEMY

851 Orange Street
Macon, Georgia 31201
Head of School: Mr. David Held

General Information Coeducational day college-preparatory, arts, religious studies, and technology school, affiliated with Roman Catholic Church. Grades 6–12. Founded: 1876. Setting: urban. 72-acre campus. 10 buildings on campus. Approved or accredited by Mercy Secondary Education Association, National Catholic Education Association, Southern Association of Colleges and Schools, Southern Association of Independent Schools, The College Board, and Georgia Department of Education. Member of National Association of Independent Schools. Endowment: $400,000. Total enrollment: 601. Upper school average class size: 19. Upper school faculty-student ratio: 1:9. There are 180 required school days per year for Upper School students. Upper School students typically attend 5 days per week. The average school day consists of 7 hours.

Upper School Student Profile Grade 6: 44 students (26 boys, 18 girls); Grade 7: 73 students (36 boys, 37 girls); Grade 8: 79 students (43 boys, 36 girls); Grade 9: 104 students (36 boys, 68 girls); Grade 10: 111 students (51 boys, 60 girls); Grade 11: 94 students (46 boys, 48 girls); Grade 12: 94 students (46 boys, 48 girls). 45% of students are Roman Catholic.

Faculty School total: 64. In upper school: 26 men, 17 women; 30 have advanced degrees.

Subjects Offered 20th century world history, advanced biology, advanced chemistry, advanced computer applications, advanced math, Advanced Placement courses, advanced studio art-AP, African American studies, algebra, American Civil War, American government, American history, American history-AP, American literature, American literature-AP, anatomy and physiology, art history-AP, astronomy, athletic training, band, biology, biology-AP, British literature, calculus, calculus-AP, chemistry, chemistry-AP, choral music, chorus, Christian education, Christian scripture, computer applications, computer multimedia, computer programming-AP, drawing and design, economics, English, English language and composition-AP, English literature. and composition-AP, European history-AP, forensics, French, government, government and politics-AP, health, Holocaust studies, honors algebra, honors English, honors geometry, New Testament, physical education, physics-AP, portfolio art, pre-calculus, programming, psychology, psychology-AP, Spanish-AP, speech, statistics, statistics-AP, studio art, U.S. government, U.S. government and politics-AP, U.S. history, U.S. history-AP, visual arts, World War II, yearbook.

Graduation Requirements 1 1/2 elective credits, algebra, American government, American history, arts and fine arts (art, music, dance, drama), biology, chemistry, computer applications, economics, English, foreign language, government, health education, physical education (includes health), physics, religion (includes Bible studies and theology), theology, U.S. history, world history.

Special Academic Programs Honors section; study at local college for college credit.

College Admission Counseling 111 students graduated in 2014; all went to college, including Georgia Institute of Technology; Georgia Southern University; Middle Georgia State University; University of Georgia. Mean SAT critical reading: 710, mean SAT math: 700, mean SAT writing: 720, mean combined SAT: 2130.

Student Life Upper grades have specified standards of dress, student council, honor system. Discipline rests primarily with faculty. Attendance at religious services is required.

Tuition and Aid Day student tuition: $11,590. Tuition installment plan (FACTS Tuition Payment Plan, monthly payment plans, individually arranged payment plans). Merit scholarship grants, need-based scholarship grants available. In 2014–15, 30% of upper-school students received aid; total upper-school merit-scholarship money awarded: $122,000. Total amount of financial aid awarded in 2014–15: $813,771.

Admissions Traditional secondary-level entrance grade is 9. For fall 2014, 92 students applied for upper-level admission, 68 were accepted, 46 enrolled. Naglieri Nonverbal School Ability Test required. Deadline for receipt of application materials: none. Application fee required: $50.

Athletics Interscholastic: baseball (boys), basketball (b,g), cheering (g), cross-country running (b,g), dance team (g), fitness (b,g), football (b), lacrosse (b), physical fitness (b,g), physical training (b,g), soccer (b,g), softball (g), strength & conditioning (b,g), swimming and diving (b,g), tennis (b,g), track and field (b,g), volleyball (g), weight training (b,g), wrestling (b); coed interscholastic: golf. 3 coaches.

Computers Computers are regularly used in all classes. Computer network features include on-campus library services, Internet access, wireless campus network, Internet filtering or blocking technology. Campus intranet, student e-mail accounts, and computer access in designated common areas are available to students. Students grades are available online. The school has a published electronic and media policy.

Contact Mrs. Ashley Griffin, Director of Admissions. 478-751-3244. Fax: 478-751-3241. E-mail: agriffin@mountdesales.net. Website: www.mountdesales.net

MOUNT DORA CHRISTIAN ACADEMY

301 West 13th Avenue
Mount Dora, Florida 32757

Head of School: Dr. Brad Moser

General Information Coeducational day college-preparatory, general academic, arts, religious studies, and technology school, affiliated with Church of Christ. Grades PK–12. Founded: 1945. Setting: small town. Nearest major city is Orlando. 70-acre campus. 10 buildings on campus. Approved or accredited by National Christian School Association, Southern Association of Colleges and Schools, and Florida Department of Education. Total enrollment: 557. Upper school average class size: 20. Upper school faculty-student ratio: 1:13. There are 180 required school days per year for Upper School students. Upper School students typically attend 5 days per week. The average school day consists of 6 hours and 30 minutes.

Upper School Student Profile Grade 6: 44 students (23 boys, 21 girls); Grade 7: 36 students (22 boys, 14 girls); Grade 8: 46 students (26 boys, 20 girls); Grade 9: 44 students (22 boys, 22 girls); Grade 10: 50 students (29 boys, 21 girls); Grade 11: 36 students (21 boys, 15 girls); Grade 12: 46 students (19 boys, 27 girls). 20% of students are members of Church of Christ.

Faculty School total: 45. In upper school: 9 men, 12 women; 11 have advanced degrees.

Subjects Offered Algebra, American government, American history, anatomy and physiology, art, band, Bible, biology, calculus-AP, career technology, ceramics, chemistry, computer skills, consumer mathematics, creative writing, drawing, earth and space science, economics, English, English literature-AP, English-AP, environmental science, geography, geometry, government, health, honors algebra, honors English, honors geometry, honors world history, journalism, life science, life skills, math applications, painting, photography, physical education, physical science, physics, pre-algebra, pre-calculus, probability and statistics, sculpture, Spanish, speech, statistics, technology/design, television, U.S. history, U.S. history-AP, video communication, video film production, weight training, world history, zoology.

Graduation Requirements Advanced biology, advanced math, algebra, American government, American history, American literature-AP, art history, arts and fine arts (art, music, dance, drama), Bible, biology, chemistry, economics, electives, English, foreign language, lab science, life skills, physical education (includes health), physical science, world history, 100 hours of community service.

Special Academic Programs 4 Advanced Placement exams for which test preparation is offered; honors section; independent study; study at local college for college credit.

College Admission Counseling 35 students graduated in 2015; 32 went to college, including Harding University; Lipscomb University; Seminole State College of Florida; The University of Alabama; University of Central Florida. Other: 1 went to work, 2 had other specific plans. Median SAT critical reading: 495, median SAT math: 470, median SAT writing: 490, median combined SAT: 1465, median composite ACT: 20. 16.6% scored over 600 on SAT math, 16.6% scored over 26 on composite ACT.

Student Life Upper grades have specified standards of dress, student council. Discipline rests primarily with faculty. Attendance at religious services is required.

Summer Programs Remediation programs offered; session focuses on math; held on campus; accepts boys and girls; not open to students from other schools. 10 students usually enrolled. 2016 schedule: June 5 to June 20.

Tuition and Aid Day student tuition: $9504. Tuition installment plan (FACTS Tuition Payment Plan). Tuition reduction for siblings, need-based scholarship grants, discount for members of the Churches of Christ available. In 2015–16, 30% of upper-school students received aid.

Admissions Traditional secondary-level entrance grade is 9. For fall 2015, 54 students applied for upper-level admission, 39 were accepted, 39 enrolled. School placement exam required. Deadline for receipt of application materials: none. Application fee required: $125. On-campus interview required.

Athletics Interscholastic: baseball (boys), basketball (b,g), bowling (b,g), cheering (g), cross-country running (b,g), fitness (b,g), football (b), golf (b,g), physical fitness (b,g), physical training (b,g), softball (g), tennis (b,g), track and field (b,g), volleyball (g), weight training (b,g). 3 coaches.

Computers Computers are regularly used in all academic, independent study, journalism, library, mathematics, publications, reading, video film production, Web site design, yearbook classes. Computer network features include on-campus library services, Internet access, wireless campus network, Internet filtering or blocking technology, NetClassroom communication for students and parents, desk top monitoring and manage software, Accelerated Reader Access. Campus intranet, student e-mail accounts, and computer access in designated common areas are available to students. Students grades are available online. The school has a published electronic and media policy.

Contact Natalie Yawn, Admissions Director. 352-383-2155 Ext. 261. Fax: 352-383-0098. E-mail: natalie.yawn@mdcacademy.org. Website: www.mdcacademy.org

MOUNT MERCY ACADEMY

88 Red Jacket Parkway
Buffalo, New York 14220

Head of School: Mrs. Margaret Staszak

General Information Girls' day college-preparatory, arts, and religious studies school, affiliated with Roman Catholic Church. Grades 9–12. Founded: 1904. Setting: urban. 1-acre campus. 2 buildings on campus. Approved or accredited by Middle States Association of Colleges and Schools and New York Department of Education. Total enrollment: 229. Upper school average class size: 20. Upper school faculty-student ratio: 1:20. There are 180 required school days per year for Upper School students. Upper School students typically attend 5 days per week. The average school day consists of 6 hours and 45 minutes.

Upper School Student Profile Grade 9: 59 students (59 girls); Grade 10: 58 students (58 girls); Grade 11: 52 students (52 girls); Grade 12: 60 students (60 girls). 97% of students are Roman Catholic.

Faculty School total: 30. In upper school: 6 men, 24 women; 23 have advanced degrees.

Subjects Offered 1 1/2 elective credits.

Special Academic Programs Advanced Placement exam preparation; honors section; independent study.

College Admission Counseling 58 students graduated in 2015; all went to college.

Student Life Upper grades have uniform requirement, student council, honor system. Discipline rests equally with students and faculty. Attendance at religious services is required.

Summer Programs Enrichment programs offered; session focuses on Regents review; held on campus; accepts boys and girls; open to students from other schools. 2016 schedule: July to August.

Tuition and Aid Day student tuition: $9450. Tuition installment plan (FACTS Tuition Payment Plan). Tuition reduction for siblings, merit scholarship grants, need-based scholarship grants, paying campus jobs available.

Admissions Traditional secondary-level entrance grade is 9. For fall 2015, 229 students applied for upper-level admission, 229 were accepted, 229 enrolled. Admissions testing or High School Placement Test (closed version) from Scholastic Testing Service required. Deadline for receipt of application materials: none. Application fee required: $20. On-campus interview required.

Athletics Interscholastic: basketball, bowling, cheering, crew, cross-country running, golf, hockey, lacrosse, skiing (downhill), soccer, softball, tennis, volleyball. 1 PE instructor, 13 coaches.

Computers Computers are regularly used in art, business, desktop publishing, keyboarding, study skills, yearbook classes. Computer network features include on-campus library services, Internet access, wireless campus network, Internet filtering or blocking technology. Campus intranet, student e-mail accounts, and computer access in designated common areas are available to students. Students grades are available online. The school has a published electronic and media policy.

Contact Miss Molly Gasuik, Recruiter. 716-825-8796 Ext. 310. Fax: 716-825-0976. E-mail: mgasuik@mtmercy.org. Website: www.mtmercy.org

MOUNT NOTRE DAME HIGH SCHOOL

711 East Columbia Avenue
Cincinnati, Ohio 45215

Head of School: Mr. Larry Mock

General Information College-preparatory, arts, business, religious studies, bilingual studies, and technology school, affiliated with Roman Catholic Church. Founded: 1860. 1 building on campus. Approved or accredited by Ohio Department of Education. Upper school average class size: 700. Upper school faculty-student ratio: 1:15.

Upper School Student Profile 85% of students are Roman Catholic.

Special Academic Programs International Baccalaureate program; 20 Advanced Placement exams for which test preparation is offered; honors section; study at local college for college credit; study abroad.

College Admission Counseling 168 students graduated in 2014; 166 went to college. Other: 2 went to work.

Student Life Upper grades have uniform requirement. Attendance at religious services is required.

Tuition and Aid Tuition reduction for siblings, merit scholarship grants, need-based scholarship grants available.

Admissions Deadline for receipt of application materials: January. Application fee required.

Computers Computer resources include on-campus library services, Internet access, wireless campus network, Internet filtering or blocking technology, submitting homework, taking exams. Campus intranet, student e-mail accounts, and computer access in designated common areas are available to students. Students grades are available online. The school has a published electronic and media policy.

Contact Mrs. Donna Groene, Director of Admissions. 513-821-3044 Ext. 164. Fax: 513-821-6068. E-mail: dgroene@mndhs.org. Website: www.mndhs.org

MOUNT PARAN CHRISTIAN SCHOOL

1275 Stanley Road
Kennesaw, Georgia 30152

Head of School: Dr. David Tilley

General Information Coeducational day college-preparatory and religious studies school, affiliated with Christian faith; primarily serves students with learning disabilities and individuals with Attention Deficit Disorder. Grades K–12. Founded: 1976. Setting: suburban. Nearest major city is Marietta. 65-acre campus. 3 buildings on campus. Approved or accredited by Georgia Independent School Association and Southern Association of Independent Schools. Total enrollment: 1,120. Upper school average class size: 17. There are 178 required school days per year for Upper School students. Upper School students typically attend 5 days per week. The average school day consists of 7 hours and 15 minutes.

Upper School Student Profile 100% of students are Christian faith.

Subjects Offered Advanced Placement courses.

Special Academic Programs 18 Advanced Placement exams for which test preparation is offered; honors section; study at local college for college credit; study abroad; academic accommodation for the gifted, the musically talented, and the artistically talented; remedial reading and/or remedial writing; remedial math; programs in English, general development for dyslexic students; special instructional classes for deaf students.

College Admission Counseling Colleges students went to include Auburn University; Georgia Institute of Technology; University of Georgia; Wheaton College.

Student Life Upper grades have uniform requirement. Discipline rests primarily with faculty. Attendance at religious services is required.

Tuition and Aid Day student tuition: $15,476. Tuition installment plan (monthly payment plans). Need-based scholarship grants available.

Admissions Any standardized test or Cognitive Abilities Test required. Deadline for receipt of application materials: none. Application fee required: $75. Interview required.

Athletics Interscholastic: baseball (boys), basketball (b,g), cheering (g), cross-country running (b,g), equestrian sports (g), football (b), golf (b,g), lacrosse (b), soccer (b,g), softball (g), strength & conditioning (b,g), tennis (b,g), track and field (b,g), volleyball (g), weight training (b), wrestling (b); coed interscholastic: aquatics, ballet, dance, physical fitness, physical training, strength & conditioning, swimming and diving; coed intramural: fly fishing.

Computers Computers are regularly used in all academic, college planning, creative writing, current events, graphic design, keyboarding, research skills, yearbook classes. Computer network features include on-campus library services, online commercial services, Internet access, wireless campus network, Internet filtering or blocking technology. Campus intranet, student e-mail accounts, and computer access in designated common areas are available to students. Students grades are available online. The school has a published electronic and media policy.

Contact Mrs. Shaunda Brooks, Director of Admission. 770-578-0182 Ext. 2046. Fax: 770-977-9284. E-mail: sbrooks@mtparanschool.com. Website: www.mtparanschool.com

MOUNT SAINT CHARLES ACADEMY

800 Logee Street
Woonsocket, Rhode Island 02895-5599

Head of School: Mr. Herve E. Richer Jr.

General Information Coeducational day college-preparatory, arts, and religious studies school, affiliated with Roman Catholic Church. Grades 6–12. Founded: 1924. Setting: suburban. Nearest major city is Providence. 22-acre campus. 2 buildings on campus. Approved or accredited by New England Association of Schools and Colleges and Rhode Island Department of Education. Total enrollment: 627. Upper school average class size: 25. Upper school faculty-student ratio: 1:14. There are 180 required school days per year for Upper School students. Upper School students typically attend 5 days per week. The average school day consists of 6 hours and 15 minutes.

Upper School Student Profile Grade 6: 23 students (14 boys, 9 girls); Grade 7: 54 students (29 boys, 25 girls); Grade 8: 72 students (32 boys, 40 girls); Grade 9: 109 students (38 boys, 71 girls); Grade 10: 118 students (50 boys, 68 girls); Grade 11: 138 students (58 boys, 80 girls); Grade 12: 113 students (55 boys, 58 girls). 85% of students are Roman Catholic.

Faculty School total: 54. In upper school: 27 men, 27 women; 34 have advanced degrees.

Subjects Offered Advanced computer applications, algebra, American literature, architecture, art, band, biology, biology-AP, British literature, calculus, calculus-AP, chemistry, chorus, computer science, creative writing, dance, drama, economics, English, English language and composition-AP, English literature, English literature and composition-AP, English literature-AP, environmental science, environmental science-AP, European history, European history-AP, fine arts, forensics, French, geography, geometry, government, government and politics-AP, government/civics, handbells, health education, history, history of the Catholic Church, honors U.S. history, honors world history, jazz band, mathematics, mathematics-AP, modern European history, music, music theory-AP, physical education, physics, physiology, psychology, psychology-AP, religion, science, social studies, Spanish, theater, trigonometry, U.S. history, U.S. history-AP, world history, world literature, writing, yearbook.

Graduation Requirements Arts and fine arts (art, music, dance, drama), computer science, English, foreign language, mathematics, physical education (includes health), religion (includes Bible studies and theology), science, social studies (includes history).

Special Academic Programs 13 Advanced Placement exams for which test preparation is offered; honors section.

College Admission Counseling 153 students graduated in 2015; all went to college.

Student Life Upper grades have uniform requirement, student council, honor system. Discipline rests primarily with faculty. Attendance at religious services is required.

Summer Programs Sports, art/fine arts programs offered; session focuses on fine arts, soccer, hockey, basketball, baseball, volleyball; held on campus; accepts boys and girls; open to students from other schools. 350 students usually enrolled. 2016 schedule: July to August. Application deadline: none.

Tuition and Aid Day student tuition: $12,900. Tuition installment plan (FACTS Tuition Payment Plan, full payment discount plan). Need-based scholarship grants available. In 2015–16, 38% of upper-school students received aid. Total amount of financial aid awarded in 2015–16: $750,000.

Admissions Traditional secondary-level entrance grade is 9. For fall 2015, 150 students applied for upper-level admission, 100 were accepted, 70 enrolled. Diocesan Entrance Exam, ISEE, SAS, STS-HSPT, SSAT or STS required. Deadline for receipt of application materials: none. Application fee required: $30.

Athletics Interscholastic: baseball (boys), basketball (b,g), cross-country running (b,g), gymnastics (g), ice hockey (b,g), indoor track (b,g), lacrosse (b,g), soccer (b,g), softball (g), swimming and diving (b,g), tennis (b,g), track and field (b,g), volleyball (b,g), winter (indoor) track (b,g); intramural: aerobics/dance (g), basketball (b,g), dance (g); coed interscholastic: cheering, golf; coed intramural: billiards, bowling, dance team, equestrian sports, flag football, indoor soccer, lacrosse, physical training, soccer, strength & conditioning, touch football. 3 PE instructors, 15 coaches, 1 athletic trainer.

Computers Computers are regularly used in accounting, architecture, art, computer applications, desktop publishing, graphic design, science, yearbook classes. Computer network features include on-campus library services, online commercial services, Internet access, wireless campus network, Internet filtering or blocking technology. Campus intranet, student e-mail accounts, and computer access in designated common areas are available to students. Students grades are available online. The school has a published electronic and media policy.

Contact Joseph J. O'Neill Jr., Registrar/Director of Admissions. 401-769-0310 Ext. 137. Fax: 401-762-2327. E-mail: oneillj@faculty.mountsaintcharles.org. Website: www.mountsaintcharles.org

MOUNT SAINT JOSEPH ACADEMY

120 West Wissahickon Avenue
Flourtown, Pennsylvania 19031

Head of School: Sr. Kathleen Brabson, SSJ

General Information Girls' day college-preparatory, arts, business, and technology school, affiliated with Roman Catholic Church. Grades 9–12. Founded: 1858. Setting: suburban. Nearest major city is Philadelphia. 78-acre campus. 1 building on campus. Approved or accredited by Middle States Association of Colleges and Schools, Missouri Independent School Association, National Catholic Education Association, and Pennsylvania Department of Education. Member of National Association of Independent Schools. Endowment: $4 million. Total enrollment: 531. Upper school average class size: 19. Upper school faculty-student ratio: 1:10. There are 180 required school days per year for Upper School students. Upper School students typically attend 5 days per week. The average school day consists of 6 hours and 45 minutes.

Upper School Student Profile Grade 9: 122 students (122 girls); Grade 10: 139 students (139 girls); Grade 11: 137 students (137 girls); Grade 12: 133 students (133 girls). 91% of students are Roman Catholic.

Faculty School total: 63. In upper school: 15 men, 47 women; 49 have advanced degrees.

Graduation Requirements Arts and fine arts (art, music, dance, drama), computer science, English, foreign language, mathematics, physical education (includes health), religion (includes Bible studies and theology), science, social studies (includes history).

Special Academic Programs 13 Advanced Placement exams for which test preparation is offered; honors section; independent study; study at local college for college credit; academic accommodation for the gifted, the musically talented, and the artistically talented.

College Admission Counseling 142 students graduated in 2015; all went to college, including Drexel University; Fordham University; Loyola University Maryland; Penn State University Park; Temple University; Villanova University. Mean SAT critical reading: 632, mean SAT math: 610, mean SAT writing: 655, mean combined SAT: 1897. 60% scored over 600 on SAT critical reading, 57% scored over 600 on SAT math, 68% scored over 600 on SAT writing, 60% scored over 1800 on combined SAT.

Student Life Upper grades have uniform requirement, student council, honor system. Discipline rests primarily with faculty. Attendance at religious services is required.

Tuition and Aid Day student tuition: $17,350. Tuition installment plan (Higher Education Service, Inc, semester payment plan). Tuition reduction for siblings, merit scholarship grants, need-based scholarship grants available. In 2015–16, 26% of upper-school students received aid; total upper-school merit-scholarship money awarded: $398,900. Total amount of financial aid awarded in 2015–16: $699,113.

Admissions Traditional secondary-level entrance grade is 9. For fall 2015, 248 students applied for upper-level admission. High School Placement Test, SAS, STS-HSPT or school's own test required. Deadline for receipt of application materials: October 30. Application fee required: $75.

Athletics Interscholastic: basketball, crew, cross-country running, diving, field hockey, golf, indoor track, lacrosse, soccer, softball, swimming and diving, tennis, track and field, volleyball. 2 PE instructors, 24 coaches, 1 athletic trainer.

Computers Computers are regularly used in art, business studies, career exploration, college planning, commercial art, computer applications, desktop publishing, English, foreign language, graphic design, history, mathematics, music, science, theater arts, writing, writing, yearbook classes. Computer network features include on-campus library services, online commercial services, Internet access, wireless campus network, Internet filtering or blocking technology, video conferencing, SmartBoards, iPads. Campus intranet, student e-mail accounts, and computer access in designated common areas are available to students. Students grades are available online. The school has a published electronic and media policy.

Contact Ms. Carol Finney, Director of Admissions. 215-233-9133. Fax: 215-233-5887. E-mail: cfinney@msjacad.org. Website: www.msjacad.org

MOUNT VERNON PRESBYTERIAN SCHOOL

471 Mt. Vernon Highway NE
Atlanta, Georgia 30328

Head of School: Dr. Brett Jacobsen

General Information Coeducational day college-preparatory, arts, religious studies, technology, and design thinking school, affiliated with Presbyterian Church. Grades PK–12. Founded: 1972. Setting: suburban. 37-acre campus. 3 buildings on campus. Approved or accredited by Southern Association of Colleges and Schools, Southern Association of Independent Schools, and Georgia Department of Education. Member of National Association of Independent Schools and Secondary School Admission Test Board. Total enrollment: 932. Upper school average class size: 15. Upper school faculty-student ratio: 1:10. There are 175 required school days per year for Upper School students. Upper School students typically attend 5 days per week. The average school day consists of 7 hours.

Upper School Student Profile Grade 6: 87 students (48 boys, 39 girls); Grade 7: 73 students (39 boys, 34 girls); Grade 8: 84 students (48 boys, 36 girls); Grade 9: 81 students (39 boys, 42 girls); Grade 10: 84 students (38 boys, 46 girls); Grade 11: 81 students (48 boys, 33 girls); Grade 12: 62 students (30 boys, 32 girls). 15% of students are Presbyterian.

Faculty School total: 165. In upper school: 40 have advanced degrees.

Special Academic Programs Advanced Placement exam preparation; honors section; term-away projects; study abroad; ESL (12 students enrolled).

College Admission Counseling 55 went to college. Other: 55 went to work.

Student Life Upper grades have uniform requirement, student council, honor system. Discipline rests primarily with faculty. Attendance at religious services is required.

Summer Programs Remediation, enrichment, advancement, sports, art/fine arts programs offered; session focuses on enrichment; held on campus; accepts boys and girls; open to students from other schools. 100 students usually enrolled. 2016 schedule: May 25 to August 5. Application deadline: May 1.

Tuition and Aid Tuition installment plan (monthly payment plans). Need-based scholarship grants available. In 2015–16, 20% of upper-school students received aid.

Admissions Traditional secondary-level entrance grade is 9. ISEE, SSAT and Wechsler Intelligence Scale for Children required. Deadline for receipt of application materials: February 1. Application fee required: $100. Interview required.

Athletics Interscholastic: baseball (boys), basketball (b,g), cheering (g), dance (b,g), fitness (b,g), football (b,g), lacrosse (b,g), modern dance (b,g), physical fitness (b,g), physical training (b,g), soccer (b,g), softball (g), volleyball (g), wrestling (b), yoga (b); intramural: baseball (b), basketball (b,g), cheering (g), dance squad (g), dance team (g), flag football (b), football (b,g), jogging (b,g), running (b,g), soccer (b,g), softball (g); coed interscholastic: basketball, cross-country running, dance, diving, fitness, football, golf, lacrosse, modern dance, physical fitness, physical training, swimming and diving, tennis, track and field, weight lifting, weight training; coed intramural: basketball, football, golf, jogging, running, soccer, tennis, track and field, volleyball.

Computers Computer network features include on-campus library services, online commercial services, Internet access, wireless campus network, Internet filtering or blocking technology. Student e-mail accounts and computer access in designated common areas are available to students. Students grades are available online. The school has a published electronic and media policy.

Contact Kirsten Beard, Chief Admissions Officer. 404-252-3448 Ext. 2401. Fax: 404-252-7154. E-mail: kbeard@mountvernonschool.org. Website: www.mountvernonschool.org/

MU HIGH SCHOOL

306 Clark Hall
Columbia, Missouri 65211

Head of School: Zac March

General Information Coeducational day college-preparatory, general academic, and distance learning school. Grades 9–12. Founded: 1999. Setting: suburban. Nearest major city is St. Louis. Approved or accredited by Missouri Independent School Association and North Central Association of Colleges and Schools.

Subjects Offered 1 1/2 elective credits, 20th century American writers, 20th century physics, 20th century world history, 3-dimensional art, accounting, advanced math, Advanced Placement courses, African-American literature, agriculture, Alabama history and geography, algebra, American biography, American Civil War, American culture, American democracy, American foreign policy, American government, American history, American history-AP, ancient world history, art, art appreciation, art history-AP, astronomy, basic language skills, Basic programming, biology, business applications, business skills, business studies, calculus, calculus-AP, career education, career exploration, career planning, career/college preparation, careers, character education, chemistry, child development, Chinese, civics, college planning, communication arts, comparative politics, comparative religion, computer applications, computer literacy, computer programming, computer science-AP, conservation, consumer economics, consumer education, consumer mathematics, contemporary history, contemporary issues, creative writing, decision making skills, economics, English, English literature and composition-AP, entrepreneurship, environmental science, European history-AP, European literature, family and consumer science, family living, family studies, female experience in America, fiction, film and literature, fitness, food and nutrition, French, general science, geography, geology, geometry, German, government, government and politics-AP, grammar, health and safety, health and wellness, history, independent study, integrated mathematics, interpersonal skills, Japanese, keyboarding, language, language arts, Latin, law and the legal system, literature, literature and composition-AP, literature by women, math applications, mathematics, media studies, medieval history, modern history, modern world history, music appreciation, mythology, newspaper, North American literature, novels, parent/child development, personal and social education, personal development, personal finance, personal fitness, personal money management, photography, poetry, political science, pre-algebra, pre-calculus, psychology, psychology-AP, reading/study skills, religious studies, science fiction, Shakespeare, short story, skills for success, social studies, sociology, Spanish, state history, statistics, study skills, trigonometry, U.S. constitutional history, U.S. government, U.S. government and politics, U.S. government and politics-AP, U.S. history, U.S. history-AP, U.S. literature, women's literature, world geography, world history, world religions, writing.

Graduation Requirements Missouri Department of Elementary and Secondary Education requirements.

Special Academic Programs Advanced Placement exam preparation; accelerated programs; independent study; study at local college for college credit; academic accommodation for the gifted, the musically talented, and the artistically talented; remedial reading and/or remedial writing.

College Admission Counseling 120 students graduated in 2014.

Admissions Deadline for receipt of application materials: none. Application fee required: $25.

Athletics 1 PE instructor.

Computers Computers are regularly used in accounting, art, business, business applications, business education, business skills, business studies, career education, career exploration, classics, college planning, computer applications, creative writing, current events, digital applications, economics, English, foreign language, French, French as a second language, geography, health, historical foundations for arts, history, humanities, independent study, information technology, journalism, keyboarding, language development, Latin, life skills, mathematics, media, music, news writing, occupational education, photography, programming, psychology, reading, religious studies, research skills, science, social sciences, social studies, Spanish, study skills, theater, theater arts, typing, writing, writing classes. Computer resources include on-campus library services, INET Library, Britannica Online School Edition, course access. Computer access in designated common areas is available to students. Students grades are available online. The school has a published electronic and media policy.

Contact Alicia Bixby, Counselor. 573-882-7208. Fax: 573-884-9665. E-mail: bixbya@missouri.edu. Website: www.mizzouk12online.missouri.edu

NAMPA CHRISTIAN SCHOOLS

11920 W. Flamingo Ave.
Nampa, Idaho 83651

Head of School: Dr. Greg Wiles

General Information Coeducational day college-preparatory, general academic, religious studies, and technology school, affiliated with Christian faith. Grades PK–12. Founded: 1959. Setting: suburban. Nearest major city is Boise. 17-acre campus. 1 building on campus. Approved or accredited by Association of Christian Schools International, Northwest Association of Schools and Colleges, and Idaho Department of Education. Endowment: $275,000. Total enrollment: 586. Upper school average class size: 15. Upper school faculty-student ratio: 1:18. There are 171 required school days per year for Upper School students. Upper School students typically attend 5 days per week. The average school day consists of 6 hours and 2 minutes.

Upper School Student Profile Grade 9: 42 students (25 boys, 17 girls); Grade 10: 56 students (38 boys, 18 girls); Grade 11: 47 students (25 boys, 22 girls); Grade 12: 51 students (31 boys, 20 girls). 99% of students are Christian faith.

Faculty School total: 42. In upper school: 9 men, 7 women; 6 have advanced degrees.

Subjects Offered Algebra, American history, American literature, art, art history, band, Bible studies, biology, calculus, ceramics, chemistry, choir, computer science, computer skills, creative writing, debate, drama, earth science, economics, English, English literature, environmental science, geography, geometry, government/civics, grammar, health, history, humanities, mathematics, music, physical education, physics, reading, religion, science, social sciences, social studies, Spanish, speech, theater, trigonometry, typing, world history.

Graduation Requirements Economics, English, mathematics, physical education (includes health), reading, religion (includes Bible studies and theology), science, social sciences, speech.

Special Academic Programs Honors section; independent study; study at local college for college credit.

College Admission Counseling 52 students graduated in 2015; 50 went to college, including Boise State University; Dordt College; George Fox University; Grand Canyon University; Northwest Nazarene University; The College of Idaho. Other: 1 went to work, 1 entered military service. Median SAT critical reading: 563, median SAT math: 554, median composite ACT: 24.

Student Life Upper grades have specified standards of dress, student council. Discipline rests primarily with faculty. Attendance at religious services is required.

Tuition and Aid Day student tuition: $6055. Tuition installment plan (monthly payment plans, individually arranged payment plans). Tuition reduction for siblings, need-based scholarship grants available. In 2015–16, 12% of upper-school students received aid. Total amount of financial aid awarded in 2015–16: $15,000.

Admissions Traditional secondary-level entrance grade is 9. Deadline for receipt of application materials: none. Application fee required: $25. On-campus interview required.

Athletics Interscholastic: baseball (boys), basketball (b,g), cheering (g), cross-country running (b,g), football (b), softball (g), volleyball (g); coed interscholastic: alpine skiing, fitness, freestyle skiing, golf, physical fitness, skiing (downhill), track and field, weight lifting, weight training. 2 PE instructors, 5 coaches.

Computers Computers are regularly used in all academic classes. Computer network features include on-campus library services, Internet access, Internet filtering or blocking technology. Student e-mail accounts are available to students. Students grades are available online. The school has a published electronic and media policy.

Contact Tracie Johanson, Registrar. 208-475-1711. Fax: 208-466-8452. E-mail: tjohanson@nampachristianschools.com. Website: www.nampachristianschools.com

NASHVILLE CHRISTIAN SCHOOL

7555 Sawyer Brown Road
Nashville, Tennessee 37221

Head of School: Mrs. Connie Jo Shelton

General Information Coeducational day college-preparatory, arts, and religious studies school, affiliated with Christian faith. Grades K–12. Founded: 1971. Setting: suburban. 45-acre campus. 2 buildings on campus. Approved or accredited by National Christian School Association, North Central Association of Colleges and Schools, Southern Association of Colleges and Schools, and Tennessee Department of Education. Total enrollment: 467. Upper school average class size: 18. Upper school faculty-student ratio: 1:18. There are 176 required school days per year for Upper School students. Upper School students typically attend 5 days per week. The average school day consists of 7 hours and 15 minutes.

Upper School Student Profile Grade 6: 49 students (26 boys, 23 girls); Grade 7: 34 students (19 boys, 15 girls); Grade 8: 30 students (12 boys, 18 girls); Grade 9: 63 students (45 boys, 18 girls); Grade 10: 44 students (36 boys, 8 girls); Grade 11: 64 students (34 boys, 30 girls); Grade 12: 62 students (41 boys, 21 girls). 90% of students are Christian.

Faculty School total: 44. In upper school: 11 men, 14 women; 15 have advanced degrees.

Subjects Offered Advanced Placement courses, algebra, American history, art, Bible, Bible studies, biology, calculus, chemistry, chorus, computer science, economics, English, fine arts, general science, geometry, government/civics, health, journalism, keyboarding, Latin, Mandarin, mathematics, music, physical education, physical science, physics, pre-algebra, pre-calculus, science, social sciences, social studies, Spanish, speech.

Graduation Requirements American history, American history-AP, arts and fine arts (art, music, dance, drama), Bible, computer science, English, foreign language, mathematics, physical education (includes health), science, social sciences, social studies (includes history).

Special Academic Programs Advanced Placement exam preparation; honors section; independent study; study at local college for college credit; remedial reading and/or remedial writing; remedial math; programs in English, mathematics, general development for dyslexic students; special instructional classes for students with Attention Deficit Disorder.

College Admission Counseling 48 students graduated in 2015; 45 went to college, including Freed-Hardeman University; The University of Tennessee; The University of Tennessee at Chattanooga; The University of Tennessee at Martin; University of Mississippi; Western Kentucky University. Other: 2 went to work, 1 entered military service.

Student Life Upper grades have uniform requirement, student council, honor system. Discipline rests primarily with faculty. Attendance at religious services is required.

Summer Programs Remediation, sports, art/fine arts programs offered; held on campus; accepts boys and girls; open to students from other schools.

Tuition and Aid Day student tuition: $7790. Guaranteed tuition plan. Tuition installment plan (FACTS Tuition Payment Plan). Tuition reduction for siblings, need-based scholarship grants, paying campus jobs available. In 2015–16, 3% of upper-school students received aid. Total amount of financial aid awarded in 2015–16: $3000.

Admissions Traditional secondary-level entrance grade is 9. For fall 2015, 52 students applied for upper-level admission, 37 were accepted, 35 enrolled. Stanford Diagnostic Test required. Deadline for receipt of application materials: none. Application fee required: $100. Interview required.

Athletics Interscholastic: baseball (boys), basketball (b,g), bowling (b,g), cheering (g), cross-country running (b,g), football (b), golf (b,g), riflery (b,g), soccer (b,g), softball (g), strength & conditioning (b,g), track and field (b,g), volleyball (g), weight lifting (b,g), weight training (b,g), wrestling (b); intramural: aerobics/dance (g); coed interscholastic: fitness, physical fitness, physical training, soccer; coed intramural: archery. 2 PE instructors, 6 coaches, 1 athletic trainer.

Computers Computers are regularly used in all academic classes. Computer network features include on-campus library services, Internet access, wireless campus network,

Internet filtering or blocking technology. Student e-mail accounts and computer access in designated common areas are available to students. Students grades are available online. The school has a published electronic and media policy.

Contact Mrs. Wendy Paszek, Admissions Coordinator. 615-356-5600 Ext. 162. Fax: 615-352-1324. E-mail: paszekw@nashvillechristian.org. Website: www.nashvillechristian.org/

NATIONAL CATHEDRAL SCHOOL

3612 Woodley Road NW
Washington, District of Columbia 20016-5000

Head of School: Mrs. Kathleen O'Neill Jamieson

General Information Girls' day college-preparatory school, affiliated with Episcopal Church. Grades 4–12. Founded: 1900. Setting: urban. 59-acre campus. 7 buildings on campus. Approved or accredited by Association of Independent Maryland Schools, Association of Independent Schools of Greater Washington, Middle States Association of Colleges and Schools, National Association of Episcopal Schools, and District of Columbia Department of Education. Member of National Association of Independent Schools and Secondary School Admission Test Board. Endowment: $19 million. Total enrollment: 590. Upper school average class size: 14. Upper school faculty-student ratio: 1:7.

Upper School Student Profile Grade 9: 93 students (93 girls); Grade 10: 74 students (74 girls); Grade 11: 73 students (73 girls); Grade 12: 73 students (73 girls).

Faculty School total: 101. In upper school: 11 men, 34 women; 36 have advanced degrees.

Subjects Offered Advanced Placement courses, African American history, African-American literature, algebra, American history, American literature, art, art history, art history-AP, biology, calculus, ceramics, chemistry, Chinese, community service, computer programming, computer science, creative writing, dance, drama, earth science, economics, English, English literature, ethics, European history, expository writing, fine arts, French, geography, geometry, government/civics, Greek, history, Japanese, Latin, mathematics, music, photography, physical education, physics, political science, psychology, public speaking, religion, science, social studies, Spanish, statistics, theater, trigonometry, world history, writing.

Graduation Requirements Arts and fine arts (art, music, dance, drama), English, foreign language, mathematics, physical education (includes health), religion (includes Bible studies and theology), science, social studies (includes history). Community service is required.

Special Academic Programs 17 Advanced Placement exams for which test preparation is offered; honors section; independent study; term-away projects; study abroad; academic accommodation for the gifted.

College Admission Counseling 73 students graduated in 2015; all went to college, including Brown University; Dartmouth College; Princeton University; Stanford University; University of Pennsylvania; Yale University. Mean SAT critical reading: 718, mean SAT math: 698, mean SAT writing: 724.

Student Life Upper grades have specified standards of dress, student council, honor system. Discipline rests equally with students and faculty. Attendance at religious services is required.

Summer Programs Enrichment, sports, art/fine arts programs offered; held on campus; accepts boys and girls; open to students from other schools. 2016 schedule: June 11 to July 30. Application deadline: June 1.

Tuition and Aid Day student tuition: $38,850. Tuition installment plan (FACTS Tuition Payment Plan). Need-based scholarship grants available. In 2015–16, 22% of upper-school students received aid. Total amount of financial aid awarded in 2015–16: $1,604,156.

Admissions Traditional secondary-level entrance grade is 9. For fall 2015, 111 students applied for upper-level admission, 60 were accepted, 32 enrolled. ISEE or SSAT required. Deadline for receipt of application materials: January 15. Application fee required: $75. Interview required.

Athletics Interscholastic: basketball, crew, dance team, field hockey, ice hockey, indoor soccer, indoor track, indoor track & field, lacrosse, Nautilus, rowing, soccer, softball, tennis, track and field, volleyball, winter (indoor) track; intramural: aerobics, aerobics/dance, aerobics/Nautilus, backpacking, ballet, canoeing/kayaking, climbing, dance, fitness, hiking/backpacking, independent competitive sports, kayaking, modern dance, mountain biking, outdoor adventure, physical fitness, rafting, rappelling, rock climbing, strength & conditioning, weight lifting, weight training, yoga; coed interscholastic: cross-country running, diving, swimming and diving. 11 PE instructors, 11 coaches, 1 athletic trainer.

Computers Computers are regularly used in art, English, foreign language, mathematics, multimedia, science classes. Computer network features include on-campus library services, online commercial services, Internet access, wireless campus network, Internet filtering or blocking technology. Student e-mail accounts and computer access in designated common areas are available to students. The school has a published electronic and media policy.

Contact Ms. Elizabeth Wilson, Admission Assistant. 202-537-6374. Fax: 202-537-2382. E-mail: ncs_admissions@cathedral.org. Website: www.ncs.cathedral.org

NAZARETH ACADEMY

1209 West Ogden Avenue
LaGrange Park, Illinois 60526

Head of School: Mrs. Deborah A. Tracy

General Information Coeducational day college-preparatory school, affiliated with Roman Catholic Church. Grades 9–12. Founded: 1900. Setting: suburban. Nearest major city is Chicago. 20-acre campus. 3 buildings on campus. Approved or accredited by North Central Association of Colleges and Schools, The College Board, and Illinois Department of Education. Total enrollment: 763. Upper school average class size: 24. Upper school faculty-student ratio: 1:17. There are 180 required school days per year for Upper School students. Upper School students typically attend 5 days per week. The average school day consists of 7 hours.

Upper School Student Profile Grade 9: 216 students (107 boys, 109 girls); Grade 10: 170 students (97 boys, 73 girls); Grade 11: 193 students (83 boys, 110 girls); Grade 12: 184 students (94 boys, 90 girls). 85% of students are Roman Catholic.

Faculty School total: 49. In upper school: 19 men, 30 women; 45 have advanced degrees.

Subjects Offered 3-dimensional design, acting, algebra, American government, American literature, art, biology, biology-AP, calculus-AP, chemistry, chemistry-AP, Chinese, computer programming, computer science-AP, concert band, concert choir, creative writing, drawing and design, economics, English, English language and composition-AP, English literature and composition-AP, environmental science, French, geometry, health, Italian, music theory, photography, physical education, physics, physics-AP, pre-calculus, psychology, religion, scripture, Spanish, speech, studio art, theater, trigonometry, U.S. history, U.S. history-AP, Western civilization, wind ensemble, world history, world literature, world religions.

Graduation Requirements Advanced math, algebra, American literature, arts and fine arts (art, music, dance, drama), biology, chemistry, church history, English, foreign language, geometry, physical education (includes health), physics, religion (includes Bible studies and theology), scripture, U.S. history, Western civilization, world literature, world religions, world studies, service hours, off-campus retreat for juniors.

Special Academic Programs 12 Advanced Placement exams for which test preparation is offered; honors section.

College Admission Counseling 162 students graduated in 2015; 161 went to college, including Loyola University Chicago; Marquette University; Northwestern University; University of Illinois at Chicago; University of Illinois at Urbana–Champaign; University of Notre Dame. Other: 1 entered military service. Median composite ACT: 25. 40% scored over 26 on composite ACT.

Student Life Upper grades have uniform requirement, student council, honor system. Discipline rests primarily with faculty. Attendance at religious services is required.

Summer Programs Enrichment, advancement, sports, art/fine arts programs offered; session focuses on athletic camps and academic enrichment; held on campus; accepts boys and girls; open to students from other schools.

Tuition and Aid Day student tuition: $12,770. Tuition installment plan (monthly payment plans). Tuition reduction for siblings, merit scholarship grants, need-based scholarship grants available. In 2015–16, 22% of upper-school students received aid; total upper-school merit-scholarship money awarded: $60,000. Total amount of financial aid awarded in 2015–16: $300,000.

Admissions Traditional secondary-level entrance grade is 9. For fall 2015, 340 students applied for upper-level admission, 216 enrolled. High School Placement Test or TOEFL required. Deadline for receipt of application materials: June 30. No application fee required. Interview recommended.

Athletics Interscholastic: baseball (boys), basketball (b,g), cheering (g), cross-country running (b,g), football (b), golf (b,g), hockey (b), lacrosse (b,g), pom squad (g), soccer (b,g), softball (g), tennis (b,g), track and field (b,g), volleyball (b,g), wrestling (b); intramural: weight training (b,g). 1 PE instructor, 1 coach, 1 athletic trainer.

Computers Computers are regularly used in all academic classes. Computer network features include on-campus library services, Internet access, wireless campus network, Internet filtering or blocking technology. Student e-mail accounts and computer access in designated common areas are available to students. Students grades are available online. The school has a published electronic and media policy.

Contact Mr. John Bonk, Recruitment Director. 708-387-8538. Fax: 708-354-0109. E-mail: jbonk@nazarethacademy.com. Website: www.nazarethacademy.com

NEBRASKA CHRISTIAN SCHOOLS

1847 Inskip Avenue
Central City, Nebraska 68826

Head of School: Mr. Josh Cumpston

General Information Coeducational boarding and day college-preparatory school, affiliated with Protestant-Evangelical faith. Boarding grades 7–12, day grades K–12. Founded: 1959. Setting: rural. Nearest major city is Lincoln. Students are housed in single-sex dormitories. 27-acre campus. 7 buildings on campus. Approved or accredited by Association of Christian Schools International and Nebraska Department of Education. Total enrollment: 201. Upper school average class size: 15. Upper school faculty-student ratio: 1:10. There are 155 required school days per year for Upper School students. Upper School students typically attend 4 days per week. The average school day consists of 8 hours and 5 minutes.

Upper School Student Profile Grade 6: 12 students (9 boys, 3 girls); Grade 7: 11 students (7 boys, 4 girls); Grade 8: 18 students (10 boys, 8 girls); Grade 9: 31 students (15 boys, 16 girls); Grade 10: 32 students (17 boys, 15 girls); Grade 11: 29 students (12 boys, 17 girls); Grade 12: 27 students (16 boys, 11 girls). 27% of students are boarding students. 77% are state residents. 1 state is represented in upper school student body. 23% are international students. International students from China, Republic of Korea, Taiwan, Thailand, and Viet Nam. 85% of students are Protestant-Evangelical faith.

Faculty School total: 23. In upper school: 13 men, 7 women; 4 have advanced degrees; 5 reside on campus.

Subjects Offered Accounting, ACT preparation, advanced math, algebra, American government, American history, American literature, anatomy and physiology, ancient world history, art, band, Bible, biology, business, business law, calculus, chemistry, choir, Christian doctrine, Christian ethics, Christian studies, composition, computer applications, computer programming, concert band, consumer mathematics, creation science, desktop publishing, economics, economics and history, English, English composition, ESL, family living, fitness, general math, geography, geometry, health and safety, history, keyboarding, lab science, language arts, Life of Christ, life science, literature, mathematics, music, music theory, physical education, physical fitness, physical science, physics, pre-calculus, SAT preparation, SAT/ACT preparation, science, science project, social studies, Spanish, speech, trigonometry, U.S. government, vocal ensemble, vocal music, Web site design, word processing, world geography, world history, writing, yearbook.

Graduation Requirements Algebra, American government, American history, American literature, art, Bible, biology, calculus-AP, chemistry, Christian doctrine, economics, English, family living, geometry, history, keyboarding, Life of Christ, music, physical education (includes health), physical science, public speaking, Spanish, vocal music, world history.

Special Academic Programs Independent study; study at local college for college credit; ESL (26 students enrolled).

College Admission Counseling 36 students graduated in 2015; 33 went to college, including South Dakota School of Mines and Technology; University of Illinois at Urbana–Champaign; University of Nebraska–Lincoln; University of Nebraska at Kearney; University of Nebraska at Omaha; University of Wisconsin–Madison. Other: 2 went to work, 1 entered military service. Median composite ACT: 22. 55% scored over 26 on composite ACT.

Student Life Upper grades have specified standards of dress, student council, honor system. Discipline rests primarily with faculty. Attendance at religious services is required.

Tuition and Aid Day student tuition: $5000; 5-day tuition and room/board: $8000; 7-day tuition and room/board: $27,500. Guaranteed tuition plan. Tuition installment plan (FACTS Tuition Payment Plan, individually arranged payment plans). Tuition reduction for siblings, merit scholarship grants, need-based scholarship grants available. In 2015–16, 26% of upper-school students received aid; total upper-school merit-scholarship money awarded: $10,000. Total amount of financial aid awarded in 2015–16: $140,000.

Admissions Traditional secondary-level entrance grade is 9. For fall 2015, 43 students applied for upper-level admission, 35 were accepted, 35 enrolled. SLEP for foreign students or TOEFL or SLEP required. Deadline for receipt of application materials: none. Application fee required: $100. Interview recommended.

Athletics Interscholastic: basketball (boys, girls), cross-country running (b,g), football (b), soccer (b), track and field (b,g), volleyball (g), wrestling (b). 3 PE instructors, 7 coaches.

Computers Computers are regularly used in business applications, desktop publishing, Web site design, yearbook classes. Computer network features include Internet access, wireless campus network, Internet filtering or blocking technology. Students grades are available online.

Contact Mr. Larry Hoff, Director, International Programs. 308-946-3836. Fax: 308-946-3837. E-mail: lhoff@nebraskachristian.org. Website: www.nebraskachristian.org

NERINX HALL

530 East Lockwood Avenue
Webster Groves, Missouri 63119

Head of School: Mr. John Gabriel

General Information Girls' day college-preparatory and arts school, affiliated with Roman Catholic Church. Grades 9–12. Founded: 1924. Setting: suburban. Nearest major city is St. Louis. 7-acre campus. 4 buildings on campus. Approved or accredited by National Catholic Education Association, North Central Association of Colleges and Schools, and Missouri Department of Education. Endowment: $6 million. Total enrollment: 597. Upper school average class size: 19. Upper school faculty-student ratio: 1:9. There are 176 required school days per year for Upper School students. Upper School students typically attend 5 days per week. The average school day consists of 6 hours and 25 minutes.

Upper School Student Profile Grade 9: 168 students (168 girls); Grade 10: 160 students (160 girls); Grade 11: 120 students (120 girls); Grade 12: 149 students (149 girls). 84% of students are Roman Catholic.

Faculty School total: 54. In upper school: 14 men, 40 women; 48 have advanced degrees.

Subjects Offered Accounting, acting, advanced math, American government, American history, American literature, anatomy, anthropology, art, art-AP, astronomy,

athletics, biology, biology-AP, business, calculus, ceramics, chemistry, computer applications, computer graphics, computer science, conceptual physics, creative writing, death and loss, drawing and design, Eastern world civilizations, economics, English composition, English literature, English literature-AP, environmental science, film appreciation, French, French-AP, gender issues, geology, German, graphics, health, history, Holocaust, honors algebra, honors English, honors geometry, honors U.S. history, instrumental music, jazz band, keyboarding, lab science, Latin, Latin-AP, media, Middle East, model United Nations, multimedia, orchestra, painting, performing arts, personal finance, physics, pre-calculus, psychology, religious education, science and technology, Spanish, Spanish-AP, theology, Web site design, world history-AP, world religions.

Graduation Requirements Algebra, arts and fine arts (art, music, dance, drama), biology, chemistry, computer applications, foreign language, geometry, physical education (includes health), physical fitness, physics, theology, U.S. government and politics, U.S. history, U.S. literature, world history, writing. Community service is required.

Special Academic Programs 11 Advanced Placement exams for which test preparation is offered; honors section; study at local college for college credit.

College Admission Counseling 149 students graduated in 2015; 147 went to college, including Loyola University Chicago; Missouri State University; Rockhurst University; Saint Louis University; University of Missouri. Other: 2 entered a postgraduate year. Mean composite ACT: 27.

Student Life Upper grades have uniform requirement, student council, honor system. Discipline rests primarily with faculty. Attendance at religious services is required.

Summer Programs Advancement, art/fine arts, computer instruction programs offered; session focuses on advancement; held on campus; accepts girls; not open to students from other schools. 175 students usually enrolled.

Tuition and Aid Day student tuition: $12,850. Tuition installment plan (SMART Tuition Payment Plan). Tuition reduction for siblings, merit scholarship grants, need-based scholarship grants, paying campus jobs available. In 2015–16, 31% of upper-school students received aid; total upper-school merit-scholarship money awarded: $124,000. Total amount of financial aid awarded in 2015–16: $826,135.

Admissions Traditional secondary-level entrance grade is 9. For fall 2015, 205 students applied for upper-level admission, 185 were accepted, 169 enrolled. Any standardized test or CTBS (or similar from their school) required. Deadline for receipt of application materials: December 11. Application fee required: $10. On-campus interview required.

Athletics Interscholastic: basketball, cross-country running, diving, field hockey, golf, lacrosse, racquetball, soccer, softball, swimming and diving, tennis, track and field, volleyball. 3 PE instructors, 25 coaches, 1 athletic trainer.

Computers Computers are regularly used in graphics, humanities, keyboarding, mathematics, science, speech, writing, writing classes. Computer network features include on-campus library services, Internet access, wireless campus network, Internet filtering or blocking technology. Student e-mail accounts are available to students. Students grades are available online. The school has a published electronic and media policy.

Contact Mrs. Monica Sullivan, Admissions. 314-968-1505 Ext. 115. Fax: 314-962-6556. E-mail: msullivan@ncrinxhs.org. Website: www.nerinxhs.org

NEUCHATEL JUNIOR COLLEGE

Cret-Taconnet 4
Neuchâtel 2002, Switzerland

Head of School: Mr. William S. Boyer

General Information Coeducational boarding college-preparatory, arts, business, bilingual studies, and international development school. Grade 12. Founded: 1956. Setting: urban. Nearest major city is Berne, Switzerland. Students are housed in homes of host families. 1-acre campus. 3 buildings on campus. Approved or accredited by California Association of Independent Schools, Canadian Association of Independent Schools, Canadian Educational Standards Institute, and state department of education. Languages of instruction: English and French. Endowment: CAN$450,000. Total enrollment: 59. Upper school average class size: 15. Upper school faculty-student ratio: 1:10. Upper School students typically attend 5 days per week. The average school day consists of 5 hours and 15 minutes.

Upper School Student Profile Grade 12: 40 students (14 boys, 26 girls); Postgraduate: 19 students (5 boys, 14 girls). 100% of students are boarding students. 3% are international students. International students from Canada, France, Germany, Sweden, United Kingdom, and United States.

Faculty School total: 8. In upper school: 3 men, 4 women; 6 have advanced degrees; 1 resides on campus.

Subjects Offered 20th century world history, advanced chemistry, advanced math, Advanced Placement courses, advanced studio art-AP, algebra, analysis and differential calculus, ancient world history, applied arts, art, art history, art history-AP, athletics, biology, biology-AP, British history, calculus, calculus-AP, Canadian history, Canadian law, Canadian literature, chemistry, chemistry-AP, classical civilization, comparative government and politics-AP, comparative politics, debate, dramatic arts, earth science, economics, economics-AP, English, English language and composition-AP, English literature-AP, environmental science, European history, European history-AP, finite math, French as a second language, French language-AP, French literature-AP, German-

AP, government and politics-AP, human geography - AP, law, personal and social education, physics, physics-AP, public speaking, studio art-AP, United Nations and international issues, world history-AP, world issues.

Graduation Requirements English, minimum of 6 senior year university prep level courses.

Special Academic Programs 8 Advanced Placement exams for which test preparation is offered; study abroad.

College Admission Counseling 75 students graduated in 2014; 73 went to college, including Dalhousie University; McGill University; Queen's University at Kingston; The University of Western Ontario; University of Guelph; University of Toronto. Other: 2 had other specific plans.

Student Life Upper grades have specified standards of dress, student council, honor system. Discipline rests primarily with faculty.

Tuition and Aid 7-day tuition and room/board: 54,500 Swiss francs. Tuition installment plan (individually arranged payment plans). Tuition reduction for siblings, bursaries, merit scholarship grants available. In 2014–15, 10% of upper-school students received aid; total upper-school merit-scholarship money awarded: CAN$2000. Total amount of financial aid awarded in 2014–15: CAN$60,000.

Admissions Traditional secondary-level entrance grade is 12. For fall 2014, 72 students applied for upper-level admission, 70 were accepted, 59 enrolled. Deadline for receipt of application materials: February 9. Application fee required: CAN$175. Interview recommended.

Athletics Interscholastic: field hockey (boys, girls), rugby (b,g), soccer (b,g); intramural: hockey (b,g), ice hockey (b,g), indoor hockey (b,g), rugby (b,g), soccer (b,g); coed interscholastic: alpine skiing, aquatics, badminton, golf, skiing (downhill), snowboarding, swimming and diving; coed intramural: alpine skiing, aquatics, basketball, bicycling, cross-country running, curling, equestrian sports, fitness, floor hockey, hiking/backpacking, horseback riding, jogging, outdoor adventure, physical fitness, rafting, sailing, skiing (cross-country), skiing (downhill), snowboarding, tennis, volleyball.

Computers Computer network features include on-campus library services, Internet access, wireless campus network. Campus intranet, student e-mail accounts, and computer access in designated common areas are available to students. The school has a published electronic and media policy.

Contact Ms. Brenda Neil, Director of Admission. 416-368-8169 Ext. 222. Fax: 416-368-0956. E-mail: admissions@neuchatel.org. Website: www.njc.ch

NEWARK ACADEMY

91 South Orange Avenue
Livingston, New Jersey 07039-4989

Head of School: M. Donald M. Austin

General Information Coeducational day college-preparatory, arts, technology, and International Baccalaureate school. Grades 6–12. Founded: 1774. Setting: suburban. Nearest major city is Morristown. 68-acre campus. 1 building on campus. Approved or accredited by Middle States Association of Colleges and Schools and New Jersey Department of Education. Member of National Association of Independent Schools and Secondary School Admission Test Board. Endowment: $25 million. Total enrollment: 580. Upper school average class size: 13. Upper school faculty-student ratio: 1:12. There are 165 required school days per year for Upper School students. Upper School students typically attend 5 days per week. The average school day consists of 6 hours.

Upper School Student Profile Grade 9: 104 students (45 boys, 59 girls); Grade 10: 104 students (55 boys, 49 girls); Grade 11: 102 students (54 boys, 48 girls); Grade 12: 93 students (48 boys, 45 girls).

Faculty School total: 75. In upper school: 32 men, 35 women; 67 have advanced degrees.

Subjects Offered Accounting, acting, advanced biology, advanced chemistry, advanced computer applications, advanced math, Advanced Placement courses, advanced studio art-AP, algebra, American history, American literature, anatomy, art, art history, arts, biology, botany, calculus, ceramics, chemistry, chorus, community service, computer programming, computer science, creative writing, drama, driver education, ecology, economics, English, English literature, European history, film studies, filmmaking, finance, fine arts, French, geometry, government/civics, grammar, health, history, history-AP, Holocaust studies, honors algebra, honors geometry, humanities, International Baccalaureate courses, jazz band, leadership, Mandarin, mathematics, mechanical drawing, model United Nations, modern dance, money management, music, musical theater, newspaper, oil painting, participation in sports, peer counseling, philosophy, physical education, physical science, physics, play production, playwriting and directing, poetry, political science, pottery, pre-algebra, pre-calculus, probability and statistics, SAT/ACT preparation, science, Spanish, theater, theory of knowledge, trigonometry, world history, world literature, writing.

Graduation Requirements Arts and fine arts (art, music, dance, drama), computer science, English, foreign language, mathematics, physical education (includes health), science, social studies (includes history), 40-hour senior service project, community service.

Special Academic Programs International Baccalaureate program; 5 Advanced Placement exams for which test preparation is offered; honors section; accelerated programs; independent study; term-away projects; study abroad; academic accommodation for the gifted, the musically talented, and the artistically talented.

College Admission Counseling 101 students graduated in 2015; all went to college, including Cornell University; Georgetown University; Harvard University; New York University; The George Washington University; University of Pennsylvania. Median SAT critical reading: 697, median SAT math: 688, median SAT writing: 703, median combined SAT: 2088, median composite ACT: 30.

Student Life Upper grades have specified standards of dress, student council, honor system. Discipline rests primarily with faculty.

Summer Programs Remediation, enrichment, advancement, sports, art/fine arts, computer instruction programs offered; session focuses on enrichment and advancement; held on campus; accepts boys and girls; open to students from other schools. 1,250 students usually enrolled.

Tuition and Aid Day student tuition: $34,760. Tuition installment plan (Insured Tuition Payment Plan, Key Tuition Payment Plan, monthly payment plans). Need-based scholarship grants available. In 2015–16, 17% of upper-school students received aid. Total amount of financial aid awarded in 2015–16: $1,729,521.

Admissions Traditional secondary-level entrance grade is 9. For fall 2015, 574 students applied for upper-level admission, 94 were accepted, 52 enrolled. ISEE or SSAT required. Deadline for receipt of application materials: December 7. Application fee required: $75. On-campus interview required.

Athletics Interscholastic: baseball (boys), basketball (b,g), cross-country running (b,g), fencing (b,g), field hockey (g), football (b), golf (b,g), lacrosse (b,g), running (b,g), skiing (downhill) (b,g), soccer (b,g), softball (g), swimming and diving (b,g), tennis (b,g), track and field (b,g), volleyball (g), wrestling (b); intramural: aerobics/dance (b,g), aerobics/Nautilus (b,g), baseball (b), basketball (b,g), bicycling (b,g), cross-country running (b,g), dance (b,g), dance team (b,g), field hockey (g), fitness (b,g), football (b), golf (b,g), hockey (b), ice hockey (b), lacrosse (b,g), modern dance (b,g), soccer (b,g), softball (g), swimming and diving (b,g), tennis (b,g), track and field (b,g), volleyball (g), weight lifting (b,g), wrestling (b), yoga (b,g); coed intramural: aerobics/dance, aerobics/Nautilus, bicycling, cricket, dance, dance team, fitness, modern dance, mountain biking, skiing (downhill), table tennis, ultimate Frisbee, weight lifting, yoga. 5 PE instructors, 10 coaches, 1 athletic trainer.

Computers Computers are regularly used in all academic classes. Computer network features include on-campus library services, online commercial services, Internet access, wireless campus network, Internet filtering or blocking technology. Campus intranet and student e-mail accounts are available to students. Students grades are available online. The school has a published electronic and media policy.

Contact Mrs. Dana Pomykala, Admission Office Manager. 973-992-7000 Ext. 323. Fax: 973-488-0040. E-mail: dpomykala@newarka.edu. Website: www.newarka.edu

NEW COVENANT ACADEMY

3304 South Cox Road
Springfield, Missouri 65807

Head of School: Mr. Matt Searson

General Information Coeducational day college-preparatory, arts, business, religious studies, technology, and science, math, foreign language, language arts school, affiliated with Christian faith. Grades JK–12. Founded: 1979. Setting: suburban. 27-acre campus. 1 building on campus. Approved or accredited by North Central Association of Colleges and Schools. Total enrollment: 478. Upper school faculty-student ratio: 1:10. There are 167 required school days per year for Upper School students. Upper School students typically attend 5 days per week. The average school day consists of 7 hours and 30 minutes.

Upper School Student Profile 99% of students are Christian.

Faculty School total: 30. In upper school: 7 men, 10 women.

Subjects Offered Advanced math, algebra, American government, American history, American literature, anatomy and physiology, ancient world history, art, athletics, Bible, biology, British literature, business, calculus, chemistry, Christianity, comparative government and politics, computer processing, computer technologies, computers, concert choir, economics, English, English composition, geology, geometry, health, history, independent study, Life of Christ, literature, mathematics, music appreciation, New Testament, oceanography, physical education, physics, pre-algebra, robotics, science, scripture, Spanish, trigonometry, world history, yearbook.

Special Academic Programs Study at local college for college credit.

College Admission Counseling 16 students graduated in 2015.

Student Life Upper grades have specified standards of dress, student council, honor system. Discipline rests primarily with faculty. Attendance at religious services is required.

Tuition and Aid Guaranteed tuition plan. Tuition installment plan (monthly payment plans, individually arranged payment plans). Need-based scholarship grants available.

Admissions Otis-Lennon School Ability Test, Stanford Achievement Test or TOEFL Junior required. Deadline for receipt of application materials: none. Application fee required: $50. Interview required.

Athletics Interscholastic: baseball (boys, girls), basketball (b,g), cheering (g), cross-country running (b,g), golf (b), soccer (b,g), swimming and diving (g), track and field (b,g), volleyball (g); intramural: basketball (b,g), soccer (b,g); coed interscholastic: golf. 1 PE instructor, 11 coaches.

Computers Computers are regularly used in computer applications, journalism, technology, word processing, yearbook classes. Computer network features include Internet access, wireless campus network, Internet filtering or blocking technology.

Student e-mail accounts and computer access in designated common areas are available to students. Students grades are available online.

Contact Mrs. Delana Reynolds, Admissions Officer. 417-887-9848 Ext. 6. Fax: 417-887-2419. E-mail: dreynolds@newcovenant.net. Website: www.newcovenant.net

NEWTON COUNTRY DAY SCHOOL OF THE SACRED HEART

785 Centre Street
Newton, Massachusetts 02458

Head of School: Barbara Rogers, RSCJ

General Information Girls' day college-preparatory, arts, religious studies, and technology school, affiliated with Roman Catholic Church. Grades 5–12. Founded: 1880. Setting: suburban. Nearest major city is Boston. 20-acre campus. 6 buildings on campus. Approved or accredited by Association of Independent Schools in New England, Network of Sacred Heart Schools, New England Association of Schools and Colleges, and Massachusetts Department of Education. Member of National Association of Independent Schools and Secondary School Admission Test Board. Endowment: $18.9 million. Total enrollment: 409. Upper school average class size: 15. Upper school faculty-student ratio: 1:7. Upper School students typically attend 5 days per week. The average school day consists of 8 hours.

Upper School Student Profile Grade 9: 69 students (69 girls); Grade 10: 66 students (66 girls); Grade 11: 66 students (66 girls); Grade 12: 62 students (62 girls). 70% of students are Roman Catholic.

Faculty School total: 74. In upper school: 20 men, 37 women; 45 have advanced degrees.

Subjects Offered Algebra, American history, American history-AP, American literature, anatomy, art, art history, art-AP, biology, biology-AP, calculus, calculus-AP, chemistry, chemistry-AP, Chinese, community service, comparative government and politics, comparative government and politics-AP, creative writing, dance, drama, earth science, economics, English, English language-AP, English literature, English literature-AP, environmental science, environmental science-AP, European history-AP, expository writing, French, French language-AP, geography, geometry, government/civics, grammar, history, Latin, Latin-AP, mathematics, music, music theory, photography, physical education, physics, physics-AP, physiology, psychology, public speaking, religion, science, social sciences, social studies, Spanish, Spanish language-AP, Spanish literature-AP, statistics, statistics-AP, technology, theater, theology, trigonometry, U.S. government and politics-AP, world history, world literature, writing.

Graduation Requirements Arts and fine arts (art, music, dance, drama), English, foreign language, mathematics, physical education (includes health), religion (includes Bible studies and theology), science, senior project, social sciences, social studies (includes history). Community service is required.

Special Academic Programs 21 Advanced Placement exams for which test preparation is offered; honors section; independent study; term-away projects; study at local college for college credit; domestic exchange program (with Network of Sacred Heart Schools); study abroad.

College Admission Counseling 67 students graduated in 2014; all went to college, including Boston College; College of the Holy Cross; Georgetown University; Harvard University; Johns Hopkins University; Villanova University.

Student Life Upper grades have specified standards of dress, student council, honor system. Discipline rests equally with students and faculty. Attendance at religious services is required.

Tuition and Aid Day student tuition: $43,500. Tuition installment plan (Academic Management Services Plan, monthly payment plans). Need-based scholarship grants available. In 2014–15, 22% of upper-school students received aid. Total amount of financial aid awarded in 2014–15: $1,070,000.

Admissions Traditional secondary-level entrance grade is 9. For fall 2014, 50 students applied for upper-level admission, 25 were accepted, 15 enrolled. ISEE or SSAT required. Deadline for receipt of application materials: February 1. Application fee required: $50. On-campus interview required.

Athletics Interscholastic: basketball, cross-country running, dance team, field hockey, golf, ice hockey, lacrosse, sailing, soccer, softball, squash, tennis, volleyball; intramural: aerobics, aerobics/dance, ballet, basketball, cooperative games, crew, cross-country running, dance, dance team, fitness, flag football, modern dance, outdoor adventure, outdoor education, outdoor recreation, outdoor skills, physical fitness, physical training, soccer, softball, swimming and diving, tennis, volleyball. 1 PE instructor, 1 coach, 1 athletic trainer.

Computers Computers are regularly used in all academic classes. Computer network features include on-campus library services, online commercial services, Internet access, wireless campus network, Internet filtering or blocking technology. Student e-mail accounts are available to students. The school has a published electronic and media policy.

Contact Clare Martin, Director of Admissions. 617-244-4246. Fax: 617-965-5313. E-mail: cmartin@newtoncountryday.org. Website: www.newtoncountryday.org

NEWTON'S GROVE SCHOOL

1 City View Drive
Toronto, Ontario M9W 5A5, Canada

Head of School: Mrs. Gabrielle Bush

General Information Coeducational day college-preparatory, arts, business, technology, science, humanities, and math school. Grades JK–12. Founded: 1977. Setting: urban. 1 building on campus. Approved or accredited by Ontario Ministry of Education and Ontario Department of Education. Language of instruction: English. Total enrollment: 249. Upper school average class size: 18. Upper school faculty-student ratio: 1:18. There are 192 required school days per year for Upper School students. Upper School students typically attend 5 days per week. The average school day consists of 6 hours and 30 minutes.

Upper School Student Profile Grade 9: 17 students (10 boys, 7 girls); Grade 10: 29 students (21 boys, 8 girls); Grade 11: 36 students (22 boys, 14 girls); Grade 12: 28 students (14 boys, 14 girls).

Faculty School total: 35. In upper school: 8 men, 10 women; 2 have advanced degrees.

Subjects Offered Accounting, anthropology, biology, Canadian geography, Canadian history, Canadian law, chemistry, civics, communications, data processing, discrete mathematics, dramatic arts, English, film, French, functions, geometry, healthful living, information technology, learning strategies, mathematics, organizational studies, personal finance, philosophy, physics, psychology, reading, science, society challenge and change, sociology, visual arts, world history, writing.

Graduation Requirements English, Ontario Ministry of Education requirements.

Special Academic Programs 2 Advanced Placement exams for which test preparation is offered; ESL (15 students enrolled).

College Admission Counseling 28 students graduated in 2014; all went to college, including McMaster University; Ryerson University; University of Guelph; University of Toronto; University of Waterloo; York University.

Student Life Upper grades have uniform requirement, student council, honor system. Discipline rests primarily with faculty.

Tuition and Aid Day student tuition: CAN$14,800. Tuition installment plan (individually arranged payment plans, MPS Payment Plan). Tuition reduction for siblings, early payment discount available.

Admissions Traditional secondary-level entrance grade is 9. Admissions testing required. Deadline for receipt of application materials: October 31. No application fee required. Interview required.

Athletics Interscholastic: ball hockey (boys, girls), baseball (b,g), basketball (b,g), flag football (b,g), football (b), golf (b), indoor track & field (b,g), running (b,g), soccer (b,g), swimming and diving (b,g), track and field (b,g), volleyball (b,g); intramural: basketball (b,g), flag football (b,g), floor hockey (b,g), Frisbee (b,g), indoor hockey (b,g), physical fitness (b,g), rhythmic gymnastics (b,g), running (b,g), soccer (b,g), swimming and diving (b,g), touch football (b,g), track and field (b,g), ultimate Frisbee (b,g), volleyball (b,g), winter (indoor) track (b,g), winter soccer (b,g); coed interscholastic: aquatics, badminton, bowling, cross-country running, field hockey, flag football, Frisbee, track and field; coed intramural: badminton, ball hockey, baseball, basketball, bowling, cooperative games, cross-country running, flag football, tennis, track and field. 2 PE instructors.

Computers Computers are regularly used in art, business education, computer applications, graphic arts, media arts, photography classes. Computer resources include Internet access, Internet filtering or blocking technology. Student e-mail accounts are available to students. The school has a published electronic and media policy.

Contact Mrs. Gabrielle Bush, Director. 416-745-1328. Fax: 416-745-4168. E-mail: gabriellebush@newtonsgroveschool.com. Website: www.newtonsgroveschool.com

NEW YORK MILITARY ACADEMY

78 Academy Avenue
Cornwall-on-Hudson, New York 12520

Head of School: Maj. Gen. William G. Beard, US Army-Retd.

General Information Coeducational boarding and day college-preparatory, Junior ROTC, ESL, and military school. Grades 8–12. Founded: 1889. Setting: small town. Nearest major city is New York. Students are housed in single-sex dormitories. 140-acre campus. 11 buildings on campus. Approved or accredited by Middle States Association of Colleges and Schools, New York State Association of Independent Schools, The Association of Boarding Schools, and New York Department of Education. Member of National Association of Independent Schools and Secondary School Admission Test Board. Endowment: $2.6 million. Total enrollment: 141. Upper school average class size: 8. Upper school faculty-student ratio: 1:8. There are 189 required school days per year for Upper School students. Upper School students typically attend 5 days per week. The average school day consists of 6 hours and 30 minutes.

Upper School Student Profile Grade 9: 17 students (13 boys, 4 girls); Grade 10: 28 students (22 boys, 6 girls); Grade 11: 38 students (31 boys, 7 girls); Grade 12: 41 students (29 boys, 12 girls); Grade 13: 124 students (95 boys, 29 girls). 82% of students are boarding students. 66% are state residents. 8 states are represented in upper school student body. 13% are international students. International students from Ethiopia, Guadeloupe, Hong Kong, Mexico, Republic of Korea, and Venezuela; 3 other countries represented in student body.

Faculty School total: 15. In upper school: 8 men, 7 women; 14 have advanced degrees; all reside on campus.

Subjects Offered Algebra, American history, American history-AP, art, biology, business mathematics, chemistry, computer literacy, criminology, earth science, economics, English, English-AP, environmental science, geography, geometry, government, health, JROTC, physical science, physics, pre-calculus, social studies, Spanish, trigonometry, world history.

Graduation Requirements American history, art, biology, calculus, chemistry, computer science, economics, English, English composition, English literature, foreign language, global studies, government, JROTC or LEAD (Leadership Education and Development), mathematics, physical education (includes health), science, trigonometry. Community service is required.

Special Academic Programs International Baccalaureate program; 9 Advanced Placement exams for which test preparation is offered; honors section; study at local college for college credit; ESL (12 students enrolled).

College Admission Counseling 40 students graduated in 2014; 38 went to college, including American University; Boston University; Drexel University; Embry-Riddle Aeronautical University–Daytona; Stony Brook University, State University of New York; United States Military Academy. Other: 2 had other specific plans.

Student Life Upper grades have uniform requirement, student council, honor system. Discipline rests primarily with faculty. Attendance at religious services is required.

Tuition and Aid Day student tuition: $13,890; 7-day tuition and room/board: $36,190. Tuition installment plan (individually arranged payment plans). Tuition reduction for siblings, merit scholarship grants, need-based scholarship grants, Sallie Mae loans available. In 2014–15, 74% of upper-school students received aid; total upper-school merit-scholarship money awarded: $36,000. Total amount of financial aid awarded in 2014–15: $355,000.

Admissions Traditional secondary-level entrance grade is 10. For fall 2014, 51 students applied for upper-level admission, 42 were accepted, 36 enrolled. California Achievement Test, Cooperative Entrance Exam (McGraw-Hill), Iowa Tests of Basic Skills, Otis-Lennon School Ability Test, PSAT and SAT for applicants to grade 11 and 12, SLEP, SSAT, Stanford Achievement Test or TOEFL required. Deadline for receipt of application materials: none. Application fee required: $100. On-campus interview required.

Athletics Interscholastic: baseball (boys), basketball (b,g), football (b), ice hockey (b), lacrosse (b), soccer (b), softball (g), volleyball (g), wrestling (b); intramural: hockey (b); coed interscholastic: cross-country running, drill team, fencing, golf, JROTC drill, marksmanship, martial arts, paint ball, project adventure, riflery, tennis, track and field, weight lifting; coed intramural: dance, dance team, equestrian sports, handball, ice skating, martial arts. 1 PE instructor, 1 coach, 1 athletic trainer.

Computers Computers are regularly used in all academic classes. Computer network features include on-campus library services, Internet access, Internet filtering or blocking technology. Student e-mail accounts are available to students. Students grades are available online. The school has a published electronic and media policy.

Contact Capt. Michael J. Broderick, US Army-Retd., Director of Admissions. 845-534-3710 Ext. 4272. Fax: 845-534-7699. E-mail: mbroderick@nyma.org. Website: www.nyma.org

NIAGARA CHRISTIAN COMMUNITY OF SCHOOLS

2619 Niagara Boulevard
Fort Erie, Ontario L2A 5M4, Canada

Head of School: Mr. Mark Thiessen

General Information Coeducational boarding and day college-preparatory, general academic, arts, business, vocational, religious studies, and technology school, affiliated with Brethren in Christ Church. Boarding grades 9–12, day grades 6–12. Founded: 1932. Setting: rural. Nearest major city is Niagara Falls, Canada. Students are housed in single-sex dormitories. 121-acre campus. 16 buildings on campus. Approved or accredited by Ontario Department of Education. Language of instruction: English. Total enrollment: 205. Upper school average class size: 18. Upper school faculty-student ratio: 1:16. There are 170 required school days per year for Upper School students. Upper School students typically attend 5 days per week. The average school day consists of 6 hours.

Upper School Student Profile Grade 9: 21 students (11 boys, 10 girls); Grade 10: 24 students (16 boys, 8 girls); Grade 11: 55 students (34 boys, 21 girls); Grade 12: 80 students (47 boys, 33 girls). 80% of students are boarding students. 20% are province residents. 2 provinces are represented in upper school student body. 85% are international students. International students from Brazil, China, Hong Kong, Japan, Nigeria, and Saudi Arabia; 4 other countries represented in student body. 35% of students are Brethren in Christ Church.

Faculty School total: 24. In upper school: 8 men, 16 women; 2 have advanced degrees.

Subjects Offered Accounting, advanced chemistry, advanced math, algebra, analysis and differential calculus, analytic geometry, anthropology, art, art history, athletics, Bible, biology, business, business applications, business education, business mathematics, business technology, calculus, Canadian geography, Canadian history, Canadian literature, career education, chemistry, choir, civics, computer applications, computer programming, concert choir, data processing, early childhood, economics, English, English literature, ESL, exercise science, family studies, French as a second language, general math, geography, geometry, guidance, health education, history,

information technology, instrumental music, integrated science, international affairs, leadership education training, Life of Christ, mathematics, media studies, modern world history, music, parenting, physical education, physics, politics, pre-calculus, science, Spanish, world history, world issues, writing, writing.

Special Academic Programs Special instructional classes for students with learning disabilities; ESL (60 students enrolled).

College Admission Counseling 78 students graduated in 2015; 14 went to college, including Queen's University at Kingston; University of Guelph; University of Ottawa; University of Toronto; University of Waterloo. Other: 4 went to work, 60 entered a postgraduate year.

Student Life Upper grades have uniform requirement, student council, honor system. Discipline rests primarily with faculty. Attendance at religious services is required.

Summer Programs ESL programs offered; session focuses on ESL; held on campus; accepts boys and girls; not open to students from other schools. 100 students usually enrolled. 2016 schedule: July 7 to August 27. Application deadline: none.

Tuition and Aid Day student tuition: CAN$9050; 5-day tuition and room/board: CAN$29,895; 7-day tuition and room/board: CAN$38,840. Tuition installment plan (monthly payment plans, individually arranged payment plans, quarterly payment plan). Tuition reduction for siblings, bursaries, merit scholarship grants, need-based scholarship grants, paying campus jobs available. In 2015–16, 10% of upper-school students received aid; total upper-school merit-scholarship money awarded: CAN$50,000. Total amount of financial aid awarded in 2015–16: CAN$400,000.

Admissions Traditional secondary-level entrance grade is 9. For fall 2015, 210 students applied for upper-level admission, 200 were accepted, 197 enrolled. Admissions testing and English proficiency required. Deadline for receipt of application materials: none. Application fee required: CAN$100. Interview required.

Athletics Interscholastic: badminton (boys, girls), baseball (g), basketball (b,g), cross-country running (b,g), golf (b), soccer (b,g), track and field (b,g), volleyball (b,g); coed interscholastic: badminton, swimming and diving; coed intramural: aerobics, alpine skiing, aquatics, badminton, ball hockey, bowling, canoeing/kayaking, cross-country running, fitness, fitness walking, floor hockey, golf, ice skating, skiing (downhill), soccer. 2 PE instructors.

Computers Computers are regularly used in accounting, all academic, business, data processing, economics, ESL, mathematics, science, yearbook classes. Computer network features include on-campus library services, Internet access, wireless campus network, Internet filtering or blocking technology. Campus intranet and computer access in designated common areas are available to students. Students grades are available online. The school has a published electronic and media policy.

Contact Mrs. Lesley Burrison, Enrolment Specialist. 905-871-6980. Fax: 905-871-9260. E-mail: enrol@niagaracc.com. Website: www.niagaracc.com

NICHOLS SCHOOL

1250 Amherst St.
Buffalo, New York 14216

Head of School: Mr. William Clough

General Information Coeducational day college preparatory, arts, and technology school. Grades 5–12. Founded: 1892. Setting: urban. 30-acre campus. 8 buildings on campus. Approved or accredited by New York Department of Education and New York Department of Education. Member of National Association of Independent Schools. Endowment: $25 million. Total enrollment: 574. Upper school average class size: 14. Upper school faculty-student ratio: 1:8. Upper School students typically attend 5 days per week. The average school day consists of 7 hours.

Upper School Student Profile Grade 9: 104 students (61 boys, 43 girls); Grade 10: 91 students (50 boys, 41 girls); Grade 11: 96 students (40 boys, 56 girls); Grade 12: 94 students (55 boys, 39 girls).

Faculty School total: 76. In upper school: 29 men, 21 women; 39 have advanced degrees.

Subjects Offered Algebra, American history, American literature, anatomy, art, art history, biology, calculus, chemistry, Chinese, community service, computer graphics, computer math, computer programming, computer science, creative writing, dance, drama, driver education, earth science, economics, engineering, English, English literature, environmental science, European history, expository writing, fine arts, French, geology, geometry, government/civics, history, Latin, mathematics, music, photography, physical education, physics, psychology-AP, science, social studies, Spanish, speech, theater, trigonometry, world history, world literature.

Graduation Requirements Arts and fine arts (art, music, dance, drama), English, foreign language, mathematics, physical education (includes health), science, social studies (includes history).

Special Academic Programs Advanced Placement exam preparation; honors section; independent study; study abroad.

College Admission Counseling 105 students graduated in 2014; 98 went to college, including Colgate University; Harvard University; John Carroll University; The George Washington University; University at Buffalo, the State University of New York; Williams College. Other: 2 entered a postgraduate year, 5 had other specific plans. Median SAT critical reading: 620, median SAT math: 640, median SAT writing: 620, median composite ACT: 27. 59% scored over 600 on SAT critical reading, 57% scored over 600 on SAT math, 55% scored over 600 on SAT writing, 58% scored over 26 on composite ACT.

Student Life Upper grades have specified standards of dress, student council, honor system. Discipline rests equally with students and faculty.

Tuition and Aid Day student tuition: $19,725–$21,175. Tuition installment plan (Insured Tuition Payment Plan, monthly payment plans). Need-based scholarship grants available. In 2014–15, 30% of upper-school students received aid. Total amount of financial aid awarded in 2014–15: $1,800,000.

Admissions Traditional secondary-level entrance grade is 9. For fall 2014, 237 students applied for upper-level admission, 225 were accepted, 137 enrolled. Otis-Lennon and 2 sections of ERB required. Deadline for receipt of application materials: none. Application fee required: $50. On-campus interview required.

Athletics Interscholastic: baseball (boys), basketball (b,g), crew (b,g), cross-country running (b,g), field hockey (g), football (b), golf (b,g), hockey (b,g), ice hockey (b,g), lacrosse (b,g), soccer (b,g), softball (g), squash (b,g), tennis (b,g), volleyball (g); coed interscholastic: aerobics, aerobics/dance, dance, modern dance; coed intramural: aerobics/dance. 21 coaches, 1 athletic trainer.

Computers Computers are regularly used in art, library skills, newspaper, photography, science, technology, yearbook classes. Computer network features include on-campus library services, online commercial services, Internet access. Student e-mail accounts are available to students. The school has a published electronic and media policy.

Contact Mrs. Nina Barone, Director of Admissions. 716-332-6325. Fax: 716-875-6474. E-mail: nbarone@nicholsschool.org. Website: www.nicholsschool.org

NOAH WEBSTER CHRISTIAN SCHOOL

3411 Cleveland Avenue
PO Box 21239
Cheyenne, Wyoming 82003

Head of School: Mrs. DeAnn Gomez

General Information Coeducational day college-preparatory and general academic school, affiliated with Christian faith. Grades K–12. Founded: 1987. Setting: suburban. Nearest major city is Denver, CO. 8-acre campus. 1 building on campus. Approved or accredited by Association of Christian Schools International. Endowment: $30,000. Total enrollment: 52. Upper school average class size: 12. Upper school faculty-student ratio: 1:12. There are 175 required school days per year for Upper School students. Upper School students typically attend 5 days per week. The average school day consists of 6 hours and 30 minutes.

Upper School Student Profile Grade 10: 2 students (2 boys); Grade 11: 1 student (1 boy). 100% of students are Christian faith.

Faculty School total: 6. In upper school: 2 women.

Special Academic Programs Accelerated programs; independent study; academic accommodation for the gifted.

Student Life Upper grades have specified standards of dress, honor system. Discipline rests primarily with faculty. Attendance at religious services is required.

Tuition and Aid Day student tuition: $3450. Tuition installment plan (monthly payment plans). Tuition reduction for siblings, need-based scholarship grants available.

Admissions Traditional secondary-level entrance grade is 9. For fall 2015, 1 student applied for upper-level admission, 1 was accepted, 1 enrolled. Admissions testing required. Deadline for receipt of application materials: none. Application fee required: $50. On-campus interview required.

Athletics Coed Interscholastic: archery. 1 PE instructor.

Computers Computer resources include Internet access, Internet filtering or blocking technology. Computer access in designated common areas is available to students. The school has a published electronic and media policy.

Contact 307-635-2175. Fax: 307-773-8523.
Website: www.noahwebsterchristianschool.com

NOBLE ACADEMY

Greensboro, North Carolina
See Special Needs Schools section.

NOBLE AND GREENOUGH SCHOOL

10 Campus Drive
Dedham, Massachusetts 02026-4099

Head of School: Mr. Robert P. Henderson Jr.

General Information Coeducational boarding and day college-preparatory school. Boarding grades 9–12, day grades 7–12. Founded: 1866. Setting: suburban. Nearest major city is Boston. Students are housed in single-sex dormitories. 187-acre campus. 12 buildings on campus. Approved or accredited by New England Association of Schools and Colleges and Massachusetts Department of Education. Member of National Association of Independent Schools and Secondary School Admission Test Board. Endowment: $122 million. Total enrollment: 615. Upper school average class size: 14. Upper school faculty-student ratio: 1:7. There are 162 required school days per year for Upper School students. Upper School students typically attend 5 days per week. The average school day consists of 7 hours and 5 minutes.

Upper School Student Profile Grade 9: 133 students (65 boys, 68 girls); Grade 10: 108 students (45 boys, 63 girls); Grade 11: 133 students (70 boys, 63 girls); Grade 12: 124 students (59 boys, 65 girls). 8% of students are boarding students. 100% are state residents. 1 state is represented in upper school student body.

Faculty School total: 127. In upper school: 61 men, 66 women; 36 reside on campus.

Subjects Offered 20th century history, Advanced Placement courses, African-American literature, algebra, American history, American literature, anatomy, ancient history, art, art history, astronomy, biology, calculus, ceramics, chemistry, community service, computer programming, computer science, concert band, creative writing, drama, drawing, earth science, ecology, economics, English, English literature, environmental science, ethics, European history, expository writing, fine arts, French, genetics, geography, geometry, government/civics, grammar, health, history, independent study, Japanese, journalism, Latin, Latin American history, marine biology, mathematics, music, painting, philosophy, photography, physics, physiology, printmaking, psychology, Roman civilization, science, senior internship, senior project, social studies, Spanish, speech, statistics, theater, trigonometry, Vietnam, world history, world literature, writing.

Graduation Requirements Arts and fine arts (art, music, dance, drama), computer science, English, foreign language, mathematics, performing arts, physical education (includes health), science, social studies (includes history), 80 hours of community service must be completed.

Special Academic Programs Advanced Placement exam preparation; honors section; independent study; term-away projects; study abroad; academic accommodation for the gifted, the musically talented, and the artistically talented.

College Admission Counseling 124 students graduated in 2015; all went to college. 82% scored over 600 on SAT critical reading, 81% scored over 600 on SAT math, 83% scored over 600 on SAT writing, 87% scored over 1800 on combined SAT, 79% scored over 26 on composite ACT.

Student Life Upper grades have specified standards of dress, student council, honor system. Discipline rests equally with students and faculty.

Tuition and Aid Day student tuition: $44,400; 5-day tuition and room/board: $50,200. Tuition installment plan (FACTS Tuition Payment Plan, Tuition Management Systems). Need-based scholarship grants available. In 2015–16, 24% of upper-school students received aid. Total amount of financial aid awarded in 2015–16: $3,985,500.

Admissions Traditional secondary-level entrance grade is 9. For fall 2015, 578 students applied for upper-level admission, 121 were accepted, 78 enrolled. ISEE or SSAT required. Deadline for receipt of application materials: January 15. Application fee required: $60. On-campus interview required.

Athletics Interscholastic: baseball (boys), basketball (b,g), crew (b,g), cross-country running (b,g), dance (b,g), field hockey (g), football (b), golf (b), hockey (b,g), outdoor adventure (b,g), sailing (b,g), skiing (cross-country) (b,g), soccer (b,g), softball (b,g), squash (b,g), strength & conditioning (b,g), tennis (b,g), volleyball (g), wrestling (b); coed intramural: aerobics/dance, dance. 12 coaches, 2 athletic trainers.

Computers Computers are regularly used in English, foreign language, history, journalism, Latin, mathematics, music, science classes. Computer network features include on-campus library services, online commercial services, Internet access, Internet filtering or blocking technology, NoblesNet (first class email and bulletin board with electronic conferencing capability), wireless iBooks. Campus intranet, student e-mail accounts, and computer access in designated common areas are available to students. The school has a published electronic and media policy.

Contact Ms. Jennifer Hines, Dean of Enrollment Management. 781-320-7100. Fax: 781-320-1329. E-mail: admission@nobles.edu. Website: www.nobles.edu

THE NORA SCHOOL

955 Sligo Avenue
Silver Spring, Maryland 20910

Head of School: David E. Mullen

General Information Coeducational day college-preparatory, arts, and technology school. Grades 9–12. Founded: 1964. Setting: urban. Nearest major city is Washington, DC. 1-acre campus. 1 building on campus. Approved or accredited by Association of Independent Schools of Greater Washington, Middle States Association of Colleges and Schools, and Maryland Department of Education. Member of National Association of Independent Schools. Endowment: $250,000. Total enrollment: 66. Upper school average class size: 8. Upper school faculty-student ratio: 1:5. There are 175 required school days per year for Upper School students. Upper School students typically attend 5 days per week. The average school day consists of 5 hours and 35 minutes.

Upper School Student Profile Grade 9: 12 students (8 boys, 4 girls); Grade 10: 18 students (8 boys, 10 girls); Grade 11: 16 students (7 boys, 9 girls); Grade 12: 16 students (10 boys, 6 girls).

Faculty School total: 11. In upper school: 7 men, 4 women; all have advanced degrees.

Subjects Offered African-American literature, algebra, American literature, American studies, architecture, art, art history, astronomy, biology, British literature, calculus, ceramics, chemistry, college writing, community service, computer graphics, conceptual physics, conflict resolution, crafts, creative writing, economics, English composition, environmental science, expository writing, film and literature, forensics, geography, geometry, German, graphic design, illustration, integrated science, peace studies, peer counseling, photo shop, photography, physical education, physics, political science, pre-algebra, pre-calculus, psychology, sculpture, social justice, Spanish, statistics, street law, studio art, trigonometry, U.S. history, wilderness education, women's literature, world history, world religions, writing.

Graduation Requirements Arts and fine arts (art, music, dance, drama), English, foreign language, lab science, mathematics, personal fitness, science, social studies (includes history), sports, U.S. history, wilderness education, writing, graduation portfolio. Community service is required.

Special Academic Programs Independent study; term-away projects; study at local college for college credit; academic accommodation for the gifted and the artistically talented; remedial reading and/or remedial writing; remedial math; programs in English, mathematics, general development for dyslexic students; special instructional classes for students with Attention Deficit Disorder and learning disabilities, students who have been unsuccessful in a traditional learning environment.

College Admission Counseling 17 students graduated in 2015; all went to college, including Bard College; Dickinson College; Goucher College; Guilford College; Loyola University Maryland; University of Vermont.

Student Life Upper grades have student council. Discipline rests primarily with faculty.

Tuition and Aid Day student tuition: $26,700. Tuition installment plan (monthly payment plans). Need-based scholarship grants, Black Student Fund, Latino Student Fund, Washington Scholarship Fund available. In 2015–16, 24% of upper-school students received aid. Total amount of financial aid awarded in 2015–16: $167,000.

Admissions Traditional secondary-level entrance grade is 9. For fall 2015, 70 students applied for upper-level admission, 67 were accepted, 65 enrolled. Writing sample required. Deadline for receipt of application materials: none. Application fee required: $75. On-campus interview required.

Athletics Interscholastic: basketball (boys, girls); intramural: cheering (g); coed interscholastic: soccer, softball; coed intramural: alpine skiing, backpacking, bicycling, bowling, canoeing/kayaking, climbing, cooperative games, dance, Frisbee, hiking/backpacking, ice skating, kayaking, life saving, outdoor activities, outdoor adventure, rafting, rock climbing, ropes courses, running, skiing (downhill), table tennis, volleyball, wilderness, winter walking, yoga. 2 coaches.

Computers Computers are regularly used in art, college planning, creative writing, design, drawing and design, English, graphic arts, graphic design, independent study, literary magazine, mathematics, photography, SAT preparation, writing, writing, yearbook classes. Computer network features include on-campus library services, online commercial services, Internet access, wireless campus network, Internet filtering or blocking technology. Students grades are available online. The school has a published electronic and media policy.

Contact Marcia D. Miller, Director of Admissions. 301-495-6672. Fax: 301-495-7829. E-mail: marcia@nora-school.org. Website: www.nora-school.org

NORFOLK ACADEMY

1585 Wesleyan Drive
Norfolk, Virginia 23502

Head of School: Mr. Dennis G. Manning

General Information Coeducational day college-preparatory school. Grades 1–12. Founded: 1728. Setting: suburban. 70-acre campus. 14 buildings on campus. Approved or accredited by Southern Association of Colleges and Schools, Southern Association of Independent Schools, The College Board, and Virginia Department of Education. Member of National Association of Independent Schools and Secondary School Admission Test Board. Endowment: $50 million. Total enrollment: 1,241. Upper school average class size: 15. Upper school faculty-student ratio: 1:10. There are 175 required school days per year for Upper School students. Upper School students typically attend 5 days per week. The average school day consists of 7 hours.

Upper School Student Profile Grade 10: 115 students (57 boys, 58 girls); Grade 11: 139 students (77 boys, 62 girls); Grade 12: 121 students (65 boys, 56 girls).

Faculty School total: 124. In upper school: 27 men, 17 women; 37 have advanced degrees.

Subjects Offered Algebra, American history, American literature, art, art history, band, biology, calculus, chemistry, chorus, computer math, computer programming, computer science, dance, driver education, economics, English, English literature, environmental science, European history, film studies, fine arts, French, geography, geometry, German, government/civics, health, history, instrumental music, Italian, Latin, mathematics, music, music history, music theory, physical education, physics, science, social studies, Spanish, speech, statistics, studio art, theater arts, world history.

Graduation Requirements Arts and fine arts (art, music, dance, drama), English, foreign language, mathematics, physical education (includes health), science, social studies (includes history), 8-minute senior speech, seminar program. Community service is required.

Special Academic Programs Advanced Placement exam preparation; independent study; study abroad; academic accommodation for the gifted, the musically talented, and the artistically talented.

College Admission Counseling 130 students graduated in 2014; all went to college, including Hampden-Sydney College; James Madison University; The College of William and Mary; University of Virginia; Virginia Polytechnic Institute and State University. Mean SAT critical reading: 618, mean SAT math: 646, mean SAT writing: 628, mean composite ACT: 26.

Student Life Upper grades have specified standards of dress, student council, honor system. Discipline rests equally with students and faculty.

Tuition and Aid Day student tuition: $22,200. Tuition installment plan (monthly payment plans, individually arranged payment plans). Need-based scholarship grants available. In 2014–15, 20% of upper-school students received aid.

Admissions Traditional secondary-level entrance grade is 10. For fall 2014, 11 students applied for upper-level admission, 7 were accepted, 5 enrolled. ERB Achievement Test, ERB CTP IV, essay, Individual IQ, Otis-Lennon School Ability Test or SSAT required. Deadline for receipt of application materials: January 30. Application fee required: $50. On-campus interview required.

Athletics Interscholastic: baseball (boys), basketball (b,g), cheering (g), crew (b,g), cross-country running (b,g), dance (b,g), diving (b,g), field hockey (g), football (b), golf (b,g), indoor track (b,g), lacrosse (b,g), sailing (b,g), soccer (b,g), softball (g), swimming and diving (b,g), tennis (b,g), track and field (b,g), volleyball (g), winter (indoor) track (b,g), wrestling (b); intramural: dance (g), dance team (g). 2 PE instructors, 3 athletic trainers.

Computers Computers are regularly used in all academic classes. Computer network features include on-campus library services, online commercial services, Internet access, wireless campus network, Internet filtering or blocking technology, online library resources, video production, curriculum-based software, desktop publishing, campus-wide media distribution system. Campus intranet, student e-mail accounts, and computer access in designated common areas are available to students. Students grades are available online. The school has a published electronic and media policy.

Contact Mr. James H. Lasley Jr., Director of Admissions. 757-455-5582 Ext. 5337. Fax: 757-455-3199. E-mail: jlasley@norfolkacademy.org. Website: www.norfolkacademy.org

NORMAN HOWARD SCHOOL

Rochester, New York
See Special Needs Schools section.

THE NORTH BROWARD PREPARATORY UPPER SCHOOL

7600 Lyons Road
Coconut Creek, Florida 33073

Head of School: Elise R. Ecoff, EdD

General Information Coeducational boarding and day college-preparatory, arts, and technology school; primarily serves students with learning disabilities, individuals with Attention Deficit Disorder, and dyslexic students. Boarding grades 6–12, day grades PK–12. Founded: 1957. Setting: suburban. Students are housed in single-sex dormitories. 75-acre campus. 10 buildings on campus. Approved or accredited by Florida Council of Independent Schools and Southern Association of Colleges and Schools. Total enrollment: 1,550. Upper school average class size: 18. Upper school faculty-student ratio: 1:18. There are 172 required school days per year for Upper School students. Upper School students typically attend 5 days per week. The average school day consists of 6 hours and 20 minutes.

Upper School Student Profile Grade 6: 105 students (56 boys, 49 girls); Grade 7: 115 students (75 boys, 40 girls); Grade 8: 127 students (64 boys, 63 girls); Grade 9: 205 students (126 boys, 79 girls); Grade 10: 219 students (133 boys, 86 girls); Grade 11: 254 students (135 boys, 119 girls); Grade 12: 217 students (129 boys, 88 girls). 30% of students are boarding students. 85% are state residents. 3 states are represented in upper school student body. 30% are international students. International students from Brazil, China, Germany, Italy, Republic of Korea, and Russian Federation; 20 other countries represented in student body.

Faculty School total: 110. In upper school: 37 men, 73 women; 73 have advanced degrees.

Subjects Offered Algebra, American history-AP, analysis and differential calculus, analytic geometry, ancient world history, art, art history, audio visual/media, Basic programming, biology, biology-AP, British literature, broadcast journalism, business, calculus, calculus-AP, chemistry, chemistry-AP, choir, choral music, college counseling, computer applications, computer graphics, computer programming, computer programming-AP, computers, concert band, concert choir, contemporary women writers, drama workshop, dramatic arts, ecology, environmental systems, economics, English, English composition, English literature, English literature and composition-AP, environmental science, environmental science-AP, ESL, European history, European history-AP, forensics, French, French language-AP, French literature-AP, geometry, guitar, honors algebra, honors English, honors geometry, honors U.S. history, honors world history, jazz band, jazz dance, jazz ensemble, keyboarding, Latin, model United Nations, modern European history, modern European history-AP, music, music appreciation, performing arts, physical education, physical fitness, physics-AP, psychology-AP, robotics, SAT preparation, Shakespeare, skills for success, sociology, Spanish, Spanish language-AP, Spanish literature, Spanish literature-AP, U.S. government, U.S. government and politics-AP, U.S. history, U.S. literature, wind ensemble, wind instruments, women in literature, world history-AP.

Graduation Requirements Algebra, American history, American literature, biology, calculus, chemistry, computer applications, electives, English, European history, foreign language, geometry, performing arts, physical education (includes health), physics, U.S. government, U.S. literature, world cultures. Community service is required.

Special Academic Programs International Baccalaureate program; Advanced Placement exam preparation; honors section; independent study; study at local college for college credit; academic accommodation for the gifted, the musically talented, and the artistically talented; remedial reading and/or remedial writing; remedial math; programs in English, mathematics, general development for dyslexic students; ESL (80 students enrolled).

College Admission Counseling 210 students graduated in 2015; all went to college, including Boston University; Duke University; Florida State University; University of Florida; University of Miami; University of Pennsylvania. Mean SAT critical reading: 525, mean SAT math: 571, mean SAT writing: 525. 27% scored over 600 on SAT critical reading, 29% scored over 600 on SAT math, 25% scored over 600 on SAT writing, 23% scored over 1800 on combined SAT, 26% scored over 26 on composite ACT.

Student Life Upper grades have uniform requirement, student council, honor system. Discipline rests primarily with faculty.

Summer Programs Remediation, enrichment, advancement, sports, art/fine arts, computer instruction programs offered; session focuses on enrichment; held on campus; accepts boys and girls; open to students from other schools. 750 students usually enrolled. 2016 schedule: June 13 to August 7.

Tuition and Aid Day student tuition: $23,250–$25,900; 7-day tuition and room/board: $52,500. Tuition installment plan (monthly payment plans). Tuition reduction for siblings, merit scholarship grants available. In 2015–16, 22% of upper-school students received aid; total upper-school merit-scholarship money awarded: $1,360,000. Total amount of financial aid awarded in 2015–16: $2,400,000.

Admissions Traditional secondary-level entrance grade is 9. For fall 2015, 828 students applied for upper-level admission, 632 were accepted, 446 enrolled. Deadline for receipt of application materials: none. Application fee required: $150. Interview required.

Athletics Interscholastic: aquatics (boys, girls), baseball (b), basketball (b,g), cross-country running (b,g), dance (g), dance squad (g), dance team (g), flag football (g), football (b), golf (b,g), ice hockey (b), lacrosse (b,g), physical fitness (b,g), soccer (b,g), softball (g), swimming and diving (b,g), tennis (b,g), track and field (b,g), volleyball (g), water polo (b,g), winter soccer (b,g); coed interscholastic: aquatics, cheering, cross-country running, dance, dressage, fencing, golf, physical fitness; coed intramural: basketball, flag football, scuba diving, strength & conditioning. 4 PE instructors, 18 coaches, 1 athletic trainer.

Computers Computers are regularly used in all academic classes. Computer network features include on-campus library services, online commercial services, Internet access, wireless campus network, Internet filtering or blocking technology. Campus intranet, student e-mail accounts, and computer access in designated common areas are available to students. Students grades are available online. The school has a published electronic and media policy.

Contact Jackie Fagan, Director of Admissions. 954-247-0011 Ext. 303. Fax: 954-247-0012. E-mail: faganj@nbps.org. Website: www.nbps.org

NORTH CENTRAL TEXAS ACADEMY

3846 North Highway 144
Granbury, Texas 76048

Head of School: Mrs. Jennifer Smith

General Information Coeducational boarding and day and distance learning college-preparatory, arts, and agriculture/FFA school, affiliated with Christian faith. Grades PK–12. Distance learning grade X. Founded: 1975. Setting: rural. Nearest major city is Dallas. Students are housed in single-sex residences. 500-acre campus. 1 building on campus. Approved or accredited by Association of Christian Schools International, Southern Association of Colleges and Schools, and The Association of Boarding Schools. Member of National Association of Independent Schools. Total enrollment: 175. Upper school average class size: 8. Upper school faculty-student ratio: 1:7. There are 186 required school days per year for Upper School students. Upper School students typically attend 5 days per week. The average school day consists of 6 hours and 30 minutes.

Upper School Student Profile 70% of students are boarding students. 70% are state residents. 8 states are represented in upper school student body. 10% are international students. International students from Brazil, China, Democratic People's Republic of Korea, Hong Kong, Serbia and Montenegro, and Taiwan; 4 other countries represented in student body. 65% of students are Christian.

Faculty School total: 33. In upper school: 6 men, 18 women; 7 have advanced degrees; 10 reside on campus.

Subjects Offered 1 1/2 elective credits, advanced math, Advanced Placement courses, agriculture, algebra, American history, American literature, animal husbandry, animal science, applied music, art, athletics, basketball, Bible, biology, calculus, cheerleading, chemistry, choir, classical music, computer education, computer literacy, computer skills, concert choir, desktop publishing, drawing, driver education, economics, economics-AP, electives, English, English literature, English-AP, fine arts, gardening, general math, general science, geometry, golf, government, government-AP, guitar, health, history, horticulture, instruments, journalism, language arts, library, life

science, mathematics, mathematics-AP, music, music appreciation, music performance, music theory, newspaper, physical education, physics, pottery, pre-algebra, pre-calculus, science, scripture, social studies, Spanish, speech, sports, tennis, track and field, trigonometry, U.S. government, U.S. history, vocal ensemble, volleyball, weight training, world history, yearbook.

Special Academic Programs Honors section; independent study; study at local college for college credit; academic accommodation for the gifted, the musically talented, and the artistically talented; ESL (15 students enrolled).

College Admission Counseling 21 students graduated in 2015; all went to college, including Hardin-Simmons University; Southwestern University; Texas A&M University; Texas Christian University; Texas Wesleyan University; United States Air Force Academy.

Student Life Upper grades have uniform requirement, student council, honor system. Discipline rests primarily with faculty.

Summer Programs Remediation, enrichment, ESL, sports, art/fine arts programs offered; session focuses on enrichment; held on campus; accepts boys and girls; not open to students from other schools. 160 students usually enrolled. 2016 schedule: June 6 to July 15.

Tuition and Aid Day student tuition: $8800; 7-day tuition and room/board: $49,000. Tuition installment plan (monthly payment plans, individually arranged payment plans). Tuition reduction for siblings, need-based scholarship grants available. In 2015–16, 90% of upper-school students received aid.

Admissions Traditional secondary-level entrance grade is 10. Achievement tests, English for Non-native Speakers, Stanford Achievement Test or writing sample required. Deadline for receipt of application materials: none. Application fee required: $95. Interview required.

Athletics Interscholastic: baseball (boys), basketball (b,g), cheering (g), cross-country running (b,g), football (b), golf (b,g), horseback riding (b,g), outdoor education (b,g), physical fitness (b,g), running (b,g), soccer (g), softball (g), strength & conditioning (b,g), tennis (b,g), track and field (b,g), volleyball (g), weight training (b,g). 2 PE instructors, 4 coaches.

Computers Computers are regularly used in computer applications, creative writing, desktop publishing, English, journalism, library, newspaper, yearbook classes. Computer resources include on-campus library services, Internet access, wireless campus network, Internet filtering or blocking technology. Computer access in designated common areas is available to students. Students grades are available online. **Contact** Mr. Todd L. Shipman, President/Chief Financial Officer. 254-897-4822. Fax: 254-897-7650. E-mail: todd@northcentraltexasacademy.org. Website: www.NorthCentralTexasAcademy.org

NORTH CLACKAMAS CHRISTIAN SCHOOL

19575 Sebastian Way
Oregon City, Oregon 97045

Head of School: Mr. Tim Tutty

General Information Coeducational day college-preparatory, arts, religious studies, bilingual studies, and technology school, affiliated with Christian faith. Grades PK–12. Founded: 1973. Setting: suburban. Nearest major city is Portland. 5-acre campus. 3 buildings on campus. Approved or accredited by Association of Christian Schools International, Northwest Accreditation Commission, and Oregon Department of Education. Total enrollment: 258. Upper school average class size: 22. Upper school faculty-student ratio: 1:20. There are 168 required school days per year for Upper School students. Upper School students typically attend 5 days per week. The average school day consists of 7 hours.

Upper School Student Profile Grade 6: 28 students (17 boys, 11 girls); Grade 7: 14 students (9 boys, 5 girls); Grade 8: 19 students (9 boys, 10 girls); Grade 9: 16 students (6 boys, 10 girls); Grade 10: 18 students (11 boys, 7 girls); Grade 11: 15 students (7 boys, 8 girls); Grade 12: 14 students (7 boys, 7 girls). 100% of students are Christian faith.

Faculty School total: 22. In upper school: 4 men, 7 women; 7 have advanced degrees.

Subjects Offered Art, ASB Leadership, band, basketball, Bible, Bible studies, biology, calculus, calligraphy, chemistry, choir, computer skills, economics, electives, English, government, honors U.S. history, library, mathematics, meteorology, music, physical fitness, physics, pre-calculus, publications, SAT/ACT preparation, science, Spanish, speech, track and field, U.S. history, U.S. history-AP, volleyball, world geography, writing, yearbook.

Graduation Requirements Arts and fine arts (art, music, dance, drama), Bible, electives, English, foreign language, health, leadership, mathematics, physical education (includes health), science, social sciences, speech.

College Admission Counseling 15 students graduated in 2015; 12 went to college, including Corban University; George Fox University; LeTourneau University; Oregon State University; University of Oregon; University of Portland. Other: 1 went to work, 2 had other specific plans.

Student Life Upper grades have specified standards of dress, student council, honor system. Discipline rests primarily with faculty. Attendance at religious services is required.

Tuition and Aid Day student tuition: $6693. Tuition installment plan (monthly payment plans, individually arranged payment plans). Tuition reduction for siblings, need-based scholarship grants available. In 2015–16, 25% of upper-school students received aid.

Admissions Traditional secondary-level entrance grade is 9. Terra Nova-CTB required. Deadline for receipt of application materials: none. Application fee required: $100. On-campus interview required.

Athletics Interscholastic: basketball (boys, girls), cross-country running (b,g), track and field (b,g), volleyball (g); intramural: basketball (b,g), cross-country running (b,g), track and field (b,g), volleyball (g); coed interscholastic: soccer; coed intramural: soccer. 1 PE instructor, 10 coaches.

Computers Computers are regularly used in all academic, Bible studies, writing classes. Computer resources include on-campus library services, Internet access, Internet filtering or blocking technology. Computer access in designated common areas is available to students. Students grades are available online.

Contact Mrs. Julie Gatewood, Office Manager. 503-655-5961 Ext. 100. Fax: 503-655-4875. E-mail: julie_gatewood@ncchristianschool.com. Website: www.ncchristianschool.com

NORTH COUNTRY SCHOOL

Lake Placid, New York
See Junior Boarding Schools section.

NORTHFIELD MOUNT HERMON SCHOOL

One Lamplighter Way
Mount Hermon, Massachusetts 01354

Head of School: Peter B. Fayroian

General Information Coeducational boarding and day college-preparatory and college model academic planning school. Grades 9–PG. Founded: 1879. Setting: rural. Nearest major city is Hartford, CT. Students are housed in single-sex by floor dormitories and single-sex dormitories. 1,565-acre campus. 35 buildings on campus. Approved or accredited by Association of Independent Schools in New England, New England Association of Schools and Colleges, and Massachusetts Department of Education. Member of National Association of Independent Schools and Secondary School Admission Test Board. Endowment: $120 million. Total enrollment: 650. Upper school average class size: 11. Upper school faculty-student ratio: 1:5. There are 158 required school days per year for Upper School students. Upper School students typically attend 5 days per week. The average school day consists of 8 hours.

Upper School Student Profile Grade 9: 92 students (40 boys, 52 girls); Grade 10: 168 students (83 boys, 85 girls); Grade 11: 181 students (100 boys, 81 girls); Grade 12: 183 students (88 boys, 95 girls); Postgraduate: 27 students (19 boys, 8 girls). 80% of students are boarding students. 34 states are represented in upper school student body. 24% are international students. International students from Canada, China, Nigeria, Republic of Korea, Russian Federation, and Viet Nam; 46 other countries represented in student body.

Faculty School total: 121. In upper school: 63 men, 58 women; 85 have advanced degrees; all reside on campus.

Subjects Offered 3-dimensional art, acting, Advanced Placement courses, aerobics, algebra, American history, American history-AP, American literature, American literature-AP, analytic geometry, anatomy, anatomy and physiology, ancient history, applied music, Arabic, art, art-AP, arts, astronomy, athletics, ballet, band, baseball, Basic programming, basketball, Bible, bioethics, biology, biology-AP, botany, broadcasting, calculus, calculus-AP, campus ministry, cell biology, ceramics, chamber groups, chemistry, chemistry-AP, Chinese, Chinese literature, choir, choral music, choreography, chorus, Christian doctrine, Christianity, Civil War, collage and assemblage, college admission preparation, college counseling, community service, computers, concert band, concert choir, creative writing, dance, dance performance, debate, digital imaging, digital music, digital photography, drama, drama performance, drama workshop, dramatic arts, drawing, driver education, earth science, economics, economics-AP, electives, English, English composition, English language-AP, English literature and composition-AP, English-AP, English/composition-AP, ensembles, environmental science, environmental science-AP, environmental studies, epic literature, equality and freedom, ESL, ethics, European history, European history-AP, European literature, expository writing, fiction, film, film and literature, film history, film studies, fine arts, fitness, foreign language, French, French language-AP, French-AP, functions, general science, genetics, geology, geometry, global issues, global studies, golf, government, graphic design, great books, guitar, Harlem Renaissance, health, health and wellness, health education, history, history of jazz, history of music, history of religion, history-AP, honors algebra, honors English, honors geometry, honors U.S. history, honors world history, human anatomy, humanities, independent study, instrumental music, instruments, introduction to literature, introduction to theater, jazz, jazz band, jewelry making, journalism, language-AP, languages, Latin, Latin-AP, life science, linear algebra, literary magazine, literature, literature seminar, literature-AP, macro/microeconomics-AP, Mandarin, martial arts, mathematics, mathematics-AP, mechanics of writing, media arts, meditation, microeconomics, model United Nations, modern dance, modern European history, modern European history-AP, modern history, modern Western civilization, modern world history, music, music history, music performance, music theater, music theory, music theory-AP, musical productions, musical theater, musicianship, New Testament, news writing, newspaper,

non-Western literature, non-Western societies, North American literature, novels, oral communications, oral expression, orchestra, outdoor education, painting, performing arts, philosophy, photography, physical education, physical fitness, physical science, physics, physics-AP, physiology, piano, play production, poetry, political science, portfolio art, pottery, pre-calculus, printmaking, programming, psychology-AP, public speaking, publications, radio broadcasting, religion, religion and culture, religious studies, research skills, robotics, Russian studies, SAT preparation, SAT/ACT preparation, science, science research, scripture, sculpture, Shakespeare, short story, social studies, society, politics and law, Spanish, Spanish language-AP, Spanish literature, Spanish-AP, speech, speech and debate, stage design, stagecraft, statistics, statistics-AP, strings, student government, student publications, studio art, studio art-AP, study skills, swimming, tennis, The 20th Century, theater, theater arts, theater design and production, theater production, topics in dramatic literature, track and field, travel, trigonometry, Turkish history, U.S. history, U.S. history-AP, U.S. literature, United States government-AP, video, video film production, visual and performing arts, visual arts, vocal ensemble, vocal music, voice ensemble, volleyball, Western religions, wilderness experience, wind ensemble, work experience, work-study, world cultures, world governments, world history, world issues, world literature, world religions, world religions, world studies, wrestling, writing, writing, writing workshop, yearbook, yoga.

Graduation Requirements Arts and fine arts (art, music, dance, drama), English, foreign language, mathematics, physical education (includes health), religion (includes Bible studies and theology), science, social studies (includes history), participation in work program.

Special Academic Programs Advanced Placement exam preparation; honors section; independent study; term-away projects; study abroad; academic accommodation for the gifted, the musically talented, and the artistically talented; ESL.

College Admission Counseling 188 students graduated in 2015; 183 went to college, including Boston University; Connecticut College; Hobart and William Smith Colleges; New York University; Trinity College; United States Naval Academy. Other: 1 entered a postgraduate year, 4 had other specific plans.

Student Life Upper grades have specified standards of dress, student council, honor system. Discipline rests primarily with faculty.

Summer Programs Remediation, enrichment, ESL, art/fine arts programs offered; session focuses on intense academic preparation; held on campus; accepts boys and girls; open to students from other schools. 2016 schedule: June to August.

Tuition and Aid Day student tuition: $38,900; 7-day tuition and room/board: $57,100. Tuition installment plan (Tuition Pay 10-Month). Need-based scholarship grants, need-based loans, Sallie Mae K-12 Family Education loans, Your Solution Education available. In 2015–16, 31% of upper-school students received aid. Total amount of financial aid awarded in 2015–16: $8,400,000.

Admissions Traditional secondary-level entrance grade is 9. For fall 2015, 1,467 students applied for upper-level admission, 227 enrolled. ACT, ISEE, PSAT, SAT, SSAT or TOEFL required. Deadline for receipt of application materials: February 1. Application fee required: $50. Interview recommended.

Athletics Interscholastic: alpine skiing (boys, girls), baseball (b), basketball (b,g), crew (b,g), cross-country running (b,g), field hockey (g), Frisbee (b,g), hockey (b,g), ice hockey (b,g), lacrosse (b,g), nordic skiing (b,g), skiing (cross-country) (b,g), skiing (downhill) (b,g), soccer (b,g), softball (g), swimming and diving (b,g), tennis (b,g), track and field (b,g), ultimate Frisbee (b,g), volleyball (b,g), wrestling (b); coed interscholastic: golf, modern dance; coed intramural: aerobics, aerobics/dance, alpine skiing, aquatics, backpacking, badminton, ballet, basketball, bicycling, canoeing/kayaking, climbing, dance, dance team, fencing, fitness, Frisbee, hiking/backpacking, kayaking, lacrosse, martial arts, modern dance, mountain biking, nordic skiing, outdoor activities, outdoor education, physical fitness, physical training, rock climbing, running, sailing, skiing (cross-country), skiing (downhill), snowboarding, soccer, softball, strength & conditioning, ultimate Frisbee, volleyball, weight training, yoga.

Computers Computers are regularly used in all academic classes. Computer network features include on-campus library services, online commercial services, Internet access, wireless campus network, Internet filtering or blocking technology. Campus intranet, student e-mail accounts, and computer access in designated common areas are available to students. Students grades are available online. The school has a published electronic and media policy.

Contact Office of Admission. 413-498-3227. Fax: 413-498-3152. E-mail: admission@nmhschool.org. Website: www.nmhschool.org

NORTHPOINT CHRISTIAN SCHOOL

7400 Getwell Road
Southaven, Mississippi 38672

Head of School: Mr. David H. Manley

General Information Coeducational day college-preparatory, arts, religious studies, technology, and chorus and band school, affiliated with Christian faith, Baptist Church. Grades PK–12. Founded: 1972. Setting: suburban. Nearest major city is Memphis, TN. 61-acre campus. 4 buildings on campus. Approved or accredited by Southern Association of Colleges and Schools and Southern Association of Independent Schools. Member of National Association of Independent Schools. Total enrollment: 1,084. Upper school average class size: 21. Upper school faculty-student ratio: 1:13. There are 176 required school days per year for Upper School students. Upper School students typically attend 5 days per week. The average school day consists of 7 hours and 5 minutes.

Upper School Student Profile Grade 7: 82 students (44 boys, 38 girls); Grade 8: 69 students (33 boys, 36 girls); Grade 9: 90 students (39 boys, 51 girls); Grade 10: 86 students (43 boys, 43 girls); Grade 11: 69 students (34 boys, 35 girls); Grade 12: 80 students (46 boys, 34 girls). 90% of students are Christian, Baptist.

Faculty School total: 101. In upper school: 17 men, 31 women; 17 have advanced degrees.

Subjects Offered Acting, advanced biology, advanced chemistry, advanced math, Advanced Placement courses, algebra, American government, American history, anatomy and physiology, art, art-AP, arts, band, Bible, Bible studies, biology, biotechnology, calculus, calculus-AP, chemistry, computer programming, computer science, drafting, drama, driver education, economics, English, English-AP, geometry, home economics, journalism, keyboarding, Latin, physical education, physics, pre-algebra, psychology, sociology, Spanish, U.S. government and politics-AP, vocal music, world history, yearbook.

Graduation Requirements 20th century world history, advanced math, algebra, American history, anatomy and physiology, Bible, chemistry, Christian studies, economics, education, English, geometry, Latin, physics, psychology, Spanish, U.S. government and politics-AP, world history.

Special Academic Programs 5 Advanced Placement exams for which test preparation is offered; honors section; academic accommodation for the gifted; remedial reading and/or remedial writing; remedial math; programs in English, mathematics, general development for dyslexic students.

College Admission Counseling 60 students graduated in 2015; all went to college, including Belmont University; Mississippi College; Mississippi State University; University of Memphis; University of Mississippi; Vanderbilt University. Mean composite ACT: 26. 32% scored over 26 on composite ACT.

Student Life Upper grades have uniform requirement, student council, honor system. Discipline rests primarily with faculty. Attendance at religious services is required.

Summer Programs Sports programs offered; session focuses on driver's education and sports camps; held both on and off campus; held at classroom portion done on campus; driving portion and done on the highways and towns in north Mississippi, all sports on campus; accepts boys and girls; not open to students from other schools. 100 students usually enrolled. 2016 schedule: May 31 to August 10. Application deadline: July 15.

Tuition and Aid Day student tuition: $8295–$9325. Tuition installment plan (SMART Tuition Payment Plan). Tuition reduction for siblings, need-based scholarship grants available. In 2015–16, 15% of upper-school students received aid. Total amount of financial aid awarded in 2015–16: $70,000.

Admissions Traditional secondary-level entrance grade is 9. For fall 2015, 57 students applied for upper-level admission, 57 were accepted, 50 enrolled. Admissions testing, Individual IQ, math and English placement tests and Math Placement Exam required. Deadline for receipt of application materials: none. Application fee required: $225. On-campus interview required.

Athletics Interscholastic: baseball (boys), basketball (b,g), cheering (g), combined training (b), cross-country running (b,g), drill team (g), football (b), golf (b,g), soccer (b,g), softball (g), strength & conditioning (b,g), swimming and diving (b,g), tennis (b,g), track and field (b,g), volleyball (g), weight lifting (b,g). 2 PE instructors, 10 coaches, 2 athletic trainers.

Computers Computers are regularly used in computer applications, keyboarding, mathematics, science, word processing, writing, yearbook classes. Computer network features include on-campus library services, Internet access, wireless campus network, Internet filtering or blocking technology. Student e-mail accounts and computer access in designated common areas are available to students. Students grades are available online. The school has a published electronic and media policy.

Contact Mrs. Sheila Sheron, Director of Admission. 662-349-5127. Fax: 662-349-4962. E-mail: ssheron@ncstrojans.com. Website: www.ncstrojans.com/

NORTH SHORE COUNTRY DAY SCHOOL

310 Green Bay Road
Winnetka, Illinois 60093-4094

Head of School: Mr. Tom Doar III

General Information Coeducational day college-preparatory, arts, technology, and global education school. Grades PK–12. Founded: 1919. Setting: suburban. Nearest major city is Chicago. 16-acre campus. 6 buildings on campus. Approved or accredited by Independent Schools Association of the Central States and Illinois Department of Education. Member of National Association of Independent Schools and Secondary School Admission Test Board. Endowment: $23 million. Total enrollment: 525. Upper school average class size: 14. Upper school faculty-student ratio: 1:8. Upper School students typically attend 5 days per week. The average school day consists of 6 hours and 30 minutes.

Upper School Student Profile Grade 9: 51 students (23 boys, 28 girls); Grade 10: 51 students (28 boys, 23 girls); Grade 11: 51 students (27 boys, 24 girls); Grade 12: 47 students (24 boys, 23 girls).

Faculty School total: 80. In upper school: 27 men, 35 women; 42 have advanced degrees.

Subjects Offered Algebra, American history, American literature, anatomy and physiology, art, Asian studies, biology, biology-AP, calculus, calculus-AP, ceramics, chemistry, chemistry-AP, creative writing, drama, earth science, ecology, economics, English, English literature, English-AP, European history, expository writing, fine arts, French, French-AP, geography, geometry, government/civics, grammar, journalism, Mandarin, mathematics, music, photography, physical education, physics, physics-AP, printmaking, science, social studies, Spanish, Spanish-AP, speech, statistics, statistics-AP, technology, theater, trigonometry, U.S. history-AP, world history, world literature, writing.

Graduation Requirements Arts and fine arts (art, music, dance, drama), English, foreign language, mathematics, physical education (includes health), physical fitness, science, service learning/internship, social studies (includes history), technology, one stage performance in four years, completion of senior service project in May, completion of one-week community service project in four years.

Special Academic Programs Advanced Placement exam preparation; independent study; term-away projects; study at local college for college credit; study abroad.

College Admission Counseling 56 students graduated in 2015; all went to college, including University of Notre Dame.

Student Life Upper grades have specified standards of dress, student council, honor system. Discipline rests primarily with faculty.

Tuition and Aid Day student tuition: $12,000–$28,350. Tuition installment plan (Insured Tuition Payment Plan, Key Tuition Payment Plan, monthly payment plans, individually arranged payment plans, trimester payment plan). Merit scholarship grants, need-based scholarship grants, need-based loans, middle-income loans available. In 2015–16, 19% of upper-school students received aid. Total amount of financial aid awarded in 2015–16: $1,500,000.

Admissions Traditional secondary-level entrance grade is 9. SSAT and writing sample required. Deadline for receipt of application materials: January 31. Application fee required: $75. On-campus interview required.

Athletics Interscholastic: baseball (boys), basketball (b,g), cross-country running (b,g), field hockey (g), football (b), golf (b,g), indoor track & field (b,g), soccer (b,g), tennis (b,g), track and field (b,g), volleyball (g); intramural: physical training (b,g), weight lifting (b,g); coed intramural: dance, sailing. 4 PE instructors, 24 coaches, 1 athletic trainer.

Computers Computers are regularly used in all academic classes. Computer network features include on-campus library services, online commercial services, Internet access, wireless campus network, Internet filtering or blocking technology. Campus intranet and student e-mail accounts are available to students. The school has a published electronic and media policy.

Contact Ms. Leonie O'Donohoe, Admissions Associate. 847 881 8887. Fax: 847 446-0675. E-mail: lodonohoe@nscds.org. Website: www.nscds.org

NORTH TORONTO CHRISTIAN SCHOOL

255 Yorkland Boulevard
Toronto, Ontario M2J 1S3, Canada

Head of School: Mr. Allen Schenk

General Information Coeducational day college-preparatory and religious studies school, affiliated with Protestant-Evangelical faith. Grades JK–12. Founded: 1981. Setting: urban. 6-acre campus. 1 building on campus. Approved or accredited by Association of Christian Schools International and Ontario Department of Education. Language of instruction: English. Total enrollment: 407. Upper school average class size: 25. Upper school faculty-student ratio: 1:15. There are 184 required school days per year for Upper School students. Upper School students typically attend 5 days per week. The average school day consists of 6 hours.

Faculty School total: 31. In upper school: 11 men, 11 women; 8 have advanced degrees.

Subjects Offered Accounting, biology, business, calculus, Canadian geography, Canadian law, career exploration, chemistry, civics, computer applications, discrete mathematics, English, French, functions, geography, geometry, healthful living, information technology, instrumental music, marketing, physics, visual arts, world history, world issues, world religions.

Graduation Requirements 40 hours of community service, successful completion of the Ontario Secondary School Literacy Test.

Special Academic Programs Independent study; ESL (21 students enrolled).

College Admission Counseling 43 students graduated in 2015; 42 went to college, including Brock University; McMaster University; Queen's University at Kingston; The University of Western Ontario; University of Toronto; York University. Other: 1 had other specific plans.

Student Life Upper grades have uniform requirement. Discipline rests primarily with faculty. Attendance at religious services is required.

Summer Programs ESL programs offered; held on campus; accepts boys and girls; open to students from other schools. 20 students usually enrolled.

Tuition and Aid Day student tuition: CAN$8496. Tuition installment plan (monthly payment plans, individually arranged payment plans). Tuition reduction for siblings available.

Admissions Traditional secondary-level entrance grade is 9. Deadline for receipt of application materials: none. Application fee required: CAN$150. On-campus interview required.

Athletics Interscholastic: rugby (girls); coed interscholastic: aquatics, badminton, ball hockey, basketball, cross-country running, golf, soccer, softball, squash, swimming and diving, table tennis, tennis, track and field, volleyball; coed intramural: alpine skiing, canoeing/kayaking, diving, fitness, floor hockey, judo, kayaking, outdoor education, outdoor skills, street hockey, water polo. 6 PE instructors.

Computers Computers are regularly used in business applications, information technology, introduction to technology, keyboarding, mathematics, programming, science, typing, word processing classes. Computer network features include Internet access, wireless campus network. The school has a published electronic and media policy.

Contact Mr. Gordon Cooke, Administrator. 416-491-7667. Fax: 416-491-3806. E-mail: gcooke@ntcs.on.ca. Website: www.ntcs.on.ca

NORTHWEST ACADEMY

1130 Southwest Main Street
Portland, Oregon 97205

Head of School: Mary Vinton Folberg

General Information Coeducational day college-preparatory, arts, and bilingual studies school. Grades 6–12. Founded: 1996. Setting: urban. 5 buildings on campus. Approved or accredited by Northwest Association of Independent Schools and Oregon Department of Education. Member of National Association of Independent Schools. Total enrollment: 211. Upper school average class size: 15. Upper school faculty-student ratio: 1:5. Upper School students typically attend 5 days per week. The average school day consists of 7 hours and 30 minutes.

Upper School Student Profile Grade 6: 30 students (12 boys, 18 girls); Grade 7: 37 students (17 boys, 20 girls); Grade 8: 40 students (13 boys, 27 girls); Grade 9: 31 students (18 boys, 13 girls); Grade 10: 32 students (18 boys, 14 girls); Grade 11: 26 students (9 boys, 17 girls); Grade 12: 15 students (5 boys, 10 girls).

Faculty School total: 44. In upper school: 15 men, 29 women; 23 have advanced degrees.

Subjects Offered 20th century history, acting, algebra, anatomy and physiology, animation, art history, ballet, biology, calculus, career/college preparation, chemistry, comparative government and politics, comparative politics, comparative religion, computer animation, computer literacy, computer music, creative writing, critical thinking, dance performance, desktop publishing, digital art, drama workshop, drawing, earth and space science, ecology, environmental systems, English literature, European civilization, film studies, French, geometry, history of music, human anatomy, humanities, illustration, independent study, internship, introduction to digital multitrack recording techniques, jazz band, jazz dance, jazz ensemble, journalism, keyboarding, media arts, medieval/Renaissance history, multimedia design, music composition, music history, music performance, musical theater, painting, photo shop, physics, play/screen writing, political systems, pre-calculus, printmaking, senior thesis, Shakespeare, social sciences, Spanish, student publications, tap dance, theater, trigonometry, U.S. government and politics, U.S. history, video film production, visual arts, vocal ensemble, vocal jazz, world cultures, world history, world wide web design, writing, yearbook, yoga.

Graduation Requirements Senior thesis, 4 years of English/humanities, senior thesis seminar, 3 years of both math and science, 2 years of foreign language, 7 units of credit of arts electives, community service, computer literacy, physical education.

Special Academic Programs Accelerated programs; independent study; study at local college for college credit; academic accommodation for the gifted, the musically talented, and the artistically talented.

College Admission Counseling 14 students graduated in 2015; 12 went to college, including Macalester College; Occidental College; Wellesley College; Whitman College. Other: 1 went to work, 1 had other specific plans. Median SAT critical reading: 610, median SAT math: 570, median SAT writing: 570, median combined SAT: 1749. 57% scored over 600 on SAT critical reading, 43% scored over 600 on SAT math, 36% scored over 600 on SAT writing, 43% scored over 1800 on combined SAT.

Student Life Upper grades have student council, honor system. Discipline rests primarily with faculty.

Tuition and Aid Day student tuition: $20,500. Tuition installment plan (FACTS Tuition Payment Plan). Need-based scholarship grants available. In 2015–16, 20% of upper-school students received aid. Total amount of financial aid awarded in 2015–16: $500,000.

Admissions Traditional secondary-level entrance grade is 9. For fall 2015, 117 students applied for upper-level admission, 96 were accepted, 60 enrolled. Admissions testing, placement test and writing sample required. Deadline for receipt of application materials: January 29. Application fee required: $100. Interview required.

Athletics Coed Intramural: aerobics, aerobics/dance, artistic gym, ballet, combined training, cooperative games, dance, dance squad, fitness, modern dance, outdoor activities, tai chi, yoga.

Computers Computers are regularly used in all academic, yearbook classes. Computer network features include Internet access, wireless campus network, film and audio editing, sound design, animation, Flash. Campus intranet, student e-mail accounts, and computer access in designated common areas are available to students. Students grades are available online. The school has a published electronic and media policy.

Contact Lainie Keslin Ettinger, Director of Admissions and Marketing. 503-223-3367 Ext. 104. Fax: 503-402-1043. E-mail: lettinger@nwacademy.org. Website: www.nwacademy.org

NORTHWEST CATHOLIC HIGH SCHOOL

29 Wampanoag Drive
West Hartford, Connecticut 06117

Head of School: Mr. David Eustis

General Information Coeducational day college-preparatory and religious studies school, affiliated with Roman Catholic Church. Grades 9–12. Founded: 1961. Setting: suburban. Nearest major city is Hartford. 1 building on campus. Approved or accredited by New England Association of Schools and Colleges and Connecticut Department of Education. Total enrollment: 587. Upper school average class size: 18. Upper school faculty-student ratio: 1:12. There are 180 required school days per year for Upper School students. Upper School students typically attend 5 days per week. The average school day consists of 6 hours and 18 minutes.

Upper School Student Profile Grade 9: 146 students (80 boys, 66 girls); Grade 10: 125 students (71 boys, 54 girls); Grade 11: 168 students (77 boys, 91 girls); Grade 12: 146 students (70 boys, 76 girls). 79% of students are Roman Catholic.

Faculty School total: 51. In upper school: 18 men, 33 women; 37 have advanced degrees.

Subjects Offered Biology-AP, calculus-AP, chemistry-AP, computer science-AP, English language and composition-AP, English literature and composition-AP, French language-AP, Latin-AP, music theory-AP, physics-AP, Spanish-AP, statistics-AP, studio art-AP, U.S. government and politics-AP, U.S. history-AP.

Graduation Requirements Arts and fine arts (art, music, dance, drama), English, foreign language, health education, mathematics, physical education (includes health), religion (includes Bible studies and theology), science, social studies (includes history), 25 hours of community service.

Special Academic Programs 15 Advanced Placement exams for which test preparation is offered; honors section; study at local college for college credit.

College Admission Counseling 141 students graduated in 2015; 138 went to college, including Assumption College; Fairfield University; Providence College; Quinnipiac University; University of Connecticut; University of Hartford. Other: 1 entered military service, 1 entered a postgraduate year, 1 had other specific plans. Mean SAT critical reading: 577, mean SAT math: 574, mean SAT writing: 573.

Student Life Upper grades have uniform requirement, student council, honor system. Discipline rests primarily with faculty. Attendance at religious services is required.

Summer Programs Sports programs offered; session focuses on grades 3-8; held both on and off campus; held at Northwest Catholic High facilities and St.Thomas Seminary fields; accepts boys and girls; open to students from other schools. 100 students usually enrolled. 2016 schedule: June to August. Application deadline: May 31.

Tuition and Aid Day student tuition: $14,300. Tuition installment plan (monthly payment plans). Tuition reduction for siblings, merit scholarship grants, need-based scholarship grants available. Total upper-school merit-scholarship money awarded for 2015–16: $90,000. Total amount of financial aid awarded in 2015–16: $2,034,000.

Admissions Traditional secondary-level entrance grade is 9. High School Placement Test required. Deadline for receipt of application materials: March 1. Application fee required: $25.

Athletics Interscholastic: baseball (boys), basketball (b,g), cross-country running (b,g), field hockey (g), golf (b,g), ice hockey (b,g), indoor track & field (b,g), lacrosse (b,g), soccer (b,g), softball (g), tennis (b,g), track and field (b,g), volleyball (g), winter (indoor) track (b,g); intramural: basketball (b,g); coed interscholastic: cheering, diving, football, swimming and diving; coed intramural: canoeing/kayaking, climbing, fitness, flag football, hiking/backpacking, indoor soccer, outdoor adventure, rappelling, rock climbing, skiing (downhill), snowboarding, snowshoeing, strength & conditioning, ultimate Frisbee, weight training, whiffle ball. 1 PE instructor, 1 athletic trainer.

Computers Computers are regularly used in all academic classes. Computer network features include on-campus library services, Internet access, wireless campus network, Internet filtering or blocking technology, many software programs, 1:1 iPad program. Student e-mail accounts and computer access in designated common areas are available to students. Students grades are available online. The school has a published electronic and media policy.

Contact Mrs. Nancy Scully Bannon, Director of Admissions. 860-236-4221 Ext. 124. Fax: 860-570-0080. E-mail: nbannon@nwcath.org. Website: www.northwestcatholic.org

THE NORTHWEST SCHOOL

1415 Summit Avenue
Seattle, Washington 98122

Head of School: Mike McGill

General Information Coeducational boarding and day college-preparatory, arts, and ESL school. Boarding grades 9–12, day grades 6–12. Founded: 1978. Setting: urban. Students are housed in coed dormitories. 1-acre campus. 4 buildings on campus. Approved or accredited by Northwest Association of Independent Schools and

Washington Department of Education. Member of National Association of Independent Schools. Endowment: $4.8 million. Total enrollment: 506. Upper school average class size: 17. Upper school faculty-student ratio: 1:9. There are 168 required school days per year for Upper School students. Upper School students typically attend 5 days per week. The average school day consists of 7 hours and 20 minutes.

Upper School Student Profile Grade 9: 90 students (44 boys, 46 girls); Grade 10: 88 students (44 boys, 44 girls); Grade 11: 93 students (36 boys, 57 girls); Grade 12: 79 students (38 boys, 41 girls). 16% of students are boarding students. 80% are state residents. 2 states are represented in upper school student body. 17% are international students. International students from China, Japan, Republic of Korea, Taiwan, Thailand, and Viet Nam; 6 other countries represented in student body.

Faculty School total: 76. In upper school: 22 men, 33 women; 40 have advanced degrees.

Subjects Offered Advanced chemistry, algebra, astronomy, biology, calculus, ceramics, chemistry, Chinese, chorus, computer skills, contemporary problems, dance, drama, drawing, earth science, English, ESL, evolution, fiber arts, film, fine arts, French, geometry, health, history, humanities, illustration, improvisation, jazz dance, jazz ensemble, journalism, life science, literature, math analysis, mathematics, mentorship program, musical theater, orchestra, outdoor education, painting, performing arts, philosophy, photography, physical education, physical science, physics, play production, pre-algebra, pre-calculus, printmaking, Spanish, statistics, strings, textiles, theater, trigonometry, U.S. government and politics, U.S. history, visual arts, Washington State and Northwest History, water color painting, wilderness education, world history, writing.

Graduation Requirements English, foreign language, history, humanities, mathematics, physical education (includes health), science, senior project, social studies (includes history), visual and performing arts, participation in environmental maintenance program.

Special Academic Programs Term-away projects; ESL (50 students enrolled).

College Admission Counseling 92 students graduated in 2015; 86 went to college, including Boston University; Haverford College; Macalester College; Reed College; University of Washington; Western Washington University. Other: 6 had other specific plans.

Student Life Upper grades have honor system. Discipline rests primarily with faculty.

Summer Programs Enrichment, ESL, sports, art/fine arts, computer instruction programs offered; session focuses on global connections with international students; held on campus; accepts boys and girls; open to students from other schools. 350 students usually enrolled. 2016 schedule: July 11 to August 19. Application deadline: June 27.

Tuition and Aid Day student tuition: $34,150–$37,995; 7-day tuition and room/board: $49,660–$53,505. Tuition installment plan (school's own payment plan). Need-based scholarship grants available. In 2015–16, 14% of upper-school students received aid. Total amount of financial aid awarded in 2015–16: $1,340,175.

Admissions Traditional secondary-level entrance grade is 9. For fall 2015, 159 students applied for upper-level admission, 86 were accepted, 40 enrolled. ISEE, SSAT or TOEFL required. Deadline for receipt of application materials: January 14. Application fee required: $70. Interview required.

Athletics Interscholastic: basketball (boys, girls), cross-country running (b,g), soccer (b,g), track and field (b,g), ultimate Frisbee (b,g), volleyball (g); coed intramural: fitness, hiking/backpacking, outdoor education, physical fitness, physical training, rock climbing, ropes courses, skiing (cross-country), skiing (downhill), snowboarding. 2 PE instructors, 30 coaches.

Computers Computers are regularly used in art, English, ESL, foreign language, graphic design, health, history, humanities, journalism, library, mathematics, music, science, social studies, theater, video film production, writing, yearbook classes. Computer network features include on-campus library services, Internet access, wireless campus network, ProQuest, ABC-Cleo, JSTOR, eLibrary, CultureGrams, World Conflicts and Online Encyclopedias. Student e-mail accounts and computer access in designated common areas are available to students. Students grades are available online. The school has a published electronic and media policy.

Contact Douglas Leek, Director of Admissions and Enrollment Management. 206-682-7309. Fax: 206-467-7353. E-mail: douglas.leek@northwestschool.org. Website: www.northwestschool.org

NORTHWEST YESHIVA HIGH SCHOOL

5017 90th Avenue Southeast
Mercer Island, Washington 98040

Head of School: Rabbi Bernie Fox

General Information Coeducational day college-preparatory and religious studies school, affiliated with Jewish faith. Grades 9–12. Founded: 1974. Setting: suburban. Nearest major city is Seattle. 2-acre campus. 3 buildings on campus. Approved or accredited by Northwest Association of Schools and Colleges and Washington Department of Education. Languages of instruction: English, Hebrew, and Spanish. Endowment: $1.2 million. Total enrollment: 60. Upper school average class size: 12. Upper school faculty-student ratio: 1:4. There are 180 required school days per year for Upper School students. Upper School students typically attend 5 days per week. The average school day consists of 8 hours.

Upper School Student Profile Grade 9: 22 students (11 boys, 11 girls); Grade 10: 14 students (7 boys, 7 girls); Grade 11: 18 students (8 boys, 10 girls); Grade 12: 5 students (2 boys, 3 girls). 100% of students are Jewish.

Faculty School total: 22. In upper school: 12 men, 10 women; 18 have advanced degrees.

Subjects Offered 20th century history, algebra, American legal systems, art, art history, biology, calculus, chemistry, college admission preparation, college counseling, drama, economics, English, film appreciation, fine arts, geometry, Hebrew, Hebrew scripture, integrated mathematics, Jewish history, Judaic studies, lab science, language arts, modern Western civilization, newspaper, philosophy, physical education, physics, prayer/spirituality, pre-algebra, pre-calculus, psychology, Rabbinic literature, religious studies, Spanish, Talmud, U.S. government, U.S. history, U.S. literature, Western civilization, world history, writing, yearbook.

Graduation Requirements Advanced math, arts and fine arts (art, music, dance, drama), biology, conceptual physics, Hebrew, integrated mathematics, Judaic studies, language arts, physics, Spanish, Talmud, U.S. government, U.S. history, world history. Community service is required.

Special Academic Programs Honors section; independent study; study at local college for college credit; academic accommodation for the gifted; remedial reading and/or remedial writing; remedial math; special instructional classes for deaf students, blind students; ESL (2 students enrolled).

College Admission Counseling 22 students graduated in 2015; 16 went to college, including American University; Brandeis University; University of Washington; Yeshiva University. Other: 6 had other specific plans. Median SAT critical reading: 620, median SAT math: 620, median SAT writing: 630, median combined SAT: 1870. 53% scored over 600 on SAT critical reading, 67% scored over 600 on SAT math, 60% scored over 600 on SAT writing, 53% scored over 1800 on combined SAT.

Student Life Upper grades have specified standards of dress, student council, honor system. Discipline rests primarily with faculty. Attendance at religious services is required.

Tuition and Aid Day student tuition: $17,940. Tuition installment plan (monthly payment plans, individually arranged payment plans). Need-based scholarship grants available. In 2015–16, 50% of upper-school students received aid. Total amount of financial aid awarded in 2015–16: $348,936.

Admissions Traditional secondary-level entrance grade is 9. For fall 2015, 22 students applied for upper-level admission, 22 were accepted, 22 enrolled. Deadline for receipt of application materials: none. Application fee required: $100. Interview required.

Athletics Interscholastic: basketball (boys, girls), crew (b,g), cross-country running (b,g), golf (b,g), volleyball (g); coed interscholastic: cross-country running, softball. 5 PE instructors, 5 coaches.

Computers Computers are regularly used in all classes. Computer network features include Internet access, wireless campus network, Internet filtering or blocking technology. Student e-mail accounts are available to students. Students grades are available online.

Contact Mr. Ian Weiner, Director of Student Services. 206-232-5272. Fax: 206-232-2711. E-mail: iw@nyhs.net. Website: www.nyhs.net

NORTH YARMOUTH ACADEMY

148 Main Street
Yarmouth, Maine 04096

Head of School: Mr. John Drisko

General Information Coeducational day college-preparatory, arts, and technology school. Grades PK–12. Founded: 1814. Setting: suburban. Nearest major city is Portland. 25-acre campus. 9 buildings on campus. Approved or accredited by Association of Independent Schools in New England, Independent Schools of Northern New England, New England Association of Schools and Colleges, and Maine Department of Education. Member of National Association of Independent Schools and Secondary School Admission Test Board. Total enrollment: 345. Upper school average class size: 15. Upper school faculty-student ratio: 1:6. There are 165 required school days per year for Upper School students. Upper School students typically attend 5 days per week. The average school day consists of 6 hours and 45 minutes.

Upper School Student Profile Grade 9: 36 students (22 boys, 14 girls); Grade 10: 43 students (28 boys, 15 girls); Grade 11: 43 students (16 boys, 27 girls); Grade 12: 48 students (16 boys, 32 girls).

Faculty School total: 63. In upper school: 16 men, 26 women; 26 have advanced degrees.

Subjects Offered Algebra, American government, American history, American history-AP, ancient world history, art, art history-AP, art-AP, biology-AP, calculus-AP, chemistry, chorus, classical language, college counseling, composition-AP, computer graphics, contemporary issues, drama, drawing and design, earth science, English, English composition, English literature, English literature and composition-AP, English-AP, environmental science-AP, European history, European history-AP, experiential education, fine arts, French, French-AP, genetics, geometry, history, instrumental music, jazz, language-AP, Latin, Latin-AP, Mandarin, mathematical modeling, mathematics, meditation, model United Nations, modern European history, modern European history-AP, music, music theory-AP, music-AP, painting, photography, physical education, physical science, physics, physics-AP, pottery, pre-algebra, pre-calculus, psychology, science, senior project, social issues, social studies, society challenge and change, Spanish, Spanish-AP, speech and debate, statistics, statistics-AP, student publications, studio art, studio art-AP, study skills, technology, theater, trigonometry, U.S. government and politics-AP, U.S. history, U.S. history-AP, visual and performing arts, vocal music, world history.

Graduation Requirements Arts and fine arts (art, music, dance, drama), English, foreign language, history, mathematics, science, senior project, speech, two-week volunteer senior service project, senior speech, participation in athletics or performing arts program each season (3).

Special Academic Programs 17 Advanced Placement exams for which test preparation is offered; honors section; independent study; study abroad; ESL (5 students enrolled).

College Admission Counseling 36 students graduated in 2014; all went to college, including Boston College; Quinnipiac University; University of Maine.

Student Life Upper grades have specified standards of dress, student council, honor system. Discipline rests equally with students and faculty.

Tuition and Aid Day student tuition: $26,700; 7-day tuition and room/board: $36,500. Tuition installment plan (Insured Tuition Payment Plan, monthly payment plans). Need-based scholarship grants available. In 2014–15, 40% of upper-school students received aid. Total amount of financial aid awarded in 2014–15: $900,000.

Admissions Traditional secondary-level entrance grade is 9. School placement exam, SSAT or writing sample required. Deadline for receipt of application materials: February 1. Application fee required: $50. Interview required.

Athletics Interscholastic: baseball (boys), basketball (b,g), cross-country running (b,g), dance (g), field hockey (g), golf (b,g), ice hockey (b,g), indoor track (b,g), indoor track & field (b,g), lacrosse (b,g), nordic skiing (b,g), physical training (b,g), sailing (b,g), skiing (cross-country) (b,g), soccer (b,g), softball (g), strength & conditioning (b,g), swimming and diving (b,g), tennis (b,g), track and field (b,g), weight lifting (b,g), weight training (b,g). 3 PE instructors, 17 coaches, 1 athletic trainer.

Computers Computers are regularly used in English, foreign language, graphic design, history, mathematics, science, technology classes. Computer network features include on-campus library services, Internet access, wireless campus network, Internet filtering or blocking technology. Campus intranet, student e-mail accounts, and computer access in designated common areas are available to students. The school has a published electronic and media policy.

Contact Ms. Leslie Durgin, Associate Director of Admission. 207-846-2376. E-mail: admission@nya.org. Website: www.nya.org

THE NORWICH FREE ACADEMY

305 Broadway
Norwich, Connecticut 06360

Head of School: Mr. David J. Klein

General Information Coeducational day college-preparatory, general academic, arts, business, vocational, bilingual studies, and technology school. Grades 9–12. Founded: 1856. Setting: suburban. 15-acre campus. 11 buildings on campus. Approved or accredited by New England Association of Schools and Colleges and Connecticut Department of Education. Member of National Association of Independent Schools. Total enrollment: 2,280. Upper school average class size: 24. Upper school faculty-student ratio: 1:13. There are 181 required school days per year for Upper School students. Upper School students typically attend 5 days per week. The average school day consists of 7 hours.

Upper School Student Profile Grade 9: 549 students (269 boys, 280 girls); Grade 10: 565 students (284 boys, 281 girls); Grade 11: 615 students (279 boys, 336 girls); Grade 12: 553 students (265 boys, 288 girls).

Faculty School total: 171. In upper school: 60 men, 111 women.

Subjects Offered 3-dimensional art, 3-dimensional design, accounting, advanced biology, advanced chemistry, advanced computer applications, advanced math, Advanced Placement courses, advanced studio art-AP, advanced TOEFL/grammar, algebra, American history, American history-AP, American literature, American sign language, anatomy and physiology, Arabic, architectural drawing, art, art history-AP, audio visual/media, band, biology, biology-AP, biotechnology, British literature, British literature-AP, business technology, calculus-AP, chemistry, chemistry-AP, child development, Chinese, choir, choral music, chorus, civics, classical language, clayworking, composition-AP, computer science-AP, computer-aided design, consumer mathematics, creative writing, culinary arts, dance, digital photography, discrete mathematics, drafting, drama, drawing, drawing and design, early childhood, economics, economics-AP, English language and composition-AP, English language-AP, English literature, English literature and composition-AP, English literature-AP, environmental science, environmental science-AP, ESL, European history-AP, exercise science, family and consumer science, finance, food and nutrition, foods, forensics, French, French language-AP, French studies, geometry, government/civics, graphic design, Greek, health, health and wellness, human anatomy, integrated science, international foods, Italian, jazz band, jazz dance, journalism, kinesiology, Latin, Latin-AP, marching band, marine biology, marketing, metalworking, microeconomics-AP, modern European history-AP, modern history, music theory, oceanography, personal finance, photo shop, photography, physical education, physical fitness, physics, physics-AP, piano, political science, politics, pre-calculus, printmaking, probability and statistics, psychology, psychology-AP, public speaking, Spanish language-AP, speech,

speech communications, sports science, television, U.S. history, U.S. history-AP, visual arts, vocal ensemble, woodworking, zoology.

Special Academic Programs 20 Advanced Placement exams for which test preparation is offered; honors section; study at local college for college credit; remedial reading and/or remedial writing; remedial math; special instructional classes for students with learning disabilities, Attention Deficit Disorder, emotional and behavioral problems, and dyslexia; ESL (90 students enrolled).

College Admission Counseling 537 students graduated in 2015; 421 went to college, including Central Connecticut State University; Eastern Connecticut State University; Rhode Island College; Southern Connecticut State University; University of Connecticut; University of New Hampshire. Other: 40 went to work, 14 entered military service, 22 entered a postgraduate year, 30 had other specific plans. Mean SAT critical reading: 498, mean SAT math: 490, mean SAT writing: 491, mean composite ACT: 22.

Student Life Upper grades have specified standards of dress, student council, honor system. Discipline rests primarily with faculty.

Summer Programs Remediation, enrichment, ESL, sports programs offered; held on campus; accepts boys and girls; not open to students from other schools. 250 students usually enrolled. 2016 schedule: July 1 to July 29. Application deadline: June 1.

Tuition and Aid Day student tuition: $12,710.

Admissions Traditional secondary-level entrance grade is 9. Deadline for receipt of application materials: none. No application fee required. Interview required.

Athletics Interscholastic: baseball (boys), basketball (b,g), cheering (b,g), cross-country running (b,g), fencing (b,g), field hockey (g), football (b), golf (b,g), gymnastics (g), hockey (b), ice hockey (b), indoor track (b,g), indoor track & field (b,g), lacrosse (b,g), running (b,g), soccer (b,g), softball (g), Special Olympics (b,g), swimming and diving (b,g), tennis (b,g), track and field (b,g), volleyball (b,g), winter (indoor) track (b,g), wrestling (b); intramural: skiing (downhill) (b,g), snowboarding (b); coed interscholastic: drill team; coed intramural: dance, dance team, physical fitness, physical training, power lifting, skateboarding, snowboarding, strength & conditioning, weight lifting, weight training. 6 PE instructors, 25 coaches, 5 athletic trainers.

Computers Computer network features include on-campus library services, Internet access, wireless campus network, Internet filtering or blocking technology. Student e-mail accounts are available to students. The school has a published electronic and media policy.

Contact Mr. John Iovino, Director of Student Affairs. 860-425-5510. Fax: 860-889-7124. E-mail: iovinoj@nfaschool.org. Website: www.nfaschool.org

NOTRE DAME ACADEMY

2851 Overland Avenue
Los Angeles, California 90064

Head of School: Ms. Lilliam Paetzold

General Information Girls' day college-preparatory, arts, religious studies, technology, and athletics school, affiliated with Roman Catholic Church. Grades 9–12. Founded: 1949. Setting: urban. 4-acre campus. 1 building on campus. Approved or accredited by Western Association of Schools and Colleges, Western Catholic Education Association, and California Department of Education. Total enrollment: 380. Upper school average class size: 23. Upper school faculty-student ratio: 1:12.

Upper School Student Profile 75% of students are Roman Catholic.

Faculty School total: 35. In upper school: 11 men, 24 women; 21 have advanced degrees.

Subjects Offered Advanced studio art-AP, algebra, American history, art, art history-AP, athletic training, biology, biology-AP, calculus, calculus-AP, campus ministry, chemistry, chemistry-AP, choir, Christian and Hebrew scripture, community service, computer science, dance, design, digital photography, drama, drama performance, economics, English, English language and composition-AP, English literature and composition-AP, environmental science-AP, European history-AP, French, French-AP, geometry, government and politics-AP, government/civics, health, history, honors geometry, Japanese, law, leadership, photography, physical education, physics, pre-calculus, psychology, psychology-AP, religion, Spanish, Spanish language-AP, speech and oral interpretations, statistics, trigonometry, U.S. government and politics-AP, U.S. history-AP, world civilizations, world history-AP.

Graduation Requirements Arts and fine arts (art, music, dance, drama), computer science, English, foreign language, mathematics, physical education (includes health), religion (includes Bible studies and theology), science, social studies (includes history), speech. Community service is required.

Special Academic Programs 16 Advanced Placement exams for which test preparation is offered; honors section.

College Admission Counseling 95 students graduated in 2014; all went to college, including Loyola Marymount University; Santa Clara University; University of California, Berkeley; University of California, Davis; University of California, Los Angeles; University of Southern California. Median SAT critical reading: 580, median SAT math: 540, median SAT writing: 570. Mean combined SAT: 1683, mean composite ACT: 25.

Student Life Upper grades have uniform requirement, student council, honor system. Discipline rests primarily with faculty. Attendance at religious services is required.

Tuition and Aid Day student tuition: $12,500. Tuition installment plan (FACTS Tuition Payment Plan, monthly payment plans). Merit scholarship grants, need-based scholarship grants, paying campus jobs available. In 2014–15, 30% of upper-school students received aid.

Admissions Traditional secondary-level entrance grade is 9. High School Placement Test (closed version) from Scholastic Testing Service or ISEE required. Deadline for receipt of application materials: January 12. Application fee required: $75. On-campus interview required.

Athletics Interscholastic: basketball, cross-country running, dance, equestrian sports, soccer, softball, swimming and diving, tennis, track and field, volleyball. 1 PE instructor, 18 coaches, 1 athletic trainer.

Computers Computers are regularly used in all academic, computer applications, design, journalism, photography, yearbook classes. Computer network features include on-campus library services, online commercial services, Internet access, wireless campus network, Internet filtering or blocking technology, 1:1 iPad program. Campus intranet, student e-mail accounts, and computer access in designated common areas are available to students. Students grades are available online. The school has a published electronic and media policy.

Contact Ms. Brigid Williams, Director of Admissions. 310 839 5289 Ext. 218. Fax: 310-839-7957. E-mail: bwilliams@ndala.com. Website: www.ndala.com

NOTRE DAME-CATHEDRAL LATIN SCHOOL

13000 Auburn Road

Chardon, Ohio 44024

Head of School: Mr. Joseph Waler

General Information Coeducational day college-preparatory school, affiliated with Roman Catholic Church. Grades 9–12. Founded: 1988. Setting: suburban. Nearest major city is Cleveland. 75-acre campus. 2 buildings on campus. Approved or accredited by North Central Association of Colleges and Schools and Ohio Department of Education. Total enrollment: 678. Upper school average class size: 20. Upper school faculty-student ratio: 1:15. Upper School students typically attend 5 days per week. The average school day consists of 6 hours and 50 minutes.

Upper School Student Profile 88% of students are Roman Catholic.

Faculty School total: 59.

Subjects Offered Algebra, American history, American literature, anatomy, art, biology, business, calculus, ceramics, chemistry, Chinese, community service, computer programming, computer science-AP, creative writing, desktop publishing, drawing, economics, electronic research, English, English literature, environmental science, film studies, fine arts, French, geography, geometry, government/civics, health, history, home economics, journalism, keyboarding, mathematics, music, music theory, photography, physical education, physical science, physics, physiology, religion, science, social studies, sociology, Spanish, speech, statistics, studio art-AP, theology, trigonometry, world affairs, world history, world literature.

Special Academic Programs Advanced Placement exam preparation; honors section; study at local college for college credit; ESL.

Student Life Upper grades have uniform requirement, student council, honor system. Discipline rests primarily with faculty. Attendance at religious services is required.

Summer Programs Enrichment, advancement, sports, art/fine arts programs offered; held on campus; accepts boys and girls; open to students from other schools.

Tuition and Aid Day student tuition: $11,400. Tuition installment plan (FACTS Tuition Payment Plan, bank-arranged 10-month plan). Merit scholarship grants, need-based scholarship grants available. In 2015–16, 47% of upper-school students received aid.

Admissions Otis-Lennon School Ability Test required. Deadline for receipt of application materials: none. No application fee required.

Athletics Interscholastic: baseball (boys), basketball (b,g), bowling (b,g), cheering (g), cross-country running (b,g), dance team (g), drill team (g), football (b), golf (b,g), gymnastics (g), lacrosse (b,g), physical fitness (b,g), physical training (b,g), soccer (b,g), softball (g), swimming and diving (b,g), tennis (b,g), track and field (b,g), volleyball (b,g), wrestling (b); intramural: skiing (downhill) (b,g), snowboarding (b,g), strength & conditioning (b,g), table tennis (b,g), weight training (b,g); coed interscholastic: diving, gymnastics, hockey, ice hockey, indoor track & field, physical fitness, physical training, winter (indoor) track; coed intramural: skiing (downhill), snowboarding, strength & conditioning, table tennis. 3 PE instructors.

Computers Computer network features include Internet access, wireless campus network. Campus intranet and student e-mail accounts are available to students. Students grades are available online.

Contact Mr. Michael Suso, Director of Admissions. 440-279-1088. Fax: 440-286-7199. E-mail: michael.suso@ndcl.org. Website: www.ndcl.org

NOTRE DAME HIGH SCHOOL

1540 Ralston Avenue

Belmont, California 94002-1995

Head of School: Ms. Maryann Osmond

General Information Girls' day college-preparatory, arts, religious studies, technology, and visual and performing arts school, affiliated with Roman Catholic Church; primarily serves students with learning disabilities, individuals with Attention Deficit Disorder, and dyslexic students. Grades 9–12. Founded: 1851. Setting: suburban. Nearest major city is San Francisco. 11-acre campus. 1 building on campus. Approved or accredited by Western Association of Schools and Colleges, Western Catholic Education Association, and California Department of Education. Member of National Association of Independent Schools. Total enrollment: 450. Upper school average class size: 23. Upper school faculty-student ratio: 1:14. There are 180 required school days per year for Upper School students. Upper School students typically attend 5 days per week. The average school day consists of 6 hours.

Upper School Student Profile Grade 9: 115 students (115 girls); Grade 10: 110 students (110 girls); Grade 11: 100 students (100 girls); Grade 12: 125 students (125 girls). 66% of students are Roman Catholic.

Faculty School total: 45. In upper school: 12 men, 33 women; 37 have advanced degrees.

Subjects Offered Advanced chemistry, advanced computer applications, advanced math, Advanced Placement courses, advanced studio art-AP, algebra, American government, American history, American literature, art, art history, art history-AP, art-AP, band, bioethics, biology, biology-AP, British literature, British literature-AP, calculus, calculus-AP, chemistry, chemistry-AP, choir, choral music, chorus, Christian and Hebrew scripture, church history, computer applications, computer literacy, computer science, creative writing, dance, decision making skills, digital photography, driver education, economics, economics and history, economics-AP, English, English literature, English literature-AP, environmental science, ethics, European history, French, French language-AP, geometry, government and politics-AP, government-AP, health, Hebrew scripture, history, honors English, honors geometry, honors U.S. history, honors world history, integrated science, jazz band, journalism, leadership, leadership and service, modern world history, moral reasoning, newspaper, orchestra, photography, physical education, physical science, physics, physics-AP, pre-calculus, psychology, relationships, religion, science, sculpture, self-defense, social justice, social sciences, Spanish, Spanish language-AP, Spanish-AP, sports conditioning, sports medicine, studio art-AP, television, trigonometry, U.S. government, U.S. government and politics-AP, U.S. history-AP, video film production, weight training, world history, world literature, world religions, yearbook.

Graduation Requirements Arts and fine arts (art, music, dance, drama), English, foreign language, mathematics, physical education (includes health), religion (includes Bible studies and theology), science, social sciences, social studies (includes history), 80 hours community service.

Special Academic Programs 12 Advanced Placement exams for which test preparation is offered; honors section; independent study; study at local college for college credit; special instructional classes for deaf students, blind students, students with learning differences.

College Admission Counseling 100 students graduated in 2015; all went to college, including Loyola Marymount University; Santa Clara University; University of California, Davis; University of California, Santa Barbara; University of Oregon; University of Southern California. Mean SAT critical reading: 543, mean SAT math: 533, mean SAT writing: 558.

Student Life Upper grades have uniform requirement, student council, honor system. Discipline rests primarily with faculty. Attendance at religious services is required.

Summer Programs Remediation, enrichment, advancement, sports, art/fine arts, computer instruction programs offered; session focuses on enrichment for grades 6-9; held on campus; accepts boys and girls; open to students from other schools. 150 students usually enrolled. 2016 schedule: June 15 to July 10. Application deadline: May 1.

Tuition and Aid Day student tuition: $20,440. Tuition installment plan (FACTS Tuition Payment Plan, individually arranged payment plans). Merit scholarship grants, need-based scholarship grants available. In 2014–15, 24% of upper-school students received aid; total upper-school merit-scholarship money awarded: $200,000. Total amount of financial aid awarded in 2014–15: $10,000,000.

Admissions Traditional secondary-level entrance grade is 9. For fall 2015, 250 students applied for upper-level admission, 225 were accepted, 115 enrolled. High School Placement Test (closed version) from Scholastic Testing Service and writing sample required. Deadline for receipt of application materials: January 8. Application fee required: $110. On-campus interview required.

Athletics Interscholastic: aquatics, basketball, cheering, cross-country running, dance, dance team, golf, modern dance, physical fitness, physical training, pom squad, running, soccer, softball, strength & conditioning, swimming and diving, tennis, track and field, volleyball, water polo, weight training, yoga; intramural: cheering, touch football, ultimate Frisbee. 1 PE instructor, 33 coaches, 2 athletic trainers.

Computers Computers are regularly used in college planning, creative writing, English, foreign language, health, history, independent study, journalism, mathematics, media production, newspaper, photography, publishing, religious studies, SAT preparation, science, social studies, video film production, yearbook classes. Computer network features include on-campus library services, Internet access, wireless campus network, Internet filtering or blocking technology. Student e-mail accounts and computer access in designated common areas are available to students. Students grades are available online. The school has a published electronic and media policy.

Contact Mrs. Wendy Bell, Associate Director of Admissions. 650-595-1913 Ext. 310. Fax: 650-595-2116. E-mail: wbell@ndhsb.org. Website: www.ndhsb.org

NOTRE DAME HIGH SCHOOL

7085 Brockton Avenue
Riverside, California 92506

Head of School: Mr. Matthew M. Luttringer

General Information Coeducational day college-preparatory, arts, business, religious studies, and technology school, affiliated with Roman Catholic Church; primarily serves individuals with Attention Deficit Disorder. Grades 9–12. Founded: 1956. Setting: small town. Nearest major city is Los Angeles. 4-acre campus. 7 buildings on campus. Approved or accredited by Western Association of Schools and Colleges and California Department of Education. Endowment: $10,000. Total enrollment: 629. Upper school average class size: 20. Upper school faculty-student ratio: 1:19. There are 181 required school days per year for Upper School students. Upper School students typically attend 5 days per week. The average school day consists of 7 hours.

Upper School Student Profile Grade 9: 223 students (116 boys, 107 girls); Grade 10: 151 students (69 boys, 82 girls); Grade 11: 117 students (59 boys, 58 girls); Grade 12: 138 students (76 boys, 62 girls). 80% of students are Roman Catholic.

Faculty School total: 39. In upper school: 23 men, 16 women; 35 have advanced degrees.

Subjects Offered Advanced computer applications, advanced math, algebra, anatomy and physiology, ancient world history, art, ASB Leadership, audio visual/media, Basic programming, biology, British literature, British literature (honors), business law, calculus, campus ministry, Catholic belief and practice, chemistry, choir, choral music, church history, comparative religion, composition-AP, computer education, computer programming, computer programming-AP, computers, consumer mathematics, drama, drama performance, driver education, economics, economics-AP, English literature and composition-AP, fine arts, finite math, foreign language, French, geometry, government, health, history, history of the Catholic Church, honors algebra, honors English, honors geometry, honors U.S. history, humanities, independent study, intro to computers, journalism, keyboarding, martial arts, moral theology, music history, musical productions, peer ministry, philosophy, physical education, physical science, physics, play production, pre-algebra, pre-calculus, psychology, psychology-AP, public speaking, religion, science, scripture, Shakespeare, social sciences, social studies, sociology, Spanish, speech, sports conditioning, sports team management, stage design, student government, student publications, study skills, theology, training, trigonometry, U.S. government, U.S. government and politics-AP, U.S. history, U.S. history-AP, U.S. literature, video, weight training, word processing, work experience, world history, world literature, yearbook.

Special Academic Programs Advanced Placement exam preparation; honors section; independent study; study at local college for college credit; ESL (14 students enrolled).

College Admission Counseling 143 students graduated in 2015; 140 went to college, including Cornell University. Other: 1 went to work, 2 entered military service. Median SAT critical reading: 500, median SAT math: 470. 13% scored over 600 on SAT critical reading, 16% scored over 600 on SAT math.

Student Life Upper grades have uniform requirement, student council. Discipline rests primarily with faculty. Attendance at religious services is required.

Summer Programs Remediation, enrichment, advancement, sports, art/fine arts programs offered; session focuses on remediation and advancement; held on campus; accepts boys and girls; open to students from other schools. 300 students usually enrolled. 2016 schedule: June 26 to July 30. Application deadline: May 20.

Tuition and Aid Day student tuition: $7100–$14,000. Tuition installment plan (Insured Tuition Payment Plan, FACTS Tuition Payment Plan, monthly payment plans, individually arranged payment plans, discounts for annual and semi-annual payments). Tuition reduction for siblings, need-based scholarship grants available. In 2015–16, 11% of upper-school students received aid. Total amount of financial aid awarded in 2015–16: $120,000.

Admissions Traditional secondary-level entrance grade is 9. For fall 2015, 275 students applied for upper-level admission, 238 were accepted, 212 enrolled. High School Placement Test required. Deadline for receipt of application materials: none. Application fee required: $130. On-campus interview recommended.

Athletics Interscholastic: baseball (boys), basketball (b,g), cheering (g), cross-country running (b,g), football (b), golf (b,g), soccer (b,g), softball (g), swimming and diving (b,g), tennis (b,g), track and field (b,g), volleyball (b,g), wrestling (b); coed interscholastic: cross-country running, equestrian sports, weight lifting. 3 PE instructors, 15 coaches.

Computers Computers are regularly used in journalism, newspaper, video film production, yearbook classes. Computer resources include on-campus library services, Internet access, wireless campus network, Internet filtering or blocking technology, iPad school. Campus intranet and computer access in designated common areas are available to students. Students grades are available online. The school has a published electronic and media policy.

Contact Ms. Beverly A. Wilson, Director of Tuition and Enrollment. 951-275-5861. Fax: 951-781-9020. E-mail: bwilson@ndhsriverside.org. Website: www.notredameriverside.org

NOTRE DAME HIGH SCHOOL

596 South Second Street
San Jose, California 95112

Head of School: Mrs. Mary Elizabeth Riley

General Information Girls' day college-preparatory, arts, religious studies, and technology school, affiliated with Roman Catholic Church. Grades 9–12. Founded: 1851. Setting: urban. 2-acre campus. 4 buildings on campus. Approved or accredited by Western Association of Schools and Colleges, Western Catholic Education Association, and California Department of Education. Endowment: $8.8 million. Total enrollment: 631. Upper school average class size: 24. Upper school faculty-student ratio: 1:11. There are 204 required school days per year for Upper School students. Upper School students typically attend 5 days per week. The average school day consists of 6 hours and 55 minutes.

Upper School Student Profile Grade 9: 166 students (166 girls); Grade 10: 168 students (168 girls); Grade 11: 148 students (148 girls); Grade 12: 149 students (149 girls). 51% of students are Roman Catholic.

Faculty School total: 56. In upper school: 8 men, 48 women; 52 have advanced degrees.

Subjects Offered Advanced biology, advanced chemistry, Advanced Placement courses, algebra, art, ASB Leadership, athletics, band, Basic programming, biology, biology-AP, calculus-AP, campus ministry, ceramics, chemistry, chorus, Christian and Hebrew scripture, college admission preparation, computer programming, computer science, creative writing, dance, decision making skills, digital photography, drama, drama performance, economics, English, English language and composition-AP, English literature, English literature and composition-AP, environmental science-AP, film and literature, fine arts, French, French language-AP, French literature-AP, geography, geometry, global studies, government/civics, healthful living, honors algebra, honors English, honors geometry, honors U.S. history, honors world history, journalism, library research, library skills, mathematics, modern world history, moral and social development, musical theater, painting, peer counseling, peer ministry, philosophy, photography, physical education, physical fitness, physics, post-calculus, pre-calculus, psychology, psychology-AP, public speaking, religion, research skills, robotics, science, service learning/internship, social justice, social psychology, social studies, Spanish, Spanish language-AP, Spanish literature-AP, speech and debate, statistics, study skills, theater, trigonometry, U.S. government, U.S. government and politics-AP, U.S. history, U.S. history-AP, video film production, Web site design, women in society, world history, world history-AP, world religions, yearbook.

Graduation Requirements Arts and fine arts (art, music, dance, drama), English, foreign language, mathematics, physical education (includes health), religion (includes Bible studies and theology), science, social studies (includes history), community service learning program.

Special Academic Programs 11 Advanced Placement exams for which test preparation is offered; honors section; independent study; study at local college for college credit.

College Admission Counseling 155 students graduated in 2015; 153 went to college, including Chapman University; Loyola Marymount University; San Jose State University; Seattle University. Other: 1 entered military service, 1 had other specific plans. Mean SAT critical reading: 590, mean SAT math: 567, mean SAT writing: 607. 47% scored over 600 on SAT critical reading, 43% scored over 600 on SAT math, 54% scored over 600 on SAT writing.

Student Life Upper grades have uniform requirement, student council, honor system. Discipline rests primarily with faculty. Attendance at religious services is required.

Summer Programs Remediation, enrichment, advancement programs offered; session focuses on enrichment/advancement; held on campus; accepts boys and girls; open to students from other schools. 125 students usually enrolled. 2016 schedule: June to July.

Tuition and Aid Day student tuition: $16,470. Tuition installment plan (FACTS Tuition Payment Plan, annual payment plan, 2-payment plan). Merit scholarship grants, need-based scholarship grants, individual sponsored grants available. In 2015–16, 23% of upper-school students received aid; total upper-school merit-scholarship money awarded: $8000. Total amount of financial aid awarded in 2015–16: $1,200,000.

Admissions Traditional secondary-level entrance grade is 9. For fall 2015, 432 students applied for upper-level admission, 327 were accepted, 169 enrolled. High School Placement Test required. Deadline for receipt of application materials: January 13. Application fee required: $100.

Athletics Interscholastic: basketball, cross-country running, golf, lacrosse, soccer, softball, swimming and diving, tennis, track and field, volleyball; intramural: badminton, basketball, cheering, volleyball. 2 PE instructors, 25 coaches, 2 athletic trainers.

Computers Computers are regularly used in all academic, computer applications, English, foreign language, graphic design, history, journalism, mathematics, religious studies, science, social studies, Web site design, yearbook classes. Computer network features include on-campus library services, online commercial services, Internet access, wireless campus network, Internet filtering or blocking technology. Student e-mail accounts are available to students. Students grades are available online. The school has a published electronic and media policy.

Contact Ms. Susana Garcia, Vice Principal, Enrollment and Public Relations. 408-294-1113 Ext. 2159. Fax: 408-293-9779. E-mail: sgarcia@ndsj.org. Website: www.ndsj.org

NOTRE DAME HIGH SCHOOL

910 North Eastern Avenue
Crowley, Louisiana 70526

Head of School: Mrs. Cindy Istre

General Information Coeducational day college-preparatory, arts, vocational, religious studies, and technology school, affiliated with Roman Catholic Church. Grades 9–12. Founded: 1967. Setting: small town. Nearest major city is Lafayette. 10-acre campus. 7 buildings on campus. Approved or accredited by Southern Association of Colleges and Schools and Louisiana Department of Education. Total enrollment: 450. Upper school average class size: 25. Upper school faculty-student ratio: 1:25. There are 178 required school days per year for Upper School students. Upper School students typically attend 5 days per week. The average school day consists of 7 hours and 15 minutes.

Upper School Student Profile 99% of students are Roman Catholic.

Faculty School total: 38. In upper school: 13 men, 25 women; 9 have advanced degrees.

Subjects Offered Accounting, adolescent issues, advanced math, agriculture, algebra, American history, anatomy and physiology, ancient world history, art, athletics, baseball, basketball, biology, calculus, chemistry, civics/free enterprise, computer applications, computer technologies, dance, drama, driver education, early childhood, English, environmental science, family and consumer science, fine arts, food and nutrition, French, geometry, health education, honors algebra, honors English, honors geometry, honors U.S. history, honors world history, keyboarding, physical education, physical science, physics, pre-calculus, psychology, publications, religion, softball, Spanish, speech, study skills, swimming, tennis, theater, track and field, U.S. history, volleyball, world history, yearbook.

Special Academic Programs Honors section; independent study; study at local college for college credit; academic accommodation for the gifted.

College Admission Counseling 108 students graduated in 2015; 104 went to college, including Louisiana State University and Agricultural & Mechanical College; Louisiana State University at Eunice; University of Louisiana at Lafayette. Other: 3 went to work, 1 entered military service.

Student Life Upper grades have uniform requirement, student council. Discipline rests primarily with faculty. Attendance at religious services is required.

Summer Programs Sports programs offered; session focuses on training and fitness; held on campus; accepts boys and girls; not open to students from other schools.

Tuition and Aid Tuition installment plan (The Tuition Plan, monthly payment plans). Tuition reduction for siblings available.

Admissions ACT or Explore required. Deadline for receipt of application materials: none. No application fee required. Interview required.

Athletics Interscholastic: baseball (boys), basketball (b,g), cheering (g), cross-country running (b,g), dance squad (g), football (b), softball (g), tennis (b,g), track and field (b,g), volleyball (g); coed interscholastic: drill team, golf, soccer, swimming and diving. 12 coaches, 2 athletic trainers.

Computers Computers are regularly used in computer applications, English classes. Computer network features include on-campus library services, Internet access, Internet filtering or blocking technology. Students grades are available online.

Contact Mr. Nolan Theriot, Dean of Students. 337-783-3519. Fax: 337-788-2115. Website: www.ndpios.com

NOTRE DAME HIGH SCHOOL

320 East Ripa Avenue
St. Louis, Missouri 63125-2897

Head of School: Dr. Meghan Bohac

General Information Girls' day college-preparatory, arts, business, religious studies, bilingual studies, and technology school, affiliated with Roman Catholic Church; primarily serves students with learning disabilities, individuals with Attention Deficit Disorder, individuals with emotional and behavioral problems, and dyslexic students. Grades 9–12. Founded: 1934. Setting: suburban. 40-acre campus. 3 buildings on campus. Approved or accredited by North Central Association of Colleges and Schools and Missouri Department of Education. Total enrollment: 205. Upper school average class size: 16. Upper school faculty-student ratio: 1:12. There are 180 required school days per year for Upper School students. Upper School students typically attend 5 days per week. The average school day consists of 7 hours.

Upper School Student Profile Grade 9: 55 students (55 girls); Grade 10: 50 students (50 girls); Grade 11: 49 students (49 girls); Grade 12: 51 students (51 girls). 89% of students are Roman Catholic.

Faculty School total: 44. In upper school: 8 men, 36 women; 20 have advanced degrees.

Subjects Offered 3-dimensional art, ACT preparation, acting, advanced biology, advanced chemistry, advanced math, African-American literature, algebra, American history, American history-AP, American literature, analytic geometry, anatomy and physiology, applied music, art, arts, basketball, Bible studies, biology, botany, British literature, broadcast journalism, business, business education, business law, calculus, calculus-AP, career/college preparation, ceramics, chemistry, chemistry-AP, child development, Chinese, choir, choral music, choreography, chorus, Christian and Hebrew scripture, Christian education, Christian ethics, Christian scripture, Christian studies, Christian testament, Christianity, church history, civics, civil rights, Civil War, civil war history, college admission preparation, college counseling, college placement, college planning, college writing, communication arts, communication skills, communications, community service, composition-AP, computer applications, computer art, computer education, computer graphics, computer literacy, computer multimedia, computer programming, computer science, computer skills, computer technologies, concert choir, constitutional history of U.S., contemporary issues, costumes and make-up, creative writing, culinary arts, dance, death and loss, debate, developmental language skills, developmental math, digital art, digital imaging, digital photography, drama, drama workshop, drawing, drawing and design, early childhood, earth science, ecology, economics, economics and history, English, English literature, English literature and composition-AP, English literature-AP, environmental geography, environmental science, ethics, European history, exercise science, expository writing, fabric arts, family and consumer science, family living, family studies, fashion, fiction, film and literature, finance, fine arts, food and nutrition, foods, foreign language, forensics, French as a second language, freshman seminar, gardening, general science, geography, geology, geometry, global studies, government, government and politics-AP, government/civics, grammar, graphic design, guidance, health, health education, health enhancement, health science, histology, historical research, history, history of architecture, history-AP, home economics, honors English, honors U.S. history, human sexuality, independent study, interdisciplinary studies, intro to computers, journalism, keyboarding, law, leadership, leadership and service, library, library research, library skills, literary genres, marketing, mathematics, media literacy, music, music appreciation, music for dance, music theater, musical productions, musical theater, musical theater dance, newspaper, novels, nutrition, oral communications, parent/child development, participation in sports, peace education, peer ministry, performing arts, personal finance, photography, physical education, physics, playwriting and directing, practical arts, pre-calculus, public speaking, reading/study skills, religion, religious education, religious studies, science, science and technology, sculpture, senior seminar, social studies, society, politics and law, sociology, softball, sophomore skills, Spanish, Spanish-AP, speech, speech and debate, sports, stage design, statistics, student government, study skills, theater, theater arts, trigonometry, typing, U.S. government, U.S. government and politics, U.S. history, U.S. history-AP, vocal music, volleyball, wind ensemble, world civilizations, world cultures, world geography, world governments, world history, world history-AP, world literature, world religions, world religions, world studies, writing, writing, yearbook, zoology.

Graduation Requirements Arts and fine arts (art, music, dance, drama), athletics, business skills (includes word processing), computer science, English, mathematics, physical education (includes health), religion (includes Bible studies and theology), science, social studies (includes history), service hour requirement. Community service is required.

Special Academic Programs Advanced Placement exam preparation; honors section; accelerated programs; independent study; study at local college for college credit; academic accommodation for the gifted, the musically talented, and the artistically talented; remedial reading and/or remedial writing; remedial math; programs in English, mathematics; general development for dyslexic students.

College Admission Counseling 61 students graduated in 2015; all went to college, including Fontbonne University; Missouri State University; Rockhurst University; St. Louis Community College at Meramec; University of Missouri; Webster University.

Student Life Upper grades have uniform requirement, student council, honor system. Discipline rests primarily with faculty. Attendance at religious services is required.

Summer Programs Enrichment, sports, art/fine arts programs offered; held on campus; accepts girls; open to students from other schools. 2016 schedule: June 6 to July 15.

Tuition and Aid Day student tuition: $11,300. Tuition installment plan (FACTS Tuition Payment Plan, monthly payment plans, individually arranged payment plans, quarterly payment plan). Tuition reduction for siblings, merit scholarship grants, need-based scholarship grants, tuition reduction for children of faculty and staff, reciprocal tuition agreement consortium, tuition reduction for local Emergency Responders available. In 2015–16, 31% of upper-school students received aid; total upper-school merit-scholarship money awarded: $10,000.

Admissions Traditional secondary-level entrance grade is 9. Any standardized test or Iowa Tests of Basic Skills required. Deadline for receipt of application materials: none. No application fee required. Interview required.

Athletics Interscholastic: basketball, cheering, cross-country running, diving, field hockey, golf, lacrosse, racquetball, soccer, softball, swimming and diving, tennis, track and field, volleyball; intramural: aerobics/dance, cheering, cross-country running, dance, fitness, flag football, modern dance, walking. 2 PE instructors, 9 coaches, 1 athletic trainer.

Computers Computers are regularly used in business skills, English, journalism, mathematics, newspaper, writing, yearbook classes. Computer network features include on-campus library services, online commercial services, Internet access, wireless campus network, Internet filtering or blocking technology. Campus intranet, student e-mail accounts, and computer access in designated common areas are available to students. Students grades are available online. The school has a published electronic and media policy.

Contact Ms. Katie Mallette, Director of Admissions. 314-544-1015 Ext. 1104. Fax: 314-544-8003. E-mail: mallk@ndhs.net. Website: www.ndhs.net

NOTRE DAME HIGH SCHOOL

601 Lawrence Road
Lawrenceville, New Jersey 08648

Head of School: Mr. Barry Edward Breen and Ms. Mary Liz Ivins

General Information Coeducational day college-preparatory school, affiliated with Roman Catholic Church. Grades 9–12. Founded: 1957. Setting: suburban. Nearest major city is Trenton. 100-acre campus. 1 building on campus. Approved or accredited by National Catholic Education Association and New Jersey Department of Education. Total enrollment: 1,292. Upper school average class size: 23. Upper school faculty-student ratio: 1:13. There are 180 required school days per year for Upper School students. Upper School students typically attend 5 days per week. The average school day consists of 6 hours and 30 minutes.

Upper School Student Profile Grade 9: 324 students (183 boys, 141 girls); Grade 10: 269 students (124 boys, 145 girls); Grade 11: 359 students (178 boys, 181 girls); Grade 12: 340 students (169 boys, 171 girls). 80% of students are Roman Catholic.

Faculty School total: 82. In upper school: 34 men, 48 women; 41 have advanced degrees.

Subjects Offered 20th century history, 3-dimensional art, 3-dimensional design, accounting, acting, advanced chemistry, advanced computer applications, advanced math, Advanced Placement courses, algebra, American government, American literature, ancient world history, applied music, art, art and culture, art-AP, athletics, Basic programming, Bible studies, biology, biology-AP, British literature, business, business applications, business studies, calculus, calculus-AP, campus ministry, Catholic belief and practice, ceramics, chemistry, chemistry-AP, choir, chorus, Christian doctrine, community service, comparative religion, computer applications, computer science, concert band, concert choir, constitutional law, contemporary issues, creative writing, dance, dance performance, digital music, discrete mathematics, drama, driver education, ecology, environmental systems, economics, economics-AP, English, English composition, English language and composition-AP, English literature and composition-AP, English literature-AP, environmental science-AP, etymology, European history-AP, exercise science, film appreciation, film studies, filmmaking, finance, first aid, French, French-AP, geometry, German, German literature, government-AP, health education, honors algebra, honors English, honors world history, independent study, Italian, Japanese, jazz band, journalism, kinesiology, language-AP, Latin, law, law and the legal system, leadership and service, leadership education training, literature and composition-AP, literature-AP, macro/microeconomics-AP, madrigals, Mandarin, math review, media communications, media literacy, music theory, newspaper, orchestra, painting, peer counseling, peer ministry, personal finance, philosophy, photography, physical education, physics, physics-AP, piano, portfolio art, pottery, pre-algebra, pre-calculus, probability and statistics, psychology, psychology-AP, public speaking, reading/study skills, religion, religion and culture, robotics, Russian, SAT preparation, scripture, senior internship, senior project, service learning/internship, sociology, Spanish, Spanish literature, Spanish-AP, speech and debate, sports medicine, statistics-AP, strings, studio art-AP, U.S. government, U.S. government and politics-AP, U.S. history, U.S. history-AP, U.S. literature, United States government-AP, Web site design, weight training, women spirituality and faith, world history, world literature, writing.

Graduation Requirements Biology, English, foreign language, integrated technology fundamentals, lab science, mathematics, physical education (includes health), religion (includes Bible studies and theology), U.S. history, world history, service-learning. Community service is required.

Special Academic Programs 15 Advanced Placement exams for which test preparation is offered; honors section; independent study; study at local college for college credit; remedial reading and/or remedial writing; remedial math; ESL (19 students enrolled).

College Admission Counseling 322 students graduated in 2015; 319 went to college, including Penn State University Park; Rutgers, The State University of New Jersey, New Brunswick; Saint Joseph's University; Seton Hall University; University of Pittsburgh. Other: 1 went to work, 2 entered military service. Mean SAT critical reading: 536, mean SAT math: 536, mean SAT writing: 531, mean combined SAT: 1603.

Student Life Upper grades have uniform requirement, student council, honor system. Discipline rests primarily with faculty. Attendance at religious services is required.

Summer Programs Enrichment, advancement, sports, art/fine arts, computer instruction programs offered; session focuses on sports, arts, academic and writing camps, college application seminar; held on campus; accepts boys and girls; open to students from other schools. 775 students usually enrolled. 2016 schedule: June 20 to August 19. Application deadline: June 17.

Tuition and Aid Day student tuition: $12,965. Tuition installment plan (Private School Aid Service). Tuition reduction for siblings, need-based scholarship grants

available. In 2015–16, 10% of upper-school students received aid. Total amount of financial aid awarded in 2015–16: $700,000.

Admissions Traditional secondary-level entrance grade is 9. For fall 2015, 550 students applied for upper-level admission, 430 were accepted, 324 enrolled. Scholastic Testing Service High School Placement Test required. Deadline for receipt of application materials: December 1. Application fee required: $50. On-campus interview required.

Athletics Interscholastic: baseball (boys), basketball (b,g), cheering (g), cross-country running (b,g), dance (g), field hockey (g), football (b), golf (b,g), ice hockey (b), indoor track (b,g), lacrosse (b,g), soccer (b,g), softball (g), swimming and diving (b,g), tennis (b,g), track and field (b,g), volleyball (g), winter (indoor) track (b,g), wrestling (b); intramural: touch football (g), volleyball (b,g); coed interscholastic: cheering, dance, diving, fitness, strength & conditioning; coed intramural: crew, Frisbee, outdoor activities, outdoor recreation, physical fitness, ultimate Frisbee, volleyball, weight lifting, weight training. 10 PE instructors, 86 coaches, 1 athletic trainer.

Computers Computers are regularly used in all academic classes. Computer network features include on-campus library services, online commercial services, Internet access, wireless campus network, Internet filtering or blocking technology. Campus intranet, student e-mail accounts, and computer access in designated common areas are available to students. Students grades are available online. The school has a published electronic and media policy.

Contact Ms. Peggy Miller, Director of Enrollment Management. 609-882-7900 Ext. 139. Fax: 609-882-6599. E-mail: miller@ndnj.org. Website: www.ndnj.org

NOTRE DAME HIGH SCHOOL

1400 Maple Avenue
Elmira, New York 14904

Head of School: Sr. Mary Walter Hickey

General Information Coeducational day college-preparatory, arts, religious studies, and technology school, affiliated with Roman Catholic Church. Grades 7–12. Founded: 1954. Setting: suburban. Nearest major city is Binghamton. 30-acre campus. 1 building on campus. Approved or accredited by Mercy Secondary Education Association, Middle States Association of Colleges and Schools, National Catholic Education Association, and New York Department of Education. Member of Secondary School Admission Test Board. Total enrollment: 373. Upper school average class size: 20. Upper school faculty-student ratio: 1:15. There are 180 required school days per year for Upper School students. Upper School students typically attend 5 days per week. The average school day consists of 5 hours and 30 minutes.

Upper School Student Profile Grade 7: 50 students (22 boys, 28 girls); Grade 8: 58 students (33 boys, 25 girls); Grade 9: 66 students (30 boys, 36 girls); Grade 10: 75 students (40 boys, 35 girls); Grade 11: 67 students (33 boys, 34 girls); Grade 12: 57 students (23 boys, 34 girls). 80% of students are Roman Catholic.

Faculty School total: 35. In upper school: 13 men, 22 women; 19 have advanced degrees.

Subjects Offered Art, arts, band, biology, calculus, ceramics, chemistry, chemistry-AP, Chinese, choir, computer literacy, creative writing, drama, drawing, earth science, English, English-AP, fine arts, government/civics, health, human development, mathematics, multimedia, music history, music theory, painting, physical education, physics, portfolio art, pre-calculus, psychology, public speaking, religion, science, social studies, Spanish, studio art, theology.

Graduation Requirements Arts and fine arts (art, music, dance, drama), English, language, mathematics, physical education (includes health), religion (includes Bible studies and theology), science, social studies (includes history).

Special Academic Programs Advanced Placement exam preparation; honors section; study at local college for college credit; academic accommodation for the gifted and the artistically talented; remedial reading and/or remedial writing; remedial math.

College Admission Counseling 55 students graduated in 2015; 54 went to college, including Cornell University; Harvard University; Rochester Institute of Technology; The Catholic University of America; University of Notre Dame. Other: 1 entered military service. Median SAT critical reading: 563, median SAT math: 582, median SAT writing: 547, median composite ACT: 26.

Student Life Upper grades have uniform requirement, student council. Discipline rests primarily with faculty. Attendance at religious services is required.

Tuition and Aid Day student tuition: $8650. Tuition installment plan (monthly payment plans, local bank-arranged plan). Tuition reduction for siblings, merit scholarship grants, need-based scholarship grants available. In 2015–16, 60% of upper-school students received aid; total upper-school merit-scholarship money awarded: $2000. Total amount of financial aid awarded in 2015–16: $600,000.

Admissions Traditional secondary-level entrance grade is 9. Scholastic Testing Service High School Placement Test required. Deadline for receipt of application materials: none. Application fee required: $100. Interview recommended.

Athletics Interscholastic: baseball (boys), basketball (b,g), bowling (b,g), cross-country running (b,g), football (b), golf (b), lacrosse (b), soccer (b,g), softball (g), swimming and diving (b,g), tennis (b,g), track and field (b,g). 3 PE instructors, 27 coaches, 1 athletic trainer.

Computers Computer network features include on-campus library services, Internet access, wireless campus network, Internet filtering or blocking technology. Campus intranet, student e-mail accounts, and computer access in designated common areas are

available to students. Students grades are available online. The school has a published electronic and media policy.

Contact Mrs. Jennifer Roberts-O'Brian, Director of Admissions. 607-734-2267 Ext. 316. Fax: 607-737-8903. E-mail: obrianj@notredamehighschool.com. Website: www.notredamehighschool.com

NOTRE DAME HIGH SCHOOL

2701 Vermont Avenue

Chattanooga, Tennessee 37404

Head of School: Mr. George D. Valadie

General Information Coeducational day college-preparatory, arts, religious studies, technology, and Microsoft IT Academy Certification school, affiliated with Roman Catholic Church. Grades 9–12. Founded: 1876. Setting: urban. 22-acre campus. 3 buildings on campus. Approved or accredited by Southern Association of Colleges and Schools and Tennessee Department of Education. Endowment: $750,000. Total enrollment: 423. Upper school average class size: 20. Upper school faculty-student ratio: 1:10. There are 180 required school days per year for Upper School students. Upper School students typically attend 5 days per week. The average school day consists of 5 hours and 50 minutes.

Upper School Student Profile Grade 9: 113 students (53 boys, 60 girls); Grade 10: 115 students (58 boys, 57 girls); Grade 11: 99 students (43 boys, 56 girls); Grade 12: 96 students (42 boys, 54 girls). 77% of students are Roman Catholic.

Faculty School total: 39. In upper school: 15 men, 24 women; 25 have advanced degrees.

Subjects Offered 3-dimensional art, ACT preparation, Advanced Placement courses, algebra, American history-AP, American literature, anatomy, anatomy and physiology, art-AP, band, biology, biology-AP, British literature, calculus, Catholic belief and practice, chemistry, choir, civics, conceptual physics, creative dance, drama, economics, electives, English composition, English literature, English-AP, environmental science-AP, European history-AP, foreign language, French, geometry, German, government, government/civics, health and wellness, history-AP, honors algebra, honors English, honors geometry, honors U.S. history, honors world history, Latin, physics, religion, Spanish, U.S. government and politics-AP, weight training, wellness, world geography, world history, world history-AP, writing, yoga.

Special Academic Programs Advanced Placement exam preparation; honors section; independent study; study at local college for college credit.

College Admission Counseling 104 students graduated in 2015; all went to college, including Auburn University; Middle Tennessee State University; The University of Tennessee; The University of Tennessee at Chattanooga; University of Georgia.

Student Life Upper grades have uniform requirement, student council, honor system. Discipline rests primarily with faculty. Attendance at religious services is required.

Summer Programs Enrichment, sports, art/fine arts programs offered; session focuses on enrichment; held on campus; accepts boys and girls; open to students from other schools. 250 students usually enrolled. 2016 schedule: June 1 to July 24. Application deadline: April 1.

Tuition and Aid Day student tuition: $11,038–$14,592. Tuition installment plan (Insured Tuition Payment Plan, FACTS Tuition Payment Plan, monthly payment plans, individually arranged payment plans). Tuition reduction for siblings, need-based scholarship grants available. In 2015–16, 30% of upper-school students received aid. Total amount of financial aid awarded in 2015–16: $378,271.

Admissions Traditional secondary-level entrance grade is 9. ACT-Explore required. Deadline for receipt of application materials: none. Application fee required: $125. On-campus interview required.

Athletics Interscholastic: aerobics/dance (girls), baseball (b), basketball (b,g), bowling (b,g), cross-country running (b,g), dance (g), dance squad (g), dance team (g), diving (b,g), football (b), golf (b,g), modern dance (g), physical training (b,g), running (b,g), soccer (b,g), softball (g), swimming and diving (b,g), tennis (b,g), track and field (b,g), volleyball (g), weight training (b,g), wrestling (b); intramural: aerobics/dance (g), cheering (g), indoor soccer (b), indoor track (b,g), lacrosse (b,g); coed interscholastic: cheering, yoga; coed intramural: backpacking, canoeing/kayaking, climbing, crew, hiking/backpacking, kayaking, mountaineering, outdoors, rafting, rappelling, rock climbing, rowing, skiing (downhill), snowboarding, wall climbing. 3 PE instructors, 43 coaches, 1 athletic trainer.

Computers Computers are regularly used in information technology classes. Computer network features include on-campus library services, Internet access, wireless campus network, Internet filtering or blocking technology, language software labs, Microsoft IT Academy Training. Student e-mail accounts and computer access in designated common areas are available to students. Students grades are available online. The school has a published electronic and media policy.

Contact Ms. Laura Goodhard, Admissions Director. 423-624-4618 Ext. 1004. Fax: 423-624-4621. E-mail: admissions@myndhs.com. Website: www.myndhs.com

NOTRE DAME JUNIOR/SENIOR HIGH SCHOOL

60 Spangenburg Avenue

East Stroudsburg, Pennsylvania 18301-2799

Head of School: Mr. Jeffrey Neill Lyons

General Information Coeducational day college-preparatory, arts, and religious studies school, affiliated with Roman Catholic Church. Grades 7–12. Founded: 1967. Setting: suburban. 40-acre campus. 4 buildings on campus. Approved or accredited by Middle States Association of Colleges and Schools, National Catholic Education Association, and Pennsylvania Department of Education. Total enrollment: 317. Upper school average class size: 25. Upper school faculty-student ratio: 1:15. There are 180 required school days per year for Upper School students. Upper School students typically attend 5 days per week. The average school day consists of 6 hours and 30 minutes.

Upper School Student Profile Grade 7: 38 students (15 boys, 23 girls); Grade 8: 44 students (22 boys, 22 girls); Grade 9: 59 students (34 boys, 25 girls); Grade 10: 49 students (22 boys, 27 girls); Grade 11: 52 students (17 boys, 35 girls); Grade 12: 75 students (35 boys, 40 girls). 75% of students are Roman Catholic.

Faculty School total: 24. In upper school: 5 men, 18 women; 12 have advanced degrees.

Graduation Requirements Lab/keyboard, mathematics, moral theology, physical education (includes health), physical science, religion (includes Bible studies and theology), senior project, U.S. history, U.S. literature, word processing, world cultures, world religions.

Special Academic Programs Advanced Placement exam preparation; honors section; study at local college for college credit.

College Admission Counseling 43 students graduated in 2015; 42 went to college, including Marywood University; Mount St. Mary's University; Penn State University Park; Saint Joseph's University; Temple University; The University of Scranton. Other: 1 entered a postgraduate year. Median SAT critical reading: 500, median SAT math: 460, median SAT writing: 500, median combined SAT: 1460. 10% scored over 600 on SAT critical reading, 15% scored over 600 on SAT math, 10% scored over 600 on SAT writing, 25% scored over 1800 on combined SAT.

Student Life Upper grades have uniform requirement, student council. Discipline rests primarily with faculty. Attendance at religious services is required.

Tuition and Aid Tuition installment plan (FACTS Tuition Payment Plan). Tuition reduction for siblings, need-based scholarship grants available. In 2015–16, 35% of upper-school students received aid.

Admissions Traditional secondary-level entrance grade is 7. Achievement tests or TerraNova required. Deadline for receipt of application materials: May 1. No application fee required. Interview required.

Athletics Interscholastic: baseball (boys), basketball (b,g), field hockey (g), soccer (b,g), softball (g), tennis (b,g); coed interscholastic: golf, soccer; coed intramural: cross-country running, strength & conditioning. 2 PE instructors, 15 coaches, 1 athletic trainer.

Computers Computer network features include on-campus library services, Internet access, Internet filtering or blocking technology. The school has a published electronic and media policy.

Contact Mr. Jeffrey Neill Lyons, Principal. 570-421-0466. Fax: 570-476-0629. E-mail: principal@ndhigh.org. Website: www.ndhigh.org

OAK GROVE SCHOOL

220 West Lomita Avenue

Ojai, California 93023

Head of School: Meredy Benson Rice

General Information Coeducational boarding and day college-preparatory and arts school. Boarding grades 9–12, day grades PK–12. Founded: 1975. Setting: small town. Nearest major city is Los Angeles. Students are housed in coed dormitories. 150-acre campus. 6 buildings on campus. Approved or accredited by The Association of Boarding Schools, Western Association of Schools and Colleges, and California Department of Education. Member of National Association of Independent Schools and Secondary School Admission Test Board. Endowment: $1.2 million. Total enrollment: 227. Upper school average class size: 15. Upper school faculty-student ratio: 1:7. There are 170 required school days per year for Upper School students. Upper School students typically attend 5 days per week. The average school day consists of 8 hours and 30 minutes.

Upper School Student Profile 35% of students are boarding students. 83% are state residents. 2 states are represented in upper school student body. 23% are international students. International students from China, India, Japan, Mexico, Republic of Korea, and Viet Nam.

Faculty School total: 35. In upper school: 6 men, 5 women; 7 have advanced degrees; 2 reside on campus.

Subjects Offered Algebra, American history, American literature, anatomy, art, art history, biology, calculus, ceramics, chemistry, communications, community service, comparative religion, computer science, drama, earth science, economics, English, English literature, ethics, film and new technologies, fine arts, gardening, geography, geometry, global studies, history, horticulture, human development, inquiry into relationship, mathematics, music, permaculture, photography, physical education, physics, relationships, religion and culture, science, social studies, Spanish, studio art, theater, world cultures, world history, world literature.

Graduation Requirements Algebra, American history, arts and fine arts (art, music, dance, drama), backpacking, biology, chemistry, college admission preparation, comparative religion, economics and history, English, ethics and responsibility, foreign language, geometry, mathematics, science, social studies (includes history), Spanish, world religions, participation in camping and travel programs and sports, one year of visual and performing arts. Community service is required.

Special Academic Programs 3 Advanced Placement exams for which test preparation is offered; honors section; ESL (4 students enrolled).

College Admission Counseling 11 students graduated in 2014; 10 went to college, including Reed College; University of California, Berkeley; University of California, Davis; University of California, Santa Cruz; Washington University in St. Louis; Willamette University. Other: 1 had other specific plans. Mean SAT critical reading: 627, mean SAT math: 580, mean SAT writing: 617. 57% scored over 600 on SAT critical reading, 28% scored over 600 on SAT math, 42% scored over 600 on SAT writing.

Student Life Upper grades have student council, honor system. Discipline rests equally with students and faculty.

Tuition and Aid Day student tuition: $17,500; 7-day tuition and room/board: $39,320. Tuition installment plan (FACTS Tuition Payment Plan, annual and semiannual payment plans). Need-based scholarship grants, African-American scholarships available. In 2014–15, 40% of upper-school students received aid. Total amount of financial aid awarded in 2014–15: $80,000.

Admissions Traditional secondary-level entrance grade is 9. For fall 2014, 40 students applied for upper-level admission, 28 were accepted, 10 enrolled. SSAT or TOEFL or SLEP required. Deadline for receipt of application materials: none. Application fee required: $50. Interview required.

Athletics Interscholastic: soccer (boys, girls), volleyball (b,g); intramural: equestrian sports (g), soccer (b,g), volleyball (b,g); coed intramural: backpacking, fitness, hiking/backpacking, outdoor activities, outdoor education, outdoor skills, physical fitness, ropes courses, skiing (downhill), table tennis, tennis, wilderness. 1 PE instructor, 3 coaches.

Computers Computers are regularly used in art, ESL, graphic arts, history, independent study, library, mathematics, multimedia, photography, SAT preparation, science, technology, typing, writing, yearbook classes. Computer network features include on-campus library services, online commercial services, Internet access, wireless campus network, Internet filtering or blocking technology. Computer access in designated common areas is available to students.

Contact Joy Maguire-Parsons, Director of Admissions. 805-646-8236 Ext. 109. Fax: 805-646-6509. E-mail: enroll@oakgroveschool.org. Website: www.oakgroveschool.org

OAK HILL SCHOOL

86397 Eldon Schafer Drive
Eugene, Oregon 97405-9647

Head of School: Bob Sarkisian

General Information Coeducational day college-preparatory, arts, and technology school. Grades K–12. Founded: 1994. Setting: small town. 72-acre campus. 2 buildings on campus. Approved or accredited by Northwest Accreditation Commission, Northwest Association of Independent Schools, Northwest Association of Schools and Colleges, and Oregon Department of Education. Member of National Association of Independent Schools. Endowment: $100,000. Total enrollment: 151. Upper school average class size: 13. Upper school faculty-student ratio: 1:10. There are 177 required school days per year for Upper School students. Upper School students typically attend 5 days per week. The average school day consists of 7 hours.

Faculty School total: 26. In upper school: 6 men, 7 women; 10 have advanced degrees.

Subjects Offered Acting, advanced math, algebra, American literature, analytic geometry, anatomy, art, arts, band, calculus-AP, ceramics, chemistry, comparative government and politics, composition, computer education, drama performance, drawing and design, economics, English composition, English literature, English literature-AP, fitness, French, geometry, health education, history, independent study, Mandarin, outdoor education, physical education, pre-calculus, probability and statistics, Spanish, Spanish language-AP, Spanish literature-AP, speech communications, theater arts, U.S. government and politics, U.S. history, world history, writing.

Graduation Requirements Algebra, American government, American history, arts, computer skills, economics, English, English composition, foreign language, French, lab science, mathematics, physical education (includes health), science, Spanish, world history, 70 community service hours.

Special Academic Programs Advanced Placement exam preparation; honors section; academic accommodation for the gifted; ESL (13 students enrolled).

College Admission Counseling 6 students graduated in 2015; all went to college, including Oregon State University; Pomona College; Savannah College of Art and Design; Southern Oregon University; University of California, Berkeley; University of Oregon. Median SAT critical reading: 547, median SAT math: 612, median SAT writing: 547. 28% scored over 600 on SAT critical reading, 27% scored over 600 on SAT math, 28% scored over 600 on SAT writing.

Student Life Upper grades have specified standards of dress, student council, honor system. Discipline rests equally with students and faculty.

Summer Programs Remediation, enrichment, advancement, art/fine arts, computer instruction programs offered; session focuses on academics/curiosity; held on campus; accepts boys and girls; open to students from other schools. 2016 schedule: June 15 to August 28. Application deadline: none.

Tuition and Aid Day student tuition: $5000–$16,600. Tuition installment plan (monthly payment plans). Merit scholarship grants, need-based scholarship grants available. In 2015–16, 51% of upper-school students received aid; total upper-school merit-scholarship money awarded: $12,000. Total amount of financial aid awarded in 2015–16: $106,000.

Admissions Traditional secondary-level entrance grade is 9. Admissions testing or comprehensive educational evaluation required. Deadline for receipt of application materials: none. Application fee required: $100. Interview required.

Athletics Interscholastic: basketball (boys), volleyball (g); intramural: basketball (g), indoor soccer (b), volleyball (g); coed interscholastic: backpacking, canoeing/kayaking, cooperative games, cross-country running, fitness, hiking/backpacking, indoor track & field, juggling, kickball, outdoor skills, ropes courses, running, snowshoeing, touch football, track and field, wilderness survival; coed intramural: golf, outdoor education, physical training, strength & conditioning. 2 PE instructors, 1 coach.

Computers Computers are regularly used in desktop publishing, graphic arts, graphic design, information technology, introduction to technology, multimedia, publications, technology, video film production, Web site design, writing classes. Computer network features include Internet access, wireless campus network, Internet filtering or blocking technology, online homework calendars for each upper school class. Campus intranet, student e-mail accounts, and computer access in designated common areas are available to students. The school has a published electronic and media policy.

Contact James Pearson, Admissions Director. 541-744-0954 Ext. 105. Fax: 541-741-6968. E-mail: jpearson@oakhillschool.net. Website: www.oakhillschool.com

OAKLAND SCHOOL

Troy, Virginia
See Special Needs Schools section.

THE OAKRIDGE SCHOOL

5900 West Pioneer Parkway
Arlington, Texas 76013-2899

Head of School: Mr. Jonathan Kellam

General Information Coeducational day college-preparatory, arts, and technology school. Grades PS–12. Founded: 1979. Setting: suburban. 100-acre campus. 12 buildings on campus. Approved or accredited by Independent Schools Association of the Southwest, Independent Schools Council (UK), Independent Schools Joint Council, and Texas Department of Education. Member of National Association of Independent Schools. Endowment: $700,000. Total enrollment: 869. Upper school average class size: 16. Upper school faculty-student ratio: 1:11. There are 171 required school days per year for Upper School students. Upper School students typically attend 5 days per week. The average school day consists of 7 hours.

Upper School Student Profile Grade 6: 64 students (33 boys, 31 girls); Grade 7: 70 students (34 boys, 36 girls); Grade 8: 72 students (35 boys, 37 girls); Grade 9: 82 students (41 boys, 41 girls); Grade 10: 75 students (38 boys, 37 girls); Grade 11: 83 students (36 boys, 47 girls); Grade 12: 74 students (42 boys, 32 girls).

Faculty School total: 82. In upper school: 12 men, 14 women; 26 have advanced degrees.

Subjects Offered 3-dimensional art, acting, Advanced Placement courses, advanced studio art-AP, algebra, American history, American history-AP, American literature, anatomy, ancient world history, anthropology, archaeology, art, art history-AP, athletics, biology, British literature, calculus, calculus-AP, chemistry, chemistry-AP, Chinese, choir, choral music, college admission preparation, college counseling, college writing, community service, comparative religion, composition-AP, computer art, computer graphics, computer literacy, computer multimedia, computer science-AP, concert choir, creative writing, current events, desktop publishing, digital applications, digital art, digital imaging, digital photography, discrete mathematics, drama, drama performance, drama workshop, dramatic arts, drawing, drawing and design, economics, economics and history, English, English language and composition-AP, English literature and composition-AP, environmental science-AP, European civilization, European history-AP, expository writing, film and literature, fine arts, fractal geometry, French, French language-AP, French-AP, geometry, golf, government, government and politics-AP, government-AP, government/civics, graphic arts, graphic design, graphics, honors algebra, honors English, honors geometry, honors world history, human biology, independent study, language and composition, language arts, literature and composition-AP, modern European history-AP, modern world history, music theory, music theory-AP, musical productions, physics, physics-AP, play production, poetry, portfolio art, portfolio writing, pre-algebra, pre-calculus, probability and statistics, programming, public service, public speaking, reading/study skills, SAT preparation, SAT/ACT preparation, Spanish, Spanish-AP, strings, theater, track and field, U.S. government, U.S. government and politics, U.S. government and politics-AP, U.S. history, U.S. history-AP, United States government-AP, video, video communication, video film production, visual and performing arts, voice, voice ensemble, Web site design, weightlifting, world history.

Graduation Requirements Arts and fine arts (art, music, dance, drama), English, foreign language, mathematics, physical education (includes health), science, social studies (includes history), participation in six seasons of athletics, 60 hours of community service. Community service is required.

Special Academic Programs 21 Advanced Placement exams for which test preparation is offered; honors section; independent study; study at local college for college credit; study abroad; academic accommodation for the gifted, the musically talented, and the artistically talented.

College Admission Counseling 80 students graduated in 2014; all went to college, including Austin College; Oklahoma State University; Texas A&M University; Texas Christian University; The University of Texas at Austin; Vassar College. Mean SAT critical reading: 600, mean SAT math: 619, mean SAT writing: 595, mean combined SAT: 1814, mean composite ACT: 27.

Student Life Upper grades have uniform requirement, student council, honor system. Discipline rests primarily with faculty.

Tuition and Aid Day student tuition: $18,300. Tuition installment plan (FACTS Tuition Payment Plan, early discount option). Need-based scholarship grants available. In 2014–15, 22% of upper-school students received aid. Total amount of financial aid awarded in 2014–15: $523,375.

Admissions Traditional secondary-level entrance grade is 9. For fall 2014, 43 students applied for upper-level admission, 27 were accepted, 22 enrolled. ERB Reading and Math, ISEE, Otis-Lennon School Ability Test or SSAT, ERB, PSAT, SAT, PLAN or ACT required. Deadline for receipt of application materials: March 1. Application fee required: $75. Interview required.

Athletics Interscholastic: baseball (boys), basketball (b,g), cheering (b,g), cross-country running (b,g), equestrian sports (b,g), field hockey (g), football (b), golf (b,g), physical fitness (b,g), physical training (b,g), power lifting (b), soccer (b,g), softball (g), strength & conditioning (b,g), swimming and diving (b,g), tennis (b,g), track and field (b,g), volleyball (g), weight lifting (b), wrestling (b); intramural: equestrian sports (b,g), fitness (b,g), physical fitness (b,g), physical training (b,g), strength & conditioning (b,g), weight lifting (b), weight training (b); coed interscholastic: horseback riding; coed intramural: archery, horseback riding, outdoor activities, outdoor education, sailing. 7 PE instructors, 10 coaches, 2 athletic trainers.

Computers Computers are regularly used in art, English, foreign language, history, mathematics, programming, science, stock market, technology, video film production, Web site design, writing, yearbook classes. Computer network features include on-campus library services, online commercial services, Internet access, wireless campus network, Internet filtering or blocking technology. Campus intranet, student e-mail accounts, and computer access in designated common areas are available to students. Students grades are available online. The school has a published electronic and media policy.

Contact Dr. David Michael "Mike" Cobb Jr., Director of Admissions. 817-451-4994 Ext. 2708. Fax: 817-457-6681. E-mail: mcobb@theoakridgeschool.org. Website: www.theoakridgeschool.org

OAKWOOD FRIENDS SCHOOL

22 Spackenkill Road
Poughkeepsie, New York 12603

Head of School: Peter F. Baily

General Information Coeducational boarding and day college-preparatory and arts school, affiliated with Society of Friends. Boarding grades 9–12, day grades 6–12. Founded: 1796. Setting: suburban. Nearest major city is New York. Students are housed in single-sex dormitories. 63-acre campus. 22 buildings on campus. Approved or accredited by Friends Council on Education, New York State Association of Independent Schools, New York State Board of Regents, The Association of Boarding Schools, and New York Department of Education. Member of National Association of Independent Schools and Secondary School Admission Test Board. Endowment: $3 million. Total enrollment: 150. Upper school average class size: 12. Upper school faculty-student ratio: 1:4. There are 167 required school days per year for Upper School students. Upper School students typically attend 5 days per week. The average school day consists of 8 hours and 30 minutes.

Upper School Student Profile Grade 6: 6 students (2 boys, 4 girls); Grade 7: 6 students (5 boys, 1 girl); Grade 8: 5 students (3 boys, 2 girls); Grade 9: 32 students (14 boys, 18 girls); Grade 10: 40 students (20 boys, 20 girls); Grade 11: 36 students (24 boys, 12 girls); Grade 12: 25 students (10 boys, 15 girls). 58% of students are boarding students. 59% are state residents. 5 states are represented in upper school student body. 37% are international students. International students from China, Ghana, Russian Federation, Rwanda, Turkey, and Viet Nam; 5 other countries represented in student body. 1% of students are members of Society of Friends.

Faculty School total: 31. In upper school: 13 men, 18 women; 23 have advanced degrees; 24 reside on campus.

Subjects Offered 20th century American writers, 20th century world history, 3-dimensional design, acting, advanced biology, advanced chemistry, advanced math, Advanced Placement courses, algebra, American culture, American democracy, American foreign policy, American government, American history, American literature, American sign language, ancient history, anthropology, art, art history, biology, biology-

AP, calculus, ceramics, chemistry, chemistry-AP, community service, computer applications, conceptual physics, critical thinking, directing, drama, drawing, ecology, English, English literature, English-AP, ensembles, environmental science, ESL, ESL, European history, existentialism, expository writing, fashion, fine arts, French, French-AP, geometry, global studies, graphic arts, graphic design, Greek culture, health, health science, history, interdisciplinary studies, introduction to theater, Mandarin, mathematics, mathematics-AP, media arts, music, music theater, painting, photography, physical education, physics, playwriting and directing, pre-calculus, programming, psychology, public speaking, Quakerism and ethics, robotics, science, sculpture, social studies, Spanish, Spanish-AP, stage design, stagecraft, statistics-AP, theater, Web site design, world history, writing, yoga.

Graduation Requirements 3-dimensional design, advanced math, algebra, American history, arts and fine arts (art, music, dance, drama), biology, chemistry, computer literacy, conceptual physics, English, foreign language, geometry, health, interdisciplinary studies, physical education (includes health), Quakerism and ethics, U.S. history, world history, senior orientation trip in September, senior evaluation trip in June, community service. Community service is required.

Special Academic Programs 7 Advanced Placement exams for which test preparation is offered; independent study; programs in English, mathematics, general development for dyslexic students; special instructional classes for students with mild learning differences; ESL (20 students enrolled).

College Admission Counseling 31 students graduated in 2014; all went to college, including Boston University; Oberlin College; Penn State University Park; Rochester Institute of Technology; University of Southern California; Washington and Lee University. Mean SAT critical reading: 516, mean SAT math: 567, mean SAT writing: 538.

Student Life Upper grades have specified standards of dress, student council, honor system. Discipline rests equally with students and faculty. Attendance at religious services is required.

Tuition and Aid Day student tuition: $27,859; 5-day tuition and room/board: $42,422; 7-day tuition and room/board: $49,743. Tuition installment plan (FACTS Tuition Payment Plan, monthly payment plans). Tuition reduction for siblings, need-based scholarship grants available. In 2014–15, 38% of upper-school students received aid.

Admissions Traditional secondary-level entrance grade is 9. For fall 2014, 130 students applied for upper-level admission, 91 were accepted, 44 enrolled. TOEFL or writing sample required. Deadline for receipt of application materials: none. Application fee required: $50. Interview required.

Athletics Interscholastic: baseball (boys), basketball (b,g), cross-country running (b,g), Frisbee (b,g), independent competitive sports (b,g), running (b,g), soccer (b,g), softball (g), tennis (b,g), ultimate Frisbee (b,g), volleyball (g); coed interscholastic: cross-country running, Frisbee, running, swimming and diving, ultimate Frisbee; coed intramural: basketball, billiards, bowling, cooperative games, cross-country running, curling, fitness, fitness walking, hiking/backpacking, indoor soccer, jogging, kickball, martial arts, outdoor activities, physical fitness, physical training, ropes courses, running, skiing (downhill), snowboarding, strength & conditioning, table tennis, tai chi, ultimate Frisbee, volleyball, walking, weight lifting, weight training, whiffle ball, yoga.

Computers Computers are regularly used in English, foreign language, graphic design, history, photography, programming, science, Web site design, writing classes. Computer network features include on-campus library services, online commercial services, Internet access, wireless campus network, Internet filtering or blocking technology. Computer access in designated common areas is available to students. Students grades are available online. The school has a published electronic and media policy.

Contact Barbara Lonczak, Director of Admissions. 845-462-4200 Ext. 215. Fax: 845-462-4251. E-mail: blonczak@oakwoodfriends.org. Website: www.oakwoodfriends.org

OLDENBURG ACADEMY

1 Twister Circle
P.O.Box 200
Oldenburg, Indiana 47036

Head of School: Ms. Diane H. Laake

General Information Coeducational day college-preparatory, arts, and religious studies school, affiliated with Roman Catholic Church. Grades 9–12. Founded: 1852. Setting: small town. Nearest major city is Cincinnati, OH. 23-acre campus. 3 buildings on campus. Approved or accredited by North Central Association of Colleges and Schools and Indiana Department of Education. Total enrollment: 198. Upper school average class size: 15. Upper school faculty-student ratio: 1:12. There are 180 required school days per year for Upper School students. The average school day consists of 7 hours.

Upper School Student Profile Grade 9: 43 students (23 boys, 20 girls); Grade 10: 60 students (30 boys, 30 girls); Grade 11: 51 students (23 boys, 28 girls); Grade 12: 48 students (21 boys, 27 girls). 80% of students are Roman Catholic.

Faculty School total: 17. In upper school: 8 men, 9 women; 13 have advanced degrees.

Graduation Requirements 40 hours of community service.

Special Academic Programs Advanced Placement exam preparation; honors section; ESL (8 students enrolled).

College Admission Counseling Colleges students went to include Butler University; Indiana University Bloomington; Purdue University.

Student Life Upper grades have uniform requirement, student council, honor system. Discipline rests primarily with faculty. Attendance at religious services is required.

Tuition and Aid Day student tuition: $7925. Tuition installment plan (FACTS Tuition Payment Plan). Tuition reduction for siblings, merit scholarship grants, need-based scholarship grants available. In 2014–15, 57% of upper-school students received aid; total upper-school merit-scholarship money awarded: $25,000. Total amount of financial aid awarded in 2014–15: $65,000.

Admissions Traditional secondary-level entrance grade is 9. High School Placement Test (closed version) from Scholastic Testing Service required. Deadline for receipt of application materials: none. Application fee required: $350. Interview recommended.

Athletics Interscholastic: baseball (boys), basketball (b,g), cheering (g), cross-country running (b,g), dance (b,g), dance team (g), football (b), physical fitness (b,g), soccer (b,g), softball (g), swimming and diving (b,g), tennis (b,g), track and field (b,g), volleyball (g), weight lifting (b,g), weight training (b,g). 1 PE instructor, 9 coaches, 1 athletic trainer.

Computers Computer network features include on-campus library services, Internet access, wireless campus network, Internet filtering or blocking technology, one-to-one student iPad program. Campus intranet, student e-mail accounts, and computer access in designated common areas are available to students. Students grades are available online. The school has a published electronic and media policy.

Contact Mrs. Bettina Rose, Principal. 812-934-4440 Ext. 223. Fax: 812-934-4838. E-mail: brose@oldenburgacademy.org. Website: www.oldenburgacademy.org/

OLNEY FRIENDS SCHOOL

61830 Sandy Ridge Road
Barnesville, Ohio 43713

Head of School: Charlie Szumilas

General Information Coeducational boarding and day college-preparatory and technology school, affiliated with Society of Friends. Grades 9–12. Founded: 1837. Setting: small town. Nearest major city is Pittsburgh, PA. Students are housed in single-sex dormitories. 350-acre campus. 11 buildings on campus. Approved or accredited by Friends Council on Education, Independent Schools Association of the Central States, Midwest Association of Boarding Schools, Ohio Association of Independent Schools, The Association of Boarding Schools, and Ohio Department of Education. Member of National Association of Independent Schools. Endowment: $600,000. Total enrollment: 43. Upper school average class size: 8. Upper school faculty-student ratio: 1:3. There are 181 required school days per year for Upper School students. Upper School students typically attend 5 days per week. The average school day consists of 8 hours and 15 minutes.

Upper School Student Profile Grade 9: 6 students (3 boys, 3 girls); Grade 10: 8 students (5 boys, 3 girls); Grade 11: 12 students (9 boys, 3 girls); Grade 12: 17 students (9 boys, 8 girls). 97% of students are boarding students. 25% are state residents. 13 states are represented in upper school student body. 25% are international students. International students from China, Ecuador, Ethiopia, Germany, Republic of Korea, and Viet Nam; 1 other country represented in student body. 21% of students are members of Society of Friends.

Faculty School total: 13. In upper school: 9 men, 4 women; 8 have advanced degrees; 12 reside on campus.

Subjects Offered Advanced math, agriculture, agroecology, algebra, alternative physical education, ancient history, art, biology, calculus, calculus-AP, ceramics, chemistry, clayworking, college counseling, community service, drawing, engineering, English, English literature, English literature-AP, environmental science, ESL, fine arts, folk art, gardening, general science, geometry, global issues, government/civics, guitar, health, history, library research, library skills, mathematics, personal finance, photography, physical education, physics, religion, social studies, Spanish, theater, weight training, welding, wellness, Western civilization, woodworking, world literature.

Graduation Requirements Algebra, arts and fine arts (art, music, dance, drama), English, foreign language, general science, geometry, humanities, lab science, mathematics, physical education (includes health), pre-calculus, religion (includes Bible studies and theology), science, social studies (includes history), research graduation essay, practical skills and religion electives, must be accepted to a four year college or university. Community service is required.

Special Academic Programs Independent study; term-away projects; academic accommodation for the gifted, the musically talented, and the artistically talented; remedial reading and/or remedial writing; remedial math; ESL.

College Admission Counseling 13 students graduated in 2014; all went to college, including Earlham College; Goshen College; Marquette University; Rochester Institute of Technology; The Ohio State University. Median SAT critical reading: 540, median SAT math: 560. 33% scored over 600 on SAT critical reading, 33% scored over 600 on SAT math.

Student Life Upper grades have specified standards of dress, student council, honor system. Discipline rests equally with students and faculty. Attendance at religious services is required.

Tuition and Aid Day student tuition: $8900; 7-day tuition and room/board: $32,300. Tuition installment plan (FACTS Tuition Payment Plan, monthly payment plans, individually arranged payment plans). Merit scholarship grants, need-based scholarship grants, tuition discounts for children of faculty, tuition discounts for children of alumni, tuition discounts for students with a Quaker background available. In 2014–15, 65% of upper-school students received aid; total upper-school merit-scholarship money awarded: $40,000. Total amount of financial aid awarded in 2014–15: $411,900.

Admissions Traditional secondary-level entrance grade is 9. For fall 2014, 41 students applied for upper-level admission, 35 were accepted, 22 enrolled. TOEFL or SLEP required. Deadline for receipt of application materials: none. Application fee required: $50. Interview required.

Athletics Interscholastic: basketball (boys); intramural: basketball (b,g), volleyball (b,g); coed interscholastic: soccer; coed intramural: aerobics/dance, artistic gym, backpacking, ball hockey, bicycling, cooperative games, cross-country running, dance, fitness, fitness walking, Frisbee, gymnastics, hiking/backpacking, indoor soccer, jump rope, outdoor activities, outdoor adventure, outdoor education, outdoor recreation, outdoor skills, outdoors, running, soccer, tennis, ultimate Frisbee, walking, yoga. 5 PE instructors, 3 coaches.

Computers Computers are regularly used in art, college planning, engineering, English, ESL, history, humanities, music, photography, social studies classes. Computer network features include on-campus library services, online commercial services, Internet access, wireless campus network, Internet filtering or blocking technology, PC computer classroom with a multimedia presentation system, Mac computers in designated areas. Campus intranet, student e-mail accounts, and computer access in designated common areas are available to students. Students grades are available online. The school has a published electronic and media policy.

Contact Joe Sullivan, Director of Admissions. 740-425-3655 Ext. 214. Fax: 740-425-3202. E-mail: admissions@olneyfriends.org. Website: www.olneyfriends.org

THE O'NEAL SCHOOL

3300 Airport Road
PO Box 290
Southern Pines, North Carolina 28388-0290

Head of School: Mr. John Elmore

General Information Coeducational day college-preparatory school. Grades PK–12. Founded: 1971. Setting: small town. Nearest major city is Raleigh. 40-acre campus. 3 buildings on campus. Approved or accredited by North Carolina Association of Independent Schools, Southern Association of Colleges and Schools, Southern Association of Independent Schools, and North Carolina Department of Education. Member of National Association of Independent Schools. Endowment: $1 million. Total enrollment: 411. Upper school average class size: 15. Upper school faculty-student ratio: 1:12. There are 174 required school days per year for Upper School students. Upper School students typically attend 5 days per week. The average school day consists of 6 hours and 15 minutes.

Upper School Student Profile Grade 9: 46 students (22 boys, 24 girls); Grade 10: 36 students (19 boys, 17 girls); Grade 11: 40 students (17 boys, 23 girls); Grade 12: 32 students (11 boys, 21 girls).

Faculty School total: 51. In upper school: 9 men, 12 women; 12 have advanced degrees.

Subjects Offered Algebra, American history, American literature, art, art history, art history-AP, biology, biology-AP, calculus-AP, chemistry, community service, computer science, drama, economics, English, English language-AP, English literature, English literature-AP, environmental science, environmental science-AP, European history, European history-AP, expository writing, film, filmmaking, fine arts, French, geometry, government-AP, mathematics, photography, physical education, physics-AP, pottery, pre-calculus, robotics, science, social studies, Spanish, statistics-AP, U.S. history-AP, world history, world literature, yearbook.

Graduation Requirements Arts and fine arts (art, music, dance, drama), English, foreign language, mathematics, physical education (includes health), science, social studies (includes history), 36 hours of community service.

Special Academic Programs 13 Advanced Placement exams for which test preparation is offered; independent study; study at local college for college credit.

College Admission Counseling 40 students graduated in 2015; all went to college, including Appalachian State University; Liberty University; North Carolina State University; Southern Methodist University; The University of North Carolina at Charlotte; University of Mississippi. Median SAT critical reading: 580, median SAT math: 580, median SAT writing: 540, median combined SAT: 1700, median composite ACT: 26. 20% scored over 600 on SAT critical reading, 15% scored over 600 on SAT math, 25% scored over 600 on SAT writing, 25% scored over 1800 on combined SAT, 35% scored over 26 on composite ACT.

Student Life Upper grades have specified standards of dress, student council, honor system. Discipline rests primarily with faculty.

Tuition and Aid Day student tuition: $16,990. Tuition installment plan (Insured Tuition Payment Plan, monthly payment plans, individually arranged payment plans). Merit scholarship grants, need-based scholarship grants available. In 2015–16, 37% of upper-school students received aid; total upper-school merit-scholarship money awarded: $38,223. Total amount of financial aid awarded in 2015–16: $505,932.

Admissions Traditional secondary-level entrance grade is 9. For fall 2015, 24 students applied for upper-level admission, 23 were accepted, 22 enrolled. Admissions testing, essay, OLSAT, Stanford Achievement Test, PSAT and SAT for applicants to grade 11

and 12, WRAT or writing sample required. Deadline for receipt of application materials: none. Application fee required: $100. On-campus interview required.

Athletics Interscholastic: baseball (boys), basketball (b,g), cross-country running (b,g), soccer (b,g), swimming and diving (b,g), tennis (b,g), track and field (b,g), volleyball (g); coed interscholastic: cheering, golf. 2 PE instructors, 2 coaches, 1 athletic trainer.

Computers Computers are regularly used in all academic classes. Computer network features include on-campus library services, Internet access, wireless campus network, Internet filtering or blocking technology, EBSCO, World Book Online. Student e-mail accounts and computer access in designated common areas are available to students. The school has a published electronic and media policy.

Contact Mrs. Alice Droppers, Director of Admissions and Financial Aid. 910-692-6920 Ext. 103. Fax: 910-692-6930. E-mail: adroppers@onealschool.org. Website: www.onealschool.org

ONEIDA BAPTIST INSTITUTE

11 Mulberry Street
Oneida, Kentucky 40972

Head of School: Mr. Larry A. Gritton Jr.

General Information Coeducational boarding and day college-preparatory, general academic, arts, vocational, religious studies, bilingual studies, and agriculture school, affiliated with Southern Baptist Convention. Grades 6–12. Founded: 1899. Setting: rural. Nearest major city is Lexington. Students are housed in single-sex dormitories. 200-acre campus. 15 buildings on campus. Approved or accredited by The Kentucky Non-Public School Commission, The National Non-Public School Commission, and Kentucky Department of Education. Endowment: $28 million. Total enrollment: 320. Upper school average class size: 11. Upper school faculty-student ratio: 1:11. There are 170 required school days per year for Upper School students. Upper School students typically attend 5 days per week. The average school day consists of 6 hours.

Upper School Student Profile Grade 9: 42 students (19 boys, 23 girls); Grade 10: 59 students (32 boys, 27 girls); Grade 11: 47 students (28 boys, 19 girls); Grade 12: 58 students (41 boys, 17 girls). 84% of students are boarding students. 41% are state residents. 28 states are represented in upper school student body. 24% are international students. International students from China, Ethiopia, Nigeria, Papua New Guinea, Republic of Korea, and Thailand; 20 other countries represented in student body. 25% of students are Southern Baptist Convention.

Faculty School total: 40. In upper school: 13 men, 15 women; 11 have advanced degrees; 36 reside on campus.

Subjects Offered Agriculture, algebra, band, Bible, biology, biology-AP, calculus-AP, careers, chemistry, child development, choir, commercial art, computer skills, culinary arts, English, English-AP, ESL, European history-AP, fashion, geography, geometry, government, government-AP, guitar, health, language arts, leadership, life skills, literature, mathematics, media production, physical education, physical science, physics, piano, Spanish, stagecraft, U.S. history, U.S. history-AP, vocal ensemble, world history.

Graduation Requirements Arts and fine arts (art, music, dance, drama), Bible, computer literacy, English, foreign language, mathematics, physical education (includes health), science, social studies (includes history), field placement.

Special Academic Programs 6 Advanced Placement exams for which test preparation is offered; independent study; remedial reading and/or remedial writing; remedial math; ESL (15 students enrolled).

College Admission Counseling 51 students graduated in 2015; 48 went to college, including Berea College; Eastern Kentucky University; Lindsey Wilson College; University of Kentucky; University of the Cumberlands; Western Kentucky University. Other: 3 went to work.

Student Life Upper grades have specified standards of dress. Discipline rests primarily with faculty. Attendance at religious services is required.

Summer Programs Remediation, enrichment, advancement programs offered; session focuses on remediation and make-up courses; held on campus; accepts boys and girls; open to students from other schools. 125 students usually enrolled. 2016 schedule: May 16 to June 17. Application deadline: none.

Tuition and Aid 7-day tuition and room/board: $6250–$13,500. Tuition installment plan (monthly payment plans). Need-based scholarship grants available. In 2015–16, 100% of upper-school students received aid.

Admissions Traditional secondary-level entrance grade is 9. Deadline for receipt of application materials: none. Application fee required: $50. On-campus interview required.

Athletics Interscholastic: baseball (boys), basketball (b,g), cheering (g), cross-country running (b,g), golf (b,g), soccer (b,g), softball (g), swimming and diving (b,g), tennis (b,g), track and field (b,g), volleyball (g). 2 PE instructors.

Computers Computers are regularly used in commercial art, media production classes. Computer resources include Internet access, Internet filtering or blocking technology. The school has a published electronic and media policy.

Contact Admissions. 606-847-4111 Ext. 233. Fax: 606-847-4496. E-mail: admissions@oneidaschool.org. Website: www.oneidaschool.org

ORANGEBURG PREPARATORY SCHOOLS, INC.

2651 North Road
Orangeburg, South Carolina 29118

Head of School: Dr. Brian Newsome

General Information Coeducational day college-preparatory and arts school. Grades K4–12. Founded: 1986. Setting: small town. Nearest major city is Columbia. 40-acre campus. 7 buildings on campus. Approved or accredited by South Carolina Independent School Association, Southern Association of Colleges and Schools, and South Carolina Department of Education. Endowment: $500,000. Total enrollment: 678. Upper school average class size: 20. Upper school faculty-student ratio: 1:12. Upper School students typically attend 5 days per week. The average school day consists of 6 hours and 40 minutes.

Upper School Student Profile Grade 9: 63 students (35 boys, 28 girls); Grade 10: 49 students (26 boys, 23 girls); Grade 11: 40 students (18 boys, 22 girls); Grade 12: 38 students (15 boys, 23 girls).

Faculty School total: 30. In upper school: 9 men, 20 women; 10 have advanced degrees.

Subjects Offered Acting, advanced chemistry, advanced computer applications, advanced math, algebra, American government, American history, American literature-AP, analysis and differential calculus, analytic geometry, anatomy and physiology, ancient world history, applied arts, art, automated accounting, baseball, Basic programming, basketball, biology, British literature, British literature-AP, calculus-AP, career/college preparation, cheerleading, chemistry, chemistry-AP, choral music, civics, college admission preparation, college counseling, college placement, college planning, composition, computer studies, desktop publishing, English literature and composition-AP, fencing, forensics, four units of summer reading, French, golf, government, grammar, history, honors algebra, honors English, honors geometry, honors U.S. history, honors world history, Internet, introduction to theater, musical theater, physical education, physical fitness, physical science, physics, pre-algebra, pre-calculus, probability and statistics, psychology, SAT preparation, senior composition, softball, Spanish, speech and debate, speech and oral interpretations, tennis, theater, track and field, U.S. history-AP, volleyball, weight training.

Graduation Requirements Algebra, American government, American history, American literature, analytic geometry, biology, British literature, chemistry, computer studies, economics, English literature, foreign language.

Special Academic Programs Advanced Placement exam preparation; honors section; independent study; study at local college for college credit; ESL (10 students enrolled).

College Admission Counseling 48 students graduated in 2015; all went to college, including Clemson University; College of Charleston; Presbyterian College; The Citadel, The Military College of South Carolina; University of South Carolina; Wofford College.

Student Life Upper grades have specified standards of dress, student council, honor system. Discipline rests primarily with faculty.

Summer Programs Remediation, sports programs offered; session focuses on remediation; held on campus; accepts boys and girls; open to students from other schools. 50 students usually enrolled. 2016 schedule: June 3 to July 19. Application deadline: June 3.

Tuition and Aid Day student tuition: $4428–$5880. Tuition installment plan (monthly payment plans). Tuition reduction for siblings, merit scholarship grants, need-based scholarship grants available. In 2015–16, 6% of upper-school students received aid; total upper-school merit-scholarship money awarded: $6600. Total amount of financial aid awarded in 2015–16: $20,370.

Admissions Traditional secondary-level entrance grade is 9. For fall 2015, 7 students applied for upper-level admission, 7 were accepted, 7 enrolled. Achievement tests, PSAT and SAT for applicants to grade 11 and 12 or Stanford Achievement Test required. Deadline for receipt of application materials: none. Application fee required: $150. Interview recommended.

Athletics Interscholastic: baseball (boys), basketball (b,g), cheering (g), softball (g), track and field (b,g), volleyball (g); coed interscholastic: cross-country running, golf, soccer; coed intramural: archery, badminton, cooperative games, fencing, fitness, physical fitness, physical training, strength & conditioning. 3 PE instructors, 8 coaches, 1 athletic trainer.

Computers Computers are regularly used in all classes. Computer network features include on-campus library services, online commercial services, Internet access, wireless campus network, Internet filtering or blocking technology. Campus intranet is available to students. Students grades are available online. The school has a published electronic and media policy.

Contact 803-534-7970. Fax: 803-535-2190.
Website: http://www.orangeburgprep.com/

ORANGEWOOD ADVENTIST ACADEMY

13732 Clinton Street
Garden Grove, California 92843

Head of School: Ms. Datha S. Tickner

General Information Coeducational day college-preparatory and religious studies school, affiliated with Seventh-day Adventist Church. Grades PK–12. Founded: 1956.

Setting: urban. Nearest major city is Anaheim. 11-acre campus. 6 buildings on campus. Approved or accredited by Board of Regents, General Conference of Seventh-day Adventists, Western Association of Schools and Colleges, and California Department of Education. Total enrollment: 261. Upper school average class size: 24. Upper school faculty-student ratio: 1:10. There are 180 required school days per year for Upper School students. Upper School students typically attend 5 days per week. The average school day consists of 7 hours.

Upper School Student Profile Grade 9: 22 students (9 boys, 13 girls); Grade 10: 25 students (11 boys, 14 girls); Grade 11: 22 students (13 boys, 9 girls); Grade 12: 26 students (16 boys, 10 girls). 80% of students are Seventh-day Adventists.

Faculty School total: 20. In upper school: 4 men, 7 women; 4 have advanced degrees.

Subjects Offered Algebra, arts, biology, calculus, career education, chemistry, choir, computer science, computers, drama, English, family studies, fine arts, geometry, government, health, journalism, life skills, mathematics, physical education, physical science, physics, pre-calculus, religion, science, social studies, Spanish, typing, U.S. history, world history, yearbook.

Graduation Requirements Arts and fine arts (art, music, dance, drama), business skills (includes word processing), career education, computer science, economics, English, foreign language, government, health, mathematics, physical education (includes health), religion (includes Bible studies and theology), science, social studies (includes history), work experience, community service.

Special Academic Programs Advanced Placement exam preparation; honors section; ESL (21 students enrolled).

College Admission Counseling 24 students graduated in 2014; 22 went to college, including California State University; La Sierra University; Loma Linda University. Other: 1 went to work, 1 had other specific plans.

Student Life Upper grades have uniform requirement, student council, honor system. Discipline rests primarily with faculty.

Tuition and Aid Day student tuition: $10,830. Tuition installment plan (monthly payment plans). Tuition reduction for siblings, merit scholarship grants, need-based scholarship grants, paying campus jobs available. In 2014–15, 52% of upper-school students received aid; total upper-school merit-scholarship money awarded: $150,000. Total amount of financial aid awarded in 2014–15: $200,000.

Admissions Traditional secondary-level entrance grade is 9. TOEFL required. Deadline for receipt of application materials: none. Application fee required: $250. Interview required.

Athletics Interscholastic: basketball (boys, girls), cheering (g), flag football (b), soccer (b), softball (g), volleyball (b,g); intramural: basketball (b,g), flag football (b), softball (g), volleyball (b,g); coed interscholastic: badminton, fitness, golf, physical fitness, running, soccer; coed intramural: golf, gymnastics, running. 1 PE instructor, 5 coaches.

Computers Computers are regularly used in accounting, all academic, art, Bible studies, business applications, career education, college planning, computer applications, economics, English, geography, health, independent study, introduction to technology, journalism, keyboarding, mathematics, media production, music, newspaper, photography, photojournalism, religion, SAT preparation, science, social sciences, study skills, typing, word processing, writing, yearbook classes. Computer network features include on-campus library services, online commercial services, Internet access, wireless campus network, Internet filtering or blocking technology. Students grades are available online. The school has a published electronic and media policy.

Contact Mrs. Aime Cuevas, Vice Principal and Registrar. 714-534-4694 Ext. 207. Fax: 714-534-5931. E-mail: acuevas@orangewoodacademy.com. Website: www.orangewoodacademy.com

ORANGEWOOD CHRISTIAN SCHOOL

1300 West Maitland Boulevard
Maitland, Florida 32751

Head of School: Donald M. Larson, PhD

General Information Coeducational day college-preparatory, arts, religious studies, and technology school, affiliated with Presbyterian Church, Christian faith. Grades K4–12. Founded: 1980. Setting: suburban. Nearest major city is Orlando. 8-acre campus. 2 buildings on campus. Approved or accredited by Association of Christian Schools International, Christian Schools of Florida, National Council for Private School Accreditation, and Southern Association of Colleges and Schools. Total enrollment: 732. Upper school average class size: 14. Upper school faculty-student ratio: 1:11. The average school day consists of 7 hours.

Upper School Student Profile 100% of students are Presbyterian, Christian.

Faculty School total: 65. In upper school: 18 have advanced degrees.

Subjects Offered Advanced Placement courses, algebra, American culture, American government, American history, American history-AP, anatomy and physiology, art, art-AP, astronomy, Bible, biology, biology-AP, calculus-AP, career exploration, ceramics, chemistry, choir, commercial art, computer applications, computer graphics, creative writing, drama, drawing, economics, English, English language and composition-AP, English literature and composition-AP, environmental science, foreign language, geometry, graphic design, honors algebra, honors English, honors geometry, honors U.S. history, honors world history, Latin, life management skills, marine science, meteorology, oceanography, painting, personal fitness, photography, physics, physics-AP, pre-calculus, psychology, SAT preparation, sculpture, senior seminar, Spanish,

Spanish language-AP, speech, studio art-AP, television, trigonometry, weight training, world geography, world history, world religions, yearbook.

Graduation Requirements Algebra, American government, American history, arts and fine arts (art, music, dance, drama), Bible, biology, computer applications, economics, electives, English, foreign language, life management skills, mathematics, personal fitness, physical education (includes health), science, senior seminar, world history.

Special Academic Programs Advanced Placement exam preparation; honors section; accelerated programs; independent study; study at local college for college credit.

College Admission Counseling 68 students graduated in 2015; 67 went to college, including Covenant College; Florida State University; Palm Beach Atlantic University; University of Central Florida; University of Florida; University of North Florida. Median SAT critical reading: 550, median SAT math: 550, median SAT writing: 525. 32% scored over 600 on SAT critical reading, 27% scored over 600 on SAT math, 22% scored over 600 on SAT writing.

Student Life Upper grades have specified standards of dress, student council, honor system. Discipline rests primarily with faculty. Attendance at religious services is required.

Summer Programs Remediation, enrichment, advancement, sports, art/fine arts, rigorous outdoor training, computer instruction programs offered; session focuses on enrichment, sports, fine arts; held both on and off campus; held at various team camps; accepts boys and girls; open to students from other schools. 200 students usually enrolled. 2016 schedule: June to August. Application deadline: April 1.

Tuition and Aid Tuition installment plan (SMART Tuition Payment Plan, 4% discount if paid in full). Tuition reduction for siblings, need-based scholarship grants available. In 2015–16, 11% of upper-school students received aid. Total amount of financial aid awarded in 2015–16: $124,000.

Admissions Traditional secondary-level entrance grade is 9. Admissions testing and ISEE required. Deadline for receipt of application materials: none. Application fee required: $125. Interview required.

Athletics Interscholastic: baseball (boys), basketball (b,g), cheering (g), cross-country running (b,g), flag football (b), football (b), golf (b,g), lacrosse (b,g), physical fitness (b,g), physical training (b,g), soccer (b,g), strength & conditioning (b,g), tennis (b,g), track and field (b,g), volleyball (g), weight lifting (b,g), weight training (b,g); intramural: yoga (g); coed intramural: bowling, fishing, sailing, table tennis, ultimate Frisbee. 2 PE instructors, 8 coaches, 2 athletic trainers.

Computers Computers are regularly used in all classes. Computer network features include on-campus library services, Internet access, wireless campus network, Internet filtering or blocking technology. Campus intranet, student e-mail accounts, and computer access in designated common areas are available to students. Students grades are available online. The school has a published electronic and media policy.

Contact Mrs. Joyce McDonald, Director of Admissions. 407-339-0223. Fax: 407-339-4148. E-mail: jmcdonald@ocsrams.org. Website: www.ocsrams.org

ORATORY PREPARATORY SCHOOL

1 Beverly Road
Summit, New Jersey 07901

Head of School: Mr. Robert Costello

General Information Boys' day college-preparatory school, affiliated with Roman Catholic Church. Grades 7–12. Founded: 1907. Setting: suburban. Nearest major city is Newark. 10-acre campus. 2 buildings on campus. Approved or accredited by Middle States Association of Colleges and Schools, National Catholic Education Association, New Jersey Association of Independent Schools, and New Jersey Department of Education. Endowment: $2 million. Total enrollment: 359. Upper school average class size: 14. Upper school faculty-student ratio: 1:9. There are 170 required school days per year for Upper School students. Upper School students typically attend 5 days per week. The average school day consists of 6 hours and 35 minutes.

Upper School Student Profile Grade 7: 26 students (26 boys); Grade 8: 16 students (16 boys); Grade 9: 86 students (86 boys); Grade 10: 91 students (91 boys); Grade 11: 73 students (73 boys); Grade 12: 67 students (67 boys). 72% of students are Roman Catholic.

Faculty School total: 40. In upper school: 25 men, 15 women; 18 have advanced degrees.

Subjects Offered Algebra, American history, American literature, art, art-AP, biology, British literature, calculus, chemistry, computer applications, computer math, computer programming, computer science, conceptual physics, creative writing, economics, English, English literature, English-AP, expository writing, finite math, first aid, foreign language, geography, geometry, grammar, health, history, history-AP, honors algebra, honors English, honors geometry, honors U.S. history, honors world history, journalism, language-AP, Latin, mathematics, mathematics-AP, media, music appreciation, philosophy, physical education, physics, pre-algebra, probability, religion, rhetoric, science, social sciences, social studies, sociology, Spanish, statistics, theology, trigonometry, U.S. history, U.S. history-AP, world cultures, world geography, world history, world history-AP, world literature, writing.

Graduation Requirements English, foreign language, mathematics, physical education (includes health), religion (includes Bible studies and theology), science, social sciences, social studies (includes history). Community service is required.

Special Academic Programs Advanced Placement exam preparation; honors section; independent study; study at local college for college credit.

College Admission Counseling 66 students graduated in 2015; all went to college, including Boston College; Bucknell University; Fairfield University; Fairleigh Dickinson University, College at Florham; University of Pennsylvania; Villanova University. Mean SAT critical reading: 616, mean SAT math: 608, mean SAT writing: 615, mean composite ACT: 27.

Student Life Upper grades have specified standards of dress, student council, honor system. Discipline rests primarily with faculty. Attendance at religious services is required.

Summer Programs Enrichment, sports, art/fine arts, computer instruction programs offered; session focuses on enrichment; held on campus; accepts boys and girls; open to students from other schools. 30 students usually enrolled. 2016 schedule: June 1 to July 31. Application deadline: none.

Tuition and Aid Day student tuition: $19,650. Tuition installment plan (monthly payment plans, individually arranged payment plans). Merit scholarship grants, need-based scholarship grants available. In 2015–16, 41% of upper-school students received aid; total upper-school merit-scholarship money awarded: $381,300. Total amount of financial aid awarded in 2015–16: $542,300.

Admissions Traditional secondary-level entrance grade is 9. For fall 2015, 196 students applied for upper-level admission, 172 were accepted, 84 enrolled. Admissions testing or independent norms required. Deadline for receipt of application materials: none. Application fee required: $50. On-campus interview required.

Athletics Interscholastic: baseball, basketball, bowling, cross-country running, fencing, golf, hockey, ice hockey, indoor track, indoor track & field, lacrosse, soccer, swimming and diving, tennis, track and field, winter (indoor) track; intramural: basketball, combined training, fishing, flag football, football, Frisbee, kickball, physical training, skiing (downhill), snowboarding, strength & conditioning, tennis, ultimate Frisbee, volleyball. 3 PE instructors, 12 coaches, 1 athletic trainer.

Computers Computers are regularly used in English, foreign language, history, Latin, mathematics, religious studies, science, Spanish, technology, yearbook classes. Computer network features include on-campus library services, online commercial services, Internet access, wireless campus network, Internet filtering or blocking technology, laptop program, wireless campus network. Student e-mail accounts are available to students. Students grades are available online. The school has a published electronic and media policy.

Contact Mr. Thomas R. Boniello, Director of Admissions. 908-273-5771 Ext. 11. Fax: 908-273-1554. E-mail: admissions@oratoryprep.org. Website: www.oratoryprep.org

OREGON EPISCOPAL SCHOOL

6300 Southwest Nicol Road
Portland, Oregon 97223-7566

Head of School: Mrs. Mo Copeland

General Information Coeducational boarding and day college-preparatory, arts, religious studies, technology, and science school, affiliated with Episcopal Church. Boarding grades 9–12, day grades PK–12. Founded: 1869. Setting: suburban. Students are housed in single-sex dormitories. 59-acre campus. 9 buildings on campus. Approved or accredited by National Association of Episcopal Schools, Northwest Association of Independent Schools, Northwest Association of Schools and Colleges, and Oregon Department of Education. Member of National Association of Independent Schools and Secondary School Admission Test Board. Endowment: $24.4 million. Total enrollment: 870. Upper school average class size: 15. Upper school faculty-student ratio: 1:7. There are 175 required school days per year for Upper School students. Upper School students typically attend 5 days per week. The average school day consists of 7 hours.

Upper School Student Profile Grade 9: 77 students (34 boys, 43 girls); Grade 10: 82 students (37 boys, 45 girls); Grade 11: 75 students (40 boys, 35 girls); Grade 12: 78 students (44 boys, 34 girls). 18% of students are boarding students. 81% are state residents. 4 states are represented in upper school student body. 16% are international students. International students from China, Jamaica, Republic of Korea, Taiwan, Thailand, and Viet Nam; 5 other countries represented in student body. 10% of students are members of Episcopal Church.

Faculty School total: 123. In upper school: 19 men, 28 women; 38 have advanced degrees; 6 reside on campus.

Subjects Offered Advanced biology, advanced chemistry, advanced math, Advanced Placement courses, algebra, American Civil War, American history, American literature, American studies, anatomy, anatomy and physiology, Ancient Greek, ancient history, ancient/medieval philosophy, animation, Arabic studies, art, Asian history, astronomy, athletic training, backpacking, Basic programming, biology, Buddhism, calculus, calculus-AP, ceramics, chemistry, Chinese, chorus, Christian studies, Christianity, college counseling, college planning, college writing, community service, computer graphics, computer science, computer science-AP, constitutional law, creative writing, dance, debate, discrete mathematics, drama, drawing, East Asian history, ecology, electronics, engineering, English, English literature, environmental science, ESL, ESL, European history, fencing, film, film and literature, filmmaking, fine arts, finite math, foreign language, foreign policy, French, French language-AP, French-AP, freshman seminar, functions, geology, geometry, graphic arts, graphic design, graphics, health, health and wellness, history, human anatomy, human relations, human sexuality,

humanities, independent study, international affairs, international relations, jazz band, jazz ensemble, journalism, literature, marine biology, marine ecology, mathematics, mathematics-AP, microbiology, model United Nations, music, music history, music technology, musical productions, musical theater, newspaper, painting, personal finance, personal fitness, philosophy, photography, photojournalism, physical education, physical fitness, physics, playwriting and directing, poetry, pre-algebra, pre-calculus, psychology, psychology-AP, religion, religion and culture, research, science, science project, science research, service learning/internship, sex education, sexuality, Shakespeare, social studies, Spanish, Spanish language-AP, Spanish literature, Spanish-AP, speech, stagecraft, statistics, statistics-AP, tennis, theater, theater design and production, track and field, trigonometry, U.S. history, U.S. history-AP, urban studies, video and animation, video film production, visual arts, vocal ensemble, vocal music, weight training, weightlifting, wellness, wilderness education, wilderness experience, world history, world literature, world religions, world religions, yearbook, yoga, zoology.

Graduation Requirements Arts and fine arts (art, music, dance, drama), electives, English, foreign language, health education, humanities, mathematics, philosophy, physical education (includes health), religion (includes Bible studies and theology), science, service learning/internship, U.S. history, Winterim—experiential education on and off campus in March.

Special Academic Programs Advanced Placement exam preparation; honors section; independent study; term-away projects; study abroad; academic accommodation for the gifted; ESL (9 students enrolled).

College Admission Counseling 80 students graduated in 2015; 79 went to college, including Brown University; Dartmouth College; Gonzaga University; Haverford College; University of California, Berkeley; University of Southern California. Other: 1 had other specific plans. Median SAT critical reading: 680, median SAT math: 690, median SAT writing: 690, median combined SAT: 2050, median composite ACT: 29. 75% scored over 600 on SAT critical reading, 81% scored over 600 on SAT math, 75% scored over 600 on SAT writing, 81% scored over 1800 on combined SAT, 74% scored over 26 on composite ACT.

Student Life Upper grades have specified standards of dress, student council. Discipline rests equally with students and faculty. Attendance at religious services is required.

Summer Programs Remediation, enrichment, advancement, sports, art/fine arts, computer instruction programs offered; session focuses on a variety of academic, sports, and artistic enrichment programs; held both on and off campus; held at local/regional trips are offered through summer programs for experiential education and science and research, marine ecology trip on Oregon Coast, backpacking on Mt. Hood, etc; accepts boys and girls; open to students from other schools. 2,500 students usually enrolled. 2016 schedule: June 15 to August 25.

Tuition and Aid Day student tuition: $29,300; 7-day tuition and room/board: $55,900. Tuition installment plan (Insured Tuition Payment Plan, monthly payment plans). Need-based scholarship grants available. In 2015–16, 16% of upper-school students received aid. Total amount of financial aid awarded in 2015–16: $1,121,623.

Admissions Traditional secondary-level entrance grade is 9. For fall 2015, 186 students applied for upper-level admission, 79 were accepted, 43 enrolled. SSAT or TOEFL required. Deadline for receipt of application materials: January 20. Application fee required: $75. Interview required.

Athletics Interscholastic: alpine skiing (boys, girls), basketball (b,g), cross-country running (b,g), fencing (b,g), golf (b,g), lacrosse (b,g), skiing (downhill) (b,g), soccer (b,g), tennis (b,g), track and field (b,g), volleyball (g); intramural: backpacking (b,g), hiking/backpacking (b,g), outdoor activities (b,g), yoga (b,g); coed intramural: outdoor education, physical fitness, physical training, rock climbing, ropes courses. 2 PE instructors, 47 coaches, 1 athletic trainer.

Computers Computers are regularly used in art, English, foreign language, history, humanities, independent study, mathematics, music, philosophy, religion, science, social sciences, technology classes. Computer network features include on-campus library services, online commercial services, Internet access, wireless campus network, Internet filtering or blocking technology, one-to-one laptop program. Campus intranet, student e-mail accounts, and computer access in designated common areas are available to students. Students grades are available online. The school has a published electronic and media policy.

Contact Carla Zilaff, Admissions Assistant. 503-768-3115. Fax: 503-768-3140. E-mail: admit@oes.edu. Website: www.oes.edu

ORINDA ACADEMY

19 Altarinda Road
Orinda, California 94563-2602

Head of School: Ron Graydon

General Information Coeducational day college-preparatory, general academic, and arts school. Grades 8–12. Founded: 1982. Setting: suburban. Nearest major city is Walnut Creek. 1-acre campus. 2 buildings on campus. Approved or accredited by East Bay Independent Schools Association, The College Board, and Western Association of Schools and Colleges. Total enrollment: 78. Upper school average class size: 9. Upper school faculty-student ratio: 1:9. There are 180 required school days per year for Upper School students. Upper School students typically attend 5 days per week. The average school day consists of 6 hours and 30 minutes.

Upper School Student Profile Grade 9: 15 students (11 boys, 4 girls); Grade 10: 20 students (10 boys, 10 girls); Grade 11: 17 students (13 boys, 4 girls); Grade 12: 23 students (13 boys, 10 girls).

Faculty School total: 21. In upper school: 8 men, 12 women; 9 have advanced degrees.

Subjects Offered Algebra, American history, American literature, American sign language, art, basketball, biology, calculus, chemistry, community service, computer graphics, computer multimedia, computer music, contemporary issues, creative writing, dance, drama, earth science, economics, English, English literature, English literature and composition-AP, ensembles, environmental science, ESL, European history, film history, fine arts, French, geography, geometry, government/civics, health, history, history of music, introduction to theater, journalism, mathematics, music, music performance, musical productions, performing arts, physical education, physics, science, social studies, Spanish, Spanish language-AP, theater, trigonometry, visual arts, yearbook.

Graduation Requirements Algebra, biology, civics, composition, economics, English, foreign language, geometry, physical education (includes health), science, trigonometry, U.S. history, visual and performing arts. Community service is required.

Special Academic Programs 2 Advanced Placement exams for which test preparation is offered; honors section; accelerated programs; academic accommodation for the gifted; ESL (15 students enrolled).

College Admission Counseling 16 students graduated in 2015; 12 went to college, including California Polytechnic State University, San Luis Obispo; Hampshire College; Linfield College; University of Minnesota, Twin Cities Campus; University of Redlands; Willamette University. Other: 4 had other specific plans. Mean SAT critical reading: 599, mean SAT math: 588, mean SAT writing: 564, mean combined SAT: 1751, mean composite ACT: 24. 50% scored over 600 on SAT critical reading, 58% scored over 600 on SAT math, 2% scored over 600 on SAT writing, 25% scored over 1800 on combined SAT, 50% scored over 26 on composite ACT.

Student Life Upper grades have specified standards of dress, student council, honor system. Discipline rests primarily with faculty.

Summer Programs Remediation, enrichment, advancement programs offered; session focuses on academics; held on campus; accepts boys and girls; open to students from other schools. 30 students usually enrolled. 2016 schedule: June 20 to July 29. Application deadline: none.

Tuition and Aid Day student tuition: $34,980. Tuition installment plan (FACTS Tuition Payment Plan). Tuition reduction for siblings, need-based scholarship grants available. In 2015–16, 25% of upper-school students received aid. Total amount of financial aid awarded in 2015–16: $400,000.

Admissions Traditional secondary-level entrance grade is 9. For fall 2015, 70 students applied for upper-level admission, 46 were accepted, 26 enrolled. Any standardized test, ISEE, SSAT or Star-9 required. Deadline for receipt of application materials: January 15. Application fee required: $75. On-campus interview required.

Athletics Interscholastic: baseball (boys), basketball (b,g); intramural: volleyball (g); coed interscholastic: soccer; coed intramural: soccer, softball. 1 PE instructor, 1 coach.

Computers Computers are regularly used in English, French, media arts, social sciences, Spanish, writing, yearbook classes. Computer network features include Internet access, Internet filtering or blocking technology. Student e-mail accounts and computer access in designated common areas are available to students. The school has a published electronic and media policy.

Contact Laurel Evans, Director of Admissions. 925-254-7553 Ext. 305. Fax: 925-254-4768. E-mail: laurel@orindaacademy.org. Website: www.orindaacademy.org

THE ORME SCHOOL

HC 63, Box 3040
1000
Mayer, Arizona 86333

Head of School: Mr. Bruce Sanborn

General Information Coeducational boarding and day college-preparatory, arts, bilingual studies, ESL, and horsemanship school; primarily serves individuals with Attention Deficit Disorder and dyslexic students. Grades 8–PG. Founded: 1929. Setting: rural. Nearest major city is Phoenix. Students are housed in single-sex dormitories. 360-acre campus. 30 buildings on campus. Approved or accredited by Arizona Association of Independent Schools, North Central Association of Colleges and Schools, The Association of Boarding Schools, and Arizona Department of Education. Member of National Association of Independent Schools and Secondary School Admission Test Board. Endowment: $2 million. Total enrollment: 75. Upper school average class size: 6. Upper school faculty-student ratio: 1:4. There are 179 required school days per year for Upper School students. Upper School students typically attend 5 days per week. The average school day consists of 7 hours.

Upper School Student Profile Grade 8: 9 students (5 boys, 4 girls); Grade 9: 22 students (12 boys, 10 girls); Grade 10: 27 students (16 boys, 11 girls); Grade 11: 26 students (14 boys, 12 girls); Grade 12: 23 students (14 boys, 9 girls); Postgraduate: 2 students (1 boy, 1 girl). 98% of students are boarding students. 60% are state residents. 15 states are represented in upper school student body. 33% are international students. International students from China, Colombia, Germany, Norway, Russian Federation, and Turkey; 5 other countries represented in student body.

Faculty School total: 25. In upper school: 10 men, 12 women; 15 have advanced degrees; 20 reside on campus.

Subjects Offered Advanced Placement courses, advanced TOEFL/grammar, algebra, American history, American history-AP, American literature, American literature-AP, ancient world history, art, art history, astronomy, band, biology, British literature (honors), calculus, calculus-AP, ceramics, chemistry, choir, college admission preparation, college counseling, community service, computer programming, computer science, creative writing, drama, drama performance, ecology, English, English language and composition-AP, English literature, English literature and composition-AP, European history, European history-AP, fine arts, French, geography, geology, geometry, government, grammar, history, history of music, honors English, honors U.S. history, humanities, Latin, mathematics, music, performing arts, photography, physics, physics-AP, psychology, science, social sciences, social studies, Spanish, statistics-AP, student government, theater, trigonometry, U.S. history, U.S. history-AP, weightlifting, world cultures, world history, world literature, writing.

Graduation Requirements Advanced Placement courses, arts and fine arts (art, music, dance, drama), computer science, English, equine science, ESL, foreign language, humanities, mathematics, science, social sciences, social studies (includes history), students must participate annually in Caravan and the Fine Arts Festival. All students also take "sustainability". Community service is required.

Special Academic Programs 8 Advanced Placement exams for which test preparation is offered; independent study; ESL (20 students enrolled).

College Admission Counseling 33 students graduated in 2014; all went to college, including Arizona State University at the Tempe campus; Boston University; Columbia University; Cornell University; Dartmouth College; Northern Arizona University. Mean SAT critical reading: 500, mean SAT math: 533, mean SAT writing: 495, mean combined SAT: 1528, mean composite ACT: 21. 19% scored over 600 on SAT critical reading, 12% scored over 1800 on combined SAT, 9% scored over 26 on composite ACT.

Student Life Upper grades have specified standards of dress, student council, honor system. Discipline rests equally with students and faculty.

Tuition and Aid Day student tuition: $20,650; 5-day tuition and room/board: $36,000; 7-day tuition and room/board: $41,400. Tuition installment plan (individually arranged payment plans). Need-based scholarship grants available. In 2014–15, 60% of upper-school students received aid. Total amount of financial aid awarded in 2014–15: $1,200,000.

Admissions Traditional secondary-level entrance grade is 8. For fall 2014, 91 students applied for upper-level admission, 66 were accepted, 33 enrolled. PSAT and SAT for applicants to grade 11 and 12, SSAT, standardized test scores, TOEFL or SLEP and writing sample required. Deadline for receipt of application materials: none. Application fee required: $50. Interview required.

Athletics Interscholastic: baseball (boys), basketball (b,g), cross-country running (b,g), equestrian sports (b,g), football (b), pom squad (g), rodeo (b,g), running (b,g), softball (g), tennis (b,g), track and field (b,g), volleyball (g); intramural: aerobics/dance (g), fitness (b,g), physical training (b,g), rappelling (b,g), rock climbing (b,g), rodeo (b,g), strength & conditioning (b,g), wall climbing (b,g), weight lifting (b,g), weight training (b,g), wilderness (b,g), wilderness survival (b,g), wrestling (b); coed interscholastic: aquatics, dressage, equestrian sports, horseback riding, rodeo, soccer, swimming and diving; coed intramural: alpine skiing, aquatics, archery, backpacking, bicycling, billiards, canoeing/kayaking, climbing, fishing, fitness, fitness walking, fly fishing, freestyle skiing, Frisbee, hiking/backpacking, horseback riding, ice skating, life saving, marksmanship, mountain biking, mountaineering, nordic skiing, outdoor activities, outdoor adventure, outdoor recreation, outdoor skills, outdoors, paddle tennis, physical training, power lifting, rappelling, rock climbing, rodeo, ropes courses, skiing (cross-country), skiing (downhill), snowboarding, soccer, strength & conditioning, table tennis, tennis, ultimate Frisbee, volleyball, walking, wall climbing, weight lifting, weight training, wilderness, wilderness survival, yoga. 1 coach.

Computers Computers are regularly used in all academic classes. Computer network features include on-campus library services, Internet access, wireless campus network, Internet filtering or blocking technology. Campus intranet, student e-mail accounts, and computer access in designated common areas are available to students. Students grades are available online. The school has a published electronic and media policy.

Contact Ms. Marney Babbitt, Associate Director of Admission. 928-632-1562. Fax: 928-632-7605. E-mail: mbabbitt@ormeschool.org. Website: www.ormeschool.org

OUR LADY OF GOOD COUNSEL HIGH SCHOOL

17301 Old Vic Boulevard
Olney, Maryland 20832

Head of School: Dr. Paul G. Barker, EdD

General Information Coeducational day college-preparatory, arts, religious studies, technology, International Baccalaureate, and STEM program school, affiliated with Roman Catholic Church. Grades 9–12. Founded: 1958. Setting: suburban. Nearest major city is Washington, DC. 52-acre campus. 1 building on campus. Approved or accredited by Middle States Association of Colleges and Schools and Maryland Department of Education. Member of National Association of Independent Schools. Total enrollment: 1,240. Upper school average class size: 22. Upper school faculty-student ratio: 1:13. There are 185 required school days per year for Upper School students. Upper School students typically attend 5 days per week. The average school day consists of 6 hours and 45 minutes.

Upper School Student Profile Grade 9: 307 students (144 boys, 163 girls); Grade 10: 327 students (157 boys, 170 girls); Grade 11: 317 students (162 boys, 155 girls); Grade 12: 298 students (161 boys, 137 girls). 70% of students are Roman Catholic.

Faculty School total: 86. In upper school: 48 men, 38 women; 61 have advanced degrees.

Subjects Offered 20th century world history, accounting, algebra, American history, American history-AP, American literature, American literature-AP, art, art history, athletic training, Bible studies, biology, biology-AP, business law, business skills, calculus, calculus-AP, chemistry, chemistry-AP, choral music, college admission preparation, comparative government and politics-AP, composition-AP, computer applications, computer math, computer programming, computer science, creative writing, drama, economics, economics-AP, English, English literature, English literature and composition-AP, environmental science, ethics, European history, European history-AP, fine arts, French, French language-AP, general science, geometry, government/civics, health, health education, history, HTML design, International Baccalaureate courses, keyboarding, Latin, Latin American history, mathematics, music, music performance, physical education, physics, programming, psychology, religion, science, social sciences, social studies, Spanish, Spanish language-AP, speech, trigonometry, typing, world history, world literature.

Graduation Requirements All academic, service requirements for each grade.

Special Academic Programs International Baccalaureate program; 18 Advanced Placement exams for which test preparation is offered; honors section; academic accommodation for the gifted; remedial reading and/or remedial writing; programs in English, mathematics for dyslexic students; special instructional classes for students with learning disabilities (Ryken Program).

College Admission Counseling 282 students graduated in 2015; all went to college, including Towson University; University of Dayton; University of Maryland, College Park; University of South Carolina; University of Virginia; Virginia Polytechnic Institute and State University.

Student Life Upper grades have uniform requirement, student council, honor system. Discipline rests primarily with faculty. Attendance at religious services is required.

Summer Programs Enrichment, sports, art/fine arts, computer instruction programs offered; session focuses on English and mathematics skill enrichment for students with learning disabilities, computer courses, robotics; held on campus; accepts boys and girls; open to students from other schools. 80 students usually enrolled. 2016 schedule: June 10 to August 15. Application deadline: none.

Tuition and Aid Day student tuition: $19,500. Tuition installment plan (FACTS Tuition Payment Plan). Merit scholarship grants, need-based scholarship grants available. In 2015–16, 25% of upper-school students received aid; total upper-school merit-scholarship money awarded: $500,000. Total amount of financial aid awarded in 2015–16: $2,000,000.

Admissions Traditional secondary-level entrance grade is 9. For fall 2015, 704 students applied for upper-level admission, 477 were accepted, 307 enrolled. High School Placement Test required. Deadline for receipt of application materials: December 11. Application fee required: $50. On-campus interview required.

Athletics Interscholastic: baseball (boys), basketball (b,g), cheering (g), cross-country running (b,g), dance squad (g), dance team (g), diving (b,g), dressage (g), equestrian sports (b,g), field hockey (g), football (b), indoor track & field (b,g), lacrosse (b,g), pom squad (g), rugby (b), soccer (b,g), softball (g), swimming and diving (b,g), tennis (b,g), track and field (b,g), volleyball (g); intramural: basketball (b,g), equestrian sports (g), softball (b); coed interscholastic: aquatics, golf, ice hockey, indoor track & field, winter (indoor) track, wrestling; coed intramural: aerobics, aerobics/dance, martial arts, physical training, skiing (downhill), strength & conditioning, weight training. 5 PE instructors, 73 coaches, 3 athletic trainers.

Computers Computers are regularly used in all academic classes. Computer network features include on-campus library services, online commercial services, Internet access, wireless campus network, Internet filtering or blocking technology. Student e-mail accounts are available to students. Students grades are available online. The school has a published electronic and media policy.

Contact Emmy McNamara, Assistant Director of Admissions. 240-283-3235. Fax: 240-283-3250. E-mail: admissions@olgchs.org. Website: www.olgchs.org

OUR LADY OF MERCY ACADEMY

1001 Main Road
Newfield, New Jersey 08344

Head of School: Sr. Grace Marie Scandale

General Information Girls' day college-preparatory, arts, business, religious studies, bilingual studies, and technology school, affiliated with Roman Catholic Church. Grades 9–12. Founded: 1962. Setting: rural. Nearest major city is Vineland. 58-acre campus. 2 buildings on campus. Approved or accredited by Middle States Association of Colleges and Schools and National Catholic Education Association. Endowment: $255,000. Total enrollment: 128. Upper school average class size: 20. Upper school faculty-student ratio: 1:11. There are 180 required school days per year for Upper School students. Upper School students typically attend 5 days per week. The average school day consists of 6 hours and 30 minutes.

Upper School Student Profile Grade 9: 44 students (44 girls); Grade 10: 28 students (28 girls); Grade 11: 20 students (20 girls); Grade 12: 35 students (35 girls); Postgraduate: 128 students (128 girls). 90% of students are Roman Catholic.

Faculty School total: 20. In upper school: 20 women; 10 have advanced degrees.

Subjects Offered Algebra, American history, American literature, art, biology, botany, British literature (honors), career and personal planning, Catholic belief and practice, chemistry, choral music, chorus, Christian ethics, Christian scripture, Christian testament, Christianity, college counseling, computer technologies, CPR, current events, death and loss, driver education, electronic publishing, English literature, first aid, food and nutrition, French, graphic design, honors algebra, honors geometry, Middle Eastern history, physics, pre-calculus, probability and statistics, psychology, publications, religion, social justice, sociology, technology, Western civilization.

Graduation Requirements Algebra, biology, chemistry, English, geometry, physical education (includes health), religion (includes Bible studies and theology), religious studies, technology, U.S. history, Western civilization.

Special Academic Programs 1 Advanced Placement exam for which test preparation is offered; honors section; study at local college for college credit.

College Admission Counseling 43 students graduated in 2015; 25 went to college, including Rutgers, The State University of New Jersey, New Brunswick; Saint Joseph's University; Seton Hall University.

Student Life Upper grades have uniform requirement, student council, honor system. Discipline rests primarily with faculty. Attendance at religious services is required.

Tuition and Aid Day student tuition: $10,950. Tuition installment plan (SMART Tuition Payment Plan, monthly payment plans, individually arranged payment plans). Tuition reduction for siblings, merit scholarship grants, need-based scholarship grants, paying campus jobs available. In 2015–16, 15% of upper-school students received aid; total upper-school merit-scholarship money awarded: $34,500. Total amount of financial aid awarded in 2015–16: $35,000.

Admissions Traditional secondary-level entrance grade is 9. For fall 2015, 52 students applied for upper-level admission, 52 were accepted, 44 enrolled. High School Placement Test (closed version) from Scholastic Testing Service required. Deadline for receipt of application materials: none. Application fee required: $200.

Athletics Interscholastic: basketball, cheering, crew, lacrosse, soccer, softball, strength & conditioning, swimming and diving, tennis, track and field, volleyball; intramural: badminton, basketball, flag football, golf, gymnastics, physical fitness, soccer, softball, synchronized swimming, volleyball. 2 PE instructors, 12 coaches, 1 athletic trainer.

Computers Computers are regularly used in all academic, career exploration, college planning, creative writing, graphic design, graphics, library, library skills, photography, publications, research skills, technology, typing, Web site design, word processing, yearbook classes. Computer network features include on-campus library services, Internet access, wireless campus network, Internet filtering or blocking technology. Computer access in designated common areas is available to students. Students grades are available online. The school has a published electronic and media policy.

Contact Mrs. Natalie Cusick, Secretary. 856-697-2008 Ext. 120. Fax: 856-697-2887. E-mail: ncusick@olmanj.org. Website: www.olmanj.org

OUT-OF-DOOR-ACADEMY

5950 Deer Drive
Sarasota, Florida 34240

Head of School: Mr. David Mahler

General Information Coeducational day college-preparatory school. Grades PK–12. Founded: 1924. Setting: suburban. Nearest major city is Tampa. 85-acre campus. 10 buildings on campus. Approved or accredited by Florida Council of Independent Schools and National Independent Private Schools Association. Member of National Association of Independent Schools. Endowment: $16 million. Total enrollment: 723. Upper school average class size: 16. Upper school faculty-student ratio: 1:7. There are 172 required school days per year for Upper School students. Upper School students typically attend 5 days per week. The average school day consists of 7 hours.

Upper School Student Profile Grade 9: 83 students (50 boys, 33 girls); Grade 10: 68 students (34 boys, 34 girls); Grade 11: 77 students (43 boys, 34 girls); Grade 12: 46 students (22 boys, 24 girls).

Faculty School total: 88. In upper school: 13 men, 23 women; 20 have advanced degrees.

Subjects Offered Advanced Placement courses, advanced studio art-AP, algebra, American history-AP, art history, biology, biology-AP, British literature, calculus, calculus-AP, chemistry, chemistry-AP, college counseling, computers, drama, drama performance, dramatic arts, English, English composition, English language and composition-AP, English literature, English literature and composition-AP, English-AP, European history-AP, expository writing, French, French language-AP, geometry, graphic design, health and wellness, history-AP, honors algebra, honors geometry, Latin, Latin-AP, literature, literature and composition-AP, music, newspaper, photography, portfolio art, robotics, Spanish, Spanish language-AP, studio art, studio art-AP, U.S. government, U.S. history, U.S. history-AP, women's studies, world cultures, world literature, world studies, yearbook, zoology.

Graduation Requirements Arts and fine arts (art, music, dance, drama), electives, English, foreign language, health, history, mathematics, performing arts, personal fitness, science. Community service is required.

Special Academic Programs 21 Advanced Placement exams for which test preparation is offered; honors section; independent study.

College Admission Counseling 61 students graduated in 2015; 60 went to college, including Duke University; Florida State University; New York University; Rollins

College; Stanford University; University of Florida. Mean SAT critical reading: 611, mean SAT math: 611, mean SAT writing: 612, mean combined SAT: 1222.

Student Life Upper grades have specified standards of dress, student council, honor system. Discipline rests equally with students and faculty.

Summer Programs Enrichment, sports, art/fine arts' programs offered; held on campus; accepts boys and girls; open to students from other schools. 150 students usually enrolled. 2016 schedule: June 6 to July 29. Application deadline: May 1.

Tuition and Aid Day student tuition: $19,700. Tuition installment plan (FACTS Tuition Payment Plan). Need-based scholarship grants, faculty/staff tuition remission available. In 2015–16, 30% of upper-school students received aid. Total amount of financial aid awarded in 2015–16: $1,133,313.

Admissions Traditional secondary-level entrance grade is 9. For fall 2015, 90 students applied for upper-level admission, 47 were accepted, 34 enrolled. ERB or SSAT required. Deadline for receipt of application materials: March 1. Application fee required: $100. Interview required.

Athletics Interscholastic: baseball (boys), basketball (b,g), cheering (g), cross-country running (b,g), football (b), golf (b,g), independent competitive sports (b,g), lacrosse (b,g), soccer (b,g), softball (g), swimming and diving (b,g), tennis (b,g), track and field (b,g), volleyball (g); intramural: fitness (b,g); coed interscholastic: sailing; coed intramural: physical fitness, physical training, strength & conditioning, weight training. 4 PE instructors, 35 coaches, 1 athletic trainer.

Computers Computers are regularly used in all academic, computer applications, English, foreign language, French, graphic design, history, Latin, mathematics, newspaper, science, senior seminar, social studies, Spanish, yearbook classes. Computer network features include on-campus library services, online commercial services, Internet access, wireless campus network, Internet filtering or blocking technology, digital video production. Campus intranet, student e-mail accounts, and computer access in designated common areas are available to students. Students grades are available online. The school has a published electronic and media policy.

Contact Mr. Michael Salmon, Director of Middle and Upper School Admissions. 941-554-5955. Fax: 941-907-1251. E-mail: msalmon@oda.edu. Website: www.oda.edu

THE OXFORD ACADEMY

1393 Boston Post Road
Westbrook, Connecticut 06498-0685

Head of School: Mr. Philip B. Cocchiola

General Information Boys' boarding college-preparatory, general academic, arts, bilingual studies, and ESL school; primarily serves students with learning disabilities and individuals with Attention Deficit Disorder. Grades 9–PG. Founded: 1906. Setting: small town. Nearest major city is New Haven. Students are housed in single-sex dormitories. 13-acre campus. 8 buildings on campus. Approved or accredited by Connecticut Association of Independent Schools, New England Association of Schools and Colleges, The Association of Boarding Schools, and Connecticut Department of Education. Member of National Association of Independent Schools and Secondary School Admission Test Board. Endowment: $250,000. Total enrollment: 45. Upper school average class size: 1. Upper school faculty-student ratio: 1:1. There are 150 required school days per year for Upper School students. Upper School students typically attend 5 days per week. The average school day consists of 7 hours.

Upper School Student Profile Grade 9: 3 students (3 boys); Grade 10: 10 students (10 boys); Grade 11: 17 students (17 boys); Grade 12: 14 students (14 boys); Grade 13: 1 student (1 boy). 100% of students are boarding students. 22% are state residents. 11 states are represented in upper school student body. 28% are international students. International students from China, Egypt, India, Rwanda, Saudi Arabia, and Turks and Caicos Islands; 1 other country represented in student body.

Faculty School total: 22. In upper school: 13 men, 7 women; 12 have advanced degrees; 11 reside on campus.

Subjects Offered Algebra, American history, American history-AP, American literature, anatomy, art, astronomy, biology, biology-AP, botany, calculus, calculus-AP, chemistry, chemistry-AP, creative writing, drawing, earth science, ecology, economics, English, English as a foreign language, English literature, English literature-AP, environmental science, ESL, European history, expository writing, French, geography, geology, geometry, government/civics, grammar, history, Latin, marine biology, mathematics, oceanography, paleontology, philosophy, physical education, physics, physiology, psychology, science, social studies, sociology, Spanish, study skills, trigonometry, world history, world literature, writing, zoology.

Graduation Requirements English, foreign language, mathematics, science, social studies (includes history). Community service is required.

Special Academic Programs Advanced Placement exam preparation; honors section; accelerated programs; independent study; academic accommodation for the gifted; remedial reading and/or remedial writing; remedial math; ESL (10 students enrolled).

College Admission Counseling 11 students graduated in 2015; all went to college. 20% scored over 600 on SAT critical reading, 20% scored over 600 on SAT math, 20% scored over 600 on SAT writing.

Student Life Upper grades have specified standards of dress, student council, honor system. Discipline rests equally with students and faculty.

Summer Programs Remediation, enrichment, advancement, ESL, sports, art/fine arts programs offered; session focuses on acceleration of academics, study skills, ESL; held

on campus; accepts boys; open to students from other schools. 35 students usually enrolled. 2016 schedule: June 20 to July 22. Application deadline: none.

Tuition and Aid 5-day tuition and room/board: $50,000; 7-day tuition and room/board: $58,600. Guaranteed tuition plan. Tuition installment plan (individually arranged payment plans). Tuition reduction for siblings, need-based scholarship grants available. In 2015–16, 17% of upper-school students received aid.

Admissions For fall 2015, 33 students applied for upper-level admission, 30 were accepted, 15 enrolled. English proficiency, psychoeducational evaluation, TOEFL, Wechsler Individual Achievement Test or WISC-III and Woodcock-Johnson required. Deadline for receipt of application materials: none. Application fee required: $65. Interview required.

Athletics Interscholastic: basketball, soccer, tennis; intramural: alpine skiing, badminton, baseball, basketball, bicycling, bowling, cross-country running, fishing, fitness, flag football, floor hockey, Frisbee, golf, hiking/backpacking, kickball, lacrosse, outdoor activities, paint ball, physical fitness, running, sailing, skiing (downhill), snowboarding, soccer, strength & conditioning, table tennis, tennis, ultimate Frisbee, weight lifting, weight training, whiffle ball.

Computers Computers are regularly used in mathematics classes. Computer network features include on-campus library services, online commercial services, Internet access, wireless campus network, Internet filtering or blocking technology. Student e-mail accounts and computer access in designated common areas are available to students. The school has a published electronic and media policy.

Contact Ms. Hilary L. Holmes, Assistant Director of Admissions. 860-399-6247 Ext. 100. Fax: 860-399-5555. E-mail: admissions@oxfordacademy.net. Website: www.oxfordacademy.net

PACE ACADEMY

966 West Paces Ferry Road NW
Atlanta, Georgia 30327

Head of School: Mr. Frederick G. Assaf

General Information Coeducational day college-preparatory, arts, and technology school. Grades K–12. Founded: 1958. Setting: suburban. 63-acre campus. 7 buildings on campus. Approved or accredited by Southern Association of Colleges and Schools and Southern Association of Independent Schools. Member of National Association of Independent Schools and Secondary School Admission Test Board. Endowment: $50.6 million. Total enrollment: 1,015. Upper school average class size: 12. Upper school faculty-student ratio: 1:7. There are 180 required school days per year for Upper School students. Upper School students typically attend 5 days per week. The average school day consists of 6 hours and 50 minutes.

Upper School Student Profile Grade 9: 102 students (49 boys, 53 girls); Grade 10: 91 students (48 boys, 43 girls); Grade 11: 86 students (40 boys, 46 girls); Grade 12: 93 students (47 boys, 46 girls).

Faculty School total: 178. In upper school: 34 men, 35 women; 51 have advanced degrees.

Subjects Offered Acting, adolescent issues, advanced math, advanced studio art-AP, algebra, American history, American history-AP, American literature, ancient world history, architectural drawing, art, art history, art history-AP, arts, band, biology, biology-AP, British literature, British literature (honors), calculus, calculus-AP, ceramics, chemistry, chemistry-AP, Chinese history, chorus, community service, comparative government and politics-AP, comparative politics, computer science-AP, computer skills, creative writing, debate, digital imaging, digital photography, directing, drawing, earth science, economics, English, English literature, English-AP, environmental science-AP, European history, fine arts, French, French language-AP, geometry, history, honors algebra, honors English, honors geometry, honors U.S. history, honors world history, Japanese history, keyboarding, Latin, Latin-AP, leadership education training, mathematics, modern European history-AP, music history, music theory-AP, painting, photography, physical education, physics, physics-AP, political science, pre-algebra, psychology, public speaking, religion, science, social sciences, Spanish, Spanish language-AP, stagecraft, statistics-AP, student publications, trigonometry, world history, world literature, yearbook.

Graduation Requirements Arts and fine arts (art, music, dance, drama), English, foreign language, mathematics, physical education (includes health), science, social sciences, social studies (includes history), 40 hours of community service, one semester of public speaking.

Special Academic Programs 17 Advanced Placement exams for which test preparation is offered; honors section; independent study; term-away projects; study abroad; academic accommodation for the gifted, the musically talented, and the artistically talented.

College Admission Counseling 98 students graduated in 2015; all went to college, including Emory University; Georgia Institute of Technology; Miami University; Southern Methodist University; Tulane University; University of Georgia. Mean SAT critical reading: 642, mean SAT math: 641, mean SAT writing: 635, mean combined SAT: 1918, mean composite ACT: 30.

Student Life Upper grades have specified standards of dress, student council, honor system. Discipline rests equally with students and faculty.

Summer Programs Remediation, enrichment, advancement, sports, art/fine arts, computer instruction programs offered; session focuses on traditional day camp with specialty academic, activity, and athletic camps; held on campus; accepts boys and girls; open to students from other schools. 1,200 students usually enrolled. 2016 schedule: June 1 to July 30.

Tuition and Aid Day student tuition: $25,170. Tuition installment plan (FACTS Tuition Payment Plan). Need-based scholarship grants available. In 2015–16, 12% of upper-school students received aid. Total amount of financial aid awarded in 2015–16: $1,400,000.

Admissions Traditional secondary-level entrance grade is 9. For fall 2015, 190 students applied for upper-level admission, 62 were accepted, 41 enrolled. SSAT required. Deadline for receipt of application materials: February 1. Application fee required: $95. On-campus interview required.

Athletics Interscholastic: baseball (boys), basketball (b,g), cheering (g), cross-country running (b,g), diving (b,g), fitness (b,g), football (b), golf (b,g), gymnastics (g), lacrosse (b,g), soccer (b,g), softball (g), swimming and diving (b,g), tennis (b,g), track and field (b,g), volleyball (g), wrestling (b); intramural: squash (b), water polo (b); coed interscholastic: physical training, strength & conditioning; coed intramural: equestrian sports, flag football, mountain biking, ultimate Frisbee. 8 PE instructors, 6 coaches, 4 athletic trainers.

Computers Computers are regularly used in all classes. Computer network features include on-campus library services, online commercial services, Internet access, wireless campus network, Internet filtering or blocking technology, classroom SmartBoards and ActivBoards, student laptop/iPad loaner program. Campus intranet, student e-mail accounts, and computer access in designated common areas are available to students. Students grades are available online. The school has a published electronic and media policy.

Contact Mrs. Ashley Stafford, Admissions Database Manager. 404-240-7412. Fax: 404-240-9124. E-mail: astafford@paceacademy.org. Website: www.paceacademy.org

PACE/BRANTLEY HALL HIGH SCHOOL

Longwood, Florida
See Special Needs Schools section.

PACELLI CATHOLIC HIGH SCHOOL

2020 Kay Circle
Columbus, Georgia 31907
Head of School: Mrs. Kristin Turner

General Information Coeducational day college-preparatory, arts, religious studies, and technology school, affiliated with Roman Catholic Church. Grades 9–12. Founded: 1958. Setting: urban. Nearest major city is Atlanta. 26-acre campus. 4 buildings on campus. Approved or accredited by National Catholic Education Association, Southern Association of Colleges and Schools, and Georgia Department of Education. Total enrollment: 598. Upper school average class size: 15. Upper school faculty-student ratio: 1:11. There are 180 required school days per year for Upper School students. Upper School students typically attend 5 days per week. The average school day consists of 6 hours and 35 minutes.

Upper School Student Profile 55% of students are Roman Catholic.

Faculty School total: 17. In upper school: 6 men, 11 women; 1 has an advanced degree.

Subjects Offered American history, American literature, anatomy, Bible studies, creative writing, earth science, economics, geology, mathematics, psychology, social sciences, world history, world literature.

Graduation Requirements English, foreign language, mathematics, physical education (includes health), religion (includes Bible studies and theology), science, social sciences, social studies (includes history), world history.

Special Academic Programs Advanced Placement exam preparation; honors section.

College Admission Counseling 35 students graduated in 2014; 34 went to college, including Auburn University; Columbus State University; Georgia Institute of Technology; University of Georgia. Other: 1 entered military service. Mean SAT critical reading: 530, mean SAT math: 545, mean SAT writing: 506, mean combined SAT: 1581, mean composite ACT: 24.

Student Life Upper grades have uniform requirement, student council. Discipline rests primarily with faculty. Attendance at religious services is required.

Tuition and Aid Day student tuition: $7300. Tuition installment plan (FACTS Tuition Payment Plan). Tuition reduction for siblings, merit scholarship grants, need-based scholarship grants available. In 2014–15, 12% of upper-school students received aid; total upper-school merit-scholarship money awarded: $22,000. Total amount of financial aid awarded in 2014–15: $65,000.

Admissions Traditional secondary-level entrance grade is 9. For fall 2014, 50 students applied for upper-level admission, 35 were accepted, 28 enrolled. STS required. Deadline for receipt of application materials: none. Application fee required: $50.

Athletics Interscholastic: baseball (boys), basketball (b,g), cheering (g), cross-country running (b,g), dance (g), football (b), soccer (b,g), softball (g), tennis (b,g), volleyball (g), wrestling (b); coed interscholastic: golf. 1 PE instructor.

Computers Computer network features include Internet access, wireless campus network. Students grades are available online. The school has a published electronic and media policy.

Contact Mrs. Julie Davis, Director of Admissions & Communications. 706-561-8232 Ext. 271. Fax: 706-563-0211. E-mail: jdavis@sasphs.net. Website: www.BeAViking.com

PACIFIC CREST COMMUNITY SCHOOL

116 Northeast 29th Street
Portland, Oregon 97232
Head of School: Jenny Osborne

General Information Coeducational day college-preparatory and arts school. Grades 6–12. Founded: 1993. Setting: urban. 1 building on campus. Approved or accredited by Northwest Accreditation Commission, Northwest Association of Schools and Colleges, and Oregon Department of Education. Total enrollment: 95. Upper school average class size: 10. Upper school faculty-student ratio: 1:9. There are 180 required school days per year for Upper School students. Upper School students typically attend 5 days per week. The average school day consists of 6 hours.

Faculty School total: 14. In upper school: 6 men, 8 women; 11 have advanced degrees.

Subjects Offered Acting, advanced math, African drumming, algebra, American government, American history, American literature, animal behavior, anthropology, art history, Asian history, bioethics, botany, calculus, cell biology, chemistry, civil war history, comparative religion, computer applications, creative writing, cultural criticism, current events, drama, drawing, ecology, economics, English literature, entomology, ethics, European history, filmmaking, foreign language, geometry, government, health, history of mathematics, HTML design, Japanese studies, linear algebra, literature by women, logic, marine biology, medieval history, Pacific Island studies, personal finance, philosophy, physical education, physics, play/screen writing, pre-algebra, precalculus, printmaking, probability and statistics, psychology, public speaking, SAT preparation, science fiction, senior seminar, service learning/internship, set design, Shakespeare, short story, sociology, Spanish, stage design, theater arts, U.S. government, U.S. history, visual literacy, Web site design, women's literature, writing.

Graduation Requirements Senior seminar/dissertation.

Special Academic Programs Independent study; study at local college for college credit; academic accommodation for the gifted.

College Admission Counseling 16 students graduated in 2015; 13 went to college. Other: 3 had other specific plans.

Student Life Discipline rests equally with students and faculty.

Tuition and Aid Day student tuition: $13,000. Tuition installment plan (FACTS Tuition Payment Plan, monthly payment plans). Need-based scholarship grants available. In 2015–16, 15% of upper-school students received aid. Total amount of financial aid awarded in 2015–16: $60,000.

Admissions Traditional secondary-level entrance grade is 9. For fall 2015, 22 students applied for upper-level admission, 19 were accepted, 19 enrolled. Deadline for receipt of application materials: March 1. Application fee required: $100. Interview required.

Athletics Coed Intramural: basketball, bicycling, bowling, canoeing/kayaking, hiking/backpacking, outdoor adventure, outdoor education, outdoor skills, rock climbing, running, skiing (cross-country). 2 PE instructors.

Computers Computers are regularly used in all academic classes. Computer network features include Internet access, wireless campus network. Student e-mail accounts are available to students.

Contact Jenny Osborne, Director. 503-234-2826. Fax: 503-234-3186. E-mail: Jenny@pcrest.org. Website: www.pcrest.org

PACIFIC LUTHERAN HIGH SCHOOL

2814 Manhattan Beach Blvd.
Gardena, California 90249
Head of School: Mr. Lucas Michael Fitzgerald

General Information Coeducational day college-preparatory, general academic, and religious studies school, affiliated with Lutheran Church–Missouri Synod; primarily serves underachievers. Grades 9–12. Founded: 1997. Setting: suburban. Nearest major city is Los Angeles. 2-acre campus. 1 building on campus. Approved or accredited by Western Association of Schools and Colleges and California Department of Education. Upper school average class size: 15. Upper school faculty-student ratio: 1:10. Upper School students typically attend 5 days per week. The average school day consists of 6 hours and 30 minutes.

Upper School Student Profile Grade 9: 31 students (20 boys, 11 girls); Grade 10: 22 students (11 boys, 11 girls); Grade 11: 28 students (10 boys, 18 girls); Grade 12: 22 students (10 boys, 12 girls). 15% of students are Lutheran Church–Missouri Synod.

Faculty In upper school: 5 men, 5 women; 6 have advanced degrees.

Subjects Offered 1 1/2 elective credits, 1968, 3-dimensional art, 3-dimensional design, accounting, ACT preparation, acting, addiction, ADL skills, advanced biology, advanced chemistry, advanced computer applications, advanced studio art-AP, advanced TOEFL/grammar, advertising design, aerobics, aerospace education, aerospace science, aesthetics, African American history, African American studies, African dance, African drumming, African history, African literature, African studies.

Graduation Requirements Students are required to take four years of theology courses.

Special Academic Programs International Baccalaureate program; Advanced Placement exam preparation; academic accommodation for the gifted; remedial reading and/or remedial writing.

College Admission Counseling 26 students graduated in 2014; 23 went to college. Other: 3 went to work.

Student Life Upper grades have specified standards of dress, student council, honor system. Discipline rests equally with students and faculty.

Tuition and Aid Day student tuition: $7000. Tuition installment plan (monthly payment plans, individually arranged payment plans). Tuition reduction for siblings, merit scholarship grants, need-based scholarship grants, middle-income loans, we work with families to arrange payment plans where/if necessary available. In 2014–15, 5% of upper-school students received aid; total upper-school merit-scholarship money awarded: $10,000. Total amount of financial aid awarded in 2014–15: $20,000.

Admissions Traditional secondary-level entrance grade is 9. Iowa Test of Educational Development required. Deadline for receipt of application materials: none. Application fee required: $50. Interview required.

Athletics Interscholastic: basketball (boys, girls), football (b), volleyball (b,g); coed interscholastic: baseball, cheering, cross-country running, golf, winter soccer; coed intramural: flag football, outdoor activities, outdoor education, outdoor recreation, ropes courses, strength & conditioning, touch football. 1 PE instructor, 4 coaches.

Computers Computer network features include Internet access, wireless campus network, Internet filtering or blocking technology. Students grades are available online.

Contact Mrs. Denise Spartalis, Office Manager. 310-538-6863 Ext. 1000. Fax: 310-510-6761. E-mail: pacificlutheranhigh@yahoo.com. Website: www.pacificlutheranhigh.com/

THE PACKER COLLEGIATE INSTITUTE

170 Joralemon Street
Brooklyn, New York 11201

Head of School: Dr. Bruce L. Dennis

General Information Coeducational day college-preparatory, arts, and technology school. Grades PK–12. Founded: 1845. Setting: urban. Nearest major city is New York. 5 buildings on campus. Approved or accredited by New York State Association of Independent Schools and New York Department of Education. Member of National Association of Independent Schools and Secondary School Admission Test Board. Endowment: $16 million. Total enrollment: 941. Upper school average class size: 15. Upper school faculty-student ratio: 1:7.

Upper School Student Profile Grade 9: 66 students (34 boys, 32 girls); Grade 10: 87 students (45 boys, 42 girls); Grade 11: 70 students (36 boys, 34 girls); Grade 12: 83 students (38 boys, 45 girls).

Faculty School total: 149. In upper school: 27 men, 42 women; 48 have advanced degrees.

Subjects Offered African literature, algebra, American history, American literature, art, art history, biology, calculus, chemistry, community service, computer math, computer programming, computer science, creative writing, dance, drama, English, English literature, ethics, European history, expository writing, fine arts, French, geometry, government/civics, health, history, Latin, music, philosophy, photography, physical education, physics, science, sociology, Spanish, theater, trigonometry, women's studies, world history, world literature.

Graduation Requirements Arts and fine arts (art, music, dance, drama), English, foreign language, mathematics, physical education (includes health), science, social studies (includes history). Community service is required.

Special Academic Programs Honors section; independent study; term-away projects; study at local college for college credit; study abroad.

College Admission Counseling 90 students graduated in 2015; all went to college, including Brown University; Skidmore College; Wesleyan College; Williams College; Yale University.

Student Life Upper grades have student council. Discipline rests equally with students and faculty.

Tuition and Aid Day student tuition: $40,000. Tuition installment plan (monthly payment plans). Need-based scholarship grants available. In 2015–16, 30% of upper-school students received aid. Total amount of financial aid awarded in 2015–16: $7,400,000.

Admissions Traditional secondary-level entrance grade is 9. For fall 2015, 400 students applied for upper-level admission, 80 were accepted, 35 enrolled. ISEE or SSAT required. Deadline for receipt of application materials: December 1. Application fee required: $60. On-campus interview required.

Athletics Interscholastic: baseball (boys), basketball (b,g), cross-country running (b,g), dance (b,g). 10 PE instructors, 4 coaches, 2 athletic trainers.

Computers Computers are regularly used in mathematics, science, writing classes. Computer network features include on-campus library services, online commercial services, Internet access, laptop program (grades 6-12).

Contact Sara Goin, Admissions Coordinator. 718-250-0385. Fax: 718-875-1363. E-mail: sgoin@packer.edu. Website: www.packer.edu

PADUA ACADEMY

905 North Broom Street
Wilmington, Delaware 19806

Head of School: Mrs. Cindy Hayes Mann

General Information Girls' day college-preparatory, general academic, arts, business, religious studies, and technology school, affiliated with Roman Catholic Church. Grades 9–12. Founded: 1954. Setting: urban. 2 buildings on campus. Approved or accredited by Middle States Association of Colleges and Schools and Delaware Department of Education. Member of Secondary School Admission Test Board. Endowment: $1 million. Total enrollment: 600. Upper school average class size: 23. Upper school faculty-student ratio: 1:11. There are 180 required school days per year for Upper School students. Upper School students typically attend 5 days per week. The average school day consists of 5 hours and 50 minutes.

Upper School Student Profile Grade 9: 150 students (150 girls); Grade 10: 150 students (150 girls); Grade 11: 150 students (150 girls); Grade 12: 150 students (150 girls). 80% of students are Roman Catholic.

Faculty School total: 57. In upper school: 18 men, 39 women; 42 have advanced degrees.

Subjects Offered Advanced Placement courses, algebra, American history, American literature, anatomy, art, art history, biology, business, calculus, chemistry, computer programming, computer science, English, English literature, environmental science, European history, fine arts, French, geometry, government/civics, health, history, home economics, Italian, mathematics, physical education, physics, religion, science, social studies, Spanish, statistics, theology, trigonometry, world history, world literature.

Graduation Requirements Arts and fine arts (art, music, dance, drama), electives, English, foreign language, mathematics, physical education (includes health), religion (includes Bible studies and theology), science, social studies (includes history). Community service is required.

Special Academic Programs Advanced Placement exam preparation; honors section; study at local college for college credit.

College Admission Counseling 154 students graduated in 2015; 153 went to college, including Cabrini College; Saint Joseph's University; University of Delaware; West Chester University of Pennsylvania; Widener University. Other: 1 went to work. Mean SAT critical reading: 550, mean SAT math: 510, mean SAT writing: 550, mean combined SAT: 1610.

Student Life Upper grades have uniform requirement, student council, honor system. Discipline rests primarily with faculty. Attendance at religious services is required.

Tuition and Aid Day student tuition: $6797. Tuition installment plan (monthly payment plans). Tuition reduction for siblings, merit scholarship grants, need-based scholarship grants available. In 2015–16, 25% of upper-school students received aid; total upper-school merit-scholarship money awarded: $50,000. Total amount of financial aid awarded in 2015–16: $500,000.

Admissions Traditional secondary-level entrance grade is 9. For fall 2015, 250 students applied for upper-level admission, 180 were accepted, 154 enrolled. High School Placement Test (closed version) from Scholastic Testing Service required. Deadline for receipt of application materials: July 1. Application fee required: $100. On-campus interview recommended.

Athletics Interscholastic: aerobics/dance, basketball, cross-country running, dance squad, diving, field hockey, golf, indoor track, soccer, softball, swimming and diving, track and field, volleyball, winter (indoor) track; intramural: bowling, volleyball. 3 PE instructors, 10 coaches, 1 athletic trainer.

Computers Computers are regularly used in business studies, career exploration, Christian doctrine, college planning, desktop publishing, foreign language, health, library science, library skills, literary magazine, newspaper, psychology, religious studies, SAT preparation, social studies, yearbook classes. Computer network features include on-campus library services, Internet access, wireless campus network. Student e-mail accounts are available to students. Students grades are available online. The school has a published electronic and media policy.

Contact Ms. Shana L. Maguire, Director of Admission. 302-421-3765. Fax: 302-421-3763. E-mail: smaguire@paduaacademy.org. Website: www.paduaacademy.org

PADUA FRANCISCAN HIGH SCHOOL

6740 State Road
Parma, Ohio 44134-4598

Head of School: Mr. David Stec

General Information Coeducational day college-preparatory, arts, business, religious studies, and technology school, affiliated with Roman Catholic Church; primarily serves students with learning disabilities. Grades 9–12. Founded: 1961. Setting: suburban. Nearest major city is Cleveland. 40-acre campus. 1 building on campus. Approved or accredited by North Central Association of Colleges and Schools, Ohio Catholic Schools Accreditation Association (OCSAA), and Ohio Department of Education. Endowment: $3 million. Total enrollment: 773. Upper school average class size: 23. Upper school faculty-student ratio: 1:15. There are 179 required school days per year for Upper School students. Upper School students typically attend 5 days per week. The average school day consists of 6 hours and 30 minutes.

Upper School Student Profile Grade 9: 191 students (91 boys, 100 girls); Grade 10: 174 students (83 boys, 91 girls); Grade 11: 187 students (90 boys, 97 girls); Grade 12: 221 students (129 boys, 92 girls). 92% of students are Roman Catholic.

Faculty School total: 55. In upper school: 22 men, 32 women; 30 have advanced degrees.

Subjects Offered Accounting, algebra, American government, art appreciation, biology-AP, business, calculus-AP, chemistry, child development, Christian ethics, church history, computers, concert band, concert choir, consumer economics, current events, design, drawing, earth science, economics, English, English language-AP, ensembles, fitness, food and nutrition, French, French-AP, geography, geometry, German, German-AP, honors algebra, honors English, honors geometry, honors U.S. history, integrated science, interior design, Italian, Latin, Latin-AP, marching band, marketing, math analysis, music appreciation, music theory, orchestra, painting, photography, physics, pre-calculus, programming, psychology, social issues, social justice, sociology, Spanish, Spanish-AP, stagecraft, symphonic band, theater, trigonometry, U.S. history, U.S. history-AP, world cultures, world history.

Graduation Requirements Arts and fine arts (art, music, dance, drama), computer science, English, foreign language, lab science, mathematics, physical education (includes health), social studies (includes history), theology, four years of service projects.

Special Academic Programs Advanced Placement exam preparation; honors section; accelerated programs; study at local college for college credit; study abroad; remedial reading and/or remedial writing; remedial math; programs in English, mathematics for dyslexic students; special instructional classes for students with learning disabilities.

College Admission Counseling 178 students graduated in 2014; 172 went to college, including Cleveland State University; John Carroll University; Kent State University; Miami University; The University of Akron. Other: 3 went to work, 1 entered military service, 2 had other specific plans. Median combined SAT: 1610, median composite ACT: 24. Mean SAT critical reading: 539, mean SAT math: 541, mean SAT writing: 530. 25% scored over 600 on SAT critical reading, 23% scored over 600 on SAT math, 28% scored over 600 on SAT writing, 37.6% scored over 26 on composite ACT.

Student Life Upper grades have specified standards of dress, student council, honor system. Discipline rests primarily with faculty. Attendance at religious services is required.

Tuition and Aid Day student tuition: $9985. Tuition installment plan (monthly payment plans, individually arranged payment plans). Tuition reduction for siblings, merit scholarship grants, need-based scholarship grants, paying campus jobs, early payment discount, music scholarships available. In 2014–15, 45% of upper-school students received aid; total upper-school merit-scholarship money awarded: $415,000. Total amount of financial aid awarded in 2014–15: $540,000.

Admissions Traditional secondary-level entrance grade is 9. For fall 2014, 235 students applied for upper-level admission, 230 were accepted, 191 enrolled. High School Placement Test or STS required. Deadline for receipt of application materials: January 31. Application fee required: $50.

Athletics Interscholastic: aquatics (boys, girls), baseball (b), basketball (b,g), bowling (b,g), cheering (g), combined training (b,g), cross-country running (b,g), dance team (g), diving (b,g), football (b), golf (b,g), ice hockey (b), lacrosse (b), physical fitness (b,g), soccer (b,g), softball (g), strength & conditioning (b,g), swimming and diving (b,g), tennis (b,g), track and field (b,g), volleyball (g), wrestling (b); intramural: basketball (b), flag football (b), football (b), freestyle skiing (b,g), golf (g), gymnastics (g), power lifting (b), touch football (b), weight lifting (b), weight training (b), winter soccer (b), yoga (b); coed interscholastic: figure skating, fitness; coed intramural: alpine skiing, backpacking, canoeing/kayaking, fishing, hiking/backpacking, skiing (downhill), snowboarding, wilderness, wilderness survival, wildernessways. 3 PE instructors, 30 coaches, 5 athletic trainers.

Computers Computers are regularly used in all academic classes. Computer network features include on-campus library services, online commercial services, Internet access, wireless campus network, all students received a Chromebook for 2014-15. Student e-mail accounts and computer access in designated common areas are available to students. Students grades are available online. The school has a published electronic and media policy.

Contact Mrs. Rachel DeGirolamo, Admissions Coordinator. 440-845-2444 Ext. 112. Fax: 440-845-5710. E-mail: rdegirolamo@paduafranciscan.com. Website: www.paduafranciscan.com

THE PAIDEIA SCHOOL
1509 Ponce de Leon Avenue
Atlanta, Georgia 30307
Head of School: Paul F. Bianchi
General Information Coeducational day college-preparatory, arts, and technology school. Grades PK–12. Founded: 1971. Setting: urban. 28-acre campus. 13 buildings on campus. Approved or accredited by Georgia Independent School Association, Southern Association of Colleges and Schools, Southern Association of Independent Schools, and Georgia Department of Education. Member of National Association of Independent Schools. Endowment: $15.8 million. Total enrollment: 991. Upper school average class size: 14. Upper school faculty-student ratio: 1:9. There are 177 required school days per year for Upper School students. Upper School students typically attend 5 days per week. The average school day consists of 5 hours.

Upper School Student Profile Grade 9: 114 students (48 boys, 66 girls); Grade 10: 109 students (50 boys, 59 girls); Grade 11: 101 students (50 boys, 51 girls); Grade 12: 100 students (54 boys, 46 girls).

Faculty School total: 157. In upper school: 34 men, 36 women; 62 have advanced degrees.

Subjects Offered 20th century American writers, 20th century history, 3-dimensional design, acting, African drumming, African-American history, African-American literature, algebra, American culture, American government, American literature, anatomy, anatomy and physiology, art, art history, Asian history, Asian studies, athletic training, auto mechanics, bioethics, biology, biology-AP, calculus, calculus-AP, ceramics, chemistry, chemistry-AP, chorus, community service, comparative religion, computer programming, computer science, creative writing, drama, drawing, ecology, environmental systems, economics, English, English literature, environmental science, ethics, expository writing, filmmaking, fine arts, forensics, French, French studies, gardening, geography, geology, geometry, government/civics, health, health and wellness, history, humanities, jazz band, jewelry making, journalism, literary magazine, literature, mathematics, medieval history, music theory, Native American studies, newspaper, orchestra, peer counseling, photography, physical education, physics, physics-AP, play production, playwriting and directing, poetry, pre-calculus, psychology, Shakespeare, social studies, Spanish, Spanish literature, speech, stage design, statistics, statistics-AP, studio art, theater, theater arts, trigonometry, U.S. history, Web site design, weight training, women's health, women's studies, world civilizations, world history, world literature, writing, yearbook.

Graduation Requirements Arts and fine arts (art, music, dance, drama), English, foreign language, mathematics, physical education (includes health), science, social studies (includes history), 60 hours of community service with local non-profit agency. Community service is required.

Special Academic Programs 6 Advanced Placement exams for which test preparation is offered; honors section; independent study; special instructional classes for deaf students.

College Admission Counseling 103 students graduated in 2014; 101 went to college, including Emory University; Georgia Institute of Technology; Georgia State University; Oberlin College; Tulane University; University of Georgia. Other: 1 went to work, 1 had other specific plans.

Student Life Upper grades have student council, honor system. Discipline rests equally with students and faculty.

Tuition and Aid Day student tuition: $21,564. Tuition installment plan (Bank-arranged tuition loan program). Need-based scholarship grants, need-based tuition assistance available. In 2014–15, 21% of upper-school students received aid. Total amount of financial aid awarded in 2014–15: $1,481,011.

Admissions Traditional secondary-level entrance grade is 9. Deadline for receipt of application materials: January 26. Application fee required: $75. On-campus interview required.

Athletics Interscholastic: baseball (boys), basketball (b,g), cross-country running (b,g), diving (b,g), golf (b), soccer (b,g), softball (g), swimming and diving (b,g), tennis (b,g), track and field (b,g), ultimate Frisbee (b,g), volleyball (g); coed intramural: basketball, bicycling, bocce, fitness, flag football, horseshoes, kickball, outdoor education, running, soccer, softball, strength & conditioning, tai chi, ultimate Frisbee, volleyball, weight lifting, weight training, yoga. 3 PE instructors, 2 coaches, 1 athletic trainer.

Computers Computers are regularly used in all classes. Computer network features include on-campus library services, online commercial services, Internet access, wireless campus network, Internet filtering or blocking technology, technology specialist program, computer borrowing program for students, all students have iPads. Campus intranet, student e-mail accounts, and computer access in designated common areas are available to students. The school has a published electronic and media policy.

Contact Admissions Office. 404-270-2312. Fax: 404-270-2666. E-mail: admissions@paideiaschool.org. Website: www.paideiaschool.org

PALMA SCHOOL
919 Iverson Street
Salinas, California 93901
Head of School: Br. Patrick D. Dunne, CFC
General Information Boys' day college-preparatory and religious studies school, affiliated with Roman Catholic Church. Grades 7–12. Founded: 1951. Setting: suburban. 25-acre campus. 16 buildings on campus. Approved or accredited by Western Association of Schools and Colleges, Western Catholic Education Association, and California Department of Education. Total enrollment: 428. Upper school average class size: 25. Upper school faculty-student ratio: 1:15. Upper School students typically attend 5 days per week. The average school day consists of 6 hours.

Upper School Student Profile Grade 9: 83 students (83 boys); Grade 10: 80 students (80 boys); Grade 11: 85 students (85 boys); Grade 12: 78 students (78 boys). 69% of students are Roman Catholic.

Faculty School total: 28. In upper school: 23 men, 5 women; 19 have advanced degrees.

Palma School

Subjects Offered Agriculture, algebra, American history, American literature, anatomy, art, art history, band, biology, biology-AP, business, calculus, calculus-AP, chemistry, Chinese, Christian and Hebrew scripture, church history, civics, community service, computer applications, computer art, computer math, computer multimedia, computer programming, computer programming-AP, computer science, computer-aided design, creative writing, debate, digital art, driver education, earth science, economics, English, English language and composition-AP, English language-AP, English literature, English literature and composition-AP, English literature-AP, English/composition-AP, ethics, European history, European history-AP, expository writing, film, film studies, fine arts, finite math, French, geography, geometry, government and politics-AP, government/civics, grammar, health, health education, history, honors algebra, honors geometry, jazz, jazz ensemble, journalism, Latin, mathematics, music, oceanography, participation in sports, physical education, physical science, physics, physics-AP, pre-algebra, pre-calculus, psychology, religion, SAT/ACT preparation, science, social studies, Spanish, Spanish language-AP, Spanish-AP, speech, statistics-AP, student government, studio art-AP, study skills, symphonic band, theology, trigonometry, typing, U.S. government and politics-AP, U.S. history-AP, United States government-AP, video film production, world history, world history-AP, world literature, world religions, world religions, writing, yearbook.

Graduation Requirements Advanced biology, arts and fine arts (art, music, dance, drama), chemistry, English, foreign language, mathematics, physical education (includes health), religion (includes Bible studies and theology), science, social studies (includes history), religious retreat (8th, 9th, 10th grades), 60 hours of community service, must take the ACT College Entrance Exam.

Special Academic Programs Advanced Placement exam preparation; honors section.

College Admission Counseling 97 students graduated in 2015; 96 went to college, including California Polytechnic State University, San Luis Obispo; California State University, Fresno; California State University, Monterey Bay; Saint Mary's College of California; Santa Clara University; University of California, Davis. Other: 1 went to work.

Student Life Upper grades have specified standards of dress, student council, honor system. Discipline rests primarily with faculty. Attendance at religious services is required.

Summer Programs Remediation, enrichment, advancement, sports, art/fine arts programs offered; session focuses on remediation, advancement, and enrichment; held on campus; accepts boys and girls; open to students from other schools. 150 students usually enrolled. 2016 schedule: June 15 to July 25. Application deadline: May 1.

Tuition and Aid Day student tuition: $15,000. Tuition installment plan (Insured Tuition Payment Plan, monthly payment plans, 2-payment plan). Merit scholarship grants, need-based scholarship grants available. In 2015–16, 15% of upper-school students received aid. Total amount of financial aid awarded in 2015–16: $700,000.

Admissions Traditional secondary-level entrance grade is 9. For fall 2015, 54 students applied for upper-level admission, 47 were accepted, 33 enrolled. ETS high school placement exam and ETS HSPT (closed) required. Deadline for receipt of application materials: none. Application fee required: $75. On-campus interview required.

Athletics Interscholastic: baseball, basketball, cross-country running, field hockey, football, golf, mountain biking, soccer, swimming and diving, tennis, track and field, volleyball, water polo, winter soccer, wrestling; intramural: basketball, bicycling, indoor soccer, kayaking, mountain biking, physical training, power lifting, skiing (downhill), snowboarding, strength & conditioning, ultimate Frisbee, weight lifting, weight training, whiffle ball. 5 PE instructors, 15 coaches, 1 athletic trainer.

Computers Computers are regularly used in art, economics, English, foreign language, history, mathematics, multimedia, music, newspaper, photography, science, social sciences, video film production, writing, yearbook classes. Computer network features include on-campus library services, online commercial services, Internet access, wireless campus network, Internet filtering or blocking technology. Campus intranet, student e-mail accounts, and computer access in designated common areas are available to students. Students grades are available online. The school has a published electronic and media policy.

Contact Mr. Raul Rico, Director of Admissions. 831-422-6391. Fax: 831-422-5065. E-mail: rico@palmahschool.org. Website: www.palmaschool.org

PALO ALTO PREPARATORY SCHOOL

2462 Wyandotte Street
Mountain View, California 94043

Head of School: Christopher Morley Keck

General Information Coeducational day and distance learning college-preparatory and arts school; primarily serves students with learning disabilities, individuals with Attention Deficit Disorder, individuals with emotional and behavioral problems, and dyslexic students. Grades 8–12. Distance learning grades 9–12. Founded: 1986. Setting: suburban. 1 building on campus. Approved or accredited by Western Association of Schools and Colleges and California Department of Education. Total enrollment: 75. Upper school average class size: 8. Upper school faculty-student ratio: 1:8. There are 180 required school days per year for Upper School students. Upper School students typically attend 5 days per week. The average school day consists of 6 hours.

Upper School Student Profile Grade 8: 2 students (2 boys); Grade 9: 16 students (11 boys, 5 girls); Grade 10: 19 students (13 boys, 6 girls); Grade 11: 14 students (9 boys, 5 girls); Grade 12: 24 students (16 boys, 8 girls).

Faculty School total: 14. In upper school: 7 men, 4 women; 5 have advanced degrees.

Subjects Offered 20th century world history, African American history, African American studies, algebra, American government, American history, American history-AP, American sign language, applied arts, applied music, art, ASB Leadership, biology, calculus, chemistry, chemistry-AP, civics, computer art, digital art, economics, English, English composition, English literature, environmental science, geometry, government, health, marine biology, modern civilization, music, music performance, pre-algebra, senior project, Spanish, study skills.

Graduation Requirements African American history, art, biology, economics, English, geometry, government, health, senior project, U.S. history, world civilizations.

Special Academic Programs 3 Advanced Placement exams for which test preparation is offered; honors section; accelerated programs; independent study; term-away projects; study at local college for college credit; study abroad; programs in English, mathematics for dyslexic students.

College Admission Counseling 15 students graduated in 2015; 13 went to college, including California Polytechnic State University, San Luis Obispo; California State University Channel Islands; Lewis & Clark College; The Evergreen State College; University of California, Davis; University of California, Santa Cruz. Other: 1 went to work, 1 had other specific plans.

Student Life Upper grades have specified standards of dress, student council, honor system. Discipline rests primarily with faculty.

Summer Programs Remediation, advancement, rigorous outdoor training programs offered; session focuses on outdoor excursions and classes for makeup or to get ahead; held on campus; accepts boys and girls; open to students from other schools. 40 students usually enrolled. 2016 schedule: July 1 to August 9. Application deadline: May 15.

Tuition and Aid Day student tuition: $27,500. Tuition installment plan (SMART Tuition Payment Plan). Need-based scholarship grants available. In 2015–16, 1% of upper-school students received aid.

Admissions Traditional secondary-level entrance grade is 9. Deadline for receipt of application materials: none. No application fee required. On-campus interview required.

Computers Computers are regularly used in all classes. Computer network features include Internet access, wireless campus network, Internet filtering or blocking technology. Campus intranet, student e-mail accounts, and computer access in designated common areas are available to students. Students grades are available online. The school has a published electronic and media policy.

Contact Lisa Ohearn-Keck, Dean of Students. 650-493-7071 Ext. 102. Fax: 650-493-7073. E-mail: lisa@paloaltoprep.com. Website: www.paloaltoprep.com

PARADISE ADVENTIST ACADEMY

5699 Academy Drive
PO Box 2169
Paradise, California 95969

Head of School: Mr. Monte Nystrom

General Information Coeducational day college-preparatory school, affiliated with Seventh-day Adventists. Grades K–12. Founded: 1908. Setting: small town. Nearest major city is Sacramento. 12-acre campus. 6 buildings on campus. Approved or accredited by Western Association of Schools and Colleges and California Department of Education. Endowment: $200,000. Total enrollment: 143. Upper school average class size: 20. Upper school faculty-student ratio: 1:6. There are 180 required school days per year for Upper School students. Upper School students typically attend 5 days per week. The average school day consists of 8 hours and 5 minutes.

Upper School Student Profile Grade 9: 19 students (9 boys, 10 girls); Grade 10: 8 students (5 boys, 3 girls); Grade 11: 10 students (3 boys, 7 girls); Grade 12: 14 students (11 boys, 3 girls). 80% of students are Seventh-day Adventists.

Faculty School total: 13. In upper school: 5 men, 3 women; 3 have advanced degrees.

Subjects Offered Advanced biology, advanced computer applications, advanced math, algebra, American government, American history, band, basketball, Bible, biology, career education, chemistry, choir, computer applications, computers, drama, earth science, English, geometry, health, keyboarding, military history, physical education, physical science, physics, pre-algebra, pre-calculus, Spanish, U.S. government, U.S. history, volleyball, weightlifting, world history, yearbook.

Graduation Requirements Advanced computer applications, algebra, American government, American history, arts and fine arts (art, music, dance, drama), Bible, biology, career and personal planning, career education, chemistry, computer literacy, electives, English, keyboarding, languages, life skills, physical education (includes health), physics, Spanish, world history, 25 hours of community service per year of attendance, 20 credits of fine arts, 10 credits of Religion for each year of attendance.

Special Academic Programs Accelerated programs; independent study; remedial math.

College Admission Counseling 21 students graduated in 2015; all went to college, including California State University, Chico; Pacific Union College; Southern Adventist University; University of Illinois at Chicago; Walla Walla University. Median SAT critical reading: 547, median SAT math: 574, median SAT writing: 530, median combined SAT: 1618, median composite ACT: 24. 36% scored over 600 on SAT critical reading, 50% scored over 600 on SAT math, 14% scored over 600 on SAT writing, 29% scored over 1800 on combined SAT, 33% scored over 26 on composite ACT.

Student Life Upper grades have specified standards of dress, student council. Discipline rests primarily with faculty. Attendance at religious services is required.

Summer Programs Sports programs offered; session focuses on basketball; held on campus; accepts boys and girls; open to students from other schools. 30 students usually enrolled. 2016 schedule: June 15 to June 19. Application deadline: June 15.

Tuition and Aid Day student tuition: $9230. Tuition installment plan (monthly payment plans, individually arranged payment plans, 10 or 12 month plan, automatic bank withdrawal). Tuition reduction for siblings, merit scholarship grants, need-based scholarship grants, paying campus jobs available. In 2015–16, 25% of upper-school students received aid; total upper-school merit-scholarship money awarded: $800. Total amount of financial aid awarded in 2015–16: $110,000.

Admissions Traditional secondary-level entrance grade is 9. For fall 2015, 5 students applied for upper-level admission, 5 were accepted, 5 enrolled. Deadline for receipt of application materials: none. Application fee required: $50. Interview required.

Athletics Interscholastic: basketball (boys, girls), football (b,g), volleyball (g); coed interscholastic: soccer. 1 PE instructor, 3 coaches.

Computers Computers are regularly used in all academic, computer applications, Web site design, word processing, yearbook classes. Computer network features include on-campus library services, Internet access, wireless campus network, Internet filtering or blocking technology. Campus intranet, student e-mail accounts, and computer access in designated common areas are available to students. Students grades are available online. The school has a published electronic and media policy.

Contact Mrs. Brenda Muth, Registrar. 530-877-6540 Ext. 3010. Fax: 530-877-0870. E-mail: bmuth@mypaa.net. Website: www.mypaa.net

THE PARK SCHOOL OF BALTIMORE

2425 Old Court Road
Baltimore, Maryland 21208

Head of School: Mr. Daniel Paradis

General Information Coeducational day college-preparatory school. Grades PK–12. Founded: 1912. Setting: suburban. 100-acre campus. 4 buildings on campus. Approved or accredited by Association of Independent Maryland Schools and Maryland Department of Education. Member of National Association of Independent Schools. Endowment: $37.4 million. Total enrollment: 788. Upper school average class size: 15. Upper school faculty-student ratio: 1:7. There are 170 required school days per year for Upper School students. Upper School students typically attend 5 days per week. The average school day consists of 7 hours.

Upper School Student Profile Grade 9: 92 students (43 boys, 49 girls); Grade 10: 89 students (44 boys, 45 girls); Grade 11: 83 students (41 boys, 42 girls); Grade 12: 69 students (34 boys, 35 girls).

Faculty School total: 124. In upper school: 30 men, 29 women; 46 have advanced degrees.

Subjects Offered 20th century world history, 3-dimensional art, acting, advanced chemistry, advanced math, African studies, anatomy, animal behavior, anthropology, architectural drawing, art history, astronomy, audio visual/media, biochemistry, bioethics, DNA and culture, biology, British literature, calculus, ceramics, chemistry, Chinese, Chinese history, Chinese literature, choir, choral music, computer animation, computer programming, criminal justice, criminology, debate, design, digital art, digital music, digital photography, discrete mathematics, drama workshop, drawing, ecology, economics, English, English composition, English literature, environmental science, equality and freedom, etymology, European history, film studies, filmmaking, French, French studies, functions, Greek drama, health education, human sexuality, illustration, independent study, Islamic studies, jazz ensemble, jewelry making, keyboarding, madrigals, mathematics, Middle East, modern languages, multicultural studies, music composition, music performance, musical theater, organic chemistry, painting, photography, physical education, physics, playwriting and directing, poetry, publications, sculpture, senior project, set design, Shakespeare, social justice, Spanish, Spanish literature, statistics, studio art, theater, theater arts, U.S. history, visual and performing arts, vocal ensemble, Web site design, women in literature, woodworking, world religions, World War II, World-Wide-Web publishing, writing workshop.

Graduation Requirements Art, English, history, mathematics, modern languages, physical education (includes health), science.

Special Academic Programs Advanced Placement exam preparation; independent study; term-away projects; study abroad; academic accommodation for the gifted, the musically talented, and the artistically talented.

College Admission Counseling 90 students graduated in 2015; all went to college, including American University; Bard College; Brown University; Dickinson College; University of Maryland, College Park; Washington University in St. Louis.

Student Life Upper grades have student council, honor system. Discipline rests equally with students and faculty.

Summer Programs Held on campus; accepts boys and girls; open to students from other schools. 2016 schedule: June 13 to July 29.

Tuition and Aid Day student tuition: $28,540. Tuition installment plan (The Tuition Plan, Insured Tuition Payment Plan, FACTS Tuition Payment Plan, monthly payment plans). Need-based scholarship grants available. In 2015–16, 27% of upper-school students received aid. Total amount of financial aid awarded in 2015–16: $1,683,076.

Admissions Traditional secondary-level entrance grade is 9. For fall 2015, 94 students applied for upper-level admission, 65 were accepted, 32 enrolled. Deadline for receipt of application materials: January 1. Application fee required: $50. Interview required.

Athletics Interscholastic: baseball (boys), basketball (b,g), cross-country running (b,g), field hockey (g), indoor soccer (g), lacrosse (b,g), soccer (b,g), softball (g), tennis (b,g), winter soccer (g); coed interscholastic: squash; coed intramural: climbing, strength & conditioning, ultimate Frisbee, wall climbing, yoga. 3 PE instructors, 19 coaches, 1 athletic trainer.

Computers Computers are regularly used in art, computer applications, creative writing, desktop publishing, English, foreign language, French, graphic design, history, journalism, library skills, mathematics, media production, music, music technology, news writing, newspaper, photojournalism, programming, publications, science, Spanish, theater, theater arts, video film production, woodworking, writing, writing, yearbook classes. Computer network features include on-campus library services, online commercial services, Internet access, wireless campus network, Internet filtering or blocking technology, access to course materials and assignments through faculty Web pages and wikis, discounted software purchase plan. Campus intranet, student e-mail accounts, and computer access in designated common areas are available to students. Students grades are available online. The school has a published electronic and media policy.

Contact Rachel Hockett, Administrative Assistant. 410-339-4130. Fax: 410-339-4127. E-mail: admission@parkschool.net. Website: www.parkschool.net

THE PARK SCHOOL OF BUFFALO

4625 Harlem Road
Snyder, New York 14226

Head of School: Christopher J. Lauricella

General Information Coeducational boarding and day college-preparatory and arts school. Boarding grades 9–12, day grades PK–12. Founded: 1912. Setting: suburban. Nearest major city is Buffalo. Students are housed in host families. 34-acre campus. 13 buildings on campus. Approved or accredited by New York Department of Education, New York State Association of Independent Schools, and New York Department of Education. Member of National Association of Independent Schools. Endowment: $1.9 million. Total enrollment: 298. Upper school average class size: 16. Upper school faculty-student ratio: 1:8. There are 164 required school days per year for Upper School students. Upper School students typically attend 5 days per week. The average school day consists of 7 hours.

Upper School Student Profile Grade 9: 28 students (14 boys, 14 girls); Grade 10: 31 students (11 boys, 20 girls); Grade 11: 39 students (17 boys, 22 girls); Grade 12: 30 students (17 boys, 13 girls). 18% of students are boarding students. 82% are state residents. International students from Canada, China, Germany, Panama, and Republic of Korea.

Faculty School total: 43. In upper school: 14 men, 12 women; 20 have advanced degrees.

Subjects Offered Advanced studio art-AP, algebra, American history, American history-AP, American literature, American literature-AP, art, band, biology, biology-AP, calculus, calculus-AP, ceramics, chemistry, chorus, college admission preparation, college counseling, community service, computer applications, computer programming, critical thinking, drama, drawing, economics, English, environmental science, fine arts, forensics, French, French language-AP, freshman seminar, geometry, government/civics, health, junior and senior seminars, marine biology, media, media production, metalworking, music, orchestra, organic chemistry, photography, physical education, physics, senior project, senior seminar, senior thesis, sophomore skills, Spanish, Spanish-AP, studio art-AP, trigonometry, U.S. government and politics-AP, woodworking, world history, yearbook.

Graduation Requirements Arts and fine arts (art, music, dance, drama), computer science, English, foreign language, mathematics, physical education (includes health), science, senior project, senior thesis, social sciences, social studies (includes history). Community service is required.

Special Academic Programs Advanced Placement exam preparation; honors section; accelerated programs; independent study; study at local college for college credit; study abroad; academic accommodation for the gifted; ESL (27 students enrolled).

College Admission Counseling 26 students graduated in 2014; 21 went to college, including Florida Atlantic University; Nazareth College of Rochester; University at Buffalo, the State University of New York. Other: 5 had other specific plans. Median SAT critical reading: 580, median SAT math: 560, median SAT writing: 610, median combined SAT: 1754, median composite ACT: 24. 37% scored over 600 on SAT critical reading, 36% scored over 600 on SAT math, 47% scored over 600 on SAT writing, 36% scored over 1800 on combined SAT, 38% scored over 26 on composite ACT.

Student Life Upper grades have specified standards of dress, student council, honor system. Discipline rests equally with students and faculty.

Tuition and Aid Day student tuition: $19,570–$20,575; 5-day tuition and room/board: $28,000; 7-day tuition and room/board: $32,000. Tuition installment plan (Insured Tuition Payment Plan, FACTS Tuition Payment Plan). Tuition reduction for siblings, merit scholarship grants, need-based scholarship grants available. In 2014–15, 48% of upper-school students received aid; total upper-school merit-scholarship money awarded: $173,382. Total amount of financial aid awarded in 2014–15: $533,061.

Admissions Traditional secondary-level entrance grade is 9. For fall 2014, 51 students applied for upper-level admission, 40 were accepted, 30 enrolled. ERB Reading and Math, Otis-Lennon School Ability Test or TOEFL required. Deadline for receipt of application materials: none. Application fee required: $50. Interview required.

Athletics Interscholastic: basketball (boys, girls), bowling (b,g), golf (b), lacrosse (b), soccer (b,g), tennis (b,g); coed interscholastic: soccer; coed intramural: bicycling, cooperative games, cross-country running, fitness, flag football, floor hockey, Frisbee, hiking/backpacking, indoor soccer, outdoor activities, outdoor adventure, outdoor education, outdoor recreation, outdoor skills, outdoors, physical fitness, running, skiing (downhill), snowboarding, snowshoeing, soccer, strength & conditioning, weight lifting, weight training, winter walking, yoga. 2 PE instructors, 14 coaches.

Computers Computers are regularly used in creative writing, current events, data processing, English, graphic arts, independent study, keyboarding, mathematics, media, media arts, media production, media services, music technology, newspaper, photography, science, technical drawing, technology, typing, Web site design, word processing, yearbook classes. Computer network features include on-campus library services, online commercial services, Internet access, wireless campus network, Internet filtering or blocking technology. Campus intranet, student e-mail accounts, and computer access in designated common areas are available to students. Students grades are available online. The school has a published electronic and media policy.

Contact Marnie Cerrato, Director of Enrollment Management. 716-839-1242 Ext. 107. Fax: 716-408-9511. E-mail: mcerrato@theparkschool.org. Website: www.theparkschool.org

PARKVIEW ADVENTIST ACADEMY

6940 University Drive
Lacombe, Alberta T4L 2E7, Canada

Head of School: Ms. Angie Bishop

General Information Coeducational boarding and day college-preparatory, general academic, arts, vocational, religious studies, and technology school, affiliated with Seventh-day Adventist Church. Grades 10–12. Founded: 1907. Setting: small town. Nearest major city is Edmonton, Canada. Students are housed in single-sex by floor dormitories. 160-acre campus. 11 buildings on campus. Approved or accredited by National Council for Private School Accreditation and Alberta Department of Education. Language of instruction: English. Endowment: CAN$10 million. Upper school average class size: 20. Upper school faculty-student ratio: 1:10. There are 188 required school days per year for Upper School students. Upper School students typically attend 5 days per week. The average school day consists of 5 hours and 50 minutes.

Upper School Student Profile Grade 10: 30 students (15 boys, 15 girls); Grade 11: 32 students (17 boys, 15 girls); Grade 12: 45 students (24 boys, 21 girls). 40% of students are boarding students. 70% are province residents. 4 provinces are represented in upper school student body. 1% are international students. International students from China and Rwanda; 3 other countries represented in student body. 80% of students are Seventh-day Adventists.

Faculty School total: 9. In upper school: 3 men, 6 women; 2 have advanced degrees; 1 resides on campus.

Subjects Offered Advanced math, art, arts, band, biology, career and technology systems, chemistry, choir, choral music, English, fine arts, foods, French, home economics, industrial arts, instrumental music, language arts, mathematics, mechanics, metalworking, music, photography, physical education, physics, religion, religious studies, science, social sciences, social studies, welding, woodworking.

Graduation Requirements Computer processing, keyboarding, physical education (includes health), word processing.

Special Academic Programs ESL.

College Admission Counseling 36 went to college. Other: 3 went to work.

Student Life Upper grades have specified standards of dress, student council, honor system. Discipline rests primarily with faculty. Attendance at religious services is required.

Tuition and Aid Day student tuition: CAN$7500; 7-day tuition and room/board: CAN$14,000. Tuition installment plan (monthly payment plans, individually arranged payment plans). Tuition reduction for siblings, merit scholarship grants available.

Admissions Traditional secondary-level entrance grade is 10. Deadline for receipt of application materials: none. Application fee required: CAN$20. Interview required.

Athletics Interscholastic: aquatics (boys), basketball (b,g), hockey (b), soccer (b), volleyball (b,g); intramural: basketball (b,g), football (b), softball (g), volleyball (b,g); coed interscholastic: baseball, basketball, soccer; coed intramural: baseball, basketball. 1 PE instructor, 3 coaches.

Computers Computer network features include on-campus library services, Internet access, wireless campus network, Internet filtering or blocking technology. Student e-mail accounts are available to students. Students grades are available online. The school has a published electronic and media policy.

Contact Mr. Rodney Jamieson, Vice Principal. 403-782-3381 Ext. 4111. Fax: 866-931-2652. E-mail: rjamieso@paa.ca. Website: http://www.paa.ca/

PARKVIEW BAPTIST SCHOOL

5750 Parkview Church Road
Baton Rouge, Louisiana 70816

Head of School: Ben D. Haindel

General Information College-preparatory school, affiliated with Baptist Church. Founded: 1981. Setting: urban. 21-acre campus. 2 buildings on campus. Approved or accredited by Southern Association of Colleges and Schools, Southern Association of Independent Schools, and Louisiana Department of Education. Member of National Association of Independent Schools and Secondary School Admission Test Board. Upper school average class size: 22. Upper school faculty-student ratio: 1:21. There are 175 required school days per year for Upper School students. The average school day consists of 8 hours.

Upper School Student Profile 30% of students are Baptist.

Faculty School total: 40. In upper school: 10 have advanced degrees.

Student Life Upper grades have uniform requirement, honor system. Discipline rests primarily with faculty. Attendance at religious services is required.

Tuition and Aid Day student tuition: $8960. Tuition installment plan (FACTS Tuition Payment Plan). Tuition reduction for siblings, need-based scholarship grants available.

Admissions ISEE required. Deadline for receipt of application materials: none. Application fee required: $150. Interview required.

Contact Cindy K. Harrison, Admissions Coordinator. 225-291-2500 Ext. 104. Fax: 225-293-4135. E-mail: admissions@Parkviewbaptist.com. Website: www.parkviewbaptist.com/

THE PATHWAY SCHOOL

Jeffersonville, Pennsylvania
See Special Needs Schools section.

PATTEN ACADEMY OF CHRISTIAN EDUCATION

2430 Coolidge Avenue
Oakland, California 94601

Head of School: Dr. Sharon Anderson

General Information Coeducational day college-preparatory, arts, religious studies, and bilingual studies school, affiliated with Christian faith. Grades K–12. Founded: 1944. Setting: urban. Nearest major city is San Francisco. 3 buildings on campus. Approved or accredited by Association of Christian Schools International, Western Association of Schools and Colleges, and California Department of Education. Total enrollment: 119. Upper school average class size: 14. Upper school faculty-student ratio: 1:8. There are 175 required school days per year for Upper School students. Upper School students typically attend 5 days per week. The average school day consists of 6 hours and 45 minutes.

Upper School Student Profile Grade 9: 12 students (3 boys, 9 girls); Grade 10: 17 students (7 boys, 10 girls); Grade 11: 12 students (9 boys, 3 girls); Grade 12: 13 students (7 boys, 6 girls). 14% of students are Christian faith.

Faculty School total: 16. In upper school: 6 men, 1 woman; 5 have advanced degrees.

Subjects Offered Algebra, American literature, band, Bible studies, biology, chemistry, choir, community service, computer science, economics, English, English literature, fine arts, geometry, health, instrumental music, introduction to literature, language arts, life skills, mathematics, music, physical education, physical science, physics, piano, pre-calculus, religion, science, sign language, social studies, Spanish, statistics, strings, U.S. government, U.S. history, vocal music, world geography, world history, world literature, writing.

Graduation Requirements Arts and fine arts (art, music, dance, drama), English, environmental science, foreign language, mathematics, science, social studies (includes history). Community service is required.

College Admission Counseling 7 students graduated in 2015; 5 went to college, including California State University, East Bay; University of California, Davis; University of California, Riverside. Other: 1 went to work, 1 had other specific plans.

Student Life Upper grades have uniform requirement, student council, honor system. Discipline rests primarily with faculty. Attendance at religious services is required.

Tuition and Aid Day student tuition: $5999. Tuition installment plan (monthly payment plans). Tuition reduction for siblings, need-based scholarship grants available. In 2015–16, 22% of upper-school students received aid. Total amount of financial aid awarded in 2015–16: $22,650.

Admissions Traditional secondary-level entrance grade is 9. For fall 2015, 13 students applied for upper-level admission, 13 were accepted, 13 enrolled. Deadline for receipt of application materials: none. Application fee required: $50. On-campus interview required.

Athletics Interscholastic: basketball (boys, girls), cross-country running (b), track and field (b,g), volleyball (b,g). 1 PE instructor.

Computers Computers are regularly used in all academic classes. Computer network features include Internet access.

Contact Mrs. Sharon Moncher, Coordinator. 510-533-3121. E-mail: smoncher@pattenceca.org. Website: pattenacademy.org

PEDDIE SCHOOL
201 South Main Street
Hightstown, New Jersey 08520
Head of School: Peter Quinn

General Information Coeducational boarding and day college-preparatory, arts, and technology school. Grades 9–PG. Founded: 1864. Setting: small town. Nearest major city is Princeton. Students are housed in single-sex dormitories. 280-acre campus. 53 buildings on campus. Approved or accredited by Middle States Association of Colleges and Schools, The Association of Boarding Schools, and New Jersey Department of Education. Member of National Association of Independent Schools and Secondary School Admission Test Board. Endowment: $326.7 million. Total enrollment: 542. Upper school average class size: 12. Upper school faculty-student ratio: 1:6. There are 180 required school days per year for Upper School students. Upper School students typically attend 6 days per week. The average school day consists of 7 hours.

Upper School Student Profile Grade 9: 106 students (56 boys, 50 girls); Grade 10: 138 students (73 boys, 65 girls); Grade 11: 144 students (78 boys, 66 girls); Grade 12: 141 students (61 boys, 80 girls); Postgraduate: 13 students (10 boys, 3 girls). 62% of students are boarding students. 29 states are represented in upper school student body. 17% are international students. International students from China, Hong Kong, Japan, Republic of Korea, Thailand, and United Kingdom; 29 other countries represented in student body.

Faculty School total: 84. In upper school: 43 men, 36 women; 74 have advanced degrees; 72 reside on campus.

Subjects Offered Acting, African studies, algebra, American history, American literature, American studies, anatomy, architecture, art, art history, art history-AP, Asian studies, astronomy, Bible studies, biology, biology-AP, calculus, calculus-AP, chemistry, Chinese, comedy, comparative religion, computer programming, computer science, creative writing, debate, digital imaging, DNA, DNA science lab, drama, earth science, ecology, economics, English, English literature, environmental science, environmental science-AP, European history, European history-AP, expository writing, film history, fine arts, forensics, French, French language-AP, French literature-AP, geometry, global issues, global science, government/civics, health, history, information technology, Latin, Latin-AP, mathematics, Middle East, music, music theory-AP, neuroscience, philosophy, photography, physical education, physics, physics-AP, psychology, psychology-AP, robotics, science, Shakespeare, social studies, Spanish, Spanish language-AP, Spanish literature-AP, speech, statistics, statistics-AP, studio art-AP, theater, trigonometry, U.S. history, U.S. history-AP, video film production, world history, world literature, World War I, World War II, writing.

Graduation Requirements Arts and fine arts (art, music, dance, drama), computer science, English, foreign language, history, mathematics, physical education (includes health), science. Community service is required.

Special Academic Programs 18 Advanced Placement exams for which test preparation is offered; honors section; independent study; term-away projects; study abroad.

College Admission Counseling 140 students graduated in 2015; all went to college, including Carnegie Mellon University; Cornell University; Johns Hopkins University; New York University; The George Washington University; United States Naval Academy. Mean SAT critical reading: 616, mean SAT math: 646, mean SAT writing: 622, mean combined SAT: 1844, mean composite ACT: 27.

Student Life Upper grades have specified standards of dress, student council. Discipline rests primarily with faculty.

Summer Programs Enrichment, advancement, sports, art/fine arts, computer instruction programs offered; session focuses on enrichment; held on campus; accepts boys and girls; open to students from other schools. 175 students usually enrolled. 2016 schedule: June 29 to August 7. Application deadline: none.

Tuition and Aid Day student tuition: $44,800; 7-day tuition and room/board: $53,900. Tuition installment plan (Academic Management Services Plan, individually arranged payment plans). Merit scholarship grants, need-based scholarship grants, need-based loans available. In 2015–16, 40% of upper-school students received aid; total upper-school merit-scholarship money awarded: $70,000. Total amount of financial aid awarded in 2015–16: $6,800,000.

Admissions Traditional secondary-level entrance grade is 9. For fall 2015, 1,480 students applied for upper-level admission, 325 were accepted, 171 enrolled. ISEE or SSAT required. Deadline for receipt of application materials: January 15. Application fee required: $50. Interview required.

Athletics Interscholastic: aquatics (boys, girls), baseball (b), basketball (b,g), crew (b,g), cross-country running (b,g), field hockey (g), football (b), golf (b,g), indoor track & field (b,g), lacrosse (b,g), soccer (b,g), softball (g), swimming and diving (b,g), tennis (b,g), track and field (b,g), winter (indoor) track (b,g), wrestling (b); intramural: fitness (b,g), strength & conditioning (b,g), weight lifting (b,g), weight training (b,g), yoga (b,g); coed intramural: bicycling, dance, physical fitness, physical training, softball. 9 coaches, 3 athletic trainers.

Computers Computers are regularly used in English, foreign language, history, mathematics, science classes. Computer network features include on-campus library services, online commercial services, Internet access, wireless campus network, Internet filtering or blocking technology, NewsBank, Britannica, GaleNet, Electric Library. Student e-mail accounts are available to students. Students grades are available online. The school has a published electronic and media policy.

Contact Raymond H. Cabot, Director of Admission. 609-944-7501. Fax: 609-944-7901. E-mail: admission@peddie.org. Website: www.peddie.org

THE PENNINGTON SCHOOL
112 West Delaware Avenue
Pennington, New Jersey 08534-1601
Head of School: Dr. William S. Hawkey

General Information Coeducational boarding and day college-preparatory, arts, religious studies, technology, and 20 AP classes and a Global Studies Certificate Program school, affiliated with Methodist Church; primarily serves students with learning disabilities, dyslexic students, and Approximately 15% of our students are enrolled in our Cervone Center for Learning focusing on Language Based LD. Boarding grades 8–12, day grades 6–12. Founded: 1838. Setting: suburban. Nearest major city is Philadelphia, PA. Students are housed in single-sex dormitories. 54-acre campus. 17 buildings on campus. Approved or accredited by Middle States Association of Colleges and Schools, National Independent Private Schools Association, New Jersey Association of Independent Schools, The Association of Boarding Schools, The College Board, University Senate of United Methodist Church, and New Jersey Department of Education. Member of National Association of Independent Schools and Secondary School Admission Test Board. Endowment: $35 million. Total enrollment: 500. Upper school average class size: 12. Upper school faculty-student ratio: 1:6. There are 180 required school days per year for Upper School students. Upper School students typically attend 5 days per week. The average school day consists of 7 hours.

Upper School Student Profile Grade 9: 87 students (48 boys, 39 girls); Grade 10: 108 students (54 boys, 54 girls); Grade 11: 103 students (54 boys, 49 girls); Grade 12: 102 students (60 boys, 42 girls). 30% of students are boarding students. 61% are state residents. 7 states are represented in upper school student body. 12% are international students. International students from Brazil, China, Finland, Germany, Republic of Korea, and Taiwan; 15 other countries represented in student body. 5% of students are Methodist.

Faculty School total: 87. In upper school: 31 men, 38 women; 55 have advanced degrees; 50 reside on campus.

Subjects Offered Advanced studio art-AP, advanced TOEFL/grammar, African-American history, algebra, American history, American literature, anatomy, anatomy and physiology, art, bioethics, DNA and culture, biology, British literature-AP, calculus-AP, cheerleading, chemistry, chemistry-AP, Chinese, chorus, computer applications, computer skills, drama, economics, English, English literature, English literature-AP, English-AP, environmental science, ESL, fine arts, forensics, French, French language-AP, genetics, geometry, German, government and politics-AP, Greek, Greek culture, health, history-AP, honors algebra, honors English, honors geometry, honors U.S. history, jazz ensemble, Latin, macroeconomics AP, music, music history, music theory, organic chemistry, photography, physics, physics-AP, pottery, pre-calculus, psychology, public speaking, religion, robotics, senior internship, Spanish, Spanish literature, Spanish-AP, stage design, stagecraft, technical theater, U.S. government and politics-AP, Web site design, weight training, world history, world history AP.

Graduation Requirements Algebra, American history, arts and fine arts (art, music, dance, drama), athletics, biology, chemistry, computer education, English, foreign language, geometry, health education, public speaking, religion (includes Bible studies and theology), religion and culture, world history.

Special Academic Programs 20 Advanced Placement exams for which test preparation is offered; honors section; independent study; term-away projects; study at local college for college credit; study abroad; academic accommodation for the gifted; programs in English, mathematics, general development for dyslexic students; special instructional classes for students with LD enroll through our Cervone Center for Learning and receive individualized support.; ESL (7 students enrolled).

College Admission Counseling 91 students graduated in 2015; all went to college, including Colgate University; Columbia University; Dickinson State University; Franklin & Marshall College; Georgetown University; Quinnipiac University. Mean combined SAT: 1695, mean composite ACT: 25.

Student Life Upper grades have specified standards of dress, student council, honor system. Discipline rests primarily with faculty. Attendance at religious services is required.

Summer Programs Enrichment, sports, art/fine arts programs offered; session focuses on enrichment; held on campus; accepts boys and girls; open to students from other schools. 300 students usually enrolled. 2016 schedule: June 29 to August 6. Application deadline: none.

Tuition and Aid Day student tuition: $32,900–$34,600; 7-day tuition and room/board: $51,400. Tuition installment plan (monthly payment plans). Merit scholarship grants, need-based scholarship grants available. In 2015–16, 28% of upper-school students received aid; total upper-school merit-scholarship money awarded: $30,000. Total amount of financial aid awarded in 2015–16: $4,000,000.

Admissions Traditional secondary-level entrance grade is 9. For fall 2015, 650 students applied for upper-level admission, 240 were accepted, 126 enrolled. SSAT or TOEFL required. Deadline for receipt of application materials: February 1. Application fee required: $50. Interview required.

Athletics Interscholastic: baseball (boys), basketball (b,g), cheering (g), field hockey (g), football (b), ice hockey (b), softball (g); intramural: aquatics (b,g), bowling (b,g);

coed interscholastic: cross-country running, golf, indoor track, lacrosse, soccer, swimming and diving, tennis, track and field, water polo, weight training, winter (indoor) track; coed intramural: dance team, fitness, physical training, strength & conditioning, weight training. 3 coaches, 2 athletic trainers.

Computers Computers are regularly used in art, college planning, computer applications, creative writing, current events, data processing, desktop publishing, drawing and design, economics, English, ESL, ethics, foreign language, French, graphic design, health, history, library, literary magazine, mathematics, music, newspaper, photography, psychology, religious studies, research skills, science, Spanish, technology, theater, video film production, word processing, writing, yearbook classes. Computer network features include on-campus library services, online commercial services, Internet access, wireless campus network, Internet filtering or blocking technology, one to one iPad program; iPads are issued to each student and are included in tuition. Campus intranet, student e-mail accounts, and computer access in designated common areas are available to students. Students grades are available online. The school has a published electronic and media policy.

Contact Ms. Lynn Zahn, Admission Officer. 609-737-6128. Fax: 609-730-1405. E-mail: lzahn@pennington.org. Website: www.pennington.org

PENSACOLA CATHOLIC HIGH SCHOOL

3043 West Scott Street
Pensacola, Florida 32505

Head of School: Sr. Kierstin Martin

General Information Coeducational day college-preparatory and technology school, affiliated with Roman Catholic Church. Grades 9–12. Founded: 1941. Setting: urban. 25-acre campus. 5 buildings on campus. Approved or accredited by Southern Association of Colleges and Schools. Total enrollment: 599. Upper school average class size: 25. Upper school faculty-student ratio: 1:18. There are 180 required school days per year for Upper School students. Upper School students typically attend 5 days per week. The average school day consists of 7 hours.

Upper School Student Profile Grade 9: 175 students (97 boys, 78 girls); Grade 10: 144 students (79 boys, 65 girls); Grade 11: 133 students (77 boys, 56 girls); Grade 12: 147 students (88 boys, 59 girls). 60% of students are Roman Catholic.

Faculty School total: 50. In upper school: 15 men, 35 women; 15 have advanced degrees.

Subjects Offered Advanced math, Advanced Placement courses, African literature, algebra, American government, American history, American history-AP, American literature, analysis and differential calculus, analytic geometry, anatomy and physiology, art, art appreciation, arts and crafts, athletics, band, baseball, basketball, Bible, Bible studies, biology, botany, British literature, broadcast journalism, business law, calculus, calculus-AP, campus ministry, Catholic belief and practice, chemistry, Christian ethics, Christian scripture, Christian studies, Christian testament, church history, college counseling, composition, composition-AP, computer applications, computer graphics, CPR, creative arts, digital photography, drawing, earth science, economics, electives, English, English composition, English language and composition-AP, English literature, English literature and composition-AP, environmental science, fabric arts, film appreciation, film history, filmmaking, foreign language, French, genetics, geography, geometry, government, government-AP, grammar, guidance, health education, history, history of the Catholic Church, honors algebra, honors English, honors geometry, honors U.S. history, honors world history, journalism, lab science, library, library assistant, Life of Christ, literature and composition-AP, marine biology, music appreciation, music history, physical education, physical science, physics, pottery, pre-algebra, pre-calculus, probability and statistics, reading, religion, sex education, social studies, Spanish, student government, student publications, telecommunications and the Internet, television, trigonometry, U.S. government, U.S. government and politics-AP, U.S. history, U.S. literature, weight training, Western civilization, world geography, world history, world religions.

Graduation Requirements American government, American history, American literature, art appreciation, biology, economics, personal fitness, U.S. history, world geography, students must have earned 26 credits in order to graduate, and many of those credits are specific to specific courses.

Special Academic Programs Advanced Placement exam preparation; honors section; independent study; study at local college for college credit; academic accommodation for the gifted; programs in English, mathematics, general development for dyslexic students; special instructional classes for deaf students, blind students.

College Admission Counseling 153 students graduated in 2015; 150 went to college, including Florida State University; Mississippi State University; Pensacola State College; The University of Alabama; University of Florida. Other: 1 went to work, 2 entered military service. Mean SAT critical reading: 536, mean SAT math: 521, mean SAT writing: 526, mean combined SAT: 1583, mean composite ACT: 23.

Student Life Upper grades have specified standards of dress, student council. Discipline rests primarily with faculty. Attendance at religious services is required.

Summer Programs Remediation; enrichment programs offered; session focuses on religion courses, enrichment, and study skills; held on campus; accepts boys and girls; not open to students from other schools.

Tuition and Aid Guaranteed tuition plan. Tuition installment plan (individually arranged payment plans). Tuition reduction for siblings, need-based scholarship grants available.

Admissions Traditional secondary-level entrance grade is 9. Achievement tests, any standardized test, ETS high school placement exam or High School Placement Test (closed version) from Scholastic Testing Service required. Deadline for receipt of application materials: none. Application fee required: $125. On-campus interview required.

Athletics Interscholastic: baseball (boys), basketball (b,g), cheering (b,g), dance team (g), diving (b,g), football (b), golf (b,g), lacrosse (b), soccer (b,g), softball (g), swimming and diving (b,g), tennis (b,g), track and field (b,g), volleyball (g), weight lifting (b); coed interscholastic: physical fitness.

Computers Computers are regularly used in Bible studies, computer applications, creative writing, desktop publishing, foreign language, French, geography, graphic design, history, independent study, keyboarding, mathematics, publications, reading, religion, science, social studies, Spanish, stock market, study skills, video film production, Web site design, word processing, yearbook classes. Computer network features include on-campus library services, online commercial services, Internet access, wireless campus network, Internet filtering or blocking technology. Student e-mail accounts and computer access in designated common areas are available to students. Students grades are available online. The school has a published electronic and media policy.

Contact Mary Kyte, Junior and Senior Counselor. 850-436-6400 Ext. 120. Fax: 850-436-6405. E-mail: mkyte@pensacolachs.org. Website: www.pensacolachs.org

PEOPLES CHRISTIAN ACADEMY

245 Renfrew Drive
Markham, Ontario L3R 6G3, Canada

Head of School: Mr. David Broomer

General Information Coeducational day college-preparatory and religious studies school, affiliated with Christian faith. Grades JK–12. Founded: 1971. Setting: urban. Nearest major city is Toronto, Canada. 5-acre campus. 1 building on campus. Approved or accredited by Association of Christian Schools International, Christian Schools International, Ontario Ministry of Education, and Ontario Department of Education. Language of instruction: English. Endowment: CAN$15,000. Total enrollment: 376. Upper school average class size: 20. Upper school faculty-student ratio: 1:10. There are 194 required school days per year for Upper School students. Upper School students typically attend 5 days per week. The average school day consists of 7 hours.

Upper School Student Profile Grade 9: 17 students (9 boys, 8 girls); Grade 10: 29 students (11 boys, 18 girls); Grade 11: 25 students (14 boys, 11 girls); Grade 12: 37 students (15 boys, 22 girls). 85% of students are Christian.

Faculty School total: 40. In upper school: 8 men, 10 women; 8 have advanced degrees.

Subjects Offered Accounting, Bible, biology, calculus, Canadian geography, Canadian history, Canadian law, careers, chemistry, civics, discrete mathematics, dramatic arts, economics, English, exercise science, family studies, French, functions, geography, geometry, health education, healthful living, ideas, information technology, instrumental music, journalism, keyboarding, literature, mathematics, media arts, organizational studies, philosophy, physical education, physics, psychology, science, sociology, visual arts, vocal music, world history, world religions, writing.

Graduation Requirements Arts, Canadian geography, Canadian history, careers, civics, English, French as a second language, mathematics, physical education (includes health), science, must complete Bible course curriculum for all grades.

Special Academic Programs Advanced Placement exam preparation; independent study.

College Admission Counseling 29 students graduated in 2015; 27 went to college, including McMaster University; The University of Western Ontario; University of Guelph; University of Toronto; Wilfrid Laurier University; York University. Other: 2 had other specific plans.

Student Life Upper grades have uniform requirement, student council, honor system. Discipline rests primarily with faculty. Attendance at religious services is required.

Tuition and Aid Day student tuition: CAN$10,120. Tuition installment plan (monthly payment plans). Tuition reduction for siblings, bursaries, need-based scholarship grants, alumni scholarships, prepayment tuition reduction available. In 2015–16, 2% of upper-school students received aid. Total amount of financial aid awarded in 2015–16: CAN$30,000.

Admissions Traditional secondary-level entrance grade is 9. For fall 2015, 18 students applied for upper-level admission, 18 were accepted, 18 enrolled. CTBS (or similar from their school) required. Deadline for receipt of application materials: none. Application fee required: CAN$150. Interview required.

Athletics Interscholastic: badminton (boys, girls), baseball (b,g), basketball (b,g), cross-country running (b,g), Frisbee (b,g), running (b,g), track and field (b,g), volleyball (b,g); intramural: badminton (b,g), basketball (b,g), cross-country running (b,g), floor hockey (b,g), running (b,g); coed interscholastic: badminton, baseball, basketball, cross-country running, Frisbee, running, track and field; coed intramural: badminton, basketball, cross-country running, floor hockey, running, volleyball. 2 PE instructors.

Computers Computers are regularly used in business studies, drawing and design, graphics, information technology, introduction to technology, journalism, mathematics, yearbook classes. Computer network features include Internet access, Internet filtering or blocking technology. The school has a published electronic and media policy.

Contact School Office. 416-733-2010 Ext. 204. Fax: 416-733-2011. E-mail: admissions@pca.ca. Website: www.pca.ca

PERKIOMEN SCHOOL

200 Seminary Street
Pennsburg, Pennsylvania 18073

Head of School: Mr. Mark A. Devey

General Information Coeducational boarding and day college-preparatory school. Grades 6–PG. Founded: 1875. Setting: small town. Nearest major city is Philadelphia. Students are housed in single-sex dormitories. 172-acre campus. 25 buildings on campus. Approved or accredited by Middle States Association of Colleges and Schools, Pennsylvania Association of Independent Schools, The Association of Boarding Schools, The College Board, and Pennsylvania Department of Education. Member of National Association of Independent Schools and Secondary School Admission Test Board. Endowment: $7 million. Total enrollment: 350. Upper school average class size: 12. Upper school faculty-student ratio: 1:7. There are 180 required school days per year for Upper School students. Upper School students typically attend 5 days per week. The average school day consists of 6 hours and 45 minutes.

Upper School Student Profile Grade 9: 64 students (41 boys, 23 girls); Grade 10: 72 students (43 boys, 29 girls); Grade 11: 79 students (50 boys, 29 girls); Grade 12: 85 students (54 boys, 31 girls). 11 states are represented in upper school student body.

Subjects Offered African history, algebra, American history, American literature, art, art history, astronomy, biology, calculus, ceramics, chemistry, computer graphics, computer programming, computer science, creative writing, current events, developmental language skills, drama, earth science, economics, English, English literature, environmental science, ESL, ethics, European history, fine arts, geometry, government/civics, grammar, health, history, humanities, journalism, Latin, mathematics, music, painting, philosophy, photography, physics, physics-AP, psychology, religion, science, social studies, sociology, Spanish, Spanish-AP, speech, statistics, statistics-AP, studio art-AP, theater, trigonometry, world history, world literature.

Graduation Requirements Arts and fine arts (art, music, dance, drama), computer studies, English, foreign language, mathematics, physical education (includes health), religion (includes Bible studies and theology), science, social studies (includes history). Community service is required.

Special Academic Programs Advanced Placement exam preparation; honors section; independent study; academic accommodation for the gifted, the musically talented, and the artistically talented; programs in English, general development for dyslexic students; ESL.

College Admission Counseling 77 students graduated in 2015; all went to college. Mean SAT critical reading: 550, mean SAT math: 600, mean SAT writing: 560.

Student Life Upper grades have uniform requirement, student council, honor system. Discipline rests primarily with faculty.

Summer Programs Enrichment, ESL, sports, art/fine arts programs offered; held on campus; accepts boys and girls; open to students from other schools.

Tuition and Aid Day student tuition: $29,950; 7-day tuition and room/board: $52,500. Tuition installment plan (monthly payment plans). Merit scholarship grants, need-based scholarship grants available. In 2015–16, 40% of upper-school students received aid.

Admissions ISEE, SSAT, TOEFL Junior or TOEFL or SLEP required. Deadline for receipt of application materials: February 1. Application fee required: $50. Interview required.

Athletics Interscholastic: baseball (boys), basketball (b,g), field hockey (g), football (b), lacrosse (b,g), soccer (b,g), softball (g), tennis (b,g); coed interscholastic: badminton, boxing, cross-country running, dance, golf, martial arts, strength & conditioning, swimming and diving, winter (indoor) track; coed intramural: dance, skateboarding.

Computers Computers are regularly used in all academic, art classes. Computer network features include on-campus library services, online commercial services, Internet access, wireless campus network, Internet filtering or blocking technology. Campus intranet, student e-mail accounts, and computer access in designated common areas are available to students. The school has a published electronic and media policy.

Contact Ms. Abby P. Moser, Director of Admissions and Financial Aid. 215-679-9511. Fax: 215-679-5202. E-mail: amoser@perkiomen.org. Website: www.perkiomen.org

THE PHELPS SCHOOL

583 Sugartown Road
Malvern, Pennsylvania 19355

Head of School: Mr. Daniel E. Knopp

General Information Boys' boarding and day college-preparatory, Academic Support Program (ASP), and ESL program school. Boarding grades 7–PG, day grades 6–PG. Founded: 1946. Setting: suburban. Nearest major city is Philadelphia. Students are housed in single-sex dormitories. 70-acre campus. 18 buildings on campus. Approved or accredited by Academy of Orton-Gillingham Practitioners and Educators, Middle States Association of Colleges and Schools, Pennsylvania Association of Independent Schools, The Association of Boarding Schools, and Pennsylvania Department of Education. Member of National Association of Independent Schools and Secondary School Admission Test Board. Total enrollment: 97. Upper school average class size: 7. Upper school faculty-student ratio: 1:4. There are 160 required school days

per year for Upper School students. Upper School students typically attend 5 days per week. The average school day consists of 7 hours.

Upper School Student Profile Grade 6: 2 students (2 boys); Grade 7: 2 students (2 boys); Grade 8: 9 students (9 boys); Grade 9: 13 students (13 boys); Grade 10: 21 students (21 boys); Grade 11: 20 students (20 boys); Grade 12: 22 students (22 boys); Postgraduate: 8 students (8 boys). 81% of students are boarding students. 32% are state residents. 10 states are represented in upper school student body. 40% are international students. International students from China, Ghana, Lithuania, Saudi Arabia, Spain, and Taiwan; 8 other countries represented in student body.

Faculty School total: 23. In upper school: 12 men, 8 women; 9 have advanced degrees; 16 reside on campus.

Subjects Offered Advanced Placement courses, algebra, American government, American history, American literature, art, baseball, basketball, biology, biology-AP, British literature, calculus-AP, chemistry, chemistry-AP, college admission preparation, college counseling, computer technologies, culinary arts, earth science, English, English literature and composition-AP, environmental science, environmental science-AP, ESL, ethics, finance, fitness, gardening, general math, general science, geography, geometry, health, information technology, learning strategies, life science, mathematics, participation in sports, photography, physical education, physical science, physics, physics-AP, pre-algebra, pre-calculus, psychology, psychology-AP, public speaking, reading, reading/study skills, SAT preparation, sociology, Spanish, Spanish language-AP, sports, statistics-AP, study skills, TOEFL preparation, U.S. government and politics-AP, U.S. history-AP, world history, world history-AP, wrestling, writing, yearbook.

Graduation Requirements English, health, mathematics, physical education (includes health), science, social studies (includes history). Community service is required.

Special Academic Programs Advanced Placement exam preparation; academic accommodation for the gifted; remedial reading and/or remedial writing; remedial math; programs in English, mathematics, general development for dyslexic students; ESL (30 students enrolled).

College Admission Counseling 30 students graduated in 2015; 28 went to college, including Drexel University; Ithaca College; Michigan State University; Penn State University Park; Saint Joseph's University; Temple University. Other: 1 went to work, 1 entered a postgraduate year.

Student Life Upper grades have uniform requirement, student council. Discipline rests primarily with faculty.

Tuition and Aid Day student tuition: $25,800; 7-day tuition and room/board: $46,800. Tuition installment plan (FACTS Tuition Payment Plan). Merit scholarship grants, need-based scholarship grants available. In 2015–16, 45% of upper-school students received aid. Total amount of financial aid awarded in 2015–16: $1,100,000.

Admissions Deadline for receipt of application materials: none. Application fee required: $50. Interview required.

Athletics Interscholastic: baseball, basketball, cross-country running, golf, lacrosse, soccer, tennis, wrestling; intramural: bowling, cooperative games, fitness, Frisbee, golf, indoor soccer, jump rope, outdoor activities, outdoor adventure, outdoor education, outdoor recreation, outdoor skills, paint ball, physical fitness, street hockey, strength & conditioning, table tennis, weight lifting, weight training, whiffle ball, winter soccer. 2 PE instructors, 16 coaches, 2 athletic trainers.

Computers Computers are regularly used in all classes. Computer network features include Internet access, wireless campus network, Internet filtering or blocking technology, all students are provided a laptop with the option to buy. Campus intranet, student e-mail accounts, and computer access in designated common areas are available to students. Students grades are available online. The school has a published electronic and media policy.

Contact Mrs. Lisa Ballard, Admissions Associate. 610-644-1754. Fax: 610-644-6679. E-mail: admis@thephelpsschool.org. Website: www.thephelpsschool.org

PHILADELPHIA-MONTGOMERY CHRISTIAN ACADEMY

35 Hillcrest Avenue
Erdenheim, Pennsylvania 19038

Head of School: Mr. Donald B. Beebe

General Information Coeducational day college-preparatory, arts, and religious studies school, affiliated with Christian faith. Grades K–12. Founded: 1943. Setting: suburban. Nearest major city is Philadelphia. 1-acre campus. 1 building on campus. Approved or accredited by Association of Christian Schools International, Christian Schools International, and Middle States Association of Colleges and Schools. Endowment: $150,205. Total enrollment: 252. Upper school average class size: 16. Upper school faculty-student ratio: 1:10. There are 178 required school days per year for Upper School students. Upper School students typically attend 5 days per week. The average school day consists of 6 hours and 50 minutes.

Upper School Student Profile Grade 9: 38 students (18 boys, 20 girls); Grade 10: 21 students (13 boys, 8 girls); Grade 11: 27 students (11 boys, 16 girls); Grade 12: 38 students (21 boys, 17 girls). 99% of students are Christian.

Faculty School total: 33. In upper school: 10 men, 8 women; 8 have advanced degrees.

Subjects Offered Algebra, American history, American literature, art, art history, biology, calculus, ceramics, chemistry, creative writing, drama, English, English literature, ethics, European history, fine arts, geography, geometry, German, government/civics, grammar, health, history, mathematics, music, physical education, physics, religion, science, social studies, sociology, Spanish, theater, trigonometry, typing, world history, writing.

Graduation Requirements Arts and fine arts (art, music, dance, drama), Bible, English, languages, mathematics, physical education (includes health), science, social studies (includes history), 4 years of Bible instruction are required to graduate if student attends from grades 9-12.

Special Academic Programs 4 Advanced Placement exams for which test preparation is offered; honors section; academic accommodation for the gifted, the musically talented, and the artistically talented; ESL (10 students enrolled).

College Admission Counseling 31 students graduated in 2015; 30 went to college, including Eastern University; Montgomery County Community College; Penn State University Park; Temple University. Other: 1 went to work. Median SAT critical reading: 559, median SAT math: 600, median SAT writing: 551, median combined SAT: 1710.

Student Life Upper grades have uniform requirement, student council. Discipline rests primarily with faculty. Attendance at religious services is required.

Summer Programs ESL, sports programs offered; session focuses on intensive English and cultural immersion; held both on and off campus; held at the bulk of the program is via email correspondence with a day of orientation on campus at the end; accepts boys and girls; not open to students from other schools. 5 students usually enrolled. 2016 schedule: August 1 to August 31.

Tuition and Aid Day student tuition: $14,085. Tuition installment plan (FACTS Tuition Payment Plan). Tuition reduction for siblings, need-based scholarship grants available. In 2015–16, 100% of upper-school students received aid. Total amount of financial aid awarded in 2015–16: $600,000.

Admissions Traditional secondary-level entrance grade is 9. For fall 2015, 19 students applied for upper-level admission, 19 were accepted, 15 enrolled. Brigance Test of Basic Skills or Iowa Tests of Basic Skills required. Deadline for receipt of application materials: none. Application fee required: $100. Interview required.

Athletics Interscholastic: baseball (boys), basketball (b,g), soccer (b,g), softball (b,g), tennis (g), track and field (b,g), wrestling (b); coed interscholastic: cross-country running; coed intramural: tennis. 2 PE instructors, 6 coaches.

Computers Computers are regularly used in art, Bible studies, Christian doctrine, creative writing, drawing and design, English, ESL, foreign language, graphic design, history, life skills, mathematics, music, religious studies, research skills, science, Spanish, theater, theater arts, theology, yearbook classes. Computer network features include on-campus library services, Internet access, Internet filtering or blocking technology, online college search. Campus intranet, student e-mail accounts, and computer access in designated common areas are available to students. The school has a published electronic and media policy.

Contact Phil VanVeldhuizen, Admissions and Marketing Manager. 215-233-0782 Ext. 408. Fax: 215-233-0829. E-mail: admissions@phil-mont.com. Website: www.phil-mont.com

PHILLIPS ACADEMY (ANDOVER)

180 Main Street
Andover, Massachusetts 01810-4161

Head of School: John G. Palfrey Jr.

General Information Coeducational boarding and day college-preparatory school. Grades 9–PG. Founded: 1778. Setting: suburban. Nearest major city is Boston. Students are housed in single-sex dormitories and 9th graders housed separately from other students. 500-acre campus. 160 buildings on campus. Approved or accredited by New England Association of Schools and Colleges and The Association of Boarding Schools. Member of National Association of Independent Schools and Secondary School Admission Test Board. Endowment: $1 billion. Total enrollment: 1,131. Upper school average class size: 13. Upper school faculty-student ratio: 1:5. There are 154 required school days per year for Upper School students. Upper School students typically attend 5 days per week. The average school day consists of 7 hours.

Upper School Student Profile Grade 9: 228 students (110 boys, 118 girls); Grade 10: 300 students (150 boys, 150 girls); Grade 11: 284 students (139 boys, 145 girls); Grade 12: 289 students (144 boys, 145 girls); Postgraduate: 30 students (20 boys, 10 girls). 74% of students are boarding students. 40% are state residents. 45 states are represented in upper school student body. 10% are international students. International students from Canada, China, Hong Kong, Republic of Korea, Thailand, and United Kingdom; 39 other countries represented in student body.

Faculty School total: 217. In upper school: 103 men, 114 women; 181 have advanced degrees; 185 reside on campus.

Subjects Offered Algebra, American history, American literature, ancient history, animal behavior, animation, architecture, art, art history, astronomy, band, Bible studies, biology, calculus, ceramics, chamber groups, chemistry, Chinese, chorus, computer graphics, computer programming, computer science, creative writing, dance, drama, drawing, ecology, economics, English, English literature, environmental science, ethics, European history, expository writing, film, fine arts, French, geology, geometry, German, government/civics, grammar, Greek, health, history, international relations,

Japanese, jazz, Latin, Latin American studies, life issues, literature, mathematics, Middle Eastern history, music, mythology, oceanography, painting, philosophy, photography, physical education, physics, physiology, printmaking, psychology, religion, Russian, Russian studies, science, sculpture, social sciences, social studies, sociology, Spanish, speech, swimming, theater, trigonometry, video, world history, writing.

Graduation Requirements Arts and fine arts (art, music, dance, drama), English, foreign language, history, life issues, mathematics, philosophy, physical education (includes health), religion (includes Bible studies and theology), science, social sciences, swimming test.

Special Academic Programs Advanced Placement exam preparation; honors section; independent study; term-away projects; study abroad; academic accommodation for the gifted, the musically talented, and the artistically talented; programs in English, mathematics, general development for dyslexic students; special instructional classes for deaf students, blind students.

College Admission Counseling 328 students graduated in 2015; 324 went to college, including Boston College; Cornell University; Harvard University; Stanford University; University of Chicago; University of Pennsylvania. Other: 4 had other specific plans. Mean SAT critical reading: 703, mean SAT math: 714, mean SAT writing: 695.

Student Life Upper grades have student council, honor system. Discipline rests primarily with faculty.

Summer Programs Remediation, enrichment, advancement, ESL, sports, art/fine arts, computer instruction programs offered; session focuses on academics; held on campus; accepts boys and girls; open to students from other schools. 550 students usually enrolled. 2016 schedule: June 27 to July 31. Application deadline: none.

Tuition and Aid Day student tuition: $39,100; 7-day tuition and room/board: $50,300. Tuition installment plan (individually arranged payment plans, The Andover Plan). Need-based scholarship grants available. In 2015–16, 47% of upper-school students received aid. Total amount of financial aid awarded in 2015–16: $20,195,000.

Admissions For fall 2015, 3,040 students applied for upper-level admission, 436 were accepted, 365 enrolled. ISEE or SSAT required. Deadline for receipt of application materials: February 1. Application fee required: $40. Interview required.

Athletics Interscholastic: baseball (boys), basketball (b,g), bicycling (b,g), crew (b,g), cross-country running (b,g), diving (b,g), field hockey (g), football (b), golf (b,g), ice hockey (b,g), indoor track & field (b,g), lacrosse (b,g), nordic skiing (b,g), skiing (cross-country) (b,g), soccer (b,g), softball (g), squash (b,g), swimming and diving (b,g), tennis (b,g), track and field (b,g), volleyball (b,g), water polo (b,g), winter (indoor) track (b,g); intramural: aerobics/dance (b,g), backpacking (b,g), basketball (b,g), crew (b,g), martial arts (b,g), physical fitness (b,g), physical training (b,g); coed interscholastic: bicycling, Frisbee, golf, ultimate Frisbee, wrestling; coed intramural: badminton, ballet, canoeing/kayaking, cheering, cross-country running, dance, fencing, fitness, fitness walking, hiking/backpacking, martial arts, modern dance, outdoor adventure, outdoor education, physical fitness, physical training, rappelling, rock climbing, ropes courses, soccer, softball, strength & conditioning, tennis, wall climbing. 7 PE instructors, 25 coaches, 3 athletic trainers.

Computers Computers are regularly used in animation, architecture, art, classics, computer applications, digital applications, English, foreign language, history, mathematics, music, photography, psychology, religious studies, science, theater, video film production classes. Computer network features include on-campus library services, online commercial services, Internet access, wireless campus network. Campus intranet and student e-mail accounts are available to students. Students grades are available online. The school has a published electronic and media policy.

Contact Jim Ventre, Dean of Admission and Director of Financial Aid. 978-749-4050. Fax: 978-749-4068. E-mail: admissions@andover.edu. Website: www.andover.edu

PHOENIX CHRISTIAN UNIFIED SCHOOLS

1751 West Indian School Road
Phoenix, Arizona 85015

Head of School: Mr. Joe Bradley

General Information Coeducational day college-preparatory, general academic, religious studies, and AP/honors school, affiliated with Christian faith. Grades PS–12. Founded: 1949. Setting: urban. 12-acre campus. 10 buildings on campus. Approved or accredited by Association of Christian Schools International, North Central Association of Colleges and Schools, and Arizona Department of Education. Total enrollment: 385. Upper school average class size: 24. Upper school faculty-student ratio: 1:24. There are 179 required school days per year for Upper School students. Upper School students typically attend 5 days per week. The average school day consists of 6 hours and 40 minutes.

Upper School Student Profile Grade 9: 37 students (16 boys, 21 girls); Grade 10: 48 students (27 boys, 21 girls); Grade 11: 44 students (18 boys, 26 girls); Grade 12: 56 students (28 boys, 28 girls). 85% of students are Christian faith.

Faculty School total: 31. In upper school: 11 men, 10 women; 19 have advanced degrees.

Subjects Offered Advanced computer applications, algebra, American literature, American literature-AP, anatomy, art, arts, band, Bible, biology, biology-AP, calculus, calculus-AP, career and personal planning, chemistry, choir, choral music, computer applications, computers, creative writing, drama, drama performance, drawing, economics, English, English literature, English literature-AP, English-AP, film studies, geometry, government, government-AP, instrumental music, integrated science, intro to computers, language-AP, literature, literature-AP, marching band, photography, physical education, physics, pre-algebra, pre-calculus, psychology, religious education, sociology, Spanish, Spanish language-AP, statistics, student government, study skills, U.S. government, U.S. history, U.S. history-AP, Web site design, world history, yearbook.

Graduation Requirements Advanced math, Advanced Placement courses, algebra, American literature, arts and fine arts (art, music, dance, drama), biology, British literature, chemistry, computer education, economics, English, English composition, English literature, foreign language, geometry, government, integrated science, pre-calculus, religious studies, study skills, U.S. history, world history, world literature, a Bible class must be taken every semester while attending.

Special Academic Programs 7 Advanced Placement exams for which test preparation is offered; honors section; independent study; study at local college for college credit.

College Admission Counseling 39 students graduated in 2015; 37 went to college, including Arizona Christian University; Arizona State University at the Tempe campus; Grand Canyon University; Northern Arizona University; The University of Arizona. Other: 2 went to work. Mean SAT critical reading: 545, mean SAT math: 572, mean SAT writing: 508, mean composite ACT: 23.

Student Life Upper grades have uniform requirement, student council, honor system. Discipline rests primarily with faculty.

Summer Programs Remediation, advancement, sports programs offered; session focuses on advance education, redemption, refine skills; held on campus; accepts boys and girls; open to students from other schools. 60 students usually enrolled. 2016 schedule: June 1 to July 15. Application deadline: May 15.

Tuition and Aid Day student tuition: $9362. Tuition installment plan (FACTS Tuition Payment Plan, monthly payment plans, individually arranged payment plans). Tuition reduction for siblings, allow families to use state tax credits available. In 2014–15, 75% of upper-school students received aid.

Admissions Traditional secondary-level entrance grade is 9. For fall 2015, 40 students applied for upper-level admission, 36 were accepted, 36 enrolled. Achievement tests, any standardized test or placement test required. Deadline for receipt of application materials: none. Application fee required: $50. Interview required.

Athletics Interscholastic: baseball (boys), basketball (b,g), cheering (g), football (b), softball (g), volleyball (g), wrestling (h); intramural: flag football (g), volleyball (b); coed interscholastic: golf, soccer, tennis, track and field. 2 PE instructors, 25 coaches, 1 athletic trainer.

Computers Computers are regularly used in career exploration, college planning, computer applications, keyboarding, library, media services, Web site design, yearbook classes. Computer network features include on-campus library services, Internet access, wireless campus network, Internet filtering or blocking technology. Student e-mail accounts and computer access in designated common areas are available to students. Students grades are available online. The school has a published electronic and media policy.

Contact Mrs. Gretchen Janes, Admissions Director. 602-265-4707 Ext. 270. Fax: 602-277-7170. E-mail: gjanes@phoenixchristian.org. Website: www.phoenixchristian.org

PHOENIX COUNTRY DAY SCHOOL

3901 East Stanford Drive
Paradise Valley, Arizona 85253

Head of School: Mr. Andrew Rodin

General Information Coeducational day college-preparatory, arts, performing and studio arts, extensive athletics, and community service, global citizenship, and travel school. Grades PK–12. Founded: 1961. Setting: suburban. Nearest major city is Phoenix. 40-acre campus. 8 buildings on campus. Approved or accredited by Independent Schools Association of the Southwest and National Independent Private Schools Association. Member of National Association of Independent Schools. Endowment: $15 million. Total enrollment: 750. Upper school average class size: 15. Upper school faculty-student ratio: 1:8. There are 173 required school days per year for Upper School students. Upper School students typically attend 5 days per week. The average school day consists of 5 hours.

Faculty School total: 110. In upper school: 17 men, 13 women; 23 have advanced degrees.

Subjects Offered Acting, advanced biology, advanced chemistry, advanced math, Advanced Placement courses, African-American literature, algebra, American government, American history, American history-AP, American literature, anatomy, anatomy and physiology, anthropology, art, art history, art history-AP, astronomy, band, baseball, basketball, biology, biology-AP, British literature, calculus, calculus-AP, ceramics, chemistry, chemistry-AP, Chinese, Chinese studies, choir, chorus, computer programming, computer science, creative writing, digital photography, directing, discrete mathematics, drawing, ecology, English, English composition, English literature, environmental science, environmental science-AP, ethics, European history, evolution, fine arts, French, French-AP, geography, geology, geometry, government/civics, history, Holocaust studies, jazz band, journalism, Latin, Latin American literature, Latin-AP, literature, Mandarin, marine biology, mathematics, music, oceanography, orchestra, painting, photography, physical education, physics,

physics-AP, physiology, pre-calculus, probability and statistics, psychology, scene study, science, Shakespeare, social sciences, social studies, Spanish, Spanish-AP, speech, statistics, statistics-AP, theater, theater arts, trigonometry, world history, world literature, world religions.

Graduation Requirements Advanced biology, American history, American literature, ancient world history, arts and fine arts (art, music, dance, drama), biology, chemistry, English, foreign language, mathematics, physical education (includes health), physics, science, U.S. history, Western civilization, world history, 40 hours of community service.

Special Academic Programs 15 Advanced Placement exams for which test preparation is offered; honors section; independent study; study abroad.

College Admission Counseling 63 students graduated in 2015; 62 went to college, including Arizona State University at the Tempe campus; Harvard University; Massachusetts Institute of Technology; New York University; Southern Methodist University; University of Southern California. Other: 1 had other specific plans. Median SAT critical reading: 670, median SAT math: 680, median SAT writing: 690, median combined SAT: 2010, median composite ACT: 29. 77% scored over 600 on SAT critical reading, 86% scored over 600 on SAT math, 86% scored over 600 on SAT writing, 86% scored over 1800 on combined SAT, 78% scored over 26 on composite ACT.

Student Life Upper grades have specified standards of dress, student council, honor system. Discipline rests primarily with faculty.

Summer Programs Enrichment, advancement, sports, art/fine arts, computer instruction programs offered; session focuses on academics/sports camp/arts program; held on campus; accepts boys and girls; open to students from other schools. 500 students usually enrolled. 2016 schedule: June 4 to July 13. Application deadline: none.

Tuition and Aid Day student tuition: $24,000. Tuition installment plan (Insured Tuition Payment Plan, monthly payment plans, individually arranged payment plans, 10 months, quarterly, semiannual, and yearly payment plans). Need-based scholarship grants available. In 2015–16, 21% of upper-school students received aid. Total amount of financial aid awarded in 2015–16: $1,016,600.

Admissions Traditional secondary-level entrance grade is 9. For fall 2015, 90 students applied for upper-level admission, 30 were accepted, 18 enrolled. Achievement/Aptitude/Writing, ERB CTP IV, Math Placement Exam, Otis-Lennon IQ or writing sample required. Deadline for receipt of application materials: February 1. Application fee required: $75. Interview required.

Athletics Interscholastic: baseball (boys), basketball (b,g), cheering (g), diving (b,g), flag football (b), golf (b,g), lacrosse (b,g), soccer (b,g), softball (g), winter soccer (g); intramural: archery (b,g), badminton (b,g), basketball (b,g), lacrosse (b,g), outdoor education (b,g), outdoor recreation (b,g), physical fitness (b,g), softball (g), strength & conditioning (b,g), yoga (b,g); coed interscholastic: cheering, diving, swimming and diving, tennis, volleyball; coed intramural: basketball, cross-country running, flag football, golf, hiking/backpacking, running, soccer, swimming and diving, tennis, volleyball, weight lifting, winter soccer. 5 PE instructors, 23 coaches, 1 athletic trainer.

Computers Computers are regularly used in art, college planning, creative writing, data processing, desktop publishing, economics, engineering, English, foreign language, French, history, humanities, independent study, information technology, keyboarding, library, library skills, literary magazine, mathematics, news writing, newspaper, photography, programming, publications, research skills, science, social sciences, social studies, Spanish, stock market, Web site design, writing, yearbook classes. Computer network features include on-campus library services, online commercial services, Internet access, wireless campus network, Internet filtering or blocking technology. Campus intranet, student e-mail accounts, and computer access in designated common areas are available to students. Students grades are available online. The school has a published electronic and media policy.

Contact Blake Howard, Assistant Director of Admissions. 602-955-8200 Ext. 2255. Fax: 602-381-4554. E-mail: Blake.Howard@pcds.org. Website: www.pcds.org

PICKENS ACADEMY

225 Ray Bass Road
Carrollton, Alabama 35447

Head of School: Mr. Brach White

General Information Coeducational day college-preparatory, general academic, and technology school. Grades K4–12. Founded: 1970. Setting: rural. Nearest major city is Tuscaloosa. 3 buildings on campus. Approved or accredited by Distance Education Accrediting Commission, Southern Association of Colleges and Schools, and Alabama Department of Education. Total enrollment: 267. Upper school average class size: 25. Upper school faculty-student ratio: 1:20. There are 180 required school days per year for Upper School students. Upper School students typically attend 5 days per week. The average school day consists of 7 hours.

Upper School Student Profile Grade 7: 25 students (11 boys, 14 girls); Grade 8: 28 students (11 boys, 17 girls); Grade 9: 15 students (7 boys, 8 girls); Grade 10: 26 students (13 boys, 13 girls); Grade 11: 19 students (7 boys, 12 girls); Grade 12: 34 students (15 boys, 19 girls).

Faculty School total: 21. In upper school: 5 men, 16 women; 8 have advanced degrees.

Subjects Offered 20th century history, 20th century world history, advanced chemistry, advanced computer applications, advanced math, Alabama history and geography, algebra, American democracy, American government, American history, American literature, anatomy and physiology, ancient history, ancient world history,

www.petersons.com 399

applied music, art, band, baseball, basketball, biology, British literature, business mathematics, calculus, career/college preparation, cheerleading, chemistry, civics, college admission preparation, composition, computer literacy, consumer economics, CPR, creative writing, desktop publishing, economics, English composition, English literature, environmental science, family and consumer science, French, geography, government, grammar, health education, history, keyboarding, land management, leadership education training, library assistant, Microsoft, music, music appreciation, physical education, physical science, physics, research skills, science, student government, trigonometry, U.S. government and politics, Web site design, weight training, weightlifting.

Graduation Requirements 20th century world history, advanced math, American government, American history, anatomy and physiology, calculus, economics, English, English composition, English literature, physics, research skills, trigonometry.

Special Academic Programs Study at local college for college credit.

College Admission Counseling 24 students graduated in 2015; 17 went to college, including Auburn University; Mississippi State University; The University of Alabama. Other: 1 went to work, 1 entered military service. Median composite ACT: 21. 4% scored over 26 on composite ACT.

Student Life Upper grades have specified standards of dress, student council. Discipline rests primarily with faculty.

Summer Programs Sports programs offered; session focuses on conditioning; held on campus; accepts boys and girls; not open to students from other schools. 2016 schedule: June 1 to July 30. Application deadline: May 15.

Tuition and Aid Day student tuition: $3000. Guaranteed tuition plan. Tuition installment plan (Insured Tuition Payment Plan, monthly payment plans).

Admissions Traditional secondary-level entrance grade is 9. PSAT or Stanford Achievement Test, Otis-Lennon School Ability Test required. Deadline for receipt of application materials: none. No application fee required. On-campus interview required.

Athletics Interscholastic: baseball (boys), basketball (b,g), cheering (g), cross-country running (b,g), danceline (g), football (b), golf (b,g), softball (g), volleyball (g), weight lifting (b,g); coed interscholastic: tennis, track and field. 1 PE instructor, 2 coaches.

Computers Computers are regularly used in all academic classes. Computer network features include on-campus library services, Internet access, Internet filtering or blocking technology. Student e-mail accounts are available to students. Students grades are available online. The school has a published electronic and media policy.

Contact Admissions. 205-367-8144. Fax: 205-367-8145. Website: www.pickensacademy.com

PICKERING COLLEGE

16945 Bayview Avenue
Newmarket, Ontario L3Y 4X2, Canada

Head of School: Mr. Peter C. Sturrup

General Information Coeducational boarding and day college-preparatory, arts, technology, film studies and radio station, and leadership school. Boarding grades 7–12, day grades JK–12. Founded: 1842. Setting: suburban. Nearest major city is Toronto, Canada. Students are housed in single-sex dormitories. 42-acre campus. 6 buildings on campus. Approved or accredited by Canadian Association of Independent Schools, Canadian Educational Standards Institute, National Independent Private Schools Association, Ontario Ministry of Education, The Association of Boarding Schools, and Ontario Department of Education. Affiliate member of National Association of Independent Schools; member of Secondary School Admission Test Board. Language of instruction: English. Total enrollment: 423. Upper school average class size: 18. Upper school faculty-student ratio: 1:8. There are 164 required school days per year for Upper School students. Upper School students typically attend 5 days per week. The average school day consists of 8 hours.

Upper School Student Profile 35% of students are boarding students. 60% are province residents. 40% are international students. International students from Barbados, China, Germany, Japan, Mexico, and Russian Federation; 18 other countries represented in student body.

Faculty School total: 51. In upper school: 12 men, 20 women; 8 have advanced degrees; 16 reside on campus.

Subjects Offered Algebra, art, art history, biology, business, business skills, business studies, calculus, Canadian geography, Canadian history, careers, chemistry, community service, computer applications, computer multimedia, computer programming, computer science, concert band, creative writing, drama, dramatic arts, economics, English, English composition, English literature, entrepreneurship, environmental science, ESL, experiential education, family studies, filmmaking, fine arts, finite math, French, geography, geometry, government/civics, guitar, health, health education, history, instrumental music, jazz band, law, leadership, literature, mathematics, media studies, music, physical education, physics, politics, science, social sciences, social studies, theater, video film production, visual arts, vocal music, world history.

Graduation Requirements English, 60 hours of community service completed over 4 years before graduation.

Special Academic Programs Advanced Placement exam preparation; independent study; ESL (30 students enrolled).

College Admission Counseling 69 students graduated in 2015; 67 went to college, including Dalhousie University; McGill University; Queen's University at Kingston; The University of Western Ontario; University of Toronto; University of Waterloo. Other: 2 had other specific plans.

Student Life Upper grades have uniform requirement, student council, honor system. Discipline rests equally with students and faculty.

Summer Programs ESL programs offered; session focuses on ESL summer camp; held on campus; accepts boys and girls; open to students from other schools. 70 students usually enrolled. 2016 schedule: June 26 to August 19. Application deadline: May 1.

Tuition and Aid Day student tuition: CAN$19,130–CAN$23,000; 7-day tuition and room/board: CAN$47,700–CAN$49,930. Tuition installment plan (Insured Tuition Payment Plan, monthly payment plans). Tuition reduction for siblings, bursaries, merit scholarship grants, need-based scholarship grants available. In 2015–16, 4% of upper-school students received aid; total upper-school merit-scholarship money awarded: CAN$13,000. Total amount of financial aid awarded in 2015–16: CAN$125,000.

Admissions Traditional secondary-level entrance grade is 9. For fall 2015, 109 students applied for upper-level admission, 52 enrolled. CAT, International English Language Test, SLEP for foreign students or TOEFL required. Deadline for receipt of application materials: none. Application fee required: CAN$200. Interview required.

Athletics Interscholastic: badminton (boys, girls), basketball (b,g), cross-country running (b,g), figure skating (b,g), hockey (b), horseback riding (b,g), ice hockey (b), ice skating (b,g), rugby (b,g), skiing (downhill) (b,g), snowboarding (b,g), soccer (b,g), softball (b,g), swimming and diving (b,g), tennis (b,g), track and field (b,g), volleyball (b,g); intramural: badminton (b,g), ball hockey (b,g), combined training (b,g), figure skating (b,g), floor hockey (b,g), hockey (b,g), horseback riding (b,g), ice skating (b,g), outdoor activities (b,g), outdoor adventure (b,g), outdoor recreation (b,g), paddle tennis (b,g), physical training (b,g), running (b,g), skiing (downhill) (b,g), soccer (b,g), strength & conditioning (b,g), swimming and diving (b,g), tennis (b,g), track and field (b,g), volleyball (b,g); coed interscholastic: alpine skiing, aquatics, badminton, cross-country running, equestrian sports, figure skating, hockey, horseback riding, ice hockey, ice skating, mountain biking, skiing (downhill), snowboarding, soccer, swimming and diving, tennis, track and field; coed intramural: aerobics/dance, badminton, ball hockey, basketball, bowling, broomball, canoeing/kayaking, cooperative games, cross-country running, curling, dance squad, equestrian sports, figure skating, fitness, floor hockey, Frisbee, golf, hockey, horseback riding, ice skating, indoor soccer, mountain biking, nordic skiing, outdoor adventure, outdoor education, paint ball, rock climbing, skiing (downhill), soccer, strength & conditioning, swimming and diving, table tennis, tennis, touch football, track and field, volleyball, wall climbing, wilderness survival, yoga. 3 PE instructors, 3 coaches, 1 athletic trainer.

Computers Computers are regularly used in all classes. Computer network features include on-campus library services, Internet access, wireless campus network, Internet filtering or blocking technology. Student e-mail accounts are available to students. Students grades are available online. The school has a published electronic and media policy.

Contact Mrs. Susan Hundert, Admission Associate, Day and North American Boarding. 905-895-1700 Ext. 259. Fax: 905-895-1306. E-mail: admission@pickeringcollege.on.ca. Website: www.pickeringcollege.on.ca

PIEDMONT ACADEMY

PO Box 231
126 Highway 212 West
Monticello, Georgia 31064

Head of School: Mr. Tony Tanner

General Information Coeducational day college-preparatory, arts, business, vocational, religious studies, bilingual studies, and technology school, affiliated with Protestant faith. Grades 1–12. Founded: 1970. Setting: rural. Nearest major city is Macon. 22-acre campus. 8 buildings on campus. Approved or accredited by Georgia Accrediting Commission, Georgia Independent School Association, and Southern Association of Independent Schools. Total enrollment: 259. Upper school average class size: 13. Upper school faculty-student ratio: 1:13. There are 180 required school days per year for Upper School students. Upper School students typically attend 5 days per week. The average school day consists of 7 hours.

Upper School Student Profile Grade 6: 26 students (12 boys, 14 girls); Grade 7: 18 students (8 boys, 10 girls); Grade 8: 20 students (12 boys, 8 girls); Grade 9: 30 students (10 boys, 20 girls); Grade 10: 32 students (15 boys, 17 girls); Grade 11: 27 students (15 boys, 12 girls); Grade 12: 29 students (16 boys, 13 girls). 98% of students are Protestant.

Faculty School total: 31. In upper school: 6 men, 15 women; 15 have advanced degrees.

Subjects Offered Advanced chemistry, advanced computer applications, advanced math, algebra, American government, American history, American history-AP, anatomy and physiology, band, biology, business law, calculus, calculus-AP, chemistry, chemistry-AP, civics, computer science, computer science-AP, computers, concert band, concert choir, consumer economics, consumer law, economics, English, English-AP, geometry, government and politics-AP, government-AP, government/civics, grammar, health education, honors algebra, honors English, honors geometry, Internet, intro to computers, keyboarding, language arts, leadership and service, literature, mathematics, performing arts, personal finance, physical fitness, physical science, physics, pre-calculus, science, sociology, Spanish, student government, wind instruments, world history, yearbook.

Graduation Requirements Algebra, American government, American literature, biology, calculus, chemistry, civics, English composition, English literature, geometry, government, grammar, history, keyboarding, mathematics, physical education (includes health), physical science, science, Spanish.

Special Academic Programs Study at local college for college credit.

College Admission Counseling 33 went to college, including Georgia Institute of Technology; Georgia Perimeter College; University of Georgia; University of North Georgia. Other: 33 entered a postgraduate year.

Student Life Upper grades have uniform requirement, student council, honor system. Discipline rests primarily with faculty.

Tuition and Aid Day student tuition: $6730–$6910. Guaranteed tuition plan. Tuition installment plan (monthly payment plans, individually arranged payment plans, APOGEE School Choice Scholarship, Financial Assistance (Grant)). Tuition reduction for siblings, need-based scholarship grants available. In 2015–16, 8% of upper-school students received aid. Total amount of financial aid awarded in 2015–16: $30,000.

Admissions Traditional secondary-level entrance grade is 9. For fall 2015, 30 students applied for upper-level admission, 23 were accepted, 23 enrolled. Cognitive Abilities Test, OLSAT, Stanford Achievement Test or WAIS, WICS required. Deadline for receipt of application materials: none. Application fee required: $75. Interview required.

Athletics Interscholastic: baseball (boys), basketball (b,g), cheering (b,g), fitness (b,g), flag football (b,g), football (b), golf (b,g), power lifting (b,g); coed interscholastic: cross-country running, skeet shooting; coed intramural: cross-country running, flag football. 6 PE instructors, 14 coaches, 1 athletic trainer.

Computers Computers are regularly used in all academic classes. Computer network features include on-campus library services, online commercial services, Internet access, wireless campus network, Internet filtering or blocking technology. Campus intranet is available to students. Students grades are available online. The school has a published electronic and media policy.

Contact Judy M. Nelson, Director of Admissions/Public and Alumni Relations. 706-468-8818 Ext. 304. Fax: 706-468-2409. E-mail: judy_nelson@piedmontacademy.com. Website: www.piedmontacademy.com

PINECREST ACADEMY

955 Peachtree Parkway
Cumming, Georgia 30041

Head of School: Mr. Paul Parker

General Information Coeducational day college-preparatory, arts, religious studies, and technology school, affiliated with Roman Catholic Church. Grades PK–12. Founded: 1993. Setting: suburban. Nearest major city is Atlanta. 79-acre campus. 3 buildings on campus. Approved or accredited by Georgia Independent School Association, National Catholic Education Association, Southern Association of Colleges and Schools, Southern Association of Independent Schools, The College Board, and Georgia Department of Education. Member of National Association of Independent Schools and Secondary School Admission Test Board. Total enrollment: 807. Upper school average class size: 18. Upper school faculty-student ratio: 1:8. There are 180 required school days per year for Upper School students. Upper School students typically attend 5 days per week. The average school day consists of 7 hours and 30 minutes.

Upper School Student Profile Grade 9: 71 students (34 boys, 37 girls); Grade 10: 74 students (31 boys, 43 girls); Grade 11: 73 students (38 boys, 35 girls); Grade 12: 67 students (35 boys, 32 girls). 79% of students are Roman Catholic.

Faculty School total: 93. In upper school: 17 men, 17 women; 10 have advanced degrees.

Subjects Offered Advanced chemistry, advanced math, Advanced Placement courses, advanced studio art-AP, algebra, American history, American history-AP, American literature, anatomy and physiology, art, art history-AP, art-AP, arts, band, biology, biology-AP, British literature, British literature-AP, calculus, calculus-AP, chemistry, chemistry-AP, chorus, Christian ethics, church history, composition, composition-AP, computer science-AP, concert band, creative writing, debate, digital imaging, drama, dramatic arts, drawing, drawing and design, economics, electives, engineering, English, English composition, English language and composition-AP, English language-AP, English literature, English literature and composition-AP, English literature-AP, English-AP, English/composition-AP, environmental science, ESL, ESL, European history-AP, general science, geometry, government and politics-AP, health education, history of the Catholic Church, history-AP, honors algebra, honors English, honors geometry, honors U.S. history, honors world history, instrumental music, instruments, journalism, language, language and composition, language arts, language-AP, languages, Latin, Latin-AP, Life of Christ, literature and composition-AP, macroeconomics-AP, microeconomics-AP, music, music theory-AP, painting, personal fitness, philosophy, physical education, physics, play production, pre-algebra, pre-calculus, psychology, psychology-AP, SAT preparation, SAT/ACT preparation, science, scripture, sculpture, Spanish, Spanish language-AP, Spanish literature, Spanish literature-AP, Spanish-AP, speech and debate, statistics, statistics-AP, studio art, studio art-AP, symphonic band, technology, theater arts, theology, U.S. government and politics, U.S. government and politics-AP, U.S. history, U.S. history-AP, weight fitness,

weight training, weightlifting, world history, world history-AP, world literature, yearbook.

Special Academic Programs 17 Advanced Placement exams for which test preparation is offered; honors section; ESL (15 students enrolled).

College Admission Counseling 66 students graduated in 2015; 64 went to college, including Auburn University; Georgia Institute of Technology; Georgia State University; Kennesaw State University; University of Georgia; University of North Georgia. Other: 2 had other specific plans. Median SAT critical reading: 580, median SAT math: 600, median SAT writing: 570, median combined SAT: 1730, median composite ACT: 26. 39% scored over 600 on SAT critical reading, 46% scored over 600 on SAT math, 39% scored over 600 on SAT writing, 35% scored over 1800 on combined SAT, 47% scored over 26 on composite ACT.

Student Life Upper grades have uniform requirement, student council, honor system. Discipline rests primarily with faculty. Attendance at religious services is required.

Summer Programs Advancement programs offered; session focuses on math programs; held on campus; accepts boys and girls; not open to students from other schools. 10 students usually enrolled.

Tuition and Aid Day student tuition: $15,345. Tuition installment plan (monthly payment plans). Tuition reduction for siblings, need-based scholarship grants available.

Admissions Traditional secondary-level entrance grade is 9. For fall 2015, 29 students applied for upper-level admission, 22 were accepted, 17 enrolled. Admissions testing, Individual IQ, Achievement and behavior rating scale, PSAT or SAT for applicants to grade 11 and 12, psychoeducational evaluation, school's own exam, SSAT or TOEFL required. Deadline for receipt of application materials: none. Application fee required: $150. Interview required.

Athletics Interscholastic: baseball (boys), basketball (b,g), cheering (g), cross-country running (b,g), fencing (b,g), football (b), golf (b), lacrosse (b,g), soccer (b,g), swimming and diving (b,g), tennis (b,g), volleyball (g); coed interscholastic: cross-country running, fencing, lacrosse, soccer, swimming and diving, tennis. 1 PE instructor.

Computers Computers are regularly used in accounting classes. Computer network features include on-campus library services, online commercial services, Internet access, wireless campus network, Internet filtering or blocking technology, homework is available online. Campus intranet, student e-mail accounts, and computer access in designated common areas are available to students. Students grades are available online. The school has a published electronic and media policy.

Contact Ms. Melissa McWaters, Admissions Coordinator. 770-888-4477 Ext. 245. Fax: 770-888-0404. E-mail: mmcwaters@pinecrestacademy.org. Website: www.pinecrestacademy.org/

THE PINE SCHOOL

12350 SE Federal Highway
Hobe Sound, Florida 33455

Head of School: Mrs. Phyllis Parker

General Information Coeducational day college-preparatory school. Grades PK–12. Founded: 1969. Setting: small town. Nearest major city is West Palm Beach. Approved or accredited by Florida Department of Education. Member of National Association of Independent Schools. Upper school average class size: 9. Upper school faculty-student ratio: 1:9. Upper School students typically attend 5 days per week.

Special Academic Programs Advanced Placement exam preparation; honors section; study abroad.

Student Life Upper grades have uniform requirement, student council, honor system. Discipline rests primarily with faculty.

Tuition and Aid Financial aid available to upper-school students. In 2014–15, 29% of upper-school students received aid. Total amount of financial aid awarded in 2014–15: $1,000,000.

Admissions Deadline for receipt of application materials: none. Application fee required: $60. Interview required.

Athletics Intramural: basketball (boys, girls), cheering (g), cross-country running (b,g), diving (b,g), golf (b,g), lacrosse (b), sailing (b,g), soccer (b,g), tennis (b,g), volleyball (g).

Computers Computer network features include on-campus library services, Internet access, wireless campus network, Internet filtering or blocking technology. Student e-mail accounts and computer access in designated common areas are available to students. Students grades are available online. The school has a published electronic and media policy.

Contact 772-675-7005. Website: www.thepineschool.org

PINE TREE ACADEMY

67 Pownal Road
Freeport, Maine 04032

Head of School: Mr. Brendan Krueger

General Information Coeducational boarding and day college-preparatory school, affiliated with Seventh-day Adventist Church. Boarding grades 9–12, day grades K–12. Founded: 1961. Setting: small town. Nearest major city is Portland. Students are housed in single-sex dormitories. 80-acre campus. 4 buildings on campus. Approved or accredited by Middle States Association of Colleges and Schools, National Council for Private School Accreditation, and Maine Department of Education. Total enrollment: 121. Upper school average class size: 15. Upper school faculty-student ratio: 1:6. There are 180 required school days per year for Upper School students. Upper School students typically attend 5 days per week. The average school day consists of 7 hours.

Upper School Student Profile Grade 9: 17 students (11 boys, 6 girls); Grade 10: 12 students (6 boys, 6 girls); Grade 11: 17 students (7 boys, 10 girls); Grade 12: 15 students (9 boys, 6 girls). 36% of students are boarding students. 75% are state residents. 7 states are represented in upper school student body. 3% are international students. International students from Nicaragua, Republic of Korea, and United States. 80% of students are Seventh-day Adventists.

Faculty School total: 11. In upper school: 5 men, 6 women; 5 have advanced degrees; 4 reside on campus.

Subjects Offered Agriculture, algebra, American government, American history, American literature, ancient world history, archaeology, art, auto mechanics, band, basketball, bell choir, Bible, Bible studies, biology, British literature, calculus, chemistry, choir, church history, composition, computer science, concert band, concert bell choir, concert choir, driver education, earth science, economics, French, general math, geometry, German, government, health, instruments, keyboarding, Life of Christ, music, personal finance, personal fitness, physical education, physics, piano, pre-algebra, pre-calculus, Spanish, voice, woodworking, world history, world religions, yearbook.

College Admission Counseling 21 students graduated in 2015; 19 went to college, including Andrews University; High Point University; Southern Maine Community College; University of Maine at Farmington; Walla Walla University; Westmont College. Other: 1 went to work, 1 entered military service. Median SAT critical reading: 630, median SAT math: 530, median SAT writing: 540, median combined SAT: 1700, median composite ACT: 27. 53% scored over 600 on SAT critical reading, 13% scored over 600 on SAT math, 27% scored over 600 on SAT writing, 20% scored over 1800 on combined SAT, 100% scored over 26 on composite ACT.

Student Life Upper grades have uniform requirement, honor system. Discipline rests primarily with faculty. Attendance at religious services is required.

Tuition and Aid Tuition installment plan (FACTS Tuition Payment Plan). Tuition reduction for siblings, need-based scholarship grants, paying campus jobs available. In 2015–16, 23% of upper-school students received aid.

Admissions Traditional secondary-level entrance grade is 9. Deadline for receipt of application materials: none. Application fee required: $25. Interview required.

Athletics Interscholastic: basketball (boys, girls), soccer (b,g); coed intramural: basketball. 2 PE instructors.

Computers Computer resources include Internet access, Internet filtering or blocking technology. Student e-mail accounts and computer access in designated common areas are available to students. Students grades are available online. The school has a published electronic and media policy.

Contact Mrs. Barb Glover, Office Manager. 207-865-4747. Fax: 207-865-1768. E-mail: bglover@pinetreeacademy.org. Website: www.pinetreeacademy.org

PINEWOOD - THE INTERNATIONAL SCHOOL OF THESSALONIKI, GREECE

14th KM Thessalonikis-N. Moudanion
Thermi
PO Box 60606
Thessaloniki 57001, Greece

Head of School: Dr. Robin Roxanne Giampapa

General Information Coeducational boarding and day college-preparatory, arts, and bilingual studies school. Boarding grades 7–12, day grades PK–12. Founded: 1950. Setting: suburban. Students are housed in coed dormitories. 4-acre campus. 2 buildings on campus. Approved or accredited by International Baccalaureate Organization, Middle States Association of Colleges and Schools, The College Board, US Department of State, and state department of education. Affiliate member of National Association of Independent Schools; member of European Council of International Schools. Language of instruction: English. Total enrollment: 250. Upper school average class size: 15. Upper school faculty-student ratio: 1:5. There are 174 required school days per year for Upper School students. Upper School students typically attend 5 days per week. The average school day consists of 6 hours and 30 minutes.

Upper School Student Profile 10% of students are boarding students. 80% are international students. International students from Bulgaria, China, Italy, Russian Federation, Spain, and United States; 20 other countries represented in student body.

Faculty School total: 35. In upper school: 7 men, 14 women; 14 have advanced degrees.

Subjects Offered Algebra, art, biology, chemistry, computer applications, computer science, computers, economics, electives, English, English literature, ESL, European history, French, general science, geography, geometry, Greek, Greek culture, history, honors English, honors U.S. history, library, literature, math methods, mathematics, modern European history, music, physical education, physical science, physics, pre-algebra, psychology, science, social sciences, social studies, U.S. history, world cultures, world geography, world history, world literature, yearbook.

Graduation Requirements Electives, English, European history, foreign language, mathematics, physical education (includes health), science, social studies (includes history), world history.

Special Academic Programs International Baccalaureate program; honors section; accelerated programs; independent study; study at local college for college credit; ESL (30 students enrolled).

College Admission Counseling 28 students graduated in 2014; 27 went to college, including Bard College; Cornell University; Franklin & Marshall College; John Carroll University; Quinnipiac University; Rutgers, The State University of New Jersey, Newark. Other: 1 had other specific plans.

Student Life Upper grades have specified standards of dress, student council, honor system. Discipline rests primarily with faculty.

Tuition and Aid Day student tuition: €10,812; 7-day tuition and room/board: €22,500. Tuition installment plan (monthly payment plans, individually arranged payment plans, 3-payment plan). Tuition reduction for siblings, merit scholarship grants, need-based scholarship grants available. In 2014–15, 20% of upper-school students received aid.

Admissions Traditional secondary-level entrance grade is 10. English entrance exam, English language or Math Placement Exam required. Deadline for receipt of application materials: none. No application fee required. Interview recommended.

Athletics Interscholastic: aerobics/dance (girls), basketball (b,g), dance (g), fitness (b,g), football (b), soccer (b,g), volleyball (b,g); intramural: basketball (b,g), cheering (g), flag football (b,g), floor hockey (b,g), football (b), soccer (b,g), table tennis (b,g), tennis (b,g), volleyball (b,g); coed interscholastic: gymnastics, indoor soccer, juggling; coed intramural: baseball, gymnastics, juggling, softball, table tennis. 2 PE instructors, 3 coaches, 2 athletic trainers.

Computers Computers are regularly used in English, science, word processing, yearbook classes. Computer network features include on-campus library services, Internet access, wireless campus network. Student e-mail accounts are available to students. Students grades are available online. The school has a published electronic and media policy.

Contact Ms. Petroula Rosiou, Admissions and Administrative Officer. 30-2310-301221 Ext. 13. Fax: 30-2310-323196. E-mail: admissions@pinewood.gr. Website: www.pinewood.gr

THE PINGREE SCHOOL

537 Highland Street
South Hamilton, Massachusetts 01982

Head of School: Dr. Timothy M. Johnson

General Information Coeducational day college-preparatory school. Grades 9–12. Founded: 1961. Setting: suburban. Nearest major city is Boston. 100-acre campus. 3 buildings on campus. Approved or accredited by Association of Independent Schools in New England, National Independent Private Schools Association, and New England Association of Schools and Colleges. Member of National Association of Independent Schools and Secondary School Admission Test Board. Endowment: $11 million. Total enrollment: 364. Upper school average class size: 15. Upper school faculty-student ratio: 1:6. There are 162 required school days per year for Upper School students. Upper School students typically attend 5 days per week. The average school day consists of 8 hours.

Upper School Student Profile Grade 9: 103 students (47 boys, 56 girls); Grade 10: 82 students (39 boys, 43 girls); Grade 11: 91 students (38 boys, 53 girls); Grade 12: 88 students (45 boys, 43 girls).

Faculty School total: 58. In upper school: 22 men, 34 women; 45 have advanced degrees.

Subjects Offered Algebra, American history, American literature, American studies, art, art history, astronomy, biology, calculus, ceramics, chemistry, computer programming, computer science, creative writing, dance, drama, driver education, earth science, ecology, economics, engineering, English, English literature, European history, fine arts, French, geometry, history, Latin, mathematics, music, oceanography, philosophy, photography, physics, psychology, Russian literature, science, social studies, Spanish, theater, trigonometry, writing.

Graduation Requirements Arts and fine arts (art, music, dance, drama), English, foreign language, mathematics, science, social studies (includes history), senior projects.

Special Academic Programs Advanced Placement exam preparation; honors section; independent study; term-away projects.

College Admission Counseling 80 students graduated in 2015; 79 went to college, including Boston College; Boston University; Colby College; Northeastern University; Pitzer College; University of Southern California. Other: 1 entered military service. Median SAT critical reading: 621, median SAT math: 633, median SAT writing: 630, median combined SAT: 1884, median composite ACT: 27. 60% scored over 600 on SAT critical reading, 70% scored over 600 on SAT math, 68% scored over 600 on SAT writing, 66% scored over 1800 on combined SAT.

Student Life Upper grades have specified standards of dress, student council, honor system. Discipline rests equally with students and faculty.

Tuition and Aid Day student tuition: $40,750. Tuition installment plan (FACTS Tuition Payment Plan). Merit scholarship grants, need-based scholarship grants, need-based loans available. In 2015–16, 35% of upper-school students received aid; total upper-school merit-scholarship money awarded: $140,690. Total amount of financial aid awarded in 2015–16: $3,080,000.

Admissions Traditional secondary-level entrance grade is 9. For fall 2015, 410 students applied for upper-level admission, 200 were accepted, 111 enrolled. ISEE or SSAT required. Deadline for receipt of application materials: January 15. Application fee required: $50. On-campus interview required.

Athletics Interscholastic: baseball (boys), basketball (b,g), cross-country running (b,g), field hockey (g), football (b), golf (b,g), ice hockey (b,g), lacrosse (b,g), running (b,g), soccer (b,g), softball (g), swimming and diving (b,g), tennis (b,g), volleyball (g); coed interscholastic: Frisbee, sailing, ultimate Frisbee; coed intramural: dance, fitness, golf, hiking/backpacking, modern dance, mountaineering, outdoor adventure, outdoor education, outdoor skills, physical fitness, physical training, skiing (downhill), strength & conditioning, weight lifting, weight training, wilderness. 24 coaches, 2 athletic trainers.

Computers Computers are regularly used in college planning, computer applications, desktop publishing, digital applications, drawing and design, English, foreign language, graphic arts, graphic design, independent study, information technology, mathematics, programming, publications, science, technology, Web site design, word processing, writing, yearbook classes. Computer network features include on-campus library services, online commercial services, Internet access, wireless campus network, Internet filtering or blocking technology. Campus intranet, student e-mail accounts, and computer access in designated common areas are available to students. Students grades are available online. The school has a published electronic and media policy.

Contact Mrs. Denise DeChristoforo, Admission Office Coordinator. 978-468-4415 Ext. 262. Fax: 978-468-3758. E-mail: ddechristoforo@pingree.org. Website: www.pingree.org

THE PINGRY SCHOOL

Martinsville Road
131 Martinsville Road
Basking Ridge, New Jersey 07920

Head of School: Mr. Nathaniel Conard

General Information Coeducational day college-preparatory, arts, and technology school. Grades K–12. Founded: 1861. Setting: suburban. Nearest major city is New York, NY. 240-acre campus. 1 building on campus. Approved or accredited by Middle States Association of Colleges and Schools and New Jersey Department of Education. Member of National Association of Independent Schools. Endowment: $80 million. Total enrollment: 1,116. Upper school average class size: 13. Upper school faculty-student ratio: 1:7. There are 168 required school days per year for Upper School students. Upper School students typically attend 5 days per week. The average school day consists of 6 hours and 15 minutes.

Upper School Student Profile Grade 9: 148 students (74 boys, 74 girls); Grade 10: 141 students (76 boys, 65 girls); Grade 11: 139 students (81 boys, 58 girls); Grade 12: 129 students (62 boys, 67 girls).

Faculty School total: 120. In upper school: 47 men, 37 women; 61 have advanced degrees.

Subjects Offered Algebra, American literature, analysis, analysis and differential calculus, anatomy, architecture, art, art history-AP, biology, biology-AP, brass choir, calculus, chemistry, chemistry-AP, Chinese, clayworking, comparative cultures, computer science-AP, creative writing, drafting, drama, driver education, English, ethics, European literature, filmmaking, French, French-AP, geometry, German, German-AP, Greek drama, health, jazz band, jewelry making, Latin, literature by women, macro/microeconomics-AP, macroeconomics-AP, modern European history, music theory, mythology, orchestra, painting, peer counseling, photography, physics, physics-AP, physiology, psychology, psychology-AP, sculpture, Shakespeare, Spanish, Spanish-AP, studio art-AP, trigonometry, U.S. government and politics-AP, U.S. history-AP, wind ensemble, world literature, yearbook.

Graduation Requirements Arts and fine arts (art, music, dance, drama), English, foreign language, mathematics, physical education (includes health), science, social studies (includes history). Community service is required.

Special Academic Programs 20 Advanced Placement exams for which test preparation is offered; honors section; independent study; term-away projects; study abroad; academic accommodation for the gifted.

College Admission Counseling 142 students graduated in 2015; all went to college, including Carnegie Mellon University; Harvard University; Lehigh University; New York University; University of Pennsylvania; Washington University in St. Louis. Mean SAT critical reading: 681, mean SAT math: 696, mean SAT writing: 695, mean composite ACT: 30.

Student Life Upper grades have specified standards of dress, student council, honor system. Discipline rests equally with students and faculty.

Summer Programs Enrichment, sports programs offered; session focuses on enrichment, writing, and study skills; held on campus; accepts boys and girls; open to students from other schools. 30 students usually enrolled. 2016 schedule: June 27 to August 12.

Tuition and Aid Day student tuition: $31,504–$37,062. Tuition installment plan (individually arranged payment plans, My Tuition Solutions). Need-based scholarship grants available. In 2015–16, 15% of upper-school students received aid. Total amount of financial aid awarded in 2015–16: $2,711,787.

Admissions Traditional secondary-level entrance grade is 9. For fall 2015, 328 students applied for upper-level admission, 98 were accepted, 68 enrolled. ERB, ISEE, SSAT or Wechsler Intelligence Scale for Children required. Deadline for receipt of application materials: January 3. Application fee required: $75. On-campus interview required.

Athletics Interscholastic: alpine skiing (boys, girls), baseball (b), basketball (b,g), cross-country running (b,g), fencing (b,g), field hockey (g), football (b), golf (b,g), ice hockey (b,g), indoor track & field (b,g), lacrosse (b,g), skiing (downhill) (b,g), soccer (b,g), softball (g), squash (b,g), swimming and diving (b,g), tennis (b,g), track and field (b,g), wrestling (b); intramural: fitness (b,g), yoga (b,g); coed interscholastic: dance, physical fitness, physical training, water polo. 3 PE instructors, 15 coaches, 1 athletic trainer.

Computers Computers are regularly used in all academic classes. Computer network features include on-campus library services, online commercial services, Internet access, wireless campus network, Internet filtering or blocking technology. Campus intranet, student e-mail accounts, and computer access in designated common areas are available to students. The school has a published electronic and media policy.

Contact Mr. George Mihalik, Admission Coordinator. 908-647-5555 Ext. 1221. Fax: 908-647-4395. E-mail: gmihalik@pingry.org. Website: www.pingry.org

PIONEER VALLEY CHRISTIAN ACADEMY

965 Plumtree Road
Springfield, Massachusetts 01119

Head of School: Mr. Timothy L. Duff

General Information Coeducational day college-preparatory, religious studies, bilingual studies, and technology school, affiliated with Protestant faith, Evangelical faith. Grades PS–12. Founded: 1972. Setting: suburban. 25-acre campus. 1 building on campus. Approved or accredited by Association of Christian Schools International, New England Association of Schools and Colleges, and Massachusetts Department of Education. Total enrollment: 293. Upper school average class size: 11. Upper school faculty-student ratio: 1:6. There are 181 required school days per year for Upper School students. Upper School students typically attend 5 days per week. The average school day consists of 6 hours and 40 minutes.

Upper School Student Profile Grade 9: 29 students (16 boys, 13 girls); Grade 10: 20 students (10 boys, 10 girls); Grade 11: 19 students (12 boys, 7 girls); Grade 12: 22 students (11 boys, 11 girls). 95% of students are Protestant, members of Evangelical faith.

Faculty School total: 29. In upper school: 6 men, 9 women; 8 have advanced degrees.

Subjects Offered Advanced math, algebra, American literature, American literature-AP, anatomy, art, athletics, baseball, basketball, bell choir, Bible studies, biology, British literature, British literature-AP, calculus-AP, chemistry, choir, choral music, Christian education, drama, economics, English, English-AP, French, geometry, government, history, instrumental music, music, physical education, physical science, physics, pre-algebra, sociology, softball, Spanish, speech, sports, technology, tennis, U.S. history, volleyball, weight training, Western civilization, world history, yearbook.

Graduation Requirements Algebra, American literature, arts and fine arts (art, music, dance, drama), Bible, biology, British literature, economics, English, foreign language, government, physical education (includes health), physical science, sociology, speech, U.S. history, Christian/community service hours.

Special Academic Programs Advanced Placement exam preparation; honors section; remedial reading and/or remedial writing; remedial math; programs in English, mathematics, general development for dyslexic students; special instructional classes for students with learning disabilities, Attention Deficit Disorder, and dyslexia.

College Admission Counseling 19 students graduated in 2015; all went to college, including Anderson University; Cedarville University; University of Massachusetts Boston; Western New England University. Median SAT critical reading: 540, median SAT math: 520, median SAT writing: 520.

Student Life Upper grades have uniform requirement, honor system. Discipline rests primarily with faculty. Attendance at religious services is required.

Tuition and Aid Day student tuition: $11,750. Tuition installment plan (monthly payment plans, Electronic Funds Transfer, weekly, biweekly, monthly). Need-based scholarship grants, need-based financial aid and scholarship available. In 2015–16, 51% of upper-school students received aid. Total amount of financial aid awarded in 2015–16: $215,125.

Admissions Traditional secondary-level entrance grade is 9. For fall 2015, 11 students applied for upper-level admission, 11 were accepted, 11 enrolled. Admissions testing required. Deadline for receipt of application materials: none. Application fee required: $100. Interview required.

Athletics Interscholastic: baseball (boys), basketball (b,g), softball (g), tennis (b,g), volleyball (g); intramural: soccer (b,g); coed interscholastic: soccer, weight training; coed intramural: combined training, physical training, soccer, strength & conditioning. 2 PE instructors, 8 coaches.

Computers Computers are regularly used in all academic classes. Computer network features include Internet access, Internet filtering or blocking technology, homework assignments available online.

Contact Mrs. Denise Richards, Director of Admissions. 413-782-8031. Fax: 413-782-8033. E-mail: drichards@pvcama.org. Website: www.pvcama.org

PIUS X HIGH SCHOOL

6000 A Street

Lincoln, Nebraska 68510

Head of School: Fr. James J. Meysenburg

General Information Coeducational day college-preparatory, general academic, and religious studies school, affiliated with Roman Catholic Church; primarily serves students with learning disabilities, individuals with Attention Deficit Disorder, and individuals with emotional and behavioral problems. Grades 9–12. Founded: 1956. Setting: urban. 30-acre campus. 1 building on campus. Approved or accredited by North Central Association of Colleges and Schools, Western Catholic Education Association, and Nebraska Department of Education. Endowment: $14 million. Total enrollment: 1,224. Upper school average class size: 26. Upper school faculty-student ratio: 1:23. There are 182 required school days per year for Upper School students. Upper School students typically attend 5 days per week. The average school day consists of 6 hours.

Upper School Student Profile Grade 9: 319 students (154 boys, 165 girls); Grade 10: 324 students (154 boys, 170 girls); Grade 11: 311 students (155 boys, 156 girls); Grade 12: 267 students (140 boys, 127 girls). 97.5% of students are Roman Catholic.

Faculty School total: 81. In upper school: 40 men, 41 women; 51 have advanced degrees.

Subjects Offered Accounting, acting, advanced chemistry, advanced computer applications, advanced math, algebra, American government, American literature, anatomy, applied arts, applied music, architectural drawing, art, art appreciation, art history, Bible studies, biology, biology-AP, British literature, business, business law, calculus, calculus-AP, carpentry, Catholic belief and practice, chemistry, chemistry-AP, choir, choral music, civics, comparative government and politics-AP, comparative religion, composition, computer applications, computer graphics, computer literacy, concert band, concert choir, drafting, drama, drawing, drawing and design, English, English composition, English literature, English literature-AP, family living, fitness, food and nutrition, French, general math, geography, government and politics-AP, government-AP, graphic design, health, history of music, history of the Catholic Church, human anatomy, industrial arts, instrumental music, integrated science, interior design, jazz band, journalism, keyboarding, literature-AP, marching band, marketing, mechanical drawing, moral theology, music appreciation, personal money management, photography, physical education, physical science, physics, physics-AP, play production, pre-algebra, pre-calculus, psychology, religion, small engine repair, social justice, Spanish, speech and debate, stage design, student publications, studio art, symphonic band, textiles, U.S. government and politics-AP, U.S. history, U.S. history-AP, vocal music, world geography, world history, yearbook.

Graduation Requirements Arts and fine arts (art, music, dance, drama), civics, computer literacy, electives, English, geography, mathematics, physical education (includes health), religion (includes Bible studies and theology), science, speech communications, U.S. history, world history, senior service requirement, all-school retreat attendance.

Special Academic Programs 13 Advanced Placement exams for which test preparation is offered; independent study; study at local college for college credit; remedial reading and/or remedial writing; remedial math.

College Admission Counseling 269 students graduated in 2015; 251 went to college, including Benedictine College; Creighton University; University of Nebraska–Lincoln; University of Nebraska at Kearney; University of Nebraska at Omaha; Wesleyan University. Other: 2 went to work, 5 entered military service, 1 entered a postgraduate year, 6 had other specific plans. Mean SAT critical reading: 628, mean SAT math: 622, mean SAT writing: 610, mean composite ACT: 24. 64% scored over 600 on SAT critical reading, 61% scored over 600 on SAT math, 54% scored over 600 on SAT writing, 32% scored over 26 on composite ACT.

Student Life Upper grades have uniform requirement, student council. Discipline rests primarily with faculty. Attendance at religious services is required.

Tuition and Aid Day student tuition: $1500. Guaranteed tuition plan. Tuition installment plan (monthly payment plans, individually arranged payment plans). Need-based scholarship grants available. In 2015–16, 5% of upper-school students received aid. Total amount of financial aid awarded in 2015–16: $10,000.

Admissions Traditional secondary-level entrance grade is 9. Deadline for receipt of application materials: none. Application fee required: $70.

Athletics Interscholastic: baseball (boys), basketball (b,g), cheering (g), cross-country running (b,g), dance team (g), drill team (g), football (b), golf (b,g), soccer (b,g), softball (g), swimming and diving (b,g), tennis (b,g), track and field (b,g), volleyball (g), wrestling (b); intramural: running (g); coed interscholastic: weight training; coed intramural: basketball, bowling, running. 4 PE instructors, 2 coaches, 1 athletic trainer.

Computers Computers are regularly used in accounting, business, business applications, business education, business skills, business studies, computer applications, creative writing, drafting, journalism, multimedia, Web site design, yearbook classes. Computer network features include on-campus library services,

Internet access, wireless campus network, Internet filtering or blocking technology. Computer access in designated common areas is available to students. Students grades are available online. The school has a published electronic and media policy.

Contact Mrs. Jan Frayser, Director of Guidance. 402-488-0931. Fax: 402-488-1061. E-mail: jan.frayser@piusx.net. Website: www.piusx.net

POLYTECHNIC SCHOOL

1030 East California Boulevard

Pasadena, California 91106-4099

Head of School: Mr. John Bracker

General Information Coeducational day college-preparatory school. Grades K–12. Founded: 1907. Setting: suburban. 15-acre campus. 7 buildings on campus. Approved or accredited by California Association of Independent Schools, The College Board, Western Association of Schools and Colleges, and California Department of Education. Member of National Association of Independent Schools. Endowment: $62.3 million. Total enrollment: 858. Upper school average class size: 17. Upper school faculty-student ratio: 1:6. There are 170 required school days per year for Upper School students. Upper School students typically attend 5 days per week. The average school day consists of 6 hours and 30 minutes.

Upper School Student Profile Grade 9: 96 students (50 boys, 46 girls); Grade 10: 93 students (52 boys, 41 girls); Grade 11: 98 students (53 boys, 45 girls); Grade 12: 87 students (43 boys, 44 girls).

Faculty School total: 64. In upper school: 25 men, 35 women; 41 have advanced degrees.

Subjects Offered Acting, algebra, American history, American history-AP, analytic geometry, art history, athletics, audio visual/media, Basic programming, batik, biology, biology-AP, calculus, calculus-AP, ceramics, chamber groups, chemistry, chemistry-AP, choral music, communications, computer art, computer science, constitutional law, data analysis, drama, drama performance, drawing, East Asian history, economics, English, English language and composition-AP, English literature and composition-AP, ensembles, ethics, filmmaking, French, French literature-AP, functions, geometry, guitar, improvisation, jazz dance, jazz ensemble, Latin, Latin-AP, madrigals, math analysis, mathematical modeling, music history, music theory, musical productions, musical theater, orchestra, painting, photography, physical science, physics, physics-AP, Roman civilization, sculpture, silk screening, society, Spanish, Spanish literature-AP, statistics, tap dance, technical theater, theater, theater design and production, theater history, trigonometry, U.S. government and politics, U.S. history-AP, Vietnam War, visual arts, Western civilization, woodworking, world cultures, world religions.

Special Academic Programs 12 Advanced Placement exams for which test preparation is offered; honors section; independent study; study abroad.

College Admission Counseling 98 students graduated in 2015; 95 went to college, including Cornell University; Harvard University; New York University; Stanford University; University of Southern California. Other: 3 had other specific plans. 91% scored over 600 on SAT critical reading, 92% scored over 600 on SAT math, 92% scored over 600 on SAT writing, 91% scored over 1800 on combined SAT, 92% scored over 26 on composite ACT.

Student Life Upper grades have specified standards of dress, student council, honor system. Discipline rests equally with students and faculty.

Summer Programs Remediation, enrichment, advancement, art/fine arts, computer instruction programs offered; session focuses on For students to have a fun and balanced summer experience.; held on campus; accepts boys and girls; open to students from other schools. 600 students usually enrolled. 2016 schedule: June 13 to July 29. Application deadline: May 1.

Tuition and Aid Day student tuition: $33,500. Tuition installment plan (monthly payment plans). Need-based scholarship grants available. In 2015–16, 25% of upper-school students received aid. Total amount of financial aid awarded in 2015–16: $2,040,187.

Admissions Traditional secondary-level entrance grade is 9. For fall 2015, 246 students applied for upper-level admission, 49 were accepted, 38 enrolled. ISEE required. Deadline for receipt of application materials: January 8. Application fee required: $100. Interview required.

Athletics Interscholastic: aquatics (boys, girls), baseball (b), basketball (b,g), cross-country running (b,g), diving (b,g), football (b), golf (b,g), soccer (b,g), softball (g), swimming and diving (b,g), tennis (b,g), track and field (b,g), volleyball (b,g), water polo (b,g); coed interscholastic: badminton, dance team, equestrian sports, fencing, outdoor education, physical fitness, physical training, strength & conditioning, weight lifting, weight training, yoga. 6 PE instructors, 42 coaches, 2 athletic trainers.

Computers Computers are regularly used in all classes. Computer network features include on-campus library services, Internet access, wireless campus network, Internet filtering or blocking technology, Bring Your Own Device program, faculty web pages, library resources online, Global Online Academy. Student e-mail accounts are available to students. Students grades are available online. The school has a published electronic and media policy.

Contact Ms. Sally Jeanne McKenna, Director of Admission. 626-396-6300. Fax: 626-396-6591. E-mail: sjmckenna@polytechnic.org. Website: www.polytechnic.org

POPE JOHN PAUL II HIGH SCHOOL

1901 Jaguar Drive
Slidell, Louisiana 70461-0000

Head of School: Mrs. Martha M. Mundine

General Information Coeducational day college-preparatory, arts, and religious studies school, affiliated with Roman Catholic Church. Grades 8–12. Founded: 1980. Setting: suburban. Nearest major city is New Orleans. 2 buildings on campus. Approved or accredited by National Catholic Education Association, Southern Association of Colleges and Schools, and Louisiana Department of Education. Total enrollment: 346. Upper school average class size: 24. Upper school faculty-student ratio: 1:11. Upper School students typically attend 5 days per week. The average school day consists of 7 hours and 15 minutes.

Upper School Student Profile 97% of students are Roman Catholic.

Special Academic Programs Advanced Placement exam preparation; honors section; study at local college for college credit.

College Admission Counseling 78 students graduated in 2015; 76 went to college. Other: 1 went to work, 1 entered military service.

Student Life Upper grades have uniform requirement, student council, honor system. Discipline rests primarily with faculty. Attendance at religious services is required.

Tuition and Aid Need-based scholarship grants available. In 2015–16, 18% of upper-school students received aid.

Admissions Traditional secondary-level entrance grade is 8. Deadline for receipt of application materials: none. Application fee required: $300. Interview required.

Athletics Interscholastic: aerobics/dance (girls), baseball (b), dance team (g), football (b), softball (g), volleyball (g); coed interscholastic: basketball, cheering, cross-country running, fitness, golf, physical fitness, power lifting, soccer, strength & conditioning, swimming and diving, tennis, track and field.

Computers Computer network features include on-campus library services, Internet access, wireless campus network, Internet filtering or blocking technology. Campus intranet and student e-mail accounts are available to students. Students grades are available online. The school has a published electronic and media policy.

Contact Ms. Lise Bremond, Assistant Principal. 504-649-0914. Fax: 504-649-5494. E-mail: lbremond@pjp.org. Website: www.pjp.org

POPE JOHN XXIII REGIONAL HIGH SCHOOL

28 Andover Road
Sparta, New Jersey 07871

Head of School: Mr. Thomas J. Costello

General Information Coeducational day college-preparatory, arts, business, religious studies, and technology school, affiliated with Roman Catholic Church. Grades 8–12. Founded: 1956. Setting: suburban. Nearest major city is New York, NY. 15-acre campus. 1 building on campus. Approved or accredited by New Jersey Department of Education. Total enrollment: 953. Upper school average class size: 20. Upper school faculty-student ratio: 1:12. There are 180 required school days per year for Upper School students. Upper School students typically attend 5 days per week. The average school day consists of 5 hours and 42 minutes.

Upper School Student Profile Grade 8: 145 students (76 boys, 69 girls); Grade 9: 187 students (101 boys, 86 girls); Grade 10: 214 students (121 boys, 93 girls); Grade 11: 209 students (114 boys, 95 girls); Grade 12: 198 students (92 boys, 106 girls). 73% of students are Roman Catholic.

Faculty School total: 98. In upper school: 50 men, 48 women; 32 have advanced degrees.

Subjects Offered Advanced chemistry, advanced computer applications, advanced math, Advanced Placement courses, algebra, American literature, American studies, anatomy and physiology, art, biology, biology-AP, British literature, business, business law, calculus, calculus-AP, chemistry, chemistry-AP, choral music, computer science, computer science-AP, conceptual physics, concert choir, earth science, economics, English, English language-AP, English literature, English literature and composition-AP, environmental science, environmental science-AP, European history-AP, fine arts, French, French-AP, geometry, German, global issues, government and politics-AP, graphic arts, health and safety, history-AP, honors algebra, honors English, honors geometry, honors U.S. history, honors world history, human geography - AP, Italian, Japanese, jazz band, journalism, lab science, Latin, macroeconomics-AP, microeconomics-AP, modern politics, music theory, physical education, physics, physics-AP, pre-calculus, psychology, psychology-AP, reading/study skills, robotics, Spanish, Spanish language-AP, statistics, statistics-AP, theater arts, theology, U.S. government, U.S. government and politics-AP, U.S. history, U.S. history-AP, world cultures, world history-AP, zoology.

Graduation Requirements Arts and fine arts (art, music, dance, drama), English, foreign language, health and safety, mathematics, science, social studies (includes history), theology, 60 hours of community service (15 hours per year).

Special Academic Programs 22 Advanced Placement exams for which test preparation is offered; honors section.

College Admission Counseling 208 students graduated in 2015; 200 went to college, including High Point University; Loyola University Maryland; Quinnipiac University; Rowan University; The University of Scranton; University of Delaware. Other: 1 entered military service, 4 entered a postgraduate year, 3 had other specific

plans. Mean SAT critical reading: 560, mean SAT math: 560, mean SAT writing: 550, mean combined SAT: 1670.

Student Life Upper grades have uniform requirement, student council. Discipline rests primarily with faculty. Attendance at religious services is required.

Summer Programs Remediation, enrichment, sports programs offered; session focuses on sports; held on campus; accepts boys and girls; open to students from other schools. 200 students usually enrolled.

Tuition and Aid Day student tuition: $15,000. Guaranteed tuition plan. Tuition installment plan (FACTS Tuition Payment Plan). Need-based scholarship grants available.

Admissions Traditional secondary-level entrance grade is 9. CTB/McGraw-Hill/Macmillan Co-op Test, Math Placement Exam, placement test and writing sample required. Deadline for receipt of application materials: none. No application fee required. Interview required.

Athletics Interscholastic: baseball (boys), basketball (b,g), cheering (g), cross-country running (b,g), field hockey (g), football (b), ice hockey (b), indoor track & field (b,g), lacrosse (b,g), running (b,g), skiing (downhill) (b,g), softball (g), swimming and diving (b,g), tennis (b,g), track and field (b,g), volleyball (b,g), winter (indoor) track (b,g), wrestling (b); coed interscholastic: golf.

Computers Computers are regularly used in all academic classes. Computer network features include Internet access, wireless campus network, Internet filtering or blocking technology, Naviance Succeed. Computer access in designated common areas is available to students. Students grades are available online. The school has a published electronic and media policy.

Contact Mrs. Anne Kaiser, Administrative Assistant for Admissions. 973-729-6125 Ext. 255. Fax: 973-729-4536. E-mail: annekaiser@popejohn.org. Website: www.popejohn.org

PORTLEDGE SCHOOL

355 Duck Pond Road
Locust Valley, New York 11560

Head of School: Mr. Simon Owen Williams

General Information Coeducational day college-preparatory school. Grades N–12. Founded: 1965. Setting: suburban. Nearest major city is New York. 62-acre campus. 4 buildings on campus. Approved or accredited by New York State Board of Regents. Member of National Association of Independent Schools and Secondary School Admission Test Board. Endowment: $2.5 million. Total enrollment: 475. Upper school average class size: 16. Upper school faculty-student ratio: 1:8. There are 170 required school days per year for Upper School students. Upper School students typically attend 5 days per week. The average school day consists of 6 hours and 55 minutes.

Upper School Student Profile Grade 6: 26 students (13 boys, 13 girls); Grade 7: 47 students (26 boys, 21 girls); Grade 8: 34 students (17 boys, 17 girls); Grade 9: 50 students (25 boys, 25 girls); Grade 10: 52 students (29 boys, 23 girls); Grade 11: 54 students (25 boys, 29 girls); Grade 12: 54 students (28 boys, 26 girls).

Faculty School total: 83. In upper school: 19 men, 18 women; 21 have advanced degrees.

Subjects Offered 3-dimensional art, advanced biology, advanced chemistry, advanced computer applications, advanced math, Advanced Placement courses, advanced studio art-AP, algebra, American history, American history-AP, American literature, American literature-AP, ancient history, architectural drawing, architecture, art, art appreciation, art history, art-AP, Basic programming, biology, calculus, calculus-AP, ceramics, chemistry, chemistry-AP, chorus, community service, computer programming, computer science, computers, creative writing, digital music, drama, drama workshop, driver education, earth science, economics, English, English literature, English literature-AP, environmental science, European history, expository writing, fine arts, foreign language, French, French-AP, geography, geometry, government/civics, grammar, graphic design, health, health education, history, honors algebra, honors English, honors geometry, honors U.S. history, independent study, instrumental music, jazz ensemble, journalism, keyboarding, Mandarin, mathematics, music, Native American history, photography, physical education, physics, psychology, public policy, public service, public speaking, science, senior project, social sciences, social studies, sociology, Spanish, Spanish-AP, theater, trigonometry, U.S. history-AP, world history.

Graduation Requirements Arts and fine arts (art, music, dance, drama), computer science, English, foreign language, mathematics, performing arts, physical education (includes health), public speaking, science, senior project, social sciences, social studies (includes history). Community service is required.

Special Academic Programs Academic accommodation for the gifted, the musically talented, and the artistically talented.

College Admission Counseling 55 students graduated in 2015; 53 went to college. Other: 2 entered a postgraduate year. Median SAT critical reading: 580, median SAT math: 610, median SAT writing: 590, median composite ACT: 28.

Student Life Upper grades have specified standards of dress, student council, honor system. Discipline rests primarily with faculty.

Summer Programs Enrichment, sports, art/fine arts, computer instruction programs offered; session focuses on chess, computers, tennis, field hockey, lacrosse, soccer; held on campus; accepts boys and girls; open to students from other schools. 300 students usually enrolled. 2016 schedule: June 21 to August 21.

Portledge School

Tuition and Aid Day student tuition: $29,950. Tuition installment plan (Tuition Management Systems). Tuition reduction for siblings, need-based scholarship grants available. In 2015–16, 26% of upper-school students received aid.

Admissions Traditional secondary-level entrance grade is 9. For fall 2015, 225 students applied for upper-level admission, 102 enrolled. SSAT required. Deadline for receipt of application materials: February 5. Application fee required: $75. On-campus interview required.

Athletics Interscholastic: baseball (boys), basketball (b,g), fencing (b,g), flag football (b), hockey (b,g), lacrosse (b,g), soccer (b,g), softball (g), tennis (b,g); intramural: ballet (g), cheering (g), tennis (g); coed interscholastic: cross-country running, golf, squash. 3 PE instructors, 3 coaches.

Computers Computers are regularly used in art, English, foreign language, history, mathematics, music, science classes. Computer network features include on-campus library services, online commercial services, Internet access, wireless campus network, Internet filtering or blocking technology. Computer access in designated common areas is available to students. The school has a published electronic and media policy.

Contact Mr. Michael Coope, Director of Admissions. 516-750-3203. Fax: 516-674-7063. E-mail: mcoope@portledge.org. Website: www.portledge.org

PORTSMOUTH ABBEY SCHOOL

285 Cory's Lane
Portsmouth, Rhode Island 02871

Head of School: Mr. Daniel McDonough

General Information Coeducational boarding and day college-preparatory school, affiliated with Roman Catholic Church. Grades 9–12. Founded: 1926. Setting: small town. Nearest major city is Providence. Students are housed in single-sex dormitories. 525-acre campus. 36 buildings on campus. Approved or accredited by Association of Independent Schools in New England, National Independent Private Schools Association, New England Association of Schools and Colleges, and The Association of Boarding Schools. Member of National Association of Independent Schools and Secondary School Admission Test Board. Endowment: $46 million. Total enrollment: 354. Upper school average class size: 13. Upper school faculty-student ratio: 1:7. There are 180 required school days per year for Upper School students. Upper School students typically attend 6 days per week. The average school day consists of 7 hours.

Upper School Student Profile Grade 9: 84 students (41 boys, 43 girls); Grade 10: 87 students (47 boys, 40 girls); Grade 11: 86 students (46 boys, 40 girls); Grade 12: 97 students (53 boys, 44 girls). 70% of students are boarding students. 35% are state residents. 24 states are represented in upper school student body. 16% are international students. International students from China, Dominican Republic, Guatemala, Republic of Korea, Spain, and Trinidad and Tobago; 15 other countries represented in student body. 60% of students are Roman Catholic.

Faculty School total: 79. In upper school: 31 men, 19 women; 40 have advanced degrees; 58 reside on campus.

Subjects Offered Algebra, American literature, art, art history, art history-AP, art-AP, biology, biology-AP, calculus, calculus-AP, chemistry, chemistry-AP, Chinese, Christian doctrine, Christian ethics, computer programming-AP, computer science, computer science-AP, creative writing, drama, drama workshop, economics, English, English language and composition-AP, English literature, English literature and composition-AP, fine arts, French, French language-AP, French literature-AP, geometry, government/civics, Greek, health, history, history-AP, humanities, international relations, Latin, Latin-AP, Mandarin, marine biology, mathematics, mathematics-AP, modern European history-AP, music, music composition, music theory, music theory-AP, philosophy, photography, physics, physics-AP, physiology, political science, religion, science, social sciences, Spanish, Spanish language-AP, Spanish literature-AP, statistics-AP, studio art-AP, theater, theology, trigonometry, U.S. history, U.S. history-AP, world history, writing workshop.

Graduation Requirements Arts and fine arts (art, music, dance, drama), English, foreign language, history, Latin, mathematics, religion (includes Bible studies and theology), science, humanities.

Special Academic Programs 17 Advanced Placement exams for which test preparation is offered; honors section; independent study; study abroad; academic accommodation for the gifted.

College Admission Counseling 118 students graduated in 2015; all went to college, including Boston College; Brown University; Georgetown University; New York University; Northeastern University; The George Washington University. Mean SAT critical reading: 618, mean SAT math: 616, mean SAT writing: 619, mean combined SAT: 1853.

Student Life Upper grades have specified standards of dress, student council, honor system. Discipline rests primarily with faculty. Attendance at religious services is required.

Summer Programs Enrichment, advancement, ESL, sports, art/fine arts programs offered; session focuses on academic; held on campus; accepts boys and girls; open to students from other schools. 90 students usually enrolled. 2016 schedule: June 30 to July 30. Application deadline: none.

Tuition and Aid Day student tuition: $35,860; 7-day tuition and room/board: $54,630. Tuition installment plan (FACTS Tuition Payment Plan, monthly payment plans). Merit scholarship grants, need-based scholarship grants available. In 2015–16,

36% of upper-school students received aid; total upper-school merit-scholarship money awarded: $300,000. Total amount of financial aid awarded in 2015–16: $4,000,000.

Admissions Traditional secondary-level entrance grade is 9. For fall 2015, 550 students applied for upper-level admission, 208 were accepted, 114 enrolled. PSAT or SAT for applicants to grade 11 and 12, SSAT and TOEFL required. Deadline for receipt of application materials: January 31. Application fee required: $50. Interview required.

Athletics Interscholastic: baseball (boys), basketball (b,g), cross-country running (b,g), field hockey (g), football (b), golf (b,g), ice hockey (b,g), lacrosse (b,g), soccer (b,g), softball (g), squash (b,g), swimming and diving (b,g), tennis (b,g), track and field (b,g), wrestling (g); coed interscholastic: cross-country running, sailing, swimming and diving, track and field; coed intramural: ballet, dance, equestrian sports, fitness, horseback riding, modern dance, strength & conditioning, weight training. 1 athletic trainer.

Computers Computer network features include on-campus library services, online commercial services, Internet access, wireless campus network. Campus intranet and student e-mail accounts are available to students. Students grades are available online.

Contact Mrs. Ann Motta, Admissions Coordinator. 401-643-1248. Fax: 401-643-1355. E-mail: admissions@portsmouthabbey.org. Website: www.portsmouthabbey.org

PORTSMOUTH CHRISTIAN ACADEMY

20 Seaborne Drive
Dover, New Hampshire 03820

Head of School: Dr. John Engstrom

General Information Coeducational day college-preparatory, arts, religious studies, technology, and science/mathematics/fine arts school, affiliated with Christian faith. Grades K–12. Founded: 1979. Setting: rural. Nearest major city is Portsmouth. 50-acre campus. 2 buildings on campus. Approved or accredited by Association of Christian Schools International, New England Association of Schools and Colleges, and New Hampshire Department of Education. Total enrollment: 551. Upper school average class size: 17. Upper school faculty-student ratio: 1:9. There are 176 required school days per year for Upper School students. Upper School students typically attend 5 days per week. The average school day consists of 7 hours and 10 minutes.

Upper School Student Profile 70% of students are Christian faith.

Faculty School total: 55. In upper school: 13 men, 9 women; 16 have advanced degrees.

Subjects Offered 3-dimensional art, 3-dimensional design, ACT preparation, advanced chemistry, advanced math, Advanced Placement courses, advanced studio art-AP, algebra, American history, American literature, American literature-AP, anatomy and physiology, art, art education, art history, art history-AP, athletic training, athletics, band, baseball, basketball, Bible, biology, British literature, calculus, calculus-AP, chemistry, chemistry-AP, choir, choral music, chorus, Christian doctrine, Christian ethics, Christian studies, Christianity, church history, civics, college admission preparation, college awareness, college counseling, college placement, college planning, college writing, comparative religion, composition, computer applications, computer-aided design, debate, digital photography, drama, drama performance, drama workshop, drawing, drawing and design, economics, economics and history, English, English as a foreign language, English composition, English language and composition-AP, English literature and composition-AP, English literature-AP, English-AP, European history, film and literature, foreign language, French, French language-AP, geometry, government, government/civics, guitar, health and wellness, honors algebra, honors English, honors geometry, honors world history, human anatomy, instrumental music, integrated physics, jazz band, lab science, literature, literature and composition-AP, literature-AP, logic, rhetoric, and debate, marine science, mathematics, modern European history, music, musical productions, musical theater, New Testament, performing arts, photography, physics, physics-AP, pre-calculus, rhetoric, SAT preparation, SAT/ACT preparation, Shakespeare, Spanish, Spanish language-AP, Spanish-AP, student government, symphonic band, theater arts, theology, U.S. history, U.S. history-AP, world history, World War II, writing, writing workshop, yearbook.

Graduation Requirements Arts and fine arts (art, music, dance, drama), Bible, electives, English, foreign language, mathematics, physical education (includes health), science, social sciences, 1 Bible course for each year of Upper School attendance, service hours, participate in athletics.

Special Academic Programs 15 Advanced Placement exams for which test preparation is offered; honors section; accelerated programs; independent study; study at local college for college credit; academic accommodation for the gifted and the musically talented; special instructional classes for deaf students, blind students, students with Attention Deficit Disorder and Dyslexia; ESL (12 students enrolled).

College Admission Counseling 45 students graduated in 2015; 44 went to college, including Boston College; Boston University; New York University; Penn State University Park; University of New Hampshire; Villanova University. Other: 1 entered military service. Mean SAT critical reading: 585, mean SAT math: 576, mean SAT writing: 579.

Student Life Upper grades have specified standards of dress, student council, honor system. Discipline rests primarily with faculty.

Summer Programs Remediation, enrichment, ESL, sports, art/fine arts programs offered; session focuses on soccer, basketball, and volleyball; ESL, instrumental, enrichment, remediation; held on campus; accepts boys and girls; open to students from other schools. 100 students usually enrolled. 2016 schedule: June 13 to August 19. Application deadline: May 15.

Tuition and Aid Day student tuition: $10,250–$20,000. Tuition installment plan (SMART Tuition Payment Plan, monthly payment plans). Need-based scholarship grants, Tuition Assistance available. In 2015–16, 28% of upper-school students received aid. Total amount of financial aid awarded in 2015–16: $218,000.

Admissions Traditional secondary-level entrance grade is 9. Achievement tests, PSAT or SAT, PSAT or SAT for applicants to grade 11 and 12, SAT, standardized test scores, Stanford Achievement Test, Test of Achievement and Proficiency, TOEFL or writing sample required. Deadline for receipt of application materials: none. Application fee required: $100. Interview required.

Athletics Interscholastic: baseball (boys), basketball (b,g), cross-country running (b,g), gymnastics (g), horseback riding (g), indoor track & field (b,g), soccer (b,g), softball (g), swimming and diving (g), tennis (b,g), track and field (b,g), volleyball (g), winter (indoor) track (b,g); intramural: bicycling (b,g), golf (b,g), skiing (cross-country) (b,g), skiing (downhill) (b,g), snowboarding (b,g), table tennis (b,g), tennis (b,g); coed interscholastic: cross-country running, fitness, indoor track & field, track and field, winter (indoor) track; coed intramural: alpine skiing, bicycling, skiing (cross-country), skiing (downhill), snowboarding, table tennis, tennis. 1 PE instructor, 14 coaches.

Computers Computers are regularly used in college planning, graphic design, library, SAT preparation, yearbook classes. Computer network features include on-campus library services, online commercial services, Internet access, wireless campus network, Internet filtering or blocking technology. Computer access in designated common areas is available to students. Students grades are available online. The school has a published electronic and media policy.

Contact Mrs. Wendy Moran, Director of Admissions. 603-742-3617 Ext. 116. Fax: 603-750-0490. E-mail: wmoran@pcaschool.org. Website: www.pcaschool.org

THE POTOMAC SCHOOL

1301 Potomac School Road
McLean, Virginia 22101

Head of School: John Kowalik

General Information Coeducational day college-preparatory and liberal arts, arts, athletics, and character education school. Grades K–12. Founded: 1904. Setting: suburban. Nearest major city is Washington, DC. 90-acre campus. Approved or accredited by Association of Independent Schools of Greater Washington and Virginia Association of Independent Schools. Member of National Association of Independent Schools and Secondary School Admission Test Board. Endowment: $36 million. Total enrollment: 1,032. Upper school average class size: 14. Upper school faculty-student ratio: 1:6.

Upper School Student Profile Grade 9: 115 students (62 boys, 53 girls); Grade 10: 116 students (56 boys, 60 girls); Grade 11: 113 students (59 boys, 54 girls); Grade 12: 97 students (54 boys, 43 girls).

Faculty School total: 160. In upper school: 32 men, 38 women.

Subjects Offered 20th century American writers, 20th century world history, 3-dimensional art, 3-dimensional design, acting, advanced computer applications, advanced math, Advanced Placement courses, advanced studio art-AP, African-American studies, algebra, American literature, anatomy and physiology, ancient world history, art, art history, band, bell choir, biology, biology-AP, British literature, calculus, calculus-AP, ceramics, chamber groups, character education, chemistry, chemistry-AP, Chinese history, choral music, civics, civil rights, community service, comparative religion, computer programming, computer programming-AP, computer science, conceptual physics, concert band, creative writing, debate, directing, drama, drawing and design, economics and history, engineering, English, English literature, environmental science, European history, expository writing, fine arts, foreign policy, French, French language-AP, French literature-AP, French-AP, geometry, global studies, government, government/civics, handbells, history of music, independent study, jazz band, Latin, Latin American history, Latin-AP, leadership, literary magazine, madrigals, mathematics, Middle Eastern history, model United Nations, modern European history, music, music composition, music history, music theory-AP, newspaper, painting, performing arts, photography, physical education, physics, physics-AP, portfolio art, pre-calculus, psychology, robotics, science, science and technology, sculpture, senior project, Shakespeare, short story, Spanish, Spanish language-AP, Spanish literature-AP, stagecraft, statistics-AP, strings, student government, studio art-AP, theater arts, trigonometry, U.S. government and politics, U.S. history-AP, vocal music, yearbook.

Graduation Requirements Arts and fine arts (art, music, dance, drama), English, foreign language, history, mathematics, physical education (includes health), science, senior project, month-long senior project.

Special Academic Programs Advanced Placement exam preparation; honors section; independent study.

College Admission Counseling 114 students graduated in 2015; 112 went to college, including Georgetown University; New York University; The College of William and Mary; Tufts University; University of Virginia; Wake Forest University. Other: 2 entered a postgraduate year. Median SAT critical reading: 690, median SAT math: 710, median SAT writing: 695.

Student Life Upper grades have specified standards of dress, student council, honor system. Discipline rests equally with students and faculty.

Summer Programs Enrichment, advancement, sports, art/fine arts programs offered; session focuses on academics and enrichment; held on campus; accepts boys and girls; open to students from other schools. 2016 schedule: June 20 to August 26. Application deadline: none.

Tuition and Aid Day student tuition: $37,095. Tuition installment plan (Insured Tuition Payment Plan, FACTS Tuition Payment Plan, monthly payment plans). Need-based scholarship grants available. In 2015–16, 18% of upper-school students received aid.

Admissions Traditional secondary-level entrance grade is 9. ISEE or SSAT required. Deadline for receipt of application materials: January 8. Application fee required: $65. Interview required.

Athletics Interscholastic: baseball (boys), basketball (b,g), cross-country running (b,g), field hockey (g), football (b), lacrosse (b,g), soccer (b,g), softball (g), squash (b,g), tennis (b,g), track and field (b,g), volleyball (g), wrestling (b); intramural: independent competitive sports (b,g); coed interscholastic: golf, ice hockey, indoor track & field, swimming and diving, winter (indoor) track; coed intramural: dance, fitness, physical fitness, physical training, sailing, strength & conditioning, weight training, yoga. 5 PE instructors, 60 coaches, 2 athletic trainers.

Computers Computers are regularly used in all academic, computer applications, independent study, literary magazine, newspaper, photography, programming, yearbook classes. Computer network features include on-campus library services, online commercial services, Internet access, wireless campus network, Internet filtering or blocking technology, eBooks. Campus intranet, student e-mail accounts, and computer access in designated common areas are available to students. Students grades are available online. The school has a published electronic and media policy.

Contact Ellen Fitzpatrick, Admission Services Coordinator. 703-749-6313. Fax: 703-356-1764. E-mail: admission@potomacschool.org. Website: www.potomacschool.org

POUGHKEEPSIE DAY SCHOOL

260 Boardman Road
Poughkeepsie, New York 12603

Head of School: Josie Holford

General Information Coeducational day college-preparatory, arts, and technology school. Grades PK–12. Founded: 1934. Setting: suburban. Nearest major city is New York. 35-acre campus. 2 buildings on campus. Approved or accredited by New York State Association of Independent Schools and New York Department of Education. Member of National Association of Independent Schools. Endowment: $4.1 million. Total enrollment: 264. Upper school average class size: 12. Upper school faculty-student ratio: 1:7. There are 165 required school days per year for Upper School students. Upper School students typically attend 5 days per week. The average school day consists of 7 hours.

Upper School Student Profile Grade 9: 30 students (14 boys, 16 girls); Grade 10: 24 students (13 boys, 11 girls); Grade 11: 22 students (10 boys, 12 girls); Grade 12: 30 students (14 boys, 16 girls).

Faculty School total: 45. In upper school: 9 men, 11 women; 10 have advanced degrees.

Subjects Offered 3-dimensional art, acting, advanced math, Advanced Placement courses, African drumming, algebra, American literature, American literature-AP, analysis and differential calculus, analytic geometry, anatomy, anatomy and physiology, ancient history, ancient world history, art history, arts, Basic programming, bioethics, biology, calculus, calculus-AP, chamber groups, chemistry, collage and assemblage, college admission preparation, college planning, community service, computer programming, computer science, computer-aided design, conflict resolution, contemporary art, creative arts, creative drama, creative writing, decision making skills, desktop publishing, digital art, digital music, digital photography, discrete mathematics, drama, drama performance, drawing, ecology, economics, English, English literature, English literature-AP, English-AP, ensembles, European civilization, European history, fiction, filmmaking, fine arts, French, French language-AP, French-AP, geology, geometry, guitar, history, Holocaust and other genocides, Holocaust studies, independent study, instrumental music, integrated arts, interdisciplinary studies, Islamic studies, jazz band, jazz ensemble, lab science, leadership, life saving, life skills, linear algebra, literary magazine, literature, literature-AP, mathematics, modern European history, multicultural literature, multicultural studies, music, music appreciation, music composition, music performance, music theory, music theory-AP, musical productions, oil painting, painting, peer counseling, performing arts, photography, physical education, physical science, physics, physiology, play production, playwriting and directing, pre-calculus, printmaking, probability and statistics, religion and culture, SAT preparation, science, senior internship, service learning/internship, social issues, social studies, Spanish, Spanish language-AP, Spanish-AP, stained glass, statistics, strings, studio art, theater arts, theater production, trigonometry, U.S. history, video film production, visual arts, voice ensemble, Western civilization, wind ensemble, writing workshop, yearbook, zoology.

Graduation Requirements Algebra, arts, biology, chemistry, college planning, electives, English, English literature, foreign language, geometry, interdisciplinary studies, life skills, mathematics, music, performing arts, physical education (includes health), physics, physiology, pre-calculus, SAT preparation, senior internship, senior thesis, trigonometry, visual arts, four-week off-campus senior internship. Community service is required.

Special Academic Programs 10 Advanced Placement exams for which test preparation is offered; honors section; independent study; term-away projects; study at local college for college credit; academic accommodation for the gifted, the musically talented, and the artistically talented; ESL (17 students enrolled).

College Admission Counseling 38 students graduated in 2015; all went to college, including Earlham College; Hobart and William Smith Colleges; Ithaca College; Johns Hopkins University; Rensselaer Polytechnic Institute; Rhode Island School of Design. Mean SAT critical reading: 653, mean SAT math: 620, mean SAT writing: 637, mean combined SAT: 1910. 90% scored over 600 on SAT critical reading, 90% scored over 600 on SAT math, 90% scored over 600 on SAT writing, 90% scored over 1800 on combined SAT.

Student Life Upper grades have student council, honor system. Discipline rests primarily with faculty.

Summer Programs Enrichment, art/fine arts programs offered; session focuses on visual and performing arts, enrichment, jazz; held on campus; accepts boys and girls; open to students from other schools. 200 students usually enrolled. 2016 schedule: June 15 to August 21. Application deadline: June 1.

Tuition and Aid Day student tuition: $26,220. Tuition installment plan (FACTS Tuition Payment Plan, The Tuition Refund Plan). Need-based scholarship grants, tuition reduction for children of full-time faculty and staff available. In 2015–16, 43% of upper-school students received aid. Total amount of financial aid awarded in 2015–16: $550,000.

Admissions Traditional secondary-level entrance grade is 9. For fall 2015, 35 students applied for upper-level admission, 24 were accepted, 13 enrolled. School's own exam required. Deadline for receipt of application materials: none. Application fee required: $50. On-campus interview required.

Athletics Interscholastic: baseball (boys), basketball (b,g), cross-country running (b,g), soccer (b,g), softball (g), volleyball (g); intramural: basketball (b,g), softball (g); coed interscholastic: cross-country running, Frisbee, soccer, ultimate Frisbee; coed intramural: alpine skiing, basketball, cooperative games, cross-country running, dance, fitness, fitness walking, Frisbee, hiking/backpacking, ice skating, jogging, life saving, outdoor education, outdoor skills, outdoors, skiing (downhill), snowboarding, soccer, ultimate Frisbee, volleyball, walking, yoga. 2 PE instructors, 12 coaches.

Computers Computers are regularly used in all academic, college planning, desktop publishing, journalism, library skills, literary magazine, media, music, newspaper, photography, photojournalism, programming, SAT preparation, video film production, Web site design, yearbook classes. Computer network features include on-campus library services, online commercial services, Internet access, wireless campus network, EBSCOhost, Maps101, Web Feet Guides, Gale databases, ProQuest, unitedstreaming, Britannica Online, World Book Online, Grolier Online. Campus intranet, student e-mail accounts, and computer access in designated common areas are available to students. Students grades are available online. The school has a published electronic and media policy.

Contact Tammy Reilly, Advancement Associate for Admissions. 845-462-7600 Ext. 201. Fax: 845-462-7602. E-mail: treilly@poughkeepsieday.org. Website: www.poughkeepsieday.org/

POWERS CATHOLIC HIGH SCHOOL

1505 West Court Street
Flint, Michigan 48503

Head of School: Mrs. Sally Bartos

General Information Coeducational day college-preparatory, arts, business, religious studies, and technology school, affiliated with Roman Catholic Church. Grades 9–12. Founded: 1970. Setting: urban. 80-acre campus. 1 building on campus. Approved or accredited by National Catholic Education Association, North Central Association of Colleges and Schools, and Michigan Department of Education. Endowment: $3 million. Total enrollment: 605. Upper school average class size: 25. Upper school faculty-student ratio: 1:17. There are 188 required school days per year for Upper School students. Upper School students typically attend 5 days per week. The average school day consists of 6 hours and 51 minutes.

Upper School Student Profile Grade 9: 186 students (96 boys, 90 girls); Grade 10: 183 students (101 boys, 82 girls); Grade 11: 144 students (69 boys, 75 girls); Grade 12: 138 students (75 boys, 63 girls). 75% of students are Roman Catholic.

Faculty School total: 35. In upper school: 15 men, 20 women; 26 have advanced degrees.

Subjects Offered Art, art-AP, biology, biology-AP, calculus-AP, ceramics, chemistry, choir, computer skills, concert band, drafting, economics, English, English literature and composition-AP, European history-AP, French, geometry, government, government-AP, health, honors algebra, honors English, honors geometry, integrated science, interdisciplinary studies, macroeconomics-AP, marching band, math analysis, math applications, mechanical drawing, physics, pre-algebra, pre-calculus, psychology, psychology-AP, public speaking, religion, social justice, Spanish, state history, studio art-AP, theology, trigonometry, U.S. history, wind ensemble, world geography, world history, world religions, yearbook.

Graduation Requirements American history, English, government, health, mathematics, science, theology, world history, 40 hours of community service (5 hours for each semester in attendance at Powers).

Special Academic Programs 7 Advanced Placement exams for which test preparation is offered; honors section; remedial reading and/or remedial writing; remedial math.

College Admission Counseling 161 students graduated in 2015; 159 went to college, including Central Michigan University; Grand Valley State University; Michigan State University; Saginaw Valley State University; University of Michigan; University of Michigan–Dearborn. Mean composite ACT: 23.

Student Life Upper grades have uniform requirement, student council. Discipline rests primarily with faculty. Attendance at religious services is required.

Tuition and Aid Day student tuition: $8200. Tuition installment plan (SMART Tuition Payment Plan). Tuition reduction for siblings, need-based scholarship grants available. In 2015–16, 50% of upper-school students received aid. Total amount of financial aid awarded in 2015–16: $450,000.

Admissions Traditional secondary-level entrance grade is 9. ACT-Explore or admissions testing required. Deadline for receipt of application materials: none. Application fee required: $100. Interview required.

Athletics Interscholastic: alpine skiing (boys, girls), baseball (b), basketball (b,g), bowling (b,g), cross-country running (b,g), dance squad (g), dance team (g), diving (b,g), football (b), golf (b,g), ice hockey (b), lacrosse (b,g), skiing (downhill) (b,g), soccer (b,g), softball (g), swimming and diving (g), tennis (b,g), track and field (b,g), volleyball (g), wrestling (b); coed interscholastic: cheering, equestrian sports, indoor track, power lifting, skeet shooting, strength & conditioning, weight lifting; coed intramural: ultimate Frisbee, weight training. 1 PE instructor.

Computers Computers are regularly used in accounting, business applications, drafting, graphic design, keyboarding, yearbook classes. Computer network features include on-campus library services, Internet access, wireless campus network, Internet filtering or blocking technology. Computer access in designated common areas is available to students. Students grades are available online. The school has a published electronic and media policy.

Contact Mr. Brian Sheeran, Assistant Principal/Athletic Director. 810-591-4741. Fax: 810-591-1794. E-mail: bsheeran@powerscatholic.org. Website: www.powerscatholic.org/

PRESBYTERIAN PAN AMERICAN SCHOOL

PO Box 1578
223 North FM Road 772
Kingsville, Texas 78364-1578

Head of School: Dr. Doug Dalglish

General Information Coeducational boarding and day and distance learning college-preparatory, career, Human Anatomy & Physiology, Intro. To Business, and Principles of Engineering school, affiliated with Presbyterian Church (U.S.A.). Grades 9–12. Distance learning grades 9–12. Founded: 1912. Setting: rural. Nearest major city is Corpus Christi. Students are housed in single-sex dormitories. 670-acre campus. 23 buildings on campus. Approved or accredited by Southern Association of Colleges and Schools, Texas Private School Accreditation Commission, and Texas Department of Education. Endowment: $8.9 million. Total enrollment: 168. Upper school average class size: 22. Upper school faculty-student ratio: 1:10. There are 180 required school days per year for Upper School students. Upper School students typically attend 5 days per week. The average school day consists of 8 hours.

Upper School Student Profile Grade 9: 39 students (12 boys, 27 girls); Grade 10: 43 students (20 boys, 23 girls); Grade 11: 34 students (20 boys, 14 girls); Grade 12: 48 students (19 boys, 29 girls); Grade 13: 4 students (2 boys, 2 girls). 100% of students are boarding students. 2% are state residents. 1 state is represented in upper school student body. 98% are international students. International students from Mexico, Republic of Korea, and Rwanda; 9 other countries represented in student body. 34% of students are Presbyterian Church (U.S.A.).

Faculty School total: 18. In upper school: 8 men, 10 women; 6 have advanced degrees; 2 reside on campus.

Subjects Offered Algebra, American history, American literature, anatomy and physiology, animal science, art, arts, Bible studies, biology, business, calculus, career exploration, chemistry, choir, communications, computer science, debate, economics, engineering, English, English literature, ESL, geography, geometry, government/civics, health, horticulture, journalism, literary genres, mathematical modeling, physical education, physics, pre-calculus, religion, Spanish, theater arts, U.S. history, world history, world literature, yearbook.

Graduation Requirements Algebra, arts and fine arts (art, music, dance, drama), Bible, biology, career/college preparation, chemistry, communications, economics, electives, English, ESL, foreign language, government, health, junior and senior seminars, mathematical modeling, physical education (includes health), physics, pre-calculus, science, social studies (includes history), U.S. history, world geography, world history, TOEFL score of 550, or SAT Reading of 550.

Special Academic Programs 3 Advanced Placement exams for which test preparation is offered; honors section; independent study; study at local college for college credit; ESL (39 students enrolled).

College Admission Counseling 33 students graduated in 2015; all went to college, including Schreiner University; Texas A&M University; Texas A&M University–Kingsville; The University of Texas at Austin; The University of Texas at San Antonio.

Median SAT critical reading: 420, median SAT math: 460, median SAT writing: 420. 4% scored over 600 on SAT critical reading, 5% scored over 600 on SAT math.

Student Life Upper grades have uniform requirement, student council, honor system. Discipline rests primarily with faculty. Attendance at religious services is required.

Tuition and Aid Day student tuition: $10,000; 7-day tuition and room/board: $18,000. Guaranteed tuition plan. Tuition installment plan (monthly payment plans, individually arranged payment plans, quarterly payment plan, semester payment plan). Tuition reduction for siblings, merit scholarship grants, need-based scholarship grants, need-based financial aid, discounts tied to enrollment referred by current student families available. In 2015–16, 92% of upper-school students received aid. Total amount of financial aid awarded in 2015–16: $1,460,500.

Admissions For fall 2015, 123 students applied for upper-level admission, 85 were accepted, 69 enrolled. PSAT, SAT, or ACT for applicants to grade 11 and 12, TerraNova and TOEFL required. Deadline for receipt of application materials: none. Application fee required: $75. Interview recommended.

Athletics Interscholastic: baseball (boys), basketball (b,g), cheering (b,g), cross-country running (b,g), soccer (b,g), track and field (b,g), volleyball (g); intramural: billiards (b), jogging (b,g), life saving (b,g), paddle tennis (b,g), physical fitness (b,g), strength & conditioning (b,g), table tennis (b,g), tennis (b,g), volleyball (b), walking (b,g), winter walking (b,g); coed intramural: aquatics, fitness walking, jogging, life saving, paddle tennis, strength & conditioning, table tennis, volleyball, walking, winter walking. 1 PE instructor, 2 coaches, 1 athletic trainer.

Computers Computers are regularly used in all academic, art, Bible studies, business, career exploration, college planning, economics, engineering, English, ESL, geography, health, history, journalism, mathematics, publications, religion, SAT preparation, science, senior seminar, social sciences, theater arts, yearbook classes. Computer network features include on-campus library services, Internet access, wireless campus network, Internet filtering or blocking technology. Campus intranet, student e-mail accounts, and computer access in designated common areas are available to students. Students grades are available online. The school has a published electronic and media policy.

Contact Joe L. Garcia, Director of Admissions. 361-592-4307 Ext. 1004. Fax: 361-592-6126. E-mail: jlgarcia@ppas.org. Website: www.ppas.org

PRESTON HIGH SCHOOL

2780 Schurz Avenue
Bronx, New York 10465

Head of School: Mrs. Jane Grendell

General Information Girls' day college-preparatory, arts, religious studies, and technology school, affiliated with Roman Catholic Church. Grades 9–12. Founded: 1947. Setting: urban. Nearest major city is New York. 2-acre campus. 2 buildings on campus. Approved or accredited by Middle States Association of Colleges and Schools, New York Department of Education, New York State Board of Regents, and New York Department of Education. Total enrollment: 511. Upper school average class size: 25. Upper school faculty-student ratio: 1:25. There are 180 required school days per year for Upper School students. Upper School students typically attend 5 days per week. The average school day consists of 6 hours and 14 minutes.

Upper School Student Profile Grade 9: 121 students (121 girls); Grade 10: 112 students (112 girls); Grade 11: 147 students (147 girls); Grade 12: 131 students (131 girls). 74% of students are Roman Catholic.

Faculty School total: 47. In upper school: 13 men, 34 women; 31 have advanced degrees.

Subjects Offered 1 1/2 elective credits, advanced computer applications, advanced math, advanced studio art-AP, advertising design, algebra, American government, American history, American history-AP, American legal systems, American literature, anatomy, anatomy and physiology, art, art appreciation, art education, art history, art-AP, arts, athletic training, band, Basic programming, biology, biology-AP, British literature, British literature (honors), broadcast journalism, calculus, Catholic belief and practice, chamber groups, character education, chemistry, choir, Christian doctrine, civics, classical language, college admission preparation, college counseling, college planning, college writing, commercial art, communication skills, communications, community service, comparative religion, composition, computer animation, computer art, computer graphics, computer literacy, computer multimedia, computer processing, computer programming, computer skills, concert choir, constitutional law, consumer economics, consumer mathematics, creative drama, design, digital art, drama, drama workshop, dramatic arts, earth science, economics, economics and history, electives, English, English composition, English language and composition-AP, English language-AP, English literature, English literature and composition-AP, English literature-AP, English-AP, ensembles, film, film studies, fine arts, fitness, folk dance, forensics, gender and religion, gender issues, general science, geometry, global studies, government, government/civics, graphic arts, graphic design, guidance, health, health education, Hispanic literature, history, history of the Catholic Church, history-AP, honors algebra, honors English, honors geometry, honors U.S. history, humanities, instruments, integrated mathematics, introduction to literature, introduction to theater, lab science, language, language arts, language-AP, Latin, law, law and the legal system, life science, literacy, literature, literature and composition-AP, literature-AP, marketing, mathematics, modern civilization, modern European history, modern history, modern languages, modern Western civilization, moral and social development, music, music

appreciation, music performance, music theory, musical productions, musical theater dance, mythology, New Testament, peer ministry, personal fitness, philosophy, physical education, physical fitness, physical science, physics, physiology, play production, play/screen writing, portfolio art, pre-calculus, psychology, public speaking, reading, reading/study skills, religion, religion and culture, religious education, religious studies, SAT preparation, science, scripture, senior humanities, senior project, senior seminar, senior thesis, service learning/internship, social sciences, social studies, socioeconomic problems, sociology, Spanish, Spanish language-AP, Spanish literature, Spanish literature-AP, Spanish-AP, speech, speech and oral interpretations, speech communications, telecommunications, television, theater arts, theology, trigonometry, U.S. constitutional history, U.S. government, U.S. government and politics, U.S. history, U.S. history-AP, U.S. literature, video, video and animation, video communication, video film production, visual and performing arts, vocal ensemble, vocal music, voice, voice ensemble, weight fitness, weight training, Western civilization, Western literature, wilderness education, wind ensemble, women in society, women spirituality and faith, world history, world literature, world religions, world religions, writing, writing, writing workshop, yearbook.

Graduation Requirements All academic, religion (includes Bible studies and theology), students must complete an Independent Senior Project.

Special Academic Programs Advanced Placement exam preparation; honors section; independent study; study at local college for college credit.

College Admission Counseling 133 students graduated in 2015; 132 went to college, including City College of the City University of New York; Fordham University; Iona College; Manhattan College; Pace University; St. John's University. Other: 1 went to work. Mean SAT critical reading: 525, mean SAT math: 507, mean SAT writing: 528, mean combined SAT: 1560. 20% scored over 600 on SAT critical reading, 18% scored over 600 on SAT math, 22% scored over 600 on SAT writing.

Student Life Upper grades have uniform requirement, student council, honor system. Discipline rests equally with students and faculty. Attendance at religious services is required.

Summer Programs Remediation, enrichment programs offered; session focuses on enrichment for incoming freshmen; held on campus; accepts girls; not open to students from other schools. 60 students usually enrolled. 2016 schedule: August 1 to August 15.

Tuition and Aid Day student tuition: $9345. Tuition installment plan (FACTS Tuition Payment Plan, monthly payment plans). Tuition reduction for siblings, merit scholarship grants, need-based scholarship grants available. In 2015–16, 25% of upper-school students received aid; total upper-school merit-scholarship money awarded: $477,500. Total amount of financial aid awarded in 2015–16: $555,000.

Admissions Traditional secondary-level entrance grade is 9. For fall 2015, 553 students applied for upper-level admission, 432 were accepted, 121 enrolled. Math, reading, and mental ability tests, school placement exam and writing sample required. Deadline for receipt of application materials: none. No application fee required.

Athletics Interscholastic: basketball, cheering, fitness, soccer, softball, volleyball; intramural: yoga. 2 PE instructors, 9 coaches.

Computers Computers are regularly used in all academic, graphic design, programming, video film production, Web site design, yearbook classes. Computer network features include on-campus library services, Internet access, Internet filtering or blocking technology. Students grades are available online. The school has a published electronic and media policy.

Contact Mrs. Cristina Fragale, Director of Admissions. 718-863-9134 Ext. 132. Fax: 718-863-6125. E-mail: cfragale@prestonhs.org. Website: www.prestonhs.org

PRESTONWOOD CHRISTIAN ACADEMY

6801 West Park Boulevard
Plano, Texas 75093

Head of School: Dr. Larry Taylor

General Information Coeducational day and distance learning college-preparatory and Bible courses school, affiliated with Southern Baptist Convention. Grades PK–12. Distance learning grades 6–12. Founded: 1997. Setting: suburban. Nearest major city is Dallas. 44-acre campus. 2 buildings on campus. Approved or accredited by Southern Association of Colleges and Schools and Texas Department of Education. Total enrollment: 1,551. Upper school average class size: 18. Upper school faculty-student ratio: 1:12. There are 172 required school days per year for Upper School students. Upper School students typically attend 5 days per week. The average school day consists of 7 hours and 35 minutes.

Upper School Student Profile Grade 9: 130 students (75 boys, 55 girls); Grade 10: 123 students (66 boys, 57 girls); Grade 11: 125 students (62 boys, 63 girls); Grade 12: 129 students (71 boys, 58 girls). 66% of students are Southern Baptist Convention.

Faculty School total: 128. In upper school: 13 men, 25 women; 20 have advanced degrees.

Subjects Offered 20th century history, 20th century physics, advanced chemistry, advanced math, Advanced Placement courses, algebra, American history-AP, American literature, anatomy and physiology, art, art-AP, band, Bible, biology, biology-AP, British literature, calculus-AP, ceramics, chemistry, choir, Christian doctrine, computer applications, conceptual physics, debate, drama, drawing, economics, ethics, fine arts, fitness, geometry, government, government-AP, health, honors algebra, honors English, honors geometry, honors U.S. history, honors world history, internship, language-AP, leadership education training, learning lab, literature-AP, logic, multimedia, multimedia design, newspaper, painting, performing arts, personal fitness, philosophy, photo shop, physical fitness, physics, physics-AP, pre-calculus, printmaking, sculpture, service learning/internship, Spanish, Spanish-AP, speech, statistics, strings, student government, studio art, U.S. government and politics-AP, U.S. history, Web site design, Western literature, world history, world religions, yearbook.

Graduation Requirements 1 1/2 elective credits, algebra, arts and fine arts (art, music, dance, drama), Bible, biology, British literature, chemistry, Christian doctrine, computer applications, economics, English, English literature, ethics, foreign language, geometry, government, mathematics, philosophy, physical education (includes health), physics, speech, U.S. history, Western literature, world history, mission trip.

Special Academic Programs Advanced Placement exam preparation; honors section; academic accommodation for the gifted.

College Admission Counseling 130 students graduated in 2015; all went to college, including Baylor University; Oklahoma State University; Southern Methodist University; Texas A&M University; The University of Texas at Austin; University of Oklahoma. Median SAT critical reading: 560, median SAT math: 550, median SAT writing: 550, median combined SAT: 1540, median composite ACT: 24. 37% scored over 600 on SAT critical reading, 35% scored over 600 on SAT math, 31% scored over 600 on SAT writing, 47% scored over 1800 on combined SAT, 38% scored over 26 on composite ACT.

Student Life Upper grades have uniform requirement, student council, honor system. Discipline rests primarily with faculty.

Summer Programs Remediation, enrichment, advancement, sports, art/fine arts, rigorous outdoor training, computer instruction programs offered; held on campus; accepts boys and girls; open to students from other schools. 800 students usually enrolled. 2016 schedule: June 1 to August 5. Application deadline: May 1.

Tuition and Aid Day student tuition: $18,535–$19,100. Tuition installment plan (FACTS Tuition Payment Plan, monthly payment plans, individually arranged payment plans). Tuition reduction for siblings, need-based scholarship grants available. In 2015–16, 21% of upper-school students received aid. Total amount of financial aid awarded in 2015–16: $734,381.

Admissions Traditional secondary-level entrance grade is 9. For fall 2015, 109 students applied for upper-level admission, 65 were accepted, 54 enrolled. ISEE or Stanford Achievement Test required. Deadline for receipt of application materials: none. Application fee required: $100. Interview required.

Athletics Interscholastic: baseball (boys), basketball (b,g), cheering (g), cross-country running (b,g), drill team (g), football (b), golf (b,g), soccer (b,g), softball (g), swimming and diving (b,g), tennis (b,g), track and field (b,g), volleyball (g). 7 PE instructors, 42 coaches.

Computers Computers are regularly used in all academic, technology classes. Computer network features include on-campus library services, Internet access, wireless campus network, Internet filtering or blocking technology. Student e-mail accounts are available to students. Students grades are available online. The school has a published electronic and media policy.

Contact Mrs. Allison P. Taylor, Admissions Assistant. 972-930-4010. Fax: 972-930-4008. E-mail: aptaylor@prestonwoodchristian.org. Website: www.prestonwoodchristian.org

PROCTOR ACADEMY

PO Box 500
204 Main Street
Andover, New Hampshire 03216

Head of School: Mr. Michael Henriques

General Information Coeducational boarding and day college-preparatory, arts, technology, environmental studies, and experiential learning programs school. Grades 9–12. Founded: 1848. Setting: small town. Nearest major city is Concord. Students are housed in single-sex dormitories. 3,000-acre campus. 46 buildings on campus. Approved or accredited by Association for Experiential Education, Association of Independent Schools in New England, Independent Schools of Northern New England, New England Association of Schools and Colleges, The Association of Boarding Schools, and New Hampshire Department of Education. Member of National Association of Independent Schools and Secondary School Admission Test Board. Endowment: $25 million. Total enrollment: 360. Upper school average class size: 12. Upper school faculty-student ratio: 1:5. There are 170 required school days per year for Upper School students. Upper School students typically attend 6 days per week. The average school day consists of 5 hours and 35 minutes.

Upper School Student Profile Grade 9: 81 students (51 boys, 30 girls); Grade 10: 78 students (48 boys, 30 girls); Grade 11: 114 students (68 boys, 46 girls); Grade 12: 96 students (59 boys, 37 girls). 78% of students are boarding students. 31% are state residents. 30 states are represented in upper school student body. 7% are international students. International students from China, Hong Kong, Mexico, Republic of Korea, Spain, and Viet Nam; 9 other countries represented in student body.

Faculty School total: 85. In upper school: 39 men, 46 women; 66 have advanced degrees; 35 reside on campus.

Subjects Offered Algebra, American history, American literature, art, art history, biology, boat building, calculus, ceramics, chemistry, computer math, computer programming, creative writing, drama, economics, English, English literature, environmental science, European history, fine arts, finite math, forestry, French,

genetics, geometry, health, history, industrial arts, mathematics, Middle Eastern history, music, music history, music technology, Native American history, performing arts, photography, physical education, physics, piano, play/screen writing, poetry, political thought, probability and statistics, psychology, public speaking, publications, science, senior project, social sciences, Spanish, sports medicine, studio art, study skills, the Web, theater, theater history, U.S. government and politics-AP, U.S. history-AP, Vietnam history, voice, voice ensemble, wilderness experience, woodworking, world literature, writing, writing workshop.

Graduation Requirements Arts and fine arts (art, music, dance, drama), English, foreign language, mathematics, science, social sciences.

Special Academic Programs 14 Advanced Placement exams for which test preparation is offered; honors section; independent study; term-away projects; study at local college for college credit; study abroad; academic accommodation for the gifted; programs in general development for dyslexic students.

College Admission Counseling 104 students graduated in 2015; 96 went to college, including Connecticut College; Elon University; Endicott College; St. Lawrence University; University of Denver; University of New Hampshire. Other: 8 had other specific plans. Mean SAT critical reading: 555, mean SAT math: 560, mean SAT writing: 545, mean combined SAT: 1660, mean composite ACT: 23. 20% scored over 600 on SAT critical reading, 24% scored over 600 on SAT math, 22% scored over 600 on SAT writing, 24% scored over 26 on composite ACT.

Student Life Upper grades have student council, honor system. Discipline rests equally with students and faculty.

Tuition and Aid Day student tuition: $33,400; 7-day tuition and room/board: $55,500. Tuition installment plan (Academic Management Services Plan, FACTS Tuition Payment Plan, monthly payment plans). Need-based scholarship grants available. In 2015–16, 33% of upper-school students received aid. Total amount of financial aid awarded in 2015–16: $3,200,000.

Admissions Traditional secondary-level entrance grade is 9. For fall 2015, 600 students applied for upper-level admission, 287 were accepted, 140 enrolled. ISEE, PSAT or SAT for applicants to grade 11 and 12, SSAT, TOEFL or SLEP, WISC/Woodcock-Johnson or writing sample required. Deadline for receipt of application materials: February 1. Application fee required: $50. Interview required.

Athletics Interscholastic: alpine skiing (boys, girls), archery (b,g), baseball (b), basketball (b,g), bicycling (b,g), canoeing/kayaking (b,g), cross-country running (b,g), field hockey (g), football (b), hockey (b,g), ice hockey (b,g), lacrosse (b,g), nordic skiing (b,g); intramural: alpine skiing (b,g); coed interscholastic: crew, dance, freestyle skiing, golf, horseback riding, kayaking; coed intramural: aerobics/dance, aerobics/Nautilus, backpacking, ballet, broomball, canoeing/kayaking, climbing, combined training, dance, equestrian sports, fencing, fitness, Frisbee, hiking/backpacking, horseback riding, kayaking, martial arts, modern dance, mountain biking, mountaineering, outdoor activities, outdoor adventure, outdoor education, outdoor recreation, outdoor skills, outdoors, paint ball, rock climbing. 5 coaches, 2 athletic trainers.

Computers Computers are regularly used in all academic classes. Computer network features include on-campus library services, online commercial services, Internet access, wireless campus network, Internet filtering or blocking technology. Campus intranet and student e-mail accounts are available to students. Students grades are available online. The school has a published electronic and media policy.

Contact Lisa Tanguay, Admissions Coordinator. 603-735-6312. Fax: 603-735-6284. E-mail: tanguayli@proctoracademy.org. Website: www.proctoracademy.org

PROFESSIONAL CHILDREN'S SCHOOL

132 West 60th Street
New York, New York 10023

Head of School: Dr. James Dawson

General Information Coeducational day college-preparatory school. Grades 6–12. Founded: 1914. Setting: urban. 1 building on campus. Approved or accredited by New York State Association of Independent Schools. Member of National Association of Independent Schools. Endowment: $2.7 million. Total enrollment: 198. Upper school average class size: 16. Upper school faculty-student ratio: 1:8. There are 167 required school days per year for Upper School students. Upper School students typically attend 5 days per week. The average school day consists of 7 hours.

Upper School Student Profile Grade 6: 5 students (3 boys, 2 girls); Grade 7: 10 students (6 boys, 4 girls); Grade 8: 15 students (9 boys, 6 girls); Grade 9: 39 students (27 boys, 12 girls); Grade 10: 44 students (29 boys, 15 girls); Grade 11: 41 students (24 boys, 17 girls); Grade 12: 44 students (30 boys, 14 girls).

Faculty School total: 29. In upper school: 13 men, 12 women; 20 have advanced degrees.

Subjects Offered Advanced math, algebra, American government, American history, biology, calculus, chemistry, chorus, computer education, constitutional history of U.S., constitutional law, creative writing, drama, English, English literature, environmental science, ESL, foreign language, French, general math, geometry, health education, introduction to literature, keyboarding, library research, library skills, physical education, physics, pre-algebra, pre-calculus, Spanish, studio art, U.S. government, U.S. history.

Graduation Requirements Art, English, foreign language, health, history, mathematics, science.

Special Academic Programs ESL (35 students enrolled).

College Admission Counseling 52 students graduated in 2015; 37 went to college. Other: 3 went to work, 1 entered military service, 6 entered a postgraduate year, 5 had other specific plans.

Student Life Upper grades have student council, honor system. Discipline rests primarily with faculty.

Summer Programs Accepts boys and girls; not open to students from other schools.

Tuition and Aid Day student tuition: $38,300. Tuition installment plan (Tuition Management Systems). Need-based scholarship grants available. In 2015–16, 30% of upper-school students received aid. Total amount of financial aid awarded in 2015–16: $795,802.

Admissions Traditional secondary-level entrance grade is 9. For fall 2015, 85 students applied for upper-level admission, 75 were accepted, 55 enrolled. Deadline for receipt of application materials: none. Application fee required: $75. Interview required.

Athletics 1 PE instructor.

Computers Computers are regularly used in all academic classes. Computer network features include on-campus library services, Internet access, wireless campus network, Internet filtering or blocking technology. Student e-mail accounts and computer access in designated common areas are available to students. The school has a published electronic and media policy.

Contact Ms. Shari Honig, Director of Admissions. 212-582-3116 Ext. 112. Fax: 212-307-6542. E-mail: admissions@pcs-nyc.org. Website: www.pcs-nyc.org

THE PROUT SCHOOL

4640 Tower Hill Road
Wakefield, Rhode Island 02879

Head of School: Mr. David Estes

General Information Coeducational day college-preparatory, arts, religious studies, and technology school, affiliated with Roman Catholic Church. Grades 9–12. Founded: 1966. Setting: small town. Nearest major city is Providence. 25-acre campus. 1 building on campus. Approved or accredited by International Baccalaureate Organization, New England Association of Schools and Colleges, Rhode Island State Certified Resource Progam, and Rhode Island Department of Education. Member of National Association of Independent Schools. Total enrollment: 500. Upper school average class size: 23. Upper school faculty-student ratio: 1:18. There are 182 required school days per year for Upper School students. Upper School students typically attend 5 days per week. The average school day consists of 6 hours and 30 minutes.

Upper School Student Profile 75% of students are Roman Catholic.

Faculty School total: 48. In upper school: 20 men, 28 women; 40 have advanced degrees.

Subjects Offered Acting, American literature, anatomy and physiology, art education, art history, athletic training, ballet, ballet technique, band, biology, calculus, chemistry, choir, chorus, Christian doctrine, Christian education, Christian ethics, Christian scripture, Christian studies, Christianity, church history, clayworking, college planning, college writing, community service, comparative religion, computer applications, computer art, computer education, computer graphics, computer multimedia, computer programming, computer science, computer skills, computer studies, contemporary history, contemporary issues, costumes and make-up, CPR, creative dance, creative drama, creative thinking, critical studies in film, critical writing, dance performance, drama performance, drama workshop, dramatic arts, drawing, drawing and design, earth science, economics, economics and history, English, English composition, English literature, environmental science, environmental studies, first aid, fitness, food and nutrition, foreign language, French, general science, government, graphic arts, graphic design, health, health and wellness, history, history of the Catholic Church, honors English, honors U.S. history, honors world history, human anatomy, instruments, introduction to theater, Italian, jazz band, keyboarding, lab science, language, language and composition, law and the legal system, life science, marine science, mathematics, modern history, music performance, music theater, musical theater, musical theater dance, oceanography, personal fitness, physical fitness, physics, play production, portfolio art, pre-calculus, public service, religion, religion and culture, religious education, religious studies, scene study, science, science research, scripture, set design, Spanish, sports nutrition, stage and body movement, stage design, theater, theater arts, theater design and production, theater history, visual and performing arts, yearbook.

Graduation Requirements Computers, English, foreign language, health education, history, lab science, mathematics, oceanography, physical education (includes health), religion (includes Bible studies and theology), science.

Special Academic Programs International Baccalaureate program; Advanced Placement exam preparation; honors section.

College Admission Counseling 140 students graduated in 2015; 137 went to college, including Northeastern University; Providence College; Roger Williams University; University of New Hampshire; University of Rhode Island. Other: 1 entered a postgraduate year, 2 had other specific plans.

Student Life Upper grades have uniform requirement, student council, honor system. Discipline rests primarily with faculty. Attendance at religious services is required.

Tuition and Aid Day student tuition: $12,975. Tuition installment plan (FACTS Tuition Payment Plan). Tuition reduction for siblings, need-based scholarship grants available. In 2015–16, 35% of upper-school students received aid.

Admissions Traditional secondary-level entrance grade is 9. Admissions testing, essay and High School Placement Test required. Deadline for receipt of application materials: December 22. Application fee required: $45.

Athletics Interscholastic: baseball (boys), basketball (b,g), cheering (g), cross-country running (b,g), gymnastics (g), lacrosse (b,g), soccer (b,g), softball (g), swimming and diving (b,g), tennis (b,g), track and field (b,g), volleyball (g); intramural: dance (g), outdoor recreation (b,g); coed interscholastic: aquatics, golf, ice hockey; coed intramural: aerobics, aerobics/dance, ballet, bicycling, fitness, outdoor recreation, sailing, strength & conditioning, table tennis, weight lifting, weight training. 3 PE instructors, 14 coaches, 1 athletic trainer.

Computers Computers are regularly used in all academic classes. Computer network features include on-campus library services, Internet access, Internet filtering or blocking technology. Computer access in designated common areas is available to students. The school has a published electronic and media policy.

Contact Ms. Sharon DeLuca, Director of Admissions. 401-789-9262 Ext. 514. Fax: 401-782-2262. E-mail: sdeluca@theproutschool.org. Website: www.theproutschool.org

PROVIDENCE ACADEMY

15100 Schmidt Lake Road
Plymouth, Minnesota 55446

Head of School: Dr. Todd Flanders

General Information Coeducational day college-preparatory, arts, and religious studies school, affiliated with Roman Catholic Church. Grades PK–12. Founded: 2001. Setting: suburban. Nearest major city is Minneapolis. 42-acre campus. 1 building on campus. Approved or accredited by Minnesota Department of Education. Member of National Association of Independent Schools. Total enrollment: 847. Upper school average class size: 19. Upper school faculty-student ratio: 1:11. There are 172 required school days per year for Upper School students. Upper School students typically attend 5 days per week. The average school day consists of 6 hours and 45 minutes.

Upper School Student Profile Grade 9: 87 students (43 boys, 44 girls); Grade 10: 77 students (34 boys, 43 girls); Grade 11: 90 students (42 boys, 48 girls); Grade 12: 77 students (38 boys, 39 girls); Grade 13: 73 students (38 boys, 35 girls). 67% of students are Roman Catholic.

Faculty School total: 74. In upper school: 14 men, 12 women; 17 have advanced degrees.

Subjects Offered ACT preparation, advanced biology, advanced chemistry, math analysis.

Special Academic Programs 14 Advanced Placement exams for which test preparation is offered; honors section; study at local college for college credit; study abroad.

College Admission Counseling 77 students graduated in 2014; 75 went to college, including Boston College; Marquette University; Miami University; North Dakota State University; University of Notre Dame; University of St. Thomas. Other: 2 entered a postgraduate year. Median SAT critical reading: 670, median SAT math: 660, median SAT writing: 630, median combined SAT: 1970, median composite ACT: 28. 76% scored over 600 on SAT critical reading, 61% scored over 600 on SAT math, 66% scored over 600 on SAT writing, 66% scored over 1800 on combined SAT, 55% scored over 26 on composite ACT.

Student Life Upper grades have uniform requirement, student council, honor system. Discipline rests primarily with faculty. Attendance at religious services is required.

Tuition and Aid Day student tuition: $17,385. Tuition installment plan (individually arranged payment plans). Merit scholarship grants, need-based scholarship grants available. In 2014–15, 32% of upper-school students received aid; total upper-school merit-scholarship money awarded: $60,000. Total amount of financial aid awarded in 2014–15: $1,200,000.

Admissions Traditional secondary-level entrance grade is 9. For fall 2014, 44 students applied for upper-level admission, 44 were accepted, 33 enrolled. ISEE required. Deadline for receipt of application materials: January 17. Application fee required: $25. Interview required.

Athletics Interscholastic: baseball (boys), basketball (b,g), cross-country running (b,g), football (b), golf (b,g), hockey (b,g), lacrosse (b), soccer (b,g), softball (g), swimming and diving (b,g), tennis (b,g), track and field (b,g), volleyball (g); coed intramural: sailing, skiing (cross-country), skiing (downhill). 4 PE instructors, 80 coaches, 1 athletic trainer.

Computers Computer resources include on-campus library services, Internet access, wireless campus network, Internet filtering or blocking technology. Campus intranet, student e-mail accounts, and computer access in designated common areas are available to students. Students grades are available online. The school has a published electronic and media policy.

Contact Mrs. Susan Truax, Admissions Assistant. 763-258-2502. Fax: 763-258-2503. E-mail: susan.truax@providenceacademy.org. Website: www.providenceacademy.org/

PROVIDENCE CATHOLIC SCHOOL, THE COLLEGE PREPARATORY SCHOOL FOR GIRLS GRADES 6-12

1215 North St. Mary's
San Antonio, Texas 78215-1787

Head of School: Ms. Alicia Garcia

General Information Girls' day college-preparatory, arts, and religious studies school, affiliated with Roman Catholic Church. Grades 6–12. Founded: 1951. Setting: urban. 3-acre campus. 4 buildings on campus. Approved or accredited by Southern Association of Colleges and Schools, Southern Association of Independent Schools, Texas Catholic Conference, and Texas Education Agency. Endowment: $500,000. Total enrollment: 301. Upper school average class size: 22. Upper school faculty-student ratio: 1:12. There are 186 required school days per year for Upper School students. Upper School students typically attend 5 days per week. The average school day consists of 7 hours.

Upper School Student Profile Grade 9: 37 students (37 girls); Grade 10: 49 students (49 girls); Grade 11: 53 students (53 girls); Grade 12: 44 students (44 girls). 80% of students are Roman Catholic.

Faculty School total: 30. In upper school: 6 men, 21 women; 20 have advanced degrees.

Subjects Offered Acting, advanced biology, advanced chemistry, advanced math, Advanced Placement courses, aerobics, algebra, American history, American history-AP, American literature, American literature-AP, anatomy, ancient world history, art, athletics, audio visual/media, band, biology, biology-AP, British literature, British literature-AP, broadcast journalism, broadcasting, calculus-AP, career education internship, Catholic belief and practice, cheerleading, chemistry, choir, choral music, church history, composition-AP, computer information systems, concert band, concert choir, conflict resolution, creative writing, dance, dance performance, desktop publishing, drama, drama performance, drama workshop, economics, English, English language and composition-AP, English language-AP, English literature, English literature and composition-AP, English literature-AP, English-AP, film, fitness, foreign language, French, geography, government, government and politics-AP, history, history-AP, human anatomy, jazz band, journalism, JROTC, JROTC or LEAD (Leadership Education and Development), Latin, law, leadership, literature and composition-AP, music theory, newspaper, peer ministry, personal fitness, photography, photojournalism, physical education, physical fitness, physical science, physics, play production, psychology, social justice, sociology, softball, Spanish, Spanish language-AP, Spanish-AP, speech, sports, statistics-AP, student government, student publications, swimming, swimming competency, tennis, Texas history, the Web, theater, theater arts, theater design and production, theater production, theology, track and field, U.S. government and politics, U.S. government and politics-AP, U.S. history, U.S. history-AP, volleyball, Web site design, world geography, world history, yearbook.

Graduation Requirements All academic, 100 hours of community service completed by grade 12, senior retreat participation.

Special Academic Programs International Baccalaureate program; 13 Advanced Placement exams for which test preparation is offered; honors section; independent study; study at local college for college credit.

College Admission Counseling 46 students graduated in 2015; all went to college, including St. Mary's University; Texas A&M University; The University of Texas at Austin; The University of Texas at San Antonio; University of the Incarnate Word.

Student Life Upper grades have uniform requirement, student council, honor system. Discipline rests primarily with faculty. Attendance at religious services is required.

Summer Programs Remediation, enrichment, advancement, sports, art/fine arts, computer instruction programs offered; session focuses on getting ahead (improvement); held on campus; accepts girls; open to students from other schools. 100 students usually enrolled. 2016 schedule: June 6 to July 24. Application deadline: May 27.

Tuition and Aid Day student tuition: $7842. Tuition installment plan (FACTS Tuition Payment Plan, Middle School tuition $4,748). Tuition reduction for siblings, merit scholarship grants, need-based scholarship grants available. In 2015–16, 12% of upper-school students received aid; total upper-school merit-scholarship money awarded: $58,550. Total amount of financial aid awarded in 2015–16: $214,713.

Admissions Traditional secondary-level entrance grade is 9. For fall 2015, 51 students applied for upper-level admission, 43 were accepted, 43 enrolled. High School Placement Test or QUIC required. Deadline for receipt of application materials: none. No application fee required. On-campus interview recommended.

Athletics Interscholastic: aerobics, aerobics/dance, basketball, bowling, cheering, cross-country running, dance, dance team, JROTC drill, physical fitness, physical training, running, soccer, softball, tennis, track and field, volleyball, weight training, winter soccer; coed interscholastic: aquatics. 1 PE instructor, 7 coaches, 1 athletic trainer.

Computers Computers are regularly used in desktop publishing, journalism, newspaper, Web site design, yearbook classes. Computer network features include on-campus library services, online commercial services, Internet access, Internet filtering or blocking technology, online classrooms. Campus intranet and student e-mail accounts are available to students. Students grades are available online. The school has a published electronic and media policy.

Contact Mrs. Stephanie Takas-Mercer, Admissions Director. 210-224-6651 Ext. 210. Fax: 210-224-9242. E-mail: stakas-mercer@providencehs.net. Website: www.providencehs.net

PROVIDENCE COUNTRY DAY SCHOOL

660 Waterman Avenue
East Providence, Rhode Island 02914-1724

Head of School: Mr. Vince Watchorn

General Information Coeducational day college-preparatory and arts school. Grades 6–12. Founded: 1923. Setting: suburban. Nearest major city is Providence. 31-acre campus. 6 buildings on campus. Approved or accredited by Association of Independent Schools in New England, New England Association of Schools and Colleges, The College Board, and Rhode Island Department of Education. Member of National Association of Independent Schools and Secondary School Admission Test Board. Endowment: $1.7 million. Total enrollment: 208. Upper school average class size: 12. Upper school faculty-student ratio: 1:8. There are 166 required school days per year for Upper School students. Upper School students typically attend 5 days per week. The average school day consists of 6 hours and 30 minutes.

Upper School Student Profile Grade 9: 43 students (26 boys, 17 girls); Grade 10: 42 students (25 boys, 17 girls); Grade 11: 43 students (31 boys, 12 girls); Grade 12: 37 students (22 boys, 15 girls).

Faculty School total: 36. In upper school: 13 men, 20 women; 21 have advanced degrees.

Subjects Offered 3-dimensional art, Advanced Placement courses, algebra, American government, American history, American history-AP, American literature, ancient history, art, art history-AP, Asian studies, band, Bible as literature, bioethics, biology, biology-AP, British literature, calculus, calculus-AP, ceramics, chemistry, choir, computer graphics, computer science, conceptual physics, creative writing, drama, drawing, electives, English, English literature, English literature-AP, environmental science, European civilization, European history, European history-AP, evolution, expository writing, fiction, fine arts, foreign language, forensics, geometry, government/civics, graphic design, health, history, independent study, jazz ensemble, Latin, Latin-AP, mathematics, media production, modern European history, music, painting, performing arts, photography, physical education, physics, politics, pottery, pre-calculus, printmaking, public speaking, SAT/ACT preparation, science, sculpture, senior internship, senior project, Shakespeare, short story, social studies, Spanish, Spanish language-AP, sports, studio art, theater, trigonometry, U.S. government and politics-AP, U.S. history-AP, visual and performing arts, visual arts, water color painting, Western literature, world history, world literature, writing, yearbook.

Graduation Requirements Arts and fine arts (art, music, dance, drama), English, foreign language, history, mathematics, performing arts, science, senior independent project, community service, athletics.

Special Academic Programs 10 Advanced Placement exams for which test preparation is offered; honors section; independent study; term-away projects; study abroad; academic accommodation for the gifted, the musically talented, and the artistically talented.

College Admission Counseling 42 students graduated in 2015; 40 went to college, including Brown University; Denison University; Rhode Island College; University of Rhode Island. Other: 1 entered a postgraduate year, 1 had other specific plans. Mean SAT critical reading: 593, mean SAT math: 583, mean SAT writing: 571, mean combined SAT: 1747, mean composite ACT: 25.

Student Life Upper grades have specified standards of dress, student council, honor system. Discipline rests equally with students and faculty.

Summer Programs Sports, art/fine arts programs offered; held on campus; accepts boys and girls; open to students from other schools.

Tuition and Aid Day student tuition: $33,200–$33,500. Tuition installment plan (FACTS Tuition Payment Plan, monthly payment plans, Tuition Refund Insurance). Merit scholarship grants, need-based scholarship grants available. In 2015–16, 45% of upper-school students received aid; total upper-school merit-scholarship money awarded: $129,900. Total amount of financial aid awarded in 2015–16: $1,945,025.

Admissions Traditional secondary-level entrance grade is 9. For fall 2015, 165 students applied for upper-level admission, 113 were accepted, 49 enrolled. ISEE or SSAT required. Deadline for receipt of application materials: February 1. Application fee required: $55. On-campus interview required.

Athletics Interscholastic: basketball (boys, girls), football (b), ice hockey (b), lacrosse (b,g), soccer (b,g), tennis (b,g); coed interscholastic: baseball, cross-country running, golf, ice hockey, independent competitive sports, sailing, squash, swimming and diving, track and field; coed intramural: physical fitness, rock climbing, strength & conditioning, weight training, yoga. 1 PE instructor, 21 coaches, 1 athletic trainer.

Computers Computers are regularly used in art, English, foreign language, history, mathematics, music, science classes. Computer network features include on-campus library services, online commercial services, Internet access, wireless campus network, Internet filtering or blocking technology. Campus intranet, student e-mail accounts, and computer access in designated common areas are available to students. The school has a published electronic and media policy.

Contact Mr. Dave Provost, Director of Admissions and Financial Aid. 401-438-5170 Ext. 102. Fax: 401-435-4514. E-mail: provost@providencecountryday.org. Website: www.providencecountryday.org

PROVIDENCE DAY SCHOOL

5800 Sardis Road
Charlotte, North Carolina 28270

Head of School: Dr. Glyn Cowlishaw

General Information Coeducational day college-preparatory and global studies diploma program school. Grades PK–12. Founded: 1970. Setting: suburban. 44-acre campus. 18 buildings on campus. Approved or accredited by Southern Association of Independent Schools and North Carolina Department of Education. Member of National Association of Independent Schools. Endowment: $8 million. Total enrollment: 1,580. Upper school average class size: 18. Upper school faculty-student ratio: 1:9. There are 176 required school days per year for Upper School students. Upper School students typically attend 5 days per week. The average school day consists of 7 hours and 10 minutes.

Upper School Student Profile Grade 9: 143 students (71 boys, 72 girls); Grade 10: 143 students (73 boys, 70 girls); Grade 11: 142 students (70 boys, 72 girls); Grade 12: 142 students (71 boys, 71 girls).

Faculty School total: 148. In upper school: 46 men, 34 women; 56 have advanced degrees.

Subjects Offered 3-dimensional design, accounting, African-American history, algebra, American history, American literature, art, art history-AP, Asian history, band, biology, biology-AP, calculus-AP, chemistry, chemistry-AP, chorus, Civil War, composition, computer graphics, computer programming, computer science, computer science-AP, drama, economics, English, English literature, English-AP, environmental science, environmental science-AP, fine arts, French, French-AP, geometry, German, German-AP, government-AP, government/civics, health, history, history-AP, instrumental music, international relations, journalism, Judaic studies, keyboarding, Latin, Latin-AP, literature, Mandarin, mathematics, music-AP, photography, physical education, physical science, physics, physics-AP, political science, pre-calculus, psychology, science, set design, social studies, Spanish, Spanish-AP, sports medicine, statistics-AP, theater, word processing, world history, writing, yearbook.

Graduation Requirements Arts and fine arts (art, music, dance, drama), computer science, English, foreign language, mathematics, physical education (includes health), science, social studies (includes history), Global Studies Diploma.

Special Academic Programs 24 Advanced Placement exams for which test preparation is offered; honors section; accelerated programs; domestic exchange program; study abroad; academic accommodation for the gifted, the musically talented, and the artistically talented.

College Admission Counseling 141 students graduated in 2015; all went to college, including Appalachian State University; Duke University; North Carolina State University; The University of North Carolina at Chapel Hill; Vanderbilt University; Wake Forest University. Median SAT critical reading: 650, median SAT math: 660, median SAT writing: 650, median combined SAT: 1960, median composite ACT: 28. 73% scored over 600 on SAT critical reading, 80% scored over 600 on SAT math, 71% scored over 600 on SAT writing, 73% scored over 1800 on combined SAT.

Student Life Upper grades have specified standards of dress, student council, honor system. Discipline rests equally with students and faculty.

Summer Programs Remediation, enrichment, advancement, sports, art/fine arts, computer instruction programs offered; session focuses on academics, enrichment; held both on and off campus; held at various parks, recreation centers, museums; accepts boys and girls; open to students from other schools. 2,500 students usually enrolled. 2016 schedule: June 7 to August 6. Application deadline: none.

Tuition and Aid Day student tuition: $23,935. Tuition installment plan (Academic Management Services Plan, SMART Tuition Payment Plan, monthly payment plans). Need-based scholarship grants available. In 2015–16, 14% of upper-school students received aid. Total amount of financial aid awarded in 2015–16: $1,106,585.

Admissions Traditional secondary-level entrance grade is 9. For fall 2015, 113 students applied for upper-level admission, 65 were accepted, 39 enrolled. Cognitive Abilities Test, ERB CTP IV, ISEE, SSAT, ERB, PSAT, SAT, PLAN or ACT or Woodcock-Johnson Educational Evaluation, WISC III required. Deadline for receipt of application materials: January 15. Application fee required: $90. Interview required.

Athletics Interscholastic: aerobics/dance (girls), aquatics (b,g), baseball (b), basketball (b,g), cheering (g), cross-country running (b,g), dance squad (g), field hockey (g), football (b), golf (b,g), lacrosse (b,g), soccer (b,g), softball (g), swimming and diving (b,g), tennis (b,g), track and field (b,g), volleyball (g), wrestling (b); intramural: indoor hockey (b,g), indoor soccer (b,g), Newcombe ball (b,g), physical fitness (b,g), pillo polo (b,g), soccer (b,g), softball (b,g), strength & conditioning (b,g), volleyball (b,g); coed intramural: indoor hockey, indoor soccer, Newcombe ball, physical fitness, pillo polo, soccer, softball, strength & conditioning, tennis, volleyball. 4 PE instructors, 36 coaches, 2 athletic trainers.

Computers Computers are regularly used in English, mathematics, science, technology, word processing classes. Computer network features include on-campus library services, online commercial services, Internet access, wireless campus network, Internet filtering or blocking technology, wireless iBook lab available for individual student check-out, iPads. Student e-mail accounts and computer access in designated common areas are available to students. Students grades are available online. The school has a published electronic and media policy.

Contact Mrs. Carissa Goddard, Admissions Assistant. 704-887-7040. Fax: 704-887-7520 Ext. 7041. E-mail: carissa.goddard@providenceday.org. Website: www.providenceday.org

PROVIDENCE HIGH SCHOOL

511 South Buena Vista Street
Burbank, California 91505-4865

Head of School: Mr. Joe Sciuto

General Information Coeducational day college-preparatory, arts, religious studies, and technology school, affiliated with Roman Catholic Church. Grades 9–12. Founded: 1955. Setting: urban. Nearest major city is Los Angeles. 4-acre campus. 7 buildings on campus. Approved or accredited by California Association of Independent Schools, National Catholic Education Association, Western Association of Schools and Colleges, Western Catholic Education Association, and California Department of Education. Endowment: $1.6 million. Total enrollment: 435. Upper school average class size: 17. Upper school faculty-student ratio: 1:8. There are 177 required school days per year for Upper School students. Upper School students typically attend 5 days per week. The average school day consists of 7 hours and 15 minutes.

Upper School Student Profile Grade 9: 107 students (53 boys, 54 girls); Grade 10: 121 students (55 boys, 66 girls); Grade 11: 104 students (42 boys, 62 girls); Grade 12: 103 students (49 boys, 54 girls). 73% of students are Roman Catholic.

Faculty School total: 52. In upper school: 26 men, 26 women; 25 have advanced degrees.

Subjects Offered 3-dimensional art, accounting, advanced computer applications, Advanced Placement courses, advanced studio art-AP, algebra, American history, American history-AP, American literature, American literature-AP, anatomy and physiology, ASB Leadership, athletics, audio visual/media, Basic programming, basketball, Bible studies, biology, biology-AP, biotechnology, British literature, British literature (honors), British literature-AP, business mathematics, calculus, calculus-AP, Catholic belief and practice, ceramics, chemistry, chemistry-AP, Chinese, choir, choral music, chorus, Christian and Hebrew scripture, community service, computer animation, computer art, computer programming, computer science, computer science-AP, digital photography, drama, economics, economics-AP, electives, English, English language and composition-AP, English literature, English literature and composition-AP, English literature-AP, environmental science, environmental science-AP, ethics, film, fine arts, French, geometry, government and politics-AP, graphic arts, history, instruments, journalism, language-AP, Latin, law, leadership, macroeconomics-AP, Mandarin, mathematics, media studies, music, photography, physical education, physics, physics-AP, pre-calculus, psychology, psychology-AP, public speaking, religion, robotics, science, social studies, Spanish, Spanish language-AP, Spanish-AP, theater, trigonometry, U.S. government, U.S. government and politics-AP, U.S. history-AP, United States government-AP, video, video and animation, video film production, visual and performing arts, volleyball, world history, world history-AP, world religions, world religions, writing, yearbook, yoga.

Graduation Requirements Advanced math, American government, American history, American literature, art, biology, British literature, chemistry, comparative religion, computer science, economics, electives, English, foreign language, mathematics, physical education (includes health), religion (includes Bible studies and theology), science, social studies (includes history), world history, world literature, completion of Christian Service hours.

Special Academic Programs 15 Advanced Placement exams for which test preparation is offered; honors section; academic accommodation for the musically talented and the artistically talented.

College Admission Counseling 112 students graduated in 2015; 110 went to college, including Arizona State University at the Tempe campus; California State University, Long Beach; California State University, Northridge; Pasadena City College; San Francisco State University; University of California, Los Angeles. Other: 2 had other specific plans. Mean SAT critical reading: 537, mean SAT math: 530, mean SAT writing: 541, mean combined SAT: 1608, mean composite ACT: 25.

Student Life Upper grades have uniform requirement, student council. Discipline rests equally with students and faculty. Attendance at religious services is required.

Summer Programs Remediation, enrichment, advancement, sports, art/fine arts, computer instruction programs offered; session focuses on enrichment, remediation, and extracurricular activities; held on campus; accepts boys and girls; open to students from other schools. 300 students usually enrolled.

Tuition and Aid Day student tuition: $15,450. Tuition installment plan (SMART Tuition Payment Plan, annual payment ($15,450): 100% due on June 1, semi-annual installment ($15,700): 60% due on June 1; 40% due on Dec. 1, monthly Installment (11 payments; $15,950): $1,450/month from June 1, 2015-April 1, 2016). Merit scholarship grants, need-based scholarship grants available. In 2015–16, 46% of upper-school students received aid; total upper-school merit-scholarship money awarded: $214,000. Total amount of financial aid awarded in 2015–16: $942,250.

Admissions Traditional secondary-level entrance grade is 9. For fall 2015, 249 students applied for upper-level admission, 221 were accepted, 114 enrolled. Admissions testing, High School Placement Test and Math Placement Exam required. Deadline for receipt of application materials: January 14. Application fee required: $75. On-campus interview required.

Athletics Interscholastic: baseball (boys), basketball (b,g), cheering (g), cross-country running (b,g), golf (b), soccer (b,g), softball (g), track and field (b,g), volleyball (b,g). 4 PE instructors, 25 coaches, 1 athletic trainer.

Computers Computers are regularly used in accounting, animation, computer applications, desktop publishing, digital applications, information technology, journalism, library, literary magazine, media, media production, newspaper, photography, programming, publications, video film production, Web site design, writing, yearbook classes. Computer network features include on-campus library services, online commercial services, Internet access, wireless campus network, Internet filtering or blocking technology, Adobe Creative Cloud 2014, Microsoft Office Suite 2013, campus Extranet portal. Campus intranet, student e-mail accounts, and computer access in designated common areas are available to students. Students grades are available online. The school has a published electronic and media policy.

Contact Mrs. Judy Umeck, Director of Admissions. 818-846-8141 Ext. 14501. Fax: 818-843-8421. E-mail: judy.umeck@providencehigh.org. Website: www.providencehigh.org

PUNAHOU SCHOOL

1601 Punahou Street
Honolulu, Hawaii 96822

Head of School: Dr. James K. Scott

General Information Coeducational day and distance learning college-preparatory, arts, and technology school. Grades K–12. Distance learning grades 9–12. Founded: 1841. Setting: urban. 76-acre campus. 21 buildings on campus. Approved or accredited by Western Association of Schools and Colleges. Member of National Association of Independent Schools and Secondary School Admission Test Board. Endowment: $231 million. Total enrollment: 3,768. Upper school average class size: 21. Upper school faculty-student ratio: 1:11. There are 174 required school days per year for Upper School students. Upper School students typically attend 5 days per week. The average school day consists of 7 hours.

Upper School Student Profile Grade 9: 440 students (216 boys, 224 girls); Grade 10: 439 students (217 boys, 222 girls); Grade 11: 430 students (211 boys, 219 girls); Grade 12: 432 students (210 boys, 222 girls).

Faculty School total: 335. In upper school: 80 men, 90 women; 134 have advanced degrees.

Subjects Offered Acting, advanced biology, advanced chemistry, advanced math, Advanced Placement courses, algebra, American history, American literature, American studies, anatomy and physiology, anthropology, art, Asian history, astronomy, athletics, ballet, band, Bible as literature, bioethics, bioethics, DNA and culture, biology, biology-AP, biotechnology, British literature, business studies, calculus, calculus-AP, career/college preparation, ceramics, character education, chemistry, chemistry-AP, child development, Chinese, choir, choral music, chorus, clayworking, college admission preparation, college counseling, college planning, college writing, community garden, composition, computer science, computer science-AP, concert band, contemporary issues, CPR, creative writing, dance, digital art, digital photography, drama performance, drawing, driver education, economics, engineering, English, English composition, environmental science, environmental science-AP, environmental studies, European history, European history-AP, film and literature, filmmaking, foreign language, French, French language-AP, geometry, glassblowing, government and politics-AP, graphic design, guitar, Hawaiian history, Hawaiian language, humanities, independent study, Japanese, jewelry making, journalism, JROTC or LEAD (Leadership Education and Development), law, Mandarin, marching band, marine biology, mechanical drawing, medieval history, medieval/Renaissance history, microeconomics, money management, music, music theory, musical theater, oceanography, organic chemistry, painting, peer counseling, photography, physical education, physics, physics-AP, poetry, pre-calculus, psychology, psychology-AP, religion, robotics, SAT preparation, science fiction, sculpture, self-defense, Shakespeare, social studies, Spanish, Spanish-AP, sports psychology, statistics-AP, studio art, studio art-AP, symphonic band, technical theater, tennis, theater design and production, U.S. government and politics, U.S. government and politics-AP, U.S. history, U.S. history-AP, video, video film production, Western literature, wind ensemble, wind instruments, world civilizations, world literature, writing, yoga.

Graduation Requirements Electives, English, foreign language, mathematics, physical education (includes health), science, social studies (includes history), visual and performing arts, seniors are required to take a Capstone course that combines economics and community service, one course with the Spiritual, Ethical, Community Responsibility (SECR) designation.

Special Academic Programs 17 Advanced Placement exams for which test preparation is offered; honors section; independent study; study abroad.

College Admission Counseling 419 students graduated in 2015; 409 went to college, including Boston University; Chapman University; New York University; Seattle University; University of Hawaii at Manoa; University of San Francisco. Other: 10 had other specific plans. Median SAT critical reading: 600, median SAT math: 660, median SAT writing: 630, median combined SAT: 1880. 49% scored over 600 on SAT critical reading, 76% scored over 600 on SAT math, 57% scored over 600 on SAT writing, 63% scored over 1800 on combined SAT.

Student Life Upper grades have specified standards of dress, student council, honor system. Discipline rests primarily with faculty. Attendance at religious services is required.

Summer Programs Enrichment, advancement, sports, art/fine arts programs offered; session focuses on enrichment and graduation credit; held both on and off campus; held at Japan, China, Alaska; accepts boys and girls; open to students from other schools. 1,521 students usually enrolled. 2016 schedule: June 13 to July 15. Application deadline: April 8.

Tuition and Aid Day student tuition: $22,050. Tuition installment plan (Insured Tuition Payment Plan, monthly payment plans, semester payment plan, annual payment plan). Merit scholarship grants, need-based scholarship grants available. In 2015–16, 18% of upper-school students received aid; total upper-school merit-scholarship money awarded: $264,600. Total amount of financial aid awarded in 2015–16: $3,073,375.

Admissions Traditional secondary-level entrance grade is 9. For fall 2015, 331 students applied for upper-level admission, 127 were accepted, 89 enrolled. SAT or SSAT required. Deadline for receipt of application materials: November 15. Application fee required: $125. Interview required.

Athletics Interscholastic: baseball (boys), basketball (b,g), bowling (b,g), canoeing/kayaking (b,g), cheering (g), cross-country running (b,g), football (b), golf (b,g), judo (b,g), kayaking (b,g), paddling (b,g), riflery (b,g), sailing (b,g), soccer (b,g), softball (g), swimming and diving (b,g), tennis (b,g), track and field (b,g), volleyball (b,g), water polo (b,g), wrestling (b,g); coed interscholastic: canoeing/kayaking, paddling. 4 PE instructors, 303 coaches, 4 athletic trainers.

Computers Computers are regularly used in all academic classes. Computer network features include on-campus library services, online commercial services, Internet access, wireless campus network, Internet filtering or blocking technology. Campus intranet, student e-mail accounts, and computer access in designated common areas are available to students. The school has a published electronic and media policy.

Contact Mrs. Betsy S. Hata, Director of Admission and Financial Aid. 808-944-5714. Fax: 808-943-3602. E-mail: admission@punahou.edu. Website: www.punahou.edu

PURNELL SCHOOL

Pottersville, New Jersey
See Special Needs Schools section.

PUSCH RIDGE CHRISTIAN ACADEMY

9500 North Oracle Road
Tucson, Arizona 85704

Head of School: Dr. Rodney Marshall

General Information Coeducational day college-preparatory, arts, and religious studies school, affiliated with Presbyterian Church in America. Grades 6–12. Founded: 2000. Setting: suburban. Nearest major city is Oro Valley. 48-acre campus. 2 buildings on campus. Approved or accredited by Arizona Department of Education. Endowment: $40,000. Upper school average class size: 22. Upper school faculty-student ratio: 1:16. There are 176 required school days per year for Upper School students. Upper School students typically attend 5 days per week. The average school day consists of 6 hours and 30 minutes.

Upper School Student Profile Grade 9: 81 students (38 boys, 43 girls); Grade 10: 79 students (41 boys, 38 girls); Grade 11: 73 students (48 boys, 25 girls); Grade 12: 78 students (31 boys, 47 girls). 15% of students are Presbyterian Church in America.

Faculty School total: 29. In upper school: 13 men, 16 women; 13 have advanced degrees.

Subjects Offered 3-dimensional art, acting, advanced biology, advanced chemistry, advanced math, Advanced Placement courses, algebra, American Civil War, American government, American history, American history-AP, American literature, American literature-AP, analytic geometry, anatomy, art, ASB Leadership, athletics, band, Bible, biology, chemistry, chemistry-AP, choir, choral music, chorus, college admission preparation, college counseling, college placement, college planning, computer-aided design, concert band, concert choir, creative writing, drama performance, drawing and design, economics, economics-AP, electives, English, English composition, English language and composition-AP, English language-AP, English literature, English literature and composition-AP, English literature-AP, English-AP, English/composition-AP, environmental science, geometry, government, government-AP, graphic arts, honors algebra, honors English, honors geometry, introduction to theater, Latin, leadership, New Testament, physics, SAT preparation, Spanish, Spanish language-AP, statistics, U.S. government, U.S. history, U.S. history-AP, Web site design, world geography, world history.

Graduation Requirements Algebra, American government, American history, American literature, Bible, biology, electives, English, geography, geometry, U.S. government, U.S. history, world history.

Special Academic Programs Advanced Placement exam preparation; honors section; study at local college for college credit.

College Admission Counseling 57 students graduated in 2014; 55 went to college. Other: 1 entered military service. 46% scored over 600 on SAT critical reading, 38% scored over 600 on SAT math, 43% scored over 600 on SAT writing, 41% scored over 1800 on combined SAT.

Student Life Upper grades have specified standards of dress, student council, honor system. Discipline rests primarily with faculty. Attendance at religious services is required.

Tuition and Aid Day student tuition: $8437. Tuition installment plan (monthly payment plans). Tuition reduction for siblings, need-based scholarship grants available. In 2014–15, 85% of upper-school students received aid. Total amount of financial aid awarded in 2014–15: $2,000,000.

Admissions Traditional secondary-level entrance grade is 9. For fall 2014, 40 students applied for upper-level admission, 33 were accepted, 32 enrolled. Admissions testing,

Gates MacGinite Reading Tests and school's own exam required. Deadline for receipt of application materials: none. Application fee required: $100. Interview required.
Athletics Interscholastic: baseball (boys), basketball (b,g), cheering (g), flagball (b), soccer (b,g), softball (g), swimming and diving (b,g), tennis (b,g), track and field (b,g), volleyball (g); coed interscholastic: cross-country running, golf. 1 PE instructor, 38 coaches, 1 athletic trainer.
Computers Computers are regularly used in college planning, graphic arts, photography, SAT preparation, science, wilderness education classes. Computer network features include Internet access, Internet filtering or blocking technology. Campus intranet is available to students. The school has a published electronic and media policy.
Contact Mrs. Casey Robinson, Director of Admissions. 520-797-0107 Ext. 502. Fax: 520-797-0598. E-mail: casey.robinson@prca-tucson.org. Website: www.prca-cca.com/

QUEEN MARGARET'S SCHOOL

660 Brownsey Avenue
Duncan, British Columbia V9L 1C2, Canada

Head of School: Mrs. Wilma Jamieson

General Information Girls' boarding and coeducational day college-preparatory, arts, technology, equestrian studies, and STEM school, affiliated with Anglican Church of Canada. Boarding girls grades 6–12, day boys grades PS–7, day girls grades PS–12. Founded: 1921. Setting: small town. Nearest major city is Victoria, Canada. Students are housed in single-sex dormitories. 27-acre campus. 9 buildings on campus. Approved or accredited by Canadian Association of Independent Schools, Canadian Educational Standards Institute, The Association of Boarding Schools, and British Columbia Department of Education. Affiliate member of National Association of Independent Schools; member of Secondary School Admission Test Board and Canadian Association of Independent Schools. Language of instruction: English. Endowment: CAN$500,000. Total enrollment: 339. Upper school average class size: 18. Upper school faculty-student ratio: 1:8. There are 168 required school days per year for Upper School students. Upper School students typically attend 5 days per week. The average school day consists of 7 hours.
Upper School Student Profile Grade 8: 23 students (23 girls); Grade 9: 18 students (18 girls); Grade 10: 39 students (39 girls); Grade 11: 26 students (26 girls); Grade 12: 35 students (35 girls). 3 provinces are represented in upper school student body.
Faculty School total: 45. In upper school: 3 men, 18 women; 9 have advanced degrees; 3 reside on campus.
Subjects Offered Acting, advanced math, advanced studio art-AP, animal science, applied skills, art, athletics, band, biology, business education, business skills, calculus, calculus-AP, Canadian history, career and personal planning, career exploration, chemistry, choir, chorus, college planning, communications, computer science, creative writing, diversity studies, drama, drama performance, dramatic arts, engineering, English, English language-AP, English literature, English-AP, environmental science-AP, equestrian sports, equine management, equine science, equitation, ESL, finance, fine arts, food and nutrition, French, geography, grammar, guitar, health, history, home economics, information technology, instrumental music, international relations, international studies, Japanese, jazz ensemble, journalism, law, leadership, leadership and service, Mandarin, mathematics, media, media arts, music, music composition, music theory, outdoor education, photography, physical education, physics, science, social issues, social studies, society, politics and law, speech, sports, sports psychology, textiles, theater, visual arts, world history, writing, yearbook.
Graduation Requirements Applied skills, arts and fine arts (art, music, dance, drama), career and personal planning, English, language arts, life skills, mathematics, physical education (includes health), science, social studies (includes history). Community service is required.
Special Academic Programs Advanced Placement exam preparation; independent study; study at local college for college credit; academic accommodation for the gifted, the musically talented, and the artistically talented; ESL (39 students enrolled).
College Admission Counseling 31 students graduated in 2015; all went to college, including Queen's University at Kingston; The University of Western Ontario; University of Alberta; University of Guelph; University of Toronto; University of Victoria.
Student Life Upper grades have uniform requirement, student council, honor system. Discipline rests primarily with faculty. Attendance at religious services is required.
Summer Programs Enrichment, ESL, sports programs offered; session focuses on ESL group camps and equestrian riding; held on campus; accepts boys and girls; open to students from other schools. 15 students usually enrolled. 2016 schedule: June 25 to August 29. Application deadline: April 10.
Tuition and Aid Day student tuition: CAN$11,300–CAN$13,500; 5-day tuition and room/board: CAN$36,700; 7-day tuition and room/board: CAN$43,100–CAN$59,200. Tuition installment plan (Insured Tuition Payment Plan, monthly payment plans, individually arranged payment plans). Tuition reduction for siblings, bursaries, merit scholarship grants, need-based scholarship grants, staff tuition discount available. In 2015–16, 33% of upper-school students received aid; total upper-school merit-scholarship money awarded: CAN$50,000. Total amount of financial aid awarded in 2015–16: CAN$150,000.
Admissions Traditional secondary-level entrance grade is 8. Deadline for receipt of application materials: none. Application fee required: CAN$200. Interview required.

Athletics Interscholastic: aquatics, badminton, basketball (b), cross-country running (b), dressage, equestrian sports (b), field hockey, golf, horseback riding (b), running (b), soccer (b), swimming and diving, track and field (b), volleyball (b); intramural: aerobics, aerobics/dance, football (b), modern dance, rafting, rappelling, rugby (b), sailing, scuba diving, sea rescue, snowshoeing, surfing, track and field (b), ultimate Frisbee, volleyball (b), wrestling (b), yoga (b); coed intramural: alpine skiing, aquatics, archery, backpacking, badminton, ball hockey, baseball, basketball, bowling, canoeing/kayaking, climbing, cooperative games, cross-country running, curling, dance, dressage, equestrian sports, field hockey, figure skating, fitness, flag football, floor hockey, freestyle skiing, Frisbee, golf, gymnastics, hiking/backpacking, hockey, horseback riding, ice skating, kayaking, martial arts, ocean paddling, outdoor activities, outdoor adventure, outdoor education, outdoor recreation, outdoor skills, outdoors, paddling, physical fitness, physical training, rock climbing, ropes courses, rounders, rugby, skiing (downhill), snowboarding, soccer, softball, street hockey, strength & conditioning, swimming and diving, touch football, walking, weight training. 1 PE instructor, 4 coaches, 2 athletic trainers.
Computers Computers are regularly used in all academic, art, career education, career exploration, college planning, creative writing, English, ESL, French, information technology, introduction to technology, journalism, mathematics, media arts, media production, science, social sciences, technology classes. Computer network features include on-campus library services, Internet access, wireless campus network, Internet filtering or blocking technology. Campus intranet and student e-mail accounts are available to students. The school has a published electronic and media policy.
Contact Admissions Coordinator. 250-746-4185 Ext. 237. Fax: 250-746-4187. E-mail: admissions@qms.bc.ca. Website: www.qms.bc.ca

QUINTE CHRISTIAN HIGH SCHOOL

138 Wallbridge-Loyalist Road
RR 2
Belleville, Ontario K8N 4Z2, Canada

Head of School: Mr. John VanderWindt

General Information Coeducational day college-preparatory, general academic, arts, business, vocational, religious studies, bilingual studies, and technology school, affiliated with Christian faith, Protestant faith. Grades 9–12. Founded: 1977. Setting: suburban. Nearest major city is Toronto, Canada. 25-acre campus. 1 building on campus. Approved or accredited by Christian Schools International, Ontario Ministry of Education, and Ontario Department of Education. Language of instruction: English. Total enrollment: 148. Upper school average class size: 15. Upper school faculty-student ratio: 1:15. There are 176 required school days per year for Upper School students. Upper School students typically attend 5 days per week. The average school day consists of 6 hours and 10 minutes.
Upper School Student Profile 90% of students are Christian, Protestant.
Faculty School total: 16. In upper school: 9 men, 7 women; 2 have advanced degrees.
Subjects Offered Accounting, art, Bible, biology, calculus, careers, chemistry, Christian education, civics, computers, drama, English, English literature, ESL, French, geography, history, law, leadership education training, mathematics, mathematics-AP, media, music, peer counseling, physical education, physics, religious education, science, shop, society challenge and change, technical education, transportation technology, world issues, world religions.
Graduation Requirements Accounting, applied arts, careers, Christian education, civics, computers, English, French, geography, mathematics, physical education (includes health), religious education, science, social studies (includes history), world religions, Ontario Christian School diploma requirements.
Special Academic Programs Special instructional classes for students with learning disabilities.
College Admission Counseling Colleges students went to include Calvin College; Dordt College; Queen's University at Kingston; Redeemer University College; University of Guelph; University of Waterloo. 100% scored over 26 on composite ACT.
Student Life Upper grades have specified standards of dress, student council, honor system. Discipline rests primarily with faculty. Attendance at religious services is required.
Tuition and Aid Day student tuition: CAN$12,200. Tuition installment plan (monthly payment plans, individually arranged payment plans). Tuition reduction for siblings, need-based scholarship grants available. In 2015–16, 18% of upper-school students received aid.
Admissions Traditional secondary-level entrance grade is 9. Deadline for receipt of application materials: March 31. Application fee required: CAN$500. Interview required.
Athletics Interscholastic: badminton (boys, girls), basketball (b,g), cross-country running (b,g), track and field (b,g), volleyball (b,g); coed interscholastic: badminton; coed intramural: badminton, basketball, fitness walking, indoor soccer, physical training, volleyball. 3 PE instructors.
Computers Computers are regularly used in all classes. Computer network features include on-campus library services, Internet access, wireless campus network, Internet filtering or blocking technology. Campus intranet, student e-mail accounts, and computer access in designated common areas are available to students. The school has a published electronic and media policy.

Contact Mrs. Sharon Siderius, Administrative Assistant. 613-968-7870. Fax: 613-968-7970. E-mail: admin@qchs.ca. Website: www.qchs.ca

RABUN GAP-NACOOCHEE SCHOOL

339 Nacoochee Drive
Rabun Gap, Georgia 30568
Head of School: Dr. Anthony Sgro

General Information Coeducational boarding and day college-preparatory, arts, ESL, and performing arts school, affiliated with Presbyterian Church. Boarding grades 7–12, day grades 5–12. Founded: 1903. Setting: rural. Nearest major city is Atlanta. Students are housed in single-sex dormitories. 1,400-acre campus. 14 buildings on campus. Approved or accredited by North Carolina Association of Independent Schools, Southern Association of Colleges and Schools, Southern Association of Independent Schools, The Association of Boarding Schools, and Georgia Department of Education. Member of National Association of Independent Schools and Secondary School Admission Test Board. Endowment: $50 million. Total enrollment: 423. Upper school average class size: 16. Upper school faculty-student ratio: 1:10. There are 172 required school days per year for Upper School students. Upper School students typically attend 5 days per week. The average school day consists of 6 hours and 15 minutes.

Upper School Student Profile Grade 9: 69 students (39 boys, 30 girls); Grade 10: 81 students (44 boys, 37 girls); Grade 11: 93 students (46 boys, 47 girls); Grade 12: 76 students (44 boys, 32 girls). 63% of students are boarding students. 65% are state residents. 15 states are represented in upper school student body. 26% are international students. International students from Bahamas, China, Germany, Mexico, Republic of Korea, and Taiwan; 22 other countries represented in student body. 10% of students are Presbyterian.

Faculty School total: 54. In upper school: 19 men, 21 women; 26 have advanced degrees; 49 reside on campus.

Subjects Offered Advanced Placement courses, algebra, American literature, anatomy, ancient world history, art, art history, art history-AP, band, Bible studies, biology, biology-AP, botany, calculus-AP, chemistry, chemistry-AP, chorus, computer-aided design, creative writing, economics, English language-AP, English literature-AP, environmental science, environmental science-AP, ESL, European history-AP, French, French-AP, geography, geometry, government, government-AP, health, health education, history-AP, honors algebra, honors English, honors U.S. history, honors world history, industrial arts, journalism, life science, mathematics, modern European history-AP, modern world history, music, orchestra, physical education, physical science, physics, physics-AP, pre-algebra, pre-calculus, probability and statistics, psychology, science, Spanish, Spanish language-AP, Spanish-AP, studio art-AP, theater, U.S. government and politics-AP, U.S. history, U.S. history-AP, wind ensemble, world geography, world history, world literature, yearbook.

Graduation Requirements Algebra, ancient world history, arts and fine arts (art, music, dance, drama), biology, chemistry, English, foreign language, geometry, mathematics, modern world history, physical education (includes health), physics, religion (includes Bible studies and theology), science, social studies (includes history), U.S. history, participation in Intersession/G.A.P. week, science symposium, Project Eagle.

Special Academic Programs 12 Advanced Placement exams for which test preparation is offered; honors section; independent study; study abroad; ESL (16 students enrolled).

College Admission Counseling 75 students graduated in 2015; 72 went to college, including Berry College; Emory University; Georgia Institute of Technology; The University of North Carolina at Chapel Hill; Vanderbilt University. Other: 3 went to work. Mean SAT critical reading: 503, mean SAT math: 544, mean SAT writing: 506, mean combined SAT: 1553, mean composite ACT: 23.

Student Life Upper grades have uniform requirement, student council, honor system. Discipline rests equally with students and faculty. Attendance at religious services is required.

Summer Programs Remediation, advancement, sports programs offered; session focuses on fall sports team preparation, math remedial, and enrichment programs; held both on and off campus; held at online; accepts boys and girls; not open to students from other schools. 130 students usually enrolled. 2016 schedule: June 1 to August 22.

Tuition and Aid Day student tuition: $18,390; 7-day tuition and room/board: $46,610. Tuition installment plan (monthly payment plans, semester payment plan). Merit scholarship grants, need-based scholarship grants, tuition remission for children of faculty and staff available. In 2015–16, 76% of upper-school students received aid; total upper-school merit-scholarship money awarded: $300,000. Total amount of financial aid awarded in 2015–16: $5,000,000.

Admissions Traditional secondary-level entrance grade is 9. For fall 2015, 365 students applied for upper-level admission, 196 were accepted, 81 enrolled. ISEE, SSAT or TOEFL required. Deadline for receipt of application materials: February 5. Application fee required: $85. Interview required.

Athletics Interscholastic: baseball (boys), basketball (b,g), cross-country running (b,g), football (b), soccer (b,g), softball (g), swimming and diving (b,g), tennis (b,g), volleyball (g), wrestling (b); intramural: soccer (b,g), swimming and diving (b,g), tennis (b,g); coed interscholastic: Circus, dance team, golf, marksmanship, riflery, skeet shooting, tennis; coed intramural: aerobics/dance, backpacking, ballet, basketball,

bicycling, canoeing/kayaking, Circus, climbing, combined training, dance, dance team, fitness, fitness walking, hiking/backpacking, kayaking, modern dance, mountain biking, Nautilus, outdoor activities, physical training, rafting, rock climbing, strength & conditioning, swimming and diving, tennis, triathlon, ultimate Frisbee, wall climbing, weight lifting, weight training, yoga. 1 PE instructor, 22 coaches, 1 athletic trainer.

Computers Computers are regularly used in English, library skills, literary magazine, technical drawing, theater arts, writing, yearbook classes. Computer network features include on-campus library services, online commercial services, Internet access, wireless campus network, Internet filtering or blocking technology, application and re-enrollment online services. Campus intranet, student e-mail accounts, and computer access in designated common areas are available to students. Students grades are available online. The school has a published electronic and media policy.

Contact Mrs. Kathy Watts, Admission Assistant. 706-746-7720. Fax: 706-746-7797. E-mail: kwatts@rabungap.org. Website: www.rabungap.org

RACINE LUTHERAN HIGH SCHOOL

251 Luedtke Avenue
Racine, Wisconsin 53405
Head of School: Mr. David S. Burgess

General Information College-preparatory and general academic school, affiliated with Lutheran Church–Missouri Synod. Founded: 1944. Setting: urban. Nearest major city is Milwaukee. 1 building on campus. Approved or accredited by North Central Association of Colleges and Schools and Wisconsin Department of Education. Upper school average class size: 15.

Upper School Student Profile 46% of students are Lutheran Church–Missouri Synod.

Faculty School total: 18. In upper school: 11 men, 7 women; 5 have advanced degrees.

Special Academic Programs 4 Advanced Placement exams for which test preparation is offered; study at local college for college credit.

Student Life Upper grades have specified standards of dress, student council, honor system. Discipline rests primarily with faculty.

Tuition and Aid Tuition installment plan (FACTS Tuition Payment Plan, monthly payment plans). Tuition reduction for siblings, merit scholarship grants, need-based scholarship grants, Government-funded school choice vouchers, Church grants available. In 2015–16, 75% of upper-school students received aid.

Admissions Deadline for receipt of application materials: none. No application fee required. Interview recommended.

Athletics Interscholastic: baseball (boys), basketball (b,g), cheering (b,g), football (b), golf (b), soccer (b,g), softball (g), strength & conditioning (b,g), track and field (b,g), trap and skeet (b,g), volleyball (b,g).

Contact Mrs. Susie Drummond, Director of Admissions. 262-637-6538. Fax: 262-637-6601. E-mail: sdrummond@racinelutheran.org. Website: www.racinelutheran.org/

RAMONA CONVENT SECONDARY SCHOOL

1701 West Ramona Road
Alhambra, California 91803-3080
Head of School: Ms. Mary E. Mansell

General Information Girls' day college-preparatory, arts, business, religious studies, bilingual studies, and technology school, affiliated with Roman Catholic Church. Grades 9–12. Founded: 1889. Setting: suburban. Nearest major city is Los Angeles. 19-acre campus. 10 buildings on campus. Approved or accredited by Western Association of Schools and Colleges, Western Catholic Education Association, and California Department of Education. Endowment: $2 million. Upper school average class size: 22. Upper school faculty-student ratio: 1:9. There are 180 required school days per year for Upper School students. Upper School students typically attend 5 days per week. The average school day consists of 6 hours and 30 minutes.

Upper School Student Profile Grade 9: 65 students (65 girls); Grade 10: 60 students (60 girls); Grade 11: 65 students (65 girls); Grade 12: 60 students (60 girls). 80% of students are Roman Catholic.

Faculty School total: 30. In upper school: 6 men, 24 women; all have advanced degrees.

Subjects Offered Advanced Placement courses, advanced studio art-AP, algebra, American history, American literature, art history, Bible studies, biology, biology-AP, calculus, calculus-AP, ceramics, chemistry, chemistry-AP, computer programming, computer science, dance, drama, economics, English, English literature, environmental science, European history, European history-AP, fine arts, French, French-AP, geography, geometry, government/civics, grammar, graphic arts, health, history, honors English, honors geometry, mathematics, music, photography, physical education, physics, pre-calculus, religion, science, social sciences, social studies, Spanish, Spanish language-AP, Spanish literature-AP, speech, theater, theology, trigonometry, U.S. government and politics-AP, visual arts, word processing, world history, world literature.

Graduation Requirements Arts and fine arts (art, music, dance, drama), business skills (includes word processing), computer science, English, foreign language, mathematics, physical education (includes health), religion (includes Bible studies and theology), science, social studies (includes history), speech.

Special Academic Programs Advanced Placement exam preparation; honors section; independent study; study abroad; academic accommodation for the gifted, the musically talented, and the artistically talented.

College Admission Counseling 89 students graduated in 2015; all went to college, including California State University, Los Angeles; Loyola Marymount University; Mount Saint Mary's University; Pitzer College; University of California, Irvine; University of California, Los Angeles. Mean SAT critical reading: 532, mean SAT math: 511, mean SAT writing: 536.

Student Life Upper grades have uniform requirement, student council, honor system. Discipline rests primarily with faculty. Attendance at religious services is required.

Summer Programs Remediation, enrichment, advancement, sports, art/fine arts, computer instruction programs offered; session focuses on academics; held on campus; accepts boys and girls; open to students from other schools. 200 students usually enrolled. 2016 schedule: June 27 to July 22. Application deadline: June 1.

Tuition and Aid Day student tuition: $13,025. Tuition installment plan (monthly payment plans, quarterly and semester payment plans). Merit scholarship grants, need-based scholarship grants, paying campus jobs available. In 2015–16, 33% of upper-school students received aid; total upper-school merit-scholarship money awarded: $18,000. Total amount of financial aid awarded in 2015–16: $350,000.

Admissions Traditional secondary-level entrance grade is 9. High School Placement Test required. Deadline for receipt of application materials: January 20. Application fee required: $100. On-campus interview required.

Athletics Interscholastic: basketball, cross-country running, soccer, softball, swimming and diving, tennis, track and field, volleyball. 1 PE instructor, 9 coaches.

Computers Computers are regularly used in all academic classes. Computer network features include on-campus library services, Internet access, wireless campus network, Internet filtering or blocking technology. Student e-mail accounts and computer access in designated common areas are available to students. Students grades are available online. The school has a published electronic and media policy.

Contact Mrs. Veronica Fernandez, Associate Director of Enrollment and Public Relations. 626-282-4151 Ext. 168. Fax: 626-281-0797. E-mail: vfernandez@ramonaconvent.org. Website: www.ramonaconvent.org

RANDOLPH-MACON ACADEMY

200 Academy Drive
Front Royal, Virginia 22630

Head of School: Brig. Gen. David Wesley

General Information Coeducational boarding and day college-preparatory, religious studies, technology, Air Force Junior ROTC, ESL, and military school, affiliated with Methodist Church. Grades 6–PG. Founded: 1892. Setting: small town. Nearest major city is Washington, DC. Students are housed in single-sex dormitories. 135-acre campus. 9 buildings on campus. Approved or accredited by Southern Association of Colleges and Schools, The Association of Boarding Schools, University Senate of United Methodist Church, Virginia Association of Independent Schools, and Virginia Department of Education. Member of National Association of Independent Schools. Languages of instruction: English and French. Endowment: $6.7 million. Total enrollment: 293. Upper school average class size: 12. Upper school faculty-student ratio: 1:7. There are 180 required school days per year for Upper School students. Upper School students typically attend 5 days per week. The average school day consists of 7 hours.

Upper School Student Profile Grade 6: 7 students (7 boys); Grade 7: 17 students (10 boys, 7 girls); Grade 8: 29 students (23 boys, 6 girls); Grade 9: 39 students (24 boys, 15 girls); Grade 10: 71 students (49 boys, 22 girls); Grade 11: 70 students (53 boys, 17 girls); Grade 12: 76 students (52 boys, 24 girls); Postgraduate: 5 students (2 boys, 3 girls). 81% of students are boarding students. 39% are state residents. 20 states are represented in upper school student body. 29% are international students. International students from Angola, China, Democratic People's Republic of Korea, Nigeria, Saudi Arabia, and Viet Nam; 15 other countries represented in student body. 13.6% of students are Methodist.

Faculty School total: 34. In upper school: 24 men, 10 women; 23 have advanced degrees; 15 reside on campus.

Subjects Offered Advanced math, aerospace science, algebra, American government, American history, American history-AP, American literature, American literature-AP, anatomy, anatomy and physiology, art, art history, art history-AP, Asian history, aviation, band, Bible studies, biology, biology-AP, British literature, calculus, calculus-AP, career education, chemistry, chorus, college counseling, comparative religion, composition-AP, computer applications, computer literacy, conceptual physics, concert band, concert choir, critical thinking, desktop publishing, discrete mathematics, drama, English, English composition, English literature, English literature and composition-AP, English-AP, epic literature, ESL, flight instruction, geography, geometry, German, German-AP, government/civics, handbells, history, honors algebra, honors English, honors geometry, honors U.S. history, independent study, journalism, JROTC, keyboarding, life management skills, mathematics, music, music appreciation, New Testament, personal finance, personal fitness, photography, physical education, physics, physics-AP, physiology, pre-algebra, pre-calculus, psychology, religion, SAT preparation, science, senior seminar, Shakespeare, social studies, Spanish, Spanish literature-AP, speech and debate, statistics-AP, studio art, theater arts, trigonometry, U.S. government, U.S. history, world history, yearbook.

Graduation Requirements Aerospace science, arts and fine arts (art, music, dance, drama), computer science, English, foreign language, mathematics, physical education (includes health), religion (includes Bible studies and theology), science, social studies (includes history), Air Force Junior ROTC for each year student is enrolled.

Special Academic Programs Advanced Placement exam preparation; honors section; independent study; study at local college for college credit; study abroad; academic accommodation for the gifted; ESL (18 students enrolled).

College Admission Counseling 66 students graduated in 2015; all went to college, including George Mason University; Howard University; Michigan State University; The College of William and Mary; Virginia Military Institute; Virginia Polytechnic Institute and State University. Median SAT critical reading: 486, median SAT math: 557, median SAT writing: 485, median combined SAT: 1582, median composite ACT: 22.

Student Life Upper grades have uniform requirement, student council, honor system. Discipline rests equally with students and faculty. Attendance at religious services is required.

Summer Programs Remediation, enrichment, advancement, ESL, art/fine arts, computer instruction programs offered; session focuses on remediation, new courses, ESL, flight, college counseling; held on campus; accepts boys and girls; open to students from other schools. 180 students usually enrolled. 2016 schedule: July 3 to July 29. Application deadline: June 1.

Tuition and Aid Day student tuition: $17,814; 7-day tuition and room/board: $34,565. Tuition installment plan (monthly payment plans, 2-payment plan). Tuition reduction for siblings, merit scholarship grants, need-based scholarship grants, paying campus jobs, Methodist Church scholarships available. In 2015–16, 36% of upper-school students received aid; total upper-school merit-scholarship money awarded: $70,000. Total amount of financial aid awarded in 2015–16: $304,242.

Admissions Traditional secondary-level entrance grade is 9. For fall 2015, 157 students applied for upper-level admission, 147 were accepted, 110 enrolled. Any standardized test or SSAT required. Deadline for receipt of application materials: none. Application fee required: $75. Interview required.

Athletics Interscholastic: baseball (boys), basketball (b,g), cross-country running (b,g), football (b), lacrosse (b), soccer (b,g), softball (g), swimming and diving (b,g), tennis (b,g), track and field (b,g), volleyball (b,g), wrestling (b); intramural: basketball (b,g), horseback riding (g), independent competitive sports (b,g), soccer (b,g), softball (g), strength & conditioning (b,g), swimming and diving (b,g), tennis (b,g), track and field (b,g), volleyball (b,g); coed interscholastic: cheering, drill team, golf, JROTC drill; coed intramural: golf, horseback riding, indoor soccer, jogging, JROTC drill, outdoor activities, outdoor recreation, physical fitness, soccer, strength & conditioning, swimming and diving, table tennis, volleyball, weight lifting, weight training. 2 PE instructors, 1 athletic trainer.

Computers Computers are regularly used in aerospace science, aviation, English, ESL, foreign language, independent study, mathematics, science, yearbook classes. Computer network features include on-campus library services, online commercial services, Internet access, wireless campus network, Internet filtering or blocking technology. Campus intranet and student e-mail accounts are available to students. Students grades are available online. The school has a published electronic and media policy.

Contact Ms. Juliette Michael, Admission Assistant. 540-636-5484. Fax: 540-636-5419. E-mail: jmichael@rma.edu. Website: www.rma.edu

RANDOLPH SCHOOL

1005 Drake Avenue SE
Huntsville, Alabama 35802

Head of School: Mr. James E. Rainey Jr.

General Information Coeducational day college-preparatory and arts school. Grades K–12. Founded: 1959. Setting: suburban. 67-acre campus. 3 buildings on campus. Approved or accredited by Southern Association of Colleges and Schools, Southern Association of Independent Schools, and The College Board. Member of National Association of Independent Schools. Endowment: $16 million. Total enrollment: 969. Upper school average class size: 13. Upper school faculty-student ratio: 1:10. There are 182 required school days per year for Upper School students. Upper School students typically attend 5 days per week. The average school day consists of 7 hours.

Upper School Student Profile Grade 9: 95 students (40 boys, 55 girls); Grade 10: 94 students (45 boys, 49 girls); Grade 11: 86 students (39 boys, 47 girls); Grade 12: 101 students (50 boys, 51 girls).

Faculty School total: 140. In upper school: 18 men, 22 women; 32 have advanced degrees.

Subjects Offered 3-dimensional art, acting, algebra, American history, American history-AP, American literature, anatomy, art, art-AP, band, biology, biology-AP, calculus, calculus-AP, ceramics, chemistry, chemistry-AP, comparative government and politics-AP, computer math, concert choir, creative writing, drama, drama workshop, economics, English, English literature, English-AP, environmental science, European history, European history-AP, film appreciation, filmmaking, fine arts, French, French-AP, geometry, history, journalism, Latin, marine biology, mathematics, music, music theory-AP, physical education, physics, physics-AP, physiology, psychology, science, social studies, Southern literature, Spanish, Spanish-AP, speech, stage design, stagecraft, student publications, studio art-AP, theater, trigonometry, U.S. government and politics-AP, U.S. history-AP, world history, world history-AP, world literature, writing, yearbook.

Graduation Requirements Algebra, arts and fine arts (art, music, dance, drama), biology, chemistry, English, foreign language, geometry, health, literature, mathematics, science, social studies (includes history), U.S. history, world history.

Special Academic Programs 12 Advanced Placement exams for which test preparation is offered; honors section; independent study; study at local college for college credit.

College Admission Counseling 91 students graduated in 2015; 89 went to college, including Auburn University; Birmingham-Southern College; Emory University; Oxford College; Samford University; Texas Christian University; The University of Alabama. Other: 2 had other specific plans. Mean SAT critical reading: 575, mean SAT math: 581, mean SAT writing: 584, mean combined SAT: 1741, mean composite ACT: 28. 38% scored over 600 on SAT critical reading, 41% scored over 600 on SAT math, 46% scored over 600 on SAT writing, 41% scored over 1800 on combined SAT, 40% scored over 26 on composite ACT.

Student Life Upper grades have specified standards of dress, student council, honor system. Discipline rests equally with students and faculty.

Summer Programs Enrichment, sports, art/fine arts programs offered; session focuses on sports, arts, academics; held on campus; accepts boys and girls; open to students from other schools. 140 students usually enrolled. 2016 schedule: June 1 to June 30. Application deadline: none.

Tuition and Aid Day student tuition: $13,890–$18,990. Tuition installment plan (Insured Tuition Payment Plan, 2- and 10-month payment plans). Need-based scholarship grants, middle-income loans available. In 2014–15, 9% of upper-school students received aid. Total amount of financial aid awarded in 2014–15: $258,240.

Admissions Traditional secondary-level entrance grade is 9. For fall 2015, 30 students applied for upper-level admission, 24 were accepted, 21 enrolled. ISEE, PSAT and SAT for applicants to grade 11 and 12, SSAT or writing sample required. Deadline for receipt of application materials: none. No application fee required. On-campus interview required.

Athletics Interscholastic: baseball (boys), basketball (b,g), bowling (b,g), cheering (g), cross-country running (b,g), diving (b,g), football (b), golf (b,g), indoor track & field (b,g), physical fitness (b,g), physical training (b,g), soccer (b,g), softball (g), swimming and diving (b,g), tennis (b,g), track and field (b,g), volleyball (g), winter (indoor) track (b,g); coed interscholastic: diving. 2 PE instructors, 19 coaches, 2 athletic trainers.

Computers Computers are regularly used in all academic classes. Computer network features include on-campus library services, online commercial services, Internet access, wireless campus network, Internet filtering or blocking technology, laptops, netbooks, iPads. Campus intranet, student e-mail accounts, and computer access in designated common areas are available to students. Students grades are available online. The school has a published electronic and media policy.

Contact Glynn Below, Director of Admissions. 256-799-6104. Fax: 256-881-1784. E-mail: gbelow@randolphschool.net. Website: www.randolphschool.net

RANSOM EVERGLADES SCHOOL

3575 Main Highway
Miami, Florida 33133

Head of School: Mrs. Stephanie G. Townsend

General Information Coeducational day college-preparatory school. Grades 6–12. Founded: 1903. Setting: urban. 11-acre campus. 19 buildings on campus. Approved or accredited by Southern Association of Colleges and Schools, Southern Association of Independent Schools, and Florida Department of Education. Member of National Association of Independent Schools and Secondary School Admission Test Board. Endowment: $28.6 million. Total enrollment: 1,085. Upper school average class size: 15. Upper school faculty-student ratio: 1:9. There are 172 required school days per year for Upper School students. Upper School students typically attend 5 days per week. The average school day consists of 5 hours and 40 minutes.

Upper School Student Profile Grade 9: 156 students (82 boys, 74 girls); Grade 10: 150 students (85 boys, 65 girls); Grade 11: 159 students (84 boys, 75 girls); Grade 12: 147 students (75 boys, 72 girls).

Faculty School total: 112. In upper school: 27 men, 30 women; 41 have advanced degrees.

Subjects Offered Advanced Placement courses, algebra, American history, American history-AP, American literature, anatomy and physiology, art, art history, art history-AP, Asian studies, astronomy, band, biology, calculus, calculus-AP, ceramics, chemistry, chemistry-AP, Chinese, choir, chorus, college counseling, comparative government and politics-AP, computer math, computer programming, computer science, computer science-AP, computer-aided design, concert band, creative writing, dance, dance performance, debate, digital photography, drama, earth science, ecology, economics, economics-AP, engineering, English, English literature, English literature and composition-AP, English-AP, environmental science, environmental science-AP, environmental studies, ethical decision making, ethics, ethics and responsibility, European history, European history-AP, experiential education, fine arts, French, French language-AP, French-AP, geography, geology, geometry, government and politics-AP, government/civics, grammar, graphic design, guitar, health, health and wellness, history, history-AP, human anatomy, interdisciplinary studies, jazz ensemble, journalism, macro/microeconomics-AP, macroeconomics-AP, Mandarin, marine

biology, mathematics, mathematics-AP, music, music theory, music theory-AP, music-AP, mythology, philosophy, photography, physical education, physics, physics-AP, probability and statistics, psychology, psychology-AP, robotics, science, sculpture, social studies, sociology, Spanish, Spanish language-AP, Spanish literature-AP, speech, speech and debate, statistics, statistics-AP, strings, theater, theory of knowledge, trigonometry, U.S. government and politics-AP, U.S. history, U.S. history-AP, world history, world history-AP, world literature, writing, yearbook.

Graduation Requirements Arts and fine arts (art, music, dance, drama), computer science, English, foreign language, mathematics, physical education (includes health), science, social studies (includes history).

Special Academic Programs 26 Advanced Placement exams for which test preparation is offered; honors section.

College Admission Counseling 153 students graduated in 2015; all went to college, including Columbia University; New York University; The George Washington University; University of Miami; University of Pennsylvania. Median SAT critical reading: 660, median SAT math: 675, median SAT writing: 675, median combined SAT: 2020, median composite ACT: 31. 81% scored over 600 on SAT critical reading, 90% scored over 600 on SAT math, 88% scored over 600 on SAT writing, 86% scored over 1800 on combined SAT, 92% scored over 26 on composite ACT.

Student Life Upper grades have specified standards of dress, student council, honor system. Discipline rests primarily with faculty.

Summer Programs Enrichment, advancement, computer instruction programs offered; session focuses on enrichment to reinforce basic skills and advancement for credit; held on campus; accepts boys and girls; open to students from other schools. 90 students usually enrolled. 2016 schedule: June 20 to July 29. Application deadline: May 29.

Tuition and Aid Day student tuition: $34,100. Tuition installment plan (monthly payment plans, 60%/40% payment plan). Need-based scholarship grants available. In 2015–16, 17% of upper-school students received aid. Total amount of financial aid awarded in 2015–16: $3,130,377.

Admissions Traditional secondary-level entrance grade is 9. For fall 2015, 103 students applied for upper-level admission, 18 were accepted, 15 enrolled. SSAT required. Deadline for receipt of application materials: December 1. Application fee required: $100. On-campus interview required.

Athletics Interscholastic: baseball (boys), basketball (b,g), canoeing/kayaking (b,g), cheering (g), crew (b,g), cross-country running (b,g), dance (g), dance team (g), football (b), golf (b,g), kayaking (b,g), lacrosse (b,g), physical training (b,g), sailing (b,g), soccer (b,g), softball (g), swimming and diving (b,g), tennis (b,g), track and field (b,g), volleyball (b,g), water polo (b,g), wrestling (b); coed interscholastic: crew, kayaking, sailing. 4 PE instructors, 80 coaches, 2 athletic trainers.

Computers Computers are regularly used in all classes. Computer network features include on-campus library services, online commercial services, Internet access, wireless campus network, Internet filtering or blocking technology. Student e-mail accounts and computer access in designated common areas are available to students. Students grades are available online. The school has a published electronic and media policy.

Contact Amy Sayfie Zichella, Director of Admission. 305-250-6875. Fax: 305-854-1846. E-mail: asayfie@ransomeverglades.org. Website: www.ransomeverglades.org

RAVENSCROFT SCHOOL

7409 Falls of the Neuse Road
Raleigh, North Carolina 27615

Head of School: Mrs. Doreen C. Kelly

General Information Coeducational day college-preparatory, arts, and technology school. Grades PK–12. Founded: 1862. Setting: suburban. 127-acre campus. 13 buildings on campus. Approved or accredited by Southern Association of Colleges and Schools, Southern Association of Independent Schools, and North Carolina Department of Education. Member of National Association of Independent Schools. Endowment: $15 million. Total enrollment: 1,169. Upper school average class size: 13. Upper school faculty-student ratio: 1:8. There are 176 required school days per year for Upper School students. Upper School students typically attend 5 days per week. The average school day consists of 7 hours and 30 minutes.

Upper School Student Profile Grade 6: 105 students (42 boys, 63 girls); Grade 7: 101 students (54 boys, 47 girls); Grade 8: 106 students (56 boys, 50 girls); Grade 9: 130 students (66 boys, 64 girls); Grade 10: 112 students (57 boys, 55 girls); Grade 11: 110 students (58 boys, 52 girls); Grade 12: 111 students (62 boys, 49 girls).

Faculty School total: 156. In upper school: 28 men, 26 women; 42 have advanced degrees.

Subjects Offered Advanced Placement courses, algebra, American history, American literature, anatomy, art, art history, astronomy, biology, biotechnology, calculus, chemistry, computer programming, computer science, discrete mathematics, drama, economics, engineering, English, English literature, environmental science, environmental science-AP, European history, expository writing, fine arts, French, geometry, government/civics, health, history, journalism, Latin, mathematics, music, photography, physical education, physics, psychology, science, social sciences, social studies, Spanish, speech, sports medicine, stagecraft, statistics-AP, theater, world history, writing.

Graduation Requirements Arts and fine arts (art, music, dance, drama), composition, English, foreign language, mathematics, physical education (includes health), science, social sciences, social studies (includes history). Community service is required.

Special Academic Programs 24 Advanced Placement exams for which test preparation is offered; honors section; independent study; term-away projects; study at local college for college credit; study abroad; academic accommodation for the gifted, the musically talented, and the artistically talented.

College Admission Counseling 119 students graduated in 2015; all went to college, including East Carolina University; Elon University; High Point University; North Carolina State University; The University of North Carolina at Chapel Hill; University of South Carolina. Median SAT critical reading: 610, median SAT math: 630, median SAT writing: 610, median combined SAT: 1860, median composite ACT: 27. 50% scored over 600 on SAT critical reading, 63% scored over 600 on SAT math, 55% scored over 600 on SAT writing, 62% scored over 1800 on combined SAT, 57% scored over 26 on composite ACT.

Student Life Upper grades have specified standards of dress, student council, honor system. Discipline rests equally with students and faculty.

Summer Programs Enrichment, advancement, sports, art/fine arts, computer instruction programs offered; session focuses on enrichment; held on campus; accepts boys and girls; open to students from other schools. 2,000 students usually enrolled. 2016 schedule: June 15 to August 7. Application deadline: none.

Tuition and Aid Day student tuition: $21,720. Tuition installment plan (individually arranged payment plans). Merit scholarship grants, need-based scholarship grants, need-based loans available. In 2015–16, 19% of upper-school students received aid.

Admissions Traditional secondary-level entrance grade is 9. For fall 2015, 184 students applied for upper-level admission, 88 were accepted, 57 enrolled. ERB and SSAT required. Deadline for receipt of application materials: none. Application fee required: $70. On-campus interview required.

Athletics Interscholastic: baseball (boys), basketball (b,g), cheering (g), cross-country running (b,g), dance squad (g), field hockey (g), fitness (b,g), football (b), golf (b,g), lacrosse (b,g), physical training (b,g), soccer (b,g), softball (g), strength & conditioning (b,g), swimming and diving (b,g), tennis (b,g), track and field (b,g), volleyball (g), weight training (b,g), wrestling (b); intramural: baseball (b), basketball (b,g), cheering (g), dance team (g), football (b,g), lacrosse (b), soccer (b,g), softball (g), strength & conditioning (b,g), swimming and diving (b,g), tennis (b,g), track and field (b,g), volleyball (g), wrestling (b); coed interscholastic: life saving. 10 PE instructors, 68 coaches, 2 athletic trainers.

Computers Computers are regularly used in economics, English, foreign language, history, mathematics, science, social studies, writing classes. Computer network features include on-campus library services, online commercial services, Internet access, wireless campus network, Internet filtering or blocking technology, Campus intranet, student e-mail accounts, and computer access in designated common areas are available to students. Students grades are available online. The school has a published electronic and media policy.

Contact Mrs. Toni V. Katen, Assistant to the Director of Admissions. 919-847-0900 Ext. 2227. Fax: 919 846 2371. E mail: admissions@ravenscroft.org. Website: www.ravenscroft.org

REALMS OF INQUIRY

4998 S. Galleria Drive
Murray, Utah 84123

Head of School: Mr. Peter Westman

General Information Coeducational day college-preparatory, general academic, arts, bilingual studies, and outdoor education school; primarily serves gifted students. Grades 6–12. Founded: 1972. Setting: suburban. Nearest major city is Salt Lake City. 2 buildings on campus. Approved or accredited by Northwest Accreditation Commission and Northwest Association of Independent Schools. Total enrollment: 32. Upper school average class size: 20. Upper school faculty-student ratio: 1:8. There are 180 required school days per year for Upper School students. Upper School students typically attend 5 days per week. The average school day consists of 6 hours and 15 minutes.

Upper School Student Profile Grade 6: 4 students (2 boys, 2 girls); Grade 7: 2 students (1 boy, 1 girl); Grade 8: 5 students (2 boys, 3 girls); Grade 9: 7 students (5 boys, 2 girls); Grade 10: 4 students (2 boys, 2 girls); Grade 11: 5 students (5 boys); Grade 12: 5 students (4 boys, 1 girl).

Faculty School total: 4. In upper school: 3 men, 1 woman; 2 have advanced degrees.

Subjects Offered Algebra, art, band, biology, calculus, chemistry, computer literacy, drama, earth science, English, geometry, history, life skills, outdoor education, photography, physical education, physics, pre-calculus, Spanish, writing.

Graduation Requirements Arts and fine arts (art, music, dance, drama), computer science, English, foreign language, mathematics, outdoor education, physical education (includes health), science, social sciences, social studies (includes history), 30 volunteer service hours per year.

Special Academic Programs Accelerated programs; independent study; study at local college for college credit; study abroad; academic accommodation for the gifted,

the musically talented, and the artistically talented; programs in English, mathematics, general development for dyslexic students.

College Admission Counseling 3 students graduated in 2015; 1 went to college, including The University of Montana Western; University of Utah; Westminster College. Other: 2 went to work. Median SAT critical reading: 690, median SAT math: 640, median SAT writing: 670, median combined SAT: 2000, median composite ACT: 28. 100% scored over 600 on SAT critical reading, 100% scored over 600 on SAT math, 100% scored over 600 on SAT writing, 100% scored over 1800 on combined SAT, 100% scored over 26 on composite ACT.

Student Life Upper grades have specified standards of dress, student council, honor system. Discipline rests equally with students and faculty.

Tuition and Aid Day student tuition: $12,900. Tuition installment plan (monthly payment plans, individually arranged payment plans). Tuition reduction for siblings, need-based scholarship grants available. In 2015–16, 10% of upper-school students received aid. Total amount of financial aid awarded in 2015–16: $6600.

Admissions Traditional secondary-level entrance grade is 9. For fall 2015, 6 students applied for upper-level admission, 6 were accepted, 5 enrolled. Admissions testing, WISC-III and Woodcock-Johnson, WISC/Woodcock-Johnson or Woodcock-Johnson required. Deadline for receipt of application materials: none. Application fee required: $25. Interview required.

Athletics Coed Interscholastic: backpacking, bicycling, canoeing/kayaking, climbing, combined training, cooperative games, cross-country running, fishing, fitness, flag football, Frisbee, gymnastics, hiking/backpacking, kayaking, life saving, martial arts, mountain biking, mountaineering, nordic skiing, outdoor activities, outdoor adventure, outdoor education, outdoor recreation, outdoor skills, outdoors, paddling, physical fitness, physical training, project adventure, rafting, rappelling, rock climbing, running, skiing (cross-country), skiing (downhill), snowboarding, snowshoeing, strength & conditioning, swimming and diving, touch football, ultimate Frisbee, walking, wall climbing, weight lifting, weight training, wilderness, wilderness survival, wildernessways, winter walking, yoga.

Computers Computers are regularly used in all academic, career exploration, college planning, commercial art, computer applications, creative writing, current events, design, desktop publishing, digital applications, drafting, drawing and design, engineering, English, foreign language, graphic design, graphics, history, independent study, mathematics, media, media arts, media production, media services, music, photography, photojournalism, publishing, research skills, SAT preparation, science, social sciences, social studies classes. Computer network features include Internet access, wireless campus network. Computer access in designated common areas is available to students. Students grades are available online. The school has a published electronic and media policy.

Contact Karri Van Tongeren, Administrator. 801-467-5911. Fax: 801-590-7701. E-mail: frontdesk@realmsofinquiry.org. Website: www.realmsofinquiry.org

THE RECTORY SCHOOL

Pomfret, Connecticut
See Junior Boarding Schools section.

REDEEMER CHRISTIAN HIGH SCHOOL

82 Colonnade Road North
Ottawa, Ontario K2E 7L2, Canada

Head of School: Mr. Paul Oucis

General Information Coeducational day college-preparatory, general academic, and religious studies school, affiliated with Christian faith. Grades 9–12. Founded: 1975. Setting: urban. 2-acre campus. 1 building on campus. Approved or accredited by Christian Schools International, Ontario Ministry of Education, and Ontario Department of Education. Language of instruction: English. Total enrollment: 149. Upper school average class size: 20. Upper school faculty-student ratio: 1:9. There are 186 required school days per year for Upper School students. Upper School students typically attend 5 days per week. The average school day consists of 6 hours and 20 minutes.

Upper School Student Profile Grade 9: 28 students (8 boys, 20 girls); Grade 10: 42 students (17 boys, 25 girls); Grade 11: 44 students (17 boys, 27 girls); Grade 12: 35 students (17 boys, 18 girls). 95% of students are Christian faith.

Faculty School total: 18. In upper school: 10 men, 8 women; 5 have advanced degrees.

Graduation Requirements Graduating students must have proof they have completed a minimum of 60 volunteer hours in the community.

Student Life Upper grades have uniform requirement, student council, honor system. Discipline rests primarily with faculty. Attendance at religious services is required.

Admissions Traditional secondary-level entrance grade is 9. For fall 2015, 30 students applied for upper-level admission, 29 were accepted, 28 enrolled. Deadline for receipt of application materials: none. Application fee required: CAN$250. Interview required.

Contact Mrs. Mary Joustra, Office Administrator. 613-723-9262 Ext. 21. Fax: 613-723-9321. E-mail: info@rchs.on.ca. Website: www.rchs.on.ca

REDEMPTION CHRISTIAN ACADEMY

154 South Mountain Road
P.O. Box 183
Northfield, Massachusetts 01360

Head of School: Elder John Massey Jr.

General Information Coeducational boarding and day college-preparatory, Agricultural Engineering, and career development school, affiliated with Pentecostal Church. Boarding grades 7–PG, day grades K–PG. Founded: 1979. Setting: rural. Nearest major city is Boston. Students are housed in single-sex dormitories. 100-acre campus. 6 buildings on campus. Approved or accredited by American Association of Christian Schools, Association of Christian Schools International, and Massachusetts Department of Education. Upper school average class size: 10. Upper school faculty-student ratio: 1:8. There are 180 required school days per year for Upper School students. Upper School students typically attend 5 days per week. The average school day consists of 6 hours and 30 minutes.

Upper School Student Profile 100% of students are boarding students. 5% are state residents. 6 states are represented in upper school student body. 45% are international students. International students from Bahamas, Czech Republic, Germany, Ghana, Jamaica, and Venezuela; 4 other countries represented in student body. 31% of students are Pentecostal.

Faculty School total: 8. In upper school: 4 men, 4 women; 2 have advanced degrees; 6 reside on campus.

Subjects Offered African-American literature, algebra, American history, American literature, art, athletic training, basketball, Bible studies, biology, chemistry, choir, communication skills, computer science, current events, earth science, economics, English, English literature, French, geometry, government/civics, health, keyboarding, life skills, mathematics, music, physical education, physics, religion, SAT preparation, science, social sciences, social studies, Spanish, study skills, trigonometry, world history, writing.

Graduation Requirements Art, English, foreign language, health science, keyboarding, mathematics, physical education (includes health), science, social studies (includes history).

Special Academic Programs 6 Advanced Placement exams for which test preparation is offered; accelerated programs; independent study; academic accommodation for the gifted; remedial reading and/or remedial writing; remedial math; programs in English, mathematics, general development for dyslexic students; special instructional classes for students with learning disabilities, Attention Deficit Disorder, emotional and behavioral problems, dyslexia; ESL (5 students enrolled).

College Admission Counseling 7 students graduated in 2015; all went to college.

Student Life Upper grades have uniform requirement, student council, honor system. Discipline rests primarily with faculty.

Summer Programs Remediation, enrichment, advancement, ESL, sports, computer instruction programs offered; session focuses on program for new students and credit recovery; held on campus; accepts boys and girls; open to students from other schools. 2016 schedule: July 5 to August 12. Application deadline: none.

Tuition and Aid Day student tuition: $7000; 5-day tuition and room/board: $19,500; 7-day tuition and room/board: $24,500. Tuition installment plan (individually arranged payment plans, 2-installment payment plan). Tuition reduction for siblings, merit scholarship grants, need-based scholarship grants, tuition work credit, parent fundraiser program available. In 2015–16, 80% of upper-school students received aid; total upper-school merit-scholarship money awarded: $300,000. Total amount of financial aid awarded in 2015–16: $700,000.

Admissions For fall 2015, 20 students applied for upper-level admission, 17 were accepted, 17 enrolled. Deadline for receipt of application materials: none. Application fee required: $50. Interview required.

Athletics Interscholastic: basketball (boys); intramural: aerobics (g), basketball (b,g), outdoor recreation (b,g), physical fitness (b,g), soccer (b,g), volleyball (b,g); coed intramural: archery. 2 PE instructors, 4 coaches, 1 athletic trainer.

Computers Computers are regularly used in English, social sciences classes. Computer network features include Internet access, wireless campus network, Internet filtering or blocking technology. The school has a published electronic and media policy.

Contact Laura Holmes, Vice Principal. 518-272-6679. Fax: 518-270-8039. E-mail: admissions@redemptionchristianacademy.org. Website: www.redemptionchristianacademy.org

REDWOOD CHRISTIAN SCHOOLS

4200 James Avenue
Castro Valley, California 94546

Head of School: Mr. Bruce D. Johnson

General Information Coeducational day college-preparatory and religious studies school, affiliated with Christian faith. Grades K–12. Founded: 1970. Setting: urban. Nearest major city is Oakland. 10-acre campus. 11 buildings on campus. Approved or accredited by Association of Christian Schools International, Western Association of Schools and Colleges, and California Department of Education. Total enrollment: 650. Upper school average class size: 20. Upper school faculty-student ratio: 1:14. There are 175 required school days per year for Upper School students. Upper School students

typically attend 5 days per week. The average school day consists of 6 hours and 50 minutes.

Upper School Student Profile Grade 9: 70 students (43 boys, 27 girls); Grade 10: 70 students (41 boys, 29 girls); Grade 11: 71 students (40 boys, 31 girls); Grade 12: 70 students (36 boys, 34 girls). 50% of students are Christian.

Faculty School total: 30. In upper school: 16 men, 14 women; 9 have advanced degrees.

Subjects Offered Advanced math, Advanced Placement courses, algebra, art, athletics, band, baseball, basketball, Bible studies, biology, calculus-AP, chemistry, choir, civics, computer literacy, concert band, creative writing, drama, drama performance, economics, English, English language and composition-AP, English literature and composition-AP, ensembles, European history-AP, fitness, geometry, honors English, keyboarding, macro/microeconomics-AP, physical education, physical science, physics, softball, Spanish, speech, track and field, trigonometry, U.S. government, U.S. history, vocal music, woodworking, world history, world history-AP, yearbook.

Graduation Requirements Arts and fine arts (art, music, dance, drama), Bible, computer literacy, electives, English, foreign language, mathematics, physical education (includes health), science, speech, world history.

Special Academic Programs Advanced Placement exam preparation; honors section; study at local college for college credit; remedial reading and/or remedial writing; remedial math; programs in English, mathematics, general development for dyslexic students; ESL (26 students enrolled).

College Admission Counseling 76 students graduated in 2015; 71 went to college, including Grand Canyon University; Pepperdine University; University of California, Irvine; University of California, San Diego; University of California, Santa Barbara; University of the Pacific. Other: 2 went to work, 3 entered military service. Mean SAT critical reading: 586, mean SAT math: 555, mean SAT writing: 573, mean combined SAT: 1713.

Student Life Upper grades have specified standards of dress, student council, honor system. Discipline rests primarily with faculty.

Tuition and Aid Day student tuition: $10,029–$25,400. Tuition installment plan (FACTS Tuition Payment Plan, monthly payment plans, individually arranged payment plans). Tuition reduction for siblings, need-based scholarship grants, paying campus jobs available. In 2015–16, 40% of upper-school students received aid. Total amount of financial aid awarded in 2015–16: $420,000.

Admissions Traditional secondary-level entrance grade is 9. For fall 2015, 83 students applied for upper-level admission, 68 were accepted, 54 enrolled. Stanford Achievement Test required. Deadline for receipt of application materials: none. Application fee required: $175. On-campus interview required.

Athletics Interscholastic: baseball (boys), basketball (b,g), cross-country running (b,g), soccer (b,g), softball (g), tennis (b,g), track and field (b,g), volleyball (b,g). 2 PE instructors, 1 coach.

Computers Computers are regularly used in computer applications, keyboarding, yearbook classes. Computer network features include on-campus library services, Internet access, wireless campus network, 1:1 iPad Initiative for grades 9-12. Campus intranet and student e-mail accounts are available to students. Students grades are available online. The school has a published electronic and media policy.

Contact Mrs. Deborah Wright, Administrative Assistant. 510-889-7526. Fax: 510-881-0127. E-mail: deborahwright@rcs.edu. Website: www.rcs.edu

REGIS HIGH SCHOOL

55 East 84th Street
New York, New York 10028-0884

Head of School: Dr. Gary J. Tocchet

General Information Boys' day college-preparatory school, affiliated with Roman Catholic Church. Grades 9–12. Founded: 1914. Setting: urban. 3-acre campus. 1 building on campus. Approved or accredited by Jesuit Secondary Education Association, Middle States Association of Colleges and Schools, and New York Department of Education. Total enrollment: 532. Upper school average class size: 15. Upper school faculty-student ratio: 1:15. There are 180 required school days per year for Upper School students. Upper School students typically attend 5 days per week. The average school day consists of 6 hours and 50 minutes.

Upper School Student Profile Grade 9: 136 students (136 boys); Grade 10: 131 students (131 boys); Grade 11: 134 students (134 boys); Grade 12: 131 students (131 boys). 100% of students are Roman Catholic.

Faculty School total: 54. In upper school: 35 men, 19 women; 48 have advanced degrees.

Subjects Offered Algebra, American history, American literature, art, art history, band, biology, calculus, chemistry, Chinese, computer programming, computer science, creative writing, drama, driver education, economics, English, English literature, ethics, European history, expository writing, film, French, geometry, German, health, history, Latin, mathematics, music, physical education, physics, psychology, social studies, Spanish, speech, statistics, theater, theology, trigonometry, writing.

Graduation Requirements Art, computer literacy, English, foreign language, history, mathematics, music, physical education (includes health), science, theology, Christian service program.

Special Academic Programs 14 Advanced Placement exams for which test preparation is offered; independent study; study abroad.

College Admission Counseling Colleges students went to include Boston College; Cornell University; Fordham University; Georgetown University; New York University; Northeastern University. Mean SAT critical reading: 721, mean SAT math: 722, mean SAT writing: 724, mean combined SAT: 2163.

Student Life Upper grades have specified standards of dress, student council. Discipline rests primarily with faculty. Attendance at religious services is required.

Tuition and Aid Tuition-free school available.

Admissions Traditional secondary-level entrance grade is 9. For fall 2015, 772 students applied for upper-level admission, 140 were accepted, 136 enrolled. Admissions testing required. Deadline for receipt of application materials: October 23. Application fee required: $85. On-campus interview required.

Athletics Interscholastic: baseball, basketball, cross-country running, fencing, floor hockey, indoor track & field, track and field, volleyball; intramural: baseball, basketball, cross-country running, floor hockey, indoor soccer. 2 PE instructors, 10 coaches.

Computers Computers are regularly used in all academic classes. Computer network features include on-campus library services, Internet access, wireless campus network, Internet filtering or blocking technology. Campus intranet, student e-mail accounts, and computer access in designated common areas are available to students.

Contact Mr. Eric P. DiMichele, Director of Admissions. 212-288-1100 Ext. 2057. Fax: 212-794-1221. E-mail: edimiche@regis.org. Website: www.regis.org

REGIS JESUIT HIGH SCHOOL, BOYS DIVISION
6400 South Lewiston Way
Aurora, Colorado 80016
Head of School: Mr. Alan Carruthers

General Information Boys' day college-preparatory, arts, and religious studies school, affiliated with Roman Catholic Church (Jesuit order). Grades 9–12. Founded: 1877. Setting: suburban. 64-acre campus. 4 buildings on campus. Approved or accredited by Jesuit Secondary Education Association, North Central Association of Colleges and Schools, and Colorado Department of Education. Member of National Association of Independent Schools. Endowment: $13 million. Total enrollment: 944. Upper school average class size: 26. Upper school faculty-student ratio: 1:12. There are 181 required school days per year for Upper School students. Upper School students typically attend 5 days per week. The average school day consists of 6 hours and 45 minutes.

Upper School Student Profile Grade 9: 257 students (257 boys); Grade 10: 255 students (255 boys); Grade 11: 209 students (209 boys); Grade 12: 233 students (233 boys). 70% of students are Roman Catholic Church (Jesuit order).

Faculty School total: 82. In upper school: 62 have advanced degrees.

Subjects Offered Algebra, American literature, anatomy, art, band, biology, British literature, calculus, chemistry, chorus, Colorado ecology, computer applications, computer graphics, computer literacy, computer programming, earth science, economics, English, English literature, fine arts, French, geography, geometry, history, integrated science, international relations, Latin, Mandarin, math analysis, mathematics, mechanical drawing, media studies, music, physical education, physics, physiology, social studies, sociology, Spanish, speech, statistics, theater, theology, trigonometry, U.S. government, U.S. history, Western civilization, world history.

Graduation Requirements Arts and fine arts (art, music, dance, drama), computer science, English, foreign language, mathematics, physical education (includes health), religion (includes Bible studies and theology), science, social sciences, social studies (includes history). Community service is required.

Special Academic Programs 19 Advanced Placement exams for which test preparation is offered; honors section; academic accommodation for the gifted; remedial reading and/or remedial writing; remedial math; programs in English, mathematics, general development for dyslexic students.

College Admission Counseling 310 students graduated in 2015; 203 went to college, including Colorado School of Mines; Colorado State University; Creighton University; Gonzaga University; Santa Clara University; University of Denver. Other: 3 entered military service, 7 had other specific plans. Mean SAT critical reading: 585, mean SAT math: 600, mean SAT writing: 561, mean composite ACT: 26.

Student Life Upper grades have specified standards of dress, student council, honor system. Discipline rests primarily with faculty. Attendance at religious services is required.

Summer Programs Remediation, enrichment, advancement, sports, art/fine arts, computer instruction programs offered; held on campus; accepts boys and girls; not open to students from other schools. 75 students usually enrolled. 2016 schedule: June 1 to July 31.

Tuition and Aid Day student tuition: $14,625. Tuition installment plan (FACTS Tuition Payment Plan). Merit scholarship grants, need-based scholarship grants, work grant tuition exchange program available. In 2015–16, 23% of upper-school students received aid; total upper-school merit-scholarship money awarded: $15,000. Total amount of financial aid awarded in 2015–16: $1,600,000.

Admissions Traditional secondary-level entrance grade is 9. High School Placement Test required. Deadline for receipt of application materials: December 9. No application fee required.

Athletics Interscholastic: aquatics, baseball, basketball, cross-country running, diving, football, golf, ice hockey, lacrosse, rugby, soccer, swimming and diving, tennis, track and field, volleyball, wrestling; intramural: basketball, bicycling, bowling, fly fishing, golf, kickball, power lifting, rock climbing, rugby, self defense, skateboarding, soccer, Special Olympics (g), table tennis (g), ultimate Frisbee, volleyball, water polo, weight lifting, weight training, whiffle ball, yoga; coed intramural: climbing, fencing, rowing. 4 PE instructors, 75 coaches, 2 athletic trainers.

Computers Computers are regularly used in all academic classes. Computer network features include on-campus library services, online commercial services, Internet access, wireless campus network, Internet filtering or blocking technology. Campus intranet and student e-mail accounts are available to students. Students grades are available online. The school has a published electronic and media policy.

Contact Mr. Paul Muller, Director of Admissions. 303-269-8064. Fax: 303-766-2240. E-mail: pmuller@regisjesuit.com. Website: www.regisjesuit.com

REGIS JESUIT HIGH SCHOOL, GIRLS DIVISION
6300 South Lewiston Way
Aurora, Colorado 80016
Head of School: Ms. Gretchen M. Kessler

General Information Girls' day college-preparatory, arts, and religious studies school, affiliated with Roman Catholic Church (Jesuit order). Grades 9–12. Founded: 1877. Setting: suburban. 64-acre campus. 3 buildings on campus. Approved or accredited by Jesuit Secondary Education Association, North Central Association of Colleges and Schools, and Colorado Department of Education. Endowment: $13 million. Total enrollment: 738. Upper school average class size: 20. Upper school faculty-student ratio: 1:12. There are 182 required school days per year for Upper School students. Upper School students typically attend 5 days per week. The average school day consists of 6 hours and 45 minutes.

Upper School Student Profile Grade 9: 202 students (202 girls); Grade 10: 186 students (186 girls); Grade 11: 171 students (171 girls); Grade 12: 179 students (179 girls). 70% of students are Roman Catholic Church (Jesuit order).

Faculty School total: 65. In upper school: 53 have advanced degrees.

Subjects Offered ACT preparation, acting, advanced biology, advanced chemistry, advanced computer applications, advanced math, Advanced Placement courses, advanced studio art-AP, algebra, American government, American history, American history-AP, American literature, American literature-AP, American studies, analysis and differential calculus, analytic geometry, anatomy and physiology, Ancient Greek, architecture, art, art-AP, athletic training, biology, biology-AP, British literature, British literature (honors), British literature-AP, broadcast journalism, business, calculus, calculus-AP, campus ministry, ceramics, chemistry-AP, Chinese, choir, choral music, chorus, Christian doctrine, Christian ethics, Christian studies, Christianity, church history, classical studies, classics, communication skills, communications, community service, computer applications, computer art, computer graphics, concert band, dance, debate, drama, drama performance, earth science, English, English composition, English language and composition-AP, English language-AP, English literature, English literature and composition-AP, English literature-AP, English-AP, English/composition-AP, fine arts, French, French language-AP, geometry, history, Latin, Latin-AP, mathematics-AP, physics-AP, public speaking, religion, social studies, Spanish, Spanish language-AP, speech and debate, theater, yoga.

Graduation Requirements Arts and fine arts (art, music, dance, drama), computer education, English, foreign language, mathematics, physical education (includes health), religious studies, science, social studies (includes history). Community service is required.

Special Academic Programs 19 Advanced Placement exams for which test preparation is offered; honors section; independent study; remedial reading and/or remedial writing; remedial math; programs in English, mathematics, general development for dyslexic students.

College Admission Counseling 162 students graduated in 2015; 157 went to college, including Colorado State University; Creighton University; Gonzaga University; University of Colorado Boulder; University of Denver; University of Northern Colorado. Other: 1 entered military service. Mean SAT critical reading: 267, mean SAT math: 237, mean SAT writing: 557, mean composite ACT: 25.

Student Life Upper grades have specified standards of dress, student council, honor system. Discipline rests primarily with faculty. Attendance at religious services is required.

Summer Programs Remediation, enrichment, advancement, sports, art/fine arts, computer instruction programs offered; held on campus; accepts boys and girls; not open to students from other schools. 50 students usually enrolled. 2016 schedule: June 1 to July 31.

Tuition and Aid Day student tuition: $14,625. Tuition installment plan (FACTS Tuition Payment Plan). Merit scholarship grants, need-based scholarship grants, work grant tuition exchange program available. In 2015–16, 23% of upper-school students received aid; total upper-school merit-scholarship money awarded: $15,000. Total amount of financial aid awarded in 2015–16: $1,600,000.

Admissions Traditional secondary-level entrance grade is 9. High School Placement Test required. Deadline for receipt of application materials: December 9. No application fee required.

Athletics Interscholastic: aerobics/dance, aquatics, baseball, basketball, cheering, cross-country running, dance, dance team, field hockey, fitness, golf, modern dance, pom squad, rugby, soccer, softball, swimming and diving, tennis, track and field, volleyball; intramural: basketball, golf, Special Olympics, table tennis, ultimate Frisbee, weight lifting, whiffle ball (b), yoga. 4 PE instructors, 40 coaches, 2 athletic trainers.

Computers Computers are regularly used in all classes. Computer network features include on-campus library services, Internet access, wireless campus network, Internet filtering or blocking technology. Campus intranet, student e-mail accounts, and computer access in designated common areas are available to students. Students grades are available online. The school has a published electronic and media policy.

Contact Ms. Patricia Long, Director of Admissions. 303-269-8164. Fax: 303-221-4772. E-mail: plong@regisjesuit.com. Website: www.regisjesuit.com

REJOICE CHRISTIAN SCHOOLS

12200 East 86th Street North

Owasso, Oklahoma 74055

Head of School: Dr. Craig D. Shaw

General Information Coeducational day college-preparatory school, affiliated with Free Will Baptist Church. Grades P3–12. Founded: 1992. Setting: suburban. Nearest major city is Tulsa. 1 building on campus. Approved or accredited by Association of Christian Schools International and Oklahoma Department of Education. Total enrollment: 873. Upper school average class size: 15. Upper school faculty-student ratio: 1:15. There are 175 required school days per year for Upper School students. The average school day consists of 7 hours.

Upper School Student Profile Grade 6: 43 students (23 boys, 20 girls); Grade 7: 52 students (22 boys, 30 girls); Grade 8: 46 students (30 boys, 16 girls); Grade 9: 44 students (20 boys, 24 girls); Grade 10: 47 students (27 boys, 20 girls); Grade 11: 42 students (24 boys, 18 girls); Grade 12: 38 students (21 boys, 17 girls). 30% of students are Free Will Baptist Church.

Faculty School total: 75. In upper school: 11 men, 23 women; 10 have advanced degrees.

Subjects Offered Advanced biology, advanced chemistry, Advanced Placement courses, algebra, American democracy, American government, American history, American history-AP, anatomy, anatomy and physiology, art, art appreciation, art education, art history, athletic training, athletics, band, basketball, Bible, Bible studies, biology, biology-AP, business, business education, calculus, calculus-AP, cheerleading, chemistry, chemistry-AP, choir, chorus, Christian education, civics, computer skills, electives, English, English language-AP, English literature and composition-AP, English literature-AP, English-AP, English/composition-AP, fitness, general business, general math, geography, geometry, golf, government, government and politics-AP, government-AP, government/civics, government/civics-AP, history, honors algebra, honors English, honors geometry, honors U.S. history, honors world history, journalism, language, language arts, library, mathematics, mathematics-AP, media, music, novels, physical education, physical fitness, physical science, pre-algebra, pre-calculus, Spanish, Spanish language-AP, speech, speech and debate, sports, sports conditioning, state history, technology, track and field, trigonometry, U.S. government, U.S. government and politics-AP, U.S. history, U.S. history-AP, weight training, world history, world history-AP, yearbook.

Special Academic Programs Honors section; study at local college for college credit.

College Admission Counseling 23 students graduated in 2015.

Student Life Upper grades have student council, honor system. Discipline rests primarily with faculty.

Tuition and Aid Tuition installment plan (SMART Tuition Payment Plan, monthly payment plans, annual payment plans, semi-annual payment plans). Need-based scholarship grants available. Total amount of financial aid awarded in 2015–16: $15,000.

Admissions PSAT, Stanford Achievement Test or TerraNova required. Deadline for receipt of application materials: none. Application fee required: $25. Interview required.

Athletics Interscholastic: baseball (boys), basketball (b,g), cheering (g), cross-country running (b,g), football (b), golf (b,g), physical fitness (b,g), soccer (b,g), tennis (b,g), track and field (b,g), volleyball (g).

Computers Computers are regularly used in English, journalism, library, media, newspaper, yearbook classes. Computer network features include on-campus library services, Internet access, wireless campus network, Internet filtering or blocking technology. Campus intranet and student e-mail accounts are available to students. Students grades are available online. The school has a published electronic and media policy.

Contact Mrs. Julie Long, High School Registrar. 918-516-0050. Fax: 918-516-0299. E-mail: jlong@rejoiceschool.com. Website: www.rejoiceschool.com

RIDLEY COLLEGE

2 Ridley Road

St. Catharines, Ontario L2R7C3, Canada

Head of School: Mr. Edward Kidd

General Information Coeducational boarding and day college-preparatory, arts, business, and technology school, affiliated with Church of England (Anglican). Boarding grades 5–PG, day grades JK–PG. Founded: 1889. Setting: suburban. Nearest major city is Buffalo, NY. Students are housed in single-sex dormitories. 90-acre campus. 13 buildings on campus. Approved or accredited by Canadian Association of Independent Schools, Canadian Educational Standards Institute, Conference of Independent Schools of Ontario, Headmasters' Conference, International Baccalaureate Organization, National Independent Private Schools Association, Ontario Ministry of Education, The Association of Boarding Schools, and Ontario Department of Education. Affiliate member of National Association of Independent Schools; member of Secondary School Admission Test Board. Language of instruction: English. Endowment: CAN$29 million. Total enrollment: 649. Upper school average class size: 17. Upper school faculty-student ratio: 1:8. There are 232 required school days per year for Upper School students. Upper School students typically attend 6 days per week. The average school day consists of 6 hours.

Upper School Student Profile Grade 9: 38 students (13 boys, 25 girls); Grade 10: 62 students (36 boys, 26 girls); Grade 11: 110 students (61 boys, 49 girls); Grade 12: 123 students (75 boys, 48 girls); Postgraduate: 2 students (2 boys). 68% of students are boarding students. 56% are province residents. 15 provinces are represented in upper school student body. 30% are international students. International students from China, Germany, Mexico, Nigeria, Russian Federation, and United States; 38 other countries represented in student body. 20% of students are members of Church of England (Anglican).

Faculty School total: 77. In upper school: 37 men, 40 women; 26 have advanced degrees; 40 reside on campus.

Subjects Offered Accounting, algebra, American history, anthropology, art, art history, biology, business mathematics, business skills, calculus, Canadian history, Canadian law, chemistry, computer multimedia, computer programming, computer science, creative writing, drafting, drama, dramatic arts, driver education, economics, English, English literature, environmental science, ESL, exercise science, finance, fine arts, French, geography, German, health education, health science, instrumental music, International Baccalaureate courses, kinesiology, Latin, Mandarin, mathematics, music, philosophy, physical education, physics, science, social sciences, social studies, Spanish, sports science, theater, world history, world religions, writing.

Graduation Requirements Arts and fine arts (art, music, dance, drama), business skills (includes word processing), English, foreign language, mathematics, physical education (includes health), science, social sciences, social studies (includes history).

Special Academic Programs International Baccalaureate program; honors section; independent study; study abroad; academic accommodation for the gifted, the musically talented, and the artistically talented; ESL (20 students enrolled).

College Admission Counseling 131 students graduated in 2015; 122 went to college, including Brock University; Carleton University; Queen's University at Kingston; The University of Western Ontario; University of Guelph; University of Toronto. Other: 9 had other specific plans.

Student Life Upper grades have uniform requirement, student council, honor system. Discipline rests primarily with faculty. Attendance at religious services is required.

Summer Programs ESL programs offered; session focuses on improvement of English language skills; held on campus; accepts boys and girls; open to students from other schools.

Tuition and Aid Day student tuition: CAN$13,770–CAN$30,465; 5-day tuition and room/board: CAN$47,890–CAN$50,280; 7-day tuition and room/board: CAN$54,010–CAN$59,465. Tuition installment plan (monthly payment plans, individually arranged payment plans). Bursaries, merit scholarship grants, need-based scholarship grants, need-based loans available. In 2015–16, 33% of upper-school students received aid.

Admissions Traditional secondary-level entrance grade is 9. For fall 2015, 537 students applied for upper-level admission, 305 were accepted, 194 enrolled. Deadline for receipt of application materials: none. Application fee required: CAN$150. Interview required.

Athletics Interscholastic: artistic gym (girls), baseball (b,g), basketball (b,g), crew (b,g), cross-country running (b,g), field hockey (g), fitness walking (g), gymnastics (g), hockey (b,g), ice hockey (b,g), rowing (b,g), rugby (b,g), running (b,g), soccer (b,g), softball (b,g), squash (b,g), swimming and diving (b,g), tennis (b,g), track and field (b,g), volleyball (g); intramural: hockey (b,g), ice hockey (b,g), running (b,g); coed interscholastic: golf, tennis; coed intramural: aerobics, aerobics/dance, alpine skiing, aquatics, backpacking, badminton, ball hockey, ballet, baseball, basketball, bicycling, billiards, bowling, broomball, canoeing/kayaking, climbing, cooperative games, Cosom hockey, cross-country running, curling, dance, dance squad, dance team, drill team, equestrian sports, fencing, fitness, flag football, Frisbee, golf, hiking/backpacking, horseback riding, ice skating, indoor soccer, jogging, life saving, martial arts, modern dance, outdoor activities, outdoor education, outdoor recreation, outdoor skills, physical fitness, physical training, power lifting, racquetball, rock climbing, ropes courses, sailing, scuba diving, self defense, skiing (cross-country), skiing (downhill), snowboarding, snowshoeing, soccer, softball, squash, strength & conditioning, swimming and diving, table tennis, tennis, track and field, triathlon, ultimate Frisbee, volleyball, walking, wall climbing, weight lifting, weight training, wilderness survival, yoga. 8 coaches, 3 athletic trainers.

Computers Computers are regularly used in all academic classes. Computer network features include on-campus library services, online commercial services, Internet access, wireless campus network, Internet filtering or blocking technology. Student e-mail accounts and computer access in designated common areas are available to students. Students grades are available online. The school has a published electronic and media policy.

Contact Mrs. Stephanie Park, Admissions Administrative Assistant. 905-684-1889 Ext. 2207. Fax: 905-684-8875. E-mail: admissions@ridleycollege.com. Website: www.ridleycollege.com

RIVERDALE COUNTRY SCHOOL

5250 Fieldston Road
Bronx, New York 10471-2999

Head of School: Dominic A.A. Randolph

General Information Coeducational day college-preparatory school. Grades PK–12. Founded: 1907. Setting: suburban. Nearest major city is New York. 27-acre campus. 9 buildings on campus. Approved or accredited by New York State Association of Independent Schools and New York Department of Education. Member of National Association of Independent Schools and Secondary School Admission Test Board. Endowment: $63 million. Total enrollment: 1,150. Upper school average class size: 16. Upper school faculty-student ratio: 1:8. Upper School students typically attend 5 days per week.

Faculty School total: 185.

Subjects Offered Algebra, American literature, anatomy, art, art history, biology, calculus, ceramics, chemistry, community service, computer math, computer programming, computer science, creative writing, drama, driver education, earth science, ecology, economics, English, English literature, environmental science, European history, expository writing, fine arts, French, geology, geometry, government/civics, grammar, health, history, history of science, introduction to liberal studies, Japanese, journalism, Latin, Mandarin, marine biology, mathematics, music, oceanography, philosophy, photography, physical education, physics, psychology, science, social studies, Spanish, speech, statistics, theater, theory of knowledge, trigonometry, world history, writing.

Graduation Requirements American studies, arts and fine arts (art, music, dance, drama), computer science, English, foreign language, mathematics, physical education (includes health), science, social studies (includes history), integrated liberal studies. Community service is required.

Special Academic Programs Honors section; independent study; term-away projects; study abroad; academic accommodation for the gifted, the musically talented, and the artistically talented.

College Admission Counseling 131 students graduated in 2015; all went to college, including Columbia University; Cornell University; Dartmouth College; Johns Hopkins University; University of Pennsylvania; Yale University.

Student Life Upper grades have student council, honor system. Discipline rests equally with students and faculty.

Summer Programs Enrichment programs offered; session focuses on science research; held both on and off campus; held at campus and NYC; accepts boys and girls; open to students from other schools.

Tuition and Aid Day student tuition: $47,660. Tuition installment plan (monthly payment plans). Need-based scholarship grants available. In 2015–16, 20% of upper-school students received aid.

Admissions Traditional secondary-level entrance grade is 9. ISEE or SSAT required. Deadline for receipt of application materials: November 16. Application fee required: $60. On-campus interview required.

Athletics Interscholastic: baseball (boys), basketball (b,g), crew (b,g), field hockey (g), football (b), lacrosse (b,g), soccer (b,g), softball (g), tennis (b,g), volleyball (g); intramural: baseball (b), basketball (b,g), field hockey (g), football (b), lacrosse (b,g), soccer (b,g), softball (g), tennis (b,g), volleyball (g); coed interscholastic: cross-country running, fencing, golf, squash, swimming and diving, track and field, ultimate Frisbee; coed intramural: cross-country running, dance, fencing, fitness, physical fitness, squash, swimming and diving, tennis, track and field, ultimate Frisbee, yoga. 7 PE instructors, 31 coaches, 1 athletic trainer.

Computers Computers are regularly used in art, English, foreign language, history, mathematics, music, science classes. Computer network features include on-campus library services, online commercial services, Internet access, wireless campus network, Internet filtering or blocking technology, off-campus email, off-campus library services. Student e-mail accounts and computer access in designated common areas are available to students. The school has a published electronic and media policy.

Contact Jenna Rogers King, Director of Admission and Enrollment. 718-519-2715. Fax: 718-519-2793. E-mail: jrking@riverdale.edu. Website: www.riverdale.edu

RIVER OAKS ACADEMY

Houston, Texas
See Special Needs Schools section.

RIVER OAKS BAPTIST SCHOOL

2300 Willowick
Houston, Texas 77027

Head of School: Mrs. Leanne Reynolds

General Information Coeducational day college-preparatory and character education school, affiliated with Christian faith. Grades PK–8. Founded: 1955. Setting: urban. Approved or accredited by Accreditation Commission of the Texas Association of Baptist Schools, Independent Schools Association of the Southwest, and Texas Department of Education. Member of National Association of Independent Schools. Endowment: $30 million. Total enrollment: 732. Upper school faculty-student ratio: 1:16. There are 187 required school days per year for Upper School students. The average school day consists of 6 hours and 10 minutes.

Upper School Student Profile Grade 6: 80 students (40 boys, 40 girls); Grade 7: 80 students (40 boys, 40 girls); Grade 8: 80 students (40 boys, 40 girls). 95% of students are Christian.

Faculty School total: 91. In upper school: 11 men, 31 women; 21 have advanced degrees.

Student Life Upper grades have uniform requirement, honor system. Discipline rests primarily with faculty. Attendance at religious services is required.

Tuition and Aid Tuition installment plan (monthly payment plans). Need-based scholarship grants available.

Admissions Individual IQ, ISEE and OLSAT, Stanford Achievement Test required. Deadline for receipt of application materials: December 10. Application fee required: $100. On-campus interview required.

Computers Computer network features include on-campus library services, wireless campus network, Internet filtering or blocking technology. Campus intranet and student e-mail accounts are available to students. Students grades are available online. The school has a published electronic and media policy.

Contact Mrs. Kristin Poe, Director of Admission. 713-623-6938. Fax: 713-623-0650. E-mail: kpoe@robs.org. Website: www.robs.org

RIVERSIDE CHRISTIAN SCHOOLS

8775 Magnolia Ave
Riverside, California 92503

Head of School: Pastor John Moran

General Information Coeducational day college-preparatory and religious studies school. Grades K–12. Founded: 1958. Setting: urban. Students are housed in homes. 5-acre campus. 2 buildings on campus. Approved or accredited by Association of Christian Schools International and Western Association of Schools and Colleges. Total enrollment: 253. Upper school average class size: 25. Upper school faculty-student ratio: 1:10. There are 5 required school days per year for Upper School students. Upper School students typically attend 5 days per week. The average school day consists of 6 hours and 45 minutes.

Upper School Student Profile Grade 6: 14 students (6 boys, 8 girls); Grade 7: 15 students (8 boys, 7 girls); Grade 8: 19 students (12 boys, 7 girls); Grade 9: 14 students (9 boys, 5 girls); Grade 10: 31 students (18 boys, 13 girls); Grade 11: 31 students (21 boys, 10 girls); Grade 12: 17 students (7 boys, 10 girls).

Faculty School total: 20. In upper school: 5 men, 9 women; 6 have advanced degrees.

Subjects Offered Advanced biology, advanced chemistry, advanced math, Advanced Placement courses, American government, American history, American history-AP, American literature, American literature-AP, anatomy and physiology, ancient history, area studies, biology, biology-AP, biotechnology, British literature, British literature (honors), British literature-AP, calculus, calculus-AP, chemistry, chemistry-AP, choir, Christian and Hebrew scripture, Christian doctrine, Christian education, Christian scripture, Christian studies, Christian testament, drama, drama performance, economics, English, English language and composition-AP, English language-AP, English literature, English literature and composition-AP, English literature-AP, English-AP, fine arts, general science, government, government-AP, history-AP, honors algebra, honors English, honors geometry, honors U.S. history, honors world history, language and composition, life science, modern world history, New Testament, physical fitness, physical science, physics, physics-AP, pre-algebra, pre-calculus, science, U.S. government, U.S. history, U.S. history-AP, U.S. literature, video film production, visual arts, world cultures, world geography, world history, world studies, yearbook.

Graduation Requirements All academic, 4 years of Bible.

Special Academic Programs 8 Advanced Placement exams for which test preparation is offered; study at local college for college credit; remedial reading and/or remedial writing; remedial math; ESL (10 students enrolled).

College Admission Counseling 36 students graduated in 2015; 35 went to college, including California State University, San Bernardino; Fullerton College; Grand Canyon University; University of California, Riverside. Other: 1 went to work.

Student Life Upper grades have specified standards of dress, student council, honor system. Discipline rests primarily with faculty.

Tuition and Aid Tuition installment plan (monthly payment plans, international students paid in full at beginning of school year). Tuition reduction for siblings available.

Admissions TOEFL or SLEP required. Deadline for receipt of application materials: none. Application fee required: $25. Interview required.

Athletics Interscholastic: baseball (boys), basketball (b,g), football (b), softball (g), swimming and diving (b,g), volleyball (g); coed interscholastic: soccer, swimming and diving. 2 PE instructors, 1 athletic trainer.

Computers Computers are regularly used in Bible studies, English, ESL, geography, history, mathematics, social studies, Spanish, technology, yearbook classes. Computer network features include Internet access, iPads. Campus intranet, student e-mail accounts, and computer access in designated common areas are available to students. The school has a published electronic and media policy.

Contact 909-687-0077. Fax: 909-687-3340. Website: www.rivchristian.org/

RIVERSIDE MILITARY ACADEMY

2001 Riverside Drive
Gainesville, Georgia 30501

Head of School: Dr. James H. Benson, Col., USMC-Retd.

General Information Boys' boarding and day college-preparatory, arts, technology, JROTC (grades 9-12), and military school, affiliated with Christian faith. Grades 7–12. Founded: 1907. Setting: suburban. Nearest major city is Atlanta. Students are housed in single-sex dormitories. 206-acre campus. 9 buildings on campus. Approved or accredited by Southern Association of Colleges and Schools, Southern Association of Independent Schools, and Georgia Department of Education. Member of National Association of Independent Schools. Endowment: $42 million. Total enrollment: 500. Upper school average class size: 15. Upper school faculty-student ratio: 1:15. There are 180 required school days per year for Upper School students. Upper School students typically attend 5 days per week. The average school day consists of 5 hours and 45 minutes.

Upper School Student Profile Grade 7: 62 students (62 boys); Grade 8: 55 students (55 boys); Grade 9: 100 students (100 boys); Grade 10: 75 students (75 boys); Grade 11: 102 students (102 boys); Grade 12: 98 students (98 boys). 99% of students are boarding students. 56% are state residents. 30 states are represented in upper school student body. 29% are international students. International students from China, Colombia, Dominican Republic, Kazakhstan, Mexico, and Republic of Korea; 26 other countries represented in student body. 80% of students are Christian faith.

Faculty School total: 45. In upper school: 35 men, 10 women; 40 have advanced degrees; 20 reside on campus.

Subjects Offered Algebra, American literature, art, art appreciation, band, biology, biology-AP, calculus, calculus-AP, ceramics, chemistry, chemistry-AP, chorus, computer applications, computer education, computer programming, computer science, computer skills, computer studies, computer technologies, desktop publishing, drama, drawing, earth science, economics, English, English composition, English literature, English/composition-AP, ESL, ethics, European history, fine arts, geography, geometry, government/civics, grammar, health, history-AP, honors English, honors geometry, honors U.S. history, honors world history, JROTC, keyboarding, Latin, leadership, mathematics, military science, modern world history, music, music technology, music theory, painting, physical education, physics, physics-AP, pre-algebra, pre-calculus, science, social studies, Spanish, statistics, swimming, theater, U.S. government, U.S. government and politics-AP, U.S. history, U.S. history-AP, U.S. literature, visual arts, weight training, world geography, world history, world history-AP, world literature, yearbook.

Graduation Requirements Arts and fine arts (art, music, dance, drama), computer science, electives, English, foreign language, JROTC, lab science, mathematics, military science, physical education (includes health), science, social studies (includes history).

Special Academic Programs 8 Advanced Placement exams for which test preparation is offered; honors section; independent study; special instructional classes for students with Attention Deficit Hyperactivity Disorder, students with Attention Deficit Disorder; ESL (35 students enrolled).

College Admission Counseling 93 students graduated in 2014; 89 went to college, including The Citadel, The Military College of South Carolina; The University of Alabama; United States Military Academy; University of Georgia; University of North Georgia. Other: 1 went to work, 3 entered military service. Median SAT critical reading: 484, median SAT math: 511, median SAT writing: 462, median combined SAT: 1458, median composite ACT: 20.

Student Life Upper grades have uniform requirement, student council, honor system. Discipline rests equally with students and faculty. Attendance at religious services is required.

Tuition and Aid Day student tuition: $19,000; 7-day tuition and room/board: $31,550. Tuition installment plan (Key Tuition Payment Plan, FACTS Tuition Payment Plan, monthly payment plans, individually arranged payment plans). Tuition reduction for siblings, need-based scholarship grants available. In 2014–15, 40% of upper-school students received aid. Total amount of financial aid awarded in 2014–15: $2,000,000.

Admissions Traditional secondary-level entrance grade is 10. For fall 2014, 180 students applied for upper-level admission, 170 were accepted, 135 enrolled. Any standardized test required. Deadline for receipt of application materials: none. Application fee required: $100. Interview required.

Athletics Interscholastic: aquatics, baseball, basketball, crew, cross-country running, drill team, football, golf, JROTC drill, lacrosse, marksmanship, outdoor adventure, outdoor skills, paint ball, riflery, ropes courses, rowing, soccer, strength & conditioning, swimming and diving, tennis, track and field, weight lifting, weight training, wrestling;

intramural: aquatics, backpacking, baseball, basketball, billiards, canoeing/kayaking, cheering, climbing, combined training, crew, cross-country running, fencing, fishing, fitness, flag football, football, hiking/backpacking, horseback riding, indoor soccer, indoor track, indoor track & field, jogging, JROTC drill, kayaking, marksmanship, mountaineering, outdoor activities, paddle tennis, physical fitness, physical training, rafting, rappelling, riflery, rock climbing, ropes courses, rowing, running, skateboarding, soccer, softball, swimming and diving, table tennis, tennis, volleyball, wall climbing, water polo, water volleyball, weight lifting, wilderness. 5 PE instructors, 20 coaches, 1 athletic trainer.

Computers Computers are regularly used in college planning, desktop publishing, English, ESL, foreign language, library, mathematics, multimedia, music, SAT preparation, science, Spanish, technology, theater, yearbook classes. Computer network features include on-campus library services, Internet access, wireless campus network, Internet filtering or blocking technology. Campus intranet, student e-mail accounts, and computer access in designated common areas are available to students. Students grades are available online. The school has a published electronic and media policy.

Contact Admissions Office. 800-462-2338. Fax: 678-291-3364. E-mail: apply@riversidemilitary.com. Website: www.riversidemilitary.com

THE RIVERS SCHOOL

333 Winter Street
Weston, Massachusetts 02493-1040

Head of School: Edward V. Parsons

General Information Coeducational day college-preparatory and arts school. Grades 6–12. Founded: 1915. Setting: suburban. Nearest major city is Boston. 53-acre campus. 8 buildings on campus. Approved or accredited by Association of Independent Schools in New England and New England Association of Schools and Colleges. Member of National Association of Independent Schools and Secondary School Admission Test Board. Endowment: $22.3 million. Total enrollment: 490. Upper school average class size: 12. Upper school faculty-student ratio: 1:6. Upper School students typically attend 5 days per week. The average school day consists of 7 hours and 15 minutes.

Upper School Student Profile Grade 9: 90 students (43 boys, 47 girls); Grade 10: 94 students (42 boys, 52 girls); Grade 11: 90 students (50 boys, 40 girls); Grade 12: 93 students (41 boys, 52 girls).

Faculty School total: 86. In upper school: 43 men, 43 women; 56 have advanced degrees.

Subjects Offered Advanced Placement courses, algebra, American history, American literature, art, art history, art history-AP, astronomy, biochemistry, biology, biology-AP, calculus, calculus-AP, ceramics, chamber groups, chemistry, chemistry-AP, chorus, civil rights, Civil War, computer graphics, computer science, computer science-AP, creative writing, drama, earth science, economics-AP, English, English language and composition-AP, English literature, English literature and composition-AP, environmental science-AP, European history, expository writing, film studies, filmmaking, fine arts, French, French-AP, geography, geometry, history, Holocaust, jazz band, journalism, kinesiology, Latin, Latin-AP, Mandarin, mathematics, modern European history-AP, music, photography, physics, physics-AP, playwriting, science, Spanish, Spanish-AP, statistics-AP, the Presidency, theater, theater arts, trigonometry, U.S. history-AP, world history, world literature.

Graduation Requirements Algebra, athletics, biology, chemistry, English, foreign language, geometry, history, mathematics, modern European history, science, U.S. history, visual and performing arts, participation in athletics. Community service is required.

Special Academic Programs Advanced Placement exam preparation; honors section; independent study; study at local college for college credit.

College Admission Counseling 84 students graduated in 2015; all went to college, including Boston College; Colby College; Colgate University; Connecticut College; Tufts University; Yale University. Median SAT critical reading: 650, median SAT math: 690, median SAT writing: 680, median combined SAT: 2000, median composite ACT: 31. 82% scored over 600 on SAT critical reading, 75% scored over 600 on SAT math, 76% scored over 600 on SAT writing, 82% scored over 1800 on combined SAT.

Student Life Upper grades have specified standards of dress, student council, honor system. Discipline rests primarily with faculty.

Tuition and Aid Day student tuition: $43,680. Tuition installment plan (Academic Management Services Plan, Key Tuition Payment Plan, monthly payment plans). Need-based scholarship grants available. In 2015–16, 26% of upper-school students received aid. Total amount of financial aid awarded in 2015–16: $3,727,504.

Admissions Traditional secondary-level entrance grade is 9. ISEE or SSAT required. Deadline for receipt of application materials: January 15. Application fee required: $50. On-campus interview required.

Athletics Interscholastic: alpine skiing (boys, girls), baseball (b), basketball (b,g), cross-country running (b,g), field hockey (g), football (b), ice hockey (b,g), lacrosse (b,g), skiing (downhill) (b,g), soccer (b,g), softball (g), strength & conditioning (b,g), tennis (b,g); intramural: basketball (b,g), tennis (g); coed interscholastic: fitness, golf, nordic skiing, physical training, track and field, weight lifting, weight training; coed intramural: fencing, strength & conditioning. 4 coaches, 2 athletic trainers.

Computers Computers are regularly used in art, English, foreign language, history, humanities, language development, mathematics, newspaper, publications, science, writing, yearbook classes. Computer network features include on-campus library services, online commercial services, Internet access, wireless campus network, Internet filtering or blocking technology, language lab. Campus intranet, student e-mail accounts, and computer access in designated common areas are available to students. Students grades are available online. The school has a published electronic and media policy.

Contact Gillian Lloyd, Director of Admissions. 781-235-9300. Fax: 781-239-3614. E-mail: g.lloyd@rivers.org. Website: www.rivers.org

RIVERSTONE INTERNATIONAL SCHOOL

5521 Warm Springs Avenue
Boise, Idaho 83716

Head of School: Mr. Bob Carignan

General Information Coeducational day college-preparatory and International Baccalaureate Programmes school. Grades PS–12. Founded: 1997. Setting: suburban. 14-acre campus. 6 buildings on campus. Approved or accredited by International Baccalaureate Organization, Northwest Accreditation Commission, Northwest Association of Independent Schools, Northwest Association of Schools and Colleges, and Idaho Department of Education. Member of National Association of Independent Schools and Secondary School Admission Test Board. Endowment: $750,000. Total enrollment: 325. Upper school average class size: 12. Upper school faculty-student ratio: 1:5. There are 170 required school days per year for Upper School students. Upper School students typically attend 5 days per week. The average school day consists of 6 hours and 45 minutes.

Upper School Student Profile Grade 9: 28 students (11 boys, 17 girls); Grade 10: 14 students (5 boys, 9 girls); Grade 11: 34 students (17 boys, 17 girls); Grade 12: 27 students (14 boys, 13 girls).

Faculty School total: 45. In upper school: 6 men, 11 women; 12 have advanced degrees.

Subjects Offered International Baccalaureate courses.

Graduation Requirements Art, English, foreign language, history, mathematics, science.

Special Academic Programs International Baccalaureate program; study abroad; ESL (15 students enrolled).

College Admission Counseling 18 students graduated in 2015; 17 went to college, including Claremont McKenna College; Linfield College; Stanford University; University of Chicago; University of Southern California. Other: 1 had other specific plans. Mean SAT critical reading: 655, mean SAT math: 621, mean SAT writing: 617, mean combined SAT: 1832, mean composite ACT: 27.

Student Life Upper grades have specified standards of dress, student council, honor system. Discipline rests primarily with faculty.

Summer Programs Enrichment, ESL, sports, art/fine arts, rigorous outdoor training programs offered; session focuses on camps, ESL, and outdoor education; held both on and off campus; held at Boise River, Boise foothills, and Sawtooth and White Cloud Mountains; accepts boys and girls; open to students from other schools. 100 students usually enrolled. 2016 schedule: June 11 to August 16. Application deadline: June 1.

Tuition and Aid Day student tuition: $17,120. Tuition installment plan (monthly payment plans). Need-based scholarship grants available. In 2015–16, 20% of upper-school students received aid.

Admissions Traditional secondary-level entrance grade is 9. For fall 2015, 21 students applied for upper-level admission, 18 were accepted, 15 enrolled. Deadline for receipt of application materials: none. Application fee required: $75. Interview required.

Athletics Interscholastic: basketball (boys, girls), volleyball (g); coed interscholastic: alpine skiing, nordic skiing, skiing (cross-country), skiing (downhill), snowboarding, soccer; coed intramural: backpacking, canoeing/kayaking, climbing, hiking/backpacking, kayaking, nordic skiing, outdoor activities, outdoor adventure, outdoor education, outdoor recreation, outdoor skills, outdoors, physical fitness, rafting, rock climbing, skiing (cross-country), skiing (downhill), snowboarding, snowshoeing, wilderness, yoga. 1 PE instructor, 10 coaches.

Computers Computers are regularly used in art, business, college planning, English, ESL, foreign language, French, history, humanities, lab/keyboard, mathematics, music, research skills, science, Spanish, technology, writing, yearbook classes. Computer network features include online commercial services, Internet access, wireless campus network. Campus intranet and student e-mail accounts are available to students. Students grades are available online. The school has a published electronic and media policy.

Contact Ms. Rachel Pusch, Director of Enrollment Management and Administration. 208-424-5000 Ext. 3. Fax: 208-424-0033. E-mail: rpusch@riverstoneschool.org. Website: www.riverstoneschool.org

ROBERT LAND ACADEMY

Wellandport, Ontario, Canada
See Special Needs Schools section.

ROBERT LOUIS STEVENSON SCHOOL

New York, New York
See Special Needs Schools section.

ROCKHURST HIGH SCHOOL

9301 State Line Road
Kansas City, Missouri 64114-3299

Head of School: Rev. Terrence Baum

General Information Boys' day college-preparatory, arts, religious studies, and technology school, affiliated with Roman Catholic Church. Grades 9–12. Founded: 1910. Setting: suburban. 36-acre campus. 3 buildings on campus. Approved or accredited by Jesuit Secondary Education Association, North Central Association of Colleges and Schools, and Missouri Department of Education. Member of National Association of Independent Schools. Endowment: $16 million. Upper school average class size: 23. Upper school faculty-student ratio: 1:13. There are 172 required school days per year for Upper School students. Upper School students typically attend 5 days per week. The average school day consists of 7 hours.

Upper School Student Profile Grade 9: 251 students (251 boys); Grade 10: 266 students (266 boys); Grade 11: 247 students (247 boys); Grade 12: 252 students (252 boys). 78.5% of students are Roman Catholic.

Faculty School total: 79. In upper school: 69 men, 10 women; 57 have advanced degrees.

Subjects Offered Algebra, American history, American literature, anatomy, art, biology, business, calculus, ceramics, chemistry, Christian and Hebrew scripture, computer math, computer programming, computer science, creative writing, drama, economics, English, English literature, European history, fine arts, forensics, French, geography, geometry, government/civics, Greek, history, journalism, Latin, mathematics, music, photography, physical education, physics, physiology, religion, science, social studies, Spanish, speech, theater, theology, trigonometry.

Graduation Requirements Arts and fine arts (art, music, dance, drama), computer science, English, foreign language, mathematics, physical education (includes health), religion (includes Bible studies and theology), science, social studies (includes history), attendance at retreats, community service hours.

Special Academic Programs 16 Advanced Placement exams for which test preparation is offered; honors section; study at local college for college credit.

College Admission Counseling 252 students graduated in 2015; all went to college, including Creighton University; Kansas State University; Miami University; Rockhurst University; The University of Kansas; University of Missouri. Mean SAT critical reading: 650, mean SAT math: 655, mean SAT writing: 645, mean combined SAT: 1950, mean composite ACT: 27.

Student Life Upper grades have specified standards of dress, student council. Discipline rests primarily with faculty. Attendance at religious services is required.

Summer Programs Remediation, enrichment, advancement, sports, art/fine arts, computer instruction programs offered; session focuses on transition to high school and enrichment; held on campus; accepts boys and girls; open to students from other schools. 350 students usually enrolled. 2016 schedule: June 6 to July 1. Application deadline: none.

Tuition and Aid Day student tuition: $12,050. Tuition installment plan (monthly payment plans, individually arranged payment plans). Merit scholarship grants, need-based scholarship grants, paying campus jobs available. In 2015–16, 40% of upper-school students received aid; total upper-school merit-scholarship money awarded: $22,000. Total amount of financial aid awarded in 2015–16: $2,100,000.

Admissions Traditional secondary-level entrance grade is 9. For fall 2015, 312 students applied for upper-level admission, 301 were accepted, 251 enrolled. High School Placement Test (closed version) from Scholastic Testing Service required. Deadline for receipt of application materials: December 15. No application fee required.

Athletics Interscholastic: baseball, basketball, cross-country running, diving, football, golf, ice hockey, lacrosse, soccer, swimming and diving, tennis, track and field, wrestling; intramural: basketball, football, juggling, racquetball, soccer, softball, ultimate Frisbee, volleyball, weight lifting, weight training. 2 PE instructors, 17 coaches, 1 athletic trainer.

Computers Computers are regularly used in mathematics, science, technology classes. Computer network features include on-campus library services, online commercial services, Internet access, wireless campus network. Campus intranet, student e-mail accounts, and computer access in designated common areas are available to students. Students grades are available online. The school has a published electronic and media policy.

Contact Mr. Jack Reichmeier, Director of Admission and Financial Aid. 816-363-2036 Ext. 558. Fax: 816-363-3764. E-mail: jreichme@rockhursths.edu. Website: www.rockhursths.edu

ROCKLAND COUNTRY DAY SCHOOL

34 Kings Highway

Congers, New York 10920-2253

Head of School: Ms. Kimberly A. Morcate

General Information Coeducational boarding and day college-preparatory and arts school. Boarding grades 8–12, day grades PK–12. Founded: 1959. Setting: suburban. Students are housed in coed dormitories. 22-acre campus. 5 buildings on campus. Approved or accredited by New York State Association of Independent Schools and New York Department of Education. Member of National Association of Independent Schools. Total enrollment: 117. Upper school average class size: 15. Upper school faculty-student ratio: 1:8. There are 176 required school days per year for Upper School students. Upper School students typically attend 5 days per week. The average school day consists of 7 hours and 30 minutes.

Upper School Student Profile Grade 9: 12 students (6 boys, 6 girls); Grade 10: 13 students (5 boys, 8 girls); Grade 11: 18 students (7 boys, 11 girls); Grade 12: 21 students (11 boys, 10 girls). 33% of students are boarding students. 45% are state residents. 3 states are represented in upper school student body. 55% are international students. International students from China and Republic of Korea; 2 other countries represented in student body.

Faculty School total: 31. In upper school: 10 men, 11 women; 11 have advanced degrees; 2 reside on campus.

Subjects Offered Algebra, American history, American literature, art, art history, band, biology, biology-AP, calculus, calculus-AP, career exploration, ceramics, chemistry, chorus, college admission preparation, college counseling, college placement, community service, computers, creative arts, creative writing, dance, debate, digital photography, drama, drama performance, dramatic arts, drawing, earth science, economics, electives, English, English literature, English-AP, environmental science, environmental studies, European history, European history-AP, fine arts, French, French-AP, gardening, geometry, global studies, guitar, health, health education, history, honors English, humanities, independent study, instrumental music, internship, jazz ensemble, lab science, language-AP, literature-AP, madrigals, mathematics, mathematics-AP, modern European history-AP, music, music theory-AP, painting, performing arts, philosophy, photography, physical education, physics, physics-AP, pre-algebra, pre-calculus, science, social studies, Spanish, Spanish-AP, student government, studio art, theater, theater arts, U.S. history-AP, visual arts, voice ensemble, world history, world literature, writing, yearbook.

Graduation Requirements Arts and fine arts (art, music, dance, drama), computer science, English, experiential education, foreign language, mathematics, music, physical education (includes health), science, social studies (includes history), WISE Program, off-campus senior independent senior project. Community service is required.

Special Academic Programs 15 Advanced Placement exams for which test preparation is offered; honors section; independent study; study at local college for college credit; academic accommodation for the gifted, the musically talented, and the artistically talented.

College Admission Counseling 18 students graduated in 2015; all went to college, including Boston University; New York University; Purchase College, State University of New York; Smith College; University of California, Berkeley; University of California, San Diego. Median SAT critical reading: 470, median SAT math: 560, median SAT writing: 460, median composite ACT: 25. 20% scored over 26 on composite ACT.

Student Life Upper grades have specified standards of dress, student council, honor system. Discipline rests primarily with faculty.

Tuition and Aid Day student tuition: $32,410; 7-day tuition and room/board: $52,410. Tuition installment plan (Insured Tuition Payment Plan, monthly payment plans, individually arranged payment plans, TADS). Tuition reduction for siblings, need-based scholarship grants available. In 2015–16, 18% of upper-school students received aid. Total amount of financial aid awarded in 2015–16: $367,421.

Admissions Traditional secondary-level entrance grade is 9. For fall 2015, 85 students applied for upper-level admission, 42 were accepted, 22 enrolled. Any standardized test and writing sample required. Deadline for receipt of application materials: none. Application fee required: $75. Interview required.

Athletics Interscholastic: basketball (boys, girls); coed interscholastic: aerobics/dance, soccer; coed intramural: bowling, dance, golf, jogging, lacrosse, outdoor adventure, tennis. 3 PE instructors, 3 coaches.

Computers Computers are regularly used in art, desktop publishing, English, foreign language, history, humanities, independent study, keyboarding, lab/keyboard, literary magazine, mathematics, music, newspaper, photography, research skills, SAT preparation, science, theater, video film production, word processing, writing, yearbook classes. Computer network features include online commercial services, Internet access, wireless campus network, Internet filtering or blocking technology, eLibrary. The school has a published electronic and media policy.

Contact Ms. Tricia Mayer, Admissions Coordinator. 845-268-6802 Ext. 206. Fax: 845-268-4644. E-mail: tmayer@rocklandcds.org. Website: www.rocklandcds.org

ROCK POINT SCHOOL

1 Rock Point Road

Burlington, Vermont 05408

Head of School: C.J. Spirito

General Information Coeducational boarding and day college-preparatory and arts school, affiliated with Episcopal Church; primarily serves students with learning disabilities, individuals with Attention Deficit Disorder, individuals with emotional and behavioral problems, and dyslexic students. Grades 9–12. Founded: 1928. Setting: small town. Students are housed in single-sex by floor dormitories. 130-acre campus. 3 buildings on campus. Approved or accredited by Association of Independent Schools in New England, Independent Schools of Northern New England, National Association of Episcopal Schools, New England Association of Schools and Colleges, The Association of Boarding Schools, and Vermont Department of Education. Member of National Association of Independent Schools. Endowment: $2.5 million. Total enrollment: 26. Upper school average class size: 10. Upper school faculty-student ratio: 1:5. There are 167 required school days per year for Upper School students. Upper School students typically attend 5 days per week. The average school day consists of 6 hours and 45 minutes.

Upper School Student Profile Grade 9: 1 student (1 boy); Grade 10: 9 students (5 boys, 4 girls); Grade 11: 9 students (5 boys, 4 girls); Grade 12: 7 students (3 boys, 4 girls). 80% of students are boarding students. 15% are state residents. 9 states are represented in upper school student body. 7% of students are members of Episcopal Church.

Faculty School total: 11. In upper school: 5 men, 6 women; 4 have advanced degrees; 4 reside on campus.

Subjects Offered Agriculture, algebra, American history, American literature, ancient history, animation, art, art history, biology, calculus, chemistry, community service, creative thinking, critical thinking, drawing, earth science, English, geometry, health, historical foundations for arts, history, mathematics, painting, photography, physical education, poetry, portfolio art, pre-calculus, science, stained glass, Western civilization, world history, world literature.

Graduation Requirements Art, art history, English, history, mathematics, physical education (includes health), science. Community service is required.

Special Academic Programs Independent study; study at local college for college credit; academic accommodation for the gifted and the artistically talented; special instructional classes for students who need structure and personal attention; ESL.

College Admission Counseling 4 students graduated in 2015; 3 went to college, including Cornell College. Other: 1 went to work. Median SAT critical reading: 540, median SAT math: 490, median SAT writing: 490, median combined SAT: 1500. 29% scored over 600 on SAT critical reading, 14% scored over 600 on SAT math, 14% scored over 600 on SAT writing, 29% scored over 1800 on combined SAT.

Student Life Upper grades have specified standards of dress. Discipline rests primarily with faculty.

Summer Programs Remediation, art/fine arts programs offered; session focuses on explore outdoor education, earn credits, and have fun in Vermont; held both on and off campus; held at day trips outside into Burlington, Vermont, throughout the state, and beyond; accepts boys and girls; open to students from other schools. 10 students usually enrolled. 2016 schedule: July 5 to August 12. Application deadline: June 30.

Tuition and Aid Day student tuition: $28,400; 7-day tuition and room/board: $57,700. Tuition installment plan (individually arranged payment plans, deposit and two installment plan (September 1 and December 1), other specially created plans with a family). Need-based scholarship grants available. In 2015–16, 31% of upper-school students received aid. Total amount of financial aid awarded in 2015–16: $150,000.

Admissions Traditional secondary-level entrance grade is 10. For fall 2015, 20 students applied for upper-level admission, 15 were accepted, 12 enrolled. Essay or writing sample required. Deadline for receipt of application materials: none. Application fee required: $50. On-campus interview required.

Athletics Coed Interscholastic: basketball, ultimate Frisbee; coed intramural: alpine skiing, backpacking, ball hockey, basketball, bicycling, billiards, broomball, canoeing/kayaking, climbing, cooperative games, fitness, fitness walking, Frisbee, hiking/backpacking, jogging, kickball, martial arts, nordic skiing, outdoor activities, outdoor adventure, outdoor recreation, physical fitness, physical training, rock climbing, ropes courses, running, skateboarding, skiing (downhill), snowboarding, soccer, softball, touch football, ultimate Frisbee, walking, weight lifting, winter walking, yoga. 7 PE instructors.

Computers Computers are regularly used in all academic, animation, art, college planning, creative writing, media, music, photography, video film production, word processing classes. Computer network features include Internet access, Internet filtering or blocking technology. Student e-mail accounts are available to students.

Contact Hillary Kramer, Director of Admissions. 802-863-1104 Ext. 12. Fax: 802-863-6628. E-mail: hkramer@rockpoint.org. Website: www.rockpoint.org

ROCKWAY MENNONITE COLLEGIATE

110 Doon Road
Kitchener, Ontario N2G 3C8, Canada

Head of School: Ms. Ann Schultz

General Information Coeducational boarding and day college-preparatory, arts, religious studies, and technology school, affiliated with Mennonite Church. Grades 7–12. Founded: 1945. Setting: suburban. Nearest major city is Toronto, Canada. Students are housed in host family homes. 14-acre campus. 7 buildings on campus. Approved or accredited by Mennonite Schools Council and Ontario Department of Education. Language of instruction: English. Endowment: CAN$735,000. Total enrollment: 265. Upper school average class size: 21. Upper school faculty-student ratio: 1:10. There are 194 required school days per year for Upper School students. Upper School students typically attend 5 days per week. The average school day consists of 6 hours.

Upper School Student Profile Grade 9: 50 students (25 boys, 25 girls); Grade 10: 37 students (21 boys, 16 girls); Grade 11: 62 students (33 boys, 29 girls); Grade 12: 71 students (34 boys, 37 girls). 1% of students are boarding students. 85% are province residents. 1 province is represented in upper school student body. 15% are international students. International students from China, Democratic People's Republic of Korea, Germany, Hong Kong, Japan, and Taiwan; 2 other countries represented in student body. 38% of students are Mennonite.

Faculty School total: 35. In upper school: 12 men, 18 women; 8 have advanced degrees.

Subjects Offered Algebra, auto mechanics, Bible, biology, calculus, Canadian history, career education, chemistry, choral music, civics, computer science, computer studies, construction, dramatic arts, English, entrepreneurship, ESL, family studies, finite math, food and nutrition, French, functions, geography, geometry, German, guidance, health, healthful living, history, information technology, instrumental music, integrated technology fundamentals, mathematics, music, orchestra, parenting, personal finance, philosophy, physical education, physics, religious studies, science, strings, technology/design, transportation technology, visual arts, vocal music, wind instruments, world history, world religions.

Graduation Requirements Ontario Ministry of Education requirements, 2 credits in a language other than English, religious studies courses through grade 10.

Special Academic Programs Independent study; ESL (34 students enrolled).

College Admission Counseling 64 students graduated in 2015; 47 went to college, including Carleton University; The University of Western Ontario; University of Guelph; University of Toronto; University of Waterloo; Wilfrid Laurier University. Other: 13 went to work, 4 had other specific plans.

Student Life Upper grades have specified standards of dress, student council. Discipline rests primarily with faculty. Attendance at religious services is required.

Tuition and Aid Day student tuition: CAN$14,680; 7-day tuition and room/board: CAN$29,500. Tuition installment plan (monthly payment plans, individually arranged payment plans). Tuition reduction for siblings, bursaries, need-based scholarship grants, paying campus jobs available. In 2015–16, 20% of upper-school students received aid. Total amount of financial aid awarded in 2015–16: CAN$186,927.

Admissions Traditional secondary-level entrance grade is 9. For fall 2015, 60 students applied for upper-level admission, 56 were accepted, 55 enrolled. Deadline for receipt of application materials: none. Application fee required: CAN$100.

Athletics Interscholastic: badminton (boys, girls), baseball (b,g), basketball (b,g), cross-country running (b,g), track and field (b,g), volleyball (b,g), wrestling (b,g); intramural: ball hockey (b,g), baseball (b,g), basketball (b,g), cooperative games (b,g), dance (b,g), flag football (h,g), flagball (b,g), floor hockey (b,g), indoor soccer (b,g), outdoor education (b,g), physical training (b,g), power lifting (b,g), rock climbing (b,g), rugby (b,g), soccer (b,g), strength & conditioning (b,g), volleyball (b,g); coed interscholastic: Frisbee; coed intramural: baseball, cooperative games, outdoor education, street hockey, table tennis, track and field. 3 PE instructors.

Computers Computers are regularly used in Bible studies, business, career technology, college planning, construction, drafting, English, geography, library, mathematics, religious studies, science, typing, Web site design, yearbook classes. Computer resources include on-campus library services, Internet access, wireless campus network. Campus intranet, student e-mail accounts, and computer access in designated common areas are available to students. The school has a published electronic and media policy.

Contact Director of Admissions and Recruitment. 519-743-5209 Ext. 3029. Fax: 519-743-5935. E-mail: admissions@rockway.ca. Website: www.rockway.ca

THE ROEPER SCHOOL

41190 Woodward Avenue
Bloomfield Hills, Michigan 48304

Head of School: David Feldman

General Information Coeducational day college-preparatory and gifted education school. Grades PK–12. Founded: 1941. Setting: urban. Nearest major city is Birmingham. 1-acre campus. 1 building on campus. Approved or accredited by Independent Schools Association of the Central States. Member of National Association of Independent Schools. Endowment: $8 million. Total enrollment: 579. Upper school average class size: 14. Upper school faculty-student ratio: 1:8. There are 165 required school days per year for Upper School students. Upper School students typically attend 5 days per week. The average school day consists of 7 hours and 10 minutes.

Upper School Student Profile Grade 9: 40 students (26 boys, 14 girls); Grade 10: 31 students (18 boys, 13 girls); Grade 11: 41 students (28 boys, 13 girls); Grade 12: 37 students (17 boys, 20 girls).

Faculty School total: 79. In upper school: 17 men, 29 women; 27 have advanced degrees.

Subjects Offered 20th century American writers, 20th century history, 3-dimensional art, acting, advanced biology, advanced chemistry, advanced math, Advanced Placement courses, African-American history, African-American literature, algebra, American history, American literature, anatomy, architecture, art, art history, athletics, audition methods, band, bioethics, biology, calculus, calculus-AP, cartooning/animation, ceramics, chamber groups, chemistry, chemistry-AP, Chinese, choir, choreography, communications, comparative government and politics, computer programming, concert band, constitutional law, costumes and make-up, creative writing, dance, debate, digital photography, drama, drawing and design, economics, English, English literature, English-AP, European history, European history-AP, film, fine arts, first aid, fitness, forensics, French, geometry, government, government/civics, graphic design, health, health education, history, independent study, jazz band, journalism, Latin, mathematics, model United Nations, music, music theory, musical theater, newspaper, philosophy, photography, physical education, physical fitness, physics, poetry, programming, science, senior project, social studies, Spanish, speech, stagecraft, statistics, strings, taxonomy, theater, trigonometry, world history, world literature, writing, yearbook.

Graduation Requirements Arts and fine arts (art, music, dance, drama), computer science, English, foreign language, government, health, mathematics, science, social studies (includes history).

Special Academic Programs 13 Advanced Placement exams for which test preparation is offered; independent study; academic accommodation for the gifted, the musically talented, and the artistically talented; programs in English, mathematics, general development for dyslexic students.

College Admission Counseling 42 students graduated in 2015; all went to college, including Kalamazoo College; Northwestern University; University of Chicago; University of Michigan; Western Michigan University.

Student Life Upper grades have student council, honor system. Discipline rests primarily with faculty.

Summer Programs Art/fine arts programs offered; session focuses on theater; held on campus; accepts boys and girls; open to students from other schools. 75 students usually enrolled. 2016 schedule: June 22 to July 31.

Tuition and Aid Day student tuition: $26,100. Tuition installment plan (FACTS Tuition Payment Plan, individually arranged payment plans). Need-based scholarship grants available. In 2014–15, 40% of upper-school students received aid. Total amount of financial aid awarded in 2014–15: $533,656.

Admissions Traditional secondary-level entrance grade is 9. For fall 2015, 30 students applied for upper-level admission, 26 were accepted, 20 enrolled. Individual IQ and TOEFL or SLEP required. Deadline for receipt of application materials: none. Application fee required: $75. On-campus interview required.

Athletics Interscholastic: baseball (boys), basketball (b,g), cross-country running (b,g), golf (b,g), physical training (b,g), soccer (b,g), strength & conditioning (b,g), track and field (b,g), volleyball (g), weight lifting (b,g); intramural: indoor soccer (b,g); coed intramural: physical training, strength & conditioning, weight lifting. 4 PE instructors, 30 coaches.

Computers Computers are regularly used in English, foreign language, graphic design, journalism, library, mathematics, photography, programming, publishing, science, yearbook classes. Computer network features include on-campus library services, online commercial services, Internet access, wireless campus network. Student e-mail accounts and computer access in designated common areas are available to students. Students grades are available online.

Contact Lori Zinser, Director of Admissions. 248-203-7302. Fax: 248-203-7310. E-mail: lori.zinser@roeper.org. Website: www.roeper.org

ROLAND PARK COUNTRY SCHOOL

5204 Roland Avenue
Baltimore, Maryland 21210

Head of School: Mrs. Jean Waller Brune

General Information Coeducational day (boys only in lower grades) and distance learning college-preparatory and arts school. Boys grade PS, girls grades PS–12. Distance learning grades 9–12. Founded: 1901. Setting: suburban. 21-acre campus. 1 building on campus. Approved or accredited by Association of Independent Maryland Schools. Member of National Association of Independent Schools and Secondary School Admission Test Board. Endowment: $58.3 million. Total enrollment: 644. Upper school average class size: 14. Upper school faculty-student ratio: 1:7. There are 177 required school days per year for Upper School students. Upper School students typically attend 5 days per week. The average school day consists of 7 hours and 45 minutes.

Upper School Student Profile Grade 6: 35 students (35 girls); Grade 7: 35 students (35 girls); Grade 8: 59 students (59 girls); Grade 9: 65 students (65 girls); Grade 10: 86 students (86 girls); Grade 11: 79 students (79 girls); Grade 12: 80 students (80 girls).

Faculty School total: 107. In upper school: 11 men, 41 women; 40 have advanced degrees.

Subjects Offered 3-dimensional art, advanced biology, advanced chemistry, advanced math, Advanced Placement courses, advanced studio art-AP, algebra, American history-AP, American literature, American literature-AP, anatomy, ancient world history, Arabic, archaeology, art, art history, art history-AP, astronomy, biology, biology-AP, calculus, calculus-AP, ceramics, chemistry, chemistry-AP, Chesapeake Bay studies, Chinese, community service, computer programming, computer science, creative writing, dance, drama, ecology, economics, engineering, English, English language-AP, English literature, English literature-AP, English-AP, environmental science, environmental studies, European civilization, European history, European history-AP, French, French language-AP, French literature-AP, geometry, German, government/civics, Greek, health, integrated mathematics, Latin, music, philosophy, photography, physical education, physics, physiology, religion, Russian, science, social studies, Spanish, speech, statistics, theater, trigonometry, world history.

Graduation Requirements Adolescent issues, arts and fine arts (art, music, dance, drama), biology, chemistry, English, foreign language, history, mathematics, physical education (includes health), physics, public speaking, science. Community service is required.

Special Academic Programs Advanced Placement exam preparation; honors section; independent study; term-away projects; study abroad.

College Admission Counseling 81 students graduated in 2015; all went to college, including Boston University; Clemson University; Georgetown University; Penn State University Park; University of Maryland, College Park; Villanova University. Mean SAT critical reading: 601, mean SAT math: 618, mean SAT writing: 625, mean combined SAT: 1844, mean composite ACT: 26.

Student Life Upper grades have uniform requirement, student council, honor system. Discipline rests equally with students and faculty.

Summer Programs Remediation, enrichment, advancement, sports, art/fine arts programs offered; session focuses on summer camp, arts, some academics; held both on and off campus; held at off-site pool and venues for outdoor education programs and various sites around Baltimore for art projects; accepts boys and girls; open to students from other schools. 600 students usually enrolled. 2016 schedule: June 13 to August 22. Application deadline: none.

Tuition and Aid Day student tuition: $26,995. Tuition installment plan (FACTS Tuition Payment Plan, individually arranged payment plans). Need-based scholarship grants, paying campus jobs available. In 2015–16, 36% of upper-school students received aid. Total amount of financial aid awarded in 2015–16: $1,516,770.

Admissions Traditional secondary-level entrance grade is 9. For fall 2015, 112 students applied for upper-level admission, 68 were accepted, 36 enrolled. ISEE required. Deadline for receipt of application materials: December 18. Application fee required: $60. Interview required.

Athletics Interscholastic: badminton, basketball, crew, cross-country running, field hockey, golf, independent competitive sports, indoor soccer, indoor track, lacrosse, soccer, softball, squash, swimming and diving, tennis, track and field, volleyball, winter (indoor) track, winter soccer; intramural: dance, fitness, modern dance, outdoor education, physical fitness, rock climbing, strength & conditioning. 7 PE instructors, 1 athletic trainer.

Computers Computers are regularly used in all classes. Computer network features include on-campus library services, online commercial services, Internet access, wireless campus network, Internet filtering or blocking technology, online database. Campus intranet, student e-mail accounts, and computer access in designated common areas are available to students. Students grades are available online. The school has a published electronic and media policy.

Contact Kathleen Curtis, Director of Admissions and Enrollment Management. 410-323-5500. Fax: 410-323-2164. E-mail: admissions@rpcs.org. Website: www.rpcs.org

ROLLING HILLS PREPARATORY SCHOOL

One Rolling Hills Prep Way
San Pedro, California 90732

Head of School: Peter McCormack

General Information Coeducational day college-preparatory, arts, and technology school. Grades 6–12. Founded: 1981. Setting: suburban. Nearest major city is Los Angeles. 21-acre campus. 20 buildings on campus. Approved or accredited by California Association of Independent Schools, Western Association of Schools and Colleges, and California Department of Education. Member of National Association of Independent Schools. Endowment: $100,000. Total enrollment: 256. Upper school average class size: 17. Upper school faculty-student ratio: 1:9. There are 180 required school days per year for Upper School students. Upper School students typically attend 5 days per week. The average school day consists of 6 hours.

Upper School Student Profile Grade 9: 60 students (35 boys, 25 girls); Grade 10: 33 students (16 boys, 17 girls); Grade 11: 50 students (25 boys, 25 girls); Grade 12: 35 students (18 boys, 17 girls).

Faculty School total: 36. In upper school: 10 men, 19 women; 14 have advanced degrees.

Subjects Offered Algebra, American history, American literature, American sign language, anatomy, art, biology, calculus, ceramics, chemistry, Chinese, computer science, creative writing, drama, economics, English, English literature, European history, fine arts, French, geography, geometry, government/civics, history, mathematics, music, photography, physical education, physics, pre-calculus, psychology-AP, robotics, science, social studies, Spanish, speech, statistics, theater, trigonometry, world history.

Graduation Requirements Arts and fine arts (art, music, dance, drama), English, foreign language, mathematics, outdoor education, physical education (includes health), science, social studies (includes history), two-week senior internship, senior speech.

Special Academic Programs 10 Advanced Placement exams for which test preparation is offered; honors section; independent study; academic accommodation for the gifted; programs in general development for dyslexic students; ESL (20 students enrolled).

College Admission Counseling 43 students graduated in 2015; all went to college, including Carnegie Mellon University; Lewis & Clark College; University of California, Berkeley; University of California, Los Angeles; University of Southern California; University of Washington. Mean SAT critical reading: 620, mean SAT math: 600, mean SAT writing: 610. 45% scored over 600 on SAT critical reading, 40% scored over 600 on SAT math, 45% scored over 600 on SAT writing.

Student Life Upper grades have specified standards of dress, student council, honor system. Discipline rests primarily with faculty.

Summer Programs Enrichment, art/fine arts programs offered; session focuses on algebra and photography; held on campus; accepts boys and girls; open to students from other schools. 30 students usually enrolled. 2016 schedule: June 26 to August 28. Application deadline: June 1.

Tuition and Aid Day student tuition: $27,900. Tuition installment plan (Insured Tuition Payment Plan, Key Tuition Payment Plan, monthly payment plans). Merit scholarship grants, need-based scholarship grants available. In 2014–15, 40% of upper-school students received aid. Total amount of financial aid awarded in 2014–15: $1,000,000.

Admissions Traditional secondary-level entrance grade is 9. For fall 2015, 55 students applied for upper-level admission, 40 were accepted, 30 enrolled. ISEE, TOEFL, TOEFL Junior or writing sample required. Deadline for receipt of application materials: none. Application fee required: $125. Interview required.

Athletics Interscholastic: baseball (boys), basketball (b,g), cheering (g), football (b), soccer (b,g), softball (g), track and field (g), volleyball (b,g); intramural: cheering (g), dance (g); coed interscholastic: cross-country running, golf, roller hockey, running, sailing, track and field; coed intramural: backpacking, climbing, fitness, hiking/backpacking, outdoor education, physical fitness, rock climbing, ropes courses. 4 PE instructors, 10 coaches, 1 athletic trainer.

Computers Computers are regularly used in English, foreign language, history, mathematics, photography, science classes. Computer network features include on-campus library services, Internet access, wireless campus network. The school has a published electronic and media policy.

Contact Ryan Tillson, Director of Admission. 310-791-1101 Ext. 148. Fax: 310-373-4931. E-mail: rtillson@rollinghillsprep.org. Website: www.rollinghillsprep.org

ROSATI-KAIN HIGH SCHOOL

4389 Lindell Boulevard
St. Louis, Missouri 63108

Head of School: Dr. Elizabeth Ann Goodwin

General Information Girls' day college-preparatory and arts school, affiliated with Roman Catholic Church. Grades 9–12. Founded: 1911. Setting: urban. Nearest major city is Saint Louis. Students are housed in No housing. 1 building on campus. Approved or accredited by Missouri Department of Education. Upper school average class size: 300. Upper school faculty-student ratio: 1:12. There are 180 required school days per year for Upper School students. Upper School students typically attend 5 days per week. The average school day consists of 6 hours and 45 minutes.

Upper School Student Profile Grade 9: 70 students (70 girls); Grade 10: 66 students (66 girls); Grade 11: 92 students (92 girls); Grade 12: 72 students (72 girls). 75% of students are Roman Catholic.

Faculty School total: 35. In upper school: 5 men, 30 women; 20 have advanced degrees.

Subjects Offered Accounting, advanced biology, advanced chemistry, advanced computer applications, advanced math, Advanced Placement courses, algebra, American government, American history, American history-AP, American literature, American literature-AP, analysis and differential calculus, ancient world history, art, art history, audio visual/media, biology, biology-AP, business skills, calculus, calculus-AP, career/college preparation, Catholic belief and practice, chemistry, chemistry-AP, chorus, Christianity, civics, college planning, communications, community service, comparative government and politics, comparative government and politics-AP, composition, composition-AP, computer applications, computer art, computer education, computer graphics, computer information systems, computer literacy, computer math, computer multimedia, computer processing, computer programming, computer programming-AP, computer science, computer science-AP, computer studies, concert band, constitutional history of U.S., contemporary art, CPR, creative arts, creative writing, debate, dramatic arts, drawing and design, ecology, ecology, environmental systems, economics, economics-AP, English language and composition-AP, English literature, English literature and composition-AP, English literature-AP, English/composition-AP, environmental education, environmental science, fine arts,

French, French language-AP, French-AP, geometry, government and politics-AP, government/civics, government/civics-AP, graphic arts, graphic design, health and wellness, health education, history-AP, Holocaust and other genocides, humanities, language-AP, literature and composition-AP, literature-AP, mathematics-AP, media production, microeconomics, music, music appreciation, musical theater, nature study, news writing, newspaper, nutrition, personal finance, personal money management, photography, photojournalism, physical education, physical fitness, physics, physics-AP, play production, poetry, political science, portfolio art, pottery, pre-calculus, probability and statistics, psychology, public speaking, publications, reading/study skills, SAT/ACT preparation, sculpture, sociology, Spanish language-AP, sports, statistics, statistics-AP, student government, studio art, telecommunications and the Internet, theater arts, theater production, theology, trigonometry, U.S. government, U.S. government and politics, U.S. government and politics-AP, U.S. history, U.S. history-AP, United States government-AP, visual and performing arts, women's studies, world history-AP, writing, yearbook.

Special Academic Programs Advanced Placement exam preparation; independent study; study at local college for college credit; academic accommodation for the gifted, the musically talented, and the artistically talented; special instructional classes for deaf students, blind students.

College Admission Counseling 88 students graduated in 2015; all went to college, including Fontbonne University; Kansas State University; Loyola University Chicago; Mercer University; Stanford University; University of Missouri. Median composite ACT: 27.

Student Life Upper grades have specified standards of dress, student council, honor system. Discipline rests primarily with faculty. Attendance at religious services is required.

Tuition and Aid Day student tuition: $10,000. Tuition installment plan (FACTS Tuition Payment Plan, monthly payment plans, individually arranged payment plans). Tuition reduction for siblings, merit scholarship grants, need-based scholarship grants, paying campus jobs available. In 2015–16, 40% of upper-school students received aid; total upper-school merit-scholarship money awarded: $5000. Total amount of financial aid awarded in 2015–16: $100,000.

Admissions Traditional secondary-level entrance grade is 9. For fall 2015, 95 students applied for upper-level admission, 75 were accepted, 70 enrolled. Deadline for receipt of application materials: none. No application fee required. Interview recommended.

Athletics Interscholastic: aquatics, basketball, bocce, cheering, cross-country running, dance, dance team, field hockey, Frisbee, lacrosse, pom squad, soccer, softball, swimming and diving, tennis, track and field, ultimate Frisbee. 1 PE instructor, 10 coaches, 5 athletic trainers.

Computers Computers are regularly used in all classes. Computer network features include on-campus library services, online commercial services, Internet access, wireless campus network, Internet filtering or blocking technology, personal student laptops provided at no charge. Campus intranet, student e-mail accounts, and computer access in designated common areas are available to students. Students grades are available online. The school has a published electronic and media policy.

Contact Mrs. Laura A. Schulte, Director of Enrollment Management. 314-533-8513 Ext. 2215. Fax: 314-533-1618. E-mail: lschulte@rosati-kain.org. Website: www.rosati-kain.org/

ROSSEAU LAKE COLLEGE

1967 Bright Street
Rosseau, Ontario P0C 1J0, Canada

Head of School: Mr. Lance Postma

General Information Coeducational boarding and day college-preparatory, arts, business, and technology school. Grades 7–12. Founded: 1967. Setting: rural. Nearest major city is Toronto, Canada. Students are housed in single-sex dormitories. 53-acre campus. 13 buildings on campus. Approved or accredited by Canadian Association of Independent Schools, Canadian Educational Standards Institute, Ontario Ministry of Education, The Association of Boarding Schools, and Ontario Department of Education. Languages of instruction: English and French. Endowment: CAN$100,000. Total enrollment: 84. Upper school average class size: 15. Upper school faculty-student ratio: 1:6. There are 176 required school days per year for Upper School students. Upper School students typically attend 5 days per week. The average school day consists of 7 hours and 30 minutes.

Upper School Student Profile Grade 7: 2 students (1 boy, 1 girl); Grade 8: 10 students (9 boys, 1 girl); Grade 9: 16 students (11 boys, 5 girls); Grade 10: 21 students (9 boys, 12 girls); Grade 11: 26 students (19 boys, 7 girls); Grade 12: 20 students (13 boys, 7 girls). 62% of students are boarding students. 54% are province residents. 2 provinces are represented in upper school student body. 46% are international students. International students from Brazil, China, Guyana, Japan, Mexico, and Republic of Korea.

Faculty School total: 16. In upper school: 7 men, 9 women; 3 have advanced degrees; 9 reside on campus.

Subjects Offered Accounting, algebra, art, art history, biology, business, calculus, Canadian law, career and personal planning, chemistry, civics, computer programming, computer science, data analysis, economics, English, entrepreneurship, ESL, European history, experiential education, fine arts, French, geography, geometry, health, history, information technology, marketing, mathematics, music, outdoor education, physical

education, physics, political science, science, social sciences, trigonometry, visual arts, world governments, writing.

Graduation Requirements Arts and fine arts (art, music, dance, drama), business skills (includes word processing), career planning, civics, computer science, English, foreign language, mathematics, physical education (includes health), science, social studies (includes history).

Special Academic Programs Independent study; term-away projects; study abroad; ESL (18 students enrolled).

College Admission Counseling 15 students graduated in 2015; all went to college, including McMaster University; Queen's University at Kingston; The University of Western Ontario; University of Guelph; University of Toronto; York University.

Student Life Upper grades have uniform requirement, student council, honor system. Discipline rests equally with students and faculty.

Summer Programs Remediation, enrichment, advancement programs offered; session focuses on academics; held on campus; accepts boys and girls; open to students from other schools. 10 students usually enrolled. 2016 schedule: July 1 to July 30. Application deadline: June 15.

Tuition and Aid Day student tuition: CAN$18,800; 7-day tuition and room/board: CAN$47,500. Tuition installment plan (individually arranged payment plans). Merit scholarship grants, need-based scholarship grants available. In 2015–16, 10% of upper-school students received aid; total upper-school merit-scholarship money awarded: CAN$40,000. Total amount of financial aid awarded in 2015–16: CAN$160,000.

Admissions Traditional secondary-level entrance grade is 9. For fall 2015, 69 students applied for upper-level admission, 42 were accepted, 42 enrolled. Admissions testing and English Composition Test for ESL students required. Deadline for receipt of application materials: none. Application fee required: CAN$300. Interview required.

Athletics Interscholastic: baseball (boys), basketball (b,g), cross-country running (b,g), field hockey (g), hockey (b), ice hockey (b), mountain biking (b,g), nordic skiing (b,g), rugby (b), running (b,g), skiing (cross-country) (b,g), snowboarding (b,g), soccer (b,g), softball (b), swimming and diving (b,g), tennis (b,g), track and field (b,g), volleyball (b,g); intramural: alpine skiing (b,g), baseball (b), basketball (b,g), cross-country running (b,g), field hockey (g), hockey (b,g), ice hockey (b,g), rugby (b), running (b,g), skiing (cross-country) (b,g), snowboarding (b,g); coed interscholastic: bicycling, canoeing/kayaking, climbing, golf, kayaking, mountain biking, nordic skiing, running, skiing (cross-country), skiing (downhill), snowboarding, softball, track and field; coed intramural: aerobics, aerobics/dance, aquatics, backpacking, ball hockey, baseball, basketball, bicycling, bowling, broomball, canoeing/kayaking, climbing, combined training, cooperative games, Cosom hockey, cross-country running, equestrian sports, fishing, fitness, fitness walking, flag football, floor hockey, fly fishing, freestyle skiing, Frisbee, golf, hiking/backpacking, horseback riding, ice skating, indoor hockey, indoor soccer, jogging, kayaking, life saving, mountain biking, mountaineering, nordic skiing, outdoor activities, paddle tennis, paddling, physical fitness, physical training, rappelling, rock climbing, ropes courses, sailboarding, sailing, scuba diving, skateboarding, skiing (cross-country), skiing (downhill), snowboarding, snowshoeing, soccer, softball, squash, street hockey, strength & conditioning, swimming and diving, table tennis, tennis, track and field, triathlon, ultimate Frisbee, volleyball, walking, wall climbing, water skiing, weight lifting, weight training, wilderness, wilderness survival, wildernessways, windsurfing, winter walking, yoga. 2 PE instructors, 2 coaches.

Computers Computers are regularly used in geography, graphic arts, information technology classes. Computer network features include on-campus library services, Internet access, wireless campus network, Internet filtering or blocking technology. Campus intranet, student e-mail accounts, and computer access in designated common areas are available to students. The school has a published electronic and media policy.

Contact Ms. Lynda G. Marshall, Director of Admissions. 705-732-4351 Ext. 12. Fax: 705-732-6319. E-mail: lynda.marshall@rosseaulakecollege.com. Website: www.rosseaulakecollege.com

ROSS SCHOOL

18 Goodfriend Drive
East Hampton, New York 11937

Head of School: Ms. Patricia Lein

General Information Coeducational boarding and day college-preparatory, technology, Globally-focused, integrated curriculum, and ESOL curriculum school; primarily serves students with learning disabilities and individuals with emotional and behavioral problems. Boarding grades 7–12, day grades N–12. Founded: 1991. Setting: small town. Nearest major city is New York City. Students are housed in single-sex dormitories. 100-acre campus. 7 buildings on campus. Approved or accredited by Middle States Association of Colleges and Schools, New York State Association of Independent Schools, The Association of Boarding Schools, and New York Department of Education. Member of National Association of Independent Schools and Secondary School Admission Test Board. Total enrollment: 521. Upper school average class size: 15. Upper school faculty-student ratio: 1:7. There are 175 required school days per year for Upper School students. Upper School students typically attend 5 days per week. The average school day consists of 8 hours.

Upper School Student Profile 66% of students are boarding students. 6 states are represented in upper school student body. 60% are international students. International students from Brazil, China, Germany, Republic of Korea, Russian Federation, and Taiwan; 19 other countries represented in student body.

Faculty School total: 94. In upper school: 21 men, 33 women; 41 have advanced degrees; 19 reside on campus.

Subjects Offered 20th century world history, 3-dimensional design, acting, advanced biology, advanced chemistry, advanced computer applications, advanced math, African drumming, algebra, American history, art history, athletics, audio visual/media, biology, calculus, chemistry, Chinese, chorus, college counseling, computer multimedia, concert band, contemporary issues, creative writing, current events, dance, digital imaging, drawing, electives, English, English literature, entrepreneurship, ESL, filmmaking, French, geometry, global issues, health, health and wellness, history, independent study, integrated arts, interdisciplinary studies, jazz band, literature by women, marine biology, mathematics, media arts, media production, media studies, model United Nations, music, musical productions, performing arts, philosophy, photography, physics, pre-algebra, pre-calculus, probability and statistics, psychology, religion, SAT preparation, science, science and technology, senior internship, senior project, Spanish, studio art, technological applications, theater arts, United Nations and international issues, visual arts, Web site design, wood lab, world history.

Graduation Requirements 60 hours of community service.

Special Academic Programs 9 Advanced Placement exams for which test preparation is offered; honors section; independent study; term-away projects; ESL (158 students enrolled).

College Admission Counseling 68 students graduated in 2014; all went to college, including Boston University; Cornell University; New York University; Parsons School of Design; Purdue University; Stanford University. Median SAT critical reading: 520, median SAT math: 560, median SAT writing: 510.

Student Life Upper grades have uniform requirement, student council, honor system. Discipline rests primarily with faculty.

Tuition and Aid Day student tuition: $37,300; 7-day tuition and room/board: $55,900. Tuition installment plan (monthly payment plans). Need-based scholarship grants available. In 2014–15, 35% of upper-school students received aid.

Admissions Traditional secondary-level entrance grade is 9. Any standardized test, SSAT, TOEFL, TOEFL Junior or TOEFL or SLEP required. Deadline for receipt of application materials: none. Application fee required: $100. Interview required.

Athletics Interscholastic: baseball (boys), basketball (b,g), cross-country running (b,g), golf (b,g), soccer (b,g), softball (g), tennis (b,g), track and field (b,g), volleyball (g); coed interscholastic: cheering, rowing, sailing; coed intramural: archery, dance, kayaking, modern dance, mountain biking, sailing, strength & conditioning, surfing, tai chi, yoga. 6 PE instructors, 8 coaches, 1 athletic trainer.

Computers Computers are regularly used in all classes. Computer network features include on-campus library services, online commercial services, Internet access, wireless campus network, Internet filtering or blocking technology. Campus intranet and student e-mail accounts are available to students. Students grades are available online. The school has a published electronic and media policy.

Contact Ms. Kristin Eberstadt, Director of Admissions. 631-907-5205. Fax: 631-907-5563. E-mail: keberstadt@ross.org. Website: www.ross.org

ROTHESAY NETHERWOOD SCHOOL

40 College Hill Road
Rothesay, New Brunswick E2E 5H1, Canada

Head of School: Mr. Paul G. Kitchen

General Information Coeducational boarding and day college-preparatory, arts, and technology school, affiliated with Anglican Church of Canada. Grades 6–12. Founded: 1877. Setting: small town. Nearest major city is Saint John, Canada. Students are housed in single-sex dormitories. 260-acre campus. 26 buildings on campus. Approved or accredited by Canadian Association of Independent Schools, Conference of Independent Schools of Ontario, International Baccalaureate Organization, The Association of Boarding Schools, and New Brunswick Department of Education. Affiliate member of National Association of Independent Schools; member of Secondary School Admission Test Board. Languages of instruction: English and French. Endowment: CAN$3.5 million. Total enrollment: 271. Upper school average class size: 16. Upper school faculty-student ratio: 1:8. There are 176 required school days per year for Upper School students. Upper School students typically attend 5 days per week. The average school day consists of 7 hours and 45 minutes.

Upper School Student Profile Grade 9: 42 students (23 boys, 19 girls); Grade 10: 57 students (33 boys, 24 girls); Grade 11: 56 students (28 boys, 28 girls); Grade 12: 60 students (27 boys, 33 girls). 58% of students are boarding students. 66% are province residents. 9 provinces are represented in upper school student body. 17% are international students. International students from China, Germany, Ireland, Mexico, Nigeria, and United States; 8 other countries represented in student body. 30% of students are members of Anglican Church of Canada.

Faculty School total: 42. In upper school: 15 men, 15 women; 6 have advanced degrees; 35 reside on campus.

Subjects Offered Advanced biology, advanced chemistry, art, biology, Canadian history, chemistry, computer programming, CPR, digital art, drama, English, English literature, ESL, European history, fine arts, French, geography, geometry, health, history, information technology, International Baccalaureate courses, leadership, math

applications, mathematics, music, outdoor education, physical education, physics, science, social studies, Spanish, theater arts, world history, writing.

Graduation Requirements Arts and fine arts (art, music, dance, drama), computer science, English, foreign language, mathematics, physical education (includes health), science, social sciences, social studies (includes history), International Baccalaureate Theory of Knowledge, IB designation CAS hours (creativity, action, service), Extended Essay, Outward Bound adventure.

Special Academic Programs International Baccalaureate program; honors section; independent study; term-away projects; study at local college for college credit; academic accommodation for the gifted, the musically talented, and the artistically talented; ESL (10 students enrolled).

College Admission Counseling 58 students graduated in 2015; all went to college, including Acadia University; Dalhousie University; Mount Allison University; Queen's University at Kingston; St. Francis Xavier University; University of Toronto.

Student Life Upper grades have uniform requirement, student council, honor system. Discipline rests primarily with faculty. Attendance at religious services is required.

Summer Programs ESL, sports programs offered; session focuses on preparing ESL students for high school and sports camps; held on campus; accepts boys and girls; open to students from other schools. 2016 schedule: July 18 to August 5. Application deadline: May 31.

Tuition and Aid Day student tuition: CAN$21,480; 7-day tuition and room/board: CAN$35,550. Tuition installment plan (monthly payment plans, individually arranged payment plans). Tuition reduction for siblings, bursaries, merit scholarship grants, need-based scholarship grants available. In 2015–16, 34% of upper-school students received aid; total upper-school merit-scholarship money awarded: CAN$99,740. Total amount of financial aid awarded in 2015–16: CAN$1,029,195.

Admissions Traditional secondary-level entrance grade is 9. For fall 2015, 91 students applied for upper-level admission, 82 were accepted, 63 enrolled. Deadline for receipt of application materials: none. Application fee required: CAN$100. Interview required.

Athletics Interscholastic: basketball (boys, girls), crew (b,g), cross-country running (b,g), field hockey (g), ice hockey (b,g), rowing (b,g), rugby (b,g), running (b,g), soccer (b,g), squash (b,g), tennis (b,g), track and field (b,g), volleyball (b,g); intramural: crew (b,g), cross-country running (b,g), ice hockey (b,g), indoor soccer (b), squash (b,g), tennis (b,g), track and field (b,g), yoga (g); coed interscholastic: badminton, crew, cross-country running, ice hockey, rowing, tennis, track and field; coed intramural: aerobics, aerobics/dance, backpacking, badminton, bicycling, billiards, broomball, canoeing/kayaking, climbing, cooperative games, crew, cross-country running, fitness, fitness walking, floor hockey, hiking/backpacking, ice hockey, ice skating, indoor soccer, jogging, kayaking, outdoor activities, outdoor education, physical fitness, physical training, rock climbing, running, skiing (cross-country), skiing (downhill), snowboarding, snowshoeing, squash, street hockey, strength & conditioning, tennis, track and field, ultimate Frisbee, volleyball, walking, wall climbing, weight training. 3 PE instructors.

Computers Computers are regularly used in all classes. Computer network features include on-campus library services, Internet access, wireless campus network, Internet filtering or blocking technology, Web site for each academic course, informative, interactive online community for parents, teachers, and students. Campus intranet and student e-mail accounts are available to students. Students grades are available online. The school has a published electronic and media policy.

Contact Mrs. Elizabeth Kitchen, Director of Admission. 506-848-0866. Fax: 506-848-0851. E-mail: Elizabeth.Kitchen@rns.cc. Website: www.rns.cc

ROTTERDAM INTERNATIONAL SECONDARY SCHOOL, WOLFERT VAN BORSELEN

Bentincklaan 294
Rotterdam 3039 KK, Netherlands

Head of School: Ms. Jane Forrest

General Information Coeducational day college-preparatory, bilingual studies, and languages school. Grades 6–12. Founded: 1987. Setting: urban. 2-hectare campus. 1 building on campus. Approved or accredited by Council of International Schools, International Baccalaureate Organization, and New England Association of Schools and Colleges. Member of European Council of International Schools. Language of instruction: English. Total enrollment: 278. Upper school average class size: 15. Upper school faculty-student ratio: 1:10. There are 190 required school days per year for Upper School students. Upper School students typically attend 5 days per week. The average school day consists of 6 hours.

Upper School Student Profile Grade 6: 29 students (15 boys, 14 girls); Grade 7: 24 students (14 boys, 10 girls); Grade 8: 46 students (20 boys, 26 girls); Grade 9: 48 students (24 boys, 24 girls); Grade 10: 50 students (25 boys, 25 girls); Grade 11: 46 students (24 boys, 22 girls); Grade 12: 35 students (14 boys, 21 girls).

Faculty School total: 35. In upper school: 11 men, 24 women; 16 have advanced degrees.

Special Academic Programs International Baccalaureate program; ESL.

College Admission Counseling 29 students graduated in 2015; all went to college.

Student Life Upper grades have student council. Discipline rests primarily with faculty.

Tuition and Aid Day student tuition: €6800–€8500. Tuition installment plan (monthly payment plans, eight yearly payments).

Admissions Admissions testing required. Deadline for receipt of application materials: none. Application fee required: €250. On-campus interview required.

Athletics Coed Interscholastic: basketball, soccer; coed intramural: baseball, basketball, bicycling, rugby, soccer, table tennis, track and field, volleyball. 2 PE instructors.

Computers Computers are regularly used in all academic classes. Computer network features include on-campus library services, online commercial services, Internet access, wireless campus network. Student e-mail accounts are available to students. Students grades are available online. The school has a published electronic and media policy.

Contact Kathy Vos, Admissions Officer. 31-10 890 7743. Fax: 31-10 8907755. E-mail: kvo@wolfert.nl. Website: www.wolfert.nl/riss/

ROUTT CATHOLIC HIGH SCHOOL

500 East College
Jacksonville, Illinois 62650

Head of School: Mr. Nick Roscetti

General Information Coeducational day college-preparatory, arts, business, and religious studies school, affiliated with Roman Catholic Church; primarily serves students with learning disabilities and individuals with Attention Deficit Disorder. Grades 9–12. Founded: 1902. Setting: small town. Nearest major city is Springfield. 3-acre campus. 1 building on campus. Approved or accredited by Illinois Department of Education. Total enrollment: 118. Upper school average class size: 15. Upper school faculty-student ratio: 1:8. There are 176 required school days per year for Upper School students. Upper School students typically attend 5 days per week. The average school day consists of 6 hours and 30 minutes.

Upper School Student Profile Grade 9: 34 students (15 boys, 19 girls); Grade 10: 28 students (19 boys, 9 girls); Grade 11: 31 students (15 boys, 16 girls); Grade 12: 23 students (9 boys, 14 girls). 75% of students are Roman Catholic.

Faculty School total: 18. In upper school: 6 men, 12 women; 5 have advanced degrees.

Subjects Offered Advanced computer applications, Advanced Placement courses, algebra, American history-AP, American literature-AP, band, biology, calculus, Catholic belief and practice, chemistry, composition, drama, earth science, economics-AP, English, English literature-AP, environmental science, geography, geometry, government, health, history of the Catholic Church, Life of Christ, physical education, physics, psychology, public speaking, sociology, Spanish, U.S. history-AP, world history, world religions.

Graduation Requirements 1968, 15 community service hours per year (60 total).

Special Academic Programs 2 Advanced Placement exams for which test preparation is offered; honors section; study at local college for college credit; remedial reading and/or remedial writing; remedial math.

College Admission Counseling 21 students graduated in 2014; 18 went to college. Other: 1 went to work, 1 had other specific plans. Median composite ACT: 20. 16% scored over 26 on composite ACT.

Student Life Upper grades have uniform requirement, student council, honor system. Discipline rests primarily with faculty. Attendance at religious services is required.

Tuition and Aid Day student tuition: $3700. Tuition installment plan (FACTS Tuition Payment Plan). Tuition reduction for siblings, merit scholarship grants, need-based scholarship grants available. In 2014–15, 44% of upper-school students received aid; total upper-school merit-scholarship money awarded: $3500.

Admissions Traditional secondary-level entrance grade is 9. High School Placement Test (closed version) from Scholastic Testing Service required. Deadline for receipt of application materials: none. No application fee required. Interview required.

Athletics Interscholastic: baseball (boys), basketball (b,g), cheering (g), football (b), golf (b,g), softball (g), swimming and diving (b,g), track and field (b,g), volleyball (g); coed intramural: bowling. 1 PE instructor, 10 coaches.

Computers Computers are regularly used in computer applications, desktop publishing, journalism, keyboarding, media production, photojournalism, Web site design, word processing, yearbook classes. Computer network features include Internet access, Internet filtering or blocking technology. The school has a published electronic and media policy.

Contact Mrs. Betty Kuvinka, Development Director. 217-243-8563 Ext. 6. Fax: 217-243-3138. E-mail: bkuvinka@routtcatholic.com. Website: www.routtcatholic.com

ROWLAND HALL

843 South Lincoln Street
Salt Lake City, Utah 84102

Head of School: Mr. Alan C. Sparrow

General Information Coeducational day college-preparatory school. Grades PK–12. Founded: 1867. Setting: urban. 4-acre campus. 1 building on campus. Approved or accredited by Northwest Association of Independent Schools, Northwest Association of Schools and Colleges, The College Board, and Utah Department of Education. Member of National Association of Independent Schools. Endowment: $10 million. Total enrollment: 918. Upper school average class size: 16. Upper school faculty-student ratio: 1:7. There are 170 required school days per year for Upper School students.

Upper School students typically attend 5 days per week. The average school day consists of 6 hours.

Upper School Student Profile Grade 9: 73 students (33 boys, 40 girls); Grade 10: 88 students (41 boys, 47 girls); Grade 11: 72 students (26 boys, 46 girls); Grade 12: 67 students (25 boys, 42 girls).

Faculty School total: 130. In upper school: 21 men, 22 women; 32 have advanced degrees.

Subjects Offered Adolescent issues, algebra, biology, biology-AP, calculus, calculus-AP, ceramics, chemistry, chemistry-AP, Chinese, chorus, computer graphics, creative writing, dance, debate, drama, English, English language and composition-AP, English literature and composition-AP, environmental science, ethics, European history-AP, French, geometry, graphic arts, graphic design, history, human development, jazz band, math applications, modern European history-AP, music theory, newspaper, orchestra, photography, physical education, physics, physics-AP, political science, pre-calculus, psychology-AP, Spanish, Spanish-AP, statistics-AP, studio art, studio art-AP, theater, trigonometry, U.S. history, U.S. history-AP, weight training, Western civilization, world cultures, world religions, yearbook.

Graduation Requirements American history, arts and fine arts (art, music, dance, drama), biology, chemistry, English, ethics, foreign language, health education, mathematics, physical education (includes health), physics, science, social studies (includes history), world religions.

Special Academic Programs 17 Advanced Placement exams for which test preparation is offered; honors section; independent study.

College Admission Counseling 69 students graduated in 2014; 68 went to college, including Boston College; California Polytechnic State University, San Luis Obispo; New York University; University of Southern California; University of Utah; Wesleyan University. Other: 1 had other specific plans. Median SAT critical reading: 630, median SAT math: 620, median SAT writing: 620, median combined SAT: 1870, median composite ACT: 29. 59% scored over 600 on SAT critical reading, 57% scored over 600 on SAT math, 51% scored over 600 on SAT writing, 56% scored over 1800 on combined SAT, 65% scored over 26 on composite ACT.

Student Life Upper grades have specified standards of dress, student council, honor system. Discipline rests equally with students and faculty.

Tuition and Aid Day student tuition: $19,515. Tuition installment plan (monthly payment plans, individually arranged payment plans, 2-installment plan). Merit scholarship grants, need-based scholarship grants, ethnic/racial diversity scholarship grants, Malone Family Foundation Academically Talented/need-based scholarships available. In 2014–15, 20% of upper-school students received aid; total upper-school merit-scholarship money awarded: $37,500. Total amount of financial aid awarded in 2014–15: $867,697.

Admissions Traditional secondary-level entrance grade is 9. For fall 2014, 87 students applied for upper-level admission, 56 were accepted, 37 enrolled. ACT-Explore, ERB CTP IV, ISEE, PSAT, TOEFL or writing sample required. Deadline for receipt of application materials: March 1. Application fee required: $60. Interview required.

Athletics Interscholastic: alpine skiing (boys, girls), baseball (b), basketball (b,g), golf (b,g), skiing (downhill) (b,g), soccer (b,g), softball (g), swimming and diving (b,g), tennis (b,g), volleyball (g); intramural: skiing (downhill) (b,g); coed interscholastic: alpine skiing, cross-country running, dance, modern dance, skiing (downhill), track and field; coed intramural: climbing, deck hockey, hiking/backpacking, mountain biking, outdoor activities, outdoor education, physical fitness, physical training, rock climbing, ropes courses, skiing (cross-country), skiing (downhill), snowboarding, strength & conditioning, swimming and diving, telemark skiing, weight training, yoga. 6 PE instructors, 22 coaches, 1 athletic trainer.

Computers Computers are regularly used in desktop publishing, graphic design, yearbook classes. Computer network features include on-campus library services, Internet access, wireless campus network, Internet filtering or blocking technology, all students have their own laptop computer. Campus intranet, student e-mail accounts, and computer access in designated common areas are available to students. Students grades are available online. The school has a published electronic and media policy.

Contact Kathryn B. Gundersen, Director of Admission. 801-924-2950. Fax: 801-363-5521. E-mail: kathygundersen@rowlandhall.org. Website: www.rowlandhall.org

THE ROXBURY LATIN SCHOOL

101 St. Theresa Avenue
West Roxbury, Massachusetts 02132

Head of School: Mr. Kerry Paul Brennan

General Information Boys' day college-preparatory school. Grades 7–12. Founded: 1645. Setting: urban. Nearest major city is Boston. 117-acre campus. 10 buildings on campus. Approved or accredited by Association of Independent Schools in New England, Headmasters' Conference, and New England Association of Schools and Colleges. Member of National Association of Independent Schools and Secondary School Admission Test Board. Endowment: $135 million. Total enrollment: 303. Upper school average class size: 13. Upper school faculty-student ratio: 1:7. There are 176 required school days per year for Upper School students. Upper School students typically attend 5 days per week. The average school day consists of 6 hours and 30 minutes.

The Roxbury Latin School

Upper School Student Profile Grade 7: 46 students (46 boys); Grade 8: 43 students (43 boys); Grade 9: 55 students (55 boys); Grade 10: 52 students (52 boys); Grade 11: 53 students (53 boys); Grade 12: 52 students (52 boys).

Faculty School total: 43. In upper school: 37 men, 6 women; 33 have advanced degrees.

Subjects Offered Advanced biology, advanced chemistry, advanced math, algebra, American Civil War, American government, American history, American literature, American studies, analysis, analytic geometry, Ancient Greek, ancient history, ancient world history, applied arts, art, art history, art history-AP, arts, biology, calculus, calculus-AP, chemistry, classical Greek literature, classical language, college counseling, college placement, computer science, computer science-AP, creative writing, design, drama, earth science, English, English literature, environmental science, European history, expository writing, fine arts, French, French language-AP, geometry, global studies, government/civics, grammar, history, Indian studies, Latin, Latin-AP, life science, macro/microeconomics-AP, mathematics, Middle East, model United Nations, modern European history-AP, music, music theory-AP, personal development, photography, physical education, physical science, physics, pre-algebra, science, senior project, Spanish, Spanish language-AP, Spanish-AP, statistics-AP, studio art, theater, trigonometry, U.S. history, visual arts, water color painting, Western civilization, world history, writing.

Graduation Requirements Arts, English, foreign language, history, Latin, mathematics, science, U.S. history, Western civilization, independent senior project.

Special Academic Programs 13 Advanced Placement exams for which test preparation is offered; honors section; independent study; academic accommodation for the gifted, the musically talented, and the artistically talented.

College Admission Counseling 56 students graduated in 2015; all went to college, including Boston College; Columbia University; Dartmouth College; Georgetown University; Harvard University; Princeton University. Median SAT critical reading: 720, median SAT math: 750, median SAT writing: 740, median combined SAT: 2210. 96% scored over 600 on SAT critical reading, 98% scored over 600 on SAT math, 98% scored over 600 on SAT writing, 98% scored over 1800 on combined SAT.

Student Life Upper grades have specified standards of dress, student council, honor system. Discipline rests equally with students and faculty.

Summer Programs Enrichment, sports, computer instruction programs offered; held on campus; accepts boys and girls; open to students from other schools. 200 students usually enrolled. 2016 schedule: June 30 to July 31. Application deadline: none.

Tuition and Aid Day student tuition: $29,300. Tuition installment plan (Insured Tuition Payment Plan, Key Tuition Payment Plan, 2-payment plan). Need-based scholarship grants available. In 2015–16, 36% of upper-school students received aid. Total amount of financial aid awarded in 2015–16: $2,266,575.

Admissions Traditional secondary-level entrance grade is 7. For fall 2015, 515 students applied for upper-level admission, 64 were accepted, 58 enrolled. ISEE or SSAT required. Deadline for receipt of application materials: January 6. No application fee required. On-campus interview required.

Athletics Interscholastic: baseball, basketball, cross-country running, football, ice hockey, lacrosse, soccer, tennis, track and field, wrestling. 7 coaches, 1 athletic trainer.

Computers Computers are regularly used in all academic, desktop publishing, literary magazine, newspaper, yearbook classes. Computer network features include on-campus library services, online commercial services, Internet access, wireless campus network, Internet filtering or blocking technology. Campus intranet, student e-mail accounts, and computer access in designated common areas are available to students. The school has a published electronic and media policy.

Contact Ms. Lindsay Schuyler, Assistant Director of Admission. 617-325-4920. Fax: 617-325-3585. E-mail: admission@roxburylatin.org. Website: www.roxburylatin.org

ROYAL CANADIAN COLLEGE

8610 Ash Street
Vancouver, British Columbia V6P 3M2, Canada

Head of School: Mr. Howard H. Jiang

General Information Coeducational day college-preparatory and general academic school. Grades 8–12. Founded: 1989. Setting: suburban. 1-acre campus. 2 buildings on campus. Approved or accredited by British Columbia Department of Education. Language of instruction: English. Total enrollment: 149. Upper school average class size: 20. Upper school faculty-student ratio: 1:20. There are 197 required school days per year for Upper School students. Upper School students typically attend 5 days per week. The average school day consists of 5 hours and 30 minutes.

Upper School Student Profile Grade 11: 49 students (32 boys, 17 girls); Grade 12: 73 students (40 boys, 33 girls).

Faculty School total: 9. In upper school: 7 men, 2 women; 2 have advanced degrees.

Subjects Offered Applied skills, biology, business education, calculus, Canadian history, career planning, chemistry, communications, drama, economics, English, ESL, fine arts, general science, history, Mandarin, marketing, mathematics, physical education, physics, pre-calculus, social sciences, world history, writing.

Graduation Requirements Applied skills, arts and fine arts (art, music, dance, drama), career and personal planning, language arts, mathematics, science, social studies (includes history).

Special Academic Programs ESL (14 students enrolled).

College Admission Counseling 66 students graduated in 2015; 62 went to college, including McGill University; Simon Fraser University; The University of British Columbia; University of Toronto; University of Victoria. Other: 4 had other specific plans.

Student Life Upper grades have student council, honor system. Discipline rests primarily with faculty.

Tuition and Aid Day student tuition: CAN$13,900. Merit scholarship grants available. In 2015–16, 4% of upper-school students received aid; total upper-school merit-scholarship money awarded: CAN$10,000. Total amount of financial aid awarded in 2015–16: CAN$18,000.

Admissions Traditional secondary-level entrance grade is 11. For fall 2015, 18 students applied for upper-level admission, 16 were accepted, 16 enrolled. English language required. Deadline for receipt of application materials: none. Application fee required: CAN$200. Interview recommended.

Athletics Intramural: badminton (boys, girls), baseball (b,g), basketball (b,g), Frisbee (b,g), soccer (b,g), table tennis (b,g), ultimate Frisbee (b,g), volleyball (b,g); coed intramural: badminton, baseball, Frisbee, soccer, table tennis, ultimate Frisbee, volleyball. 1 PE instructor.

Computers Computers are regularly used in career exploration, English, science, social studies classes. Computer network features include Internet access, Internet filtering or blocking technology. Computer access in designated common areas is available to students.

Contact Ms. Alice Syn, Admissions Manager. 604-738-2221. Fax: 604-738-2282. E-mail: alice.syn@royalcanadiancollege.com. Website: www.royalcanadiancollege.com

ROYCEMORE SCHOOL

1200 Davis Street
Evanston, Illinois 60201

Head of School: Mr. Kevin Smith

General Information Coeducational day college-preparatory and arts school. Grades PK–12. Founded: 1915. Setting: suburban. Nearest major city is Chicago. 2-acre campus. 1 building on campus. Approved or accredited by Independent Schools Association of the Central States and Illinois Department of Education. Member of National Association of Independent Schools. Endowment: $11,000. Total enrollment: 271. Upper school average class size: 8. Upper school faculty-student ratio: 1:5. There are 172 required school days per year for Upper School students. Upper School students typically attend 5 days per week. The average school day consists of 7 hours.

Upper School Student Profile Grade 9: 19 students (7 boys, 12 girls); Grade 10: 18 students (10 boys, 8 girls); Grade 11: 31 students (18 boys, 13 girls); Grade 12: 30 students (14 boys, 16 girls).

Faculty School total: 41. In upper school: 4 men, 17 women; 14 have advanced degrees.

Subjects Offered African-American literature, algebra, American literature, art, biology, biology-AP, calculus-AP, chemistry, Chinese, choir, comedy, composition, drawing, English language and composition-AP, English literature, environmental science, European history-AP, French, French-AP, geometry, government/civics, human development, independent study, international relations, introduction to theater, literature-AP, microeconomics, modern European history, music composition, music history, music theory, music theory-AP, mythology, painting, physical education, physics, physics-AP, pottery, public speaking, sculpture, society, politics and law, sociology, Spanish, Spanish-AP, studio art-AP, trigonometry, U.S. history, U.S. history-AP, world history, world literature, world religions, yearbook.

Graduation Requirements Arts and fine arts (art, music, dance, drama), English, foreign language, mathematics, physical education (includes health), science, social studies (includes history), participation in a 3-week January short-term project each year.

Special Academic Programs 10 Advanced Placement exams for which test preparation is offered; accelerated programs; independent study; study at local college for college credit.

College Admission Counseling 30 students graduated in 2014; all went to college, including DePaul University; Knox College; Marquette University; New York University; Ohio Wesleyan University; University of Illinois at Urbana–Champaign. Median SAT critical reading: 550, median SAT math: 540, median SAT writing: 545, median combined SAT: 1600, median composite ACT: 24. 26% scored over 600 on SAT critical reading, 42% scored over 600 on SAT math, 32% scored over 600 on SAT writing, 37% scored over 1800 on combined SAT, 50% scored over 26 on composite ACT.

Student Life Upper grades have specified standards of dress, student council, honor system. Discipline rests primarily with faculty.

Tuition and Aid Day student tuition: $26,550. Tuition installment plan (individually arranged payment plans, semi-annual payment plan, 9-month payment plan). Merit scholarship grants, need-based scholarship grants, discounts for children of Northwestern University and NorthShore University HealthSystem employees available. In 2014–15, 35% of upper-school students received aid.

Admissions Traditional secondary-level entrance grade is 9. Any standardized test or writing sample required. Deadline for receipt of application materials: none. Application fee required: $75. Interview required.

Athletics Interscholastic: basketball (boys, girls), cross-country running (b,g), volleyball (g); intramural: strength & conditioning (b); coed interscholastic: soccer; coed intramural: gymnastics, table tennis. 3 PE instructors, 2 coaches.

Computers Computers are regularly used in all academic classes. Computer network features include on-campus library services, Internet access, wireless campus network. Student e-mail accounts are available to students. The school has a published electronic and media policy.

Contact Ms. Amanda Avery, Director of Admissions and Financial Aid. 847-866-6055. Fax: 847-866-6545. E-mail: aavery@roycemoreschool.org. Website: www.roycemoreschool.org

RUDOLF STEINER SCHOOL OF ANN ARBOR

2230 Pontiac Trail
Ann Arbor, Michigan 48105

Head of School: Ms. Sandra Greenstone

General Information Coeducational day college-preparatory and arts school; primarily serves students with learning disabilities, individuals with Attention Deficit Disorder, individuals with emotional and behavioral problems, and dyslexic students. Grades 9–12. Founded: 1980. Setting: suburban. 6-acre campus. 3 buildings on campus. Approved or accredited by Association of Waldorf Schools of North America and Michigan Department of Education. Member of National Association of Independent Schools. Languages of instruction: German, Mandarin, and Spanish. Total enrollment: 345. Upper school average class size: 20. Upper school faculty-student ratio: 1:10. There are 175 required school days per year for Upper School students. Upper School students typically attend 5 days per week. The average school day consists of 7 hours and 10 minutes.

Upper School Student Profile Grade 9: 26 students (11 boys, 15 girls); Grade 10: 22 students (7 boys, 15 girls); Grade 11: 31 students (16 boys, 15 girls); Grade 12: 30 students (11 boys, 19 girls).

Faculty School total: 42. In upper school: 10 men, 22 women; 15 have advanced degrees.

Special Academic Programs Study abroad; ESL (8 students enrolled).

College Admission Counseling 27 students graduated in 2015; 26 went to college, including Bryn Mawr College; Grand Valley State University; Kalamazoo College; Macalester College; Michigan State University; University of Michigan. Other: 1 had other specific plans. Median SAT critical reading: 590, median SAT math: 540, median SAT writing: 580, median composite ACT: 25. 45% scored over 600 on SAT critical reading, 25% scored over 600 on SAT math, 55% scored over 600 on SAT writing, 40% scored over 26 on composite ACT.

Student Life Discipline rests primarily with faculty.

Tuition and Aid Day student tuition: $17,400. Tuition installment plan (FACTS Tuition Payment Plan). Need-based scholarship grants available. In 2015–16, 25% of upper-school students received aid.

Admissions Traditional secondary-level entrance grade is 9. For fall 2015, 15 students applied for upper-level admission, 12 were accepted, 11 enrolled. Deadline for receipt of application materials: none. Application fee required: $60. Interview required.

Athletics Interscholastic: basketball (boys, girls), ice hockey (b), lacrosse (b), soccer (b,g), volleyball (g); coed interscholastic: cross-country running, golf, running, tennis; coed intramural: backpacking, crew, freestyle skiing, hiking/backpacking, outdoor activities, outdoor adventure, outdoor education, outdoor recreation, outdoor skills, outdoors, rowing, skiing (downhill). 3 PE instructors, 4 coaches.

Computers Computer resources include Internet access, Internet filtering or blocking technology. Computer access in designated common areas is available to students. The school has a published electronic and media policy.

Contact Dr. Sian Owen-Cruise, High School Coordinator. 734-669-9394. Fax: 734-669-9394. E-mail: sowen-cruise@steinerschool.org. Website: www.steinerschool.org/

RUMSEY HALL SCHOOL

Washington Depot, Connecticut
See Junior Boarding Schools section.

RUNDLE COLLEGE

7375 17th Avenue SW
Calgary, Alberta T3H 3W5, Canada

Head of School: Mr. Jason Rogers

General Information Coeducational day college-preparatory, arts, business, bilingual studies, and technology school. Grades K–12. Founded: 1985. Setting: suburban. 20-acre campus. 1 building on campus. Approved or accredited by Canadian Association of Independent Schools and Alberta Department of Education. Member of Secondary School Admission Test Board. Language of instruction: English. Total enrollment: 811. Upper school average class size: 14. Upper school faculty-student ratio: 1:14. There are 187 required school days per year for Upper School students. Upper School students typically attend 5 days per week. The average school day consists of 7 hours.

Upper School Student Profile Grade 10: 84 students (37 boys, 47 girls); Grade 11: 94 students (46 boys, 48 girls); Grade 12: 78 students (41 boys, 37 girls).

Faculty School total: 45. In upper school: 14 men, 31 women; 15 have advanced degrees.

Subjects Offered Accounting, art, band, biology, calculus, chemistry, computer science, drama, English, French, general science, mathematics, physical education, physics, science, social studies, Spanish, theater.

Graduation Requirements Career and personal planning, English, mathematics, physical education (includes health), science, social sciences.

Special Academic Programs Honors section; study abroad.

College Admission Counseling 84 students graduated in 2015; 82 went to college, including Queen's University at Kingston; St. Francis Xavier University; The University of British Columbia; University of Alberta; University of Calgary; University of Victoria. Other: 1 went to work, 1 had other specific plans.

Student Life Upper grades have uniform requirement, student council, honor system. Discipline rests primarily with faculty.

Tuition and Aid Day student tuition: CAN$12,000. Tuition installment plan (monthly payment plans). Bursaries, merit scholarship grants available. In 2015–16, 1% of upper-school students received aid; total upper-school merit-scholarship money awarded: CAN$24,000. Total amount of financial aid awarded in 2015–16: CAN$90,000.

Admissions Traditional secondary-level entrance grade is 10. For fall 2015, 50 students applied for upper-level admission, 25 were accepted, 20 enrolled. Achievement tests and SSAT or WISC III required. Deadline for receipt of application materials: none. Application fee required: CAN$100. Interview required.

Athletics Interscholastic: badminton (boys, girls), basketball (b,g), cross-country running (b,g), curling (b,g), dance squad (b,g), flag football (b,g), floor hockey (b,g), football (b), golf (b,g), rugby (b,g), soccer (b,g), track and field (b,g), volleyball (b,g), wrestling (b); intramural: aerobics (g), badminton (b,g), dance (g), football (b); coed interscholastic: badminton, softball; coed intramural: badminton, baseball, basketball, cross-country running, flag football, football, lacrosse, outdoor recreation, skiing (downhill), soccer, table tennis, track and field, volleyball, weight lifting, wrestling. 4 PE instructors.

Computers Computers are regularly used in technology classes. Computer network features include Internet access, wireless campus network, Web page hosting, multimedia productions, streaming video student news. Student e-mail accounts and computer access in designated common areas are available to students. Students grades are available online. The school has a published electronic and media policy.

Contact Ms. Nicola Spencer, Director of Admissions. 403-291-3866 Ext. 106. Fax: 403-291-5458. E-mail: spencer@rundle.ab.ca. Website: www.rundle.ab.ca

RUTGERS PREPARATORY SCHOOL

1345 Easton Avenue
Somerset, New Jersey 08873

Head of School: Dr. Steven A. Loy

General Information Coeducational day college-preparatory school. Grades PK–12. Founded: 1766. Setting: suburban. Nearest major city is New York, NY. 41-acre campus. 8 buildings on campus. Approved or accredited by Council of International Schools and New Jersey Association of Independent Schools. Member of National Association of Independent Schools and Secondary School Admission Test Board. Total enrollment: 640. Upper school average class size: 14. Upper school faculty-student ratio: 1:7. There are 165 required school days per year for Upper School students. Upper School students typically attend 5 days per week. The average school day consists of 6 hours and 45 minutes.

Upper School Student Profile Grade 6: 25 students (12 boys, 13 girls); Grade 7: 46 students (30 boys, 16 girls); Grade 8: 59 students (29 boys, 30 girls); Grade 9: 88 students (51 boys, 37 girls); Grade 10: 94 students (53 boys, 41 girls); Grade 11: 105 students (63 boys, 42 girls); Grade 12: 93 students (44 boys, 49 girls).

Faculty School total: 98. In upper school: 23 men, 31 women; 41 have advanced degrees.

Subjects Offered 3-dimensional art, acting, advanced chemistry, advanced computer applications, Advanced Placement courses, algebra, American history, American history-AP, American literature, Arabic, architecture, art, art history, astronomy, band, baseball, basketball, biology, biology-AP, business mathematics, calculus, calculus-AP, career/college preparation, ceramics, chemistry, choir, classics, college admission preparation, college placement, comedy, community service, comparative religion, computer art, computer multimedia, computer programming, computer science, computer science-AP, creative arts, creative writing, digital photography, discrete mathematics, drama, driver education, economics, economics-AP, English, English literature, entrepreneurship, environmental science, European history, fine arts, foundations of civilization, French, French-AP, geometry, government/civics, health, health education, history, history-AP, Holocaust studies, independent study, Japanese, jazz ensemble, Latin, literary magazine, literature, literature-AP, marching band, mathematics, media, model United Nations, multimedia, multimedia design, music, mythology, peer counseling, photography, physical education, physical fitness, physical science, physics, physics-AP, poetry, post-calculus, pre-calculus, probability and statistics, psychology, psychology-AP, SAT/ACT preparation, scene study, science, science research, senior project, sex education, Shakespeare, social studies, softball, software design, Spanish, Spanish literature-AP, Spanish-AP, stage design, statistics, statistics-AP, swimming, tennis, theater, theater design and production, U.S. government and politics-AP, U.S. history-AP, United States government-AP, vocal music, volleyball, word processing, world history, world history-AP, wrestling, writing, yearbook.

Special Academic Programs 22 Advanced Placement exams for which test preparation is offered; honors section; independent study; term-away projects; academic accommodation for the gifted, the musically talented, and the artistically talented.

College Admission Counseling 91 students graduated in 2015; all went to college, including Bucknell University; Emory University; New York University; Northeastern University; Rutgers, The State University of New Jersey, Rutgers College; University of Michigan. Mean SAT critical reading: 608, mean SAT math: 647, mean SAT writing: 617, mean combined SAT: 1871, mean composite ACT: 26. 60.7% scored over 600 on SAT critical reading, 64% scored over 600 on SAT math, 65% scored over 600 on SAT writing.

Student Life Upper grades have specified standards of dress, student council, honor system. Discipline rests primarily with faculty.

Summer Programs Remediation, enrichment, advancement, sports, art/fine arts, computer instruction programs offered; session focuses on academic summer school, multiple camps; held on campus; accepts boys and girls; open to students from other schools. 2016 schedule: June 8 to August 21.

Tuition and Aid Day student tuition: $34,000. Tuition installment plan (RPS Tuition Plan). Need-based financial aid available. In 2015–16, 31% of upper-school students received aid.

Admissions Iowa Tests of Basic Skills, ISEE or SSAT required. Deadline for receipt of application materials: none. Application fee required: $75. Interview required.

Athletics Interscholastic: baseball (boys), basketball (b,g), lacrosse (b,g), soccer (b,g), softball (g), tennis (b,g), volleyball (g), wrestling (b); intramural: dance team (g); coed interscholastic: cross-country running, golf, swimming and diving; coed intramural: croquet, dance, Frisbee, ice hockey, jogging, physical fitness, power lifting, strength & conditioning, ultimate Frisbee, wall climbing, weight training. 6 PE instructors, 9 coaches, 2 athletic trainers.

Computers Computers are regularly used in all academic, college planning, publications classes. Computer network features include on-campus library services, online commercial services, Internet access, wireless campus network, Internet filtering or blocking technology, laptops, iPads, iPad minis, Apple TV, Smartboards. Student e-mail accounts and computer access in designated common areas are available to students. The school has a published electronic and media policy.

Contact Audrey Forte, Admission Assistant. 732-545-5600 Ext. 261. Fax: 732-214-1819. E-mail: forte@rutgersprep.org. Website: www.rutgersprep.org

RYE COUNTRY DAY SCHOOL

Cedar Street
Rye, New York 10580-2034

General Information Coeducational day college-preparatory, arts, and technology school. Grades PK–12. Founded: 1869. Setting: suburban. Nearest major city is New York. 30-acre campus. 8 buildings on campus. Approved or accredited by New York Department of Education. Member of National Association of Independent Schools and Secondary School Admission Test Board. Endowment: $29 million. Total enrollment: 886. Upper school average class size: 13. Upper school faculty-student ratio: 1:7. There are 165 required school days per year for Upper School students. Upper School students typically attend 5 days per week. The average school day consists of 6 hours and 50 minutes.

See Display on this page and Close-Up on page 614.

SACRAMENTO COUNTRY DAY SCHOOL

2636 Latham Drive
Sacramento, California 95864-7198

Head of School: Stephen T. Repsher

General Information Coeducational day college-preparatory, arts, and technology school. Grades PK–12. Founded: 1964. Setting: suburban. 12-acre campus. 8 buildings on campus. Approved or accredited by California Association of Independent Schools and Western Association of Schools and Colleges. Member of National Association of Independent Schools. Endowment: $2.8 million. Total enrollment: 503. Upper school average class size: 12. Upper school faculty-student ratio: 1:9. There are 175 required school days per year for Upper School students. Upper School students typically attend 5 days per week. The average school day consists of 6 hours and 25 minutes.

Upper School Student Profile Grade 9: 39 students (17 boys, 22 girls); Grade 10: 37 students (19 boys, 18 girls); Grade 11: 32 students (17 boys, 15 girls); Grade 12: 34 students (17 boys, 17 girls).

Faculty School total: 65. In upper school: 18 men, 10 women; 19 have advanced degrees.

Subjects Offered Acting, algebra, American history, American literature, ancient history, ancient/medieval philosophy, art, art history, art history-AP, art-AP, band, biology, biology-AP, British literature, calculus, calculus-AP, ceramics, chamber groups, chemistry, chemistry-AP, community service, computer skills, computer

technologies, concert band, creative writing, digital imaging, drama, drama performance, drawing, earth science, economics, English, English literature, European history, fine arts, French, French-AP, geography, geometry, government/civics, grammar, history, international relations, jazz band, journalism, language and composition, Latin, Latin-AP, mathematics, microeconomics, newspaper, nutrition, orchestra, physical education, physics, physics-AP, physiology, pre-calculus, public speaking, science, social studies, Spanish, Spanish-AP, speech, studio art, studio art-AP, technology/design, theater, trigonometry, U.S. history, U.S. history-AP, world history, world literature, writing.

Graduation Requirements Arts and fine arts (art, music, dance, drama), computer science, electives, English, foreign language, history, interdisciplinary studies, mathematics, physical education (includes health), science, Senior Seminars. Community service is required.

Special Academic Programs Advanced Placement exam preparation; honors section; independent study; study at local college for college credit.

College Admission Counseling 29 students graduated in 2015; all went to college, including Harvard University; Occidental College; University of California, San Diego; University of Pennsylvania. Median SAT critical reading: 609, median SAT math: 643, median SAT writing: 641, median combined SAT: 1893. 100% scored over 600 on SAT critical reading, 100% scored over 600 on SAT math, 100% scored over 600 on SAT writing, 100% scored over 1800 on combined SAT.

Student Life Upper grades have specified standards of dress, student council, honor system. Discipline rests primarily with faculty.

Summer Programs Enrichment, advancement programs offered; held on campus; accepts boys and girls; open to students from other schools. 250 students usually enrolled. 2016 schedule: June 20 to July 28. Application deadline: June 20.

Tuition and Aid Day student tuition: $17,900–$23,300. Tuition installment plan (Insured Tuition Payment Plan, monthly payment plans, individually arranged payment plans). Need-based scholarship grants available. In 2015–16, 35% of upper-school students received aid. Total amount of financial aid awarded in 2015–16: $45,000.

Admissions Traditional secondary-level entrance grade is 9. For fall 2015, 37 students applied for upper-level admission, 19 were accepted, 13 enrolled. ERB, Otis-Lennon Mental Ability Test and writing sample required. Deadline for receipt of application materials: none. Application fee required: $125. Interview required.

Athletics Interscholastic: baseball (boys), basketball (b,g), flag football (b), lacrosse (b), soccer (b,g), softball (g), swimming and diving (b,g), track and field (b,g), volleyball (b,g); coed interscholastic: cross-country running, golf, skiing (downhill), snowboarding, tennis, wrestling. 3 PE instructors, 14 coaches.

Computers Computers are regularly used in all academic classes. Computer network features include on-campus library services, online commercial services, Internet access, wireless campus network, Internet filtering or blocking technology. Campus intranet and student e-mail accounts are available to students. The school has a published electronic and media policy.

Contact Lonna Bloedau, Director of Admission. 916-481-8811. Fax: 916-481-6016. E-mail: lbloedau@saccds.org. Website: www.saccds.org

SACRAMENTO WALDORF SCHOOL

3750 Bannister Road
Fair Oaks, California 95628

Head of School: Marcela Iglesias

General Information Coeducational day college-preparatory, general academic, and arts school. Grades PK–12. Founded: 1959. Setting: suburban. Nearest major city is Sacramento. 22-acre campus. 8 buildings on campus. Approved or accredited by Association of Waldorf Schools of North America, Western Association of Schools and Colleges, and California Department of Education. Endowment: $50,000. Total enrollment: 441. Upper school average class size: 25. Upper school faculty-student ratio: 1:6. There are 170 required school days per year for Upper School students. Upper School students typically attend 5 days per week. The average school day consists of 6 hours and 30 minutes.

Upper School Student Profile Grade 6: 30 students (12 boys, 18 girls); Grade 7: 29 students (11 boys, 18 girls); Grade 8: 29 students (14 boys, 15 girls); Grade 9: 52 students (28 boys, 24 girls); Grade 10: 38 students (18 boys, 20 girls); Grade 11: 39 students (20 boys, 19 girls); Grade 12: 33 students (16 boys, 17 girls).

Faculty School total: 52. In upper school: 13 men, 15 women; 11 have advanced degrees.

Subjects Offered 20th century American writers, 20th century history, 20th century world history, 3-dimensional art, acting, advanced math, algebra, American government, American history, American literature, anatomy, applied arts, applied music, architectural drawing, architecture, art, art history, arts, astronomy, bacteriology, band, biology, bookbinding, botany, British literature, calculus, calligraphy, career/college preparation, chemistry, choir, choral music, chorus, civics, classical Greek literature, college admission preparation, college awareness, college counseling, college placement, college planning, communication skills, community service, computer literacy, computer skills, concert choir, conflict resolution, crafts, creative arts, creative thinking, drama, drama performance, drama workshop, dramatic arts, drawing, electives, English, English composition, English literature, ensembles, European civilization, European history, European literature, eurythmy, expressive arts, fiber arts, fine arts, freshman seminar, gardening, general math, general science,

geography, geology, geometry, German, government/civics, grammar, Greek drama, health, history, history of the Americas, human anatomy, human sexuality, language arts, literature, mathematics, medieval history, medieval literature, medieval/Renaissance history, multicultural studies, music, music appreciation, music performance, musical productions, mythology, orchestra, organic gardening, participation in sports, performing arts, physical education, physical science, physics, physiology, play production, pottery, pre-calculus, printmaking, projective geometry, Russian literature, science, sculpture, senior career experience, senior project, sex education, sexuality, Shakespeare, Shakespearean histories, social sciences, social studies, Spanish, speech, strings, student publications, theater, theater arts, theater design and production, theater production, theory of knowledge, trigonometry, U.S. government, U.S. history, U.S. literature, visual and performing arts, visual arts, vocal ensemble, vocal jazz, vocal music, woodworking, world arts, world civilizations, world cultures, world geography, world history, world literature, writing, writing, writing workshop, yearbook, zoology.

Graduation Requirements Aesthetics, algebra, American government, American history, anatomy and physiology, ancient world history, architecture, art history, arts and crafts, arts and fine arts (art, music, dance, drama), biochemistry, biology, bookbinding, botany, calligraphy, cell biology, ceramics, chemistry, civics, computer literacy, computer skills, English, foreign language, mathematics, physical education (includes health), science, senior project, social sciences, social studies (includes history). Community service is required.

Special Academic Programs Independent study; term-away projects; study abroad.

College Admission Counseling 28 students graduated in 2015; 25 went to college, including Occidental College; Saint Mary's College of California; University of California, Berkeley; University of Puget Sound; University of Redlands. Other: 1 went to work, 2 had other specific plans. Median SAT critical reading: 648, median SAT math: 580, median SAT writing: 590, median combined SAT: 1680, median composite ACT: 25. 40% scored over 600 on SAT critical reading, 40% scored over 600 on SAT math, 40% scored over 600 on SAT writing, 20% scored over 1800 on combined SAT.

Student Life Upper grades have specified standards of dress, student council. Discipline rests primarily with faculty.

Tuition and Aid Day student tuition: $10,420–$19,500. Tuition installment plan (Insured Tuition Payment Plan, monthly payment plans, semiannual and annual payment plans). Tuition reduction for siblings, need-based scholarship grants available. In 2015–16, 56% of upper-school students received aid. Total amount of financial aid awarded in 2015–16: $180,474.

Admissions Traditional secondary-level entrance grade is 9. For fall 2015, 42 students applied for upper-level admission, 22 were accepted, 22 enrolled. Math Placement Exam or TOEFL required. Deadline for receipt of application materials: none. Application fee required: $75. Interview required.

Athletics Interscholastic: baseball (boys), basketball (b,g), cross-country running (b,g), golf (b), soccer (b,g), volleyball (g); coed interscholastic: aerobics/Nautilus, climbing, combined training, cooperative games, flag football, mountain biking, physical fitness, physical training, rock climbing, skiing (downhill), track and field, ultimate Frisbee, winter soccer. 1 PE instructor, 8 coaches.

Computers Computers are regularly used in college planning, independent study, introduction to technology, mathematics, photography, word processing, yearbook classes. Computer network features include Internet access, wireless campus network, Internet filtering or blocking technology, online college and career searches. Campus intranet and computer access in designated common areas are available to students. Students grades are available online. The school has a published electronic and media policy.

Contact Marcela Iglesias, High School Coordinator. 916-860-2525. Fax: 916-961-3970. E-mail: miglesias@sacwaldorf.org. Website: www.sacwaldorf.org

SACRED HEART ACADEMY

3175 Lexington Road
Louisville, Kentucky 40206

Head of School: Ms. Mary Lee McCoy

General Information Girls' day college-preparatory, arts, business, religious studies, and technology school, affiliated with Roman Catholic Church. Grades 9–12. Founded: 1877. Setting: suburban. 46-acre campus. 2 buildings on campus. Approved or accredited by Southern Association of Colleges and Schools and Kentucky Department of Education. Upper school average class size: 21. Upper school faculty-student ratio: 1:15.

Upper School Student Profile 87% of students are Roman Catholic.

Faculty School total: 87. In upper school: 9 men, 78 women; 48 have advanced degrees.

Subjects Offered Algebra, American history, American literature, anatomy, art, art history, biology, business, calculus, ceramics, chemistry, computer graphics, computer programming, computer science, creative writing, drama, English, English literature, environmental science, ethics, European history, French, geography, geometry, government/civics, grammar, health, history, journalism, marketing, mathematics, music, nutrition, physical education, physics, physiology, psychology, religion, science, social studies, sociology, Spanish, speech, statistics, theater, theology, trigonometry, video, world history, writing.

Graduation Requirements Computer science, English, foreign language, mathematics, physical education (includes health), religion (includes Bible studies and theology), science, social studies (includes history).

Special Academic Programs Advanced Placement exam preparation; honors section; independent study; study at local college for college credit; academic accommodation for the gifted, the musically talented, and the artistically talented.

College Admission Counseling 211 students graduated in 2015; 100 went to college, including Bellarmine University; Miami University; Saint Louis University; University of Kentucky; University of Louisville; Xavier University.

Student Life Upper grades have uniform requirement, student council. Discipline rests primarily with faculty. Attendance at religious services is required.

Tuition and Aid Day student tuition: $5035. Merit scholarship grants, need-based scholarship grants, paying campus jobs available. In 2015–16, 86% of upper-school students received aid; total upper-school merit-scholarship money awarded: $10,500.

Admissions High School Placement Test required. Deadline for receipt of application materials: none. No application fee required. On-campus interview required.

Athletics Interscholastic: archery, basketball, cross-country running, diving, field hockey, golf, soccer, softball, swimming and diving, tennis, track and field, volleyball; intramural: basketball, volleyball. 1 PE instructor, 14 coaches, 1 athletic trainer.

Computers Computers are regularly used in English, mathematics classes. Computer network features include on-campus library services, Internet access, Internet filtering or blocking technology. Campus intranet, student e-mail accounts, and computer access in designated common areas are available to students. Students grades are available online. The school has a published electronic and media policy.

Contact Dean of Studies. 502-897-6097. Fax: 502-896-3935. Website: www.sacredheartschools.org

SACRED HEART/GRIFFIN HIGH SCHOOL

1200 West Washington
Springfield, Illinois 62702-4794

Head of School: Sr. Margaret Joanne Grueter, OP

General Information Coeducational day college-preparatory school, affiliated with Roman Catholic Church. Grades 9–12. Founded: 1895. Setting: urban. 13-acre campus. 2 buildings on campus. Approved or accredited by National Catholic Education Association, North Central Association of Colleges and Schools, and Illinois Department of Education. Endowment: $12 million. Total enrollment: 725. Upper school average class size: 24. Upper school faculty-student ratio: 1:15. There are 176 required school days per year for Upper School students. Upper School students typically attend 5 days per week. The average school day consists of 7 hours.

Upper School Student Profile Grade 9: 174 students (84 boys, 90 girls); Grade 10: 169 students (93 boys, 76 girls); Grade 11: 196 students (90 boys, 106 girls); Grade 12: 186 students (95 boys, 91 girls). 88% of students are Roman Catholic.

Faculty School total: 49. In upper school: 23 men, 26 women; 26 have advanced degrees.

Subjects Offered Advanced biology.

Graduation Requirements 80 hours of service to community or approved organizations.

Special Academic Programs 9 Advanced Placement exams for which test preparation is offered; honors section; study at local college for college credit; academic accommodation for the gifted, the musically talented, and the artistically talented.

College Admission Counseling 214 students graduated in 2015; 210 went to college, including Saint Louis University. Other: 1 went to work, 2 entered military service, 1 had other specific plans. Median composite ACT: 24.

Student Life Upper grades have uniform requirement, student council, honor system. Discipline rests primarily with faculty. Attendance at religious services is required.

Summer Programs Remediation, enrichment, advancement, sports programs offered; session focuses on physical education and health; held on campus; accepts boys and girls; open to students from other schools. 300 students usually enrolled. 2016 schedule: June 1 to June 26. Application deadline: April 15.

Tuition and Aid Day student tuition: $7925. Tuition installment plan (FACTS Tuition Payment Plan, monthly payment plans, individually arranged payment plans). Tuition reduction for siblings, merit scholarship grants, need-based scholarship grants available. In 2015–16, 40% of upper-school students received aid; total upper-school merit-scholarship money awarded: $12,000. Total amount of financial aid awarded in 2015–16: $608,284.

Admissions Traditional secondary-level entrance grade is 9. For fall 2015, 174 students applied for upper-level admission, 174 were accepted, 174 enrolled. Explore required. Deadline for receipt of application materials: none. Application fee required: $275. Interview recommended.

Athletics Interscholastic: aquatics (boys, girls), baseball (b), basketball (b,g), cheering (g), cross-country running (b,g), diving (b,g), football (b), golf (b,g), hockey (b), pom squad (g), soccer (b,g), softball (g), swimming and diving (b,g), tennis (b,g), track and field (b,g), volleyball (g); intramural: basketball (b,g). 1 PE instructor, 3 coaches, 1 athletic trainer.

Computers Computers are regularly used in all academic classes. Computer network features include on-campus library services, Internet access, wireless campus network, Internet filtering or blocking technology. Students grades are available online. The school has a published electronic and media policy.

Contact Taylor Fishburn, Marketing/Communications. 217-787-9732. Fax: 217-726-9791. E-mail: Fishburn@shg.org. Website: www.shg.org

SACRED HEART HIGH SCHOOL

2111 Griffin Avenue
Los Angeles, California 90031

Head of School: Mr. Raymond Saborio

General Information Girls' day college-preparatory, general academic, arts, and religious studies school, affiliated with Roman Catholic Church. Grades 9–12. Founded: 1907. Setting: urban. 1-acre campus. 2 buildings on campus. Approved or accredited by Western Association of Schools and Colleges, Western Catholic Education Association, and California Department of Education. Language of instruction: Spanish. Total enrollment: 250. Upper school average class size: 25. Upper school faculty-student ratio: 1:20.

Upper School Student Profile Grade 9: 70 students (70 girls); Grade 10: 55 students (55 girls); Grade 11: 60 students (60 girls); Grade 12: 41 students (41 girls). 95% of students are Roman Catholic.

Faculty School total: 25. In upper school: 4 men, 21 women; 2 have advanced degrees.

Graduation Requirements Arts and fine arts (art, music, dance, drama), business skills (includes word processing), computer science, English, foreign language, mathematics, physical education (includes health), religion (includes Bible studies and theology), science, social studies (includes history). Community service is required.

Special Academic Programs 9 Advanced Placement exams for which test preparation is offered; honors section; independent study.

College Admission Counseling 77 students graduated in 2015; 70 went to college, including California State University, Los Angeles; California State University, Northridge; Loyola Marymount University; University of California, Irvine; University of California, Los Angeles. Other: 7 went to work.

Student Life Upper grades have uniform requirement, student council, honor system. Discipline rests primarily with faculty. Attendance at religious services is required.

Summer Programs Remediation, advancement programs offered; held on campus; accepts girls; not open to students from other schools. 60 students usually enrolled. 2016 schedule: June 21 to July 23. Application deadline: June 1.

Tuition and Aid Day student tuition: $7125. Tuition installment plan (FACTS Tuition Payment Plan, monthly payment plans, individually arranged payment plans). Tuition reduction for siblings, merit scholarship grants, need-based scholarship grants, paying campus jobs available. In 2015–16, 90% of upper-school students received aid. Total amount of financial aid awarded in 2015–16: $800,000.

Admissions Traditional secondary-level entrance grade is 9. For fall 2015, 130 students applied for upper-level admission, 100 were accepted, 70 enrolled. High School Placement Test (closed version) from Scholastic Testing Service required. Deadline for receipt of application materials: August 15. Application fee required: $25. Interview required.

Athletics Interscholastic: basketball, cross-country running, soccer, softball, track and field, volleyball. 1 PE instructor, 6 coaches.

Computers Computers are regularly used in remedial study skills classes. Computer network features include on-campus library services, Internet access, wireless campus network, Internet filtering or blocking technology. Student e-mail accounts are available to students. Students grades are available online. The school has a published electronic and media policy.

Contact Ms. Jennifer Beltran, Admissions Coordinator. 323-225-2209. Fax: 323-225-5046. E-mail: admissions@shhsla.org. Website: www.shhsla.org

SACRED HEART SCHOOL OF HALIFAX

5820 Spring Garden Road
Halifax, Nova Scotia B3H 1X8, Canada

Head of School: Sr. Anne Wachter

General Information Coeducational day college-preparatory and religious studies school, affiliated with Roman Catholic Church. Grades K–12. Founded: 1849. Setting: urban. 1 building on campus. Approved or accredited by Canadian Association of Independent Schools, Network of Sacred Heart Schools, and Nova Scotia Department of Education. Language of instruction: English. Total enrollment: 490. Upper school average class size: 18. Upper school faculty-student ratio: 1:10. There are 175 required school days per year for Upper School students. Upper School students typically attend 5 days per week. The average school day consists of 7 hours.

Upper School Student Profile Grade 7: 35 students (10 boys, 25 girls); Grade 8: 45 students (18 boys, 27 girls); Grade 9: 57 students (12 boys, 45 girls); Grade 10: 43 students (17 boys, 26 girls); Grade 11: 52 students (22 boys, 30 girls); Grade 12: 37 students (11 boys, 26 girls). 60% of students are Roman Catholic.

Faculty School total: 65. In upper school: 7 men, 28 women; 22 have advanced degrees.

Subjects Offered 20th century history, 20th century world history, algebra, art, Bible studies, biology, calculus, Canadian history, chemistry, creative writing, earth science, economics, English, English literature, environmental science, European history, expository writing, French, geography, geometry, government/civics, grammar, health, history, mathematics, music, physical education, physics, religion, science, social studies, sociology, Spanish, theater, trigonometry, world history, writing.

Graduation Requirements Arts and fine arts (art, music, dance, drama), English, foreign language, history, mathematics, physical education (includes health), religion (includes Bible studies and theology), science. Community service is required.

Special Academic Programs 8 Advanced Placement exams for which test preparation is offered; honors section; domestic exchange program (with Network of Sacred Heart Schools); study abroad; ESL (27 students enrolled).

College Admission Counseling 36 students graduated in 2014; 35 went to college, including Acadia University; Dalhousie University; Mount Allison University; Queen's University at Kingston; Saint Mary's University; St. Francis Xavier University. Other: 1 had other specific plans.

Student Life Upper grades have uniform requirement, student council, honor system. Discipline rests primarily with faculty. Attendance at religious services is required.

Tuition and Aid Day student tuition: CAN$12,977. Tuition installment plan (monthly payment plans, individually arranged payment plans). Tuition reduction for siblings, bursaries, merit scholarship grants, need-based scholarship grants available. In 2014–15, 12% of upper-school students received aid; total upper-school merit-scholarship money awarded: CAN$106,000. Total amount of financial aid awarded in 2014–15: CAN$300,000.

Admissions Traditional secondary-level entrance grade is 7. Otis-Lennon School Ability Test and school's own test required. Deadline for receipt of application materials: none. No application fee required. On-campus interview required.

Athletics Interscholastic: aquatics (girls), badminton (b,g), basketball (b,g), cross-country running (b,g), field hockey (g), ice hockey (b), soccer (b,g), swimming and diving (b,g), tennis (g), volleyball (g); intramural: alpine skiing (b,g), badminton (b,g), basketball (b,g), cross-country running (b,g), curling (g), fitness walking (g), jogging (b,g), running (b,g), skiing (downhill) (b,g), soccer (b,g), swimming and diving (b), tennis (g), track and field (g), volleyball (g). 3 PE instructors.

Computers Computer network features include on-campus library services, Internet access, wireless campus network, Internet filtering or blocking technology. Campus intranet and student e-mail accounts are available to students. Students grades are available online. The school has a published electronic and media policy.

Contact Ms. Robyn Erickson, Director of Admissions. 902-422-4459 Ext. 210. Fax: 902-423-7691. E-mail: rerickson@shsh.ca. Website: www.sacredheartschool.ns.ca

SADDLEBACK VALLEY CHRISTIAN SCHOOL

26333 Oso Road
San Juan Capistrano, California 92675

Head of School: Mr. Edward Carney

General Information Coeducational day college-preparatory, general academic, arts, religious studies, and technology school, affiliated with Christian faith. Grades PK–12. Founded: 1997. Setting: suburban. Nearest major city is Irvine/Anaheim. 69-acre campus. 6 buildings on campus. Approved or accredited by Association of Christian Schools International, Western Association of Schools and Colleges, and California Department of Education. Total enrollment: 828. Upper school average class size: 24. Upper school faculty-student ratio: 1:15. There are 180 required school days per year for Upper School students. Upper School students typically attend 5 days per week. The average school day consists of 6 hours and 35 minutes.

Upper School Student Profile Grade 6: 56 students (33 boys, 23 girls); Grade 7: 66 students (33 boys, 33 girls); Grade 8: 81 students (37 boys, 44 girls); Grade 9: 71 students (35 boys, 36 girls); Grade 10: 77 students (47 boys, 30 girls); Grade 11: 94 students (57 boys, 37 girls); Grade 12: 99 students (46 boys, 53 girls). 75% of students are Christian faith.

Faculty School total: 75. In upper school: 12 men, 22 women; 10 have advanced degrees.

Subjects Offered 1 1/2 elective credits, algebra, American history, American history-AP, American literature, American sign language, anatomy and physiology, applied arts, art, ASB Leadership, athletic training, Bible, Bible as literature, biology, biology-AP, British literature, business mathematics, calculus-AP, chemistry, computers, concert choir, English language and composition-AP, English literature and composition-AP, environmental science, ESL, geography, geometry, government and politics-AP, history, honors English, music, oceanography, psychology-AP, public speaking, religious studies, science, senior project, Spanish, Spanish language-AP, sports, statistics-AP, studio art-AP, trigonometry, U.S. government and politics, U.S. government and politics-AP, U.S. history, U.S. history-AP, visual and performing arts, world history, world literature, world religions, yearbook.

Graduation Requirements Algebra, American history, American literature, anatomy and physiology, art, Bible, biology, British literature, earth science, English, English literature, foreign language, geometry, history, life science, physical education (includes health), physical science, science, Spanish, trigonometry, U.S. history, visual arts, world history.

Special Academic Programs 11 Advanced Placement exams for which test preparation is offered; honors section; independent study; study at local college for college credit; study abroad; remedial reading and/or remedial writing; remedial math; programs in English, mathematics, general development for dyslexic students; special instructional classes for students with learning disabilities; ESL (24 students enrolled).

College Admission Counseling 64 students graduated in 2014; 50 went to college, including Biola University; California Polytechnic State University, San Luis Obispo; Grand Canyon University; Point Loma Nazarene University; University of California, Los Angeles; University of California, San Diego. Other: 10 went to work, 4 had other specific plans. Median SAT critical reading: 540, median SAT math: 540, median SAT writing: 540, median combined SAT: 1620. 29% scored over 600 on SAT critical reading, 44% scored over 600 on SAT math, 29% scored over 600 on SAT writing, 26% scored over 1800 on combined SAT.

Student Life Upper grades have uniform requirement, student council, honor system. Discipline rests primarily with faculty. Attendance at religious services is required.

Tuition and Aid Day student tuition: $8600. Tuition installment plan (monthly payment plans). Tuition reduction for siblings, need-based scholarship grants available. In 2014–15, 25% of upper-school students received aid. Total amount of financial aid awarded in 2014–15: $175,000.

Admissions Traditional secondary-level entrance grade is 9. For fall 2014, 70 students applied for upper-level admission, 65 were accepted, 60 enrolled. Placement test required. Deadline for receipt of application materials: none. Application fee required: $200. Interview required.

Athletics Interscholastic: aquatics (boys, girls), baseball (b), basketball (b,g), cheering (g), cross-country running (b,g), football (b), golf (b,g), soccer (b,g), softball (g), swimming and diving (b,g), tennis (g), track and field (b,g), volleyball (b,g), wrestling (b); intramural: equestrian sports (g); coed interscholastic: dance team. 5 PE instructors, 15 coaches, 4 athletic trainers.

Computers Computers are regularly used in computer applications classes. Computer network features include Internet access, Internet filtering or blocking technology. Student e-mail accounts are available to students. Students grades are available online. The school has a published electronic and media policy.

Contact Mrs. Heather Vreeland, Registrar. 949-443-4050 Ext. 1201. Fax: 949-443-3941. E-mail: hvreeland@svcschools.org. Website: www.svcschools.org

SADDLEBROOK PREPARATORY SCHOOL

5700 Saddlebrook Way
Wesley Chapel, Florida 33543

Head of School: Mr. Larry W. Robison

General Information Coeducational boarding and day college-preparatory school. Boarding grades 6–12, day grades 3–12. Founded: 1993. Setting: suburban. Nearest major city is Tampa. Students are housed in single-sex dormitories. 50-acre campus. 8 buildings on campus. Approved or accredited by Southern Association of Colleges and Schools and Florida Department of Education. Total enrollment: 80. Upper school average class size: 8. Upper school faculty-student ratio: 1:8. There are 175 required school days per year for Upper School students. Upper School students typically attend 5 days per week. The average school day consists of 7 hours and 15 minutes.

Upper School Student Profile Grade 9: 14 students (12 boys, 2 girls); Grade 10: 18 students (13 boys, 5 girls); Grade 11: 13 students (10 boys, 3 girls); Grade 12: 18 students (13 boys, 5 girls); Postgraduate: 3 students (3 boys). 55% of students are boarding students. 20% are state residents. 12 states are represented in upper school student body. 69% are international students. International students from Brazil, Canada, China, Germany, India, and Mexico; 17 other countries represented in student body.

Faculty School total: 12. In upper school: 1 man, 6 women; 6 have advanced degrees.

Subjects Offered Algebra, American government, American history, biology, calculus, chemistry, economics, English, French, geometry, marine biology, physical science, physics, pre-algebra, pre-calculus, probability and statistics, SAT preparation, Spanish, world geography, world history.

Graduation Requirements Algebra, American government, American history, biology, chemistry, economics, English, geometry, mathematics, physical education (includes health), physical science, science, social studies (includes history), world history.

Special Academic Programs Honors section; ESL (20 students enrolled).

College Admission Counseling 14 students graduated in 2015; 12 went to college, including College of Charleston; Francis Marion University; Johns Hopkins University; Northwestern University; The University of Tampa; University of Richmond. Other: 2 had other specific plans.

Student Life Upper grades have uniform requirement, student council, honor system. Discipline rests primarily with faculty.

Summer Programs Remediation, enrichment, advancement, ESL, sports, art/fine arts programs offered; session focuses on academics; held on campus; accepts boys and girls; open to students from other schools. 8 students usually enrolled. 2016 schedule: June 16 to August 18. Application deadline: May 25.

Tuition and Aid Day student tuition: $16,885; 7-day tuition and room/board: $32,885. Tuition installment plan (individually arranged payment plans). Tuition reduction for siblings available.

Admissions Traditional secondary-level entrance grade is 12. For fall 2015, 60 students applied for upper-level admission, 51 were accepted, 46 enrolled. Deadline for receipt of application materials: none. Application fee required: $50. Interview recommended.

Athletics 28 coaches, 3 athletic trainers.

Computers Computers are regularly used in English, foreign language, history, mathematics, science classes. Computer network features include on-campus library services, online commercial services, Internet access, wireless campus network, Internet filtering or blocking technology, RenWeb. Student e-mail accounts and computer access in designated common areas are available to students. Students grades are available online. The school has a published electronic and media policy.

Contact Ms. Donna Claggett, Administrative Manager. 813-907-4525. Fax: 813-991-4713. E-mail: dclaggett@saddlebrook.com. Website: www.saddlebrookprep.com

SAGE HILL SCHOOL

20402 Newport Coast Drive
Newport Coast, California 92657-0300

Head of School: Ms. Patricia Merz

General Information Coeducational day college-preparatory and arts school. Grades 9–12. Founded: 2000. Setting: suburban. Nearest major city is Newport Beach. 30-acre campus. 7 buildings on campus. Approved or accredited by California Association of Independent Schools, Western Association of Schools and Colleges, and California Department of Education. Member of National Association of Independent Schools. Endowment: $13.4 million. Total enrollment: 521. Upper school average class size: 16. Upper school faculty-student ratio: 1:10. There are 162 required school days per year for Upper School students. Upper School students typically attend 5 days per week. The average school day consists of 6 hours and 20 minutes.

Upper School Student Profile Grade 9: 138 students (74 boys, 64 girls); Grade 10: 131 students (66 boys, 65 girls); Grade 11: 126 students (65 boys, 61 girls); Grade 12: 126 students (62 boys, 64 girls).

Faculty School total: 52. In upper school: 28 men, 24 women; 28 have advanced degrees.

Subjects Offered Advanced biology, advanced chemistry, advanced math, Advanced Placement courses, algebra, American history, American history-AP, art, athletics, biology, biology-AP, British literature, calculus, calculus-AP, ceramics, chemistry, chemistry-AP, Chinese, choral music, computer science-AP, dance, dance performance, digital art, economics-AP, engineering, English, English literature and composition AP, English-AP, environmental science-AP, forensics, French, geometry, honors algebra, honors English, honors geometry, instrumental music, international relations, Latin, marine science, modern dance, modern world history, music, music theory-AP, physical science, physics-AP, pre-calculus, psychology, psychology-AP, science research, Spanish, Spanish-AP, statistics-AP, studio art-AP, theater, theater design and production, U.S. history, U.S. history-AP, United States government-AP, wind ensemble.

Graduation Requirements Arts, English, history, languages, mathematics, physical education (includes health), science.

Special Academic Programs 20 Advanced Placement exams for which test preparation is offered; honors section; independent study; academic accommodation for the gifted, the musically talented, and the artistically talented.

College Admission Counseling 116 students graduated in 2015; all went to college, including Massachusetts Institute of Technology; New York University; Southern Methodist University; University of California, Berkeley; University of California, Los Angeles; University of Michigan. Mean SAT critical reading: 665, mean SAT math: 678, mean SAT writing: 673, mean combined SAT: 2016, mean composite ACT: 30.

Student Life Upper grades have specified standards of dress, student council, honor system. Discipline rests equally with students and faculty.

Summer Programs Remediation, enrichment, advancement, sports, art/fine arts programs offered; session focuses on academics; held on campus; accepts boys and girls; open to students from other schools. 345 students usually enrolled. 2016 schedule: June to July.

Tuition and Aid Day student tuition: $34,640. Tuition installment plan (SMART Tuition Payment Plan, monthly payment plans). Need-based scholarship grants available. In 2015–16, 13% of upper-school students received aid. Total amount of financial aid awarded in 2015–16: $2,170,550.

Admissions Traditional secondary-level entrance grade is 9. ISEE required. Deadline for receipt of application materials: February 15. Application fee required: $100. On-campus interview required.

Athletics Interscholastic: baseball (boys), basketball (b,g), cross-country running (b,g), diving (b,g), football (b), golf (b,g), lacrosse (b,g), soccer (b,g), swimming and diving (b,g), tennis (b,g), track and field (b,g), volleyball (b,g), water polo (b); intramural: sand volleyball (g); coed intramural: equestrian sports, strength & conditioning. 2 PE instructors, 53 coaches, 1 athletic trainer.

Computers Computers are regularly used in computer applications, digital applications, video film production classes. Computer network features include on-campus library services, online commercial services, Internet access, wireless campus network, Internet filtering or blocking technology. Student e-mail accounts and computer access in designated common areas are available to students. Students grades are available online. The school has a published electronic and media policy.

Contact Mrs. Tina McDaniel, Admission Coordinator. 949-219-1337. Fax: 949-219-1399. E-mail: mcdanielt@sagehillschool.org. Website: www.sagehillschool.org

SAGE RIDGE SCHOOL

2515 Crossbow Court
Reno, Nevada 89511

Head of School: Mr. Norm Colb

General Information Coeducational day college-preparatory, arts, and technology school. Grades 5–12. Founded: 1997. Setting: suburban. 44-acre campus. 2 buildings on campus. Approved or accredited by Northwest Association of Independent Schools and Nevada Department of Education. Member of National Association of Independent Schools. Total enrollment: 220. Upper school average class size: 15. Upper school faculty-student ratio: 1:8. There are 180 required school days per year for Upper School students. Upper School students typically attend 5 days per week. The average school day consists of 7 hours and 10 minutes.

Upper School Student Profile Grade 9: 21 students (11 boys, 10 girls); Grade 10: 18 students (9 boys, 9 girls); Grade 11: 31 students (17 boys, 14 girls); Grade 12: 28 students (13 boys, 15 girls).

Faculty School total: 32. In upper school: 8 men, 8 women; 9 have advanced degrees.

Subjects Offered Advanced chemistry, algebra, American history-AP, American literature, American literature-AP, analytic geometry, anatomy and physiology, ancient world history, art history, biology, biology-AP, British literature, British literature-AP, calculus, calculus-AP, ceramics, chemistry, choir, classical language, college counseling, conceptual physics, creative writing, debate, drama performance, electives, English language and composition-AP, English language-AP, English literature and composition-AP, English literature-AP, European history, European literature, foreign language, geometry, honors English, honors algebra, honors English, lab science, language-AP, Latin, Latin-AP, medieval history, modern European history, music history, music performance, music theory, outdoor education, philosophy, physical education, physical fitness, physics, playwriting and directing, poetry, pre-algebra, pre-calculus, probability and statistics, public speaking, senior internship, senior seminar, senior thesis, Spanish, Spanish language-AP, Spanish literature, Spanish literature-AP, Spanish-AP, statistics, studio art, studio art-AP, theater, theater arts, theater history, theory of knowledge, trigonometry, U.S. government and politics-AP, U.S. history, U.S. history-AP, Western literature, world history.

Graduation Requirements 20th century world history, algebra, American history, American literature, analytic geometry, ancient world history, art history, biology, British literature, chemistry, conceptual physics, English composition, European history, foreign language, history of music, modern European history, music, outdoor education, participation in sports, pre-calculus, public speaking, science, senior internship, senior thesis, speech, theater history, trigonometry, U.S. history, 15 hours of community service per year, senior thesis and senior internship, two mini-semester seminars per year.

Special Academic Programs 16 Advanced Placement exams for which test preparation is offered; honors section; independent study; ESL (5 students enrolled).

College Admission Counseling 14 students graduated in 2015; all went to college, including Boston College; Emory University; New York University; Stanford University; University of San Diego; University of Southern California. Mean SAT critical reading: 609, mean SAT math: 604, mean SAT writing: 644, mean combined SAT: 1857, mean composite ACT: 27.

Student Life Upper grades have uniform requirement, student council, honor system. Discipline rests equally with students and faculty.

Summer Programs Enrichment, art/fine arts programs offered; session focuses on enrichment for elementary and middle school students; held on campus; accepts boys and girls; open to students from other schools. 150 students usually enrolled. 2016 schedule: July 12 to July 30.

Tuition and Aid Day student tuition: $20,300. Tuition installment plan (Insured Tuition Payment Plan). Need-based scholarship grants available. In 2015–16, 13% of upper-school students received aid. Total amount of financial aid awarded in 2015–16: $179,225.

Admissions Traditional secondary-level entrance grade is 9. ISEE required. Deadline for receipt of application materials: none. Application fee required: $50. Interview required.

Athletics Interscholastic: alpine skiing (boys, girls), basketball (b,g), cross-country running (b,g), golf (b), skiing (downhill) (b,g), track and field (b,g), volleyball (g), wrestling (b,g); intramural: alpine skiing (b,g), basketball (b,g), cross-country running (b,g), golf (b,g), skiing (downhill) (b,g), swimming and diving (b,g), track and field (b,g), volleyball (g); coed intramural: bicycling, Frisbee, lacrosse, outdoor education, ropes courses, soccer. 2 PE instructors, 13 coaches.

Computers Computers are regularly used in art, classics, college planning, current events, English, foreign language, history, humanities, independent study, Latin, literary magazine, mathematics, newspaper, publications, SAT preparation, science, senior seminar, social sciences, social studies, Spanish, speech, word processing, writing, yearbook classes. Computer network features include on-campus library services, online commercial services, Internet access, wireless campus network, Internet filtering or blocking technology. Student e-mail accounts are available to students. Students grades are available online. The school has a published electronic and media policy.

Contact Ms. Kendra Moore, Director of Admissions. 775-852-6222 Ext. 509. Fax: 775-852-6228. E-mail: kmoore@sageridge.org. Website: www.sageridge.org

SAINT AGNES ACADEMIC HIGH SCHOOL

13-20 124th Street
College Point, New York 11356
General Information College-preparatory and general academic school, affiliated with Roman Catholic Church. Approved or accredited by New York Department of Education. Upper school average class size: 350.
Student Life Attendance at religious services is required.
Admissions Deadline for receipt of application materials: none. No application fee required.
Contact 718-353-6276. Fax: 718-353-6068. Website: http://www.stagneshs.org/

SAINT AGNES ACADEMY–ST. DOMINIC SCHOOL

4830 Walnut Grove Road
Memphis, Tennessee 38117
Head of School: Mrs. Barbara H. Daush
General Information Coeducational day college-preparatory, arts, religious studies, bilingual studies, technology, and music school, affiliated with Roman Catholic Church. Boys grades PK–8, girls grades PK–12. Founded: 1851. Setting: suburban. 25-acre campus. 3 buildings on campus. Approved or accredited by Southern Association of Colleges and Schools and Tennessee Department of Education. Member of National Association of Independent Schools. Total enrollment: 847. Upper school average class size: 18. Upper school faculty-student ratio: 1:8. There are 178 required school days per year for Upper School students. Upper School students typically attend 5 days per week. The average school day consists of 7 hours and 15 minutes.
Upper School Student Profile Grade 9: 81 students (81 girls); Grade 10: 89 students (89 girls); Grade 11: 89 students (89 girls); Grade 12: 87 students (87 girls). 64% of students are Roman Catholic.
Faculty School total: 42. In upper school: 7 men, 35 women; 27 have advanced degrees.
Subjects Offered Advanced Placement courses, algebra, American history, anatomy, art, arts, biology, calculus-AP, chemistry, computer science, drama, English, environmental science, fine arts, French, German, government/civics, health, journalism, mathematics, music, physical education, physical science, physics, psychology, religion, science, social sciences, social studies, Spanish, theater, trigonometry, world history.
Graduation Requirements Arts and fine arts (art, music, dance, drama), computer science, English, etymology, foreign language, mathematics, physical education (includes health), religion (includes Bible studies and theology), science, social sciences, social studies (includes history).
Special Academic Programs Advanced Placement exam preparation; honors section; study at local college for college credit; academic accommodation for the gifted and the artistically talented.
College Admission Counseling 92 students graduated in 2015; all went to college, including The University of Tennessee; University of New Mexico. Median SAT critical reading: 580, median SAT math: 555, median composite ACT: 26.
Student Life Upper grades have uniform requirement, student council, honor system. Discipline rests equally with students and faculty. Attendance at religious services is required.
Summer Programs Remediation, enrichment, computer instruction programs offered; held on campus; accepts boys and girls; open to students from other schools. 35 students usually enrolled. 2016 schedule: June to July. Application deadline: none.
Tuition and Aid Day student tuition: $14,800. Tuition installment plan (Insured Tuition Payment Plan, FACTS Tuition Payment Plan, monthly payment plans, individually arranged payment plans, 2- or 8-payment plans). Merit scholarship grants, need-based scholarship grants available. In 2015–16, 33% of upper-school students received aid.
Admissions Traditional secondary-level entrance grade is 9. High School Placement Test and ISEE required. Deadline for receipt of application materials: none. Application fee required: $75. Interview recommended.
Athletics Interscholastic: basketball, bowling, cross-country running, golf, lacrosse, soccer, softball, swimming and diving, tennis, track and field, volleyball. 2 PE instructors, 5 coaches, 1 athletic trainer.
Computers Computers are regularly used in all classes. Computer network features include on-campus library services, Internet access.
Contact Mrs. Jean Skorupa-Moore, Director of Upper School Admissions. 901-435-5858. Fax: 901-435-5866. E-mail: jmoore@saa-sds.org. Website: www.saa-sds.org

ST. ALBANS SCHOOL

Mount Saint Alban
Washington, District of Columbia 20016
Head of School: Mr. Vance Wilson
General Information Boys' boarding and day college-preparatory school, affiliated with Episcopal Church. Boarding grades 9–12, day grades 4–12. Founded: 1909. Setting: urban. Students are housed in single-sex dormitories. 54-acre campus. 7 buildings on campus. Approved or accredited by Association of Independent Maryland Schools, Association of Independent Schools of Greater Washington, The Association of Boarding Schools, and District of Columbia Department of Education. Member of National Association of Independent Schools and Secondary School Admission Test Board. Endowment: $64.6 million. Total enrollment: 593. Upper school average class size: 13. Upper school faculty-student ratio: 1:7. There are 175 required school days per year for Upper School students. Upper School students typically attend 5 days per week. The average school day consists of 9 hours and 30 minutes.
Upper School Student Profile Grade 9: 84 students (84 boys); Grade 10: 82 students (82 boys); Grade 11: 80 students (80 boys); Grade 12: 77 students (77 boys). 9% of students are boarding students. 47% are state residents. 5 states are represented in upper school student body. 2% are international students. International students from China, Nigeria, and United Kingdom. 20% of students are members of Episcopal Church.
Faculty School total: 80. In upper school: 49 men, 21 women; 45 have advanced degrees; 6 reside on campus.
Subjects Offered Advanced Placement courses, algebra, American history, American literature, Ancient Greek, art, art history, art history-AP, Bible studies, biology, biotechnology, calculus, ceramics, chemistry, Chinese, community service, computer math, computer programming, computer science, creative writing, dance, directing, drama, earth science, economics, engineering, English, English literature, ethics, European history, expository writing, filmmaking, fine arts, French, geography, geology, geometry, government/civics, Greek, history, Japanese, Latin, marine biology, mathematics, music, photography, physical education, physics, religion, science, sculpture, social studies, Spanish, speech, stagecraft, theater, zoology.
Graduation Requirements American history, ancient history, arts and fine arts (art, music, dance, drama), English, ethics, foreign language, mathematics, physical education (includes health), religious studies, science, participation in athletic program, participation in community service. Community service is required.
Special Academic Programs Advanced Placement exam preparation; honors section; independent study; term-away projects; study abroad.
College Admission Counseling 77 students graduated in 2015; all went to college, including Columbia University; Harvard University; Indiana University Bloomington; The George Washington University; University of Chicago; University of Miami.
Student Life Upper grades have specified standards of dress, student council, honor system. Discipline rests equally with students and faculty. Attendance at religious services is required.
Summer Programs Remediation, enrichment, advancement, ESL, sports, art/fine arts, rigorous outdoor training, computer instruction programs offered; session focuses on academics, day camp, and sports camps; held on campus; accepts boys and girls; open to students from other schools. 1,500 students usually enrolled. 2016 schedule: June 8 to August 21. Application deadline: none.
Tuition and Aid Day student tuition: $39,411; 7-day tuition and room/board: $55,750. Tuition installment plan (Insured Tuition Payment Plan, monthly payment plans, individually arranged payment plans). Need-based scholarship grants, need-based loans available. In 2015–16, 24% of upper-school students received aid. Total amount of financial aid awarded in 2015–16: $4,034,535.
Admissions Traditional secondary-level entrance grade is 9. For fall 2015, 167 students applied for upper-level admission, 55 were accepted, 24 enrolled. Admissions testing, ISEE or SSAT required. Deadline for receipt of application materials: January 8. Application fee required: $80. Interview required.
Athletics Interscholastic: aquatics, baseball, basketball, canoeing/kayaking, climbing, crew, cross-country running, diving, football, golf, ice hockey, independent competitive sports, indoor soccer, indoor track, indoor track & field, kayaking, lacrosse, rappelling, rock climbing, soccer, swimming and diving, tennis, track and field, wall climbing, weight training, winter (indoor) track, winter soccer, wrestling; intramural: aquatics, basketball, combined training, dance, fitness, indoor soccer, outdoor activities, physical training, tennis, track and field, weight lifting, yoga. 5 coaches, 2 athletic trainers.
Computers Computers are regularly used in all academic, mathematics, programming, science classes. Computer network features include on-campus library services, online commercial services, Internet access, wireless campus network. Campus intranet and student e-mail accounts are available to students. The school has a published electronic and media policy.
Contact Ms. Lily Fardshisheh, Admissions and Financial Aid Coordinator. 202-537-6440. Fax: 202-537-2225. E-mail: lfardshisheh@cathedral.org. Website: www.stalbansschool.org/

SAINT ALBERT JUNIOR-SENIOR HIGH SCHOOL

400 Gleason Avenue
Council Bluffs, Iowa 51503
Head of School: Mr. David M. Schweitzer
General Information Coeducational day college-preparatory school, affiliated with Roman Catholic Church. Grades PK–12. Founded: 1963. Setting: suburban. 5-acre campus. 1 building on campus. Approved or accredited by North Central Association of Colleges and Schools and Iowa Department of Education. Endowment: $1 million. Total enrollment: 720. Upper school average class size: 20. Upper school faculty-student ratio: 1:11. There are 176 required school days per year for Upper School students. Upper School students typically attend 5 days per week. The average school day consists of 7 hours.

Upper School Student Profile Grade 6: 50 students (24 boys, 26 girls); Grade 7: 48 students (24 boys, 24 girls); Grade 8: 51 students (29 boys, 22 girls); Grade 9: 64 students (32 boys, 32 girls); Grade 10: 45 students (18 boys, 27 girls); Grade 11: 55 students (24 boys, 31 girls); Grade 12: 56 students (32 boys, 24 girls).

Faculty School total: 32. In upper school: 12 men, 18 women; 18 have advanced degrees.

Subjects Offered U.S. history.

Graduation Requirements World religions.

Special Academic Programs 9 Advanced Placement exams for which test preparation is offered; honors section; study at local college for college credit; academic accommodation for the gifted; remedial reading and/or remedial writing; remedial math; special instructional classes for deaf students.

College Admission Counseling 54 students graduated in 2015; 52 went to college, including Iowa State University of Science and Technology; Northwest Missouri State University; The University of Iowa; University of Nebraska–Lincoln; University of Nebraska at Omaha; University of Northern Iowa. Other: 2 went to work. Median composite ACT: 23. 50% scored over 26 on composite ACT.

Student Life Upper grades have uniform requirement, student council. Discipline rests primarily with faculty. Attendance at religious services is required.

Summer Programs Remediation programs offered; session focuses on learning recovery; held on campus; accepts boys and girls; not open to students from other schools. 10 students usually enrolled. 2016 schedule: June 1 to June 30.

Tuition and Aid Day student tuition: $7500. Tuition installment plan (FACTS Tuition Payment Plan, monthly payment plans, individually arranged payment plans). Tuition reduction for siblings, merit scholarship grants, need-based scholarship grants, paying campus jobs available. In 2014–15, 30% of upper-school students received aid; total upper-school merit-scholarship money awarded: $15,000. Total amount of financial aid awarded in 2014–15: $380,000.

Admissions Traditional secondary-level entrance grade is 9. For fall 2015, 30 students applied for upper-level admission, 28 were accepted, 28 enrolled. Deadline for receipt of application materials: none. No application fee required. Interview recommended.

Athletics Interscholastic: baseball (boys), basketball (b,g), bowling (b,g), cheering (g), cross-country running (b,g), dance (g), dance squad (g), dance team (g), football (b), golf (b,g), soccer (b,g), softball (g), swimming and diving (b,g), tennis (b,g), track and field (b,g), wrestling (b). 2 PE instructors, 53 coaches, 1 athletic trainer.

Computers Computers are regularly used in all classes. Computer network features include Internet access, wireless campus network, Internet filtering or blocking technology. Campus intranet and student e-mail accounts are available to students. Students grades are available online. The school has a published electronic and media policy.

Contact Ms. Abby Jares, Admissions Coordinator. 712-328-2316. Fax: 712-328-0228. E-mail: jaresa@saintalbertschools.org. Website: www.saintalbertschools.org/

ST. ANDREW'S COLLEGE

15800 Yonge Street
Aurora, Ontario L4G 3H7, Canada

Head of School: Mr. Kevin R. McHenry

General Information Boys' boarding and day college-preparatory, arts, business, religious studies, bilingual studies, and technology school. Grades 5–12. Founded: 1899. Setting: small town. Nearest major city is Toronto, Canada. Students are housed in single-sex dormitories. 110-acre campus. 25 buildings on campus. Approved or accredited by Canadian Association of Independent Schools, Canadian Educational Standards Institute, Conference of Independent Schools of Ontario, Ontario Ministry of Education, The Association of Boarding Schools, and Ontario Department of Education. Affiliate member of National Association of Independent Schools; member of Secondary School Admission Test Board. Language of instruction: English. Endowment: CAN$28.6 million. Total enrollment: 626. Upper school average class size: 17. Upper school faculty-student ratio: 1:8. There are 158 required school days per year for Upper School students. Upper School students typically attend 5 days per week. The average school day consists of 5 hours and 20 minutes.

Upper School Student Profile Grade 9: 103 students (103 boys); Grade 10: 110 students (110 boys); Grade 11: 122 students (122 boys); Grade 12: 124 students (124 boys). 49% of students are boarding students. 75% are province residents. 10 provinces are represented in upper school student body. 25% are international students. International students from China, Germany, Hong Kong, Mexico, Republic of Korea, and United States represented in student body.

Faculty School total: 73. In upper school: 45 men, 10 women; 23 have advanced degrees; 35 reside on campus.

Subjects Offered Accounting, Advanced Placement courses, algebra, American history, art, biology, business, calculus, chemistry, communications, community service, computer science, creative writing, drama, economics, English, English literature, environmental science, fine arts, French, geography, geometry, German, health, history, Mandarin, mathematics, music, physical education, physics, physiology, science, social sciences, social studies, sociology, Spanish, statistics, world history, world religions.

Graduation Requirements Arts, arts and fine arts (art, music, dance, drama), business, careers, civics, computer science, drama, English, foreign language, French, geography, health education, history, mathematics, physical education (includes health),

science, science and technology, social sciences, Cadet program. Community service is required.

Special Academic Programs 10 Advanced Placement exams for which test preparation is offered; honors section; accelerated programs; independent study; term-away projects; study abroad; ESL (68 students enrolled).

College Admission Counseling 97 students graduated in 2014; 85 went to college, including Dalhousie University; McMaster University; Queen's University at Kingston; Ryerson University; University of Toronto; Wilfrid Laurier University. Other: 1 entered military service, 3 entered a postgraduate year, 8 had other specific plans.

Student Life Upper grades have uniform requirement, student council, honor system. Discipline rests equally with students and faculty. Attendance at religious services is required.

Tuition and Aid Day student tuition: CAN$31,865; 7-day tuition and room/board: CAN$51,210. Tuition installment plan (monthly payment plans, one-time payment, three installments plan, Plastiq). Bursaries, merit scholarship grants, need-based scholarship grants available. In 2014–15, 26% of upper-school students received aid; total upper-school merit-scholarship money awarded: CAN$410,500. Total amount of financial aid awarded in 2014–15: CAN$1,909,000.

Admissions Traditional secondary-level entrance grade is 9. For fall 2014, 161 students applied for upper-level admission, 102 were accepted, 85 enrolled. CAT, SSAT, TOEFL or TOEFL Junior required. Deadline for receipt of application materials: none. Application fee required: CAN$175. Interview required.

Athletics Interscholastic: alpine skiing, aquatics, badminton, baseball, basketball, biathlon, cricket, cross-country running, curling, fencing, football, golf, ice hockey, indoor track, indoor track & field, lacrosse, marksmanship, nordic skiing, rugby, running, skiing (cross-country), skiing (downhill), soccer, softball, squash, swimming and diving, table tennis, tennis, track and field, triathlon, volleyball, winter (indoor) track; intramural: aquatics, archery, backpacking, badminton, baseball, basketball, canoeing/kayaking, climbing, cooperative games, cross-country running, curling, fencing, fitness, floor hockey, football, golf, hiking/backpacking, ice hockey, ice skating, jogging, kayaking, lacrosse, marksmanship, mountain biking, nordic skiing, outdoor activities, outdoor education, outdoor recreation, outdoor skills, physical fitness, riflery, rock climbing, ropes courses, running, scuba diving, self defense, skiing (cross-country), skiing (downhill), soccer, softball, squash, strength & conditioning, swimming and diving, table tennis, tennis, touch football, track and field, triathlon, ultimate Frisbee, volleyball, wall climbing, water polo, weight lifting, weight training, wilderness survival, yoga. 2 PE instructors, 6 athletic trainers.

Computers Computers are regularly used in all academic classes. Computer network features include on-campus library services, online commercial services, Internet access, wireless campus network, Internet filtering or blocking technology. Campus intranet and student e-mail accounts are available to students. Students grades are available online. The school has a published electronic and media policy.

Contact Mrs. Wendy Coates, Admission Associate. 905-727-3178 Ext. 303. Fax: 905-727-9032. E-mail: admission@sac.on.ca. Website: www.sac.on.ca

ST. ANDREW'S EPISCOPAL SCHOOL

8804 Postoak Road
Potomac, Maryland 20854

Head of School: Mr. Robert Kosasky

General Information Coeducational day college-preparatory school, affiliated with Episcopal Church. Grades PS–12. Founded: 1978. Setting: suburban. Nearest major city is Washington, DC. 19-acre campus. 5 buildings on campus. Approved or accredited by Association of Independent Maryland Schools, Association of Independent Schools of Greater Washington, and National Association of Episcopal Schools. Member of National Association of Independent Schools and Secondary School Admission Test Board. Endowment: $10 million. Total enrollment: 553. Upper school average class size: 14. Upper school faculty-student ratio: 1:7. There are 172 required school days per year for Upper School students. Upper School students typically attend 5 days per week. The average school day consists of 6 hours and 40 minutes.

Upper School Student Profile Grade 6: 31 students (16 boys, 15 girls); Grade 7: 41 students (23 boys, 18 girls); Grade 8: 29 students (16 boys, 13 girls); Grade 9: 68 students (28 boys, 40 girls); Grade 10: 88 students (47 boys, 41 girls); Grade 11: 80 students (41 boys, 39 girls); Grade 12: 61 students (38 boys, 23 girls). 15% of students are members of Episcopal Church.

Faculty School total: 66. In upper school: 23 men, 24 women; 27 have advanced degrees.

Subjects Offered 20th century history, 3-dimensional art, 3-dimensional design, acting, Advanced Placement courses, advanced studio art-AP, algebra, American history, American literature, art, art history, art history-AP, art-AP, athletics, band, Bible, biology, biology-AP, British literature, calculus, calculus-AP, ceramics, chemistry, Chinese studies, chorus, civics, college counseling, composition-AP, computer animation, computer art, computer graphics, computer science, creative writing, dance, digital photography, drama, dramatic arts, earth science, English, English literature, English literature and composition-AP, English-AP, ethics, European history, fine arts, French, French language-AP, French literature-AP, geography, geometry, global studies, government/civics, guitar, health, history, instrumental music, jazz band, journalism, Latin, Latin American studies, Latin-AP, mathematics, modern European history, music, musical theater, newspaper, orchestra, organic biochemistry, painting, photography, physical education, physical science, physics, physics-AP, pre-algebra, pre-calculus, public speaking, religion, robotics, science, service learning/internship, Spanish, Spanish language-AP, Spanish literature-AP, Spanish-AP, sports, stage design, statistics, student publications, studio art, studio art-AP, theater, theater design and production, theology, trigonometry, U.S. history, U.S. history-AP, video, visual and performing arts, vocal music, world cultures, world history, world religions, writing, yearbook.

Graduation Requirements English, foreign language, history, mathematics, performing arts, physical education (includes health), religion (includes Bible studies and theology), science, senior thesis, visual arts. Community service is required.

Special Academic Programs Advanced Placement exam preparation; independent study; special instructional classes for deaf students; ESL (4 students enrolled).

College Admission Counseling 72 students graduated in 2015; all went to college, including American University; University of Pittsburgh.

Student Life Upper grades have specified standards of dress, student council, honor system. Discipline rests primarily with faculty. Attendance at religious services is required.

Summer Programs Enrichment, advancement, sports, art/fine arts, computer instruction programs offered; session focuses on advancement and enrichment; held both on and off campus; held at Washington DC and surrounding area; accepts boys and girls; open to students from other schools. 2,000 students usually enrolled. 2016 schedule: June 20 to August 5. Application deadline: none.

Tuition and Aid Day student tuition: $37,990. Tuition installment plan (FACTS Tuition Payment Plan, monthly payment plans). Need-based scholarship grants available. In 2014–15, 25% of upper-school students received aid. Total amount of financial aid awarded in 2014–15: $2,708,400.

Admissions Traditional secondary-level entrance grade is 9. ISEE or SSAT required. Deadline for receipt of application materials: January 15. Application fee required: $50. On-campus interview required.

Athletics Interscholastic: baseball (boys), basketball (b,g), cross-country running (b,g), lacrosse (b,g), soccer (b,g), softball (g), tennis (b,g), volleyball (g); coed interscholastic: equestrian sports, golf, indoor track & field, track and field, wrestling; coed intramural: dance, fitness, physical fitness, strength & conditioning, weight training, winter (indoor) track, yoga. 12 coaches, 1 athletic trainer.

Computers Computers are regularly used in English, foreign language, graphic arts, history, journalism, mathematics, music, science classes. Computer network features include on-campus library services, online commercial services, Internet access, wireless campus network, Internet filtering or blocking technology. Campus intranet and student e-mail accounts are available to students. Students grades are available online. The school has a published electronic and media policy.

Contact Mrs. Aileen Moodic, Associate Director of Admission/Admission Office Coordinator. 240-477-1700. Fax: 301-765-8912. E-mail: admission@saes.org. Website: www.saes.org

ST. ANDREW'S EPISCOPAL SCHOOL

370 Old Agency Road
Ridgeland, Mississippi 39157

Head of School: Dr. George D. Penick Jr.

General Information Coeducational day college-preparatory, arts, religious studies, technology, and global studies school, affiliated with Episcopal Church. Grades PK–12. Founded: 1947. Setting: suburban. Nearest major city is Jackson. 108-acre campus. 12 buildings on campus. Approved or accredited by National Association of Episcopal Schools, Southern Association of Colleges and Schools, and Southern Association of Independent Schools. Member of National Association of Independent Schools. Endowment: $8 million. Total enrollment: 1,217. Upper school average class size: 18. Upper school faculty-student ratio: 1:9. Upper School students typically attend 5 days per week. The average school day consists of 7 hours and 30 minutes.

Upper School Student Profile Grade 9: 77 students (31 boys, 46 girls); Grade 10: 93 students (43 boys, 50 girls); Grade 11: 90 students (40 boys, 50 girls); Grade 12: 86 students (42 boys, 44 girls). 29% of students are members of Episcopal Church.

Faculty School total: 138. In upper school: 21 men, 23 women; 32 have advanced degrees.

Subjects Offered 3-dimensional design, algebra, American history, American literature, art, art history-AP, astronomy, biology, biology-AP, calculus, calculus-AP, chemistry, chemistry-AP, community service, computer programming, computers, creative writing, drama, driver education, engineering, English, English literature, English literature-AP, English-AP, European history, European literature, film, French, French language-AP, freshman seminar, geometry, government-AP, government/civics, grammar, history-AP, honors algebra, honors English, honors geometry, honors U.S. history, international studies, Latin, Latin-AP, literature-AP, Mandarin, mathematics, modern European history, music, physics, physics-AP, probability and statistics, psychology, Spanish, Spanish language-AP, speech, speech and debate, studio art-AP, theater arts, U.S. government and politics-AP, U.S. history-AP, visual arts, world history, world literature.

Graduation Requirements Arts and fine arts (art, music, dance, drama), English, foreign language, mathematics, science, social studies (includes history), speech, 100 community service hours. Community service is required.

Special Academic Programs Advanced Placement exam preparation; honors section; study abroad; academic accommodation for the gifted, the musically talented, and the artistically talented.

College Admission Counseling 85 students graduated in 2015; all went to college, including Harvard University; Millsaps College; Mississippi State University; Southern Methodist University; University of Mississippi; Vanderbilt University. Mean SAT critical reading: 657, mean SAT math: 626, mean SAT writing: 665, mean combined SAT: 1948, mean composite ACT: 30.

Student Life Upper grades have specified standards of dress, student council, honor system. Discipline rests equally with students and faculty. Attendance at religious services is required.

Summer Programs Enrichment, sports programs offered; held on campus; accepts boys and girls; open to students from other schools. 300 students usually enrolled. 2016 schedule: June 7 to August 5. Application deadline: June 7.

Tuition and Aid Day student tuition: $16,480. Tuition installment plan (monthly payment plans, individually arranged payment plans, semester payment plan). Tuition reduction for siblings, merit scholarship grants, need-based scholarship grants available. In 2015–16, 21% of upper-school students received aid; total upper-school merit-scholarship money awarded: $104,509. Total amount of financial aid awarded in 2015–16: $300,000.

Admissions Traditional secondary-level entrance grade is 9. For fall 2015, 38 students applied for upper-level admission, 30 were accepted, 23 enrolled. ERB Reading and Math, PSAT, SAT, or ACT for applicants to grade 11 and 12 or writing sample required. Deadline for receipt of application materials: none. Application fee required: $35. On-campus interview required.

Athletics Interscholastic: baseball (boys), basketball (b,g), bowling (b,g), cross-country running (b,g), dance squad (g), dance team (g), fitness (b,g), football (b), golf (b,g), lacrosse (b), power lifting (b,g), running (b,g), soccer (b,g), softball (g), swimming and diving (b,g), tennis (b,g), track and field (b,g), volleyball (g); coed interscholastic: archery, cheering, physical fitness, physical training, weight training, yoga; coed intramural: equestrian sports. 10 coaches.

Computers Computers are regularly used in all academic, college planning, geography, journalism, newspaper, theater, yearbook classes. Computer network features include on-campus library services, online commercial services, Internet access, wireless campus network, Internet filtering or blocking technology, laptop requirement for all students in grades 9 through 12. Student e-mail accounts and computer access in designated common areas are available to students. Students grades are available online. The school has a published electronic and media policy.

Contact Mrs. Mary Purvis, Director of Admissions. 601-853-6042. Fax: 601-853-6001. E-mail: purvism@gosaints.org. Website: www.gosaints.org

ST. ANDREW'S REGIONAL HIGH SCHOOL

880 Mckenzie Avenue
Victoria, British Columbia V8X 3G5, Canada

Head of School: Mr. Andrew Keleher

General Information Coeducational day college-preparatory, general academic, and religious studies school, affiliated with Roman Catholic Church. Grades 8–12. Founded: 1983. Setting: urban. 2-acre campus. 1 building on campus. Approved or accredited by British Columbia Department of Education. Language of instruction: English. Total enrollment: 335. Upper school average class size: 24. Upper school faculty-student ratio: 1:14. There are 178 required school days per year for Upper School students. Upper School students typically attend 5 days per week. The average school day consists of 5 hours.

Upper School Student Profile 65% of students are Roman Catholic.

Faculty School total: 25. In upper school: 11 men, 13 women; 12 have advanced degrees.

Subjects Offered Advanced Placement courses, religious education.

Graduation Requirements Religious studies.

Special Academic Programs 2 Advanced Placement exams for which test preparation is offered; honors section.

College Admission Counseling 72 students graduated in 2015; 45 went to college, including University of Victoria. Other: 20 went to work, 7 had other specific plans.

Student Life Upper grades have uniform requirement, student council, honor system. Discipline rests primarily with faculty. Attendance at religious services is required.

Tuition and Aid Day student tuition: CAN$7608. Tuition installment plan (monthly payment plans). Tuition reduction for siblings, bursaries, merit scholarship grants available. In 2015–16, 15% of upper-school students received aid; total upper-school merit-scholarship money awarded: CAN$25,000. Total amount of financial aid awarded in 2015–16: CAN$100,000.

Admissions Traditional secondary-level entrance grade is 12. For fall 2015, 5 students applied for upper-level admission, 5 were accepted, 5 enrolled. Deadline for receipt of application materials: February 28. Application fee required: CAN$50. Interview required.

Athletics Interscholastic: badminton (boys, girls), basketball (b,g), cross-country running (b,g), golf (b), rowing (b,g), track and field (b,g), volleyball (b,g); intramural: basketball (b,g); coed interscholastic: aquatics, rowing, track and field; coed intramural: dance team, floor hockey, indoor soccer. 4 PE instructors, 2 coaches.

Computers Computers are regularly used in business education, computer applications, digital applications, photography classes. Computer resources include on-campus library services, Internet access, Internet filtering or blocking technology. Student e-mail accounts are available to students. The school has a published electronic and media policy.

Contact Mr. Ciaran McLaverty, Vice Principal. 250-479-1414. Fax: 250-479-5356. E-mail: cmclaverty@cisdv.bc.ca. Website: www.standrewshigh.ca/

ST. ANDREW'S SCHOOL

350 Noxontown Road
Middletown, Delaware 19709

Head of School: Daniel T. Roach

General Information Coeducational boarding college-preparatory, arts, religious studies, and technology school, affiliated with Episcopal Church. Grades 9–12. Founded: 1929. Setting: small town. Nearest major city is Wilmington. Students are housed in single-sex dormitories. 2,100-acre campus. 16 buildings on campus. Approved or accredited by Middle States Association of Colleges and Schools, National Association of Episcopal Schools, The Association of Boarding Schools, The College Board, and Delaware Department of Education. Member of National Association of Independent Schools and Secondary School Admission Test Board. Endowment: $190 million. Total enrollment: 310. Upper school average class size: 11. Upper school faculty-student ratio: 1:5. Upper School students typically attend 6 days per week.

Upper School Student Profile Grade 9: 66 students (34 boys, 32 girls); Grade 10: 83 students (41 boys, 42 girls); Grade 11: 84 students (41 boys, 43 girls); Grade 12: 77 students (42 boys, 35 girls). 100% of students are boarding students. 12% are state residents. 26 states are represented in upper school student body. 17% are international students. International students from Bermuda, China, India, Philippines, Republic of Korea, and Viet Nam; 10 other countries represented in student body. 30% of students are members of Episcopal Church.

Faculty School total: 70. In upper school: 35 men, 35 women; 57 have advanced degrees; all reside on campus.

Subjects Offered 20th century world history, acting, advanced chemistry, advanced math, algebra, American history, American literature, art, art history, art history-AP, Asian history, biology, calculus, calculus-AP, ceramics, chemistry, Chinese, choir, choral music, college counseling, comparative religion, computer literacy, computer programming, concert choir, creative writing, digital music, drama, drawing, driver education, East Asian history, English, English literature, English literature-AP, environmental science, ethics, European history, European history-AP, film, film studies, fine arts, French, French literature-AP, geometry, Greek, history, honors geometry, improvisation, Islamic history, Latin, Latin-AP, mathematics, Middle Eastern history, modern European history, music, music theory, organic chemistry, painting, philosophy, photography, physics, physics-AP, poetry, pottery, psychology, religion, religious studies, science, science research, Spanish, Spanish literature-AP, speech, statistics-AP, theater, trigonometry, U.S. history, Western religions.

Graduation Requirements Arts and fine arts (art, music, dance, drama), English, foreign language, history, mathematics, religion (includes Bible studies and theology), science.

Special Academic Programs Honors section; independent study; academic accommodation for the gifted, the musically talented, and the artistically talented.

College Admission Counseling 70 students graduated in 2015; 68 went to college, including Davidson College; Duke University; Harvard University; New York University; Wesleyan University; Williams College. Other: 1 entered a postgraduate year, 1 had other specific plans. Mean SAT critical reading: 629, mean SAT math: 651, mean SAT writing: 625.

Student Life Upper grades have specified standards of dress, student council, honor system. Discipline rests equally with students and faculty. Attendance at religious services is required.

Tuition and Aid 7-day tuition and room/board: $55,500. Tuition installment plan (monthly payment plans). Need-based scholarship grants available. In 2015–16, 46% of upper-school students received aid. Total amount of financial aid awarded in 2015–16: $6,066,500.

Admissions Traditional secondary-level entrance grade is 9. For fall 2015, 546 students applied for upper-level admission, 148 were accepted, 90 enrolled. ISEE, SSAT or TOEFL required. Deadline for receipt of application materials: January 15. Application fee required: $60. On-campus interview required.

Athletics Interscholastic: aquatics (boys, girls), baseball (b), basketball (b,g), crew (b,g), cross-country running (b,g), field hockey (g), football (b), lacrosse (b,g), rowing (b,g), soccer (b,g), squash (b,g), swimming and diving (b,g), tennis (b,g), volleyball (g), wrestling (b); coed intramural: aerobics, aerobics/dance, canoeing/kayaking, dance, fencing, fishing, fitness, Frisbee, indoor soccer, kayaking, outdoors, paddle tennis, physical training, rowing, sailboarding, sailing, weight lifting, weight training, windsurfing, yoga. 1 athletic trainer.

Computers Computers are regularly used in English, foreign language, history, mathematics, science classes. Computer network features include on-campus library services, online commercial services, Internet access, wireless campus network, Internet filtering or blocking technology. Campus intranet, student e-mail accounts, and computer access in designated common areas are available to students. The school has a published electronic and media policy.

Contact Louisa H. Zendt, Director of Admission. 302-285-4230. Fax: 302-378-7120. E-mail: lzendt@standrews-de.org. Website: www.standrews-de.org

SAINT ANDREW'S SCHOOL

3900 Jog Road
Boca Raton, Florida 33434

Head of School: Mr. Peter Benedict

General Information Coeducational boarding and day college-preparatory school, affiliated with Episcopal Church. Boarding grades 9–12, day grades JK–12. Founded: 1961. Setting: suburban. Nearest major city is West Palm Beach. Students are housed in single-sex dormitories. 82-acre campus. 18 buildings on campus. Approved or accredited by Florida Council of Independent Schools, Southern Association of Colleges and Schools, The Association of Boarding Schools, and Florida Department of Education. Member of National Association of Independent Schools and Secondary School Admission Test Board. Endowment: $16 million. Total enrollment: 1,285. Upper school average class size: 14. Upper school faculty-student ratio: 1:9. There are 180 required school days per year for Upper School students. Upper School students typically attend 5 days per week. The average school day consists of 7 hours and 30 minutes.

Upper School Student Profile Grade 9: 138 students (68 boys, 70 girls); Grade 10: 148 students (76 boys, 72 girls); Grade 11: 163 students (88 boys, 75 girls); Grade 12: 153 students (77 boys, 76 girls). 17% of students are boarding students. 82% are state residents. 7 states are represented in upper school student body. 12% are international students. International students from Bahamas, China, Germany, Republic of Korea, Russian Federation, and Viet Nam; 25 other countries represented in student body. 5% of students are members of Episcopal Church.

Faculty School total: 210. In upper school: 55 men, 75 women; 80 have advanced degrees; 38 reside on campus.

Subjects Offered Advanced studio art-AP, algebra, American history, American literature, American studies, anatomy, archaeology, art, art history, Bible studies, biology, biology-AP, calculus, calculus-AP, chemistry, chemistry-AP, Chinese, community service, computer math, computer programming, computer science, computer science-AP, creative writing, drafting, drama, earth science, ecology, economics, English, English literature, English-AP, environmental science, ethics, European history, expository writing, fine arts, French, French-AP, geography, geometry, German, German-AP, government/civics, grammar, history, journalism, Latin, marine biology, mathematics, music, photography, physical education, physics, physics-AP, pre-calculus, psychology, science, social studies, Spanish, Spanish-AP, speech, statistics, theater, theology, trigonometry, U.S. history-AP, world history, world history-AP, world literature, writing.

Graduation Requirements Arts and fine arts (art, music, dance, drama), computer science, English, foreign language, mathematics, physical education (includes health), religion (includes Bible studies and theology), science, social studies (includes history), speech, visual and performing arts, participation in sports, community service hours. Community service is required.

Special Academic Programs 25 Advanced Placement exams for which test preparation is offered; honors section; academic accommodation for the gifted; ESL (20 students enrolled).

College Admission Counseling 141 students graduated in 2015; all went to college, including Florida State University; The George Washington University; University of Florida; University of Miami; Vanderbilt University. Mean SAT critical reading: 608, mean SAT math: 624, mean SAT writing: 616, mean combined SAT: 1848, mean composite ACT: 27. 50% scored over 600 on SAT critical reading, 60% scored over 600 on SAT math, 57% scored over 600 on SAT writing, 59% scored over 1800 on combined SAT, 58% scored over 26 on composite ACT.

Student Life Upper grades have specified standards of dress, student council, honor system. Discipline rests primarily with faculty. Attendance at religious services is required.

Summer Programs Remediation, enrichment, advancement, ESL, sports, art/fine arts, computer instruction programs offered; session focuses on academics; held on campus; accepts boys and girls; open to students from other schools. 225 students usually enrolled. 2016 schedule: June 10 to July 20. Application deadline: none.

Tuition and Aid Day student tuition: $28,940; 7-day tuition and room/board: $50,840. Tuition installment plan (Insured Tuition Payment Plan, FACTS Tuition Payment Plan, monthly payment plans, individually arranged payment plans). Merit scholarship grants, need-based scholarship grants available. In 2015–16, 15% of upper-school students received aid; total upper-school merit-scholarship money awarded: $110,000. Total amount of financial aid awarded in 2015–16: $3,000,000.

Admissions Traditional secondary-level entrance grade is 9. For fall 2015, 397 students applied for upper-level admission, 198 were accepted, 124 enrolled. SSAT and TOEFL or SLEP required. Deadline for receipt of application materials: February 1. Application fee required: $75. Interview required.

Athletics Interscholastic: baseball (boys), basketball (b,g), cheering (g), cross-country running (b,g), dance (b,g), danceline (g), diving (b,g), fitness (b,g), football (b), golf (b,g), ice hockey (b,g), lacrosse (b,g), soccer (b,g), softball (g), swimming and diving (b,g), tennis (b,g), track and field (b,g), volleyball (g), water polo (b,g), wrestling (b), yoga (b,g); intramural: weight lifting (b,g); coed interscholastic: bowling, water polo. 48 coaches.

Computers Computers are regularly used in college planning, English, foreign language, history, mathematics, science classes. Computer network features include on-campus library services, online commercial services, Internet access, wireless campus network, Internet filtering or blocking technology. Campus intranet, student e-mail accounts, and computer access in designated common areas are available to students. Students grades are available online. The school has a published electronic and media policy.

Contact Kilian J. Forgus, Associate Headmaster for Enrollment and Planning. 561-210-2000. Fax: 561-210-2027. E-mail: admission@saintandrews.net. Website: www.saintandrews.net

ST. ANDREW'S SCHOOL

601 Penn Waller Road
Savannah, Georgia 31410

Head of School: Mr. Mark Toth

General Information Coeducational day college-preparatory, arts, bilingual studies, and technology school. Grades PK–12. Founded: 1947. Setting: suburban. 28-acre campus. 4 buildings on campus. Approved or accredited by Georgia Independent School Association, South Carolina Independent School Association, Southern Association of Colleges and Schools, and Southern Association of Independent Schools. Member of National Association of Independent Schools. Endowment: $400,000. Total enrollment: 457. Upper school average class size: 16. Upper school faculty-student ratio: 1:6. There are 180 required school days per year for Upper School students. Upper School students typically attend 5 days per week. The average school day consists of 7 hours and 25 minutes.

Upper School Student Profile Grade 6: 40 students (21 boys, 19 girls); Grade 7: 31 students (16 boys, 15 girls); Grade 8: 51 students (26 boys, 25 girls); Grade 9: 32 students (16 boys, 16 girls); Grade 10: 41 students (21 boys, 20 girls); Grade 11: 33 students (16 boys, 17 girls); Grade 12: 30 students (14 boys, 16 girls).

Faculty School total: 72. In upper school: 11 men, 14 women; 21 have advanced degrees.

Subjects Offered 3-dimensional design, acting, advanced biology, advanced chemistry, advanced math, advanced studio art-AP, advertising design, algebra, American government, American history, American legal systems, American literature, anatomy, animation, art, art history, arts, band, Basic programming, biology, calculus, chemistry, choir, classical studies, communication skills, community service, computer art, computer programming, computer science, computer skills, computer-aided design, costumes and make-up, creative writing, current history, digital art, drafting, drama, drama performance, drama workshop, drawing, drawing and design, earth science, economics, electives, English, English as a foreign language, English literature, environmental science, ESL, European history, fine arts, geography, geometry, government/civics, health, history, Mandarin, mathematics, music, physical education, physics, psychology, science, social studies, Spanish, theater, trigonometry, Web site design, world history.

Graduation Requirements Arts and fine arts (art, music, dance, drama), computer science, English, foreign language, mathematics, physical education (includes health), science, social studies (includes history), community service. Community service is required.

Special Academic Programs International Baccalaureate program; honors section; accelerated programs; independent study; study at local college for college credit; study abroad; academic accommodation for the gifted, the musically talented, and the artistically talented; remedial reading and/or remedial writing; remedial math; ESL (15 students enrolled).

College Admission Counseling 38 students graduated in 2015; all went to college, including Georgia Institute of Technology; Georgia Southern University; Savannah College of Art and Design; University of Georgia; University of South Carolina; Wake Forest University. Median SAT critical reading: 541, median SAT math: 547, median SAT writing: 535.

Student Life Upper grades have specified standards of dress, student council, honor system. Discipline rests equally with students and faculty.

Summer Programs Remediation, enrichment, sports, art/fine arts programs offered; session focuses on enrichment; held on campus; accepts boys and girls; open to students from other schools. 339 students usually enrolled. 2016 schedule: June 14 to July 30.

Tuition and Aid Day student tuition: $10,220. Tuition installment plan (monthly payment plans). Need-based scholarship grants, need-based grants available. In 2015–16, 25% of upper-school students received aid. Total amount of financial aid awarded in 2015–16: $150,000.

Admissions Traditional secondary-level entrance grade is 9. For fall 2015, 30 students applied for upper-level admission, 10 were accepted, 9 enrolled. Deadline for receipt of application materials: none. Application fee required: $150. Interview required.

Athletics Interscholastic: aerobics/dance (girls), baseball (b), basketball (b,g), cheering (g), cross-country running (b,g), dance team (g), football (b), golf (b,g), physical fitness (b,g), physical training (b,g), soccer (b,g), softball (g), strength & conditioning (b,g), swimming and diving (b,g), tennis (b,g), track and field (b,g), volleyball (g), weight lifting (b,g), weight training (b,g); intramural: basketball (b,g), cheering (b,g), cross-country running (b,g), football (b), golf (b), lacrosse (b), physical fitness (b,g), physical training (b,g), soccer (b,g), softball (g), swimming and diving (b,g), tennis (b,g), track and field (b,g), volleyball (g), weight lifting (b,g), weight training (b,g); coed interscholastic: cheering, cross-country running, physical fitness, physical training, weight lifting, weight training; coed intramural: physical fitness, physical training. 2 PE instructors, 3 coaches, 1 athletic trainer.

Computers Computers are regularly used in all classes. Computer network features include on-campus library services, online commercial services, Internet access, wireless campus network, Internet filtering or blocking technology. Campus intranet, student e-mail accounts, and computer access in designated common areas are available to students. Students grades are available online. The school has a published electronic and media policy.

Contact Mrs. Casey Awad, Director of Admissions. 912-897-4941 Ext. 402. Fax: 912-897-4943. E-mail: awadc@saintschool.com. Website: www.saintschool.com

ST. ANDREW'S SCHOOL

63 Federal Road
Barrington, Rhode Island 02806

Head of School: Mr. David Tinagero

General Information Coeducational boarding and day college-preparatory and arts school. Boarding grades 9–12, day grades 6–12. Founded: 1893. Setting: suburban. Nearest major city is Providence. Students are housed in single-sex dormitories. 100-acre campus. 33 buildings on campus. Approved or accredited by Massachusetts Department of Education, National Association of Episcopal Schools, New England Association of Schools and Colleges, Rhode Island State Certified Resource Progam, The Association of Boarding Schools, and Rhode Island Department of Education. Member of National Association of Independent Schools and Secondary School Admission Test Board. Endowment: $16.4 million. Total enrollment: 205. Upper school average class size: 10. Upper school faculty-student ratio: 1:5. There are 150 required school days per year for Upper School students. Upper School students typically attend 5 days per week. The average school day consists of 8 hours.

Upper School Student Profile Grade 9: 34 students (23 boys, 11 girls); Grade 10: 40 students (22 boys, 18 girls); Grade 11: 47 students (31 boys, 16 girls); Grade 12: 51 students (32 boys, 19 girls); Postgraduate: 3 students (3 boys). 31% of students are boarding students. 59% are state residents. 8 states are represented in upper school student body. 18% are international students. International students from China, India, Republic of Korea, South Africa, Taiwan, and United Kingdom; 2 other countries represented in student body.

Faculty School total: 42. In upper school: 14 men, 24 women; 25 have advanced degrees; 21 reside on campus.

Subjects Offered Advanced biology, Advanced Placement courses, algebra, American history, ancient history, art, astronomy, biology, calculus, calculus-AP, ceramics, chemistry, chorus, college counseling, computer applications, creative writing, digital applications, digital photography, drawing, English, environmental science, ESL, European history, French, geometry, human anatomy, humanities, jewelry making, lab science, music history, music theory, music theory-AP, oceanography, oral communications, physical education, physics, pre-calculus, printmaking, probability and statistics, remedial study skills, Spanish, stagecraft, statistics-AP, studio art, study skills, technical theater, theater, TOEFL preparation, trigonometry, water color painting, yearbook.

Graduation Requirements Arts and fine arts (art, music, dance, drama), English, mathematics, physical education (includes health), science, social studies (includes history), community service.

Special Academic Programs Advanced Placement exam preparation; honors section; independent study; remedial reading and/or remedial writing; programs in English for dyslexic students; special instructional classes for deaf students, blind students, students with mild language-based learning disabilities, students with attention/organizational issues (ADHD); ESL (24 students enrolled).

College Admission Counseling 47 students graduated in 2015; 44 went to college, including Bard College; Brandeis University; Emory University; Fordham University; Gettysburg College; Worcester Polytechnic Institute. Other: 3 went to work. Median SAT critical reading: 480, median SAT math: 520, median SAT writing: 490, median combined SAT: 1540, median composite ACT: 20. 10% scored over 600 on SAT critical reading, 21% scored over 600 on SAT math, 10% scored over 600 on SAT writing, 10% scored over 1800 on combined SAT.

Student Life Upper grades have specified standards of dress, student council. Discipline rests primarily with faculty.

Summer Programs Remediation, enrichment, advancement, ESL, sports, art/fine arts, rigorous outdoor training, computer instruction programs offered; session focuses on skills development; held on campus; accepts boys and girls; open to students from other schools. 800 students usually enrolled. 2016 schedule: June 23 to August 15. Application deadline: none.

Tuition and Aid Day student tuition: $35,500; 7-day tuition and room/board: $53,700. Tuition installment plan (Key Tuition Payment Plan). Need-based scholarship grants, need-based loans available. In 2015–16, 47% of upper-school students received aid. Total amount of financial aid awarded in 2015–16: $2,117,710.

Admissions Traditional secondary-level entrance grade is 9. For fall 2015, 291 students applied for upper-level admission, 137 were accepted, 52 enrolled. Any standardized test required. Deadline for receipt of application materials: January 15. Application fee required: $50. Interview required.

Athletics Interscholastic: basketball (boys, girls), cross-country running (b,g), golf (b), lacrosse (b,g), soccer (b,g), tennis (b,g); coed interscholastic: soccer; coed intramural: badminton, ball hockey, basketball, bicycling, billiards, bocce, cooperative games, croquet, dance, fitness, fitness walking, flag football, floor hockey, Frisbee, horseshoes, jogging, physical fitness, project adventure, ropes courses, running, soccer, strength & conditioning, tennis, touch football, ultimate Frisbee, walking, weight lifting, weight training, yoga. 1 PE instructor, 20 coaches, 1 athletic trainer.

Computers Computers are regularly used in all academic, computer applications, library skills, multimedia, photography, SAT preparation, yearbook classes. Computer network features include on-campus library services, Internet access, wireless campus network, Internet filtering or blocking technology, NetClassroom is available for parents and students. Campus intranet, student e-mail accounts, and computer access in designated common areas are available to students. Students grades are available online. The school has a published electronic and media policy.

Contact Kristel Dunphy, Associate Director to Admissions. 401-246-1230 Ext. 3053. Fax: 401-246-0510. E-mail: kdunphy@standrews-ri.org. Website: www.standrews-ri.org

ST. ANDREW'S–SEWANEE SCHOOL

290 Quintard Road
Sewanee, Tennessee 37375-3000

Head of School: Mrs. Judy Chamberlain

General Information Coeducational boarding and day college-preparatory, arts, and science school, affiliated with Episcopal Church. Boarding grades 9–12, day grades 6–12. Founded: 1868. Setting: small town. Nearest major city is Chattanooga. Students are housed in single-sex dormitories. 550-acre campus. 19 buildings on campus. Approved or accredited by National Association of Episcopal Schools, Southern Association of Colleges and Schools, Southern Association of Independent Schools, Tennessee Association of Independent Schools, The Association of Boarding Schools, and Tennessee Department of Education. Member of National Association of Independent Schools and Secondary School Admission Test Board. Endowment: $12.9 million. Total enrollment: 230. Upper school average class size: 12. Upper school faculty-student ratio: 1:6. There are 168 required school days per year for Upper School students. Upper School students typically attend 5 days per week. The average school day consists of 4 hours and 30 minutes.

Upper School Student Profile Grade 9: 23 students (15 boys, 8 girls); Grade 10: 45 students (23 boys, 22 girls); Grade 11: 47 students (19 boys, 28 girls); Grade 12: 33 students (18 boys, 15 girls). 40% of students are boarding students. 72% are state residents. 10 states are represented in upper school student body. 16% are international students. International students from China, Cuba, Germany, Jamaica, Japan, and Spain; 5 other countries represented in student body. 34% of students are members of Episcopal Church.

Faculty School total: 36. In upper school: 15 men, 20 women; 29 have advanced degrees; 19 reside on campus.

Subjects Offered 20th century American writers, 20th century history, 20th century world history, 3-dimensional art, 3-dimensional design, acting, adolescent issues, advanced biology, advanced chemistry, advanced math, advanced TOEFL/grammar, aerobics, African history, African literature, African-American literature, algebra, American history, American literature, American studies, art, Asian history, Asian literature, band, biology, British literature, British literature (honors), calculus, chamber groups, chemistry, Chinese, choir, college counseling, community service, comparative religion, creative writing, drama, dramatic arts, ecology, English, English literature, environmental systems, ESL, European literature, filmmaking, fine arts, general science, geometry, history, humanities, Latin, Latin American literature, leadership, literature, mathematics, minority studies, music, philosophy, physical education, physics, poetry, pottery, pre-algebra, psychology, religion, religious studies, science, social studies, Southern literature, Spanish, statistics, theater, trigonometry, world history, yearbook.

Graduation Requirements Arts and fine arts (art, music, dance, drama), English, foreign language, mathematics, physical education (includes health), religion (includes Bible studies and theology), science, social studies (includes history), senior lecture series, creedal statement. Community service is required.

Special Academic Programs 13 Advanced Placement exams for which test preparation is offered; independent study; term-away projects; study at local college for college credit; study abroad; academic accommodation for the gifted, the musically talented, and the artistically talented; remedial reading and/or remedial writing; remedial math; ESL (10 students enrolled).

College Admission Counseling 55 students graduated in 2015; 53 went to college, including Agnes Scott College; Middle Tennessee State University; Sewanee: The University of the South; Tennessee Technological University; The University of Tennessee; The University of Tennessee at Chattanooga. Other: 2 went to work.

Student Life Upper grades have specified standards of dress, student council, honor system. Discipline rests equally with students and faculty. Attendance at religious services is required.

Summer Programs Sports, art/fine arts programs offered; session focuses on sports, outdoor adventure, art; held both on and off campus; held at surrounding natural areas; accepts boys and girls; open to students from other schools. 140 students usually enrolled. 2016 schedule: May 20 to July 22. Application deadline: none.

Tuition and Aid Day student tuition: $17,950; 7-day tuition and room/board: $43,725. Tuition installment plan (monthly payment plans). Merit scholarship grants, need-based scholarship grants available. In 2015–16, 46% of upper-school students received aid; total upper-school merit-scholarship money awarded: $84,296. Total amount of financial aid awarded in 2015–16: $1,576,449.

Admissions Traditional secondary-level entrance grade is 9. For fall 2015, 133 students applied for upper-level admission, 110 were accepted, 64 enrolled. SLEP, TOEFL or writing sample required. Deadline for receipt of application materials: none. Application fee required: $50. Interview required.

Athletics Interscholastic: baseball (boys), basketball (b,g), cross-country running (b,g), diving (b,g), football (b), soccer (b,g), swimming and diving (b,g), tennis (b,g), track and field (b,g), volleyball (g), wrestling (b,g); intramural: ballet (g); coed interscholastic: bicycling, climbing, cross-country running, diving, golf, mountain biking, tennis, track and field; coed intramural: aerobics, aerobics/dance, backpacking, billiards, canoeing/kayaking, combined training, fitness, hiking/backpacking, independent competitive sports, modern dance, mountaineering, outdoor activities, outdoor adventure, outdoor education, outdoor recreation, outdoor skills, outdoors, physical fitness, physical training, rafting, rock climbing, running, strength & conditioning, table tennis, walking, wall climbing, weight training, wilderness, wilderness survival, yoga. 8 coaches.

Computers Computers are regularly used in all academic, art, college planning, creative writing, design, desktop publishing, digital applications, English, foreign language, graphic arts, graphic design, history, humanities, introduction to technology, Latin, literary magazine, mathematics, religion, SAT preparation, science, Spanish, yearbook classes. Computer network features include on-campus library services, online commercial services, Internet access, wireless campus network, Internet filtering or blocking technology, access to University of the South technology facilities. Student e-mail accounts and computer access in designated common areas are available to students. Students grades are available online.

Contact Mr. David Mendlewski, Director of Admission and Financial Aid. 931-598-5651 Ext. 2117. Fax: 931-914-1222. E-mail: admission@sasweb.org. Website: www.sasweb.org

ST. ANNE'S–BELFIELD SCHOOL

2132 Ivy Road
Charlottesville, Virginia 22903

Head of School: Mr. David S. Lourie

General Information Coeducational boarding and day college-preparatory, arts, religious studies, and ESL school, affiliated with Christian faith. Boarding grades 9–12, day grades PK–12. Founded: 1910. Setting: small town. Nearest major city is Washington, DC. Students are housed in coed dormitories. 49-acre campus. 6 buildings on campus. Approved or accredited by The Association of Boarding Schools, Virginia Association of Independent Schools, and Virginia Department of Education. Member of National Association of Independent Schools and Secondary School Admission Test Board. Endowment: $31 million. Total enrollment: 910. Upper school average class size: 13. Upper school faculty-student ratio: 1:8. There are 180 required school days per year for Upper School students. Upper School students typically attend 5 days per week. The average school day consists of 7 hours and 30 minutes.

Upper School Student Profile Grade 9: 82 students (40 boys, 42 girls); Grade 10: 87 students (43 boys, 44 girls); Grade 11: 100 students (54 boys, 46 girls); Grade 12: 89 students (41 boys, 48 girls). 18% of students are boarding students. 87% are state residents. 7 states are represented in upper school student body. 9% are international students. International students from Azerbaijan, China, Ethiopia, Republic of Korea, Saint Kitts and Nevis, and South Africa; 22 other countries represented in student body.

Faculty School total: 111. In upper school: 16 men, 25 women; 35 have advanced degrees; 7 reside on campus.

Subjects Offered 1968, algebra, art, biology, biology-AP, calculus-AP, ceramics, chemistry, chemistry-AP, choir, conceptual physics, drama, economics, English, environmental science-AP, ESL, French, French language-AP, geometry, honors algebra, honors geometry, humanities, Latin, Latin-AP, modern European history-AP, modern world history, music theory, music theory-AP, orchestra, photography, physics, physics-AP, pre-calculus, religion, sculpture, Spanish, Spanish language-AP, statistics, statistics-AP, theology, trigonometry, U.S. history, U.S. history-AP, video, world history, writing workshop.

Graduation Requirements Art, English, foreign language, history, mathematics, physical education (includes health), religion (includes Bible studies and theology), science. Community service is required.

Special Academic Programs 14 Advanced Placement exams for which test preparation is offered; honors section; independent study; study at local college for college credit; ESL (12 students enrolled).

College Admission Counseling 358 students graduated in 2015; they went to James Madison University; Lynchburg College; The College of William and Mary; University of Mary Washington; University of Virginia; Virginia Commonwealth University. Other: 1 had other specific plans. Median SAT critical reading: 630, median SAT math: 620. Mean SAT writing: 622. 59% scored over 600 on SAT critical reading, 57% scored over 600 on SAT math, 68% scored over 600 on SAT writing, 72% scored over 1800 on combined SAT.

Student Life Upper grades have uniform requirement, student council, honor system. Discipline rests primarily with faculty. Attendance at religious services is required.

Summer Programs Remediation, enrichment, ESL, sports programs offered; session focuses on academic enrichment and remediation through 8th grade, ESL Summer Program; held on campus; accepts boys and girls; open to students from other schools. 350 students usually enrolled. 2016 schedule: June 15 to July 31. Application deadline: none.

Tuition and Aid Day student tuition: $24,600; 5-day tuition and room/board: $40,500; 7-day tuition and room/board: $51,500. Tuition installment plan (Insured Tuition Payment Plan, FACTS Tuition Payment Plan, monthly payment plans). Need-based scholarship grants, need-based financial aid available. In 2015–16, 39% of upper-school students received aid. Total amount of financial aid awarded in 2015–16: $4,700,000.

Admissions Traditional secondary-level entrance grade is 9. For fall 2015, 213 students applied for upper-level admission, 81 were accepted, 53 enrolled. ERB verbal, ERB math, SSAT, TOEFL or writing sample required. Deadline for receipt of application materials: February 5. No application fee required. Interview required.

Athletics Interscholastic: baseball (boys), basketball (b,g), cross-country running (b,g), field hockey (g), football (b), golf (b,g), lacrosse (b,g), soccer (b,g), softball (g), squash (b,g), swimming and diving (b,g), tennis (b,g), track and field (b,g), volleyball (g), wrestling (b); coed interscholastic: cross-country running, golf, squash, swimming and diving, track and field; coed intramural: aerobics, aerobics/dance, alpine skiing, dance, fitness, physical fitness, yoga. 6 PE instructors, 8 coaches, 2 athletic trainers.

Computers Computers are regularly used in all academic classes. Computer network features include on-campus library services, online commercial services, Internet access, wireless campus network. Student e-mail accounts and computer access in designated common areas are available to students. Students grades are available online. The school has a published electronic and media policy.

Contact Mr. Sintayehu Taye, Assistant Director of Admission for Grades 5-12. 434-296-5106. Fax: 434-979-1486. E-mail: staye@stab.org. Website: www.stab.org

SAINT ANTHONY HIGH SCHOOL

304 East Roadway Avenue
Effingham, Illinois 62401

Head of School: Mr. Greg Fearday

General Information Coeducational day college-preparatory, arts, business, religious studies, bilingual studies, and technology school, affiliated with Roman Catholic Church. Grades 9–12. Setting: small town. Nearest major city is St. Louis, MO. 1 building on campus. Approved or accredited by National Catholic Education Association and Illinois Department of Education. Total enrollment: 190. Upper school average class size: 20. Upper school faculty-student ratio: 1:10. There are 176 required school days per year for Upper School students. Upper School students typically attend 5 days per week. The average school day consists of 5 hours and 42 minutes.

Upper School Student Profile Grade 9: 50 students (26 boys, 24 girls); Grade 10: 56 students (29 boys, 27 girls); Grade 11: 42 students (23 boys, 19 girls); Grade 12: 42 students (16 boys, 26 girls). 97% of students are Roman Catholic.

Faculty School total: 21. In upper school: 6 men, 15 women; 8 have advanced degrees.

Subjects Offered Accounting, advanced math, algebra, American government, anatomy, art appreciation, band, biology, British literature, calculus-AP, career exploration, Catholic belief and practice, ceramics, chemistry, chorus, communications, composition, computer applications, conceptual physics, concert band, consumer education, current events, earth science, English literature, English-AP, environmental science, finite math, general math, geography, geometry, health, microbiology, music appreciation, physical education, physical science, physics, pre-algebra, psychology, publications, Spanish, statistics-AP, U.S. history, world history, world wide web design.

Graduation Requirements American government, arts and fine arts (art, music, dance, drama), computer science, consumer education, English, mathematics, physical education (includes health), religion (includes Bible studies and theology), science, social sciences, speech, U.S. history, world history.

Special Academic Programs International Baccalaureate program; 3 Advanced Placement exams for which test preparation is offered; independent study; study at local college for college credit; remedial math; special instructional classes for deaf students.

College Admission Counseling 48 students graduated in 2015; 47 went to college, including Eastern Illinois University; Southern Illinois University Edwardsville; University of Illinois at Urbana–Champaign. Other: 1 entered military service. Median composite ACT: 25.

Student Life Upper grades have specified standards of dress, student council. Discipline rests primarily with faculty. Attendance at religious services is required.

Tuition and Aid Tuition installment plan (monthly payment plans). Need-based scholarship grants available.

Admissions Traditional secondary-level entrance grade is 9. Deadline for receipt of application materials: none. No application fee required.

Athletics Interscholastic: baseball (boys), basketball (b,g), cheering (g), dance team (g), golf (b,g), soccer (b,g), softball (g), tennis (b,g), track and field (b,g), volleyball (g), wrestling (b); coed interscholastic: cross-country running. 1 PE instructor, 19 coaches.

Computers Computers are regularly used in publications, yearbook classes. Computer network features include on-campus library services, Internet access, Internet filtering or blocking technology. Student e-mail accounts are available to students. Students grades are available online. The school has a published electronic and media policy.

Contact Mr. Greg Fearday, Principal. 217-342-6969. Fax: 217-342-6997. E-mail: gfearday@stanthony.com. Website: www.stanthony.com

ST. AUGUSTINE HIGH SCHOOL

3266 Nutmeg Street
San Diego, California 92104-5199

Head of School: James Horne

General Information Boys' day college-preparatory and religious studies school, affiliated with Roman Catholic Church. Grades 9–12. Founded: 1922. Setting: urban. 7-acre campus. 10 buildings on campus. Approved or accredited by National Catholic Education Association, Western Association of Schools and Colleges, and Western Catholic Education Association. Endowment: $1 million. Total enrollment: 700. Upper school average class size: 25. Upper school faculty-student ratio: 1:25. There are 180 required school days per year for Upper School students. Upper School students typically attend 5 days per week. The average school day consists of 5 hours and 50 minutes.

Upper School Student Profile Grade 9: 190 students (190 boys); Grade 10: 180 students (180 boys); Grade 11: 170 students (170 boys); Grade 12: 160 students (160 boys). 92% of students are Roman Catholic.

Faculty School total: 50. In upper school: 38 men, 10 women; 41 have advanced degrees.

Subjects Offered Algebra, American history, American literature, anatomy, art, art history, arts, Bible studies, biology, calculus, chemistry, computer science, driver education, economics, economics-AP, English, English literature, English-AP, ethics, fine arts, French, geometry, government/civics, grammar, health, history, Latin, Latin-AP, mathematics, music, philosophy, physical education, physics, physiology, psychology, religion, science, social studies, Spanish, speech, theology, trigonometry, world history, world literature, writing.

Graduation Requirements Arts and fine arts (art, music, dance, drama), English, foreign language, mathematics, physical education (includes health), religion (includes Bible studies and theology), science, social studies (includes history), speech, 100 hours of Christian service over four years.

Special Academic Programs Advanced Placement exam preparation; honors section; study abroad; academic accommodation for the gifted; remedial reading and/or remedial writing; remedial math; programs in English, mathematics, general development for dyslexic students; special instructional classes for blind students.

College Admission Counseling 169 students graduated in 2014; all went to college, including Gonzaga University; San Diego State University; University of California, Los Angeles; University of California, San Diego; University of Notre Dame; University of San Diego. 45% scored over 600 on SAT critical reading, 45% scored over 600 on SAT math, 45% scored over 600 on SAT writing, 55% scored over 26 on composite ACT.

Student Life Upper grades have specified standards of dress, student council, honor system. Discipline rests primarily with faculty. Attendance at religious services is required.

Tuition and Aid Day student tuition: $16,500. Tuition installment plan (SMART Tuition Payment Plan, monthly payment plans, quarterly and annual payment plans). Merit scholarship grants, need-based scholarship grants, paying campus jobs available. In 2014–15, 50% of upper-school students received aid. Total amount of financial aid awarded in 2014–15: $2,100,000.

Admissions Traditional secondary-level entrance grade is 9. For fall 2014, 320 students applied for upper-level admission, 220 were accepted, 190 enrolled. ETS HSPT (closed) required. Deadline for receipt of application materials: January 24. Application fee required: $50. Interview required.

Athletics Interscholastic: baseball, basketball, cross-country running, diving, football, golf, in-line hockey, lacrosse, roller hockey, rugby, running, soccer, surfing, swimming and diving, tennis, track and field, volleyball, winter soccer, wrestling; intramural: basketball, bicycling, crew, fishing, fitness, flag football, Frisbee, kickball, mountain biking, ocean paddling, outdoor activities, outdoor adventure, outdoor education, outdoor recreation, physical fitness, physical training, racquetball, scuba diving, speedball, street hockey, strength & conditioning, table tennis, ultimate Frisbee, volleyball, weight lifting, weight training, yoga. 5 PE instructors, 26 coaches, 1 athletic trainer.

Computers Computers are regularly used in foreign language, mathematics, science, Web site design, writing classes. Computer network features include on-campus library services, online commercial services, Internet access, wireless campus network, Internet filtering or blocking technology, online databases, remote access. Campus intranet, student e-mail accounts, and computer access in designated common areas are available to students. Students grades are available online. The school has a published electronic and media policy.

Contact Jeannie Oliwa, Registrar. 619-282-2184 Ext. 5512. Fax: 619-282-1203. E-mail: joliwa@sahs.org. Website: www.sahs.org

SAINT AUGUSTINE PREPARATORY SCHOOL

611 Cedar Avenue
PO Box 279
Richland, New Jersey 08350

Head of School: Rev. Donald F. Reilly, OSA

General Information Boys' day college-preparatory, arts, business, religious studies, bilingual studies, and technology school, affiliated with Roman Catholic Church. Grades 9–12. Founded: 1959. Setting: rural. Nearest major city is Vineland. 120-acre campus. 4 buildings on campus. Approved or accredited by Middle States Association of Colleges and Schools, National Catholic Education Association, New Jersey Association of Independent Schools, and New Jersey Department of Education. Member of National Association of Independent Schools. Endowment: $750,000. Total enrollment: 695. Upper school average class size: 17. Upper school faculty-student ratio: 1:12. There are 180 required school days per year for Upper School students. Upper School students typically attend 5 days per week. The average school day consists of 6 hours and 8 minutes.

Upper School Student Profile Grade 9: 185 students (185 boys); Grade 10: 194 students (194 boys); Grade 11: 150 students (150 boys); Grade 12: 166 students (166 boys). 78% of students are Roman Catholic.

Faculty School total: 63. In upper school: 48 men, 15 women; 36 have advanced degrees.

Subjects Offered 20th century history, 20th century world history, accounting, advanced chemistry, Advanced Placement courses, advanced studio art-AP, algebra, American Civil War, American government, American history, American history-AP, American literature, analysis and differential calculus, anatomy and physiology, ancient world history, Arabic, Arabic studies, art, art appreciation, art education, arts, band, Bible, biology, biology-AP, British literature, British literature (honors), British literature-AP, business education, business studies, calculus, calculus-AP, Catholic belief and practice, chemistry, chemistry-AP, choir, Christian and Hebrew scripture, Christian doctrine, Christian ethics, church history, Civil War, classical language, college counseling, college planning, community service, comparative religion, computer applications, computer programming, computer science, computer science-AP, computer-aided design, concert choir, culinary arts, current events, drama, drama performance, driver education, economics, engineering, English, English composition, English literature, English literature-AP, environmental education, ethics and responsibility, European history, European history-AP, finance, French, geometry, German, grammar, guitar, history, history-AP, Holocaust, Holocaust and other genocides, honors algebra, honors English, honors geometry, honors U.S. history, independent study, jazz band, jazz ensemble, lab science, language-AP, Latin, marine biology, mathematics-AP, model United Nations, moral theology, music theory, music theory-AP, peer ministry, philosophy, photojournalism, physical education, physics, physics-AP, political science, pre-calculus, psychology, psychology-AP, public speaking, religion, religious studies, SAT preparation, scripture, service learning/internship, social skills, sociology, Spanish, Spanish language-AP, Spanish literature-AP, Spanish-AP, studio art, theater, travel, U.S. history-AP, vocal music, Web site design, world cultures, world religions, writing.

Graduation Requirements Electives, English, foreign language, lab science, mathematics, religion (includes Bible studies and theology), science, service learning/internship, U.S. history, world cultures, social service project (approximately 100 hours), retreat experiences, third semester experiences (travel; hands-on learning.

Special Academic Programs 18 Advanced Placement exams for which test preparation is offered; honors section; independent study; term-away projects; study at local college for college credit; study abroad; academic accommodation for the gifted, the musically talented, and the artistically talented; programs in general development for dyslexic students; special instructional classes for deaf students, blind students.

College Admission Counseling 171 students graduated in 2015; all went to college, including Drexel University; La Salle University; Rowan University; Saint Joseph's University; University of Delaware; Villanova University. Mean SAT critical reading: 553, mean SAT math: 591, mean SAT writing: 567, mean combined SAT: 1711, mean composite ACT: 25. 32% scored over 600 on SAT critical reading, 43% scored over 600 on SAT math, 31% scored over 600 on SAT writing, 31% scored over 1800 on combined SAT, 31% scored over 26 on composite ACT.

Student Life Upper grades have uniform requirement, student council, honor system. Discipline rests primarily with faculty. Attendance at religious services is required.

Summer Programs Enrichment, advancement, sports, art/fine arts, rigorous outdoor training programs offered; session focuses on academic enrichment, community relations, sports camps; held both on and off campus; held at crew camp on nearby lake; accepts boys and girls; open to students from other schools. 700 students usually enrolled. 2016 schedule: July 1 to August 15. Application deadline: June 1.

Tuition and Aid Day student tuition: $16,100. Tuition installment plan (FACTS Tuition Payment Plan, individually arranged payment plans, credit card payment). Merit scholarship grants, need-based scholarship grants available. In 2015–16, 38% of upper-school students received aid; total upper-school merit-scholarship money awarded: $215,000. Total amount of financial aid awarded in 2015–16: $1,100,000.

Admissions Traditional secondary-level entrance grade is 9. For fall 2015, 302 students applied for upper-level admission, 250 were accepted, 185 enrolled. School's own exam required. Deadline for receipt of application materials: January 31. Application fee required: $75. On-campus interview required.

Athletics Interscholastic: baseball, basketball, bowling, crew, cross-country running, fencing, football, golf, ice hockey, indoor track, lacrosse, rowing, rugby, sailing, soccer, squash, surfing, swimming and diving, tennis, track and field, volleyball, winter (indoor) track, wrestling; intramural: basketball, flag football, physical training, soccer, ultimate Frisbee, volleyball, weight training. 2 PE instructors, 12 coaches, 1 athletic trainer.

Computers Computers are regularly used in all academic, art, career education, computer applications, design, photojournalism, SAT preparation classes. Computer network features include on-campus library services, online commercial services, Internet access, wireless campus network, Internet filtering or blocking technology, syllabus, current grades, and assignments available online for all courses. Student e-mail accounts and computer access in designated common areas are available to students. Students grades are available online. The school has a published electronic and media policy.

Contact Mr. Stephen Cappuccio, Dean of Enrollment Management. 856-697-2600 Ext. 112. Fax: 856-285-7108. E-mail: mr.cappuccio@hermits.com. Website: www.hermits.com

ST. BENEDICT AT AUBURNDALE

8250 Varnavas Drive
Cordova, Tennessee 38016

Head of School: Mrs. Sondra Morris

General Information Coeducational day college-preparatory, arts, business, religious studies, bilingual studies, and technology school, affiliated with Roman Catholic Church. Grades 9–12. Founded: 1966. Setting: suburban. Nearest major city is Memphis. 40-acre campus. 1 building on campus. Approved or accredited by National Catholic Education Association, Southern Association of Colleges and Schools, and Tennessee Department of Education. Endowment: $200,000. Total enrollment: 945. Upper school average class size: 26. Upper school faculty-student ratio: 1:16. There are 186 required school days per year for Upper School students. Upper School students typically attend 5 days per week. The average school day consists of 7 hours and 15 minutes.

Upper School Student Profile Grade 9: 230 students (110 boys, 120 girls); Grade 10: 252 students (122 boys, 130 girls); Grade 11: 240 students (110 boys, 130 girls); Grade 12: 223 students (100 boys, 123 girls). 85% of students are Roman Catholic.

Faculty School total: 65. In upper school: 15 men, 50 women; 40 have advanced degrees.

Subjects Offered Accounting, acting, algebra, American government, American history, American history-AP, American literature-AP, anatomy and physiology, applied music, art, art appreciation, art education, art history, art-AP, astronomy, band, biology, calculus, calculus-AP, Catholic belief and practice, chemistry, choir, choral music, choreography, chorus, church history, cinematography, clayworking, comparative religion, composition-AP, computer graphics, computer multimedia, computers, creative writing, dance, digital art, digital photography, drama, drama performance, drawing, driver education, ecology, economics, economics-AP, English, English language-AP, English literature-AP, English-AP, English/composition-AP, etymology, European history, film, filmmaking, fine arts, first aid, fitness, forensics, French, French-AP, general business, geometry, German, government, government-AP, graphic arts, graphic design, health and wellness, health education, history, history of the Catholic Church, history-AP, honors algebra, honors English, honors geometry, honors U.S. history, human anatomy, human biology, instrumental music, internship, jazz band, jazz dance, journalism, keyboarding, lab/keyboard, Latin, literature-AP, macroeconomics-AP, marketing, modern history, music appreciation, music history, music theory, newspaper, performing arts, personal finance, photography, physical education, physical science, physics, play production, pre-algebra, pre-calculus, psychology, religion, set design, sociology, Spanish, Spanish-AP, speech, sports conditioning, stage design, statistics-AP, student publications, U.S. government and politics-AP, U.S. history-AP, world geography, world history, yearbook.

Graduation Requirements Arts and fine arts (art, music, dance, drama), economics, English, foreign language, government, mathematics, physical education (includes health), religion (includes Bible studies and theology), science, social studies (includes history), technology, theology.

Special Academic Programs 10 Advanced Placement exams for which test preparation is offered; study at local college for college credit; academic accommodation for the gifted, the musically talented, and the artistically talented; remedial reading and/or remedial writing; remedial math; programs in English, mathematics, general development for dyslexic students; special instructional classes for students with diagnosed learning disabilities and Attention Deficit Disorder.

College Admission Counseling 243 students graduated in 2015; all went to college, including Christian Brothers University; Middle Tennessee State University; Mississippi State University; The University of Alabama; The University of Tennessee; University of Memphis. Mean SAT critical reading: 570, mean SAT math: 560, mean composite ACT: 24. 38% scored over 600 on SAT critical reading, 37% scored over 600 on SAT math, 30% scored over 26 on composite ACT.

Student Life Upper grades have uniform requirement, student council, honor system. Discipline rests primarily with faculty. Attendance at religious services is required.

Summer Programs Remediation, enrichment programs offered; session focuses on enrichment for math and language; held on campus; accepts boys and girls; not open to students from other schools. 30 students usually enrolled. 2016 schedule: July 5 to July 29. Application deadline: none.

Tuition and Aid Day student tuition: $8600. Tuition installment plan (FACTS Tuition Payment Plan, monthly payment plans, individually arranged payment plans). Merit scholarship grants, need-based scholarship grants available. In 2014–15, 4% of upper-school students received aid; total upper-school merit-scholarship money awarded: $30,000. Total amount of financial aid awarded in 2014–15: $35,000.

Admissions Traditional secondary-level entrance grade is 9. For fall 2015, 270 students applied for upper-level admission, 270 were accepted, 260 enrolled. High School Placement Test required. Deadline for receipt of application materials: none. Application fee required: $75. Interview required.

Athletics Interscholastic: baseball (boys), basketball (b,g), bowling (b,g), cheering (g), cross-country running (b,g), dance (g), dance squad (g), dance team (g), football (b), Frisbee (b,g), golf (b,g), lacrosse (b,g), pom squad (g), soccer (b,g), softball (g), strength & conditioning (b), swimming and diving (b,g), tennis (b,g), track and field (b,g), volleyball (g), weight lifting (b), weight training (b), wrestling (b); coed interscholastic: water polo; coed intramural: Frisbee. 4 PE instructors, 17 coaches, 1 athletic trainer.

Computers Computers are regularly used in all academic, art, business, commercial art, current events, dance, design, desktop publishing, economics, French, graphic arts, graphic design, health, history, journalism, lab/keyboard, Latin, mathematics, music, newspaper, photography, psychology, publications, religion, science, social sciences, social studies, Spanish, speech, study skills, technology, theater, theater arts, theology, Web site design, writing, yearbook classes. Computer network features include on-campus library services, Internet access, wireless campus network, Internet filtering or blocking technology. Campus intranet and student e-mail accounts are available to students. Students grades are available online. The school has a published electronic and media policy.

Contact Mrs. Terri Heath, Director of Admissions. 901-260-2873. Fax: 901-260-2850. E-mail: heatht@sbaeagles.org. Website: www.sbaeagles.org

ST. BERNARD HIGH SCHOOL

9100 Falmouth Avenue
Playa del Rey, California 90293-8299

Head of School: Dr. Patrick Lynch

General Information Coeducational day college-preparatory, arts, and religious studies school, affiliated with Roman Catholic Church. Grades 9–12. Founded: 1957. Setting: suburban. Nearest major city is Los Angeles. 14-acre campus. 5 buildings on campus. Approved or accredited by National Catholic Education Association, Western Association of Schools and Colleges, Western Catholic Education Association, and California Department of Education. Endowment: $1.2 million. Total enrollment: 260. Upper school average class size: 20. Upper school faculty-student ratio: 1:20.

Upper School Student Profile 65% of students are Roman Catholic.

Faculty School total: 20. In upper school: 9 men, 9 women; 14 have advanced degrees.

Subjects Offered Advanced math, algebra, American literature, American minority experience, ancient history, applied music, band, Bible, biology, biology-AP, British literature, British literature (honors), broadcasting, business law, calculus, campus ministry, Catholic belief and practice, chemistry, chemistry-AP, choir, choral music, Christian and Hebrew scripture, church history, college counseling, comparative religion, competitive science projects, computer literacy, concert band, concert choir, CPR, dance, drama, drawing and design, driver education, earth science, economics, economics-AP, English, English composition, English language and composition-AP, English literature-AP, entrepreneurship, ethics, European history, European history-AP, first aid, French, government, health, history of the Catholic Church, honors algebra, honors English, honors geometry, honors U.S. history, honors world history, human biology, instrumental music, introduction to theater, Life of Christ, literary magazine, marine biology, modern European history-AP, music appreciation, physics, play production, psychology, social sciences, Spanish, Spanish language-AP, speech, study skills, U.S. government, U.S. government and politics-AP, U.S. history, U.S. history-AP, yearbook.

Graduation Requirements 60 hours of community service.

Special Academic Programs Advanced Placement exam preparation; honors section; study at local college for college credit.

College Admission Counseling 65 students graduated in 2015; 62 went to college, including California State University, Dominguez Hills; California State University, Long Beach; California State University, Northridge; Loyola Marymount University; St. John's University; University of California, Los Angeles. Other: 3 went to work.

Student Life Upper grades have uniform requirement, student council, honor system. Discipline rests primarily with faculty. Attendance at religious services is required.

Summer Programs Remediation, enrichment, advancement, sports, art/fine arts, computer instruction programs offered; held on campus; accepts boys and girls; open to students from other schools. 300 students usually enrolled. 2016 schedule: June 16 to July 29. Application deadline: June 5.

Tuition and Aid Day student tuition: $8435. Tuition installment plan (FACTS Tuition Payment Plan). Tuition reduction for siblings, merit scholarship grants, need-based scholarship grants, Catholic Education Foundation available. In 2014–15, 60% of upper-school students received aid.

Admissions Traditional secondary-level entrance grade is 9. Catholic High School Entrance Examination required. Deadline for receipt of application materials: January 16. Application fee required: $79. On-campus interview required.

Athletics Interscholastic: baseball (boys), basketball (b,g), cheering (g), cross-country running (b,g), dance team (g), football (b), golf (b), soccer (b,g), softball (g), track and field (b,g), volleyball (b,g), wrestling (b); coed interscholastic: aerobics/dance, basketball, cross-country running, dance, modern dance; coed intramural: aerobics/dance, bowling, dance, dance squad, jogging, physical fitness, strength & conditioning, surfing, weight training. 1 PE instructor, 15 coaches, 1 athletic trainer.

Computers Computers are regularly used in all classes. Computer network features include on-campus library services, Internet access, Internet filtering or blocking technology. The school has a published electronic and media policy.

Contact Ms. Christina McCole, Director of Admissions. 310-823-4651 Ext. 113. Fax: 310-827-3365. E-mail: cmccole@stbernardhs.org. Website: www.stbernardhs.org

ST. BERNARD HIGH SCHOOL

1593 Norwich-New London Turnpike
Uncasville, Connecticut 06382

Head of School: Mr. Donald Macrino Sr.

General Information Coeducational day college-preparatory school, affiliated with Roman Catholic Church. Grades 6–12. Founded: 1956. Setting: suburban. Nearest major city is Hartford. 119-acre campus. 2 buildings on campus. Approved or accredited by New England Association of Schools and Colleges and Connecticut Department of Education. Member of National Association of Independent Schools. Endowment: $1 million. Total enrollment: 322. Upper school average class size: 19. Upper school faculty-student ratio: 1:10. There are 177 required school days per year for Upper School students. Upper School students typically attend 5 days per week. The average school day consists of 6 hours.

Upper School Student Profile Grade 6: 25 students (11 boys, 14 girls); Grade 7: 23 students (11 boys, 12 girls); Grade 8: 42 students (22 boys, 20 girls); Grade 9: 54 students (28 boys, 26 girls); Grade 10: 66 students (23 boys, 43 girls); Grade 11: 70 students (34 boys, 36 girls); Grade 12: 54 students (27 boys, 27 girls). 60% of students are Roman Catholic.

Faculty School total: 39. In upper school: 16 men, 23 women; 32 have advanced degrees.

Subjects Offered 3-dimensional art, accounting, acting, advanced biology, advanced chemistry, advanced computer applications, advanced math, Advanced Placement courses, advanced studio art-AP, algebra, American history, American history-AP, American literature, American literature-AP, analysis, analysis and differential calculus, analytic geometry, anatomy and physiology, art history-AP, art-AP, athletic training, band, biology, biology-AP, British literature, British literature (honors), British literature-AP, calculus, calculus-AP, chemistry, chemistry-AP, choir, Christian doctrine, Christian ethics, Christian scripture, church history, composition-AP, conceptual physics, concert band, concert choir, creative writing, design, drawing and design, economics, English, English language and composition-AP, English literature and composition-AP, environmental science, ESL, European history-AP, fine arts, forensics, French, French-AP, geometry, global issues, health, honors algebra, honors English, honors geometry, honors U.S. history, honors world history, integrated science, intro to computers, modern European history-AP, modern world history, moral theology, music, music theory, music theory-AP, music-AP, Native American studies, nutrition, organic chemistry, painting, peace and justice, peer counseling, peer ministry, performing arts, personal finance, personal fitness, philosophy, photography, physical education, physics, pottery, pre-algebra, pre-calculus, printmaking, psychology-AP, public speaking, religion and culture, religious studies, scripture, sociology, Spanish, Spanish-AP, sports conditioning, sports nutrition, statistics, street law, strings, studio art, studio art-AP, technology, theater arts, U.S. history, U.S. history-AP, world history.

Graduation Requirements Art, biology, chemistry, English, health education, history, intro to computers, mathematics, physical education (includes health), theology, U.S. history, world history, all students are required to complete 100 hours of community service prior to high school graduation.

Special Academic Programs Honors section; study at local college for college credit; ESL (16 students enrolled).

College Admission Counseling 74 students graduated in 2015; 72 went to college, including Providence College; Saint Michael's College; University of Connecticut; Worcester Polytechnic Institute. Other: 2 entered military service. Mean SAT critical reading: 550, mean SAT math: 526, mean SAT writing: 568, mean combined SAT: 1644. 10% scored over 1800 on combined SAT.

Student Life Upper grades have uniform requirement, student council, honor system. Discipline rests primarily with faculty. Attendance at religious services is required.

Summer Programs Advancement, art/fine arts, computer instruction programs offered; held on campus; accepts boys and girls; not open to students from other schools. 2016 schedule: June to August. Application deadline: January 15.

Tuition and Aid Day student tuition: $11,400. Tuition installment plan (SMART Tuition Payment Plan, FACTS Tuition Payment Plan, monthly payment plans, individually arranged payment plans). Tuition reduction for siblings, merit scholarship grants, need-based scholarship grants available. In 2014–15, 35% of upper-school students received aid; total upper-school merit-scholarship money awarded: $166,050. Total amount of financial aid awarded in 2014–15: $354,257.

Admissions Traditional secondary-level entrance grade is 9. For fall 2015, 136 students applied for upper-level admission, 120 were accepted, 110 enrolled. High School Placement Test (closed version) from Scholastic Testing Service and Scholastic Testing Service required. Deadline for receipt of application materials: January 15. Application fee required. On-campus interview recommended.

Athletics Interscholastic: baseball (boys), basketball (b,g), cheering (g), cross-country running (b,g), diving (b,g), fencing (b,g), football (b), golf (b,g), ice hockey (b), indoor track & field (b,g), lacrosse (b,g), physical fitness (b,g), soccer (b,g), softball (g), swimming and diving (b,g), tennis (b,g), track and field (b,g), wrestling (b,g); intramural: dance squad (g); coed interscholastic: cheering, cross-country running, fencing, golf, physical fitness, soccer, swimming and diving, wrestling; coed intramural: skiing (cross-country), skiing (downhill), snowboarding, strength & conditioning, volleyball, weight training. 2 PE instructors, 50 coaches, 1 athletic trainer.

Computers Computers are regularly used in computer applications, design classes. Computer resources include on-campus library services, Internet access, wireless campus network, Internet filtering or blocking technology. Campus intranet, student e-mail accounts, and computer access in designated common areas are available to students. Students grades are available online. The school has a published electronic and media policy.

Contact Mrs. Catherine Brown, Director of Admissions (Gr. 6-8) and International Programs. 860-848-1271 Ext. 102. Fax: 860-848-1274. E-mail: Admissions@Saint-Bernard.com. Website: www.saint-bernard.com

ST. BERNARD'S CATHOLIC SCHOOL

222 Dollison Street
Eureka, California 95501

Head of School: Mr. Paul Shanahan

General Information Coeducational boarding and day college-preparatory and religious studies school, affiliated with Roman Catholic Church. Boarding grades 9–12, day grades 7–12. Founded: 1912. Setting: small town. Nearest major city is San Francisco. 5-acre campus. 4 buildings on campus. Approved or accredited by National Catholic Education Association, Western Association of Schools and Colleges, Western Catholic Education Association, and California Department of Education. Endowment: $63,000. Total enrollment: 231. Upper school average class size: 20. Upper school faculty-student ratio: 1:12. There are 180 required school days per year for Upper School students. Upper School students typically attend 5 days per week. The average school day consists of 6 hours.

Upper School Student Profile 15% of students are boarding students. 85% are state residents. 15% are international students. International students from China, Republic of Korea, and Viet Nam. 35% of students are Roman Catholic.

Faculty School total: 25. In upper school: 9 men, 11 women; 5 have advanced degrees.

Subjects Offered Arts, community service, English, fine arts, mathematics, physical education, religion, science, social studies.

Graduation Requirements Arts and fine arts (art, music, dance, drama), English, foreign language, mathematics, physical education (includes health), science, social studies (includes history), theology, follow the University of California requirements (250 units). Community service is required.

Special Academic Programs Advanced Placement exam preparation; honors section; remedial reading and/or remedial writing; remedial math; special instructional classes for students with learning disabilities.

College Admission Counseling 43 students graduated in 2015; 40 went to college, including College of the Redwoods; Humboldt State University; Sonoma State University; University of California, Davis; University of California, Los Angeles. Other: 2 went to work, 1 entered military service.

Student Life Upper grades have specified standards of dress, student council. Discipline rests equally with students and faculty. Attendance at religious services is required.

Summer Programs Remediation programs offered; session focuses on make-up work; held on campus; accepts boys and girls; open to students from other schools. 10 students usually enrolled.

Tuition and Aid Day student tuition: $6300. Tuition installment plan (monthly payment plans, individually arranged payment plans, 3% reduction if paid in full by July 10). Tuition reduction for siblings, merit scholarship grants, need-based scholarship grants, paying campus jobs available. In 2015–16, 47% of upper-school students received aid; total upper-school merit-scholarship money awarded: $2500. Total amount of financial aid awarded in 2015–16: $55,000.

Admissions Traditional secondary-level entrance grade is 9. Admissions testing or TOEFL required. Deadline for receipt of application materials: none. Application fee required: $40. Interview required.

Athletics Interscholastic: baseball (boys), basketball (b,g), football (b), golf (b,g), soccer (b,g), softball (g), tennis (b,g), volleyball (g), wrestling (b); intramural: cheering (g); coed interscholastic: track and field. 2 PE instructors, 15 coaches, 1 athletic trainer.

Computers Computers are regularly used in graphic design, journalism, yearbook classes. Computer network features include on-campus library services, Internet access, wireless campus network, Internet filtering or blocking technology. Students grades are available online. The school has a published electronic and media policy.

Contact Mr. David Sharp, Director of Admissions. 707-443-2735 Ext. 115. Fax: 707-443-4723. E-mail: sharp@saintbernards.us. Website: www.saintbernards.us/

ST. BRENDAN HIGH SCHOOL

2950 Southwest 87th Avenue
Miami, Florida 33165-3295

Head of School: Mr. Jose Rodelgo-Bueno

General Information Coeducational day college-preparatory, general academic, arts, business, religious studies, bilingual studies, and technology school, affiliated with Roman Catholic Church. Grades 9–12. Founded: 1975. Setting: urban. 34-acre campus. 4 buildings on campus. Approved or accredited by Southern Association of Colleges and Schools and Florida Department of Education. Total enrollment: 1,145. Upper school average class size: 27. Upper school faculty-student ratio: 1:16. There are 180 required school days per year for Upper School students. Upper School students typically attend 5 days per week. The average school day consists of 6 hours and 45 minutes.

Upper School Student Profile 98% of students are Roman Catholic.

Faculty School total: 73. In upper school: 25 men, 47 women; 35 have advanced degrees.

Graduation Requirements Algebra, students must complete 100 learning community service hours in their four years of high school.

Special Academic Programs 10 Advanced Placement exams for which test preparation is offered; honors section; study at local college for college credit; academic accommodation for the gifted; remedial reading and/or remedial writing; remedial math.

College Admission Counseling 258 students graduated in 2015; all went to college, including Florida International University; Florida State University; Miami Dade College; University of Central Florida; University of Florida; University of Miami. Median SAT critical reading: 500, median SAT math: 490, median SAT writing: 500, median combined SAT: 1490, median composite ACT: 22. 12% scored over 600 on SAT critical reading, 10% scored over 600 on SAT math, 9% scored over 26 on composite ACT.

Student Life Upper grades have uniform requirement, student council, honor system. Discipline rests primarily with faculty. Attendance at religious services is required.

Summer Programs Enrichment, advancement, sports, computer instruction programs offered; held on campus; accepts boys and girls; not open to students from other schools. 270 students usually enrolled. 2016 schedule: June 13 to August.

Tuition and Aid Tuition installment plan (FACTS Tuition Payment Plan, monthly payment plans). Tuition reduction for siblings, need-based scholarship grants, paying campus jobs available. In 2015–16, 23% of upper-school students received aid. Total amount of financial aid awarded in 2015–16: $266,000.

Admissions Traditional secondary-level entrance grade is 9. Catholic High School Entrance Examination or placement test required. Deadline for receipt of application materials: none. Application fee required: $50.

Athletics Interscholastic: baseball (boys), basketball (b,g), cheering (g), cross-country running (b,g), dance (g), dance team (g), lacrosse (b), physical fitness (b,g), physical training (b,g), soccer (b,g), softball (g), swimming and diving (b,g), tennis (b,g), track and field (b,g), volleyball (b,g). 1 PE instructor, 17 coaches, 1 athletic trainer.

Computers Computers are regularly used in business, computer applications, graphic design, mathematics, media arts, media production, newspaper, programming, reading, remedial study skills, research skills, science, speech, Web site design, word processing, yearbook classes. Computer network features include on-campus library services, Internet access, wireless campus network, Internet filtering or blocking technology, 1:1 iPad program. Campus intranet and computer access in designated common areas are available to students. Students grades are available online. The school has a published electronic and media policy.

Contact Melissa Ferrer. 305-223-5181 Ext. 578. Fax: 305-220-7434. E-mail: mferrer@stbhs.org. Website: www.stbrendanhigh.org

ST. CATHERINE'S ACADEMY

Anaheim, California
See Junior Boarding Schools section.

ST. CATHERINE'S SCHOOL

6001 Grove Avenue
Richmond, Virginia 23226

Head of School: Dr. Terrie Hale Scheckelhoff

General Information Girls' day college-preparatory school, affiliated with Episcopal Church. Grades JK–12. Founded: 1890. Setting: urban. Nearest major city is Washington, DC. 16-acre campus. 22 buildings on campus. Approved or accredited by National Association of Episcopal Schools, Virginia Association of Independent Schools, and Virginia Department of Education. Member of National Association of Independent Schools and Secondary School Admission Test Board. Endowment: $46 million. Total enrollment: 985. Upper school average class size: 16. Upper School students typically attend 5 days per week. The average school day consists of 7 hours and 30 minutes.

Upper School Student Profile Grade 6: 79 students (79 girls); Grade 7: 87 students (87 girls); Grade 8: 90 students (90 girls); Grade 9: 71 students (71 girls); Grade 10: 82

students (82 girls); Grade 11: 75 students (75 girls); Grade 12: 85 students (85 girls). 35.5% of students are members of Episcopal Church.

Subjects Offered Acting, adolescent issues, advanced chemistry, advanced computer applications, advanced math, algebra, American government, American history, American history-AP, American literature, ancient history, architecture, art, art and culture, art history, art history-AP, band, Bible, biology, British literature-AP, calculus, calculus-AP, ceramics, chamber groups, chemistry, chemistry-AP, Chinese, choir, choral music, choreography, chorus, comparative government and politics-AP, comparative religion, computer applications, computer math, computer programming, computer science, computer science-AP, constitutional law, creative writing, dance, dance performance, desktop publishing, drama, driver education, economics, economics-AP, English, English language and composition-AP, English literature, English literature and composition-AP, environmental science, environmental science-AP, ethics, ethics and responsibility, European history, expository writing, film and literature, fine arts, French, French language-AP, French literature-AP, gender issues, geography, geometry, government and politics-AP, government/civics, grammar, Greek, guitar, health and wellness, health education, history, history of jazz, honors algebra, honors English, honors geometry, independent study, Latin, Latin-AP, macro/microeconomics-AP, mathematics, modern dance, moral and social development, moral theology, music, music history, music theory, music theory-AP, orchestra, painting, performing arts, philosophy, photography, physical education, physical fitness, physics, physics-AP, playwriting and directing, portfolio art, post-calculus, pre-calculus, printmaking, regional literature, religion, rhetoric, robotics, science, sculpture, short story, social studies, Southern literature, Spanish, Spanish language-AP, Spanish literature, Spanish literature-AP, speech, speech communications, statistics, statistics-AP, theater, theater arts, theology, trigonometry, U.S. government and politics-AP, world cultures, world geography, world history, world literature, writing.

Graduation Requirements Arts and fine arts (art, music, dance, drama), computer science, English, foreign language, health, mathematics, physical education (includes health), religion (includes Bible studies and theology), science, social sciences, social studies (includes history), community service requirement.

Special Academic Programs 23 Advanced Placement exams for which test preparation is offered; honors section; independent study; term-away projects; study abroad.

College Admission Counseling 67 students graduated in 2015; all went to college, including James Madison University; The College of William and Mary; University of Virginia; Virginia Commonwealth University; Washington and Lee University. Median SAT critical reading: 600, median SAT math: 580, median SAT writing: 610, median combined SAT: 1800, median composite ACT: 25. 53% scored over 600 on SAT critical reading, 48% scored over 600 on SAT math, 59% scored over 600 on SAT writing, 53% scored over 1800 on combined SAT, 47% scored over 26 on composite ACT.

Student Life Upper grades have specified standards of dress, student council, honor system. Discipline rests equally with students and faculty. Attendance at religious services is required.

Summer Programs Enrichment, advancement, sports, art/fine arts programs offered; session focuses on creative arts program, enrichment, and sports camps; held both on and off campus; held at James River (rafting) outdoor adventures; accepts boys and girls; open to students from other schools. 1,700 students usually enrolled. 2016 schedule: June 27 to August 5. Application deadline: February 1.

Tuition and Aid Day student tuition: $14,500–$24,980. Tuition installment plan (SMART Tuition Payment Plan, Tuition Management Systems Plan). Need-based scholarship grants available. In 2015–16, 23% of upper-school students received aid. Total amount of financial aid awarded in 2015–16: $917,330.

Admissions Traditional secondary-level entrance grade is 9. For fall 2015, 51 students applied for upper-level admission, 29 were accepted, 17 enrolled. Achievement tests, SSAT and Wechsler Intelligence Scale for Children required. Deadline for receipt of application materials: none. Application fee required: $50. On-campus interview required.

Athletics Interscholastic: basketball, cross-country running, diving, field hockey, golf, indoor track, indoor track & field, lacrosse, soccer, softball, squash, swimming and diving, tennis, track and field, volleyball, winter (indoor) track; intramural: aerobics, aerobics/dance, aerobics/Nautilus, aquatics, ballet, basketball, canoeing/kayaking, climbing, dance, equestrian sports, field hockey, golf, lacrosse, martial arts, modern dance, physical fitness, physical training, soccer, softball, strength & conditioning, swimming and diving, tennis, track and field, volleyball, weight lifting, weight training, wilderness, yoga; coed interscholastic: indoor track & field, track and field; coed intramural: aerobics/dance, backpacking, ballet, canoeing/kayaking, climbing, dance, modern dance, outdoor adventure, wilderness. 7 PE instructors, 87 coaches, 3 athletic trainers.

Computers Computers are regularly used in all classes. Computer network features include on-campus library services, online commercial services, Internet access, wireless campus network, Internet filtering or blocking technology. Campus intranet and student e-mail accounts are available to students. Students grades are available online. The school has a published electronic and media policy.

Contact Jennifer Cullinan, Director of Admissions. 804-288-2804. Fax: 804-285-8169. E-mail: jcullinan@st.catherines.org. Website: www.st.catherines.org

ST. CHRISTOPHER'S SCHOOL

711 St. Christopher's Road
Richmond, Virginia 23226

Head of School: Mr. Charles M. Stillwell

General Information Boys' day college-preparatory school, affiliated with Episcopal Church. Grades JK–12. Founded: 1911. Setting: suburban. 60-acre campus. 9 buildings on campus. Approved or accredited by National Association of Episcopal Schools and Virginia Association of Independent Schools. Member of National Association of Independent Schools and Secondary School Admission Test Board. Endowment: $61 million. Total enrollment: 1,006. Upper school average class size: 16. Upper school faculty student ratio: 1:6. Upper School students typically attend 5 days per week. The average school day consists of 7 hours and 30 minutes.

Upper School Student Profile Grade 9: 87 students (87 boys); Grade 10: 84 students (84 boys); Grade 11: 80 students (80 boys); Grade 12: 86 students (86 boys). 45% of students are members of Episcopal Church.

Faculty School total: 170. In upper school: 34 men, 20 women; 36 have advanced degrees.

Subjects Offered Algebra, American history, American literature, ancient history, architecture, art, art history, astronomy, Bible studies, biology, calculus, ceramics, chemistry, Chinese, communications, community service, computer math, computer programming, computer science, creative thinking, creative writing, current events, dance, digital photography, drama, driver education, ecology, economics, English, English literature, environmental science, ethics, European history, expository writing, fine arts, French, geography, geology, geometry, government/civics, grammar, Greek, health, history, industrial arts, journalism, Latin, mathematics, music, philosophy, photography, physics, public speaking, religion, robotics, science, social studies, Spanish, speech, statistics, theater, theology, trigonometry, typing, video film production, woodworking, writing.

Graduation Requirements 1 1/2 elective credits, algebra, American history, American literature, ancient history, arts and fine arts (art, music, dance, drama), biology, British literature, chemistry, church history, computer science, current events, English, English literature, European history, foreign language, geometry, physical education (includes health), physics, public speaking, religion (includes Bible studies and theology), speech, U.S. history. Community service is required.

Special Academic Programs 23 Advanced Placement exams for which test preparation is offered; honors section; independent study; academic accommodation for the gifted, the musically talented, and the artistically talented.

College Admission Counseling 82 students graduated in 2015; all went to college, including Clemson University; James Madison University; The College of William and Mary; University of Richmond; University of Virginia; Virginia Polytechnic Institute and State University.

Student Life Upper grades have specified standards of dress, student council, honor system. Discipline rests equally with students and faculty. Attendance at religious services is required.

Summer Programs Enrichment, advancement, sports, art/fine arts programs offered; session focuses on enrichment, sports, day camp, leadership; held on campus; accepts boys and girls; open to students from other schools. 500 students usually enrolled. 2016 schedule: June 20 to July 29. Application deadline: none.

Tuition and Aid Day student tuition: $25,475. Tuition installment plan (Academic Management Services Plan, monthly payment plans, individually arranged payment plans, Tuition Refund Plan). Need-based scholarship grants available. In 2015–16, 29% of upper-school students received aid. Total amount of financial aid awarded in 2015–16: $783,200.

Admissions Traditional secondary-level entrance grade is 9. For fall 2015, 47 students applied for upper-level admission, 31 were accepted, 22 enrolled. SSAT and writing sample required. Deadline for receipt of application materials: none. Application fee required: $50. On-campus interview required.

Athletics Interscholastic: baseball, basketball, bicycling, cross-country running, diving, football, golf, indoor soccer, indoor track & field, lacrosse, mountain biking, physical training, sailing, soccer, squash, strength & conditioning, swimming and diving, tennis, track and field, weight lifting, weight training, winter (indoor) track, wrestling; coed interscholastic: canoeing/kayaking, climbing, dance, outdoor adventure, rappelling. 6 coaches, 1 athletic trainer.

Computers Computers are regularly used in all classes. Computer network features include on-campus library services, online commercial services, Internet access, wireless campus network, Internet filtering or blocking technology. Campus intranet, student e-mail accounts, and computer access in designated common areas are available to students. Students grades are available online. The school has a published electronic and media policy.

Contact Cary C. Mauck, Director of Admission. 804-282-3185 Ext. 2388. Fax: 804-673-6632. E-mail: mauckc@stcva.org. Website: www.stchristophers.com

St. Clement's School

ST. CLEMENT'S SCHOOL

21 St. Clements Avenue
Toronto, Ontario M4R 1G8, Canada

Head of School: Ms. Martha Perry

General Information Girls' day college-preparatory, arts, business, and technology school, affiliated with Anglican Church of Canada. Grades 1–12. Founded: 1901. Setting: urban. 1-acre campus. 1 building on campus. Approved or accredited by Canadian Educational Standards Institute and Ontario Department of Education. Affiliate member of National Association of Independent Schools; member of Secondary School Admission Test Board. Language of instruction: English. Total enrollment: 470. Upper school average class size: 16. Upper school faculty-student ratio: 1:7. Upper School students typically attend 5 days per week.

Subjects Offered Accounting, Advanced Placement courses, algebra, Ancient Greek, ancient world history, art, art history-AP, art-AP, band, biology, biology-AP, business, business studies, calculus, calculus-AP, Canadian geography, Canadian history, Canadian law, Canadian literature, career and personal planning, career education, character education, chemistry, chemistry-AP, civics, classics, college admission preparation, communication arts, computer science, creative writing, dance, data processing, design, drama, economics, economics-AP, English, English language-AP, English literature, English literature and composition-AP, environmental science, environmental science-AP, European history, European history-AP, exercise science, film studies, fine arts, finite math, French, French-AP, geography, geometry, grammar, graphic design, guidance, health, history, history-AP, human geography - AP, instrumental music, interdisciplinary studies, jazz ensemble, keyboarding, kinesiology, language and composition, language arts, Latin, Latin-AP, law, leadership and service, library, macro/microeconomics-AP, Mandarin, mathematics, modern Western civilization, music, music theory-AP, musical theater, philosophy, photography, physical education, physics, physics-AP, physiology, religion, science, social sciences, social studies, Spanish, Spanish-AP, statistics-AP, studio art-AP, theater, trigonometry, U.S. history-AP, Western civilization, world history, world issues, writing workshop.

Graduation Requirements Arts, business skills (includes word processing), career/college preparation, civics, computer science, English, foreign language, geography, mathematics, physical education (includes health), science, social studies (includes history).

Special Academic Programs 20 Advanced Placement exams for which test preparation is offered; independent study.

College Admission Counseling 64 students graduated in 2015; all went to college, including Dalhousie University; McGill University; Queen's University at Kingston; The University of British Columbia; The University of Western Ontario; University of Toronto.

Student Life Upper grades have uniform requirement, student council, honor system. Discipline rests equally with students and faculty. Attendance at religious services is required.

Summer Programs Session focuses on cooperative program and summer school credit courses; held on campus; accepts boys and girls; open to students from other schools. 15 students usually enrolled. 2016 schedule: June 20 to July 22. Application deadline: May 1.

Tuition and Aid Day student tuition: CAN$26,675. Tuition installment plan (monthly payment plans). Bursaries, merit scholarship grants, need-based scholarship grants available. In 2015–16, 8% of upper-school students received aid.

Admissions SSAT required. Deadline for receipt of application materials: December 4. Application fee required: CAN$175. Interview required.

Athletics Interscholastic: alpine skiing, aquatics, badminton, basketball, cross-country running, dance, dance team, field hockey, golf, hockey, ice hockey, skiing (downhill), soccer, softball, tennis, track and field, volleyball; intramural: aerobics/dance, ballet, basketball, canoeing/kayaking, cooperative games, dance, dance team, fitness, floor hockey, jogging, life saving, outdoor education, running, table tennis, yoga. 5 PE instructors, 12 coaches.

Computers Computers are regularly used in all academic classes. Computer network features include on-campus library services, online commercial services, Internet access, wireless campus network, Internet filtering or blocking technology. Campus intranet, student e-mail accounts, and computer access in designated common areas are available to students. The school has a published electronic and media policy.

Contact Ms. Elena Holeton, Director of Admissions. 416-483-4414 Ext. 2227. Fax: 416-483-8242. E-mail: elena.holeton@scs.on.ca. Website: www.scs.on.ca

ST. CROIX SCHOOLS

1200 Oakdale Avenue
West St. Paul, Minnesota 55118

Head of School: Pres. Todd Russ

General Information Coeducational boarding and day college-preparatory, general academic, arts, business, vocational, religious studies, bilingual studies, technology, and ESL school, affiliated with Wisconsin Evangelical Lutheran Synod, Christian faith. Grades 6–12. Founded: 1958. Setting: suburban. Nearest major city is St. Paul. Students are housed in single-sex dormitories. 30-acre campus. 4 buildings on campus. Approved or accredited by Minnesota Non-Public School Accrediting Association and Minnesota Department of Education. Endowment: $1.9 million. Total enrollment: 500.

Upper school average class size: 19. Upper school faculty-student ratio: 1:13. There are 176 required school days per year for Upper School students. Upper School students typically attend 5 days per week. The average school day consists of 5 hours and 30 minutes.

Upper School Student Profile Grade 9: 110 students (52 boys, 58 girls); Grade 10: 110 students (57 boys, 53 girls); Grade 11: 110 students (56 boys, 54 girls); Grade 12: 110 students (53 boys, 57 girls). 30% of students are boarding students. 74% are state residents. 5 states are represented in upper school student body. 25% are international students. International students from China, Japan, Republic of Korea, Taiwan, Thailand, and Viet Nam; 10 other countries represented in student body. 57% of students are Wisconsin Evangelical Lutheran Synod, Christian.

Faculty School total: 38. In upper school: 24 men, 11 women; 26 have advanced degrees; 5 reside on campus.

Subjects Offered Accounting, advanced biology, advanced chemistry, advanced math, Advanced Placement courses, algebra, American history, American literature, applied skills, art, band, Bible studies, biology, biology-AP, business skills, calculus, chemistry, choir, chorus, composition-AP, computer programming, computer science, drama, economics, engineering, English, English literature, environmental science, general science, geography, geology, geometry, German, home economics, keyboarding, Latin, literature, Mandarin, mathematics, music, physical education, physics, pre-algebra, reading, religion, science, social sciences, social studies, Spanish, speech, trigonometry, world history, writing.

Graduation Requirements Algebra, arts and fine arts (art, music, dance, drama), biology, chemistry, English, English composition, English literature, foreign language, geometry, government, grammar, literature, physical education (includes health), physics, religion (includes Bible studies and theology), science, social studies (includes history), speech, world geography.

Special Academic Programs 14 Advanced Placement exams for which test preparation is offered; honors section; independent study; academic accommodation for the gifted, the musically talented, and the artistically talented; remedial reading and/or remedial writing; remedial math; programs in English for dyslexic students; special instructional classes for students with learning disabilities; ESL (30 students enrolled).

College Admission Counseling 118 students graduated in 2015; 114 went to college, including Bethany Lutheran College; Cornell College; Martin Luther College; Minnesota State University Mankato; University of Minnesota, Twin Cities Campus; University of Wisconsin–Madison. Other: 1 went to work, 2 entered military service, 1 had other specific plans. Mean composite ACT: 25.

Student Life Upper grades have specified standards of dress, student council, honor system. Discipline rests equally with students and faculty.

Summer Programs ESL, sports programs offered; session focuses on ESL and activities, and a variety of sports camps; held on campus; accepts boys and girls; open to students from other schools. 80 students usually enrolled. 2016 schedule: July 17 to August 21. Application deadline: May 15.

Tuition and Aid 7-day tuition and room/board: $32,400. Merit scholarship grants, need-based scholarship grants available. In 2015–16, 40% of upper-school students received aid; total upper-school merit-scholarship money awarded: $80,000. Total amount of financial aid awarded in 2015–16: $850,000.

Admissions Traditional secondary-level entrance grade is 9. For fall 2015, 177 students applied for upper-level admission, 122 were accepted, 102 enrolled. Secondary Level English Proficiency or writing sample required. Deadline for receipt of application materials: none. Application fee required: $100. Interview recommended.

Athletics Interscholastic: baseball (boys), basketball (b,g), bowling (b,g), cheering (g), cross-country running (b,g), dance team (g), football (b), golf (b,g), hockey (b,g), ice hockey (b,g), lacrosse (b), soccer (b,g), softball (g), swimming and diving (b,g), tennis (b,g), track and field (b,g), volleyball (g), wrestling (b); intramural: badminton (b,g), basketball (b,g); coed interscholastic: riflery; coed intramural: alpine skiing, ball hockey, basketball, bowling, cheering, cross-country running, dance team, flag football, floor hockey, Frisbee, jogging, juggling, kickball, physical fitness, physical training, power lifting, skiing (downhill), snowboarding, softball, strength & conditioning, swimming and diving, table tennis, tennis, touch football, track and field, ultimate Frisbee, volleyball, weight lifting, weight training, whiffle ball. 3 PE instructors, 3 coaches, 2 athletic trainers.

Computers Computers are regularly used in accounting, computer applications, desktop publishing, economics, graphic design, keyboarding, media arts, media production, writing, yearbook classes. Computer network features include on-campus library services, online commercial services, Internet access, wireless campus network, Internet filtering or blocking technology. Student e-mail accounts and computer access in designated common areas are available to students. Students grades are available online. The school has a published electronic and media policy.

Contact Dr. Jeff Lemke, Admissions Director. 651-455-1521. Fax: 651-451-3968. E-mail: international@stcroixlutheran.org. Website: www.stcroixlutheran.org

ST. DAVID'S SCHOOL

3400 White Oak Road
Raleigh, North Carolina 27609

Head of School: Mr. Kevin J. Lockerbie

General Information Coeducational day college-preparatory, arts, religious studies, and technology school, affiliated with Episcopal Church, Christian faith. Grades PK–

12. Founded: 1972. Setting: suburban. 15-acre campus. 7 buildings on campus. Approved or accredited by National Association of Episcopal Schools, North Carolina Association of Independent Schools, Southern Association of Colleges and Schools, Southern Association of Independent Schools, and North Carolina Department of Education. Member of National Association of Independent Schools and Secondary School Admission Test Board. Endowment: $1.6 million. Total enrollment: 625. Upper school average class size: 12. Upper school faculty-student ratio: 1:6. There are 180 required school days per year for Upper School students. Upper School students typically attend 5 days per week. The average school day consists of 7 hours and 10 minutes.

Upper School Student Profile Grade 9: 53 students (23 boys, 30 girls); Grade 10: 68 students (37 boys, 31 girls); Grade 11: 58 students (30 boys, 28 girls); Grade 12: 47 students (24 boys, 23 girls).

Faculty School total: 85. In upper school: 21 men, 19 women; 29 have advanced degrees.

Subjects Offered 20th century history, algebra, American history, American literature, art, band, Bible, biology, biology-AP, calculus, calculus-AP, ceramics, chemistry, chemistry-AP, choir, composition, computer programming, computer-aided design, drama, drawing, earth science, English, English literature, English literature-AP, English/composition-AP, European history, European history-AP, French, French language-AP, French-AP, geography, geometry, Greek, Homeric Greek, honors algebra, honors English, honors geometry, independent study, introduction to theater, Latin, Latin-AP, mathematics, media production, modern European history-AP, music theory-AP, personal finance, physical education, physical science, physics, physics-AP, pre-calculus, psychology-AP, public speaking, robotics, science, social studies, Spanish, Spanish-AP, statistics-AP, studio art, studio art-AP, theater, U.S. history-AP, vocal ensemble, Web site design, weight training, wind ensemble, world history, world literature.

Graduation Requirements Arts and fine arts (art, music, dance, drama), English, foreign language, mathematics, physical education (includes health), religion (includes Bible studies and theology), science, social studies (includes history), 80 hours of community service, senior seminar.

Special Academic Programs 19 Advanced Placement exams for which test preparation is offered; honors section; independent study.

College Admission Counseling 43 students graduated in 2014; all went to college, including North Carolina State University; The University of North Carolina at Chapel Hill; The University of North Carolina Wilmington; Wake Forest University. Mean SAT critical reading: 617, mean SAT math: 605, mean SAT writing: 618, mean combined SAT: 1840, mean composite ACT: 27. 65% scored over 600 on SAT critical reading, 53% scored over 600 on SAT math, 56% scored over 600 on SAT writing, 56% scored over 1800 on combined SAT, 42% scored over 26 on composite ACT.

Student Life Upper grades have specified standards of dress, student council, honor system. Discipline rests equally with students and faculty. Attendance at religious services is required.

Tuition and Aid Day student tuition: $20,000. Tuition installment plan (Insured Tuition Payment Plan, monthly payment plans, 10-month payment plan). Need-based scholarship grants available. In 2014–15, 16% of upper-school students received aid. Total amount of financial aid awarded in 2014–15: $519,550.

Admissions Traditional secondary-level entrance grade is 9. For fall 2014, 42 students applied for upper-level admission, 34 were accepted, 24 enrolled. ISEE and writing sample required. Deadline for receipt of application materials: February 20. Application fee required: $75. On-campus interview required.

Athletics Interscholastic: baseball (boys), basketball (b,g), cheering (g), cross-country running (b,g), football (b), golf (b,g), lacrosse (b,g), soccer (b,g), softball (g), tennis (b,g), track and field (b,g), volleyball (g); coed interscholastic: swimming and diving. 2 coaches, 1 athletic trainer.

Computers Computers are regularly used in all academic, graphic design, media production, video film production, yearbook classes. Computer network features include on-campus library services, online commercial services, Internet access, wireless campus network, Internet filtering or blocking technology. Campus intranet, student e-mail accounts, and computer access in designated common areas are available to students. Students grades are available online. The school has a published electronic and media policy.

Contact Mrs. Teresa Wilson, Director of Admissions. 919-782-3331 Ext. 230. Fax: 919-232-5053. E-mail: twilson@sdsw.org. Website: www.sdsw.org

SAINT DOMINIC ACADEMY

Bishop Joseph OSB Boulevard
121 Gracelawn Road
Auburn, Maine 04210

Head of School: Mr. Donald Fournier

General Information Coeducational day and distance learning college-preparatory, arts, business, and religious studies school, affiliated with Roman Catholic Church. Grades PK–12. Distance learning grades 11–12. Founded: 1941. Setting: suburban. 70-acre campus. 1 building on campus. Approved or accredited by Maine Department of Education. Total enrollment: 571. Upper school average class size: 18. Upper school faculty-student ratio: 1:12. There are 175 required school days per year for Upper

School students. Upper School students typically attend 5 days per week. The average school day consists of 6 hours and 15 minutes.

Upper School Student Profile 70% of students are Roman Catholic.

Faculty School total: 25. In upper school: 10 men, 15 women.

Subjects Offered Advanced Placement courses.

Special Academic Programs Advanced Placement exam preparation; honors section; independent study.

College Admission Counseling 63 students graduated in 2015; 60 went to college. Other: 1 went to work, 2 entered military service. Median SAT critical reading: 542, median SAT math: 534, median SAT writing: 524, median combined SAT: 1600.

Student Life Upper grades have specified standards of dress, student council, honor system. Discipline rests primarily with faculty. Attendance at religious services is required.

Summer Programs Enrichment, sports, art/fine arts programs offered; session focuses on recreation/theater/math and science; held both on and off campus; held at various venues; accepts boys and girls; open to students from other schools.

Tuition and Aid Day student tuition: $11,414. Tuition installment plan (FACTS Tuition Payment Plan). Merit scholarship grants, need-based scholarship grants available. In 2015–16, 55% of upper-school students received aid. Total amount of financial aid awarded in 2015–16: $600,000.

Admissions Traditional secondary-level entrance grade is 9. Scholastic Testing Service High School Placement Test required. Deadline for receipt of application materials: none. Application fee required: $50. Interview required.

Athletics Interscholastic: baseball (boys), basketball (b,g), field hockey (g), ice hockey (b,g), indoor track & field (b,g), soccer (b,g), softball (b,g), swimming and diving (b); coed interscholastic: alpine skiing, cheering, cross-country running, dance team, golf, nordic skiing. 1 PE instructor, 30 coaches, 1 athletic trainer.

Computers Computer network features include on-campus library services, online commercial services, Internet access, wireless campus network, Internet filtering or blocking technology. Campus intranet, student e-mail accounts, and computer access in designated common areas are available to students. Students grades are available online. The school has a published electronic and media policy.

Contact Ms. Marianne Pelletier, Director of Admissions. 207-782-6911 Ext. 2110. Fax: 207-795-6439. E-mail: Marianne.pelletier@portlanddiocese.org. Website: www.stdomsmaine.org

SAINT ELIZABETH HIGH SCHOOL

1530 34th Avenue
Oakland, California 94601

Head of School: Mr. Martin Procaccio

General Information Coeducational day college-preparatory, arts, and religious studies school, affiliated with Roman Catholic Church; primarily serves students with learning disabilities. Grades 9–12. Founded: 1921. Setting: urban. Nearest major city is Berkeley. 2-acre campus. 1 building on campus. Approved or accredited by National Catholic Education Association, Western Association of Schools and Colleges, and California Department of Education. Endowment: $100,000. Total enrollment: 159. Upper school average class size: 16. Upper school faculty-student ratio: 1:15. There are 180 required school days per year for Upper School students. Upper School students typically attend 5 days per week. The average school day consists of 6 hours and 48 minutes.

Upper School Student Profile Grade 9: 52 students (26 boys, 26 girls); Grade 10: 50 students (28 boys, 22 girls); Grade 11: 31 students (18 boys, 13 girls); Grade 12: 26 students (14 boys, 12 girls). 80% of students are Roman Catholic.

Faculty School total: 17. In upper school: 5 men, 10 women; 8 have advanced degrees.

Subjects Offered Advanced math, algebra, American literature, American literature-AP, anatomy and physiology, art and culture, biology, business mathematics, calculus-AP, Catholic belief and practice, chemistry, Christian and Hebrew scripture, Christian testament, civics, composition, computer applications, computer graphics, computer literacy, creative writing, drawing and design, economics, economics and history, English, English literature and composition-AP, geometry, journalism, learning strategies, moral and social development, physical education, physical science, physics, pre-algebra, pre-calculus, psychology, social justice, Spanish, Spanish language-AP, Spanish literature-AP, speech, speech communications, trigonometry, U.S. history, world cultures, world geography, world history, world religions.

Graduation Requirements Arts and fine arts (art, music, dance, drama), electives, English, foreign language, mathematics, physical education (includes health), religious studies, science, social sciences, 100 hours of community service.

Special Academic Programs 3 Advanced Placement exams for which test preparation is offered; honors section; remedial reading and/or remedial writing; remedial math; programs in English, mathematics for dyslexic students; special instructional classes for students with learning disabilities, Attention Deficit Disorder, dyslexia, and emotional and behavioral problems.

College Admission Counseling 42 students graduated in 2014; all went to college, including California State University, East Bay; Holy Names University; San Francisco State University; San Jose State University; University of California, Berkeley; University of California, Davis.

Student Life Upper grades have specified standards of dress, honor system. Discipline rests primarily with faculty. Attendance at religious services is required.

Tuition and Aid Day student tuition: $11,200. Tuition installment plan (SMART Tuition Payment Plan). Tuition reduction for siblings, merit scholarship grants, need-based scholarship grants available. In 2014–15, 90% of upper-school students received aid.

Admissions Traditional secondary-level entrance grade is 9. For fall 2014, 97 students applied for upper-school admission, 70 were accepted, 52 enrolled. High School Placement Test required. Deadline for receipt of application materials: none. Application fee required: $75. Interview required.

Athletics Interscholastic: baseball (boys), basketball (b,g), soccer (b,g), track and field (b,g), volleyball (b,g). 1 PE instructor, 9 coaches.

Computers Computer network features include on-campus library services, Internet access, wireless campus network, Internet filtering or blocking technology. Students grades are available online. The school has a published electronic and media policy.

Contact Claudia Briones, Admissions. 510-532-8947 Ext. 9121. Fax: 510-532-9754. E-mail: cbriones@stliz-hs.org. Website: www.stliz-hs.org

ST. FRANCIS DE SALES HIGH SCHOOL

2323 West Bancroft Street
Toledo, Ohio 43607

Head of School: Mr. Eric J. Smola

General Information Boys' day college-preparatory, religious studies, AP courses, and community service school, affiliated with Roman Catholic Church. Grades 9–12. Founded: 1955. Setting: urban. Nearest major city is Cleveland. 25-acre campus. 1 building on campus. Approved or accredited by Ohio Catholic Schools Accreditation Association (OCSAA) and Ohio Department of Education. Endowment; $7.9 million. Total enrollment: 592. Upper school average class size: 22. Upper school faculty-student ratio: 1:14. There are 180 required school days per year for Upper School students. Upper School students typically attend 5 days per week. The average school day consists of 6 hours and 30 minutes.

Upper School Student Profile Grade 9: 151 students (151 boys); Grade 10: 167 students (167 boys); Grade 11: 126 students (126 boys); Grade 12: 148 students (148 boys). 69% of students are Roman Catholic.

Faculty School total: 47. In upper school: 35 men, 12 women; 28 have advanced degrees.

Subjects Offered Advanced Placement courses, advanced studio art-AP, algebra, American history, American history-AP, American literature, American literature-AP, anatomy, animation, art, art history, biology, biology-AP, British literature, calculus, calculus-AP, chemistry, chemistry-AP, Chinese, chorus, church history, community service, computer science, computer science-AP, computer skills, computer-aided design, creative writing, criminal justice, drawing, economics, English literature, English-AP, environmental science, ESL, expository writing, French, French-AP, geometry, government/civics, grammar, graphic design, health, journalism, Latin, Latin-AP, macroeconomics-AP, math analysis, mathematics, microeconomics-AP, military history, music, mythology, New Testament, performing arts, physical education, physical science, physics, physics-AP, pre-calculus, psychology, psychology-AP, public speaking, science, social justice, social studies, sociology, Spanish, Spanish-AP, statistics, theology, trigonometry, U.S. government, U.S. government and politics-AP, U.S. history-AP, Web site design, world geography, world history, yearbook.

Graduation Requirements Art, computer science, English, foreign language, mathematics, physical education (includes health), religion (includes Bible studies and theology), science, social studies (includes history), participation in religious retreats four of 4 years. Community service is required.

Special Academic Programs Advanced Placement exam preparation; honors section; study at local college for college credit; ESL (5 students enrolled).

College Admission Counseling 151 students graduated in 2014; all went to college, including Bowling Green State University; Miami University; The Ohio State University; The University of Toledo; University of Cincinnati; University of Dayton. Mean SAT critical reading: 580, mean SAT math: 580, mean SAT writing: 540, mean composite ACT: 25.

Student Life Upper grades have specified standards of dress, student council. Discipline rests primarily with faculty. Attendance at religious services is required.

Tuition and Aid Day student tuition: $10,920. Tuition installment plan (monthly payment plans, quarterly payment plan). Tuition reduction for siblings, merit scholarship grants, need-based scholarship grants, paying campus jobs available. In 2014–15, 66% of upper-school students received aid; total upper-school merit-scholarship money awarded: $394,500. Total amount of financial aid awarded in 2014–15: $1,655,000.

Admissions Traditional secondary-level entrance grade is 9. For fall 2014, 199 students applied for upper-level admission, 173 were accepted, 151 enrolled. STS required. Deadline for receipt of application materials: none. No application fee required. On-campus interview required.

Athletics Interscholastic: baseball, basketball, bowling, crew, cross-country running, diving, football, golf, ice hockey, lacrosse, soccer, swimming and diving, tennis, track and field, water polo, winter (indoor) track, wrestling; intramural: basketball, football. 2 PE instructors, 51 coaches, 2 athletic trainers.

Computers Computers are regularly used in animation, art, desktop publishing, English, mathematics, science, Web site design classes. Computer network features

include Internet access, Internet filtering or blocking technology. Student e-mail accounts and computer access in designated common areas are available to students. Students grades are available online. The school has a published electronic and media policy.

Contact Mrs. Jacqueline VanDemark, Administrative Assistant. 419-531-1618. Fax: 419-531-9740. E-mail: jvandemark@sfstoledo.org. Website: www.sfstoledo.org

SAINT FRANCIS HIGH SCHOOL

200 Foothill Boulevard
La Canada Flintridge, California 91011

Head of School: Fr. Antonio Marti

General Information Boys' day college-preparatory and religious studies school, affiliated with Roman Catholic Church. Grades 9–12. Founded: 1946. Setting: suburban. Nearest major city is Los Angeles. 19-acre campus. 5 buildings on campus. Approved or accredited by Western Association of Schools and Colleges and Western Catholic Education Association. Total enrollment: 663. Upper school average class size: 28. Upper school faculty-student ratio: 1:12. There are 182 required school days per year for Upper School students. Upper School students typically attend 5 days per week. The average school day consists of 6 hours.

Upper School Student Profile Grade 9: 184 students (184 boys); Grade 10: 153 students (153 boys); Grade 11: 163 students (163 boys); Grade 12: 163 students (163 boys). 65% of students are Roman Catholic.

Faculty School total: 48. In upper school: 38 men, 10 women; 25 have advanced degrees.

Subjects Offered Advanced Placement courses, computer skills, English, fine arts, foreign language, history, mathematics, physical education, religion, science, social sciences, technology.

Graduation Requirements Arts and fine arts (art, music, dance, drama), English, foreign language, mathematics, physical education (includes health), religion (includes Bible studies and theology), science, social sciences, technology, Christian service hours, retreat each year of attendance. Community service is required.

Special Academic Programs Advanced Placement exam preparation; honors section.

College Admission Counseling 162 students graduated in 2015; 160 went to college, including California Polytechnic State University, San Luis Obispo; California State University, Northridge; Loyola Marymount University. Other: 2 had other specific plans. Mean SAT critical reading: 567, mean SAT math: 570, mean SAT writing: 549, mean composite ACT: 25.

Student Life Upper grades have specified standards of dress, student council. Discipline rests primarily with faculty. Attendance at religious services is required.

Summer Programs Remediation, enrichment, sports, art/fine arts, computer instruction programs offered; session focuses on remediation and enrichment; held on campus; accepts boys and girls; open to students from other schools. 400 students usually enrolled. 2016 schedule: June 20 to July 22. Application deadline: June 13.

Tuition and Aid Day student tuition: $14,400. Tuition installment plan (FACTS Tuition Payment Plan, monthly payment plans). Merit scholarship grants, need-based scholarship grants available. In 2015–16, 20% of upper-school students received aid; total upper-school merit-scholarship money awarded: $90,000. Total amount of financial aid awarded in 2015–16: $900,000.

Admissions Traditional secondary-level entrance grade is 9. For fall 2015, 360 students applied for upper-level admission, 210 were accepted, 184 enrolled. High School Placement Test required. Deadline for receipt of application materials: January 23. Application fee required: $75. On-campus interview required.

Athletics Interscholastic: baseball, basketball, cross-country running, football, golf, lacrosse, soccer, swimming and diving, tennis, track and field, volleyball, water polo. 3 PE instructors, 14 coaches, 2 athletic trainers.

Computers Computers are regularly used in all academic, yearbook classes. Computer network features include on-campus library services, Internet access, wireless campus network, Internet filtering or blocking technology, students purchase iPads. Students grades are available online. The school has a published electronic and media policy.

Contact Mrs. Betty Dowling, Registrar. 818-790-0325 Ext. 502. Fax: 818-790-5542. E-mail: dowlingb@sfhs.net. Website: www.sfhs.net

SAINT FRANCIS HIGH SCHOOL

1885 Miramonte Avenue
Mountain View, California 94040

Head of School: Mr. Simon Chiu

General Information Coeducational day college-preparatory, arts, religious studies, and technology school, affiliated with Roman Catholic Church, Roman Catholic Church. Grades 9–12. Founded: 1954. Setting: suburban. Nearest major city is San Jose. 25-acre campus. 10 buildings on campus. Approved or accredited by Western Association of Schools and Colleges and California Department of Education. Total enrollment: 1,761. Upper school average class size: 27. Upper school faculty-student ratio: 1:27. There are 180 required school days per year for Upper School students.

Upper School students typically attend 5 days per week. The average school day consists of 6 hours and 30 minutes.

Upper School Student Profile Grade 9: 466 students (257 boys, 209 girls); Grade 10: 445 students (218 boys, 227 girls); Grade 11: 427 students (211 boys, 216 girls); Grade 12: 423 students (213 boys, 210 girls). 70% of students are Roman Catholic, Roman Catholic.

Faculty School total: 103. In upper school: 56 men, 47 women; 63 have advanced degrees.

Subjects Offered 20th century American writers, 3-dimensional design, algebra, American literature, analytic geometry, anatomy and physiology, band, biology, biology-AP, British literature, British literature (honors), business, calculus-AP, chemistry, chemistry-AP, Christianity, computer graphics, computer literacy, computer programming, computer science, computer science-AP, concert band, concert choir, contemporary issues, contemporary problems, creative writing, design, drama, drawing, economics, electronic music, English, English literature-AP, film and literature, French, French-AP, geography, geometry, German-AP, global science, graphics, health science, human biology, information technology, jazz band, jazz ensemble, journalism, music, oil painting, philosophy, physical education, physical science, pre-calculus, printmaking, psychology, religious studies, science fiction, social justice, Spanish, Spanish-AP, speech, speech communications, statistics, symphonic band, technology, trigonometry, U.S. government, U.S. government and politics-AP, U.S. history, U.S. history-AP, water color painting, world history, world religions.

Graduation Requirements Computer literacy, English, foreign language, human biology, mathematics, physical education (includes health), religious studies, science, social studies (includes history).

Special Academic Programs Advanced Placement exam preparation; honors section; study at local college for college credit.

College Admission Counseling 430 students graduated in 2015; 425 went to college, including Loyola Marymount University; Stanford University; University of California, Berkeley; University of California, Los Angeles; University of Southern California. Mean SAT critical reading: 711, mean SAT math: 743, mean SAT writing: 742.

Student Life Upper grades have specified standards of dress, student council, honor system. Discipline rests primarily with faculty. Attendance at religious services is required.

Summer Programs Remediation, enrichment, advancement, sports, art/fine arts, computer instruction programs offered; session focuses on academics and enrichment; held on campus; accepts boys and girls; open to students from other schools. 1,000 students usually enrolled. 2016 schedule: June 15 to July 15. Application deadline: June 15.

Tuition and Aid Day student tuition: $16,700. Tuition installment plan (SMART Tuition Payment Plan, monthly payment plans, individually arranged payment plans). Need-based scholarship grants, paying campus jobs available. In 2015–16, 18% of upper school students received aid. Total amount of financial aid awarded in 2015–16: $3,000,000.

Admissions Traditional secondary-level entrance grade is 9. For fall 2015, 1,500 students applied for upper-level admission, 800 were accepted, 495 enrolled. High School Placement Test required. Deadline for receipt of application materials: December 11. Application fee required: $75. On-campus interview required.

Athletics Interscholastic: aquatics (boys, girls), baseball (b,g), basketball (b,g), cheering (g), cross-country running (b,g), dance squad (g), diving (b,g), drill team (b,g), field hockey (g), football (b), golf (b,g), gymnastics (g), ice hockey (b,g), lacrosse (b,g), soccer (b,g), softball (g), strength & conditioning (b,g), swimming and diving (b,g), track and field (b,g), volleyball (b,g), water polo (b,g), wrestling (b); intramural: cooperative games (b,g), flag football (b,g), indoor soccer (b,g), physical fitness (b,g), rugby (b,g), soccer (b,g), strength & conditioning (b,g), swimming and diving (b,g), table tennis (b,g), volleyball (b,g), whiffle ball (b,g); coed interscholastic: cheering, ice hockey, roller hockey; coed intramural: basketball, cooperative games, flag football, indoor soccer, soccer, volleyball, whiffle ball. 6 PE instructors, 51 coaches, 1 athletic trainer.

Computers Computers are regularly used in creative writing, current events, digital applications, graphic arts, graphic design, photography, publications classes. Computer network features include on-campus library services, Internet access, wireless campus network, Internet filtering or blocking technology. Campus intranet, student e-mail accounts, and computer access in designated common areas are available to students. Students grades are available online.

Contact Mr. Simon Raines, Director of Admissions. 650-968-1213 Ext. 213. Fax: 650-968-1706. E-mail: simonraines@sfhs.com. Website: www.sfhs.com

ST. FRANCIS HIGH SCHOOL
233 West Broadway
Louisville, Kentucky 40202
Head of School: Ms. Alexandra Schreiber Thurstone

General Information Coeducational day college-preparatory and arts school. Grades 9–12. Founded: 1976. Setting: urban. 2-acre campus. 1 building on campus. Approved or accredited by Independent Schools Association of the Central States and Kentucky Department of Education. Member of National Association of Independent Schools. Endowment: $1 million. Total enrollment: 154. Upper school average class size: 12.

Upper school faculty-student ratio: 1:9. There are 174 required school days per year for Upper School students. Upper School students typically attend 5 days per week. The average school day consists of 7 hours.

Upper School Student Profile Grade 9: 34 students (17 boys, 17 girls); Grade 10: 41 students (17 boys, 24 girls); Grade 11: 48 students (20 boys, 28 girls); Grade 12: 29 students (11 boys, 18 girls).

Faculty School total: 20. In upper school: 12 men, 8 women; 15 have advanced degrees.

Subjects Offered African studies, algebra, American history, ancient history, ancient world history, art, biology, biology-AP, business, calculus, calculus-AP, chemistry, chemistry-AP, Chinese, Chinese history, civil rights, community service, creative writing, drama, drawing, English, English literature, English literature-AP, environmental science, environmental science-AP, European history, European history-AP, film studies, filmmaking, fine arts, finite math, French, French language-AP, French literature-AP, French-AP, gender and religion, gender issues, geometry, health, history-AP, journalism, law, medieval history, modern civilization, photography, physical education, physics, physics-AP, playwriting, pre-calculus, senior project, Spanish, Spanish language-AP, Spanish literature-AP, Spanish-AP, statistics, statistics-AP, The 20th Century, U.S. history-AP, video film production, world history, writing, zoology.

Graduation Requirements Arts and fine arts (art, music, dance, drama), English, foreign language, history, mathematics, physical education (includes health), science, senior project (year-long research project on a topic of student's choice). Community service is required.

Special Academic Programs Advanced Placement exam preparation; independent study; study abroad; academic accommodation for the gifted and the artistically talented.

College Admission Counseling 35 students graduated in 2014; all went to college.

Student Life Upper grades have student council. Discipline rests equally with students and faculty.

Tuition and Aid Day student tuition: $19,950. Tuition installment plan (Insured Tuition Payment Plan, FACTS Tuition Payment Plan, monthly payment plans). Merit scholarship grants, need-based scholarship grants, tuition remission for children of faculty and staff available. In 2014–15, 52% of upper-school students received aid.

Admissions Traditional secondary-level entrance grade is 9. For fall 2014, 47 students applied for upper-level admission, 42 were accepted, 39 enrolled. Deadline for receipt of application materials: January 15. Application fee required: $50. On-campus interview required.

Athletics Interscholastic: basketball (boys, girls), bicycling (b,g), bowling (b,g), field hockey (g), fitness (b,g), running (b,g), tennis (b,g), track and field (b,g); intramural: indoor hockey (g), indoor soccer (b); coed interscholastic: indoor track & field, soccer; coed intramural: dance team, fitness, physical fitness, physical training, power lifting, racquetball, rowing, ultimate Frisbee, wall climbing, wallyball, weight lifting, weight training, yoga. 1 PE instructor, 12 coaches.

Computers Computers are regularly used in English, French, history, mathematics, science, Spanish classes. Computer network features include Internet access, wireless campus network, word processing, publishing, and Web page programs. Student e-mail accounts and computer access in designated common areas are available to students. The school has a published electronic and media policy.

Contact Ms. Lucy Wathen, Director of Admissions. 502-736-1009. Fax: 502-736-1049. E-mail: lwathen@stfrancisschool.org. Website: www.stfrancisschool.org

ST. FRANCIS SCHOOL
13440 Cogburn Road
Milton, Georgia 30004
Head of School: Drew Buccellato

General Information Coeducational day college-preparatory, arts, technology, and Science Technology Engineering Arts and Mathematics (STEAM) school. Grades K–12. Founded: 1976. Setting: suburban. Nearest major city is Atlanta. 47-acre campus. 8 buildings on campus. Approved or accredited by Georgia Accrediting Commission, Georgia Independent School Association, Southern Association of Colleges and Schools, Southern Association of Independent Schools, and Georgia Department of Education. Endowment: $2 million. Total enrollment: 778. Upper school average class size: 14. Upper school faculty-student ratio: 1:14. There are 180 required school days per year for Upper School students. Upper School students typically attend 5 days per week. The average school day consists of 5 hours and 45 minutes.

Upper School Student Profile Grade 9: 78 students (40 boys, 38 girls); Grade 10: 74 students (44 boys, 30 girls); Grade 11: 69 students (38 boys, 31 girls); Grade 12: 95 students (60 boys, 35 girls).

Faculty School total: 40. In upper school: 15 men, 25 women; 22 have advanced degrees.

Subjects Offered 3-dimensional art, 3-dimensional design, acting, Advanced Placement courses, algebra, American literature, art-AP, arts, biology, British literature, calculus, character education, cheerleading, chemistry, chorus, Civil War, college counseling, computer processing, computer programming, computer science-AP, computers, drama, drawing, economics, engineering, English, English literature-AP, English-AP, environmental science, geography, geometry, government, graphic arts, graphic design, health, history-AP, honors algebra, honors English, honors geometry, honors U.S. history, honors world history, instrumental music, journalism, keyboarding, Latin, mathematics, newspaper, painting, performing arts, physical education, physical science, physics, play production, psychology, public speaking, SAT preparation, science, social studies, Spanish, studio art, studio art-AP, study skills, trigonometry, U.S. government, U.S. government and politics-AP, U.S. history, U.S. history-AP, word processing, world history, writing, yearbook.

Graduation Requirements Arts and fine arts (art, music, dance, drama), electives, English, foreign language, mathematics, physical education (includes health), science, social studies (includes history), technology, writing, community service hours.

Special Academic Programs Advanced Placement exam preparation; honors section; remedial reading and/or remedial writing; remedial math; special instructional classes for students with learning disabilities and Attention Deficit Disorder.

College Admission Counseling 61 students graduated in 2015; all went to college, including Georgia College & State University; Kennesaw State University; The University of Alabama; University of Georgia.

Student Life Upper grades have uniform requirement, student council, honor system. Discipline rests primarily with faculty.

Summer Programs Held on campus; accepts boys and girls; not open to students from other schools. 40 students usually enrolled.

Tuition and Aid Day student tuition: $20,000. Tuition installment plan (monthly payment plans). Tuition reduction for siblings, need-based scholarship grants available.

Admissions Traditional secondary-level entrance grade is 9. For fall 2015, 95 students applied for upper-level admission, 39 were accepted, 28 enrolled. School placement exam required. Deadline for receipt of application materials: March 4. Application fee required: $150. On-campus interview required.

Athletics Interscholastic: baseball (boys), basketball (b,g), cheering (g), cross-country running (b,g), equestrian sports (b,g), football (b), golf (b,g), horseback riding (b,g), physical fitness (b,g), soccer (b,g), softball (g), strength & conditioning (b,g), swimming and diving (b,g), tennis (b,g), track and field (b,g), volleyball (g), weight lifting (b,g), weight training (b,g), wrestling (b); intramural: equestrian sports (g), horseback riding (g); coed interscholastic: swimming and diving, tennis, track and field. 3 PE instructors, 6 coaches, 1 athletic trainer.

Computers Computers are regularly used in all classes. Computer network features include on-campus library services, online commercial services, Internet access, wireless campus network, Internet filtering or blocking technology. Campus intranet, student e-mail accounts, and computer access in designated common areas are available to students. Students grades are available online. The school has a published electronic and media policy.

Contact Brandon Bryan, High School Admissions. 678-339-9989 Ext. 33. Fax: 678-339-0473. E-mail: bbryan@sfschools.net. Website: www.SaintFrancisSchools.com

ST. GEORGE'S INDEPENDENT SCHOOL
1880 Wolf River Road
Collierville, Tennessee 38017

Head of School: Mr. J. Ross Peters

General Information Coeducational day college-preparatory school, affiliated with Christian faith. Grades PK–12. Founded: 1959. Setting: suburban. Nearest major city is Memphis. 250-acre campus. 5 buildings on campus. Approved or accredited by National Association of Episcopal Schools, Southern Association of Colleges and Schools, and Southern Association of Independent Schools. Member of National Association of Independent Schools. Endowment: $7.2 million. Total enrollment: 1,188. Upper school average class size: 19. Upper school faculty-student ratio: 1:9. There are 175 required school days per year for Upper School students. Upper School students typically attend 5 days per week. The average school day consists of 7 hours and 18 minutes.

Faculty In upper school: 60 have advanced degrees.

Subjects Offered Algebra, band, biology, biology-AP, calculus, calculus-AP, chemistry, chemistry-AP, chorus, computer programming, drawing, English, English language and composition-AP, English literature and composition-AP, environmental science, European history-AP, film, French, French language-AP, geometry, global issues, global studies, government and politics-AP, government/civics, honors algebra, honors geometry, human anatomy, independent study, journalism, Latin, Latin-AP, Mandarin, painting, philosophy, photography, physics, physics-AP, pottery, pre-calculus, psychology, psychology-AP, religion, social justice, Spanish, Spanish language-AP, Spanish literature-AP, statistics-AP, theater, trigonometry, U.S. history, U.S. history-AP, visual arts, wellness, world history, world history-AP, writing, yearbook.

Graduation Requirements Art, electives, English, history, independent study, language, mathematics, religion (includes Bible studies and theology), science, wellness, senior independent study, senior Global Challenge.

Special Academic Programs 17 Advanced Placement exams for which test preparation is offered; honors section; independent study.

College Admission Counseling 98 students graduated in 2015; they went to Mississippi State University; The University of Alabama; The University of Tennessee; The University of Tennessee at Chattanooga; University of Arkansas; University of Mississippi. Mean SAT critical reading: 615, mean SAT math: 591, mean SAT writing: 601, mean combined SAT: 1807, mean composite ACT: 26.

Student Life Upper grades have specified standards of dress, student council, honor system. Discipline rests equally with students and faculty. Attendance at religious services is required.

Summer Programs Remediation, enrichment, advancement, sports, art/fine arts, computer instruction programs offered; session focuses on enrichment; held on campus; accepts boys and girls; open to students from other schools. 2016 schedule: June to August. Application deadline: June 1.

Tuition and Aid Day student tuition: $13,510–$19,500. Tuition installment plan (individually arranged payment plans, One payment per year, two payments per year, and four payments per year.). Need-based scholarship grants available. In 2015–16, 29% of upper-school students received aid. Total amount of financial aid awarded in 2015–16: $975,000.

Admissions Traditional secondary-level entrance grade is 9. Admissions testing or ISEE required. Deadline for receipt of application materials: none. Application fee required: $50. Interview required.

Athletics Interscholastic: baseball (boys), basketball (b,g), cheering (g), cross-country running (b,g), football (b), lacrosse (b,g), pom squad (g), soccer (b,g), softball (g), tennis (b,g), track and field (b,g), volleyball (g), wrestling (b); intramural: bowling (b); coed interscholastic: golf, swimming and diving, trap and skeet, water polo; coed intramural: equestrian sports.

Computers Computers are regularly used in all classes. Computer network features include on-campus library services, Internet access, wireless campus network, Internet filtering or blocking technology. Campus intranet, student e-mail accounts, and computer access in designated common areas are available to students. Students grades are available online. The school has a published electronic and media policy.

Contact Mrs. Olivia Hammond, Director of Admission. 901-457-2000. Fax: 901-457-2111. E-mail: obuffington@sgis.org. Website: www.sgis.org

ST. GEORGE'S SCHOOL
372 Purgatory Road
Middletown, Rhode Island 02842-5984

Head of School: Eric F. Peterson

General Information Coeducational boarding and day college-preparatory, arts, religious studies, technology, and marine sciences school, affiliated with Episcopal Church. Grades 9–12. Founded: 1896. Setting: suburban. Nearest major city is Providence. Students are housed in single-sex dormitories. 125-acre campus. 47 buildings on campus. Approved or accredited by Association of Independent Schools in New England, National Association of Episcopal Schools, New England Association of Schools and Colleges, The Association of Boarding Schools, and Rhode Island Department of Education. Member of National Association of Independent Schools and Secondary School Admission Test Board. Endowment: $120 million. Total enrollment: 370. Upper school average class size: 11. Upper school faculty-student ratio: 1:6. Upper School students typically attend 6 days per week. The average school day consists of 6 hours and 50 minutes.

Upper School Student Profile Grade 9: 67 students (33 boys, 34 girls); Grade 10: 95 students (44 boys, 51 girls); Grade 11: 111 students (55 boys, 56 girls); Grade 12: 97 students (53 boys, 44 girls). 85% of students are boarding students. 20% are state residents. 31 states are represented in upper school student body. 15% are international students. International students from Bermuda, China, Kazakhstan, Mexico, Republic of Korea, and Switzerland; 18 other countries represented in student body.

Faculty School total: 70. In upper school: 32 men, 37 women; 55 have advanced degrees; 65 reside on campus.

Subjects Offered 3-dimensional art, 3-dimensional design, acting, advanced biology, advanced chemistry, advanced computer applications, advanced math, Advanced Placement courses, advanced studio art-AP, African American history, African American studies, algebra, American history, American history-AP, American literature, American literature-AP, American studies, analytic geometry, architectural drawing, architecture, art, art history, art-AP, Asian studies, Bible, Bible as literature, Bible studies, biology, biology-AP, calculus, calculus-AP, ceramics, chemistry, chemistry-AP, Chinese, computer graphics, computer math, computer programming, computer science, computer science-AP, creative writing, dance, DNA, drama, dramatic arts, drawing, ecology, economics, economics-AP, English, English language and composition-AP, English literature, English literature-AP, environmental science, environmental science-AP, ethics, European history, European history-AP, expository writing, fine arts, French, French language-AP, geometry, global studies, government/civics, grammar, health, history, journalism, Latin, Latin-AP, law, logic, macro/microeconomics-AP, Mandarin, marine biology, mathematics, microbiology, music, music theory-AP, navigation, oceanography, philosophy, photography, physics, physics-AP, psychology, public speaking, religion, robotics, science, sculpture, social studies, Spanish, Spanish language-AP, Spanish literature-AP, statistics, studio art-AP, theater, theology, trigonometry, U.S. government and politics-AP, veterinary science, world history, world history-AP, world literature, writing.

Graduation Requirements Arts and fine arts (art, music, dance, drama), computer science, English, foreign language, mathematics, physical education (includes health), religion (includes Bible studies and theology), science, social studies (includes history).

Special Academic Programs Advanced Placement exam preparation; honors section; independent study; term-away projects; study abroad; academic accommodation for the gifted, the musically talented, and the artistically talented.

College Admission Counseling 90 students graduated in 2015; 87 went to college, including Brown University; Dartmouth College; Georgetown University; Middlebury College; The George Washington University; Wake Forest University. Other: 3 had other specific plans. Mean SAT critical reading: 630, mean SAT math: 655, mean SAT writing: 630, mean combined SAT: 1915.

Student Life Upper grades have specified standards of dress, student council, honor system. Discipline rests primarily with faculty. Attendance at religious services is required.

Tuition and Aid Day student tuition: $38,500; 7-day tuition and room/board: $56,000. Tuition installment plan (Insured Tuition Payment Plan, monthly payment plans, individually arranged payment plans). Need-based scholarship grants, need-based loans, middle-income loans available. In 2015–16, 33% of upper-school students received aid. Total amount of financial aid awarded in 2015–16: $4,000,000.

Admissions Traditional secondary-level entrance grade is 9. For fall 2015, 800 students applied for upper-level admission, 210 were accepted, 101 enrolled. ISEE, PSAT, SSAT or TOEFL required. Deadline for receipt of application materials: February 1. Application fee required: $50. Interview recommended.

Athletics Interscholastic: baseball (boys), basketball (b,g), cross-country running (b,g), field hockey (g), football (b), hockey (b,g), ice hockey (b,g), lacrosse (b,g), sailing (b,g), soccer (b,g), softball (g), squash (b,g), swimming and diving (b,g), tennis (b,g), track and field (b,g); coed interscholastic: dance, golf, sailing; coed intramural: aerobics/dance, dance, modern dance, mountain biking, Nautilus, soccer, softball, squash, strength & conditioning. 3 coaches, 3 athletic trainers.

Computers Computers are regularly used in art, English, foreign language, history, mathematics, music, religion, science, theater classes. Computer network features include on-campus library services, online commercial services, Internet access, wireless campus network, Internet filtering or blocking technology, scanners, digital cameras, and access to printers. Campus intranet, student e-mail accounts, and computer access in designated common areas are available to students. Students grades are available online. The school has a published electronic and media policy.

Contact Ryan P. Mulhern, Director of Admission. 401-842-6600. Fax: 401-842-6696. E-mail: admission@stgeorges.edu. Website: www.stgeorges.edu

ST. GEORGE'S SCHOOL

4175 West 29th Avenue
Vancouver, British Columbia V6S 1V1, Canada

Head of School: Dr. Tom Matthews

General Information Boys' boarding and day college-preparatory, arts, business, bilingual studies, and technology school. Boarding grades 8–12, day grades 1–12. Founded: 1930. Setting: urban. Students are housed in single-sex dormitories. 27-acre campus. 2 buildings on campus. Approved or accredited by Canadian Association of Independent Schools, Northwest Association of Independent Schools, The Association of Boarding Schools, and British Columbia Department of Education. Affiliate member of National Association of Independent Schools; member of Secondary School Admission Test Board. Language of instruction: English. Endowment: CAN$22 million. Total enrollment: 1,150. Upper school average class size: 19. Upper school faculty-student ratio: 1:8. There are 157 required school days per year for Upper School students. Upper School students typically attend 5 days per week. The average school day consists of 6 hours.

Upper School Student Profile Grade 8: 139 students (139 boys); Grade 9: 155 students (155 boys); Grade 10: 156 students (156 boys); Grade 11: 160 students (160 boys); Grade 12: 164 students (164 boys). 18% of students are boarding students. 91% are province residents. 9 provinces are represented in upper school student body. 9% are international students. International students from Canada, China, Hong Kong, Jamaica, Mexico, and United States; 13 other countries represented in student body.

Faculty School total: 130. In upper school: 62 men, 31 women; 55 have advanced degrees; 15 reside on campus.

Subjects Offered Advanced chemistry, advanced computer applications, advanced math, algebra, analysis and differential calculus, applied arts, applied music, applied skills, architecture, art, art history, art history-AP, biology, biology-AP, business, business skills, calculus, calculus-AP, Canadian geography, Canadian history, Canadian literature, career and personal planning, ceramics, chemistry, chemistry-AP, comparative government and politics-AP, computer graphics, computer programming, computer programming-AP, computer science, computer science-AP, creative writing, critical thinking, debate, drama, drama performance, dramatic arts, earth science, economics, economics-AP, English, English literature, English literature-AP, environmental science, European history, expository writing, film, fine arts, French, French-AP, geography, geology, geometry, German, German-AP, government/civics, grammar, history, industrial arts, introduction to theater, Japanese, journalism, Latin, Latin-AP, law, library, Mandarin, mathematics, mathematics-AP, music, music-AP, performing arts, photography, physical education, physical fitness, physics, physics-AP, psychology, psychology-AP, science, social studies, society, politics and law, Spanish, Spanish-AP, speech and debate, studio art, studio art-AP, technical theater, theater, trigonometry, typing, U.S. history-AP, United States government-AP, Western civilization, world history, world literature, writing.

Graduation Requirements Arts and fine arts (art, music, dance, drama), business skills (includes word processing), career planning, English, foreign language, guidance,

mathematics, physical education (includes health), science, social studies (includes history), volunteer/work experience.

Special Academic Programs Advanced Placement exam preparation; honors section; remedial reading and/or remedial writing.

College Admission Counseling 160 students graduated in 2015; 153 went to college, including McGill University; New York University; Queen's University at Kingston; The University of British Columbia; The University of Western Ontario; University of Toronto. Other: 7 had other specific plans.

Student Life Upper grades have uniform requirement, student council, honor system. Discipline rests primarily with faculty.

Summer Programs Enrichment, ESL, sports, art/fine arts, computer instruction programs offered; session focuses on recreation and enrichment; held both on and off campus; held at other schools in area (outdoor education); accepts boys and girls; open to students from other schools. 1,000 students usually enrolled. 2016 schedule: July 2 to August 15. Application deadline: none.

Tuition and Aid Day student tuition: CAN$22,115–CAN$32,120; 7-day tuition and room/board: CAN$44,300–CAN$58,275. Tuition installment plan (monthly payment plans, individually arranged payment plans, term payment plan, one-time payment plan). Tuition reduction for siblings, bursaries, merit scholarship grants, need-based scholarship grants available. In 2015–16, 7% of upper-school students received aid; total upper-school merit-scholarship money awarded: CAN$250,000. Total amount of financial aid awarded in 2015–16: CAN$1,000,000.

Admissions Traditional secondary-level entrance grade is 8. For fall 2015, 225 students applied for upper-level admission, 92 were accepted, 51 enrolled. CAT, school's own exam and SSAT required. Deadline for receipt of application materials: February 1. Application fee required: CAN$250. Interview required.

Athletics Interscholastic: badminton, basketball, cricket, cross-country running, curling, field hockey, Frisbee, golf, hockey, ice hockey, rowing, rugby, soccer, squash, swimming and diving, table tennis, tennis, track and field, triathlon, ultimate Frisbee, volleyball, water polo; intramural: archery, badminton, ball hockey, basketball, bicycling, canoeing/kayaking, cross-country running, curling, fitness, flag football, floor hockey, freestyle skiing, golf, hiking/backpacking, ice hockey, jogging, kayaking, martial arts, outdoor education, outdoor recreation, physical fitness, rock climbing, rugby, running, sailing, scuba diving, skiing (downhill), snowboarding, soccer, softball, strength & conditioning, swimming and diving, table tennis, tennis, track and field, volleyball, water polo, weight training, yoga. 10 PE instructors, 3 coaches, 2 athletic trainers.

Computers Computers are regularly used in desktop publishing, history, information technology, mathematics, media, publications, science, technology classes. Computer network features include on-campus library services, online commercial services, Internet access, wireless campus network, Internet filtering or blocking technology. Campus intranet, student e-mail accounts, and computer access in designated common areas are available to students. Students grades are available online. The school has a published electronic and media policy.

Contact Mr. Gordon C. Allan, Director of Admissions. 604-221-3881. Fax: 604-221-3893. E-mail: gallan@stgeorges.bc.ca. Website: www.stgeorges.bc.ca

SAINT GERTRUDE HIGH SCHOOL

3215 Stuart Avenue
Richmond, Virginia 23221

Head of School: Mrs. Renata Rafferty

General Information Girls' day college-preparatory and religious studies school, affiliated with Roman Catholic Church. Grades 9–12. Founded: 1922. Setting: urban. 1 building on campus. Approved or accredited by National Catholic Education Association, Southern Association of Colleges and Schools, and Virginia Department of Education. Member of National Association of Independent Schools. Total enrollment: 247. Upper school average class size: 15. Upper school faculty-student ratio: 1:9. There are 180 required school days per year for Upper School students. Upper School students typically attend 5 days per week. The average school day consists of 7 hours.

Upper School Student Profile Grade 9: 53 students (53 girls); Grade 10: 68 students (68 girls); Grade 11: 67 students (67 girls); Grade 12: 59 students (59 girls). 67% of students are Roman Catholic.

Faculty School total: 37. In upper school: 4 men, 33 women.

Subjects Offered Advanced Placement courses, algebra, American history, American history-AP, American literature, American literature-AP, anatomy, art, bell choir, Bible studies, biology, calculus, calculus-AP, ceramics, chemistry, chemistry-AP, chorus, church history, community service, computer science, computer technologies, drama, drawing, driver education, English, English language and composition-AP, English language-AP, English literature, English literature and composition-AP, environmental science, European history, expository writing, fine arts, French, geometry, government and politics-AP, government/civics, grammar, history, honors algebra, honors English, honors world history, humanities, keyboarding, Latin, mathematics, media, music, painting, physical education, physics, physics-AP, pre-calculus, probability and statistics, psychology, religion, science, social sciences, social studies, sociology, Spanish, Spanish literature, studio art-AP, theater, theology, trigonometry, U.S. government and politics-AP, world history, world literature, writing, yearbook.

Graduation Requirements Arts and fine arts (art, music, dance, drama), computer science, English, keyboarding, mathematics, physical education (includes health), religion (includes Bible studies and theology), science, social sciences, social studies (includes history), 4 years of theology. Community service is required.

Special Academic Programs Advanced Placement exam preparation; honors section.

College Admission Counseling Colleges students went to include James Madison University; The College of William and Mary; University of Virginia; Virginia Commonwealth University; Virginia Polytechnic Institute and State University.

Student Life Upper grades have uniform requirement, student council, honor system. Discipline rests equally with students and faculty. Attendance at religious services is required.

Summer Programs Sports, art/fine arts programs offered; held both on and off campus; held at both the main building and the Outdoor Athletic Center; accepts girls; open to students from other schools. 2016 schedule: June to August.

Tuition and Aid Day student tuition: $16,200. Tuition installment plan (FACTS Tuition Payment Plan, monthly payment plans). Merit scholarship grants, need-based scholarship grants available. In 2015–16, 30% of upper-school students received aid.

Admissions Traditional secondary-level entrance grade is 9. For fall 2015, 114 students applied for upper-level admission, 101 were accepted, 63 enrolled. Admissions testing, latest standardized score from previous school, Otis-Lennon School Ability Test and writing sample required. Deadline for receipt of application materials: January 31. Application fee required: $50. On-campus interview required.

Athletics Interscholastic: basketball, cross-country running, field hockey, golf, indoor track, lacrosse, soccer, softball, swimming and diving, tennis, track and field, volleyball; coed interscholastic: swimming and diving, track and field. 1 PE instructor, 14 coaches, 1 athletic trainer.

Computers Computers are regularly used in all academic classes. Computer network features include on-campus library services, Internet access, wireless campus network, Internet filtering or blocking technology. Campus intranet, student e-mail accounts, and computer access in designated common areas are available to students. Students grades are available online. The school has a published electronic and media policy.

Contact Meredith McNamara, Director of Admission. 804-822-3955. Fax: 804-353-8929. E-mail: mmcnamara@saintgertrude.org. Website: www.saintgertrude.org

SAINT JAMES SCHOOL

17641 College Road

Hagerstown, Maryland 21740

Head of School: Rev. Dr. D. Stuart Dunnan

General Information Coeducational boarding and day college-preparatory school, affiliated with Episcopal Church. Grades 8–12. Founded: 1842. Setting: rural. Nearest major city is Washington, DC. Students are housed in single-sex dormitories. 1,000-acre campus. 36 buildings on campus. Approved or accredited by Association of Independent Maryland Schools, Association of Independent Schools of Greater Washington, Middle States Association of Colleges and Schools, National Association of Episcopal Schools, The Association of Boarding Schools, and Maryland Department of Education. Member of National Association of Independent Schools and Secondary School Admission Test Board. Endowment: $25 million. Total enrollment: 237. Upper school average class size: 12. Upper school faculty-student ratio: 1:7. There are 180 required school days per year for Upper School students. Upper School students typically attend 5 days per week. The average school day consists of 6 hours and 30 minutes.

Upper School Student Profile Grade 8: 29 students (16 boys, 13 girls); Grade 9: 54 students (33 boys, 21 girls); Grade 10: 54 students (37 boys, 17 girls); Grade 11: 53 students (33 boys, 20 girls); Grade 12: 47 students (27 boys, 20 girls). 75% of students are boarding students. 40% are state residents. 17 states are represented in upper school student body. 22% are international students. International students from China, Ghana, Hong Kong, Mexico, Nigeria, and Republic of Korea; 12 other countries represented in student body. 38% of students are members of Episcopal Church.

Faculty School total: 31. In upper school: 17 men, 14 women; 16 have advanced degrees; all reside on campus.

Subjects Offered Algebra, American history-AP, American literature, ancient history, art, art history, art-AP, biology-AP, calculus-AP, chemistry, chemistry-AP, choir, community service, economics, English, English literature, environmental science, European history-AP, fine arts, French-AP, geography, geometry, government-AP, keyboarding, Latin-AP, mathematics, modern European history, music, music history, physical science, physics, physics-AP, political science, science, Spanish-AP, theology, voice, world literature, writing workshop.

Graduation Requirements Arts and fine arts (art, music, dance, drama), English, foreign language, history, mathematics, science. Community service is required.

Special Academic Programs 14 Advanced Placement exams for which test preparation is offered; honors section; academic accommodation for the musically talented.

College Admission Counseling 57 students graduated in 2015; all went to college, including Cornell University; Davidson College; Sewanee: The University of the South; The George Washington University; University of Virginia.

Student Life Upper grades have specified standards of dress, student council, honor system. Discipline rests equally with students and faculty. Attendance at religious services is required.

Tuition and Aid Day student tuition: $29,300; 7-day tuition and room/board: $44,000. Tuition installment plan (SMART Tuition Payment Plan, individually arranged payment plans). Need-based scholarship grants available. In 2015–16, 33% of upper-school students received aid. Total amount of financial aid awarded in 2015–16: $2,500,000.

Admissions Traditional secondary-level entrance grade is 9. For fall 2015, 300 students applied for upper-level admission, 110 were accepted, 80 enrolled. PSAT or SAT, SSAT or TOEFL required. Deadline for receipt of application materials: January 31. Application fee required: $65. Interview required.

Athletics Interscholastic: baseball (boys), basketball (b,g), cross-country running (b), field hockey (g), football (b), golf (b), lacrosse (b,g), soccer (b,g), softball (g), tennis (b,g), volleyball (g), wrestling (b); intramural: aerobics/dance (g), ballet (g), dance (g), modern dance (g), weight training (b,g); coed intramural: alpine skiing, fitness, indoor soccer, martial arts, physical fitness, skiing (downhill), snowboarding, strength & conditioning, weight training, winter (indoor) track. 2 coaches, 2 athletic trainers.

Computers Computers are regularly used in all academic classes. Computer network features include on-campus library services, online commercial services, Internet access, wireless campus network, Internet filtering or blocking technology. Student e-mail accounts are available to students. The school has a published electronic and media policy.

Contact Mrs. Karla R. McNamee, Admission Assistant. 301-733-9330. Fax: 301-739-1310. E-mail: admissions@stjames.edu. Website: www.stjames.edu

SAINT JOAN ANTIDA HIGH SCHOOL

1341 North Cass Street

Milwaukee, Wisconsin 53202

Head of School: Mr. Paul Gessner

General Information Girls' day college-preparatory, arts, business, religious studies, technology, and engineering school, affiliated with Roman Catholic Church. Grades 9–12. Founded: 1954. Setting: urban. 2 buildings on campus. Approved or accredited by International Baccalaureate Organization, North Central Association of Colleges and Schools, and Wisconsin Department of Education. Total enrollment: 163. Upper school average class size: 25. Upper school faculty-student ratio: 1:14. Upper School students typically attend 5 days per week.

Upper School Student Profile Grade 9: 66 students (66 girls); Grade 10: 26 students (26 girls); Grade 11: 40 students (40 girls); Grade 12: 31 students (31 girls). 50% of students are Roman Catholic.

Faculty School total: 20. In upper school: 4 men, 16 women; 9 have advanced degrees.

Subjects Offered Advanced biology, advanced chemistry, advanced math, algebra, architecture, art, Bible, biology, biotechnology, calculus, chemistry, Christianity, engineering, English, environmental science, geometry, global studies, health, history of the Americas, moral theology, physical education, physical fitness, pre-calculus, Spanish, theology, U.S. government, U.S. history, world history, world literature.

Graduation Requirements Algebra, American history, art, biology, chemistry, Christian studies, church history, composition, electives, engineering, English, English composition, English literature, geometry, history, literature, physical education (includes health), physics, religion (includes Bible studies and theology), science, Spanish, U.S. history, world history.

Special Academic Programs International Baccalaureate program; study at local college for college credit; remedial reading and/or remedial writing; remedial math.

College Admission Counseling 27 students graduated in 2015; 23 went to college, including Milwaukee Area Technical College; University of Wisconsin–Milwaukee. Other: 4 had other specific plans. Median composite ACT: 18.

Student Life Upper grades have uniform requirement, student council, honor system. Discipline rests primarily with faculty. Attendance at religious services is required.

Tuition and Aid Day student tuition: $7900. Tuition installment plan (SMART Tuition Payment Plan, monthly payment plans, individually arranged payment plans). Merit scholarship grants, need-based scholarship grants available. In 2015–16, 98% of upper-school students received aid.

Admissions Traditional secondary-level entrance grade is 9. For fall 2015, 150 students applied for upper-level admission, 120 were accepted, 118 enrolled. Admissions testing required. Deadline for receipt of application materials: none. No application fee required. On-campus interview required.

Athletics Interscholastic: cross-country running, soccer, volleyball. 1 PE instructor.

Computers Computers are regularly used in architecture, career exploration, college planning, engineering classes. Computer network features include on-campus library services, Internet access, wireless campus network, Internet filtering or blocking technology. Student e-mail accounts are available to students. Students grades are available online. The school has a published electronic and media policy.

Contact Ms. Mary Fowler, Front Desk Receptionist. 414-272-8423. Fax: 414-272-3135. Website: www.saintjoanantida.org/

ST. JOHN NEUMANN HIGH SCHOOL

3000 53rd Street SW
Naples, Florida 34116-8018

Head of School: Sr. Patricia Roche, FMA

General Information Coeducational day college-preparatory and religious studies school, affiliated with Roman Catholic Church. Grades 9–12. Founded: 1980. Setting: suburban. 5 buildings on campus. Approved or accredited by Southern Association of Colleges and Schools and Florida Department of Education. Endowment: $225. Total enrollment: 213. Upper school average class size: 20. Upper school faculty-student ratio: 1:12. There are 182 required school days per year for Upper School students. Upper School students typically attend 5 days per week. The average school day consists of 6 hours and 45 minutes.

Upper School Student Profile Grade 9: 40 students (20 boys, 20 girls); Grade 10: 55 students (28 boys, 27 girls); Grade 11: 65 students (33 boys, 32 girls); Grade 12: 53 students (26 boys, 27 girls). 80% of students are Roman Catholic.

Faculty School total: 25. In upper school: 12 men, 13 women.

Subjects Offered Advanced Placement courses, algebra, American history, American history-AP, anatomy and physiology, art, band, biology, biology-AP, business, calculus-AP, campus ministry, chemistry, choir, chorus, church history, college admission preparation, concert band, creative arts, drama, drawing, economics, electives, English, English language-AP, English literature-AP, environmental science-AP, geometry, government, health, history, history of music, history of the Catholic Church, honors algebra, honors English, honors geometry, honors U.S. history, honors world history, human anatomy, human geography - AP, independent study, jazz band, language-AP, law studies, leadership, marine biology, marketing, media production, music appreciation, music technology, New Testament, newspaper, orchestra, peer ministry, physical education, physics-AP, pre-algebra, pre-calculus, psychology-AP, reading, religion, SAT preparation, social justice, Spanish-AP, speech and debate, U.S. history, U.S. history-AP, weightlifting, world history, world history-AP, yearbook.

Graduation Requirements Arts and fine arts (art, music, dance, drama), English, foreign language, health, mathematics, physical education (includes health), science, social studies (includes history), theology.

Special Academic Programs 11 Advanced Placement exams for which test preparation is offered; honors section; independent study; study at local college for college credit; remedial reading and/or remedial writing; remedial math; special instructional classes for deaf students.

College Admission Counseling 62 students graduated in 2015; 61 went to college, including Auburn University; Florida Atlantic University; Florida State University; The University of Tampa; University of Central Florida; University of Florida. Other: 1 went to work. Mean SAT critical reading: 672, mean SAT math: 670, mean SAT writing: 650, mean combined SAT: 1992, mean composite ACT: 31.

Student Life Upper grades have uniform requirement, student council, honor system. Discipline rests primarily with faculty. Attendance at religious services is required.

Tuition and Aid Day student tuition: $11,250. Tuition installment plan (FACTS Tuition Payment Plan). Merit scholarship grants, need-based scholarship grants available. In 2015–16, 60% of upper-school students received aid; total upper-school merit-scholarship money awarded: $10,000. Total amount of financial aid awarded in 2015–16: $400,000.

Admissions Traditional secondary-level entrance grade is 9. STS required. Deadline for receipt of application materials: February 22. Application fee required: $30. On-campus interview recommended.

Athletics Interscholastic: baseball (boys), basketball (b,g), cheering (g), cross-country running (b,g), football (b), golf (b,g), soccer (b,g), softball (g), strength & conditioning (b,g), swimming and diving (b,g), tennis (b,g), track and field (b,g), volleyball (g). 1 PE instructor, 14 coaches.

Computers Computer network features include Internet access, wireless campus network, Internet filtering or blocking technology, iPads. Campus intranet, student e-mail accounts, and computer access in designated common areas are available to students. Students grades are available online. The school has a published electronic and media policy.

Contact Mrs. Betsi Jones, Director of Admissions. 239-455-3044 Ext. 201. Fax: 239-455-2966. E-mail: ejones@sjnceltics.org. Website: www.sjnceltics.org

ST. JOHN'S CATHOLIC PREP

3989 Buckeystown Pike
P.O. Box 909
Buckeystown, Maryland 21717

Head of School: Dr. Thomas Powell

General Information Coeducational day college-preparatory school, affiliated with Roman Catholic Church. Grades 9–12. Founded: 1829. Setting: rural. Nearest major city is Baltimore. 65-acre campus. 1 building on campus. Approved or accredited by Association of Independent Maryland Schools, Southern Association of Colleges and Schools, and Maryland Department of Education. Total enrollment: 260. Upper school average class size: 15. Upper school faculty-student ratio: 1:9. The average school day consists of 6 hours and 45 minutes.

Upper School Student Profile 65% of students are Roman Catholic.

Faculty School total: 31. In upper school: 14 men, 17 women.

Special Academic Programs Advanced Placement exam preparation; honors section; study at local college for college credit.

College Admission Counseling 65 students graduated in 2015; all went to college, including University of Maryland, College Park. Median SAT critical reading: 602, median SAT math: 596, median SAT writing: 576.

Student Life Upper grades have uniform requirement, honor system. Discipline rests primarily with faculty. Attendance at religious services is required.

Summer Programs Sports programs offered; held on campus; accepts boys and girls; open to students from other schools. 2016 schedule: June to August.

Tuition and Aid Day student tuition: $15,785. Tuition installment plan (FACTS Tuition Payment Plan). Tuition reduction for siblings, merit scholarship grants, need-based scholarship grants available. In 2015–16, 50% of upper-school students received aid; total upper-school merit-scholarship money awarded: $20,000. Total amount of financial aid awarded in 2015–16: $788,000.

Admissions Traditional secondary-level entrance grade is 9. For fall 2015, 126 students applied for upper-level admission, 123 were accepted, 60 enrolled. High School Placement Test (closed version) from Scholastic Testing Service required. Deadline for receipt of application materials: none. Application fee required: $105. On-campus interview required.

Athletics Interscholastic: baseball (boys), basketball (b,g), cheering (g), cross-country running (b,g), football (b), golf (b,g), lacrosse (b,g), soccer (b,g), softball (g), swimming and diving (b,g), tennis (b,g), volleyball (g), wrestling (b); coed interscholastic: indoor track & field, track and field; coed intramural: equestrian sports, horseback riding, indoor hockey, skiing (downhill), snowboarding, strength & conditioning, weight training. 2 PE instructors, 17 coaches, 1 athletic trainer.

Computers Computer network features include on-campus library services, Internet access. Student e-mail accounts are available to students.

Contact Mr. Michael W. Schultz, Director of Enrollment Management. 301-662-4210 Ext. 121. Fax: 301-892-6877. E-mail: mschultz@saintjohnsprep.org. Website: www.saintjohnsprep.org

ST. JOHN'S PREPARATORY SCHOOL

72 Spring Street
Danvers, Massachusetts 01923

Head of School: Dr. Edward P. Hardiman

General Information Boys' day college-preparatory, arts, religious studies, and technology school, affiliated with Roman Catholic Church. Grades 6–12. Founded: 1907. Setting: suburban. Nearest major city is Boston. 175-acre campus. 11 buildings on campus. Approved or accredited by Association of Independent Schools in New England, National Catholic Education Association, and New England Association of Schools and Colleges. Member of National Association of Independent Schools. Endowment: $16.1 million. Total enrollment: 1,450. Upper school average class size: 18. Upper school faculty-student ratio: 1:11. There are 161 required school days per year for Upper School students. Upper School students typically attend 5 days per week. The average school day consists of 6 hours and 9 minutes.

Upper School Student Profile Grade 6: 100 students (100 boys); Grade 7: 100 students (100 boys); Grade 8: 100 students (100 boys); Grade 9: 300 students (300 boys); Grade 10: 300 students (300 boys); Grade 11: 300 students (300 boys); Grade 12: 300 students (300 boys). 70% of students are Roman Catholic.

Faculty School total: 150. In upper school: 75 men, 40 women; 80 have advanced degrees.

Subjects Offered Accounting, acting, aerospace science, algebra, American history, American history-AP, American literature, anatomy and physiology, art, biology, biology-AP, business, calculus, calculus-AP, ceramics, chemistry, chemistry-AP, Chinese, chorus, computer programming, computer science, computer science-AP, desktop publishing, drama, driver education, economics, economics-AP, English, English literature, English-AP, environmental science, environmental studies, ethics, European history, European history-AP, geometry, German, German-AP, government/civics, Holocaust, human geography - AP, jazz ensemble, Latin, Latin-AP, law studies, mathematics, music, music technology, neuroscience, physical education, physics, physics-AP, psychology-AP, religion, robotics, science, sculpture, social studies, society, politics and law, Spanish, Spanish-AP, statistics, statistics-AP, studio art, technology, trigonometry, U.S. government and politics-AP, U.S. history-AP, video, world history, world religions.

Graduation Requirements Arts and fine arts (art, music, dance, drama), computer science, English, foreign language, mathematics, physical education (includes health), religion (includes Bible studies and theology), science, social studies (includes history).

Special Academic Programs Advanced Placement exam preparation; honors section; independent study; academic accommodation for the gifted, the musically talented, and the artistically talented.

College Admission Counseling 265 students graduated in 2015; 261 went to college, including Boston College; Northeastern University; Syracuse University; University of Massachusetts Amherst; University of New Hampshire; University of Vermont. Other: 3 entered a postgraduate year, 1 had other specific plans.

Student Life Upper grades have specified standards of dress, student council. Discipline rests primarily with faculty. Attendance at religious services is required.

Summer Programs Enrichment, advancement, sports, art/fine arts, computer instruction programs offered; session focuses on academic enrichment, study skills, arts, fitness; held on campus; accepts boys and girls; open to students from other schools.

Tuition and Aid Day student tuition: $21,170. Tuition installment plan (SMART Tuition Payment Plan). Merit scholarship grants, need-based scholarship grants available. In 2015–16, 31% of upper-school students received aid. Total amount of financial aid awarded in 2015–16: $3,800,000.

Admissions Traditional secondary-level entrance grade is 9. SSAT or STS, Diocese Test required. Deadline for receipt of application materials: December 20. Application fee required: $50. Interview recommended.

Athletics Interscholastic: alpine skiing, baseball, basketball, cross-country running, fencing, football, Frisbee, golf, hockey, ice hockey, indoor track, lacrosse, rugby, sailing, skiing (downhill), soccer, swimming and diving, tennis, track and field, ultimate Frisbee, volleyball, water polo, winter (indoor) track, wrestling; intramural: baseball, basketball, bicycling, bocce, bowling, boxing, climbing, combined training, cooperative games, crew, fitness, flag football, floor hockey, Frisbee, golf, hiking/backpacking, ice hockey, judo, martial arts, mountain biking, Nautilus, outdoor adventure, physical fitness, power lifting, rowing, sailing, skiing (downhill), snowboarding, strength & conditioning, surfing, table tennis, tennis, touch football, ultimate Frisbee, volleyball, weight lifting, weight training, whiffle ball, yoga. 4 PE instructors, 120 coaches, 2 athletic trainers.

Computers Computers are regularly used in all academic, career exploration, college planning, research skills classes. Computer network features include on-campus library services, Internet access, wireless campus network, Internet filtering or blocking technology, student access to 300 computer workstations. Student e-mail accounts are available to students. Students grades are available online. The school has a published electronic and media policy.

Contact Mrs. Joan Spencer, Administrative Assistant. 978-624-1301. Fax: 978-624-1315. E-mail: jspencer@stjohnsprep.org. Website: www.stjohnsprep.org

SAINT JOHN'S PREPARATORY SCHOOL

Box 4000
2280 Watertower Road
Collegeville, Minnesota 56321

Head of School: Fr. Jonathan Licari, OSB

General Information Coeducational boarding and day college-preparatory, arts, religious studies, and bilingual studies school, affiliated with Roman Catholic Church. Boarding grades 9–PG, day grades 6–PG. Founded: 1857. Setting: rural. Nearest major city is Minneapolis/St. Paul. Students are housed in single-sex dormitories. 2,700-acre campus. 23 buildings on campus. Approved or accredited by Minnesota Department of Education. Member of National Association of Independent Schools. Endowment: $12.5 million. Total enrollment: 285. Upper school average class size: 15. Upper school faculty-student ratio: 1:10. There are 172 required school days per year for Upper School students. Upper School students typically attend 5 days per week. The average school day consists of 5 hours and 35 minutes.

Upper School Student Profile Grade 8: 34 students (18 boys, 16 girls); Grade 9: 40 students (19 boys, 21 girls); Grade 10: 72 students (35 boys, 37 girls); Grade 11: 52 students (25 boys, 27 girls); Grade 12: 47 students (25 boys, 22 girls). 33% of students are boarding students. 63% are state residents. 4 states are represented in upper school student body. 25% are international students. International students from Austria, China, Hong Kong, Mexico, Republic of Korea, and Taiwan; 14 other countries represented in student body. 50% of students are Roman Catholic.

Faculty School total: 34. In upper school: 18 men, 16 women; 24 have advanced degrees; 2 reside on campus.

Subjects Offered 3-dimensional design, advanced chemistry, Advanced Placement courses, algebra, American history, American literature, art, art history, band, Bible studies, biology, biology-AP, British literature, calculus, ceramics, chemistry, Chinese, choir, civics, conceptual physics, creative writing, current events, drawing, earth science, economics, English, English literature, English-AP, environmental science-AP, ESL, European history, fine arts, geometry, German, government/civics, health, history, International Baccalaureate courses, mathematics, music, orchestra, photography, physical education, physics, pre-calculus, religion, science, social studies, Spanish, speech, statistics, theology, trigonometry, world history, world literature, writing.

Graduation Requirements American literature, British literature, English, theology and the arts, world literature.

Special Academic Programs International Baccalaureate program; Advanced Placement exam preparation; honors section; independent study; term-away projects; study at local college for college credit; study abroad; ESL (23 students enrolled).

College Admission Counseling 71 students graduated in 2015; 69 went to college, including Babson College; Boston College; College of Saint Benedict; Penn State University Park; St. John's University; University of Minnesota, Twin Cities Campus. Other: 2 had other specific plans. Mean SAT critical reading: 559, mean SAT math: 660, mean SAT writing: 574, mean combined SAT: 1793, mean composite ACT: 27.

Student Life Upper grades have specified standards of dress, student council, honor system. Discipline rests primarily with faculty. Attendance at religious services is required.

Summer Programs Enrichment, advancement, art/fine arts programs offered; session focuses on academic focus in a fun camp environment; held on campus; accepts boys

and girls; open to students from other schools. 250 students usually enrolled. 2016 schedule: June 16 to August 8. Application deadline: June 1.

Tuition and Aid Day student tuition: $15,448; 5-day tuition and room/board: $32,178; 7-day tuition and room/board: $35,945. Tuition installment plan (monthly payment plans, individually arranged payment plans, semester payment plan). Merit scholarship grants, need-based scholarship grants, paying campus jobs available. In 2015–16, 46% of upper-school students received aid; total upper-school merit-scholarship money awarded: $30,000. Total amount of financial aid awarded in 2015–16: $896,000.

Admissions Traditional secondary-level entrance grade is 9. For fall 2015, 127 students applied for upper-level admission, 85 were accepted, 56 enrolled. International English Language Test or TOEFL required. Deadline for receipt of application materials: none. Application fee required: $25. Interview required.

Athletics Interscholastic: alpine skiing (boys, girls), aquatics (g), baseball (b), basketball (b,g), cross-country running (b,g), diving (g), football (b), gymnastics (g), ice hockey (b,g), indoor track & field (b,g), nordic skiing (b,g), soccer (b,g), softball (g), swimming and diving (g), tennis (b,g), track and field (b,g); intramural: aerobics (g), aerobics/dance (g), dance (g), figure skating (g), golf (b,g), ice skating (g); coed intramural: bicycling, canoeing/kayaking, cross-country running, fitness, fitness walking, flag football, floor hockey, Frisbee, indoor soccer, mountain biking, nordic skiing, physical fitness, physical training, racquetball, rock climbing, roller blading, skiing (cross-country), skiing (downhill), soccer, strength & conditioning, swimming and diving, ultimate Frisbee, volleyball, walking, wall climbing, wallyball, weight lifting, weight training, winter (indoor) track, winter soccer, winter walking, yoga. 1 PE instructor, 21 coaches.

Computers Computers are regularly used in all academic, English, science classes. Computer network features include on-campus library services, Internet access, wireless campus network, Internet filtering or blocking technology. Campus intranet, student e-mail accounts, and computer access in designated common areas are available to students. Students grades are available online. The school has a published electronic and media policy.

Contact Mr. Jeremy Meyer, Assistant Director of Admissions. 320-363-3320. Fax: 320-363-3322. E-mail: jmeyer@sjprep.net. Website: www.sjprep.net

ST. JOHN'S-RAVENSCOURT SCHOOL

400 South Drive
Winnipeg, Manitoba R3T 3K5, Canada

Head of School: Mr. Jim Keefe

General Information Coeducational boarding and day college-preparatory school. Boarding grades 8–12, day grades K–12. Founded: 1820. Setting: suburban. Students are housed in single-sex dormitories. 23-acre campus. 6 buildings on campus. Approved or accredited by Canadian Association of Independent Schools, Canadian Educational Standards Institute, The Association of Boarding Schools, and Manitoba Department of Education. Language of instruction: English. Endowment: CAN$8.3 million. Total enrollment: 822. Upper school average class size: 20. Upper school faculty-student ratio: 1:10. There are 172 required school days per year for Upper School students.

Upper School Student Profile Grade 9: 96 students (49 boys, 47 girls); Grade 10: 88 students (53 boys, 35 girls); Grade 11: 100 students (60 boys, 40 girls); Grade 12: 89 students (47 boys, 42 girls). 9% of students are boarding students. 96% are province residents. 5 provinces are represented in upper school student body. 5% are international students. International students from China, Democratic People's Republic of Korea, Hong Kong, Mexico, Nepal, and Taiwan; 2 other countries represented in student body.

Faculty School total: 78. In upper school: 25 men, 23 women; 16 have advanced degrees; 4 reside on campus.

Subjects Offered Advanced Placement courses, algebra, American history, animation, art, biology, biology-AP, calculus, calculus-AP, Canadian geography, Canadian history, chemistry, chemistry-AP, computer science, debate, drama, driver education, economics, English, English literature, European history, European history-AP, French, French-AP, geography, geometry, history, information technology, law, linear algebra, mathematics, music, physical education, physics, physics-AP, pre-calculus, psychology, psychology-AP, science, social studies, Spanish, theater, visual arts, Web site design, world issues.

Graduation Requirements Canadian geography, Canadian history, computer science, English, French, geography, history, mathematics, physical education (includes health), pre-calculus, science, social sciences.

Special Academic Programs Advanced Placement exam preparation; honors section; independent study; study at local college for college credit; ESL (27 students enrolled).

College Admission Counseling 99 students graduated in 2014; 98 went to college, including McGill University; Queen's University at Kingston; The University of British Columbia; The University of Western Ontario; University of Manitoba; University of Toronto.

Student Life Upper grades have uniform requirement, student council, honor system. Discipline rests equally with students and faculty.

Tuition and Aid Day student tuition: CAN$18,650; 7-day tuition and room/board: CAN$34,790–CAN$45,400. Tuition installment plan (monthly payment plans, individually arranged payment plans). Bursaries, merit scholarship grants available. In 2014–15, 21% of upper-school students received aid; total upper-school merit-scholarship money awarded: CAN$95,000. Total amount of financial aid awarded in 2014–15: CAN$262,250.

Admissions Traditional secondary-level entrance grade is 9. For fall 2014, 72 students applied for upper-level admission, 47 were accepted, 39 enrolled. Otis-Lennon School Ability Test, school's own exam or TOEFL or SLEP required. Deadline for receipt of application materials: none. Application fee required: CAN$125. Interview recommended.

Athletics Interscholastic: aerobics (boys, girls), badminton (b,g), basketball (b,g), cross-country running (b,g), Frisbee (b,g), golf (b), hockey (b,g), ice hockey (b,g), indoor track (b,g), indoor track & field (b,g), lacrosse (b,g); intramural: badminton (b,g), basketball (b,g), cross-country running (b,g), dance (b,g), hockey (b,g); coed interscholastic: badminton, Frisbee, physical fitness; coed intramural: badminton, flag football, floor hockey. 6 PE instructors.

Computers Computers are regularly used in business skills, career exploration, college planning, creative writing, English, history, library skills, newspaper, science, social studies, yearbook classes. Computer network features include on-campus library services, Internet access, wireless campus network, Internet filtering or blocking technology, EBSCO. Campus intranet and student e-mail accounts are available to students. The school has a published electronic and media policy.

Contact Mr. Paul Prieur, Director of Admissions and Marketing. 204-477-2400. Fax: 204-477-2429. E-mail: admissions@sjr.mb.ca. Website: www.sjr.mb.ca

SAINT JOSEPH ACADEMY

500 Las Flores Drive
San Marcos, California 92078

Head of School: Mr. Anthony Biese

General Information Coeducational day college-preparatory and religious studies school, affiliated with Roman Catholic Church. Grades K–12. Founded: 1995. Setting: suburban. Nearest major city is San Diego. 6-acre campus. 2 buildings on campus. Approved or accredited by Western Association of Schools and Colleges and California Department of Education. Total enrollment: 302. Upper school average class size: 16. Upper school faculty-student ratio: 1:16. There are 176 required school days per year for Upper School students. Upper School students typically attend 5 days per week. The average school day consists of 6 hours and 30 minutes.

Upper School Student Profile Grade 9: 15 students (9 boys, 6 girls); Grade 10: 16 students (6 boys, 10 girls); Grade 11: 20 students (9 boys, 11 girls); Grade 12: 14 students (9 boys, 5 girls). 99.7% of students are Roman Catholic.

Faculty School total: 25. In upper school: 6 men, 9 women; 7 have advanced degrees.

Subjects Offered Acting, Advanced Placement courses, algebra, American history-AP, American literature, American literature-AP, art history, art history-AP, ASB Leadership, athletics, Bible, biology, British literature, British literature-AP, calculus, calculus-AP, Catholic belief and practice, Christian ethics, church history, composition, composition-AP, economics, English composition, English language-AP, general math, geography, geometry, government/civics-AP, health, physical education, physics, physics-AP, Spanish, speech and debate, U.S. government and politics-AP, world history, world history-AP, yearbook.

Graduation Requirements Christian service hours.

Special Academic Programs 4 Advanced Placement exams for which test preparation is offered; honors section; independent study.

College Admission Counseling 12 students graduated in 2015; all went to college, including California State University, San Marcos; Palomar College; University of Dallas; University of Mary. Mean SAT critical reading: 580, mean SAT math: 620, mean SAT writing: 630, mean combined SAT: 615. 27% scored over 600 on SAT critical reading, 45% scored over 600 on SAT math, 55% scored over 600 on SAT writing, 45% scored over 1800 on combined SAT.

Student Life Upper grades have uniform requirement, student council, honor system. Discipline rests primarily with faculty. Attendance at religious services is required.

Summer Programs Remediation, enrichment programs offered; session focuses on remediation; held on campus; accepts boys and girls; open to students from other schools. 5 students usually enrolled. 2016 schedule: June 13 to August 12.

Tuition and Aid Day student tuition: $9700. Tuition installment plan (FACTS Tuition Payment Plan, monthly payment plans). Tuition reduction for siblings, need-based scholarship grants available. In 2015–16, 54% of upper-school students received aid. Total amount of financial aid awarded in 2015–16: $80,112.

Admissions Traditional secondary-level entrance grade is 9. For fall 2015, 10 students applied for upper-level admission, 10 were accepted, 8 enrolled. Catholic High School Entrance Examination required. Deadline for receipt of application materials: none. Application fee required: $60. On-campus interview required.

Athletics Interscholastic: basketball (boys, girls), football (b), volleyball (g); coed interscholastic: golf; coed intramural: snowboarding. 9 coaches.

Computers Computer network features include Internet access, wireless campus network, Internet filtering or blocking technology. Campus intranet and student e-mail accounts are available to students. Students grades are available online. The school has a published electronic and media policy.

Contact Mrs. Patti Terich, Business Manager. 760-305-8505 Ext. 1121. Fax: 760-305-8466. E-mail: pterich@saintjosephacademy.org. Website: www.saintjosephacademy.org

ST. JOSEPH ACADEMY

155 State Road 207
St. Augustine, Florida 32084

Head of School: Mr. Todd DeClemente

General Information Coeducational day college-preparatory, arts, religious studies, and technology school, affiliated with Roman Catholic Church. Grades 9–12. Founded: 1866. Setting: suburban. 33-acre campus. 13 buildings on campus. Approved or accredited by National Catholic Education Association, Southern Association of Colleges and Schools, and Florida Department of Education. Total enrollment: 318. Upper school average class size: 14. Upper school faculty-student ratio: 1:11. There are 180 required school days per year for Upper School students. Upper School students typically attend 5 days per week. The average school day consists of 6 hours and 40 minutes.

Upper School Student Profile Grade 9: 83 students (39 boys, 44 girls); Grade 10: 82 students (40 boys, 42 girls); Grade 11: 82 students (43 boys, 39 girls); Grade 12: 71 students (37 boys, 34 girls). 84% of students are Roman Catholic.

Faculty School total: 22. In upper school: 12 men, 10 women; 18 have advanced degrees.

Subjects Offered Advanced computer applications, advanced math, Advanced Placement courses, advanced studio art-AP, algebra, American government, American history, American sign language, anatomy and physiology, ancient world history, applied arts, art, art history, Bible studies, biology, calculus-AP, career education, career exploration, career planning, Catholic belief and practice, chemistry, Christianity, church history, clayworking, college counseling, college placement, college planning, community service, computer applications, computer education, computer skills, costumes and make-up, creative drama, drama, drama performance, drama workshop, drawing, English, English composition, English language-AP, environmental science, government, history of the Catholic Church, honors algebra, honors English, honors geometry, honors U.S. history, honors world history, integrated mathematics, Internet research, life management skills, marine biology, Microsoft, moral theology, peer ministry, personal fitness, physical education, physics, play production, portfolio art, pottery, pre-calculus, psychology, religious education, Shakespeare, Spanish, Spanish language-AP, Spanish literature-AP, theology, U.S. history, weight training.

Graduation Requirements Advanced Placement courses, career/college preparation, Catholic belief and practice, college writing, computer literacy, dramatic arts, economics, English, environmental science, foreign language, government, mathematics, physical education (includes health), religion (includes Bible studies and theology), social studies (includes history), theology.

Special Academic Programs Advanced Placement exam preparation; honors section; study at local college for college credit; academic accommodation for the gifted and the artistically talented; special instructional classes for students with Attention Deficit Disorder.

College Admission Counseling 73 students graduated in 2015; all went to college, including Florida Atlantic University; Florida State University; Florida State University; University of Central Florida; University of Florida; University of North Florida. 25% scored over 1800 on combined SAT, 45% scored over 26 on composite ACT.

Student Life Upper grades have uniform requirement, student council, honor system. Discipline rests primarily with faculty. Attendance at religious services is required.

Summer Programs Sports, computer instruction programs offered; session focuses on football conditioning, weight training, basketball clinics and tournaments; held on campus; accepts boys and girls; not open to students from other schools. 86 students usually enrolled. 2016 schedule: June 1 to July 31.

Tuition and Aid Day student tuition: $8570–$9950. Tuition installment plan (FACTS Tuition Payment Plan). Tuition reduction for siblings, need-based scholarship grants available. In 2015–16, 41% of upper-school students received aid. Total amount of financial aid awarded in 2015–16: $120,000.

Admissions Traditional secondary-level entrance grade is 9. For fall 2015, 122 students applied for upper-level admission, 118 were accepted, 114 enrolled. High School Placement Test, Iowa Tests of Basic Skills, Iowa Tests of Basic Skills-Grades 7-8, Archdiocese HSEPT-Grade 9, PSAT or SAT required. Deadline for receipt of application materials: none. Application fee required: $600. Interview recommended.

Athletics Interscholastic: baseball (boys), basketball (b,g), cheering (g), cross-country running (b,g), football (b), golf (b,g), physical fitness (b,g), physical training (b,g), soccer (b,g), softball (g), swimming and diving (b,g), tennis (b,g), track and field (b,g), volleyball (g), weight training (b), winter soccer (b,g); intramural: lacrosse (b,g). 2 PE instructors, 3 coaches, 1 athletic trainer.

Computers Computers are regularly used in all academic, animation, computer applications, media classes. Computer network features include on-campus library services, Internet access, wireless campus network, Internet filtering or blocking technology. Student e-mail accounts and computer access in designated common areas are available to students. Students grades are available online. The school has a published electronic and media policy.

Contact Mr. Patrick M. Keane, Director of Admissions. 904-824-0431 Ext. 305. Fax: 904-824-4412. E-mail: patrick.keane@sjaweb.org. Website: www.sjaweb.org

SAINT JOSEPH ACADEMY HIGH SCHOOL

3470 Rocky River Drive
Cleveland, Ohio 44111

Head of School: Mr. Jeff Sutliff

General Information Girls' day college-preparatory, arts, religious studies, technology, Pre-engineering; Health Sciences Honors Program;, and Mandarin Chinese; AVID Program school, affiliated with Roman Catholic Church. Grades 9–12. Founded: 1890. Setting: urban. 21-acre campus. 1 building on campus. Approved or accredited by North Central Association of Colleges and Schools, Ohio Catholic Schools Accreditation Association (OCSAA), and Ohio Department of Education. Endowment: $8.3 million. Total enrollment: 710. Upper school average class size: 23. Upper school faculty-student ratio: 1:12. There are 169 required school days per year for Upper School students. Upper School students typically attend 5 days per week. The average school day consists of 7 hours.

Upper School Student Profile Grade 9: 192 students (192 girls); Grade 10: 180 students (180 girls); Grade 11: 169 students (169 girls); Grade 12: 169 students (169 girls). 84% of students are Roman Catholic.

Faculty School total: 62. In upper school: 16 men, 46 women; 43 have advanced degrees.

Subjects Offered ACT preparation, acting, advanced biology, advanced chemistry, Advanced Placement courses, advanced studio art-AP, algebra, American history, art, biology-AP, calculus, calculus-AP, chemistry, chemistry-AP, Chinese, chorus, composition-AP, creative writing, digital photography, drama, drawing and design, English language-AP, English literature and composition-AP, English/composition-AP, environmental science, European history-AP, film studies, filmmaking, French-AP, geometry, government and politics-AP, graphic arts, graphic design, health and wellness, Holocaust studies, honors algebra, honors English, honors geometry, honors U.S. history, honors world history, human anatomy, instrumental music, jazz band, Latin, Latin-AP, model United Nations, personal finance, physical education, physics, psychology-AP, religion, Spanish, Spanish-AP, speech and debate, statistics-AP, studio art-AP, U.S. history-AP, Vietnam War, world history-AP.

Graduation Requirements 4 credits of Theology, 4 credits of mathematics.

Special Academic Programs 15 Advanced Placement exams for which test preparation is offered; honors section; independent study; study abroad.

College Admission Counseling 145 students graduated in 2014; 140 went to college, including Cleveland State University; Miami University; Ohio University; The Ohio State University. Other: 4 went to work, 1 entered military service. Median SAT critical reading: 540, median SAT math: 530, median SAT writing: 530, median combined SAT: 1530, median composite ACT: 23.

Student Life Upper grades have uniform requirement, student council, honor system. Discipline rests primarily with faculty. Attendance at religious services is required.

Tuition and Aid Day student tuition: $12,040. Tuition installment plan (monthly payment plans, Semi-annual Payment Plan). Tuition reduction for siblings, merit scholarship grants, need-based scholarship grants, need-based loans, paying campus jobs available. In 2014–15, 64% of upper-school students received aid; total upper-school merit-scholarship money awarded: $205,000. Total amount of financial aid awarded in 2014–15: $1,215,000.

Admissions Traditional secondary-level entrance grade is 9. For fall 2014, 268 students applied for upper-level admission, 208 were accepted, 192 enrolled. High School Placement Test (closed version) from Scholastic Testing Service required. Deadline for receipt of application materials: none. No application fee required. Interview required.

Athletics Interscholastic: aquatics, basketball, cheering, crew, cross-country running, diving, golf, rugby, soccer, softball, swimming and diving, tennis, track and field, volleyball; intramural: aerobics, alpine skiing, dance team, physical fitness, strength & conditioning. 2 PE instructors, 32 coaches, 1 athletic trainer.

Computers Computers are regularly used in all classes. Computer network features include on-campus library services, Internet access, wireless campus network, Internet filtering or blocking technology, Each student has a Chrome Book laptop computer. Campus intranet, student e-mail accounts, and computer access in designated common areas are available to students. Students grades are available online. The school has a published electronic and media policy.

Contact Ms. Diane Marie Kanney, Vice President of Enrollment and Marketing. 216-251-4868 Ext. 220. Fax: 216-251-5809. E-mail: admissions@sja1890.org. Website: www.sja1890.org

ST. JOSEPH HIGH SCHOOL

2320 Huntington Turnpike
Trumbull, Connecticut 06611

Head of School: Pres. William J. Fitzgerald, PhD

General Information Coeducational day college-preparatory, arts, business, religious studies, and technology school, affiliated with Roman Catholic Church. Grades 9–12. Founded: 1962. Setting: suburban. Nearest major city is Bridgeport. 25-acre campus. 4 buildings on campus. Approved or accredited by New England Association of Schools and Colleges and Connecticut Department of Education. Upper school average class size: 22. Upper school faculty-student ratio: 1:11. There are 183 required school days per year for Upper School students. Upper School students typically attend 5 days per week. The average school day consists of 6 hours.

Upper School Student Profile Grade 9: 200 students (100 boys, 100 girls); Grade 10: 200 students (100 boys, 100 girls); Grade 11: 200 students (100 boys, 100 girls); Grade 12: 200 students (100 boys, 100 girls). 85% of students are Roman Catholic.

Faculty School total: 69. In upper school: 29 men, 40 women; 55 have advanced degrees.

Subjects Offered Advanced Placement courses, algebra, American government, American history, American history-AP, anatomy, art, art history, biology, biology-AP, business skills, calculus, calculus-AP, Catholic belief and practice, current events, design, dramatic arts, ecology, English, English literature, ESL, French, geometry, government, health, human anatomy, human biology, integrated science, Italian, journalism, microbiology, music, New Testament, personal finance, physical education, physics, pottery, pre-calculus, religion, religious studies, science, social sciences, social studies, Spanish, Spanish language-AP, Spanish-AP, trigonometry, U.S. government, U.S. history, U.S. history-AP.

Graduation Requirements Arts and fine arts (art, music, dance, drama), English, foreign language, mathematics, physical education (includes health), religion (includes Bible studies and theology), science, social studies (includes history). Community service is required.

Special Academic Programs 11 Advanced Placement exams for which test preparation is offered; study at local college for college credit; academic accommodation for the gifted; special instructional classes for students with learning disabilities and Attention Deficit Disorder; ESL (18 students enrolled).

College Admission Counseling 210 students graduated in 2015; 205 went to college, including Fairfield University; Providence College; Quinnipiac University; Sacred Heart University; Southern Connecticut State University; University of Connecticut. Other: 5 entered military service. Mean SAT critical reading: 529, mean SAT math: 520, mean SAT writing: 533, mean combined SAT: 1597, mean composite ACT: 22.

Student Life Upper grades have uniform requirement, student council. Discipline rests primarily with faculty. Attendance at religious services is required.

Summer Programs Remediation, enrichment, advancement, sports, art/fine arts, computer instruction programs offered; session focuses on academics, athletics, enrichment; held on campus; accepts boys and girls; open to students from other schools. 150 students usually enrolled. 2016 schedule: July 1 to August 20.

Tuition and Aid Day student tuition: $14,450. Tuition installment plan (monthly payment plans, one lump sum payment with discount by June 1 or two payments by semester, payment plan through People's Bank). Tuition reduction for siblings, merit scholarship grants, need-based scholarship grants available. In 2015–16, 50% of upper-school students received aid; total upper-school merit-scholarship money awarded: $440,000. Total amount of financial aid awarded in 2015–16: $1,200,000.

Admissions Traditional secondary-level entrance grade is 9. For fall 2015, 500 students applied for upper-level admission, 430 were accepted, 223 enrolled. Admissions testing, High School Placement Test or STS - Educational Development Series required. Deadline for receipt of application materials: November 14. Application fee required: $50.

Athletics Interscholastic: baseball (boys), basketball (b,g), cheering (g), cross-country running (b,g), diving (g), field hockey (g), football (b), ice hockey (b,g), indoor track & field (b,g), lacrosse (b,g), softball (g), swimming and diving (b,g), tennis (b,g), track and field (b,g), volleyball (b,g); coed interscholastic: bowling, golf. 2 PE instructors, 80 coaches, 2 athletic trainers.

Computers Computers are regularly used in all classes. Computer network features include on-campus library services, online commercial services, Internet access, wireless campus network, Internet filtering or blocking technology, Internet access throughout the building. Campus intranet, student e-mail accounts, and computer access in designated common areas are available to students. Students grades are available online. The school has a published electronic and media policy.

Contact Linda Lucy, Admissions Operation Manager. 203-378-9378 Ext. 455. Fax: 203-378-7306. E-mail: llucy@sjcadets.org. Website: www.sjcadets.org

SAINT JOSEPH HIGH SCHOOL

10900 West Cermak Road
Westchester, Illinois 60154-4299

Head of School: Mr. Ronald Hoover

General Information Coeducational day college-preparatory, arts, business, vocational, religious studies, bilingual studies, and technology school, affiliated with Roman Catholic Church. Grades 9–12. Founded: 1960. Setting: suburban. Nearest major city is Chicago. 21-acre campus. 2 buildings on campus. Approved or accredited by Christian Brothers Association, North Central Association of Colleges and Schools, and Illinois Department of Education. Total enrollment: 470. Upper school average class size: 25. Upper school faculty-student ratio: 1:16. There are 176 required school days per year for Upper School students. Upper School students typically attend 5 days per week. The average school day consists of 6 hours and 30 minutes.

Upper School Student Profile Grade 9: 154 students (86 boys, 68 girls); Grade 10: 114 students (67 boys, 47 girls); Grade 11: 88 students (50 boys, 38 girls); Grade 12: 114 students (60 boys, 54 girls). 45% of students are Roman Catholic.

Faculty School total: 32. In upper school: 17 men, 13 women; 15 have advanced degrees.

Subjects Offered Accounting, ACT preparation, acting, algebra, American history, anatomy and physiology, art, band, biology, business law, calculus, calculus-AP, chemistry, Christian ethics, computer applications, computer programming, computer-aided design, creative writing, current events, digital photography, economics, English, English-AP, film studies, fine arts, geometry, graphic arts, health, human biology, Italian, journalism, moral and social development, music appreciation, peace and justice, peer ministry, photography, physical education, physics, pre-algebra, pre-calculus, reading, reading/study skills, sociology, Spanish, Spanish-AP, speech, sports conditioning, studio art, theater production, U.S. history, video and animation, video film production, Web site design, world cultures, world religions.

Graduation Requirements Arts and fine arts (art, music, dance, drama), economics, English, foreign language, health, mathematics, physical education (includes health), religion (includes Bible studies and theology), science, social studies (includes history), each student must complete 40 community service hours.

Special Academic Programs 4 Advanced Placement exams for which test preparation is offered; honors section; independent study; study at local college for college credit; remedial reading and/or remedial writing; remedial math; special instructional classes for deaf students, blind students.

College Admission Counseling 114 students graduated in 2014; 104 went to college, including Illinois State University; Saint Mary's University of Minnesota; Saint Xavier University; Triton College; University of Illinois at Urbana–Champaign; Western Illinois University. Other: 10 went to work. Median composite ACT: 20. 11% scored over 26 on composite ACT.

Student Life Upper grades have uniform requirement, student council, honor system. Discipline rests primarily with faculty. Attendance at religious services is required.

Tuition and Aid Day student tuition: $9400. Tuition installment plan (monthly payment plans, individually arranged payment plans, based on parents income special arrangements are made with income tax return). Tuition reduction for siblings, merit scholarship grants, need-based scholarship grants, paying campus jobs available. In 2014–15, 65% of upper-school students received aid; total upper-school merit-scholarship money awarded: $110,000. Total amount of financial aid awarded in 2014–15: $1,000,000.

Admissions Traditional secondary-level entrance grade is 9. For fall 2014, 253 students applied for upper-level admission, 253 were accepted, 154 enrolled. High School Placement Test (closed version) from Scholastic Testing Service required. Deadline for receipt of application materials: none. Application fee required: $300. On-campus interview required.

Athletics Interscholastic: aerobics/dance (girls), baseball (b), basketball (b,g), bowling (b,g), cheering (g), cross-country running (b,g), dance team (g), football (b), golf (b,g), hockey (g), indoor soccer (b,g), indoor track (b,g), soccer (b,g), softball (g), strength & conditioning (b,g), tennis (b,g), track and field (b,g), volleyball (b,g), wrestling (b); coed intramural: yoga. 3 PE instructors, 30 coaches, 1 athletic trainer.

Computers Computers are regularly used in business applications, current events, economics, English, graphic arts, graphic design, health, history, journalism, mathematics, music, newspaper, photography, reading, religion, science, social studies, Spanish, speech, technology, theater arts, video film production, writing, yearbook classes. Computer network features include Internet access, wireless campus network, Internet filtering or blocking technology, 10th, 11th, and 12th have a laptop computer with wireless access to the Internet, anywhere on campus, 9th graders take part in a digital citizenship course in which they learn about the computers. Campus intranet and student e-mail accounts are available to students. Students grades are available online. The school has a published electronic and media policy.

Contact Mrs. Tricia McGleam, Admissions Director. 708-562-4433 Ext. 117. Fax: 708-562-4459. E-mail: tmcgleam@stjoeshs.org. Website: www.stjoeshs.org/

SAINT JOSEPH HIGH SCHOOL

145 Plainfield Avenue
Metuchen, New Jersey 08840

Head of School: Mr. Justin J. Fleetwood

General Information Boys' day college-preparatory, arts, religious studies, and technology school, affiliated with Roman Catholic Church. Grades 9–12. Founded: 1961. Setting: suburban. Nearest major city is New York, NY. 68-acre campus. 8 buildings on campus. Approved or accredited by Middle States Association of Colleges and Schools and New Jersey Department of Education. Endowment: $2 million. Total enrollment: 683. Upper school average class size: 24. Upper school faculty-student ratio: 1:12. There are 178 required school days per year for Upper School students. Upper School students typically attend 5 days per week. The average school day consists of 6 hours and 12 minutes.

Upper School Student Profile Grade 9: 180 students (180 boys); Grade 10: 172 students (172 boys); Grade 11: 154 students (154 boys); Grade 12: 177 students (177 boys). 75% of students are Roman Catholic.

Faculty School total: 68. In upper school: 30 men, 20 women; 27 have advanced degrees.

Subjects Offered Acting, Advanced Placement courses, algebra, American Civil War, American government, American history, American literature, art, astronomy, biology, biology-AP, calculus, calculus-AP, campus ministry, career education, Catholic

belief and practice, chemistry, chemistry-AP, Christian doctrine, Christian education, Christian ethics, Christian scripture, Christian studies, Christianity, church history, community service, computer animation, computer applications, computer programming, computer science, computer science-AP, constitutional law, desktop publishing, digital applications, digital imaging, digital photography, discrete mathematics, driver education, economics, economics and history, English, English literature, English-AP, European civilization, European history, European history-AP, film, forensics, French, French as a second language, French-AP, geometry, German, German literature, government and politics-AP, government/civics-AP, guitar, health, history, lab science, Latin, math methods, mathematics-AP, meteorology, music, personal finance, photography, physical education, physics, physics-AP, pre-calculus, probability, probability and statistics, public speaking, religion, SAT preparation, SAT/ACT preparation, social justice, social studies, Spanish, Spanish-AP, statistics, technical drawing, theology, U.S. government and politics-AP, U.S. history-AP, Web site design, world history, world literature, writing.

Graduation Requirements Arts and fine arts (art, music, dance, drama), career education, computer science, English, foreign language, lab science, mathematics, physical education (includes health), religion (includes Bible studies and theology), science, social studies (includes history). Community service is required.

Special Academic Programs 12 Advanced Placement exams for which test preparation is offered; honors section; independent study; study at local college for college credit; academic accommodation for the gifted.

College Admission Counseling 185 students graduated in 2015; all went to college, including Penn State University Park; Rutgers, The State University of New Jersey, Rutgers College; Stevens Institute of Technology; The Catholic University of America; University of Pittsburgh; Villanova University. Mean SAT critical reading: 580, mean SAT math: 619, mean SAT writing: 580. 42% scored over 600 on SAT critical reading, 64% scored over 600 on SAT math, 48% scored over 600 on SAT writing, 52% scored over 1800 on combined SAT, 38% scored over 26 on composite ACT.

Student Life Upper grades have specified standards of dress, student council, honor system. Discipline rests primarily with faculty. Attendance at religious services is required.

Summer Programs Remediation, enrichment, advancement, sports, computer instruction programs offered; session focuses on remediation and enrichment; held on campus; accepts boys and girls; open to students from other schools. 225 students usually enrolled. 2016 schedule: June 28 to July 26. Application deadline: June 1.

Tuition and Aid Day student tuition: $13,100. Tuition installment plan (FACTS Tuition Payment Plan, monthly payment plans). Merit scholarship grants, need-based scholarship grants available. In 2015–16, 15% of upper-school students received aid; total upper-school merit-scholarship money awarded: $250,000. Total amount of financial aid awarded in 2015–16: $750,000.

Admissions Traditional secondary-level entrance grade is 9. For fall 2015, 340 students applied for upper-level admission, 335 were accepted, 183 enrolled. High School Placement Test required. Deadline for receipt of application materials: none. No application fee required. On-campus interview recommended.

Athletics Interscholastic: baseball, basketball, bowling, cross-country running, football, golf, ice hockey, indoor track & field, lacrosse, soccer, swimming and diving, tennis, track and field, volleyball, winter (indoor) track; intramural: crew, flag football, Frisbee, skiing (downhill), snowboarding, strength & conditioning, ultimate Frisbee, weight lifting, weight training. 3 PE instructors, 41 coaches, 1 athletic trainer.

Computers Computers are regularly used in animation, computer applications, desktop publishing, desktop publishing, ESL, drawing and design, graphic design, graphics, journalism, mathematics, news writing, newspaper, photography, publications, publishing, science, technical drawing, technology, Web site design, word processing, yearbook classes. Computer network features include on-campus library services, online commercial services, Internet access, wireless campus network, Internet filtering or blocking technology. Campus intranet, student e-mail accounts, and computer access in designated common areas are available to students. Students grades are available online. The school has a published electronic and media policy.

Contact Mr. Casey Ransone, Director of Admissions. 732-549-7600 Ext. 221. Fax: 732-549-0282. E-mail: admissions@stjoes.org. Website: www.stjoes.org

SAINT JOSEPH REGIONAL HIGH SCHOOL

40 Chestnut Ridge Road
Montvale, New Jersey 07645

Head of School: Mr. Barry Donnelly

General Information Boys' day college-preparatory school, affiliated with Roman Catholic Church. Grades 9–12. Founded: 1962. Setting: suburban. Nearest major city is New York, NY. 33-acre campus. 1 building on campus. Approved or accredited by Middle States Association of Colleges and Schools and New Jersey Department of Education. Total enrollment: 516. Upper school average class size: 23. Upper school faculty-student ratio: 1:12. There are 176 required school days per year for Upper School students. Upper School students typically attend 5 days per week. The average school day consists of 6 hours.

Upper School Student Profile Grade 9: 146 students (146 boys); Grade 10: 121 students (121 boys); Grade 11: 123 students (123 boys); Grade 12: 126 students (126 boys).

Faculty School total: 38. In upper school: 28 men, 10 women; 27 have advanced degrees.

Subjects Offered Accounting, advanced chemistry, advanced math, Advanced Placement courses, algebra, American government, American history, American history-AP, American literature, anatomy, art, art appreciation, Bible studies, biology, biology-AP, British literature, calculus, calculus-AP, Catholic belief and practice, chemistry, chemistry-AP, Christian doctrine, church history, computer applications, computer science, driver education, economics, English, English-AP, European history-AP, French, geography, geometry, health education, honors algebra, honors English, honors geometry, honors U.S. history, honors world history, keyboarding, Latin, law, New Testament, physical education, physics, physics-AP, pre-calculus, psychology, religion, science, social studies, Spanish, Spanish-AP, studio art, The 20th Century, theology, U.S. government, U.S. history, U.S. history-AP, Western civilization, word processing, world cultures, world geography, world history.

Special Academic Programs Advanced Placement exam preparation; honors section; study at local college for college credit.

College Admission Counseling 116 students graduated in 2015; all went to college, including Fairfield University; Iona College; Penn State University Park; Rutgers, The State University of New Jersey, New Brunswick; The University of Scranton.

Student Life Upper grades have specified standards of dress, student council, honor system. Discipline rests primarily with faculty. Attendance at religious services is required.

Tuition and Aid Day student tuition: $12,700. Tuition installment plan (FACTS Tuition Payment Plan). Tuition reduction for siblings, merit scholarship grants, need-based scholarship grants, need-based loans available.

Admissions Traditional secondary-level entrance grade is 9. Cooperative Entrance Exam (McGraw-Hill) required. Deadline for receipt of application materials: none. No application fee required. Interview required.

Athletics Interscholastic: baseball, basketball, bowling, cross-country running, football, golf, hockey, ice hockey, indoor hockey, indoor track, indoor track & field, lacrosse, physical fitness, running, soccer, tennis, track and field, weight lifting, weight training, winter (indoor) track, wrestling; intramural: basketball, floor hockey, Frisbee, indoor soccer, skiing (downhill), strength & conditioning, ultimate Frisbee, volleyball. 1 athletic trainer.

Computers Computers are regularly used in accounting classes. Computer network features include on-campus library services, Internet access, wireless campus network, Internet filtering or blocking technology. Campus intranet, student e-mail accounts, and computer access in designated common areas are available to students. Students grades are available online. The school has a published electronic and media policy.

Contact Mr. Michael J. Doherty, Director of Admissions. 201-391-3300 Ext. 41. Fax: 201-391-8073. E-mail: dohertym@saintjosephregional.org. Website: www.saintjosephregional.org

ST. JOSEPH'S ACADEMY

3015 Broussard Street
Baton Rouge, Louisiana 70808

Head of School: Dr. Michele Lambert

General Information Girls' day college-preparatory, arts, religious studies, and technology school, affiliated with Roman Catholic Church. Grades 9–12. Founded: 1868. Setting: urban. 14-acre campus. 8 buildings on campus. Approved or accredited by National Catholic Education Association, Southern Association of Colleges and Schools, Southern Association of Independent Schools, and Louisiana Department of Education. Endowment: $2.5 million. Total enrollment: 1,070. Upper school average class size: 20. Upper school faculty-student ratio: 1:15. There are 178 required school days per year for Upper School students. Upper School students typically attend 5 days per week. The average school day consists of 7 hours and 20 minutes.

Upper School Student Profile Grade 9: 252 students (252 girls); Grade 10: 272 students (272 girls); Grade 11: 281 students (281 girls); Grade 12: 265 students (265 girls). 92.1% of students are Roman Catholic.

Faculty School total: 71. In upper school: 8 men, 63 women; 35 have advanced degrees.

Subjects Offered Accounting, acting, advanced biology, advanced chemistry, advanced computer applications, advanced math, Advanced Placement courses, algebra, American history, American history-AP, American literature, American literature-AP, analysis, analysis and differential calculus, art, art appreciation, art history-AP, band, Basic programming, biology, biology-AP, business law, calculus-AP, campus ministry, Catholic belief and practice, chemistry, child development, choir, choral music, chorus, Christian and Hebrew scripture, church history, civics, civics/free enterprise, computer applications, computer information systems, computer multimedia, computer programming, computer technologies, computer technology certification, CPR, critical studies in film, dance, desktop publishing, drama, drama performance, economics, English, English literature-AP, English-AP, environmental science, European history-AP, family and consumer science, film and literature, fine arts, foreign language, French, French as a second language, geometry, grammar, health, health and safety, health education, Hebrew scripture, honors algebra, honors English, honors geometry, human sexuality, independent study, information technology, Latin, marching band, media arts, media production, music, novels, physical education,

physical fitness, physics, poetry, pre-calculus, public speaking, religion, research, Shakespeare, social justice, Spanish, speech, speech communications, technology, the Web, transition mathematics, U.S. history, U.S. history-AP, U.S. literature, visual arts, vocal ensemble, vocal music, Web authoring, Web site design, world history-AP.

Graduation Requirements Advanced math, algebra, American history, arts and fine arts (art, music, dance, drama), biology, chemistry, civics, computer applications, English, foreign language, geometry, physical education (includes health), physical science, physics, religion (includes Bible studies and theology), world history, service hours.

Special Academic Programs Advanced Placement exam preparation; honors section; independent study; study at local college for college credit.

College Admission Counseling 241 students graduated in 2015; 240 went to college, including Louisiana State University and Agricultural & Mechanical College; Louisiana Tech University; Southeastern Louisiana University; Spring Hill College; Tulane University; University of Louisiana at Lafayette. Other: 1 went to work. 66% scored over 26 on composite ACT.

Student Life Upper grades have uniform requirement, student council, honor system. Discipline rests primarily with faculty. Attendance at religious services is required.

Summer Programs Computer instruction programs offered; session focuses on computer orientation for incoming 9th grade students; held on campus; accepts girls; not open to students from other schools. 260 students usually enrolled. 2016 schedule: July 20 to July 31. Application deadline: November 20.

Tuition and Aid Day student tuition: $10,330. Tuition installment plan (monthly debit plan). Need-based scholarship grants available. In 2015–16, 11% of upper-school students received aid. Total amount of financial aid awarded in 2015–16: $513,581.

Admissions Traditional secondary-level entrance grade is 9. ACT-Explore required. Deadline for receipt of application materials: November 20. Application fee required: $65. On-campus interview required.

Athletics Interscholastic: ballet, basketball, bowling, cheering, cross-country running, dance squad, golf, gymnastics, indoor track, physical fitness, physical training, running, soccer, softball, strength & conditioning, swimming and diving, tennis, track and field, volleyball, weight training, winter (indoor) track, winter soccer; coed intramural: volleyball. 6 PE instructors, 7 coaches, 1 athletic trainer.

Computers Computers are regularly used in all classes. Computer network features include on-campus library services, online commercial services, Internet access, wireless campus network, Internet filtering or blocking technology, administrative software/grading/scheduling. Campus intranet and student e-mail accounts are available to students. Students grades are available online. The school has a published electronic and media policy.

Contact Mrs. Sheri Gillio, Admissions Director. 225-388-2243. Fax: 225-344-5714. E-mail: gillios@sjabr.org. Website: www.sjabr.org

ST. JOSEPH'S CATHOLIC SCHOOL

100 St. Joseph's Drive
Greenville, South Carolina 29607

Head of School: Mr. Keith F. Kiser

General Information Coeducational day college-preparatory school, affiliated with Roman Catholic Church. Grades 6–12. Founded: 1993. Setting: suburban. 36-acre campus. 3 buildings on campus. Approved or accredited by South Carolina Independent School Association, Southern Association of Colleges and Schools, and South Carolina Department of Education. Total enrollment: 677. Upper school average class size: 18. Upper school faculty-student ratio: 1:10. There are 175 required school days per year for Upper School students. Upper School students typically attend 5 days per week. The average school day consists of 7 hours and 10 minutes.

Upper School Student Profile Grade 9: 110 students (52 boys, 58 girls); Grade 10: 113 students (58 boys, 55 girls); Grade 11: 98 students (46 boys, 52 girls); Grade 12: 102 students (54 boys, 48 girls). 70% of students are Roman Catholic.

Faculty School total: 56. In upper school: 15 men, 24 women; 17 have advanced degrees.

Subjects Offered Advanced Placement courses, algebra, American history, American literature, anatomy and physiology, ancient world history, art, art history-AP, arts appreciation, astronomy, band, bioethics, biology, biology-AP, calculus, calculus-AP, chemistry, chemistry-AP, choral music, chorus, Christian doctrine, Christian ethics, church history, composition, computer applications, computer graphics, creative writing, dance, digital photography, directing, drama workshop, dramatic arts, drawing, economics, English language and composition-AP, English literature and composition-AP, ensembles, environmental science, European history, European history-AP, European literature, exercise science, film, film studies, fine arts, forensics, French, genetics, geometry, government, government-AP, honors algebra, honors English, honors geometry, honors U.S. history, human movement and its application to health, improvisation, instrumental music, keyboarding, Latin, literary magazine, literature, media, medieval/Renaissance history, moral theology, newspaper, personal finance, physical education, physics, physics-AP, pre-algebra, pre-calculus, psychology, Shakespeare, Spanish, Spanish language-AP, Spanish-AP, speech, sports conditioning, statistics, statistics-AP, strings, theater arts, theater production, U.S. history, U.S. history-AP, yearbook.

Graduation Requirements 65 hours of community service.

Special Academic Programs 14 Advanced Placement exams for which test preparation is offered; honors section; independent study.

College Admission Counseling 94 students graduated in 2015; 93 went to college, including Clemson University; College of Charleston; Furman University; University of South Carolina; Wofford College. Other: 1 had other specific plans. Mean SAT critical reading: 605, mean SAT math: 598, mean SAT writing: 588, mean combined SAT: 1791, mean composite ACT: 27.

Student Life Upper grades have uniform requirement, student council, honor system. Discipline rests primarily with faculty. Attendance at religious services is required.

Summer Programs Enrichment, sports, art/fine arts programs offered; held on campus; accepts boys and girls; open to students from other schools. 216 students usually enrolled. 2016 schedule: June 1 to August 16.

Tuition and Aid Day student tuition: $12,175. Tuition installment plan (monthly payment plans, yearly payment plan, semiannual payment plan). Tuition reduction for siblings, merit scholarship grants, need-based scholarship grants, tuition reduction for staff available. In 2015–16, 37% of upper-school students received aid; total upper-school merit-scholarship money awarded: $48,000. Total amount of financial aid awarded in 2015–16: $760,000.

Admissions Traditional secondary-level entrance grade is 9. For fall 2015, 82 students applied for upper-level admission, 65 were accepted, 47 enrolled. Scholastic Testing Service High School Placement Test (open version) required. Deadline for receipt of application materials: none. Application fee required: $150. On-campus interview required.

Athletics Interscholastic: baseball (boys), basketball (b,g), cheering (g), cross-country running (b,g), football (b), golf (b), lacrosse (b,g), soccer (b,g), softball (g), swimming and diving (b,g), tennis (b,g), track and field (b,g), volleyball (g), wrestling (b); intramural: basketball (b,g), flag football (b), soccer (b,g), volleyball (g); coed interscholastic: golf. 1 PE instructor, 21 coaches, 1 athletic trainer.

Computers Computers are regularly used in computer applications, graphic design, photography, programming, yearbook classes. Computer network features include on-campus library services, Internet access, wireless campus network, Internet filtering or blocking technology. Student e-mail accounts and computer access in designated common areas are available to students. Students grades are available online. The school has a published electronic and media policy.

Contact Mrs. Barbara L. McGrath, Director of Admissions. 864-234-9009 Ext. 104. Fax: 864-234-5516. E-mail: bmcgrath@sjcatholicschool.org. Website: www.sjcatholicschool.org

ST. JOSEPH'S PREPARATORY SCHOOL

1733 Girard Avenue
Philadelphia, Pennsylvania 19130

Head of School: Rev. John W. Swope, SJ

General Information Boys' day college-preparatory, arts, and religious studies school, affiliated with Roman Catholic Church. Grades 9–12. Founded: 1851. Setting: urban, 7-acre campus. 3 buildings on campus. Approved or accredited by Jesuit Secondary Education Association, Middle States Association of Colleges and Schools, National Catholic Education Association, and Pennsylvania Department of Education. Member of National Association of Independent Schools. Endowment: $16 million. Total enrollment: 890. Upper school average class size: 22. Upper school faculty-student ratio: 1:16. There are 180 required school days per year for Upper School students. Upper School students typically attend 5 days per week. The average school day consists of 6 hours.

Upper School Student Profile Grade 9: 211 students (211 boys); Grade 10: 237 students (237 boys); Grade 11: 225 students (225 boys); Grade 12: 217 students (217 boys). 95% of students are Roman Catholic.

Faculty School total: 80. In upper school: 60 men, 20 women; 65 have advanced degrees.

Subjects Offered Algebra, American history, American literature, anatomy, archaeology, art, biology, business, calculus, chemistry, classics, computer math, computer programming, computer science, earth science, economics, English, English literature, environmental science, ethics, European history, fine arts, French, geometry, German, government/civics, Greek, history, Latin, Mandarin, marine biology, mathematics, photography, physical education, physics, physiology, religion, science, social sciences, social studies, Spanish, speech, trigonometry, world history, world literature.

Graduation Requirements Arts and fine arts (art, music, dance, drama), classics, computer science, English, foreign language, mathematics, physical education (includes health), religion (includes Bible studies and theology), science, social sciences, social studies (includes history), Christian service hours in junior and senior year.

Special Academic Programs International Baccalaureate program; 15 Advanced Placement exams for which test preparation is offered; honors section; independent study; study at local college for college credit; study abroad; academic accommodation for the gifted, the musically talented, and the artistically talented.

College Admission Counseling 241 students graduated in 2015; all went to college. Mean SAT critical reading: 615, mean SAT math: 623, mean SAT writing: 606, mean combined SAT: 1847. 57% scored over 600 on SAT critical reading, 67% scored over 600 on SAT math, 53% scored over 600 on SAT writing, 61% scored over 1800 on combined SAT.

Student Life Upper grades have specified standards of dress, student council. Discipline rests primarily with faculty. Attendance at religious services is required.

Summer Programs Remediation, enrichment, advancement, sports, art/fine arts, computer instruction programs offered; session focuses on pre-8th grade enrichment; held on campus; accepts boys and girls; open to students from other schools. 300 students usually enrolled. 2016 schedule: June 20 to July 15. Application deadline: none.

Tuition and Aid Day student tuition: $21,500. Tuition installment plan (monthly payment plans). Tuition reduction for siblings, merit scholarship grants, need-based scholarship grants, need-based loans, middle-income loans, paying campus jobs available. In 2015–16, 42% of upper-school students received aid; total upper-school merit-scholarship money awarded: $500,000. Total amount of financial aid awarded in 2015–16: $3,900,000.

Admissions Traditional secondary-level entrance grade is 9. For fall 2015, 650 students applied for upper-level admission, 320 were accepted, 248 enrolled. High School Placement Test or High School Placement Test (closed version) from Scholastic Testing Service required. Deadline for receipt of application materials: November 6. Application fee required: $50. On-campus interview recommended.

Athletics Interscholastic: baseball, basketball, bowling, crew, cross-country running, diving, football, Frisbee, golf, ice hockey, indoor track & field, lacrosse, rowing, rugby, running, soccer, squash, swimming and diving, tennis, track and field, ultimate Frisbee, volleyball, winter (indoor) track, wrestling; intramural: basketball, bicycling, climbing, fishing, flag football, handball, martial arts, paint ball, physical fitness, table tennis, team handball, volleyball, water polo. 35 coaches, 1 athletic trainer.

Computers Computers are regularly used in all academic classes. Computer network features include on-campus library services, online commercial services, Internet access, wireless campus network, Internet filtering or blocking technology, Chromebook-approved Helpdesk to repair all student machines. Campus intranet, student e-mail accounts, and computer access in designated common areas are available to students. Students grades are available online. The school has a published electronic and media policy.

Contact Jason M. Zazyczny, Director of Admission. 215-978-1958. Fax: 215-978-1920. E-mail: jzazyczny@sjprep.org. Website: www.sjprep.org

ST. JUDE'S SCHOOL

888 Trillium Drive
Kitchener, Ontario N2R 1K4, Canada

Head of School: Mr. Frederick T. Gore

General Information Coeducational day college-preparatory, arts, and bright learning disabled school; primarily serves underachievers, students with learning disabilities, individuals with Attention Deficit Disorder, and dyslexic students. Grades 1–12. Founded: 1982. Setting: small town. Nearest major city is Toronto, Canada. 10-acre campus. 1 building on campus. Approved or accredited by Ontario Ministry of Education and Ontario Department of Education. Language of instruction: English. Total enrollment: 30. Upper school average class size: 6. Upper school faculty student ratio: 1:6. There are 200 required school days per year for Upper School students. Upper School students typically attend 5 days per week. The average school day consists of 7 hours.

Upper School Student Profile Grade 10: 2 students (2 boys); Grade 11: 1 student (1 boy).

Faculty School total: 6. In upper school: 3 men, 3 women; 3 have advanced degrees.

Subjects Offered 20th century history, 20th century physics, 20th century world history, accounting, acting, adolescent issues, advanced chemistry, advanced math, algebra, analytic geometry, ancient history, ancient world history, ancient/medieval philosophy, anthropology, applied arts, art, art appreciation, art education, art history, basic skills, biology, bookkeeping, business education, business law, business mathematics, business studies, calculus, Canadian history, Canadian law, Canadian literature, career and personal planning, career education, chemistry, civics, college counseling, communication skills, computer literacy, computer science, computer skills, computer studies, discrete mathematics, dramatic arts, drawing and design, earth and space science, ecology, ecology, environmental systems, economics, economics and history, English, English literature, environmental studies, ESL, family studies, fencing, finite math, general science, geography, health, health education, history, honors algebra, honors English, honors geometry, independent study, intro to computers, keyboarding, law, law studies, marketing, media studies, modern Western civilization, modern world history, philosophy, physical education, physical fitness, remedial study skills, remedial/makeup course work, science, science and technology, society, politics and law, sociology, Spanish, study skills, visual arts, Western philosophy, world issues.

Graduation Requirements Ontario requirements.

Special Academic Programs Remedial reading and/or remedial writing; remedial math; programs in English, mathematics, general development for dyslexic students; special instructional classes for students with learning disabilities, Attention Deficit Disorder, and dyslexia; ESL (2 students enrolled).

College Admission Counseling 5 students graduated in 2014; all went to college, including University of Waterloo; Wilfrid Laurier University.

Student Life Upper grades have uniform requirement, student council, honor system. Discipline rests primarily with faculty.

Tuition and Aid Day student tuition: CAN$16,900. Tuition installment plan (monthly payment plans, individually arranged payment plans).

Admissions For fall 2014, 5 students applied for upper-level admission, 5 were accepted, 5 enrolled. Academic Profile Tests, achievement tests, Woodcock Reading Mastery Key Math and Woodcock-Johnson Educational Evaluation, WISC III required. Deadline for receipt of application materials: none. No application fee required. Interview required.

Athletics Interscholastic: synchronized swimming (girls); coed interscholastic: basketball, bowling, cross-country running, fencing, golf; coed intramural: badminton, ball hockey, baseball, basketball, bowling, cross-country running, curling, fencing, fitness, floor hockey, golf, martial arts. 2 PE instructors.

Computers Computers are regularly used in all classes. Computer network features include Internet access, Internet filtering or blocking technology.

Contact Frederick T. Gore, Director of Education. 519-888-0807. Fax: 519-888-0316. E-mail: director@stjudes.com. Website: www.stjudes.com

ST. LAWRENCE SEMINARY HIGH SCHOOL

301 Church Street
Mount Calvary, Wisconsin 53057

Head of School: Fr. John Holly, OFMCAP

General Information Boys' boarding college-preparatory and religious studies school, affiliated with Roman Catholic Church. Grades 9–12. Founded: 1860. Setting: rural. Nearest major city is Milwaukee. Students are housed in single-sex dormitories. 150-acre campus. 11 buildings on campus. Approved or accredited by National Catholic Education Association, North Central Association of Colleges and Schools, and Wisconsin Department of Education. Total enrollment: 203. Upper school average class size: 17. Upper school faculty-student ratio: 1:9. There are 167 required school days per year for Upper School students. Upper School students typically attend 5 days per week. The average school day consists of 7 hours and 45 minutes.

Upper School Student Profile Grade 9: 55 students (55 boys); Grade 10: 58 students (58 boys); Grade 11: 44 students (44 boys); Grade 12: 46 students (46 boys); Postgraduate: 203 students (203 boys). 100% of students are boarding students. 30% are state residents. 16 states are represented in upper school student body. 10% are international students. International students from Ghana, India, Republic of Korea, Saudi Arabia, United Arab Emirates, and Viet Nam. 100% of students are Roman Catholic.

Faculty School total: 23. In upper school: 18 men, 5 women; 12 have advanced degrees; 5 reside on campus.

Subjects Offered Accounting, advanced chemistry, advanced computer applications, advanced math, algebra, American government, American history, American literature, art, biology, business, business law, calculus, chemistry, classical studies, computer applications, computer science, economics, English, English literature, fine arts, geometry, German, government/civics, guidance, health, health and wellness, humanities, industrial arts, Latin, literary genres, mathematics, mechanical drawing, music, music appreciation, music theory, physical education, physics, pre-calculus, probability and statistics, psychology, religion, science, socioeconomic problems, Spanish, theology, trigonometry, U.S. history, woodworking, world history, world literature, writing.

Graduation Requirements Arts and fine arts (art, music, dance, drama), business skills (includes word processing), computer science, English, foreign language, health education, humanities, mathematics, physical education (includes health), religion (includes Bible studies and theology), science, social studies (includes history), study skills, ministry hours.

Special Academic Programs Independent study; study at local college for college credit.

College Admission Counseling 45 students graduated in 2015; 44 went to college, including Creighton University; University of Illinois at Chicago; University of Illinois at Urbana–Champaign; University of Wisconsin–Madison; University of Wisconsin–Milwaukee. Other: 1 entered military service. Median SAT critical reading: 550, median SAT math: 600, median SAT writing: 540, median combined SAT: 1630, median composite ACT: 23. 10% scored over 600 on SAT critical reading, 50% scored over 600 on SAT math, 20% scored over 600 on SAT writing, 30% scored over 1800 on combined SAT, 23% scored over 26 on composite ACT.

Student Life Upper grades have specified standards of dress, student council, honor system. Discipline rests primarily with faculty. Attendance at religious services is required.

Tuition and Aid 7-day tuition and room/board: $13,000. Tuition installment plan (SMART Tuition Payment Plan, monthly payment plans, individually arranged payment plans). Need-based scholarship grants available. In 2015–16, 73% of upper-school students received aid. Total amount of financial aid awarded in 2015–16: $778,110.

Admissions Traditional secondary-level entrance grade is 9. For fall 2015, 85 students applied for upper-level admission, 70 were accepted, 70 enrolled. 3-R Achievement Test and any standardized test required. Deadline for receipt of application materials: none. Application fee required: $300. Interview recommended.

Athletics Interscholastic: baseball, basketball, cross-country running, soccer, tennis, track and field, wrestling; intramural: basketball, bicycling, billiards, bowling, floor hockey, Frisbee, handball, kickball, outdoor activities, outdoor recreation, physical fitness, physical training, racquetball, skiing (downhill), softball, table tennis, tennis, volleyball, wallyball, weight lifting, winter soccer. 3 PE instructors, 8 coaches, 1 athletic trainer.

Computers Computers are regularly used in accounting, business education, classics, creative writing, drafting, economics, English, keyboarding, mathematics, psychology, science, typing, writing, yearbook classes. Computer network features include on-campus library services, Internet access, Internet filtering or blocking technology. Campus intranet, student e-mail accounts, and computer access in designated common areas are available to students. The school has a published electronic and media policy.

Contact Mrs. Deann Sippel, Administrative Assistant to Admissions. 920-753-7570. Fax: 920-753-7507. E-mail: dsippel@stlawrence.edu. Website: www.stlawrence.edu

ST. LOUIS UNIVERSITY HIGH SCHOOL

4970 Oakland Avenue
St. Louis, Missouri 63110

Head of School: Mr. David J. Laughlin

General Information Boys' day college-preparatory school, affiliated with Roman Catholic Church (Jesuit order). Grades 9–12. Founded: 1818. Setting: urban. 27-acre campus. 2 buildings on campus. Approved or accredited by Jesuit Secondary Education Association, North Central Association of Colleges and Schools, and Missouri Department of Education. Member of National Association of Independent Schools. Upper school average class size: 21. Upper school faculty-student ratio: 1:12. There are 167 required school days per year for Upper School students. Upper School students typically attend 5 days per week. The average school day consists of 7 hours and 10 minutes.

Upper School Student Profile 87% of students are Roman Catholic Church (Jesuit order).

Faculty School total: 95. In upper school: 70 men, 25 women; 90 have advanced degrees.

Special Academic Programs 20 Advanced Placement exams for which test preparation is offered; honors section; study at local college for college credit; study abroad.

College Admission Counseling 268 students graduated in 2015; 267 went to college, including Dalhousie University. Mean SAT critical reading: 659, mean SAT math: 686, mean SAT writing: 650, mean composite ACT: 30.

Student Life Upper grades have specified standards of dress, student council, honor system. Discipline rests primarily with faculty. Attendance at religious services is required.

Summer Programs Remediation, enrichment, sports, computer instruction programs offered; held on campus; accepts boys; not open to students from other schools.

Tuition and Aid Day student tuition: $15,400. Tuition installment plan (FACTS Tuition Payment Plan, quarterly, semi-annually). Need-based scholarship grants available. In 2015–16, 40% of upper-school students received aid. Total amount of financial aid awarded in 2015–16: $3,246,000.

Admissions Traditional secondary-level entrance grade is 9. For fall 2015, 320 students applied for upper-level admission, 286 were accepted, 260 enrolled. Scholastic Achievement Test required. Deadline for receipt of application materials: November 19. Application fee required: $7. Interview required.

Athletics Interscholastic: baseball, basketball, cross-country running, football, golf, ice hockey, in-line hockey, lacrosse, racquetball, riflery, rugby, soccer, swimming and diving, tennis, track and field, ultimate Frisbee, volleyball, water polo, wrestling; intramural: bicycling, billiards, bocce, Circus, climbing, dance, fishing, hiking/backpacking, juggling, outdoor adventure, table tennis, ultimate Frisbee, weight lifting. 58 coaches, 1 athletic trainer.

Computers Computer network features include on-campus library services, online commercial services, Internet access, wireless campus network, Internet filtering or blocking technology. Campus intranet, student e-mail accounts, and computer access in designated common areas are available to students. Students grades are available online. The school has a published electronic and media policy.

Contact Dr. John Moran, Principal. 314-531-0330 Ext. 2125. E-mail: jmoran@sluh.org. Website: www.sluh.org

ST. LUKE'S SCHOOL

377 North Wilton Road
New Canaan, Connecticut 06840

Head of School: Mr. Mark C. Davis

General Information Coeducational day college-preparatory, arts, and technology school. Grades 5–12. Founded: 1928. Setting: suburban. Nearest major city is New York, NY. 40-acre campus. 5 buildings on campus. Approved or accredited by Connecticut Association of Independent Schools, New England Association of Schools and Colleges, and Connecticut Department of Education. Member of National Association of Independent Schools. Endowment: $26 million. Upper school average class size: 11. Upper school faculty-student ratio: 1:8. There are 180 required school days per year for Upper School students. Upper School students typically attend 5 days per week. The average school day consists of 9 hours.

Upper School Student Profile Grade 9: 72 students (37 boys, 35 girls); Grade 10: 90 students (45 boys, 45 girls); Grade 11: 81 students (47 boys, 34 girls); Grade 12: 65 students (37 boys, 28 girls)..

Faculty School total: 75. In upper school: 34 men, 28 women; 60 have advanced degrees.

Subjects Offered 20th century American writers, 20th century history, 20th century world history, acting, advanced chemistry, advanced computer applications, advanced math, Advanced Placement courses, advanced studio art-AP, African American studies, algebra, American Civil War, American foreign policy, American history, American literature, anatomy and physiology, Ancient Greek, ancient history, art, art history, biology, biology-AP, British literature (honors), calculus, calculus-AP, ceramics, chemistry, chemistry-AP, choral music, chorus, classical civilization, classical language, classical studies, classics, college counseling, community service, computer applications, computer art, computer education, computer graphics, computer information systems, computer math, computer programming, computer science, computer science-AP, concert band, creative writing, digital art, digital photography, discrete mathematics, drama, drawing, earth science, economics, engineering, English, English language and composition-AP, English literature, environmental science, environmental science-AP, European history, European history-AP, expository writing, fine arts, French, French-AP, geography, geometry, government and politics-AP, government/civics, grammar, health education, honors algebra, honors English, honors geometry, honors U.S. history, honors world history, human geography - AP, humanities, journalism, Latin, Latin-AP, leadership, literature and composition-AP, literature-AP, Mandarin, marine biology, marine science, mathematics, modern European history-AP, music, photography, physical education, physics, physics-AP, pre-calculus, psychology, religion and culture, robotics, Roman civilization, Roman culture, science, social sciences, social studies, Spanish, Spanish-AP, sports medicine, statistics, statistics-AP, studio art, studio art-AP, technical theater, the Sixties, theater, trigonometry, U.S. government and politics-AP, U.S. history, U.S. history-AP, Vietnam, Vietnam War, Western civilization, world history, world history-AP, writing, yearbook.

Graduation Requirements Arts and fine arts (art, music, dance, drama), computer science, English, foreign language, mathematics, music, science, social studies (includes history), 20 hours of community service per year.

Special Academic Programs Advanced Placement exam preparation; honors section; independent study; term-away projects; study abroad; academic accommodation for the gifted.

College Admission Counseling 71 students graduated in 2015; all went to college, including Boston University; Bucknell University; Colby College; Dartmouth College; Tulane University; Yale University. Median SAT critical reading: 660, median SAT math: 650, median SAT writing: 650, median composite ACT: 29.

Student Life Upper grades have specified standards of dress, student council, honor system. Discipline rests equally with students and faculty.

Summer Programs Enrichment, advancement, sports, art/fine arts, computer instruction programs offered; session focuses on enrichment; held on campus; accepts boys and girls; open to students from other schools. 500 students usually enrolled. 2016 schedule: June 19 to August 12. Application deadline: April 1.

Tuition and Aid Day student tuition: $37,820–$39,570. Tuition installment plan (The Tuition Plan, Insured Tuition Payment Plan, monthly payment plans). Need-based scholarship grants available. In 2015–16, 15% of upper-school students received aid. Total amount of financial aid awarded in 2015–16: $749,850.

Admissions Traditional secondary-level entrance grade is 9. For fall 2015, 329 students applied for upper-level admission, 134 were accepted, 98 enrolled. ISEE or SSAT required. Deadline for receipt of application materials: February 1. Application fee required: $75. On-campus interview required.

Athletics Interscholastic: baseball (boys), basketball (b,g), crew (b,g), cross-country running (b,g), field hockey (g), football (b), golf (b), hockey (b), lacrosse (b,g), soccer (b,g), softball (g), squash (b,g), tennis (b,g), volleyball (g); intramural: equestrian sports (g), fitness (b,g), physical training (b,g), skiing (downhill) (b,g); coed interscholastic: crew, cross-country running, golf, hockey, squash; coed intramural: bicycling, physical training, skiing (downhill), weight training. 4 PE instructors, 2 coaches, 2 athletic trainers.

Computers Computers are regularly used in art, college planning, design, English, foreign language, graphic design, library, mathematics, media, science, social sciences, technology, yearbook classes. Computer network features include on-campus library services, online commercial services, Internet access, wireless campus network, Internet filtering or blocking technology. Student e-mail accounts are available to students. Students grades are available online. The school has a published electronic and media policy.

Contact Ginny Bachman, Director of Admission and Financial Aid. 203-801-4833. Fax: 203-972-5353. E-mail: bachmanv@stlukesct.org. Website: www.stlukesct.org

ST. MARGARET'S SCHOOL

1080 Lucas Avenue
Victoria, British Columbia V8X 3P7, Canada

Head of School: Cathy Thornicroft

General Information Girls' boarding and day college-preparatory, general academic, arts, technology, and ESL school. Boarding grades 7–12, day grades JK–12. Founded: 1908. Setting: suburban. Students are housed in single-sex dormitories. 22-acre campus.

10 buildings on campus. Approved or accredited by Canadian Association of Independent Schools, The Association of Boarding Schools, and British Columbia Department of Education. Language of instruction: English. Total enrollment: 346. Upper school average class size: 18. Upper school faculty-student ratio: 1:8.

Upper School Student Profile Grade 6: 20 students (20 girls); Grade 7: 18 students (18 girls); Grade 8: 18 students (18 girls); Grade 9: 15 students (15 girls); Grade 10: 32 students (32 girls); Grade 11: 46 students (46 girls); Grade 12: 34 students (34 girls). 55% of students are boarding students. 45% are province residents. 6 provinces are represented in upper school student body. 55% are international students. International students from China, Hong Kong, Japan, Mexico, Republic of Korea, and Taiwan; 6 other countries represented in student body.

Faculty School total: 38. In upper school: 7 men, 30 women; 12 have advanced degrees.

Subjects Offered 1968, Advanced Placement courses, algebra, applied skills, art, biology, calculus, Canadian geography, Canadian history, career and personal planning, chemistry, Chinese, choir, communications, comparative civilizations, computer science, creative writing, dance, drama, English, English literature, ESL, fine arts, French, geography, history, information technology, Japanese, journalism, law, leadership, Mandarin, mathematics, music, music appreciation, outdoor education, performing arts, photography, physical education, physics, science, social studies, Spanish, theater, Western civilization, writing.

Graduation Requirements Applied skills, arts and fine arts (art, music, dance, drama), English, foreign language, mathematics, science, social studies (includes history).

Special Academic Programs 4 Advanced Placement exams for which test preparation is offered; ESL (38 students enrolled).

College Admission Counseling 44 students graduated in 2015; 42 went to college, including McGill University; Simon Fraser University; The University of British Columbia; University of Toronto; University of Victoria; University of Waterloo. Other: 2 had other specific plans.

Student Life Upper grades have uniform requirement, student council. Discipline rests primarily with faculty.

Summer Programs ESL programs offered; session focuses on ESL, combined with recreational activities and sightseeing; held both on and off campus; held at various locations for the local homestay program; accepts girls; open to students from other schools. 20 students usually enrolled. 2016 schedule: August 17 to August 31. Application deadline: May 1.

Tuition and Aid Day student tuition: CAN$6054–CAN$16,301; 7-day tuition and room/board: CAN$31,831–CAN$39,411. Tuition installment plan (Insured Tuition Payment Plan, monthly payment plans). Tuition reduction for siblings, bursaries, merit scholarship grants, need-based scholarship grants available. In 2015–16, 17% of upper-school students received aid; total upper-school merit-scholarship money awarded: CAN$30,000. Total amount of financial aid awarded in 2015–16: CAN$70,000.

Admissions Traditional secondary-level entrance grade is 7. For fall 2015, 115 students applied for upper-level admission, 97 were accepted, 92 enrolled. School's own exam required. Deadline for receipt of application materials: none. Application fee required: CAN$225. Interview required.

Athletics Interscholastic: aerobics/dance, aquatics, badminton, basketball, cross-country running, dance, field hockey, fitness, rowing, running, soccer, swimming and diving, synchronized swimming, track and field, volleyball; intramural: aerobics, aerobics/dance, alpine skiing, aquatics, backpacking, badminton, baseball, basketball, bicycling, canoeing/kayaking, climbing, cooperative games, cross-country running, dance, equestrian sports, field hockey, figure skating, fitness, floor hockey, Frisbee, golf, gymnastics, hiking/backpacking, horseback riding, ice skating, indoor soccer, jogging, jump rope, kayaking, martial arts, modern dance, mountain biking, ocean paddling, outdoor activities, paddle tennis, physical fitness, rock climbing, ropes courses, rugby, running, sailing, skiing (cross-country), skiing (downhill), snowboarding, soccer, softball, squash, strength & conditioning, surfing, swimming and diving, table tennis, tennis, track and field, ultimate Frisbee, volleyball, wallyball, weight training, wilderness, wilderness survival, yoga. 4 PE instructors, 10 coaches, 2 athletic trainers.

Computers Computers are regularly used in career exploration, English, ESL, foreign language, French, history, journalism, mathematics, science classes. Computer network features include Internet access, wireless campus network, Internet filtering or blocking technology. Student e-mail accounts and computer access in designated common areas are available to students.

Contact Ms. Kathy Charleson, Director of Admissions. 250-479-7171. Fax: 250-479-8976. E-mail: stmarg@stmarg.ca. Website: www.stmarg.ca

ST. MARK'S SCHOOL OF TEXAS

10600 Preston Road
Dallas, Texas 75230-4000

Head of School: Mr. David W. Dini

General Information Boys' day college-preparatory, arts, technology, and Advanced Placement school. Grades 1–12. Founded: 1906. Setting: urban. 40-acre campus. 13 buildings on campus. Approved or accredited by Independent Schools Association of the Southwest. Member of National Association of Independent Schools and Secondary School Admission Test Board. Endowment: $130 million. Total enrollment: 863. Upper school average class size: 14. Upper school faculty-student ratio: 1:8. There are 172 required school days per year for Upper School students. Upper School students typically attend 5 days per week. The average school day consists of 7 hours and 55 minutes.

Upper School Student Profile Grade 9: 99 students (99 boys); Grade 10: 93 students (93 boys); Grade 11: 92 students (92 boys); Grade 12: 88 students (88 boys).

Subjects Offered 3-dimensional art, acting, algebra, American history-AP, ancient world history, art, art history, astronomy, Basic programming, biology, biology-AP, calculus, calculus-AP, ceramics, chemistry, chemistry-AP, Chinese, choir, civil rights, community service, computer programming, computer science, computer science-AP, conceptual physics, concert band, creative drama, creative writing, debate, digital art, digital photography, directing, DNA science lab, drama, drama workshop, economics, economics-AP, English, English literature and composition-AP, English literature-AP, environmental science-AP, European history, European history-AP, film studies, fine arts, gender issues, geology, geometry, history, honors English, honors geometry, humanities, independent study, Japanese, journalism, Latin, Latin-AP, macroeconomics-AP, marine ecology, mathematics, microeconomics-AP, modern European history-AP, modern world history, music, oceanography, photography, physical education, physics, physics-AP, piano, science, science fiction, sculpture, senior project, Spanish, Spanish language-AP, Spanish literature-AP, statistics-AP, strings, theater, trigonometry, U.S. history, video film production, Web site design, woodworking, world history, world religions.

Graduation Requirements Arts and fine arts (art, music, dance, drama), English, foreign language, mathematics, physical education (includes health), science, social studies (includes history), senior exhibition. Community service is required.

Special Academic Programs Advanced Placement exam preparation; honors section; independent study; term-away projects; study abroad; academic accommodation for the gifted.

College Admission Counseling 91 students graduated in 2015; all went to college, including Dartmouth College; Georgetown University; Southern Methodist University; Texas A&M University; The University of Texas at Austin; University of Pennsylvania. Mean SAT critical reading: 699, mean SAT math: 724, mean SAT writing: 688, mean combined SAT: 2111, mean composite ACT: 32.

Student Life Upper grades have uniform requirement, student council, honor system. Discipline rests primarily with faculty. Attendance at religious services is required.

Tuition and Aid Day student tuition: $23,525. Tuition installment plan (Insured Tuition Payment Plan, individually arranged payment plans, financial aid student monthly payment plan). Need-based scholarship grants, tuition remission for sons of faculty and staff, need-based middle-income financial aid available. In 2015–16, 17% of upper-school students received aid. Total amount of financial aid awarded in 2015–16: $1,170,052.

Admissions Traditional secondary-level entrance grade is 9. For fall 2015, 100 students applied for upper-level admission, 17 were accepted, 14 enrolled. ISEE required. Deadline for receipt of application materials: January 5. Application fee required: $175. Interview required.

Athletics Interscholastic: backpacking, baseball, basketball, cheering, climbing, crew, cross-country running, diving, fencing, football, golf, hiking/backpacking, hockey, ice hockey, lacrosse, outdoor education, outdoor skills, physical fitness, physical training, soccer, strength & conditioning, swimming and diving, tennis, track and field, volleyball, wall climbing, water polo, weight training, wilderness, winter soccer, wrestling; intramural: basketball, bicycling, cooperative games, cross-country running, fitness, flag football, floor hockey, jump rope, kickball, lacrosse, physical fitness, physical training, soccer, softball, swimming and diving, table tennis, team handball, tennis, track and field, volleyball, water polo, weight training, winter soccer, wrestling. 11 PE instructors, 69 coaches, 2 athletic trainers.

Computers Computers are regularly used in English, foreign language, humanities, mathematics, science classes. Computer network features include on-campus library services, online commercial services, Internet access, wireless campus network, Internet filtering or blocking technology. Student e-mail accounts and computer access in designated common areas are available to students. Students grades are available online. The school has a published electronic and media policy.

Contact Mr. David P. Baker, Director of Admission and Financial Aid. 214-346-8171. Fax: 214-346-8701. E-mail: admission@smtexas.org. Website: www.smtexas.org

ST. MARTIN'S EPISCOPAL SCHOOL

225 Green Acres Road
Metairie, Louisiana 70003

Head of School: Merry Sorrells

General Information Coeducational day college-preparatory, arts, religious studies, bilingual studies, and technology school, affiliated with Episcopal Church. Grades PK–12. Founded: 1947. Setting: suburban. Nearest major city is New Orleans. 18-acre campus. 13 buildings on campus. Approved or accredited by Independent Schools Association of the Southwest, National Association of Episcopal Schools, Southwest Association of Episcopal Schools, The College Board, and Louisiana Department of Education. Member of National Association of Independent Schools. Endowment: $6.7

million. Total enrollment: 473. Upper school average class size: 15. Upper school faculty-student ratio: 1:6. There are 178 required school days per year for Upper School students. Upper School students typically attend 5 days per week. The average school day consists of 5 hours and 30 minutes.

Upper School Student Profile Grade 9: 45 students (23 boys, 22 girls); Grade 10: 40 students (22 boys, 18 girls); Grade 11: 42 students (28 boys, 14 girls); Grade 12: 47 students (28 boys, 19 girls). 11% of students are members of Episcopal Church.

Faculty School total: 87. In upper school: 9 men, 18 women; 23 have advanced degrees.

Subjects Offered Advanced chemistry, advanced math, Advanced Placement courses, advanced studio art-AP, algebra, American history, American history-AP, American literature, American literature-AP, art, art history, band, baseball, basketball, Bible studies, biology, biology-AP, calculus, calculus-AP, career education internship, career/college preparation, ceramics, cheerleading, chemistry, chemistry-AP, Chinese studies, chorus, civics, college counseling, community garden, community service, computer literacy, creative writing, current events, digital photography, drama, earth science, economics, economics and history, English, English as a foreign language, English composition, English language and composition-AP, English literature, English literature and composition-AP, English literature-AP, environmental science, ethics, European history-AP, fine arts, French, French-AP, geography, geology, geometry, grammar, history-AP, honors algebra, honors English, honors geometry, humanities, internship, journalism, lab science, Latin, Latin-AP, life management skills, life skills, literary magazine, Mandarin, mathematics, model United Nations, music, music appreciation, music-AP, musical productions, newspaper, philosophy, physical education, physics, pre-algebra, publications, religion, SAT preparation, science, scripture, senior internship, social studies, softball, Spanish, Spanish-AP, speech, statistics-AP, student government, studio art, studio art-AP, swimming, tennis, theater, theater design and production, theology, track and field, trigonometry, U.S. history-AP, volleyball, world history, world literature, world religions, writing.

Graduation Requirements Arts and fine arts (art, music, dance, drama), electives, English, foreign language, life skills, mathematics, physical education (includes health), religion (includes Bible studies and theology), science, senior internship, social studies (includes history), senior intern program, 50 hours of community service.

Special Academic Programs 12 Advanced Placement exams for which test preparation is offered; honors section; independent study; ESL (9 students enrolled).

College Admission Counseling 58 students graduated in 2015; 57 went to college, including Chapman University; Louisiana State University and Agricultural & Mechanical College; Savannah College of Art and Design; St. Edward's University; Texas A&M University; Texas Christian University. Median SAT critical reading: 560, median SAT math: 570, median SAT writing: 570, median combined SAT: 1740, median composite ACT: 26. 24% scored over 600 on SAT critical reading, 41% scored over 600 on SAT math, 32% scored over 600 on SAT writing, 32% scored over 1800 on combined SAT, 40% scored over 26 on composite ACT.

Student Life Upper grades have specified standards of dress, student council, honor system. Discipline rests primarily with faculty. Attendance at religious services is required.

Summer Programs Remediation, enrichment, advancement, sports, art/fine arts, computer instruction programs offered; session focuses on academics, athletics, creative arts, and enrichment; held on campus; accepts boys and girls; open to students from other schools. 438 students usually enrolled. 2016 schedule: June 1 to August 7. Application deadline: May 15.

Tuition and Aid Day student tuition: $19,950. Tuition installment plan (local bank-arranged plan). Merit scholarship grants, need-based scholarship grants available. In 2015–16, 47% of upper-school students received aid; total upper-school merit-scholarship money awarded: $239,042. Total amount of financial aid awarded in 2015–16: $349,973.

Admissions Traditional secondary-level entrance grade is 9. For fall 2015, 41 students applied for upper-level admission, 31 were accepted, 23 enrolled. Admissions testing, ISEE, Kaufman Test of Educational Achievement, math and English placement tests, WISC III or other aptitude measures; standardized achievement test or writing sample required. Deadline for receipt of application materials: none. Application fee required: $50. Interview required.

Athletics Interscholastic: baseball (boys), basketball (b,g), cheering (g), cross-country running (b,g), football (b), golf (b,g), soccer (b,g), softball (g), swimming and diving (b,g), tennis (b,g), track and field (b,g), volleyball (g), winter (indoor) track (b); intramural: basketball (b,g), lacrosse (b,g), ropes courses (b,g), soccer (b,g), swimming and diving (b,g), tennis (b,g), track and field (b,g), volleyball (g); coed intramural: project adventure. 2 PE instructors, 5 coaches, 1 athletic trainer.

Computers Computers are regularly used in all academic classes. Computer network features include on-campus library services, online commercial services, Internet access, wireless campus network, Internet filtering or blocking technology, vpn for teachers, staff, and students. Campus intranet, student e-mail accounts, and computer access in designated common areas are available to students. Students grades are available online. The school has a published electronic and media policy.

Contact Mrs. DeAnna Tillery, Admission Assistant. 504-736-9917. Fax: 504-736-8802. E-mail: deanna.tillery@stmsaints.com. Website: www.stmsaints.com

ST. MARY'S EPISCOPAL SCHOOL

60 Perkins Extended
Memphis, Tennessee 38117-3199

Head of School: Mr. Albert L. Throckmorton

General Information Girls' day college-preparatory, arts, technology, and STEM (Science, Technology, Engineering, Math) school, affiliated with Episcopal Church. Grades PK–12. Founded: 1847. Setting: urban. 27-acre campus. 8 buildings on campus. Approved or accredited by National Association of Episcopal Schools, Southern Association of Colleges and Schools, Southern Association of Independent Schools, Tennessee Association of Independent Schools, The College Board, and Tennessee Department of Education. Member of National Association of Independent Schools. Endowment: $21.7 million. Total enrollment: 837. Upper school average class size: 12. Upper school faculty-student ratio: 1:9. There are 175 required school days per year for Upper School students. Upper School students typically attend 5 days per week. The average school day consists of 6 hours and 25 minutes.

Upper School Student Profile Grade 9: 60 students (60 girls); Grade 10: 66 students (66 girls); Grade 11: 63 students (63 girls); Grade 12: 65 students (65 girls). 11.4% of students are members of Episcopal Church.

Faculty School total: 108. In upper school: 6 men, 29 women; 29 have advanced degrees.

Subjects Offered Algebra, anatomy and physiology, art history, art history-AP, biology, biology-AP, calculus, calculus-AP, chamber groups, chemistry, chemistry-AP, choir, comparative religion, economics, English, English language and composition-AP, English literature and composition-AP, ethics, French, French-AP, geography, geometry, global issues, global studies, guitar, health, humanities, instrumental music, Latin, Latin-AP, Mandarin, microbiology, music theory-AP, performing arts, physical education, physics, physics-AP, pre-calculus, psychology, religion, robotics, Spanish, Spanish-AP, speech, studio art, studio art-AP, technology, theater, U.S. government, U.S. history, U.S. history-AP, wind ensemble, world history, world history-AP.

Graduation Requirements 1 1/2 elective credits, algebra, arts and fine arts (art, music, dance, drama), biology, calculus, chemistry, computer skills, economics, English, English language-AP, English literature-AP, foreign language, geometry, physical education (includes health), physics, pre-calculus, religion (includes Bible studies and theology), social studies (includes history), U.S. history, world history, each student is required to complete one online class.

Special Academic Programs 16 Advanced Placement exams for which test preparation is offered; honors section; independent study; academic accommodation for the gifted, the musically talented, and the artistically talented.

College Admission Counseling 56 students graduated in 2015; all went to college, including New York University; Northwestern University; Sewanee: The University of the South; Tulane University; University of Mississippi; University of Southern California. Median SAT critical reading: 610, median SAT math: 600, median SAT writing: 640, median combined SAT: 1820, median composite ACT: 29. 50% scored over 600 on SAT critical reading, 45% scored over 600 on SAT math, 68% scored over 600 on SAT writing, 61% scored over 1800 on combined SAT, 87% scored over 26 on composite ACT.

Student Life Upper grades have specified standards of dress, student council, honor system. Discipline rests equally with students and faculty. Attendance at religious services is required.

Summer Programs Enrichment, sports, art/fine arts programs offered; session focuses on summer enrichment, reading; held both on and off campus; held at predominantly held on the school campus; swimming component at a neighborhood pool; accepts boys and girls; open to students from other schools. 600 students usually enrolled. 2016 schedule: May 31 to August 12. Application deadline: none.

Tuition and Aid Day student tuition: $19,280. Tuition installment plan (monthly payment plans, credit card payment). Need-based scholarship grants available. In 2015–16, 16% of upper-school students received aid. Total amount of financial aid awarded in 2015–16: $381,400.

Admissions Traditional secondary-level entrance grade is 9. For fall 2015, 23 students applied for upper-level admission, 21 were accepted, 15 enrolled. ISEE and writing sample required. Deadline for receipt of application materials: none. Application fee required: $75. On-campus interview required.

Athletics Interscholastic: basketball, bowling, cross-country running, dance team, fencing, golf, lacrosse, soccer, softball, swimming and diving, tennis, track and field, trap and skeet, volleyball. 1 PE instructor, 20 coaches, 1 athletic trainer.

Computers Computers are regularly used in all academic classes. Computer network features include on-campus library services, Internet access, wireless campus network, Internet filtering or blocking technology, online database services for research available at school and at home. Campus intranet, student e-mail accounts, and computer access in designated common areas are available to students. Students grades are available online. The school has a published electronic and media policy.

Contact Ms. Nicole Hernandez, Director of Admission and Financial Aid. 901-537-1405. Fax: 901-685-1098. E-mail: nhernandez@stmarysschool.org. Website: www.stmarysschool.org

SAINT MARY'S HALL

9401 Starcrest Drive
San Antonio, Texas 78217

Head of School: Mr. Jonathan Eades

General Information Coeducational day college-preparatory and arts school. Grades PK–12. Founded: 1879. Setting: suburban. 60-acre campus. 15 buildings on campus. Approved or accredited by Independent Schools Association of the Southwest. Member of National Association of Independent Schools. Endowment: $40 million. Total enrollment: 996. Upper school average class size: 15. Upper school faculty-student ratio: 1:6. There are 173 required school days per year for Upper School students. Upper School students typically attend 5 days per week. The average school day consists of 7 hours and 15 minutes.

Upper School Student Profile Grade 9: 96 students (50 boys, 46 girls); Grade 10: 96 students (42 boys, 54 girls); Grade 11: 96 students (52 boys, 44 girls); Grade 12: 94 students (53 boys, 41 girls).

Faculty School total: 56. In upper school: 28 men, 20 women; 40 have advanced degrees.

Subjects Offered 3-dimensional art, Advanced Placement courses, algebra, American history-AP, American literature, anatomy and physiology, art, art history, art history-AP, art-AP, athletic training, ballet, baseball, basketball, biology, biology-AP, British literature, calculus, calculus-AP, cell biology, ceramics, chemistry, chemistry-AP, choir, college counseling, composition, computer science, computer science-AP, concert choir, creative writing, dance, digital photography, directing, drama, drawing, drawing and design, economics, economics-AP, English language and composition-AP, English literature and composition-AP, environmental science-AP, European history, European history-AP, fitness, French, French language-AP, genetics, geology, geometry, golf, government/civics, great books, guitar, health, human geography - AP, jazz band, Latin, Latin-AP, literary magazine, marine biology, model United Nations, music theory, painting, photography, physical education, physics, physics-AP, piano, pre-calculus, religious studies, science research, sculpture, set design, softball, Spanish, Spanish language-AP, Spanish literature-AP, speech, statistics-AP, swimming, technical theater, tennis, track and field, U.S. history, voice, volleyball, Web site design, world geography, world history, world literature, world religions, yearbook, zoology.

Graduation Requirements Arts and fine arts (art, music, dance, drama), athletics, electives, English, foreign language, mathematics, physical education (includes health), science, social studies (includes history), 40 hours of community service.

Special Academic Programs 25 Advanced Placement exams for which test preparation is offered; honors section; independent study; study abroad.

College Admission Counseling 94 students graduated in 2014; all went to college, including Emory University, Oxford College; Texas A&M University; Texas Christian University; The University of Texas at Austin; Trinity University; University of Southern California. Median SAT critical reading: 650, median SAT math: 654, median SAT writing: 671.

Student Life Upper grades have uniform requirement, student council, honor system. Discipline rests primarily with faculty. Attendance at religious services is required.

Tuition and Aid Day student tuition: $22,770. Tuition installment plan (monthly payment plans, individually arranged payment plans, full-year payment plan, 2-payment plan, monthly payment plan). Merit scholarship grants, need-based scholarship grants available. In 2014–15, 22% of upper-school students received aid; total upper-school merit-scholarship money awarded: $382,320. Total amount of financial aid awarded in 2014–15: $621,990.

Admissions Traditional secondary-level entrance grade is 9. For fall 2014, 94 students applied for upper-level admission, 54 were accepted, 46 enrolled. ISEE required. Deadline for receipt of application materials: November 14. Application fee required: $50. Interview required.

Athletics Interscholastic: ballet (boys, girls), baseball (b), basketball (b,g), cheering (g), dance (b,g), field hockey (g), fitness (b,g), football (b), golf (b,g), independent competitive sports (b,g), lacrosse (b), soccer (b,g), softball (g), volleyball (b,g); coed interscholastic: cross-country running, physical fitness, physical training, strength & conditioning, tennis, track and field, weight training. 14 coaches, 2 athletic trainers.

Computers Computers are regularly used in all academic, media arts classes. Computer network features include on-campus library services, Internet access, wireless campus network, Internet filtering or blocking technology, SmartBoards. Student e-mail accounts are available to students. Students grades are available online. The school has a published electronic and media policy.

Contact Mrs. Julie Hellmund, Director of Admission. 210-483-9234. Fax: 210-655-5211. E-mail: jhellmund@smhall.org. Website: www.smhall.org

SAINT MARY'S HIGH SCHOOL

2525 North Third Street
Phoenix, Arizona 85004

Head of School: Mrs. Suzanne M. Fessler

General Information Coeducational day college-preparatory, arts, and religious studies school, affiliated with Roman Catholic Church. Grades 9–12. Founded: 1917. Setting: urban. 6-acre campus. 5 buildings on campus. Approved or accredited by North Central Association of Colleges and Schools, Western Catholic Education Association, and Arizona Department of Education. Endowment: $1 million. Total enrollment: 541.

Upper school average class size: 22. Upper school faculty-student ratio: 1:15. There are 180 required school days per year for Upper School students. Upper School students typically attend 5 days per week. The average school day consists of 6 hours and 45 minutes.

Upper School Student Profile Grade 9: 154 students (89 boys, 65 girls); Grade 10: 152 students (84 boys, 68 girls); Grade 11: 134 students (62 boys, 72 girls); Grade 12: 101 students (55 boys, 46 girls). 88% of students are Roman Catholic.

Faculty School total: 39. In upper school: 19 men, 20 women; 20 have advanced degrees.

Subjects Offered Advanced Placement courses, algebra, American government, American history, American history-AP, American literature, art, band, biology, British literature, British literature (honors), calculus-AP, Catholic belief and practice, chemistry, Christian and Hebrew scripture, composition, dance, drama, economics, electives, English, English composition, English literature, English literature and composition-AP, fine arts, foreign language, French, geometry, health, history, history of the Catholic Church, honors algebra, honors English, honors geometry, honors U.S. history, Latin, Life of Christ, physical education, physical science, physics, prayer/spirituality, pre-calculus, religious education, social studies, Spanish, Spanish language-AP, standard curriculum, state government, state history, theology, trigonometry, world geography, world history, world religions, yearbook.

Graduation Requirements Advanced math, algebra, American government, American history, American literature, anatomy and physiology, arts and fine arts (art, music, dance, drama), biology, British literature, Catholic belief and practice, chemistry, Christian and Hebrew scripture, composition, economics, electives, English, foreign language, geometry, health education, history of the Catholic Church, language and composition, physical education (includes health), physics, pre-calculus, theology, trigonometry, world history, world literature, 90 hours of Christian community service, 4 credtis of Catholic Theology courses.

Special Academic Programs 5 Advanced Placement exams for which test preparation is offered; honors section; study at local college for college credit; remedial reading and/or remedial writing; remedial math.

College Admission Counseling 106 students graduated in 2015; 105 went to college, including Arizona State University at the Tempe campus; Grand Canyon University; Northern Arizona University; The University of Arizona. Other: 1 entered military service. 8% scored over 600 on SAT critical reading, 9% scored over 600 on SAT math, 9% scored over 600 on SAT writing, 3% scored over 1800 on combined SAT, 3% scored over 26 on composite ACT.

Student Life Upper grades have uniform requirement, student council. Discipline rests primarily with faculty. Attendance at religious services is required.

Summer Programs Remediation, enrichment, advancement, sports, art/fine arts programs offered; session focuses on high school preparation for incoming freshmen and advancement for upper classmen; held on campus; accepts boys and girls; open to students from other schools. 200 students usually enrolled. 2016 schedule: May 31 to July 1. Application deadline: May 13.

Tuition and Aid Day student tuition: $13,800. Tuition installment plan (monthly payment plans, individually arranged payment plans, quarterly and semester payment plans). Need-based scholarship grants, paying campus jobs available. In 2015–16, 80% of upper-school students received aid. Total amount of financial aid awarded in 2015–16: $3,800,000.

Admissions Traditional secondary level entrance grade is 9. For fall 2015, 180 students applied for upper-level admission, 170 were accepted, 160 enrolled. High School Placement Test required. Deadline for receipt of application materials: none. Application fee required: $300. On-campus interview required.

Athletics Interscholastic: baseball (boys), basketball (b,g), cheering (g), football (b), golf (b,g), physical fitness (b,g), soccer (b,g), softball (g), strength & conditioning (b,g), tennis (b,g), volleyball (b,g), weight training (b,g), winter soccer (b,g); intramural: dance (g); coed interscholastic: cross-country running, physical fitness, strength & conditioning, swimming and diving, track and field, weight training. 2 PE instructors, 20 coaches, 1 athletic trainer.

Computers Computers are regularly used in digital applications, graphics, yearbook classes. Computer resources include on-campus library services, online commercial services, Internet access, wireless campus network, Internet filtering or blocking technology. Students grades are available online. The school has a published electronic and media policy.

Contact Ms. Allison Madigan, Director of Admissions. 602-251-2515. Fax: 602-251-2595. E-mail: amadigan@smknights.org. Website: www.smknights.org

SAINT MARY'S HIGH SCHOOL

113 Duke of Gloucester Street
Annapolis, Maryland 21401

Head of School: Mrs. Mindi Imes

General Information Coeducational day college-preparatory, arts, religious studies, bilingual studies, and technology school, affiliated with Roman Catholic Church. Grades 9–12. Founded: 1946. Setting: small town. 5-acre campus. 3 buildings on campus. Approved or accredited by Southern Association of Independent Schools and Maryland Department of Education. Total enrollment: 500. Upper school average class size: 22. Upper school faculty-student ratio: 1:15. Upper School students typically attend 5 days per week. The average school day consists of 6 hours and 25 minutes.

Upper School Student Profile 80% of students are Roman Catholic.

Faculty School total: 33. In upper school: 12 men, 21 women.

Subjects Offered Accounting, algebra, American government, American literature, art, art history, art history-AP, biology, biology-AP, British literature, calculus-AP, Catholic belief and practice, chemistry, chemistry-AP, Christian scripture, Christianity, cinematography, computer applications, creative writing, current events, drama, economics, environmental science, European history-AP, fiction, forensics, French, geography, geometry, health, integrated mathematics, interdisciplinary studies, Irish literature, Latin, literature and composition-AP, math analysis, mathematics, mechanical drawing, microbiology, musical theater, peace and justice, physical education, physical science, physics, physics-AP, pre-calculus, psychology, public speaking, relationships, religion, religion and culture, senior project, Shakespeare, social justice, sociology, Spanish, sports conditioning, studio art, trigonometry, U.S. government and politics-AP, U.S. history, U.S. history-AP, weight training, world arts, world history, world literature, writing, zoology.

Graduation Requirements Arts and fine arts (art, music, dance, drama), computers, English, foreign language, mathematics, physical education (includes health), religion (includes Bible studies and theology), science, social studies (includes history).

Special Academic Programs Advanced Placement exam preparation; honors section; study at local college for college credit; study abroad; academic accommodation for the gifted.

College Admission Counseling 110 students graduated in 2014; all went to college.

Student Life Upper grades have uniform requirement, student council, honor system. Discipline rests primarily with faculty. Attendance at religious services is required.

Tuition and Aid Day student tuition: $14,230. Tuition installment plan (monthly payment plans). Merit scholarship grants, need-based scholarship grants available. In 2014–15, 25% of upper-school students received aid; total upper-school merit-scholarship money awarded: $30,000. Total amount of financial aid awarded in 2014–15: $250,000.

Admissions Traditional secondary-level entrance grade is 9. For fall 2014, 285 students applied for upper-level admission, 138 enrolled. High School Placement Test required. Deadline for receipt of application materials: January 7. Application fee required: $75.

Athletics Interscholastic: baseball (boys), basketball (b,g), cross-country running (b,g), field hockey (g), football (b), golf (b,g), indoor track (b,g), lacrosse (b,g), soccer (b,g), swimming and diving (b,g), tennis (b,g), track and field (b,g), volleyball (g), wrestling (b); intramural: crew (g); coed intramural: dance team, fishing, Frisbee, sailing, weight training, yoga. 2 PE instructors, 56 coaches, 1 athletic trainer.

Computers Computers are regularly used in all classes. Computer network features include on-campus library services, online commercial services, Internet access, wireless campus network. Student e-mail accounts are available to students. Students grades are available online. The school has a published electronic and media policy.

Contact Ms. Jennifer Shelsby, Director of Admissions. 410-990-4236. Fax: 410-269-7843. E-mail: jshelsby@stmarysannapolis.org. Website: www.stmarysannapolis.org

ST. MARY'S PREPARATORY SCHOOL

3535 Indian Trail
Orchard Lake, Michigan 48324

Head of School: Cormac Lynn

General Information Boys' boarding and day college-preparatory school, affiliated with Roman Catholic Church. Grades 9–12. Founded: 1885. Setting: suburban. Nearest major city is Detroit. Students are housed in single-sex dormitories. 80-acre campus. 12 buildings on campus. Approved or accredited by Michigan Association of Non-Public Schools and Michigan Department of Education. Total enrollment: 540. Upper school average class size: 18. Upper school faculty-student ratio: 1:10. There are 185 required school days per year for Upper School students. Upper School students typically attend 5 days per week. The average school day consists of 7 hours.

Upper School Student Profile Grade 9: 133 students (133 boys); Grade 10: 137 students (137 boys); Grade 11: 126 students (126 boys); Grade 12: 127 students (127 boys). 15% of students are boarding students. 80% are state residents. 5 states are represented in upper school student body. 15% are international students. International students from Brazil, China, Poland, Republic of Korea, Russian Federation, and Taiwan. 80% of students are Roman Catholic.

Faculty School total: 58. In upper school: 43 men, 15 women; 16 have advanced degrees; 6 reside on campus.

Subjects Offered Algebra, American history, American literature, art, band, Bible studies, biology, business, business skills, calculus, chemistry, Chinese, computer programming, computer science, creative writing, drafting, driver education, earth science, ecology, economics, English, English literature, expository writing, fine arts, French, geometry, government/civics, grammar, health, history, journalism, law, mathematics, music technology, mythology, physical education, physics, Polish, psychology, religion, robotics, science, social sciences, social studies, Spanish, speech, theology, trigonometry, world history, writing.

Graduation Requirements Arts and fine arts (art, music, dance, drama), business skills (includes word processing), computer science, English, foreign language, mathematics, physical education (includes health), religion (includes Bible studies and theology), science, social sciences, social studies (includes history).

Special Academic Programs Advanced Placement exam preparation; honors section; study at local college for college credit; academic accommodation for the musically talented and the artistically talented; programs in general development for dyslexic students; special instructional classes for students with learning disabilities, Attention Deficit Disorder, and dyslexia; ESL (50 students enrolled).

College Admission Counseling 103 students graduated in 2015; 95 went to college, including Michigan State University; Oakland University; University of Detroit Mercy; University of Michigan; Wayne State University; Western Michigan University. Other: 2 went to work, 1 entered military service, 5 had other specific plans. Median SAT critical reading: 503, median SAT math: 600, median SAT writing: 510, median combined SAT: 1613, median composite ACT: 24. 5% scored over 600 on SAT critical reading, 15% scored over 600 on SAT math, 40% scored over 26 on composite ACT.

Student Life Upper grades have specified standards of dress, student council, honor system. Discipline rests primarily with faculty. Attendance at religious services is required.

Summer Programs Sports programs offered; session focuses on football, basketball, and lacrosse, hockey; held on campus; accepts boys and girls; open to students from other schools. 400 students usually enrolled. 2016 schedule: June to August. Application deadline: June 1.

Tuition and Aid Day student tuition: $11,000; 5-day tuition and room/board: $20,000; 7-day tuition and room/board: $30,000. Tuition installment plan (SMART Tuition Payment Plan, individually arranged payment plans). Tuition reduction for siblings, merit scholarship grants, need-based scholarship grants available. In 2015–16, 80% of upper-school students received aid.

Admissions Traditional secondary-level entrance grade is 9. For fall 2015, 300 students applied for upper-level admission, 200 were accepted, 150 enrolled. STS and TOEFL required. Deadline for receipt of application materials: none. Application fee required: $35. Interview recommended.

Athletics Interscholastic: alpine skiing, baseball, basketball, crew, cross-country running, football, freestyle skiing, golf, hockey, ice hockey, indoor track, indoor track & field, jogging, lacrosse, rowing, skiing (downhill), soccer, track and field, wrestling; intramural: aerobics/Nautilus, aquatics, basketball, bicycling, billiards, bowling, broomball, fitness, Frisbee, golf, hockey, ice hockey, ice skating, indoor hockey, indoor soccer, indoor track, jogging, lacrosse, mountain biking, Nautilus, physical fitness, physical training, rowing, running, skeet shooting, skiing (downhill), snowboarding, soccer, strength & conditioning, swimming and diving, table tennis, tennis, weight lifting, weight training, whiffle ball. 2 PE instructors, 25 coaches, 3 athletic trainers.

Computers Computers are regularly used in desktop publishing, drafting, engineering, yearbook classes. Computer network features include on-campus library services, Internet access, Internet filtering or blocking technology. Campus intranet and student e-mail accounts are available to students. Students grades are available online.

Contact Candace Knight, Dean of Admissions. 248-683-0514. Fax: 248-683-1740. E-mail: cknight@stmarysprep.com. Website: www.stmarysprep.com/

SAINT MARY'S SCHOOL
900 Hillsborough Street
Raleigh, North Carolina 27603-1689
Head of School: Dr. Monica M. Gillespie

General Information Girls' boarding and day college-preparatory, arts, religious studies, bilingual studies, and technology school, affiliated with Episcopal Church. Grades 9–12. Founded: 1842. Setting: urban. Students are housed in single-sex dormitories. 23-acre campus. 26 buildings on campus. Approved or accredited by National Association of Episcopal Schools, North Carolina Association of Independent Schools, Southern Association of Colleges and Schools, Southern Association of Independent Schools, and The Association of Boarding Schools. Member of National Association of Independent Schools and Secondary School Admission Test Board. Total enrollment: 262. Upper school average class size: 12. Upper school faculty-student ratio: 1:8. Upper School students typically attend 5 days per week. The average school day consists of 7 hours.

Upper School Student Profile Grade 9: 56 students (56 girls); Grade 10: 67 students (67 girls); Grade 11: 78 students (78 girls); Grade 12: 61 students (61 girls). 49% of students are boarding students. 78% are state residents. 12 states are represented in upper school student body. 11% are international students. International students from China, Nigeria, Poland, Republic of Korea, United Kingdom, and Viet Nam; 1 other country represented in student body.

Faculty School total: 40. In upper school: 10 men, 30 women; 30 have advanced degrees; 36 reside on campus.

Subjects Offered 3-dimensional art, acting, advanced chemistry, advanced math, Advanced Placement courses, algebra, American government, American history, American history-AP, American literature, anatomy, art, astronomy, athletics, ballet, biology, biology-AP, calculus, calculus-AP, ceramics, chemistry, chemistry-AP, choir, choral music, computer science, dance, drama, drama performance, drawing, drawing and design, earth science, ecology, English, English literature, English literature-AP, European history, French, French language-AP, geometry, government, government-AP, government/civics, honors English, honors geometry, honors U.S. history, honors world history, Latin, Latin-AP, mathematics, philosophy, physical education, physics, physics-AP, piano, psychology-AP, religion, senior project, Spanish, Spanish language-

AP, speech, U.S. government and politics-AP, U.S. history, U.S. history-AP, Western civilization, world literature, yearbook, yoga.

Graduation Requirements Algebra, arts and fine arts (art, music, dance, drama), biology, electives, English, foreign language, geometry, government, physical education (includes health), physical science, religion (includes Bible studies and theology), social sciences, U.S. history, Western civilization.

Special Academic Programs Advanced Placement exam preparation; honors section; independent study; study at local college for college credit; study abroad; academic accommodation for the gifted, the musically talented, and the artistically talented.

College Admission Counseling 73 students graduated in 2015; all went to college.

Student Life Upper grades have specified standards of dress, student council, honor system. Discipline rests equally with students and faculty. Attendance at religious services is required.

Summer Programs Enrichment, sports, art/fine arts, computer instruction programs offered; held on campus; accepts boys and girls; open to students from other schools. 2016 schedule: June 1 to July 31.

Tuition and Aid Day student tuition: $24,850; 7-day tuition and room/board: $49,500. Tuition installment plan (FACTS Tuition Payment Plan, monthly payment plans). Merit scholarship grants, need-based scholarship grants available. In 2015–16, 32% of upper-school students received aid.

Admissions Traditional secondary-level entrance grade is 9. For fall 2015, 178 students applied for upper-level admission, 123 were accepted, 77 enrolled. SSAT and TOEFL required. Deadline for receipt of application materials: none. Application fee required: $100. Interview required.

Athletics Interscholastic: basketball, cross-country running, field hockey, golf, lacrosse, soccer, softball, swimming and diving, tennis, track and field, volleyball; intramural: ballet, dance, dance team, modern dance. 2 PE instructors, 32 coaches, 1 athletic trainer.

Computers Computers are regularly used in dance, English, foreign language, history, introduction to technology, mathematics, newspaper, publications, science, senior seminar, writing, yearbook classes. Computer network features include on-campus library services, online commercial services, Internet access, wireless campus network, Internet filtering or blocking technology. Campus intranet, student e-mail accounts, and computer access in designated common areas are available to students. Students grades are available online. The school has a published electronic and media policy.

Contact Mrs. Elizabeth Lynnes, Manager of Admission Systems and Data. 919-424-4003. Fax: 919-424-4122. E-mail: admission@sms.edu. Website: www.sms.edu

ST. MARY'S SCHOOL
816 Black Oak Drive
Medford, Oregon 97504-8504
Head of School: Mr. Frank Phillips

General Information Coeducational boarding and day college-preparatory, arts, religious studies, and ESL school, affiliated with Roman Catholic Church. Boarding grades 9–12, day grades 6–12. Founded: 1865. Setting: small town. Nearest major city is Eugene. Students are housed in single-sex dormitories. 24-acre campus. 9 buildings on campus. Approved or accredited by National Catholic Education Association, Northwest Accreditation Commission, Northwest Association of Independent Schools, Northwest Association of Schools and Colleges, Office for Standards in Education (OFSTED), and Oregon Department of Education. Member of National Association of Independent Schools. Total enrollment: 467. Upper school average class size: 20. Upper school faculty-student ratio: 1:10. There are 180 required school days per year for Upper School students. Upper School students typically attend 5 days per week. The average school day consists of 7 hours and 15 minutes.

Upper School Student Profile Grade 9: 78 students (44 boys, 34 girls); Grade 10: 88 students (50 boys, 38 girls); Grade 11: 68 students (38 boys, 30 girls); Grade 12: 88 students (52 boys, 36 girls). 15% of students are boarding students. 85% are state residents. 2 states are represented in upper school student body. 15% are international students. International students from China, Republic of Korea, and Thailand; 5 other countries represented in student body. 35% of students are Roman Catholic.

Faculty School total: 48. In upper school: 22 men, 26 women; 21 have advanced degrees; 2 reside on campus.

Subjects Offered Advanced Placement courses, advanced TOEFL/grammar, algebra, American history, American history-AP, American literature, ancient history, art, art history-AP, biology, biology-AP, calculus-AP, chamber groups, chemistry, chemistry-AP, chorus, community service, computer programming-AP, computer science, creative writing, drama, earth science, economics-AP, English, English-AP, environmental science-AP, ESL, ethics, European history, European history-AP, expository writing, fine arts, general science, geometry, German, government/civics, government/civics-AP, grammar, health, history, human geography - AP, instrumental music, jazz band, Latin, Latin-AP, mathematics, music theory-AP, physical education, physics, physics-AP, playwriting and directing, religion, science, social sciences, social studies, Spanish, Spanish-AP, speech, studio art-AP, trigonometry, world history, world literature, writing.

Graduation Requirements Arts and fine arts (art, music, dance, drama), electives, English, foreign language, mathematics, physical education (includes health), religion (includes Bible studies and theology), science, social sciences, social studies (includes history), 28 credits required for graduation, 100 hours of community service (25 each year in Upper School).

Special Academic Programs 24 Advanced Placement exams for which test preparation is offered; independent study; study at local college for college credit; academic accommodation for the gifted, the musically talented, and the artistically talented; ESL (60 students enrolled).

College Admission Counseling 76 students graduated in 2015; all went to college, including Oregon State University; Portland State University; Santa Clara University; University of Oregon; University of Portland; University of San Diego. Mean SAT critical reading: 603, mean SAT math: 565, mean SAT writing: 601, mean combined SAT: 1769, mean composite ACT: 25.

Student Life Upper grades have specified standards of dress, student council, honor system. Discipline rests equally with students and faculty. Attendance at religious services is required.

Summer Programs Enrichment, advancement, sports programs offered; session focuses on enrichment and SAT prep; held both on and off campus; held at various camp locations; accepts boys and girls; open to students from other schools. 75 students usually enrolled. 2016 schedule: June 15 to August 20. Application deadline: none.

Tuition and Aid Tuition installment plan (monthly payment plans, annual payment plan). Need-based scholarship grants available. In 2015–16, 47% of upper-school students received aid. Total amount of financial aid awarded in 2015–16: $1,000,000.

Admissions Traditional secondary-level entrance grade is 9. PSAT required. Deadline for receipt of application materials: February 15. Application fee required: $50. Interview required.

Athletics Interscholastic: baseball (boys), basketball (b,g), combined training (b,g), cross-country running (b,g), football (b), golf (b,g), independent competitive sports (b,g), soccer (b,g), softball (g), swimming and diving (b,g), tennis (b,g), track and field (b,g), volleyball (g); intramural: alpine skiing (b,g), canoeing/kayaking (b,g), equestrian sports (b,g), flag football (g), hiking/backpacking (b,g); coed interscholastic: martial arts; coed intramural: backpacking, bicycling, fencing, fitness, floor hockey, kayaking, outdoor activities, outdoor adventure, rafting, skiing (downhill), strength & conditioning, tennis, weight lifting. 2 PE instructors.

Computers Computers are regularly used in English, history, mathematics, science, speech classes. Computer network features include on-campus library services, online commercial services, Internet access, wireless campus network, Internet filtering or blocking technology, access to homework, daily bulletins, and teachers via email, WiFi. Campus intranet and computer access in designated common areas are available to students. Students grades are available online. The school has a published electronic and media policy.

Contact Ms. Rebecca Naumes Vega, Director of Admissions. 541-773-7877. Fax: 541-772-8973. E-mail: admissions@smschool.us. Website: www.smschool.us

SAINT MAUR INTERNATIONAL SCHOOL

83 Yamate-cho, Naka-ku
Yokohama 231-8654, Japan

Head of School: Mrs. Catherine Osias Endo

General Information Coeducational day college-preparatory, general academic, arts, religious studies, and technology school, affiliated with Roman Catholic Church. Grades PK–12. Founded: 1872. Setting: urban. 1.1-hectare campus. 7 buildings on campus. Approved or accredited by Council of International Schools, East Asia Regional Council of Schools, International Baccalaureate Organization, Ministry of Education, Japan, and New England Association of Schools and Colleges. Language of instruction: English. Total enrollment: 446. Upper school average class size: 36. Upper school faculty-student ratio: 1:4. There are 175 required school days per year for Upper School students. Upper School students typically attend 5 days per week. The average school day consists of 5 hours and 30 minutes.

Upper School Student Profile Grade 9: 39 students (18 boys, 21 girls); Grade 10: 29 students (16 boys, 13 girls); Grade 11: 38 students (16 boys, 22 girls); Grade 12: 37 students (18 boys, 19 girls). 31% of students are Roman Catholic.

Faculty School total: 64. In upper school: 15 men, 17 women; 18 have advanced degrees.

Subjects Offered Algebra, art, biology, calculus, calculus-AP, chemistry, computer science, drama, drama performance, economics, economics-AP, English, fine arts, French, geography, geometry, information technology, Japanese, Japanese history, mathematics, modern Chinese history, modern European history, music, music performance, physical education, physics, psychology, religious studies, science, social studies, Spanish, theory of knowledge, TOEFL preparation, trigonometry, visual arts, world history.

Graduation Requirements Arts and fine arts (art, music, dance, drama), English, foreign language, mathematics, physical education (includes health), religion (includes Bible studies and theology), science, social studies (includes history).

Special Academic Programs International Baccalaureate program; 10 Advanced Placement exams for which test preparation is offered; independent study; academic accommodation for the gifted; ESL.

College Admission Counseling 33 students graduated in 2015; all went to college, including Boston University; Savannah College of Art and Design; Tokyo International University; The University of British Columbia; and Waseda University, Tokyo. Median SAT critical reading: 500, median SAT math: 630, median SAT writing: 540,

median combined SAT: 1670. 20% scored over 600 on SAT critical reading, 67% scored over 600 on SAT math, 23% scored over 600 on SAT writing, 23% scored over 1800 on combined SAT.

Student Life Upper grades have uniform requirement, student council. Discipline rests primarily with faculty. Attendance at religious services is required.

Summer Programs Enrichment, advancement, ESL, sports, art/fine arts, computer instruction programs offered; session focuses on TOEFL and SAT preparation, pre-IB, math, technology; held both on and off campus; held at various off-campus locations; accepts boys and girls; open to students from other schools. 130 students usually enrolled. 2016 schedule: June 15 to July 8. Application deadline: May 15.

Tuition and Aid Day student tuition: ¥2,145,000. Tuition installment plan (tuition installment upon request).

Admissions For fall 2015, 30 students applied for upper-level admission, 21 were accepted, 18 enrolled. School's own test required. Deadline for receipt of application materials: none. Application fee required: ¥20,000. Interview required.

Athletics Interscholastic: baseball (boys), basketball (b,g), cross-country running (b,g), soccer (b,g), volleyball (g); intramural: soccer (b); coed interscholastic: cross-country running, table tennis. 2 PE instructors.

Computers Computers are regularly used in art, computer applications, economics, English, foreign language, French, geography, independent study, mathematics, music, psychology, SAT preparation, science, social studies, Spanish, technology classes. Computer network features include on-campus library services, Internet access, wireless campus network, Internet filtering or blocking technology, iPad. Campus intranet, student e-mail accounts, and computer access in designated common areas are available to students. Students grades are available online. The school has a published electronic and media policy.

Contact Mr. Richard B. Rucci, Director of Admissions. 81-(0) 45-641-5751. Fax: 81-(0) 45-641-6688. E-mail: rrucci@stmaur.ac.jp. Website: www.stmaur.ac.jp

ST. MICHAEL'S COLLEGE SCHOOL

1515 Bathurst Street
Toronto, Ontario M5P 3H4, Canada

Head of School: Fr. Jefferson Thomson, CSB

General Information Boys' day college-preparatory and religious studies school, affiliated with Roman Catholic Church. Grades 7–12. Founded: 1852. Setting: urban. 10-acre campus. 2 buildings on campus. Approved or accredited by Ontario Ministry of Education and Ontario Department of Education. Member of Secondary School Admission Test Board. Language of instruction: English. Total enrollment: 1,029. Upper school average class size: 24. Upper school faculty-student ratio: 1:16. There are 184 required school days per year for Upper School students. Upper School students typically attend 5 days per week. The average school day consists of 6 hours and 19 minutes.

Upper School Student Profile Grade 9: 212 students (212 boys); Grade 10: 193 students (193 boys); Grade 11: 208 students (208 boys); Grade 12: 211 students (211 boys). 90% of students are Roman Catholic.

Faculty School total: 70. In upper school: 62 men, 8 women; 20 have advanced degrees.

Subjects Offered Advanced Placement courses, American history, anatomy and physiology, ancient history, art, biology, calculus, calculus-AP, Canadian geography, Canadian history, Canadian law, Canadian literature, career and personal planning, career education, chemistry, civics, computer multimedia, economics, English, English composition, English literature, finite math, French, functions, geography, history, history-AP, Italian, Latin, leadership, mathematics, media arts, modern Western civilization, outdoor education, physical education, religion, robotics, science, Spanish, theology, world religions.

Graduation Requirements English, religion (includes Bible studies and theology), 20 hours of community service, 20 hours of Christian service must be completed over the 4 years of high school.

Special Academic Programs 3 Advanced Placement exams for which test preparation is offered.

College Admission Counseling 205 students graduated in 2015; 200 went to college, including Queen's University at Kingston; Ryerson University; The University of Western Ontario; University of Guelph; University of Toronto; York University. Other: 5 entered a postgraduate year.

Student Life Upper grades have uniform requirement, student council, honor system. Discipline rests primarily with faculty. Attendance at religious services is required.

Summer Programs Sports programs offered; session focuses on hockey and lacrosse; held on campus; accepts boys; open to students from other schools. 2016 schedule: July 4 to August 12. Application deadline: June 17.

Tuition and Aid Day student tuition: CAN$18,100. Tuition installment plan (monthly payment plans, individually arranged payment plans). Bursaries, merit scholarship grants, need-based scholarship grants available. In 2015–16, 15% of upper-school students received aid; total upper-school merit-scholarship money awarded: CAN$105,000. Total amount of financial aid awarded in 2015–16: CAN$1,800,000.

Admissions Traditional secondary-level entrance grade is 9. For fall 2015, 268 students applied for upper-level admission, 244 were accepted, 122 enrolled. SSAT required. Deadline for receipt of application materials: none. Application fee required: CAN$125.

Athletics Interscholastic: alpine skiing, aquatics, archery, badminton, baseball, basketball, cross-country running, football, golf, ice hockey, indoor track & field, lacrosse, mountain biking, nordic skiing, rugby, skiing (cross-country), skiing (downhill), snowboarding, soccer, softball, swimming and diving, tennis, track and field, volleyball; intramural: archery, badminton, ball hockey, basketball, fishing, fitness, flag football, ice hockey, indoor soccer, outdoor education, soccer, tennis, touch football. 2 athletic trainers.

Computers Computers are regularly used in all academic, media arts classes. Computer network features include on-campus library services, Internet access, wireless campus network, Internet filtering or blocking technology. Student e-mail accounts and computer access in designated common areas are available to students. The school has a published electronic and media policy.

Contact Ms. Marilyn Furgiuele, Admissions Assistant. 416-653-3180 Ext. 438. Fax: 416-653-7704. E-mail: furgiuele@smcsmail.com. Website: www.stmichaelscollegeschool.com

ST. MICHAEL'S PREPARATORY SCHOOL OF THE NORBERTINE FATHERS

19292 El Toro Road
Silverado, California 92676-9710

Head of School: Rev. Victor J. Szczurek, OPRAEM

General Information Boys' boarding college-preparatory and religious studies school, affiliated with Roman Catholic Church. Grades 9–12. Founded: 1961. Setting: suburban. Nearest major city is Los Angeles. Students are housed in single-sex dormitories. 35-acre campus. 4 buildings on campus. Approved or accredited by National Catholic Education Association, Western Association of Schools and Colleges, and California Department of Education. Total enrollment: 64. Upper school average class size: 12. Upper school faculty-student ratio: 1:3. There are 180 required school days per year for Upper School students. Upper School students typically attend 5 days per week. The average school day consists of 7 hours.

Upper School Student Profile Grade 9: 16 students (16 boys); Grade 10: 16 students (16 boys); Grade 11: 16 students (16 boys); Grade 12: 16 students (16 boys). 100% of students are boarding students. 95% are state residents. 5% are international students. International students from China, France, Hong Kong, Mexico, Spain, and Viet Nam. 95% of students are Roman Catholic.

Faculty School total: 24. In upper school: 24 men; 18 have advanced degrees; 15 reside on campus.

Subjects Offered Advanced Placement courses, algebra, American history, American history-AP, American literature, ancient history, art history, Bible studies, biology, calculus-AP, chemistry, chorus, economics, economics-AP, English, English literature, ethics, fine arts, geography, geometry, government-AP, government/civics, Greek, health, history, Latin, Latin-AP, mathematics, philosophy, physical education, physical science, physics, pre-calculus, religion, science, social studies, theology, trigonometry, world literature.

Graduation Requirements Arts and fine arts (art, music, dance, drama), English, foreign language, mathematics, physical education (includes health), religion (includes Bible studies and theology), science, social studies (includes history), Senior Matura.

Special Academic Programs Advanced Placement exam preparation; honors section; independent study; academic accommodation for the gifted; ESL.

College Admission Counseling 17 students graduated in 2015; all went to college, including California State University, Fullerton; California State University, Long Beach; Thomas Aquinas College; University of California, Davis; University of Dallas; University of Notre Dame. Median combined SAT: 1844, median composite ACT: 28.

Student Life Upper grades have uniform requirement, student council, honor system. Discipline rests equally with students and faculty. Attendance at religious services is required.

Tuition and Aid 5-day tuition and room/board: $22,785. Tuition installment plan (FACTS Tuition Payment Plan, monthly payment plans, individually arranged payment plans). Need-based scholarship grants available. In 2015–16, 80% of upper-school students received aid. Total amount of financial aid awarded in 2015–16: $500,000.

Admissions Traditional secondary-level entrance grade is 9. High School Placement Test required. Deadline for receipt of application materials: none. Application fee required: $100. Interview required.

Athletics Interscholastic: baseball, basketball, cross-country running, football, running, soccer; intramural: archery, field hockey, outdoor activities, outdoor recreation, physical fitness, physical training, skateboarding, strength & conditioning, surfing, swimming and diving, table tennis, volleyball, weight lifting. 2 PE instructors, 7 coaches, 5 athletic trainers.

Computers Computers are regularly used in creative writing, English, mathematics, science, writing classes. Computer network features include on-campus library services, Internet access, Internet filtering or blocking technology. Campus intranet, student e-mail accounts, and computer access in designated common areas are available to students. Students grades are available online. The school has a published electronic and media policy.

Contact Mrs. Pamela M. Christian, School Secretary. 949-858-0222 Ext. 237. Fax: 949-858-7365. E-mail: admissions@stmichaelsprep.org. Website: www.stmichaelsprep.org

ST. PATRICK CATHOLIC HIGH SCHOOL

18300 St. Patrick Road
Biloxi, Mississippi 39532

Head of School: Mrs. J. Renee McDaniel

General Information Coeducational day college-preparatory and religious studies school, affiliated with Roman Catholic Church; primarily serves dyslexic students. Grades 7–12. Founded: 2007. Setting: rural. 32-acre campus. 7 buildings on campus. Approved or accredited by Southern Association of Colleges and Schools and Mississippi Department of Education. Endowment: $400,000. Total enrollment: 441. Upper school average class size: 20. Upper school faculty-student ratio: 1:13. There are 180 required school days per year for Upper School students. Upper School students typically attend 5 days per week. The average school day consists of 6 hours and 45 minutes.

Upper School Student Profile Grade 7: 87 students (39 boys, 48 girls); Grade 8: 53 students (29 boys, 24 girls); Grade 9: 60 students (25 boys, 35 girls); Grade 10: 86 students (42 boys, 44 girls); Grade 11: 61 students (22 boys, 39 girls); Grade 12: 90 students (47 boys, 43 girls); Postgraduate: 440 students (204 boys, 236 girls). 80% of students are Roman Catholic.

Faculty School total: 37. In upper school: 14 men, 20 women; 16 have advanced degrees.

Subjects Offered Accounting, advanced chemistry, advanced computer applications, advanced math, Advanced Placement courses, algebra, American government, American history, American literature, analytic geometry, anatomy and physiology, art, athletics, band, baseball, Basic programming, basketball, biology, British literature, business applications, business law, calculus, calculus-AP, campus ministry, Catholic belief and practice, cheerleading, chemistry, chemistry-AP, choral music, Christian and Hebrew scripture, church history, civics, college counseling, college placement, college planning, composition-AP, computer applications, creative writing, desktop publishing, drama, driver education, earth science, economics, English, English literature and composition-AP, environmental science, French, geometry, global studies, health, humanities, introduction to theater, journalism, keyboarding, law, Life of Christ, marching band, marine biology, marine science, oral communications, physical education, physical science, pre-algebra, pre-calculus, probability and statistics, psychology, softball, Spanish, track and field, trigonometry, U.S. government, U.S. history, U.S. history-AP, volleyball, Web site design, weight fitness, weight training, weightlifting, wood processing, world geography, world history, yearbook.

Graduation Requirements Algebra, American literature, American literature, art, biology, British literature, cell biology, chemistry, computer applications, English literature, foreign language, physical education (includes health), state history, U.S. government, U.S. history, world geography, world history, world literature, religion.

Special Academic Programs International Baccalaureate program; Advanced Placement exam preparation; independent study; study at local college for college credit; programs in general development for dyslexic students.

College Admission Counseling 70 students graduated in 2015; all went to college, including Louisiana State University and Agricultural & Mechanical College; Millsaps College; Mississippi State University; University of Mississippi; University of South Alabama; University of Southern Mississippi. Mean SAT critical reading: 647, mean SAT math: 623, mean SAT writing: 617, mean composite ACT: 24. 67% scored over 600 on SAT critical reading, 83% scored over 600 on SAT math, 67% scored over 600 on SAT writing, 37% scored over 26 on composite ACT.

Student Life Upper grades have uniform requirement, student council, honor system. Discipline rests primarily with faculty. Attendance at religious services is required.

Summer Programs Remediation, sports, art/fine arts, computer instruction programs offered; session focuses on robotics/sports; held on campus; accepts boys and girls; open to students from other schools. 100 students usually enrolled. 2016 schedule: June 1 to July 17. Application deadline: May 31.

Tuition and Aid Day student tuition: $7150. Tuition installment plan (monthly payments through local bank). Tuition reduction for siblings, need-based scholarship grants available. In 2015–16, 25% of upper-school students received aid. Total amount of financial aid awarded in 2015–16: $168,524.

Admissions Traditional secondary-level entrance grade is 7. For fall 2015, 443 students applied for upper-level admission, 443 were accepted, 441 enrolled. PSAT required. Deadline for receipt of application materials: none. No application fee required. Interview required.

Athletics Interscholastic: baseball (boys), basketball (b,g), cheering (g), cross-country running (b,g), dance team (g), football (b), golf (b,g), power lifting (b,g), soccer (b,g), softball (g), strength & conditioning (b), swimming and diving (b,g), tennis (b,g), track and field (b,g), volleyball (g), weight lifting (b,g), weight training (b,g); coed interscholastic: sailing; coed intramural: sailing. 2 PE instructors, 26 coaches, 1 athletic trainer.

Computers Computers are regularly used in accounting, business applications, business education, computer applications, desktop publishing, journalism, mathematics, newspaper, Web site design, word processing, yearbook classes. Computer network features include on-campus library services, Internet access, Internet filtering or blocking technology. Campus intranet and computer access in designated common areas are available to students. Students grades are available online. The school has a published electronic and media policy.

Contact Mrs. Theresa Whiteside, Records Clerk. 228-702-0500. Fax: 228-702-0511. E-mail: twhiteside@stpatrickhighschool.net. Website: www.stpatrickhighschool.net

SAINT PATRICK HIGH SCHOOL

5900 West Belmont Avenue
Chicago, Illinois 60634

Head of School: Dr. Joseph G. Schmidt, EdD

General Information Boys' day college-preparatory, arts, and religious studies school, affiliated with Roman Catholic Church. Grades 9–12. Founded: 1861. Setting: urban. 1 building on campus. Approved or accredited by Christian Brothers Association, National Catholic Education Association, North Central Association of Colleges and Schools, and Illinois Department of Education. Endowment: $5.3 million. Total enrollment: 648. Upper school average class size: 21. Upper school faculty-student ratio: 1:17. There are 180 required school days per year for Upper School students. Upper School students typically attend 5 days per week. The average school day consists of 6 hours and 40 minutes.

Upper School Student Profile Grade 9: 157 students (157 boys); Grade 10: 196 students (196 boys); Grade 11: 160 students (160 boys); Grade 12: 135 students (135 boys). 77% of students are Roman Catholic.

Faculty School total: 55. In upper school: 36 men, 19 women; 39 have advanced degrees.

Subjects Offered Accounting, algebra, American history, American literature, anatomy, art, art history, biology, broadcasting, business, business skills, calculus, chemistry, Chinese, chorus, computer graphics, computer science, creative writing, drama, driver education, ecology, economics, English, English as a foreign language, English literature, ethics, European history, fine arts, French, geography, geometry, government/civics, grammar, health, history, journalism, keyboarding, mathematics, music, physical education, physics, psychology, religion, science, social sciences, social studies, sociology, Spanish, speech, theater, trigonometry, word processing, world history, writing.

Graduation Requirements Arts and fine arts (art, music, dance, drama), business skills (includes word processing), computer science, English, mathematics, physical education (includes health), religion (includes Bible studies and theology), science, service learning/internship, social sciences, social studies (includes history), participation in a retreat program. Community service is required.

Special Academic Programs Advanced Placement exam preparation; honors section; study at local college for college credit; remedial reading and/or remedial writing; remedial math.

College Admission Counseling 178 students graduated in 2015; 168 went to college, including DePaul University; Loyola University Chicago; Northeastern Illinois University; Northern Illinois University; University of Illinois at Chicago; University of Illinois at Urbana–Champaign. Other: 2 went to work, 4 entered military service, 4 had other specific plans. Mean composite ACT: 21. 26% scored over 26 on composite ACT.

Student Life Upper grades have specified standards of dress, student council, honor system. Discipline rests primarily with faculty. Attendance at religious services is required.

Summer Programs Remediation, enrichment, advancement, sports, art/fine arts, computer instruction programs offered; session focuses on remediation and enrichment; held on campus; accepts boys and girls; open to students from other schools. 160 students usually enrolled. 2016 schedule: June 6 to July 29. Application deadline: June 1.

Tuition and Aid Day student tuition: $11,000. Guaranteed tuition plan. Tuition installment plan (monthly payment plans, quarterly payment plan). Merit scholarship grants, need-based scholarship grants, legacy (sons and grandsons of alumni) available. In 2015–16, 48% of upper-school students received aid; total upper-school merit-scholarship money awarded: $180,000. Total amount of financial aid awarded in 2015–16: $1,170,000.

Admissions Traditional secondary-level entrance grade is 9. For fall 2015, 284 students applied for upper-level admission, 282 were accepted, 157 enrolled. ACT-Explore or any standardized test required. Deadline for receipt of application materials: none. No application fee required. On-campus interview required.

Athletics Interscholastic: baseball, basketball, bowling, cross-country running, diving, fishing, football, golf, ice hockey, indoor track & field, soccer, swimming and diving, tennis, track and field, volleyball, water polo, wrestling; intramural: basketball, flagball, football, kickball, life saving, volleyball. 2 PE instructors, 2 coaches, 1 athletic trainer.

Computers Computers are regularly used in business, English, foreign language, geography, graphic arts, graphic design, graphics, history, information technology, introduction to technology, library skills, mathematics, media arts, media production, media services, newspaper, photojournalism, religion, remedial study skills, research skills, science, typing, word processing, yearbook classes. Computer network features include on-campus library services, online commercial services, Internet access, wireless campus network, Internet filtering or blocking technology. Student e-mail accounts are available to students. Students grades are available online. The school has a published electronic and media policy.

Contact Brian O'Connor, Admissions Counselor. 773-282-8844 Ext. 286. Fax: 773-282-2361. E-mail: boconnor@stpatrick.org. Website: www.stpatrick.org

ST. PATRICK'S REGIONAL SECONDARY

115 East 11th Avenue
Vancouver, British Columbia V5T 2C1, Canada

Head of School: Mr. Ralph J. Gabriele

General Information Coeducational day college-preparatory, general academic, arts, business, religious studies, and technology school, affiliated with Roman Catholic Church. Grades 8–12. Founded: 1923. Setting: urban. 2 buildings on campus. Approved or accredited by British Columbia Department of Education. Language of instruction: English. Total enrollment: 500. Upper school average class size: 25. There are 180 required school days per year for Upper School students. Upper School students typically attend 5 days per week. The average school day consists of 6 hours.

Upper School Student Profile Grade 8: 100 students (50 boys, 50 girls); Grade 9: 87 students (37 boys, 50 girls); Grade 10: 99 students (41 boys, 58 girls); Grade 11: 104 students (35 boys, 69 girls); Grade 12: 100 students (34 boys, 66 girls). 97% of students are Roman Catholic.

Faculty School total: 35. In upper school: 15 men, 15 women; 8 have advanced degrees.

Special Academic Programs Advanced Placement exam preparation; ESL (15 students enrolled).

College Admission Counseling 100 students graduated in 2015; all went to college, including University of Alaska Fairbanks.

Student Life Upper grades have uniform requirement. Attendance at religious services is required.

Tuition and Aid Tuition installment plan (monthly payment plans).

Admissions Application fee required: CAN$100. Interview required.

Athletics Interscholastic: basketball (boys, girls), dance squad (b,g), soccer (b,g), track and field (b,g), volleyball (g), wrestling (b,g); intramural: dance squad (b,g); coed interscholastic: dance squad; coed intramural: badminton, ball hockey, dance squad. 5 PE instructors, 5 coaches.

Computers The school has a published electronic and media policy.

Contact Mr. Ralph J. Gabriele, Principal. 604-874-6422. Fax: 604-874-5176. E-mail: administration@stpats.bc.ca. Website: www.stpats.bc.ca

ST. PAUL ACADEMY AND SUMMIT SCHOOL

1712 Randolph Avenue
St. Paul, Minnesota 55105

Head of School: Bryn S. Roberts

General Information Coeducational day college-preparatory school. Grades K–12. Founded: 1900. Setting: urban. 32-acre campus. 4 buildings on campus. Approved or accredited by Independent Schools Association of the Central States, National Independent Private Schools Association, and Minnesota Department of Education. Member of National Association of Independent Schools. Endowment: $42.3 million. Total enrollment: 918. Upper school average class size: 15. Upper school faculty-student ratio: 1:8. Upper School students typically attend 5 days per week.

Upper School Student Profile Grade 9: 109 students (55 boys, 54 girls); Grade 10: 101 students (52 boys, 49 girls); Grade 11: 113 students (59 boys, 54 girls); Grade 12: 96 students (42 boys, 54 girls).

Faculty School total: 109. In upper school: 19 men, 25 women; 36 have advanced degrees.

Subjects Offered Algebra, American literature, art, biology, calculus, ceramics, chemistry, Chinese, creative writing, current events, debate, drama, earth science, economics, English, English literature, European history, expository writing, fine arts, French, geometry, German, journalism, law and the legal system, marine biology, mathematics, multicultural studies, music, music theory, newspaper, photography, physical education, physics, psychology, science, senior project, Shakespeare, social psychology, social studies, sociology, space and physical sciences, Spanish, trigonometry, world history, world literature, world religions, yearbook.

Graduation Requirements Arts and fine arts (art, music, dance, drama), English, foreign language, mathematics, physical education (includes health), science, social studies (includes history), month-long senior project, senior speech.

Special Academic Programs Honors section; independent study; term-away projects; study abroad.

College Admission Counseling 89 students graduated in 2015; all went to college, including Carleton College; Northeastern University; St. Olaf College; University of Minnesota, Twin Cities Campus; University of Wisconsin–Madison. Median SAT critical reading: 640, median SAT math: 650, median SAT writing: 620, median combined SAT: 1870, median composite ACT: 30. 62% scored over 600 on SAT critical reading, 68% scored over 600 on SAT math, 57% scored over 600 on SAT writing, 64% scored over 1800 on combined SAT, 78% scored over 26 on composite ACT.

Student Life Upper grades have specified standards of dress, student council. Discipline rests equally with students and faculty.

Summer Programs Enrichment programs offered; held on campus; accepts boys and girls; open to students from other schools.

Tuition and Aid Day student tuition: $27,500. Tuition installment plan (Insured Tuition Payment Plan, monthly payment plans). Need-based scholarship grants available. In 2015–16, 23% of upper-school students received aid. Total amount of financial aid awarded in 2015–16: $3,200,000.

Admissions Traditional secondary-level entrance grade is 9. For fall 2015, 82 students applied for upper-level admission, 46 were accepted, 32 enrolled. SSAT, ERB, PSAT, SAT, PLAN or ACT or writing sample required. Deadline for receipt of application materials: February 1. Application fee required: $75. Interview required.

Athletics Interscholastic: alpine skiing (boys, girls), baseball (b), basketball (b,g), cross-country running (b,g), dance team (g), diving (b,g), fencing (b,g), football (b), golf (b,g), ice hockey (b,g), lacrosse (g), skiing (cross-country) (b,g), skiing (downhill) (b,g), soccer (b,g), softball (g), swimming and diving (b,g), tennis (b,g), volleyball (g); intramural: outdoor adventure (b,g); coed interscholastic: strength & conditioning, track and field; coed intramural: hiking/backpacking, physical fitness, snowboarding, table tennis. 3 PE instructors, 90 coaches, 1 athletic trainer.

Computers Computers are regularly used in all academic classes. Computer network features include on-campus library services, online commercial services, Internet access, wireless campus network, Internet filtering or blocking technology, laptop program (beginning in grade 6). Student e-mail accounts and computer access in designated common areas are available to students. The school has a published electronic and media policy.

Contact Mrs. Heather Cameron Ploen, Director of Admission and Financial Aid. 651-698-2451. Fax: 651-698-6787. E-mail: hploen@spa.edu. Website: www.spa.edu

SAINT PAUL LUTHERAN HIGH SCHOOL

205 South Main Street
PO Box 719
Concordia, Missouri 64020

Head of School: Rev. Paul M. Mehl

General Information Coeducational boarding and day college-preparatory, general academic, arts, and religious studies school, affiliated with Lutheran Church–Missouri Synod. Grades 9–12. Founded: 1883. Setting: small town. Nearest major city is Kansas City. Students are housed in single-sex dormitories. 50-acre campus. 9 buildings on campus. Approved or accredited by Lutheran School Accreditation Commission, Midwest Association of Boarding Schools, North Central Association of Colleges and Schools, and Missouri Department of Education. Endowment: $2.5 million. Total enrollment: 189. Upper school average class size: 20. Upper school faculty-student ratio: 1:9. There are 173 required school days per year for Upper School students. Upper School students typically attend 5 days per week. The average school day consists of 6 hours.

Upper School Student Profile Grade 9: 40 students (24 boys, 16 girls); Grade 10: 29 students (14 boys, 15 girls); Grade 11: 72 students (31 boys, 41 girls); Grade 12: 48 students (24 boys, 24 girls). 43% are state residents. 15 states are represented in upper school student body. 40% are international students. 60% of students are Lutheran Church–Missouri Synod.

Faculty School total: 21. In upper school: 12 men, 9 women; 18 have advanced degrees; 9 reside on campus.

Subjects Offered Accounting, ADL skills, advanced biology, algebra, American history, American literature, analytic geometry, art, athletic training, band, Bible studies, biology, business law, calculus, ceramics, chemistry, child development, chorus, Christian doctrine, church history, community service, comparative religion, composition, computer science, concert choir, creative writing, current events, drama, drawing, economics, English, English literature, ESL, family studies, freshman seminar, general science, geography, geometry, German, government/civics, health, human anatomy, music appreciation, music theory, novels, painting, physical education, physical science, physics, poetry, pre-algebra, psychology, religion, Shakespeare, sociology, Spanish, speech, statistics, theology, trigonometry, world history, world literature, writing.

Graduation Requirements Arts and fine arts (art, music, dance, drama), computer science, English, foreign language, mathematics, physical education (includes health), practical arts, religion (includes Bible studies and theology), science, social studies (includes history), 3.0 grade point average on a 4.0 scale for college preparatory students, above (national) average score on ACT or SAT. Community service is required.

Special Academic Programs International Baccalaureate program; independent study; study at local college for college credit.

College Admission Counseling 40 students graduated in 2015; 38 went to college, including Concordia University Irvine; Rockhurst University; University of Central Missouri; University of Missouri. Other: 2 went to work. Median SAT critical reading: 450, median SAT math: 650, median SAT writing: 490, median combined SAT: 1590, median composite ACT: 24. 15% scored over 600 on SAT critical reading, 66% scored over 600 on SAT math, 14% scored over 600 on SAT writing, 26% scored over 1800 on combined SAT, 40% scored over 26 on composite ACT.

Student Life Upper grades have specified standards of dress, student council, honor system. Discipline rests primarily with faculty. Attendance at religious services is required.

Tuition and Aid Day student tuition: $10,700; 7-day tuition and room/board: $15,950. Guaranteed tuition plan. Tuition installment plan (monthly payment plans, individually arranged payment plans, lump sum payment discount plan). Tuition reduction for siblings, need-based scholarship grants, paying campus jobs, LCMS Grants for church vocation students, early bird tuition grants available. In 2015–16, 54% of upper-school students received aid. Total amount of financial aid awarded in 2015–16: $273,555.

Admissions Traditional secondary-level entrance grade is 9. For fall 2015, 106 students applied for upper-level admission, 105 were accepted, 96 enrolled. School placement exam and SLEP for foreign students required. Deadline for receipt of application materials: none. Application fee required: $100. On-campus interview recommended.

Athletics Interscholastic: baseball (boys), basketball (b,g), cheering (g), cross-country running (b,g), football (b), golf (b,g), soccer (b,g), softball (g), track and field (b,g), volleyball (g); intramural: baseball (b), basketball (b,g), dance team (g), football (b), golf (b,g), jogging (b,g), roller blading (b,g), running (b,g), soccer (b,g), softball (g), strength & conditioning (b,g), tennis (b,g), volleyball (b,g), weight lifting (b,g); coed interscholastic: cross-country running, track and field; coed intramural: jogging, roller blading, running, soccer, table tennis, ultimate Frisbee. 2 PE instructors, 1 coach.

Computers Computers are regularly used in Christian doctrine, creative writing, data processing, English, freshman foundations, history, keyboarding, lab/keyboard, library skills, religious studies, speech, study skills, word processing, writing, writing classes. Computer resources include Internet access, wireless campus network. Students grades are available online. The school has a published electronic and media policy.

Contact Mr. Clint Colwell, Director of Recruitment. 660-463-2238 Ext. 245. Fax: 660-463-7621. E-mail: admissions@splhs.org. Website: www.splhs.org

ST. PAUL PREPARATORY SCHOOL

380 Jackson Street
Suite 100
Saint Paul, Minnesota 55101

Head of School: Mr. John Belpedio

General Information Coeducational day college-preparatory, general academic, arts, business, bilingual studies, technology, and Liberal Arts school. Grades 9–12. Founded: 2003. Setting: urban. Nearest major city is St. Paul. 2-acre campus. 1 building on campus. Approved or accredited by North Central Association of Colleges and Schools and Minnesota Department of Education. Total enrollment: 166. Upper school average class size: 13. Upper school faculty-student ratio: 1:12. There are 175 required school days per year for Upper School students. Upper School students typically attend 5 days per week. The average school day consists of 6 hours and 44 minutes.

Upper School Student Profile Grade 9: 1 student (1 girl); Grade 10: 27 students (16 boys, 11 girls); Grade 11: 40 students (21 boys, 19 girls); Grade 12: 98 students (53 boys, 45 girls).

Faculty School total: 19. In upper school: 9 men, 9 women; 9 have advanced degrees.

Subjects Offered Advanced Placement courses, algebra, American history, American literature, art, art history, aviation, biology, calculus, chemistry, chemistry-AP, Chinese, college admission preparation, composition, computer science, computer science-AP, creative writing, drama, drawing, economics, English as a foreign language, English composition, English literature and composition-AP, ESL, fitness, French, geography, geometry, guitar, health, internship, intro to computers, introduction to literature, life science, literature, music, music theory-AP, painting, physical education, physical fitness, physical science, physics, pre-calculus, psychology, robotics, SAT preparation, sociology, Spanish, Spanish literature, speech, statistics-AP, theater, U.S. history, U.S. history-AP, world history, world history-AP, world literature, writing, writing, writing workshop, yearbook.

Special Academic Programs International Baccalaureate program; 9 Advanced Placement exams for which test preparation is offered; honors section; accelerated programs; study at local college for college credit; study abroad; academic accommodation for the musically talented and the artistically talented; ESL (100 students enrolled).

College Admission Counseling 78 students graduated in 2015; 70 went to college, including Hamline University; University of Minnesota, Twin Cities Campus; University of St. Thomas. Other: 8 had other specific plans. Mean SAT critical reading: 494, mean SAT math: 476, mean SAT writing: 532, mean combined SAT: 1502, mean composite ACT: 23.

Student Life Upper grades have specified standards of dress, student council, honor system. Discipline rests equally with students and faculty.

Summer Programs Enrichment, advancement, ESL programs offered; session focuses on language and culture; held both on and off campus; held at various international countries; accepts boys and girls; open to students from other schools. 30 students usually enrolled. 2016 schedule: July 8 to August 3. Application deadline: May 1.

Tuition and Aid Day student tuition: $10,500. Tuition installment plan (monthly payment plans, individually arranged payment plans, Admissions & Enrollment Financial Aid Assessment Tuition Management (TADS)). Merit scholarship grants, need-based scholarship grants available. In 2015–16, 60% of upper-school students received aid; total upper-school merit-scholarship money awarded: $4500. Total amount of financial aid awarded in 2015–16: $5500.

Admissions Traditional secondary-level entrance grade is 11. For fall 2015, 2,180 students applied for upper-level admission, 167 were accepted, 166 enrolled. Iowa Tests of Basic Skills, Stanford Achievement Test or TOEFL or SLEP required. Deadline for receipt of application materials: none. No application fee required. Interview required.

Athletics Interscholastic: basketball (boys, girls), soccer (b,g); coed interscholastic: track and field; coed intramural: badminton, Frisbee, table tennis, ultimate Frisbee, volleyball. 1 PE instructor, 4 coaches.

Computers Computers are regularly used in aviation, college planning, creative writing, English, ESL, foreign language, mathematics, SAT preparation, science, social sciences, Web site design, writing, yearbook classes. Computer network features include Internet access, wireless campus network, Internet filtering or blocking technology, PowerSchool Database Host. Computer access in designated common areas is available to students. Students grades are available online. The school has a published electronic and media policy.

Contact Annika Bowers, Admissions Director. 651-288-4610. Fax: 651-288-4616. E-mail: abowers@stpaulprep.org. Website: www.stpaulprep.org

ST. PAUL'S HIGH SCHOOL

2200 Grant Avenue
Winnipeg, Manitoba R3P 0P8, Canada

Head of School: Fr. Len Altilia, SJ

General Information Boys' day college-preparatory, arts, religious studies, and technology school, affiliated with Roman Catholic Church. Grades 9–12. Founded: 1926. Setting: suburban. 18-acre campus. 6 buildings on campus. Approved or accredited by Jesuit Secondary Education Association and Manitoba Department of Education. Language of instruction: English. Endowment: CAN$7.5 million. Total enrollment: 554. Upper school average class size: 26. Upper school faculty-student ratio: 1:14. There are 196 required school days per year for Upper School students. Upper School students typically attend 5 days per week. The average school day consists of 5 hours and 50 minutes.

Upper School Student Profile Grade 9: 125 students (125 boys); Grade 10: 145 students (145 boys); Grade 11: 139 students (139 boys); Grade 12: 145 students (145 boys). 68% of students are Roman Catholic.

Faculty School total: 44. In upper school: 32 men, 10 women; 19 have advanced degrees.

Subjects Offered Algebra, American history, art, biology, calculus, chemistry, classics, computer science, current events, economics, English, ethics, French, geography, geometry, history, law, mathematics, media, multimedia, multimedia design, music, Native American studies, physical education, physics, political science, psychology, religion, science, social studies, speech, theology, world wide web design.

Graduation Requirements English, mathematics, physical education (includes health), religion (includes Bible studies and theology), science, social studies (includes history), completion of Christian service program.

Special Academic Programs Advanced Placement exam preparation; honors section; remedial math.

College Admission Counseling 147 students graduated in 2015; 117 went to college, including McGill University; Queen's University at Kingston; The University of British Columbia; The University of Winnipeg; University of Manitoba; University of Toronto. Other: 30 had other specific plans.

Student Life Upper grades have specified standards of dress, student council, honor system. Discipline rests primarily with faculty. Attendance at religious services is required.

Summer Programs Sports programs offered; session focuses on sport skills and relationship building; held on campus; accepts boys; open to students from other schools. 80 students usually enrolled. 2016 schedule: August 19 to September 1.

Tuition and Aid Day student tuition: CAN$8300. Tuition installment plan (Insured Tuition Payment Plan, monthly payment plans, individually arranged payment plans). Bursaries, need-based loans available. In 2015–16, 14% of upper-school students received aid. Total amount of financial aid awarded in 2015–16: CAN$355,200.

Admissions Traditional secondary-level entrance grade is 9. Achievement tests and STS required. Deadline for receipt of application materials: February 1. Application fee required: CAN$100. On-campus interview required.

Athletics Interscholastic: badminton, basketball, cross-country running, curling, football, golf, ice hockey, indoor track, indoor track & field, rugby, soccer, track and field, ultimate Frisbee, volleyball, wrestling; intramural: badminton, basketball, curling, fitness, flag football, golf, physical fitness, physical training, skiing (downhill), strength & conditioning, table tennis, volleyball, weight training. 4 PE instructors, 1 athletic trainer.

Computers Computers are regularly used in French, French as a second language, geography, mathematics, multimedia, religious studies, science, Web site design classes. Computer network features include on-campus library services, online commercial services, Internet access, wireless campus network, Internet filtering or blocking technology. Campus intranet, student e-mail accounts, and computer access in designated common areas are available to students. Students grades are available online. The school has a published electronic and media policy.

Contact Mr. Bob Lewin, Principal. 204-831-2300. Fax: 204-831-2340. E-mail: blewin@stpauls.mb.ca. Website: www.stpauls.mb.ca

ST. PAUL'S SCHOOL

325 Pleasant Street
Concord, New Hampshire 03301-2591

Head of School: Mr. Michael G. Hirschfeld

General Information Coeducational boarding college-preparatory and arts school, affiliated with Episcopal Church. Grades 9–12. Founded: 1856. Setting: suburban. Students are housed in single-sex dormitories. 2,000-acre campus. 75 buildings on campus. Approved or accredited by Association of Independent Schools in New England, National Association of Episcopal Schools, New England Association of Schools and Colleges, The Association of Boarding Schools, and New Hampshire Department of Education. Member of National Association of Independent Schools and Secondary School Admission Test Board. Endowment: $573 million. Total enrollment: 541. Upper school average class size: 11. Upper school faculty-student ratio: 1:5. Upper School students typically attend 5 days per week. The average school day consists of 6 hours.

Upper School Student Profile Grade 9: 115 students (60 boys, 55 girls); Grade 10: 139 students (68 boys, 71 girls); Grade 11: 148 students (76 boys, 72 girls); Grade 12: 139 students (71 boys, 68 girls). 100% of students are boarding students. 11% are state residents. 30 states are represented in upper school student body. 17% are international students. International students from Canada, China, Democratic People's Republic of Korea, Hong Kong, Japan, and United Kingdom; 16 other countries represented in student body. 33% of students are members of Episcopal Church.

Faculty School total: 121. In upper school: 46 men, 33 women; 71 have advanced degrees; 109 reside on campus.

Subjects Offered 3-dimensional design, algebra, American history, American literature, applied arts, applied music, architecture, art, art history, astronomy, ballet, biology, calculus, ceramics, chemistry, Chinese, classical civilization, classical Greek literature, classical language, computer math, computer programming, computer science, creative writing, drama, driver education, ecology, English, English literature, environmental science, ethics, European history, fine arts, French, geometry, German, government/civics, grammar, Greek, health, history, humanities, independent study, instrumental music, Japanese, Latin, mathematics, music, photography, physical education, physics, religion, robotics, science, social studies, Spanish, speech, statistics, theater, trigonometry, writing.

Graduation Requirements Art, athletics, humanities, language, mathematics, music, religion (includes Bible studies and theology), science, residential life. Community service is required.

Special Academic Programs 9 Advanced Placement exams for which test preparation is offered; honors section; accelerated programs; independent study; term-away projects; study abroad; academic accommodation for the gifted, the musically talented, and the artistically talented.

College Admission Counseling 158 students graduated in 2015; 154 went to college, including Boston College; Brown University; Columbia University; Dartmouth College; Georgetown University; Harvard University. Median SAT critical reading: 683, median SAT math: 683, median SAT writing: 681.

Student Life Upper grades have specified standards of dress, student council, honor system. Discipline rests primarily with faculty.

Summer Programs Enrichment programs offered; session focuses on enrichment for New Hampshire public high school juniors only; held on campus; accepts boys and girls; open to students from other schools. 245 students usually enrolled. 2016 schedule: June 28 to August 1. Application deadline: December 1.

Tuition and Aid 7-day tuition and room/board: $54,290. Tuition installment plan (Academic Management Services Plan, monthly payment plans). Need-based scholarship grants, tuition remission for children of faculty and staff available. In 2015–16, 38% of upper-school students received aid. Total amount of financial aid awarded in 2015–16: $7,200,000.

Admissions Traditional secondary-level entrance grade is 9. For fall 2015, 1,524 students applied for upper-level admission, 243 were accepted, 187 enrolled. SSAT required. Deadline for receipt of application materials: January 15. Application fee required: $75. Interview required.

Athletics Interscholastic: alpine skiing (boys, girls), baseball (b), basketball (b,g), crew (b,g), cross-country running (b,g), field hockey (g), football (b), ice hockey (b,g), lacrosse (b,g), rowing (b,g), skiing (cross-country) (b,g), skiing (downhill) (b,g), soccer (b,g), softball (g), squash (b,g), tennis (b,g), track and field (b,g), volleyball (g), wrestling (b); intramural: crew (b,g), ice hockey (b,g), rowing (b,g), soccer (b,g); coed interscholastic: ballet; coed intramural: aerobics, aerobics/Nautilus, alpine skiing, backpacking, baseball, basketball, crew, equestrian sports, fitness, fly fishing, horseback riding, ice hockey, physical fitness, rowing, skeet shooting, skiing (cross-country), skiing (downhill), snowboarding, soccer, squash, tai chi, tennis, weight training, wrestling. 2 coaches, 2 athletic trainers.

Computers Computers are regularly used in English, foreign language, humanities, mathematics, science classes. Computer network features include on-campus library services, online commercial services, Internet access, wireless campus network, Internet filtering or blocking technology. Campus intranet, student e-mail accounts, and computer access in designated common areas are available to students. Students grades are available online. The school has a published electronic and media policy.

Contact Ms. Holly Foote, Assistant Director of Admission Operations. 603-229-4700. Fax: 603-229-4771. E-mail: admissions@sps.edu. Website: www.sps.edu

ST. PAUL'S SCHOOL FOR GIRLS

11232 Falls Road

Brooklandville, Maryland 21022

Head of School: Mrs. Penny B. Evins

General Information Girls' day college-preparatory, arts, religious studies, technology, and AP and honors, leadership school, affiliated with Episcopal Church. Grades 5–12. Founded: 1959. Setting: suburban. Nearest major city is Baltimore. 38-acre campus. 4 buildings on campus. Approved or accredited by Association of Independent Maryland Schools, National Association of Episcopal Schools, and Maryland Department of Education. Member of National Association of Independent Schools. Endowment: $13.2 million. Total enrollment: 417. Upper school average class size: 15. Upper school faculty-student ratio: 1:6. There are 170 required school days per year for Upper School students. Upper School students typically attend 5 days per week. The average school day consists of 7 hours.

Upper School Student Profile Grade 9: 65 students (65 girls); Grade 10: 68 students (68 girls); Grade 11: 65 students (65 girls); Grade 12: 72 students (72 girls).

Faculty School total: 71. In upper school: 14 men, 36 women; 37 have advanced degrees.

Subjects Offered Algebra, American history, American literature, anatomy, ancient history, art, biology, biology-AP, biotechnology, calculus, calculus-AP, chemistry, chemistry-AP, Chinese, chorus, community service, computer science, dance, drama, economics, economics-AP, English, English language and composition-AP, English literature and composition-AP, English-AP, environmental science, environmental science-AP, ethics, fine arts, forensics, French, French-AP, genetics, geography, geometry, German, German-AP, health, history, Japanese, journalism, leadership and service, literary magazine, literature, mathematics, mechanics, medieval history, modern history, music, newspaper, optics, photography, physical education, physics, physics-AP, physiology, pre-calculus, programming, psychology-AP, religion, research skills, science, senior project, social studies, Spanish, Spanish language-AP, speech, statistics, studio art-AP, theater, trigonometry, U.S. history-AP, world cultures, world history.

Graduation Requirements Arts and fine arts (art, music, dance, drama), English, foreign language, mathematics, physical education (includes health), religion (includes Bible studies and theology), science, social studies (includes history), senior work project, senior speech. Community service is required.

Special Academic Programs 17 Advanced Placement exams for which test preparation is offered; honors section; independent study; term-away projects; domestic exchange program; study abroad; academic accommodation for the gifted, the musically talented, and the artistically talented.

College Admission Counseling 62 students graduated in 2014; all went to college, including Bucknell University; Franklin & Marshall College; James Madison University; The College of William and Mary; University of Maryland, College Park; University of Virginia.

Student Life Upper grades have uniform requirement, student council, honor system. Discipline rests equally with students and faculty. Attendance at religious services is required.

Tuition and Aid Day student tuition: $25,765. Tuition installment plan (FACTS Tuition Payment Plan, monthly payment plans). Merit scholarship grants, need-based scholarship grants, paying campus jobs available. In 2014–15, 30% of upper-school students received aid; total upper-school merit-scholarship money awarded: $30,765. Total amount of financial aid awarded in 2014–15: $1,427,445.

Admissions Traditional secondary-level entrance grade is 9. ISEE required. Deadline for receipt of application materials: December 31. Application fee required: $50. On-campus interview required.

Athletics Interscholastic: aerobics/dance, aquatics, badminton, ballet, basketball, crew, cross-country running, dance, field hockey, golf, indoor soccer, lacrosse, modern dance, physical fitness, rowing, soccer, softball, squash, swimming and diving, tennis, volleyball; coed intramural: sailing. 2 PE instructors, 12 coaches, 1 athletic trainer.

Computers Computers are regularly used in college planning, creative writing, current events, English, French, geography, history, introduction to technology, journalism, language development, library science, literary magazine, mathematics, newspaper, photography, psychology, religious studies, research skills, SAT preparation, science, Spanish, study skills, technology, yearbook classes. Computer network features include on-campus library services, online commercial services, Internet access, wireless campus network, Internet filtering or blocking technology, LMS, Senior Systems, 1 to 1 laptops for grade 8-12. Campus intranet, student e-mail accounts, and computer access in designated common areas are available to students. Students grades are available online. The school has a published electronic and media policy.

Contact Debbie Awalt, Assistant Director of Admission. 443-632-1002. Fax: 410-828-7238. E-mail: dawalt@spsfg.org. Website: www.spsfg.org

ST. PETER'S PREPARATORY SCHOOL

144 Grand Street

Jersey City, New Jersey 07302

Head of School: Rev. Kenneth J. Boller, SJ

General Information Boys' day college-preparatory, arts, technology, and music school, affiliated with Roman Catholic Church. Grades 9–12. Founded: 1872. Setting: urban. Nearest major city is New York, NY. 7-acre campus. 8 buildings on campus. Approved or accredited by Jesuit Secondary Education Association, Middle States Association of Colleges and Schools, New Jersey Association of Independent Schools, and New Jersey Department of Education. Member of National Association of Independent Schools. Endowment: $22.5 million. Total enrollment: 931. Upper school average class size: 22. Upper school faculty-student ratio: 1:12. There are 176 required school days per year for Upper School students. Upper School students typically attend 5 days per week. The average school day consists of 6 hours and 10 minutes.

Upper School Student Profile Grade 9: 260 students (260 boys); Grade 10: 248 students (248 boys); Grade 11: 234 students (234 boys); Grade 12: 189 students (189 boys). 78% of students are Roman Catholic.

Faculty School total: 77. In upper school: 52 men, 23 women; 60 have advanced degrees.

Subjects Offered Advanced Placement courses, algebra, American history, American history-AP, American legal systems, American literature, Ancient Greek, architecture, art, art history, biology, biology-AP, calculus, calculus-AP, ceramics, chemistry, chemistry-AP, choir, Christian ethics, community service, computer programming, computer science, concert band, creative writing, drawing, English, English language-AP, English literature, English literature-AP, European history, forensics, French, French language-AP, geometry, German, German-AP, government and politics-AP, health, history, human anatomy, Italian, jazz band, Latin, Latin-AP, Mandarin, mathematics, music, music theory, physical education, physics, religion, sculpture, social justice, Spanish, Spanish language-AP, Spanish literature-AP, statistics, statistics-AP, studio art, theology, trigonometry, Web site design, world civilizations, world history, world literature, writing.

Graduation Requirements Algebra, American history, American literature, ancient world history, art, biology, British literature, chemistry, English, geometry, Latin, modern languages, music, physical education (includes health), physics, religion (includes Bible studies and theology), U.S. history, world civilizations, 20 hours of community service in freshman and sophomore years, 60 hours in the third (junior) year.

Special Academic Programs 18 Advanced Placement exams for which test preparation is offered; honors section; study at local college for college credit; study abroad.

College Admission Counseling 248 students graduated in 2015; all went to college, including Fordham University; Loyola University Maryland; New Jersey Institute of Technology; Rutgers, The State University of New Jersey, Rutgers College; Saint Peter's University; Seton Hall University. Median SAT critical reading: 576, median SAT math: 593. Mean SAT writing: 574, mean combined SAT: 1731. 44% scored over 600 on SAT critical reading, 48% scored over 600 on SAT math, 50% scored over 600 on SAT writing, 50% scored over 1800 on combined SAT.

Student Life Upper grades have specified standards of dress, student council. Discipline rests primarily with faculty.

Summer Programs Remediation, enrichment, sports, art/fine arts programs offered; session focuses on make-up course work for failed classes and enrichment for students trying to advance their studies; held on campus; accepts boys and girls; open to students from other schools. 180 students usually enrolled. 2016 schedule: June 27 to July 29. Application deadline: June 13.

Tuition and Aid Day student tuition: $15,150. Tuition installment plan (FACTS Tuition Payment Plan, monthly payment plans). Merit scholarship grants, need-based scholarship grants, paying campus jobs available. In 2015–16, 51% of upper-school students received aid; total upper-school merit-scholarship money awarded: $721,500. Total amount of financial aid awarded in 2015–16: $1,718,000.

Admissions Traditional secondary-level entrance grade is 9. For fall 2015, 960 students applied for upper-level admission, 449 were accepted, 264 enrolled. Cooperative Entrance Exam (McGraw-Hill) or SSAT required. Deadline for receipt of application materials: November 15. No application fee required.

Athletics Interscholastic: baseball, basketball, bowling, crew, cross-country running, diving, fencing, football, golf, ice hockey, indoor track, indoor track & field, lacrosse, rugby, soccer, swimming and diving, tennis, track and field, volleyball, water polo, winter (indoor) track, wrestling; intramural: basketball, flag football, Frisbee, handball, indoor soccer, outdoor recreation, team handball, touch football, ultimate Frisbee, whiffle ball. 4 PE instructors, 23 coaches, 1 athletic trainer.

Computers Computers are regularly used in all academic classes. Computer network features include on-campus library services, online commercial services, Internet access, wireless campus network, Internet filtering or blocking technology. Campus intranet and student e-mail accounts are available to students. Students grades are available online. The school has a published electronic and media policy.

Contact Mr. John T. Irvine, Director of Admissions. 201-547-6389. Fax: 201-547-2341. E-mail: Irvinej@spprep.org. Website: www.spprep.org

ST. PIUS X HIGH SCHOOL

5301 St. Joseph Drive NW

Albuquerque, New Mexico 87120

Head of School: Dr. Barbara M. Rothweiler

General Information Coeducational day college-preparatory, arts, religious studies, and technology school, affiliated with Roman Catholic Church; primarily serves students with learning disabilities, individuals with Attention Deficit Disorder, and dyslexic students. Grades 9–12. Founded: 1956. Setting: urban. 57-acre campus. 6 buildings on campus. Approved or accredited by National Catholic Education Association, North Central Association of Colleges and Schools, and New Mexico Department of Education. Endowment: $3 million. Total enrollment: 722. Upper school average class size: 22. Upper school faculty-student ratio: 1:13. There are 180 required school days per year for Upper School students. Upper School students typically attend 5 days per week. The average school day consists of 7 hours.

Upper School Student Profile Grade 9: 187 students (88 boys, 99 girls); Grade 10: 185 students (87 boys, 98 girls); Grade 11: 156 students (67 boys, 89 girls); Grade 12: 194 students (88 boys, 106 girls). 95% of students are Roman Catholic.

Faculty School total: 54. In upper school: 23 men, 31 women; 49 have advanced degrees.

Subjects Offered 20th century American writers, 20th century history, 20th century physics, 3-dimensional art, accounting, acting, algebra, American government, American history, American history-AP, American literature, American literature-AP, anatomy, anatomy and physiology, applied arts, applied music, art, art and culture, art appreciation, art history-AP, band, Bible, biology, biology-AP, business law, calculus, calculus-AP, campus ministry, chemistry, child development, choir, chorus, church history, community service, comparative religion, computer art, computer literacy, computer programming, conceptual physics, concert band, creative writing, culinary arts, drafting, drama, drawing, economics, English language-AP, English literature-AP, environmental science-AP, French, geometry, government, government-AP, health, history of the Catholic Church, honors algebra, honors geometry, human anatomy, independent living, math analysis, mechanical drawing, model United Nations, moral theology, music appreciation, newspaper, orchestra, painting, peer ministry, photography, physical education, physics, play production, pre-calculus, printmaking, probability and statistics, psychology, set design, social justice, softball, Spanish, Spanish language-AP, sports medicine, statistics-AP, studio art, study skills, swimming, theology, trigonometry, U.S. government and politics-AP, weight training, world geography, world history, yearbook.

Graduation Requirements Algebra, American government, American history, American literature, art, biology, computer skills, English, foreign language, geometry, history, language and composition, literature, music, physical education (includes health), physical science, science, theology, world history.

Special Academic Programs Advanced Placement exam preparation; honors section; remedial reading and/or remedial writing.

College Admission Counseling 190 students graduated in 2014; 185 went to college, including New Mexico State University; University of New Mexico. Other: 2 went to work, 3 entered military service. Median composite ACT: 23. 25% scored over 26 on composite ACT.

Student Life Upper grades have uniform requirement, student council, honor system. Discipline rests primarily with faculty. Attendance at religious services is required.

Tuition and Aid Day student tuition: $10,900. Tuition installment plan (FACTS Tuition Payment Plan). Tuition reduction for siblings, merit scholarship grants, need-based scholarship grants available. In 2014–15, 50% of upper-school students received aid; total upper-school merit-scholarship money awarded: $27,000. Total amount of financial aid awarded in 2014–15: $600,000.

Admissions Traditional secondary-level entrance grade is 9. For fall 2014, 250 students applied for upper-level admission, 230 were accepted, 205 enrolled. High School Placement Test required. Deadline for receipt of application materials: none. No application fee required.

Athletics Interscholastic: baseball (boys), basketball (b,g), cheering (g), cross-country running (b,g), drill team (g), football (b), ice hockey (b), physical fitness (b,g), soccer (b,g), softball (g), swimming and diving (b,g), tennis (b,g), track and field (b,g), volleyball (g), weight lifting (b,g), weight training (b,g), wrestling (b); intramural: basketball (b,g), flag football (b,g), soccer (b,g); coed interscholastic: diving, golf; coed intramural: softball, table tennis. 2 PE instructors, 1 athletic trainer.

Computers Computers are regularly used in graphic arts, journalism, multimedia, newspaper, programming, writing, yearbook classes. Computer network features include on-campus library services, online commercial services, Internet access, wireless campus network, Internet filtering or blocking technology. Computer access in designated common areas is available to students. Students grades are available online. The school has a published electronic and media policy.

Contact Mr. Jeff Turcotte, Director of Enrollment. 505-831-8417. Fax: 505-831-8413. E-mail: jturcotte@spx.k12.nm.us. Website: www.saintpiusx.com/

ST. PIUS X HIGH SCHOOL

811 West Donovan Street
Houston, Texas 77091-5699

Head of School: Sr. Donna M. Pollard, OP

General Information Coeducational day college-preparatory, arts, business, religious studies, and technology school, affiliated with Roman Catholic Church. Grades 9–12. Founded: 1956. Setting: urban. 28-acre campus. 1 building on campus. Approved or accredited by Southern Association of Colleges and Schools, Texas Catholic Conference, The College Board, and Texas Department of Education. Member of National Association of Independent Schools. Endowment: $4 million. Total enrollment: 682. Upper school average class size: 18. Upper school faculty-student ratio: 1:13. There are 180 required school days per year for Upper School students. Upper School students typically attend 5 days per week. The average school day consists of 7 hours.

Upper School Student Profile Grade 9: 173 students (105 boys, 68 girls); Grade 10: 179 students (104 boys, 75 girls); Grade 11: 176 students (92 boys, 84 girls); Grade 12: 154 students (85 boys, 69 girls). 60% of students are Roman Catholic.

Faculty School total: 53. In upper school: 23 men, 29 women; 45 have advanced degrees.

Subjects Offered Advanced chemistry, advanced computer applications, advanced math, Advanced Placement courses, algebra, American history-AP, American literature, art, band, biology, biology-AP, business law, calculus, calculus-AP, campus ministry, Catholic belief and practice, chemistry, choir, chorus, Christian ethics, church history, college counseling, communications, community service, computer applications, computer multimedia, computer programming, computer science-AP, earth and space science, economics, English language-AP, English literature-AP, environmental science, film history, fine arts, foreign language, French, geometry, graphic design, health, health education, history of the Catholic Church, honors geometry, honors world history, introduction to theater, jewelry making, language arts, Latin, Latin-AP, library assistant, marching band, modern world history, moral and social development, moral theology, musical productions, painting, personal finance, photography, physical education, physics, physics-AP, psychology, reading/study skills, SAT/ACT preparation, Shakespeare, social justice, Spanish, Spanish language-AP, Spanish-AP, speech, speech communications, stagecraft, student government, student publications, technical theater, theology, U.S. government, U.S. government and politics-AP, U.S. history, U.S. history-AP, Web site design, world history, world religions, world wide web design, yearbook.

Graduation Requirements Advanced math, Advanced Placement courses, algebra, American government, American history, ancient world history, art, arts and fine arts (art, music, dance, drama), athletic training, band, biology, biology-AP, British literature-AP, calculus-AP, career exploration, chemistry, Christian education, communications, computer science-AP, concert band, concert bell choir, concert choir, dance performance, digital photography, drama, drama performance, earth and space science, economics, economics-AP, electives, English, English language-AP, English literature-AP, environmental science, film history, foreign language, French studies, geometry, government, handbells, health, health education, history-AP, honors algebra, honors English, honors geometry, honors U.S. history, honors world history, integrated physics, introduction to theater, jewelry making, Latin-AP, leadership and service, marching band, New Testament, personal finance, philosophy, physical education (includes health), physics, physics-AP, psychology, reading/study skills, religious education, Shakespeare, social issues, social justice, Spanish-AP, stagecraft, student government, theater, theater arts, theater production, theology, U.S. history-AP, video film production, vocal music, voice ensemble, weight training, weightlifting, world history-AP, 2 years of foreign language or reading development, Christian Service Learning (100 hours of community service), 4 years of theology.

Special Academic Programs 10 Advanced Placement exams for which test preparation is offered; honors section; study at local college for college credit; remedial reading and/or remedial writing; remedial math; programs in English, mathematics, general development for dyslexic students.

College Admission Counseling 179 students graduated in 2015; all went to college, including Sam Houston State University; Texas A&M University; Texas State University; Texas Tech University; The University of Texas at Austin; University of Houston. Mean SAT critical reading: 515, mean SAT math: 518, mean SAT writing: 508, mean combined SAT: 1541, mean composite ACT: 23. 17% scored over 600 on SAT critical reading, 21% scored over 600 on SAT math, 20% scored over 600 on SAT writing, 19% scored over 1800 on combined SAT, 21% scored over 26 on composite ACT.

Student Life Upper grades have uniform requirement, student council, honor system. Discipline rests primarily with faculty. Attendance at religious services is required.

Summer Programs Remediation, enrichment, advancement, sports, art/fine arts, computer instruction programs offered; session focuses on enrichment and remediation; held on campus; accepts boys and girls; not open to students from other schools. 200 students usually enrolled. 2016 schedule: June 8 to July 30. Application deadline: May 1.

Tuition and Aid Day student tuition: $13,900. Tuition installment plan (monthly payment plans, individually arranged payment plans). Tuition reduction for siblings, merit scholarship grants, need-based scholarship grants available. In 2015–16, 25% of upper-school students received aid; total upper-school merit-scholarship money awarded: $63,250. Total amount of financial aid awarded in 2015–16: $806,450.

Admissions Traditional secondary-level entrance grade is 9. For fall 2015, 375 students applied for upper-level admission, 275 were accepted, 199 enrolled. Catholic High School Entrance Examination or ISEE required. Deadline for receipt of application materials: January 15. Application fee required: $50. Interview required.

Athletics Interscholastic: baseball (boys), basketball (b,g), cheering (g), cross-country running (b,g), dance squad (g), dance team (b,g), drill team (g), football (b), golf (b,g), rugby (b,g), soccer (b,g), softball (g), strength & conditioning (b,g), swimming and diving (b,g), tennis (b,g), track and field (b,g), volleyball (g), weight training (b,g), wrestling (b). 1 PE instructor, 1 athletic trainer.

Computers Computers are regularly used in art, career exploration, career technology, desktop publishing, drawing and design, graphic design, mathematics, multimedia, news writing, publications, social studies, technology, video film production, yearbook classes. Computer network features include on-campus library services, Internet access, wireless campus network, Internet filtering or blocking technology, Learning Management System with online classrooms. Student e-mail accounts and computer access in designated common areas are available to students. Students grades are available online. The school has a published electronic and media policy.

Contact Ms. Susie Kramer, Admissions Director. 713-579-7507. Fax: 713-692-5725. E-mail: kramers@stpiusx.org. Website: www.stpiusx.org

SAINTS PETER AND PAUL HIGH SCHOOL

900 High Street
Easton, Maryland 21601

Head of School: Mr. James Edward Nemeth

General Information Coeducational day college-preparatory school, affiliated with Roman Catholic Church. Grades 9–12. Founded: 1958. Setting: small town. Nearest major city is Baltimore. 4-acre campus. 4 buildings on campus. Approved or accredited by Middle States Association of Colleges and Schools, National Catholic Education Association, and Maryland Department of Education. Endowment: $285,000. Total enrollment: 187. Upper school average class size: 14. Upper school faculty-student ratio: 1:8. There are 180 required school days per year for Upper School students. Upper School students typically attend 5 days per week. The average school day consists of 6 hours and 30 minutes.

Upper School Student Profile Grade 9: 62 students (37 boys, 25 girls); Grade 10: 51 students (29 boys, 22 girls); Grade 11: 49 students (23 boys, 26 girls); Grade 12: 52 students (17 boys, 35 girls). 67% of students are Roman Catholic.

Faculty School total: 21. In upper school: 9 men, 12 women; 11 have advanced degrees.

Subjects Offered Advanced computer applications, Advanced Placement courses, algebra, American government, American history-AP, American literature, anatomy and physiology, art and culture, Basic programming, biology, biology-AP, British literature, British literature (honors), British literature-AP, calculus, calculus-AP, campus ministry, Catholic belief and practice, chemistry, chemistry-AP, choir, Christian and Hebrew scripture, Christian ethics, Christianity, church history, computer multimedia, computer programming, computer science, conceptual physics, creative writing, drama, earth science, economics, English language and composition-AP, English language-AP, English literature and composition-AP, English literature-AP, environmental science, European history-AP, film and literature, geography, geometry, government and politics-AP, health and wellness, Hebrew scripture, honors algebra, honors English, honors geometry, honors U.S. history, honors world history, Latin, Microsoft, moral theology, music theory, philosophy, physical education, physics, pre-calculus, probability and statistics, Spanish, Spanish literature-AP, speech, street law, studio art-AP, theology, U.S. government, U.S. government and politics-AP, U.S. history, U.S. history-AP, Web site design, world geography, world history, yearbook.

Graduation Requirements Algebra, American literature, arts and fine arts (art, music, dance, drama), biology, British literature, Catholic belief and practice, chemistry, Christian and Hebrew scripture, Christianity, computer applications, computer science, English, foreign language, geometry, history of the Catholic Church, mathematics, moral theology, physical education (includes health), physics, pre-algebra, social justice, U.S. government, U.S. history, world history.

Special Academic Programs 9 Advanced Placement exams for which test preparation is offered; honors section; independent study.

College Admission Counseling 48 students graduated in 2014; all went to college, including Salisbury University; University of Maryland, College Park; University of South Carolina; Villanova University; Virginia Polytechnic Institute and State University. Median SAT critical reading: 530, median SAT math: 520, median SAT writing: 520. 18% scored over 600 on SAT critical reading, 18% scored over 600 on SAT math, 30% scored over 600 on SAT writing.

Student Life Upper grades have uniform requirement. Discipline rests primarily with faculty. Attendance at religious services is required.

Tuition and Aid Day student tuition: $11,900. Tuition installment plan (FACTS Tuition Payment Plan). Tuition reduction for siblings, need-based scholarship grants, parish subsidies available. In 2014–15, 5% of upper-school students received aid. Total amount of financial aid awarded in 2014–15: $35,000.

Admissions Traditional secondary-level entrance grade is 9. For fall 2014, 65 students applied for upper-level admission, 55 were accepted, 52 enrolled. Diocesan Entrance Exam required. Deadline for receipt of application materials: none. Application fee required: $50. On-campus interview required.

Athletics Interscholastic: baseball (boys), basketball (b,g), cross-country running (b,g), field hockey (g), golf (b), lacrosse (b,g), soccer (b,g), softball (g), swimming and diving (b,g), tennis (b,g); coed interscholastic: sailing. 1 PE instructor, 23 coaches.

Computers Computers are regularly used in all academic classes. Computer network features include on-campus library services, Internet access, wireless campus network, Internet filtering or blocking technology. Students grades are available online. The school has a published electronic and media policy.

Contact Mrs. Deborah Morton, Administrative Assistant. 410-822-2275 Ext. 150. Fax: 410-822-1767. E-mail: dmorton@ssppeaston.org. Website: www.ssppeaston.org

ST. STANISLAUS COLLEGE

304 South Beach Boulevard
Bay St. Louis, Mississippi 39520

Head of School: Br. Francis David, SC

General Information Boys' boarding and day college-preparatory, business, religious studies, technology, and ESL school, affiliated with Roman Catholic Church. Grades 7–12. Founded: 1854. Setting: small town. Nearest major city is New Orleans, LA. Students are housed in single-sex dormitories. 30-acre campus. 8 buildings on campus. Approved or accredited by National Catholic Education Association, Southern Association of Colleges and Schools, Southern Association of Independent Schools, and Mississippi Department of Education. Member of National Association of Independent Schools. Endowment: $5 million. Total enrollment: 352. Upper school average class size: 22. Upper school faculty-student ratio: 1:12. There are 180 required school days per year for Upper School students. Upper School students typically attend 5 days per week. The average school day consists of 6 hours and 23 minutes.

Upper School Student Profile Grade 9: 65 students (65 boys); Grade 10: 64 students (64 boys); Grade 11: 66 students (66 boys); Grade 12: 55 students (55 boys). 25% of students are boarding students. 90% are state residents. 6 states are represented in upper school student body. 1% are international students. International students from Angola, China, Mexico, Republic of Korea, Senegal, and Venezuela; 1 other country represented in student body. 80% of students are Roman Catholic.

Faculty School total: 34. In upper school: 28 men, 6 women; 21 have advanced degrees; 8 reside on campus.

Subjects Offered Accounting, ACT preparation, advanced biology, advanced chemistry, advanced computer applications, advanced math, Advanced Placement courses, algebra, American history, American history-AP, American literature, anatomy, art, astronomy, biology, biology-AP, business, business education, business law, calculus, calculus-AP, campus ministry, ceramics, chemistry, chemistry-AP, computer programming, computer science, computer science-AP, creative writing, desktop publishing, drama, economics, economics and history, English, English language and composition-AP, English literature, English literature and composition-AP, environmental science, ESL, finance, French, French as a second language, genetics, geography, geology, geometry, government, government/civics, grammar, guidance, health, health education, history, journalism, law, marine biology, marine science, mathematics, music, music performance, physical education, physics, physics-AP, pre-calculus, psychology, psychology-AP, religion, science, scuba diving, short story, social sciences, social studies, sociology, Spanish, speech, swimming, symphonic band, theater, theater arts, theology, track and field, trigonometry, typing, U.S. history-AP, world history, world literature.

Graduation Requirements Arts and fine arts (art, music, dance, drama), computer science, English, foreign language, mathematics, physical education (includes health), religion (includes Bible studies and theology), science, social sciences, social studies (includes history), volunteer service hours are required.

Special Academic Programs 4 Advanced Placement exams for which test preparation is offered; honors section; study at local college for college credit; remedial reading and/or remedial writing; remedial math; ESL (16 students enrolled).

College Admission Counseling 59 students graduated in 2014; all went to college, including Louisiana State University and Agricultural & Mechanical College; Mississippi State University; University of Mississippi; University of New Orleans; University of South Alabama; University of Southern Mississippi. Median SAT critical reading: 520, median SAT math: 620, median SAT writing: 570, median composite ACT: 24. 40% scored over 600 on SAT critical reading, 50% scored over 600 on SAT math, 35% scored over 600 on SAT writing, 22% scored over 1800 on combined SAT, 17% scored over 26 on composite ACT.

Student Life Upper grades have uniform requirement, student council, honor system. Discipline rests primarily with faculty. Attendance at religious services is required.

Tuition and Aid Day student tuition: $6290; 7-day tuition and room/board: $24,257. Tuition installment plan (monthly payment plans, individually arranged payment plans). Need-based scholarship grants, paying campus jobs available.

Admissions Traditional secondary-level entrance grade is 9. For fall 2014, 100 students applied for upper-level admission, 90 were accepted, 80 enrolled. Deadline for receipt of application materials: none. Application fee required: $100. Interview required.

Athletics Interscholastic: baseball, basketball, cross-country running, football, golf, power lifting, soccer, track and field; intramural: baseball, basketball, billiards, croquet, fishing, flag football, floor hockey, football, hiking/backpacking, jogging, outdoor activities, outdoor adventure, outdoor education, outdoor recreation, outdoor skills, outdoors, physical fitness, physical training, power lifting, scuba diving, swimming and diving, table tennis, tennis, touch football, volleyball, water polo, water skiing, weight lifting, weight training; coed interscholastic: cheering, sailing, swimming and diving, tennis. 5 PE instructors, 16 coaches, 1 athletic trainer.

Computers Computers are regularly used in accounting, English, mathematics, religion, SAT preparation, science, Spanish classes. Computer resources include on-campus library services, online commercial services, Internet access, wireless campus network, Internet filtering or blocking technology. Computer access in designated common areas is available to students. Students grades are available online.

Contact Mr. Richard Gleber, Assistant Director of Admissions. 228-467-9057 Ext. 249. Fax: 228-466-2972. E-mail: richard@ststan.com. Website: www.ststan.com

ST. STEPHEN'S & ST. AGNES SCHOOL

1000 St. Stephen's Road
Alexandria, Virginia 22304

Head of School: Mrs. Kirsten Prettyman Adams

General Information Coeducational day college-preparatory, arts, religious studies, and technology school, affiliated with Episcopal Church. Grades JK–12. Founded: 1924. Setting: suburban. Nearest major city is Washington, DC. 58-acre campus. 5 buildings on campus. Approved or accredited by Association of Independent Schools of Greater Washington, National Association of Episcopal Schools, and Virginia Association of Independent Schools. Member of National Association of Independent Schools and Secondary School Admission Test Board. Endowment: $28 million. Total enrollment: 1,152. Upper school average class size: 14. Upper school faculty-student ratio: 1:9. There are 170 required school days per year for Upper School students. Upper School students typically attend 5 days per week. The average school day consists of 7 hours and 10 minutes.

Upper School Student Profile Grade 9: 111 students (59 boys, 52 girls); Grade 10: 113 students (60 boys, 53 girls); Grade 11: 119 students (60 boys, 59 girls); Grade 12: 107 students (50 boys, 57 girls). 23% of students are members of Episcopal Church.

Faculty School total: 142. In upper school: 24 men, 29 women; 41 have advanced degrees.

Subjects Offered 1 1/2 elective credits, Advanced Placement courses, algebra, American history, American literature, art, art history, art history-AP, bioethics, biology, biology-AP, calculus, calculus-AP, ceramics, chemistry, chemistry-AP, Christian education, Christian ethics, Christian scripture, Christian testament, comparative government and politics-AP, concert choir, directing, drama, drawing, economics, English, English-AP, ensembles, environmental science-AP, ethics, European history, European history-AP, forensics, French, French language-AP, geometry, government/civics-AP, history, honors English, honors geometry, honors U.S. history, honors world history, instrumental music, jazz ensemble, Latin, Latin-AP, macro/microeconomics-AP, Mandarin, mathematics, medieval history, medieval/Renaissance history, microeconomics-AP, music, music theory-AP, newspaper, painting, physical education, physics, physics-AP, playwriting and directing, pre-calculus, psychology-AP, religion, robotics, sculpture, senior project, Spanish, Spanish language-AP, Spanish literature-AP, sports, sports medicine, statistics-AP, studio art, studio art-AP, technical theater, theater, theater arts, trigonometry, U.S. history-AP, world history, writing, yearbook, yoga.

Graduation Requirements Arts and fine arts (art, music, dance, drama), English, family studies, foreign language, history, mathematics, physical education (includes health), religion (includes Bible studies and theology), science, technological applications, senior year independent off-campus project, 40 hours of community service.

Special Academic Programs 22 Advanced Placement exams for which test preparation is offered; honors section; independent study; term-away projects; study abroad; academic accommodation for the gifted, the musically talented, and the artistically talented.

College Admission Counseling 119 students graduated in 2014; all went to college, including Boston University; The College of William and Mary; University of Virginia; Virginia Polytechnic Institute and State University; Wake Forest University; Washington and Lee University. Mean SAT critical reading: 639, mean SAT math: 642, mean SAT writing: 631, mean combined SAT: 1912.

Student Life Upper grades have specified standards of dress, student council, honor system. Discipline rests equally with students and faculty. Attendance at religious services is required.

Tuition and Aid Day student tuition: $33,520. Tuition installment plan (FACTS Tuition Payment Plan). Need-based scholarship grants available. In 2014–15, 26% of upper-school students received aid. Total amount of financial aid awarded in 2014–15: $2,304,268.

Admissions Traditional secondary-level entrance grade is 9. ISEE or SSAT required. Deadline for receipt of application materials: January 15. Application fee required: $70. Interview required.

Athletics Interscholastic: baseball (boys), basketball (b,g), field hockey (g), football (b), ice hockey (b), lacrosse (b,g), soccer (b,g), softball (g), swimming and diving (b,g), tennis (b,g), track and field (b,g), volleyball (g), winter soccer (g), wrestling (b); intramural: dance team (g), independent competitive sports (b,g); coed interscholastic: cross-country running, diving, golf, winter (indoor) track; coed intramural: basketball, fitness, independent competitive sports, jogging, physical fitness, physical training,

strength & conditioning, weight lifting, weight training, yoga. 6 PE instructors, 14 coaches, 2 athletic trainers.

Computers Computers are regularly used in all academic classes. Computer network features include on-campus library services, online commercial services, Internet access, wireless campus network, Internet filtering or blocking technology, computer labs for foreign language, math, technology, library, newspaper, physics, and chemistry, homework assignments posted online, mobile wireless laptop cart, iPads, computers available in study hall and library. Campus intranet, student e-mail accounts, and computer access in designated common areas are available to students. Students grades are available online. The school has a published electronic and media policy.

Contact Mr. Jon Kunz, Director of Admission, Grades 6-12. 703-212-2706. Fax: 703-212-2788. E-mail: jkunz@sssas.org. Website: www.sssas.org

ST. STEPHEN'S EPISCOPAL SCHOOL

6500 St. Stephen's Drive
Austin, Texas 78746

Head of School: Mr. Robert Kirkpatrick

General Information Coeducational boarding and day college-preparatory, arts, and theater focus school, affiliated with Episcopal Church. Boarding grades 8–12, day grades 6–12. Founded: 1950. Setting: suburban. Students are housed in single-sex dormitories. 370-acre campus. 45 buildings on campus. Approved or accredited by Independent Schools Association of the Southwest, National Association of Episcopal Schools, Southern Association of Colleges and Schools, The Association of Boarding Schools, and Texas Department of Education. Member of National Association of Independent Schools and Secondary School Admission Test Board. Endowment: $13 million. Total enrollment: 688. Upper school average class size: 17. Upper school faculty-student ratio: 1:8. There are 165 required school days per year for Upper School students. Upper School students typically attend 5 days per week. The average school day consists of 7 hours and 35 minutes.

Upper School Student Profile Grade 9: 114 students (53 boys, 61 girls); Grade 10: 125 students (66 boys, 59 girls); Grade 11: 125 students (65 boys, 60 girls); Grade 12: 126 students (69 boys, 57 girls). 35% of students are boarding students. 80% are state residents. 11 states are represented in upper school student body. 20% are international students. International students from Bahamas, China, Hong Kong, Mexico, Saudi Arabia, and Taiwan; 7 other countries represented in student body. 18% of students are members of Episcopal Church.

Faculty School total: 98. In upper school: 40 men, 35 women; 45 have advanced degrees; 40 reside on campus.

Subjects Offered 3-dimensional design, acting, algebra, American history, American history-AP, anthropology, art, art history, astrophysics, ballet, band, biology, calculus, ceramics, chamber groups, chemistry, Chinese, choreography, classics, computer applications, computer math, computer science, computer studies, creative writing, directing, drama, English, English literature, environmental science, European history, fine arts, French, geology, geometry, government/civics, graphic design, history, jazz band, Latin, mathematics, music, musical theater, photography, physical education, physics, physics-AP, play/screen writing, pre-calculus, psychology, public policy issues and action, public speaking, religion, science, social studies, Spanish, theater arts, theology, video, world history, world literature.

Graduation Requirements Arts and fine arts (art, music, dance, drama), electives, English, foreign language, mathematics, physical education (includes health), religion (includes Bible studies and theology), science, social studies (includes history), community service requirement in middle and upper schools.

Special Academic Programs Advanced Placement exam preparation; honors section; independent study; study abroad.

College Admission Counseling 107 students graduated in 2015; all went to college, including Cornell University; New York University; Southern Methodist University; The University of Texas at Austin; Trinity University; University of California, San Diego. Mean SAT critical reading: 611, mean SAT math: 651, mean SAT writing: 642, mean combined SAT: 1904, mean composite ACT: 29.

Student Life Upper grades have specified standards of dress, student council. Discipline rests equally with students and faculty. Attendance at religious services is required.

Summer Programs Sports, art/fine arts programs offered; session focuses on soccer, tennis, travel abroad, foreign language/culture, fine arts, community service; held both on and off campus; held at locations in Europe, El Salvador, Nicaragua, Costa Rica, American wilderness areas; accepts boys and girls; open to students from other schools. 120 students usually enrolled. 2016 schedule: June 1 to July 1. Application deadline: none.

Tuition and Aid Day student tuition: $24,750; 7-day tuition and room/board: $51,460. Tuition installment plan (individually arranged payment plans). Need-based scholarship grants available. In 2015–16, 12% of upper-school students received aid. Total amount of financial aid awarded in 2015–16: $2,460,000.

Admissions Traditional secondary-level entrance grade is 9. For fall 2015, 213 students applied for upper-level admission, 84 were accepted, 43 enrolled. ISEE or SSAT required. Deadline for receipt of application materials: January 25. Application fee required: $100. Interview required.

Athletics Interscholastic: baseball (boys), basketball (b,g), crew (b,g), cross-country running (b,g), field hockey (g), football (b), golf (b,g), lacrosse (b,g), running (b,g), soccer (b,g), softball (g), swimming and diving (b,g), tennis (b,g), track and field (b,g), volleyball (g), winter soccer (b,g); intramural: bicycling (b,g), climbing (b,g), combined training (b,g), dance (b,g), fitness (b,g), hiking/backpacking (b,g), independent competitive sports (b,g), indoor hockey (b,g), modern dance (b,g), mountain biking (b,g), mountaineering (b,g), outdoor adventure (b,g), outdoor education (b,g), paddle tennis (b,g), physical fitness (b,g), physical training (b,g), rappelling (b,g), rock climbing (b,g), ropes courses (b,g), strength & conditioning (b,g), surfing (b,g), wall climbing (b,g), weight training (b,g); coed interscholastic: aerobics/dance, badminton, bicycling, climbing, mountain biking. 2 PE instructors, 5 coaches, 2 athletic trainers.

Computers Computer network features include on-campus library services, online commercial services, Internet access, wireless campus network, Internet filtering or blocking technology, online schedules, syllabi, homework, examples, and links to information sources. Campus intranet, student e-mail accounts, and computer access in designated common areas are available to students. Students grades are available online. The school has a published electronic and media policy.

Contact Lawrence Sampleton, Director of Admission. 512-327-1213 Ext. 210. Fax: 512-327-6771. E-mail: admission@sstx.org. Website: www.sstx.org

ST. STEPHEN'S SCHOOL, ROME

Via Aventina 3
Rome 00153, Italy

Head of School: Mr. Eric J. Mayer

General Information Coeducational boarding and day college-preparatory and arts school. Grades 9–PG. Founded: 1964. Setting: urban. Students are housed in single-sex by floor dormitories. 2-acre campus. 2 buildings on campus. Approved or accredited by International Baccalaureate Organization, New England Association of Schools and Colleges, and US Department of State. Affiliate member of National Association of Independent Schools; member of European Council of International Schools. Language of instruction: English. Endowment: $7 million. Total enrollment: 287. Upper school average class size: 13. Upper school faculty-student ratio: 1:7. There are 175 required school days per year for Upper School students. Upper School students typically attend 5 days per week. The average school day consists of 7 hours.

Upper School Student Profile Grade 9: 58 students (24 boys, 34 girls); Grade 10: 73 students (38 boys, 35 girls); Grade 11: 86 students (49 boys, 37 girls); Grade 12: 70 students (39 boys, 31 girls). 16% of students are boarding students. 61% are international students. International students from Canada, China, France, Germany, United Kingdom, and United States; 24 other countries represented in student body.

Faculty School total: 55. In upper school: 14 men, 41 women; 45 have advanced degrees; 10 reside on campus.

Subjects Offered 20th century history, algebra, American literature, art history, biology, calculus, chemistry, chorus, classical studies, creative writing, dance, drama, drawing, economics, English, English literature, environmental systems, European history, French, geometry, health, instrumental music, Islamic studies, Italian, Latin, music theory, painting, photography, physical education, physics, pre-calculus, Roman civilization, sculpture, Spanish, theory of knowledge, trigonometry, world literature.

Graduation Requirements Arts and fine arts (art, music, dance, drama), English, foreign language, mathematics, physical education (includes health), science, social studies (includes history), senior research paper, computer proficiency examination, service project.

Special Academic Programs International Baccalaureate program; 9 Advanced Placement exams for which test preparation is offered; domestic exchange program (with Buckingham Browne & Nichols School, Choate Rosemary Hall).

College Admission Counseling 72 students graduated in 2015; 71 went to college, including Brown University; Georgetown University; Macalester College; New York University; Northeastern University; University of California, Berkeley. Other: 1 entered military service. Mean SAT critical reading: 606, mean SAT math: 604, mean SAT writing: 606, mean combined SAT: 1866.

Student Life Upper grades have student council. Discipline rests equally with students and faculty.

Summer Programs Enrichment, art/fine arts programs offered; session focuses on liberal arts/pre-college; held both on and off campus; held at off-campus sites include museum visits and visits to various historical sites within the city; accepts boys and girls; open to students from other schools. 50 students usually enrolled. 2016 schedule: June 20 to August 4. Application deadline: May 19.

Tuition and Aid Day student tuition: €24,750–€25,250; 7-day tuition and room/board: €37,750–€38,250. Tuition installment plan (individually arranged payment plans). Tuition reduction for siblings, need-based scholarship grants available. In 2015–16, 19% of upper-school students received aid. Total amount of financial aid awarded in 2015–16: €562,000.

Admissions Traditional secondary-level entrance grade is 9. For fall 2015, 179 students applied for upper-level admission, 123 were accepted, 101 enrolled. School's own exam required. Deadline for receipt of application materials: February 9. Application fee required: €150. Interview required.

Athletics Interscholastic: basketball (boys, girls), soccer (b,g), volleyball (b,g); intramural: basketball (b,g), soccer (b,g), volleyball (b,g); coed interscholastic: tennis, track and field; coed intramural: dance, tennis, track and field, yoga. 1 PE instructor, 6 coaches.

Computers Computers are regularly used in English, foreign language, mathematics, photography, science, social studies classes. Computer network features include on-campus library services, Internet access, wireless campus network, Internet filtering or blocking technology, in-house technical assistance. Campus intranet, student e-mail accounts, and computer access in designated common areas are available to students. Students grades are available online. The school has a published electronic and media policy.

Contact Ms. Alex Perniciaro, Admissions Coordinator. 39-06-575-0605. Fax: 39-06-574-1941. E-mail: alex.perniciaro@sssrome.it. Website: www.sssrome.it

SAINT TERESA'S ACADEMY

5600 Main Street
Kansas City, Missouri 64113

Head of School: Mrs. Nan Tiehen Bone

General Information Girls' day college-preparatory school, affiliated with Roman Catholic Church. Grades 9–12. Founded: 1866. Setting: urban. 20-acre campus. 4 buildings on campus. Approved or accredited by National Catholic Education Association, North Central Association of Colleges and Schools, and Missouri Department of Education. Endowment: $150,000. Total enrollment: 596. Upper school average class size: 21. Upper school faculty-student ratio: 1:12. There are 174 required school days per year for Upper School students. Upper School students typically attend 5 days per week. The average school day consists of 6 hours and 40 minutes.

Upper School Student Profile Grade 9: 163 students (163 girls); Grade 10: 128 students (128 girls); Grade 11: 153 students (153 girls); Grade 12: 152 students (152 girls). 87% of students are Roman Catholic.

Faculty School total: 52. In upper school: 9 men, 40 women; 35 have advanced degrees.

Subjects Offered Advanced chemistry, advanced math, algebra, American government, American history, American history-AP, American literature, American literature-AP, analysis, anatomy and physiology, art, athletics, basketball, biology, biology-AP, botany, British literature, calculus, career/college preparation, chamber groups, chemistry, chemistry-AP, choir, chorus, computer graphics, computer programming, current events, dance, directing, drama, drawing, ecology, English, English language and composition-AP, English language-AP, English literature, European history-AP, fiber arts, fitness, foreign language, forensics, French, French language-AP, French-AP, freshman seminar, geometry, golf, graphic design, health, independent study, journalism, keyboarding, language arts, Latin, Latin History, music-AP, newspaper, painting, physical education, physics, piano, playwriting, portfolio art, pre-calculus, probability and statistics, psychology, psychology-AP, Shakespeare, social issues, social studies, sociology, softball, Spanish, Spanish language-AP, Spanish literature-AP, Spanish-AP, speech, speech and debate, speech communications, sports conditioning, sports performance development, stagecraft, swimming, technical theater, tennis, theater, theology and the arts, track and field, trigonometry, U.S. government, U.S. government and politics, U.S. government and politics-AP, U.S. history, U.S. history-AP, volleyball, Western civilization, women in literature, women spirituality and faith, world geography, world history-AP, world religions, world religions, writing, writing, yearbook.

Graduation Requirements Arts and fine arts (art, music, dance, drama), computer science, electives, English, foreign language, mathematics, physical education (includes health), science, social studies (includes history), theology. Community service is required.

Special Academic Programs 10 Advanced Placement exams for which test preparation is offered; honors sections; study at local college for college credit.

College Admission Counseling 144 students graduated in 2015; all went to college, including Kansas State University; Saint Louis University; The University of Kansas; University of Arkansas; University of Missouri. Mean SAT critical reading: 600, mean SAT math: 580, mean SAT writing: 610, mean combined SAT: 1780, mean composite ACT: 26.

Student Life Upper grades have uniform requirement, student council. Discipline rests primarily with faculty. Attendance at religious services is required.

Summer Programs Enrichment, sports, art/fine arts, computer instruction programs offered; session focuses on fine arts, sports, credit bearing courses, and enrichment summer school programs; held on campus; accepts girls; open to students from other schools. 135 students usually enrolled. 2016 schedule: June 6 to July 1. Application deadline: March 1.

Tuition and Aid Day student tuition: $11,650. Tuition installment plan (SMART Tuition Payment Plan). Tuition reduction for siblings, merit scholarship grants, need-based scholarship grants available. In 2015–16, 25% of upper-school students received aid; total upper-school merit-scholarship money awarded: $60,000. Total amount of financial aid awarded in 2015–16: $150,000.

Admissions Traditional secondary-level entrance grade is 9. For fall 2015, 178 students applied for upper-level admission, 166 were accepted, 163 enrolled. Placement test required. Deadline for receipt of application materials: February 27. Application fee required: $350.

Athletics Interscholastic: aerobics/dance, basketball, cross-country running, diving, drill team, golf, lacrosse, soccer, softball, swimming and diving, tennis, track and field, volleyball; intramural: aerobics/dance, badminton, fitness, fitness walking, jogging, physical fitness, physical training, running, strength & conditioning, table tennis, volleyball, walking, weight lifting, weight training. 1 PE instructor, 25 coaches, 1 athletic trainer.

Computers Computers are regularly used in business education, creative writing, desktop publishing, graphic arts, graphic design, graphics, journalism, library, literary magazine, newspaper, photography, research skills, science, writing, yearbook classes. Computer network features include on-campus library services, Internet access, wireless campus network, Internet filtering or blocking technology. Campus intranet and student e-mail accounts are available to students. Students grades are available online. The school has a published electronic and media policy.

Contact Mrs. Roseann Hudnall, Admissions Director. 816-501-0011 Ext. 135. Fax: 816-523-0232. E-mail: rhudnall@stteresasacademy.org.

Website: www.stteresasacademy.org

ST. THOMAS AQUINAS HIGH SCHOOL

2801 Southwest 12th Street
Fort Lauderdale, Florida 33312-2999

Head of School: Dr. Denise Aloma

General Information Coeducational day college-preparatory, arts, religious studies, technology, campus ministry, and college preparatory school, affiliated with Roman Catholic Church. Grades 9–12. Founded: 1936. Setting: suburban. 24-acre campus. 23 buildings on campus. Approved or accredited by National Catholic Education Association, Southern Association of Colleges and Schools, and Florida Department of Education. Total enrollment: 2,171. Upper school average class size: 25. Upper school faculty-student ratio: 1:18. There are 180 required school days per year for Upper School students. Upper School students typically attend 5 days per week. The average school day consists of 6 hours and 30 minutes.

Upper School Student Profile Grade 9: 538 students (273 boys, 265 girls); Grade 10: 557 students (259 boys, 298 girls); Grade 11: 546 students (256 boys, 290 girls); Grade 12: 530 students (272 boys, 258 girls). 85% of students are Roman Catholic.

Faculty School total: 138. In upper school: 60 men, 70 women; 73 have advanced degrees.

Subjects Offered 20th century history, 20th century world history, 3-dimensional art, ACT preparation, acting, advanced biology, advanced chemistry, advanced computer applications, advanced math, Advanced Placement courses, advanced studio art-AP, aerobics, algebra, American government, American history, American history-AP, American literature, anatomy, anatomy and physiology, animation, art, art appreciation, art history, art history-AP, art-AP, athletics, audio visual/media, audition methods, ballet, baseball, Bible, biology, biology-AP, bowling, British literature, British literature (honors), British literature-AP, broadcast journalism, broadcasting, Broadway dance, calculus, calculus-AP, campus ministry, cartooning/animation, Catholic belief and practice, cheerleading, chemistry, chemistry-AP, Chinese, choir, choral music, choreography, chorus, Christian scripture, Christianity, church history, comparative government and politics-AP, comparative political systems-AP, composition-AP, computer applications, computer art, computer graphics, computer programming-AP, computer science, computer science-AP, computer skills, concert band, concert choir, creative dance, creative drama, debate, desktop publishing, digital art, digital imaging, directing, drama, drama performance, drama workshop, dramatic arts, drawing, drawing and design, driver education, earth science, economics, economics-AP, electives, English, English composition, English language and composition-AP, English language-AP, English literature, English literature and composition-AP, English literature-AP, English-AP, English/composition-AP, environmental science, environmental science-AP, environmental studies, ethics, European history, European history-AP, fiction, film, film and literature, film and new technologies, film appreciation, film history, fitness, food science, foreign language, forensics, French, French language-AP, French literature-AP, French-AP, general science, genetics, geography, geometry, government, government and politics-AP, government-AP, government/civics-AP, grammar, graphic arts, graphic design, health, health and safety, health and wellness, health education, health enhancement, health science, healthful living, Hispanic literature, history, history of drama, history-AP, Holocaust, honors algebra, honors English, honors geometry, honors U.S. history, honors world history, human anatomy, human geography - AP, instrumental music, Italian, Italian history, jazz, jazz band, jazz ensemble, jazz theory, journalism, keyboarding, lab science, language, language and composition, language arts, language-AP, Latin, Latin-AP, leadership, leadership and service, leadership education training, library skills, Life of Christ, literature, literature and composition-AP, literature-AP, macro/microeconomics-AP, macroeconomics-AP, marching band, marine biology, marine science, marine studies, mathematics, mathematics-AP, media, microeconomics, microeconomics-AP, model United Nations, modern dance, modern European history, modern European history-AP, music, music appreciation, music composition, music performance, music theory, musical theater, New Testament, news writing, newspaper, nutrition, oral communications, oral expression, orchestra, painting, peace and justice, peace education, peace studies, performing arts, photography, photojournalism, physical education, physical fitness, physical science, physics, physics-AP, play production, playwriting and directing, poetry, political systems, pottery, prayer/spirituality, pre-algebra, pre-calculus, probability, probability and statistics, psychology, psychology-AP, public speaking, publications, reading, religion, religion and culture, religious education, religious studies, robotics, SAT preparation, SAT/ACT preparation, science, science and technology, science project, science research, Shakespeare, Shakespearean

histories, Spanish, Spanish language-AP, Spanish literature, Spanish literature-AP, Spanish-AP, speech, speech and debate, speech and oral interpretations, speech communications, sports team management, stage and body movement, stage design, stagecraft, statistics, statistics-AP, student government, student publications, studio art, study skills, swimming, technical theater, television, tennis, theater arts, theater design and production, theater history, theater production, theology, trigonometry, U.S. government, U.S. government and politics, U.S. government and politics-AP, U.S. history, U.S. history-AP, U.S. literature, U.S. Presidents, United States government-AP, vocal ensemble, vocal jazz, vocal music, voice, voice and diction, voice ensemble, volleyball, water color painting, water polo, weight training, weightlifting, Western civilization, women's studies, world history, world history-AP.

Graduation Requirements Arts and fine arts (art, music, dance, drama), computer science, electives, English, foreign language, health, mathematics, personal fitness, science, social sciences, theology.

Special Academic Programs Advanced Placement exam preparation; honors section; study at local college for college credit; remedial reading and/or remedial writing; remedial math.

College Admission Counseling 532 students graduated in 2015; 527 went to college, including Florida Atlantic University; Florida State University; University of Central Florida; University of Florida; University of Miami; University of North Florida. Other: 1 entered military service, 4 had other specific plans. Mean SAT critical reading: 568, mean SAT math: 562, mean SAT writing: 577, mean composite ACT: 24.

Student Life Upper grades have uniform requirement, honor system. Discipline rests primarily with faculty. Attendance at religious services is required.

Summer Programs Remediation, enrichment, advancement, art/fine arts, computer instruction programs offered; session focuses on enrichment; held on campus; accepts boys and girls; open to students from other schools. 1,000 students usually enrolled. 2016 schedule: June 13 to June 29. Application deadline: June 13.

Tuition and Aid Tuition installment plan (TADS). Need-based scholarship grants available.

Admissions Traditional secondary-level entrance grade is 9. For fall 2015, 754 students applied for upper-level admission, 578 were accepted, 560 enrolled. High School Placement Test required. Deadline for receipt of application materials: none. Application fee required: $50. Interview required.

Athletics Interscholastic: aerobics/dance (girls), baseball (b), basketball (b,g), bowling (b,g), cheering (g), cross-country running (b,g), dance (b,g), dance squad (g), dance team (g), diving (b,g), drill team (g), football (b), golf (b,g), lacrosse (b,g), physical fitness (b,g), running (b,g), sailing (b,g), soccer (b,g), softball (g), swimming and diving (b,g), tennis (b,g), track and field (b,g), volleyball (b,g), water polo (b,g), wrestling (b); intramural: dance team (g), danceline (g), drill team (g); coed interscholastic: ballet, bowling, hockey, ice hockey, indoor hockey, physical training; coed intramural: physical training, running. 2 PE instructors, 39 coaches, 1 athletic trainer.

Computers Computers are regularly used in all academic, data processing, desktop publishing, graphic arts, graphic design, graphics, journalism, keyboarding, lab/keyboard, media, media arts, media production, media services, news writing, newspaper, programming, publications, publishing, technology, video film production, Web site design, word processing classes. Computer network features include on-campus library services, online commercial services, Internet access, wireless campus network, Internet filtering or blocking technology. Campus intranet, student e-mail accounts, and computer access in designated common areas are available to students. Students grades are available online. The school has a published electronic and media policy.

Contact Admissions Office. 954-581-2127 Ext. 8623. Fax: 954-327-2193. E-mail: mary.facella@aquinas-sta.org. Website: www.aquinas-sta.org

SAINT THOMAS AQUINAS HIGH SCHOOL

11411 Pflumm Road
Overland Park, Kansas 66215-4816

Head of School: Dr. William P. Ford

General Information Coeducational day college-preparatory, religious studies, and technology school, affiliated with Roman Catholic Church. Grades 9–12. Founded: 1988. Setting: suburban. Nearest major city is Kansas City, MO. 44-acre campus. 2 buildings on campus. Approved or accredited by National Catholic Education Association, North Central Association of Colleges and Schools, and Kansas Department of Education. Total enrollment: 900. Upper school average class size: 24. Upper school faculty-student ratio: 1:15. There are 180 required school days per year for Upper School students. Upper School students typically attend 5 days per week. The average school day consists of 7 hours.

Upper School Student Profile Grade 9: 250 students (135 boys, 115 girls); Grade 10: 206 students (86 boys, 120 girls); Grade 11: 223 students (106 boys, 117 girls); Grade 12: 225 students (110 boys, 115 girls). 97% of students are Roman Catholic.

Faculty School total: 66. In upper school: 30 men, 36 women; 64 have advanced degrees.

Graduation Requirements Arts and fine arts (art, music, dance, drama), computer technologies, electives, English, Latin, mathematics, modern languages, physical education (includes health), science, social studies (includes history), speech, theology, service (one fourth credit each of 4 years).

Special Academic Programs Advanced Placement exam preparation; honors section; study at local college for college credit; academic accommodation for the gifted; remedial reading and/or remedial writing; remedial math.

College Admission Counseling 220 students graduated in 2015; 219 went to college, including Benedictine College; Johnson County Community College; Kansas State University; The University of Kansas; University of Arkansas; University of Notre Dame. Other: 1 entered military service. Mean SAT critical reading: 619, mean SAT math: 638, mean SAT writing: 603, mean composite ACT: 25.

Student Life Upper grades have uniform requirement, student council. Discipline rests primarily with faculty. Attendance at religious services is required.

Summer Programs Remediation, advancement, sports, computer instruction programs offered; session focuses on sports camps and selected academic coursework; held on campus; accepts boys and girls; open to students from other schools.

Tuition and Aid Day student tuition: $8400–$9500. Tuition installment plan (SMART Tuition Payment Plan). Tuition reduction for siblings, merit scholarship grants, need-based scholarship grants available. In 2015–16, 30% of upper-school students received aid. Total amount of financial aid awarded in 2015–16: $1,000,000.

Admissions Traditional secondary-level entrance grade is 9. High School Placement Test required. Deadline for receipt of application materials: none. Application fee required: $200. Interview required.

Athletics Interscholastic: baseball (boys), basketball (b,g), bowling (b,g), cross-country running (b,g), dance team (g), diving (b,g), football (b), golf (b,g), soccer (b,g), softball (g), swimming and diving (b,g), tennis (b,g), track and field (b,g), volleyball (g), wrestling (b); intramural: field hockey (g), lacrosse (b); coed interscholastic: cheering; coed intramural: table tennis, ultimate Frisbee. 3 PE instructors, 1 athletic trainer.

Computers Computers are regularly used in all academic, computer applications, desktop publishing, programming, video film production, Web site design classes. Computer network features include on-campus library services, Internet access, wireless campus network, computer labs and laptop carts. Student e-mail accounts and computer access in designated common areas are available to students. Students grades are available online. The school has a published electronic and media policy.

Contact Mrs. Diane Pyle, Director of Admissions. 913-319-2423. Fax: 913-345-2319. E-mail: dpyle@stasaints.net. Website: www.stasaints.net

ST. THOMAS AQUINAS HIGH SCHOOL

197 Dover Point Road
Dover, New Hampshire 03820

Head of School: Mr. Kevin Collins

General Information Coeducational day college-preparatory and religious studies school, affiliated with Roman Catholic Church. Grades 9–12. Founded: 1960. Setting: small town. Nearest major city is Boston, MA. 11-acre campus. 2 buildings on campus. Approved or accredited by New England Association of Schools and Colleges and New Hampshire Department of Education. Total enrollment: 526. Upper school average class size: 18. Upper school faculty-student ratio: 1:13. There are 186 required school days per year for Upper School students. Upper School students typically attend 5 days per week. The average school day consists of 6 hours and 25 minutes.

Subjects Offered 3-dimensional design, advanced math, algebra, American history-AP, American literature-AP, anatomy and physiology, biology, biology-AP, biotechnology, British literature, British literature (honors), calculus, calculus-AP, chemistry, chorus, Christian ethics, civics, concert band, drawing, economics, English, English language-AP, English literature-AP, environmental science-AP, French, freshman seminar, geography, geometry, government-AP, health education, honors algebra, honors English, honors geometry, honors U.S. history, humanities, international relations, introduction to technology, jazz band, Latin, marine biology, math applications, media arts, music appreciation, music theory, painting, physics, prayer/spirituality, pre-calculus, psychology, public speaking, science, scripture, sculpture, social justice, sociology, Spanish, statistics-AP, studio art, theology, trigonometry, U.S. government and politics-AP, U.S. history, U.S. history-AP, wellness, Western civilization, world religions.

Graduation Requirements Arts and fine arts (art, music, dance, drama), Christian ethics, electives, English, foreign language, freshman seminar, mathematics, prayer/spirituality, science, scripture, social justice, social studies (includes history), theology, world religions, 40 hour community service requirement.

Special Academic Programs Advanced Placement exam preparation; honors section; independent study.

College Admission Counseling 132 students graduated in 2015; 122 went to college, including Plymouth State University; Saint Anselm College; Simmons College; Suffolk University; University of New Hampshire. Other: 3 entered military service, 2 entered a postgraduate year, 5 had other specific plans. Mean SAT critical reading: 553, mean SAT math: 555, mean SAT writing: 544, mean composite ACT: 24.

Student Life Upper grades have specified standards of dress, student council. Discipline rests primarily with faculty. Attendance at religious services is required.

Summer Programs Enrichment programs offered; held on campus; accepts boys and girls; not open to students from other schools.

Tuition and Aid Day student tuition: $12,100. Tuition installment plan (annual, semiannual, and 10-month payment plans). Need-based scholarship grants available. In 2015–16, 33% of upper-school students received aid.

Admissions Traditional secondary-level entrance grade is 9. Scholastic Testing Service High School Placement Test required. Deadline for receipt of application materials: December 18. Application fee required: $40.

Athletics Interscholastic: baseball (boys), basketball (b,g), cross-country running (b,g), field hockey (g), football (b), golf (b,g), ice hockey (b,g), lacrosse (b,g), skiing (downhill) (b,g), soccer (b,g), softball (g), swimming and diving (b,g), tennis (b,g), track and field (b,g), volleyball (g), winter (indoor) track (b,g); intramural: dance team (g). 51 coaches, 1 athletic trainer.

Computers Computers are regularly used in animation, design, introduction to technology, media arts, programming classes. Computer network features include on-campus library services, Internet access, wireless campus network. Student e-mail accounts and computer access in designated common areas are available to students. Students grades are available online.

Contact Mr. Keith Adams, Director of Admissions. 603-742-3206. Fax: 603-749-7822. E-mail: kadams@stalux.org. Website: www.stalux.org

ST. THOMAS CHOIR SCHOOL

New York, New York
See Junior Boarding Schools section.

ST. THOMAS HIGH SCHOOL

4500 Memorial Drive
Houston, Texas 77007-7332

Head of School: Rev. Patrick Fulton, CSB

General Information Boys' day college-preparatory and religious studies school, affiliated with Roman Catholic Church. Grades 9–12. Founded: 1900. Setting: urban. 37-acre campus. 6 buildings on campus. Approved or accredited by Southern Association of Colleges and Schools, Texas Catholic Conference, Texas Education Agency, and Texas Department of Education. Member of National Association of Independent Schools. Endowment: $12 million. Total enrollment: 774. Upper school average class size: 19. Upper school faculty-student ratio: 1:14. There are 185 required school days per year for Upper School students. Upper School students typically attend 5 days per week. The average school day consists of 7 hours and 20 minutes.

Upper School Student Profile Grade 9: 226 students (226 boys); Grade 10: 190 students (190 boys); Grade 11: 201 students (201 boys); Grade 12: 157 students (157 boys). 70% of students are Roman Catholic.

Faculty School total: 56. In upper school: 35 men, 21 women; 26 have advanced degrees.

Subjects Offered Algebra, American government, American history, American history-AP, American literature, anatomy and physiology, ancient history, art, arts, Basic programming, Bible studies, bioethics, biology, biology-AP, British literature, calculus, calculus-AP, ceramics, chemistry, chemistry-AP, civics/free enterprise, classical civilization, college counseling, comparative government and politics-AP, computer applications, computer information systems, computer programming, computer studies, creative writing, critical thinking, critical writing, decision making skills, desktop publishing, digital photography, drama, drawing, ecology, environmental systems, economics, economics-AP, English, English language-AP, English literature, English literature-AP, environmental education, environmental science, ethics, European history, fine arts, forensics, French, geography, geology, geometry, government and politics-AP, government/civics, grammar, guidance, health, health education, history of the Catholic Church, Holocaust studies, instrumental music, jazz band, journalism, Latin, marine biology, mathematics, military history, oceanography, oral communications, orchestra, painting, photography, physical education, physics, physics-AP, pre-calculus, programming, public speaking, publications, religion, social studies, Spanish, Spanish language-AP, speech, student government, student publications, theater, theology, trigonometry, U.S. government and politics-AP, world history, world literature.

Graduation Requirements Arts and fine arts (art, music, dance, drama), computer applications, English, foreign language, mathematics, physical education (includes health), religion (includes Bible studies and theology), science, social studies (includes history).

Special Academic Programs 10 Advanced Placement exams for which test preparation is offered; honors section.

College Admission Counseling 177 students graduated in 2014; 176 went to college, including Louisiana State University and Agricultural & Mechanical College; Texas A&M University; Texas Tech University; The University of Texas at Austin; The University of Texas at San Antonio; University of Houston. Other: 1 entered military service. Mean composite ACT: 26.

Student Life Upper grades have specified standards of dress, student council, honor system. Discipline rests primarily with faculty. Attendance at religious services is required.

Tuition and Aid Day student tuition: $14,500. Tuition installment plan (monthly payment plans). Merit scholarship grants, need-based scholarship grants, middle-income loans available. In 2014–15, 30% of upper-school students received aid; total upper-school merit-scholarship money awarded: $200,000. Total amount of financial aid awarded in 2014–15: $1,200,000.

Admissions Traditional secondary-level entrance grade is 9. For fall 2014, 561 students applied for upper-level admission, 325 were accepted, 229 enrolled. High School Placement Test required. Deadline for receipt of application materials: January 15. Application fee required: $75.

Athletics Interscholastic: baseball, basketball, cross-country running, football, golf, lacrosse, rugby, soccer, swimming and diving, tennis, track and field, wrestling; intramural: basketball, bowling, flag football, Frisbee, roller hockey, table tennis, weight lifting. 2 PE instructors, 2 coaches, 1 athletic trainer.

Computers Computers are regularly used in data processing, desktop publishing, multimedia, newspaper, photography, programming, publications, Web site design, word processing classes. Computer network features include on-campus library services, Internet access, wireless campus network, Internet filtering or blocking technology. Campus intranet, student e-mail accounts, and computer access in designated common areas are available to students. Students grades are available online. The school has a published electronic and media policy.

Contact Ms. Christine Westman, Assistant Principal. 713-864-6348. Fax: 713-864-5750. E-mail: chris.westman@sths.org. Website: www.sths.org

SAINT THOMAS MORE CATHOLIC HIGH SCHOOL

450 East Farrel Road
Lafayette, Louisiana 70508

Head of School: Mr. Richard Lavergne

General Information Coeducational day college-preparatory, arts, business, religious studies, bilingual studies, and technology school, affiliated with Roman Catholic Church. Grades 9–12. Founded: 1982. Setting: suburban. Nearest major city is Baton Rouge. 45-acre campus. 1 building on campus. Approved or accredited by National Catholic Education Association, Southern Association of Colleges and Schools, and Louisiana Department of Education. Endowment: $3 million. Total enrollment: 1,050. Upper school average class size: 24. Upper school faculty-student ratio: 1:12. There are 179 required school days per year for Upper School students. Upper School students typically attend 5 days per week. The average school day consists of 7 hours.

Upper School Student Profile Grade 9: 279 students (127 boys, 152 girls); Grade 10: 256 students (125 boys, 131 girls); Grade 11: 249 students (127 boys, 122 girls); Grade 12: 266 students (128 boys, 138 girls). 93% of students are Roman Catholic.

Faculty School total: 93. In upper school: 30 men, 63 women; 44 have advanced degrees.

Subjects Offered ACT preparation, advanced chemistry, advanced math, Advanced Placement courses, advanced studio art-AP, algebra, American history, anatomy and physiology, applied music, art, athletics, band, biology, biology-AP, business, calculus-AP, campus ministry, chemistry, chemistry-AP, choir, civics/free enterprise, computer literacy, computer multimedia, computer science, computer skills, creative writing, debate, desktop publishing, drama, English, English language and composition-AP, English literature and composition-AP, environmental science, European history-AP, fitness, French, geography, geometry, health, honors algebra, honors English, honors U.S. history, honors world history, independent study, kinesiology, Latin, mathematics, newspaper, photography, physical education, physical science, physics, play production, pre-calculus, psychology, psychology-AP, public speaking, religion, Spanish, speech, speech and debate, studio art-AP, study skills, trigonometry, U.S. government and politics-AP, U.S. history-AP, Web site design, weight training, world history, yearbook.

Graduation Requirements Arts and fine arts (art, music, dance, drama), business applications, English, French, keyboarding, mathematics, physical education (includes health), religion (includes Bible studies and theology), science, social studies (includes history), Spanish, world history.

Special Academic Programs 10 Advanced Placement exams for which test preparation is offered; honors section; independent study; study at local college for college credit; academic accommodation for the gifted; remedial reading and/or remedial writing; remedial math.

College Admission Counseling 258 students graduated in 2015; 254 went to college, including Louisiana State University and Agricultural & Mechanical College; Spring Hill College; Tulane University; University of Louisiana at Lafayette; University of Mississippi. Other: 2 went to work, 2 had other specific plans. Median composite ACT: 24. 26.5% scored over 26 on composite ACT.

Student Life Upper grades have uniform requirement, student council, honor system. Discipline rests primarily with faculty. Attendance at religious services is required.

Tuition and Aid Day student tuition: $6070–$6270. Tuition installment plan (monthly payment plans, individually arranged payment plans). Merit scholarship grants, need-based scholarship grants, paying campus jobs available. In 2015–16, 5% of upper-school students received aid; total upper-school merit-scholarship money awarded: $98,000. Total amount of financial aid awarded in 2015–16: $100,000.

Admissions Traditional secondary-level entrance grade is 9. Achievement tests, ACT-Explore, any standardized test, Explore, High School Placement Test, latest standardized score from previous school and standardized test scores required. Deadline for receipt of application materials: none. No application fee required.

Athletics Interscholastic: aquatics (boys, girls), baseball (b), basketball (b,g), bowling (b,g), cross-country running (b,g), dance squad (g), dance team (g), football (b), golf (b), indoor track (b,g), indoor track & field (b,g), physical training (b,g), soccer (b,g), softball (g), strength & conditioning (b,g), tennis (b,g), track and field (b,g), volleyball (g), weight lifting (b,g), weight training (b,g), winter (indoor) track (b,g), wrestling (b); intramural: flag football (b,g), lacrosse (b); coed interscholastic: cheering, Special Olympics. 4 PE instructors, 4 coaches.

Computers Computers are regularly used in all academic, library classes. Computer network features include on-campus library services, online commercial services, Internet access, wireless campus network, Internet filtering or blocking technology, computer access in the library before and after school and during lunch. Campus intranet, student e-mail accounts, and computer access in designated common areas are available to students. Students grades are available online. The school has a published electronic and media policy.

Contact Ms. Natalie D. Broussard '00, Assistant Director of Admissions. 337-988-7779. Fax: 337-988-2911. E-mail: natalie.broussard@stmcougars.net. Website: www.stmcougars.net

ST. TIMOTHY'S SCHOOL

8400 Greenspring Avenue
Stevenson, Maryland 21153

Head of School: Randy S. Stevens

General Information Girls' boarding and day college-preparatory, arts, and International Baccalaureate school, affiliated with Episcopal Church. Grades 9–12. Founded: 1882. Setting: suburban. Nearest major city is Baltimore. Students are housed in single-sex dormitories. 145-acre campus. 24 buildings on campus. Approved or accredited by Association of Independent Maryland Schools, International Baccalaureate Organization, Middle States Association of Colleges and Schools, National Association of Episcopal Schools, The Association of Boarding Schools, and Maryland Department of Education. Member of National Association of Independent Schools and Secondary School Admission Test Board. Endowment: $10 million. Total enrollment: 199. Upper school average class size: 12. Upper school faculty-student ratio: 1:6. There are 175 required school days per year for Upper School students. Upper School students typically attend 5 days per week. The average school day consists of 7 hours.

Upper School Student Profile Grade 9: 40 students (40 girls); Grade 10: 52 students (52 girls); Grade 11: 57 students (57 girls); Grade 12: 50 students (50 girls). 69% of students are boarding students, 37% are state residents. 20 states are represented in upper school student body. 31% are international students. International students from China, Germany, Ghana, Japan, Mexico, and Nigeria; 21 other countries represented in student body.

Faculty School total: 27. In upper school: 11 men, 15 women; 17 have advanced degrees; 22 reside on campus.

Subjects Offered Algebra, American literature, art, art history, bell choir, biology, British literature, calculus, chemistry, Chinese, choir, college counseling, comparative politics, creative writing, dance, drama, drama performance, drama workshop, economics, English, English composition, English literature, ESL, ethics, European history, fine arts, foreign language, French, geometry, history, integrated mathematics, International Baccalaureate courses, Mandarin, mathematics, modern dance, music, photography, physics, piano, SAT preparation, science, Spanish, U.S. history, world history, world literature, writing.

Graduation Requirements Arts and fine arts (art, music, dance, drama), English, foreign language, history, mathematics, physical education (includes health), science, Theory of Knowledge course, extended essay, Community, Action, and Service (CAS). Community service is required.

Special Academic Programs International Baccalaureate program; independent study; ESL (21 students enrolled).

College Admission Counseling 39 students graduated in 2015; all went to college, including Haverford College; Syracuse University; University of California, Los Angeles; University of Maryland, College Park; Wake Forest University.

Student Life Upper grades have uniform requirement, student council, honor system. Discipline rests equally with students and faculty. Attendance at religious services is required.

Summer Programs ESL programs offered; session focuses on global immersion/intensive language; held on campus; accepts boys and girls; open to students from other schools. 2016 schedule: July 31 to August 27.

Tuition and Aid Day student tuition: $29,300; 7-day tuition and room/board: $51,800. Tuition installment plan (FACTS Tuition Payment Plan). Merit scholarship grants, need-based scholarship grants, need-based loans available. In 2015–16, 51% of upper-school students received aid; total upper-school merit-scholarship money awarded: $445,000. Total amount of financial aid awarded in 2015–16: $3,257,000.

Admissions Traditional secondary-level entrance grade is 9. For fall 2015, 229 students applied for upper-level admission, 121 were accepted, 65 enrolled. ISEE, SLEP for foreign students, SSAT or TOEFL required. Deadline for receipt of application materials: February 1. Application fee required: $50. Interview required.

Athletics Interscholastic: badminton, basketball, cross-country running, dressage, equestrian sports, field hockey, golf, horseback riding, ice hockey, indoor soccer, lacrosse, soccer, softball, squash, swimming and diving, tennis, volleyball; intramural: ballet, dance, dance squad, equestrian sports, horseback riding, modern dance, outdoor adventure, weight training, yoga. 8 coaches, 1 athletic trainer.

Computers Computers are regularly used in art, college planning, English, mathematics, publications, SAT preparation, science, yearbook classes. Computer network features include on-campus library services, online commercial services, Internet access, wireless campus network, Internet filtering or blocking technology. Student e-mail accounts are available to students. The school has a published electronic and media policy.

Contact Kimberly Coughlin, Director of Admissions. 410-486-7401. Fax: 410-486-1167. E-mail: kcoughlin@stt.org. Website: www.stt.org

SAINT URSULA ACADEMY

1339 East McMillan Street
Cincinnati, Ohio 45206

Head of School: Mr. Craig Maliborski

General Information Girls' day college preparatory, arts, religious studies, and technology school, affiliated with Roman Catholic Church; primarily serves students with learning disabilities, individuals with Attention Deficit Disorder, and dyslexic students. Grades 9–12. Founded: 1910. Setting: urban. 10-acre campus. Approved or accredited by Ohio Catholic Schools Accreditation Association (OCSAA) and Ohio Department of Education. Upper school average class size: 665.

Upper School Student Profile Grade 6: 665 students (665 girls). 90% of students are Roman Catholic.

College Admission Counseling 170 students graduated in 2015; all went to college.

Student Life Upper grades have uniform requirement, honor system. Attendance at religious services is required.

Tuition and Aid Merit scholarship grants, need-based scholarship grants available.

Admissions Traditional secondary-level entrance grade is 9. Deadline for receipt of application materials: November 19. No application fee required.

Computers The school has a published electronic and media policy.

Contact Ms. Michelle Dellecave, Director of Admissions. 513-961-3410 Ext. 183. Fax: 513-961-3856. E-mail: mdellecave@saintursula.org. Website: www.saintursula.org

SAINT URSULA ACADEMY

4025 Indian Road
Toledo, Ohio 43606

Head of School: Mrs. Mary Werner

General Information Girls' day college-preparatory, arts, business, religious studies, bilingual studies, technology, and college preparatory school, affiliated with Roman Catholic Church. Grades 6–12. Founded: 1854. Setting: suburban. 16-acre campus. 1 building on campus. Approved or accredited by National Catholic Education Association, North Central Association of Colleges and Schools, Ohio Catholic Schools Accreditation Association (OCSAA), and Ohio Department of Education. Total enrollment: 552. Upper school average class size: 17. Upper school faculty-student ratio: 1:10. There are 185 required school days per year for Upper School students. Upper School students typically attend 5 days per week. The average school day consists of 7 hours.

Upper School Student Profile Grade 6: 22 students (22 girls); Grade 7: 34 students (34 girls); Grade 8: 49 students (49 girls); Grade 9: 105 students (105 girls); Grade 10: 100 students (100 girls); Grade 11: 111 students (111 girls); Grade 12: 131 students (131 girls). 70% of students are Roman Catholic.

Faculty School total: 51. In upper school: 9 men, 41 women; 32 have advanced degrees.

Subjects Offered 3-dimensional art, accounting, Advanced Placement courses, advanced studio art-AP, algebra, American government, American history, American history-AP, American literature, anatomy, anatomy and physiology, art, art-AP, ballet, biology, British literature, British literature-AP, business law, calculus-AP, career exploration, Catholic belief and practice, ceramics, chemistry, chemistry-AP, choral music, choreography, chorus, church history, comparative government and politics-AP, comparative religion, composition-AP, computer applications, computer graphics, concert choir, dance, digital photography, drama, drawing, economics, electives, engineering, English language and composition-AP, English literature and composition-AP, fashion, female experience in America, film history, foreign language, French language-AP, geometry, government, government and politics-AP, graphic arts, health, history of the Catholic Church, honors algebra, honors English, honors geometry, honors world history, human geography - AP, instrumental music, Latin, Latin-AP, literature, literature and composition-AP, Mandarin, marketing, mathematics-AP, microeconomics, music, music theory-AP, New Testament, orchestra, painting, personal finance, photography, physical education, physics, physiology, pre-calculus, printmaking, probability and statistics, psychology, psychology-AP, religion and culture, religious education, sculpture, single survival, social psychology, Spanish, Spanish language-AP, speech, statistics, statistics-AP, student publications, studio art-AP, symphonic band, theology, trigonometry, U.S. government and politics, U.S. government and politics-AP, U.S. history, U.S. history-AP, U.S. literature, United States government-AP, vocal music, women's health, women's studies, yearbook.

Graduation Requirements Arts and fine arts (art, music, dance, drama), computers, English, foreign language, mathematics, physical education (includes health), science, social studies (includes history), theology, community service, career exploration experience.

Special Academic Programs 15 Advanced Placement exams for which test preparation is offered; honors section; study at local college for college credit.

College Admission Counseling 127 students graduated in 2015; all went to college, including Miami University; The Ohio State University; The University of Toledo; University of Cincinnati; University of Dayton. Mean SAT critical reading: 570, mean SAT math: 551, mean SAT writing: 543, mean composite ACT: 24. 40% scored over 600 on SAT critical reading, 25% scored over 600 on SAT math, 58% scored over 600 on SAT writing, 37% scored over 26 on composite ACT.

Student Life Upper grades have uniform requirement, student council, honor system. Discipline rests primarily with faculty. Attendance at religious services is required.

Summer Programs Enrichment, advancement, sports, art/fine arts, computer instruction programs offered; session focuses on athletics and academics; held both on and off campus; held at golf course; accepts girls; open to students from other schools. 300 students usually enrolled. 2016 schedule: June 6 to July 29. Application deadline: June 1.

Tuition and Aid Day student tuition: $10,400. Tuition installment plan (SMART Tuition Payment Plan). Tuition reduction for siblings, merit scholarship grants, need-based scholarship grants, paying campus jobs available. In 2015–16, 75% of upper-school students received aid; total upper-school merit-scholarship money awarded: $200,000. Total amount of financial aid awarded in 2015–16: $1,420,000.

Admissions Traditional secondary-level entrance grade is 9. High School Placement Test or placement test required. Deadline for receipt of application materials: none. No application fee required.

Athletics Interscholastic: aerobics/dance, ballet, basketball, bowling, broomball, cheering, crew, cross-country running, dance team, diving, equestrian sports, fencing, golf, gymnastics, horseback riding, independent competitive sports, lacrosse, modern dance, physical fitness, physical training, rowing, soccer, softball, swimming and diving, tennis, track and field, volleyball, water polo, weight training; intramural: badminton, cooperative games, volleyball. 1 PE instructor, 32 coaches, 1 athletic trainer.

Computers Computers are regularly used in accounting, computer applications, graphic arts, newspaper, Web site design, yearbook classes. Computer network features include on-campus library services, Internet access, wireless campus network, Internet filtering or blocking technology. Campus intranet, student e-mail accounts, and computer access in designated common areas are available to students. Students grades are available online. The school has a published electronic and media policy.

Contact Mrs. Nichole Flores, Principal. 419-329-2279. Fax: 419-531-4575. E-mail: nflores@toledosua.org. Website: www.toledosua.org

SAINT XAVIER HIGH SCHOOL

600 North Bend Road
Cincinnati, Ohio 45224

Head of School: Rev. Timothy A. Howe, SJ

General Information Boys' day college-preparatory, arts, religious studies, technology, and service learning school, affiliated with Roman Catholic Church. Grades 9–12. Founded: 1831. Setting: suburban. 114-acre campus. 1 building on campus. Approved or accredited by Jesuit Secondary Education Association, North Central Association of Colleges and Schools, Ohio Catholic Schools Accreditation Association (OCSAA), and Ohio Department of Education. Endowment: $45 million. Total enrollment: 1,600. Upper school average class size: 25. Upper school faculty-student ratio: 1:15. There are 185 required school days per year for Upper School students. Upper School students typically attend 5 days per week. The average school day consists of 7 hours and 5 minutes.

Upper School Student Profile Grade 9: 411 students (411 boys); Grade 10: 409 students (409 boys); Grade 11: 382 students (382 boys); Grade 12: 392 students (392 boys). 80% of students are Roman Catholic.

Faculty School total: 132. In upper school: 88 men, 44 women; 88 have advanced degrees.

Subjects Offered Arts, biology, chemistry, Chinese, computer science, English, fine arts, French, German, Greek, health, Latin, mathematics, physical education, physics, religion, science, social studies, Spanish.

Graduation Requirements Arts and fine arts (art, music, dance, drama), computer science, English, foreign language, forensics, mathematics, physical education (includes health), religion (includes Bible studies and theology), science, social studies (includes history).

Special Academic Programs Advanced Placement exam preparation; independent study; term-away projects; study at local college for college credit.

College Admission Counseling 378 students graduated in 2015; 377 went to college, including Miami University; Saint Louis University; The Ohio State University; University of Cincinnati; University of Notre Dame; Xavier University. Other: 1 went to work. Median SAT critical reading: 630, median SAT math: 640, median composite ACT: 29. 64% scored over 600 on SAT critical reading, 72% scored over 600 on SAT math, 60% scored over 26 on composite ACT.

Student Life Upper grades have specified standards of dress, student council. Discipline rests primarily with faculty. Attendance at religious services is required.

Tuition and Aid Day student tuition: $13,870. Tuition installment plan (FACTS Tuition Payment Plan, monthly payment plans, individually arranged payment plans). Merit scholarship grants, need-based scholarship grants, paying campus jobs available. In 2015–16, 40% of upper-school students received aid; total upper-school merit-scholarship money awarded: $50,000. Total amount of financial aid awarded in 2015–16: $3,800,000.

Admissions Traditional secondary-level entrance grade is 9. For fall 2015, 800 students applied for upper-level admission, 450 were accepted, 390 enrolled. High School Placement Test required. Deadline for receipt of application materials: December 1. Application fee required: $30.

Athletics Interscholastic: baseball, basketball, bowling, cheering, crew, cross-country running, diving, football, golf, ice hockey, lacrosse, rugby, soccer, swimming and diving, tennis, track and field, volleyball, water polo, weight training, wrestling; intramural: basketball, football, golf, soccer, table tennis, tennis, volleyball. 3 PE instructors, 2 athletic trainers.

Computers Computers are regularly used in art, design, drawing and design, foreign language, graphic arts, graphic design, graphics, keyboarding, lab/keyboard, language development, library, programming, research skills, science classes. Computer network features include on-campus library services, online commercial services, Internet access, wireless campus network, Internet filtering or blocking technology. Campus intranet, student e-mail accounts, and computer access in designated common areas are available to students. Students grades are available online. The school has a published electronic and media policy.

Contact Mr. Roderick D. Hinton, Assistant Vice President and Director of Enrollment. 513-761-7815 Ext. 106. Fax: 513-761-3811. E-mail: rhinton@stxavier.org. Website: www.stxavier.org

SALEM ACADEMY

500 Salem Avenue
Winston-Salem, North Carolina 27101-0578

Head of School: Mr. Karl Sjolund

General Information Girls' boarding and day college-preparatory and arts school, affiliated with Moravian Church. Grades 9–12. Founded: 1772. Setting: urban. Students are housed in single-sex dormitories. 60-acre campus. 4 buildings on campus. Approved or accredited by Southern Association of Colleges and Schools, The Association of Boarding Schools, and North Carolina Department of Education. Member of National Association of Independent Schools and Secondary School Admission Test Board. Endowment: $7 million. Total enrollment: 160. Upper school average class size: 10. Upper school faculty-student ratio: 1:7. There are 172 required school days per year for Upper School students. Upper School students typically attend 5 days per week. The average school day consists of 7 hours and 30 minutes.

Upper School Student Profile Grade 9: 31 students (31 girls); Grade 10: 39 students (39 girls); Grade 11: 44 students (44 girls); Grade 12: 38 students (38 girls). 60% of students are boarding students. 30% are state residents. 11 states are represented in upper school student body. 33% are international students. International students from China, Germany, and Republic of Korea; 3 other countries represented in student body. 4% of students are Moravian.

Faculty School total: 24. In upper school: 2 men, 22 women; 13 have advanced degrees; 3 reside on campus.

Subjects Offered Algebra, American history, art, biology, calculus, chemistry, dance, drama, economics, English, European history, fine arts, French, geometry, government/civics, Latin, mathematics, music, physical education, physics, pre-calculus, psychology, religion, science, social sciences, social studies, Spanish, theater, trigonometry, world history.

Graduation Requirements Arts and fine arts (art, music, dance, drama), English, foreign language, mathematics, physical education (includes health), religion (includes Bible studies and theology), science, social sciences, social studies (includes history), completion of January term.

Special Academic Programs 8 Advanced Placement exams for which test preparation is offered; honors section; term-away projects; study at local college for college credit; study abroad; programs in general development for dyslexic students; ESL (8 students enrolled).

College Admission Counseling 40 students graduated in 2015; all went to college, including New York University; Penn State University Park; The University of North Carolina at Chapel Hill; The University of North Carolina at Greensboro. Mean SAT critical reading: 575, mean SAT math: 631, mean SAT writing: 598, mean combined SAT: 1876.

Student Life Upper grades have specified standards of dress, student council, honor system. Discipline rests equally with students and faculty.

Tuition and Aid Day student tuition: $19,940; 7-day tuition and room/board: $40,490. Tuition installment plan (Key Tuition Payment Plan, monthly payment plans). Merit scholarship grants, need-based scholarship grants available. In 2015–16, 45% of upper-school students received aid; total upper-school merit-scholarship money awarded: $123,100. Total amount of financial aid awarded in 2015–16: $1,033,794.

Admissions Traditional secondary-level entrance grade is 9. For fall 2015, 160 students applied for upper-level admission, 85 were accepted, 65 enrolled. ACT, PSAT,

SAT, SSAT or TOEFL required. Deadline for receipt of application materials: none. Application fee required: $50. Interview required.

Athletics Interscholastic: basketball, cross-country running, fencing, field hockey, golf, soccer, softball, swimming and diving, tennis, track and field, volleyball; intramural: aerobics/dance, archery, badminton, dance, fitness, flag football, floor hockey, golf, horseback riding, indoor hockey, indoor soccer, self defense. 2 PE instructors, 15 coaches, 1 athletic trainer.

Computers Computers are regularly used in all academic classes. Computer network features include on-campus library services, online commercial services, Internet access, wireless campus network. Student e-mail accounts and computer access in designated common areas are available to students. Students grades are available online.

Contact C. Lucia Higgins, Director of Admissions. 336-721-2643. Fax: 336-917-5340. E-mail: academy@salem.edu. Website: www.salemacademy.com

SALEM ACADEMY

942 Lancaster Drive NE
Salem, Oregon 97301

Head of School: Micah Powers

General Information Coeducational day college-preparatory, general academic, arts, business, vocational, religious studies, bilingual studies, and technology school, affiliated with Protestant Church. Grades K–12. Founded: 1945. Setting: suburban. 34-acre campus. 6 buildings on campus. Approved or accredited by Northwest Accreditation Commission and Oregon Department of Education. Total enrollment: 646. Upper school average class size: 20. Upper school faculty-student ratio: 1:13. Upper School students typically attend 5 days per week. The average school day consists of 7 hours and 15 minutes.

Upper School Student Profile 90% of students are Protestant.

Faculty School total: 51. In upper school: 13 men, 14 women; 16 have advanced degrees.

Subjects Offered Advanced chemistry, Advanced Placement courses, algebra, American history, American literature, American sign language, anatomy and physiology, art, astronomy, athletics, auto mechanics, baseball, Bible, Bible studies, biology, business, calculus, ceramics, cheerleading, chemistry, choir, college counseling, college writing, computer programming, computer science, drama, drama performance, economics, English, English literature, English literature and composition-AP, English literature-AP, ESL, foods, geography, geometry, government/civics, grammar, health, history, history-AP, home economics, honors English, industrial arts, Japanese, mathematics, music, physical education, physical science, physics, psychology, religion, SAT preparation, science, shop, social sciences, social studies, softball, Spanish, speech, track and field, typing, U.S. history-AP, video film production, vocal music, volleyball, weight training, woodworking, world history, world literature, writing.

Graduation Requirements English, foreign language, mathematics, physical education (includes health), religion (includes Bible studies and theology), science, social sciences, social studies (includes history), one credit in biblical studies for each year attended, 10 hours of community service per year (high school).

Special Academic Programs 7 Advanced Placement exams for which test preparation is offered; honors section; independent study; study at local college for college credit; academic accommodation for the musically talented and the artistically talented; ESL.

College Admission Counseling 54 students graduated in 2015; 49 went to college, including Chemeketa Community College; Corban University; George Fox University; Grand Canyon University; Oregon State University; University of Oregon. Other: 2 entered military service. Mean SAT critical reading: 521, mean SAT math: 495, mean SAT writing: 510, mean combined SAT: 1520, mean composite ACT: 25.

Student Life Upper grades have specified standards of dress, student council, honor system. Discipline rests primarily with faculty.

Tuition and Aid Tuition installment plan (FACTS Tuition Payment Plan). Tuition reduction for siblings, need-based scholarship grants available. In 2015–16, 25% of upper-school students received aid.

Admissions Traditional secondary-level entrance grade is 9. For fall 2015, 36 students applied for upper-level admission, 33 were accepted, 32 enrolled. Math Placement Exam, Reading for Understanding, school's own exam and writing sample required. Deadline for receipt of application materials: none. Application fee required: $50. Interview required.

Athletics Interscholastic: baseball (boys), basketball (b,g), cheering (g), cross-country running (b,g), football (b), golf (b,g), soccer (b,g), softball (g), track and field (b,g), volleyball (g); coed interscholastic: equestrian sports, swimming and diving; coed intramural: jump rope, racquetball. 2 PE instructors, 36 coaches.

Computers Computers are regularly used in computer applications, design, digital applications, media, media production, multimedia, music technology, photography, photojournalism, video film production, yearbook classes. Computer network features include on-campus library services, Internet access, wireless campus network, Internet filtering or blocking technology. Students grades are available online. The school has a published electronic and media policy.

Contact Mrs. Stephanie Jorgensen, Director of Admissions. 503-378-1219. Fax: 503-375-3522. E-mail: sjorgensen@salemacademy.org. Website: www.salemacademy.org

SALESIANUM SCHOOL

1801 North Broom Street
Wilmington, Delaware 19802-3891

Head of School: Rev. J. Christian Beretta, OSFS

General Information Boys' day college-preparatory school, affiliated with Roman Catholic Church. Grades 9–12. Founded: 1903. Setting: suburban. 22-acre campus. 1 building on campus. Approved or accredited by Middle States Association of Colleges and Schools and Delaware Department of Education. Total enrollment: 1,035. Upper school average class size: 20. Upper school faculty-student ratio: 1:12.

Upper School Student Profile Grade 9: 264 students (264 boys); Grade 10: 272 students (272 boys); Grade 11: 260 students (260 boys); Grade 12: 239 students (239 boys). 86% of students are Roman Catholic.

Faculty School total: 92. In upper school: 67 men, 25 women; 53 have advanced degrees.

Subjects Offered Algebra, American history, American history-AP, American literature, anatomy, architecture, art, art-AP, band, biology, biology-AP, business, business law, calculus, calculus-AP, career/college preparation, chemistry, chemistry-AP, chorus, community service, computer applications, computer programming, computer science, computer science-AP, drafting, driver education, ecology, economics, English, English literature, English-AP, ensembles, environmental science-AP, European history-AP, fine arts, foreign policy, French, French-AP, geometry, government/civics, health, journalism, Latin, law, literature, Mandarin, marketing, mathematics, physical education, physics, physics-AP, pre-calculus, psychology, psychology-AP, religion, science, social sciences, social studies, Spanish, Spanish-AP, statistics, statistics-AP, television, trigonometry, U.S. government and politics-AP, video, Western literature, world affairs, world history, world literature.

Graduation Requirements Arts and fine arts (art, music, dance, drama), college planning, computer science, driver education, electives, English, foreign language, mathematics, physical education (includes health), religion (includes Bible studies and theology), science, social sciences, social studies (includes history). Community service is required.

Special Academic Programs Advanced Placement exam preparation; honors section; independent study; study at local college for college credit; domestic exchange program (with Ursuline Academy, Padua Academy); academic accommodation for the gifted; remedial reading and/or remedial writing; remedial math.

College Admission Counseling 238 students graduated in 2015; 236 went to college, including Penn State University Park; Saint Joseph's University; University of Delaware; University of South Carolina; Villanova University. Other: 1 went to work, 1 entered military service.

Student Life Upper grades have specified standards of dress, student council. Discipline rests primarily with faculty. Attendance at religious services is required.

Summer Programs Enrichment, art/fine arts, computer instruction programs offered; session focuses on freshman transition and technology; held on campus; accepts boys; not open to students from other schools.

Tuition and Aid Day student tuition: $14,200. Tuition installment plan (Insured Tuition Payment Plan, monthly payment plans, semester payment plan, annual payment plan, monthly payment plan). Merit scholarship grants, need-based scholarship grants, paying campus jobs available. In 2015–16, 30% of upper-school students received aid; total upper-school merit-scholarship money awarded: $375,000. Total amount of financial aid awarded in 2015–16: $1,000,000.

Admissions Traditional secondary-level entrance grade is 9. Scholastic Testing Service High School Placement Test required. Deadline for receipt of application materials: November 20. Application fee required: $65. Interview recommended.

Athletics Interscholastic: baseball, basketball, cross-country running, diving, football, golf, ice hockey, lacrosse, rugby, soccer, swimming and diving, tennis, track and field, volleyball, wrestling; intramural: basketball, bowling, flag football, Frisbee, lacrosse, roller hockey, rowing, skateboarding, tennis, ultimate Frisbee, weight lifting. 4 PE instructors, 58 coaches, 1 athletic trainer.

Computers Computers are regularly used in architecture, college planning, drafting, English, foreign language, mathematics, science, social studies classes. Computer network features include on-campus library services, online commercial services, Internet access, wireless campus network, Internet filtering or blocking technology. Campus intranet, student e-mail accounts, and computer access in designated common areas are available to students. Students grades are available online. The school has a published electronic and media policy.

Contact Mrs. Barbara Palena, Admissions Associate. 302-654-2495 Ext. 148. Fax: 302-654-7767. E-mail: bpalena@salesianum.org. Website: www.salesianum.org

SALPOINTE CATHOLIC HIGH SCHOOL

1545 East Copper Street
Tucson, Arizona 85719-3199

Head of School: Mrs. Kay Sullivan

General Information Coeducational day college-preparatory, religious studies, humanities, and STEM school, affiliated with Roman Catholic Church. Grades 9–12. Founded: 1950. Setting: urban. 40-acre campus. 12 buildings on campus. Approved or accredited by National Catholic Education Association, North Central Association of Colleges and Schools, Western Catholic Education Association, and Arizona Department of Education. Endowment: $3.9 million. Total enrollment: 1,093. Upper school average class size: 24. Upper school faculty-student ratio: 1:15. There are 180 required school days per year for Upper School students. Upper School students typically attend 5 days per week. The average school day consists of 6 hours and 50 minutes.

Upper School Student Profile Grade 9: 307 students (157 boys, 150 girls); Grade 10: 286 students (148 boys, 138 girls); Grade 11: 242 students (125 boys, 117 girls); Grade 12: 258 students (129 boys, 129 girls). 79% of students are Roman Catholic.

Faculty School total: 83. In upper school: 27 men, 49 women; 66 have advanced degrees.

Subjects Offered 3-dimensional art, 3-dimensional design, accounting, acting, advanced biology, advanced chemistry, advanced math, Advanced Placement courses, advanced studio art-AP, aerobics, algebra, American culture, American government, American history, American history-AP, American literature, American literature-AP, American studies, analysis and differential calculus, animation, art, art appreciation, art history, art history-AP, art-AP, arts, athletic training, athletics, band, Bible studies, biology, biology-AP, British literature, British literature (honors), business, calculus, calculus-AP, career and personal planning, career and technology systems, career technology, career/college preparation, Catholic belief and practice, ceramics, chemistry, chemistry-AP, choir, choral music, classics, comparative religion, composition, computer animation, computer art, computer programming, computer science, computer skills, computer-aided design, computers, concert band, concert choir, constitutional history of U.S., consumer economics, creative writing, dance, desktop publishing, digital art, digital photography, discrete mathematics, drama, drama performance, drawing and design, earth science, economics, electives, electronic publishing, engineering, English, English literature, English literature and composition-AP, English literature-AP, environmental science, environmental science-AP, European history, finance, fitness, French, French language-AP, French literature-AP, French-AP, geography, geometry, government, government and politics-AP, government/civics, history, honors algebra, honors English, honors geometry, honors U.S. history, humanities, instrumental music, jazz band, jazz ensemble, journalism, language arts, Latin, Latin-AP, law, leadership, leadership and service, learning lab, Life of Christ, literary magazine, macroeconomics-AP, marching band, marketing, music history, newspaper, non-Western literature, orchestra, painting, performing arts, personal fitness, photo shop, photography, photojournalism, physical fitness, physics, physics-AP, play production, politics, pottery, pre-algebra, pre-calculus, probability and statistics, programming, psychology, rhetoric, robotics, SAT/ACT preparation, scripture, sculpture, Shakespeare, social justice, space and physical sciences, Spanish, Spanish language-AP, Spanish literature, Spanish literature-AP, Spanish-AP, sports conditioning, sports medicine, statistics, statistics-AP, student government, student publications, studio art, studio art-AP, symphonic band, theater, theology, trigonometry, U.S. government and politics, U.S. history-AP, United States government-AP, visual and performing arts, visual arts, vocal music, voice ensemble, water color painting, weight fitness, weight training, weightlifting, world history, world history-AP, world literature, world religions, world studies, writing, writing workshop, yearbook.

Graduation Requirements Arts and fine arts (art, music, dance, drama), career and technology systems, English, exercise science, mathematics, modern languages, science, social studies (includes history), theology.

Special Academic Programs 18 Advanced Placement exams for which test preparation is offered; honors section; study at local college for college credit; remedial reading and/or remedial writing; remedial math; programs in English, mathematics, general development for dyslexic students.

College Admission Counseling 245 students graduated in 2015; 237 went to college, including Arizona State University at the Tempe campus; Gonzaga University; Grand Canyon University; Northern Arizona University; Pima Community College; The University of Arizona. Other: 3 went to work, 4 entered military service, 1 had other specific plans. Median SAT critical reading: 540, median SAT math: 520, median SAT writing: 510, median combined SAT: 1590, median composite ACT: 23. 28% scored over 600 on SAT critical reading, 24% scored over 600 on SAT math, 19% scored over 600 on SAT writing, 22% scored over 1800 on combined SAT, 28% scored over 26 on composite ACT.

Student Life Upper grades have specified standards of dress, student council, honor system. Discipline rests primarily with faculty. Attendance at religious services is required.

Summer Programs Remediation, enrichment, advancement, sports, computer instruction programs offered; session focuses on advancement, remediation, sports camps; held on campus; accepts boys and girls; open to students from other schools. 329 students usually enrolled. 2016 schedule: May 23 to June 29. Application deadline: May 19.

Tuition and Aid Day student tuition: $8200. Tuition installment plan (monthly payment plans, individually arranged payment plans). Merit scholarship grants, need-based scholarship grants, USS Education Loan Program available. In 2015–16, 52% of upper-school students received aid; total upper-school merit-scholarship money awarded: $62,000. Total amount of financial aid awarded in 2015–16: $1,848,925.

Admissions Traditional secondary-level entrance grade is 9. For fall 2015, 401 students applied for upper-level admission, 372 were accepted, 309 enrolled. High School Placement Test or TOEFL required. Deadline for receipt of application materials: none. Application fee required: $60. On-campus interview required.

Athletics Interscholastic: aerobics/dance (girls), baseball (b), basketball (b,g), cheering (g), cross-country running (b,g), dance team (g), diving (b,g), football (b), golf (b,g), lacrosse (b), soccer (b,g), softball (g), swimming and diving (b,g), tennis (b,g), track and field (b,g), volleyball (b,g), wrestling (b). 3 PE instructors, 110 coaches, 2 athletic trainers.

Computers Computers are regularly used in all academic classes. Computer network features include on-campus library services, Internet access, wireless campus network, Internet filtering or blocking technology. Campus intranet, student e-mail accounts, and computer access in designated common areas are available to students. Students grades are available online. The school has a published electronic and media policy.

Contact Mr. Michael Fisher, Director of Admission. 520-547-4460. Fax: 520-327-8477. E-mail: mfisher@salpointe.org. Website: www.salpointe.org

SAN DIEGO JEWISH ACADEMY

11860 Carmel Creek Road
San Diego, California 92130

Head of School: Chaim Heller

General Information Coeducational day college-preparatory, arts, and religious studies school, affiliated with Jewish faith. Grades K–12. Founded: 1979. Setting: suburban. 56-acre campus. 3 buildings on campus. Approved or accredited by California Association of Independent Schools, Western Association of Schools and Colleges, and California Department of Education. Member of National Association of Independent Schools. Languages of instruction: English and Hebrew. Endowment: $2.5 million. Total enrollment: 477. Upper school average class size: 20. Upper school faculty-student ratio: 1:18. Upper School students typically attend 5 days per week. The average school day consists of 7 hours and 15 minutes.

Upper School Student Profile Grade 6: 36 students (19 boys, 17 girls); Grade 7: 40 students (14 boys, 26 girls); Grade 8: 49 students (26 boys, 23 girls); Grade 9: 40 students (17 boys, 23 girls); Grade 10: 47 students (28 boys, 19 girls); Grade 11: 51 students (27 boys, 24 girls); Grade 12: 47 students (22 boys, 25 girls). 99% of students are Jewish.

Faculty School total: 35. In upper school: 12 men, 19 women; 17 have advanced degrees.

Subjects Offered 20th century history, 20th century world history, advanced biology, advanced chemistry, Advanced Placement courses, algebra, American government, American history, American history-AP, American literature, American literature-AP, American sign language, analytic geometry, art, art history-AP, arts and crafts, ASB Leadership, athletic training, athletics, baseball, Basic programming, basketball, Bible, Bible studies, biology, biology-AP, British history, British literature, British literature (honors), calculus, calculus-AP, chemistry, chorus, college admission preparation, college counseling, community service, comparative religion, competitive science projects, composition, composition-AP, computer programming, conceptual physics, creative drama, creative writing, digital photography, dramatic arts, earth science, economics, economics and history, electives, English, English composition, English language and composition-AP, English language-AP, English literature, English literature and composition-AP, English literature-AP, English-AP, English/composition-AP, environmental science-AP, European history, European history-AP, European literature, fitness, foreign language, French, golf, government, government-AP, government/civics, guitar, Hebrew, Hebrew scripture, history, Holocaust, Holocaust studies, honors algebra, honors English, honors geometry, honors world history, humanities, independent study, instrumental music, instruments, integrated physics, Israeli studies, Jewish history, Jewish studies, Judaic studies, languages, literature and composition-AP, literature-AP, Mandarin, mathematics-AP, music, musical theater dance, photography, physical education, physics, physics-AP, prayer/spirituality, pre-algebra, pre-calculus, pre-college orientation, psychology, Rabbinic literature, religious education, religious studies, social sciences, Spanish, standard curriculum, statistics-AP, student government, Talmud, theater, trigonometry, U.S. government, U.S. history, U.S. history-AP, U.S. literature, video film production, visual arts, volleyball, weight fitness, weightlifting, world history, world literature, yearbook.

Special Academic Programs 19 Advanced Placement exams for which test preparation is offered; honors section; independent study.

College Admission Counseling 38 students graduated in 2014; 37 went to college, including Chapman University; University of California, Berkeley; University of California, San Diego; University of California, Santa Barbara; University of Southern California. Other: 1 had other specific plans. Mean SAT critical reading: 592, mean SAT math: 593, mean SAT writing: 606, mean composite ACT: 26.

Student Life Upper grades have specified standards of dress, student council, honor system. Discipline rests primarily with faculty. Attendance at religious services is required.

Tuition and Aid Day student tuition: $22,775. Tuition installment plan (FACTS Tuition Payment Plan, monthly payment plans). Tuition reduction for siblings, merit scholarship grants, need-based scholarship grants available. In 2014–15, 30% of upper-school students received aid; total upper-school merit-scholarship money awarded: $50,000. Total amount of financial aid awarded in 2014–15: $553,000.

Admissions Traditional secondary-level entrance grade is 9. For fall 2014, 36 students applied for upper-level admission, 25 were accepted, 17 enrolled. Deadline for receipt of application materials: none. Application fee required: $100. On-campus interview required.

Athletics Interscholastic: aquatics (boys, girls), baseball (b), basketball (b,g), cross-country running (b,g), football (b), golf (b), independent competitive sports (b,g),

soccer (b,g), softball (g), tennis (b,g), volleyball (g), winter soccer (b,g); coed interscholastic: flag football, track and field; coed intramural: baseball, basketball, dance, fencing, fitness, flag football, football, martial arts, physical fitness, physical training, self defense, soccer, softball, strength & conditioning, tennis, track and field, volleyball, weight lifting, weight training, winter soccer. 4 PE instructors, 50 coaches, 2 athletic trainers.

Computers Computers are regularly used in college planning, economics, English, foreign language, French, graphic design, history, humanities, mathematics, newspaper, photography, psychology, religious studies, science, social studies, video film production, writing, yearbook classes. Computer network features include on-campus library services, online commercial services, Internet access, wireless campus network, Internet filtering or blocking technology. Student e-mail accounts are available to students. Students grades are available online.

Contact Leslie Cohen Kastner, Admissions Director. 858-704-3716. Fax: 858-704-3850. E-mail: lkastner@sdja.com. Website: www.sdja.com

SAN DOMENICO SCHOOL

1500 Butterfield Road
San Anselmo, California 94960

Head of School: Ms. Cecily Stock

General Information Coeducational boarding and day college-preparatory, arts, religious studies, music, theater arts, dance, and social justice school, affiliated with Roman Catholic Church. Boarding grades 9–12, day grades K–12. Founded: 1850. Setting: suburban. Nearest major city is San Francisco. Students are housed in single-sex by floor dormitories. 515-acre campus. 4 buildings on campus. Approved or accredited by California Association of Independent Schools, New Jersey Association of Independent Schools, The Association of Boarding Schools, Western Association of Schools and Colleges, and Western Catholic Education Association. Member of National Association of Independent Schools. Endowment: $9 million. Total enrollment: 621. Upper school average class size: 12. Upper school faculty-student ratio: 1:5. There are 180 required school days per year for Upper School students. Upper School students typically attend 5 days per week. The average school day consists of 7 hours.

Upper School Student Profile Grade 6: 73 students (30 boys, 43 girls); Grade 7: 73 students (31 boys, 42 girls); Grade 8: 69 students (25 boys, 44 girls); Grade 9: 45 students (45 girls); Grade 10: 52 students (52 girls); Grade 11: 40 students (40 girls); Grade 12: 46 students (46 girls). 53% of students are boarding students. 57% are state residents. 2 states are represented in upper school student body. 43% are international students. International students from China, Hong Kong, Japan, Mexico, Republic of Korea, and Taiwan. 25% of students are Roman Catholic.

Faculty School total: 35. In upper school: 7 men, 28 women; 17 have advanced degrees; 7 reside on campus.

Subjects Offered Acting, advanced studio art-AP, algebra, American history, American literature, art, art history, biology, biology-AP, calculus, calculus-AP, ceramics, chemistry, chemistry-AP, community service, drama, English, English language and composition-AP, English literature, English literature-AP, environmental science, environmental science-AP, ESL, ethics, European history, expository writing, fine arts, geometry, government/civics, grammar, history, Mandarin, mathematics, modern world history, music, music composition, music theater, music theory, music theory-AP, musical productions, musicianship, photography, physical education, physics, physics-AP, psychology-AP, religion, science, social studies, sociology, Spanish, Spanish language-AP, statistics-AP, studio art-AP, theater, theology, trigonometry, U.S. history-AP, world history, world literature.

Graduation Requirements Arts and fine arts (art, music, dance, drama), English, foreign language, health, mathematics, physical education (includes health), religion (includes Bible studies and theology), science, social studies (includes history). Community service is required.

Special Academic Programs Advanced Placement exam preparation; honors section; independent study; study abroad; academic accommodation for the musically talented; ESL (18 students enrolled).

College Admission Counseling 30 students graduated in 2015; all went to college, including Boston University; California Polytechnic State University, San Luis Obispo; Lehigh University; Stanford University; The Juilliard School; University of California, Berkeley. Mean SAT critical reading: 584, mean SAT math: 606, mean SAT writing: 592, mean combined SAT: 1782, mean composite ACT: 29.

Student Life Upper grades have specified standards of dress, student council, honor system. Discipline rests primarily with faculty.

Tuition and Aid Day student tuition: $36,100; 7-day tuition and room/board: $52,600. Tuition installment plan (Insured Tuition Payment Plan, monthly payment plans). Need-based scholarship grants available. In 2015–16, 46% of upper-school students received aid. Total amount of financial aid awarded in 2015–16: $2,000,000.

Admissions Traditional secondary-level entrance grade is 9. For fall 2015, 155 students applied for upper-level admission, 103 were accepted, 54 enrolled. High School Placement Test, ISEE or SSAT required. Deadline for receipt of application materials: January 15. Application fee required: $100. Interview required.

Athletics Interscholastic: badminton (girls), basketball (b,g), cross-country running (b,g), equestrian sports (b,g), flag football (b,g), horseback riding (b,g), mountain biking (b,g), soccer (b,g), swimming and diving (b,g), tennis (b,g), volleyball (g);

intramural: dance (g), golf (b,g), modern dance (g); coed interscholastic: cross-country running; coed intramural: dance, modern dance. 1 PE instructor, 5 coaches.

Computers Computers are regularly used in English, mathematics, science, social studies, yearbook classes. Computer network features include on-campus library services, online commercial services, Internet access, wireless campus network, Internet filtering or blocking technology. Student e-mail accounts are available to students. Students grades are available online. The school has a published electronic and media policy.

Contact Mr. Dan Babior, Director of Upper School Admissions and Marketing/Communications. 415-258-1905. Fax: 415-258-1906. E-mail: dbabior@ sandomenico.org. Website: www.sandomenico.org/

SANDY SPRING FRIENDS SCHOOL

16923 Norwood Road
Sandy Spring, Maryland 20860

Head of School: Thomas R. Gibian

General Information Coeducational boarding and day college-preparatory, arts, and ESL school, affiliated with Society of Friends. Boarding grades 9–12, day grades PK–12. Founded: 1961. Setting: suburban. Nearest major city is Washington, DC. Students are housed in single-sex by floor dormitories. 140-acre campus. 15 buildings on campus. Approved or accredited by Association of Independent Maryland Schools, Association of Independent Schools of Greater Washington, Friends Council on Education, The Association of Boarding Schools, and Maryland Department of Education. Member of National Association of Independent Schools and Secondary School Admission Test Board. Endowment: $1.1 million. Total enrollment: 577. Upper school average class size: 14. Upper school faculty-student ratio: 1:8. There are 171 required school days per year for Upper School students. Upper School students typically attend 5 days per week. The average school day consists of 7 hours and 30 minutes.

Upper School Student Profile Grade 9: 61 students (34 boys, 27 girls); Grade 10: 71 students (41 boys, 30 girls); Grade 11: 82 students (44 boys, 38 girls); Grade 12: 71 students (41 boys, 30 girls). 31% of students are boarding students. 71% are state residents. 6 states are represented in upper school student body. 24% are international students. International students from China, Thailand, and Viet Nam; 2 other countries represented in student body. 11% of students are members of Society of Friends.

Faculty School total: 68. In upper school: 12 men, 20 women; 22 have advanced degrees; 6 reside on campus.

Subjects Offered Algebra, American history, American literature, art, biology, British literature-AP, calculus, calculus-AP, ceramics, chemistry, chemistry-AP, choral music, creative writing, cultural geography, dance, dance performance, desktop publishing, drama, drawing, English, English as a foreign language, English literature and composition-AP, English literature-AP, environmental science-AP, ESL, ESL, French, French language-AP, geology, geometry, grammar, history, mathematics, music, music theory-AP, Native American history, painting, photography, physical education, physics, poetry, Quakerism and ethics, Russian literature, science, Spanish, Spanish language-AP, statistics-AP, trigonometry, U.S. history-AP, weaving, Western civilization, world literature.

Graduation Requirements Art, English, foreign language, history, mathematics, physical education (includes health), religion (includes Bible studies and theology), science. Community service is required.

Special Academic Programs 15 Advanced Placement exams for which test preparation is offered; honors section; independent study; academic accommodation for the gifted, the musically talented, and the artistically talented; ESL (25 students enrolled).

College Admission Counseling 72 students graduated in 2015; 70 went to college, including McDaniel College; Penn State University Park; Purdue University; St. Mary's College of Maryland; Syracuse University; Washington College. Other: 1 entered a postgraduate year, 1 had other specific plans. Median SAT critical reading: 580, median SAT math: 590, median SAT writing: 580, median combined SAT: 1750, median composite ACT: 24. 23% scored over 600 on SAT critical reading, 20% scored over 600 on SAT math, 19% scored over 600 on SAT writing, 23% scored over 1800 on combined SAT, 4% scored over 26 on composite ACT.

Student Life Upper grades have specified standards of dress, student council, honor system. Discipline rests equally with students and faculty. Attendance at religious services is required.

Summer Programs Enrichment, ESL, sports, art/fine arts programs offered; session focuses on recreational and enrichment; held on campus; accepts boys and girls; open to students from other schools. 1,200 students usually enrolled. 2016 schedule: June 20 to August 12. Application deadline: May 1.

Tuition and Aid Day student tuition: $31,400; 5-day tuition and room/board: $46,225; 7-day tuition and room/board: $57,825. Tuition installment plan (FACTS Tuition Payment Plan). Need-based scholarship grants available. In 2015–16, 31% of upper-school students received aid. Total amount of financial aid awarded in 2015–16: $3,035,000.

Admissions Traditional secondary-level entrance grade is 9. For fall 2015, 198 students applied for upper-level admission, 106 were accepted, 57 enrolled. ISEE, PSAT, SSAT or TOEFL or SLEP required. Deadline for receipt of application materials: January 1. Application fee required: $75. Interview required.

Athletics Interscholastic: baseball (boys), basketball (b,g), cross-country running (b,g), ice hockey (b), lacrosse (b,g), soccer (b,g), softball (g), tennis (b,g), volleyball (g); coed interscholastic: cooperative games, golf, kickball, modern dance, running, track and field; coed intramural: basketball, cooperative games, dance, Frisbee, hiking/backpacking, jogging, outdoor activities, outdoor adventure, outdoor education, outdoor recreation, outdoor skills, outdoors, physical fitness, physical training, rappelling, rock climbing, ropes courses, running, skiing (downhill), snowboarding, strength & conditioning, table tennis, track and field, ultimate Frisbee, walking, wall climbing, weight lifting, weight training, wilderness, wilderness survival, wrestling, yoga. 5 PE instructors, 3 coaches, 1 athletic trainer.

Computers Computers are regularly used in all academic classes. Computer network features include on-campus library services, Internet access, wireless campus network. Student e-mail accounts and computer access in designated common areas are available to students. Students grades are available online.

Contact Tony McCudden, Director of Enrollment Management. 301-774-7455 Ext. 182. Fax: 301-576-8664. E-mail: tony.mccudden@ssfs.org. Website: www.ssfs.org

SANFORD SCHOOL

6900 Lancaster Pike
Hockessin, Delaware 19707

Head of School: Mark J. Anderson

General Information Coeducational day college-preparatory and arts school. Grades PK–12. Founded: 1930. Setting: suburban. Nearest major city is Wilmington. 100-acre campus. 6 buildings on campus. Approved or accredited by Middle States Association of Colleges and Schools, Pennsylvania Association of Independent Schools, and Delaware Department of Education. Member of National Association of Independent Schools and Secondary School Admission Test Board. Endowment: $7 million. Total enrollment: 585. Upper school average class size: 13. Upper school faculty-student ratio: 1:8. There are 169 required school days per year for Upper School students. Upper School students typically attend 5 days per week. The average school day consists of 6 hours.

Upper School Student Profile Grade 9: 54 students (24 boys, 30 girls); Grade 10: 57 students (27 boys, 30 girls); Grade 11: 57 students (25 boys, 32 girls); Grade 12: 65 students (32 boys, 33 girls).

Faculty School total: 85. In upper school: 12 men, 22 women; 23 have advanced degrees.

Subjects Offered Algebra, American literature, anatomy and physiology, art, art history-AP, biology, biology-AP, business, calculus-AP, ceramics, chemistry, chemistry-AP, choir, collage and assemblage, computer art, computer graphics, computer science-AP, concert band, drawing, driver education, ecology, environmental systems, economics, engineering, English, English language-AP, English literature, English literature-AP, environmental science-AP, fine arts, French, French-AP, functions, geometry, German, German-AP, graphic design, health, history, jazz band, Latin, Latin-AP, leadership, mathematics, music, music appreciation, painting, philosophy, photography, physics, physics-AP, pre-calculus, printmaking, psychology, social studies, Spanish, Spanish-AP, statistics, statistics-AP, studio art-AP, technology, trigonometry, U.S. history, U.S. history-AP, video film production, visual arts, vocal ensemble, voice, world civilizations, world history, world history-AP, world literature, writing, yearbook.

Graduation Requirements Arts and fine arts (art, music, dance, drama), athletics, computer science, electives, English, foreign language, health, lab science, mathematics, music, social sciences, 2-week senior project/internship in May.

Special Academic Programs Advanced Placement exam preparation; honors section; independent study.

College Admission Counseling 49 students graduated in 2014; all went to college, including Harvard University; Loyola University Maryland; Rensselaer Polytechnic Institute; Stanford University; University of Delaware.

Student Life Upper grades have specified standards of dress, student council, honor system. Discipline rests equally with students and faculty.

Tuition and Aid Day student tuition: $20,850–$24,375. Tuition installment plan (Tuition Management System (TMS)). Merit scholarship grants, need-based scholarship grants available. In 2014–15, 46% of upper-school students received aid. Total amount of financial aid awarded in 2014–15: $1,375,825.

Admissions Traditional secondary-level entrance grade is 9. For fall 2014, 73 students applied for upper-level admission, 62 were accepted, 36 enrolled. ERB CTP IV, ISEE or SSAT required. Deadline for receipt of application materials: January 5. Application fee required: $40. Interview required.

Athletics Interscholastic: baseball (boys), basketball (b,g), cross-country running (b,g), field hockey (g), lacrosse (b,g), soccer (b,g), swimming and diving (b,g), tennis (b,g), volleyball (g), wrestling (b); coed interscholastic: golf, indoor track; coed intramural: physical fitness. 27 coaches, 1 athletic trainer.

Computers Computers are regularly used in art, computer applications, English, foreign language, history, mathematics, newspaper, science, yearbook classes. Computer network features include on-campus library services, online commercial services, Internet access, wireless campus network, Internet filtering or blocking technology. Campus intranet and student e-mail accounts are available to students. Students grades are available online. The school has a published electronic and media policy.

Contact Ceil Baum, Admission Assistant. 302-235-6503. Fax: 302-239-5389. E-mail: admission@sanfordschool.org. Website: www.sanfordschool.org

SAN FRANCISCO UNIVERSITY HIGH SCHOOL

3065 Jackson Street

San Francisco, California 94115

Head of School: Mrs. Julia Eells

General Information Coeducational day college-preparatory, arts, technology, and community service school. Grades 9–12. Founded: 1973. Setting: urban. 2-acre campus. 4 buildings on campus. Approved or accredited by California Association of Independent Schools, Western Association of Schools and Colleges, and California Department of Education. Member of National Association of Independent Schools and Secondary School Admission Test Board. Endowment: $20.5 million. Total enrollment: 403. Upper school average class size: 14. Upper school faculty-student ratio: 1:8.

Upper School Student Profile Grade 9: 104 students (51 boys, 53 girls); Grade 10: 104 students (52 boys, 52 girls); Grade 11: 100 students (49 boys, 51 girls); Grade 12: 95 students (45 boys, 50 girls).

Faculty School total: 53. In upper school: 25 men, 28 women; 43 have advanced degrees.

Subjects Offered 20th century physics, adolescent issues, advanced chemistry, advanced math, advanced studio art-AP, African American studies, African-American literature, algebra, American history, American literature, American literature-AP, analysis and differential calculus, anatomy, art, art history, Asian history, astronomy, band, Bible as literature, biochemistry, biology, calculus, calculus-AP, cell biology, ceramics, chamber groups, chemistry, chemistry-AP, chorus, clayworking, college counseling, community service, computer programming, computer science, creative writing, drawing, economics, economics and history, economics-AP, electronic music, English, English language and composition-AP, English literature, English literature-AP, environmental science, environmental science-AP, European history, European history-AP, film, fine arts, fractal geometry, French, French language-AP, French literature-AP, French-AP, genetics, geography, geometry, global issues, grammar, health education, instrumental music, introduction to theater, jazz band, jazz ensemble, Latin, Latin-AP, marine biology, mathematics, mathematics-AP, Mexican history, microbiology, music, music theory, music theory-AP, music-AP, musical productions, musical theater, orchestra, peer counseling, philosophy, photography, physical education, physics, physics-AP, physiology, pre-calculus, probability and statistics, psychology, science, senior internship, senior project, senior seminar, social studies, Spanish, Spanish language-AP, Spanish literature, Spanish literature-AP, Spanish-AP, studio art-AP, theater, trigonometry, U.S. government and politics-AP, U.S. history-AP, Western civilization, world history, world literature, writing.

Graduation Requirements American history-AP, art, English, foreign language, mathematics, physical education (includes health), science, social studies (includes history). Community service is required.

Special Academic Programs Advanced Placement exam preparation; honors section; independent study; term-away projects; domestic exchange program (with The Masters School); study abroad; academic accommodation for the gifted, the musically talented, and the artistically talented.

College Admission Counseling Colleges students went to include Brown University; New York University; Stanford University; Tufts University; University of California, Berkeley; University of California, Los Angeles. Mean SAT critical reading: 720, mean SAT math: 710, mean SAT writing: 710.

Student Life Upper grades have student council, honor system. Discipline rests equally with students and faculty.

Tuition and Aid Day student tuition: $40,850. Tuition installment plan (monthly payment plans). Need-based scholarship grants available. In 2015–16, 22% of upper-school students received aid. Total amount of financial aid awarded in 2015–16: $2,500,000.

Admissions Traditional secondary-level entrance grade is 9. For fall 2015, 550 students applied for upper-level admission. ISEE, SSAT or TOEFL required. Deadline for receipt of application materials: January 14. Application fee required: $90. On-campus interview required.

Athletics Interscholastic: baseball (boys), basketball (b,g), cross-country running (b,g), fencing (b,g), field hockey (g), lacrosse (b), soccer (b,g), swimming and diving (b,g), tennis (b,g), track and field (b,g), volleyball (g); intramural: basketball (b,g), cross-country running (b,g), field hockey (g), lacrosse (b), soccer (b,g), strength & conditioning (b,g), volleyball (g); coed interscholastic: badminton; coed intramural: archery, bowling, canoeing/kayaking, climbing, crew, dance, fencing, fitness, golf, hiking/backpacking, outdoor education, yoga. 4 PE instructors, 43 coaches.

Computers Computers are regularly used in all academic classes. Computer network features include on-campus library services, online commercial services, Internet access.

Contact Admissions Assistant. 415-447-3100. Fax: 415-447-5801. E-mail: admissions@sfuhs.org. Website: www.sfuhs.org

SAN MARCOS BAPTIST ACADEMY

2801 Ranch Road Twelve

San Marcos, Texas 78666-9406

Head of School: Mr. Jimmie W. Scott

General Information Coeducational boarding and day and distance learning college-preparatory, arts, business, religious studies, technology, learning skills, and ESL school, affiliated with Baptist General Conference. Boarding grades 7–12, day grades 6–12. Distance learning grades 6–12. Founded: 1907. Setting: small town. Nearest major city is Austin. Students are housed in single-sex dormitories. 220-acre campus. 10 buildings on campus. Approved or accredited by Accreditation Commission of the Texas Association of Baptist Schools, Southern Association of Colleges and Schools, Texas Education Agency, and Texas Department of Education. Member of National Association of Independent Schools. Endowment: $6 million. Total enrollment: 270. Upper school average class size: 12. Upper school faculty-student ratio: 1:9. There are 180 required school days per year for Upper School students. Upper School students typically attend 5 days per week. The average school day consists of 7 hours and 40 minutes.

Upper School Student Profile Grade 9: 39 students (22 boys, 17 girls); Grade 10: 61 students (35 boys, 26 girls); Grade 11: 48 students (34 boys, 14 girls); Grade 12: 59 students (41 boys, 18 girls). 60% of students are boarding students. 60% are state residents. 10 states are represented in upper school student body. 34% are international students. International students from Angola, China, Mexico, Nigeria, Saudi Arabia, and Viet Nam; 6 other countries represented in student body. 20% of students are Baptist General Conference.

Faculty School total: 37. In upper school: 14 men, 17 women; 18 have advanced degrees; 2 reside on campus.

Subjects Offered Advanced math, Advanced Placement courses, algebra, American government, American history, American literature, analysis and differential calculus, analytic geometry, anatomy and physiology, ancient world history, applied arts, applied music, art, athletic training, athletics, band, baseball, Basic programming, basketball, Bible, Bible studies, biology, biology-AP, British literature, British literature (honors), British literature-AP, business applications, calculus, calculus-AP, career/college preparation, character education, cheerleading, chemistry, choir, Christian scripture, Christian testament, Christianity, civics, civics/free enterprise, clayworking, college admission preparation, college counseling, college planning, communication skills, community service, comparative religion, computer applications, computer information systems, computer programming, computer science, computers, concert band, concert choir, contemporary art, critical thinking, desktop publishing, digital photography, drama, drama performance, drama workshop, dramatic arts, drawing, driver education, earth and space science, earth science, economics, economics and history, English, English as a foreign language, English composition, English literature, English literature and composition-AP, English literature-AP, English-AP, ESL, family and consumer science, fine arts, foreign language, French, geography, geometry, golf, government/civics, grammar, guidance, health, health education, history, history of the Americas, honors algebra, honors geometry, honors U.S. history, honors world history, HTML design, human anatomy, human biology, instrumental music, instruments, intro to computers, introduction to theater, jazz band, journalism, JROTC, JROTC or LEAD (Leadership Education and Development), keyboarding, language and composition, language arts, Latin, leadership, leadership and service, leadership education training, learning strategies, library, library skills, library studies, Life of Christ, life skills, literature, literature and composition-AP, literature-AP, logic, mathematical modeling, mathematics, mathematics-AP, military science, music, music appreciation, music performance, music theory, musical productions, musical theater, musicianship, New Testament, news writing, newspaper, novels, painting, participation in sports, personal and social education, personal fitness, personal growth, photography, photojournalism, physical education, physical fitness, physical science, physics, piano, play production, pottery, prayer/spirituality, pre-calculus, psychology, public speaking, reading, reading/study skills, religion, religious education, remedial study skills, research skills, SAT preparation, SAT/ACT preparation, science, social skills, social studies, society and culture, sociology, softball, Spanish, speech, speech and debate, speech communications, sports, sports conditioning, sports performance development, sports team management, state government, state history, stock market, student government, student publications, study skills, swimming, tennis, Texas history, theater, theater arts, theater production, theology, TOEFL preparation, track and field, U.S. government, U.S. government and politics, U.S. history, U.S. literature, visual arts, vocal ensemble, vocal jazz, vocal music, voice, voice and diction, voice ensemble, volleyball, Web site design, weight training, weightlifting, Western civilization, world civilizations, world cultures, world geography, world history, world issues, world literature, world religions, world religions, world studies, world wide web design, yearbook.

Graduation Requirements Arts and fine arts (art, music, dance, drama), computer science, economics, electives, English, foreign language, government, JROTC or LEAD (Leadership Education and Development), mathematics, physical education (includes health), religion (includes Bible studies and theology), science, social studies (includes history), speech.

Special Academic Programs 6 Advanced Placement exams for which test preparation is offered; honors section; accelerated programs; independent study; study at local college for college credit; academic accommodation for the gifted, the musically talented, and the artistically talented; programs in English, mathematics, general development for dyslexic students; special instructional classes for students with Section 504 learning disabilities, Attention Deficit Disorder, and dyslexia; ESL (50 students enrolled).

College Admission Counseling 73 students graduated in 2015; 70 went to college, including Baylor University; Indiana University Bloomington; Penn State University Park; Texas A&M University; Texas State University; The University of Texas at Austin. Other: 1 went to work, 1 entered military service, 1 had other specific plans. Median SAT critical reading: 480, median SAT math: 510, median SAT writing: 480, median combined SAT: 1470, median composite ACT: 21. 19% scored over 600 on SAT critical reading, 42% scored over 600 on SAT math, 19% scored over 600 on SAT writing, 17% scored over 1800 on combined SAT, 11% scored over 26 on composite ACT.

Student Life Upper grades have uniform requirement, student council, honor system. Discipline rests primarily with faculty. Attendance at religious services is required.

Tuition and Aid Day student tuition: $9828; 5-day tuition and room/board: $23,900; 7-day tuition and room/board: $31,500. Guaranteed tuition plan. Tuition installment plan (monthly payment plans, individually arranged payment plans). Need-based scholarship grants available. In 2015–16, 45% of upper-school students received aid. Total amount of financial aid awarded in 2015–16: $70,000.

Admissions Traditional secondary-level entrance grade is 9. For fall 2015, 100 students applied for upper-level admission, 85 were accepted, 55 enrolled. Deadline for receipt of application materials: none. Application fee required: $100. Interview required.

Athletics Interscholastic: baseball (boys), basketball (b,g), cross-country running (b,g), football (b), golf (b,g), JROTC drill (b,g), power lifting (b,g), riflery (b,g), softball (g), swimming and diving (b,g), tennis (b,g), track and field (b,g), volleyball (g), weight lifting (b,g); coed interscholastic: equestrian sports, flag football, marksmanship, soccer, winter soccer; coed intramural: cheering, Frisbee, horseback riding, ropes courses, table tennis, weight lifting, weight training. 3 PE instructors, 20 coaches, 1 athletic trainer.

Computers Computer network features include on-campus library services, online commercial services, Internet access, wireless campus network, Internet filtering or blocking technology, 1:1 computer device program for high school students. Student e-mail accounts and computer access in designated common areas are available to students. Students grades are available online. The school has a published electronic and media policy.

Contact Mrs. Shelley Henry, Director of Admissions and Communications. 800-428-5120. Fax: 512-753-8031. E-mail: admissions@smabears.org. Website: www.smabears.org

SANTA CATALINA SCHOOL

1500 Mark Thomas Drive
Monterey, California 93940-5291

Head of School: Sr. Claire Barone

General Information Girls' boarding and day college-preparatory, liberal arts, and marine biology school, affiliated with Roman Catholic Church. Grades 9–12. Founded: 1950. Setting: small town. Nearest major city is San Francisco. Students are housed in single-sex dormitories. 36-acre campus. 21 buildings on campus. Approved or accredited by California Association of Independent Schools, National Catholic Education Association, The Association of Boarding Schools, The College Board, Western Association of Schools and Colleges, and California Department of Education. Member of National Association of Independent Schools and Secondary School Admission Test Board. Endowment: $29 million. Total enrollment: 244. Upper school average class size: 12. Upper school faculty-student ratio: 1:8. There are 170 required school days per year for Upper School students. Upper School students typically attend 5 days per week. The average school day consists of 6 hours and 10 minutes.

Upper School Student Profile Grade 9: 57 students (57 girls); Grade 10: 72 students (72 girls); Grade 11: 59 students (59 girls); Grade 12: 56 students (56 girls). 46% of students are boarding students. 79% are state residents. 13 states are represented in upper school student body. 13% are international students. International students from China, Democratic People's Republic of Korea, Indonesia, Mexico, Saudi Arabia, and Singapore; 4 other countries represented in student body. 45% of students are Roman Catholic.

Faculty School total: 34. In upper school: 14 men, 20 women; 26 have advanced degrees; 11 reside on campus.

Subjects Offered Algebra, American literature, art, art history-AP, ballet, biology, biology-AP, British literature, calculus, calculus-AP, ceramics, chemistry, chemistry-AP, Chinese, choir, college counseling, computer science, computer technologies, conceptual physics, creative writing, dance, digital art, drama, drama performance, economics-AP, English, English composition, English language and composition-AP, English literature, English literature and composition-AP, ensembles, European history, finance, fine arts, French, French language-AP, geometry, global issues, grammar, health, honors algebra, honors English, honors geometry, human geography - AP, jazz dance, Latin, Latin-AP, macro/microeconomics-AP, Mandarin, marine ecology, marine science, media arts, music, music performance, music theory-AP, peace and justice, philosophy, photography, physical education, physics, physics-AP, pre-calculus, social justice, Spanish, Spanish language-AP, Spanish literature-AP, statistics, statistics-AP, studio art, studio art-AP, theater, theater arts, theater design and production, theology,

trigonometry, U.S. history, U.S. history-AP, women spirituality and faith, world history, world history-AP, world issues, world literature, world religions.

Graduation Requirements Arts, English, foreign language, history, lab science, mathematics, physical education (includes health), religious studies.

Special Academic Programs 21 Advanced Placement exams for which test preparation is offered; honors section; academic accommodation for the gifted, the musically talented, and the artistically talented.

College Admission Counseling 55 students graduated in 2015; all went to college, including Boston University; California Polytechnic State University, San Luis Obispo; Emory University; New York University; Pace University; University of San Diego. Mean SAT critical reading: 621, mean SAT math: 621, mean SAT writing: 634, mean composite ACT: 27.

Student Life Upper grades have uniform requirement, student council, honor system. Discipline rests equally with students and faculty. Attendance at religious services is required.

Summer Programs Enrichment, sports, art/fine arts programs offered; session focuses on recreation and enrichment fun; held on campus; accepts girls; open to students from other schools. 210 students usually enrolled. 2016 schedule: June 26 to July 30. Application deadline: none.

Tuition and Aid Day student tuition: $33,000; 7-day tuition and room/board: $50,300. Need-based scholarship grants available. In 2014–15, 42% of upper-school students received aid. Total amount of financial aid awarded in 2014–15: $1,964,000.

Admissions Traditional secondary-level entrance grade is 9. For fall 2015, 181 students applied for upper-level admission, 102 were accepted, 71 enrolled. ISEE, SSAT or TOEFL required. Deadline for receipt of application materials: February 1. Application fee required: $75. Interview required.

Athletics Interscholastic: basketball, cross-country running, diving, equestrian sports, field hockey, golf, lacrosse, soccer, softball, swimming and diving, tennis, track and field, volleyball, water polo; intramural: ballet, canoeing/kayaking, dance, fencing, fitness, horseback riding, kayaking, modern dance, outdoor activities, physical fitness, rafting, rock climbing, self defense, strength & conditioning, surfing, weight training, yoga. 1 PE instructor, 26 coaches.

Computers Computers are regularly used in English, foreign language, mathematics, media arts, science, yearbook classes. Computer network features include on-campus library services, Internet access, wireless campus network, Internet filtering or blocking technology, iPads for juniors, sophomores, and freshmen. Campus intranet, student e-mail accounts, and computer access in designated common areas are available to students. The school has a published electronic and media policy.

Contact Mrs. Jamie Buffington Browne '85, Director of Admission. 831-655-9356. Fax: 831-655-7535. E-mail: jamie.brown@santacatalina.org. Website: www.santacatalina.org

SANTA FE PREPARATORY SCHOOL

1101 Camino de la Cruz Blanca
Santa Fe, New Mexico 87505

Head of School: Mr. James W. Leonard

General Information Coeducational day college-preparatory, arts, and community service school. Grades 7–12. Founded: 1961. Setting: suburban. 33-acre campus. 4 buildings on campus. Approved or accredited by Independent Schools Association of the Southwest and New Mexico Department of Education. Member of National Association of Independent Schools. Endowment: $12.5 million. Total enrollment: 317. Upper school average class size: 13. Upper school faculty-student ratio: 1:16. There are 171 required school days per year for Upper School students. Upper School students typically attend 5 days per week. The average school day consists of 6 hours and 23 minutes.

Upper School Student Profile Grade 9: 61 students (37 boys, 24 girls); Grade 10: 44 students (25 boys, 19 girls); Grade 11: 51 students (28 boys, 23 girls); Grade 12: 67 students (29 boys, 38 girls).

Faculty School total: 48. In upper school: 19 men, 20 women; 27 have advanced degrees.

Subjects Offered Acting, advanced chemistry, advanced computer applications, advanced math, algebra, American Civil War, American culture, American democracy, American government, American history, American history-AP, American literature, analytic geometry, art, art appreciation, art history, art history-AP, arts, athletics, basketball, biology, calculus, calculus-AP, ceramics, chemistry, chemistry-AP, chorus, clayworking, college counseling, community service, computer applications, computer graphics, computer literacy, computer programming, computer science, conceptual physics, creative writing, drama, drama performance, dramatic arts, driver education, earth science, English, English literature, environmental science, European history, fine arts, French, geography, geometry, health, history, humanities, journalism, keyboarding, Latin, mathematics, music, photography, physical education, physics, psychology, science, social studies, Spanish, theater, trigonometry, world history, world literature, writing.

Graduation Requirements Arts and fine arts (art, music, dance, drama), computer science, English, foreign language, history, humanities, mathematics, physical education (includes health), science, social studies (includes history), senior seminar program. Community service is required.

Special Academic Programs 5 Advanced Placement exams for which test preparation is offered; honors section; independent study; study at local college for college credit; study abroad; academic accommodation for the gifted.

College Admission Counseling 37 students graduated in 2014; all went to college, including Dartmouth College; Middlebury College; Princeton University; University of Denver; University of New Mexico; Whitman College. Median SAT critical reading: 620, median SAT math: 610, median SAT writing: 600, median combined SAT: 1850, median composite ACT: 28. 61% scored over 600 on SAT critical reading, 61% scored over 600 on SAT math, 54% scored over 600 on SAT writing, 61% scored over 1800 on combined SAT, 58% scored over 26 on composite ACT.

Student Life Upper grades have specified standards of dress, student council. Discipline rests equally with students and faculty.

Tuition and Aid Day student tuition: $18,906. Tuition installment plan (individually arranged payment plans, Tuition Management Systems Plan). Need-based scholarship grants, tuition remission for faculty available. In 2014–15, 40% of upper-school students received aid.

Admissions Traditional secondary-level entrance grade is 9. For fall 2014, 34 students applied for upper-level admission, 31 were accepted, 17 enrolled. Mathematics proficiency exam required. Deadline for receipt of application materials: none. Application fee required: $55. Interview required.

Athletics Interscholastic: basketball (boys, girls), cross-country running (b,g), diving (b,g), fencing (b,g), lacrosse (b,g), soccer (b,g), swimming and diving (b,g), tennis (b,g), track and field (b,g), volleyball (g); intramural: basketball (b,g), cross-country running (b,g), football (b,g), Frisbee (b,g), hiking/backpacking (b,g), martial arts (b,g), outdoor activities (b,g), soccer (b,g), tennis (b,g), track and field (b,g), ultimate Frisbee (b,g), volleyball (g); coed interscholastic: baseball; coed intramural: basketball, skiing (downhill), snowshoeing, swimming and diving. 1 PE instructor, 16 coaches, 1 athletic trainer.

Computers Computers are regularly used in current events, English, geography, graphic arts, history, humanities, journalism, library, literary magazine, mathematics, newspaper, photography, photojournalism, science, social sciences, writing, yearbook classes. Computer network features include on-campus library services, Internet access, wireless campus network, Internet filtering or blocking technology. Campus intranet, student e-mail accounts, and computer access in designated common areas are available to students. The school has a published electronic and media policy.

Contact Michael Multari, Director of Admissions. 505-982-1829 Ext. 1212. Fax: 505-982-2897. E-mail: mmultari@sfprep.org. Website: www.santafeprep.org

SANTA MARGARITA CATHOLIC HIGH SCHOOL

22062 Antonio Parkway
Rancho Santa Margarita, California 92688

Head of School: Mr. Ray Dunne

General Information Coeducational day college-preparatory, arts, religious studies, technology, International Baccalaureate, and auxiliary studies program school, affiliated with Roman Catholic Church. Grades 9–12. Founded: 1987. Setting: suburban. 42-acre campus. 18 buildings on campus. Approved or accredited by International Baccalaureate Organization, National Catholic Education Association, Western Association of Schools and Colleges, Western Catholic Education Association, and California Department of Education. Total enrollment: 1,755. Upper school average class size: 28. Upper school faculty-student ratio: 1:15. There are 180 required school days per year for Upper School students. Upper School students typically attend 5 days per week. The average school day consists of 5 hours and 30 minutes.

Upper School Student Profile Grade 9: 430 students (218 boys, 212 girls); Grade 10: 465 students (225 boys, 240 girls); Grade 11: 413 students (179 boys, 234 girls); Grade 12: 426 students (203 boys, 223 girls). 61% of students are Roman Catholic.

Faculty School total: 109. In upper school: 65 have advanced degrees.

Subjects Offered Accounting, ACT preparation, advanced biology, advanced chemistry, advanced math, Advanced Placement courses, algebra, American Civil War, American government, American history, American history-AP, American literature, anatomy and physiology, art, art education, art history, art history-AP, art-AP, audio visual/media, Bible studies, biology, biology-AP, business communications, business studies, calculus, calculus-AP, campus ministry, career/college preparation, Catholic belief and practice, ceramics, chamber groups, chemistry, chemistry-AP, choir, chorus, Christian doctrine, Christian education, Christian studies, Christianity, cinematography, classical music, classical studies, community service, comparative government and politics, comparative government and politics-AP, comparative political systems-AP, comparative politics, comparative religion, composition, computer education, computer programming, computer science, computer science-AP, concert band, creative arts, current events, debate, drama, drawing, earth science, East European studies, economics, economics and history, economics-AP, English, English composition, English language-AP, English literature, English literature and composition-AP, English literature-AP, English-AP, English/composition-AP, environmental science, environmental science-AP, ethics, European civilization, European history, European history-AP, European literature, finance, fine arts, forensics, French, French language-AP, French literature-AP, French-AP, geography, geology, geometry, government and politics-AP, government-AP, government/civics, government/civics-AP, graphic arts, graphic design, health and wellness, health education, health science, history, history of religion, history of the Catholic Church, history-AP, honors algebra, honors English,

honors geometry, honors U.S. history, honors world history, human biology, instrumental music, international relations, jazz band, jazz ensemble, journalism, language and composition, language arts, language-AP, Latin, Latin-AP, law studies, literature and composition-AP, literature-AP, macro/microeconomics-AP, macroeconomics-AP, marine biology, mathematics, mathematics-AP, microeconomics-AP, model United Nations, music, music theory-AP, musical theater, newspaper, nutrition, oceanography, orchestra, painting, philosophy, photography, physical science, physics, physics-AP, physiology, poetry, political science, politics, pre-algebra, pre-calculus, probability, probability and statistics, psychology, psychology-AP, public speaking, reading/study skills, religion, religious education, remedial/makeup course work, SAT preparation, SAT/ACT preparation, social studies, sociology, Spanish, Spanish language-AP, Spanish literature, Spanish literature-AP, Spanish-AP, speech, speech and debate, speech communications, sports, statistics, statistics-AP, student government, student publications, studio art, theater arts, trigonometry, U.S. government, U.S. government and politics, U.S. government and politics-AP, U.S. history, U.S. history-AP, United States government-AP, vocal music, weight training, world governments, world history, world history-AP, world issues, world literature, world religions, World War I, World War II, writing, yearbook.

Graduation Requirements Foreign language, health, science, social sciences.

Special Academic Programs International Baccalaureate program; 19 Advanced Placement exams for which test preparation is offered; honors section; independent study; study at local college for college credit; academic accommodation for the gifted, the musically talented, and the artistically talented; remedial reading and/or remedial writing; remedial math; programs in English, mathematics, general development for dyslexic students; special instructional classes for deaf students, blind students, students with learning disabilities, Attention Deficit Disorder, and dyslexia.

College Admission Counseling 406 students graduated in 2015; 404 went to college, including Arizona State University at the Tempe campus; San Diego State University; Southern Methodist University; Texas Christian University; The University of Arizona; University of Oregon. Other: 1 went to work, 1 had other specific plans. Mean SAT critical reading: 556, mean SAT math: 574, mean SAT writing: 559, mean combined SAT: 1689, mean composite ACT: 25.

Student Life Upper grades have uniform requirement, student council, honor system. Discipline rests primarily with faculty. Attendance at religious services is required.

Summer Programs Remediation, enrichment, advancement, sports, art/fine arts, computer instruction programs offered; session focuses on enrichment; held on campus; accepts boys and girls; open to students from other schools. 1,272 students usually enrolled. 2016 schedule: June to July. Application deadline: none.

Tuition and Aid Day student tuition: $13,425. Tuition installment plan (monthly payment plans, annual payment, semi-annual). Tuition reduction for siblings, need-based scholarship grants available. In 2015–16, 20% of upper-school students received aid. Total amount of financial aid awarded in 2015–16: $1,500,000.

Admissions Traditional secondary-level entrance grade is 9. For fall 2015, 670 students applied for upper-level admission, 557 were accepted, 435 enrolled. High School Placement Test required. Deadline for receipt of application materials: none. Application fee required: $50.

Athletics Interscholastic: aerobics/dance (girls), aquatics (b,g), ballet (g), baseball (b), basketball (b,g), cheering (g), cross-country running (b,g), dance (b,g), dance squad (g), dance team (g), diving (b,g), dressage (b,g), drill team (g), equestrian sports (b,g), fitness (b,g), football (b), golf (b,g), hockey (b), ice hockey (b), in-line hockey (b), lacrosse (b,g), modern dance (g), physical fitness (b,g), physical training (b,g), power lifting (b), roller hockey (b), running (b,g), soccer (b,g), softball (g), surfing (b,g), swimming and diving (b,g), tennis (b,g), track and field (b,g), volleyball (b,g), water polo (b,g), wrestling (b); intramural: fitness (b,g), power lifting (b), running (b,g), self defense (b,g), weight lifting (b,g), weight training (b,g); coed interscholastic: aerobics/dance; coed intramural: dance, Special Olympics. 4 PE instructors, 27 coaches, 2 athletic trainers.

Computers Computers are regularly used in all academic classes. Computer network features include on-campus library services, online commercial services, Internet access, wireless campus network, Internet filtering or blocking technology, custom learning portal, Aeries, DyKnow, Windows 8 for Education. Campus intranet and student e-mail accounts are available to students. Students grades are available online. The school has a published electronic and media policy.

Contact Mr. Ron Blanc, Admissions Director. 949-766-6076. Fax: 949-766-6005. E-mail: admissions@smhs.org. Website: www.smhs.org

SAVANNAH CHRISTIAN PREPARATORY SCHOOL

PO Box 2848
Savannah, Georgia 31402-2848

Head of School: Dr. David Pitre

General Information Coeducational day college-preparatory school, affiliated with Christian faith. Grades PK–12. Founded: 1951. Setting: suburban. 236-acre campus. 6 buildings on campus. Approved or accredited by Georgia Independent School Association, Southern Association of Colleges and Schools, and Georgia Department of Education. Endowment: $1.1 million. Total enrollment: 1,227. Upper school average class size: 17. Upper school faculty-student ratio: 1:14. There are 180 required school days per year for Upper School students. Upper School students typically attend 5 days per week. The average school day consists of 6 hours and 35 minutes.

Upper School Student Profile Grade 9: 129 students (68 boys, 61 girls); Grade 10: 118 students (61 boys, 57 girls); Grade 11: 126 students (75 boys, 51 girls); Grade 12: 104 students (42 boys, 62 girls). 95% of students are Christian faith.

Faculty School total: 125. In upper school: 10 men, 25 women; 26 have advanced degrees.

Subjects Offered 20th century history, accounting, advanced TOEFL/grammar, algebra, American Civil War, American history, American history-AP, art, astronomy, band, Bible, biology, botany, business law, calculus-AP, chemistry, chemistry-AP, chorus, Christian ethics, computer applications, computer-aided design, creative writing, design, drama, driver education, earth science, ecology, economics, English, English-AP, European history-AP, French, geometry, government/civics, graphic arts, health, marine biology, mathematics, mechanical drawing, music appreciation, physical education, physics, probability and statistics, psychology, science, social studies, sociology, Spanish, speech, technical theater, theater, trigonometry, typing, world history, yearbook.

Graduation Requirements Accounting, algebra, biology, chemistry, economics, English, foreign language, geometry, mathematics, physical education (includes health), religion (includes Bible studies and theology), science, social studies (includes history).

Special Academic Programs Advanced Placement exam preparation; honors section; study at local college for college credit.

College Admission Counseling 108 students graduated in 2015; 107 went to college, including Armstrong State University; Georgia College & State University; Georgia Southern University; University of Georgia; University of South Carolina; Valdosta State University. Other: 1 entered military service. Mean SAT critical reading: 545, mean SAT math: 551, mean SAT writing: 545, mean combined SAT: 1641, mean composite ACT: 24.

Student Life Upper grades have uniform requirement, student council, honor system. Discipline rests primarily with faculty.

Tuition and Aid Day student tuition: $8167. Tuition installment plan (monthly payment plans). Merit scholarship grants, need-based scholarship grants available. In 2015–16, 15% of upper-school students received aid; total upper-school merit-scholarship money awarded: $35,000. Total amount of financial aid awarded in 2015–16: $110,000.

Admissions Traditional secondary-level entrance grade is 9. For fall 2015, 61 students applied for upper-level admission, 58 were accepted, 58 enrolled. Stanford Achievement Test and writing sample required. Deadline for receipt of application materials: none. Application fee required: $125.

Athletics Interscholastic: baseball (boys), basketball (b,g), cheering (g), cross-country running (b,g), dance team (g), football (b), golf (b,g), lacrosse (b,g), soccer (b,g), softball (g), tennis (b,g), track and field (b,g), volleyball (g), wrestling (b); coed intramural: sailing. 3 PE instructors, 3 coaches, 1 athletic trainer.

Computers Computers are regularly used in accounting, business applications, computer applications, English, graphic arts, history, science, word processing, yearbook classes. Computer network features include on-campus library services, Internet access, wireless campus network, Internet filtering or blocking technology. Computer access in designated common areas is available to students. Students grades are available online. The school has a published electronic and media policy.

Contact Mrs. Debbie Fairbanks, Director of Admissions. 912-721-2114. Fax: 912-234-0491. E-mail: dfairbanks@savcps.com. Website: www.savcps.com

THE SAVANNAH COUNTRY DAY SCHOOL

824 Stillwood Drive
Savannah, Georgia 31419-2643

Head of School: Mr. Kcf Wilson

General Information Coeducational day college-preparatory, arts, and technology school. Grades PK–12. Founded: 1955. Setting: suburban. 65-acre campus. 11 buildings on campus. Approved or accredited by Georgia Independent School Association, Southern Association of Colleges and Schools, and Southern Association of Independent Schools. Member of National Association of Independent Schools. Endowment: $32.2 million. Total enrollment: 893. Upper school average class size: 6. Upper school faculty-student ratio: 1:6. There are 180 required school days per year for Upper School students. Upper School students typically attend 5 days per week. The average school day consists of 7 hours.

Faculty School total: 81. In upper school: 21 men, 18 women; 24 have advanced degrees.

Subjects Offered Advanced Placement courses, algebra, American history, American literature, analysis and differential calculus, anatomy and physiology, art, art history, biology, biology-AP, British literature-AP, calculus, calculus-AP, ceramics, chemistry, chemistry-AP, chorus, composition, computer education, computer science, dance, drama, drama performance, economics and history, English, English literature, English-AP, environmental science, environmental science-AP, European history, European history-AP, fine arts, French, geometry, government-AP, government/civics, guidance, health, honors algebra, honors English, honors geometry, honors U.S. history, honors world history, independent study, instrumental music, intro to computers, jazz band, language-AP, Latin, Latin-AP, music, photography, physical education, physics, physics-AP, pre-calculus, public speaking, Spanish, Spanish language-AP, statistics, studio art-AP, theater, U.S. history-AP, world history, world history-AP, yearbook.

Graduation Requirements Arts and fine arts (art, music, dance, drama), English, foreign language, health education, history, mathematics, physical education (includes health), science, speech.

Special Academic Programs Advanced Placement exam preparation; honors section; independent study; study at local college for college credit; ESL.

College Admission Counseling 55 students graduated in 2015; 54 went to college. Other: 1 entered military service.

Student Life Upper grades have uniform requirement, student council, honor system. Discipline rests equally with students and faculty.

Summer Programs Remediation, enrichment, advancement, sports, art/fine arts, computer instruction programs offered; session focuses on recreation and enrichment; held both on and off campus; held at the beach (Coastal Ecology); accepts boys and girls; open to students from other schools. 1,400 students usually enrolled. 2016 schedule: May 31 to August 18.

Tuition and Aid Tuition installment plan (Insured Tuition Payment Plan, FACTS Tuition Payment Plan, monthly payment plans, individually arranged payment plans). Need-based scholarship grants available.

Admissions Traditional secondary-level entrance grade is 9. ERB Reading and Math, Math Placement Exam, Otis-Lennon Mental Ability Test or writing sample required. Deadline for receipt of application materials: none. Application fee required: $175. Interview required.

Athletics Interscholastic: baseball (boys), basketball (b,g), cheering (g), cross-country running (b,g), football (b), golf (b,g), soccer (b,g), softball (g), tennis (b,g), track and field (b,g), volleyball (g); intramural: basketball (b,g), bocce (b,g), cheering (g), climbing (b,g), cross-country running (b,g), dance (b,g), outdoor adventure (b,g), outdoor education (b,g), physical training (b,g), power lifting (b,g), project adventure (b,g), ropes courses (b,g), strength & conditioning (b,g), track and field (b,g), volleyball (g), weight lifting (b,g), weight training (b,g); coed interscholastic: swimming and diving; coed intramural: archery, sailing, soccer, strength & conditioning. 6 PE instructors, 6 coaches, 2 athletic trainers.

Computers Computers are regularly used in college planning, creative writing, English, foreign language, history, library skills, mathematics, publications, publishing, research skills, SAT preparation, science, yearbook classes. Computer network features include on-campus library services, online commercial services, Internet access, wireless campus network, Internet filtering or blocking technology. Campus intranet and student e-mail accounts are available to students. The school has a published electronic and media policy.

Contact Mrs. Amy Pinckney, Assistant Director of Admissions. 912-961-8700. Fax: 912-920-7800. E-mail: pinckney@savcds.org. Website: www.savcds.org

SCATTERGOOD FRIENDS SCHOOL

1951 Delta Avenue
West Branch, Iowa 52358-8507

Head of School: Mr. Thomas Weber

General Information Coeducational boarding and day college-preparatory, arts, sustainable agriculture, and writing school, affiliated with Society of Friends. Boarding grades 9–PG, day grades 9–12. Founded: 1890. Setting: rural. Nearest major city is Iowa City. Students are housed in single-sex dormitories. 126-acre campus. 15 buildings on campus. Approved or accredited by Friends Council on Education, Independent Schools Association of the Central States, and The Association of Boarding Schools. Member of National Association of Independent Schools. Endowment: $5 million. Total enrollment: 35. Upper school average class size: 10. Upper school faculty-student ratio: 1:3. There are 180 required school days per year for Upper School students. Upper School students typically attend 5 days per week. The average school day consists of 7 hours.

Upper School Student Profile Grade 9: 7 students (3 boys, 4 girls); Grade 10: 8 students (5 boys, 3 girls); Grade 11: 7 students (3 boys, 4 girls); Grade 12: 13 students (6 boys, 7 girls). 94% of students are boarding students. 29% are state residents. 11 states are represented in upper school student body. 20% are international students. International students from Afghanistan, China, Colombia, Ethiopia, Rwanda, and Taiwan; 1 other country represented in student body. 20% of students are members of Society of Friends.

Faculty School total: 13. In upper school: 8 men, 5 women; 8 have advanced degrees; 10 reside on campus.

Subjects Offered Agriculture, algebra, alternative physical education, American culture, American government, American history, animal husbandry, art, biology, calculus, career/college preparation, ceramics, chemistry, college admission preparation, college counseling, college placement, college planning, college writing, community service, creative writing, critical thinking, digital art, drama, drama performance, drawing and design, ecology, environmental systems, environmental science, ESL, ethics, expository writing, fencing, fine arts, geometry, government/civics, history, independent study, Internet research, mathematics, organic gardening, photography, physics, portfolio writing, pottery, Quakerism and ethics, religion, research seminar, science, science research, senior seminar, social studies, Spanish, studio art, U.S. history, writing workshop, yearbook, yoga.

Graduation Requirements Algebra, biology, chemistry, English, foreign language, geometry, government, health and wellness, history, humanities, junior and senior seminars, physical education (includes health), physics, Quakerism and ethics, religious studies, U.S. government, U.S. history, world literature, 30 hours of community service per year in attendance, 20-page senior research paper with a thesis defense presentation, acceptance to an accredited 4-year college or university.

Special Academic Programs Honors section; independent study; academic accommodation for the gifted; ESL (7 students enrolled).

College Admission Counseling 12 students graduated in 2015; 9 went to college, including Cornell College; Iowa State University of Science and Technology; Oberlin College; The University of Iowa; University of South Florida. Other: 2 went to work, 1 had other specific plans.

Student Life Upper grades have specified standards of dress, student council. Discipline rests equally with students and faculty. Attendance at religious services is required.

Summer Programs Art/fine arts programs offered; session focuses on organic farming; held on campus; accepts boys and girls; open to students from other schools. 8 students usually enrolled. 2016 schedule: June to August.

Tuition and Aid Day student tuition: $17,800; 5-day tuition and room/board: $28,980; 7-day tuition and room/board: $28,980. Tuition installment plan (monthly payment plans, individually arranged payment plans). Need-based scholarship grants available. In 2015–16, 60% of upper-school students received aid. Total amount of financial aid awarded in 2015–16: $499,528.

Admissions Traditional secondary-level entrance grade is 9. Deadline for receipt of application materials: none. Application fee required: $65. Interview required.

Athletics Coed Interscholastic: basketball, cross-country running, fencing, soccer; coed intramural: archery, backpacking, bicycling, canoeing/kayaking, combined training, cooperative games, dance, fishing, fitness, fitness walking, Frisbee, hiking/backpacking, jogging, juggling, kayaking, martial arts, modern dance, outdoor activities, outdoor recreation, outdoors, physical fitness, running, ultimate Frisbee, walking.

Computers Computers are regularly used in all classes. Computer network features include on-campus library services, online commercial services, Internet access, wireless campus network, Internet filtering or blocking technology, laptop for each student. Campus intranet, student e-mail accounts, and computer access in designated common areas are available to students. Students grades are available online.

Contact Ms. Alicia Streeter, Director of Admissions. 319-643-7628. Fax: 319-643-7485. E-mail: admissions@scattergood.org. Website: www.scattergood.org

SCHECK HILLEL COMMUNITY SCHOOL

19000 25th Avenue
North Miami Beach, Florida 33180

Head of School: Dr. Ezra Levy

General Information Coeducational day and distance learning college-preparatory, arts, religious studies, bilingual studies, and technology school, affiliated with Jewish faith; primarily serves students with learning disabilities and dyslexic students. Grades PK–12. Distance learning grades 9–12. Founded: 1970. Setting: suburban. 14-acre campus. 3 buildings on campus. Approved or accredited by Florida Department of Education. Member of National Association of Independent Schools and Secondary School Admission Test Board. Total enrollment: 1,045. Upper school average class size: 20. Upper school faculty-student ratio: 1:15. There are 180 required school days per year for Upper School students. Upper School students typically attend 5 days per week. The average school day consists of 8 hours.

Upper School Student Profile 100% of students are Jewish.

Faculty School total: 250.

Subjects Offered Studio art, studio art-AP, tennis, the Web, theater, track and field, U.S. government, U.S. government and politics-AP, U.S. history-AP, United States government-AP, Web site design, world history, world history-AP.

Graduation Requirements Jewish studies.

Special Academic Programs International Baccalaureate program; Advanced Placement exam preparation; honors section; study at local college for college credit; academic accommodation for the gifted and the artistically talented; remedial reading and/or remedial writing; remedial math; programs in English, mathematics, general development for dyslexic students; ESL (100 students enrolled).

College Admission Counseling 70 students graduated in 2015; all went to college, including Florida International University; Florida State University; University of Central Florida; University of Florida; University of Maryland, Baltimore County; University of Miami. Mean SAT critical reading: 577, mean SAT math: 612, mean SAT writing: 574, mean composite ACT: 24.

Student Life Upper grades have uniform requirement, student council, honor system. Discipline rests primarily with faculty. Attendance at religious services is required.

Summer Programs Remediation, enrichment, advancement, ESL programs offered; session focuses on academics; held on campus; accepts boys and girls; open to students from other schools. 50 students usually enrolled. 2016 schedule: June to July. Application deadline: May.

Tuition and Aid Day student tuition: $24,700–$30,000. Tuition installment plan (FACTS Tuition Payment Plan). Tuition reduction for siblings, merit scholarship grants, need-based scholarship grants available. In 2015–16, 25% of upper-school students received aid; total upper-school merit-scholarship money awarded: $100,000. Total amount of financial aid awarded in 2015–16: $1,000,000.

Admissions Traditional secondary-level entrance grade is 9. For fall 2015, 200 students applied for upper-level admission, 180 were accepted, 170 enrolled. SSAT required. Deadline for receipt of application materials: February 15. Application fee required: $200. Interview required.

Athletics Interscholastic: basketball (boys, girls), crew (b,g), cross-country running (b,g), fitness (b,g), flag football (b,g), football (b), golf (b,g), running (b,g), soccer (b,g), strength & conditioning (b,g), tennis (b,g), volleyball (b,g), winter soccer (b,g); coed interscholastic: crew, cross-country running, fitness, tennis. 10 PE instructors.

Computers Computer network features include on-campus library services, Internet access, Internet filtering or blocking technology. Campus intranet, student e-mail accounts, and computer access in designated common areas are available to students. Students grades are available online. The school has a published electronic and media policy.

Contact Mrs. Betty Salinas, Director of Admissions. 305-931-2831 Ext. 173. Fax: 305-932-7463. E-mail: salinas@ehillel.org. Website: www.hillel-nmb.org/

SCHOLAR'S HALL PREPARATORY SCHOOL

888 Trillium Drive
Kitchener, Ontario N2R 1K4, Canada

Head of School: Mr. Frederick T. Gore

General Information Coeducational day college-preparatory, general academic, arts, and business school. Grades JK–12. Founded: 1997. Setting: small town. Nearest major city is Toronto, Canada. 10-acre campus. 1 building on campus. Approved or accredited by Ontario Department of Education. Language of instruction: English. Total enrollment: 105. Upper school average class size: 15. Upper school faculty-student ratio: 1:10. There are 200 required school days per year for Upper School students. Upper School students typically attend 5 days per week. The average school day consists of 7 hours.

Upper School Student Profile Grade 6: 10 students (5 boys, 5 girls); Grade 7: 10 students (5 boys, 5 girls); Grade 8: 10 students (5 boys, 5 girls); Grade 9: 10 students (5 boys, 5 girls); Grade 10: 10 students (5 boys, 5 girls); Grade 11: 10 students (5 boys, 5 girls); Grade 12: 10 students (5 boys, 5 girls).

Faculty School total: 10. In upper school: 5 men, 5 women; 5 have advanced degrees.

Special Academic Programs ESL (20 students enrolled).

College Admission Counseling 10 students graduated in 2014; 2 went to college, including The University of Western Ontario; University of Waterloo; Wilfrid Laurier University. Other: 8 entered a postgraduate year.

Student Life Upper grades have uniform requirement, student council, honor system. Discipline rests primarily with faculty.

Tuition and Aid Day student tuition: CAN$10,900. Guaranteed tuition plan. Tuition installment plan (The Tuition Plan, monthly payment plans, individually arranged payment plans). Tuition reduction for siblings, bursaries available. In 2014–15, 10% of upper-school students received aid. Total amount of financial aid awarded in 2014–15: CAN$20,000.

Admissions Traditional secondary-level entrance grade is 9. For fall 2014, 20 students applied for upper-level admission, 15 were accepted, 15 enrolled. Woodcock-Johnson Educational Evaluation, WISC III required. Deadline for receipt of application materials: June 1. No application fee required. Interview required.

Athletics Coed Interscholastic: badminton, ball hockey, baseball, basketball, cross-country running, fencing, fitness, fitness walking, flag football, floor hockey, Frisbee, golf, independent competitive sports, martial arts, outdoor activities, outdoor education, physical fitness, self defense, soccer, softball, table tennis, volleyball; coed intramural: badminton, ball hockey, baseball, basketball, bowling, cross-country running, fencing, fitness, fitness walking, flag football, floor hockey, Frisbee, golf, martial arts, outdoor activities, outdoor education, physical fitness, self defense, soccer, softball, table tennis, volleyball. 2 PE instructors.

Computers Computers are regularly used in all classes. Computer network features include Internet access, wireless campus network, Internet filtering or blocking technology. Campus intranet is available to students. The school has a published electronic and media policy.

Contact 519-888-6620. Fax: 519-884-0316. Website: www.scholarshall.com

SCHULE SCHLOSS SALEM

Schlossbezirk 1
Salem 88682, Germany

Head of School: Mr. Bernd Westermeyer

General Information Coeducational boarding and day college-preparatory, general academic, bilingual studies, German Abitur, and International Baccalaureate school. Grades 5–12. Founded: 1920. Setting: small town. Nearest major city is Stuttgart, Germany. Students are housed in single-sex dormitories. 32-hectare campus. 14 buildings on campus. Approved or accredited by International Baccalaureate Organization. Member of European Council of International Schools. Languages of instruction: English and German. Endowment: €45 million. Total enrollment: 675. Upper school average class size: 15. Upper school faculty-student ratio: 1:5. There are 200 required school days per year for Upper School students. Upper School students typically attend 6 days per week. The average school day consists of 6 hours.

Upper School Student Profile Grade 11: 130 students (67 boys, 63 girls); Grade 12: 157 students (81 boys, 76 girls); Grade 13: 161 students (86 boys, 75 girls). 95% of students are boarding students. 21% are international students. International students from Austria, China, Russian Federation, Spain, and Switzerland; 33 other countries represented in student body.

Faculty School total: 125. In upper school: 35 men, 30 women; 60 have advanced degrees; 40 reside on campus.

Subjects Offered Art history, biology, chemistry, computer science, economics, English, ethics, French, geography, German, Greek, history, Latin, mathematics, music, philosophy, physical education, physics, political science, religion, Russian, science, Spanish, theater arts, visual arts.

Graduation Requirements Arts and fine arts (art, music, dance, drama), English, foreign language, German, mathematics, physical education (includes health), science, social sciences, theory of knowledge, 2 hours of community service per week, academic requirements vary depending upon academic program pursued.

Special Academic Programs International Baccalaureate program; independent study; term-away projects; domestic exchange program (with Bishop's College School, Sedbergh School, The Athenian School, Choate Rosemary Hall); study abroad; academic accommodation for the gifted, the musically talented, and the artistically talented; ESL.

College Admission Counseling 132 students graduated in 2014; 128 went to college, including Harvard University; London School of Economics and Political Science; University of Chicago; University of Oxford; University of St. Andrews.

Student Life Upper grades have student council. Discipline rests equally with students and faculty.

Tuition and Aid Day student tuition: €12,000; 7-day tuition and room/board: €28,000. Guaranteed tuition plan. Tuition installment plan (monthly payment plans, individually arranged payment plans, trimester payment plan, annual payment plan). Tuition reduction for siblings, merit scholarship grants, need-based scholarship grants, need-based loans available. In 2014–15, 30% of upper-school students received aid; total upper-school merit-scholarship money awarded: €2,000,000.

Admissions School's own exam or school's own test required. Deadline for receipt of application materials: none. Application fee required: €1200. Interview required.

Athletics Interscholastic: basketball (boys, girls), field hockey (b,g), gymnastics (b,g), indoor hockey (b,g), rugby (b), volleyball (b,g); intramural: aerobics/dance (g); basketball (b,g), field hockey (b,g), gymnastics (b,g), indoor hockey (b,g), rowing (b,g), rugby (b), soccer (b,g), softball (b,g), track and field (b,g), ultimate Frisbee (b,g), volleyball (b,g); coed interscholastic: sailing, volleyball; coed intramural: alpine skiing, archery, backpacking, badminton, bicycling, canoeing/kayaking, Circus, climbing, cross-country running, equestrian sports, fitness, golf, handball, hiking/backpacking, horseback riding, independent competitive sports, jogging, kayaking, life saving, mountain biking, nordic skiing, outdoor activities, rock climbing, running, sailing, sea rescue, skiing (cross-country), skiing (downhill), snowboarding, snowshoeing, squash, strength & conditioning, swimming and diving, table tennis, tennis, volleyball, wall climbing, water polo, weight training, windsurfing, yoga. 7 PE instructors, 7 coaches.

Computers Computers are regularly used in economics classes. Computer network features include on-campus library services, Internet access, Internet filtering or blocking technology. The school has a published electronic and media policy.

Contact Ms. Dagmar Berger, Director of Admissions. 49-7553-919 Ext. 337. Fax: 49-7553-919 Ext. 303. E-mail: dagmar.berger@salem-net.de. Website: www.salem-net.de

SCICORE ACADEMY

156 Maxwell Ave.
Hightstown, New Jersey 08520

Head of School: Arthur T. Poulos, PhD

General Information Coeducational day college-preparatory and technology school. Grades K–12. Founded: 2002. Setting: small town. Nearest major city is Trenton. 5-acre campus. 1 building on campus. Approved or accredited by Middle States Association of Colleges and Schools. Total enrollment: 95. Upper school average class size: 11. Upper school faculty-student ratio: 1:7. There are 170 required school days per year for Upper School students. Upper School students typically attend 5 days per week. The average school day consists of 6 hours and 30 minutes.

Faculty School total: 16. In upper school: 8 men, 3 women; 5 have advanced degrees.

Subjects Offered Advanced biology, advanced chemistry, advanced math, algebra, American government, American history, American literature, anatomy and physiology, art, biology, biology-AP, biotechnology, British literature, calculus, chemistry, chemistry-AP, Chinese, choir, drama, electronics, English composition, French, history of science, lab science, logic, rhetoric, and debate, microcomputer technology applications, music appreciation, physics, pre-calculus, programming, public speaking, SAT preparation, science project, senior project, Spanish, speech and debate, U.S. history, Western civilization, world literature.

Graduation Requirements Advanced math, algebra, American government, American history, American literature, biology, British literature, chemistry, civics, computer programming, English composition, foreign language, geometry, lab science, logic, rhetoric, and debate, physical education (includes health), physics, programming, SAT preparation, science project, U.S. history, Western civilization, world literature.

Special Academic Programs 3 Advanced Placement exams for which test preparation is offered; honors section; independent study; academic accommodation for the gifted and the artistically talented; ESL (4 students enrolled).

College Admission Counseling 11 students graduated in 2015; all went to college, including Cornell University; Emory University, Oxford College; Rutgers, The State University of New Jersey, New Brunswick; Tulane University.

Student Life Upper grades have uniform requirement, honor system. Discipline rests primarily with faculty.

Summer Programs Enrichment, advancement, computer instruction programs offered; session focuses on science, math, writing, and computer camps; held on campus; accepts boys and girls; open to students from other schools. 90 students usually enrolled. 2016 schedule: June 21 to August 20. Application deadline: none.

Tuition and Aid Day student tuition: $9120. Tuition installment plan (monthly payment plans). Tuition reduction for siblings available.

Admissions Traditional secondary-level entrance grade is 9. Admissions testing required. Deadline for receipt of application materials: none. No application fee required. Interview required.

Athletics Interscholastic: basketball (boys); intramural: aerobics/dance (g); coed interscholastic: cross-country running, golf, soccer, volleyball; coed intramural: cross-country running, equestrian sports, fencing, horseback riding. 2 PE instructors, 1 coach.

Computers Computers are regularly used in English, foreign language, French, programming, science, Spanish, yearbook classes. Computer resources include Internet access, wireless campus network. Student e-mail accounts and computer access in designated common areas are available to students. Students grades are available online. The school has a published electronic and media policy.

Contact Mrs. Danette N. Poulos, Vice Principal. 609-448-8950. Fax: 609-448-8952. E-mail: atpoulos@scicore.org. Website: www.scicore.org/

SCOTUS CENTRAL CATHOLIC HIGH SCHOOL

1554 18th Avenue
Columbus, Nebraska 68601-5132

Head of School: Mr. Wayne Morfeld

General Information Coeducational day college-preparatory, arts, business, religious studies, and technology school, affiliated with Roman Catholic Church. Grades 7–12. Founded: 1884. Setting: small town. Nearest major city is Omaha. 1-acre campus. 1 building on campus. Approved or accredited by National Catholic Education Association, North Central Association of Colleges and Schools, and Nebraska Department of Education. Endowment: $8.4 million. Total enrollment: 364. Upper school average class size: 20. Upper school faculty-student ratio: 1:14. There are 174 required school days per year for Upper School students. Upper School students typically attend 5 days per week. The average school day consists of 6 hours and 40 minutes.

Upper School Student Profile Grade 9: 63 students (31 boys, 32 girls); Grade 10: 68 students (37 boys, 31 girls); Grade 11: 68 students (39 boys, 29 girls); Grade 12: 49 students (24 boys, 25 girls). 95% of students are Roman Catholic.

Faculty School total: 32. In upper school: 12 men, 18 women; 9 have advanced degrees.

Subjects Offered Accounting, ACT preparation, advanced biology, advanced chemistry, advanced math, Advanced Placement courses, algebra, American government, American history, art, astronomy, band, Bible studies, biology, bookkeeping, calculus, calculus-AP, campus ministry, career and personal planning, career exploration, career/college preparation, Catholic belief and practice, character education, chemistry, child development, choir, choral music, chorus, community service, computer applications, computer multimedia, computer studies, computer technologies, concert band, concert choir, consumer economics, consumer mathematics, contemporary problems, CPR, current events, digital applications, drama, earth science, economics, English, English-AP, fabric arts, family and consumer science, fitness, food and nutrition, geography, government, guidance, health and safety, history, history-AP, human development, instrumental music, jazz band, jazz ensemble, journalism, keyboarding, life management skills, life skills, marching band, modern world history, personal fitness, physical education, physical science, physics, physiology, psychology, reading/study skills, sociology, Spanish, speech, speech and debate, speech communications, student publications, textiles, theater, U.S. history, vocal ensemble, voice, weight training, world history, yearbook.

Graduation Requirements Algebra, American government, American history, biology, chemistry, computer applications, electives, English, geometry, mathematics, modern history, physical education (includes health), religion (includes Bible studies and theology), Spanish, speech, U.S. history, world history, 80 hours of Living the Faith community/church/school service.

Special Academic Programs Study at local college for college credit.

College Admission Counseling 61 students graduated in 2014; all went to college, including Iowa State University of Science and Technology; University of Nebraska–Lincoln; University of Nebraska at Kearney; University of Nebraska at Omaha. Median composite ACT: 23. 21% scored over 26 on composite ACT.

Student Life Upper grades have uniform requirement, student council, honor system. Discipline rests equally with students and faculty. Attendance at religious services is required.

Tuition and Aid Day student tuition: $2550–$2650. Tuition installment plan (monthly payment plans). Need-based scholarship grants, paying campus jobs available. In 2014–15, 28% of upper-school students received aid. Total amount of financial aid awarded in 2014–15: $106,956.

Admissions Traditional secondary-level entrance grade is 9. Deadline for receipt of application materials: none. No application fee required. Interview recommended.

Athletics Interscholastic: baseball (boys), basketball (b,g), cheering (g), cross-country running (b,g), football (b), golf (b,g), soccer (b,g), softball (g), swimming and diving (b,g), tennis (b,g), track and field (b,g), volleyball (g), wrestling (b). 3 PE instructors, 15 coaches, 3 athletic trainers.

Computers Computers are regularly used in business, computer applications, English, graphic design, history, journalism, keyboarding, lab/keyboard, news writing, newspaper, photography, publications, religion, social sciences, speech, technology, Web site design, word processing, writing, yearbook classes. Computer network features include on-campus library services, Internet access, wireless campus network, Internet filtering or blocking technology. Campus intranet, student e-mail accounts, and computer access in designated common areas are available to students. Students grades are available online. The school has a published electronic and media policy.

Contact Mrs. Pamela K. Weir, 7-12 Guidance Counselor. 402-564-7165 Ext. 121. Fax: 402-564-6004. E-mail: pweir@scotuscc.org. Website: www.scotuscc.org

SEABURY HALL

480 Olinda Road
Makawao, Hawaii 96768-9399

Head of School: Ms. Sarah Bakhiet

General Information Coeducational day college-preparatory, arts, and technology school, affiliated with Episcopal Church. Grades 6–12. Founded: 1964. Setting: rural. Nearest major city is Kahului. 65-acre campus. 8 buildings on campus. Approved or accredited by Western Association of Schools and Colleges. Member of National Association of Independent Schools and Secondary School Admission Test Board. Endowment: $36.2 million. Total enrollment: 455. Upper school average class size: 15. Upper school faculty-student ratio: 1:11. There are 175 required school days per year for Upper School students. Upper School students typically attend 5 days per week. The average school day consists of 7 hours and 30 minutes.

Upper School Student Profile Grade 9: 88 students (43 boys, 45 girls); Grade 10: 82 students (36 boys, 46 girls); Grade 11: 78 students (41 boys, 37 girls); Grade 12: 73 students (44 boys, 29 girls). 5% of students are members of Episcopal Church.

Faculty School total: 56. In upper school: 23 men, 15 women; 23 have advanced degrees.

Subjects Offered Acting, algebra, American history, American history-AP, American literature, American literature-AP, art, band, biology, biology-AP, calculus-AP, ceramics, chemistry, chorus, college counseling, college placement, college planning, community service, comparative religion, computer programming, dance, drawing, economics, engineering, English, English literature, ethics, European history-AP, expository writing, fine arts, geometry, global issues, government, Hawaiian history, Hawaiian language, history, Japanese, keyboarding, mathematics, mythology, painting, philosophy, physical education, physics, physics-AP, political science, pre-algebra, pre-calculus, religion, SAT preparation, science, set design, social studies, Spanish, Spanish-AP, speech, studio art-AP, yearbook.

Graduation Requirements Arts and fine arts (art, music, dance, drama), English, foreign language, mathematics, physical education (includes health), religion (includes Bible studies and theology), science, social studies (includes history), speech. Community service is required.

Special Academic Programs 13 Advanced Placement exams for which test preparation is offered; honors section; independent study; academic accommodation for the gifted.

College Admission Counseling 78 students graduated in 2015; 73 went to college, including California Polytechnic State University, San Luis Obispo; Chapman University; Colorado State University; Gonzaga University; University of Hawaii at Manoa; University of San Diego. Mean SAT critical reading: 550, mean SAT math: 570, mean SAT writing: 565, mean combined SAT: 1685, mean composite ACT: 25.

Student Life Upper grades have specified standards of dress, student council, honor system. Discipline rests primarily with faculty.

Summer Programs Enrichment, sports, art/fine arts programs offered; session focuses on enrichment; held on campus; accepts boys and girls; open to students from other schools. 180 students usually enrolled. 2016 schedule: June 6 to July 8. Application deadline: June 6.

Tuition and Aid Day student tuition: $18,950. Tuition installment plan (FACTS Tuition Payment Plan). Need-based scholarship grants available. In 2015–16, 32% of upper-school students received aid. Total amount of financial aid awarded in 2015–16: $987,400.

Admissions Traditional secondary-level entrance grade is 9. For fall 2015, 96 students applied for upper-level admission, 75 were accepted, 49 enrolled. ERB CTP III, ISEE or SSAT required. Deadline for receipt of application materials: February 20. Application fee required: $75. Interview required.

Athletics Interscholastic: ballet (boys, girls), baseball (b), basketball (b,g), cross-country running (b,g), dance (g), diving (g), football (b), golf (b,g), independent competitive sports (b,g), modern dance (b,g), paddling (b,g), physical fitness (b,g), riflery (b,g), soccer (b,g), softball (g), surfing (b,g), swimming and diving (b,g), tennis (b,g), track and field (b,g), volleyball (b,g), water polo (g); intramural: basketball (b,g), fitness (b,g), strength & conditioning (b,g); coed interscholastic: dance, paddling, physical fitness; coed intramural: fitness, outdoor adventure, outdoor education, track and field, volleyball. 4 PE instructors, 12 coaches, 1 athletic trainer.

Computers Computers are regularly used in art, economics, English, foreign language, history, journalism, mathematics, newspaper, science, speech, yearbook classes. Computer network features include on-campus library services, online commercial services, Internet access, wireless campus network, Internet filtering or blocking technology. Campus intranet, student e-mail accounts, and computer access in designated common areas are available to students. Students grades are available online. The school has a published electronic and media policy.

Contact Elaine V. Nelson, Director of Admissions. 808-572-0807. Fax: 808-572-2042. E-mail: enelson@seaburyhall.org. Website: www.seaburyhall.org

SEACREST COUNTRY DAY SCHOOL

7,100 Davis Boulevard
Naples, Florida 34104

Head of School: Dr. John Watson, PhD

General Information Coeducational day college-preparatory school. Grades 9–12. Founded: 1983. Setting: suburban. Students are housed in day school. 40-acre campus. 3 buildings on campus. Approved or accredited by Florida Council of Independent Schools, Southern Association of Colleges and Schools, and Florida Department of Education. Member of National Association of Independent Schools and Secondary School Admission Test Board. Total enrollment: 399. Upper school average class size: 18. Upper school faculty-student ratio: 1:9. There are 181 required school days per year for Upper School students. Upper School students typically attend 5 days per week. The average school day consists of 7 hours and 45 minutes.

Upper School Student Profile Grade 6: 31 students (15 boys, 16 girls); Grade 7: 34 students (23 boys, 11 girls); Grade 8: 31 students (19 boys, 12 girls); Grade 9: 48 students (30 boys, 18 girls); Grade 10: 34 students (14 boys, 20 girls); Grade 11: 35 students (16 boys, 19 girls); Grade 12: 34 students (14 boys, 20 girls).

Faculty School total: 25. In upper school: 10 men, 14 women; 16 have advanced degrees.

College Admission Counseling 35 students graduated in 2014; all went to college. Mean SAT critical reading: 572, mean SAT math: 555, mean SAT writing: 591, mean composite ACT: 25.

Student Life Upper grades have specified standards of dress, student council, honor system. Discipline rests primarily with faculty.

Tuition and Aid Day student tuition: $20,500. Tuition installment plan (FACTS Tuition Payment Plan, monthly payment plans).

Admissions Traditional secondary-level entrance grade is 9. For fall 2014, 23 students applied for upper-level admission, 16 were accepted, 12 enrolled. ISEE required. Deadline for receipt of application materials: none. Application fee required: $75. Interview required.

Athletics Interscholastic: aquatics (boys, girls), baseball (b), basketball (b,g), cross-country running (b,g), diving (b,g), golf (b,g), soccer (b,g), softball (g), tennis (b,g), track and field (b,g), volleyball (g); intramural: flag football (b); coed interscholastic: sailing; coed intramural: fishing.

Computers Computer resources include on-campus library services, online commercial services, Internet access, wireless campus network, Internet filtering or blocking technology. Campus intranet and student e-mail accounts are available to students.

Contact Mrs. Erin Duffy, Head of Upper School. 239-793-1986. Fax: 239-793-1460. E-mail: eduffy@seacrest.org. Website: www.seacrest.org/

SEATTLE ACADEMY OF ARTS AND SCIENCES

1201 East Union Street
Seattle, Washington 98122

Head of School: Joe Puggelli

General Information Coeducational day college-preparatory, arts, and technology school. Grades 6–12. Founded: 1983. Setting: urban. 3-acre campus. 6 buildings on campus. Approved or accredited by Northwest Association of Independent Schools and Washington Department of Education. Member of National Association of Independent Schools. Endowment: $14.8 million. Total enrollment: 764. Upper school average class size: 18. Upper school faculty-student ratio: 1:6. There are 172 required school days per year for Upper School students. Upper School students typically attend 5 days per week. The average school day consists of 6 hours and 45 minutes.

Upper School Student Profile Grade 9: 142 students (63 boys, 79 girls); Grade 10: 122 students (60 boys, 62 girls); Grade 11: 118 students (56 boys, 62 girls); Grade 12: 111 students (59 boys, 52 girls).

Faculty School total: 125. In upper school: 62 men, 62 women; 83 have advanced degrees.

Subjects Offered 20th century world history, acting, advanced chemistry, algebra, American history, American literature, Asian studies, biology, biotechnology, calculus, chemistry, choir, civics, community service, dance, debate, drawing, economics,

English, environmental systems, French, geometry, health, history, humanities, independent study, instrumental music, lab science, literature, Mandarin, marine science, math analysis, musical productions, painting, physical education, physics, printmaking, robotics, sculpture, Spanish, speech, stagecraft, statistics, visual arts, vocal music, world literature, yearbook.

Graduation Requirements Arts and fine arts (art, music, dance, drama), English, foreign language, history, mathematics, physical education (includes health), science, social studies (includes history). Community service is required.

Special Academic Programs Honors section; independent study; term-away projects; study abroad; academic accommodation for the gifted, the musically talented, and the artistically talented; remedial reading and/or remedial writing; remedial math; programs in English, mathematics, general development for dyslexic students.

College Admission Counseling 110 students graduated in 2015; 109 went to college, including New York University; Santa Clara University; The George Washington University; University of Colorado Boulder; University of Washington; Western Washington University. Other: 1 had other specific plans. Mean SAT critical reading: 601, mean SAT math: 585, mean SAT writing: 584, mean combined SAT: 1770, mean composite ACT: 27.

Student Life Upper grades have student council, honor system. Discipline rests equally with students and faculty.

Summer Programs Enrichment, sports, art/fine arts programs offered; held both on and off campus; held at outdoor trips to various national and international locations; accepts boys and girls; open to students from other schools. 100 students usually enrolled. 2016 schedule: June 20 to August 12.

Tuition and Aid Day student tuition: $30,990. Tuition installment plan (Academic Management Services Plan, monthly payment plans). Need-based scholarship grants available. In 2015–16, 20% of upper-school students received aid.

Admissions Traditional secondary-level entrance grade is 9. ISEE or SSAT required. Deadline for receipt of application materials: January 14. Application fee required: $100. Interview required.

Athletics Interscholastic: basketball (boys, girls), cross-country running (b,g), Frisbee (b,g), golf (b,g), soccer (b,g), tennis (b,g), track and field (b,g), ultimate Frisbee (b,g), volleyball (g); coed interscholastic: dance, dance squad, dance team, wrestling; coed intramural: alpine skiing, climbing, fitness, outdoor activities, outdoor recreation, paint ball, physical fitness, skiing (cross-country), skiing (downhill), snowboarding, snowshoeing, squash, weight training. 5 PE instructors, 30 coaches, 2 athletic trainers.

Computers Computers are regularly used in all academic, computer applications, English, foreign language, graphic design, history, mathematics, newspaper, science, speech, study skills, theater arts, video film production, Web site design, yearbook classes. Computer network features include on-campus library services, online commercial services, Internet access, wireless campus network, Internet filtering or blocking technology. Student e-mail accounts are available to students. Students grades are available online. The school has a published electronic and media policy.

Contact Jim Rupp, Admission Director. 206-324-7227. Fax: 206-323-6618. E-mail: jrupp@seattleacademy.org. Website: www.seattleacademy.org

SEATTLE LUTHERAN HIGH SCHOOL

4100 SW Genesee Street
Seattle, Washington 98116

Head of School: Dave Meyer

General Information Coeducational day college-preparatory, general academic, arts, and religious studies school, affiliated with Lutheran Church; primarily serves students with learning disabilities and dyslexic students. Grades 9–12. Founded: 1977. Setting: urban. 2-acre campus. 1 building on campus. Approved or accredited by Lutheran School Accreditation Commission, National Lutheran School Accreditation, Northwest Accreditation Commission, and Washington Department of Education. Endowment: $385,000. Total enrollment: 128. Upper school average class size: 18. Upper school faculty-student ratio: 1:9. There are 180 required school days per year for Upper School students. Upper School students typically attend 5 days per week. The average school day consists of 6 hours and 45 minutes.

Upper School Student Profile Grade 9: 27 students (17 boys, 10 girls); Grade 10: 37 students (26 boys, 11 girls); Grade 11: 28 students (15 boys, 13 girls); Grade 12: 36 students (21 boys, 15 girls). 20% of students are Lutheran.

Faculty School total: 16. In upper school: 8 men, 6 women; 5 have advanced degrees.

Subjects Offered 3-dimensional art, Advanced Placement courses, algebra, American government, American history, American history-AP, American literature, American sign language, art, art history, band, biology, boating, British literature (honors), British literature-AP, calculus, calculus-AP, ceramics, chemistry, choir, Christian doctrine, Christian education, Christian ethics, community service, design, drama, earth science, economics, English, English composition, English literature, ESL, French, geography, geometry, handbells, health, history, jazz band, journalism, keyboarding, life skills, newspaper, painting, physical education, physics, portfolio art, pre-algebra, pre-calculus, psychology, publications, religion, robotics, science, senior project, social sciences, social studies, Spanish, Spanish-AP, state history, student government, study skills, world cultures, world history, world literature.

Graduation Requirements American government, American history, arts and fine arts (art, music, dance, drama), biology, English, foreign language, keyboarding, life skills, mathematics, physical education (includes health), religion (includes Bible

studies and theology), science, senior project, social sciences, world cultures. Community service is required.

Special Academic Programs 3 Advanced Placement exams for which test preparation is offered; honors section; independent study; remedial reading and/or remedial writing; remedial math; programs in English, mathematics, general development for dyslexic students; ESL (1 student enrolled).

College Admission Counseling 32 students graduated in 2015; 31 went to college, including Concordia University Irvine; Pacific Lutheran University; Seattle Pacific University; South Seattle College; University of Washington; Western Washington University. Other: 1 went to work.

Student Life Upper grades have specified standards of dress, student council, honor system. Discipline rests equally with students and faculty. Attendance at religious services is required.

Summer Programs Sports programs offered; session focuses on basketball, volleyball, soccer; held both on and off campus; held at Fairmount Park; accepts boys and girls; not open to students from other schools. 50 students usually enrolled. 2016 schedule: June 2 to July 31.

Tuition and Aid Day student tuition: $8900. Tuition installment plan (SMART Tuition Payment Plan, monthly payment plans). Tuition reduction for siblings, merit scholarship grants, need-based scholarship grants, honors scholarship at entrance to incoming valedictorians of 8th grade class available. In 2015–16, 21% of upper-school students received aid; total upper-school merit-scholarship money awarded: $1000. Total amount of financial aid awarded in 2015–16: $92,710.

Admissions Traditional secondary-level entrance grade is 9. For fall 2015, 42 students applied for upper-level admission, 40 were accepted, 32 enrolled. School's own exam and TAP required. Deadline for receipt of application materials: February 12. Application fee required: $50. Interview required.

Athletics Interscholastic: baseball (boys), basketball (b,g), cheering (b,g), cross-country running (b,g), football (b), physical training (b,g), soccer (g), softball (g), strength & conditioning (b,g), tennis (g), track and field (b,g), volleyball (g), weight training (b,g); intramural: yoga (g); coed interscholastic: golf; coed intramural: fencing, fitness, sailing. 3 PE instructors, 25 coaches.

Computers Computers are regularly used in English, keyboarding, life skills, newspaper, publications, social sciences, study skills, yearbook classes. Computer network features include on-campus library services, Internet access, wireless campus network, Internet filtering or blocking technology. Computer access in designated common areas is available to students. Students grades are available online. The school has a published electronic and media policy.

Contact Rachel Bigliardi, Director of Admission. 206-937-7722 Ext. 18. Fax: 206-937-6781. E-mail: rbigliardi@seattlelutheran.org. Website: www.seattlelutheran.org

SEDONA SKY ACADEMY

Rimrock, Arizona
See Special Needs Schools section.

SEISEN INTERNATIONAL SCHOOL

1-12-15 Yoga, Setagaya-ku
Tokyo 158-0097, Japan

Head of School: Ms. Colette Rogers

General Information Coeducational day (boys' only in lower grades) college-preparatory school, affiliated with Roman Catholic Church. Boys grade K, girls grades K–12. Founded: 1962. Setting: urban. 1-hectare campus. 3 buildings on campus. Approved or accredited by Council of International Schools, Department of Defense Dependents Schools, International Baccalaureate Organization, Ministry of Education, Japan, National Catholic Education Association, and New England Association of Schools and Colleges. Member of Secondary School Admission Test Board. Language of instruction: English. Total enrollment: 646. Upper school average class size: 20. Upper school faculty-student ratio: 1:6. There are 170 required school days per year for Upper School students. Upper School students typically attend 5 days per week. The average school day consists of 6 hours.

Upper School Student Profile Grade 9: 43 students (43 girls); Grade 10: 43 students (43 girls); Grade 11: 57 students (57 girls); Grade 12: 51 students (51 girls). 13% of students are Roman Catholic.

Faculty School total: 95. In upper school: 18 men, 32 women; 28 have advanced degrees.

Subjects Offered 3-dimensional art, advanced math, art, bell choir, biology, business, career planning, chemistry, Chinese, choir, college planning, computer graphics, computers, Danish, drama, English, environmental studies, environmental systems, ESL, filmmaking, French, geography, geometry, health education, history, honors algebra, honors geometry, information technology, International Baccalaureate courses, Japanese, journalism, Korean, library, library science, math methods, mathematics, model United Nations, music, music composition, music performance, painting, performing arts, personal and social education, physical education, physics, pottery, psychology, religion, robotics, science, social sciences, social studies, Spanish, speech, study skills, theory of knowledge, trigonometry, visual arts, world history, yearbook.

Graduation Requirements Electives, English, experiential education, mathematics, modern languages, physical education (includes health), religion (includes Bible studies and theology), science, social studies (includes history).

Special Academic Programs International Baccalaureate program; honors section; independent study; remedial reading and/or remedial writing; remedial math; ESL (10 students enrolled).

College Admission Counseling 44 students graduated in 2015; all went to college, including Carnegie Mellon University; New York University; The University of British Columbia; University of California, San Diego; University of Pennsylvania; University of Southern California. Median SAT critical reading: 575, median SAT math: 655, median SAT writing: 605, median combined SAT: 1805. 44% scored over 600 on SAT critical reading, 74% scored over 600 on SAT math, 59% scored over 600 on SAT writing, 52% scored over 1800 on combined SAT.

Student Life Upper grades have uniform requirement, student council, honor system. Discipline rests primarily with faculty.

Summer Programs Remediation, ESL programs offered; session focuses on remedial work only; held on campus; accepts girls; not open to students from other schools. 8 students usually enrolled. 2016 schedule: June 6 to June 24. Application deadline: May 1.

Tuition and Aid Day student tuition: ¥2,070,000. Tuition installment plan (monthly payment plans, individually arranged payment plans). Tuition reduction for siblings, need-based scholarship grants available. In 2015–16, 2% of upper-school students received aid. Total amount of financial aid awarded in 2015–16: ¥4,500,000.

Admissions Traditional secondary-level entrance grade is 9. For fall 2015, 37 students applied for upper-level admission, 21 were accepted, 16 enrolled. Admissions testing, mathematics proficiency exam, Reading for Understanding or writing sample required. Deadline for receipt of application materials: none. Application fee required: ¥20,000. Interview required.

Athletics Interscholastic: basketball, cross-country running, running, soccer, swimming and diving, tennis, track and field, volleyball, winter soccer; intramural: badminton, outdoor activities, running, soccer, table tennis, tennis. 3 PE instructors.

Computers Computers are regularly used in art, business studies, career education, college planning, economics, English, foreign language, graphic design, history, information technology, journalism, library science, mathematics, music, psychology, science, study skills, writing, yearbook classes. Computer network features include on-campus library services, online commercial services, Internet access, wireless campus network, Internet filtering or blocking technology. Campus intranet, student e-mail accounts, and computer access in designated common areas are available to students.

Contact Ms. Sung Hee Kim, Admissions and Student Records. 81-3-3704-2661 Ext. 1461. Fax: 81-3-3701-1033. E-mail: skim@seisen.com. Website: www.seisen.com

SERVITE HIGH SCHOOL

1952 West La Palma Avenue
Anaheim, California 92801-3595

Head of School: Mr. Michael P. Brennan

General Information Boys' day college preparatory, arts, business, religious studies, and technology school, affiliated with Roman Catholic Church. Grades 9–12. Founded: 1958. Setting: suburban. 14-acre campus. 9 buildings on campus. Approved or accredited by Western Association of Schools and Colleges and Western Catholic Education Association. Total enrollment: 905. Upper school average class size: 23. Upper school faculty-student ratio: 1:15. There are 187 required school days per year for Upper School students. Upper School students typically attend 5 days per week. The average school day consists of 6 hours and 55 minutes.

Upper School Student Profile Grade 9: 236 students (236 boys); Grade 10: 238 students (238 boys); Grade 11: 224 students (224 boys); Grade 12: 207 students (207 boys). 80% of students are Roman Catholic.

Faculty School total: 60. In upper school: 36 men, 22 women; 50 have advanced degrees.

Subjects Offered Advanced Placement courses, algebra, American government, American history, American history-AP, American literature, anatomy, ancient world history, art, art history, art history-AP, band, biology, calculus, calculus-AP, Catholic belief and practice, chemistry, chemistry-AP, Christian and Hebrew scripture, Christianity, computer science, computer science-AP, drama, drawing, driver education, economics, economics-AP, English, English literature, English literature-AP, English-AP, European history, European history-AP, fine arts, French, general science, geometry, government/civics, guitar, health, health education, history, history of the Catholic Church, honors algebra, honors English, honors geometry, honors U.S. history, instrumental music, journalism, Latin, Latin-AP, mathematics, modern European history-AP, music, music appreciation, performing arts, philosophy, physical education, physical science, physics-AP, physiology, pre-calculus, religion, science, social studies, Spanish, Spanish-AP, studio art, theater, trigonometry, U.S. government and politics-AP, U.S. history, U.S. history-AP, word processing, world cultures.

Graduation Requirements ADL skills, algebra, ancient/medieval philosophy, arts and fine arts (art, music, dance, drama), biology, Catholic belief and practice, church history, English, English composition, English literature, foreign language, geometry, government, language, mathematics, moral theology, physical education (includes health), religion (includes Bible studies and theology), science, social studies (includes history), theology and the arts, U.S. history, 100 hours of Christian service.

Special Academic Programs Advanced Placement exam preparation; honors section; study at local college for college credit; study abroad; special instructional classes for deaf students, blind students.

College Admission Counseling 220 students graduated in 2015; all went to college. Mean SAT critical reading: 538, mean SAT math: 553, mean SAT writing: 522, mean composite ACT: 25.

Student Life Upper grades have specified standards of dress, student council, honor system. Discipline rests equally with students and faculty. Attendance at religious services is required.

Summer Programs Remediation, enrichment, advancement, sports programs offered; session focuses on enrichment for incoming students, advancement for current students, and sports training; held on campus; accepts boys and girls; open to students from other schools. 900 students usually enrolled. 2016 schedule: June 20 to July 22. Application deadline: January 29.

Tuition and Aid Day student tuition: $15,275. Tuition installment plan (FACTS Tuition Payment Plan, monthly payment plans, individually arranged payment plans, paid in full or semester payments). Tuition reduction for siblings, merit scholarship grants, need-based scholarship grants, need-based loans, middle-income loans, paying campus jobs available. In 2015–16, 30% of upper-school students received aid; total upper-school merit-scholarship money awarded: $5000. Total amount of financial aid awarded in 2015–16: $1,500,000.

Admissions Traditional secondary-level entrance grade is 9. High School Placement Test or STS required. Deadline for receipt of application materials: January 29. Application fee required: $65. On-campus interview required.

Athletics Interscholastic: aquatics, baseball, basketball, cross-country running, football, golf, lacrosse, soccer, swimming and diving, tennis, track and field, volleyball, water polo, wrestling; intramural: ice hockey, rugby. 2 PE instructors, 101 coaches, 2 athletic trainers.

Computers Computers are regularly used in accounting, art, Bible studies, business, computer applications, economics, English, ethics, history, journalism, Latin, mathematics, music, philosophy, photojournalism, religion, science, social studies, Spanish, technology, theology, video film production, yearbook classes. Computer network features include on-campus library services, online commercial services, Internet access, wireless campus network, Internet filtering or blocking technology, student server profile account and data storage space, homework posting online. Campus intranet, student e-mail accounts, and computer access in designated common areas are available to students. Students grades are available online. The school has a published electronic and media policy.

Contact Mr. Chris Weir '97, Director of Admissions. 714-774-7575 Ext. 1170. Fax: 714-774-1404. E-mail: admissions@servitehs.org. Website: www.servitehs.org

SETON CATHOLIC CENTRAL HIGH SCHOOL

70 Seminary Avenue
Binghamton, New York 13905

Head of School: Mr. Richard Bucci

General Information Coeducational day college-preparatory, arts, business, religious studies, technology, and cybersecurity school, affiliated with Roman Catholic Church. Grades 7–12. Founded: 1963. Setting: suburban. 4-acre campus. 1 building on campus. Approved or accredited by Middle States Association of Colleges and Schools, National Catholic Education Association, New York State Board of Regents, The College Board, and New York Department of Education. Endowment: $1.5 million. Upper school average class size: 23. Upper school faculty-student ratio: 1:23. There are 185 required school days per year for Upper School students. Upper School students typically attend 5 days per week. The average school day consists of 6 hours and 45 minutes.

Upper School Student Profile 90% of students are Roman Catholic.

Faculty School total: 43. In upper school: 16 men, 19 women; 27 have advanced degrees.

Subjects Offered 3-dimensional design, accounting, advanced computer applications, Advanced Placement courses, advertising design, algebra, alternative physical education, American government, American history-AP, American legal systems, American literature, American literature-AP, ancient world history, applied music, architectural drawing, art-AP, band, Bible, biology, biology-AP, business, business law, business mathematics, calculus, calculus-AP, chemistry, chemistry-AP, chorus, Christian scripture, church history, comparative religion, computer applications, computer programming, computer programming-AP, creative drama, criminal justice, dramatic arts, economics, engineering, English, English language and composition-AP, English literature and composition-AP, entrepreneurship, environmental science, ethical decision making, ethics and responsibility, European history-AP, food and nutrition, foreign language, forensics, French, government/civics, guitar, health, honors English, honors geometry, instrumental music, integrated mathematics, keyboarding, Latin, Latin-AP, law and the legal system, literature and composition-AP, math applications, mathematics-AP, music theater, music theory, performing arts, photography, physical education, physics, physics-AP, pre-algebra, religion, social psychology, Spanish, Spanish-AP, studio art-AP, theater arts, theology, U.S. history, U.S. history-AP, wood processing, work-study, world history-AP, world religions.

Graduation Requirements Arts and fine arts (art, music, dance, drama), English, foreign language, mathematics, physical education (includes health), science, social studies (includes history), theology.

Special Academic Programs 18 Advanced Placement exams for which test preparation is offered; honors section; study at local college for college credit; academic accommodation for the gifted and the artistically talented; remedial reading and/or remedial math.

College Admission Counseling 70 students graduated in 2014; all went to college, including Binghamton University, State University of New York; Le Moyne College; St. Bonaventure University; The University of Scranton. Mean SAT critical reading: 561, mean SAT math: 587, mean SAT writing: 561.

Student Life Upper grades have uniform requirement, student council, honor system. Discipline rests primarily with faculty. Attendance at religious services is required.

Tuition and Aid Day student tuition: $6500. Tuition installment plan (monthly payment plans). Tuition reduction for siblings, merit scholarship grants, need-based scholarship grants available. In 2014–15, 40% of upper-school students received aid; total upper-school merit-scholarship money awarded: $10,000. Total amount of financial aid awarded in 2014–15: $200,000.

Admissions Traditional secondary-level entrance grade is 9. Deadline for receipt of application materials: none. Application fee required: $100. Interview required.

Athletics Interscholastic: baseball (boys), basketball (b,g), cross-country running (b,g), field hockey (g), football (b), ice hockey (b), indoor track & field (b,g), lacrosse (b,g), soccer (b,g), softball (g), swimming and diving (b,g), tennis (b,g), track and field (b,g), winter (indoor) track (b,g); intramural: snowboarding (b,g), strength & conditioning (b,g), weight training (b,g); coed interscholastic: cheering, golf; coed intramural: alpine skiing. 2 PE instructors, 25 coaches, 1 athletic trainer.

Computers Computers are regularly used in business applications, computer applications, desktop publishing, economics, engineering, English, foreign language, history, keyboarding, Latin, mathematics, science, social studies, Spanish, technology, yearbook classes. Computer network features include on-campus library services, online commercial services, Internet access, wireless campus network, Internet filtering or blocking technology. Computer access in designated common areas is available to students. The school has a published electronic and media policy.

Contact Mr. John Kiereck, Director of Admissions. 607-748-7423 Ext. 3. Fax: 607-474-9576. E-mail: jkiereck@syrdiocese.org. Website: www.setoncchs.com

SETON CATHOLIC HIGH SCHOOL
1150 North Dobson Road
Chandler, Arizona 85224
Head of School: Patricia L. Collins

General Information Coeducational day college-preparatory, arts, religious studies, technology, and dual enrollment school, affiliated with Roman Catholic Church. Grades 9–12. Founded: 1954. Setting: suburban. Nearest major city is Phoenix. 30-acre campus. 11 buildings on campus. Approved or accredited by North Central Association of Colleges and Schools, Western Catholic Education Association, and Arizona Department of Education. Endowment: $342,000. Total enrollment: 563. Upper school average class size: 21. Upper school faculty-student ratio: 1:13. There are 182 required school days per year for Upper School students. Upper School students typically attend 5 days per week. The average school day consists of 6 hours and 55 minutes.

Upper School Student Profile Grade 9: 147 students (73 boys, 74 girls); Grade 10: 145 students (70 boys, 75 girls); Grade 11: 151 students (76 boys, 75 girls); Grade 12: 120 students (65 boys, 55 girls). 96% of students are Roman Catholic.

Faculty School total: 45. In upper school: 21 men, 24 women; 29 have advanced degrees.

Subjects Offered Aerobics, algebra, American government, American history, anatomy, art, athletic training, Basic programming, biology, biology-AP, calculus, chemistry, chemistry-AP, choir, Christian and Hebrew scripture, Christian scripture, church history, computer applications, dance, drama, drawing, economics, English, English-AP, European history-AP, fitness, foreign language, French, geometry, government, guitar, health, honors English, honors geometry, honors U.S. history, keyboarding, Latin, Latin-AP, personal fitness, photography, physics, pre-calculus, psychology, reading/study skills, religion, scripture, social justice, Spanish, Spanish-AP, study skills, television, theology, U.S. government, U.S. history, video film production, weight training, world history, world religions, yearbook.

Graduation Requirements Arts and fine arts (art, music, dance, drama), computer applications, computer literacy, English, foreign language, mathematics, physical education (includes health), religion (includes Bible studies and theology), science, social studies (includes history), study skills.

Special Academic Programs 11 Advanced Placement exams for which test preparation is offered; honors section.

College Admission Counseling 137 students graduated in 2014; 136 went to college, including Arizona State University at the Tempe campus; Northern Arizona University; The University of Arizona. Other: 1 had other specific plans. Mean SAT critical reading: 573, mean SAT math: 567, mean SAT writing: 543, mean composite ACT: 25. 26% scored over 600 on SAT critical reading, 31% scored over 600 on SAT math, 20% scored over 600 on SAT writing.

Student Life Upper grades have uniform requirement, student council, honor system. Discipline rests primarily with faculty. Attendance at religious services is required.

Tuition and Aid Day student tuition: $13,690. Tuition installment plan (FACTS Tuition Payment Plan, monthly payment plans). Merit scholarship grants, need-based scholarship grants, Catholic Tuition Organization of Diocese of Phoenix available. In 2014–15, 50% of upper-school students received aid; total upper-school merit-scholarship money awarded: $44,000. Total amount of financial aid awarded in 2014–15: $705,000.

Admissions Traditional secondary-level entrance grade is 9. For fall 2014, 249 students applied for upper-level admission, 185 were accepted, 159 enrolled. Catholic High School Entrance Examination or Scholastic Testing Service High School Placement Test required. Deadline for receipt of application materials: January 31. Application fee required: $75. Interview required.

Athletics Interscholastic: baseball (boys), basketball (b,g), cheering (g), cross-country running (b,g), dance squad (g), danceline (g), diving (b,g), football (b), golf (b,g), soccer (b,g), softball (g), swimming and diving (b,g), tennis (b,g), track and field (b,g), volleyball (b,g), wrestling (b); coed interscholastic: aerobics/dance, dance, dance team, football, physical fitness, strength & conditioning, weight training. 2 PE instructors, 70 coaches, 1 athletic trainer.

Computers Computers are regularly used in all academic, religious studies, yearbook classes. Computer network features include on-campus library services, Internet access, wireless campus network, Internet filtering or blocking technology, Turnitin®. Campus intranet and student e-mail accounts are available to students. Students grades are available online. The school has a published electronic and media policy.

Contact Mr. Chris Moore, Director of Admission. 480-963-1900 Ext. 2008. Fax: 480-963-1974. E-mail: cmoore@setoncatholic.org. Website: www.setoncatholic.org

THE SEVEN HILLS SCHOOL
5400 Red Bank Road
Cincinnati, Ohio 45227
Head of School: Mr. Christopher P. Garten

General Information Coeducational day college-preparatory, arts, and technology school. Grades PK–12. Founded: 1974. Setting: suburban. 35-acre campus. 16 buildings on campus. Approved or accredited by Independent Schools Association of the Central States, Ohio Association of Independent Schools, and Ohio Department of Education. Member of National Association of Independent Schools and Secondary School Admission Test Board. Endowment: $19.2 million. Total enrollment: 1,017. Upper school average class size: 15. Upper school faculty-student ratio: 1:9. There are 180 required school days per year for Upper School students. Upper School students typically attend 5 days per week. The average school day consists of 7 hours and 5 minutes.

Upper School Student Profile Grade 9: 80 students (42 boys, 38 girls); Grade 10: 92 students (44 boys, 48 girls); Grade 11: 84 students (48 boys, 36 girls); Grade 12: 84 students (38 boys, 46 girls).

Faculty School total: 128. In upper school: 26 men, 32 women; 49 have advanced degrees

Subjects Offered Acting, advanced computer applications, Advanced Placement courses, algebra, American history, American literature, ancient history, art, art history, biology, British literature, calculus, ceramics, chemistry, computer programming, computer science, economics, English, European history, fine arts, French, geometry, journalism, Latin, linear algebra, Mandarin, medieval/Renaissance history, modern political theory, music, physical education, physics, pre-calculus, psychology, Spanish, speech, theater, world history, world literature, writing.

Graduation Requirements Algebra, arts and fine arts (art, music, dance, drama), biology, chemistry, computer science, English, foreign language, geometry, performing arts, physical education (includes health), physics, U.S. history, U.S. literature, completion of a personal challenge project, successfully pass writing competency exam, 30 hours of community service.

Special Academic Programs 16 Advanced Placement exams for which test preparation is offered; honors section; independent study; term-away projects; study abroad; academic accommodation for the gifted.

College Admission Counseling 79 students graduated in 2015; all went to college, including Duke University; Massachusetts Institute of Technology; Miami University; Northwestern University; University of Michigan; Washington University in St. Louis. Median SAT critical reading: 661, median SAT math: 663, median SAT writing: 666, median composite ACT: 29. 74% scored over 600 on SAT critical reading, 87% scored over 600 on SAT math, 84% scored over 600 on SAT writing.

Student Life Upper grades have specified standards of dress, student council. Discipline rests primarily with faculty.

Summer Programs Enrichment programs offered; session focuses on SAT review, sports clinics, and acting workshop; held on campus; accepts boys and girls; open to students from other schools. 400 students usually enrolled. 2016 schedule: June 13 to August 5. Application deadline: none.

Tuition and Aid Day student tuition: $22,476–$23,222. Tuition installment plan (monthly payment plans, individually arranged payment plans). Merit scholarship grants, need-based scholarship grants available. In 2015–16, 16% of upper-school students received aid; total upper-school merit-scholarship money awarded: $455,600. Total amount of financial aid awarded in 2015–16: $710,453.

Admissions Traditional secondary-level entrance grade is 9. For fall 2015, 77 students applied for upper-level admission, 60 were accepted, 34 enrolled. ISEE required.

Deadline for receipt of application materials: November 24. Application fee required: $50. On-campus interview required.

Athletics Interscholastic: baseball (boys), basketball (b,g), bowling (b,g), cheering (g), cross-country running (b,g), golf (b), gymnastics (g), lacrosse (b,g), soccer (b,g), softball (g), swimming and diving (b,g), tennis (b,g), volleyball (g); coed interscholastic: track and field. 3 PE instructors, 9 coaches.

Computers Computers are regularly used in foreign language, mathematics, science classes. Computer network features include on-campus library services, online commercial services, Internet access, wireless campus network, Internet filtering or blocking technology. Student e-mail accounts and computer access in designated common areas are available to students. Students grades are available online. The school has a published electronic and media policy.

Contact Mrs. Janet S. Hill, Director of Admission and Financial Aid. 513-728-2405. Fax: 513-728-2409. E-mail: janet.hill@7hills.org. Website: www.7hills.org

SEVERN SCHOOL

201 Water Street
Severna Park, Maryland 21146

Head of School: Douglas H. Lagarde

General Information Coeducational day college-preparatory, arts, and technology school. Grades PS–12. Founded: 1914. Setting: suburban. Nearest major city is Annapolis. 19-acre campus. 8 buildings on campus. Approved or accredited by Association of Independent Maryland Schools and Maryland Department of Education. Member of National Association of Independent Schools and Secondary School Admission Test Board. Endowment: $11.3 million. Total enrollment: 843. Upper school average class size: 12. Upper school faculty-student ratio: 1:8. There are 175 required school days per year for Upper School students. Upper School students typically attend 5 days per week. The average school day consists of 6 hours and 35 minutes.

Upper School Student Profile Grade 9: 105 students (51 boys, 54 girls); Grade 10: 109 students (58 boys, 51 girls); Grade 11: 105 students (57 boys, 48 girls); Grade 12: 99 students (60 boys, 39 girls).

Faculty School total: 115. In upper school: 27 men, 30 women; 38 have advanced degrees.

Subjects Offered Algebra, American history, American literature, art, biology, calculus, ceramics, chemistry, community service, computer programming, computer science, CPR, creative writing, dance, desktop publishing, digital art, digital imaging, digital photography, discrete mathematics, drama, drama performance, dramatic arts, drawing, drawing and design, earth science, ecology, economics, economics-AP, English, English literature, environmental science, environmental systems, European civilization, European history, European history-AP, expository writing, fine arts, forensics, French, French language-AP, French literature-AP, geometry, government/civics, grammar, graphic arts, health, history, journalism, Latin, marine biology, mathematics, multimedia, music, photography, physical education, physics, psychology, science, social studies, Spanish, speech, theater, trigonometry, world history, world literature, writing.

Graduation Requirements Arts and fine arts (art, music, dance, drama), computer science, CPR, English, foreign language, mathematics, physical education (includes health), science, social studies (includes history). Community service is required.

Special Academic Programs Advanced Placement exam preparation; honors section; independent study; study abroad; academic accommodation for the gifted, the musically talented, and the artistically talented.

College Admission Counseling 99 students graduated in 2015; 98 went to college, including Boston University; Elon University; Johns Hopkins University; The George Washington University; The University of Alabama; University of Maryland, College Park. Other: 1 entered a postgraduate year. Median SAT critical reading: 600, median SAT math: 630, median SAT writing: 620, median combined SAT: 1860, median composite ACT: 26. 47% scored over 600 on SAT critical reading, 56% scored over 600 on SAT math, 55% scored over 600 on SAT writing, 58% scored over 1800 on combined SAT, 47% scored over 26 on composite ACT.

Student Life Upper grades have uniform requirement, student council, honor system. Discipline rests primarily with faculty.

Summer Programs Enrichment, sports, art/fine arts, computer instruction programs offered; session focuses on day camp, and sports camps; held both on and off campus; held at SPY swimming pool; accepts boys and girls; open to students from other schools. 500 students usually enrolled. 2016 schedule: June 23 to August 1.

Tuition and Aid Day student tuition: $24,575. Tuition installment plan (FACTS Tuition Payment Plan). Need-based scholarship grants available. In 2015–16, 28% of upper-school students received aid. Total amount of financial aid awarded in 2015–16: $1,800,000.

Admissions Traditional secondary-level entrance grade is 9. For fall 2015, 131 students applied for upper-level admission, 70 were accepted, 45 enrolled. ISEE required. Deadline for receipt of application materials: January 19. Application fee required: $60. On-campus interview required.

Athletics Interscholastic: baseball (boys), basketball (b,g), combined training (b,g), field hockey (g), football (b), lacrosse (b,g), soccer (b,g), tennis (b,g), wrestling (b); coed interscholastic: cross-country running, dance, diving, fitness, golf, outdoor education, physical fitness, ropes courses, sailing, strength & conditioning, swimming and diving, track and field, weight training, yoga; coed intramural: aerobics/dance, ice hockey, outdoor adventure, paint ball. 4 PE instructors, 56 coaches, 2 athletic trainers.

Computers Computers are regularly used in all academic classes. Computer network features include on-campus library services, online commercial services, Internet access, wireless campus network, Internet filtering or blocking technology. Campus intranet, student e-mail accounts, and computer access in designated common areas are available to students. Students grades are available online. The school has a published electronic and media policy.

Contact Ellen Murray, Associate Director of Admissions. 410-647-7701 Ext. 2266. Fax: 410-544-9451. E-mail: e.murray@severnschool.com. Website: www.severnschool.com

SEWICKLEY ACADEMY

315 Academy Avenue
Sewickley, Pennsylvania 15143

Head of School: Mr. Kolia J. O'Connor

General Information Coeducational day college-preparatory, arts, and technology school. Grades PK–12. Founded: 1838. Setting: suburban. Nearest major city is Pittsburgh. 30-acre campus. 10 buildings on campus. Approved or accredited by Pennsylvania Department of Education. Member of National Association of Independent Schools. Endowment: $31 million. Total enrollment: 657. Upper school average class size: 15. Upper school faculty-student ratio: 1:7. There are 167 required school days per year for Upper School students. Upper School students typically attend 5 days per week. The average school day consists of 7 hours.

Upper School Student Profile Grade 9: 72 students (40 boys, 32 girls); Grade 10: 59 students (30 boys, 29 girls); Grade 11: 70 students (39 boys, 31 girls); Grade 12: 66 students (31 boys, 35 girls).

Faculty School total: 106. In upper school: 28 men, 28 women; 32 have advanced degrees.

Subjects Offered Advanced chemistry, advanced studio art-AP, African studies, algebra, American history, American history-AP, American literature, American literature-AP, art, art-AP, astronomy, band, biology, biology-AP, calculus, calculus-AP, ceramics, chemistry, chemistry-AP, choral music, chorus, clayworking, computer applications, computer art, computer programming, computer science, computer science-AP, concert band, concert choir, contemporary issues, creative writing, dance, dance performance, digital art, drama, drama performance, drama workshop, drawing, driver education, economics, English, English literature, environmental science, ethics, European history, European history-AP, expository writing, fine arts, French, French language-AP, French literature-AP, geometry, German, German-AP, government/civics, health, health education, history, Italian, keyboarding, Mandarin, music, musical theater, performing arts, photography, physical education, physics, physics-AP, pre-calculus, psychology, psychology-AP, senior project, Spanish, Spanish literature, Spanish-AP, speech and debate, statistics, statistics-AP, studio art, theater, trigonometry, U.S. history-AP, U.S. literature, Vietnam War, world history, world literature, writing.

Graduation Requirements Arts and fine arts (art, music, dance, drama), English, foreign language, health education, mathematics, physical education (includes health), science, social studies (includes history), U.S. history, world cultures, world studies. Community service is required.

Special Academic Programs Advanced Placement exam preparation; honors section; independent study; term-away projects; study at local college for college credit; study abroad.

College Admission Counseling 77 students graduated in 2015; all went to college, including Carnegie Mellon University; New York University; Penn State University Park; University of Virginia; Virginia Polytechnic Institute and State University; Wake Forest University.

Student Life Upper grades have specified standards of dress, student council, honor system. Discipline rests equally with students and faculty.

Summer Programs Enrichment, advancement, sports, art/fine arts programs offered; session focuses on academics, athletics, and musical theater; held on campus; accepts boys and girls; open to students from other schools. 150 students usually enrolled. Application deadline: none.

Tuition and Aid Day student tuition: $25,705. Tuition installment plan (monthly payment plans). Need-based scholarship grants available.

Admissions Traditional secondary-level entrance grade is 9. ISEE or SSAT required. Deadline for receipt of application materials: February 8. Application fee required: $50. Interview required.

Athletics Interscholastic: baseball (boys), basketball (b,g), cross-country running (b,g), golf (b,g), ice hockey (b), lacrosse (b,g), physical fitness (b,g), soccer (b,g), softball (g), tennis (b,g); coed interscholastic: bowling, diving, field hockey, physical fitness, swimming and diving, track and field. 5 PE instructors, 5 coaches, 1 athletic trainer.

Computers Computers are regularly used in all academic classes. Computer network features include on-campus library services, online commercial services, Internet access, wireless campus network, Internet filtering or blocking technology. Campus intranet, student e-mail accounts, and computer access in designated common areas are available to students. The school has a published electronic and media policy.

Contact Ms. Wendy Berns, Admission Assistant. 412-741-2235. Fax: 412-741-1411. E-mail: wberns@sewickley.org. Website: www.sewickley.org

SHADES MOUNTAIN CHRISTIAN SCHOOL

2290 Old Tyler Road
Hoover, Alabama 35226

Head of School: Mr. Rick Gardner

General Information Coeducational day college-preparatory and Biblical studies school, affiliated with Christian faith. Grades K–12. Founded: 1974. Setting: suburban. Nearest major city is Birmingham. 30-acre campus. 3 buildings on campus. Approved or accredited by Association of Christian Schools International, Southern Association of Colleges and Schools, and Alabama Department of Education. Total enrollment: 311. Upper school average class size: 20. Upper school faculty-student ratio: 1:9. There are 178 required school days per year for Upper School students. Upper School students typically attend 5 days per week. The average school day consists of 6 hours and 35 minutes.

Upper School Student Profile Grade 7: 30 students (17 boys, 13 girls); Grade 8: 30 students (15 boys, 15 girls); Grade 9: 22 students (13 boys, 9 girls); Grade 10: 21 students (12 boys, 9 girls); Grade 11: 20 students (13 boys, 7 girls); Grade 12: 26 students (16 boys, 10 girls). 50% of students are Christian faith.

Faculty School total: 31. In upper school: 7 men, 11 women; 10 have advanced degrees.

Subjects Offered Advanced chemistry, advanced math, algebra, American government, American literature, anatomy and physiology, ancient world history, art, band, Bible studies, business applications, calculus-AP, character education, chemistry, choir, choral music, Christian doctrine, Christian education, Christian ethics, Christian scripture, Christian studies, Christianity, civics, competitive science projects, composition, composition-AP, computer applications, computer literacy, consumer economics, creative thinking, creative writing, decision making skills, driver education, earth and space science, economics, English, English composition, English language and composition-AP, English literature, ensembles, ethics and responsibility, finance, general science, geography, geometry, government/civics, guitar, instruments, jazz band, junior and senior seminars, keyboarding, leadership, Life of Christ, marching band, math applications, math methods, math review, mathematics, mathematics-AP, music appreciation, mythology, news writing, personal finance, philosophy, physical education, physical science, physics, pre-algebra, pre-calculus, psychology, reading/study skills, relationships, religion, research and reference, research skills, rhetoric, science, science project, science research, social sciences, social skills, social studies, Spanish, sports medicine, technology, trigonometry, typing, U.S. government and politics, U.S. history, values and decisions, world history, yearbook.

Graduation Requirements American history, Bible, computers, economics, English, foreign language, government, mathematics, philosophy, physical education (includes health), science, world history.

Special Academic Programs 3 Advanced Placement exams for which test preparation is offered; honors section; independent study; programs in English, mathematics, general development for dyslexic students; special instructional classes for students with learning disabilities.

College Admission Counseling 30 students graduated in 2014; 27 went to college, including Auburn University; Birmingham-Southern College; Samford University; The University of Alabama; The University of Alabama at Birmingham; University of Montevallo. Other: 2 went to work, 1 entered military service. Median composite ACT: 24. 25% scored over 26 on composite ACT.

Student Life Upper grades have specified standards of dress, student council, honor system. Discipline rests primarily with faculty. Attendance at religious services is required.

Tuition and Aid Day student tuition: $6875. Tuition installment plan (monthly payment plans, individually arranged payment plans). Tuition reduction for siblings, need-based scholarship grants available. In 2014–15, 12% of upper-school students received aid. Total amount of financial aid awarded in 2014–15: $40,000.

Admissions Traditional secondary-level entrance grade is 9. For fall 2014, 24 students applied for upper-level admission, 17 were accepted, 17 enrolled. Any standardized test required. Deadline for receipt of application materials: none. Application fee required: $75. Interview required.

Athletics Interscholastic: baseball (boys), basketball (b,g), cheering (g), cross-country running (b,g), football (b), golf (b,g), independent competitive sports (b,g), physical fitness (b,g), physical training (b,g), soccer (b,g), softball (g), strength & conditioning (b,g), swimming and diving (b,g), tennis (b,g), volleyball (g), wrestling (b). 2 PE instructors, 5 coaches, 1 athletic trainer.

Computers Computers are regularly used in Bible studies, Christian doctrine, college planning, English, geography, history, keyboarding, library, mathematics, science, social sciences, social studies, Spanish, theater arts, word processing, yearbook classes. Computer resources include on-campus library services, Internet access, wireless campus network, Internet filtering or blocking technology. Campus intranet and computer access in designated common areas are available to students. Students grades are available online. The school has a published electronic and media policy.

Contact Mrs. Beth Buyck, School Secretary. 205-978-6001. Fax: 205-978-9120. E-mail: bethbuyck@smcs.org. Website: www.smcs.org/

SHADY SIDE ACADEMY

423 Fox Chapel Road
Pittsburgh, Pennsylvania 15238

Head of School: Mr. Thomas Cangiano

General Information Coeducational boarding and day college-preparatory school. Boarding grades 9–12, day grades PK–12. Founded: 1883. Setting: suburban. Students are housed in single-sex dormitories. 130-acre campus. 26 buildings on campus. Approved or accredited by Middle States Association of Colleges and Schools, Pennsylvania Association of Independent Schools, The Association of Boarding Schools, and Pennsylvania Department of Education. Member of National Association of Independent Schools. Endowment: $55 million. Total enrollment: 945. Upper school average class size: 13. Upper school faculty-student ratio: 1:8. There are 172 required school days per year for Upper School students. Upper School students typically attend 5 days per week. The average school day consists of 8 hours and 15 minutes.

Upper School Student Profile Grade 9: 124 students (71 boys, 53 girls); Grade 10: 132 students (72 boys, 60 girls); Grade 11: 125 students (73 boys, 52 girls); Grade 12: 128 students (70 boys, 58 girls). 12% of students are boarding students. 96% are state residents. 5 states are represented in upper school student body. 2% are international students. International students from Bulgaria, China, Germany, and Republic of Korea; 4 other countries represented in student body.

Faculty School total: 118. In upper school: 35 men, 28 women; 41 have advanced degrees; 22 reside on campus.

Subjects Offered 3-dimensional art, advanced biology, advanced chemistry, advanced computer applications, advanced math, Advanced Placement courses, algebra, American history, American literature, architectural drawing, architecture, art, art history, band, biology, calculus, calculus-AP, ceramics, chemistry, Chinese, Chinese history, choir, college counseling, computer graphics, computer math, computer programming, computer science, computer science-AP, concert band, creative writing, drama, economics, English, English literature, environmental science, ethics, European history, expository writing, film and literature, fine arts, fractal geometry, French, French-AP, gender issues, geography, geometry, German, German-AP, health, history, introduction to theater, jazz ensemble, Latin, linear algebra, logic, mathematics, modern dance, music, music technology, musical theater, philosophy, photography, physical education, physics, pre-calculus, probability and statistics, religion and culture, science, senior project, social studies, Spanish, Spanish-AP, speech, statistics, studio art, technical theater, theater arts, trigonometry, world history, world literature, writing.

Graduation Requirements Art, athletics, computer science, English, foreign language, history, mathematics, physical education (includes health), science, participation in five seasons of athletics.

Special Academic Programs 6 Advanced Placement exams for which test preparation is offered; honors section; accelerated programs; independent study; term-away projects; study at local college for college credit; study abroad; academic accommodation for the gifted, the musically talented, and the artistically talented.

College Admission Counseling 119 students graduated in 2015; 118 went to college, including Emory University; Kenyon College; New York University; University of Pennsylvania; University of Pittsburgh; Washington University in St. Louis. Other: 1 entered a postgraduate year. Median SAT critical reading: 620, median SAT math: 630, median SAT writing: 630, median combined SAT: 1920, median composite ACT: 28. 59% scored over 600 on SAT critical reading, 60% scored over 600 on SAT math, 61% scored over 600 on SAT writing, 61% scored over 1800 on combined SAT, 53% scored over 26 on composite ACT.

Student Life Upper grades have specified standards of dress, student council. Discipline rests primarily with faculty.

Summer Programs Remediation, enrichment, advancement, sports, art/fine arts, computer instruction programs offered; session focuses on academic and non-academic enrichment; held on campus; accepts boys and girls; open to students from other schools. 1,200 students usually enrolled. 2016 schedule: June 13 to August 19. Application deadline: none.

Tuition and Aid Day student tuition: $28,950; 5-day tuition and room/board: $40,950; 7-day tuition and room/board: $43,950. Tuition installment plan (monthly payment plans, Tuition Refund Plan available through Dewar's). Tuition reduction for siblings, merit scholarship grants, need-based scholarship grants, merit-based scholarships for grades 6-10 and boarding, FAME awards (Fund for the Advancement of Minorities Through Education), partial tuition remission for children of full-time employees available. In 2015–16, 20% of upper-school students received aid; total upper-school merit-scholarship money awarded: $81,000. Total amount of financial aid awarded in 2015–16: $2,287,075.

Admissions Traditional secondary-level entrance grade is 9. For fall 2015, 131 students applied for upper-level admission, 96 were accepted, 65 enrolled. ISEE, SSAT or TOEFL required. Deadline for receipt of application materials: February 6. Application fee required: $50. On-campus interview required.

Athletics Interscholastic: baseball (boys), basketball (b,g), cheering (g), crew (b,g), cross-country running (b,g), field hockey (g), football (b), golf (b,g), ice hockey (b,g), lacrosse (b,g), soccer (b,g), softball (g), squash (b,g), swimming and diving (b,g), tennis (b,g), track and field (b,g); intramural: volleyball (g); coed interscholastic: ultimate Frisbee; coed intramural: badminton, bowling, fitness, outdoor adventure, ultimate Frisbee, weight lifting. 1 PE instructor, 47 coaches, 2 athletic trainers.

Computers Computers are regularly used in all classes. Computer network features include on-campus library services, online commercial services, Internet access, wireless campus network, Internet filtering or blocking technology, report cards are available in the parent portal four times a year. Student e-mail accounts and computer access in designated common areas are available to students. The school has a published electronic and media policy.

Contact Ms. Katherine H. Mihm, Director of Enrollment Management and Marketing. 412-968-3179. Fax: 412-968-3213. E-mail: kmihm@shadysideacademy.org. Website: www.shadysideacademy.org

SHANLEY HIGH SCHOOL

5600 25th Street South
Fargo, North Dakota 58104

Head of School: Mrs. Sarah Crary

General Information Coeducational day college-preparatory, business, and religious studies school, affiliated with Roman Catholic Church. Grades 9–12. Founded: 1882. Setting: suburban. 1 building on campus. Approved or accredited by North Central Association of Colleges and Schools and North Dakota Department of Education. Total enrollment: 327. Upper school average class size: 20. Upper school faculty-student ratio: 1:18. There are 175 required school days per year for Upper School students. Upper School students typically attend 5 days per week. The average school day consists of 7 hours and 30 minutes.

Upper School Student Profile Grade 9: 93 students (46 boys, 47 girls); Grade 10: 82 students (45 boys, 37 girls); Grade 11: 80 students (36 boys, 44 girls); Grade 12: 72 students (45 boys, 27 girls). 90% of students are Roman Catholic.

Faculty School total: 24. In upper school: 10 men, 14 women; 12 have advanced degrees.

Subjects Offered Accounting, advanced chemistry, advanced math, Advanced Placement courses, algebra, American history, anatomy and physiology, art, band, biology, business applications, business law, calculus-AP, ceramics, chemistry, chemistry-AP, choir, computer applications, economics, English, English literature-AP, general math, geography, global issues, health, journalism, Latin, leadership, modern European history-AP, physical education, physics, pre-algebra, pre-calculus, psychology-AP, religion, science, social studies, U.S. government, U.S. history, world history.

Special Academic Programs International Baccalaureate program; 5 Advanced Placement exams for which test preparation is offered; honors section; independent study.

College Admission Counseling 69 students graduated in 2015; 66 went to college, including Concordia College; North Dakota State University; University of Mary; University of North Dakota. Other: 2 went to work, 1 entered military service. Median composite ACT: 24.

Student Life Upper grades have specified standards of dress, student council, honor system. Discipline rests primarily with faculty. Attendance at religious services is required.

Tuition and Aid Tuition installment plan (monthly payment plans). Tuition reduction for siblings, merit scholarship grants, need-based scholarship grants available. In 2015–16, 20% of upper-school students received aid.

Admissions Traditional secondary-level entrance grade is 9. For fall 2015, 29 students applied for upper-level admission, 29 were accepted, 29 enrolled. Deadline for receipt of application materials: none. Application fee required: $50. Interview required.

Athletics Interscholastic: aquatics (boys, girls), baseball (b), basketball (b,g), cheering (g), cross-country running (b,g), diving (b,g), football (b), golf (b,g), hockey (b), swimming and diving (b,g), tennis (b,g), track and field (b,g), volleyball (g), weight training (b,g).

Computers Computers are regularly used in all academic classes. Computer resources include on-campus library services, Internet access, wireless campus network, Internet filtering or blocking technology. Campus intranet and student e-mail accounts are available to students. Students grades are available online.

Contact Ms. Lori K. Hager, Director of Admissions, Marketing and Recruitment. 701-893-3271. Fax: 701-356-0473. E-mail: lori.hager@jp2schools.org. Website: www.jp2schools.org

SHAWE MEMORIAL JUNIOR/SENIOR HIGH SCHOOL

201 West State Street
Madison, Indiana 47250-2899

Head of School: Mr. Steven J. Hesse

General Information Coeducational day college-preparatory and religious studies school, affiliated with Roman Catholic Church. Grades 7–12. Founded: 1954. Setting: small town. 30-acre campus. 1 building on campus. Approved or accredited by North Central Association of Colleges and Schools and Indiana Department of Education. Total enrollment: 342. Upper school average class size: 12. Upper school faculty-student ratio: 1:8. There are 180 required school days per year for Upper School students. Upper School students typically attend 5 days per week. The average school day consists of 7 hours and 15 minutes.

Upper School Student Profile Grade 9: 25 students (12 boys, 13 girls); Grade 10: 23 students (11 boys, 12 girls); Grade 11: 41 students (22 boys, 19 girls); Grade 12: 19 students (11 boys, 8 girls). 70% of students are Roman Catholic.

Faculty School total: 19. In upper school: 3 men, 16 women; 10 have advanced degrees.

Special Academic Programs International Baccalaureate program; 6 Advanced Placement exams for which test preparation is offered; honors section; independent study; study at local college for college credit; academic accommodation for the gifted; remedial reading and/or remedial writing; special instructional classes for deaf students, some students with special needs can be accommodated on an individual basis.

College Admission Counseling 39 students graduated in 2014; 37 went to college. Other: 2 went to work. Mean SAT critical reading: 534, mean SAT math: 516, mean SAT writing: 515, mean combined SAT: 1565. 24% scored over 600 on SAT critical reading, 19% scored over 600 on SAT math, 27% scored over 600 on SAT writing.

Student Life Upper grades have uniform requirement, student council, honor system. Discipline rests primarily with faculty. Attendance at religious services is required.

Tuition and Aid Day student tuition: $5915. Tuition installment plan (The Tuition Plan, FACTS Tuition Payment Plan, individually arranged payment plans, multiple options). Tuition reduction for siblings, need-based scholarship grants available. In 2014–15, 35% of upper-school students received aid. Total amount of financial aid awarded in 2014–15: $161,537.

Admissions Traditional secondary-level entrance grade is 9. Deadline for receipt of application materials: none. Application fee required: $150. Interview required.

Athletics Interscholastic: baseball (boys), basketball (b,g), cheering (g), cross-country running (b,g), fencing (b), golf (b,g), soccer (b,g), softball (g), tennis (b,g), track and field (b,g), volleyball (g); coed interscholastic: archery. 2 PE instructors, 10 coaches, 1 athletic trainer.

Computers Computer network features include on-campus library services, Internet access, wireless campus network, Internet filtering or blocking technology. Campus intranet is available to students. Students grades are available online.

Contact Mr. Philip J. Kahn, President. 812-273-5835 Ext. 245. Fax: 812-273-8975. E-mail: poppresident@popeace.org. Website: www.popeaceschools.org/

SHAWNIGAN LAKE SCHOOL

1975 Renfrew Road
Shawnigan Lake, British Columbia V0R 2W1, Canada

Head of School: Mr. David Robertson

General Information Coeducational boarding and day college-preparatory, arts, athletics, leadership, citizenship, and entrepreneurship, and language studies school. Grades 8–12. Founded: 1916. Setting: rural. Nearest major city is Victoria, Canada. Students are housed in single-sex dormitories. 380-acre campus. Approved or accredited by British Columbia Independent Schools Association, Canadian Association of Independent Schools, The Association of Boarding Schools, Western Boarding Schools Association, and British Columbia Department of Education. Affiliate member of National Association of Independent Schools; member of Secondary School Admission Test Board. Languages of instruction: English and French. Endowment: CAN$13.5 million. Total enrollment: 493. Upper school average class size: 16. Upper school faculty student ratio: 1:8. There are 168 required school days per year for Upper School students. Upper School students typically attend 6 days per week. The average school day consists of 6 hours and 30 minutes.

Upper School Student Profile Grade 8: 40 students (20 boys, 20 girls); Grade 9: 67 students (44 boys, 23 girls); Grade 10: 116 students (68 boys, 48 girls); Grade 11: 135 students (81 boys, 54 girls); Grade 12: 135 students (74 boys, 61 girls). 90% of students are boarding students. 60% are province residents. 13 provinces are represented in upper school student body. 20% are international students. International students from China, Democratic People's Republic of Korea, Germany, Hong Kong, Mexico, and United States; 19 other countries represented in student body.

Faculty School total: 79. In upper school: 50 men, 29 women; 29 have advanced degrees; 32 reside on campus.

Subjects Offered Advanced Placement courses, advanced studio art-AP, algebra, architectural drawing, art, art history, biology, biology-AP, business skills, calculus, calculus-AP, career and personal planning, ceramics, chemistry, chemistry-AP, choir, comparative civilizations, computer science, computer science-AP, creative writing, earth science, economics, economics and history, English, English language and composition-AP, English literature, English literature and composition-AP, English-AP, entrepreneurship, environmental science, European history, European history-AP, fine arts, French, French language-AP, French literature-AP, French-AP, geography, geometry, German-AP, health, history, human geography - AP, industrial arts, information technology, law, mathematics, media studies, music, philosophy, physical education, physics, physics-AP, robotics, science, social studies, Spanish, Spanish language-AP, sports science, study skills, theater, trigonometry, U.S. history-AP, woodworking, writing.

Graduation Requirements Arts and fine arts (art, music, dance, drama), career and personal planning, English, mathematics, physical education (includes health), science, social studies (includes history), graduation requirements are mandated by the BC Provincial Government and include English 12 plus 4 additional grade 12 courses, and 30 hours of work experience, refer to the curriculum courses to see the subject offerings.

Special Academic Programs Advanced Placement exam preparation; honors section; academic accommodation for the gifted; remedial reading and/or remedial writing; remedial math; programs in English, mathematics, general development for dyslexic students; ESL (37 students enrolled).

College Admission Counseling 129 students graduated in 2015; 124 went to college, including Dalhousie University; McGill University; Queen's University at Kingston; The University of British Columbia; University of Toronto; University of Victoria. Other: 5 had other specific plans.

Student Life Upper grades have uniform requirement, student council, honor system. Discipline rests primarily with faculty.

Summer Programs Sports programs offered; session focuses on squash, ice hockey, rugby; held on campus; accepts boys and girls; open to students from other schools. 180 students usually enrolled. 2016 schedule: July 1 to July 31.

Tuition and Aid Day student tuition: CAN$23,800; 7-day tuition and room/board: CAN$44,200–CAN$58,300. Tuition installment plan (monthly payment plans). Tuition reduction for siblings, bursaries, merit scholarship grants available. In 2014–15, 25% of upper-school students received aid; total upper-school merit-scholarship money awarded: CAN$1,000,000. Total amount of financial aid awarded in 2014–15: CAN$1,500,000.

Admissions Traditional secondary-level entrance grade is 8. For fall 2015, 412 students applied for upper-level admission, 209 were accepted, 169 enrolled. English entrance exam and Math Placement Exam required. Deadline for receipt of application materials: none. Application fee required: CAN$200. Interview required.

Athletics Interscholastic: basketball (boys, girls), crew (b,g), cross-country running (b,g), field hockey (g), figure skating (g), golf (b,g), hockey (b), ice hockey (b), rowing (b,g), rugby (b,g), soccer (b,g), squash (b,g), tennis (b,g), volleyball (g); intramural: ballet (g), basketball (b,g), crew (b,g), field hockey (g), golf (b,g), rowing (b,g), rugby (b,g), soccer (b,g), squash (b,g), strength & conditioning (b,g), tennis (b,g), volleyball (g), weight training (b,g), winter soccer (g); coed interscholastic: hockey, ice hockey; coed intramural: aerobics, aerobics/dance, alpine skiing, aquatics, backpacking, badminton, canoeing/kayaking, climbing, cross-country running, dance, fitness, fly fishing, golf, hiking/backpacking, jogging, kayaking, modern dance, nordic skiing, ocean paddling, outdoor activities, outdoor adventure, outdoor education, outdoor recreation, outdoor skills, outdoors, physical fitness, physical training, rock climbing, running, skiing (cross-country), skiing (downhill), snowboarding, snowshoeing, swimming and diving, track and field, triathlon, wilderness survival, yoga. 8 PE instructors, 34 coaches.

Computers Computers are regularly used in animation, architecture, art, business, college planning, computer applications, design, drafting, drawing and design, foreign language, graphic arts, history, information technology, library, mathematics, photography, research skills, science, social studies, video film production, yearbook classes. Computer network features include on-campus library services, online commercial services, Internet access, wireless campus network, Internet filtering or blocking technology. Campus intranet and student e-mail accounts are available to students. Students grades are available online. The school has a published electronic and media policy.

Contact Ms. Gaynor Samuel, Director of Admissions. 250-743-6207. Fax: 250-743-6280. E-mail: admissions@shawnigan.ca. Website: www.shawnigan.ca

SHELTON SCHOOL AND EVALUATION CENTER

Dallas, Texas
See Special Needs Schools section.

SHORECREST PREPARATORY SCHOOL

5101 First Street NE
Saint Petersburg, Florida 33703

Head of School: Mr. Michael A. Murphy

General Information Coeducational day college-preparatory and arts school. Grades PK–12. Founded: 1923. Setting: suburban. Nearest major city is Tampa. 28-acre campus. 3 buildings on campus. Approved or accredited by Florida Council of Independent Schools, Southern Association of Colleges and Schools, Southern Association of Independent Schools, The College Board, and Florida Department of Education. Member of National Association of Independent Schools and Secondary School Admission Test Board. Endowment: $4.1 million. Total enrollment: 940. Upper school average class size: 15. Upper school faculty-student ratio: 1:12. There are 175 required school days per year for Upper School students. Upper School students typically attend 5 days per week. The average school day consists of 6 hours and 45 minutes.

Upper School Student Profile Grade 9: 82 students (39 boys, 43 girls); Grade 10: 67 students (31 boys, 36 girls); Grade 11: 76 students (35 boys, 41 girls); Grade 12: 84 students (35 boys, 49 girls).

Faculty School total: 97. In upper school: 21 men, 14 women; 24 have advanced degrees.

Subjects Offered 3-dimensional design, algebra, American literature, anatomy and physiology, ancient history, art, art history, art history-AP, band, biology, biology-AP, calculus, calculus-AP, chemistry, chemistry-AP, computer graphics, computer music,

computer science, computer science-AP, conceptual physics, contemporary issues, creative writing, dance, digital imaging, drama, drawing and design, economics, economics-AP, English, English language-AP, English literature-AP, European history, European history-AP, film history, fine arts, fitness, French, French language-AP, French literature-AP, geometry, guitar, health, history of ideas, history of rock and roll, human geography - AP, humanities, journalism, Latin, Latin-AP, macroeconomics-AP, marine biology, music, music theory-AP, musical productions, musical theater, photography, physical education, physics, physics-AP, play/screen writing, political science, portfolio art, pre-calculus, probability and statistics, psychology, psychology-AP, social studies, Spanish, Spanish language-AP, studio art-AP, theater, trigonometry, U.S. history, U.S. history-AP, video film production, Web site design, weight training, Western civilization, world civilizations, world history, world history-AP, world literature, world religions, world wide web design, writing, yearbook.

Graduation Requirements Arts and fine arts (art, music, dance, drama), English, foreign language, health education, mathematics, science, social studies (includes history).

Special Academic Programs 22 Advanced Placement exams for which test preparation is offered; honors section; independent study; academic accommodation for the gifted.

College Admission Counseling 84 students graduated in 2015; all went to college, including Boston University; Brown University; Columbia University; Florida State University; University of Florida; University of South Florida. Mean SAT critical reading: 602, mean SAT math: 620, mean SAT writing: 605, mean combined SAT: 1828, mean composite ACT: 28.

Student Life Upper grades have specified standards of dress, student council, honor system. Discipline rests primarily with faculty.

Summer Programs Enrichment, sports, art/fine arts programs offered; session focuses on arts, academic enrichment, athletics and recreational activities; held on campus; accepts boys and girls; open to students from other schools. 2016 schedule: June 6 to August 12.

Tuition and Aid Day student tuition: $21,050. Tuition installment plan (monthly payment plans, semiannual payment plan). Need-based scholarship grants available. In 2015–16, 23% of upper-school students received aid. Total amount of financial aid awarded in 2015–16: $1,150,000.

Admissions Traditional secondary-level entrance grade is 9. For fall 2015, 61 students applied for upper-level admission, 40 were accepted, 21 enrolled. ACT, ISEE, PSAT or SAT or SSAT required. Deadline for receipt of application materials: none. Application fee required: $75. Interview recommended.

Athletics Interscholastic: baseball (boys), basketball (b,g), cheering (g), cross-country running (b,g), diving (b,g), football (b), golf (b,g), soccer (b,g), softball (g), swimming and diving (b,g), tennis (b,g), track and field (b,g), volleyball (g); coed interscholastic: sailing. 4 PE instructors, 28 coaches, 1 athletic trainer.

Computers Computers are regularly used in all academic classes. Computer network features include on-campus library services, online commercial services, Internet access, wireless campus network, Internet filtering or blocking technology. Campus intranet, student e-mail accounts, and computer access in designated common areas are available to students. Students grades are available online. The school has a published electronic and media policy.

Contact Dr. Jean Spencer Carnes, Director of Admissions. 727-456-7511. Fax: 727-527-4191. E-mail: admissions@shorecrest.org. Website: www.shorecrest.org

SHORELINE CHRISTIAN

2400 Northeast 147th Street
Shoreline, Washington 98155

Head of School: Mr. Timothy E. Visser

General Information Coeducational day college-preparatory, general academic, and religious studies school, affiliated with Christian faith. Grades PS–12. Founded: 1952. Setting: suburban. Nearest major city is Seattle. 7-acre campus. 3 buildings on campus. Approved or accredited by Christian Schools International, Northwest Accreditation Commission, Northwest Association of Independent Schools, Northwest Association of Schools and Colleges, and Washington Department of Education. Total enrollment: 199. Upper school average class size: 16. Upper school faculty-student ratio: 1:8. There are 180 required school days per year for Upper School students. Upper School students typically attend 5 days per week. The average school day consists of 6 hours and 30 minutes.

Upper School Student Profile Grade 6: 6 students (3 boys, 3 girls); Grade 7: 11 students (4 boys, 7 girls); Grade 8: 10 students (6 boys, 4 girls); Grade 9: 17 students (10 boys, 7 girls); Grade 10: 12 students (8 boys, 4 girls); Grade 11: 12 students (5 boys, 7 girls); Grade 12: 14 students (6 boys, 8 girls). 100% of students are Christian faith.

Faculty School total: 25. In upper school: 5 men, 6 women; 6 have advanced degrees.

Subjects Offered 20th century history, advanced math, Advanced Placement courses, algebra, American history, American literature, art, band, Bible, biology, British literature, calculus, calculus-AP, chemistry, choir, Christian doctrine, college writing, composition, computer applications, consumer education, current events, current history, drama, drawing, English, English composition, English literature, fine arts, geography, geometry, global studies, government, health, human anatomy, jazz band, keyboarding, language arts, life science, life skills, literature, mathematics, mathematics-AP, music appreciation, physical education, physical science, physics, pre-calculus, psychology, sculpture, sociology, Spanish, speech, study skills, U.S. history, Washington State and Northwest History, weight training, Western civilization, world literature, world religions, yearbook.

Graduation Requirements American government, American literature, Bible, British literature, composition, electives, English, global issues, keyboarding, mathematics, occupational education, physical education (includes health), portfolio art, portfolio writing, science, social sciences, speech, U.S. history, Washington State and Northwest History, Western civilization, world literature.

Special Academic Programs Honors section; independent study; study at local college for college credit; remedial reading and/or remedial writing; programs in English for dyslexic students.

College Admission Counseling 15 students graduated in 2015; 12 went to college, including Edmonds Community College; Seattle Pacific University; University of Washington; Washington State University; Western Washington University; Whitworth University. Other: 3 went to work. Median SAT critical reading: 521, median SAT math: 512, median SAT writing: 528, median combined SAT: 1561, median composite ACT: 26. 32% scored over 600 on SAT critical reading, 28% scored over 600 on SAT math, 33% scored over 600 on SAT writing, 31% scored over 1800 on combined SAT, 67% scored over 26 on composite ACT.

Student Life Upper grades have specified standards of dress, student council, honor system. Discipline rests primarily with faculty. Attendance at religious services is required.

Tuition and Aid Day student tuition: $10,200–$11,975. Tuition installment plan (monthly payment plans, individually arranged payment plans, prepaid cash tuition discount, quarterly or semi-annual payment plans). Tuition reduction for siblings, need-based scholarship grants, discount for qualifying Pastor families, discount for staff available. In 2015–16, 30% of upper-school students received aid. Total amount of financial aid awarded in 2015–16: $170,000.

Admissions Traditional secondary-level entrance grade is 9. Deadline for receipt of application materials: none. Application fee required: $125. Interview required.

Athletics Interscholastic: baseball (boys), basketball (b,g), soccer (b), volleyball (g); coed interscholastic: golf, soccer, track and field. 1 PE instructor, 17 coaches.

Computers Computers are regularly used in all academic, art, computer applications, library, music, occupational education, research skills, yearbook classes. Computer network features include on-campus library services, Internet access, wireless campus network, Internet filtering or blocking technology. Campus intranet, student e-mail accounts, and computer access in designated common areas are available to students. Students grades are available online. The school has a published electronic and media policy.

Contact Ms. Tassie DeMoney, Director of Development and Marketing. 206-364-7777 Ext. 312. Fax: 206-364-0349. E-mail: tdemoney@shorelinechristian.org. Website: www.shorelinechristian.org

SIERRA CANYON SCHOOL

20801 Rinaldi Street
Chatsworth, California 91311

Head of School: Mr. Jim Skrumbis

General Information College-preparatory, arts, technology, 23 Advanced Placement courses and 32 Honors courses, and traditional liberal arts curriculum school. Founded: 1978. Setting: suburban. Nearest major city is Los Angeles. 6 buildings on campus. Approved or accredited by California Association of Independent Schools, Western Association of Schools and Colleges, and California Department of Education. Member of National Association of Independent Schools and Secondary School Admission Test Board. Total enrollment: 1,000. Upper school average class size: 14. Upper school faculty-student ratio: 1:11. There are 170 required school days per year for Upper School students. Upper School students typically attend 5 days per week. The average school day consists of 7 hours.

Upper School Student Profile 11% are international students.

Faculty School total: 89. In upper school: 27 men, 20 women; 47 have advanced degrees.

Subjects Offered 20th century history, 20th century world history, 3-dimensional art, 3-dimensional design, acting, advanced biology, advanced chemistry, advanced computer applications, advanced math, Advanced Placement courses, advanced studio art-AP, African-American history, algebra, American government, American history-AP, American literature-AP, anatomy and physiology, ancient world history, architecture, art history-AP, art-AP, band, calculus, calculus-AP, ceramics, chemistry, chemistry-AP, Chinese, choir, choreography, chorus, civil rights, Civil War, comparative government and politics-AP, computer programming, computer programming-AP, computer science, computer science-AP, conceptual physics, dance, debate, digital art, digital photography, drama, drama performance, drawing and design, economics, economics and history, economics-AP, electives, English, English language and composition-AP, English language-AP, English literature, English literature and composition-AP, English literature-AP, English-AP, English/composition-AP, environmental science, environmental science-AP, environmental studies, equality and freedom, ethics, ethics and responsibility, ethnic studies, European history-AP, experiential education, experimental science, film, filmmaking, fitness, foreign language, forensics, foundations of civilization, French, French as a second language, French language-AP, French literature-AP, French studies, French-AP, functions,

geometry, global studies, government, government and politics-AP, government-AP, government/civics, government/civics-AP, grammar, graphic arts, health, history, history of architecture, history of rock and roll, history-AP, Holocaust, Holocaust and other genocides, Holocaust legacy, Holocaust seminar, Holocaust studies, honors algebra, honors English, honors geometry, honors U.S. history, honors world history, independent study, information technology, introduction to theater, journalism, lab science, language, language and composition, language arts, language-AP, languages, Latin, Latin-AP, leadership and service, life science, literature and composition-AP, literature seminar, literature-AP, logarithms, macro/microeconomics-AP, macroeconomics-AP, Mandarin, mathematics, mathematics-AP, modern European history, modern European history-AP, music, music theory, music theory-AP, musical theater, newspaper, orchestra, painting, performing arts, personal development, photography, physical education, physical fitness, physics, physics-AP, poetry, politics, pottery, pre-algebra, pre-calculus, programming, psychology, research seminar, Roman civilization, science, science research, sculpture, senior seminar, service learning/internship, Shakespeare, short story, Spanish language-AP, Spanish literature-AP, Spanish-AP, speech and debate, student government, student publications, studio art, studio art-AP, The 20th Century, theater arts, theater design and production, trigonometry, U.S. constitutional history, U.S. government, U.S. government and politics, U.S. government and politics-AP, U.S. history, U.S. history-AP, visual and performing arts, visual arts, vocal music, yoga.

Graduation Requirements English, history, language, mathematics, science, visual and performing arts, Students are required to take 4 years of English, 2 years of Science and Visual/Performing Arts (3 or more recommended), and 3 years of History (4 recommended), Math (minimum of Pre-Calculus recommended), and World Languages.

Special Academic Programs 23 Advanced Placement exams for which test preparation is offered; honors section; independent study; academic accommodation for the gifted, the musically talented, and the artistically talented.

College Admission Counseling 96 students graduated in 2015; all went to college, including New York University; The University of Arizona; University of California, Davis; University of California, Los Angeles; University of Southern California; University of Washington. Mean SAT critical reading: 573, mean SAT math: 598, mean SAT writing: 590, mean combined SAT: 1761, mean composite ACT: 27.

Student Life Upper grades have specified standards of dress, student council, honor system. Discipline rests primarily with faculty.

Tuition and Aid Tuition installment plan (SMART Tuition Payment Plan). Need-based scholarship grants available. In 2015–16, 37% of upper-school students received aid.

Admissions Traditional secondary-level entrance grade is 9. Admissions testing, ISEE or school placement exam required. Deadline for receipt of application materials: January 15. Application fee required: $150. Interview required.

Athletics Interscholastic: baseball (boys), basketball (b,g), cheering (g), dance (g), dance squad (g), dance team (g), flag football (b), football (b), golf (b), lacrosse (b), modern dance (g), sand volleyball (g), soccer (b,g), softball (g), tennis (b), volleyball (g); coed interscholastic: cross-country running, dressage, equestrian sports, golf, swimming and diving, track and field. 4 PE instructors, 34 coaches, 1 athletic trainer.

Computers Computers are regularly used in all classes. Computer network features include on-campus library services, Internet access, wireless campus network, Internet filtering or blocking technology, iPads. Campus intranet, student e-mail accounts, and computer access in designated common areas are available to students. Students grades are available online. The school has a published electronic and media policy.

Contact 818-882-8121. Website: https://www.sierracanyonschool.org/

SIGNET CHRISTIAN SCHOOL

95 Jonesville Crescent
North York, Ontario M4A 1H2, Canada

Head of School: Mrs. Catherine Dume

General Information Coeducational day college-preparatory, business, and science school, affiliated with Christian faith. Grades JK–12. Founded: 1975. Setting: urban. Nearest major city is Toronto, Canada. 1-acre campus. 1 building on campus. Approved or accredited by Association of Christian Schools International and Ontario Department of Education. Language of instruction: English. Total enrollment: 30. Upper school average class size: 6. Upper school faculty-student ratio: 1:5. There are 176 required school days per year for Upper School students. Upper School students typically attend 5 days per week. The average school day consists of 6 hours and 30 minutes.

Upper School Student Profile Grade 9: 3 students (2 boys, 1 girl); Grade 10: 1 student (1 boy); Grade 11: 2 students (1 boy, 1 girl); Grade 12: 4 students (2 boys, 2 girls). 80% of students are Christian.

Faculty School total: 11. In upper school: 2 men, 3 women; 1 has an advanced degree.

Subjects Offered Biology, business studies, calculus, Canadian geography, Canadian history, career education, chemistry, civics, English, ESL, French as a second language, math analysis, math applications, physics, science, visual arts.

Graduation Requirements English, Ontario Ministry of Education requirements.

Special Academic Programs Independent study; ESL (3 students enrolled).

College Admission Counseling 5 students graduated in 2015; all went to college.

Student Life Upper grades have uniform requirement, student council. Discipline rests primarily with faculty. Attendance at religious services is required.

Tuition and Aid Day student tuition: CAN$7000. Tuition installment plan (individually arranged payment plans). Tuition reduction for siblings available.

Admissions SLEP required. Deadline for receipt of application materials: none. No application fee required.

Athletics Coed Intramural: basketball, bowling, cross-country running, ice skating, skiing (downhill), snowboarding, soccer, table tennis, track and field.

Computers Computers are regularly used in English, mathematics, technology classes. Computer network features include Internet access.

Contact Admissions. 416-750-7515. Fax: 416-750-7720. E-mail: info@signetschool.ca. Website: www.signetschool.ca

SMITH SCHOOL

New York, New York
See Special Needs Schools section.

SMITHVILLE CHRISTIAN HIGH SCHOOL

6488 Smithville Townline Road
Smithville, Ontario L0R 2A0, Canada

Head of School: Mr. Ted W. Harris

General Information Coeducational day college-preparatory, general academic, arts, business, vocational, religious studies, bilingual studies, and technology school, affiliated with Christian faith, Christian faith. Grades 9–12. Founded: 1980. Setting: small town. Nearest major city is Hamilton, Canada. 4-acre campus. 1 building on campus. Approved or accredited by Christian Schools International, Ontario Ministry of Education, and Ontario Department of Education. Language of instruction: English. Endowment: CAN$500,000. Total enrollment: 220. Upper school average class size: 18. Upper school faculty-student ratio: 1:11. The average school day consists of 5 hours and 20 minutes.

Upper School Student Profile 95% of students are Christian, Christian.

Faculty School total: 18. In upper school: 12 men, 6 women; 7 have advanced degrees.

Subjects Offered 20th century history, accounting, advanced math, ancient history, arts, athletics, Bible, biology, business, calculus, Canadian geography, Canadian history, careers, chemistry, civics, computer applications, computer information systems, computer science, construction, data analysis, discrete mathematics, drama, dramatic arts, English, finance, fitness, food and nutrition, French, French as a second language, functions, general math, geography, geometry, health, health education, healthful living, history, instrumental music, integrated technology fundamentals, mathematics, media, parenting, personal finance, physical education, physics, science, society challenge and change, transportation technology, urban studies, visual arts, world geography, world history, writing.

Graduation Requirements Arts, Bible, Canadian geography, Canadian history, careers, civics, electives, English, French, mathematics, physical education (includes health), science, society challenge and change.

Special Academic Programs Independent study; remedial reading and/or remedial writing; remedial math; programs in English for dyslexic students; special instructional classes for students with learning disabilities, Attention Deficit Disorder, emotional and behavioral problems; ESL (20 students enrolled).

College Admission Counseling 65 students graduated in 2015; 55 went to college, including Calvin College; Carleton University; Dordt College; Redeemer University College; University of Toronto; University of Waterloo. Other: 5 went to work, 5 had other specific plans.

Student Life Upper grades have uniform requirement, student council, honor system. Discipline rests primarily with faculty.

Tuition and Aid Day student tuition: CAN$13,500. Tuition installment plan (monthly payment plans, individually arranged payment plans). Tuition reduction for siblings, bursaries, need-based scholarship grants available. In 2015–16, 25% of upper-school students received aid. Total amount of financial aid awarded in 2015–16: CAN$150,000.

Admissions Traditional secondary-level entrance grade is 9. Deadline for receipt of application materials: none. Application fee required: CAN$500. Interview recommended.

Athletics Interscholastic: badminton (boys, girls), basketball (b,g), cross-country running (b,g), soccer (b,g), track and field (b,g), volleyball (b,g); coed interscholastic: badminton; coed intramural: backpacking, ball hockey, basketball, floor hockey, hiking/backpacking, hockey, outdoor education, outdoor skills, winter soccer. 2 PE instructors, 10 coaches.

Computers Computers are regularly used in all academic, Bible studies, business education, college planning, construction, current events, data processing, design, drafting, English, geography, history, independent study, introduction to technology, keyboarding, library, occupational education, photography, reading, social sciences, social studies, technical drawing, word processing, writing, writing, yearbook classes. Computer network features include Internet access, wireless campus network, one-to-one program, starting September 2016, all incoming students will be issued a laptop. Student e-mail accounts are available to students. Students grades are available online. The school has a published electronic and media policy.

Contact Mr. Will Lammers, Director of Program. 905-957-3255. Fax: 905-957-3431. E-mail: wlammers@smithvillechristian.ca. Website: www.smithvillechristian.ca

SOLEBURY SCHOOL

6832 Phillips Mill Road
New Hope, Pennsylvania 18938-9682

Head of School: Mr. Thomas G. Wilschutz

General Information Coeducational boarding and day college-preparatory, arts, and technology school. Boarding grades 9–12, day grades 7–12. Founded: 1925. Setting: small town. Nearest major city is Philadelphia. Students are housed in single-sex dormitories. 90-acre campus. 25 buildings on campus. Approved or accredited by Pennsylvania Association of Independent Schools and Pennsylvania Department of Education. Member of National Association of Independent Schools and Secondary School Admission Test Board. Endowment: $6.2 million. Total enrollment: 223. Upper school average class size: 11. Upper school faculty-student ratio: 1:12. Upper School students typically attend 5 days per week. The average school day consists of 9 hours and 30 minutes.

Upper School Student Profile Grade 9: 46 students (27 boys, 19 girls); Grade 10: 53 students (31 boys, 22 girls); Grade 11: 56 students (31 boys, 25 girls); Grade 12: 50 students (25 boys, 25 girls). 35% of students are boarding students. 39% are state residents. 7 states are represented in upper school student body. 20% are international students. International students from China, Republic of Korea, Rwanda, South Africa, and Taiwan; 3 other countries represented in student body.

Faculty School total: 70. In upper school: 28 men, 21 women; 34 have advanced degrees; 24 reside on campus.

Subjects Offered 20th century world history, 3-dimensional art, 3-dimensional design, acting, advanced biology, advanced chemistry, advanced computer applications, advanced math, Advanced Placement courses, advanced studio art-AP, advanced TOEFL/grammar, algebra, American government, American history-AP, American studies, anatomy, anatomy and physiology, ancient history, anthropology, applied music, art, art education, art history, art history-AP, art-AP, astronomy, audio visual/media, biology, biology-AP, calculus, calculus-AP, ceramics, chemistry, chemistry-AP, chorus, comparative government and politics, comparative government and politics-AP, computer art, computer education, computer graphics, computer math, computer music, computer programming, computer skills, computer-aided design, conceptual physics, concert choir, creative writing, criminal justice, current events, digital photography, drama, drawing, English, English-AP, environmental science-AP, ESL, ethics, fine arts, food and nutrition, forensics, fractal geometry, French, French-AP, geometry, government and politics-AP, health, honors geometry, jazz band, Middle East, music, painting, performing arts, photography, physical education, pre-algebra, pre-calculus, printmaking, psychology, public speaking, sculpture, senior project, Shakespeare, Spanish, Spanish-AP, statistics-AP, studio art, theater, theater design and production, trigonometry, U.S. government and politics-AP, U.S. history, world history, writing.

Graduation Requirements Art, computers, electives, English, foreign language, health, mathematics, science, social studies (includes history), 10 hours of community service per year.

Special Academic Programs 10 Advanced Placement exams for which test preparation is offered; honors section; independent study; term-away projects; academic accommodation for the gifted, the musically talented, and the artistically talented; remedial reading and/or remedial writing; remedial math; programs in English, general development for dyslexic students; ESL (26 students enrolled).

College Admission Counseling 53 students graduated in 2015; 51 went to college, including American University; Brown University; Dickinson College; Drexel University; Purdue University; The George Washington University. Other: 1 went to work, 1 entered a postgraduate year. Median SAT critical reading: 575, median SAT math: 560, median SAT writing: 575, median combined SAT: 1750, median composite ACT: 22. 37% scored over 600 on SAT critical reading, 37% scored over 600 on SAT math, 41% scored over 600 on SAT writing, 43% scored over 1800 on combined SAT, 32% scored over 26 on composite ACT.

Student Life Upper grades have student council. Discipline rests equally with students and faculty.

Tuition and Aid Day student tuition: $35,950; 7-day tuition and room/board: $51,995. Tuition installment plan (monthly payment plans). Merit scholarship grants, need-based scholarship grants available. In 2015–16, 40% of upper-school students received aid; total upper-school merit-scholarship money awarded: $117,500. Total amount of financial aid awarded in 2015–16: $1,975,000.

Admissions Traditional secondary-level entrance grade is 9. For fall 2015, 340 students applied for upper-level admission, 136 were accepted, 79 enrolled. ACT, any standardized test, International English Language Test, SSAT or TOEFL Junior required. Deadline for receipt of application materials: January 15. Application fee required: $50. Interview required.

Athletics Interscholastic: baseball (boys), basketball (b,g), field hockey (g), lacrosse (g), soccer (b,g), softball (g), wrestling (b); coed interscholastic: cross-country running, golf, tennis, track and field; coed intramural: bicycling, canoeing/kayaking, cheering, dance, dance team, fitness, fitness walking, hiking/backpacking, horseback riding, independent competitive sports, modern dance, outdoor activities, outdoor education, rock climbing, skiing (downhill), snowboarding, tennis, ultimate Frisbee, walking, wall climbing, weight lifting, weight training, yoga. 1 PE instructor, 1 coach, 2 athletic trainers.

Computers Computers are regularly used in art, college planning, English, ESL, foreign language, independent study, language development, literary magazine, mathematics, music, news writing, newspaper, research skills, science, social studies, technical drawing, theater, theater arts, video film production, yearbook classes. Computer network features include on-campus library services, online commercial services, Internet access, wireless campus network, Internet filtering or blocking technology, audio-visual room/library, mobile computer carts. Campus intranet, student e-mail accounts, and computer access in designated common areas are available to students. Students grades are available online. The school has a published electronic and media policy.

Contact Mr. Scott Eckstein, Director of Admission. 215-862-5261. Fax: 215-862-3366. E-mail: admissions@solebury.org. Website: www.solebury.org

SONOMA ACADEMY

2500 Farmers Lane
Santa Rosa, California 95404

Head of School: Janet Durgin

General Information Coeducational day college-preparatory and Environmental Leadership a Global Citizenship concentrations school. Grades 9–12. Founded: 1999. Setting: suburban. Nearest major city is San Francisco. 34-acre campus. 3 buildings on campus. Approved or accredited by Western Association of Schools and Colleges and California Department of Education. Member of National Association of Independent Schools. Total enrollment: 284. Upper school average class size: 15. Upper school faculty-student ratio: 1:10. Upper School students typically attend 5 days per week. The average school day consists of 6 hours and 30 minutes.

Faculty School total: 28. In upper school: 13 men, 15 women; 22 have advanced degrees.

Subjects Offered 3-dimensional design, acting, advanced math, Advanced Placement courses, African studies, algebra, alternative physical education, American history, American literature, anatomy and physiology, art, art history, arts, athletic training, athletics, audio visual/media, baseball, Basic programming, basketball, biology, calculus, calculus-AP, chemistry, chemistry-AP, choir, college admission preparation, college awareness, college counseling, college placement, college planning, college writing, comparative cultures, computer programming, constitutional law, costumes and make-up, creative writing, digital photography, drama, drama performance, dramatic arts, drawing, East European studies, ecology, environmental systems, economics, economics and history, engineering, English, English language and composition-AP, English literature and composition-AP, English literature-AP, environmental education, environmental studies, equestrian sports, expository writing, fine arts, fitness, foreign language, forensics, French, genetics, geometry, health and wellness, historiography, history of rock and roll, honors algebra, honors geometry, instrumental music, international relations, journalism, literature, Mandarin, music history, Native American studies, oceanography, philosophy, physics, physics-AP, public speaking, Russian history, Shakespeare, Spanish, Spanish language-AP, sports, studio art, theater, theater arts, theater design and production, theater production, track and field, visual arts, weight training.

Graduation Requirements Participation in intersession each year; senior speech.

Special Academic Programs 7 Advanced Placement exams for which test preparation is offered; honors section; independent study; study abroad.

College Admission Counseling 70 students graduated in 2015; 68 went to college, including Stanford University; University of Chicago; University of Washington. Other: 2 had other specific plans. Mean combined SAT: 1884.

Student Life Upper grades have student council, honor system. Discipline rests equally with students and faculty.

Tuition and Aid Day student tuition: $38,700. Tuition installment plan (Insured Tuition Payment Plan, monthly payment plans). Need-based scholarship grants, STEM scholarships, Davis Scholarship, Lytton Rancheria Scholarship available. In 2014–15, 50% of upper-school students received aid. Total amount of financial aid awarded in 2014–15: $3,000,000.

Admissions Traditional secondary-level entrance grade is 9. SSAT required. Deadline for receipt of application materials: January 11. Application fee required: $90. Interview required.

Athletics Interscholastic: baseball (boys), basketball (b,g), cross-country running (b,g), equestrian sports (b,g), lacrosse (b,g), soccer (b,g), track and field (b,g), volleyball (g); coed intramural: aerobics/dance, combined training, dance, fencing, fitness, flag football, Frisbee, kickball, martial arts, outdoor education, physical fitness, physical training, power lifting, rock climbing, softball, strength & conditioning, tai chi, ultimate Frisbee, weight training, yoga.

Computers Computers are regularly used in all academic classes. Computer network features include on-campus library services, online commercial services, Internet access, wireless campus network, Internet filtering or blocking technology, one-to-one laptop program, digital technology center, broadcast studio. Campus intranet and student e-mail accounts are available to students. Students grades are available online. The school has a published electronic and media policy.

Contact Sandy Stack, Director of Enrollment and Marketing. 707-545-1770. Fax: 707-636-2474. E-mail: sandy.stack@sonomaacademy.org. Website: www.sonomaacademy.org/

SOUNDVIEW PREPARATORY SCHOOL

370 Underhill Avenue
Yorktown Heights, New York 10598

Head of School: W. Glyn Hearn

General Information Coeducational day college-preparatory, arts, and technology school. Grades 6–PG. Founded: 1989. Setting: suburban. Nearest major city is New York. 13-acre campus. 7 buildings on campus. Approved or accredited by New York Department of Education, New York State Association of Independent Schools, and New York Department of Education. Member of National Association of Independent Schools. Total enrollment: 70. Upper school average class size: 7. Upper school faculty-student ratio: 1:5. There are 164 required school days per year for Upper School students. Upper School students typically attend 5 days per week. The average school day consists of 6 hours and 47 minutes.

Upper School Student Profile Grade 9: 9 students (4 boys, 5 girls); Grade 10: 12 students (7 boys, 5 girls); Grade 11: 17 students (9 boys, 8 girls); Grade 12: 19 students (11 boys, 8 girls).

Faculty School total: 14. In upper school: 5 men, 9 women; 12 have advanced degrees.

Subjects Offered Advanced Placement courses, advanced studio art-AP, algebra, American history, American literature, art, art-AP, biology, calculus, calculus-AP, chemistry, chemistry-AP, computer science, computer science-AP, earth science, English, English literature, English-AP, environmental science, European history-AP, forensics, French, geometry, government-AP, health, Italian, Latin, mathematics, music, physical education, physics, physics-AP, pottery, psychology-AP, science, social studies, Spanish, study skills, U.S. history-AP, world history.

Graduation Requirements Art, electives, English, foreign language, health, history, mathematics, physical education (includes health), science.

Special Academic Programs 9 Advanced Placement exams for which test preparation is offered; honors section; accelerated programs; independent study; academic accommodation for the gifted, the musically talented, and the artistically talented; special instructional classes for students needing wheelchair accessibility.

College Admission Counseling 7 students graduated in 2015; 6 went to college, including Clark University; Curry College; Merrimack College; New York University. Other: 1 had other specific plans. Mean SAT critical reading: 610, mean SAT math: 619, mean SAT writing: 525, mean composite ACT: 26. 50% scored over 600 on SAT critical reading, 50% scored over 600 on SAT math, 50% scored over 600 on SAT writing.

Student Life Discipline rests primarily with faculty.

Tuition and Aid Day student tuition: $36,500–$38,000. Need-based scholarship grants available. In 2015–16, 30% of upper-school students received aid. Total amount of financial aid awarded in 2015–16: $569,000.

Admissions Traditional secondary-level entrance grade is 9. For fall 2015, 41 students applied for upper-level admission, 28 were accepted, 19 enrolled. Deadline for receipt of application materials: none. Application fee required: $50. On-campus interview required.

Athletics Interscholastic: basketball (boys, girls); coed interscholastic: bowling, soccer, ultimate Frisbee. 1 PE instructor, 1 coach.

Computers Computers are regularly used in all academic classes. Computer network features include Internet access, wireless campus network, Internet filtering or blocking technology. Campus intranet and student e-mail accounts are available to students. The school has a published electronic and media policy.

Contact Mary E. Ivanyi, Assistant Head. 914-962-2780. Fax: 914-302-2769. E-mail: mivanyi@soundviewprep.org. Website: www.soundviewprep.org

See Display on next page and Close-Up on page 616.

SOUTHERN ONTARIO COLLEGE

28 Rebecca Street
Hamilton, Ontario L8R 1B4, Canada

Head of School: Susan J. Woods

General Information Coeducational day college-preparatory school. Grades 9–12. Founded: 1980. Setting: urban. 1 building on campus. Approved or accredited by Ontario Ministry of Education and Ontario Department of Education. Language of instruction: English. Upper school average class size: 20. Upper school faculty-student ratio: 1:15. Upper School students typically attend 5 days per week.

Faculty School total: 7. In upper school: 3 men, 3 women; 3 have advanced degrees.

Special Academic Programs ESL (15 students enrolled).

College Admission Counseling 50 students graduated in 2015; 5 went to college, including Penn State University Park. Other: 45 entered a postgraduate year.

Student Life Upper grades have uniform requirement, honor system. Discipline rests primarily with faculty.

Tuition and Aid Guaranteed tuition plan.

Admissions Application fee required: CAN$150.

Computers Computers are regularly used in accounting, career education, computer applications classes. Computer resources include Internet access, wireless campus network, Internet filtering or blocking technology.

Contact Mrs. Maryam Yussuf, Admissions Officer. 905-546-1501. Fax: 866-875-2619. E-mail: admin@mysoc.ca. Website: www.mysoc.ca

SOUTHFIELD CHRISTIAN HIGH SCHOOL

28650 Lahser Road

Southfield, Michigan 48034-2099

Head of School: Mrs. Sue Hoffenbacher

General Information Coeducational day college preparatory, arts, religious studies, and technology school, affiliated with Christian faith, Evangelical faith. Grades PK–12. Founded: 1970. Setting: suburban. Nearest major city is Detroit. 28-acre campus. 1 building on campus. Approved or accredited by Association of Christian Schools International, Independent Schools Association of the Central States, North Central Association of Colleges and Schools, and Michigan Department of Education. Endowment: $1.5 million. Total enrollment: 588. Upper school average class size: 22. Upper school faculty-student ratio: 1:20. There are 180 required school days per year for Upper School students. Upper School students typically attend 5 days per week. The average school day consists of 7 hours.

Upper School Student Profile Grade 9: 44 students (25 boys, 19 girls); Grade 10: 43 students (20 boys, 23 girls); Grade 11: 48 students (17 boys, 31 girls); Grade 12: 46 students (26 boys, 20 girls). 100% of students are Christian faith, members of Evangelical faith.

Faculty School total: 55. In upper school: 14 men, 14 women; 13 have advanced degrees.

Subjects Offered Accounting, Advanced Placement courses, algebra, American government, American history, American history-AP, American literature, American literature-AP, ancient world history, art, band, Bible, biology, biology-AP, British literature, calculus-AP, chemistry, chemistry-AP, choir, chorus, communication arts, composition-AP, computer applications, computer programming, conceptual physics, creative writing, drawing and design, economics, English language-AP, English literature and composition-AP, film and literature, French, geography, geometry, government, graphic design, health, instrumental music, Life of Christ, literature and composition-AP, Middle Eastern history, New Testament, organic chemistry, photography, physical education, physics-AP, pre-calculus, probability and statistics, Russian history, senior project, Spanish, speech and debate, U.S. history, vocal music, Web site design, world studies, yearbook.

Special Academic Programs Advanced Placement exam preparation; honors section; independent study.

College Admission Counseling 44 students graduated in 2015; all went to college, including Grand Valley State University; Hope College; Michigan State University; Oakland University; University of Michigan; Wheaton College. Median SAT critical reading: 460, median SAT math: 430, median SAT writing: 480, median composite ACT: 24. 25% scored over 26 on composite ACT.

Student Life Upper grades have uniform requirement, student council. Discipline rests primarily with faculty. Attendance at religious services is required.

Summer Programs Session focuses on physical education; held on campus; accepts boys and girls; not open to students from other schools. 10 students usually enrolled. 2016 schedule: June 15 to June 26. Application deadline: May 1.

Tuition and Aid Day student tuition: $9520. Tuition installment plan (FACTS Tuition Payment Plan). Tuition reduction for siblings, need-based scholarship grants available. In 2015–16, 10% of upper-school students received aid.

Admissions Traditional secondary-level entrance grade is 9. For fall 2015, 65 students applied for upper-level admission, 25 were accepted, 19 enrolled. Any standardized test required. Deadline for receipt of application materials: none. No application fee required. On-campus interview required.

Athletics Interscholastic: baseball (boys), basketball (b,g), cheering (g), cross-country running (b,g), football (b), soccer (b,g), softball (g), track and field (b,g), volleyball (g); coed interscholastic: golf; coed intramural: skiing (downhill), weight lifting. 1 PE instructor, 1 athletic trainer.

Computers Computers are regularly used in art, commercial art, computer applications, creative writing, drawing and design, graphic arts, graphic design, independent study, media production, programming, publishing, Web site design, writing, yearbook classes. Computer network features include on-campus library services, Internet access, wireless campus network, Internet filtering or blocking technology. Student e-mail accounts are available to students. Students grades are available online. The school has a published electronic and media policy.

Contact Mrs. Alisa Ruffin, High School Principal. 248-357-3660 Ext. 278. Fax: 248-357-5271. E-mail: aruffin@southfieldchristian.org. Website: www.southfieldchristian.org

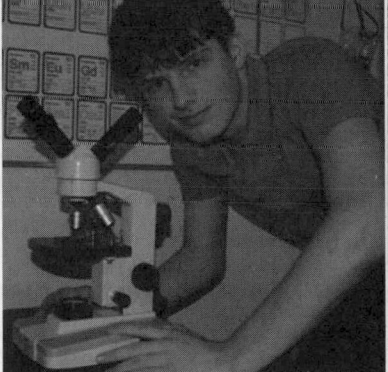

SOUTH KENT SCHOOL

40 Bulls Bridge Road
South Kent, Connecticut 06785

Head of School: Mr. Andrew J. Vadnais

General Information Boys' boarding and day college-preparatory, arts, and technology school, affiliated with Episcopal Church. Grades 9–PG. Founded: 1923. Setting: rural. Nearest major city is New York, NY. Students are housed in single-sex dormitories. 650-acre campus. 30 buildings on campus. Approved or accredited by National Association of Episcopal Schools, New England Association of Schools and Colleges, The Association of Boarding Schools, and Connecticut Department of Education. Member of National Association of Independent Schools and Secondary School Admission Test Board. Endowment: $14 million. Total enrollment: 178. Upper school average class size: 10. Upper school faculty-student ratio: 1:6. Upper School students typically attend 6 days per week. The average school day consists of 6 hours.

Upper School Student Profile Grade 9: 34 students (34 boys); Grade 10: 30 students (30 boys); Grade 11: 45 students (45 boys); Grade 12: 46 students (46 boys); Postgraduate: 22 students (22 boys). 86% of students are boarding students. 20% are state residents. 22 states are represented in upper school student body. 42% are international students. International students from Bermuda, Canada, China, Republic of Korea, Russian Federation, and Taiwan; 14 other countries represented in student body. 35% of students are members of Episcopal Church.

Faculty School total: 38. In upper school: 24 men, 11 women; 23 have advanced degrees; 26 reside on campus.

Subjects Offered Advanced biology, Advanced Placement courses, advanced studio art-AP, algebra, American history, American literature, art, biology, calculus, calculus-AP, chemistry, creative writing, digital applications, driver education, ecology, economics-AP, English, English language and composition-AP, English literature, entrepreneurship, environmental science, environmental studies, ESL, European history, expository writing, finance, fine arts, French, French-AP, functions, geography, geometry, government and politics-AP, grammar, history, Latin, marketing, mathematics, Native American history, photography, physics, physiology, pre-calculus, psychology, psychology-AP, robotics, science, Spanish, Spanish-AP, statistics, statistics-AP, trigonometry, U.S. history-AP, world history, writing.

Graduation Requirements Art, English, foreign language, lab science, mathematics, U.S. history.

Special Academic Programs Advanced Placement exam preparation; honors section; independent study; study at local college for college credit; ESL (30 students enrolled).

College Admission Counseling 65 students graduated in 2014; 59 went to college, including Brown University; DePaul University; Hobart and William Smith Colleges; Rutgers, The State University of New Jersey, New Brunswick; Tufts University; University of New Hampshire. Other: 3 entered a postgraduate year, 3 had other specific plans. Median SAT critical reading: 520, median SAT math: 500. 18% scored over 600 on SAT critical reading, 24% scored over 600 on SAT math.

Student Life Upper grades have specified standards of dress, student council, honor system. Discipline rests equally with students and faculty. Attendance at religious services is required.

Tuition and Aid Day student tuition: $28,000; 7-day tuition and room/board: $48,500. Tuition installment plan (The Tuition Plan, Insured Tuition Payment Plan, monthly payment plans). Merit scholarship grants, need-based scholarship grants available. In 2014–15, 35% of upper-school students received aid. Total amount of financial aid awarded in 2014–15: $1,900,000.

Admissions Traditional secondary-level entrance grade is 9. PSAT or SAT, SSAT or writing sample required. Deadline for receipt of application materials: none. Application fee required: $50. Interview required.

Athletics Interscholastic: baseball, basketball, crew, cross-country running, golf, ice hockey, lacrosse, soccer, tennis; intramural: baseball, basketball, bicycling, canoeing/kayaking, climbing, crew, golf, hiking/backpacking, ice hockey, mountain biking, outdoor activities, skiing (cross-country), skiing (downhill), snowboarding, soccer, strength & conditioning, ultimate Frisbee, wall climbing, weight lifting, weight training, yoga. 28 coaches, 2 athletic trainers.

Computers Computers are regularly used in all classes. Computer network features include on-campus library services, online commercial services, Internet access, wireless campus network, Internet filtering or blocking technology, 1:1 iPad program. Student e-mail accounts and computer access in designated common areas are available to students. Students grades are available online. The school has a published electronic and media policy.

Contact Ms. Kathy McCann, Associate Director of Admissions. 860-927-3539 Ext. 253. Fax: 888-803-0140. E-mail: mccannk@southkentschool.org. Website: www.southkentschool.org

SOUTHWEST CHRISTIAN SCHOOL, INC.

6901 Altamesa Boulevard
Fort Worth, Texas 76123

Head of School: Dr. Shane Naterman

General Information Coeducational day college-preparatory, arts, religious studies, and technology school, affiliated with Christian faith. Grades PK–12. Founded: 1969. Setting: suburban. 39-acre campus. 3 buildings on campus. Approved or accredited by Southern Association of Colleges and Schools and Texas Department of Education. Member of National Association of Independent Schools. Total enrollment: 820. Upper school average class size: 15. Upper school faculty-student ratio: 1:10. There are 176 required school days per year for Upper School students. Upper School students typically attend 5 days per week. The average school day consists of 7 hours.

Faculty School total: 130. In upper school: 13 men, 35 women; 34 have advanced degrees.

Subjects Offered 1 1/2 elective credits, advanced math, algebra, American government, American literature, American literature-AP, anatomy and physiology, art, Bible studies, biology, biology-AP, British literature, British literature-AP, calculus, calculus-AP, chemistry, chemistry-AP, choir, drama, English, English literature-AP, English-AP, foreign language, French, geometry, government, history, honors algebra, honors English, honors geometry, honors U.S. history, honors world history, journalism, keyboarding, lab science, leadership, literature and composition-AP, physics, physics-AP, pre-algebra, pre-calculus, psychology, SAT preparation, Spanish, speech, technology, U.S. history, U.S. history-AP, Web site design.

Graduation Requirements 4 years of Bible courses.

Special Academic Programs Advanced Placement exam preparation; honors section; accelerated programs; study at local college for college credit; study abroad; academic accommodation for the gifted.

College Admission Counseling 77 students graduated in 2015.

Student Life Upper grades have uniform requirement, student council, honor system. Discipline rests primarily with faculty. Attendance at religious services is required.

Summer Programs Enrichment, sports, art/fine arts, computer instruction programs offered; session focuses on enrichment, athletics; held on campus; accepts boys and girls; open to students from other schools. 2016 schedule: June to June. Application deadline: June 1.

Tuition and Aid Day student tuition: $10,275–$13,700. Tuition installment plan (FACTS Tuition Payment Plan). Need-based scholarship grants available. In 2015–16, 20% of upper-school students received aid. Total amount of financial aid awarded in 2015–16: $455,000.

Admissions Traditional secondary-level entrance grade is 9. Stanford 9 required. Deadline for receipt of application materials: none. No application fee required. Interview required.

Athletics Interscholastic: baseball (boys), basketball (b,g), cheering (g), cross-country running (b,g), dance (g), dance team (g), equestrian sports (b,g), football (b), golf (b,g), soccer (b,g), softball (g), track and field (b,g), volleyball (g), wrestling (b); intramural: physical training (b,g); coed interscholastic: aquatics, equestrian sports, paint ball, rodeo; coed intramural: aquatics, fitness, strength & conditioning, weight training. 2 PE instructors, 12 coaches, 1 athletic trainer.

Computers Computers are regularly used in all academic classes. Computer network features include on-campus library services, online commercial services, Internet access, wireless campus network, Internet filtering or blocking technology, computer carts for classroom use. Student e-mail accounts and computer access in designated common areas are available to students. Students grades are available online. The school has a published electronic and media policy.

Contact Mr. Travis Crow, Dean of Student Services. 817-294-9596 Ext. 207. Fax: 817-294-9603. E-mail: tcrow@southwestchristian.org. Website: www.southwestchristian.org

SOUTHWESTERN ACADEMY

8800 East Ranch Campus Road
Rimrock, Arizona 86335

Head of School: Mr. Kenneth Veronda

General Information Coeducational boarding and day college-preparatory, general academic, and arts school. Grades 6–PG. Founded: 1924. Setting: suburban. Nearest major city is Los Angeles, CA. Students are housed in single-sex dormitories. 8-acre campus. 24 buildings on campus. Approved or accredited by The Association of Boarding Schools, Western Association of Schools and Colleges, and Arizona Department of Education. Member of Secondary School Admission Test Board. Endowment: $10 million. Total enrollment: 1,161. Upper school average class size: 6. Upper school faculty-student ratio: 1:6. There are 184 required school days per year for Upper School students. Upper School students typically attend 5 days per week. The average school day consists of 8 hours.

Upper School Student Profile Grade 7: 2 students (2 boys); Grade 8: 11 students (5 boys, 6 girls); Grade 9: 27 students (14 boys, 13 girls); Grade 10: 31 students (24 boys, 7 girls); Grade 11: 46 students (30 boys, 16 girls); Grade 12: 37 students (22 boys, 15 girls); Postgraduate: 1 student (1 girl). 98% of students are boarding students. 25% are state residents. 4 states are represented in upper school student body. 75% are international students. International students from China, Japan, Mexico, Russian Federation, Serbia and Montenegro, and Viet Nam; 10 other countries represented in student body.

Faculty School total: 22. In upper school: 5 men, 17 women; 14 have advanced degrees; 6 reside on campus.

Subjects Offered Advanced math, Advanced Placement courses, algebra, American history, American literature, American literature-AP, art, art appreciation, art history, astronomy, biology, biology-AP, British literature, calculus, chemistry, earth science, ecology, economics, English, English composition, environmental education, environmental science, environmental studies, ESL, fashion, fine arts, general math, geometry, health, integrated science, math review, mathematics, music, music appreciation, outdoor education, physics, pre-algebra, Spanish, studio art, U.S. government, world cultures, yearbook.

Graduation Requirements Algebra, American government, American history, American literature, British literature, computer literacy, economics, electives, English, foreign language, geometry, lab science, mathematics, physical education (includes health), visual and performing arts, world cultures, 20 hours per school year of community service. Community service is required.

Special Academic Programs 12 Advanced Placement exams for which test preparation is offered; honors section; independent study; study at local college for college credit; academic accommodation for the musically talented and the artistically talented; ESL (65 students enrolled).

College Admission Counseling 8 students graduated in 2014; all went to college, including Boston University; Drexel University; The University of Arizona. Median SAT critical reading: 550, median SAT math: 700, median SAT writing: 550, median combined SAT: 1800.

Student Life Upper grades have specified standards of dress, student council, honor system. Discipline rests primarily with faculty.

Tuition and Aid Day student tuition: $18,550; 7-day tuition and room/board: $35,750. Tuition installment plan (monthly payment plans, individually arranged payment plans). Need-based scholarship grants available. In 2014–15, 30% of upper-school students received aid. Total amount of financial aid awarded in 2014–15: $240,000.

Admissions Traditional secondary-level entrance grade is 9. For fall 2014, 199 students applied for upper-level admission, 133 were accepted, 47 enrolled. English language, English proficiency, ESL, High School Placement Test, International English Language Test, international math and English tests, SLEP, SLEP for foreign students, TOEFL or writing sample required. Deadline for receipt of application materials: none. Application fee required: $100. Interview required.

Athletics Interscholastic: basketball (boys, girls), golf (b,g), volleyball (b,g); coed interscholastic: baseball, golf, soccer; coed intramural: alpine skiing, aquatics, archery, backpacking, badminton, baseball, basketball, bicycling, billiards, canoeing/kayaking, climbing, croquet, cross-country running, equestrian sports, fishing, fitness, fitness walking, flag football, flagball, Frisbee, golf, hiking/backpacking, horseback riding, horseshoes, ice skating, mountain biking, outdoor activities, outdoor adventure, outdoor education, outdoor recreation, outdoor skills, outdoors, paint ball, physical fitness, rafting, rock climbing, ropes courses, running, skiing (cross-country), skiing (downhill), snowboarding, soccer, softball, swimming and diving, table tennis, tennis, touch football, track and field, volleyball, walking, weight lifting, weight training, wilderness. 1 PE instructor, 7 coaches.

Computers Computers are regularly used in all academic, animation, architecture, art, basic skills, career education, career exploration, classics, college planning, commercial art, computer applications, creative writing, current events, data processing, design, digital applications, drafting, drawing and design, economics, English, ESL, ethics, foreign language, geography, graphic arts, graphic design, graphics, health, historical foundations for arts, history, humanities, independent study, information technology, journalism, keyboarding, lab/keyboard, language development, learning cognition, library, life skills, literacy, literary magazine, mathematics, media, media arts, media production, media services, mentorship program, multimedia, music, music technology, news writing, newspaper, occupational education, philosophy, photography, photojournalism, programming, psychology, publications, publishing, reading, research skills, SAT preparation, science, senior seminar, social sciences, social studies, Spanish, speech, stock market, study skills, technical drawing, technology, theater, theater arts, typing, video film production, vocational-technical courses, Web site design, wilderness education, word processing, writing, writing, yearbook classes. Computer network features include on-campus library services, Internet access, wireless campus network, Internet filtering or blocking technology. Student e-mail accounts and computer access in designated common areas are available to students.

Contact Mr. Joseph M. Blake, Director of Admissions and Outreach. 626-799-5010 Ext. 203. Fax: 626-799-0407. E-mail: jblake@southwesternacademy.edu. Website: www.southwesternacademy.edu

SOUTHWESTERN ACADEMY

2800 Monterey Road
San Marino, California 91108

Head of School: Mr. Kenneth R. Veronda

General Information Coeducational boarding and day college-preparatory, general academic, arts, and ESL school. Grades 6–PG. Founded: 1924. Setting: suburban. Nearest major city is Los Angeles. Students are housed in single-sex dormitories. 8-acre campus. 9 buildings on campus. Approved or accredited by The Association of Boarding Schools, Western Association of Schools and Colleges, and California Department of Education. Member of Secondary School Admission Test Board. Endowment: $9 million. Total enrollment: 134. Upper school average class size: 12. Upper school faculty-student ratio: 1:6. There are 184 required school days per year for Upper School students. Upper School students typically attend 5 days per week. The average school day consists of 8 hours.

Upper School Student Profile Grade 7: 2 students (2 boys); Grade 8: 11 students (6 boys, 5 girls); Grade 9: 23 students (12 boys, 11 girls); Grade 10: 27 students (22 boys, 5 girls); Grade 11: 36 students (24 boys, 12 girls); Grade 12: 32 students (19 boys, 13 girls); Postgraduate: 1 student (1 girl). 75% of students are boarding students. 29% are state residents. 7 states are represented in upper school student body. 55% are international students. International students from China, Germany, Japan, Russian Federation, Taiwan, and Viet Nam; 11 other countries represented in student body.

Faculty School total: 27. In upper school: 12 men, 11 women; 15 have advanced degrees; 10 reside on campus.

Subjects Offered Algebra, American history, American literature, animation, art, art history, audio visual/media, biology, calculus, calculus-AP, chemistry, college counseling, creative writing, drama, earth science, economics, English, English literature, ESL, European history, expository writing, fashion, fine arts, geography, geology, geometry, government/civics, grammar, health, history, journalism, mathematics, music, photography, physical education, physics, psychology, science, social sciences, social studies, Spanish, speech, world cultures, world history, world literature, writing.

Graduation Requirements Algebra, American government, American history, American literature, biology, British literature, computer literacy, economics, electives, English, foreign language, geometry, lab science, mathematics, physical education (includes health), visual and performing arts, world cultures, 100 hours of community service. Community service is required.

Special Academic Programs Advanced Placement exam preparation; honors section; independent study; study at local college for college credit; academic accommodation for the musically talented and the artistically talented; ESL (39 students enrolled).

College Admission Counseling 36 students graduated in 2014; all went to college, including Drexel University; Marymount California University; Pepperdine University; Syracuse University; University of California, Los Angeles; University of Virginia.

Student Life Upper grades have specified standards of dress, student council, honor system. Discipline rests primarily with faculty.

Tuition and Aid Day student tuition: $18,550; 7-day tuition and room/board: $36,500. Tuition installment plan (monthly payment plans, individually arranged payment plans). Need-based scholarship grants available. In 2014–15, 20% of upper-school students received aid. Total amount of financial aid awarded in 2014–15: $600,000.

Admissions Traditional secondary-level entrance grade is 9. For fall 2014, 192 students applied for upper-level admission, 88 were accepted, 43 enrolled. TOEFL or SLEP or writing sample required. Deadline for receipt of application materials: none. Application fee required: $100. Interview required.

Athletics Interscholastic: baseball (boys), basketball (b,g), track and field (b,g), volleyball (b,g); intramural: baseball (b), basketball (b,g), track and field (b,g), volleyball (b,g); coed interscholastic: baseball, bowling, climbing, cross-country running, fishing, fitness, fitness walking, flag football, horseback riding, soccer, tennis, walking, weight lifting; coed intramural: archery, backpacking, baseball, bicycling, bowling, climbing, cross-country running, fishing, fitness, fitness walking, golf, hiking/backpacking, horseback riding, jogging, mountain biking, outdoor activities, outdoor adventure, outdoor education, outdoor recreation, outdoor skills, outdoors, paddle tennis, physical fitness, physical training, skiing (downhill), snowboarding, soccer, table tennis, tennis, walking, weight lifting. 2 PE instructors, 4 coaches, 1 athletic trainer.

Computers Computers are regularly used in all academic, animation, art, career exploration, classics, college planning, computer applications, creative writing, current events, design, desktop publishing, digital applications, economics, English, ESL, foreign language, geography, graphic arts, graphic design, graphics, historical foundations for arts, history, humanities, independent study, journalism, language development, library, life skills, literary magazine, mathematics, media, media arts, media production, media services, mentorship program, multimedia, music, music technology, news writing, photography, photojournalism, publications, publishing, reading, SAT preparation, science, senior seminar, social sciences, social studies, Spanish, speech, study skills, technology, theater, theater arts, typing, video film production, word processing, writing, writing, yearbook classes. Computer network features include on-campus library services, online commercial services, Internet access, wireless campus network, Internet filtering or blocking technology. Student e-mail accounts and computer access in designated common areas are available to students. The school has a published electronic and media policy.

Contact Mr. Joseph M. Blake, Director of Admissions and Outreach. 626-799-5010 Ext. 1203. Fax: 626-799-0407. E-mail: jblake@southwesternacademy.edu. Website: www.SouthwesternAcademy.edu

THE SPENCE SCHOOL

22 East 91st Street
New York, New York 10128-0657

Head of School: Ellanor (Bodie) N. Brizendine

General Information Girls' day college-preparatory, arts, and technology school. Grades K–12. Founded: 1892. Setting: urban. 2 buildings on campus. Approved or accredited by New York State Association of Independent Schools. Member of National Association of Independent Schools and Secondary School Admission Test Board.

Total enrollment: 738. Upper school average class size: 14. Upper school faculty-student ratio: 1:6. There are 164 required school days per year for Upper School students. Upper School students typically attend 5 days per week. The average school day consists of 7 hours.

Upper School Student Profile Grade 9: 68 students (68 girls); Grade 10: 69 students (69 girls); Grade 11: 57 students (57 girls); Grade 12: 55 students (55 girls).

Faculty School total: 127. In upper school: 20 men, 50 women; 54 have advanced degrees.

Subjects Offered 20th century American writers, 20th century history, 20th century world history, 3-dimensional design, acting, addiction, advanced chemistry, advanced math, aerobics, African history, African literature, African-American literature, algebra, alternative physical education, American culture, American history, American literature, art, art and culture, art history, art-AP, Asian history, Asian literature, bioethics, bioethics, DNA and culture, biology, calculus, ceramics, chemistry, Chinese, Chinese history, Chinese literature, civil rights, college admission preparation, composition, computer programming, computer science, constitutional law, CPR, critical writing, dance, dance performance, design, digital imaging, digital photography, discrete mathematics, drama, drama performance, dramatic arts, drawing, earth science, economics, English, environmental science, equality and freedom, European history, exercise science, female experience in America, fiber arts, film studies, first aid, fitness, foreign language, French, geometry, global studies, health, health and wellness, history, instrumental music, Israeli studies, Japanese history, Japanese literature, Latin, Latin American history, Latin American literature, Latin American studies, linear algebra, literature, mathematics, media literacy, Middle East, modern European history, multimedia, music, music composition, music theory, non-Western literature, novels, painting, performing arts, photo shop, photography, physical education, physics, poetry, pre-algebra, printmaking, psychology, robotics, science, science research, sculpture, self-defense, Shakespeare, South African history, Spanish, Spanish literature, speech, statistics, technology, theater production, U.S. history, video film production, visual and performing arts, women's studies, world history, world religions, world studies, yoga.

Graduation Requirements Advanced math, algebra, American literature, art, biology, chemistry, computer science, dance, English, European history, foreign language, geometry, global studies, health, history, languages, music, non-Western societies, performing arts, physical education (includes health), physics, science, Shakespeare, speech, technology, U.S. history, visual and performing arts, visual arts, world religions, world studies.

Special Academic Programs 1 Advanced Placement exam for which test preparation is offered; independent study; term-away projects; study abroad.

College Admission Counseling 60 students graduated in 2015; all went to college, including Bowdoin College; Cornell University; Duke University; Harvard University; University of Pennsylvania; University of Southern California. Median SAT critical reading: 690, median SAT math: 690, median SAT writing: 720, median combined SAT: 2150, median composite ACT: 32. 90% scored over 600 on SAT critical reading, 79% scored over 600 on SAT math, 88% scored over 600 on SAT writing, 90% scored over 1800 on combined SAT, 96% scored over 26 on composite ACT.

Student Life Upper grades have uniform requirement, student council. Discipline rests primarily with faculty.

Tuition and Aid Day student tuition: $45,150. Need-based scholarship grants available. In 2015–16, 23% of upper-school students received aid.

Admissions Traditional secondary-level entrance grade is 9. ISEE, school's own exam or SSAT required. Deadline for receipt of application materials: December 1. Application fee required: $65. On-campus interview required.

Athletics Interscholastic: badminton, basketball, cross-country running, field hockey, indoor track & field, lacrosse, soccer, softball, squash, swimming and diving, tennis, track and field, volleyball, winter (indoor) track. 9 PE instructors, 30 coaches, 2 athletic trainers.

Computers Computers are regularly used in all classes. Computer network features include on-campus library services, online commercial services, Internet access, wireless campus network, all classrooms equipped with Smart Boards. Campus intranet, student e-mail accounts, and computer access in designated common areas are available to students. The school has a published electronic and media policy.

Contact Susan Parker, Director of Admissions. 212-710-8140. Fax: 212-289-6025. E-mail: sparker@spenceschool.org. Website: www.spenceschool.org

SPRING CREEK ACADEMY

6000 Custer Road
Building 5
Plano, Texas 75023

Head of School: Matt Thomas

General Information Coeducational boarding and day and distance learning college-preparatory and general academic school. Grades 2–12. Distance learning grade X. Founded: 1997. Setting: suburban. Nearest major city is Dallas. 3 buildings on campus. Approved or accredited by Southern Association of Colleges and Schools, Texas Education Agency, Texas Private School Accreditation Commission, and Texas Department of Education. Upper school average class size: 6. Upper school faculty-student ratio: 1:6. There are 180 required school days per year for Upper School students. Upper School students typically attend 5 days per week. The average school day consists of 3 hours.

Faculty School total: 20. In upper school: 6 men, 14 women; 12 have advanced degrees.

Special Academic Programs Advanced Placement exam preparation; honors section; study at local college for college credit.

College Admission Counseling 15 students graduated in 2015; all went to college.

Student Life Upper grades have specified standards of dress, student council, honor system. Discipline rests primarily with faculty.

Summer Programs Remediation, enrichment, advancement, art/fine arts programs offered; held on campus; accepts boys and girls; open to students from other schools. 70 students usually enrolled. 2016 schedule: June 6 to July 21. Application deadline: May 15.

Admissions Traditional secondary-level entrance grade is 9. Iowa Tests of Basic Skills required. Deadline for receipt of application materials: none. Application fee required: $750. On-campus interview recommended.

Computers Computer network features include Internet access, wireless campus network, Internet filtering or blocking technology. Student e-mail accounts and computer access in designated common areas are available to students. Students grades are available online. The school has a published electronic and media policy.

Contact 972-517-6730. Fax: 972-517-8750. Website: www.springcreekacademy.com/

SPRINGSIDE CHESTNUT HILL ACADEMY

500 West Willow Grove Avenue
Philadelphia, Pennsylvania 19118

Head of School: Dr. Mark Segar, EdD

General Information Coeducational day college-preparatory, arts, technology, science, and math school. Grades PK–12. Founded: 1861. Setting: suburban. 62-acre campus. 4 buildings on campus. Approved or accredited by Pennsylvania Association of Independent Schools and Pennsylvania Department of Education. Member of National Association of Independent Schools and Secondary School Admission Test Board. Endowment: $41 million. Total enrollment: 1,059. Upper school average class size: 18. Upper school faculty-student ratio: 1:9. There are 172 required school days per year for Upper School students. Upper School students typically attend 5 days per week. The average school day consists of 7 hours and 40 minutes.

Upper School Student Profile Grade 9: 118 students (64 boys, 54 girls); Grade 10: 104 students (53 boys, 51 girls); Grade 11: 120 students (57 boys, 63 girls); Grade 12: 115 students (44 boys, 71 girls).

Faculty School total: 156. In upper school: 26 men, 40 women; 43 have advanced degrees.

Subjects Offered Advanced biology, advanced chemistry, advanced math, Advanced Placement courses, African studies, algebra, American history, architecture, art, art history, biology, biology-AP, calculus, calculus-AP, ceramics, chamber groups, chemistry, Chinese, choral music, college counseling, communications, community service, computer animation, computer programming, computer science, constitutional law, dance, dance performance, digital art, digital music, digital photography, drama, drawing and design, East Asian history, engineering, English, English literature, English-AP, entrepreneurship, environmental science, ethics and responsibility, European history, fine arts, forensics, French, French language-AP, gardening, geometry, handbells, health, independent study, international relations, jazz ensemble, Latin, Latin American studies, mathematics, Middle Eastern history, money management, music, oceanography, orchestra, painting, peer counseling, photography, physical education, physics, physics-AP, physiology, playwriting and directing, pre-calculus, printmaking, robotics, science, senior project, social studies, Spanish, Spanish-AP, statistics, statistics-AP, studio art, the Sixties, theater, trigonometry, U.S. government and politics-AP, U.S. history, U.S. history-AP, video, video and animation, video communication, video film production, weight reduction, woodworking, world history, world history-AP, World War II, writing, writing workshop, yearbook.

Graduation Requirements Arts, English, foreign language, health, history, mathematics, physical education (includes health), science, senior project, sports, senior speech, Center for Entrepreneurial Leadership seminars.

Special Academic Programs 12 Advanced Placement exams for which test preparation is offered; honors section; independent study; term-away projects; academic accommodation for the gifted, the musically talented, and the artistically talented.

College Admission Counseling 119 students graduated in 2015; 118 went to college, including Drexel University; Johns Hopkins University; Northeastern University; Penn State University Park; Rensselaer Polytechnic Institute; University of Pennsylvania. Other: 1 entered a postgraduate year. Mean SAT critical reading: 613, mean SAT math: 617, mean SAT writing: 616, mean composite ACT: 27.

Student Life Upper grades have specified standards of dress, student council, honor system. Discipline rests equally with students and faculty.

Summer Programs Enrichment, sports programs offered; session focuses on to offer a variety of interesting opportunities for kids of all ages and interests; held on campus; accepts boys and girls; open to students from other schools. 490 students usually enrolled. 2016 schedule: June 13 to August 19.

Tuition and Aid Day student tuition: $33,200. Tuition installment plan (FACTS Tuition Payment Plan, monthly payment plans, Higher Education Service, Inc). Need-based scholarship grants available. In 2015–16, 41% of upper-school students received aid. Total amount of financial aid awarded in 2015–16: $4,176,875.

Admissions Traditional secondary-level entrance grade is 9. For fall 2015, 171 students applied for upper-level admission, 104 were accepted, 44 enrolled. ISEE or SSAT required. Deadline for receipt of application materials: January 15. Application fee required: $50. On-campus interview required.

Athletics Interscholastic: baseball (boys), basketball (b,g), crew (b,g), cross-country running (b,g), field hockey (g), football (b), golf (b,g), ice hockey (b), independent competitive sports (b,g), indoor track & field (b,g), lacrosse (b,g), rowing (b,g), soccer (b,g), softball (g), squash (b,g), swimming and diving (b,g), table tennis (b,g), tennis (b,g), track and field (b,g), volleyball (g), winter (indoor) track (b,g), wrestling (b). 2 PE instructors, 57 coaches, 2 athletic trainers.

Computers Computers are regularly used in all classes. Computer network features include on-campus library services, online commercial services, Internet access, wireless campus network, Internet filtering or blocking technology, SCH is a 1:1 school in grades 3-12, and 1:2 in PK-2, many faculty are 1+1 with iPads and laptops. Campus intranet, student e-mail accounts, and computer access in designated common areas are available to students. Students grades are available online. The school has a published electronic and media policy.

Contact Ms. Murielle Telemaque, Admissions Office Manager. 215-247-7007. Fax: 215-242-4055. E-mail: mtelemaque@sch.org. Website: www.sch.org

SQUAW VALLEY ACADEMY

235 Squaw Valley Road
Olympic Valley, California 96146

Head of School: Mr. Donald Rees

General Information Coeducational boarding and day college-preparatory and arts school; primarily serves students with learning disabilities, individuals with Attention Deficit Disorder, and individuals with emotional and behavioral problems. Grades 9–12. Founded: 1978. Setting: rural. Nearest major city is Reno, NV. Students are housed in single-sex by floor dormitories and single-sex dormitories. 3-acre campus. 4 buildings on campus. Approved or accredited by National Independent Private Schools Association, Western Association of Schools and Colleges, and California Department of Education. Member of National Association of Independent Schools and Secondary School Admission Test Board. Total enrollment: 100. Upper school average class size: 8. Upper school faculty-student ratio: 1:8. Upper School students typically attend 5 days per week. The average school day consists of 8 hours.

Upper School Student Profile 100% of students are boarding students. 70% are international students. International students from Bangladesh, China, Japan, Kyrgyzstan, Republic of Korea, and Russian Federation; 8 other countries represented in student body.

Faculty School total: 12. In upper school: 9 men, 3 women; all have advanced degrees; 10 reside on campus.

Subjects Offered Addiction, advanced biology, advanced chemistry, advanced math, Advanced Placement courses, advanced TOEFL/grammar, algebra, American democracy, American government, American history, American history-AP, American literature, American literature-AP, anatomy, applied arts, applied music, art, art education, art history, backpacking, band, biology, biology-AP, calculus, calculus-AP, ceramics, chemistry, civics, college admission preparation, college counseling, college placement, college planning, college writing, computer science, computers, creative writing, drama, English, English literature, environmental science, expository writing, fine arts, French, geography, geometry, government/civics, grammar, health, history, history-AP, instruments, Internet, Internet research, jazz, language-AP, linear algebra, literature-AP, martial arts, mathematics, mathematics-AP, music, music appreciation, music history, music performance, music theory, novels, outdoor education, photography, physical education, physics, physics-AP, pre-calculus, psychology, publications, research and reference, SAT preparation, SAT/ACT preparation, science, social sciences, social studies, Spanish, Spanish-AP, student government, student publications, studio art, surfing, swimming, TOEFL preparation, travel, trigonometry, typing, video, visual and performing arts, weight fitness, world history, world history-AP, writing, yearbook, yoga.

Graduation Requirements Arts and fine arts (art, music, dance, drama), college admission preparation, English, foreign language, mathematics, physical education (includes health), science, social sciences, participation in skiing and snowboarding, seniors must gain acceptance into a minimum of one (1) college or university.

Special Academic Programs 15 Advanced Placement exams for which test preparation is offered; honors section; accelerated programs; independent study; study at local college for college credit; academic accommodation for the gifted, the musically talented, and the artistically talented; programs in English, mathematics for dyslexic students; special instructional classes for students with ADD and dyslexia; ESL (15 students enrolled).

College Admission Counseling 22 students graduated in 2015; all went to college, including Johns Hopkins University; Michigan State University; Penn State University Park; University of California, Davis; University of Colorado Boulder; University of Oregon. Median combined SAT: 1650. 20% scored over 600 on SAT critical reading, 40% scored over 600 on SAT math, 20% scored over 600 on SAT writing, 20% scored over 1800 on combined SAT.

Student Life Upper grades have uniform requirement, student council, honor system. Discipline rests primarily with faculty.

Summer Programs Remediation, enrichment, advancement, ESL, sports, art/fine arts programs offered; session focuses on academics and mountain sports; held both on and off campus; held at Lake Tahoe; accepts boys and girls; open to students from other schools. 25 students usually enrolled. 2016 schedule: June 30 to August 10. Application deadline: none.

Tuition and Aid 7-day tuition and room/board: $52,950. Tuition installment plan (individually arranged payment plans). Tuition reduction for siblings, merit scholarship grants, need-based scholarship grants available. In 2015–16, 10% of upper-school students received aid; total upper-school merit-scholarship money awarded: $175,000. Total amount of financial aid awarded in 2015–16: $175,000.

Admissions Traditional secondary-level entrance grade is 10. For fall 2015, 120 students applied for upper-level admission, 110 were accepted, 80 enrolled. Math Placement Exam and writing sample required. Deadline for receipt of application materials: none. Application fee required: $100. Interview required.

Athletics Interscholastic: alpine skiing (boys, girls), freestyle skiing (b,g), skiing (downhill) (b,g), snowboarding (b,g); intramural: aerobics (b,g), aerobics/Nautilus (b,g), alpine skiing (b,g), aquatics (b,g), backpacking (b,g), badminton (b,g), basketball (b,g), bicycling (b,g), billiards (b,g), blading (b,g), bowling (b,g), canoeing/kayaking (b,g), climbing (b,g), combined training (b,g), croquet (b,g), cross-country running (b,g), field hockey (b,g), fishing (b,g), fitness (b,g), fitness walking (b,g), flag football (b,g), fly fishing (b,g), freestyle skiing (b,g), Frisbee (b,g), golf (b,g), hiking/backpacking (b,g), horseback riding (b,g), ice skating (b,g), jogging (b,g), kayaking (b,g), mountain biking (b,g), mountaineering (b,g), nordic skiing (b,g), outdoor activities (b,g), outdoor adventure (b,g), outdoor education (b,g), outdoor recreation (b,g), outdoor skills (b,g), outdoors (b,g), paddling (b,g), paint ball (b,g), physical fitness (b,g), physical training (b,g), rafting (b,g), rock climbing (b,g), ropes courses (b,g), running (b,g), self defense (b,g), skateboarding (b,g), skiing (cross-country) (b,g), skiing (downhill) (b,g), snowboarding (b,g), snowshoeing (b,g), strength & conditioning (b,g), swimming and diving (b,g), table tennis (b,g), telemark skiing (b,g), tennis (b,g), ultimate Frisbee (b,g), volleyball (b,g), walking (b,g), wall climbing (b,g), weight lifting (b,g), weight training (b,g), yoga (b,g); coed interscholastic: alpine skiing, freestyle skiing, skiing (downhill), snowboarding, soccer; coed intramural: aerobics, aerobics/Nautilus, alpine skiing, aquatics, backpacking, badminton, baseball, basketball, bicycling, billiards, blading, bowling, canoeing/kayaking, climbing, combined training, croquet, cross-country running, field hockey, fishing, fitness, fitness walking, flag football, fly fishing, freestyle skiing, Frisbee, golf, hiking/backpacking, horseback riding, ice skating, jogging, kayaking, mountain biking, mountaineering, nordic skiing, outdoor activities, outdoor adventure, outdoor education, outdoor recreation, outdoor skills, outdoors, paddling, paint ball, physical fitness, physical training, rafting, rock climbing, ropes courses, running, self defense, skateboarding, skiing (cross-country), skiing (downhill), snowboarding, snowshoeing, soccer, softball, strength & conditioning, swimming and diving, table tennis, telemark skiing, tennis, ultimate Frisbee, volleyball, walking, wall climbing, weight lifting, weight training, yoga.

Computers Computers are regularly used in all academic classes. Computer network features include on-campus library services, online commercial services, Internet access, wireless campus network, Internet filtering or blocking technology. Computer access in designated common areas is available to students. The school has a published electronic and media policy.

Contact Adrienne Forbes, M.Ed., Admissions Director. 530-583-9393 Ext. 105. Fax: 530-581-1111. E-mail: enroll@sva.org. Website: www.sva.org

STANBRIDGE ACADEMY

San Mateo, California
See Special Needs Schools section.

STANSTEAD COLLEGE

450 Dufferin Street
Stanstead, Quebec J0B 3E0, Canada

Head of School: Mr. Michael Wolfe

General Information Coeducational boarding and day college-preparatory and bilingual studies school, affiliated with Christian faith. Grades 7–12. Founded: 1872. Setting: rural. Nearest major city is Montreal, Canada. Students are housed in single-sex dormitories. 720-acre campus. 10 buildings on campus. Approved or accredited by Canadian Association of Independent Schools, Canadian Educational Standards Institute, New England Association of Schools and Colleges, Quebec Association of Independent Schools, and Quebec Department of Education. Affiliate member of National Association of Independent Schools; member of Secondary School Admission Test Board. Language of instruction: English. Endowment: CAN$5 million. Total enrollment: 220. Upper school average class size: 12. Upper school faculty-student ratio: 1:8. There are 180 required school days per year for Upper School students. Upper School students typically attend 5 days per week. The average school day consists of 5 hours and 30 minutes.

Upper School Student Profile Grade 10: 52 students (24 boys, 28 girls); Grade 11: 47 students (28 boys, 19 girls); Grade 12: 58 students (41 boys, 17 girls). 75% of students are boarding students. 50% are province residents. 12 provinces are represented in upper school student body. 40% are international students. International students from China, Germany, Japan, Mexico, Saudi Arabia, and United States; 22 other countries represented in student body.

Faculty School total: 35. In upper school: 16 men, 14 women; 7 have advanced degrees; 20 reside on campus.

Subjects Offered Advanced Placement courses, algebra, art, athletic training, biology, calculus, career planning, chemistry, college admission preparation, college counseling, college placement, college planning, comparative politics, computer programming, computer science, drama, ecology, economics, English, English literature, environmental science, ESL, ethics, French, French as a second language, geography, geometry, history, mathematics, music, philosophy, physics, political science, psychology, science, social studies, sociology, statistics, technology, theater, trigonometry, world history.

Graduation Requirements English, foreign language, mathematics, science, social studies (includes history).

Special Academic Programs Advanced Placement exam preparation; honors section; independent study; study at local college for college credit; study abroad; special instructional classes for students with mild learning disorders; ESL (5 students enrolled).

College Admission Counseling 54 students graduated in 2015; 52 went to college, including Carleton University; Harvard University; McGill University; University of Ottawa; University of Toronto; University of Vermont. Other: 2 entered a postgraduate year.

Student Life Upper grades have uniform requirement, student council, honor system. Discipline rests primarily with faculty.

Summer Programs ESL, sports, art/fine arts programs offered; session focuses on English, French, and Spanish; held both on and off campus; held at nearby lakes, mountains, local attractions; accepts boys and girls; open to students from other schools. 130 students usually enrolled. 2016 schedule: July 3 to July 31. Application deadline: none.

Tuition and Aid Day student tuition: CAN$19,990; 7-day tuition and room/board: CAN$44,300. Tuition installment plan (monthly payment plans, monthly or term payment plans). Tuition reduction for siblings, merit scholarship grants, need-based scholarship grants, need-based loans available. In 2015–16, 40% of upper-school students received aid; total upper-school merit-scholarship money awarded: CAN$200,000. Total amount of financial aid awarded in 2015–16: CAN$1,400,000.

Admissions Traditional secondary-level entrance grade is 10. OLSAT, Stanford Achievement Test or SSAT required. Deadline for receipt of application materials: none. Application fee required: CAN$50. Interview required.

Athletics Interscholastic: basketball (boys, girls), cross-country running (b,g), football (b), ice hockey (b,g), lacrosse (b), physical fitness (b,g), physical training (b,g), rugby (b,g), soccer (b,g), squash (b,g), strength & conditioning (b,g), swimming and diving (b,g), tennis (b,g), track and field (b,g); coed interscholastic: aquatics, curling, golf, skiing (cross-country); coed intramural: alpine skiing, archery, backpacking, badminton, basketball, broomball, canoeing/kayaking, dance, equestrian sports, fishing, fitness, freestyle skiing, hiking/backpacking, horseback riding, kayaking, life saving, nordic skiing, outdoor activities, outdoor education, outdoor recreation, outdoor skills, skiing (cross-country), skiing (downhill), snowboarding, softball, swimming and diving, track and field, volleyball, walking, weight training, yoga. 1 PE instructor, 3 coaches, 1 athletic trainer.

Computers Computers are regularly used in English, mathematics, science classes. Computer network features include on-campus library services, Internet access, wireless campus network, Internet filtering or blocking technology. Student e-mail accounts and computer access in designated common areas are available to students. The school has a published electronic and media policy.

Contact Joanne Tracy Carruthers, Director of Admissions. 819-876-2223. Fax: 819-876-5891. E-mail: admissions@stansteadcollege.com.
Website: www.stansteadcollege.com

THE STANWICH SCHOOL

257 Stanwich Road
Greenwich, Connecticut 06830

Head of School: Mr. Paul Geise

General Information Coeducational day college-preparatory, arts, and technology school. Grades PK–12. Founded: 1998. Setting: suburban. Nearest major city is Stamford. 40-acre campus. 2 buildings on campus. Approved or accredited by Association of Independent Schools in New England, Connecticut Association of Independent Schools, New England Association of Schools and Colleges, and Connecticut Department of Education. Member of National Association of Independent Schools and Secondary School Admission Test Board. Total enrollment: 345. Upper school average class size: 7. Upper school faculty-student ratio: 1:6. There are 170 required school days per year for Upper School students. Upper School students typically attend 5 days per week. The average school day consists of 6 hours and 15 minutes.

Upper School Student Profile Grade 7: 35 students (21 boys, 14 girls); Grade 8: 34 students (23 boys, 11 girls); Grade 9: 11 students (9 boys, 2 girls); Grade 10: 10 students (8 boys, 2 girls); Grade 11: 17 students (9 boys, 8 girls).

Faculty School total: 60. In upper school: 18 men, 13 women; 30 have advanced degrees.

Subjects Offered Accounting, American government, American history, American history-AP, American literature, American literature-AP, American studies, applied arts, art, art history-AP, art-AP, athletics, band, baseball, basketball, bell choir, biology, biology-AP, British literature, British literature (honors), British literature-AP, calculus, calculus-AP, chemistry, chemistry-AP, choir, choral music, chorus, college admission preparation, college counseling, comparative government and politics-AP, composition, composition-AP, computer programming, computers, concert band, concert bell choir, CPR, debate, democracy in America, digital photography, drama, earth science, economics, economics-AP, electives, English, English composition, English language and composition-AP, English language-AP, English literature, English literature and composition-AP, English literature-AP, English-AP, English/composition-AP, entrepreneurship, ethics and responsibility, European history, European history-AP, European literature, French, French language-AP, French-AP, general science, golf, government and politics-AP, government-AP, grammar, graphic arts, Greek culture, handbells, health, history, history-AP, honors algebra, honors English, honors geometry, instrumental music, instruments, internship, introduction to theater, jazz, jazz band, journalism, language arts, language-AP, languages, Latin, Latin-AP, leadership and service, linear algebra, literature, literature and composition-AP, literature seminar, marine biology, marine science, mathematics-AP, medieval history, modern European history, modern European history-AP, music, musical productions, musical theater, news writing, newspaper, painting, participation in sports, performing arts, photography, physical fitness, physics, piano, politics, probability and statistics, public speaking, reading/study skills, robotics, SAT preparation, SAT/ACT preparation, Shakespeare, Shakespearean histories, softball, Spanish, Spanish language-AP, Spanish-AP, squash, statistics-AP, student government, studio art, studio art-AP, study skills, tennis, theater, U.S. government and politics, U.S. government and politics-AP, U.S. history, U.S. history-AP, U.S. literature, visual and performing arts, voice, volleyball, writing, writing, yearbook.

Graduation Requirements American history, American literature, art, biology, British literature, calculus, chemistry, college counseling, computers, economics, English, geometry, government/civics, health, history, independent study, language, literature, mathematics, physics, public speaking, U.S. history, U.S. literature, Moral Leadership Program.

Special Academic Programs 12 Advanced Placement exams for which test preparation is offered; honors section; accelerated programs; independent study; study abroad; academic accommodation for the gifted, the musically talented, and the artistically talented.

College Admission Counseling 16 students graduated in 2014; all went to college, including Fordham University; Lehigh University; University of Connecticut; Vanderbilt University; Washington and Lee University; Wesleyan University.

Student Life Upper grades have uniform requirement, student council. Discipline rests primarily with faculty.

Tuition and Aid Day student tuition: $29,000–$37,000. Tuition installment plan (Insured Tuition Payment Plan, monthly payment plans, individually arranged payment plans). Need-based scholarship grants available. In 2014–15, 30% of upper-school students received aid.

Admissions Traditional secondary-level entrance grade is 7. For fall 2014, 52 students applied for upper-level admission, 22 were accepted, 17 enrolled. Admissions testing, ERB (grade level), ERB CTP IV, ISEE, TOEFL, TOEFL Junior or writing sample required. Deadline for receipt of application materials: none. Application fee required: $80. Interview required.

Athletics Interscholastic: baseball (boys), basketball (b,g), field hockey (g), football (b), lacrosse (b), soccer (b,g), softball (g); intramural: softball (g), volleyball (g); coed interscholastic: crew, cross-country running, golf, physical training, sailing, squash, tennis; coed intramural: climbing, dance, fitness, flag football, golf, ice hockey, ice skating, outdoor adventure, outdoors, physical fitness, rock climbing, running. 6 PE instructors, 6 coaches, 6 athletic trainers.

Computers Computers are regularly used in all academic, art, college planning, computer applications, data processing, design, economics, English, foreign language, French, graphic arts, graphic design, health, history, independent study, journalism, Latin, literacy, mathematics, music, news writing, newspaper, photography, programming, SAT preparation, science, Spanish, theater, video film production, writing, yearbook classes. Computer network features include on-campus library services, online commercial services, Internet access, wireless campus network, Internet filtering or blocking technology. Campus intranet, student e-mail accounts, and computer access in designated common areas are available to students. Students grades are available online. The school has a published electronic and media policy.

Contact Jessie Drennen, Assistant Director of Admissions. 203-542-0035. Fax: 203-542-0025. E-mail: jdrennen@stanwichschool.org. Website: www.stanwichschool.org/

STEAMBOAT MOUNTAIN SCHOOL

42605 County Road 36
Steamboat Springs, Colorado 80487

Head of School: Meg Morse

General Information Coeducational boarding and day college-preparatory school. Grades 9–12. Founded: 1957. Setting: rural. Nearest major city is Denver. Students are housed in single-sex dormitories. 140-acre campus. 10 buildings on campus. Approved or accredited by Association of Colorado Independent Schools, The Association of Boarding Schools, and Colorado Department of Education. Member of National Association of Independent Schools and Secondary School Admission Test Board. Endowment: $1 million. Upper school average class size: 8. Upper school faculty-student ratio: 1:8. There are 175 required school days per year for Upper School students. Upper School students typically attend 5 days per week. The average school day consists of 7 hours.

Upper School Student Profile Grade 9: 12 students (2 boys, 10 girls); Grade 10: 7 students (6 boys, 1 girl); Grade 11: 16 students (12 boys, 4 girls); Grade 12: 9 students (5 boys, 4 girls). 50% of students are boarding students. 52% are state residents. 14 states are represented in upper school student body. 14% are international students. International students from Australia, Canada, China, Mexico, Mexico, and Sweden.

Faculty School total: 14. In upper school: 5 men, 9 women; 7 have advanced degrees; 11 reside on campus.

Subjects Offered 20th century history, algebra, American history, American literature, American studies, anatomy, art, art history, biology, calculus, chemistry, computer math, computer programming, computer science, creative writing, drama, economics, English, English literature, expository writing, film, fine arts, French, geography, geology, geometry, government/civics, grammar, mathematics, physical education, physics, science, social sciences, social studies, Spanish, theater, trigonometry, typing, world history, writing.

Graduation Requirements Algebra, arts and fine arts (art, music, dance, drama), chemistry, computer science, English, foreign language, geography, geometry, mathematics, physical education (includes health), science, social sciences, social studies (includes history), Western civilization, foreign travel program, competitive ski/snowboarding program, outdoor program.

Special Academic Programs Advanced Placement exam preparation; honors section; independent study; study abroad; academic accommodation for the gifted.

College Admission Counseling 12 students graduated in 2015; all went to college, including Colorado State University; Hobart and William Smith Colleges; Pepperdine University; University of Colorado Boulder; University of Denver.

Student Life Upper grades have student council, honor system. Discipline rests equally with students and faculty.

Tuition and Aid Day student tuition: $22,240; 7-day tuition and room/board: $42,075. Tuition installment plan (individually arranged payment plans, school's own payment plan). Merit scholarship grants, need-based scholarship grants available. In 2015–16, 36% of upper-school students received aid; total upper-school merit-scholarship money awarded: $10,000. Total amount of financial aid awarded in 2015–16: $220,000.

Admissions Traditional secondary-level entrance grade is 9. For fall 2015, 29 students applied for upper-level admission, 27 were accepted, 21 enrolled. Deadline for receipt of application materials: February. Application fee required: $100. Interview recommended.

Athletics Interscholastic: alpine skiing (boys, girls), biathlon (b,g), cheering (g), cross-country running (b,g), dance team (g), freestyle skiing (b,g), hockey (b,g), ice hockey (b,g), indoor hockey (b,g), mountain biking (b,g), mountaineering (b,g), nordic skiing (b,g), outdoor adventure (b,g), ski jumping (b,g), skiing (cross-country) (b,g), skiing (downhill) (b,g), snowboarding (b,g), soccer (b,g); intramural: backpacking (b,g), bicycling (b,g), ice hockey (b,g), ice skating (b,g), independent competitive sports (b,g), indoor hockey (b,g), jogging (b,g), lacrosse (g), mountain biking (b,g), mountaineering (b,g), outdoor adventure (b,g), rock climbing (b,g), skiing (cross-country) (b,g), skiing (downhill) (b,g), snowboarding (b,g), soccer (b,g); coed interscholastic: alpine skiing, biathlon, climbing, cross-country running, freestyle skiing, ice hockey, indoor hockey, kayaking, mountain biking, mountaineering, nordic skiing, outdoor adventure, outdoor education, outdoor recreation, outdoor skills, rock climbing, ski jumping, skiing (cross-country), skiing (downhill), snowboarding, soccer, telemark skiing, wall climbing; coed intramural: aerobics, backpacking, badminton, bicycling, canoeing/kayaking, climbing, figure skating, fitness, flag football, Frisbee, golf, hiking/backpacking, horseback riding, ice hockey, ice skating, independent competitive sports, indoor hockey, jogging, judo, juggling, kayaking, lacrosse, mountain biking, mountaineering, nordic skiing, outdoor adventure, outdoor education, outdoor recreation, outdoor skills, physical fitness, physical training, rafting, rappelling, rock climbing, running, skateboarding, skiing (cross-country), skiing (downhill), snowboarding, snowshoeing, soccer, strength & conditioning, telemark skiing, volleyball, wall climbing, weight lifting, weight training, wilderness, wilderness survival, wildernessways, winter walking, yoga.

Computers Computers are regularly used in all academic classes. Computer network features include on-campus library services, online commercial services, Internet access, wireless campus network, Internet filtering or blocking technology. Campus intranet and student e-mail accounts are available to students. The school has a published electronic and media policy.

Contact Pearson Alspach, Director of Admissions. 970-879-1350 Ext. 18. Fax: 970-879-0506. E-mail: alspachp@steamboatmountainschoo.org. Website: www.steamboatmountainschool.org

STEPHEN T. BADIN HIGH SCHOOL

571 New London Road
Hamilton, Ohio 45013

Head of School: Mr. Brian Pendergest

General Information Coeducational day college-preparatory, general academic, arts, business, vocational, religious studies, and technology school, affiliated with Roman Catholic Church; primarily serves students with learning disabilities and individuals with Attention Deficit Disorder. Grades 9–12. Founded: 1966. Setting: urban. Nearest major city is Cincinnati. 22-acre campus. 2 buildings on campus. Approved or accredited by National Catholic Education Association and Ohio Department of Education. Endowment: $120,000. Total enrollment: 543. Upper school average class size: 22. Upper school faculty-student ratio: 1:19. There are 187 required school days per year for Upper School students. Upper School students typically attend 5 days per week. The average school day consists of 7 hours.

Upper School Student Profile Grade 9: 147 students (73 boys, 74 girls); Grade 10: 122 students (76 boys, 46 girls); Grade 11: 134 students (75 boys, 59 girls); Grade 12: 140 students (76 boys, 64 girls). 85% of students are Roman Catholic.

Faculty School total: 41. In upper school: 17 men, 24 women; 23 have advanced degrees.

Subjects Offered Accounting, algebra, American history, American literature, art, band, biology, British literature, calculus, calculus-AP, chemistry, chorus, computer programming, computer resources, consumer economics, economics, English, English literature, English-AP, French, geometry, government-AP, government/civics, history, integrated science, intro to computers, journalism, marketing, mathematics, music, music theory, physical education, physical science, physics, physiology, pre-calculus, publications, religion, science, social studies, Spanish, Web site design, Western literature, world history.

Graduation Requirements Computer science, English, mathematics, physical education (includes health), religion (includes Bible studies and theology), science, social studies (includes history), 15 hours of community service per year for seniors.

Special Academic Programs 8 Advanced Placement exams for which test preparation is offered; honors section; study at local college for college credit; study abroad; remedial reading and/or remedial writing; remedial math.

College Admission Counseling 119 students graduated in 2015; 118 went to college, including Miami University; Mount St. Joseph University; Ohio University; The Ohio State University; University of Cincinnati; Xavier University. Other: 1 entered military service. Median SAT critical reading: 526, median SAT math: 521, median SAT writing: 529, median combined SAT: 1574, median composite ACT: 24. 21% scored over 600 on SAT critical reading, 11% scored over 600 on SAT math, 16% scored over 600 on SAT writing, 20% scored over 1800 on combined SAT, 25% scored over 26 on composite ACT.

Student Life Upper grades have uniform requirement, student council. Discipline rests primarily with faculty. Attendance at religious services is required.

Tuition and Aid Day student tuition: $8840. Tuition installment plan (monthly payment plans, individually arranged payment plans, quarterly payment plan). Merit scholarship grants, need-based scholarship grants, paying campus jobs available. In 2015–16, 43% of upper-school students received aid; total upper-school merit-scholarship money awarded: $334,800. Total amount of financial aid awarded in 2015–16: $688,200.

Admissions Traditional secondary-level entrance grade is 9. Deadline for receipt of application materials: none. No application fee required. On-campus interview recommended.

Athletics Interscholastic: baseball (boys), basketball (b,g), bowling (b,g), cheering (g), diving (b), football (b), golf (b,g), gymnastics (g), soccer (b,g), softball (g), swimming and diving (b,g), tennis (b,g), volleyball (b,g). 1 PE instructor, 59 coaches, 1 athletic trainer.

Computers Computers are regularly used in all academic, mathematics, music, science, Web site design classes. Computer network features include on-campus library services, Internet access, wireless campus network, Internet filtering or blocking technology, scanners, travelling laptops, digital cameras. Campus intranet, student e-mail accounts, and computer access in designated common areas are available to students. Students grades are available online. The school has a published electronic and media policy.

Contact Mrs. Angie Gray, Director of Recruitment. 513-863-3993 Ext. 145. Fax: 513-785-2844. E-mail: agray@mail.badinhs.org. Website: http://www.badinhs.org/

STEVENSON SCHOOL

3152 Forest Lake Road
Pebble Beach, California 93953

Head of School: Dr. Kevin Hicks

General Information Coeducational boarding and day college-preparatory and arts school. Boarding grades 9–12, day grades PK–12. Founded: 1952. Setting: suburban. Nearest major city is San Francisco. Students are housed in single-sex dormitories and single-sex by wing. 65-acre campus. 24 buildings on campus. Approved or accredited by The Association of Boarding Schools, Western Association of Schools and Colleges, and California Department of Education. Member of National Association of Independent Schools and Secondary School Admission Test Board. Endowment: $31 million. Total enrollment: 747. Upper school average class size: 14. Upper school faculty-student ratio: 1:10. There are 160 required school days per year for Upper School students. Upper School students typically attend 5 days per week. The average school day consists of 6 hours and 30 minutes.

Upper School Student Profile Grade 9: 104 students (49 boys, 55 girls); Grade 10: 135 students (71 boys, 64 girls); Grade 11: 132 students (60 boys, 72 girls); Grade 12: 127 students (67 boys, 60 girls). 60% of students are boarding students. 57% are state residents. 19 states are represented in upper school student body. 25% are international students. International students from China, Hong Kong, Japan, Republic of Korea, Taiwan, and Viet Nam; 19 other countries represented in student body.

Faculty School total: 95. In upper school: 42 men, 20 women; 46 have advanced degrees; 38 reside on campus.

Subjects Offered 3-dimensional art, advanced chemistry, Advanced Placement courses, algebra, American history, American literature, American literature-AP, architecture, art, art history, art-AP, biology, biology-AP, broadcasting, calculus, calculus-AP, ceramics, chemistry, chemistry-AP, Chinese, computer programming, computer science, concert band, creative writing, dance, dance performance, drama, drama performance, drama workshop, dramatic arts, drawing, drawing and design, driver education, economics, economics-AP, English, English literature, English-AP, environmental science, environmental science-AP, ethics, European civilization, European history, expository writing, fine arts, French, French-AP, geometry, government/civics, grammar, history of ideas, history-AP, honors algebra, honors English, honors geometry, honors U.S. history, Japanese, jazz, jazz band, jazz ensemble, jazz theory, journalism, Latin, Latin-AP, macroeconomics-AP, marine biology, mathematics, mathematics-AP, microbiology, music, musical productions, musical theater, ornithology, photography, physical education, physics, physics-AP, portfolio art, pre-calculus, psychology, science, social studies, Spanish, Spanish-AP, speech, stage design, stagecraft, studio art-AP, tap dance, theater, trigonometry, U.S. history-AP, visual and performing arts, visual arts, vocal ensemble, wilderness education, wilderness experience, wind ensemble, world cultures, world history, world literature, world studies, writing, yearbook.

Graduation Requirements Arts and fine arts (art, music, dance, drama), athletics, English, foreign language, history, mathematics, science.

Special Academic Programs 23 Advanced Placement exams for which test preparation is offered; honors section; independent study; term-away projects; study abroad.

College Admission Counseling 135 students graduated in 2015; 128 went to college, including New York University; Northwestern University; Pepperdine University; The University of Arizona; University of California, Santa Barbara; University of Oregon. Other: 1 entered military service, 3 had other specific plans. Median SAT critical reading: 620, median SAT math: 640, median SAT writing: 610, median combined SAT: 1870. Mean composite ACT: 28. 59% scored over 600 on SAT critical reading, 60% scored over 600 on SAT math, 56% scored over 600 on SAT writing, 58% scored over 1800 on combined SAT.

Student Life Upper grades have specified standards of dress, student council, honor system. Discipline rests equally with students and faculty.

Summer Programs Enrichment, advancement, sports, art/fine arts programs offered; held on campus; accepts boys and girls; open to students from other schools. 140 students usually enrolled. 2016 schedule: June 26 to August 29. Application deadline: May 15.

Tuition and Aid Day student tuition: $36,200; 7-day tuition and room/board: $59,800. Tuition installment plan (Insured Tuition Payment Plan). Need-based scholarship grants available. In 2015–16, 35% of upper-school students received aid. Total amount of financial aid awarded in 2015–16: $3,475,000.

Admissions Traditional secondary-level entrance grade is 9. For fall 2015, 458 students applied for upper-level admission, 267 were accepted, 135 enrolled. ISEE, PSAT, SSAT, TOEFL or writing sample required. Deadline for receipt of application materials: February 1. Application fee required: $75. Interview required.

Athletics Interscholastic: baseball (boys), basketball (b,g), cross-country running (b,g), diving (b,g), field hockey (g), football (b), golf (b,g), lacrosse (b,g), sailing (b,g), soccer (b,g), softball (g), swimming and diving (b,g), tennis (b,g), track and field (b,g), volleyball (g), water polo (b,g); intramural: ballet (g), dance (b,g), golf (b,g), horseback riding (b,g), independent competitive sports (b,g), kayaking (b,g), modern dance (b,g), mountaineering (b,g), outdoor education (b,g), outdoors (b,g), rock climbing (b,g), strength & conditioning (b,g), table tennis (b,g), weight lifting (b,g), wilderness (b,g), yoga (b,g); coed interscholastic: sailing; coed intramural: backpacking, ballet, bicycling, climbing, dance, equestrian sports, fitness walking, hiking/backpacking, horseback riding, independent competitive sports, kayaking, modern dance, mountaineering, outdoor education, outdoors, rock climbing, sailing, softball, strength & conditioning, table tennis, weight lifting, weight training, wilderness, yoga. 30 coaches.

Computers Computers are regularly used in all classes. Computer network features include on-campus library services, online commercial services, Internet access, wireless campus network, Internet filtering or blocking technology. Campus intranet and student e-mail accounts are available to students. Students grades are available online. The school has a published electronic and media policy.

Contact Mrs. Melissa Schuette, Associate Director of Admission. 831-625-8309. Fax: 831-625-5208. E-mail: info@stevensonschool.org. Website: www.stevensonschool.org

ST LEONARDS SCHOOL AND SIXTH FORM COLLEGE

St. Andrews

Fife, Scotland KY16 9QJ, United Kingdom

Head of School: Dr. Michael Carslaw

General Information Coeducational boarding and day college-preparatory, general academic, arts, business, religious studies, bilingual studies, and technology school. Boarding grades 8–13, day grades 1–13. Founded: 1877. Setting: small town. Nearest major city is St, Andrews (Near Edinburgh), United Kingdom. Students are housed in single-sex dormitories. 26-acre campus. 8 buildings on campus. Approved or accredited by Boarding Schools Association (UK), Headmasters' Conference, Independent Schools Council (UK), International Baccalaureate Organization, and Scottish Education Department. Language of instruction: English. Total enrollment: 453. Upper school average class size: 16. Upper school faculty-student ratio: 1:9. The average school day consists of 8 hours.

Upper School Student Profile Grade 8: 39 students (18 boys, 21 girls); Grade 9: 33 students (14 boys, 19 girls); Grade 10: 40 students (17 boys, 23 girls); Grade 11: 45 students (19 boys, 26 girls); Grade 12: 73 students (38 boys, 35 girls); Grade 13: 53 students (27 boys, 26 girls). 65% of students are boarding students. 40% are international students. International students from Austria, China, Germany, Hong Kong, and Russian Federation; 11 other countries represented in student body.

Faculty In upper school: 21 men, 30 women; 9 have advanced degrees; 8 reside on campus.

Subjects Offered 20th century physics, 20th century world history, 3-dimensional art, 3-dimensional design, acting, adolescent issues, advanced chemistry, advanced computer applications, advanced math, advanced TOEFL/grammar, Ancient Greek, art, art history, arts, biology, British history, business, career and personal planning, chemistry, classics, computer literacy, computer skills, creative arts, design, drama, economics, English, English as a foreign language, European history, geography, German, Greek, history, humanities, Latin, mathematics, modern history, modern languages, music, personal and social education, physics, politics, psychology, religious studies, science, theater design and production, vocal ensemble, voice, wind ensemble, wind instruments, word processing, work experience, world geography, world history.

Special Academic Programs International Baccalaureate program; study at local college for college credit; academic accommodation for the gifted, the musically talented, and the artistically talented; programs in English, mathematics, general development for dyslexic students; ESL (25 students enrolled).

College Admission Counseling 56 students graduated in 2015; 54 went to college. Other: 2 had other specific plans.

Student Life Upper grades have specified standards of dress, student council, honor system. Discipline rests equally with students and faculty.

Tuition and Aid Day student tuition: £9297; 7-day tuition and room/board: £30,957. Tuition installment plan (monthly payment plans, individually arranged payment plans). Need-based scholarship grants available.

Admissions For fall 2015, 74 students applied for upper-level admission, 70 were accepted, 70 enrolled. School's own exam required. Deadline for receipt of application materials: none. Application fee required: £100. Interview required.

Athletics Interscholastic: cricket (boys), golf (b,g), hockey (b,g), lacrosse (g), netball (g), rugby (b), running (b,g), squash (b,g), swimming and diving (b,g), tennis (b,g); intramural: aerobics (g), aerobics/dance (g), ballet (g), cricket (b), football (b), lacrosse (g), netball (g), rounders (b,g), rugby (b), running (b,g), squash (b,g), tennis (b,g), yoga (g); coed interscholastic: alpine skiing, cross-country running, equestrian sports, freestyle skiing, golf, hockey, horseback riding, judo, physical fitness, rounders, running, skiing (downhill), squash, swimming and diving, tennis, track and field, winter soccer; coed intramural: alpine skiing, archery, backpacking, badminton, ball hockey, basketball, bicycling, canoeing/kayaking, climbing, cross-country running, dance, equestrian sports, fencing, field hockey, fitness, freestyle skiing, golf, gymnastics, hiking/backpacking, hockey, horseback riding, indoor hockey, indoor soccer, judo, kayaking, lacrosse, life saving, outdoor activities, physical fitness, rock climbing, rounders, running, sailing, self defense, skiing (downhill), soccer, squash, surfing, swimming and diving, table tennis, tennis, track and field, volleyball, wall climbing, weight training, wilderness survival, windsurfing, winter soccer. 4 PE instructors, 13 coaches.

Computers Computers are regularly used in art, career exploration, English, French, geography, history, information technology, language development, library skills, mathematics, music, research skills, Spanish, technical drawing classes. Computer network features include on-campus library services, Internet access, wireless campus network, Internet filtering or blocking technology. Campus intranet, student e-mail accounts, and computer access in designated common areas are available to students. The school has a published electronic and media policy.

Contact Dr. Caroline Routledge, Registrar. 44-1334-472126. Fax: 44-1334 476152. E-mail: info@stleonards-fife.org. Website: www.stleonards-fife.org/

STONELEIGH–BURNHAM SCHOOL

574 Bernardston Road
Greenfield, Massachusetts 01301

Head of School: Sally Mixsell

General Information Girls' boarding and day college-preparatory and arts school. Grades 7–PG. Founded: 1869. Setting: small town. Nearest major city is Boston. Students are housed in single-sex dormitories. 100-acre campus. 7 buildings on campus. Approved or accredited by Association of Independent Schools in New England, International Baccalaureate Organization, New England Association of Schools and Colleges, The Association of Boarding Schools, and Massachusetts Department of Education. Member of National Association of Independent Schools. Endowment: $2.8 million. Total enrollment: 155. Upper school average class size: 9. Upper school faculty-student ratio: 1:5. Upper School students typically attend 5 days per week. The average school day consists of 8 hours.

Upper School Student Profile Grade 9: 22 students (22 girls); Grade 10: 34 students (34 girls); Grade 11: 24 students (24 girls); Grade 12: 28 students (28 girls). 70% of students are boarding students. 38% are state residents. 18 states are represented in upper school student body. 40% are international students. International students from China, Germany, Japan, Mexico, and Republic of Korea; 2 other countries represented in student body.

Faculty School total: 35. In upper school: 7 men, 16 women; 14 have advanced degrees; 13 reside on campus.

Subjects Offered Acting, algebra, American history, art, band, biology, calculus, ceramics, chemistry, Chinese, conceptual physics, dance, desktop publishing, drama, drawing, English, equine science, ESL, fine arts, French, geometry, graphic arts, history, International Baccalaureate courses, mathematics, music, music theory, photography, physics, poetry, psychology, public speaking, science, senior seminar, social studies, Spanish, theater, values and decisions, water color painting, weaving, yearbook.

Graduation Requirements Art, arts and fine arts (art, music, dance, drama), English, foreign language, history, mathematics, physical education (includes health), science, U.S. history.

Special Academic Programs International Baccalaureate program; honors section; independent study; ESL (15 students enrolled).

College Admission Counseling 30 students graduated in 2014; all went to college.

Student Life Upper grades have specified standards of dress, student council, honor system. Discipline rests equally with students and faculty.

Tuition and Aid Day student tuition: $30,947; 7-day tuition and room/board: $51,892. Tuition installment plan (monthly payment plans). Merit scholarship grants, need-based scholarship grants available. In 2014–15, 50% of upper-school students received aid; total upper-school merit-scholarship money awarded: $20,000. Total amount of financial aid awarded in 2014–15: $904,000.

Admissions Traditional secondary-level entrance grade is 9. For fall 2014, 102 students applied for upper-level admission, 66 were accepted, 28 enrolled. ISEE, SSAT or TOEFL or SLEP required. Deadline for receipt of application materials: February 15. Application fee required: $50. Interview required.

Athletics Interscholastic: aerobics/dance, ballet, basketball, cross-country running, dance, dressage, equestrian sports, horseback riding, lacrosse, modern dance, soccer, softball, tennis, volleyball; intramural: alpine skiing, cross-country running, fitness, golf, horseback riding, ice skating, skiing (downhill), snowboarding, strength & conditioning, tennis. 1 athletic trainer.

Computers Computers are regularly used in all classes. Computer network features include on-campus library services, Internet access, wireless campus network, Internet filtering or blocking technology. Campus intranet, student e-mail accounts, and computer access in designated common areas are available to students. Students grades are available online. The school has a published electronic and media policy.

Contact Sharon Weyers, Associate Director of Admissions. 413-774-2711 Ext. 257. Fax: 413-772-2602. E-mail: admissions@sbschool.org. Website: www.sbschool.org

STONE RIDGE SCHOOL OF THE SACRED HEART

9101 Rockville Pike
Bethesda, Maryland 20814

Head of School: Mrs. Catherine Ronan Karrels

General Information Coeducational day (boys' only in lower grades) college-preparatory, arts, religious studies, and technology school, affiliated with Roman Catholic Church. Boys grades PS–K, girls grades PS–12. Founded: 1923. Setting: suburban. Nearest major city is Washington, DC. 35-acre campus. 12 buildings on campus. Approved or accredited by Association of Independent Schools of Greater Washington, Middle States Association of Colleges and Schools, National Catholic Education Association, Network of Sacred Heart Schools, and Maryland Department of Education. Member of National Association of Independent Schools and Secondary School Admission Test Board. Endowment: $37 million. Total enrollment: 719. Upper school average class size: 15. Upper school faculty-student ratio: 1:7. Upper School students typically attend 5 days per week. The average school day consists of 5 hours and 20 minutes.

Upper School Student Profile 75% of students are Roman Catholic.

Faculty School total: 84. In upper school: 21 men, 35 women; 56 have advanced degrees.

Subjects Offered Advanced chemistry, advanced math, Advanced Placement courses, algebra, American history, American literature, art, art history, biochemistry, biology, ceramics, chemistry, chorus, community service, computer graphics, computer programming, computer science, creative writing, drama, economics, economics and history, English, English literature, environmental science, ethics, European history, film, fine arts, French, geometry, history, independent study, journalism, Latin, mathematics, media arts, microbiology, music, photography, physical science, physics, pre-calculus, religion, science, social studies, Spanish, theater, theology, trigonometry, women's studies, world history, world literature, world religions, writing.

Graduation Requirements Arts and fine arts (art, music, dance, drama), English, foreign language, mathematics, physical education (includes health), science, social studies (includes history), theology. Community service is required.

Special Academic Programs Advanced Placement exam preparation; honors section; independent study; term-away projects; domestic exchange program (with Network of Sacred Heart Schools); study abroad; academic accommodation for the gifted and the artistically talented.

College Admission Counseling 80 students graduated in 2015; all went to college, including Boston College; Elon University; Georgetown University; University of Maryland, College Park; University of Notre Dame; University of Virginia.

Student Life Upper grades have uniform requirement, student council, honor system. Discipline rests primarily with faculty. Attendance at religious services is required.

Summer Programs Remediation, enrichment, advancement, sports, art/fine arts, computer instruction programs offered; session focuses on recreation, academic, and enrichment; held on campus; accepts boys and girls; open to students from other schools. 700 students usually enrolled. 2016 schedule: June 20 to July 29. Application deadline: none.

Tuition and Aid Day student tuition: $309,000. Tuition installment plan (Key Tuition Payment Plan, FACTS Tuition Payment Plan). Merit scholarship grants, need-based scholarship grants available. In 2015–16, 30% of upper-school students received aid; total upper-school merit-scholarship money awarded: $85,000. Total amount of financial aid awarded in 2015–16: $2,600,000.

Admissions Traditional secondary-level entrance grade is 9. ERB, SSAT or Wechsler Intelligence Scale for Children required. Deadline for receipt of application materials: December 4. Application fee required: $50. On-campus interview required.

Athletics Interscholastic: aquatics (girls), basketball (g), cross-country running (g), diving (g), field hockey (g), lacrosse (g), soccer (g), softball (g), swimming and diving (g), tennis (g), track and field (g), volleyball (g); intramural: aerobics (g), aerobics/dance (g), aerobics/Nautilus (g), aquatics (g), dance (g), equestrian sports (g), fitness (g), golf (g), ice hockey (g), independent competitive sports (g), modern dance (g), running (g), squash (g), synchronized swimming (g), wall climbing (g), weight training (g), yoga (g). 3 PE instructors, 28 coaches, 1 athletic trainer.

Computers Computers are regularly used in all academic classes. Computer network features include on-campus library services, online commercial services, Internet access, wireless campus network, Internet filtering or blocking technology. Campus intranet, student e-mail accounts, and computer access in designated common areas are available to students. Students grades are available online. The school has a published electronic and media policy.

Contact Ms. Mary Tobias, Director of Admission. 301-657-4322 Ext. 321. Fax: 301-657-4393. E-mail: admissions@stoneridgeschool.org. Website: www.stoneridgeschool.org

THE STONY BROOK SCHOOL

1 Chapman Parkway
Stony Brook, New York 11790

Head of School: Mr. Joshua Crane

General Information Coeducational boarding and day college-preparatory, arts, religious studies, and technology school, affiliated with Christian faith. Grades 7–12. Founded: 1922. Setting: suburban. Nearest major city is New York. Students are housed in single-sex dormitories. 55-acre campus. 15 buildings on campus. Approved or accredited by Middle States Association of Colleges and Schools, New York State Association of Independent Schools, The Association of Boarding Schools, and New York Department of Education. Member of National Association of Independent Schools and Secondary School Admission Test Board. Endowment: $14 million. Total enrollment: 360. Upper school average class size: 14. Upper school faculty-student ratio: 1:7. There are 162 required school days per year for Upper School students. Upper School students typically attend 5 days per week. The average school day consists of 7 hours and 30 minutes.

Upper School Student Profile Grade 9: 77 students (44 boys, 33 girls); Grade 10: 74 students (32 boys, 42 girls); Grade 11: 76 students (41 boys, 35 girls); Grade 12: 66 students (25 boys, 41 girls). 47% of students are boarding students. 45% are state residents. 12 states are represented in upper school student body. 33% are international students. International students from China, Germany, Jamaica, Republic of Korea, Russian Federation, and Saudi Arabia; 17 other countries represented in student body. 60% of students are Christian.

Faculty School total: 45. In upper school: 22 men, 18 women; 37 have advanced degrees; 41 reside on campus.

Subjects Offered Algebra, American history, American history-AP, ancient history, art, art-AP, Bible, Bible studies, biology, biology-AP, calculus, calculus-AP, ceramics, chamber groups, character education, chemistry, chemistry-AP, Chinese studies, chorus, Christian studies, computer applications, concert choir, creative writing, critical thinking, design, digital imaging, drawing, English, English literature, English-AP, environmental science-AP, ESL, ethics, European history, European history-AP, expository writing, fine arts, French, French-AP, general science, geometry, health, history, honors English, humanities, instrumental music, instruments, intro to computers, Latin, Latin-AP, marine science, mathematics, modern European history, music, orchestra, painting, photography, physical education, physics, physics-AP, piano, political thought, pre-algebra, pre-calculus, psychology, psychology-AP, science, social studies, Spanish, Spanish-AP, statistics-AP, studio art-AP, study skills, theater arts, U.S. history, U.S. history-AP, visual arts, world history, writing.

Graduation Requirements Algebra, arts and fine arts (art, music, dance, drama), Bible, English, European history, foreign language, geometry, health, mathematics, physical education (includes health), science, social studies (includes history), U.S. history.

Special Academic Programs Advanced Placement exam preparation; honors section; independent study; study at local college for college credit; ESL (20 students enrolled).

College Admission Counseling 58 students graduated in 2015; all went to college, including Boston University; Emory University, Oxford College; Gordon College; Johns Hopkins University; New York University; Northwestern University. Mean SAT critical reading: 602, mean SAT math: 660, mean SAT writing: 630, mean combined SAT: 1892.

Student Life Upper grades have specified standards of dress, student council, honor system. Discipline rests equally with students and faculty. Attendance at religious services is required.

Summer Programs Enrichment, sports, art/fine arts, rigorous outdoor training, computer instruction programs offered; session focuses on athletics, recreation, and/or writing; held both on and off campus; held at sailing programs in Port Jefferson Harbor and local beaches, rivers, upstate NY, NYC, depending on the program; accepts boys and girls; open to students from other schools. 2016 schedule: July 5 to August 5. Application deadline: May 1.

Tuition and Aid Day student tuition: $26,800; 5-day tuition and room/board: $42,300; 7-day tuition and room/board: $49,500. Tuition installment plan (FACTS Tuition Payment Plan, Tuition Management Systems). Need-based scholarship grants available. In 2015–16, 40% of upper-school students received aid.

Admissions Traditional secondary-level entrance grade is 9. For fall 2015, 364 students applied for upper-level admission, 117 were accepted, 72 enrolled. SSAT or TOEFL required. Deadline for receipt of application materials: none. Application fee required: $100. Interview required.

Athletics Interscholastic: baseball (boys), basketball (b,g), cross-country running (b,g), lacrosse (g), soccer (b,g), swimming and diving (b,g), tennis (b,g), track and field (b,g), volleyball (g), wrestling (b); coed interscholastic: badminton, golf, sailing; coed intramural: baseball, flag football, Frisbee, outdoor adventure, physical fitness, physical training, ultimate Frisbee, weight lifting. 1 PE instructor, 15 coaches.

Computers Computers are regularly used in computer applications, digital applications, foreign language, photography, programming classes. Computer network features include Internet access, wireless campus network, Internet filtering or blocking technology. Campus intranet and student e-mail accounts are available to students. Students grades are available online. The school has a published electronic and media policy.

Contact Mrs. Molly Shteierman, Admissions Counselor. 631-751-1800 Ext. 1. Fax: 631-751-4211. E-mail: admissions@stonybrookschool.org. Website: www.stonybrookschool.org

THE STORM KING SCHOOL

314 Mountain Road
Cornwall-on-Hudson, New York 12520-1899

Head of School: Mr. Jonathan W.R. Lamb

General Information Coeducational boarding and day college-preparatory and arts school. Grades 8–PG. Founded: 1867. Setting: small town. Nearest major city is New York. Students are housed in single-sex dormitories. 55-acre campus. 24 buildings on campus. Approved or accredited by Middle States Association of Colleges and Schools, New York State Association of Independent Schools, The Association of Boarding Schools, and New York Department of Education. Member of National Association of Independent Schools and Secondary School Admission Test Board. Endowment: $1 million. Total enrollment: 167. Upper school average class size: 12. Upper school faculty-student ratio: 1:4. There are 169 required school days per year for Upper School students. Upper School students typically attend 5 days per week. The average school day consists of 6 hours and 50 minutes.

Upper School Student Profile Grade 8: 13 students (4 boys, 9 girls); Grade 9: 37 students (20 boys, 17 girls); Grade 10: 30 students (21 boys, 9 girls); Grade 11: 42 students (26 boys, 16 girls); Grade 12: 45 students (31 boys, 14 girls). 82% of students

are boarding students. 24% are state residents. 5 states are represented in upper school student body. 65% are international students. International students from China, Germany, Ghana, Republic of Korea, Russian Federation, and Spain; 19 other countries represented in student body.

Faculty School total: 44. In upper school: 22 men, 20 women; 28 have advanced degrees; 19 reside on campus.

Subjects Offered 3-dimensional art, acting, Advanced Placement courses, advanced studio art-AP, advanced TOEFL/grammar, algebra, American history, American literature, American sign language, art, art history-AP, art-AP, astronomy, athletics, biology, biology-AP, British literature (honors), calculus, calculus-AP, chemistry, Chinese, choir, college counseling, college planning, community service, computer graphics, computer programming, computer programming-AP, computer science-AP, creative writing, dance, dance performance, digital art, drama, drawing, earth science, economics, economics-AP, English, English literature, English literature-AP, English-AP, environmental science, ESL, ESL, fine arts, foreign language, geometry, government/civics, guitar, health education, high adventure outdoor program, history, humanities, literacy, literature, macro/microeconomics-AP, macroeconomics-AP, Mandarin, mathematics, music, music composition, musical productions, outdoor education, painting, performing arts, photography, physics, physics-AP, piano, pre-calculus, psychology, psychology-AP, SAT preparation, science, Spanish, stage design, stagecraft, statistics-AP, student government, studio art-AP, theater, theater design and production, U.S. history, world history, world literature, writing, yearbook.

Graduation Requirements Biology, English, foreign language, mathematics, performing arts, science, social studies (includes history), visual arts, at least two community service, outdoor adventure, and cultural experiences per year. Community service is required.

Special Academic Programs 10 Advanced Placement exams for which test preparation is offered; honors section; academic accommodation for the gifted, the musically talented, and the artistically talented; remedial reading and/or remedial writing; programs in English, mathematics, general development for dyslexic students; ESL (69 students enrolled).

College Admission Counseling 38 students graduated in 2015; all went to college, including Bryn Mawr College; New York University; Pace University; Parsons School of Design; Penn State University Park; The University of Alabama. Median SAT critical reading: 480, median SAT math: 590, median SAT writing: 500, median combined SAT: 1570. 20% scored over 600 on SAT critical reading, 49% scored over 600 on SAT math, 26% scored over 600 on SAT writing, 34% scored over 1800 on combined SAT.

Student Life Upper grades have uniform requirement, student council, honor system. Discipline rests primarily with faculty.

Summer Programs ESL programs offered; session focuses on ESL and outdoor activities; held on campus; accepts boys and girls; open to students from other schools. 30 students usually enrolled. 2016 schedule: June 21 to August 6. Application deadline: April 1.

Tuition and Aid Day student tuition: $28,816; 7-day tuition and room/board: $53,945. Tuition installment plan (individually arranged payment plans). Merit scholarship grants, need based scholarship grants available. In 2015–16, 39% of upper-school students received aid; total upper-school merit-scholarship money awarded: $150,000. Total amount of financial aid awarded in 2015–16: $1,234,117.

Admissions Traditional secondary-level entrance grade is 9. For fall 2015, 236 students applied for upper-level admission, 136 were accepted, 59 enrolled. SSAT or WISC III or TOEFL or SLEP required. Deadline for receipt of application materials: none. Application fee required: $85. Interview required.

Athletics Interscholastic: baseball (boys), basketball (b,g), lacrosse (b,g), soccer (b,g), softball (g), tennis (b,g), volleyball (g), wrestling (b); coed interscholastic: crew, cross-country running, fencing, golf, mountain biking, rowing, running, skiing (downhill), snowboarding, ultimate Frisbee; coed intramural: aerobics/dance, alpine skiing, backpacking, ballet, bowling, canoeing/kayaking, climbing, dance, fitness, fitness walking, freestyle skiing, golf, hiking/backpacking, ice skating, jogging, kayaking, modern dance, mountaineering, Nautilus, outdoor activities, outdoor adventure, outdoor education, outdoor recreation, outdoor skills, outdoors, paddle tennis, physical fitness, physical training, power lifting, project adventure, rappelling, rock climbing, ropes courses, sailing, skiing (cross-country), skiing (downhill), snowboarding, snowshoeing, strength & conditioning, table tennis, tennis, touch football, walking, wall climbing, weight lifting, weight training, wilderness, winter walking, yoga. 3 coaches, 1 athletic trainer.

Computers Computers are regularly used in all academic, art, college planning, computer applications, drawing and design, economics, English, ESL, foreign language, graphic design, history, mathematics, music technology, photography, psychology, publications, video film production, writing, yearbook classes. Computer network features include on-campus library services, online commercial services, Internet access, wireless campus network, Internet filtering or blocking technology, parent/student/teacher communication portal. Campus intranet, student e-mail accounts, and computer access in designated common areas are available to students. Students grades are available online. The school has a published electronic and media policy.

Contact Mr. Marek Pramuka, Director of Admissions and Marketing. 845-458-7542. Fax: 845-534-4128. E-mail: mpramuka@sks.org. Website: www.sks.org

STRATFORD ACADEMY

6010 Peake Road
Macon, Georgia 31220-3903
Head of School: Dr. Robert E. Veto
General Information Coeducational day college-preparatory, arts, and technology school. Grades 1–12. Founded: 1960. Setting: suburban. Nearest major city is Atlanta. 70-acre campus. 4 buildings on campus. Approved or accredited by Georgia Independent School Association, Southern Association of Colleges and Schools, Southern Association of Independent Schools, and Georgia Department of Education. Member of National Association of Independent Schools. Endowment: $1 million. Total enrollment: 896. Upper school average class size: 17. Upper school faculty-student ratio: 1:13. There are 180 required school days per year for Upper School students. Upper School students typically attend 5 days per week. The average school day consists of 6 hours.
Faculty School total: 101. In upper school: 24 men, 23 women; 26 have advanced degrees.
Subjects Offered Advanced Placement courses, algebra, American history, American literature, anatomy, art, art history, art-AP, athletics, baseball, basketball, biology, biology-AP, calculus, calculus-AP, chemistry, chemistry-AP, community service, comparative government and politics-AP, computer programming, computer science, creative writing, drama, drama performance, driver education, earth science, economics, English, English literature, English literature-AP, English-AP, European history, European history-AP, expository writing, French, French-AP, geography, geometry, government/civics, grammar, history, history-AP, humanities, journalism, keyboarding, Latin, Latin-AP, Mandarin, mathematics, mathematics-AP, music, physical education, physical science, physics, pre-calculus, science, social sciences, social studies, sociology, Spanish, Spanish-AP, speech, speech and debate, theater, trigonometry, U.S. government and politics-AP, water color painting, world history, world literature, writing.
Graduation Requirements English, foreign language, math applications, mathematics, science, senior seminar, social sciences, social studies (includes history), community service. Community service is required.
Special Academic Programs Advanced Placement exam preparation; independent study; special instructional classes for students with learning disabilities, Attention Deficit Disorder, and dyslexia.
College Admission Counseling 72 students graduated in 2015; all went to college, including Auburn University; Brown University; Georgia Institute of Technology; Georgia Southern University; Mercer University; University of Georgia.
Student Life Upper grades have uniform requirement, student council, honor system. Discipline rests primarily with faculty.
Summer Programs Enrichment, sports, art/fine arts programs offered; held on campus; accepts boys and girls; open to students from other schools. 250 students usually enrolled.
Tuition and Aid Day student tuition: $13,640. Tuition installment plan (Insured Tuition Payment Plan, monthly payment plans, individually arranged payment plans). Merit scholarship grants, need-based scholarship grants available. Total upper-school merit-scholarship money awarded for 2015–16: $13,640.
Admissions Traditional secondary-level entrance grade is 9. ERB or Iowa Tests of Basic Skills required. Deadline for receipt of application materials: none. Application fee required: $50. On-campus interview required.
Athletics Interscholastic: aerobics (girls), aquatics (b,g), baseball (b), basketball (b,g), cheering (g), cross-country running (b,g), dance team (g), drill team (g), fitness (b,g), football (b), horseback riding (b,g), lacrosse (b,g), physical training (b,g), soccer (b,g), softball (b), tennis (b,g), track and field (b,g), volleyball (b), wrestling (b), yoga (g); coed interscholastic: badminton, golf, skeet shooting. 9 PE instructors, 6 coaches, 2 athletic trainers.
Computers Computers are regularly used in art, creative writing, English, French, graphics, information technology, Spanish classes. Computer network features include on-campus library services, Internet access, wireless campus network. Computer access in designated common areas is available to students. The school has a published electronic and media policy.
Contact Ms. Lori Palmer, Director of Admissions. 478-477-8073 Ext. 203. Fax: 478-477-0299. E-mail: lori.palmer@stratford.org. Website: www.stratford.org

STRATHCONA-TWEEDSMUIR SCHOOL

RR 2
Okotoks, Alberta T1S 1A2, Canada
Head of School: Mr. William Jones
General Information Coeducational day college-preparatory, arts, and technology school. Grades 1–12. Founded: 1905. Setting: rural. Nearest major city is Calgary, Canada. 200-acre campus. 1 building on campus. Approved or accredited by Canadian Association of Independent Schools, Canadian Educational Standards Institute, International Baccalaureate Organization, and Alberta Department of Education. Affiliate member of National Association of Independent Schools; member of Secondary School Admission Test Board. Language of instruction: English. Endowment: CAN$5 million. Total enrollment: 672. Upper school average class size: 20. Upper school faculty-student ratio: 1:9. There are 174 required school days per year

for Upper School students. Upper School students typically attend 5 days per week. The average school day consists of 6 hours and 40 minutes.
Upper School Student Profile Grade 10: 79 students (36 boys, 43 girls); Grade 11: 70 students (30 boys, 40 girls); Grade 12: 81 students (43 boys, 38 girls).
Faculty School total: 80. In upper school: 24 men, 19 women; 15 have advanced degrees.
Subjects Offered Art, band, biology, calculus, chemistry, computer science, design, drama, English, fine arts, French, Latin, mathematics, music, outdoor education, physical education, physics, science, social sciences, social studies, Spanish, theater.
Graduation Requirements Arts and fine arts (art, music, dance, drama), business skills (includes word processing), English, foreign language, mathematics, physical education (includes health), science, social sciences, social studies (includes history).
Special Academic Programs International Baccalaureate program; term-away projects.
College Admission Counseling 69 students graduated in 2014; 66 went to college, including Dalhousie University; Queen's University at Kingston; The University of British Columbia; The University of Western Ontario; University of Alberta; University of Victoria. Other: 3 had other specific plans.
Student Life Upper grades have uniform requirement, student council, honor system. Discipline rests primarily with faculty.
Tuition and Aid Day student tuition: CAN$15,760–CAN$18,090. Tuition installment plan (monthly payment plans). Bursaries, merit scholarship grants, need-based scholarship grants available. In 2014–15, 10% of upper-school students received aid; total upper-school merit-scholarship money awarded: CAN$167,000.
Admissions Traditional secondary-level entrance grade is 10. CTBS, OLSAT, Differential Aptitude Test, Henmon-Nelson or SSAT required. Deadline for receipt of application materials: none. Application fee required: CAN$100. Interview required.
Athletics Interscholastic: badminton (boys, girls), basketball (b,g), canoeing/kayaking (b,g), cross-country running (b,g), fencing (b,g), field hockey (g), golf (b,g), hiking/backpacking (b,g), jump rope (b,g), nordic skiing (b,g), outdoor activities (b,g), outdoor education (b,g), rugby (b), soccer (g), telemark skiing (b,g), track and field (b,g), triathlon (b,g), volleyball (b,g), wall climbing (b,g); coed interscholastic: alpine skiing, backpacking, badminton, canoeing/kayaking, climbing, cross-country running, hiking/backpacking, jump rope, mountain biking, mountaineering, nordic skiing, outdoor activities, outdoor education; coed intramural: badminton, basketball, volleyball. 10 PE instructors, 38 coaches, 2 athletic trainers.
Computers Computers are regularly used in all classes. Computer network features include on-campus library services, online commercial services, Internet access, wireless campus network, Internet filtering or blocking technology. Campus intranet and student e-mail accounts are available to students. Students grades are available online. The school has a published electronic and media policy.
Contact Ms. Lydia J. Hawkins, Director of Enrollment. 403-938-8303. Fax: 403-938-4492. E-mail: hawkinl@sts.ab.ca. Website: www.sts.ab.ca

STRATTON MOUNTAIN SCHOOL

World Cup Circle
Stratton Mountain, Vermont 05155
Head of School: Christopher G. Kaltsas
General Information Coeducational boarding and day college-preparatory, arts, bilingual studies, and technology school. Grades 7–PG. Founded: 1972. Setting: rural. Nearest major city is Albany, NY. Students are housed in single-sex by floor dormitories. 12-acre campus. 7 buildings on campus. Approved or accredited by New England Association of Schools and Colleges and Vermont Department of Education. Member of National Association of Independent Schools. Endowment: $2.4 million. Total enrollment: 134. Upper school average class size: 10. Upper school faculty-student ratio: 1:6. There are 170 required school days per year for Upper School students. Upper School students typically attend 5 days per week. The average school day consists of 5 hours.
Upper School Student Profile Grade 9: 21 students (11 boys, 10 girls); Grade 10: 28 students (18 boys, 10 girls); Grade 11: 28 students (14 boys, 14 girls); Grade 12: 29 students (18 boys, 11 girls); Postgraduate: 5 students (3 boys, 2 girls). 57% of students are boarding students. 46% are state residents. 22 states are represented in upper school student body. 5% are international students. International students from Australia, Canada, Italy, Japan, Poland, and Russian Federation; 3 other countries represented in student body.
Faculty School total: 21. In upper school: 7 men, 10 women; 8 have advanced degrees; 8 reside on campus.
Subjects Offered Algebra, American history, American literature, art, biology, calculus, chemistry, computer science, English, English literature, environmental science, French, geography, geometry, grammar, health, history, journalism, mathematics, nutrition, physical education, physics, science, social studies, Spanish, world history.
Graduation Requirements Arts and fine arts (art, music, dance, drama), computer education, English, foreign language, health education, mathematics, science, social studies (includes history), superior competence in winter sports (skiing/snowboarding). Community service is required.
Special Academic Programs Honors section; independent study; ESL (3 students enrolled).

College Admission Counseling 15 students graduated in 2014; 13 went to college, including Dartmouth College; Harvard University; Middlebury College; University of Colorado Boulder; University of New Hampshire; University of Vermont. Other: 2 entered a postgraduate year. Mean SAT critical reading: 580, mean SAT math: 570, mean SAT writing: 600, mean combined SAT: 1750. 32% scored over 600 on SAT critical reading, 21% scored over 600 on SAT math, 47% scored over 600 on SAT writing, 42% scored over 1800 on combined SAT.

Student Life Upper grades have specified standards of dress, student council, honor system. Discipline rests primarily with faculty.

Tuition and Aid Day student tuition: $35,000; 7-day tuition and room/board: $48,000. Tuition installment plan (choice of one or two tuition installments plus advance deposit). Need-based scholarship grants, need-based loans available. In 2014–15, 46% of upper-school students received aid. Total amount of financial aid awarded in 2014–15: $760,000.

Admissions Traditional secondary-level entrance grade is 9. For fall 2014, 70 students applied for upper-level admission, 46 were accepted, 38 enrolled. Math Placement Exam required. Deadline for receipt of application materials: March 15. Application fee required: $100. On-campus interview required.

Athletics Interscholastic: alpine skiing (boys, girls), bicycling (b,g), cross-country running (b,g), freestyle skiing (b,g), golf (b,g), lacrosse (b,g), mountain biking (b,g), nordic skiing (b,g), skiing (cross-country) (b,g), skiing (downhill) (b,g), snowboarding (b,g), soccer (b,g), tennis (b,g); intramural: strength & conditioning (b,g), tennis (b,g), yoga (b,g); coed intramural: skateboarding, tennis, yoga. 24 coaches, 1 athletic trainer.

Computers Computers are regularly used in computer applications, graphic design, mathematics, media production, research skills, science, Web site design, yearbook classes. Computer network features include on-campus library services, online commercial services, Internet access, wireless campus network, Internet filtering or blocking technology. Campus intranet, student e-mail accounts, and computer access in designated common areas are available to students. Students grades are available online. The school has a published electronic and media policy.

Contact Mrs. Kate Nolan Joyce, Director of Admissions. 802-856-1124. Fax: 802-297-0020. E-mail: knolan@gosms.org. Website: www.gosms.org

STUART HALL

235 West Frederick Street
PO Box 210
Staunton, Virginia 24401

Head of School: Mr. Mark H. Eastham

General Information Coeducational boarding and day college-preparatory, arts, and technology school, affiliated with Episcopal Church. Boarding grades 8–12, day grades PK–12. Founded: 1844. Setting: small town. Nearest major city is Richmond. Students are housed in single-sex dormitories. 8-acre campus. 7 buildings on campus. Approved or accredited by National Association of Episcopal Schools, Virginia Association of Independent Schools, and Virginia Department of Education. Member of National Association of Independent Schools and Secondary School Admission Test Board. Endowment: $5.5 million. Total enrollment: 302. Upper school average class size: 12. Upper school faculty-student ratio: 1:8. There are 172 required school days per year for Upper School students. Upper School students typically attend 5 days per week. The average school day consists of 7 hours and 20 minutes.

Upper School Student Profile Grade 9: 39 students (18 boys, 21 girls); Grade 10: 38 students (15 boys, 23 girls); Grade 11: 30 students (9 boys, 21 girls); Grade 12: 32 students (12 boys, 20 girls). 60% of students are boarding students. 46% are state residents. 14 states are represented in upper school student body. 43% are international students. International students from China, Rwanda, and Viet Nam; 13 other countries represented in student body. 10% of students are members of Episcopal Church.

Faculty School total: 38. In upper school: 9 men, 14 women; 20 have advanced degrees; 15 reside on campus.

Subjects Offered Algebra, American literature, ancient world history, applied arts, applied music, art appreciation, art history, biology, biology-AP, British literature, calculus-AP, career education, career/college preparation, ceramics, chamber groups, chemistry, chemistry-AP, choir, choral music, chorus, civics, college counseling, composition, creative writing, drama, drama performance, dramatic arts, English, English composition, English language and composition-AP, English literature-AP, English-AP, entrepreneurship, environmental science, environmental science-AP, ESL, fine arts, French, geometry, grammar, guitar, health education, history of drama, history of music, history-AP, honors algebra, honors English, honors geometry, honors world history, instrumental music, lab science, language and composition, leadership, learning lab, mathematics, modern world history, music, music composition, music history, music performance, music theater, music theory, philosophy, photography, physical education, physical fitness, physics, piano, playwriting and directing, portfolio art, pre-algebra, pre-calculus, probability and statistics, religion, SAT preparation, science, social studies, Spanish, Spanish language-AP, Spanish-AP, stage and body movement, stage design, strings, student government, student publications, study skills, theater, theater arts, theater history, theater production, trigonometry, U.S. government, U.S. government and politics-AP, U.S. history, U.S. history-AP, visual and performing arts, visual arts, vocal ensemble, vocal music, voice, voice ensemble, world geography, world history, world history-AP, world literature, yearbook.

Graduation Requirements Arts and fine arts (art, music, dance, drama), English, foreign language, mathematics, philosophy, physical education (includes health), religion (includes Bible studies and theology), SAT preparation, science, social studies (includes history).

Special Academic Programs Advanced Placement exam preparation; honors section; study at local college for college credit; academic accommodation for the gifted, the musically talented, and the artistically talented; ESL (24 students enrolled).

College Admission Counseling 33 students graduated in 2015; all went to college, including James Madison University; Roanoke College; The College of William and Mary; University of Virginia; Virginia Commonwealth University; Virginia Polytechnic Institute and State University. Mean SAT critical reading: 577, mean SAT math: 567, mean SAT writing: 561.

Student Life Upper grades have specified standards of dress, student council, honor system. Discipline rests equally with students and faculty.

Tuition and Aid Day student tuition: $15,100; 5-day tuition and room/board: $33,000; 7-day tuition and room/board: $48,000. Tuition installment plan (Insured Tuition Payment Plan, monthly payment plans, individually arranged payment plans). Merit scholarship grants, need-based scholarship grants available. In 2015–16, 37% of upper-school students received aid; total upper-school merit-scholarship money awarded: $30,000. Total amount of financial aid awarded in 2015–16: $1,400,000.

Admissions Traditional secondary-level entrance grade is 9. For fall 2015, 50 students applied for upper-level admission, 40 were accepted, 34 enrolled. SSAT, TOEFL Junior or TOEFL or SLEP required. Deadline for receipt of application materials: none. Application fee required: $45. Interview required.

Athletics Interscholastic: basketball (boys, girls), cheering (g), golf (b,g), jogging (b,g), soccer (b,g), volleyball (g); intramural: cheering (g), skiing (downhill) (b,g), snowboarding (b,g); coed interscholastic: cross-country running, running, soccer; coed intramural: golf. 1 PE instructor, 1 coach.

Computers Computers are regularly used in all classes. Computer network features include on-campus library services, Internet access, wireless campus network, Internet filtering or blocking technology. Student e-mail accounts and computer access in designated common areas are available to students. Students grades are available online. The school has a published electronic and media policy.

Contact Ms. Alisa Loughlin, Enrollment and Database Coordinator. 540-213-3726. Fax: 540-886-2275. E-mail: aloughlin@stuart-hall.org. Website: www.stuarthallschool.org

THE STUDY

3233 The Boulevard
Westmount, Montreal, Quebec H3Y 1S4, Canada

Head of School: Nancy Sweer

General Information Girls' day college-preparatory, arts, bilingual studies, technology, and science school. Grades K–11. Founded: 1915. Setting: urban. Nearest major city is Montreal, Canada. 2 buildings on campus. Approved or accredited by Canadian Association of Independent Schools, Quebec Association of Independent Schools, and Quebec Department of Education. Affiliate member of National Association of Independent Schools. Languages of instruction: English and French. Endowment: CAN$8 million. Total enrollment: 327. Upper school average class size: 18. Upper school faculty-student ratio: 1:8. There are 180 required school days per year for Upper School students. Upper School students typically attend 5 days per week. The average school day consists of 7 hours.

Faculty School total: 60. In upper school: 1 man, 28 women; 8 have advanced degrees.

Subjects Offered Algebra, art, art history, arts appreciation, biology, chemistry, computer science, ecology, economics, English, entrepreneurship, environmental science, ethics, European history, French, gender issues, geography, geometry, history, Mandarin, mathematics, music, philosophy, physical education, physics, religion and culture, science, social studies, Spanish, stagecraft, technology, theater, world history.

Graduation Requirements English, ethics, foreign language, French, mathematics, physical education (includes health), science, social studies (includes history), technology. Community service is required.

Special Academic Programs Advanced Placement exam preparation; academic accommodation for the gifted.

Student Life Upper grades have uniform requirement, student council, honor system. Discipline rests primarily with faculty.

Tuition and Aid Day student tuition: CAN$17,285. Tuition installment plan (monthly payment plans, individually arranged payment plans, 2-payment plan). Tuition reduction for siblings, bursaries, merit scholarship grants, need-based scholarship grants available. In 2015–16, 15% of upper-school students received aid. Total amount of financial aid awarded in 2015–16: CAN$400,000.

Admissions Traditional secondary-level entrance grade is 7. Admissions testing, CAT, common entrance examinations, English, French, and math proficiency or school's own test required. Deadline for receipt of application materials: none. Application fee required: CAN$50. Interview required.

Athletics Interscholastic: alpine skiing, badminton, basketball, crew, cross-country running, flag football, golf, hockey, ice hockey, rowing, running, skiing (cross-country), soccer, swimming and diving, tennis, touch football, track and field, volleyball; intramural: aerobics, aerobics/dance, aerobics/Nautilus, aquatics, badminton, ballet, basketball, bicycling, cooperative games, dance, fitness, ice hockey, indoor hockey,

jump rope, martial arts, outdoor activities, soccer, squash, swimming and diving, tennis, touch football, track and field, ultimate Frisbee, volleyball. 4 PE instructors, 8 coaches.
Computers Computers are regularly used in art, college planning, engineering, English, French, history, mathematics, photography, science, technology, video film production classes. Computer network features include on-campus library services, Internet access, wireless campus network, Internet filtering or blocking technology. Campus intranet, student e-mail accounts, and computer access in designated common areas are available to students. Students grades are available online. The school has a published electronic and media policy.
Contact Antonia Zannis, Deputy Head of School. 514-935-9352 Ext. 260. Fax: 514-935-1721. E-mail: admissions@thestudy.qc.ca. Website: www.thestudy.qc.ca

SUBIACO ACADEMY
405 North Subiaco Avenue
Subiaco, Arkansas 72865
Head of School: Mr. Matthew C. Stengel
General Information Boys' boarding and day college-preparatory, arts, religious studies, bilingual studies, technology, and art and performing art school, affiliated with Roman Catholic Church. Grades 7–12. Founded: 1887. Setting: rural. Nearest major city is Fort Smith. Students are housed in single-sex dormitories. 100-acre campus. 10 buildings on campus. Approved or accredited by Independent Schools Association of the Central States, National Catholic Education Association, North Central Association of Colleges and Schools, The Association of Boarding Schools, and Arkansas Department of Education. Member of National Association of Independent Schools. Endowment: $3.5 million. Total enrollment: 199. Upper school average class size: 15. Upper school faculty-student ratio: 1:9. There are 179 required school days per year for Upper School students. Upper School students typically attend 5 days per week. The average school day consists of 6 hours and 25 minutes.
Upper School Student Profile Grade 7: 10 students (10 boys); Grade 8: 15 students (15 boys); Grade 9: 37 students (37 boys); Grade 10: 47 students (47 boys); Grade 11: 50 students (50 boys); Grade 12: 40 students (40 boys). 60% of students are boarding students. 57% are state residents. 18 states are represented in upper school student body. 17% are international students. International students from China, Japan, Mexico, Nigeria, Republic of Korea, and Viet Nam; 3 other countries represented in student body. 65% of students are Roman Catholic.
Faculty School total: 31. In upper school: 21 men, 10 women; 18 have advanced degrees; 9 reside on campus.
Subjects Offered Algebra, American history, American history-AP, art, art-AP, band, biology, biology-AP, broadcasting, calculus, calculus-AP, chemistry, chemistry-AP, choral music, chorus, Christian doctrine, Christian education, Christian scripture, Christian studies, Christian testament, church history, communications, computer art, computer science, drama, drama workshop, driver education, earth and space science, earth science, economics, English, English literature, English literature and composition-AP, English-AP, finance, fine arts, geography, geometry, government/civics, jazz ensemble, journalism, Latin, mathematics-AP, music, physical education, physics, piano, psychology, religion, sociology, Spanish, speech, statistics-AP, Western civilization, world history.
Graduation Requirements Arts and fine arts (art, music, dance, drama), computer science, English, foreign language, mathematics, physical education (includes health), religion (includes Bible studies and theology), science, social studies (includes history), Western civilization. Community service is required.
Special Academic Programs 8 Advanced Placement exams for which test preparation is offered; honors section; academic accommodation for the gifted, the musically talented, and the artistically talented; ESL (11 students enrolled).
College Admission Counseling 35 students graduated in 2014; all went to college, including Hendrix College; Penn State University Park; Rhodes College; Texas Christian University; University of Arkansas; University of Dallas. Median SAT critical reading: 544, median SAT math: 672, median SAT writing: 544, median combined SAT: 1760, median composite ACT: 25.
Student Life Upper grades have uniform requirement, student council, honor system. Discipline rests primarily with faculty. Attendance at religious services is required.
Tuition and Aid Day student tuition: $7250; 5-day tuition and room/board; $21,500; 7-day tuition and room/board: $24,000. Tuition installment plan (monthly payment plans, individually arranged payment plans). Need-based scholarship grants available. In 2014–15, 35% of upper-school students received aid. Total amount of financial aid awarded in 2014–15: $425,610.
Admissions Traditional secondary-level entrance grade is 9. For fall 2014, 70 students applied for upper-level admission, 54 were accepted, 46 enrolled. International English Language Test or TOEFL required. Deadline for receipt of application materials: none. Application fee required: $50. Interview required.
Athletics Interscholastic: baseball, basketball, cross-country running, football, golf, soccer, tennis, track and field; intramural: backpacking, cross-country running, fishing, Frisbee, handball, hiking/backpacking, outdoor activities, skateboarding, soccer. 1 PE instructor, 12 coaches.
Computers Computers are regularly used in art, Christian doctrine, commercial art, creative writing, desktop publishing, digital applications, drawing and design, economics, English, geography, graphic arts, history, journalism, keyboarding, literary magazine, mathematics, news writing, newspaper, photography, photojournalism,

publications, religion, religious studies, SAT preparation, science, Spanish, stock market, video film production, word processing, writing, yearbook classes. Computer network features include on-campus library services, Internet access, wireless campus network, Internet filtering or blocking technology. Computer access in designated common areas is available to students. Students grades are available online. The school has a published electronic and media policy.
Contact Ms. Evelyn Bauer, Assistant Director of Admissions. 479-934-1034. Fax: 479-934-1033. E-mail: ebauer@subi.org. Website: www.SubiacoAcademy.us

THE SUDBURY VALLEY SCHOOL
2 Winch Street
Framingham, Massachusetts 01701
Head of School: Olivia Charles
General Information Coeducational day college-preparatory and general academic school. Grades PS–12. Founded: 1968. Setting: suburban. Nearest major city is Boston. 10-acre campus. 2 buildings on campus. Approved or accredited by Massachusetts Department of Education. Total enrollment: 160. Upper school faculty-student ratio: 1:16. There are 180 required school days per year for Upper School students. Upper School students typically attend 5 days per week. The average school day consists of 6 hours.
Faculty School total: 9. In upper school: 4 men, 5 women; 3 have advanced degrees.
Subjects Offered Algebra, American history, American literature, anatomy, anthropology, archaeology, art, art history, Bible studies, biology, botany, business, calculus, ceramics, chemistry, computer programming, computer science, creative writing, dance, drama, economics, English, English literature, ethics, European history, expository writing, French, geography, geometry, German, government/civics, grammar, Hebrew, history, history of ideas, history of science, home economics, Latin, mathematics, music, philosophy, photography, physical education, physics, physiology, psychology, religion, social studies, Spanish, speech, theater, trigonometry, typing, world history, world literature, writing.
Graduation Requirements Students must justify the proposition that they have developed the problem solving skill, the adaptability, and the abilities needed to function, independently in the world.
Special Academic Programs Independent study.
College Admission Counseling 6 students graduated in 2015; 4 went to college. Other: 2 went to work.
Student Life Upper grades have student council, honor system. Discipline rests equally with students and faculty.
Tuition and Aid Day student tuition: $8700. Tuition reduction for siblings available.
Admissions Deadline for receipt of application materials: none. Application fee required: $50. On-campus interview required.
Computers Computer network features include on-campus library services, Internet access. Student e-mail accounts are available to students. The school has a published electronic and media policy.
Contact Hanna Greenberg, Admissions Clerk. 508-877-3030. Fax: 508-788-0674. E-mail: office@sudval.org. Website: www.sudval.org

SUMMERFIELD WALDORF SCHOOL
655 Willowside Road
Santa Rosa, California 95401
Head of School: Mr. Bob Flagg
General Information Coeducational day college-preparatory, arts, and Waldorf curriculum school. Grades K–12. Founded: 1974. Setting: rural. 38-acre campus. 8 buildings on campus. Approved or accredited by Association of Waldorf Schools of North America, Western Association of Schools and Colleges, and California Department of Education. Total enrollment: 409. Upper school average class size: 28. Upper school faculty-student ratio: 1:7. Upper School students typically attend 5 days per week. The average school day consists of 7 hours.
Faculty School total: 23. In upper school: 11 men, 12 women; all have advanced degrees.
Subjects Offered Advanced chemistry, arts, history, humanities, literature, mathematics, music, science.
Graduation Requirements All, senior thesis project.
Special Academic Programs Honors section; study abroad.
College Admission Counseling 22 students graduated in 2015; 21 went to college, including Bennington College; Cornell University; Oberlin College; Sonoma State University; University of California, Davis; University of Redlands. Other: 1 went to work.
Student Life Upper grades have specified standards of dress, student council, honor system. Discipline rests primarily with faculty.
Tuition and Aid Day student tuition: $17,000. Tuition installment plan (FACTS Tuition Payment Plan, monthly payment plans). Tuition reduction for siblings, need-based scholarship grants available. In 2015–16, 40% of upper-school students received aid.

Admissions Traditional secondary-level entrance grade is 9. For fall 2015, 56 students applied for upper-level admission, 38 were accepted, 34 enrolled. Deadline for receipt of application materials: January 16. Application fee required: $75. On-campus interview required.

Athletics Interscholastic: basketball (boys, girls), soccer (b,g), volleyball (b,g); coed interscholastic: tennis. 5 PE instructors, 5 coaches.

Computers The school has a published electronic and media policy.

Contact Ms. Sallie Miller, Admissions Director. 707-575-7194 Ext. 102. Fax: 707-575-3217. E-mail: sallie@summerfieldwaldof.org. Website: http://www.summerfieldws.org/home/

THE SUMMIT COUNTRY DAY SCHOOL

2161 Grandin Road
Cincinnati, Ohio 45208-3300

Head of School: Mr. Rich Wilson

General Information Coeducational day college-preparatory school, affiliated with Roman Catholic Church. Grades PK–12. Founded: 1890. Setting: suburban. 24-acre campus. 4 buildings on campus. Approved or accredited by Independent Schools Association of the Central States, Ohio Association of Independent Schools, The College Board, and Ohio Department of Education. Member of National Association of Independent Schools. Endowment: $20 million. Total enrollment: 1,011. Upper school average class size: 16. Upper school faculty-student ratio: 1:9. There are 187 required school days per year for Upper School students. Upper School students typically attend 5 days per week. The average school day consists of 7 hours.

Upper School Student Profile Grade 9: 108 students (61 boys, 47 girls); Grade 10: 107 students (58 boys, 49 girls); Grade 11: 90 students (46 boys, 44 girls); Grade 12: 93 students (36 boys, 57 girls). 60% of students are Roman Catholic.

Faculty School total: 136. In upper school: 14 men, 23 women; 33 have advanced degrees.

Subjects Offered Advanced Placement courses, algebra, American history, American history-AP, American literature, anatomy and physiology, archaeology, art, biology, biology-AP, business law, calculus, calculus-AP, ceramics, chemistry, chemistry-AP, chorus, college admission preparation, college placement, community service, computer applications, computer science, computer science-AP, concert choir, critical studies in film, drama, economics, English, English literature, English-AP, environmental science, European history, European history-AP, fine arts, French, French-AP, geometry, government-AP, government/civics, grammar, graphic design, Greek, health, history, history of science, history-AP, Holocaust studies, language-AP, Latin, Latin-AP, leadership, leadership and service, leadership education training, literary magazine, mathematics, music, music theory-AP, music-AP, philosophy, physical education, physics, physics-AP, pre-calculus, psychology, psychology-AP, public speaking, religion, religious studies, science, senior career experience, service learning/internship, social studies, Spanish, Spanish language-AP, Spanish-AP, speech, speech communications, statistics-AP, student government, studio art, studio art-AP, study skills, theater, trigonometry, U.S. government and politics-AP, world history, world history-AP, world literature, world religions, writing.

Graduation Requirements Arts and fine arts (art, music, dance, drama), computer applications, computer science, English, foreign language, mathematics, physical education (includes health), religion (includes Bible studies and theology), science, social sciences, social studies (includes history), speech communications, junior year leadership course (one semester), junior year speech course, 40 hours of community service, senior search (2-week field experience in career of interest area).

Special Academic Programs 19 Advanced Placement exams for which test preparation is offered; honors section; independent study; study abroad; academic accommodation for the gifted and the artistically talented.

College Admission Counseling 98 students graduated in 2015; 97 went to college, including Boston College; Miami University; The Ohio State University; University of Cincinnati; University of Richmond; Vanderbilt University. Other: 1 entered a postgraduate year. Median SAT critical reading: 631, median SAT math: 609, median composite ACT: 28.

Student Life Upper grades have uniform requirement, student council, honor system. Discipline rests equally with students and faculty. Attendance at religious services is required.

Summer Programs Enrichment, advancement, sports, art/fine arts, computer instruction programs offered; session focuses on enrichment, academic advancement; held both on and off campus; held at 16-acre athletic sports complex; accepts boys and girls; open to students from other schools. 2016 schedule: June 7 to August 15. Application deadline: none.

Tuition and Aid Day student tuition: $19,825–$20,550. Tuition installment plan (Insured Tuition Payment Plan, monthly payment plans, individually arranged payment plans). Merit scholarship grants, need-based scholarship grants available. In 2015–16, 50% of upper-school students received aid.

Admissions Traditional secondary-level entrance grade is 9. For fall 2015, 285 students applied for upper-level admission, 173 were accepted, 50 enrolled. High School Placement Test or ISEE required. Deadline for receipt of application materials: December 15. Application fee required: $50. On-campus interview required.

Athletics Interscholastic: baseball (boys, girls), basketball (b,g), bowling (b,g), cheering (g), cross-country running (b,g), diving (b,g), field hockey (g), football (b),

golf (b,g), lacrosse (b), soccer (b,g), softball (g), swimming and diving (b,g), tennis (b,g), track and field (b,g), volleyball (g), wrestling (b); intramural: dance team (g); coed interscholastic: weight lifting. 52 coaches, 1 athletic trainer.

Computers Computers are regularly used in all classes. Computer network features include on-campus library services, online commercial services, Internet access, wireless campus network, Internet filtering or blocking technology, mobile laptop computer lab, school-wide PORTAL/grades, Sketchpad, 8 full-text databases including Big Chalk, World Book, Children's Lit, SIRS, Biography Resource Center, Wilson Web, INFOhio, JSTOR. Campus intranet, student e-mail accounts, and computer access in designated common areas are available to students. Students grades are available online. The school has a published electronic and media policy.

Contact Mrs. Kelley Schiess, Assistant Head of School for Enrollment Management and Special Projects. 513-871-4700 Ext. 207. Fax: 513-533-5350. E-mail: schiess_k@summitcds.org. Website: www.summitcds.org

SUMMIT PREPARATORY SCHOOL

Kalispell, Montana
See Special Needs Schools section.

SUNSHINE BIBLE ACADEMY

400 Sunshine Drive
Miller, South Dakota 57362-6821

Head of School: Mr. Jason Watson

General Information Coeducational boarding and day college-preparatory, general academic, arts, business, vocational, religious studies, bilingual studies, and technology school, affiliated with Christian faith. Boarding grades 8–12, day grades K–12. Founded: 1951. Setting: rural. Nearest major city is Pierre. Students are housed in single-sex dormitories. 160-acre campus. 6 buildings on campus. Approved or accredited by Association of Christian Schools International and South Dakota Department of Education. Total enrollment: 85. Upper school average class size: 28. Upper school faculty-student ratio: 1:9. There are 175 required school days per year for Upper School students. Upper School students typically attend 5 days per week. The average school day consists of 6 hours and 40 minutes.

Upper School Student Profile Grade 9: 16 students (8 boys, 8 girls); Grade 10: 15 students (5 boys, 10 girls); Grade 11: 17 students (7 boys, 10 girls); Grade 12: 10 students (4 boys, 6 girls). 91% of students are boarding students. 70% are state residents. 6 states are represented in upper school student body. 15% are international students. International students from Ethiopia and Republic of Korea; 2 other countries represented in student body. 100% of students are Christian faith.

Faculty School total: 15. In upper school: 8 men, 3 women; 4 have advanced degrees; all reside on campus.

Subjects Offered Accounting, advanced math, agriculture, algebra, American history, American literature, band, bell choir, Bible, Bible studies, biology, chemistry, choir, Christian doctrine, Christian ethics, computer science, creative writing, drama, drama performance, economics, English, English literature, ethics, fine arts, geography, geometry, government/civics, grammar, health, history, HTML design, journalism, mathematics, music, music appreciation, music composition, music history, music performance, newspaper, physical education, physics, science, social sciences, social studies, Spanish, speech, speech and oral interpretations, trigonometry, typing, U.S. government, U.S. history, vocal music, world geography, world history, writing, yearbook.

Graduation Requirements Arts and fine arts (art, music, dance, drama), Bible, computer science, English, mathematics, science, social sciences, social studies (includes history).

Special Academic Programs Independent study; study at local college for college credit; academic accommodation for the musically talented; remedial math.

College Admission Counseling 18 students graduated in 2015; 16 went to college, including Dordt College; South Dakota State University; The University of South Dakota; University of Sioux Falls. Other: 2 went to work. Median composite ACT: 23. 25% scored over 26 on composite ACT.

Student Life Upper grades have specified standards of dress, student council, honor system. Discipline rests primarily with faculty. Attendance at religious services is required.

Tuition and Aid Day student tuition: $5965; 5-day tuition and room/board: $8350; 7-day tuition and room/board: $8350. Tuition installment plan (monthly payment plans). Tuition reduction for siblings, need-based scholarship grants available. In 2015–16, 20% of upper-school students received aid. Total amount of financial aid awarded in 2015–16: $38,520.

Admissions Traditional secondary-level entrance grade is 9. For fall 2015, 32 students applied for upper-level admission, 31 were accepted, 27 enrolled. Deadline for receipt of application materials: none. Application fee required: $50. On-campus interview required.

Athletics Interscholastic: basketball (boys, girls), cheering (g), cross-country running (b,g), football (b), track and field (b,g), volleyball (g), wrestling (b); intramural: physical fitness (b,g), physical training (b,g), strength & conditioning (b,g), weight lifting (b,g), weight training (b,g). 1 PE instructor, 6 coaches.

Computers Computers are regularly used in art, journalism, newspaper, publications, publishing, research skills, speech, typing, Web site design, writing, yearbook classes. Computer resources include on-campus library services, Internet access, wireless campus network, Internet filtering or blocking technology. Student e-mail accounts are available to students.

Contact Mr. Wes McClure, Dean of Students. 605-853-3071 Ext. 227. Fax: 605-853-3072. E-mail: wes.mcclure@k12.sd.us. Website: www.sunshinebible.org

THE TAFT SCHOOL
110 Woodbury Road
Watertown, Connecticut 06795
Head of School: Mr. William R. MacMullen

General Information Coeducational boarding and day college-preparatory, arts, and humanities school. Grades 9–PG. Founded: 1890. Setting: small town. Nearest major city is Waterbury. Students are housed in single-sex dormitories. 226-acre campus. 20 buildings on campus. Approved or accredited by New England Association of Schools and Colleges, The Association of Boarding Schools, The College Board, and Connecticut Department of Education. Member of National Association of Independent Schools and Secondary School Admission Test Board. Endowment: $236 million. Total enrollment: 594. Upper school average class size: 11. Upper school faculty-student ratio: 1:5. There are 176 required school days per year for Upper School students. Upper School students typically attend 6 days per week. The average school day consists of 7 hours.

Upper School Student Profile Grade 9: 108 students (51 boys, 57 girls); Grade 10: 150 students (75 boys, 75 girls); Grade 11: 157 students (77 boys, 80 girls); Grade 12: 178 students (89 boys, 89 girls). 82% of students are boarding students. 37% are state residents. 47 states are represented in upper school student body. 20% are international students. International students from Bermuda, Canada, China, Hong Kong, Republic of Korea, and Viet Nam; 41 other countries represented in student body.

Faculty School total: 124. In upper school: 65 men, 59 women; 97 have advanced degrees; 118 reside on campus.

Subjects Offered Acting, adolescent issues, advanced biology, advanced chemistry, advanced computer applications, advanced math, Advanced Placement courses, advanced studio art-AP, African-American literature, algebra, American history, American history-AP, American literature, anatomy, anatomy and physiology, animal behavior, architectural drawing, architecture, art, art history, art history-AP, astronomy, biology, biology-AP, calculus, calculus-AP, ceramics, chamber groups, character education, chemistry, chemistry-AP, Chinese, computer math, computer programming, computer science, computer science-AP, concert choir, creative writing, dance, design, digital imaging, drama, drawing, ecology, economics, economics-AP, English, English literature, English literature-AP, environmental science, environmental science AP, ethics, European history, European history-AP, expository writing, film studies, fine arts, forensics, French, French language-AP, geography, geology, geometry, government-AP, government/civics, grammar, Greek, history, history of rock and roll, history of science, honors algebra, honors English, honors geometry, human rights, humanities, Islamic studies, Japanese, jazz band, Latin, Mandarin, marine biology, mathematics, music, music theory-AP, philosophy, photography, physical education, physics, physics-AP, physiology, pre-calculus, psychology, religion, science, senior project, senior thesis, service learning/internship, sex education, South African history, Spanish, Spanish literature-AP, Spanish-AP, speech, statistics, statistics-AP, studio art-AP, theater, theology, trigonometry, U.S. government and politics-AP, U.S. history-AP, video film production, world history, world literature, writing, zoology.

Graduation Requirements American history, arts and fine arts (art, music, dance, drama), English, foreign language, mathematics, science, social studies (includes history), three semesters of arts.

Special Academic Programs 29 Advanced Placement exams for which test preparation is offered; honors section; independent study; term-away projects; study abroad; academic accommodation for the gifted, the musically talented, and the artistically talented.

College Admission Counseling 177 students graduated in 2015; 175 went to college, including Cornell University; Georgetown University; Trinity College; Tufts University; University of Southern California; Wesleyan University. Other: 1 entered a postgraduate year, 1 had other specific plans. Mean SAT critical reading: 590, mean SAT math: 610, mean SAT writing: 600.

Student Life Upper grades have specified standards of dress, student council, honor system. Discipline rests equally with students and faculty.

Summer Programs Enrichment, ESL, sports, art/fine arts programs offered; session focuses on academic enrichment; held on campus; accepts boys and girls; open to students from other schools. 150 students usually enrolled. 2016 schedule: June 26 to July 30. Application deadline: none.

Tuition and Aid Day student tuition: $39,950; 7-day tuition and room/board: $53,850. Tuition installment plan (SMART Tuition Payment Plan). Need-based scholarship grants, need-based loans available. In 2015–16, 36% of upper-school students received aid. Total amount of financial aid awarded in 2015–16: $7,700,000.

Admissions Traditional secondary-level entrance grade is 9. For fall 2015, 1,706 students applied for upper-level admission, 358 were accepted, 195 enrolled. SSAT required. Deadline for receipt of application materials: January 15. Application fee required: $50. Interview required.

Athletics Interscholastic: alpine skiing (boys, girls), baseball (b), basketball (b,g), crew (b,g), cross-country running (b,g), field hockey (g), football (b), golf (b,g), hockey (b,g), ice hockey (b,g), lacrosse (b,g), rowing (b,g), soccer (b,g), softball (g), squash (b,g), tennis (b,g), track and field (b,g), ultimate Frisbee (b,g), volleyball (g), wrestling (b); coed interscholastic: dressage, equestrian sports, horseback riding; coed intramural: aerobics, aerobics/dance, ballet, basketball, climbing, cross-country running, dance, dressage, equestrian sports, figure skating, fitness, fitness walking, Frisbee, hockey, horseback riding, ice hockey, ice skating, jogging, martial arts, modern dance, outdoor activities, physical fitness, rock climbing, rowing, running, sailing, self defense, soccer, squash, strength & conditioning, tennis, track and field, ultimate Frisbee, walking, wall climbing, weight lifting, weight training, yoga. 1 coach, 3 athletic trainers.

Computers Computers are regularly used in art, English, foreign language, geography, history, mathematics, music, science classes. Computer network features include on-campus library services, online commercial services, Internet access, wireless campus network, Internet filtering or blocking technology. Campus intranet, student e-mail accounts, and computer access in designated common areas are available to students. The school has a published electronic and media policy.

Contact Mr. Peter A. Frew, Director of Admissions. 860-945-7700. Fax: 860-945-7808. E-mail: admissions@taftschool.org. Website: www.taftschool.org

TAIPEI AMERICAN SCHOOL
800 Chung Shan North Road, Section 6
Taipei 11152, Taiwan
Head of School: Dr. Sharon Hennessy

General Information Coeducational day college-preparatory, arts, bilingual studies, technology, fine and performing arts, STEM, robotics, public speaking, and character education school. Grades PK–12. Founded: 1949. Setting: urban. 15-acre campus. 5 buildings on campus. Approved or accredited by International Baccalaureate Organization, US Department of State, and Western Association of Schools and Colleges. Affiliate member of National Association of Independent Schools. Language of instruction: English. Total enrollment: 2,323. Upper school average class size: 17. Upper school faculty-student ratio: 1:8. There are 180 required school days per year for Upper School students. Upper School students typically attend 5 days per week. The average school day consists of 6 hours and 40 minutes.

Upper School Student Profile Grade 9: 233 students (127 boys, 106 girls); Grade 10: 211 students (112 boys, 99 girls); Grade 11: 225 students (119 boys, 106 girls); Grade 12: 218 students (117 boys, 101 girls).

Faculty School total: 282. In upper school: 62 men, 57 women; 94 have advanced degrees.

Subjects Offered 20th century history, advanced math, Advanced Placement courses, advanced studio art-AP, algebra, American literature, art history-AP, Asian history, Asian studies, astronomy, band, biology, biology-AP, business, calculus, calculus-AP, ceramics, chemistry, chemistry-AP, choir, classics, comparative government and politics AP, computer graphics, computer science, computer science-AP, conceptual physics, concert choir, dance, debate, digital photography, economics-AP, electronics, English, English language-AP, English literature-AP, entrepreneurship, environmental science, environmental science-AP, ethics, European history, European history-AP, expository writing, fitness, forensics, French, French-AP, geometry, health, International Baccalaureate courses, international relations, Japanese, jazz ensemble, journalism, Latin, linear algebra, macro/microeconomics-AP, Mandarin, marketing, music, music theater, music theory, music theory-AP, orchestra, philosophy, physical education, physics, physics-AP, piano, political science, pre-algebra, pre-calculus, programming, psychology, research seminar, rhetoric, robotics, science fiction, Shakespeare, Spanish, Spanish literature-AP, Spanish-AP, speech and debate, stagecraft, statistics-AP, studio art-AP, symphonic band, technical theater, theater, theory of knowledge, U.S. history, U.S. history-AP, video film production, visual arts, wind ensemble, world history-AP, world literature, yearbook.

Graduation Requirements English, mathematics, modern languages, performing arts, physical education (includes health), public speaking, science, social studies (includes history).

Special Academic Programs International Baccalaureate program; 29 Advanced Placement exams for which test preparation is offered; honors section; ESL.

College Admission Counseling 225 students graduated in 2015; 223 went to college, including Emory University; New York University; University of Illinois at Urbana–Champaign; University of Southern California; University of Toronto; University of Washington. Other: 2 entered military service. Mean SAT critical reading: 626, mean SAT math: 697, mean SAT writing: 636, mean combined SAT: 1959.

Student Life Upper grades have specified standards of dress, student council, honor system. Discipline rests primarily with faculty.

Summer Programs Remediation, enrichment, advancement, computer instruction programs offered; session focuses on internships, advancement, and make-up courses; honors math and science, robotics, writing, public speaking; held on campus; accepts boys and girls; open to students from other schools. 400 students usually enrolled. 2016 schedule: June to July. Application deadline: May 1.

Tuition and Aid Day student tuition: 658,755 Taiwan dollars. Tuition installment plan (individually arranged payment plans).

Admissions For fall 2015, 122 students applied for upper-level admission, 87 were accepted, 75 enrolled. California Achievement Test, English for Non-native Speakers,

Taipei American School

ERB CTP IV, Iowa Tests of Basic Skills, ISEE, latest standardized score from previous school, PSAT, SAT, SSAT or Stanford Achievement Test required. Deadline for receipt of application materials: none. Application fee required: 10,000 Taiwan dollars.

Athletics Interscholastic: badminton (boys, girls), basketball (b,g), cross-country running (b,g), dance (b,g), golf (b,g), rugby (b,g), soccer (b,g), softball (b,g), swimming and diving (b,g), tennis (b,g), track and field (b,g), volleyball (b,g); intramural: basketball (b,g), cross-country running (b,g), soccer (b,g), softball (b,g), swimming and diving (b,g), tennis (b,g), volleyball (b,g). 6 PE instructors, 1 athletic trainer.

Computers Computers are regularly used in all academic classes. Computer network features include on-campus library services, online commercial services, Internet access, wireless campus network, Internet filtering or blocking technology. Campus intranet, student e-mail accounts, and computer access in designated common areas are available to students. Students grades are available online. The school has a published electronic and media policy.

Contact Dr. Winnie Tang, Director of Admissions. 886-2-2873-9900 Ext. 328. Fax: 886-2-2873-1641. E-mail: admissions@tas.edu.tw. Website: www.tas.edu.tw

TAKOMA ACADEMY

8120 Carroll Avenue

Takoma Park, Maryland 20912-7397

Head of School: Mrs. Carla Thrower

General Information Coeducational day college-preparatory, arts, religious studies, and technology school, affiliated with Seventh-day Adventist Church. Grades 9–12. Founded: 1904. Setting: urban. 10-acre campus. 1 building on campus. Approved or accredited by Middle States Association of Colleges and Schools, National Council for Private School Accreditation, and Maryland Department of Education. Endowment: $400,000. Total enrollment: 226. Upper school average class size: 20. Upper school faculty-student ratio: 1:11. There are 180 required school days per year for Upper School students. Upper School students typically attend 5 days per week. The average school day consists of 7 hours.

Upper School Student Profile Grade 9: 59 students (27 boys, 32 girls); Grade 10: 49 students (26 boys, 23 girls); Grade 11: 62 students (34 boys, 28 girls); Grade 12: 56 students (23 boys, 33 girls). 80% of students are Seventh-day Adventists.

Faculty School total: 23. In upper school: 10 men, 11 women; 11 have advanced degrees.

Subjects Offered Accounting, Advanced Placement courses, algebra, American government, American history, anatomy and physiology, art and culture, band, Bible, biology, calculus-AP, career and personal planning, chemistry, choir, computer applications, computer skills, conceptual physics, critical thinking, earth science, English, English-AP, geography, geometry, graphic design, health education, honors algebra, honors English, honors geometry, honors U.S. history, honors world history, physical education, physics, pre-calculus, Spanish, U.S. government and politics, U.S. government and politics-AP, world history.

Special Academic Programs Advanced Placement exam preparation; honors section; study at local college for college credit; remedial reading and/or remedial writing.

College Admission Counseling 59 students graduated in 2015; 57 went to college, including Andrews University; Oakwood University; Pacific Union College; Southern Adventist University; University of Maryland, College Park; Washington Adventist University. Other: 1 entered military service, 1 entered a postgraduate year.

Student Life Upper grades have uniform requirement, student council, honor system. Discipline rests primarily with faculty. Attendance at religious services is required.

Summer Programs Remediation, enrichment programs offered; held both on and off campus; held at via computer; accepts boys and girls. 2016 schedule: June 29 to August 10.

Tuition and Aid Day student tuition: $13,695. Tuition installment plan (SMART Tuition Payment Plan). Tuition reduction for siblings, merit scholarship grants, need-based scholarship grants available.

Admissions Traditional secondary-level entrance grade is 9. Deadline for receipt of application materials: none. Application fee required: $100. On-campus interview required.

Athletics Interscholastic: basketball (boys, girls), cross-country running (b,g), soccer (b,g), volleyball (g); intramural: basketball (b,g); coed interscholastic: track and field. 1 PE instructor.

Computers Computers are regularly used in accounting, computer applications, graphic design, journalism, music, music technology classes. Computer resources include on-campus library services, Internet access, wireless campus network, Internet filtering or blocking technology. Campus intranet, student e-mail accounts, and computer access in designated common areas are available to students. Students grades are available online. The school has a published electronic and media policy.

Contact Mrs. Kelli Collins, Data Specialist. 301-434-4700 Ext. 743. Fax: 301-434-4814. E-mail: kcollins@ta.edu. Website: www.ta.edu

TAMPA PREPARATORY SCHOOL

727 West Cass Street

Tampa, Florida 33606

Head of School: Mr. Kevin M. Plummer

General Information Coeducational day college-preparatory, arts, and technology school. Grades 6–12. Founded: 1974. Setting: urban. 12-acre campus. 4 buildings on campus. Approved or accredited by Florida Council of Independent Schools, Southern Association of Colleges and Schools, Southern Association of Independent Schools, and Florida Department of Education. Member of National Association of Independent Schools and Secondary School Admission Test Board. Endowment: $10 million. Total enrollment: 650. Upper school average class size: 16. Upper school faculty-student ratio: 1:16. There are 180 required school days per year for Upper School students. Upper School students typically attend 5 days per week. The average school day consists of 6 hours and 40 minutes.

Upper School Student Profile Grade 6: 60 students (41 boys, 19 girls); Grade 7: 65 students (38 boys, 27 girls); Grade 8: 67 students (41 boys, 26 girls); Grade 9: 121 students (69 boys, 52 girls); Grade 10: 111 students (56 boys, 55 girls); Grade 11: 114 students (57 boys, 57 girls); Grade 12: 109 students (61 boys, 48 girls).

Faculty School total: 52. In upper school: 27 men, 25 women; 41 have advanced degrees.

Subjects Offered 3-dimensional design, Advanced Placement courses, aerospace science, computer science-AP, engineering, global studies, marine biology, music theater, music theory-AP, music-AP, orchestra, physics-AP, robotics, SAT preparation, Spanish literature-AP, speech and oral interpretations, sports medicine, statistics-AP, theater arts, TOEFL preparation, U.S. government and politics-AP, video and animation, video film production, world religions.

Graduation Requirements Arts and fine arts (art, music, dance, drama), English, foreign language, history, mathematics, physical education (includes health), science.

Special Academic Programs 21 Advanced Placement exams for which test preparation is offered; honors section; independent study; study abroad; academic accommodation for the gifted, the musically talented, and the artistically talented.

College Admission Counseling 110 students graduated in 2015; all went to college, including Elon University; Florida State University; Southern Methodist University; University of Central Florida; University of Florida.

Student Life Upper grades have specified standards of dress, student council, honor system. Discipline rests primarily with faculty.

Summer Programs Remediation, enrichment, advancement, sports, computer instruction programs offered; session focuses on grades 8-12 summer camp, accelerated academics, enrichment classes; held on campus; accepts boys and girls; open to students from other schools. 400 students usually enrolled. 2016 schedule: June 8 to July 31. Application deadline: none.

Tuition and Aid Day student tuition: $20,090. Tuition installment plan (FACTS Tuition Payment Plan, monthly payment plans, individually arranged payment plans). Merit scholarship grants, need-based scholarship grants available. In 2015–16, 21% of upper-school students received aid; total upper-school merit-scholarship money awarded: $90,500. Total amount of financial aid awarded in 2015–16: $1,000,000.

Admissions Traditional secondary-level entrance grade is 9. For fall 2015, 273 students applied for upper-level admission, 175 were accepted, 153 enrolled. ISEE, PSAT or SAT for applicants to grade 11 and 12, SSAT, TOEFL or writing sample required. Deadline for receipt of application materials: February 15. Application fee required: $75. On-campus interview recommended.

Athletics Interscholastic: aquatics (boys, girls), baseball (b), basketball (b,g), bowling (b,g), crew (b,g), cross-country running (b,g), diving (b,g), golf (b,g), lacrosse (b), rowing (b,g), running (b,g), soccer (b,g), softball (g), swimming and diving (b,g), tennis (b,g), track and field (b,g), volleyball (b,g), wrestling (b). 4 PE instructors, 65 coaches, 2 athletic trainers.

Computers Computers are regularly used in aerospace science classes. Computer network features include on-campus library services, online commercial services, Internet access, wireless campus network, Internet filtering or blocking technology. Student e-mail accounts and computer access in designated common areas are available to students. Students grades are available online. The school has a published electronic and media policy.

Contact Mrs. Linda Y. Quinn, Admissions Assistant. 813-251-8481 Ext. 4011. Fax: 813-254-2106. E-mail: lquinn@tampaprep.org. Website: www.tampaprep.org

TANDEM FRIENDS SCHOOL

279 Tandem Lane

Charlottesville, Virginia 22902

Head of School: Andy Jones-Wilkins

General Information Coeducational day college-preparatory and arts school, affiliated with Society of Friends. Grades 5–12. Founded: 1970. Setting: small town. Nearest major city is Richmond. 23-acre campus. 7 buildings on campus. Approved or accredited by Friends Council on Education and Virginia Association of Independent Schools. Member of National Association of Independent Schools. Endowment: $3.3 million. Upper school average class size: 12. Upper school faculty-student ratio: 1:6. There are 180 required school days per year for Upper School students. Upper School students typically attend 5 days per week. The average school day consists of 7 hours.

Upper School Student Profile Grade 9: 24 students (11 boys, 13 girls); Grade 10: 28 students (13 boys, 15 girls); Grade 11: 24 students (11 boys, 13 girls); Grade 12: 34 students (12 boys, 22 girls). 3% of students are members of Society of Friends.

Faculty School total: 36. In upper school: 7 men, 10 women; 10 have advanced degrees.

Subjects Offered Algebra, American literature, anatomy, art, bioethics, biology, biology-AP, calculus, calculus-AP, ceramics, chemistry, chemistry-AP, college counseling, computer applications, creative writing, cultural geography, discrete mathematics, drama, economics, economics and history, English, English-AP, environmental science-AP, expository writing, fine arts, French, French-AP, geometry, health and wellness, jazz ensemble, Latin, Latin-AP, marine biology, media studies, modern world history, music, musical productions, performing arts, photo shop, photography, physics, Quakerism and ethics, senior project, Spanish, Spanish-AP, statistics, statistics-AP, student government, student publications, studio art, theater, trigonometry, U.S. government, U.S. history, U.S. history-AP, weaving, world history, world literature, writing, yearbook.

Graduation Requirements Arts and fine arts (art, music, dance, drama), computer science, English, foreign language, government/civics, history, mathematics, science, senior year independent experiential learning project. Community service is required.

Special Academic Programs Advanced Placement exam preparation; independent study; academic accommodation for the gifted; remedial reading and/or remedial writing; remedial math.

College Admission Counseling 28 students graduated in 2015; 27 went to college, including James Madison University; The College of William and Mary; University of California, Berkeley; University of Virginia; Virginia Polytechnic Institute and State University. Other: 1 had other specific plans. Median SAT critical reading: 670, median SAT math: 605, median SAT writing: 620, median composite ACT: 28.

Student Life Upper grades have student council, honor system. Discipline rests equally with students and faculty. Attendance at religious services is required.

Summer Programs Art/fine arts programs offered; session focuses on arts, grades K-8; held on campus; accepts boys and girls; open to students from other schools. 125 students usually enrolled. 2016 schedule: June 13 to July 22. Application deadline: May 1.

Tuition and Aid Day student tuition: $20,000. Tuition installment plan (Insured Tuition Payment Plan, monthly payment plans, individually arranged payment plans). Need-based scholarship grants, tuition remission for children of full-time faculty available. In 2015–16, 37% of upper-school students received aid.

Admissions Traditional secondary-level entrance grade is 9. Woodcock-Johnson required. Deadline for receipt of application materials: none. Application fee required: $50. Interview required.

Athletics Interscholastic: basketball (boys, girls), lacrosse (b,g), soccer (b,g), tennis (b), volleyball (g); coed interscholastic: cross-country running, fencing, golf, outdoor education, track and field; coed intramural: fencing. 2 PE instructors, 24 coaches, 1 athletic trainer.

Computers Computers are regularly used in all academic classes. Computer network features include on-campus library services, online commercial services, Internet access, wireless campus network, Internet filtering or blocking technology, virtual classroom, iPad program for grades 5-9. Student e-mail accounts and computer access in designated common areas are available to students. Students grades are available online. The school has a published electronic and media policy.

Contact Emily Robey Morrison, Director of Admissions. 434-951-9314. Fax: 434-296-1886. E-mail: emorrison@tandemfs.org. Website: www.tandemfs.org

TAPPLY BINET COLLEGE

245 Garner Road West
Ancaster, Ontario L9G 3K9, Canada

Head of School: Ms. Sue Davidson

General Information Coeducational day college-preparatory and general academic school. Grades 7–12. Founded: 1997. Setting: small town. Nearest major city is Hamilton, Canada. 1-acre campus. 1 building on campus. Approved or accredited by Ontario Ministry of Education and Ontario Department of Education. Language of instruction: English. Total enrollment: 17. Upper school average class size: 6. Upper school faculty-student ratio: 1:3.

Upper School Student Profile Grade 9: 2 students (1 boy, 1 girl); Grade 10: 3 students (2 boys, 1 girl); Grade 11: 2 students (1 boy, 1 girl); Grade 12: 10 students (7 boys, 3 girls).

Faculty School total: 6. In upper school: 1 man, 3 women; 3 have advanced degrees.

College Admission Counseling 4 students graduated in 2015; they went to Brock University; Trent University; Wilfrid Laurier University.

Student Life Upper grades have uniform requirement, student council, honor system. Discipline rests primarily with faculty.

Admissions Battery of testing done through outside agency required. Deadline for receipt of application materials: none. No application fee required.

Athletics Coed Interscholastic: aerobics/Nautilus. 1 PE instructor.

Contact Ms. Sue Davidson, Principal. 905-648-2737. Fax: 905-648-8762. E-mail: tapplybinetcollege@cogeco.net. Website: www.tapplybinetcollege.com

TASIS THE AMERICAN SCHOOL IN ENGLAND

Coldharbour Lane
Thorpe, Surrey TW20 8TE, United Kingdom

Head of School: Dr. Mindy Hong

General Information Coeducational boarding and day college-preparatory and arts school. Boarding grades 9–13, day grades N–13. Founded: 1976. Setting: rural. Nearest major city is London, United Kingdom. Students are housed in single-sex dormitories. 46-acre campus. 26 buildings on campus. Approved or accredited by Council of International Schools, International Baccalaureate Organization, New England Association of Schools and Colleges, Office for Standards in Education (OFSTED), and state department of education. Affiliate member of National Association of Independent Schools; member of Secondary School Admission Test Board and European Council of International Schools. Language of instruction: English. Total enrollment: 750. Upper school average class size: 15. Upper school faculty-student ratio: 1:7. There are 171 required school days per year for Upper School students. Upper School students typically attend 5 days per week. The average school day consists of 6 hours.

Upper School Student Profile Grade 9: 78 students (41 boys, 37 girls); Grade 10: 108 students (50 boys, 58 girls); Grade 11: 112 students (57 boys, 55 girls); Grade 12: 100 students (45 boys, 55 girls); Grade 13: 2 students (2 girls). 50% of students are boarding students. 44% are international students. International students from Canada, Germany, Italy, Japan, Spain, and United States; 36 other countries represented in student body.

Faculty School total: 138. In upper school: 26 men, 33 women; 42 have advanced degrees; 21 reside on campus.

Subjects Offered 20th century history, acting, algebra, American government, American history, American history-AP, American literature, ancient history, art, art history, art history-AP, biology, biology-AP, British history, calculus-AP, ceramics, chamber groups, chemistry, chemistry-AP, choir, computer graphics, computer science-AP, debate, drawing, economics, economics-AP, English, English language and composition-AP, English literature, English literature and composition-AP, ensembles, environmental science, environmental science-AP, ESL, European history, European history-AP, French, geometry, German, health and wellness, humanities, jazz ensemble, journalism, keyboarding, Latin, mathematics, music, music technology, music theory, music theory-AP, painting, photography, physical education, physics, physics-AP, pre-calculus, printmaking, psychology, public speaking, Russian, sculpture, senior humanities, Shakespeare, Spanish, Spanish-AP, statistics-AP, theater arts, theory of knowledge, U.S. government and politics-AP, visual arts, weight training, Western civilization, word processing, world history, yearbook.

Graduation Requirements American history, arts and fine arts (art, music, dance, drama), computer science, English, foreign language, history, lab science, mathematics, physical education (includes health), senior humanities, sports. Community service is required.

Special Academic Programs International Baccalaureate program; 15 Advanced Placement exams for which test preparation is offered; independent study; study abroad; academic accommodation for the gifted; remedial reading and/or remedial writing; ESL (76 students enrolled).

College Admission Counseling 116 students graduated in 2015; 106 went to college, including New York University; Northeastern University; Northwestern University; Penn State University Park; University of Miami. Other: 10 had other specific plans.

Student Life Upper grades have uniform requirement, student council. Discipline rests primarily with faculty.

Summer Programs Remediation, enrichment, advancement, ESL, sports, art/fine arts, computer instruction programs offered; session focuses on ESL, academics, enrichment, and theater; held on campus; accepts boys and girls; open to students from other schools. 420 students usually enrolled. 2016 schedule: June 25 to August 6. Application deadline: none.

Tuition and Aid Day student tuition: £22,070; 7-day tuition and room/board: £38,350. Tuition installment plan (individually arranged payment plans). Need-based scholarship grants available. In 2015–16, 9% of upper-school students received aid.

Admissions TOEFL or SLEP required. Deadline for receipt of application materials: none. Application fee required: £125. Interview recommended.

Athletics Interscholastic: baseball (boys), basketball (b,g), cross-country running (b,g), lacrosse (b,g), rugby (b), soccer (b,g), softball (g), tennis (b,g), volleyball (b,g); intramural: aerobics (g), aerobics/dance (g), badminton (b,g), ballet (g), dance (g), dance team (g), field hockey (b,g), fitness (b,g), floor hockey (b,g), gymnastics (b,g), indoor soccer (b,g), lacrosse (b,g), physical fitness (b,g), physical training (b,g), rhythmic gymnastics (b,g), rugby (b), running (b,g), soccer (b,g), softball (b,g), strength & conditioning (b,g), weight training (b,g), winter soccer (b,g); coed interscholastic: cheering, golf; coed intramural: basketball, bicycling, golf, gymnastics, horseback riding, indoor soccer, lacrosse, martial arts, modern dance, outdoor activities, outdoor adventure, squash, strength & conditioning, swimming and diving, table tennis, tennis, track and field, ultimate Frisbee, volleyball, weight training, winter soccer, yoga. 5 PE instructors, 10 coaches, 1 athletic trainer.

Computers Computers are regularly used in all academic classes. Computer network features include on-campus library services, online commercial services, Internet access, wireless campus network, Internet filtering or blocking technology. Campus intranet, student e-mail accounts, and computer access in designated common areas are

available to students. Students grades are available online. The school has a published electronic and media policy.

Contact Ms. Karen House, Director of Admissions and Enrollment Management. 44-1932-582316. Fax: 44-1932-564644. E-mail: ukadmissions@tasisengland.org. Website: www.tasisengland.org

TASIS, THE AMERICAN SCHOOL IN SWITZERLAND

Via Collina d'Oro
Montagnola-Lugano CH-6926; Switzerland

Head of School: Dr. Lyle Rigg

General Information Coeducational boarding and day college-preparatory, arts, bilingual studies, and sports school. Boarding grades 7–PG, day grades K–PG. Founded: 1956. Setting: small town. Nearest major city is Lugano, Switzerland. Students are housed in single-sex dormitories. 9-acre campus. 19 buildings on campus. Approved or accredited by New England Association of Schools and Colleges and Swiss Federation of Private Schools. Affiliate member of National Association of Independent Schools; member of Secondary School Admission Test Board. Language of instruction: English. Total enrollment: 722. Upper school average class size: 15. Upper school faculty-student ratio: 1:6. Upper School students typically attend 5 days per week. The average school day consists of 6 hours.

Upper School Student Profile 75% of students are boarding students. 82% are international students. International students from Brazil, Italy, Russian Federation, Turkey, and United States; 50 other countries represented in student body.

Faculty In upper school: 31 men, 42 women; 45 have advanced degrees; 33 reside on campus.

Subjects Offered Advanced Placement courses, algebra, American history, American literature, ancient history, art, art history, art history-AP, biology, biology-AP, calculus, calculus-AP, ceramics, chemistry, chemistry-AP, digital photography, drama, economics, economics-AP, English, English language and composition-AP, English literature, English literature and composition-AP, environmental science, ESL, European history, European history-AP, fine arts, French, French language-AP, geography, geometry, German, German-AP, graphic design, health, history, international relations, Italian, mathematics, medieval/Renaissance history, music, photography, physical education, physics, science, social studies, Spanish, Spanish language-AP, theater, theory of knowledge, U.S. government, U.S. history-AP, world cultures, world history, world literature.

Graduation Requirements Arts, English, European history, foreign language, mathematics, science, senior humanities, sports, U.S. history. Community service is required.

Special Academic Programs International Baccalaureate program; Advanced Placement exam preparation; honors section; independent study; study abroad; academic accommodation for the gifted, the musically talented, and the artistically talented; ESL (200 students enrolled).

College Admission Counseling 108 students graduated in 2015; 106 went to college, including Pace University; The American University of Paris; The George Washington University. Other: 2 entered a postgraduate year. Median SAT critical reading: 570, median SAT math: 570. 30% scored over 600 on SAT critical reading, 22% scored over 600 on SAT math.

Student Life Upper grades have uniform requirement, student council, honor system. Discipline rests equally with students and faculty.

Summer Programs ESL, sports, art/fine arts, rigorous outdoor training programs offered; session focuses on languages, sports, and arts, outdoor leadership; held both on and off campus; held at TASIS Lugano Campus and Chateau d'Oex; accepts boys and girls; open to students from other schools. 650 students usually enrolled. 2016 schedule: June 26 to August 12. Application deadline: none.

Tuition and Aid Day student tuition: 45,200 Swiss francs; 7-day tuition and room/board: 78,000 Swiss francs. Tuition installment plan (individually arranged payment plans). Need-based scholarship grants available. In 2015–16, 15% of upper-school students received aid.

Admissions TOEFL or SLEP required. Deadline for receipt of application materials: none. Application fee required: 300 Swiss francs. Interview recommended.

Athletics Interscholastic: alpine skiing (boys, girls), badminton (b,g), basketball (b,g), golf (b), rugby (b), soccer (b,g), swimming and diving (b,g), tennis (b,g), track and field (b,g), volleyball (b,g); intramural: basketball (b,g), rugby (b); coed interscholastic: skiing (downhill), softball, swimming and diving, track and field; coed intramural: aerobics, aerobics/dance, aerobics/Nautilus, badminton, basketball, climbing, combined training, cross-country running, dance, fitness, flag football, floor hockey, golf, horseback riding, indoor soccer, jogging, lacrosse, martial arts, modern dance, physical fitness, physical training, rock climbing, running, sailing, skiing (downhill), soccer, softball, squash, strength & conditioning, swimming and diving, tennis, ultimate Frisbee, volleyball, weight lifting, weight training. 3 PE instructors.

Computers Computers are regularly used in art, English, ESL, foreign language, history, photography, science classes. Computer network features include on-campus library services, Internet access, wireless campus network, Internet filtering or blocking technology. Student e-mail accounts are available to students. Students grades are available online. The school has a published electronic and media policy.

Contact William E. Eichner, Director of Admissions. 41-91-960-5151. Fax: 41-91-993-2979. E-mail: admissions@tasis.ch. Website: www.tasis.com

See Display below and Close-Up on page 618.

THE AMERICAN SCHOOL IN SWITZERLAND

TASIS INSPIRES

www.tasis.ch

TELLURIDE MOUNTAIN SCHOOL

200 San Miguel River Drive
Telluride, Colorado 81435

Head of School: Mrs. Karen Walker

General Information Coeducational day college-preparatory, arts, technology, and music, visual, and dramatic arts school. Grades PK–12. Founded: 1999. Setting: small town. Nearest major city is Denver. 1 building on campus. Approved or accredited by Association of Colorado Independent Schools and Colorado Department of Education. Member of National Association of Independent Schools. Total enrollment: 104. Upper school average class size: 5. Upper school faculty-student ratio: 1:5. There are 165 required school days per year for Upper School students. Upper School students typically attend 5 days per week. The average school day consists of 6 hours and 30 minutes.

Upper School Student Profile Grade 6: 8 students (3 boys, 5 girls); Grade 7: 8 students (3 boys, 5 girls); Grade 8: 9 students (6 boys, 3 girls); Grade 9: 8 students (7 boys, 1 girl); Grade 10: 2 students (2 boys); Grade 11: 7 students (4 boys, 3 girls); Grade 12: 2 students (1 boy, 1 girl).

Faculty School total: 17. In upper school: 4 men, 4 women; 5 have advanced degrees.

Subjects Offered Algebra, alternative physical education, American Civil War, American history, American literature, ancient world history, applied music, art, backpacking, biology, calculus, character education, chemistry, civil rights, college admission preparation, college counseling, college planning, community service, computer education, computer literacy, computer multimedia, computer music, CPR, creative writing, critical thinking, critical writing, digital music, drama, dramatic arts, English composition, English literature, environmental education, European history, film studies, geography, geology, geometry, grammar, guitar, history, history of rock and roll, instrumental music, Internet research, keyboarding, Latin American literature, leadership, leadership and service, music, music performance, music technology, outdoor education, painting, physics, portfolio writing, pre-algebra, pre-calculus, public speaking, reading/study skills, Spanish, Spanish literature, studio art, trigonometry, video film production, visual arts, white-water trips, wilderness education, world history.

Graduation Requirements Algebra, biology, chemistry, college admission preparation, college counseling, dramatic arts, English, English composition, English literature, geometry, grammar, history, music, physics, pre-calculus, Spanish, trigonometry, U.S. history, visual arts, wilderness education, world history.

Special Academic Programs Honors section; independent study; study abroad.

Student Life Upper grades have specified standards of dress. Discipline rests primarily with faculty.

Tuition and Aid Day student tuition: $23,150. Tuition installment plan (monthly payment plans, individually arranged payment plans). Merit scholarship grants, need-based scholarship grants available. In 2014–15, 58% of upper-school students received aid. Total amount of financial aid awarded in 2014–15: $162,120.

Admissions Traditional secondary-level entrance grade is 9. For fall 2014, 2 students applied for upper-level admission, 2 were accepted, 2 enrolled. Deadline for receipt of application materials: none. Application fee required: $50. Interview required.

Athletics Interscholastic: alpine skiing (boys, girls), freestyle skiing (b,g), skiing (cross-country) (b,g), skiing (downhill) (b,g), snowboarding (b,g); coed interscholastic: backpacking, bicycling, canoeing/kayaking, climbing, cooperative games, hiking/backpacking, ice skating, kayaking, mountaineering, nordic skiing, outdoor activities, outdoor adventure, outdoor education, outdoor recreation, outdoor skills, outdoors, paddle tennis, rafting, rappelling, rock climbing, skateboarding, telemark skiing, wilderness, wilderness survival, yoga; coed intramural: alpine skiing. 1 PE instructor.

Computers Computers are regularly used in all classes. Computer network features include Internet access, wireless campus network. Campus intranet, student e-mail accounts, and computer access in designated common areas are available to students. The school has a published electronic and media policy.

Contact Mrs. Jamie Intemann, Program Coordinator. 970-728-1969. Fax: 970-369-4412. E-mail: jintemann@telluridemtnschool.org. Website: www.telluridemtnschool.org/

THE TENNEY SCHOOL

3500 South Gessner
Houston, Texas 77063

Head of School: Mr. Michael E. Tenney

General Information Coeducational day college-preparatory and general academic school; primarily serves individuals with Attention Deficit Disorder. Grades 6–12. Founded: 1973. Setting: suburban. 2-acre campus. 1 building on campus. Approved or accredited by Southern Association of Colleges and Schools and Texas Department of Education. Total enrollment: 57. Upper school average class size: 1. Upper school faculty-student ratio: 1:2. There are 170 required school days per year for Upper School students. Upper School students typically attend 5 days per week. The average school day consists of 5 hours.

Upper School Student Profile Grade 6: 6 students (4 boys, 2 girls); Grade 7: 5 students (3 boys, 2 girls); Grade 8: 9 students (3 boys, 6 girls); Grade 9: 6 students (3

boys, 3 girls); Grade 10: 13 students (7 boys, 6 girls); Grade 11: 11 students (7 boys, 4 girls); Grade 12: 7 students (4 boys, 3 girls).

Faculty School total: 27. In upper school: 3 men, 24 women; 14 have advanced degrees.

Subjects Offered Accounting, algebra, American history, American literature, biology, British literature, business law, calculus, chemistry, computer programming, computer studies, creative writing, economics, English, fine arts, geometry, government, health, independent study, journalism, keyboarding, mathematics, microcomputer technology applications, physical education, physical science, physics, pre-calculus, psychology, science, social studies, sociology, Spanish, studio art, study skills, world geography, world history, world literature, yearbook.

Graduation Requirements American government, American history.

Special Academic Programs Advanced Placement exam preparation; honors section; academic accommodation for the gifted, the musically talented, and the artistically talented; remedial reading and/or remedial writing; remedial math; special instructional classes for deaf students, ESL (10 students enrolled).

College Admission Counseling 10 students graduated in 2015; all went to college, including Houston Baptist University; St. Thomas University; Texas A&M University; The University of Texas at Austin; University of Houston.

Student Life Upper grades have specified standards of dress. Discipline rests primarily with faculty.

Summer Programs Remediation, enrichment, advancement programs offered; session focuses on academic course work; held on campus; accepts boys and girls; open to students from other schools. 45 students usually enrolled. 2016 schedule: June 9 to July 1. Application deadline: June 1.

Tuition and Aid Day student tuition: $23,000.

Admissions Traditional secondary-level entrance grade is 9. For fall 2015, 40 students applied for upper-level admission, 18 were accepted, 17 enrolled. Naglieri Nonverbal School Ability Test, Otis-Lennon School Ability Test or Scholastic Achievement Test required. Deadline for receipt of application materials: none. Application fee required: $100. On-campus interview required.

Athletics 1 PE instructor.

Computers Computers are regularly used in computer applications, creative writing, desktop publishing, English, foreign language, journalism, keyboarding, speech, word processing, yearbook classes. Computer network features include on-campus library services, Internet access, wireless campus network, Internet filtering or blocking technology. Campus intranet, student e-mail accounts, and computer access in designated common areas are available to students. Students grades are available online.

Contact Mr. Michael E. Tenney, Head of School. 713-783-6990. Fax: 713-783-0786. E-mail: mtenney@tenneyschool.com. Website: www.tenneyschool.com

TEURLINGS CATHOLIC HIGH SCHOOL

139 Teurlings Drive
Lafayette, Louisiana 70501-3832

Head of School: Mr. Michael Harrison Boyer

General Information Coeducational day college-preparatory, religious studies, and dual enrollment partnerships with local universities school, affiliated with Roman Catholic Church. Grades 9–12. Founded: 1955. Setting: urban. Nearest major city is Baton Rouge. 33-acre campus. 13 buildings on campus. Approved or accredited by Southern Association of Colleges and Schools and Louisiana Department of Education. Endowment: $140,000. Total enrollment: 779. Upper school average class size: 17. Upper school faculty-student ratio: 1:17. There are 179 required school days per year for Upper School students. Upper School students typically attend 5 days per week. The average school day consists of 6 hours and 50 minutes.

Upper School Student Profile Grade 9: 218 students (107 boys, 111 girls); Grade 10: 212 students (106 boys, 106 girls); Grade 11: 196 students (93 boys, 103 girls); Grade 12: 153 students (80 boys, 73 girls). 95% of students are Roman Catholic.

Faculty School total: 46. In upper school: 16 men, 28 women; 16 have advanced degrees.

Subjects Offered Acting, advanced math, algebra, American history, American literature, anatomy and physiology, art, biology, calculus, campus ministry, Catholic belief and practice, chemistry, civics/free enterprise, drama, English, environmental science, fine arts, French, geography, geometry, health, honors algebra, honors English, honors geometry, honors U.S. history, honors world history, interpersonal skills, physical education, physical science, physics, psychology, publications, sociology, Spanish, speech, sports medicine, theology, world history.

Graduation Requirements Advanced math, algebra, American history, American literature, biology, chemistry, civics, civics/free enterprise, electives, English, geometry, literature, physical education (includes health), physical science, theology, world geography, world history.

Special Academic Programs Honors section; study at local college for college credit.

College Admission Counseling 164 students graduated in 2015; 148 went to college, including Louisiana State University and Agricultural & Mechanical College; Louisiana State University at Eunice; Northwestern State University of Louisiana; Tulane University; University of Louisiana at Lafayette. Other: 13 went to work, 2 entered military service, 1 had other specific plans. Median composite ACT: 23. 22% scored over 26 on composite ACT.

Student Life Upper grades have uniform requirement, student council. Discipline rests equally with students and faculty. Attendance at religious services is required.

Tuition and Aid Day student tuition: $5400. Tuition installment plan (monthly payment plans). Need-based scholarship grants, paying campus jobs available. In 2015–16, 20% of upper-school students received aid. Total amount of financial aid awarded in 2015–16: $84,000.

Admissions Traditional secondary-level entrance grade is 9. For fall 2015, 286 students applied for upper-level admission, 275 were accepted, 275 enrolled. ACT, ACT-Explore, Explore, PSAT or Stanford Achievement Test required. Deadline for receipt of application materials: January 27. No application fee required.

Athletics Interscholastic: baseball (boys), basketball (b,g), bowling (b,g), cheering (g), cross-country running (b,g), dance team (g), football (b), golf (b,g), gymnastics (b,g), indoor track & field (b,g), soccer (b,g), softball (g), strength & conditioning (b,g), swimming and diving (b,g), tennis (b,g), track and field (b,g), volleyball (g), winter (indoor) track (b,g), wrestling (b); coed interscholastic: riflery, skeet shooting, trap and skeet. 3 coaches.

Computers Computers are regularly used in business applications, English, French, geography, history, mathematics, publications, science, Spanish, theater classes. Computer network features include on-campus library services, Internet access, wireless campus network, Internet filtering or blocking technology. Student e-mail accounts and computer access in designated common areas are available to students. Students grades are available online. The school has a published electronic and media policy.

Contact Mrs. Maria L. Hanes, Admissions Director. 337-235-5711 Ext. 128. Fax: 337-234-8057. E-mail: mhanes@tchs.net. Website: www.tchs.net

THE THACHER SCHOOL

5025 Thacher Road
Ojai, California 93023

Head of School: Mr. Michael K. Mulligan

General Information Coeducational boarding and day college-preparatory, arts, and technology school. Grades 9–12. Founded: 1889. Setting: small town. Nearest major city is Santa Barbara. Students are housed in single-sex dormitories. 450-acre campus. 89 buildings on campus. Approved or accredited by Georgia Association of Private Schools for Exceptional Children, The Association of Boarding Schools, Western Association of Schools and Colleges, and California Department of Education. Member of National Association of Independent Schools and Secondary School Admission Test Board. Endowment: $138.8 million. Total enrollment: 252. Upper school average class size: 11. Upper school faculty-student ratio: 1:5. Upper School students typically attend 5 days per week. The average school day consists of 7 hours.

Upper School Student Profile Grade 9: 67 students (33 boys, 34 girls); Grade 10: 64 students (32 boys, 32 girls); Grade 11: 63 students (33 boys, 30 girls); Grade 12: 63 students (31 boys, 32 girls). 91% of students are boarding students. 51% are state residents. 25 states are represented in upper school student body. 14% are international students. International students from Australia, China, Hong Kong, Japan, Republic of Korea, and Saudi Arabia; 4 other countries represented in student body.

Faculty School total: 51. In upper school: 27 men, 24 women; 33 have advanced degrees; 49 reside on campus.

Subjects Offered 3-dimensional art, ACT preparation, acting, advanced chemistry, advanced math, Advanced Placement courses, advanced studio art-AP, algebra, American history, American history-AP, American literature, art, art history, art history-AP, astronomy, biology, biology-AP, calculus, calculus-AP, ceramics, chemistry, chemistry-AP, Chinese, computer math, computer science, computer science-AP, conceptual physics, creative writing, dance, drama, ecology, economics, economics and history, electronic music, English, English literature, English literature-AP, English/composition-AP, environmental science, environmental science-AP, European history, European history-AP, film, fine arts, French, French language-AP, French literature-AP, geography, geometry, health, history, journalism, Latin, logic, marine biology, mathematics, music, music theory-AP, philosophy, photography, physical education, physics, physics-AP, psychology, religion, science, social studies, Spanish, Spanish language-AP, Spanish literature-AP, statistics, studio art-AP, theater, trigonometry, U.S. history-AP, world history, world literature, writing.

Graduation Requirements Arts and fine arts (art, music, dance, drama), English, foreign language, mathematics, physical education (includes health), science, social studies (includes history), senior exhibition program (students choose an academic topic of interest and study it for one year, culminating in a school-wide presentation).

Special Academic Programs 17 Advanced Placement exams for which test preparation is offered; honors section; independent study; study abroad; academic accommodation for the gifted, the musically talented, and the artistically talented.

College Admission Counseling 67 students graduated in 2015; all went to college, including Columbia College; Middlebury College; New York University; Stanford University; University of Southern California.

Student Life Upper grades have specified standards of dress, student council, honor system. Discipline rests equally with students and faculty.

Tuition and Aid Day student tuition: $36,800; 7-day tuition and room/board: $55,600. Tuition installment plan (monthly payment plans). Need-based scholarship grants available. In 2015–16, 28% of upper-school students received aid. Total amount of financial aid awarded in 2015–16: $2,818,894.

Admissions Traditional secondary-level entrance grade is 9. For fall 2015, 670 students applied for upper-level admission, 82 were accepted, 71 enrolled. ACT-Explore, ISEE, PSAT or SSAT required. Deadline for receipt of application materials: January 15. Application fee required: $75. Interview required.

Athletics Interscholastic: baseball (boys), basketball (b,g), cross-country running (b,g), dance (b,g), football (b), lacrosse (b,g), soccer (b,g), tennis (b,g), track and field (b,g), volleyball (g); intramural: aerobics (b,g), backpacking (b,g), ballet (b,g), bicycling (b,g), canoeing/kayaking (b,g), climbing (b,g), dance (b,g), dance squad (b,g), horseback riding (b,g), outdoor activities (b,g), weight training (b,g), wilderness (b,g), wilderness survival (b,g), yoga (b,g); coed interscholastic: dance, equestrian sports; coed intramural: aerobics, backpacking, ballet, bicycling, bowling, canoeing/kayaking, climbing, dance, equestrian sports, fencing, Frisbee, golf, handball, hiking/backpacking, horseback riding, kayaking, modern dance, mountain biking, outdoor activities, paddle tennis, pistol, polo, Polocrosse, riflery, rock climbing, rodeo, skiing (downhill), surfing, trap and skeet, ultimate Frisbee, wall climbing, weight lifting, yoga. 18 coaches, 1 athletic trainer.

Computers Computers are regularly used in English, foreign language, history, mathematics, science classes. Computer network features include on-campus library services, online commercial services, Internet access, wireless campus network, Internet filtering or blocking technology. Campus intranet, student e-mail accounts, and computer access in designated common areas are available to students. Students grades are available online. The school has a published electronic and media policy.

Contact Ms. Yung Roman, Admission Office Manager. 805-640-3210. Fax: 805-640-9377. E-mail: admission@thacher.org. Website: www.thacher.org

THINK GLOBAL SCHOOL

1562 First Avenue #205-3296
New York, New York 10028

Head of School: Mr. James Steckart

General Information Coeducational boarding college-preparatory and International Baccalaureate curriculum school. Grades 10–12. Founded: 2009. Setting: suburban. Students are housed in coed facilities in host city. Approved or accredited by International Baccalaureate Organization and Western Association of Schools and Colleges. Endowment: $50 million. Total enrollment: 44. Upper school average class size: 12. Upper school faculty-student ratio: 1:3. There are 193 required school days per year for Upper School students. Upper School students typically attend 5 days per week. The average school day consists of 6 hours and 45 minutes.

Upper School Student Profile Grade 10: 14 students (7 boys, 7 girls); Grade 11: 16 students (4 boys, 12 girls); Grade 12: 14 students (5 boys, 9 girls). 100% of students are boarding students. 10 states are represented in upper school student body. 100% are international students. International students from Bhutan, Ecuador, Germany, India, New Zealand, and South Africa; 15 other countries represented in student body.

Faculty School total: 14. In upper school: 7 men, 7 women; 10 have advanced degrees; 13 reside on campus.

Subjects Offered All academic.

Graduation Requirements International Baccalaureate courses.

Special Academic Programs International Baccalaureate program; study abroad.

College Admission Counseling 13 students graduated in 2015; 11 went to college, including Clark University; Columbia University; Georgetown University; Harvard University; New York University; Syracuse University. Other: 2 had other specific plans.

Student Life Upper grades have specified standards of dress, student council, honor system. Discipline rests equally with students and faculty.

Tuition and Aid 7-day tuition and room/board: $79,000. Tuition installment plan (monthly payment plans, individually arranged payment plans). Need-based scholarship grants available. In 2015–16, 90% of upper-school students received aid. Total amount of financial aid awarded in 2015–16: $2,649,200.

Admissions Traditional secondary-level entrance grade is 10. For fall 2015, 93 students applied for upper-level admission, 16 were accepted, 14 enrolled. Admissions testing or English proficiency required. Deadline for receipt of application materials: March 1. No application fee required. Interview required.

Athletics Coed Intramural: soccer.

Computers Computers are regularly used in all classes. Computer network features include Internet access, wireless campus network, Internet filtering or blocking technology, all students are provided with laptops, iPads, and phones. Campus intranet and student e-mail accounts are available to students. Students grades are available online. The school has a published electronic and media policy.

Contact Mrs. Melanie Anderson, Admissions Associate. 646-504-6924. E-mail: manderson@thinkglobalschool.org. Website: www.thinkglobalschool.org

THOMAS JEFFERSON SCHOOL

4100 South Lindbergh Boulevard
St. Louis, Missouri 63127

Head of School: Dr. Elizabeth L. Holekamp

General Information Coeducational boarding and day college-preparatory and classical liberal arts education school. Grades 7–PG. Founded: 1946. Setting: suburban. Students are housed in single-sex dormitories. 20-acre campus. 12 buildings on campus. Approved or accredited by Independent Schools Association of the Central States and The Association of Boarding Schools. Member of National Association of Independent Schools and Secondary School Admission Test Board. Endowment: $1.5 million. Total enrollment: 91. Upper school average class size: 14. Upper school faculty-student ratio: 1:7. There are 140 required school days per year for Upper School students. Upper School students typically attend 5 days per week. The average school day consists of 8 hours and 30 minutes.

Upper School Student Profile Grade 9: 15 students (10 boys, 5 girls); Grade 10: 17 students (13 boys, 4 girls); Grade 11: 13 students (7 boys, 6 girls); Grade 12: 16 students (9 boys, 7 girls). 57% of students are boarding students. 43% are state residents. 10 states are represented in upper school student body. 30% are international students. International students from Canada, China, Japan, Poland, Republic of Korea, and Taiwan; 3 other countries represented in student body.

Faculty School total: 22. In upper school: 6 men, 7 women; 11 have advanced degrees; 5 reside on campus.

Subjects Offered Advanced Placement courses, algebra, American history-AP, ancient history, ancient world history, art, art history, biology, biology-AP, calculus, calculus-AP, ceramics, chemistry, chemistry-AP, dance, earth science, English, English language-AP, English literature-AP, ESL, fine arts, French, geography, geometry, government and politics-AP, government/civics, Greek, history, Homeric Greek, Italian, Latin, life science, mathematics, music, physical science, physics, physics-AP, science, social studies, trigonometry, U.S. history-AP, world history, world history-AP.

Graduation Requirements Arts and fine arts (art, music, dance, drama), English, foreign language, mathematics, science, social studies (includes history). Community service is required.

Special Academic Programs 10 Advanced Placement exams for which test preparation is offered; honors section; academic accommodation for the gifted; ESL (10 students enrolled).

College Admission Counseling 16 students graduated in 2015; all went to college, including Beloit College; Boston University; Knox College; New York University; Pomona College; Smith College. Median SAT critical reading: 680, median SAT math: 700, median SAT writing: 680, median combined SAT: 2050.

Student Life Upper grades have specified standards of dress, student council, honor system. Discipline rests equally with students and faculty.

Tuition and Aid Day student tuition: $26,100; 5-day tuition and room/board: $41,000; 7-day tuition and room/board: $44,000. Tuition installment plan (SMART Tuition Payment Plan, monthly payment plans, individually arranged payment plans, Sallie Mae TuitionPay). Merit scholarship grants, need-based scholarship grants, paying campus jobs available. In 2015–16, 40% of upper-school students received aid; total upper-school merit-scholarship money awarded: $25,000. Total amount of financial aid awarded in 2015–16: $640,000.

Admissions Traditional secondary-level entrance grade is 9. For fall 2015, 31 students applied for upper-level admission, 18 were accepted, 14 enrolled. SSAT or TOEFL required. Deadline for receipt of application materials: February 15. Application fee required: $40. Interview required.

Athletics Interscholastic: basketball (boys, girls), soccer (b,g), volleyball (b,g); intramural: basketball (b,g), soccer (b,g), volleyball (b,g); coed interscholastic: soccer; coed intramural: dance, fitness, physical fitness, tennis, weight training, yoga.

Computers Computers are regularly used in foreign language, mathematics, science, yearbook classes. Computer network features include online commercial services, Internet access, wireless campus network, Internet filtering or blocking technology. Campus intranet, student e-mail accounts, and computer access in designated common areas are available to students. The school has a published electronic and media policy.

Contact Mr. Stephen Held, Director of Admissions. 314-843-4151 Ext. 2340. Fax: 314-843-3527. E-mail: sheld@tjs.org. Website: www.tjs.org

See Display below and Close-Up on page 620.

TIDEWATER ACADEMY

217 West Church Street
Wakefield, Virginia 23888

Head of School: Ms. Frances Joyner

General Information Coeducational day college-preparatory, arts, and technology school. Grades PK–12. Founded: 1964. Setting: rural. Nearest major city is Richmond. 10-acre campus. 4 buildings on campus. Approved or accredited by Virginia Association of Independent Schools. Total enrollment: 154. Upper school average class size: 15. Upper school faculty-student ratio: 1:15. There are 180 required school days per year for Upper School students. Upper School students typically attend 5 days per week. The average school day consists of 7 hours.

Upper School Student Profile Grade 9: 10 students (7 boys, 3 girls); Grade 10: 12 students (6 boys, 6 girls); Grade 11: 11 students (10 boys, 1 girl); Grade 12: 13 students (7 boys, 6 girls).

Faculty School total: 25. In upper school: 4 men, 6 women; 3 have advanced degrees.

Subjects Offered Algebra, American history, American literature, art, arts, biology, calculus, chemistry, computer applications, creative writing, driver education, earth science, English, English literature, English-AP, fine arts, geography, geometry, government/civics, grammar, health, history, life skills, mathematics, music, physical education, science, social sciences, social studies, Spanish, world history, world literature, writing.

Graduation Requirements Arts and fine arts (art, music, dance, drama), business skills (includes word processing), computer science, English, foreign language, mathematics, physical education (includes health), science, social sciences, social studies (includes history).

Special Academic Programs 6 Advanced Placement exams for which test preparation is offered; honors section; independent study.

College Admission Counseling 11 students graduated in 2014; 10 went to college, including James Madison University; Lynchburg College; Radford University; Randolph-Macon College. Other: 1 entered military service. Median SAT critical reading: 516, median SAT math: 501. 5% scored over 600 on SAT critical reading.

Student Life Upper grades have specified standards of dress, student council, honor system. Discipline rests primarily with faculty.

Tuition and Aid Day student tuition: $6800. Tuition installment plan (FACTS Tuition Payment Plan, monthly payment plans, individually arranged payment plans). Need-based scholarship grants available. In 2014–15, 40% of upper-school students received aid. Total amount of financial aid awarded in 2014–15: $125,000.

Admissions Traditional secondary-level entrance grade is 10. For fall 2014, 3 students applied for upper-level admission, 3 were accepted, 3 enrolled. Any standardized test required. Deadline for receipt of application materials: none. Application fee required: $25. On-campus interview required.

Athletics Interscholastic: baseball (boys), basketball (b,g), cheering (g), football (b), softball (g), tennis (b,g), volleyball (g). 2 PE instructors, 2 coaches.

Computers Computers are regularly used in career education, yearbook classes. Computer network features include on-campus library services, Internet access, wireless campus network. Campus intranet is available to students.

Contact Mrs. Brandee R. Phillips, Admissions Director. 757-899-5401. Fax: 757-899-2521. E-mail: b_phillips@tawarriors.org. Website: www.tawarriors.org

TILTON SCHOOL

30 School Street
Tilton, New Hampshire 03276

Head of School: Peter Saliba

General Information Coeducational boarding and day college-preparatory school; primarily serves students with learning disabilities, individuals with Attention Deficit Disorder, and dyslexic students. Grades 9–PG. Founded: 1845. Setting: small town. Nearest major city is Concord. Students are housed in single-sex by floor dormitories and single-sex dormitories. 150-acre campus. 30 buildings on campus. Approved or accredited by Association of Independent Schools in New England, Independent Schools of Northern New England, New England Association of Schools and Colleges, The Association of Boarding Schools, and New Hampshire Department of Education. Member of National Association of Independent Schools and Secondary School Admission Test Board. Endowment: $1.6 million. Total enrollment: 233. Upper school average class size: 12. Upper school faculty-student ratio: 1:6. There are 187 required school days per year for Upper School students. Upper School students typically attend 6 days per week. The average school day consists of 7 hours.

Upper School Student Profile Grade 9: 37 students (18 boys, 19 girls); Grade 10: 46 students (25 boys, 21 girls); Grade 11: 83 students (56 boys, 27 girls); Grade 12: 73 students (49 boys, 24 girls); Postgraduate: 16 students (12 boys, 4 girls). 75% of students are boarding students. 35% are state residents. 17 states are represented in upper school student body. 27% are international students. International students from Canada, China, Japan, Republic of Korea, Spain, and Taiwan; 8 other countries represented in student body.

Faculty School total: 40. In upper school: 25 men, 15 women; 19 have advanced degrees; 34 reside on campus.

Subjects Offered Advanced chemistry, advanced math, advanced studio art-AP, advertising design, algebra, American history, American literature, anatomy and physiology, art, biology, biology-AP, calculus, calculus-AP, ceramics, chemistry, chemistry-AP, clayworking, college counseling, computer graphics, criminal justice, criminology, dance, digital art, drama, drawing, ecology, economics, English, English language and composition-AP, English literature-AP, ESL, European history, European history-AP, forensics, French, French literature-AP, French-AP, functions, geology, geometry, global studies, graphic arts, graphic design, guitar, honors algebra, honors English, honors geometry, independent study, Indian studies, integrated mathematics, integrated science, Japanese, leadership, marine ecology, music, music appreciation, music theory, musical productions, painting, photography, physics, physics-AP, politics, pre-calculus, psychology, psychology-AP, Russian, SAT preparation, sociology, Spanish, Spanish literature-AP, Spanish-AP, statistics, studio art, studio art-AP, theater, trigonometry, wilderness education, world cultures, world literature, world religions, yearbook.

Graduation Requirements American history, arts and fine arts (art, music, dance, drama), English, foreign language, history, lab science, mathematics, science, annual

participation in Plus/5 (including activities in art and culture, athletics, community service, leadership, and outdoor experience).

Special Academic Programs 11 Advanced Placement exams for which test preparation is offered; honors section; independent study; ESL (15 students enrolled).

College Admission Counseling 81 students graduated in 2015; 78 went to college, including Connecticut College; Ithaca College; Northeastern University; Norwich University; University of New Hampshire. Mean SAT critical reading: 515, mean SAT math: 557, mean SAT writing: 527, mean combined SAT: 1599.

Student Life Upper grades have specified standards of dress, student council, honor system. Discipline rests primarily with faculty.

Summer Programs Enrichment, advancement, ESL, sports, art/fine arts, computer instruction programs offered; held both on and off campus; held at mountain bike park a few miles away; accepts boys and girls; open to students from other schools. 2016 schedule: June 20 to August 26.

Tuition and Aid Day student tuition: $31,750; 7-day tuition and room/board: $55,250. Tuition installment plan (FACTS Tuition Payment Plan, individually arranged payment plans). Merit scholarship grants, need-based scholarship grants, need-based loans available. In 2015–16, 53% of upper-school students received aid; total upper-school merit-scholarship money awarded: $506,750. Total amount of financial aid awarded in 2015–16: $3,416,870.

Admissions Traditional secondary-level entrance grade is 9. For fall 2015, 507 students applied for upper-level admission, 307 were accepted, 101 enrolled. ACT, PSAT, PSAT or SAT for applicants to grade 11 and 12, SAT, SLEP, SSAT, SSAT, ERB, PSAT, SAT, PLAN or ACT, TOEFL, TOEFL or SLEP, WAIS, WICS or writing sample required. Deadline for receipt of application materials: February 1. Application fee required: $50. Interview required.

Athletics Interscholastic: baseball (boys), basketball (b,g), field hockey (g), football (b), ice hockey (b,g), lacrosse (b,g), soccer (b,g), softball (g), tennis (b,g); coed interscholastic: alpine skiing, cross-country running, golf, mountain biking, skiing (downhill), snowboarding, weight lifting, weight training, wrestling; coed intramural: canoeing/kayaking, hiking/backpacking, outdoor activities, outdoor education, outdoor skills, rock climbing, squash, strength & conditioning, wall climbing, weight training, wilderness survival. 60 coaches, 1 athletic trainer.

Computers Computers are regularly used in English, foreign language, graphic arts, history, mathematics, newspaper, science, yearbook classes. Computer network features include on-campus library services, online commercial services, Internet access, wireless campus network, Internet filtering or blocking technology, USB ports, Smart Media Readers. Campus intranet, student e-mail accounts, and computer access in designated common areas are available to students. Students grades are available online. The school has a published electronic and media policy.

Contact Sharon Trudel, Admissions Assistant. 603-286-1733. Fax: 603-286-1705. E-mail: admissions@tiltonschool.org. Website: www.tiltonschool.org

TIMOTHY CHRISTIAN HIGH SCHOOL

1061 South Prospect Avenue
Elmhurst, Illinois 60126

Head of School: Mr. Bradford Mitchell

General Information Coeducational day college-preparatory, general academic, arts, business, vocational, religious studies, and technology school, affiliated with Christian faith. Grades K–12. Founded: 1911. Setting: suburban. Nearest major city is Chicago. 26-acre campus. 1 building on campus. Approved or accredited by North Central Association of Colleges and Schools and Illinois Department of Education. Total enrollment: 990. Upper school average class size: 20. Upper school faculty-student ratio: 1:10. There are 176 required school days per year for Upper School students. Upper School students typically attend 5 days per week. The average school day consists of 6 hours and 45 minutes.

Upper School Student Profile 99% of students are Christian.

Faculty School total: 29. In upper school: 14 men, 15 women; 18 have advanced degrees.

Subjects Offered Advanced math, algebra, American literature, anatomy and physiology, art, band, Bible, biology, biology-AP, British literature, business studies, calculus-AP, ceramics, chemistry, child development, choir, Christian doctrine, Christian ethics, church history, communication skills, community service, computer applications, computer art, computer graphics, computer-aided design, concert choir, desktop publishing, drawing and design, economics, electives, English, English literature-AP, expository writing, food and nutrition, geometry, health, home economics, honors algebra, honors geometry, human anatomy, independent living, industrial arts, industrial technology, instrumental music, interior design, jazz ensemble, music, music appreciation, music theory, New Testament, oral communications, orchestra, parent/child development, photography, physical education, physics, physics-AP, pre-calculus, psychology, sewing, Spanish, Spanish language-AP, trigonometry, U.S. government, U.S. history, U.S. history-AP, United States government-AP, Western civilization, world cultures, world literature.

Graduation Requirements Computer processing, English, mathematics, music, physical education (includes health), religious studies, science, social studies (includes history), 8-day Winterim (Renew).

Special Academic Programs 7 Advanced Placement exams for which test preparation is offered; honors section; remedial reading and/or remedial writing.

College Admission Counseling 81 students graduated in 2015; 79 went to college, including Baylor University; Calvin College; Dordt College; Hope College; Trinity Christian College; University of Illinois at Urbana–Champaign. Other: 1 went to work, 1 entered military service.

Student Life Upper grades have specified standards of dress, student council, honor system. Discipline rests primarily with faculty. Attendance at religious services is required.

Summer Programs Advancement, sports, art/fine arts programs offered; session focuses on athletic and art camps for any student, along with academic summer school program for TC students; held on campus; accepts boys and girls; open to students from other schools. 136 students usually enrolled.

Tuition and Aid Day student tuition: $9730–$23,500. Tuition installment plan (FACTS Tuition Payment Plan, FACTS is required unless paying the total tuition at once, additional application fee of $50, $100, or $200 app, depending upon date of submission., Capital maintenance fee of $525 required annually per family). Need-based scholarship grants, some need-based financial assistance available through school foundation available. In 2015–16, 13% of upper-school students received aid.

Admissions Traditional secondary-level entrance grade is 9. ITBS-TAP, Scholastic Testing Service High School Placement Test, school's own exam, TOEFL or TOEFL Junior required. Deadline for receipt of application materials: none. Application fee required: $50. On-campus interview required.

Athletics Interscholastic: baseball (boys), basketball (b,g), cross-country running (b,g), pom squad (g), soccer (b,g), softball (g), tennis (b,g), track and field (b,g), volleyball (g); intramural: basketball (b), flag football (b); coed interscholastic: cheering, golf; coed intramural: volleyball. 2 PE instructors, 1 athletic trainer.

Computers Computers are regularly used in art, business education, Christian doctrine, computer applications, engineering, English, foreign language, graphic design, keyboarding, mathematics, science, Spanish, technology, theology, word processing, writing classes. Computer network features include on-campus library services, Internet access, wireless campus network, Internet filtering or blocking technology. Student e-mail accounts are available to students. Students grades are available online. The school has a published electronic and media policy.

Contact Mr. Dan Quist, Director of Admissions and Student Recruitment. 630-782-4043. Fax: 630-833-9238. E-mail: quist@timothychristian.com. Website: www.timothychristian.com

TIMOTHY CHRISTIAN SCHOOL

2008 Ethel Road
Piscataway, New Jersey 08854

Head of School: Dr. Hubert Hartzler

General Information Coeducational day college-preparatory, arts, business, religious studies, bilingual studies, and technology school, affiliated with Christian faith. Grades PK–12. Founded: 1949. Setting: suburban. Nearest major city is New Brunswick. 25-acre campus. 7 buildings on campus. Approved or accredited by Association of Christian Schools International and Middle States Association of Colleges and Schools. Endowment: $76,000. Total enrollment: 465. Upper school average class size: 18. Upper school faculty-student ratio: 1:11. There are 175 required school days per year for Upper School students. Upper School students typically attend 5 days per week. The average school day consists of 6 hours and 30 minutes.

Upper School Student Profile Grade 9: 38 students (14 boys, 24 girls); Grade 10: 25 students (13 boys, 12 girls); Grade 11: 45 students (27 boys, 18 girls); Grade 12: 40 students (23 boys, 17 girls). 100% of students are Christian faith.

Faculty School total: 62. In upper school: 7 men, 10 women; 15 have advanced degrees.

Subjects Offered Accounting, acting, advanced biology, advanced chemistry, advanced computer applications, advanced math, Advanced Placement courses, advanced studio art-AP, advanced TOEFL/grammar, algebra, American government, American history, American history-AP, American literature, American literature-AP, American studies, art, band, Bible, Bible studies, biology, biology-AP, British literature, calculus, calculus-AP, chamber groups, chemistry, chemistry-AP, computer applications, computer programming, computer science, computer science-AP, concert choir, creative writing, critical thinking, debate, earth science, English, English language-AP, home economics, journalism, keyboarding, music, music theory, physics, pre-algebra, pre-calculus, programming, psychology, Spanish, technical theater, theater arts, trigonometry, woodworking, yearbook.

Graduation Requirements Algebra, American literature, Bible, Bible studies, biology, British literature, chemistry, composition, earth science, geometry, health, introduction to literature, physical education (includes health), trigonometry, U.S. history, world history, world literature, worldview studies.

Special Academic Programs 6 Advanced Placement exams for which test preparation is offered; honors section; independent study; study at local college for college credit; remedial reading and/or remedial writing; programs in English, mathematics, general development for dyslexic students; ESL (20 students enrolled).

College Admission Counseling 45 students graduated in 2015; they went to Gordon College; Liberty University; Messiah College; Rutgers, The State University of New Jersey, New Brunswick; Virginia Polytechnic Institute and State University; Wheaton College. Median SAT critical reading: 556, median SAT math: 524.

Student Life Upper grades have uniform requirement, student council, honor system. Discipline rests primarily with faculty. Attendance at religious services is required.

Summer Programs Remediation, enrichment, ESL, sports programs offered; session focuses on remedial work and athletics; held on campus; accepts boys and girls; open to students from other schools. 30 students usually enrolled. 2016 schedule: June 28 to August 6. Application deadline: April 15.

Tuition and Aid Tuition installment plan (FACTS Tuition Payment Plan). Need-based scholarship grants available. In 2015–16, 30% of upper-school students received aid. Total amount of financial aid awarded in 2015–16: $100,000.

Admissions Traditional secondary-level entrance grade is 9. For fall 2015, 26 students applied for upper-level admission, 16 were accepted, 16 enrolled. Admissions testing, TerraNova and TOEFL required. Deadline for receipt of application materials: none. Application fee required: $95. On-campus interview required.

Athletics Interscholastic: baseball (boys), basketball (b,g), cheering (g), golf (b,g), soccer (b,g), softball (g), track and field (b,g), volleyball (g), weight training (b,g). 2 PE instructors, 20 coaches, 1 athletic trainer.

Computers Computers are regularly used in foreign language, yearbook classes. Computer network features include on-campus library services, Internet access, Internet filtering or blocking technology. Computer access in designated common areas is available to students. Students grades are available online. The school has a published electronic and media policy.

Contact Mrs. Ella Mendalski, Admissions Secretary. 732-985-0300 Ext. 613. Fax: 732-985-8008. E-mail: emendalski@timothychristian.org. Website: www.timothychristian.org

TMI - THE EPISCOPAL SCHOOL OF TEXAS

20955 West Tejas Trail
San Antonio, Texas 78257

Head of School: Dr. John W. Cooper

General Information Coeducational boarding and day college-preparatory, arts, religious studies, technology, military/leadership, and military school, affiliated with Episcopal Church, Christian faith. Boarding grades 8–12, day grades 6–12. Founded: 1893. Setting: suburban. Students are housed in single-sex dormitories. 80-acre campus. 18 buildings on campus. Approved or accredited by Independent Schools Association of the Southwest, Southwest Association of Episcopal Schools, and Texas Department of Education. Member of National Association of Independent Schools. Total enrollment: 472. Upper school average class size: 16. Upper school faculty-student ratio: 1:9. There are 168 required school days per year for Upper School students. Upper School students typically attend 5 days per week. The average school day consists of 6 hours and 10 minutes.

Upper School Student Profile 84% of students are members of Episcopal Church, Christian.

Faculty School total: 64. In upper school: 43 have advanced degrees; 16 reside on campus.

Subjects Offered 20th century history, acting, Advanced Placement courses, algebra, American Civil War, American history, American literature, anatomy and physiology, astronomy, athletics, biology, British literature, calculus, ceramics, chemistry, choir, computer programming, conceptual physics, earth science, economics, English, English literature, environmental science, fine arts, geometry, government, history, JROTC, Latin, meteorology, military history, philosophy, photography, physics, playwriting, religion, Spanish, statistics, studio art, theater arts, theater design and production, world history, writing.

Graduation Requirements Arts and fine arts (art, music, dance, drama), electives, English, foreign language, history, mathematics, philosophy, physical education (includes health), religion (includes Bible studies and theology), science, community service requirement, senior chapel talk.

Special Academic Programs Advanced Placement exam preparation; honors section; independent study; ESL.

College Admission Counseling 80 students graduated in 2015; all went to college, including Baylor University; Southern Methodist University; Southwestern University; Texas A&M University; Texas Christian University; United States Military Academy.

Student Life Upper grades have uniform requirement, student council, honor system. Discipline rests equally with students and faculty. Attendance at religious services is required.

Summer Programs Enrichment, advancement, sports, art/fine arts, rigorous outdoor training programs offered; session focuses on academics, sports and enrichment; held on campus; accepts boys and girls; open to students from other schools. 150 students usually enrolled. 2016 schedule: June to July. Application deadline: May 1.

Tuition and Aid Day student tuition: $22,145–$23,450; 5-day tuition and room/board: $42,425; 7-day tuition and room/board: $46,525. Tuition installment plan (FACTS Tuition Payment Plan). Merit scholarship grants, need-based scholarship grants available.

Admissions Traditional secondary-level entrance grade is 9. ERB, ISEE, PSAT or SAT, SSAT or TOEFL required. Deadline for receipt of application materials: none. Application fee required: $75. Interview required.

Athletics Interscholastic: baseball (boys), basketball (b,g), cheering (b,g), cross-country running (b,g), dance (g), fitness (b,g), football (b), golf (b,g), independent competitive sports (b,g), lacrosse (b,g), soccer (b,g), softball (g), strength &

conditioning (b,g), swimming and diving (b,g), tennis (b,g), track and field (b,g), volleyball (g), weight training (b,g); coed interscholastic: JROTC drill, marksmanship, outdoor education, physical fitness, physical training, riflery, strength & conditioning.

Computers Computers are regularly used in digital applications, graphic arts, graphic design, graphics, journalism, language development, library, literary magazine, mathematics, media production, multimedia, newspaper, photography, programming, science, video film production, yearbook classes. Computer network features include on-campus library services, online commercial services, Internet access, wireless campus network, Internet filtering or blocking technology. Campus intranet, student e-mail accounts, and computer access in designated common areas are available to students. Students grades are available online. The school has a published electronic and media policy.

Contact Mr. Aaron Hawkins, Director of Admissions. 210-564-6152. Fax: 210-698-0715. E-mail: a.hawkins@tmi-sa.org. Website: www.tmi-sa.org

TOME SCHOOL

581 South Maryland Avenue
North East, Maryland 21901

Head of School: Christine Szymanski

General Information Coeducational day college-preparatory school. Grades K–12. Founded: 1889. Setting: small town. Nearest major city is Baltimore. 100-acre campus. 1 building on campus. Approved or accredited by Maryland Department of Education. Endowment: $3 million. Total enrollment: 480. Upper school average class size: 16. Upper school faculty-student ratio: 1:10. There are 170 required school days per year for Upper School students. Upper School students typically attend 5 days per week. The average school day consists of 6 hours and 35 minutes.

Upper School Student Profile Grade 9: 39 students (16 boys, 23 girls); Grade 10: 45 students (19 boys, 26 girls); Grade 11: 29 students (13 boys, 16 girls); Grade 12: 36 students (18 boys, 18 girls).

Faculty School total: 50. In upper school: 5 men, 10 women; 9 have advanced degrees.

Subjects Offered Advanced biology, algebra, American history, American literature, ancient history, ancient world history, biology, British literature (honors), calculus, chemistry, composition-AP, English, English language and composition-AP, English literature, English literature and composition-AP, environmental science, forensics, French, geometry, government/civics, grammar, history, mathematics, physical education, physics, pre-calculus, Spanish, statistics, world history, world literature.

Graduation Requirements English, foreign language, mathematics, science, social sciences, social studies (includes history), 4 credits in Literature, 4 credits in composition.

Special Academic Programs Advanced Placement exam preparation; honors section; study at local college for college credit.

College Admission Counseling 32 students graduated in 2015; 31 went to college, including Salisbury University; Towson University; University of Maryland, Baltimore County; University of Maryland, College Park; University of South Florida. Other: 1 entered military service. Median SAT critical reading: 620, median SAT math: 610, median SAT writing: 640, median combined SAT: 1870, median composite ACT: 26. 60% scored over 600 on SAT critical reading, 54% scored over 600 on SAT math, 79% scored over 600 on SAT writing, 53% scored over 26 on composite ACT.

Student Life Upper grades have uniform requirement, student council, honor system. Discipline rests primarily with faculty.

Summer Programs Remediation, enrichment programs offered; session focuses on math remediation/SAT Prep; held on campus; accepts boys and girls; not open to students from other schools. 10 students usually enrolled. 2016 schedule: June 20 to July 30. Application deadline: June 1.

Tuition and Aid Day student tuition: $7500. Tuition installment plan (SMART Tuition Payment Plan). Merit scholarship grants, need-based scholarship grants available. In 2015–16, 30% of upper-school students received aid; total upper-school merit-scholarship money awarded: $25,000.

Admissions Traditional secondary-level entrance grade is 9. For fall 2015, 24 students applied for upper-level admission, 20 were accepted, 15 enrolled. Otis-Lennon School Ability Test and Stanford Achievement Test required. Deadline for receipt of application materials: none. Application fee required: $50. On-campus interview required.

Athletics Interscholastic: baseball (boys), basketball (b,g), field hockey (g), lacrosse (b), soccer (b,g), softball (g), tennis (b,g), volleyball (g); coed interscholastic: cheering, cross-country running, tennis; coed intramural: baseball, basketball, cross-country running, fitness walking, flag football, football, Frisbee, paddle tennis, speedball, table tennis, tennis, ultimate Frisbee, volleyball, weight lifting, yoga. 2 PE instructors, 12 coaches.

Computers Computers are regularly used in English, mathematics classes. Computer resources include on-campus library services, Internet access, wireless campus network, Internet filtering or blocking technology. Students grades are available online. The school has a published electronic and media policy.

Contact Christine Szymanski, Head of School. 410-287-2050. Fax: 410-287-8999. E-mail: c.szymanski@tomeschool.org. Website: www.tomeschool.org

TOWER HILL SCHOOL

2813 West 17th Street
Wilmington, Delaware 19806

Head of School: Mrs. Elizabeth Speers

General Information Coeducational day college-preparatory, arts, and technology school. Grades PS–12. Founded: 1919. Setting: suburban. Nearest major city is Philadelphia, PA. 44-acre campus. 4 buildings on campus. Approved or accredited by Middle States Association of Colleges and Schools, Pennsylvania Association of Independent Schools, and Delaware Department of Education. Member of National Association of Independent Schools and Secondary School Admission Test Board. Endowment: $34.4 million. Total enrollment: 703. Upper school average class size: 14. Upper school faculty-student ratio: 1:6. There are 162 required school days per year for Upper School students. Upper School students typically attend 5 days per week. The average school day consists of 7 hours.

Upper School Student Profile Grade 9: 59 students (27 boys, 32 girls); Grade 10: 67 students (33 boys, 34 girls); Grade 11: 74 students (37 boys, 37 girls); Grade 12: 60 students (33 boys, 27 girls).

Faculty School total: 97. In upper school: 23 men, 23 women; 29 have advanced degrees.

Subjects Offered Acting, advanced biology, advanced chemistry, advanced computer applications, advanced math, advanced studio art-AP, algebra, American government, American literature, art, art history, astronomy, band, biology, British literature, calculus, calculus-AP, chemistry, chemistry-AP, China/Japan history, chorus, civil rights, community service, computer science, digital imaging, drama, drawing, driver education, engineering, English, English literature, European history, film, fine arts, French, geometry, health and wellness, historical research, history, human anatomy, jazz band, Latin, Latin American literature, mathematics, music, music theory, painting, photography, physical science, physics, poetry, politics, pre-calculus, Roman culture, SAT preparation, science, set design, Shakespeare, social issues, social justice, Spanish, Spanish literature, strings, theater, theater design and production, U.S. constitutional history, U.S. history, U.S. history-AP, woodworking, world history, writing, writing, yearbook.

Graduation Requirements Arts, athletics, English, foreign language, mathematics, science, social studies (includes history). Community service is required.

Special Academic Programs Advanced Placement exam preparation; honors section; independent study; academic accommodation for the gifted, the musically talented, and the artistically talented.

College Admission Counseling 64 students graduated in 2015; all went to college, including Boston College; Johns Hopkins University; New York University; Tufts University; University of Delaware. Median SAT critical reading: 650, median SAT math: 660, median SAT writing: 640, median composite ACT: 30. 67% scored over 600 on SAT critical reading, 75% scored over 600 on SAT math, 60% scored over 600 on SAT writing, 71% scored over 1800 on combined SAT, 73% scored over 26 on composite ACT.

Student Life Upper grades have specified standards of dress, student council, honor system. Discipline rests equally with students and faculty.

Summer Programs Sports programs offered; session focuses on sports camps; held on campus; accepts boys and girls; open to students from other schools. 60 students usually enrolled. 2016 schedule: June 13 to August 5. Application deadline: June 10.

Tuition and Aid Day student tuition: $27,125. Tuition installment plan (monthly payment plans, 60/40). Merit scholarship grants, need-based scholarship grants available. In 2015–16, 24% of upper-school students received aid; total upper-school merit-scholarship money awarded: $131,000. Total amount of financial aid awarded in 2015–16: $1,284,750.

Admissions Traditional secondary-level entrance grade is 9. For fall 2015, 80 students applied for upper-level admission, 55 were accepted, 26 enrolled. ISEE, PSAT or SAT for applicants to grade 11 and 12, SSAT, TOEFL or writing sample required. Deadline for receipt of application materials: January 2. Application fee required: $40. On-campus interview required.

Athletics Interscholastic: baseball (boys), basketball (b,g), cross-country running (b,g), field hockey (g), football (b), indoor track (b,g), lacrosse (b,g), soccer (b,g), swimming and diving (b,g), tennis (b,g), track and field (b,g), volleyball (g), winter (indoor) track (b,g), wrestling (b); intramural: dance (g), fitness (g), physical fitness (g), self defense (g), yoga (g); coed interscholastic: golf; coed intramural: aerobics/Nautilus, physical training, strength & conditioning, weight lifting. 27 coaches, 2 athletic trainers.

Computers Computers are regularly used in all academic classes. Computer network features include on-campus library services, Internet access, wireless campus network, Internet filtering or blocking technology. Campus intranet, student e-mail accounts, and computer access in designated common areas are available to students. Students grades are available online. The school has a published electronic and media policy.

Contact Mr. William R. Ushler, Associate Director of Admission. 302-657-8350. Fax: 302-657-8377. E-mail: wushler@towerhill.org. Website: www.towerhill.org

TRADITIONAL LEARNING ACADEMY

1189 Rochester Avenue
Coquitlam, British Columbia V3K 2X3, Canada

Head of School: Mr. Martin Charles Postgate Dale

General Information Coeducational day college-preparatory and general academic school, affiliated with Roman Catholic Church. Grades K–12. Founded: 1991. Setting: suburban. Nearest major city is Vancouver, Canada. 4-acre campus. 1 building on campus. Approved or accredited by home study and British Columbia Department of Education. Language of instruction: English. Total enrollment: 200. Upper school average class size: 10. Upper school faculty-student ratio: 1:10. There are 185 required school days per year for Upper School students. Upper School students typically attend 5 days per week. The average school day consists of 5 hours and 55 minutes.

Upper School Student Profile Grade 8: 17 students (7 boys, 10 girls); Grade 9: 5 students (3 boys, 2 girls); Grade 10: 9 students (7 boys, 2 girls); Grade 11: 7 students (3 boys, 4 girls); Grade 12: 8 students (6 boys, 2 girls). 85% of students are Roman Catholic.

Faculty School total: 17. In upper school: 6 men, 4 women; 2 have advanced degrees.

Subjects Offered 20th century world history, art, art education, athletic training, Bible studies, biology, British literature, calculus, Canadian geography, Canadian history, career planning, Catholic belief and practice, chaplaincy, chemistry, choir, choral music, Christian doctrine, college admission preparation, computer education, dance, drama performance, English, English literature, French, French as a second language, grammar, history, Latin, mathematics, oral expression, participation in sports, physical education, physics, play production, prayer/spirituality, pre-algebra, pre-calculus, religion, religious education, science, scripture, social studies, speech, vocal music.

Graduation Requirements High School students must take a full schedule of all the courses offered. In grades 11 & 12, some choice of subjects may be offered.

College Admission Counseling 3 students graduated in 2015; 2 went to college, including Simon Fraser University; The University of British Columbia. Other: 1 entered military service.

Student Life Upper grades have uniform requirement, honor system. Discipline rests equally with students and faculty. Attendance at religious services is required.

Tuition and Aid Day student tuition: CAN$4000. Tuition installment plan (monthly payment plans, individually arranged payment plans). Tuition reduction for siblings, bursaries, need-based scholarship grants available. In 2015–16, 90% of upper-school students received aid. Total amount of financial aid awarded in 2015–16: CAN$25,000.

Admissions Traditional secondary-level entrance grade is 8. For fall 2015, 10 students applied for upper-level admission, 10 were accepted, 10 enrolled. English entrance exam required. Deadline for receipt of application materials: none. Application fee required: CAN$50. On-campus interview required.

Athletics Interscholastic: basketball (boys, girls), floor hockey (b), soccer (b,g), softball (b,g), track and field (b,g), volleyball (b,g); intramural: basketball (b,g), floor hockey (b), volleyball (g); coed interscholastic: Frisbee, ultimate Frisbee; coed intramural: alpine skiing, badminton, canoeing/kayaking, dance, hiking/backpacking, kayaking, tennis, ultimate Frisbee. 1 PE instructor.

Computers Computers are regularly used in career education classes. Computer resources include Internet access, Internet filtering or blocking technology.

Contact Mrs. Rina Caan, Secretary. 604-931-7265. Fax: 604-931-3432. E-mail: tlaoffice@traditionallearning.com. Website: www.traditionallearning.com

TREVOR DAY SCHOOL

1 West 88th Street
New York, New York 10024

Head of School: Scott R. Reisinger

General Information Coeducational day college-preparatory, arts, and technology school. Grades N–12. Founded: 1930. Setting: urban. 1 building on campus. Approved or accredited by New York State Association of Independent Schools and New York Department of Education. Member of National Association of Independent Schools and Secondary School Admission Test Board. Endowment: $19.3 million. Total enrollment: 795. Upper school average class size: 15. Upper school faculty-student ratio: 1:7. There are 178 required school days per year for Upper School students. Upper School students typically attend 5 days per week. The average school day consists of 6 hours and 45 minutes.

Upper School Student Profile Grade 6: 65 students (34 boys, 31 girls); Grade 7: 68 students (38 boys, 30 girls); Grade 8: 64 students (26 boys, 38 girls); Grade 9: 79 students (36 boys, 43 girls); Grade 10: 70 students (36 boys, 34 girls); Grade 11: 63 students (34 boys, 29 girls); Grade 12: 55 students (22 boys, 33 girls).

Faculty School total: 150. In upper school: 26 men, 36 women; 44 have advanced degrees.

Subjects Offered Advanced chemistry, advanced computer applications, advanced math, African-American literature, algebra, American history, American literature, ancient world history, animation, art, art history, Asian literature, Basic programming, biology, British literature, calculus, calculus-AP, ceramics, chemistry, choreography, chorus, college counseling, community service, computer programming, computer science, computer studies, concert band, creative writing, dance, discrete mathematics, drama, drama performance, drawing, economics, English, English literature, environmental science, equality and freedom, ethics, European history, expository writing, film and literature, filmmaking, fine arts, foreign language, forensics, French, genetics, geometry, grammar, Harlem Renaissance, health, Hispanic literature, history, honors English, independent study, intro to computers, jazz ensemble, literary magazine, madrigals, mathematics, model United Nations, music, musical productions, newspaper, peer counseling, performing arts, photography, photojournalism, physical education, physics, play production, playwriting, poetry, pottery, pre-calculus, science, senior internship, Shakespeare, Shakespearean histories, social studies, Spanish, stained glass, statistics, statistics-AP, student government, studio art, technical theater, theater, U.S. history-AP, video, Web site design, wilderness education, world history, world literature, writing, yearbook.

Graduation Requirements Arts and fine arts (art, music, dance, drama), computer science, English, ethics, foreign language, mathematics, physical education (includes health), science, social studies (includes history), 80 hours of community service.

Special Academic Programs Advanced Placement exam preparation; honors section; independent study; term-away projects; study at local college for college credit; study abroad; academic accommodation for the gifted, the musically talented, and the artistically talented.

College Admission Counseling 63 students graduated in 2014; 62 went to college, including New York University; Oberlin College; Rice University; University of Pennsylvania; Washington University in St. Louis; Wesleyan University. Other: 1 entered a postgraduate year.

Student Life Upper grades have student council. Discipline rests equally with students and faculty.

Tuition and Aid Day student tuition: $34,650–$41,600. Tuition installment plan (FACTS Tuition Payment Plan, plan A: balance (85%) due August 15, plan B: 45% due July 24 - balance due December 30, plan C: 9-monthly installments). Need-based scholarship grants available. In 2014–15, 18% of upper-school students received aid. Total amount of financial aid awarded in 2014–15: $4,700,000.

Admissions Traditional secondary-level entrance grade is 9. ISEE, PSAT, SAT, or ACT for applicants to grade 11 and 12 or SSAT required. Deadline for receipt of application materials: January 1. Application fee required: $60. On-campus interview required.

Athletics Interscholastic: baseball (boys), basketball (b,g), soccer (b,g), softball (g), tennis (b,g), volleyball (g), wrestling (b,g); coed interscholastic: cross-country running, dance, fitness walking, modern dance, outdoor education, track and field. 4 PE instructors, 12 coaches.

Computers Computers are regularly used in art, English, foreign language, history, mathematics, music, science classes. Computer network features include on-campus library services, online commercial services, Internet access, wireless campus network, Internet filtering or blocking technology, personal portals with homework and schedules for each student. Campus intranet and student e-mail accounts are available to students. The school has a published electronic and media policy.

Contact Kristin Harman, Director of Admissions and Financial Aid for the Upper School. 212-426-3362. Fax: 646-672-5579. E-mail: kharman@trevor.org. Website: www.trevor.org

TRI-CITY CHRISTIAN ACADEMY

2211 W Germann Road
Chandler, Arizona 85286

Head of School: Pastor Thad E. Todd

General Information Coeducational day college-preparatory, religious studies, and music school, affiliated with Baptist Church. Grades K–12. Founded: 1971. Setting: suburban. Nearest major city is Phoenix. 9-acre campus. 1 building on campus. Approved or accredited by Association of Christian Schools International. Total enrollment: 276. Upper school average class size: 23. Upper school faculty-student ratio: 1:7. There are 174 required school days per year for Upper School students. Upper School students typically attend 5 days per week. The average school day consists of 7 hours and 5 minutes.

Upper School Student Profile Grade 9: 28 students (16 boys, 12 girls); Grade 10: 26 students (15 boys, 11 girls); Grade 11: 24 students (14 boys, 10 girls); Grade 12: 28 students (13 boys, 15 girls). 40% of students are Baptist.

Faculty School total: 24. In upper school: 8 men, 7 women; 4 have advanced degrees.

Subjects Offered 20th century history, 20th century world history, algebra, American government, American history, American literature, applied music, athletic training, athletics, band, basic language skills, basketball, bell choir, Bible, Bible studies, biology, brass choir, business mathematics, calculus, career and personal planning, career/college preparation, cheerleading, chemistry, choir, choral music, chorus, Christian doctrine, Christian education, Christian ethics, Christian scripture, civics, computer applications, computer studies, computers, concert choir, debate, drama, drama performance, dramatic arts, English, English composition, English literature, ESL, foreign language, geometry, government, journalism, keyboarding, library skills, public speaking, Spanish, strings, U.S. history, voice and diction, volleyball, wind instruments, world history, yearbook.

Special Academic Programs Honors section; independent study; study at local college for college credit; ESL (10 students enrolled).

College Admission Counseling 16 students graduated in 2015; all went to college, including Arizona State University at the Tempe campus; Bob Jones University; Grand

Canyon University; Northern Arizona University; The University of Arizona. Median SAT critical reading: 520, median SAT math: 620, median SAT writing: 560, median combined SAT: 1750, median composite ACT: 28. 36% scored over 600 on SAT critical reading, 57% scored over 600 on SAT math, 36% scored over 600 on SAT writing, 36% scored over 1800 on combined SAT, 50% scored over 26 on composite ACT.

Student Life Upper grades have uniform requirement, student council, honor system. Discipline rests primarily with faculty.

Tuition and Aid Day student tuition: $5515. Tuition installment plan (monthly payment plans). Tuition reduction for siblings, tuition tax scholarships available. In 2015–16, 30% of upper-school students received aid. Total amount of financial aid awarded in 2015–16: $25,000.

Admissions Traditional secondary-level entrance grade is 9. For fall 2015, 12 students applied for upper-level admission, 12 were accepted, 12 enrolled. Deadline for receipt of application materials: none. Application fee required: $225. On-campus interview required.

Athletics Interscholastic: baseball (boys), basketball (b,g), soccer (b,g), volleyball (g); coed interscholastic: golf. 2 PE instructors.

Computers Computers are regularly used in ESL, foreign language classes. Computer resources include Internet access. Students grades are available online.

Contact 480-245-7902. Fax: 480-245-7908. Website: www.tcawarriors.org

TRINITY CATHOLIC HIGH SCHOOL

926 Newfield Avenue
Stamford, Connecticut 06905

Head of School: Dr. Joseph Gerics

General Information Coeducational day college-preparatory school, affiliated with Roman Catholic Church. Grades 9–12. Founded: 1956. Setting: suburban. 27-acre campus. 1 building on campus. Approved or accredited by New England Association of Schools and Colleges and Connecticut Department of Education. Total enrollment: 429. Upper school average class size: 24. Upper school faculty-student ratio: 1:13. There are 180 required school days per year for Upper School students. Upper School students typically attend 5 days per week. The average school day consists of 6 hours and 10 minutes.

Upper School Student Profile Grade 9: 98 students (56 boys, 42 girls); Grade 10: 96 students (57 boys, 39 girls); Grade 11: 133 students (68 boys, 65 girls); Grade 12: 102 students (51 boys, 51 girls). 60% of students are Roman Catholic.

Faculty School total: 32. In upper school: 13 men, 19 women; 24 have advanced degrees.

Subjects Offered Advanced Placement courses, algebra, American history, American history-AP, American literature, anatomy, art, art appreciation, art history, arts, audio visual/media, Bible studies, biology, British literature, calculus, calculus-AP, Catholic belief and practice, chemistry, chemistry-AP, civics, community service, computer art, computer literacy, computer science, digital art, earth science, economics, engineering, English, English language-AP, English literature, English literature-AP, environmental science, environmental studies, European civilization, European history, European history-AP, fine arts, forensics, geography, geometry, government, government/civics, health, language arts, mathematics, New Testament, physical education, physical science, physics, physics-AP, pre-calculus, psychology, religion, social studies, sociology, Spanish, Spanish-AP, speech, trigonometry, video film production, visual arts, vocational arts, word processing, world history, world literature, writing.

Graduation Requirements Arts and fine arts (art, music, dance, drama), computer science, English, foreign language, mathematics, physical education (includes health), religion (includes Bible studies and theology), science, social studies (includes history). Community service is required.

Special Academic Programs 9 Advanced Placement exams for which test preparation is offered; honors section; study at local college for college credit; ESL (32 students enrolled).

College Admission Counseling 117 students graduated in 2015; 112 went to college, including Bryant University; Fordham University; Michigan State University; Sacred Heart University; Southern Connecticut State University; University of Connecticut. Other: 1 entered military service, 3 entered a postgraduate year, 1 had other specific plans. Mean SAT critical reading: 524, mean SAT math: 527, mean SAT writing: 531, mean combined SAT: 1490, mean composite ACT: 22. 18% scored over 600 on SAT critical reading, 26% scored over 600 on SAT math, 25% scored over 600 on SAT writing, 18% scored over 1800 on combined SAT, 18% scored over 26 on composite ACT.

Student Life Upper grades have uniform requirement, student council. Discipline rests primarily with faculty. Attendance at religious services is required.

Summer Programs Remediation programs offered; session focuses on remediation; held both on and off campus; held at online; accepts boys and girls; open to students from other schools. 40 students usually enrolled. 2016 schedule: June 27 to August 5. Application deadline: June 24.

Tuition and Aid Day student tuition: $12,860. Tuition installment plan (FACTS Tuition Payment Plan, monthly payment plans). Tuition reduction for siblings, merit scholarship grants, need-based scholarship grants available. In 2015–16, 32% of upper-school students received aid; total upper-school merit-scholarship money awarded: $121,000. Total amount of financial aid awarded in 2015–16: $472,490.

Admissions Traditional secondary-level entrance grade is 9. For fall 2015, 178 students applied for upper-level admission, 176 were accepted, 97 enrolled. High School Placement Test required. Deadline for receipt of application materials: none. Application fee required: $50. On-campus interview recommended.

Athletics Interscholastic: baseball (boys), basketball (b,g), cheering (g), diving (g), football (b), ice hockey (b), lacrosse (b), soccer (b,g), softball (g), tennis (b,g), volleyball (g); coed interscholastic: cross-country running, golf. 1 PE instructor, 11 coaches, 1 athletic trainer.

Computers Computers are regularly used in all classes. Computer network features include online commercial services, Internet access, wireless campus network, Internet filtering or blocking technology. Student e-mail accounts are available to students. Students grades are available online. The school has a published electronic and media policy.

Contact Mrs. Christine Green, Director of Admissions. 203-322-3401 Ext. 302. Fax: 203-322-5330. E-mail: cgreen@trinitycatholic.org. Website: www.trinitycatholic.org

TRINITY COLLEGE SCHOOL

55 Deblaquire Street North
Port Hope, Ontario L1A 4K7, Canada

Head of School: Mr. Stuart K.C. Grainger

General Information Coeducational boarding and day college-preparatory and liberal arts school, affiliated with Church of England (Anglican). Boarding grades 9–12, day grades 5–12. Founded: 1865. Setting: small town. Nearest major city is Toronto, Canada. Students are housed in single-sex dormitories. 100-acre campus. 15 buildings on campus. Approved or accredited by Canadian Association of Independent Schools, Conference of Independent Schools of Ontario, The Association of Boarding Schools, and Ontario Department of Education. Affiliate member of National Association of Independent Schools; member of Secondary School Admission Test Board. Language of instruction: English. Endowment: CAN$40.2 million. Total enrollment: 562. Upper school average class size: 16. Upper school faculty-student ratio: 1:8. There are 165 required school days per year for Upper School students. Upper School students typically attend 5 days per week. The average school day consists of 6 hours.

Upper School Student Profile Grade 9: 82 students (44 boys, 38 girls); Grade 10: 114 students (64 boys, 50 girls); Grade 11: 132 students (75 boys, 57 girls); Grade 12: 125 students (73 boys, 52 girls). 78% of students are boarding students. 41% are province residents. 8 provinces are represented in upper school student body. 48% are international students. International students from Bermuda, Cayman Islands, China, Mexico, Nigeria, and Saudi Arabia; 24 other countries represented in student body. 30% of students are members of Church of England (Anglican).

Faculty School total: 79. In upper school: 32 men, 29 women; 16 have advanced degrees; 13 reside on campus.

Subjects Offered Algebra, American history, art, art history-AP, astronomy, biology, biology-AP, calculus, calculus-AP, Canadian geography, Canadian history, Canadian law, career education, career/college preparation, chemistry, chemistry-AP, civics, classical civilization, community service, comparative government and politics-AP, computer programming, computer science, computer science-AP, creative writing, dramatic arts, earth science, economics, English, English language-AP, English literature, English literature-AP, environmental science, environmental science-AP, environmental studies, ESL, fine arts, finite math, French, French-AP, general science, geography, geometry, German, guidance, health education, history, human geography - AP, independent study, Latin, law, mathematics, microeconomics-AP, music, music theory-AP, outdoor education, philosophy, physical education, physics, physics-AP, political science, politics, research seminar, society challenge and change, Spanish, statistics-AP, studio art-AP, world history, world history-AP.

Graduation Requirements Arts, Canadian geography, Canadian history, civics, English, French, guidance, mathematics, physical education (includes health), science, social sciences, technology, minimum 40 hours of community service, provincial literacy test completion, addtional arts and language credits.

Special Academic Programs 16 Advanced Placement exams for which test preparation is offered; term-away projects; study abroad; ESL (27 students enrolled).

College Admission Counseling 130 students graduated in 2015; 124 went to college, including McGill University; Queen's University at Kingston; The University of Western Ontario; University of Guelph; University of Toronto; University of Waterloo. Other: 1 entered military service, 5 had other specific plans. Mean SAT critical reading: 539, mean SAT math: 596, mean SAT writing: 552, mean combined SAT: 539.

Student Life Upper grades have uniform requirement, student council, honor system. Discipline rests primarily with faculty. Attendance at religious services is required.

Summer Programs Enrichment, advancement, ESL programs offered; session focuses on advancement through cultural enrichment; held both on and off campus; held at England; accepts boys and girls; open to students from other schools. 30 students usually enrolled. 2016 schedule: July 4 to July 26. Application deadline: May 1.

Tuition and Aid Day student tuition: CAN$22,950–CAN$31,850; 7-day tuition and room/board: CAN$38,950–CAN$56,950. Tuition installment plan (monthly payment plans, quarterly payment plan (domestic students only), three payment option (international students)). Bursaries, merit scholarship grants, need-based scholarship grants available. In 2015–16, 30% of upper-school students received aid; total upper-school merit-scholarship money awarded: CAN$156,100. Total amount of financial aid awarded in 2015–16: CAN$2,407,200.

Admissions Traditional secondary-level entrance grade is 9. For fall 2015, 309 students applied for upper-level admission, 272 were accepted, 176 enrolled. Otis-Lennon Ability or Stanford Achievement Test, SSAT or TOEFL required. Deadline for receipt of application materials: none. Application fee required: CAN$150. Interview required.

Athletics Interscholastic: baseball (boys), basketball (b,g), cricket (b), field hockey (g), football (b), ice hockey (b,g), rugby (b,g), soccer (b,g), squash (b,g), tennis (b,g), volleyball (g); coed interscholastic: badminton, cross-country running, golf, nordic skiing, outdoor education, rowing, swimming and diving, track and field; coed intramural: aerobics, aerobics/dance, badminton, basketball, cooperative games, cricket, cross-country running, dance, dance squad, equestrian sports, fitness, fitness walking, golf, ice hockey, ice skating, skiing (downhill), snowboarding, soccer, softball, squash, strength & conditioning, swimming and diving, table tennis, tennis, ultimate Frisbee, weight lifting, weight training, yoga. 4 PE instructors, 5 coaches, 2 athletic trainers.

Computers Computers are regularly used in all academic classes. Computer network features include on-campus library services, Internet access, wireless campus network, Internet filtering or blocking technology. Campus intranet and student e-mail accounts are available to students. Students grades are available online. The school has a published electronic and media policy.

Contact Ms. Kathryn A. LaBranche, Director of Admissions. 905-885-3217 Ext. 1208. Fax: 905-885-7444. E-mail: admissions@tcs.on.ca. Website: www.tcs.on.ca

TRINITY EPISCOPAL SCHOOL
3850 Pittaway Drive
Richmond, Virginia 23235

Head of School: Mr. Robert A. Short

General Information Coeducational day college-preparatory, arts, and International Baccalaureate school, affiliated with Episcopal Church. Grades 8–12. Founded: 1972. Setting: suburban. 40-acre campus. 6 buildings on campus. Approved or accredited by National Association of Episcopal Schools, Virginia Association of Independent Schools, and Virginia Department of Education. Member of National Association of Independent Schools. Endowment: $300,000. Total enrollment: 495. Upper school average class size: 14. Upper school faculty-student ratio: 1:9. There are 180 required school days per year for Upper School students. Upper School students typically attend 5 days per week. The average school day consists of 7 hours and 10 minutes.

Upper School Student Profile Grade 8: 14 students (8 boys, 6 girls); Grade 9: 115 students (62 boys, 53 girls); Grade 10: 120 students (73 boys, 47 girls); Grade 11: 72 students (11 boys, 61 girls); Grade 12: 115 students (53 boys, 62 girls).

Faculty School total: 53. In upper school: 30 have advanced degrees.

Subjects Offered 20th century history, 20th century world history, 3-dimensional art, Advanced Placement courses, advanced studio art-AP, algebra, American government, American history, American history-AP, American literature, American politics in film, anatomy, art, astronomy, band, Bible studies, biology, biology-AP, calculus, calculus-AP, chemistry, chemistry-AP, chorus, computer graphics, computer programming, computer science, concert band, concert choir, creative writing, digital music, drama, driver education, earth science, economics, English, English literature, English-AP, environmental science, European history, European history-AP, foreign policy, French, French-AP, geography, geology, geometry, German, German-AP, government-AP, government/civics, International Baccalaureate courses, jazz band, keyboarding, Latin, math analysis, mathematics, music, physics, physics-AP, pre-calculus, religion, science, social sciences, social studies, Southern literature, Spanish, studio art-AP, theater, theology, theory of knowledge, trigonometry, U.S. government and politics-AP, U.S. history-AP, Web site design, word processing, world history, world literature, world religions, writing.

Graduation Requirements Arts and fine arts (art, music, dance, drama), athletics, English, foreign language, mathematics, religion (includes Bible studies and theology), science, social studies (includes history), Junior Work Week. Community service is required.

Special Academic Programs International Baccalaureate program; 10 Advanced Placement exams for which test preparation is offered; honors section; independent study; academic accommodation for the gifted, the musically talented, and the artistically talented.

College Admission Counseling 100 students graduated in 2015; 99 went to college, including James Madison University; Longwood University; The College of William and Mary; University of Virginia; Virginia Commonwealth University; Virginia Polytechnic Institute and State University. Other: 1 entered a postgraduate year. Median SAT critical reading: 560, median SAT math: 580, median SAT writing: 560.

Student Life Upper grades have specified standards of dress, student council, honor system. Discipline rests equally with students and faculty. Attendance at religious services is required.

Summer Programs Enrichment, advancement, sports, art/fine arts, computer instruction programs offered; held on campus; accepts boys and girls; open to students from other schools. 250 students usually enrolled. 2016 schedule: June 1 to August 10. Application deadline: April 1.

Tuition and Aid Day student tuition: $21,400. Tuition installment plan (Insured Tuition Payment Plan, FACTS Tuition Payment Plan). Merit scholarship grants, need-based scholarship grants available. In 2015–16, 25% of upper-school students received aid.

Admissions Traditional secondary-level entrance grade is 9. Otis-Lennon, Stanford Achievement Test required. Deadline for receipt of application materials: February 12. Application fee required: $50. On-campus interview recommended.

Athletics Interscholastic: baseball (boys), basketball (b,g), cross-country running (b,g), field hockey (g), football (b), indoor soccer (b,g), lacrosse (b,g), soccer (b,g), softball (g), tennis (b,g), track and field (b,g), volleyball (b,g), winter soccer (b,g); coed interscholastic: aquatics, canoeing/kayaking, diving, golf, indoor track, kayaking, mountain biking, paddling, running, swimming and diving, winter (indoor) track, wrestling; coed intramural: aerobics/dance, backpacking, canoeing/kayaking, climbing, dance, fitness, outdoor activities, outdoor adventure, outdoor education, outdoor recreation, outdoor skills, physical fitness, physical training, rappelling, rock climbing, scuba diving, strength & conditioning, table tennis, wall climbing, weight lifting, weight training, yoga. 1 PE instructor, 14 coaches, 2 athletic trainers.

Computers Computers are regularly used in animation, graphic design, library, library skills, music technology, photography, science, social studies, video film production, word processing, writing, yearbook classes. Computer resources include on-campus library services, online commercial services, Internet access, wireless campus network, Internet filtering or blocking technology, 1:1 Apple laptop program. Campus intranet and student e-mail accounts are available to students. Students grades are available online. The school has a published electronic and media policy.

Contact Mrs. Margie Snead, Director of Admission. 804-327-3151. Fax: 804-272-4652. E-mail: margiesnead@trinityes.org. Website: www.trinityes.org

TRINITY HIGH SCHOOL
4011 Shelbyville Road
Louisville, Kentucky 40207-9427

Head of School: Robert J. Mullen, EdD

General Information Boys' day college-preparatory, arts, business, religious studies, and technology school, affiliated with Roman Catholic Church. Grades 9–12. Founded: 1953. Setting: suburban. 110-acre campus. 11 buildings on campus. Approved or accredited by National Catholic Education Association, Southern Association of Colleges and Schools, Southern Association of Independent Schools, and Kentucky Department of Education. Member of National Association of Independent Schools. Endowment: $21 million. Total enrollment: 1,230. Upper school average class size: 20. Upper school faculty-student ratio: 1:12. There are 175 required school days per year for Upper School students. Upper School students typically attend 5 days per week. The average school day consists of 7 hours.

Upper School Student Profile Grade 9: 320 students (320 boys); Grade 10: 300 students (300 boys); Grade 11: 310 students (310 boys); Grade 12: 300 students (300 boys). 84% of students are Roman Catholic.

Faculty School total: 120. In upper school: 88 men, 30 women; 110 have advanced degrees.

Subjects Offered 20th century history, 3-dimensional art, accounting, acting, adolescent issues, advanced chemistry, advanced computer applications, advanced math, Advanced Placement courses, advanced studio art-AP, algebra, American Civil War, American democracy, American foreign policy, American government, American history, American history-AP, American literature, American literature-AP, analysis and differential calculus, analysis of data, anatomy and physiology, ancient history, ancient world history, applied arts, applied music, art, art and culture, art appreciation, art education, art history, art-AP, arts, arts appreciation, athletic training, athletics, band, banking, Basic programming, Bible as literature, biology, biology-AP, broadcasting, business, business education, business law, business mathematics, business studies, business technology, calculus, calculus-AP, campus ministry, career exploration, career planning, career/college preparation, cell biology, character education, cheerleading, chemistry, chemistry-AP, choir, choral music, chorus, Christian doctrine, Christian ethics, Christian scripture, church history, cinematography, civics, Civil War, classical civilization, classical Greek literature, classical music, college admission preparation, college awareness, college counseling, college placement, college planning, communication arts, communication skills, community service, comparative cultures, comparative government and politics, composition-AP, computer animation, computer applications, computer art, computer education, computer graphics, computer information systems, computer literacy, computer math, computer multimedia, computer music, computer processing, computer programming, computer science, computer skills, computer studies, computer technologies, computer technology certification, computer tools, computers, concert band, concert choir, conflict resolution, constitutional law, contemporary art, CPR, creative writing, critical studies in film, critical thinking, critical writing, data analysis, data processing, death and loss, decision making skills, developmental math, digital photography, DNA research, drama, drama performance, drawing, drawing and design, earth and space science, earth science, ecology, economics, economics and history, economics-AP, English, English language and composition-AP, English literature, English-AP, environmental studies, European civilization, European history, evolution, family living, fencing, film, film studies, finite math, first aid, forensics, French, general science, geography, geometry, German, health, health science, Hebrew scripture, Holocaust studies, HTML design, humanities, independent study, information technology, instrumental music, integrated mathematics, interdisciplinary studies, Internet, jazz band, journalism, keyboarding, language arts, leadership and service, literature, literature-AP, martial arts, mathematics, modern civilization, moral and social development, multimedia design, music performance, musical theater, New Testament, news writing, newspaper, oil painting, painting, peace and justice, philosophy, photography, photojournalism, physical education, physical fitness, physical science, physics, physics-AP, post-calculus, pottery, pre-algebra, pre-calculus, probability and statistics, programming, psychology, public speaking, religion, religious studies, Roman civilization, Romantic period literature, Russian history, SAT/ACT preparation, science, sculpture, senior seminar, social justice, social psychology, social sciences, social studies, sociology, software design, space and physical sciences, Spanish, Spanish literature, Spanish-AP, speech and debate, sports medicine, sports nutrition, stage design, stained glass, statistics, student government, student publications, technology, trigonometry, U.S. government and politics-AP, U.S. history-AP, video film production, Web site design, weight training, Western civilization, work-study, world civilizations, world history, world history-AP, yearbook.

Graduation Requirements ACT preparation, algebra, biology, chemistry, Christian and Hebrew scripture, Christian ethics, church history, civics, communication arts, computer education, English, English literature, European literature, foreign language, grammar, health and wellness, humanities, lab science, mathematics, physical education (includes health), physics, pre-calculus, reading, religion (includes Bible studies and theology), science, social justice, social studies (includes history), U.S. history, world geography, several elective offerings, must have taken the ACT. Community service is required.

Special Academic Programs Advanced Placement exam preparation; honors section; independent study; study at local college for college credit; study abroad; academic accommodation for the gifted, the musically talented, and the artistically talented; remedial reading and/or remedial writing; remedial math; programs in English, mathematics, general development for dyslexic students; special instructional classes for deaf students, blind students.

College Admission Counseling 295 students graduated in 2015; 291 went to college, including Bellarmine University; Eastern Kentucky University; Indiana University Bloomington; University of Dayton; University of Kentucky; University of Louisville. Other: 2 went to work, 2 entered military service. Mean combined SAT: 1817, mean composite ACT: 24.

Student Life Upper grades have specified standards of dress, student council, honor system. Discipline rests primarily with faculty. Attendance at religious services is required.

Summer Programs Remediation, enrichment, advancement, sports, art/fine arts, computer instruction programs offered; session focuses on academic advancement and enrichment/sports camps; held on campus; accepts boys; not open to students from other schools. 1,000 students usually enrolled. 2016 schedule: June 1 to August 3. Application deadline: May 15.

Tuition and Aid Day student tuition: $12,700. Guaranteed tuition plan. Tuition installment plan (monthly payment plans, individually arranged payment plans, Tuition Management Systems). Merit scholarship grants, need-based scholarship grants, paying campus jobs available. In 2015–16, 44% of upper-school students received aid; total upper-school merit-scholarship money awarded: $120,000. Total amount of financial aid awarded in 2015–16: $2,700,000.

Admissions Traditional secondary-level entrance grade is 9. High School Placement Test required. Deadline for receipt of application materials: none. Application fee required: $75. Interview required.

Athletics Interscholastic: archery, baseball, basketball, bicycling, bowling, cheering, crew, cross-country running, diving, fishing, football, golf, hockey, ice hockey, lacrosse, power lifting, rugby, soccer, swimming and diving, tennis, track and field, volleyball, weight lifting, wrestling; intramural: alpine skiing, basketball, bocce, climbing, cricket, fencing, fishing, flag football, freestyle skiing, Frisbee, golf, hiking/backpacking, judo, kickball, life saving, martial arts, mountain biking, outdoor adventure, paddle tennis, rock climbing, skiing (downhill), snowboarding, strength & conditioning, table tennis, ultimate Frisbee, volleyball, water polo, weight lifting, weight training; coed intramural: bowling. 5 PE instructors, 30 coaches, 3 athletic trainers.

Computers Computers are regularly used in all classes. Computer network features include on-campus library services, online commercial services, Internet access, wireless campus network, Internet filtering or blocking technology, free use of Office 365, cloud-based document storage. Campus intranet, student e-mail accounts, and computer access in designated common areas are available to students. Students grades are available online. The school has a published electronic and media policy.

Contact Mr. Joseph M. Porter Jr., Vice President for Advancement. 502-736-2119. Fax: 502-899-2052. E-mail: porter@thsrock.net. Website: www.trinityrocks.com

TRINITY HIGH SCHOOL

581 Bridge Street
Manchester, New Hampshire 03104

Head of School: Mr. Denis Mailloux

General Information Coeducational day college-preparatory, arts, religious studies, and technology school, affiliated with Roman Catholic Church. Grades 9–12. Founded: 1886. Setting: urban. Nearest major city is Boston, MA. 5-acre campus. 2 buildings on campus. Approved or accredited by National Catholic Education Association, New England Association of Schools and Colleges, and New Hampshire Department of Education. Total enrollment: 398. Upper school average class size: 15. Upper school faculty-student ratio: 1:12. There are 180 required school days per year for Upper School students. Upper School students typically attend 5 days per week. The average school day consists of 6 hours and 40 minutes.

Upper School Student Profile Grade 9: 91 students (46 boys, 45 girls); Grade 10: 85 students (38 boys, 47 girls); Grade 11: 110 students (65 boys, 45 girls); Grade 12: 112 students (63 boys, 49 girls). 80% of students are Roman Catholic.

Faculty School total: 34. In upper school: 20 men, 14 women; 25 have advanced degrees.

Subjects Offered 3-dimensional art, advanced biology, advanced math, Advanced Placement courses, algebra, American government, American history, American history-AP, American literature, analysis, anatomy and physiology, art, Bible studies, biology, calculus, calculus-AP, chemistry, computer science, driver education, English, English literature, English-AP, ethics, French, geometry, grammar, health, history, human development, journalism, Latin, mathematics, physical education, physics, psychology, psychology-AP, religion, science, social studies, sociology, Spanish, theology, trigonometry, U.S. history-AP, world history, world literature.

Special Academic Programs 5 Advanced Placement exams for which test preparation is offered; honors section; study at local college for college credit.

College Admission Counseling 101 students graduated in 2015; 95 went to college, including Boston University; Keene State College; Northeastern University; Saint Anselm College; Stonehill College; University of New Hampshire. Other: 4 went to work, 2 entered a postgraduate year.

Student Life Upper grades have specified standards of dress, student council, honor system. Discipline rests primarily with faculty. Attendance at religious services is required.

Tuition and Aid Day student tuition: $10,875. Tuition installment plan (FACTS Tuition Payment Plan). Need-based scholarship grants available. In 2015–16, 10% of upper-school students received aid.

Admissions Traditional secondary-level entrance grade is 9. STS required. Deadline for receipt of application materials: none. Application fee required: $50. Interview recommended.

Athletics Interscholastic: baseball (boys), basketball (b,g), cheering (g), crew (b,g), cross-country running (b,g), football (b), gymnastics (g), hockey (b), ice hockey (b), indoor track & field (b,g), lacrosse (b), skiing (cross-country) (b,g), skiing (downhill) (b,g), soccer (b,g), softball (g), swimming and diving (b,g), tennis (b,g), volleyball (g), winter (indoor) track (b,g), wrestling (b); coed interscholastic: alpine skiing, golf, track and field; coed intramural: gymnastics. 1 PE instructor, 25 coaches, 1 athletic trainer.

Computers Computers are regularly used in all academic, English, journalism, science, social sciences, yearbook classes. Computer network features include Internet access, wireless campus network. Campus intranet and student e-mail accounts are available to students. Students grades are available online.

Contact Mr. Patrick Smith, Dean of Students and Director of Admissions. 603-668-2910 Ext. 218. Fax: 603-668-2913. E-mail: psmith@trinity-hs.org. Website: www.trinity-hs.org

TRINITY HIGH SCHOOL

12425 Granger Road
Garfield Heights, Ohio 44125

Head of School: Mrs. Linda Bacho

General Information Coeducational day college-preparatory, arts, business, religious studies, technology, technical, and medical school, affiliated with Roman Catholic Church. Grades 9–12. Founded: 1926. Setting: suburban. Nearest major city is Cleveland. 26-acre campus. 3 buildings on campus. Approved or accredited by National Catholic Education Association, North Central Association of Colleges and Schools, Ohio Catholic Schools Accreditation Association (OCSAA), and Ohio Department of Education. Total enrollment: 327. Upper school average class size: 17. Upper school faculty-student ratio: 1:10. There are 199 required school days per year for Upper School students. Upper School students typically attend 5 days per week. The average school day consists of 7 hours.

Upper School Student Profile Grade 9: 68 students (33 boys, 35 girls); Grade 10: 89 students (43 boys, 46 girls); Grade 11: 75 students (36 boys, 39 girls); Grade 12: 95 students (37 boys, 58 girls). 78% of students are Roman Catholic.

Faculty School total: 32. In upper school: 10 men, 22 women; 13 have advanced degrees.

Subjects Offered 3-dimensional art, accounting, advanced biology, advanced chemistry, advanced computer applications, advanced math, Advanced Placement courses, advanced studio art-AP, algebra, American government, American history, American history-AP, American literature, analysis and differential calculus, anatomy and physiology, animation, art, athletics, automated accounting, band, Bible, Bible studies, biology, bookkeeping, British literature, British literature (honors), business applications, business skills, business technology, calculus-AP, campus ministry, career and personal planning, career education, career education internship, career experience, career exploration, career planning, career/college preparation, Catholic belief and practice, ceramics, chemistry, choir, Christian and Hebrew scripture, Christian doctrine, Christian ethics, Christian scripture, Christian testament, church history, college admission preparation, college awareness, college counseling, college placement, college planning, college writing, communication skills, community service, comparative religion, competitive science projects, computer animation, computer applications, computer art, computer education, computer graphics, computer information systems, computer multimedia, computer technologies, computer technology certification, computer-aided design, concert band, concert choir, consumer economics, creative writing, critical thinking, critical writing, culinary arts, digital applications, drama performance, drawing and design, earth science, economics and history, electives, English, English literature and composition-AP, environmental science, ethics, European history, food and nutrition, foods, foreign language, four units of summer reading, geometry, global studies, government-AP, graphic arts, graphic design, graphics, guidance, health education, honors algebra, honors English, honors geometry, human anatomy, human biology, instrumental music, integrated mathematics, Internet research, internship, lab science, library, life issues, Life of Christ, marching band, marine biology, Microsoft, moral theology, musical theater, neuroscience, oral communications, participation in sports, peace and justice, peer ministry, personal finance, photo shop, physical education, physics, play production, portfolio art, prayer/spirituality, pre-algebra, pre-calculus, psychology, public speaking, SAT/ACT preparation, speech, sports, studio art-AP, study skills, symphonic band, theology, U.S. government and politics-AP, video, video and animation, vocal ensemble, Web site design, wind ensemble, word processing, world history, yearbook.

Graduation Requirements Arts and fine arts (art, music, dance, drama), electives, English, government, human relations, mathematics, physical education (includes health), science, social studies (includes history), theology, Western civilization, service hours, internship.

Special Academic Programs Advanced Placement exam preparation; honors section; independent study; academic accommodation for the gifted and the artistically talented; remedial math; programs in English, mathematics, general development for dyslexic students.

College Admission Counseling 60 students graduated in 2015; 57 went to college, including John Carroll University; Kent State University; Miami University; Ohio University; The Ohio State University; University of Dayton. Other: 2 went to work, 1 entered military service. Median composite ACT: 23.

Student Life Upper grades have uniform requirement, student council. Discipline rests primarily with faculty. Attendance at religious services is required.

Summer Programs Enrichment, advancement, sports, art/fine arts programs offered; session focuses on recruitment; held both on and off campus; held at other schools; accepts boys and girls; open to students from other schools. 125 students usually enrolled. 2016 schedule: June 8 to June 30. Application deadline: May 30.

Tuition and Aid Day student tuition: $11,100. Guaranteed tuition plan. Tuition installment plan (individually arranged payment plans, private bank loans). Tuition reduction for siblings, need-based scholarship grants, middle-income loans, private bank loans available. In 2015–16, 25% of upper-school students received aid. Total amount of financial aid awarded in 2015–16: $150,000.

Admissions Traditional secondary-level entrance grade is 9. For fall 2015, 75 students applied for upper-level admission, 72 were accepted, 68 enrolled. Scholastic Testing Service High School Placement Test required. Deadline for receipt of application materials: none. Application fee required: $20. On-campus interview required.

Athletics Interscholastic: baseball (boys), basketball (b,g), cheering (g), cross-country running (b,g), danceline (g), football (b), soccer (b,g), softball (g), track and field (b,g), volleyball (g), wrestling (b); coed interscholastic: golf, indoor track & field; coed intramural: skiing (downhill), snowboarding. 1 PE instructor, 34 coaches, 1 athletic trainer.

Computers Computers are regularly used in all academic classes. Computer network features include on-campus library services, online commercial services, Internet access, wireless campus network, Internet filtering or blocking technology, network printing, personal storage on network, weekly email grade reports, electronic newsletters, remote access, school Web site, online homework tracking system. Computer access in designated common areas is available to students. Students grades are available online. The school has a published electronic and media policy.

Contact Sr. Dian Majsterek, Administrative Assistant, Admissions and Marketing. 216-581-1061. Fax: 216-581-9348. E-mail: SisterDian@ths.org. Website: www.ths.org

TRINITY-PAWLING SCHOOL

700 Route 22
Pawling, New York 12564

Head of School: Mr. William W. Taylor

General Information Boys' boarding and day college-preparatory, arts, religious studies, technology, and English Language Program school, affiliated with Episcopal Church. Boarding grades 9–PG, day grades 7–PG. Founded: 1907. Setting: small town. Nearest major city is New York. Students are housed in single-sex dormitories. 140-acre campus. 31 buildings on campus. Approved or accredited by New York State Association of Independent Schools. Member of National Association of Independent Schools and Secondary School Admission Test Board. Endowment: $35 million. Total enrollment: 285. Upper school average class size: 12. Upper school faculty-student ratio: 1:8. There are 186 required school days per year for Upper School students.

Upper School students typically attend 6 days per week. The average school day consists of 6 hours and 30 minutes.

Upper School Student Profile Grade 9: 32 students (32 boys); Grade 10: 61 students (61 boys); Grade 11: 89 students (89 boys); Grade 12: 61 students (61 boys); Postgraduate: 21 students (21 boys). 80% of students are boarding students. 20% are state residents. 28 states are represented in upper school student body. 25% are international students. International students from Canada, China, Hong Kong, Republic of Korea, Taiwan, and Viet Nam; 8 other countries represented in student body. 20% of students are members of Episcopal Church.

Faculty School total: 56. In upper school: 37 men, 19 women; 37 have advanced degrees; 52 reside on campus.

Subjects Offered Advanced Placement courses, advanced studio art-AP, algebra, American government, American history, American legal systems, American literature, American studies, anatomy, anatomy and physiology, architectural drawing, art, art history, art history-AP, Asian history, Asian studies, astronomy, Bible, biology, biology-AP, calculus, calculus-AP, ceramics, chemistry, chemistry-AP, choir, chorus, Christian ethics, civil rights, composition-AP, computer applications, computer information systems, computer math, computer music, computer programming, computer science, computer science-AP, computer technologies, constitutional history of U.S., data analysis, drafting, drama, drama performance, earth science, East Asian history, ecology, economics, economics-AP, English, English language-AP, English literature, English literature-AP, English-AP, English/composition-AP, environmental science, environmental science-AP, environmental studies, ESL, ethics, European history, European history-AP, fine arts, French, French language-AP, French studies, geology, geometry, government, government and politics-AP, government/civics, grammar, health science, history, honors algebra, honors English, honors geometry, honors U.S. history, honors world history, human anatomy, keyboarding, Latin, Latin American literature, Latin-AP, law and the legal system, literature, literature and composition-AP, Mandarin, mathematics, mechanical drawing, model United Nations, music, philosophy, photography, physical education, physics, physics-AP, physiology, political science, pre-calculus, probability and statistics, psychology, public speaking, reading/study skills, religion, religious education, religious studies, SAT preparation, science, Shakespeare, social justice, social sciences, social studies, Spanish, Spanish language-AP, Spanish literature-AP, statistics-AP, studio art, studio art-AP, study skills, theater, theology, trigonometry, U.S. government and politics, U.S. history, U.S. history-AP, Vietnam War, word processing, world history, writing, yearbook.

Graduation Requirements Arts and fine arts (art, music, dance, drama), English, foreign language, mathematics, religion (includes Bible studies and theology), science, social studies (includes history).

Special Academic Programs 17 Advanced Placement exams for which test preparation is offered; honors section; remedial reading and/or remedial writing; programs in English for dyslexic students; ESL (25 students enrolled).

College Admission Counseling 102 students graduated in 2015; all went to college, including Bowdoin College; Carnegie Mellon University; Cornell University; Emory University; Northwestern University; University of California, Berkeley. Mean SAT critical reading: 580, mean SAT math: 570.

Student Life Upper grades have specified standards of dress, student council, honor system. Discipline rests equally with students and faculty. Attendance at religious services is required.

Tuition and Aid Day student tuition: $38,850; 7-day tuition and room/board: $54,900. Tuition installment plan (monthly payment plans, individually arranged payment plans, payment plans are arranged directly with the school business office). Need-based scholarship grants, need-based loans, middle-income loans, loans are arranged directly through the Your Tuition Solution Plan available. In 2015–16, 40% of upper-school students received aid. Total amount of financial aid awarded in 2015–16: $3,500,000.

Admissions Traditional secondary-level entrance grade is 9. For fall 2015, 411 students applied for upper-level admission, 280 were accepted, 108 enrolled. PSAT or SAT, SSAT, TOEFL, Wechsler Intelligence Scale for Children III or WISC-R required. Deadline for receipt of application materials: January 15. Application fee required: $50. On-campus interview required.

Athletics Interscholastic: alpine skiing, baseball, basketball, cross-country running, football, golf, hockey, ice hockey, lacrosse, ropes courses, skiing (downhill), soccer, squash, strength & conditioning, tennis, track and field, weight lifting, weight training, wrestling; intramural: alpine skiing, basketball, bicycling, climbing, fishing, fitness, floor hockey, fly fishing, Frisbee, golf, hiking/backpacking, ice skating, mountain biking, outdoor education, outdoor recreation, physical training, polo, rock climbing, running, skiing (downhill), snowboarding, soccer, softball, squash, strength & conditioning, tennis, trap and skeet, ultimate Frisbee, wall climbing, weight lifting. 30 coaches, 2 athletic trainers.

Computers Computers are regularly used in English, history, mathematics, remedial study skills, science classes. Computer network features include on-campus library services, online commercial services, Internet access, wireless campus network, Internet filtering or blocking technology. Campus intranet, student e-mail accounts, and computer access in designated common areas are available to students. Students grades are available online. The school has a published electronic and media policy.

Contact Ms. Amy Heinrich, Admission Office Manager. 845-855-4825. Fax: 845-855-4827. E-mail: aheinrich@trinitypawling.org. Website: www.trinitypawling.org

TRINITY PREPARATORY SCHOOL

5700 Trinity Prep Lane
Winter Park, Florida 32792

Head of School: Craig S. Maughan

General Information Coeducational day college-preparatory, arts, technology, and Stanford Online video conferencing courses school, affiliated with Episcopal Church. Grades 6–12. Founded: 1966. Setting: suburban. Nearest major city is Orlando. 100-acre campus. 12 buildings on campus. Approved or accredited by Florida Council of Independent Schools and Florida Department of Education. Member of National Association of Independent Schools and Secondary School Admission Test Board. Endowment: $9.2 million. Total enrollment: 861. Upper school average class size: 18. Upper school faculty-student ratio: 1:10. There are 175 required school days per year for Upper School students. Upper School students typically attend 5 days per week. The average school day consists of 5 hours and 45 minutes.

Upper School Student Profile Grade 9: 131 students (65 boys, 66 girls); Grade 10: 129 students (66 boys, 63 girls); Grade 11: 129 students (74 boys, 55 girls); Grade 12: 127 students (72 boys, 55 girls). 7% of students are members of Episcopal Church.

Faculty School total: 75. In upper school: 23 men, 34 women; 34 have advanced degrees.

Subjects Offered 20th century American writers, 20th century world history, 3-dimensional art, advanced math, Advanced Placement courses, advanced studio art-AP, algebra, American history, American literature, anatomy, animal science, art, athletic training, audio visual/media, band, Basic programming, Bible, biology, biology-AP, calculus, calculus-AP, character education, chemistry, chemistry-AP, chorus, civics, comparative religion, computer graphics, computer multimedia, computer processing, computer programming, computer programming-AP, concert band, concert choir, creative writing, critical studies in film, digital photography, drama, drawing, economics, economics-AP, English, English language and composition-AP, English literature, English literature and composition-AP, environmental science, environmental science-AP, ethics, European history, European history-AP, filmmaking, fine arts, forensics, French, French language-AP, French literature-AP, geography, geometry, government and politics-AP, health, honors algebra, honors English, honors geometry, journalism, Latin, Latin-AP, life management skills, mathematics, music, music theory-AP, newspaper, painting, physical education, physics, physics-AP, portfolio art, pottery, pre-algebra, pre-calculus, probability and statistics, psychology, psychology-AP, robotics, science, sculpture, social studies, Spanish, Spanish language-AP, Spanish literature-AP, speech, strings, studio art-AP, theater, trigonometry, U.S. government and politics-AP, U.S. history-AP, weight training, world history, world wide web design, writing, yearbook.

Graduation Requirements 1 1/2 elective credits, arts and fine arts (art, music, dance, drama), computer science, electives, English, foreign language, life management skills, mathematics, physical education (includes health), science, social sciences, 1/2 additional social studies credit.

Special Academic Programs 26 Advanced Placement exams for which test preparation is offered; honors section; independent study; study at local college for college credit; study abroad; academic accommodation for the gifted, the musically talented, and the artistically talented.

College Admission Counseling 130 students graduated in 2015; all went to college, including Florida State University; Furman University; Northwestern University; The University of Alabama in Huntsville; University of Florida.

Student Life Upper grades have specified standards of dress, student council, honor system. Discipline rests primarily with faculty. Attendance at religious services is required.

Summer Programs Remediation, enrichment, advancement, sports, art/fine arts, computer instruction programs offered; session focuses on enrichment; held on campus; accepts boys and girls; open to students from other schools. 300 students usually enrolled. 2016 schedule: June 14 to August 8. Application deadline: none.

Tuition and Aid Day student tuition: $19,450. Tuition installment plan (Insured Tuition Payment Plan, monthly payment plans, semiannual and annual payment plans). Need-based scholarship grants available. In 2015–16, 25% of upper-school students received aid. Total amount of financial aid awarded in 2015–16: $2,670,890.

Admissions Traditional secondary-level entrance grade is 9. For fall 2015, 74 students applied for upper-level admission, 41 were accepted, 29 enrolled. CTP, ISEE, PSAT, SAT or SSAT required. Deadline for receipt of application materials: February 5. Application fee required: $75. Interview required.

Athletics Interscholastic: baseball (boys), basketball (b,g), bowling (b,g), cheering (g), cross-country running (b,g), diving (b,g), fitness (b,g), football (b), golf (b,g), lacrosse (b,g), physical fitness (b,g), soccer (b,g), softball (g), strength & conditioning (b,g), swimming and diving (b,g), tennis (b,g), track and field (b,g), volleyball (g), weight lifting (b,g), weight training (b,g); intramural: ropes courses (b,g), strength & conditioning (b,g). 5 PE instructors, 48 coaches, 1 athletic trainer.

Computers Computer network features include on-campus library services, online commercial services, Internet access, wireless campus network, Internet filtering or blocking technology. Student e-mail accounts and computer access in designated common areas are available to students. Students grades are available online. The school has a published electronic and media policy.

Contact Catherine Hay, Associate Director of Admission. 321-282-2545. Fax: 407-671-6935. E-mail: hayc@trinityprep.org. Website: www.trinityprep.org

TRINITY SCHOOL

139 West 91st Street
New York, New York 10024

Head of School: Allman John

General Information Coeducational day college-preparatory school, affiliated with Episcopal Church. Grades K–12. Founded: 1709. Setting: urban. 1 building on campus. Approved or accredited by National Association of Private Schools for Exceptional Children, New York State Association of Independent Schools, and New York Department of Education. Member of National Association of Independent Schools. Endowment: $50 million. Total enrollment: 990. Upper school average class size: 16. Upper school faculty-student ratio: 1:7. Upper School students typically attend 5 days per week.

Upper School Student Profile Grade 9: 110 students (55 boys, 55 girls); Grade 10: 110 students (55 boys, 55 girls); Grade 11: 110 students (55 boys, 55 girls); Grade 12: 110 students (55 boys, 55 girls). 5% of students are members of Episcopal Church.

Faculty School total: 165. In upper school: 52 men, 45 women; 74 have advanced degrees.

Subjects Offered Algebra, American history, American literature, art, art history, biology, calculus, ceramics, chemistry, computer math, computer programming, computer science, creative writing, dance, drama, driver education, economics, English, English literature, environmental science, ethics, European history, expository writing, fine arts, French, geometry, German, government/civics, Greek, history, Latin, marine biology, mathematics, music, photography, physical education, physics, psychology, religion, science, social studies, Spanish, speech, statistics, theater, trigonometry.

Graduation Requirements Arts and fine arts (art, music, dance, drama), English, foreign language, mathematics, physical education (includes health), religion (includes Bible studies and theology), science, social studies (includes history).

Special Academic Programs Honors section; independent study.

College Admission Counseling 110 students graduated in 2014; all went to college, including Brown University; Columbia College; Harvard University; Princeton University; University of Pennsylvania.

Student Life Upper grades have specified standards of dress, student council. Discipline rests equally with students and faculty.

Tuition and Aid Day student tuition: $40,895. Middle-income loans, need-based grants available. In 2014–15, 23% of upper-school students received aid. Total amount of financial aid awarded in 2014–15: $2,500,000.

Admissions Traditional secondary-level entrance grade is 9. For fall 2014, 500 students applied for upper-level admission, 90 were accepted, 55 enrolled. SSAT required. Deadline for receipt of application materials: January 12. Application fee required: $60. On-campus interview required.

Athletics Interscholastic: baseball (boys), basketball (b,g), golf (b,g), indoor track & field (b,g), lacrosse (b,g), soccer (b,g), softball (g), tennis (b,g), track and field (b,g), volleyball (g), winter (indoor) track (b,g), wrestling (b); coed interscholastic: cross-country running, swimming and diving, water polo. 16 PE instructors, 45 coaches, 1 athletic trainer.

Computers Computers are regularly used in art, mathematics, science classes. Computer network features include on-campus library services, Internet access. Student e-mail accounts are available to students. The school has a published electronic and media policy.

Contact Danielle Considine Rettinger, Associate Director of Admissions. 212-932-6823. Fax: 212-932-6812 Ext. 6819. E-mail: danielle.rettinger@trinityschoolnyc.org. Website: www.trinityschoolnyc.org

TRINITY SCHOOL OF TEXAS

215 Teague Street
Longview, Texas 75601

Head of School: Mr. Gary L. Whitwell

General Information Coeducational day college-preparatory, arts, religious studies, and technology school, affiliated with Episcopal Church. Grades PK–12. Founded: 1957. Setting: small town. Nearest major city is Dallas. 14-acre campus. 4 buildings on campus. Approved or accredited by National Association of Episcopal Schools, Southern Association of Colleges and Schools, Southwest Association of Episcopal Schools, and Texas Department of Education. Endowment: $315,000. Total enrollment: 265. Upper school average class size: 12. Upper school faculty-student ratio: 1:8. There are 174 required school days per year for Upper School students. Upper School students typically attend 5 days per week. The average school day consists of 6 hours and 20 minutes.

Upper School Student Profile Grade 9: 15 students (9 boys, 6 girls); Grade 10: 15 students (9 boys, 6 girls); Grade 11: 12 students (5 boys, 7 girls); Grade 12: 18 students (9 boys, 9 girls). 11% of students are members of Episcopal Church.

Faculty School total: 38. In upper school: 3 men, 13 women; 3 have advanced degrees.

Subjects Offered Advanced studio art-AP, algebra, American history, art, astronomy, athletics, biology, biology-AP, calculus, calculus-AP, Central and Eastern European history, character education, chemistry, chemistry-AP, choral music, college admission preparation, college writing, community service, computer applications, computer literacy, conflict resolution, creative writing, desktop publishing, digital photography, drama performance, earth science, economics, English-AP, environmental studies,

European history-AP, geography, geometry, government, government/civics, grammar, health, junior and senior seminars, keyboarding, language and composition, language arts, leadership and service, library, life science, literature and composition-AP, mathematics, modern European history, modern Western civilization, modern world history, music, music performance, mythology, newspaper, participation in sports, personal finance, photography, photojournalism, physical education, physical fitness, physical science, physics, pre-algebra, pre-calculus, probability and statistics, psychology, psychology-AP, religious studies, research seminar, research skills, SAT preparation, SAT/ACT preparation, sociology, Spanish, Spanish language-AP, sports, statistics, student publications, studio art, Texas history, U.S. government, U.S. history, world geography, world history, world religions, yearbook.

Graduation Requirements Arts and fine arts (art, music, dance, drama), computers, English, government/civics, languages, mathematics, physical education (includes health), science, social sciences, speech, theology.

Special Academic Programs Advanced Placement exam preparation; accelerated programs; independent study; term-away projects; study at local college for college credit; study abroad; academic accommodation for the gifted, the musically talented, and the artistically talented; programs in English, mathematics for dyslexic students.

College Admission Counseling 18 students graduated in 2015; all went to college, including Louisiana State University and Agricultural & Mechanical College; Texas A&M University; The University of Texas at Austin. Median SAT critical reading: 530, median SAT math: 620, median SAT writing: 535, median combined SAT: 1690, median composite ACT: 23. 18% scored over 600 on SAT critical reading, 23% scored over 600 on SAT math, 13% scored over 600 on SAT writing, 42% scored over 26 on composite ACT.

Student Life Upper grades have specified standards of dress, student council, honor system. Discipline rests primarily with faculty. Attendance at religious services is required.

Summer Programs Remediation, enrichment, advancement programs offered; session focuses on broad, age-appropriate opportunities for child development; held both on and off campus; held at a wide variety of excursions related to weekly themes; accepts boys and girls; open to students from other schools. 47 students usually enrolled. 2016 schedule: May 31 to July 29. Application deadline: April 15.

Tuition and Aid Day student tuition: $8500. Tuition installment plan (FACTS Tuition Payment Plan, monthly payment plans, individually arranged payment plans, semester payment plan). Merit scholarship grants, need-based scholarship grants available. In 2015–16, 22% of upper-school students received aid; total upper-school merit-scholarship money awarded: $650,000.

Admissions Traditional secondary-level entrance grade is 9. For fall 2015, 12 students applied for upper-level admission, 12 were accepted, 12 enrolled. Otis-Lennon, Stanford Achievement Test, PSAT or SAT for applicants to grade 11 and 12, Woodcock-Johnson Revised Achievement Test and writing sample required. Deadline for receipt of application materials: none. Application fee required: $850. On-campus interview required.

Athletics Interscholastic: baseball (boys), basketball (b,g), cheering (g), football (b), golf (b,g), physical fitness (b), power lifting (b), tennis (b,g), track and field (b,g), volleyball (g); intramural: football (b), physical fitness (b,g), tennis (b,g), volleyball (g); coed interscholastic: soccer; coed intramural: soccer, track and field, weight training. 2 PE instructors, 4 coaches.

Computers Computers are regularly used in college planning, computer applications, creative writing, English, geography, history, journalism, keyboarding, library, mathematics, newspaper, photography, photojournalism, psychology, publications, publishing, research skills, SAT preparation, science, senior seminar, Spanish, technology, writing, yearbook classes. Computer network features include on-campus library services, online commercial services, Internet access, Internet filtering or blocking technology. The school has a published electronic and media policy.

Contact Mrs. Cissy Abernathy, Director of Admission. 903-753-0612 Ext. 236. Fax: 903-753-4812. E-mail: cabernathy@trinityschooloftexas.com. Website: www.trinityschooloftexas.com

TRINITY VALLEY SCHOOL

7500 Dutch Branch Road
Fort Worth, Texas 76132

Head of School: Dr. Gary Krahn

General Information Coeducational day college-preparatory school. Grades K–12. Founded: 1959. Setting: urban. 75-acre campus. 7 buildings on campus. Approved or accredited by Independent Schools Association of the Southwest and Texas Department of Education. Member of National Association of Independent Schools. Endowment: $38 million. Total enrollment: 962. Upper school average class size: 16. Upper school faculty-student ratio: 1:8. There are 170 required school days per year for Upper School students. Upper School students typically attend 5 days per week. The average school day consists of 7 hours and 45 minutes.

Upper School Student Profile Grade 9: 95 students (42 boys, 53 girls); Grade 10: 90 students (46 boys, 44 girls); Grade 11: 89 students (50 boys, 39 girls); Grade 12: 80 students (39 boys, 41 girls).

Faculty School total: 115. In upper school: 27 men, 36 women; 44 have advanced degrees.

Subjects Offered Algebra, American culture, American history, American history-AP, ancient history, ancient world history, art, Asian history, biology, biology-AP, British history, calculus, calculus-AP, ceramics, chemistry, chemistry-AP, Chinese, choir, computer graphics, computer science, computer science-AP, constitutional law, creative writing, debate, digital imaging, economics, economics-AP, English, English language-AP, English literature-AP, environmental science, French, French-AP, geometry, government/civics, humanities, journalism, Latin, Latin-AP, leadership, modern European history, photography, physical education, physics, physics-AP, psychology-AP, Spanish, Spanish-AP, statistics, statistics-AP, technical theater, theater arts, U.S. government, U.S. government and politics-AP, video film production, writing workshop, yearbook.

Graduation Requirements Algebra, American government, American history, arts and fine arts (art, music, dance, drama), biology, chemistry, economics, English, foreign language, geometry, physical education (includes health), physics, pre-calculus, Western civilization, students must complete 60 hours of community service in the U.S. Community service is required.

Special Academic Programs 22 Advanced Placement exams for which test preparation is offered; honors section; academic accommodation for the gifted, the musically talented, and the artistically talented.

College Admission Counseling 88 students graduated in 2014; all went to college, including Southern Methodist University; Texas A&M University; Texas Christian University; The University of Texas at Austin; Tulane University; University of Oklahoma. Mean SAT critical reading: 613, mean SAT math: 610, mean SAT writing: 604, mean composite ACT: 28.

Student Life Upper grades have uniform requirement, student council, honor system. Discipline rests equally with students and faculty.

Tuition and Aid Day student tuition: $19,970. Tuition installment plan (monthly payment plans). Need-based scholarship grants available. In 2014–15, 17% of upper-school students received aid. Total amount of financial aid awarded in 2014–15: $916,480.

Admissions Traditional secondary-level entrance grade is 9. For fall 2014, 36 students applied for upper-level admission, 22 were accepted, 13 enrolled. ISEE required. Deadline for receipt of application materials: February 28. Application fee required: $75. Interview required.

Athletics Interscholastic: baseball (boys), basketball (b,g), cross-country running (b,g), field hockey (g), football (b), golf (b,g), lacrosse (b), soccer (b,g), softball (g), tennis (b,g), track and field (b,g), volleyball (b,g). 11 coaches, 2 athletic trainers.

Computers Computers are regularly used in all academic classes. Computer network features include on-campus library services, online commercial services, Internet access, wireless campus network, Internet filtering or blocking technology. Campus intranet, student e-mail accounts, and computer access in designated common areas are available to students. Students grades are available online. The school has a published electronic and media policy.

Contact Judith Kinser, Director of Admissions and Financial Aid. 817-321-0116. Fax: 817-321-0105. E-mail: kinserj@trinityvalleyschool.org. Website: www.trinityvalleyschool.org

TUSCALOOSA ACADEMY

420 Rice Valley Road North
Tuscaloosa, Alabama 35406

Head of School: Dr. Isaac Espy

General Information Coeducational day college-preparatory, arts, bilingual studies, technology, and ESL school. Grades PK–12. Founded: 1967. Setting: suburban. Nearest major city is Birmingham. 35-acre campus. 2 buildings on campus. Approved or accredited by Southern Association of Colleges and Schools and Southern Association of Independent Schools. Member of National Association of Independent Schools. Total enrollment: 438. Upper school average class size: 15. Upper school faculty-student ratio: 1:15. There are 177 required school days per year for Upper School students. Upper School students typically attend 5 days per week. The average school day consists of 6 hours and 55 minutes.

Upper School Student Profile Grade 9: 38 students (17 boys, 21 girls); Grade 10: 35 students (24 boys, 11 girls); Grade 11: 39 students (18 boys, 21 girls); Grade 12: 42 students (26 boys, 16 girls).

Faculty School total: 56. In upper school: 10 men, 12 women; 11 have advanced degrees.

Subjects Offered ACT preparation, advanced math, Advanced Placement courses, algebra, American government, American history, American history-AP, American literature, American literature-AP, anatomy, art, art history, art-AP, baseball, basketball, biology, biology-AP, calculus, calculus-AP, cheerleading, chemistry, chemistry-AP, choir, choral music, chorus, college counseling, computer programming, computer science, computer studies, creative writing, drama, earth science, economics, English, English literature, English-AP, English/composition-AP, European history, expository writing, fine arts, French, French language-AP, French-AP, geography, geometry, German, golf, government-AP, government/civics, grammar, health, history, history-AP, journalism, Latin, Latin-AP, literature-AP, mathematics, mathematics-AP, music, physical education, pre-calculus, psychology, psychology-AP, SAT preparation, SAT/ACT preparation, science, senior thesis, social studies, sociology, softball, Spanish, Spanish language-AP, Spanish-AP, speech, sports conditioning, studio art, studio art-AP, theater, track and field, trigonometry, U.S. history-AP, world history, world literature, yearbook.

Graduation Requirements Algebra, American government, American history, arts and fine arts (art, music, dance, drama), biology, chemistry, computer science, electives, English, foreign language, geometry, literature, mathematics, modern European history, physical education (includes health), physical science, pre-calculus, science, social studies (includes history), speech, U.S. history, 80 community service hours.

Special Academic Programs Advanced Placement exam preparation; honors section; independent study; study at local college for college credit; study abroad; academic accommodation for the gifted; ESL (81 students enrolled).

College Admission Counseling 31 students graduated in 2015; all went to college, including Auburn University; Birmingham-Southern College; Shelton State Community College; The University of Alabama; University of Mississippi.

Student Life Upper grades have specified standards of dress, student council, honor system. Discipline rests primarily with faculty.

Summer Programs Enrichment, sports, art/fine arts, computer instruction programs offered; session focuses on enrichment and sports; held on campus; accepts boys and girls; open to students from other schools. 250 students usually enrolled. 2016 schedule: June 1 to July 30. Application deadline: none.

Tuition and Aid Day student tuition: $7334–$9388. Guaranteed tuition plan. Tuition installment plan (Insured Tuition Payment Plan, monthly payment plans, semester payment plan, annual payment plan). Tuition reduction for siblings, need-based scholarship grants available. In 2015–16, 20% of upper-school students received aid. Total amount of financial aid awarded in 2015–16: $160,000.

Admissions Traditional secondary-level entrance grade is 9. For fall 2015, 27 students applied for upper-level admission, 24 were accepted, 16 enrolled. Any standardized test, Star-9 and writing sample required. Deadline for receipt of application materials: none. Application fee required: $100. Interview required.

Athletics Interscholastic: baseball (boys), basketball (b,g), cheering (g), cross-country running (b,g), dance team (g), football (b), golf (b,g), softball (g), strength & conditioning (b), tennis (b,g), track and field (b,g), volleyball (g), weight training (b); coed interscholastic: soccer. 1 PE instructor, 2 coaches, 6 athletic trainers.

Computers Computers are regularly used in journalism, keyboarding, yearbook classes. Computer network features include on-campus library services, online commercial services, Internet access, wireless campus network, Internet filtering or blocking technology, laptop program. Campus intranet, student e-mail accounts, and computer access in designated common areas are available to students. Students grades are available online. The school has a published electronic and media policy.

Contact Niccole Poole, Director of Admission. 205-758-4462 Ext. 202. Fax: 205-758-4418. E-mail: npoole@tuscaloosaacademy.org. Website: www.tuscaloosaacademy.org

TYLER STREET CHRISTIAN ACADEMY

915 West 9th Street
Dallas, Texas 75208

Head of School: Dr. Karen J. Egger

General Information Coeducational day college-preparatory, general academic, arts, religious studies, and technology school, affiliated with Christian faith. Boys grades P3–5, girls grades P3–1. Founded: 1972. Setting: urban. 5-acre campus. 2 buildings on campus. Approved or accredited by Association of Christian Schools International, Southern Association of Colleges and Schools, Texas Private School Accreditation Commission, and Texas Department of Education. Endowment: $45,000. Total enrollment: 161. Upper school average class size: 10. Upper school faculty-student ratio: 1:11. There are 176 required school days per year for Upper School students. Upper School students typically attend 5 days per week. The average school day consists of 7 hours and 40 minutes.

Upper School Student Profile Grade 9: 13 students (8 boys, 5 girls); Grade 10: 8 students (3 boys, 5 girls); Grade 11: 13 students (8 boys, 5 girls); Grade 12: 11 students (4 boys, 7 girls). 75% of students are Christian faith.

Faculty School total: 25. In upper school: 8 men, 8 women; 5 have advanced degrees.

Subjects Offered Advanced Placement courses, algebra, American government, American history, art, art appreciation, art history, arts and crafts, athletic training, ballet, band, bell choir, Bible studies, biology, British literature, British literature (honors), calculus, calculus-AP, cheerleading, chemistry, choir, choral music, Christian education, college admission preparation, college counseling, college planning, community service, composition, computer applications, computer literacy, computer skills, computer technologies, computer-aided design, concert band, concert bell choir, CPR, critical writing, economics, English literature, family living, freshman seminar, geography, geometry, government, grammar, guidance, health, history, Holocaust studies, honors algebra, honors English, honors geometry, human anatomy, human biology, integrated physics, keyboarding, lab science, lab/keyboard, leadership, leadership and service, literature, mathematics-AP, musical productions, physical education, physical science, physics, physiology, pre-calculus, religion, robotics, science, social studies, Spanish, speech communications, student government, track and field, U.S. government, U.S. history, U.S. literature, volleyball, weight training, world geography, world history, world literature, yearbook.

Graduation Requirements Algebra, American government, arts and fine arts (art, music, dance, drama), Bible, biology, calculus, chemistry, computer science, economics, English, geometry, physical education (includes health), physical science,

physics, Spanish, speech communications, U.S. history, world geography, world history.

Special Academic Programs International Baccalaureate program; 1 Advanced Placement exam for which test preparation is offered; honors section; independent study; study at local college for college credit.

College Admission Counseling 11 students graduated in 2015; 9 went to college, including Baylor University; Prairie View A&M University; Texas A&M University–Commerce; University of North Texas. Other: 2 had other specific plans. Median composite ACT: 26.

Student Life Upper grades have uniform requirement, student council, honor system. Discipline rests primarily with faculty. Attendance at religious services is required.

Tuition and Aid Day student tuition: $8700. Tuition installment plan (FACTS Tuition Payment Plan). Merit scholarship grants, need-based scholarship grants available. In 2015–16, 80% of upper-school students received aid; total upper-school merit-scholarship money awarded: $2500. Total amount of financial aid awarded in 2015–16: $92,000.

Admissions Traditional secondary-level entrance grade is 9. Admissions testing, English entrance exam, mathematics proficiency exam and writing sample required. Deadline for receipt of application materials: none. Application fee required: $75. On-campus interview required.

Athletics Interscholastic: basketball (boys, girls), cheering (g), dance squad (b,g), football (b), independent competitive sports (b,g), life saving (b,g), physical training (b,g), strength & conditioning (b,g), track and field (b,g), volleyball (g), weight lifting (b,g), weight training (b,g); coed interscholastic: cooperative games, life saving, physical training. 1 PE instructor, 2 coaches.

Computers Computers are regularly used in business applications, business skills, career exploration, Christian doctrine, college planning, computer applications, data processing, desktop publishing, digital applications, engineering, graphic arts, information technology, introduction to technology, journalism, keyboarding, lab/keyboard, library, library skills, literacy, photojournalism, reading, technology, word processing, yearbook classes. Computer network features include on-campus library services, Internet access, wireless campus network, Internet filtering or blocking technology, on-campus library services for Accelerated Reader Program. Student e-mail accounts and computer access in designated common areas are available to students. Students grades are available online. The school has a published electronic and media policy.

Contact Mrs. Jennifer Pena, Registrar. 214-941-9717 Ext. 200. Fax: 214-941-0324. E-mail: jenniferpena@tsca.org. Website: www.tsca.org

UNITED MENNONITE EDUCATIONAL INSTITUTE

614 Mersea Road 6, RR 5
Leamington, Ontario N8H 3V8, Canada

Head of School: Mrs. Sonya A. Bedal

General Information Coeducational day college-preparatory, arts, religious studies, and technology school, affiliated with Mennonite Church; primarily serves students with learning disabilities. Grades 9–12. Founded: 1945. Setting: rural. Nearest major city is Windsor, Canada. 12-acre campus. 1 building on campus. Approved or accredited by Mennonite Education Agency, Mennonite Schools Council, and Ontario Department of Education. Language of instruction: English. Total enrollment: 48. Upper school average class size: 15. Upper school faculty-student ratio: 1:8. There are 194 required school days per year for Upper School students. Upper School students typically attend 5 days per week. The average school day consists of 6 hours.

Upper School Student Profile Grade 9: 14 students (4 boys, 10 girls); Grade 10: 18 students (8 boys, 10 girls); Grade 11: 14 students (6 boys, 8 girls); Grade 12: 7 students (6 boys, 1 girl). 58% of students are Mennonite.

Faculty School total: 7. In upper school: 4 men, 3 women.

Subjects Offered 20th century physics, accounting, advanced chemistry, advanced math, algebra, American history, ancient world history, art, Bible, biology, business studies, career exploration, chemistry, choir, choral music, Christian ethics, church history, civics, communication arts, computer applications, computer studies, computer technologies, creative writing, English, environmental geography, family studies, film and new technologies, French as a second language, instrumental music, introduction to theater, leadership and service, literacy, mathematics, media arts, orchestra, parenting, peace studies, philosophy, physical education, physics, religious studies, robotics, society challenge and change, theater arts.

Graduation Requirements Arts, Canadian geography, Canadian history, careers, civics, English, French, mathematics, physical education (includes health), science.

College Admission Counseling 11 students graduated in 2015; 8 went to college, including University of Guelph; University of Waterloo; University of Windsor; Wilfrid Laurier University. Other: 3 went to work.

Student Life Upper grades have specified standards of dress, student council. Discipline rests equally with students and faculty. Attendance at religious services is required.

Tuition and Aid Day student tuition: CAN$7500. Tuition installment plan (monthly payment plans). Tuition reduction for siblings, bursaries, need-based scholarship grants, need-based loans available. In 2015–16, 23% of upper-school students received aid. Total amount of financial aid awarded in 2015–16: CAN$46,000.

Admissions Traditional secondary-level entrance grade is 9. For fall 2015, 14 students applied for upper-level admission, 14 were accepted, 14 enrolled. Deadline for receipt of application materials: none. Application fee required: CAN$200. Interview recommended.

Athletics Interscholastic: badminton (boys, girls), baseball (b,g), basketball (b,g), cross-country running (b,g), floor hockey (b,g), golf (b,g), soccer (b), softball (g), track and field (b,g), volleyball (b,g); intramural: badminton (b,g), baseball (b,g), basketball (b,g), bicycling (b), fitness (b,g), football (b), indoor hockey (b,g), indoor soccer (b,g), outdoor activities (b,g), soccer (b,g), track and field (b,g), volleyball (b,g); coed intramural: ultimate Frisbee, weight lifting, yoga. 1 PE instructor, 4 coaches.

Computers Computers are regularly used in all classes. Computer network features include on-campus library services, Internet access, wireless campus network, Internet filtering or blocking technology. The school has a published electronic and media policy.

Contact Ms. Chrissy Kelton, Admissions Director. 519-326 7448. Fax: 519-326 0278. E-mail: chrissy.kelton@umei.ca. Website: www.umei.ca

UNITED NATIONS INTERNATIONAL SCHOOL

24-50 Franklin D. Roosevelt Drive
New York, New York 10010-4046

Head of School: Ms. Jane Camblin

General Information Coeducational day college-preparatory, arts, technology, English Language Learners and Eight Mother Tongue programs, and International Baccalaureate, Eight 3rd Language Programs school. Grades K–12. Founded: 1947. Setting: urban. 3-acre campus. 1 building on campus. Approved or accredited by Council of International Schools, International Baccalaureate Organization, New York State Association of Independent Schools, and New York Department of Education. Member of National Association of Independent Schools and European Council of International Schools. Endowment: $19 million. Total enrollment: 1,570. Upper school average class size: 22. Upper school faculty-student ratio: 1:4. There are 171 required school days per year for Upper School students. Upper School students typically attend 5 days per week. The average school day consists of 6 hours and 40 minutes.

Upper School Student Profile Grade 9: 119 students (58 boys, 61 girls); Grade 10: 113 students (52 boys, 61 girls); Grade 11: 107 students (46 boys, 61 girls); Grade 12: 114 students (53 boys, 61 girls).

Faculty School total: 221. In upper school: 51 men, 54 women; 83 have advanced degrees.

Subjects Offered 3-dimensional art, algebra, American history, American literature, American studies, anthropology, Arabic, art, biology, calculus, chemistry, Chinese, community service, computer applications, computer science, creative writing, drama, economics, English, English literature, ESL, European history, expository writing, film, film studies, fine arts, French, geometry, German, history, humanities, Italian, Japanese, journalism, languages, library, mathematics, media production, modern languages, music, philosophy, photography, physical education, physics, psychology, Russian, science, social sciences, social studies, Spanish, theater arts, theory of knowledge, United Nations and international issues, video, video and animation, video communication, video film production, world history, world literature, writing.

Graduation Requirements Art, electives, English, health and wellness, humanities, independent study, mathematics, modern languages, music, physical education (includes health), science, International Baccalaureate, Theory of Knowledge, extended essay, Creative Aesthetic Service, individual project. Community service is required.

Special Academic Programs International Baccalaureate program; independent study; academic accommodation for the gifted, the musically talented, and the artistically talented; ESL (185 students enrolled).

College Admission Counseling 113 students graduated in 2015; 111 went to college, including Emory University; Fordham University; Harvard University; McGill University; New York University; Northeastern University. Other: 2 had other specific plans. Median SAT critical reading: 620, median SAT math: 600, median SAT writing: 610, median combined SAT: 1830, median composite ACT: 27. 62% scored over 600 on SAT critical reading, 54% scored over 600 on SAT math, 63% scored over 600 on SAT writing, 60% scored over 1800 on combined SAT, 67% scored over 26 on composite ACT.

Student Life Upper grades have student council. Discipline rests primarily with faculty.

Summer Programs Enrichment, ESL, sports, art/fine arts, computer instruction programs offered; session focuses on recreational program for students 4 to 14 years old; held on campus; accepts boys and girls; open to students from other schools. 300 students usually enrolled. 2016 schedule: June 22 to July 31. Application deadline: May 15.

Tuition and Aid Day student tuition: $35,320–$36,200. Tuition installment plan (Tuition Management System). Bursaries available. In 2014–15, 7% of upper-school students received aid. Total amount of financial aid awarded in 2014–15: $32,580.

Admissions Traditional secondary-level entrance grade is 9. For fall 2015, 247 students applied for upper-level admission, 82 were accepted, 58 enrolled. ISEE, PSAT and SAT for applicants to grade 11 and 12 or SSAT required. Deadline for receipt of application materials: November 15. Application fee required: $75. On-campus interview required.

Athletics Interscholastic: baseball (boys), basketball (b,g), cross-country running (b,g), indoor track (b,g), indoor track & field (b,g), soccer (b,g), softball (g), track and field (b,g), volleyball (b,g); intramural: volleyball (b,g); coed interscholastic: swimming and diving; coed intramural: aerobics, aerobics/dance, aerobics/Nautilus, aquatics, badminton, ball hockey, basketball, canoeing/kayaking, climbing, cooperative games, cross-country running, dance, field hockey, fitness, flag football, floor hockey, gymnastics, handball, hiking/backpacking, independent competitive sports, indoor hockey, indoor soccer, indoor track, indoor track & field, jogging, jump rope, life saving, martial arts, modern dance, outdoor activities, physical fitness, physical training, rock climbing, ropes courses, rounders, running, soccer, softball, strength & conditioning, swimming and diving, table tennis, team handball, tennis, touch football, track and field, volleyball, wall climbing, weight training. 10 PE instructors, 25 coaches.

Computers Computers are regularly used in all academic, animation, art, basic skills, career education, career exploration, career technology, classics, college planning, computer applications, creative writing, current events, data processing, desktop publishing, desktop publishing, ESL, digital applications, drawing and design, economics, English, ESL, foreign language, French, French as a second language, graphic arts, graphic design, graphics, health, history, humanities, independent study, information technology, introduction to technology, journalism, keyboarding, lab/keyboard, learning cognition, library, library science, library skills, life skills, literacy, literary magazine, mathematics, media, media arts, media production, media services, multimedia, music, music technology, news writing, newspaper, philosophy, photography, photojournalism, programming, publications, publishing, research skills, science, social sciences, social studies, Spanish, study skills, technology, theater, theater arts, video film production, Web site design, writing, yearbook classes. Computer network features include on-campus library services, online commercial services, Internet access, wireless campus network, Internet filtering or blocking technology, media lab, TV studio, Web portal, film production, digital video streaming, digital video editing. Campus intranet, student e-mail accounts, and computer access in designated common areas are available to students. Students grades are available online. The school has a published electronic and media policy.

Contact Admissions Office. 212-584-3071. Fax: 212-685-5023. E-mail: admissions@unis.org. Website: www.unis.org

THE UNITED WORLD COLLEGE - USA

PO Box 248
State Road 65
Montezuma, New Mexico 87731

Head of School: Dr. Mukul Kumar

General Information Coeducational boarding college-preparatory, arts, bilingual studies, wilderness, search and rescue, conflict resolution, and service, science, humanities school. Grades 11–12. Founded: 1982. Setting: small town. Nearest major city is Santa Fe. Students are housed in single-sex dormitories. 320-acre campus. 20 buildings on campus. Approved or accredited by Independent Schools Association of the Southwest and New Mexico Department of Education. Member of National Association of Independent Schools. Endowment: $120 million. Upper school average class size: 15. Upper school faculty-student ratio: 1:9. There are 245 required school days per year for Upper School students. Upper School students typically attend 5 days per week. The average school day consists of 6 hours and 30 minutes.

Upper School Student Profile Grade 11: 118 students (48 boys, 70 girls); Grade 12: 111 students (57 boys, 54 girls). 100% of students are boarding students. 1% are state residents. 28 states are represented in upper school student body. 81% are international students. International students from China, Denmark, Germany, Mexico, Senegal, and Spain; 70 other countries represented in student body.

Faculty School total: 30. In upper school: 15 men, 15 women; 25 have advanced degrees; 18 reside on campus.

Subjects Offered Anthropology, art, biology, calculus, chemistry, community service, conflict resolution, economics, English, environmental geography, environmental science, environmental studies, environmental systems, fine arts, French, German, history, information technology, International Baccalaureate courses, mathematics, music, physics, science, social sciences, social studies, Spanish, theater arts, theory of knowledge, voice, voice and diction, voice ensemble, weight fitness, weight training, welding, Western civilization, wilderness education, wilderness experience, wind ensemble, wind instruments, women in literature, women in society, world affairs, world cultures, world history, world issues, world literature, world religions, world studies.

Graduation Requirements Arts and fine arts (art, music, dance, drama), biology, calculus, chemistry, economics, English literature, environmental geography, environmental systems, European history, foreign language, French, French as a second language, geography, German, German literature, history of the Americas, International Baccalaureate courses, literature, math methods, mathematics, music, music theory, organic chemistry, physics, post-calculus, pre-algebra, pre-calculus, research, science, senior thesis, Spanish, Spanish literature, statistics, studio art, theater, theater arts, theory of knowledge, visual arts, extended essay, independent research, theory of knowledge.

Special Academic Programs International Baccalaureate program; honors section; independent study; academic accommodation for the musically talented and the artistically talented; ESL (43 students enrolled).

College Admission Counseling 104 students graduated in 2015; 98 went to college, including Harvard University; Middlebury College; St. Lawrence University; Stanford University; University of Florida; Williams College. Other: 3 entered military service, 3 had other specific plans. 35% scored over 600 on SAT critical reading, 75% scored over 600 on SAT math, 50% scored over 600 on SAT writing, 50% scored over 1800 on combined SAT, 95% scored over 26 on composite ACT.

Student Life Upper grades have student council, honor system. Discipline rests equally with students and faculty.

Summer Programs Enrichment, rigorous outdoor training programs offered; session focuses on leadership and social activism; wilderness; held both on and off campus; held at northern New Mexico; accepts boys and girls; open to students from other schools. 30 students usually enrolled. 2016 schedule: June 18 to July 5.

Tuition and Aid 7-day tuition and room/board: $36,750. Guaranteed tuition plan. Tuition installment plan (all accepted U.S. students are awarded full merit scholarships, need-based aid available to all other students). Merit scholarship grants, need-based scholarship grants, full tuition merit scholarships awarded to all admitted U.S. citizens available. In 2015–16, 85% of upper-school students received aid; total upper-school merit-scholarship money awarded: $6,800,000. Total amount of financial aid awarded in 2015–16: $6,800,000.

Admissions Traditional secondary-level entrance grade is 11. For fall 2015, 486 students applied for upper-level admission, 52 were accepted, 52 enrolled. ACT, PSAT or SAT or PSAT, SAT, or ACT for applicants to grade 11 and 12 required. Deadline for receipt of application materials: November 5. No application fee required. Interview required.

Athletics Coed Intramural: aerobics, aerobics/dance, aerobics/Nautilus, alpine skiing, aquatics, backpacking, badminton, ballet, baseball, basketball, bicycling, billiards, canoeing/kayaking, climbing, combined training, cooperative games, cricket, cross-country running, dance, fitness, Frisbee, hiking/backpacking, jogging, modern dance, mountaineering, nordic skiing, outdoor activities, physical training, racquetball, rock climbing, ropes courses, running, sailing, skiing (cross-country), skiing (downhill), snowboarding, snowshoeing, soccer, softball, squash, strength & conditioning, swimming and diving, table tennis, tennis, ultimate Frisbee, volleyball, walking, weight lifting, weight training, wilderness, wilderness survival, yoga. 1 PE instructor, 12 athletic trainers.

Computers Computers are regularly used in art, English, ESL, foreign language, mathematics, music, science classes. Computer network features include on-campus library services, Internet access, wireless campus network, Internet filtering or blocking technology. Campus intranet, student e-mail accounts, and computer access in designated common areas are available to students. Students grades are available online.

Contact Ms. Kathy Gonzales, Assistant to the Director of Admission. 505-454-4245. Fax: 505-454-4294. E-mail: kathy.gonzales@uwc-usa.org. Website: www.uwc-usa.org

UNIVERSITY LAKE SCHOOL

4024 Nagawicka Road
Hartland, Wisconsin 53029

Head of School: Mr. Ronald Smyczek

General Information Coeducational day college-preparatory and arts school. Grades PK–12. Founded: 1956. Setting: small town. Nearest major city is Milwaukee. 180-acre campus. 4 buildings on campus. Approved or accredited by Independent Schools Association of the Central States. Member of National Association of Independent Schools. Endowment: $2.4 million. Total enrollment: 258. Upper school average class size: 12. Upper school faculty-student ratio: 1:9. Upper School students typically attend 5 days per week. The average school day consists of 3 hours and 20 minutes.

Upper School Student Profile Grade 6: 19 students (10 boys, 9 girls); Grade 7: 22 students (15 boys, 7 girls); Grade 8: 18 students (6 boys, 12 girls); Grade 9: 20 students (9 boys, 11 girls); Grade 10: 30 students (13 boys, 17 girls); Grade 11: 14 students (7 boys, 7 girls); Grade 12: 19 students (9 boys, 10 girls).

Faculty School total: 41. In upper school: 11 men, 4 women; 11 have advanced degrees.

Subjects Offered Advanced Placement courses, algebra, American history, American literature, art, biology, calculus, chemistry, cinematography, computer science, creative writing, design, drama, English, English literature, environmental science, fine arts, French, geometry, government/civics, journalism, mathematics, music, photography, physical education, physics, science, social studies, Spanish, speech, statistics, theater, Web site design, world history, world literature, writing.

Graduation Requirements Art, arts and fine arts (art, music, dance, drama), English, foreign language, health education, literature, mathematics, physical education (includes health), science, social studies (includes history).

Special Academic Programs Advanced Placement exam preparation; honors section; independent study; study at local college for college credit; academic accommodation for the gifted, the musically talented, and the artistically talented; remedial reading and/or remedial writing; remedial math; programs in English for dyslexic students; special instructional classes for blind students.

College Admission Counseling 23 students graduated in 2014; all went to college, including Montana State University Billings; University of Wisconsin–Madison. Median SAT critical reading: 560, median SAT math: 550, median composite ACT: 27.

Student Life Upper grades have specified standards of dress, student council, honor system. Discipline rests equally with students and faculty.

Tuition and Aid Day student tuition: $17,980. Tuition installment plan (Insured Tuition Payment Plan, FACTS Tuition Payment Plan, monthly payment plans, individually arranged payment plans). Merit scholarship grants, need-based scholarship grants available. In 2014–15, 37% of upper-school students received aid; total upper-school merit-scholarship money awarded: $80,000. Total amount of financial aid awarded in 2014–15: $272,000.

Admissions Traditional secondary-level entrance grade is 9. For fall 2014, 13 students applied for upper-level admission, 13 were accepted, 13 enrolled. Admissions testing, Kuhlmann-Anderson and Kulhmann-Anderson Level G (for grades 7-9) or Level H (for grades 10-12) required. Deadline for receipt of application materials: none. Application fee required: $25. On-campus interview recommended.

Athletics Interscholastic: basketball (boys, girls), field hockey (g), lacrosse (b), skiing (downhill) (b,g), soccer (b,g), tennis (b,g), volleyball (g); coed interscholastic: alpine skiing, aquatics, cross-country running, golf, ice hockey, swimming and diving; coed intramural: volleyball, wall climbing. 2 PE instructors, 7 coaches.

Computers Computers are regularly used in all academic classes. Computer network features include on-campus library services, Internet access, wireless campus network, Internet filtering or blocking technology, one-to-one notebook computing program. Campus intranet and student e-mail accounts are available to students. Students grades are available online. The school has a published electronic and media policy.

Contact Deb Smith, Director of Admissions. 262-367-6011 Ext. 1455. Fax: 262-367-3146. E-mail: deb.smith@universitylake.org. Website: www.universitylake.org

UNIVERSITY LIGGETT SCHOOL

1045 Cook Road
Grosse Pointe Woods, Michigan 48236

Head of School: Dr. Joseph P. Healey

General Information Coeducational day college-preparatory, arts, and technology school. Grades PK–12. Founded: 1878. Setting: suburban. Nearest major city is Detroit. 50-acre campus. 4 buildings on campus. Approved or accredited by Independent Schools Association of the Central States. Member of National Association of Independent Schools. Total enrollment: 606. Upper school average class size: 14. Upper school faculty-student ratio: 1:8. There are 170 required school days per year for Upper School students. Upper School students typically attend 5 days per week. The average school day consists of 7 hours.

Upper School Student Profile Grade 9: 74 students (37 boys, 37 girls); Grade 10: 76 students (37 boys, 39 girls); Grade 11: 67 students (34 boys, 33 girls); Grade 12: 68 students (34 boys, 34 girls).

Faculty School total: 100. In upper school: 23 men, 16 women; 27 have advanced degrees.

Subjects Offered Algebra, American history, American literature, art, art history, biology, calculus, ceramics, chemistry, creative writing, drama, engineering, English, English literature, environmental science-AP, European history, fine arts, French, geology, geometry, government/civics, Greek, health and wellness, history of jazz, instrumental music, Latin, mathematics, media arts, modern languages, photography, physical education, physical fitness, physics, physiology, psychology, SAT preparation, science, social studies, Spanish, technology, theater, Vietnam, world history.

Graduation Requirements Algebra, arts and fine arts (art, music, dance, drama), biology, chemistry, computer science, English, foreign language, geometry, government, mathematics, physical education (includes health), science, U.S. history, world history, advanced research project. Community service is required.

Special Academic Programs Honors section; independent study; term-away projects; study abroad; academic accommodation for the gifted, the musically talented, and the artistically talented; special instructional classes for deaf students.

College Admission Counseling 77 students graduated in 2014; all went to college, including Boston College; Kalamazoo College; Michigan State University; University of Michigan; Western Michigan University; Williams College. Mean SAT critical reading: 610, mean SAT math: 590, mean SAT writing: 590, mean composite ACT: 27. 54% scored over 600 on SAT critical reading, 43% scored over 600 on SAT math, 54% scored over 600 on SAT writing.

Student Life Upper grades have specified standards of dress, student council, honor system. Discipline rests primarily with faculty.

Tuition and Aid Day student tuition: $24,260. Tuition installment plan (Insured Tuition Payment Plan, individually arranged payment plans, 2- and 4-payment plans). Tuition reduction for siblings, merit scholarship grants, need-based scholarship grants, scholarships for children of alumni available. In 2014–15, 35% of upper-school students received aid; total upper-school merit-scholarship money awarded: $400,000. Total amount of financial aid awarded in 2014–15: $2,000,000.

Admissions Traditional secondary-level entrance grade is 9. For fall 2014, 105 students applied for upper-level admission, 48 were accepted, 38 enrolled. ERB CTP III or SSAT required. Deadline for receipt of application materials: none. Application fee required: $50. Interview required.

Athletics Interscholastic: baseball (boys), basketball (b,g), field hockey (g), football (b), golf (b), ice hockey (b,g), lacrosse (b,g), outdoor education (b,g), soccer (b,g), softball (g), tennis (b,g), volleyball (g); coed interscholastic: physical training, swimming and diving; coed intramural: aerobics/dance, ultimate Frisbee, weight lifting. 4 PE instructors, 15 coaches, 1 athletic trainer.

Computers Computers are regularly used in all academic classes. Computer network features include on-campus library services, online commercial services, Internet access, wireless campus network, Internet filtering or blocking technology. Campus intranet, student e-mail accounts, and computer access in designated common areas are available to students. Students grades are available online. The school has a published electronic and media policy.

Contact Ms. Anne Sheppard, Assistant Head of Enrollment/Director of Admissions and Financial Aid. 313-884-4444 Ext. 405. Fax: 313-884-1775. E-mail: asheppard@uls.org. Website: www.uls.org

UNIVERSITY OF CHICAGO LABORATORY SCHOOLS

1362 East 59th Street
Chicago, Illinois 60637

Head of School: Ms. Robin Appleby

General Information Coeducational day college-preparatory school. Grades N–12. Founded: 1896. Setting: urban. 15-acre campus. 4 buildings on campus. Approved or accredited by Independent Schools Association of the Central States, North Central Association of Colleges and Schools, and Illinois Department of Education. Member of National Association of Independent Schools. Endowment: $21 million. Total enrollment: 2,007. Upper school average class size: 15. Upper school faculty-student ratio: 1:10. There are 170 required school days per year for Upper School students. Upper School students typically attend 5 days per week. The average school day consists of 7 hours and 5 minutes.

Upper School Student Profile Grade 9: 129 students (61 boys, 68 girls); Grade 10: 127 students (58 boys, 69 girls); Grade 11: 128 students (56 boys, 72 girls); Grade 12: 132 students (64 boys, 68 girls).

Faculty School total: 251. In upper school: 35 men, 42 women; 67 have advanced degrees.

Subjects Offered Acting, advanced biology, advanced chemistry, African-American history, algebra, American history, art, art history, band, biology, calculus, calculus-AP, chemistry, Chinese, choir, community service, computer science, computer science-AP, CPR, creative writing, discrete mathematics, drama, drawing, driver education, English, English literature, European history, expository writing, fine arts, French, French-AP, geometry, German, German-AP, government/civics, history, Holocaust, honors geometry, jazz band, journalism, Latin, Mandarin, mathematics, modern European history, music, music theory, music theory-AP, newspaper, orchestra, painting, photography, photojournalism, physical education, physics, play production, post-calculus, science, sculpture, social studies, Spanish, Spanish language-AP, Spanish-AP, statistics, statistics-AP, studio art, theater, trigonometry, U.S. history, video film production, Web site design, Western civilization, world history, writing, yearbook.

Graduation Requirements Arts and fine arts (art, music, dance, drama), computer science, English, foreign language, mathematics, music, physical education (includes health), science, social studies (includes history). Community service is required.

Special Academic Programs 8 Advanced Placement exams for which test preparation is offered; accelerated programs; independent study; study at local college for college credit.

College Admission Counseling 113 students graduated in 2015; 110 went to college, including Columbia University; Macalester College; Northwestern University; University of Chicago; University of Illinois at Urbana–Champaign; Yale University. Other: 1 went to work, 2 had other specific plans. Median SAT critical reading: 696, median SAT math: 708, median SAT writing: 684, median combined SAT: 2088, median composite ACT: 30.

Student Life Upper grades have student council. Discipline rests primarily with faculty.

Summer Programs Enrichment, advancement, sports programs offered; session focuses on advancement of placement in courses; held on campus; accepts boys and girls; open to students from other schools. 125 students usually enrolled. 2016 schedule: June 20 to July 29. Application deadline: May 15.

Tuition and Aid Day student tuition: $30,618. Tuition installment plan (monthly payment plans, quarterly payment plan). Need-based scholarship grants available. In 2015–16, 13% of upper-school students received aid. Total amount of financial aid awarded in 2015–16: $1,044,409.

Admissions Traditional secondary-level entrance grade is 9. For fall 2015, 174 students applied for upper-level admission, 67 were accepted, 32 enrolled. ISEE required. Deadline for receipt of application materials: November 30. Application fee required: $80. On-campus interview required.

Athletics Interscholastic: baseball (boys), basketball (b,g), cross-country running (b,g), indoor track & field (b,g), soccer (b,g), swimming and diving (b,g), tennis (b,g), track and field (b,g), volleyball (g), winter (indoor) track (b,g); intramural: dance squad (g), weight training (b,g); coed interscholastic: cross-country running, fencing, golf, sailing; coed intramural: life saving. 14 PE instructors, 33 coaches, 1 athletic trainer.

Computers Computers are regularly used in business applications, mathematics, music, newspaper, science, writing, yearbook classes. Computer network features include on-campus library services, Internet access, wireless campus network. Student e-mail accounts and computer access in designated common areas are available to students. Students grades are available online. The school has a published electronic and media policy.

Contact Irene Reed, Executive Director of Admissions and Financial Aid. 773-702-9451. Fax: 773-702-7455. E-mail: ireed@ucls.uchicago.edu. Website: www.ucls.uchicago.edu/

See Close-Up on page 622.

UNIVERSITY PREP

8000 25th Avenue NE
Seattle, Washington 98115

Head of School: Matt Levinson

General Information Coeducational day college-preparatory, arts, bilingual studies, technology, and global education school. Grades 6–12. Founded: 1976. Setting: urban. 6-acre campus. 5 buildings on campus. Approved or accredited by Northwest Association of Independent Schools and Washington Department of Education. Member of National Association of Independent Schools and Secondary School Admission Test Board. Endowment: $10 million. Total enrollment: 545. Upper school average class size: 17. Upper school faculty-student ratio: 1:9. There are 169 required school days per year for Upper School students. Upper School students typically attend 5 days per week. The average school day consists of 6 hours and 50 minutes.

Faculty School total: 68. In upper school: 33 men, 35 women; 45 have advanced degrees.

Subjects Offered 3-dimensional art, advanced chemistry, advanced math, African-American studies, algebra, American government, American history, American literature, applied arts, applied music, art, art and culture, art history, Asian literature, Asian studies, astronomy, athletics, audio visual/media, band, biology, British literature, calculus, career and personal planning, career planning, career/college preparation, chemistry, Chinese, Chinese studies, choir, chorus, civil rights, classical civilization, college counseling, college placement, college planning, community service, comparative government and politics, comparative religion, composition, computer art, computer literacy, computer science, conceptual physics, creative dance, creative drama, creative writing, critical thinking, critical writing, dance, decision making skills, democracy in America, design, digital art, digital photography, diversity studies, drafting, drama, drama performance, dramatic arts, drawing, ecology, economics, electives, English, English composition, English literature, ensembles, environmental education, environmental science, environmental studies, ethnic studies, European history, expository writing, film studies, fine arts, fitness, foreign language, French, freshman seminar, geography, geometry, global studies, golf, government, government/civics, graphic design, health, history, history of religion, independent study, information technology, introduction to technology, Japanese, Japanese history, Japanese studies, jazz ensemble, journalism, languages, Latin American studies, library, life skills, literary magazine, mathematics, media, medieval/Renaissance history, minority studies, multicultural studies, music, music performance, music theory, orchestra, Pacific Northwest seminar, painting, performing arts, personal fitness, philosophy, photography, physical education, physical fitness, physics, play production, play/screen writing, poetry, political science, politics, psychology, public policy, publishing, research, Russian studies, science, senior thesis, social justice, Spanish, stagecraft, statistics, student publications, theater, theater arts, theater design and production, trigonometry, vocal ensemble, weight training, weightlifting, wilderness education, wilderness experience, women in society, world literature, yearbook.

Graduation Requirements American history, arts and fine arts (art, music, dance, drama), biology, chemistry, English, foreign language, life skills, mathematics, Pacific Northwest seminar, physical education (includes health), physics, science, senior thesis, social studies (includes history). Community service is required.

Special Academic Programs Independent study; term-away projects; study abroad; programs in English, mathematics, general development for dyslexic students; special instructional classes for college-bound students with high intellectual potential who have diagnosed specific learning disability.

College Admission Counseling 78 students graduated in 2015; all went to college, including Gonzaga University; Santa Clara University; University of Denver; University of Southern California; University of Washington; Whitman College. Median SAT critical reading: 620, median SAT math: 610, median SAT writing: 620, median combined SAT: 1855, median composite ACT: 28. 60% scored over 600 on SAT critical reading, 52% scored over 600 on SAT math, 60% scored over 600 on SAT writing, 57% scored over 1800 on combined SAT, 64% scored over 26 on composite ACT.

Student Life Upper grades have student council, honor system. Discipline rests equally with students and faculty.

Tuition and Aid Day student tuition: $28,080. Tuition installment plan (Insured Tuition Payment Plan, Key Tuition Payment Plan, monthly payment plans, individually arranged payment plans, Dewar Tuition Refund Plan). Need-based scholarship grants available. In 2015–16, 21% of upper-school students received aid. Total amount of financial aid awarded in 2015–16: $1,392,423.

Admissions Traditional secondary-level entrance grade is 9. For fall 2015, 206 students applied for upper-level admission, 43 were accepted, 23 enrolled. ISEE required. Deadline for receipt of application materials: January 14. Application fee required: $80. On-campus interview required.

Athletics Interscholastic: baseball (boys), basketball (b,g), cross-country running (b,g), flag football (b), Frisbee (b,g), soccer (b,g), softball (g), tennis (b,g), track and field (b,g), volleyball (g); intramural: golf (b,g), ultimate Frisbee (b,g); coed interscholastic: ultimate Frisbee; coed intramural: aerobics, aerobics/dance, backpacking, climbing, dance, fitness, hiking/backpacking, modern dance, outdoor activities, outdoor adventure, outdoor education, outdoor skills, outdoors, rock climbing, skiing (downhill), snowboarding, strength & conditioning, ultimate Frisbee, wall climbing, weight training, wilderness, yoga. 5 PE instructors, 65 coaches, 1 athletic trainer.

Computers Computers are regularly used in all academic, art, creative writing, English, foreign language, geography, history, information technology, journalism, library, mathematics, media, music, photography, publications, publishing, research skills, science, technology, writing, writing, yearbook classes. Computer network features include on-campus library services, online commercial services, Internet access, wireless campus network, Internet filtering or blocking technology, RYOD—Required Your On Device. Campus intranet, student e-mail accounts, and computer access in designated common areas are available to students. Students grades are available online. The school has a published electronic and media policy.

Contact Melaine Taylor, Associate Director of Admission. 206-523-6407. Fax: 206-525-5320. E-mail: admissionoffice@universityprep.org. Website: www.universityprep.org

UNIVERSITY SCHOOL OF JACKSON

232/240 McClellan Road
Jackson, Tennessee 38305

Head of School: Stuart Hirstein

General Information Coeducational day college-preparatory, arts, and technology school. Grades PK–12. Founded: 1970. Setting: suburban. 130-acre campus. 4 buildings on campus. Approved or accredited by Southern Association of Colleges and Schools and Tennessee Department of Education. Member of National Association of Independent Schools. Endowment: $85,000. Total enrollment: 1,124. Upper school average class size: 20. Upper school faculty-student ratio: 1:13. There are 180 required school days per year for Upper School students. Upper School students typically attend 5 days per week. The average school day consists of 7 hours and 10 minutes.

Upper School Student Profile Grade 9: 68 students (39 boys, 29 girls); Grade 10: 94 students (56 boys, 38 girls); Grade 11: 86 students (44 boys, 42 girls); Grade 12: 85 students (39 boys, 46 girls).

Faculty School total: 94. In upper school: 15 men, 20 women; 30 have advanced degrees.

Subjects Offered 3-dimensional art, 3-dimensional design, accounting, acting, advanced biology, advanced chemistry, advanced math, Advanced Placement courses, advanced studio art-AP, algebra, American history, American literature, anatomy, anatomy and physiology, art, band, biology, biology-AP, broadcast journalism, calculus, calculus-AP, character education, chemistry, chemistry-AP, chorus, computer applications, computer programming, computer science, creative writing, current events, dramatic arts, ecology, economics, economics and history, English, English language-AP, English literature and composition-AP, English literature-AP, environmental science, environmental science-AP, European history, fine arts, French, geography, geology, geometry, government, government/civics, honors algebra, honors English, honors geometry, humanities, keyboarding, macroeconomics-AP, mathematics, music theory, music theory-AP, music-AP, performing arts, photography, physical education, physical science, physics, pre-calculus, psychology, science, social studies, Spanish, Spanish language-AP, studio art-AP, trigonometry, U.S. history, U.S. history-AP, vocal ensemble, world history, world religions, yearbook.

Graduation Requirements Arts and fine arts (art, music, dance, drama), computer science, English, foreign language, mathematics, science, social studies (includes history), 50 hours of community service.

Special Academic Programs 11 Advanced Placement exams for which test preparation is offered; honors section; academic accommodation for the gifted, the musically talented, and the artistically talented; ESL (10 students enrolled).

College Admission Counseling 88 students graduated in 2015; all went to college, including Mississippi State University; Rhodes College; Tennessee Technological University; The University of Tennessee; Union University; University of Arkansas. Median SAT critical reading: 550, median SAT math: 588, median SAT writing: 536, median combined SAT: 1674, median composite ACT: 26. 20% scored over 600 on SAT critical reading, 20% scored over 600 on SAT math, 20% scored over 600 on SAT writing, 20% scored over 1800 on combined SAT, 57% scored over 26 on composite ACT.

Student Life Upper grades have uniform requirement, student council, honor system. Discipline rests equally with students and faculty.

Summer Programs Remediation, enrichment, sports, art/fine arts, computer instruction programs offered; session focuses on enrichment and remediation; held on campus; accepts boys and girls; open to students from other schools. 500 students usually enrolled. 2016 schedule: June 1 to July 31. Application deadline: none.

Tuition and Aid Day student tuition: $7251–$9950. Tuition installment plan (FACTS Tuition Payment Plan, monthly payment plans, quarterly payment plan). Tuition reduction for siblings, need-based scholarship grants, need-based financial aid available. In 2015–16, 3% of upper-school students received aid. Total amount of financial aid awarded in 2015–16: $180,000.

Admissions Traditional secondary-level entrance grade is 9. For fall 2015, 14 students applied for upper-level admission, 13 were accepted, 10 enrolled. Math Placement Exam, Otis-Lennon School Ability Test and writing sample required. Deadline for receipt of application materials: none. Application fee required: $50. On-campus interview required.

Athletics Interscholastic: baseball (boys), basketball (b,g), cheering (g), cross-country running (b,g), fitness (b,g), football (b), golf (b,g), physical fitness (b,g), soccer (b,g), softball (g), tennis (b,g), track and field (b,g), volleyball (g), weight lifting (g), weight training (b,g); intramural: bowling (b,g), in-line hockey (b); coed intramural: bowling. 2 coaches, 1 athletic trainer.

Computers Computers are regularly used in art, English, foreign language, history, journalism, keyboarding, music, science, technology, theater arts, word processing, writing, yearbook classes. Computer network features include on-campus library services, online commercial services, Internet access, wireless campus network, Internet filtering or blocking technology. Campus intranet and computer access in designated common areas are available to students. Students grades are available online. The school has a published electronic and media policy.

Contact Kay Shearin, Director of Admissions. 731-660-1692. Fax: 731-668-6910. E-mail: kshearin@usjbruins.org. Website: www.usjbruins.org

UPPER CANADA COLLEGE

200 Lonsdale Road
Toronto, Ontario M4V 1W6, Canada

Head of School: Dr. James Power

General Information Boys' boarding and day college-preparatory, arts, bilingual studies, technology, and International Baccalaureate school. Boarding grades 8–12, day grades K–12. Founded: 1829. Setting: urban. Students are housed in single-sex dormitories. 16-hectare campus. 4 buildings on campus. Approved or accredited by Canadian Association of Independent Schools, Conference of Independent Schools of Ontario, International Baccalaureate Organization, Ontario Ministry of Education, The Association of Boarding Schools, and Ontario Department of Education. Affiliate member of National Association of Independent Schools; member of Secondary School Admission Test Board. Language of instruction: English. Endowment: CAN$40 million. Total enrollment: 1,166. Upper school average class size: 20. Upper school faculty-student ratio: 1:8. There are 210 required school days per year for Upper School students. Upper School students typically attend 5 days per week. The average school day consists of 6 hours and 30 minutes.

Upper School Student Profile Grade 6: 80 students (80 boys); Grade 7: 120 students (120 boys); Grade 8: 125 students (125 boys); Grade 9: 145 students (145 boys); Grade 10: 159 students (159 boys); Grade 11: 165 students (165 boys); Grade 12: 165 students (165 boys). 15% of students are boarding students. 90% are province residents. 3 provinces are represented in upper school student body. 10% are international students. International students from Bangladesh, China, Hong Kong, Russian Federation, and United States; 21 other countries represented in student body.

Faculty School total: 138. In upper school: 57 men, 28 women; 35 have advanced degrees; 17 reside on campus.

Subjects Offered 3-dimensional design, advanced biology, advanced chemistry, advanced math, algebra, American history, art, athletics, biology, calculus, career and personal planning, chemistry, Chinese, civics, community service, computer multimedia, computer programming, computer science, creative arts, creative writing, digital art, drama, economics, English, English literature, environmental science, equality and freedom, European history, expository writing, film, film studies, fine arts, French, functions, geography, geometry, German, health, history, instrumental music, International Baccalaureate courses, Latin, mathematics, music, physical education, physics, science, social sciences, social studies, Spanish, theater, theater arts, theory of knowledge, trigonometry, visual arts, world history, writing.

Graduation Requirements English, foreign language, mathematics, science, social sciences, IB diploma requirements. Community service is required.

Special Academic Programs International Baccalaureate program; honors section; term-away projects; study abroad.

College Admission Counseling 165 students graduated in 2015; 157 went to college, including Dalhousie University; McGill University; Queen's University at Kingston; The University of Western Ontario; University of Toronto; University of Waterloo. Other: 3 had other specific plans.

Student Life Upper grades have specified standards of dress, student council. Discipline rests equally with students and faculty.

Summer Programs Enrichment, advancement, art/fine arts, computer instruction programs offered; session focuses on enrichment and credit courses; held on campus; accepts boys and girls; open to students from other schools. 300 students usually enrolled. 2016 schedule: June 15 to August 30. Application deadline: none.

Tuition and Aid Day student tuition: CAN$33,550; 7-day tuition and room/board: CAN$54,510–CAN$61,010. Tuition installment plan (twice annual payment plan or full-payment discount plan). Merit scholarship grants, need-based scholarship grants, need-based financial assistance available. In 2015–16, 18% of upper-school students received aid; total upper-school merit-scholarship money awarded: CAN$50,000. Total amount of financial aid awarded in 2015–16: CAN$4,500,000.

Admissions Traditional secondary-level entrance grade is 9. SSAT or SSAT, ERB, PSAT, SAT, PLAN or ACT required. Deadline for receipt of application materials: none. Application fee required: CAN$200. Interview required.

Athletics Interscholastic: aquatics, badminton, baseball, basketball, crew, cricket, cross-country running, dance, football, golf, hockey, ice hockey, lacrosse, rowing, rugby, running, soccer, softball, squash, swimming and diving, tennis, track and field, volleyball; intramural: alpine skiing, backpacking, ball hockey, basketball, bicycling, canoeing/kayaking, climbing, combined training, cooperative games, fencing, field hockey, floor hockey, hiking/backpacking, hockey, ice hockey, in-line hockey, indoor hockey, indoor soccer, kayaking, martial arts, mountain biking, outdoor activities, outdoor adventure, outdoor education, outdoor recreation, outdoor skills, physical training, power lifting, rock climbing, ropes courses, self defense, skiing (downhill), snowboarding, soccer, softball, street hockey, strength & conditioning, tai chi, volleyball, weight training, wilderness, winter soccer. 4 coaches, 1 athletic trainer.

Computers Computers are regularly used in business education, computer applications, digital applications, graphic arts, graphic design, graphics, media arts, technology classes. Computer network features include on-campus library services, online commercial services, Internet access, wireless campus network, Internet filtering or blocking technology, laptop school; laptop used across all subjects. Campus intranet, student e-mail accounts, and computer access in designated common areas are available to students. The school has a published electronic and media policy.

Contact Tricia Rankin, Associate Director of Admission. 416-488-1125 Ext. 2221. Fax: 416-484-8618. E-mail: trankin@ucc.on.ca. Website: www.ucc.on.ca

THE URSULINE ACADEMY OF DALLAS

4900 Walnut Hill Lane
Dallas, Texas 75229
Head of School: Mrs. Andrea Shurley

General Information Girls' day college-preparatory, arts, religious studies, and technology school, affiliated with Roman Catholic Church. Grades 9–12. Founded: 1874. Setting: urban. 26-acre campus. 5 buildings on campus. Approved or accredited by Independent Schools Association of the Southwest, National Catholic Education Association, Texas Catholic Conference, The College Board, and Texas Department of Education. Member of National Association of Independent Schools. Total enrollment: 843. Upper school average class size: 18. Upper school faculty-student ratio: 1:10.

Upper School Student Profile Grade 9: 222 students (222 girls); Grade 10: 223 students (223 girls); Grade 11: 194 students (194 girls); Grade 12: 204 students (204 girls). 77% of students are Roman Catholic.

Faculty School total: 89. In upper school: 20 men, 69 women; 74 have advanced degrees.

Subjects Offered 20th century history, Advanced Placement courses, algebra, anatomy, anatomy and physiology, Arabic, band, biology, calculus, ceramics, chemistry, Chinese, choir, Christian and Hebrew scripture, community service, comparative government and politics, comparative religion, computer programming, computer science, concert choir, creative writing, current events, dance, design, digital imaging, digital photography, discrete mathematics, drama, drawing, economics, English literature, environmental science, ethics, European history, fitness, French, geography, geology, geometry, government, government/civics, health and wellness, journalism, Mandarin, newspaper, oceanography, orchestra, painting, peer ministry, photography, physical education, physics, pre-calculus, printmaking, psychology, social justice, Spanish, speech, statistics, theater, theology, U.S. history, U.S. literature, Web authoring, Western civilization, world history, world literature, yearbook.

Graduation Requirements Arts and fine arts (art, music, dance, drama), computer science, English, foreign language, mathematics, physical education (includes health), religion (includes Bible studies and theology), science, social studies (includes history), speech. Community service is required.

Special Academic Programs Advanced Placement exam preparation; honors section.

College Admission Counseling 196 students graduated in 2015; 191 went to college. Other: 1 entered a postgraduate year, 4 had other specific plans. Mean SAT critical reading: 593, mean SAT math: 594, mean SAT writing: 611, mean combined SAT: 1798, mean composite ACT: 27.

Student Life Upper grades have uniform requirement, student council, honor system. Discipline rests equally with students and faculty. Attendance at religious services is required.

Summer Programs Remediation, advancement, art/fine arts, computer instruction programs offered; session focuses on remediation and advancement; held on campus; accepts girls; not open to students from other schools. 200 students usually enrolled. 2016 schedule: June 6 to July 1. Application deadline: February 19.

Tuition and Aid Day student tuition: $19,100. Tuition installment plan (individually arranged payment plans, annual, semi-annual, and monthly (by bank draft) payment plans). Merit scholarship grants, need-based scholarship grants available. In 2015–16, 24% of upper-school students received aid; total upper-school merit-scholarship money awarded: $88,500. Total amount of financial aid awarded in 2015–16: $1,065,000.

Admissions Traditional secondary-level entrance grade is 9. For fall 2015, 400 students applied for upper-level admission, 220 enrolled. ISEE required. Deadline for receipt of application materials: January 8. Application fee required: $100. Interview required.

Athletics Interscholastic: basketball, cheering, crew, cross-country running, diving, drill team, golf, lacrosse, soccer, softball, swimming and diving, tennis, track and field, volleyball. 3 PE instructors, 15 coaches, 1 athletic trainer.

Computers Computers are regularly used in all classes. Computer network features include on-campus library services, online commercial services, Internet access, wireless campus network. Campus intranet and student e-mail accounts are available to students. Students grades are available online. The school has a published electronic and media policy.

Contact Mrs. Jill Tilden, Admissions Assistant. 469-232-1804. Fax: 469-232-1836. E-mail: jtilden@ursulinedallas.org. Website: www.ursulinedallas.org

VACAVILLE CHRISTIAN SCHOOLS

1117 Davis Street
Vacaville, California 95687
Head of School: Mr. Paul Harrell

General Information Coeducational day college-preparatory, general academic, arts, religious studies, bilingual studies, and technology school, affiliated with Christian faith, Christian faith. Grades K–12. Founded: 1975. Setting: suburban. Nearest major city is Sacramento. 24-acre campus. 11 buildings on campus. Approved or accredited by Association of Christian Schools International, Western Association of Schools and Colleges, and California Department of Education. Total enrollment: 812. Upper school average class size: 25. Upper school faculty-student ratio: 1:10. There are 176 required school days per year for Upper School students. Upper School students typically attend 5 days per week. The average school day consists of 7 hours.

Upper School Student Profile Grade 6: 52 students (21 boys, 31 girls); Grade 7: 51 students (25 boys, 26 girls); Grade 8: 57 students (27 boys, 30 girls); Grade 9: 61 students (41 boys, 20 girls); Grade 10: 68 students (32 boys, 36 girls); Grade 11: 61 students (28 boys, 33 girls); Grade 12: 62 students (33 boys, 29 girls). 80% of students are Christian, Christian faith.

Faculty School total: 56. In upper school: 11 men, 16 women; 8 have advanced degrees.

Subjects Offered Algebra, American literature, art, band, Bible, biology, broadcasting, calculus-AP, chemistry, choir, college planning, computer applications, computer graphics, conceptual physics, digital photography, drama, economics, English, English literature, French, geometry, graphic arts, health, instrumental music, jazz band, journalism, media production, Microsoft, newspaper, participation in sports, performing arts, physical education, physics, physics-AP, pre-calculus, psychology, psychology-AP, radio broadcasting, Spanish, speech, sports, student government, study skills, symphonic band, U.S. government, U.S. government and politics-AP, U.S. history, Web site design, weight training, world history, yearbook.

Graduation Requirements Algebra, American government, arts and fine arts (art, music, dance, drama), Bible, biology, British literature, chemistry, conceptual physics, economics, electives, English, foreign language, geometry, government, physical education (includes health), practical arts, statistics, U.S. history, world history, 20 community service hours.

Special Academic Programs 17 Advanced Placement exams for which test preparation is offered; honors section; study at local college for college credit; programs in English, mathematics for dyslexic students.

College Admission Counseling 60 students graduated in 2014; 48 went to college, including California State University, Long Beach; California State University, Sacramento; Sonoma State University; University of California, Davis; University of California, Irvine; University of California, Santa Cruz. Other: 10 went to work, 2 entered military service. Median SAT critical reading: 540, median SAT math: 585, median SAT writing: 560, median combined SAT: 1805. 22% scored over 600 on SAT critical reading, 19% scored over 600 on SAT math, 22% scored over 600 on SAT writing.

Student Life Upper grades have specified standards of dress, student council, honor system. Discipline rests primarily with faculty. Attendance at religious services is required.

Tuition and Aid Day student tuition: $10,000. Tuition installment plan (SMART Tuition Payment Plan, monthly payment plans). Tuition reduction for siblings, merit scholarship grants, need-based scholarship grants available. In 2014–15, 10% of upper-school students received aid; total upper-school merit-scholarship money awarded: $5000. Total amount of financial aid awarded in 2014–15: $5000.

Admissions Traditional secondary-level entrance grade is 9. For fall 2014, 28 students applied for upper-level admission, 26 were accepted, 26 enrolled. Any standardized test required. Deadline for receipt of application materials: none. Application fee required: $300. Interview required.

Athletics Interscholastic: baseball (boys), basketball (b,g), football (b), wrestling (b,g); coed interscholastic: cheering, cross-country running, golf. 3 PE instructors, 20 coaches.

Computers Computers are regularly used in graphic arts, graphic design, journalism, media production, newspaper, Web site design, yearbook classes. Computer network features include on-campus library services, Internet access, wireless campus network,

Internet filtering or blocking technology. Campus intranet is available to students. Students grades are available online. The school has a published electronic and media policy.

Contact Mrs. Maylene Ripley, Director of Admissions. 707-446-1776 Ext. 2102. Fax: 707-446-1514. E-mail: maylene.ripley@go-vcs.com. Website: www.go-vcs.com

VALLE CATHOLIC HIGH SCHOOL

40 North Fourth Street
Ste. Genevieve, Missouri 63670

Head of School: Dr. Mark Gilligan

General Information Coeducational day college-preparatory, arts, business, vocational, religious studies, and technology school, affiliated with Roman Catholic Church. Grades 9–12. Founded: 1837. Setting: small town. Nearest major city is St. Louis. 3-acre campus. 4 buildings on campus. Approved or accredited by North Central Association of Colleges and Schools and Missouri Department of Education. Endowment: $2 million. Total enrollment: 134. Upper school average class size: 15. Upper school faculty-student ratio: 1:9. There are 171 required school days per year for Upper School students. Upper School students typically attend 5 days per week. The average school day consists of 6 hours and 30 minutes.

Upper School Student Profile Grade 9: 26 students (14 boys, 12 girls); Grade 10: 40 students (19 boys, 21 girls); Grade 11: 26 students (17 boys, 9 girls); Grade 12: 42 students (23 boys, 19 girls). 98% of students are Roman Catholic.

Faculty School total: 16. In upper school: 9 men, 7 women; 8 have advanced degrees.

Subjects Offered Accounting, advanced chemistry, advanced computer applications, advanced math, algebra, American democracy, American history, American literature, analysis and differential calculus, anatomy and physiology, architectural drawing, art, art history, band, biology, British literature, business, business applications, business law, business studies, calculus, calculus-AP, Catholic belief and practice, chemistry-AP, Christian and Hebrew scripture, Christian scripture, church history, civics, civics/free enterprise, classics, communications, comparative religion, composition, computer applications, computer multimedia, computer science, computer skills, concert band, consumer economics, consumer law, drafting, drama, drama performance, drawing, economics, economics and history, English, entrepreneurship, environmental science, foreign language, geography, geometry, history of the Catholic Church, honors algebra, honors English, honors U.S. history, human anatomy, marching band, math analysis, mathematics, media communications, moral theology, novels, orchestra, painting, peace and justice, physical education, physics, practical arts, psychology, religion, science, social studies, sociology, Spanish, technical drawing, U.S. government, values and decisions, visual arts, Western civilization, yearbook.

Graduation Requirements Advanced math, algebra, American history, American literature, biology, Catholic belief and practice, chemistry, Christian and Hebrew scripture, civics, English, English composition, ethical decision making, foreign language, geometry, government/civics, history of the Catholic Church, mathematics, physical education (includes health), practical arts, religion (includes Bible studies and theology), science, senior composition, social justice, social studies (includes history), Spanish, 80 hours of community service.

Special Academic Programs Honors section; study at local college for college credit; academic accommodation for the gifted, the musically talented, and the artistically talented; remedial reading and/or remedial writing; remedial math.

College Admission Counseling 39 students graduated in 2014; all went to college, including Fontbonne University; Missouri State University; Saint Louis University; Southeast Missouri State University; Truman State University; University of Missouri. Mean SAT critical reading: 720, mean SAT math: 780, mean composite ACT: 24. 100% scored over 600 on SAT critical reading, 100% scored over 600 on SAT math, 26% scored over 26 on composite ACT.

Student Life Upper grades have uniform requirement, student council, honor system. Discipline rests primarily with faculty. Attendance at religious services is required.

Tuition and Aid Day student tuition: $3800. Tuition installment plan (The Tuition Plan, monthly payment plans, individually arranged payment plans, tuition assistance through the St. Louis Archdiocese and Scholarships available through the School). Tuition reduction for siblings, merit scholarship grants, need-based scholarship grants, tuition relief funds available from St. Louis Archdiocese available. In 2014–15, 25% of upper-school students received aid; total upper-school merit-scholarship money awarded: $10,000. Total amount of financial aid awarded in 2014–15: $165,000.

Admissions Traditional secondary-level entrance grade is 9. For fall 2014, 26 students applied for upper-level admission, 26 were accepted, 26 enrolled. Any standardized test, school placement exam and writing sample required. Deadline for receipt of application materials: none. Application fee required: $25. Interview recommended.

Athletics Interscholastic: baseball (boys), basketball (b,g), dance team (g), drill team (g), football (b), softball (g), track and field (b,g), volleyball (g), weight training (b); coed interscholastic: cheering, cross-country running, golf, physical training, strength & conditioning, weight lifting. 1 PE instructor.

Computers Computers are regularly used in accounting, business, career exploration, college planning, English, geography, history, humanities, journalism, mathematics, psychology, science, Spanish, writing, yearbook classes. Computer network features include Internet access, wireless campus network, Internet filtering or blocking technology. Student e-mail accounts and computer access in designated common areas

are available to students. Students grades are available online. The school has a published electronic and media policy.

Contact Mrs. Dawn C. Basler, Registrar. 573-883-7496 Ext. 242. Fax: 573-883-9142. E-mail: baslerd@valleschools.org. Website: www.valleschools.org

VALLEY CHRISTIAN HIGH SCHOOL

100 Skyway Drive
San Jose, California 95111

Head of School: Dr. Clifford Daugherty

General Information Coeducational day college-preparatory, arts, religious studies, technology, Conservatory of the Arts, and Applied Math, Science and Engineering Institute school, affiliated with Christian faith. Grades K–12. Founded: 1960. Setting: suburban. 53-acre campus. 6 buildings on campus. Approved or accredited by Association of Christian Schools International, Western Association of Schools and Colleges, and California Department of Education. Total enrollment: 2,668. Upper school average class size: 27. Upper school faculty-student ratio: 1:11. There are 175 required school days per year for Upper School students. Upper School students typically attend 5 days per week. The average school day consists of 6 hours and 45 minutes.

Upper School Student Profile Grade 9: 418 students (223 boys, 195 girls); Grade 10: 403 students (200 boys, 203 girls); Grade 11: 370 students (198 boys, 172 girls); Grade 12: 323 students (161 boys, 162 girls). 80% of students are Christian.

Faculty School total: 127. In upper school: 48 men, 59 women; 35 have advanced degrees.

Subjects Offered 20th century American writers, acting, advanced chemistry, advanced computer applications, advanced math, Advanced Placement courses, advanced studio art-AP, aerospace science, algebra, American history, American literature, American sign language, anatomy and physiology, ancient world history, applied music, art, art history-AP, art-AP, astronomy, audio visual/media, ballet, Basic programming, basketball, Bible, Bible studies, biology, biology-AP, British literature, broadcasting, calculus-AP, career and personal planning, ceramics, chemistry, chemistry-AP, Chinese, choral music, choreography, chorus, Christian doctrine, Christian ethics, Christian scripture, Christian studies, church history, college admission preparation, college counseling, college planning, comparative political systems-AP, composition-AP, computer animation, computer art, computer music, computer programming, computer science-AP, computer-aided design, computers, concert band, concert choir, creative writing, critical studies in film, dance, dance performance, debate, digital art, digital music, digital photography, drama performance, drawing, economics, economics-AP, electronic publishing, electronics, engineering, English, English language and composition-AP, English language-AP, English literature-AP, English-AP, English/composition-AP, environmental science-AP, ethics, film appreciation, filmmaking, finite math, foreign language, French, French studies, geometry, global studies, government, government-AP, grammar, guitar, health education, history, history of music, honors English, honors geometry, honors world history, HTML design, human anatomy, human geography - AP, instrumental music, introduction to theater, Japanese, jazz band, jazz dance, jazz ensemble, journalism, keyboarding, lab science, Latin, leadership, leadership and service, literature and composition-AP, macro/microeconomics-AP, macroeconomics-AP, Mandarin, marching band, marine biology, microeconomics-AP, modern world history, music history, music theater, music theory-AP, musical productions, musical theater, New Testament, philosophy, photo shop, photography, photojournalism, physical science, physics, physics-AP, play/screen writing, pre-algebra, pre-calculus, programming, radio broadcasting, religion and culture, SAT preparation, SAT/ACT preparation, science research, sign language, Spanish, Spanish language-AP, Spanish-AP, speech and debate, sports conditioning, stage design, stagecraft, statistics, statistics-AP, student government, studio art, studio art-AP, symphonic band, tap dance, technical theater, technological applications, telecommunications, television, theater arts, theater design and production, theater history, theology and the arts, trigonometry, U.S. government, U.S. government and politics-AP, U.S. history, U.S. history-AP, video and animation, video film production, visual arts, vocal ensemble, vocal jazz, weight training, wind ensemble, world history, world religions, yearbook.

Graduation Requirements American literature, art appreciation, arts and fine arts (art, music, dance, drama), Bible studies, biology, Christian and Hebrew scripture, Christian doctrine, Christian studies, computers, economics, economics and history, English, English composition, English literature, foreign language, global studies, health and wellness, mathematics, physical education (includes health), physical science, U.S. government, U.S. history, world history, world literature.

Special Academic Programs 23 Advanced Placement exams for which test preparation is offered; honors section; academic accommodation for the musically talented and the artistically talented; remedial math; programs in English, mathematics, general development for dyslexic students.

College Admission Counseling 350 students graduated in 2015; all went to college, including California Polytechnic State University, San Luis Obispo; California State University, Chico; Pepperdine University; San Jose State University; University of California, Berkeley; University of California, Davis. Mean SAT critical reading: 570, mean SAT math: 580, mean SAT writing: 570, mean combined SAT: 1720, mean composite ACT: 26.

Student Life Upper grades have specified standards of dress, student council, honor system. Discipline rests primarily with faculty.

Summer Programs Remediation, enrichment, advancement, sports, art/fine arts, computer instruction programs offered; session focuses on advancement, remediation, and enrichment; held on campus; accepts boys and girls; open to students from other schools. 500 students usually enrolled. 2016 schedule: June 13 to July 29. Application deadline: June 1.

Tuition and Aid Day student tuition: $18,834. Tuition installment plan (FACTS Tuition Payment Plan). Need-based scholarship grants available. In 2015–16, 15% of upper-school students received aid. Total amount of financial aid awarded in 2015–16: $2,500,000.

Admissions Traditional secondary-level entrance grade is 9. For fall 2015, 572 students applied for upper-level admission, 423 were accepted, 229 enrolled. Admissions testing, essay, Iowa Subtests, mathematics proficiency exam, school's own test, TOEFL or TOEFL Junior required. Deadline for receipt of application materials: February 1. Application fee required: $70. Interview required.

Athletics Interscholastic: aquatics (boys, girls), badminton (b,g), baseball (b), basketball (b,g), cheering (b), cross-country running (b,g), dance squad (b,g), dance team (b), diving (b,g), football (b), golf (b,g), ice hockey (b,g), in-line hockey (b,g), lacrosse (b,g), soccer (b,g), softball (g), swimming and diving (b,g), tennis (b,g), track and field (b,g), volleyball (b,g), water polo (b,g), weight training (b,g), wrestling (b); intramural: weight training (b,g); coed intramural: drill team. 7 PE instructors, 46 coaches, 2 athletic trainers.

Computers Computers are regularly used in aerospace science, all academic, Bible studies, college planning, computer applications, desktop publishing, digital applications, engineering, foreign language, graphic arts, graphic design, journalism, keyboarding, lab/keyboard, library, mathematics, media arts, music, music technology, news writing, newspaper, photography, photojournalism, research skills, science, technology, theater arts, typing, video film production, Web site design, word processing, writing, yearbook classes. Computer network features include on-campus library services, Internet access, wireless campus network, Internet filtering or blocking technology, two online classes, through two online learning labs. Campus intranet, student e-mail accounts, and computer access in designated common areas are available to students. Students grades are available online. The school has a published electronic and media policy.

Contact Alana James, High School Admissions Coordinator. 408-513-2512. Fax: 408-513-2527. E-mail: ajames@vcs.net. Website: www.vcs.net

VALLEY FORGE MILITARY ACADEMY & COLLEGE

1001 Eagle Road
Wayne, Pennsylvania 19087-3695

Head of School: Mrs. Sandra Young

General Information Boys' boarding and day college-preparatory, arts, business, religious studies, bilingual studies, technology, music, and military school. Grades 7–12. Founded: 1928. Setting: suburban. Nearest major city is Philadelphia. Students are housed in single-sex dormitories. 100-acre campus. 83 buildings on campus. Approved or accredited by Middle States Association of Colleges and Schools, The Association of Boarding Schools, and Pennsylvania Department of Education. Member of National Association of Independent Schools and Secondary School Admission Test Board. Endowment: $8.1 million. Total enrollment: 311. Upper school average class size: 12. Upper school faculty-student ratio: 1:11. There are 169 required school days per year for Upper School students. Upper School students typically attend 5 days per week. The average school day consists of 6 hours and 30 minutes.

Upper School Student Profile Grade 7: 9 students (9 boys); Grade 8: 28 students (28 boys); Grade 9: 45 students (45 boys); Grade 10: 77 students (77 boys); Grade 11: 75 students (75 boys); Grade 12: 77 students (77 boys). 95% of students are boarding students. 28% are state residents. 19 states are represented in upper school student body. 32% are international students. International students from China, Egypt, Mexico, Republic of Korea, United Arab Emirates, and Yemen; 7 other countries represented in student body.

Faculty School total: 29. In upper school: 13 men, 13 women; 14 have advanced degrees; 4 reside on campus.

Subjects Offered ACT preparation, algebra, American government, American history-AP, anatomy and physiology, ancient world history, applied music, art, biology, calculus, chemistry, Chinese, computer programming, creative writing, driver education, earth science, English, English literature and composition-AP, ESL, ESL, European history, French, French studies, geometry, government/civics, health, health education, honors geometry, honors U.S. history, instrumental music, Latin, mathematics, modern world history, music, music theory, physical education, physics, physics-AP, pre-algebra, Russian, social sciences, sociology, Spanish, speech, statistics-AP, TOEFL preparation, U.S. government, U.S. history, U.S. history-AP, world history, world religions, world religions.

Special Academic Programs Advanced Placement exam preparation; honors section; independent study; study at local college for college credit; study abroad; academic accommodation for the musically talented and the artistically talented; remedial reading and/or remedial writing; remedial math; ESL (24 students enrolled).

College Admission Counseling 70 students graduated in 2014; all went to college. Median SAT critical reading: 485, median SAT math: 530, median SAT writing: 465,

median combined SAT: 1495, median composite ACT: 22. 15% scored over 600 on SAT critical reading, 29% scored over 600 on SAT math, 8% scored over 600 on SAT writing, 10% scored over 1800 on combined SAT, 17% scored over 26 on composite ACT.

Student Life Upper grades have uniform requirement, student council, honor system. Discipline rests equally with students and faculty.

Tuition and Aid Day student tuition: $27,370; 5-day tuition and room/board: $42,840; 7-day tuition and room/board: $42,840. Tuition installment plan (monthly payment plans, individually arranged payment plans, Higher Education Services (HES)). Tuition reduction for siblings, merit scholarship grants, need-based scholarship grants available. In 2014–15, 58% of upper-school students received aid; total upper-school merit-scholarship money awarded: $510,500. Total amount of financial aid awarded in 2014–15: $3,427,722.

Admissions Traditional secondary-level entrance grade is 9. For fall 2014, 403 students applied for upper-level admission, 144 were accepted, 132 enrolled. TOEFL or SLEP required. Deadline for receipt of application materials: none. Application fee required: $100. Interview required.

Athletics Interscholastic: baseball, basketball, climbing, cross-country running, dressage, drill team, equestrian sports, fitness, football, golf, horseback riding, indoor track, judo, lacrosse, marksmanship, outdoor activities, outdoor recreation, physical fitness, physical training, soccer, swimming and diving, weight lifting, weight training, wrestling; intramural: boxing, fencing, hockey, indoor hockey, indoor soccer, life saving, martial arts, paint ball, physical training, rugby, scuba diving, soccer, street hockey, ultimate Frisbee. 3 PE instructors, 12 coaches, 2 athletic trainers.

Computers Computers are regularly used in all classes. Computer network features include on-campus library services, Internet access, wireless campus network, Internet filtering or blocking technology, Blackboard. Campus intranet, student e-mail accounts, and computer access in designated common areas are available to students. Students grades are available online. The school has a published electronic and media policy.

Contact Ms. Mary Pontius, Academy Admissions Receptionist. 610-989-1200. Fax: 610-340-2194. E-mail: admissions@vfmac.edu. Website: www.vfmac.edu

THE VALLEY SCHOOL

5255 S. Linden Rd.
Swartz Creek, Michigan 48473

Head of School: Kaye C. Panchula

General Information Coeducational day college-preparatory, arts, and technology school. Grades PK–12. Founded: 1970. Setting: urban. Nearest major city is Flint. 5-acre campus. 1 building on campus. Candidate for accreditation by Independent Schools Association of the Central States. Total enrollment: 64. Upper school average class size: 19. Upper school faculty-student ratio: 1:8. There are 170 required school days per year for Upper School students. Upper School students typically attend 5 days per week. The average school day consists of 5 hours and 30 minutes.

Upper School Student Profile Grade 9: 5 students (2 boys, 3 girls); Grade 10: 4 students (2 boys, 2 girls); Grade 11: 4 students (2 boys, 2 girls); Grade 12: 6 students (3 boys, 3 girls).

Faculty School total: 13. In upper school: 4 men, 3 women; 4 have advanced degrees.

Subjects Offered Algebra, American history, American literature, anatomy, art, art history, biology, chemistry, current events, earth science, English, English literature, European history, expository writing, fine arts, geometry, government/civics, grammar, history, mathematics, music, physical education, physics, probability and statistics, SAT/ACT preparation, science, social sciences, Spanish, trigonometry, world cultures, world history, world literature, world religions.

Graduation Requirements Arts and fine arts (art, music, dance, drama), biology, college counseling, English, foreign language, mathematics, science, social sciences, social studies (includes history), senior project off campus.

Special Academic Programs Honors section; study at local college for college credit; academic accommodation for the gifted and the artistically talented.

Student Life Upper grades have student council. Discipline rests equally with students and faculty.

Tuition and Aid Day student tuition: $9899. Tuition installment plan (FACTS Tuition Payment Plan). Tuition reduction for siblings, merit scholarship grants, need-based scholarship grants available. In 2015–16, 75% of upper-school students received aid; total upper-school merit-scholarship money awarded: $31,500. Total amount of financial aid awarded in 2015–16: $200,000.

Admissions Traditional secondary-level entrance grade is 9. For fall 2015, 5 students applied for upper-level admission, 3 were accepted, 2 enrolled. Brigance Test of Basic Skills, PSAT or school's own exam required. Deadline for receipt of application materials: none. No application fee required. On-campus interview required.

Athletics Interscholastic: basketball (boys, girls), golf (b), outdoor skills (b,g), outdoors (b,g), physical fitness (b,g), soccer (b,g), tennis (g), volleyball (g). 2 PE instructors, 3 coaches.

Computers Computers are regularly used in art, English, mathematics, science, social sciences, stock market, study skills, writing classes. Computer resources include Internet access, wireless campus network. Computer access in designated common areas is available to students.

Contact Ms. Minka Owens, Director of Admissions. 810-767-4004. Fax: 810-655-0853. E-mail: email@valleyschool.org. Website: www.valleyschool.org

VALLEY VIEW SCHOOL

North Brookfield, Massachusetts
See Special Needs Schools section.

VALWOOD SCHOOL

4380 US Highway 41 North
Hahira, Georgia 31632

Head of School: Darren Pascavage

General Information Coeducational day college-preparatory school. Grades PK–12. Founded: 1969. Setting: rural. Nearest major city is Jacksonville, FL. 45-acre campus. 7 buildings on campus. Approved or accredited by Georgia Accrediting Commission, Georgia Independent School Association, Southern Association of Colleges and Schools, and Southern Association of Independent Schools. Member of National Association of Independent Schools and Secondary School Admission Test Board. Total enrollment: 509. Upper school average class size: 20. Upper school faculty-student ratio: 1:12. There are 180 required school days per year for Upper School students. Upper School students typically attend 5 days per week. The average school day consists of 7 hours and 30 minutes.

Upper School Student Profile Grade 6: 32 students (15 boys, 17 girls); Grade 7: 40 students (16 boys, 24 girls); Grade 8: 38 students (25 boys, 13 girls); Grade 9: 43 students (22 boys, 21 girls); Grade 10: 44 students (25 boys, 19 girls); Grade 11: 43 students (23 boys, 20 girls); Grade 12: 44 students (26 boys, 18 girls).

Faculty School total: 45. In upper school: 7 men, 8 women; 6 have advanced degrees.

Subjects Offered Algebra, American history, anatomy and physiology, art, biology, business skills, calculus, calculus-AP, chemistry, chemistry-AP, composition, drama, economics, English, English language-AP, English literature-AP, fitness, French, French-AP, geography, geometry, global issues, government/civics, health, honors algebra, honors English, honors geometry, instruments, Latin, literature, mathematics, model United Nations, music, music appreciation, physical education, physical science, physics, physics-AP, pre-calculus, psychology, science, senior project, Spanish, speech, strings, technology, trigonometry, U.S. history, U.S. history-AP, world history, world history-AP, yearbook.

Graduation Requirements Arts and fine arts (art, music, dance, drama), composition, computer science, English, foreign language, mathematics, physical education (includes health), science, social sciences, social studies (includes history), speech, technology, 20 hours of community service annually.

Special Academic Programs 15 Advanced Placement exams for which test preparation is offered; honors section; independent study; academic accommodation for the gifted and the musically talented.

College Admission Counseling 45 students graduated in 2015; all went to college, including Georgia Southern University; University of Georgia; Valdosta State University. Mean SAT critical reading: 554, mean SAT math: 528, mean SAT writing: 559, mean combined SAT: 1641, mean composite ACT: 24.

Student Life Upper grades have specified standards of dress, student council, honor system. Discipline rests equally with students and faculty.

Tuition and Aid Day student tuition: $12,703. Tuition installment plan (monthly payment plans). Tuition reduction for siblings, merit scholarship grants, need-based scholarship grants available.

Admissions Traditional secondary-level entrance grade is 9. For fall 2015, 32 students applied for upper-level admission, 24 were accepted, 20 enrolled. ACT, Explore, latest standardized score from previous school, PSAT or SAT or Stanford Achievement Test required. Deadline for receipt of application materials: none. Application fee required: $50. Interview recommended.

Athletics Interscholastic: baseball (boys), basketball (b,g), cheering (g), cross-country running (b,g), football (b), golf (b,g), soccer (b,g), softball (g), tennis (b,g), track and field (b,g), volleyball (g), wrestling (b). 3 coaches, 1 athletic trainer.

Computers Computers are regularly used in creative writing, mathematics, science, technology, writing classes. Computer network features include on-campus library services, Internet access, wireless campus network, Internet filtering or blocking technology. Student e-mail accounts are available to students. Students grades are available online.

Contact Val Gallahan, Admissions Coordinator. 229-242-8491. Fax: 229-245-7894. E-mail: admissions@valwood.org. Website: www.valwood.org

THE VANGUARD SCHOOL

Lake Wales, Florida
See Special Needs Schools section.

VENTA PREPARATORY SCHOOL

2013 Old Carp Road
Ottawa, Ontario K0A 1L0, Canada

Head of School: Ms. Marilyn Mansfield

General Information Coeducational boarding and day college-preparatory, arts, and music school. Boarding grades 1–10, day grades JK–10. Founded: 1981. Setting: small town. Students are housed in single-sex by floor dormitories. 50-acre campus. 8 buildings on campus. Approved or accredited by Ontario Ministry of Education and Ontario Department of Education. Member of Secondary School Admission Test Board. Language of instruction: English. Total enrollment: 66. Upper school average class size: 12. Upper school faculty-student ratio: 1:6. There are 167 required school days per year for Upper School students. Upper School students typically attend 5 days per week. The average school day consists of 8 hours and 30 minutes.

Upper School Student Profile Grade 8: 11 students (7 boys, 4 girls). 90% are province residents. 2 provinces are represented in upper school student body.

Faculty School total: 18. In upper school: 4 men, 4 women; 7 have advanced degrees; 6 reside on campus.

Special Academic Programs Independent study; academic accommodation for the gifted; remedial reading and/or remedial writing; remedial math; programs in English, mathematics, general development for dyslexic students.

Student Life Upper grades have uniform requirement, honor system. Discipline rests primarily with faculty.

Tuition and Aid Day student tuition: CAN$17,070–CAN$18,585; 5-day tuition and room/board: CAN$30,965–CAN$33,895; 7-day tuition and room/board: CAN$34,465–CAN$37,395. Tuition installment plan (monthly payment plans, individually arranged payment plans). Tuition reduction for siblings, merit scholarship grants available. Total upper-school merit-scholarship money awarded for 2014–15: CAN$6000.

Admissions Traditional secondary-level entrance grade is 8. For fall 2015, 1 student applied for upper-level admission, 1 was accepted, 1 enrolled. Psychoeducational evaluation, Wechsler Individual Achievement Test or Wechsler Intelligence Scale for Children III required. Deadline for receipt of application materials: none. Application fee required: CAN$150. On-campus interview required.

Athletics Coed Interscholastic: basketball, rugby, soccer; coed intramural: ball hockey, baseball, basketball, canoeing/kayaking, fitness, football, golf, handball, ice hockey, jogging, outdoor recreation, physical fitness, physical training, running, soccer, track and field, ultimate Frisbee. 1 PE instructor.

Computers Computers are regularly used in current events, geography, keyboarding, mathematics, research skills, science classes. Computer network features include Internet access, wireless campus network, Internet filtering or blocking technology. The school has a published electronic and media policy.

Contact Ms. Elizabeth Barnes, Manager of Admissions. 613-839-2175 Ext. 240. Fax: 613-839-1956. E-mail: info@ventaprep.com. Website: www.ventapreparatoryschool.com

VICKSBURG CATHOLIC SCHOOL

1900 Grove Street
Vicksburg, Mississippi 39183

Head of School: Mr. Virgil "Buddy" Strickland

General Information Coeducational day college-preparatory and religious studies school, affiliated with Roman Catholic Church. Grades PK–12. Founded: 1860. Setting: urban. Nearest major city is Jackson. 8-acre campus. 2 buildings on campus. Approved or accredited by National Catholic Education Association, Southern Association of Colleges and Schools, and Mississippi Department of Education. Endowment: $350,000. Total enrollment: 536. Upper school average class size: 17. Upper school faculty-student ratio: 1:11. There are 180 required school days per year for Upper School students. Upper School students typically attend 5 days per week. The average school day consists of 5 hours and 50 minutes.

Upper School Student Profile Grade 7: 40 students (13 boys, 27 girls); Grade 8: 50 students (27 boys, 23 girls); Grade 9: 49 students (21 boys, 28 girls); Grade 10: 40 students (19 boys, 21 girls); Grade 11: 43 students (21 boys, 22 girls); Grade 12: 42 students (26 boys, 16 girls). 50% of students are Roman Catholic.

Faculty School total: 28. In upper school: 9 men, 19 women; 9 have advanced degrees.

Subjects Offered ACT preparation, algebra, anatomy and physiology, art, band, biology, biology-AP, calculus-AP, chemistry, chemistry-AP, choir, computer applications, desktop publishing, drama, earth science, economics, English, English language and composition-AP, environmental science, geography, geology, geometry, health, honors algebra, honors English, honors geometry, honors U.S. history, keyboarding, law, learning lab, literature, music, personal finance, physical education, physical science, physics-AP, pre-algebra, pre-calculus, psychology, sociology, Spanish, speech, state history, statistics, theology, trigonometry, U.S. government, U.S. history, world history, yearbook.

Graduation Requirements ACT preparation, algebra, American government, American history, art, biology, computer skills, economics, English, foreign language, geography, geometry, health, history, lab science, personal finance, physical education (includes health), state history, theology, U.S. government, U.S. history, world history, Mississippi state requirements.

Special Academic Programs 5 Advanced Placement exams for which test preparation is offered; honors section; study at local college for college credit; special instructional classes for students with learning disabilities, Attention Deficit Disorder, dyslexia, emotional and behavioral problems.

College Admission Counseling 42 students graduated in 2015; all went to college, including Hinds Community College; Louisiana State University and Agricultural & Mechanical College; Louisiana Tech University; Mississippi State University;

University of Mississippi; University of Southern Mississippi. Median composite ACT: 25. 40% scored over 26 on composite ACT.

Student Life Upper grades have uniform requirement, student council, honor system. Discipline rests primarily with faculty. Attendance at religious services is required.

Tuition and Aid Day student tuition: $6650. Tuition installment plan (FACTS Tuition Payment Plan). Tuition reduction for siblings, need-based scholarship grants available. In 2015–16, 13% of upper-school students received aid. Total amount of financial aid awarded in 2015–16: $75,000.

Admissions Traditional secondary-level entrance grade is 7. For fall 2015, 13 students applied for upper-level admission, 13 were accepted, 13 enrolled. Admissions testing required. Deadline for receipt of application materials: none. Application fee required: $75. Interview required.

Athletics Interscholastic: baseball (boys), basketball (b,g), cheering (g), cross-country running (b,g), dance squad (g), football (b), golf (b,g), power lifting (b), soccer (b,g), softball (g), swimming and diving (b,g), tennis (b,g), track and field (b,g); coed interscholastic: swimming and diving, tennis. 1 PE instructor, 1 coach.

Computers Computers are regularly used in computer applications, desktop publishing, keyboarding, yearbook classes. Computer network features include on-campus library services, online commercial services, Internet access, Internet filtering or blocking technology, library. Students grades are available online. The school has a published electronic and media policy.

Contact Mrs. Patricia Rabalais, Registrar. 601-636-2256 Ext. 16. Fax: 601-631-0430. E-mail: patricia.rabalais@vicksburgcatholic.org. Website: www.vicksburgcatholic.org

VICTOR VALLEY CHRISTIAN SCHOOL

15260 Nisqualli Road
Victorville, California 92395

Head of School: Mrs. Deb Clarkson

General Information Coeducational day college-preparatory, arts, religious studies, and bilingual studies school, affiliated with Assemblies of God. Grades K–12. Founded: 1972. Setting: suburban. Nearest major city is Ontario. 8-acre campus. 5 buildings on campus. Approved or accredited by Association of Christian Schools International and Western Association of Schools and Colleges. Languages of instruction: English and Spanish. Total enrollment: 275. Upper school average class size: 20. Upper school faculty-student ratio: 1:20. There are 176 required school days per year for Upper School students. Upper School students typically attend 5 days per week. The average school day consists of 7 hours and 15 minutes.

Upper School Student Profile 20% of students are Assemblies of God.

Faculty School total: 18. In upper school: 4 men, 6 women; 5 have advanced degrees.

Subjects Offered Algebra, American history, art, arts, Bible studies, biology, biology-AP, calculus-AP, chemistry, chorus, Christian education, computer literacy, computer science, drama, English, English as a foreign language, English language and composition-AP, English literature-AP, fine arts, geometry, government, health, mathematics, physical education, physics, pre-calculus, psychology-AP, religion, science, social sciences, social studies, Spanish, U.S. history, U.S. history-AP, word processing, world history, world history-AP, yearbook.

Graduation Requirements Arts and fine arts (art, music, dance, drama), English, foreign language, government, health, mathematics, religion (includes Bible studies and theology), science, social sciences, community service.

Special Academic Programs 5 Advanced Placement exams for which test preparation is offered; honors section; accelerated programs; independent study; study at local college for college credit; special instructional classes for students with learning disabilities; ESL (18 students enrolled).

College Admission Counseling 30 students graduated in 2015; all went to college, including California State University, Fullerton; California State University, San Bernardino; The University of Arizona; University of California, Irvine. Mean SAT critical reading: 480, mean SAT math: 470, mean SAT writing: 475, mean composite ACT: 22. 10% scored over 600 on SAT math.

Student Life Upper grades have uniform requirement, student council. Discipline rests primarily with faculty.

Summer Programs Remediation, enrichment programs offered; held on campus; accepts boys and girls; open to students from other schools. 8 students usually enrolled. 2016 schedule: June to August. Application deadline: June 1.

Tuition and Aid Tuition installment plan (FACTS Tuition Payment Plan, monthly payment plans, individually arranged payment plans). Tuition reduction for siblings, need-based scholarship grants available. In 2015–16, 20% of upper-school students received aid.

Admissions Traditional secondary-level entrance grade is 9. Deadline for receipt of application materials: none. No application fee required. Interview required.

Athletics Interscholastic: baseball (boys), basketball (b,g), cheering (g), cross-country running (b,g), football (b), softball (g), track and field (b,g), volleyball (g), weight lifting (b); coed interscholastic: golf, self defense, soccer. 1 PE instructor, 10 coaches, 1 athletic trainer.

Computers Computers are regularly used in desktop publishing, graphic arts, journalism, yearbook classes. Computer resources include on-campus library services, Internet access, wireless campus network, Internet filtering or blocking technology. Campus intranet is available to students. Students grades are available online.

Contact Mrs. Page Porter, Secretary. 760-241-8827. Fax: 760-243-0654. E-mail: pporter@vfassembly.org. Website: www.vvcs.org

VIEWPOINT SCHOOL

23620 Mulholland Highway
Calabasas, California 91302

Head of School: Mr. Mark McKee

General Information Coeducational day college-preparatory, arts, and technology school. Grades K–12. Founded: 1961. Setting: suburban. Nearest major city is Los Angeles. 40-acre campus. 5 buildings on campus. Approved or accredited by California Association of Independent Schools, Western Association of Schools and Colleges, and California Department of Education. Member of National Association of Independent Schools and Secondary School Admission Test Board. Endowment: $12 million. Total enrollment: 1,215. Upper school average class size: 18. Upper school faculty-student ratio: 1:10. There are 180 required school days per year for Upper School students. Upper School students typically attend 5 days per week. The average school day consists of 7 hours.

Upper School Student Profile Grade 9: 149 students (79 boys, 70 girls); Grade 10: 127 students (68 boys, 59 girls); Grade 11: 145 students (70 boys, 75 girls); Grade 12: 124 students (63 boys, 61 girls).

Faculty School total: 213. In upper school: 23 men, 37 women; 39 have advanced degrees.

Subjects Offered Adolescent issues, advanced chemistry, advanced computer applications, advanced studio art-AP, African literature, algebra, American history, American history-AP, American literature, American literature-AP, ancient history, ancient world history, animation, art, art appreciation, art history, art history-AP, art-AP, Asian history, Asian studies, ballet, Basic programming, basic skills, Bible as literature, biology, biology-AP, British literature, business skills, calculus, calculus-AP, California writers, ceramics, character education, chemistry, chemistry-AP, Chinese, Chinese studies, choir, choreography, chorus, college admission preparation, community service, comparative government and politics, comparative government and politics-AP, comparative political systems-AP, comparative politics, computer animation, computer programming, computer science, computer science-AP, concert band, contemporary women writers, CPR, creative writing, critical studies in film, dance, debate, decision making skills, diversity studies, drama, drama performance, dramatic arts, drawing and design, earth science, economics, English, English language-AP, English literature, English literature-AP, ensembles, environmental education, environmental science, environmental science-AP, European history, European history-AP, film, film appreciation, filmmaking, fine arts, French, French language-AP, French literature-AP, geometry, global science, government/civics, history, history-AP, Holocaust and other genocides, honors algebra, honors English, honors geometry, human development, humanities, instrumental music, international relations, jazz, jazz band, jazz dance, jazz ensemble, journalism, keyboarding, Latin, Latin American history, Latin History, Latin-AP, library skills, literary magazine, literature by women, mathematics, medieval history, multicultural literature, music, music composition, music history, music theory-AP, newspaper, oceanography, outdoor education, painting, performing arts, photography, physical education, physics, physics-AP, physiology, poetry, probability and statistics, psychology, psychology-AP, public speaking, robotics, science, sculpture, senior project, Shakespeare, short story, social studies, sociology, Spanish, Spanish language-AP, Spanish literature-AP, Spanish-AP, speech and debate, student publications, studio art, studio art-AP, study skills, swimming, theater, trigonometry, U.S. government and politics-AP, U.S. history-AP, video, vocal jazz, women's literature, word processing, world history, yearbook.

Graduation Requirements Arts and fine arts (art, music, dance, drama), computer science, English, foreign language, global studies, mathematics, physical education (includes health), science, social studies (includes history). Community service is required.

Special Academic Programs 28 Advanced Placement exams for which test preparation is offered; honors section; independent study; study abroad.

College Admission Counseling 111 students graduated in 2015; all went to college, including New York University; Stanford University; University of California, Berkeley; University of California, Los Angeles; University of Southern California; Washington University in St. Louis. Mean SAT critical reading: 653, mean SAT math: 651, mean SAT writing: 671, mean combined SAT: 1975, mean composite ACT: 30.

Student Life Upper grades have specified standards of dress, student council, honor system. Discipline rests primarily with faculty.

Summer Programs Enrichment, advancement, sports, art/fine arts, computer instruction programs offered; session focuses on academics, arts, sports, and recreation; held on campus; accepts boys and girls; open to students from other schools. 600 students usually enrolled. 2016 schedule: June 20 to August 12. Application deadline: none.

Tuition and Aid Day student tuition: $35,325. Tuition installment plan (Insured Tuition Payment Plan, monthly payment plans). Need-based scholarship grants available. In 2015–16, 20% of upper-school students received aid. Total amount of financial aid awarded in 2015–16: $2,801,010.

Admissions Traditional secondary-level entrance grade is 9. For fall 2015, 159 students applied for upper-level admission, 75 were accepted, 43 enrolled. ISEE or

SSAT required. Deadline for receipt of application materials: December 15. Application fee required: $125. Interview required.

Athletics Interscholastic: baseball (boys), basketball (b,g), flag football (b), football (b), lacrosse (b), soccer (b,g), softball (g), volleyball (b,g); intramural: aerobics/dance (g), backpacking (b,g), ball hockey (b,g), ballet (b,g), baseball (b), basketball (b,g), soccer (b,g), volleyball (b,g); coed interscholastic: cross-country running, dance, dance squad, dressage, drill team, equestrian sports, golf, horseback riding, swimming and diving, tennis, track and field; coed intramural: cheering, cooperative games, cross-country running, dance, dance squad, dance team, football, hiking/backpacking, modern dance, outdoor activities, outdoor adventure, outdoor education, outdoor recreation, outdoor skills, outdoors, physical fitness, physical training, power lifting, strength & conditioning, table tennis, weight training, yoga. 14 PE instructors, 51 coaches, 2 athletic trainers.

Computers Computers are regularly used in animation, basic skills, college planning, English, foreign language, history, keyboarding, library skills, mathematics, multimedia, music, newspaper, publications, science, video film production, Web site design, word processing, yearbook classes. Computer network features include on-campus library services, online commercial services, Internet access, wireless campus network, Internet filtering or blocking technology, virtual desktop. Campus intranet, student e-mail accounts, and computer access in designated common areas are available to students. Students grades are available online. The school has a published electronic and media policy.

Contact Mr. Patrick LaBo, Admission and Financial Aid Coordinator. 818-591-6560. Fax: 818-591-0834. E-mail: admission@viewpoint.org. Website: www.viewpoint.org

VILLA ANGELA-ST. JOSEPH HIGH SCHOOL

18491 Lakeshore Boulevard
Cleveland, Ohio 44119-1212

Head of School: Mr. David Csank

General Information Coeducational day college-preparatory, general academic, arts, business, vocational, religious studies, bilingual studies, and technology school, affiliated with Roman Catholic Church. Grades 9–12. Founded: 1990. Setting: urban. 5-acre campus. 2 buildings on campus. Approved or accredited by North Central Association of Colleges and Schools and Ohio Department of Education. Endowment: $3 million. Total enrollment: 375. Upper school average class size: 22. Upper school faculty-student ratio: 1:18. There are 179 required school days per year for Upper School students. Upper School students typically attend 5 days per week. The average school day consists of 7 hours and 8 minutes.

Upper School Student Profile 40% of students are Roman Catholic.

Faculty School total: 32. In upper school: 14 men, 17 women; 27 have advanced degrees.

Subjects Offered 20th century American writers, 20th century history, 20th century physics, 20th century world history, 3-dimensional art, 3-dimensional design, accounting, ACT preparation, advanced chemistry, advanced computer applications, advanced math, Advanced Placement courses, African American history, African-American history, algebra, alternative physical education, American Civil War, American culture, American democracy, American government, American history, American history-AP, American literature, analysis, analytic geometry, anatomy, anatomy and physiology, applied skills, architectural drawing, art, art appreciation, art education, art history, arts and crafts, audio visual/media, auto mechanics, band, Bible, Bible studies, biology, biology-AP, British literature, British literature (honors), business, business skills, business studies, calculus, calculus-AP, campus ministry, career and personal planning, career education, career exploration, career/college preparation, carpentry, cartooning/animation, Catholic belief and practice, chemistry, chemistry-AP, child development, choir, choral music, chorus, Christian doctrine, Christian education, Christian ethics, Christian scripture, Christian studies, Christian testament, Christianity, church history, civics, Civil War, civil war history, college admission preparation, community service, composition, computer education, computer information systems, computer literacy, computer programming, computer science, computer studies, computer technologies, computer tools, computer-aided design, conceptual physics, concert band, creative arts, creative writing, critical thinking, critical writing, culinary arts, current events, current history, debate, design, desktop publishing, diversity studies, drawing and design, early childhood, engineering, English, English composition, English language and composition-AP, English language-AP, English literature, English literature and composition-AP, English literature-AP, English-AP, English/composition-AP, environmental education, environmental geography, environmental science, environmental studies, epic literature, ethnic literature, ethnic studies, European civilization, European history, expressive arts, family and consumer science, family living, family studies, fiction, fine arts, food and nutrition, foreign language, French, freshman foundations, gender and religion, general business, general math, general science, geography, geometry, global issues, global science, government-AP, government/civics, health, health education, health science, history, history of religion, history of the Catholic Church, history-AP, honors algebra, honors English, honors geometry, honors U.S. history, honors world history, human development, human relations, human sexuality, independent living, industrial arts, industrial technology, instrumental music, interactive media, Internet research, intro to computers, introduction to literature, keyboarding, lab science, lab/keyboard, language and composition, language arts, languages, Latin, life

management skills, life science, life skills, literary genres, literary magazine, literature, literature and composition-AP, literature-AP, logic, rhetoric, and debate, math analysis, math applications, math methods, math review, mathematics, mathematics-AP, minority studies, modern civilization, modern European history, modern history, modern politics, modern Western civilization, modern world history, moral and social development, multicultural studies, multimedia design, music, music performance, musical productions, musical theater, newspaper, nutrition, painting, parent/child development, peer ministry, performing arts, personal and social education, physical education, physical science, physics, physics-AP, prayer/spirituality, pre-algebra, pre-calculus, programming, publications, reading, reading/study skills, religion, religion and culture, religious education, religious studies, research skills, Romantic period literature, SAT preparation, SAT/ACT preparation, science, science and technology, scripture, sculpture, sewing, sex education, social education, social justice, social sciences, social studies, society, politics and law, space and physical sciences, Spanish, Spanish literature, speech and debate, student government, student publications, studio art, study skills, technology, technology/design, theology, trigonometry, typing, U.S. government and politics, U.S. government and politics-AP, U.S. history, U.S. literature, United Nations and international issues, United States government-AP, Vietnam history, visual and performing arts, visual arts, vocal ensemble, vocal music, vocational skills, vocational-technical courses, Web authoring, Web site design, Western civilization, Western literature, woodworking, word processing, world civilizations, world cultures, world geography, world governments, world history, world literature, world religions, world religions, world studies, World War I, World War II, writing, writing, yearbook.

Graduation Requirements Students are required to complete a total of 50 hours of service work to be eligible for graduation.

Special Academic Programs Advanced Placement exam preparation; honors section; study at local college for college credit; remedial reading and/or remedial writing; remedial math.

College Admission Counseling 55 students graduated in 2014; all went to college, including Bowling Green State University; John Carroll University; Kent State University; Ohio University; The Ohio State University; University of Dayton.

Student Life Upper grades have uniform requirement, student council, honor system. Discipline rests primarily with faculty. Attendance at religious services is required.

Tuition and Aid Day student tuition: $8250. Tuition installment plan (monthly payment plans). Merit scholarship grants, need-based scholarship grants available. In 2014–15, 85% of upper-school students received aid.

Admissions Traditional secondary-level entrance grade is 9. Deadline for receipt of application materials: none. No application fee required. On-campus interview required.

Athletics Interscholastic: baseball (boys), basketball (b,g), cheering (g), cross-country running (b,g), dance team (g), football (b), golf (b,g), hockey (b), ice hockey (b), indoor track (b,g), indoor track & field (b,g), soccer (b,g), softball (g), track and field (b,g), volleyball (g), wrestling (g); intramural: basketball (b,g), flag football (g); coed interscholastic: bowling; coed intramural: flag football, Frisbee, touch football, ultimate Frisbee, volleyball. 1 PE instructor, 60 coaches, 2 athletic trainers.

Computers Computers are regularly used in architecture, business, career education, career exploration, college planning, creative writing, data processing, design, desktop publishing, drafting, drawing and design, English, industrial technology, information technology, introduction to technology, keyboarding, lab/keyboard, literary magazine, newspaper, publications, publishing, research skills, science, technical drawing, technology, typing, vocational-technical courses, Web site design, word processing, writing, writing, yearbook classes. Computer network features include on-campus library services, online commercial services, Internet access, wireless campus network, Internet filtering or blocking technology, Schoology (online learning information system). Campus intranet, student e-mail accounts, and computer access in designated common areas are available to students. Students grades are available online. The school has a published electronic and media policy.

Contact Mr. Kevin Flynt, Director of Admissions. 216-481-8414 Ext. 254. Fax: 216-486-1035. E-mail: kflynt@vasj.com. Website: www.vasj.com

VILLA DUCHESNE AND OAK HILL SCHOOL

801 S. Spoede Road
St. Louis, Missouri 63131

Head of School: Mrs. Elizabeth Miller

General Information Coeducational day college-preparatory, arts, religious studies, and technology school, affiliated with Roman Catholic Church. Boys grades JK–6, girls grades JK–12. Founded: 1929. Setting: suburban. 60-acre campus. 2 buildings on campus. Approved or accredited by Independent Schools Association of the Central States, National Catholic Education Association, Network of Sacred Heart Schools, and Missouri Department of Education. Member of National Association of Independent Schools. Total enrollment: 585. Upper school average class size: 15. Upper school faculty-student ratio: 1:8. There are 180 required school days per year for Upper School students. Upper School students typically attend 5 days per week. The average school day consists of 7 hours.

Upper School Student Profile 88% of students are Roman Catholic.

Faculty School total: 89. In upper school: 13 men, 44 women; 40 have advanced degrees.

Subjects Offered American government, American literature, American literature-AP, anatomy and physiology, art, biology, biology-AP, British literature, calculus,

calculus-AP, campus ministry, ceramics, chemistry, chorus, civics, computers, creative writing, discrete mathematics, drawing, economics, English, European history, European history-AP, Far Eastern history, French, geography, geometry, health, integrated physics, math analysis, Middle East, music, newspaper, painting, personal development, physical education, physics, pre-algebra, pre-calculus, printmaking, psychology, public speaking, religion, scripture, sculpture, social justice, Spanish, studio art, studio art-AP, theater arts, U.S. history, U.S. history-AP, Western civilization, women's studies, world literature, yearbook.

Graduation Requirements All academic, students must perform community service to graduate.

Special Academic Programs International Baccalaureate program; 13 Advanced Placement exams for which test preparation is offered; honors section; independent study; term-away projects; study at local college for college credit; domestic exchange program (with Network of Sacred Heart Schools); study abroad; remedial reading and/or remedial writing; remedial math.

College Admission Counseling 69 students graduated in 2015; all went to college, including Miami University; Saint Louis University; Texas Christian University; Truman State University; University of Dayton; University of Missouri. Mean SAT critical reading: 568, mean SAT math: 549, mean SAT writing: 580, mean combined SAT: 1697, mean composite ACT: 27.

Student Life Upper grades have uniform requirement, student council, honor system. Discipline rests primarily with faculty. Attendance at religious services is required.

Summer Programs Enrichment, advancement, sports, art/fine arts, computer instruction programs offered; session focuses on enrichment and college preparation; held on campus; accepts boys and girls; open to students from other schools. 200 students usually enrolled. 2016 schedule: June 1 to August 14. Application deadline: May 1.

Tuition and Aid Day student tuition: $20,250. Tuition installment plan (SMART Tuition Payment Plan). Tuition reduction for siblings, merit scholarship grants, need-based scholarship grants available. In 2015–16, 24% of upper-school students received aid.

Admissions Traditional secondary-level entrance grade is 9. SSAT required. Deadline for receipt of application materials: none. Application fee required: $50. On-campus interview required.

Athletics Interscholastic: basketball (girls), cross-country running (g), diving (g), field hockey (g), golf (g), lacrosse (g), racquetball (g), soccer (g), swimming and diving (g), tennis (g), track and field (g), volleyball (g). 5 PE instructors, 34 coaches, 1 athletic trainer.

Computers Computers are regularly used in all academic classes. Computer network features include on-campus library services, online commercial services, Internet access, wireless campus network, Internet filtering or blocking technology, students in grades 7 to 12 have personal tablet PCs. Campus intranet, student e-mail accounts, and computer access in designated common areas are available to students. Students grades are available online. The school has a published electronic and media policy.

Contact Mrs. Elaine Brooks, Admissions Assistant. 314-810-3566. Fax: 314-432-0199. E-mail: ebrooks@vdoh.org. Website: www.vdoh.org

VILLA MADONNA ACADEMY

2500 Amsterdam Road
Covington, Kentucky 41017

Head of School: Mrs. Pamela McQueen

General Information Coeducational day college-preparatory school, affiliated with Roman Catholic Church. Grades 7–12. Founded: 1904. Setting: suburban. Nearest major city is Cincinnati, OH. 234-acre campus. 3 buildings on campus. Approved or accredited by Commission on Secondary and Middle Schools, Southern Association of Colleges and Schools, and Kentucky Department of Education. Total enrollment: 421. Upper school average class size: 11. Upper school faculty-student ratio: 1:8. There are 177 required school days per year for Upper School students. Upper School students typically attend 5 days per week. The average school day consists of 6 hours and 30 minutes.

Upper School Student Profile Grade 7: 38 students (22 boys, 16 girls); Grade 8: 28 students (14 boys, 14 girls); Grade 9: 28 students (8 boys, 20 girls); Grade 10: 41 students (16 boys, 25 girls); Grade 11: 28 students (16 boys, 12 girls); Grade 12: 42 students (11 boys, 31 girls). 70% of students are Roman Catholic.

Faculty School total: 26. In upper school: 10 men, 16 women; 18 have advanced degrees.

Subjects Offered Advanced biology, advanced chemistry, Advanced Placement courses, advanced studio art-AP, algebra, American history, American history-AP, art, art history, biology, calculus, calculus-AP, chemistry, chorus, computer programming-AP, computer science, contemporary studies, digital photography, drama, economics and history, English, English language and composition-AP, English literature and composition-AP, English-AP, European history, French, French-AP, geometry, government/civics, graphic arts, health, honors English, human geography - AP, Latin, Latin-AP, macro/microeconomics-AP, media production, music, music theory-AP, photography, physical education, physics, physics-AP, pre-calculus, psychology-AP, religion, Spanish, Spanish-AP, speech communications, stagecraft, theater, U.S. history-AP.

Special Academic Programs Advanced Placement exam preparation; independent study; study at local college for college credit.

College Admission Counseling 33 students graduated in 2015; 32 went to college. Other: 1 entered military service. Mean composite ACT: 28.

Student Life Upper grades have uniform requirement, student council, honor system. Discipline rests primarily with faculty. Attendance at religious services is required.

Tuition and Aid Tuition installment plan (FACTS Tuition Payment Plan). Tuition reduction for siblings, merit scholarship grants, need-based scholarship grants available.

Admissions Traditional secondary-level entrance grade is 9. Diocesan Entrance Exam and High School Placement Test required. Deadline for receipt of application materials: none. No application fee required. On-campus interview recommended.

Athletics Interscholastic: baseball (boys), basketball (b,g), bowling (b,g), cross-country running (b,g), golf (b,g), running (b,g), soccer (b,g), softball (g), swimming and diving (b,g), tennis (b,g), track and field (b,g), volleyball (g).

Computers Computers are regularly used in all academic classes. Computer network features include on-campus library services, Internet access, wireless campus network, Internet filtering or blocking technology. Student e-mail accounts are available to students. Students grades are available online. The school has a published electronic and media policy.

Contact Mrs. Janet Baugh, Director of Admissions. 859-331-6333 Ext. 139. Fax: 859-331-8615. E-mail: admissions@villamadonna.net. Website: www.villamadonna.org/

VILLA VICTORIA ACADEMY

376 West Upper Ferry Road
Ewing, New Jersey 08628

Head of School: Sr. Lillian Harrington, MPF

General Information Girls' day college-preparatory, arts, religious studies, and technology school, affiliated with Roman Catholic Church. Grades PK–12. Founded: 1933. Setting: suburban. Nearest major city is Trenton. 44-acre campus. 7 buildings on campus. Approved or accredited by Middle States Association of Colleges and Schools, National Catholic Education Association, New Jersey Association of Independent Schools, and New Jersey Department of Education. Member of National Association of Independent Schools. Total enrollment: 162. Upper school average class size: 12. Upper school faculty-student ratio: 1:8. There are 180 required school days per year for Upper School students. Upper School students typically attend 5 days per week. The average school day consists of 6 hours and 20 minutes.

Upper School Student Profile Grade 9: 16 students (16 girls); Grade 10: 14 students (14 girls); Grade 11: 12 students (12 girls); Grade 12: 13 students (13 girls). 65% of students are Roman Catholic.

Faculty School total: 32. In upper school: 3 men, 16 women; 14 have advanced degrees.

Subjects Offered Algebra, American literature, art, art history, art-AP, arts, arts appreciation, athletics, Bible studies, biology, calculus, calculus-AP, campus ministry, career and personal planning, career exploration, career planning, career/college preparation, Catholic belief and practice, ceramics, character education, chemistry, chemistry-AP, Chinese studies, choir, choral music, chorus, Christian education, Christian ethics, Christianity, church history, clayworking, college admission preparation, college awareness, college counseling, college placement, college planning, college writing, communication skills, community service, computer science, concert band, concert choir, creative thinking, creative writing, critical thinking, critical writing, cultural arts, current events, drama, drawing, drawing and design, earth science, English, English composition, English language and composition-AP, English literature, English literature-AP, English-AP, ethics and responsibility, European history, fiction, fine arts, French, French language AP, French studies, French-AP, gender and religion, general business, general math, general science, geography, geometry, global issues, government, government and politics-AP, government-AP, government/civics, government/civics-AP, grammar, health, health and safety, health and wellness, health education, history, history of music, history of religion, history of the Americas, history of the Catholic Church, history-AP, honors algebra, honors English, honors geometry, honors U.S. history, honors world history, humanities, independent study, interdisciplinary studies, Internet, Internet research, interpersonal skills, language and composition, Latin, leadership, leadership and service, library research, library skills, life management skills, Life of Christ, linguistics, literary magazine, literature, literature-AP, math analysis, math applications, math methods, math review, mathematics, mathematics-AP, mechanics of writing, modern history, modern languages, modern world history, money management, moral and social development, moral reasoning, moral theology, multimedia, music, music appreciation, music history, music performance, music theater, music theory, musical productions, musical theater, musical theater dance, oil painting, painting, participation in sports, peer ministry, performing arts, personal development, personal finance, personal fitness, personal money management, photography, physical education, physics, physics-AP, play production, poetry, portfolio art, pottery, prayer/spirituality, pre-algebra, pre-calculus, public service, public speaking, qualitative analysis, reading/study skills, religion, religion and culture, religious education, research, research skills, rhetoric, SAT preparation, SAT/ACT preparation, science, science and technology, sculpture, senior humanities, senior project, senior seminar, set design, Shakespeare, skills for success, social skills, social studies, society and culture, Spanish, Spanish language-AP, Spanish-AP, sports, sports conditioning, stage design, stagecraft, strategies for success, student government, student publications, theater, theater design and production, trigonometry, U.S. history, United States government-AP, values and decisions, visual and performing arts, visual arts, vocal ensemble, world civilizations, world cultures, world history, world issues, world literature, world religions, writing.

Graduation Requirements American literature, art history, arts and fine arts (art, music, dance, drama), biology, British literature, chemistry, computer science, English, foreign language, mathematics, physical education (includes health), physics, religion (includes Bible studies and theology), SAT/ACT preparation, science, social studies (includes history), world cultures, world literature, interdisciplinary humanities. Community service is required.

Special Academic Programs Advanced Placement exam preparation; honors section; independent study; academic accommodation for the gifted, the musically talented, and the artistically talented.

College Admission Counseling 12 students graduated in 2014; all went to college, including Boston University; Fordham University; New York University; The George Washington University; University of Pennsylvania; Villanova University. Median combined SAT: 1814.

Student Life Upper grades have uniform requirement, student council, honor system. Discipline rests primarily with faculty. Attendance at religious services is required.

Tuition and Aid Day student tuition: $12,500. Tuition installment plan (FACTS Tuition Payment Plan, individually arranged payment plans, 2-payment plan). Tuition reduction for siblings, merit scholarship grants, need-based scholarship grants available. In 2014–15, 30% of upper-school students received aid; total upper-school merit-scholarship money awarded: $50,000.

Admissions Traditional secondary-level entrance grade is 9. High School Placement Test (closed version) from Scholastic Testing Service or school placement exam required. Deadline for receipt of application materials: none. Application fee required: $50. On-campus interview required.

Athletics Interscholastic: basketball, cross-country running, soccer, softball, tennis, track and field; intramural: dance, outdoor activities, outdoor education, walking. 1 PE instructor, 4 coaches.

Computers Computers are regularly used in art, English, foreign language, history, mathematics, music, SAT preparation, science, theater classes. Computer network features include on-campus library services, Internet access, wireless campus network, Internet filtering or blocking technology, each student in 9-11 grade have their own NetBook for use in school and home. Computer access in designated common areas is available to students. Students grades are available online. The school has a published electronic and media policy.

Contact Ms. Lori Hoffman, Director of Admissions. 609-882-1700 Ext. 19. Fax: 609-882-8421. E-mail: lhoffman@villavictoria.org. Website: www.villavictoria.org

VILLA WALSH ACADEMY

455 Western Avenue
Morristown, New Jersey 07960

Head of School: Sr. Patricia Pompa

General Information Girls' day college-preparatory, arts, religious studies, and technology school, affiliated with Roman Catholic Church. Grades 7–12. Founded: 1967. Setting: suburban. Nearest major city is New York, NY. 130-acre campus. 4 buildings on campus. Approved or accredited by Middle States Association of Colleges and Schools, National Catholic Education Association, New Jersey Department of Education, and New Jersey Department of Education. Endowment: $6 million. Total enrollment: 238. Upper school average class size: 12. Upper school faculty-student ratio: 1:8. There are 176 required school days per year for Upper School students. Upper School students typically attend 5 days per week. The average school day consists of 6 hours and 30 minutes.

Upper School Student Profile Grade 9: 51 students (51 girls); Grade 10: 49 students (49 girls); Grade 11: 55 students (55 girls); Grade 12: 53 students (53 girls). 90% of students are Roman Catholic.

Faculty School total: 36. In upper school: 4 men, 32 women; 21 have advanced degrees.

Subjects Offered Advanced Placement courses, algebra, American history, American literature, anatomy and physiology, art, Bible as literature, biology, biology-AP, British literature, British literature (honors), calculus, calculus-AP, career/college preparation, chemistry, chemistry-AP, choral music, chorus, church history, college admission preparation, computer applications, computer graphics, computer literacy, computer processing, computer programming, computer science, computer skills, CPR, creative writing, desktop publishing, driver education, economics, English, English language and composition-AP, English literature, English literature-AP, ethics, European civilization, European history-AP, family living, first aid, French, French language-AP, French-AP, geometry, health education, honors English, honors geometry, honors U.S. history, Italian, mathematics, modern European history, moral theology, philosophy, physical education, physics, physics-AP, pre-calculus, psychology, psychology-AP, Spanish, Spanish-AP, statistics-AP, studio art, theology, U.S. government and politics, U.S. history, U.S. history-AP, voice ensemble, Web site design, world history, world literature.

Graduation Requirements Arts and fine arts (art, music, dance, drama), English, foreign language, mathematics, physical education (includes health), science, social studies (includes history), theology.

Special Academic Programs 14 Advanced Placement exams for which test preparation is offered; honors section; independent study; academic accommodation for the gifted, the musically talented, and the artistically talented.

College Admission Counseling 55 students graduated in 2015; all went to college, including Brown University; Bucknell University; Penn State University Park; University of Michigan; University of Notre Dame; University of Richmond. Mean SAT critical reading: 650, mean SAT math: 650, mean SAT writing: 660, mean combined SAT: 1960.

Student Life Upper grades have uniform requirement, student council, honor system. Discipline rests primarily with faculty. Attendance at religious services is required.

Tuition and Aid Day student tuition: $19,000. Tuition installment plan (Insured Tuition Payment Plan, individually arranged payment plans). Merit scholarship grants, need-based scholarship grants available. In 2015–16, 11% of upper-school students received aid; total upper-school merit-scholarship money awarded: $10,000. Total amount of financial aid awarded in 2015–16: $110,000.

Admissions Traditional secondary-level entrance grade is 9. For fall 2015, 140 students applied for upper-level admission, 60 were accepted, 51 enrolled. Math, reading, and mental ability tests and writing sample required. Deadline for receipt of application materials: none. Application fee required: $50. On-campus interview required.

Athletics Interscholastic: basketball, cross-country running, indoor track, lacrosse, soccer, softball, swimming and diving, tennis, track and field, volleyball, winter (indoor) track. 1 PE instructor, 32 coaches, 1 athletic trainer.

Computers Computers are regularly used in college planning, desktop publishing, independent study, keyboarding, library science, mathematics, newspaper, programming, SAT preparation, science, technology, Web site design, word processing, yearbook classes. Computer network features include on-campus library services, Internet access, wireless campus network, Internet filtering or blocking technology. Campus intranet is available to students. The school has a published electronic and media policy.

Contact Sr. Doris Lavinthal, Director. 973-538-3680 Ext. 175. Fax: 973-538-6733. E-mail: lavinthald@aol.com. Website: www.villawalsh.org

VISITATION ACADEMY

3020 North Ballas Road
St. Louis, Missouri 63131

Head of School: Mrs. Rosalie Henry

General Information Coeducational day (boys' only in lower grades) college-preparatory, arts, business, and technology school, affiliated with Roman Catholic Church. Boys grades PK–K, girls grades PK–12. Founded: 1833. Setting: suburban. 30-acre campus. 1 building on campus. Approved or accredited by Independent Schools Association of the Central States and Missouri Department of Education. Member of National Association of Independent Schools. Total enrollment: 553. Upper school average class size: 16. Upper school faculty-student ratio: 1:6. There are 176 required school days per year for Upper School students. Upper School students typically attend 5 days per week. The average school day consists of 7 hours.

Upper School Student Profile Grade 9: 53 students (53 girls); Grade 10: 87 students (87 girls); Grade 11: 82 students (82 girls); Grade 12: 84 students (84 girls). 81% of students are Roman Catholic.

Faculty School total: 80. In upper school: 8 men, 40 women.

Subjects Offered Adolescent issues, advanced biology, advanced chemistry, advanced math, Advanced Placement courses, algebra, American history, American history-AP, American literature, American literature-AP, anatomy, anatomy and physiology, art, art appreciation, art history, bell choir, biology, biology-AP, calculus, calculus-AP, character education, chemistry, chemistry-AP, choral music, chorus, church history, civics, classical language, computer math, computer programming, computer science, computer science-AP, concert choir, creative writing, digital applications, digital photography, drama, drawing and design, earth science, economics, engineering, English, English literature, English literature-AP, environmental science, European history, European history-AP, expository writing, fine arts, French, French-AP, genetics, geography, geometry, government/civics, grammar, graphic arts, graphic design, health, history, independent study, keyboarding, Latin, mathematics, music, music theory-AP, New Testament, photo shop, photography, physical education, physical science, physics, pre-calculus, psychology, robotics, science, social studies, Spanish, speech, statistics-AP, theater, theology, trigonometry, U.S. history-AP, Web site design, world geography, world literature.

Graduation Requirements Arts and fine arts (art, music, dance, drama), computers, electives, English, foreign language, mathematics, physical education (includes health), science, service learning/internship, social studies (includes history), theology, 120 hours of community service.

Special Academic Programs 13 Advanced Placement exams for which test preparation is offered; honors section; independent study; study at local college for college credit; special instructional classes for students with mild learning differences.

College Admission Counseling 99 students graduated in 2015; all went to college, including Emory University; Miami University; Saint Louis University; Texas Christian University; University of Arkansas; University of Missouri. Median SAT critical reading: 603, median SAT math: 593, median SAT writing: 591, median combined SAT: 1815, median composite ACT: 29.

Student Life Upper grades have uniform requirement, student council. Discipline rests primarily with faculty. Attendance at religious services is required.

Summer Programs Enrichment, sports programs offered; session focuses on athletics—basketball, soccer, volleyball, cheerleading; held on campus; accepts girls; open to students from other schools. 200 students usually enrolled.

Tuition and Aid Day student tuition: $18,860. Tuition installment plan (FACTS Tuition Payment Plan). Merit scholarship grants, need-based scholarship grants available. In 2015–16, 18% of upper-school students received aid. Total amount of financial aid awarded in 2015–16: $660,000.

Admissions Traditional secondary-level entrance grade is 9. For fall 2015, 37 students applied for upper-level admission, 33 were accepted, 23 enrolled. SSAT required. Deadline for receipt of application materials: January 15. Application fee required: $75. On-campus interview required.

Athletics Interscholastic: basketball, cheering, cross-country running, dance, diving, field hockey, golf, lacrosse, racquetball, soccer, swimming and diving, tennis, track and field, volleyball; intramural: cheering, dance. 4 PE instructors, 17 coaches, 1 athletic trainer.

Computers Computers are regularly used in all academic, art, English, foreign language, history, mathematics, science, theology classes. Computer network features include on-campus library services, online commercial services, Internet access, wireless campus network, Internet filtering or blocking technology. Campus intranet, student e-mail accounts, and computer access in designated common areas are available to students. Students grades are available online. The school has a published electronic and media policy.

Contact Mrs. Ashley Giljum, Director of Admission. 314-625-9102. Fax: 314-432-7210. E-mail: agiljum@visitationacademy.org. Website: www.visitationacademy.org

THE WALDORF SCHOOL OF SARATOGA SPRINGS

122 Regent Street
Saratoga Springs, New York 12866
Head of School: Mrs. Anne Maguire

General Information Coeducational day college-preparatory, general academic, and arts school. Grades PK–12. Founded: 1981. Setting: suburban. 5-acre campus. 1 building on campus. Approved or accredited by Association of Waldorf Schools of North America, New York State Association of Independent Schools, and New York Department of Education. Total enrollment: 248. Upper school average class size: 13. Upper school faculty-student ratio: 1:13. There are 170 required school days per year for Upper School students. Upper School students typically attend 5 days per week. The average school day consists of 7 hours and 20 minutes.

Upper School Student Profile Grade 9: 13 students (4 boys, 9 girls); Grade 10: 6 students (2 boys, 4 girls); Grade 11: 16 students (7 boys, 9 girls); Grade 12: 8 students (2 boys, 6 girls).

Faculty School total: 40. In upper school: 7 men, 11 women; 5 have advanced degrees.

Subjects Offered All academic.

Graduation Requirements American history, American literature, analytic geometry, anatomy and physiology, Ancient Greek, ancient history, art, art history, astronomy, Bible as literature, biology, botany, calculus, calligraphy, career education internship, chemistry, choir, chorus, creative writing, critical writing, drama performance, drawing, earth science, English, English literature, eurythmy, foreign language, French, geology, geometry, German, history, history of architecture, human anatomy, human biology, human development, hydrology, life science, mathematics, medieval/Renaissance history, meteorology, modern world history, music, orchestra, organic chemistry, physical education (includes health), physics, printmaking, psychology, senior internship, Shakespeare, trigonometry, U.S. history, world cultures, zoology, juniors must complete an internship program, seniors must complete a senior project. Community service is required.

Special Academic Programs Independent study; study abroad; remedial reading and/or remedial writing; remedial math.

College Admission Counseling 13 students graduated in 2015; 12 went to college, including Bryn Mawr College; University at Albany, State University of New York; University of California, Irvine. Other: 1 went to work.

Student Life Upper grades have specified standards of dress, honor system. Discipline rests primarily with faculty.

Tuition and Aid Day student tuition: $16,245. Tuition installment plan (monthly payment plans). Tuition reduction for siblings, need-based scholarship grants, tuition assistance program available. In 2015–16, 30% of upper-school students received aid.

Admissions Traditional secondary-level entrance grade is 9. For fall 2015, 9 students applied for upper-level admission, 9 were accepted, 9 enrolled. Non-standardized placement tests required. Deadline for receipt of application materials: none. No application fee required. Interview required.

Athletics Interscholastic: cross-country running (boys, girls), rowing (b,g), track and field (b,g); coed intramural: archery, climbing, golf, hiking/backpacking, mountain biking, outdoor activities, outdoor adventure, outdoor education, outdoor recreation, outdoor skills, rock climbing, skiing (downhill), tennis, ultimate Frisbee, walking, yoga. 1 PE instructor.

Computers Computers are regularly used in computer applications, graphic design, yearbook classes. Students grades are available online. The school has a published electronic and media policy.

Contact Mr. Richard Youmans, Enrollment Director. 518-587-2224. Fax: 518-581-1466. E-mail: admissions@waldorfsaratoga.org. Website: www.waldorfsaratoga.org/

THE WALKER SCHOOL

700 Cobb Parkway North
Marietta, Georgia 30062
Head of School: Jack Hall

General Information Coeducational day college-preparatory, arts, and technology school. Grades PK–12. Founded: 1957. Setting: suburban. Nearest major city is Atlanta. 32-acre campus. 3 buildings on campus. Approved or accredited by Southern Association of Independent Schools. Member of National Association of Independent Schools and Secondary School Admission Test Board. Endowment: $1.3 million. Total enrollment: 982. Upper school average class size: 13. Upper school faculty-student ratio: 1:15. There are 170 required school days per year for Upper School students. Upper School students typically attend 5 days per week. The average school day consists of 7 hours.

Faculty School total: 117. In upper school: 28 men, 19 women; 34 have advanced degrees.

Subjects Offered Acting, algebra, American history, American literature, analysis, anatomy, ancient world history, art, art-AP, astronomy, band, biology, biology-AP, calculus, calculus-AP, chemistry, chemistry-AP, chorus, comparative government and politics-AP, computer science, computer science-AP, dance, drama, economics, engineering, English, English composition, English language and composition-AP, English literature, English literature and composition-AP, English-AP, European history, fine arts, fitness, French, French language-AP, French literature-AP, genetics, geometry, German, German-AP, government and politics-AP, government-AP, history, history-AP, honors English, honors geometry, Latin, Latin-AP, linear algebra, literature and composition-AP, macro/microeconomics-AP, mathematics, modern world history, multimedia design, music, music theory-AP, musical theater, newspaper, oceanography, orchestra, philosophy, physical education, physics, physics-AP, play production, post-calculus, psychology, public speaking, science, science research, social studies, Spanish, Spanish-AP, stagecraft, statistics, statistics-AP, trigonometry, U.S. history-AP, Web site design, world history, world history-AP, world literature, writing.

Graduation Requirements Advanced Placement courses, American government, arts and fine arts (art, music, dance, drama), computer science, English, English composition, English literature, foreign language, mathematics, physical education (includes health), science, social studies (includes history).

Special Academic Programs 25 Advanced Placement exams for which test preparation is offered; honors section; independent study; study abroad; academic accommodation for the gifted, the musically talented, and the artistically talented.

College Admission Counseling 85 students graduated in 2014; all went to college, including Auburn University; Elon University; Georgia College & State University; Georgia Institute of Technology; Georgia Southern University; University of Georgia. 43% scored over 1800 on combined SAT, 41% scored over 26 on composite ACT.

Student Life Upper grades have specified standards of dress, student council, honor system. Discipline rests equally with students and faculty.

Tuition and Aid Day student tuition: $20,100. Tuition installment plan (school's own payment plan (1, 3, or 7 payments)). Need-based scholarship grants available. In 2014–15, 14% of upper-school students received aid. Total amount of financial aid awarded in 2014–15: $577,767.

Admissions Traditional secondary-level entrance grade is 9. For fall 2014, 77 students applied for upper-level admission, 52 were accepted, 30 enrolled. Otis-Lennon School Ability Test, SSAT or WISC III or Stanford Achievement Test required. Deadline for receipt of application materials: February 18. Application fee required: $85. On-campus interview required.

Athletics Interscholastic: baseball (boys), basketball (b,g), cheering (g), cross-country running (b,g), football (b), golf (b,g), lacrosse (b,g), physical training (b,g), soccer (b,g), softball (g), swimming and diving (b,g), tennis (b,g), track and field (b,g), volleyball (g), wrestling (b); intramural: aerobics/dance (b,g), fitness (b,g), physical fitness (b,g), physical training (b,g), strength & conditioning (b,g), weight training (b,g), yoga (b,g); coed interscholastic: cross-country running, swimming and diving; coed intramural: aerobics/dance, fitness, physical fitness, physical training, weight training, yoga. 4 PE instructors, 7 coaches, 2 athletic trainers.

Computers Computers are regularly used in art, drawing and design, English, foreign language, history, information technology, introduction to technology, literary magazine, mathematics, news writing, newspaper, science, writing classes. Computer network features include on-campus library services, online commercial services, Internet access, wireless campus network, Internet filtering or blocking technology. Student e-mail accounts are available to students. Students grades are available online. The school has a published electronic and media policy.

Contact Brad Brown, Director of Admission. 678-581-6923. Fax: 770-514-8122. E-mail: brad.brown@thewalkerschool.org. Website: www.thewalkerschool.org

WALLA WALLA VALLEY ACADEMY

300 South West Academy Way
College, Washington 99324-1283

Head of School: Brian Harris

General Information Coeducational day college-preparatory, arts, religious studies, and technology school, affiliated with Seventh-day Adventists. Grades 9–12. Founded: 1886. Setting: small town. Nearest major city is Tri Cities. 15-acre campus. 2 buildings on campus. Approved or accredited by National Council for Private School Accreditation and Washington Department of Education. Total enrollment: 178. Upper school average class size: 25. Upper school faculty-student ratio: 1:9. There are 180 required school days per year for Upper School students. Upper School students typically attend 5 days per week. The average school day consists of 7 hours and 30 minutes.

Upper School Student Profile 90% of students are Seventh-day Adventists.

Faculty School total: 16. In upper school: 10 men, 6 women; 7 have advanced degrees.

Subjects Offered Accounting.

Special Academic Programs Advanced Placement exam preparation; study at local college for college credit; remedial reading and/or remedial writing; remedial math; ESL (9 students enrolled).

Student Life Upper grades have uniform requirement, student council, honor system. Discipline rests primarily with faculty. Attendance at religious services is required.

Tuition and Aid Day student tuition: $9500. Tuition installment plan (monthly payment plans, individually arranged payment plans). Tuition reduction for siblings, merit scholarship grants, need-based scholarship grants, paying campus jobs available.

Admissions Traditional secondary-level entrance grade is 9. For fall 2015, 195 students applied for upper-level admission, 185 were accepted, 178 enrolled. High School Placement Test required. Deadline for receipt of application materials: June 1. Application fee required: $2000. Interview required.

Athletics Interscholastic: baseball (boys), basketball (b,g), cross-country running (b,g), golf (b,g), soccer (b,g), softball (g), track and field (b,g), volleyball (g); coed interscholastic: gymnastics, soccer; coed intramural: backpacking, basketball, flag football, ultimate Frisbee. 1 PE instructor, 12 coaches.

Computers Computer network features include on-campus library services, Internet access, wireless campus network, Internet filtering or blocking technology. Student e-mail accounts and computer access in designated common areas are available to students. Students grades are available online. The school has a published electronic and media policy.

Contact Elaine Hinshaw, Director of Recruitment & Marketing. 509-525-1050 Ext. 234. Fax: 509-525-1056. E-mail: hinsel@wwva.org. Website: www.wwva.org

WALNUT HILL SCHOOL FOR THE ARTS

12 Highland Street
Natick, Massachusetts 01760-2199

Head of School: Mr. Antonio Viva

General Information Coeducational boarding and day college-preparatory and arts school. Grades 9–PG. Founded: 1893. Setting: suburban. Nearest major city is Boston. Students are housed in single-sex dormitories. 45-acre campus. 19 buildings on campus. Approved or accredited by Association of Independent Schools in New England, New England Association of Schools and Colleges, and Massachusetts Department of Education. Member of National Association of Independent Schools and Secondary School Admission Test Board. Endowment: $16 million. Total enrollment: 285. Upper school average class size: 16. Upper school faculty-student ratio: 1:6. Upper School students typically attend 5 days per week. The average school day consists of 8 hours.

Upper School Student Profile Grade 9: 43 students (15 boys, 28 girls); Grade 10: 76 students (17 boys, 59 girls); Grade 11: 85 students (17 boys, 68 girls); Grade 12: 80 students (33 boys, 47 girls). 75% of students are boarding students. 33% are state residents. 23 states are represented in upper school student body. 30% are international students. International students from China, Ecuador, Germany, Republic of Korea, Russian Federation, and Taiwan; 8 other countries represented in student body.

Faculty School total: 51. In upper school: 24 men, 27 women; 47 have advanced degrees; 30 reside on campus.

Subjects Offered 20th century world history, 3-dimensional art, acting, advanced chemistry, advanced math, algebra, American history, American literature, art history, arts, ballet, ballet technique, biology, calculus, ceramics, chemistry, choral music, choreography, chorus, classical music, college counseling, community service, creative writing, dance, directing, drama, drawing, English, English literature, ESL, fine arts, French, geometry, health, history, history of dance, jazz dance, mathematics, modern dance, music history, music theory, musical theater, musical theater dance, opera, orchestra, painting, photography, physics, piano, poetry, pre-calculus, research seminar, science, sculpture, set design, Shakespeare, social studies, Spanish, stage design, technical theater, theater, theater design and production, theater production, U.S. history, visual and performing arts, visual arts, vocal music, voice, voice ensemble, world history, writing.

Graduation Requirements Arts, English, foreign language, mathematics, science, social studies (includes history), U.S. history, completion of arts portfolio, body of writing, or participation in performing arts ensembles and/or solo recital.

Special Academic Programs Study at local college for college credit; academic accommodation for the gifted, the musically talented, and the artistically talented; ESL (30 students enrolled).

College Admission Counseling 96 students graduated in 2015; 91 went to college, including Berklee College of Music; McGill University; New England Conservatory of Music; School of the Art Institute of Chicago; The Juilliard School; University of Cincinnati. Other: 1 entered military service, 4 had other specific plans.

Student Life Upper grades have student council. Discipline rests equally with students and faculty.

Summer Programs Art/fine arts programs offered; session focuses on theater, ballet, visual art, writing & film; held on campus; accepts boys and girls; open to students from other schools. 300 students usually enrolled. 2016 schedule: June 20 to August 15. Application deadline: none.

Tuition and Aid Day student tuition: $41,900; 7-day tuition and room/board: $55,520. Tuition installment plan (SMART Tuition Payment Plan, Tuition Refund Plan). Need-based scholarship grants available. In 2015–16, 39% of upper-school students received aid. Total amount of financial aid awarded in 2015–16: $3,500,000.

Admissions Traditional secondary-level entrance grade is 9. For fall 2015, 304 students applied for upper-level admission, 191 were accepted, 117 enrolled. Any standardized test, audition, TOEFL or SLEP or writing sample required. Deadline for receipt of application materials: January 15. Application fee required: $65. Interview required.

Athletics Coed Intramural: aerobics, aerobics/dance, ballet, basketball, boxing, combined training, dance, fitness, fitness walking, Frisbee, modern dance, outdoor activities, paddle tennis, physical training, strength & conditioning, yoga. 2 athletic trainers.

Computers Computer network features include on-campus library services, Internet access, wireless campus network, Internet filtering or blocking technology. Student e-mail accounts and computer access in designated common areas are available to students. Students grades are available online. The school has a published electronic and media policy.

Contact Jason Hersom, Director of Admission and Financial Aid. 508-650-5020. Fax: 508-655-3726. E-mail: admissions@walnuthillarts.org. Website: www.walnuthillarts.org/

WASATCH ACADEMY

120 South 100 West
Mt. Pleasant, Utah 84647

Head of School: Mr. Joseph Loftin

General Information Coeducational boarding and day college-preparatory, arts, bilingual studies, technology, and debate school. Grades 7–PG. Founded: 1875. Setting: small town. Nearest major city is Provo. Students are housed in single-sex dormitories. 40-acre campus. 31 buildings on campus. Approved or accredited by Northwest Accreditation Commission, Northwest Association of Independent Schools, Northwest Association of Schools and Colleges, The Association of Boarding Schools, and Utah Department of Education. Member of National Association of Independent Schools. Endowment: $2 million. Total enrollment: 319. Upper school average class size: 12. Upper school faculty-student ratio: 1:10. There are 165 required school days per year for Upper School students. Upper School students typically attend 5 days per week. The average school day consists of 7 hours.

Upper School Student Profile Grade 9: 40 students (30 boys, 10 girls); Grade 10: 61 students (39 boys, 22 girls); Grade 11: 93 students (52 boys, 41 girls); Grade 12: 101 students (64 boys, 37 girls). 78% of students are boarding students. 23% are state residents. 30 states are represented in upper school student body. 50% are international students. International students from China, Germany, Japan, Taiwan, Turkey, and Viet Nam; 28 other countries represented in student body.

Faculty School total: 53. In upper school: 25 men, 26 women; 19 have advanced degrees; 48 reside on campus.

Subjects Offered 3-dimensional art, 3-dimensional design, acting, advanced computer applications, Advanced Placement courses, advanced studio art-AP, advanced TOEFL/grammar, algebra, American Civil War, American history, American history-AP, American literature-AP, anatomy, animation, art, athletic training, audio visual/media, ballet, biology, biology-AP, broadcast journalism, business mathematics, calculus-AP, ceramics, chemistry, chemistry-AP, Chinese, choir, cinematography, Civil War, college counseling, college placement, comedy, community garden, community service, dance, design, drama, drawing, drawing and design, driver education, earth science, electronic music, emerging technology, English, English language and composition-AP, English literature and composition-AP, English-AP, ensembles, environmental science-AP, equestrian sports, equine science, ESL, ESL, European history, European history-AP, film, filmmaking, fine arts, forensics, French, geography, geology, global issues, golf, guitar, honors algebra, honors English, honors U.S. history, jazz ensemble, jewelry making, Latin, learning strategies, martial arts, math applications, music, music theory, outdoor education, painting, performing arts, philosophy, photography, physical education, physical science, physics, physics-AP, piano, play production, pottery, pre-calculus, reading, SAT/ACT preparation, Spanish, Spanish-AP, speech and debate, stained glass, statistics-AP, student government, studio art-AP, study skills, theater, theater arts, theater design and production, TOEFL preparation, U.S. government, U.S. history, U.S. history-AP, United Nations and international issues, Vietnam War, weightlifting, Western civilization, woodworking, world religions, yearbook, yoga.

Graduation Requirements Arts and fine arts (art, music, dance, drama), computer literacy, English, foreign language, mathematics, physical education (includes health), science, social sciences, social studies (includes history), U.S. history, outdoor, cultural, community service, and recreational requirements.

Special Academic Programs 16 Advanced Placement exams for which test preparation is offered; honors section; accelerated programs; independent study; study at local college for college credit; programs in English, mathematics, general development for dyslexic students; ESL (29 students enrolled).

College Admission Counseling 105 students graduated in 2015; 100 went to college, including Boston University; Michigan State University; Parsons School of Design; Penn State University Park; Smith College; University of Utah. Median SAT critical reading: 500, median SAT math: 480, median composite ACT: 22. Mean SAT writing: 564, mean combined SAT: 1892. 13% scored over 600 on SAT critical reading, 9% scored over 600 on SAT math, 27% scored over 26 on composite ACT.

Student Life Upper grades have specified standards of dress, student council, honor system. Discipline rests primarily with faculty.

Summer Programs Remediation, enrichment, advancement, ESL programs offered; session focuses on academics and recreation; held on campus; accepts boys and girls; open to students from other schools. 50 students usually enrolled. 2016 schedule: June 26 to August 6. Application deadline: none.

Tuition and Aid Day student tuition: $28,700; 5-day tuition and room/board: $49,300; 7-day tuition and room/board: $52,300. Tuition installment plan (The Tuition Plan, individually arranged payment plans). Merit scholarship grants, need-based scholarship grants, need-based loans available. In 2015–16, 44% of upper-school students received aid; total upper-school merit-scholarship money awarded: $134,300. Total amount of financial aid awarded in 2015–16: $3,857,580.

Admissions Traditional secondary-level entrance grade is 11. For fall 2015, 212 students applied for upper-level admission, 178 were accepted, 120 enrolled. Deadline for receipt of application materials: none. Application fee required: $100. On-campus interview required.

Athletics Interscholastic: alpine skiing (boys, girls), baseball (b), basketball (b,g), climbing (b,g), cross-country running (b,g), dance (b,g), dressage (b,g), equestrian sports (b,g), golf (b,g), horseback riding (b,g), outdoor activities (b,g), outdoor education (b,g), paint ball (b,g), physical training (b,g), rodeo (b,g), running (b,g), skiing (cross-country) (b,g), skiing (downhill) (b,g), snowboarding (b,g), snowshoeing (b,g), soccer (b,g), tennis (b,g), track and field (b,g), volleyball (g), weight training (b,g); intramural: alpine skiing (b,g), dance (g), skiing (downhill) (b,g), soccer (b,g), table tennis (b,g); coed interscholastic: aerobics/dance, backpacking, ballet, bicycling, canoeing/kayaking, cheering, climbing, combined training, cross-country running, dance, dressage, equestrian sports, fishing, golf, hiking/backpacking, horseback riding, kayaking, martial arts, modern dance, mountain biking, nordic skiing, outdoor activities, paint ball, physical training, rock climbing, rodeo, running, ski jumping, skiing (cross-country), skiing (downhill), snowboarding, snowshoeing, swimming and diving, table tennis, telemark skiing, tennis, track and field, weight training, yoga; coed intramural: aerobics/dance, aquatics, backpacking, badminton, ballet, bicycling, billiards, blading, bowling, canoeing/kayaking, climbing, combined training, cooperative games, dance team, equestrian sports, fishing, fitness, flag football, freestyle skiing, Frisbee, golf, hiking/backpacking, horseback riding, horseshoes, jogging, lacrosse, modern dance, mountain biking, nordic skiing, outdoor activities, paint ball, physical training, power lifting, rafting, rappelling, rock climbing, running, skateboarding, skiing (downhill), snowshoeing, swimming and diving, table tennis, telemark skiing, ultimate Frisbee, volleyball, weight lifting, weight training, yoga. 2 coaches, 1 athletic trainer.

Computers Computers are regularly used in all academic classes. Computer network features include on-campus library services, online commercial services, Internet access, wireless campus network, Internet filtering or blocking technology. Campus intranet and student e-mail accounts are available to students. Students grades are available online. The school has a published electronic and media policy.

Contact Mrs. Brian McCauley, Director of Admissions. 435-462-1400. Fax: 435-462-1450. E-mail: brian.mccauley@wasatchacademy.org. Website: www.wasatchacademy.org

WASHINGTON INTERNATIONAL SCHOOL

3100 Macomb Street NW
Washington, District of Columbia 20008

Head of School: Clayton W. Lewis

General Information Coeducational day college-preparatory, bilingual studies, and International Baccalaureate school. Grades PS–12. Founded: 1966. Setting: urban. 6-acre campus. 8 buildings on campus. Approved or accredited by Council of International Schools, International Baccalaureate Organization, Middle States Association of Colleges and Schools, and District of Columbia Department of Education. Member of National Association of Independent Schools, Secondary School Admission Test Board, and European Council of International Schools. Languages of instruction: English, French, and Spanish. Endowment: $5.5 million. Total enrollment: 920. Upper school average class size: 10. Upper school faculty-student ratio: 1:7. There are 176 required school days per year for Upper School students. Upper School students

typically attend 5 days per week. The average school day consists of 5 hours and 25 minutes.

Faculty School total: 105. In upper school: 16 men, 20 women.

Subjects Offered Advanced chemistry, advanced math, art, arts, biology, calculus, chemistry, chorus, community service, comparative government and politics, computer multimedia, computer science, contemporary history, drama, Dutch, economics, English, English literature, environmental science, fine arts, French, geography, history, information technology, integrated mathematics, International Baccalaureate courses, literature seminar, music, musical productions, physical education, physics, psychology, robotics, science, social sciences, Spanish, theater, theory of knowledge, world history.

Graduation Requirements Algebra, arts, arts and fine arts (art, music, dance, drama), biology, calculus, chemistry, economics, English, environmental science, foreign language, geography, geometry, physical education (includes health), physics, trigonometry, world history, world literature, International Baccalaureate program. Community service is required.

Special Academic Programs International Baccalaureate program.

College Admission Counseling 64 students graduated in 2015; all went to college, including Columbia University; Georgetown University; Princeton University; University of California, Los Angeles; University of Pennsylvania; Wesleyan University. Mean SAT critical reading: 658, mean SAT math: 667, mean SAT writing: 662, mean combined SAT: 1988.

Student Life Upper grades have student council. Discipline rests primarily with faculty.

Summer Programs ESL programs offered; held on campus; accepts boys and girls; open to students from other schools. 2016 schedule: June 27 to August 5. Application deadline: July 30.

Tuition and Aid Day student tuition: $37,030. Tuition installment plan (monthly payment plans, 2-payment plan). Need-based scholarship grants available.

Admissions School's own exam required. Deadline for receipt of application materials: January 5. Application fee required: $75. Interview required.

Athletics Interscholastic: basketball (boys, girls), soccer (b,g), softball (g), tennis (b,g), track and field (b,g), volleyball (b,g); coed interscholastic: cross-country running, golf; coed intramural: swimming and diving. 3 PE instructors, 1 athletic trainer.

Computers Computers are regularly used in all classes. Computer network features include on-campus library services, online commercial services, Internet access, wireless campus network, Internet filtering or blocking technology. Campus intranet and student e-mail accounts are available to students. The school has a published electronic and media policy.

Contact Ms. Mary Hastings Moore, Director of Admissions and Financial Aid. 202-243-1831. Fax: 202-243-1807. E-mail: moore@wis.edu. Website: www.wis.edu

WASHINGTON WALDORF SCHOOL

4800 Sangamore Road
Bethesda, Maryland 20816

Head of School: Ms. Jennifer Page

General Information Coeducational day college-preparatory and arts school. Grades PS–12. Founded: 1969. Setting: suburban. Nearest major city is Washington, DC. 6-acre campus. 1 building on campus. Approved or accredited by Association of Independent Maryland Schools, Association of Waldorf Schools of North America, Middle States Association of Colleges and Schools, and Maryland Department of Education. Member of National Association of Independent Schools. Total enrollment: 242. Upper school average class size: 18. Upper school faculty-student ratio: 1:7. There are 175 required school days per year for Upper School students. Upper School students typically attend 5 days per week. The average school day consists of 7 hours.

Upper School Student Profile Grade 9: 18 students (6 boys, 12 girls); Grade 10: 17 students (9 boys, 8 girls); Grade 11: 10 students (3 boys, 7 girls); Grade 12: 8 students (5 boys, 3 girls).

Faculty School total: 38. In upper school: 8 men, 8 women; 9 have advanced degrees.

Subjects Offered 3-dimensional art, African-American history, algebra, American Civil War, American literature, anatomy and physiology, ancient world history, art, art and culture, art history, biochemistry, biology, bookbinding, botany, British literature, calculus, calculus-AP, chamber groups, chemistry, choir, chorus, civil rights, classical civilization, crafts, critical thinking, critical writing, drama performance, ecology, epic literature, eurythmy, fine arts, general math, general science, geology, geometry, German, grammar, history of architecture, history of music, human anatomy, human development, lab science, medieval literature, metalworking, modern history, modern world history, mythology, oil painting, optics, physical education, pre-calculus, printmaking, research skills, sculpture, Shakespeare, Spanish, stone carving, trigonometry, U.S. constitutional history, weaving, Western literature, writing, zoology.

Graduation Requirements Arts and fine arts (art, music, dance, drama), comparative religion, constitutional history of U.S., crafts, English, eurythmy, foreign language, history of drama, history of music, mathematics, physical education (includes health), science, social studies (includes history).

Special Academic Programs 1 Advanced Placement exam for which test preparation is offered; study abroad; academic accommodation for the musically talented and the artistically talented.

College Admission Counseling 9 students graduated in 2014; 7 went to college, including Bates College; Bennington College; Emerson College; Johnson & Wales

University; Oberlin College; The Colorado College. Other: 2 went to work. Median SAT critical reading: 648, median SAT math: 578, median SAT writing: 652.

Student Life Upper grades have specified standards of dress, student council. Discipline rests primarily with faculty.

Tuition and Aid Day student tuition: $25,200. Tuition installment plan (FACTS Tuition Payment Plan, monthly payment plans, individually arranged payment plans, self-insured tuition insurance). Tuition reduction for siblings, need-based scholarship grants, need-based assistance grants, tuition remission for children of faculty, one full scholarship for an inner-city student available. In 2014–15, 25% of upper-school students received aid. Total amount of financial aid awarded in 2014–15: $38,000.

Admissions Traditional secondary-level entrance grade is 9. For fall 2014, 9 students applied for upper-level admission, 7 were accepted, 5 enrolled. Math and English placement tests required. Deadline for receipt of application materials: none. Application fee required: $60. On-campus interview required.

Athletics Interscholastic: baseball (boys), basketball (b,g), cross-country running (b,g), soccer (b,g), softball (g); coed intramural: golf, outdoor education, table tennis, volleyball, yoga. 1 PE instructor, 3 coaches.

Computers Computers are regularly used in graphic design, technology classes. Computer resources include Internet access.

Contact Ms. Lezlie Lawson, Admissions/Enrollment Director. 301-229-6107 Ext. 154. Fax: 301-229-9379. E-mail: llawson@washingtonwaldorf.org. Website: www.washingtonwaldorf.org

THE WATERFORD SCHOOL

1480 East 9400 South
Sandy, Utah 84093

Head of School: Dr. Brandon Bennett

General Information Coeducational day college-preparatory, arts, technology, and visual arts, music, photography, dance, and theater school. Grades PK–12. Founded: 1981. Setting: suburban. Nearest major city is Salt Lake City. 40-acre campus. 10 buildings on campus. Approved or accredited by Northwest Accreditation Commission, Northwest Association of Independent Schools, and Utah Department of Education. Member of National Association of Independent Schools. Endowment: $3 million. Total enrollment: 880. Upper school average class size: 16. Upper school faculty-student ratio: 1:4. There are 169 required school days per year for Upper School students. Upper School students typically attend 5 days per week. The average school day consists of 6 hours.

Upper School Student Profile Grade 9: 76 students (40 boys, 36 girls); Grade 10: 64 students (28 boys, 36 girls); Grade 11: 75 students (33 boys, 42 girls); Grade 12: 72 students (43 boys, 29 girls).

Faculty School total: 122. In upper school: 41 men, 37 women; 59 have advanced degrees.

Subjects Offered 20th century history, 3-dimensional design, acting, advanced math, Advanced Placement courses, aerobics, algebra, American history, American history-AP, American literature, art, Asian history, basketball, biology, biology-AP, British literature, calculus, calculus-AP, ceramics, chemistry, chemistry-AP, chorus, computer applications, computer art, computer graphics, computer programming, computer science, computer science-AP, creative writing, debate, drama, drama performance, drama workshop, drawing, ecology, economics, English-AP, European history, European history-AP, French, French-AP, genetics, geology, geometry, German, German-AP, Japanese, jazz ensemble, Latin, Latin American literature, music history, music performance, music theater, outdoor education, painting, philosophy, photography, physical education, physics, physics-AP, pre-calculus, probability and statistics, psychology, robotics, sculpture, Spanish, Spanish-AP, statistics-AP, strings, studio art-AP, trigonometry, voice ensemble, volleyball, weight training, wind ensemble, world literature, writing workshop, yearbook, zoology.

Graduation Requirements 20th century world history, algebra, American history, American literature, biology, British literature, calculus, chemistry, computer science, English, European history, foreign language, geometry, music performance, physics, pre-calculus, trigonometry, visual arts, world history, writing workshop, six terms of physical education or participation on athletic teams.

Special Academic Programs 15 Advanced Placement exams for which test preparation is offered; honors section; independent study; term-away projects; academic accommodation for the gifted, the musically talented, and the artistically talented.

College Admission Counseling 64 students graduated in 2015; 63 went to college. Other: 1 entered military service. Mean SAT critical reading: 637, mean SAT math: 664, mean SAT writing: 618, mean combined SAT: 1919, mean composite ACT: 28.

Student Life Upper grades have uniform requirement, student council, honor system. Discipline rests equally with students and faculty.

Summer Programs Enrichment, advancement, sports, art/fine arts, rigorous outdoor training programs offered; session focuses on enrichment and advancement; held both on and off campus; held at various locations in Utah and abroad; accepts boys and girls; not open to students from other schools. 100 students usually enrolled. 2016 schedule: June 10 to August 15. Application deadline: March 15.

Tuition and Aid Day student tuition: $21,000. Tuition installment plan (Insured Tuition Payment Plan, monthly payment plans). Tuition reduction for siblings, need-

based scholarship grants available. In 2015–16, 10% of upper-school students received aid. Total amount of financial aid awarded in 2015–16: $1,500,000.

Admissions Traditional secondary-level entrance grade is 9. For fall 2015, 42 students applied for upper-level admission, 32 were accepted, 25 enrolled. ERB CTP IV, school's own test or TOEFL required. Deadline for receipt of application materials: none. Application fee required: $35. On-campus interview required.

Athletics Interscholastic: basketball (boys, girls), crew (b,g), cross-country running (b,g), golf (b,g), lacrosse (b,g), soccer (b,g), tennis (b,g), volleyball (g); coed interscholastic: alpine skiing, ballet, dance, Frisbee, racquetball, ultimate Frisbee; coed intramural: aerobics, backpacking, climbing, crew, hiking/backpacking, outdoor activities, outdoor adventure, outdoor education, outdoor recreation, outdoor skills, outdoors, rock climbing, snowshoeing, strength & conditioning, weight training, yoga. 6 PE instructors, 15 coaches.

Computers Computers are regularly used in all academic, animation, college planning, graphic design, library, literary magazine, newspaper, photography, programming, publications, writing, yearbook classes. Computer network features include on-campus library services, online commercial services, Internet access, wireless campus network, Internet filtering or blocking technology. Campus intranet, student e-mail accounts, and computer access in designated common areas are available to students. Students grades are available online. The school has a published electronic and media policy.

Contact Mr. Todd Winters, Director of Admissions. 801-816-2213. Fax: 801-572-1787. E-mail: toddwinters@waterfordschool.org. Website: www.waterfordschool.org

WATKINSON SCHOOL

180 Bloomfield Avenue
Hartford, Connecticut 06105

Head of School: Mrs. Teriann Schrader

General Information Coeducational day college-preparatory, arts, and athletics, global studies school. Grades 6–PG. Founded: 1881. Setting: suburban. 40-acre campus. 5 buildings on campus. Approved or accredited by Association of Independent Schools in New England, New England Association of Schools and Colleges, and Connecticut Department of Education. Member of National Association of Independent Schools and Secondary School Admission Test Board. Endowment: $4.4 million. Total enrollment: 240. Upper school average class size: 12. Upper school faculty-student ratio: 1:6. There are 165 required school days per year for Upper School students. Upper School students typically attend 5 days per week. The average school day consists of 7 hours and 30 minutes.

Upper School Student Profile Grade 9: 40 students (19 boys, 21 girls); Grade 10: 45 students (26 boys, 19 girls); Grade 11: 45 students (20 boys, 25 girls); Grade 12: 45 students (23 boys, 22 girls); Postgraduate: 5 students (4 boys, 1 girl).

Faculty School total: 56. In upper school: 13 men, 30 women; 21 have advanced degrees.

Subjects Offered African history, algebra, American history, American literature, American sign language, anatomy, ancient world history, art, Asian history, biology, calculus, ceramics, chemistry, creative writing, dance, drama, drawing, earth science, English, English literature, environmental science, European history, expository writing, fine arts, forensics, French, geography, geometry, health, history, internship, mathematics, modern European history, painting, photography, physics, pottery, science, social studies, Spanish, theater, U.S. history, world history, world literature, writing.

Graduation Requirements Arts and fine arts (art, music, dance, drama), English, foreign language, health and wellness, mathematics, science, social studies (includes history), technology.

Special Academic Programs Independent study; study at local college for college credit; academic accommodation for the gifted, the musically talented, and the artistically talented; programs in English, mathematics, general development for dyslexic students; special instructional classes for deaf students.

College Admission Counseling 53 students graduated in 2015; 51 went to college, including Emerson College; Hampshire College; McGill University; Quinnipiac University; Salve Regina University; University of Connecticut. Other: 1 went to work, 1 had other specific plans. Median SAT critical reading: 530, median SAT math: 520, median SAT writing: 540, median combined SAT: 1615, median composite ACT: 25. 32% scored over 600 on SAT critical reading, 25% scored over 600 on SAT math, 32% scored over 600 on SAT writing, 20% scored over 1800 on combined SAT, 47% scored over 26 on composite ACT.

Student Life Upper grades have specified standards of dress, student council. Discipline rests equally with students and faculty.

Summer Programs Remediation, enrichment programs offered; session focuses on academics; held on campus; accepts boys and girls; open to students from other schools. 10 students usually enrolled. 2016 schedule: June 30 to August 1. Application deadline: none.

Tuition and Aid Day student tuition: $37,000. Tuition installment plan (Insured Tuition Payment Plan, SMART Tuition Payment Plan). Need-based scholarship grants available. In 2015–16, 41% of upper-school students received aid. Total amount of financial aid awarded in 2015–16: $1,650,522.

Admissions Traditional secondary-level entrance grade is 9. For fall 2015, 107 students applied for upper-level admission, 45 were accepted, 24 enrolled. ISEE, SSAT,

TOEFL or TOEFL Junior required. Deadline for receipt of application materials: February 1. Application fee required: $50. On-campus interview required.

Athletics Interscholastic: baseball (boys), basketball (b,g), crew (b,g), cross-country running (b,g), lacrosse (b,g), rowing (b,g), soccer (b,g), softball (g), tennis (b,g), track and field (b,g), volleyball (g); coed interscholastic: crew, cross-country running, tennis, ultimate Frisbee; coed intramural: alpine skiing, ballet, Circus, climbing, combined training, dance, fencing, fitness, Frisbee, golf, horseback riding, outdoor activities, outdoor adventure, physical fitness, physical training, strength & conditioning, tennis, ultimate Frisbee, volleyball, weight lifting, yoga. 4 coaches.

Computers Computers are regularly used in college planning, computer applications, desktop publishing classes. Computer network features include on-campus library services, online commercial services, Internet access, wireless campus network, Internet filtering or blocking technology. Campus intranet, student e-mail accounts, and computer access in designated common areas are available to students. Students grades are available online. The school has a published electronic and media policy.

Contact Mrs. Maryann Dupuis, Admissions Office Assistant. 860-236-5618 Ext. 136. Fax: 860-986-6146. E-mail: Maryann_Dupuis@watkinson.org. Website: www.watkinson.org

WAYNFLETE SCHOOL
360 Spring Street
Portland, Maine 04102

Head of School: Geoffrey Wagg

General Information Coeducational day college-preparatory school. Grades PK–12. Founded: 1898. Setting: urban. Nearest major city is Boston, MA. 37-acre campus. 10 buildings on campus. Approved or accredited by Association of Independent Schools in New England, Independent Schools of Northern New England, New England Association of Schools and Colleges, The College Board, and Maine Department of Education. Member of National Association of Independent Schools. Endowment: $23.7 million. Total enrollment: 583. Upper school average class size: 12. Upper school faculty-student ratio: 1:12. There are 172 required school days per year for Upper School students. Upper School students typically attend 5 days per week. The average school day consists of 7 hours and 15 minutes.

Upper School Student Profile Grade 9: 73 students (37 boys, 36 girls); Grade 10: 58 students (26 boys, 32 girls); Grade 11: 69 students (27 boys, 42 girls); Grade 12: 63 students (31 boys, 32 girls).

Faculty School total: 85. In upper school: 22 men, 33 women; 34 have advanced degrees.

Subjects Offered 20th century American writers, 20th century history, 3-dimensional art, 3-dimensional design, acting, advanced biology, advanced math, African literature, algebra, American history, American literature, ancient/medieval philosophy, art history, astrophysics, bioethics, biology, British literature (honors), Buddhism, calculus, ceramics, chemistry, computer studies, constitutional history of U.S., creative writing, drama, drama workshop, English, English composition, English literature, environmental science, environmental studies, equality and freedom, European history, expository writing, French, geometry, government/civics, health, Irish literature, Islamic studies, Latin, Mandarin, marine biology, Middle Eastern history, modern European history, music, physical education, physics, pre-calculus, printmaking, psychology, Russian history, Spanish, statistics, studio art, trigonometry, U.S. constitutional history, Vietnam, world history, world literature.

Graduation Requirements Arts, biology, English, foreign language, history, mathematics, performing arts, physical education (includes health), science, U.S. history, Seniors may design a month-long Senior Project, which allows them to pursue academic interests, potential careers, fine arts, or community service. Community service is required.

Special Academic Programs Independent study; term-away projects; study abroad.

College Admission Counseling 68 students graduated in 2015; 67 went to college, including Bowdoin College; Connecticut College; Cornell University; Franklin & Marshall College; Oberlin College; Saint Joseph's College of Maine. Other: 1 went to work. Median SAT critical reading: 620, median SAT math: 590, median SAT writing: 600, median combined SAT: 1820, median composite ACT: 29. 62% scored over 600 on SAT critical reading, 37% scored over 600 on SAT math, 49% scored over 600 on SAT writing, 54% scored over 1800 on combined SAT, 62% scored over 26 on composite ACT.

Student Life Upper grades have student council. Discipline rests primarily with faculty.

Summer Programs Enrichment, sports, art/fine arts programs offered; session focuses on sports, gymnastics, martial arts, robotics, fine/performing arts, technology, sustainable ocean studies; held both on and off campus; held at Fore River Fields, Portland, ME and Pensobscot Bay, Darling Marine Center, Mt. Desert Island; accepts boys and girls; open to students from other schools. 750 students usually enrolled. 2016 schedule: June 13 to July 29. Application deadline: none.

Tuition and Aid Day student tuition: $28,265. Tuition installment plan (Insured Tuition Payment Plan, FACTS Tuition Payment Plan). Need-based scholarship grants available. In 2015–16, 38% of upper-school students received aid. Total amount of financial aid awarded in 2015–16: $2,067,247.

Admissions Traditional secondary-level entrance grade is 9. For fall 2015, 76 students applied for upper-level admission, 43 were accepted, 35 enrolled. Deadline for receipt

---

of application materials: February 10. Application fee required: $40. Interview required.

Athletics Interscholastic: baseball (boys), basketball (b,g), cross-country running (b,g), field hockey (g), golf (b), ice hockey (b,g), lacrosse (b,g), nordic skiing (b,g), skiing (cross-country) (b,g), soccer (b,g), tennis (b,g); coed interscholastic: crew, rowing, sailing, swimming and diving, track and field; coed intramural: dance, fitness walking, golf, modern dance, physical fitness, sailing, swimming and diving, tennis, weight lifting, weight training, yoga. 3 PE instructors, 20 coaches, 1 athletic trainer.

Computers Computers are regularly used in computer applications, information technology, introduction to technology, programming classes. Computer network features include on-campus library services, online commercial services, Internet access, wireless campus network, Internet filtering or blocking technology, Google doc accounts; academic databases, including JSTOR and Schoology; Quizlet; and Noodle Tools. Student e-mail accounts and computer access in designated common areas are available to students. The school has a published electronic and media policy.

Contact Admission Office. 207-774-5721 Ext. 1224. Fax: 207-772-4782. E-mail: admissionoffice@waynflete.org. Website: www.waynflete.org

WEBB SCHOOL OF KNOXVILLE
9800 Webb School Drive
Knoxville, Tennessee 37923-3399

Head of School: Mr. Michael V. McBrien

General Information Coeducational day college-preparatory, arts, religious studies, and technology school. Grades K–12. Founded: 1955. Setting: urban. Nearest major city is Chattanooga. 114-acre campus. 8 buildings on campus. Approved or accredited by Southern Association of Colleges and Schools, Southern Association of Independent Schools, and Tennessee Department of Education. Member of National Association of Independent Schools and Secondary School Admission Test Board. Endowment: $39.7 million. Total enrollment: 989. Upper school average class size: 16. Upper school faculty-student ratio: 1:11. There are 172 required school days per year for Upper School students. Upper School students typically attend 5 days per week. The average school day consists of 8 hours and 5 minutes.

Upper School Student Profile Grade 9: 113 students (54 boys, 59 girls); Grade 10: 125 students (64 boys, 61 girls); Grade 11: 111 students (51 boys, 60 girls); Grade 12: 99 students (49 boys, 50 girls).

Faculty School total: 92. In upper school: 15 men, 27 women; 41 have advanced degrees.

Subjects Offered 3-dimensional design, algebra, anatomy and physiology, art history-AP, biology, biology-AP, calculus, calculus-AP, ceramics, chamber groups, chemistry, chemistry-AP, computer science-AP, concert choir, digital imaging, drama, drawing, economics, English, English language and composition-AP, English literature and composition-AP, English-AP, French, French-AP, geometry, government and politics-AP, history of rock and roll, honors algebra, honors English, honors geometry, honors world history, journalism, Latin, Latin-AP, macroeconomics-AP, Mandarin, microeconomics-AP, modern European history-AP, modern world history, music theory-AP, painting, philosophy, photo shop, photography, physics, physics-AP, pre-calculus, printmaking, probability and statistics, psychology-AP, robotics, sculpture, Spanish, Spanish-AP, stage design, statistics-AP, strings, studio art-AP, trigonometry, U.S. history, U.S. history-AP, video communication, wind ensemble, world history, world history-AP, world issues, world religions, yearbook.

Graduation Requirements Algebra, American history, arts and fine arts (art, music, dance, drama), biology, chemistry, English, foreign language, geometry, history, mathematics, physical education (includes health), public service, science, world history, world religions, public speaking (two chapel talks), 15 hours of community service per year.

Special Academic Programs 25 Advanced Placement exams for which test preparation is offered; honors section; independent study; study abroad; remedial reading and/or remedial writing; remedial math.

College Admission Counseling 136 students graduated in 2015; all went to college, including Auburn University; Belmont University; The University of Alabama; The University of Tennessee; University of Georgia; Virginia Polytechnic Institute and State University. Mean SAT critical reading: 622, mean SAT math: 605, mean SAT writing: 608, mean combined SAT: 1877, mean composite ACT: 27. 62% scored over 600 on SAT critical reading, 50% scored over 600 on SAT math, 58% scored over 600 on SAT writing, 54% scored over 26 on composite ACT.

Student Life Upper grades have uniform requirement, student council, honor system. Discipline rests equally with students and faculty.

Summer Programs Remediation, enrichment, advancement, art/fine arts programs offered; session focuses on academic; held on campus; accepts boys and girls; not open to students from other schools. 86 students usually enrolled. 2016 schedule: June 1 to July 31. Application deadline: June 1.

Tuition and Aid Day student tuition: $18,600. Tuition installment plan (monthly payment plans, individually arranged payment plans, tuition payments can also be paid in two installments-last calendar day in July and November). Need-based scholarship grants available. In 2015–16, 19% of upper-school students received aid. Total amount of financial aid awarded in 2015–16: $860,000.

Admissions Traditional secondary-level entrance grade is 9. For fall 2015, 49 students applied for upper-level admission, 44 were accepted, 36 enrolled. ISEE required.

Deadline for receipt of application materials: January 31. Application fee required: $75. On-campus interview required.

Athletics Interscholastic: baseball (boys), basketball (b,g), bowling (b,g), cheering (g), cross-country running (b,g), dance squad (g), diving (b,g), field hockey (g), football (b), golf (b,g), lacrosse (b), soccer (b,g), softball (g), swimming and diving (b,g), tennis (b,g), track and field (b,g), volleyball (g), wrestling (b); intramural: archery (b,g), climbing (b,g), dance (b,g), fly fishing (b,g), Frisbee (b,g), hiking/backpacking (b,g); coed interscholastic: sailing. 48 coaches, 1 athletic trainer.

Computers Computers are regularly used in all classes. Computer network features include on-campus library services, Internet access, wireless campus network, Internet filtering or blocking technology, all students in grades 4-12 own/lease iPads for school. Student e-mail accounts are available to students. Students grades are available online. The school has a published electronic and media policy.

Contact Mrs. Christy Widener, Admissions Administrative Assistant. 865-291-3830. Fax: 865-291-1532. E-mail: christy_widener@webbschool.org. Website: www.webbschool.org

THE WEBB SCHOOLS

1175 West Baseline Road ·
Claremont, California 91711

Head of School: Mr. Taylor Stockdale

General Information Coeducational boarding and day college-preparatory school. Grades 9–12. Founded: 1922. Setting: suburban. Nearest major city is Los Angeles. Students are housed in single-sex dormitories. 70-acre campus. Approved or accredited by The Association of Boarding Schools, Western Association of Schools and Colleges, Western Catholic Education Association, and California Department of Education. Member of National Association of Independent Schools and Secondary School Admission Test Board. Endowment: $32 million. Upper school average class size: 16. Upper school faculty-student ratio: 1:8.

Upper School Student Profile Grade 9: 88 students (43 boys, 45 girls); Grade 10: 108 students (55 boys, 53 girls); Grade 11: 114 students (61 boys, 53 girls); Grade 12: 98 students (51 boys, 47 girls). 65% of students are boarding students. 70% are state residents. 13 states are represented in upper school student body. 20% are international students. International students from China, Hong Kong, Indonesia, Republic of Korea, Russian Federation, and Saudi Arabia; 18 other countries represented in student body.

Faculty School total: 58. In upper school: 47 have advanced degrees; 47 reside on campus.

Subjects Offered Algebra, American literature, art, astronomy, biology, biology-AP, calculus, calculus-AP, chamber groups, chemistry, chemistry-AP, Chinese, chorus, composition, computer programming, drawing, economics, English, English language and composition-AP, English literature and composition-AP, environmental science, environmental science-AP, foundations of civilization, French, French language-AP, health and wellness, history, humanities, integrated mathematics, introduction to literature, journalism, linear algebra, media arts, modern world history, oceanography, orchestra, painting, paleontology, physics, physics-AP, pre-calculus, psychology, sculpture, Spanish, Spanish language-AP, Spanish literature-AP, statistics, statistics-AP, theater, U.S. history, U.S. history-AP, world history-AP.

Graduation Requirements Arts and fine arts (art, music, dance, drama), English, foreign language, health, history, mathematics, physical education (includes health), science.

Special Academic Programs 15 Advanced Placement exams for which test preparation is offered; honors section; academic accommodation for the gifted.

College Admission Counseling 100 students graduated in 2015; 99 went to college, including Cornell University; Loyola Marymount University; New York University; Scripps College; University of California, San Diego; University of Southern California. Other: 1 had other specific plans. Median combined SAT: 2015.

Student Life Upper grades have specified standards of dress, student council, honor system. Discipline rests equally with students and faculty.

Summer Programs Enrichment programs offered; session focuses on academic enrichment; held on campus; accepts boys and girls; open to students from other schools. 2016 schedule: July to July.

Tuition and Aid Day student tuition: $39,815; 7-day tuition and room/board: $55,985. Tuition installment plan (Insured Tuition Payment Plan, monthly payment plans). Need-based scholarship grants available. In 2015–16, 34% of upper-school students received aid. Total amount of financial aid awarded in 2015–16: $4,100,000.

Admissions Traditional secondary-level entrance grade is 9. ISEE, SSAT or TOEFL required. Deadline for receipt of application materials: January 15. Application fee required: $75. Interview required.

Athletics Interscholastic: baseball (boys), basketball (b,g), cross-country running (b,g), diving (b,g), football (b), golf (b,g), soccer (b,g), softball (g), swimming and diving (b,g), tennis (b,g), track and field (b,g), volleyball (b,g), water polo (b,g), wrestling (b); coed interscholastic: badminton; coed intramural: dance, fitness, outdoor activities, triathlon, yoga.

Computers Computers are regularly used in all academic classes. Computer network features include on-campus library services, online commercial services, Internet access, wireless campus network, Internet filtering or blocking technology. Campus intranet and student e-mail accounts are available to students. Students grades are available online. The school has a published electronic and media policy.

Contact Mr. Heidi Marti, Assistant Director of Admission. 909-482-5214. Fax: 909-445-8269. E-mail: hmarti@webb.org. Website: www.webb.org/admission

THE WEBER SCHOOL

6751 Roswell Road
Sandy Springs, Georgia 30328

Head of School: Rabbi Edward Harwitz

General Information Coeducational day college-preparatory, arts, religious studies, bilingual studies, and technology school, affiliated with Jewish faith. Grades 9–12. Founded: 1997. Setting: suburban. Nearest major city is Atlanta. 20-acre campus. 2 buildings on campus. Approved or accredited by Georgia Independent School Association, Southern Association of Colleges and Schools, Southern Association of Independent Schools, The College Board, and Georgia Department of Education. Member of National Association of Independent Schools and Secondary School Admission Test Board. Languages of instruction: English, Hebrew, and Spanish. Total enrollment: 226. Upper school average class size: 15. Upper school faculty-student ratio: 1:8. There are 180 required school days per year for Upper School students. Upper School students typically attend 5 days per week. The average school day consists of 8 hours.

Upper School Student Profile Grade 9: 54 students (27 boys, 27 girls); Grade 10: 60 students (31 boys, 29 girls); Grade 11: 56 students (23 boys, 33 girls); Grade 12: 56 students (28 boys, 28 girls). 100% of students are Jewish.

Faculty School total: 38. In upper school: 12 men, 26 women; 35 have advanced degrees.

Subjects Offered Advanced chemistry, advanced computer applications, advanced math, Advanced Placement courses, advanced studio art-AP, algebra, American government, American history, American history-AP, American literature, American literature-AP, ancient history, art, Bible, Bible studies, biology, biology-AP, British literature, British literature (honors), calculus, calculus-AP, chemistry, chemistry-AP, choir, college admission preparation, college awareness, college counseling, college placement, college planning, composition, composition-AP, computer applications, computer multimedia, critical thinking, digital photography, drama, economics, electives, English, English language and composition-AP, English language-AP, English literature, English literature and composition-AP, environmental science, European history, European history-AP, evolution, experiential education, fine arts, geometry, Hebrew, Hebrew scripture, history, history-AP, Holocaust, honors algebra, honors English, honors geometry, honors U.S. history, honors world history, integrated arts, jazz ensemble, Jewish history, Jewish studies, Judaic studies, literature, literature and composition-AP, literature-AP, mathematics, modern European history, multimedia, peer counseling, physics, physics-AP, pre-calculus, Rabbinic literature, Spanish, Spanish-AP, student government, studio art, Talmud, U.S. history, U.S. history-AP.

Graduation Requirements Jewish Studies requirements, Hebrew language, Capstone Honors thesis.

Special Academic Programs 17 Advanced Placement exams for which test preparation is offered; honors section; independent study; study at local college for college credit; study abroad.

College Admission Counseling 55 students graduated in 2015; 50 went to college, including Boston University; Tulane University; University of Georgia; University of Michigan; Washington University in St. Louis. Other: 1 entered military service, 4 had other specific plans. Mean SAT critical reading: 599, mean SAT math: 589, mean SAT writing: 617, mean combined SAT: 1805, mean composite ACT: 26.

Student Life Upper grades have specified standards of dress, student council. Discipline rests primarily with faculty.

Summer Programs Enrichment, advancement programs offered; session focuses on Academic subjects; held on campus; accepts boys and girls; open to students from other schools. 20 students usually enrolled. 2016 schedule: June 10 to July 20. Application deadline: June 1.

Tuition and Aid Day student tuition: $26,000. Tuition installment plan (FACTS Tuition Payment Plan, monthly payment plans, individually arranged payment plans, supplemental tuition assistance). Tuition reduction for siblings, need-based scholarship grants available. In 2015–16, 40% of upper-school students received aid.

Admissions Traditional secondary-level entrance grade is 9. For fall 2015, 118 students applied for upper-level admission, 104 were accepted, 54 enrolled. PSAT and SAT for applicants to grade 11 and 12 or SSAT required. Deadline for receipt of application materials: February 1. Application fee required: $125. On-campus interview required.

Athletics Interscholastic: baseball (boys), basketball (b,g), soccer (b,g), softball (g), tennis (b,g), volleyball (g), wrestling (b); coed interscholastic: cross-country running, golf, swimming and diving, track and field; coed intramural: aerobics/Nautilus, dance, dance team, fitness, modern dance, ultimate Frisbee, yoga. 14 coaches, 1 athletic trainer.

Computers Computers are regularly used in all academic classes. Computer network features include on-campus library services, online commercial services, Internet access, wireless campus network, Internet filtering or blocking technology, wireless lab, learning center. Campus intranet, student e-mail accounts, and computer access in designated common areas are available to students. Students grades are available online. The school has a published electronic and media policy.

Contact Ms. Rise Arkin, Director of Admissions. 404-917-2500 Ext. 101. Fax: 404-917-2501. E-mail: risearkin@weberschool.org. Website: www.weberschool.org

THE WELLINGTON SCHOOL

3650 Reed Road
Columbus, Ohio 43220

Head of School: Mr. Robert D. Brisk

General Information Coeducational day college-preparatory, arts, business, and technology school. Grades PK–12. Founded: 1982. Setting: suburban. 21-acre campus. 1 building on campus. Approved or accredited by Independent Schools Association of the Central States, Ohio Association of Independent Schools, and Ohio Department of Education. Member of National Association of Independent Schools. Total enrollment: 668. Upper school average class size: 15. Upper school faculty-student ratio: 1:8. Upper School students typically attend 5 days per week. The average school day consists of 7 hours and 30 minutes.

Faculty School total: 83. In upper school: 24 have advanced degrees.

Subjects Offered Algebra, art and culture, band, biology, business skills, calculus, ceramics, chemistry, choir, chorus, computer graphics, creative arts, drama, drawing, earth and space science, economics, English, film, French, geometry, government, journalism, Latin, mathematics, modern history, music appreciation, painting, photography, physical education, physics, printmaking, Spanish, speech, strings, studio art-AP, U.S. history, visual arts, voice, Western civilization, word processing, writing, yearbook.

Graduation Requirements 3-dimensional art, arts and fine arts (art, music, dance, drama), English, foreign language, government, lab science, mathematics, physical education (includes health), science, social sciences, social studies (includes history), speech, senior independent project. Community service is required.

Special Academic Programs Advanced Placement exam preparation; honors section; accelerated programs; independent study; study at local college for college credit; study abroad; academic accommodation for the gifted, the musically talented, and the artistically talented; ESL.

College Admission Counseling Colleges students went to include Emory University.

Student Life Upper grades have uniform requirement, student council, honor system. Discipline rests equally with students and faculty.

Tuition and Aid Day student tuition: $11,200–$21,425. Tuition installment plan (monthly payment plans, individually arranged payment plans, 2-, 6-, and 10-month payment plans). Merit scholarship grants, need-based scholarship grants available.

Admissions Traditional secondary-level entrance grade is 9. Admissions testing or ERB required. Deadline for receipt of application materials: none. Application fee required: $50. On-campus interview required.

Athletics Interscholastic: baseball (boys), basketball (b,g), diving (b,g), fencing (b,g), golf (b,g), lacrosse (b,g), soccer (b,g), softball (g), tennis (b,g); intramural: basketball (b,g), independent competitive sports (g), lacrosse (g); coed interscholastic: fencing, swimming and diving; coed intramural: canoeing/kayaking, climbing, flag football, martial arts. 2 PE instructors, 15 coaches, 1 athletic trainer.

Computers Computer network features include on-campus library services, online commercial services, Internet access, wireless campus network, Internet filtering or blocking technology, SmartBoards. Campus intranet, student e-mail accounts, and computer access in designated common areas are available to students. Students grades are available online. The school has a published electronic and media policy.

Contact Ms. Lynne Steger, Assistant Director of Admissions. 614-324-1647. Fax: 614-442-3286. E-mail: steger@wellington.org. Website: www.wellington.org

WELLSPRING FOUNDATION

Bethlehem, Connecticut
See Special Needs Schools section.

WESLEYAN ACADEMY

PO Box 1489
Guaynabo, Puerto Rico 00970-1489

Head of School: Rev. Fernando Vazquez

General Information Coeducational day college-preparatory and arts school, affiliated with Wesleyan Church. Grades PK–12. Founded: 1955. Setting: urban. Nearest major city is San Juan. 6-acre campus. 1 building on campus. Approved or accredited by Association of Christian Schools International, Middle States Association of Colleges and Schools, and Puerto Rico Department of Education. Total enrollment: 903. Upper school average class size: 25. Upper school faculty-student ratio: 1:25. There are 180 required school days per year for Upper School students. Upper School students typically attend 6 days per week. The average school day consists of 7 hours.

Upper School Student Profile Grade 9: 69 students (33 boys, 36 girls); Grade 10: 66 students (28 boys, 38 girls); Grade 11: 54 students (28 boys, 26 girls); Grade 12: 57 students (29 boys, 28 girls). 40% of students are members of Wesleyan Church.

Faculty School total: 74. In upper school: 12 men, 14 women; 5 have advanced degrees.

Subjects Offered Accounting, advanced math, algebra, American history, anatomy and physiology, art, athletics, Bible, biology, calculus, career and personal planning, career planning, chemistry, choir, Christian education, college planning, computer skills, critical writing, dance, drama, earth science, English, English literature, French, general math, general science, geography, geometry, global studies, golf, guidance, guitar, handbells, health, history, Internet, intro to computers, keyboarding, lab science, library, mathematics, music, music appreciation, personal development, piano, poetry, pre-algebra, pre-calculus, pre-college orientation, Puerto Rican history, science, social sciences, Spanish, swimming, trigonometry, U.S. government, volleyball, world affairs, world history, yearbook.

Graduation Requirements American government, American history, Bible, computer science, electives, English, foreign language, geometry, health, history, lab science, mathematics, physical education (includes health), science, service learning/internship, social sciences, social studies (includes history), Spanish, 84 accumulative hours of community service during high school years.

Special Academic Programs 3 Advanced Placement exams for which test preparation is offered; honors section; independent study.

College Admission Counseling 51 students graduated in 2015; all went to college, including Georgetown University; University of Puerto Rico, Mayagüez Campus; University of Puerto Rico, Río Piedras Campus; University of Puerto Rico in Cayey; University of Puerto Rico in Humacao. Median SAT critical reading: 540, median SAT math: 500, median SAT writing: 490, median combined SAT: 1560. 21% scored over 600 on SAT critical reading, 13% scored over 600 on SAT math, 11% scored over 600 on SAT writing, 16% scored over 1800 on combined SAT.

Student Life Upper grades have uniform requirement, student council, honor system. Discipline rests primarily with faculty.

Summer Programs Remediation, enrichment programs offered; session focuses on remediation and enrichment classes; held on campus; accepts boys and girls; open to students from other schools. 100 students usually enrolled. 2016 schedule: June 2 to June 29. Application deadline: May 31.

Tuition and Aid Day student tuition: $6700. Guaranteed tuition plan. Tuition installment plan (monthly payment plans, full payment discount plan, semester payment plan). Need-based scholarship grants, need-based financial aid available. In 2015–16, 2% of upper-school students received aid. Total amount of financial aid awarded in 2015–16: $1000.

Admissions Traditional secondary-level entrance grade is 9. For fall 2015, 150 students applied for upper-level admission, 105 were accepted, 96 enrolled. Academic Profile Tests, admissions testing, mathematics proficiency exam and Metropolitan Achievement Test required. Deadline for receipt of application materials: none. Application fee required: $100. On-campus interview required.

Athletics Interscholastic: basketball (boys, girls), cheering (b,g), cross-country running (b,g), dance team (b,g), golf (b,g), indoor soccer (b,g), soccer (b,g), swimming and diving (b,g), tennis (b,g), track and field (b,g), volleyball (b,g); intramural: basketball (b,g), cheering (b,g), indoor soccer (b,g), soccer (b,g), track and field (b,g), volleyball (b,g); coed interscholastic: tennis. 2 PE instructors, 6 coaches.

Computers Computers are regularly used in all academic classes. Computer network features include on-campus library services, Internet access, wireless campus network, Internet filtering or blocking technology. Student e-mail accounts and computer access in designated common areas are available to students. Students grades are available online. The school has a published electronic and media policy.

Contact Mrs. Mae Ling Cardona, Admissions Clerk. 787-720-8959 Ext. 1235. Fax: 787-790-0730. E-mail: maeling.cardona@wesleyanacademy.org. Website: www.wesleyanacademy.org

WESLEYAN SCHOOL

5405 Spalding Drive
Peachtree Corners, Georgia 30092

Head of School: Mr. Chris Cleveland

General Information Coeducational day college-preparatory, arts, religious studies, and technology school, affiliated with Christian faith. Grades K–12. Founded: 1963. Setting: suburban. Nearest major city is Atlanta. 85-acre campus. 9 buildings on campus. Approved or accredited by Association of Christian Schools International, Georgia Independent School Association, Southern Association of Colleges and Schools, Southern Association of Independent Schools, and Georgia Department of Education. Member of National Association of Independent Schools and Secondary School Admission Test Board. Endowment: $16.5 million. Total enrollment: 1,132. Upper school average class size: 16. Upper school faculty-student ratio: 1:14. There are 180 required school days per year for Upper School students. Upper School students typically attend 5 days per week. The average school day consists of 6 hours and 55 minutes.

Upper School Student Profile Grade 6: 100 students (49 boys, 51 girls); Grade 7: 111 students (50 boys, 61 girls); Grade 8: 101 students (51 boys, 50 girls); Grade 9: 114 students (61 boys, 53 girls); Grade 10: 128 students (61 boys, 67 girls); Grade 11: 129 students (54 boys, 75 girls); Grade 12: 112 students (63 boys, 49 girls).

Faculty School total: 167. In upper school: 38 men, 37 women; 55 have advanced degrees.

Wesleyan School

Subjects Offered 20th century history, 20th century world history, 3-dimensional art, acting, advanced chemistry, advanced computer applications, advanced math, algebra, American government, American literature, art, art history-AP, band, Basic programming, Bible, biology, biology-AP, British literature, British literature (honors), calculus, calculus-AP, chemistry, chemistry-AP, choral music, chorus, Christian doctrine, Christian education, Christian ethics, Christian studies, computer science-AP, economics, English literature and composition-AP, English literature-AP, environmental science, European history-AP, French, geometry, government, health and wellness, Latin, literary genres, modern world history, New Testament, photography, physical education, physics, pre-calculus, public speaking, Spanish, Spanish language-AP, studio art-AP, theater, U.S. history, U.S. history-AP, vocal ensemble, weight training, word processing, world literature.

Graduation Requirements Algebra, American history, American literature, analysis, arts and fine arts (art, music, dance, drama), Bible, biology, British literature, chemistry, economics, environmental science, foreign language, geometry, government, modern world history, physical education (includes health), physics, pre-calculus, statistics, world literature, writing.

Special Academic Programs Advanced Placement exam preparation; honors section.

College Admission Counseling 105 students graduated in 2015; all went to college, including Auburn University; Clemson University; Georgia College & State University; Samford University; University of Georgia; University of Mississippi. Median SAT critical reading: 580, median SAT math: 580, median SAT writing: 580, median composite ACT: 27. Mean combined SAT: 1791. 42% scored over 600 on SAT critical reading, 44% scored over 600 on SAT math, 47% scored over 600 on SAT writing, 63% scored over 26 on composite ACT.

Student Life Upper grades have uniform requirement, student council, honor system. Discipline rests equally with students and faculty. Attendance at religious services is required.

Summer Programs Enrichment, sports, art/fine arts, computer instruction programs offered; session focuses on sports, arts, and academics; held on campus; accepts boys and girls; open to students from other schools. 800 students usually enrolled. 2016 schedule: June 1 to July 31.

Tuition and Aid Day student tuition: $21,700. Tuition installment plan (Insured Tuition Payment Plan). Need-based scholarship grants available. In 2015–16, 22% of upper-school students received aid. Total amount of financial aid awarded in 2015–16: $1,551,511.

Admissions Traditional secondary-level entrance grade is 9. For fall 2015, 102 students applied for upper-level admission, 67 were accepted, 41 enrolled. PSAT, SSAT and writing sample required. Deadline for receipt of application materials: February 17. Application fee required: $85. Interview required.

Athletics Interscholastic: baseball (boys), basketball (b,g), cross-country running (b,g), diving (b,g), football (b), golf (b,g), lacrosse (b,g), soccer (b,g), softball (g), swimming and diving (b,g), tennis (b,g), track and field (b,g), volleyball (g), wrestling (b); intramural: cheering (g); coed intramural: strength & conditioning, water polo. 2 PE instructors, 2 athletic trainers.

Computers Computers are regularly used in all classes. Computer network features include on-campus library services, Internet access, wireless campus network, Internet filtering or blocking technology. Student e-mail accounts are available to students. Students grades are available online. The school has a published electronic and media policy.

Contact Mrs. Sylvia Pryor, Admissions Coordinator. 770-448-7640 Ext. 2267. Fax: 770-448-3699. E-mail: spryor@wesleyanschool.org. Website: www.wesleyanschool.org

WESTBURY CHRISTIAN SCHOOL

10420 Hillcroft
Houston, Texas 77096

Head of School: Mr. Michael D. White

General Information Coeducational day college-preparatory, arts, business, religious studies, and technology school, affiliated with Church of Christ. Grades PK–12. Founded: 1975. Setting: urban. 13-acre campus. 1 building on campus. Approved or accredited by National Christian School Association, Southern Association of Colleges and Schools, Texas Private School Accreditation Commission, The College Board, and Texas Department of Education. Endowment: $300,000. Total enrollment: 464. Upper school average class size: 22. Upper school faculty-student ratio: 1:10. There are 180 required school days per year for Upper School students. Upper School students typically attend 5 days per week. The average school day consists of 7 hours and 45 minutes.

Upper School Student Profile Grade 9: 56 students (34 boys, 22 girls); Grade 10: 55 students (34 boys, 21 girls); Grade 11: 50 students (23 boys, 27 girls); Grade 12: 62 students (33 boys, 29 girls). 18% of students are members of Church of Christ.

Faculty School total: 52. In upper school: 16 men, 15 women; 10 have advanced degrees.

Subjects Offered Accounting, algebra, anatomy and physiology, art, athletics, band, basketball, Bible, biology, biology-AP, business, calculus-AP, cheerleading, chemistry, chemistry-AP, community service, computer applications, drama, economics, English, English language and composition-AP, English literature and composition-AP,

geography, geometry, government, government-AP, health, human geography - AP, macro/microeconomics-AP, photography, physical education, physical science, physics, pre-calculus, psychology-AP, robotics, Spanish, speech, statistics-AP, studio art-AP, U.S. history, U.S. history-AP, vocal music, weight training, world history, world history-AP.

Graduation Requirements Arts and fine arts (art, music, dance, drama), Bible, electives, English, foreign language, geometry, mathematics, physical education (includes health), science, social studies (includes history), speech, continuous participation in student activities programs, community service each semester.

Special Academic Programs 15 Advanced Placement exams for which test preparation is offered; independent study; ESL (10 students enrolled).

College Admission Counseling 63 students graduated in 2015; 62 went to college, including Harding University; Houston Baptist University; Texas A&M University; Texas Tech University; The University of Texas at Austin; University of Houston. Other: 1 entered a postgraduate year. Mean SAT critical reading: 496, mean SAT math: 545, mean SAT writing: 495, mean combined SAT: 1536, mean composite ACT: 21. 9% scored over 600 on SAT critical reading, 25% scored over 600 on SAT math, 17% scored over 600 on SAT writing, 48% scored over 1800 on combined SAT, 36% scored over 26 on composite ACT.

Student Life Upper grades have uniform requirement, student council, honor system. Discipline rests primarily with faculty.

Summer Programs Enrichment, sports, art/fine arts programs offered; session focuses on week-long basketball, football, and volleyball instruction camps; held both on and off campus; held at Wildcat athletic complex, 10402 Fondren, Houston; accepts boys and girls; open to students from other schools. 200 students usually enrolled. 2016 schedule: June 3 to July 26. Application deadline: none.

Tuition and Aid Day student tuition: $13,860. Tuition installment plan (FACTS Tuition Payment Plan). Merit scholarship grants, need-based scholarship grants available. In 2015–16, 15% of upper-school students received aid; total upper-school merit-scholarship money awarded: $43,000. Total amount of financial aid awarded in 2015–16: $204,206.

Admissions Traditional secondary-level entrance grade is 9. For fall 2015, 84 students applied for upper-level admission, 72 were accepted, 61 enrolled. ISEE, Otis-Lennon School Ability Test and SLEP for foreign students required. Deadline for receipt of application materials: none. Application fee required: $75. Interview required.

Athletics Interscholastic: ballet (girls), baseball (b), basketball (b,g), cheering (g), cross-country running (b,g), football (b), golf (b,g), soccer (b,g), softball (g), strength & conditioning (b,g), swimming and diving (b,g), tennis (b,g), track and field (b,g), volleyball (g). 1 PE instructor, 4 coaches, 1 athletic trainer.

Computers Computers are regularly used in all academic classes. Computer network features include on-campus library services, online commercial services, Internet access, wireless campus network, Internet filtering or blocking technology. Campus intranet and student e-mail accounts are available to students. Students grades are available online. The school has a published electronic and media policy.

Contact Mrs. Phylis Frye, Director of Admissions. 713-551-8100 Ext. 1018. Fax: 713-551-8117. E-mail: admissions@westburychristian.org. Website: www.westburychristian.org

WEST CATHOLIC HIGH SCHOOL

1801 Bristol Avenue NW
Grand Rapids, Michigan 49504

Head of School: Mrs. Cynthia Kneibel

General Information Coeducational day college-preparatory and religious studies school, affiliated with Roman Catholic Church. Grades 9–12. Founded: 1962. Setting: urban. 20-acre campus. 1 building on campus. Approved or accredited by National Catholic Education Association, North Central Association of Colleges and Schools, and Michigan Department of Education. Endowment: $1 million. Total enrollment: 442. Upper school average class size: 30. Upper school faculty-student ratio: 1:30. There are 181 required school days per year for Upper School students. Upper School students typically attend 5 days per week. The average school day consists of 6 hours.

Upper School Student Profile Grade 9: 112 students (54 boys, 58 girls); Grade 10: 91 students (45 boys, 46 girls); Grade 11: 120 students (65 boys, 55 girls); Grade 12: 115 students (72 boys, 43 girls). 95% of students are Roman Catholic.

Faculty School total: 26. In upper school: 11 men, 15 women; 16 have advanced degrees.

Subjects Offered 20th century world history, acting, advanced chemistry, advanced computer applications, advanced math, American government, American literature, anatomy, art, band, Basic programming, biology, biology-AP, calculus, calculus-AP, career planning, chemistry, choir, Christian doctrine, composition, composition-AP, computer applications, computer programming, concert band, desktop publishing, drama, drawing, earth science, economics, economics-AP, English, English language and composition-AP, English literature, English literature and composition-AP, English literature-AP, environmental science, family living, French, general math, geometry, government, government and politics-AP, government-AP, government/civics, history, history of the Catholic Church, honors algebra, honors English, honors geometry, honors world history, human anatomy, intro to computers, jazz band, journalism, marching band, physics, pre-algebra, pre-calculus, psychology, sexuality, social justice, sociology, Spanish, U.S. government and politics-AP, U.S. history, Web site design, world history, yearbook.

Graduation Requirements Economics, electives, English composition, foreign language, government, health, mathematics, religion (includes Bible studies and theology), science, social studies (includes history), U.S. history, visual arts.

Special Academic Programs Advanced Placement exam preparation; honors section; independent study; study at local college for college credit; remedial reading and/or remedial writing.

College Admission Counseling 120 students graduated in 2014; 117 went to college, including Central Michigan University; Grand Valley State University; University of Notre Dame. Other: 1 went to work, 2 entered military service. Median SAT critical reading: 685, median SAT math: 710, median SAT writing: 680, median combined SAT: 2110, median composite ACT: 23. 83% scored over 600 on SAT critical reading, 100% scored over 600 on SAT math, 83% scored over 600 on SAT writing, 83% scored over 1800 on combined SAT, 35% scored over 26 on composite ACT.

Student Life Upper grades have uniform requirement, student council, honor system. Discipline rests primarily with faculty. Attendance at religious services is required.

Tuition and Aid Day student tuition: $8605. Tuition installment plan (FACTS Tuition Payment Plan, individually arranged payment plans). Need-based scholarship grants available. In 2014–15, 50% of upper-school students received aid. Total amount of financial aid awarded in 2014–15: $30,000.

Admissions Traditional secondary-level entrance grade is 9. For fall 2014, 8 students applied for upper-level admission, 8 were accepted, 8 enrolled. Essay and High School Placement Test required. Deadline for receipt of application materials: February 1. Application fee required: $150.

Athletics Interscholastic: baseball (boys), basketball (b,g), bowling (b,g), cheering (g), cross-country running (b,g), diving (b,g), football (b), golf (b,g), gymnastics (g), hockey (b), ice hockey (b), pom squad (g), skiing (downhill) (b,g), soccer (b,g), softball (g), swimming and diving (b,g), tennis (b,g), track and field (b,g), volleyball (g), weight lifting (b), weight training (b), wrestling (b); intramural: basketball (b,g). 1 PE instructor, 66 coaches, 2 athletic trainers.

Computers Computers are regularly used in all academic classes. Computer network features include Internet access, wireless campus network, Internet filtering or blocking technology. Student e-mail accounts and computer access in designated common areas are available to students. Students grades are available online. The school has a published electronic and media policy.

Contact Mrs. Lauri Ford, Guidance Secretary. 616-233-5909. Fax: 616-453-4320. E-mail: lauriford@grcss.org. Website: www.grwestcatholic.org

WESTCHESTER COUNTRY DAY SCHOOL

2045 North Old Greensboro Road
High Point, North Carolina 27265

Head of School: Mr. Cobb Atkinson

General Information Coeducational day and distance learning college-preparatory, arts, bilingual studies, and technology school. Grades PK–12. Distance learning grades 6–12. Founded: 1967. Setting: rural. 53-acre campus. 6 buildings on campus. Approved or accredited by North Carolina Association of Independent Schools, Southern Association of Colleges and Schools, Southern Association of Independent Schools, and North Carolina Department of Education. Member of National Association of Independent Schools. Endowment: $2.5 million. Total enrollment: 372. Upper school average class size: 16. Upper school faculty-student ratio: 1:5. There are 176 required school days per year for Upper School students. Upper School students typically attend 5 days per week. The average school day consists of 5 hours and 40 minutes.

Upper School Student Profile Grade 9: 33 students (22 boys, 11 girls); Grade 10: 36 students (17 boys, 19 girls); Grade 11: 36 students (23 boys, 13 girls); Grade 12: 23 students (12 boys, 11 girls).

Faculty School total: 53. In upper school: 9 men, 17 women; 18 have advanced degrees.

Subjects Offered Advanced chemistry, Advanced Placement courses, advanced studio art-AP, algebra, American history, American literature, American literature-AP, art, art history-AP, art-AP, athletics, biology, biology-AP, British literature, calculus, calculus-AP, chamber groups, character education, chemistry, chemistry-AP, Chinese, choral music, chorus, college admission preparation, college counseling, college placement, college planning, college writing, computer science, creative writing, dance, debate, earth science, economics, English, English language-AP, English literature, English literature-AP, environmental science, European history, European history-AP, exercise science, film and literature, fine arts, geography, geometry, global studies, government/civics, grammar, health, health education, history, Mandarin, mathematics, music, physical education, physics, probability and statistics, science, social studies, Spanish, Spanish language-AP, statistics-AP, theater, U.S. history-AP, voice ensemble, Web site design, world history, world literature, writing.

Graduation Requirements Arts and fine arts (art, music, dance, drama), civics, English, foreign language, mathematics, physical education (includes health), science, social studies (includes history), community service project, senior speech.

Special Academic Programs 13 Advanced Placement exams for which test preparation is offered; honors section; independent study.

College Admission Counseling 38 students graduated in 2014; all went to college, including East Carolina University; High Point University; North Carolina State

University; The University of North Carolina at Charlotte; The University of North Carolina Wilmington; Virginia Polytechnic Institute and State University. Median SAT critical reading: 590, median SAT math: 590, median SAT writing: 550, median combined SAT: 1180.

Student Life Upper grades have specified standards of dress, student council, honor system. Discipline rests primarily with faculty.

Tuition and Aid Day student tuition: $5250–$15,720. Guaranteed tuition plan. Tuition installment plan (monthly payment plans, TADS). Tuition reduction for siblings, merit scholarship grants, need-based scholarship grants available. In 2014–15, 32% of upper-school students received aid; total upper-school merit-scholarship money awarded: $68,000. Total amount of financial aid awarded in 2014–15: $450,000.

Admissions Traditional secondary-level entrance grade is 9. Brigance Test of Basic Skills, ERB CTP IV, grade equivalent tests, Metropolitan Achievement Test, placement test, Wide Range Achievement Test or Woodcock-Johnson Revised Achievement Test required. Deadline for receipt of application materials: none. Application fee required: $75. Interview recommended.

Athletics Interscholastic: baseball (boys), basketball (b,g), cheering (g), dance (g), dance team (g), soccer (b,g), softball (g), tennis (b,g), volleyball (g); coed interscholastic: aquatics, cross-country running, golf, physical fitness, swimming and diving, track and field. 2 PE instructors, 15 coaches.

Computers Computers are regularly used in English, foreign language, history, library science, mathematics, science, Web site design, yearbook classes. Computer network features include on-campus library services, Internet access, wireless campus network, Internet filtering or blocking technology. Campus intranet, student e-mail accounts, and computer access in designated common areas are available to students. Students grades are available online. The school has a published electronic and media policy.

Contact Mrs. Kerie Beth Scott, Director of Admissions. 336-822-4005. Fax: 336-869-6685. E-mail: kcriebeth.scott@westchestercds.org. Website: www.westchestercds.org

WESTERN MENNONITE SCHOOL

9045 Wallace Road NW
Salem, Oregon 97304-9716

Head of School: Zig Derochowski

General Information Coeducational boarding and day college-preparatory, general academic, and religious studies school, affiliated with Mennonite Church USA. Boarding grades 9–12, day grades 6–12. Founded: 1945. Setting: rural. Students are housed in single-sex dormitories. 45-acre campus. 10 buildings on campus. Approved or accredited by Association of Christian Schools International, Mennonite Education Agency, Mennonite Schools Council, and Oregon Department of Education. Endowment: $1 million. Total enrollment: 202. Upper school average class size: 16. Upper school faculty-student ratio: 1:14. There are 173 required school days per year for Upper School students. Upper School students typically attend 5 days per week. The average school day consists of 5 hours and 25 minutes.

Upper School Student Profile Grade 9: 32 students (18 boys, 14 girls); Grade 10: 41 students (24 boys, 17 girls); Grade 11: 28 students (15 boys, 13 girls); Grade 12: 41 students (23 boys, 18 girls). 12% of students are boarding students. 85% are state residents. 4 states are represented in upper school student body. 12% are international students. International students from China, Ethiopia, Japan, Republic of Korea, Rwanda, and Taiwan; 7 other countries represented in student body. 10% of students are Mennonite Church USA.

Faculty School total: 26. In upper school: 12 men, 14 women; 8 have advanced degrees; 10 reside on campus.

Subjects Offered Accounting, advanced math, algebra, anatomy and physiology, art, Bible studies, biology, calculus, career and personal planning, career education, chemistry, choral music, Christian education, Christian scripture, church history, computer applications, computer programming, drawing and design, economics, English, English composition, English literature, general math, geography, geometry, government, health education, human anatomy, instrumental music, intro to computers, keyboarding, mathematics, music, music performance, novels, physical education, physical fitness, physical science, physics, pre-algebra, pre-calculus, psychology, religious education, religious studies, research, science, Spanish, U.S. government, U.S. history, U.S. literature, woodworking, yearbook.

Graduation Requirements Algebra, applied arts, Bible studies, biology, career education, chemistry, choir, economics, English, English literature, geometry, global studies, music, physical education (includes health), Spanish, U.S. government, U.S. history, U.S. literature, world geography, Mini-Term—one week of co-curricular activity at end of academic year (sophomore through senior year).

Special Academic Programs Independent study; term-away projects; study at local college for college credit.

College Admission Counseling 31 students graduated in 2014; 26 went to college, including Chemeketa Community College; Corban University; Eastern Mennonite University; Hesston College; Oregon State University; Western Oregon University. Median SAT math: 520, median composite ACT: 27. 11% scored over 600 on SAT math, 50% scored over 26 on composite ACT.

Student Life Upper grades have specified standards of dress, student council, honor system. Discipline rests primarily with faculty. Attendance at religious services is required.

Tuition and Aid Day student tuition: $8600; 5-day tuition and room/board: $13,779; 7-day tuition and room/board: $15,977. Tuition installment plan (monthly payment plans, individually arranged payment plans). Tuition reduction for siblings, merit scholarship grants, need-based scholarship grants, paying campus jobs available. In 2014–15, 41% of upper-school students received aid.

Admissions Traditional secondary-level entrance grade is 9. Deadline for receipt of application materials: none. Application fee required: $50. Interview recommended.

Athletics Interscholastic: baseball (boys, girls), basketball (b,g), cross-country running (b), soccer (b,g), volleyball (g); coed intramural: softball. 5 PE instructors, 8 coaches.

Computers Computers are regularly used in independent study, introduction to technology, keyboarding, yearbook classes. Computer network features include on-campus library services, online commercial services, Internet access, wireless campus network, Internet filtering or blocking technology. Campus intranet, student e-mail accounts, and computer access in designated common areas are available to students. Students grades are available online. The school has a published electronic and media policy.

Contact Mr. Rich Martin, Admissions Coordinator. 503-363-2000 Ext. 121. Fax: 503-370-9455. E-mail: rmartin@westernmenniteschool.org.
Website: www.westernmenniteschool.org

WESTERN RESERVE ACADEMY

115 College Street
Hudson, Ohio 44236

Head of School: Christopher D. Burner

General Information Coeducational boarding and day college-preparatory and arts school. Grades 9–PG. Founded: 1826. Setting: small town. Nearest major city is Cleveland. Students are housed in single-sex dormitories. 190-acre campus. 49 buildings on campus. Approved or accredited by Midwest Association of Boarding Schools, Ohio Association of Independent Schools, The Association of Boarding Schools, and Ohio Department of Education. Member of National Association of Independent Schools and Secondary School Admission Test Board. Endowment: $11.3 million. Total enrollment: 389. Upper school average class size: 12. Upper school faculty-student ratio: 1:6. There are 182 required school days per year for Upper School students. Upper School students typically attend 6 days per week. The average school day consists of 7 hours and 15 minutes.

Upper School Student Profile Grade 9: 80 students (45 boys, 35 girls); Grade 10: 94 students (52 boys, 42 girls); Grade 11: 98 students (53 boys, 45 girls); Grade 12: 117 students (59 boys, 58 girls); Postgraduate: 3 students (2 boys, 1 girl). 70% of students are boarding students. 50% are state residents. 21 states are represented in upper school student body. 22% are international students. International students from China, Germany, Hong Kong, Mexico, Republic of Korea, and Saudi Arabia; 16 other countries represented in student body.

Faculty School total: 64. In upper school: 39 men, 25 women; 54 have advanced degrees; 58 reside on campus.

Subjects Offered Algebra, American history, American literature, architecture, art, art history, astronomy, band, biology, calculus, ceramics, chemistry, chorus, computer programming, creative writing, dance, drafting, drama, economics, engineering, English, English literature, environmental science, European history, fine arts, French, geometry, German, health, history, humanities, independent study, industrial arts, Latin, Mandarin, mathematics, mechanical drawing, music, music history, music theory, orchestra, photography, physical education, physics, science, social studies, Spanish, speech, statistics, theater, trigonometry, world history, zoology.

Graduation Requirements Arts and fine arts (art, music, dance, drama), English, foreign language, history, mathematics, physical education (includes health), science, senior seminar, senior thesis.

Special Academic Programs 20 Advanced Placement exams for which test preparation is offered; honors section; independent study; term-away projects; study at local college for college credit; study abroad; academic accommodation for the gifted, the musically talented, and the artistically talented.

College Admission Counseling 101 students graduated in 2014; all went to college, including Boston College; Case Western Reserve University; Cornell University; Dartmouth College; New York University; The Ohio State University.

Student Life Upper grades have specified standards of dress, student council. Discipline rests equally with students and faculty.

Tuition and Aid Day student tuition: $33,400; 7-day tuition and room/board: $49,700. Tuition installment plan (The Tuition Plan, Insured Tuition Payment Plan, Key Tuition Payment Plan, monthly payment plans, individually arranged payment plans). Need-based scholarship grants available. In 2014–15, 40% of upper-school students received aid.

Admissions Traditional secondary-level entrance grade is 9. For fall 2014, 489 students applied for upper-level admission, 179 were accepted, 122 enrolled. SSAT or TOEFL required. Deadline for receipt of application materials: January 15. Application fee required: $50. Interview required.

Athletics Interscholastic: baseball (boys), basketball (b,g), cross-country running (b,g), diving (b,g), field hockey (g), football (b), golf (b), ice hockey (b), lacrosse (b,g), soccer (b,g), softball (g), swimming and diving (b,g), tennis (b,g), track and field (b,g), volleyball (g), wrestling (b); intramural: basketball (b); coed interscholastic: marksmanship, riflery; coed intramural: aerobics, aerobics/dance, aerobics/Nautilus,

backpacking, bicycling, dance, fitness, hiking/backpacking, jogging, martial arts, modern dance, Nautilus, outdoor recreation, paddle tennis, physical fitness, physical training, running, skeet shooting, skiing (downhill), snowboarding, soccer, strength & conditioning, weight lifting, weight training, winter (indoor) track, yoga. 1 coach, 2 athletic trainers.

Computers Computers are regularly used in architecture, drawing and design, economics, engineering, English, foreign language, history, mathematics, science, technical drawing classes. Computer network features include on-campus library services, online commercial services, Internet access, wireless campus network, Internet filtering or blocking technology. Campus intranet and student e-mail accounts are available to students. The school has a published electronic and media policy.

Contact Mr. Dan Morrissey, Dean of Admission and Financial Aid. 330-650-9716. Fax: 330-650-9754. E-mail: admission@wra.net. Website: www.wra.net

WEST ISLAND COLLEGE

7410 Blackfoot Trail SE
Calgary, Alberta T2H IM5, Canada

Head of School: Ms. Carol Grant-Watt

General Information Coeducational day college-preparatory, arts, business, bilingual studies, technology, and Advanced Placement school. Grades 7–12. Founded: 1982. Setting: urban. 18-acre campus. 2 buildings on campus. Approved or accredited by Canadian Association of Independent Schools and Alberta Department of Education. Languages of instruction: English and French. Total enrollment: 533. Upper school average class size: 21. Upper school faculty-student ratio: 1:17. There are 182 required school days per year for Upper School students. Upper School students typically attend 5 days per week. The average school day consists of 6 hours and 13 minutes.

Upper School Student Profile Grade 10: 81 students (40 boys, 41 girls); Grade 11: 65 students (33 boys, 32 girls); Grade 12: 83 students (41 boys, 42 girls).

Faculty School total: 45. In upper school: 20 men, 21 women; 15 have advanced degrees.

Subjects Offered Advanced Placement courses, anthropology, art, arts, biology, business, chemistry, choral music, communications, debate, drama, English, European history, experiential education, French, French studies, health, information processing, information technology, leadership, literature, mathematics, modern languages, music, outdoor education, philosophy, physical education, physics, political thought, politics, psychology, public speaking, science, social sciences, social studies, sociology, Spanish, standard curriculum, study skills, world geography, world history, world religions.

Graduation Requirements Alberta education requirements.

Special Academic Programs 10 Advanced Placement exams for which test preparation is offered; honors section; independent study; study abroad; academic accommodation for the gifted.

College Admission Counseling 67 students graduated in 2015; 66 went to college, including McGill University; Queen's University at Kingston; The University of British Columbia; University of Alberta; University of Calgary; University of Victoria. Other: 1 had other specific plans.

Student Life Upper grades have uniform requirement, student council, honor system. Discipline rests equally with students and faculty.

Summer Programs Enrichment, advancement, sports, computer instruction programs offered; session focuses on study skills and academic preparedness; held both on and off campus; held at various public parks in the city; accepts boys and girls; not open to students from other schools. 50 students usually enrolled. 2016 schedule: August 19 to August 23. Application deadline: May 30.

Tuition and Aid Day student tuition: CAN$12,800. Tuition installment plan (monthly payment plans).

Admissions Traditional secondary-level entrance grade is 10. For fall 2015, 24 students applied for upper-level admission, 23 were accepted, 19 enrolled. 3-R Achievement Test, CCAT, CTBS, OLSAT, Gates MacGinite Reading Tests or Otis-Lennon IQ Test required. Deadline for receipt of application materials: none. Application fee required: CAN$100. Interview required.

Athletics Interscholastic: basketball (boys, girls), field hockey (g), rugby (b), track and field (b,g), volleyball (b,g); intramural: aquatics (b,g), basketball (b,g), floor hockey (b,g), track and field (b,g), volleyball (b,g); coed interscholastic: badminton, climbing, cross-country running, soccer; coed intramural: alpine skiing, backpacking, badminton, bicycling, bowling, canoeing/kayaking, climbing, cross-country running, curling, dance, fitness, golf, hiking/backpacking, kayaking, mountaineering, nordic skiing, outdoor activities, outdoor education, physical fitness, physical training, rock climbing, sailing, skiing (cross-country), skiing (downhill), snowboarding, soccer, wilderness survival, wildernessways. 4 PE instructors, 10 coaches, 2 athletic trainers.

Computers Computers are regularly used in business, career education, career exploration, career technology, economics, English, French, independent study, mathematics, media arts, media production, multimedia, science, social studies, technology, word processing classes. Computer network features include on-campus library services, online commercial services, Internet access, wireless campus network, Internet filtering or blocking technology. Campus intranet, student e-mail accounts, and computer access in designated common areas are available to students. Students grades are available online. The school has a published electronic and media policy.

Contact Ms. Nicole Bernard, Director of Admissions. 403-444-0023. Fax: 403-444-2820. E-mail: admissions@westislandcollege.ab.ca. Website: www.westislandcollege.ab.ca

WESTMARK SCHOOL
Encino, California
See Special Needs Schools section.

WESTMINSTER ACADEMY
5601 North Federal Highway
Fort Lauderdale, Florida 33308

Head of School: Dr. Leo Orsino

General Information College-preparatory, arts, religious studies, and technology school, affiliated with Presbyterian Church in America. Founded: 1971. 3 buildings on campus. Approved or accredited by Christian Schools of Florida, Middle States Association of Colleges and Schools, National Independent Private Schools Association, Southern Association of Colleges and Schools, and Florida Department of Education. Total enrollment: 966. Upper school average class size: 18. Upper school faculty-student ratio: 1:11.

Upper School Student Profile 30% of students are Presbyterian Church in America.

Student Life Upper grades have uniform requirement, student council. Attendance at religious services is required.

Admissions Application fee required: $100. Interview required.

Athletics Interscholastic: baseball (boys), basketball (b,g), cheering (g), cross-country running (b,g), diving (b,g), football (b), golf (b,g), soccer (b,g), softball (g), swimming and diving (b,g), tennis (b,g), track and field (b,g), volleyball (g), water polo (b,g).

Contact Mr. Jeffrey Jacques, Director of Admissions. 954-771-4615 Ext. 2529. E-mail: jacquesj@wa.edu. Website: www.wa.edu

WESTMINSTER CHRISTIAN ACADEMY
186 Westminster Drive
Opelousas, Louisiana 70570

Head of School: Mrs. Merida Brooks

General Information Coeducational day college-preparatory, arts, religious studies, bilingual studies, and technology school, affiliated with Protestant-Evangelical faith, Christian faith. Grades PK–12. Founded: 1978. Setting: rural. Nearest major city is Lafayette. 30-acre campus. 6 buildings on campus. Approved or accredited by Association of Christian Schools International and Louisiana Department of Education. Endowment: $400,000. Total enrollment: 1,059. Upper school average class size: 23. Upper school faculty-student ratio: 1:13. There are 175 required school days per year for Upper School students. Upper School students typically attend 5 days per week. The average school day consists of 7 hours.

Upper School Student Profile Grade 9: 68 students (42 boys, 26 girls); Grade 10: 50 students (26 boys, 24 girls); Grade 11: 54 students (25 boys, 29 girls); Grade 12: 59 students (30 boys, 29 girls). 95% of students are Protestant-Evangelical faith, Christian faith.

Faculty School total: 66. In upper school: 15 men, 15 women; 5 have advanced degrees.

Subjects Offered ACT preparation, advanced math, Advanced Placement courses, algebra, American history, art, athletics, Bible, biology, calculus, calculus-AP, ceramics, chemistry, chemistry-AP, civics, computer education, computer literacy, computer multimedia, concert choir, creative writing, desktop publishing, drama, drama workshop, economics, English, English-AP, fine arts, French, geometry, guitar, history, history-AP, honors English, Latin, music, physics, religion, Spanish, world history, yearbook.

Graduation Requirements Arts and fine arts (art, music, dance, drama), Bible, computer literacy, English, foreign language, mathematics, physical education (includes health), religion (includes Bible studies and theology), science, social studies (includes history).

Special Academic Programs 6 Advanced Placement exams for which test preparation is offered; honors section; accelerated programs; study at local college for college credit; special instructional classes for students with mild learning disabilities and Attention Deficit Disorder.

College Admission Counseling 47 students graduated in 2015; 45 went to college, including Baylor University; Columbia University; Louisiana State University and Agricultural & Mechanical College; Louisiana State University at Eunice; Louisiana Tech University; University of Louisiana at Lafayette. Other: 1 went to work, 1 had other specific plans. Mean composite ACT: 26. 28% scored over 26 on composite ACT.

Student Life Upper grades have uniform requirement, student council. Discipline rests primarily with faculty. Attendance at religious services is required.

Tuition and Aid Day student tuition: $6480. Tuition installment plan (monthly payment plans, individually arranged payment plans, annual and biannual payment plans). Need-based scholarship grants, pastor discounts available. In 2015–16, 10% of upper-school students received aid. Total amount of financial aid awarded in 2015–16: $50,000.

Admissions Traditional secondary-level entrance grade is 9. For fall 2015, 19 students applied for upper-level admission, 13 were accepted, 12 enrolled. School's own exam and Terra Nova-CTB required. Deadline for receipt of application materials: none. Application fee required: $150. On-campus interview required.

Athletics Interscholastic: baseball (boys), basketball (b,g), cheering (g), cross-country running (b,g), football (b), soccer (b,g), softball (g), swimming and diving (b,g), tennis (b,g), track and field (b,g), volleyball (g); coed interscholastic: golf, hiking/backpacking, soccer, wilderness survival; coed intramural: archery, outdoor adventure. 3 PE instructors, 2 coaches, 1 athletic trainer.

Computers Computers are regularly used in computer applications classes. Computer network features include on-campus library services, Internet access, wireless campus network, Internet filtering or blocking technology, one-to-one iPad program for grades 9-12. Student e-mail accounts and computer access in designated common areas are available to students. Students grades are available online. The school has a published electronic and media policy.

Contact Mrs. Michelle Nezat, Director of Institutional Advancement. 337-948-4623 Ext. 123. Fax: 337-948-4090. E-mail: mnezat@wcala.org. Website: www.wcala.org

WESTMINSTER CHRISTIAN SCHOOL
6855 Southwest 152nd Street
Palmetto Bay, Florida 33157

Head of School: Mr. Peter Cabrera

General Information Coeducational day college-preparatory, arts, religious studies, and technology school, affiliated with Christian faith. Grades PK–12. Founded: 1961. Setting: suburban. Nearest major city is Miami. 31-acre campus. 9 buildings on campus. Approved or accredited by Christian Schools of Florida, Florida Council of Independent Schools, Southern Association of Colleges and Schools, and Florida Department of Education. Endowment: $2.2 million. Total enrollment: 1,244. Upper school average class size: 20. Upper school faculty-student ratio: 1:15. There are 175 required school days per year for Upper School students. Upper School students typically attend 5 days per week. The average school day consists of 7 hours.

Upper School Student Profile Grade 9: 107 students (55 boys, 52 girls); Grade 10: 128 students (58 boys, 70 girls); Grade 11: 132 students (62 boys, 70 girls); Grade 12: 134 students (71 boys, 63 girls). 100% of students are Christian.

Faculty School total: 120. In upper school: 26 men, 26 women; 40 have advanced degrees.

Subjects Offered Advanced Placement courses, algebra, American history, American literature, anatomy, art, Bible studies, biology, biology-AP, business law, business skills, calculus, ceramics, chemistry, chemistry-AP, community service, computer programming, computer science, creative writing, drama, economics, English, English literature, fine arts, French, French-AP, geometry, government-AP, government/civics, health, macroeconomics-AP, marine biology, mathematics, musical theater, organic chemistry, photography, physical education, physics, physiology, psychology, religion, SAT preparation, sculpture, sociology, softball, Spanish, Spanish-AP, speech, sports, statistics-AP, strings, study skills, swimming, theater, track and field, trigonometry, U.S. government, U.S. government and politics-AP, U.S. history, U.S. history-AP, vocal ensemble, volleyball, weightlifting, world history, world history-AP, world literature, wrestling, yearbook.

Graduation Requirements Arts and fine arts (art, music, dance, drama), Bible, electives, English, foreign language, health science, lab science, mathematics, physical education (includes health), science, social studies (includes history), speech. Community service is required.

Special Academic Programs 21 Advanced Placement exams for which test preparation is offered; honors section; independent study; academic accommodation for the gifted, the musically talented, and the artistically talented; programs in English, mathematics for dyslexic students.

College Admission Counseling 122 students graduated in 2015; all went to college, including Florida International University; Florida State University; University of Central Florida; University of Florida; University of Miami. Mean SAT critical reading: 549, mean SAT math: 549, mean SAT writing: 536, mean combined SAT: 1634, mean composite ACT: 23. 50% scored over 600 on SAT critical reading, 50% scored over 600 on SAT math, 50% scored over 600 on SAT writing, 50% scored over 1800 on combined SAT, 50% scored over 26 on composite ACT.

Student Life Upper grades have uniform requirement, student council, honor system. Discipline rests primarily with faculty. Attendance at religious services is required.

Summer Programs Remediation, advancement, sports programs offered; session focuses on academics and athletics; held on campus; accepts boys and girls; not open to students from other schools. 50 students usually enrolled. 2016 schedule: June 7 to July 30.

Tuition and Aid Day student tuition: $17,900. Tuition installment plan (monthly payment plans, semiannual and annual payment plans). Need-based scholarship grants available. In 2015–16, 20% of upper-school students received aid. Total amount of financial aid awarded in 2015–16: $750,000.

Admissions Traditional secondary-level entrance grade is 9. For fall 2015, 150 students applied for upper-level admission, 81 were accepted, 61 enrolled. Iowa Tests of Basic Skills and writing sample required. Deadline for receipt of application materials: none. Application fee required: $125. On-campus interview required.

Athletics Interscholastic: baseball (boys), basketball (b,g), cheering (g), cross-country running (b,g), football (b), golf (b,g), lacrosse (b), physical fitness (b,g), physical training (b,g), sailing (b,g), soccer (b,g), softball (g), swimming and diving (b,g), tennis (b,g), track and field (b,g), volleyball (b,g), weight lifting (b,g), weight training (b,g), wrestling (b). 5 PE instructors, 50 coaches, 2 athletic trainers.

Computers Computers are regularly used in all academic classes. Computer network features include on-campus library services, online commercial services, Internet access, wireless campus network, Internet filtering or blocking technology. Campus intranet, student e-mail accounts, and computer access in designated common areas are available to students. Students grades are available online. The school has a published electronic and media policy.

Contact Mrs. Lisa North, Director of Admission. 305-233-2030 Ext. 1246. Fax: 305-253-9623. E-mail: lnorth@wcsmiami.org. Website: www.wcsmiami.org

WESTMINSTER SCHOOL

995 Hopmeadow Street
Simsbury, Connecticut 06070

Head of School: Mr. William V.N. Philip

General Information Coeducational boarding and day college-preparatory, arts, and technology school. Grades 9–PG. Founded: 1888. Setting: suburban. Nearest major city is Hartford. Students are housed in single-sex dormitories. 230-acre campus. 39 buildings on campus. Approved or accredited by Connecticut Association of Independent Schools, New England Association of Schools and Colleges, The Association of Boarding Schools, Virginia Association of Independent Specialized Education Facilities, and Connecticut Department of Education. Member of National Association of Independent Schools and Secondary School Admission Test Board. Endowment: $95 million. Total enrollment: 394. Upper school average class size: 12. Upper school faculty-student ratio: 1:5. There are 182 required school days per year for Upper School students. Upper School students typically attend 6 days per week. The average school day consists of 6 hours and 30 minutes.

Upper School Student Profile Grade 9: 72 students (35 boys, 37 girls); Grade 10: 108 students (59 boys, 49 girls); Grade 11: 100 students (55 boys, 45 girls); Grade 12: 109 students (57 boys, 52 girls); Postgraduate: 7 students (6 boys, 1 girl). 70% of students are boarding students. 48% are state residents. 25 states are represented in upper school student body. 15% are international students. International students from Bermuda, Canada, China, Mexico, Republic of Korea, and Russian Federation; 18 other countries represented in student body.

Faculty School total: 59. In upper school: 30 men, 29 women; 43 have advanced degrees; 50 reside on campus.

Subjects Offered Acting, advanced chemistry, advanced computer applications, advanced math, Advanced Placement courses, advanced studio art-AP, African American history, algebra, American history, American history-AP, American literature, American literature-AP, anatomy and physiology, architecture, art, art history, art history-AP, art-AP, Asian history, astronomy, athletics, band, biology, biology-AP, calculus, calculus-AP, character education, chemistry, chemistry-AP, Chinese, choir, choral music, comparative government and politics-AP, computer programming, computer science-AP, creative writing, dance, discrete mathematics, drama, drama workshop, drawing, drawing and design, driver education, ecology, economics, economics-AP, English, English literature, English-AP, English/composition-AP, environmental science-AP, ethics, ethics and responsibility, European history, European history-AP, female experience in America, fine arts, French, French language-AP, French literature-AP, geometry, graphic design, history, honors algebra, honors English, honors geometry, illustration, Latin, Latin-AP, literature and composition-AP, macro/microeconomics-AP, mathematics, mathematics-AP, mechanical drawing, modern European history-AP, music, music appreciation, music composition, music theory-AP, musical theater, painting, philosophy, photography, physics, physics-AP, pre-calculus, probability and statistics, psychology-AP, SAT preparation, SAT/ACT preparation, science, set design, social studies, Spanish, Spanish language-AP, Spanish literature, Spanish literature-AP, stagecraft, statistics, statistics-AP, student government, studio art-AP, theater, trigonometry, U.S. history-AP, world history, writing.

Graduation Requirements Arts, English, foreign language, history, mathematics, science.

Special Academic Programs 23 Advanced Placement exams for which test preparation is offered; honors section; independent study; term-away projects; study abroad.

College Admission Counseling 108 students graduated in 2015; all went to college, including Amherst College; Boston College; Trinity College; University of Richmond; Williams College. Median SAT critical reading: 623, median SAT math: 620, median SAT writing: 648, median combined SAT: 1871.

Student Life Upper grades have specified standards of dress, student council. Discipline rests primarily with faculty.

Summer Programs Sports programs offered; session focuses on soccer, lacrosse; held on campus; accepts boys and girls; open to students from other schools. 400 students usually enrolled. 2016 schedule: July 3 to August 4.

Tuition and Aid Day student tuition: $42,100; 7-day tuition and room/board: $56,100. Tuition installment plan (SMART Tuition Payment Plan). Need-based scholarship grants available. In 2015–16, 31% of upper-school students received aid. Total amount of financial aid awarded in 2015–16: $4,760,560.

Admissions Traditional secondary-level entrance grade is 9. For fall 2015, 1,107 students applied for upper-level admission, 276 were accepted, 122 enrolled. PSAT and SAT for applicants to grade 11 and 12, SSAT or TOEFL required. Deadline for receipt of application materials: January 15. Application fee required: $75. Interview required.

Athletics Interscholastic: baseball (boys), basketball (b,g), cross-country running (b,g), diving (b,g), field hockey (g), football (b), golf (b,g), hockey (b,g), ice hockey (b,g), lacrosse (b,g), soccer (b,g), softball (g), squash (b,g), swimming and diving (b,g), tennis (b,g), track and field (b,g); intramural: strength & conditioning (b,g); coed interscholastic: dance, martial arts, modern dance; coed intramural: aerobics/dance, ballet, canoeing/kayaking, dance, fly fishing, freestyle skiing, hiking/backpacking, ice skating, kayaking, modern dance, mountain biking, outdoor activities, rugby, skiing (cross-country), skiing (downhill), snowboarding, table tennis, unicycling, weight lifting, weight training. 2 athletic trainers.

Computers Computers are regularly used in English, foreign language, history, mathematics, science classes. Computer network features include on-campus library services, online commercial services, Internet access, wireless campus network, Internet filtering or blocking technology. Campus intranet, student e-mail accounts, and computer access in designated common areas are available to students. Students grades are available online. The school has a published electronic and media policy.

Contact Mrs. Rhonda Smith, Admissions Assistant. 860-408-3060. Fax: 860-408-3042. E-mail: admit@westminster-school.org. Website: www.westminster-school.org

THE WESTMINSTER SCHOOLS

1424 West Paces Ferry Road NW
Atlanta, Georgia 30327

Head of School: Mr. Keith Evans

General Information Coeducational day college-preparatory, arts, business, religious studies, bilingual studies, and technology school, affiliated with Christian faith. Grades K–12. Founded: 1951. Setting: suburban. 180-acre campus. 7 buildings on campus. Approved or accredited by Georgia Independent School Association, Southern Association of Colleges and Schools, and Southern Association of Independent Schools. Member of National Association of Independent Schools and Secondary School Admission Test Board. Endowment: $260.8 million. Total enrollment: 1,858. Upper school average class size: 16. Upper school faculty-student ratio: 1:8. There are 175 required school days per year for Upper School students. Upper School students typically attend 5 days per week. The average school day consists of 6 hours.

Upper School Student Profile Grade 9: 211 students (108 boys, 103 girls); Grade 10: 203 students (95 boys, 108 girls); Grade 11: 189 students (98 boys, 91 girls); Grade 12: 209 students (99 boys, 110 girls). 80% of students are Christian.

Faculty School total: 277. In upper school: 58 men, 57 women; 91 have advanced degrees.

Subjects Offered 3-dimensional art, 3-dimensional design, acting, advanced chemistry, advanced math, Advanced Placement courses, advanced studio art-AP, African American history, algebra, American history, American history-AP, American literature-AP, architecture, art, art history, Basic programming, Bible studies, biology, biology-AP, British literature-AP, calculus, calculus-AP, ceramics, chemistry, chemistry-AP, Chinese, choral music, Christian education, civil rights, computer math, computer programming, computer science, drama, driver education, earth science, economics, English, English language and composition-AP, English literature, English literature and composition-AP, entrepreneurship, environmental science-AP, ethics, European history, European history-AP, fine arts, French, French language-AP, French literature-AP, geometry, grammar, graphic design, health, history, Holocaust seminar, internship, Latin, Latin-AP, leadership education training, Mandarin, marine biology, mathematics, mathematics-AP, music, natural history, outdoor education, philosophy, photography, physical education, physics, physics-AP, political systems, psychology, religion, robotics, science, social studies, sociology, Spanish, Spanish language-AP, Spanish literature-AP, speech, speech and debate, statistics, statistics-AP, studio art-AP, theater, theater arts, trigonometry, U.S. history-AP, video film production, visual and performing arts, world history, writing.

Graduation Requirements Arts and fine arts (art, music, dance, drama), English, experiential education, foreign language, history, mathematics, physical education (includes health), religion (includes Bible studies and theology), science.

Special Academic Programs Advanced Placement exam preparation; honors section; independent study; term-away projects; study abroad; academic accommodation for the gifted, the musically talented, and the artistically talented.

College Admission Counseling 200 students graduated in 2015; all went to college, including Auburn University; Georgia Institute of Technology; University of Georgia; University of Virginia; Wake Forest University; Washington University in St. Louis.

Student Life Upper grades have specified standards of dress, student council, honor system. Discipline rests equally with students and faculty.

Summer Programs Remediation, enrichment, advancement, sports, art/fine arts, rigorous outdoor training, computer instruction programs offered; session focuses on academics and sports/arts camps, philanthropy; held on campus; accepts boys and girls; open to students from other schools. 400 students usually enrolled. 2016 schedule: May 31 to July 8. Application deadline: February 2.

Tuition and Aid Day student tuition: $25,660. Tuition installment plan (Key Tuition Payment Plan, monthly payment plans). Need-based scholarship grants available. In

2015–16, 14% of upper-school students received aid. Total amount of financial aid awarded in 2015–16: $4,000,000.

Admissions Traditional secondary-level entrance grade is 9. For fall 2015, 181 students applied for upper-level admission, 36 were accepted, 23 enrolled. Admissions testing, Individual IQ, PSAT or SAT for applicants to grade 11 and 12 or SSAT required. Deadline for receipt of application materials: January 29. Application fee required: $75. On-campus interview required.

Athletics Interscholastic: baseball (boys), basketball (b,g), cheering (g), crew (g), cross-country running (b,g), diving (b,g), football (b), golf (b,g), gymnastics (g), lacrosse (b,g), soccer (b,g), softball (g), swimming and diving (b,g), tennis (b,g), track and field (b,g), volleyball (g), wrestling (b); intramural: crew (g), dance (g), equestrian sports (g), physical fitness (b,g), strength & conditioning (b,g); coed intramural: backpacking, climbing, dance squad, dance team, hiking/backpacking, paddle tennis, rappelling, rock climbing, ropes courses, squash, table tennis, tennis, ultimate Frisbee, water polo. 2 PE instructors, 4 coaches, 4 athletic trainers.

Computers Computers are regularly used in art, Bible studies, desktop publishing, economics, English, foreign language, history, mathematics, multimedia, music, religion, science, technology, video film production, writing classes. Computer network features include on-campus library services, online commercial services, Internet access, wireless campus network, Internet filtering or blocking technology, Math Lab staffed with faculty, Writing Lab staffed with students and faculty. Campus intranet, student e-mail accounts, and computer access in designated common areas are available to students. The school has a published electronic and media policy.

Contact Mrs. Julie Williams, Assistant Director of Admissions. 404-609-6202. Fax: 404-367-7894. E-mail: admissions@westminster.net. Website: www.westminster.net

WESTMINSTER SCHOOLS OF AUGUSTA

3067 Wheeler Road
Augusta, Georgia 30909

Head of School: Mr. Stephen D. O'Neil

General Information Coeducational day college-preparatory, arts, religious studies, bilingual studies, technology, and music, debate and drama school, affiliated with Presbyterian Church in America. Grades PK–12. Founded: 1972. Setting: suburban. 34-acre campus. 6 buildings on campus. Approved or accredited by Georgia Independent School Association, Southern Association of Colleges and Schools, and Southern Association of Independent Schools. Member of National Association of Independent Schools. Endowment: $290,000. Total enrollment: 605. Upper school average class size: 14. Upper school faculty-student ratio: 1:7. There are 180 required school days per year for Upper School students. Upper School students typically attend 5 days per week. The average school day consists of 7 hours and 30 minutes.

Upper School Student Profile Grade 9: 59 students (32 boys, 27 girls); Grade 10: 52 students (17 boys, 35 girls); Grade 11: 47 students (25 boys, 22 girls); Grade 12: 59 students (32 boys, 27 girls). 40% of students are Presbyterian Church in America.

Faculty School total: 63. In upper school: 20 men, 10 women; 16 have advanced degrees.

Subjects Offered 3-dimensional art, ACT preparation, advanced biology, advanced chemistry, Advanced Placement courses, advanced studio art-AP, algebra, analysis and differential calculus, analytic geometry, Ancient Greek, art, arts, band, Bible studies, biology, biology-AP, British literature (honors), calculus, calculus-AP, chemistry, chemistry-AP, choir, chorus, Christian scripture, classical Greek literature, computer programming, computer skills, computers, concert choir, drama, drama performance, dramatic arts, earth science, English, English language and composition-AP, English language-AP, English literature, English literature and composition-AP, English literature-AP, environmental science, family living, French, French language-AP, French-AP, geography, geometry, government/civics, Greek, guidance, health, health education, history, history-AP, honors algebra, honors English, honors geometry, honors U.S. history, keyboarding, lab science, Latin, Latin-AP, mathematics, modern European history-AP, modern history, modern world history, music, physical education, physical science, physics, physics-AP, pre-algebra, pre-calculus, religion, SAT preparation, science, social studies, Spanish, Spanish language-AP, Spanish-AP, speech, statistics-AP, studio art, study skills, swimming, trigonometry, U.S. government and politics-AP, U.S. history, U.S. history-AP, U.S. literature, United States government-AP, weight training, word processing, world history, world literature, writing, yearbook.

Graduation Requirements Arts and fine arts (art, music, dance, drama), electives, English, foreign language, mathematics, physical education (includes health), religion (includes Bible studies and theology), science, social studies (includes history).

Special Academic Programs 19 Advanced Placement exams for which test preparation is offered; honors section; study abroad; academic accommodation for the gifted; programs in general development for dyslexic students.

College Admission Counseling 42 students graduated in 2015; all went to college, including Augusta State University; Georgia Southern University; Kennesaw State University; Presbyterian College; University of Georgia; University of South Carolina. Median SAT critical reading: 580, median SAT math: 620, median SAT writing: 600, median combined SAT: 1800, median composite ACT: 25. 37% scored over 600 on SAT critical reading, 56% scored over 600 on SAT math, 37% scored over 600 on SAT writing, 49% scored over 1800 on combined SAT, 38% scored over 26 on composite ACT.

Student Life Upper grades have specified standards of dress, honor system. Discipline rests primarily with faculty.

Summer Programs Remediation, enrichment, sports, art/fine arts programs offered; session focuses on sports and academics; held on campus; accepts boys and girls; open to students from other schools. 244 students usually enrolled. 2016 schedule: June 6 to July 29. Application deadline: May 31.

Tuition and Aid Day student tuition: $13,900. Tuition installment plan (monthly payment plans). Tuition reduction for siblings, merit scholarship grants, need-based scholarship grants available. In 2015–16, 27% of upper-school students received aid. Total amount of financial aid awarded in 2015–16: $250,000.

Admissions Traditional secondary-level entrance grade is 9. For fall 2015, 36 students applied for upper-level admission, 27 were accepted, 22 enrolled. ERB - verbal abilities, reading comprehension, quantitative abilities (level F, form 1), mathematics proficiency exam and writing sample required. Deadline for receipt of application materials: none. Application fee required: $75. On-campus interview required.

Athletics Interscholastic: baseball (boys), basketball (b,g), cheering (g), cross-country running (b,g), football (b), golf (b,g), soccer (b,g), swimming and diving (b,g), tennis (b,g), track and field (b,g). 3 PE instructors, 4 coaches, 1 athletic trainer.

Computers Computers are regularly used in college planning, keyboarding, programming, SAT preparation, technology, yearbook classes. Computer network features include Internet access, wireless campus network, Internet filtering or blocking technology. Campus intranet, student e-mail accounts, and computer access in designated common areas are available to students. Students grades are available online. The school has a published electronic and media policy.

Contact Mrs. Aimee C. Lynch, Director of Admissions. 706-731-5260 Ext. 2220. Fax: 706-261-7786. E-mail: alynch@wsa.net. Website: www.wsa.net

WESTOVER SCHOOL

1237 Whittemore Road
Middlebury, Connecticut 06762

Head of School: Ms. Julie Faulstich

General Information Girls' boarding and day college-preparatory, arts, business, technology, science and engineering, and art history school. Grades 9–12. Founded: 1909. Setting: small town. Nearest major city is New York, NY. Students are housed in single-sex dormitories. 145-acre campus. 11 buildings on campus. Approved or accredited by Association of Independent Schools in New England, Connecticut Association of Independent Schools, New England Association of Schools and Colleges, The Association of Boarding Schools, and Connecticut Department of Education. Member of National Association of Independent Schools and Secondary School Admission Test Board. Endowment: $61.9 million. Total enrollment: 210. Upper school average class size: 11. Upper school faculty-student ratio: 1:8. There are 183 required school days per year for Upper School students. Upper School students typically attend 6 days per week. The average school day consists of 6 hours.

Upper School Student Profile Grade 9: 53 students (53 girls); Grade 10: 54 students (54 girls); Grade 11: 50 students (50 girls); Grade 12: 53 students (53 girls). 59% of students are boarding students. 55% are state residents. 19 states are represented in upper school student body. 19% are international students. International students from China, Japan, Mexico, Russian Federation, Rwanda, and Spain; 13 other countries represented in student body.

Faculty School total: 42. In upper school: 36 have advanced degrees.

Subjects Offered Advanced chemistry, Advanced Placement courses, African-American studies, algebra, American history, American history-AP, American literature, art, art history, art-AP, astronomy, ballet technique, bell choir, biology, biology-AP, calculus, calculus-AP, ceramics, chemistry, clayworking, community service, computer literacy, computer science, computer science-AP, creative writing, dance, drama, drawing, English, English language and composition-AP, English literature, environmental science, ESL, etymology, European history, European history-AP, filmmaking, fine arts, French, French-AP, geography, geometry, grammar, health and wellness, journalism, Latin, mathematics, music, music theory-AP, musical productions, painting, performing arts, photo shop, photography, physics, physics-AP, poetry, politics, portfolio art, pre-calculus, religion, robotics, science, sculpture, Shakespeare, short story, social studies, Spanish, Spanish-AP, speech, studio art-AP, theater, trigonometry, wilderness education, women's studies, world history, writing.

Graduation Requirements Art, athletics, English, foreign language, lab science, mathematics. Community service is required.

Special Academic Programs 25 Advanced Placement exams for which test preparation is offered; honors section; independent study; term-away projects; study abroad; academic accommodation for the gifted, the musically talented, and the artistically talented; special instructional classes for deaf students; ESL (3 students enrolled).

College Admission Counseling 51 students graduated in 2015; all went to college, including College of Charleston; Ithaca College; St. Lawrence University; The College of William and Mary; The George Washington University. Median SAT critical reading: 625, median SAT math: 675, median SAT writing: 710, median combined SAT: 2205, median composite ACT: 27.

Student Life Upper grades have specified standards of dress, student council, honor system. Discipline rests equally with students and faculty.

Summer Programs Enrichment, sports, art/fine arts programs offered; session focuses on Science & Engineering, Invest in Girls & Finance, Model UN, photography, drama, ceramics; held on campus; accepts girls; open to students from other schools. 30 students usually enrolled. 2016 schedule: July 5 to July 17.

Tuition and Aid Day student tuition: $37,650; 7-day tuition and room/board: $52,350. Tuition installment plan (SMART Tuition Payment Plan). Need-based scholarship grants available. In 2014–15, 50% of upper-school students received aid. Total amount of financial aid awarded in 2014–15: $3,200,000.

Admissions Traditional secondary-level entrance grade is 9. For fall 2015, 235 students applied for upper-level admission, 140 were accepted, 62 enrolled. ISEE, SSAT or TOEFL required. Deadline for receipt of application materials: January 15. Application fee required: $50. On-campus interview required.

Athletics Interscholastic: basketball, crew, cross-country running, field hockey, golf, independent competitive sports, lacrosse, rowing, soccer, softball, squash, swimming and diving, tennis, volleyball; intramural: aerobics, aerobics/dance, backpacking, ballet, canoeing/kayaking, climbing, dance, fitness, hiking/backpacking, jogging, kayaking, modern dance, outdoor activities, outdoor adventure, outdoor education, outdoor recreation, outdoor skills, outdoors, paddle tennis, physical fitness, physical training, rappelling, rock climbing, running, self defense, skiing (downhill), snowboarding, strength & conditioning, tennis, ultimate Frisbee, walking, wall climbing, weight lifting, weight training, wilderness, yoga. 2 PE instructors, 10 coaches, 1 athletic trainer.

Computers Computers are regularly used in all academic classes. Computer network features include on-campus library services, online commercial services, Internet access, wireless campus network, Internet filtering or blocking technology. Campus intranet, student e-mail accounts, and computer access in designated common areas are available to students. Students grades are available online. The school has a published electronic and media policy.

Contact Ms. Dawn Curtis, Associate Director of Admission. 203-577-4521. Fax: 203-577-4588. E-mail: admission@westoverschool.org. Website: www.westoverschool.org

WEST SOUND ACADEMY

16571 Creative Drive NE
Poulsbo, Washington 98370

Head of School: Barrie Hillman

General Information Coeducational boarding and day college-preparatory, arts, technology, and International Baccalaureate school. Boarding grades 8–12, day grades 6–12. Founded: 1998. Setting: rural. Nearest major city is Seattle. Students are housed in coed dormitories. 20-acre campus. 4 buildings on campus. Approved or accredited by International Baccalaureate Organization, Northwest Accreditation Commission, Northwest Association of Independent Schools, and Washington Department of Education. Total enrollment: 113. Upper school average class size: 13. Upper school faculty-student ratio: 1:6. There are 173 required school days per year for Upper School students. Upper School students typically attend 5 days per week. The average school day consists of 6 hours and 5 minutes.

Upper School Student Profile Grade 9: 20 students (7 boys, 13 girls); Grade 10: 15 students (4 boys, 11 girls); Grade 11: 18 students (7 boys, 11 girls); Grade 12: 17 students (13 boys, 4 girls). 20% of students are boarding students. 70% are state residents. 1 state is represented in upper school student body. 30% are international students. International students from Bangladesh, China, Finland, Germany, and Sweden.

Faculty School total: 17. In upper school: 4 men, 9 women; 10 have advanced degrees.

Subjects Offered Biology, chemistry, community service, electives, English, experiential education, foreign language, history, mathematics, physics, senior project, theory of knowledge, visual arts.

Graduation Requirements Biology, chemistry, electives, English, experiential education, foreign language, history, mathematics, physics, senior project, theory of knowledge, visual arts. West Sound Academy has a 4-1-4 academic calendar; students complete a Jan-Term course each year., Jan Term has 3-week-long short courses of intense study in a variety of subjects outside the usual curriculum. Fall retreats, along with spring trips to varied locations, teach leadership, environmental ethics, and technical skills.

Special Academic Programs International Baccalaureate program; independent study; term-away projects; academic accommodation for the gifted, the musically talented, and the artistically talented; ESL (12 students enrolled).

College Admission Counseling 17 students graduated in 2015; 15 went to college, including Lewis & Clark College; Michigan State University; Mount Holyoke College; Reed College; University of Washington; Willamette University. Other: 2 entered a postgraduate year. Median SAT critical reading: 550, median SAT math: 670, median SAT writing: 590, median combined SAT: 1750, median composite ACT: 23. 31% scored over 600 on SAT critical reading, 77% scored over 600 on SAT math, 46% scored over 600 on SAT writing, 46% scored over 1800 on combined SAT, 20% scored over 26 on composite ACT.

Student Life Upper grades have specified standards of dress, student council, honor system. Discipline rests primarily with faculty.

Tuition and Aid Day student tuition: $16,770; 5-day tuition and room/board: $31,645; 7-day tuition and room/board: $43,995. Tuition installment plan (Insured Tuition Payment Plan, monthly payment plans). Merit scholarship grants, need-based scholarship grants available. In 2015–16, 36% of upper-school students received aid;

total upper-school merit-scholarship money awarded: $106,540. Total amount of financial aid awarded in 2015–16: $185,412.

Admissions Traditional secondary-level entrance grade is 9. For fall 2015, 36 students applied for upper-level admission, 24 were accepted, 20 enrolled. International English Language Test or TOEFL required. Deadline for receipt of application materials: none. Application fee required: $175. Interview required.

Athletics Interscholastic: cross-country running (boys), football (b), golf (g), soccer (b,g), track and field (b), volleyball (g); intramural: ballet (g), dance team (g), gymnastics (g), horseback riding (g), lacrosse (b,g); coed intramural: hiking/backpacking, outdoor activities, outdoor education, outdoor recreation, rafting, rappelling, rock climbing, yoga.

Computers Computers are regularly used in all classes. Computer network features include on-campus library services, Internet access, wireless campus network, Internet filtering or blocking technology. Student e-mail accounts are available to students. Students grades are available online. The school has a published electronic and media policy.

Contact Lisa Gsellman, Director of Admissions. 360-598-5954. Fax: 360-598-5494. E-mail: lgsellman@westsoundacademy.org. Website: www.westsoundacademy.org/

WESTTOWN SCHOOL

975 Westtown Road
West Chester, Pennsylvania 19382-5700

Head of School: John W. Baird

General Information Coeducational boarding and day college-preparatory, arts, religious studies, and bilingual studies school, affiliated with Society of Friends. Boarding grades 9–12, day grades PK–12. Founded: 1799. Setting: suburban. Nearest major city is Philadelphia. Students are housed in single-sex by floor dormitories and single-sex dormitories. 600-acre campus. 38 buildings on campus. Approved or accredited by Friends Council on Education, Middle States Association of Colleges and Schools, Pennsylvania Association of Independent Schools, and Pennsylvania Department of Education. Member of National Association of Independent Schools and Secondary School Admission Test Board. Endowment: $70 million. Total enrollment: 636. Upper school average class size: 15. Upper school faculty-student ratio: 1:8. Upper School students typically attend 5 days per week. The average school day consists of 9 hours and 20 minutes.

Upper School Student Profile Grade 9: 74 students (33 boys, 41 girls); Grade 10: 89 students (52 boys, 37 girls); Grade 11: 105 students (43 boys, 62 girls); Grade 12: 98 students (45 boys, 53 girls). 78% of students are boarding students. 58% are state residents. 19 states are represented in upper school student body. 16% are international students. International students from China, Germany, Republic of Korea, Spain, Thailand, and Turkey; 13 other countries represented in student body. 15% of students are members of Society of Friends.

Faculty School total: 112. In upper school: 32 men, 34 women; 52 have advanced degrees; 62 reside on campus.

Subjects Offered 3-dimensional art, ACT preparation, advanced biology, advanced chemistry, advanced math, algebra, American culture, American foreign policy, American history, American literature, ancient history, art, Asian history, band, baseball, basketball, Bible, Bible studies, biology, botany, British literature, calculus, choir, choral music, Christian and Hebrew scripture, classical language, classical studies, comparative religion, computer applications, concert band, concert choir, crafts, creative dance, creative writing, dance, dance performance, digital art, drama, drama performance, drama workshop, drawing, drawing and design, earth science, Eastern religion and philosophy, ecology, ecology, environmental systems, electives, engineering, English, English as a foreign language, English composition, English literature, environmental science, environmental studies, environmental systems, ESL, European history, film and literature, folk art, foreign language, foreign policy, fractal geometry, French, functions, geometry, graphic design, Holocaust and other genocides, honors algebra, honors geometry, honors U.S. history, honors world history, jazz, jazz dance, jazz ensemble, lab science, language, Latin, Latin American history, leadership, library research, linear algebra, literature, literature seminar, Mandarin, mathematics, model United Nations, modern dance, music, music composition, music performance, music theater, musical theater, mythology, nature writers, non-Western literature, peace and justice, physics, piano, play production, playwriting and directing, pre-algebra, pre-calculus, Quakerism and ethics, religion, robotics, SAT preparation, science, senior project, senior seminar, set design, Shakespeare, Spanish, Spanish literature, stage design, statistics, student government, student publications, studio art, swimming, tennis, theater, theater design and production, theater history, theater production, trigonometry, U.S. history, U.S. literature, visual and performing arts, visual arts, vocal ensemble, vocal music, water color painting, weight fitness, Western civilization, Western literature, Western religions, woodworking, world history, world literature, world religions, wrestling, writing, writing workshop, yearbook.

Graduation Requirements Arts and fine arts (art, music, dance, drama), English, foreign language, health education, history, mathematics, physical education (includes health), religion (includes Bible studies and theology), religious studies, science, senior project, service learning/internship, social sciences.

Special Academic Programs Advanced Placement exam preparation; honors section; independent study; study abroad; academic accommodation for the gifted, the musically talented, and the artistically talented; remedial math; ESL (18 students enrolled).

College Admission Counseling 77 students graduated in 2015; all went to college, including Guilford College; Hamilton College; Haverford College; University of Pennsylvania; University of Pittsburgh; Wesleyan University. Median SAT critical reading: 620, median SAT math: 630, median SAT writing: 610, median combined SAT: 1865, median composite ACT: 28.

Student Life Upper grades have specified standards of dress, student council, honor system. Discipline rests equally with students and faculty. Attendance at religious services is required.

Tuition and Aid Day student tuition: $32,820; 7-day tuition and room/board: $52,360. Tuition installment plan (monthly payment plans). Merit scholarship grants, need-based scholarship grants available. In 2014–15, 51% of upper-school students received aid; total upper-school merit-scholarship money awarded: $153,500. Total amount of financial aid awarded in 2014–15: $5,567,170.

Admissions Traditional secondary-level entrance grade is 9. For fall 2015, 410 students applied for upper-level admission, 162 were accepted, 76 enrolled. SSAT or TOEFL required. Deadline for receipt of application materials: none. Application fee required: $50. Interview required.

Athletics Interscholastic: baseball (boys), basketball (b,g), cross-country running (b,g), field hockey (g), independent competitive sports (b,g), lacrosse (b,g), soccer (b,g), softball (g), swimming and diving (b,g), tennis (b,g), track and field (b,g), volleyball (g); coed interscholastic: dance, dance team, golf, independent competitive sports, indoor track, indoor track & field; coed intramural: aquatics, ballet, basketball, canoeing/kayaking, combined training, dance, fitness, hiking/backpacking, indoor soccer, life saving, modern dance, outdoor activities, outdoor education, outdoor recreation, physical fitness, physical training, ropes courses, running, strength & conditioning, weight training, yoga. 18 coaches, 2 athletic trainers.

Computers Computers are regularly used in all academic, art, career exploration, college planning, current events, desktop publishing, digital applications, introduction to technology, library, library skills, literary magazine, publications, research skills, theater classes. Computer network features include on-campus library services, online commercial services, Internet access, wireless campus network, Internet filtering or blocking technology. Campus intranet, student e-mail accounts, and computer access in designated common areas are available to students. Students grades are available online. The school has a published electronic and media policy.

Contact Nathan Bohn, Director of Admission. 610-399-7900. Fax: 610-399-7909. E-mail: admissions@westtown.edu. Website: www.westtown.edu

WESTVIEW SCHOOL

Los Angeles, California
See Special Needs Schools section.

WHEATON ACADEMY

900 Prince Crossing Road
West Chicago, Illinois 60185

Head of School: Dr. Gene Frost

General Information Coeducational day college-preparatory and religious studies school, affiliated with Christian faith. Grades 9–12. Founded: 1853. Setting: suburban. Nearest major city is Chicago. 43-acre campus. 8 buildings on campus. Approved or accredited by Association of Christian Schools International, North Central Association of Colleges and Schools, and Illinois Department of Education. Total enrollment: 640. Upper school average class size: 21. Upper school faculty-student ratio: 1:15. There are 175 required school days per year for Upper School students. Upper School students typically attend 5 days per week. The average school day consists of 6 hours and 30 minutes.

Upper School Student Profile Grade 9: 167 students (81 boys, 86 girls); Grade 10: 164 students (77 boys, 87 girls); Grade 11: 160 students (78 boys, 82 girls); Grade 12: 165 students (81 boys, 84 girls). 96% of students are Christian faith.

Faculty School total: 55. In upper school: 29 men, 26 women; 33 have advanced degrees.

Subjects Offered ACT preparation, algebra, art, arts and crafts, band, Bible, Bible studies, biology, biology-AP, British literature, business, business applications, calculus, calculus-AP, ceramics, chemistry, chemistry-AP, child development, choir, Christian doctrine, Christian education, classics, comparative government and politics-AP, computer art, computer education, computer graphics, computer multimedia, computer processing, computer programming-AP, computer science, concert choir, consumer economics, creative writing, debate, desktop publishing, drama, drama workshop, drawing, driver education, earth science, economics, engineering, English, English language and composition-AP, English literature, English literature and composition-AP, environmental science, environmental science-AP, European history, European history-AP, family living, fiber arts, fine arts, foods, French, French language-AP, freshman seminar, geology, geometry, government/civics, graphic design, Greek, health, health and wellness, history, honors English, honors geometry, honors U.S. history, industrial arts, internship, journalism, keyboarding, leadership, literature, mathematics, multimedia design, music, music theory-AP, novels, orchestra, personal

growth, physical education, physics, physics-AP, portfolio art, pre-algebra, psychology, publications, science, social sciences, social studies, sociology, Spanish, Spanish language-AP, speech, statistics, statistics-AP, student publications, theater, theology, trigonometry, U.S. government, U.S. government and politics-AP, U.S. history, U.S. history-AP, U.S. literature, world history, world history-AP, world literature, writing.

Graduation Requirements Arts and fine arts (art, music, dance, drama), English, mathematics, physical education (includes health), religion (includes Bible studies and theology), science, social sciences, social studies (includes history), Winterim (2-week period during January allowing students to take two classes beyond the typical curriculum).

Special Academic Programs 17 Advanced Placement exams for which test preparation is offered; honors section; independent study; term-away projects; study at local college for college credit; academic accommodation for the gifted, the musically talented, and the artistically talented; remedial reading and/or remedial writing; remedial math; special instructional classes for students with learning disabilities; ESL (50 students enrolled).

College Admission Counseling 164 students graduated in 2015; 160 went to college, including Biola University; Calvin College; Hope College; Taylor University; University of Illinois at Urbana–Champaign; Wheaton College. Other: 1 went to work, 3 had other specific plans. Median composite ACT: 25. 45% scored over 26 on composite ACT.

Student Life Upper grades have specified standards of dress, student council, honor system. Discipline rests primarily with faculty. Attendance at religious services is required.

Summer Programs Enrichment, advancement, sports, art/fine arts, computer instruction programs offered; held on campus; accepts boys and girls; open to students from other schools. 75 students usually enrolled. 2016 schedule: June 15 to July 3.

Tuition and Aid Day student tuition: $15,000. Tuition installment plan (monthly payment plans, semester payment plan). Tuition reduction for siblings, merit scholarship grants, need-based scholarship grants, paying campus jobs available. In 2015–16, 35% of upper-school students received aid; total upper-school merit-scholarship money awarded: $15,000. Total amount of financial aid awarded in 2015–16: $700,000.

Admissions Traditional secondary-level entrance grade is 9. ACT-Explore and placement test required. Deadline for receipt of application materials: January 31. Application fee required: $50. On-campus interview required.

Athletics Interscholastic: baseball (boys), basketball (b,g), cheering (g), cross-country running (b,g), dance team (g), football (b), golf (b,g), ice hockey (b), lacrosse (b), pom squad (g), soccer (b,g), softball (g), tennis (b,g), track and field (b,g), volleyball (b,g); intramural: aerobics (g), flagball (g), ice hockey (b), wilderness survival (b); coed interscholastic: modern dance, physical training, running; coed intramural: climbing, floor hockey, hiking/backpacking, outdoor education, outdoor skills, power lifting, project adventure, riflery, rock climbing, skiing (cross-country), strength & conditioning, wall climbing, weight lifting, weight training. 2 PE instructors, 6 coaches, 1 athletic trainer.

Computers Computers are regularly used in Bible studies, graphic design, independent study, mathematics, multimedia, writing, yearbook classes. Computer network features include on-campus library services, online commercial services, Internet access, wireless campus network, Internet filtering or blocking technology. Student e-mail accounts are available to students. Students grades are available online. The school has a published electronic and media policy.

Contact Mr. Ryan Hall, Admissions Director. 630-562-7500 Ext. 7501. Fax: 630-231-1469. E-mail: rhall@wheatonacademy.org. Website: www.wheatonacademy.org

THE WHEELER SCHOOL

216 Hope Street
Providence, Rhode Island 02906

Head of School: Mr. Dan Miller, PhD

General Information Coeducational day college-preparatory, arts, Community Action Program (service-based learning), and AERIE Program (individual academic enrichment grades 9-12) school. Grades N–12. Founded: 1889. Setting: urban. 5-acre campus. 8 buildings on campus. Approved or accredited by Association of Independent Schools in New England, New England Association of Schools and Colleges, and Rhode Island Department of Education. Member of National Association of Independent Schools. Endowment: $21.3 million. Total enrollment: 819. Upper school average class size: 15. Upper school faculty-student ratio: 1:7. There are 165 required school days per year for Upper School students. Upper School students typically attend 5 days per week. The average school day consists of 6 hours and 25 minutes.

Upper School Student Profile Grade 9: 95 students (47 boys, 48 girls); Grade 10: 90 students (45 boys, 45 girls); Grade 11: 92 students (54 boys, 38 girls); Grade 12: 94 students (53 boys, 41 girls).

Faculty School total: 124. In upper school: 29 men, 46 women; 36 have advanced degrees.

Subjects Offered 20th century American writers, 20th century world history, acting, Advanced Placement courses, advanced studio art-AP, algebra, American history, anatomy, art, art history, biology, biology-AP, biotechnology, Black history, broadcasting, business skills, calculus, calculus-AP, ceramics, chemistry, Chinese, Chinese studies, choral music, civil rights, computer programming, computer science, contemporary issues, dance, drama, drawing, economics, engineering, English, English literature, English-AP, environmental science, environmental science-AP, European history, film studies, fine arts, forensics, French, geometry, guitar, Japanese, jazz ensemble, kinesiology, Latin, Latin American history, Latin American studies, mathematics, Middle Eastern history, music, nutrition, photography, physical education, physics, physiology, pre-calculus, printmaking, psychology, research, science, sculpture, social studies, Spanish, statistics, theater, trigonometry, Web site design, Western civilization.

Graduation Requirements Arts and fine arts (art, music, dance, drama), English, foreign language, history, mathematics, performing arts, physical education (includes health), science, community service, Unity and Diversity Curriculum.

Special Academic Programs 20 Advanced Placement exams for which test preparation is offered; honors section; independent study; term-away projects; study at local college for college credit; study abroad; academic accommodation for the gifted; programs in general development for dyslexic students.

College Admission Counseling 83 students graduated in 2015; all went to college, including Boston University; Brown University; Harvard University; The George Washington University; University of Rhode Island. Mean SAT critical reading: 611, mean SAT math: 624, mean SAT writing: 628, mean combined SAT: 1863, mean composite ACT: 27.

Student Life Upper grades have specified standards of dress, student council. Discipline rests equally with students and faculty.

Summer Programs Enrichment, sports, art/fine arts programs offered; session focuses on jazz camp, basketball camp, kayaking/voyager camps, sports academy; held on campus; accepts boys and girls; open to students from other schools. 175 students usually enrolled. 2016 schedule: June 18 to August 12. Application deadline: none.

Tuition and Aid Day student tuition: $32,565. Tuition installment plan (Key Tuition Payment Plan, monthly payment plans). Need-based scholarship grants available. In 2015–16, 24% of upper-school students received aid. Total amount of financial aid awarded in 2015–16: $1,975,505.

Admissions Traditional secondary-level entrance grade is 9. For fall 2015, 146 students applied for upper-level admission, 43 were accepted, 28 enrolled. ISEE or SSAT required. Deadline for receipt of application materials: January 15. Application fee required: $60. On-campus interview required.

Athletics Interscholastic: baseball (boys), basketball (b,g), cross-country running (b,g), field hockey (g), football (b), ice hockey (b,g), lacrosse (b,g), soccer (b,g), softball (g), swimming and diving (b,g), tennis (b,g), track and field (b,g), winter (indoor) track (b,g); coed interscholastic: golf, squash. 6 PE instructors, 48 coaches, 1 athletic trainer.

Computers Computers are regularly used in all classes. Computer network features include on-campus library services, online commercial services, Internet access, wireless campus network. Campus intranet, student e-mail accounts, and computer access in designated common areas are available to students. Students grades are available online. The school has a published electronic and media policy.

Contact Mrs. Jeanette Epstein, Director of Admission. 401-421-8100 Ext. 119. Fax: 401-751-7674. E-mail: jeanetteepstein@wheelerschool.org. Website: www.wheelerschool.org

WHITEFIELD ACADEMY

7711 Fegenbush Lane
Louisville, Kentucky 40228

Head of School: Mr. Gary W. Mounce

General Information Coeducational day college-preparatory, arts, religious studies, and technology school, affiliated with Baptist Church. Grades PS–12. Founded: 1976. Setting: suburban. 30-acre campus. 2 buildings on campus. Approved or accredited by Association of Christian Schools International, CITA (Commission on International and Trans-Regional Accreditation), Christian Schools International, Council of Accreditation and School Improvement, Southern Association of Colleges and Schools, and Kentucky Department of Education. Total enrollment: 711. Upper school average class size: 20. Upper school faculty-student ratio: 1:11. There are 179 required school days per year for Upper School students. Upper School students typically attend 5 days per week. The average school day consists of 6 hours and 25 minutes.

Upper School Student Profile Grade 9: 55 students (35 boys, 20 girls); Grade 10: 39 students (18 boys, 21 girls); Grade 11: 47 students (25 boys, 22 girls); Grade 12: 51 students (29 boys, 22 girls). 35% of students are Baptist.

Faculty School total: 47. In upper school: 9 men, 9 women; 12 have advanced degrees.

Subjects Offered Adolescent issues, advanced math, algebra, anatomy, art, arts, band, Bible studies, biology, calculus-AP, chemistry, choir, Christian education, Christian studies, college placement, college planning, college writing, composition, computer education, computers, drama, drama performance, economics, English, English composition, English literature, English literature-AP, foreign language, geometry, history, honors English, library, mathematics, music, political science, pre-calculus, reading, SAT/ACT preparation, science, science project, sex education, social sciences, Spanish, speech and debate, student government, student publications, U.S. history, U.S. history-AP.

Graduation Requirements Arts and fine arts (art, music, dance, drama), Bible, electives, English, foreign language, health, mathematics, physical education (includes health), science, social studies (includes history), religious studies.

Special Academic Programs 7 Advanced Placement exams for which test preparation is offered; honors section; independent study; study at local college for college credit; academic accommodation for the gifted.

College Admission Counseling 51 students graduated in 2015; 48 went to college, including Bellarmine University; Eastern Kentucky University; Jefferson Community and Technical College; University of Kentucky; University of Louisville; Western Kentucky University. Other: 1 went to work, 2 entered military service. Median composite ACT: 24. 20% scored over 26 on composite ACT.

Student Life Upper grades have uniform requirement, student council, honor system. Discipline rests primarily with faculty. Attendance at religious services is required.

Summer Programs Enrichment, sports, art/fine arts programs offered; session focuses on academic enrichment; held on campus; accepts boys and girls; open to students from other schools. 60 students usually enrolled.

Tuition and Aid Day student tuition: $6900. Tuition installment plan (FACTS Tuition Payment Plan, annual payment in full plan). Tuition reduction for siblings, need-based scholarship grants available. In 2015–16, 8% of upper-school students received aid. Total amount of financial aid awarded in 2015–16: $42,175.

Admissions Traditional secondary-level entrance grade is 9. For fall 2015, 17 students applied for upper-level admission, 13 were accepted, 13 enrolled. TerraNova required. Deadline for receipt of application materials: none. Application fee required: $100. On-campus interview required.

Athletics Interscholastic: aquatics (boys, girls), baseball (b), basketball (b,g), cheering (b,g), cross-country running (b,g), golf (b,g), soccer (b,g), softball (g), swimming and diving (b,g), tennis (b,g), track and field (b,g), volleyball (g); intramural: aerobics (g), fitness (b,g), outdoor activities (b,g), physical fitness (b,g), volleyball (g), weight lifting (b,g). 2 PE instructors.

Computers Computers are regularly used in all academic, college planning, library, newspaper, SAT preparation, theater arts, yearbook classes. Computer network features include on-campus library services, Internet access, wireless campus network, Internet filtering or blocking technology. Computer access in designated common areas is available to students. Students grades are available online. The school has a published electronic and media policy.

Contact Mrs. Lisa Sexton, Admissions Coordinator. 502-231-6261. Fax: 502-239-3144. E-mail: lisa.sexton@whitefield.org. Website: www.whitefield.org/

WHITFIELD SCHOOL

175 South Mason Road
St. Louis, Missouri 63141

Head of School: Mr. John Delautre

General Information Coeducational day college-preparatory school. Grades 6–12. Founded: 1952. Setting: suburban. 25-acre campus. 3 buildings on campus. Approved or accredited by Independent Schools Association of the Central States. Member of National Association of Independent Schools. Endowment: $7.7 million. Total enrollment: 409. Upper school average class size: 14. Upper school faculty-student ratio: 1:7.

Faculty School total: 55. In upper school: 17 men, 22 women; 28 have advanced degrees.

Subjects Offered Advanced chemistry, algebra, American history, American literature, art, biology, calculus, calculus-AP, ceramics, chemistry, chemistry-AP, choir, college counseling, college placement, college planning, community service, concert band, earth science, English, European history, fine arts, French, French-AP, geometry, health, history, junior and senior seminars, Latin, Mandarin, mathematics, modern world history, music, painting, photography, physical education, physics, pre-algebra, pre-calculus, science, senior internship, social studies, sophomore skills, Spanish, Spanish-AP, symphonic band, theater, trigonometry, visual and performing arts, Western civilization, world cultures, world history, world literature.

Graduation Requirements Arts and fine arts (art, music, dance, drama), English, foreign language, mathematics, physical education (includes health), science, social studies (includes history), sophomore, junior, senior seminars and intersession.

Special Academic Programs Advanced Placement exam preparation; honors section; independent study; academic accommodation for the gifted, the musically talented, and the artistically talented; ESL (6 students enrolled).

College Admission Counseling 61 students graduated in 2015; all went to college. Mean composite ACT: 27.

Student Life Upper grades have specified standards of dress, student council, honor system. Discipline rests primarily with faculty.

Tuition and Aid Day student tuition: $24,500. Tuition installment plan (Insured Tuition Payment Plan, monthly payment plans, 1-, 2-, and 10-payment plans). Merit scholarship grants, need-based scholarship grants available. In 2015–16, 26% of upper-school students received aid; total upper-school merit-scholarship money awarded: $35,500. Total amount of financial aid awarded in 2015–16: $1,379,000.

Admissions Traditional secondary-level entrance grade is 9. SSAT required. Deadline for receipt of application materials: January 15. Application fee required: $75. On-campus interview required.

Athletics Interscholastic: baseball (boys), basketball (b,g), cheering (g), cross-country running (b,g), dance team (g), field hockey (g), golf (b), ice hockey (b), lacrosse (b,g), soccer (b,g), squash (b,g), tennis (b), track and field (b,g), volleyball (g), wrestling (b); intramural: baseball (b), basketball (b,g), cheering (g), cross-country running (b,g), dance team (g), field hockey (g), soccer (b,g), volleyball (g), wrestling (b); coed interscholastic: dance team, golf, ice hockey, tennis; coed intramural: climbing, ice hockey, independent competitive sports, outdoor education, outdoor skills, wall climbing, yoga. 3 PE instructors, 2 coaches, 1 athletic trainer.

Computers Computers are regularly used in all classes. Computer network features include on-campus library services, online commercial services, Internet access, wireless campus network, off-campus library and database searches, tablet PC program running Microsoft Windows. Campus intranet and student e-mail accounts are available to students. Students grades are available online. The school has a published electronic and media policy.

Contact Emily Chrysler, Director of Admission. 314-415-1270. Fax: 314-434-6193. E-mail: emily.chrysler@whitfieldschool.org. Website: www.whitfieldschool.org

WHITINSVILLE CHRISTIAN SCHOOL

279 Linwood Avenue
Whitinsville, Massachusetts 01588

Head of School: Lance B. Engbers

General Information Coeducational day college-preparatory school, affiliated with Christian Reformed Church. Grades PK–12. Founded: 1928. Setting: small town. Nearest major city is Worcester. 40-acre campus. 1 building on campus. Approved or accredited by Christian Schools International, New England Association of Schools and Colleges, and Massachusetts Department of Education. Endowment: $1.4 million. Total enrollment: 474. Upper school average class size: 13. Upper school faculty-student ratio: 1:8. There are 180 required school days per year for Upper School students. The average school day consists of 6 hours and 15 minutes.

Upper School Student Profile Grade 9: 44 students (21 boys, 23 girls); Grade 10: 48 students (18 boys, 30 girls); Grade 11: 51 students (19 boys, 32 girls); Grade 12: 33 students (16 boys, 17 girls). 35% of students are members of Christian Reformed Church.

Faculty School total: 60. In upper school: 14 have advanced degrees.

Special Academic Programs 5 Advanced Placement exams for which test preparation is offered; honors section; ESL (18 students enrolled).

College Admission Counseling 35 students graduated in 2015; 33 went to college, including Calvin College; Cedarville University; Gordon College; Messiah College; Palm Beach Atlantic University; University of Massachusetts Amherst. Other: 2 entered military service.

Student Life Upper grades have specified standards of dress, student council. Discipline rests primarily with faculty. Attendance at religious services is required.

Tuition and Aid Tuition installment plan (monthly payment plans). Tuition reduction for siblings available.

Admissions Deadline for receipt of application materials: none. Application fee required: $75. Interview required.

Athletics Interscholastic: baseball (boys), basketball (b,g), cross-country running (b,g), golf (b), indoor track & field (b,g), soccer (b,g), softball (g), tennis (b,g), track and field (b,g), volleyball (g). 2 PE instructors.

Computers Computer resources include Internet access, wireless campus network, Internet filtering or blocking technology. Student e-mail accounts are available to students. Students grades are available online. The school has a published electronic and media policy.

Contact 508-234-8211. Fax: 508-234-0624. Website: www.whitinsvillechristian.org

WICHITA COLLEGIATE SCHOOL

9115 East 13th Street
Wichita, Kansas 67206

Head of School: Mr. Tom Davis

General Information Coeducational day college-preparatory, arts, and technology school. Grades PS–12. Founded: 1963. Setting: urban. 42-acre campus. 1 building on campus. Approved or accredited by Independent Schools Association of the Southwest. Member of National Association of Independent Schools. Endowment: $7.8 million. Total enrollment: 935. Upper school average class size: 14. Upper school faculty-student ratio: 1:8. There are 174 required school days per year for Upper School students. Upper School students typically attend 5 days per week. The average school day consists of 7 hours.

Upper School Student Profile Grade 6: 65 students (37 boys, 28 girls); Grade 7: 69 students (31 boys, 38 girls); Grade 8: 50 students (25 boys, 25 girls); Grade 9: 70 students (33 boys, 37 girls); Grade 10: 68 students (40 boys, 28 girls); Grade 11: 73 students (42 boys, 31 girls); Grade 12: 78 students (36 boys, 42 girls).

Faculty School total: 108. In upper school: 16 men, 15 women; 17 have advanced degrees.

Subjects Offered Advanced Placement courses, algebra, American history, American history-AP, American literature, art, biology, biology-AP, calculus, calculus-AP, chemistry, chemistry-AP, computer programming, computer science-AP, drama, economics, economics-AP, English, English literature, English-AP, environmental science, European history, fine arts, French, French-AP, geometry, global studies, government-AP, government/civics, history, humanities, journalism, Latin, Latin-AP,

macroeconomics-AP, mathematics, medieval/Renaissance history, music, photography, physical education, physics, physics-AP, science, social studies, Spanish, Spanish-AP, statistics, statistics-AP, theater, U.S. history-AP, United States government-AP, video, video film production, world history, writing, yearbook.

Graduation Requirements Arts and fine arts (art, music, dance, drama), computer science, economics, English, foreign language, humanities, mathematics, science, social studies (includes history).

Special Academic Programs 18 Advanced Placement exams for which test preparation is offered; study at local college for college credit; academic accommodation for the gifted.

College Admission Counseling 51 students graduated in 2015; all went to college, including Baylor University; Boston University; Kansas State University; The University of Kansas. Median SAT critical reading: 640, median SAT math: 660, median SAT writing: 640, median combined SAT: 1865, median composite ACT: 28. 62% scored over 600 on SAT critical reading, 76% scored over 600 on SAT math, 59% scored over 600 on SAT writing, 68% scored over 1800 on combined SAT, 81% scored over 26 on composite ACT.

Student Life Upper grades have specified standards of dress, student council, honor system. Discipline rests primarily with faculty.

Summer Programs Remediation, enrichment, sports, art/fine arts programs offered; held on campus; accepts boys and girls; open to students from other schools. 700 students usually enrolled. 2016 schedule: June 6 to August 5. Application deadline: none.

Tuition and Aid Day student tuition: $16,840. Tuition installment plan (monthly payment plans, individually arranged payment plans, 3-payment plan). Need-based scholarship grants available. In 2015–16, 20% of upper-school students received aid. Total amount of financial aid awarded in 2015–16: $670,000.

Admissions Traditional secondary-level entrance grade is 9. Iowa Tests of Basic Skills, Otis-Lennon School Ability Test and writing sample required. Deadline for receipt of application materials: none. Application fee required: $35. Interview recommended.

Athletics Interscholastic: baseball (boys), basketball (b,g), cross-country running (b,g), dance squad (g), dance team (g), football (b), golf (b,g), soccer (g), strength & conditioning (b,g), swimming and diving (b,g), tennis (b,g), track and field (b,g), volleyball (g); coed interscholastic: bowling, cheering. 2 PE instructors, 16 coaches, 1 athletic trainer.

Computers Computers are regularly used in video film production, yearbook classes. Computer network features include on-campus library services, Internet access, wireless campus network. Student e-mail accounts and computer access in designated common areas are available to students. Students grades are available online. The school has a published electronic and media policy.

Contact Ms. Susie Steed, Director of Admission. 316-771-2203. Fax: 316-634-0598. E-mail: ssteed@wcsks.com. Website: www.wcsks.com

WILBRAHAM & MONSON ACADEMY

423 Main Street
Wilbraham, Massachusetts 01095

Head of School: Mr. Brian Easler

General Information Coeducational boarding and day college-preparatory, arts, business, and technology school. Boarding grades 8–PG, day grades 6–12. Founded: 1804. Setting: small town. Nearest major city is Springfield. Students are housed in single-sex by floor dormitories and single-sex dormitories. 300-acre campus. 24 buildings on campus. Approved or accredited by Arizona Association of Independent Schools, Association of Independent Schools in New England, New England Association of Schools and Colleges, The Association of Boarding Schools, and Massachusetts Department of Education. Member of National Association of Independent Schools and Secondary School Admission Test Board. Endowment: $10 million. Total enrollment: 455. Upper school average class size: 15. Upper school faculty-student ratio: 1:6. There are 180 required school days per year for Upper School students. Upper School students typically attend 5 days per week. The average school day consists of 7 hours.

Upper School Student Profile Grade 6: 18 students (12 boys, 6 girls); Grade 7: 25 students (16 boys, 9 girls); Grade 8: 26 students (19 boys, 7 girls); Grade 9: 67 students (40 boys, 27 girls); Grade 10: 80 students (49 boys, 31 girls); Grade 11: 91 students (60 boys, 31 girls); Grade 12: 122 students (71 boys, 51 girls); Postgraduate: 14 students (11 boys, 3 girls). 57% of students are boarding students. 73% are state residents. 11 states are represented in upper school student body. 30% are international students. International students from Bermuda, China, Democratic People's Republic of Korea, Italy, and Russian Federation; 31 other countries represented in student body.

Faculty School total: 71. In upper school: 34 men, 27 women; 41 have advanced degrees; 26 reside on campus.

Subjects Offered Advanced Placement courses, advanced studio art-AP, algebra, American history, American literature, art, art history, biology, biology-AP, bookmaking, calculus, calculus-AP, ceramics, chemistry, chemistry-AP, college admission preparation, computer programming, computer science, computer-aided design, conceptual physics, creative writing, critical studies in film, decision making skills, desktop publishing, drama, driver education, economics, economics-AP, English, English literature, English-AP, entrepreneurship, environmental science, environmental science-AP, ESL, ethical decision making, European history, European history-AP, finance, fine arts, French, French-AP, geometry, global studies, honors algebra, honors geometry, honors U.S. history, honors world history, human geography - AP, humanities, instrumental music, instruments, Internet research, Irish literature, Latin, Latin-AP, leadership, literature and composition-AP, macro/microeconomics-AP, Mandarin, mathematics, microeconomics-AP, modern European history, modern European history-AP, music theory-AP, music-AP, painting, performing arts, personal finance, photography, physical education, physics, physics-AP, play/screen writing, poetry, pre-algebra, pre-calculus, pre-college orientation, probability and statistics, public speaking, research and reference, SAT preparation, science, sculpture, Shakespeare, short story, social studies, sociology, Spanish, Spanish language-AP, Spanish-AP, statistics-AP, studio art, studio art-AP, the Web, theater, U.S. history, U.S. history-AP, Vietnam War, visual arts, vocal ensemble, Web site design, world history, world history-AP, world literature, writing, writing workshop.

Graduation Requirements Algebra, American history, arts and fine arts (art, music, dance, drama), English, foreign language, geometry, lab science, physical education (includes health).

Special Academic Programs Advanced Placement exam preparation; honors section; independent study; academic accommodation for the musically talented and the artistically talented; ESL (20 students enrolled).

College Admission Counseling 94 students graduated in 2014; all went to college, including Babson College; Boston University; Clark University; Connecticut College; Northeastern University; Worcester Polytechnic Institute. Mean SAT critical reading: 549, mean SAT math: 627, mean SAT writing: 594, mean combined SAT: 1770.

Student Life Upper grades have specified standards of dress, student council, honor system. Discipline rests equally with students and faculty.

Tuition and Aid Day student tuition: $35,640; 7-day tuition and room/board: $52,985. Tuition installment plan (The Tuition Plan, Academic Management Services Plan, SMART Tuition Payment Plan, monthly payment plans, Your Tuition Solution). Need-based scholarship grants, need-based loans available. In 2014–15, 37% of upper-school students received aid.

Admissions Traditional secondary-level entrance grade is 9. For fall 2014, 611 students applied for upper-level admission, 287 were accepted, 148 enrolled. SSAT, TOEFL or TOEFL Junior required. Deadline for receipt of application materials: February 1. Application fee required: $75. Interview required.

Athletics Interscholastic: baseball (boys), basketball (b,g), cross-country running (b,g), field hockey (g), football (b), independent competitive sports (b,g), lacrosse (b,g), rugby (b), soccer (b,g), softball (g), swimming and diving (b,g), tennis (b,g), track and field (b,g), volleyball (b,g), wrestling (b); intramural: basketball (b,g); coed interscholastic: alpine skiing, crew, dance, golf, independent competitive sports, indoor track, modern dance, riflery, skiing (downhill), water polo, winter (indoor) track; coed intramural: aerobics, aerobics/dance, aerobics/Nautilus, backpacking, canoeing/kayaking, climbing, fitness, hiking/backpacking, jogging, kayaking, life saving, outdoor adventure, physical fitness, physical training, rock climbing, running, snowboarding, strength & conditioning, tai chi, tennis, weight lifting, weight training, yoga. 1 PE instructor, 11 coaches, 1 athletic trainer.

Computers Computers are regularly used in all academic, architecture, art, college planning, drawing and design, English, graphic design, library skills, literary magazine, mathematics, music, newspaper, research skills, science, Web site design, yearbook classes. Computer network features include on-campus library services, online commercial services, Internet access, wireless campus network, Internet filtering or blocking technology. Campus intranet and student e-mail accounts are available to students. Students grades are available online. The school has a published electronic and media policy.

Contact Ms. Elyse Dunbar, Administrative Assistant, Admission. 413-596-6811 Ext. 107. Fax: 413-599-1749. E-mail: edunbar@wma.us. Website: www.wma.us

THE WILLISTON NORTHAMPTON SCHOOL

19 Payson Avenue

Easthampton, Massachusetts 01027

Head of School: Mr. Robert W. Hill III

General Information Coeducational boarding and day college-preparatory school. Boarding grades 9–PG, day grades 7–12. Founded: 1841. Setting: small town. Nearest major city is Northampton. Students are housed in single-sex dormitories. 125-acre campus. 57 buildings on campus. Approved or accredited by Association of Independent Schools in New England, New England Association of Schools and Colleges, and The Association of Boarding Schools. Member of National Association of Independent Schools and Secondary School Admission Test Board. Endowment: $44 million. Total enrollment: 528. Upper school average class size: 13. Upper school faculty-student ratio: 1:6. There are 160 required school days per year for Upper School students. Upper School students typically attend 5 days per week. The average school day consists of 8 hours and 30 minutes.

Upper School Student Profile Grade 9: 66 students (29 boys, 37 girls); Grade 10: 98 students (58 boys, 40 girls); Grade 11: 125 students (62 boys, 63 girls); Grade 12: 130 students (69 boys, 61 girls); Postgraduate: 12 students (11 boys, 1 girl). 67% of

students are boarding students. 51% are state residents. 27 states are represented in upper school student body. 19% are international students. International students from Canada, China, Japan, Nigeria, Republic of Korea, and Taiwan; 26 other countries represented in student body.

Faculty School total: 73. In upper school: 35 men, 38 women; 48 have advanced degrees; 57 reside on campus.

Subjects Offered African-American history, algebra, American history, American literature, anatomy and physiology, animal behavior, art, art history, astronomy, biology, biology-AP, calculus, calculus-AP, chemistry, chemistry-AP, China/Japan history, Chinese, choral music, choreography, Christian and Hebrew scripture, comparative government and politics-AP, comparative politics, computer math, computer programming, computer science, computer science-AP, constitutional law, creative writing, dance, discrete mathematics, drama, economics, economics and history, economics-AP, English, English language-AP, English literature, English literature-AP, environmental science, ESL, ethics, European history, expository writing, fine arts, French, French language-AP, French literature-AP, French-AP, genetics, geometry, global studies, government/civics, health, history, history of jazz, honors algebra, honors English, honors geometry, Islamic studies, Latin, Latin American history, Latin-AP, mathematics, music, music theory, organic biochemistry, organic chemistry, philosophy, photography, photojournalism, physics, physics-AP, play production, playwriting, poetry, psychology, psychology-AP, religion, religion and culture, Russian history, science, sculpture, social studies, Spanish, Spanish language-AP, Spanish literature-AP, statistics-AP, theater, theology, trigonometry, U.S. history-AP, world history, world literature, writing workshop.

Graduation Requirements Arts and fine arts (art, music, dance, drama), English, foreign language, history, mathematics, science, participation in afternoon program.

Special Academic Programs 19 Advanced Placement exams for which test preparation is offered; honors section; independent study; term-away projects; study abroad; academic accommodation for the gifted, the musically talented, and the artistically talented; special instructional classes for deaf students; ESL (12 students enrolled).

College Admission Counseling 139 students graduated in 2015; 135 went to college, including Connecticut College; Cornell University; Hobart and William Smith Colleges; Syracuse University; The George Washington University; Trinity College. Other: 1 entered a postgraduate year, 3 had other specific plans. Median SAT critical reading: 580, median SAT math: 600, median SAT writing: 580, median combined SAT: 1770, median composite ACT: 25. 43% scored over 600 on SAT critical reading, 57% scored over 600 on SAT math, 45% scored over 600 on SAT writing, 47% scored over 1800 on combined SAT, 48% scored over 26 on composite ACT.

Student Life Upper grades have specified standards of dress, student council, honor system. Discipline rests equally with students and faculty.

Tuition and Aid Day student tuition: $37,500; 7-day tuition and room/board: $55,300. Tuition installment plan (Insured Tuition Payment Plan, monthly payment plans, individually arranged payment plans, Tuition Management Systems). Merit scholarship grants, need-based scholarship grants available. In 2015–16, 48% of upper-school students received aid; total upper school merit-scholarship money awarded: $213,000. Total amount of financial aid awarded in 2015–16: $6,458,850.

Admissions Traditional secondary-level entrance grade is 9. For fall 2015, 873 students applied for upper-level admission, 313 were accepted, 113 enrolled. ACT, ISEE, PSAT or SAT for applicants to grade 11 and 12, SSAT or TOEFL required. Deadline for receipt of application materials: January 15. Application fee required: $50. Interview required.

Athletics Interscholastic: alpine skiing (boys, girls), baseball (b), basketball (b,g), crew (b,g), cross-country running (b,g), field hockey (g), football (b), golf (b,g), ice hockey (b,g), lacrosse (b,g), soccer (b,g), softball (g), squash (b,g), strength & conditioning (b,g), swimming and diving (b,g), tennis (b,g), track and field (b,g), volleyball (g), water polo (b,g), wrestling (b); intramural: self defense (g); coed interscholastic: dance, diving, physical training, ultimate Frisbee; coed intramural: aerobics, aerobics/dance, dance, dance team, equestrian sports, fitness, horseback riding, judo, martial arts, modern dance, mountain biking, snowboarding, weight lifting, weight training, yoga. 1 PE instructor, 5 coaches, 2 athletic trainers.

Computers Computers are regularly used in college planning, geography, graphic design, history, library, mathematics, newspaper, photography, photojournalism, programming, science, yearbook classes. Computer network features include on-campus library services, online commercial services, Internet access, wireless campus network, Internet filtering or blocking technology. Campus intranet, student e-mail accounts, and computer access in designated common areas are available to students. Students grades are available online. The school has a published electronic and media policy.

Contact Mr. Derek Cunha, Associate Director of Admission. 413-529-3241. Fax: 413-527-9494. E-mail: dcunha@williston.com. Website: www.williston.com

WILLOW HILL SCHOOL

Sudbury, Massachusetts

See Special Needs Schools section.

THE WILLOWS ACADEMY

1015 Rose Avenue
Des Plaines, Illinois 60016
Head of School: Mrs. Jeanne Petros
General Information Girls' day college-preparatory, arts, religious studies, technology, and college preparatory school, affiliated with Roman Catholic Church. Grades 6–12. Founded: 1974. Setting: suburban. Nearest major city is Chicago. 4-acre campus. 1 building on campus. Approved or accredited by Illinois Department of Education. Total enrollment: 230. Upper school average class size: 18. Upper school faculty-student ratio: 1:10. Upper School students typically attend 5 days per week. The average school day consists of 6 hours and 30 minutes.
Upper School Student Profile Grade 6: 21 students (21 girls); Grade 7: 30 students (30 girls); Grade 8: 21 students (21 girls); Grade 9: 30 students (30 girls); Grade 10: 38 students (38 girls); Grade 11: 39 students (39 girls); Grade 12: 43 students (43 girls). 85% of students are Roman Catholic.
Faculty School total: 35. In upper school: 27 women; 15 have advanced degrees.
Subjects Offered Algebra, American history, American literature, art, biology, calculus, chemistry, choir, choral music, computer graphics, computer programming, computer science, economics, English, English literature, ethics, European history, fine arts, four units of summer reading, French, geography, geometry, government/civics, grammar, health, history, instrumental music, Latin, mathematics, music, music history, music theory, musical productions, philosophy, physical education, physics, pre-calculus, science, social studies, Spanish, statistics, theology, visual arts, vocal music, world history, world literature, writing.
Graduation Requirements Arts and fine arts (art, music, dance, drama), English, foreign language, four units of summer reading, mathematics, physical education (includes health), religion (includes Bible studies and theology), science, social studies (includes history), 40 hours of service work per year.
Special Academic Programs Advanced Placement exam preparation; honors section.
College Admission Counseling 33 students graduated in 2015; all went to college, including Marquette University; Northwestern University; University of Chicago; University of Dallas; University of Illinois at Urbana–Champaign; University of Notre Dame. Mean SAT critical reading: 690, mean SAT math: 670, mean SAT writing: 717, mean composite ACT: 28.
Student Life Upper grades have uniform requirement, student council, honor system. Discipline rests primarily with faculty.
Summer Programs Enrichment, sports programs offered; session focuses on athletic camps and enrichment; held on campus; accepts girls; open to students from other schools. 30 students usually enrolled. 2016 schedule: June 1 to July 31. Application deadline: none.
Tuition and Aid Day student tuition: $14,000. Tuition installment plan (Insured Tuition Payment Plan, monthly payment plans, quarterly, semiannual, and annual payment plans). Tuition reduction for siblings, need-based scholarship grants available. In 2015–16, 30% of upper-school students received aid.
Admissions Traditional secondary-level entrance grade is 9. For fall 2015, 51 students applied for upper-level admission, 49 were accepted, 46 enrolled. Any standardized test, ISEE or school's own exam required. Deadline for receipt of application materials: none. Application fee required: $50. On-campus interview required.
Athletics Interscholastic: basketball, cross-country running, dance team, soccer, softball, swimming and diving, volleyball; intramural: strength & conditioning. 1 PE instructor, 8 coaches.
Computers Computers are regularly used in graphic design, history, mathematics, music, music technology, science classes. Computer network features include Internet access, Internet filtering or blocking technology. Computer access in designated common areas is available to students. Students grades are available online.
Contact Mrs. Kathryn Ferry, Director of Admissions. 847-824-6900 Ext. 208. Fax: 847-824-7089. E-mail: ferry@willowsacademy.org. Website: www.willowsacademy.org

WILMINGTON CHRISTIAN SCHOOL

825 Loveville Road
Hockessin, Delaware 19707
Head of School: Mr. William F. Stevens Jr.
General Information Coeducational day college-preparatory, arts, religious studies, and technology school, affiliated with Protestant faith. Grades PK–12. Founded: 1946. Setting: suburban. Nearest major city is Wilmington. 15-acre campus. 1 building on campus. Approved or accredited by Association of Christian Schools International, Middle States Association of Colleges and Schools, and Delaware Department of Education. Endowment: $400,000. Total enrollment: 500. Upper school average class size: 20. Upper school faculty-student ratio: 1:15. There are 177 required school days per year for Upper School students. Upper School students typically attend 5 days per week. The average school day consists of 6 hours and 40 minutes.
Upper School Student Profile Grade 9: 41 students (20 boys, 21 girls); Grade 10: 55 students (25 boys, 30 girls); Grade 11: 50 students (24 boys, 26 girls); Grade 12: 64 students (30 boys, 34 girls). 99% of students are Protestant.
Faculty School total: 57. In upper school: 13 men, 22 women; 15 have advanced degrees.

Subjects Offered Accounting, advanced math, algebra, American history, American history-AP, American minority experience, anatomy and physiology, art, band, biology, calculus, calculus-AP, chemistry, chorus, Christian doctrine, Christian ethics, church history, civics, computer applications, consumer mathematics, creative writing, democracy in America, driver education, ecology, economics, English, geometry, German, health, honors algebra, honors English, honors geometry, information processing, journalism, lab science, library assistant, marine biology, modern history, music theory, novels, physical education, physical science, physics, pre-calculus, Spanish, speech, study skills, trigonometry, world civilizations, world religions, yearbook.
Graduation Requirements Bible studies, English, foreign language, health education, mathematics, physical education (includes health), science, social studies (includes history), 40 hours of community service.
Special Academic Programs Advanced Placement exam preparation; honors section; study at local college for college credit; remedial reading and/or remedial writing; remedial math; ESL (9 students enrolled).
College Admission Counseling 64 students graduated in 2015; 62 went to college, including Drexel University; Eastern University; Gordon College; Liberty University; Messiah College; University of Delaware. Other: 2 had other specific plans.
Student Life Upper grades have uniform requirement, student council, honor system. Discipline rests primarily with faculty. Attendance at religious services is required.
Summer Programs Remediation, advancement programs offered; session focuses on to attract more students to the school; held on campus; accepts boys and girls; open to students from other schools. 12 students usually enrolled. 2016 schedule: June 15 to August 5.
Tuition and Aid Day student tuition: $12,290. Tuition installment plan (STEP Plan (monthly deduction from a checking account)). Tuition reduction for siblings, need-based scholarship grants available. In 2015–16, 47% of upper-school students received aid. Total amount of financial aid awarded in 2015–16: $292,720.
Admissions Traditional secondary-level entrance grade is 9. For fall 2015, 68 students applied for upper-level admission, 35 were accepted, 32 enrolled. Stanford Achievement Test required. Deadline for receipt of application materials: August 1. Application fee required: $125. On-campus interview required.
Athletics Interscholastic: baseball (boys), basketball (b,g), cheering (g), field hockey (g), lacrosse (b), soccer (b,g), softball (g), volleyball (g), wrestling (b); coed interscholastic: cross-country running, golf, running. 2 PE instructors, 16 coaches, 1 athletic trainer.
Computers Computers are regularly used in accounting, business education, data processing, information technology, newspaper, yearbook classes. Computer network features include on-campus library services, Internet access. The school has a published electronic and media policy.
Contact Mrs. Carol Allston-Stiles, Director of Enrollment. 302-239-2121 Ext. 3205. Fax: 302-239-2778. E-mail: admissions@WilmingtonChristian.org. Website: www.wilmingtonchristian.org

WILMINGTON FRIENDS SCHOOL

101 School Road
Wilmington, Delaware 19803
Head of School: Kenneth E. Aldridge
General Information Coeducational day college-preparatory school, affiliated with Society of Friends. Grades PS–12. Founded: 1748. Setting: suburban. Nearest major city is Philadelphia, PA. 57-acre campus. 4 buildings on campus. Approved or accredited by Friends Council on Education, International Baccalaureate Organization, Middle States Association of Colleges and Schools, Pennsylvania Association of Independent Schools, and Delaware Department of Education. Member of National Association of Independent Schools. Endowment: $27.6 million. Total enrollment: 736. Upper school average class size: 15. Upper school faculty-student ratio: 1:10. There are 169 required school days per year for Upper School students. Upper School students typically attend 5 days per week. The average school day consists of 7 hours.
Upper School Student Profile Grade 9: 63 students (37 boys, 26 girls); Grade 10: 80 students (39 boys, 41 girls); Grade 11: 76 students (36 boys, 40 girls); Grade 12: 69 students (37 boys, 32 girls). 4.3% of students are members of Society of Friends.
Faculty School total: 89. In upper school: 13 men, 13 women; 24 have advanced degrees.
Subjects Offered 3-dimensional art, advanced chemistry, art, biology, calculus, chemistry, community service, computer art, driver education, English, environmental science, European history, French, history, human development, improvisation, independent study, integrated mathematics, jazz ensemble, journalism, Mandarin, mathematics, music, music theory, peace and justice, physical education, physics, pre-calculus, programming, Quakerism and ethics, religion, science, social sciences, Spanish, studio art, theater, theater arts, theory of knowledge, U.S. history, Web site design, wellness, wind ensemble, world history.
Graduation Requirements Computer literacy, English, foreign language, history, mathematics, performing arts, Quakerism and ethics, science, social sciences, sports, 50 hours of community service (single organization) before senior year, Global Peace and Justice course, Visual and Performing Arts courses, Human Dynamics and Development course.

Special Academic Programs International Baccalaureate program; 2 Advanced Placement exams for which test preparation is offered; honors section; independent study; term-away projects; study abroad; academic accommodation for the gifted, the musically talented, and the artistically talented.

College Admission Counseling 56 students graduated in 2015; all went to college, including Georgetown University; University of Delaware; University of Miami; University of Pittsburgh; University of Virginia; Wake Forest University. Median SAT critical reading: 590, median SAT math: 620, median SAT writing: 590, median combined SAT: 1790, median composite ACT: 29. 44% scored over 600 on SAT critical reading, 60% scored over 600 on SAT math, 44% scored over 600 on SAT writing, 46% scored over 1800 on combined SAT, 65% scored over 26 on composite ACT.

Student Life Upper grades have specified standards of dress, student council. Discipline rests primarily with faculty. Attendance at religious services is required.

Tuition and Aid Day student tuition: $26,075. Tuition installment plan (Tuition Management Systems (purchased Key Tuition Plan)). Need-based scholarship grants available. In 2014–15, 38% of upper-school students received aid. Total amount of financial aid awarded in 2014–15: $1,596,299.

Admissions Traditional secondary-level entrance grade is 9. For fall 2015, 80 students applied for upper-level admission, 44 were accepted, 27 enrolled. CTP, ERB or ISEE required. Deadline for receipt of application materials: none. Application fee required: $50. Interview required.

Athletics Interscholastic: baseball (boys), basketball (b,g), cross-country running (b,g), field hockey (g), football (b), lacrosse (b,g), soccer (b,g), swimming and diving (b,g), tennis (b,g), track and field (b,g), volleyball (g), wrestling (b); intramural: strength & conditioning (b,g); coed interscholastic: winter (indoor) track; coed intramural: aerobics. 3 PE instructors, 43 coaches, 1 athletic trainer.

Computers Computers are regularly used in art, English, French, library skills, literary magazine, mathematics, music, newspaper, science, social studies, Spanish, yearbook classes. Computer network features include on-campus library services, online commercial services, Internet access, wireless campus network, Internet filtering or blocking technology, 1:1 laptop program, Google Docs account, off-campus library services, online access to attendance, personalized Web site login for data driven Web site, open wireless network for personal devices, document storage, backup, and security. Campus intranet and computer access in designated common areas are available to students. Students grades are available online. The school has a published electronic and media policy.

Contact Ms. Melissa Brown, Acting Director of Admissions and Financial Aid. 302-576-2932. Fax: 302-576-2939. E-mail: mbrown@wilmingtonfriends.org. Website: www.wilmingtonfriends.org/

WILSON HALL

520 Wilson Hall Road
Sumter, South Carolina 29150

Head of School: Mr. Frederick B. Moulton Sr.

General Information Coeducational day college-preparatory, arts, and technology school. Grades PS–12. Founded: 1966. Setting: small town. Nearest major city is Columbia. 17-acre campus. 6 buildings on campus. Approved or accredited by Southern Association of Colleges and Schools, Southern Association of Independent Schools, and South Carolina Department of Education. Endowment: $280,000. Total enrollment: 781. Upper school average class size: 18. Upper school faculty-student ratio: 1:13. There are 177 required school days per year for Upper School students. Upper School students typically attend 5 days per week. The average school day consists of 6 hours and 20 minutes.

Upper School Student Profile Grade 9: 50 students (30 boys, 20 girls); Grade 10: 66 students (26 boys, 40 girls); Grade 11: 65 students (32 boys, 33 girls); Grade 12: 64 students (32 boys, 32 girls).

Faculty School total: 83. In upper school: 15 men, 28 women; 23 have advanced degrees.

Subjects Offered 3-dimensional design, algebra, anatomy, biology-AP, calculus-AP, chemistry-AP, computer applications, computer programming, computer programming-AP, drawing, economics, English, English language-AP, English literature-AP, environmental science, European history-AP, French, French language-AP, government, government-AP, journalism, Latin, Latin-AP, Middle Eastern history, multimedia, music theory-AP, philosophy, physical education, physical science, physics-AP, pottery, sculpture, Spanish, Spanish language-AP, studio art-AP, trigonometry, U.S. history-AP, world history.

Graduation Requirements Arts and fine arts (art, music, dance, drama), computer science, English, foreign language, mathematics, physical education (includes health), science, social studies (includes history), acceptance into four-year college or university, 40 hours community service.

Special Academic Programs 17 Advanced Placement exams for which test preparation is offered; honors section.

College Admission Counseling 60 students graduated in 2015; all went to college, including Clemson University; College of Charleston; Duke University; Furman University; The Citadel, The Military College of South Carolina; University of South Carolina. Mean SAT critical reading: 610, mean SAT math: 606, mean SAT writing: 605, mean combined SAT: 1821, mean composite ACT: 26.

Student Life Upper grades have specified standards of dress, honor system. Discipline rests primarily with faculty.

Summer Programs Remediation, enrichment, sports, art/fine arts, computer instruction programs offered; session focuses on enrichment; held on campus; accepts boys and girls; open to students from other schools. 250 students usually enrolled. 2016 schedule: June 1 to July 31. Application deadline: May 20.

Tuition and Aid Day student tuition: $4650–$6595. Tuition installment plan (monthly payment plans). Need-based scholarship grants available. In 2015–16, 4% of upper-school students received aid. Total amount of financial aid awarded in 2015–16: $145,000.

Admissions Traditional secondary-level entrance grade is 9. For fall 2015, 121 students applied for upper-level admission, 113 were accepted, 113 enrolled. ACT, CTBS, OLSAT, Iowa Tests of Basic Skills, PSAT and SAT for applicants to grade 11 and 12, school's own test or Stanford Achievement Test, Otis-Lennon School Ability Test required. Deadline for receipt of application materials: none. Application fee required: $150. Interview recommended.

Athletics Interscholastic: baseball (boys), basketball (b,g), bowling (b,g), cheering (g), cross-country running (b,g), fishing (b), football (b), golf (b,g), marksmanship (b), Nautilus (b,g), riflery (b), running (b,g), skeet shooting (b), softball (g), strength & conditioning (b,g), swimming and diving (b,g), tennis (b,g), track and field (b,g), trap and skeet (b), volleyball (g), wrestling (b); intramural: table tennis (b), weight lifting (b,g), weight training (b,g); coed interscholastic: climbing, equestrian sports, outdoor adventure, outdoor education, paint ball, riflery, skeet shooting, soccer; coed intramural: archery, outdoor adventure, rafting, rock climbing, ropes courses, table tennis. 4 PE instructors, 13 coaches.

Computers Computers are regularly used in computer applications, English, journalism, literary magazine, technology, yearbook classes. Computer network features include on-campus library services, online commercial services, Internet access, wireless campus network, Internet filtering or blocking technology. Students grades are available online. The school has a published electronic and media policy.

Contact Mr. Sean Hoskins, Director of Admissions and Public Relations. 803-469-3475 Ext. 107. Fax: 803-469-3477. E-mail: sean_hoskins@hotmail.com. Website: www.wilsonhall.org

WINCHESTER THURSTON SCHOOL

555 Morewood Avenue
Pittsburgh, Pennsylvania 15213-2899

Head of School: Mr. Gary J. Niels

General Information Coeducational day college-preparatory and arts school. Grades PK–12. Founded: 1887. Setting: urban. 5-acre campus. 2 buildings on campus. Approved or accredited by Pennsylvania Association of Independent Schools, The College Board, and Pennsylvania Department of Education. Member of National Association of Independent Schools and Secondary School Admission Test Board. Endowment: $12 million. Total enrollment: 670. Upper school average class size: 15. Upper school faculty-student ratio: 1:8. There are 175 required school days per year for Upper School students. Upper School students typically attend 5 days per week. The average school day consists of 6 hours and 50 minutes.

Upper School Student Profile Grade 9: 60 students (33 boys, 27 girls); Grade 10: 64 students (28 boys, 36 girls); Grade 11: 57 students (30 boys, 27 girls); Grade 12: 56 students (32 boys, 24 girls).

Faculty School total: 91. In upper school: 16 men, 16 women; 18 have advanced degrees.

Subjects Offered Algebra, American history, American history-AP, American literature, animal behavior, art, art history, biology, biology-AP, calculus, calculus-AP, ceramics, chemistry, Chinese, choir, chorus, classics, composition-AP, computer programming, computer science, computer science-AP, creative writing, dance, drama, drawing, economics, economics-AP, English, English literature, English literature-AP, English-AP, European history, European history-AP, expository writing, filmmaking, French, French-AP, geometry, government/civics, health, history, journalism, Latin, Latin-AP, linear algebra, mathematics, music, music theory, philosophy, photography, physical education, physics, physics-AP, psychology, SAT preparation, science, social studies, Spanish, Spanish-AP, speech, statistics-AP, visual arts, world history, world literature, writing, yearbook.

Graduation Requirements Arts and fine arts (art, music, dance, drama), computer science, English, foreign language, mathematics, physical education (includes health), science, social studies (includes history), speech, City As Our Campus coursework, a unique program which connects our students with various educational opportunities within the city of Pittsburgh, (examples of these opportunities include internships, research programs, and service learning options).

Special Academic Programs Advanced Placement exam preparation; independent study; term-away projects; study at local college for college credit; study abroad; academic accommodation for the gifted, the musically talented, and the artistically talented; ESL (2 students enrolled).

College Admission Counseling 60 students graduated in 2015; all went to college, including Boston University; Carnegie Mellon University; Harvard University; University of Pittsburgh. Mean SAT critical reading: 627, mean SAT math: 620, mean SAT writing: 613, mean combined SAT: 1860, mean composite ACT: 26. 76% scored over 600 on SAT critical reading, 73% scored over 600 on SAT math, 67% scored over 600 on SAT writing.

Student Life Upper grades have specified standards of dress, student council. Discipline rests equally with students and faculty.

Tuition and Aid Day student tuition: $25,500–$27,700. Tuition installment plan (monthly payment plans). Need-based scholarship grants available. In 2015–16, 30% of upper-school students received aid. Total amount of financial aid awarded in 2015–16: $1,450,000.

Admissions Traditional secondary-level entrance grade is 9. For fall 2015, 106 students applied for upper-level admission, 50 were accepted, 29 enrolled. ISEE, SSAT, TOEFL or TOEFL Junior required. Deadline for receipt of application materials: December 15. Application fee required: $50. Interview required.

Athletics Interscholastic: basketball (boys, girls), drill team (g), field hockey (g), lacrosse (b,g), rowing (b,g), running (b,g), tennis (b,g); intramural: squash (b); coed interscholastic: crew, cross-country running, fencing, golf, soccer, squash, track and field; coed intramural: basketball, dance, Frisbee, independent competitive sports, outdoor activities, physical fitness, physical training, soccer, strength & conditioning, ultimate Frisbee, weight training, winter soccer, yoga. 4 PE instructors, 24 coaches, 1 athletic trainer.

Computers Computers are regularly used in art, college planning, computer applications, creative writing, English, foreign language, history, library, mathematics, music, photography, science, senior seminar, social studies, writing, writing, yearbook classes. Computer network features include on-campus library services, online commercial services, Internet access, wireless campus network, Internet filtering or blocking technology. Campus intranet, student e-mail accounts, and computer access in designated common areas are available to students. Students grades are available online. The school has a published electronic and media policy.

Contact Mr. Scot Lorenzi, Director of Upper School Admission. 412-578-3738. Fax: 412-578-7504. E-mail: lorenzis@winchesterthurston.org. Website: www.winchesterthurston.org

WINDERMERE PREPARATORY SCHOOL

6189 Winter Garden-Vineland Road
Windermere, Florida 34786

Head of School: Thomas L. Marcy, EdD

General Information Boys' boarding and coeducational day college-preparatory and arts school. Boarding boys grades 9–12, day boys grades PK–12, day girls grades PK–12. Founded: 2000. Setting: suburban. Nearest major city is Orlando. Students are housed in single-sex dormitories. 48-acre campus. 3 buildings on campus. Approved or accredited by International Baccalaureate Organization, Southern Association of Colleges and Schools, Southern Association of Independent Schools, and Florida Department of Education. Upper school average class size: 18. Upper school faculty-student ratio: 1:14. There are 180 required school days per year for Upper School students. Upper School students typically attend 5 days per week. The average school day consists of 7 hours and 45 minutes.

Upper School Student Profile Grade 6: 88 students (43 boys, 45 girls); Grade 7: 87 students (42 boys, 45 girls); Grade 8: 78 students (44 boys, 34 girls); Grade 9: 118 students (66 boys, 52 girls); Grade 10: 116 students (57 boys, 59 girls); Grade 11: 105 students (66 boys, 39 girls); Grade 12: 123 students (68 boys, 55 girls). 19% of students are boarding students. 80% are state residents. 20% are international students. International students from Brazil, China, India, United Kingdom, Venezuela, and Viet Nam; 57 other countries represented in student body.

Faculty School total: 200. In upper school: 16 men, 23 women; 22 have advanced degrees; 1 resides on campus.

Subjects Offered 20th century history, 3-dimensional art, 3-dimensional design, acting, advanced biology, advanced chemistry, advanced math, Advanced Placement courses, advanced TOEFL/grammar, algebra, American government, American history, American literature, anatomy and physiology, art, band, biology, business, calculus, ceramics, chemistry, Chinese, choir, chorus, creative writing, dance, dance performance, digital art, digital imaging, drama, drama performance, economics, electives, English, English composition, English literature, entrepreneurship, environmental science, ESL, film, French, French as a second language, geometry, graphic design, honors algebra, honors English, honors U.S. history, honors world history, International Baccalaureate courses, jazz ensemble, Latin, life skills, marine science, music, music theory, personal fitness, physical education, physical fitness, physics, piano, pre-calculus, psychology, public speaking, social sciences, Spanish, speech and debate, sports medicine, theory of knowledge, U.S. history, weight training, wind ensemble, world history, world literature, writing, yearbook.

Graduation Requirements Arts and fine arts (art, music, dance, drama), biology, chemistry, electives, English, foreign language, mathematics, performing arts, physical fitness, science, social sciences, U.S. history, 26 credits are required for graduation. This is 2 credits higher than the State of Florida graduation requirement. Community service is required.

Special Academic Programs International Baccalaureate program; 2 Advanced Placement exams for which test preparation is offered; honors section; independent study; study abroad; academic accommodation for the musically talented and the artistically talented; ESL (22 students enrolled).

College Admission Counseling 132 students graduated in 2015; all went to college, including Florida State University; Penn State University Park; Rollins

College; University of Central Florida; University of Florida. Mean SAT critical reading: 536, mean SAT math: 573, mean SAT writing: 536, mean combined SAT: 1645, mean composite ACT: 24.

Student Life Upper grades have uniform requirement, student council, honor system. Discipline rests primarily with faculty.

Summer Programs Enrichment, advancement, ESL, sports programs offered; session focuses on enrichment and academics; held on campus; accepts boys and girls; open to students from other schools. 50 students usually enrolled. 2016 schedule: June 20 to July 20. Application deadline: June 6.

Tuition and Aid Day student tuition: $18,950; 7-day tuition and room/board: $54,500. Tuition installment plan (monthly payment plans). Merit scholarship grants, need-based scholarship grants available. In 2015–16, 8% of upper-school students received aid; total upper-school merit-scholarship money awarded: $175,000. Total amount of financial aid awarded in 2015–16: $425,000.

Admissions Traditional secondary-level entrance grade is 9. For fall 2015, 153 students applied for upper-level admission, 110 were accepted, 76 enrolled. ERB (grade level), ISEE, school placement exam or TOEFL required. Deadline for receipt of application materials: none. Application fee required: $85. Interview recommended.

Athletics Interscholastic: baseball (boys), basketball (b,g), cheering (g), dance (g), football (b), golf (b,g), lacrosse (b,g), physical training (b,g), soccer (b,g), softball (g), strength & conditioning (b,g), swimming and diving (b,g), tennis (b,g), track and field (b,g), volleyball (g), weight lifting (b), weight training (b,g); coed interscholastic: aerobics/dance, aquatics, archery, crew, cross-country running, dance, dance team, track and field; coed intramural: flag football, golf. 9 PE instructors, 48 coaches, 1 athletic trainer.

Computers Computers are regularly used in all academic classes. Computer network features include on-campus library services, online commercial services, Internet access, wireless campus network, Internet filtering or blocking technology. Campus intranet and student e-mail accounts are available to students. Students grades are available online. The school has a published electronic and media policy.

Contact Mrs. Laura Lykins, Director of Admissions. 407-905-7737 Ext. 3228. Fax: 407-905-7710. E-mail: laura.lykins@windmereprep.com. Website: www.windmereprep.com

THE WINDSOR SCHOOL

37-02 Main St. / 3rd Floor
Flushing, New York 11354

Head of School: Mr. James Seery

General Information Coeducational day college-preparatory and arts school. Grades 6–PG. Founded: 1969. Setting: urban. Nearest major city is New York. 1 building on campus. Approved or accredited by Middle States Association of Colleges and Schools, New York Department of Education, New York State Board of Regents, The College Board, and New York Department of Education. Total enrollment: 110. Upper school average class size: 14. Upper school faculty-student ratio: 1:14. There are 185 required school days per year for Upper School students. Upper School students typically attend 5 days per week. The average school day consists of 6 hours and 5 minutes.

Upper School Student Profile Grade 8: 10 students (4 boys, 6 girls); Grade 9: 12 students (7 boys, 5 girls); Grade 10: 23 students (10 boys, 13 girls); Grade 11: 32 students (18 boys, 14 girls); Grade 12: 33 students (16 boys, 17 girls).

Faculty School total: 12. In upper school: 6 men, 6 women; 10 have advanced degrees.

Subjects Offered Advanced Placement courses, algebra, American history, American literature, art, basic skills, biology, business, calculus, chemistry, computer skills, creative writing, economics, English, English literature, environmental science, ESL, European history, fine arts, geometry, government/civics, grammar, health, marketing, mathematics, music, physical education, physics, pre-calculus, psychology, science, social sciences, social studies, Spanish, trigonometry, world affairs, world history.

Graduation Requirements Arts and fine arts (art, music, dance, drama), English, foreign language, health education, mathematics, physical education (includes health), science, social studies (includes history).

Special Academic Programs Advanced Placement exam preparation; honors section; accelerated programs; independent study; academic accommodation for the gifted, the musically talented, and the artistically talented; remedial reading and/or remedial writing; remedial math; ESL (27 students enrolled).

College Admission Counseling 34 students graduated in 2015; all went to college, including City College of the City University of New York; Michigan State University; Pace University; St. John's University; Stony Brook University, State University of New York. Median SAT critical reading: 440, median SAT math: 550, median SAT writing: 460. 10% scored over 600 on SAT critical reading, 35% scored over 600 on SAT math, 10% scored over 600 on SAT writing.

Student Life Upper grades have specified standards of dress, student council. Discipline rests primarily with faculty.

Summer Programs Remediation, enrichment, advancement, ESL programs offered; session focuses on advancement, enrichment, remediation; held on campus; accepts boys and girls; open to students from other schools. 450 students usually enrolled. 2016 schedule: July 1 to August 18. Application deadline: June 30.

Tuition and Aid Day student tuition: $26,000. Tuition installment plan (individually arranged payment plans). Tuition reduction for siblings available. In 2014–15, 5% of upper-school students received aid. Total amount of financial aid awarded in 2014–15: $20,000.

Admissions Traditional secondary-level entrance grade is 10. For fall 2015, 80 students applied for upper-level admission, 76 were accepted, 73 enrolled. Achievement tests and school's own exam required. Deadline for receipt of application materials: none. No application fee required. On-campus interview recommended.

Athletics Interscholastic: basketball (boys, girls), soccer (b,g), table tennis (b,g), track and field (b,g); intramural: basketball (b,g), cooperative games (b,g), fitness (b,g), jump rope (g), physical fitness (b,g), soccer (b,g), strength & conditioning (b,g), table tennis (b,g), tennis (b,g), volleyball (b,g), yoga (b,g); coed interscholastic: basketball, soccer, table tennis, track and field; coed intramural: basketball, fitness, jump rope, physical fitness, soccer, strength & conditioning, table tennis, tennis, volleyball, yoga. 2 PE instructors, 2 coaches.

Computers Computers are regularly used in art, mathematics, research skills, yearbook classes. Computer network features include Internet access, Internet filtering or blocking technology. Campus intranet and computer access in designated common areas are available to students. The school has a published electronic and media policy.

Contact Ms. Emily Yu, Director of Admissions. 718-359-8300. Fax: 718-359-1876. E-mail: admin@thewindsorschool.com. Website: www.windsorschool.com

WINDWARD SCHOOL

11350 Palms Boulevard
Los Angeles, California 90066

Head of School: Tom Gilder

General Information Coeducational day college-preparatory school. Grades 7–12. Founded: 1971. Setting: urban. 9-acre campus. 11 buildings on campus. Approved or accredited by California Association of Independent Schools and Western Association of Schools and Colleges. Member of National Association of Independent Schools. Total enrollment: 541. Upper school average class size: 16. Upper school faculty-student ratio: 1:7. There are 165 required school days per year for Upper School students. Upper School students typically attend 5 days per week. The average school day consists of 7 hours.

Upper School Student Profile Grade 9: 80 students (38 boys, 42 girls); Grade 10: 94 students (46 boys, 48 girls); Grade 11: 91 students (48 boys, 43 girls); Grade 12: 89 students (43 boys, 46 girls).

Faculty School total: 65. In upper school: 32 men, 27 women; 37 have advanced degrees.

Subjects Offered 3-dimensional art, acting, advanced biology, advanced chemistry, Advanced Placement courses, algebra, American history, American literature, art, art history, ballet, biology, calculus, ceramics, chemistry, Chinese, chorus, computer science, creative writing, dance, drama, English, English literature, environmental science, European history, fine arts, French, geometry, government/civics, health, history, journalism, Latin, marine biology, mathematics, music, performing arts, photography, photojournalism, physical education, physiology, robotics, science, senior internship, social studies, Spanish, theater, trigonometry, world history.

Graduation Requirements Arts and fine arts (art, music, dance, drama), English, foreign language, mathematics, physical education (includes health), science, social studies (includes history).

Special Academic Programs 16 Advanced Placement exams for which test preparation is offered; honors section; independent study; study at local college for college credit.

College Admission Counseling 88 students graduated in 2014; all went to college, including Dartmouth College; Northwestern University; Tufts University; University of California, Berkeley; Williams College; Yale University. Mean SAT critical reading: 650, mean SAT math: 645, mean SAT writing: 671, mean combined SAT: 1966.

Student Life Upper grades have specified standards of dress, student council, honor system. Discipline rests primarily with faculty.

Tuition and Aid Day student tuition: $34,215. Tuition installment plan (Key Tuition Payment Plan, monthly payment plans). Need-based scholarship grants, need-based loans available. In 2014–15, 17% of upper-school students received aid. Total amount of financial aid awarded in 2014–15: $1,980,066.

Admissions Traditional secondary-level entrance grade is 9. For fall 2014, 177 students applied for upper-level admission, 30 were accepted, 23 enrolled. ISEE required. Deadline for receipt of application materials: December 11. Application fee required: $100. On-campus interview required.

Athletics Interscholastic: baseball (boys), basketball (b,g), football (b); coed interscholastic: cross-country running, flag football. 5 PE instructors, 15 coaches, 2 athletic trainers.

Computers Computers are regularly used in art, English, history, mathematics, science classes. Computer network features include on-campus library services, online commercial services, Internet access, wireless campus network, Internet filtering or blocking technology. Student e-mail accounts are available to students. The school has a published electronic and media policy.

Contact Sharon Pearline, Director of Admissions. 310-391-7127. Fax: 310-397-5655. Website: www.windwardschool.org

WINSTON PREPARATORY SCHOOL

New York, New York
See Special Needs Schools section.

THE WINSTON SCHOOL

Dallas, Texas
See Special Needs Schools section.

THE WINSTON SCHOOL SAN ANTONIO

San Antonio, Texas
See Special Needs Schools section.

THE WOODHALL SCHOOL

PO Box 550
58 Harrison Lane
Bethlehem, Connecticut 06751

Head of School: Matthew C. Woodhall

General Information Boys' boarding and day college-preparatory and arts school; primarily serves students with above-average intellectual ability who have had difficulties in traditional school environments. Grades 9–PG. Founded: 1983. Setting: rural. Nearest major city is Waterbury. Students are housed in single-sex dormitories. 38-acre campus. 5 buildings on campus. Approved or accredited by Association of Independent Schools in New England, Connecticut Association of Independent Schools, New England Association of Schools and Colleges, and Connecticut Department of Education. Member of National Association of Independent Schools. Endowment: $450,000. Total enrollment: 42. Upper school average class size: 4. Upper school faculty-student ratio: 1:3. There are 184 required school days per year for Upper School students. Upper School students typically attend 6 days per week. The average school day consists of 6 hours.

Upper School Student Profile Grade 9: 4 students (4 boys); Grade 10: 13 students (13 boys); Grade 11: 16 students (16 boys); Grade 12: 9 students (9 boys). 100% of students are boarding students. 6% are state residents. 17 states are represented in upper school student body. 1% are international students. International students from Brazil.

Faculty School total: 16. In upper school: 14 men, 2 women; 15 have advanced degrees; 13 reside on campus.

Subjects Offered Algebra, American history, anatomy, art, biology, calculus, chemistry, comparative government and politics, drama, English, environmental science, geometry, Greek, language and composition, Latin, physics, pre-calculus, Spanish, world civilizations.

Graduation Requirements Arts and fine arts (art, music, dance, drama), communication skills, English, foreign language, mathematics, physical education (includes health), science, social studies (includes history).

Special Academic Programs 6 Advanced Placement exams for which test preparation is offered; independent study; special instructional classes for students with Attention Deficit Disorder and non-verbal learning disabilities; ESL.

College Admission Counseling 13 students graduated in 2015; 11 went to college, including Goucher College; Ursinus College. Other: 2 entered a postgraduate year. Median SAT critical reading: 560, median SAT math: 615, median SAT writing: 565, median combined SAT: 1695, median composite ACT: 26. 50% scored over 600 on SAT critical reading, 60% scored over 600 on SAT math, 30% scored over 600 on SAT writing, 40% scored over 1800 on combined SAT, 60% scored over 26 on composite ACT.

Student Life Upper grades have specified standards of dress, student council, honor system. Discipline rests primarily with faculty.

Tuition and Aid Day student tuition: $48,750; 7-day tuition and room/board: $65,000. Tuition installment plan (individually arranged payment plans).

Admissions Traditional secondary-level entrance grade is 10. For fall 2015, 59 students applied for upper-level admission, 20 were accepted, 20 enrolled. Deadline for receipt of application materials: none. Application fee required: $100. On-campus interview required.

Athletics Interscholastic: basketball, cross-country running, lacrosse, soccer, wrestling; intramural: basketball, canoeing/kayaking, cross-country running, fishing, fitness, fitness walking, hiking/backpacking, jogging, lacrosse, outdoor activities, outdoor education, outdoor recreation, physical fitness, physical training, rafting, running, skiing (cross-country), soccer, strength & conditioning, volleyball, walking, wall climbing, weight lifting, winter walking, wrestling. 10 coaches, 1 athletic trainer.

Computers Computers are regularly used in art, English, foreign language, history, mathematics, science, social sciences classes. Computer resources include Internet access. The school has a published electronic and media policy.

Contact Matthew C. Woodhall, Head of School. 203-266-7788. Fax: 203-266-5896. E-mail: mwoodhall@woodhallschool.org. Website: www.woodhallschool.org

THE WOODLANDS CHRISTIAN ACADEMY

5800 Academy Way
The Woodlands, Texas 77384

Head of School: Mrs. Julie Ambler

General Information Coeducational day college-preparatory, arts, religious studies, bilingual studies, and technology school, affiliated with Christian faith. Grades PK–12. Founded: 1993. Setting: suburban. Nearest major city is Houston. 40-acre campus. 6 buildings on campus. Approved or accredited by Association of Christian Schools International, Southern Association of Colleges and Schools, and Texas Department of Education. Member of Secondary School Admission Test Board. Endowment: $100,000. Total enrollment: 579. Upper school average class size: 16. Upper school faculty-student ratio: 1:7. There are 177 required school days per year for Upper School students. Upper School students typically attend 5 days per week. The average school day consists of 7 hours and 30 minutes.

Upper School Student Profile Grade 6: 48 students (23 boys, 25 girls); Grade 7: 37 students (22 boys, 15 girls); Grade 8: 42 students (25 boys, 17 girls); Grade 9: 44 students (26 boys, 18 girls); Grade 10: 47 students (25 boys, 22 girls); Grade 11: 44 students (21 boys, 23 girls); Grade 12: 36 students (21 boys, 15 girls). 100% of students are Christian.

Faculty School total: 62. In upper school: 8 men, 16 women; 11 have advanced degrees.

Subjects Offered Advanced Placement courses, athletics, band, Bible, choir, computer applications, theater arts.

Special Academic Programs Advanced Placement exam preparation; honors section; study at local college for college credit.

College Admission Counseling 36 students graduated in 2015; all went to college, including Baylor University; Oklahoma State University; Texas A&M University; Texas Christian University; Texas Tech University; Wheaton College.

Student Life Upper grades have uniform requirement, student council, honor system. Discipline rests primarily with faculty. Attendance at religious services is required.

Tuition and Aid Day student tuition: $16,495–$18,995. Tuition installment plan (Insured Tuition Payment Plan, FACTS Tuition Payment Plan, monthly payment plans, biannual payment plan). Need-based scholarship grants available. In 2015–16, 10% of upper-school students received aid.

Admissions Traditional secondary-level entrance grade is 9. For fall 2015, 69 students applied for upper-level admission, 44 were accepted, 42 enrolled. ISEE or SSAT, ERB, PSAT, SAT, PLAN or ACT required. Deadline for receipt of application materials: January 28. Application fee required: $275. Interview required.

Athletics Interscholastic: baseball (boys), basketball (b,g), cheering (g), cross-country running (b,g), football (b), golf (b,g), physical training (b,g), softball (g), swimming and diving (b,g), tennis (b,g), track and field (b,g), volleyball (g), weight training (b,g). 4 PE instructors, 17 coaches, 1 athletic trainer.

Computers Computers are regularly used in all academic classes. Computer network features include on-campus library services, Internet access, wireless campus network, Internet filtering or blocking technology. Student e-mail accounts are available to students. Students grades are available online. The school has a published electronic and media policy.

Contact D'Anne Surber, Director of Admissions. 936-273-2555. Fax: 936-271-3115. E-mail: dsurber@twca.net. Website: www.twca.net

WOODLYNDE SCHOOL

445 Upper Gulph Road
Strafford, Pennsylvania 19087

Head of School: Dr. Christopher M. Fulco, EdD

General Information Coeducational day college-preparatory, arts, and technology school; primarily serves students with learning disabilities, individuals with Attention Deficit Disorder, dyslexic students, Executive Function Disorder, and Auditory Processing Disorder. Grades K–12. Founded: 1976. Setting: suburban. Nearest major city is Philadelphia. 8-acre campus. 2 buildings on campus. Approved or accredited by Pennsylvania Association of Independent Schools and Pennsylvania Department of Education. Member of National Association of Independent Schools. Endowment: $559,699. Total enrollment: 270. Upper school average class size: 10. Upper school faculty-student ratio: 1:5. There are 168 required school days per year for Upper School students. Upper School students typically attend 5 days per week. The average school day consists of 6 hours and 55 minutes.

Upper School Student Profile Grade 9: 45 students (30 boys, 15 girls); Grade 10: 32 students (23 boys, 9 girls); Grade 11: 36 students (25 boys, 11 girls); Grade 12: 38 students (22 boys, 16 girls).

Faculty School total: 63. In upper school: 17 men, 19 women; 16 have advanced degrees.

Subjects Offered Advanced Placement courses, algebra, American history, American literature, art, art-AP, arts, biology, chemistry, creative writing, earth science, English, English literature, English-AP, European history, fine arts, French, geometry, government/civics, health, history, journalism, mathematics, music, photography, physical education, physics, political science, psychology, science, sign language, social studies, Spanish, studio art, world history, world literature, writing.

Graduation Requirements Arts and fine arts (art, music, dance, drama), English, foreign language, internship, mathematics, physical education (includes health), science, social studies (includes history), community service, senior project, senior speech.

Special Academic Programs Advanced Placement exam preparation; honors section; study at local college for college credit; remedial reading and/or remedial writing; remedial math; programs in English, mathematics, general development for dyslexic students.

College Admission Counseling 42 students graduated in 2015; 41 went to college, including Albright College; Cabrini College; High Point University; Oberlin College; Saint Joseph's University. Other: 1 entered a postgraduate year.

Student Life Upper grades have uniform requirement, student council. Discipline rests primarily with faculty.

Summer Programs Remediation, enrichment, advancement, sports, art/fine arts programs offered; session focuses on mathematics and reading enrichment; held both on and off campus; held at Camp Nock-A-Mixon; accepts boys and girls; open to students from other schools. 75 students usually enrolled. 2016 schedule: June 20 to July 22. Application deadline: May 30.

Tuition and Aid Day student tuition: $34,000. Tuition installment plan (FACTS Tuition Payment Plan, monthly payment plans). Need-based scholarship grants available. In 2015–16, 38% of upper-school students received aid. Total amount of financial aid awarded in 2015–16: $525,475.

Admissions Traditional secondary-level entrance grade is 9. For fall 2015, 30 students applied for upper-level admission, 20 were accepted, 19 enrolled. Individual IQ required. Deadline for receipt of application materials: none. Application fee required: $100. On-campus interview required.

Athletics Interscholastic: basketball (boys, girls), lacrosse (b,g), softball (g), tennis (b,g), volleyball (g); coed interscholastic: cross-country running, golf, indoor track, soccer; coed intramural: fitness, horseback riding, outdoor adventure, outdoors, physical fitness, strength & conditioning. 3 PE instructors, 12 coaches, 1 athletic trainer.

Computers Computers are regularly used in all academic, art, college planning, creative writing, drawing and design, English, foreign language, French, graphic arts, graphic design, health, history, journalism, Latin, learning cognition, mathematics, music, newspaper, photography, psychology, publications, science, social studies, Spanish, study skills, technology, word processing, writing, writing, yearbook classes. Computer network features include on-campus library services, online commercial services, Internet access, wireless campus network, Internet filtering or blocking technology. Campus intranet and student e-mail accounts are available to students. Students grades are available online. The school has a published electronic and media policy.

Contact Kristen Tabun, Director of Admissions. 610-687-9660 Ext. 624. Fax: 610-687-4752. E-mail: tabun@woodlynde.org. Website: www.woodlynde.org

WOODSIDE PRIORY SCHOOL

302 Portola Road
Founders Hall
Portola Valley, California 94028-7897

Head of School: Mr. Tim J. Molak

General Information Coeducational boarding and day college-preparatory, arts, religious studies, and technology school, affiliated with Roman Catholic Church, Jewish faith. Boarding grades 9–12, day grades 6–12. Founded: 1957. Setting: suburban. Nearest major city is San Francisco/San Jose. Students are housed in single-sex dormitories. 50-acre campus. 25 buildings on campus. Approved or accredited by California Association of Independent Schools, National Catholic Education Association, The Association of Boarding Schools, The College Board, Western Association of Schools and Colleges, Western Catholic Education Association, and California Department of Education. Member of National Association of Independent Schools and Secondary School Admission Test Board. Endowment: $1.3 million. Total enrollment: 386. Upper school average class size: 18. Upper school faculty-student ratio: 1:9. There are 175 required school days per year for Upper School students. Upper School students typically attend 5 days per week. The average school day consists of 6 hours and 30 minutes.

Upper School Student Profile Grade 9: 79 students (41 boys, 38 girls); Grade 10: 70 students (37 boys, 33 girls); Grade 11: 61 students (34 boys, 27 girls); Grade 12: 68 students (29 boys, 39 girls). 18% of students are boarding students. 88% are state residents. 2 states are represented in upper school student body. 12% are international students. International students from China, Hungary, Nigeria, Republic of Korea, Taiwan, and Thailand; 6 other countries represented in student body. 40% of students are Roman Catholic, Jewish.

Faculty School total: 70. In upper school: 28 men, 27 women; 48 have advanced degrees; 16 reside on campus.

Subjects Offered 20th century physics, 3-dimensional art, 3-dimensional design, acting, advanced chemistry, advanced computer applications, advanced math, Advanced Placement courses, advanced studio art-AP, algebra, American democracy, American government, American history, American literature, analysis and differential calculus, animation, architecture, art, art history, art-AP, ASB Leadership, astronomy, Basic programming, biology, biology-AP, British literature, calculus, calculus-AP, ceramics, chemistry, chemistry-AP, choir, choral music, Christian and Hebrew scripture, church history, classics, college admission preparation, college counseling, community garden, community service, comparative cultures, computer applications, computer art, computer graphics, computer math, computer programming, computer science, computer science-AP, computer technologies, computers, constitutional history of U.S., contemporary issues, creative arts, creative writing, desktop publishing, drama, drama performance, earth and space science, earth science, ecology, economics, economics-AP, English, English composition, English literature, English literature-AP, English-AP, environmental science-AP, ethics, European history, European history-AP, expository writing, fine arts, French, French-AP, geography, geometry, government/civics, grammar, health and wellness, history of ideas, honors English, humanities, journalism, keyboarding, life science, mathematics, music, music appreciation, music performance, peer counseling, personal fitness, philosophy, photography, physical education, physics, physics-AP, play production, portfolio art, pre-algebra, pre-calculus, probability and statistics, psychology, religion, science, social sciences, social studies, sociology, Spanish, Spanish language-AP, Spanish literature-AP, speech, studio art-AP, theater, theology, trigonometry, typing, U.S. history-AP, world history, world literature, world religions, writing.

Graduation Requirements 3-dimensional art, algebra, arts and fine arts (art, music, dance, drama), biology, British literature, calculus, chemistry, Christian and Hebrew scripture, comparative religion, computer science, earth science, English, environmental science, expository writing, foreign language, geometry, mathematics, physical education (includes health), physics, science, social sciences, social studies (includes history), theology. Community service is required.

Special Academic Programs 20 Advanced Placement exams for which test preparation is offered; honors section; independent study; academic accommodation for the gifted, the musically talented, and the artistically talented.

College Admission Counseling 65 students graduated in 2015; all went to college, including Massachusetts Institute of Technology; Santa Clara University; Stanford University; University of California, Berkeley; University of California, Los Angeles. Median SAT critical reading: 633, median SAT math: 641, median SAT writing: 653, median combined SAT: 1927. 31% scored over 600 on SAT critical reading, 31% scored over 600 on SAT math, 34% scored over 600 on SAT writing, 32% scored over 1800 on combined SAT.

Student Life Upper grades have specified standards of dress, student council, honor system. Discipline rests primarily with faculty.

Tuition and Aid Day student tuition: $39,900; 7-day tuition and room/board: $59,890. Tuition installment plan (monthly payment plans, individually arranged payment plans). Need-based scholarship grants available. In 2015–16, 21% of upper-school students received aid. Total amount of financial aid awarded in 2015–16: $2,170,538.

Admissions Traditional secondary-level entrance grade is 9. For fall 2015, 369 students applied for upper-level admission, 104 were accepted, 55 enrolled. High School Placement Test (closed version) from Scholastic Testing Service, ISEE, PSAT or SAT for applicants to grade 11 and 12, SSAT, TOEFL or writing sample required. Deadline for receipt of application materials: January 14. Application fee required: $95. On-campus interview required.

Athletics Interscholastic: baseball (boys), basketball (b,g), cross-country running (b,g), flag football (b), football (b), golf (b,g), soccer (b,g), softball (g), swimming and diving (g), track and field (b,g), volleyball (g), water polo (b); intramural: alpine skiing (b,g); coed interscholastic: cross-country running, dance, golf, outdoor education, tennis; coed intramural: alpine skiing, bowling, canoeing/kayaking, cross-country running, fitness, ropes courses. 4 PE instructors, 10 coaches, 1 athletic trainer.

Computers Computers are regularly used in all academic, animation, art, college planning, drafting, library, literary magazine, media arts, research skills, senior seminar, study skills, technology, yearbook classes. Computer network features include on-campus library services, online commercial services, Internet access, wireless campus network, Internet filtering or blocking technology. Campus intranet and student e-mail accounts are available to students. Students grades are available online. The school has a published electronic and media policy.

Contact Mr. Al Zappelli, Dean of Admissions and Financial Aid. 650-851-6101. Fax: 650-851-2839. E-mail: azappelli@prioryca.org. Website: www.PrioryCA.org

WOODSTOCK ACADEMY
57 Academy Rd
Woodstock, Connecticut 06281

Head of School: Mr. Christopher Sandford

General Information Coeducational boarding and day college-preparatory, arts, and technology school; primarily serves students with learning disabilities and individuals with Attention Deficit Disorder. Grades 9–12. Founded: 1801. Setting: rural. Nearest major city is Hartford. Students are housed in host families. 30-acre campus. 6 buildings on campus. Approved or accredited by New England Association of Schools and Colleges and Connecticut Department of Education. Member of National Association of Independent Schools and Secondary School Admission Test Board. Endowment: $3 million. Total enrollment: 1,025. Upper school average class size: 20. Upper school faculty-student ratio: 1:14. There are 182 required school days per year for Upper School students. Upper School students typically attend 5 days per week. The average school day consists of 6 hours and 45 minutes.

Upper School Student Profile Grade 9: 250 students (125 boys, 125 girls); Grade 10: 250 students (125 boys, 125 girls); Grade 11: 250 students (125 boys, 125 girls); Grade 12: 250 students (125 boys, 125 girls). 10% of students are boarding students. 90% are state residents. 3 states are represented in upper school student body. 10% are international students. International students from China, India, Republic of Korea, and Rwanda.

Faculty School total: 90. In upper school: 45 men, 45 women; 75 have advanced degrees.

Special Academic Programs Advanced Placement exam preparation; honors section; independent study; study at local college for college credit; study abroad; academic accommodation for the musically talented and the artistically talented; remedial reading and/or remedial writing; remedial math; ESL (33 students enrolled).

College Admission Counseling 277 students graduated in 2014; 250 went to college, including University of Connecticut. Other: 10 went to work, 7 entered military service, 10 had other specific plans. Mean SAT critical reading: 511, mean SAT math: 511, mean SAT writing: 521.

Student Life Upper grades have specified standards of dress, student council. Discipline rests equally with students and faculty.

Tuition and Aid Day student tuition: $13,500; 7-day tuition and room/board: $44,722. Guaranteed tuition plan. Tuition reduction for siblings, merit scholarship grants, need-based scholarship grants available. In 2014–15, 3% of upper-school students received aid. Total amount of financial aid awarded in 2014–15: $10,000.

Admissions Traditional secondary-level entrance grade is 10. For fall 2014, 215 students applied for upper-level admission, 180 were accepted, 90 enrolled. Deadline for receipt of application materials: none. Application fee required: $100. Interview required.

Athletics Interscholastic: baseball (boys), basketball (b,g), cross-country running (b,g), field hockey (g), football (b), golf (b,g), ice hockey (b), indoor track & field (b,g), lacrosse (b,g), soccer (b,g), softball (g), tennis (b,g), volleyball (b,g), winter (indoor) track (b,g); coed interscholastic: cheering, gymnastics, wrestling; coed intramural: badminton, bicycling, climbing, dance squad, fishing, project adventure, table tennis, ultimate Frisbee, weight lifting. 4 PE instructors, 75 coaches, 1 athletic trainer.

Computers Computer network features include on-campus library services, online commercial services, Internet access, wireless campus network, Internet filtering or blocking technology. Campus intranet and student e-mail accounts are available to students. Students grades are available online. The school has a published electronic and media policy.

Contact Mrs. Amy W. Favreau, Assistant Headmaster for Admissions and Special Programs. 860-928-6575 Ext. 142. Fax: 860-963-7222. E-mail: afavreau@woodstockacademy.org. Website: www.woodstockacademy.org

THE WOODWARD SCHOOL
1102 Hancock Street
Quincy, Massachusetts 02169

Head of School: Carol Andrews, JD

General Information Girls' day college-preparatory, arts, and technology school. Grades 6–12. Founded: 1869. Setting: urban. Nearest major city is Boston. 2-acre campus. 2 buildings on campus. Approved or accredited by Association of Independent Schools in New England, New England Association of Schools and Colleges, and Massachusetts Department of Education. Member of Secondary School Admission Test Board. Total enrollment: 120. Upper school average class size: 12. Upper school faculty-student ratio: 1:8. There are 165 required school days per year for Upper School students. Upper School students typically attend 5 days per week. The average school day consists of 6 hours and 50 minutes.

Upper School Student Profile Grade 9: 18 students (18 girls); Grade 10: 22 students (22 girls); Grade 11: 18 students (18 girls); Grade 12: 19 students (19 girls).

Faculty School total: 21. In upper school: 6 men, 15 women; 15 have advanced degrees.

Subjects Offered Advanced computer applications, algebra, American history, American literature, anatomy, art, arts, biology, calculus, calculus-AP, chemistry, chorus, classical studies, classics, community service, computer graphics, computer math, computer science, computer skills, constitutional law, drama, ecology, English, English language and composition-AP, environmental science, filmmaking, fine arts, French, health and wellness, health science, language arts, Latin, Latin-AP, law and the legal system, literature, literature and composition-AP, mathematics, media studies, music, music appreciation, physics, physics-AP, physiology, political science, portfolio art, pre-algebra, psychology, rhetoric, SAT preparation, science, senior project, social sciences, social studies, sociology, Spanish, study skills, theater arts, U.S. government, U.S. history, Web authoring, Web site design, world history, world literature, World War II, writing.

Graduation Requirements Arts and fine arts (art, music, dance, drama), computer science, English, foreign language, mathematics, science, senior project, social studies (includes history). Community service is required.

Special Academic Programs 5 Advanced Placement exams for which test preparation is offered; honors section; independent study; ESL (15 students enrolled).

College Admission Counseling 18 students graduated in 2015; all went to college, including Boston College; Boston University; Brandeis University; Brown University; Georgetown University; Northeastern University.

Student Life Upper grades have specified standards of dress, student council, honor system. Discipline rests primarily with faculty.

Tuition and Aid Day student tuition: $13,625. Tuition installment plan (SMART Tuition Payment Plan, monthly payment plans, individually arranged payment plans, Tuition Management Systems). Tuition reduction for siblings, merit scholarship grants, need-based scholarship grants, prepGATE K-12 education loan available. In 2015–16, 34% of upper-school students received aid; total upper-school merit-scholarship money awarded: $15,000. Total amount of financial aid awarded in 2015–16: $227,569.

Admissions Traditional secondary-level entrance grade is 9. For fall 2015, 29 students applied for upper-level admission, 27 were accepted, 15 enrolled. ERB, ISEE, school's own exam, SSAT or writing sample required. Deadline for receipt of application materials: none. Application fee required: $50. Interview required.

Athletics Interscholastic: basketball, soccer, softball. 2 PE instructors, 5 coaches, 1 athletic trainer.

Computers Computers are regularly used in all classes. Computer network features include on-campus library services, Internet access, wireless campus network, Internet filtering or blocking technology. Computer access in designated common areas is available to students. The school has a published electronic and media policy.

Contact Katie Carroll, Director of Admissions. 617-773-5610. Fax: 617-770-1551. E-mail: kcarroll@thewoodwardschool.org. Website: www.thewoodwardschool.org

WOOSTER SCHOOL

91 Miry Brook Road
Danbury, Connecticut 06810

Head of School: Mr. Matthew J Byrnes

General Information Coeducational day college-preparatory, arts, and technology school, affiliated with Episcopal Church. Grades PK–12. Founded: 1926. Setting: suburban. 100-acre campus. 15 buildings on campus. Approved or accredited by Connecticut Association of Independent Schools, National Association of Episcopal Schools, New England Association of Schools and Colleges, and Connecticut Department of Education. Member of National Association of Independent Schools. Endowment: $8 million. Total enrollment: 383. Upper school average class size: 12. Upper school faculty-student ratio: 1:10. There are 173 required school days per year for Upper School students. Upper School students typically attend 5 days per week.

Upper School Student Profile Grade 9: 35 students (20 boys, 15 girls); Grade 10: 48 students (29 boys, 19 girls); Grade 11: 32 students (13 boys, 19 girls); Grade 12: 32 students (16 boys, 16 girls).

Faculty School total: 97. In upper school: 13 men, 11 women; 14 have advanced degrees.

Subjects Offered Accounting, algebra, American government, American history, American history-AP, ancient history, Arabic, art, art history-AP, art-AP, biology, biology-AP, calculus, calculus-AP, chemistry, community service, computer animation, computer science, computer science-AP, earth science, economics, English, English literature-AP, English/composition-AP, ESL, ethics, European history-AP, fine arts, French, French-AP, general science, geography, geometry, mathematics, music, music-AP, Pacific art, photography, physical education, physics, political science, pottery, religion, science, social studies, Spanish, Spanish-AP, statistics, statistics-AP, U.S. history-AP.

Graduation Requirements 20th century history, arts and fine arts (art, music, dance, drama), computer science, English, foreign language, mathematics, physical education (includes health), religion (includes Bible studies and theology), science, social studies (includes history), 100 hours of community service, senior independent study and Senior Seminar, Leadership in Self-help (jobs) program.

Special Academic Programs Advanced Placement exam preparation; honors section; accelerated programs; independent study; programs in English, mathematics, general development for dyslexic students.

College Admission Counseling 39 students graduated in 2015; all went to college, including Carnegie Mellon University; Sarah Lawrence College; Skidmore College; Tufts University; Vassar College. Mean SAT critical reading: 626, mean SAT math: 616, mean SAT writing: 638, mean combined SAT: 1881.

Student Life Upper grades have specified standards of dress, student council, honor system. Discipline rests equally with students and faculty. Attendance at religious services is required.

Tuition and Aid Day student tuition: $20,100–$34,350. Tuition installment plan (The Tuition Plan, Insured Tuition Payment Plan, monthly payment plans, individually arranged payment plans, school's own payment plan). Need-based scholarship grants available. In 2015–16, 28% of upper-school students received aid.

Admissions Traditional secondary-level entrance grade is 9. For fall 2015, 66 students applied for upper-level admission, 47 were accepted, 19 enrolled. ISEE or SSAT required. Deadline for receipt of application materials: February 1. Application fee required: $65. On-campus interview required.

Athletics Interscholastic: baseball (boys), basketball (b,g), cross-country running (b,g), football (b), ice hockey (b), lacrosse (b,g), soccer (b,g), tennis (b,g), volleyball (g); intramural: dance (g), weight training (g); coed interscholastic: alpine skiing, Frisbee, golf, outdoor education, skiing (downhill), strength & conditioning, yoga; coed intramural: outdoor education, ropes courses, weight lifting, weight training. 3 PE instructors, 15 coaches, 1 athletic trainer.

Computers Computers are regularly used in all classes. Computer network features include on-campus library services, Internet access, wireless campus network, Internet filtering or blocking technology. Campus intranet, student e-mail accounts, and computer access in designated common areas are available to students. The school has a published electronic and media policy.

Contact Ms. Melissa Haas, Database Manager and Admission Assistant. 203-830-3916. Fax: 203-790-7147. E-mail: melissa.haas@woosterschool.org. Website: www.woosterschool.org

WORCESTER PREPARATORY SCHOOL

508 South Main Street
PO Box 1006
Berlin, Maryland 21811

Head of School: Dr. Barry W. Tull

General Information Coeducational day college-preparatory, arts, and technology school. Grades PK–12. Founded: 1970. Setting: small town. Nearest major city is Ocean City. 45-acre campus. 7 buildings on campus. Approved or accredited by Association of Independent Maryland Schools, Middle States Association of Colleges and Schools, and Maryland Department of Education. Member of National Association of Independent Schools. Total enrollment: 542. Upper school average class size: 15. Upper school faculty-student ratio: 1:9. There are 173 required school days per year for Upper School students. Upper School students typically attend 5 days per week. The average school day consists of 6 hours and 30 minutes.

Upper School Student Profile Grade 6: 42 students (22 boys, 20 girls); Grade 7: 48 students (27 boys, 21 girls); Grade 8: 51 students (24 boys, 27 girls); Grade 9: 54 students (35 boys, 19 girls); Grade 10: 51 students (15 boys, 36 girls); Grade 11: 55 students (29 boys, 26 girls); Grade 12: 47 students (24 boys, 23 girls).

Faculty School total: 62. In upper school: 12 men, 22 women; 29 have advanced degrees.

Subjects Offered Advanced Placement courses, algebra, American history, American literature, art, art history, biology, biology-AP, calculus, calculus-AP, chemistry, chemistry-AP, computer programming, computer programming-AP, computer science, computer science-AP, creative writing, dance, dance performance, digital applications, digital photography, drama, earth science, economics, English, English literature, English literature and composition-AP, English-AP, European history, fine arts, French, geography, geometry, government/civics, keyboarding, Latin, literature and composition-AP, literature-AP, mathematics, music, music theory, physical education, physics, physics-AP, programming, psychology, SAT preparation, science, social sciences, social studies, Spanish, speech, statistics, technological applications, technology/design, theater, U.S. history-AP, vocal music, world history, world history-AP, world literature, writing.

Graduation Requirements Art appreciation, arts and fine arts (art, music, dance, drama), computer science, English, foreign language, mathematics, music appreciation, physical education (includes health), science, social sciences.

Special Academic Programs 9 Advanced Placement exams for which test preparation is offered; honors section; independent study; academic accommodation for the gifted, the musically talented, and the artistically talented.

College Admission Counseling 47 students graduated in 2015; all went to college, including College of Charleston; Cornell University; Tufts University; University of Delaware; University of Maryland, College Park; University of Virginia.

Student Life Upper grades have uniform requirement, student council, honor system. Discipline rests primarily with faculty.

Tuition and Aid Day student tuition: $14,100. Tuition installment plan (The Tuition Plan, Insured Tuition Payment Plan, monthly payment plans, individually arranged payment plans). Need-based scholarship grants available. In 2015–16, 1% of upper-school students received aid.

Admissions Traditional secondary-level entrance grade is 9. For fall 2015, 21 students applied for upper-level admission, 16 were accepted, 14 enrolled. Achievement/Aptitude/Writing and writing sample required. Deadline for receipt of application materials: none. Application fee required: $50. On-campus interview required.

Athletics Interscholastic: basketball (boys, girls), cross-country running (b,g), field hockey (g), lacrosse (b,g), soccer (b,g), tennis (b,g), volleyball (g), weight training (b,g), winter soccer (b,g); intramural: basketball (b,g), dance (b,g), dance squad (b,g), flag football (b,g), soccer (b,g); coed interscholastic: cheering, golf, tennis; coed intramural: dance, dance squad. 3 PE instructors, 21 coaches, 1 athletic trainer.

Computers Computers are regularly used in all classes. Computer network features include on-campus library services, online commercial services, Internet access, wireless campus network, Internet filtering or blocking technology. Campus intranet, student e-mail accounts, and computer access in designated common areas are available to students. The school has a published electronic and media policy.

Contact Tara F. Becker, Director of Admissions. 410-641-3575 Ext. 107. Fax: 410-641-3586. E-mail: tbecker@worcesterprep.org. Website: www.worcesterprep.org

WYOMING SEMINARY

201 North Sprague Avenue
Kingston, Pennsylvania 18704-3593

Head of School: Mr. Kevin Rea

General Information Coeducational boarding and day college-preparatory school, affiliated with United Methodist Church. Grades 9–PG. Founded: 1844. Setting: suburban. Nearest major city is Wilkes-Barre. Students are housed in single-sex dormitories. 22-acre campus. 13 buildings on campus. Approved or accredited by Middle States Association of Colleges and Schools, Pennsylvania Association of Independent Schools, The Association of Boarding Schools, The College Board, University Senate of United Methodist Church, and Pennsylvania Department of Education. Member of National Association of Independent Schools and Secondary School Admission Test Board. Endowment: $56.7 million. Total enrollment: 790. Upper school average class size: 13. Upper school faculty-student ratio: 1:8. There are 170 required school days per year for Upper School students. Upper School students typically attend 5 days per week. The average school day consists of 7 hours.

Upper School Student Profile Grade 9: 89 students (49 boys, 40 girls); Grade 10: 104 students (58 boys, 46 girls); Grade 11: 127 students (77 boys, 50 girls); Grade 12: 109 students (50 boys, 59 girls); Postgraduate: 13 students (11 boys, 2 girls). 28% of students are boarding students. 63% are state residents. 19 states are represented in upper school student body. 25% are international students. International students from Canada, China, Japan, Republic of Korea, Taiwan, and Viet Nam; 11 other countries represented in student body. 10% of students are United Methodist Church.

Faculty School total: 58. In upper school: 31 men, 27 women; 46 have advanced degrees; 35 reside on campus.

Subjects Offered 20th century world history, 3-dimensional design, algebra, alternative physical education, American Civil War, American history, American literature, analysis and differential calculus, analytic geometry, anatomy and physiology, ancient world history, art, art appreciation, art history, art history-AP, Bible studies, biology, biology-AP, botany, British literature, calculus, calculus-AP, ceramics, chemistry, chemistry-AP, choral music, college admission preparation, college counseling, computer programming, computer science, conceptual physics, creative writing, critical writing, discrete mathematics, drama, drawing and design, ecology, English, English literature, environmental science, environmental science-AP, ESL, European history, European history-AP, expository writing, fine arts, forensics, French, French-AP, geometry, health education, history, history of music, independent study, Judaic studies, Latin, Latin-AP, mathematics, music, music theory, music theory-AP, philosophy, photography, physics, poetry, pre-calculus, printmaking, psychology, psychology-AP, public speaking, religion, Russian, science, science research, Shakespeare, social studies, sociology, Spanish, Spanish-AP, statistics, statistics-AP, studio art-AP, theater, trigonometry, U.S. government and politics-AP, U.S. history-AP, women in literature, world civilizations, world cultures, world history, world literature, world religions, World War II, zoology.

Graduation Requirements Art history, Bible as literature, biology, computer science, English, foreign language, health education, mathematics, music history, physical education (includes health), public speaking, science, social studies (includes history), U.S. history, world civilizations, 40 hours of community service, extracurricular participation.

Special Academic Programs 21 Advanced Placement exams for which test preparation is offered; honors section; independent study; term-away projects; study at local college for college credit; study abroad; ESL (47 students enrolled).

College Admission Counseling 120 students graduated in 2015; 119 went to college, including Columbia University; Cornell University; New York University; United States Naval Academy; University of Pennsylvania; University of Pittsburgh. Other: 1 went to work. Mean SAT critical reading: 598, mean SAT math: 638, mean SAT writing: 610, mean combined SAT: 1846, mean composite ACT: 26.

Student Life Upper grades have specified standards of dress, student council, honor system. Discipline rests equally with students and faculty.

Summer Programs Enrichment, advancement, ESL, sports, art/fine arts programs offered; session focuses on performing arts and ESL; held on campus; accepts boys and girls; open to students from other schools. 400 students usually enrolled. 2016 schedule: June 22 to August 12. Application deadline: June 1.

Tuition and Aid Day student tuition: $23,700; 7-day tuition and room/board: $48,900. Tuition installment plan (FACTS Tuition Payment Plan, monthly payment plans). Merit scholarship grants, need-based scholarship grants, need-based loans, prepGATE loans, Your Tuition Solution available. In 2015–16, 47% of upper-school students received aid; total upper-school merit-scholarship money awarded: $400,000. Total amount of financial aid awarded in 2015–16: $6,500,000.

Admissions Traditional secondary-level entrance grade is 9. For fall 2015, 571 students applied for upper-level admission, 373 were accepted, 195 enrolled. ACT, PSAT or SAT for applicants to grade 11 and 12, SSAT or TOEFL or SLEP required. Deadline for receipt of application materials: none. Application fee required: $75. Interview required.

Athletics Interscholastic: baseball (boys), basketball (b,g), cross-country running (b,g), diving (b,g), field hockey (g), football (b), ice hockey (b,g), lacrosse (b,g), soccer (b,g), softball (g), swimming and diving (b,g), tennis (b,g), wrestling (b); coed interscholastic: golf, strength & conditioning; coed intramural: ballet, combined training, dance, fitness, martial arts, modern dance, outdoor activities, outdoor recreation, physical training, wall climbing. 2 PE instructors, 6 coaches, 2 athletic trainers.

Computers Computers are regularly used in art, English, foreign language, history, mathematics, music, science classes. Computer network features include on-campus library services, online commercial services, Internet access, wireless campus network, Internet filtering or blocking technology. Campus intranet, student e-mail accounts, and computer access in designated common areas are available to students. Students grades are available online. The school has a published electronic and media policy.

Contact Mr. Eric Turner, Director of Enrollment Management. 570-270-2160. Fax: 570-270-2191. E-mail: admission@wyomingseminary.org. Website: www.wyomingseminary.org

XAVIER COLLEGE PREPARATORY

4710 North Fifth Street
Phoenix, Arizona 85012

Head of School: Sr. Joan Fitzgerald, BVM

General Information Girls' day college-preparatory, arts, religious studies, technology, Great Books, Advanced Placement, Dual College Enrollment, and STEM education school, affiliated with Roman Catholic Church. Grades 9–12. Founded: 1943. Setting: urban. 20-acre campus. 10 buildings on campus. Approved or accredited by National Catholic Education Association, North Central Association of Colleges and Schools, Western Catholic Education Association, and Arizona Department of Education. Endowment: $2.5 million. Total enrollment: 1,196. Upper school average class size: 24. Upper school faculty-student ratio: 1:22. There are 181 required school days per year for Upper School students. Upper School students typically attend 5 days per week. The average school day consists of 5 hours.

Upper School Student Profile Grade 9: 308 students (308 girls); Grade 10: 315 students (315 girls); Grade 11: 287 students (287 girls); Grade 12: 286 students (286 girls). 75% of students are Roman Catholic.

Faculty School total: 95. In upper school: 20 men, 75 women; 70 have advanced degrees.

Subjects Offered Accounting, advanced biology, advanced chemistry, advanced computer applications, advanced math, Advanced Placement courses, advanced studio art-AP, algebra, American government, American history, American history-AP, American literature, analysis and differential calculus, anatomy, anatomy and physiology, architecture, art, art history, art history-AP, astronomy, athletic training, audition methods, band, Basic programming, biology, biology-AP, calculus, calculus-AP, ceramics, cheerleading, chemistry, chemistry-AP, child development, Chinese, choir, church history, community service, computer programming-AP, computer science, computer studies, concert choir, contemporary issues, dance, dance performance, digital photography, drama, economics, English, English language and composition-AP, English literature-AP, environmental science-AP, ethics, European history-AP, family and consumer science, film studies, fine arts, French, French language-AP, geography, geometry, graphic design, great books, jazz band, Latin, Latin-AP, music, music theory-AP, musical theater, New Testament, newspaper, philosophy, physical education, physics, physics-AP, pre-calculus, psychology, sociology, Spanish, Spanish language-AP, Spanish literature-AP, sports medicine, stagecraft, statistics-AP, student government, theology, trigonometry, U.S. government and politics-AP, video and animation, visual arts, weight training, world history-AP, world literature.

Graduation Requirements American literature, arts and fine arts (art, music, dance, drama), computer programming, English, English literature-AP, foreign language, mathematics, physical education (includes health), religion (includes Bible studies and theology), science, social studies (includes history), Arizona History and Free Enterprise independent study, summer reading program, 50 hours of community service.

Special Academic Programs 24 Advanced Placement exams for which test preparation is offered; honors section; independent study; study at local college for college credit; study abroad; academic accommodation for the gifted and the artistically talented.

College Admission Counseling 286 students graduated in 2015; all went to college, including Arizona State University at the Tempe campus; Creighton University; Northern Arizona University; Santa Clara University; The University of Arizona; University of Southern California. Median composite ACT: 26. Mean SAT critical reading: 572, mean SAT math: 550, mean SAT writing: 567.

Student Life Upper grades have uniform requirement, student council, honor system. Discipline rests primarily with faculty. Attendance at religious services is required.

Summer Programs Enrichment, advancement, sports, art/fine arts, computer instruction programs offered; session focuses on academic advancement; held on campus; accepts girls; not open to students from other schools. 700 students usually enrolled. 2016 schedule: May 23 to June 29. Application deadline: April 1.

Tuition and Aid Day student tuition: $14,316–$18,312. Tuition installment plan (monthly payment plans, semester payment plan). Need-based scholarship grants, reduced tuition rate for Catholic families registered in Catholic parishes of the Diocese of Phoenix available. In 2015–16, 40% of upper-school students received aid. Total amount of financial aid awarded in 2015–16: $2,000,000.

Admissions Traditional secondary-level entrance grade is 9. For fall 2015, 500 students applied for upper-level admission, 360 were accepted, 325 enrolled. High

School Placement Test required. Deadline for receipt of application materials: January 28. Application fee required: $50.

Athletics Interscholastic: aerobics/dance, badminton, basketball, cheering, crew, cross-country running, dance squad, dance team, danceline, diving, golf, lacrosse, pom squad, rowing, sand volleyball, soccer, softball, swimming and diving, tennis, track and field, volleyball, winter soccer; intramural: archery, crew, dance, fitness, floor hockey, modern dance, skeet shooting, strength & conditioning, tennis, weight training, yoga; coed interscholastic: ice hockey; coed intramural: flag football, mountain biking, tennis, volleyball. 4 PE instructors, 30 coaches, 2 athletic trainers.

Computers Computers are regularly used in all classes. Computer network features include on-campus library services, online commercial services, Internet access, wireless campus network, Internet filtering or blocking technology, Canvas, Naviance, Google Apps for Education. Student e-mail accounts and computer access in designated common areas are available to students. Students grades are available online. The school has a published electronic and media policy.

Contact Mrs. Paula Petrowski, Director of Admissions. 602-277-3772 Ext. 3104. Fax: 602-240-3175. E-mail: ppetrowski@xcp.org. Website: www.xcp.org

YOKOHAMA INTERNATIONAL SCHOOL

258 Yamate-cho, Naka-ku
Yokohama 231-0862, Japan

Head of School: Mr. Craig Coutts

General Information Coeducational day college-preparatory, arts, bilingual studies, and technology school. Grades N–12. Founded: 1924. Setting: urban. 3-acre campus. 8 buildings on campus. Approved or accredited by Council of International Schools, International Baccalaureate Organization, and New England Association of Schools and Colleges. Language of instruction: English. Total enrollment: 644. Upper school average class size: 18. Upper school faculty-student ratio: 1:8. There are 179 required school days per year for Upper School students. Upper School students typically attend 5 days per week. The average school day consists of 7 hours.

Upper School Student Profile Grade 6: 39 students (19 boys, 20 girls); Grade 7: 53 students (28 boys, 25 girls); Grade 8: 61 students (32 boys, 29 girls); Grade 9: 63 students (37 boys, 26 girls); Grade 10: 60 students (34 boys, 26 girls); Grade 11: 55 students (29 boys, 26 girls); Grade 12: 66 students (39 boys, 27 girls).

Faculty School total: 78. In upper school: 25 men, 23 women; 27 have advanced degrees.

Subjects Offered Advanced chemistry, advanced math, art, band, biology, chemistry, choir, dance, drama, Dutch, economics, English, English literature, environmental science, French, geography, German, International Baccalaureate courses, Japanese, mathematics, modern languages, music composition, music theory, physical education, physics, psychology, Spanish, studio art, theater, theater arts, theory of knowledge, world history, world literature.

Graduation Requirements Arts, English, foreign language, information technology, mathematics, physical education (includes health), science, senior thesis, social studies (includes history), theory of knowledge.

Special Academic Programs International Baccalaureate program; ESL.

College Admission Counseling 56 students graduated in 2014; 50 went to college, including Berklee College of Music; Johns Hopkins University; New York University; Princeton University; University of Southern California. Other: 6 had other specific plans. Mean SAT critical reading: 537, mean SAT math: 585, mean SAT writing: 538.

Student Life Upper grades have specified standards of dress, student council. Discipline rests primarily with faculty.

Tuition and Aid Day student tuition: ¥2,498,000.

Admissions Traditional secondary-level entrance grade is 9. For fall 2014, 123 students applied for upper-level admission, 108 were accepted, 85 enrolled. School's own test required. Deadline for receipt of application materials: none. Application fee required: ¥20,000. Interview recommended.

Athletics Interscholastic: baseball (boys), basketball (b,g), cross-country running (b,g), field hockey (g), soccer (b,g), track and field (b,g), volleyball (b,g); coed interscholastic: tennis; coed intramural: skateboarding, yoga. 4 PE instructors.

Computers Computers are regularly used in all academic classes. Computer network features include on-campus library services, online commercial services, Internet access, wireless campus network, Internet filtering or blocking technology. Campus intranet, student e-mail accounts, and computer access in designated common areas are available to students. Students grades are available online. The school has a published electronic and media policy.

Contact Ms. Susan Chen, Administrative Officer. 81-45-622-0084. Fax: 81-45-621-0379. E-mail: admissions@yis.ac.jp. Website: www.yis.ac.jp

YORK COUNTRY DAY SCHOOL

1071 Regents Glen Boulevard
York, Pennsylvania 17403

Head of School: Dr. Christine Heine

General Information Coeducational day college-preparatory, arts, and bilingual studies school. Grades PS–12. Founded: 1953. Setting: suburban. Nearest major city is Baltimore, MD. 15-acre campus. 1 building on campus. Approved or accredited by Middle States Association of Colleges and Schools, National Independent Private Schools Association, Pennsylvania Association of Independent Schools, and Pennsylvania Department of Education. Member of National Association of Independent Schools. Endowment: $1.3 million. Total enrollment: 246. Upper school average class size: 12. Upper school faculty-student ratio: 1:6. There are 170 required school days per year for Upper School students. Upper School students typically attend 5 days per week. The average school day consists of 7 hours and 30 minutes.

Upper School Student Profile Grade 9: 16 students (11 boys, 5 girls); Grade 10: 18 students (13 boys, 5 girls); Grade 11: 14 students (9 boys, 5 girls); Grade 12: 15 students (5 boys, 10 girls).

Faculty School total: 42. In upper school: 10 men, 9 women; 15 have advanced degrees.

Subjects Offered Advanced biology, advanced chemistry, advanced studio art-AP, algebra, American history, American literature, art, art history, biochemistry, biology, calculus, chemistry, choral music, community service, creative writing, drama, English, English literature, European history, fine arts, French, geography, geometry, government/civics, health, history, Latin, literature, mathematics, music, physical education, physics, psychology, public speaking, robotics, SAT preparation, science, social studies, Spanish, studio art-AP, theater, world history, yearbook.

Graduation Requirements Arts and fine arts (art, music, dance, drama), English, foreign language, history, independent study, mathematics, physical education (includes health), public speaking, science, visual arts, 4 college classes. Community service is required.

Special Academic Programs Advanced Placement exam preparation; honors section; independent study; study at local college for college credit; academic accommodation for the gifted, the musically talented, and the artistically talented.

College Admission Counseling 12 students graduated in 2015; all went to college, including American University; Gettysburg College; Penn State University Park; University of Pittsburgh; University of Richmond; Ursinus College. Mean SAT critical reading: 537, mean SAT math: 552, mean SAT writing: 533, mean combined SAT: 1638.

Student Life Upper grades have specified standards of dress, student council, honor system. Discipline rests equally with students and faculty.

Summer Programs Sports, art/fine arts programs offered; session focuses on providing sports, arts, crafts, and swimming; held off campus; held at York College of Pennsylvania; accepts boys and girls; open to students from other schools. 35 students usually enrolled. 2016 schedule: June 20 to July 31. Application deadline: June 15.

Tuition and Aid Day student tuition: $19,530. Tuition installment plan (Insured Tuition Payment Plan, monthly payment plans, semester payment plan). Need-based scholarship grants available. In 2015–16, 41% of upper-school students received aid. Total amount of financial aid awarded in 2015–16: $339,000.

Admissions Traditional secondary level entrance grade is 9. Academic Profile Tests, ISEE or PSAT and SAT for applicants to grade 11 and 12 required. Deadline for receipt of application materials: none. Application fee required: $35. On-campus interview required.

Athletics Interscholastic: baseball (boys), basketball (b,g), cross-country running (b,g), field hockey (g), football (b), golf (b,g), soccer (b,g), softball (g), swimming and diving (b,g), tennis (b,g), volleyball (g), wrestling (b); intramural: basketball (b,g), soccer (b,g); coed intramural: soccer. 2 PE instructors, 6 coaches.

Computers Computers are regularly used in all academic classes. Computer network features include on-campus library services, online commercial services, Internet access, wireless campus network, Internet filtering or blocking technology. Student e-mail accounts are available to students. Students grades are available online.

Contact Mrs. Hannah Holliway, Director of Admission and Financial Aid. 717-815-6700. Fax: 717-815-6769. E-mail: hholliwa@ycds.org. Website: www.ycds.org

YORK PREPARATORY SCHOOL

40 West 68th Street
New York, New York 10023-6092

General Information Coeducational day college-preparatory, arts, technology, music (practical and theory), and drama school. Grades 6–12. Founded: 1969. Setting: urban. 1 building on campus. Approved or accredited by Middle States Association of Colleges and Schools, National Independent Private Schools Association, and New York Department of Education. Member of National Association of Independent Schools. Total enrollment: 358. Upper school average class size: 15. Upper school faculty-student ratio: 1:6. There are 158 required school days per year for Upper School students. Upper School students typically attend 5 days per week. The average school day consists of 6 hours and 30 minutes.

See Display on next page and Close-Up on page 624.

YORK SCHOOL

9501 York Road
Monterey, California 93940

Head of School: Chuck Harmon

General Information Coeducational day college-preparatory, arts, bilingual studies, and technology school. Grades 8–12. Founded: 1959. Setting: suburban. Nearest major city is San Jose. 126-acre campus. 6 buildings on campus. Approved or accredited by California Association of Independent Schools, National Association of Episcopal Schools, Western Association of Schools and Colleges, and California Department of Education. Member of National Association of Independent Schools. Endowment: $8 million. Total enrollment: 228. Upper school average class size: 13. Upper school faculty-student ratio: 1:7. Upper School students typically attend 5 days per week. The average school day consists of 7 hours.

Upper School Student Profile Grade 8: 22 students (9 boys, 13 girls); Grade 9: 55 students (25 boys, 30 girls); Grade 10: 56 students (20 boys, 36 girls); Grade 11: 55 students (22 boys, 33 girls); Grade 12: 50 students (24 boys, 26 girls).

Faculty School total: 33. In upper school: 18 men, 15 women; 26 have advanced degrees.

Subjects Offered Advanced studio art-AP, algebra, American history-AP, anatomy, ancient history, art, art history, Asian history, band, biology, biology-AP, calculus, calculus-AP, chemistry, chemistry-AP, choir, community service, computer science, creative writing, digital art, drama, English, English-AP, environmental science, film, fine arts, French, French language-AP, geometry, Greek, jazz, Latin, Latin-AP, marine biology, mathematics, music, music theory-AP, orchestra, painting, philosophy, photography, physical education, physical science, physics, physics-AP, physiology, pre-calculus, psychology-AP, science, social studies, Spanish, Spanish language-AP, statistics, studio art, U.S. history, U.S. history-AP, world history, yearbook.

Graduation Requirements Arts and fine arts (art, music, dance, drama), computer science, English, foreign language, mathematics, physical education (includes health), science, social studies (includes history), ensemble participation. Community service is required.

Special Academic Programs Advanced Placement exam preparation; honors section; independent study.

College Admission Counseling 47 students graduated in 2015; all went to college, including California Polytechnic State University, San Luis Obispo; University of California, Santa Barbara. Mean SAT critical reading: 649, mean SAT math: 635, mean SAT writing: 616, mean combined SAT: 1900.

Student Life Upper grades have specified standards of dress, student council, honor system. Discipline rests primarily with faculty.

Tuition and Aid Day student tuition: $31,150. Tuition installment plan (individually arranged payment plans, 2 payments, 10 payments). Need-based scholarship grants available. In 2015–16, 42% of upper-school students received aid. Total amount of financial aid awarded in 2015–16: $1,436,650.

Admissions Traditional secondary-level entrance grade is 9. For fall 2015, 115 students applied for upper-level admission, 92 were accepted, 61 enrolled. Admissions testing required. Deadline for receipt of application materials: February 1. Application fee required: $80. Interview required.

Athletics Interscholastic: basketball (boys, girls), cross-country running (b,g), diving (b,g), field hockcy (g), golf (b,g), soccer (b,g), softball (g), swimming and diving (b,g), tennis (b,g), volleyball (g); coed interscholastic: dance, lacrosse; coed intramural: badminton, basketball, fitness walking, independent competitive sports, jogging, soccer, ultimate Frisbee, volleyball, walking, weight training, yoga. 18 coaches.

Computers Computers are regularly used in art, computer applications, technology, yearbook classes. Computer network features include on-campus library services, Internet access, wireless campus network. The school has a published electronic and media policy.

Contact Rebecca Geldmacher, Admission Associate and Registrar. 831-372-7338 Ext. 116. Fax: 831-372-8055. E-mail: becca@york.org. Website: www.york.org

THE YORK SCHOOL

1320 Yonge Street
Toronto, Ontario M4T 1X2, Canada

Head of School: Mr. Conor Jones

General Information Coeducational day college-preparatory and International Baccalaureate school. Grades JK–12. Founded: 1965. Setting: urban. 1-acre campus. 1 building on campus. Approved or accredited by Canadian Association of Independent Schools, Canadian Educational Standards Institute, Conference of Independent Schools of Ontario, International Baccalaureate Organization, and Ontario Department of Education. Member of Secondary School Admission Test Board. Language of instruction: English. Total enrollment: 600. Upper school average class size: 18. Upper school faculty-student ratio: 1:16. Upper School students typically attend 5 days per week. The average school day consists of 7 hours.

Faculty School total: 80. In upper school: 12 men, 20 women.

Subjects Offered 20th century history, American history, biology, calculus, Canadian geography, Canadian history, Canadian law, careers, chemistry, civics, discrete mathematics, dramatic arts, economics, English, environmental systems, French, functions, geography, geometry, global issues, healthful living, instrumental music,

Mandarin, physical education, physics, social sciences, society challenge and change, Spanish, theater arts, theory of knowledge, visual arts, vocal music, world history, world religions.

Graduation Requirements International Baccalaureate diploma exams.

Special Academic Programs International Baccalaureate program; honors section; independent study; study abroad; academic accommodation for the gifted, the musically talented, and the artistically talented.

College Admission Counseling 66 students graduated in 2015; all went to college, including Dalhousie University; McGill University; Queen's University at Kingston; The University of British Columbia; The University of Western Ontario; University of Toronto.

Student Life Upper grades have uniform requirement, student council, honor system. Discipline rests primarily with faculty.

Tuition and Aid Day student tuition: CAN$27,000. Tuition installment plan (monthly payment plans, individually arranged payment plans). Merit scholarship grants, need-based scholarship grants available. In 2015–16, 5% of upper-school students received aid.

Admissions Traditional secondary-level entrance grade is 9. For fall 2015, 100 students applied for upper-level admission, 81 were accepted, 34 enrolled. School's own exam required. Deadline for receipt of application materials: December 4. Application fee required: CAN$200. Interview recommended.

Athletics Interscholastic: aerobics/dance (boys, girls), aerobics/Nautilus (b,g), alpine skiing (b,g), badminton (b,g), baseball (b,g), basketball (b,g), cooperative games (b,g), cross-country running (b,g), fitness (b,g), floor hockey (b,g), outdoor activities (b,g), outdoor education (b,g), running (b,g), soccer (b,g), softball (b,g), strength & conditioning (b,g), track and field (b,g); intramural: aerobics/Nautilus (b,g), badminton (b,g), baseball (b,g), basketball (b,g), outdoor education (b,g), volleyball (b,g); coed interscholastic: badminton, cooperative games, cross-country running, floor hockey, ice skating, outdoor activities, outdoor education, running, strength & conditioning, track and field, ultimate Frisbee; coed intramural: backpacking, badminton, curling, Frisbee, hiking/backpacking, outdoor adventure, outdoor education, outdoor skills, track and field, ultimate Frisbee. 4 PE instructors.

Computers Computers are regularly used in all academic classes. Computer network features include on-campus library services, Internet access, wireless campus network, Internet filtering or blocking technology. Campus intranet, student e-mail accounts, and computer access in designated common areas are available to students. Students grades are available online. The school has a published electronic and media policy.

Contact Ms. Julia Gordon, Admission Assistant. 416-646-5275. Fax: 416-926-9592. E-mail: admission@yorkschool.com. Website: www.yorkschool.com

ZURICH INTERNATIONAL SCHOOL

Steinacherstrasse 140
Wädenswil 8820, Switzerland

Head of School: Jeff Paulson

General Information Coeducational day college-preparatory, technology, and International Baccalaureate Diploma and Advanced Placement school. Grades PS–13. Founded: 1963. Setting: suburban. Nearest major city is Zurich, Switzerland. 6-acre campus. 1 building on campus. Approved or accredited by International Baccalaureate Organization, New England Association of Schools and Colleges, and Swiss Federation of Private Schools. Member of European Council of International Schools. Language of instruction: English. Total enrollment: 1,422. Upper school average class size: 16. Upper school faculty-student ratio: 1:7. There are 175 required school days per year for Upper School students. Upper School students typically attend 5 days per week. The average school day consists of 7 hours.

Upper School Student Profile Grade 9: 124 students (66 boys, 58 girls); Grade 10: 124 students (57 boys, 67 girls); Grade 11: 137 students (70 boys, 67 girls); Grade 12: 112 students (50 boys, 62 girls).

Faculty School total: 224. In upper school: 33 men, 37 women; 40 have advanced degrees.

Subjects Offered Acting, Advanced Placement courses, art history, art history-AP, art-AP, biology, biology-AP, calculus, calculus-AP, chemistry-AP, computer programming-AP, concert band, concert choir, digital photography, drama, drama performance, economics, economics-AP, English, English language and composition-AP, English literature, English literature and composition-AP, ESL, European history-AP, fine arts, French, French language-AP, German, German-AP, health, history, history-AP, International Baccalaureate courses, journalism, macro/microeconomics-AP, macroeconomics-AP, mathematics, microeconomics-AP, music, philosophy, photography, physical education, physics-AP, pre-calculus, psychology-AP, public speaking, robotics, science, social studies, Spanish language-AP, statistics-AP, studio art, studio art-AP, theater, U.S. history-AP, visual arts, world history, world history-AP, writing.

Graduation Requirements Arts and fine arts (art, music, dance, drama), English, foreign language, mathematics, physical education (includes health), science, social studies (includes history), completion of a yearly service project. Community service is required.

Special Academic Programs International Baccalaureate program; 22 Advanced Placement exams for which test preparation is offered; honors section; independent study; remedial reading and/or remedial writing; remedial math; ESL (12 students enrolled).

College Admission Counseling 111 students graduated in 2015; 100 went to college, including Calvin College; Cornell University; Florida Institute of Technology; Northwestern University; Syracuse University; University of California, Los Angeles. Other: 2 went to work, 4 entered military service, 5 had other specific plans. Mean SAT critical reading: 579, mean SAT math: 595, mean SAT writing: 577, mean combined SAT: 1751. 36% scored over 600 on SAT critical reading, 46% scored over 600 on SAT math, 36% scored over 600 on SAT writing.

Student Life Upper grades have specified standards of dress, student council. Discipline rests primarily with faculty.

Summer Programs Held both on and off campus; held at in and around the greater Zurich area; accepts boys and girls; open to students from other schools.

Tuition and Aid Day student tuition: 33,900 Swiss francs. Tuition installment plan (monthly payment plans). Need-based scholarship grants available. In 2015–16, 2% of upper-school students received aid. Total amount of financial aid awarded in 2015–16: 27,000 Swiss francs.

Admissions Traditional secondary-level entrance grade is 9. For fall 2015, 139 students applied for upper-level admission, 86 were accepted, 64 enrolled. English for Non-native Speakers or math and English placement tests required. Deadline for receipt of application materials: none. Application fee required: 500 Swiss francs.

Athletics Interscholastic: basketball (boys, girls), rugby (b), soccer (b,g), softball (g), tennis (b,g), volleyball (g); coed interscholastic: alpine skiing, cross-country running, Frisbee, golf, nordic skiing, skiing (cross-country), skiing (downhill), swimming and diving, track and field, ultimate Frisbee; coed intramural: basketball, canoeing/kayaking, climbing, fitness, Frisbee, hiking/backpacking, indoor soccer, indoor track & field, juggling, kayaking, outdoor activities, rock climbing, running, snowboarding, wall climbing, yoga. 5 PE instructors, 8 coaches.

Computers Computers are regularly used in all classes. Computer network features include on-campus library services, online commercial services, Internet access, wireless campus network, one-to-one tablet program, Moodle, VHS, MAC lab, iPad pilot in upper school. Campus intranet, student e-mail accounts, and computer access in designated common areas are available to students. Students grades are available online. The school has a published electronic and media policy.

Contact James Cooper, Head Admissions. 41-58 750 2531. Fax: 41-58 750 2501. E-mail: jcooper@zis.ch. Website: www.zis.ch

Traditional Day and Boarding School Close-Ups

AMERICAN HERITAGE SCHOOL

Plantation and Delray Beach, Florida

Type: Coeducational, day, independent, nonsectarian
Grades: PK-3–Grade 12
Enrollment: 2,400—Plantation campus; 1,300—Boca/Delray campus
Head of School: William Laurie, President and Founder

THE SCHOOL
American Heritage School's mission is to graduate students who are prepared in mind, body, and spirit to meet the requirements of the colleges of their choice. To this end, American Heritage School strives to offer a challenging college preparatory curriculum, opportunities for leadership, and superior programs in the arts and athletics. American Heritage is committed to providing a safe and nurturing environment for learning so that children of average to gifted intelligence may achieve their full potential to be intelligent, creative, and contributing members of society. Students receive a well-rounded education that provides opportunities for leadership; character building; and growth in academics, new technology, the arts, and athletics.

ACADEMIC PROGRAM
The curriculum for the pre-primary child is developmental and age appropriate at each level. Daily language, speech, and auditory development activities help children to listen, understand, speak, and learn effectively. The program seeks to maximize the academic potential of each child, while fostering a positive self-image and providing the skills necessary for the next level of education.

The Lower School is committed to developing a student's basic skills, helping the student master content areas, and maintaining the student's enthusiasm for learning. Students learn the fundamentals of reading, process writing, mathematics, and English through a logical progressive sequence, and they learn social studies, handwriting, spelling, science, and health, with an emphasis on the development of good study skills. In math, language arts, and science, students are grouped at different grade levels according to ability. The Stanford University math program is offered for accelerated math students in fourth through sixth grades.

In 2016, American Heritage Lower School was the **#1 private school in elementary math competition in the state of Florida,** and one out of four students in fifth and sixth grade qualified for Duke University's Talent Identification Program.

The core curriculum is supplemented with over fifteen elective classes integrated into all students' daily schedules, including computer education, investigative science lab, library and media center, Spanish, Chinese, 2-D and 3-D art, music, drama, dance, chorus, orchestra, band, and physical education. Field trips, special projects and events, and assemblies supplement the work introduced in class.

In junior high school, **two students are in the top 1 percent in the nation in math, and the Geometry Team is #1 in Central and South Florida.** Math, reading, grammar, literature, social studies, and science are the core subjects of the curriculum, where critical-thinking skills become increasingly important. Writing skills are emphasized, helping students become literate and articulate thinkers and writers. Enrichment courses are an important part of the junior high curriculum, with courses rotated on a nine-week basis. Honors classes are available in all core subject areas.

At the high school level, emphasis is placed on college preparation and on higher-level thinking skills. Students are challenged by required research and speech and writing assignments in all subject areas. An extensive variety of classes in all areas of the fine arts are available. A selection of electives—from marine biology to Advanced Placement Chinese to stagecraft—rounds out the students' schedules, allowing them to explore other interests and talents. In addition to traditional lecture and discussion, teachers supplement the text curriculum with activities, projects, and field trips that make subjects more relevant and meaningful to the students.

Ninety-four honors courses and 27 Advanced Placement (AP) courses are available to qualified students. Students may gain college credit as a benefit of the successful completion of AP courses, which include American government, American history, biology, calculus, chemistry, economics, English language, English literature, environmental studies, European history, French, music theory, physics, psychology, Spanish, and world history.

American Heritage School offers unique **pre-medical, pre-law, pre-engineering, and biomedical engineering programs** to qualified high school students. The pre-professional programs challenge those ninth- through twelfth-grade students who have an interest in these fields of study and encourage students to consider these areas as potential career choices. The many course offerings are most often taught by working professionals in each area. In addition to course work for both programs, there are required internships that match students with professionals in their area of study.

In 2016, American Heritage School had **69 National Merit Scholar Semifinalists and a total of 121 nationally recognized scholars** among both campuses, which makes American Heritage the **#1 high school in the state of Florida, the #1 private school in the nation, and 7th out of 22,000 high schools in the United States.** American Heritage School is the #1 private school in the U.S. in national math competitions, #1 science research school at the Florida State Science Fair, #1 in robotics in the Southeast Region and 16th in the world, #1 private school in the U.S. in Model U.N., and #1 high school in the state in Mock Trial.

Through the International Program, in addition to an international student's regular academic classes, one to two hours of English language instruction is provided daily. Living with an American family produces more opportunity for language development and practice.

FACULTY AND ADVISERS
The students at American Heritage in Plantation are served by a faculty of 296 teachers, assistants, specialists, and counselors, and there are 154 faculty members at the Delray campus. Over 62 percent hold master's or doctoral degrees. Teachers actively seek out workshops to attend, and they return with creative ideas for their teaching. Faculty turnover is minimal and average teacher tenure exceeds ten years. The faculty is also committed to the Heritage philosophy of developing good character and self-esteem, as well as the reinforcement of traditional values in students. Teachers maintain close communication with parents regarding their child's progress through frequent written progress reports, phone calls, and scheduled conference days. The school provides a web-based service where students and parents can access information ranging from general school, club, and sports information to specific content for individual classes. Classes are small, and the student to faculty ratio is 8:1.

COLLEGE ADMISSION COUNSELING
One-hundred percent of American Heritage graduates are accepted to four-year colleges and universities every year. At American Heritage, the goal is to send seniors to colleges that match their goals and expectations for college life. There are 18 full-time guidance counselors in the high schools between both campuses, including a Director of College Planning and an International Counselor.

The college placement process begins in seventh grade with academic advising about curriculum and course selection and continues through high school with college preparation advising. The counselors stay informed of current admissions trends through attendance at national and local conferences and frequent contact with college admissions representatives.

The preparation for college intensifies as students in grades 9 through 12 follow a program designed to help them score well on the SATs. The program includes SAT prep mini-exercises in their English and math classes. In tenth grade and above, students may take an intensive daily SAT prep class taught on campus during the regular school day.

At this level, academic counseling gives consideration to graduation requirements and course selection, study skills and time management, leadership and club involvement, and referral to mentoring or professional tutoring, if needed. College advising is offered in the classroom on topics such as standardized test taking, the college application process, resume and essay writing, and searching for colleges and majors. The school reviews all college applications sent, writes letters of recommendation, finds scholarships for students, prepares students for college interviews, invites college admission representatives to campus, hosts a college fair, and proctors AP exams.

Virtually all graduates continue their education and are admitted to the nation's finest colleges and universities. Over 200 colleges and universities visit American Heritage School each year, and students participate in school-chaperoned college visits throughout the country as well. In recent years, graduates have been admitted to schools such as Berkeley, Boston University, Brown, Caltech, Carnegie Mellon, Colgate, Columbia, Cornell, Dartmouth, Duke, Georgetown, Harvard, Johns Hopkins, MIT, Northwestern, NYU, Princeton, Rutgers, Stanford, Tufts, Tulane, UCLA, University of Chicago, University of Michigan, University of North Carolina, University of Pennsylvania, University of Virginia, Vanderbilt, Wake Forest, West Point, Washington University, and Yale.

STUDENT BODY AND CONDUCT
In the Lower School, PK-3 through grade 6, each classroom has a teacher and a full-time assistant. The approximate number of students in each classroom are as follows: PK-3: 16 students, PK-4, 17; Kindergarten, 18; grades 1 and 2, 21; grades 3 and 4, 22; and grades 5 and 6, 23. In preschool through grade six, each class has a teacher and a full-time assistant. Grades 7 through 12 in the Upper School average 17 students in each class.

The Plantation campus has 2,400 students, with 733 in the Lower School and 1,667 in the Upper School. The Boca/Delray student population totals 1,300 with 270 students in the Lower School and 1,030 in the Upper School. American Heritage School's day population is culturally diverse, with students representing forty-three countries from around the world.

ACADEMIC FACILITIES
The American Heritage Plantation campus includes three fully equipped investigative science labs, fifteen state-of-the-art computer rooms, a courtroom, Engineering and Robotics Lab, an outdoor Environmental Education Center with a certified natural habitat and amphitheater, and a $25-million Center for the Arts that houses a state-of-the-art 800-seat theater, a black-box theater, spacious art studios, a graphic design lab, choral and band rooms, and individual practice rooms. Two new library/media centers have been built, one that services the Lower School and another that meets all the technological requirements of students in the Upper School. Heritage has an excellent physical education center that includes an Olympic-sized swimming and diving facility, a gymnasium, six tennis courts, a track, four modern locker rooms, a weight-training room, and acres of well-maintained athletic fields.

The American Heritage Boca/Delray campus provides seven state-of-the-art iMac computer labs, fully equipped science labs, a courtroom, Engineering and Robotics lab, a butterfly garden with an aquaponics growing system, art studios, a college guidance computer lab, a library/media center and research lab, a new

$8-million elementary/junior high classroom building, a $20-million Center for the Arts, an Olympic-sized swimming pool with eight racing lanes, a 2,600-square-foot teaching pool, a 25,000-square-foot gymnasium/auditorium, six lighted tennis courts, a football and soccer field, fully equipped weight training room, locker rooms, two well-equipped playgrounds, acres of well-maintained baseball and softball fields, practice fields for soccer and football, and beautifully landscaped grounds and courtyards.

THE ARTS
The Arts Department is recognized internationally and provides an outstanding program to students in PK3 through grade 12 with all abilities in the arts. Teachers are experts in their fields and they enable students to develop skills at their own pace and become masters in their work. The Center for the Arts is a beautiful, specially designed facility that enhances the arts program. Performance techniques are taught along with hands-on applications and theory in all disciplines of study. Students discover hidden talents and have the opportunity to display their talents both on campus and throughout the region, country, and world at various competitions, festivals, and events.

The arts programs include many areas: visual arts with classes in drawing, painting, fashion design, and photography; theater with classes in musical theater, sound and lighting, stagecraft, and theater history; music with chorus, band, orchestra, guitar, piano, and music theory classes; and dance with dance competition and dance conditioning classes. **Students participating in art, music, and drama programs have won awards at local, state, and national levels of competition in recent years.** Some of these recognitions include: All-Florida rating by the Florida Scholastic Press Association; 11 Critics' Choice awards at the District Thespian convention; featured choir at the National Youth Choir at Carnegie Hall in New York; superior ratings for choir, solo, and ensemble from the Florida Vocal Association; superior ratings for solo and ensemble/guitar and strings from the Florida Orchestra Association; American Choral Directors award; and gold and silver medals from the National Scholastic Art competition.

ATHLETICS
The athletics program is an important part of the sense of community that has developed at American Heritage. Parents, teachers, administrators, and students develop a special kind of camaraderie while cheering on the Patriot and Stallion teams. Heritage offers a complete competitive sports program. A "no-cut" policy allows every student who wants to participate an opportunity to play on the Patriot team of his or her choice. Coaches provide high-quality instruction in all sports. Sportsmanship, teamwork, recognition of effort, and training and preparation are the goals toward which American Heritage works every day. Each year, a number of student athletes receive financial assistance for their college education based on their athletic ability and their performance. More importantly, however, for those who do not have the ability—or maybe the desire—to participate at the collegiate level, athletic opportunities offer a very enjoyable and memorable experience, with accomplishments and friendships that last a lifetime. **American Heritage competes as a member of the Florida High School Activities Association, and the athletics programs are consistently ranked in the top ten in the state of Florida.**

EXTRACURRICULAR OPPORTUNITIES
American Heritage offers over 70 extracurricular activities for students, which serve several purposes. Primarily, they assist in the growth and development of students, and they also provide opportunities for leadership and excellence, which are increasingly required for college admission. Among some of the activities and clubs offered to high school students are the National Honor Society; Student Council; Spanish/French Honor Society; Pre-Med, Pre-Law, and Pre-Engineering Clubs; the Modern Language Club; Mu Alpha Theta (math club); astronomy; marine biology; chess; yearbook; newspaper; literary magazine; thespians; marching band; orchestra; jazz band; and chorus. Lower School students can take after-school classes in art, dance, instrumental music, karate, cooking, computers, and other areas of interest. Students may also participate in Student Council, Junior Thespians, and advanced math competitions.

Many students participate in enrichment and leadership programs offered in Broward County, including the National Conference for Community and Justice, Leadership Broward, Boys and Girls Clubs, Silver Knight, and the Institute for Math and Computer Science. Nationally, students have participated in the Hugh O'Brian Youth Foundation, Freedoms Foundation, Presidential Classroom, and Global Young Leaders Conference. In addition, American Heritage School is home to the Center for the Arts Scholarship Foundation, a nonprofit fundraising organization that awards scholarships to talented students in the arts.

SUMMER PROGRAMS
American Heritage has provided summer fun for young campers from throughout the community and all over the world since 1981. Summer camp offers activities that help build confidence and self-esteem. Campers enjoy the challenges and rewards of teamwork in one of nine different camp opportunities. **Day Camp offers a variety of summer activities that keep campers active and engaged from morning through the end of the day. Specialty Camps and Sports Camps fulfill passions and inspire young enthusiasts creating unforgettable experiences.** The Specialty Camps include: robotics, science adventure, theater, video production, and young artists; the Sports Camps include: lacrosse, soccer, and tennis. Campers continue to develop the socialization skills initiated in school and enjoy good relationships with the high school and college counselors, who serve as role models for them. American Heritage Summer Day Camp sessions are available for students 13 years old and under.

American Heritage also offers the Summer Institute, a program for high achievers in grades PK3–12. Dedicated faculty is comprised of career educators, as well as professionals currently practicing in their fields, who teach students desiring to pursue an existing passion, explore something new, or simply improve upon an important academic skill. Courses range from computer coding, robotics, math, and creative writing to pre-medical, pre-law, leadership, and SAT prep.

American Heritage Summer School is also offered to students in PK3–12 from throughout South Florida for grade promotion and early elementary readiness. Class sizes are small (8–12) students, teachers are certified and highly experienced, weekly progress reports are provided, and free bus transportation is available. For more information, please contact American Heritage School.

COSTS AND FINANCIAL AID
In 2015–16, tuition and fees total between $20,662 for preschoolers and $26,008 for students in twelfth grade. An international program is available at an additional cost for the academic school year—August through May—and includes tuition, housing, three meals a day, books, uniforms, and two hours each day of English language study.

American Heritage offers financial grants to parents who qualify.

ADMISSIONS INFORMATION
Enrollment at American Heritage School is limited to students who are above average to gifted in intelligence and who are working at or above grade level. Math, reading, vocabulary, and IQ tests are administered and are used to determine if the student has the background and basic skills necessary to be successful. The results of these entrance exams are discussed with the parents at a conference following the testing. I-20 visas are granted to international students who are accepted. Details are available from the Director of Admissions. Students are admitted without regard to race, creed, or national origin.

For acceptance into American Heritage's international program, families must supply complete academic records from the age of 12, translated into English; two teacher letters of recommendation, translated into English; copies of the student's passport; and a completed American Heritage School application form. The American Heritage Admissions Committee reviews the student's records and determines suitable placement. Full tuition for the school year is due upon acceptance. After tuition has been received, the School issues an I-20 form, which must be taken to the U.S. Embassy in the student's country to obtain a student visa.

APPLICATION TIMETABLE
First-semester classes begin in late August. Information regarding specific deadlines can be obtained by contacting American Heritage School's Plantation campus.

ADMISSIONS CORRESPONDENCE
Plantation Campus
American Heritage School
Admissions Department
12200 West Broward Boulevard
Plantation, Florida 33325
United States
Phone: 954-472-0022
E-mail: admissions@ahschool.com
Website: http://www.ahschool.com

Boca/Delray Campus
American Heritage School
Admissions Department
6200 Linton Boulevard
Delray Beach, Florida 33484
United States
Phone: 561-495-7272
E-mail: admissions.bd@ahschool.com
Website: http://www.ahschool.com

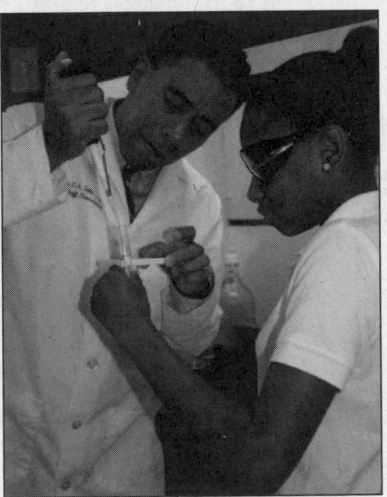

BERKELEY PREPARATORY SCHOOL
Tampa, Florida

Type: Coeducational, independent, Episcopal-affiliated, college-preparatory day school
Grades: PK–12: Lower Division, Pre-Kindergarten–5; Middle Division, 6–8; Upper Division, 9–12
Enrollment: School total: 1,300; Lower Division: 400; Middle Division: 325; Upper Division: 575
Head of School: Joseph W. Seivold, Headmaster

THE SCHOOL

The Latin words *Disciplina, Diligentia,* and *Integritas* in Berkeley's motto describe the school's mission to nurture students' intellectual, emotional, spiritual and physical development so they can achieve their highest potential. Episcopal in heritage, Berkeley was founded in 1960 and opened for grades 7–12 the following year. Kindergarten through grade 6 was added in 1967, and Pre-Kindergarten began in 1988. Berkeley's purpose is to enable its students to achieve academic excellence in preparation for higher education and to instill in students a strong sense of morality, ethics, and social responsibility.

Berkeley is located on an 84-acre campus in Tampa, Florida, a location that attracts students from Hillsborough, Pinellas, Pasco, Polk, and Hernando Counties and throughout the greater Tampa Bay area. Private bus transportation is available.

Berkeley is incorporated as a nonprofit institution and is governed by a 27-member Board of Trustees that includes alumni, parents of current students, and parents of alumni. The presidents of the Alumni Association and Parents' Club are also members of the Board.

ACADEMIC PROGRAM

The school year runs from the end of August to the first week of June and includes Thanksgiving, Christmas, and spring vacations. The curriculum naturally varies within each division.

In the Lower Division, the program seeks to provide appropriate, challenging learning experiences in a safe environment that reflects the academic, social, moral, and ethical values the school espouses in its philosophy. Curricular emphasis is on core subjects of reading and mathematics. An interdisciplinary approach is used in world language and social studies, and manipulatives are used extensively in the science and mathematics programs. Each student also receives instruction in library skills and integration of technology and learning.

Academic requirements in the Middle Division, where classes average 16 to 20 students, are English, English expression, mathematics, global studies, world language, science, technology, physical education, art, drama, and music. Classes meet five days a week on a rotating schedule. Extra help is available from teachers, and grades are sent to parents four times a year.

The Upper Division program, with an average class size of 15 to 20 students, requires students to take four or five credit courses a year, in addition to fine arts and physical education requirements. To graduate, a student must complete 23 credits, including 4 in English, 4 in mathematics, and 3 in history, science, and foreign language. Students must also complete one year of personal fitness/health and an additional year of physical education, two years of fine arts, and two electives. In addition, Berkeley students are required to take a semester of religious studies each year and complete 76 hours of community service. More than 20 Advanced Placement courses are offered. The Upper Division program is designed to provide students with the atmosphere and advantages of a small liberal arts college. Students are offered a choice of 100 student activities and clubs, and they may be selected to join several nationally recognized academic honor groups, including the Cum Laude Society and National Honor Society.

FACULTY AND ADVISERS

There are 245 full-time faculty members and administrators. They hold baccalaureate, more than 100 graduate, and several doctoral degrees. Headmaster Joseph Seivold graduated Phi Beta Kappa from the University of North Carolina at Chapel Hill with a degree in history. He holds a master's degree in education administration from St. Mary's University of Minnesota. He came to Berkeley from The Blake School in Minnesota.

In addition to teaching responsibilities, faculty members are involved in Berkeley's co-curricular programs as coaches and student activity advisers. Berkeley faculty members receive support for professional development opportunities and several faculty members have been recognized as some of the top teachers among their peers nationally.

COLLEGE ADMISSION COUNSELING

Traditionally, 100 percent of Berkeley's graduating class goes on to attend college. Although Berkeley does not rank its students, more than 130 colleges visit the school each year to recruit its graduates. Berkeley's college counseling department works to assist students and their families in selecting colleges that best suit their academic, financial, and social needs.

Recent graduates are attending Boston College, Brown, Cornell, Dartmouth, Duke, Emory, Georgetown, Harvard, Northwestern, Notre Dame, NYU, Princeton, Stanford, Vanderbilt, Villanova, Yale, and the Universities of Florida, Miami, Michigan, North Carolina, Pennsylvania, and Virginia. Scholarship offers totaling more than $9 million were made to the Class of 2015.

STUDENT BODY AND CONDUCT

In all divisions, Berkeley students are expected to maintain high standards. Mature conduct and use of manners are expected, and an honor code outlines students' responsibilities. In exchange, students are entrusted with certain privileges, such as direct access to the administration and the opportunity to initiate school-sponsored clubs. Students wear uniforms to class.

CAMPUS FACILITIES

The 84-acre campus is located in Town and Country, a suburb of Tampa. The campus consists of classrooms; two libraries; technology labs; general convocation rooms; physical education fields; a 19,000-square-foot student center; the 425-seat Berkeley Café; a Pre-Kindergarten wing; and administrative offices for the Lower, Middle, and Upper Divisions. The new 78,000-square-foot Gries Center for the Arts and Sciences is the home for the Middle and Upper Division fine and visual arts and for Upper Division math and science, and includes a state-of-the-art design technology center, digital media lab, and recital hall.

The fine arts program is enhanced by the Lykes Center for the Arts, a 634-seat performing arts center, which also includes a gallery for visual arts displays, a flex studio for dance and small drama productions, dressing rooms, and an orchestra pit.

ATHLETICS

Varsity sports for boys include baseball, basketball, crew, cross-country, diving, football, golf, hockey, lacrosse, soccer, hockey, swimming, tennis, track, and wrestling. Girls compete in basketball, crew, cross-country, diving, golf, lacrosse, soccer, softball, swimming, tennis, track, and volleyball. Berkeley has been recognized as the Florida High School Athletic Association's overall 4A state academic champion for four consecutive years and has several individual and team champions.

Berkeley's athletic facilities include the 53,000 square-foot Straz Family Field House, two gymnasiums, a junior Olympic swimming pool, a wrestling/gymnastics room, a weight room, a rock-climbing wall, a varsity level soccer field, a tennis complex, a high- and low-ropes course, a baseball and softball complex, a state-of-the-art track, and practice fields for football, soccer, and lacrosse. Seasonal sports award banquets and a homecoming football game are scheduled annually.

EXTRACURRICULAR OPPORTUNITIES

In addition to its broad-based commitment to student organizations and clubs and its community service requirements, Berkeley offers its students a vast array of possibilities beyond the classrooms. Student artwork is accepted each year into national art shows and exhibits, and several students receive Gold Key Awards each year from the Alliance for Young Artists and Writers. An after-school Lower Division chess club attracts close to 100 students from Kindergarten through grade 5. Middle and Upper Division students, as well as many faculty members, participate in several international experiences, visiting countries such as England, New Zealand, the Dominican Republic, Ghana, Australia, China, France, Italy, Switzerland, and Spain.

DAILY LIFE

Students in Pre-Kindergarten through grade 5 attend classes from 8:00 a.m. to 3:05 p.m. Middle and Upper Division students also begin at 8:00 a.m. and end at 3:20 p.m. Teachers are available to assist students and offer extra help during activity periods, which are scheduled into each class day. Supervised study halls are also scheduled for some students.

SUMMER PROGRAMS

Berkeley hosts more than 100 sports, academic, and professional development camps and sessions during a six-week summer program for Bay-area students, prekindergarten through grade 12. More information is available online at www.berkeleyprep.org/summer.

COSTS AND FINANCIAL AID

The tuition schedule for 2015–16 is as follows: $17,460 for Pre-Kindergarten and Kindergarten, $19,060 for grades 1–5, $21,060 for grades 6–8, and $22,710 for grades 9–12. Tuition is payable in eight installments and must be paid in full by January 1. Tuition payments do not cover costs of uniforms, laptops, supplies, transportation, special event admission fees, or other expenses incurred in the ordinary course of student activities at Berkeley.

Berkeley makes all admission decisions without regard to financial status. Families who have reviewed their financial situation and feel that help may be needed in paying tuition should apply for aid. Financial aid awards are available at any grade level to students who demonstrate need. In determining need, the guidelines of the School and Student Service for Financial Aid (SSS) are used. Each award is individualized based upon the financial assessment of each applicant. It is important to note that Berkeley may not be able to accommodate all financial aid applications in a given year.

Berkeley is also fortunate to have a number of scholarships available to students. In addition to demonstrated financial need, specific criteria such as academic achievement and leadership potential are also components of a separate scholarship application process. Receiving a scholarship is a great honor; therefore, the process is both competitive and selective. A selection committee will review the completed applications and announce the scholarship recipients in early March.

ADMISSIONS INFORMATION

In considering applicants, Berkeley evaluates a student's talent, academic skills, personal interests, motivation to learn, and desire to attend.

Lower Division candidates visit age-appropriate classrooms and are evaluated through grade level assessments. Middle and Upper Division candidates are required to take the Secondary School Admissions Test (SSAT) and generally register for a November, December, or January test date. In addition to the SSAT, all applicants schedule an appointment with the Admissions Office for Otis-Lennon testing and a writing sample. Entering juniors and seniors may submit PSAT, SAT, PLAN, or ACT scores in place of sitting for the SSAT.

The admission process is selective and is based on information gathered from the application form, interviews, the candidate's record, admission tests, and teacher recommendations.

Berkeley admits students of any race, color, sex, religion, and national or ethnic origin and does not discriminate on the basis of any category protected by law in the administration of its educational policies, admission policies, and scholarship, financial aid, athletic, and other school-administered programs.

APPLICATION TIMETABLE

Applications should be submitted by the fall one year prior to the student's entrance into Berkeley. The Lower and Upper Division Admissions Committees begin evaluation of applicants in mid-February and decisions are made in March. The Middle Division Admissions Committee begins evaluation of completed files in mid-January with notification on a rolling basis from the end of January until vacancies are filled. All applications after the initial selection process are considered on a space-available basis.

Berkeley welcomes inquiries from families throughout the year. However, because of the competitive nature of the admission process, families are encouraged to visit the campus as early as possible to become familiar with the school, its programs, and its admission procedure.

ADMISSIONS CORRESPONDENCE

Janie McIlvaine
Director of Admissions
Berkeley Preparatory School
4811 Kelly Road
Tampa, Florida 33615
United States
Phone: 813-885-1673
Fax: 813-886-6933
E-mail: mcilvjan@berkeleyprep.org
Website: www.berkeleyprep.org/admissions

BERKSHIRE SCHOOL

Sheffield, Massachusetts

Type: Coeducational boarding and day college-preparatory school
Grades: 9–12 (Forms III–VI), postgraduate year
Enrollment: 405
Head of School: Pieter M. Mulder

THE SCHOOL

Berkshire School is a coed, college preparatory boarding and day school that prepares 405 ninth through twelfth graders and postgraduates for a global future. Pioneering programs—such as Advanced Math/Science Research, Advanced Humanities Research, and Sustainability and Resource Management—coexist with advanced sections and AP offerings in all disciplines. With a range of artistic and athletic offerings, a new Fine Arts Center, a state-of-the-art math and science center, a 117,000-square-foot athletic facility, and national recognition for its efforts in environmental conservation, Berkshire School is an extraordinary setting in which students are encouraged to embrace the school motto: *Pro Vita Non Pro Schola Discimus,* "Learning—not just for school but for life."

In 1907, Mr. and Mrs. Seaver B. Buck, graduates of Harvard and Smith respectively, rented the building of Glenny Farm at the foot of Mt. Everett and founded Berkshire School. The Bucks devoted themselves to educating young men with the values of academic excellence, physical vigor, and high personal standards. In 1969, this commitment to excellence was extended to include girls.

Situated at the base of Mt. Everett, Berkshire's campus spans 400 acres. It is a 75-minute drive to both Albany International Airport and Hartford's Bradley International Airport and just over 2 hours from Boston and New York City.

Berkshire School is incorporated as a not-for-profit institution, governed by a 26-member self-perpetuating Board of Trustees. The School has a $123-million endowment. Annual operating expenses exceed $26 million. Annual Giving in 2014–15 exceeded $2.6 million. The Berkshire Chapter of the Cum Laude Society was established in 1942.

Berkshire School is accredited by the New England Association of Schools and Colleges and holds memberships in the Independent School Association of Massachusetts, the National Association of Independent Schools, the College Entrance Examination Board, the National Association for College Admission Counseling, the Secondary School Admission Test Board, and the Association of Boarding Schools.

ACADEMIC PROGRAM

Berkshire's academic program is firmly rooted in a college-preparatory curriculum that features advanced and AP courses across all disciplines. In addition, unique opportunities in math/science research, student-directed independent study, and electives in science, humanities, and fine arts allow students to pursue advanced study. As creative and agile problem solvers, strong critical thinkers, persuasive communicators, and active global citizens, Berkshire students are equipped with the skills required for the twenty-first century. The School's balance between academic rigor and possibility allows students to flourish as independent learners and community members.

Believing that the best preparation for college is learning from a variety of disciplines, Berkshire requires the following credits: 4 years of English; 3 years each of mathematics, a foreign language, and history; 2 years of science; and 1 year of the visual or performing arts. All students are placed at a level commensurate with their skills and talent. Many take one or more of the seventeen Advanced Placement courses offered.

Most students carry five courses. The average number of students in a class is 12, and the student-teacher ratio is 5:1. The academic year is divided into two semesters, each culminating with an assessment period. Students receive grades and teacher comments twice a semester, and advisor letters twice a year. Berkshire uses a traditional letter-grading system of A–F (D is passing).

In 2007, Berkshire introduced its Advanced Math/Science Research course in which students use the strong foundation of knowledge acquired in the regular Berkshire curriculum as a springboard for beyond-the-curriculum projects in areas of cutting-edge research. Students work closely with mentors in the fields of their choice for 4 to 8 hours a week. The course concludes with a critical review and a scientific research paper.

Berkshire's signature programs are wide-ranging and appeal to a variety of students. The Aviation Science program consists of a combination of classroom and flight-based instruction during a semester-long class that prepares students to pass the Federal Aviation Administration's (FAA) Ground School Certification Exam. The course focuses on the study of aerodynamics, meteorology, navigation, radio communication, and instrumentation; each student takes flight training at the nearby Great Barrington Airport. Pro Vita Winter Session allows Berkshire students, for one week each winter, to move beyond the core curriculum by participating in three unique, intensive courses of their choosing, taught by Berkshire faculty, parents, alumni and friends. Pro Vita offers over 80 course options, including trips to places like Ghana and Germany.

FACULTY AND ADVISORS

The Berkshire faculty numbers 59, 86 including nonteaching faculty. Forty-three teachers hold a master's degree and 7 hold doctorates. Faculty members contribute to both the academic and personal development of each student. Each student is paired with a faculty advisor who provides guidance, monitors academic progress, and serves as a liaison with the student's family. Berkshire also retains the services of 4 pediatricians, 5 full-time registered nurses, and 2 certified athletic trainers.

In November 2013, Pieter M. Mulder was named Berkshire's sixteenth head of school. He holds a bachelor's degree in American studies from Williams College with minors in architecture and environmental science, and a master's degree in mathematics with a concentration in creative writing from Wesleyan University. Mr. Mulder is in his eleventh year at Berkshire. He lives on campus with his wife, Lucia, and their two children.

COLLEGE ADMISSION COUNSELING

Berkshire School's five college counselors work closely with students and their parents in the search for an appropriate college or university. The formal process begins in sophomore year, with individual conferences with counselors, and the opportunity to meet with selected members of the approximately 100 college admissions representatives who visit the campus. Parents of sophomores are welcomed into the process with an overview from the College Counseling Office during Fall Parents' Weekend. In February, juniors and their parents attend a two-day seminar on the college admission process, in which admission strategies are discussed and specific institutions are identified for each student's consideration. During the summer, students are encouraged to visit colleges and draft their college application essays, while completing the Common Application. The application process is generally completed by winter vacation in the senior year.

Members of the classes of 2012–2015 enrolled at a variety of four-year colleges or universities, including: Amherst, Bates, Berkeley, Boston College, Boston University, Bowdoin, Brown, Bucknell, Colby, Colgate, College of Charleston, Colorado College, Columbia, Cornell, Dartmouth, Davidson, Denison, Dickinson, Duke, Elon, Emory, Franklin & Marshall, George Washington, Hamilton, Harvard, Johns Hopkins, Kenyon, Lafayette, Lehigh, Middlebury, NYU, Northeastern, Northwestern, Occidental, Pitzer, Princeton, Providence College, RIT, Savannah College of Art and Design, Skidmore, Smith, SMU, St. Lawrence, Syracuse, Trinity, Tufts, Union, United States Military Academy, United States Naval Academy, Vassar, Wake Forest, Wesleyan, Wheaton, Whitman, William and Mary, Williams, Yale, and the Universities of Connecticut, Colorado, Illinois, Miami, Michigan, New Hampshire, Pennsylvania, Richmond, Vermont, Virginia, and Wisconsin.

STUDENT BODY AND CONDUCT

In the 2015–16 academic year, there are 368 boarders and 37 day students. The student body is drawn from 29 states and 30 countries.

Students contribute directly to the life of the school community through involvement in Student Government, the Prefect Program, dormitory life, and various clubs and activities. Participation gives students a positive growth experience in keeping with the School's motto, *Pro Vita Non Pro Schola Discimus,* "Learning—not just for school but for life." The rules at Berkshire are simple and straightforward and are consistent with the values and ideals of the School. They are designed to help students live orderly lives within an environment of mutual trust and respect.

ACADEMIC FACILITIES

Berkshire Hall, the School's primary academic facility, built in 1930 and the centerpiece of the campus, reopened in the fall of 2008 after a full renovation. It houses larger classrooms with state-of-the-art technology, new administrative offices, a two-story atrium, and a Great Room for student study and special functions. A new music center and dance center opened in the fall of 2010, while in the fall of 2011, Allen Theater reopened after a complete renovation. This included new academic spaces for the Kenefick Center for Learning, classrooms for the theater and film department and the SAT tutoring program, and a studio for WBSL, the School's own radio station.

In October 2012, Berkshire inaugurated the state-of-the-art Bellas/Dixon Math and Science Center. This 48,000-square-foot LEED-Certified Gold building provides facilities that allow students to pursue academic excellence and innovation at the highest level while adhering to the School's commitment to sustainability. The 2013 school year saw the opening of the School's new Fine Arts Center, which includes a gallery, department offices, and classrooms for studio and digital art and ceramics.

In the fall of 2015, Berkshire completed a full renovation of its Geier Library, creating a comfortable, quiet study space of about 17,000 square feet, featuring ten Mac computers, half of which contain the Adobe Creative Cloud for design work. The space is flooded with natural light and equipped with WiFi. Research is facilitated by access to JSTOR, an online database of more than 1,000 academic journals, containing literally millions of peer-reviewed articles, images, reviews, and primary sources. The library also holds a wide-ranging print collection that is easily augmented by interlibrary loan.

At the Dixon Observatory, computer-synchronized telescopes make it possible to view and photograph objects in the solar system and beyond. Given the combination of equipment, software, and location, Berkshire's observatory is among the best in New England.

BOARDING AND GENERAL FACILITIES

Berkshire has ten residential houses, including two girls' dormitories completed in the fall of 2002. Three faculty families typically reside in each house, along with 2 prefects—seniors, whose primary responsibility is to assist dorm parents with daily routines, including study hall and room inspection. Dorm rooms all have Internet access and private phone lines. There is a common room in each house, where students may relax or study. Benson Commons features a dining hall, a post office, the School bookstore, the Music Center, the Student Life Office, and recreational spaces. In 2011 an 8-acre solar field was built on campus; it now provides approximately 40 percent of the School's energy needs. In the summer of 2015, Berkshire completed a project begun by students in the Sustainability class, installing an electric car charger on campus and making it available to the community.

ATHLETICS

Berkshire enjoys a proud tradition of athletic excellence. The School provides competition in 27 interscholastic sports, including baseball, basketball, crew, cross-country running, field hockey, football, golf, ice hockey, lacrosse, mountain biking, skiing, soccer, softball, squash, tennis, track and field, and volleyball. Students may also choose to participate in the Ritt Kellogg Mountain Program, utilizing Berkshire's natural environment and proximity to the Appalachian Trail to offer athletic challenges, teach leadership, and foster environmental responsibility.

In January 2009, the 117,000-square-foot Jackman L. Stewart Athletic Center opened. The facility offers two ice rinks (one Olympic-size), 14 locker rooms, seating for 800 spectators, a 34-machine fitness center and athletic training rooms. It can also be used for indoor tennis and can accommodate all-school functions. A second athletic center features full-size courts for basketball and volleyball, four international

squash courts, a climbing wall, and a dance studio. Other athletic facilities include the Thomas H. Young Field for baseball, softball fields, an all-weather track, a lighted football field, and two synthetic-turf fields. A twelve-court tennis facility was completed in the fall of 2010.

EXTRACURRICULAR OPPORTUNITIES

Berkshire offers students a variety of opportunities to express their talents and passions. Students publish a newspaper, a yearbook, and both literary and scholarly journals featuring student writing, art, and photography. The Ritt Kellogg Mountain Program offers backcountry skills, boatbuilding, fly fishing, hiking, kayaking, rock climbing, and winter mountaineering.

There are a number of active clubs, including ArtsReach, the International and Investment Clubs, Kids 4 Kids, Maple Syrup Corporation, the Philanthropy Society, Student Activities Committee, and Gay/Straight Alliance.

A student-run FM radio station, WBSL, operates with a power of 250 watts and is capable of reaching 10,000 listeners. Berkshire is one of the few secondary schools to hold membership in the Intercollegiate Broadcasting System and the only one affiliated with both the Associated Press wire and radio services.

Berkshire students pursue the arts in the classroom and through extracurricular activities. The theater program offers a play in the fall and another in the spring, as well as a winter musical. There are four choral groups: Bear Tones, a coed a capella group; Ursa Major, an all-school chorus; Ursa Minor, a girls' a cappella group; and Greensleeves, an all-male chorus. There are two music groups: jazz band and the chamber music ensemble. Students can also take private voice and instrument lessons. Each season, the Berkshire community looks forward to various performances, such as dance and music recitals, a jazz café, and open mic nights. Visual arts include painting, drawing, sculpture, digital art, photography, and ceramics. Students display their work in the Student Center, and in the Atrium and the Warren Family Gallery in Berkshire Hall.

DAILY LIFE

The first of the six class periods in a school day begins at 8 a.m., and the final class concludes at 2:45 p.m., except on Wednesday and Saturday, when the last class ends by 11:35 a.m. Berkshire follows a rotating schedule in which classes meet at different times each day.

Athletics, outdoor experiences, and art activities occupy the afternoon. Clubs often meet after dinner, before the two-hour study period, which begins at 8 p.m.

WEEKEND LIFE

Weekend activities are planned by a Director of Student Activities and include first-run movies, dances with live bands, and DJs. There are trips to local amusement parks and theaters, as well as shopping trips to Hartford and Albany. In addition, students and faculty members journey to New York and Boston to visit museums,

attend theater and music productions, and take in professional sports events.

COSTS AND FINANCIAL AID

For the 2015–16 academic year, tuition is $56,150 for boarding students and $44,700 for day students. For most students, $100 a month is sufficient personal spending money. Ten percent of the tuition is paid upon enrollment, 50 percent is payable on June 30, and 40 percent is payable by October 31. Two tuition payment plans are available.

Financial aid is awarded on the basis of need to about 30 percent of the student body. The total financial aid spent in 2014–15 was $4.9 million. The School and Student Service (SSS) Parents Financial Statement and a 1040 form are required.

ADMISSIONS INFORMATION

Berkshire adheres to the principle that in diversity there is strength and therefore, actively seeks students from a broad range of geographic, ethnic, religious, and socioeconomic backgrounds. Admission is most common in the freshman and sophomore years, and the School enrolls a small number of juniors and postgraduates each year.

In order to assess a student's academic record, potential, character, and contributions to his or her school, Berkshire requires a personal interview, a transcript, test scores, and recommendations from English and mathematics teachers, along with the actual application. Candidates should have their Secondary School Admission Test (SSAT) scores forwarded to Berkshire School (school code 1612). International students are required to have their Test of English as a Foreign Language (TOEFL) scores forwarded in addition to their SSAT (school code 3252).

APPLICATION TIMETABLE

Interested families are encouraged to visit the campus in the fall or winter preceding the September in which admission is desired. Visits are arranged according to the academic schedule, Monday, Tuesday, Thursday, and Friday, from 8 a.m. to 2 p.m. and Wednesday and Saturday from 8 a.m. to 10:45 a.m. January 15 is the deadline for submitting applications; late applications are accepted as long as space is anticipated. Berkshire adheres to the standard notification date of March 10 and the families' reply date of April 10. Depending on availability, late applications are processed on a rolling basis. Applications to Berkshire School can be submitted using Gateway to Prep Schools and SSAT Standard Application Online.

ADMISSIONS CORRESPONDENCE

Andrew Bogardus, Director of Admission
Berkshire School
245 North Undermountain Road
Sheffield, Massachusetts 01257
United States
Phone: 413-229-1003
Fax: 413-229-1016
E-mail: admission@berkshireschool.org
Website: http://www.berkshireschool.org

CANTERBURY SCHOOL

Fort Myers, Florida

Type: Coeducational, day, college-preparatory
Grades: Prekindergarten–12: Lower School, Pre-K–3; Intermediate School, 4–6; Middle School, 7–8; Upper School, 9–12
Enrollment: 625; Upper School, 235
Head of School: Richard Kirschner

THE SCHOOL

Founded in 1964, the Canterbury School sits on 32 acres located on College Parkway between U.S. 41 and McGregor Boulevard. The School is dedicated to academic excellence within a caring and supportive community, preparing students of ability, promise, and diverse backgrounds for selective colleges. Canterbury's motto, "Education, character, leadership, service," defines the focus of the School's program and underscores all that its students do in and out of the classroom.

There are four divisions—Lower (grades prekindergarten–3), Intermediate (grades 4–6), Middle (grades 7–8), and Upper (grades 9–12). At all levels, the academic program emphasizes individual growth, skill development, collaboration, a high caliber of instruction, and high standards. Canterbury provides all students with an opportunity to challenge themselves and take risks in an atmosphere of mutual respect and partnership among students, parents, and teachers. Canterbury's integrated, innovative curriculum emphasizes group and individual study of the liberal arts, in addition to experiential learning and community service opportunities. Canterbury Advantage focuses on developing scholars, artists, and athletes of character.

The Canterbury School is accredited by the Southern Association of Independent Schools (SAIS), Southern Association of Colleges and Schools/Council on Accreditation and School Improvement (SACS/CASI), Florida Council of Independent Schools (FCIS), the College Board, and the Florida Kindergarten Council (FKC).

ACADEMIC PROGRAM

All students pursue a demanding schedule of college-preparatory classes for four years in the Upper School, earning a minimum of 25 credits to graduate. Students play an active role in their course of study, and juniors and seniors may pursue advanced work in areas of significant interest or expertise. Although Honors and Advanced Placement courses, as well as independent studies, give students extra challenges, even the standard-level courses thoroughly prepare students for college work. Offering a rigorous and rewarding liberal arts curriculum, the Upper School program is rich in math, science, modern and classical languages, music, visual arts, social sciences, foreign language, and drama, with a special emphasis on writing, research, and the discourse of ideas. Study strategies, self-discipline, academic responsibility, and fluency in technology are underscored in each content area. Students learn academic honesty, competitive fair play, and good citizenship through a respected honor code. Students master key skills that will serve them well in their college careers as they actively participate in intellectual inquiry, analysis, and evaluation.

Middle School students take one course in each of the major disciplines every year—English, mathematics, science, social studies, and foreign language—and classes in the arts and in physical education/health, as well as other electives.

Canterbury's Intermediate School offers instruction in a math, science, and technology triad, as well as the Writing Across the Curriculum initiative, which links critical thinking and written expression in every curriculum area. Lower School celebrates childhood in an age-appropriate, developmental learning environment for students in prekindergarten 3 and 4 through third grade; a balance between hard work and fun creates an environment where children are encouraged to take risks and assume personal responsibility for their learning as they embark upon their learning journey.

FACULTY AND ADVISERS

There are 80 faculty members, 38 of whom teach in the Upper School. Canterbury's talented and dedicated faculty seeks to inspire young minds through a rigorous and rewarding curriculum. Passionate about ideas and mentoring, instructors understand how students learn most effectively. Teaching is more than facts, figures, and formulas—it's a way of life. Canterbury's teachers personalize their approach to meet individual student needs. Small class sizes allow one-on-one time for personal attention, challenging and supporting students as they stretch their minds and their opportunities.

COLLEGE ADMISSION COUNSELING

College preparation is a primary focus of Canterbury's curriculum, so students receive the highly personalized direction and encouragement they need to choose the undergraduate institution with the right fit. An experienced college counselor guides juniors and seniors, as well as their families, through the process—helping them gain a comprehensive understanding of college acceptance practices. The result? An ongoing tradition of a 100 percent college-acceptance rate among Canterbury graduates. Recent graduates have been accepted to such distinguished institutions as Carnegie Mellon, Dartmouth, Davidson, Duke, Georgetown, Harvard, Princeton, Penn State, and Yale.

STUDENT BODY AND CONDUCT

Six hundred twenty-five students are enrolled in grades pre-K3–12. They come from diverse backgrounds, but the majority live in Fort Myers, Cape Coral, Estero, Sanibel, and the surrounding area.

ACADEMIC FACILITIES

The Canterbury School Libraries offer instruction, materials, and technology to promote the skills of information literacy and fluency, the love of reading, and the joy of intellectual discovery. By providing resources for both academic and recreational reading needs, the libraries help students develop research competencies for college and facilitate lifelong learning. The libraries also provide space for individual reflection and creation, as well as a forum for the sharing of ideas within the Canterbury community. The Ellenberg Library (grades 6–12) has established several special collections, in addition to the familiar biography, fiction, nonfiction, periodical, reference, and story collections. The Hilliard Library serves students from pre-K through fifth grade and their teachers. The library collection, of both print and nonprint resources, includes books, videotapes, magazines, Internet access, professional resources, and online subscription databases.

The Lower and Intermediate schools have dedicated art and music classrooms, science laboratories, computer labs and classrooms. They share a library. The Middle and Upper schools share a library, a language listening lab, and music and art classrooms, but they have separate science laboratories, computer labs, classrooms, and commons areas. The entire school shares the dining hall, two gymnasiums and a sports center, an outdoor marine biology touch tank and classroom, and the Performing Arts Center. The Middle School has a new technology learning environment, the Cougar Den, complete with mobile furniture, interactive whiteboards, and a media scape allowing for increased innovation and student-teacher collaboration.

ATHLETICS

At Canterbury, the life of the mind is complemented by a strong athletic program. Canterbury School fields teams in soccer, basketball, baseball, football, volleyball, swimming, tennis, golf, cross-country, track and field, and lacrosse. Students are encouraged to become involved with athletics; around 85 percent of all Middle and Upper School students participate in interscholastic sports. Canterbury School is a member of the Florida High School Athletic Association (FHSAA) and is accredited by the Southern Association of Schools and Colleges (SACS). The Middle School belongs to the Suncoast Middle School League.

CO-CURRICULAR OPPORTUNITIES

Clubs and organizations play key roles in student life. Students can choose from more than 20 active clubs on campus, including yearbook, newspaper, chess, mock trial, and Model UN, which meet regularly throughout the year. Students can also participate in a variety of local, state, national, and international scholastic competitions.

DAILY LIFE

Students spend their days in class, followed by after-school activities ranging from community service, student government, and athletics to clubs and study groups.

SUMMER PROGRAMS

Summer academic, arts, athletic, and enrichment programs are available to students of all ages. Students can brush up their math, writing, or Spanish skills or take SAT-prep courses. Canterbury provides a recommended summer reading list for

prekindergarten to fifth grade students so that they can begin, continue, and support the process of developing comprehension and analytical skills. Students in grades 6–12 receive a required summer reading list to support their academic course selection for the following year.

COSTS AND FINANCIAL AID

Upper School students pay $22,220 per academic year. Tuition is $16,320 for pre-K 4 and kindergarten; $20,220 for grades 1–5, and $22,220 for grades 6–12. In 2015–16, Canterbury provided more than $2.3 million in financial assistance to 28 percent of the student body, with awards ranging from 20 percent to 95 percent of tuition.

Tuition payments include both a nonrefundable deposit and the remaining tuition balance. The nonrefundable 20 percent deposit is due upon enrollment and must accompany the student's enrollment contract. On July 1, another 30 percent of tuition is due, and the remaining 50 percent is due October 1. With this plan, tuition refund insurance is optional. Additional payment plans include monthly and quarterly options.

ADMISSIONS INFORMATION

As a college-preparatory school with high academic standards, Canterbury seeks students of demonstrated abilities with

potential for intellectual growth. Boys and girls entering the prekindergartens through grade eleven are invited to apply, beginning the fall prior to the school year they wish to attend. Applications can be submitted online and must include the $100 application fee.

Applicants are first evaluated by testing, using the ERB, CTP 4 Test, or the SSAT in grades 4–11. Next, candidates' files are forwarded to the Admission Committee, which assesses each application based on the student's past academic achievement, performance on the admission test, a written essay, personal recommendations, and an interview with the division head and director of admission.

APPLICATION TIMETABLE

Open houses are scheduled October through March; attendees must reserve a space by contacting the admission office. Applications are accepted continually.

ADMISSIONS CORRESPONDENCE

Julie Peters, Director of Admissions
Canterbury School
8141 College Parkway
Fort Myers, Florida 33919
United States
Phone: 239-415-8945
Fax: 239-481-8339
E-mail: jpeters@canterburyfortmyers.org
Website: http://www.canterburyfortmyers.org/

THE CASCADILLA SCHOOL

Ithaca, New York

Type: Coeducational boarding and day college-preparatory school
Grades: 9–12, postgraduate year
Enrollment: 60
Head of School: Patricia A. Kendall, Headmistress

THE SCHOOL

The Cascadilla School was founded in 1870 as a preparatory school for Cornell University. In 1939, it was reorganized as a nonprofit corporation under a Board of Trustees and granted an absolute charter by the Board of Regents of the State of New York.

The philosophy of education at Cascadilla is to provide a flexible, accelerated program within which each individual can achieve his or her goals in preparation for a successful college career. This learning experience emphasizes the steady development of an adult viewpoint and a mature approach to life.

The School is located in the heart of the Finger Lakes region in Ithaca, a city of 50,000 people, 20,000 of whom are college and university students. This scenic college town provides many cultural activities as well as athletics events. The School is located on the edge of the Cornell University campus, and students are encouraged to take advantage of the community's outstanding offerings, which include restaurants, shops, theater, and recreational facilities. There is direct air and bus service to and from New York City and other major U.S. cities.

The Cascadilla School is run by a 5-member Board of Trustees that is drawn from the business and professional community. Patricia A. Kendall is currently President of the Board and also Headmistress.

The School is privately endowed and nondenominational and has assets of approximately $1.2 million. Tuition charges provide more than 90 percent of its funding, and gifts from alumni and friends make up the remainder.

The Cascadilla School is registered with the New York State Board of Regents.

ACADEMIC PROGRAM

The Cascadilla School offers a complete high school curriculum. The School's goal is to prepare students for college in a flexible program that includes accelerated courses. In the accelerated program, full-unit high school courses are taught by the semester; the typical student completes between 7 and 8 units per year.

Twenty-three units are required for graduation, including 5 in English, 4 in social sciences, 3 in math, 3 in science, 1 in a language other than English, 1 in art and/or music, 2 in physical education, ½ in health, and 3½ in electives. All courses are taught on the New York State Regents level. In addition to taking Advanced Placement courses, seniors may enroll in actual college course work at Cornell, Ithaca College, or Tompkins Cortland Community College.

Extra help and supervised study are available in the afternoon until 5 p.m. The library and the laboratories are open until then. No evening study hall is required unless a student's academic performance falls below acceptable standards.

All class grouping is heterogeneous. Class size averages 8 students, and the student-teacher ratio is 5:1.

The Cascadilla School uses a numerical grading system that runs from 0 to 100, with 70 the minimum passing grade and 75 the start of college-recommending grades. Reports, with individual comments, are sent home monthly; more frequent reports are developed in special situations. Certain reading and writing skills are required for entrance into English III. A three-level skills program is used for students who do not meet these requirements. All students are assisted in their process of application to American universities and colleges.

FACULTY AND ADVISERS

The Cascadilla School has 10 full-time and 4 part-time teachers. All have bachelor's degrees, and 5 have master's degrees. The small size and personal nature of the School make every teacher an adviser. An attempt is made to make time in the school day for personal contact outside of regularly scheduled classes.

There is very little turnover in the full-time staff. The part-time staff is drawn from the Cornell and Ithaca college communities and changes as courses demand.

The Headmistress's academic background includes a B.S. degree from Syracuse University, an M.S. degree from Nazareth College, and an administrative degree in education from the State University of New York at Cortland. Mrs. Kendall brings nearly forty years of experience in education to Cascadilla School.

COLLEGE ADMISSION COUNSELING

Planning for college begins almost as soon as a student enters Cascadilla. A section of the library is devoted to college catalogs and career information. College visits are encouraged, and the School provides transportation for them. Involvement with the Cornell University community provides valuable stimulation for most Cascadilla students.

SAT scores for 2014–15 ranged from 1430 to 2010. Approximately one third of the graduating seniors also took the ACT.

The School averages 13 graduates per year. Each of the 12 members of the class of 2015 entered a four-year college. Recent graduates are attending Columbia, Cornell, Hamilton, MIT, Northwestern, NYU, various SUNY colleges and universities, and the Universities of Arizona, Colorado, Georgia, Illinois, Massachusetts, Michigan, Missouri, and Wisconsin.

STUDENT BODY AND CONDUCT

The Cascadilla School attracts students from a wide geographic area. Since 2008, students have come from the U.S. and eight other countries. The School has room for 25–30 boarders; day students make up the rest of the School population. Sixty percent of the students are juniors, seniors, and postgraduates; Cascadilla is interested primarily in students who are planning to be at the School for two to three years. The accelerated program works best when the students have the emotional maturity to establish goals and work toward them.

ACADEMIC FACILITIES

The classroom building was opened in 1890. It contains eight classrooms, a science laboratory, a language laboratory, a computer room, and a library of nearly 9,000 volumes.

Students who are interested in music or the visual arts may use the programs and facilities of Cornell University or Ithaca College.

BOARDING AND GENERAL FACILITIES

The two dormitories are designed to bring together the elements of a family environment, college life, and apartment living. Single and double rooms are available, each with its own refrigerator; each dormitory has a snack kitchen. Supervision is provided by dorm parents. The School tries to create a living environment that reinforces its academic programs.

Cascadilla boarding students are enrolled in a customized meal plan that includes a Cornell University dining account. The City Bucks card allows Cascadilla students to purchase additional meals at local restaurants and food stores.

ATHLETICS

The Cascadilla Gryphons soccer team provides an interscholastic athletic program throughout the academic year. Club sports include basketball, tennis, and equestrian activities. Cascadilla's physical education program offers bowling, cross-country skiing, rowing, and sailboarding. Students are also encouraged to join the YMCA, which includes the weight room and aerobics, swimming, and racquetball facilities.

EXTRACURRICULAR OPPORTUNITIES

Most extracurricular opportunities are available through the university and the community. The area is rich in cultural events that range from lectures and plays to musical performances of all types.

DAILY LIFE

Most students have 6 hours of academic course work between 9 a.m. and 4 p.m. All students and faculty members share a common lunch period. The afternoon program varies from day to day and may include physical education, student clubs, and opportunities to get extra help or tutoring. Many students also work on the School's news magazine and yearbook, which utilize their photography, graphic design, and journalism skills. After dinner, evenings typically involve study, recreation, a movie, or other extracurricular activities.

WEEKEND LIFE

The School sponsors movies and occasional parties. There may also be ski trips that include transportation, instruction, and rental of equipment. In addition, as is true of extracurricular activities during the week, students may take advantage of the wide range of opportunities at Cornell and other local schools and colleges.

COSTS AND FINANCIAL AID

Tuition, a double room, and board fees for the 2015–16 school year are $39,950. Additional charges are made for single rooms and for unusually heavy course loads.

The Cascadilla School is interested in attracting good students from all cultures and socioeconomic groups. Last year, 40 percent of the School's students received some type of financial aid or scholarship. There are also several opportunities for part-time work at the School.

ADMISSIONS INFORMATION

The Cascadilla School is looking for students who are ready to put their high school program together and prepare for college. The School, however, seeks students with academic potential, if not achievement. An admission interview is required for all U.S. applicants, and a $50 application fee is required of all U.S. applicants. An application fee is also required of international applicants.

The Cascadilla School admits students of any race, color, and national or ethnic origin to all the rights, privileges, programs, and activities generally accorded or made available to students at the School. It does not discriminate on the basis of race, color, or national and ethnic origin in administration of its educational policies, admissions policies, and scholarship, athletic, and other School-administered programs.

APPLICATION TIMETABLE

The Cascadilla School has a rolling admission process; however, the recommended application deadlines are January 15, June 30, and September 1, depending on the term in which a student wishes to begin. A $5,000 deposit is required upon acceptance. It is strongly suggested that applications be submitted by June 1 for September entrance, as the amount of dormitory space is extremely limited.

ADMISSIONS CORRESPONDENCE

Patricia A. Kendall, Headmistress
The Cascadilla School
116 Summit Street
Ithaca, New York 14850
United States
Phone: 607-272-3110
Fax: 607-272-0747
E-mail: admissions@cascadillaschool.org
Website: http://www.cascadillaschool.org

CHARLOTTE LATIN SCHOOL

Charlotte, North Carolina

Type: Independent, college-preparatory, nonsectarian, coeducational day school
Grades: Transitional kindergarten–Grade 12
Enrollment: 1,410
Head of School: Arch N. McIntosh, Jr., Headmaster

THE SCHOOL

Founded in 1970, Charlotte Latin School (CLS) is located on a 122-acre campus in southeast Charlotte, North Carolina. The school community, which includes students, parents, alumni, and faculty and staff members, embraces a shared mission, core values, and a commitment to academic excellence. Latin is a school that is traditional by design yet innovative in implementation. The School's emphasis is for its students to maintain balance in their lives, which is enhanced by a curriculum built upon a foundation of academic rigor, the arts, and athletics. Students are presented with many growth-promoting opportunities to explore and develop their interests, including a variety of co-curricular options and a TK–12 community service program that fosters a lifelong commitment to service through age-appropriate activities. Students also are encouraged to explore their world and are supported in this endeavor through active international sister schools, study-abroad, and global studies programs.

Charlotte Latin remains true to its founding parents' original vision as a place where a stimulating learning environment is united with a vibrant family life. Named for America's early Latin schools, in which colonial children pursued classical studies under the careful tutelage of their teachers, Charlotte Latin similarly fosters a close relationship between its faculty and students. With their teachers' guidance, students of all ages study and serve the community that surrounds them and the world that beckons them, in preparation to care for and succeed in the global community they will inherit as adults. Their parents, too, are partners with the School in their education and are frequently seen on campus attending special events, cheering on a Hawks athletic team, sharing lunch with their children in Founders' Hall, or serving on the Board of Trustees, Parents' Council, or one of the many volunteer committees that make Charlotte Latin a special place. Alumni, too, often return to campus to visit former teachers, and in some cases, to visit their own children at Latin. More than 3,700 alumni are members of the active CLS Alumni Association.

Charlotte Latin School is accredited by and is a member of the National, Southern, and North Carolina Associations of Independent Schools. The most recent reaccreditation by SAIS-SACS (the Southern Association of Independent Schools and Southern Association of Colleges and Schools) was in 2015. The School is also accredited by the North Carolina Department of Public Instruction. Latin is the youngest school in the United States to receive a Cum Laude Society chapter, and it has been named a Blue Ribbon School of Excellence three times by the U.S. Department of Education.

ACADEMIC PROGRAM

Charlotte Latin is organized into three divisions: the Lower School includes transitional kindergarten through fifth grade; the Middle School encompasses the sixth through eighth grades; and the Upper School is composed of the ninth through twelfth grades.

The academic program prepares students to succeed in college and beyond by instilling a lifelong love of learning. Charlotte Latin School's curriculum is designed so that each successive grade adds to the students' mastery of skills and continued maturation. Through the leadership of the Division Heads and curriculum development staff, the curriculum is constantly reviewed and refined to ensure that best practices are adopted to create a strong academic foundation and to offer students a variety of experiential learning opportunities.

The class of 2015's SAT scores reflect this academic strength. The middle 50 percent of scores are 570–710 for critical reading, 600–700 for mathematics, and 580–700 for writing. The SAT combined middle 50 percent range is 1760–2070, with a mean combined score of 1928. The class's middle 50 percent ACT composite score is 26–31.

While Latin has high expectations for its students, the School provides a nurturing environment and individual support, including a learning resources coordinator and a guidance counselor for each division.

FACULTY AND ADVISORS

At Latin's core is a dedicated faculty composed of more than 175 experienced educators. The School's low student-teacher ratios and considerable professional development resources demonstrate that Latin values its teachers and celebrates learning. Active Middle School and Upper School advisory programs foster strong ties between faculty members and students, which enable these adults to serve as positive role models for maturing adolescents.

COLLEGE ADMISSION COUNSELING

As a college preparatory school, Charlotte Latin provides a College Center that guides students and their families through every step of the college admission process. The College Center is staffed by three full-time college counselors and a full-time registrar who work actively with both students and their families throughout the Upper School years. The support is individualized and proactive, and it is designed to empower the student to take ownership of the process. The success of Latin's approach to college admissions is evidenced annually; 100 percent of the School's graduates are accepted to prestigious colleges and universities across the United States and beyond.

STUDENT BODY AND CONDUCT

The Charlotte Latin community is guided by the CLS Honor Code. A plaque bearing the inscription "Honor above all" is proudly displayed in every classroom as a constant reminder of the importance of this creed in the life of Charlotte Latin School. Adherence to the Honor Pledge is a condition of enrollment in the Upper School. Students may participate with administrators and faculty members as representatives of the Upper School Honor Council after demonstrating successive levels of leadership and personally modeling honorable conduct.

ACADEMIC FACILITIES

Latin's campus features distinct areas and buildings for each of the three divisions as well as shared facilities, such as the 17,630-square-foot Media Center and 13,275-square-foot Founders' Hall dining facility. Connected by covered walkways, each area of campus is appropriate for the developmental stage of the students while also enhancing a sense of school unity. The Horne Performing Arts Center, which opened in 2011, provides state-of-the-art instructional and performance spaces for the vocal and instrumental music programs. The theater program benefits from the performing arts center's 740-seat Thies Auditorium and Anne's Black Box Theater.

Wired and wireless computer connectivity is available in every building via a campus-wide fiber-optic network and a dedicated 300bps line for high-speed data transmission. Computer labs and mobile laptop labs are utilized by students at all grade levels, while third through twelfth grade students participate in an iPad 1:1 program. Internet access via the academic network is filtered by the School to ensure that students view only appropriate online content.

The Science, Art, and Technology Building houses shared lab spaces where engineering, computer science, and visual arts students collaborate on projects, including creating virtual reality environments. In 2015, the School was granted certification as a Fab Lab School according to criteria developed by the Massachusetts Institute of Technology. The Fab Lab features equipment such as 3-D printers and laser cutters to facilitate rapid prototyping and to encourage the design thinking that sparks students' creativity and critical thinking skills.

To help ensure a balance between instructional screen time and hands-on activities, the Hawks Quest low ropes challenge course was opened in 2013 to enhance students' experiential and outdoor learning opportunities.

ATHLETICS

Interscholastic athletics have a long and rich tradition at Charlotte Latin School. Throughout its more than forty-year history, students have proven they can compete on the playing field as well as in the classroom. Along with the many conference and state titles earned over the years, the School has always placed a premium on the values instilled and the life lessons learned from athletic competition.

Latin sponsors more than sixty-nine athletic teams in twenty-three men's and women's sports, and more than 90 percent of students in grades 7–12 participate in at least one sport.

Athletic facilities include three gymnasiums, an all-weather track surrounding the 1,450-seat Patten Stadium; six tennis courts; seven playing fields; an Olympic-quality natatorium; a cross-country course; and the Beck Student Activities Center, which includes an arena, fitness facility, indoor track, and dedicated wrestling room.

The Charlotte Latin Hawks have won the Wells Fargo/Wachovia Cup for overall excellence in high school athletics sixteen times. A commitment to athletic excellence is not only reflected in the many championship banners collected over the years but also through Latin's adherence to high standards of personal conduct and good sportsmanship on the part of student athletes, coaches, and fans.

CO-CURRICULAR OPPORTUNITIES

Charlotte Latin offers a balanced program that provides creative outlets for students' intellectual and physical energies. Beginning in the fourth grade, a broad selection of clubs and organizations is available to encourage students to pursue their interests and explore new opportunities. Leadership development is a key component of participation, with students accepting increasing responsibility for managing organizations such as the Student Council, Service Program, Model United Nations Club, and the Mosaic Club, which fosters inclusiveness and promotes awareness of diversity issues.

SUMMER PROGRAMS

The goal of Charlotte Latin Summer Programs is to provide an environment that promotes a joy for learning, where campers can develop cognitively, socially, emotionally, and physically through growth-promoting experiences. A professional and caring staff sustains a safe, structured, and innovative environment that sparks children's excitement about exploring new possibilities. Enrichment and sports camps are available for boys and girls of all ages. Fees vary depending on the camp(s) selected. For more information, call 704-846-7277.

COSTS AND FINANCIAL AID

Tuition for the 2015–16 school year is as follows: transitional kindergarten and kindergarten, $16,850; grades 1–5, $19,650; and grades 6–12, $21,280.

Charlotte Latin has need-based financial aid funds available for qualified families. Application for financial aid is made during the admissions application process. Charlotte Latin is a Malone Scholar School, and other scholarships are available to students based upon specific qualifying criteria.

ADMISSIONS INFORMATION

Charlotte Latin School's admission policies were established to fulfill the School's philosophy: to initiate in its students a love of and a respect for learning, to help them develop self-discipline, and to encourage creativity. The School seeks to attract a variety of students who demonstrate motivation and the ability to respond to the total School program. Charlotte Latin welcomes students who indicate a willingness to participate and a desire to do their best. The School believes that students with a breadth of talents and interests will contribute to the creation of a dynamic learning environment. Charlotte Latin School does not discriminate on the basis of sex, race, color, religion, sexual orientation, or national origin in the administration of its educational programs, admissions policies, financial aid policies, employment practices, or other School-administered programs.

APPLICATION TIMETABLE

Key dates and additional information about Charlotte Latin School's admissions process are available online at www.charlottelatin.org/admissions.

ADMISSIONS CORRESPONDENCE

Charlotte Latin School
9502 Providence Road
Charlotte, North Carolina 28277
United States
Phone: 704-846-1100
E-mail: inquiries@charlottelatin.org
Website: http://www.charlottelatin.org

DEERFIELD ACADEMY
Deerfield, Massachusetts

Type: Independent coeducational boarding and day school
Grades: 9–12, postgraduate year
Enrollment: 638
Head of School: Dr. Margarita O'Byrne Curtis

THE SCHOOL

Founded in 1797, Deerfield Academy offers a modern, vibrant curriculum that supports curiosity, exploration, and entrepreneurial leadership while nurturing high standards of scholarship, citizenship, and personal responsibility. Through a unique liberal arts curriculum, extensive cocurricular programs, and a supportive residential environment, Deerfield students develop inquisitive and creative minds, sound bodies, strong moral characters, and a commitment to service as they break new ground together and cultivate ideas with the potential to solve the world's most pressing problems.

The school's 330-acre campus is located in the center of Historic Deerfield, a restored Colonial village in western Massachusetts, 90 miles from Boston, Massachusetts, and 55 miles from Hartford, Connecticut. Rich in tradition and beauty, Deerfield's campus is the setting for an inclusive educational community; it inspires reflection, study and play, and the cultivation of friendships. Only 20 minutes south is the Five College area that includes Amherst, Smith, Mount Holyoke, and Hampshire colleges and the University of Massachusetts, Amherst, providing rich cultural and intellectual resources.

A 30-member Board of Trustees is the Academy's governing body. The endowment is valued at approximately $532 million. In 2013–14, operating expenses totaled $52 million, capital gifts amounted to $18.7 million, and Annual Giving was $5.5 million.

Deerfield Academy is accredited by the New England Association of Schools and Colleges. It is a member of the National Association of Independent Schools, the Independent School Association of Massachusetts, and the Secondary School Admission Test Board.

ACADEMIC PROGRAM

Deerfield's curriculum is designed to enable its graduates to assume active and intelligent roles in the world community. Courses and teaching methods are aimed at developing logical and imaginative thinking, systematic approaches to problem solving, clear and correct expression in writing and speech, and the confidence to pursue creatively personal interests and talents. Students take five courses per trimester. Their schedules are planned individually in consultation with advisors and the Academic Dean.

Graduation requirements include 4 years of English, 3 years of mathematics, 3 years of a foreign language (Arabic, Chinese, French, Greek, Latin, or Spanish), 2 years of history (including 1 year of U.S. history), 2 years of a laboratory science, 2 terms of fine arts, and 1 term of philosophy and religious studies. All tenth-graders take a 1-term course in health issues and all new students take a required course in library skills. Honors and Advanced Placement (AP) courses are offered in nineteen subject areas. Last year, 312 students sat for 713 AP exams; 93 percent of the tests received qualifying scores of 3 or better. Independent study is offered in all departments.

During the spring term, seniors may engage in off-campus alternate-studies projects, or the Directed Study Program, which offers them the opportunity to design part of their course of study. Tenth-graders and juniors also have many opportunities for off-campus study, such as

School Year Abroad: the Maine Coast Semester, which combines regular classes with studies of environmental issues; the Mountain School in Vermont; or a peer boarding school in South Africa, Botswana, Kenya, or Jordan, among other opportunities. Students may also choose from many exchange programs, including those in Australia, Hong Kong, Jordan, New Zealand, or through the Round Square organization. Summer opportunities are available in China, the Dominican Republic, France, Greece, Italy, Spain, Uruguay, and Tanzania. By challenging students to consider new perspectives and different cultures, these off-campus experiences help to integrate a Deerfield education with the shifting realities of the wider world.

The average class size is 12 and the overall student-teacher ratio is 5:1. Placement in AP courses, honors sections, and accelerated courses is based upon preparedness, ability, and interest. All students have study hours Sunday through Thursday evenings.

The school year is divided into three 11-week terms. Grades are sent at the end of each term and at midterm. In the fall and spring, academic advisors prepare written reports and comment extensively on their students' academic performance, attitude, work habits, dormitory life, participation in athletics and cocurricular activities, and as citizens of the school.

Grading is based on a numerical scale of 0 to 100. The Honor Roll is made up of students with minimum averages of 90, and the High Honor Roll recognizes students with averages of 93 and above. Students in academic difficulty are reviewed by the Academic Standing Committee at the end of each term. Teachers are available during evenings, weekends, and free periods to assist students individually. Students can also get help from the Study Skills Coordinator and/or Peer Tutors.

FACULTY AND ADVISORS

Deerfield's faculty is the school's greatest endowment. It is exceptional in its intellectual breadth and depth, its dedication to the education of young people, and its belief in the Academy's motto: "Be worthy of your heritage."

The faculty consists of 125 members; 70 percent hold advanced degrees. Ninety-eight percent reside on campus or live in the village of Deerfield. All faculty members act as advisors to students, coach sports, head tables in the Dining Hall, and serve on various committees. Teachers receive summer grants and time away from the Academy for advanced study, travel, and exchange teaching.

Dr. Margarita O'Byrne Curtis was appointed Head of School in July 2006. She earned her B.A. from Tulane, her B.S. from Mankato State, and a Ph.D. in Romance languages and literature from Harvard.

COLLEGE ADMISSION COUNSELING

Beginning in their junior year, all students attend small-group discussions that help them make informed decisions about college. In mid-winter, every junior is assigned to an individual college advisor, who further develops, with parental consultation, a list of prospective colleges. In the fall of senior year, college advisors assist students in narrowing their college choices and in making the most effective presentation of their strengths. At that time, representatives of approximately 160

colleges visit the Academy for presentations and interviews.

Normally, tenth-graders and juniors take the PSAT in October. Juniors take the SAT in January; SAT Subject Tests in December, May, and June; and Advanced Placement (AP) tests in May. Seniors, whenever advisable, take the SAT in the fall and additional AP tests later in the year. Average SAT scores for the class of 2015 were: 663 critical reading, 679 math, and 666 writing.

Of the 192 graduates in 2014, 185 are attending college, 7 students deferred admission to college for a year. Colleges attended by 5 or more graduates are: Bowdoin, Brown, Bucknell, Cornell, Georgetown, Harvard, NYU, Trinity, Virginia, and Yale.

STUDENT BODY AND CONDUCT

In fall 2015, Deerfield enrolled 638 students: 307 girls and 331 boys. This included 87 boarders and 13 day students in the ninth grade, 151 boarders and 18 day students in the tenth grade, 149 boarders and 18 day students in the eleventh grade, and 169 boarders and 24 day students in the twelfth grade (including 20 postgraduates). Part of what makes boarding school so rewarding is the experience of learning alongside students from different cultures and backgrounds. To that end, international students make up 11 percent of the student body, and those from minority groups made up 28.5 percent. Deerfield students came from 35 states and 34 countries.

In all communities, a healthy tension exists between the need for individuality and the need for common values and standards. A community's shared values define the place, giving it a distinct sense of itself. In all facets of school life, Deerfield strives to teach that honesty, tolerance, compassion, and responsibility are essential to the well-being of the individual, the school, and society. Deerfield is a residential community in which students learn to conduct themselves according to high standards of citizenship. Expectations are clear, and the response to misbehavior is timely and as supportive as possible of the students involved.

ACADEMIC FACILITIES

Deerfield's campus has 81 buildings, including the newly redesigned Boyden Library, which offers spaces for independent and group study, and houses an Innovation Laboratory, Global Studies, and College Advising; the Koch Center, a state-of-the-art 80,000-square-foot center for science, mathematics, and technology that includes a planetarium, 30 classroom and laboratory spaces, a 225-seat auditorium, the Star Terrace, and a central atrium; and the Hess Center for the Arts, which was completed in 2014 and includes the Hess Auditorium, the von Auersperg Gallery, the Elizabeth Wachsman Concert Hall, an acting lab, a cutting-edge recording studio, and several visual and performing arts spaces.

BOARDING AND GENERAL FACILITIES

There are eighteen dormitories, including the Ninth-Grade Village, which houses all ninth-grade students and features structured study experiences and extracurricular opportunities to help new students get off to a strong start. Faculty members live in apartments attached to each dorm corridor and maintain a close, supportive relationship with students. Two senior proctors also live on ninth-grade and tenth-grade corridors. Ninth-graders typically live in double rooms, and most older students live in single rooms.

The health center, Dewey House, is staffed by a full-time physician and registered nurses who specialize in adolescent care.

ATHLETICS

Participation in sports—at the student's level of ability—is the athletic program's central focus. The Academy fields interscholastic teams in baseball, basketball, crew, cross-country, diving, field hockey, football, golf, ice hockey, lacrosse, skiing, soccer, softball, squash, swimming, tennis, track, volleyball, water polo, and wrestling. Noncompetitive athletic programs include Ultimate disc, yoga, dance, skiing, squash, strength training, tennis, an outdoor skills program, and more.

Deerfield's athletics complex contains three basketball courts, a wrestling arena, an indoor hockey rink, a 5,500-square-foot fitness center with state-of-the-art cardiovascular and weight lifting equipment, trainer's room, and locker rooms; the Dewey Squash Center, a 16,000-square-foot facility housing ten international squash courts and tournament seating; and the David H. Koch Natatorium, which includes an eight-lane, 25-yard pool with a separate diving well. Ninety acres of playing fields include three football fields, twelve soccer/lacrosse fields, three field hockey fields, twenty-one tennis courts, a major-league-quality baseball field, a softball field, paddle tennis courts, the Hammerschlag Family Boathouse and crew facility, and an eight-lane 10mm full-pour track surface with two synthetic turf fields.

COCURRICULAR OPPORTUNITIES

Deerfield students and faculty members are extraordinarily productive in the performing and visual arts. Musical groups include wind ensemble, chamber music, string orchestra, jazz ensemble, the Deerfield Choral Society, a cappella groups, and the Academy Chorus. Many opportunities exist for acting as well: Deerfield is proud of its award-winning, active theater program. In addition to three major productions each year, plays and scenes are also performed by advanced acting classes. In a typical year, over 100 students participate as actors and technicians and more than 2,500 patrons attend productions.

Deerfield's comprehensive dance program provides training in modern, jazz, ballet, pointe, hip-hop, and contemporary dance techniques as well as instruction in the craft of choreography and improvisation. Classes are tailored to meet the needs of all experience levels—from complete beginners to preprofessional dancers.

Cocurricular organizations include Peer Counselors, the Diversity Task Force, Amnesty International, debate, photography, political clubs, and many more; students are welcome to start a club or alliance if they have an interest that isn't represented. Outing groups offer opportunities to ski, rock climb, and bike on weekends. Publications include an award-winning campus newspaper, the yearbook, and literary publications.

Deerfield has a tradition of service, and the Community Service Program offers a range of opportunities for students to serve the school and local and global communities.

On campus they provide service as tutors, dormitory proctors, tour guides, and waiters in the Dining Hall. They also serve on various standing and ad hoc administrative committees and play an especially important role on the Disciplinary Committee. Off-campus, ongoing projects include mentoring at nearby schools, volunteering in day-care centers, tutoring, organic farming, visiting nursing homes, working at the local animal shelter, serving meals at Second Helpings (a local soup kitchen), and sponsoring Red Cross blood drives. Some students also serve as Big Brothers or Big Sisters to local youth. Many one-time opportunities such as Habitat for Humanity work days, Relay for Life, and other special projects are offered on a sign-up basis. In addition, every ninth-grader also participates in the Deerfield Academy Perspectives Program, an on-campus service program.

DAILY LIFE

Students normally take five courses each term, and each course meets four times per week. The length of a class period ranges from 45 to 70 minutes. Classes begin at 8:30 a.m. and end at 3:05 p.m., except on Wednesdays, when classes end at 12:45 p.m. and are followed by interscholastic athletics and cocurricular activities. Classes do not meet on Saturdays. One morning a week, students and faculty members gather together for School Meeting, and students and faculty members attend seven family-style meals per week. All sports and drama activities take place after classes. Clubs and cocurricular groups meet between dinner and study hours or on weekends.

Students study in their dormitory rooms between 7:45 and 9:45 p.m., Sunday through Thursday. They may also study in the library, perform laboratory experiments, or seek help from a faculty member or Peer Tutor. During the school week, curfew for ninth- and tenth-graders is 7:45 p.m.; for juniors and seniors, it is 9:45 p.m.

WEEKEND LIFE

In addition to athletic events on Saturday afternoons, there are films, theatrical productions, and musical performances. Deerfield students spend most of their free time on campus because there always seems to be something happening. Events that are sponsored by the Student Activities Committee and chaperoned by faculty members include coffeehouses, talent shows, concerts, poetry slams, and dances. Deerfield's rural setting and extensive athletic facilities are ideal for recreational hiking, rock climbing, skiing, swimming, ice skating, and other activities, including, but not limited to ping-pong tournaments and dodgeball competitions.

The Academy Events Committee brings performers and artists to campus throughout the school year. Recent visitors include filmmaker Ken Burns and the Alvin Ailey American Dance Theater. In the winter of 2015, Deerfield held its first-ever TEDxDeerfield Academy event organized around the theme of "time." TEDxDeerfield Academy will be an annual occurrence going forward. Various lecture series bring leaders in politics, government, education, science, and journalism to campus. Students attend concerts and film series, and art exhibitions and numerous dramatic productions provide recognition for promising young artists,

photographers, and actors. Students also have access to cultural programs in the Five College area.

Ninth-graders may take two weekends off campus in the fall term and three each in the winter and spring terms; tenth-graders may take two weekends in fall, three in winter, and an unlimited number in spring; juniors and seniors in good standing may take unlimited weekends. On weekends, the curfew for ninth- and tenth-graders is 10:30 p.m. on Fridays and 11 p.m. on Saturdays. For juniors and seniors, Friday curfew is at 11 p.m.; Saturday curfew is at 11:30 p.m.

COSTS AND FINANCIAL AID

For the 2015–16 school year, the cost for boarding students was $54,720; for day students, it was $39,220. Additional fees included $2,320 for books, infirmary, and technology. Tuition is payable in two installments, on August 1 and December 1. A $2,500 deposit (credited to the August tuition bill) is due within four weeks of a student's acceptance by Deerfield.

Deerfield awards financial aid to 33 percent of its students; financial aid totaled more than $8.9 million for the 2015–16 academic year. Grants, based on demonstrated need and procedures established by the School and Student Service for Financial Aid, range from $2,500 to full tuition.

ADMISSIONS INFORMATION

Deerfield maintains rigorous academic standards and seeks a diverse student body. Selection is based upon academic ability and performance, character and maturity, and promise as a positive community citizen. The Admission Committee also closely examines candidates' teacher and school recommendations and personal essays. Students who are admitted to Deerfield are intellectually alive and highly curious about the world they live in; they seek deeper intellectual understanding and are committed to shaping their education at Deerfield and beyond.

The SSAT or ISEE is required of applicants for grades 9 and 10 and should be taken during an applicant's current academic year. The SSAT, ISEE, or PSAT is required for eleventh-grade applicants, and the PSAT, SAT or ACT is required for twelfth-grade and postgraduate candidates. In additional, the TOEFL must be taken by students for whom English is not their first language.

Deerfield Academy does not discriminate against any individual on the basis of race, color, religion, sex, sexual orientation, transgender status, marital status, national origin, ancestry, genetic information, age, disability, status as a veteran or being a member of the Reserves or National Guard, or any other classification protected under state or federal law in its admission policies or financial aid program.

APPLICATION TIMETABLE

Applicants normally visit Deerfield the year before they would begin classes. Campus tours and interviews are conducted from 8:30 a.m. to 2:20 p.m. on Monday, Tuesday, Thursday, and Friday; from 8:15 a.m. to noon on Wednesday; and at 9:00, 10:00, and 11:00 a.m. on Saturday. Weekday appointments are preferable so applicants may observe students in class. The completed application—including teacher recommendations, school transcript(s), and essays—should be submitted no later than January 15. Applicants receive notification of the admission decisions on March 10. The candidate reply date is April 10. Specific dates and more information can be found on the Academy's website at deerfield.edu/apply.

ADMISSIONS CORRESPONDENCE

Pamela Safford
Dean of Admission and Financial Aid
Deerfield Academy
Deerfield, Massachusetts 01342
United States
Phone: 413-774-1400
E-mail: admission@deerfield.edu
Website: deerfield.edu

DELBARTON SCHOOL
Morristown, New Jersey

Type: Boys' day college-preparatory school
Grades: 7–12: Middle School, 7–8; Upper School, 9–12
Enrollment: School total: 572; Upper School: 506
Head of School: Br. Paul Diveny, O.S.B., Headmaster

THE SCHOOL

Delbarton School was established in 1939 by the Benedictine monks of Saint Mary's Abbey as an independent boarding and day school. Now a day school, Delbarton is located on a 200-acre woodland campus 3 miles west of historic Morristown and 30 miles west of New York City. Adjacent to the campus is Jockey Hollow, a national historic park.

Delbarton School seeks to enroll boys of good character who have demonstrated scholastic achievement and the capacity for further growth. The faculty strives to support each boy's efforts toward intellectual development and to reinforce his commitment to help build a community of responsible individuals. The faculty encourages each boy to become an independent seeker of information, not a passive recipient, and to assume responsibility for gaining both knowledge and judgment that will strengthen his contribution to the life of the School and his later contribution to society. While the School offers much, it also seeks boys who are willing to give much and who are eager to understand as well as to be understood.

The School is governed by the 9-member Board of Trustees of the Order of Saint Benedict of New Jersey, located at Saint Mary's Abbey in Morristown. Delbarton's 2015–16 annual operating expenses totaled $21.22 million. It has an endowment of $35 million. This includes annual fund-raising support from 44 percent of the alumni.

Delbarton School is accredited by the Middle States Association of Colleges and Schools and approved by the Department of Education of the State of New Jersey. It is a member of the National Association of Independent Schools, the New Jersey Association of Independent Schools, the Council for Advancement and Support of Education, the National Catholic Educational Association, and the New Jersey State Interscholastic Athletic Association.

ACADEMIC PROGRAM

The academic program in the Upper School is college preparatory. The course of study offers preparation in all major academic subjects and a number of electives. The studies are intended to help a boy shape a thought and a sentence, speak clearly about ideas and effectively about feelings, and suspend judgment until all the facts are known. Course work, on the whole, is intensive and involves about 20 hours of outside preparation each week. The curriculum contains both a core of required subjects that are fundamental to a liberal education and various elective courses that are designed to meet the individual interests of the boys. Instruction is given in all areas that are necessary for gaining admission to liberal arts or technical institutions of higher learning.

The school year is divided into three academic terms. In each term, every boy must take five major courses, physical education, and religious studies. The specific departmental requirements in grades 9 through 12 are English (4 years), mathematics (4 years), foreign language (3 years), science (3 years), history (3 years), religious studies (2 terms in each of 4 years), physical education and health (4 years), fine arts (1 major course, 1 term of art, and 1 term of music), and computer technology (2 terms). For qualified boys in the junior and senior years, all departments offer Advanced Placement courses, and it is also possible in certain instances to pursue work through independent study or to study at neighboring colleges.

The grading system uses A to F (failing) designations with pluses and minuses. Advisory reports are sent to parents in the middle of each term as well as at the end of the three terms. Parents are also contacted when a student has received an academic warning or is placed on probation. The average class size is 15, and the student-teacher ratio is about 7:1, which fosters close student-faculty relations.

FACULTY AND ADVISERS

In 2015–16 the faculty consisted of 4 Benedictine monks and 74 lay teachers. Sixty-three are full-time members, with 57 holding advanced degrees.

Br. Paul Diveny, O.S.B., became Headmaster in July 2007. Br. Paul received his B.A. from the Catholic University of America in 1975; his diploma in Monastic Studies from the Pontificio Ateneo Sant'Anselmo in Rome, Italy in 1982; and his M.A. in German from Middlebury College in 1987. He has served the School previously as a teacher of Latin, German, ancient history, and religious studies, and as Assistant Headmaster.

The teaching tradition of the School has called upon faculty members to serve as coaches, counselors, or administrators. A genuine interest in the development of people leads the faculty to be involved in many student activities. Every boy is assigned to a guidance counselor, who advises in the selection of courses that meet School and college requirements as well as personal interests. Individual conferences are regularly arranged to discuss academic and personal development. The counselor also contacts the boy's parents when it seems advisable.

COLLEGE ADMISSION COUNSELING

Preparation for college begins when a boy enters Delbarton. The PSAT is given to everyone in the tenth and eleventh grades. Guidance for admission to college is directed by the senior class counselor. This process generally begins in the fall of the junior year, when the junior class counselor meets

with each boy to help clarify his goals and interests. Many college admissions officers visit the School annually for conferences. Every effort is made to direct each boy toward an institution that will challenge his abilities and satisfy his interests.

The mean SAT critical reading and math score for the class of 2015 was 1310. More than 25 percent of the young men in the classes of 2012, 2013, 2014, and 2015 have been named National Merit Scholars, Semifinalists, or Commended Students. In addition, 95 percent of the members of the class of 2015 were enrolled in at least one AP course.

All of the graduates of the classes of 2012, 2013, 2014, and 2015 went on to college, with 3 or more attending such schools as Boston College, Columbia, Cornell, Dartmouth, Duke, Georgetown, Harvard, Holy Cross, Johns Hopkins, Middlebury, Notre Dame, Princeton, Villanova, Williams, Yale, and the Universities of Pennsylvania and Virginia.

STUDENT BODY AND CONDUCT

The 2015–16 Upper School student body consisted of 134 ninth graders, 129 tenth graders, 126 eleventh graders, and 117 twelfth graders. The Middle School has 35 seventh and 31 eighth graders. All of the students are from New Jersey, particularly the counties of Morris, Essex, Somerset, Union, Bergen, Hunterdon, Passaic, and Sussex.

Regulations, academic and social, are relatively few. The School eschews the manipulative, the coercive, the negative, or the merely punitive approach to discipline. The basic understanding underlying the School's regulations is that each boy, entering with others in a common educational enterprise, shares responsibility with his fellow students and with faculty members for developing and maintaining standards that contribute to the welfare of the entire School community. Moreover, shared responsibility is essential to the growth of the community; at the same time, much of an individual boy's growth, the increase in his capacity for self-renewal, his sense of belonging, and his sense of identity spring from his eagerness and willingness to contribute to the life of the School. Each class has a moderator, who is available for advice and assistance. The moderator works closely with the boys, assisting them in their progress.

ACADEMIC FACILITIES

The physical facilities include two classroom buildings, a fine arts center, a science pavilion, a greenhouse, the church, and the dining hall. Academic facilities include thirty-seven classrooms, six science laboratories, art and music studios, and a library of more than 20,000 volumes. The five computer laboratories consist of 250 workstations in a networked system. The school recently adopted a one-to-one laptop program for the students and provides several charging stations throughout the campus. Three computer laboratories and dedicated classroom computers also provide over 100 workstations in a networked system. Some individual academic departments offer personal computers for advanced study in their discipline as well.

ATHLETICS

Sports at the School are an integral part of student life. The School holds the traditional belief that much can be learned about cooperation, competition, and character through participating in sports. Almost 85 percent of the boys participate on one or more interscholastic athletics teams. Varsity sports offered in the fall term are football, soccer, and cross-country; in the winter term, basketball, wrestling, track, hockey, squash, bowling, and swimming (in an off-campus pool); and in the spring, baseball, track, lacrosse, tennis, and golf. In most of these sports, there are junior varsity, freshman, and Middle School teams. Some intramural sports are available, depending upon interest, every year.

The facilities consist of two gymnasiums, eight athletics fields, six tennis courts, and an outdoor pool for swimming during warm weather. Students who join the golf team are able to play at nearby golf clubs.

EXTRACURRICULAR OPPORTUNITIES

The School provides opportunities for individual development outside the classroom as well as within. The faculty encourages the boys to express their intellectual, cultural, social, and recreational interests through a variety of activities and events. For example, fine arts at Delbarton are available both within and outside the curriculum. Studio hours accommodate boys after school, and students visit galleries and museums. In the music department, vocal and instrumental instruction is available. Performing ensembles include an orchestra, band, and chorus and smaller vocal and instrumental ensembles. Under the aegis of the Abbey Players, drama productions are staged three times a year, involving boys in a wide variety of experiences.

Other activities include Deaneries (student support groups promoting School unity and spirit), the *Courier* (the School newspaper), the *Archway* (the yearbook), *Schola Cantorum* (a vocal ensemble), the Abbey Orchestra, and the Model UN, Mock Trial, Speech and Debate, Junior Statesmen, Art, History, Chess, Cycling, Stock Exchange, and Future Business Leaders clubs. In addition, faculty moderators of the Ski Club

regularly organize and chaperone trips during School vacations.

To expose students to other cultures and to enhance their understanding of the world, faculty members have organized trips to Europe, Africa, and Latin America. The Campus Ministry office is active in sponsoring several outreach programs that lead boys to an awareness of the needs of others and the means to answer calls for help. The outreach programs include community soup kitchens, Big Brothers of America, Adopt-a-Grandparent, and Basketball Clinic for exceptional children.

Students' imagination and initiative are also given opportunities for expression through Student Council committees and assemblies. The students are also offered School-sponsored trips to cultural and recreational events at area colleges and in nearby cities.

DAILY LIFE

Classes begin at 8:15 a.m. and end at 2:34 p.m. The average number of classes per day for each student is six. Two classes are an hour long, while the remainder are 40 minutes each. The School operates on a six-day cycle, and each class meets five days per cycle. Physical education classes are held during the school day. After classes, students are involved in athletics and the arts. Clubs and organizations also meet after school, while many meet at night.

COSTS AND FINANCIAL AID

Charges at Delbarton for the 2015–16 academic year are $35,500. These are comprehensive fees that include a daily hot lunch as well as library and athletics fees. The only other major expenses are the bookstore bill and transportation, the cost of which varies. Optional expenses may arise for such items as the yearbook, music lessons, or trips.

Because of the School's endowment and generous alumni and parent support, a financial aid program enables many boys to attend the School. All awards are based on financial need, as determined by the criteria set by the School and Student Service for Financial Aid. No academic or athletics scholarships are awarded. Financial aid is granted to boys in grades 7 through 12. This year, the School was able to grant $2.3 million to students.

ADMISSIONS INFORMATION

Delbarton School selects students whose academic achievement and personal promise indicate that they are likely to become positive members of the community. The object of the admissions procedure is for the School and prospective student to learn as much

as possible about each other. Admission is based on the candidate's overall qualifications, without regard to race, color, religion, or national or ethnic origin.

The typical applicant takes one of the three entrance tests administered by the School in October, November, and December. Candidates are considered on the basis of their transcript, recommendations, test results, and personal interview in addition to the formal application. In 2015–16, 401 students were tested for entrance in grades 7 and 9; of these, 155 were accepted. Ninety-four percent of the students who were accepted for the seventh grade were enrolled; 85 percent of those accepted for the ninth grade were enrolled. Delbarton does not admit postgraduate students or students who are entering the twelfth grade.

APPLICATION TIMETABLE

The School welcomes inquiries at any time during the year. Students who apply are invited to spend a day at Delbarton attending classes with a School host. Interested applicants should arrange this day visit through the Admissions Office. Tours of the campus are generally given in conjunction with interviews, from 9 a.m. to noon on Saturdays in the fall, or by special arrangement. The formal application for admission must be accompanied by a nonrefundable fee of $65. Application fee waivers are available upon request.

It is advisable to initiate the admissions process in the early fall. Acceptance notifications for applicants to grades 7 and 9 are made by the end of January. Applicants to all remaining grades, as well as students placed in a wait pool, are given acceptance notification as late as June. Parents are expected to reply to acceptances two to three weeks after notification. A refundable deposit is also required. Application for financial aid should be made as early as possible; the committee hopes to notify financial aid applicants by the middle of March.

ADMISSIONS CORRESPONDENCE

Dr. David Donovan
Dean of Admissions
Delbarton School
Morristown, New Jersey 07960
United States
Phone: 973-538-3231 Ext. 3019
Fax: 973-538-8836
E-mail: admissions@delbarton.org
Website: http://www.delbarton.org/
   admissions

THE DERRYFIELD SCHOOL

Manchester, New Hampshire

Type: Coeducational, college-preparatory day school
Grades: Grades 6–12
Enrollment: Total: 388; Middle School: 124; Upper School: 264
Head of School: Mary Halpin Carter, Ph.D.

THE SCHOOL

The Derryfield School is an independent, coeducational, college-preparatory day school. It was founded by a group of Manchester families in 1964 to provide an outstanding secondary education, on par with the best boarding schools, where students could still be home for dinner each night.

Derryfield is a school built around its students—a school that cares about their points of view, their interests, how they learn, and their passions. Small enough and smart enough to truly personalize each learning experience, Derryfield invites students to come together to grow as individuals; to gain the skills and experience to be valued, dynamic, confident and purposeful members of any community.

Derryfield is accredited by the New England Association of Schools and Colleges and is a member of the National Association of Independent Schools (NAIS), the Association of Independent Schools of New England (AISNE), and the Independent Schools Association of Northern New England (ISANNE).

ACADEMIC PROGRAM

The promise of Derryfield's academic program is realized every day through small, engaged classes, taught by dynamic, dedicated teachers. In Derryfield classrooms, students feel safe to take intellectual risks. And what happens in the classroom is only the beginning. Derryfield's active style of learning brings Middle School science students into the woods, looking for animal tracks in the snow. It sends Upper School students to Manchester's immigrant communities for service learning. It encourages seniors to complete Independent Senior Projects that take them, in some cases, all over the world.

Derryfield's Middle School curriculum combines a seriousness of purpose with a sense of fun and love of learning, providing a firm background in skills and basic discipline areas in preparation for Upper School courses. All students in grades 6, 7, and 8 take English, mathematics, science, history, and a foreign language. In addition, all Middle School students participate in drama, music, wellness, physical education, and art.

Upper School students (grades 9–12) plan their course of study in the context of graduation requirements, college plans, and interests. A total of 18 academic credits is required with the following departmental distribution: 4 credits in English, 2 credits in history, 3 credits in mathematics, 3 credits in a world language, 2-1/3 credits in science, 1 credit in fine arts, and participation in either the alternative sports program or a team sport two seasons per year. Each student carries a minimum of five courses each term. The academic year consists of three terms.

The Independent Senior Project is an option for seniors during the final six weeks of the spring term. The project allows students to explore their interests and to gain practical experience outside of the classroom.

FACULTY AND ADVISERS

The Derryfield faculty consists of 47 members (25 men and 22 women). Master's degrees are held by 27 members and Ph.D.'s are held by 5 members. Twenty-five faculty members have taught at Derryfield for ten or more years, and annual faculty turnover is low. The student-faculty ratio is 8:1.

Faculty members are hired on the basis of a high level of expertise in their academic areas as well as enthusiasm to contribute to the overall success of their students and the School. In addition to their classroom obligations, faculty members advise approximately 8 students, coach Derryfield's athletic and academic teams, advise student activities, and make themselves available to counsel students in other areas of student life.

COLLEGE ADMISSION COUNSELING

The unique educational experience of Derryfield is evident in its graduates. Academically excellent, they are also energetic, empowered individuals. They've learned how to learn and how to make more of their college experiences and their lives.

A dedicated college counselor begins working with students in the fall of their junior year. College counseling is an active process that includes group seminars and individual meetings with students and their families. More than 100 college representatives visit Derryfield each year.

The average SAT scores for the class of 2015 were 600 in critical reading, 612 in math, and 602 in the writing section. Sixty-seven students graduated in 2015, with 100 percent of the class going to college. A sampling of the colleges and universities currently attended by 2 or more Derryfield graduates includes American, Bates, Boston College, Brown, Colby, Cornell, Dartmouth, Elon, George Washington, Georgetown, Goucher, Holy Cross, Johns Hopkins, Middlebury, NYU, Northeastern, Providence, Quinnipiac, RIT, St. Lawrence, Syracuse, Tufts, William and Mary, and the Universities of Colorado–Boulder, Michigan, Vermont, and Virginia.

STUDENT BODY AND CONDUCT

Of the 388 students enrolled at The Derryfield School, 124 students attend the Middle School and 264 students attend the Upper School. Students come from fifty communities in New Hampshire and northern Massachusetts, as well as several foreign countries. To make the commute easier, bus transportation is available to five different regions of the state, including a route to the Seacoast.

Students are guided by five Fundamental Standards, and five Daily Guidelines for success at Derryfield. The Standards are:

1. Be honest.
2. Treat people and property with care and respect.
3. Take care of yourself in body, mind, and spirit.
4. Obey federal, state, and local laws.
5. Maintain the reputation and good nature of the school.

The Guidelines are:

1. Be present and engaged.
2. Be timely.
3. Be responsible, both on and off campus.
4. Dress appropriately.
5. Put forth your best effort.

While there is a dress code, it is not formal, and there is no uniform. Certain days during the year are dress-up days (Grandparents' Day in the fall, and sports teams' away games, for example), and there are also Spirit Days, on which students are invited to be creative in their dress.

ACADEMIC FACILITIES

Derryfield's academic facilities include classroom buildings with five fully equipped science laboratories, a STEM classroom, a technology center with workstations and laptops, a 95-seat multimedia lyceum, a 20,000-volume library with a large subscription database, two art studios, an art gallery, and a 400-seat performing arts center. Outdoor classroom facilities include several miles of cross-country trails, high and low ropes courses, and many acres of woods. A turf field, a full-sized gymnasium, weight-training area, and trainer's room are also valuable learning sites for courses in physical education and health and wellness. In addition, the School opened the 8,000-square-foot Gateway Building in 2011, which houses administrative offices, the Breakthrough Manchester Program, and additional teaching spaces.

ATHLETICS

"A sound mind in a healthy body" defined the Greek ideal and is the concept at the core of Derryfield's physical education, health and wellness, and athletics philosophy.

All Middle Schoolers (grades 6–8) take physical education and health and wellness. Seventh and eighth graders also have competitive athletic requirements. Offerings include alpine skiing, baseball, basketball, cross-country running, field hockey, lacrosse, Nordic skiing, soccer, softball, and tennis.

In the Upper School (grades 9–12), two levels of competitive sports teams (junior varsity and varsity), as well as some alternative physical activities (e.g., yoga, dance, weight training) are offered. Upper School athletics include alpine skiing, baseball, basketball, crew, cross-country running, equestrian, field hockey, golf, hockey, lacrosse, Nordic skiing, soccer, softball, swimming, bass fishing, and tennis. The School also honors areas of physical interest that it does not offer on site; students may request that an independent physical activity be a replacement for one of the two required seasons.

Derryfield is a member of the New Hampshire Interscholastic Athletic Association, participating in Divisions I, II, III, and IV, according to sport. Derryfield currently has the most athletic offerings of any Division IV school in New Hampshire and has garnered more than thirty-five state championships in the last ten years.

ARTS

Derryfield believes that an education designed to bring out the best in every student would not be complete without the arts, so the School's commitment to the arts is strong. Upper School students perform two large-scale theater productions each year, one musical and one play, while seventh and eighth graders stage their own musical. Each sixth grade drama class produces a junior musical. Instrumental ensembles that include classical, jazz, and orchestral instruments are active in both the Middle and Upper School. There are vocal groups in both schools, and Upper School students may audition for a select chorus or a cappella groups for men and women. All musicians participate in two concerts per year and frequently in talent shows and assemblies. Students are encouraged to audition for the New Hampshire All-State Chorus and Band. Visual art students regularly submit materials to the New Hampshire Student Artist Awards and the Boston Globe Scholastic Art Awards, and help organize displays of their own work in Derryfield's art gallery openings. Derryfield's campus also includes a sculpture garden, where student work is displayed each year.

EXTRACURRICULAR AND GLOBAL OPPORTUNITIES

In each of the two schools, Middle and Upper, students participate in more than a dozen student-organized clubs. Choices include School Council, Conservation Club, Art Club, Gay/Straight Alliance, Empower Women Club, Robotics Club, Social Media Ambassadors, and Chinese Culture Club, among others. Derryfield also offers competitive clubs, including Math Team, Mock Trial, Granite State Challenge, and Model United Nations. Student publications include newspapers, literary magazines, academic journals, and a yearbook.

Field trips, organized through classes or clubs, include regular visits to New York City, Boston, and Manchester museums, theaters, courtrooms, and outdoor areas of interest. Each year, different faculty members lead groups of students on cultural or service-learning outings. Upper School trips for the 2015–16 school year include two weeks exploring the language and culture of Spain, a Habitat for Humanity work project in North Carolina, and service-oriented trips to Eleuthera, Bahamas and a Native American reservation. Middle School opportunities include trips to Washington D.C. or Costa Rica. Derryfield has also established an exchange program for ninth and tenth grade students with two South African high schools, the Durban Girls' College in Durban and the Wynberg Boys' School in Cape Town.

In its dedication to local and global communities, Derryfield's Key Club actively partners with more than a dozen organizations, including the New Hampshire Food Bank, the American Cancer Society, New Horizons Soup Kitchen, Boys and Girls Club, Special Olympics, and local immigrant/refugee programs.

Breakthrough Manchester, a year-round, tuition-free academic program, is also an important part of The Derryfield School. Breakthrough offers motivated students from Manchester's public middle schools the

opportunity to learn from outstanding high school and college students. Several Derryfield faculty members work as mentor teachers, while a large number of Derryfield students teach for Breakthrough.

Traditional Derryfield events and celebrations include Founders' Day, Winter Carnival, Grandparents' Day, Head's Holiday, Country Fair, Moose Revue talent show, and the Prom.

DAILY LIFE

Because Derryfield students come from approximately fifty different surrounding towns, the School itself becomes a hub for learning, playing, serving, and socializing.

The school day begins at 7:55 a.m. and ends between 2:45 and 3:20 p.m. Departure times vary, depending on grade, a student's grade, level of involvement in extracurricular activities, or desire to obtain extra help from a teacher, use the library, or attend study hall.

The class schedule is a seven-period, seven-"day," rotating schedule, with blocks set aside each day for extracurricular meetings. Homeroom gatherings occur three mornings per week, and advisory groups meet three times per week. Monday's extracurricular block is an all-school assembly; the Tuesday and Friday blocks allow time for an activities period, during which clubs meet; and Thursday's is an academic block, when students may study independently, or seek extra help from their teachers. Athletic practices and games are held after the academic day ends.

SUMMER PROGRAMS

The Derryfield campus continues to be busy over the summer, when summer programs take over, including lacrosse, soccer, and a very popular theater camp. There are also a number of academic options, featuring robotics, academic skills, SAT preparation, creative writing, and writing for the college process.

COSTS AND FINANCIAL AID

Tuition and fees for 2015–16 are $30,500. In addition to the need-based Financial Aid Program and the Merit and Malone Scholarship Programs, which offer direct grants, the School offers installment payment options.

The Financial Aid Program is designed to make a Derryfield education accessible to qualified students who could not otherwise afford the cost of attending. On average, Derryfield provides financial assistance to 23 percent of the

student body, with awards that vary from 5 to 95 percent of tuition. Derryfield awards nearly $2 million in financial aid grants annually.

The Merit Scholarship Program is designed to recognize students who demonstrate qualities that will add meaning and vitality to Derryfield's core values or are distinguished by a commitment to purposeful involvement in both the local and global community. Awards of up to $15,000 are made annually.

The Malone Scholars Program was established in 2012 with a $2 million award from the Malone Foundation in recognition of the School's academic program. The Foundation's goal is to improve access to quality education for gifted students who lack the financial resources to develop their talents. Currently, the school has five Malone Scholars, and anticipates an additional Scholar will be added for the 2016–17 school year.

ADMISSIONS INFORMATION

The Admission Committee considers applications from students entering grades 6 through 12. Although the largest number of students enters in grades 6, 7, and 9, spaces are often available in other grades as well.

Applicants are required to complete an on-campus interview and an online written application. The SSAT is required for all applications to grades 6 through 9. Applicants to grade 10, 11, and 12 have the option to submit their PSAT or SAT scores.

APPLICATION TIMETABLE

The priority deadline for applications is February 1. Tours and interviews are offered through the Admission Office. There is a $50 preliminary application fee for applicants.

Notification of acceptance is mailed on March 10, and families are expected to reply by April 10.

ADMISSION CORRESPONDENCE

Admission Office
The Derryfield School
2108 River Road
Manchester, New Hampshire 03104-1396
United States
Phone: 603-669-4524
Fax: 603-641-9521
E-mail: admission@derryfield.org
Website: http://www.derryfield.org

GRIER SCHOOL
Tyrone, Pennsylvania

Type: Girls' boarding and day college-preparatory school
Grades: 7–PG: Middle School, 7–8; Upper School: 9–12, postgraduate year
Enrollment: School total: 308
Heads of School: Douglas A. Grier, Director; Gina Borst, Head of School

THE SCHOOL

Grier School was founded in 1853 as the Mountain Female Seminary and was reincorporated in 1857 under the direction of Dr. Lemuel Grier. The School has been successfully operated under the management of four generations of the Grier family. In 1957, the School was reincorporated as a nonprofit foundation administered by an alumnae Board of Trustees. Grier is located on a 300-acre campus in the country, 3 miles from Tyrone, Pennsylvania, and halfway between State College (where Penn State University is located) and Altoona.

The School is committed to a highly supportive philosophy aimed at developing each girl's full potential as an individual. Competitive sports are offered but do not overshadow the many intramural, life-sports, and creative arts opportunities available to each girl. Grier does not seek an elitist or high-pressure label and is proud of its family-like environment. "Friendliness" is the word most often used by visitors to describe the atmosphere.

The current endowment stands at approximately $20 million, supplemented by $750,000 raised through the most recent Annual and Capital Giving program.

Grier School is accredited by the Middle States Association of Colleges and Schools. It has memberships in the National Association of Independent Schools, the Pennsylvania Association of Independent Schools, and the Secondary School Admission Test Board.

ACADEMIC PROGRAM

Grier offers a multi-track academic program. The Elite Scholars Program is well suited for high-achieving students interested in honors and AP courses. AP courses are offered in all subject areas as twenty class offerings. While all classes are college preparatory in nature, the Learning Skills and Student Support programs ensure that all students receive the support they need to empower themselves as learners. Every attempt is made to pace the curriculum to the needs of individual students, and crossover is encouraged between the academic tracks according to the abilities of the students.

Learning Skills, a course taught by 3 specialists, is available for students who require additional academic structure and provides opportunities for tutoring and the development of strong study habits. This program serves the needs of approximately 50 students at Grier. A comprehensive English as a second language program is offered to international students. Girls who test below 100 on the TOEFL Internet-based test are required to attend an intensive summer session.

Students are encouraged to take at least one elective in the arts each year. The variety of course offerings is designed to provide students with the opportunity to pursue areas of interest and to develop and enhance their individual talents. Strong programs are offered in studio art, ceramics, jewelry making, photography, weaving, costume design, dance, music, and drama. Art faculty members help students assemble portfolios in preparation for higher education.

FACULTY AND ADVISERS

The full-time faculty consists of 47 women and 19 men, more than half of whom have received advanced degrees.

Douglas A. Grier, Director of the School for the past thirty years, is a graduate of Princeton and has an M.A. and a Ph.D. from the University of Michigan. Gina Borst is the Head of School. She has a B.S. and an M.Ed. from Penn State University. She has worked at Grier for twenty-three years.

Many faculty members live on campus, and 22 housemothers supervise the dormitories. Faculty members are available for extra academic help on a daily basis. Faculty members also serve as advisers to students and participate in various clubs and sports activities.

COLLEGE ADMISSION COUNSELING

The School has two full-time college counselors who work with students in their junior and senior years. College counseling begins in the winter term of the junior year with class discussions about colleges, admissions requirements, and application procedures. The college counselors then discuss specific colleges with each student individually and help the student develop a preliminary list of colleges to investigate and visit over the summer, thus refining the list. In the fall of the senior year, the counselors review each student's list again and encourage the student to apply to at least six colleges. Applications are usually sent by Thanksgiving (or before Christmas break at the latest).

Graduates of the class of 2015 were accepted at various colleges and universities, including Bates, Berkeley, Boston College, Bryn Mawr, Carnegie Mellon, Cornell, Harvey Mudd, Smith, and the University of Virginia.

STUDENT BODY AND CONDUCT

Students come from nineteen states and seventeen other countries.

Students are expected to follow the rules as defined in the student handbook. A Discipline Committee composed of students,

faculty members, and administrators handles all infractions. Grier believes that good citizenship should be encouraged through incentive, and girls earn merits for good conduct, honors grades, and academic effort.

The student government consists of a Student Council with representatives from each class. The council serves as a forum for student concerns and helps plan the weekend programs.

ACADEMIC FACILITIES

Trustees Building is a modern classroom facility that was completely remodeled in summer 2002. It houses academic classrooms and art studios for ceramics, batik, and photo printmaking. Adjoining buildings house computer studios, language classrooms, and the Landon Library, which houses 16,000 volumes. The Fine Arts Center, housing extensive facilities for music and art classes, opened in January 2002. The Science Center opened in August 2003. Grier's Performing Arts Center, containing practice and performance space for dance and drama, opened in June 2006. Four new classrooms were added to the academic facilities when a new dormitory was completed in September 2012. The Music Building opened in September 2015 and features classrooms for instrumental music, two grand piano studios, an orchestra rehearsal room, and a computer lab for video and music production.

BOARDING AND GENERAL FACILITIES

The living quarters consist of seven dormitory areas and seven cottages. The dorms and cottages provide a modern private bath for every two rooms. Two girls share a room, and each combination of two rooms and bath is called a suite. All students must leave the campus for Thanksgiving, Christmas, and spring break, though the School does sponsor trips during Thanksgiving and spring break.

Multiple student lounges with TVs and games are available, and a School-operated snack bar is located in a remodeled eighteenth-century log cabin.

The Health Center is located on the campus and is staffed with registered nurses at all times for emergencies or any medical concern that may arise.

ATHLETICS

Students of all ability levels are encouraged to participate in either the interscholastic sports program, which includes riding, dance, basketball, soccer, volleyball, and tennis, or the life-sports program of riding, dance, swimming, tennis, fencing, archery, badminton, yoga, body sculpting, scuba diving, and skiing/snowboarding. Grier has an excellent horseback riding program with 3 full-time instructors and 2 part-time instructors. Four stables accommodate 33 School horses and up to 15 privately owned horses. Two indoor and two outdoor rings are located on the campus within an easy walking distance of the dorm. Grier's Western indoor ring was completed in September of 2012.

The School's gymnasium is well suited for basketball and volleyball. Grier's state-of-the-art fitness center opened in September 2006. Five tennis courts and ample playing fields round out the School's physical education facilities.

EXTRACURRICULAR OPPORTUNITIES

Student groups active on campus include Grier Dance; Grier Equestrians; the Athletic Association; drama, cooking, baking, outing, ecology, modern languages, and community service clubs; and the yearbook and School newspaper. In addition, students participate in "Green and Gold" intramural sports, which often include soccer, volleyball, basketball, softball, and horseback riding.

Creative arts play an important part in school life, and girls can participate in several activities for enjoyment and credit, including drama, photography, art, instrumental music, voice, and dance.

DAILY LIFE

Classes begin at 8 and run until 2:37, Monday through Friday; sports activities are scheduled during the next 3 hours. A 40-minute period is set aside daily for student-teacher conferences, and an all-school meeting is held monthly. Students have a 105-minute supervised study period in the dormitories Sunday through Thursday nights.

WEEKEND LIFE

Because most of Grier's students are boarders, a comprehensive program of weekend activities is planned. Approximately eight dances are planned annually, usually for Saturday evenings. The Outing Club uses the nearby facilities of Raystown Lake for camping and hiking, and canoeing and white-water rafting on the Youghiogheny River are also popular. Tussey Mountain Ski Resort is 40 minutes away.

Nearby Penn State University provides many cultural, social, and educational opportunities. A wide variety of field trips are offered each year, ranging from rock concerts to ski weekends to trips to Washington, D.C., Pittsburgh, and New York City. A regular schedule of visiting artists and a movie series complete the social activities.

COSTS AND FINANCIAL AID

Tuition, room, and board for the 2015–16 school year was $50,500. Books cost approximately $500 per year. Off-campus entertainment is optional, with additional costs charged based on individual participation. A deposit of $5,000 is due with the Enrollment Contract. Parents may elect to pay the entire tuition by July 1 or pay 75 percent in July and the balance in December.

Financial aid is based primarily on need. To apply, parents must submit the Parents' Financial Statement to the School and Student Service for Financial Aid in Princeton, New Jersey. In 2014–15, 50 percent of the student body received a total of $2.5 million in financial aid.

ADMISSIONS INFORMATION

Grier seeks college-bound students of average to above-average ability who possess interest in sports and the arts as well as a desire to work in a challenging yet supportive academic atmosphere. Applicants are accepted in grades 7 through 12 (and occasionally for a postgraduate year) on the basis of previous record, recommendations, and an interview. Grier School admits students of any race, nationality, religion, or ethnic background.

Approximately 50 percent of all applicants are accepted for admission.

APPLICATION TIMETABLE

Grier has rolling admissions, and the Selection Committee meets on a regular basis to consider students whose files are complete. Candidates are asked to file an application and transcript release form with a $50 application fee, submit two teacher's recommendations, and have a personal interview on campus. The Admissions Office is open for interviews and tours during both the academic year and the summer.

ADMISSIONS CORRESPONDENCE

Jennifer Neely, Director of Admissions
Grier School
Tyrone, Pennsylvania 16686
United States
Phone: 814-684-3000
Fax: 814-684-2177
E-mail: admissions@grier.org
Website: http://www.grier.org

LAURALTON HALL, THE ACADEMY OF OUR LADY OF MERCY

Milford, Connecticut

Lauralton Hall
Connecticut's First Catholic College-Prep School for Girls

Type: Girls college-preparatory day school
Grades: 9–12
Enrollment: 465+
Head of School: Antoinette Iadarola, Ph.D., President

THE ACADEMY

Lauralton Hall, the Academy of Our Lady of Mercy, is a Catholic college-preparatory high school, founded in 1905 by the Sisters of Mercy. The first Catholic college-prep school for young women in Connecticut, it is over 100 years old—a major milestone for any school and even more significant for a Catholic girls' school. A member of the National Coalition of Girls' Schools, Lauralton Hall is accredited by the New England Association of Schools and Colleges and the Connecticut Department of Education.

Lauralton Hall is one of a select group of Catholic girls' schools that has remained true to its original mission. Inspired by the Mercy Tradition, Lauralton Hall empowers young women to pursue their highest potential through lifelong learning, compassionate service, and responsible leadership in a global society. This empowers young women to excel in any endeavor, to find their own voices, and to be bearers of mercy for others. Since Lauralton believes character formation is as essential as academic achievement, the core values of a Mercy education play an integral role in a Lauralton Hall education: compassion and service, educational excellence, concern for women and women's issues, global vision and responsibility, spiritual growth and development, and collaboration.

A Lauralton education is transformational; girls learn to take risks and forge lasting friendships. They will learn to be concerned not only for their own well-being, but for the well-being of others. The school's goal is to graduate competent, confident, and compassionate young women empowered for life in the twenty-first century.

ACADEMIC PROGRAM

The well-rounded Lauralton Hall curriculum fully prepares students for college study, with demanding honors and advanced placement classes offered in all academic disciplines. In keeping with the tradition of the Sisters of Mercy, students are constantly challenged to think of others and to reach out to those in need. They are expected to become Renaissance women for the twenty-first century—articulate and poised, confident and compassionate, gracious in their strength, at home in their own times, respectful of the past, and fully prepared to embrace the future.

Lauralton strives to develop clear, independent thinkers who appreciate knowledge and the learning process. The school offers a solid and well-balanced college-preparatory curriculum, which emphasizes a mastery of analytical and critical thinking

skills, problem solving, and the ability to communicate ideas effectively. Challenging and demanding college-preparatory, honors, and advanced placement courses are offered. Courses are also available through the UConn Early College Experience (ECE), a concurrent enrollment program that allows motivated high school students to take UConn courses at their high schools for both high school and college credit. Every course taken through the UConn ECE is equivalent to the same course at the University of Connecticut. Established in 1955, the UConn ECE is the nation's longest running concurrent enrollment program and is nationally accredited by the National Alliance of Concurrent Enrollment Partnerships (NACEP).

Lauralton Hall offers Advanced Placement (AP) courses in calculus, chemistry, English language and composition, English literature and composition, European history, French, Spanish, Environmental Science, and United States history. UConn ECE courses are offered in biology, elementary discrete mathematics, European history, fundamentals of music theory, environmental science, and U.S. history.

In order to graduate, a minimum of 25 credits must be earned, which must include six major subject areas (English, world languages, history, mathematics, science, and religion), one credit in fine arts, physical education, and 75 hours of community service.

FACULTY AND ADMINISTRATION

There are 43 faculty members, 7 administrators, 4 guidance counselors, and 2 library media specialists. About 81 percent of the faculty members hold advanced degrees.

COLLEGE ADMISSION COUNSELING

Individual conferences and group sessions are an integral, ongoing part of each student's guidance experience during her four years at Lauralton Hall. The counselors guide students in making appropriate college choices and help students with the application process.

In recent years, Lauralton Hall graduates have attended top-tier institutions such as Boston College, Brown, Carnegie Mellon, College of the Holy Cross, Columbia, Dartmouth, Duke, Georgetown, Harvard, Rensselaer Polytechnic Institute, the United States Military Academy, the United States Naval Academy, the University of Pennsylvania, Vanderbilt, and Vassar, to name a few.

STUDENT BODY AND CONDUCT

Centrally located in historic downtown Milford, more than 460 young women from 40 Connecticut towns commute by bus, train, or car to attend Lauralton Hall. They come seeking the same rigorous preparation for college as the more than 6,000 alumnae who have passed through Lauralton's halls for over 100 years. The students are from diverse socioeconomic, religious, and ethnic backgrounds; about 76 percent are Catholic, and 20 percent are students of color.

ACADEMIC FACILITIES

The beautiful 30-acre campus surrounds a Victorian mansion built in 1864. The mansion and its property were purchased by the Sisters of Mercy in 1905 for use as a school. The administrative building, known as Mercy Hall, and the St. Joseph school building were added to provide classrooms, offices, an auditorium, a library/media center, and the school chapel. The school also has a music building, an athletic center, five new state-of-the-art science labs, and art rooms.

ATHLETICS

At Lauralton Hall, students have the opportunity to participate in many different interscholastic athletics and are required to take physical education classes. "We've got the spirit!" summarizes what student athletes at Lauralton Hall experience: the joy of competition, pride in school and personal accomplishments, and the ability to win or lose with heads held high. Lauralton Hall athletes are expected to play fair, enjoy honest competition, and demonstrate sportsmanship, dedication, and compassion for one another, opponents, officials, and spectators. The school is a member of the Connecticut Interscholastic Athletic Conference (CIAC) and the Southern Connecticut Conference (SCC). There are fifteen varsity sports: basketball, cheerleading, cross-country, field hockey, golf, gymnastics, ice hockey, lacrosse, skiing, soccer, softball, swimming and diving, tennis, track and field, and volleyball. The campus has its own playing fields and an athletic center, which houses a basketball court as well as a fully equipped fitness center.

EXTRACURRICULAR OPPORTUNITIES

In preparing its young women to become visionary leaders and active members of their communities, Lauralton encourages each student to become involved in at least one extracurricular activity. Clubs, organizations, and activities bring new experiences, new challenges, and new friends. With more than thirty clubs and organizations to choose from, there is something to fit the interest of every young woman. Extracurricular activities include culture trips, student council, national and language honor societies, a fall musical, a spring play, Christmas and spring concerts, art club, youth and government, environmental club, percussion ensemble, Shakespeare club, humanities, classic film, dance club, Key club, debate club, world language clubs, student literary publications, yearbook, and school mixers/dances. New groups and activities are added yearly, based on student interest.

CAMPUS MINISTRY

Lauralton students are sisters in faith. They help the less fortunate and are stewards of the earth. They have retreats, liturgies, and prayer services.

The Office of Campus Ministry annually sponsors special collections to benefit those less fortunate. Lauralton's students generously embrace these initiatives. The four-year service program builds compassion and links the school to the global community through national and international mission trips.

The Lauralton Hall Women of Mercy award was created in 2004 to recognize young women, chosen by their peers, who exemplify the qualities of mercy established by Catherine McAuley: compassion, kindness, honesty, integrity, and care for the least of God's people.

DAILY LIFE

Classes begin at 8 a.m. with homeroom and end at 2:20 p.m., Monday through Friday. Sports and activities are offered after school.

SUMMER PROGRAMS

Lauralton Hall offers summer sports and enrichment programs for girls and boys. A qualified adult staff guides children through a week of learning and fun in a safe environment. Open to students ages 6 and up, these high-quality, educational, fun programs offer participants an opportunity to experience community and engage in diverse activities on the beautiful Lauralton Hall campus at various times and dates from the end of June through August.

Enrichment programs include a variety of offerings in art, sports, science, writing, cooking, and more. Recent sessions have included STEM Gems, video making, baking, all levels of cooking, Art Adventure, Fun Adventures, creative writing, CSI, physics, soccer, basketball, baseball, field hockey, lacrosse, softball, and cheerleading.

COSTS AND FINANCIAL AID

Tuition for 2015–16 is $18,750, plus the cost of books and uniform. There is also a $150 athletics fee per sport per athlete. Financial aid and scholarships are available. About 24 percent of students receive financial aid.

ADMISSIONS INFORMATION

Interested parents and prospective students, including transfer students, may request information by contacting Mrs. Kathleen O.

Shine, Director of Enrollment Management at kshine@lauraltonhall.org or 203-877-2786. Information can also be accessed on the school website, www.lauraltonhall.org. Prospective students are also welcome to spend a day at the school.

APPLICATION TIMETABLE

Inquiries are welcome anytime. Applications should be submitted online by November 15, but they are accepted later, space permitting. The application fee is $60.

ADMISSIONS CORRESPONDENCE

Admissions Office
Lauralton Hall
200 High Street
Milford, Connecticut 06460
United States
Phone: 203-877-2786
Fax: 203-876-9760
E-mail: admission@lauraltonhall.org
Website: http://www.lauraltonhall.org

THE LAWRENCEVILLE SCHOOL

Lawrenceville, New Jersey

Type: Coeducational boarding and day college-preparatory school
Grades: 9–PG (Second–Fifth Forms): Lower School, Second Form; Circle/Crescent Level, Third–Fourth Forms; Fifth Form
Enrollment: 817
Head of School: Stephen S. Murray, Head Master

THE SCHOOL

The Lawrenceville School was founded in 1810 by Isaac Van Arsdale Brown as the Maidenhead Academy. Throughout the 1900s, Lawrenceville continued to develop as a leader in academic innovation, including early adoption of Advanced Placement (AP) courses and the introduction of nationally and internationally known guest speakers designed to broaden the intellectual horizons of young Lawrentians. Among the most-lasting changes was the introduction in 1936 of the Harkness method of education, which sought to bring the benefits of the House system to the classroom by providing an intimate environment for intellectual discourse.

Discussion of coeducation began in earnest in the 1970s, and after a lengthy, but thoughtful analysis of what it would mean both pedagogically and practically to the School, the Board elected to accept female students in 1985. The first girls arrived on campus in 1987 and brought a new vitality to the campus community. As the twentieth century drew to a close, the School embraced the ever-increasing diversity of its students in gender, geography, faith, race, and socioeconomic status, focusing on the need for a Lawrentian education to include broad exposure to all facets of the global community and an appreciation for and understanding of multiculturalism.

For more than 200 years, Lawrenceville graduates have gone on to success in their chosen fields, prepared by their education for the changing world around them. As the School enters its third century of educating students, it welcomes new students to join the legacy of Lawrenceville and discover what it means to be a Lawrentian in the 21st century.

The Lawrenceville School is located on 700 acres in the historic village of Lawrenceville, New Jersey.

The mission of the School is to inspire and educate promising young people from diverse backgrounds for responsible leadership, personal fulfillment, and enthusiastic participation in the world. Through its unique House system, collaborative Harkness approach to teaching and learning, close mentoring relationships, and extensive co-curricular opportunities, Lawrenceville helps students to develop high standards of character and scholarship; a passion for learning; an appreciation for diversity; a global perspective; and strong commitments to personal, community, and environmental responsibility.

Lawrenceville is accredited by the Middle States Association of Colleges and Schools and is a member of the Secondary School Admission Test Board, the National Association of Independent Schools, the New Jersey Association of Independent Schools, and the Council for Religion in Independent Schools.

ACADEMIC PROGRAM

The School's graduation requirements are designed to ensure students receive a strong foundation in all disciplines during their first two years that can be built upon in the upper forms. The requirements meet NCAA standards and are aligned with standard requirements for college admissions.

The requirements for entering Second Formers are: arts, 3 terms; English, 9 terms; history, 6 terms; humanities–English, 3 terms; humanities–cultural studies, 3 terms; interdisciplinary, 2 terms (at the advanced level); language through Level 3*; mathematics through advanced algebra or precalculus*; religion and philosophy, 2 terms; and science, 9 terms*. Students are also required to give at least 40 hours of community service before they graduate. (*Students may opt to finish their course work in one of these disciplines at the foundational level with approval.)

Individual participation is encouraged in small classroom sections that average 12 students. Classes are grouped randomly and are taught around a large oval table called the Harkness table. Evening study periods, held in the Houses, are supervised by the Housemaster, the Assistant Housemaster, or an Associate Housemaster.

Students may also apply for independent study, off-campus projects, or the Lawrenceville international programs. Recent destinations include China, the Dominican Republic, Mexico, Japan, France, Peru, Nicaragua, Ghana, the Galapagos, Great Britain, South Africa, and Tanzania. Other opportunities include language immersion trips, where students reside with host families. Driver's education is also available.

Lawrenceville uses a letter grading system (A–F) in which D– is passing and B+ qualifies for honors.

The school year is divided into three 10-week terms. Full reports are sent home at the end of each term, with interim reports at midterm. The full reports include comments and grades from each of a student's teachers indicating his or her accomplishments, efforts, and attitudes. Less formal progress reports are also written by teachers throughout the term as needed. Students in academic difficulty are placed on academic review, which entails close supervision and additional communication with parents.

FACULTY AND ADVISERS

There are 102 full-time and two part-time faculty members, and eight teaching fellows, all of whom hold numerous degrees: 15 doctorates (13 Ph.D.'s, 2 J.D.'s); 70 master's; and 17 bachelor's. Most faculty members reside on the campus, and many serve as residential Housemasters, coaches, and club advisers. All are active in advising and counseling students.

Stephen S. Murray H'55 '65 P'16 became the Lawrenceville School's 13th Head Master on July 1, 2015. Murray came to the Lawrenceville School with deep independent school leadership experience. In his most recent role as Headmaster of University School in Shaker Heights and Hunting Valley, Ohio (a position he held for a decade), Murray was responsible for the overall management of the two-campus K–12 boys' school of 875 students and 235 faculty and staff. From 1990–2005, Murray led a distinguished career at Deerfield Academy including serving as Assistant Headmaster, Academic Dean, Dean of Students, and as teacher, coach, and faculty resident.

Murray received a B.A. in French and Political Science with honors in 1985 from Williams College, an Ed.M. from the Harvard Graduate School of Education in 1987, an M.A. in French Literature from the Harvard Graduate School of Arts and Sciences in 1990, and is a 1981 graduate of Phillips Exeter Academy.

Murray currently serves or has served on the boards of numerous nonprofit and civic institutions, including chairing the Board of the Center for the Study of Boys' and Girls' Lives (in collaboration with the University of Pennsylvania), chairing the Board of Citizens' Academy Charter School in Cleveland, and chairing and/or serving on the boards of the Cleveland Council of Independent Schools, the International Boys' School Coalition, and Camp Agawam, and was invited to participate in the civic engagement program Leadership Cleveland.

COLLEGE ADMISSION COUNSELING

The College Counseling Office supports, informs, and encourages students and their families as they navigate the exciting, complex, and ever-changing process of college admissions. The counselors educate students and families about the nuances of admissions, advise students about college options that best suit their individual needs, and support and encourage students as they complete the application process.

Lawrenceville's college counselors offer students decades of professional experience as college counselors and college admissions officers. The counseling staff provides valuable and timely advice to families as the process unfolds and helps students present their abilities, talents, and experiences to colleges in the most appropriate manner. The five counselors carry a small average case load of 45 students, which allows for personal attention and sustained involvement in all aspects of the residential school community. Over the course of their Lawrenceville careers, families and students receive information through form-specific newsletters, class-wide meetings, and Parents' Weekend programming. They also have access to Naviance, an online college admission management tool. All of these resources help ensure that students and their families are well prepared to embrace the college counseling process when students are officially assigned to individual counselors in the middle of their Fourth Form year.

Median SAT scores are: 690 critical reading, 700 math, and 700 writing. Between 2013 and 2015, the twenty colleges most attended by Lawrenceville students were the following: Princeton, Georgetown, NYU, Columbia, University of Pennsylvania, Brown, Yale, Duke, University of Virginia, Stanford, Colgate, Davidson, Dartmouth, Trinity, Williams, University of Chicago, Bucknell, Johns Hopkins, Boston College, and University of Michigan.

STUDENT BODY AND CONDUCT

For 2015–16, there are 817 students: boarding 561, day 256, male 427, and female 390. Students are from 34 states and 40 countries.

Lawrenceville expects its students to achieve good records and develop self-control, systematic study habits, and a clear sense of responsibility. The School has a high regard for energy, initiative, a positive attitude, and active cooperation. Students accepting this premise have no trouble following the basic regulations.

The student body elects five governing officers from among students in the Fifth Form, and each House elects its own Student Council.

ACADEMIC FACILITIES

Lawrenceville's first rate, state-of-the art academic facilities, which include Fathers' Building, the Kirby Arts Center, Gruss Center of Visual Arts, the F. M. Kirby Math and Science Center, the Juliet Lyell Staunton Clark Music Center, Bunn Library, and the Noyes History Center, offer a unique opportunity for all students. Each building houses an entire academic discipline, so students are immersed within a particular subject from the minute they enter the building until the minute they leave.

Lawrenceville supports excellent teaching with outstanding educational and campus resources. The Bicentennial Campaign, completed in 2010 in honor of the School's 200th anniversary, demonstrated the intense willingness of alumni, parents, and friends to provide the absolute best facilities and support for students and faculty. This most ambitious campaign raised $218.5 million, exceeding the $200 million goal, for student financial aid, faculty support, academic programs, and student life. Among the campaign's successes were the new Al Rashid Health and Wellness Center, a state-of-the-art facility for both treatment and prevention; Carter House, a Crescent girls' residential house; and lighted turf fields of the Getz Sports Complex.

BOARDING AND GENERAL FACILITIES

Lawrenceville's most distinguishing feature is its House system. In each of the twenty Houses, the Housemaster maintains close contact with the residents. House athletics teams compete on an intramural level, and House identity is maintained through separate dining rooms in the Irwin Dining

Center for the underformers. This distinctive system provides a small social environment in which each student's contribution is important and measurable.

Services in the Edith Memorial Chapel are nondenominational. The Al Rashid Health and Wellness Center offers inpatient and outpatient medical care, including psychological counseling services, and a consulting staff who offer gynecological care, orthopedic/sports medicine, and nutrition. Certified athletic trainers provide rehabilitation services for injuries. The Center's health professionals seek to educate and encourage students to develop the knowledge and skills needed to sustain a lifetime of healthy function.

ATHLETICS

Lawrenceville regards athletics as yet another educational opportunity for students and a valuable complement to the School's rigorous academic expectations. The importance of commitment; satisfaction of teamwork; hard lessons of failure; courage to surmount pain, fatigue, and frustration for a common goal; the virtue of physical conditioning; imperatives of sportsmanship; and the sheer joy of healthy competition are values Lawrenceville's athletic program is uniquely suited to teach. In addition, the School's proud interscholastic tradition and comprehensive intramural program, along with instruction in lifetime sports, ensure that each student experiences the challenge and reward of athletic competition.

The School takes pride in its first-class outdoor sports facilities: two FieldTurf artificial playing surfaces with lights for field hockey, lacrosse, and soccer; and eighteen other multipurpose natural grass athletic fields, including five intramural fields and two softball and two baseball diamonds. There are also twelve tennis courts, a nine-hole golf course, and a quarter-mile all-weather track. The crew program enjoys the use of a bay and other facilities at the Mercer Lake Rowing Association boathouse.

The Edward J. Lavino Field House is one of the finest athletic facilities at any independent school. The main arena has a Mondo surface with three combination basketball-volleyball-tennis courts; a four-lane 200-meter banked indoor track, with an eight-lane straightaway; and long jump, shot put, pole vault, and high jump areas. Along each side of the arena are two gymnasiums, a six-lane competition swimming pool, a wrestling room, a performance center, and an athletic training wellness room. A modern, enclosed ice hockey rink is attached to the Lavino Field House, and there are ten Anderson international squash courts. Nearby, a separate building houses the state-of-the-art, 4,500-square-foot Al Rashid Strength and Conditioning Center that is supervised by two certified coaches.

Students must participate in an approved form of athletic activity each term. Rehabilitation of athletic injuries and fitness testing are an important part of the athletic program and are available to students by Lawrenceville's two certified athletic trainers.

The School's outdoor, experientially based programs and initiatives educate students in responsible leadership, community membership, and character development and provide interactions in the outdoor environment, enhancing both academic and nonacademic skills development. Lawrentians have traveled the globe through outdoor program courses, scaling glaciers in Patagonia, trekking through the desert in South Africa, and sea kayaking among icebergs in Newfoundland. Athletic credit is given to participants.

Lawrenceville's ropes course offers students the opportunity to accept a challenge and work toward conquering it as a group. The course, created and built by an outdoor experiential education expert, is designed to help students listen to each other, trust each other, and work toward a common goal.

EXTRACURRICULAR OPPORTUNITIES

Lawrenceville provides a numerous opportunities for students to explore outside the classroom. There are more than 155 clubs and organizations specializing in interests such as writing, acting, debate, music, art, history, religion, science, photography, woodworking, and scuba diving.

Through the required Community Service Program, students serve as tutors, elementary school study center supervisors, and group activity counselors. The School sponsors organized educational and cultural trips to New York City and Washington, D.C.

Exhibits occur throughout the year. Several lecture programs bring speakers and artists to the campus. Annual events include Parents' Weekend in the fall, Parents' Winter Gathering, and Alumni Weekend in the spring.

DAILY LIFE

Lawrenceville students have their schedules packed full of classes, study hours, athletic practice, rehearsals, and time for friends, special events, eating, and sleeping. Students learn to manage their time, meet their commitments, and enjoy their friendships.

Classes begin at 8 a.m. on most days, and the dining center opens at 7 a.m. for breakfast. Each class meets four times a week for 55-minute sessions. Science and advanced classes have an additional 55-minute period each week for labs, extended discussions, test practice, writing workshops, etc. There are also three 40-minute periods each week for student-teacher consultations. Students are highly encouraged to take advantage of consultation periods.

The entire School eats lunch at the same time, and each House dines together. This tradition is yet another example of how the House system defines the Lawrenceville experience. On Mondays, students take lunch with their academic advisers. Each advisee group shares a table, and time is spent discussing both individual and group concerns; if needed, students can schedule a private meeting with their adviser.

The entire School assembles once a week for an all-School community meeting. These gatherings feature readings, reflections, and announcements. School meeting agendas include outside speakers, special guests, musical presentations, and opportunities to examine student issues.

Classes end at 3:05 p.m., but then there is more to do—sports or community service. On Wednesdays, classes end at 12:20 p.m., and students have the option of studying, rehearsing, practicing sports, working on publications, or fulfilling their community service requirement. Saturday classes end at 11:30 a.m.

Dinner is served from 5:30 to 7 p.m. All Forms eat in the Irwin Dining Center, except for the Fifth Form, which takes meals in the Abbott Dining Room. After dinner, there is time for clubs, activities, homework, and socializing. Check-in is at 8 p.m. for Lower School, 8:30 p.m. for Crescent and Circle Houses, and 9 p.m. for the Fifth Form, Sunday–Friday. Permission to leave the House after check-in to go to the library, rehearsals, club meetings, or to meet a teacher for consultation is granted after check-in time, but students must check back in with the Housemaster on duty by 10 p.m. (11 p.m. on Saturday).

WEEKEND LIFE

On weekends, at least one House sponsors an all-School social event, which may include carnivals, concerts, formal dinners, and dances. Faculty members are on hand to take trips to local shopping areas and movie theaters. Reach Out to the Arts is a faculty-led club that takes weekly trips to cultural events in New York. Day students are encouraged to attend all-campus activities.

COSTS AND FINANCIAL AID

The annual charges for 2015–16 are $57,840 for boarding students and $47,550 for day students.

Through the generosity of alumni, friends, and foundations, approximately $11.7 million in funds are available to provide financial assistance to qualified students. Currently, 33 percent of the student body receives assistance. Awards are made on the basis of character, ability, past performance, and future promise. Amounts are based solely on need and are determined by procedures established by the School and Student Service for Financial Aid.

ADMISSIONS INFORMATION

All students who enter must be able to meet the academic standards. Lawrenceville also looks for students who possess the potential to become vitally interested members of the student body—students who make individual contributions.

Selection is based on all-around qualifications without regard to race, creed, or national origin. Character, seriousness of purpose, and future promise as well as past performance, the recommendation of a headmaster or principal, and SSAT results are all taken into consideration by the Admission Committee.

For fall 2015, 2,068 applications were submitted for grades 9–12, of which 252 enrolled. Required for admission is the formal application, which includes a written essay, a transcript of the applicant's school record, a letter of recommendation from the head of the current school, three reference letters, SSAT or ISEE and/or TOEFL scores, and an on-campus interview.

APPLICATION TIMETABLE

Campus interviews are conducted during the week from 9 a.m. to 2 p.m. Monday, Tuesday, Thursday, and Friday. Applicants can also interview on Wednesdays from 9 a.m. to 10:30 a.m. and on Saturdays from 8:30 a.m. to 11:30 a.m. Interviews are not conducted on Saturdays during the summer months.

The application deadline is January 15 for boarding and day students, at which time all application materials must be submitted and interviews completed. The notification date is March 10, and parents reply by April 10.

ADMISSIONS CORRESPONDENCE

Dean of Admission
The Lawrenceville School
2500 Main Street
P.O. Box 6008
Lawrenceville, New Jersey 08648
United States
Phone: 609-895-2030
800-735-2030 (toll-free outside New Jersey)
Fax: 609-895-2217
E-mail: admission@lawrenceville.org
Website: http://www.lawrenceville.org

MAINE CENTRAL INSTITUTE
Pittsfield, Maine

Type: Coeducational traditional boarding and day college-preparatory and comprehensive curriculum
Grades: 9–12, postgraduate year
Enrollment: 500
Head of School: Christopher Hopkins

THE SCHOOL

Founded in 1866 by Free Will Baptists, Maine Central Institute (MCI) retains the inventive spirit and philosophy of its founders but no longer has a formal affiliation with the church. During the school's pioneer years, MCI served as a feeder school to Bates College in nearby Lewiston, Maine. Although adhering to upstanding and traditional educational values, MCI is progressive and broadminded, pledging to provide a comprehensive college-preparatory education to a multicultural student body diverse in talents, abilities, and interests.

MCI regards each student as an individual with individual needs and aspirations. In keeping with its belief in individuality, MCI strives to foster an overall environment of mutual respect, cooperation, and tolerance among all of its members and with the surrounding community. In a safe and caring atmosphere, students are encouraged to develop a moral and social consciousness, self-esteem, and social responsibility and to become globally aware, lifelong learners.

The rural town of Pittsfield (population 4,500) is nestled in between the Atlantic Ocean and the mountains of western Maine. The region of central Maine provides prime opportunities for hiking, skiing, biking, fishing, skating, and snowmobiling. The campus is within walking distance of local eateries, recreational parks, shopping, hiking trails, and a movie theater.

Maine Central Institute is accredited by the New England Association of Schools and Colleges and approved by the State of Maine Department of Education. MCI is also a member of the College Board and the National Association of Independent Schools.

ACADEMIC PROGRAM

MCI offers a rigorous comprehensive curriculum to accommodate various learning styles and academic abilities. MCI fosters the intellectual curiosities of its student body by offering accelerated and advanced placement courses in all core subject areas.

For grades 9–12, 20 credits are required for graduation. Students must successfully complete units in English (4), mathematics (4), social studies (3, including U.S. history), science (4), physical education (1), fine arts (1), computer science (½), and health (½). Students are required to take the equivalent of at least 6 units each semester. MCI also offers a postgraduate academic year with college prep and advanced placement courses.

MCI's math and science programs exceed national standards and utilize state-of-the-art technology and academic facilities.

Students in MCI's well-known humanities program understand the culture of an era through a study of its history, literature, and art. The school has an award-winning music program.

The world language program includes four levels of French and Spanish. In 2009, MCI added a Chinese Mandarin program to the world languages, which is taught by a teacher from China. In addition to the traditional offerings, students may take courses in psychology, guitar, business, sociology, public speaking, computer-assisted drawing, vocational subjects, and piano.

MCI offers a structured ESL program for the international student who is planning for a university education. Students receive individual testing before placement at one of four levels of ESL. The extensive ESL program includes American history for international students and carefully structured math classes that focus on the development of math language skills. MCI also offers a two-week summer program for ESL which is required for all new international students.

FACULTY AND ADVISERS

The 2015–16 faculty consists of 60 full-time members. More than a quarter of the faculty and staff members reside on campus, while the rest live in nearby towns such as Newport, Waterville, and Bangor.

Faculty members are selected on the basis of three main criteria. They must possess a strong subject-matter background, the ability to relate to students, and an educational philosophy consistent with that of the institution and its mission. Faculty members are also expected to become actively involved in coaching, supervising dormitories, advising, counseling, and student affairs.

COLLEGE ADMISSION COUNSELING

A guidance team of 5 professionals is available for students. Counselors are responsible primarily for helping students with post-secondary placement and academic program planning. Approximately 75 college admissions representatives visit MCI's campus annually. Career counseling is also an integral part of the counseling department. Financial aid workshops for seniors, postgraduates, and their parents are offered. Preparation for the SAT and ACT is offered within the math and English curricula. Supplemental SAT preparation is offered outside of the school day.

MCI has a strong history of placing students in post-secondary schools. Schools attended by recent graduates include Bates, Boston College, Boston University, Brown, Colby, Columbia, Cornell, Emerson, Emory, George Mason, George Washington, Hofstra, Husson, Maine Maritime Academy, Michigan State, Muhlenberg, Northeastern, NYU, Pace, Penn State, Princeton, Simmons, Syracuse, Tufts, UCLA, and the Universities of Connecticut, California, Maine, New England, New Hampshire, North Carolina–Chapel Hill, Rhode Island, Virginia, and Washington.

STUDENT BODY AND CONDUCT

The 2015–16 enrollment of 500 includes day and boarding students. Students come to MCI from six states and thirteen countries.

Students at MCI are expected to be good citizens and are held responsible for their behavior. The rules that provide the structure for the school community are written in the student handbook. Disciplinary issues are the responsibility of the administration, the faculty, and the residence hall staff.

ACADEMIC FACILITIES

There are seventeen buildings housed on the 23-acre campus. Visitors are greeted upon entrance with the stoic simplicity of the campus with its brick-front buildings and the historic bell tower of Founder's Hall.

The Math and Science Center is a 23,000-square-foot recent addition to MCI, including fifteen instructional spaces, a computer classroom, and a nearby greenhouse. MCI adopted a one-to-one computer program in 2013, providing every student with an iPad for use at school and at home. Students can access Wi-Fi throughout campus and the dormitories. The school also has 100 additional computers are available for student use. Students have access to both the Powell Memorial Library and the Pittsfield Public Library.

BOARDING AND GENERAL FACILITIES

Boarding students reside in single-sex residence halls on campus, supervised by resident faculty and staff members. There is also an option for the highest-achieving residential students to live in the Honors Dormitory. Each residence hall has its own recreation room and laundry facilities. The Trustee Memorial Student Center was recently added to the MCI campus. It is home to the dining hall, student lounge, and garden sitting area, including a performance stage, food court, garden benches, and game room.

Weymouth Hall houses the ESL Center, the Wellness Center, the school bookstore, and an additional student lounge.

MCI offers a unique Host Family Program. Participating students are paired with a family from the community that makes the student a part of its family for the school year. Students may spend time with their host family on weekends, after school, and during vacations.

ATHLETICS

MCI believes that athletics are an important part of the education process, a dynamic lesson in teamwork, and a hallmark of personal dedication. The school offers a comprehensive athletic program for student-athletes of varying levels of ability by offering JV, varsity, and club-level sports.

There are eighteen sports teams for boys and girls, including baseball, basketball, cheering, field hockey, football, golf, lacrosse, rifle, soccer, softball, tennis, track, and wrestling.

Wright Gymnasium and Parks Gymnasium are multiple-use athletic facilities, and each contains a weight room and locker facilities. Located on the main campus are a football field, a practice field, a ¼-mile track, and a rifle range. Manson Park has fields for soccer, field hockey, baseball, and softball as well as three tennis courts. The school has the use of a local golf course and ski areas for competitive teams and recreation.

EXTRACURRICULAR OPPORTUNITIES

MCI students may choose from among thirty-nine campus organizations, which represent some of the following interests: drama production; world languages and travel to places such as Costa Rica, Spain, France, Italy, and Russia; chess; robotics; Kindness Krew; Outdoor adventure team, which includes hiking, biking, canoeing, and other activities; weight lifting; Key Club, which is the school's community service organization; computer science; and public speaking. Students may participate in Student Council; MCI's strong, award-winning music program includes concert band, concert choir, chamber choir, vocal jazz ensemble, instrumental jazz ensemble,

jazz combo, percussion ensemble, and pep band; and the Math Team which competes locally and statewide.

Bossov Ballet Theatre offers MCI students a unique opportunity to study classical ballet as part of the academic curriculum. Ballet classes are taught by Natalya Nikolaevna Getman, a former dancer with the Moscow Ballet. The program allows students to earn full academic credit for ballet training. Students who complete the program are uniquely positioned either to matriculate to an outstanding college or join a professional ballet company.

DAILY LIFE

The school day begins at 7:45 a.m. and ends at 2:45 p.m., with a 40-minute lunch break.

Classes run from Monday through Friday, with dinner served from 5 to 6:30 p.m. Sunday through Thursday, there is a mandatory supervised study hall from 7 to 8:30 p.m. for all boarding students. Honors Study is available to high-achieving students.

WEEKEND LIFE

Supervised weekend activities include trips to Canada, Boston, the nearby capital of Augusta, the city of Portland, historic ports, lighthouses and coastal towns along the Atlantic shoreline, and cultural and athletic events both on and off campus. Activities such as whale watching, white-water rafting, and skiing at Sugarloaf Resort are also offered. With parental permission, students are allowed to go home on weekends or visit the home of their host family.

COSTS AND FINANCIAL AID

The 2015–16 tuition, room, and board are $42,000 for boarding students, and tuition is $10,000 for private day students. The cost for ESL support is $3,000 for the first class and $2,000 for each additional class. The nonrefundable deposit of $5,000 is due within two weeks of an offer of admission. A variety of payment plans are available.

Financial aid is awarded on a need basis, determined by information shown on the Parents' Confidential Statement and any additional financial information that is requested.

ADMISSIONS INFORMATION

MCI's Admissions Committee screens all applicants to determine their compatibility with MCI's philosophy that students should assume a mature responsibility for their own education. No entrance tests are required, but an on-campus or online video conference interview with each student and his or her parents is strongly recommended. School transcripts and results of standardized tests are used to determine academic ability and appropriate academic placement in classes in accordance with the student's individual needs, abilities, and interests.

Maine Central Institute does not discriminate on the basis of race, sex, age, religion, sexual preference, disability, or national or ethnic origin in the administration of its educational and admission policies, financial aid programs, and athletic or other school-administered programs and activities.

APPLICATION TIMETABLE

Inquiries and applications are welcome at any time; however, applying by June 1 is recommended. Visits may be scheduled at any time during the year but are most effective when school is in session. Tours and interviews can be arranged by calling the Admissions Office, which is open Monday through Friday from 8 a.m. to 4:30 p.m. A nonrefundable application fee of $75 is required.

ADMISSIONS CORRESPONDENCE

Clint M. Williams, Dean of Admission
Maine Central Institute
295 Main Street
Pittsfield, Maine 04967
United States
Phone: 207-487-2282
Fax: 207-487-3512
E-mail: cwilliams@mci-school.org
Website: http://www.mci-school.org
Twitter: mciadmissions
Facebook: https://www.facebook.com/pages/
    MCI-Admissions/732239663517712
Skype: mciadmissions

MARYMOUNT SCHOOL OF NEW YORK

New York, New York

Type: Girls' independent college-preparatory Catholic day school
Grades: N–XII: Lower School, Nursery–II; Lower Middle School, III–V; Upper Middle School, VI–VIII, Upper School, IX–XII
Enrollment: School total: 749; Upper School: 230
Head of School: Concepcion R. Alvar

THE SCHOOL

Marymount School of New York is an independent Catholic day school that educates girls in a tradition of academic excellence and moral values. The School promotes in each student a respect for her own unique abilities and provides a foundation for exploring and acting on questions of integrity and ethical decision-making. Founded by Mother Marie Joseph Butler in 1926 as part of a worldwide network of schools directed by the Religious of the Sacred Heart of Mary, Marymount remains faithful to its mission "to educate young women who question, risk, and grow; young women who care, serve, and lead; young women prepared to challenge, shape, and change the world." Committed to its Catholic heritage, the School welcomes and values the religious diversity of its student body and seeks to give all students a deeper understanding of the role of the spiritual in life. The School also has an active social service program and integrates social justice and human rights into the curriculum.

Marymount occupies three adjoining landmark *Beaux Arts* mansions, located on Fifth Avenue's historic Museum Mile, a fourth mansion on East 82nd Street, and a recently renovated 42,000-square-foot facility on East 97th Street. The Metropolitan Museum of Art and Central Park, both located directly across the street from the Fifth Avenue Campus, provide resources that are integral to the School's academic and extracurricular programs. Several studio art classes meet in the Museum's Carroll Classroom. As part of the Class IX humanities curriculum and in advanced art history courses, Upper School students have classes in the Museum weekly. Central Park is used for science and fitness classes as well as extracurricular activities. Other city sites, such as the United Nations, Carnegie Hall, the American Museum of Natural History, MoMA, and the Guggenheim, are also frequent extensions of the classroom for Marymount students.

Since 1969, the School has been independently incorporated under the direction of a 30-member Board of Trustees made up of parents, alumnae, educators, and members of the founding order. The School benefits from a strong Parents' Association; an active Alumnae Association; the involvement of parents, alumnae, and student volunteers; and a successful Annual Giving Program.

Marymount is accredited by the New York State Association of Independent Schools (NYSAIS). The School holds membership in the National Association of Independent Schools (NAIS), NYSAIS, the Independent Schools Admissions Association of Greater New York (ISAAGNY), the National Catholic Education Association, the National Coalition of Girls' Schools (NCGS), and the Educational Records Bureau (ERB).

ACADEMIC PROGRAM

The study of classic disciplines at Marymount is dynamic and innovative. The rigorous college-preparatory curriculum emphasizes critical thinking, collaboration, communication, and creativity. Students are encouraged to question and explore topics in depth, to take intellectual risks, and to work independently and collaboratively to find alternative approaches to problems. With its focus on the education of young women, Marymount allows each student to find her own voice. Students develop the skills necessary to succeed in competitive colleges and in life beyond the classroom: self-confidence, leadership ability, a risk-taking spirit, and joy in learning.

A commitment to the study of science, technology, engineering, art, and mathematics (STEAM) is reflected in Marymount's curriculum, which fully integrates information and communication technologies into all subject areas. Students have access to desktop and laptop computers, iPads, and other mobile computing devices throughout the School. Students in Classes K through V use iPads for individual and collaborative exploration, creation, and communication. Students in Classes VI through XII and staff members each have a school-supplied MacBook, school email, and Google account and use digital media to carry out research, create presentations, publish work, communicate, and demonstrate ideas and concepts. Students learn a wide variety of authoring tools as well as programming languages to create and publish digital media. Using an array of interactive media, students extend discussions and collaborations beyond the classroom. Using online tools and video-conferencing, students collaborate on projects with other Marymount Schools and with students and researchers around the globe.

Marymount's position at the forefront of educational technology relies on more than the investment in laptops, iPads, interactive displays, software, and networks. To maintain its cutting-edge program—which has been recognized for excellence by NAIS, NCGS, littleBits, and Apple Inc.—the School offers technology workshops throughout the school year for the faculty and other NAIS-school faculty members. Sponsored in part by a generous grant from the E. E. Ford Foundation, Marymount established the Making and Learning Institute in 2014 to offer professional development to teachers in New York City interested in hands-on learning and innovative teaching.

The School offers honors and Advanced Placement courses as well as electives and studio courses, including art history, economics, classical Greek, introduction to acting, advanced drawing portfolio, 2-D design, critical thinking in the arts, Middle Eastern studies, physical computing, and data visualization. In senior English, students choose from seminars that cover topics from slave narratives to contemporary American drama to women's literature. Most students elect to take a fourth year of math; advanced offerings include AP calculus AB, AP calculus BC, AP statistics, and calculus. Fourth-year science courses include advanced or AP courses in biology, chemistry, and physics, as well as molecular biology, atmospheric science, and engineering. The science program connects with and utilizes the research of numerous institutions, including Cold Spring Harbor Laboratory's DNA Learning Center in Manhattan, the New York Academy of Sciences, and Princeton University. The School also participates in the STEM Internship Program and the STEM Research Program. Class XII students may elect to take AP psychology or other advanced courses through Marymount's affiliate membership in Online School for Girls.

While a leader in science and technological education, Marymount is also committed to the study of humanities. All Class IX students take part in the Integrated Humanities program, an interdisciplinary curriculum that focuses on history, literature, and art history in the study of ancient civilizations. Classes are held at the Metropolitan Museum of Art at least once a week. The program includes a performance-based World Civilizations Festival and collaborative research projects in history and art history. As a culminating project, seniors submit an interdisciplinary writing portfolio of selected work from their last three years of high school.

The visual and performing arts offerings include studio art, media arts, AP 2-D design, AP drawing, ensemble music, choral music, chamber choir, and introduction to acting. The after-school chorus, Marymount Singers, performs regularly at masses and concerts, and the Marymount Players stage two productions annually.

The religious studies program includes comparative religions, Hebrew scriptures, the New Testament, social justice, and ethics. With a focus on moral and ethical decision-making, students analyze systemic social issues and immerse themselves in the community through numerous service projects, as well as the Marymount Philanthropy and Community Transformation (M-PACT) program. The Catholic-Jewish Initiative provides students with a deeper understanding of the Judeo-Christian tradition and includes Holocaust studies and a trip to the National Holocaust Museum in Washington, D.C.

High school graduation requirements include satisfactory completion of 4 years of English, 3 years of history, 3 years of math, 3 years of laboratory science, a 3-year sequence of a world language, 4 years of religious studies, 4 years of physical education, 3 semesters of visual/performing arts, and 2 semesters of health education. These requirements provide a broad, solid base of knowledge while sharpening problem-solving and research skills and promoting critical and creative thinking. Upper School students are formally evaluated four times a year, using an A–F grading scale. The evaluation process includes written reports and biannual parent/student/teacher conferences.

During the summer after junior year, each student participates in an off-campus internship to gain exposure to a career of interest. Students have interned at hospitals, research laboratories, law firms, financial organizations, theaters, schools, nonprofit organizations, and corporations. They also attend a career day, with visiting alumnae as guest speakers. A financial literacy program prepares graduates for the financial challenges of college and life.

As members of a worldwide network of schools, students may opt to spend the second semester of their sophomore year at a Marymount International School in London or Rome. There are also opportunities for shorter cultural or language exchanges at schools in Brazil, Colombia, Spain, and France. Annual concert and study tours and service trips extend the curriculum. Recent study tours have included researching sea turtles with Earthwatch in the Bahamas and discovering scientists and poets in England and Scotland. Recent service trips have brought students to advocate for Typhoon Haiyan victims on Capitol Hill and to build affordable housing in Florida. The Marymount Singers enjoy an annual concert tour and have performed domestically and abroad.

Housed in a newly renovated facility on East 97th Street, the Upper Middle School encourages, supports, and challenges early adolescent students as they continue to develop independence, leadership, and achievement. Experiential, inquiry-based learning offers students opportunities to question their thinking, shape their understanding, and explore varied points of view as they become critical thinkers and innovative problem-solvers. Studio courses allow students to tinker, explore, and practice creative expression. Students in the Upper Mid are expected to be both independent and collaborative, curious and compassionate, bold and reflective.

The Lower Middle School curriculum welcomes the diverse interests of young adolescents and is structured to channel their energy and natural love of learning. The integrated core curriculum gradually increases in the degree of departmentalization at each grade level, and challenging learning activities and flexible groupings in main subject areas ensure that the students achieve their full potential. Speech classes prepare the girls for dramatic presentations reflective of their social studies and literature curriculum, and Class V students visit the Metropolitan Museum of Art for studio art and social studies classes. Uptown Broadway, an extracurricular option, allows the students to participate in a full-scale musical production.

The Lower School provides child-centered, creative learning within a challenging, structured environment. The curriculum focuses on the acquisition of foundational skills, often through an interdisciplinary approach. Programs engage students in the exciting process of learning about themselves, their surroundings, and the larger world. Introductory lessons in Spanish complement the social studies curriculum. A hands-on science program; an emphasis on technology integration, including a study of robotics and coding; a popular School chorus; and an extensive after-school program are some highlights of the Lower School.

FACULTY AND ADVISORS

There are 120 full-time and 17 part-time faculty members, allowing for a 5:1 student-teacher ratio. Eighty-eight percent of the faculty members hold master's degrees, and 7 percent hold doctoral degrees. In Nursery through Class II, each class has a head teacher and at least one assistant teacher. In Classes III through V, each class has three homeroom teachers. In Classes VI–XII, each student has a homeroom teacher and an advisor, usually one of her teachers, who follows her academic progress and provides guidance and support. Learning resource specialists, school nurses, an athletic trainer, artists-in-residence, and school psychologists work with students throughout the School.

Concepcion R. Alvar was appointed Headmistress in 2004 after serving thirteen years as the Director of Admissions and three years as a head teacher. She also served as the Director and Supervisor of Marymount Summer for sixteen years. Mrs. Alvar holds a B.S. from Maryknoll College (Philippines) and an M.A. from Columbia University, Teachers College.

COLLEGE ADMISSION COUNSELING

Under the guidance of the Director of College Counseling, Marymount's formal college counseling program begins during the junior year. Two College Nights are held for Class XI students and parents. Individual counseling throughout the semester directs each student to those colleges that best match her achievements and interests. Students participate in weekly guidance classes to learn about general requirements for college admission, the application process, and standardized tests. During the fall of their senior year, students continue the weekly sessions, focusing on essay writing, admissions interviews, and financial aid applications.

Graduates from recent classes are attending the following colleges and universities: Amherst, Barnard, Boston College, Boston University, Bowdoin, Brown, Columbia, Connecticut College, Cornell, Dartmouth, Davidson, Duke, Fairfield, Fordham, George Washington, Georgetown, Harvard, Holy Cross, Kenyon, Middlebury, NYU, Oberlin, Oxford University, Princeton, Sewanee, Skidmore, Smith, Stanford, Trinity, Tufts, Vanderbilt, Villanova, Wake Forest, Washington (St. Louis), Wellesley, Wesleyan, Wheaton, Williams, Yale, and the Universities of Notre Dame, Pennsylvania, St. Andrew's (Scotland), and Virginia.

STUDENT BODY AND CONDUCT

Marymount's enrollment is 749 students in Nursery through Class XII, with 230 girls in the Upper School. Most students reside in the five boroughs of New York City; however, Upper School students also commute from Long Island, New Jersey, and Westchester County. Students wear uniforms, except on special days; participate in athletic and extracurricular activities; and attend weekly chapel services, all-school masses, and annual class retreats.

Marymount encourages students to be active participants in their education and in the life of the School community. Students seek out leadership and volunteer opportunities, serving as advocates for one another through peer mentoring, retreat teams, and the Big Sister/Little Sister program. Student government and campus ministry provide social and service opportunities that enable students to broaden their perspectives, develop as leaders, sharpen public-speaking skills, and form lasting friendships. Teachers and administrators encourage each student to respect herself and others and to be responsible members of the community.

ACADEMIC FACILITIES

The *Beaux Arts* mansions on Fifth Avenue provide rooms for Lower and Upper School classes, and include four science laboratories, two art studios, a math center, an idea lab and tinker space, a gymnasium, an auditorium, a courtyard play area, a chapel, and a library complex. The East 82nd Street facility is the home of the Lower Middle School. Students in the Lower Mid, Upper Mid, and Upper Schools also attend classes at the East 97th Street campus. This renovated facility is the home of the Upper Middle School and includes a gymnasium, cafeteria, and three floors of classrooms. The fourth floor of the 97th Street Campus features several science classrooms and laboratories as well as a media-production lab and a fab lab where students can design, engineer, and fabricate an array of objects and solutions using 3-D printers, laser cutters, and other fabrication tools. The additional campus also offers space for visual and performing arts, dance, and fitness. All classrooms feature interactive boards and multimedia displays.

ATHLETICS

The athletics program promotes good health, physical fitness, coordination, skill development, confidence, and a spirit of competition and collaboration through its physical education classes, the electives program for Classes X–XII, and individual and team sports.

Marymount provides a full schedule for varsity and junior varsity sports, as well as competitive teams at the V/VI and VII/VIII class levels. Participants in Classes V/VI stay two days per week for an after-school sports program; students in Classes VII/VIII commit to three afternoons per week. The junior varsity and varsity teams compete within the Athletic Association of Independent Schools League (AAIS) in badminton, basketball, cross-country, fencing, field hockey, lacrosse, soccer, softball, swimming, tennis, track and field, and volleyball.

In addition to its gymnasia, Marymount has an athletics field and tennis court on East 97th Street for PE classes and sports practices, and the School uses facilities and field throughout New York City for some practices and competitions in field sports, track and field, tennis, and swimming.

EXTRACURRICULAR OPPORTUNITIES

A wide range of clubs and activities complement the academic program, promote student initiative, and provide opportunities to contribute to the School community and develop communication, cooperation, and leadership skills. Student-led clubs include Amnesty International, book club, digital photography, science and the environment club, film club, finance club, forensics team, Mathletes, philosophy club, set design/tech crew, student government, and women in action. Campus Ministry, CAMBIAS (Cultural Awareness Club), Marymount Singers, Marymount Players, Mock Trial, Model UN, and National Honor Society offer additional opportunities for student service, leadership, and performance. Student publications include a yearbook (*Marifia*), a newspaper (*Joritan*), and an award-winning literary/arts journal (*Muse*).

Each year, the Upper School presents two dramatic productions, including a musical; organizes either a Harambee Celebration or a Bias Awareness Day; sponsors an Art Festival; and participates in numerous community service projects, local and national competitions, and conferences with other schools, including Model UN, Mock Trial, and the International Student Technology Conference. Students have the opportunity to interact with boys from neighboring schools through most of these activities, as well as at dances and other student-run social activities.

DAILY LIFE

Upper School classes are held from 8:00 a.m. to 2:50 p.m. Class periods are 45, 60, or 75 minutes in length and typically meet four days in an eight-day cycle. After classes have ended, most students remain for sports, extracurricular activities, and/or independent study.

COSTS AND FINANCIAL AID

The tuition for the 2015–16 academic year ranges from $25,400 for Nursery to $44,630 for Class XII. In February, parents are required to make a deposit of $6,500, which is credited toward the November tuition. The Tuition Management System payment plan is available.

Roughly $4 million in financial aid was awarded in 2015–16 to students after establishing need through TADS. Twenty-two percent of Marymount students receive need-based financial aid.

ADMISSIONS INFORMATION

As a college-preparatory school, Marymount aims to enroll young women of academic promise and sound character who seek a challenging educational environment and opportunities for learning outside the classroom. Educational Records Bureau tests, school records, and interviews are used in selecting students.

The School admits students of any race, color, and national or ethnic origin to all the rights, privileges, programs, and activities generally accorded or made available to students at the School and does not discriminate on these bases in the administration of its educational policies, admissions policies, scholarship or loan programs, athletic programs, or other School programs.

APPLICATION TIMETABLE

Interested students are encouraged to contact the Admissions Office early in the fall for admission the following year. The application deadline is November 30, but may be changed at the discretion of the Director of Admissions. Notification of admissions decisions is sent in February, according to the dates established by the Independent School Admissions Association of Greater New York.

ADMISSIONS CORRESPONDENCE

Lillian Issa
Deputy Head/Director of Admissions
Marymount School of New York
1026 Fifth Avenue
New York, New York 10028
United States
Phone: 212-744-4486
Fax: 212-744-0716 (admissions)
E-mail: admissions@marymountnyc.org
Website: http://marymountnyc.org

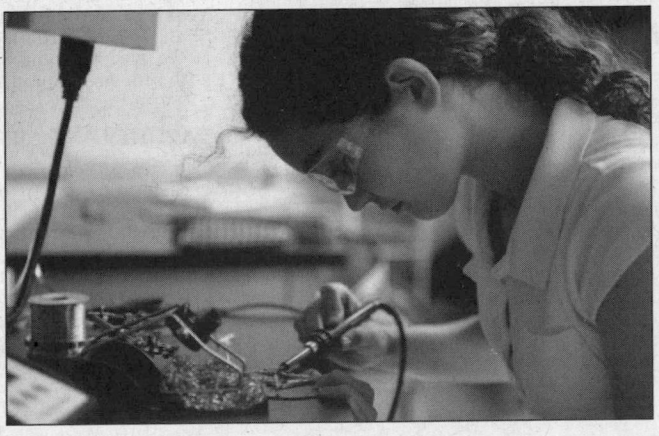

MILTON ACADEMY

Milton, Massachusetts

Type: Coeducational boarding and day college-preparatory school
Grades: K–12: (Lower School: K–5; Middle School: 6–8; Upper School: 9–12)
Enrollment: School total: 1,000; Upper School: 700
Head of School: Todd Bland

THE SCHOOL

The Academy received its charter in 1798 under the Massachusetts land-grant policy. It bequeathed to the school a responsibility to "open the way for all the people to a higher order of education than the common schools can supply." Milton's motto, "Dare to be true," not only states a core value, it describes Milton's culture. Milton fosters intellectual inquiry and encourages initiative and the open exchange of ideas. Teaching and learning at Milton are active processes that recognize the intelligence, talents, and potential of each member of the Academy.

For more than 200 years, Milton has developed confident, independent thinkers in an intimate, friendly setting where students and faculty members understand that the life of the mind is the pulse of the school. A gifted and dedicated faculty motivates a diverse student body, providing students with the structure to learn and the support to take risks. The faculty's teaching expertise and passion for scholarship generates extraordinary growth in students who learn to expect the most of themselves. The Milton community connects purposefully with world issues. Students graduate with a clear sense of themselves, their world, and how to contribute.

From Milton Academy's suburban 125-acre campus, 8 miles south of Boston in the town of Milton (population 26,000), students and faculty members access the vast cultural resources of Boston and Cambridge. Minutes from campus is the Blue Hills Reservation, 6,000 wooded acres of hiking trails and ski slopes.

Milton Academy is a nonprofit organization with a self-perpetuating Board of Trustees. Its endowment is $268 million (as of June 2015).

Milton Academy is accredited by the New England Association of Schools and Colleges and holds memberships in the National Association of Independent Schools, the Cum Laude Society, and the Association of Independent Schools in New England.

ACADEMIC PROGRAM

Milton students and faculty members are motivated participants in the world of ideas, concepts, and values. Milton's curriculum provides rigorous preparation for college and includes more than 182 courses in nine academic departments. For students entering Milton in the ninth grade, a minimum of 18 credits are required for graduation. This includes 4 years of English, 2 years of history (including U.S. and modern world history), 2 years of science, 1 year of an arts course, and successful completion of algebra II, geometry, and a level III foreign language course. Noncredit requirements include current events/public speaking, physical education, a ninth-grade arts course (music/drama/visual arts), and a four-year affective education curriculum that includes health, values, social awareness, and senior transitions.

Electives are offered in all academic areas. Examples of electives include computer programming, comparative government, performing literature, Spanish film and social change, advanced architecture, philosophy and literature, choreography, film and video production, psychology, engineering, nuclear physics, issues in environmental science, creative writing, music theory, observational astronomy, and marine biology. Students may petition to take independent study courses, and Advanced Placement courses leading to college credit are offered.

In January, seniors submit a proposal for a five-week spring independent project, on or off campus. Senior projects give students the opportunity to pursue in-depth interests stemming from their work at Milton.

The typical class size is 14 students, and the overall student-teacher ratio is 5:1. Nightly 2-hour study periods in the houses are supervised for boarding students.

Faculty members are available for individual help throughout the day and in the houses at night. Students seeking assistance with assignments or help with specific skills, organization, and/or time management visit the Academic Skills Center, which is staffed throughout the day.

The school year, which is divided into two semesters, runs from early September to early June with an examination period at the end of January. Students typically take five courses per semester. Students earn letter grades from E (failure) through A+, and comments prepared by each student's teachers and adviser are sent to parents three times a year in November, February, and June.

All academic buildings and residential houses are part of a campuswide computer network. MiltONline, the Academy's e-mail and conferencing system, allows students to join conference discussions for many classes and extracurricular activities, communicate with faculty members and friends, and submit assignments. Students have access to the Milton Intranet as well as the Internet.

Class II students (eleventh graders) may apply to spend either the fall or spring semester at the Mountain School Program of Milton Academy (an interdisciplinary academic program set on a working 300-acre farm in Vermont); at CITYterm at the Master's School in Dobbs Ferry, New York; or at the Maine Coast Semester at Chewonki. Through School Year Abroad, Milton provides opportunities in Spain, France, Italy, and China. Milton also offers six- to eight-week exchange programs with schools in Spain, France, and China.

FACULTY AND ADVISERS

The deep commitment of a learned and experienced group of teachers is Milton's greatest treasure. Teaching in Classes IV-I (grades 9–12) are 140 full-time faculty members, 75 percent of whom hold advanced degrees (Ph.D. and master's degrees). Eighty-five percent of faculty members live on campus.

In addition to teaching, faculty members also serve as house parents and coaches, as well as advisers to student clubs, organizations, publications, and activities. Each faculty member is an adviser to a group of 6 to 8 students and supports the students' emotional, social, and academic well-being at Milton.

COLLEGE ADMISSION COUNSELING

Four college counselors work one-on-one with students, beginning in their Class II (eleventh grade) year, in a highly personal and effective approach toward the college admissions process.

For the graduating classes of 2013, 2014, and 2015 the top college enrollments were Brown (26), Harvard (23), Chicago (21), NYU (18), Cornell (17), Columbia (14), Trinity (14), and Tufts (14).

STUDENT BODY AND CONDUCT

Of the 700 students in the Upper School, 50 percent are boys and 50 percent are girls; 50 percent are boarding students and 50 percent are day students. Forty-one percent of Milton's enrolled students are students of color. Thirteen percent of the Upper School students are international, coming from twenty-four countries across the globe. Thirty-five percent of Milton students receive financial aid, and the average grants account for 75 percent of tuition.

All Upper School students from Classes IV-I (grades 9–12) participate in the Self-Governing Association, led by 2 elected student representatives, 1 senior girl and 1 senior boy. Elected class representatives serve with faculty members on the Discipline Committee, which recommends to the Head of School appropriate responses when infractions of major school rules occur. Rules at Milton Academy foster the cohesion and morale of the community and enhance education by upholding standards of conduct developed by generations of students and faculty members.

ACADEMIC FACILITIES

Among the prominent buildings on the Milton campus are three primarily academic buildings: Warren Hall (English), Wigglesworth Hall (history), and Ware Hall (math and foreign languages); the Kellner Performing Arts Center, with a 350-seat teaching theater, a studio theater, dressing rooms, scene shop, practice rooms, orchestral rehearsal room, dance studio, and speech/debate room; the Athletic and Convocation Center, with a hockey rink, a fitness center, three basketball courts, and an indoor track; the Williams Squash Courts; the Ayer Observatory; and Apthorp Chapel. The Pritzker Science Center, which opened in 2010, integrates classroom areas with laboratory tables and equipment to create an environment that allows students to work collaboratively and move seamlessly between discussion and hands-on lab work. The Art and Media Center is home to numerous visual art studios and public display spaces, including the Nesto Gallery and the Greely auditorium.

Cox Library contains more than 46,000 volumes, more than 150 periodicals with back issues on microfilm, and a newspaper collection dating back to 1704. It also provides CD-ROM sources, Internet access and online search capabilities. Within Cox Library is one of several computer laboratories.

BOARDING AND GENERAL FACILITIES

Milton Academy students live in one of eight single-sex houses ranging in size from 31 to 48 students; four for boys and four for girls. Single rooms house one third of the students, while the other two thirds of the students reside in double rooms. Milton houses include all four classes as well as faculty members' families. Students spend all their Milton years in one house, experiencing a family-at-school context for developing close relationships with valued adults, learning about responsibility to the community, taking leadership roles with peers, and sharing social and cultural traditions. All rooms are networked, and school computers are available for student use in the house common rooms.

The Health and Counseling Center and the Academic Skills Center, as well as house parents in each residential house, class deans, and the office of the school chaplain, are available to meet students' needs.

ATHLETICS

Milton believes that teamwork, sportsmanship, and the pursuit of excellence are important values and that regular vigorous exercise is a foundation of good health. Milton offers a comprehensive athletic program that includes physical education classes and a range of intramural and interscholastic sports geared to the needs and interests of every student.

The school's offerings in interscholastic sports are Alpine skiing, baseball, basketball, cross-country, field hockey, football, golf, ice hockey, lacrosse, sailing, soccer, softball, squash, swimming and diving, tennis, track, volleyball, and wrestling.

Intramural offerings include the outdoor program, Pilates, soccer, squash, strength and conditioning, tennis, Ultimate (Frisbee), and yoga.

Sports facilities include four athletic buildings, an ice hockey rink and fitness center, two indoor climbing walls, twelve playing fields, seventeen tennis courts, seven international squash courts, an all-weather track, a cross-country course, and a ropes course.

EXTRACURRICULAR OPPORTUNITIES

The breadth of extracurricular opportunities means that every student finds a niche—a comfortable place to develop new skills, take on leadership, show commitment, make friends, and have fun. Clubs and organizations include cultural groups such as the Asian Society, Latino Association, Onyx, and Common Ground (an umbrella organization for the various groups); the Arts Board; the Outdoor Club; the Chinese, French, and Spanish clubs; the debate, math, and speech teams; and Students for Gender Equality. There are eleven student publications, among them *The Asian, La Voz, MAGUS/MABUS, Mille Tonnes, Milton Measure, Milton Paper,* and the yearbook. Music programs include the chamber singers, the gospel choir, the glee club, the orchestra, improvisational jazz combos, and five a cappella groups. The performing arts are an important part of the extracurricular offerings at Milton. Main stage theater productions, studio theater productions, play readings, and speech and debate team are a few of the available opportunities. Milton stages twelve major theater productions each year, including a Class IV (ninth grade) play, student directed one-act plays, a dance concert, and a biennial musical. Service opportunities include the audiovisual crew, community service, Lorax (environmental group), Orange and Blue Key (admission tour guides and leaders), and the Public Issues Board.

DAILY LIFE

The academic day runs from 8 a.m. to 2:55 p.m., except on Wednesday, when classes end at 1:15 p.m. There are no classes on Saturday or Sunday. Cafeteria-style lunch is served from 11 a.m. to 1:30 p.m., and students eat during a free period within that time. The students' activities period is from 3 to 3:30 p.m. Athletics and extracurricular activities take place from 3:30 to 5:30 p.m. Family-style dinner is at 6 p.m., and the evening study period runs from 7:30 to 9:30 p.m. Lights-out time depends on the grade level of each student.

WEEKEND LIFE

Interscholastic games are held on Wednesday, Friday, and Saturday afternoons. Social activities on Friday and Saturday evenings are planned by the Student Activities Association. Day students join boarders every weekend for events such as dances with live or recorded music, classic and new films, concerts, plays, drama readings, dormitory open houses, and trips to professional sports events, arts events, or local museums.

Prior to leaving campus, students must check their plans with house parents, who must approve their whereabouts and any overnight plans.

SUMMER PROGRAMS

Milton Academy does not run its own summer programs on campus. Professional development opportunities are made available to faculty members, including the Cultural Diversity Institute and the Boarding Staff Conference for teachers from across the country. In addition, Milton hosts many outside programs, including sports camps and academic enrichment programs.

COSTS AND FINANCIAL AID

For the 2015–16 academic year, tuition is $53,330 for boarding students and $43,780 for day students.

Milton seeks to enroll the most qualified applicants regardless of their financial circumstances. To that end, more than $9.6 million in financial aid will be provided to students in the 2016–17 school year. All financial aid at Milton is awarded on the basis of need. In addition to the program of direct grants, the school offers installment payment options and two low-interest loan programs.

ADMISSIONS INFORMATION

Milton Academy seeks students who are able, energetic, intellectually curious, and have strong values and a willingness to grow. Applicants must submit the Secondary School Admission Test (SSAT) scores (students applying for eleventh grade may submit PSAT or SAT scores if applicable). All applicants must also submit a school transcript, teacher recommendations, parental statement, and two essays. An interview, on or off campus, is also required.

APPLICATION TIMETABLE

The deadline for applying is January 15. Notification letters are sent out March 10; the reply date is April 10. There is a $50 application fee for U.S. applicants and a $100 fee for international applicants.

ADMISSIONS CORRESPONDENCE

Paul Rebuck, Dean of Enrollment and Financial Aid
Milton Academy
170 Centre Street
Milton, Massachusetts 02186
United States
Phone: 617-898-2227
Fax: 617-898-1701
E-mail: admissions@milton.edu
Website: http://www.milton.edu

MILTON HERSHEY SCHOOL

Hershey, Pennsylvania

Type: Coeducational, residential, college-preparatory, career and technical education school
Grades: PK–12: (Elementary School, PK–4; Middle School, 5–8; High School, 9–12)
Enrollment: School total: 2,000; High School: 945
Head of School: Peter Gurt, President

THE SCHOOL

Milton Hershey School (MHS), a cost-free educational boarding school, was founded in 1909 by Milton S. Hershey and his wife, Catherine. Milton and Catherine were unable to have children of their own and wanted to provide a home and school for children in need. In 1918, three years after Mrs. Hershey's death, Milton Hershey pledged his entire fortune derived from his chocolate business toward the support of the School. His generosity continues to provide a cost-free education and home for children from families of limited income. The School offers a secure, nurturing environment in which students of character and ability can learn and develop the skills necessary to prepare them for meaningful, productive, and successful lives. The comprehensive program supports each child's educational and growth needs to allow the student to reach his or her fullest potential.

The School's 4,200-acre campus is located in Derry Township in Dauphin County, Pennsylvania. The School is 12 miles east of the state capital of Harrisburg, 90 miles west of Philadelphia, 130 miles northwest of Washington, D.C., and 185 miles southwest of New York City. There are many cultural, amusement, and sports attractions in the Hershey/Harrisburg area. These include a nationally recognized theme park, HERSHEYPARK; a professional American League hockey team, the Hershey Bears; orchestral concerts and Broadway shows in the Hershey Theatre; a Museum of American History; and, of course, the largest chocolate manufacturing facility in the world. All of these attractions are located within a 3-mile radius of the Milton Hershey School campus. The community of Hershey is home to the Milton S. Hershey Medical Center and Medical School of The Pennsylvania State University. These excellent facilities are available to the students of Milton Hershey School should medical care be necessary.

Milton Hershey School is governed by a Board of Managers, with representation from the alumni and the Hershey enterprises. The School is totally funded by income generated by the trust established by the founders in 1909. The trust is administered by the Hershey Trust Company, established by Mr. Hershey in 1905.

Milton Hershey School is accredited by the Middle States Association of Colleges and Schools and the Pennsylvania Association of Private Academic Schools. The School is affiliated with the major associations of private schools in the United States, including the National Association of Independent Schools, the Pennsylvania Association of Independent Schools, the Pennsylvania Association of Private Academic Schools, the Association of Boarding Schools, and the National Middle School Association.

ACADEMIC PROGRAM

The strength of the Milton Hershey School experience is a strong, comprehensive, standards-based educational program with an emphasis on applied and experiential learning within a caring, family-like residential community.

Elementary students benefit from cooperative learning, individualized assistance, technology applications, field trips, and extracurricular activities. They attend classes in an elementary school equipped with the latest technology, two science labs, an outdoor atrium classroom, a library, a swimming pool, and age-appropriate play areas. Hands-on, activity-based experiential learning is the basis of the curriculum. The average class size is 15–17 students.

In the Middle School, students enhance their educational development through team-learning experiences from teachers of various disciplines. In addition, students learn the importance of goal setting, organizational skills, and time management. Students have the opportunity to explore career fields of their choice from a number of categories that represent diverse occupational clusters such as manufacturing, air and land transportation, industrial arts, communications, and consumer science, among others.

High school students engage in comprehensive, in-depth studies through the enhanced learning opportunities. The High School program provides all students with basic and advanced academic and career-technical courses (eleven career pathways) and offers applied learning, including internships, to prepare each student for entry-level work and further study. Temple University provides college classes on campus for high-achieving students.

From prekindergarten to grade 12, all students are involved in experiences to prepare them for the world of work. Practical and age-appropriate career technical exploratory experiences and hands-on curriculum activities broaden each student's understanding of the world of work and his or her own aptitudes and interests. Eleven career technical programs are offered to high school students, who gain entry-level job skills. Career and postsecondary counseling begins in the Middle School and continues into the High School.

Students also participate in the Agricultural and Environmental Education program, through which they learn about land use, animals, plants, and related resources. As an example, at the School's Environmental Center, students learn how to care for, conserve, and appreciate nature. As part of the career technical program, high school students can begin to focus their career paths in horticultural science occupations.

Because Milton Hershey School believes that all students can achieve at high levels, every student participates in a standards-based environment, where teaching and learning are tied to specific outcomes. Each program has an age-appropriate curriculum that is linked to national standards, which are designed to help children become productive, purposeful adults.

FACULTY AND ADVISERS

All of the 190 teachers hold baccalaureate degrees, and many have earned advanced degrees. Married houseparent couples staff 163 student homes, and guide and nurture an average of 8–12 students of similar ages. They are employed full-time and serve as the primary advocates and caregivers for the children in their care.

The School provides on-campus professional services for medical, dental, and counseling care for all students. The School also employs a staff for orientation of new students and for enrollment and family relations.

COLLEGE PLACEMENT

Once a student reaches high school, a counselor keeps him or her thinking about life after graduation. The counselor helps the student decide whether it would be best to attend college or a trade, technical, or business school; join the armed services; or enter the job market directly.

In 2014, 85 percent of the graduating seniors continued their education at postsecondary schools.

STUDENT BODY AND CONDUCT

Milton Hershey School seeks to maintain a diverse population among the School's students. The student body comes predominantly from Pennsylvania and the mid-Atlantic region and represents more than thirty states.

From the day they arrive at MHS, students are getting themselves ready for the day they graduate. Classroom learning builds knowledge. A solid home life and leadership experiences build character and confidence. Activities and other experiences build teamwork and time-management skills. Guided and nurtured at every step, MHS students are provided everything they need to succeed.

ACADEMIC FACILITIES

Milton Hershey School's campus includes three major classroom buildings, one each for elementary, middle, and high school; a Learning Resource Center; a student services center; a visual arts building; a performance gym; and agricultural and environmental education learning centers located near fields, streams, and woodland.

From high-tech smart classrooms to laptops and tablets for students, MHS is committed to providing the tools and the technological education each student needs to learn and prepare for the future.

BOARDING AND GENERAL FACILITIES

In each of approximately 163 student homes, an average of 10 students live with houseparents who have received specialized training in child care and child development. These adults play an important role in each student's development. In the student homes, students are responsible for doing household chores, participating in family activities, and completing homework. They also learn to respect the values and traditions of other cultures and gain life experiences through a wide range of opportunities and activities.

Students participate in planned activities and enjoy free and quiet times during the day for study and relaxation.

ATHLETICS

MHS fields varsity and junior varsity teams in baseball, basketball, cross-country (boys and girls), field hockey, volleyball, football, soccer, ice hockey, softball, swimming (boys and girls), track (boys and girls), and wrestling. Milton Hershey School teams compete locally with both public and private schools. Intramural and recreational athletics are offered as well.

In addition to a football stadium seating 7,000; the School has eight tennis courts, three indoor swimming pools, an ice skating rink, an all-weather track, field hockey and soccer fields, baseball and softball diamonds, and three gymnasiums. The Spartan Center is a state-of-the-art sports complex with tennis courts, strength-training and aerobics rooms, and an indoor jogging track. The center, with a seating capacity of 1,800, is also the venue for basketball games and wrestling matches and hosts competitive athletic events for both middle and high school teams.

EXTRACURRICULAR OPPORTUNITIES

The School offers a wide variety of activities, including a student yearbook; computer, environmental, animal, photography, science, and math clubs; Boy Scouts and Girl Scouts; and a number of music groups, ranging from a jazz ensemble and band to a varsity choir.

Community service programs, off-campus study, internships, and work programs are offered through several businesses and community organizations.

The Copenhaver Center includes a natatorium, providing swimming facilities for both middle and high school students; an ice skating rink; a social room; student government and club rooms; a student store; a snack area; student television production and radio studios; dance, drama, and music studios and theater; medical, dental, and psychological services; and the Religious Programs Office. Outdoor tennis courts and bicycle pathways are nearby. At no cost, students may enjoy the Hershey Museum, Hershey Gardens, and HERSHEYPARK in season, which is from May through September.

DAILY LIFE

The typical day for high school students begins at 6 a.m. Students eat the morning and evening meals as a family group in the student residence. Classes begin at 7:30 and end between 2:30 and 2:45 p.m. A healthy lunch is provided for all students. The afternoon includes academic classes, a tutoring period, time for sports and activities, and afternoon chores. Following dinner and study hour, students may have free time if all homework is completed.

WEEKEND LIFE

Many students enjoy visiting hours with their parents and other approved visitors over the weekend. Students may participate in a wide variety of organized activities as their schedules permit. Students are encouraged to participate in as many activities as their schedules permit. Attendance at a nondenominational Sunday morning chapel service is required of all students.

SUMMER PROGRAMS

Because MHS provides a year-round experience, students have the option of remaining on campus during six weeks of the summer and attending a variety of educational programs and enjoyable activities, such as sports camps, field trips and camping, community service activities, part-time work, and internship and career exploration. Students who need extra help with classroom studies can take advantage of the program's tutoring and study skills offerings.

COSTS AND FINANCIAL AID

Milton Hershey School provides, at no cost, an education, housing in a student home, clothing, meals, medical and dental care, and recreational activities.

The Continuing Education Scholarship program provides graduates the opportunity to earn scholarship money, approximately $80,000, by solid academic achievement and good citizenship. This scholarship award may be applied to all kinds of accredited postsecondary education, including colleges, universities, trade and technical institutes, and business and computer schools.

ADMISSIONS INFORMATION

To be considered for enrollment, children must come from a family with limited income. (For example, the current income guideline for a family of three is $40,180.) Applicants must also be between the ages of 4 and 15 at the time of enrollment, have the potential for scholastic achievement, and be free of serious behavioral problems that disrupt life in the classroom or the home. Students must also be able to participate fully in the program offered.

Enrollment preference is given first to children born in the Pennsylvania counties of Dauphin, Lebanon, and Lancaster; followed by those from within the state of Pennsylvania; and then those from outside of Pennsylvania. Milton Hershey School does not discriminate in admissions or in the administration of its policies and programs.

APPLICATION TIMETABLE

Enrollment takes place primarily in August, September, and January. If space is available, students may enroll in October, November, February or March. Students accepted for August enrollment are notified between May and July.

ADMISSIONS CORRESPONDENCE

Admissions Office
Milton Hershey School
P.O. Box 830
Hershey, Pennsylvania 17033-0830
United States
Phone: 717-520-3600
800-322-3248 (toll-free)
Fax: 717-520-2117
E-mail: mhs-admissions@mhs-pa.org
Website: mhskids.org

MORAVIAN ACADEMY

Bethlehem, Pennsylvania

MORAVIAN
ACADEMY

Type: Day college-preparatory school
Grades: PK–12: Lower School, Primer–5; Middle School, 6–8; Upper School, 9–12
Enrollment: School total: 734; Upper School: 314
Head of School: Jeffrey M. Zemsky, Headmaster

THE SCHOOL

Moravian Academy (MA) traces its origin back to 1742 and the Moravians who settled Bethlehem. Guided by the wisdom of John Amos Comenius, Moravian bishop and renowned educator, the Moravian Church established schools in every community in which it settled. Moravian Academy became incorporated in 1971 when Moravian Seminary for Girls and Moravian Preparatory School were merged. The school has two campuses: the Lower–Middle School campus in the historic downtown area of Bethlehem and the Upper School campus on a 120-acre estate 6 miles to the east.

For about 274 years, Moravian Academy has encouraged sound innovations to meet contemporary challenges while recognizing the permanence of basic human values. The school seeks to promote young people's full development in mind, body, and spirit by fostering a love for learning, respect for others, joy in participation and service, and skill in decision-making. Preparation for college occurs in an atmosphere characterized by an appreciation for the individual.

Moravian Academy is governed by a Board of Trustees. Six members are representatives of the Moravian Church. As of June 30, 2015, the net asset value of the Academy is $40.8 million, of which $19 million is endowment. In 2014–15, Annual Giving was $453,327, and operating expenses were $16.5 million.

Moravian Academy is accredited by the Middle States Association of Colleges and Schools and the Pennsylvania Association of Independent Schools. The school is a member of the National Association of Independent Schools, the Association of Delaware Valley Independent Schools, the College Board, the Council for Spiritual and Ethical Education, the School and Student Service for Financial Aid, and the Secondary School Admission Test Board.

Moravian Academy does not discriminate on the basis of race, nationality, sex, sexual orientation, religious affiliation, or ethnic origin in the administration of its educational and admission policies, financial aid awards, and athletic or other school-administered programs. Applicants who are disabled (or applicants' family members who are disabled) and require any type of accommodation during the application process, or at any other time, are encouraged to identify themselves and indicate what type of accommodation is needed.

ACADEMIC PROGRAM

Students are required to carry five major courses per year. Minimum graduation requirements include English, 4 credits; mathematics, 3 credits; lab sciences, 3 credits; global language, 3 credits; social studies, 3 credits; fine arts, 2 credits; and physical education and health. All students must successfully complete a semester course in world religions or ethics. Community service is an integral part of the curriculum. Electives are offered in all areas, including fine and performing arts, sciences, English, math, history, and global languages. Moravian Academy offers Advanced Placement courses, numerous honors courses, and the opportunity to pursue an honors independent study project under the mentorship of a faculty member. The Academy also participates in a high school scholars program that enables a small number of highly qualified students to take college courses at no cost. The overall student-faculty ratio is about 8:1, with classes ranging from 10 to 18 students.

Grades in most courses are A–F; D is a passing grade. However, a C- is required to advance to the next level in math and global languages. Reports are sent to parents on a monthly basis, and parent-conference opportunities are scheduled in the fall semester. Faculty and staff members are available for additional conferences whenever necessary. Examinations are held at the end of each seventeen-week semester in all major subjects. In the senior year, final examinations are given in May to allow seniors time for a two-week Post Term Experience before graduation.

There are three formal school exchange programs; France, Guatemala, and Spain. All of the programs provide complete immersion in the daily life of that country, including living with a family, attending high school classes, and participating in cultural events. The length of each program varies from one to two months.

FACULTY AND ADVISORS

The Upper School has 39 full-time and 9 part-time faculty members. Ninety-four percent of the full-time Upper School faculty members have advanced degrees. Several faculty members have degrees in counseling in addition to other subjects, and the entire faculty shares in counseling through the Faculty-Student Advisor Program.

Jeffrey M. Zemsky was appointed Headmaster in 2016. He previously served as Head of Middle School at Sewickley Academy in Sewickley, Pennsylvania and Head of Middle and Upper School at York Country Day School in York, Pennsylvania. Mr. Zemsky received his B.A. from Carleton College and his M.A. from Columbia University.

COLLEGE ADMISSION COUNSELING

The Director of College Counseling begins group work in college guidance in the tenth grade. Tenth graders take a practice PSAT and repeat it the following year. Sophomore Seminar encourages students to familiarize themselves with the college application process; the focus is on understanding academic options and participation in school and community life. College Night is held annually for juniors and their parents. Junior Seminar meets weekly in small groups for college counseling during the second semester and includes an individual family conference in the spring. They take the PSAT, SAT, and Subject Tests. Some students also elect to take the ACT in their junior or senior year. Senior Seminar meets weekly in small groups during the first semester for additional guidance and seniors are led through the college application process. They take the SAT and Subject Tests again, if necessary. In recent years, approximately 85 to 90 percent of the senior class takes at least one Advanced Placement exam and earns a score of 3 or higher.

Average SAT scores of 2015 graduates were 627 critical reading, 653 math, and 639 writing. Graduates of 2015 are attending Babson, Barnard, Bates, Boston University, Bucknell, Carnegie Mellon, Colby, Cornell, Eckerd, Elon, Emory, Franklin and Marshall, George Washington, Georgetown, Gettysburg, Hamilton, Harvard, High Point, Hobart and William Smith, Lafayette, Lehigh, Loughborough University (UK) Loyola University Maryland, McDaniel, Muhlenberg, North Carolina State, Northeastern, Penn State, Rensselaer Polytechnic Institute, Saint Joseph's (Pennsylvania), Smith, Stetson, Syracuse, Tufts, Tulane, Wake Forest, William and Mary, and the Universities of Michigan, Pennsylvania, Pittsburgh, Rochester, and Scranton. Some students participate in travel abroad or gap year programs before attending college.

STUDENT BODY AND CONDUCT

The Upper School has 314 students. The school understands the value of diversity in the educational setting. In all divisions, students and faculty members from a variety of ethnic, cultural, religious, and socioeconomic backgrounds carry on this commitment. Through classroom activities, nondenominational services discussing many faiths, and active engagement with each other, students are encouraged to appreciate one another's individuality.

Students enjoy the small classes and the opportunity for participation in sports and other activities. Students are expected to wear clothing that is neat and appropriate for school. Denim is not permitted during the school day, and a school uniform is required for members of performing groups. Students participate actively in a Student Council. Serious matters of discipline come before a faculty-student discipline committee.

ACADEMIC FACILITIES

Snyder House, Walter Hall, Couch Fine Arts Center, the Heath Science Complex, and the Athletic and Wellness Center hold the classrooms, studios, and laboratories (environmental science, physics, and biology). The Academy's arts program is enhanced by the courses offered in the Van S. Merle-Smith Woodworking Studio. All of the library's resources are integrated with the instructional program to intensify and individualize the educational experience. Technology plays an important role in enhancing learning and students get hands-on experience with the latest equipment in classrooms and labs. The 1:1 program gives all students their own MacBook Air laptop; use of the laptop is integrated into the curriculum and is an integral part of the learning program. SmartBoards and Smart TVs are used in all divisions to enhance the learning process. The Couch Fine Arts Center houses the studio arts department. A 350-seat auditorium enhances the music and theater programs. Students can also use the resources and facilities of the seven colleges and universities in the area.

ATHLETICS

A strong athletics program meets the guidelines of the school's philosophy that a person must be nurtured in body, as well as in mind and spirit, and that respect for others and participation are important goals. A new 40,000 square-foot athletic and wellness center, completed in March 2014, has a competition court, two practice courts, a multipurpose gym, and a fitness/weight training space. In addition, eight athletics fields, and six tennis courts provide the school with facilities for varsity and junior varsity teams in boys' and girls' lacrosse; girls' field hockey; boys' and girls' baseball, basketball, cross-country, soccer, and tennis; coeducational golf; and a girls' varsity softball team. Students also have the opportunity to participate in girls' volleyball,

football, track, swimming, and wrestling in co-operative programs with local schools. An outdoor recreational pool is available for special student functions as well as the Academy's summer programs.

All students take part in team sports. In any given athletic season, more than one third of the Upper School student body participates in after-school athletics at the Academy.

EXTRACURRICULAR OPPORTUNITIES

Moravian Academy's activity program provides opportunities for varied interests and talents. Included are service projects, outdoor education, International Club, *Legacy* (yearbook), *Green Ponderer* (literary magazine), Model Congress, Model UN, PJAS, Scholastic Scrimmage, and a variety of activities that change in response to student interests. A fine arts series combines music, art, drama, and dance. In addition, the Academy's outdoor education program offers a variety of off-campus experiences in hiking, rock climbing, and white water rafting/kayaking. The annual Country Fair gives students an opportunity to work with the Parents' Association to create a family fun day for the school and Lehigh Valley community. Rooted in Moravian tradition, a strong appreciation of music has continued. There are several student musical groups, including chorale, MA Chamber Singers, Coda Red (an a cappella group), handbell choirs, and instrumental ensembles. Highlights of the year include the Christmas Vespers Service and the spring concert.

DAILY LIFE

A typical school day begins at 8 a.m., and classes run until 3:15 p.m. on Monday, Tuesday, Wednesday, and Friday. On Thursday, classes conclude at 2:55. The average length of class periods is about 40 minutes. Students usually take five major classes daily along with courses in the fine and performing arts, physical education, and health/driver's education.

A weekly nondenominational chapel service is held on Friday mornings. On Monday, Tuesday, Wednesday, and Thursday, there is a period for class meetings, all-school meetings, advisory meetings, or activity periods.

COSTS AND FINANCIAL AID

Tuition for 2015–16 was $26,790. There is an additional dining fee for students. An initial deposit of $1,000 is required upon acceptance. The remainder of the tuition and fees can be paid through various payment plans. An additional fee for tuition insurance is recommended for all new students.

Financial aid is available. Moravian Academy uses the services of the School and Student Service for Financial Aid by NAIS. Aid is awarded on the basis of demonstrated financial need. Aid is received by approximately 32 percent of Upper School students.

ADMISSIONS INFORMATION

Students are admitted in grades 9–11. Each applicant is carefully considered. Students who demonstrate an ability and willingness to handle a rigorous academic program as well as such qualities as intellectual curiosity, responsibility, creativity, and enthusiasm for school and community life, are encouraged to apply. Scores on tests administered by the school are also used in the admission process. In addition, school records, recommendations, and a personal interview are required. Admissions are usually completed by May, but there are sometimes openings available after that time.

APPLICATION TIMETABLE

Inquiries are welcome at any time. The Admission Office makes arrangements for tours and classroom visits during the school week. If necessary, other arrangements for tours can be made. The application fee is $65. Test dates are scheduled on specified Saturday mornings from December through March. Notifications are sent after February 15, and families are asked to respond within two weeks.

ADMISSIONS CORRESPONDENCE

Daniel J. Axford
Director of Admissions, Upper School
Moravian Academy
4313 Green Pond Road
Bethlehem, Pennsylvania 18020
United States
Phone: 610-691-1600
Website: http://www.moravianacademy.org

RYE COUNTRY DAY SCHOOL

Rye, New York

Type: Coeducational day college-preparatory school
Grades: P–12: Lower School, Prekindergarten–4; Middle School, 5–8; Upper School, 9–12
Enrollment: School total: 894; Upper School: 403; Middle School: 291; Lower School: 200.
Head of School: Scott A. Nelson, Headmaster

THE SCHOOL

Founded in 1869, Rye Country Day School (RCDS) is nearing its 150th year. Reflecting and reaffirming the School's purposes, the RCDS mission statement states, "Rye Country Day School is a coeducational, college-preparatory school dedicated to providing students from Pre-Kindergarten through Grade Twelve with an excellent education using both traditional and innovative approaches. In a nurturing and supportive environment, we offer a challenging program that stimulates individuals to achieve their maximum potential through academic, athletic, creative, and social endeavors. We are actively committed to diversity. We expect and promote moral responsibility, and strive to develop strength of character within a respectful school community. Our goal is to foster a lifelong passion for learning, understanding, and service in an ever-changing world."

Rye Country Day School acts consciously and deliberately in order to create and sustain an inclusive community. According to the School's diversity mission statement, "At Rye Country Day, we believe that diversity is the existence of human variety. As such, each one of us is diverse in multiple ways and in a variety of contexts. We recognize diversity as including, but not limited to, differences in ability/disability, age, ethnicity, family structures, gender, geographic origin, life experiences, physical appearance, race, religion, sexual orientation, and socioeconomic status. As educators, we are committed to creating and sustaining a school community that is diverse and inclusive, one in which all members can participate fully and maximize their potential. We believe that only an inclusive school community can be equitable and just. We are proactive about teaching our students the importance of diversity and inclusion in an increasingly interconnected, multicultural, and ever-changing world. As we prepare our students for leadership in the world beyond Rye Country Day, we are responsible for teaching them how to communicate with and be respectful of others—beginning with those in our school community and extending to those who live beyond our nation's borders. Every global citizen should be able to thrive in a diverse and interconnected society. Our commitment to inclusion enriches our community with diverse ideas and perspectives. Students grow and flourish in this type of environment, where they can safely explore their individual identity while developing and exercising strength of character, healthy self-esteem, and confidence. Through our commitment to diversity and inclusion, we strive to be good role models for the individuals in our care so that their present and future actions and choices may positively impact the world."

The 26-acre campus is located in Rye at the junction of routes I-95 and I-287, one block from the train station. The School's location, 25 miles from Manhattan, provides easy access to both New York City and to a suburban setting with ample playing fields and open spaces. Through frequent community service and partnership projects, field trips, and internships, the School takes considerable advantage of the cultural opportunities in the New York metropolitan area.

A nonprofit, nonsectarian institution, Rye Country Day is governed by a 26-member Board of Trustees that includes parents and alumni. The annual operating budget is $34.6 million, and the physical plant assets have a value in excess of $52.4 million. Annual gifts from parents, alumni, and friends amount to more than $4.2 million. The endowment of the School is valued at more than $48 million.

Rye Country Day School is accredited by the Middle States Association of Colleges and Schools and the New York State Association of Independent Schools and is chartered and registered by the New York State Board of Regents. It is a member of the National Association of Independent Schools, the New York State Association of Independent Schools, the Educational Records Bureau, the College Board, and the National Association for College Admission Counseling.

ACADEMIC PROGRAM

Leading to the college-preparatory program of the Upper School, the program in the Middle School (grades 5–8) emphasizes the development of skills and the acquisition of information needed for success at the secondary school level by exposing students to a wide range of opportunities. The academic program is fully departmentalized. Spanish or French is offered to all students in grades 2–5. Starting in grade 6, students may choose Latin or Mandarin Chinese or continue with Spanish or French. The math, foreign language, and writing programs lead directly into the Upper School curriculum. Programs in art, music (vocal and instrumental), computer use, and dramatics are offered in all grades. Students in kindergarten through grade 6 are scheduled for sports for 45 to 75 minutes daily, and a full interscholastic sports program is available to both boys and girls in grades 7 and 8, and in the Upper School.

Sixteen courses are required for Upper School graduation, including 4 years of English, mathematics through algebra II and trigonometry, completion of Level 3 of one foreign language, 2 years of science (one biological, one physical), and 2 years of history. Students entering the School by grade 9 must complete 1.5 units in the arts and a tenth-grade health class. In addition, a student must either play on a sports team or be enrolled in a physical education class for each athletic season. Students are expected to carry five academic courses per year.

Full-year courses in English include English 9, 10, and 11; major American writers; English and American literature; and creative and expository writing. Required mathematics courses are algebra I, algebra II, trigonometry, and geometry. Regular course work extends through calculus BC, and tutorials are available for more advanced students. Yearlong courses in science are environmental science, biology, chemistry, and physics. Science courses are laboratory based. The computer science department offers beginning and advanced programming, software applications courses, desktop publishing, and independent study opportunities.

The modern language department offers five years of Mandarin Chinese, French, and Spanish, and the classics department teaches five years of Latin. History courses include world civilizations, U.S. history, government, and modern European history. Semester electives in the humanities include philosophy, psychology, government, and economics.

In the arts, full-year courses in studio art, art history, and music theory are available. Participation in the Concert Choir and Wind Ensemble earns students full academic credit. Semester courses in drawing, printmaking, sculpture, graphic design, ceramics, and photography are available. The drama department offers electives in technique, history, oral presentation, technical theater, and dance.

Advanced Placement courses leading to the AP examinations are offered in biology, environmental science, chemistry, physics, psychology, economics, statistics, calculus, English, U.S. government, U.S. and modern European history, Mandarin Chinese, French, Spanish, Latin, music theory, photography, studio art, history of art, and computer science. In 2015, 79 percent of students taking AP exams received a 4 or a 5. Honors sections are scheduled in tenth- and eleventh-grade English, math, physics, biology, and chemistry, and in foreign languages at all levels. Independent study is available in grades 11 and 12 in all disciplines.

The student-teacher ratio is 8:1, and the average class size in the Upper School is 12. Extra help is provided for students as needed.

The year is divided into two semesters. Examinations are given in March. Grades are scaled from A to F and are given four times a year. Written comments accompany grades at the end of each quarter.

Academic classes travel to New York City and other areas to supplement classroom work. Although not a graduation requirement, all students are involved in community service programs. Class projects, club-based programs, and individual service experiences involve work with Achilles International, Adopt-A-Dog, Carver Center, Ferncliff Manor School for Adaptive and Integrative Learning (SAIL), God's Love We Deliver, Greenwich Audubon, Let's Get Ready, MetLife Stadium, Mianus River Park, Miracle League, Our New Way Garden, REACH Prep, Rye Historical Society, SquirrelWood Sanctuary, The Sharing Shelf, United Minds of America/Yale University School of Medicine, and numerous local community partners.

All students in grades 7–12 have laptop computers. The campus supports wireless Internet connection and provides appropriate filters for student and faculty educational use. A technology department supports and updates the network and assists students with software and hardware issues. Students receiving financial aid awards receive new laptop computers from the school which are replaced every three years.

FACULTY AND ADVISORS

The Upper School faculty consists of 65 full-time teachers—35 men and 30 women, the large majority of whom hold at least one advanced degree. The average length of service is eight years, and annual faculty turnover averages fewer than 6 teachers.

Scott A. Nelson became Headmaster in 1993. He holds a B.A. from Brown University and an M.A. from Fordham University. Prior to his appointment at Rye, he served as Upper School Director both at the Marlborough School in Los Angeles and at the Hackley School in Tarrytown, New York. Mr. Nelson and his family reside on campus.

Nearly all faculty members in the Middle and Upper Schools serve as advisors for 5 to 12 students each. In addition to helping students select courses, faculty advisors monitor student progress in all areas of school life and provide ongoing support. The advisors also meet with students' parents at various times throughout the year.

Rye Country Day seeks faculty members who are effective teachers in their field and who, by virtue of their sincere interest in students' overall well-being, will further the broad goals of the School's philosophy. The School supports the continuing education of its faculty through grants and summer sabbaticals totaling more than $477,500 a year.

COLLEGE ADMISSION COUNSELING

The college selection process is supervised by a team, which includes a Director of College Counseling and two Associate Directors, with support provided by an administrative assistant. Counseling is done in groups and on an individual basis, with the staff meeting with both students and their families. More than 100 college representatives visit the campus each year.

The 99 graduates of the class of 2015 enrolled in forty-nine colleges and universities, with two or more attending Amherst, Brown, Bucknell, Colgate, Cornell, Dartmouth, Duke, Georgetown, Hamilton, Harvard, NYU, St. Andrews, Stanford, Tufts, Notre Dame, USC, Vanderbilt, Wake Forest, Washington University (St. Louis), Wesleyan, Williams, and the Universities of Michigan, Pennsylvania, and Wisconsin. .

STUDENT BODY AND CONDUCT

The Upper School enrollment for 2015–16 totaled 403: 214 boys and 184 girls. Thirty-one percent of the student body in grades 5–12 self-identified as students of color. Students came from roughly forty different school districts in Westchester and Fairfield counties as well as New York City. Students holding citizenship in twenty countries were enrolled.

While School regulations are few, the School consciously and directly emphasizes a cooperative, responsible, and healthy community life. The Student Council plays a major role in administering School organizations and activities. Minor disciplinary problems are handled by the Division Principal or Grade Level Dean; more serious matters in the Upper School may be brought before the Disciplinary Committee. There is student representation on the Academic Affairs and other major committees.

ACADEMIC FACILITIES

Academic facilities at Rye Country Day School include the Main Building (1927) and Main Building Addition (2002), with separate areas for kindergarten through grade 4, grades 5 and 6, and grades 7 and 8. The Lower and Middle School divisions have separate art, computer, and science facilities.

The Upper School is housed in the Pinkham Building (1964), which was completely renovated in 2010. Also in 2010, a 14,000-square-foot addition was built that includes a 140-seat auditorium, a college counseling center, faculty offices, classrooms, and three science labs.

There are two libraries on campus—the Lower School Library (2002) and the Klingenstein Library (1984), which serves the Middle and Upper School divisions. The Klingenstein Library, which was renovated in 2014, contains more than 25,000 volumes with fully automated circulation and collection management technology. Resources include significant periodical and reference materials that are available via direct online services and the Internet, CD-ROM, and substantial video collection.

The School has invested in technology infrastructure and classroom SmartBoards in all three divisions. Laptop computers, which are required for all students in grades 7 through 12, are used extensively throughout the curriculum. Access to the RCDS network and Internet is via a campuswide wireless network. In total, there are over 650 networked computers on campus.

The performing arts programs are housed in the Dunn Performing Arts Center (1990), which includes a 400-seat theater-auditorium and classroom spaces for vocal music, instrumental music, and a dance studio. There also are five music practice rooms with adjunct faculty use for private music lessons.

ATHLETICS

Rye Country Day's athletic program offers seventy-two interscholastic teams for students in grades 7 through 12. Varsity competition includes boys' and girls' teams in soccer, cross-country, basketball, ice hockey, fencing, squash, tennis, golf, track and field, sailing, and lacrosse, as well as football, field hockey, wrestling, baseball, and softball. Approximately 70 percent of the students participate in at least one team sport.

The physical education department offers classes throughout the year in fitness center training, yoga, boot camp, kickboxing, Zumba, tennis, squash, dance, running, and skating.

Athletic facilities include the LaGrange Field House (1972) with its indoor ice rink/tennis courts; a multipurpose gymnasium which serves as the home for the wrestling and fencing programs; the Scott A. Nelson Athletic Center (2000), which houses a two-court gymnasium, four squash courts, four locker rooms, and an athletic training facility; a multipurpose room; and a state-of-the-art fitness center. Between 2007 and 2009, the School installed four artificial turf fields, making it the premier outdoor athletic facility in the area.

EXTRACURRICULAR OPPORTUNITIES

More than fifty extracurricular activities are available. Students can choose vocal music (Concert Choir, Madrigal Singers, and solfeggio classes) and instrumental music (Wind Ensemble, Concert Band, and Jazz Band). Many of these offerings have curricular status. The performance groups give local concerts and occasionally travel to perform at schools and universities here and abroad. In addition, professional instructors offer private instrumental and voice lessons during and after the school day. The drama department presents major productions three times a year. Recent productions have included *The Laramie Project, South Pacific, Dark of the Moon, The Mystery of Edwin Drood, Macbeth, The Pajama Game, The Arabian Nights, Anything Goes, Alice in Wonderland, Urinetown, Museum, Bye Bye Birdie, The Comedy of Errors, The Boys from Syracuse, Working, The Miracle Worker, Guys and Dolls, Dracula,* and *Footloose.*

Student publications include a yearbook, newspaper, literary magazine, graphic arts and photography magazines, and a public affairs journal, each of which is composed using student publications desktop publishing facilities. The School's website (http://www.ryecountryday.org) is an ever-changing location for student- and staff-provided information on and perspectives of the School. Students participate in Model Congress programs on campus and at other schools and colleges.

The School's new focus on public purpose goes beyond community service by challenging community members to use rich and varied methods to identify, examine, and research social inequities and plan a partnership-based course of action that is responsive to community needs. Using an interdisciplinary service-learning approach, the School encourages students to question their assumptions, integrate community and global themes into their academic work, and realize their potential to empower others and themselves as empathetic, interconnected citizens. Rye Country Day is committed to leveraging its human and educational resources to co-create sustainable solutions to real-world problems. The School's public purpose mission statement reads: "Since 1869, Rye Country Day School's motto, 'Not for self, but for service,' has been integral to the culture of the School. The Rye Country Day School philosophy states, 'A superior education embraces the concept that to educate is to do more than to teach.' Through service learning, we will provide transformative educational opportunities that prepare our students to be responsible citizens with an ethic of service and empathy for our shared human experience. We believe that meaningful and mutually beneficial partnerships emanate from a curriculum enhanced by community engagement. Rye Country Day School's sustained commitment to making a positive impact on the community and contributing to the common good defines our public purpose."

DAILY LIFE

Beginning each day at 8:05, the Upper School utilizes a six-day schedule cycle. Most courses meet five of the six days, with one or two longer, 70-minute periods per cycle. The day includes an activity/meeting period and two lunch periods as well as seven class periods. Class periods end at 2:50, and team sport practices and games begin at 3:30. Breakfast and lunch may be purchased in the school dining room; seniors may have lunch off campus. Study halls are required for grade 9.

SUMMER PROGRAMS

The Rye Country Day Summer School enrolls approximately 100 students—rising students to grades 6 to postgraduate—in remedial, enrichment, and advanced-standing courses. Some courses prepare students for the New York State Regents exams that may be taken at the local public schools. The program is six weeks long and runs on a five-period schedule from 8 a.m. to noon, Monday through Friday. Tuition averages $1,300 per course. A brochure is available after April 1 on the Summer School page of the School's website.

In addition to the Summer School, Rye conducts a summer program, the ACTION Program, an academic enrichment program at Rye for highly motivated public school students who will be entering grades 7, 8, and 9. The ACTION Program seeks to expand the academic and intellectual horizons of very capable and responsible students from local communities who may not have the resources available to provide such summer programs. The program promotes confidence and strength of character while helping students grow academically and develop as leaders.

The ACTION Program runs for four weeks in July. Its philosophy emphasizes learning for the sake of learning. All students take project-based courses in math, science, history, leadership, Presidential election coverage, creative writing, drama, and yoga/kickboxing. Once a week, the curriculum is reinforced with experiential learning opportunities outside the classroom. Field trips include seeing a Broadway musical, participating in a high ropes adventures program, and sailing aboard a schooner in the Long Island Sound.

COSTS AND FINANCIAL AID

Tuition for grade 9 for 2015–16 is $37,700. Additional charges are made for textbooks, lunches, sports, field trips, and private music lessons, as appropriate.

Financial aid is available on a need basis. For the 2015–16 academic year, 16 percent of students received a total of more than $4.9 million in aid. All aid applications are processed through the School and Student Service for Financial Aid.

ADMISSIONS INFORMATION

Students are accepted in all grades. In 2015–16, 22 new students enrolled in the ninth grade, 6 in the tenth grade, and 2 in the eleventh grade. Academic readiness is a prerequisite; a diversity of skills and interests, as well as general academic aptitude, is eagerly sought. The School seeks and enrolls students of all backgrounds; a diverse student body is an important part of the School's educational environment.

Required in the admissions process are the results of the Educational Records Bureau's Independent School Entrance Examination (ISEE) or the Secondary School Admission Test (SSAT); the student's school record; and school and faculty recommendations. A visit to the campus and an interview are also required.

APPLICATION TIMETABLE

Inquiries are welcome throughout the year. Interviews and tours of the campus begin in late September. To be considered in initial admissions decisions, applicants must fully complete the Application by December 15. All other parts of the Application Folder (transcripts, testing, recommendation forms, interview, etc.) are due by January 15. Candidates whose Application Folders are complete by that date are notified by approximately February 15. Applications received after December 15 are evaluated on a rolling basis. All application materials are available online (www.ryecountryday.org/admissions).

ADMISSIONS CORRESPONDENCE

Matthew J. M. Suzuki, Director of Admissions
Rye Country Day School
Cedar Street
Rye, New York 10580-2034
United States
Phone: 914-925-4513
Fax: 914-921-2147
E-mail: matt_suzuki@ryecountryday.org
Website: http://www.ryecountryday.org

SOUNDVIEW PREPARATORY SCHOOL

Yorktown Heights, New York

Type: Coeducational day college-preparatory school
Grades: Middle School, 6–8; Upper School, 9–12
Enrollment: Total, 70; Middle School, 13; Upper School, 57
Head of School: W. Glyn Hearn, Head of School

THE SCHOOL

Soundview Preparatory School, a coeducational, college-preparatory school for grades 6 through 12, was founded in 1989 on the belief that the best environment for students is one where classes are small, teachers know the learning style and interests of each student, and an atmosphere of mutual trust prevails. At Soundview, students and teachers work in close collaboration in classes with an average size of 7 students.

The School's mission is to provide a college-preparatory education in a supportive and noncompetitive environment that requires rigorous application to academics, instills respect for ethical values, and fosters self-confidence by helping each student feel recognized and valued. Soundview empowers students to develop their potential and reach their own goals in a setting that promotes respect for others and a sense of community.

Soundview Prep opened its doors with 13 students in the spring of 1989. In the spring of 1998, having outgrown its original quarters in Pocantico Hills, New York, the School moved to a larger facility in Mount Kisco, New York. On January 14, 2008, Soundview moved to its first permanent home, a 13.8-acre campus in Yorktown Heights, New York. New York City, only an hour away, provides a wealth of cultural opportunities for Soundview students to explore on class trips.

The School is governed by a 10-member Board of Trustees. The current operating budget is $2 million. In 2014–15, Soundview raised a gross total amount of $176,508 through the Annual Fund and a Gala and Auction. Donations were made by parents, alumni families, grandparents, friends, foundations, and corporations.

Soundview is chartered by the New York State Board of Regents and is accredited by the New York State Association of Independent Schools. The School is a member of the National Association of Independent Schools, the Education Records Bureau, and the Council for Advancement and Support of Education.

ACADEMIC PROGRAM

Soundview provides a rigorous academic program to ensure that students not only develop the skills and acquire the knowledge needed for college work but also have the opportunity to pursue their own personal goals and interests.

The academic day is carefully structured but informal, with nurture a crucial ingredient. Soundview's student-teacher ratio of 5:1 guarantees that students are monitored closely and receive the support they need. At the same time, the School provides advanced courses for students who wish to go beyond the high school level or take a subject that is not usually offered, allowing students to soar academically and truly develop their potential.

The Middle School curriculum is designed to establish a foundation of knowledge and skills in each academic discipline, strong comprehension and communication skills, good work habits and study skills, confidence in using technology, and creativity in the arts.

The Upper School curriculum provides a traditional college-preparatory education in academics and the arts. In addition to the core subjects—English, history, math, and science—Soundview offers four languages (Latin, French, Spanish, and Italian); studio art; music; and electives that vary from year to year (recent offerings have included history of philosophy, forensics, computer science, astronomy, journalism, environmental science, and human anatomy and physiology).

AP courses are made available according to students' abilities and interests. Recently, AP courses have been offered in calculus, biology, physics, U.S. history, European history, government, English, psychology, computer science, and art.

Academic requirements for graduation are 4 years each of English and history, 3 years each of math and science, 3 years of one foreign language or 2 years each of two different languages, 1 year of art or music, and ½ year of health.

Computer technology at Soundview is integrated into the curriculum. Teachers post assignments on the School's website, and students upload completed work into teachers' folders. The School is wired for wireless technology and has a well-equipped computer lab.

The School's annual 10-day trips abroad (to England, Ireland, Spain, Austria, Germany, and Italy in recent years) offer students experience with other cultures. The School's academic curriculum is supplemented throughout the year by a variety of trips within the New York metropolitan area, to museums, nature centers, science labs, and other educational venues.

The school year is divided into two semesters, with letter grades sent out at the end of each. Individual conferences with parents, students, faculty members, and the Head of School are arranged throughout the year.

FACULTY AND ADVISERS

The faculty consists of 14 teachers (9 women and 5 men); the majority hold advanced degrees. Two teachers are part-time; the rest, full-time. Turnover is low, with an average of one replacement or addition every other year.

Each teacher serves as adviser to up to 5 students. Most faculty members supervise a club or publication or coach an athletic team.

W. Glyn Hearn has served as Head of School since Soundview was founded in 1989. He obtained his B.A. in English at the University of Texas at Austin and his M.A. in American literature at Texas Tech University. He spent twelve years at the Awty International School of Houston, Texas, where he served as Principal of the Lower, Middle, and Upper Schools and Head of the American Section, before becoming Assistant Headmaster and then Headmaster of the American Renaissance School in Westchester County in 1987.

COLLEGE ADMISSION COUNSELING

College placement at Soundview is directed by Carol Gill, one of the nation's leading college counseling experts. The process starts early on, when eighth, ninth, and tenth graders plan and

refine a course sequence that is appropriate for a competitive college. In the junior year, students and their parents begin meeting with Ms. Gill to discuss the college application process, develop lists of colleges, and plan college visits. The meetings continue through the senior year to complete applications. Representatives from approximately fifteen colleges visit Soundview every year to speak with students.

Because of the School's small size, the faculty and staff members know each student well and are able to assist students in selecting colleges that are the right match for them. The Head of School writes a personal recommendation for each senior.

College acceptances in recent years include Bard, Barnard, Bates, Boston University, Brown, Carnegie Mellon, Champlain, Clark, Columbia, Dickinson, Duke, Emerson, Franklin & Marshall, Gettysburg, Hampshire, Hartwick, High Point, Hobart, Ithaca, Manhattanville, Maryland Institute College of Art, Muhlenberg, Northeastern, NYU, Oberlin, Reed, Rensselaer, Rhode Island School of Design, R.I.T., Roger Williams, Sarah Lawrence, St. John's (Santa Fe), Skidmore, SUNY, Susquehanna, Vassar, Williams, and the Universities of Maine, Massachusetts, New Haven, and Vermont.

STUDENT BODY AND CONDUCT

Soundview reflects the diversity—ethnic, religious, and economic—of American society. The 36 boys and 34 girls come from Westchester, Fairfield, Rockland, and Putnam Counties and New York City. Approximately 13 percent of the student body are members of minority groups.

Respect for ethical values such as kindness, honesty, and respect for others are paramount at Soundview, where individual responsibility and a sense of community are stressed.

The School's disciplinary structure is informal, since it is based on the assumption that students attending the School desire to be there and are therefore willing to adhere to a code of conduct that demonstrates awareness that the community is based upon a shared sense of purpose and commitment. Despite the cordiality of its atmosphere, Soundview has high expectations of personal conduct. The result of this policy is a remarkably cooperative, considerate group of students who value each other and who appreciate their teachers.

Attire appropriate for a school is expected of all students, although there is no formal dress code.

ACADEMIC FACILITIES

Soundview's campus consists of 13.8 rustic acres with a historic main house, numerous outbuildings, a large pond, meadows, and woods, all in the heart of the village of Yorktown Heights, New York. The main house, the former Underhill mansion built by Yorktown's leading family in the nineteenth century, contains classrooms, administrative offices, the computer lab, and meeting rooms. A large barn houses the science lab, art studios, additional classrooms, and a meeting hall, while a third building is home to the Middle School. A fourth building provides another meeting and performance space, while a former chapel is used for the music program. Woodland paths and footbridges lead across streams and around the property. The campus is woven into the academic program in a variety of ways: students test pond water as part of environmental science, draw from nature in art, or enjoy a class outdoors on an especially fine day.

ATHLETICS

Physical education and sports at Soundview offer students the opportunity to develop leadership and teamwork skills as well as to excel in individual sports. Students participate on coed soccer, basketball, bowling, and Ultimate Frisbee teams that compete against other independent schools in the Hudson Valley region. Depending upon student interest in a given year, other sports, such as tennis, softball, and baseball may also be offered. Any student who wishes to play is accepted, regardless of ability.

For physical education, students play intramural sports and exercise at Soundview's home gym, the Solaris Sports Club in Yorktown Heights, a state-of-the-art multisport center just blocks from the School. The facility includes tennis courts, a large indoor basketball court, and exercise equipment.

EXTRACURRICULAR OPPORTUNITIES

Soundview offers a wide range of clubs and activities, with additional choices added each year by students themselves. Current clubs include yearbook; literary magazine; the Westchester County Mock Trial program; A Capella; and clubs for chess, 3-D design, knitting, gardening and composting, and community service.

The School sponsors activities to expose students to other cultures and experiences, such as trips to art exhibitions, dance performances, concerts, and plays. Students have the opportunity to perform music and drama at the annual talent show and at more informal coffeehouses throughout the year.

Major annual events at Soundview include the Back-to-School Picnic; Back-to-School Night, when parents learn about their student's classes; the Maple Syrup project, when students and faculty tap trees, boil sap into syrup, and serve a pancake breakfast; Texas Day, a lighthearted event featuring a barbecue, games, and spoofs on the Headmaster's home state; and the Graduation Dinner, an evening for Soundview parents to honor the graduating class. A parent-run Spring Gala and Auction fundraiser is held every other year. In 2014, the School celebrated a milestone with a 25th Anniversary Festival on campus, which drew over 200 alumni, current families, friends, and local officials to commemorate the school's founding.

DAILY LIFE

The school day begins at 8:10 with Morning Meeting, when the entire student body, faculty, and staff assemble to hear announcements about ongoing clubs, listen to presentations by clubs, and discuss the day's national and international news. The Head of School encourages students to express their views and helps them to assess events that are unfolding in the world around them.

Classes begin at 8:25 and end at 3:25. There are eight academic periods plus lunch.

SUMMER PROGRAMS

Occasionally, Soundview offers a small summer school for secondary school students on an as-needed basis, with classes that vary each year. A typical offering includes English, writing, math, history, a science, and a language. Students have the opportunity to work one-on-one with a teacher or in small classes to skip ahead in a given subject or fulfill a requirement. In addition, Soundview offers a S.T.E.A.M. (science, technology, engineering, art, and math) enrichment program for elementary school children.

COSTS AND FINANCIAL AID

Tuition and fees for 2015–16 are $40,000 for Middle School and $41,500 for Upper School. Fees include gym, books, art and lab fees, ERB exams, and literary publications.

In 2014–15, the School provided a total of $569,000 in financial aid to 30 percent of the student body.

ADMISSIONS INFORMATION

Soundview operates on a rolling admissions policy, with students accepted throughout the year in all grades except twelfth. Families of prospective students meet with the Admissions Director, after which the student spends a day at the School. The SSAT is not required, but portions of the ERB standardized examination are administered (unless the applicant provides the School with sufficient, current test data).

Students of all backgrounds are welcomed. The academic program is demanding, but the School's small size allows it to work with each individual student in order to develop strategies for success.

APPLICATION TIMETABLE

Soundview accepts applications on a rolling basis throughout the year. The application fee is $50.

ADMISSIONS CORRESPONDENCE

Mary E. Ivanyi
Director of Admissions and Assistant Head
Soundview Preparatory School
370 Underhill Road
Yorktown Heights, New York 10598
United States
Phone: 914-962-2780
E-mail: info@soundviewprep.org
Website: http://www.soundviewprep.org

TASIS THE AMERICAN SCHOOL IN SWITZERLAND

Montagnola-Lugano, Switzerland

Type: Coeducational boarding and day college preparatory school
Grades: Pre-Kindergarten–Postgraduate: Elementary School, pre-K–5; Middle School, 6–8; High School, 9–12, postgraduate year
Enrollment: School total: 730; High School: 380; Middle School: 150; Elementary School: 200
Head of School: Lyle D. Rigg

THE SCHOOL

TASIS The American School in Switzerland was founded in 1956 by Mrs. M. Crist Fleming to offer a strong American college-preparatory education in a European setting. TASIS was the first American boarding school established in Europe. Over time, it has become a school for students from more than 65 countries seeking an American independent school experience. Both the Advanced Placement (AP) and the International Baccalaureate (IB) programs are offered in the High School.

The objective of the School is to foster both a vital enthusiasm for learning and habits that are essential to a full realization of each student's moral and intellectual potential. The curriculum gives special emphasis to the achievements of the Western heritage, many elements of which are easily accessible from the School's location. By providing an international dimension to education, TASIS stresses the need for young people to mature with confidence and competence in an increasingly interrelated world.

The beautiful campus is in the village of Montagnola, overlooking the city and the lake of Lugano, nestled among the southernmost of the Swiss Alps in the Italian-speaking canton of Ticino. Ideally situated in the heart of Europe, the School makes the most of its location by introducing students to European cultures and languages through extensive travel programs.

The TASIS Foundation, a not-for-profit foundation, owns the School. The TASIS Foundation also has a school near London and offers summer programs in England, Spain, and Italy as well as Switzerland. Alumni provide enthusiastic support for the School's activities and participate in annual reunions and other special events.

TASIS is accredited by the Council of International Schools (CIS) and the New England Association of Schools and Colleges (NEASC) and is a member of the National Association of Independent Schools and the Swiss Group of International Schools.

ACADEMIC PROGRAM

The minimum requirements for graduation from the High School college-preparatory program are 4 years of English, 3 years of history (including modern history and U.S. history), a third-year proficiency in a modern foreign language, 3 years of mathematics (through algebra II), 3 years of laboratory science (including physical and biological sciences), and 1 year of fine arts, plus senior humanities, sports/physical education, and service learning requirements. Students must satisfactorily complete a minimum of 19 credits and are required to enroll in a minimum of five full-credit courses per year or the equivalent.

TASIS offers an extensive English as an Additional Language program that focuses on oral and written academic English skills and competence in a high school curriculum leading to the TASIS college preparatory diploma.

TASIS offers a diverse and challenging curriculum, including the Advanced Placement Program (AP), the International Baccalaureate Diploma Program (IBDP), and a wide range of required and elective courses. In 2015, students took 162 AP exams; 37 percent of the scores were 4 or above, and 20 percent were the top score of 5. Students may also select IB courses and can earn subject-specific certificates or the full diploma. In 2015, 88 students took 440 IB exams; 90 percent of scores were 4 or above, 64 percent 5 or above, and 38 percent 6 or better.

The average class size is 15; the student-teacher ratio is 6:1. The student's day is fully structured, including time for academics, sports and activities, meals and socializing, and supervised evening study hours. The grading system uses A to F for performance and assigns effort grades of 1 to 5, reflecting students' attitudes and application to their work. The academic year is divided into two semesters and grades and comment reports are e-mailed to parents four times a year.

The postgraduate year presents an additional opportunity to high school graduates who wish to spend an interim year in Europe before going on to college. With assistance from the Academic Dean, each postgraduate student can design a tailor-made course of study that enables him or her to explore and develop new interests, strengthen academic weaknesses, or concentrate in areas of strength or particular interest. The postgraduate year includes a course-related Academic Travel program.

FACULTY AND ADVISORS

The faculty represents one of the School's strongest assets. Its members are a group of dedicated professionals who are enthusiastic about working with young people. There are 65 faculty members in the High School, 73 percent of whom hold advanced degrees and 60 percent of whom come from the United States. More than 30 faculty members live on campus; the rest live nearby and participate in most campus activities. In addition to teaching, faculty members act as advisors, sports coaches, trip chaperones, and dormitory residents, helping create a warm, family-like atmosphere.

COLLEGE ADMISSION COUNSELING

The School employs three full-time college counselors, who meet with students individually and in groups throughout their High School years. The College Counseling Office maintains a reference library of university catalogs from around the world so that students can familiarize themselves with the wide variety of opportunities that are open to them. As a counseling resource, the School provides a small computer lab for college research. Many college admissions officers from universities in the U.S. and Europe visit the School and speak to students. TASIS is an official testing center for the PSAT, SAT, SAT Subject Tests, ACT, PLAN, TOEFL, and all AP and IB examinations.

Recent graduates have been accepted to such institutions as Oxford, Cambridge, California–Berkeley, Imperial College London, UCLA, Johns Hopkins, Northwestern, Michigan, Middlebury, Davidson, Washington and Lee, and Bates.

STUDENT BODY AND CONDUCT

Each student is honor bound to abide by the rules, as defined in the TASIS *Student Handbook*. The School employs a variety of counseling, disciplinary, and administrative responses to rules violations, determined on a case-by-case basis. The School administration and Conduct Review Board handle more serious offenses. All responses take into account the seriousness of the offense, the number of previous offenses, any mitigating circumstances, and the student's record as a member of the TASIS community.

Students at TASIS bear a serious responsibility to conduct themselves not only in a way that does credit to them, to their School, and to their country of origin, but also in a way that is consistent with the high standards set by the citizens of the European countries they visit. For this reason, TASIS has established reasonable but definitive standards of behavior, attitude, and appearance for all of its students. The School reserves the right to ask any student to withdraw for failure to maintain these standards.

ACADEMIC FACILITIES

The campus comprises twenty-five buildings—a combination of historical villas restored for school use and new, purpose-built facilities. The seventeenth-century Villa De Nobili was the School's original building and houses the dining hall, dormitories, and administrative offices. Hadsall House contains Elementary School classrooms and a High School dormitory. Villa Monticello contains classrooms, a computer center, a computer-based language lab, and a dormitory. Next to Villa Monticello is the 22,000-volume M. Crist Fleming Library. Villa Aurora provides classrooms for both the Elementary and Middle School. Middle School classes are also held in Belvedere. The Palestra houses a sports complex with a gymnasium, fitness center, dance studio, locker rooms, student lounge with café, and music rooms. In the past five years the School completed the John E. Palmer Cultural Center, which includes a state-of-the-art theater; Fiammetta, which houses classrooms; and Lanterna, which houses both a dormitory and classrooms. The newly renovated Casa Al Focolare houses Elementary School students from Pre-Kindergarten to first grade. The Ferit Sahenk ('83) Arts Center provides space for art studios, architecture and design, painting/drawing, ceramics/sculpture, and photography. This building also houses the Palestrina, a second gymnasium. Campo Science, the newest addition to the Global Village, opened in September 2014.

BOARDING AND GENERAL FACILITIES

The campus includes ten dormitories, each of which houses from 6 to 43 students. Dormitories are located in the Villa De Nobili, Villa Monticello, Hadsall House, Villa Del Sole, Balmelli, Giani, Belvedere, and Lanterna buildings. All dormitories are supervised, and some faculty members live in the dormitories. Rooms accommodate from 2 to 4 students each. Although School facilities are closed during the winter and spring vacations, optional faculty-chaperoned trips are sometimes offered for students who are unable to return home.

Two recreation centers and a snack bar serve as focal points for student social activities. Three nurses are in residence.

ATHLETICS

Students are required to participate in either a varsity sport three days a week or recreational sports after classes. Sports available include soccer, basketball, fitness training, volleyball, rugby, tennis, track and field, lacrosse, skiing, swimming, cross-country, horseback riding, and aerobics. On weekends, students often go on hiking and mountain climbing trips in the Swiss Alps during the fall and spring and go skiing during the winter. During Ski Week in Crans-Montana (High School) or St. Moritz (Middle School), every student takes lessons in downhill or snowboarding.

Varsity sports give students the opportunity to compete against many schools in Switzerland and other countries and to take part in tournaments sponsored by the Swiss Group of International Schools (NISSA, ESC). Varsity sports include soccer, rugby, volleyball, basketball, tennis, badminton, swimming, lacrosse, and track and field. Students also have the opportunity to enroll in the AC Milan soccer program, run by the coaches of the renowned Italian soccer team AC Milan.

Facilities include a playing field, two gymnasiums, and an outdoor basketball/volleyball area. The newly constructed Palestra sports complex includes a gymnasium with seating for up to 400 spectators, a dance studio, a fitness center, changing rooms, and a student lounge with a café.

EXTRACURRICULAR OPPORTUNITIES

The School's location in central Europe offers an enviable range of cultural opportunities. Trips to concerts, art galleries, and museums in Lugano, Locarno, and Milan extend education beyond the classroom. All students participate in the Academic Travel program, a four-day, faculty-chaperoned trip in the fall and a seven-day, faculty-chaperoned trip in the spring to such cities as Athens, Barcelona, Florence, Madrid, Munich, Nice, Paris, Prague, Rome, Venice, and Vienna.

On-campus activities include drama productions, choral and instrumental music, Model UN, Student Council, Film Club, and yearbook. The Service Learning program focuses on the TASIS community, the local community, the interschool community, and the global community. Opportunities include peer tutoring, volunteering at a local domestic violence shelter, and participating in Model UN. TASIS also offers an annual summer service trip to Africa. Special annual social events include Family Weekend, dinner dances at the beginning of the academic year and at Christmas, prom, and the Spring Arts Festival, along with a special graduation banquet and ceremony for seniors.

The TASIS Global Service Program transforms lives by providing every High School student with a unique opportunity to connect across borders—whether geographic, economic, or social—through comprehensive experiences that build empathy and encourage personal responsibility. The program awakens students to humanitarian needs; inspires them to build enduring, mutually beneficial relationships; and leads them toward a life of active citizenship and committed service.

DAILY LIFE

Classes start at 8 a.m. and follow a rotating schedule. Classes meet from 50 to 65 minutes. There are weekly all-School assemblies. Sports and activities take place after school until 6 p.m. Meals are served buffet-style except for some Wednesday evenings, when students share a formal dinner with their advisor group. Evening study is from 7 until 10.

WEEKEND LIFE

Both day and boarding students are encouraged to participate in organized events on weekends, including mountain climbing and camping trips to scenic areas in Switzerland, shopping trips to open-air markets in northern Italy, and sightseeing excursions to Zurich, Milan, Venice, or Florence. On-campus events include talent shows, open-mic coffeehouse afternoons, films, and discotheque dances.

On weekends, students have Lugano town privileges if they have no School commitments and are in good academic and social standing. All excursions beyond Lugano are chaperoned by a member of the faculty, except those for seniors and some juniors, who, with parental permission, enjoy the privilege of independent travel in groups of two or more.

COSTS AND FINANCIAL AID

The all-inclusive tuition fee for boarding students is CHF 78,000 for the 2015–16 academic year, with an enrollment deposit of CHF 3000. This includes all fees that are necessary for attendance: room, board, tuition, eleven days of academic travel, Ski Week, all textbooks, laundry, activities, and most lab fees. A monthly personal allowance of CHF 250–300 is recommended. Seventy percent of the tuition is due by July 1 and the remainder by November 15.

Students may apply for financial assistance, which is granted on the basis of merit, need, and the student's ability to contribute to the School community.

ADMISSIONS INFORMATION

All applicants are considered on the basis of previous academic records, three teachers' evaluations, a personal statement, and a parental statement. The SSAT is recommended, and the Cambridge or TOEFL test is required for students whose native language is not English. TASIS does not discriminate on the basis of race, color, nationality, or ethnic origin in its admissions policies and practices.

Application for entrance is recommended only for those students with sufficient academic interest and motivation to benefit from the program. The School accepts students from Pre-Kindergarten to grade 12 and at the postgraduate level.

APPLICATION TIMETABLE

TASIS has a rolling admissions policy and considers applications throughout the year. Applicants are encouraged to make an appointment to visit the campus. Within ten days of receipt of a completed application, the CHF 300 application fee, an official transcript from the previous school, and three teachers' evaluations, the Admissions Committee notifies the parents of its decision.

ADMISSIONS CORRESPONDENCE

Mr. William E. Eichner, Director of Admissions
TASIS The American School in Switzerland
CH-6926 Montagnola-Lugano
Switzerland
Phone: +41-91-960-5151
Fax: +41-91-993-2979
E-mail: admissions@tasis.ch
Website: http://www.tasis.ch

or

The TASIS Schools
112 South Royal Street
Alexandria, Virginia 22314
United States
Phone: 703-299-8150
     800-442-6005
Fax: 703-299-8157
E-mail: usadmissions@tasis.com

THOMAS JEFFERSON SCHOOL

St. Louis, Missouri

Type: Coeducational boarding and day college-preparatory school
Grades: 7–12
Enrollment: 74
Head of School: Elizabeth L. Holekamp, Ph.D.

THE SCHOOL

Thomas Jefferson School (TJ) was founded in 1946. It is known for its academic excellence and its commitment to enrolling students from all over the world since its inception. The School became coeducational in 1971. The campus is a 20-acre estate in Sunset Hills, a suburb 15 miles southwest of downtown St. Louis.

The School's mission is to give its students the strongest possible academic background through a classical education. Within a nurturing community, students develop a responsibility for their own learning and a desire to lift up the world with beauty and intellect. Many of the School's distinctive features, such as its size, its program, and even its daily schedule, are outgrowths of this mission.

The School has an active parent organization as well as an alumni association that bridges generations and continents and maintains a link with current students in an effort to ready them for life after TJ.

Thomas Jefferson School is a member of the National Association of Independent Schools, the Association of Boarding Schools, the Independent Schools Association of the Central States, Midwest Boarding Schools, and the School and Student Service for Financial Aid.

ACADEMIC PROGRAM

Thomas Jefferson offers a challenging approach to learning, with the emphasis on the student's own efforts. Class periods are short, and the teachers seldom lecture; instead, all students are called on to answer questions and generate discussion. During afternoon and evening study time, the students have a good deal of freedom in choosing when and where to do their homework, with help readily available from faculty members.

Seventh and eighth graders take English, mathematics, science, social studies, and Latin. In the ninth through twelfth grades, students take 4 years of English; 4 years of mathematics through calculus; 2 years of Ancient Greek (ninth and tenth grades); 2 years of Italian or French (tenth and eleventh); at least 3 years of science, including an AP course; and at least 2 years of history, including AP U.S. History. Electives include additional language, science, and history courses. Advanced Placement exams are a standard part of the courses in the social sciences, calculus, biology, physics, chemistry, advanced languages, and junior and senior English. Faculty members also help students work toward AP exams in other subject areas.

The English curriculum gives students intensive training in grammar, vocabulary, and writing skills. They also read and discuss a great deal of literature, including recognized classics (Shakespeare, the Bible, and epics), time-tested authors (Austen, Dickens, Dostoyevsky, Fitzgerald, Manzoni, Melville, and Shaw), and more contemporary major authors, such as Amy Tan, Ralph Ellison, and Chaim Potok.

A special feature is the study of classical Greek, which contributes to intellectual development (including concrete benefits such as enhanced vocabulary) and cultural knowledge.

The typical class size is 15, and the overall student-teacher ratio is 7:1. During the day, teachers are accessible to everyone and are ready to help; a teacher is on duty each evening and is available to assist with homework. Younger new students and those having academic difficulty are placed in supervised afternoon or evening study halls for additional support.

The grading system uses letter grades of A, B, C, D, and E. An average of B– is Honors; an average of A– is High Honors. To remain in good standing, a student must have no more than one D in any grading period; students in their first year, however, are allowed extra time to adjust. One-hour examinations are given at the end of the first and third quarters (October and April), and 2- to 3-hour examinations are given at midyear and at the end of the year. Following each exam period, a student's adviser sends the parents an individualized grade letter discussing the student's progress and giving the latest grades and teachers' comments.

The nearly month-long winter and spring vacations give students an opportunity to unwind, spend time with their families, and do independent work.

FACULTY AND ADVISERS

The faculty, including the Head of School, consists of 22 full-time and part-time adjunct members, 13 women and 9 men. Faculty members hold twenty-two baccalaureate degrees, nine master's degrees, one law degree, and four Ph.D.'s.

Dr. Elizabeth Holekamp became the fourth Head of School in the summer of 2011. Dr. Holekamp attended the University of Missouri and holds a Ph.D. from Indiana University.

All faculty members are expected to continue educating themselves through a variety of professional development activities, including regular reading, both within and outside the subject areas they teach.

Currently, 2 faculty members live on the campus, along with 5 resident assistants and a full-time Director of Residence Life. Each faculty member, whether resident or not, has several duties besides teaching, such as athletics supervision, evening study help, and advising students. Teachers meet with each of their advisees regularly to check the student's grades and to keep in touch with his or her personal development.

COLLEGE ADMISSION COUNSELING

Excellent preparation for college is the School's primary objective. An experienced faculty member serves as the Director of College Counseling, guiding seniors through the application and admissions process (including a College Boot Camp at the beginning of the senior year), helping them develop a realistic list of choices, and offering advice on writing personal essays. Faculty members support the director by writing letters of recommendation, attesting to student performance, and preparing Secondary School Reports. They also spend many hours following up with colleges by phone and e-mail. College admissions recruiters come to campus to talk with students virtually every week during each fall semester.

In sixty-eight years, the School has had 646 graduates; all have gone to college—many to well-known, selective institutions. Among the colleges and universities attended by recent Thomas Jefferson graduates are Beloit, Boston University, Brown, Caltech, Carnegie Mellon, Carleton, Claremont-McKenna, Columbia, Cornell, Duke, Emory, Harvard, Haverford, Johns Hopkins, Lawrence College, New York University–Stern, Northwestern, Penn State, Pitzer, Pomona, Reed, Rensselaer, Rhodes, Smith, Stanford, Swarthmore, Vanderbilt, Washington (St. Louis), Wesleyan, the University of Chicago, The University of Delaware, the University of Missouri, and the University of Pennsylvania.

The School consistently maintains first-tier SAT scores among U.S. boarding schools as listed by Boarding School Review.com.

STUDENT BODY AND CONDUCT

In 2014–15, the School had 74 students (38 boarding, 36 day). Domestic students come primarily from the region between the Appalachians and the Great Plains. Approximately one third of all students are international students from various countries (ESL instruction is available, although good English proficiency is required for admission). Most grades have girls and boys in about equal numbers.

A Student Council, whose members are elected twice a year, brings student concerns before the faculty and helps maintain a healthy, studious atmosphere. Collectively, the council has one vote in faculty meetings on many decisions concerning student life. A student prefect system gives students an additional layer of peer support.

Demerits are given for misconduct, lateness, and other routine matters; a student who receives too many demerits in one week has to do chores around the campus on Saturday. Students may appeal any demerits, even those given by the Head of School, before a Student Appeals Court.

ACADEMIC FACILITIES

The Charles E. Merrill, Jr. Building, built as a gracious family home on the original estate, provides a comfortable setting for classes and meals; it also contains faculty and administrative offices, the library collections, and an art gallery. The adjoining Sayers Hall provides science laboratories and classrooms. A dedicated arts facility provides classroom and studio space for the fine arts, including a print-making shop. The recent addition to the gymnasium provides weight-training and yoga facilities.

BOARDING AND GENERAL FACILITIES

Boarders live in the Gables—a brick outbuilding from the original estate—and in six cottages constructed as on-campus living quarters. Each cottage has four double rooms; each room has an outside entrance, a private bath, large windows, wall-to-wall carpeting, air conditioning, and wireless Internet access. The cottages were designed to provide quiet, privacy, and independence. Normally, 2 or 3 boarding students share a room with 1 or 2 day students.

ATHLETICS

Thomas Jefferson School athletics are designed to support the physical and mental well-being of students. Outdoor sports include intramural tennis (five courts), varsity soccer, and fitness; indoor sports are volleyball and basketball (both varsity and JV), yoga, and general fitness. Athletics are required on Monday, Tuesday, Thursday, and Friday afternoons. Teams compete with other local schools in basketball, soccer, and volleyball. Some students with specialized interests fulfill this requirement off campus.

EXTRACURRICULAR OPPORTUNITIES

The St. Louis area has a wealth of resources in art, music, and theater, as well as an internationally recognized zoo, a science museum, and a world-renowned botanical garden. The School keeps the students informed about opportunities around town and helps with transportation and tickets whenever possible. Teachers often take groups of students on informal weekend field trips. In recent years, groups have gone to the Ozarks for camping, to the Mississippi River to see bald eagles, and to many symphony concerts, ballets, and plays. Students also attend movies, sports events, and concerts.

Service learning is an integral part of the program, and the School helps students find opportunities for volunteering. All students must plan and complete a required amount of voluntary community service before they graduate. Students are encouraged to pursue their own interests, such as music lessons or studying a language that is not part of the curriculum, and the School helps make arrangements. A piano is available for anyone to use for lessons or for personal enjoyment. Over the years, students have initiated and sustained major activities, such as the School yearbook, a student newspaper, mock trial, and the all-school play. Clubs include Robotics, Equality, Green, Chess, Dungeons and Dragons, and Pandora.

DAILY LIFE

A school day begins with breakfast at 7:45. Eight 35-minute class periods (and lunch) take place between 8:30 and 1:10. In grades 11 and 12, students take four classes and in grades 7 through 10, they take five. Classes meet daily, but AP classes, which have longer assignments, may meet only four days a week. After lunch, a student may have a science lab, a language lab, or other supplementary academic work. Then students have an hour of athletics, perhaps a meeting with their adviser or study help from another teacher, and some independent time in which they are expected to start their homework for the next day. Day students generally leave around 5:00. Dinner is at 6:00, and evenings are devoted to study. On Wednesday and Friday afternoons, there are fine-arts classes in such subjects as drawing, photography, ceramics, digital art, and art and music appreciation, and students may leave the campus for nearby shopping centers.

WEEKEND LIFE

Weekends are loosely structured. As long as students are in good standing academically, they have considerable freedom and may leave the campus for movies, shopping, and the like. A driver is employed on the weekends to provide student transportation. Older students may keep cars on campus at the discretion of the School. The sports facilities are available for weekend use. Events and outings are organized almost every weekend by the Student Council, the Student Activities Committee, and the Residence Life staff.

SUMMER PROGRAMS

The School organizes both domestic and international study trips during school breaks or the summer, often led by faculty members. Trips may augment a particular field of study or present a new challenge. Some students choose to attend college classes during the summer months, work at internships, or volunteer over an extended period of time in their home community.

COSTS AND FINANCIAL AID

Charges for 2015–16 are $45,500 for full boarding international students, $44,800 for full boarding U.S. students, $42,250 for weekday boarding, and $25,000 for day students. This includes room plus all meals for boarders and all lunches for day students. An additional $1,800 should cover the cost of books, supplies, activity and technology fees, and other school expenses. This figure does not include travel expenses, weekly allowances, or College Board and Advanced Placement examinations for juniors. In addition, international students will be charged approximately $1,200 for health insurance.

A $2,000 nonrefundable deposit (credited to tuition), is required when a student enrolls. The balance of the tuition is paid through various payment plans.

Financial aid is available, based on a family's need. More than 40 percent of the student body currently receives some financial aid; the total amount awarded is in excess of $590,000. An applicant's family must file a statement with the School and Student Service, and this information is used in judging need. Many middle-income families receive some assistance.

ADMISSIONS INFORMATION

The School looks for evidence of strong intellect, liveliness, energy, ambition, and curiosity. Strong grades and test scores are important considerations but not always the deciding factors. A candidate should submit the results of the Secondary School Admission Test (SSAT); international students submit the results of the TOEFL. About 60 percent of those who complete the application process are accepted.

APPLICATION TIMETABLE

Inquiries and applications are welcome at any time, but the School has three rounds of admissions: early decision applicants submit their materials by mid-December and receive an answer in early January; regular decision applicants submit their materials by mid-February and receive an answer in early March; after April, applications for any remaining openings are considered as they are received. As part of the application process, prospective students usually spend a day at the School visiting classes, having lunch, and spending time with the admissions staff to ask questions and have an interview. Skype interviews are conducted with out-of-town applicants. There is a $40 fee for domestic applications, and a $100 fee for international applications.

ADMISSIONS CORRESPONDENCE

Stephen Held, Director of Admissions
Thomas Jefferson School
4100 South Lindbergh Boulevard
St. Louis, Missouri 63127
United States
Phone: 314-843-4151
Fax: 314-843-3527
E-mail: admissions@tjs.org
Website: http://www.tjs.org

THE UNIVERSITY OF CHICAGO LABORATORY SCHOOLS

Chicago, Illinois

THE UNIVERSITY OF **CHICAGO** | **Laboratory Schools**

Type: Coeducational, day, college-preparatory school
Grades: N–12
Enrollment: Approximately 1,965
Head of School: Robin Appleby

THE SCHOOL

Founded by the renowned educator John Dewey in 1896, the University of Chicago Laboratory Schools (Lab) are among the nation's best. The Laboratory Schools are home to the youngest members of the University of Chicago's academic community. Lab strives to ignite and nurture an enduring spirit of scholarship, curiosity, creativity, and confidence. The Schools value learning experientially, exhibiting kindness, and honoring diversity. Being part of the University of Chicago means that the importance of intellectual life—of thought and exploration—infuses everything Lab does across all aspects of its curriculum. Families who choose Lab care deeply about curiosity, inquiry, and creativity. All are attracted to a diverse community and an environment that creates and nurtures habits of expansive thinking and complex problem-solving.

Lab is approved or accredited by the Independent Schools Association of the Central States, North Central Association of Colleges and Schools, and the Illinois Department of Education. Lab is a member of the National Association of Independent Schools and the Council of International Schools.

ACADEMIC PROGRAM

The Laboratory Schools do not specialize in a particular academic area. Rather, Lab prepares students to be creative, in-depth thinkers who are lifelong learners, ready to face the challenges of an increasingly complex global society. For the younger learners, Lab provides a play-based curriculum and teachers encourage choice, initiative, exploration, and collaboration. New skills and challenges are added in developmentally appropriate ways to provide each child with opportunities to investigate, inquire, experiment, and exchange ideas. Formal instruction in art, music, physical education, and computers is added during Primary School and world language is added in third grade (French, German, Mandarin, or Spanish; the high school also offers Latin).

The high school curriculum emphasizes analytical reading, writing, research, strong math and science skills, and broad access to the arts and music. U-High has more than 150 different classes—all are college-preparatory and should be considered equivalent to honors-level classes in most public school systems. In addition, U-High also offers 17 Advanced Placement and advanced-topic classes. Starting in the tenth grade, U-Highers have access to University of Chicago libraries and resources. Qualified students may also take college courses at the University of Chicago at no extra charge.

FACULTY AND ADVISERS

Lab's 255 teachers (of whom 80 percent hold advanced degrees) are best-in-class and possess the background and skills to inspire and engage students. Faculty are chosen for their experience with students at a specific grade level, and all educators come to the Schools with at least several years of teaching experience. Ten Lab teachers have won Chicago's prestigious Golden Apple Award for excellence in teaching—more than any other school in the city.

COLLEGE ADMISSION COUNSELING

Virtually every graduate from the Laboratory Schools High School graduates from a four-year college. They gain acceptance to outstanding colleges around Chicago and the country: from the University of Chicago, University of Illinois at Urbana–Champaign, Northwestern, and DePaul, to Harvard, Emory, University of Southern California, and many more. During junior year, each U-Higher begins working with one of three full-time college counselors who oversee the college application process. The counselor focuses on helping each student gain acceptance at a college that will fit his or her unique needs and Lab's counseling program supports families as they navigate the financial aspects of a college education.

STUDENT BODY AND CONDUCT

Lab enrolls approximately 1,965 students in fifteen grades, with a largely equal number of boys and girls. Lab students speak more than forty languages at home, and identify themselves as having fifty-nine different nationalities. The Nursery/Kindergarten program enrolls approximately 400 students, the Primary School (grades 1 and 2) enrolls approximately 280 students, the Lower School (grades 3–5) enrolls approximately 400 students, and the Middle School (grades 6–8) enrolls approximately 360 students. Lab's high school, University High (U-High), enrolls approximately 500 students. Lab students live throughout the greater Chicago area, with approximately half coming from the Hyde Park/Kenwood area. Approximately 50 percent of Lab students have parents who are affiliated with the University of Chicago.

ACADEMIC FACILITIES

Within 615,000 square feet of space (about 11 football fields of indoor space), students take full advantage of facilities. Grades N–2 occupy the newly built Earl Shapiro Hall, a light-filled building designed to maximize the independence a child feels during the school day and to seamlessly connect indoor and outdoor learning. ESH features multiple outdoor play spaces, art and music rooms, a library, and a gymnasium.

Two blocks to the west is Lab's Historic Campus. Covering two city blocks, it is home to grades 3–12. The architecturally impressive buildings date from the early 1900s and are undergoing a once-in-a-lifetime restoration and renovation.

The Historic Campus includes five connected buildings and a gym complex; 13 wet science labs, 4 computer labs, and a digital language lab; full wireless capability, 1,250+ regularly upgraded desk and laptop computers, and iPads for in-school use; and libraries with more than 100,000 volumes.

The most dramatic change to the Historic Campus is the new Gordon Parks Arts Hall. With 94,000 square feet on three stories, Lab's arts spaces match the talent of the students and teachers who will use them and support drama, art, music, film, photography, and digital music and media.

Expansive athletic facilities including a soccer field, tennis courts, a pool, and multiple gymnasiums and training spaces are on the Historic Campus. Some high school teams benefit from University of Chicago's athletic facilities.

ATHLETICS

Athletics draw hundreds of participants for the love of the game—and to win. The Middle School has fifteen sports teams and U-High fields thirty-one sports teams that compete in the Independent School League and the Illinois High School Association (IHSA). Over the past decade, Lab's teams have competed—and won—at high levels of competition, including fifty IHSA regional and sectional championships in twelve different sports. They achieve this within a "no cut" policy system that encourages students to participate (nearly 65 percent of U-Highers play on at least one team) and distinguishes Lab from most athletic programs in the country.

EXTRACURRICULAR OPPORTUNITIES

In the high school, students run more than forty school-sponsored organizations, ranging from religious and ethnic clubs to activities in the arts, culture, academics, philanthropy, and social activism. University High students devote significant time to many different extracurricular activities: joining sports, math, science, debate, or

Model UN teams; writing and publishing the School's newspaper or yearbook; serving in student government or community service roles; and participating in theater productions or musical performances. Many of these extracurricular activities begin in the Middle School.

DAILY LIFE

Because Lab begins with children who are 3 years old, and slightly over half continue at Lab until they graduate from U-High in twelfth grade, there are enormous variances in the students' daily schedules and activities.

The nursery and kindergarten classrooms at Lab are busy, with many different activities going on at one time. This is Lab's negotiated curriculum in action: teachers prepare an environment filled with possibilities and encourage choice, initiative, exploration, and collaboration.

Lab's Primary and Lower School curricula (first through fifth grades) are designed to help children master the skills that will serve as the foundation to their intellectual life. Children entering the Middle School years (sixth through eighth grade) begin an intense period of social, emotional, physical, moral, and intellectual growth.

U-Highers are an independent group whose high expectations go hand in hand with a demanding workload and a great deal of personal freedom. Each year, Lab students are better able to think for themselves, challenge assumptions, and, most importantly, take on increasing levels of responsibility for their own education.

SUMMER PROGRAMS

Summer Lab is a six-week program that includes Summer School, Adventure Kids Day Camp, Sports Camps, Fun in the Sun, and Summer Lab on Stage. Summer Lab Field Study stages domestic and international summer travel. Summer Lab embodies the notion that love of learning never goes on vacation. Approximately 1,000 students, from ages 3 to 18, participated last summer in the rich and diverse program, mixing Labbies with children from all around the city of Chicago, the United States, and the world.

COSTS AND FINANCIAL AID

Tuition costs for the 2015–16 academic year are as follows: $19,302 for the nursery school half-day program; $27,384 for the nursery and kindergarten full-day program; $27,384 for grades 1–5; $29,328 for grades 6–8; and $30,618 for grades 9–12.

Lab welcomes all applicants, regardless of financial need. Having the best and brightest students in its classrooms is part of what makes the Lab experience special, so the Schools strive to make its educational program affordable for as many families as possible through scholarship and financial aid. Those who wish to apply for financial aid should do so in tandem with the school admission process. Financial aid awards are not automatically renewed; families are required to reapply for aid each year. Awards are recalculated annually based on the most recent financial data.

In keeping with long-standing traditions and policies, the University of Chicago Laboratory Schools considers students for admission on the basis of individual merit and does not discriminate based on race, color, religion, sex, sexual orientation, gender identity, national or ethnic origin, disability, or any other protected class under the law in its admissions policies, scholarship and loan programs, educational policies, and other administered programs.

ADMISSIONS INFORMATION

Every applicant family receives personal attention, including a meeting with an admissions officer, a tour of the schools, and an opportunity to interact with other students and faculty. Lab believes that each applicant is unique and possesses special qualities that cannot always be captured by test scores and applications alone. Lab learns about its applicants through playgroups, classroom visits, interviews, shadow days, and tours. Applicant families also learn more about Lab's special character through this process.

APPLICATION TIMETABLE

Historically, most students enter Lab at either Nursery 3 (3 years old), sixth grade, or ninth grade and begin the application process in August or September of the year prior to enrollment. Admissions deadlines and details on the application process for all grades are available on Lab's website at www.ucls.uchicago.edu.

ADMISSIONS CORRESPONDENCE

Irene M. Reed, Executive Director
Admissions and Financial Aid
University of Chicago Laboratory Schools
1362 East 59th Street
Chicago, Illinois 60637
United States
Phone: 773-702-9451
Fax: 773-702-1520
E-mail: admissions@ucls.uchicago.edu
Website: http://www.ucls.uchicago.edu

YORK PREPARATORY SCHOOL

New York, New York

Type: Coeducational day college preparatory school
Grades: 6–12: Middle School, 6–8; Upper School, 9–12
Enrollment: 350
Head of School: Ronald P. Stewart, Headmaster

THE SCHOOL

York Prep is a college preparatory school with a strong, academically challenging, traditional curriculum. In a city known for its diversity of private schools, York Prep has developed a unique program that leads students to their highest potential. The School's responsive approach emphasizes independent thought, builds confidence, and sends graduates on to the finest colleges and universities. At York, every student finds opportunities to flourish. York Prep believes that success breeds success, and excellence in academics, arts, or sports creates self-confidence that enhances all aspects of life, both in and out of the classroom.

York Prep was established in 1969 by its current Headmaster, Ronald P. Stewart, and his wife, Jayme Stewart, Director of College Guidance. Situated on West 68th Street between Columbus Avenue and Central Park West, the School is well served by public transportation. Therefore, it attracts students from all over the metropolitan area, creating a diverse community. York Prep takes full advantage of the prime location, with regular visits to museums, parks, and theaters, all of which are easily accessible.

York Prep is approved by the New York State Board of Regents and accredited by the Middle States Association of Colleges and Schools.

ACADEMIC PROGRAM

The curriculum is designed to develop the superior academic skills necessary for future success. Close attention to each student's needs ensures that progress toward personal excellence is carefully guided.

Students must complete 20 credits for graduation: 4 in English, 4 in math, 4 in science, 4 in history, and 4 in foreign language.

Eleventh and twelfth graders choose from a number of course offerings in every subject area. In addition to selecting one course from each required category, a student must choose an elective from a variety of options that range from the creative and performing arts to the analytical sciences.

York Prep is proud of its commitment to community service. Student volunteer work benefits others, helps students realize their full potential, builds a well-rounded individual, and establishes a closer relationship between the School and community. Colleges expect students to have volunteer experience and York Prep College Guidance strongly urges students to perform 25 hours of community service per year during high school as a mark of integrity, responsibility, and citizenship.

Classes at York are small—the average class has 15 students. There are close student-teacher relations and all students begin their day with a morning "house" period. Each student's academic and social progress is carefully monitored by the teachers, advisers, and deans of the Upper and Middle Schools. The deans, in turn, keep the Headmaster, Associate Head, and Principal informed at weekly meetings. In addition, the Administration maintains close relationships with the students. All of York's administrators teach courses and are readily available to students and parents alike. At the close of each day, there is a period when students may go to faculty members or advisers for help.

Parents are kept informed of a student's progress through individual reports posted every Friday on "Edline," a component of the York Prep website. Each family signs in with a unique password to see their child's progress in all academic subjects. The annual Curriculum Night, during which parents become students for an evening by attending their child's abbreviated classes, provides a good overview of the course work and the faculty members. Parent involvement is encouraged, and there is an active Parents' Association.

FACULTY AND ADVISERS

York Prep is proud of having maintained a stable faculty of outstanding and dedicated individuals. New teachers join the staff periodically, creating a nice balance between youth and experience.

There are 70 full-time faculty members, including 2 college guidance counselors, an IT specialist, and reading and learning specialists.

Mr. Ronald P. Stewart, the founding Headmaster, is a graduate of Oxford University (B.A., 1965; M.A., 1966; B.C.L., 1968), where he also taught.

COLLEGE ADMISSION COUNSELING

York Prep has a notable college guidance program. Mrs. Jayme Stewart and Janet Rooney, Co-Directors of College Guidance, are well known for their expertise and experience. Jayme Stewart is the author of *How to Get into the College of Your Choice*. They meet with all ninth- and tenth-graders to outline the program and then meet individually with eleventh graders. Extensive meetings continue through the twelfth grade on an individual basis. In addition, the eleventh and twelfth graders take college guidance as a course where they write their essays, research colleges, and

complete their applications during school hours.

One hundred percent of York Prep's graduating students are accepted to college. The ultimate aim of the college guidance program is the placement of each student in the college best suited to him or her. More than 85 percent of York Prep graduates are accepted to, attend, and finish at their first- or second-choice college. Graduates are currently attending schools that include Barnard, Brandeis, Brown, Colgate, Cornell, Dickinson, Franklin and Marshall, Georgetown, Hamilton, Harvard, Johns Hopkins, MIT, Oberlin, Skidmore, UPENN, University of Edinburgh (UK), University of Wisconsin, Vassar, and the University of Michigan. Numerous college representatives visit the School regularly to meet with interested students.

YORK PREP SCHOLARS AND JUMP START

York Prep Scholars is an enrichment program designed to address the needs of students who are already excelling in their standard honors curriculum. The York Scholars program provides a rich variety of opportunities to broaden and deepen students' academic perspectives. Courses include Contemporary Poetry, Linear Algebra through Matrices, Modern Political Philosophy, The Battle of Brooklyn, Euclid in the New World, and Microbiology.

York Prep's Jump Start Program enables students with different learning styles or specific learning differences to function successfully in an academically challenging mainstream setting. Students in the program work with a specialist in one or more of the following areas: language processing, reading, writing, math, and organizational skills.

STUDENT BODY AND CONDUCT

There are 350 students enrolled at York Prep. York students reside in all five boroughs of New York City as well as Long Island, northern New Jersey, and Westchester County. The School has a student code of conduct and a dress code. The elected student council is also an integral part of life at York Prep.

ACADEMIC FACILITIES

York is located near Lincoln Center on a safe and lovely tree-lined street, just steps from Central Park at 40 West 68th Street, in a seven-story granite building housing science laboratories, performance and art studios, and a sprung hardwood gymnasium with weight and locker room facilities. All classrooms have computers, audiovisual (AV) projectors, and interactive white boards. Wireless Internet access is available throughout the School and enables students to e-mail their teachers, review homework assignments, and extend learning to all areas of the School. Dance classes are held at a professional dance studio next to the School. The building is wheelchair accessible and meets ADA requirements.

ATHLETICS

All students are required to take courses in physical education and health each year. A varied and extensive athletic program offers students the opportunity to participate in competitive, noncompetitive, team, and individual sports. Sports include soccer, volleyball, basketball, golf, swimming, baseball, softball, track and field, and cross-country. York Prep participates in the ISAL, which it founded.

EXTRACURRICULAR OPPORTUNITIES

The School provides over sixty extracurricular activities, including Math Competition Club, Model UN, Broadway Club, chess and backgammon, Young Doctors Club, vocal and instrumental groups (including ukelele), beekeeping, hiking, improv, pottery, trapeze, literary magazine, and a drama club. Upper School students also have the opportunity to travel internationally to countries in Asia, Europe, and South America.

DAILY LIFE

The school day begins at 8:40 with a 10-minute house period. Academic classes of 42-minute duration begin at 8:54. There is a midmorning break at 10:22. Lunch period is from 12:06 to 12:58, Mondays through Thursdays, and classes end at 3:12. Following dismissal, teachers are available for extra help. During this time, clubs and sports teams also meet. On Fridays the school day ends at 1:38.

SUMMER PROGRAMS

The School provides workshops during the summer, both in study skills and in academic courses, most of which are set up on an individual tutorial basis. In addition, the athletic department provides summer sports camps.

COSTS AND FINANCIAL AID

Tuition for the 2016–17 academic year ranges from $46,725 to $47,450. More than 12 percent of the student body receives some financial assistance. During the previous year, $1 million was offered in scholarship assistance.

ADMISSIONS INFORMATION

York Prep seeks to enroll students of above-average intelligence with the will and ability to complete college preparatory work. Students are accepted on the basis of their applications, teacher recommendations, ISEE or SSAT test scores, writing samples, and interviews.

APPLICATION TIMETABLE

York conforms to the notification guidelines established by the Independent Schools Admissions Association of Greater New York. Subsequent applications are processed on a rolling admissions basis. Requests for financial aid should be made at the time of application for entrance.

ADMISSIONS CORRESPONDENCE

Elizabeth Norton, Director of Enrollment
Cathy Minaudo, Director of Admissions
York Preparatory School
40 West 68th Street
New York, New York 10023
United States
Phone: 212-362-0400
Fax: 212-362-7424
E-mail: enorton@yorkprep.org
        cminaudo@yorkprep.org
Website: http://www.yorkprep.org

Special Needs Schools

ALPINE ACADEMY

1280 Whispering Horse Drive
Erda, Utah 84074

Head of School: Michele Boguslofski

General Information Girls' boarding college-preparatory, general academic, arts, vocational, bilingual studies, and equestrian, consumer sciences school; primarily serves underachievers, students with learning disabilities, individuals with Attention Deficit Disorder, individuals with emotional and behavioral problems, and dyslexic students. Grades 7–12. Founded: 2001. Setting: rural. Nearest major city is Salt Lake City. Students are housed in single-sex dormitories. 35-acre campus. 10 buildings on campus. Approved or accredited by Northwest Accreditation Commission and Utah Department of Education. Total enrollment: 61. Upper school average class size: 8. Upper school faculty-student ratio: 1:4. There are 210 required school days per year for Upper School students. Upper School students typically attend 5 days per week. The average school day consists of 5 hours and 50 minutes.

Upper School Student Profile Grade 8: 3 students (3 girls); Grade 9: 12 students (12 girls); Grade 10: 17 students (17 girls); Grade 11: 8 students (8 girls); Grade 12: 21 students (21 girls). 100% of students are boarding students. 10 states are represented in upper school student body.

Faculty School total: 10. In upper school: 1 man, 9 women; 1 has an advanced degree.

Subjects Offered ACT preparation, algebra, American government, American history, art, arts, basic skills, biology, botany, chemistry, college admission preparation, costumes and make-up, CPR, dance, debate, drama, earth science, electives, English, equine science, geography, geometry, government, health, health education, history, honors English, journalism, life skills, mathematics, personal money management, physical education, pre-algebra, pre-calculus, psychology, SAT preparation, science, Spanish, weight training, women in world history.

Graduation Requirements Graduation is therapeutically, rather than academically, indicated.

Special Academic Programs Honors section; accelerated programs; independent study; study at local college for college credit; academic accommodation for the gifted; remedial reading and/or remedial writing; remedial math; special instructional classes for blind students.

College Admission Counseling 15 students graduated in 2015; 5 went to college. Other: 3 went to work.

Student Life Upper grades have specified standards of dress. Discipline rests primarily with faculty.

Summer Programs Remediation, enrichment, advancement, sports, art/fine arts programs offered; session focuses on making up or getting ahead on credits toward graduation (Year Round School); held on campus; accepts girls; not open to students from other schools. 65 students usually enrolled. 2016 schedule: May 2 to July 15. Application deadline: none.

Tuition and Aid Guaranteed tuition plan. Tuition installment plan (monthly payment plans, individually arranged payment plans). Need-based scholarship grants available. In 2015–16, 2% of upper-school students received aid.

Admissions Traditional secondary-level entrance grade is 10. Achievement tests or psychoeducational evaluation required. Deadline for receipt of application materials: none. No application fee required.

Athletics Interscholastic: aerobics, aerobics/dance, basketball, bicycling, climbing, cooperative games, dance, equestrian sports, fitness, fitness walking, Frisbee, golf, hiking/backpacking, horseback riding, outdoor activities, outdoor adventure, outdoor recreation, physical fitness, physical training, racquetball, rafting, rock climbing, running, snowshoeing, soccer, softball, strength & conditioning, swimming and diving, tennis, ultimate Frisbee, volleyball, walking, wall climbing, weight lifting, weight training, yoga. 1 PE instructor.

Computers Computers are regularly used in English, history, writing classes. Computer network features include on-campus library services, Internet access, Internet filtering or blocking technology. Campus intranet and computer access in designated common areas are available to students. Students grades are available online.

Contact Christian Egan, Admissions Director. 800-244-1113. Fax: 435-843-5416. E-mail: cegan@alpineacademy.org. Website: www.alpineacademy.org

AMERICAN ACADEMY

12200 West Broward Boulevard
Plantation, Florida 33325

Head of School: Mr. William R. Laurie

General Information Coeducational day college-preparatory, arts, and technology school; primarily serves underachievers, students with learning disabilities, individuals with Attention Deficit Disorder, dyslexic students, and slow learners and those with lowered self-esteem and confidence. Grades K–12. Founded: 1965. Setting: suburban. Nearest major city is Fort Lauderdale. 40-acre campus. 7 buildings on campus. Approved or accredited by Association of Independent Schools of Florida, National Council for Private School Accreditation, Southern Association of Independent Schools, and Florida Department of Education. Total enrollment: 328. Upper school average class size: 14. Upper school faculty-student ratio: 1:14. There are 175 required school days per year for Upper School students. Upper School students typically attend 5 days per week. The average school day consists of 7 hours and 15 minutes.

Upper School Student Profile Grade 7: 33 students (24 boys, 9 girls); Grade 8: 28 students (19 boys, 9 girls); Grade 9: 37 students (28 boys, 9 girls); Grade 10: 42 students (26 boys, 16 girls); Grade 11: 40 students (25 boys, 15 girls); Grade 12: 50 students (36 boys, 14 girls).

Faculty School total: 32. In upper school: 5 men, 16 women; 18 have advanced degrees.

Subjects Offered Algebra, American history, American literature, anatomy, art, band, biology, business mathematics, ceramics, chemistry, chorus, computer graphics, computer science, creative writing, drafting, drama, drawing, earth science, English, English literature, environmental science, fine arts, French, geometry, health, jazz, mathematics, music appreciation, oceanography, orchestra, photography, physical education, physical science, science, sculpture, Spanish, theater, vocal music, weight training, word processing, world geography, world history, world literature, writing, yearbook.

Graduation Requirements 20th century history, arts and fine arts (art, music, dance, drama), computer science, English, mathematics, physical education (includes health), science, social studies (includes history), must be accepted to a college, 120 community service hours over 4 years of high school. Community service is required.

Special Academic Programs Honors section; independent study; academic accommodation for the gifted, the musically talented, and the artistically talented; remedial reading and/or remedial writing; remedial math; programs in English, mathematics, general development for dyslexic students; ESL (2 students enrolled).

College Admission Counseling 49 students graduated in 2014; 46 went to college, including Broward College; Florida Atlantic University; Lynn University; Nova Southeastern University; Palm Beach State College.

Student Life Upper grades have uniform requirement, student council. Discipline rests primarily with faculty.

Tuition and Aid Day student tuition: $25,418–$29,399. Tuition installment plan (monthly payment plans, semester payment plan, annual payment plan). Tuition reduction for siblings, need-based scholarship grants available.

Admissions Traditional secondary-level entrance grade is 9. Psychoeducational evaluation, SAT and Slosson Intelligence required. Deadline for receipt of application materials: none. Application fee required: $100. On-campus interview required.

Athletics Interscholastic: baseball (boys), basketball (b,g), cheering (g), cross-country running (b,g), dance (g), dance squad (g), diving (b,g), football (b), golf (b,g), lacrosse (b,g), roller hockey (b), soccer (b,g), softball (g), swimming and diving (b,g), tennis (b,g), track and field (b,g), volleyball (b,g), weight lifting (b), weight training (b,g), winter soccer (b,g), wrestling (b). 7 PE instructors, 4 coaches, 1 athletic trainer.

Computers Computers are regularly used in graphic arts, literary magazine, newspaper, Web site design, word processing, writing, yearbook classes. Computer network features include on-campus library services, online commercial services, Internet access, Internet filtering or blocking technology. Student e-mail accounts and computer access in designated common areas are available to students. Students grades are available online. The school has a published electronic and media policy.

Contact William R. Laurie, President. 954-472-0022. Fax: 954-472-3088. Website: www.ahschool.com

ASSETS SCHOOL

One Ohana Nui Way
Honolulu, Hawaii 96818

Head of School: Mr. Paul Singer

General Information Coeducational day college-preparatory, arts, and technology school; primarily serves students with learning disabilities, individuals with Attention Deficit Disorder, dyslexic students, and gifted/talented students. Grades K–12. Founded: 1955. Setting: urban. 3-acre campus. 12 buildings on campus. Approved or accredited by The Hawaii Council of Private Schools, Western Association of Schools and Colleges, and Hawaii Department of Education. Member of National Association of Independent Schools. Endowment: $3.1 million. Total enrollment: 323. Upper school average class size: 8. Upper school faculty-student ratio: 1:8. There are 168 required school days per year for Upper School students. Upper School students typically attend 5 days per week. The average school day consists of 5 hours and 58 minutes.

Upper School Student Profile Grade 9: 40 students (32 boys, 8 girls); Grade 10: 40 students (25 boys, 15 girls); Grade 11: 23 students (13 boys, 10 girls); Grade 12: 19 students (14 boys, 5 girls).

Faculty School total: 68. In upper school: 7 men, 17 women; 18 have advanced degrees.

Subjects Offered 1 1/2 elective credits, algebra, American history, art, biology, business skills, calculus, chemistry, computer science, consumer education, creative writing, current events, earth science, economics, English, fine arts, fitness, general science, geometry, government/civics, health, humanities, independent study, integrated science, keyboarding, literature, marine biology, marine science, mathematics, music, music appreciation, philosophy, physical education, physics, pre-calculus, psychology, sign language, social studies, Spanish, statistics, theater, trigonometry, women's health, woodworking, word processing, world history, world literature.

Graduation Requirements Arts and fine arts (art, music, dance, drama), biology, business skills (includes word processing), computer science, English, foreign language, mathematics, physical education (includes health), science, social studies (includes history), study skills, participation in mentorship program in 9th-12th grades.

Special Academic Programs Academic accommodation for the gifted; remedial reading and/or remedial writing; remedial math; programs in English, mathematics, general development for dyslexic students.

College Admission Counseling 30 students graduated in 2015; 27 went to college, including Chaminade University of Honolulu; Hawai`i Pacific University; Oregon State University; University of Hawaii at Manoa; Washington State University. Other: 3 had other specific plans.

Student Life Upper grades have specified standards of dress, student council, honor system. Discipline rests primarily with faculty.

Summer Programs Advancement programs offered; session focuses on learning strategies for students in the 9th and 10th grades; held on campus; accepts boys and girls; open to students from other schools. 40 students usually enrolled. 2016 schedule: June 10 to July 19. Application deadline: none.

Tuition and Aid Day student tuition: $23,180. Tuition installment plan (FACTS Tuition Payment Plan, monthly payment plans, individually arranged payment plans, semester payment plan). Need-based scholarship grants, partial tuition remission for children of staff available. In 2015–16, 37% of upper-school students received aid. Total amount of financial aid awarded in 2015–16: $170,000.

Admissions Traditional secondary-level entrance grade is 9. WISC III or other aptitude measures; standardized achievement test required. Deadline for receipt of application materials: none. Application fee required: $75. On-campus interview required.

Athletics Interscholastic: baseball (boys), basketball (b,g), bowling (b,g), canoeing/kayaking (b,g), cheering (g), cross-country running (b,g), diving (b,g), football (b), golf (b,g), gymnastics (g), judo (b,g), kayaking (b,g), sailing (b,g), soccer (b,g), softball (g), swimming and diving (b,g), tennis (b,g), track and field (b,g), volleyball (b,g), water polo (b,g), wrestling (b,g); intramural: basketball (b,g), volleyball (b,g); coed intramural: basketball, dance, flag football, kickball, Newcombe ball, soccer, softball, tai chi, touch football, ultimate Frisbee, volleyball, whiffle ball, yoga. 2 PE instructors, 4 coaches.

Computers Computers are regularly used in English, mathematics, photography, science classes. Computer network features include on-campus library services, Internet access, wireless campus network, Internet filtering or blocking technology, assistive technology for learning differences. Student e-mail accounts and computer access in designated common areas are available to students. The school has a published electronic and media policy.

Contact Ms. Sandi Tadaki, Director of Admissions. 808-423-1356. Fax: 808-422-1920. E-mail: stadaki@assets-school.net. Website: www.assets-school.net

ATLANTIS ACADEMY
9600 Southwest 107th Avenue
Miami, Florida 33176

Head of School: Mr. Carlos Aballi

General Information Coeducational day general academic school; primarily serves underachievers, students with learning disabilities, individuals with Attention Deficit Disorder, individuals with emotional and behavioral problems, dyslexic students, and Autism Spectrum Disorder. Ungraded, ages 5–18. Founded: 1976. Setting: suburban. 3-acre campus. 1 building on campus. Approved or accredited by Florida Council of Independent Schools, Southern Association of Colleges and Schools, and Florida Department of Education. Total enrollment: 156. Upper school average class size: 9. Upper school faculty-student ratio: 1:8. The average school day consists of 6 hours and 15 minutes.

Faculty School total: 26. In upper school: 5 men, 9 women; 3 have advanced degrees.

Subjects Offered Art, computer skills, language arts, mathematics, physical education, reading, science, social studies, Spanish.

Special Academic Programs Remedial reading and/or remedial writing; remedial math; programs in English, mathematics, general development for dyslexic students; ESL (3 students enrolled).

College Admission Counseling 12 students graduated in 2015; 8 went to college, including Florida International University; Lynn University; Miami Dade College; New York Institute of Technology. Other: 4 went to work.

Student Life Upper grades have uniform requirement. Discipline rests primarily with faculty.

Summer Programs Remediation, ESL, art/fine arts, computer instruction programs offered; session focuses on remediation; held on campus; accepts boys and girls; open to students from other schools. 60 students usually enrolled. 2016 schedule: June 13 to August 6. Application deadline: March 1.

Tuition and Aid Day student tuition: $16,700–$18,100. Tuition installment plan (FACTS Tuition Payment Plan, monthly payment plans, semi-annual and annual payment plans). Need-based scholarship grants available. In 2015–16, 90% of upper-school students received aid. Total amount of financial aid awarded in 2015–16: $12,000.

Admissions Traditional secondary-level entrance age is 14. For fall 2015, 15 students applied for upper-level admission, 15 were accepted, 15 enrolled. Psychoeducational evaluation or school's own exam required. Deadline for receipt of application materials: none. No application fee required. On-campus interview required.

Athletics Interscholastic: basketball (boys, girls), flag football (b), tennis (b,g), volleyball (b,g); intramural: flag football (b); coed interscholastic: soccer, softball; coed intramural: basketball, golf, soccer, tennis, volleyball. 1 PE instructor, 2 coaches.

Computers Computers are regularly used in art, English, foreign language, history, mathematics, science, social sciences classes. Computer network features include Internet access.

Contact Mr. Eric Smith, Assistant Director/Director of Admissions. 305-271-9771. Fax: 305-271-7078. E-mail: esmith@esa-education.com. Website: www.atlantisacademy.com/

BALBOA CITY SCHOOL
525 Hawthorn Street
San Diego, California 92101

Head of School: Mr. Zachary Jones

General Information Coeducational day college-preparatory, general academic, and bilingual studies school; primarily serves underachievers, students with learning disabilities, individuals with Attention Deficit Disorder, and dyslexic students. Grades K–12. Founded: 1993. Setting: urban. 4 buildings on campus. Approved or accredited by Western Association of Schools and Colleges and California Department of Education. Total enrollment: 75. Upper school average class size: 6. Upper school faculty-student ratio: 1:6. There are 180 required school days per year for Upper School students. Upper School students typically attend 5 days per week.

Faculty School total: 26. In upper school: 11 men, 15 women; 5 have advanced degrees.

Subjects Offered Algebra, American literature, American sign language, art, arts, astronomy, biology, British literature, calculus, chemistry, computer graphics, computer literacy, construction, crafts, creative writing, drama, economics, English, foreign language, geometry, government, guitar, health, history, history of rock and roll, journalism, language, life science, life skills, literature, marine biology, mathematics, multicultural studies, music, outdoor education, painting, physical education, physical science, physics, piano, pre-calculus, psychology, reading, science, social sciences, social studies, sociology, Spanish, speech therapy, study skills, U.S. history, video film production, visual arts, vocational arts, world history, world literature, yearbook.

Graduation Requirements Arts and fine arts (art, music, dance, drama), computer science, English, foreign language, mathematics, physical education (includes health), science, social sciences, social studies (includes history). Community service is required.

Special Academic Programs Accelerated programs; independent study; academic accommodation for the gifted, the musically talented, and the artistically talented; remedial reading and/or remedial writing; remedial math; programs in English, mathematics, general development for dyslexic students; ESL (20 students enrolled).

Student Life Upper grades have specified standards of dress, student council, honor system. Discipline rests primarily with faculty.

Tuition and Aid Day student tuition: $11,500. Guaranteed tuition plan. Tuition installment plan (monthly payment plans, individually arranged payment plans). Tuition reduction for siblings, merit scholarship grants, need-based scholarship grants available. In 2014–15, 5% of upper-school students received aid.

Admissions Deadline for receipt of application materials: none. No application fee required. On-campus interview required.

Athletics Interscholastic: basketball (boys). 6 PE instructors, 2 coaches.

Computers Computers are regularly used in English, foreign language, history, mathematics, music, science classes. Computer network features include on-campus library services, Internet access, Internet filtering or blocking technology. Computer access in designated common areas is available to students. The school has a published electronic and media policy.

Contact Ms. Monica Castro, Registrar. 619-298-2990. Fax: 619-295-8886. E-mail: mcastro@balboaschool.com. Website: www.balboaschool.com

BRANDON HALL SCHOOL
1701 Brandon Hall Drive
Atlanta, Georgia 30350-3706

Head of School: Mr. Johnny Graham

General Information Coeducational boarding and day college-preparatory, arts, business, bilingual studies, technology, and ESL school. Boarding grades 7–12, day grades 6–12. Founded: 1959. Setting: suburban. Students are housed in coed dormitories. 27-acre campus. 5 buildings on campus. Approved or accredited by Georgia Independent School Association, Southern Association of Colleges and Schools, Southern Association of Independent Schools, and Georgia Department of Education. Member of National Association of Independent Schools. Endowment: $100,000. Total enrollment: 155. Upper school average class size: 6. Upper school faculty-student ratio: 1:8. There are 180 required school days per year for Upper School students. Upper School students typically attend 5 days per week. The average school day consists of 7 hours and 15 minutes.

Upper School Student Profile Grade 9: 18 students (12 boys, 6 girls); Grade 10: 29 students (15 boys, 14 girls); Grade 11: 46 students (29 boys, 17 girls); Grade 12: 46

students (25 boys, 21 girls). 46% of students are boarding students. 25% are state residents. 20 states are represented in upper school student body. 23% are international students. International students from China, Democratic People's Republic of Korea, France, Mexico, Nigeria, and Viet Nam; 9 other countries represented in student body.

Faculty School total: 40. In upper school: 21 men, 11 women; 16 have advanced degrees; 17 reside on campus.

Subjects Offered 20th century history, 3-dimensional art, acting, advanced biology, advanced chemistry, advanced math, Advanced Placement courses, advanced studio art-AP, advanced TOEFL/grammar, African American history, algebra, American government, American history-AP, American literature, American literature-AP, American sign language, analysis and differential calculus, anatomy and physiology, art, Asian history, astronomy, athletic training, audio visual/media, ballet, biology, British literature, British literature (honors), British literature-AP, calculus, calculus-AP, career/college preparation, chemistry, chemistry-AP, choral music, chorus, cinematography, college admission preparation, college awareness, college counseling, college placement, college planning, college writing, computer science, computer science-AP, computer-aided design, contemporary issues, dance, desktop publishing, digital photography, drama, drama performance, driver education, earth science, economics, English, English as a foreign language, English composition, English literature and composition-AP, environmental science, environmental studies, ESL, ESL, fine arts, French, French as a second language, French-AP, geometry, government/civics, grammar, health education, history, honors English, honors geometry, honors U.S. history, honors world history, human anatomy, information technology, intro to computers, introduction to technology, introduction to theater, keyboarding, Latin, linear algebra, mathematics, microeconomics-AP, music, music history, music performance, musical theater, organic chemistry, painting, performing arts, philosophy, photography, physical education, physical fitness, physical science, physics, physics-AP, play production, play/screen writing, playwriting, playwriting and directing, poetry, politics, pre-algebra, pre-calculus, printmaking, probability and statistics, psychology, public speaking, reading/study skills, research skills, SAT/ACT preparation, science, sculpture, senior project, senior seminar, set design, sign language, social studies, Spanish, Spanish-AP, statistics-AP, student government, student publications, student teaching, technical theater, theater, TOEFL preparation, trigonometry, U.S. government, U.S. history, U.S. literature, video film production, word processing, world history, world literature, writing, yearbook.

Graduation Requirements American government, arts and fine arts (art, music, dance, drama), computer applications, economics, English, foreign language, mathematics, physical education (includes health), science, social studies (includes history).

Special Academic Programs 12 Advanced Placement exams for which test preparation is offered; honors section; accelerated programs; study at local college for college credit; study abroad; ESL (10 students enrolled).

College Admission Counseling 43 students graduated in 2015; 40 went to college, including Emory University; Georgia College & State University; Savannah College of Art and Design; The University of Alabama; University of Mississippi; Young Harris College. Other: 1 entered a postgraduate year, 2 had other specific plans.

Student Life Upper grades have uniform requirement, student council, honor system. Discipline rests primarily with faculty.

Summer Programs Remediation, enrichment, advancement, ESL, sports, art/fine arts, computer instruction programs offered; session focuses on general academics; held on campus; accepts boys and girls; open to students from other schools. 150 students usually enrolled. 2016 schedule: May 30 to August 5.

Tuition and Aid Day student tuition: $31,940; 7-day tuition and room/board: $60,800. Tuition installment plan (Insured Tuition Payment Plan, monthly payment plans, individually arranged payment plans). Need-based scholarship grants available. In 2015–16, 10% of upper-school students received aid. Total amount of financial aid awarded in 2015–16: $250,000.

Admissions Traditional secondary-level entrance grade is 9. SSAT and TOEFL required. Deadline for receipt of application materials: none. No application fee required. Interview required.

Athletics Interscholastic: baseball (boys), basketball (b,g), tennis (b,g), volleyball (g), wrestling (b); coed interscholastic: cheering, cross-country running, dance, equestrian sports, golf, soccer, swimming and diving, track and field; coed intramural: physical training. 1 PE instructor.

Computers Computers are regularly used in all classes. Computer network features include on-campus library services, Internet access, wireless campus network, Internet filtering or blocking technology. Campus intranet, student e-mail accounts, and computer access in designated common areas are available to students. Students grades are available online. The school has a published electronic and media policy.

Contact Ms. Kirsten Knowles, Director of Admissions. 770-394-8177 Ext. 201. Fax: 678-848-1444. E-mail: knowles@brandonhall.org. Website: www.brandonhall.org

BREHM PREPARATORY SCHOOL

950 S. Brehm Lane
Carbondale, Illinois 62901

Head of School: Mr. Brian P. Brown, PhD

General Information Coeducational boarding and day college-preparatory, general academic, arts, and technology school; primarily serves students with learning disabilities, individuals with Attention Deficit Disorder, dyslexic students, and language-based learning differences. Grades 6–PG. Founded: 1982. Setting: small town. Nearest major city is St. Louis, MO. Students are housed in single-sex dormitories. 100-acre campus. 13 buildings on campus. Approved or accredited by Independent Schools Association of the Central States, North Central Association of Colleges and Schools, and Illinois Department of Education. Member of National Association of Independent Schools. Endowment: $900,000. Total enrollment: 85. Upper school average class size: 8. Upper school faculty-student ratio: 1:4. There are 185 required school days per year for Upper School students. Upper School students typically attend 5 days per week. The average school day consists of 7 hours and 30 minutes.

Upper School Student Profile Grade 9: 13 students (12 boys, 1 girl); Grade 10: 15 students (12 boys, 3 girls); Grade 11: 19 students (14 boys, 5 girls); Grade 12: 20 students (15 boys, 5 girls); Postgraduate: 8 students (8 boys). 86% of students are boarding students. 23% are state residents. 24 states are represented in upper school student body. 8% are international students. International students from Cameroon, Canada, India, Latvia, Nigeria, and Norway.

Faculty School total: 24. In upper school: 8 men, 16 women; 15 have advanced degrees.

Subjects Offered 20th century American writers, 20th century history, ACT preparation, algebra, American history, American literature, anatomy and physiology, art, biology, British literature, calculus, career exploration, chemistry, communication skills, composition, computer graphics, computer programming, computer science, computer skills, consumer education, creative writing, current events, current history, desktop publishing, digital imaging, digital photography, earth science, economics, English, English literature, environmental science, geometry, government/civics, health, keyboarding, language, learning cognition, mathematics, photography, physical education, pragmatics, pre-algebra, pre-calculus, psychology, reading/study skills, science, Shakespeare, social studies, sociology, Spanish, speech, trigonometry, video and animation, weight training, world history, writing.

Graduation Requirements ACT preparation, computer science, consumer education, English, government, learning cognition, mathematics, physical education (includes health), science, social studies (includes history).

Special Academic Programs Study at local college for college credit; academic accommodation for the gifted; remedial reading and/or remedial writing; remedial math; programs in English, mathematics, general development for dyslexic students.

College Admission Counseling 24 students graduated in 2015; 10 went to college, including John A. Logan College; Lynn University; Marshall University; Southern Illinois University Edwardsville. Other: 10 entered a postgraduate year, 4 had other specific plans. Median composite ACT: 17. 7% scored over 26 on composite ACT.

Student Life Upper grades have specified standards of dress, student council, honor system. Discipline rests equally with students and faculty.

Summer Programs Remediation, enrichment, art/fine arts programs offered; session focuses on experiential learning/PBL; held on campus; accepts boys and girls; open to students from other schools. 32 students usually enrolled. 2016 schedule: June 26 to July 23. Application deadline: May 1.

Tuition and Aid Day student tuition: $44,000; 7-day tuition and room/board: $73,100. Tuition installment plan (individually arranged payment plans, Tuition Solution). Need-based scholarship grants available. In 2015–16, 8% of upper-school students received aid. Total amount of financial aid awarded in 2015–16: $99,300.

Admissions Traditional secondary-level entrance grade is 9. For fall 2015, 33 students applied for upper-level admission, 30 were accepted, 24 enrolled. Wechsler Individual Achievement Test, WISC or WAIS and Woodcock-Johnson required. Deadline for receipt of application materials: none. Application fee required: $75. On-campus interview required.

Athletics Interscholastic: basketball (boys, girls); coed interscholastic: soccer; coed intramural: aerobics, aerobics/dance, archery, basketball, billiards, bowling, dance, fishing, flag football, Frisbee, golf, hiking/backpacking, horseback riding, outdoor skills, paint ball, physical fitness, soccer, softball, strength & conditioning. 1 PE instructor, 1 coach.

Computers Computers are regularly used in all academic, career exploration, college planning, creative writing, design, desktop publishing, graphic arts, graphic design, keyboarding, learning cognition, photography, reading, remedial study skills, research skills, study skills, typing, word processing, writing, writing, yearbook classes. Computer network features include Internet access, wireless campus network, Internet filtering or blocking technology. Student e-mail accounts are available to students. Students grades are available online. The school has a published electronic and media policy.

Contact Mr. Brian Taylor, Director of Admissions. 618-457-0371 Ext. 1303. Fax: 618-529-1248. E-mail: brian.taylor@brehm.org. Website: www.brehm.org

BRIDGES ACADEMY

3921 Laurel Canyon Boulevard
Studio City, California 91604

Head of School: Carl Sabatino

General Information Coeducational day college-preparatory, arts, technology, and music, drama, talent development school; primarily serves students with learning disabilities, individuals with Attention Deficit Disorder, and gifted students with non-verbal learning differences. Grades 4–12. Founded: 1994. Setting: suburban. Nearest major city is Los Angeles. 4-acre campus. 3 buildings on campus. Approved or accredited by California Association of Independent Schools, Western Association of Schools and Colleges, and California Department of Education. Total enrollment: 170. Upper school average class size: 8. Upper school faculty-student ratio: 1:8. There are 174 required school days per year for Upper School students. Upper School students typically attend 5 days per week. The average school day consists of 5 hours and 15 minutes.

Upper School Student Profile Grade 9: 24 students (22 boys, 2 girls); Grade 10: 19 students (17 boys, 2 girls); Grade 11: 23 students (21 boys, 2 girls); Grade 12: 21 students (16 boys, 5 girls).

Faculty School total: 28. In upper school: 19 men, 9 women; 10 have advanced degrees.

Subjects Offered 20th century history, algebra, American government, American literature, anatomy and physiology, art, biology, calculus, chemistry, drama, economics, European history, European literature, film, genetics, geometry, Japanese, modern European history, music, non-Western literature, photography, physics, pre-calculus, robotics, senior project, Spanish, statistics, study skills, technology, U.S. history, world history.

Graduation Requirements Economics, English, foreign language, government, history, mathematics, performing arts, science, senior seminar, visual arts.

Special Academic Programs Honors section; academic accommodation for the gifted.

College Admission Counseling 18 students graduated in 2015; 14 went to college, including California State University, Northridge; Occidental College; Pitzer College; University of California, Berkeley; University of California, San Diego; University of Colorado Boulder. Other: 4 had other specific plans. 57% scored over 600 on SAT critical reading, 23% scored over 600 on SAT math.

Student Life Discipline rests primarily with faculty.

Summer Programs Enrichment, sports, art/fine arts, computer instruction programs offered; session focuses on enrichment; held both on and off campus; held at outdoor recreation and field trips—arts/sciences; accepts boys and girls; open to students from other schools. 2016 schedule: June 1 to June 30. Application deadline: none.

Tuition and Aid Day student tuition: $35,910. Tuition installment plan (Insured Tuition Payment Plan, monthly payment plans). Need-based scholarship grants available. In 2015–16, 15% of upper-school students received aid.

Admissions Traditional secondary-level entrance grade is 9. For fall 2015, 21 students applied for upper-level admission, 17 were accepted, 14 enrolled. Deadline for receipt of application materials: March 1. Application fee required: $150. On-campus interview required.

Athletics Coed Interscholastic: basketball, cross-country running, track and field. 3 PE instructors, 2 coaches.

Computers Computers are regularly used in all classes. Computer network features include Internet access, wireless campus network, Internet filtering or blocking technology. Campus intranet and student e-mail accounts are available to students. Students grades are available online.

Contact Doug Lenzini, Director of Admissions. 818-506-1091. Fax: 818-506-8094. E-mail: doug@bridges.edu. Website: www.bridges.edu

CAMPHILL SPECIAL SCHOOL
1784 Fairview Road
Glenmoore, Pennsylvania 19343
Head of School: Mr. Bernard Wolf

General Information Coeducational boarding and day general academic, arts, and vocational school; primarily serves underachievers, intellectual and developmental disabilities, and mental retardation. Grades K–13. Founded: 1963. Setting: rural. Nearest major city is Philadelphia. Students are housed in on-campus single family homes. 85-acre campus. 1 building on campus. Approved or accredited by Association of Waldorf Schools of North America, Middle States Association of Colleges and Schools, National Council for Private School Accreditation, and Pennsylvania Department of Education. Total enrollment: 120. Upper school average class size: 11. Upper school faculty-student ratio: 1:7. There are 180 required school days per year for Upper School students. Upper School students typically attend 5 days per week. The average school day consists of 8 hours.

Upper School Student Profile Grade 9: 11 students (8 boys, 3 girls); Grade 10: 12 students (4 boys, 8 girls); Grade 11: 11 students (6 boys, 5 girls); Grade 12: 10 students (6 boys, 4 girls); Grade 13: 23 students (14 boys, 9 girls). 62% of students are boarding students. 64% are state residents. 12 states are represented in upper school student body. 6% are international students. International students from India, Jamaica, Nigeria, and Saudi Arabia.

Faculty In upper school: 2 men, 2 women; 2 have advanced degrees; 70 reside on campus.

Subjects Offered 20th century American writers, 20th century history, 20th century physics, 20th century world history, acting, agriculture, alternative physical education, American Civil War, American culture, American democracy, American government, American history, anatomy, Ancient Greek, ancient history, ancient world history, ancient/medieval philosophy, animal husbandry, animal science, art, art and culture, art appreciation, art history, astronomy, bell choir, biology, body human, bookbinding, botany, chemistry, choir, civil rights, Civil War, drama, drama performance, ecology,

environmental education, eurythmy, gardening, geography, geometry, government, handbells, health and wellness, history, instruments, life skills, mathematics, medieval history, medieval literature, medieval/Renaissance history, meteorology, music, mythology, natural history, painting, physics, poetry, pottery, reading, science, Shakespeare, woodworking, zoology.

Special Academic Programs Remedial reading and/or remedial writing; remedial math.

Student Life Upper grades have student council. Discipline rests primarily with faculty.

Summer Programs Enrichment programs offered; session focuses on Extended School Year (ESY); held on campus; accepts boys and girls; not open to students from other schools. 45 students usually enrolled. 2016 schedule: July 2 to July 30.

Tuition and Aid Need-based scholarship grants available.

Admissions Traditional secondary-level entrance grade is 9. Deadline for receipt of application materials: none. No application fee required. On-campus interview required.

Contact 610-469-9236. Website: www.camphillspecialschool.org

CHATHAM ACADEMY
4 Oglethorpe Professional Boulevard
Savannah, Georgia 31406
Head of School: Mrs. Carolyn M. Hannaford

General Information Coeducational day college-preparatory, general academic, and technology school; primarily serves underachievers, students with learning disabilities, individuals with Attention Deficit Disorder, dyslexic students, and different learning styles. Grades 1–12. Founded: 1978. Setting: suburban. 5-acre campus. 2 buildings on campus. Approved or accredited by Southern Association of Colleges and Schools, Southern Association of Independent Schools, and Georgia Department of Education. Endowment: $100,000. Upper school average class size: 10. Upper school faculty-student ratio: 1:10. There are 180 required school days per year for Upper School students. Upper School students typically attend 5 days per week. The average school day consists of 6 hours.

Upper School Student Profile Grade 9: 11 students (9 boys, 2 girls); Grade 10: 10 students (9 boys, 1 girl); Grade 11: 5 students (5 boys); Grade 12: 12 students (9 boys, 3 girls).

Faculty School total: 15. In upper school: 2 men, 6 women; 6 have advanced degrees.

Subjects Offered Algebra, American history, American literature, analytic geometry, ancient world history, art, basic skills, biology, body human, British literature, business communications, business mathematics, business studies, career exploration, career/college preparation, chemistry, college awareness, computer literacy, consumer economics, consumer mathematics, creative writing, earth science, ecology, ecology, environmental systems, economics, English, English literature, environmental science, expository writing, general math, geography, geology, geometry, government/civics, grammar, health and wellness, health education, health science, history, human biology, keyboarding, kinesiology, life science, life skills, literacy, literature, math applications, mathematics, organic chemistry, personal finance, personal fitness, personal money management, physical education, physical fitness, physical science, physics, pre-algebra, reading, reading/study skills, remedial study skills, remedial/makeup course work, SAT/ACT preparation, science, social sciences, social skills, social studies, Spanish, speech and debate, sports, U.S. history, weightlifting, work-study, world history, world literature, writing.

Graduation Requirements Algebra, American government, American history, biology, British literature, chemistry, civics, composition, consumer economics, earth science, economics, electives, English, English composition, English literature, foreign language, French, grammar, marine biology, mathematics, physical education (includes health), physical science, reading/study skills, science, social studies (includes history), U.S. history.

Special Academic Programs Independent study; study at local college for college credit; remedial reading and/or remedial writing; remedial math; programs in English, mathematics, general development for dyslexic students.

College Admission Counseling 9 students graduated in 2015; 3 went to college, including Armstrong State University; College of Charleston; Savannah College of Art and Design. Other: 4 went to work, 2 had other specific plans.

Student Life Upper grades have uniform requirement, student council, honor system. Discipline rests primarily with faculty.

Tuition and Aid Day student tuition: $16,274. Tuition installment plan (monthly payment plans, individually arranged payment plans). Tuition reduction for siblings, need-based scholarship grants, Georgia Special Needs Scholarship available. In 2015–16, 33% of upper-school students received aid. Total amount of financial aid awarded in 2015–16: $90,200.

Admissions Traditional secondary-level entrance grade is 10. For fall 2015, 10 students applied for upper-level admission, 7 were accepted, 5 enrolled. Achievement tests, Individual IQ, Achievement and behavior rating scale, school's own test, Stanford Binet, Wechsler Individual Achievement Test, Wechsler Intelligence Scale for Children III, WISC or WAIS, WISC-R, Woodcock-Johnson, Woodcock-Johnson Revised Achievement Test or writing sample required. Deadline for receipt of application materials: none. Application fee required: $50. Interview required.

Athletics Interscholastic: basketball (boys), flag football (b,g), yoga (g); intramural: soccer (b,g); coed interscholastic: basketball, cheering, fitness, fitness walking, flag football; coed intramural: canoeing/kayaking, cheering, cooperative games, fitness, fitness walking, flag football, jump rope, kickball, Newcombe ball, outdoor activities, outdoor recreation, paddle tennis, physical fitness, physical training, soccer, whiffle ball. 1 PE instructor, 2 coaches.

Computers Computers are regularly used in all academic classes. Computer network features include Internet access, Internet filtering or blocking technology. The school has a published electronic and media policy.

Contact Mrs. Carolyn M. Hannaford, Principal. 912-354-4047. Fax: 912-354-4633. E-mail: channaford@chathamacademy.com. Website: www.chathamacademy.com

CHELSEA SCHOOL

2970 Belcrest Center Drive, Suite 300
Hyattsville, Maryland 20782

Head of School: Katherine Fedalen

General Information Coeducational day college-preparatory, general academic, arts, and technology school; primarily serves students with learning disabilities, individuals with Attention Deficit Disorder, and dyslexic students. Grades 5–12. Founded: 1976. Setting: suburban. 1 building on campus. Approved or accredited by Maryland Department of Education. Total enrollment: 65. Upper school average class size: 8. Upper school faculty-student ratio: 1:8. There are 184 required school days per year for Upper School students. Upper School students typically attend 5 days per week. The average school day consists of 6 hours and 30 minutes.

Upper School Student Profile Grade 6: 7 students (5 boys, 2 girls); Grade 7: 5 students (4 boys, 1 girl); Grade 8: 9 students (4 boys, 5 girls); Grade 9: 12 students (8 boys, 4 girls); Grade 10: 12 students (11 boys, 1 girl); Grade 11: 4 students (4 boys); Grade 12: 15 students (12 boys, 3 girls).

Faculty School total: 20. In upper school: 8 men, 12 women; 14 have advanced degrees.

Subjects Offered Algebra, American history, American literature, art, biology, calculus, career/college preparation, chemistry, community service, composition, computer graphics, computer technologies, computers, earth and space science, earth science, English, English literature, environmental science, foreign language, geometry, health, health and wellness, information technology, math review, music, personal fitness, physical education, pre-algebra, pre-calculus, reading, reading/study skills, remedial study skills, science, social skills, Spanish, state government, U.S. government, U.S. history, U.S. literature.

Graduation Requirements 20th century world history, algebra, American government, American history, art, biology, career/college preparation, chemistry, earth science, electives, English, English composition, English literature, general math, geometry, health and wellness, physical education (includes health), pre-algebra, Spanish, U.S. history.

Special Academic Programs Remedial reading and/or remedial writing; remedial math; programs in English, mathematics, general development for dyslexic students.

College Admission Counseling 11 students graduated in 2015; 9 went to college, including Eastern Connecticut State University. Other: 2 went to work.

Student Life Upper grades have student council. Discipline rests primarily with faculty.

Summer Programs Remediation, enrichment, computer instruction programs offered; session focuses on remediation; held on campus; accepts boys and girls; open to students from other schools. 30 students usually enrolled. 2016 schedule: July to August. Application deadline: none.

Tuition and Aid Day student tuition: $37,357. Tuition installment plan (individually arranged payment plans). Need-based scholarship grants available.

Admissions Academic Profile Tests, Wechsler Individual Achievement Test, Wide Range Achievement Test, WISC III or other aptitude measures; standardized achievement test, WISC or WAIS, WISC-R or Woodcock-Johnson required. Deadline for receipt of application materials: none. Application fee required: $50. On-campus interview required.

Athletics Interscholastic: basketball (boys, girls); coed interscholastic: soccer, softball, track and field. 1 PE instructor.

Computers Computer network features include on-campus library services, Internet access, wireless campus network, Internet filtering or blocking technology. Campus intranet, student e-mail accounts, and computer access in designated common areas are available to students. The school has a published electronic and media policy.

Contact Debbie Lourie, Director of Admissions. 240-467-2100 Ext. 303. Fax: 240-467-2120. E-mail: dlourie@chelseaschool.edu. Website: www.chelseaschool.edu

COMMUNITY HIGH SCHOOL

1135 Teaneck Road
Teaneck, New Jersey 07666

Head of School: Scott Parisi

General Information Coeducational day college-preparatory school; primarily serves students with learning disabilities, individuals with Attention Deficit Disorder, and dyslexic students. Founded: 1968. Setting: suburban. Nearest major city is Hackensack. 1 building on campus. Approved or accredited by New Jersey Association of Independent Schools, New York Department of Education, and New Jersey Department of Education. Total enrollment: 181. Upper school faculty-student ratio: 1:5. There are 180 required school days per year for Upper School students. Upper School students typically attend 5 days per week. The average school day consists of 6 hours and 30 minutes.

Upper School Student Profile Grade 9: 51 students (36 boys, 15 girls); Grade 10: 45 students (31 boys, 14 girls); Grade 11: 42 students (30 boys, 12 girls); Grade 12: 42 students (30 boys, 12 girls).

Faculty School total: 45. In upper school: 9 men, 35 women.

Subjects Offered Algebra, American history, American literature, art, biology, business, calculus, chemistry, computer science, creative writing, drama, driver education, English, English literature, European history, expository writing, fine arts, forensics, geography, geometry, government/civics, grammar, history, journalism, mathematics, music, photography, physical education, physics, psychology, science, social sciences, social studies, sociology, Spanish, speech, study skills, theater, trigonometry, writing.

Graduation Requirements Arts and fine arts (art, music, dance, drama), English, mathematics, physical education (includes health), science, social sciences, social studies (includes history).

Special Academic Programs Remedial reading and/or remedial writing; remedial math; programs in English, mathematics, general development for dyslexic students.

College Admission Counseling 49 students graduated in 2015.

Student Life Upper grades have specified standards of dress, student council, honor system. Discipline rests primarily with faculty.

Tuition and Aid Day student tuition: $45,983.

Admissions Traditional secondary-level entrance grade is 9. For fall 2015, 200 students applied for upper-level admission, 60 were accepted, 51 enrolled. Deadline for receipt of application materials: none. Application fee required: $65. On-campus interview required.

Athletics Interscholastic: baseball (boys), basketball (b), soccer (b), softball (g); intramural: baseball (b), basketball (b,g), softball (g), table tennis (b,g), track and field (b,g), volleyball (b,g). 5 PE instructors, 8 coaches.

Computers Computers are regularly used in all academic classes. Computer network features include online commercial services, voice recognition systems. The school has a published electronic and media policy.

Contact Toby Braunstein, Director of Education. 201-862-1796 Ext. 18. Fax: 201-862-1791. E-mail: tbraunstein@communityhighschool.org. Website: www.communityschool.k12.nj.us

DELAWARE VALLEY FRIENDS SCHOOL

19 East Central Avenue
Paoli, Pennsylvania 19301-1345

Head of School: Mr. Kirk Smothers

General Information Coeducational day college-preparatory, arts, technology, and Orton-Gillingham based reading instruction school, affiliated with Society of Friends; primarily serves students with learning disabilities, individuals with Attention Deficit Disorder, dyslexic students, Dysgraphia, Dyscalculia, and Executive Function Challenges. Grades 6–12. Founded: 1986. Setting: suburban. Nearest major city is Philadelphia. 8-acre campus. 1 building on campus. Approved or accredited by Pennsylvania Association of Independent Schools and Pennsylvania Department of Education. Member of National Association of Independent Schools. Endowment: $7 million. Total enrollment: 149. Upper school average class size: 12. Upper school faculty-student ratio: 1:5. There are 171 required school days per year for Upper School students. Upper School students typically attend 5 days per week. The average school day consists of 6 hours and 17 minutes.

Upper School Student Profile Grade 9: 27 students (20 boys, 7 girls); Grade 10: 27 students (19 boys, 8 girls); Grade 11: 33 students (20 boys, 13 girls); Grade 12: 27 students (10 boys, 17 girls). 6% of students are members of Society of Friends.

Faculty School total: 37. In upper school: 12 men, 18 women; 16 have advanced degrees.

Subjects Offered 20th century world history, algebra, American history, Asian studies, astronomy, biology, calculus, ceramics, chemistry, college counseling, college placement, computer-aided design, crafts, culinary arts, electives, English, first aid, geometry, health and wellness, human development, internship, language arts, language development, language structure, learning strategies, music, photography, physical education, physics, pre-calculus, printmaking, psychology, robotics, SAT/ACT preparation, science, sign language, social studies, sociology, Spanish, studio art, study skills, trigonometry, video and animation, world history, writing.

Graduation Requirements Arts and fine arts (art, music, dance, drama), English, lab science, language arts, mathematics, physical education (includes health), senior internship, social studies (includes history), at least one Adventure Based Learning (A.B.L.E.) course. Community service is required.

Special Academic Programs Study at local college for college credit; academic accommodation for the artistically talented; remedial reading and/or remedial writing; remedial math; programs in English, mathematics, general development for dyslexic students.

College Admission Counseling 34 students graduated in 2015; 32 went to college, including Cabrini College; Drexel University; High Point University; Johnson & Wales

University; Shippensburg University of Pennsylvania; West Chester University of Pennsylvania. Other: 2 went to work.

Student Life Upper grades have specified standards of dress, student council. Discipline rests primarily with faculty. Attendance at religious services is required.

Summer Programs Remediation, enrichment, art/fine arts, computer instruction programs offered; session focuses on individualized reading skills/writing tutoring using Orton-Gillingham methods; held on campus; accepts boys and girls; open to students from other schools. 50 students usually enrolled. 2016 schedule: June 27 to July 29. Application deadline: May 31.

Tuition and Aid Day student tuition: $37,950. Tuition installment plan (Insured Tuition Payment Plan, FACTS Tuition Payment Plan, monthly payment plans, individually arranged payment plans, 2-payment plan (66% due May 1, 34% due January 1)). Tuition reduction for siblings, need-based scholarship grants, need-based loans, middle-income loans available. In 2015–16, 38% of upper-school students received aid. Total amount of financial aid awarded in 2015–16: $791,663.

Admissions Traditional secondary-level entrance grade is 9. For fall 2015, 62 students applied for upper-level admission, 30 were accepted, 21 enrolled. Psychoeducational evaluation and WISC or WAIS required. Deadline for receipt of application materials: none. Application fee required: $100. On-campus interview required.

Athletics Interscholastic: basketball (boys, girls), cross-country running (b,g), lacrosse (b,g), soccer (b,g), tennis (b,g); coed interscholastic: golf, ultimate Frisbee; coed intramural: backpacking, bicycling, canoeing/kayaking, climbing, hiking/backpacking, rock climbing, ropes courses, sailing, skiing (cross-country), volleyball, yoga. 2 PE instructors, 5 coaches.

Computers Computers are regularly used in all classes. Computer network features include online commercial services, Internet access, wireless campus network, Internet filtering or blocking technology, adaptive technologies such as Kurzweil, Dragon/Mac Speech Dictate, etc., homework site, all students have school-supplied laptops (no additional cost). Student e-mail accounts and computer access in designated common areas are available to students. Students grades are available online. The school has a published electronic and media policy.

Contact Mary Ellen Trent, Director of Admissions. 610-640-4150 Ext. 2162. Fax: 610-560-4336. E-mail: maryellen.trent@dvfs.org. Website: www.dvfs.org

DENVER ACADEMY
4400 East Iliff Avenue
Denver, Colorado 80222
Head of School: Mark Twarogowski

General Information Coeducational day college-preparatory, general academic, arts, vocational, and technology school; primarily serves underachievers, students with learning disabilities, individuals with Attention Deficit Disorder, dyslexic students, and unique learning styles. Grades 1–12. Founded: 1972. Setting: urban. 22-acre campus. 19 buildings on campus. Approved or accredited by Association of Colorado Independent Schools and Colorado Department of Education. Member of National Association of Independent Schools. Endowment: $3 million. Total enrollment: 378. Upper school average class size: 14. Upper school faculty student ratio: 1:8. There are 169 required school days per year for Upper School students. Upper School students typically attend 5 days per week. The average school day consists of 6 hours and 15 minutes.

Upper School Student Profile Grade 9: 49 students (33 boys, 16 girls); Grade 10: 55 students (42 boys, 13 girls); Grade 11: 55 students (33 boys, 22 girls); Grade 12: 47 students (29 boys, 18 girls).

Faculty School total: 63. In upper school: 20 men, 23 women; 18 have advanced degrees.

Subjects Offered ACT preparation, adolescent issues, algebra, American history, American literature, anatomy, art, art history, arts, baseball, basic skills, basketball, biology, botany, business, calculus, ceramics, chemistry, comparative cultures, computer applications, computer graphics, computer math, computer processing, computer programming, computer science, computer skills, creative writing, drama, dramatic arts, earth science, English, English literature, environmental science, ethics, European history, film, filmmaking, fine arts, geography, geometry, government/civics, grammar, health, history, life skills, mathematics, music, philosophy, photography, physical education, physics, physiology, psychology, science, social sciences, social studies, Spanish, speech, theater, trigonometry, values and decisions, world history, world literature, writing, yearbook.

Graduation Requirements Arts and fine arts (art, music, dance, drama), English, mathematics, physical education (includes health), science, social sciences, social studies (includes history).

Special Academic Programs Independent study; academic accommodation for the gifted; remedial reading and/or remedial writing; remedial math; programs in English, mathematics, general development for dyslexic students.

College Admission Counseling 48 students graduated in 2015; they went to Arapahoe Community College; Metropolitan State University of Denver; University of Colorado Boulder; University of Denver; University of Northern Colorado.

Student Life Upper grades have specified standards of dress, student council, honor system. Discipline rests primarily with faculty.

Summer Programs Remediation, enrichment, advancement, art/fine arts, rigorous outdoor training, computer instruction programs offered; session focuses on academics,

remediation, and summer fun camp; held both on and off campus; held at various locations around the city and the Rocky Mountains; accepts boys and girls; open to students from other schools. 150 students usually enrolled. 2016 schedule: June to July. Application deadline: June 1.

Tuition and Aid Day student tuition: $26,125. Tuition installment plan (monthly payment plans). Tuition reduction for siblings, need-based scholarship grants available. In 2015–16, 30% of upper-school students received aid.

Admissions For fall 2015, 38 students applied for upper-level admission, 34 were accepted, 29 enrolled. WISC or WAIS, Woodcock-Johnson and Woodcock-Johnson Revised Achievement Test required. Deadline for receipt of application materials: none. Application fee required: $75. On-campus interview required.

Athletics Interscholastic: baseball (boys), basketball (b,g), cross-country running (b,g), golf (b), soccer (b,g), track and field (b), volleyball (g); intramural: volleyball (g); coed interscholastic: physical fitness, physical training; coed intramural: backpacking, basketball, boxing, canoeing/kayaking, climbing, cooperative games, fishing, flag football, golf, indoor hockey, indoor soccer, indoor track, jump rope, mountaineering, outdoor activities, rafting, rock climbing, skiing (downhill), soccer, swimming and diving, track and field, wall climbing. 4 PE instructors, 4 coaches.

Computers Computers are regularly used in basic skills, career exploration, career technology, college planning, drawing and design, English, foreign language, independent study, introduction to technology, mathematics, media arts, media production, media services, multimedia, music, occupational education, SAT preparation, science, writing, yearbook classes. Computer network features include on-campus library services, online commercial services, Internet access, wireless campus network, Internet filtering or blocking technology. Student e-mail accounts and computer access in designated common areas are available to students. Students grades are available online. The school has a published electronic and media policy.

Contact Janet Woolley, Director of Admissions. 303-777-5161. Fax: 303-777-5893. E-mail: jwoolley@denveracademy.org. Website: www.denveracademy.org

EAGLE HILL SCHOOL
45 Glenville Road
Greenwich, Connecticut 06831
Head of School: Dr. Marjorie E. Castro

General Information Coeducational boarding and day college-preparatory, general academic, arts, and technology school; primarily serves students with learning disabilities, dyslexic students, and language-based learning disabilities. Boarding grades 5–9, day grades 1–9. Founded: 1975. Setting: suburban. Nearest major city is New York, NY. Students are housed in single-sex by floor dormitories. 16-acre campus. 3 buildings on campus. Approved or accredited by Connecticut Department of Education. Member of National Association of Independent Schools and Secondary School Admission Test Board. Total enrollment: 250. Upper school average class size: 6. Upper school faculty-student ratio: 1:4. There are 180 required school days per year for Upper School students. Upper School students typically attend 5 days per week. The average school day consists of 7 hours and 40 minutes.

Upper School Student Profile 30% of students are boarding students. 50% are state residents. 4 states are represented in upper school student body.

Faculty School total: 65. In upper school: 15 men, 20 women; 33 have advanced degrees; 28 reside on campus.

Subjects Offered Art, English, health, history, mathematics, music, physical education, science, technology.

Graduation Requirements Arts and fine arts (art, music, dance, drama), computer science, English, mathematics, physical education (includes health), science, social sciences, social studies (includes history), study skills.

Special Academic Programs Remedial reading and/or remedial writing; remedial math; programs in English, mathematics, general development for dyslexic students.

College Admission Counseling 60 students graduated in 2015.

Student Life Upper grades have specified standards of dress, student council, honor system. Discipline rests primarily with faculty.

Tuition and Aid Day student tuition: $64,450; 5-day tuition and room/board: $85,365. Tuition installment plan (monthly payment plans). Need-based scholarship grants available.

Admissions For fall 2015, 179 students applied for upper-level admission, 90 were accepted, 70 enrolled. Psychoeducational evaluation and Wechsler Intelligence Scale for Children III required. Deadline for receipt of application materials: none. Application fee required: $100. On-campus interview required.

Athletics Interscholastic: baseball (boys), basketball (b,g), cheering (g), field hockey (g), lacrosse (b,g); intramural: aerobics (g), aerobics/dance (g), aerobics/Nautilus (b), flag football (b), football (b), lacrosse (g); coed interscholastic: basketball, cross-country running, ice hockey; coed intramural: basketball, bicycling, billiards, canoeing/kayaking, dance, fitness, fitness walking, floor hockey, Frisbee, golf, gymnastics, ice skating, jogging, judo, lacrosse, martial arts, outdoor activities, outdoor education, outdoor recreation, physical fitness, physical training, volleyball, yoga. 1 PE instructor, 1 athletic trainer.

Computers Computers are regularly used in English, history, mathematics, science classes. Computer network features include on-campus library services, online commercial services, Internet access, wireless campus network, Internet filtering or blocking technology, digital lab, iMovie, Active Boards, Intranet. The school has a published electronic and media policy.

Contact Mr. Thomas Cone, Director of Admissions and Placement. 203-622-9240 Ext. 648. Fax: 203-622-0914. E-mail: t.cone@eaglehill.org. Website: www.eaglehillschool.org

EDMONTON ACADEMY

Unit 2, 810 Saddleback Road
Edmonton, Alberta T6J 4W4, Canada

Head of School: Laurie Oakes

General Information Coeducational day college-preparatory and arts school; primarily serves students with learning disabilities, individuals with Attention Deficit Disorder, and dyslexic students. Grades 3–12. Founded: 1983. Setting: urban. Approved or accredited by Association of Independent Schools and Colleges of Alberta and Alberta Department of Education. Language of instruction: English. Total enrollment: 62. Upper school average class size: 12. Upper school faculty-student ratio: 1:6. There are 175 required school days per year for Upper School students. Upper School students typically attend 5 days per week. The average school day consists of 7 hours and 10 minutes.

Upper School Student Profile Grade 10: 3 students (3 boys); Grade 11: 9 students (5 boys, 4 girls); Grade 12: 15 students (10 boys, 5 girls).

Faculty School total: 11. In upper school: 2 men, 5 women; 1 has an advanced degree.

Subjects Offered All academic.

Special Academic Programs Academic accommodation for the gifted; remedial reading and/or remedial writing; remedial math; programs in English, mathematics for dyslexic students.

Student Life Upper grades have honor system. Discipline rests primarily with faculty.

Tuition and Aid Day student tuition: CAN$9000. Tuition installment plan (The Tuition Plan, individually arranged payment plans). Tuition reduction for siblings, bursaries available. In 2014–15, 4% of upper-school students received aid. Total amount of financial aid awarded in 2014–15: CAN$6900.

Admissions Traditional secondary-level entrance grade is 10. For fall 2014, 3 students applied for upper-level admission, 3 were accepted, 3 enrolled. Battery of testing done through outside agency, Individual IQ, Achievement and behavior rating scale or WISC-R required. Deadline for receipt of application materials: August 31. Application fee required: CAN$50. Interview required.

Athletics Coed Intramural: aerobics, badminton, ball hockey, basketball, cooperative games, fitness, flag football, floor hockey, golf, life saving, outdoor education, physical fitness, volleyball. 1 PE instructor.

Computers Computers are regularly used in all academic classes. Computer network features include Internet access, wireless campus network, Internet filtering or blocking technology. Computer access in designated common areas is available to students. The school has a published electronic and media policy.

Contact Elizabeth Richards, Executive Director. 780-482-5449. Fax: 780-482-0902. E-mail: e.richards@edmontonacademy.com. Website: www.edmontonacademy.com

ETON ACADEMY

1755 Melton Street
Birmingham, Michigan 48009

Head of School: Pete Pullen

General Information Coeducational day college-preparatory, general academic, and arts school; primarily serves underachievers, students with learning disabilities, individuals with Attention Deficit Disorder, dyslexic students, and dysgraphia, auditory processing. Grades 1–12. Founded: 1986. Setting: suburban. Nearest major city is Detroit. 3-acre campus. 1 building on campus. Approved or accredited by Independent Schools Association of the Central States and Michigan Department of Education. Member of National Association of Independent Schools. Endowment: $1 million. Total enrollment: 209. Upper school average class size: 8. Upper school faculty-student ratio: 1:4. Upper School students typically attend 5 days per week. The average school day consists of 7 hours.

Faculty School total: 30. In upper school: 3 men, 8 women; 6 have advanced degrees.

Subjects Offered Algebra, American literature, art, business, ceramics, chemistry, creative writing, drama, earth science, economics, English, English literature, expository writing, geography, geometry, government/civics, grammar, health, history, keyboarding, mathematics, physical education, science, social studies, sociology, speech, trigonometry, U.S. history, writing.

Graduation Requirements Arts and fine arts (art, music, dance, drama), English, mathematics, physical education (includes health), science, social studies (includes history).

Special Academic Programs Remedial reading and/or remedial writing; remedial math; programs in English, mathematics, general development for dyslexic students; special instructional classes for deaf students, blind students.

College Admission Counseling 82 students graduated in 2014; 8 went to college, including Oakland Community College; Oakland University; University of Michigan–Dearborn; Western Michigan University. Other: 1 entered a postgraduate year.

Student Life Upper grades have specified standards of dress, student council, honor system. Discipline rests primarily with faculty.

Tuition and Aid Day student tuition: $21,000. Tuition installment plan (FACTS Tuition Payment Plan, monthly payment plans, individually arranged payment plans). Need-based scholarship grants available. In 2014–15, 12% of upper-school students received aid. Total amount of financial aid awarded in 2014–15: $150,000.

Admissions Traditional secondary-level entrance grade is 9. For fall 2014, 12 students applied for upper-level admission, 11 were accepted, 9 enrolled. Psychoeducational evaluation and Woodcock-Johnson Educational Evaluation, WISC III required. Deadline for receipt of application materials: none. Application fee required: $100. On-campus interview required.

Athletics Interscholastic: basketball (boys, girls), soccer (b,g); intramural: basketball (b,g), tennis (b,g), volleyball (b,g); coed interscholastic: basketball, cheering, soccer; coed intramural: basketball, bowling, running, tennis, volleyball. 3 PE instructors, 4 coaches.

Computers Computers are regularly used in English, history, mathematics, science classes. Computer network features include on-campus library services, Internet access, Internet filtering or blocking technology, library database is accessible from the Website, weekly progress reports accessible for parents online. Computer access in designated common areas is available to students.

Contact Blythe Moran, Director of Advancement. 248-642-1150. Fax: 248-642-3670. E-mail: BMoran@EtonAcademy.org. Website: www.EtonAcademy.org

THE FORMAN SCHOOL

12 Norfolk Road
PO Box 80
Litchfield, Connecticut 06759

Head of School: Adam K. Man

General Information Coeducational boarding and day college-preparatory, arts, and technology school; primarily serves students with learning disabilities, individuals with Attention Deficit Disorder, and dyslexic students. Grades 9–12. Founded: 1930. Setting: small town. Nearest major city is Hartford. Students are housed in single-sex dormitories. 125-acre campus. 30 buildings on campus. Approved or accredited by National Association of Episcopal Schools, New England Association of Schools and Colleges, The Association of Boarding Schools, and Connecticut Department of Education. Member of National Association of Independent Schools and Secondary School Admission Test Board. Endowment: $5 million. Total enrollment: 210. Upper school average class size: 8. Upper school faculty-student ratio: 1:4. Upper School students typically attend 6 days per week. The average school day consists of 6 hours and 30 minutes.

Upper School Student Profile 87% of students are boarding students. 31% are state residents. 24 states are represented in upper school student body. 10% are international students. International students from Bermuda, Indonesia, Italy, Saudi Arabia, Singapore, and United Kingdom; 9 other countries represented in student body.

Faculty School total: 60. In upper school: 30 men, 30 women; 33 have advanced degrees; 40 reside on campus.

Subjects Offered Algebra, American history, art, art history, band, biology, calculus, ceramics, chemistry, computer science, creative writing, driver education, ecology, English, English literature, environmental science, European history, expository writing, fine arts, French, geography, geometry, history, Holocaust seminar, human development, music, photography, physics, psychology, science, social sciences, social studies, Spanish, trigonometry, world history, writing.

Graduation Requirements Arts and fine arts (art, music, dance, drama), English, mathematics, physical education (includes health), science, social sciences, social studies (includes history).

Special Academic Programs Advanced Placement exam preparation; honors section; programs in English, mathematics, general development for dyslexic students.

College Admission Counseling 53 students graduated in 2014; 49 went to college, including Hofstra University; Montana State University; Savannah College of Art and Design; The University of Arizona. Other: 4 had other specific plans.

Student Life Upper grades have specified standards of dress, student council, honor system. Discipline rests primarily with faculty.

Tuition and Aid Day student tuition: $54,000; 7-day tuition and room/board: $66,100. Tuition installment plan (The Tuition Plan, Key Tuition Payment Plan, monthly payment plans, self-funded tuition, refund plan, Tuition Management Payment Plan). Need-based scholarship grants available. In 2014–15, 21% of upper-school students received aid. Total amount of financial aid awarded in 2014–15: $1,100,000.

Admissions Traditional secondary-level entrance grade is 9. For fall 2014, 136 students applied for upper-level admission, 96 were accepted, 53 enrolled. WISC/Woodcock-Johnson required. Deadline for receipt of application materials: none. Application fee required: $50. Interview required.

Athletics Interscholastic: baseball (boys), basketball (b,g), football (b), golf (b), ice hockey (b,g), lacrosse (b,g), soccer (b,g), tennis (b,g), ultimate Frisbee (b,g), volleyball (g), wrestling (b); coed interscholastic: alpine skiing, canoeing/kayaking, crew, cross-country running, equestrian sports, kayaking, skiing (downhill), ultimate Frisbee; coed intramural: climbing, dance, freestyle skiing, golf, horseback riding, kayaking, modern dance, outdoor activities, outdoor education, outdoor recreation, outdoor skills, physical fitness, physical training, rock climbing, ropes courses, skateboarding, skiing (cross-country), skiing (downhill), snowboarding, strength & conditioning, tennis, ultimate Frisbee, wall climbing, weight lifting, weight training, yoga. 1 athletic trainer.

Computers Computers are regularly used in English, foreign language, mathematics, music, science, writing classes. Computer network features include on-campus library services, Internet access, wireless campus network, Internet filtering or blocking technology. Campus intranet and student e-mail accounts are available to students. Students grades are available online. The school has a published electronic and media policy.

Contact Aline Rossiter, Director of Admission. 860-567-1803. Fax: 860-567-3501. E-mail: aline.rossiter@formanschool.org. Website: www.formanschool.org

FRANKLIN ACADEMY

140 River Road

East Haddam, Connecticut 06423

Head of School: A. Frederick Weissbach

General Information Coeducational boarding and day college-preparatory school; primarily serves students with learning disabilities and non-verbal learning differences (NLD), Autism Spectrum Disorder (ASD), and Asperger's Syndrome. Grades 8–PG. Founded: 2001. Setting: rural. Nearest major city is Hartford. Students are housed in single-sex by floor dormitories and single-sex dormitories. 75-acre campus. 18 buildings on campus. Approved or accredited by Connecticut Association of Independent Schools, New England Association of Schools and Colleges, and Connecticut Department of Education. Member of National Association of Independent Schools. Total enrollment: 85. Upper school average class size: 6. Upper school faculty-student ratio: 1:2. There are 180 required school days per year for Upper School students. Upper School students typically attend 6 days per week. The average school day consists of 6 hours and 30 minutes.

Upper School Student Profile 95% of students are boarding students. 20% are state residents. 19 states are represented in upper school student body. 10% are international students. International students from Croatia, Hong Kong, Mexico, Singapore, Taiwan, and Uganda; 2 other countries represented in student body.

Faculty School total: 45. In upper school: 21 men, 23 women; 32 have advanced degrees; 20 reside on campus.

Graduation Requirements Must take the "Individual and Community" or "Franklin Learning Institute "Seminar Series".

Special Academic Programs Honors section; independent study; term-away projects; study at local college for college credit; academic accommodation for the gifted; remedial reading and/or remedial writing; remedial math.

College Admission Counseling 19 students graduated in 2015; 17 went to college, including Fairleigh Dickinson University, College at Florham; Hampshire College; High Point University; Landmark College; Rochester Institute of Technology; University of Connecticut. Other: 2 entered a postgraduate year.

Student Life Upper grades have student council, honor system. Discipline rests equally with students and faculty.

Summer Programs Remediation, enrichment, art/fine arts, computer instruction programs offered; session focuses on social skills, special interest areas, summer camp; held both on and off campus; held at Mystic Aquarium, Mystic, CT; accepts boys and girls; open to students from other schools. 90 students usually enrolled. 2016 schedule: June 26 to July 23. Application deadline: June 1.

Tuition and Aid Day student tuition: $69,800; 7-day tuition and room/board: $79,800. Tuition installment plan (monthly payment plans, individually arranged payment plans, quarterly payment plans, pay in full discount). Merit scholarship grants available. In 2015–16, 5% of upper-school students received aid.

Admissions Achievement tests, Individual IQ, Achievement and behavior rating scale, psychoeducational evaluation and writing sample required. Deadline for receipt of application materials: none. Application fee required: $75. On-campus interview required.

Athletics Coed Interscholastic: aerobics/dance, archery, basketball, bicycling, billiards, canoeing/kayaking, cooperative games, cross-country running, dance, fishing, fitness, fitness walking, flag football, fly fishing, Frisbee, golf, horseback riding, ice skating, jogging, kayaking, kickball, outdoor recreation, outdoors, paddling, paint ball, physical fitness, running, sailing, soccer, softball, table tennis, ultimate Frisbee, walking, yoga.

Computers Computers are regularly used in all classes. Computer network features include on-campus library services, Internet access, wireless campus network, Internet filtering or blocking technology, Dragon Speak and other speech-to-text programs. Campus intranet, student e-mail accounts, and computer access in designated common areas are available to students. The school has a published electronic and media policy.

Contact Vincent Schmidt, Assistant Director of Admissions. 860-873-2700 Ext. 1154. Fax: 860-873-9345. E-mail: Vince@fa-ct.org. Website: www.fa-ct.org

THE FROSTIG SCHOOL

971 North Altadena Drive

Pasadena, California 91107

Head of School: Ms. Jennifer Janetzke

General Information Coeducational day arts, vocational, and technology school; primarily serves underachievers, students with learning disabilities, individuals with Attention Deficit Disorder, dyslexic students, and autism. Grades 1–12. Founded: 1951. Setting: suburban. Nearest major city is Los Angeles. 2-acre campus. 1 building on campus. Approved or accredited by Western Association of Schools and Colleges and California Department of Education. Endowment: $3 million. Total enrollment: 106. Upper school average class size: 12. Upper school faculty-student ratio: 1:6. There are 180 required school days per year for Upper School students. Upper School students typically attend 5 days per week. The average school day consists of 6 hours and 10 minutes.

Upper School Student Profile Grade 6: 15 students (11 boys, 4 girls); Grade 7: 13 students (6 boys, 7 girls); Grade 8: 14 students (9 boys, 5 girls); Grade 9: 7 students (5 boys, 2 girls); Grade 10: 14 students (12 boys, 2 girls); Grade 11: 12 students (12 boys); Grade 12: 11 students (7 boys, 4 girls).

Faculty School total: 26. In upper school: 5 men, 7 women; 4 have advanced degrees.

Subjects Offered Algebra, American government, American history, art, athletics, basic skills, career and personal planning, career education, computer animation, computer applications, consumer economics, creative drama, economics, English, filmmaking, geometry, government, health education, music, physical education, physics, U.S. history.

Special Academic Programs Remedial reading and/or remedial writing; remedial math; programs in English, mathematics, general development for dyslexic students.

College Admission Counseling 9 students graduated in 2014; 8 went to college, including Citrus College; Glendale Community College; Pasadena City College. Other: 1 entered a postgraduate year.

Student Life Upper grades have specified standards of dress, student council. Discipline rests equally with students and faculty.

Tuition and Aid Day student tuition: $30,000. Tuition installment plan (monthly payment plans, individually arranged payment plans). Need-based scholarship grants available. In 2014–15, 5% of upper-school students received aid. Total amount of financial aid awarded in 2014–15: $50,000.

Admissions Traditional secondary-level entrance grade is 9. For fall 2014, 15 students applied for upper-level admission, 11 were accepted, 11 enrolled. Admissions testing required. Deadline for receipt of application materials: none. Application fee required: $100. On-campus interview required.

Athletics Coed Interscholastic: basketball, flag football, soccer, softball, touch football. 1 PE instructor, 2 coaches.

Computers Computers are regularly used in art, career education, geography, library, library skills, media, music, occupational education, photography, remedial study skills, Web site design, yearbook classes. Computer network features include on-campus library services, Internet access, wireless campus network, Internet filtering or blocking technology, assistive technology services, laptops. Student e-mail accounts are available to students.

Contact Ms. Jacquie Knight, IEP and Admissions Administrator. 626-791-1255. Fax: 626-798-1801. E-mail: admissions@frostig.org. Website: www.frostig.org

GATEWAY SCHOOL

2570 NW Green Oaks Boulevard

Arlington, Texas 76012

Head of School: Mrs. Harriet R. Walber

General Information Coeducational day college-preparatory, general academic, arts, and technology school; primarily serves underachievers, students with learning disabilities, individuals with Attention Deficit Disorder, and dyslexic students. Grades 5–12. Founded: 1980. Setting: urban. 7-acre campus. 1 building on campus. Approved or accredited by Southern Association of Colleges and Schools, Southern Association of Independent Schools, and Texas Department of Education. Upper school average class size: 10. Upper school faculty-student ratio: 1:5. There are 176 required school days per year for Upper School students. Upper School students typically attend 5 days per week. The average school day consists of 8 hours.

Faculty School total: 5. In upper school: 5 women; 3 have advanced degrees.

Subjects Offered Algebra, American literature, art, biology, British literature, career planning, chemistry, college awareness, college counseling, community service, composition, computer education, computer literacy, computer science, computer skills, developmental math, drama, earth science, economics, English, English composition, English literature, environmental science, geometry, government, government/civics, grammar, health, health education, history, intro to computers, introduction to theater, journalism, keyboarding, language arts, literature, mathematics, music, music performance, music theater, newspaper, physical education, pre-algebra, reading, reading/study skills, science, social studies, Spanish, speech, state history, theater, U.S. government, U.S. history, word processing, world history, world literature, writing, writing workshop, yearbook.

Graduation Requirements Computer science, English, foreign language, mathematics, physical education (includes health), science, social studies (includes history). Community service is required.

Special Academic Programs Independent study; study at local college for college credit; remedial reading and/or remedial writing; remedial math; programs in English, mathematics, general development for dyslexic students.

College Admission Counseling 1 student graduated in 2014 and went to Tarrant County College District.

Student Life Upper grades have uniform requirement, student council. Discipline rests primarily with faculty.

Tuition and Aid Day student tuition: $13,500. Guaranteed tuition plan. Tuition installment plan (monthly payment plans, individually arranged payment plans, payment by the semester).

Admissions Traditional secondary-level entrance grade is 9. School's own test, Wechsler Intelligence Scale for Children and Woodcock-Johnson required. Deadline for receipt of application materials: none. Application fee required: $250. On-campus interview required.

Athletics Interscholastic: basketball (boys, girls), golf (g); intramural: basketball (b,g), bowling (b,g), golf (b,g), jogging (b,g); coed interscholastic: fitness walking, golf, jogging, scuba diving; coed intramural: bowling. 1 PE instructor.

Computers Computers are regularly used in basic skills, English, history, mathematics, science classes. Computer network features include Internet access. The school has a published electronic and media policy.

Contact Harriet R. Walber, Executive Director. 817-226-6222. Fax: 817-226-6225. E-mail: walberhr@aol.com. Website: www.gatewayschool.com

GLEN EDEN SCHOOL

#190-13151 Vanier Pl
Richmond, British Columbia V6V 2J1, Canada

Head of School: Dr. Rick Brennan

General Information Coeducational day school; primarily serves underachievers, students with learning disabilities, individuals with Attention Deficit Disorder, individuals with emotional and behavioral problems, and Autism Spectrum Disorders. Grades K–12. Founded: 1984. Setting: urban. Nearest major city is Richmond, Canada. 1 building on campus. Approved or accredited by British Columbia Department of Education. Language of instruction: English. Upper school average class size: 4. Upper school faculty-student ratio: 1:5.

Faculty School total: 5. In upper school: 2 men, 1 woman; 2 have advanced degrees.

Special Academic Programs Remedial reading and/or remedial writing; remedial math.

Tuition and Aid Tuition installment plan (monthly payment plans, individually arranged payment plans).

Admissions Deadline for receipt of application materials: none. Application fee required: CAN$1000. Interview required.

Computers Computer resources include Internet access.

Contact Dr. Rick Brennan, Director. 604-821-1457. Fax: 604-821-1527. E-mail: glenedenschool@gleneden.org. Website: www.gleneden.org

THE GLENHOLME SCHOOL, DEVEREUX CONNECTICUT

81 Sabbaday Lane
Washington, Connecticut 06793

Head of School: Maryann Campbell

General Information Coeducational boarding and day college-preparatory, arts, vocational, technology, social coaching and motivational management, and self-discipline strategies and character development school; primarily serves underachievers, students with learning disabilities, individuals with Attention Deficit Disorder, individuals with emotional and behavioral problems, High functioning ASD including Asperger's Syndrome; ADHD, PDD, and anxiet, depression and compulsive disorders. Founded: 1968. Setting: small town. Nearest major city is Hartford. Students are housed in single-sex dormitories. 105-acre campus. 30 buildings on campus. Approved or accredited by Association of Independent Schools in New England, Connecticut Department of Children and Families, Council of Accreditation and School Improvement, Massachusetts Department of Education, National Association of Private Schools for Exceptional Children, New England Association of Schools and Colleges, New Jersey Department of Education, New York Department of Education, and Connecticut Department of Education. Member of National Association of Independent Schools. Total enrollment: 95. Upper school average class size: 10. Upper school faculty-student ratio: 1:10. There are 215 required school days per year for Upper School students. Upper School students typically attend 5 days per week. The average school day consists of 5 hours and 45 minutes.

Upper School Student Profile Grade 6: 6 students (6 boys); Grade 7: 3 students (3 boys); Grade 8: 10 students (7 boys, 3 girls); Grade 9: 7 students (3 boys, 4 girls); Grade 10: 15 students (10 boys, 5 girls); Grade 11: 17 students (11 boys, 6 girls); Grade 12: 25 students (16 boys, 9 girls); Grade 13: 6 students (2 boys, 4 girls); Postgraduate: 6 students (4 boys, 2 girls). 95% of students are boarding students. 28% are state

residents. 15 states are represented in upper school student body. 5% are international students. International students from China, Costa Rica, Hong Kong, Mexico, and Panama; 4 other countries represented in student body.

Faculty School total: 22. In upper school: 4 men, 16 women; 12 have advanced degrees; 3 reside on campus.

Subjects Offered ADL skills, adolescent issues, aerobics, algebra, art, basketball, biology, career and personal planning, career education, career exploration, career/college preparation, character education, chemistry, choral music, chorus, college admission preparation, college planning, communication skills, community service, computer animation, computer applications, computer art, computer education, computer graphics, computer literacy, computer skills, creative arts, creative dance, creative drama, creative thinking, creative writing, culinary arts, dance, decision making skills, digital photography, drama, drama performance, earth science, English, equine management, fine arts, geometry, graphic arts, guidance, health, health and wellness, health education, Internet research, interpersonal skills, keyboarding, library, life skills, mathematics, media arts, moral and social development, music, participation in sports, performing arts, personal fitness, photography, physical education, piano, play production, radio broadcasting, SAT preparation, science, social sciences, Spanish, theater, U.S. history, video and animation, world history, writing, yearbook.

Graduation Requirements Art, electives, English, language, mathematics, physical education (includes health), science, social studies (includes history), students must meet either Glenholme graduation requirements or the requirements of their home state, depending on the funding source.

Special Academic Programs Academic accommodation for the gifted; remedial reading and/or remedial writing; remedial math; programs in English, mathematics, general development for dyslexic students; ESL (3 students enrolled).

College Admission Counseling 17 students graduated in 2015; 13 went to college. Other: 2 went to work, 2 entered a postgraduate year.

Student Life Upper grades have uniform requirement, student council, honor system. Discipline rests primarily with faculty.

Summer Programs Remediation, enrichment, ESL, sports, art/fine arts, computer instruction programs offered; session focuses on strengthening social skills and boosting academic proficiency; held on campus; accepts boys and girls; open to students from other schools. 90 students usually enrolled. 2016 schedule: July 5 to August 19.

Admissions Individual IQ, Achievement and behavior rating scale or psychoeducational evaluation required. Deadline for receipt of application materials: none. Application fee required: $150. On-campus interview required.

Athletics Intramural: aerobics (boys, girls), aerobics/dance (b,g), aquatics (b,g), archery (b,g), artistic gym (b,g), basketball (b,g), cheering (b,g), combined training (b,g), cooperative games (b,g), cross-country running (b,g), dance (b,g), dance team (b,g), equestrian sports (b,g), figure skating (b,g), fishing (b,g), fitness (b,g), fitness walking (b,g), flag football (b,g), Frisbee (b,g), golf (b,g), hiking/backpacking (b,g), horseback riding (b,g), ice skating (b,g), jogging (b,g), jump rope (b,g), kickball (b,g), modern dance (b,g), outdoor activities (b,g), outdoor recreation (b,g), paddle tennis (b,g), physical fitness (b,g), physical training (b,g), roller blading (b,g), ropes courses (b,g), soccer (b,g), softball (b,g), strength & conditioning (b,g), tennis (b,g), ultimate Frisbee (b,g), volleyball (b,g), walking (b,g), weight training (b,g), yoga (b,g); coed interscholastic: basketball, cross-country running, soccer, softball, tennis; coed intramural: aerobics, aerobics/dance, aquatics, archery, artistic gym, basketball, cheering, combined training, cooperative games, cross-country running, dance, dance team, equestrian sports, figure skating, fishing, fitness, fitness walking, flag football, Frisbee, golf, hiking/backpacking, horseback riding, ice skating, jogging, jump rope, kickball, modern dance, outdoor activities, outdoor recreation, paddle tennis, physical fitness, physical training, roller blading, ropes courses, soccer, softball, strength & conditioning, tennis, ultimate Frisbee, volleyball, walking, weight training, yoga. 1 PE instructor, 2 coaches, 1 athletic trainer.

Computers Computers are regularly used in all academic, technology classes. Computer network features include on-campus library services, Internet access, wireless campus network, Internet filtering or blocking technology, online learning, Web cam parent communications. Campus intranet, student e-mail accounts, and computer access in designated common areas are available to students. Students grades are available online. The school has a published electronic and media policy.

Contact Lauren Chilson, Admissions. 860-868-7377. Fax: 860-868-7413. E-mail: lchilson@devereux.org. Website: www.theglenholmeschool.org

THE GOW SCHOOL

2491 Emery Rd
South Wales, New York 14139-9778

Head of School: Mr. M. Bradley Rogers Jr.

General Information Coeducational boarding and day college-preparatory, arts, technology, and reconstructive language school; primarily serves students with learning disabilities, individuals with Attention Deficit Disorder, dyslexic students, and language-based learning disabilities. Grades 7–12. Founded: 1926. Setting: rural. Nearest major city is Buffalo. Students are housed in single-sex dormitories. 120-acre campus. 22 buildings on campus. Approved or accredited by New York State Association of Independent Schools, New York State Board of Regents, The Association of Boarding Schools, and New York Department of Education. Member of

National Association of Independent Schools. Endowment: $22 million. Total enrollment: 145. Upper school average class size: 5. Upper school faculty-student ratio: 1:4. There are 175 required school days per year for Upper School students. Upper School students typically attend 6 days per week. The average school day consists of 13 hours.

Upper School Student Profile Grade 7: 12 students (9 boys, 3 girls); Grade 8: 12 students (12 boys); Grade 9: 15 students (14 boys, 1 girl); Grade 10: 36 students (34 boys, 2 girls); Grade 11: 35 students (33 boys, 2 girls); Grade 12: 37 students (34 boys, 3 girls). 91% of students are boarding students. 28% are state residents. 19 states are represented in upper school student body. 30% are international students. International students from Bermuda, Canada, Cayman Islands, China, Hong Kong, and United Kingdom; 10 other countries represented in student body.

Faculty School total: 35. In upper school: 27 men, 7 women; 27 have advanced degrees; 29 reside on campus.

Subjects Offered Algebra, American history, American literature, art, biology, broadcast journalism, business, business applications, business skills, calculus, ceramics, chemistry, computer applications, computer literacy, computer programming, computer science, drama, earth science, economics, engineering, English, English literature, European history, expository writing, fine arts, geology, geometry, grammar, health, journalism, keyboarding, mathematics, metalworking, music, physics, reading, reconstructive language, robotics, science, social studies, theater, trigonometry, typing, video, world history, yearbook.

Graduation Requirements Arts and fine arts (art, music, dance, drama), English, mathematics, reconstructive language, research seminar, science, senior humanities, senior seminar, social studies (includes history). Community service is required.

Special Academic Programs Independent study; study at local college for college credit; academic accommodation for the musically talented; remedial reading and/or remedial writing; remedial math; programs in English, mathematics, general development for dyslexic students; ESL (5 students enrolled).

College Admission Counseling 34 students graduated in 2015; all went to college, including High Point University; Lynn University; Marshall University; Rochester Institute of Technology. Median composite ACT: 21. 1% scored over 26 on composite ACT.

Student Life Upper grades have specified standards of dress, student council. Discipline rests primarily with faculty.

Summer Programs Remediation, enrichment, advancement, ESL, sports, art/fine arts, computer instruction programs offered; session focuses on remediation and course work; held both on and off campus; held at camping sites and city venues; accepts boys and girls; open to students from other schools. 125 students usually enrolled. 2016 schedule: June 26 to July 31. Application deadline: none.

Tuition and Aid Day student tuition: $38,100; 7-day tuition and room/board: $57,300. Tuition installment plan (monthly payment plans, individually arranged payment plans). Need-based scholarship grants available. In 2015–16, 30% of upper-school students received aid. Total amount of financial aid awarded in 2015–16: $950,000.

Admissions Traditional secondary-level entrance grade is 10. For fall 2015, 39 students applied for upper-level admission, 38 were accepted, 34 enrolled. Wechsler Intelligence Scale for Children, WISC or WAIS, WISC/Woodcock-Johnson or Woodcock-Johnson Revised Achievement Test required. Deadline for receipt of application materials: none. Application fee required: $100. On-campus interview required.

Athletics Interscholastic: basketball (boys), wrestling (b); intramural: alpine skiing (b), backpacking (b), basketball (b), bowling (b), climbing (b), cross-country running (b), Frisbee (b), handball (b), hiking/backpacking (b), ice hockey (b), jump rope (b), outdoor education (b), power lifting (b), rappelling (b), rock climbing (b), soccer (b), touch football (b); coed interscholastic: alpine skiing, crew, cross-country running, lacrosse, running, skiing (downhill), soccer, squash, tennis, volleyball; coed intramural: alpine skiing, fitness, flag football, floor hockey, freestyle skiing, golf, jogging, lacrosse, mountain biking, Nautilus, nordic skiing, paint ball, physical fitness, physical training, ropes courses, running, skiing (cross-country), skiing (downhill), snowboarding, snowshoeing, squash, strength & conditioning, tennis, ultimate Frisbee, weight lifting, weight training, whiffle ball. 25 coaches.

Computers Computers are regularly used in all academic, art classes. Computer network features include on-campus library services, online commercial services, Internet access, wireless campus network, Internet filtering or blocking technology, scanners, digital photography, voice recognition. Student e-mail accounts are available to students. The school has a published electronic and media policy.

Contact Mr. Douglas B. Cotter, Director of Admissions. 716-687-2001. Fax: 716-687-2003. E-mail: admissions@gow.org. Website: www.gow.org

THE HILL CENTER, DURHAM ACADEMY

3200 Pickett Road
Durham, North Carolina 27705

Head of School: Dr. Bryan Brander

General Information Coeducational day college-preparatory school; primarily serves underachievers, students with learning disabilities, individuals with Attention Deficit Disorder, and dyslexic students. Grades K–12. Founded: 1977. Setting: small town. 5-acre campus. 1 building on campus. Approved or accredited by National

Association of Private Schools for Exceptional Children, North Carolina Association of Independent Schools, Southern Association of Colleges and Schools, Southern Association of Independent Schools, and North Carolina Department of Education. Member of National Association of Independent Schools. Endowment: $3.5 million. Total enrollment: 175. Upper school average class size: 4. Upper school faculty-student ratio: 1:4. There are 176 required school days per year for Upper School students. Upper School students typically attend 5 days per week. The average school day consists of 3 hours.

Upper School Student Profile Grade 9: 16 students (10 boys, 6 girls); Grade 10: 14 students (11 boys, 3 girls); Grade 11: 17 students (9 boys, 8 girls); Grade 12: 14 students (7 boys, 7 girls).

Faculty School total: 27. In upper school: 10 women; 9 have advanced degrees.

Subjects Offered Algebra, American literature, calculus, English, English literature, expository writing, geometry, grammar, mathematics, mechanics of writing, pre-algebra, pre-calculus, Spanish, writing.

Graduation Requirements Graduation requirements are determined by the student's home-based school.

Special Academic Programs Remedial reading and/or remedial writing; remedial math; programs in English, mathematics, general development for dyslexic students.

College Admission Counseling 10 students graduated in 2015; 8 went to college, including The University of North Carolina Wilmington. Other: 2 went to work.

Student Life Upper grades have student council. Discipline rests primarily with faculty.

Tuition and Aid Day student tuition: $18,200. Guaranteed tuition plan. Tuition installment plan (The Tuition Plan, Key Tuition Payment Plan, monthly payment plans, The Tuition Refund Plan). Need-based scholarship grants available. In 2015–16, 20% of upper-school students received aid. Total amount of financial aid awarded in 2015–16: $54,800.

Admissions Traditional secondary-level entrance grade is 9. For fall 2015, 27 students applied for upper-level admission, 23 were accepted, 19 enrolled. WISC-III and Woodcock-Johnson required. Deadline for receipt of application materials: March 15. Application fee required: $50. On-campus interview required.

Computers Computers are regularly used in English, foreign language, mathematics, writing classes. Computer network features include Internet access, wireless campus network. Campus intranet and student e-mail accounts are available to students.

Contact Ms. Wendy Speir, Director of Admissions. 919-489-7464 Ext. 7545. Fax: 919-489-7466. E-mail: wspeir@hillcenter.org. Website: www.hillcenter.org

THE HOWARD SCHOOL

1192 Foster Street
Atlanta, Georgia 30318

Head of School: Ms. Marifred Cilella

General Information Coeducational day college-preparatory, general academic, arts, and technology school; primarily serves students with learning disabilities, individuals with Attention Deficit Disorder, dyslexic students, and students with language learning disabilities and differences. Grades K–12. Founded: 1950. Setting: urban. 15-acre campus. 2 buildings on campus. Approved or accredited by Georgia Independent School Association, Southern Association of Colleges and Schools, Southern Association of Independent Schools, and Georgia Department of Education. Member of National Association of Independent Schools. Total enrollment: 264. Upper school average class size: 9. Upper school faculty-student ratio: 1:8. There are 173 required school days per year for Upper School students. Upper School students typically attend 5 days per week. The average school day consists of 6 hours and 30 minutes.

Upper School Student Profile Grade 9: 20 students (13 boys, 7 girls); Grade 10: 24 students (20 boys, 4 girls); Grade 11: 25 students (18 boys, 7 girls); Grade 12: 20 students (13 boys, 7 girls).

Faculty School total: 63. In upper school: 7 men, 15 women; 13 have advanced degrees.

Subjects Offered Algebra, American history, American literature, American sign language, art, biology, communications, computer science, creative writing, ecology, economics, English, English literature, European history, film studies, geography, geometry, government/civics, grammar, history, journalism, mathematics, music, physical education, physical science, psychology, reading, science, service learning/internship, social studies, Spanish, study skills, trigonometry, world history, world literature, writing.

Graduation Requirements English, foreign language, health, mathematics, physical education (includes health), science, social studies (includes history).

Special Academic Programs Independent study; academic accommodation for the gifted and the artistically talented; remedial reading and/or remedial writing; remedial math; programs in English, mathematics, general development for dyslexic students.

College Admission Counseling 11 students graduated in 2015; 10 went to college, including Georgia Southern University; Kennesaw State University; Lynn University; Reinhardt University; Savannah College of Art and Design; Young Harris College. Other: 1 had other specific plans.

Student Life Upper grades have specified standards of dress, student council, honor system. Discipline rests equally with students and faculty.

Summer Programs Remediation, advancement programs offered; session focuses on make-up of academic courses; held on campus; accepts boys and girls; open to students from other schools. 20 students usually enrolled. 2016 schedule: June 13 to July 29. Application deadline: April 1.

Tuition and Aid Day student tuition: $30,250. Tuition installment plan (FACTS Tuition Payment Plan, 1-, 2-, 3- and 8-payment plans). Need-based scholarship grants available. In 2015–16, 30% of upper-school students received aid.

Admissions Psychoeducational evaluation required. Deadline for receipt of application materials: none. Application fee required: $150. On-campus interview required.

Athletics Interscholastic: baseball (boys), basketball (b,g), soccer (b), track and field (b,g), volleyball (g), weight training (b,g); coed interscholastic: golf, soccer, track and field. 3 PE instructors, 6 coaches.

Computers Computers are regularly used in all academic classes. Computer network features include online commercial services, Internet access, wireless campus network. Student e-mail accounts are available to students. Students grades are available online. The school has a published electronic and media policy.

Contact Ms. Dawn Splinter, Admissions Associate. 404-377-7436 Ext. 259. Fax: 404-377-0884. E-mail: dsplinter@howardschool.org. Website: www.howardschool.org

HUMANEX ACADEMY

2700 South Zuni Street
Englewood, Colorado 80110

Head of School: Mr. Daniel R. Toomey

General Information Coeducational day college-preparatory, general academic, and arts school; primarily serves underachievers, students with learning disabilities, individuals with Attention Deficit Disorder, individuals with emotional and behavioral problems, dyslexic students, and Asperger's Syndrome, Autism Spectrum Disorder. Grades 6–12. Founded: 1983. Setting: suburban. Nearest major city is Denver. 1-acre campus. 1 building on campus. Approved or accredited by North Central Association of Colleges and Schools and Colorado Department of Education. Total enrollment: 50. Upper school average class size: 8. Upper school faculty-student ratio: 1:8. There are 172 required school days per year for Upper School students. Upper School students typically attend 5 days per week. The average school day consists of 6 hours and 30 minutes.

Upper School Student Profile Grade 6: 3 students (3 boys); Grade 7: 9 students (6 boys, 3 girls); Grade 8: 11 students (8 boys, 3 girls); Grade 9: 10 students (7 boys, 3 girls); Grade 10: 3 students (3 girls); Grade 11: 4 students (2 boys, 2 girls); Grade 12: 4 students (2 boys, 2 girls).

Faculty School total: 8. In upper school: 4 men, 4 women; all have advanced degrees.

Subjects Offered 1 1/2 elective credits, 1968, 20th century American writers, 20th century history, 20th century physics, 20th century world history, 3-dimensional art, 3-dimensional design, ACT preparation, addiction, ADL skills, adolescent issues, advanced biology, advanced math, advanced studio art-AP, advanced TOEFL/grammar, aerobics, American Civil War, American culture, American democracy, American foreign policy, American government, American history, American legal systems, American literature, American politics in film, anatomy, anatomy and physiology, ancient world history, animal behavior, animation, anthropology, art, art appreciation, art history, arts and crafts, athletic training, athletics, biology, British literature, calculus, career and personal planning, career exploration, cartooning/animation, chemistry, civics, civics/free enterprise, Civil War, civil war history, college counseling, college placement, comedy, composition, computer art, computer graphics, conflict resolution, consumer mathematics, creative writing, critical thinking, current events, drawing, English, English literature, epic literature, evolution, existentialism, expository writing, film, film and literature, fitness, foreign language, general, general math, general science, geography, geology, geometry, government, government/civics, grammar, graphic arts, graphic design, great books, Greek drama, guitar, Harlem Renaissance, health, health education, history, Holocaust, honors algebra, honors English, honors geometry, honors U.S. history, honors world history, human anatomy, human biology, human sexuality, illustration, independent living, keyboarding, language, language arts, language structure, languages, literacy, literary genres, literary magazine, literature, mathematics, media literacy, military history, newspaper, non-Western literature, North American literature, novels, nutrition, peer counseling, philosophy, physical fitness, physics, physiology, play/screen writing, poetry, politics, pottery, pre-algebra, pre-calculus, psychology, public speaking, reading, reading/study skills, remedial study skills, remedial/makeup course work, research, research skills, SAT preparation, SAT/ACT preparation, science, science fiction, sculpture, sexuality, Shakespeare, short story, speech, speech and debate, sports, statistics, U.S. government, U.S. government and politics, U.S. history, U.S. literature, Vietnam history, Vietnam War, weight training, weightlifting, Western civilization, Western literature, world geography, world governments, world history.

Graduation Requirements Career exploration, career/college preparation, research, speech. Community service is required.

Special Academic Programs Honors section; academic accommodation for the gifted; remedial reading and/or remedial writing; remedial math; programs in English, mathematics, general development for dyslexic students; special instructional classes for deaf students, blind students.

College Admission Counseling 11 students graduated in 2014; 5 went to college, including Arapahoe Community College; Colorado School of Mines; Colorado State University; Fort Lewis College; Metropolitan State University of Denver; University of Colorado Denver. Other: 4 went to work, 2 entered a postgraduate year. Median composite ACT: 24. 33% scored over 26 on composite ACT.

Student Life Upper grades have specified standards of dress, student council. Discipline rests primarily with faculty.

Tuition and Aid Day student tuition: $19,400. Tuition installment plan (FACTS Tuition Payment Plan). Tuition reduction for siblings, need-based scholarship grants, Sallie Mae loans available. In 2014–15, 25% of upper-school students received aid. Total amount of financial aid awarded in 2014–15: $6000.

Admissions Traditional secondary-level entrance grade is 9. For fall 2014, 11 students applied for upper-level admission, 9 were accepted, 9 enrolled. Wechsler Individual Achievement Test, Wechsler Intelligence Scale for Children III, WISC III or other aptitude measures; standardized achievement test, WISC or WAIS, WISC-III and Woodcock-Johnson, WISC-R, WISC-R or WISC-III and WISC/Woodcock-Johnson required. Deadline for receipt of application materials: none. Application fee required: $50. On-campus interview required.

Athletics Coed Intramural: aerobics, ball hockey, basketball, bocce, bowling, cooperative games, fitness, fitness walking, flag football, Frisbee, handball, jogging, kickball, outdoor activities, outdoor recreation, physical fitness, physical training, power lifting, ultimate Frisbee, weight lifting, weight training. 1 PE instructor.

Computers Computers are regularly used in art, English, health, history, literacy, mathematics, philosophy, psychology, reading, research skills, social studies, Spanish, speech, study skills, writing, writing classes. Computer resources include on-campus library services, online commercial services, Internet access, Internet filtering or blocking technology. Campus intranet and computer access in designated common areas are available to students. Students grades are available online. The school has a published electronic and media policy.

Contact Director of Admissions. 303-783-0187 Ext. 5006. Fax: 303-783-9159. E-mail: info@humanexacademy.com. Website: www.humanexacademy.com

THE JOHN DEWEY ACADEMY

389 Main Street
Great Barrington, Massachusetts 01230

Head of School: Dr. Kenneth M. Steiner

General Information Coeducational boarding college-preparatory and arts school; primarily serves underachievers, students with learning disabilities, individuals with Attention Deficit Disorder, individuals with emotional and behavioral problems, and gifted, underachieving, self-destructive adolescents. Grades 10–PG. Founded: 1985. Setting: small town. Nearest major city is Hartford, CT. Students are housed in single-sex by floor dormitories. 90-acre campus. 3 buildings on campus. Approved or accredited by New England Association of Schools and Colleges and Massachusetts Department of Education. Total enrollment: 20. Upper school average class size: 6. Upper school faculty-student ratio: 1:3. There are 330 required school days per year for Upper School students. Upper School students typically attend 7 days per week. The average school day consists of 6 hours.

Upper School Student Profile Grade 10: 3 students (3 boys); Grade 11: 10 students (7 boys, 3 girls); Grade 12: 7 students (5 boys, 2 girls). 100% of students are boarding students. 10% are state residents. 11 states are represented in upper school student body. 10% are international students. International students from Jordan and Russian Federation.

Faculty School total: 10. In upper school: 5 men, 5 women; 9 have advanced degrees; 2 reside on campus.

Subjects Offered Adolescent issues, algebra, American literature, art, art history, biology, calculus, chemistry, creative writing, drama, English, English literature, environmental science, ethics, European history, fine arts, French, geometry, government/civics, grammar, health, history, Italian, moral reasoning, philosophy, physical education, physics, psychology, sociology, Spanish, statistics, theater, trigonometry, world history, world literature, writing.

Graduation Requirements American history, arts and fine arts (art, music, dance, drama), biology, English, English literature, European history, foreign language, leadership, literature, mathematics, moral reasoning, physical education (includes health), science, social studies (includes history), moral leadership qualities, minimum 18 months residency, college acceptance.

Special Academic Programs Honors section; accelerated programs; independent study; study at local college for college credit; academic accommodation for the gifted and the artistically talented; remedial reading and/or remedial writing; remedial math; programs in general development for dyslexic students.

College Admission Counseling 7 students graduated in 2015; all went to college, including Northeastern University; State University of New York College at Geneseo; Swarthmore College; The University of Texas at Austin; University of Wisconsin–Madison. 95% scored over 600 on SAT critical reading, 95% scored over 600 on SAT math, 95% scored over 600 on SAT writing, 95% scored over 1800 on combined SAT.

Student Life Upper grades have specified standards of dress, student council, honor system. Discipline rests equally with students and faculty.

Summer Programs Session focuses on continuing college preparatory program; held on campus; accepts boys and girls; not open to students from other schools. 25 students usually enrolled.

Tuition and Aid 7-day tuition and room/board: $92,000. Tuition installment plan (monthly payment plans, individually arranged payment plans). Need-based scholarship grants available. In 2015–16, 25% of upper-school students received aid.
Admissions Traditional secondary-level entrance grade is 10. Deadline for receipt of application materials: none. No application fee required. On-campus interview required.
Computers Computer resources include Internet access. Computer access in designated common areas is available to students.
Contact Dr. Andrea Nathans, Executive Director/Admissions. 860-337-1104. E-mail: anathans@jda.org. Website: www.jda.org

KILDONAN SCHOOL
425 Morse Hill Road
Amenia, New York 12501
Head of School: Kevin Pendergast
General Information Coeducational boarding and day college-preparatory, general academic, arts, and technology school; primarily serves students with learning disabilities, dyslexic students, and language-based learning differences. Boarding grades 7–PG, day grades 2–PG. Founded: 1969. Setting: rural. Nearest major city is New York. Students are housed in single-sex dormitories. 350-acre campus. 19 buildings on campus. Approved or accredited by Academy of Orton-Gillingham Practitioners and Educators, New York State Association of Independent Schools, and The Association of Boarding Schools. Member of National Association of Independent Schools and Secondary School Admission Test Board. Endowment: $579,300. Total enrollment: 91. Upper school average class size: 8. Upper school faculty-student ratio: 1:2. The average school day consists of 7 hours.
Upper School Student Profile Grade 6: 5 students (1 boy, 4 girls); Grade 7: 8 students (5 boys, 3 girls); Grade 8: 7 students (3 boys, 4 girls); Grade 9: 12 students (10 boys, 2 girls); Grade 10: 12 students (9 boys, 3 girls); Grade 11: 9 students (7 boys, 2 girls); Grade 12: 16 students (11 boys, 5 girls). 68% of students are boarding students. 44% are state residents. 15 states are represented in upper school student body. 9% are international students. International students from Bermuda, Brazil, France, Mexico, Puerto Rico, and United Arab Emirates; 1 other country represented in student body.
Faculty School total: 56. In upper school: 26 men, 28 women; 11 have advanced degrees; 48 reside on campus.
Subjects Offered Algebra, American history, American literature, anthropology, art, art history, biology, botany, business skills, calculus, ceramics, chemistry, computer programming, computer science, creative writing, earth science, ecology, economics, English, English literature, environmental science, European history, expository writing, fine arts, geography, geology, geometry, government/civics, grammar, health, history, mathematics, photography, physical education, physics, science, social studies, trigonometry, typing, world history, world literature, zoology.
Graduation Requirements Arts and fine arts (art, music, dance, drama), English, mathematics, physical education (includes health), science, social studies (includes history).
Special Academic Programs Independent study; remedial reading and/or remedial writing; programs in English, mathematics, general development for dyslexic students.
College Admission Counseling 12 students graduated in 2014; 8 went to college, including Curry College; Landmark College; Mitchell College; Rhode Island School of Design; Xavier University. Other: 2 went to work, 1 entered a postgraduate year, 1 had other specific plans.
Student Life Upper grades have uniform requirement, student council, honor system. Discipline rests primarily with faculty.
Tuition and Aid Day student tuition: $49,900; 5-day tuition and room/board: $66,200; 7-day tuition and room/board: $68,900. Tuition installment plan (Tuition Management Systems). Need-based scholarship grants available. In 2014–15, 46% of upper-school students received aid. Total amount of financial aid awarded in 2014–15: $300,000.
Admissions Traditional secondary-level entrance grade is 9. For fall 2014, 60 students applied for upper-level admission, 43 were accepted, 23 enrolled. Wechsler Individual Achievement Test, WISC or WAIS, WISC/Woodcock-Johnson or Woodcock-Johnson Revised Achievement Test required. Deadline for receipt of application materials: none. Application fee required: $50. On-campus interview required.
Athletics Interscholastic: basketball (boys, girls); intramural: aerobics (g), basketball (b,g), dance (g); coed interscholastic: alpine skiing, lacrosse, skiing (downhill), snowboarding, soccer, softball, tennis, yoga; coed intramural: archery, basketball, bicycling, canoeing/kayaking, cross-country running, dressage, equestrian sports, fitness, fitness walking, flag football, freestyle skiing, golf, hiking/backpacking, horseback riding, ice skating, lacrosse, martial arts, mountain biking, outdoor activities, physical fitness, rock climbing, running, skiing (cross-country), skiing (downhill), snowboarding, soccer, strength & conditioning, table tennis, touch football, walking, water skiing, weight lifting, weight training.
Computers Computers are regularly used in English, mathematics, multimedia classes. Computer network features include on-campus library services, Internet access, wireless campus network. Student e-mail accounts and computer access in designated common areas are available to students. Students grades are available online. The school has a published electronic and media policy.
Contact Candie L. Fredritz, Admissions Assistant. 845-373-2012. Fax: 845-373-2004. E-mail: admissions@kildonan.org. Website: www.kildonan.org/

THE LAB SCHOOL OF WASHINGTON
4759 Reservoir Road NW
Washington, District of Columbia 20007
Head of School: Katherine Schantz
General Information Coeducational day college-preparatory and arts school; primarily serves students with learning disabilities, individuals with Attention Deficit Disorder, and dyslexic students. Grades 1–12. Founded: 1967. Setting: urban. 4-acre campus. 6 buildings on campus. Approved or accredited by Middle States Association of Colleges and Schools and District of Columbia Department of Education. Member of National Association of Independent Schools. Endowment: $3.5 million. Total enrollment: 375. Upper school average class size: 8. Upper school faculty-student ratio: 1:8. There are 180 required school days per year for Upper School students. Upper School students typically attend 5 days per week. The average school day consists of 6 hours and 30 minutes.
Upper School Student Profile Grade 9: 34 students (11 boys, 23 girls); Grade 10: 35 students (16 boys, 19 girls); Grade 11: 33 students (10 boys, 23 girls); Grade 12: 24 students (12 boys, 12 girls).
Faculty School total: 82. In upper school: 14 men, 13 women; 24 have advanced degrees.
Subjects Offered Algebra, American history, American literature, architecture, art, art history, biology, business, business skills, calculus, career education internship, chemistry, community service, creative writing, digital art, drama, earth science, English, English literature, environmental science, expository writing, film, fine arts, geography, geometry, government, government/civics, grammar, health, internship, Latin, mathematics, music, music appreciation, physical education, physical science, physics, public policy, rhetoric, science, social sciences, social studies, Spanish, technology, theater, trigonometry, video and animation, word processing, world history, writing.
Graduation Requirements Arts and fine arts (art, music, dance, drama), career education internship, computer science, English, foreign language, mathematics, physical education (includes health), science, social sciences, social studies (includes history), Senior Thesis. Community service is required.
Special Academic Programs Study abroad; academic accommodation for the gifted, the musically talented, and the artistically talented; remedial reading and/or remedial writing; remedial math; programs in English, mathematics, general development for dyslexic students.
College Admission Counseling 22 students graduated in 2014; 19 went to college, including American University; Davidson College; Gettysburg College; West Virginia Wesleyan College. Other: 2 went to work, 1 entered a postgraduate year.
Student Life Upper grades have specified standards of dress, student council. Discipline rests primarily with faculty.
Tuition and Aid Day student tuition: $41,995. Tuition installment plan (FACTS Tuition Payment Plan). Need-based scholarship grants, some students are funded by local public school systems available. In 2014–15, 9% of upper-school students received aid. Total amount of financial aid awarded in 2014–15: $164,700.
Admissions Traditional secondary level entrance grade is 9. For fall 2014, 30 students applied for upper-level admission, 16 were accepted, 11 enrolled. Latest standardized score from previous school, psychoeducational evaluation, WISC or WAIS or WISC-III and Woodcock-Johnson required. Deadline for receipt of application materials: January 15. Application fee required: $100. On-campus interview required.
Athletics Interscholastic: basketball (boys, girls), cross-country running (b,g), lacrosse (b,g), soccer (b,g), swimming and diving (b,g), track and field (b,g), volleyball (g); coed interscholastic: tennis. 2 PE instructors, 11 coaches.
Computers Computers are regularly used in all classes. Computer network features include on-campus library services, online commercial services, Internet access, wireless campus network, Internet filtering or blocking technology, iPads provided to all high school and eighth-grade students, Access to tech support. Student e-mail accounts and computer access in designated common areas are available to students. Students grades are available online. The school has a published electronic and media policy.
Contact Dr. Robert Lane, Director of Admissions. 202-944-2214. Fax: 202-454-2338. E-mail: robert.lane@labschool.org. Website: www.labschool.org

LA CHEIM SCHOOL
55 East 18th Street
Antioch, California 94509
Head of School: Ms. Sue Herrera
General Information Coeducational day general academic and vocational school; primarily serves underachievers, students with learning disabilities, individuals with Attention Deficit Disorder, individuals with emotional and behavioral problems, and Bipolar. Boys grades 6–12, girls grades 2–12. Founded: 1974. Setting: suburban. 1 building on campus. Approved or accredited by California Department of Education. Total enrollment: 8. Upper school average class size: 10. There are 180 required school days per year for Upper School students. Upper School students typically attend 5 days per week. The average school day consists of 6 hours.
Faculty School total: 1. In upper school: 1 woman.

Subjects Offered Adolescent issues, American government, American history, art, basic skills, biology, economics, grammar, health, language arts, life science, life skills, mathematics, physical education, physical science, science, social studies, vocational skills, world history, writing.

Special Academic Programs Remedial reading and/or remedial writing; remedial math.

College Admission Counseling 1 student graduated in 2015 and went to Baldwin Wallace University. Other: 1 had other specific plans.

Student Life Upper grades have specified standards of dress. Discipline rests primarily with faculty.

Summer Programs Remediation, enrichment, art/fine arts programs offered; session focuses on continuing education and mental health services; held on campus; accepts boys and girls; not open to students from other schools. 12 students usually enrolled. 2016 schedule: June 18 to July 31.

Tuition and Aid Tuition installment plan (expenses covered by referring district and county agencies with no cost to parents).

Admissions Traditional secondary-level entrance grade is 9. Deadline for receipt of application materials: none. No application fee required. On-campus interview required.

Athletics Intramural: basketball (boys, girls), flag football (b,g).

Computers Computers are regularly used in all academic classes. Computer resources include Internet access.

Contact Ms. Sue Herrera, Director. 925-777-1133. Fax: 925-777-9933. E-mail: sue@lacheim.org. Website: www.lacheim.org/schools/index.htm

LANDMARK EAST SCHOOL

708 Main Street
Wolfville, Nova Scotia B4P 1G4, Canada

Head of School: Peter Coll

General Information Coeducational boarding and day college-preparatory, arts, and technology school; primarily serves students with learning disabilities, individuals with Attention Deficit Disorder, and dyslexic students. Boarding grades 6–12, day grades 3–12. Founded: 1979. Setting: small town. Nearest major city is Halifax, Canada. Students are housed in single-sex dormitories. 5-acre campus. 4 buildings on campus. Approved or accredited by Nova Scotia Department of Education. Language of instruction: English. Endowment: CAN$1.3 million. Total enrollment: 71. Upper school average class size: 8. Upper school faculty-student ratio: 1:2. There are 180 required school days per year for Upper School students. Upper School students typically attend 5 days per week. The average school day consists of 6 hours and 45 minutes.

Upper School Student Profile Grade 6: 5 students (2 boys, 3 girls); Grade 7: 6 students (6 boys); Grade 8: 4 students (4 boys); Grade 9: 8 students (5 boys, 3 girls); Grade 10: 18 students (9 boys, 9 girls); Grade 11: 17 students (9 boys, 8 girls); Grade 12: 11 students (9 boys, 2 girls); Postgraduate: 1 student (1 girl). 40% of students are boarding students. 40% are province residents. 7 provinces are represented in upper school student body. 20% are international students. International students from Hong Kong, Japan, Nigeria, South Africa, Trinidad and Tobago, and United States.

Faculty School total: 35. In upper school: 10 men, 14 women; 2 have advanced degrees; 2 reside on campus.

Subjects Offered Accounting, art, biology, career and personal planning, chemistry, computer science, drama, economics, English, entrepreneurship, geography, geology, history, integrated science, law, mathematics, physics, strategies for success.

Graduation Requirements Canadian history.

Special Academic Programs Remedial reading and/or remedial writing; remedial math; programs in English, mathematics, general development for dyslexic students.

College Admission Counseling 17 students graduated in 2015; 14 went to college, including Saint Mary's University. Other: 2 went to work, 1 entered a postgraduate year.

Student Life Upper grades have uniform requirement, honor system. Discipline rests primarily with faculty.

Tuition and Aid Day student tuition: CAN$26,000–CAN$43,000; 7-day tuition and room/board: CAN$41,000–CAN$58,000. Tuition installment plan (monthly payment plans). Tuition reduction for siblings, bursaries, need-based scholarship grants available. In 2015–16, 50% of upper-school students received aid. Total amount of financial aid awarded in 2015–16: CAN$300,000.

Admissions Traditional secondary-level entrance grade is 10. Achievement tests, Cognitive Abilities Test and psychoeducational evaluation required. Deadline for receipt of application materials: none. Application fee required: CAN$100. Interview required.

Athletics Coed Interscholastic: cross-country running, running, track and field, volleyball, wrestling; coed intramural: aerobics, aerobics/dance, alpine skiing, aquatics, archery, badminton, ball hockey, basketball, bicycling, bowling, combined training, cooperative games, curling, dance, equestrian sports, fitness, fitness walking, flag football, floor hockey, Frisbee, handball, hiking/backpacking, horseback riding, ice skating, indoor soccer, jump rope, life saving, mountain biking, outdoor activities, outdoor education, outdoor recreation, rock climbing, running, skiing (cross-country), skiing (downhill), snowboarding, snowshoeing, soccer, softball, street hockey, strength & conditioning, table tennis, tennis, touch football, ultimate Frisbee, walking, weight lifting, weight training. 1 PE instructor.

Computers Computers are regularly used in art, English, mathematics, science classes. Computer network features include on-campus library services, online commercial services, Internet access, wireless campus network, Internet filtering or blocking technology. Student e-mail accounts and computer access in designated common areas are available to students. The school has a published electronic and media policy.

Contact Janet Cooper, Administrative Assistant. 902-542-2237 Ext. 227. Fax: 902-542-4147. E-mail: jcooper@landmarkeast.org. Website: www.landmarkeast.org

LANDMARK SCHOOL

PO Box 227
429 Hale Street
Prides Crossing, Massachusetts 01965-0227

Head of School: Robert J. Broudo

General Information Coeducational boarding and day college-preparatory, general academic, and language arts tutorial, skill-based curriculum school; primarily serves students with learning disabilities, dyslexic students, and language-based learning disabilities. Boarding grades 9–12, day grades 2–12. Founded: 1971. Setting: suburban. Nearest major city is Boston. Students are housed in single-sex dormitories. 50-acre campus. 23 buildings on campus. Approved or accredited by Association of Independent Schools in New England, Massachusetts Department of Education, Massachusetts Office of Child Care Services, National Association of Private Schools for Exceptional Children, New England Association of Schools and Colleges, and Massachusetts Department of Education. Member of National Association of Independent Schools. Endowment: $10 million. Total enrollment: 471. Upper school average class size: 8. Upper school faculty-student ratio: 1:3. There are 180 required school days per year for Upper School students. Upper School students typically attend 5 days per week. The average school day consists of 7 hours.

Upper School Student Profile Grade 9: 69 students (44 boys, 25 girls); Grade 10: 64 students (44 boys, 20 girls); Grade 11: 79 students (60 boys, 19 girls); Grade 12: 90 students (54 boys, 36 girls). 51% of students are boarding students. 78% are state residents. 22 states are represented in upper school student body. 3% are international students. International students from Aruba, China, India, Mexico, Oman, and Saudi Arabia.

Faculty School total: 126. In upper school: 40 men, 56 women; 50 have advanced degrees; 22 reside on campus.

Subjects Offered Advanced math, algebra, American government, American history, American literature, anatomy and physiology, art, auto mechanics, biology, boat building, calculus, calculus-AP, chemistry, chorus, communications, composition, computer science, consumer mathematics, creative writing, cultural geography, dance, drama, early childhood, environmental science, expressive arts, filmmaking, geometry, grammar, health education, integrated mathematics, language and composition, language arts, literature, marine science, modern world history, multimedia design, oral communications, oral expression, photography, physical education, physical science, portfolio art, pragmatics, pre-algebra, pre-calculus, reading, reading/study skills, senior thesis, sociology, study skills, technical theater, technology, U.S. history, woodworking, world history, yearbook.

Graduation Requirements English, mathematics, physical education (includes health), science, social studies (includes history), Landmark School competency tests, minimum grade equivalents on standardized tests in reading and reading comprehension.

Special Academic Programs Study at local college for college credit; remedial reading and/or remedial writing; remedial math; programs in English, mathematics, general development for dyslexic students; special instructional classes for deaf students.

College Admission Counseling 70 students graduated in 2015; 66 went to college, including Curry College; Endicott College; Lynn University; The University of Arizona; University of Denver; Westfield State University. Other: 1 entered military service, 3 had other specific plans. Mean SAT critical reading: 448, mean SAT math: 430, mean SAT writing: 441.

Student Life Upper grades have specified standards of dress, student council. Discipline rests primarily with faculty.

Summer Programs Remediation programs offered; session focuses on academic remediation and study skills; held on campus; accepts boys and girls; open to students from other schools. 140 students usually enrolled. 2016 schedule: June 30 to August 5. Application deadline: May 31.

Tuition and Aid Day student tuition: $52,900; 7-day tuition and room/board: $69,700. Tuition installment plan (Key Tuition Payment Plan). Need-based scholarship grants, community and staff grants available. In 2015–16, 5% of upper-school students received aid.

Admissions Traditional secondary-level entrance grade is 9. For fall 2015, 344 students applied for upper-level admission, 140 were accepted, 120 enrolled. Achievement tests, psychoeducational evaluation and WISC or WAIS required. Deadline for receipt of application materials: none. Application fee required: $150. On-campus interview required.

Athletics Interscholastic: baseball (boys), basketball (b,g), lacrosse (b,g), soccer (b,g), tennis (b,g), volleyball (g), wrestling (b); intramural: basketball (b,g), dance (g), floor hockey (b), weight lifting (b), weight training (b); coed interscholastic: cross-country running, golf, swimming and diving, track and field; coed intramural: ropes courses, sailing, skateboarding, skiing (downhill), yoga. 4 PE instructors, 1 athletic trainer.

Computers Computers are regularly used in all academic, programming, publishing, technology, yearbook classes. Computer network features include on-campus library services, Internet access, wireless campus network, Internet filtering or blocking technology. Student e-mail accounts are available to students. The school has a published electronic and media policy.

Contact Carol Bedrosian, Admission Liaison. 978-236-3420. Fax: 978-927-7268. E-mail: cbedrosian@landmarkschool.org. Website: www.landmarkschool.org

THE LAUREATE ACADEMY

100 Villa Maria Place

Winnipeg, Manitoba R3V 1A9, Canada

Head of School: Mr. Stino Siragusa

General Information Coeducational day college-preparatory school; primarily serves students with learning disabilities, individuals with Attention Deficit Disorder, and dyslexic students. Grades 1–12. Founded: 1987. Setting: suburban. 10-acre campus. 1 building on campus. Approved or accredited by Manitoba Department of Education. Language of instruction: English. Total enrollment: 80. Upper school average class size: 10. Upper school faculty-student ratio: 1:6. There are 183 required school days per year for Upper School students. Upper School students typically attend 5 days per week. The average school day consists of 6 hours and 15 minutes.

Upper School Student Profile Grade 9: 11 students (8 boys, 3 girls); Grade 10: 7 students (4 boys, 3 girls); Grade 11: 5 students (3 boys, 2 girls); Grade 12: 5 students (4 boys, 1 girl).

Faculty School total: 16. In upper school: 4 men, 3 women; 3 have advanced degrees.

Subjects Offered All academic.

Graduation Requirements Algebra, biology, Canadian geography, Canadian history, chemistry, communication skills, composition, computer skills, English, English literature, geometry, life issues, mathematics, physical education (includes health), physics, public speaking, science, social studies (includes history), writing, Department of Manitoba Education requirements, community service. Community service is required.

Special Academic Programs Academic accommodation for the gifted; remedial reading and/or remedial writing; remedial math; programs in English, mathematics for dyslexic students.

College Admission Counseling 5 students graduated in 2015; 3 went to college, including The University of Winnipeg; University of Manitoba. Other: 1 went to work, 1 entered a postgraduate year.

Student Life Upper grades have specified standards of dress, student council, honor system. Discipline rests primarily with faculty.

Summer Programs Remediation programs offered; session focuses on remedial reading; held on campus; accepts boys and girls; open to students from other schools. 8 students usually enrolled. 2016 schedule: July 6 to August 14. Application deadline: June 1.

Tuition and Aid Day student tuition: CAN$19,000. Tuition installment plan (monthly payment plans, quarterly payment plan). Tuition reduction for siblings, bursaries available. In 2015–16, 15% of upper-school students received aid. Total amount of financial aid awarded in 2015–16: CAN$60,000.

Admissions Traditional secondary-level entrance grade is 9. For fall 2015, 8 students applied for upper-level admission, 2 were accepted, 2 enrolled. WISC or WAIS, WISC-III and Woodcock-Johnson and writing sample required. Deadline for receipt of application materials: none. Application fee required: CAN$75. Interview required.

Athletics Interscholastic: basketball (boys), volleyball (b); intramural: badminton (b), ball hockey (b), basketball (b); coed interscholastic: badminton, cross-country running, soccer, track and field, volleyball; coed intramural: aerobics, alpine skiing, badminton, ball hockey, basketball, broomball, combined training, cooperative games, fitness, flag football, floor hockey, Frisbee, jogging, martial arts, outdoor activities, outdoor adventure, outdoor education, outdoor recreation, paddle tennis, physical fitness, physical training, running, self defense, skiing (downhill), snowboarding, soccer, softball, strength & conditioning, table tennis, touch football, track and field, ultimate Frisbee, volleyball, weight lifting, weight training. 2 PE instructors, 4 coaches.

Computers Computers are regularly used in career education, career exploration, computer applications, creative writing, English, mathematics, research skills, science, social studies, writing, yearbook classes. Computer network features include Internet access, wireless campus network, Internet filtering or blocking technology. Campus intranet, student e-mail accounts, and computer access in designated common areas are available to students. The school has a published electronic and media policy.

Contact Mrs. Dora Lawrie, Admissions Coordinator. 204-831-7107. Fax: 204-885-3217. E-mail: dlawrie@laureateacademy.com. Website: www.laureateacademy.com

LAWRENCE SCHOOL

Upper School

10036 Olde Eight Road

Sagamore Hills, Ohio 44067

Head of School: Mr. Lou Salza

General Information Coeducational day college-preparatory school; primarily serves students with learning disabilities, individuals with Attention Deficit Disorder, and dyslexic students. Grades K–12. Founded: 1969. Setting: suburban. Nearest major city is Cleveland. 47-acre campus. 1 building on campus. Approved or accredited by Independent Schools Association of the Central States and Ohio Department of Education. Member of National Association of Independent Schools. Endowment: $2 million. Total enrollment: 344. Upper school average class size: 11. Upper school faculty-student ratio: 1:11. There are 185 required school days per year for Upper School students. Upper School students typically attend 5 days per week. The average school day consists of 6 hours.

Faculty School total: 34. In upper school: 12 men, 22 women; 9 have advanced degrees.

Subjects Offered 20th century history, accounting, Advanced Placement courses, algebra, American history, American sign language, anatomy, art, astronomy, biology, calculus, choir, chorus, college counseling, computer applications, consumer economics, creative writing, debate, drama, earth science, economics, English, English composition, forensics, geography, geometry, global studies, government, graphic arts, graphic design, health, integrated mathematics, journalism, keyboarding, language arts, Latin, law, life science, life skills, mathematics, meteorology, military history, music, mythology, painting, physical education, physical science, physics, physics-AP, poetry, pre-algebra, psychology, research skills, sign language, society, politics and law, sociology, Spanish, speech, speech communications, The 20th Century, U.S. history, U.S. history-AP, video, video communication, Web site design, weight training, world geography, world history, yearbook.

Graduation Requirements Independent Study Project for Seniors, Service Learning Project.

Special Academic Programs Honors section; independent study; remedial reading and/or remedial writing; remedial math; programs in English, mathematics, general development for dyslexic students.

College Admission Counseling 40 students graduated in 2015; 35 went to college, including Chatham University; Cleveland State University; Kent State University; Ohio Wesleyan University; The College of Wooster; The University of Akron. Other: 1 went to work, 1 entered military service, 3 entered a postgraduate year.

Student Life Upper grades have specified standards of dress, student council, honor system. Discipline rests equally with students and faculty.

Tuition and Aid Day student tuition: $23,000–$25,434. Tuition installment plan (FACTS Tuition Payment Plan, monthly payment plans, individually arranged payment plans). Need-based scholarship grants available. In 2015–16, 30% of upper-school students received aid. Total amount of financial aid awarded in 2015–16: $900,000.

Admissions Traditional secondary-level entrance grade is 9. Admissions testing required. Deadline for receipt of application materials: none. Application fee required: $100. Interview required.

Athletics Interscholastic: baseball (boys), basketball (b,g), cross-country running (b,g); coed interscholastic: golf, swimming and diving; coed intramural: badminton, bowling, cooperative games, fishing, flag football, floor hockey, outdoor activities. 1 PE instructor.

Computers Computers are regularly used in all academic classes. Computer network features include on-campus library services, Internet access, wireless campus network, Internet filtering or blocking technology, one-to-one notebook laptop program for grades 9 to 12, laptop program for grades 7-8, school-wide social networking through Saywire. Student e-mail accounts are available to students. Students grades are available online. The school has a published electronic and media policy.

Contact Mrs. Mary Beth Petzke, Admissions Assistant. 440-526-0717. Fax: 440-526-0595. E-mail: mpetzke@lawrenceschool.org. Website: www.lawrenceschool.org

THE LEELANAU SCHOOL

One Old Homestead Road

Glen Arbor, Michigan 49636

Head of School: Mr. Matthew B. Ralston

General Information Coeducational boarding and day college-preparatory, arts, and experiential program school; primarily serves students with learning disabilities, individuals with Attention Deficit Disorder, dyslexic students, Attention Deficit Hyperactivity Disorder, language-based learning differences, and non-verbal learning disabilities. Grades 9–12. Founded: 1929. Setting: rural. Nearest major city is Traverse City. Students are housed in single-sex dormitories. 50-acre campus. 12 buildings on campus. Approved or accredited by Independent Schools Association of the Central States, Midwest Association of Boarding Schools, National Independent Private Schools Association, The Association of Boarding Schools, The College Board, and Michigan Department of Education. Member of National Association of Independent Schools and Secondary School Admission Test Board. Endowment: $435,200. Total enrollment: 50. Upper school average class size: 6. Upper school faculty-student ratio: 1:5. There are 165 required school days per year for Upper School students. Upper

School students typically attend 5 days per week. The average school day consists of 5 hours and 50 minutes.

Upper School Student Profile Grade 9: 5 students (4 boys, 1 girl); Grade 10: 6 students (5 boys, 1 girl); Grade 11: 18 students (13 boys, 5 girls); Grade 12: 21 students (18 boys, 3 girls). 93% of students are boarding students. 25% are state residents. 9 states are represented in upper school student body. 18% are international students. International students from Angola, China, Puerto Rico, Turkey, and United Kingdom; 3 other countries represented in student body.

Faculty School total: 18. In upper school: 10 men, 5 women; 9 have advanced degrees; 11 reside on campus.

Subjects Offered 20th century history, acting, Advanced Placement courses, advanced TOEFL/grammar, algebra, American Civil War, American government, American history, American literature, anatomy and physiology, ancient history, ancient world history, animation, applied arts, applied music, art, art appreciation, arts, arts and crafts, arts appreciation, astronomy, athletics, audio visual/media, backpacking, basic language skills, biology, biotechnology, boat building, botany, British literature, business studies, calculus, calculus-AP, calligraphy, career and personal planning, career exploration, career/college preparation, cartooning/animation, ceramics, character education, chemistry, civil war history, classical civilization, clayworking, college admission preparation, college awareness, college counseling, college placement, college planning, college writing, comedy, computer animation, computer science, conflict resolution, conservation, constitutional history of U.S., CPR, critical thinking, critical writing, decision making skills, developmental language skills, digital art, digital imaging, digital music, digital photography, drama, drama performance, dramatic arts, drawing, drawing and design, earth science, ecology, electives, English, English as a foreign language, English composition, English literature, entrepreneurship, environmental education, environmental science, environmental studies, environmental systems, epic literature, equestrian sports, equine management, ESL, European history, experiential education, experimental science, expository writing, family living, fiction, field ecology, film and new technologies, filmmaking, fine arts, foreign language, general science, geography, geology, geometry, golf, government/civics, grammar, great books, guitar, history, honors English, human anatomy, human biology, human relations, illustration, improvisation, independent living, independent study, instruments, integrated arts, integrated science, interpersonal skills, jazz band, jazz ensemble, jewelry making, journalism, Korean culture, language, language and composition, language arts, languages, leadership, leadership education training, learning cognition, learning lab, learning strategies, life issues, life management skills, life science, life skills, literacy, literature, literature by women, marine biology, marine ecology, marine science, marine studies, mathematics, mentorship program, modern European history, modern history, modern world history, moral and social development, moral reasoning, multicultural literature, music, music appreciation, Native American history, Native American studies, nature study, nature writers, oil painting, organizational studies, outdoor education, painting, participation in sports, photography, physics, poetry, pottery, pre-calculus, printmaking, psychology, reading/study skills, relationships, religious studies, remedial study skills, remedial/makeup course work, SAT preparation, SAT/ACT preparation, science, science and technology, science project, science research, senior thesis, Shakespeare, silk screening, social studies, Spanish, speech, sports, statistics-AP, student government, studio art, study skills, theater, TOEFL preparation, travel, trigonometry, U.S. government, U.S. government and politics, visual arts, weight training, weightlifting, wellness, wilderness education, wilderness experience, world history, writing, yearbook.

Graduation Requirements Arts and fine arts (art, music, dance, drama), CPR, English, foreign language, mathematics, science, senior thesis, social studies (includes history), senior leadership orientation.

Special Academic Programs 5 Advanced Placement exams for which test preparation is offered; honors section; independent study; term-away projects; remedial reading and/or remedial writing; remedial math; ESL (5 students enrolled).

College Admission Counseling 28 students graduated in 2015; 27 went to college, including Curry College; Michigan Technological University; The College of Wooster; The Evergreen State College. Other: 1 had other specific plans.

Student Life Upper grades have specified standards of dress, student council. Discipline rests primarily with faculty.

Summer Programs Remediation, enrichment, advancement, ESL programs offered; session focuses on remediation and advancement for students with learning differences; held on campus; accepts boys and girls; open to students from other schools. 20 students usually enrolled. 2016 schedule: July 8 to August 5. Application deadline: none.

Tuition and Aid Day student tuition: $30,625; 5-day tuition and room/board: $52,675; 7-day tuition and room/board: $61,350. Tuition installment plan (individually arranged payment plans). Tuition reduction for siblings, need-based scholarship grants, Beals Scholarship for legacy families available. In 2015–16, 25% of upper-school students received aid. Total amount of financial aid awarded in 2015–16: $200,000.

Admissions Traditional secondary-level entrance grade is 10. For fall 2015, 25 students applied for upper-level admission, 25 were accepted, 15 enrolled. Individual IQ, Achievement and behavior rating scale, psychoeducational evaluation, Stanford Test of Academic Skills, TOEFL or SLEP, Wechsler Intelligence Scale for Children, Wechsler Intelligence Scale for Children III, Woodcock-Johnson or writing sample required. Deadline for receipt of application materials: none. Application fee required: $50. On-campus interview required.

Athletics Interscholastic: basketball (boys), volleyball (g); coed interscholastic: dressage, equestrian sports, golf, soccer, tennis; coed intramural: alpine skiing, backpacking, bicycling, broomball, canoeing/kayaking, climbing, combined training, cross-country running, dance team, fishing, fitness, flag football, fly fishing, freestyle skiing, Frisbee, hiking/backpacking, horseback riding, independent competitive sports, jogging, kayaking, mountain biking, outdoor activities, outdoor adventure, outdoor education, outdoor recreation, outdoor skills, outdoors, paddling, paint ball, physical fitness, physical training, rock climbing, ropes courses, running, skiing (cross-country), skiing (downhill), snowboarding, snowshoeing, table tennis, triathlon, wall climbing, yoga. 1 PE instructor, 6 coaches, 1 athletic trainer.

Computers Computers are regularly used in all academic, animation, creative writing classes. Computer resources include on-campus library services, Internet access, wireless campus network, Internet filtering or blocking technology. Students grades are available online.

Contact Ms. Maleah R. Gluck, Director of Admission. 231-334-5824. Fax: 231-334-5898. E-mail: admissions@leelanau.org. Website: www.leelanau.org

LITTLE KESWICK SCHOOL

PO Box 24
Keswick, Virginia 22947

Head of School: Marc J. Columbus

General Information Boys' boarding arts school; primarily serves underachievers, students with learning disabilities, individuals with Attention Deficit Disorder, individuals with emotional and behavioral problems, and dyslexic students. Founded: 1963. Setting: small town. Nearest major city is Washington, DC. Students are housed in single-sex dormitories. 25-acre campus. 10 buildings on campus. Approved or accredited by Virginia Association of Independent Specialized Education Facilities and Virginia Department of Education. Total enrollment: 34. Upper school average class size: 7. Upper school faculty-student ratio: 1:3. There are 205 required school days per year for Upper School students. The average school day consists of 5 hours and 30 minutes.

Upper School Student Profile 100% of students are boarding students. 16 states are represented in upper school student body. 10% are international students. International students from Australia and Sweden.

Faculty School total: 6. In upper school: 3 men, 3 women; 5 have advanced degrees.

Subjects Offered Algebra, American history, biology, computer applications, earth science, English, geography, government/civics, health, industrial arts, mathematics, physical education, practical arts, social studies, world history.

Special Academic Programs Academic accommodation for the gifted; remedial reading and/or remedial writing; remedial math; programs in English, mathematics, general development for dyslexic students.

Student Life Upper grades have specified standards of dress. Discipline rests primarily with faculty.

Summer Programs Remediation, enrichment, sports, art/fine arts, rigorous outdoor training programs offered; session focuses on therapeutic; held on campus; accepts boys; open to students from other schools. 34 students usually enrolled. 2016 schedule: June 4 to August 20. Application deadline: June 1.

Tuition and Aid 7-day tuition and room/board: $111,028. Tuition installment plan (monthly payment plans). Need-based scholarship grants available. In 2015–16, 2% of upper-school students received aid. Total amount of financial aid awarded in 2015–16: $20,000.

Admissions Psychoeducational evaluation, Rorschach or Thematic Apperception Test and WISC/Woodcock-Johnson required. Deadline for receipt of application materials: none. Application fee required: $350. On-campus interview required.

Athletics Interscholastic: basketball (boys), combined training (b), soccer (b); intramural: aquatics (b), backpacking (b), basketball (b), bicycling (b), canoeing/kayaking (b), climbing (b), cross-country running (b), equestrian sports (b), fishing (b), fitness (b), hiking/backpacking (b), horseback riding (b), lacrosse (b), outdoor activities (b), outdoor adventure (b), outdoor education (b), outdoor recreation (b), outdoor skills (b), outdoors (b), physical fitness (b), rock climbing (b), running (b), soccer (b). 1 PE instructor, 2 coaches.

Computers Computer network features include Internet access. Computer access in designated common areas is available to students. The school has a published electronic and media policy.

Contact Ms. Terry Columbus, Director. 434-295-0457 Ext. 14. Fax: 434-977-1892. E-mail: tcolumbus@littlekeswickschool.net. Website: www.littlekeswickschool.net

MAPLEBROOK SCHOOL

5142 Route 22
Amenia, New York 12501

Head of School: Donna M. Konkolics

General Information Coeducational boarding and day general academic, vocational, technology, iPad program, and Executive Functioning school; primarily serves underachievers, students with learning disabilities, individuals with Attention Deficit Disorder, and low average cognitive ability (minimum I.Q. of 70). Ungraded, ages 11–18. Founded: 1945. Setting: small town. Nearest major city is Poughkeepsie. Students are housed in single-sex dormitories. 100-acre campus. 25 buildings on campus. Approved or accredited by Middle States Association of Colleges and Schools, National Association of Private Schools for Exceptional Children, New York Department of Education, New York State Board of Regents, US Department of State, and New York Department of Education. Member of National Association of Independent Schools. Endowment: $500,000. Total enrollment: 75. Upper school average class size: 6. Upper school faculty-student ratio: 1:8. There are 180 required school days per year for Upper School students. Upper School students typically attend 7 days per week. The average school day consists of 6 hours and 5 minutes.

Upper School Student Profile 98% of students are boarding students. 10% are state residents. 18 states are represented in upper school student body. 25% are international students. International students from Bermuda, Ghana, Hong Kong, Mexico, Nigeria, and Trinidad and Tobago; 6 other countries represented in student body.

Faculty School total: 55. In upper school: 12 men, 14 women; 26 have advanced degrees; 50 reside on campus.

Subjects Offered Algebra, American history, art, biology, business skills, computer science, consumer mathematics, creative writing, drama, driver education, earth science, English, geography, global studies, government/civics, health, home economics, industrial arts, integrated mathematics, keyboarding, mathematics, music, occupational education, performing arts, photography, physical education, physical science, science, social skills, speech, theater, world history, writing.

Graduation Requirements Career and personal planning, computer science, English, mathematics, physical education (includes health), science, social sciences, social skills, social studies (includes history), attendance at Maplebrook School for a minimum of 2 years.

Special Academic Programs Study at local college for college credit; remedial reading and/or remedial writing; remedial math; programs in English, mathematics, general development for dyslexic students; ESL (3 students enrolled).

College Admission Counseling 15 students graduated in 2015; 4 went to college, including Curry College; Dutchess Community College; Mitchell College. Other: 3 went to work, 8 entered a postgraduate year.

Student Life Upper grades have specified standards of dress, student council, honor system. Discipline rests primarily with faculty.

Summer Programs Remediation, enrichment, sports, art/fine arts, computer instruction programs offered; session focuses on preventing regression of skills; held both on and off campus; held at various locations for New York City day and overnight trips; accepts boys and girls; open to students from other schools. 70 students usually enrolled. 2016 schedule: July 3 to August 13. Application deadline: none.

Tuition and Aid Day student tuition: $35,000; 5-day tuition and room/board: $58,000; 7-day tuition and room/board: $63,000. Tuition installment plan (Key Tuition Payment Plan, individually arranged payment plans, Tuition Management Systems Plan, Sallie Mae loans). Merit scholarship grants, need-based scholarship grants, need-based loans, middle-income loans, paying campus jobs, minority and cultural diversity scholarships, day student scholarships, merit scholarships available. In 2015–16, 20% of upper-school students received aid; total upper-school merit-scholarship money awarded: $10,000. Total amount of financial aid awarded in 2015–16: $100,000.

Admissions Traditional secondary-level entrance age is 15. For fall 2015, 179 students applied for upper-level admission, 68 were accepted, 31 enrolled. Achievement tests, Bender Gestalt, TerraNova, Test of Achievement and Proficiency or WISC or WAIS required. Deadline for receipt of application materials: none. No application fee required. Interview required.

Athletics Interscholastic: basketball (boys, girls), cheering (g), field hockey (g); coed interscholastic: cooperative games, cross-country running, equestrian sports, fitness, freestyle skiing, horseback riding, running, skiing (cross-country), skiing (downhill), soccer, softball, swimming and diving, tennis, track and field, weight lifting, weight training; coed intramural: aerobics/dance, alpine skiing, basketball, bicycling, bowling, cooperative games, cricket, dance, figure skating, fitness, fitness walking, flag football, floor hockey, freestyle skiing, golf, hiking/backpacking, horseback riding, ice skating, indoor hockey, martial arts, outdoor education, outdoor recreation, roller blading, skiing (cross-country), skiing (downhill), soccer, softball, Special Olympics, swimming and diving, table tennis, tennis, volleyball, weight lifting, weight training, wrestling. 1 PE instructor, 12 coaches.

Computers Computers are regularly used in all academic classes. Computer network features include on-campus library services, Internet access, wireless campus network, Internet filtering or blocking technology. Campus intranet, student e-mail accounts, and computer access in designated common areas are available to students. Students grades are available online. The school has a published electronic and media policy.

Contact Christine Place, Assistant Director of Admissions. 845-373-8191. Fax: 845-373-7029. E-mail: admissions@maplebrookschool.org. Website: www.maplebrookschool.org

MILL SPRINGS ACADEMY

13660 New Providence Road
Alpharetta, Georgia 30004

Head of School: Mr. Robert W. Moore

General Information Coeducational day college-preparatory and arts school; primarily serves students with learning disabilities, individuals with Attention Deficit Disorder, and dyslexic students. Grades 1–12. Founded: 1981. Setting: suburban.

Nearest major city is Atlanta. 85-acre campus. 5 buildings on campus. Approved or accredited by Georgia Association of Private Schools for Exceptional Children, Georgia Independent School Association, Southern Association of Colleges and Schools, and Southern Association of Independent Schools. Member of National Association of Independent Schools. Endowment: $140,000. Total enrollment: 355. Upper school average class size: 6. Upper school faculty-student ratio: 1:6. There are 180 required school days per year for Upper School students. Upper School students typically attend 5 days per week. The average school day consists of 7 hours.

Upper School Student Profile Grade 9: 44 students (32 boys, 12 girls); Grade 10: 44 students (34 boys, 10 girls); Grade 11: 44 students (31 boys, 13 girls); Grade 12: 49 students (37 boys, 12 girls).

Faculty School total: 56. In upper school: 14 men, 18 women; 20 have advanced degrees.

Subjects Offered Algebra, American history, American literature, anatomy and physiology, art, band, biology, British literature, British literature (honors), calculus, career/college preparation, chemistry, Chinese, chorus, composition, creative writing, diversity studies, drama, ecology, economics, film, geometry, government, health, history, honors algebra, honors English, honors geometry, honors U.S. history, honors world history, journalism, literature, media, music theater, performing arts, physical education, physics, play production, play/screen writing, playwriting and directing, political science, pre-algebra, pre-calculus, psychology, sculpture, senior project, set design, Spanish, state government, studio art, symphonic band, technology, theater, theater design and production, trigonometry, U.S. history, values and decisions, visual and performing arts, voice, world literature, yearbook.

Graduation Requirements Algebra, American history, American literature, anatomy and physiology, biology, British literature, British literature (honors), calculus, chemistry, civics, ecology, economics, foreign language, geometry, physical education (includes health), physics, trigonometry, world history, world literature, senior English, 6 units of electives.

Special Academic Programs Honors section; study at local college for college credit; academic accommodation for the gifted, the musically talented, and the artistically talented; programs in English, mathematics, general development for dyslexic students.

College Admission Counseling 31 students graduated in 2015; all went to college, including Georgia College & State University; Georgia Perimeter College; Georgia State University; Reinhardt University; Savannah College of Art and Design; Young Harris College. Mean SAT critical reading: 504, mean SAT math: 477, mean SAT writing: 491, mean combined SAT: 1472, mean composite ACT: 19. 21% scored over 600 on SAT critical reading, 29% scored over 600 on SAT math, 14% scored over 600 on SAT writing, 29% scored over 1800 on combined SAT, 29% scored over 26 on composite ACT.

Student Life Upper grades have uniform requirement, student council, honor system. Discipline rests equally with students and faculty.

Summer Programs Enrichment, sports programs offered; session focuses on skills development or course credit; held on campus; accepts boys and girls; open to students from other schools. 160 students usually enrolled. 2016 schedule: June 13 to July 29. Application deadline: June 10.

Tuition and Aid Day student tuition: $22,151. Tuition installment plan (FACTS Tuition Payment Plan). Tuition reduction for siblings, need-based scholarship grants available. In 2015–16, 14% of upper-school students received aid. Total amount of financial aid awarded in 2015–16: $110,000.

Admissions Traditional secondary-level entrance grade is 9. For fall 2015, 53 students applied for upper-level admission, 29 were accepted, 26 enrolled. Psychoeducational evaluation required. Deadline for receipt of application materials: none. Application fee required: $100. On-campus interview required.

Athletics Interscholastic: baseball (boys), basketball (b,g), golf (b), lacrosse (b), tennis (b,g), volleyball (g), wrestling (b); intramural: cheering (g), strength & conditioning (b), weight lifting (b); coed interscholastic: cross-country running, soccer, swimming and diving, track and field; coed intramural: archery, dance, fencing, fishing, golf, mountain biking, outdoor activities, physical fitness, scuba diving, yoga. 1 PE instructor, 2 coaches.

Computers Computers are regularly used in all academic classes. Computer network features include on-campus library services, online commercial services, Internet access, wireless campus network, Internet filtering or blocking technology, all students 4-12th grades have laptops, electronic textbooks/literature books, assignments online. Student e-mail accounts are available to students. Students grades are available online. The school has a published electronic and media policy.

Contact Mrs. Sheila FitzGerald, Admissions Director. 770-360-1336 Ext. 1707. Fax: 770-360-1341. E-mail: sfitzgerald@millsprings.org. Website: www.millsprings.org

THE MONARCH SCHOOL

2815 Rosefield Drive
Houston, Texas 77080

Head of School: Vita Como

General Information Boys' day and distance learning college-preparatory, general academic, arts, business, vocational, and technology school; primarily serves underachievers, students with learning disabilities, individuals with Attention Deficit Disorder, individuals with emotional and behavioral problems, dyslexic students,

students with PDD spectrum disorders, mood disorders, Executive Functioning Disorder, other neurological-based disorders, and social coordination, and emotional regulation issues. Grades K–8. Distance learning grades 9–12. Founded: 1997. Setting: suburban. 11-acre campus. 5 buildings on campus. Approved or accredited by National Association of Private Schools for Exceptional Children and Southern Association of Colleges and Schools. Total enrollment: 135. Upper school average class size: 8. Upper school faculty-student ratio: 1:2. Upper School students typically attend 5 days per week. The average school day consists of 8 hours.

Faculty School total: 85. In upper school: 6 men, 12 women; 4 have advanced degrees.

Subjects Offered 20th century history, 20th century physics, 20th century world history, 3-dimensional art, 3-dimensional design, accounting, ADL skills, adolescent issues, advanced computer applications, advanced math, algebra, American Civil War, American culture, American government, American history, American legal systems, American literature, ancient history, ancient world history, animal behavior, applied music, art, art and culture, arts and crafts, athletics, automated accounting, banking, basic language skills, biology, boat building, body human, botany, business, business applications, business communications, business education, business mathematics, business skills, business studies, business technology, calculus, career and personal planning, career education, career education internship, career experience, career exploration, career planning, career/college preparation, carpentry, cell biology, chemistry, child development, civics, civics/free enterprise, civil rights, Civil War, civil war history, college admission preparation, college placement, comparative government and politics, competitive science projects, composition, computer animation, computer applications, computer education, computer graphics, computer literacy, computer skills, conflict resolution, conservation, construction, consumer economics, consumer education, consumer mathematics, contemporary history, crafts, creative arts, creative drama, culinary arts, current history, dance, decision making skills, democracy in America, developmental math, drawing, drawing and design, earth science, ecology, ecology, environmental systems, economics, English, English composition, entrepreneurship, environmental education, environmental geography, environmental science, environmental studies, epic literature, ethics, ethics and responsibility, European history, field ecology, fine arts, food and nutrition, food science, foods, foreign language, gardening, general science, geography, geology, geometry, government, government/civics, health, health and safety, health and wellness, health education, high adventure outdoor program, history, horticulture, independent living, inquiry into relationship, instrumental music, instruments, integrated physics, Internet, internship, interpersonal skills, Japanese, jewelry making, journalism, keyboarding, language arts, language development, language enhancement and development, leadership, leadership and service, leadership education training, learning lab, learning strategies, life skills, literacy, literature, logic, mathematics, mentorship program, moral and social development, moral reasoning, music appreciation, music performance, music theory, natural history, nature study, newspaper, North American literature, novels, nutrition, occupational education, outdoor education, peace and justice, peace education, personal and social education, personal development, personal finance, personal fitness, personal money management, physical education, physical fitness, physics, play production, play/screen writing, poetry, practical living, pre-algebra, pre-calculus, pre-vocational education, public speaking, publications, reading, reading/study skills, relationships, remedial study skills, SAT preparation, SAT/ACT preparation, science, senior project, service learning/internship, sexuality, skills for success, social issues, social skills, social studies, Spanish, speech communications, sports, standard curriculum, state government, strategies for success, student government, student publications, student teaching, techniques of living and coping, Texas history, the Presidency, the Sixties, transition mathematics, trigonometry, U.S. government, U.S. government and politics, U.S. history, values and decisions, video communication, vocational arts, vocational skills, vocational-technical courses, voice, wellness, Western civilization, wilderness education, wilderness experience, women's literature, wood lab, woodworking, work experience, work-study, world civilizations, world cultures, world geography, world history, writing, writing, yearbook.

Special Academic Programs International Baccalaureate program; Advanced Placement exam preparation; accelerated programs; independent study; study at local college for college credit; academic accommodation for the gifted and the artistically talented; remedial reading and/or remedial writing; remedial math; programs in English, mathematics, general development for dyslexic students; special instructional classes for Autistic.

College Admission Counseling 15 students graduated in 2015; 5 went to college, including Houston Baptist University; Houston Community College; St. Edward's University. Other: 10 went to work. Mean SAT critical reading: 690, mean SAT math: 605. 67% scored over 600 on SAT critical reading, 33% scored over 600 on SAT math.

Student Life Upper grades have uniform requirement, student council, honor system. Discipline rests primarily with students.

Summer Programs Remediation, enrichment, art/fine arts, computer instruction programs offered; session focuses on relationship development, self-esteem, and executive functioning; held both on and off campus; held at various venues (field trips); accepts boys and girls; open to students from other schools. 100 students usually enrolled. 2016 schedule: June 14 to July 15. Application deadline: March 15.

Tuition and Aid Day student tuition: $26,000–$38,000. Tuition installment plan (monthly payment plans, individually arranged payment plans, quarterly, yearly

payment plans). Need-based scholarship grants, need-based loans available. In 2015–16, 40% of upper-school students received aid. Total amount of financial aid awarded in 2015–16: $105,350.

Admissions Achievement tests and Individual IQ required. Deadline for receipt of application materials: none. Application fee required: $550. On-campus interview required.

Computers Computers are regularly used in business skills classes. Computer network features include Internet access, Internet filtering or blocking technology. Student e-mail accounts are available to students. The school has a published electronic and media policy.

Contact Ms. Jacquice Jones, Director of Admissions. 713-479-0800. Fax: 713-464-7499. E-mail: jjones@monarchschool.org. Website: www.monarchschool.org

NOBLE ACADEMY

3310 Horse Pen Creek Road
Greensboro, North Carolina 27410

Head of School: Linda Hale

General Information Coeducational day college-preparatory, arts, and technology school; primarily serves students with learning disabilities, individuals with Attention Deficit Disorder, and dyslexic students. Grades K–12. Founded: 1987. Setting: suburban. Nearest major city is Greensboro/Winston-Salem. 40-acre campus. 3 buildings on campus. Approved or accredited by North Carolina Department of Exceptional Children, Southern Association of Colleges and Schools, Southern Association of Independent Schools, and North Carolina Department of Education. Member of National Association of Independent Schools. Endowment: $2.5 million. Total enrollment: 160. Upper school average class size: 9. Upper school faculty-student ratio: 1:9. There are 180 required school days per year for Upper School students. Upper School students typically attend 5 days per week. The average school day consists of 6 hours and 45 minutes.

Upper School Student Profile Grade 10: 26 students (21 boys, 5 girls); Grade 11: 23 students (14 boys, 9 girls); Grade 12: 15 students (9 boys, 6 girls).

Faculty School total: 34. In upper school: 3 men, 14 women; 9 have advanced degrees.

Subjects Offered Algebra, American history, art, basic skills, biology, career and personal planning, career exploration, chemistry, civics, college counseling, drama, earth science, economics, English, environmental science, geometry, health, journalism, life management skills, political systems, pre-algebra, pre-calculus, reading, reading/study skills, Spanish, world history, world history-AP, yearbook.

Graduation Requirements Algebra, American history, biology, earth science, economics, English, environmental science, geometry, physical education (includes health), Spanish, world history, 8th grade end-of-grade test, 20th percentile score on standardized reading test, North Carolina Computer Competency Test.

Special Academic Programs Study at local college for college credit; remedial reading and/or remedial writing; remedial math; programs in English, mathematics, general development for dyslexic students.

College Admission Counseling 15 students graduated in 2015; all went to college, including Brevard College; Elon University; Guilford College; St. Andrews University; The University of North Carolina at Greensboro; William Peace University. Median SAT critical reading: 548, median SAT math: 454, median SAT writing: 496. Mean combined SAT: 1510. 22% scored over 600 on SAT critical reading, 11% scored over 600 on SAT writing.

Student Life Upper grades have student council, honor system. Discipline rests primarily with faculty.

Tuition and Aid Day student tuition: $19,200. Tuition installment plan (monthly payment plans, individually arranged payment plans). Need-based scholarship grants available. In 2015–16, 14% of upper-school students received aid. Total amount of financial aid awarded in 2015–16: $81,000.

Admissions Traditional secondary-level entrance grade is 10. For fall 2015, 9 students applied for upper-level admission, 5 were accepted, 3 enrolled. WISC/Woodcock-Johnson required. Deadline for receipt of application materials: none. Application fee required: $75. On-campus interview required.

Athletics Interscholastic: cheering (girls); coed interscholastic: basketball, cross-country running, flag football, Frisbee, golf, soccer, tennis, touch football, volleyball. 1 PE instructor, 7 coaches.

Computers Computers are regularly used in art, career education, career exploration, career technology, college planning, computer applications, current events, graphic arts, graphic design, history, information technology, introduction to technology, journalism, keyboarding, lab/keyboard, photography, social studies, Spanish, study skills, word processing, writing, writing, yearbook classes. Computer network features include on-campus library services, Internet access, wireless campus network, Internet filtering or blocking technology. Campus intranet and student e-mail accounts are available to students. Students grades are available online. The school has a published electronic and media policy.

Contact Christy Avent, Director of Advancement and Admissions. 336-282-7044. Fax: 336-282-2048. E-mail: cavent@nobleknights.org. Website: www.nobleknights.org

NORMAN HOWARD SCHOOL

275 Pinnacle Road
Rochester, New York 14623

Head of School: Linda Lawrence

General Information Coeducational day college-preparatory, general academic, and arts school; primarily serves underachievers, students with learning disabilities, individuals with Attention Deficit Disorder, dyslexic students, and autism (high functioning), anxiety. Grades 5–12. Founded: 1980. Setting: suburban. 2-acre campus. 1 building on campus. Approved or accredited by New York State Board of Regents and New York Department of Education. Total enrollment: 121. Upper school average class size: 10. Upper school faculty-student ratio: 1:3. There are 180 required school days per year for Upper School students. Upper School students typically attend 5 days per week. The average school day consists of 6 hours and 30 minutes.

Upper School Student Profile Grade 9: 19 students (12 boys, 7 girls); Grade 10: 26 students (20 boys, 6 girls); Grade 11: 17 students (10 boys, 7 girls); Grade 12: 20 students (15 boys, 5 girls).

Faculty School total: 42. In upper school: 13 men, 12 women; 17 have advanced degrees.

Subjects Offered Algebra, American history, American literature, art, athletics, biology, career/college preparation, chemistry, creative writing, drama, earth science, ecology, economics, English, English literature, environmental science, European history, expository writing, fine arts, geography, geometry, government/civics, history, keyboarding, life science, mathematics, photography, physical education, reading, reading/study skills, science, social studies, world history, writing.

Graduation Requirements Arts and fine arts (art, music, dance, drama), English, mathematics, physical education (includes health), science, social studies (includes history).

Special Academic Programs Independent study; study at local college for college credit; remedial reading and/or remedial writing; remedial math; programs in English, mathematics, general development for dyslexic students; special instructional classes for deaf students.

College Admission Counseling 22 students graduated in 2015; 12 went to college, including Monroe Community College. Other: 1 went to work, 9 had other specific plans.

Student Life Upper grades have uniform requirement, student council, honor system. Discipline rests equally with students and faculty.

Tuition and Aid Day student tuition: $27,500. Tuition installment plan (monthly payment plans, 60/40 payment option plan). Need-based scholarship grants, substantial financial aid to families who qualify available.

Admissions Traditional secondary-level entrance grade is 9. Deadline for receipt of application materials: none. Application fee required: $50. On-campus interview required.

Athletics Coed Intramural: outdoor adventure, outdoor education, physical fitness, skiing (downhill). 2 PE instructors.

Computers Computers are regularly used in creative writing, English, history, library skills, mathematics, photography, reading, science, social studies, writing, yearbook classes. Computer network features include on-campus library services, Internet access, wireless campus network, Internet filtering or blocking technology. Campus intranet and computer access in designated common areas are available to students. Students grades are available online. The school has a published electronic and media policy.

Contact Julie Murray, Associate Director of Admissions and Special Events. 585-334-8010 Ext. 302. Fax: 585-334-8073. E-mail: jmurray@normanhoward.org. Website: www.normanhoward.org

OAKLAND SCHOOL

128 Oakland Farm Way
Troy, Virginia 22974

Head of School: Ms. Carol Williams

General Information Coeducational boarding and day general academic school; primarily serves underachievers, students with learning disabilities, individuals with Attention Deficit Disorder, dyslexic students, processing difficulties, and organizational/executive functioning challenges. Boarding grades 4–8, day grades 1–8. Founded: 1950. Setting: rural. Nearest major city is Richmond. Students are housed in single-sex dormitories. 450-acre campus. 25 buildings on campus. Approved or accredited by Virginia Association of Independent Specialized Education Facilities. Upper school average class size: 5. Upper school faculty-student ratio: 1:5. There are 180 required school days per year for Upper School students. Upper School students typically attend 5 days per week. The average school day consists of 6 hours and 45 minutes.

Upper School Student Profile 40% of students are boarding students. 35% are state residents. 8 states are represented in upper school student body. 18% are international students. International students from Indonesia, Italy, and Oman.

Faculty School total: 10. In upper school: 2 men, 8 women; 6 have advanced degrees.

Subjects Offered Algebra, American history, art, art and culture, art appreciation, art history, computer literacy, computer skills, consumer mathematics, drama, drama performance, earth science, English, English composition, expository writing, geometry, grammar, health, health and wellness, health education, history of the Americas, keyboarding, life science, mathematics, physical education, physical science, remedial study skills, study skills, U.S. and Virginia history, world history.

Graduation Requirements Skills must be at or above grade/ability level.

Special Academic Programs Remedial reading and/or remedial writing; remedial math; programs in English, mathematics, general development for dyslexic students.

College Admission Counseling 12 students graduated in 2015.

Student Life Upper grades have specified standards of dress, student council, honor system. Discipline rests primarily with faculty.

Summer Programs Remediation, sports, art/fine arts, computer instruction programs offered; session focuses on academics; held on campus; accepts boys and girls; open to students from other schools. 110 students usually enrolled. 2016 schedule: June 27 to July 27.

Tuition and Aid Day student tuition: $28,325; 7-day tuition and room/board: $49,450. Tuition installment plan (SMART Tuition Payment Plan, individually arranged payment plans). Need-based scholarship grants available.

Admissions Wechsler Intelligence Scale for Children III required. Deadline for receipt of application materials: none. No application fee required. Interview required.

Athletics Interscholastic: basketball (boys, girls), cross-country running (b,g), fitness (g), handball (b,g), horseback riding (b,g), running (b,g), soccer (b,g), wilderness (g); intramural: cheering (g), soccer (b,g); coed interscholastic: basketball, cross-country running, handball, horseback riding, running, soccer; coed intramural: aerobics/dance, archery, basketball, bicycling, billiards, cooperative games, cross-country running, dance, drill team, equestrian sports, fishing, fitness, Frisbee, hiking/backpacking, horseback riding, in-line skating, indoor soccer, jogging, kickball, lacrosse, mountain biking, outdoor activities, outdoor adventure, outdoor education, outdoor recreation, outdoor skills, outdoors, paddle tennis, physical fitness, physical training, roller blading, roller skating, running, skateboarding, soccer, softball, swimming and diving, table tennis, tennis, volleyball, walking, wilderness, yoga. 1 PE instructor, 4 coaches.

Computers Computers are regularly used in English, literacy, reading, remedial study skills, research skills, social studies, study skills, word processing, writing classes. Computer resources include Internet access. The school has a published electronic and media policy.

Contact Mrs. Jamie Cato, Admissions Director. 434-293-9059. Fax: 434-296-8930. E-mail: admissions@oaklandschool.net. Website: www.oaklandschool.net

PACE/BRANTLEY HALL HIGH SCHOOL

3221 Sand Lake Road
Longwood, Florida 32779

Head of School: Pamela Tapley

General Information Coeducational day college-preparatory and general academic school; primarily serves underachievers, students with learning disabilities, individuals with Attention Deficit Disorder, dyslexic students, students with mild to moderate Austism, Asperger's Syndrome, and ADHD, and similar types of learning disabilities. Grades 1–12. Founded: 1972. Setting: suburban. Nearest major city is Orlando. 8-acre campus. 2 buildings on campus. Approved or accredited by Florida Council of Independent Schools. Total enrollment: 171. Upper school average class size: 10. Upper school faculty-student ratio: 1:12. There are 174 required school days per year for Upper School students. Upper School students typically attend 5 days per week. The average school day consists of 7 hours and 15 minutes.

Upper School Student Profile Grade 9: 27 students (18 boys, 9 girls); Grade 10: 22 students (13 boys, 9 girls); Grade 11: 19 students (18 boys, 1 girl); Grade 12: 15 students (10 boys, 5 girls).

Faculty School total: 24. In upper school: 2 men, 11 women; 5 have advanced degrees.

Subjects Offered 3-dimensional art, 3-dimensional design, algebra, American history, American literature, art, biology, chemistry, computer art, computer graphics, drama, English, English literature, fine arts, fitness, geography, geometry, government/civics, grammar, leadership, mathematics, photo shop, physical education, physical science, psychology, public speaking, reading, science, social sciences, social studies, speech, theater, world history, writing.

Graduation Requirements Arts and fine arts (art, music, dance, drama), English, foreign language, mathematics, physical education (includes health), reading, science, social studies (includes history), high school competency test.

Special Academic Programs 1 Advanced Placement exam for which test preparation is offered; honors section; study at local college for college credit; academic accommodation for the gifted; remedial reading and/or remedial writing; remedial math; programs in English, mathematics, general development for dyslexic students.

College Admission Counseling 13 students graduated in 2015; 8 went to college, including Beacon College; Florida Atlantic University; Seminole State College of Florida; Stetson University; University of North Florida; Valencia College. Other: 2 entered a postgraduate year, 3 had other specific plans.

Student Life Upper grades have uniform requirement, honor system. Discipline rests primarily with faculty.

Summer Programs Remediation, enrichment, advancement, art/fine arts, computer instruction programs offered; session focuses on course work and orientation for incoming students; held on campus; accepts boys and girls; open to students from other schools. 20 students usually enrolled. 2016 schedule: June 13 to July 8. Application deadline: May 1.

Tuition and Aid Day student tuition: $15,435. Tuition installment plan (monthly payment plans, individually arranged payment plans, semiannual payment plan). Tuition reduction for siblings, need-based scholarship grants, McKay Scholarship, PLSA, Step Up For Students available. In 2015–16, 98% of upper-school students received aid.

Admissions Traditional secondary-level entrance grade is 9. For fall 2015, 20 students applied for upper-level admission, 18 were accepted, 17 enrolled. Academic Profile Tests and WRAT required. Deadline for receipt of application materials: none. No application fee required. On-campus interview required.

Athletics Interscholastic: basketball (boys); coed interscholastic: fitness, physical fitness; coed intramural: ball hockey, field hockey, flag football, fly fishing, football, kickball, soccer, track and field. 1 PE instructor, 1 coach.

Computers Computers are regularly used in desktop publishing, graphic arts, keyboarding classes. Computer network features include on-campus library services, Internet access, wireless campus network, Internet filtering or blocking technology. Campus intranet, student e-mail accounts, and computer access in designated common areas are available to students. Students grades are available online. The school has a published electronic and media policy.

Contact Pamela Susan Bellet, Admission Director. 407-869-8882 Ext. 221. Fax: 407-869-8717. E-mail: pbellet@pacebrantley.org. Website: www.pacebrantley.org

THE PATHWAY SCHOOL

162 Egypt Road
Jeffersonville, Pennsylvania 19403

Head of School: Mr. David Schultheis

General Information Coeducational day general academic, life skills/functional academics, and pre-vocational/career education school; primarily serves underachievers, students with learning disabilities, individuals with Attention Deficit Disorder, individuals with emotional and behavioral problems, students w/ neurological impairment, students w/ neuropsychiatric disorders, Asperger's Syndrome, emotional disturbance, and students needing speech/language therapy and occupational therapy. Ungraded, ages 6–21. Founded: 1961. Setting: suburban. Nearest major city is Philadelphia. 12-acre campus. 12 buildings on campus. Approved or accredited by Pennsylvania Department of Education. Endowment: $1 million. Total enrollment: 135. Upper school average class size: 8. Upper school faculty-student ratio: 1:5. There are 181 required school days per year for Upper School students. Upper School students typically attend 5 days per week. The average school day consists of 5 hours and 30 minutes.

Faculty School total: 18. In upper school: 2 men, 4 women; 4 have advanced degrees.

Subjects Offered Algebra, art, biology, career education, career experience, career/college preparation, computer skills, consumer mathematics, creative arts, drama, earth science, electives, English, environmental science, general math, geometry, health education, history, horticulture, interpersonal skills, language arts, mathematics, money management, physical education, pre-vocational education, senior seminar, social skills, social studies, work experience, world history.

Graduation Requirements Graduation requirements are as specified by the sending school district.

Special Academic Programs Study at local college for college credit; remedial reading and/or remedial writing; remedial math; programs in general development for dyslexic students; special instructional classes for emotional support program.

College Admission Counseling 14 students graduated in 2015; 3 went to college. Other: 11 went to work.

Student Life Upper grades have student council, honor system. Discipline rests equally with students and faculty.

Summer Programs Remediation programs offered; session focuses on providing consistency for the entire calendar year; held on campus; accepts boys and girls; open to students from other schools. 85 students usually enrolled. 2016 schedule: July 11 to August 19.

Tuition and Aid Day student tuition: $46,790. Tuition installment plan (individually arranged payment plans).

Admissions Traditional secondary-level entrance age is 15. For fall 2015, 4 students applied for upper-level admission, 2 were accepted, 2 enrolled. Deadline for receipt of application materials: none. No application fee required. On-campus interview required.

Athletics Interscholastic: basketball (boys, girls), softball (b,g), Special Olympics (b,g); coed interscholastic: soccer, Special Olympics; coed intramural: basketball, flag football, soccer. 2 PE instructors, 2 coaches.

Computers Computers are regularly used in basic skills, business education, business skills, career education, data processing, newspaper, typing classes. Computer network features include Internet access, Internet filtering or blocking technology, computer access in classroom, tablet technology provided to all students. Student e-mail accounts and computer access in designated common areas are available to students. The school has a published electronic and media policy.

Contact Diana Phifer, Director of Admissions. 610-277-0660 Ext. 289. Fax: 610-539-1493. E-mail: dphifer@pathwayschool.org. Website: www.pathwayschool.org

PURNELL SCHOOL

51 Pottersville Road
PO Box 500
Pottersville, New Jersey 07979

Head of School: Jessica Eckert and Donna Ruggiero

General Information Girls' boarding and day college-preparatory, general academic, and arts school; primarily serves students with learning disabilities, individuals with Attention Deficit Disorder, and dyslexic students. Grades 9–12. Founded: 1963. Setting: rural. Nearest major city is New York, NY. Students are housed in single-sex dormitories. 83-acre campus. 23 buildings on campus. Approved or accredited by Middle States Association of Colleges and Schools, New Jersey Association of Independent Schools, and New Jersey Department of Education. Member of National Association of Independent Schools and Secondary School Admission Test Board. Endowment: $9 million. Total enrollment: 70. Upper school average class size: 10. Upper school faculty-student ratio: 1:4. There are 180 required school days per year for Upper School students. Upper School students typically attend 5 days per week. The average school day consists of 6 hours and 15 minutes.

Upper School Student Profile Grade 9: 15 students (15 girls); Grade 10: 15 students (15 girls); Grade 11: 22 students (22 girls); Grade 12: 18 students (18 girls). 99% of students are boarding students. 45% are state residents. 14 states are represented in upper school student body. 18% are international students. International students from China, Czech Republic, Democratic People's Republic of Korea, Kazakhstan, Mexico, and Nigeria; 2 other countries represented in student body.

Faculty School total: 19. In upper school: 2 men, 17 women; 11 have advanced degrees; 15 reside on campus.

Subjects Offered 3-dimensional art, algebra, American history, American literature, anatomy, art, art history, biology, calculus, ceramics, chemistry, creative writing, dance, drama, English, English literature, environmental science, fashion, fine arts, French, geography, geometry, government/civics, health, history, mathematics, music, photography, physical education, science, Shakespeare, social sciences, social studies, Spanish, speech, statistics, theater, trigonometry, women's studies, world history, world literature, writing.

Graduation Requirements Art history, arts and fine arts (art, music, dance, drama), English, foreign language, history, mathematics, performing arts, physical education (includes health), science, Project Exploration.

Special Academic Programs Independent study; study abroad; programs in English, mathematics, general development for dyslexic students; ESL (15 students enrolled).

College Admission Counseling 27 students graduated in 2014; 24 went to college, including Boston College; Goucher College; Hampshire College; Lynn University; Mitchell College; Savannah College of Art and Design. Other: 3 had other specific plans.

Student Life Upper grades have uniform requirement, student council. Discipline rests primarily with faculty.

Tuition and Aid Day student tuition: $41,300; 5-day tuition and room/board: $52,800; 7-day tuition and room/board: $54,700. Tuition installment plan (individually arranged payment plans). Need-based scholarship grants, prepGATE loans available. In 2014–15, 30% of upper-school students received aid. Total amount of financial aid awarded in 2014–15: $700,000.

Admissions Traditional secondary-level entrance grade is 9. For fall 2014, 80 students applied for upper-level admission, 50 were accepted, 25 enrolled. WISC/Woodcock-Johnson required. Deadline for receipt of application materials: none. Application fee required: $50. Interview required.

Athletics Interscholastic: basketball, dance, dance team, soccer, softball, tennis; intramural: aerobics, aerobics/dance, ballet, equestrian sports, fitness, horseback riding, jogging, modern dance, outdoor adventure, physical training, self defense, strength & conditioning, weight training, yoga. 1 PE instructor, 3 coaches.

Computers Computers are regularly used in English, foreign language, graphic design, history, mathematics, science classes. Computer network features include on-campus library services, Internet access, wireless campus network, Internet filtering or blocking technology. Campus intranet, student e-mail accounts, and computer access in designated common areas are available to students. Students grades are available online. The school has a published electronic and media policy.

Contact Mrs. Gena Parks, Associate Director of Admissions. 908-439-4025. Fax: 908-439-4088. E-mail: gparks@purnell.org. Website: www.purnell.org

RIVER OAKS ACADEMY

10600 Richmond Avenue
Houston, Texas 77042

Head of School: Dr. Luis A. Valdes, PhD

General Information Coeducational day college-preparatory and general academic school; primarily serves underachievers, students with learning disabilities, individuals with Attention Deficit Disorder, and individuals with emotional and behavioral problems. Grades K–12. Founded: 1998. Setting: urban. Students are housed in private homes. 1 building on campus. Approved or accredited by Southern Association of Colleges and Schools, Texas Education Agency, and Texas Department of Education. Total enrollment: 46. Upper school average class size: 7. Upper school faculty-student ratio: 1:7. There are 176 required school days per year for Upper School students. Upper School students typically attend 5 days per week. The average school day consists of 5 hours and 50 minutes.

Upper School Student Profile Grade 10: 9 students (6 boys, 3 girls); Grade 11: 8 students (3 boys, 5 girls); Grade 12: 16 students (9 boys, 7 girls).

Faculty School total: 6. In upper school: 3 men, 3 women.

Subjects Offered Algebra, art, calculus, computer technologies, dance, English, food and nutrition, French, geometry, government, integrated physics, language arts, mathematics, physical education, pre-algebra, pre-calculus, SAT preparation, social studies, U.S. government, U.S. history, vocational skills, world geography, world history.

Special Academic Programs Study at local college for college credit; special instructional classes for blind students.

College Admission Counseling 2 students graduated in 2014; 1 went to college, including Houston Community College. Other: 1 went to work.

Student Life Upper grades have student council. Discipline rests primarily with faculty.

Tuition and Aid Day student tuition: $17,000–$45,000. Guaranteed tuition plan. Tuition installment plan (monthly payment plans, individually arranged payment plans).

Admissions Traditional secondary-level entrance grade is 12. For fall 2014, 47 students applied for upper-level admission, 47 were accepted, 44 enrolled. Deadline for receipt of application materials: none. Application fee required: $300. Interview recommended.

Athletics Coed Intramural: aerobics, aerobics/dance, badminton, ballet, basketball, Cosom hockey, dance, fitness, kickball, modern dance, outdoor recreation, walking.

Computers Computers are regularly used in technology classes. Computer network features include Internet access, wireless campus network. Students grades are available online. The school has a published electronic and media policy.

Contact Mrs. Lisa Green, Assistant Principal. 713-783-7200. Fax: 713-783-7286. E-mail: roainfo@gmail.com. Website: www.riveroaksacademy.com/

ROBERT LAND ACADEMY

6727 South Chippawa Road
Wellandport, Ontario L0R 2J0, Canada

Head of School: Lt. Col. G. Scott Bowman

General Information Boys' boarding college-preparatory, arts, business, English and Math foundational building, and military school; primarily serves underachievers, students with learning disabilities, individuals with Attention Deficit Disorder, individuals with emotional and behavioral problems, dyslexic students, Oppositional Defiant Disorder, and Attention Deficit Hyperactive Disorder. Grades 5–12. Founded: 1978. Setting: rural. Nearest major city is Hamilton, Canada. Students are housed in single-sex dormitories and barracks. 168-acre campus. 14 buildings on campus. Approved or accredited by Ontario Ministry of Education and Ontario Department of Education. Language of instruction: English. Total enrollment: 125. Upper school average class size: 14. Upper school faculty-student ratio: 1:14. Upper School students typically attend 7 days per week. The average school day consists of 6 hours and 30 minutes.

Upper School Student Profile Grade 9: 20 students (20 boys); Grade 10: 33 students (33 boys); Grade 11: 29 students (29 boys); Grade 12: 15 students (15 boys). 100% of students are boarding students. 48% are province residents. 14 provinces are represented in upper school student body. 20% are international students. International students from China, Hong Kong, Mexico, Nigeria, United Arab Emirates, and United States; 3 other countries represented in student body.

Faculty School total: 14. In upper school: 14 men; 7 have advanced degrees.

Subjects Offered Advanced biology, advanced chemistry, advanced math, algebra, all academic, American history, ancient history, art, art history, athletic training, athletics, band, basic language skills, biology, bookkeeping, British history, business, calculus, Canadian geography, Canadian history, Canadian literature, career planning, career/college preparation, chemistry, civics, computer applications, computer art, computer education, computer graphics, computer information systems, computer processing, computer programming, computer science, computer skills, computer studies, computers, creative writing, economics, English, English literature, environmental geography, environmental science, environmental studies, ethical decision making, ethics, ethics and responsibility, European history, French, functions, geography, health education, history, language, language arts, leadership, life management skills, military history, navigation, nutrition, personal fitness, physical education, physical fitness, physics, reading, science, scuba diving, sports, survival training, values and decisions, volleyball, weight fitness, weight training, weightlifting, wilderness education, wilderness experience, wrestling.

Graduation Requirements Ontario Literacy Equivalence Test, minimum 40 hours of community service.

Special Academic Programs Honors section; independent study; remedial reading and/or remedial writing; remedial math; programs in general development for dyslexic students; ESL (10 students enrolled).

College Admission Counseling 21 students graduated in 2014; 20 went to college, including Carleton University; McGill University; McMaster University; Ryerson University; Wilfrid Laurier University. Other: 1 went to work.

Student Life Upper grades have uniform requirement, student council, honor system. Discipline rests primarily with faculty.

Tuition and Aid 7-day tuition and room/board: CAN$41,300. Tuition installment plan (monthly payment plans, individually arranged payment plans). Tuition reduction for siblings, bursaries, merit scholarship grants, need-based scholarship grants, middle-income loans available. In 2014–15, 5% of upper-school students received aid.

Admissions Traditional secondary-level entrance grade is 11. Deadline for receipt of application materials: none. Application fee required: CAN$250. Interview required.

Athletics Interscholastic: badminton, basketball, boxing, climbing, cross-country running, running, soccer, track and field, volleyball, wall climbing, wrestling; intramural: aerobics/Nautilus, archery, backpacking, badminton, ball hockey, baseball, basketball, bicycling, boxing, canoeing/kayaking, climbing, cross-country running, drill team, fishing, fitness, fitness walking, flag football, floor hockey, Frisbee, hiking/backpacking, hockey, ice hockey, ice skating, indoor hockey, indoor soccer, jogging, JROTC drill, life saving, marksmanship, mountain biking, Nautilus, outdoor activities, outdoor adventure, outdoor education, outdoor recreation, outdoor skills, outdoors, paddling, paint ball, physical fitness, physical training, rafting, rappelling, riflery, rock climbing, running, scuba diving, skydiving, snowshoeing, soccer, softball, strength & conditioning, touch football, track and field, volleyball, wall climbing, weight lifting, weight training, wilderness, wilderness survival, winter walking, wrestling. 2 PE instructors.

Computers Computer network features include Internet access, Internet filtering or blocking technology.

Contact Admissions Officer. 905-386-6203. Fax: 905-386-6607. E-mail: admissions@rla.ca. Website: www.robertlandacademy.com

ROBERT LOUIS STEVENSON SCHOOL

24 West 74th Street
New York, New York 10023

Head of School: Robert Cunningham

General Information Coeducational day college-preparatory school; primarily serves underachievers, students with learning disabilities, individuals with Attention Deficit Disorder, individuals with emotional and behavioral problems, and dyslexic students. Grades 7–PG. Founded: 1908. Setting: urban. 1 building on campus. Approved or accredited by New York Department of Education. Member of National Association of Independent Schools. Total enrollment: 61. Upper school average class size: 8. Upper school faculty-student ratio: 1:5. There are 165 required school days per year for Upper School students. Upper School students typically attend 5 days per week. The average school day consists of 6 hours and 30 minutes.

Upper School Student Profile Grade 8: 6 students (4 boys, 2 girls); Grade 9: 5 students (3 boys, 2 girls); Grade 10: 9 students (6 boys, 3 girls); Grade 11: 21 students (8 boys, 13 girls); Grade 12: 18 students (11 boys, 7 girls).

Faculty School total: 16. In upper school: 7 men, 9 women; 8 have advanced degrees.

Subjects Offered Algebra, American history, American literature, anatomy, ancient history, ancient world history, ancient/medieval philosophy, art, biology, calculus, ceramics, chemistry, creative writing, current history, drama, earth and space science, earth science, English, English literature, environmental science, European civilization, European history, expository writing, film appreciation, geometry, government/civics, grammar, health, history, history of ideas, mathematics, philosophy, physical education, physics, physiology, poetry, political science, political thought, pre-algebra, pre-calculus, psychology, robotics, science, senior project, sex education, Shakespeare, social sciences, social studies, theater, trigonometry, world literature, writing.

Graduation Requirements American history, computer literacy, English, health education, mathematics, physical education (includes health), science, social sciences, social studies (includes history), portfolio of work demonstrating readiness to graduate.

Special Academic Programs Accelerated programs; independent study; academic accommodation for the gifted; remedial reading and/or remedial writing; remedial math; programs in English, mathematics, general development for dyslexic students.

College Admission Counseling 17 students graduated in 2014; 15 went to college, including Bentley University; City University of New York System; Pace University; State University of New York System. Other: 1 went to work, 1 had other specific plans.

Student Life Upper grades have student council. Discipline rests primarily with faculty.

Tuition and Aid Day student tuition: $57,500. Tuition installment plan (individually arranged payment plans). Need-based scholarship grants, need-based loans available. In 2014–15, 5% of upper-school students received aid. Total amount of financial aid awarded in 2014–15: $50,000.

Admissions Traditional secondary-level entrance grade is 10. For fall 2014, 68 students applied for upper-level admission, 44 were accepted, 37 enrolled. Psychoeducational evaluation required. Deadline for receipt of application materials: none. No application fee required. On-campus interview required.

Athletics Coed Interscholastic: basketball, bowling, cross-country running, fitness, floor hockey, jogging, soccer, softball, track and field, yoga; coed intramural: aerobics, ball hockey, basketball, bicycling, blading, bowling, cooperative games, fitness, flag football, floor hockey, jogging, judo, juggling, martial arts, physical fitness, physical training, soccer, softball, strength & conditioning, table tennis, tennis, touch football, track and field, volleyball, weight lifting, weight training, yoga. 1 PE instructor.

Computers Computers are regularly used in art, English, history, mathematics, science, technology classes. Computer network features include Internet access, wireless campus network, Internet filtering or blocking technology. Student e-mail accounts and computer access in designated common areas are available to students. The school has a published electronic and media policy.

Contact Alessandro Mitrotti, Admissions Coordinator. 212-787-6400. Fax: 646-224-9466. E-mail: amitrotti@stevenson-school.org. Website: www.stevenson-school.org

SEDONA SKY ACADEMY

PO Box 230
Rimrock, Arizona 86335

Head of School: Tammy Behrmann

General Information Girls' boarding college-preparatory and general academic school; primarily serves students with learning disabilities, individuals with Attention Deficit Disorder, and individuals with emotional and behavioral problems. Grades 9–12. Founded: 1998. Setting: rural. Nearest major city is Sedona. Students are housed in single-sex dormitories. 29-acre campus. 8 buildings on campus. Approved or accredited by CITA (Commission on International and Trans-Regional Accreditation) and Arizona Department of Education. Total enrollment: 90. Upper school average class size: 10. Upper school faculty-student ratio: 1:10. Upper School students typically attend 5 days per week. The average school day consists of 6 hours.

Upper School Student Profile Grade 9: 20 students (20 girls); Grade 10: 20 students (20 girls); Grade 11: 25 students (25 girls); Grade 12: 25 students (25 girls). 100% of students are boarding students. 20% are state residents. 22 states are represented in upper school student body. 5% are international students.

Faculty School total: 12. In upper school: 5 men, 7 women; 3 have advanced degrees; 2 reside on campus.

Subjects Offered ACT preparation, acting, adolescent issues, advanced math, algebra, American Civil War, American government, American history, American literature, ancient history, ancient world history, applied arts, applied music, art, art and culture, art appreciation, art education, art history, arts, athletic training, athletics, ballet, ballet technique, basketball, biology, botany, British literature, business, business communications, business mathematics, calculus, career planning, character education, chemistry, child development, choir, chorus, civics, Civil War, civil war history, college admission preparation, college awareness, college counseling, college placement, college planning, college writing, communication skills, communications, community garden, community service, comparative civilizations, composition, computer applications, computer education, computer graphics, computer literacy, computer math, computer science, computer skills, computers, consumer mathematics, contemporary art, contemporary history, contemporary issues, creative arts, creative dance, creative writing, current events, dance, dance performance, decision making skills, drama, drama performance, drama workshop, dramatic arts, drawing, drawing and design, earth science, economics, economics and history, electives, English, English composition, English literature, equality and freedom, equestrian sports, equine management, equine science, ethical decision making, European history, European literature, experiential education, female experience in America, film appreciation, fine arts, fitness, food and nutrition, foreign language, foreign policy, French, gender issues, general science, geography, geology, geometry, global studies, government, government/civics, grammar, graphic arts, health, health and safety, health and wellness, health education, health science, heritage of American Women, history, history of dance, history of drama, home economics, human biology, human development, human sexuality, independent living, international studies, intro to computers, jazz dance, journalism, lab/keyboard, language, language and composition, language arts, leadership, leadership education training, learning strategies, library, life issues, life management skills, life skills, linear algebra, literature, literature by women, math applications, mathematics, modern dance, modern languages, moral and social development, music, music appreciation, music composition, music history, music performance, musical productions, musical theater, nature study, news writing, newspaper, non-Western literature, nutrition, oil painting, parenting, participation in sports, peer counseling, performing arts, personal development, personal growth, physical education, physics, play production, poetry, political science, political systems, portfolio art, pre-calculus, psychology, SAT preparation, SAT/ACT preparation, science, sex education, sexuality, Shakespeare, Shakespearean histories, social issues, sociology, softball, Spanish, Spanish literature, speech, speech and debate, sports, sports conditioning, stage and body movement, state history, statistics, student government, student publications, studio art, study skills, tap dance, theater, theater arts, theater history, theater production, trigonometry, U.S. government, U.S. government and politics, U.S. history, U.S. literature, visual and performing arts, visual arts, vocal music, volleyball, water color painting, weight fitness, weightlifting, wellness, Western literature, women in literature, women's health, women's literature, world civilizations, world cultures, world geography, world history, world studies, writing, writing, yoga.

Graduation Requirements Option of traditional academic graduation as well as graduation from the therapeutic side of school.

Special Academic Programs Accelerated programs; independent study; study at local college for college credit; academic accommodation for the gifted, the musically talented, and the artistically talented; programs in English, mathematics for dyslexic students.

Student Life Upper grades have uniform requirement, student council, honor system. Discipline rests primarily with faculty.

Tuition and Aid Middle-income loans available. In 2014–15, 30% of upper-school students received aid. Total amount of financial aid awarded in 2014–15: $81,600.

Admissions Traditional secondary-level entrance grade is 10. For fall 2014, 400 students applied for upper-level admission, 150 were accepted, 90 enrolled. SAT required. Deadline for receipt of application materials: none. No application fee required.

Athletics Interscholastic: basketball, soccer, softball, volleyball; intramural: aerobics, aerobics/dance, badminton, ballet, basketball, cross-country running, dance, fitness, fitness walking, horseback riding, jogging, modern dance, physical fitness, physical training, soccer, softball, track and field, walking, yoga. 2 PE instructors, 1 coach, 1 athletic trainer.

Computers Computers are regularly used in all academic classes. Computer network features include Internet access, Internet filtering or blocking technology. Student e-mail accounts are available to students. Students grades are available online. The school has a published electronic and media policy.

Contact Stephanie Coleman, Admissions Counselor. 877-617-1222 Ext. 116. Fax: 928-567-1323. E-mail: stephaniecoleman@sedonasky.org. Website: www.coppercanyonacademy.com

SHELTON SCHOOL AND EVALUATION CENTER

15720 Hillcrest Road
Dallas, Texas 75248

Head of School: Linda Kneese

General Information Coeducational day college-preparatory and general academic school; primarily serves students with learning disabilities, individuals with Attention Deficit Disorder, and dyslexic students. Grades PS–12. Founded: 1976. Setting: suburban. 1-acre campus. 1 building on campus. Approved or accredited by Independent Schools Association of the Southwest. Endowment: $6.5 million. Total enrollment: 895. Upper school average class size: 8. Upper school faculty-student ratio: 1:10. There are 166 required school days per year for Upper School students. Upper School students typically attend 5 days per week. The average school day consists of 6 hours.

Upper School Student Profile Grade 9: 72 students (41 boys, 31 girls); Grade 10: 76 students (46 boys, 30 girls); Grade 11: 70 students (44 boys, 26 girls); Grade 12: 60 students (33 boys, 27 girls).

Faculty School total: 138. In upper school: 13 men, 27 women; 17 have advanced degrees.

Subjects Offered All academic, American sign language, ethics, Spanish, theater arts.

Graduation Requirements Arts and fine arts (art, music, dance, drama), computers, English, ethics, foreign language, mathematics, physical education (includes health), reading, science, social studies (includes history), speech.

Special Academic Programs Programs in English, mathematics, general development for dyslexic students.

College Admission Counseling 51 students graduated in 2015; 49 went to college, including Albright College; Arkansas State University; Baylor University; Collin County Community College District; Savannah College of Art and Design; Texas Christian University. Other: 2 had other specific plans.

Student Life Upper grades have uniform requirement, student council, honor system. Discipline rests primarily with faculty.

Summer Programs Enrichment programs offered; session focuses on enrichment; held on campus; accepts boys and girls; open to students from other schools. 39 students usually enrolled. 2016 schedule: June 27 to July 22. Application deadline: May 6.

Tuition and Aid Day student tuition: $26,000. Tuition installment plan (SMART Tuition Payment Plan, Sallie Mae). Need-based scholarship grants available. In 2015–16, 17% of upper-school students received aid. Total amount of financial aid awarded in 2015–16: $516,800.

Admissions Traditional secondary-level entrance grade is 9. For fall 2015, 61 students applied for upper-level admission, 26 were accepted, 22 enrolled. WISC/Woodcock-Johnson required. Deadline for receipt of application materials: none. No application fee required. Interview required.

Athletics Interscholastic: baseball (boys), basketball (b,g), cheering (g), cross-country running (b,g), dance squad (g), drill team (g), football (b), tennis (b,g), track and field (b,g), volleyball (g); coed interscholastic: golf, physical training, soccer, strength & conditioning. 4 PE instructors, 2 coaches, 1 athletic trainer.

Computers Computers are regularly used in all academic, English, foreign language, information technology, lab/keyboard, library, research skills, SAT preparation, video film production classes. Computer network features include on-campus library services, Internet access, wireless campus network, Internet filtering or blocking technology. Campus intranet, student e-mail accounts, and computer access in designated common areas are available to students. Students grades are available online. The school has a published electronic and media policy.

Contact Diann Slaton, Director of Admission. 972-774-1772. Fax: 972-991-3977. E-mail: dslaton@shelton.org. Website: www.shelton.org

SMITH SCHOOL
131 West 86 Street
New York, New York 10024
Head of School: Karen Smith

General Information Coeducational day college-preparatory, arts, technology, and art, music, drama and technology programs school; primarily serves students with learning disabilities, individuals with Attention Deficit Disorder, and depression or anxiety disorders, emotional and/or motivational issues. Grades 7–12. Founded: 1990. Setting: urban. 1 building on campus. Approved or accredited by Middle States Association of Colleges and Schools, New York State Association of Independent Schools, New York State Board of Regents, and New York Department of Education. Total enrollment: 57. Upper school average class size: 4. Upper school faculty-student ratio: 1:4. There are 160 required school days per year for Upper School students. Upper School students typically attend 5 days per week. The average school day consists of 6 hours and 30 minutes.

Upper School Student Profile Grade 9: 10 students (4 boys, 6 girls); Grade 10: 11 students (4 boys, 7 girls); Grade 11: 9 students (4 boys, 5 girls); Grade 12: 12 students (5 boys, 7 girls).

Faculty School total: 14. In upper school: 6 men, 8 women; all have advanced degrees.

Subjects Offered Algebra, American history, art, biology, chemistry, computer skills, earth science, English, environmental science, European history, film, French, geometry, lab science, life science, oceanography, physical science, physics, pre-calculus, Spanish, trigonometry, U.S. government, U.S. history, world history.

Graduation Requirements Algebra, American history, art, biology, chemistry, conceptual physics, earth science, English, environmental science, European history, geometry, government, health education, languages, physical education (includes health), physical science, pre-algebra, pre-calculus, trigonometry, world history, mandatory extracurricular activity involvement, 100 hours of community service completed.

Special Academic Programs Accelerated programs; independent study; study at local college for college credit; academic accommodation for the musically talented and the artistically talented; remedial reading and/or remedial writing; remedial math; programs in English, mathematics, general development for dyslexic students; special instructional classes for peer mediation, socialization, and motivational issues.

College Admission Counseling 12 students graduated in 2015; all went to college, including American University; Emerson College; Fordham University; State University of New York at New Paltz; Syracuse University; Tulane University. Median SAT critical reading: 600, median SAT math: 620, median SAT writing: 620, median combined SAT: 600. 50% scored over 600 on SAT critical reading, 40% scored over 600 on SAT math, 50% scored over 600 on SAT writing, 45% scored over 1800 on combined SAT, 60% scored over 26 on composite ACT.

Student Life Upper grades have student council, honor system. Discipline rests primarily with faculty.

Summer Programs Remediation, enrichment, advancement, art/fine arts, computer instruction programs offered; session focuses on academic courses for enrichment, remediation, or credit; held both on and off campus; held at local colleges; accepts boys and girls; open to students from other schools. 25 students usually enrolled. 2016 schedule: June 14 to August 16. Application deadline: June 1.

Tuition and Aid Day student tuition: $42,000–$52,500. Tuition installment plan (monthly payment plans, individually arranged payment plans, quarterly payment plan). Tuition reduction for siblings available. In 2015–16, 10% of upper-school students received aid.

Admissions Traditional secondary-level entrance grade is 9. For fall 2015, 47 students applied for upper-level admission, 26 were accepted, 21 enrolled. Comprehensive educational evaluation, psychoeducational evaluation, school placement exam, Wide Range Achievement Test or writing sample required. Deadline for receipt of application materials: none. Application fee required: $50. On-campus interview required.

Athletics Coed Interscholastic: aerobics, basketball, cooperative games, dance, fitness, fitness walking, outdoor activities, physical fitness, physical training, running, ultimate Frisbee, volleyball, walking, yoga; coed intramural: basketball, cooperative games. 3 PE instructors, 3 coaches.

Computers Computers are regularly used in creative writing, English, history, research skills, writing, yearbook classes. Computer network features include Internet access, wireless campus network, Internet filtering or blocking technology, yearbook and monthly newsletter. Campus intranet and computer access in designated common areas are available to students. Students grades are available online. The school has a published electronic and media policy.

Contact Gladys Lopez, Executive Assistant. 212-879-6317. Fax: 212-879-0962. E-mail: glopez@smithschool.org. Website: www.smithschool.org

STANBRIDGE ACADEMY
515 East Poplar Avenue
San Mateo, California 94401
Head of School: Mrs. Marilyn Lynch

General Information Coeducational day general academic, arts, and technology school; primarily serves underachievers, students with learning disabilities, individuals with Attention Deficit Disorder, and Autism Spectrum Disorder. Grades K–12.

Founded: 1982. Setting: suburban. Nearest major city is San Francisco. 1-acre campus. 1 building on campus. Approved or accredited by Western Association of Schools and Colleges. Total enrollment: 98. Upper school average class size: 8. Upper school faculty-student ratio: 1:8. There are 182 required school days per year for Upper School students. Upper School students typically attend 5 days per week. The average school day consists of 7 hours and 30 minutes.

Upper School Student Profile Grade 6: 15 students (14 boys, 1 girl); Grade 7: 12 students (9 boys, 3 girls); Grade 8: 7 students (4 boys, 3 girls); Grade 9: 9 students (8 boys, 1 girl); Grade 10: 10 students (9 boys, 1 girl); Grade 11: 13 students (9 boys, 4 girls); Grade 12: 11 students (8 boys, 3 girls); Postgraduate: 3 students (2 boys, 1 girl).

Faculty School total: 30. In upper school: 10 men, 3 women; 2 have advanced degrees.

Subjects Offered Algebra, American government, biology, career/college preparation, ceramics, college planning, English, English literature, experiential education, general math, geography, geometry, health education, mathematics, physical education, physics, pragmatics, pre-algebra, pre-calculus, probability and statistics, science, social sciences, Spanish, U.S. history, world cultures, world history, yearbook.

Graduation Requirements Algebra, American government, biology, English, English composition, English literature, experiential education, foreign language, geometry, health and wellness, physical education (includes health), physical science, physics, trigonometry, U.S. history, visual and performing arts, world cultures.

Special Academic Programs Remedial reading and/or remedial writing; remedial math; programs in English, mathematics for dyslexic students.

College Admission Counseling 8 students graduated in 2014; 5 went to college, including Academy of Art University; Foothill College; Notre Dame de Namur University. Other: 3 had other specific plans. Median SAT critical reading: 600, median SAT math: 600, median SAT writing: 500.

Student Life Upper grades have specified standards of dress, student council. Discipline rests primarily with faculty.

Tuition and Aid Day student tuition: $33,300. Tuition installment plan (monthly payment plans). Need-based scholarship grants available. In 2014–15, 10% of upper-school students received aid. Total amount of financial aid awarded in 2014–15: $80,000.

Admissions Traditional secondary-level entrance grade is 9. For fall 2014, 4 students applied for upper-level admission, 3 were accepted, 3 enrolled. Math and English placement tests or psychoeducational evaluation required. Deadline for receipt of application materials: none. Application fee required: $100. On-campus interview required.

Athletics Coed Intramural: aerobics, badminton, basketball, climbing, cooperative games, cross-country running, dance, fitness walking, flag football, Frisbee, hockey, jogging, kickball, outdoor education, outdoor skills, physical fitness, physical training, soccer, Special Olympics, strength & conditioning, swimming and diving, table tennis, touch football, track and field, volleyball, walking, yoga. 3 PE instructors.

Computers Computers are regularly used in Spanish, yearbook classes. Computer network features include on-campus library services, Internet access, wireless campus network, Internet filtering or blocking technology. Campus intranet, student e-mail accounts, and computer access in designated common areas are available to students. Students grades are available online. The school has a published electronic and media policy.

Contact Ms. Susan Coyne, Director of Admissions. 650-375-5860 Ext. 202. Fax: 650-375-5861. E-mail: scoyne@stanbridgeacademy.org. Website: www.stanbridgeacademy.org

SUMMIT PREPARATORY SCHOOL
1605 Danielson Road
Kalispell, Montana 59901
Head of School: Todd Fiske, M.Ed

General Information Coeducational boarding college-preparatory and arts school; primarily serves students with learning disabilities, individuals with Attention Deficit Disorder, individuals with emotional and behavioral problems, dyslexic students, college-bound students with depression, anxiety, family conflict, and substance abuse, adoption issues, trauma, ADHD, mild learning disabilities. Grades 9–12. Founded: 2003. Setting: rural. Students are housed in single-sex dormitories. 540-acre campus. 1 building on campus. Approved or accredited by Association for Experiential Education, Northwest Association of Independent Schools, and Montana Department of Education. Total enrollment: 62. Upper school average class size: 10. Upper school faculty-student ratio: 1:8. Upper School students typically attend 5 days per week. The average school day consists of 5 hours.

Upper School Student Profile 100% of students are boarding students. 1% are state residents. 25 states are represented in upper school student body. 2% are international students. International students from Belgium, Honduras, and Mexico.

Faculty School total: 9. In upper school: 4 men, 5 women; 6 have advanced degrees.

Subjects Offered Algebra, American history, American literature, anatomy and physiology, art, astronomy, basketball, biology, British literature, calculus, ceramics, chemistry, choral music, composition, computer applications, drama, drawing, earth science, fitness, geometry, global studies, government, guitar, healthful living, interpersonal skills, journalism, painting, physical education, physics, poetry, portfolio art, pre-algebra, pre-calculus, SAT/ACT preparation, science fiction, sculpture,

Shakespeare, Spanish, speech and debate, studio art, substance abuse, swimming, trigonometry, U.S. government, weight training, wilderness experience, world history.

Graduation Requirements Electives, English, government, history, mathematics, physical fitness, science, completion of therapeutic program, which includes individual, group, and family therapy, and follows the student through a series of four therapeutic stages.

Special Academic Programs Accelerated programs; independent study; study at local college for college credit; academic accommodation for the gifted; remedial reading and/or remedial writing; remedial math; programs in general development for dyslexic students.

College Admission Counseling 20 students graduated in 2015; 19 went to college, including Mississippi State University; Montana State University; New York University; Savannah College of Art and Design; The Ohio State University; The University of Montana.

Student Life Upper grades have specified standards of dress, student council. Discipline rests primarily with faculty.

Tuition and Aid 7-day tuition and room/board: $99,600. Tuition installment plan (monthly payment plans, individually arranged payment plans). Need-based scholarship grants available. In 2015–16, 30% of upper-school students received aid. Total amount of financial aid awarded in 2015–16: $100,000.

Admissions Individual IQ, Achievement and behavior rating scale, psychoeducational evaluation, Rorschach or Thematic Apperception Test or WISC or WAIS required. Deadline for receipt of application materials: none. No application fee required. Interview recommended.

Athletics Interscholastic: basketball (boys, girls), indoor soccer (b,g), martial arts (b,g), soccer (b,g), tennis (b,g), volleyball (g), winter soccer (b,g); intramural: aerobics (b,g), alpine skiing (b,g), aquatics (b,g), backpacking (b,g), basketball (b,g), billiards (b,g), blading (b,g), bowling (b,g), broomball (b,g), canoeing/kayaking (b,g), climbing (b,g), cooperative games (b,g), cross-country running (b,g), fishing (b,g), fitness (b,g), floor hockey (b,g), fly fishing (b,g), Frisbee (b,g), golf (b,g), hiking/backpacking (b,g), horseback riding (b,g), ice skating (b,g), indoor soccer (b,g), indoor track (b,g), jogging (b,g), kayaking (b,g), lacrosse (b,g), martial arts (b,g), mountaineering (b,g), nordic skiing (b,g), outdoor activities (b,g), outdoor skills (b,g), physical fitness (b,g), physical training (b,g), rafting (b,g), rock climbing (b,g), roller blading (b,g), ropes course (b,g), running (b,g), skateboarding (b,g), skiing (cross-country) (b,g), skiing (downhill) (b,g), snowboarding (b,g), snowshoeing (b,g), soccer (b,g), softball (b,g), strength & conditioning (b,g), swimming and diving (b,g), tennis (b,g), ultimate Frisbee (b,g), volleyball (b,g), walking (b,g), wall climbing (b,g), water polo (b,g), weight lifting (b,g), weight training (b,g), winter walking (b,g), wrestling (b), yoga (b,g); coed interscholastic: indoor soccer, mountain biking, tennis, winter soccer; coed intramural: bicycling, bowling, cooperative games, cross-country running, indoor soccer, mountain biking, outdoor activities, outdoor skills, rock climbing, tennis. 1 PE instructor, 3 coaches.

Computers Computers are regularly used in all academic, business, creative writing, writing classes. Computer network features include on-campus library services, Internet filtering or blocking technology, supervised access only to Internet. Students grades are available online.

Contact Judy Heleva, M.A., Director of Admissions. 406-758-8113. Fax: 406-758-8150. E-mail: jheleva@summitprepschool.org. Website: www.summitprepschool.org

VALLEY VIEW SCHOOL

91 Oakham Road
PO Box 338
North Brookfield, Massachusetts 01535

Head of School: Dr. Philip G. Spiva

General Information Boys' boarding college-preparatory, general academic, arts, and vocational school; primarily serves underachievers, students with learning disabilities, individuals with Attention Deficit Disorder, individuals with emotional and behavioral problems, and difficulty socially adjusting to family and surroundings. Grades 6–12. Founded: 1970. Setting: small town. Nearest major city is Worcester. Students are housed in single-sex dormitories. 215-acre campus. 9 buildings on campus. Approved or accredited by Massachusetts Office of Child Care Services. Endowment: $675,000. Total enrollment: 33. Upper school average class size: 5. Upper school faculty-student ratio: 1:4. There are 191 required school days per year for Upper School students. Upper School students typically attend 5 days per week.

Upper School Student Profile 100% of students are boarding students. 10% are state residents. 25 states are represented in upper school student body. 15% are international students. International students from Canada, France, Kenya, Mexico, and United Arab Emirates; 3 other countries represented in student body.

Faculty School total: 11. In upper school: 6 men, 4 women; 4 have advanced degrees; 2 reside on campus.

Subjects Offered Algebra, American literature, anatomy, art, biology, chemistry, civics, composition, computer math, computer science, creative writing, drama, drama performance, drama workshop, dramatic arts, drawing, drawing and design, driver education, earth and space science, earth science, Eastern world civilizations, ecology, environmental systems, economics, economics and history, economics-AP, electronics, English, English composition, English language and composition-AP, English language-AP, English literature, English literature and composition-AP, English literature-AP, English-AP, English/composition-AP, environmental education, environmental geography, environmental science, environmental science-AP, epic literature, ethics and responsibility, ethnic studies, European history, European history-AP, general science, geography, geometry, government, grammar, health, history, life science, literature, mathematics, music, physical education, physical science, science, social studies, Spanish, study skills, theater, U.S. history, Western civilization, world history, world literature, writing, zoology.

Graduation Requirements English, mathematics, physical education (includes health), science, social studies (includes history).

Special Academic Programs Remedial reading and/or remedial writing; remedial math.

College Admission Counseling 1 student graduated in 2015 and went to college.

Student Life Upper grades have specified standards of dress, student council, honor system. Discipline rests primarily with faculty.

Summer Programs Remediation, sports, art/fine arts programs offered; held on campus; accepts boys; not open to students from other schools. 45 students usually enrolled. 2016 schedule: July 9 to August 22. Application deadline: none.

Tuition and Aid 7-day tuition and room/board: $73,645. Tuition installment plan (quarterly payment plan).

Admissions Academic Profile Tests required. Deadline for receipt of application materials: none. No application fee required. On-campus interview required.

Athletics Interscholastic: basketball, cross-country running, golf, lacrosse, running, soccer, softball, tennis, ultimate Frisbee; intramural: alpine skiing, archery, backpacking, baseball, basketball, bicycling, billiards, blading, bocce, bowling, canoeing/kayaking, climbing, cross-country running, fishing, fitness, flag football, floor hockey, Frisbee, golf, hiking/backpacking, ice hockey, ice skating, in-line skating, indoor hockey, martial arts, mountain biking, outdoor recreation, outdoors, physical fitness, riflery, rock climbing, roller blading, running, skateboarding, skiing (cross-country), skiing (downhill), snowboarding, softball, street hockey, swimming and diving, table tennis, touch football, ultimate Frisbee, volleyball, wall climbing, weight lifting, whiffle ball. 2 PE instructors.

Computers Computers are regularly used in art, English, mathematics, science classes. Computer network features include Internet access, wireless campus network. Student e-mail accounts are available to students.

Contact Mr. Rick Bulger, Associate Director. 508-867-6505 Ext. 213. Fax: 508-867-3300. E-mail: r.bulger@valleyviewschool.org. Website: www.valleyviewschool.org

THE VANGUARD SCHOOL

22000 Highway 27
Lake Wales, Florida 33859-6858

Head of School: Mr. Harold Maready

General Information Coeducational boarding and day and distance learning college-preparatory, general academic, arts, and vocational school; primarily serves underachievers, students with learning disabilities, individuals with Attention Deficit Disorder, dyslexic students, and non-verbal learning disabilities. Grades 6–12. Distance learning grades 9–12. Founded: 1966. Setting: small town. Nearest major city is Orlando. Students are housed in single-sex dormitories. 77-acre campus. 15 buildings on campus. Approved or accredited by Florida Council of Independent Schools, Southern Association of Colleges and Schools, The Association of Boarding Schools, and Florida Department of Education. Member of National Association of Independent Schools and Secondary School Admission Test Board. Endowment: $3.8 million. Total enrollment: 95. Upper school average class size: 6. Upper school faculty-student ratio: 1:6. There are 180 required school days per year for Upper School students. Upper School students typically attend 5 days per week. The average school day consists of 8 hours.

Upper School Student Profile Grade 6: 4 students (3 boys, 1 girl); Grade 7: 8 students (7 boys, 1 girl); Grade 8: 5 students (5 boys); Grade 9: 10 students (7 boys, 3 girls); Grade 10: 19 students (15 boys, 4 girls); Grade 11: 24 students (19 boys, 5 girls); Grade 12: 27 students (21 boys, 6 girls). 88% of students are boarding students. 50% are state residents. 11 states are represented in upper school student body. 36% are international students. International students from Bahamas, Bermuda, British Virgin Islands, Cayman Islands, China, and Mexico; 6 other countries represented in student body.

Faculty School total: 19. In upper school: 6 men, 13 women; 6 have advanced degrees; 1 resides on campus.

Subjects Offered ACT preparation, algebra, American history, American literature, art, basketball, biology, business mathematics, chemistry, choral music, creative writing, driver education, economics, economics and history, English, English literature, environmental science, fine arts, geometry, government, government/civics, grammar, history, industrial arts, language arts, life management skills, mathematics, music, physical education, physical science, physics, pre-calculus, reading, science, social studies, Spanish, speech, study skills, world history, yearbook.

Graduation Requirements Arts and fine arts (art, music, dance, drama), biology, economics, English, government, life management skills, literature, mathematics, physical education (includes health), reading, science, social studies (includes history).

Special Academic Programs Independent study; study at local college for college credit; academic accommodation for the gifted; remedial reading and/or remedial writing; remedial math; programs in English, mathematics, general development for dyslexic students; special instructional classes for deaf students, blind students.

College Admission Counseling 22 students graduated in 2015; 20 went to college, including Florida Gulf Coast University; Johnson & Wales University; Lynn University; Nova Southeastern University; Santa Fe College; Savannah College of Art and Design. Other: 2 went to work.

Student Life Upper grades have uniform requirement, student council, honor system. Discipline rests primarily with faculty.

Summer Programs Remediation, enrichment programs offered; session focuses on academic enhancement and remediation; held on campus; accepts boys and girls; open to students from other schools. 20 students usually enrolled. 2016 schedule: July 6 to August 3. Application deadline: June 24.

Tuition and Aid Day student tuition: $24,500; 5-day tuition and room/board: $40,000; 7-day tuition and room/board: $46,000. Tuition installment plan (individually arranged payment plans, Your Tuition Solution). Tuition reduction for siblings, need-based scholarship grants available. In 2015–16, 42% of upper-school students received aid. Total amount of financial aid awarded in 2015–16: $500,000.

Admissions Traditional secondary-level entrance grade is 9. For fall 2015, 50 students applied for upper-level admission, 35 were accepted, 22 enrolled. Wechsler Intelligence Scale for Children required. Deadline for receipt of application materials: none. Application fee required: $100. Interview required.

Athletics Interscholastic: basketball (boys, girls), golf (b), running (b,g), soccer (b), tennis (b), track and field (b,g), volleyball (g), weight lifting (b); intramural: basketball (b,g); coed interscholastic: cross-country running, golf, soccer, tennis; coed intramural: basketball, billiards, canoeing/kayaking, equestrian sports, fishing, fitness, fitness walking, golf, horseback riding, paint ball, physical fitness, sand volleyball, skateboarding, soccer, volleyball, walking, weight lifting, weight training. 5 coaches.

Computers Computers are regularly used in all classes. Computer network features include on-campus library services, online commercial services, Internet access, wireless campus network, Internet filtering or blocking technology. Computer access in designated common areas is available to students. Students grades are available online. The school has a published electronic and media policy.

Contact Ms. Candi Medeiros, Director of Admissions. 863-676-6091 Ext. 1025. Fax: 863-676-8297. E-mail: candi.medeiros@vanguardschool.org. Website: www.vanguardschool.org

WELLSPRING FOUNDATION

21 Arch Bridge Road
PO Box 370
Bethlehem, Connecticut 06751

Head of School: Dan Murray

General Information Coeducational boarding and day college-preparatory, general academic, and arts school; primarily serves students with learning disabilities, individuals with Attention Deficit Disorder, individuals with emotional and behavioral problems, and depression, mood disorders, eating disorders, and Bipolar Disorder. Boarding boys grades 1–6, boarding girls grades 1–12, day boys grades 1–12, day girls grades 1–12. Founded: 1977. Setting: rural. Nearest major city is Hartford. Students are housed in single-sex dormitories. 13-acre campus. 7 buildings on campus. Approved or accredited by Connecticut Association of Independent Schools, Connecticut Department of Children and Families, New England Association of Schools and Colleges, and Connecticut Department of Education. Total enrollment: 51. Upper school average class size: 6. There are 189 required school days per year for Upper School students. Upper School students typically attend 5 days per week.

Faculty School total: 20.

Special Academic Programs Independent study; academic accommodation for the gifted; remedial reading and/or remedial writing; remedial math.

Student Life Upper grades have specified standards of dress. Discipline rests primarily with faculty.

Summer Programs Enrichment programs offered; held on campus; accepts boys and girls; open to students from other schools. 36 students usually enrolled.

Admissions Deadline for receipt of application materials: none. No application fee required. On-campus interview required.

Computers Computer network features include Internet access, Internet filtering or blocking technology. Campus intranet is available to students. The school has a published electronic and media policy.

Contact Nancy Thurston. 203-266-8002. Fax: 203-266-8030. E-mail: nancy.thurston@wellspring.org. Website: www.wellspring.org

WESTMARK SCHOOL

5461 Louise Avenue
Encino, California 91316

Head of School: Claudia Koochek

General Information Coeducational day college-preparatory, general academic, arts, and technology school; primarily serves students with learning disabilities, individuals with Attention Deficit Disorder, dyslexic students, and students with language-based

learning disabilities. Grades 2–12. Founded: 1983. Setting: suburban. Nearest major city is Los Angeles. 5-acre campus. 6 buildings on campus. Approved or accredited by California Association of Independent Schools, Western Association of Schools and Colleges, and California Department of Education. Member of National Association of Independent Schools. Upper school average class size: 12. Upper school faculty-student ratio: 1:12. Upper School students typically attend 5 days per week. The average school day consists of 6 hours.

Faculty School total: 50.

Subjects Offered Algebra, American history, American literature, anatomy, art, biology, career exploration, chemistry, community service, computer science, creative writing, drama, earth science, economics, English, environmental science, European history, fine arts, general science, geography, geometry, health, history, literature, mathematics, music, physical education, physical science, physics, physiology, science, sign language, social sciences, social studies, Spanish, theater, trigonometry, video, world history, writing.

Graduation Requirements Arts and fine arts (art, music, dance, drama), English, foreign language, mathematics, physical education (includes health), science, social sciences, social studies (includes history), educational career plan. Community service is required.

Special Academic Programs Independent study; study at local college for college credit; remedial reading and/or remedial writing; remedial math; programs in English, mathematics, general development for dyslexic students.

College Admission Counseling 26 students graduated in 2015; all went to college.

Student Life Upper grades have uniform requirement, student council, honor system. Discipline rests primarily with faculty.

Summer Programs Remediation, enrichment, advancement, art/fine arts, computer instruction programs offered; session focuses on academic and social development; held on campus; accepts boys and girls; open to students from other schools. 40 students usually enrolled. 2016 schedule: July 7 to August 1. Application deadline: May 30.

Tuition and Aid Day student tuition: $39,720. Tuition installment plan (The Tuition Plan, Insured Tuition Payment Plan, monthly payment plans, individually arranged payment plans, Tuition Management Systems Plan). Need-based scholarship grants, sending district special education funding available.

Admissions Traditional secondary-level entrance grade is 9. Deadline for receipt of application materials: none. Application fee required: $125. On-campus interview required.

Athletics Interscholastic: baseball (boys), basketball (b,g), cheering (b,g), cross-country running (b,g), dance squad (g), equestrian sports (g), flag football (b), football (b,g), softball (g), volleyball (b,g); intramural: outdoor education (g); coed interscholastic: basketball, cross-country running, equestrian sports, flag football, golf, soccer, volleyball; coed intramural: fencing, outdoor education. 3 PE instructors, 6 coaches.

Computers Computers are regularly used in English, history, science, social studies classes. Computer network features include on-campus library services, Internet access, wireless campus network, Internet filtering or blocking technology. Campus intranet, student e-mail accounts, and computer access in designated common areas are available to students. Students grades are available online. The school has a published electronic and media policy.

Contact Catalina Lara, Director of Admissions. 818-986-5045 Ext. 303. Fax: 818-986-2605 Ext. 303. E-mail: clara@westmarkschool.org. Website: www.westmarkschool.org

WESTVIEW SCHOOL

12101 W. Washington Blvd.
Los Angeles, California 90066

Head of School: Ms. Jackie Strumwasser

General Information Coeducational day college-preparatory, general academic, and arts school; primarily serves underachievers, students with learning disabilities, individuals with Attention Deficit Disorder, individuals with emotional and behavioral problems, and Autism Spectrum Disorder. Grades 5–12. Founded: 1990. Setting: urban. 1 building on campus. Approved or accredited by Western Association of Schools and Colleges and California Department of Education. Total enrollment: 110. Upper school average class size: 10. Upper school faculty-student ratio: 1:8. There are 180 required school days per year for Upper School students. Upper School students typically attend 5 days per week. The average school day consists of 6 hours and 35 minutes.

Upper School Student Profile Grade 9: 22 students (12 boys, 10 girls); Grade 10: 20 students (18 boys, 2 girls); Grade 11: 25 students (11 boys, 14 girls); Grade 12: 34 students (20 boys, 14 girls).

Faculty School total: 17. In upper school: 11 men, 4 women; 5 have advanced degrees.

Subjects Offered Acting, advanced computer applications, advanced math, algebra, American government, American history, American literature, analytic geometry, applied music, art, arts, arts and crafts, athletics, baseball, biology, calculus, career planning, career/college preparation, chemistry, civics, college admission preparation, college awareness, college counseling, college placement, college planning, community service, composition, computer applications, computer art, computer literacy, computer processing, computer skills, computer technologies, conflict resolution, contemporary art, creative arts, creative drama, critical writing, culinary arts, current events, dance, data processing, desktop publishing, digital applications, drama, drama performance, drama workshop, dramatic arts, drawing, drawing and design, driver education, economics, economics and history, English, English composition, English literature, environmental science, experimental science, expository writing, expressive arts, filmmaking, fine arts, general science, geometry, golf, government, grammar, guidance, health, health education, history, independent study, information processing, instrumental music, intro to computers, introduction to theater, keyboarding, lab science, language arts, languages, leadership and service, literature, math review, mathematics, music, music performance, musicianship, painting, participation in sports, performing arts, physical education, physical science, physics, play production, pre-algebra, pre-calculus, reading/study skills, remedial study skills, remedial/makeup course work, science, Shakespeare, social sciences, social studies, Spanish, sports, statistics, student government, study skills, trigonometry, U.S. government, U.S. history, visual arts, voice, Web site design, word processing, world history, world literature, writing, writing, yearbook, yoga.

Graduation Requirements Algebra, arts and fine arts (art, music, dance, drama), biology, career/college preparation, chemistry, composition, computer skills, economics, English, foreign language, geometry, health, life skills, mathematics, performing arts, physical education (includes health), science, social sciences, social studies (includes history), Spanish, U.S. government. Community service is required.

Special Academic Programs Independent study; study at local college for college credit; remedial reading and/or remedial writing; remedial math; programs in English, mathematics, general development for dyslexic students.

College Admission Counseling 32 students graduated in 2014; 31 went to college, including California State University, Long Beach; Santa Monica College; University of California, Davis; University of California, Irvine; University of Redlands; West Los Angeles College. Other: 1 went to work. Median SAT critical reading: 560, median SAT math: 540, median SAT writing: 510, median combined SAT: 1610. 33% scored over 600 on SAT critical reading, 16% scored over 600 on SAT math, 16% scored over 1800 on combined SAT.

Student Life Upper grades have specified standards of dress, student council. Discipline rests primarily with faculty.

Tuition and Aid Tuition installment plan (monthly payment plans, individually arranged payment plans).

Admissions Kaufman Test of Educational Achievement or Wechsler Individual Achievement Test required. Deadline for receipt of application materials: none. No application fee required. On-campus interview required.

Athletics Interscholastic: baseball (boys), basketball (b,g), cross-country running (b,g), softball (g), volleyball (g), yoga (b,g); coed interscholastic: cross-country running, dance, golf, soccer, yoga. 2 PE instructors.

Computers Computers are regularly used in career exploration, college planning, computer applications, data processing, desktop publishing, keyboarding, typing, video film production, Web site design, word processing, yearbook classes. Computer resources include Internet access, Internet filtering or blocking technology. The school has a published electronic and media policy.

Contact Ms. Bonnie Aharoni, Director of Admissions. 310-478-5544 Ext. 1129. Fax: 310-397-4417. E-mail: baharoni@thehelpgroup.org. Website: www.westviewschool.com

WILLOW HILL SCHOOL

98 Haynes Road
Sudbury, Massachusetts 01776

Head of School: Marilyn G. Reid

General Information Coeducational day college-preparatory, arts, technology, and visual and performing arts school; primarily serves underachievers, students with learning disabilities, individuals with Attention Deficit Disorder, dyslexic students, non-verbal learning disabilities, and Asperger's Syndrome. Grades 6–12. Founded: 1970. Setting: suburban. Nearest major city is Boston. 26-acre campus. 4 buildings on campus. Approved or accredited by Massachusetts Department of Education, New England Association of Schools and Colleges, and Massachusetts Department of Education. Member of National Association of Independent Schools. Total enrollment: 61. Upper school average class size: 8. Upper school faculty-student ratio: 1:3. There are 180 required school days per year for Upper School students. Upper School students typically attend 5 days per week. The average school day consists of 6 hours and 45 minutes.

Upper School Student Profile Grade 9: 14 students (13 boys, 1 girl); Grade 10: 13 students (9 boys, 4 girls); Grade 11: 7 students (5 boys, 2 girls); Grade 12: 8 students (5 boys, 3 girls).

Faculty School total: 20. In upper school: 9 men, 11 women; 17 have advanced degrees.

Subjects Offered 20th century world history, algebra, American government, American history, American literature, art, biology, career/college preparation, chemistry, computer science, computer technologies, conceptual physics, consumer mathematics, creative writing, decision making skills, drama, dramatic arts, earth science, English composition, English literature, geography, geometry, grammar, integrated science, keyboarding, library studies, life science, mathematics, outdoor education, physical education, physical science, pragmatics, pre-algebra, pre-calculus, science, senior composition, social studies, study skills, technology, U.S. history, U.S. literature, world history, World War II.

Graduation Requirements Art, drama, English composition, keyboarding, literature, mathematics, physical education (includes health), science, social studies (includes history), wilderness education, students must pass the Massachusetts Comprehensive Assessment System (MCAS), a state-mandated competency requirement, for public funded students.

Special Academic Programs 1 Advanced Placement exam for which test preparation is offered; independent study; study at local college for college credit; academic accommodation for the artistically talented; remedial reading and/or remedial writing; remedial math; programs in English, mathematics, general development for dyslexic students; special instructional classes for blind students.

College Admission Counseling 11 students graduated in 2014; 10 went to college, including Curry College; Dean College; Westfield State University. Other: 1 had other specific plans.

Student Life Upper grades have student council. Discipline rests primarily with faculty.

Tuition and Aid Day student tuition: $50,205.

Admissions Traditional secondary-level entrance grade is 9. For fall 2014, 70 students applied for upper-level admission, 32 were accepted, 21 enrolled. Comprehensive educational evaluation and WISC or WAIS required. Deadline for receipt of application materials: none. No application fee required. On-campus interview required.

Athletics Coed Interscholastic: basketball, soccer, track and field, ultimate Frisbee; coed intramural: backpacking, basketball, bicycling, broomball, canoeing/kayaking, climbing, cooperative games, cricket, croquet, cross-country running, fitness, flag football, floor hockey, Frisbee, hiking/backpacking, horseshoes, ice skating, kayaking, lacrosse, martial arts, mountain biking, outdoor activities, outdoor adventure, outdoor education, outdoor recreation, outdoor skills, outdoors, paddling, physical fitness, rappelling, rock climbing, rugby, snowshoeing, soccer, strength & conditioning, track and field, ultimate Frisbee, volleyball, wall climbing. 1 PE instructor.

Computers Computers are regularly used in all academic, art, keyboarding, library science, technology classes. Computer network features include on-campus library services, Internet access, wireless campus network, Internet filtering or blocking technology. Computer access in designated common areas is available to students. The school has a published electronic and media policy.

Contact Ann Marie Reen, Director of Admissions. 978-443-2581. Fax: 978-443-7560. E-mail: amreen@willowhillschool.org. Website: www.willowhillschool.org

WINSTON PREPARATORY SCHOOL

126 West 17th Street
New York, New York 10011

Head of School: Mr. William DeHaven

General Information Coeducational day college-preparatory, general academic, and arts school; primarily serves underachievers, students with learning disabilities, individuals with Attention Deficit Disorder, dyslexic students, and non-verbal learning difficulties. Grades 4–12. Founded: 1981. Setting: urban. 1 building on campus. Approved or accredited by New England Association of Schools and Colleges and New York State Association of Independent Schools. Member of National Association of Independent Schools. Total enrollment: 227. Upper school average class size: 10. Upper school faculty-student ratio: 1:3. There are 227 required school days per year for Upper School students. Upper School students typically attend 5 days per week. The average school day consists of 6 hours and 45 minutes.

Faculty School total: 75. In upper school: 18 men, 57 women; 65 have advanced degrees.

Subjects Offered 3-dimensional art, acting, algebra, American Civil War, American history, American literature, art, athletic training, athletics, biology, community service, creative writing, drama, English, English literature, expository writing, geography, geometry, grammar, health, history, mathematics, music, physical education, science, social skills, speech, theater, trigonometry, U.S. history, writing.

Graduation Requirements Art, English, history, mathematics, physical education (includes health), science.

Special Academic Programs Study at local college for college credit; remedial reading and/or remedial writing; remedial math; programs in English, mathematics, general development for dyslexic students.

College Admission Counseling 34 students graduated in 2015; 30 went to college, including Fairleigh Dickinson University, College at Florham; Goucher College; Hofstra University; Ithaca College; State University of New York College at Cortland. Other: 2 went to work, 2 entered a postgraduate year.

Student Life Upper grades have specified standards of dress, student council. Discipline rests primarily with faculty.

Summer Programs Remediation, enrichment, sports, art/fine arts programs offered; session focuses on reading, writing, and math skill development as well as study skills; held on campus; accepts boys and girls; open to students from other schools. 35 students usually enrolled. 2016 schedule: June 30 to August 20. Application deadline: June 1.

Tuition and Aid Day student tuition: $55,200. Tuition installment plan (SMART Tuition Payment Plan, individually arranged payment plans). Need-based scholarship grants available. In 2015–16, 20% of upper-school students received aid. Total amount of financial aid awarded in 2015–16: $500,000.

Admissions Traditional secondary-level entrance grade is 9. For fall 2015, 258 students applied for upper-level admission, 116 were accepted, 70 enrolled. Achievement tests, admissions testing, battery of testing done through outside agency, Wechsler Individual Achievement Test, Wechsler Intelligence Scale for Children, Wechsler Intelligence Scale for Children III and writing sample required. Deadline for receipt of application materials: none. Application fee required: $100. On-campus interview required.

Athletics Interscholastic: basketball (boys, girls); coed interscholastic: cross-country running, soccer, softball, track and field; coed intramural: fencing, golf, outdoor education, physical fitness, physical training, sailing, skiing (cross-country), skiing (downhill), strength & conditioning, weight training, yoga. 2 PE instructors, 6 coaches.

Computers Computers are regularly used in art, English, history, science, writing classes. Computer network features include Internet access, wireless campus network, Internet filtering or blocking technology, online discussion group and course information, integrated technology—iPads, SmartBoards, etc. Computer access in designated common areas is available to students. The school has a published electronic and media policy.

Contact Ms. Medry Rodriguez, Assistant to Director of Admissions. 646-638-2705 Ext. 619. Fax: 646-839-5457. E-mail: mrodriguez@winstonprep.edu. Website: www.winstonprep.edu

THE WINSTON SCHOOL

5707 Royal Lane
Dallas, Texas 75229

Head of School: Ms. Rebbie Evans

General Information Coeducational day college-preparatory, arts, technology, and science school; primarily serves students with learning disabilities, individuals with Attention Deficit Disorder, and dyslexic students. Grades K–12. Founded: 1975. Setting: suburban. 4-acre campus. 1 building on campus. Approved or accredited by Texas Department of Education. Member of National Association of Independent Schools. Endowment: $6 million. Upper school average class size: 9. Upper school faculty-student ratio: 1:5. There are 169 required school days per year for Upper School students. Upper School students typically attend 5 days per week. The average school day consists of 6 hours and 10 minutes.

Upper School Student Profile Grade 9: 12 students (9 boys, 3 girls); Grade 10: 12 students (9 boys, 3 girls); Grade 11: 14 students (12 boys, 2 girls); Grade 12: 13 students (11 boys, 2 girls).

Faculty School total: 36. In upper school: 8 men, 9 women; 9 have advanced degrees.

Subjects Offered 3-dimensional art, algebra, American history, American literature, astronomy, athletics, biology, ceramics, chemistry, computer science, drama, economics, English, English literature, film, fine arts, foreign language, geometry, government/civics, grammar, health, keyboarding, photography, physical education, physics, Spanish, speech, student government, technical theater, theater, trigonometry, world history, world literature, writing.

Graduation Requirements Computer science, English, foreign language, mathematics, physical education (includes health), science, social sciences, social studies (includes history), 30 service hours per year (120 total).

Special Academic Programs Accelerated programs; independent study; study at local college for college credit; academic accommodation for the gifted and the artistically talented; remedial reading and/or remedial writing; remedial math; programs in English, mathematics, general development for dyslexic students.

College Admission Counseling 16 students graduated in 2015; 15 went to college, including Austin College; Fordham University; Pace University; Southern Methodist University; University of Arkansas; Westminster College. Other: 1 had other specific plans. Mean SAT critical reading: 547, mean SAT math: 510, mean SAT writing: 530, mean combined SAT: 1587, mean composite ACT: 22.

Student Life Upper grades have uniform requirement, student council, honor system. Discipline rests equally with students and faculty.

Summer Programs Remediation, enrichment, advancement, art/fine arts, computer instruction programs offered; session focuses on earning academic credit; held on campus; accepts boys and girls; open to students from other schools. 80 students usually enrolled. 2016 schedule: June 6 to July 22. Application deadline: June 1.

Tuition and Aid Day student tuition: $21,500–$28,000. Tuition installment plan (Insured Tuition Payment Plan, FACTS Tuition Payment Plan, monthly payment plans). Need-based scholarship grants available. In 2015–16, 24% of upper-school students received aid. Total amount of financial aid awarded in 2015–16: $229,000.

Admissions Traditional secondary-level entrance grade is 9. For fall 2015, 14 students applied for upper-level admission, 9 were accepted, 8 enrolled. Psychoeducational evaluation required. Deadline for receipt of application materials: none. Application fee required: $195. On-campus interview required.

Athletics Interscholastic: baseball (boys), basketball (b,g), fitness (b,g), flag football (b), football (b), indoor soccer (g), softball (g), volleyball (g), winter soccer (b,g); coed interscholastic: bowling, cross-country running, dance team, fitness, golf, independent competitive sports, physical fitness, running, soccer, strength & conditioning, tennis, weight training. 2 PE instructors, 2 coaches.

Computers Computers are regularly used in all academic classes. Computer resources include on-campus library services, online commercial services, Internet access, wireless campus network, Internet filtering or blocking technology. Students grades are available online. The school has a published electronic and media policy.

Contact Libby Powers, Director of Admission and Financial Aid. 214-691-6950. Fax: 214-691-1509. E-mail: admissions@winston-school.org. Website: www.winston-school.org

THE WINSTON SCHOOL SAN ANTONIO

8565 Ewing Halsell Drive
San Antonio, Texas 78229

Head of School: Dr. Charles J. Karulak

General Information Coeducational day college-preparatory, general academic, arts, and technology school; primarily serves students with learning disabilities, individuals with Attention Deficit Disorder, and dyslexic students. Grades K–12. Founded: 1985. Setting: urban. 15-acre campus. 2 buildings on campus. Approved or accredited by Independent Schools Association of the Southwest, Texas Education Agency, and Texas Department of Education. Total enrollment: 201. Upper school average class size: 9. Upper school faculty-student ratio: 1:8. There are 175 required school days per year for Upper School students. Upper School students typically attend 5 days per week. The average school day consists of 7 hours and 5 minutes.

Upper School Student Profile Grade 9: 21 students (15 boys, 6 girls); Grade 10: 19 students (14 boys, 5 girls); Grade 11: 27 students (19 boys, 8 girls); Grade 12: 19 students (15 boys, 4 girls).

Faculty School total: 31. In upper school: 8 men, 9 women; 11 have advanced degrees.

Subjects Offered Algebra, American history, American literature, anatomy and physiology, art, athletics, basketball, biology, calculus, cheerleading, chemistry, college counseling, college planning, community service, computer graphics, computer literacy, computer multimedia, drama, economics, English, English composition, English literature, environmental science, geography, geometry, government, graphic design, health, health education, journalism, mathematical modeling, multimedia, music, photography, physical education, physical science, physics, pre-calculus, reading, Spanish, speech, student publications, world geography, world history, yearbook.

Graduation Requirements Arts and fine arts (art, music, dance, drama), computer science, English, foreign language, history, mathematics, physical education (includes health), science, social sciences, 20 hours of community service per year, transition course, job shadowing program.

Special Academic Programs Independent study; study at local college for college credit; remedial reading and/or remedial writing; programs in English, mathematics, general development for dyslexic students.

College Admission Counseling 24 students graduated in 2015; 23 went to college, including Colorado School of Mines; San Antonio College; Texas A&M University–Kingsville; Trinity University; University of Denver; University of the Incarnate Word. Other: 1 went to work.

Student Life Upper grades have uniform requirement, student council, honor system. Discipline rests primarily with faculty.

Summer Programs Remediation, enrichment, advancement, sports, art/fine arts, computer instruction programs offered; session focuses on high school classes for credit; held on campus; accepts boys and girls; open to students from other schools. 110 students usually enrolled. 2016 schedule: June 20 to July 15. Application deadline: June 3.

Tuition and Aid Day student tuition: $17,500. Tuition installment plan (monthly payment plans, individually arranged payment plans). Need-based scholarship grants available. In 2015–16, 25% of upper-school students received aid.

Admissions Traditional secondary-level entrance grade is 9. For fall 2015, 12 students applied for upper-level admission, 11 were accepted, 9 enrolled. Achievement tests, battery of testing done through outside agency, comprehensive educational evaluation, Individual IQ, Individual IQ, Achievement and behavior rating scale, psychoeducational evaluation, Wechsler Individual Achievement Test, Wechsler Intelligence Scale for Children, Wide Range Achievement Test or WISC or WAIS required. Deadline for receipt of application materials: none. Application fee required: $150. On-campus interview required.

Athletics Interscholastic: baseball (boys), basketball (b,g), football (b), volleyball (g); coed interscholastic: cheering, cross-country running, golf, outdoor education, physical fitness, physical training, soccer, strength & conditioning, track and field; coed intramural: golf, martial arts, outdoor education, physical fitness, physical training, soccer, strength & conditioning, tennis, track and field. 2 PE instructors.

Computers Computers are regularly used in all academic classes. Computer network features include on-campus library services, online commercial services, Internet access, wireless campus network, Internet filtering or blocking technology. Campus intranet and student e-mail accounts are available to students. Students grades are available online. The school has a published electronic and media policy.

Contact Ms. Julie A. Saboe, Director of Admissions. 210-615-6544 Ext. 213. Fax: 210-615-6627. E-mail: jsaboe@winston-sa.org. Website: www.winston-sa.org

Junior Boarding Schools

ARTHUR MORGAN SCHOOL

60 AMS Circle
Burnsville, North Carolina 28714

Head of School: Jason Sterling

General Information Coeducational boarding and day college-preparatory, general academic, arts, service learning, and outdoor experiential learning school, affiliated with Society of Friends. Grades 7–9. Founded: 1962. Setting: rural. Nearest major city is Asheville. Students are housed in coed boarding homes. 100-acre campus. 7 buildings on campus. Approved or accredited by Friends Council on Education, North Carolina Department of Non-Public Schools, and North Carolina Department of Education. Member of Small Boarding School Association. Endowment: $1 million. Total enrollment: 27. Upper school average class size: 9. Upper school faculty-student ratio: 1:2. There are 180 required school days per year for Upper School students. Upper School students typically attend 5 days per week. The average school day consists of 8 hours.

Student Profile Grade 7: 8 students (4 boys, 4 girls); Grade 8: 11 students (5 boys, 6 girls); Grade 9: 3 students (3 boys). 100% of students are boarding students. 30% are state residents. 3 states are represented in upper school student body.

Faculty School total: 12. In upper school: 7 men, 5 women; 1 has an advanced degree; all reside on campus.

Subjects Offered 3-dimensional art, 3-dimensional design, acting, ADL skills, adolescent issues, African American history, African American studies, African history, agriculture, agroecology, algebra, alternative physical education, American culture, American government, American history, American literature, American minority experience, American studies, anatomy, ancient/medieval philosophy, animal behavior, animal husbandry, anthropology, applied skills, art, arts and crafts, astronomy, athletics, audio visual/media, audition methods, auto mechanics, backpacking, baseball, biology, bookbinding, botany, career education, career education internship, carpentry, ceramics, character education, chemistry, civics, civil rights, clayworking, communication skills, community garden, community service, comparative cultures, comparative politics, composition, computer skills, computers, conflict resolution, conservation, constitutional history of U.S., consumer education, crafts, creative arts, creative dance, creative drama, creative thinking, creative writing, critical thinking, culinary arts, current events, dance, debate, decision making skills, democracy in America, design, drama, drama performance, dramatic arts, drawing, earth science, ecology, English, English composition, English literature, entrepreneurship, ethical decision making, ethics, ethics and responsibility, evolution, experiential education, expressive arts, fabric arts, family and consumer science, family living, family studies, fiber arts, first aid, fitness, food and nutrition, foreign language, forestry, gardening, gender issues, general science, geography, geology, geometry, global issues, global studies, grammar, guitar, health and wellness, health education, high adventure outdoor program, history, horticulture, human rights, human sexuality, humanities, independent living, integrated mathematics, interpersonal skills, jewelry making, journalism, language arts, leadership, leadership and service, life issues, mathematics, media studies, medieval/Renaissance history, meditation, mentorship program, metalworking, music, mythology, Native American studies, natural history, natural resources management, nature study, North Carolina history, oil painting, organic gardening, outdoor education, painting, peace and justice, peace education, peace studies, peer counseling, permaculture, personal growth, photo shop, photography, physical education, physics, piano, playwriting, poetry, politics, pottery, practical living, printmaking, probability and statistics, reading/study skills, relationships, sex education, shop, social justice, social sciences, social skills, social studies, socioeconomic problems, Spanish, sports, stained glass, study skills, swimming, travel, values and decisions, Vietnam War, visual and performing arts, visual arts, weaving, wilderness education, woodworking, work experience, writing, yearbook, yoga.

Graduation Requirements Annual 18-day field service learning trip, annual 3-, 6- and 8-day outdoor education trips.

Special Academic Programs Independent study; programs in English, mathematics, general development for dyslexic students.

Secondary School Placement 9 students graduated in 2015; they went to Carolina Friends School; George School; The Meeting School; Westtown School.

Student Life Honor system. Discipline rests primarily with faculty.

Tuition and Aid Day student tuition: $13,517; 7-day tuition and room/board: $27,996. Tuition installment plan (40% by 8/15, 60% by Dec. 15; monthly payment 10% interest; full payment by 8/15- 2% discount). Need-based scholarship grants, individually negotiated barter arrangements may be made available. In 2015–16, 90% of students received aid. Total amount of financial aid awarded in 2015–16: $100,000.

Admissions Traditional entrance grade is 7. For fall 2015, 3 students applied for admission, 3 were accepted, 3 enrolled. Deadline for receipt of application materials: none. Application fee required: $35. On-campus interview required.

Athletics Coed Interscholastic: soccer; coed intramural: aquatics, backpacking, bicycling, billiards, blading, canoeing/kayaking, climbing, cooperative games, cross-country running, dance, fishing, Frisbee, hiking/backpacking, jogging, mountain biking, outdoor activities, rafting, rock climbing, running, skateboarding, soccer, swimming and diving, tai chi, ultimate Frisbee, wilderness, winter walking, wrestling, yoga.

Computers Computers are regularly used in current events, Spanish, writing, yearbook classes. Computer resources include supervised student access to computers for Web research, word processing, spreadsheet. Computer access in designated common areas is available to students.

Contact Bryan Freeborn, Admissions Coordinator. 828-675-4262. Fax: 828-675-0003. E-mail: admissions@arthurmorganschool.org. Website: www.arthurmorganschool.org

CARDIGAN MOUNTAIN SCHOOL

62 Alumni Drive
Canaan, New Hampshire 03741-9307

Head of School: Mr. David J. McCusker Jr.

General Information Boys' boarding and day college-preparatory, arts, and technology school. Grades 6–9. Founded: 1945. Setting: rural. Nearest major city is Manchester. Students are housed in single-sex dormitories. 400-acre campus. 27 buildings on campus. Approved or accredited by Association of Independent Schools in New England, Independent Schools of Northern New England, Junior Boarding Schools Association, New England Association of Schools and Colleges, The Association of Boarding Schools, and New Hampshire Department of Education. Member of National Association of Independent Schools and Secondary School Admission Test Board. Endowment: $29.5 million. Total enrollment: 215. Upper school average class size: 12. Upper school faculty-student ratio: 1:4. There are 165 required school days per year for Upper School students. Upper School students typically attend 6 days per week. The average school day consists of 5 hours and 15 minutes.

Student Profile Grade 6: 11 students (11 boys); Grade 7: 38 students (38 boys); Grade 8: 71 students (71 boys); Grade 9: 95 students (95 boys). 89% of students are boarding students. 16% are state residents. 20 states are represented in upper school student body. 40% are international students. International students from Canada, China, Hong Kong, Japan, Mexico, and Republic of Korea; 14 other countries represented in student body.

Faculty School total: 59. In upper school: 38 men, 21 women; 28 have advanced degrees; 43 reside on campus.

Subjects Offered Algebra, American history, American literature, art, biology, ceramics, computer math, computer science, creative writing, drama, earth science, ecology, English, English literature, environmental science, ethics, European history, expository writing, fine arts, French, geography, geology, geometry, grammar, health, history, industrial arts, Latin, life skills, mathematics, music, physical science, reading, science, social studies, Spanish, speech, study skills, theater, trigonometry, typing, world history, world literature, writing.

Graduation Requirements Arts and fine arts (art, music, dance, drama), computer science, English, foreign language, mathematics, reading, science, social studies (includes history), study skills.

Special Academic Programs Honors section; independent study; academic accommodation for the gifted; remedial reading and/or remedial writing; remedial math; ESL (12 students enrolled).

Secondary School Placement 63 students graduated in 2015; they went to Avon Old Farms School; Berkshire School; Kent School; Salisbury School; St. Paul's School; Tabor Academy.

Student Life Specified standards of dress, student council, honor system. Discipline rests primarily with faculty.

Summer Programs Remediation, enrichment, advancement, ESL, sports, art/fine arts, computer instruction programs offered; session focuses on academic enrichment, personal development, and summertime fun; held on campus; accepts boys and girls; open to students from other schools. 135 students usually enrolled. 2016 schedule: June 25 to August 4. Application deadline: none.

Tuition and Aid Day student tuition: $31,220; 7-day tuition and room/board: $53,785. Tuition installment plan (The Tuition Plan, Insured Tuition Payment Plan, Academic Management Services Plan, Key Tuition Payment Plan, monthly payment plans). Need-based scholarship grants, need-based loans, prepGATE loans available. In 2015–16, 27% of students received aid. Total amount of financial aid awarded in 2015–16: $1,000,000.

Admissions For fall 2015, 220 students applied for admission, 155 were accepted, 80 enrolled. ISEE, SSAT, TOEFL or Wechsler Intelligence Scale for Children III required. Deadline for receipt of application materials: none. Application fee required: $50. Interview required.

Athletics Interscholastic: alpine skiing, baseball, basketball, climbing, cross-country running, football, freestyle skiing, ice hockey, independent competitive sports, lacrosse, mountain biking, nordic skiing, outdoor adventure, physical training, rock climbing, running, sailing, skiing (cross-country), skiing (downhill), snowboarding, soccer, strength & conditioning, tennis, track and field, wall climbing, weight training, wrestling; intramural: archery, bicycling, bowling, boxing, climbing, equestrian sports, fitness, golf, ice hockey, martial arts, mountain biking, outdoor activities, physical training, riflery, rock climbing, ropes courses, sailing, skiing (downhill), snowboarding, swimming and diving, tennis, trap and skeet, weight lifting, whiffle ball. 3 coaches, 2 athletic trainers.

Computers Computers are regularly used in English, history, mathematics, science, writing classes. Computer network features include on-campus library services, online commercial services, Internet access, wireless campus network, Internet filtering or blocking technology. Campus intranet, student e-mail accounts, and computer access in designated common areas are available to students. Students grades are available online. The school has a published electronic and media policy.

Contact Mrs. Sarah Sinclair, Admissions Coordinator. 603-523-3548. Fax: 603-523-3565. E-mail: ssinclair@cardigan.org. Website: www.cardigan.org

See Display below and Close-Up on page 664.

EAGLEBROOK SCHOOL

271 Pine Nook Road
P.O. Box #7
Deerfield, Massachusetts 01342

Head of School: Mr. Andrew C. Chase

General Information Boys' boarding and day college-preparatory, arts, and technology school. Grades 6–9. Founded: 1922. Setting: rural. Nearest major city is Springfield. Students are housed in single-sex dormitories. 775-acre campus. 26 buildings on campus. Approved or accredited by Association of Independent Schools in New England, Junior Boarding Schools Association, and The Association of Boarding Schools. Member of National Association of Independent Schools and Secondary School Admission Test Board. Endowment: $75 million. Total enrollment: 250. Upper school average class size: 10. Upper school faculty-student ratio: 1:4.

Student Profile Grade 6: 20 students (20 boys); Grade 7: 51 students (51 boys); Grade 8: 87 students (87 boys); Grade 9: 92 students (92 boys). 80% of students are boarding students. 35% are state residents. 22 states are represented in upper school student body. 36% are international students. International students from Bahamas, China, Hong Kong, Mexico, Republic of Korea, and Taiwan; 18 other countries represented in student body.

Faculty School total: 84. In upper school: 48 men, 36 women; 39 have advanced degrees; 55 reside on campus.

Subjects Offered Acting, African-American history, algebra, American studies, anthropology, architectural drawing, architecture, art, astronomy, band, batik, biology, ceramics, Chinese, Chinese history, chorus, Civil War, civil war history, community service, computer art, computer science, computer-aided design, concert band, CPR, creative writing, current events, desktop publishing, digital music, digital photography, drafting, drama, drawing, drawing and design, earth science, ecology, English, English literature, environmental science, ESL, European history, expository writing, fine arts, first aid, French, general science, geography, geometry, grammar, health, history, industrial arts, instrumental music, journalism, keyboarding, Latin, mathematics, medieval history, music, newspaper, photography, physical education, pottery, pre-algebra, public speaking, publications, Russian history, science, sex education, social sciences, social studies, Spanish, study skills, swimming, theater, typing, U.S. history, Web site design, woodworking, world history, writing.

Graduation Requirements Arts and fine arts (art, music, dance, drama), English, foreign language, mathematics, physical education (includes health), science, social sciences, social studies (includes history). Community service is required.

Special Academic Programs Honors section; academic accommodation for the gifted, the musically talented, and the artistically talented; ESL (15 students enrolled).

Secondary School Placement 81 students graduated in 2015; they went to Choate Rosemary Hall; Deerfield Academy; Northfield Mount Hermon School; Phillips Exeter Academy; The Hotchkiss School; The Taft School.

Student Life Specified standards of dress, student council. Discipline rests primarily with faculty.

Summer Programs Enrichment, advancement, ESL, sports, art/fine arts, rigorous outdoor training, computer instruction programs offered; session focuses on enrichment; held on campus; accepts boys and girls; open to students from other schools. 60 students usually enrolled. 2016 schedule: July 3 to July 30. Application deadline: none.

Tuition and Aid Day student tuition: $36,100; 7-day tuition and room/board: $59,400. Tuition installment plan (individually arranged payment plans). Need-based scholarship grants available. In 2015–16, 30% of students received aid. Total amount of financial aid awarded in 2015–16: $1,650,000.

Admissions SSAT and Wechsler Intelligence Scale for Children required. Deadline for receipt of application materials: none. Application fee required: $50. On-campus interview required.

Athletics Interscholastic: alpine skiing, aquatics, baseball, basketball, cross-country running, diving, football, Frisbee, golf, hiking/backpacking, hockey, ice hockey, ice skating, in-line hockey, indoor hockey, indoor soccer, lacrosse, mountain biking, outdoor activities, outdoor recreation, ski jumping, skiing (downhill), snowboarding, soccer, squash, strength & conditioning, swimming and diving, tennis, track and field, triathlon, ultimate Frisbee, water polo, wrestling; intramural: backpacking, bicycling, broomball, canoeing/kayaking, climbing, deck hockey, fishing, fitness, floor hockey, fly fishing, hiking/backpacking, hockey, ice hockey, ice skating, in-line hockey, in-line skating, indoor hockey, indoor soccer, juggling, kayaking, life saving, mountain biking, nordic skiing, outdoor activities, physical training, rafting, riflery, rock climbing, roller blading, roller hockey, roller skating, ropes courses, scuba diving, ski jumping, skiing (cross-country), street hockey, surfing, table tennis, volleyball, wallyball, weight lifting, weight training, wilderness survival. 2 athletic trainers.

Computers Computer network features include on-campus library services, Internet access, wireless campus network, Internet filtering or blocking technology. Campus intranet, student e-mail accounts, and computer access in designated common areas are available to students. The school has a published electronic and media policy.

Contact Mr. Theodore J. Low, Director of Admission. 413-774-9111. Fax: 413-774-9119. E-mail: tlow@eaglebrook.org. Website: www.eaglebrook.org

See Display on this page and Close-Up on page 666.

FAY SCHOOL
48 Main Street
Southborough, Massachusetts 01772-9106
Head of School: Robert J. Gustavson

General Information Coeducational boarding and day college-preparatory, general academic, arts, bilingual studies, and technology school. Boarding grades 7–9, day grades PK–9. Founded: 1866. Setting: small town. Nearest major city is Boston. Students are housed in single-sex dormitories. 66-acre campus. Approved or accredited by Association of Independent Schools in New England, Junior Boarding Schools Association, The Association of Boarding Schools, and Massachusetts Department of Education. Member of National Association of Independent Schools and Secondary School Admission Test Board. Endowment: $45 million. Total enrollment: 475. Upper school faculty-student ratio: 1:6. There are 162 required school days per year for Upper School students. Upper School students typically attend 5 days per week. The average school day consists of 8 hours and 30 minutes.

Student Profile 50% of students are boarding students. 52% are state residents. 28% are international students. International students from China, Hong Kong, Mexico, Republic of Korea, Russian Federation, and Thailand; 14 other countries represented in student body.

Faculty School total: 78. In upper school: 18 men, 22 women; 35 have advanced degrees; 39 reside on campus.

Subjects Offered 3-dimensional art, algebra, American history, ancient history, art, band, biology, ceramics, choir, creative thinking, English, French, geometry, Latin, life science, Mandarin, modern history, music, musicianship, painting, physical science, pre-algebra, pre-calculus, printmaking, Spanish, strings, technology, technology/design, wellness, world history.

Special Academic Programs ESL (36 students enrolled).

Secondary School Placement 53 students graduated in 2015.

Student Life Specified standards of dress, student council, honor system. Discipline rests primarily with faculty.

Summer Programs Enrichment, ESL, sports, art/fine arts, computer instruction programs offered; held on campus; accepts boys and girls; open to students from other schools. 2016 schedule: June to August.

Tuition and Aid Day student tuition: $36,550–$38,290; 5-day tuition and room/board: $55,450–$57,190; 7-day tuition and room/board: $61,660–$63,400. Tuition installment plan (monthly payment plans). Need-based scholarship grants available. In 2015–16, 21% of students received aid. Total amount of financial aid awarded in 2015–16: $2,201,551.

Admissions Traditional entrance grade is 7. ISEE, SSAT, TOEFL or TOEFL Junior required. Deadline for receipt of application materials: none. Application fee required: $50. Interview required.

Athletics Interscholastic: baseball (boys), basketball (b,g), cross-country running (b,g), field hockey (g), football (b), ice hockey (b,g), independent competitive sports (b,g), lacrosse (b,g), soccer (b,g), softball (g), squash (b,g), tennis (b,g), track and field (b,g), volleyball (g), wrestling (b); coed intramural: dance, fitness, golf, outdoor adventure, skiing (downhill), snowboarding, tennis. 2 athletic trainers.

Computers Computers are regularly used in all classes. Computer network features include on-campus library services, online commercial services, Internet access, wireless campus network, Internet filtering or blocking technology. Campus intranet, student e-mail accounts, and computer access in designated common areas are available to students. Students grades are available online. The school has a published electronic and media policy.

Contact Sheila Olson, Admission Officer. 508-490-8201. Fax: 508-481-7872. E-mail: solson@fayschool.org. Website: www.fayschool.org

HAMPSHIRE COUNTRY SCHOOL
28 Patey Circle
Rindge, New Hampshire 03461
Head of School: Bernd Foecking

General Information Boys' boarding college-preparatory and general academic school; primarily serves underachievers, individuals with Attention Deficit Disorder, unusually high intellectual ability, and non-verbal learning disabilities and Asperger's Syndrome. Grades 3–12. Founded: 1948. Setting: rural. Nearest major city is Boston, MA. Students are housed in single-sex dormitories. 1,700-acre campus. 8 buildings on campus. Approved or accredited by New England Association of Schools and Colleges and New Hampshire Department of Education. Member of National Association of Independent Schools. Endowment: $1 million. Total enrollment: 20. Upper school average class size: 4. Upper school faculty-student ratio: 1:2. There are 180 required school days per year for Upper School students. Upper School students typically attend 5 days per week. The average school day consists of 5 hours and 30 minutes.

Student Profile Grade 6: 4 students (4 boys); Grade 7: 6 students (6 boys); Grade 8: 2 students (2 boys); Grade 10: 5 students (5 boys); Grade 11: 1 student (1 boy). 100% of

students are boarding students. 5% are state residents. 14 states are represented in upper school student body. 10% are international students. International students from Mexico.

Faculty School total: 14. In upper school: 7 men, 7 women; 3 have advanced degrees; 13 reside on campus.

Subjects Offered Algebra, civics, English, environmental science, geometry, German, history, life science, mathematics, pre-algebra, science, U.S. history, world history.

Graduation Requirements English, foreign language, mathematics, science, social studies (includes history).

Special Academic Programs Academic accommodation for the gifted; remedial reading and/or remedial writing; remedial math.

Student Life Specified standards of dress. Discipline rests primarily with faculty.

Summer Programs Session focuses on general recreation and play; held on campus; accepts boys; open to students from other schools. 12 students usually enrolled. 2016 schedule: July to July.

Tuition and Aid 7-day tuition and room/board: $56,200.

Admissions Academic Profile Tests, any standardized test or Individual IQ required. Deadline for receipt of application materials: none. No application fee required. On-campus interview required.

Athletics Intramural: archery, basketball, bicycling, canoeing/kayaking, climbing, fishing, flag football, floor hockey, Frisbee, hiking/backpacking, ice skating, kickball, outdoor activities, outdoor recreation, skiing (downhill), snowshoeing, soccer, tennis, touch football, walking, wall climbing, winter walking.

Computers Computers are regularly used in writing classes.

Contact William Dickerman, Admissions Director. 603-899-3325. Fax: 603-899-6521. E-mail: admissions@hampshirecountryschool.net. Website: www.hampshirecountryschool.org

HILLSIDE SCHOOL

404 Robin Hill Street
Marlborough, Massachusetts 01752

Head of School: David Z. Beecher

General Information Boys' boarding and day college-preparatory and leadership school; primarily serves students with learning disabilities, individuals with Attention Deficit Disorder, and dyslexic students. Grades 5–9. Founded: 1901. Setting: small town. Nearest major city is Boston. Students are housed in single-sex dormitories. 150-acre campus. 15 buildings on campus. Approved or accredited by Association of Independent Schools in New England, Junior Boarding Schools Association, The Association of Boarding Schools, and Massachusetts Department of Education. Member of National Association of Independent Schools and Secondary School Admission Test Board. Endowment: $4 million. Total enrollment: 150. Upper school average class size: 10. Upper school faculty-student ratio: 1:7. There are 160 required school days per year for Upper School students. Upper School students typically attend 5 days per week. The average school day consists of 9 hours.

Student Profile 67% of students are boarding students. 50% are state residents. 12 states are represented in upper school student body. 28% are international students. International students from Bermuda, Canada, China, Japan, Mexico, and Republic of Korea; 6 other countries represented in student body.

Faculty School total: 32. In upper school: 19 men, 13 women; 14 have advanced degrees; 25 reside on campus.

Subjects Offered Algebra, American government, American history, ancient history, art, earth science, economics, English, English literature, environmental science, ESL, French, geography, geometry, international relations, leadership, life science, mathematics, music, physical education, science, social skills, social studies, Spanish, woodworking, writing.

Graduation Requirements Art, English, foreign language, leadership, mathematics, music, science, social studies (includes history).

Special Academic Programs Honors section; academic accommodation for the gifted; remedial reading and/or remedial writing; remedial math; programs in general development for dyslexic students; ESL (20 students enrolled).

Secondary School Placement 37 students graduated in 2014; they went to Avon Old Farms School; Dublin School; New Hampton School; Phillips Exeter Academy; St. Paul's School; The Williston Northampton School.

Student Life Specified standards of dress, student council, honor system. Discipline rests primarily with faculty.

Tuition and Aid Day student tuition: $31,300; 5-day tuition and room/board: $47,300; 7-day tuition and room/board: $53,300. Tuition installment plan (SMART Tuition Payment Plan, monthly payment plans). Need-based scholarship grants available. In 2014–15, 36% of students received aid. Total amount of financial aid awarded in 2014–15: $1,500,000.

Admissions For fall 2014, 161 students applied for admission, 120 were accepted, 59 enrolled. Any standardized test, ISEE, SSAT, SSAT or WISC III, WISC III or other aptitude measures; standardized achievement test or WISC-III and Woodcock-Johnson

required. Deadline for receipt of application materials: none. Application fee required: $50. Interview required.

Athletics Interscholastic: baseball, basketball, cross-country running, hockey, ice hockey, lacrosse, running, soccer, track and field, wrestling; intramural: alpine skiing, bicycling, canoeing/kayaking, climbing, crew, fishing, fitness, flag football, floor hockey, football, Frisbee, golf, hiking/backpacking, ice skating, indoor hockey, indoor soccer, mountain biking, outdoor activities, outdoor adventure, outdoor education, outdoor recreation, outdoor skills, physical training, rock climbing, ropes courses, rowing, running, sailing, skiing (downhill), snowboarding, soccer, swimming and diving, table tennis, tennis, touch football, ultimate Frisbee, volleyball, walking, weight lifting, weight training, whiffle ball, yoga. 1 athletic trainer.

Computers Computers are regularly used in all academic, art, music classes. Computer network features include on-campus library services, Internet access, Internet filtering or blocking technology. Student e-mail accounts and computer access in designated common areas are available to students.

Contact William J. Newman, Assistant Headmaster for Enrollment. 508-485-2824. Fax: 508-485-4420. E-mail: admissions@hillsideschool.net. Website: www.hillsideschool.net

INDIAN MOUNTAIN SCHOOL

211 Indian Mountain Road
Lakeville, Connecticut 06039

Head of School: Mark A. Devey

General Information Coeducational boarding and day college-preparatory, general academic, arts, and ESL school. Boarding grades 6–9, day grades PK–9. Founded: 1922. Setting: rural. Nearest major city is Hartford. Students are housed in single-sex dormitories. 600-acre campus. 12 buildings on campus. Approved or accredited by Connecticut Association of Independent Schools, Junior Boarding Schools Association, The Association of Boarding Schools, and Connecticut Department of Education. Member of National Association of Independent Schools and Secondary School Admission Test Board. Endowment: $8 million. Total enrollment: 256. Upper school average class size: 12. Upper school faculty-student ratio: 1:4. There are 163 required school days per year for Upper School students. Upper School students typically attend 5 days per week. The average school day consists of 9 hours.

Student Profile Grade 7: 42 students (26 boys, 16 girls); Grade 8: 60 students (38 boys, 22 girls); Grade 9: 43 students (30 boys, 13 girls). 50% of students are boarding students. 21% are state residents. 8 states are represented in upper school student body. 11% are international students. International students from Bahamas, China, Jamaica, Japan, Mexico, and Republic of Korea; 6 other countries represented in student body.

Faculty School total: 51. In upper school: 20 men, 21 women; 24 have advanced degrees; 29 reside on campus.

Subjects Offered Algebra, American history, ancient history, art, biology, ceramics, Chinese, computers, earth science, English, film, fine arts, French, general science, geometry, health, history, Latin, mathematics, music, physical science, social studies, Spanish, theater.

Graduation Requirements Arts and fine arts (art, music, dance, drama), English, foreign language, mathematics, music, science, social studies (includes history).

Special Academic Programs ESL (11 students enrolled).

Secondary School Placement 47 students graduated in 2014; they went to Berkshire School; Choate Rosemary Hall; Kent School; Millbrook School; Suffield Academy; The Hotchkiss School.

Student Life Specified standards of dress, student council, honor system. Discipline rests primarily with faculty.

Tuition and Aid Day student tuition: $27,400; 7-day tuition and room/board: $52,000. Tuition installment plan (Key Tuition Payment Plan). Need-based scholarship grants available. In 2014–15, 22% of students received aid. Total amount of financial aid awarded in 2014–15: $683,914.

Admissions For fall 2014, 109 students applied for admission, 71 were accepted, 44 enrolled. WISC or WAIS, WISC-III and Woodcock-Johnson or WISC/Woodcock-Johnson required. Deadline for receipt of application materials: none. Application fee required: $50. Interview required.

Athletics Interscholastic: aerobics/dance (girls), baseball (b), basketball (b,g), football (b), golf (b,g), ice hockey (b), lacrosse (b,g), soccer (b,g), softball (g); intramural: dance (g); coed interscholastic: alpine skiing, cross-country running, golf, ice hockey, outdoor adventure, skiing (downhill), squash, tennis, volleyball; coed intramural: alpine skiing, backpacking, skiing (downhill), snowboarding, tennis, ultimate Frisbee. 20 coaches, 1 athletic trainer.

Computers Computers are regularly used in English, history, mathematics, science, social studies classes. Computer network features include on-campus library services, Internet access, Internet filtering or blocking technology. Student e-mail accounts are available to students. The school has a published electronic and media policy.

Contact Alan O'Neill, Director of Admission. 860-435-0871. Fax: 860-435-1380. E-mail: admissions@indianmountain.org. Website: www.indianmountain.org

NORTH COUNTRY SCHOOL

4382 Cascade Road
Lake Placid, New York 12946

Head of School: David Hochschartner

General Information Coeducational boarding and day college-preparatory, general academic, and arts school. Grades 4–9. Founded: 1938. Setting: rural. Nearest major city is Albany. Students are housed in coed dormitories. 220-acre campus. 11 buildings on campus. Approved or accredited by New York State Association of Independent Schools and New York Department of Education. Member of National Association of Independent Schools and Secondary School Admission Test Board. Endowment: $11 million. Total enrollment: 80. Upper school average class size: 10. Upper school faculty-student ratio: 1:3. Upper School students typically attend 5 days per week. The average school day consists of 5 hours and 15 minutes.

Student Profile Grade 6: 7 students (1 boy, 6 girls); Grade 7: 12 students (10 boys, 2 girls); Grade 8: 23 students (15 boys, 8 girls); Grade 9: 26 students (12 boys, 14 girls). 87% of students are boarding students. 33% are state residents. 13 states are represented in upper school student body. 32% are international students. International students from China, Guatemala, Japan, Mexico, South Africa, and Thailand; 1 other country represented in student body.

Faculty School total: 34. In upper school: 16 men, 18 women; 13 have advanced degrees; 30 reside on campus.

Subjects Offered 3-dimensional art, acting, advanced math, African dance, African drumming, algebra, American history, art, audio visual/media, ballet, band, batik, biology, ceramics, clayworking, collage and assemblage, computer music, computer science, creative dance, creative writing, culinary arts, dance, dance performance, digital photography, directing, drama, drama performance, drama workshop, dramatic arts, drawing, drawing and design, earth and space science, earth science, electives, English, English as a foreign language, English language and composition-AP, equestrian sports, ESL, fabric arts, fiber arts, film studies, fine arts, general science, geometry, guitar, history, instrumental music, Japanese, jazz, jewelry making, justice seminar, language arts, life science, mathematics, metalworking, modern dance, music, music composition, music performance, musical theater, painting, performing arts, photo shop, photography, physical education, physical science, piano, play production, portfolio art, pottery, pre-algebra, pre-calculus, printmaking, public speaking, reading, robotics, set design, shop, social studies, Spanish, stage design, stagecraft, stone carving, studio art, tap dance, theater, theater arts, theater design and production, typing, video, visual and performing arts, water color painting, weaving, welding, wind instruments, woodworking, world cultures, world history, writing.

Special Academic Programs Remedial reading and/or remedial writing; remedial math; ESL (11 students enrolled).

Secondary School Placement 16 students graduated in 2015; they went to Dublin School; Gould Academy; Northwood School; St. Paul's School; The Ethel Walker School; Trinity-Pawling School.

Student Life Specified standards of dress, student council. Discipline rests primarily with faculty.

Summer Programs ESL, art/fine arts programs offered; session focuses on recreation, arts, ESL, and outdoor programs; held on campus; accepts boys and girls; open to students from other schools. 180 students usually enrolled. 2016 schedule: June 27 to August 19. Application deadline: April 16.

Tuition and Aid Day student tuition: $26,400; 7-day tuition and room/board: $59,900. Tuition installment plan (monthly payment plans, individually arranged payment plans, 2-payment plan, Your Tuition Solutions). Need-based scholarship grants available. In 2015–16, 37% of students received aid. Total amount of financial aid awarded in 2015–16: $765,481.

Admissions Deadline for receipt of application materials: none. No application fee required. On-campus interview required.

Athletics Coed Interscholastic: alpine skiing, basketball, biathlon, climbing, cross-country running, freestyle skiing, Frisbee, independent competitive sports, nordic skiing, rock climbing, running, skiing (cross-country), skiing (downhill), snowboarding, soccer, track and field, ultimate Frisbee; coed intramural: aerobics/dance, backpacking, ballet, basketball, biathlon, bicycling, canoeing/kayaking, climbing, cross-country running, dance, drill team, equestrian sports, fishing, fitness walking, flag football, freestyle skiing, Frisbee, hiking/backpacking, hockey, horseback riding, ice skating, indoor soccer, jogging, martial arts, modern dance, mountain biking, mountaineering, nordic skiing, outdoor activities, outdoor adventure, outdoor education, outdoor recreation, outdoor skills, outdoors, paddle tennis, physical fitness, rock climbing, running, skateboarding, skiing (cross-country), skiing (downhill), snowboarding, snowshoeing, soccer, table tennis, telemark skiing, tennis, track and field, ultimate Frisbee, walking, winter walking, yoga.

Computers Computers are regularly used in all academic classes. Computer network features include on-campus library services, Internet access, wireless campus network, Internet filtering or blocking technology. Student e-mail accounts are available to students. The school has a published electronic and media policy.

Contact David Damico, Director of Admissions. 518-523-9329 Ext. 6000. Fax: 518-523-4858. E-mail: admissions@northcountryschool.org. Website: www.northcountryschool.org

THE RECTORY SCHOOL

528 Pomfret Street
P. O. Box 68
Pomfret, Connecticut 06258

Head of School: Fred Williams

General Information Coeducational boarding and day and distance learning college-preparatory, general academic, arts, bilingual studies, technology, and music school, affiliated with Episcopal Church; primarily serves underachievers, individuals with Attention Deficit Disorder, dyslexic students, OCD, and Executive Functioning. Boarding grades 5–9, day grades K–9. Distance learning grade 9. Founded: 1920. Setting: rural. Nearest major city is Hartford. Students are housed in single-sex dormitories. 138-acre campus. 24 buildings on campus. Approved or accredited by Junior Boarding Schools Association, National Independent Private Schools Association, The Association of Boarding Schools, and Connecticut Department of Education. Member of National Association of Independent Schools and Secondary School Admission Test Board. Endowment: $10 million. Total enrollment: 243. Upper school average class size: 12. Upper school faculty-student ratio: 1:4. There are 175 required school days per year for Upper School students. Upper School students typically attend 5 days per week. The average school day consists of 7 hours.

Student Profile Grade 6: 19 students (13 boys, 6 girls); Grade 7: 34 students (24 boys, 10 girls); Grade 8: 82 students (54 boys, 28 girls); Grade 9: 57 students (40 boys, 17 girls). 69% of students are boarding students. 30% are state residents. 13 states are represented in upper school student body. 40% are international students. International students from China, Japan, Mexico, Nigeria, and Republic of Korea; 3 other countries represented in student body. 14% of students are members of Episcopal Church.

Faculty School total: 57. In upper school: 23 men, 34 women; 25 have advanced degrees; 27 reside on campus.

Subjects Offered Algebra, American Civil War, American history, American literature, ancient world history, art, biology, chorus, creative arts, creative writing, drama, earth science, ecology, English, English literature, environmental science, expository writing, fine arts, foreign language, French, general science, geography, geometry, grammar, history, journalism, Latin, life science, Mandarin, mathematics, music, photography, physical education, physical science, reading, science, social studies, Spanish, study skills, theater, vocal music, world history, world literature, writing.

Graduation Requirements Arts and fine arts (art, music, dance, drama), literature, mathematics, physical education (includes health), science, social studies (includes history).

Special Academic Programs Honors section; academic accommodation for the gifted, the musically talented, and the artistically talented; remedial reading and/or remedial writing; remedial math; programs in English, mathematics, general development for dyslexic students; special instructional classes for students with learning disabilities, Attention Deficit Disorder, dyslexia, and Executive Functioning; ESL (25 students enrolled).

Secondary School Placement 56 students graduated in 2015; they went to Kent School; Millbrook School; Northfield Mount Hermon School; Pomfret School; Tabor Academy; The Hotchkiss School.

Student Life Specified standards of dress, student council, honor system. Discipline rests primarily with faculty.

Summer Programs Remediation, enrichment, advancement, ESL, sports, art/fine arts, computer instruction programs offered; session focuses on academics and recreational; held on campus; accepts boys and girls; open to students from other schools. 45 students usually enrolled. 2016 schedule: June 26 to July 22. Application deadline: none.

Tuition and Aid Day student tuition: $25,400; 5-day tuition and room/board: $45,600; 7-day tuition and room/board: $52,700. Tuition installment plan (monthly payment plans). Need-based scholarship grants available. In 2015–16, 38% of students received aid. Total amount of financial aid awarded in 2015–16: $1,600,000.

Admissions Traditional entrance grade is 8. For fall 2015, 225 students applied for admission, 148 were accepted, 82 enrolled. SSAT, TOEFL Junior or TOEFL or SLEP required. Deadline for receipt of application materials: none. Application fee required: $50. Interview required.

Athletics Interscholastic: baseball (boys), basketball (b,g), cross-country running (b,g), flag football (b), football (b), golf (b,g), lacrosse (b,g), soccer (b,g), softball (g), volleyball (g), wrestling (b); intramural: basketball (b,g), soccer (b); coed interscholastic: backpacking, cross-country running, dance, equestrian sports, fencing, golf, hockey, horseback riding, ice hockey, lacrosse, running, soccer, squash, strength & conditioning, tennis, track and field, yoga; coed intramural: basketball, bowling, climbing, cooperative games, cross-country running, dance, equestrian sports, fencing, fitness, flag football, golf, ice hockey, jogging, lacrosse, life saving, outdoor adventure, ropes courses, running, skiing (downhill), snowboarding, snowshoeing, soccer, softball, squash, street hockey, strength & conditioning, table tennis, tennis, touch football, ultimate Frisbee, volleyball, weight training, whiffle ball, yoga. 35 coaches, 1 athletic trainer.

Computers Computers are regularly used in English, French, history, mathematics, multimedia, music, science, Spanish, writing, yearbook classes. Computer network features include on-campus library services, online commercial services, Internet access, wireless campus network, Internet filtering or blocking technology. Campus intranet and student e-mail accounts are available to students. Students grades are available online. The school has a published electronic and media policy.

Contact John Seaward, Director of Enrollment. 860-928-1328. Fax: 860-928-4961. E-mail: admissions@rectoryschool.org. Website: www.rectoryschool.org

RUMSEY HALL SCHOOL

201 Romford Road
Washington Depot, Connecticut 06794

Head of School: Thomas W. Farmen

General Information Coeducational boarding and day college-preparatory, general academic, arts, bilingual studies, and technology school. Boarding grades 5–9, day grades K–9. Founded: 1900. Setting: rural. Nearest major city is Hartford. Students are housed in single-sex dormitories. 147-acre campus. 32 buildings on campus. Approved or accredited by Connecticut Association of Independent Schools, National Independent Private Schools Association, The Association of Boarding Schools, and Connecticut Department of Education. Member of National Association of Independent Schools and Secondary School Admission Test Board. Total enrollment: 420. Upper school average class size: 12. Upper school faculty-student ratio: 1:5. There are 180 required school days per year for Upper School students. Upper School students typically attend 6 days per week. The average school day consists of 6 hours and 40 minutes.

Student Profile 54% of students are boarding students. 21% are state residents. 15 states are represented in upper school student body. 20% are international students. International students from Bermuda, China, Japan, Mexico, Republic of Korea, and Russian Federation; 4 other countries represented in student body.

Faculty School total: 58. In upper school: 28 men, 30 women; 25 have advanced degrees; 40 reside on campus.

Subjects Offered Algebra, American history, American literature, art, art history, biology, computer science, creative writing, drama, earth science, English, English literature, environmental science, ESL, European history, fine arts, French, geography, geometry, government/civics, grammar, health, history, Japanese history, Latin, mathematics, music, physical education, science, social studies, Spanish, theater, world history, writing.

Graduation Requirements Arts and fine arts (art, music, dance, drama), computer science, English, foreign language, mathematics, physical education (includes health), science, social studies (includes history).

Special Academic Programs Academic accommodation for the gifted; remedial reading and/or remedial writing; programs in English for dyslexic students; special instructional classes for students with learning disabilities and Attention Deficit Disorder; ESL (23 students enrolled).

Secondary School Placement 78 students graduated in 2015; they went to Avon Old Farms School; Berkshire School; Kent School; St. George's School; The Gunnery; The Taft School.

Student Life Specified standards of dress, student council, honor system. Discipline rests primarily with faculty.

Summer Programs Enrichment, ESL programs offered; session focuses on academic enrichment; held on campus; accepts boys and girls; open to students from other schools. 60 students usually enrolled. 2016 schedule: June 27 to July 30. Application deadline: May 1.

Tuition and Aid Day student tuition: $25,160; 7-day tuition and room/board: $53,525. Tuition installment plan (monthly payment plans, individually arranged payment plans). Need-based scholarship grants available. In 2015–16, 24% of students received aid.

Admissions Traditional entrance grade is 8. For fall 2015, 152 students applied for admission, 85 were accepted, 60 enrolled. Psychoeducational evaluation, SLEP, SSAT, Wechsler Intelligence Scale for Children III or writing sample required. Deadline for receipt of application materials: none. Application fee required: $100. On-campus interview required.

Athletics Interscholastic: baseball (boys), basketball (b,g), crew (b,g), field hockey (g), football (b), ice hockey (b,g), lacrosse (b), soccer (b), softball (g), volleyball (g), wrestling (b); coed interscholastic: alpine skiing, cross-country running, horseback riding, skiing (downhill), soccer, tennis; coed intramural: alpine skiing, archery, backpacking, bicycling, broomball, canoeing/kayaking, climbing, cooperative games, equestrian sports, fishing, fly fishing, Frisbee, hiking/backpacking, ice skating, mountain biking, outdoor activities, outdoors, physical fitness, physical training, project adventure, roller blading, ropes courses, running, skateboarding, skiing (downhill), snowboarding, strength & conditioning, table tennis, tennis, track and field, ultimate Frisbee, wall climbing, weight lifting, weight training, whiffle ball. 1 PE instructor, 28 coaches, 1 athletic trainer.

Computers Computers are regularly used in all academic, English, history, mathematics, science classes. Computer network features include on-campus library services, Internet access, wireless campus network, Internet filtering or blocking technology. Campus intranet, student e-mail accounts, and computer access in designated common areas are available to students. The school has a published electronic and media policy.

Contact Matthew S. Hoeniger, Assistant Headmaster. 860-868-0535. Fax: 860-868-7907. E-mail: admiss@rumseyhall.org. Website: www.rumseyhall.org

See Display below and Close-Up on page 668.

RUMSEY HALL SCHOOL

An Independent, Coed, Junior Boarding (5-9) and Day School (K-9)

A TRADITION OF EFFORT, FAMILY & COMMUNITY

DIRECTOR OF ADMISSION, MATT HOENIGER '81

201 Romford Road, Washington, CT 06794 | 860.868.0535 | admiss@rumseyhall.org | rumseyhall.org

ST. CATHERINE'S ACADEMY

215 North Harbor Boulevard
Anaheim, California 92805
Head of School: Sr. Johnellen Turner, OP

General Information Boys' boarding and day college-preparatory, general academic, religious studies, leadership/military tradition, ESL, and military school, affiliated with Roman Catholic Church. Boarding grades 4–8, day grades K–8. Founded: 1889. Setting: suburban. Nearest major city is Los Angeles. Students are housed in single-sex dormitories. 8-acre campus. 8 buildings on campus. Approved or accredited by Military High School and College Association, National Catholic Education Association, The Association of Boarding Schools, Western Association of Schools and Colleges, Western Catholic Education Association, and California Department of Education. Total enrollment: 145. Upper school average class size: 16. Upper school faculty-student ratio: 1:14. There are 180 required school days per year for Upper School students. Upper School students typically attend 5 days per week. The average school day consists of 7 hours and 45 minutes.

Student Profile 74% of students are boarding students. 48% are state residents. 3 states are represented in upper school student body. 46% are international students. International students from China and Mexico. 58% of students are Roman Catholic.

Faculty School total: 21. In upper school: 2 men, 13 women; 10 have advanced degrees; 7 reside on campus.

Subjects Offered Art, band, Catholic belief and practice, character education, choir, Civil War, computer applications, computer literacy, computer skills, conflict resolution, decision making skills, English, environmental systems, ESL, ethical decision making, ethics and responsibility, fine arts, fitness, grammar, guidance, guitar, health and wellness, health education, healthful living, history, instrumental music, instruments, interpersonal skills, keyboarding, lab/keyboard, leadership, leadership education training, life skills, marching band, mathematics, military history, military science, moral and social development, music, music appreciation, music history, music performance, participation in sports, personal development, personal fitness, personal growth, physical education, physical fitness, piano, pre-algebra, reading/study skills, religion, religious education, science, service learning/internship, single survival, social studies, Spanish, sports, survival training, swimming, volleyball, wind instruments, word processing, yearbook.

Special Academic Programs Special instructional classes for students with Attention Deficit Disorder and learning disabilities; ESL (14 students enrolled).

Secondary School Placement 46 students graduated in 2014; they went to Army and Navy Academy; Mater Dei High School; New Mexico Military Institute; Servite High School.

Student Life Uniform requirement, honor system. Discipline rests equally with students and faculty. Attendance at religious services is required.

Tuition and Aid Day student tuition: $12,100; 5-day tuition and room/board: $32,150; 7-day tuition and room/board: $42,835. Tuition installment plan (FACTS Tuition Payment Plan, monthly payment plans, individually arranged payment plans, 4 payments). Tuition reduction for siblings, need-based scholarship grants available. In 2014–15, 48% of students received aid. Total amount of financial aid awarded in 2014–15: $400,000.

Admissions Any standardized test required. Deadline for receipt of application materials: none. Application fee required: $100. Interview required.

Athletics Interscholastic: basketball, flag football, volleyball; intramural: ball hockey, baseball, basketball, bowling, cooperative games, cross-country running, drill team, equestrian sports, field hockey, fitness, flag football, golf, handball, life saving, physical fitness, physical training, soccer, softball, swimming and diving, touch football, track and field, volleyball, water volleyball, weight lifting. 1 PE instructor, 7 coaches.

Computers Computers are regularly used in English, history, science, social studies classes. Computer network features include Internet access, Internet filtering or blocking technology. Students grades are available online.

Contact Graciela Salvador, Director of Admissions. 714-772-1363 Ext. 103. Fax: 714-772-3004. E-mail: admissions@stcatherinesacademy.org. Website: www.StCatherinesAcademy.org

ST. THOMAS CHOIR SCHOOL

202 West 58th Street
New York, New York 10019-1406
Head of School: Rev. Charles F. Wallace

General Information Boys' boarding college-preparatory, general academic, arts, religious studies, technology, music, and pre-preparatory school, affiliated with Episcopal Church. Grades 3–8. Founded: 1919. Setting: urban. Students are housed in single-sex dormitories. 1 building on campus. Approved or accredited by National Association of Episcopal Schools, The Association of Boarding Schools, and New York Department of Education. Member of National Association of Independent Schools and Secondary School Admission Test Board. Endowment: $18 million. Total enrollment: 29. Upper school average class size: 5. Upper school faculty-student ratio: 1:5. Upper School students typically attend 7 days per week. The average school day consists of 6 hours.

Student Profile Grade 6: 3 students (3 boys); Grade 7: 8 students (8 boys); Grade 8: 3 students (3 boys). 100% of students are boarding students. 40% are state residents. 11 states are represented in upper school student body. 85% of students are members of Episcopal Church.

Faculty School total: 8. In upper school: 6 men, 2 women; 6 have advanced degrees; 7 reside on campus.

Subjects Offered Algebra, applied music, art, choir, computers, English, French, Greek, history, Latin, mathematics, music theory, physical education, science, study skills, theology, visual arts.

Graduation Requirements Arts and fine arts (art, music, dance, drama), English, foreign language, mathematics, physical education (includes health), religion (includes Bible studies and theology), science, social studies (includes history).

Special Academic Programs Academic accommodation for the gifted and the musically talented; remedial reading and/or remedial writing; remedial math; programs in general development for dyslexic students.

Secondary School Placement 7 students graduated in 2015.

Student Life Uniform requirement. Discipline rests primarily with faculty. Attendance at religious services is required.

Tuition and Aid 7-day tuition and room/board: $14,875. Tuition installment plan (monthly payment plans, individually arranged payment plans). Need-based scholarship grants available. In 2015–16, 80% of students received aid. Total amount of financial aid awarded in 2015–16: $190,000.

Admissions Admissions testing and audition required. Deadline for receipt of application materials: none. No application fee required. On-campus interview required.

Athletics Interscholastic: basketball, soccer, track and field; intramural: baseball, basketball, fitness, flag football, floor hockey, independent competitive sports, indoor hockey, indoor soccer, kickball, lacrosse, Newcombe ball, outdoor recreation, physical fitness, running, soccer, softball, strength & conditioning, table tennis, track and field, ultimate Frisbee, volleyball. 1 PE instructor.

Computers Computers are regularly used in art, English, foreign language, history, library, mathematics, music, science classes.

Contact Mrs. Lily I. Scott, Director of Admissions. 212-247-3311 Ext. 504. Fax: 212-247-3393. E-mail: lscott@choirschool.org. Website: www.choirschool.org

Junior Boarding Schools
Close-Ups

CARDIGAN MOUNTAIN SCHOOL
Canaan, New Hampshire

Type: Boys' day and boarding junior high school
Grades: 6–9
Enrollment: 214
Head of School: David J. McCusker Jr. '80, Head of School

THE SCHOOL

Cardigan Mountain School was founded in 1945 to serve the specific educational and developmental needs of boys during their formative middle school years. Two men whose vision and belief in their goal were unshakable—Harold P. Hinman, a Dartmouth College graduate, and William R. Brewster, then Headmaster of Kimball Union Academy—joined forces with legendary Dartmouth President Ernest M. Hopkins to obtain the land that is now the site of Cardigan Mountain's campus. Cardigan Mountain School opened with 24 boys, and, in 1954, upon merging with the Clark School of Hanover, New Hampshire, the School as it is known today began to emerge. Since that time, the School has grown to its current enrollment of more than 200 boys in grades 6 through 9, while the philosophy and objectives set forth by the founders have remained unchanged.

Cardigan was built upon an educational experience that emphasized rigorous academics and study habits, as well as spiritual guidance, physical training, and social orientation. In order to accomplish this purpose, Cardigan's program was tailored to each boy so that he made the best possible use of his potential in these areas. Thus, every boy had a balanced and well-rounded life: physically, mentally, and spiritually. This philosophy is the same today as it was in 1945.

The 425-acre campus, located on Canaan Street Lake, is 18 miles from Dartmouth College. Driving time from Boston is approximately 2½ hours. Some of the finest skiing in New England is only one hour away.

The self-perpetuating Board of Trustees is instrumental in guiding the School. The School's endowment is valued at more than $29 million. In 2013–14, Annual Giving was over $1 million.

Cardigan Mountain School is accredited by the New England Association of Schools and Colleges. Its memberships include the National Association of Independent Schools (NAIS), the Junior Boarding Schools Association (JBSA), the Independent Schools Association of Northern New England (ISANNE), the Association of Independent Schools of New England (AISNE), the Secondary School Admission Test Board (SSATB), the International Boys' School Coalition (IBSC), and The Association of Boarding Schools (TABS).

ACADEMIC PROGRAM

Cardigan's curriculum is designed to both support and challenge the student as he prepares for the academic programs characteristic of most independent secondary schools most graduates attend. In all disciplines, emphasis is placed upon the mastery of fundamental skills, content, and study skills needed to become academically self-sufficient.

The curriculum provides each student with thorough instruction in all the major courses and substantial exposure to a number of other subject areas that round out a boy's education at this age. Cardigan requires all students to take yearlong courses in English, mathematics, social studies, and science. In addition, a foreign language (French, Latin, or Spanish) is required of boys not enrolled in English as a second language. The average class size ranges from 4 to 16 students, and there is ability tracking within each grade. Assignments and examinations are designed to challenge but not overwhelm students. The sixth grade is grouped heterogeneously and follows a self-contained classroom model.

Beyond these major courses, the School also requires each boy to broaden his horizons and strengthen his scholastic preparation through additional course work in music, life skills, leadership, art, inventing, and/or woodworking.

Cardigan's Global Community Initiative (GCI) is an on-campus, community-wide, integrated initiative. Designed to work toward an open and global mindset in all members of the school community, its goal is to develop awareness, understanding, acceptance, and appreciation of one another through intentional opportunities for the entire school community to learn from a wide range of perspectives shaped by life experiences and social identities.

Cardigan students also take a course called Personalized Education for the Acquisition of Knowledge and Skills (PEAKS®), which helps them become stronger learners and self-advocates. The PEAKS program provides students with guided self-development and helps each student, no matter his skill level, become a better learner and self-advocate. PEAKS facilitates collaboration among the members of the Cardigan Mountain School community to respond to the evolving needs of each student by focusing on the process of learning through the acquisition of developmentally appropriate knowledge and skills.

Cardigan believes that every student learns differently. Through the PEAKS program, each boy comes to understand how he learns best, and becomes equipped with tools to use as he goes forward, enabling him to find success as a lifelong learner. The PEAKS program also offers additional support for students in and out of the classroom.

PEAKS coaches are available for one-on-one assistance in the afternoons and evenings. Recognizing that some students require regular extra help, while others may need less-frequent support, the program is designed to maximize the accessibility of the coaches for their students.

FACULTY AND ADVISERS

The faculty consists of nearly 70 full-and part-time members, the majority of whom reside on campus. More than one quarter of the faculty members are women; more than half of the faculty members have earned advanced academic degrees. All faculty members teach, coach, supervise dormitories, and serve as advisers for the students. Cardigan has a 4:1 student-faculty ratio. Of the greatest importance to Cardigan are the faculty members who, by setting and attaining personal goals, serve as positive role models for the boys. Cardigan faculty members bring with them a love for learning and a variety of skills, experiences, and talents that broaden and enrich the educational experience and inject warmth and enthusiasm into campus life.

SECONDARY SCHOOL PLACEMENT

Cardigan offers extensive assistance to the students and their parents in selecting and then applying to independent secondary schools. The Secondary School Placement Office begins the counseling process in the spring of the eighth grade and continues to guide the student and his family throughout the application experience. The Placement Office offers workshops on interviewing techniques, SSAT preparation, and essay writing.

Over the past few years, a number of Cardigan graduates have matriculated to schools such as Avon Old Farms, Brooks, Deerfield, Groton, Holderness, Hotchkiss, Lawrence, Phillips Andover, Phillips Exeter, Pomfret, Salisbury, St. Mark's, St. Paul's, Tabor, Taft, and Westminster.

STUDENT BODY AND CONDUCT

In 2013–14, 223 boys enrolled at Cardigan. There were 82 boys in the ninth grade, 75 in the eighth, 44 in the seventh, and 22 in the sixth. Almost 90 percent of the Cardigan students were boarders. In 2013–14, students came to Cardigan from twenty-one states and twelve countries.

Cardigan has a two-tiered disciplinary status system in order to inform students, their advisers, and parents when School expectations are not being met. This disciplinary system is used to correct patterns of misbehavior and to discipline those students who commit serious offenses. The Discipline Committee meets to hear cases deemed appropriate by the assistant headmaster and the dean of student life. Student leaders and faculty members are selected to participate in this committee that hears cases and makes a recommendation for consequences to the headmaster.

Cardigan has a clearly stated Honor Code, and all students are expected to abide by the spirit of that code.

ACADEMIC FACILITIES

The numerous buildings that house academic facilities are highlighted by the Bronfman Center. Completed in 1996, Bronfman Center features, among other things, the three Freda R. Caspersen state-of-the-art science laboratories, an art studio, the Bhirombhakdi Computer Center, and a large classroom for the sixth-grade class. Stoddard Center is the home of both the Kirk Library and the Humann Theatre. Opened in 1982, the Kirk Library is a three-tiered, well-equipped multimedia resource center that offers students and faculty members computer software and audio-visual resources, in addition to more than 10,000 printed volumes and numerous journals and periodicals. Thousands of newspaper and magazine articles are available through online resources provided by the library. Computers with Internet access are available in both the Kirk Library and the adjacent PEAKS department. Affiliation with the New Hampshire State Library's Automated Information Access System enables users at the School to obtain materials through the interlibrary loan process. The library is supported by both a librarian and a technology integration specialist. A flexible access plan allows students and faculty members to work in groups, as well as individually, throughout the day and five evenings each week. Humann, the 250-seat theater, is the site of weekly All-School Meetings, lectures, films, concerts, and drama performances.

Cardigan emphasizes the visual arts. The Williams Woodshop and the Needham Gallery and art center are focal points for this important aspect of a boy's education. Opportunities for vocal and instrumental instruction are available, with the Humann Theatre and Cardigan chapel providing performance venues for individual performers, instrumental ensembles, and choral groups.

Cardigan's E.P.I.C. (Engineering, Possibilities, Imagination, Creativity) Center is designed to complement the Charles C. Gates Invention and Innovation Competition and I.D.E.A (Innovation in Design, Engineering, and the Arts) Shop, and expand and enhance the School's commitment to hands-on learning, problem solving, and creative thinking. The Center includes facilities/equipment for Lego Robotics and Arduino programs.

All dormitory rooms and many classrooms are wired for access to the Internet.

BOARDING AND GENERAL FACILITIES

Eleven dormitories house from 8 to 16 students each. Each dormitory houses faculty members and their families. Students reside in double rooms, with some singles provided. Two dormitories, referred to as "houses," were completed in fall 2000 and each houses three faculty members, their families, and 12 students. Hayward Hall, which previously served as the dining hall and a dormitory, was completely renovated in 2014. The dormitory now includes five faculty residences and houses 28 students.

The Cardigan Commons opened in May 2013 and includes a new kitchen and dining facility, a student center, a student store, and educational space—and is the hub of campus life. The next capital project underway is the construction of a new dormitory, with completion expected before the 2016–17 school year.

The School operates the on-campus Hamilton Family Foundation Student Health Center, where most of the students' medical needs can be met. For extended services, Cardigan students benefit from the Alice Peck Day Hospital and Dartmouth-Hitchcock Medical Center, both of which are located in Lebanon, New Hampshire. The campus health center has a resident nurse, several full- and part-time staff members, and a visiting physician.

ATHLETICS

The objectives of the activities program at Cardigan are to provide the boys with opportunities to experience success, to offer healthy and enjoyable activities for the boys' free-time periods and weekends, to promote the physical and athletic development of each boy, to teach cooperation with and reliance on teammates, to allow the boys to experience sports and activities that may be new or unfamiliar to them, and to encourage good sportsmanship.

Over the years, Cardigan has been fortunate to acquire extensive athletics facilities, fields, and equipment. These include five fields for soccer, football, and lacrosse; fourteen outdoor tennis courts; two baseball diamonds; a state-of-the-art hockey rink that can be converted to a multipurpose arena in the fall and spring; an on-campus ski slope; mountain biking trails; cross-country running and cross-country ski trails; ski team rooms; a wrestling room; an indoor climbing cave; a fully-equipped fitness room; and indoor and outdoor basketball courts.

As the School is situated on the shores of Canaan Street Lake, students and faculty members take full advantage of water-related activities. Sailing is pursued in the School's fleet of competition sailboats. Motorboats, rowboats, canoes, kayaks, and paddleboards provide additional opportunities for students to enjoy the water. The waterfront area is well supervised, and instruction is available in all activities.

The Sunapee Mountain ski area is close to the School and is used on weekdays by the Alpine ski team, recreational skiers, and snowboarders. On Sundays, there are day-long ski trips to major ski areas in New Hampshire and Vermont.

As in the classroom, the focus of interscholastic sports and individual activities is on learning the fundamentals. Teams are fielded on several levels in most sports, and they compete against local independent and public schools. Recreational sports are offered for the student who does not wish to compete interscholastically.

EXTRACURRICULAR OPPORTUNITIES
Many students and faculty members bring to Cardigan skills and interests that, though not included in the usual program of studies, may be pursued and developed in the informal setting of the Club Program. Clubs meet every Thursday afternoon in lieu of athletics, with the opportunity for additional meetings if the members and adviser so desire. Recent clubs have participated in community service, a rock band, technical rock-climbing, Rube Goldberg, Lego Robotics, ice fishing, kite surfing, chess, photography, SSAT prep, stained glass, Whiffle ball, broomball, and team handball.

A boy may participate in the drama program in each of the three seasons. The department mounts four productions a year: a series of one-act plays, the annual Christmas pageant, a full-length play/musical, and scenes from plays during the spring term talent show. Boys are given opportunities to act, serve backstage, learn to work lights and sound, build and decorate sets, produce, and, in some cases, direct. During the nights of performance, the student stage managers and student technical staff run the entire show. The

audition process gives boys an excellent opportunity to learn the skills required to get a part.

DAILY LIFE
The typical academic day begins six days per week with a required family-style breakfast. After room inspection in the dormitories, classes begin at 7:55 a.m. Six class periods precede a family-style lunch. On Monday, Tuesday, Thursday, and Friday, lunch is followed by an advisory/conference period and a study period. On Wednesday and Saturday, the academic day ends with lunch and is followed by a full slate of athletics and recreational activities. Dinner is a family-style meal every evening except Wednesday and Saturday, when a buffet is scheduled. A study period occurs each school night. Lights-out ranges from 9:20 to 10 p.m., depending on the evening and the age of the student.

Cardigan is nondenominational, yet the School seeks to strengthen each boy's spiritual development within his own religious heritage. All boys are required to attend the weekly Thursday afternoon Chapel service. Arrangements are made for students of different faiths to attend their own weekly services in the immediate area.

WEEKEND LIFE
In addition to the regularly scheduled vacations, all boys may take weekends away from the campus and parents are invited to the campus to share in their son's experience at any time. The majority of Cardigan students are on campus on weekends, and the School provides an exciting array of options. A typical Saturday night's schedule might include a movie, a trip off campus, various other on-campus activities and programs, or an excursion to Dartmouth College to watch a hockey game.

SUMMER PROGRAMS
The Cardigan Mountain Summer Session, a coeducational experience for 170 girls and boys, was instituted in 1951 to meet the needs of four groups of students: those who may be seeking admission to Cardigan in the fall, those who desire advanced academic work and enrichment, those who require intensive work in basic academic skills, and those who require review. The Summer Session also serves a limited number of international students for whom English is not the first language. Cardigan's outstanding range of sports and activities, along with its academic offerings, makes the Summer Session a special blend of camp and school.

Academic enrichment offerings in the sciences are a focal point for the more able students. Courses in environmental sciences were designed to better prepare youngsters for the changing world. The visual and performing arts, long a part of the Summer Session's afternoon program, achieved curricular status, allowing students to pursue drama, ceramics, and photography as part of their morning academic program of study.

The six-week program is still known for its individualized instruction, close supervision of daily

study time, and general emphasis on improving study skills. Academic offerings include English, advanced English composition, pre-algebra, algebra (I and II), geometry, study skills, French, Spanish, Latin, and Mandarin Chinese.

The Summer Session is open to students who have completed third through ninth grade. Need-based aid is available for tuition assistance.

COSTS AND FINANCIAL AID
In 2015–16, charges for boarding students were $53,785 and for day students, $31,220. There are additional charges for items such as textbooks, laundry service, and athletic equipment.

Financial aid is available to families of qualified students who complete the School and Student Service for Financial Aid forms and demonstrate need. Information about loans and payment plans is available from the Cardigan Admissions Office.

ADMISSIONS INFORMATION
Cardigan seeks to enroll students of good character and academic promise who will contribute to and benefit from the broad range of academic and extracurricular opportunities available. The Admissions Committee reviews applications on a rolling admissions basis for students wishing to enter the sixth through the ninth grades. Students in grades 3–9 are considered for the Summer Session. Decisions are based upon previous school records, teacher recommendations, aptitude testing, and a campus interview. Cardigan admits students of any race, color, nationality, or ethnic origin to all the rights, privileges, programs, and activities generally accorded or made available to students at the School.

APPLICATION TIMETABLE
Initial inquiries are welcome at any time. Office hours are 8 a.m. to 4 p.m., Monday through Friday, and 8 a.m. to noon on Saturday. School catalogs and applications can be obtained through the Admissions Office. The application fee is $50 for domestic applicants and $125 for international applicants.

ADMISSIONS CORRESPONDENCE
Chip Audett, Director of Admissions and
    Financial Aid
Cardigan Mountain School
62 Alumni Drive
Canaan, New Hampshire 03741
United States
Phone: 603-523-3510
Fax: 603-523-3565
E-mail: caudett@cardigan.org
Website: http://www.cardigan.org

Devin Clifford, Director of the Summer Session
Cardigan Mountain School
62 Alumni Drive
Canaan, New Hampshire 03741
United States
Phone: 603-523-3526
Fax: 603-523-3565
E-mail: dclifford@cardigan.org

EAGLEBROOK SCHOOL

Deerfield, Massachusetts

Type: Boys' day and boarding school
Grades: 6–9
Enrollment: 250
Head of School: Andrew C. Chase, Headmaster

THE SCHOOL

Eaglebrook School was opened in 1922 by its Headmaster and founder, Howard B. Gibbs, a former faculty member of Deerfield Academy. One of the earliest members of his faculty was C. Thurston Chase. When Mr. Gibbs died in 1928, Mr. Chase became Headmaster, a position he held for thirty-eight years. From 1966 to 2002, Stuart and Monie Chase assumed leadership of the School. While continuing to foster the School's traditional commitment to excellence, the Chases have encouraged and developed many components of a vital school: expansion of both academic and recreational facilities, emphasis on the arts, increased endowment and financial aid, student and faculty diversity, and a balanced, healthful diet. Stuart and Monie's son, Andrew C. Chase, now assumes leadership duties as Headmaster. Eaglebrook's goals are simple—to help each boy come into full and confident possession of his innate talents, to improve the skills needed for the challenges of secondary school, and to establish values that will allow him to be a person who acts with thoughtfulness and humanity.

The School owns more than 750 acres on Mt. Pocumtuck, overlooking the Deerfield Valley and the historic town of Deerfield. It is located 100 miles west of Boston and 175 miles north of New York City.

The Allen-Chase Foundation was chartered in 1937 as a charitable, educational trust. It is directed by a 40-member self-perpetuating Board of Trustees, representing alumni, parents, and outside professionals in many fields.

Eaglebrook is a member of the National Association of Independent Schools, the Association of Independent Schools of New England, the Valley Independent School Association, the Junior Boarding School Association, and the Secondary School Admissions Test Board.

ACADEMIC PROGRAM

Sixth graders are taught primarily in a self-contained setting. Subjects include English, mathematics, reading, Latin, history, science, and trimester-length courses in studio art, computers, music, and woodworking. Required classes for grades 7 through 9 each year include foreign language study in Latin, French, Mandarin Chinese, or Spanish; a full year of mathematics; a full year of Colonial history in seventh grade, followed by a self-selected history the next two years; a full year of English; two trimesters of geography; two trimesters of science in seventh grade, followed by a full-year laboratory course; one trimester of human sexuality in eighth grade; and one trimester of ethics in the ninth grade. The School offers

extensive trimester electives, including band and instrumental instruction, computer skills, word processing, current events, conditioning, chess, film classics, drama, public speaking, industrial field trips, music appreciation, first aid, publications, and an extensive variety of studio arts. Drug and alcohol education is required of all students in every grade.

Class enrollment averages 8 to 12 students. Teachers report directly to a student's adviser any time the student's work is noteworthy, either for excellence or deficiency. This allows the adviser to communicate praise or concern effectively and initiate appropriate follow-up. Midway through each trimester, teachers submit brief written evaluations to the advisers of each of their students. Advisers stay in close touch with the parents of their advisees. Grades, along with full academic reports from each of the student's teachers, are given to advisers each trimester and then sent home. The reports are accompanied by a letter from the adviser discussing the student's social adjustment progress, athletic and activity accomplishments, and academic progress and study habits.

FACULTY AND ADVISERS

Andrew C. Chase, the current Headmaster, is a graduate of Deerfield Academy and Williams College. Along with his wife, Rachel Blain, a graduate of Phillips Andover Academy and Amherst College, Andrew succeeded his father as Headmaster in 2002.

Eaglebrook's full- and part-time faculty consists of 72 men and women, 46 of whom live on campus, many with families of their own. Seventy hold undergraduate degrees, and 30 also hold graduate degrees. Leaves of absence, sabbaticals, and financial assistance for graduate study are available. The ratio of students to faculty members is 4.9:1.

Teachers endeavor to make learning an adventure and watch over each boy's personal growth. They set the academic tone, coach the teams, serve as dorm parents, and are available for a boy when he needs a friend. They help each individual establish lifelong study habits and set standards for quality. Eaglebrook's teachers have the skill not only to challenge the very able but also to make learning happen for those who need close supervision. Faculty members are chosen primarily for their appreciation of boys this age, their character and integrity as role models, and competence in their subject areas. The fact that many are married and have children of their own helps to create a warm, experienced family atmosphere.

SECONDARY SCHOOL PLACEMENT

The Director of Placement assists families in selecting, visiting, and applying to secondary schools. He meets with parents and students in the spring of a boy's eighth-grade year to discuss which schools might be appropriate based on each boy's aptitude, interests, achievements, and talent. He arranges visits from secondary schools and helps with applications. Parents and the Director of Placement work together until the boy has decided upon his secondary school in April of his ninth-grade year.

Schools frequently attended by Eaglebrook School graduates include Deerfield Academy, Choate Rosemary Hall, the Hotchkiss School, Loomis Chaffee, Northfield Mount Hermon School, Phillips Andover Academy, Phillips Exeter Academy, Pomfret School, St. George's School, St. Paul's School, Taft School, and Westminster School.

STUDENT BODY AND CONDUCT

In the 2015–16 school year, of the 200 boarding students and 50 day students, 20 are in grade 6, 52 in grade 7, 86 in grade 8, and 92 in grade 9. Twenty-five states and twenty countries are represented.

There are specified standards of dress, which are neat and informal most of the time. Discipline is handled on an individual basis by those faculty members who are closely involved with the student.

ACADEMIC FACILITIES

The newly renovated C. Thurston Chase Learning Center contains classrooms, an audiovisual center, and an assembly area. It also houses the Copley Library, which contains 18,000 volumes and subscriptions to eighty-five publications, books on CDs, newspapers, and Internet access. The computer room is equipped with state-of-the-art computers, color printers, scanners, digital cameras, and a projection board. The Bartlett Assembly Room is an all-purpose area with seats for the entire School. The campus has a high-speed fiber-optic network with e-mail and access to the Internet for research.

Construction is underway on the new Science, Art, and Music building of the Edward P. Evans Academic Center, which is due to be completed in November 2016. This will house the School's science laboratories; classrooms; studios for drawing, painting, stained glass, architectural design, computer-aided design, stone carving, ceramics, silk-screening, printmaking, and computer art; a darkroom for photography; a woodworking shop; a band rehearsal room; piano studios; piano practice rooms; musical instrument practice rooms; and a drama rehearsal room.

BOARDING AND GENERAL FACILITIES

Dormitories are relatively small; the five dormitories house between 40 students each, with at least one faculty family to every 8 to 10 boys.

Most students live in double rooms. A limited number of single rooms are available. After the first year, a boy may request a certain dormitory and adviser.

ATHLETICS

The athletics program is suitable for boys of all sizes and abilities. Teams are small enough to allow each boy a chance to play in the games, master skills, and develop a good sense of sportsmanship. The School's Athletic Director arranges a competitive schedule to ensure games with teams of equal ability. Fall sports include cross-country, tennis, mountain biking, football, water polo, and soccer. Winter sports include ice hockey, basketball, recreational and competitive skiing, ski patrol, swimming and diving, recreational and competitive snowboarding, squash, and wrestling. The School maintains the Easton Ski Area, consisting of several ski trails, the Macomber Chair Lift, and snowmaking equipment. Spring sports are baseball, track and field, golf, Ultimate Disc, lacrosse, Wilderness Rangers, and tennis. The School plays host to numerous students throughout the year in seasonal tournaments in ice hockey, soccer, skiing, basketball, Ultimate Disc, swimming, and wrestling. The Schwab Family Pool is a six-lane facility for both competitive and recreational swimming. The McFadden Rink at Alfond Arena features a state-of-the-art NHL-dimensioned 200-foot by 85-foot indoor ice surface. A multisport indoor surface is installed in the arena in the off-season to enable use of the facility for in-line skating, in-line hockey, soccer, lacrosse, and tennis. The Lewis Track and Field was dedicated in 2002.

EXTRACURRICULAR OPPORTUNITIES

Service and leadership opportunities build a sense of pride in the School and camaraderie in the student body. Elected Student Council representatives meet with the Headmaster as an advisory group and discuss School issues. Boys act as admissions guides, help with recycling, organize dances, serve as proctors in the dormitories and the dining room, act as headwaiters, and give the morning assemblies. Boys also assume responsibility, with faculty guidance, for the School newspaper, yearbook, and literary magazine.

Many of the students participate in numerous outdoor activities that are sponsored by the Mountain Club. They maintain an active weekend schedule that includes camping, hiking, backpacking, canoeing, kayaking, white-water rafting, fishing, rock climbing, and snowshoeing.

DAILY LIFE

On weekdays, students rise at 7:20 a.m.; breakfast is at 8. Academic class periods, including assembly, begin at 8:30. Lunch is at noon, and classes resume at 12:33. Study hall and special appointments begin at 2:15, athletics begin at 3:15, and tutorial periods and other activities begin at 5. Dinner is at 6, and evening activities are scheduled between 6:45 and 7:30; study hall is then held until 9:15 p.m. or later, according to the grade.

WEEKEND LIFE

A wide variety of weekend activities are available at Eaglebrook, both on campus and off, including community service, riflery, museum visits, dances, field trips, tournaments, movies, plays, concerts, town trips, Deerfield Academy games, bicycle trips, ski trips, hiking, camping, and mountain climbing. On Sunday, the Coordinator of Religion supervises a nondenominational and nonsectarian meeting for the student body. Attendance is required for boarding students. The aim is to share different beliefs and ways of worship. Transportation is provided for boys who wish to maintain their own religious commitment by attending local places of worship. Students with permission may leave the School for the weekend; 5–10 percent of the student body normally do so on a given weekend.

COSTS AND FINANCIAL AID

Eaglebrook School's tuition for the 2015–16 school year is $59,400 for boarding students and $36,100 for day students. Eaglebrook seeks to enroll boys from different backgrounds from this country and abroad, regardless of their ability to pay. Approximately 30 percent of the students receive financial aid. To apply for tuition assistance, a candidate must complete the School Scholarship Service's Parents' Financial Statement, which is obtainable from the Financial Aid Office.

ADMISSIONS INFORMATION

Most students enter in either the seventh or eighth grade, although students can be admitted to any grade. Information regarding required testing and transcripts can be obtained from the Admissions Office. A School visit and interview are required.

Eaglebrook welcomes boys of any race, color, religion, nation, or creed, and all share the same privileges and duties.

APPLICATION TIMETABLE

The School accepts applications throughout the year, but it is to the candidate's advantage to make application as early as possible. Decisions and notifications are made whenever a boy's file is complete. There is a $50 application fee ($100 for international students).

ADMISSIONS CORRESPONDENCE

Theodore J. Low
Director of Admissions
Eaglebrook School
271 Pine Nook Road, P.O. Box #7
Deerfield, Massachusetts 01342
United States
Phone: 413-774-9111 (admissions)
413-774-7411 (main)
Fax: 413-774-9119 (admissions)
413-772-2394 (main)
E-mail: admissions@eaglebrook.org
Website: http://www.eaglebrook.org

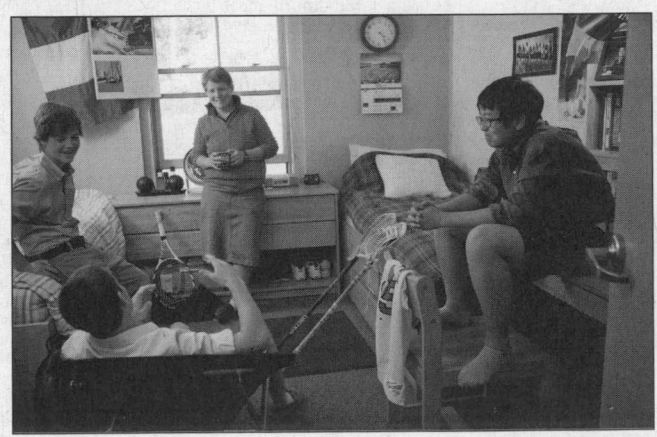

RUMSEY HALL SCHOOL

Washington Depot, Connecticut

Type: Coeducational Junior Boarding (grades 5–9) and Day Preparatory School
Grades: K–9: Lower School, K–5; Upper School, 6–9
Enrollment: School total: 335
Head of School: Thomas W. Farmen, Headmaster

THE SCHOOL

Rumsey Hall School was founded in 1900 by Mrs. Lillias Rumsey Sanford. Since its inception, Rumsey Hall School has retained its original philosophy: to help each child develop to his or her maximum stature as an individual, as a member of a family, and as a contributing member of society. The curriculum emphasizes basic academic skills, a complete athletic program, fine arts, computer literacy, and numerous extracurricular offerings, which are all designed to encourage individual responsibility for academic achievement, accomplishment in team sports, and service to the School community. The School believes that "effort is the key to success."

The 147-acre campus on the Bantam River provides landscaped and wooded areas in a rural environment located outside of Washington, Connecticut. Rumsey Hall School is 90 miles from New York City and within an hour of the major Connecticut cities of Hartford and New Haven. The School's location enables students to take advantage of major cultural and athletic events in New York City and Boston throughout the school year.

A nonprofit institution, Rumsey Hall School is governed by a 22-member Board of Trustees that meets quarterly. The 2014–15 operating budget totaled $9.3 million. Revenues include tuition and fees and contributions from alumni, parents, corporations, foundations, and friends of the School. The School's endowment is approximately $11.9 million. Annual fund giving was $1.5 million in 2014.

Rumsey Hall School is a member of the National Association of Independent Schools, the Connecticut Association of Independent Schools, the Junior Boarding Schools Association, the Educational Records Bureau, Western Connecticut Boarding Schools, and the Educational Testing Service, and is a voting member of the Secondary School Admission Test Board.

ACADEMIC PROGRAM

At Rumsey Hall, effort is as important as academic achievement. Effort as a criterion for success opens a new world to the students. Effort does not start and end with the student. It is a shared responsibility between the student and each faculty member. Just as the faculty members expect maximum effort from each student, they promise in return to give each student their very best effort.

Students in the Upper School (sixth through ninth grades) carry at least five major subjects. There are eight 40-minute periods in each day, including lunch. Extra help is available each day for students who need additional instruction or extra challenges. All classes are departmentalized.

Final examinations are given in all subjects twice a year. Report cards, with numerical grades, are sent home every other week throughout the school year. Anecdotal comments and individualized teacher, adviser, and Headmaster comments are sent home three times each academic year.

A supplementary feature of the academic program is the Language Skills Department, which is directed toward intellectually able students with dyslexia or learning differences. Students in this program carry a regular academic course load, with the exception of a foreign language. In 2014–15, 14 percent of the student body was involved in this program.

English as a Second Language (ESL) is offered to international students and is comprised of two levels with three courses in each level. The courses are designed to help students develop their conversational and academic English, reading comprehension, awareness of social and cultural differences, and to introduce them to American history.

The school year, divided into trimesters, begins in September and runs until the first weekend in June. Vacations are scheduled at Thanksgiving and Christmas and in the spring.

Class size averages between 12 and 14 students. Honors courses are offered to exceptional ninth grade students who demonstrate talent and whose scholarship indicates a strong sense of responsibility and motivation.

Students have a study hall built into their daily schedules, and there is an evening study hall for all boarding students. Study halls are supervised by faculty members, and there is ample opportunity for assistance. The library and computer facilities adjoin the formal study hall and are available at all study times.

In the Lower School (K through fifth grade), the nine daily academic periods begin at 8 a.m. after class meetings. English, reading, mathematics, science, and social studies are taught by the classroom teachers. Classes in foreign languages, language skills, health, music, art, and physical education vary the students' schedules by requiring them to move to different classrooms with specialized teachers. Normal class size is between 12 and 14 students, which makes for a dynamic learning environment where everyone's voice is heard and encouraged.

FACULTY AND ADVISERS

All 58 full- and part-time faculty members (28 men and 30 women) hold baccalaureate degrees, and half have master's degrees. Forty-two faculty members live on campus, many with their families. This enables Rumsey to provide the close supervision and warm family atmosphere that is an essential part of the School's culture.

Thomas W. Farmen was appointed Headmaster of Rumsey Hall School in 1985. He holds a Bachelor of Arts degree from New England College and a master's in school administration from Western Connecticut State University. He has served as President of the Association of Boarding Schools for the National Association of Independent Schools, President of the Junior Boarding Schools Association, and as a director of the Connecticut Association of Independent Schools.

The Dean of Students supervises and coordinates the advisory program. Each faculty member has 7 or 8 student advisees. Advisors meet with their advisees individually and in a weekly group setting. The advisor is the first link in the line of communication between school and home.

Faculty members at Rumsey Hall are encouraged to continue their professional development by taking postgraduate courses and attending seminars and conferences throughout the year. The School generously funds these programs.

SECONDARY SCHOOL PLACEMENT

The Director of Secondary School Placement supervises all facets of the secondary school search. Beginning in the eighth grade, a process of testing and interviewing with students and parents takes place that enables the placement director to highlight certain schools that seem appropriate. After visits and interviews with the schools, the list is pared down to those to which the student wishes to apply. Members of the 2014–15 class matriculated to the following secondary schools: Asheville School, NC; Avon Old Farms, CT (2); Berkshire School, MA (3); Blair Academy, NJ (2); Canterbury School, CT (10); Carol Morgan School, Dominican Republic; Choate Rosemary Hall, CT; Cushing Academy, MA; Deerfield School, MA (2); Dublin School, NH (2); Emma Willard School, NY; Ethel Walker School, CT; Forman School, CT; The Gunnery, CT (7); Hoosac School, NY; Hotchkiss School, CT (2); Kent School, CT (2); Kimball Union Academy, NH (2); Lawrence Academy, MA; Lawrenceville School, NJ (2); Loomis Chaffee School, CT (2); Mercersburg Academy, PA (2); Miss Hall's School, MA; Northfield Mount Hermon School, MA; Phillips Academy, Andover, MA; Phillips Exeter Academy, NH; Pomfret School, CT (3); St. Andrew's School, DE; Salisbury School, CT (3); Suffield Academy, CT (2); Taft School, CT (4); Vermont Academy, VT; and Westminster School, CT (4).

STUDENT BODY AND CONDUCT

In 2014–15, Rumsey Hall enrolled 335 students. The Lower School (grades K–5) enrolled 87 day and 4 boarding students. The Upper School (grades 6–9) enrolled 244 students: 105 day students and 139 boarders. The School population was 63 percent boys and 37 percent girls.

In 2015–16, Rumsey students came from fifteen states, fifteen countries, two U.S. territories, and twenty-seven local communities. International students enrolled in the ESL program composed 8 percent of the community.

The dress code requires jackets, collared shirts, and ties for boys and dresses or skirts and collared shirts or blouses for girls. In the winter term, boys may wear turtlenecks and sweaters and girls may wear slacks.

The School values of honesty, kindness, and respect comprise the yardstick by which Rumsey measures a student's thoughts and actions. Students living outside the spirit of the community are asked to meet with the Disciplinary and Senior Committees. These committees represent a cross section of administrators, faculty members, and students.

ACADEMIC FACILITIES

Situated alongside the Bantam River on a 147-acre campus, the School is housed in thirty buildings, most of which have been constructed since 1950. Nine structures house a total of thirty classrooms, including the Dane W. Dicke Family Math and Science Buildings. Other buildings include the Dicke Family Library; the Sanford House, which houses the study and meeting hall; the J. Seward Johnson Sr. Fine Arts Center, with spacious art and music rooms; the Satyvati Science Center; and a Campus Center that includes Farmen Hall—a dining hall where students and faculty members meet as a community for meals, Student Center, Health Center, School Store and Girls' Locker Room.

The Garassino Building is home to three lower school classrooms including an all-day kindergarten. The Maxwell A. Sarofim '05 Performing Arts Center (the MAX) is the setting for student performances, visiting artists, and school assemblies; students' art and exhibits of Rumsey community interest are displayed in the adjacent Allen Finkelson Gallery.

Rumsey has three fully interactive computer labs on campus and more than 120 wireless networked computers throughout the School with 34 wireless access points. The school-wide intranet system enhances communication within the community. The School network consists of a 40 gb single-mode fiber infrastructure with a 100 mb circuit that provides Internet to the School.

BOARDING AND GENERAL FACILITIES

The close relationship between teachers and students is a special part of Rumsey Hall School. Students live in dormitories with supportive dorm parents, and students become a part of their dorm parents' families.

Rumsey's boarding students live in one of eight dormitories. Dormitories are assigned by age, and most students have roommates, although single rooms are available in most dorms. Each dormitory has its own common room that is the shared living space for the dorm. A snack bar and store are open every afternoon. Laundry and dry cleaning are sent out on a weekly basis. Four registered nurses staff the School's infirmary, and the School doctor, a local pediatrician, is available on a daily basis. Emergency facilities are available at New Milford Hospital, which is 10 miles away. There are telephones in all dormitories, and every student has an e-mail account.

ATHLETICS

Athletics are a healthy and essential part of the Rumsey experience. On the playing field, lifelong attitudes, values, and habits are born. All students participate at their own level in athletics. Effort is rewarded through athletic letters and certificates at the end of the season.

Rumsey Hall fields thirty-nine interscholastic teams throughout the year. Most sports are offered on different levels so that students are able to compete with children of their own size and skill level. Over three seasons, 403 interscholastic teams are fielded in baseball, basketball, crew, cross-country, field hockey, football, boys' ice hockey, girls' ice hockey, lacrosse, skiing, soccer, softball, tennis, volleyball, and wrestling. Other activities available include horseback riding, Outdoor Club, Lower School games and activities, recreational skiing and snowboarding, biking, and ice-skating.

The John F. Schereschewsky, Sr. Memorial Center houses the Magnoli and Blue Dog Gymnasiums where basketball, volleyball, and wrestling activities are held. Recent renovations to the indoor athletic facilities include an indoor climbing wall, boys' and girls' locker rooms, and three new and improved tennis courts. The Cornell Common Room serves as the weight-training room and offers other training machines, as well as housing the athletic director and athletic training staff. Lufkin Rink is the newest of Rumsey Hall's athletic facilities. Opened in late 2008, the rink provides home ice for the boys' and girls' hockey teams. Intramural and recreational activities make the space available to skaters of all abilities.

There are several athletic fields on campus including the Pavek Athletic Field, in honor of Veronica D. and Charles H. Pavek; Scott Evans Seibert '92 Memorial Field; Paul Lincoln Cornell Athletic Field, and Roy Field. There are also three outdoor tennis courts and two ponds for outdoor recreation and winter skating.

Holt Beach at Lake Waramaug is the site for spring crew training. Off-season training is available for rowers in the state-of-the-art indoor rowing facility. Students who ski and snowboard in the winter term travel to Mohawk Mountain in nearby Cornwall, Connecticut on weekday afternoons.

EXTRACURRICULAR OPPORTUNITIES

Throughout the year, Upper School students may participate in many activities and clubs. The choices include fishing, computers, chorus, art club, bicycling, fly fishing, School newspaper, yearbook, art, swimming, hiking, rocketry, baking, community service, intramural sports, and participation in School dramatic and musical productions. The Rumsey Chamber Orchestra, Clef Club, and the a cappella singing group, Passing Notes, practice weekly and perform at various events throughout the year.

The Lower School features an exciting afternoon enrichment program for all students in kindergarten through fifth grade after their daily academic curriculum is complete. In keeping with Rumsey Hall's mission to educate the whole child, the varied activities offered each afternoon are organized to cultivate interests that can be nurtured as the children grow. Most activities are led by Rumsey teachers while others enlist the skills of specialists from surrounding communities. Activities include but are not limited to the arts (ceramics, printmaking, theater, crafts), athletics (field/gymnasium sports, martial arts), and recreational and outdoor games.

Traditional annual events for the School community include a Winter Concert, Parents' Day, Grandparents' Day, and Headmaster's Weekend and ski trip to Bromley Mountain, Vermont. Service to the School and to the greater community is encouraged throughout the year by the community service/service learning program. During the 2013–14 academic year the students amassed 903 total hours of volunteer service.

The student body is divided into red and blue color teams. These teams enjoy friendly competition throughout the school year in areas of community service, academic achievement, and athletics.

DAILY LIFE

The school day begins at 8 a.m. with an all-School meeting. All administrators, faculty members, and students are in attendance. It is a time to share the news of the School and the world as well as important information and announcements with the whole community. The rest of the academic day consists of eight 40-minute periods and supervised study halls, with a 20-minute recess in the middle of the morning. Extra help is available every day after lunch. Athletic practices or contests take place from 3 to 4:30 p.m. Dinner is served family style at 6 and is followed by study hall from 7 to 8:30. Free time follows, with bedtimes varying depending on the grade of the child.

WEEKEND LIFE

Weekends for boarding students include a variety of activities on and off campus. There are School dances, special theme weekends, off-campus trips, and intramural activities on campus. Rumsey's proximity to four major cities—New York, Boston, Hartford, and New Haven—allows for a wide variety of cultural events, sports events (collegiate and professional), and shopping excursions. All trips are fully supervised, and an appropriate student-teacher ratio is maintained. Day students are encouraged to participate in weekend activities and are also allowed to invite boarding students home with them for the weekend.

SUMMER PROGRAMS

The five-week Rumsey Hall summer session is open to students in the third through ninth grades. The program is designed for students who desire enrichment or need additional work in a subject area in order to move on to the next grade with confidence.

Special emphasis is placed on English, mathematics, study skills, and computer skills. Normal class size ranges from 6 to 10 students with individual attention and help available. Students who need support in language skills or developmental reading work daily with trained specialists. ESL is offered to international students. In the afternoon, students enjoy recreational activities such as swimming, hiking, tennis, fishing, horseback riding, baseball, soccer, lacrosse, and basketball. Off-campus trips to museums, movies, concerts, amusement parks, and sporting events occur each week. Considerable effort is made to cultivate students' interests and to expose them to new experiences. For the 2015 summer session, tuition, room, and board was $7,950 for boarding students, $2,840 for day students, and $1,845 for half-day students. There are additional fees for individual tutoring in language skills and enrollment in ESL.

COSTS AND FINANCIAL AID

In 2015–16, full-year tuition was $20,450 for kindergarten and day students in grades 1 and 2, $25,160 for day students in grades 3–9, and $53,525 for boarding students. Additional fees included books, athletic fees, school supplies, and laundry and dry cleaning. A nonrefundable deposit of $2,000 serves as the boarding student's drawing account for the year. The annual fee for language skills was $5,945. The annual fee for ESL was $7,350. Two thirds of the total tuition is due July 15 and the balance by December 15. A ten-installment payment agreement is available.

Rumsey Hall is a member of the School and Student Service for Financial Aid. In the 2014–15 academic year just over $1.15 million in tuition assistance was awarded to one third of the students.

ADMISSIONS INFORMATION

Rumsey Hall welcomes students of average to above-average intelligence and achievement. Students must show evidence of good citizenship and the willingness to live in a boarding community. Acceptance is based on past school performance, scores on standardized achievement tests, and a personal interview. Rumsey is able to accept a limited number of students with learning differences if their learning profile is compatible with the School's Orton-Gillingham–based language skills program. Rumsey Hall School admits students of any race, color, religion, or national or ethnic origin.

APPLICATION TIMETABLE

Inquiries are welcome at any time of the year, with most families beginning the admission process in the fall or winter in anticipation of September enrollment. Admission interviews and tours are scheduled throughout the year. Boarding student applications are accepted on a rolling basis. Day student applicants should complete the application process by February 15. Applicants are notified of acceptance by March 1.

ADMISSION CORRESPONDENCE

Matthew S. Hoeniger '81, Director of Admission
Rumsey Hall School
201 Romford Road
Washington, Connecticut 06794
United States
Phone: 860-868-0535
Fax: 860-868-7907
E-mail: admiss@rumseyhall.org
Website: http://www.rumseyhall.org

Specialized Directories

COEDUCATIONAL DAY SCHOOLS

The Academy at Charlemont, MA
Academy at the Lakes, FL
The Academy for Gifted Children (PACE), ON, Canada
Academy for Individual Excellence, KY
Academy of Notre Dame, MA
Academy of the Sacred Heart, MI
Académie Ste Cécile International School, ON, Canada
Admiral Farragut Academy, FL
Albuquerque Academy, NM
Alexander Dawson School, CO
Allen Academy, TX
Allentown Central Catholic High School, PA
Allison Academy, FL
All Saints' Academy, FL
Alma Heights Christian High School, CA
Alpha Omega Academy, IA
American Christian Academy, AL
American Heritage School, FL
American Heritage School, FL
American International School, Lusaka, Zambia
The American School Foundation, Mexico
The American School in Japan, Japan
The American School of Puerto Vallarta, Mexico
Andrews Osborne Academy, OH
Aquinas High School, GA
Archbishop Hoban High School, OH
Archbishop Mitty High School, CA
Archmere Academy, DE
Arendell Parrott Academy, NC
Arete Preparatory Academy, CA
Armbrae Academy, NS, Canada
Arthur Morgan School, NC
ASSETS School, HI
Athens Academy, GA
Athens Bible School, AL
Atlanta International School, GA
Atlantis Academy, FL
Augusta Christian School, GA
Austin Preparatory School, MA
Austin Waldorf School, TX
Bakersfield Christian High School, CA
The Baltimore Actors' Theatre Conservatory, MD
Banbury Crossroads School, AB, Canada
Bangor Christian School, ME
Baptist Regional School, NJ
Battle Ground Academy, TN
Bay Ridge Preparatory School, NY
The Bay School of San Francisco, CA
Bearspaw Christian School, AB, Canada
Beaufort Academy, SC
The Beekman School, NY
Ben Franklin Academy, GA
The Benjamin School, FL
Bentley School, CA
Berean Christian High School, CA
Berkeley Carroll School, NY
Berkeley Preparatory School, FL
Berkshire School, MA
Besant Hill School, CA
Beth Haven Christian School, KY
The Birch Wathen Lenox School, NY
Bishop Brady High School, NH
Bishop Brossart High School, KY
Bishop Connolly High School, MA
Bishop Denis J. O'Connell High School, VA
Bishop Eustace Preparatory School, NJ
Bishop Guertin High School, NH

Bishop Ireton High School, VA
Bishop John J. Snyder High School, FL
Bishop Kelly High School, ID
Bishop McNamara High School, MD
Bishop Miege High School, KS
Bishop Montgomery High School, CA
Bishop's College School, QC, Canada
The Bishop's School, CA
Bishop Stang High School, MA
Bishop Verot High School, FL
Bishop Walsh Middle High School, MD
Blair Academy, NJ
The Blake School, MN
Blanchet School, OR
Blessed Sacrament Huguenot Catholic School, VA
Blessed Trinity High School, GA
Boca Prep International School, FL
Bodwell High School, BC, Canada
The Bollés School, FL
Boston University Academy, MA
Boyd-Buchanan School, TN
Brandon Hall School, GA
Breck School, MN
Brehm Preparatory School, IL
Brentwood College School, BC, Canada
Brentwood School, CA
Briarcrest Christian High School, TN
Briarwood Christian High School, AL
Bridgeport International Academy, CT
Bridges Academy, CA
Brimmer and May School, MA
British International School of Boston, MA
British International School of Washington, DC
The Brook Hill School, TX
Brooks School, MA
The Buckley School, CA
Burr and Burton Academy, VT
Butte Central Catholic High School, MT
Buxton School, MA
Calgary Academy, AB, Canada
Calgary Academy Collegiate, AB, Canada
California Crosspoint High School, CA
Calvary Day School, GA
Calvin Christian High School, CA
Campbell Hall (Episcopal), CA
Campbell River Christian School, BC, Canada
Camphill Special School, PA
Canterbury School, CT
Canterbury School, FL
The Canterbury School of Florida, FL
Cape Fear Academy, NC
Cape Henry Collegiate School, VA
Capistrano Valley Christian Schools, CA
Cardinal Gibbons High School, NC
Cardinal Mooney Catholic High School, FL
Cardinal Newman High School, FL
Carlisle School, VA
Carlucci American International School of Lisbon, Portugal
Casady School, OK
Cascadilla School, NY
Cascia Hall Preparatory School, OK
Cate School, CA
Cathedral High School, MA
Catholic Central High School, NY
Catholic Central High School, WI
The Catlin Gabel School, OR
CCI The Renaissance School, Italy
Central Alberta Christian High School, AB, Canada

Central Catholic High School, CA
Central Catholic High School, MA
Chadwick School, CA
Chaminade College Preparatory, CA
Chaminade-Madonna College Preparatory, FL
Charles Finney School, NY
Charlotte Country Day School, NC
Charlotte Latin School, NC
Chatham Academy, GA
Chattanooga Christian School, TN
Chelsea School, MD
Cheverus High School, ME
Choate Rosemary Hall, CT
Christa McAuliffe Academy School of Arts and Sciences, OR
Christ Church Episcopal School, SC
Christchurch School, VA
Christian Central Academy, NY
Christian Heritage School, CT
Christopher Dock Mennonite High School, PA
Chrysalis School, WA
Clarksville Academy, TN
Colegio Bolivar, Colombia
Collegedale Academy, TN
The Collegiate School, VA
The Colorado Rocky Mountain School, CO
The Colorado Springs School, CO
Columbia Academy, TN
The Columbus Academy, OH
Commonwealth School, MA
Community Christian Academy, KY
Community High School, NJ
The Community School, ID
The Community School of Naples, FL
Concord Academy, MA
Concordia Academy, MN
Concordia Lutheran High School, IN
The Country Day School, ON, Canada
Covenant Canadian Reformed School, AB, Canada
Crawford Adventist Academy, ON, Canada
The Crenshaw School, FL
Crossroads School for Arts & Sciences, CA
Crystal Springs Uplands School, CA
C.S. Lewis Academy, OR
The Culver Academies, IN
Currey Ingram Academy, TN
Cushing Academy, MA
Darrow School, NY
Deerfield Academy, MA
De La Salle College, ON, Canada
DeLaSalle High School, MN
De La Salle North Catholic High School, OR
Delaware Valley Friends School, PA
Delphos Saint John's High School, OH
Denver Academy, CO
The Derryfield School, NH
Desert Academy, NM
Detroit Country Day School, MI
Doane Academy, NJ
The Dr. Miriam and Sheldon G. Adelson Educational Campus, The Adelson Upper School, NV
Donelson Christian Academy, TN
Donna Klein Jewish Academy, FL
The Donoho School, AL
Donovan Catholic, NJ
Dowling Catholic High School, IA
Dublin Christian Academy, NH
Dublin School, NH

Durham Academy, NC
The Dwight School, NY
Eagle Hill School, CT
Eastern Mennonite High School, VA
Eaton Academy, GA
Edison School, AB, Canada
Edmund Burke School, DC
Eldorado Emerson Private School, CA
Elgin Academy, IL
Elyria Catholic High School, OH
Episcopal Collegiate School, AR
Episcopal High School, TX
Episcopal High School of Jacksonville, FL
Erskine Academy, ME
Escuela Campo Alegre, Venezuela
Ezell-Harding Christian School, TN
Faith Lutheran High School, NV
Falmouth Academy, MA
Father Lopez High School, FL
Father Ryan High School, TN
Fayetteville Academy, NC
Fay School, MA
The First Academy, FL
First Baptist Academy, TX
First Presbyterian Day School, GA
Flint Hill School, VA
Flintridge Preparatory School, CA
Fort Worth Country Day School, TX
Foundation Academy, FL
Fountain Valley School of Colorado, CO
Fowlers Academy, PR
Franklin Academy, CT
Franklin Road Academy, TN
Fredericksburg Academy, VA
Fredericton Christian Academy, NB, Canada
Fresno Christian Schools, CA
Friends Academy, NY
Friends' Central School, PA
Friendship Christian School, TN
Friends Select School, PA
Front Range Christian High School, CO
Fuqua School, VA
Gabriel Richard Catholic High School, MI
The Galloway School, GA
Gann Academy (The New Jewish High School of Greater Boston), MA
George School, PA
George Stevens Academy, ME
George Walton Academy, GA
Glades Day School, FL
The Glenholme School, Devereux Connecticut, CT
Good Hope Country Day School, VI
The Governor French Academy, IL
The Governor's Academy, MA
The Gow School, NY
Grace Baptist Academy, TN
Grace Christian School, AK
The Grauer School, CA
Greater Atlanta Christian Schools, GA
Great Lakes Christian High School, ON, Canada
Green Fields Country Day School, AZ
Greenhill School, TX
Green Meadow Waldorf School, NY
Griggs International Academy, MD
Groton School, MA
Guamani Private School, PR
Gulliver Preparatory School, FL

The Gunnery, CT
The Gunston School, MD
Halstrom Academy, Beverly Hills, CA
Halstrom Academy, Calsbad, CA
Halstrom Academy, Cupertino, CA
Halstrom Academy, Huntington Beach, CA
Halstrom Academy, Irvine, CA
Halstrom Academy, Los Angeles, CA
Halstrom Academy, Manhattan Beach, CA
Halstrom Academy, Mission Viejo, CA
Halstrom Academy, Orange, CA
Halstrom Academy, Pasadena, CA
Halstrom Academy, San Diego, CA
Halstrom Academy, San Mateo, CA
Halstrom Academy, Walnut Creek, CA
Halstrom Academy, Westlake Village, CA
Halstrom Academy, Woodland Hills, CA
The Harker School, CA
Harrells Christian Academy, NC
Harvard-Westlake School, CA
Hawaii Baptist Academy, HI
Hawai`i Preparatory Academy, HI
Hawken School, OH
Hebrew Academy, CA
Hebrew Academy of the Five Towns & Rockaway, NY
Heritage Academy, SC
Highroad Academy, BC, Canada
The Hill Center, Durham Academy, NC
Ho'Ala School, HI
Holland Hall, OK
Holy Cross High School, CT
Holy Cross Regional Catholic School, VA
Holyoke Catholic High School, MA
Holy Savior Menard Catholic High School, LA
Holy Trinity Diocesan High School, NY
Holy Trinity High School, IL
Holy Trinity School, ON, Canada
Hope Christian School, AB, Canada
Houghton Academy, NY
Houston Academy, AL
The Howard School, GA
The Hudson School, NJ
The Hun School of Princeton, NJ
Huntington-Surrey School, TX
Hyde School, CT
Hyde School, ME
Hyman Brand Hebrew Academy of Greater Kansas City, KS
Illiana Christian High School, IL
Immaculata High School, KS
Immaculata High School, NJ
Immaculata-La Salle High School, FL
Independent School, KS
Indian Creek School, MD
Indian Springs School, AL
Institut Monte Rosa, Switzerland
International High School, CA
International School Bangkok, Thailand
International School Hamburg, Germany
The International School of Aberdeen, United Kingdom
International School of Luxembourg, Luxembourg
International School of Port-of-Spain, Trinidad and Tobago
International School of Zug and Luzern (ISZL), Switzerland
Isidore Newman School, LA
Jackson Christian School, TN
Jean and Samuel Frankel Jewish Academy of Metropolitan
    Detroit, MI
John Burroughs School, MO

John F. Kennedy Catholic High School, MO
John Hancock Academy, GA
John Paul II Catholic High School, FL
The Journeys School of Teton Science School, WY
Judge Memorial Catholic High School, UT
Kalamazoo Christian High School, MI
Kauai Christian Academy, HI
Kent Denver School, CO
Kent School, CT
Kentucky Country Day School, KY
The Key School, MD
Keystone School, TX
King Low Heywood Thomas, CT
The King's Christian High School, NJ
King's-Edgehill School, NS, Canada
Kingsway College, ON, Canada
Kingswood-Oxford School, CT
The Knox School, NY
La Cheim School, CA
La Jolla Country Day School, CA
Lakehill Preparatory School, TX
La Lumiere School, IN
Lancaster Catholic High School, PA
Lancaster Mennonite High School, PA
Landmark Christian Academy, KY
Landmark Christian School, GA
Landmark East School, NS, Canada
Landmark School, MA
Lansdale Catholic High School, PA
La Salle Academy, RI
La Salle High School, CA
The Laureate Academy, MB, Canada
Lawrence School, OH
The Lawrenceville School, NJ
Lee Academy, MS
The Leelanau School, MI
Lehigh Valley Christian High School, PA
Lehman High School, OH
Le Lycee Francais de Los Angeles, CA
Lexington Catholic High School, KY
Lexington Christian Academy, KY
Liberty Christian School, CA
Lincoln Academy, ME
Long Trail School, VT
Loudoun School for the Gifted, VA
Louisville Collegiate School, KY
The Lovett School, GA
Lutheran High School, MO
Lutheran High School North, MO
Lutheran High School Northwest, MI
Lutheran High School of Hawaii, HI
Lutheran High School of San Diego, CA
Luther College High School, SK, Canada
Lycee Claudel, ON, Canada
The Lycee International, American Section, France
Manhattan Christian High School, MT
Maplebrook School, NY
Maranatha High School, CA
Marian Central Catholic High School, IL
Marian High School, IN
Marian High School, MA
Marion Academy, AL
Marshall School, MN
Mars Hill Bible School, AL
Martin Luther High School, NY
The Marvelwood School, CT
Mary Institute and St. Louis Country Day School (MICDS), MO

Massanutten Military Academy, VA
The Masters School, NY
Matignon High School, MA
Maui Preparatory Academy, HI
Maumee Valley Country Day School, OH
Maur Hill-Mount Academy, KS
McDonogh School, MD
The Meadows School, NV
Memorial Hall School, TX
Memphis Catholic High School and Middle School, TN
Menlo School, CA
Mercersburg Academy, PA
Mesa Grande Seventh-Day Academy, CA
Miami Country Day School, FL
The Miami Valley School, OH
Middlesex School, MA
Middle Tennessee Christian School, TN
Mid-Pacific Institute, HI
Mill Springs Academy, GA
Milton Academy, MA
MMI Preparatory School, PA
Moorestown Friends School, NJ
Mooseheart High School, IL
Moravian Academy, PA
Moreau Catholic High School, CA
Mounds Park Academy, MN
Mountain View Academy, CA
Mount Dora Christian Academy, FL
Mount Saint Charles Academy, RI
Mount Vernon Presbyterian School, GA
Nampa Christian Schools, ID
Nashville Christian School, TN
Nazareth Academy, IL
Nebraska Christian Schools, NE
Newark Academy, NJ
New Covenant Academy, MO
Niagara Christian Community of Schools, ON, Canada
Noah Webster Christian School, WY
Noble Academy, NC
Noble and Greenough School, MA
The Nora School, MD
Norman Howard School, NY
The North Broward Preparatory Upper School, FL
North Clackamas Christian School, OR
North Country School, NY
Northfield Mount Hermon School, MA
Northpoint Christian School, MS
North Shore Country Day School, IL
North Toronto Christian School, ON, Canada
Northwest Academy, OR
Northwest Catholic High School, CT
The Northwest School, WA
Northwest Yeshiva High School, WA
The Norwich Free Academy, CT
Notre Dame-Cathedral Latin School, OH
Notre Dame High School, CA
Notre Dame High School, LA
Notre Dame High School, NJ
Notre Dame High School, NY
Notre Dame High School, TN
Notre Dame Junior/Senior High School, PA
Oak Hill School, OR
Oakland School, VA
The O'Neal School, NC
Oneida Baptist Institute, KY
Orangeburg Preparatory Schools, Inc., SC
Orangewood Christian School, FL

Oregon Episcopal School, OR
Orinda Academy, CA
Our Lady of Good Counsel High School, MD
Out-Of-Door-Academy, FL
Pace Academy, GA
PACE/Brantley Hall High School, FL
Pacific Crest Community School, OR
The Packer Collegiate Institute, NY
Palo Alto Preparatory School, CA
Paradise Adventist Academy, CA
The Park School of Baltimore, MD
Parkview Adventist Academy, AB, Canada
The Pathway School, PA
Patten Academy of Christian Education, CA
Peddie School, NJ
The Pennington School, NJ
Pensacola Catholic High School, FL
Peoples Christian Academy, ON, Canada
Perkiomen School, PA
Philadelphia-Montgomery Christian Academy, PA
Phillips Academy (Andover), MA
Phoenix Christian Unified Schools, AZ
Phoenix Country Day School, AZ
Pickens Academy, AL
Pickering College, ON, Canada
Piedmont Academy, GA
Pinecrest Academy, GA
Pine Tree Academy, ME
The Pingree School, MA
The Pingry School, NJ
Pioneer Valley Christian Academy, MA
Pius X High School, NE
Polytechnic School, CA
Pope John Paul II High School, LA
Pope John XXIII Regional High School, NJ
Portledge School, NY
Portsmouth Abbey School, RI
Portsmouth Christian Academy, NH
The Potomac School, VA
Poughkeepsie Day School, NY
Powers Catholic High School, MI
Prestonwood Christian Academy, TX
Proctor Academy, NH
Professional Children's School, NY
The Prout School, RI
Providence Country Day School, RI
Providence Day School, NC
Providence High School, CA
Punahou School, HI
Queen Margaret's School, BC, Canada
Quinte Christian High School, ON, Canada
Rabun Gap-Nacoochee School, GA
Randolph-Macon Academy, VA
Randolph School, AL
Ransom Everglades School, FL
Ravenscroft School, NC
Realms of Inquiry, UT
Redeemer Christian High School, ON, Canada
Redemption Christian Academy, MA
Redwood Christian Schools, CA
Rejoice Christian Schools, OK
Ridley College, ON, Canada
Riverdale Country School, NY
River Oaks Baptist School, TX
Riverside Christian Schools, CA
The Rivers School, MA
Riverstone International School, ID

Rockland Country Day School, NY
Rock Point School, VT
Rockway Mennonite Collegiate, ON, Canada
The Roeper School, MI
Rolling Hills Preparatory School, CA
Rosseau Lake College, ON, Canada
Rothesay Netherwood School, NB, Canada
Rotterdam International Secondary School, Wolfert van Borselen, Netherlands
Royal Canadian College, BC, Canada
Rudolf Steiner School of Ann Arbor, MI
Rumsey Hall School, CT
Rundle College, AB, Canada
Rutgers Preparatory School, NJ
Sacramento Country Day School, CA
Sacramento Waldorf School, CA
Sacred Heart/Griffin High School, IL
Saddlebrook Preparatory School, FL
Sage Hill School, CA
Sage Ridge School, NV
Saint Agnes Academy–St. Dominic School, TN
Saint Albert Junior-Senior High School, IA
St. Andrew's Episcopal School, MD
St. Andrew's Episcopal School, MS
St. Andrew's Regional High School, BC, Canada
Saint Andrew's School, FL
St. Andrew's School, GA
St. Andrew's School, RI
St. Andrew's–Sewanee School, TN
St. Anne's–Belfield School, VA
Saint Anthony High School, IL
St. Benedict at Auburndale, TN
St. Bernard High School, CA
St. Bernard High School, CT
St. Bernard's Catholic School, CA
St. Brendan High School, FL
St. Croix Schools, MN
Saint Dominic Academy, ME
Saint Francis High School, CA
St. Francis School, GA
St. George's Independent School, TN
St. George's School, RI
Saint James School, MD
St. John Neumann High School, FL
St. John's Catholic Prep, MD
Saint John's Preparatory School, MN
Saint Joseph Academy, CA
St. Joseph Academy, FL
St. Joseph High School, CT
St. Joseph's Catholic School, SC
St. Luke's School, CT
St. Martin's Episcopal School, LA
Saint Mary's High School, AZ
St. Mary's School, OR
Saint Maur International School, Japan
St. Patrick Catholic High School, MS
St. Patrick's Regional Secondary, BC, Canada
St. Paul Academy and Summit School, MN
Saint Paul Lutheran High School, MO
St. Paul Preparatory School, MN
St. Pius X High School, TX
St. Stephen's Episcopal School, TX
St. Stephen's School, Rome, Italy
St. Thomas Aquinas High School, FL
Saint Thomas Aquinas High School, KS
St. Thomas Aquinas High School, NH
Saint Thomas More Catholic High School, LA

Salem Academy, OR
Salpointe Catholic High School, AZ
San Domenico School, CA
Sandy Spring Friends School, MD
San Francisco University High School, CA
Santa Margarita Catholic High School, CA
Savannah Christian Preparatory School, GA
The Savannah Country Day School, GA
Scattergood Friends School, IA
Scheck Hillel Community School, FL
SciCore Academy, NJ
Seabury Hall, III
Seattle Academy of Arts and Sciences, WA
Seattle Lutheran High School, WA
The Seven Hills School, OH
Severn School, MD
Sewickley Academy, PA
Shady Side Academy, PA
Shanley High School, ND
Shawnigan Lake School, BC, Canada
Shelton School and Evaluation Center, TX
Shorecrest Preparatory School, FL
Shoreline Christian, WA
Signet Christian School, ON, Canada
Smith School, NY
Smithville Christian High School, ON, Canada
Solebury School, PA
Sonoma Academy, CA
Soundview Preparatory School, NY
Southern Ontario College, ON, Canada
Southfield Christian High School, MI
Southwest Christian School, Inc., TX
Springside Chestnut Hill Academy, PA
Squaw Valley Academy, CA
Stanstead College, QC, Canada
Steamboat Mountain School, CO
Stephen T. Badin High School, OH
Stevenson School, CA
St Leonards School and Sixth Form College, United Kingdom
The Stony Brook School, NY
The Storm King School, NY
Stratford Academy, GA
Stuart Hall, VA
The Sudbury Valley School, MA
Summerfield Waldorf School, CA
The Summit Country Day School, OH
Sunshine Bible Academy, SD
The Taft School, CT
Taipei American School, Taiwan
Takoma Academy, MD
Tampa Preparatory School, FL
Tandem Friends School, VA
Tapply Binet College, ON, Canada
TASIS The American School in England, United Kingdom
TASIS, The American School in Switzerland, Switzerland
The Tenney School, TX
Teurlings Catholic High School, LA
The Thacher School, CA
Thomas Jefferson School, MO
Tilton School, NH
Timothy Christian High School, IL
Timothy Christian School, NJ
TMI - The Episcopal School of Texas, TX
Tome School, MD
Tower Hill School, DE
Traditional Learning Academy, BC, Canada
Tri-City Christian Academy, AZ

Trinity Catholic High School, CT
Trinity College School, ON, Canada
Trinity Episcopal School, VA
Trinity High School, NH
Trinity High School, OH
Trinity Preparatory School, FL
Trinity School of Texas, TX
Tuscaloosa Academy, AL
Tyler Street Christian Academy, TX
United Mennonite Educational Institute, ON, Canada
United Nations International School, NY
University of Chicago Laboratory Schools, IL
University Prep, WA
University School of Jackson, TN
Valley Christian High School, CA
The Valley School, MI
Valwood School, GA
Venta Preparatory School, ON, Canada
Vicksburg Catholic School, MS
Victor Valley Christian School, CA
Viewpoint School, CA
Villa Duchesne and Oak Hill School, MO
Villa Madonna Academy, KY
The Waldorf School of Saratoga Springs, NY
Walla Walla Valley Academy, WA
Walnut Hill School for the Arts, MA
Wasatch Academy, UT
Washington International School, DC
The Waterford School, UT
Watkinson School, CT
Waynflete School, ME
Webb School of Knoxville, TN
The Webb Schools, CA
The Weber School, GA
Wellspring Foundation, CT
Wesleyan Academy, PR
Wesleyan School, GA
Westbury Christian School, TX
West Island College, AB, Canada
Westmark School, CA
Westminster Christian Academy, LA
Westminster Christian School, FL
Westminster School, CT
The Westminster Schools, GA
Westminster Schools of Augusta, GA
West Sound Academy, WA
Westtown School, PA
Wheaton Academy, IL
The Wheeler School, RI
Whitefield Academy, KY
Whitfield School, MO
Whitinsville Christian School, MA
Wichita Collegiate School, KS
The Williston Northampton School, MA
Wilmington Christian School, DE
Wilmington Friends School, DE
Wilson Hall, SC
Windermere Preparatory School, FL
The Windsor School, NY
Winston Preparatory School, NY
The Winston School, TX
The Winston School San Antonio, TX
The Woodlands Christian Academy, TX
Woodlynde School, PA
Wooster School, CT
Worcester Preparatory School, MD
Wyoming Seminary, PA

York Country Day School, PA
York School, CA
The York School, ON, Canada
Zurich International School, Switzerland

BOYS' DAY SCHOOLS
Academy of the New Church Boys' School, PA
All Hallows High School, NY
Archbishop Curley High School, MD
Archbishop Shaw High School, LA
Army and Navy Academy, CA
Belen Jesuit Preparatory School, FL
Benedictine High School, OH
Bishop Mora Salesian High School, CA
Brophy College Preparatory, AZ
Brother Rice High School, MI
The Browning School, NY
Brunswick School, CT
Calvert Hall College High School, MD
Cardigan Mountain School, NH
Catholic Central High School, MI
Central Catholic High School, PA
Christian Brothers Academy, NJ
Christopher Columbus High School, FL
Crescent School, ON, Canada
Damien High School, CA
De La Salle High School, CA
Delbarton School, NJ
DeMatha Catholic High School, MD
Devon Preparatory School, PA
Eaglebrook School, MA
Fairfield College Preparatory School, CT
Father Duenas Memorial School, GU
Fordham Preparatory School, NY
Gilman School, MD
Gonzaga College High School, DC
Hales Franciscan High School, IL
Hargrave Military Academy, VA
The Haverford School, PA
The Heights School, MD
Holy Cross School, LA
Holy Ghost Preparatory School, PA
Jesuit College Preparatory School, TX
Jesuit High School of Tampa, FL
Junipero Serra High School, CA
Loyola-Blakefield, MD
Malden Catholic High School, MA
Malvern Preparatory School, PA
Marquette University High School, WI
Memphis University School, TN
Missouri Military Academy, MO
Montgomery Bell Academy, TN
Oratory Preparatory School, NJ
Palma School, CA
The Phelps School, PA
Regis High School, NY
Regis Jesuit High School, Boys Division, CO
Rockhurst High School, MO
The Roxbury Latin School, MA
St. Albans School, DC
Saint Augustine Preparatory School, NJ
St. Christopher's School, VA
Saint Francis High School, CA
St. George's School, BC, Canada
St. John's Preparatory School, MA

Coeducational in lower grades

Saint Joseph High School, NJ
Saint Joseph Regional High School, NJ
St. Joseph's Preparatory School, PA
St. Louis University High School, MO
St. Mark's School of Texas, TX
St. Mary's Preparatory School, MI
St. Michael's College School, ON, Canada
Saint Patrick High School, IL
St. Paul's High School, MB, Canada
St. Peter's Preparatory School, NJ
Saint Xavier High School, OH
Salesianum School, DE
Servite High School, CA
Trinity High School, KY
Trinity-Pawling School, NY
Upper Canada College, ON, Canada
The Woodhall School, CT

GIRLS' DAY SCHOOLS

Academy of Our Lady of Peace, CA
Academy of the Holy Cross, MD
Academy of the Holy Family, CT
Academy of the New Church Girls' School, PA
The Agnes Irwin School, PA
Balmoral Hall School, MB, Canada
Branksome Hall, ON, Canada
Buffalo Seminary, NY
Carondelet High School, CA
Carrollton School of the Sacred Heart, FL
Castilleja School, CA
Cathedral High School, NY
Columbus School for Girls, OH
Dana Hall School, MA
Dominican Academy, NY
Elizabeth Seton Academy, MA
Elizabeth Seton High School, MD
The Ellis School, PA
Elmwood School, ON, Canada
Fontbonne Academy, MA
Foxcroft School, VA
Garrison Forest School, MD*
Grier School, PA
The Harpeth Hall School, TN
Holy Names Academy, WA
Immaculate Conception High School, NJ
Immaculate Heart High School and Middle School, CA
Incarnate Word Academy, TX
Josephinum Academy, IL
Lauralton Hall, CT
Louisville High School, CA
The Madeira School, VA
Marymount High School, CA
Mercy High School, CT
Merion Mercy Academy, PA
Miss Edgar's and Miss Cramp's School, QC, Canada
Miss Hall's School, MA
Miss Porter's School, CT
Montrose School, MA
Mother McAuley High School, IL
Mount Mercy Academy, NY
Mount Saint Joseph Academy, PA
National Cathedral School, DC
Nerinx Hall, MO
Notre Dame High School, CA
Notre Dame High School, CA

Notre Dame High School, MO
Our Lady of Mercy Academy, NJ
Padua Academy, DE
Preston High School, NY
Providence Catholic School, The College Preparatory School for Girls Grades 6-12, TX
Ramona Convent Secondary School, CA
Regis Jesuit High School, Girls Division, CO
Rosati-Kain High School, MO
Sacred Heart Academy, KY
Sacred Heart High School, CA
St. Catherine's School, VA
St. Clement's School, ON, Canada
Saint Gertrude High School, VA
Saint Joan Antida High School, WI
St. Joseph's Academy, LA
St. Margaret's School, BC, Canada
St. Mary's Episcopal School, TN
Saint Mary's School, NC
Saint Teresa's Academy, MO
St. Timothy's School, MD
Saint Ursula Academy, OH
Saint Ursula Academy, OH
Salem Academy, NC
Santa Catalina School, CA
The Spence School, NY
The Study, QC, Canada
The Ursuline Academy of Dallas, TX
Villa Walsh Academy, NJ
Westover School, CT
The Willows Academy, IL
The Woodward School, MA
Xavier College Preparatory, AZ

SCHOOLS ACCEPTING BOARDING BOYS AND GIRLS

Académie Ste Cécile International School, ON, Canada†
Admiral Farragut Academy, FL†
Advanced Academy of Georgia, GA
Allen Academy, TX†
Andrews Osborne Academy, OH†
Arthur Morgan School, NC†
Berkshire School, MA†
Besant Hill School, CA†
Bishop's College School, QC, Canada†
Blair Academy, NJ†
Bodwell High School, BC, Canada†
The Bolles School, FL†
Brandon Hall School, GA†
Brehm Preparatory School, IL†
Brentwood College School, BC, Canada†
Bridgeport International Academy, CT†
The Brook Hill School, TX†
Brooks School, MA†
Burr and Burton Academy, VT†
Buxton School, MA†
California Crosspoint High School, CA†
California Lutheran High School, CA
Camphill Special School, PA†
Canterbury School, CT†
Carlisle School, VA†
Cascadilla School, NY†
Cate School, CA†
CCI The Renaissance School, Italy†
Choate Rosemary Hall, CT†

Coeducational in lower grades

Christchurch School, VA†
Christopher Dock Mennonite High School, PA†
The Colorado Rocky Mountain School, CO†
Columbia International School, Japan
The Community School, ID†
Concord Academy, MA†
The Culver Academies, IN†
Cushing Academy, MA†
Darrow School, NY†
Deerfield Academy, MA†
Dublin Christian Academy, NH†
Dublin School, NH†
Eagle Hill School, CT†
Episcopal High School, VA
Fay School, MA†
First Presbyterian Day School, GA†
Forest Lake Academy, FL
Fountain Valley School of Colorado, CO†
Franklin Academy, CT†
George School, PA†
George Stevens Academy, ME†
Gilmour Academy, OH
Girard College, PA
The Glenholme School, Devereux Connecticut, CT
The Governor French Academy, IL†
The Governor's Academy, MA†
The Gow School, NY†
Great Lakes Christian High School, ON, Canada†
Groton School, MA†
The Gunnery, CT†
The Harvey School, NY
Hawai`i Preparatory Academy, HI†
Heritage Academy, SC†
Houghton Academy, NY†
The Hun School of Princeton, NJ†
Hyde School, CT†
Hyde School, ME†
Indian Springs School, AL†
Institut Monte Rosa, Switzerland†
The John Dewey Academy, MA
Kent School, CT†
King's-Edgehill School, NS, Canada†
Kingsway College, ON, Canada†
The Knox School, NY†
Lakefield College School, ON, Canada
La Lumiere School, IN†
Lancaster Mennonite High School, PA†
Landmark East School, NS, Canada†
Landmark School, MA†
The Lawrenceville School, NJ†
The Leelanau School, MI†
Leysin American School in Switzerland, Switzerland
Lincoln Academy, ME†
Luther College High School, SK, Canada†
Maplebrook School, NY
Marianapolis Preparatory School, CT
The Marvelwood School, CT†
Massanutten Military Academy, VA†
The Masters School, NY†
Maui Preparatory Academy, HI†
Maumee Valley Country Day School, OH†
Maur Hill-Mount Academy, KS†
McDonogh School, MD†
Mercersburg Academy, PA†
Middlesex School, MA†
Midland School, CA
Milton Academy, MA†

Mooseheart High School, IL†
Nebraska Christian Schools, NE†
Niagara Christian Community of Schools, ON, Canada†
Noble and Greenough School, MA†
The North Broward Preparatory Upper School, FL†
North Central Texas Academy, TX
North Country School, NY†
Northfield Mount Hermon School, MA†
The Northwest School, WA†
Oakland School, VA†
Oneida Baptist Institute, KY†
Oregon Episcopal School, OR†
Parkview Adventist Academy, AB, Canada†
Peddie School, NJ†
The Pennington School, NJ†
Perkiomen School, PA†
Phillips Academy (Andover), MA†
Pickering College, ON, Canada†
Pine Tree Academy, ME†
Portsmouth Abbey School, RI†
Presbyterian Pan American School, TX
Proctor Academy, NH†
Rabun Gap-Nacoochee School, GA†
Randolph-Macon Academy, VA†
The Rectory School, CT
Redemption Christian Academy, MA†
Ridley College, ON, Canada†
Rockland Country Day School, NY†
Rock Point School, VT†
Rockway Mennonite Collegiate, ON, Canada†
Rosseau Lake College, ON, Canada†
Rothesay Netherwood School, NB, Canada†
Rumsey Hall School, CT†
Saddlebrook Preparatory School, FL†
St. Andrew's School, DE
Saint Andrew's School, FL†
St. Andrew's School, RI†
St. Andrew's–Sewanee School, TN†
St. Anne's–Belfield School, VA†
St. Bernard's Catholic School, CA†
St. Croix Schools, MN†
St. George's School, RI†
Saint James School, MD†
Saint John's Preparatory School, MN†
St. Mary's School, OR†
Saint Paul Lutheran High School, MO†
St. Paul's School, NH
St. Stephen's Episcopal School, TX†
St. Stephen's School, Rome, Italy†
San Domenico School, CA†
Sandy Spring Friends School, MD†
San Marcos Baptist Academy, TX
Scattergood Friends School, IA†
Shady Side Academy, PA†
Shawnigan Lake School, BC, Canada†
Solebury School, PA†
Squaw Valley Academy, CA†
Stanstead College, QC, Canada†
Steamboat Mountain School, CO†
Stevenson School, CA†
St Leonards School and Sixth Form College, United Kingdom†
The Stony Brook School, NY†
The Storm King School, NY†
Stuart Hall, VA†
Summit Preparatory School, MT
Sunshine Bible Academy, SD†
The Taft School, CT†

† Accepts day students

TASIS The American School in England, United Kingdom†
TASIS, The American School in Switzerland, Switzerland†
The Thacher School, CA†
THINK Global School, NY
Thomas Jefferson School, MO†
Tilton School, NH†
TMI - The Episcopal School of Texas, TX†
Trinity College School, ON, Canada†
The United World College - USA, NM
The Vanguard School, FL
Venta Preparatory School, ON, Canada†
Walnut Hill School for the Arts, MA†
Wasatch Academy, UT†
The Webb Schools, CA†
Wellspring Foundation, CT†
Westminster School, CT†
West Sound Academy, WA†
Westtown School, PA†
The Williston Northampton School, MA†
Woodside Priory School, CA†
Wyoming Seminary, PA†

SCHOOLS ACCEPTING BOARDING BOYS
Academy of the New Church Boys' School, PA†
Army and Navy Academy, CA†
Butte Central Catholic High School, MT†
Camden Military Academy, SC
Cardigan Mountain School, NH†
Eaglebrook School, MA†
Hampshire Country School, NH
Hargrave Military Academy, VA†
Little Keswick School, VA
Marine Military Academy, TX
Missouri Military Academy, MO†
The Oxford Academy, CT
The Phelps School, PA†
St. Albans School, DC†
St. George's School, BC, Canada†
St. Lawrence Seminary High School, WI
St. Mary's Preparatory School, MI†
St. Michael's Preparatory School of the Norbertine Fathers, CA
St. Thomas Choir School, NY
Trinity-Pawling School, NY†
Upper Canada College, ON, Canada†
Valley View School, MA
Windermere Preparatory School, FL†
The Woodhall School, CT†

SCHOOLS ACCEPTING BOARDING GIRLS
Academy of the Holy Family, CT†
Academy of the New Church Girls' School, PA†
Alpine Academy, UT
Balmoral Hall School, MB, Canada†
Branksome Hall, ON, Canada†
Buffalo Seminary, NY†
Dana Hall School, MA†
Foxcroft School, VA†
Garrison Forest School, MD†
Grier School, PA†
Hebrew Academy, CA†
The Hockaday School, TX
The Madeira School, VA†

Miss Hall's School, MA†
Miss Porter's School, CT†
Queen Margaret's School, BC, Canada†
St. Margaret's School, BC, Canada†
Saint Mary's School, NC†
St. Timothy's School, MD†
Salem Academy, NC†
Santa Catalina School, CA†
Westover School, CT†

MILITARY SCHOOLS
Admiral Farragut Academy, FL
Army and Navy Academy, CA
Camden Military Academy, SC
Hargrave Military Academy, VA
Lyman Ward Military Academy, AL
Marine Military Academy, TX
Massanutten Military Academy, VA
Missouri Military Academy, MO
Randolph-Macon Academy, VA
TMI - The Episcopal School of Texas, TX

SCHOOLS WITH A RELIGIOUS AFFILIATION

Anglican Church of Canada
Holy Trinity School, ON, Canada
Queen Margaret's School, BC, Canada
Rothesay Netherwood School, NB, Canada
St. Clement's School, ON, Canada

Assemblies of God
Victor Valley Christian School, CA

Baptist Church
Bangor Christian School, ME
Berean Christian High School, CA
Beth Haven Christian School, KY
Calvary Day School, GA
Campbell River Christian School, BC, Canada
First Baptist Academy, TX
Foundation Academy, FL
Fredericton Christian Academy, NB, Canada
Grace Baptist Academy, TN
John Hancock Academy, GA
Landmark Christian Academy, KY
Liberty Christian School, CA
Northpoint Christian School, MS
Parkview Baptist School, LA
Tri-City Christian Academy, AZ
Whitefield Academy, KY

Baptist General Association of Virginia
Hargrave Military Academy, VA

Baptist General Conference
San Marcos Baptist Academy, TX

Bible Fellowship Church
California Crosspoint High School, CA

Brethren in Christ Church
Niagara Christian Community of Schools, ON, Canada

† Accepts day students

Christian

Academy of the New Church Girls' School, PA
Alma Heights Christian High School, CA
American Christian Academy, AL
Briarcrest Christian High School, TN
Christopher Dock Mennonite High School, PA
Dublin Christian Academy, NH
The First Academy, FL
First Presbyterian Day School, GA
Fowlers Academy, PR
Greater Atlanta Christian Schools, GA
Harrells Christian Academy, NC
Highroad Academy, BC, Canada
Marion Academy, AL
Mesa Grande Seventh-Day Academy, CA
Nashville Christian School, TN
New Covenant Academy, MO
North Central Texas Academy, TX
Northpoint Christian School, MS
Orangewood Christian School, FL
Peoples Christian Academy, ON, Canada
Philadelphia-Montgomery Christian Academy, PA
Quinte Christian High School, ON, Canada
Redwood Christian Schools, CA
River Oaks Baptist School, TX
St. Croix Schools, MN
Signet Christian School, ON, Canada
Smithville Christian High School, ON, Canada
The Stony Brook School, NY
Timothy Christian High School, IL
TMI - The Episcopal School of Texas, TX
Valley Christian High School, CA
Westminster Christian School, FL
The Westminster Schools, GA
The Woodlands Christian Academy, TX

Christian Nondenominational

Alpha Omega Academy, IA
Bakersfield Christian High School, CA
Bearspaw Christian School, AB, Canada
The Brook Hill School, TX
Capistrano Valley Christian Schools, CA
Charles Finney School, NY
Chattanooga Christian School, TN
Christian Central Academy, NY
C.S. Lewis Academy, OR
Donelson Christian Academy, TN
Dublin Christian Academy, NH
Friendship Christian School, TN
Front Range Christian High School, CO
Grace Christian School, AK
Houghton Academy, NY
Kauai Christian Academy, HI
The King's Christian High School, NJ
Landmark Christian School, GA
Lyman Ward Military Academy, AL
Manhattan Christian High School, MT
Maranatha High School, CA
Massanutten Military Academy, VA
Missouri Military Academy, MO
Nampa Christian Schools, ID
Noah Webster Christian School, WY
North Clackamas Christian School, OR
Patten Academy of Christian Education, CA
Phoenix Christian Unified Schools, AZ
Portsmouth Christian Academy, NH
Redeemer Christian High School, ON, Canada

St. Anne's–Belfield School, VA
St. George's Independent School, TN
Savannah Christian Preparatory School, GA
Shoreline Christian, WA
Southfield Christian High School, MI
Southwest Christian School, Inc., TX
Stanstead College, QC, Canada
Sunshine Bible Academy, SD
Timothy Christian School, NJ
Tyler Street Christian Academy, TX
Wesleyan School, GA
Westminster Christian Academy, LA
Wheaton Academy, IL

Christian Reformed Church

Central Alberta Christian High School, AB, Canada
Illiana Christian High School, IL
Kalamazoo Christian High School, MI
Manhattan Christian High School, MT
Whitinsville Christian School, MA

Church of Christ

Boyd-Buchanan School, TN
Columbia Academy, TN
Ezell-Harding Christian School, TN
Great Lakes Christian High School, ON, Canada
Jackson Christian School, TN
Mars Hill Bible School, AL
Middle Tennessee Christian School, TN
Mount Dora Christian Academy, FL
Westbury Christian School, TX

Church of England (Anglican)

Lakefield College School, ON, Canada
Ridley College, ON, Canada
Trinity College School, ON, Canada

Church of the New Jerusalem

Academy of the New Church Boys' School, PA
Academy of the New Church Girls' School, PA

Episcopal Church

All Saints' Academy, FL
Berkeley Preparatory School, FL
The Bishop's School, CA
Breck School, MN
Brooks School, MA
Campbell Hall (Episcopal), CA
The Canterbury School of Florida, FL
Casady School, OK
Christ Church Episcopal School, SC
Christchurch School, VA
Doane Academy, NJ
Episcopal Collegiate School, AR
Episcopal High School, TX
Episcopal High School, VA
Episcopal High School of Jacksonville, FL
Groton School, MA
Holland Hall, OK
Kent School, CT
National Cathedral School, DC
Oregon Episcopal School, OR
The Rectory School, CT
Rock Point School, VT
St. Albans School, DC
St. Andrew's Episcopal School, MD
St. Andrew's Episcopal School, MS

St. Andrew's School, DE
Saint Andrew's School, FL
St. Andrew's–Sewanee School, TN
St. Catherine's School, VA
St. Christopher's School, VA
St. George's School, RI
Saint James School, MD
St. Martin's Episcopal School, LA
St. Mary's Episcopal School, TN
Saint Mary's School, NC
St. Paul's School, NH
St. Stephen's Episcopal School, TX
St. Thomas Choir School, NY
St. Timothy's School, MD
Seabury Hall, HI
Stuart Hall, VA
TMI - The Episcopal School of Texas, TX
Trinity Episcopal School, VA
Trinity-Pawling School, NY
Trinity Preparatory School, FL
Trinity School of Texas, TX
Wooster School, CT

Evangelical Christian Church
Fredericton Christian Academy, NB, Canada

Evangelical
Pioneer Valley Christian Academy, MA
Southfield Christian High School, MI

Evangelical Free Church of America
Hope Christian School, AB, Canada

Evangelical/Fundamental
California Crosspoint High School, CA

Evangelical Lutheran Church in America
Faith Lutheran High School, NV

Free Will Baptist Church
Rejoice Christian Schools, OK

General Association of Regular Baptist Churches
Baptist Regional School, NJ

Jewish
The Dr. Miriam and Sheldon G. Adelson Educational Campus, The Adelson Upper School, NV
Donna Klein Jewish Academy, FL
Gann Academy (The New Jewish High School of Greater Boston), MA
Hebrew Academy, CA
Hebrew Academy of the Five Towns & Rockaway, NY
Hyman Brand Hebrew Academy of Greater Kansas City, KS☐
Jean and Samuel Frankel Jewish Academy of Metropolitan Detroit, MI
Jewish Community High School of the Bay, CA
Northwest Yeshiva High School, WA
Scheck Hillel Community School, FL
The Weber School, GA

Lutheran Church
Lutheran High School of San Diego, CA
Luther College High School, SK, Canada
Martin Luther High School, NY
Seattle Lutheran High School, WA

Lutheran Church–Missouri Synod
Concordia Academy, MN
Concordia Lutheran High School, IN
Faith Lutheran High School, NV
Lutheran High School, MO
Lutheran High School North, MO
Lutheran High School Northwest, MI
Lutheran High School of Hawaii, HI
Racine Lutheran High School, WI
Saint Paul Lutheran High School, MO

Mennonite Church
Christopher Dock Mennonite High School, PA
Eastern Mennonite High School, VA
Lancaster Mennonite High School, PA
Rockway Mennonite Collegiate, ON, Canada
United Mennonite Educational Institute, ON, Canada

Methodist Church
The Pennington School, NJ
Randolph-Macon Academy, VA

Moravian Church
Moravian Academy, PA
Salem Academy, NC

Pentecostal Church
Community Christian Academy, KY
Redemption Christian Academy, MA

Presbyterian Church
Mount Vernon Presbyterian School, GA
Orangewood Christian School, FL
Rabun Gap-Nacoochee School, GA

Presbyterian Church (U.S.A.)
Presbyterian Pan American School, TX

Presbyterian Church in America
Briarwood Christian High School, AL
First Presbyterian Day School, GA
Westminster Academy, FL
Westminster Schools of Augusta, GA

Protestant
Liberty Christian School, CA
Mooseheart High School, IL
Piedmont Academy, GA
Pioneer Valley Christian Academy, MA
Quinte Christian High School, ON, Canada
Wilmington Christian School, DE

Protestant Church
Salem Academy, OR

Protestant-Evangelical
Fresno Christian Schools, CA
Kauai Christian Academy, HI
Lehigh Valley Christian High School, PA
Nebraska Christian Schools, NE
North Toronto Christian School, ON, Canada
Westminster Christian Academy, LA

Reformed Church
Calvin Christian High School, CA
Covenant Canadian Reformed School, AB, Canada

Reformed Church in America
Illiana Christian High School, IL
Kalamazoo Christian High School, MI

Roman Catholic Church
Academy of Notre Dame, MA
Academy of Our Lady of Peace, CA
Academy of the Holy Cross, MD
Academy of the Holy Family, CT
Academy of the Sacred Heart, MI
Académie Ste Cécile International School, ON, Canada
Allentown Central Catholic High School, PA
All Hallows High School, NY
Aquinas High School, GA
Archbishop Curley High School, MD
Archbishop Hoban High School, OH
Archbishop Mitty High School, CA
Archbishop Shaw High School, LA
Archmere Academy, DE
Austin Preparatory School, MA
Belen Jesuit Preparatory School, FL
Benedictine High School, OH
Bishop Brady High School, NH
Bishop Brossart High School, KY
Bishop Connolly High School, MA
Bishop Denis J. O'Connell High School, VA
Bishop Eustace Preparatory School, NJ
Bishop Guertin High School, NH
Bishop Ireton High School, VA
Bishop John J. Snyder High School, FL
Bishop Kelly High School, ID
Bishop McCort High School, PA
Bishop McNamara High School, MD
Bishop Miege High School, KS
Bishop Montgomery High School, CA
Bishop Mora Salesian High School, CA
Bishop Stang High School, MA
Bishop Verot High School, FL
Bishop Walsh Middle High School, MD
Blanchet School, OR
Blessed Sacrament Huguenot Catholic School, VA
Blessed Trinity High School, GA
Brother Rice High School, MI
Butte Central Catholic High School, MT
Calvert Hall College High School, MD
Canterbury School, CT
Cardinal Gibbons High School, NC
Cardinal Mooney Catholic High School, FL
Cardinal Newman High School, FL
Carondelet High School, CA
Carrollton School of the Sacred Heart, FL
Cascia Hall Preparatory School, OK
Cathedral High School, MA
Cathedral High School, NY
Catholic Central High School, MI
Catholic Central High School, NY
Catholic Central High School, WI
Central Catholic High School, CA
Central Catholic High School, MA
Central Catholic High School, PA
Chaminade College Preparatory, CA
Chaminade-Madonna College Preparatory, FL
Christian Brothers Academy, NJ
Christopher Columbus High School, FL
Damien High School, CA
De La Salle College, ON, Canada
De La Salle High School, CA

DeLaSalle High School, MN
De La Salle North Catholic High School, OR
Delbarton School, NJ
Delphos Saint John's High School, OH
DeMatha Catholic High School, MD
Devon Preparatory School, PA
Dominican Academy, NY
Donovan Catholic, NJ
Dowling Catholic High School, IA
Elizabeth Seton Academy, MA
Elizabeth Seton High School, MD
Elyria Catholic High School, OH
Fairfield College Preparatory School, CT
Father Duenas Memorial School, GU
Father Lopez High School, FL
Father Ryan High School, TN
Fontbonne Academy, MA
Fordham Preparatory School, NY
Gabriel Richard Catholic High School, MI
Gilmour Academy, OH
Gonzaga College High School, DC
Hales Franciscan High School, IL
The Heights School, MD
Holy Cross High School, CT
Holy Cross Regional Catholic School, VA
Holy Cross School, LA
Holy Ghost Preparatory School, PA
Holy Names Academy, WA
Holyoke Catholic High School, MA
Holy Savior Menard Catholic High School, LA
Holy Trinity Diocesan High School, NY
Holy Trinity High School, IL
Immaculata High School, KS
Immaculata High School, NJ
Immaculata-La Salle High School, FL
Immaculate Conception High School, NJ
Immaculate Heart High School and Middle School, CA
Incarnate Word Academy, TX
Jesuit High School of Tampa, FL
John F. Kennedy Catholic High School, MO
John Paul II Catholic High School, FL
Josephinum Academy, IL
Judge Memorial Catholic High School, UT
Junipero Serra High School, CA
La Lumiere School, IN
Lancaster Catholic High School, PA
Lansdale Catholic High School, PA
La Salle Academy, RI
La Salle High School, CA
Lauralton Hall, CT
Lehman High School, OH
Lexington Catholic High School, KY
Louisville High School, CA
Loyola-Blakefield, MD
Malden Catholic High School, MA
Malvern Preparatory School, PA
Marianapolis Preparatory School, CT
Marian Central Catholic High School, IL
Marian High School, IN
Marian High School, MA
Marquette University High School, WI
Marymount High School, CA
Marymount School of New York, NY
Mater Dei High School, IL
Matignon High School, MA
Maur Hill-Mount Academy, KS
Memphis Catholic High School and Middle School, TN

Mercy High School, CT
Merion Mercy Academy, PA
Montrose School, MA
Mooseheart High School, IL
Moreau Catholic High School, CA
Mother McAuley High School, IL
Mount Mercy Academy, NY
Mount Saint Charles Academy, RI
Mount Saint Joseph Academy, PA
Nazareth Academy, IL
Nerinx Hall, MO
Northwest Catholic High School, CT
Notre Dame-Cathedral Latin School, OH
Notre Dame High School, CA
Notre Dame High School, CA
Notre Dame High School, CA
Notre Dame High School, LA
Notre Dame High School, MO
Notre Dame High School, NJ
Notre Dame High School, NY
Notre Dame High School, TN
Notre Dame Junior/Senior High School, PA
Oratory Preparatory School, NJ
Our Lady of Good Counsel High School, MD
Our Lady of Mercy Academy, NJ
Padua Academy, DE
Palma School, CA
Pensacola Catholic High School, FL
Pinecrest Academy, GA
Pius X High School, NE
Pope John Paul II High School, LA
Pope John XXIII Regional High School, NJ
Portsmouth Abbey School, RI
Powers Catholic High School, MI
Preston High School, NY
The Prout School, RI
Providence Catholic School, The College Preparatory School for
    Girls Grades 6-12, TX
Providence High School, CA
Ramona Convent Secondary School, CA
Regis High School, NY
Rockhurst High School, MO
Rosati-Kain High School, MO
Sacred Heart Academy, KY
Sacred Heart/Griffin High School, IL
Sacred Heart High School, CA
Saint Agnes Academic High School, NY
Saint Agnes Academy–St. Dominic School, TN
Saint Albert Junior-Senior High School, IA
St. Andrew's Regional High School, BC, Canada
Saint Anthony High School, IL
Saint Augustine Preparatory School, NJ
St. Benedict at Auburndale, TN
St. Bernard High School, CA
St. Bernard High School, CT
St. Bernard's Catholic School, CA
St. Brendan High School, FL
Saint Dominic Academy, ME
Saint Francis High School, CA
Saint Francis High School, CA
Saint Gertrude High School, VA
Saint Joan Antida High School, WI
St. John Neumann High School, FL
St. John's Catholic Prep, MD
St. John's Preparatory School, MA
Saint John's Preparatory School, MN
Saint Joseph Academy, CA

St. Joseph Academy, FL
St. Joseph High School, CT
Saint Joseph High School, NJ
Saint Joseph Regional High School, NJ
St. Joseph's Academy, LA
St. Joseph's Catholic School, SC
St. Joseph's Preparatory School, PA
St. Lawrence Seminary High School, WI
Saint Mary's High School, AZ
St. Mary's Preparatory School, MI
St. Mary's School, OR
Saint Maur International School, Japan
St. Michael's College School, ON, Canada
St. Michael's Preparatory School of the Norbertine Fathers, CA
St. Patrick Catholic High School, MS
Saint Patrick High School, IL
St. Patrick's Regional Secondary, BC, Canada
St. Paul's High School, MB, Canada
St. Peter's Preparatory School, NJ
St. Pius X High School, TX
Saint Teresa's Academy, MO
St. Thomas Aquinas High School, FL
Saint Thomas Aquinas High School, KS
St. Thomas Aquinas High School, NH
Saint Thomas More Catholic High School, LA
Saint Ursula Academy, OH
Saint Ursula Academy, OH
Saint Xavier High School, OH
Salesianum School, DE
Salpointe Catholic High School, AZ
San Domenico School, CA
Santa Catalina School, CA
Santa Margarita Catholic High School, CA
Seisen International School, Japan
Servite High School, CA
Shanley High School, ND
Stephen T. Badin High School, OH
Stone Ridge School of the Sacred Heart, MD
The Summit Country Day School, OH
Teurlings Catholic High School, LA
Traditional Learning Academy, BC, Canada
Trinity Catholic High School, CT
Trinity High School, KY
Trinity High School, NH
Trinity High School, OH
The Ursuline Academy of Dallas, TX
Vicksburg Catholic School, MS
Villa Duchesne and Oak Hill School, MO
Villa Madonna Academy, KY
Villa Walsh Academy, NJ
Visitation Academy, MO
The Willows Academy, IL
Woodside Priory School, CA
Xavier College Preparatory, AZ

Roman Catholic Church (Jesuit Order)

Brophy College Preparatory, AZ
Cheverus High School, ME
Jesuit College Preparatory School, TX
Regis Jesuit High School, Boys Division, CO
Regis Jesuit High School, Girls Division, CO
St. Louis University High School, MO

Seventh-day Adventist Church

Crawford Adventist Academy, ON, Canada
Griggs International Academy, MD
Mountain View Academy, CA

Parkview Adventist Academy, AB, Canada
Pine Tree Academy, ME
Takoma Academy, MD

Seventh-day Adventists

Collegedale Academy, TN
Forest Lake Academy, FL
Kingsway College, ON, Canada
Mesa Grande Seventh-Day Academy, CA
Paradise Adventist Academy, CA
Walla Walla Valley Academy, WA

Society of Friends

Arthur Morgan School, NC
Delaware Valley Friends School, PA
Friends Academy, NY
Friends' Central School, PA
Friends Select School, PA
George School, PA
Lincoln School, RI
Moorestown Friends School, NJ
Sandy Spring Friends School, MD
Scattergood Friends School, IA
Tandem Friends School, VA
Westtown School, PA
Wilmington Friends School, DE

Southern Baptist Convention

First Baptist Academy, TX
Hawaii Baptist Academy, HI
Oneida Baptist Institute, KY
Prestonwood Christian Academy, TX

United Church of Christ

Mid-Pacific Institute, HI

United Methodist Church

John Hancock Academy, GA
Wyoming Seminary, PA

Wesleyan Church

Wesleyan Academy, PR

Wisconsin Evangelical Lutheran Synod

California Lutheran High School, CA
St. Croix Schools, MN

SCHOOLS WITH ELEMENTARY DIVISIONS

The Academy at Charlemont, MA
Academy at the Lakes, FL
Admiral Farragut Academy, FL
The Agnes Irwin School, PA
Albuquerque Academy, NM
Alexander Dawson School, CO
Allen Academy, TX
All Saints' Academy, FL
American Heritage School, FL
The American School Foundation, Mexico
The American School in Japan, Japan
The American School of Puerto Vallarta, Mexico
Andrews Osborne Academy, OH
Arendell Parrott Academy, NC
Army and Navy Academy, CA
Ashley Hall, SC
ASSETS School, HI

Athens Academy, GA
Atlanta International School, GA
Austin Preparatory School, MA
Balmoral Hall School, MB, Canada
Battle Ground Academy, TN
Bay Ridge Preparatory School, NY
Beaufort Academy, SC
The Benjamin School, FL
Bentley School, CA
Berkeley Carroll School, NY
Berkeley Preparatory School, FL
The Birch Wathen Lenox School, NY
Bishop's College School, QC, Canada
The Bishop's School, CA
The Blake School, MN
The Bolles School, FL
Brandon Hall School, GA
Branksome Hall, ON, Canada
Breck School, MN
Brehm Preparatory School, IL
Brentwood School, CA
Brimmer and May School, MA
British International School of Boston, MA
British International School of Washington, DC
The Brook Hill School, TX
The Browning School, NY
Brunswick School, CT
The Bryn Mawr School for Girls, MD
The Buckley School, CA
Camden Military Academy, SC
Campbell Hall (Episcopal), CA
Canterbury School, FL
The Canterbury School of Florida, FL
Cape Fear Academy, NC
Cape Henry Collegiate School, VA
Cardigan Mountain School, NH
Carlisle School, VA
Carrollton School of the Sacred Heart, FL
Casady School, OK
Castilleja School, CA
The Catlin Gabel School, OR
Chadwick School, CA
Charlotte Country Day School, NC
Charlotte Latin School, NC
Christ Church Episcopal School, SC
Clarksville Academy, TN
The Collegiate School, VA
The Colorado Springs School, CO
The Columbus Academy, OH
Columbus School for Girls, OH
The Community School, ID
The Community School of Naples, FL
The Country Day School, ON, Canada
Crescent School, ON, Canada
Crossroads School for Arts & Sciences, CA
Crystal Springs Uplands School, CA
Currey Ingram Academy, TN
Dana Hall School, MA
Delaware Valley Friends School, PA
Delbarton School, NJ
Denver Academy, CO
The Derryfield School, NH
Desert Academy, NM
Detroit Country Day School, MI
Devon Preparatory School, PA
Doane Academy, NJ

The Dr. Miriam and Sheldon G. Adelson Educational Campus, The
   Adelson Upper School, NV
Donelson Christian Academy, TN
Donna Klein Jewish Academy, FL
The Donoho School, AL
Durham Academy, NC
The Dwight School, NY
Eaglebrook School, MA
Eagle Hill School, CT
Eastern Mennonite High School, VA
Edmund Burke School, DC
Elgin Academy, IL
The Ellis School, PA
Episcopal Collegiate School, AR
Episcopal High School of Jacksonville, FL
Falmouth Academy, MA
Fayetteville Academy, NC
Fay School, MA
The First Academy, FL
Flint Hill School, VA
Flintridge Preparatory School, CA
Fort Worth Country Day School, TX
Franklin Academy, CT
Franklin Road Academy, TN
Fredericksburg Academy, VA
Friends Academy, NY
Friends' Central School, PA
Friendship Christian School, TN
Friends Select School, PA
Fuqua School, VA
The Galloway School, GA
Garrison Forest School, MD
Gilman School, MD
Gilmour Academy, OH
Girard College, PA
Good Hope Country Day School, VI
The Gow School, NY
The Grauer School, CA
Greater Atlanta Christian Schools, GA
Green Fields Country Day School, AZ
Greenhill School, TX
Grier School, PA
Groton School, MA
Gulliver Preparatory School, FL
Hampshire Country School, NH
Hargrave Military Academy, VA
The Harker School, CA
The Harpeth Hall School, TN
Harvard-Westlake School, CA
The Harvey School, NY
Hathaway Brown School, OH
The Haverford School, PA
Hawaii Baptist Academy, HI
Hawai`i Preparatory Academy, HI
Hawken School, OH
The Heights School, MD
The Hill Center, Durham Academy, NC
The Hockaday School, TX
Holland Hall, OK
Houghton Academy, NY
Houston Academy, AL
The Howard School, GA
The Hudson School, NJ
The Hun School of Princeton, NJ
Indian Creek School, MD
Indian Springs School, AL
International High School, CA

International School Bangkok, Thailand
International School of Luxembourg, Luxembourg
Isidore Newman School, LA
John Burroughs School, MO
The Journeys School of Teton Science School, WY
Kent Denver School, CO
Kentucky Country Day School, KY
The Key School, MD
Keystone School, TX
King Low Heywood Thomas, CT
Kingswood-Oxford School, CT
The Knox School, NY
La Jolla Country Day School, CA
Lakehill Preparatory School, TX
Landmark School, MA
La Salle Academy, RI
Laurel School, OH
Lawrence School, OH
Le Lycee Francais de Los Angeles, CA
Lincoln School, RI
Long Trail School, VT
Louisville Collegiate School, KY
The Lovett School, GA
Lyman Ward Military Academy, AL
Malvern Preparatory School, PA
Marshall School, MN
Mary Institute and St. Louis Country Day School (MICDS), MO
Marymount School of New York, NY
The Masters School, NY
Maui Preparatory Academy, HI
Maumee Valley Country Day School, OH
McDonogh School, MD
The Meadows School, NV
Memphis University School, TN
Menlo School, CA
Miami Country Day School, FL
The Miami Valley School, OH
Middle Tennessee Christian School, TN
Mid-Pacific Institute, HI
Mill Springs Academy, GA
Milton Academy, MA
Miss Edgar's and Miss Cramp's School, QC, Canada
Missouri Military Academy, MO
MMI Preparatory School, PA
Montgomery Bell Academy, TN
Moorestown Friends School, NJ
Moravian Academy, PA
Mounds Park Academy, MN
Mount Vernon Presbyterian School, GA
National Cathedral School, DC
Newark Academy, NJ
Noble Academy, NC
Noble and Greenough School, MA
North Central Texas Academy, TX
North Country School, NY
Northpoint Christian School, MS
North Shore Country Day School, IL
Northwest Academy, OR
The Northwest School, WA
Oak Hill School, OR
The O'Neal School, NC
Oregon Episcopal School, OR
Out-Of-Door-Academy, FL
Pace Academy, GA
The Packer Collegiate Institute, NY
The Park School of Baltimore, MD
The Pennington School, NJ

Perkiomen School, PA
The Phelps School, PA
Phoenix Country Day School, AZ
Pickering College, ON, Canada
Pinecrest Academy, GA
The Pingry School, NJ
Polytechnic School, CA
Portledge School, NY
The Potomac School, VA
Poughkeepsie Day School, NY
Professional Children's School, NY
Providence Country Day School, RI
Providence Day School, NC
Punahou School, HI
Queen Margaret's School, BC, Canada
Rabun Gap-Nacoochee School, GA
Randolph-Macon Academy, VA
Randolph School, AL
Ransom Everglades School, FL
Ravenscroft School, NC
The Rectory School, CT
Ridley College, ON, Canada
Riverdale Country School, NY
River Oaks Baptist School, TX
The Rivers School, MA
Riverstone International School, ID
Rockland Country Day School, NY
The Roeper School, MI
Roland Park Country School, MD
Rolling Hills Preparatory School, CA
Rothesay Netherwood School, NB, Canada
The Roxbury Latin School, MA
Rumsey Hall School, CT
Rutgers Preparatory School, NJ
Sacramento Country Day School, CA
Sage Ridge School, NV
Saint Agnes Academy–St. Dominic School, TN
St. Albans School, DC
St. Andrew's Episcopal School, MD
St. Andrew's Episcopal School, MS
Saint Andrew's School, FL
St. Andrew's School, GA
St. Andrew's School, RI
St. Andrew's–Sewanee School, TN
St. Anne's–Belfield School, VA
St. Bernard High School, CT
St. Catherine's School, VA
St. Christopher's School, VA
St. Clement's School, ON, Canada
St. George's Independent School, TN
St. George's School, BC, Canada
Saint James School, MD
St. John's Preparatory School, MA
Saint John's Preparatory School, MN
St. Luke's School, CT
St. Mark's School of Texas, TX
St. Martin's Episcopal School, LA
St. Mary's Episcopal School, TN
St. Mary's School, OR
St. Paul Academy and Summit School, MN
St. Stephen's Episcopal School, TX
St. Thomas Choir School, NY
San Domenico School, CA
Sandy Spring Friends School, MD
San Marcos Baptist Academy, TX
The Savannah Country Day School, GA
Scheck Hillel Community School, FL

Seabury Hall, HI
Seattle Academy of Arts and Sciences, WA
The Seven Hills School, OH
Severn School, MD
Sewickley Academy, PA
Shady Side Academy, PA
Shawnigan Lake School, BC, Canada
Shorecrest Preparatory School, FL
Solebury School, PA
Soundview Preparatory School, NY
Southwest Christian School, Inc., TX
The Spence School, NY
Springside Chestnut Hill Academy, PA
Stanstead College, QC, Canada
Stevenson School, CA
Stone Ridge School of the Sacred Heart, MD
The Stony Brook School, NY
The Storm King School, NY
Stratford Academy, GA
Stuart Hall, VA
The Study, QC, Canada
The Summit Country Day School, OH
Taipei American School, Taiwan
Tampa Preparatory School, FL
Tandem Friends School, VA
TASIS The American School in England, United Kingdom
TASIS, The American School in Switzerland, Switzerland
Thomas Jefferson School, MO
TMI - The Episcopal School of Texas, TX
Tower Hill School, DE
Trinity College School, ON, Canada
Trinity Episcopal School, VA
Trinity-Pawling School, NY
Trinity Preparatory School, FL
Tuscaloosa Academy, AL
United Nations International School, NY
University of Chicago Laboratory Schools, IL
University Prep, WA
University School of Jackson, TN
Upper Canada College, ON, Canada
Valwood School, GA
The Vanguard School, FL
Viewpoint School, CA
Villa Duchesne and Oak Hill School, MO
Visitation Academy, MO
Wasatch Academy, UT
Washington International School, DC
The Waterford School, UT
Watkinson School, CT
Waynflete School, ME
Webb School of Knoxville, TN
Wesleyan School, GA
Westmark School, CA
The Westminster Schools, GA
Westminster Schools of Augusta, GA
Westtown School, PA
The Wheeler School, RI
Whitfield School, MO
Wichita Collegiate School, KS
The Williston Northampton School, MA
Wilmington Friends School, DE
Winston Preparatory School, NY
The Winston School, TX
Woodlynde School, PA
Woodside Priory School, CA
Wooster School, CT
Worcester Preparatory School, MD

York Country Day School, PA
York School, CA

SCHOOLS REPORTING ACADEMIC ACCOMMODATIONS FOR THE GIFTED AND TALENTED

The Academy for Gifted Children (PACE), ON, Canada	G
Academy of Notre Dame, MA	G
Academy of the Holy Cross, MD	G,A
Academy of the Holy Family, CT	G,M
Academy of the New Church Boys' School, PA	G,M,A
Academy of the New Church Girls' School, PA	G,M,A
Academy of the Sacred Heart, MI	G,M,A
Académie Ste Cécile International School, ON, Canada	G,M,A
Admiral Farragut Academy, FL	G
Advanced Academy of Georgia, GA	G,M,A
The Agnes Irwin School, PA	G
Alexander Dawson School, CO	G,M,A
Allentown Central Catholic High School, PA	G
Allison Academy, FL	G,M,A
Alpine Academy, UT	G
American Heritage School, FL	G,M,A
American Heritage School, FL	G,M,A
Andrews Osborne Academy, OH	G,M,A
Archbishop Hoban High School, OH	G,A
Archbishop Mitty High School, CA	G,M,A
Archmere Academy, DE	G,M,A
Arete Preparatory Academy, CA	G
Armbrae Academy, NS, Canada	A
Ashley Hall, SC	G,M,A
ASSETS School, HI	G
Balmoral Hall School, MB, Canada	G
The Baltimore Actors' Theatre Conservatory, MD	G,M,A
Bay Ridge Preparatory School, NY	G,M,A
Beaufort Academy, SC	G
The Beekman School, NY	G,M,A
Ben Franklin Academy, GA	G
Besant Hill School, CA	M,A
The Birch Wathen Lenox School, NY	G,M,A
Bishop Brady High School, NH	G
Bishop Denis J. O'Connell High School, VA	G
Bishop Eustace Preparatory School, NJ	G,M
Bishop Guertin High School, NH	G
Bishop Ireton High School, VA	M
Bishop McNamara High School, MD	G
Bishop Mora Salesian High School, CA	M,A
Bishop's College School, QC, Canada	G
Blueprint Education, AZ	M,A
Bodwell High School, BC, Canada	G
Boston University Academy, MA	G
Branksome Hall, ON, Canada	G,M,A
Breck School, MN	G,M,A
Brehm Preparatory School, IL	G
Brentwood School, CA	G,A
Briarcrest Christian High School, TN	G,M,A
Briarwood Christian High School, AL	G
Bridges Academy, CA	G
British International School of Boston, MA	G
The Brook Hill School, TX	G,A
The Browning School, NY	G,M
The Bryn Mawr School for Girls, MD	G,M,A
Buffalo Seminary, NY	G
Buxton School, MA	G,M,A
California Crosspoint High School, CA	G

Calvary Day School, GA	G
Calvert Hall College High School, MD	G,M,A
Cape Henry Collegiate School, VA	G,M,A
Cardigan Mountain School, NH	G
Cardinal Newman High School, FL	G
Carondelet High School, CA	G
Casady School, OK	G,M,A
Cascadilla School, NY	G,M,A
Cascia Hall Preparatory School, OK	G
Castilleja School, CA	G
Cate School, CA	G,M,A
Catholic Central High School, WI	G,A
The Catlin Gabel School, OR	G
Central Catholic High School, PA	G
Chadwick School, CA	G,M,A
Chaminade-Madonna College Preparatory, FL	G,M,A
Charlotte Country Day School, NC	G
Charlotte Latin School, NC	G
Chattanooga Christian School, TN	G,A
Choate Rosemary Hall, CT	G,M,A
Christa McAuliffe Academy School of Arts and Sciences, OR	G,M,A
Christ Church Episcopal School, SC	G
Christchurch School, VA	G
Christian Heritage School, CT	G
Christopher Columbus High School, FL	G
Chrysalis School, WA	G
The Colorado Rocky Mountain School, CO	G,M,A
The Colorado Springs School, CO	G
The Columbus Academy, OH	G
Commonwealth School, MA	G,M,A
The Community School, ID	G
The Community School of Naples, FL	G
Concord Academy, MA	G,M,A
The Crenshaw School, FL	G
Crossroads School for Arts & Sciences, CA	G,M,A
The Culver Academies, IN	G,M,A
Currey Ingram Academy, TN	G,M,A
Cushing Academy, MA	G,M,A
Darrow School, NY	M,A
Deerfield Academy, MA	G,M,A
Delaware Valley Friends School, PA	A
DeMatha Catholic High School, MD	G,M,A
Denver Academy, CO	G
Detroit Country Day School, MI	G,M,A
Doane Academy, NJ	G,M,A
The Dr. Miriam and Sheldon G. Adelson Educational Campus, The Adelson Upper School, NV	G
Donovan Catholic, NJ	G,M,A
Dowling Catholic High School, IA	G,M,A
Dublin Christian Academy, NH	M,A
Dublin School, NH	G
The Dwight School, NY	G,M,A
Eaglebrook School, MA	G,M,A
Eastern Mennonite High School, VA	G
Eaton Academy, GA	G,M,A
Edison School, AB, Canada	G
Eldorado Emerson Private School, CA	G,M,A
Elizabeth Seton High School, MD	G,M,A
The Ellis School, PA	G,M
Elmwood School, ON, Canada	G
Episcopal High School, VA	G,M,A
Episcopal High School of Jacksonville, FL	G
Explorations Academy, WA	G
Faith Lutheran High School, NV	M
Father Ryan High School, TN	G,M,A
Flint Hill School, VA	M,A

G — gifted; M — musically talented; A — artistically talented

School	
Fort Worth Country Day School, TX	G,M,A
Foxcroft School, VA	G,M,A
Franklin Academy, CT	G
Franklin Road Academy, TN	G,M,A
Fredericton Christian Academy, NB, Canada	G
Friends Select School, PA	M,A
Front Range Christian High School, CO	G
The Galloway School, GA	G,M,A
Garrison Forest School, MD	G,M,A
George Stevens Academy, ME	G,M,A
George Walton Academy, GA	G,M,A
Gilman School, MD	G,M,A
Gilmour Academy, OH	G,M,A
The Glenholme School, Devereux Connecticut, CT	G
The Governor French Academy, IL	G
The Gow School, NY	M
The Grauer School, CA	G,M,A
Greater Atlanta Christian Schools, GA	G,M,A
Grier School, PA	G,M,A
Groton School, MA	G,M,A
Gulliver Preparatory School, FL	G,M,A
The Gunnery, CT	G,M,A
The Gunston School, MD	G,M,A
Hales Franciscan High School, IL	G
Halstrom Academy, Beverly Hills, CA	G,M,A
Halstrom Academy, Calsbad, CA	G,M,A
Halstrom Academy, Cupertino, CA	G,M,A
Halstrom Academy, Huntington Beach, CA	G,M,A
Halstrom Academy, Irvine, CA	G,M,A
Halstrom Academy, Los Angeles, CA	G,M,A
Halstrom Academy, Manhattan Beach, CA	G,M,A
Halstrom Academy, Mission Viejo, CA	G,M,A
Halstrom Academy, Orange, CA	G,M,A
Halstrom Academy, Pasadena, CA	G,M,A
Halstrom Academy, San Diego, CA	G,M,A
Halstrom Academy, San Mateo, CA	G,M,A
Halstrom Academy, Walnut Creek, CA	G,M,A
Halstrom Academy, Westlake Village, CA	G,M,A
Halstrom Academy, Woodland Hills, CA	G,M,A
Hampshire Country School, NH	G
The Harker School, CA	G
The Harpeth Hall School, TN	G,M,A
Harvard-Westlake School, CA	G,M,A
Hathaway Brown School, OH	G,M
The Haverford School, PA	G
Hebrew Academy of the Five Towns & Rockaway, NY	A
The Heights School, MD	G,M,A
Heritage Academy, SC	G
Ho'Ala School, HI	G,A
Holy Cross School, LA	G,M,A
Houston Academy, AL	G,M
The Howard School, GA	G,A
The Hudson School, NJ	G,M,A
The Hun School of Princeton, NJ	G
Huntington-Surrey School, TX	G
Hyde School, ME	G,M,A
Hyman Brand Hebrew Academy of Greater Kansas City, KS	G
Immaculata High School, NJ	M
Independent School, KS	G,M,A
Indian Creek School, MD	G
Indian Springs School, AL	G,M
International High School, CA	G,M,A
Jean and Samuel Frankel Jewish Academy of Metropolitan Detroit, MI	G
The John Dewey Academy, MA	G,A
The Journeys School of Teton Science School, WY	G

School	
Kent School, CT	G,M,A
Kentucky Country Day School, KY	G,M,A
The Key School, MD	G
The Keystone School, PA	G,M,A
Keystone School, TX	G
King Low Heywood Thomas, CT	G,M,A
King's-Edgehill School, NS, Canada	G
The Knox School, NY	G
La Lumiere School, IN	G,A
Lancaster Catholic High School, PA	G,M,A
Lancaster Mennonite High School, PA	M
La Salle Academy, RI	G,M,A
The Laureate Academy, MB, Canada	G
Laurel School, OH	G,M,A
Leysin American School in Switzerland, Switzerland	G,M,A
Lincoln Academy, ME	G,M,A
Little Keswick School, VA	G
Loudoun School for the Gifted, VA	G
Loyola-Blakefield, MD	G,M,A
Lutheran High School, MO	A
Lutheran High School of Hawaii, HI	M,A
Luther College High School, SK, Canada	G
Maranatha High School, CA	A
Marine Military Academy, TX	G
Marshall School, MN	G
Mary Institute and St. Louis Country Day School (MICDS), MO	G
Marymount School of New York, NY	G
The Masters School, NY	G,M,A
Mater Dei High School, IL	G
Maumee Valley Country Day School, OH	G,M,A
Maur Hill-Mount Academy, KS	G
The Meadows School, NV	G,M,A
Memphis University School, TN	G
Mercersburg Academy, PA	G,M,A
Merion Mercy Academy, PA	G,M,A
The Miami Valley School, OH	G,M,A
Middlesex School, MA	G
Mid-Pacific Institute, HI	G,A
Mill Springs Academy, GA	G,M,A
Milton Academy, MA	G,M,A
Miss Hall's School, MA	G,M,A
Missouri Military Academy, MO	G,M,A
MMI Preparatory School, PA	G
The Monarch School, TX	G,A
Mount Saint Joseph Academy, PA	G,M,A
National Cathedral School, DC	G
Newark Academy, NJ	G,M,A
Noah Webster Christian School, WY	G
Noble and Greenough School, MA	G,M,A
The Nora School, MD	G,A
The North Broward Preparatory Upper School, FL	G,M,A
North Central Texas Academy, TX	G,M,A
Northfield Mount Hermon School, MA	G,M,A
Northpoint Christian School, MS	G
Northwest Academy, OR	G,M,A
Northwest Yeshiva High School, WA	G
Notre Dame High School, LA	G
Notre Dame High School, MO	G,M,A
Notre Dame High School, NY	G,A
Oak Hill School, OR	G
Oregon Episcopal School, OR	G
Orinda Academy, CA	G
Our Lady of Good Counsel High School, MD	G
The Oxford Academy, CT	G
Pace Academy, GA	G,M,A
PACE/Brantley Hall High School, FL	G

G — gifted; M — musically talented; A — artistically talented

Pacific Crest Community School, OR	G	St. Michael's Preparatory School of the	
The Park School of Baltimore, MD	G,M,A	Norbertine Fathers, CA	G
The Pennington School, NJ	G	St. Paul Preparatory School, MN	M,A
Pensacola Catholic High School, FL	G	St. Paul's School, NH	G,M,A
Perkiomen School, PA	G,M,A	Saint Thomas Aquinas High School, KS	G
The Phelps School, PA	G	St. Thomas Choir School, NY	G,M
Philadelphia-Montgomery Christian Academy, PA	G,M,A	Saint Thomas More Catholic High School, LA	G
Phillips Academy (Andover), MA	G,M,A	Salem Academy, OR	M,A
The Pingry School, NJ	G	Salesianum School, DE	G
Portledge School, NY	G,M,A	San Domenico School, CA	M
Portsmouth Abbey School, RI	G	Sandy Spring Friends School, MD	G,M,A
Portsmouth Christian Academy, NH	G,M	San Francisco University High School, CA	G,M,A
Poughkeepsie Day School, NY	G,M,A	San Marcos Baptist Academy, TX	G,M,A
Prestonwood Christian Academy, TX	G	Santa Catalina School, CA	G,M,A
Proctor Academy, NH	G	Santa Margarita Catholic High School, CA	G,M,A
Providence Country Day School, RI	G,M,A	Scattergood Friends School, IA	G
Providence Day School, NC	G,M,A	Scheck Hillel Community School, FL	G,A
Providence High School, CA	M,A	SciCore Academy, NJ	G,A
Queen Margaret's School, BC, Canada	G,M,A	Seabury Hall, HI	G
Ramona Convent Secondary School, CA	G,M,A	Seattle Academy of Arts and Sciences, WA	G,M,A
Randolph-Macon Academy, VA	G	The Seven Hills School, OH	G
Ravenscroft School, NC	G,M,A	Severn School, MD	G,M,A
Realms of Inquiry, UT	G,M,A	Shady Side Academy, PA	G,M,A
The Rectory School, CT	G,M,A	Shawnigan Lake School, BC, Canada	G
Redemption Christian Academy, MA	G	Shorecrest Preparatory School, FL	G
Regis Jesuit High School, Boys Division, CO	G	Sierra Canyon School, CA	G,M,A
Ridley College, ON, Canada	G,M,A	Smith School, NY	M,A
Riverdale Country School, NY	G,M,A	Solebury School, PA	G,M,A
Rockland Country Day School, NY	G,M,A	Soundview Preparatory School, NY	G,M,A
Rock Point School, VT	G,A	Southwest Christian School, Inc., TX	G
The Roeper School, MI	G,M,A	Springside Chestnut Hill Academy, PA	G,M,A
Rolling Hills Preparatory School, CA	G	Squaw Valley Academy, CA	G,M,A
Rosati-Kain High School, MO	G,M,A	Steamboat Mountain School, CO	G
Rothesay Netherwood School, NB, Canada	G,M,A	St Leonards School and Sixth Form College, United	
The Roxbury Latin School, MA	G,M,A	Kingdom	G,M,A
Rumsey Hall School, CT	G	Stone Ridge School of the Sacred Heart, MD	G,A
Rutgers Preparatory School, NJ	G,M,A	The Storm King School, NY	G,M,A
Sacred Heart Academy, KY	G,M,A	Stuart Hall, VA	G,M,A
Sacred Heart/Griffin High School, IL	G,M,A	The Study, QC, Canada	G
Sage Hill School, CA	G,M,A	The Summit Country Day School, OH	G,A
Saint Agnes Academy–St. Dominic School, TN	G,A	Summit Preparatory School, MT	G
Saint Albert Junior-Senior High School, IA	G	Sunshine Bible Academy, SD	M
St. Andrew's Episcopal School, MS	G,M,A	The Taft School, CT	G,M,A
St. Andrew's School, DE	G,M,A	Tampa Preparatory School, FL	G,M,A
Saint Andrew's School, FL	G	Tandem Friends School, VA	G
St. Andrew's School, GA	G,M,A	TASIS The American School in England, United	
St. Andrew's–Sewanee School, TN	G,M,A	Kingdom	G
Saint Augustine Preparatory School, NJ	G,M,A	TASIS, The American School in Switzerland,	
St. Benedict at Auburndale, TN	G,M,A	Switzerland	G,M,A
St. Brendan High School, FL	G	The Tenney School, TX	G,M,A
St. Christopher's School, VA	G,M,A	The Thacher School, CA	G,M,A
St. Croix Schools, MN	G,M,A	Thomas Jefferson School, MO	G
St. George's School, RI	G,M,A	Tower Hill School, DE	G,M,A
Saint James School, MD	M	Trinity Episcopal School, VA	G,M,A
St. John's Preparatory School, MA	G,M,A	Trinity High School, KY	G,M,A
St. Joseph Academy, FL	G,A	Trinity High School, OH	G,A
St. Joseph High School, CT	G	Trinity Preparatory School, FL	G,M,A
Saint Joseph High School, NJ	G	Trinity School of Texas, TX	G,M,A
St. Joseph's Preparatory School, PA	G,M,A	Tuscaloosa Academy, AL	G
St. Luke's School, CT	G	United Nations International School, NY	G,M,A
St. Mark's School of Texas, TX	G	The United World College - USA, NM	M,A
St. Mary's Episcopal School, TN	G,M,A	University School of Jackson, TN	G,M,A
St. Mary's Preparatory School, MI	M,A	Valley Christian High School, CA	M,A
Saint Mary's School, NC	G,M,A	The Valley School, MI	G,A
St. Mary's School, OR	G,M,A	Valwood School, GA	G,M
Saint Maur International School, Japan	G	The Vanguard School, FL	G
		Venta Preparatory School, ON, Canada	G

G — gifted; M — musically talented; A — artistically talented

Villa Walsh Academy, NJ	G,M,A
Walnut Hill School for the Arts, MA	G,M,A
The Waterford School, UT	G,M,A
Watkinson School, CT	G,M,A
The Webb Schools, CA	G
Wellspring Foundation, CT	G
West Island College, AB, Canada	G
Westminster Christian School, FL	G,M,A
The Westminster Schools, GA	G,M,A
Westminster Schools of Augusta, GA	G
Westover School, CT	G,M,A
West Sound Academy, WA	G,M,A
Westtown School, PA	G,M,A
Wheaton Academy, IL	G,M,A
The Wheeler School, RI	G
Whitefield Academy, KY	G
Whitfield School, MO	G,M,A
Wichita Collegiate School, KS	G
The Williston Northampton School, MA	G,M,A
Wilmington Friends School, DE	G,M,A
Windermere Preparatory School, FL	M,A
The Windsor School, NY	G,M,A
The Winston School, TX	G,A
Woodside Priory School, CA	G,M,A
Worcester Preparatory School, MD	G,M,A
Xavier College Preparatory, AZ	G,A
York Country Day School, PA	G,M,A
The York School, ON, Canada	G,M,A

SCHOOLS WITH ADVANCED PLACEMENT PREPARATION

Academy at the Lakes, FL
The Academy for Gifted Children (PACE), ON, Canada
Academy of Notre Dame, MA
Academy of Our Lady of Peace, CA
Academy of the Holy Cross, MD
Academy of the New Church Boys' School, PA
Academy of the New Church Girls' School, PA
Academy of the Sacred Heart, MI
Académie Ste Cécile International School, ON, Canada
Admiral Farragut Academy, FL
The Agnes Irwin School, PA
Albuquerque Academy, NM
Alexander Dawson School, CO
Allen Academy, TX
Allentown Central Catholic High School, PA
Allison Academy, FL
All Saints' Academy, FL
Alma Heights Christian High School, CA
American Christian Academy, AL
American Heritage School, FL
American Heritage School, FL
The American School Foundation, Mexico
The American School in Japan, Japan
The American School of Puerto Vallarta, Mexico
Andrews Osborne Academy, OH
Aquinas High School, GA
Archbishop Curley High School, MD
Archbishop Hoban High School, OH
Archbishop Mitty High School, CA
Archbishop Shaw High School, LA
Archmere Academy, DE
Arendell Parrott Academy, NC
Armbrae Academy, NS, Canada
Army and Navy Academy, CA

Ashley Hall, SC
Athens Academy, GA
Augusta Christian School, GA
Austin Preparatory School, MA
Bakersfield Christian High School, CA
Balmoral Hall School, MB, Canada
The Baltimore Actors' Theatre Conservatory, MD
Baptist Regional School, NJ
Battle Ground Academy, TN
Bay Ridge Preparatory School, NY
Beaufort Academy, SC
The Beekman School, NY
Belen Jesuit Preparatory School, FL
Benedictine High School, OH
Ben Franklin Academy, GA
The Benjamin School, FL
Bentley School, CA
Berean Christian High School, CA
Berkeley Preparatory School, FL
Berkshire School, MA
Besant Hill School, CA
The Birch Wathen Lenox School, NY
Bishop Brady High School, NH
Bishop Connolly High School, MA
Bishop Denis J. O'Connell High School, VA
Bishop Eustace Preparatory School, NJ
Bishop Guertin High School, NH
Bishop Ireton High School, VA
Bishop John J. Snyder High School, FL
Bishop Kelly High School, ID
Bishop McNamara High School, MD
Bishop Miege High School, KS
Bishop Montgomery High School, CA
Bishop's College School, QC, Canada
The Bishop's School, CA
Bishop Stang High School, MA
Bishop Verot High School, FL
Bishop Walsh Middle High School, MD
Blair Academy, NJ
The Blake School, MN
Blanchet School, OR
Blessed Sacrament Huguenot Catholic School, VA
Blessed Trinity High School, GA
Bodwell High School, BC, Canada
The Bolles School, FL
Boyd-Buchanan School, TN
Brandon Hall School, GA
Breck School, MN
Brentwood College School, BC, Canada
Brentwood School, CA
Briarcrest Christian High School, TN
Briarwood Christian High School, AL
Brimmer and May School, MA
The Brook Hill School, TX
Brooks School, MA
Brophy College Preparatory, AZ
Brother Rice High School, MI
The Browning School, NY
Brunswick School, CT
The Bryn Mawr School for Girls, MD
The Buckley School, CA
Buffalo Seminary, NY
Burr and Burton Academy, VT
Butte Central Catholic High School, MT
Calgary Academy Collegiate, AB, Canada
California Crosspoint High School, CA
California Lutheran High School, CA

Calvary Day School, GA
Calvert Hall College High School, MD
Calvin Christian High School, CA
Camden Military Academy, SC
Campbell Hall (Episcopal), CA
Canterbury School, CT
Canterbury School, FL
The Canterbury School of Florida, FL
Cape Fear Academy, NC
Cape Henry Collegiate School, VA
Capistrano Valley Christian Schools, CA
Cardinal Gibbons High School, NC
Cardinal Mooney Catholic High School, FL
Cardinal Newman High School, FL
Carlisle School, VA
Carondelet High School, CA
Carrollton School of the Sacred Heart, FL
Casady School, OK
Cascadilla School, NY
Cascia Hall Preparatory School, OK
Castilleja School, CA
Cate School, CA
Cathedral High School, NY
Catholic Central High School, MI
Catholic Central High School, NY
Catholic Central High School, WI
Central Catholic High School, CA
Central Catholic High School, MA
Central Catholic High School, PA
Chadwick School, CA
Chaminade College Preparatory, CA
Chaminade-Madonna College Preparatory, FL
Charles Finney School, NY
Charlotte Latin School, NC
Chattanooga Christian School, TN
Cheverus High School, ME
Choate Rosemary Hall, CT
Christa McAuliffe Academy School of Arts and Sciences, OR
Christchurch School, VA
Christian Brothers Academy, NJ
Christian Central Academy, NY
Christian Heritage School, CT
Christopher Columbus High School, FL
Christopher Dock Mennonite High School, PA
Clarksville Academy, TN
Colegio Bolivar, Colombia
Collegedale Academy, TN
The Collegiate School, VA
The Colorado Rocky Mountain School, CO
The Colorado Springs School, CO
Columbia Academy, TN
Columbia International School, Japan
The Columbus Academy, OH
Columbus School for Girls, OH
Commonwealth School, MA
The Community School, ID
The Community School of Naples, FL
Concordia Lutheran High School, IN
The Country Day School, ON, Canada
Crawford Adventist Academy, ON, Canada
Crescent School, ON, Canada
The Culver Academies, IN
Cushing Academy, MA
Damien High School, CA
Dana Hall School, MA
Darrow School, NY
Deerfield Academy, MA

De La Salle College, ON, Canada
De La Salle High School, CA
DeLaSalle High School, MN
De La Salle North Catholic High School, OR
Delbarton School, NJ
DeMatha Catholic High School, MD
The Derryfield School, NH
Detroit Country Day School, MI
Devon Preparatory School, PA
Doane Academy, NJ
The Dr. Miriam and Sheldon G. Adelson Educational Campus, The Adelson Upper School, NV
Dominican Academy, NY
Donelson Christian Academy, TN
Donna Klein Jewish Academy, FL
The Donoho School, AL
Donovan Catholic, NJ
Dowling Catholic High School, IA
Dublin Christian Academy, NH
Dublin School, NH
Durham Academy, NC
The Dwight School, NY
Eastern Mennonite High School, VA
Edison School, AB, Canada
Edmund Burke School, DC
Eldorado Emerson Private School, CA
Elgin Academy, IL
Elizabeth Seton High School, MD
The Ellis School, PA
Elyria Catholic High School, OH
Episcopal Collegiate School, AR
Episcopal High School, TX
Episcopal High School, VA
Episcopal High School of Jacksonville, FL
Erskine Academy, ME
Explorations Academy, WA
Ezell-Harding Christian School, TN
Fairfield College Preparatory School, CT
Faith Lutheran High School, NV
Falmouth Academy, MA
Father Duenas Memorial School, GU
Father Lopez High School, FL
Father Ryan High School, TN
Fayetteville Academy, NC
The First Academy, FL
First Baptist Academy, TX
First Presbyterian Day School, GA
Flint Hill School, VA
Flintridge Preparatory School, CA
Fontbonne Academy, MA
Fordham Preparatory School, NY
Fort Worth Country Day School, TX
Foundation Academy, FL
Fountain Valley School of Colorado, CO
Foxcroft School, VA
Franklin Road Academy, TN
Fredericksburg Academy, VA
Fresno Christian Schools, CA
Friends Academy, NY
Friendship Christian School, TN
Friends Select School, PA
Front Range Christian High School, CO
Fuqua School, VA
Gabriel Richard Catholic High School, MI
The Galloway School, GA
Gann Academy (The New Jewish High School of Greater Boston), MA

Garrison Forest School, MD
George School, PA
George Stevens Academy, ME
George Walton Academy, GA
Gilman School, MD
Gilmour Academy, OH
Girard College, PA
Glades Day School, FL
Gonzaga College High School, DC
Good Hope Country Day School, VI
The Governor French Academy, IL
The Governor's Academy, MA
Grace Baptist Academy, TN
Grace Christian School, AK
Greater Atlanta Christian Schools, GA
Green Fields Country Day School, AZ
Greenhill School, TX
Grier School, PA
Groton School, MA
Guamani Private School, PR
Gulliver Preparatory School, FL
The Gunnery, CT
The Gunston School, MD
Halstrom Academy, Beverly Hills, CA
Halstrom Academy, Calsbad, CA
Halstrom Academy, Cupertino, CA
Halstrom Academy, Huntington Beach, CA
Halstrom Academy, Irvine, CA
Halstrom Academy, Los Angeles, CA
Halstrom Academy, Manhattan Beach, CA
Halstrom Academy, Mission Viejo, CA
Halstrom Academy, Orange, CA
Halstrom Academy, Pasadena, CA
Halstrom Academy, San Diego, CA
Halstrom Academy, San Mateo, CA
Halstrom Academy, Walnut Creek, CA
Halstrom Academy, Westlake Village, CA
Halstrom Academy, Woodland Hills, CA
Hargrave Military Academy, VA
The Harker School, CA
The Harpeth Hall School, TN
Harrells Christian Academy, NC
Harvard-Westlake School, CA
The Harvey School, NY
Hathaway Brown School, OH
Hawaii Baptist Academy, HI
Hawai`i Preparatory Academy, HI
Hawken School, OH
Hebrew Academy, CA
Hebrew Academy of the Five Towns & Rockaway, NY
The Heights School, MD
Heritage Academy, SC
Ho'Ala School, HI
The Hockaday School, TX
Holland Hall, OK
Holy Cross High School, CT
Holy Cross School, LA
Holy Ghost Preparatory School, PA
Holyoke Catholic High School, MA
Holy Savior Menard Catholic High School, LA
Holy Trinity Diocesan High School, NY
Holy Trinity High School, IL
Holy Trinity School, ON, Canada
Houghton Academy, NY
Houston Academy, AL
The Hudson School, NJ
The Hun School of Princeton, NJ

Hyde School, CT
Hyde School, ME
Hyman Brand Hebrew Academy of Greater Kansas City, KS
Illiana Christian High School, IL
Immaculata High School, NJ
Immaculata-La Salle High School, FL
Immaculate Heart High School and Middle School, CA
Incarnate Word Academy, TX
Independent School, KS
Indian Creek School, MD
Indian Springs School, AL
Institut Monte Rosa, Switzerland
International School Bangkok, Thailand
International School of Port-of-Spain, Trinidad and Tobago
International School of Zug and Luzern (ISZL), Switzerland
Isidore Newman School, LA
Jean and Samuel Frankel Jewish Academy of Metropolitan
    Detroit, MI
Jesuit College Preparatory School, TX
Jesuit High School of Tampa, FL
Jewish Community High School of the Bay, CA
John Burroughs School, MO
John F. Kennedy Catholic High School, MO
John Paul II Catholic High School, FL
Josephinum Academy, IL
Judge Memorial Catholic High School, UT
Junipero Serra High School, CA
Kalamazoo Christian High School, MI
Kent Denver School, CO
Kent School, CT
Kentucky Country Day School, KY
The Key School, MD
Keystone School, TX
King Low Heywood Thomas, CT
The King's Christian High School, NJ
Kingswood-Oxford School, CT
The Knox School, NY
La Jolla Country Day School, CA
Lakefield College School, ON, Canada
Lakehill Preparatory School, TX
La Lumiere School, IN
Lancaster Catholic High School, PA
Lancaster Mennonite High School, PA
Landmark Christian School, GA
Lansdale Catholic High School, PA
La Salle Academy, RI
La Salle High School, CA
Laurel School, OH
The Leelanau School, MI
Lehigh Valley Christian High School, PA
Lehman High School, OH
Le Lycee Francais de Los Angeles, CA
Lexington Catholic High School, KY
Lexington Christian Academy, KY
Lincoln Academy, ME
Lincoln School, RI
Loudoun School for the Gifted, VA
Louisville Collegiate School, KY
Louisville High School, CA
The Lovett School, GA
Loyola-Blakefield, MD
Lutheran High School North, MO
Lutheran High School Northwest, MI
Lutheran High School of Hawaii, HI
Lutheran High School of San Diego, CA
Lycee Claudel, ON, Canada
The Lycee International, American Section, France

Lyman Ward Military Academy, AL
The Madeira School, VA
Malden Catholic High School, MA
Malvern Preparatory School, PA
Manhattan Christian High School, MT
Maranatha High School, CA
Marianapolis Preparatory School, CT
Marian Central Catholic High School, IL
Marian High School, IN
Marian High School, MA
Marine Military Academy, TX
Marquette University High School, WI
Marshall School, MN
Martin Luther High School, NY
The Marvelwood School, CT
Mary Institute and St. Louis Country Day School (MICDS), MO
Marymount High School, CA
Marymount School of New York, NY
Massanutten Military Academy, VA
The Masters School, NY
Mater Dei High School, IL
Matignon High School, MA
Maui Preparatory Academy, HI
Maumee Valley Country Day School, OH
Maur Hill-Mount Academy, KS
McDonogh School, MD
The Meadows School, NV
Memphis University School, TN
Menlo School, CA
Mercersburg Academy, PA
Mercy High School, CT
Merion Mercy Academy, PA
Miami Country Day School, FL
The Miami Valley School, OH
Middlesex School, MA
Middle Tennessee Christian School, TN
Midland School, CA
Mid-Pacific Institute, HI
Milton Academy, MA
Miss Edgar's and Miss Cramp's School, QC, Canada
Miss Hall's School, MA
Missouri Military Academy, MO
Miss Porter's School, CT
MMI Preparatory School, PA
The Monarch School, TX
Montgomery Bell Academy, TN
Montrose School, MA
Moorestown Friends School, NJ
Mooseheart High School, IL
Moravian Academy, PA
Moreau Catholic High School, CA
Mother McAuley High School, IL
Mounds Park Academy, MN
Mountain View Academy, CA
Mount Dora Christian Academy, FL
Mount Mercy Academy, NY
Mount Saint Charles Academy, RI
Mount Saint Joseph Academy, PA
Mount Vernon Presbyterian School, GA
Nashville Christian School, TN
National Cathedral School, DC
Nazareth Academy, IL
Nerinx Hall, MO
Newark Academy, NJ
Noble and Greenough School, MA
The North Broward Preparatory Upper School, FL
Northfield Mount Hermon School, MA

Northpoint Christian School, MS
North Shore Country Day School, IL
Northwest Catholic High School, CT
The Norwich Free Academy, CT
Notre Dame-Cathedral Latin School, OH
Notre Dame High School, CA
Notre Dame High School, CA
Notre Dame High School, CA
Notre Dame High School, MO
Notre Dame High School, NJ
Notre Dame High School, NY
Notre Dame High School, TN
Notre Dame Junior/Senior High School, PA
Oak Hill School, OR
The O'Neal School, NC
Oneida Baptist Institute, KY
Orangeburg Preparatory Schools, Inc., SC
Orangewood Christian School, FL
Oratory Preparatory School, NJ
Oregon Episcopal School, OR
Orinda Academy, CA
Our Lady of Good Counsel High School, MD
Our Lady of Mercy Academy, NJ
Out-Of-Door-Academy, FL
The Oxford Academy, CT
Pace Academy, GA
PACE/Brantley Hall High School, FL
Padua Academy, DE
Palma School, CA
Palo Alto Preparatory School, CA
The Park School of Baltimore, MD
Peddie School, NJ
The Pennington School, NJ
Pensacola Catholic High School, FL
Peoples Christian Academy, ON, Canada
Perkiomen School, PA
The Phelps School, PA
Philadelphia-Montgomery Christian Academy, PA
Phillips Academy (Andover), MA
Phoenix Christian Unified Schools, AZ
Phoenix Country Day School, AZ
Pickering College, ON, Canada
Pinecrest Academy, GA
The Pingree School, MA
The Pingry School, NJ
Pioneer Valley Christian Academy, MA
Pius X High School, NE
Polytechnic School, CA
Pope John Paul II High School, LA
Pope John XXIII Regional High School, NJ
Portsmouth Abbey School, RI
Portsmouth Christian Academy, NH
The Potomac School, VA
Poughkeepsie Day School, NY
Powers Catholic High School, MI
Presbyterian Pan American School, TX
Preston High School, NY
Prestonwood Christian Academy, TX
Proctor Academy, NH
The Prout School, RI
Providence Catholic School, The College Preparatory School for Girls Grades 6-12, TX
Providence Country Day School, RI
Providence Day School, NC
Providence High School, CA
Punahou School, HI
Queen Margaret's School, BC, Canada

Rabun Gap-Nacoochee School, GA
Racine Lutheran High School, WI
Ramona Convent Secondary School, CA
Randolph-Macon Academy, VA
Randolph School, AL
Ransom Everglades School, FL
Ravenscroft School, NC
Redemption Christian Academy, MA
Redwood Christian Schools, CA
Regis High School, NY
Regis Jesuit High School, Boys Division, CO
Regis Jesuit High School, Girls Division, CO
Riverside Christian Schools, CA
The Rivers School, MA
Rockhurst High School, MO
Rockland Country Day School, NY
The Roeper School, MI
Roland Park Country School, MD
Rolling Hills Preparatory School, CA
Rosati-Kain High School, MO
The Roxbury Latin School, MA
Rutgers Preparatory School, NJ
Sacramento Country Day School, CA
Sacred Heart Academy, KY
Sacred Heart/Griffin High School, IL
Sacred Heart High School, CA
Sage Hill School, CA
Sage Ridge School, NV
Saint Agnes Academy–St. Dominic School, TN
St. Albans School, DC
Saint Albert Junior-Senior High School, IA
St. Andrew's Episcopal School, MD
St. Andrew's Episcopal School, MS
St. Andrew's Regional High School, BC, Canada
Saint Andrew's School, FL
St. Andrew's School, RI
St. Andrew's–Sewanee School, TN
St. Anne's–Belfield School, VA
Saint Anthony High School, IL
Saint Augustine Preparatory School, NJ
St. Benedict at Auburndale, TN
St. Bernard High School, CA
St. Bernard's Catholic School, CA
St. Brendan High School, FL
St. Catherine's School, VA
St. Christopher's School, VA
St. Clement's School, ON, Canada
St. Croix Schools, MN
Saint Dominic Academy, ME
Saint Francis High School, CA
Saint Francis High School, CA
St. Francis School, GA
St. George's Independent School, TN
St. George's School, RI
St. George's School, BC, Canada
Saint Gertrude High School, VA
Saint James School, MD
St. John Neumann High School, FL
St. John's Catholic Prep, MD
St. John's Preparatory School, MA
Saint John's Preparatory School, MN
Saint Joseph Academy, CA
St. Joseph Academy, FL
St. Joseph High School, CT
Saint Joseph High School, NJ
Saint Joseph Regional High School, NJ
St. Joseph's Academy, LA

St. Joseph's Catholic School, SC
St. Joseph's Preparatory School, PA
St. Louis University High School, MO
St. Luke's School, CT
St. Margaret's School, BC, Canada
St. Mark's School of Texas, TX
St. Martin's Episcopal School, LA
St. Mary's Episcopal School, TN
Saint Mary's High School, AZ
St. Mary's Preparatory School, MI
Saint Mary's School, NC
St. Mary's School, OR
Saint Maur International School, Japan
St. Michael's College School, ON, Canada
St. Michael's Preparatory School of the Norbertine Fathers, CA
St. Patrick Catholic High School, MS
Saint Patrick High School, IL
St. Patrick's Regional Secondary, BC, Canada
St. Paul Preparatory School, MN
St. Paul's High School, MB, Canada
St. Paul's School, NH
St. Peter's Preparatory School, NJ
St. Pius X High School, TX
St. Stephen's Episcopal School, TX
St. Stephen's School, Rome, Italy
Saint Teresa's Academy, MO
St. Thomas Aquinas High School, FL
Saint Thomas Aquinas High School, KS
St. Thomas Aquinas High School, NH
Saint Thomas More Catholic High School, LA
Saint Ursula Academy, OH
Saint Xavier High School, OH
Salem Academy, NC
Salem Academy, OR
Salesianum School, DE
Salpointe Catholic High School, AZ
San Domenico School, CA
Sandy Spring Friends School, MD
San Francisco University High School, CA
San Marcos Baptist Academy, TX
Santa Catalina School, CA
Santa Margarita Catholic High School, CA
Savannah Christian Preparatory School, GA
The Savannah Country Day School, GA
Scheck Hillel Community School, FL
SciCore Academy, NJ
Seabury Hall, HI
Seattle Lutheran High School, WA
Servite High School, CA
The Seven Hills School, OH
Severn School, MD
Sewickley Academy, PA
Shady Side Academy, PA
Shanley High School, ND
Shawnigan Lake School, BC, Canada
Shorecrest Preparatory School, FL
Sierra Canyon School, CA
Solebury School, PA
Sonoma Academy, CA
Soundview Preparatory School, NY
Southfield Christian High School, MI
Southwest Christian School, Inc., TX
The Spence School, NY
Spring Creek Academy, TX
Springside Chestnut Hill Academy, PA
Squaw Valley Academy, CA
Stanstead College, QC, Canada

Steamboat Mountain School, CO
Stephen T. Badin High School, OH
Stevenson School, CA
Stone Ridge School of the Sacred Heart, MD
The Stony Brook School, NY
The Storm King School, NY
Stratford Academy, GA
Stuart Hall, VA
The Study, QC, Canada
The Summit Country Day School, OH
The Taft School, CT
Taipei American School, Taiwan
Takoma Academy, MD
Tampa Preparatory School, FL
Tandem Friends School, VA
TASIS The American School in England, United Kingdom
TASIS, The American School in Switzerland, Switzerland
The Tenney School, TX
The Thacher School, CA
Thomas Jefferson School, MO
Tilton School, NH
Timothy Christian High School, IL
Timothy Christian School, NJ
TMI - The Episcopal School of Texas, TX
Tome School, MD
Tower Hill School, DE
Trinity Catholic High School, CT
Trinity College School, ON, Canada
Trinity Episcopal School, VA
Trinity High School, KY
Trinity High School, NH
Trinity High School, OH
Trinity-Pawling School, NY
Trinity Preparatory School, FL
Trinity School of Texas, TX
Tuscaloosa Academy, AL
Tyler Street Christian Academy, TX
University of Chicago Laboratory Schools, IL
University School of Jackson, TN
The Ursuline Academy of Dallas, TX
Valley Christian High School, CA
Valwood School, GA
Vicksburg Catholic School, MS
Victor Valley Christian School, CA
Viewpoint School, CA
Villa Duchesne and Oak Hill School, MO
Villa Madonna Academy, KY
Villa Walsh Academy, NJ
Visitation Academy, MO
Walla Walla Valley Academy, WA
Wasatch Academy, UT
The Waterford School, UT
Webb School of Knoxville, TN
The Webb Schools, CA
The Weber School, GA
Wesleyan Academy, PR
Wesleyan School, GA
Westbury Christian School, TX
West Island College, AB, Canada
Westminster Christian Academy, LA
Westminster Christian School, FL
Westminster School, CT
The Westminster Schools, GA
Westminster Schools of Augusta, GA
Westover School, CT
Westtown School, PA
Wheaton Academy, IL

The Wheeler School, RI
Whitefield Academy, KY
Whitfield School, MO
Whitinsville Christian School, MA
Wichita Collegiate School, KS
The Williston Northampton School, MA
The Willows Academy, IL
Wilmington Christian School, DE
Wilmington Friends School, DE
Wilson Hall, SC
Windermere Preparatory School, FL
The Windsor School, NY
The Woodhall School, CT
The Woodlands Christian Academy, TX
Woodlynde School, PA
Woodside Priory School, CA
The Woodward School, MA
Wooster School, CT
Worcester Preparatory School, MD
Wyoming Seminary, PA
Xavier College Preparatory, AZ
York Country Day School, PA
York School, CA
Zurich International School, Switzerland

SCHOOLS REPORTING A POSTGRADUATE YEAR

The Academy at Charlemont, MA
The Beekman School, NY
Berkshire School, MA
Besant Hill School, CA
Blair Academy, NJ
The Bolles School, FL
Brehm Preparatory School, IL
Camden Military Academy, SC
Canterbury School, CT
Cascadilla School, NY
Choate Rosemary Hall, CT
The Culver Academies, IN
Cushing Academy, MA
Deerfield Academy, MA
Franklin Academy, CT
Grier School, PA
Griggs International Academy, MD
The Gunnery, CT
Hargrave Military Academy, VA
Hawai`i Preparatory Academy, HI
Heritage Academy, SC
The Hun School of Princeton, NJ
The John Dewey Academy, MA
Kent School, CT
La Lumiere School, IN
The Lawrenceville School, NJ
Leysin American School in Switzerland, Switzerland
Marianapolis Preparatory School, CT
Marine Military Academy, TX
Massanutten Military Academy, VA
Mercersburg Academy, PA
Miss Hall's School, MA
Missouri Military Academy, MO
Northfield Mount Hermon School, MA
The Oxford Academy, CT
Peddie School, NJ
Perkiomen School, PA
The Phelps School, PA
Phillips Academy (Andover), MA

Randolph-Macon Academy, VA
Redemption Christian Academy, MA
Ridley College, ON, Canada
Saint John's Preparatory School, MN
St. Stephen's School, Rome, Italy
Scattergood Friends School, IA
Soundview Preparatory School, NY
The Storm King School, NY
The Taft School, CT
TASIS, The American School in Switzerland, Switzerland
Thomas Jefferson School, MO
Tilton School, NH
Trinity-Pawling School, NY
Walnut Hill School for the Arts, MA
Wasatch Academy, UT
Watkinson School, CT
Westminster School, CT
The Williston Northampton School, MA
The Windsor School, NY
The Woodhall School, CT
Wyoming Seminary, PA

SCHOOLS OFFERING THE INTERNATIONAL BACCALAUREATE PROGRAM

Academy of the Holy Cross, MD
Académie Ste Cécile International School, ON, Canada
Alma Heights Christian High School, CA
American International School, Lusaka, Zambia
The American School Foundation, Mexico
Atlanta International School, GA
Boca Prep International School, FL
The Bolles School, FL
Branksome Hall, ON, Canada
British International School of Boston, MA
British International School of Washington, DC
Calgary Academy Collegiate, AB, Canada
California Lutheran High School, CA
Cardinal Newman High School, FL
Carlucci American International School of Lisbon, Portugal
Carrollton School of the Sacred Heart, FL
Central Catholic High School, MA
Charlotte Country Day School, NC
Christ Church Episcopal School, SC
Desert Academy, NM
Detroit Country Day School, MI
Dublin Christian Academy, NH
The Dwight School, NY
Elmwood School, ON, Canada
Escuela Campo Alegre, Venezuela
George School, PA
Gulliver Preparatory School, FL
Hales Franciscan High School, IL
Hebrew Academy, CA
International High School, CA
International School Bangkok, Thailand
International School Hamburg, Germany
The International School of Aberdeen, United Kingdom
International School of Luxembourg, Luxembourg
International School of Zug and Luzern (ISZL), Switzerland
John Hancock Academy, GA
The Journeys School of Teton Science School, WY
King's-Edgehill School, NS, Canada
Le Lycee Francais de Los Angeles, CA
Leysin American School in Switzerland, Switzerland
Long Trail School, VT

Luther College High School, SK, Canada
Mid-Pacific Institute, HI
The Monarch School, TX
Newark Academy, NJ
The North Broward Preparatory Upper School, FL
Our Lady of Good Counsel High School, MD
The Prout School, RI
Providence Catholic School, The College Preparatory School for Girls Grades 6-12, TX
Ridley College, ON, Canada
Riverstone International School, ID
Rothesay Netherwood School, NB, Canada
Rotterdam International Secondary School, Wolfert van Borselen, Netherlands
St. Andrew's School, GA
Saint Anthony High School, IL
Saint Joan Antida High School, WI
Saint John's Preparatory School, MN
St. Joseph's Preparatory School, PA
Saint Maur International School, Japan
St. Patrick Catholic High School, MS
Saint Paul Lutheran High School, MO
St. Paul Preparatory School, MN
St. Stephen's School, Rome, Italy
St. Timothy's School, MD
Santa Margarita Catholic High School, CA
Scheck Hillel Community School, FL
Seisen International School, Japan
Shanley High School, ND
St Leonards School and Sixth Form College, United Kingdom
Taipei American School, Taiwan
TASIS The American School in England, United Kingdom
TASIS, The American School in Switzerland, Switzerland
THINK Global School, NY
Trinity Episcopal School, VA
Tyler Street Christian Academy, TX
United Nations International School, NY
The United World College - USA, NM
Upper Canada College, ON, Canada
Villa Duchesne and Oak Hill School, MO
Washington International School, DC
West Sound Academy, WA
Wilmington Friends School, DE
Windermere Preparatory School, FL
The York School, ON, Canada
Zurich International School, Switzerland

SCHOOLS REPORTING THAT THEY AWARD MERIT SCHOLARSHIPS

Academy of Notre Dame, MA
Academy of Our Lady of Peace, CA
Academy of the Holy Cross, MD
Academy of the Sacred Heart, MI
Académie Ste Cécile International School, ON, Canada
Advanced Academy of Georgia, GA
All Hallows High School, NY
Allison Academy, FL
American Heritage School, FL
American Heritage School, FL
Andrews Osborne Academy, OH
Aquinas High School, GA
Archbishop Curley High School, MD
Archbishop Hoban High School, OH
Archbishop Shaw High School, LA
Archmere Academy, DE

Armbrae Academy, NS, Canada
Austin Preparatory School, MA
Balmoral Hall School, MB, Canada
Battle Ground Academy, TN
Bay Ridge Preparatory School, NY
The Beekman School, NY
Benedictine High School, OH
The Benjamin School, FL
Berean Christian High School, CA
Berkeley Preparatory School, FL
The Birch Wathen Lenox School, NY
Bishop Brady High School, NH
Bishop Brossart High School, KY
Bishop Connolly High School, MA
Bishop Denis J. O'Connell High School, VA
Bishop Eustace Preparatory School, NJ
Bishop Guertin High School, NH
Bishop Ireton High School, VA
Bishop McNamara High School, MD
Bishop Miege High School, KS
Bishop Montgomery High School, CA
Bishop Mora Salesian High School, CA
Bishop's College School, QC, Canada
Bishop Stang High School, MA
Bishop Verot High School, FL
Boca Prep International School, FL
Bodwell High School, BC, Canada
Branksome Hall, ON, Canada
Bridgeport International Academy, CT
British International School of Boston, MA
Brother Rice High School, MI
The Bryn Mawr School for Girls, MD
Buffalo Seminary, NY
California Crosspoint High School, CA
Calvary Day School, GA
Calvert Hall College High School, MD
Cape Fear Academy, NC
Cape Henry Collegiate School, VA
Cardinal Mooney Catholic High School, FL
Carlucci American International School of Lisbon, Portugal
Carrollton School of the Sacred Heart, FL
Casady School, OK
Cascadilla School, NY
Cathedral High School, NY
Catholic Central High School, MI
The Catlin Gabel School, OR
Central Catholic High School, CA
Central Catholic High School, MA
Central Catholic High School, PA
Chaminade College Preparatory, CA
Chaminade-Madonna College Preparatory, FL
Charlotte Latin School, NC
Cheverus High School, ME
Christ Church Episcopal School, SC
Christian Brothers Academy, NJ
Christian Central Academy, NY
The Colorado Rocky Mountain School, CO
The Colorado Springs School, CO
Columbia International School, Japan
The Columbus Academy, OH
Columbus School for Girls, OH
The Community School, ID
Concordia Academy, MN
Concordia Lutheran High School, IN
Crescent School, ON, Canada
The Culver Academies, IN
Cushing Academy, MA

Damien High School, CA
Dana Hall School, MA
DeLaSalle High School, MN
DeMatha Catholic High School, MD
The Derryfield School, NH
Desert Academy, NM
Devon Preparatory School, PA
Doane Academy, NJ
Dominican Academy, NY
Donna Klein Jewish Academy, FL
Donovan Catholic, NJ
Elgin Academy, IL
Elizabeth Seton Academy, MA
Elizabeth Seton High School, MD
The Ellis School, PA
Elmwood School, ON, Canada
Elyria Catholic High School, OH
Episcopal High School, VA
Explorations Academy, WA
Falmouth Academy, MA
Father Duenas Memorial School, GU
Father Lopez High School, FL
First Presbyterian Day School, GA
Fontbonne Academy, MA
Fordham Preparatory School, NY
Forest Lake Academy, FL
Fort Worth Country Day School, TX
Fountain Valley School of Colorado, CO
Foxcroft School, VA
Franklin Academy, CT
Fredericksburg Academy, VA
Fresno Christian Schools, CA
Front Range Christian High School, CO
Fuqua School, VA
Gabriel Richard Catholic High School, MI
Garrison Forest School, MD
George School, PA
Gilmour Academy, OH
Gonzaga College High School, DC
Good Hope Country Day School, VI
Great Lakes Christian High School, ON, Canada
Green Fields Country Day School, AZ
Grier School, PA
The Gunnery, CT
The Gunston School, MD
Hales Franciscan High School, IL
Hargrave Military Academy, VA
Hathaway Brown School, OH
The Haverford School, PA
Hawai`i Preparatory Academy, HI
Hawken School, OH
Ho'Ala School, HI
Holland Hall, OK
Holy Cross High School, CT
Holy Cross School, LA
Holy Ghost Preparatory School, PA
Holy Savior Menard Catholic High School, LA
Holy Trinity Diocesan High School, NY
Holy Trinity High School, IL
Houston Academy, AL
Hyde School, ME
Immaculata-La Salle High School, FL
Immaculate Conception High School, NJ
Immaculate Heart High School and Middle School, CA
Incarnate Word Academy, TX
Indian Creek School, MD
The International School of Aberdeen, United Kingdom

International School of Port-of-Spain, Trinidad and Tobago
Jesuit College Preparatory School, TX
Jesuit High School of Tampa, FL
John F. Kennedy Catholic High School, MO
Josephinum Academy, IL
Junipero Serra High School, CA
Kent School, CT
Kentucky Country Day School, KY
The King's Christian High School, NJ
King's-Edgehill School, NS, Canada
Kingsway College, ON, Canada
Kingswood-Oxford School, CT
Lakefield College School, ON, Canada
La Lumiere School, IN
Lancaster Mennonite High School, PA
Lansdale Catholic High School, PA
La Salle Academy, RI
La Salle High School, CA
Lauralton Hall, CT
Laurel School, OH
The Lawrenceville School, NJ
Le Lycee Francais de Los Angeles, CA
Lexington Catholic High School, KY
Leysin American School in Switzerland, Switzerland
Lincoln School, RI
Long Trail School, VT
Louisville Collegiate School, KY
Louisville High School, CA
Loyola-Blakefield, MD
Lutheran High School North, MO
Lutheran High School Northwest, MI
Lutheran High School of Hawaii, HI
Lutheran High School of San Diego, CA
Luther College High School, SK, Canada
Lyman Ward Military Academy, AL
The Madeira School, VA
Malden Catholic High School, MA
Malvern Preparatory School, PA
Maplebrook School, NY
Maranatha High School, CA
Marianapolis Preparatory School, CT
Marian High School, MA
Marine Military Academy, TX
Martin Luther High School, NY
The Marvelwood School, CT
Mary Institute and St. Louis Country Day School (MICDS), MO
Marymount High School, CA
Massanutten Military Academy, VA
Matignon High School, MA
Maui Preparatory Academy, HI
Maumee Valley Country Day School, OH
Maur Hill-Mount Academy, KS
Memphis Catholic High School and Middle School, TN
Mercersburg Academy, PA
Mercy High School, CT
Merion Mercy Academy, PA
The Miami Valley School, OH
Mid-Pacific Institute, HI
Miss Edgar's and Miss Cramp's School, QC, Canada
Miss Hall's School, MA
Missouri Military Academy, MO
Miss Porter's School, CT
MMI Preparatory School, PA
Montrose School, MA
Moorestown Friends School, NJ
Moreau Catholic High School, CA
Mother McAuley High School, IL

Mountain View Academy, CA
Mount Mercy Academy, NY
Mount Saint Joseph Academy, PA
Nazareth Academy, IL
Nebraska Christian Schools, NE
Nerinx Hall, MO
Niagara Christian Community of Schools, ON, Canada
The North Broward Preparatory Upper School, FL
North Shore Country Day School, IL
Northwest Catholic High School, CT
Notre Dame-Cathedral Latin School, OH
Notre Dame High School, CA
Notre Dame High School, CA
Notre Dame High School, MO
Notre Dame High School, NY
Oak Hill School, OR
The O'Neal School, NC
Orangeburg Preparatory Schools, Inc., SC
Oratory Preparatory School, NJ
Our Lady of Good Counsel High School, MD
Our Lady of Mercy Academy, NJ
Padua Academy, DE
Palma School, CA
Paradise Adventist Academy, CA
Parkview Adventist Academy, AB, Canada
Peddie School, NJ
The Pennington School, NJ
Perkiomen School, PA
The Phelps School, PA
Pickering College, ON, Canada
The Pingree School, MA
Portsmouth Abbey School, RI
Presbyterian Pan American School, TX
Preston High School, NY
Providence Catholic School, The College Preparatory School for
    Girls Grades 6-12, TX
Providence Country Day School, RI
Providence High School, CA
Punahou School, HI
Queen Margaret's School, BC, Canada
Rabun Gap-Nacoochee School, GA
Racine Lutheran High School, WI
Ramona Convent Secondary School, CA
Randolph-Macon Academy, VA
Ravenscroft School, NC
Redemption Christian Academy, MA
Regis Jesuit High School, Boys Division, CO
Regis Jesuit High School, Girls Division, CO
Ridley College, ON, Canada
Rockhurst High School, MO
Rolling Hills Preparatory School, CA
Rosati-Kain High School, MO
Rosseau Lake College, ON, Canada
Rothesay Netherwood School, NB, Canada
Royal Canadian College, BC, Canada
Rundle College, AB, Canada
Sacred Heart Academy, KY
Sacred Heart/Griffin High School, IL
Sacred Heart High School, CA
Saint Agnes Academy–St. Dominic School, TN
Saint Albert Junior-Senior High School, IA
St. Andrew's Episcopal School, MS
St. Andrew's Regional High School, BC, Canada
Saint Andrew's School, FL
St. Andrew's–Sewanee School, TN
Saint Augustine Preparatory School, NJ
St. Benedict at Auburndale, TN

St. Bernard High School, CA
St. Bernard High School, CT
St. Bernard's Catholic School, CA
St. Clement's School, ON, Canada
St. Croix Schools, MN
Saint Dominic Academy, ME
Saint Francis High School, CA
St. George's School, BC, Canada
Saint Gertrude High School, VA
Saint Joan Antida High School, WI
St. John Neumann High School, FL
St. John's Catholic Prep, MD
St. John's Preparatory School, MA
Saint John's Preparatory School, MN
St. Joseph High School, CT
Saint Joseph High School, NJ
Saint Joseph Regional High School, NJ
St. Joseph's Catholic School, SC
St. Joseph's Preparatory School, PA
St. Margaret's School, BC, Canada
St. Martin's Episcopal School, LA
St. Mary's Preparatory School, MI
Saint Mary's School, NC
St. Michael's College School, ON, Canada
Saint Patrick High School, IL
St. Paul Preparatory School, MN
St. Peter's Preparatory School, NJ
St. Pius X High School, TX
Saint Teresa's Academy, MO
Saint Thomas Aquinas High School, KS
Saint Thomas More Catholic High School, LA
St. Timothy's School, MD
Saint Ursula Academy, OH
Saint Ursula Academy, OH
Saint Xavier High School, OH
Salem Academy, NC
Salesianum School, DE
Salpointe Catholic High School, AZ
Savannah Christian Preparatory School, GA
Scheck Hillel Community School, FL
Seattle Lutheran High School, WA
Servite High School, CA
The Seven Hills School, OH
Shady Side Academy, PA
Shanley High School, ND
Shawnigan Lake School, BC, Canada
Solebury School, PA
Squaw Valley Academy, CA
Stanstead College, QC, Canada
Steamboat Mountain School, CO
Stephen T. Badin High School, OH
Stone Ridge School of the Sacred Heart, MD
The Storm King School, NY
Stratford Academy, GA
Stuart Hall, VA
The Study, QC, Canada
The Summit Country Day School, OH
Takoma Academy, MD
Tampa Preparatory School, FL
Thomas Jefferson School, MO
Tilton School, NH
TMI - The Episcopal School of Texas, TX
Tome School, MD
Tower Hill School, DE
Trinity Catholic High School, CT
Trinity College School, ON, Canada
Trinity Episcopal School, VA

Trinity High School, KY
Trinity School of Texas, TX
Tyler Street Christian Academy, TX
The United World College - USA, NM
Upper Canada College, ON, Canada
The Ursuline Academy of Dallas, TX
The Valley School, MI
Valwood School, GA
Venta Preparatory School, ON, Canada
Villa Duchesne and Oak Hill School, MO
Villa Madonna Academy, KY
Villa Walsh Academy, NJ
Visitation Academy, MO
Walla Walla Valley Academy, WA
Wasatch Academy, UT
Westbury Christian School, TX
Westminster Schools of Augusta, GA
West Sound Academy, WA
Westtown School, PA
Wheaton Academy, IL
Whitfield School, MO
The Williston Northampton School, MA
Windermere Preparatory School, FL
The Woodward School, MA
Wyoming Seminary, PA
The York School, ON, Canada

SCHOOLS REPORTING A GUARANTEED TUITION PLAN

Academy of the Holy Family, CT
Alpine Academy, UT
Bangor Christian School, ME
Berkeley Preparatory School, FL
Butte Central Catholic High School, MT
Christa McAuliffe Academy School of Arts and Sciences, OR
Community Christian Academy, KY
Erskine Academy, ME
Gann Academy (The New Jewish High School of Greater Boston), MA
Green Fields Country Day School, AZ
Green Meadow Waldorf School, NY
Hargrave Military Academy, VA
Hawaii Baptist Academy, HI
Hebrew Academy, CA
The Hill Center, Durham Academy, NC
Houston Academy, AL
Marion Academy, AL
Middlesex School, MA
Nashville Christian School, TN
Nebraska Christian Schools, NE
New Covenant Academy, MO
The Oxford Academy, CT
Pensacola Catholic High School, FL
Pickens Academy, AL
Piedmont Academy, GA
Pius X High School, NE
Pope John XXIII Regional High School, NJ
Presbyterian Pan American School, TX
Saint Patrick High School, IL
Saint Paul Lutheran High School, MO
San Marcos Baptist Academy, TX
Southern Ontario College, ON, Canada
Trinity High School, KY
Trinity High School, OH
Tuscaloosa Academy, AL

The United World College - USA, NM
Wesleyan Academy, PR

SCHOOLS REPORTING A TUITION INSTALLMENT PLAN

The Academy at Charlemont, MA
Academy at the Lakes, FL
The Academy for Gifted Children (PACE), ON, Canada
Academy for Individual Excellence, KY
Academy of Notre Dame, MA
Academy of Our Lady of Peace, CA
Academy of the Holy Cross, MD
Academy of the Holy Family, CT
Academy of the New Church Boys' School, PA
Academy of the New Church Girls' School, PA
Academy of the Sacred Heart, MI
Académie Ste Cécile International School, ON, Canada
Admiral Farragut Academy, FL
The Agnes Irwin School, PA
Albuquerque Academy, NM
Alexander Dawson School, CO
Allen Academy, TX
Allentown Central Catholic High School, PA
All Hallows High School, NY
Allison Academy, FL
All Saints' Academy, FL
Alma Heights Christian High School, CA
Alpha Omega Academy, IA
Alpine Academy, UT
American Christian Academy, AL
American Heritage School, FL
American Heritage School, FL
The American School Foundation, Mexico
The American School in Japan, Japan
The American School of Puerto Vallarta, Mexico
Andrews Osborne Academy, OH
Aquinas High School, GA
Archbishop Curley High School, MD
Archbishop Hoban High School, OH
Archbishop Mitty High School, CA
Archbishop Shaw High School, LA
Archmere Academy, DE
Arendell Parrott Academy, NC
Armbrae Academy, NS, Canada
Army and Navy Academy, CA
Arthur Morgan School, NC
Ashley Hall, SC
ASSETS School, HI
Athens Academy, GA
Atlanta International School, GA
Atlantis Academy, FL
Augusta Christian School, GA
Austin Preparatory School, MA
Austin Waldorf School, TX
Bakersfield Christian High School, CA
Balmoral Hall School, MB, Canada
The Baltimore Actors' Theatre Conservatory, MD
Banbury Crossroads School, AB, Canada
Bangor Christian School, ME
Baptist Regional School, NJ
Battle Ground Academy, TN
Bay Ridge Preparatory School, NY
The Bay School of San Francisco, CA
Bearspaw Christian School, AB, Canada
Beaufort Academy, SC

The Beekman School, NY
Belen Jesuit Preparatory School, FL
Benedictine High School, OH
Ben Franklin Academy, GA
The Benjamin School, FL
Bentley School, CA
Berean Christian High School, CA
Berkeley Carroll School, NY
Berkeley Preparatory School, FL
Berkshire School, MA
Besant Hill School, CA
Beth Haven Christian School, KY
The Birch Wathen Lenox School, NY
Bishop Brady High School, NH
Bishop Brossart High School, KY
Bishop Connolly High School, MA
Bishop Denis J. O'Connell High School, VA
Bishop Eustace Preparatory School, NJ
Bishop Guertin High School, NH
Bishop Ireton High School, VA
Bishop John J. Snyder High School, FL
Bishop Kelly High School, ID
Bishop McNamara High School, MD
Bishop Miege High School, KS
Bishop Montgomery High School, CA
Bishop Mora Salesian High School, CA
Bishop's College School, QC, Canada
The Bishop's School, CA
Bishop Stang High School, MA
Bishop Verot High School, FL
Bishop Walsh Middle High School, MD
Blair Academy, NJ
The Blake School, MN
Blanchet School, OR
Blessed Sacrament Huguenot Catholic School, VA
Blessed Trinity High School, GA
Boca Prep International School, FL
The Bolles School, FL
Boston University Academy, MA
Boyd-Buchanan School, TN
Brandon Hall School, GA
Branksome Hall, ON, Canada
Breck School, MN
Brehm Preparatory School, IL
Brentwood College School, BC, Canada
Brentwood School, CA
Briarcrest Christian High School, TN
Briarwood Christian High School, AL
Bridgeport International Academy, CT
Bridges Academy, CA
Brimmer and May School, MA
British International School of Boston, MA
The Brook Hill School, TX
Brooks School, MA
Brophy College Preparatory, AZ
Brother Rice High School, MI
Brunswick School, CT
The Bryn Mawr School for Girls, MD
The Buckley School, CA
Buffalo Seminary, NY
Burr and Burton Academy, VT
Butte Central Catholic High School, MT
Buxton School, MA
Calgary Academy, AB, Canada
Calgary Academy Collegiate, AB, Canada
California Crosspoint High School, CA
California Lutheran High School, CA

Calvary Day School, GA
Calvert Hall College High School, MD
Calvin Christian High School, CA
Camden Military Academy, SC
Campbell Hall (Episcopal), CA
Canterbury School, CT
Canterbury School, FL
The Canterbury School of Florida, FL
Cape Fear Academy, NC
Cape Henry Collegiate School, VA
Capistrano Valley Christian Schools, CA
Cardigan Mountain School, NH
Cardinal Gibbons High School, NC
Cardinal Mooney Catholic High School, FL
Cardinal Newman High School, FL
Carlisle School, VA
Carlucci American International School of Lisbon, Portugal
Carondelet High School, CA
Carrollton School of the Sacred Heart, FL
Casady School, OK
Cascadilla School, NY
Cascia Hall Preparatory School, OK
Castilleja School, CA
Cate School, CA
Cathedral High School, MA
Cathedral High School, NY
Catholic Central High School, MI
Catholic Central High School, NY
Catholic Central High School, WI
The Catlin Gabel School, OR
CCI The Renaissance School, Italy
Central Alberta Christian High School, AB, Canada
Central Catholic High School, CA
Central Catholic High School, MA
Central Catholic High School, PA
Chadwick School, CA
Chaminade College Preparatory, CA
Chaminade-Madonna College Preparatory, FL
Charles Finney School, NY
Charlotte Country Day School, NC
Charlotte Latin School, NC
Chatham Academy, GA
Chattanooga Christian School, TN
Chelsea School, MD
Cheverus High School, ME
Choate Rosemary Hall, CT
Christa McAuliffe Academy School of Arts and Sciences, OR
Christ Church Episcopal School, SC
Christchurch School, VA
Christian Brothers Academy, NJ
Christian Central Academy, NY
Christian Heritage School, CT
Christopher Columbus High School, FL
Christopher Dock Mennonite High School, PA
Chrysalis School, WA
Clarksville Academy, TN
Colegio Bolivar, Colombia
Collegedale Academy, TN
The Collegiate School, VA
The Colorado Rocky Mountain School, CO
The Colorado Springs School, CO
Columbia Academy, TN
Columbia International School, Japan
The Columbus Academy, OH
Commonwealth School, MA
Community Christian Academy, KY
The Community School, ID

The Community School of Naples, FL
Concord Academy, MA
Concordia Academy, MN
Concordia Lutheran High School, IN
Covenant Canadian Reformed School, AB, Canada
Crawford Adventist Academy, ON, Canada
Crescent School, ON, Canada
Crossroads School for Arts & Sciences, CA
Crystal Springs Uplands School, CA
C.S. Lewis Academy, OR
The Culver Academies, IN
Currey Ingram Academy, TN
Cushing Academy, MA
Damien High School, CA
Dana Hall School, MA
Darrow School, NY
Deerfield Academy, MA
De La Salle College, ON, Canada
De La Salle High School, CA
DeLaSalle High School, MN
De La Salle North Catholic High School, OR
Delaware Valley Friends School, PA
Delbarton School, NJ
Delphos Saint John's High School, OH
DeMatha Catholic High School, MD
Denver Academy, CO
The Derryfield School, NH
Desert Academy, NM
Detroit Country Day School, MI
Devon Preparatory School, PA
Doane Academy, NJ
The Dr. Miriam and Sheldon G. Adelson Educational Campus, The Adelson Upper School, NV
Dominican Academy, NY
Donelson Christian Academy, TN
Donna Klein Jewish Academy, FL
The Donoho School, AL
Donovan Catholic, NJ
Dowling Catholic High School, IA
Dublin Christian Academy, NH
Dublin School, NH
Durham Academy, NC
The Dwight School, NY
Eaglebrook School, MA
Eagle Hill School, CT
Eastern Mennonite High School, VA
Edison School, AB, Canada
Edmund Burke School, DC
Eldorado Emerson Private School, CA
Elgin Academy, IL
Elizabeth Seton Academy, MA
Elizabeth Seton High School, MD
The Ellis School, PA
Elmwood School, ON, Canada
Elyria Catholic High School, OH
Episcopal Collegiate School, AR
Episcopal High School, TX
Episcopal High School, VA
Episcopal High School of Jacksonville, FL
Erskine Academy, ME
Escuela Campo Alegre, Venezuela
Explorations Academy, WA
Ezell-Harding Christian School, TN
Fairfield College Preparatory School, CT
Faith Lutheran High School, NV
Father Lopez High School, FL
Father Ryan High School, TN

Fayetteville Academy, NC
Fay School, MA
The First Academy, FL
First Baptist Academy, TX
First Presbyterian Day School, GA
Flint Hill School, VA
Flintridge Preparatory School, CA
Fontbonne Academy, MA
Fordham Preparatory School, NY
Forest Lake Academy, FL
Fort Worth Country Day School, TX
Foundation Academy, FL
Fountain Valley School of Colorado, CO
Fowlers Academy, PR
Foxcroft School, VA
Franklin Academy, CT
Franklin Road Academy, TN
Fredericksburg Academy, VA
Fredericton Christian Academy, NB, Canada
Fresno Christian Schools, CA
Friends Academy, NY
Friends' Central School, PA
Friendship Christian School, TN
Friends Select School, PA
Front Range Christian High School, CO
Fuqua School, VA
Gabriel Richard Catholic High School, MI
The Galloway School, GA
Gann Academy (The New Jewish High School of Greater Boston),
    MA
Garrison Forest School, MD
George School, PA
George Stevens Academy, ME
George Walton Academy, GA
Gilman School, MD
Gilmour Academy, OH
Girard College, PA
Glades Day School, FL
Gonzaga College High School, DC
Good Hope Country Day School, VI
The Governor French Academy, IL
The Governor's Academy, MA
The Gow School, NY
Grace Baptist Academy, TN
Grace Christian School, AK
The Grauer School, CA
Greater Atlanta Christian Schools, GA
Great Lakes Christian High School, ON, Canada
Green Fields Country Day School, AZ
Green Meadow Waldorf School, NY
Grier School, PA
Griggs International Academy, MD
Groton School, MA
Gulliver Preparatory School, FL
The Gunnery, CT
The Gunston School, MD
Hales Franciscan High School, IL
Halstrom Academy, Beverly Hills, CA
Halstrom Academy, Calsbad, CA
Halstrom Academy, Cupertino, CA
Halstrom Academy, Huntington Beach, CA
Halstrom Academy, Irvine, CA
Halstrom Academy, Los Angeles, CA
Halstrom Academy, Manhattan Beach, CA
Halstrom Academy, Mission Viejo, CA
Halstrom Academy, Orange, CA
Halstrom Academy, Pasadena, CA

Halstrom Academy, San Diego, CA
Halstrom Academy, San Mateo, CA
Halstrom Academy, Walnut Creek, CA
Halstrom Academy, Westlake Village, CA
Halstrom Academy, Woodland Hills, CA
Hargrave Military Academy, VA
The Harpeth Hall School, TN
Harrells Christian Academy, NC
Harvard-Westlake School, CA
The Harvey School, NY
Hathaway Brown School, OH
The Haverford School, PA
Hawaii Baptist Academy, HI
Hawai`i Preparatory Academy, HI
Hawken School, OH
Hebrew Academy, CA
Hebrew Academy of the Five Towns & Rockaway, NY
The Heights School, MD
Heritage Academy, SC
Highroad Academy, BC, Canada
The Hill Center, Durham Academy, NC
Ho'Ala School, HI
Holland Hall, OK
Holy Cross High School, CT
Holy Cross Regional Catholic School, VA
Holy Cross School, LA
Holy Ghost Preparatory School, PA
Holyoke Catholic High School, MA
Holy Savior Menard Catholic High School, LA
Holy Trinity Diocesan High School, NY
Holy Trinity High School, IL
Houghton Academy, NY
Houston Academy, AL
The Howard School, GA
The Hudson School, NJ
The Hun School of Princeton, NJ
Huntington-Surrey School, TX
Hyde School, CT
Hyde School, ME
Hyman Brand Hebrew Academy of Greater Kansas City, KS
Illiana Christian High School, IL
Immaculata High School, NJ
Immaculata-La Salle High School, FL
Immaculate Conception High School, NJ
Immaculate Heart High School and Middle School, CA
Incarnate Word Academy, TX
Independent School, KS
Indian Creek School, MD
Indian Springs School, AL
International High School, CA
International School Bangkok, Thailand
International School Hamburg, Germany
The International School of Aberdeen, United Kingdom
International School of Zug and Luzern (ISZL), Switzerland
Isidore Newman School, LA
Jackson Christian School, TN
Jesuit College Preparatory School, TX
Jesuit High School of Tampa, FL
John Burroughs School, MO
The John Dewey Academy, MA
John F. Kennedy Catholic High School, MO
John Hancock Academy, GA
John Paul II Catholic High School, FL
Josephinum Academy, IL
The Journeys School of Teton Science School, WY
Judge Memorial Catholic High School, UT
Junipero Serra High School, CA

Kalamazoo Christian High School, MI
Kauai Christian Academy, HI
Kent Denver School, CO
Kent School, CT
Kentucky Country Day School, KY
The Key School, MD
The Keystone School, PA
Keystone School, TX
King Low Heywood Thomas, CT
The King's Christian High School, NJ
King's-Edgehill School, NS, Canada
Kingsway College, ON, Canada
Kingswood-Oxford School, CT
The Knox School, NY
La Cheim School, CA
La Jolla Country Day School, CA
Lakefield College School, ON, Canada
Lakehill Preparatory School, TX
La Lumiere School, IN
Lancaster Mennonite High School, PA
Landmark Christian Academy, KY
Landmark Christian School, GA
Landmark East School, NS, Canada
Landmark School, MA
Lansdale Catholic High School, PA
La Salle Academy, RI
La Salle High School, CA
Lauralton Hall, CT
The Laureate Academy, MB, Canada
Laurel School, OH
Lawrence School, OH
The Lawrenceville School, NJ
Lee Academy, MS
The Leelanau School, MI
Lehigh Valley Christian High School, PA
Lehman High School, OH
Le Lycee Francais de Los Angeles, CA
Lexington Catholic High School, KY
Leysin American School in Switzerland, Switzerland
Liberty Christian School, CA
Lincoln School, RI
Little Keswick School, VA
Long Trail School, VT
Loudoun School for the Gifted, VA
Louisville Collegiate School, KY
Louisville High School, CA
The Lovett School, GA
Loyola-Blakefield, MD
Lutheran High School, MO
Lutheran High School North, MO
Lutheran High School Northwest, MI
Lutheran High School of Hawaii, HI
Lutheran High School of San Diego, CA
Luther College High School, SK, Canada
Lycee Claudel, ON, Canada
The Lycee International, American Section, France
Lyman Ward Military Academy, AL
The Madeira School, VA
Malden Catholic High School, MA
Malvern Preparatory School, PA
Manhattan Christian High School, MT
Maplebrook School, NY
Maranatha High School, CA
Marianapolis Preparatory School, CT
Marian Central Catholic High School, IL
Marian High School, IN
Marian High School, MA

Marine Military Academy, TX
Marquette University High School, WI
Marshall School, MN
Mars Hill Bible School, AL
Martin Luther High School, NY
The Marvelwood School, CT
Mary Institute and St. Louis Country Day School (MICDS), MO
Marymount High School, CA
Marymount School of New York, NY
Massanutten Military Academy, VA
The Masters School, NY
Mater Dei High School, IL
Matignon High School, MA
Maui Preparatory Academy, HI
Maumee Valley Country Day School, OH
Maur Hill-Mount Academy, KS
McDonogh School, MD
The Meadows School, NV
Memorial Hall School, TX
Memphis Catholic High School and Middle School, TN
Memphis University School, TN
Menlo School, CA
Mercersburg Academy, PA
Mercy High School, CT
Merion Mercy Academy, PA
Mesa Grande Seventh-Day Academy, CA
The Miami Valley School, OH
Middlesex School, MA
Middle Tennessee Christian School, TN
Midland School, CA
Mid-Pacific Institute, HI
Mill Springs Academy, GA
Milton Academy, MA
Miss Edgar's and Miss Cramp's School, QC, Canada
Miss Hall's School, MA
Missouri Military Academy, MO
Miss Porter's School, CT
MMI Preparatory School, PA
The Monarch School, TX
Montgomery Bell Academy, TN
Montrose School, MA
Moorestown Friends School, NJ
Moravian Academy, PA
Moreau Catholic High School, CA
Mother McAuley High School, IL
Mounds Park Academy, MN
Mountain View Academy, CA
Mount Dora Christian Academy, FL
Mount Mercy Academy, NY
Mount Saint Charles Academy, RI
Mount Saint Joseph Academy, PA
Mount Vernon Presbyterian School, GA
Nampa Christian Schools, ID
Nashville Christian School, TN
National Cathedral School, DC
Nazareth Academy, IL
Nebraska Christian Schools, NE
Nerinx Hall, MO
Newark Academy, NJ
New Covenant Academy, MO
Niagara Christian Community of Schools, ON, Canada
Noah Webster Christian School, WY
Noble Academy, NC
Noble and Greenough School, MA
The Nora School, MD
Norman Howard School, NY
The North Broward Preparatory Upper School, FL

North Central Texas Academy, TX
North Clackamas Christian School, OR
North Country School, NY
Northfield Mount Hermon School, MA
Northpoint Christian School, MS
North Shore Country Day School, IL
North Toronto Christian School, ON, Canada
Northwest Academy, OR
Northwest Catholic High School, CT
The Northwest School, WA
Northwest Yeshiva High School, WA
Notre Dame-Cathedral Latin School, OH
Notre Dame High School, CA
Notre Dame High School, CA
Notre Dame High School, CA
Notre Dame High School, LA
Notre Dame High School, MO
Notre Dame High School, NJ
Notre Dame High School, NY
Notre Dame High School, TN
Notre Dame Junior/Senior High School, PA
Oak Hill School, OR
Oakland School, VA
The O'Neal School, NC
Oneida Baptist Institute, KY
Orangeburg Preparatory Schools, Inc., SC
Orangewood Christian School, FL
Oratory Preparatory School, NJ
Oregon Episcopal School, OR
Orinda Academy, CA
Our Lady of Good Counsel High School, MD
Our Lady of Mercy Academy, NJ
Out-Of-Door-Academy, FL
The Oxford Academy, CT
Pace Academy, GA
PACE/Brantley Hall High School, FL
Pacific Crest Community School, OR
The Packer Collegiate Institute, NY
Padua Academy, DE
Palma School, CA
Palo Alto Preparatory School, CA
Paradise Adventist Academy, CA
The Park School of Baltimore, MD
Parkview Adventist Academy, AB, Canada
Parkview Baptist School, LA
The Pathway School, PA
Patten Academy of Christian Education, CA
Peddie School, NJ
The Pennington School, NJ
Pensacola Catholic High School, FL
Peoples Christian Academy, ON, Canada
Perkiomen School, PA
The Phelps School, PA
Philadelphia-Montgomery Christian Academy, PA
Phillips Academy (Andover), MA
Phoenix Christian Unified Schools, AZ
Phoenix Country Day School, AZ
Pickens Academy, AL
Pickering College, ON, Canada
Piedmont Academy, GA
Pinecrest Academy, GA
Pine Tree Academy, ME
The Pingree School, MA
The Pingry School, NJ
Pioneer Valley Christian Academy, MA
Pius X High School, NE
Polytechnic School, CA

Pope John XXIII Regional High School, NJ
Portledge School, NY
Portsmouth Abbey School, RI
Portsmouth Christian Academy, NH
The Potomac School, VA
Poughkeepsie Day School, NY
Powers Catholic High School, MI
Presbyterian Pan American School, TX
Preston High School, NY
Prestonwood Christian Academy, TX
Proctor Academy, NH
Professional Children's School, NY
The Prout School, RI
Providence Catholic School, The College Preparatory School for
    Girls Grades 6-12, TX
Providence Country Day School, RI
Providence Day School, NC
Providence High School, CA
Punahou School, HI
Queen Margaret's School, BC, Canada
Quinte Christian High School, ON, Canada
Rabun Gap-Nacoochee School, GA
Racine Lutheran High School, WI
Ramona Convent Secondary School, CA
Randolph-Macon Academy, VA
Randolph School, AL
Ransom Everglades School, FL
Ravenscroft School, NC
Realms of Inquiry, UT
The Rectory School, CT
Redemption Christian Academy, MA
Redwood Christian Schools, CA
Regis Jesuit High School, Boys Division, CO
Regis Jesuit High School, Girls Division, CO
Rejoice Christian Schools, OK
Ridley College, ON, Canada
Riverdale Country School, NY
River Oaks Baptist School, TX
Riverside Christian Schools, CA
The Rivers School, MA
Riverstone International School, ID
Rockhurst High School, MO
Rockland Country Day School, NY
Rock Point School, VT
Rockway Mennonite Collegiate, ON, Canada
The Roeper School, MI
Roland Park Country School, MD
Rolling Hills Preparatory School, CA
Rosati-Kain High School, MO
Rosseau Lake College, ON, Canada
Rothesay Netherwood School, NB, Canada
Rotterdam International Secondary School, Wolfert van Borselen,
    Netherlands
The Roxbury Latin School, MA
Rudolf Steiner School of Ann Arbor, MI
Rumsey Hall School, CT
Rundle College, AB, Canada
Rutgers Preparatory School, NJ
Sacramento Country Day School, CA
Sacramento Waldorf School, CA
Sacred Heart/Griffin High School, IL
Sacred Heart High School, CA
Saddlebrook Preparatory School, FL
Sage Hill School, CA
Sage Ridge School, NV
Saint Agnes Academy–St. Dominic School, TN
St. Albans School, DC

Saint Albert Junior-Senior High School, IA
St. Andrew's Episcopal School, MD
St. Andrew's Episcopal School, MS
St. Andrew's Regional High School, BC, Canada
St. Andrew's School, DE
Saint Andrew's School, FL
St. Andrew's School, GA
St. Andrew's School, RI
St. Andrew's–Sewanee School, TN
St. Anne's–Belfield School, VA
Saint Anthony High School, IL
Saint Augustine Preparatory School, NJ
St. Benedict at Auburndale, TN
St. Bernard High School, CA
St. Bernard High School, CT
St. Bernard's Catholic School, CA
St. Brendan High School, FL
St. Catherine's School, VA
St. Christopher's School, VA
St. Clement's School, ON, Canada
Saint Dominic Academy, ME
Saint Francis High School, CA
Saint Francis High School, CA
St. Francis School, GA
St. George's Independent School, TN
St. George's School, RI
St. George's School, BC, Canada
Saint Gertrude High School, VA
Saint James School, MD
Saint Joan Antida High School, WI
St. John Neumann High School, FL
St. John's Catholic Prep, MD
St. John's Preparatory School, MA
Saint John's Preparatory School, MN
Saint Joseph Academy, CA
St. Joseph Academy, FL
St. Joseph High School, CT
Saint Joseph High School, NJ
Saint Joseph Regional High School, NJ
St. Joseph's Academy, LA
St. Joseph's Catholic School, SC
St. Joseph's Preparatory School, PA
St. Lawrence Seminary High School, WI
St. Louis University High School, MO
St. Luke's School, CT
St. Margaret's School, BC, Canada
St. Mark's School of Texas, TX
St. Martin's Episcopal School, LA
St. Mary's Episcopal School, TN
Saint Mary's High School, AZ
St. Mary's Preparatory School, MI
Saint Mary's School, NC
St. Mary's School, OR
Saint Maur International School, Japan
St. Michael's College School, ON, Canada
St. Michael's Preparatory School of the Norbertine Fathers, CA
St. Patrick Catholic High School, MS
Saint Patrick High School, IL
St. Patrick's Regional Secondary, BC, Canada
St. Paul Academy and Summit School, MN
Saint Paul Lutheran High School, MO
St. Paul Preparatory School, MN
St. Paul's High School, MB, Canada
St. Paul's School, NH
St. Peter's Preparatory School, NJ
St. Pius X High School, TX
St. Stephen's Episcopal School, TX

St. Stephen's School, Rome, Italy
Saint Teresa's Academy, MO
St. Thomas Aquinas High School, FL
Saint Thomas Aquinas High School, KS
St. Thomas Aquinas High School, NH
St. Thomas Choir School, NY
Saint Thomas More Catholic High School, LA
St. Timothy's School, MD
Saint Ursula Academy, OH
Saint Xavier High School, OH
Salem Academy, NC
Salem Academy, OR
Salesianum School, DE
Salpointe Catholic High School, AZ
San Domenico School, CA
Sandy Spring Friends School, MD
San Francisco University High School, CA
San Marcos Baptist Academy, TX
Santa Margarita Catholic High School, CA
Savannah Christian Preparatory School, GA
The Savannah Country Day School, GA
Scattergood Friends School, IA
Scheck Hillel Community School, FL
SciCore Academy, NJ
Seabury Hall, HI
Seattle Academy of Arts and Sciences, WA
Seattle Lutheran High School, WA
Seisen International School, Japan
Servite High School, CA
The Seven Hills School, OH
Severn School, MD
Sewickley Academy, PA
Shady Side Academy, PA
Shanley High School, ND
Shawnigan Lake School, BC, Canada
Shelton School and Evaluation Center, TX
Shorecrest Preparatory School, FL
Shoreline Christian, WA
Sierra Canyon School, CA
Signet Christian School, ON, Canada
Smith School, NY
Smithville Christian High School, ON, Canada
Solebury School, PA
Sonoma Academy, CA
Southfield Christian High School, MI
Southwest Christian School, Inc., TX
Springside Chestnut Hill Academy, PA
Squaw Valley Academy, CA
Stanstead College, QC, Canada
Steamboat Mountain School, CO
Stephen T. Badin High School, OH
Stevenson School, CA
St Leonards School and Sixth Form College, United Kingdom
Stone Ridge School of the Sacred Heart, MD
The Stony Brook School, NY
The Storm King School, NY
Stratford Academy, GA
Stuart Hall, VA
The Study, QC, Canada
Summerfield Waldorf School, CA
The Summit Country Day School, OH
Summit Preparatory School, MT
Sunshine Bible Academy, SD
The Taft School, CT
Taipei American School, Taiwan
Takoma Academy, MD
Tampa Preparatory School, FL

Tandem Friends School, VA
TASIS The American School in England, United Kingdom
TASIS, The American School in Switzerland, Switzerland
Teurlings Catholic High School, LA
The Thacher School, CA
THINK Global School, NY
Thomas Jefferson School, MO
Tilton School, NH
Timothy Christian High School, IL
Timothy Christian School, NJ
TMI - The Episcopal School of Texas, TX
Tome School, MD
Tower Hill School, DE
Traditional Learning Academy, BC, Canada
Tri-City Christian Academy, AZ
Trinity Catholic High School, CT
Trinity College School, ON, Canada
Trinity Episcopal School, VA
Trinity High School, KY
Trinity High School, NH
Trinity High School, OH
Trinity-Pawling School, NY
Trinity Preparatory School, FL
Trinity School of Texas, TX
Tuscaloosa Academy, AL
Tyler Street Christian Academy, TX
United Mennonite Educational Institute, ON, Canada
United Nations International School, NY
The United World College - USA, NM
University of Chicago Laboratory Schools, IL
University Prep, WA
University School of Jackson, TN
Upper Canada College, ON, Canada
The Ursuline Academy of Dallas, TX
Valley Christian High School, CA
The Valley School, MI
Valley View School, MA
Valwood School, GA
The Vanguard School, FL
Venta Preparatory School, ON, Canada
Vicksburg Catholic School, MS
Victor Valley Christian School, CA
Viewpoint School, CA
Villa Duchesne and Oak Hill School, MO
Villa Madonna Academy, KY
Villa Walsh Academy, NJ
Visitation Academy, MO
The Waldorf School of Saratoga Springs, NY
Walla Walla Valley Academy, WA
Walnut Hill School for the Arts, MA
Wasatch Academy, UT
Washington International School, DC
The Waterford School, UT
Watkinson School, CT
Waynflete School, ME
Webb School of Knoxville, TN
The Webb Schools, CA
The Weber School, GA
Wesleyan Academy, PR
Wesleyan School, GA
Westbury Christian School, TX
West Island College, AB, Canada
Westmark School, CA
Westminster Christian Academy, LA
Westminster Christian School, FL
Westminster School, CT
The Westminster Schools, GA

Westminster Schools of Augusta, GA
Westover School, CT
West Sound Academy, WA
Westtown School, PA
Wheaton Academy, IL
The Wheeler School, RI
Whitefield Academy, KY
Whitfield School, MO
Whitinsville Christian School, MA
Wichita Collegiate School, KS
The Williston Northampton School, MA
The Willows Academy, IL
Wilmington Christian School, DE
Wilmington Friends School, DE
Wilson Hall, SC
Windermere Preparatory School, FL
The Windsor School, NY
Winston Preparatory School, NY
The Winston School, TX
The Winston School San Antonio, TX
The Woodhall School, CT
The Woodlands Christian Academy, TX
Woodlynde School, PA
Woodside Priory School, CA
The Woodward School, MA
Wooster School, CT
Worcester Preparatory School, MD
Wyoming Seminary, PA
Xavier College Preparatory, AZ
York Country Day School, PA
York School, CA
The York School, ON, Canada
Zurich International School, Switzerland

SCHOOLS REPORTING THAT THEY OFFER LOANS

Alexander Dawson School, CO	N
The Benjamin School, FL	N
Bishop's College School, QC, Canada	N
Blair Academy, NJ	N
The Blake School, MN	N
Calvin Christian High School, CA	N
Canterbury School, CT	M,N
Cardigan Mountain School, NH	N
Chaminade-Madonna College Preparatory, FL	N
Commonwealth School, MA	N
Concord Academy, MA	N
Delaware Valley Friends School, PA	M,N
Episcopal High School, TX	M
Explorations Academy, WA	N
Falmouth Academy, MA	N
Friends Select School, PA	N
Gilman School, MD	N
Gilmour Academy, OH	N
Great Lakes Christian High School, ON, Canada	M,N
Grier School, PA	N
The Gunnery, CT	N
Hargrave Military Academy, VA	N
The Harker School, CA	N
Hawken School, OH	N
John Burroughs School, MO	N
Kent School, CT	N
The Madeira School, VA	M,N
Maplebrook School, NY	M,N
Marian High School, IN	N

M — middle-income loans; N — need-based loans

Massanutten Military Academy, VA	M,N
Maur Hill-Mount Academy, KS	N
McDonogh School, MD	N
Mercersburg Academy, PA	N
Mesa Grande Seventh-Day Academy, CA	M,N
Middlesex School, MA	N
Missouri Military Academy, MO	N
The Monarch School, TX	N
Moorestown Friends School, NJ	N
Northfield Mount Hermon School, MA	N
North Shore Country Day School, IL	M,N
Peddie School, NJ	N
The Pingree School, MA	N
Randolph School, AL	M
Ravenscroft School, NC	N
Ridley College, ON, Canada	N
St. Albans School, DC	N
St. Andrew's School, RI	N
St. George's School, RI	M,N
Saint Joseph Regional High School, NJ	N
St. Joseph's Preparatory School, PA	M,N
St. Paul's High School, MB, Canada	N
St. Timothy's School, MD	N
Servite High School, CA	M,N
Stanstead College, QC, Canada	N
The Taft School, CT	N
Tilton School, NH	N
Trinity High School, OH	M
Trinity-Pawling School, NY	M,N
United Mennonite Educational Institute, ON, Canada	N
Wasatch Academy, UT	N
Wyoming Seminary, PA	N

TOTAL AMOUNT OF UPPER SCHOOL FINANCIAL AID AWARDED FOR 2015–16

The Academy at Charlemont, MA	$419,375
Academy of Our Lady of Peace, CA	$2,600,000
Academy of the Holy Family, CT	$86,600
Academy of the New Church Boys' School, PA	$750,000
Academy of the New Church Girls' School, PA	$1,200,000
Academy of the Sacred Heart, MI	$626,915
Admiral Farragut Academy, FL	$500,000
Advanced Academy of Georgia, GA	$109,000
The Agnes Irwin School, PA	$176,025
Albuquerque Academy, NM	$3,526,266
Alexander Dawson School, CO	$1,450,000
Allen Academy, TX	$40,950
Allentown Central Catholic High School, PA	$923,830
Allison Academy, FL	$170,000
American Christian Academy, AL	$85,000
The American School Foundation, Mexico	13,997,103 Mexican pesos
Andrews Osborne Academy, OH	$401,000
Aquinas High School, GA	$257,379
Archbishop Mitty High School, CA	$3,750,000
Archmere Academy, DE	$2,000,000
Arendell Parrott Academy, NC	$260,000
Armbrae Academy, NS, Canada	CAN$60,000
Army and Navy Academy, CA	$382,500
Arthur Morgan School, NC	$100,000
Ashley Hall, SC	$1,215,000
ASSETS School, HI	$170,000
Athens Academy, GA	$12,000,000
Atlantis Academy, FL	$12,000
Bakersfield Christian High School, CA	$160,000

Balmoral Hall School, MB, Canada	CAN$253,096
The Baltimore Actors' Theatre Conservatory, MD	$18,000
Banbury Crossroads School, AB, Canada	CAN$10,500
Baptist Regional School, NJ	$100,000
Battle Ground Academy, TN	$657,135
Bearspaw Christian School, AB, Canada	CAN$108,314
Beaufort Academy, SC	$72,600
Belen Jesuit Preparatory School, FL	$514,810
The Benjamin School, FL	$1,388,838
Berean Christian High School, CA	$286,000
Berkeley Carroll School, NY	$2,957,561
Berkshire School, MA	$4,984,000
Besant Hill School, CA	$450,000
Beth Haven Christian School, KY	$10,150
The Birch Wathen Lenox School, NY	$1,500,000
Bishop Brady High School, NH	$550,000
Bishop Denis J. O'Connell High School, VA	$2,100,000
Bishop Eustace Preparatory School, NJ	$800,000
Bishop Guertin High School, NH	$600,000
Bishop Ireton High School, VA	$757,000
Bishop John J. Snyder High School, FL	$325,000
Bishop Kelly High School, ID	$1,412,691
Bishop Miege High School, KS	$1,000,000
Bishop Montgomery High School, CA	$68,000
Bishop Mora Salesian High School, CA	$1,548,500
Bishop's College School, QC, Canada	CAN$900,000
Bishop Stang High School, MA	$500,000
Bishop Walsh Middle High School, MD	$30,000
Blair Academy, NJ	$5,100,000
The Blake School, MN	$2,321,797
Blanchet School, OR	$250,000
Blessed Sacrament Huguenot Catholic School, VA	$150,000
The Bolles School, FL	$3,841,539
Boston University Academy, MA	$1,514,582
Boyd-Buchanan School, TN	$80,000
Brandon Hall School, GA	$250,000
Branksome Hall, ON, Canada	CAN$600,000
Brehm Preparatory School, IL	$99,300
Brentwood School, CA	$3,500,000
Briarwood Christian High School, AL	$5000
Brimmer and May School, MA	$1,606,150
The Brook Hill School, TX	$850,000
Brooks School, MA	$3,767,435
Brophy College Preparatory, AZ	$3,841,050
Brother Rice High School, MI	$900,000
The Browning School, NY	$953,900
Brunswick School, CT	$1,250,000
The Bryn Mawr School for Girls, MD	$1,797,988
The Buckley School, CA	$530,000
Buffalo Seminary, NY	$1,074,305
Butte Central Catholic High School, MT	$68,000
Buxton School, MA	$1,600,000
Calgary Academy, AB, Canada	CAN$300,000
Calgary Academy Collegiate, AB, Canada	CAN$300,000
California Crosspoint High School, CA	$205,000
Calvary Day School, GA	$183,000
Calvert Hall College High School, MD	$2,668,735
Calvin Christian High School, CA	$275,000
Campbell Hall (Episcopal), CA	$5,400,000
Canterbury School, CT	$3,500,000
Canterbury School, FL	$1,273,045
The Canterbury School of Florida, FL	$480,442
Cape Fear Academy, NC	$331,999
Capistrano Valley Christian Schools, CA	$250,000
Cardigan Mountain School, NH	$1,000,000
Cardinal Mooney Catholic High School, FL	$200,000
Carlisle School, VA	$372,479

Carondelet High School, CA	$1,300,000	Donna Klein Jewish Academy, FL	$840,465
Carrollton School of the Sacred Heart, FL	$920,000	Donovan Catholic, NJ	$400,000
Casady School, OK	$400,000	Dowling Catholic High School, IA	$1,000,000
Cascadilla School, NY	$60,000	Dublin Christian Academy, NH	$150,000
Cascia Hall Preparatory School, OK	$75,000	Dublin School, NH	$1,490,000
Castilleja School, CA	$2,200,000	Durham Academy, NC	$1,442,738
Cate School, CA	$3,200,000	Eaglebrook School, MA	$1,650,000
Catholic Central High School, MI	$1,100,000	Eastern Mennonite High School, VA	$200,000
Catholic Central High School, NY	$240,000	Edmund Burke School, DC	$978,185
Catholic Central High School, WI	$140,000	Eldorado Emerson Private School, CA	$50,000
The Catlin Gabel School, OR	$18,119	Elgin Academy, IL	$800,000
CCI The Renaissance School, Italy	€30,000	Elizabeth Seton High School, MD	$500,000
Central Catholic High School, CA	$541,705	Elmwood School, ON, Canada	CAN$250,000
Central Catholic High School, MA	$1,689,766	Elyria Catholic High School, OH	$250,300
Central Catholic High School, PA	$1,600,000	Episcopal Collegiate School, AR	$482,000
Chadwick School, CA	$1,647,415	Episcopal High School, TX	$1,700,000
Chaminade College Preparatory, CA	$2,390,407	Episcopal High School, VA	$6,000,000
Charlotte Country Day School, NC	$1,275,523	Episcopal High School of Jacksonville, FL	$2,000,000
Charlotte Latin School, NC	$1,091,140	Explorations Academy, WA	$200,000
Chatham Academy, GA	$90,200	Ezell-Harding Christian School, TN	$136,000
Chattanooga Christian School, TN	$500,000	Fairfield College Preparatory School, CT	$2,163,000
Cheverus High School, ME	$2,298,173	Faith Lutheran High School, NV	$555,000
Choate Rosemary Hall, CT	$11,300,000	Falmouth Academy, MA	$928,000
Christ Church Episcopal School, SC	$626,210	Father Lopez High School, FL	$1,230,000
Christchurch School, VA	$2,204,840	Father Ryan High School, TN	$550,000
Christian Brothers Academy, NJ	$700,000	Fayetteville Academy, NC	$204,000
Christian Central Academy, NY	$124,961	Fay School, MA	$2,201,551
Christian Heritage School, CT	$500,000	First Presbyterian Day School, GA	$874,000
Christopher Dock Mennonite High School, PA	$621,600	Flint Hill School, VA	$2,089,701
Collegedale Academy, TN	$55,000	Flintridge Preparatory School, CA	$2,286,100
The Colorado Rocky Mountain School, CO	$2,072,750	Fordham Preparatory School, NY	$2,980,000
The Colorado Springs School, CO	$347,902	Forest Lake Academy, FL	$347,000
Columbia Academy, TN	$32,250	Fort Worth Country Day School, TX	$980,225
Columbia International School, Japan	¥3,360,000	Foundation Academy, FL	$250,000
The Columbus Academy, OH	$1,000,000	Fountain Valley School of Colorado, CO	$2,354,978
Columbus School for Girls, OH	$630,518	Fowlers Academy, PR	$35,000
Commonwealth School, MA	$1,288,730	Foxcroft School, VA	$1,589,890
Community Christian Academy, KY	$9000	Franklin Road Academy, TN	$500,000
The Community School, ID	$599,175	Fredericksburg Academy, VA	$366,400
The Community School of Naples, FL	$1,199,038	Fresno Christian Schools, CA	$262,944
Concord Academy, MA	$3,900,000	Friends' Central School, PA	$2,581,380
Concordia Academy, MN	$334,804	Friendship Christian School, TN	$5000
Concordia Lutheran High School, IN	$3,163,000	Friends Select School, PA	$888,000
Crawford Adventist Academy, ON, Canada	CAN$40,000	Front Range Christian High School, CO	$181,000
Crescent School, ON, Canada	CAN$680,000	Fuqua School, VA	$67,636
Crossroads School for Arts & Sciences, CA	$3,490,851	The Galloway School, GA	$847,611
Crystal Springs Uplands School, CA	$2,200,000	Gann Academy (The New Jewish High School of	
C.S. Lewis Academy, OR	$22,113	Greater Boston), MA	$2,300,000
The Culver Academies, IN	$8,900,000	Garrison Forest School, MD	$377,600
Currey Ingram Academy, TN	$1,750,000	George School, PA	$8,500,000
Cushing Academy, MA	$3,100,000	George Stevens Academy, ME	$100,000
Damien High School, CA	$745,000	Gilman School, MD	$1,839,100
Dana Hall School, MA	$3,895,640	Gilmour Academy, OH	$3,682,304
Darrow School, NY	$1,400,000	Gonzaga College High School, DC	$2,900,000
Deerfield Academy, MA	$8,985,000	Good Hope Country Day School, VI	$311,550
De La Salle High School, CA	$2,330,000	The Governor's Academy, MA	$4,400,000
DeLaSalle High School, MN	$24,600,000	The Gow School, NY	$950,000
De La Salle North Catholic High School, OR	$294,820	Grace Christian School, AK	$200,000
Delaware Valley Friends School, PA	$791,663	The Grauer School, CA	$160,877
Delbarton School, NJ	$2,294,000	Great Lakes Christian High School, ON, Canada	CAN$225,000
DeMatha Catholic High School, MD	$1,632,348	Green Fields Country Day School, AZ	$187,987
Desert Academy, NM	$180,000	Greenhill School, TX	$1,727,046
Devon Preparatory School, PA	$1,030,000	Grier School, PA	$2,000,000
Doane Academy, NJ	$120,000	Groton School, MA	$6,200,000
The Dr. Miriam and Sheldon G. Adelson Educational		The Gunnery, CT	$3,500,000
Campus, The Adelson Upper School, NV	$1,000,000	The Gunston School, MD	$1,350,000
Donelson Christian Academy, TN	$169,053	Hales Franciscan High School, IL	$1,500,000

Hargrave Military Academy, VA	$525,000
The Harpeth Hall School, TN	$1,000,000
Harrells Christian Academy, NC	$61,378
Harvard-Westlake School, CA	$7,636,700
The Harvey School, NY	$2,080,000
Hathaway Brown School, OH	$3,100,000
The Haverford School, PA	$2,614,756
Hawaii Baptist Academy, HI	$405,465
Hawai`i Preparatory Academy, HI	$4,000,000
Hawken School, OH	$5,102,962
Hebrew Academy, CA	$30,000
The Heights School, MD	$1,000,000
The Hill Center, Durham Academy, NC	$54,800
Ho'Ala School, HI	$21,600
The Hockaday School, TX	$3,400,000
Holland Hall, OK	$928,525
Holy Cross High School, CT	$650,000
Holy Ghost Preparatory School, PA	$1,000,000
Holyoke Catholic High School, MA	$150,000
Holy Savior Menard Catholic High School, LA	$150,000
Holy Trinity High School, IL	$600,000
Holy Trinity School, ON, Canada	40,000
Houghton Academy, NY	$95,000
Houston Academy, AL	$408,049
The Hudson School, NJ	$308,710
The Hun School of Princeton, NJ	$4,000,000
Hyde School, CT	$258,000
Hyde School, ME	$1,300,000
Hyman Brand Hebrew Academy of Greater Kansas City, KS	$63,235
Immaculata-La Salle High School, FL	$490,471
Immaculate Conception High School, NJ	$155,000
Indian Springs School, AL	$1,000,000
International High School, CA	$748,000
International School of Port-of-Spain, Trinidad and Tobago	$42,000
Jackson Christian School, TN	$15,218
Jesuit College Preparatory School, TX	$1,233,850
Jesuit High School of Tampa, FL	$1,687,085
John Burroughs School, MO	$2,431,278
The Journeys School of Teton Science School, WY	$240,150
Junipero Serra High School, CA	$2,400,000
Kauai Christian Academy, HI	$40,000
Kent Denver School, CO	$2,200,000
Kent School, CT	$8,400,000
The Key School, MD	$667,300
King Low Heywood Thomas, CT	$1,490,540
King's-Edgehill School, NS, Canada	CAN$900,000
Kingsway College, ON, Canada	CAN$250,000
Kingswood-Oxford School, CT	$2,300,000
The Knox School, NY	$400,000
La Jolla Country Day School, CA	$2,285,386
Lakefield College School, ON, Canada	CAN$180,000
La Lumiere School, IN	$988,830
Lancaster Mennonite High School, PA	$3,000,000
Landmark Christian School, GA	$250,000
Landmark East School, NS, Canada	CAN$300,000
Lansdale Catholic High School, PA	$125,000
La Salle Academy, RI	$2,200,000
La Salle High School, CA	$2,000,250
Lauralton Hall, CT	$450,000
The Laureate Academy, MB, Canada	CAN$60,000
Laurel School, OH	$1,875,460
Lawrence School, OH	$900,000
The Lawrenceville School, NJ	$11,533,470
Lee Academy, MS	$35,000
The Leelanau School, MI	$200,000
Lehigh Valley Christian High School, PA	$17,387
Lehman High School, OH	$353,850
Le Lycee Francais de Los Angeles, CA	$460,024
Lexington Catholic High School, KY	$650,000
Leysin American School in Switzerland, Switzerland	600,000 Swiss francs
Liberty Christian School, CA	$70,000
Lincoln Academy, ME	$172,000
Lincoln School, RI	$2,000,000
Little Keswick School, VA	$20,000
Long Trail School, VT	$99,599
Louisville High School, CA	$564,475
The Lovett School, GA	$1,511,970
Loyola-Blakefield, MD	$2,876,095
Lutheran High School, MO	$153,000
Lutheran High School North, MO	$820,000
Lutheran High School Northwest, MI	$20,000
Lutheran High School of Hawaii, HI	$50,000
Lutheran High School of San Diego, CA	$130,000
Luther College High School, SK, Canada	CAN$165,000
The Lycee International, American Section, France	€30,000
Lyman Ward Military Academy, AL	$100,000
The Madeira School, VA	$3,043,151
Malden Catholic High School, MA	$1,105,973
Manhattan Christian High School, MT	$60,000
Maplebrook School, NY	$100,000
Marian Central Catholic High School, IL	$288,816
Marian High School, IN	$350,000
Marian High School, MA	$475,000
Marine Military Academy, TX	$760,000
Marquette University High School, WI	$2,400,000
Marshall School, MN	$1,700,000
Mars Hill Bible School, AL	$160,000
Martin Luther High School, NY	$1,955,670
The Marvelwood School, CT	$1,250,000
Mary Institute and St. Louis Country Day School (MICDS), MO	$2,512,985
Marymount High School, CA	$1,300,000
Marymount School of New York, NY	$3,000,000
The Masters School, NY	$50,400,000
Mater Dei High School, IL	$120,000
Matignon High School, MA	$600,000
Maui Preparatory Academy, HI	$261,776
Maumee Valley Country Day School, OH	$454,900
Maur Hill-Mount Academy, KS	$275,000
McDonogh School, MD	$3,340,390
The Meadows School, NV	$514,698
Memphis University School, TN	$2,475,000
Menlo School, CA	$4,200,000
Mercersburg Academy, PA	$6,178,725
Merion Mercy Academy, PA	$1,420,000
Mesa Grande Seventh-Day Academy, CA	$35,000
Miami Country Day School, FL	$3,100,000
The Miami Valley School, OH	$1,204,171
Middlesex School, MA	$5,090,000
Midland School, CA	$1,000,000
Mill Springs Academy, GA	$110,000
Miss Edgar's and Miss Cramp's School, QC, Canada	CAN$135,000
Miss Hall's School, MA	$3,000,000
Missouri Military Academy, MO	$1,200,000
Miss Porter's School, CT	$3,700,000
MMI Preparatory School, PA	$619,296
The Monarch School, TX	$105,350
Montgomery Bell Academy, TN	$2,035,000
Montrose School, MA	$500,000
Moorestown Friends School, NJ	$1,784,855

Moravian Academy, PA	$1,400,160	Portsmouth Christian Academy, NH	$218,000
Moreau Catholic High School, CA	$1,700,000	Poughkeepsie Day School, NY	$550,000
Mother McAuley High School, IL	$1,000,000	Powers Catholic High School, MI	$450,000
Mounds Park Academy, MN	$1,000,000	Presbyterian Pan American School, TX	$1,460,500
Mountain View Academy, CA	$48,500	Preston High School, NY	$555,000
Mount Saint Charles Academy, RI	$750,000	Prestonwood Christian Academy, TX	$734,381
Mount Saint Joseph Academy, PA	$699,113	Proctor Academy, NH	$3,200,000
Nampa Christian Schools, ID	$15,000	Professional Children's School, NY	$795,802
Nashville Christian School, TN	$3000	Providence Catholic School, The College Preparatory	
National Cathedral School, DC	$1,604,156	School for Girls Grades 6-12, TX	$214,713
Nazareth Academy, IL	$300,000	Providence Country Day School, RI	$1,945,025
Nebraska Christian Schools, NE	$140,000	Providence Day School, NC	$1,106,585
Nerinx Hall, MO	$826,135	Providence High School, CA	$942,250
Newark Academy, NJ	$1,729,521	Punahou School, HI	$3,073,375
Niagara Christian Community of Schools, ON,		Queen Margaret's School, BC, Canada	CAN$150,000
Canada	CAN$400,000	Rabun Gap-Nacoochee School, GA	$5,000,000
Noble Academy, NC	$81,000	Ramona Convent Secondary School, CA	$350,000
Noble and Greenough School, MA	$3,985,500	Randolph-Macon Academy, VA	$304,242
The Nora School, MD	$167,000	Randolph School, AL	$258,240
The North Broward Preparatory Upper School, FL	$2,400,000	Ransom Everglades School, FL	$3,130,377
North Country School, NY	$765,481	Realms of Inquiry, UT	$6600
Northfield Mount Hermon School, MA	$8,400,000	The Rectory School, CT	$1,600,000
Northpoint Christian School, MS	$70,000	Redemption Christian Academy, MA	$700,000
North Shore Country Day School, IL	$1,500,000	Redwood Christian Schools, CA	$420,000
Northwest Academy, OR	$500,000	Regis Jesuit High School, Boys Division, CO	$1,600,000
Northwest Catholic High School, CT	$2,034,000	Regis Jesuit High School, Girls Division, CO	$1,600,000
The Northwest School, WA	$1,340,175	Rejoice Christian Schools, OK	$15,000
Northwest Yeshiva High School, WA	$348,936	The Rivers School, MA	$3,727,504
Notre Dame High School, CA	$10,000,000	Rockhurst High School, MO	$2,100,000
Notre Dame High School, CA	$120,000	Rockland Country Day School, NY	$367,421
Notre Dame High School, CA	$1,200,000	Rock Point School, VT	$150,000
Notre Dame High School, NJ	$700,000	Rockway Mennonite Collegiate, ON, Canada	CAN$186,927
Notre Dame High School, NY	$600,000	The Roeper School, MI	$533,656
Notre Dame High School, TN	$378,271	Roland Park Country School, MD	$1,516,770
Oak Hill School, OR	$106,000	Rolling Hills Preparatory School, CA	$1,000,000
The O'Neal School, NC	$505,932	Rosati-Kain High School, MO	$100,000
Orangeburg Preparatory Schools, Inc., SC	$20,370	Rosseau Lake College, ON, Canada	CAN$160,000
Orangewood Christian School, FL	$124,000	Rothesay Netherwood School, NB, Canada	CAN$1,029,195
Oratory Preparatory School, NJ	$542,300	The Roxbury Latin School, MA	$2,266,575
Oregon Episcopal School, OR	$1,121,623	Royal Canadian College, BC, Canada	CAN$18,000
Orinda Academy, CA	$400,000	Rundle College, AB, Canada	CAN$90,000
Our Lady of Good Counsel High School, MD	$2,000,000	Sacramento Country Day School, CA	$45,000
Our Lady of Mercy Academy, NJ	$35,000	Sacramento Waldorf School, CA	$180,474
Out-Of-Door-Academy, FL	$1,133,313	Sacred Heart/Griffin High School, IL	$608,284
Pace Academy, GA	$1,400,000	Sacred Heart High School, CA	$800,000
Pacific Crest Community School, OR	$60,000	Sage Hill School, CA	$2,170,550
The Packer Collegiate Institute, NY	$7,400,000	Sage Ridge School, NV	$179,225
Padua Academy, DE	$500,000	St. Albans School, DC	$4,034,535
Palma School, CA	$700,000	Saint Albert Junior-Senior High School, IA	$380,000
Paradise Adventist Academy, CA	$110,000	St. Andrew's Episcopal School, MD	$2,708,400
The Park School of Baltimore, MD	$1,683,076	St. Andrew's Episcopal School, MS	$300,000
Patten Academy of Christian Education, CA	$22,650	St. Andrew's Regional High School, BC, Canada	CAN$100,000
Peddie School, NJ	$6,800,000	St. Andrew's School, DE	$6,066,500
The Pennington School, NJ	$4,000,000	Saint Andrew's School, FL	$3,000,000
Peoples Christian Academy, ON, Canada	CAN$30,000	St. Andrew's School, GA	$150,000
The Phelps School, PA	$1,100,000	St. Andrew's School, RI	$2,117,710
Philadelphia-Montgomery Christian Academy, PA	$600,000	St. Andrew's–Sewanee School, TN	$1,576,449
Phillips Academy (Andover), MA	$20,195,000	St. Anne's–Belfield School, VA	$4,700,000
Phoenix Country Day School, AZ	$1,016,600	Saint Augustine Preparatory School, NJ	$1,100,000
Pickering College, ON, Canada	CAN$125,000	St. Benedict at Auburndale, TN	$35,000
Piedmont Academy, GA	$30,000	St. Bernard High School, CT	$354,257
The Pingree School, MA	$3,080,000	St. Bernard's Catholic School, CA	$55,000
The Pingry School, NJ	$2,711,787	St. Brendan High School, FL	$266,000
Pioneer Valley Christian Academy, MA	$215,125	St. Catherine's School, VA	$917,330
Pius X High School, NE	$10,000	St. Christopher's School, VA	$783,200
Polytechnic School, CA	$2,040,187	St. Croix Schools, MN	$850,000
Portsmouth Abbey School, RI	$4,000,000	Saint Dominic Academy, ME	$600,000

School	Amount	School	Amount
Saint Francis High School, CA	$900,000	Shelton School and Evaluation Center, TX	$516,800
Saint Francis High School, CA	$3,000,000	Shorecrest Preparatory School, FL	$1,150,000
St. George's Independent School, TN	$975,000	Shoreline Christian, WA	$170,000
St. George's School, RI	$4,000,000	Smithville Christian High School, ON, Canada	150,000
St. George's School, BC, Canada	CAN$1,000,000	Solebury School, PA	$1,975,000
Saint James School, MD	$2,500,000	Sonoma Academy, CA	$3,000,000
St. John Neumann High School, FL	$400,000	Soundview Preparatory School, NY	$569,000
St. John's Catholic Prep, MD	$788,000	Southwest Christian School, Inc., TX	$455,000
St. John's Preparatory School, MA	$3,800,000	Springside Chestnut Hill Academy, PA	$4,176,875
Saint John's Preparatory School, MN	$896,000	Squaw Valley Academy, CA	$175,000
Saint Joseph Academy, CA	$80,112	Stanstead College, QC, Canada	CAN$1,400,000
St. Joseph Academy, FL	$120,000	Steamboat Mountain School, CO	$220,000
St. Joseph High School, CT	$1,200,000	Stephen T. Badin High School, OH	$688,200
Saint Joseph High School, NJ	$750,000	Stevenson School, CA	$3,475,000
St. Joseph's Academy, LA	$513,581	Stone Ridge School of the Sacred Heart, MD	$2,600,000
St. Joseph's Catholic School, SC	$760,000	The Storm King School, NY	$1,234,117
St. Joseph's Preparatory School, PA	$3,900,000	Stuart Hall, VA	$1,400,000
St. Lawrence Seminary High School, WI	$778,110	The Study, QC, Canada	CAN$400,000
St. Louis University High School, MO	$3,246,000	Summit Preparatory School, MT	$100,000
St. Luke's School, CT	$749,850	Sunshine Bible Academy, SD	$38,520
St. Margaret's School, BC, Canada	CAN$70,000	The Taft School, CT	$7,700,000
St. Mark's School of Texas, TX	$1,170,052	Tampa Preparatory School, FL	$1,000,000
St. Martin's Episcopal School, LA	$349,973	Teurlings Catholic High School, LA	$84,000
St. Mary's Episcopal School, TN	$381,400	The Thacher School, CA	$2,818,894
Saint Mary's High School, AZ	$3,800,000	THINK Global School, NY	$2,649,200
St. Mary's School, OR	$1,000,000	Thomas Jefferson School, MO	$640,000
St. Michael's College School, ON, Canada	CAN$1,800,000	Tilton School, NH	$3,416,870
St. Michael's Preparatory School of the Norbertine Fathers, CA	$500,000	Timothy Christian School, NJ	$100,000
St. Patrick Catholic High School, MS	$168,524	Tower Hill School, DE	$1,284,750
Saint Patrick High School, IL	$1,170,000	Traditional Learning Academy, BC, Canada	CAN$25,000
St. Paul Academy and Summit School, MN	$3,200,000	Tri-City Christian Academy, AZ	$25,000
Saint Paul Lutheran High School, MO	$273,555	Trinity Catholic High School, CT	$472,490
St. Paul Preparatory School, MN	$5500	Trinity College School, ON, Canada	CAN$2,407,200
St. Paul's High School, MB, Canada	CAN$355,200	Trinity High School, KY	$2,700,000
St. Paul's School, NH	$7,200,000	Trinity High School, OH	$150,000
St. Peter's Preparatory School, NJ	$1,718,000	Trinity-Pawling School, NY	$3,500,000
St. Pius X High School, TX	$806,450	Trinity Preparatory School, FL	$2,670,890
St. Stephen's Episcopal School, TX	$2,460,000	Tuscaloosa Academy, AL	$160,000
St. Stephen's School, Rome, Italy	€562,000	Tyler Street Christian Academy, TX	$92,000
Saint Teresa's Academy, MO	$150,000	United Mennonite Educational Institute, ON, Canada	CAN$46,000
Saint Thomas Aquinas High School, KS	$1,000,000	United Nations International School, NY	$32,580
St. Thomas Choir School, NY	$190,000	The United World College - USA, NM	$6,800,000
Saint Thomas More Catholic High School, LA	$100,000	University of Chicago Laboratory Schools, IL	$1,044,409
St. Timothy's School, MD	$3,257,000	University Prep, WA	$1,392,423
Saint Ursula Academy, OH	$1,420,000	University School of Jackson, TN	$180,000
Saint Xavier High School, OH	$3,800,000	Upper Canada College, ON, Canada	CAN$4,500,000
Salem Academy, NC	$1,033,794	The Ursuline Academy of Dallas, TX	$1,065,000
Salesianum School, DE	$1,000,000	Valley Christian High School, CA	$2,500,000
Salpointe Catholic High School, AZ	$1,848,925	The Valley School, MI	$200,000
San Domenico School, CA	$2,000,000	The Vanguard School, FL	$500,000
Sandy Spring Friends School, MD	$3,035,000	Vicksburg Catholic School, MS	$75,000
San Francisco University High School, CA	$2,500,000	Viewpoint School, CA	$2,801,010
San Marcos Baptist Academy, TX	$70,000	Villa Walsh Academy, NJ	$110,000
Santa Catalina School, CA	$1,964,000	Visitation Academy, MO	$660,000
Santa Margarita Catholic High School, CA	$1,500,000	Walnut Hill School for the Arts, MA	$3,500,000
Savannah Christian Preparatory School, GA	$110,000	Wasatch Academy, UT	$3,857,580
Scattergood Friends School, IA	$499,528	The Waterford School, UT	$1,500,000
Scheck Hillel Community School, FL	$1,000,000	Watkinson School, CT	$1,650,522
Seabury Hall, HI	$987,400	Waynflete School, ME	$2,067,247
Seattle Lutheran High School, WA	$92,710	Webb School of Knoxville, TN	$860,000
Seisen International School, Japan	¥4,500,000	The Webb Schools, CA	$4,100,000
Servite High School, CA	$1,500,000	Wesleyan Academy, PR	$1000
The Seven Hills School, OH	$710,453	Wesleyan School, GA	$1,551,511
Severn School, MD	$1,800,000	Westbury Christian School, TX	$204,206
Shady Side Academy, PA	$2,287,075	Westminster Christian Academy, LA	$50,000
Shawnigan Lake School, BC, Canada	CAN$1,500,000	Westminster Christian School, FL	$750,000
		Westminster School, CT	$4,760,560

The Westminster Schools, GA	$4,000,000
Westminster Schools of Augusta, GA	$250,000
Westover School, CT	$3,200,000
West Sound Academy, WA	$185,412
Westtown School, PA	$5,567,170
Wheaton Academy, IL	$700,000
The Wheeler School, RI	$1,975,505
Whitefield Academy, KY	$42,175
Whitfield School, MO	$1,379,000
Wichita Collegiate School, KS	$670,000
The Williston Northampton School, MA	$6,458,850
Wilmington Christian School, DE	$292,720
Wilmington Friends School, DE	$1,596,299
Wilson Hall, SC	$145,000
Windermere Preparatory School, FL	$425,000
The Windsor School, NY	$20,000
Winston Preparatory School, NY	$500,000
The Winston School, TX	$229,000
Woodlynde School, PA	$525,475
Woodside Priory School, CA	$2,170,538
The Woodward School, MA	$227,569
Wyoming Seminary, PA	$6,500,000
Xavier College Preparatory, AZ	$2,000,000
York Country Day School, PA	$339,000
York School, CA	$1,436,650
Zurich International School, Switzerland	27,000 Swiss francs

SCHOOLS REPORTING THAT THEY OFFER ENGLISH AS A SECOND LANGUAGE

The Academy at Charlemont, MA
Academy at the Lakes, FL
Academy of the Holy Family, CT
Academy of the New Church Boys' School, PA
Academy of the New Church Girls' School, PA
Académie Ste Cécile International School, ON, Canada
Admiral Farragut Academy, FL
Allen Academy, TX
Allison Academy, FL
Alma Heights Christian High School, CA
American Heritage School, FL
American Heritage School, FL
American International School, Lusaka, Zambia
The American School of Puerto Vallarta, Mexico
Andrews Osborne Academy, OH
Army and Navy Academy, CA
Atlanta International School, GA
Atlantis Academy, FL
Augusta Christian School, GA
Balmoral Hall School, MB, Canada
Banbury Crossroads School, AB, Canada
Bangor Christian School, ME
Baptist Regional School, NJ
The Beekman School, NY
Berkshire School, MA
Besant Hill School, CA
Bishop Brady High School, NH
Bishop Denis J. O'Connell High School, VA
Bishop Montgomery High School, CA
Bishop's College School, QC, Canada
Bishop Walsh Middle High School, MD
Blanchet School, OR
Bodwell High School, BC, Canada
The Bolles School, FL
Brandon Hall School, GA
Branksome Hall, ON, Canada

Bridgeport International Academy, CT
Brimmer and May School, MA
British International School of Boston, MA
British International School of Washington, DC
The Brook Hill School, TX
Burr and Burton Academy, VT
Buxton School, MA
California Crosspoint High School, CA
California Lutheran High School, CA
Canterbury School, CT
Canterbury School, FL
The Canterbury School of Florida, FL
Cape Fear Academy, NC
Cape Henry Collegiate School, VA
Capistrano Valley Christian Schools, CA
Cardigan Mountain School, NH
Carlisle School, VA
Carlucci American International School of Lisbon, Portugal
Catholic Central High School, NY
Charlotte Country Day School, NC
Christ Church Episcopal School, SC
Christchurch School, VA
Christian Heritage School, CT
Colegio Bolivar, Colombia
The Colorado Rocky Mountain School, CO
Columbia International School, Japan
The Community School, ID
Crawford Adventist Academy, ON, Canada
The Crenshaw School, FL
The Culver Academies, IN
Cushing Academy, MA
Damien High School, CA
Darrow School, NY
Deerfield Academy, MA
Desert Academy, NM
The Dr. Miriam and Sheldon G. Adelson Educational Campus, The Adelson Upper School, NV
Dominican Academy, NY
Donelson Christian Academy, TN
The Donoho School, AL
Dublin School, NH
The Dwight School, NY
Eaglebrook School, MA
Eastern Mennonite High School, VA
Eldorado Emerson Private School, CA
Elgin Academy, IL
Elmwood School, ON, Canada
Elyria Catholic High School, OH
Erskine Academy, ME
Escuela Campo Alegre, Venezuela
Father Lopez High School, FL
Fay School, MA
First Presbyterian Day School, GA
Forest Lake Academy, FL
Fountain Valley School of Colorado, CO
Foxcroft School, VA
Fredericton Christian Academy, NB, Canada
Friends Select School, PA
Fuqua School, VA
Garrison Forest School, MD
George School, PA
George Stevens Academy, ME
The Glenholme School, Devereux Connecticut, CT
The Governor French Academy, IL
The Gow School, NY
The Grauer School, CA
Great Lakes Christian High School, ON, Canada

Green Meadow Waldorf School, NY
Grier School, PA
The Gunnery, CT
The Gunston School, MD
Hargrave Military Academy, VA
Hawai`i Preparatory Academy, HI
Heritage Academy, SC
Highroad Academy, BC, Canada
The Hockaday School, TX
Holyoke Catholic High School, MA
Holy Trinity High School, IL
Houghton Academy, NY
The Hudson School, NJ
The Hun School of Princeton, NJ
Hyde School, CT
Hyde School, ME
Immaculate Conception High School, NJ
Institut Monte Rosa, Switzerland
International High School, CA
International School Bangkok, Thailand
International School Hamburg, Germany
The International School of Aberdeen, United Kingdom
International School of Luxembourg, Luxembourg
International School of Zug and Luzern (ISZL), Switzerland
Kent School, CT
The King's Christian High School, NJ
King's-Edgehill School, NS, Canada
Kingsway College, ON, Canada
The Knox School, NY
La Lumiere School, IN
Lancaster Mennonite High School, PA
The Leelanau School, MI
Le Lycee Francais de Los Angeles, CA
Leysin American School in Switzerland, Switzerland
Lincoln Academy, ME
Long Trail School, VT
Luther College High School, SK, Canada
Lycee Claudel, ON, Canada
The Madeira School, VA
Malden Catholic High School, MA
Maplebrook School, NY
Marianapolis Preparatory School, CT
Marine Military Academy, TX
The Marvelwood School, CT
Massanutten Military Academy, VA
The Masters School, NY
Matignon High School, MA
Maui Preparatory Academy, HI
Maumee Valley Country Day School, OH
Maur Hill-Mount Academy, KS
Memorial Hall School, TX
Mesa Grande Seventh-Day Academy, CA
Miami Country Day School, FL
The Miami Valley School, OH
Mid-Pacific Institute, HI
Miss Hall's School, MA
Missouri Military Academy, MO
Miss Porter's School, CT
Mooseheart High School, IL
Moreau Catholic High School, CA
Mounds Park Academy, MN
Mount Vernon Presbyterian School, GA
Nebraska Christian Schools, NE
Niagara Christian Community of Schools, ON, Canada
The North Broward Preparatory Upper School, FL
North Central Texas Academy, TX
North Country School, NY

Northfield Mount Hermon School, MA
North Toronto Christian School, ON, Canada
The Northwest School, WA
Northwest Yeshiva High School, WA
The Norwich Free Academy, CT
Notre Dame-Cathedral Latin School, OH
Notre Dame High School, CA
Notre Dame High School, NJ
Oak Hill School, OR
Oneida Baptist Institute, KY
Orangeburg Preparatory Schools, Inc., SC
Oregon Episcopal School, OR
Orinda Academy, CA
The Oxford Academy, CT
Parkview Adventist Academy, AB, Canada
The Pennington School, NJ
Perkiomen School, PA
The Phelps School, PA
Philadelphia-Montgomery Christian Academy, PA
Pickering College, ON, Canada
Pinecrest Academy, GA
Portsmouth Christian Academy, NH
Poughkeepsie Day School, NY
Presbyterian Pan American School, TX
Professional Children's School, NY
Queen Margaret's School, BC, Canada
Rabun Gap-Nacoochee School, GA
Randolph-Macon Academy, VA
The Rectory School, CT
Redemption Christian Academy, MA
Redwood Christian Schools, CA
Ridley College, ON, Canada
Riverside Christian Schools, CA
Riverstone International School, ID
Rock Point School, VT
Rockway Mennonite Collegiate, ON, Canada
Rolling Hills Preparatory School, CA
Rosseau Lake College, ON, Canada
Rothesay Netherwood School, NB, Canada
Rotterdam International Secondary School, Wolfert van Borselen, Netherlands
Royal Canadian College, BC, Canada
Rudolf Steiner School of Ann Arbor, MI
Rumsey Hall School, CT
Saddlebrook Preparatory School, FL
Sage Ridge School, NV
St. Andrew's Episcopal School, MD
Saint Andrew's School, FL
St. Andrew's School, GA
St. Andrew's School, RI
St. Andrew's–Sewanee School, TN
St. Anne's–Belfield School, VA
St. Bernard High School, CT
St. Croix Schools, MN
Saint John's Preparatory School, MN
St. Joseph High School, CT
St. Margaret's School, BC, Canada
St. Martin's Episcopal School, LA
St. Mary's Preparatory School, MI
St. Mary's School, OR
Saint Maur International School, Japan
St. Michael's Preparatory School of the Norbertine Fathers, CA
St. Patrick's Regional Secondary, BC, Canada
St. Paul Preparatory School, MN
St. Timothy's School, MD
Salem Academy, NC
Salem Academy, OR

San Domenico School, CA
Sandy Spring Friends School, MD
San Marcos Baptist Academy, TX
The Savannah Country Day School, GA
Scattergood Friends School, IA
Scheck Hillel Community School, FL
SciCore Academy, NJ
Seattle Lutheran High School, WA
Seisen International School, Japan
Shawnigan Lake School, BC, Canada
Signet Christian School, ON, Canada
Smithville Christian High School, ON, Canada
Solebury School, PA
Southern Ontario College, ON, Canada
Squaw Valley Academy, CA
Stanstead College, QC, Canada
St Leonards School and Sixth Form College, United Kingdom
The Stony Brook School, NY
The Storm King School, NY
Stuart Hall, VA
Taipei American School, Taiwan
TASIS The American School in England, United Kingdom
TASIS, The American School in Switzerland, Switzerland
The Tenney School, TX
Thomas Jefferson School, MO
Tilton School, NH
Timothy Christian School, NJ
TMI - The Episcopal School of Texas, TX
Tri-City Christian Academy, AZ
Trinity Catholic High School, CT
Trinity College School, ON, Canada
Trinity-Pawling School, NY
Tuscaloosa Academy, AL
United Nations International School, NY
The United World College - USA, NM
University School of Jackson, TN
Victor Valley Christian School, CA
Walla Walla Valley Academy, WA
Walnut Hill School for the Arts, MA
Wasatch Academy, UT
Westbury Christian School, TX
Westover School, CT
West Sound Academy, WA
Westtown School, PA
Wheaton Academy, IL
Whitfield School, MO
Whitinsville Christian School, MA
The Williston Northampton School, MA
Wilmington Christian School, DE
Windermere Preparatory School, FL
The Windsor School, NY
The Woodhall School, CT
The Woodward School, MA
Wyoming Seminary, PA
Zurich International School, Switzerland

SCHOOLS REPORTING A COMMUNITY SERVICE REQUIREMENT

The Academy for Gifted Children (PACE), ON, Canada
Academy of Our Lady of Peace, CA
Academy of the Holy Family, CT
Academy of the Sacred Heart, MI
Admiral Farragut Academy, FL
The Agnes Irwin School, PA
Allen Academy, TX

All Hallows High School, NY
Allison Academy, FL
American Christian Academy, AL
American Heritage School, FL
American Heritage School, FL
Andrews Osborne Academy, OH
Aquinas High School, GA
Archbishop Curley High School, MD
Austin Preparatory School, MA
Bakersfield Christian High School, CA
Battle Ground Academy, TN
Belen Jesuit Preparatory School, FL
Benedictine High School, OH
Berkeley Carroll School, NY
Berkeley Preparatory School, FL
Berkshire School, MA
The Birch Wathen Lenox School, NY
Bishop Brady High School, NH
Bishop Connolly High School, MA
Bishop Denis J. O'Connell High School, VA
Bishop Eustace Preparatory School, NJ
Bishop Ireton High School, VA
Bishop Kelly High School, ID
The Bishop's School, CA
Bishop Stang High School, MA
Blanchet School, OR
Blessed Sacrament Huguenot Catholic School, VA
Boston University Academy, MA
Breck School, MN
Brentwood School, CA
Briarwood Christian High School, AL
Bridgeport International Academy, CT
Brimmer and May School, MA
The Brook Hill School, TX
Brooks School, MA
Brophy College Preparatory, AZ
The Browning School, NY
Brunswick School, CT
The Bryn Mawr School for Girls, MD
The Buckley School, CA
Buffalo Seminary, NY
Burr and Burton Academy, VT
Butte Central Catholic High School, MT
Campbell Hall (Episcopal), CA
Canterbury School, FL
The Canterbury School of Florida, FL
Cape Fear Academy, NC
Cape Henry Collegiate School, VA
Cardinal Mooney Catholic High School, FL
Cardinal Newman High School, FL
Carlisle School, VA
Carrollton School of the Sacred Heart, FL
Cascadilla School, NY
Cascia Hall Preparatory School, OK
Catholic Central High School, WI
CCI The Renaissance School, Italy
Chaminade College Preparatory, CA
Chaminade-Madonna College Preparatory, FL
Charlotte Country Day School, NC
Chattanooga Christian School, TN
Cheverus High School, ME
Choate Rosemary Hall, CT
Christian Central Academy, NY
Christian Heritage School, CT
Christopher Columbus High School, FL
The Collegiate School, VA
The Colorado Rocky Mountain School, CO

The Colorado Springs School, CO
The Columbus Academy, OH
Commonwealth School, MA
The Community School of Naples, FL
Concordia Lutheran High School, IN
Crawford Adventist Academy, ON, Canada
Crossroads School for Arts & Sciences, CA
The Culver Academies, IN
Currey Ingram Academy, TN
Damien High School, CA
Dana Hall School, MA
Delaware Valley Friends School, PA
Desert Academy, NM
Devon Preparatory School, PA
Donelson Christian Academy, TN
Donna Klein Jewish Academy, FL
Dowling Catholic High School, IA
Durham Academy, NC
The Dwight School, NY
Eaglebrook School, MA
Edmund Burke School, DC
Eldorado Emerson Private School, CA
Elizabeth Seton High School, MD
Elyria Catholic High School, OH
Episcopal High School of Jacksonville, FL
Explorations Academy, WA
Fairfield College Preparatory School, CT
Faith Lutheran High School, NV
Father Lopez High School, FL
First Baptist Academy, TX
Flint Hill School, VA
Flintridge Preparatory School, CA
Fontbonne Academy, MA
Forest Lake Academy, FL
Fort Worth Country Day School, TX
Fountain Valley School of Colorado, CO
Franklin Road Academy, TN
Friends Academy, NY
Fuqua School, VA
George School, PA
Gilmour Academy, OH
Girard College, PA
Gonzaga College High School, DC
Good Hope Country Day School, VI
The Governor's Academy, MA
The Gow School, NY
The Grauer School, CA
Greenhill School, TX
Griggs International Academy, MD
Guamani Private School, PR
Gulliver Preparatory School, FL
The Gunnery, CT
The Gunston School, MD
Hales Franciscan High School, IL
Halstrom Academy, Beverly Hills, CA
Halstrom Academy, Calsbad, CA
Halstrom Academy, Cupertino, CA
Halstrom Academy, Huntington Beach, CA
Halstrom Academy, Irvine, CA
Halstrom Academy, Manhattan Beach, CA
Halstrom Academy, Mission Viejo, CA
Halstrom Academy, Orange, CA
Halstrom Academy, Pasadena, CA
Halstrom Academy, San Diego, CA
Halstrom Academy, Walnut Creek, CA
Halstrom Academy, Westlake Village, CA
Halstrom Academy, Woodland Hills, CA

The Harker School, CA
Harvard-Westlake School, CA
Hawken School, OH
Hebrew Academy of the Five Towns & Rockaway, NY
The Hockaday School, TX
Holy Cross Regional Catholic School, VA
Holy Cross School, LA
Holy Ghost Preparatory School, PA
Holyoke Catholic High School, MA
The Hudson School, NJ
The Hun School of Princeton, NJ
Hyman Brand Hebrew Academy of Greater Kansas City, KS
Immaculata-La Salle High School, FL
Immaculate Conception High School, NJ
Incarnate Word Academy, TX
Independent School, KS
International School Bangkok, Thailand
International School of Luxembourg, Luxembourg
International School of Zug and Luzern (ISZL), Switzerland
Jesuit College Preparatory School, TX
Jesuit High School of Tampa, FL
Josephinum Academy, IL
Junipero Serra High School, CA
Kalamazoo Christian High School, MI
Kent Denver School, CO
Keystone School, TX
Kingswood-Oxford School, CT
The Knox School, NY
La Jolla Country Day School, CA
La Salle Academy, RI
Lauralton Hall, CT
The Laureate Academy, MB, Canada
Laurel School, OH
The Lawrenceville School, NJ
Lincoln Academy, ME
Lincoln School, RI
Long Trail School, VT
Louisville High School, CA
Lutheran High School North, MO
Lutheran High School Northwest, MI
The Madeira School, VA
Malvern Preparatory School, PA
Manhattan Christian High School, MT
Maranatha High School, CA
Marquette University High School, WI
Marshall School, MN
Mars Hill Bible School, AL
The Marvelwood School, CT
Mary Institute and St. Louis Country Day School (MICDS), MO
Marymount School of New York, NY
Matignon High School, MA
Maui Preparatory Academy, HI
Maumee Valley Country Day School, OH
McDonogh School, MD
The Meadows School, NV
Memorial Hall School, TX
Menlo School, CA
Mercy High School, CT
Mesa Grande Seventh-Day Academy, CA
Miami Country Day School, FL
The Miami Valley School, OH
Miss Hall's School, MA
Missouri Military Academy, MO
Miss Porter's School, CT
Moorestown Friends School, NJ
Moreau Catholic High School, CA
Mounds Park Academy, MN

Mountain View Academy, CA
Mount Dora Christian Academy, FL
National Cathedral School, DC
Nerinx Hall, MO
Newark Academy, NJ
Noble and Greenough School, MA
The Nora School, MD
The North Broward Preparatory Upper School, FL
North Shore Country Day School, IL
North Toronto Christian School, ON, Canada
Northwest Academy, OR
Northwest Catholic High School, CT
Northwest Yeshiva High School, WA
Notre Dame High School, CA
Notre Dame High School, CA
Notre Dame High School, MO
Notre Dame High School, NJ
Oak Hill School, OR
The O'Neal School, NC
Oratory Preparatory School, NJ
Orinda Academy, CA
Out-Of-Door-Academy, FL
The Oxford Academy, CT
Pace Academy, GA
The Packer Collegiate Institute, NY
Padua Academy, DE
Palma School, CA
Paradise Adventist Academy, CA
Patten Academy of Christian Education, CA
Peddie School, NJ
Perkiomen School, PA
The Phelps School, PA
Phoenix Country Day School, AZ
Pickering College, ON, Canada
The Pingry School, NJ
Pioneer Valley Christian Academy, MA
Pope John XXIII Regional High School, NJ
Portledge School, NY
Poughkeepsie Day School, NY
Powers Catholic High School, MI
Providence Catholic School, The College Preparatory School for
    Girls Grades 6-12, TX
Providence Country Day School, RI
Punahou School, HI
Queen Margaret's School, BC, Canada
Ravenscroft School, NC
Regis Jesuit High School, Boys Division, CO
Regis Jesuit High School, Girls Division, CO
Riverdale Country School, NY
The Rivers School, MA
Rockhurst High School, MO
Rockland Country Day School, NY
Rock Point School, VT
Roland Park Country School, MD
Sacramento Country Day School, CA
Sacramento Waldorf School, CA
Sacred Heart High School, CA
Sage Ridge School, NV
St. Albans School, DC
St. Andrew's Episcopal School, MD
St. Andrew's Episcopal School, MS
Saint Andrew's School, FL
St. Andrew's School, GA
St. Andrew's School, RI
St. Andrew's–Sewanee School, TN
St. Anne's–Belfield School, VA
St. Bernard High School, CA

St. Bernard High School, CT
St. Bernard's Catholic School, CA
St. Brendan High School, FL
St. Catherine's School, VA
St. Christopher's School, VA
Saint Francis High School, CA
St. Francis School, GA
Saint Gertrude High School, VA
Saint James School, MD
St. Joseph High School, CT
Saint Joseph High School, NJ
St. Joseph's Catholic School, SC
St. Luke's School, CT
St. Mark's School of Texas, TX
St. Martin's Episcopal School, LA
Saint Mary's High School, AZ
St. Mary's School, OR
St. Michael's College School, ON, Canada
Saint Patrick High School, IL
Saint Paul Lutheran High School, MO
St. Paul's School, NH
St. Peter's Preparatory School, NJ
St. Pius X High School, TX
St. Stephen's Episcopal School, TX
Saint Teresa's Academy, MO
St. Thomas Aquinas High School, NH
St. Timothy's School, MD
Saint Ursula Academy, OH
Salem Academy, OR
Salesianum School, DE
San Domenico School, CA
Sandy Spring Friends School, MD
San Francisco University High School, CA
Scattergood Friends School, IA
Seabury Hall, HI
Seattle Academy of Arts and Sciences, WA
Seattle Lutheran High School, WA
The Seven Hills School, OH
Severn School, MD
Sewickley Academy, PA
Smith School, NY
Solebury School, PA
Stephen T. Badin High School, OH
Stone Ridge School of the Sacred Heart, MD
The Storm King School, NY
Stratford Academy, GA
The Study, QC, Canada
The Summit Country Day School, OH
Tandem Friends School, VA
TASIS The American School in England, United Kingdom
TASIS, The American School in Switzerland, Switzerland
Thomas Jefferson School, MO
Tilton School, NH
TMI - The Episcopal School of Texas, TX
Tower Hill School, DE
Trinity Catholic High School, CT
Trinity College School, ON, Canada
Trinity Episcopal School, VA
Trinity High School, KY
Tuscaloosa Academy, AL
United Nations International School, NY
University of Chicago Laboratory Schools, IL
University Prep, WA
University School of Jackson, TN
Upper Canada College, ON, Canada
The Ursuline Academy of Dallas, TX
Valwood School, GA

Victor Valley Christian School, CA
Viewpoint School, CA
Villa Duchesne and Oak Hill School, MO
Visitation Academy, MO
The Waldorf School of Saratoga Springs, NY
Wasatch Academy, UT
Washington International School, DC
Waynflete School, ME
Webb School of Knoxville, TN
Wesleyan Academy, PR
Westbury Christian School, TX
Westmark School, CA
Westminster Christian School, FL
Westover School, CT
The Wheeler School, RI
Wilmington Christian School, DE
Wilmington Friends School, DE
Wilson Hall, SC
Windermere Preparatory School, FL
The Winston School San Antonio, TX
Woodlynde School, PA
Woodside Priory School, CA
The Woodward School, MA
Wooster School, CT
Wyoming Seminary, PA
Xavier College Preparatory, AZ
York Country Day School, PA
York School, CA
Zurich International School, Switzerland

SCHOOLS REPORTING EXCHANGE PROGRAMS WITH OTHER U.S. SCHOOLS

Academy of the Sacred Heart, MI
Bentley School, CA
Calvary Day School, GA
Carrollton School of the Sacred Heart, FL
The Community School, ID
Crystal Springs Uplands School, CA
Josephinum Academy, IL
Maumee Valley Country Day School, OH
Montgomery Bell Academy, TN
Providence Day School, NC
St. Stephen's School, Rome, Italy
Salesianum School, DE
San Francisco University High School, CA
Stone Ridge School of the Sacred Heart, MD
Villa Duchesne and Oak Hill School, MO

SCHOOLS REPORTING PROGRAMS FOR STUDY ABROAD

The Academy at Charlemont, MA
Advanced Academy of Georgia, GA
The Agnes Irwin School, PA
Albuquerque Academy, NM
Alexander Dawson School, CO
American Christian Academy, AL
The American School Foundation, Mexico
Aquinas High School, GA
Archmere Academy, DE
Ashley Hall, SC
Atlanta International School, GA
Austin Waldorf School, TX
Beaufort Academy, SC

Benedictine High School, OH
Berkeley Carroll School, NY
Berkeley Preparatory School, FL
Berkshire School, MA
The Birch Wathen Lenox School, NY
Bishop's College School, QC, Canada
The Bishop's School, CA
Blair Academy, NJ
The Blake School, MN
Brandon Hall School, GA
Brooks School, MA
Brophy College Preparatory, AZ
Brunswick School, CT
The Bryn Mawr School for Girls, MD
The Buckley School, CA
Burr and Burton Academy, VT
California Crosspoint High School, CA
Cape Fear Academy, NC
Carrollton School of the Sacred Heart, FL
Casady School, OK
Cascia Hall Preparatory School, OK
Cate School, CA
The Catlin Gabel School, OR
CCI The Renaissance School, Italy
Chadwick School, CA
Charlotte Country Day School, NC
Charlotte Latin School, NC
Choate Rosemary Hall, CT
Columbia International School, Japan
Commonwealth School, MA
The Community School of Naples, FL
Concord Academy, MA
The Country Day School, ON, Canada
Crystal Springs Uplands School, CA
The Culver Academies, IN
Dana Hall School, MA
Deerfield Academy, MA
DeLaSalle High School, MN
The Derryfield School, NH
The Dr. Miriam and Sheldon G. Adelson Educational Campus, The Adelson Upper School, NV
Donna Klein Jewish Academy, FL
The Dwight School, NY
Eastern Mennonite High School, VA
The Ellis School, PA
Episcopal High School, VA
Episcopal High School of Jacksonville, FL
Falmouth Academy, MA
Fordham Preparatory School, NY
Fountain Valley School of Colorado, CO
Foxcroft School, VA
Friends' Central School, PA
Gann Academy (The New Jewish High School of Greater Boston), MA
George Stevens Academy, ME
The Governor's Academy, MA
The Grauer School, CA
Greater Atlanta Christian Schools, GA
Green Fields Country Day School, AZ
Greenhill School, TX
Green Meadow Waldorf School, NY
Grier School, PA
Groton School, MA
The Gunnery, CT
The Gunston School, MD
The Harpeth Hall School, TN
Harvard-Westlake School, CA

Hathaway Brown School, OH
Hawken School, OH
Hebrew Academy of the Five Towns & Rockaway, NY
The Hockaday School, TX
Holland Hall, OK
Holy Ghost Preparatory School, PA
The Hudson School, NJ
International High School, CA
Jean and Samuel Frankel Jewish Academy of Metropolitan
   Detroit, MI
Josephinum Academy, IL
Kentucky Country Day School, KY
King's-Edgehill School, NS, Canada
Kingswood-Oxford School, CT
The Knox School, NY
La Jolla Country Day School, CA
Lakefield College School, ON, Canada
Lakehill Preparatory School, TX
Laurel School, OH
The Lawrenceville School, NJ
Leysin American School in Switzerland, Switzerland
Lincoln Academy, ME
Lincoln School, RI
Louisville Collegiate School, KY
The Lovett School, GA
Luther College High School, SK, Canada
Malvern Preparatory School, PA
Marshall School, MN
Mary Institute and St. Louis Country Day School (MICDS), MO
Marymount School of New York, NY
The Masters School, NY
Matignon High School, MA
Maumee Valley Country Day School, OH
Memphis University School, TN
Mercersburg Academy, PA
The Miami Valley School, OH
Milton Academy, MA
Miss Porter's School, CT
Montgomery Bell Academy, TN
Moorestown Friends School, NJ
Mount Vernon Presbyterian School, GA
National Cathedral School, DC
Newark Academy, NJ
Noble and Greenough School, MA
Northfield Mount Hermon School, MA
North Shore Country Day School, IL
Oregon Episcopal School, OR
Pace Academy, GA
The Packer Collegiate Institute, NY
Palo Alto Preparatory School, CA
The Park School of Baltimore, MD
Peddie School, NJ
The Pennington School, NJ
Phillips Academy (Andover), MA
Phoenix Country Day School, AZ
The Pingry School, NJ
Polytechnic School, CA
Portsmouth Abbey School, RI
Proctor Academy, NH
Providence Country Day School, RI
Providence Day School, NC
Punahou School, HI
Rabun Gap-Nacoochee School, GA
Ramona Convent Secondary School, CA
Randolph-Macon Academy, VA
Ravenscroft School, NC
Realms of Inquiry, UT

Regis High School, NY
Ridley College, ON, Canada
Riverdale Country School, NY
Riverstone International School, ID
Roland Park Country School, MD
Rosseau Lake College, ON, Canada
Rudolf Steiner School of Ann Arbor, MI
Rundle College, AB, Canada
Sacramento Waldorf School, CA
St. Albans School, DC
St. Andrew's Episcopal School, MS
St. Andrew's School, GA
St. Andrew's–Sewanee School, TN
Saint Augustine Preparatory School, NJ
St. Catherine's School, VA
St. George's School, RI
Saint John's Preparatory School, MN
St. Joseph's Preparatory School, PA
St. Louis University High School, MO
St. Luke's School, CT
St. Mark's School of Texas, TX
Saint Mary's School, NC
St. Paul Academy and Summit School, MN
St. Paul Preparatory School, MN
St. Paul's School, NH
St. Peter's Preparatory School, NJ
St. Stephen's Episcopal School, TX
Salem Academy, NC
San Domenico School, CA
San Francisco University High School, CA
Seattle Academy of Arts and Sciences, WA
Servite High School, CA
The Seven Hills School, OH
Severn School, MD
Sewickley Academy, PA
Shady Side Academy, PA
Sonoma Academy, CA
Southwest Christian School, Inc., TX
The Spence School, NY
Stanstead College, QC, Canada
Steamboat Mountain School, CO
Stephen T. Badin High School, OH
Stevenson School, CA
Stone Ridge School of the Sacred Heart, MD
Summerfield Waldorf School, CA
The Summit Country Day School, OH
The Taft School, CT
Tampa Preparatory School, FL
TASIS The American School in England, United Kingdom
TASIS, The American School in Switzerland, Switzerland
The Thacher School, CA
THINK Global School, NY
Trinity College School, ON, Canada
Trinity High School, KY
Trinity Preparatory School, FL
Trinity School of Texas, TX
Tuscaloosa Academy, AL
University Prep, WA
Upper Canada College, ON, Canada
Viewpoint School, CA
Villa Duchesne and Oak Hill School, MO
The Waldorf School of Saratoga Springs, NY
Waynflete School, ME
Webb School of Knoxville, TN
The Weber School, GA
West Island College, AB, Canada
Westminster School, CT

The Westminster Schools, GA
Westminster Schools of Augusta, GA
Westover School, CT
Westtown School, PA
The Wheeler School, RI
The Williston Northampton School, MA
Wilmington Friends School, DE
Windermere Preparatory School, FL
Wyoming Seminary, PA
Xavier College Preparatory, AZ
The York School, ON, Canada

SCHOOLS REPORTING SUMMER SESSIONS OPEN TO STUDENTS FROM OTHER SCHOOLS

The Academy at Charlemont, MA	F,S,O
Academy at the Lakes, FL	A,C,F,S
Academy of Our Lady of Peace, CA	A,S,O
Academy of the Holy Cross, MD	A,C,F,S,O
Academy of the Holy Family, CT	A,O
Academy of the New Church Boys' School, PA	S
Academy of the New Church Girls' School, PA	S
Académie Ste Cécile International School, ON, Canada	A,F,O
Admiral Farragut Academy, FL	A
Advanced Academy of Georgia, GA	A,F,O
The Agnes Irwin School, PA	A,C,F,S,O
Albuquerque Academy, NM	A,C,F,S,O
Allen Academy, TX	O
Allison Academy, FL	A,O
All Saints' Academy, FL	A,C,F,S,O
Alpha Omega Academy, IA	A,C,F
The American School in Japan, Japan	A,C,F,O
The American School of Puerto Vallarta, Mexico	A,O
Andrews Osborne Academy, OH	A,S,O
Archbishop Curley High School, MD	A,C,F,S
Archbishop Mitty High School, CA	A,C,F,S,O
Arete Preparatory Academy, CA	A
Army and Navy Academy, CA	A,C,S,O
Ashley Hall, SC	A,C,F,S,O
ASSETS School, HI	A,O
Athens Academy, GA	A,C,F,S,O
Atlanta International School, GA	A,C,F,S,O
Atlantis Academy, FL	A,C,F,O
Augusta Christian School, GA	A,O
Austin Preparatory School, MA	A,F,S
Bakersfield Christian High School, CA	A,F,S
The Baltimore Actors' Theatre Conservatory, MD	A,F,O
Baptist Regional School, NJ	C,S,O
Battle Ground Academy, TN	A,C,F,S,O
Bearspaw Christian School, AB, Canada	S,O
Beaufort Academy, SC	S,O
The Beekman School, NY	A,O
Benedictine High School, OH	A,C,S,O
The Benjamin School, FL	A,C,F,S,O
Berkeley Carroll School, NY	A,C,F,S,O
Besant Hill School, CA	A,O
Bishop Brady High School, NH	A,C,F,S,O
Bishop Denis J. O'Connell High School, VA	A,C,F,S
Bishop Eustace Preparatory School, NJ	A,S,O
Bishop Ireton High School, VA	A,C,F,O
Bishop McNamara High School, MD	A,C,F,S,O
Bishop Miege High School, KS	A,C
Bishop Mora Salesian High School, CA	A,C,F,R,S,O
Bishop's College School, QC, Canada	A,O
The Bishop's School, CA	A,C,F,S

Bishop Stang High School, MA	A,C,F,S,O
The Blake School, MN	A,F,S,O
Blanchet School, OR	A,S,O
Blessed Sacrament Huguenot Catholic School, VA	A,C,F,S,O
Blueprint Education, AZ	A,O
Bodwell High School, BC, Canada	A,C,F,S,O
The Bolles School, FL	A,C,F,O
Boyd-Buchanan School, TN	A,S,O
Brandon Hall School, GA	A,C,F,S,O
Brehm Preparatory School, IL	A,F,O
Brentwood College School, BC, Canada	S,O
Brentwood School, CA	A,C,F,S,O
Bridges Academy, CA	A,C,F,S,O
Brimmer and May School, MA	A,F,S,O
The Brook Hill School, TX	A,F,S,O
Brooks School, MA	A,C,S,O
Brophy College Preparatory, AZ	A,C,F,S,O
Brother Rice High School, MI	A,F,O
Brunswick School, CT	A,O
The Bryn Mawr School for Girls, MD	A,F,S,O
The Buckley School, CA	A,C,F,O
Buffalo Seminary, NY	S,O
California Crosspoint High School, CA	A,S,O
Calvary Day School, GA	A,F,S,O
Calvert Hall College High School, MD	A,C,F,S,O
Calvin Christian High School, CA	A,S,O
Camden Military Academy, SC	A,O
Campbell Hall (Episcopal), CA	A,C,F,S,O
Canterbury School, CT	S,O
Canterbury School, FL	A,F,S,O
The Canterbury School of Florida, FL	A,C,F,S,O
Cape Fear Academy, NC	A,C,F,S,O
Cape Henry Collegiate School, VA	A,C,F,S,O
Capistrano Valley Christian Schools, CA	A,F,S,O
Cardigan Mountain School, NH	A,C,F,S,O
Cardinal Gibbons High School, NC	A,F,S,O
Carlisle School, VA	A,C,F,S,O
Carondelet High School, CA	A,S,O
Casady School, OK	A,C,F,S
Cascadilla School, NY	A,F,O
Cascia Hall Preparatory School, OK	A,F,S,O
Cathedral High School, NY	A,S
Catholic Central High School, WI	S,O
The Catlin Gabel School, OR	A,C,F,O
CCI The Renaissance School, Italy	F,O
Central Catholic High School, CA	A,O
Central Catholic High School, MA	A,C,F,O
Chadwick School, CA	C,F,S,O
Chaminade College Preparatory, CA	A,C,F,S,O
Charlotte Country Day School, NC	A,C,F,S,O
Charlotte Latin School, NC	A,C,F,S,O
Chattanooga Christian School, TN	A,F,S,O
Chelsea School, MD	A,C,O
Cheverus High School, ME	A,S,O
Choate Rosemary Hall, CT	A,F,S,O
Christa McAuliffe Academy School of Arts and Sciences, OR	A,C,O
Christ Church Episcopal School, SC	A,S,O
Christchurch School, VA	A,S,O
Chrysalis School, WA	A,C,O
Clarksville Academy, TN	A,C,F,S,O
Collegedale Academy, TN	A,O
The Collegiate School, VA	A,C,F,S,O
Columbia International School, Japan	A,C,F,S,O
The Columbus Academy, OH	A,C,F,O
Columbus School for Girls, OH	A,C,F,R,S,O
The Community School, ID	A,C,F,R,S,O

A — academic; C — computer instruction; F — art/fine arts; R — rigorous outdoor training; S — sports; O — other

The Community School of Naples, FL	A,S,O
Concordia Academy, MN	C,F,S
Concordia Lutheran High School, IN	A,C,F,S,O
The Country Day School, ON, Canada	A,F,S,O
Crescent School, ON, Canada	A,O
Crossroads School for Arts & Sciences, CA	A,C,F,S,O
The Culver Academies, IN	A,C,F,R,S,O
Currey Ingram Academy, TN	A,F,O
Cushing Academy, MA	A,C,F,S,O
Damien High School, CA	A,C,F,S,O
Dana Hall School, MA	A,O
Deerfield Academy, MA	A,O
De La Salle College, ON, Canada	A
DeLaSalle High School, MN	A
Delaware Valley Friends School, PA	A,C,F,O
Delbarton School, NJ	A,C,S,O
DeMatha Catholic High School, MD	A,C,F,S,O
Denver Academy, CO	A,C,F,R,O
Desert Academy, NM	A,C,O
Detroit Country Day School, MI	A,C,F,S,O
Dominican Academy, NY	A,O
The Donoho School, AL	A,O
Durham Academy, NC	A,C,F,S,O
Eaglebrook School, MA	A,C,F,R,S,O
Eaton Academy, GA	A,C,F,S,O
Edmund Burke School, DC	A,C,F,O
Elgin Academy, IL	A,F,S,O
Elizabeth Seton High School, MD	A,C,F,S
The Ellis School, PA	C,O
Elmwood School, ON, Canada	A,F,S
Elyria Catholic High School, OH	S,O
Episcopal Collegiate School, AR	A,C,F,S,O
Episcopal High School, TX	A,F,O
Episcopal High School, VA	A,F,S,O
Episcopal High School of Jacksonville, FL	A,C,F,R,S,O
Explorations Academy, WA	A,C,F,R,O
Fairfield College Preparatory School, CT	A,C,S,O
Falmouth Academy, MA	A,F,S
Father Duenas Memorial School, GU	A
Father Ryan High School, TN	A,C,F,S
Fayetteville Academy, NC	A,C,F,S,O
Fay School, MA	A,C,F,S
The First Academy, FL	A,F,S,O
First Presbyterian Day School, GA	A,C,F,S,O
Flint Hill School, VA	A,C,F,R,S,O
Flintridge Preparatory School, CA	A,C,F,S,O
Fontbonne Academy, MA	F,S
Forest Lake Academy, FL	A
Fort Worth Country Day School, TX	A,F,S,O
Foundation Academy, FL	A,F,S,O
Fowlers Academy, PR	A,O
Franklin Academy, CT	A,C,F,O
Franklin Road Academy, TN	A,C,F,S,O
Fredericksburg Academy, VA	A,F,S,O
Friends Academy, NY	F,O
Friends' Central School, PA	A
Friends Select School, PA	A,C,F,O
Front Range Christian High School, CO	A,F,S,O
Fuqua School, VA	A,F,S,O
The Galloway School, GA	A,C,F,S,O
Garrison Forest School, MD	F,S,O
George Walton Academy, GA	A,C,F,S,O
Gilman School, MD	A,C,F,R,S,O
Gilmour Academy, OH	A,S,O
The Glenholme School, Devereux Connecticut, CT	A,C,F,S,O
Gonzaga College High School, DC	A,O
The Governor French Academy, IL	A,O
The Governor's Academy, MA	A,F,S,O
The Gow School, NY	A,C,F,S,O
Grace Christian School, AK	A,O
The Grauer School, CA	A,C,F,R,S,O
Greater Atlanta Christian Schools, GA	A,F,S,O
Green Fields Country Day School, AZ	A,F,S,O
Greenhill School, TX	A,C,F,S,O
Grier School, PA	A,F,S,O
Griggs International Academy, MD	A
Guamani Private School, PR	A
The Gunnery, CT	S
The Gunston School, MD	A,C,S,O
Hales Franciscan High School, IL	A,C,S,O
Halstrom Academy, Beverly Hills, CA	A,F,O
Halstrom Academy, Calsbad, CA	A,F,O
Halstrom Academy, Cupertino, CA	A,F,O
Halstrom Academy, Huntington Beach, CA	A,F
Halstrom Academy, Irvine, CA	A,F
Halstrom Academy, Los Angeles, CA	A,F,O
Halstrom Academy, Manhattan Beach, CA	A,F,O
Halstrom Academy, Mission Viejo, CA	A,F,O
Halstrom Academy, Orange, CA	A,F,O
Halstrom Academy, Pasadena, CA	A,F,O
Halstrom Academy, San Diego, CA	A,C,F,O
Halstrom Academy, San Mateo, CA	A,F,O
Halstrom Academy, Walnut Creek, CA	A,F,O
Halstrom Academy, Westlake Village, CA	A,F
Halstrom Academy, Woodland Hills, CA	A,F,O
Hampshire Country School, NH	O
Hargrave Military Academy, VA	A,C,R,S,O
The Harker School, CA	A,S,O
The Harpeth Hall School, TN	A,C,F,S,O
Harvard-Westlake School, CA	A,C,F,R,S,O
The Harvey School, NY	A,O
Hathaway Brown School, OH	A,S,O
Hawaii Baptist Academy, HI	A,C,F,S,O
Hawai`i Preparatory Academy, HI	A,C,F,S,O
Hawken School, OH	A,C,O
The Heights School, MD	A,C,F,R,S,O
The Hockaday School, TX	A,C,F,S,O
Holland Hall, OK	A,C,F,S,O
Holy Cross High School, CT	F,S,O
Holy Ghost Preparatory School, PA	A,C,S,O
Holy Trinity School, ON, Canada	A,S
Houston Academy, AL	A,S,O
The Howard School, GA	A,O
The Hudson School, NJ	F,O
The Hun School of Princeton, NJ	A,C,F,S,O
Huntington-Surrey School, TX	A,O
Hyde School, CT	A,F,R,S,O
Hyde School, ME	A,C,F,R,S,O
Illiana Christian High School, IL	F,S,O
Immaculata-La Salle High School, FL	A,O
Immaculate Heart High School and Middle School, CA	A,F,S
Incarnate Word Academy, TX	S,O
Independent School, KS	A,C,F,S
Indian Creek School, MD	A,F,S
Indian Springs School, AL	A,F,S,O
Institut Monte Rosa, Switzerland	A,S,O
International High School, CA	A,O
International School Bangkok, Thailand	A,F
The International School of Aberdeen, United Kingdom	C,F,S
Isidore Newman School, LA	A,C,F,S
Jesuit College Preparatory School, TX	A,C,F,S,O
John F. Kennedy Catholic High School, MO	S

A — academic; C — computer instruction; F — art/fine arts; R — rigorous outdoor training; S — sports; O — other

John Hancock Academy, GA	A,O	Miami Country Day School, FL	A,C,F,R,S,O
Josephinum Academy, IL	A,C,F,S,O	The Miami Valley School, OH	A,F,R,S,O
Junipero Serra High School, CA	A,C,F,S,O	Mid-Pacific Institute, HI	A,C,F,O
Kent Denver School, CO	A,C,F,S,O	Mill Springs Academy, GA	A,S,O
Kent School, CT	A,O	Missouri Military Academy, MO	A,R,S,O
Kentucky Country Day School, KY	A,C,F,R,S,O	Miss Porter's School, CT	A,O
The Key School, MD	A,C,F,R,S	The Monarch School, TX	A,C,F,O
The Keystone School, PA	A,C,F,O	Montgomery Bell Academy, TN	A,C,F,R,S,O
King Low Heywood Thomas, CT	A,C,F,S,O	Montrose School, MA	A,F,S
The King's Christian High School, NJ	A,S,O	Moorestown Friends School, NJ	A,F,O
Kingswood-Oxford School, CT	A,F,S,O	Moravian Academy, PA	A,F,S,O
La Jolla Country Day School, CA	A,C,F,S,O	Moreau Catholic High School, CA	A,S,O
Lakefield College School, ON, Canada	A,O	Mother McAuley High School, IL	A,C,F,S,O
Lakehill Preparatory School, TX	A,C,F,S,O	Mounds Park Academy, MN	A,C,F,R,S
La Lumiere School, IN	A,S,O	Mount Mercy Academy, NY	A,O
Lancaster Mennonite High School, PA	A,F,S	Mount Saint Charles Academy, RI	F,S,O
Landmark School, MA	A,O	Mount Vernon Presbyterian School, GA	A,F,S,O
Lansdale Catholic High School, PA	A,F,S	Nashville Christian School, TN	A,F,S
La Salle Academy, RI	A,C,F,S	National Cathedral School, DC	A,F,S
La Salle High School, CA	A,C,F,S,O	Nazareth Academy, IL	A,F,S,O
The Laureate Academy, MB, Canada	A,O	Newark Academy, NJ	A,C,F,S,O
Laurel School, OH	A,F	The North Broward Preparatory Upper School, FL	A,C,F,S,O
The Lawrenceville School, NJ	A,C,F,S,O	North Country School, NY	A,F,O
The Leelanau School, MI	A,O	Northfield Mount Hermon School, MA	A,F,O
Le Lycee Francais de Los Angeles, CA	A,C,F,S,O	North Toronto Christian School, ON, Canada	A
Leysin American School in Switzerland, Switzerland	A,C,F,R,S,O	Northwest Catholic High School, CT	S,O
		The Northwest School, WA	A,C,F,S,O
Lincoln Academy, ME	A,F,O	Notre Dame-Cathedral Latin School, OH	A,F,S
Little Keswick School, VA	A,F,R,S,O	Notre Dame High School, CA	A,C,F,S,O
Louisville Collegiate School, KY	A,C,F,S,O	Notre Dame High School, CA	A,F,S,O
Louisville High School, CA	S,O	Notre Dame High School, CA	A,O
The Lovett School, GA	A,O	Notre Dame High School, MO	A,F,S
Loyola-Blakefield, MD	A,C,F,S	Notre Dame High School, NJ	A,C,F,S,O
Lutheran High School of Hawaii, HI	A,C,F,S,O	Notre Dame High School, TN	A,F,S,O
Luther College High School, SK, Canada	A,O	Oak Hill School, OR	A,C,F,O
Lyman Ward Military Academy, AL	A,R,O	Oakland School, VA	A,C,F,S,O
The Madeira School, VA	A,F,S,O	Oneida Baptist Institute, KY	A,O
Malden Catholic High School, MA	A,S,O	Orangeburg Preparatory Schools, Inc., SC	A,S,O
Malvern Preparatory School, PA	A,C,F,S,O	Orangewood Christian School, FL	A,C,F,R,S,O
Manhattan Christian High School, MT	A,S,O	Oratory Preparatory School, NJ	A,C,F,S,O
Maplebrook School, NY	A,C,F,S,O	Oregon Episcopal School, OR	A,C,F,S,O
Maranatha High School, CA	A,F,S,O	Orinda Academy, CA	A,O
Marianapolis Preparatory School, CT	A	Our Lady of Good Counsel High School, MD	A,C,F,S,O
Marian Central Catholic High School, IL	A,C,F,S,O	Out-Of-Door-Academy, FL	A,F,S
Marian High School, IN	C,F,S,O	The Oxford Academy, CT	A,F,S,O
Marine Military Academy, TX	A,R,S,O	Pace Academy, GA	A,C,F,S,O
Marshall School, MN	A,C,F,S,O	PACE/Brantley Hall High School, FL	A,C,F,O
Mars Hill Bible School, AL	A,F,S,O	Palma School, CA	A,F,S,O
Martin Luther High School, NY	A,C	Palo Alto Preparatory School, CA	A,R,O
The Marvelwood School, CT	A,F,O	Paradise Adventist Academy, CA	S,O
Mary Institute and St. Louis Country Day School (MICDS), MO	A,C,F,R,S,O	The Pathway School, PA	A,O
		Peddie School, NJ	A,C,F,S,O
Marymount High School, CA	A,C,F,S,O	The Pennington School, NJ	A,F,S,O
Massanutten Military Academy, VA	A,C,F,S,O	Perkiomen School, PA	A,F,S
The Masters School, NY	A,F,R,S,O	Phillips Academy (Andover), MA	A,C,F,S,O
Matignon High School, MA	A,O	Phoenix Christian Unified Schools, AZ	A,S,O
Maui Preparatory Academy, HI	A,R,S,O	Phoenix Country Day School, AZ	A,C,F,S,O
Maumee Valley Country Day School, OH	A,C,F,S,O	Pickering College, ON, Canada	A,O
Maur Hill-Mount Academy, KS	A,O	The Pingry School, NJ	A,S,O
McDonogh School, MD	A,C,F,S,O	Polytechnic School, CA	A,C,F,O
The Meadows School, NV	A,F,S,O	Pope John XXIII Regional High School, NJ	A,S,O
Memorial Hall School, TX	A,C,O	Portledge School, NY	A,C,F,S,O
Memphis University School, TN	A,C,S,O	Portsmouth Abbey School, RI	A,F,S,O
Menlo School, CA	A,O	Portsmouth Christian Academy, NH	A,F,S,O
Mercersburg Academy, PA	A,F,R,S,O	The Potomac School, VA	A,F,S,O
Merion Mercy Academy, PA	A,F,S,O	Poughkeepsie Day School, NY	A,F,O
Mesa Grande Seventh-Day Academy, CA	S,O	Prestonwood Christian Academy, TX	A,C,F,R,S

A — academic; C — computer instruction; F — art/fine arts; R — rigorous outdoor training; S — sports; O — other

Providence Catholic School, The College Preparatory School for Girls Grades 6-12, TX	A,C,F,S,O	St. Mary's Preparatory School, MI	S,O
Providence Country Day School, RI	F,S	Saint Mary's School, NC	A,C,F,S
Providence Day School, NC	A,C,F,S,O	St. Mary's School, OR	A,S,O
Providence High School, CA	A,C,F,S,O	Saint Maur International School, Japan	A,C,F,S,O
Punahou School, HI	A,F,S,O	St. Michael's College School, ON, Canada	S,O
Queen Margaret's School, BC, Canada	A,S,O	St. Patrick Catholic High School, MS	A,C,F,S,O
Ramona Convent Secondary School, CA	A,C,F,S,O	Saint Patrick High School, IL	A,C,F,S,O
Randolph-Macon Academy, VA	A,C,F,O	St. Paul Academy and Summit School, MN	A
Randolph School, AL	A,F,S,O	St. Paul Preparatory School, MN	A,O
Ransom Everglades School, FL	A,C,O	St. Paul's High School, MB, Canada	S,O
Ravenscroft School, NC	A,C,F,S,O	St. Paul's School, NH	A,O
The Rectory School, CT	A,C,F,S,O	St. Peter's Preparatory School, NJ	A,F,S,O
Redemption Christian Academy, MA	A,C,S,O	St. Stephen's Episcopal School, TX	F,S,O
Ridley College, ON, Canada	A,O	St. Stephen's School, Rome, Italy	A,F,O
Riverdale Country School, NY	A,O	Saint Teresa's Academy, MO	A,C,F,S,O
Riverstone International School, ID	A,F,R,S,O	St. Thomas Aquinas High School, FL	A,C,F,O
Rockhurst High School, MO	A,C,F,S,O	Saint Thomas Aquinas High School, KS	A,C,S,O
Rock Point School, VT	A,F,O	St. Timothy's School, MD	A,O
The Roeper School, MI	F,O	Saint Ursula Academy, OH	A,C,F,S,O
Roland Park Country School, MD	A,F,S,O	Salpointe Catholic High School, AZ	A,C,S,O
Rolling Hills Preparatory School, CA	A,F,O	Sandy Spring Friends School, MD	A,F,S,O
Rosseau Lake College, ON, Canada	A,O	Santa Catalina School, CA	A,F,S,O
Rothesay Netherwood School, NB, Canada	A,S,O	Santa Margarita Catholic High School, CA	A,C,F,S,O
The Roxbury Latin School, MA	A,C,S	The Savannah Country Day School, GA	A,C,F,S,O
Rumsey Hall School, CT	A,O	Scattergood Friends School, IA	F,O
Rutgers Preparatory School, NJ	A,C,F,S,O	Scheck Hillel Community School, FL	A,O
Sacramento Country Day School, CA	A	SciCore Academy, NJ	A,C,O
Sacred Heart/Griffin High School, IL	A,S,O	Seabury Hall, HI	A,F,S,O
Saddlebrook Preparatory School, FL	A,F,S,O	Seattle Academy of Arts and Sciences, WA	A,F,S
Sage Hill School, CA	A,F,S,O	Servite High School, CA	A,S,O
Sage Ridge School, NV	A,F,O	The Seven Hills School, OH	A,O
Saint Agnes Academy–St. Dominic School, TN	A,C	Severn School, MD	A,C,F,S,O
St. Albans School, DC	A,C,F,R,S,O	Sewickley Academy, PA	A,F,S,O
St. Andrew's Episcopal School, MD	A,C,F,S,O	Shady Side Academy, PA	A,C,F,S,O
St. Andrew's Episcopal School, MS	A,S	Shawnigan Lake School, BC, Canada	S,O
Saint Andrew's School, FL	A,C,F,S,O	Shelton School and Evaluation Center, TX	A,O
St. Andrew's School, GA	A,F,S,O	Shorecrest Preparatory School, FL	A,F,S,O
St. Andrew's School, RI	A,C,F,R,S,O	Smith School, NY	A,C,F,O
St. Andrew's–Sewanee School, TN	F,S,O	Southwest Christian School, Inc., TX	A,C,F,S,O
St. Anne's–Belfield School, VA	A,S,O	Spring Creek Academy, TX	A,F
Saint Augustine Preparatory School, NJ	A,F,R,S,O	Springside Chestnut Hill Academy, PA	A,S,O
St. Bernard High School, CA	A,C,F,S	Squaw Valley Academy, CA	A,F,S,O
St. Bernard's Catholic School, CA	A,O	Stanstead College, QC, Canada	A,F,S,O
St. Catherine's School, VA	A,F,S,O	Stevenson School, CA	A,F,S
St. Christopher's School, VA	A,F,S,O	Stone Ridge School of the Sacred Heart, MD	A,C,F,S,O
St. Clement's School, ON, Canada	O	The Stony Brook School, NY	A,C,F,R,S,O
St. Croix Schools, MN	A,S,O	The Storm King School, NY	A,O
Saint Dominic Academy, ME	A,F,S,O	Stratford Academy, GA	A,F,S
Saint Francis High School, CA	A,C,F,S,O	The Summit Country Day School, OH	A,C,F,S,O
Saint Francis High School, CA	A,C,F,S,O	The Taft School, CT	A,F,S,O
St. George's Independent School, TN	A,C,F,S,O	Taipei American School, Taiwan	A,C,O
St. George's School, BC, Canada	A,C,F,S,O	Tampa Preparatory School, FL	A,C,S,O
Saint Gertrude High School, VA	F,S	Tandem Friends School, VA	F,O
St. John's Catholic Prep, MD	S	TASIS The American School in England, United Kingdom	A,C,F,S,O
St. John's Preparatory School, MA	A,C,F,S,O	TASIS, The American School in Switzerland, Switzerland	A,F,R,S,O
Saint John's Preparatory School, MN	A,F,O		
Saint Joseph Academy, CA	A,O	The Tenney School, TX	A,O
St. Joseph High School, CT	A,C,F,S,O	Tilton School, NH	A,C,F,S
Saint Joseph High School, NJ	A,C,S,O	Timothy Christian High School, IL	A,F,S,O
St. Joseph's Catholic School, SC	A,F,S	Timothy Christian School, NJ	A,S,O
St. Joseph's Preparatory School, PA	A,C,F,S,O	TMI - The Episcopal School of Texas, TX	A,F,R,S,O
St. Luke's School, CT	A,C,F,S,O	Tower Hill School, DE	S,O
St. Margaret's School, BC, Canada	A,O	Trinity Catholic High School, CT	A,O
St. Martin's Episcopal School, LA	A,C,F,S,O	Trinity College School, ON, Canada	A,O
St. Mary's Episcopal School, TN	A,F,S,O	Trinity Episcopal School, VA	A,C,F,S
Saint Mary's High School, AZ	A,F,S,O	Trinity High School, OH	A,F,S,O

A — academic; C — computer instruction; F — art/fine arts; R — rigorous outdoor training; S — sports; O — other

Trinity Preparatory School, FL	A,C,F,S,O
Trinity School of Texas, TX	A,O
Tuscaloosa Academy, AL	A,C,F,S,O
United Nations International School, NY	A,C,F,S,O
The United World College - USA, NM	A,R,O
University of Chicago Laboratory Schools, IL	A,S,O
University School of Jackson, TN	A,C,F,S,O
Upper Canada College, ON, Canada	A,C,F,O
Valley Christian High School, CA	A,C,F,S,O
The Vanguard School, FL	A,O
Victor Valley Christian School, CA	A
Viewpoint School, CA	A,C,F,S,O
Villa Duchesne and Oak Hill School, MO	A,C,F,S,O
Visitation Academy, MO	A,S,O
Walnut Hill School for the Arts, MA	F,O
Wasatch Academy, UT	A,O
Washington International School, DC	A
Watkinson School, CT	A,O
Waynflete School, ME	A,F,S,O
The Webb Schools, CA	A,O
The Weber School, GA	A,O
Wellspring Foundation, CT	A
Wesleyan Academy, PR	A,O
Wesleyan School, GA	A,C,F,S,O
Westbury Christian School, TX	A,F,S,O
Westmark School, CA	A,C,F,O
Westminster School, CT	S,O
The Westminster Schools, GA	A,C,F,R,S,O
Westminster Schools of Augusta, GA	A,F,S,O
Westover School, CT	A,F,S,O
Wheaton Academy, IL	A,C,F,S
The Wheeler School, RI	A,F,S,O
Whitefield Academy, KY	A,F,S,O
Wichita Collegiate School, KS	A,F,S
The Willows Academy, IL	A,S,O
Wilmington Christian School, DE	A,O
Wilson Hall, SC	A,C,F,S,O
Windermere Preparatory School, FL	A,S,O
The Windsor School, NY	A,O
Winston Preparatory School, NY	A,F,S,O
The Winston School, TX	A,C,F,O
The Winston School San Antonio, TX	A,C,F,S,O
Woodlynde School, PA	A,F,S,O
Wyoming Seminary, PA	A,F,S,O
York Country Day School, PA	F,S,O

SCHOOLS REPORTING THAT THEY ACCOMMODATE UNDERACHIEVERS

Alpine Academy, UT
Atlantis Academy, FL
Calgary Academy, AB, Canada
Camphill Special School, PA
Chatham Academy, GA
Delphos Saint John's High School, OH
Denver Academy, CO
Fowlers Academy, PR
The Glenholme School, Devereux Connecticut, CT
Halstrom Academy, Beverly Hills, CA
Halstrom Academy, Cupertino, CA
Halstrom Academy, Huntington Beach, CA
Halstrom Academy, Irvine, CA
Halstrom Academy, Los Angeles, CA
Halstrom Academy, Manhattan Beach, CA
Halstrom Academy, Orange, CA
Halstrom Academy, Pasadena, CA

Halstrom Academy, San Diego, CA
Halstrom Academy, San Mateo, CA
Halstrom Academy, Walnut Creek, CA
Halstrom Academy, Westlake Village, CA
Halstrom Academy, Woodland Hills, CA
Hampshire Country School, NH
The Hill Center, Durham Academy, NC
The John Dewey Academy, MA
La Cheim School, CA
Little Keswick School, VA
Lyman Ward Military Academy, AL
Maplebrook School, NY
Marine Military Academy, TX
The Monarch School, TX
Mooseheart High School, IL
Norman Howard School, NY
Oakland School, VA
PACE/Brantley Hall High School, FL
The Pathway School, PA
The Rectory School, CT
Valley View School, MA
The Vanguard School, FL
Winston Preparatory School, NY

SCHOOLS REPORTING PROGRAMS FOR STUDENTS WITH SPECIAL NEEDS

Remedial Reading and/or Writing

Academy of the Holy Family, CT
Academy of the New Church Boys' School, PA
Academy of the New Church Girls' School, PA
Académie Ste Cécile International School, ON, Canada
Admiral Farragut Academy, FL
Alexander Dawson School, CO
All Hallows High School, NY
Allison Academy, FL
Alpine Academy, UT
American Heritage School, FL
The American School Foundation, Mexico
The American School of Puerto Vallarta, Mexico
Archbishop Curley High School, MD
Archbishop Hoban High School, OH
Arete Preparatory Academy, CA
ASSETS School, HI
Atlantis Academy, FL
Baptist Regional School, NJ
Bay Ridge Preparatory School, NY
The Beekman School, NY
Bishop Mora Salesian High School, CA
Bishop's College School, QC, Canada
Bishop Stang High School, MA
Bishop Walsh Middle High School, MD
Blueprint Education, AZ
Brehm Preparatory School, IL
Brother Rice High School, MI
Burr and Burton Academy, VT
Butte Central Catholic High School, MT
Calgary Academy, AB, Canada
California Crosspoint High School, CA
Calvary Day School, GA
Calvin Christian High School, CA
Camden Military Academy, SC
Camphill Special School, PA
Cardigan Mountain School, NH
Cardinal Mooney Catholic High School, FL

Cardinal Newman High School, FL
Cascadilla School, NY
Catholic Central High School, NY
Central Catholic High School, CA
Chaminade-Madonna College Preparatory, FL
Chatham Academy, GA
Chattanooga Christian School, TN
Chelsea School, MD
Christa McAuliffe Academy School of Arts and Sciences, OR
Christ Church Episcopal School, SC
Christopher Columbus High School, FL
Christopher Dock Mennonite High School, PA
Colegio Bolivar, Colombia
Columbia International School, Japan
Community High School, NJ
Concordia Academy, MN
Covenant Canadian Reformed School, AB, Canada
Crawford Adventist Academy, ON, Canada
Currey Ingram Academy, TN
Cushing Academy, MA
De La Salle North Catholic High School, OR
Delaware Valley Friends School, PA
DeMatha Catholic High School, MD
Denver Academy, CO
Desert Academy, NM
Doane Academy, NJ
Donovan Catholic, NJ
Dowling Catholic High School, IA
Dublin Christian Academy, NH
The Dwight School, NY
Eagle Hill School, CT
Eastern Mennonite High School, VA
Eaton Academy, GA
Elyria Catholic High School, OH
Franklin Academy, CT
Fredericton Christian Academy, NB, Canada
Fresno Christian Schools, CA
Friends Academy, NY
Front Range Christian High School, CO
George Stevens Academy, ME
Girard College, PA
The Glenholme School, Devereux Connecticut, CT
The Gow School, NY
Green Meadow Waldorf School, NY
Grier School, PA
Halstrom Academy, Beverly Hills, CA
Halstrom Academy, Calsbad, CA
Halstrom Academy, Cupertino, CA
Halstrom Academy, Huntington Beach, CA
Halstrom Academy, Irvine, CA
Halstrom Academy, Los Angeles, CA
Halstrom Academy, Manhattan Beach, CA
Halstrom Academy, Mission Viejo, CA
Halstrom Academy, Orange, CA
Halstrom Academy, Pasadena, CA
Halstrom Academy, San Diego, CA
Halstrom Academy, San Mateo, CA
Halstrom Academy, Walnut Creek, CA
Halstrom Academy, Westlake Village, CA
Halstrom Academy, Woodland Hills, CA
Hampshire Country School, NH
Hargrave Military Academy, VA
Hathaway Brown School, OH
The Haverford School, PA
Hebrew Academy, CA
The Hill Center, Durham Academy, NC
Ho'Ala School, HI

Holy Trinity High School, IL
The Howard School, GA
The Hudson School, NJ
Hyde School, CT
Hyde School, ME
Illiana Christian High School, IL
Indian Creek School, MD
Jean and Samuel Frankel Jewish Academy of Metropolitan Detroit, MI
The John Dewey Academy, MA
Josephinum Academy, IL
Kauai Christian Academy, HI
La Cheim School, CA
Lancaster Catholic High School, PA
Lancaster Mennonite High School, PA
Landmark East School, NS, Canada
Landmark School, MA
The Laureate Academy, MB, Canada
Lawrence School, OH
The Leelanau School, MI
Le Lycee Francais de Los Angeles, CA
Lincoln Academy, ME
Little Keswick School, VA
Lyman Ward Military Academy, AL
Manhattan Christian High School, MT
Maplebrook School, NY
Maranatha High School, CA
Marian Central Catholic High School, IL
Marian High School, IN
Marine Military Academy, TX
Marshall School, MN
The Marvelwood School, CT
Massanutten Military Academy, VA
Mater Dei High School, IL
Memorial Hall School, TX
Memphis University School, TN
Merion Mercy Academy, PA
Missouri Military Academy, MO
The Monarch School, TX
Mooseheart High School, IL
Nashville Christian School, TN
Noble Academy, NC
The Nora School, MD
Norman Howard School, NY
The North Broward Preparatory Upper School, FL
North Country School, NY
Northpoint Christian School, MS
Northwest Yeshiva High School, WA
The Norwich Free Academy, CT
Notre Dame High School, MO
Notre Dame High School, NJ
Notre Dame High School, NY
Oakland School, VA
Oneida Baptist Institute, KY
Our Lady of Good Counsel High School, MD
The Oxford Academy, CT
PACE/Brantley Hall High School, FL
The Pathway School, PA
The Phelps School, PA
Pioneer Valley Christian Academy, MA
Pius X High School, NE
Powers Catholic High School, MI
The Rectory School, CT
Redemption Christian Academy, MA
Redwood Christian Schools, CA
Regis Jesuit High School, Boys Division, CO
Regis Jesuit High School, Girls Division, CO

Riverside Christian Schools, CA
Rumsey Hall School, CT
Saint Albert Junior-Senior High School, IA
St. Andrew's School, GA
St. Andrew's School, RI
St. Andrew's–Sewanee School, TN
St. Benedict at Auburndale, TN
St. Bernard's Catholic School, CA
St. Brendan High School, FL
St. Croix Schools, MN
St. Francis School, GA
St. George's School, BC, Canada
Saint Joan Antida High School, WI
St. John Neumann High School, FL
Saint Mary's High School, AZ
Saint Patrick High School, IL
St. Pius X High School, TX
St. Thomas Aquinas High School, FL
Saint Thomas Aquinas High School, KS
St. Thomas Choir School, NY
Saint Thomas More Catholic High School, LA
Salesianum School, DE
Salpointe Catholic High School, AZ
Santa Margarita Catholic High School, CA
Scheck Hillel Community School, FL
Seattle Academy of Arts and Sciences, WA
Seattle Lutheran High School, WA
Seisen International School, Japan
Shawnigan Lake School, BC, Canada
Shoreline Christian, WA
Smith School, NY
Smithville Christian High School, ON, Canada
Solebury School, PA
Stephen T. Badin High School, OH
The Storm King School, NY
Summit Preparatory School, MT
Takoma Academy, MD
Tandem Friends School, VA
TASIS The American School in England, United Kingdom
The Tenney School, TX
Timothy Christian High School, IL
Timothy Christian School, NJ
Trinity High School, KY
Trinity-Pawling School, NY
Valley View School, MA
The Vanguard School, FL
Venta Preparatory School, ON, Canada
Villa Duchesne and Oak Hill School, MO
The Waldorf School of Saratoga Springs, NY
Walla Walla Valley Academy, WA
Webb School of Knoxville, TN
Wellspring Foundation, CT
Westmark School, CA
Wheaton Academy, IL
Wilmington Christian School, DE
The Windsor School, NY
Winston Preparatory School, NY
The Winston School, TX
The Winston School San Antonio, TX
Woodlynde School, PA
Zurich International School, Switzerland

Remedial Math

Academy of the Holy Family, CT
Academy of the New Church Boys' School, PA
Academy of the New Church Girls' School, PA
Académie Ste Cécile International School, ON, Canada

Admiral Farragut Academy, FL
Alexander Dawson School, CO
All Hallows High School, NY
Allison Academy, FL
Alpha Omega Academy, IA
Alpine Academy, UT
American Heritage School, FL
The American School of Puerto Vallarta, Mexico
Archbishop Curley High School, MD
Archbishop Hoban High School, OH
Arete Preparatory Academy, CA
ASSETS School, HI
Atlantis Academy, FL
Baptist Regional School, NJ
Bay Ridge Preparatory School, NY
Bearspaw Christian School, AB, Canada
The Beekman School, NY
Bishop Denis J. O'Connell High School, VA
Bishop's College School, QC, Canada
Bishop Stang High School, MA
Blueprint Education, AZ
Brehm Preparatory School, IL
Brother Rice High School, MI
Burr and Burton Academy, VT
Butte Central Catholic High School, MT
Calgary Academy, AB, Canada
Calvary Day School, GA
Camphill Special School, PA
Cardigan Mountain School, NH
Cardinal Mooney Catholic High School, FL
Cardinal Newman High School, FL
Cascadilla School, NY
Catholic Central High School, NY
Central Catholic High School, CA
Chaminade-Madonna College Preparatory, FL
Chatham Academy, GA
Chattanooga Christian School, TN
Chelsea School, MD
Christa McAuliffe Academy School of Arts and Sciences, OR
Christ Church Episcopal School, SC
Colegio Bolivar, Colombia
Columbia International School, Japan
Community High School, NJ
Concordia Academy, MN
Covenant Canadian Reformed School, AB, Canada
Cushing Academy, MA
De La Salle High School, CA
De La Salle North Catholic High School, OR
Delaware Valley Friends School, PA
Denver Academy, CO
Desert Academy, NM
Doane Academy, NJ
Donovan Catholic, NJ
Dowling Catholic High School, IA
Dublin Christian Academy, NH
The Dwight School, NY
Eagle Hill School, CT
Eastern Mennonite High School, VA
Eaton Academy, GA
Elyria Catholic High School, OH
Franklin Academy, CT
Fredericton Christian Academy, NB, Canada
Fresno Christian Schools, CA
Friends Academy, NY
Front Range Christian High School, CO
George Stevens Academy, ME
Girard College, PA

The Glenholme School, Devereux Connecticut, CT
The Gow School, NY
Green Meadow Waldorf School, NY
Grier School, PA
Halstrom Academy, Beverly Hills, CA
Halstrom Academy, Calsbad, CA
Halstrom Academy, Cupertino, CA
Halstrom Academy, Huntington Beach, CA
Halstrom Academy, Irvine, CA
Halstrom Academy, Los Angeles, CA
Halstrom Academy, Manhattan Beach, CA
Halstrom Academy, Mission Viejo, CA
Halstrom Academy, Orange, CA
Halstrom Academy, Pasadena, CA
Halstrom Academy, San Diego, CA
Halstrom Academy, San Mateo, CA
Halstrom Academy, Walnut Creek, CA
Halstrom Academy, Woodland Hills, CA
Hampshire Country School, NH
Hargrave Military Academy, VA
Hathaway Brown School, OH
The Haverford School, PA
Hebrew Academy, CA
The Hill Center, Durham Academy, NC
Ho'Ala School, HI
The Howard School, GA
The Hudson School, NJ
Hyde School, CT
Hyde School, ME
Illiana Christian High School, IL
Jean and Samuel Frankel Jewish Academy of Metropolitan
    Detroit, MI
The John Dewey Academy, MA
Josephinum Academy, IL
Kauai Christian Academy, HI
La Cheim School, CA
Lancaster Mennonite High School, PA
Landmark East School, NS, Canada
Landmark School, MA
The Laureate Academy, MB, Canada
Lawrence School, OH
The Leelanau School, MI
Le Lycee Francais de Los Angeles, CA
Lincoln Academy, ME
Little Keswick School, VA
Lutheran High School, MO
Lyman Ward Military Academy, AL
Manhattan Christian High School, MT
Maplebrook School, NY
Maranatha High School, CA
Marian Central Catholic High School, IL
Marian High School, IN
Marine Military Academy, TX
Marshall School, MN
The Marvelwood School, CT
Massanutten Military Academy, VA
Mater Dei High School, IL
Memorial Hall School, TX
Memphis University School, TN
Merion Mercy Academy, PA
Missouri Military Academy, MO
The Monarch School, TX
Mooseheart High School, IL
Mountain View Academy, CA
Nashville Christian School, TN
Noble Academy, NC
The Nora School, MD
Norman Howard School, NY

The North Broward Preparatory Upper School, FL
North Country School, NY
Northpoint Christian School, MS
Northwest Yeshiva High School, WA
The Norwich Free Academy, CT
Notre Dame High School, MO
Notre Dame High School, NJ
Notre Dame High School, NY
Oakland School, VA
Oneida Baptist Institute, KY
The Oxford Academy, CT
PACE/Brantley Hall High School, FL
Paradise Adventist Academy, CA
The Pathway School, PA
The Phelps School, PA
Pioneer Valley Christian Academy, MA
Pius X High School, NE
Powers Catholic High School, MI
The Rectory School, CT
Redemption Christian Academy, MA
Redwood Christian Schools, CA
Regis Jesuit High School, Boys Division, CO
Regis Jesuit High School, Girls Division, CO
Riverside Christian Schools, CA
Saint Albert Junior-Senior High School, IA
St. Andrew's School, GA
St. Andrew's–Sewanee School, TN
Saint Anthony High School, IL
St. Benedict at Auburndale, TN
St. Bernard's Catholic School, CA
St. Brendan High School, FL
St. Croix Schools, MN
St. Francis School, GA
Saint Joan Antida High School, WI
St. John Neumann High School, FL
Saint Mary's High School, AZ
Saint Patrick High School, IL
St. Paul's High School, MB, Canada
St. Pius X High School, TX
St. Thomas Aquinas High School, FL
Saint Thomas Aquinas High School, KS
St. Thomas Choir School, NY
Saint Thomas More Catholic High School, LA
Salesianum School, DE
Salpointe Catholic High School, AZ
Santa Margarita Catholic High School, CA
Scheck Hillel Community School, FL
Seattle Academy of Arts and Sciences, WA
Seattle Lutheran High School, WA
Seisen International School, Japan
Shawnigan Lake School, BC, Canada
Smith School, NY
Smithville Christian High School, ON, Canada
Solebury School, PA
Stephen T. Badin High School, OH
Summit Preparatory School, MT
Sunshine Bible Academy, SD
Tandem Friends School, VA
The Tenney School, TX
Trinity High School, KY
Trinity High School, OH
Valley Christian High School, CA
Valley View School, MA
The Vanguard School, FL
Venta Preparatory School, ON, Canada
Villa Duchesne and Oak Hill School, MO
The Waldorf School of Saratoga Springs, NY
Walla Walla Valley Academy, WA
Webb School of Knoxville, TN
Wellspring Foundation, CT

Westmark School, CA
Westtown School, PA
Wheaton Academy, IL
Wilmington Christian School, DE
The Windsor School, NY
Winston Preparatory School, NY
The Winston School, TX
Woodlynde School, PA
Zurich International School, Switzerland

Deaf Students

The Academy at Charlemont, MA
Alexander Dawson School, CO
Allentown Central Catholic High School, PA
American Christian Academy, AL
American Heritage School, FL
The American School Foundation, Mexico
Bishop Brady High School, NH
Blanchet School, OR
Burr and Burton Academy, VT
Cate School, CA
The Colorado Springs School, CO
Concordia Academy, MN
Eaton Academy, GA
George Stevens Academy, ME
Hathaway Brown School, OH
Jean and Samuel Frankel Jewish Academy of Metropolitan
    Detroit, MI
Lancaster Mennonite High School, PA
Landmark School, MA
The Madeira School, VA
Marian Central Catholic High School, IL
Marshall School, MN
Norman Howard School, NY
Northwest Yeshiva High School, WA
Notre Dame High School, CA
Pensacola Catholic High School, FL
Phillips Academy (Andover), MA
Portsmouth Christian Academy, NH
Rosati-Kain High School, MO

Saint Albert Junior-Senior High School, IA
St. Andrew's Episcopal School, MD
St. Andrew's School, RI
Saint Anthony High School, IL
Saint Augustine Preparatory School, NJ
St. John Neumann High School, FL
Santa Margarita Catholic High School, CA
Servite High School, CA
The Tenney School, TX
Trinity High School, KY
The Vanguard School, FL
Watkinson School, CT
Westover School, CT
The Williston Northampton School, MA

Blind Students

The Academy at Charlemont, MA
Allentown Central Catholic High School, PA
Alpine Academy, UT
American Heritage School, FL
The American School Foundation, Mexico
Burr and Burton Academy, VT
Dowling Catholic High School, IA
George Stevens Academy, ME
Jean and Samuel Frankel Jewish Academy of Metropolitan
    Detroit, MI
Lancaster Mennonite High School, PA
MMI Preparatory School, PA
Northwest Yeshiva High School, WA
Notre Dame High School, CA
Pensacola Catholic High School, FL
Phillips Academy (Andover), MA
Portsmouth Christian Academy, NH
Rosati-Kain High School, MO
St. Andrew's School, RI
Saint Augustine Preparatory School, NJ
Santa Margarita Catholic High School, CA
Servite High School, CA
Trinity High School, KY
The Vanguard School, FL

Index

Alphabetical Listing of Schools

In the index that follows, page numbers for school profiles are shown in regular type, page numbers for Close-Ups are shown in **boldface** type, and page numbers for Displays are shown in *italics*.